# HANCER'S
## PRICE GUIDE TO
# PAPERBACK
# BOOKS

# HANCER'S
## PRICE GUIDE TO
# PAPERBACK
# BOOKS
## THIRD EDITION
## KEVIN HANCER

With the assistance of
R. Reginald

Special research adviser:
Rahn Kollander

Wallace-Homestead Book Company
Radnor, Pennsylvania

Copyright © 1990 by Kevin Hancer
Third Edition   All Rights Reserved
Published in Radnor, Pennsylvania 19089, by Wallace-Homestead Book Company

Manufactured in the United States of America


Library of Congress Cataloging in Publication Data
Hancer, Kevin.
    [Price guide to paperback books]
    Hancer's price guide to paperback books / Kevin Hancer.—3rd ed.
      p.   cm.
    ISBN 0-87069-536-3
    1. Paperbacks—Collectors and collecting.  2. Paperbacks—
Bibliography.  3. Paperbacks—Prices.  4. Book collecting.
5. Books—Prices.  I. Title.  II. Title: Price guide to paperback
books.
Z1033.P3H34      1990
070.5′73—dc20                                        89-51552
                                                        CIP



1 2 3 4 5 6 7 8 9 0      9 8 7 6 5 4 3 2 1 0

# IN MEMORIAM

This book is dedicated to two men whose lives were tragically cut short.

### NORMAN H. GAULKE

*Norman H. Gaulke was my uncle and a sailor. I grew up in a loving and nurturing home where books and reading were important to my parents so we always had a large home library. Even more than books, however, Uncle Norman fanned the fires of my imagination. He told us fanciful tales of his years as a Western outlaw, outrunning sheriffs and Texas rangers on his green horse. He balanced those stories with accounts of his life in the Merchant Marine, with exciting stops in exotic ports. He was a decent and compassionate man who gave his own money to help orphans in foreign ports. He died July 17, 1966, at the age of thirty-six. All these years later my memory of him is still fresh. When the lilacs bloom in the Spring, I remember him, and as I have traveled to exotic and far places, a part of him has always been with me.*

### FRANK DONALD GOODISH

*Frank Donald Goodish was a literal giant of a man. He was a rugged individual who chose to work in one of the toughest professions and set the standard for everyone in the business. He was a professional wrestler and barking wild man, who was known as Bruiser Brody. Although there have been many leagues and many champions, few insiders would deny him the status of being the best in the business. His charisma and professionalism were the envy of his peers. He wouldn't be pushed, he wouldn't be intimidated, and he wouldn't be defeated. He was fiercely loyal to his friends and to his beloved wife and son. He supported treatment programs for youth, and single-handedly kept small wrestling promotions alive by his willingness to work for them in defiance of bigger organizations and their competition. On July 17, 1988, he died in Puerto Rico at the age of 42, of knife wounds to his abdomen, inflicted by a fellow wrestler while perhaps held by two others. His killer went free when, amidst numerous delays and reported threats to witnesses, no eye witness appeared to testify. But, for those who knew and loved him, the barking will never die.*

# CONTENTS

# ACKNOWLEDGMENTS

The following people contributed data to this edition:

Lawrence Abbott
Vince Amero
Rolf Andersen
Glenn Anderson
Red Anderson
Jeffrey Appelbaum
Mike Baka
Victor A. Berch
Mitch Berger
Mrs. Robert Black
Gary C. Bromley
Russell Brooks
B. Bruce-Briggs
Algis J. Budrys
Jeffrey L. Burk
K. E. Burke
Steve Bushakis
Dan Cataldo
Lyle Clavers
John Coltrane
Jo Cooper
Dan Crawford
Charles Culpepper
Don Davidson
Jack Deveny
Peter Donovan
James Douglas
John L. Dressig
Rim Ederveen
Steve Eichorn
Dave Farah
Deborah Finn
Florence Flynn
Jeffrey Gailiun
H. Galewitz

Robert Garlinghouse
Fred Garvin
Joyce Godsey
Mark Goodman
Bill Griffith
Brian Guidon
Joe Hagen
Nova Hamilton
Claude Held
Nadezhda R. Henry
R. C. Holland
Brian F. Hooley
Michael Houghton
C. Hughen
Richard D. Hurt
Norral Johnson
Randy Jonathan
Sam B. Jones
Edward F. Kluge, Jr
Jim Kolda
Rahn Kollander
Jan Koopmans
Ken Krueger
Robert Lambert
Philip Larson
Steve Lawson
Daniel Levitt
Dave Lewis
Marian Y. Luke
Bob Lurie
James H. Martin
David McClintock
Kelly McDowell
Jeff Melius
Vernon J. Miller

Wayne Mullins
Bob Myers
Phillip H. Nelson
Tom Nigra
Robert T. Noble
Gene Nystrom
Peter Olsen
Fred J. Olson
Randy O'Rourke
Don Osier
Wally Pattengill
David C. Peek
Dennis Petilli
Jim Reed
Ron Remitz
Rene Rendon
Jim Roberts
Craig L. Rohrer
Mark Rose
Russell C. Russ
Steve Sayles
J. J. Schmidt
Shirley Schneider
Robert Schrader
T. J. Shamon
Rickey L. Shanklin
Tim Skeffington
Mike Smith
Herb Snyder
Marvin Sommer
Jon Songas
Jane Tester
Ned Thomas
Ed Treverton
Phillip Underwood

John Unger
John Victor
The Village Bookshelf
  (Massillon, OH)

Robert Wall, Sr
Dr. Joe L. Wheeler
Chet Williamson
Thure Wilson

Michael Yoder
Edward Young
Lesley Zartens

The following publications, with the acknowledged editors and bibliographers, contributed reference data to reconfirm some of the material in this edition:

*Books Are Everything* (eds. R. C. and Elwanda Holland), Bruce Brenner, Keith Dilbone, Chris Eckhoff, Alex Henzel, Michel Lanteigne, Jim Parsons, Wally Pattengill, and Paul Payne

*Paperback Forum* (eds. Barry Kaplan, William O'Connell, and Jonathan White)

*Paperback Parade* (ed. Gary Lovisi)

I owe special thanks to Rahn Kollander. Without his voluminous and tireless research efforts, willingly and openly shared, this book would hardly be possible in its present form. Thank you, my good friend.

The reference listing of William Lyles on Dell paperbacks was a useful checking reference beyond the books Rahn and I were able to physically examine. I highly recommended his books for Dell fanciers.

The excellent reference book by Piet Schreuders was helpful in producing this price guide. His efforts overseas and in this country have certainly contributed to a greater respect for paperback cover art, and his book remains the best available reference in the field. This detailed and highly readable volume can add to anyone's knowledge, as it did to mine.

My daughter, Aileen, and my son, Colin, also helped make this book possible. It is hard to deal with a Dad who is always stopping the car at the sight of each newly discovered bookstore. These two amazing young people are great readers in their own right and fully deserving of all my pride.

My family provided unending support and patience. Especially, I thank my parents, whose affection for books and knowledge is largely responsible for my interest in these areas and the years of pleasure I have derived from them.

I want to thank some of my close friends. James May was available with photographic advice whenever I needed it, whether for this book or while we were traveling through the jungle or climbing up an active volcano. Dave Erickson always had an encouraging word, and his cheerful visits were ever welcome. John Yankovich has been a constant vocal supporter of my efforts, being one of the first to realize that the existence of this book was an inevitability. Unlike those who wanted to conceal information for the benefit of a select few, he encouraged full participation in the project so that the resultant product would be the best available.

Finally, I offer my special thanks to Jo Cooper. Without her loving, positive encouragement, I would have had considerably more difficulty facing the months of sixteen-hour days it took to complete this massive task. It is difficult for anyone to remain patient with a constantly tired, overworked, and irritable person. Thank you, Jo, for bearing with me.

# INTRODUCTION

## Historical Background

In the eleventh century A.D., a Chinese named Pi Sheng introduced movable type to the world. As the explorations of Marco Polo and others revealed the wonders of the Far East to the rest of the civilized world, Eastern technology was gradually adapted for use in Europe. Four hundred years after Pi Sheng, Johann Gutenberg's revolutionary development of movable type in Europe made books available to people who previously could not afford laboriously handwritten copies.

Books became even more accessible to the general public when cheap paperbound editions were introduced, but paperback book publication, despite a few exceptions, was not a commercial success.

In the United States, paperback popular fiction received its greatest early popularity through an author whose contributions have largely been obscured by the legends surrounding his name. The writer was Davy Crockett, and according to John Myers Myers in *The Alamo* (1948), he "emerged as the central figure of a literary fad that lasted for twenty odd years." Crockett Almanacs were the pulp magazines of their day, and the published adventures attributed to Crockett could have filled a dozen lifetimes. The imitations were numerous.

In 1860, Erastus Beadle took the paperbound format a step further and published the first American dime novel *Malaeska, the Indian Wife of the White Hunter,* by Mrs. S. Stevens. Dime novels quickly caught on, and soon a multitude of publishers were grinding out generally inaccurate stories of frontier mayhem. Mysteries, romances, and fanciful novels by authors like Horatio Alger also were very popular until the dime novel succumbed to the pulp magazine. Some dime novel publishers attempted to switch formats from a magazine size into a paperback size, but paperback publication was generally commercially unsuccessful.

It was not until the growth of leisure time for the working classes, coupled with the development of proper sales and marketing techniques, that paperback publishing became a widespread, profitable venture.

The modern era of the paperback book began in 1939 with the issuance of ten titles by Pocket Books, each in a limited test printing of no more than 10,000 copies, which were distributed only within New York City. Once the floodgates were opened, nothing could close them again.

Paperbacks have grown to become a multimillion dollar business. As inflation drives the price of hardcover books higher and higher, industry insiders predict that the future of the book industry may largely belong to the paperbound book.

Book collectors as well are gaining more respect for paperbacks. In the past collectors tended to scorn paperbound books in favor of hardcover editions. This snobbish preference has proved to be highly illogical, for the true first editions of many significant books, as well as some works by notable authors, exist solely as paperback books. Many people now realize that these fragile, paperbound volumes are worthy of inclusion in any serious book collection.

## Why People Collect Paperbacks

Anything that exists or was produced on this planet is undoubtedly collected by someone, somewhere. Collecting is a peculiar passion that affects many people in varying degrees and in many different ways.

Book collecting has been a popular hobby for many years, and paperback book collecting often follows traditional patterns.

Because books are, of course, meant to be read, many collectors collect those books that they enjoy reading. Collectors, however, generally treasure their higher grade copies and do not decrease their condition by reading them; instead, they often obtain a "reading" copy in lesser condition. A reader might collect all the books by a favorite author or group of authors, or might collect all books within a particular genre, or even books with a similar theme. Different collectors limit their reading by different degrees, so this could mean anything from a small number of books to many hundreds or even thousands.

Cover art has become a larger collecting factor in recent years and is the aspect of this hobby that seems to intrigue the media most. There are many different artists and artistic styles, but lurid cover art has been the most popular in the United States whereas fine art has been more popular in Europe. As collectors learn more about artists, this area seems to be gaining importance in the field.

Some people collect original or first editions, often within a particular genre.

Some people collect paperbacks as examples of our popular culture because the books reflect the time in which they were produced. Although a book may have been written centuries or just years earlier, the design, packaging, and cover art will reflect contemporary marketing appeal. For example, the 1932 Jacket Library edition of Rostand's *Cyrano de Bergerac* was packaged with a classic, stylish look; but when reprinted years later, the book was retitled *The Art of Love,* by "a Parisian Casanova," and the cover depicts a young couple in a heated embrace! The trend to lurid appeal perhaps reached a high (or low) point when Royal Books packaged a reprint of Mark Twain's *Pudd'nhead Wilson* as *The Unnatural Son* in order to increase its mass market appeal. America's fascination with things sexual has long been an easy mark for exploitation, and paperback publishers from 1940 to 1960 were well aware of it. This was particularly exploited in the 1940s, becoming more subdued in the 1950s as paperbacks, in much the same way as comic books, came under attack by various moral-minded groups.

Some people collect specific paperbacks because of their outrageous nature and bizarre design and packaging. Books like *Naked on Roller Skates* or *Ten Toes Up* may be utterly wretched reading, but the titles and cover art are so extreme that they have appeal for certain collectors. There are all kinds of collectors in this area. Some, for example, are especially interested in books like *Nigger Heaven* or *Hot Chocolate* that deal with blacks. Such collectors seldom take the books seriously, but rather are attracted by their very outlandishness.

## How To Start A Paperback Collection

A good place to begin collecting is your neighborhood. Local swap shops, trading posts, secondhand stores, and retail stores operated by charitable groups (such as the Salvation Army) contain many bargains for the collector. Local used book stores can also contain a lot of reasonably priced items.

Many mail-order dealers specialize in vintage paperbacks and issue catalogs periodically. There is often a charge for these catalogs, but at the current time this is the way to get the widest selection of books. Collectors should compare catalogs, the more the better, to obtain the best value. Great differences in price can exist between catalogs. This often happens when one catalog comes from a part-time dealer who sells only locally obtained items and the other catalog is from a dealer who works full time, traveling to sales as well as buying through the mail. The former has a lower overhead and offers a smaller selection at cheaper prices. The latter generally charges more but has a wider variety of items. This can become even more extreme in the case of a specialist in a particular field. The specialist may charge considerably more for the items in that field, but has invested time and effort in order to offer a wide selection. Each collector must weigh the benefits of buying a sought-after item from a specialist, usually at a higher price, against waiting for a more attractive price from another dealer.

Many dealers work from want lists. These should be submitted in a clean, orderly fashion, along with a self-addressed, stamped envelope (SASE).

Collectors have to take responsibility for keeping themselves informed. This book has been designed and created to be a valuable reference tool, and each new edition will further expand and clarify information. By examining the *Price Guide to Paperback Books* and other references such as dealer lists buyers can stay reasonably informed. Dealers may sometimes incorrectly describe their available books, or inaccurately represent values, often merely from ignorance. Collectors must remember that dealers exist with varying degrees of expertise. As in any consumer market, defensive buying makes good sense. Caveat emptor.

Another way to start collecting is at your local bookstore or newsstand. Every month new books appear that will be collector's items in the future. They include first or original editions, movie and TV tie-ins, and books with cover art by popular artists, such as Michael Whelan and Rowena Morrill.

## Taking Care of Your Paperback Collection

The physical condition of a paperback book is subject to all the ills that affect other paper collectibles, and rare or collectible books should be protected from damage that would reduce their value.

Books should be stored in a cool, dry, and dark place. The paper on which most paperbacks were printed gets brown and brittle with age. Heat, humidity, and light hasten the deterioration of books.

Many collectors use specially designed bags to protect their paperbacks. Because noninert elements in plastic bags might damage books over the years, some collectors prefer not to use them. Protective coverings made of polyester film are far preferable, although more costly.

Some collectors have coated the covers of their books with protective sprays such as Krylon Crystal Clear. This method is destructive and should not be used under any circumstances.

# The Grading of Paperback Books

The condition of a book is the most important factor affecting its value as a collectible. The following suggested guidelines represent current standards in the marketplace. Collectors and dealers should be careful not to let "wishful thinking" affect their use of these definitions.

**Mint (M).** As issued. The book is absolutely brand-new, perfect in every way, and just as clean and bright as the day it was printed. This condition grade is seldom, if ever, found.

**Near Mint (NM).** Almost perfect. The cover is bright, crisp, and unfaded. Original plastic lamination (if any) is intact. The spine is very tight, square, and clean. The pages are still largely white, with a slight darkening due to age. The book looks virtually like a perfect copy.

**Very Fine (VF).** Very minor defects. All aspects of the book are clean and fresh with no major signs of wear. There may be light fading of the cover or spine, with perhaps very minor wear spots along the book's exterior edges.

**Fine (F).** Some evidence of slight wear. This copy may have been read carefully once or twice, resulting in a light crease along the edge of the cover by the spine. There are minor stress lines on the spine. The binding is still tight. Original cover lamination (if any) may be slightly peeling at the corners. Edge staining could be slightly faded. Pages are largely white but browning around the edges. No major creases or bends are in the covers. Light wear, minor color flaking, or minor rubbing is noticeable on the extremities. An assortment of minor indications of wear are present, but the book remains a very nice copy.

**Very Good (VG).** An obviously read, but fairly tight, copy. Plastic lamination (if any) is noticeably peeling in spots. There are slight bends or creases in the cover. The pages are fairly fresh but browning. The spine is bent from several readings but not broken or torn. Wear spots, chipping, and rubbing are noticeable but are not major. Cover lustre and gloss have faded. There are no tears in the spine and no tape repairs. Very minor spine splits may be noticeable at the top and bottom.

**Good (G).** The average used copy. The cover has bends and creases and is faded. The copy is complete with no pages missing. The spine is loose and possibly splitting on either end but is still intact. The spine could be rolled. Minor tears might be present on some pages. No pieces of the cover are missing. Although this copy has been read numerous times and shows obvious signs of wear, it is still holding together.

**Fair (f).** Very heavily read and possibly soiled, but still complete and readable. Torn covers or pages are likely, as is a rolled spine. Damage from the elements or stains may be evident. This is a reading copy only.

**Poor (p).** Damaged, heavily worn, and soiled. Pages or parts of the cover may be missing. The copy is unreadable and unsuitable for collecting. Books of this quality generally belong in the garbage.

It is important to keep in mind that books that are misbound, miscut, or have covers misprinted are not worth as much as they would be without these defects. Tape repairs or colored inks to hide rubbing spots also detract from the attractiveness of a book. Condition grades are not on a sliding scale according to age. The ofttimes quoted statement, "It's very good for its age," is ridiculous and without any validity to the collector.

## A Word about Reprints

Reprint editions of most paperback books are not worth as much as first printings. Fortunately, in these cases the reprints are usually easy to detect.

Some publishers, like Pocket Books, made this quite easy. Reprints were generally noted on the indicia or copyright page of the book (almost always on the reverse side of the title page). On the subject of Pocket Books, the accuracy of their reprint information on some books has been questioned, but I have yet to hear the validity of the first printing identification made suspect.

For many publishers, it was easier to reissue a book under a new number rather than reprint it under the old number. Still others, like Dell and Popular Library, would sometimes add 1000 to the original number. For example, the reprint of Popular Library No. 392 became No. 1392.

Reprints, with a number of exceptions, are often worth 25 to 50 percent less than the original printings. Perhaps the most striking example of this exists with the first ten Pocket Book titles. Because each of the first printings was limited to no more than 10,000 copies and was distributed only within the New York City area, reprints are worth significantly less—at least 90 percent less.

## Selling Paperbacks

If you wish to sell some paperbacks, there are several methods to consider.

The easiest way to dispose of your books is to a dealer in collectible paperbacks. Often, this entails offering all your items as one group. This method, known as wholesaling, means selling books to a dealer who will try to resell them for his or her own profit. In order to understand what this involves for the dealer, a few background facts are worth discussing.

A serious book dealer is likely to be a highly individualistic businessperson. Known to other book people as a "bookman," the dealer often has begun to deal out of a love for books rather than as a means to high income. Big profits in the book business are more common in the new book field than the used book market, and used book dealers often work a 50 to 60 hour week. Many businesses are either one-person operations or center on one person. Because most of the operations reflect the owner's personality, they can differ radically from one another. They have one thing in common, however. The people who run them are entrepreneurs trying to turn a profit in an area where many businesses fail after only a few months or years. The dealer tries to buy material at a price that will allow resale at a reasonable profit. Novices need to understand that this often includes absorbing overhead, which is the cost of operating a business, such as rent, utilities, postage, advertising, and taxes.

A dealer contemplating the purchase of a group of books, is likely to consider carefully the material's desirability—how many books can be sold immediately, how many books are top-quality, what is the overall condition of the group, and so on. Collectible books are not like coins, which can be cashed in for their bullion value. In order to profit, and thereby remain in operation, the dealer must resell the books. This is the most difficult part of the business; veteran book dealers know that finding material to buy is not a problem. Any dealer who stays in business long enough, will be offered far more books than it would ever be feasible to buy. It is unrealistic for the layperson to think that it is possible to sell every book to a dealer for what might be considered a fair percentage of its value. Mediocre books exist in such profusion that no dealer has to pay a high price for them. They are extremely common and obtainable, relatively speaking, for pennies. A dealer looks for and makes a special effort to buy uncommon items. The dealer bases a wholesale offer on a percentage of the estimated retail value (which can vary a lot from one dealer to another). This can mean as high as 70 percent for extraordinarily high-quality items down to 10 percent for low-interest items. This often results in an overall percentage of 25 percent, although that certainly is not an "official" figure and can vary in either direction. To get the best price on material, especially the better books in top condition, a person trying to wholesale should find out which dealers may be interested in specific types of material. A dealer who specializes in military books, for example, would probably pay more for good books in that field than a dealer who specializes in science fiction, and so on. The dealer who specializes in

certain areas is likely to have a ready list of interested buyers within that specialty. The power of a good mailing list cannot be overemphasized, for a dealer whose ability to sell is enhanced by a healthy clientele can and will buy more material.

Wholesaling to a dealer requires the preparation of a listing with the information needed to make a meaningful bid. This includes the title, author, publisher, book number, condition, and indication of first printing (where possible). Books must be individually graded. Many novice wholesalers mistakenly provide only the most general statement of condition, such as "All books grade from good to mint." This kind of assessment is worthless, because a difference in condition on key books can mean a great difference in the wholesale price and can even determine whether the dealer wants to buy at any price. An earlier section in this book (The Grading of Paperback Books) gives detailed information that should help a lot in this area.

Some people have turned wholesaling into a profitable second income, searching at rummage sales, estate sales and farm auctions for suitable books to offer dealers with whom they are acquainted. In the trade, these people are usually referred to as "scouts." Because they don't have the contacts to sell directly to an interested public, they are content with a smaller, faster profit on their material.

If wholesaling does not appeal to a person with salable books, one alternative is trying to sell directly to the public. This also requires the preparation of a detailed listing, with books individually graded and priced. Lists can be fairly inexpensively printed at one of the many instant printing establishments throughout the country.

This method has several drawbacks. Not having an established mailing list, the seller must try to find names of interested parties wherever possible. Collector publications can be helpful but are still limited, and other dealers do not willingly share the names of their customers. Selling also involves overhead costs, because the seller is, in effect, becoming a dealer. Also, if the list does not reach interested buyers, or enough of them, many books may remain unsold. If successful, however, a higher percentage of value may be realized.

No matter which method is chosen, much trial and error is likely to occur. Experience is not only helpful in the book business, it is essential, and there are no short cuts. For the booklover, however, the learning can often be pleasurable in itself.

## State of the Market

The paperback collector's market has undergone many changes in the past several years.

Continuing publicity about the field, in publications like *The New York Times Book Review* and *The Antiquarian Bookman,* has resulted in more small caches of paperback books being uncovered and more collectors entering the marketplace. However, the value of paperback books is still unknown to many, and the systematic destruction of many older books continues. Many existing paperback exchanges refuse to handle older books because they resell for a considerably lower price, or they sell them but deface them so that they are unsuitable for collecting. The destruction hasn't ended with unimaginative booksellers either. I recall walking into a store in Milwaukee to be greeted by row upon row of gleaming spines, only to discover that each Near Mint copy was missing the back cover! The original owner had torn them off so he could squeeze an extra book or two onto each of his shelves! It was horrifying to find a beautiful copy of Vance's *The Dying Earth* so damaged.

One of the more interesting developments of the past several years was the uncovering of over 6,000 Archer paperbacks in Ohio and Indiana. Most of the books were in prime condition, and although prices slid backward as buyers learned of the quantities available, the desirability of this series was sufficient to keep the drop fairly minimal. The main effect was to stop the oftentimes feverish auctioning of several key titles like *Vice Rackets of Soho.* At slightly more modest levels, Archers remain solid.

Many early science fiction titles have stabilized because the science fiction market has been well established for quite a few years. Collectors and dealers have long since identified the quality items, precluding any major increase on those items. The exceptions to this are in more recent releases. The most sought-after contemporary author is currently Dean Koontz.

Many mystery titles, Cornell Woolrich/William Irish, early Ace titles, early Avons, early Dells, and early Popular Library titles also seem to have stabilized. Information on these titles was widely disseminated and many collectors have satisfied their wants, so that major increases in price have not been warranted.

Odd and unusual small series continued a small increase, whereas interest in paperback digests has greatly increased. Quality digests in the higher condition grades have been bringing record prices at auctions.

The most desired books appear to be those by Jim Thompson, Charles Willeford, and Richard Matheson. Interest in David Goodis, Robert Bloch, and Charles Williams has also been strong.

The most prized publisher/imprint continues to be Bantam Books of Los Angeles.

Record prices were realized on several high-grade copies that appeared in the market.

Interest in the publishers with a sexual emphasis has become very strong. With more information becoming available, some collectors began to avidly buy quality books in upper grades. This interest seems largely involved with cover art, because most of the authors involved are not of consequence. Whether this rapidly growing market starts sliding as quantities of these books appear to meet the demand remains unknown at this time, because the market is so quickly changing in this area.

In most cases westerns and literature continue to be soft markets. Notable exceptions are early Ace Louis L'amour titles and the original Ace D-15 *Junkie* by William Burroughs. These markets have considerable potential yet to be realized. Western collectors have never been as organized as science fiction and mystery collectors, and have shown an aversion to higher pricing. Literature collectors prefer hardcover editions, but this may change as they realize some of the nice items available. Quality westerns and literature remain scarce despite lower prices.

There has also been a greatly increased demand for novels involving juvenile delinquents. The prices of some volumes, especially early Ace singles and later Avons (most notably the movie tie-ins), have gone up dramatically, and there is considerably more interest in them.

One of the more interesting discussions in the paperback collecting field centered on a Canadian publisher. The discovery of an especially nice quality near-complete set of Collins White Circle created a lot of interest when a Canadian dealer stated that in his opinion the publisher was of considerably more interest and worth than had been generally believed. The debate is still unresolved, but the majority of collectors and dealers seem not to have changed their opinion in the matter. *The Price Guide to Paperbacks* has taken a conservative stand on this issue, because greater collectibility and value has yet to be proven to my satisfaction. The inclusion of Collins White Circle in this book (largely thanks to Marvin Sommer) may help resolve the matter as information is now more available.

Investors have begun to enter the collectible paperback market, and this is a sign of strength in the field. Investor interest is largely rooted in key books and publishers, helping to accelerate prices in those areas.

The existence of several stable trade publications has benefited the field of paperback collecting. After several years of subdued interest, the regular dissemination of fresh articles and increased information has given the market a boost. This should continue.

Foreign interest in American paperbacks is also noticeably growing, with some foreign collectors seeming to prefer more modestly priced Very Good copies over more expensive copies. Apparently, many foreign collectors favor a larger quantity of cheaper books still in collectible condition rather than the Near Mint copies actively sought by most American collectors.

Paperback collecting is a hobby with much growth potential. The interest is there, from established and knowledgeable collectors as well as enthusiastic newcomers. The market remains volatile, because so many areas have yet to truly develop. No better example of this from the past several years exists than the books of Charles Willeford. His titles hadn't been considered very special by most, but after some informational articles about him appeared, the prices began to jump rapidly. Many collectors and dealers are cautiously watching to see what author may be next. Meanwhile, the hobby as a whole has gained considerable strength. The very existence of this book should encourage further development, because the availability of dependable information spurs additional collector interest.

# Further Reading

For readers interested in expanding their knowledge of paperback books, the following books should be of interest:

Coser, Lewis A., Kadushin, Charles, and Powell, Walter W. *The Commerce and Culture of Publishing.* Basic Books, Inc. 1982.

Currey, L. W., ed. *Science Fiction and Fantasy Authors: A Bibliography of First Printings of Their Fiction.* G. K. Hall and Company, 1979.

Davis, Kenneth C. *Two-Bit Culture: The Paperbacking of America.* Houghton Mifflin Company, 1984.

Grier, Barbara. *The Lesbian in Literature.* Naiad Press, 1981.

Guiley, Rosemary. *Love Lines: The Romance Reader's Guide to Printed Pleasures.* Facts on File Publications, 1983.

Lyles, William H. *Dell Paperbacks, 1942 to Mid-1962: A Catalog Index.* Greenwood Press, 1983.

Lyles, William H. *Putting Dell on the Map: A History of the Dell Paperbacks.* Greenwood Press, 1983.

Milton, John R. *The Novel of the American West.* University of Nebraska Press, 1980.

O'Brien, Geoffrey. *Hardboiled America.* Van Nostrand Reinhold, 1981.

Schick, Frank L. *The Paperbound Book in America: The History of Paperbacks and Their European Background.* R. R. Bowker Company, 1959.

Schreuders, Piet. *Paperbacks, U.S.A., A Graphic History, 1939–1959.* Blue Dolphin, 1981.

Wells, Stuart W., III. *The Science Fiction and Heroic Fantasy Author Index.* Purple Unicorn Books, 1978.

A number of other periodicals cover collectible paperbacks and specialty aspects of the field. Because these publications sometimes lead an uncertain existence, they are not listed here. However, active publications are listed in my *Book Reference Report,* a frequently updated listing of all related publications currently available, as well as new and available reference books. Any publisher or editor who has a publication of interest to paperback book collectors is qualified to be listed. Fan publications offering informative articles, ads offering to sell books, or ads offering to buy books are of special interest. Readers can obtain a copy of the current *Book Reference Report* by sending $1.00 (stamps are acceptable) or can write to me for further details at the following address: 5813 York Avenue South, Edina, MN 55410.

# PAPERBACKS OF SPECIAL INTEREST

## Louis L'amour: From Pulp Writer to American Bestseller

American popular literature once flourished in a fictional wonderland known as the pulp magazine.

Called pulp magazines, or "pulps," because they were printed on cheap pulpwood paper with uneven and untrimmed pages, these magazines beckoned to the reader with lurid, sensationalistic, and often violent four-color covers that promised (and sometimes delivered) thrills and titillation on every jam-packed page. Some appeared monthly, but many titles appeared twice a month or even weekly. The variety was staggering, with readers able to stalk the darkened waterfront, stride the rolling deck of pirate ships, struggle through steaming jungles to lost cities, gallop across the plains on a wild-eyed bronc, and enter into every manner of adventure known to the imagination. Frank Gruber, in his book *The Pulp Jungle,* put it succinctly when he wrote, "Every avenue of publication was explored. Every type of writing that offered a buck was attempted."

### L'amour's Beginnings in the Western Pulps

The modern pulp magazine originated with the *Argosy* in 1896. At the high point in the mid-1930s, there were over 150 different pulp titles on the newsstands. Some lasted just one issue, and others seemed to go on forever. The western was a part of the earliest pulps, but it wasn't until Street & Smith's *Western Story Magazine* in 1919 that a pulp was totally devoted to the western genre. After 1919, however, the western pulp was a popular mainstay in the field until the demise of pulp magazines in the early 1950s. Some magazines offered a "full-length" novel and an assortment of short stories (often called "novelettes"), some preferred serials, and still others tried to imply greater reading value by cramming their pages with as many short pieces as possible. Although most stories were unrelated, there were many popular series characters, such as The Lone Ranger by Fran Striker; the Lone Ranger's popular imitator, The Masked Rider by Walker A. Tompkins; The Pecos Kid by Daniel Cushman; Pete Rice by Austin Gridley; Hopalong Cassidy, whose new adventures were written by Clarence E. Mulford under the pen name of "Tex Burns"; and a couple of stalwart Texas Rangers, Jim Hatfield by Jackson Cole and Chick Bowdrie by Louis L'amour.

Writers needed to be a hardy lot to survive, with stories being purchased for a mere fraction of a cent per word up to a dizzying three or four cents per word. Frank Gruber related how he had once existed on "tomato soup" at the Automat. The soup consisted of a bowl of hot water, filled with free crackers and ketchup. However, authors possessing either persistence and/or talent saw it as a chance to practice and improve their craft while awaiting better opportunities. Gruber was just one of the popular writers that emerged; others were Edgar Rice Burroughs, Dashiell Hammett, Max Brand (and all the other names of Frederick Faust), Erle Stanley Gardner, Raymond Chandler, H. P. Lovecraft, Robert E. Howard, Ernest Haycox, Steve Fisher, Ray Bradbury, Luke Short, and Horace McCoy.

Western writing seemed to be at the bottom, with hardcover publication of a western typically bringing the author between $100 and $250 in 1939.

As the pulps began to wane, a replacement had been developed with the mass market paperback. Paperbacked books had been around for some time, but in 1939 the format truly began to catch on. As the popularity of paperbacks grew, publishers had to acquire the reprint rights to more and more material, and it was only natural that many looked to the pulps. Many authors began to make the profitable transition from pulp to paperback, but an even greater opportunity developed when Gold Medal launched their series of original stories in paperback, making these paperbacks the genuine first editions.

Until this time, editors and publishers had generally believed that good books always appeared in hardcover first, with paperbacks reserved for reprints or inferior novels. Gold Medal proved that this didn't have to be. Mass market publication offered maximum exposure; the pay wasn't bad, starting out at $2,000 a novel; and there was still the promise of better things for those who attracted a good readership. Several writers soon emerged as top authors, and left their pulp roots behind. Mystery fans found John D. MacDonald with *The Brass Cupcake* in 1950, and western readers had Louis L'amour's *Hondo* in 1953.

## L'amour's Rise to Success

*Hondo* was L'amour's first major success, but contrary to numerous stories circulated over the years, it wasn't his first book publication. Lusk produced a volume of his poems in 1939. The English publisher Worlds Work released *Westward the Tide* in 1950, and Doubleday, in 1951 and 1952, published the four Hopalong Cassidy novels, written by L'amour under the pen name of Tex Burns. *Hondo,* however, was L'amour's real breakthrough; within four years his books had been issued by four hardcover publishers and three publishers—Gold Medal, Ace, and Bantam—were issuing his works in paperback. Initially, Gold Medal and Ace issued his paperback originals while Bantam reprinted his hardcover releases, but before long Bantam became L'amour's publisher of choice and remained so for the rest of his career.

L'amour forged a strong bond with his readership, largely by virtue of the inherent honesty of his writing. His characters, men and women alike, were not one-dimensional, nor were the stories of their lives. They were always real people, however caught up in extraordinary circumstances they might be. In *Louis L'amour: America's Storyteller* (Bantam, 1983) he is quoted as saying, "I write stories of people living out their lives against a background that demanded all they could give and often a bit more." Much as the stories of Zane Grey had decades earlier, L'amour's works realistically depicted the dramas of lifelike characters rising to the challenges of their times.

In 1960, L'amour began a series of novels that would bring him his greatest successes. *The Daybreakers* was the first of eighteen novels about the amazing Sackett clan.

Over the next twenty-eight years, he chronicled the history of this family, of Welsh and English ancestry, and two others, the Chantrys from Ireland and the Talons from France. "As they move westward in different generations," L'amour said, "they brush elbows with each other and intermarry over a period of forty years. In the end all their fates will be woven together and in the course of writing these books I plan to tell the whole story of the West" (*Louis L'amour: America's Storyteller,* Bantam, 1983).

In the 1970s, L'amour's popularity grew even greater, and he earned Bantam's claim of being the "World's Fastest Selling Western Writer," soon replaced by the title, "World's Best-Selling Western Writer." Ace and Gold Medal began to reprint the scarce twenty-year-old novels that fans had been eagerly searching for, and in 1974 L'amour started his incredible string of hardcover best-sellers, first with Saturday Review Press/E. P. Dutton and later with Bantam Books' new hardcover program. New readers discovered what old fans already knew. L'amour was a worthwhile author, no matter what his subject matter. One of his major critical successes was *The Walking Drum,* a novel of twelfth-century merchant caravans.

L'amour's success was not limited to his books. There was a series of successful calendars as well as a series of greeting cards. Over two dozen of his stories were adapted for films, beginning with *East of Sumatra* from Universal in 1953. Perhaps the most famous L'amour film was *Hondo* (1953), starring John Wayne. Early movie work was often frustrating for L'amour. He wrote *The Burning Hills* especially for Wayne, only to see Warner Brothers cast Tab Hunter in the lead role. However, with L'amour's increased popularity came more creative control, and later films, such as *The Cherokee Trail, Down the Long Hills, The Quick and the Dead, The Shadow Riders,* and an exceptional TV miniseries, *The Sacketts,* were true

to his intent. These quality productions served to increase L'amour's legion of fans. A successful series of L'amour stories has also been released on audio cassettes.

Bantam Books acknowledged L'amour's incredible popularity by beginning to issue all of his books in matched editions with quality bindings. In 1983, they celebrated his thirty years of authorship following *Hondo* by publishing a special anniversary booklet, *Louis L'amour: America's Storyteller.*

## Later Years

Bantam Books may have christened 1983 as "L'amour '83," but the year brought L'amour a great deal of frustration. The reading public was stunned by the news that L'amour had neglected to renew many early copyrights. Another publisher began to release unauthorized editions of L'amour stories that had been out of print for more than thirty years. Fans welcomed the chance to read more of L'amour's work, so L'amour responded by rushing out his own authorized editions through Bantam. Fans were further delighted when L'amour tried to remove the economic incentive for other unauthorized editions by releasing still more early stories. The last of his fifteen short story collections, *Lonigan,* appeared in 1988, and more may be forthcoming as some early stories have yet to see republication. By mid-1988 his 101 books had sold nearly 200 million copies.

L'amour was the recipient of many awards. Among them were the Spur Award from the Western Writers of America, and the Theodore Roosevelt Award, presented by the Governor of North Dakota. Perhaps his most prestigious honors were the National Gold Medal, presented by Congress in 1983 for lifetime literary achievement (he is the first and only novelist so honored), and the Medal of Freedom in 1984.

L'amour's early life was as exciting as

many of his own novels. He left home at the age of 15 to begin a boxing career that included 51 wins and 34 KOs. He worked as a barker, fruit picker, fry cook, riveter, elephant handler, miner, lumberjack, longshoreman, deckhand, hay shocker and flume builder. He was shipwrecked in the West Indies and stranded in the Mojave Desert. He operated a machine gun for Chiang Kai-shek in China, sailed a dhow on the Red Sea, stoked coal on a boat to Borneo, and was a tourist guide in Egypt. In World War II he became an officer in the Tank Destroyer and Transportation Corps and was involved in virtually all important engagements in Europe. After the war, he turned to writing, reviewing, and lecturing, and once filled in for Dorothy Kilgallen as a newspaper columnist.

An era ended June 10, 1988, when L'amour, a nonsmoker, died of lung cancer. At the time of his death he was working on a sequel to *The Walking Drum* as well as *The Sackett Companion.* His daughter Angelique has compiled a volume of quotations from her father, *A Trail of Memories.*

L'amour has left a living legacy, for as long as readers want to read exciting stories of the authentic Old West, his books will endure and continue to find new and appreciative fans.

# Edgar Rice Burroughs: Tarzan of the Paperbacks

The popularity of Edgar Rice Burroughs is an amazing phenomenon. Tarzan, and the other characters created by Burroughs, can justifiably claim the distinction of being the most successful imaginative fiction ever written.

The collectibility of Burroughs items is well known. Books, pulp magazines, movie posters, toys, novelties, and associational items of every possible kind are sought by Edgar Rice Burroughs specialists as well as by collectors in fields where Tarzan items are but a small part, such as doll collectors and gum card collectors.

Paperback editions of Edgar Rice Burroughs novels, with their interesting history, offer a wide variety of editions and publishers. Collectors of American paperbacks can choose from many interesting items.

### Early Tarzan Paperbacks

The earliest American paperbound editions are real rarities. The initial Burroughs publisher, A. C. McClurg, issued advance review copies of the first two Tarzan novels in 1914 and 1915. These were the actual hardcover edition sheets bound in pictorial paper covers.

The first American Burroughs pocket-sized paperback is the very rare *Tarzan in the Forbidden City,* published as No. 23 in the short-lived series from Bantam Books of Los Angeles, California (not to be confused with the publisher of the same name based in New York). This series was created by Western Printing and Lithographing for sales in vending machines. Wartime paper shortages are credited for causing the end of the venture, but before that happened, this Tarzan title went through at least four printings. The first three printings had unillustrated covers, varying only in the color of the ink used; the last printing featured an illustrated cover with Bantam Books' odd lamination that went on the front cover and wrapped over the spine, leaving the back cover unlaminated. This paperback series is extremely rare, and both vintage paperback and Burroughs collectors compete fiercely for any available copies of the Tarzan title. It is one of the most valuable paperbacks in existence.

The next Burroughs paperbacks were products of the U.S. Government. The Council of Books in Wartime organized a massive, morale-boosting effort that published and then gave away quality books to U.S. servicemen. These books, known as Armed Services Editions, were often read until they literally fell to pieces, so copies in respectable condition are very scarce today. Among the most desirable titles are No. M-16, *Tarzan of the Apes* (1944), and No. O-22, *The Return of Tarzan* (1945). Although not especially attractive, these two oblong volumes are very rare and very desirable items to collectors.

The Dell Publishing Company had begun publishing Tarzan items in the 1930s, and it was inevitable that Dell would publish some Burroughs paperbacks in their very successful mapback series. Dell paperbacks were produced by Western Printing and Lithographing, who had started to produce a regular Tarzan comic book series for Dell in 1947. Dell's first Burroughs book was *Cave Girl*, published in 1949 as No. 320 in the mapback series. The attractive and colorful cover illustration was by Jean des Vignes, with the detailed back cover map by Ruth Bellew. In 1951, Dell published *Tarzan and the Lost Empire* as No. 536 in the series, with another map by Ruth Bellew. The lurid cover by Robert Stanley was clearly inspired by a famous movie still of the youthful Johnny Weissmuller in *Tarzan the Ape Man* (1932). Considering the great popularity of Tarzan in movies and comics at this time, it is very puzzling that Dell released no further Burroughs volumes.

Another publisher, however, was very interested in publishing and promoting the works of Burroughs in paperback. Donald A. Wollheim was an enterprising young editor at Avon Books and was selecting classic science fiction and fantasy titles for publication as individual volumes or in anthologies like the *Avon Fantasy Reader* series. Wollheim wanted to include Burroughs in the publishing program, and collectors today may drool at the thought of what the lurid artists at Avon could have come up with for a Tarzan title, or a Barsoomian novel, or *The Monster Men*, but it wasn't to be. Wollheim's inquiries to the Burroughs estate were never answered.

### Resurgence of Tarzan Paperbacks

It seems remarkably silly today, but years and years of unavailability of Burroughs' novels ended when a misguided librarian in Downey, California, threatened to remove Tarzan books from the library shelves because, she asserted, Tarzan and Jane had never married and were living in sin. This totally unfounded charge created an enormous groundswell of interest in Burrough's books, but inquiries to his estate still went unanswered. Undaunted, legal researchers determined that the copyrights to more than two dozen Burroughs titles had not been properly renewed, and publishers rushed to publish them. The Burroughs estate disputed the claims, but books were already heading to the newsstands. Dover Books released a number of omnibus volumes, but the books that really fired the Burroughs phenomenon of the 1960s were issued by Ace Books under the editorial direction of Donald Wollheim. He had moved over from Avon but had not forgotten his desire to get Burroughs published in paperback.

Ace's Burroughs volumes were prized by readers and collectors from the very beginning, because they were excellently designed and produced. Each book in Ace's initial series featured a frontispiece by cover artist Frank Frazetta or Roy G. Krenkel, and the colorful covers were the delight of both new and old fans. Frazetta and Krenkel were as ideally suited to illustrate the Burroughs novels of this period as J. Allen St. John had been for the original hardcover editions. The talented Ed Emsh also did one cover, and the effort was so well received that Ace even added a page of congratulatory comments in subsequent releases. All of these books are very collectible today.

Meanwhile, the Burroughs estate, under the new directions of Burroughs' son Hulbert had negotiated a deal with Ballantine Books for the entire Tarzan and Mars series. Ballantine cleverly came up with the gimmick of issuing uniform, numbered volumes (a marketing idea that quickly caught on and became commonplace), and the complete Tarzan and Mars series featured stylish cover art by Richard M. Powers and Robert Abbett, respectively. Demand was so great that twice, in 1963 and 1964, Ballantine had to devote an entire month's publishing schedule to Burroughs books alone.

Ace Books, meanwhile, negotiated with Edgar Rice Burroughs, Inc., and agreed to stop publishing books that competed with the Ballantine editions while gaining the authorization to publish the entire Pellucidar and Venus series as well as most of the miscellaneous novels. Both publishers profited greatly as the Burroughs books became a national obsession, duly reported in *The Wall Street Journal, Time*, and elsewhere. Sales were further fueled by the news that President John F. Kennedy was an avid Burroughs reader.

## Other Collectible Editions

*Life* covered the amazing Burroughs revival in a special report in its November 29, 1963, issue (ironically the same issue covered President Kennedy's tragic death) and revealed a staggering statistic. According to *Life*, in the previous year Burroughs novels had accounted for nearly one-thirtieth of U.S. paperback sales! Of all paperbacks sold in the country, virtually one out of every thirty was a book by Burroughs—a popular-

ity without parallel in American popular fiction. Booksellers responded with special promotions and displays as each month's new releases sold out over and over.

The Burroughs "boom" did naturally taper off in a few years but never died, as Ace and Ballantine have continued to sell new editions successfully ever since.

In 1964, Gold Star Books, a subsidiary of Charlton, attempted to cash in on the Tarzan popularity with the first of a series of five allegedly new Tarzan books. The company's belief, apparently, was that the character of Tarzan was in the public domain, and all five books contained bits and pieces, if not long passages, from novels written by Burroughs. The heirs of the Burroughs estate filed suit and eventually prevailed. Part of the settlement called for an additional one dollar in damages to be paid for each 40-cent Gold Star title still on the stands after an appropriate recall period (as well as each of the four issues of Charlton's equally unauthorized Tarzan comic book). This certainly explains why these items are so difficult to find today.

Subsequent authorized editions are also very interesting. Ballantine published two TV tie-in editions in conjunction with the Tarzan TV series as well as the movie novelization of *Tarzan and the Valley of Gold* by Fritz Lieber in 1966. In 1970, Ace published the true first edition of *Pirate Blood*, written by Burroughs under the pen name of John Tyler Mc-Cullough, but never sold, to fill out its edition of *The Wizard of Venus*. In 1974 Ace published the first complete book edition of *The Oakdale Affair*, which had previously been published in book form missing the final two pages of text. It also published movie tie-in editions of *The Land That Time Forgot, At the Earth's Core*, and *The People That Time Forgot*, and in 1976 added to the list of Burroughs-authored Inner World novels with the publication of *Mahars of Pellucidar* by

*Ace F182, Ace F193, Ace F232.*

*Bantam Books (Los Angeles) 23, Armed Services Edition M16, Dell 536.*

John Eric Holmes. TSR, Inc., also added to the list of Tarzan volumes in 1985, publishing *Tarzan and the Well of Slaves* by Douglas Niles and *Tarzan and the Tower of Diamonds* by Richard Reinsmith.

Collectors also find interesting variety in the English language editions from overseas.

In 1929, Newnes published digest-sized paperback editions of *Tarzan of the Apes*, *The Return of Tarzan*, and *The Son of Tarzan*. These attractive books are very hard to find, even in England.

An extremely colorful and collectible paperback series was published in England by Mark Goulden and distributed by W. H. Allen. Starting in 1949, Goulden published 37 Burroughs titles. His first 25 titles were roughly the size of American digests, and subsequent volumes were a standard paperback size. Beginning with No. 20, books were identified as "A Pinnacle Book" with a Pinnacle logo. The last Pinnacle Burroughs volumes were published in 1958, and 31

years later fans are still collecting them with appreciation.

Four Square Books took over from Pinnacle and issued many colorful and attractive volumes. They continue to do so up to current times, under the New English Library imprint. Dragon Books and Flamingo Books also published very collectible editions.

Burroughs' popularity is such that some publishers have found considerable profit in the publication or creation of similar characters. England was especially active in this area, and the Tarzan-like adventures of Azan, Anjani, Jacare, and others were big sellers in the 1950s but are scarce collector's items today. The imitations do not have the staying power of the original.

Burroughs collectors seem to collect all new editions, especially those with new cover art. The durability of Burroughs' appeal will certainly maintain a demand for new printings, so collectors can look forward to new editions to collect as they complete their collections of the older ones.

# Armed Services Editions

Books can be used as a weapon, both in peace and wartime. In World War II, the United States government sponsored a publishing effort in which books became a very important weapon for democracy. The books were known as Armed Services Editions, and millions of lives were influenced by them.

### The Plan for Armed Services Editions

This incredible publishing venture was initiated through The Council on Books in Wartime,[1,2] which was an organization of

Note: The author gratefully acknowledges the following reference sources:
[1]*A History of the Council on Books in Wartime,* Robert Ballou, 1946.
[2]"Of Armed Services Editions I sing" by Max Wilk, *Publisher's Weekly,* January 2, 1981.

publishers, editors, librarians, and booksellers. In February of 1943, publisher and Council member W. W. Norton made an ambitious proposal to the organization. "It has long been felt," he wrote, "that a major contribution of the industry could properly lie along a new and completely different line, that of making freely available to our armed forces . . . the entertainment, the information, the morale, and even the inspiration, which is in books." The proposal was enthusiastically endorsed and was quickly moved from mere words to positive action.

Philip Van Doren Stern was chosen to manage the operation of Armed Services Editions. He and a small staff of eight were responsible for preparing the volumes, handling all accounts, and attending to all aspects of production—truly a Herculean effort.

The books were carefully selected. Publishers were asked to submit the titles of books that they believed would be suitable. A special committee of six people (later ten) used the publishers' lists to prepare a list of recommendations. Final selection, however, was in the hands of Lt. Col. Ray L. Trautman, of the Special Services Division of the Army, and Isabel DuBois, librarian of the United States Navy. "We tried to select a quality variety of titles from those available," recalled Trautman, "and it was no easy task."[3] That Trautman and DuBois succeeded is obvious from checking the complete listing of Armed Services Editions in this book. Armed Services Editions published more classic titles, in all fields, than any other paperback publisher.

Armed Services Editions contracted with authors in a very simple arrangement. Titles were assigned for a period extending to twelve months after repeal of the Selective Service Act. It was agreed that the books would be kept out of the private sector, so as

to not compete with regular editions of the books. Although the books were to be free to servicemen and servicewomen, a royalty of 1¢-per-copy would be paid to the publisher. This last condition was sometimes set aside. In early 1944, John Steinbeck suggested to his publisher, Viking Press, that they waive future royalties on the edition of his *Cup of Gold* . Viking Press generously agreed. Other publishers and authors, being assured that lower costs would result in the distribution of more books, agreed to waive all or part of their royalty payments.

## Production of the Books

The United States Government financed the publication of the books, which cost between four and seven cents apiece. The government's War Production Board allocated metal for printing plates, and special exemptions were secured to allow for the acquisition of paper. The project managed to work its way through wartime red tape rather quickly, as the Army and Navy were asking for a staggering 50,000 copies each of fifty different titles each month!

The first Armed Services Editions appeared in September of 1943. Thirty titles a month were initially produced, and that amount went up to forty titles a month one year later.

The books were produced in the most economical format possible, a saddle-stitched, oblong edition. The cover dimensions were either $5\frac{1}{2}'' \times 3\frac{7}{8}''$ or $6\frac{1}{2}'' \times 4\frac{1}{2}''$ depending on the length of the book. Text was printed in two columns per page. Eventually, some of the very last titles appeared in a traditional paperback format.

Concerned primarily with content, Stern's staff spent little time in the area of cover art. They were overworked to begin with, and with saleability not a factor there was no need to produce the kind of colorful covers that commercial paperback publishers were using. Covers of Armed Services Editions

[3]Personal conversations and correspondence with the late Lt. Col. Ray L. Trautman.

would either reproduce a small picture of the original hardcover dust jacket illustration or a specially designed, simple mock-up.

Once published, the books were shipped to every corner of the globe where American armed forces were stationed, as well as to military hospitals in the States. In this respect, the G.I. of World War II was far better off than his allied counterparts. One disgruntled British officer reported his dismay after a landing operation in the Pacific Theater. "There was still a lot of fierce fighting all over that island, but the Americans were already unloading beer, cigarettes, and paperback books for their soldiers."

### Results of the Program

The books were definitely a great morale booster. Any G.I. could shut out the all-too-real horrors of war by opening the pages of an Armed Services Edition. The books were highly prized and often read until they literally fell apart. Lt. Col. Trautman toured the European Theater, and recalled that some soldiers in France were willing to pay $10 just to be able to read one. "Mind you, these boys were only being paid $55 a month!" he remembered.[3] An incident in Italy was typical of how many G.I.s felt about their reading material. One G.I. had his nose broken by another, because the offending soul had torn a page out for use as a cigarette paper!

Popular author Edgar Rice Burroughs served as a war correspondent in the Pacific Theater, and received many requests for copies of his books. This was hardly unique, with many other authors receiving requests, and then thanks for the books published in Armed Services Editions. Years after the war had ended, E. B. White told an interviewer, "I still get letters."

Armed Services Editions were an exceptional effort—"one of the great altruistic movements in American publishing, which introduced millions of servicemen and servicewomen to a habit some of them never broke." When the project ended in 1947, 126 million books had been published and distributed, lifting the hearts and spirits of American troops everywhere, and the benefits didn't stop there. As troops returned home, many copies were abandoned. In this way many American authors received exposure to new readers in other lands, spreading the cream of American literature to other parts of the world.

The people involved in the Armed Services Editions project performed a great service and can be proud of their efforts. Their good work deserves the praise of booklovers everywhere.

## Foreign Editions: A Brief Look at Collectible Paperbacks from Other Countries

As I have traveled in other parts of the world, I have noticed that many paperback books from other countries are quite attractive and worthy of notice from American collectors.

Paperback publishers in other countries have as wide a diversity as American publishers. Some have extremely attractive cover designs, and some have beautiful cover art. Others reuse artwork that originally appeared on the covers of American books.

One publisher, Editormex Mexicana, is an excellent example of a publisher that should be of interest to collectors. One of its digest-sized paperbacks reprints a Barye Phillips cover from Fred Brown's *Knock Three-One-Two*, as published by Bantam. Another colorful book features a Robert Maguire cover that I had not seen before.

[3]Personal conversations and correspondence with the late Lt. Col. Ray L. Trautman.

Many popular American authors have been reprinted by foreign publishers. Mysteries, westerns, and science fiction seem to be popular in any language. Of special interest to many publishers are titles that fall into the "black novel" category, and those novels by Jim Thompson, Cornell Woolrich, and others seem to appear in every language.

Some of the most colorful and interesting books I have found have been in Third World countries, where books are often a luxury item. Excellent copies of these books are difficult to find. The print runs are small, and books have to contend with the natural elements to survive because most book stalls are out in the open air.

British paperbacks have attracted American publishers for years, with the science fiction and fantasy titles being very popular. Foreign imprints have yet to gain a foothold in this country, but this may change as collectors see what has been published.

Foreign publications, British and otherwise, are a fun part of book collecting, adding an extra dimension to a booklover's enjoyment of the hobby. They may be obscure and somewhat difficult to obtain, but they are definitely worth the effort.

Following is a listing of foreign language publishers and imprints, as well as listing of selected British publishers and imprints. Neither list should be considered definitive, but they are a start toward identifying the available material. I welcome any additions.

## Foreign Publishers

These publishers are of interest to collectors because of their subject matter or interesting cover art and design.

*Argentina*
Biblioteca de Bolsillo/Libreria Hachette (Buenos Aires)

*Brasil*
Colecao Terramarear/Compahnia Editora Nacional (Sao Paulo)

*Chile*
Coleccion "La Linterna"/Empresa Editora Zig-Zag (Santiago)

*Colombia*
Grandes Aventuras/Editorial Oveja Negra

*Denmark*
Film Bøgerne/E. M. Fallings Bogtrykkeri (Copenhagen)
Fremtids Romanen (Copenhagen)
Hudibras Pop Serie (Copenhagen)
Leopard Bøgerne (Copenhagen)
Planet Bøgerne Serien (Copenhagen)
Pyramide Bøgerne (Copenhagen)
Rekord Serien (Copenhagen)
Winters Forlag (Copenhagen)

*France*
Collection "Le Ballet Des Muses" (Paris)
Série Noire (Paris)

*Germany*
Die Gelben Ullstein-Bucher (Berlin)
Rowohlt (Hamburg)
Tauchnitz (Leipzig)

*Iceland*
Prentsmidja Austurlands (Seydisfirdi)
Utgafufelagid (Reykjavik)
Vasautgafan (Reykjavik)
Verzluna rfelagid/Leynil ogre glusogur (Reykjavik)

*India*
Jaico Books/Jaico Publishing House (Bombay)

*Indonesia*
Alam Budaya (Jakarta)

*Italy*
Ponzoni Editore (Milan)

*Mexico*
Coleccion Caiman/Editorial Diana (Tlacoquemecatl)
Editorial Novaro (Mexico City)
Editormex Mexicana (Mexico City)
Joyas de Bolsillo/Organizacion Editorial Novaro (Mexico City)

*Carcel de Mujeres (Editormex) 1257, 1303, Novelas y Cuentos 6.*

*Editorial Novaro 55, Coleccion Caiman 24, La Linterna 4.*

## Norway
Blad kompaniet A.S./Alle Tiders
    Forfattere (Oslo)
Fredhois Forlag/Norsk Pocket Bok
    (Oslo)
Gyldendals Flaggermusboker (Oslo)
Gyldendals Lommeboker (Oslo)
Naston alforlaget/Ponni-Bok (Oslo)
Roman forlaget/Coyote (Oslo)
Roman forlaget/Krone-Bokene (Oslo)
Zeniths Kriminalromaner/Zenith Forlag
    (Oslo)

## Scotland
M. C. Publications Ltd. (Glasgow)

## Spain
Coleccion Laurel/Editorial Bruguera
    (Barcelona)
Ediciones Favencia (Barcelona)
Libros de Bolsillo/Editorial Argos
    Vergara (Barcelona)
Novela Negra/Ediciones Mepora
    (Madrid)
Novela Negra/Editorial Bruguera
    (Barcelona)

## Sweden
Tiger bockerna (Stockholm)
Zebra Bok (Stockholm)

## British Publishers
W. H. Allen
Archer Press
Arrow Books
Badger Books
Blackie and Sons
T. V. Boardman and Co., Ltd.
Brown-Watson
Camden Publishing Co., Ltd.
Cherry Tree Books
Chevron Books
Chosen Books
Consul Books
Corgi Books
Curtis Warren Ltd.
Digit Books
Dragon Pub. Ltd.
Fontana Books
Four Square Books
Gaywood Press

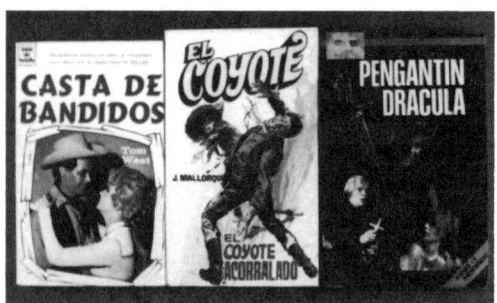

*Editorial Novaro 317, Ediciones Favencia, Alam Budaya.*

*Curtis Books unnumbered, Scion Books unnumbered, Fantasy Library 2.*

Grey Arrow
Gryphon
Guild Books
Hamilton and Co., Ltd.
Harborough Pub. Co.
Hodder and Stoughton
Horror Club
Jarrold's Novels
Jay Books
Jupiter Books
Kaner Publishing Co.
Frederick Muller Ltd.
Newnes Ltd.
Nova Novels
Odhams Press, Ltd.
Paladin Press
Pan Books
Panther Books, Ltd.
Pearson's Novels
Penguin Books, Ltd.
Pilot Press Ltd.
Pinnacle Books

Pocket Books
Red Band Mystery
Roberts and Vintner
Scion Ltd.
Scottie Books
Sexton Blake Library
Sovereign Thrillers
John Spencer and Co.
Sphere Books
Tandem Books, Ltd.
Tempest Publishing Co.
Top Fiction Press
Toucan Novels
Transworld Pub.
Utopian Pub. Ltd.
Viking Books
War Facts Press
WDL/World Distributor's, Ltd.
World-Wide Press
World's Work
Wren Books
Yellow Jacket Books

# PAPERBACK COVER ART

This book contains many illustrations of key books as well as a general sampling of the listed entries in different time periods. Cover art is very important in the field of paperback book collecting. Some books, otherwise of little interest to collectors, become valuable or sought after because a certain artist has done the cover art. Some imprints have become considerably more desirable because of the overall attractiveness of their cover designs and artistic style.

The following sections briefly discuss the artistic styles of major publishers and some of the collectible/significant artists.

## Publishers

**Ace.** Primarily known for attractive double novels, volumes that could be flipped over to reveal a second book with a second cover painting. In early books, the covers of Norman Saunders are very popular. Later books are artistically special for the artwork of Frank Frazetta, Roy Krenkel, Gray Morrow, and Jack Gaughan in their science fiction and fantasy releases.

**Archer.** Known for delicate, colorful, and beautiful covers of sexy women drawn by R. C. M. Heade.

**Avon.** Rooted in pulp magazine. Avon books were like small-size pulps. The covers were lurid, erotic, colorful, cluttered, and brash. Top authors were few, but that doesn't seem to matter because the books are so attractive. The pulp style was replaced in the mid-1950s with a tamer style characterized by some better illustrators.

**Ballantine.** Allowed artists greater freedom. This publisher had many fine illustrators, with Richard Powers' fantasy and science fiction covers a mainstay. They also published numerous quality westerns, many with nice covers by Robert Schulz and Mel Crair.

**Bantam.** Reflected several changing styles. Early covers were classically lovely, then were replaced by some very colorful and attractive pulpish covers. Later books adopted the dark Avati style, which gave way to a lighter style in 1955. Many post-1955 covers are very attractive, especially in the area of genre fiction. Bantam also did a lot of movie tie-ins with photographic covers.

**Beacon.** Outrageously sleazy. The early covers are often like the best of the earlier pulps.

**Belmont.** Currently underappreciated. High-grade early numbers are very attractive, many with jointly designed lettering and artwork.

**Berkley.** Produced many attractive

covers, especially for books packaged with a sleazy twist. Many of the best covers are by Robert Maguire.

**Crest.** Published by Fawcett. As a result, the books resemble Gold Medals. Barye Phillips and Mitch Hooks did many nice covers.

**Dell.** Known for colorful mapbacks. These books featured an airbrushed, expressionistic look on the front and a delicate and detailed map on the back. Books were designed by Western Printing and Lithographing, who also designed and produced the popular Dell comic books and the many Whitman children's books. Later covers became more realistic; Robert Stanley was the major artist. Stanley is popular with today's collectors. A later, design-oriented style was responsible for some of the most attractive books of their time. Collectors are fortunate to have the painstakingly detailed research of Bill Lyles available (see Further Reading), which identifies and credits the cover illustrators through mid-1962.

**Gold Medal.** Colorful, laminated covers. They are very popular with some collectors. Barye Phillips, Mitch Hooks, and James Meese are some of the more prolific and popular illustrators.

**Graphic.** Some good artists and better-than-average cover reproduction. Their often dark and gritty style doesn't excite many collectors today.

**Handi Books.** Started out with bold, dramatic, expressionistic and colorful covers, later replaced by more realistic covers that were also colorful and attractive.

**Harlequin.** King of romance novel publishing. Early covers are the most lurid and colorful ever produced in Canada. They are difficult to find in nice condition partially because of an inferior printing process that rubbed and damaged many copies in the binding process. A lot of historical, science fiction, mystery, and erotic titles are especially attractive. Later romance covers are extremely dull by comparison.

**Hillman.** Progressed (like many other publishers) from lurid, pulpish style to more realistic design.

**Leisure Library.** Like Archer, notable for beautiful erotic covers by R. C. M. Heade.

**Lion.** Many dark, realistic, attractive covers. There are also some very collectible cover illustrations by Robert Maguire, Earle Bergey, and Rudolph Belarski.

**Mentor.** Numerous attractive and colorful covers by Robert Jonas that fail to interest many modern collectors.

**Midwood.** Many sleazy covers; a little more daring than Beacon, a main competitor.

**Monarch.** Colorful and attractive covers. They have only recently begun to attract a lot of collector attention. Robert Maguire did many covers for this publisher.

**Novel Library.** Even more daring and lurid than releases of parent company, Avon.

**Original Novels.** Published sleazy novels. Many had very attractive covers by George Gross and Rudolph Belarski.

**Penguin.** Started out with many unimaginative covers, but moved to bold designs by artists like Robert Jonas. Some reprints have James Avati artwork.

**Perma Books (Pocket Books).** Colorful, attractively designed covers. Like later Pocket Books, these titles seem to be currently underappreciated.

**Perma Books (Perma/Doubleday).** Often rather dull, although some of the historical fiction is very attractive.

**Phantom Books.** Mystery digests with a sleazy angle, starting out with an outrageous bondage cover.

**Pocket Books.** Very classy and stylish early titles. Many artwork/design collectors aren't terribly interested in them. I personally prefer the look of the later, silver-spined titles, but collectors are not overly interested in them either.

**Popular Library.** A favorite with artwork fanciers. Early titles featured a gloomy, expressionistic style executed by H. Lawrence

Hoffman. In 1948 the publisher altered style to one almost identical to its successful pulp magazines. Pulp artists like Rudolph Belarski and Earle Bergey did many lurid and erotic covers between 1948 and 1952, and they set the tone for the rest. Later covers turn to a darker, more realistic look and are considerably less popular with collectors.

**Pyramid.** Favored an erotic emphasis, much like popular men's magazines of the day (which this publisher also produced and sometimes reprinted from them). Later cover artwork is considerably better, with some very nice covers by Robert Maguire.

**Quarter Books.** A special favorite among collectors of erotic digests. Some of the best covers were by George Gross.

**Regency.** A controversial and desirable publisher with some very attractive, expressionistic covers by Leo and Diane Dillon.

**Signet.** Notable for Avati cover art. Piet Schreuders said it best in his book (see Further Reading) when he stated, "Signet Books are paperbacks with covers by Avati." This generalization was philosophically true even if it wasn't literally so. It is quite likely that no other artist has influenced the field as did James Avati (with the possible later exception of Frank Frazetta). Avati's dark, brooding, grimly realistic covers were used extensively and heavily imitated by his own publisher's other artists as well as other publishers. Widespread collecting of his fine work has yet to catch on, possibly because he was so prolific and imitated, as well as because detailed information of his work is not widely available.

**Thrilling Books/Novels.** Resembled pulp magazines. Like the Popular Library pocketbooks, these digest paperbacks looked just like the pulp magazines also published by the company.

**Venus Books.** Publisher of erotic digests; Noted for many beautiful covers. A number of them were by George Gross and Rudolph Belarski.

# Artists

**Abbett, Robert.** Largely worked for Ballantine, Dell, and Avon. He did some excellent westerns and many of the popular Ballantine covers during the Burroughs revival.

**Avati, James.** Considered to be the very best by many of his peers. His skill and style influenced the entire paperback industry.

**Bama, James.** Has specialized in westerns. Much of his most popular and well-known art has appeared in the Doc Savage and Nevada Jim series published by Bantam.

**Belarski, Rudolph.** One of the most highly collected artists today. His flashy, colorful covers had appeared in pulps for many years before he turned to Popular Library's paperback line. His beautiful cover work influenced the publisher's entire publishing program.

**Bergey, Earle.** Another Popular Library pulp artist. His reputation today largely rests on his lurid "steel bra" cover paintings for science fiction pulps. He painted no space lovelies clad in steel bras for the paperbacks, but his colorful covers are nevertheless quite collectible.

**Bode, Vaughn.** Produced few, but very collectible, paperback covers. He is far better known for his *Deadbone Erotica* and *Cheech Wizard* comic strips.

**Cole, L. B.** Primarily a comic book artist. His popularity has helped make the paperbacks he illustrated even more collectible.

**DeSoto, Rafael.** A good artist who is beginning to attract collector attention. He did a lot of covers for Monarch.

**Finlay, Virgil.** A highly collected artist who is primarily known for his fantasy illustrations for pulp magazines.

**Frazetta, Frank.** Most popular paperback cover artist of the 1960s and 1970s. He influenced many other artists and publishers, who tried vainly to imitate him. He is best known for his covers on titles by Edgar Rice Burroughs and Robert E. Howard. His popularity led to enormously successful posters, calendars, art books, portfolios, and magazine covers. The Midwood paperbacks with his interior illustrations are highly sought after. Certainly, he is the most collected paperback cover artist today.

**Gross, George.** Primarily an illustrator of westerns; also produced some highly collectible covers for the erotic digests.

**Heade, R. C. M.** A little-known artist, with well-documented collectibility. His beautiful and erotic covers for English publishers like Archer, Harborough, and R. & L. Locker, as well as for Archer, Leisure Library, and one Checkerbook in America, are all very valuable and collectible today. Fortunately for collectors, many warehouse copies of books with his covers have surfaced in the collector market.

**Hoffman, H. Lawrence.** Very collectible early Popular Library covers (he did most of them). He was prolific and worked for many publishers.

**Hooks, Mitch.** Remains active today. His lighter style helped brighten up Gold Medal in the 1950s. One of his most recent projects was a newly illustrated volume of Sherlock Holmes stories.

**Jonas, Robert.** Abstract artist, best known for dramatic cover designs on early releases from New American Library, publishers of Pelican, Mentor, Penguin, and Signet.

**Jones, Jeff.** Started out as a Frazetta imitator, but later developed an impressive style and following of his own.

**Kinstler, Everett Raymond.** Worked primarily for Avon, both in comics and paperbacks. Today he is best known for his portraits of famous people.

**Krenkel, Roy G.** Known primarily for his fantasy illustrations for Ace's Edgar Rice Burroughs revival. Krenkel's work is ex-

tremely popular. He worked earlier for E. C. Comics and over the years collaborated several times with Frazetta. His line drawings were popular with fans.

**McCarthy, Frank C.** A very popular illustrator, primarily of western titles. His work was collected in a special art book. Today, he devotes himself to gallery art.

**McGinnis, Robert.** The most popular illustrator of the classy, elegant, sexy young woman. He illustrated many successful Mike Shayne novels for Dell, but he has done over 1,500 paperback covers by his own estimate. Some of his most recent work has been for romance novels.

**Maguire, Robert.** For a lot of collectors, the favorite illustrator of beautiful women. He was somewhat prolific, working for Signet, Berkley, Pyramid, Monarch, and others.

**Meltzoff, Stanley.** Magazine illustrator before beginning to do paperback covers. He later shared a studio with James Avati. He specialized in science fiction covers, as did Richard Powers.

**Phillips, Barye.** The primary painter of beautiful women for Gold Medal books and other Fawcett imprints.

**Powers, Richard.** Best known and well-known for abstract science fiction and fantasy covers, especially those done for Ballantine. He was the most popular science fiction and fantasy artist of the 1950s, and he was imitated by others. Tragically, much of his original artwork was destroyed by a flood in the early 1980s.

**Raboy, Mac.** Comic book artist. He did few paperback covers, but his comic book connection helps make those few desirable.

**Ross, A. Leslie.** Longtime illustrator for Street & Smith's *Western Story* pulp magazine. He did many of his distinctive western covers for Popular Library.

**Rozen, George.** Especially noted for lurid and dramatic covers for the popular *Shadow* pulp magazine. He did some attractive covers for Popular Library in the early 1950s.

**Saunders, Norman.** Very popular cover

artist, whose distinctive style was used by many publishers. Some of his most popular work was for the attractive Ace doubles, although his rarest is on the dust jacket for Ballantine 10. Ace D-1 has two of his covers, as do Ace D-25 and Ace D-26, and these books have increased popularity for that reason. He was the first artist to depict Howard's Conan the barbarian (Ace D-36), 15 years before Frazetta.

**Schomburg, Alex.** Especially noted for covers on Captain Marvel comic books and various pulp magazines. He did several cartoonlike covers for Popular Library, including the rare No. 223/*Picture Quiz Book*.

**Smith, Barry.** Known for his work on Marvel's Conan comic book. He did some collectible covers for Freeway Press.

**Stanley, Robert.** Foremost Dell artist during the 1950s. He also illustrated digest pulp magazines like *Zane Grey's Western Magazine*. Perhaps his most popular cover was Dell 536/*Tarzan and the Lost Empire*. He also was the artist involved in the unique example of a paperback cover being repainted for apparent censorship reasons. The book was Dell 542/1542 *Fools Die on Friday*, in which the reprint toned down the original erotic cover. Artwork collectors like to have copies of both versions.

**Steranko, Jim.** Another popular comics artist, who did some excellent covers for pulp magazine reprints of The Shadow and G-8.

**Tossey, Verne.** Painted for many different publishers. His covers for Pocket Books are especially nice, as are his early wraparound covers for Ballantine.

**Wood, Wally.** Started out working for E. C.

Comics along with Frank Frazetta, Roy Krenkel, Al Williamson, Reed Crandall, Jack Davis, and Graham Ingles. He did many popular science fiction comic books for Avon. In the paperback field, he is known for his covers on Avon Fantasy Readers, Galaxy, and Tower titles. His work is very popular and collectible.

**Zuckerberg, Stanley.** Another veteran pulp magazine cover artist. He worked for many publishers, and may be best known for his Signet covers. For part of his career he was favorably compared to James Avati; his work definitely showed the influence Avati had over cover art at that time.

The popularity of a certain cover artist does not necessarily mean that books featuring that artist will be especially valuable, but cover art is definitely a factor affecting price. The practical reality is that it doesn't have a direct relationship, making it easier for those who want to accumulate great paperback illustration art.

The excellent variety and quality of paperback cover art gives the illustrations a unique appeal. The paperbacks of years past, from virtually all publishers, had a charm and dramatic attraction that is generally not present today. In those days, before the research determining which colors sold well and which did not in cover designs, paperbacks often displayed a riot of color and enticement. The books retain a desirability all their own, even when the novels themselves were less than premium quality.

As more information is made available to collectors, interest will surely increase in these early paperbacks.

## You *Can* (Sometimes) Judge a Book by Its Cover: Dust-Jacketed Rarities

Most generalizations prove to be untrue. In the field of paperback book collecting, however, one generalization has no exception:

Paperback books with dust jackets are scarce and very valuable.

In U.S. publishing, dust-jacketed paperback books are rare oddities. They generally came into existence when a publisher decided to repackage an older book with numerous unsold copies on hand. In the case of Bantam Books, they also repackaged several overstocked books printed by other publishers. These repackagings often brought a distinct change in cover art, as though someone felt that the art on the earlier cover was responsible for the lack of sales. Sometimes the new art was designed to create a motion picture tie-in. In the case of the Canadian publisher Newsstand Library, dust jackets with milder art styles were placed on books with sexually oriented covers in order to overcome objections from dealers and distributors.

Dust-jacketed books hold a special fascination for collectors. They are odd, uncommon (relatively very few were produced), and attractive. Completist collectors often find these to be the last items on their want lists, for the fragile, paper dust wrappers were not designed for long-term survival, much less the collecting whims of people 20 to 40 years later.

The following is a listing of the paperback books issued in dust jacket identified to date:

Any additions to this list will be gratefully received and acknowledged.

# USING THE *PRICE GUIDE* TO PAPERBACK BOOKS

## The Format of Listings

The purpose of this book is to list all mass market paperback books published in the United States between 1939 and 1959. Many significant publishers are listed complete through 1965. Selected Canadian, pre-1939, and post-1959 books are included also, based on collector interest. Over 30,000 entries are presented in a manner designed to provide easy access to all vital information.

### Imprints, Code Numbers, and Titles

Books are listed under their imprint name, which is the identifiable series title. Imprints appear in alphabetical order. Where there is no identifiable series title, entries can be found under the publisher name (enclosed in parentheses). The publishing company is always identified below the series title and is sometimes followed by an informational note. For example, most paperbacks come in one of two sizes, but within the paperback collecting field there are many books known as "digests" because their outer dimensions resemble those of the popular *Reader's Digest*. Such size distinctions are noted, inasmuch as some collectors have a preference for digests whereas other collectors do not like them.

The vast majority of collectible paperbacks were originally published with numer-ic identification codes provided by the publisher for any given series. This Guide organizes titles according to these imprint code numbers. Where such numbers do not exist, the code "nn" has been substituted. Rather than organizing by title or author, the present listing system was chosen in order to assist those many collectors interested in obtaining all titles by particular publishers.

### Identification of Authors

The author's name, if known, appears immediately after the title. Books written by authors under other names are indicated in many cases by giving the author's real name in parentheses after the pseudonym. This has become an area of great interest, as collectors have discovered how often authors' humble beginnings included writing under pen names. Collectors of Louis L'amour, for example, want and need to know about his use of the pen names Jim Mayo and Tex Burns (the former, but not the latter, was used in early paperbacks). Information is only given when the facts are verifiable, and not merely surmised. For example, it is known that the popular mystery writers Lawrence Block and Donald Westlake used, respectively, the house names of Sheldon Lord and Alan Marshall. Just exactly which books were written by them, and which by other house authors, is not known. The publishing house kept no accurate, available records, so complete information is not available.

## Other Useful Information

### FIRST EDITIONS

In many cases, data identify books that are either original or first editions. A first edition is the first appearance of a novel or collection of short stories in book form. An original edition is the first appearance of a novel or collection of short stories in any form. An original edition is always a first edition. The identifications of first and original editions are not complete, although they are nearly complete for significant books and authors.

Publication dates are included for each identified first or original edition. Dates are also noted periodically for other entries, as a means of providing a time reference for all entries. Unfortunately, numbering sequences and publication dates do not always follow a neat pattern, and in some cases a book numbered before another will actually have been published afterward. It is worth correcting a major mistake committed by many people. The copyright date of a book is *not* the same as the publication date, because books usually do not require a new copyright each time they are published. Where a book's existence is questionable or where only certain editions have been seen by collectors, that information has also been included.

Additional informational notes include identification of movie and TV tie-in editions, where known, because a number of collectors have a special interest in them.

### COVER ART

Because cover art is of major importance to so many, selected cover artists are identified, where such knowledge is available,

based on interest in them within the collector's market. Unfortunately, such information is often limited because many publishers did not identify their artists and kept poor records. Fuller information in this area is being sought and collected for the next edition of this book. Artists, including the following, are identified in the text with a "c-" followed by the last name of the particular artist, where such information is known:

Robert K. Abbett
Rudolph Belarski
Earle K. Bergey
Vaughn Bode
L. B. Cole
Rafael De Soto
Ed Emsh
Virgil Finlay
Frank Frazetta
George Gross
R. C. M. Heade
Jeff Jones
Everett Raymond Kinstler
Roy G. Krenkel
Robert Maguire
Richard G. Powers
Mac Raboy
Norman B. Saunders
Alex Schomburg
Barry Smith
James Steranko
Wally Wood

## Pricing Codes

Each book is priced in three different condition grades—*Very Good* (V/Good), Fine, and *Near Mint* (N/Mint). These grades were chosen because, although the majority of books commonly available may be in fair, good, or very good condition, books in the upper condition grades receive the greatest interest from collectors. Many collectors are not interested in any but the rarest books in lesser condition. It is a mistake to think that the middle price—Fine—reflects the value of an average copy because it most certainly does not. The prices provide a guiding reference, an educated opinion of the average current retail value within the collector's marketplace. Prices may fluctuate higher or lower depending on the market in which they are offered. These prices are not quotations of the prices at which private parties can sell their books, unless they have access to an active, buying audience. Prices are for first printings, with the single exception of paperbacks in dust jackets. Dust-jacketed books were often reissues, and it is the dust jacket, not the book, that holds the collector value. Lesser condition copies of such books can still be salable, with a good copy worth approximately half that of a very good copy, and a fair copy perhaps half again that of a good copy. Lesser copies are in considerably less demand, and many dealers do not bother with them. Poor copies have virtually no value.

## Genre Codes

Many entries also include a one- or two-letter code in the last column. This is a genre classification to identify books that belong to a particular area within the broad scope of the book world. Some collectors limit themselves to a particular genre. The genre codes are:

A    Adventure
B    Biography
C    Combat (20th century)
E    Esoteric(a)/Exotic(a)/Exploitation. All these terms have been used by publishers and collectors to identify books that exploit a sexual emphasis. Such books should not be confused with pornographic novels, which contain explicit sexual material.
F    Fantasy
H    Humor
HO   Horror
JD   Juvenile Delinquency
M    Mystery
NF   Nonfiction
R    Romance
S    Sports
SF   Science Fiction
UF   Unidentified Flying Object
W    Western
X    Explicit Sexual Content

Some books are classifiable in more than one genre. In such cases the code shown indicates the genre of current greater interest among collectors.

# Inquiries and Further Information

Updated editions of the *Price Guide to Paperback Books* are planned. At the time you are reading this, work has already begun on the next edition. Because thoughtful, constructive comments increase the accuracy and usefulness of this book, I invite all such comments and ask that they be sent to me at the following address: 5813 York Avenue South, Edina, Minnesota, 55410. The volume of mail makes it necessary to suggest including a stamped, self-addressed envelope with your letter if you desire a reply.

The following books are missing from or are incomplete in the current edition. Information on these books is needed for the next edition. Any other additions and corrections are welcome. If available, a cover photo or photo copy is very helpful, along with the publishing date, and other information, often found on the title or copyright pages. Everyone who contributes data will be credited in the next edition.

## Information Missing and Needed
Cameo 358, 363, 364-author, 366
Carnival 944, 946, 947

I am also conducting a survey of readers, collectors, and dealers to determine which other publishers should be included in future editions and which publishers and imprints should be deleted. The very scope of the field means that some might have to be dropped in order to accommodate significant new editions, unless a two-volume set becomes feasible.

To increase pricing accuracy, I am considering the creation of a Board of Advisors to assist in refining the prices for future editions. I encourage active dealers and collectors who can contribute the necessary time and information to write for further details.

# THE
## PAPERBACK
# LISTINGS

# ACE A-SERIES
## Ace Books, Inc.

| | | V/Good | Fine | N/Mint | |
|---|---|---|---|---|---|
| A1 | The Shame and the Glory–Brigitte von Tessin; aka The Bastard | .50 | 1.00 | 1.50 | A |
| A2 | Sex and the Law–Morris Ploscowe | .50 | 1.00 | 1.50 | NF |
| A3 | Limbo–Bernard Wolfe; 1963 | 1.25 | 2.50 | 3.75 | SF |
| A4 | The Fellowship of the Ring–J.R.R. Tolkien; 1965. Note: Only paperback publication of the original hard cover text (other paperback editions were revised) | 3.00 | 6.00 | 9.00 | F |
| A5 | The Two Towers–J.R.R. Tolkien; 1965. Note: Only paperback publication of the original hard cover text (other paperback editions were revised) | 3.00 | 6.00 | 9.00 | F |
| A6 | The Return of the King–J.R.R. Tolkien; 1965. Note: Only paperback publication of the original hard cover text (other paperback editions were revised) | 3.00 | 6.00 | 9.00 | F |
| A7 | The World's Best Contemporary Short Stories | .50 | 1.00 | 1.50 | |
| A8 | Silverlock–John Myers Myers; 1966 | 2.50 | 5.00 | 7.50 | SF |
| A9 | Gold in California!–Todhunter Ballard | .75 | 1.50 | 2.25 | W |
| A10 | World's Best Science Fiction: 1967–ed. Terry Carr & Donald A. Wollheim | 1.00 | 2.00 | 3.00 | SF |
| A11 | Flying Saucers on the Attack–Harold T. Wilkins | .50 | 1.00 | 1.50 | UF |
| A12 | New Worlds of Fantasy–ed. Terry Carr | 1.00 | 2.00 | 3.00 | SF |
| A13 | The Witches of Karres–James H. Schmitz | 2.00 | 4.00 | 6.00 | SF |
| A14 | Yellow Is for Fear and Other Stories–Dorothy Eden; 1968 | .50 | 1.00 | 1.50 | R |
| A15 | World's Best Science Fiction: 1968–eds. Terry Carr & Donald A. Wollheim | 1.00 | 2.00 | 3.00 | SF |
| A16 | Rite of Passage–Alexei Panshin; 1968 | 1.50 | 3.00 | 4.50 | SF |
| A17 | The Best from Fantasy and Science Fiction, 14th Series–ed. Avram Davidson | 1.00 | 2.00 | 3.00 | SF |
| A18 | A Killing for the Hawks–Frederick E. Smith | .75 | 1.50 | 2.25 | C |
| A19 | The Ring–Piers Anthony & Robert Margroff | 1.00 | 2.00 | 3.00 | SF |
| A20 | Cookbook for Beginners–Dorothy Malone | .75 | 1.50 | 2.25 | NF |
| A21 | Eggs I Have Known–Corinne Griffith | .75 | 1.50 | 2.25 | NF |
| A22 | Cooking by the Clock–Jenn Mattimore & Clarke Mattimore | .75 | 1.50 | 2.25 | NF |
| A24 | Winged Warfare–Lt. Col. William A. Bishop | 1.00 | 2.00 | 3.00 | NF |
| A25 | The Outlaw of Torn–Edgar Rice Burroughs; c-Krenkel | 2.00 | 4.00 | 6.00 | A |
| A26 | How to Get a Good Night's Sleep–Dr. Peter J. Steincrohn; 1968 | .50 | 1.00 | 1.50 | NF |
| A27 | The Great Radio Heroes–Jim Harmon | 1.50 | 3.00 | 4.50 | NF |
| A28 | Ace of Aces–Capt. René Fonck | 1.00 | 2.00 | 3.00 | NF |
| A29 | A Torrent of Faces–James Blish & Norman L. Knight; 1968 | 1.25 | 2.50 | 3.75 | SF |

*Ace A4, Ace D1, Ace D9.*

| | | V/Good | Fine | N/Mint | |
|---|---|---|---|---|---|
| A30 | Relief Without Drugs–Ainslie Meares, MD; 1968 | .50 | 1.00 | 1.50 | NF |
| A130 | Note: This number exists as 130 in the K series and is listed there. | | | | |

# ACE D/S/G-SERIES
## Ace Books, Inc./A.A. Wynn, Inc.

| | | V/Good | Fine | N/Mint | |
|---|---|---|---|---|---|
| D1 | The Grinning Gismo–Samuel W. Taylor; c-Saunders | 50.00 | 100.00 | 150.00 | M |
| | Too Hot for Hell–Keith Vining; c-Saunders; orig. 1952 | | | | M |
| D2 | Bad Man's Return–W. Colt MacDonald | 5.00 | 10.00 | 15.00 | W |
| | Bloody Hoofs–J. Edward Leithead; c-Saunders (?); orig. 1952 | | | | W |
| D3 | Twist the Knife Slowly–Kate Clugston; aka A Murderer in the House | 6.00 | 12.00 | 18.00 | M |
| | The Big Fix–Mel Colton; orig. 1952 | | | | M |
| D4 | Rimrock Rider–Walter A. Tompkins; c-Saunders | 5.00 | 10.00 | 15.00 | W |
| | Massacre at White River–L.B. Patten; orig. 1952 | | | | W |
| D5 | Drawn to Evil–Harry Whittington; orig. 1952, c-Saunders | 7.50 | 15.00 | 22.50 | M |
| | The Scarlet Spade–Eaton K. Goldthwaite; aka Cut for Partners; c-Saunders | | | | M |
| D6 | The Branded Lawman–William E. Vance | 5.00 | 10.00 | 15.00 | W |
| | Plunder Valley–Nelson Nye | | | | W |
| D7 | So Dead My Love!–Harry Whittington | 5.00 | 10.00 | 15.00 | M |
| | I, the Executioner–Stephen Ransome; 1953 | | | | M |
| D8 | Terror Rides the Range–Alan K. Echols; orig. 1953 | 5.00 | 10.00 | 15.00 | W |
| | Gunsmoke Gold–Tom West; c-Saunders | | | | W |
| D9 | Decoy–Michael Morgan; orig. 1953 | 6.00 | 12.00 | 18.00 | M |
| | If I Die before I Wake–Sherwood King | | | | M |
| D10 | The Brazos Firebrand–Leslie Scott; orig. 1953; c-Saunders (?) | 5.00 | 10.00 | 15.00 | W |
| | Hell on Hoofs–Gordon Young; aka Quarter Horse; c-Ralph Smith | | | | W |
| D11 | Mrs. Homicide–Day Keene; orig. 1953; c-Saunders | 6.00 | 12.00 | 18.00 | M |
| | Dead Ahead–William L. Stuart; aka The Dead Lie Still | | | | M |
| D12 | The Man from Boot Hill–Dean Owen; orig. 1953 | 5.00 | 10.00 | 15.00 | W |
| | Wild Horse Range–Dan J. Stevens | | | | W |
| D13 | The Judas Goat–Leslie Edgley | 37.50 | 75.00 | 112.50 | M |
| | Cry Plague!–Theodore S. Drachman | | | | SF |
| D14 | Maverick with a Star–George Kilrain; c-Saunders | 5.00 | 10.00 | 15.00 | W |
| | Vultures on Horseback–Paul Evan Lehman | | | | W |
| D15 | Junkie–William Lee (William Burroughs); orig. 1953 | 70.00 | 140.00 | 210.00 | E |
| | Narcotic Agent–Maurice Helbrant | | | | E |
| D16 | Germinie–Jules de Goncourt & Edmond de Goncourt; c-Saunders | 5.00 | 10.00 | 15.00 | |
| | Crime d'Amour–Paul Bourget | | | | |
| D17 | Shakedown–Roney Scott (William Campbell Gault); orig. 1953; c-Saunders | 7.50 | 15.00 | 22.50 | M |
| | The Darkness Within–Walter Ericson (Howard Fast); aka Fallen Angel | | | | M |
| D18 | The Lead Slingers–J. Edward Leithead; orig. 1953; c-Saunders | 5.00 | 10.00 | 15.00 | W |
| | The Hanging Hills–Brad Ward (Samuel Peeples) | | | | W |
| D19 | Fear No More–Leslie Edgley | 5.00 | 10.00 | 15.00 | M |
| | Never Kill a Cop!–Mel Colton | | | | M |
| D20 | The Desperate Code–Roy Manning; aka Six-Gun Sheriff | 5.00 | 10.00 | 15.00 | W |
| | Double-Cross Brand–Alan K. Echols; orig. 1953 | | | | W |
| D21 | Nightshade–John N. Makris; orig. 1953; c-Saunders (?) | 6.00 | 12.00 | 18.00 | M |
| | High Stakes–Lester Dent; aka Dead at the Take-Off | | | | M |

ACE D/S/G-SERIES, *continued*

| | | V/Good | Fine | N/Mint | |
|---|---|---|---|---|---|
| D22 | Badlands Masquerader–Leslie Scott; orig. 1953 | 5.00 | 10.00 | 15.00 | W |
| | Mavericks of the Plains–Bliss Lomax | | | | W |
| D23 | Bring Back Her Body–Stuart Brock; orig. 1953 | 5.00 | 10.00 | 15.00 | M |
| | Passing Strange–Richard Sale | | | | M |
| D24 | Vulture Valley–Tom West | 5.00 | 10.00 | 15.00 | W |
| | The Sidewinders–John Callahan; orig. 1953 | | | | W |
| D25 | The Code of the Wooster–P.G. Wodehouse; c-Saunders | 6.00 | 12.00 | 18.00 | H |
| | Quick Service–P.G. Wodehouse; c-Saunders | | | | H |
| D26 | The Impotent General–Charles Pettit; c-Saunders | 6.00 | 12.00 | 18.00 | E |
| | Love in a Junk & Other Exotic Tales–Harold Acton & Lee Yi-Hsieh; aka Four Cautionary Tales, c-Saunders | | | | E |
| D27 | The Fingered Man–Bruno Fischer; c-Saunders | 5.00 | 10.00 | 15.00 | M |
| | Double Take–Mel Colton | | | | M |
| D28 | Gunsmoke Kingdom–Paul Evan; c-Saunders (?) | 5.00 | 10.00 | 15.00 | W |
| | Avenger from Nowhere–Wiliam E. Vance; orig. 1953 | | | | W |
| D29 | Dead Man Friday–J.F. Hutton; aka Too Good to Be True | 5.00 | 10.00 | 15.00 | M |
| | The Fast Buck–Ross Laurence; orig. 1953 | | | | M |
| D30 | Johnny Sundance–Brad Ward (Samuel Peeples); c-Saunders (?) | 5.00 | 10.00 | 15.00 | W |
| | South to Santa Fe–George Kilrain; orig. 1953 | | | | W |
| D31 | Universe Maker–A.E. Van Vogt; orig. 1953 | 5.00 | 10.00 | 15.00 | SF |
| | The World of Null-A–A.A. Van Vogt | | | | SF |
| D32 | Cookbook for Beginners–Dorothy Malone; aka Cookbook for Brides | 4.00 | 8.00 | 12.00 | NF |
| D33 | Murder by the Pack–Carl G. Hodges; orig. 1953; c-Saunders | 5.00 | 10.00 | 15.00 | M |
| | About Face–Frank Kane | | | | M |
| D34 | Hellion's Hole–Ken Murray; orig. 1953 | 5.00 | 10.00 | 15.00 | W |
| | Feud in Piney Flats–Ken Murray; orig. 1953; c-Saunders | | | | W |
| D35 | Open All Night–Jack Houston; orig. 1953 | 5.00 | 10.00 | 15.00 | E |
| | The Marina Street Girls–Rae Loomis | | | | E |
| D36 | Conan the Conqueror–Robert E. Howard; aka Hour of the Dragon; c-Saunders | 12.50 | 25.00 | 37.50 | SF |
| | The Sword of Rhiannon–Leigh Brackett; orig. 1953 | | | | SF |
| D37 | The Drowning Wire–Marvin Claire | 5.00 | 10.00 | 15.00 | M |
| | Departure Delayed–Will Oursler | | | | M |
| D38 | Showdown at Yellow Butte–Jim Mayo; orig. 1953 | 25.00 | 50.00 | 75.00 | W |
| | Outlaw River–Bliss Lomax; c-Saunders | | | | W |
| D39 | Quantrill's Raiders–Frank Gruber; orig. 1954; c-Saunders | 5.00 | 10.00 | 15.00 | W |
| | Rebel Road–Frank Gruber; aka Outlaw | | | | W |
| D40 | Waltz into Darkness–William Irish | 6.00 | 12.00 | 18.00 | M |
| | Scylla–Malden Grange Bishop; orig. 1954 | | | | M |
| D41 | Mourning After–Thomas B. Dewey | 5.00 | 10.00 | 15.00 | M |
| | Death House Doll–Day Keene; orig. 1954 | | | | M |
| D42 | One against a Bullet Horde–Walker A. Tompkins; c-Saunders (?) | 5.00 | 10.00 | 15.00 | W |
| | Law for Tombstone–Charles M. (Chuck) Martin | | | | W |
| D43 | Salome, My First 2,000 Years of Love–George Sylvester Viereck & Paul Eldridge | 5.00 | 10.00 | 15.00 | SF |
| D44 | Sentinels of Space–Eric Frank Russell | 5.00 | 10.00 | 15.00 | SF |
| | The Ultimate Invader–Don Wollheim; orig. 1954 | | | | SF |
| D45 | Death Hitches a Ride–Martin L. Weiss | 5.00 | 10.00 | 15.00 | M |
| | Tracked Down–Leslie Edgley; aka The Angry Heat | | | | M |
| D46 | Vengeance Valley–Roy Manning | 5.00 | 10.00 | 15.00 | W |
| | Law from Back Beyond–Chuck Martin; orig. 1954, c-Saunders (?) | | | | W |
| D47 | Kiss and Kill–Joe Barry; orig. 1954 | 5.00 | 10.00 | 15.00 | M |

| | | V/Good | Fine | N/Mint | |
|---|---|---|---|---|---|
| | On the Hook–Richard Powell; aka Shark River | | | | M |
| D48 | Utah Blaine–Jim Mayo; orig. 1954 | 25.00 | 50.00 | 75.00 | W |
| | Desert Showdown–Brad Ward; aka The Spell of the Desert; c-Saunders | | | | W |
| D49 | The Golden Temptress–Charles Grayson; aka The Broken Gate | 6.00 | 12.00 | 18.00 | E |
| | Tongking!–Dan Cushman; orig. 1954 | | | | M |
| D50 | The Mating Call–Wilene Shaw | 5.00 | 10.00 | 15.00 | E |
| | Bad 'Un–Ozro Grant | | | | E |
| D51 | Over the Edge–Lawrence Treat | 5.00 | 10.00 | 15.00 | M |
| | Switcheroo–Emmett McDowell; orig. 1954 | | | | M |
| D52 | Crossfire Trail–Louis L'amour; orig. 1954 | 25.00 | 50.00 | 75.00 | W |
| | Boomtown Buccaneers–William Colt MacDonald | | | | W |
| D53 | Gateway to Elsewhere–Murray Leinster; orig. 1954 | 3.00 | 6.00 | 9.00 | SF |
| | The Weapon Shops of Isher–A.E. Van Vogt | | | | SF |
| S54 | The Naked Fear–Carl Offord; orig. 1954 | 3.00 | 6.00 | 9.00 | E |
| D55 | Kill-box–Michael Stark; aka Run for Your Life | 4.50 | 9.00 | 13.50 | M |
| | The Tobacco Auction Murders–Robert Turner; orig. 1954 | | | | M |
| D56 | Ambush at Coffin Canyon–Bliss Lomax | 4.50 | 9.00 | 13.50 | W |
| | Hellbent for a Hangrope–Clement Hardin | | | | W |
| D57 | Treachery in Trieste–Charles L. Leonard | 4.50 | 9.00 | 13.50 | A |
| | Counterspy Express–A.S. Fleischman; orig. 1954 | | | | A |
| S58 | Vice, Inc.–Joachim Joesten | 3.00 | 6.00 | 9.00 | F |
| D59 | Spiderweb–Robert Bloch; orig. 1954 | 7.50 | 15.00 | 22.50 | M |
| | The Corpse in My Bed–David Alexander; aka Most Men Don't Kill | | | | M |
| S60 | The Marshal of Medicine Bend–Brad Ward | 3.00 | 6.00 | 9.00 | W |
| D61 | Cosmic Manhunt–L. Sprague de Camp; 1st ed. 1954 | 4.50 | 9.00 | 13.50 | SF |
| | Ring Around the Sun–Clifford D. Simak | | | | SF |
| D62 | Ken Murray's Giant Joke Book–Ken Murray | 4.00 | 8.00 | 12.00 | H |
| D63 | You'll Die Next–Harry Whittington; orig. 1954 | 5.00 | 10.00 | 15.00 | M |
| | Drag the Dark–Frederick C. Davis | | | | M |
| D64 | Bullets Don't Bluff–Paul Evan Lehman; orig. 1954 | 4.50 | 9.00 | 13.50 | W |
| | Under the Mesa Rim–Chandler Whipple | | | | W |
| D65 | Tornado–Juanita Osborne; orig. 1954 | 5.00 | 10.00 | 15.00 | E |
| | Night Fire–Edward Kimbrough | | | | E |
| S66 | Return to Tomorrow–L. Ron Hubbard | 6.00 | 12.00 | 18.00 | SF |
| S67 | The Will to Kill–Robert Bloch; orig. 1954 | 25.00 | 50.00 | 75.00 | M |
| D68 | Deadwood–Walker A. Tompkins | 4.50 | 9.00 | 13.50 | W |
| | Bullet Brand Empire–William Hopson | | | | W |
| D69 | Daybreak–2250 A.D.–Andre Norton; aka Star Man's Son | 4.00 | 8.00 | 12.00 | SF |
| | Beyond Earth's Gate–C.W. Moore & Lewis Padgett | | | | |
| S70 | Luisita–Rae Loomis | 3.00 | 6.00 | 9.00 | E |
| D71 | Drop Dead–Gordon Ashe | 4.50 | 9.00 | 13.50 | M |
| | The Case of the Hated Senator–Margaret Scherf; aka Dead: Senate Office Building | | | | M |
| D72 | Nightrider Deputy–Ralph R. Perry | 3.00 | 6.00 | 9.00 | W |
| | The Devil's Saddle–Norman A. Fox | | | | W |
| D73 | Adventures in the Far Future–D.A. Wollheim | 3.50 | 7.00 | 10.50 | SF |
| | Tales of Outer Space–Donald A. Wollheim | | | | SF |
| S74 | Heat Lightning–Wilene Shaw | 2.50 | 5.00 | 7.50 | E |
| S75 | Cartoon Annual–ed. Ralph Shikes | 4.50 | 9.00 | 13.50 | H |
| S76 | Shame–Emile Zola | 2.50 | 5.00 | 7.50 | E |
| D77 | Catch the Brass Ring–Stephen Marlow (Milton Lesser) | 10.00 | 20.00 | 30.00 | M |
| | Stranger at Home–George Sanders (Leigh Brackett) | | | | M |
| D78 | Lobo Legacy–Tom West | 3.00 | 6.00 | 9.00 | W |
| | The One-Shot Kid–Nelson Nye | | | | W |

| | | V/Good | Fine | N/Mint | |
|---|---|---|---|---|---|

ACE D/S/G-SERIES, *continued*

| | | V/Good | Fine | N/Mint | |
|---|---|---|---|---|---|
| D79 | The Brain Stealers–Murray Leinster | 3.00 | 6.00 | 9.00 | SF |
| | Atta–Francis Rufus Bellamy | | | | SF |
| S80 | The Fear and the Guilt–Wilene Shaw | 2.50 | 5.00 | 7.50 | E |
| D81 | Too Many Sinners–Sheldon Stark | 3.00 | 6.00 | 9.00 | M |
| | Liability Limited–John A. Saxon | | | | M |
| S82 | Kilkenny–Louis L'Amour | 40.00 | 80.00 | 120.00 | W |
| S83 | The Steel Noose–Arnold Drake | 2.50 | 5.00 | 7.50 | E |
| D84 | An Earth Gone Mad–Roger Dec | 2.50 | 5.00 | 7.50 | SF |
| | The Rebellious Stars–Isaac Asimov; aka The Stars, Like Dust | | | | SF |
| S85 | The Bachelor's Widow–Maurice Dekobra | 2.50 | 5.00 | 7.50 | E |
| D86 | Tangled Trail–Roy Manning | 2.50 | 5.00 | 7.50 | W |
| | Sentinel Peak–Richard Brister | | | | W |
| S87 | Why Am I So Beat–Nolan Miller; 1955 | 2.00 | 4.00 | 6.00 | E |
| D88 | The 7-Day System for Gaining Self-Confidence, Popularity and Financial Success–Dexter Davis | 2.00 | 4.00 | 6.00 | NF |
| D89 | Death Watch–Ruth Wilson & Alexander Wilson; aka The Town Is Full of Rumors | 2.50 | 5.00 | 7.50 | M |
| | Turn Left for Murder–Stephen Marlowe | | | | W |
| S90 | The Chaos Fighters–Robert Moore Williams | 2.50 | 5.00 | 7.50 | SF |
| S91 | End of the Line–Stanley Baron | 2.50 | 5.00 | 7.50 | E |
| D92 | The Drifter–Burt Arthur | 2.50 | 5.00 | 7.50 | W |
| | The Longhorn Trail–Richard Wormser & Dan Gordon | | | | W |
| S93 | Modern Casanovas Handbook–Horace T. Elmo | 3.00 | 6.00 | 9.00 | H |
| D94 | One against Eternity–A.E. Van Vogt; aka The Weapon Makers | 2.50 | 5.00 | 7.50 | SF |
| | The Other Side of Here–Murray Leinster | | | | SF |
| S95 | The Naked Jungle–Harry Whittington; orig. 1955 | 2.50 | 5.00 | 7.50 | M |
| D96 | The Last Planet–Andre Norton; aka Star Rangers | 2.50 | 5.00 | 7.50 | SF |
| | A Man Obsessed–Alan E. Nourse | | | | SF |
| D96 | The Last Planet–Andre Norton; special ed. | 2.50 | 5.00 | 7.50 | SF |
| S97 | Death Has 2 Faces–Norman Herries | 2.00 | 4.00 | 6.00 | M |
| D98 | The Lobo Horseman–Samuel Peeples | 2.50 | 5.00 | 7.50 | W |
| | The Texas Tornado–Nelson Nye; aka Rustler's Roost | | | | W |
| D99 | The Galactic Breed–Leigh Brackett; aka The Starmen | 2.50 | 5.00 | 7.50 | SF |
| | Conquest of the Space Sea–Robert Moore Williams | | | | SF |
| S100 | The Caves–Henry Lewis Nixon | 2.00 | 4.00 | 6.00 | E |
| D101 | Knock 'Em Dead–Jack Karney | 2.50 | 5.00 | 7.50 | M |
| | Point of No Escape–Mel Colton | | | | |
| S102 | Oath of Seven–George Albert Glay | 2.50 | 5.00 | 7.50 | A |
| D103 | Solar Lottery–Phillip K. Dick | 5.00 | 10.00 | 15.00 | SF |
| | The Big Jump–Leigh Brackett | | | | SF |
| S104 | Left Bank of Desire–R.V. Cassill & Eric Protter | 2.00 | 4.00 | 6.00 | E |
| S105 | The Fires of Youth–Edward DeRoo; orig. 1955 | 5.00 | 10.00 | 15.00 | JD |
| D106 | Lawman without a Badge–Dorothy L. Bonar | 2.00 | 4.00 | 6.00 | W |
| | Four Texans North–Lee Floren | | | | W |
| S107 | The Gilded Hideaway–Peter Twist | 2.00 | 4.00 | 6.00 | E |

| | | V/Good | Fine | N/Mint | |
|---|---|---|---|---|---|
| S108 | Lie Like a Lady–C.S. Cody | 2.00 | 4.00 | 6.00 | E |
| D109 | I See Red–Sterling Noel | 2.50 | 5.00 | 7.50 | M |
| | Mambo to Murder–Dale Clark | | | | M |
| D110 | No World of Their Own–Poul Anderson | 2.50 | 5.00 | 7.50 | SF |
| | The 1000 Year Plan–Isaac Asimov; aka Foundation | | | | SF |
| D110 | The 1000 Year Plan–Issac Asimov; special ed. | 2.50 | 5.00 | 7.50 | SF |
| S111 | The Smoldering Fire–Harry Harrison Kroll | 2.00 | 4.00 | 6.00 | E |
| D112 | Trigger Gospel–Henry Sinclair Drago | 2.50 | 5.00 | 7.50 | W |
| | Border Buccaneers–Frank Castle | | | | W |
| D113 | The Transposed Man–Dwight V. Swain; 1st ed. 1955 | 2.50 | 5.00 | 7.50 | SF |
| | One in 300–J.T. McIntosh | | | | |
| S114 | Living It Up–Edward Adler | 2.00 | 4.00 | 6.00 | E |
| D115 | Shady Lady–Cleve F. Adams | 2.50 | 5.00 | 7.50 | M |
| | One Got Away–Harry Whittington | | | | M |
| S116 | Words Fail Me!–ed. Brant House | 2.50 | 5.00 | 7.50 | H |
| S117 | Dark Rapture–Kim Darien | 2.00 | 4.00 | 6.00 | E |
| D118 | Dome around America–Jack Williamson | 2.50 | 5.00 | 7.50 | SF |
| | The Paradox Men–Charles L. Harness | | | | SF |
| S119 | The Driven Flesh–Lawrence Easton | 2.00 | 4.00 | 6.00 | E |
| D120 | Bounty Man–John McGreevey | 2.50 | 5.00 | 7.50 | W |
| | Call of the Gun–Samuel A. Peeples | | | | W |
| D121 | 3 Faces of Time–Sam Merwin, Jr | 2.50 | 5.00 | 7.50 | SF |
| | The Stars Are Ours!–Andre Norton | | | | SF |
| D121 | The Stars Are Ours!–Andre Norton; special ed. | 2.50 | 5.00 | 7.50 | SF |
| S122 | The Preying Streets–Ledru Baker, Jr | 4.00 | 8.00 | 12.00 | E |
| D123 | Love Me to Death–Frank Diamond | 2.00 | 4.00 | 6.00 | M |
| | The Squeeze–Gil Brewer | | | | M |
| S124 | House of Deceit–Rae Loomis | 2.00 | 4.00 | 6.00 | E |
| D125 | The Man Who Upset the Universe–Isaac Asimov; aka Foundation and Empire | 2.50 | 5.00 | 7.50 | SF |
| S126 | Washington Bachelor–A.H. Berzen | 2.00 | 4.00 | 6.00 | E |
| D127 | Alexander and the Camp Follower–Robert Payne; aka Alexander the God | 2.50 | 5.00 | 7.50 | A |
| D128 | Way Station West–William E. Vance | 2.00 | 4.00 | 6.00 | W |
| | High Saddle–William Hopson | | | | W |
| D129 | Silenced Witnesses–Norman C. Rosenthal | 2.50 | 5.00 | 7.50 | M |
| | The Dangling Carrot–Day Keene; orig. 1955 | | | | M |
| S130 | Backlash–Sidney Weissman | 2.00 | 4.00 | 6.00 | |
| D131 | The Ripening–Eugene Wyble | 2.00 | 4.00 | 6.00 | E |
| S132 | Cartoon Annual No. 2–ed. Brant House | 2.50 | 5.00 | 7.50 | H |
| S133 | Adventures on Other Planets–ed. Donald A. Wollheim | 2.50 | 5.00 | 7.50 | SF |
| D134 | Tornado on Horseback–Nelson Nye; aka Fiddle-Back Ranch | 2.00 | 4.00 | 6.00 | W |
| | The Outsiders–Gene Olson | | | | W |
| D135 | Dead Ringer–James Hadley Chase | 2.50 | 5.00 | 7.50 | M |
| | Maid for Murder–Milton K. Ozaki | | | | W |
| S136 | A Taste of Sin–R.V. Cassill | 2.00 | 4.00 | 6.00 | E |
| S137 | Violent Night–Ralph Jackson | 2.00 | 4.00 | 6.00 | E |
| D138 | Haven of the Hunted–T.V. Olsen | 2.00 | 4.00 | 6.00 | W |
| | Gunsmoke over Sabado–Paul Evan; 1956 | | | | W |
| D139 | The Atom Curtain–Nick Bodie Williams | 2.00 | 4.00 | 6.00 | SF |
| | Alien from Arcturus–Gordon R. Dickson | | | | SF |
| S140 | Honeymoon Humor–ed. Horace T. Elmo | 2.50 | 5.00 | 7.50 | H |
| S141 | Blood on the Branches–Oliver Crawford | 2.00 | 4.00 | 6.00 | |
| S142 | Masquerade in Blue–Glenn M. Barns | 2.00 | 4.00 | 6.00 | E |
| S143 | A Woman on the Place–Harry Whittington | 2.00 | 4.00 | 6.00 | E |
| D144 | The Man from Stony Lonesome–Jay Albert | 2.00 | 4.00 | 6.00 | W |
| | A Killer Comes Riding–Rod Patterson | | | | W |
| S145 | The Little Monsters–ed. Brant House | 2.50 | 5.00 | 7.50 | H |
| D146 | The Forgotten Planet–Murray Leinster | 2.50 | 5.00 | 7.50 | SF |
| | Contraband Rocket–Lee Correy | | | | SF |
| D146 | The Forgotten Planet–Murray Leinster; special ed. | 2.50 | 5.00 | 7.50 | SF |
| D147 | Prowl Cop–Gregory Jones | 2.50 | 5.00 | 7.50 | M |
| | My Private Hangman–Norman Herries | | | | M |
| S148 | The Man from Andersonville–Brad Ward | 2.00 | 4.00 | 6.00 | W |

*Ace D96, Ace S124, Ace D128.*

## ACE D/S/G-SERIES, *continued*

| ID | Title | V/Good | Fine | N/Mint | |
|---|---|---|---|---|---|
| D149 | A Run for the Money–Dale Clark | 2.00 | 4.00 | 6.00 | M |
| | The Thin Edge of Mania–Mark Macklin | | | | M |
| D150 | Agent of the Unknown–Margaret St. Clair | 2.50 | 5.00 | 7.50 | SF |
| | The World Jones Made–Philip K. Dick | | | | SF |
| S151 | Climb a Broken Ladder–Robert Novak | 1.50 | 3.00 | 4.50 | E |
| S152 | Medic Mirth–ed. Henry G. Felsen | 2.50 | 5.00 | 7.50 | H |
| S153 | The Wild Seed–Hallam Whitney (Harry Whittington) | 2.00 | 4.00 | 6.00 | E |
| D154 | Voyage to Somewhere–Sloan Wilson | 2.00 | 4.00 | 6.00 | C |
| D155 | Journey to the Center of Earth–Jules Verne | 1.50 | 3.00 | 4.50 | SF |
| D156 | Thruway West–Lee Floren; c-Leone | 2.00 | 4.00 | 6.00 | W |
| | The Naked Range–Stephen C. Lawrence | | | | W |
| D157 | Stab in the Dark–Louis Trimble | 2.00 | 4.00 | 6.00 | M |
| | Never Say No to a Killer–Jonathan Gant | | | | M |
| S158 | Golden Girl–Kim Darien | 2.00 | 4.00 | 6.00 | E |
| S159 | She Shark–John Farr | 2.00 | 4.00 | 6.00 | E |
| D160 | Decision at Sundown–Michael Carder | 2.00 | 4.00 | 6.00 | W |
| | Action along the Humboldt–Karl Kramer | | | | W |
| S161 | Gag Writer's Private Joke Book–Eddie Davis | 2.00 | 4.00 | 6.00 | H |
| D162 | The Mars Monopoly–Jerry Sohl | 2.50 | 5.00 | 7.50 | SF |
| | The Man Who Lived Forever–R. DeWitt Miller & Anna Hunger | | | | SF |
| D163 | Woman's Doctor–Russell Boltar | 2.00 | 4.00 | 6.00 | E |
| D164 | Mankind on the Run–Gordon R. Dickson | 2.50 | 5.00 | 7.50 | SF |
| | The Crossroads of Time–Andre Norton | | | | SF |
| S165 | Love and Hisses–ed. Brant House | 2.50 | 5.00 | 7.50 | H |
| D166 | Whispering Canyon–Stuart Brock | 2.00 | 4.00 | 6.00 | W |
| | Terror of Tres Alamos–Samuel A. Peeples | | | | W |
| D167 | Destroying Angel–John Creighton | 2.00 | 4.00 | 6.00 | M |
| | Never Say Die–Milton K. Ozaki | | | | M |
| S168 | Riverboat Girl–P.A. Hoover | 2.00 | 4.00 | 6.00 | E |
| D169 | Star Bridge–Jack Williamson & James E. Gunn | 2.00 | 4.00 | 6.00 | SF |
| D170 | Black Fire–Lawrence Goldman | 2.00 | 4.00 | 6.00 | |
| | Flight by Night–Day Keene; orig. 1956 | | | | |
| S171 | Campus Joke Book–ed. Eddie Davis | 2.50 | 5.00 | 7.50 | H |
| D172 | Johnny No-Name–Ben Smith | 2.00 | 4.00 | 6.00 | W |
| | Stages South–Robert Steelman | | | | W |
| D173 | Overlords from Space–Joseph E. Kelleam | 2.00 | 4.00 | 6.00 | SF |
| | The Man Who Mastered Time–Ray Cummings | | | | SF |
| S174 | B-Girl–Robert Novak | 2.00 | 4.00 | 6.00 | E |
| D175 | Best TV Humor of the Year–ed. Irving Settel | 2.00 | 4.00 | 6.00 | H |
| D176 | 3 Thousand Years–Thomas Calvert McClary | 2.00 | 4.00 | 6.00 | SF |
| | The Green Queen–Margaret St. Clair | | | | SF |
| D177 | The Girl in the Cop's Pocket–Robert Turner | 2.00 | 4.00 | 6.00 | M |
| | Violence Is Golden–C.H. Thames | | | | M |
| D178 | The Savage City–Jean Paradise | 3.00 | 6.00 | 9.00 | A |
| S179 | Squelches–ed. Brant House | 2.50 | 5.00 | 7.50 | H |
| D180 | The No-Gun Fighter–Nelson Nye | 2.00 | 4.00 | 6.00 | W |
| | One Step Ahead of the Posse–Walt Coburn | | | | W |
| D181 | The Exploits of Sherlock Holmes–John Dickson Carr & Adrian Conan Doyle | 2.50 | 5.00 | 7.50 | M |
| D182 | Shame–Emile Zola | 2.00 | 4.00 | 6.00 | E |
| | Therese Raquin–Emile Zola | | | | |
| D183 | The End of the World–Don Wollheim; orig. 1956 | 2.50 | 5.00 | 7.50 | SF |
| D184 | The Big Ivy–James McCague | 1.50 | 3.00 | 4.50 | |
| D185 | The Humming Box–Harry Whittington | 2.00 | 4.00 | 6.00 | M |
| | Build My Gallows High–Geoffrey Homes | | | | M |
| D186 | Ex-Marshal–Ray Hogan | 2.00 | 4.00 | 6.00 | W |
| | Steel Horizon–Edward Churchill | | | | W |
| D187 | The Pawns of Null-A–A.E. Van Vogt; 1st ed. 1956 | 4.50 | 9.00 | 13.50 | SF |
| S188 | They Goofed–ed. Brant House | 2.50 | 5.00 | 7.50 | H |
| D189 | Dead on Arrival–Stephen Marlowe (Milton Lesser) | 2.00 | 4.00 | 6.00 | M |
| | Weep for a Wanton–Lawrence Treat | | | | M |

| ID | Title | V/Good | Fine | N/Mint | |
|---|---|---|---|---|---|
| S190 | The Golden Couch–Henry Lewis Nixon | 1.50 | 3.00 | 4.50 | |
| D191 | Apalachee Gold–Frank G. Slaughter | 1.50 | 3.00 | 4.50 | |
| D192 | Beware of This Tenderfoot–Roy Manning | 2.00 | 4.00 | 6.00 | W |
| | Bad Blood at Black Range–John Callahan | | | | W |
| D193 | The Man Who Japed–Philip K. Dick | 5.00 | 10.00 | 15.00 | SF |
| | The Space Born–E.C. Tubb | | | | SF |
| D194 | Moscow–Theodor Plievier | 1.50 | 3.00 | 4.50 | C |
| D195 | The Deep End–Owen Dudley | 2.00 | 4.00 | 6.00 | M |
| | The Quaking Widow–Robert Colby | | | | M |
| D196 | The Night Branders–Walt Coburn | 2.00 | 4.00 | 6.00 | W |
| | The Highwayman–Frank Gruber | | | | W |
| D197 | Counterfeit Corpse–Ferguson Findley | 2.00 | 4.00 | 6.00 | M |
| | TNT for Two–James Byron | | | | M |
| S198 | Tokyo Intrigue–William Bender, Jr | 2.00 | 4.00 | 6.00 | |
| D199 | Planet of No Return–Poul Anderson | 2.50 | 5.00 | 7.50 | SF |
| | Star Guard–Andre Norton; 1957 | | | | SF |
| D200 | Report on Unidentified Flying Objects–Edward J. Ruppett | 1.25 | 2.50 | 3.75 | UF |
| D201 | Saturday Mountain–Nathaniel Jones | 2.00 | 4.00 | 6.00 | E |
| | Across That River–Harry Whittington | | | | E |
| D202 | The Color of Green–Leonard Kaufman | 1.25 | 2.50 | 3.75 | |
| D203 | Uneasy Lies the Head–William L. Rohde | 2.00 | 4.00 | 6.00 | M |
| | Cain's Girl Friend–William Grote | | | | M |
| D204 | The Desperate Donigans–Gordon Donalds | 2.00 | 4.00 | 6.00 | W |
| | John Law, Keep Out!–Paul Durst | | | | W |
| D205 | Who Speaks of Conquest?–Lan Wright | 2.00 | 4.00 | 6.00 | SF |
| | The Earth in Peril–Don A. Wollheim; c-Emsh | | | | SF |
| D206 | Great Day in the Morning–Robert Hardy Andrews | 1.50 | 3.00 | 4.50 | W |
| D207 | Hollywood Doctor–Charles Grayson | 2.00 | 4.00 | 6.00 | E |
| D208 | Blind Man's Bullets–Glenn Balch | 2.00 | 4.00 | 6.00 | W |
| | The Prodigal Gun–Barry Cord | | | | W |
| D209 | Three Times a Victim–F.L. Wallace | 3.00 | 6.00 | 9.00 | M |
| | A Night for Treason–John Jakes | | | | M |
| D210 | The Lion at Morning–Stephen Longstreet | 1.25 | 2.50 | 3.75 | E |
| D211 | Eye in the Sky–Philip K. Dick | 3.00 | 6.00 | 9.00 | SF |
| S212 | Hollywood Humor–ed. Horace T. Elmo | 2.50 | 5.00 | 7.50 | H |
| D213 | How to Stop Killing Yourself–Peter J. Steincrohn | 2.00 | 4.00 | 6.00 | NF |
| D214 | Hate Alley–Martin Weiss | 5.00 | 10.00 | 15.00 | JD |
| D215 | Three to Conquer–Eric Frank Russell | 2.50 | 5.00 | 7.50 | SF |
| | Doomsday Eve–Robert Moore Williams | | | | SF |
| D216 | Ridin' Through–William Colt MacDonald | 2.00 | 4.00 | 6.00 | W |
| | Savage Valley–Barry Cord; aka Dry Range | | | | W |
| D217 | Downwind–Bob McKnight | 2.00 | 4.00 | 6.00 | M |
| | A Rage to Kill–B.E. Lovell | | | | M |
| D218 | Tigrero!–Sasha Siemel | 1.25 | 2.50 | 3.75 | A |
| S219 | Backwater Woman–P.A. Hoover | 2.00 | 4.00 | 6.00 | E |
| D220 | Wear a Fast Gun–John Jakes | 3.00 | 6.00 | 9.00 | W |
| | The Friendless One–Ray Hogan | | | | W |
| D221 | The Terror Package–Robert Chavis | 2.00 | 4.00 | 6.00 | M |
| | You've Bet Your Life–Gordon Ashe | | | | M |
| D222 | First on the Rope–R. Frison-Roche | 1.25 | 2.50 | 3.75 | A |
| D223 | This Fortress World–James E. Gunn | 2.00 | 4.00 | 6.00 | SF |
| | The 13th Immortal–Robert Silverberg | | | | SF |
| D224 | Desire in the Ozarks–Shelby Steger | 2.00 | 4.00 | 6.00 | E |

*Ace D220, Ace D224, Ace D231.*

**ACE D/S/G-SERIES,** *continued*

| ID | Title – Author | V/Good | Fine | N/Mint | |
|---|---|---|---|---|---|
| D225 | A Lonely Walk–M.E. Chaber | 2.00 | 4.00 | 6.00 | M |
|  | Loser by a Head–Harry Giddings |  |  |  | M |
| D226 | Doc Colt–Samuel A. Peeples | 2.00 | 4.00 | 6.00 | W |
|  | Showdown at Warbird–Edwin Booth |  |  |  | W |
| D227 | Crisis in 2140–H. Beam Piper & John J. McGuire | 2.00 | 4.00 | 6.00 | SF |
|  | Gunner Cade–Cyril Judd |  |  |  | SF |
| D228 | We Die Alone–David Howarth | 1.25 | 2.50 | 3.75 | NF |
| D229 | Take It Out in Trade–Walter Whitney | 2.00 | 4.00 | 6.00 | E |
| D230 | Boss of Barbed Wire–Barry Cord | 2.00 | 4.00 | 6.00 | W |
|  | Burn 'Em Out–Lee Floren |  |  |  | W |
| D231 | Point of Peril–Edward Ronns | 2.00 | 4.00 | 6.00 | M |
|  | Murder for Charity–Owen Dudley |  |  |  | M |
| D232 | The Fixers–Willard Manus | 1.25 | 2.50 | 3.75 | E |
| D233 | First on Mars–Rex Gordon | 1.25 | 2.50 | 3.75 | SF |
| D234 | Look of the Eagle–Robert L. Scott, Jr | 1.00 | 2.00 | 3.00 | |
| D235 | The Lady and the Snake–John Farr | 1.50 | 3.00 | 4.50 | M |
|  | Nothing to Lose But My Life–Louis Trimble |  |  |  | M |
| D236 | Jinx Rider–Edwin Booth | 1.50 | 3.00 | 4.50 | W |
|  | Walk a Lonely Trail–Ray Hogan |  |  |  | W |
| D237 | The Secret Visitors–James White | 2.00 | 4.00 | 6.00 | SF |
|  | Master of Life and Death–Robert Silverberg |  |  |  | SF |
| D238 | Go–Clellon Holmes | 5.00 | 10.00 | 15.00 | JD |
| D239 | Earth Satellites and the Race for Space Superiority–G. Harry Stine | 1.00 | 2.00 | 3.00 | NF |
| D240 | Broken Wheel Ranch–Wayne C. Lee | 1.50 | 3.00 | 4.50 | W |
|  | Torture Trail–Tom West |  |  |  | W |
| D241 | The Hired Target–Wilson Tucker | 2.00 | 4.00 | 6.00 | M |
|  | One Deadly Dawn–Harry Whittington |  |  |  | M |
| D242 | Empire of the Atom–A.E. Van Vogt | 2.00 | 4.00 | 6.00 | SF |
|  | Space Station No. 1–Frank B. Long |  |  |  | SF |
| D243 | The Roving Eye–Michael Wells | 1.25 | 2.50 | 3.75 | E |
| D244 | Night Raider of the Atlantic–Terrence Robertson | 1.25 | 2.50 | 3.75 | C |
| D245 | Off on a Comet–Jules Verne | 1.00 | 2.00 | 3.00 | SF |
| D246 | The Magnate–John Harriman | 1.00 | 2.00 | 3.00 | |
| D247 | Look Out Behind You–Ken Lewis | 1.50 | 3.00 | 4.50 | M |
|  | Not So Evil as Eve–John Creighton |  |  |  | M |
| D248 | Longhorn Law–Ray Hogan | 1.50 | 3.00 | 4.50 | W |
|  | Cross Me in Gunsmoke–Clement Hardin |  |  |  | W |
| D249 | The Cosmic Puppets–Philip K. Dick | 5.00 | 10.00 | 15.00 | SF |
|  | Sargasso of Space–Andrew North (Andre Norton); c-Emsh |  |  |  | SF |
| D250 | The Terrible Swift Sword–Arthur Steuer | 1.00 | 2.00 | 3.00 | M |
| D251 | Windward Passage–Hamilton Cochran | 1.25 | 2.50 | 3.75 | A |
| D252 | The Rawhide Breed–John Callahan | 1.50 | 3.00 | 4.50 | W |
|  | Prairie Terror–Rod Patterson |  |  |  | W |
| D253 | The Buried Motive–Bruce Cassiday | 1.50 | 3.00 | 4.50 | M |
|  | Marked Down for Murder–Spencer Dean |  |  |  | M |
| D254 | The Lash of Desire–Marcos Spinelli | 2.00 | 4.00 | 6.00 | E |
| D255 | Star Ways–Poul Anderson; c-Emsh | 2.00 | 4.00 | 6.00 | SF |
|  | City under the Sea–Kenneth Bulmer |  |  |  | SF |
| S256 | The General–Karl Ludwig Opitz | 1.25 | 2.50 | 3.75 | C |
| D257 | Tiger in the Streets–Louis Malley | 5.00 | 10.00 | 15.00 | JD |
| D258 | The Long Walk–Slavomir Rawicz | 1.25 | 2.50 | 3.75 | NF |
| D259 | The Case of the Violent Virgin–Michael Avallone; 1st ed. 1957 | 2.50 | 5.00 | 7.50 | M |
| | The Case of the Bouncing Betty–Michael Avallone; 1st ed. 1957 |  |  |  | M |
| D260 | Land of the Stranger–Ray Hogan | 1.50 | 3.00 | 4.50 | W |
|  | The Saddle Wolves–Lee Floren |  |  |  | W |
| D261 | The Variable Man and Other Stories–Philip K. Dick; c-Emsh | 3.00 | 6.00 | 9.00 | SF |
| S262 | Attack!–Leland Jamieson; c-Emsh | 1.50 | 3.00 | 4.50 | C |
| S263 | See How They Run–Wilene Shaw | 1.25 | 2.50 | 3.75 | E |
| D264 | Cain Basin–Barry Cord | 1.50 | 3.00 | 4.50 | W |
|  | Brother Outlaw–Lee E. Wells |  |  |  | W |
| D265 | Terror in the Night and Other Stories–Robert Bloch | 12.50 | 25.00 | 37.50 | M |
|  | Shooting Star–Robert Bloch; 1st ed. 1958 |  |  |  | M |
| D266 | Twice upon a Time–Charles L. Fontenay; c-Emsh | 2.50 | 5.00 | 7.50 | SF |
|  | The Mechanical Monarch–E.C. Tubb |  |  |  | SF |
| D267 | Speed Demon–Jim Bosworth | 1.50 | 3.00 | 4.50 | E |
| D268 | Lincoln's Wit–ed. Brant House | 1.50 | 3.00 | 4.50 | H |
| D269 | Death in the South Atlantic; The Last Voyage of Grafspee–Michael Powell; movie tie-in | 1.25 | 2.50 | 3.75 | NF |
| D270 | D for Delinquent–Bud Clifton | 5.00 | 10.00 | 15.00 | JD |
| D271 | Lovers and Libertines–Cliff Howe | 2.00 | 4.00 | 6.00 | NF |
| D272 | Riders in the Night–Lee Floren | 1.50 | 3.00 | 4.50 | W |
|  | Backlash at Cajon Pass–William Hopson |  |  |  | W |
| D273 | The Midnight Eye–Mike Roscoe | 2.00 | 4.00 | 6.00 | M |
|  | Shakedown Hotel–Ernest Jason Fredericks |  |  |  | M |
| D274 | World without Men–Charles Eric Maine; c-Emsh | 6.00 | 12.00 | 18.00 | SF |
| S275 | Cartoon Annual No. 3–ed. Brant House | 2.50 | 5.00 | 7.50 | H |
| D276 | The Gunsmoke Trail–Barry Cord | 1.50 | 3.00 | 4.50 | W |
|  | Lead in His Fists–Tom West |  |  |  | W |
| D277 | City on the Moon–Murray Leinster; c-Emsh | 2.00 | 4.00 | 6.00 | SF |
|  | Men on the Moon–Donald A. Wollheim |  |  |  | SF |
| D278 | This Bright Sword–Donald Barr Chidsey | 1.50 | 3.00 | 4.50 | |
| D279 | Bye-Bye, Baby!–J. Harvey Bond | 2.00 | 4.00 | 6.00 | M |
|  | Murder Mutual–Bob McKnight |  |  |  | M |
| D280 | The Story of Wake Island–James P.S. Devereux | 1.25 | 2.50 | 3.75 | NF |
| D281 | Guideposts–Norman Vincent Peale | 1.00 | 2.00 | 3.00 | NF |
| D282 | Scoundrels, Fiends & Human Monsters–Cliff Howe | 2.00 | 4.00 | 6.00 | NF |
| D283 | City–Clifford D. Simak | 1.50 | 3.00 | 4.50 | SF |
| D284 | The Man Who Killed Tex–Edwin Booth | 1.50 | 3.00 | 4.50 | W |
|  | The Guns of Hammer–Barry Cord |  |  |  | W |
| D285 | The Brass Shroud–Bruce Cassiday | 1.50 | 3.00 | 4.50 | M |
|  | Odd Woman Out–Joseph Linklater |  |  |  | M |
| D286 | Invaders from Earth–Robert Silverberg; c-Emsh | 1.50 | 3.00 | 4.50 | SF |
|  | Across Time–David Grinnell |  |  |  | SF |
| D287 | Coral and Brass–Gen. Holland M. Smith & Percy Finch | 1.00 | 2.00 | 3.00 | NF |
| D288 | The Trail to Tomahawk–Edwin Booth | 1.50 | 3.00 | 4.50 | W |
|  | Law Beyond the Law–John Callahan |  |  |  | W |
| D289 | This'll Slay You–Alan Payne | 1.50 | 3.00 | 4.50 | M |
|  | Violent City–John Hawkins & Ward Hawkins; 1958 |  |  |  | M |
| D290 | A Woman Called Trouble–P.A. Hoover | 1.50 | 3.00 | 4.50 | E |

*Ace D245, Ace D257, Ace D265.*

*Ace D280, Ace D290, Ace D318.*

| | | V/Good | Fine | N/Mint | |
|---|---|---|---|---|---|

**ACE D/S/G-SERIES,** *continued*

| No. | Title | V/Good | Fine | N/Mint | |
|---|---|---|---|---|---|
| D291 | Lest We Forget Thee, Earth–Calvin M. Knox | 2.50 | 5.00 | 7.50 | SF |
| | People Minus X–Raymond Z. Gallun; c-Emsh | | | | SF |
| D292 | The Insiders–Booth Mooney | 1.50 | 3.00 | 4.50 | E |
| D293 | The Unknown Soldier–Vaino Linna | 1.50 | 3.00 | 4.50 | C |
| D294 | Beyond the Wild Missouri–Walt Coburn | 1.50 | 3.00 | 4.50 | W |
| | Bad Bunch of the Brasada–John H. Latham | | | | W |
| D295 | Big Planet–Jack Vance; c-Emsh | 5.00 | 10.00 | 15.00 | SF |
| | Slaves of the Klau–Jack Vance | | | | SF |
| D296 | Run the River Gauntlet–John Clagett | 1.50 | 3.00 | 4.50 | A |
| D297 | The Cut of the Whip–Peter Rabe | 3.50 | 7.00 | 10.50 | M |
| | Kill One, Kill Two–Robert H. Kelston | | | | M |
| D298 | Thunder Creek Range–Paul Evan | 1.50 | 3.00 | 4.50 | W |
| | Outlaw's Welcome–William E. Vance | | | | W |
| D299 | A Planet for Texans–John J. McGuire | 2.00 | 4.00 | 6.00 | SF |
| | Star Born–Andre Norton | | | | SF |
| D300 | The Dance Merchants–J. Walter Small | 1.25 | 2.50 | 3.75 | E |
| D301 | The Deadly Combo–John Farr | 2.00 | 4.00 | 6.00 | M |
| | Murder Isn't Funny–J. Harvey Bond | | | | M |
| D302 | The Iron King–Maurice Druon | 1.50 | 3.00 | 4.50 | A |
| D303 | War of the Wing-Men–Poul Anderson | 2.00 | 4.00 | 6.00 | SF |
| | The Snows of Ganymede–Poul Anderson | | | | SF |
| D304 | River to the Sunset–Archie Joscelyn | 1.50 | 3.00 | 4.50 | W |
| | Trouble at Breakdam–Ben Smith | | | | W |
| D305 | Free-Lance Murder–Vic Rodell | 1.50 | 3.00 | 4.50 | M |
| | Cornered–Louis King | | | | M |
| D306 | All Shook Up–Peyson Antholz | 5.00 | 10.00 | 15.00 | JD |
| D307 | From Eve On–ed. Brant House | 2.50 | 5.00 | 7.50 | H |
| D308 | Gunman's Gamble–Jack M. Bickham | 1.50 | 3.00 | 4.50 | W |
| | Draw and Die!–Roy Manning | | | | W |
| D309 | The Island of Dr. Moreau–H.G. Wells | 2.00 | 4.00 | 6.00 | HO |
| D310 | Mocambu–Marcus Spinell | 2.00 | 4.00 | 6.00 | E |
| D311 | Stepsons of Terra–Robert Silverberg; c-Emsh | 2.00 | 4.00 | 6.00 | SF |
| | A Man Called Destiny–Lan Wright | | | | SF |
| D312 | The Deadly Streets–Harlan Ellison; 1st ed. 1958 | 40.00 | 80.00 | 120.00 | JD |
| D313 | The Deadly Boodle–J.M. Flynn | 2.00 | 4.00 | 6.00 | M |
| | Design for Dying–Samuel A. Krasney | | | | M |
| D314 | Deeds of Darkness–Blair Ashton | 1.50 | 3.00 | 4.50 | |
| D315 | Six Worlds Yonder–Eric Frank Russell | 3.50 | 7.00 | 10.50 | SF |
| | The Space Willies–Eric Frank Russell | | | | SF |
| D316 | Mesquite Johnny–Barry Cord | 1.50 | 3.00 | 4.50 | W |
| | A Time for Guns–Rod Patterson | | | | W |
| D317 | The Wayward Blonde–John Creighton | 2.00 | 4.00 | 6.00 | M |
| | The Big Bite–Gerry Travis | | | | M |
| D318 | Captain Crossbones–Donald Barr Chidsey | 2.00 | 4.00 | 6.00 | A |
| D319 | The Man with Three Faces–Hans-Otto Meissner | 1.00 | 2.00 | 3.00 | NF |
| D320 | The Last Shoot Out–William Hopson | 1.50 | 3.00 | 4.50 | W |
| | The Rangemaster–Robert McCaig | | | | W |
| D321 | The Smell of Trouble–Louis Trimble | 1.50 | 3.00 | 4.50 | M |
| | Trial by Perjury–John Creighton | | | | M |
| D322 | The Void Beyond and Other Stories–Robert Moore Williams | 2.00 | 4.00 | 6.00 | SF |
| | The Blue Atom–Robert Moore Williams | | | | SF |
| D323 | The Violent Ones–ed. Brant House | 5.00 | 10.00 | 15.00 | JD |
| D324 | Brigands of the Moon–Ray Cummings; c-Emsh | 2.00 | 4.00 | 6.00 | SF |
| D325 | July, 1863–Irving Werstein | 1.50 | 3.00 | 4.50 | NF |
| D326 | Battling the Bombers–Wilhelm Johnen | 1.50 | 3.00 | 4.50 | C |
| D327 | First on the Moon–Jeff Satton; c-Emsh | 1.25 | 2.50 | 3.75 | SF |
| D328 | The Fourth Gunman–Merle Constiner | 1.25 | 2.50 | 3.75 | W |
| | Slick on the Draw–Tom West | | | | W |
| D329 | Stamped for Death–Emmett McDowell | 2.00 | 4.00 | 6.00 | M |
| | Three for the Gallows–Emmett McDowell | | | | M |
| D330 | Muscle Boy–Bud Clifton; c-Maguire (?) | 5.00 | 10.00 | 15.00 | E |
| D331 | The Secret of Zi–Kenneth Bultner; c-Emsh | 2.00 | 4.00 | 6.00 | SF |
| | Beyond the Vanishing Point–Ray Cummings | | | | SF |
| D332 | Stranger in Sundown–Ben Smith | 1.50 | 3.00 | 4.50 | W |
| | Blood on Boot Hill–Kermit Welles; 1959 | | | | W |
| D333 | Scream Street–Mike Brett | 2.00 | 4.00 | 6.00 | M |
| | Stranglehold–John Creighton | | | | M |

| No. | Title | V/Good | Fine | N/Mint | |
|---|---|---|---|---|---|
| D334 | Queen of the Flat-tops–Stanley Johnston | 1.50 | 3.00 | 4.50 | NF |
| D335 | War of Two Worlds–Poul Anderson | 2.00 | 4.00 | 6.00 | SF |
| | Threshold of Eternity–John Brunner; c-Emsh | | | | SF |
| D336 | Morals Squad–Samuel A. Krasney; c-Maguire (?) | 2.00 | 4.00 | 6.00 | E |
| D337 | Play It Cool–Jack Gerstine | 5.00 | 10.00 | 15.00 | JD |
| D338 | The Fires of Youth–Edward DeRoo | 5.00 | 10.00 | 15.00 | JD |
| D339 | Ring Around the Sun–Clifford D. Simak | 2.00 | 4.00 | 6.00 | SF |
| D340 | Solar Lottery–Philip K. Dick | 2.50 | 5.00 | 7.50 | SF |
| D341 | The Marina Street Girls–Rae Loomis | 2.00 | 4.00 | 6.00 | E |
| D342 | Queen's Blade–Nicholas Gorham | 1.50 | 3.00 | 4.50 | A |
| D343 | The Young Wolves–Edward DeRoo | 5.00 | 10.00 | 15.00 | JD |
| D344 | Desert Fury–Gordon Landsborough; aka Battery from Hellfire | 1.50 | 3.00 | 4.50 | C |
| D345 | Plague Ship–Andrew North (Andre Norton) | 2.00 | 4.00 | 6.00 | SF |
| | Voodoo Planet–Andrew North (Andre Norton); c-Emsh | | | | SF |
| D346 | Sheriff of Big Hat–Barry Cord | 1.50 | 3.00 | 4.50 | W |
| | Wanted! Alive!–Ray Hogan | | | | W |
| D347 | The Corpse without a Country–Louis Trimble | 2.00 | 4.00 | 6.00 | M |
| | Play for Keeps–Harry Whittington | | | | M |
| D348 | The Man from Nowhere–T.V. Olsen | 1.50 | 3.00 | 4.50 | W |
| | The Avenging Gun–John L. Shelley | | | | W |
| D349 | The Guilty Bystander–Mike Brett | 1.50 | 3.00 | 4.50 | M |
| | Kill Me with Kindness–J. Harvey Bond | | | | M |
| D350 | Red Alert–Peter Bryant | 1.00 | 2.00 | 3.00 | SF |
| D351 | The Sun Smasher–Edmond Hamilton | 2.00 | 4.00 | 6.00 | SF |
| | Star Haven–Ivar Jorgenson | | | | SF |
| G352 | Fire and Morning–Francis Leary | 1.50 | 3.00 | 4.50 | A |
| D353 | The Macabre Reader–ed. Donald A. Wollheim | 2.50 | 5.00 | 7.50 | HO |
| D354 | The Hidden Planet–Donald A. Wollheim | 2.00 | 4.00 | 6.00 | SF |
| D355 | The Beachhead Spies–Bill Strutton & Michael Pearson; aka The Secret Invaders | 1.50 | 3.00 | 4.50 | C |
| D356 | Kansas Guns–Paul Durst | 1.50 | 3.00 | 4.50 | W |
| | The Cactus Kid–Tom West | | | | W |
| D357 | Lady in Peril–Lester Dent; 1st ed. 1959 | 5.00 | 10.00 | 15.00 | M |
| | Wired for Scandal–F.L. Wallace | | | | M |
| D358 | The Plot Against Earth–Calvin M. Knox | 1.50 | 3.00 | 4.50 | SF |
| | Recruit for Andromeda–Milton Lesser | | | | SF |
| D359 | The Haunted Strangler–John C. Cooper; aka The Grip of the Strangler; movie tie-in | 5.00 | 10.00 | 15.00 | HO |
| D360 | War in Peaceful Valley–Barry Cord | 1.50 | 3.00 | 4.50 | W |
| | Johnny Sixgun–John H. Latham | | | | W |
| D361 | Murder Mistress–Robert Colby | 2.00 | 4.00 | 6.00 | M |
| | Dangerous to Know–James P. Duff | | | | M |
| D362 | The 100th Millenium–John Brunner | 2.00 | 4.00 | 6.00 | SF |
| | Edge of Time–David Grinnell; c-Emsh | | | | SF |
| D363 | The Rapist–Samuel A. Krasney | 2.00 | 4.00 | 6.00 | E |
| D364 | The Pipes Are Calling–Donald Barr Chidsey; 1st ed. 1959 | 1.50 | 3.00 | 4.50 | A |
| D365 | Mig Alley–Robert Eunson; 1st ed. 1959 | 1.25 | 2.50 | 3.75 | C |
| D366 | The Invaders Are Coming–Alan E. Nourse & J.A. Meyer; c-Emsh | 1.50 | 3.00 | 4.50 | SF |

*Ace D357, Ace D407, Ace D426.*

|  |  | V/Good | Fine | N/Mint |  |
|---|---|---|---|---|---|
| D367 | Negative of a Nude–Charles E. Fritch; 1st ed. 1959; c-Maguire (?) | 1.50 | 3.00 | 4.50 | M |
|  | Till Death Do Us Part–Louis Trimble |  |  |  | M |
| D368 | A Score to Settle–Joseph Gage | 1.50 | 3.00 | 4.50 | W |
|  | Hangman's Valley–Ray Hogan; 1st ed. 1959 |  |  |  | W |
| D369 | Vanguard from Alpha–Brian Aldiss; c-Emsh | 1.50 | 3.00 | 4.50 | SF |
|  | The Challenging Worlds–Kenneth Bulmer |  |  |  | SF |
| D370 | Cry Flood!–Ernest Jason Fredericks | 1.25 | 2.50 | 3.75 | E |
| G371 | Berlin–Theodor Plievier | 1.25 | 2.50 | 3.75 | C |
| D372 | Grass Greed–Glenn Balch | 1.50 | 3.00 | 4.50 | W |
|  | Cimarron Territory–Dan Kirby |  |  |  | W |
| D373 | Scarlet Starlet–Doug Warren | 1.50 | 3.00 | 4.50 | M |
|  | The Knave of Diamonds–Jack Karney; 1st ed. 1959 |  |  |  | M |
| D374 | The Thoroughbred and the Tramp– Burgess Leonard; 1st ed. 1959 | 1.50 | 3.00 | 4.50 | E |
| D375 | Masters of Evolution–Damon Knight; c-Emsh | 1.50 | 3.00 | 4.50 | SF |
|  | Fire in the Heavens–George O. Smith |  |  |  | SF |
| G376 | The Big Company Look–J. Harvey Howells | 1.00 | 2.00 | 3.00 |  |
| D377 | Bombs in Orbit–Jeff Sutton; 1st ed. 1959 | 1.00 | 2.00 | 3.00 | SF |
| D378 | Out for Kicks–Wilene Shaw | 5.00 | 10.00 | 15.00 | JD |
| D379 | Drink with the Dead–J.M. Flynn | 2.00 | 4.00 | 6.00 | M |
|  | Mistress of Horror House–William Woody |  |  |  | M |
| D380 | Concho Valley–Barry Cord | 1.50 | 3.00 | 4.50 | W |
|  | My Brother the Gunman–William Heuman |  |  |  | W |
| D381 | Secret of the Lost Race–Andre Norton; 1st ed. 1959 | 1.50 | 3.00 | 4.50 | SF |
|  | One Against Herculum–Jerry Sohl |  |  |  | SF |
| G382 | The Willing Maid–C.T. Ritchie | 1.50 | 3.00 | 4.50 | A |
| D383 | The Murder Specialist–Bud Clifton; 1st ed. 1959 | 1.50 | 3.00 | 4.50 | M |
| D384 | Feud Fury–Jack M. Bickham; 1st ed. 1959 | 1.50 | 3.00 | 4.50 | W |
|  | Mountain Ambush–Louis Trimble |  |  |  | W |
| D385 | Echo in the Skull–John Brunner | 1.50 | 3.00 | 4.50 | SF |
|  | Rocket to Limbo–Alan E. Nourse; c-Emsh |  |  |  | SF |
| G386 | The Sulu Sword–Richard O'Connor | 1.50 | 3.00 | 4.50 | A |
| D387 | Fare Prey–Laine Fisher | 1.50 | 3.00 | 4.50 | M |
|  | The Bikini Bombshell–Bob McKnight |  |  |  | M |
| D388 | When the Sleeper Wakes–H.G. Wells; c-Emsh | 1.25 | 2.50 | 3.75 | SF |
| D389 | No Entry–Manning Coles | 1.25 | 2.50 | 3.75 |  |
| G390 | Long Pig–Russell Foreman | 1.50 | 3.00 | 4.50 |  |
| D391 | The World Swappers–John Brunner; 1st ed. 1959 | 1.50 | 3.00 | 4.50 | SF |
|  | Seige of the Unseen–A.E. Van Vogt |  |  |  | SF |
| D392 | Twisted Trail–Tom West | 1.50 | 3.00 | 4.50 | W |
|  | The Man from Salt Creek–Archie Joscelyn |  |  |  | W |
| D393 | Dictators Die Hard–Robert A. Levey | 1.50 | 3.00 | 4.50 | M |
|  | Evil Is the Night–John Creighton; 1st ed. 1959 |  |  |  | M |
| D394 | The Flaming Island–Donald Barr Chidsey | 1.50 | 3.00 | 4.50 | A |
| D395 | Thunder at Harper's Ferry–Allan Keller | 1.25 | 2.50 | 3.75 | NF |
| D396 | Luisita–Rae Loomis | 1.25 | 2.50 | 3.75 | E |
| D397 | Journey to the Center of the Earth– Jules Verne | .75 | 1.50 | 2.25 | SF |
| D398 | Why I Am So Beat–Nolan Miller | 1.25 | 2.50 | 3.75 | E |
| D399 | Living It Up–Edward Adler | 1.25 | 2.50 | 3.75 |  |
| D400 | Last Chance at Devil's Canyon–Barry Cord | 1.50 | 3.00 | 4.50 | W |
|  | Shadow of a Gunman–Gordon D. Shirreffs |  |  |  | W |
| D401 | Obit Deferred–Louis Trimble; 1st ed. 1959 | 1.50 | 3.00 | 4.50 | M |
|  | I Want Out–Tedd Thomey |  |  |  | M |
| G402 | Kiboko–Daniel P. Mannix | 2.00 | 4.00 | 6.00 | A |
| D403 | The Pirates of Zan–Murray Leinster; 1st ed. 1959; c-Emsh | 2.00 | 4.00 | 6.00 | SF |
|  | The Mutant Weapon–Murray Leinster |  |  |  | SF |
| D404 | The Hollow Hero–Clifford Anderson; 1st ed. 1959 | 1.25 | 2.50 | 3.75 |  |

|  |  | V/Good | Fine | N/Mint |  |
|---|---|---|---|---|---|
| D405 | First to the Stars–Rex Gordon; 1st ed. 1959 | 1.25 | 2.50 | 3.75 | SF |
| D406 | Go, Man, Go!–Edward DeRoo; 1st ed. 1959 | 5.00 | 10.00 | 15.00 | JD |
| D407 | The Planet Killers–Robert Silverberg | 1.50 | 3.00 | 4.50 | SF |
|  | We Claim These Stars!–Poul Anderson |  |  |  | SF |
| D408 | Wyoming Welcome–Edwin Booth | 1.50 | 3.00 | 4.50 | W |
|  | Law of the Trigger–Giles A. Lutz |  |  |  | W |
| D409 | Terror Tournament–J.M. Flynn | 1.50 | 3.00 | 4.50 | M |
|  | Cargo for the Styx–Louis Trimble; 1st ed. 1959 |  |  |  | M |
| D410 | Buccaneer's Blade–Donald Barr Chidsey; 1st ed. 1959 | 1.50 | 3.00 | 4.50 | A |
| D411 | Swamp Sanctuary–Bob McKnight; 1st ed. 1959; c-Maguire (?) | 2.00 | 4.00 | 6.00 | E |
| D412 | Apache Butte–Gordon R. Shirreffs | 1.50 | 3.00 | 4.50 | W |
|  | Ride the Long Night–E.A. Alman; 1st ed. 1960 |  |  |  | W |
| D413 | A Touch of Infinity–Harlan Ellison | 15.00 | 30.00 | 45.00 | SF |
|  | The Man with Nine Lives–Harlan Ellison |  |  |  | SF |
| G414 | The Companions of Jehu–Alexandre Dumas | 1.50 | 3.00 | 4.50 | A |
| D415 | Dead Certain–Stewart Sterling; 1st ed. 1960 | 1.50 | 3.00 | 4.50 | M |
|  | Fire on Fear Street–Stewart Sterling |  |  |  | M |
| D416 | The Big Question–John Kenneth; 1st ed. 1960 | 1.00 | 2.00 | 3.00 | E |
| D417 | Rumble at the Housing Project–Edward DeRoo | 5.00 | 10.00 | 15.00 |  |
| D418 | Nothing But My Gun–Tom West | 1.50 | 3.00 | 4.50 | W |
|  | The Quiet Ones–C.S. Park |  |  |  | W |
| D419 | A Slice of Death–Bob McKnight; 1st ed. 1960; c-Maguire (?) | 1.50 | 3.00 | 4.50 | M |
|  | Open Season–Bernard Thielen |  |  |  | M |
| D420 | The Angry Ones–John A. Williams; 1st ed. 1960 | 1.50 | 3.00 | 4.50 | E |
| D421 | Dr. Futurity–Philip K. Dick; 1st ed. 1960 | 3.50 | 7.00 | 10.50 | SF |
|  | Slavers of Space–John Brunner |  |  |  | SF |
| D422 | The Best from Fantasy and Science Fiction, 3rd Series–ed. Anthony Boucher & J. Francis McComas | 1.50 | 3.00 | 4.50 | SF |
| D423 | Tidal Wave–Browning Norton; 1st ed. 1960 | 1.50 | 3.00 | 4.50 |  |
| D424 | Wild Justice–Robert McCaig | 1.50 | 3.00 | 4.50 | W |
|  | Shoot-out at the Way Statien–Lee Richards |  |  |  | W |
| D425 | Dig Her a Grave–Paul Kruger | 1.50 | 3.00 | 4.50 | M |
|  | A Half Interest in Murder–John Creighton; 1st ed. 1960 |  |  |  | M |
| D426 | Penal Colony–Robert S. Close; aka Eliza Callaghan | 2.50 | 5.00 | 7.50 | E |
| D427 | World of the Masterminds–Robert Moore Williams | 1.50 | 3.00 | 4.50 | SF |
|  | To the End of Time and Other Stories– Robert Moore Williams; 1st ed. 1960 |  |  |  | SF |
| D428 | Scowtown Woman–P.A. Hoover | 1.50 | 3.00 | 4.50 | E |
| D429 | The Anatomy of Violence–Charles Runyon; 1st ed. 1960 | 1.50 | 3.00 | 4.50 | E |
| D430 | Born Savage–William Hopson; c-Basil Gogos | 1.50 | 3.00 | 4.50 | W |
|  | The Hasty Hangman–Ray Hogan; 1st ed. 1960 |  |  |  | W |
| D431 | Lost in Space–George O. Smith | 1.50 | 3.00 | 4.50 | SF |
|  | Earth's Last Fortress–A.E. Van Vogt; 1st ed. 1960 |  |  |  | SF |
| D432 | Convention Queen–Donn Broward; 1st ed. 1960 | 1.50 | 3.00 | 4.50 | E |
| D433 | If Hate Could Kill–Jack Bradley; 1st ed. 1960 | 1.50 | 3.00 | 4.50 | M |
|  | The Smasher–Talmage Powell |  |  |  | M |
| D434 | The Purchase of the North Pole–Jules Verne | 1.00 | 2.00 | 3.00 | SF |
| D435 | Lady in Bondage–C.T. Ritchie; aka Black Angels | 2.00 | 4.00 | 6.00 | A |
| D436 | The Challenger–Giles A. Lutz | 1.50 | 3.00 | 4.50 | W |
|  | The Phantom Pistoleer–Tom West |  |  |  | W |
| D437 | And Then the Town Took Off–Richard Wilson | 1.50 | 3.00 | 4.50 | SF |
|  | The Sioux Spaceman–Andre Norton; 1st ed. 1960 |  |  |  | SF |

ACE D/S/G-SERIES, *continued*

| No. | Title | V/Good | Fine | N/Mint | |
|---|---|---|---|---|---|
| D438 | The Panic Button–Charles Fogg; 1st ed. 1960 | 1.00 | 2.00 | 3.00 | C |
| D439 | Run If You Can–Owen Dudley; 1st ed. 1960 | 1.50 | 3.00 | 4.50 | M |
| | The Devil's Punchbowl–Duane Decker; c-Maguire (?) | | | | M |
| G440 | Letter of Marque–Andrew Hepburn | 1.50 | 3.00 | 4.50 | A |
| D441 | Skip Bomber–Lloyd E. Olson | 1.25 | 2.50 | 3.75 | C |
| D442 | Rider of the Rincon–Rod Patterson | 1.50 | 3.00 | 4.50 | W |
| | Killer's Paradise–Jack M. Bickham | | | | W |
| D443 | Bow Down to Nul–Brian W. Aldiss; 1st ed. 1960 | 1.50 | 3.00 | 4.50 | SF |
| | The Dark Destroyers–Manly Wade Wellman | | | | SF |
| D444 | Desire Island–Shepard Rifkin; 1st ed. 1960 | 2.00 | 4.00 | 6.00 | E |
| D445 | Bloodline to Murder–Emmett McDowell | 1.50 | 3.00 | 4.50 | M |
| | In at the Kill–Emmett McDowell | | | | M |
| D446 | Flight 685 Is Overdue–Edward Moore; 1st ed. 1960 | 1.00 | 2.00 | 3.00 | M |
| D447 | The Hot Chariot–J.M. Flynn; c-Maguire (?) | 1.50 | 3.00 | 4.50 | M |
| | Kiss the Babe Goodbye–Bob McKnight; 1st ed. 1960 | | | | M |
| D448 | Pistol-Whipper–Lee Floren | 1.50 | 3.00 | 4.50 | W |
| | Winter Range–Al Cody | | | | W |
| D449 | The Genetic General–Gordon R. Dickson; 1st ed. 1960 | 3.00 | 6.00 | 9.00 | SF |
| | Time to Teleport–Gordon R. Dickson | | | | SF |
| D450 | Side Me with Sixes–Tom West | 1.50 | 3.00 | 4.50 | W |
| | The Ridgerunner–Ray Hogan | | | | W |
| D451 | Odds Against Linda–Steve Ward; 1st ed. 1960 | 1.50 | 3.00 | 4.50 | M |
| | A Key to the Morgue–Robert Martin | | | | M |
| D452 | The Color of Hate–Joe L. Hensley | 4.00 | 8.00 | 12.00 | M |
| D453 | The Games of Neith–Margaret St. Clair; 1st ed. 1960 | 1.50 | 3.00 | 4.50 | SF |
| | The Earth Gods Are Coming–Kenneth Bulmer | | | | SF |
| G454 | Ride East! Ride West!–Anne Powers; aka Rogue's Honor | 1.50 | 3.00 | 4.50 | A |
| D455 | The Best from Fantasy and Science Fiction-Fourth Series–ed. Anthony Boucher | 1.50 | 3.00 | 4.50 | SF |
| D456 | The Desperate Dude–Edwin Booth | 1.50 | 3.00 | 4.50 | W |
| | Danger Trail–Edwin Booth | | | | W |
| D457 | Vulcan's Hammer–Philip K. Dick; 1st ed. 1960 | 3.50 | 7.00 | 10.50 | SF |
| | The Skynappers–John Brunner | | | | SF |
| D458 | Womanhunt–Mark Derby | 1.50 | 3.00 | 4.50 | A |
| D459 | The Hot Diary–Howard J. Olmsted; 1st ed. 1960; c-Maguire (?) | 1.50 | 3.00 | 4.50 | M |
| | Ring Around a Rogue–J.M. Flynn | | | | M |
| D460 | When the Ship Sank–James MacGregor | 1.25 | 2.50 | 3.75 | C |
| D461 | The Time Traders–Andre Norton | 1.25 | 2.50 | 3.75 | SF |
| D462 | The Useless Gun–Jack M. Bickham | 1.50 | 3.00 | 4.50 | W |
| | The Long Fuse–John H. Latham; 1st ed. 1960 | | | | W |
| D463 | Dying Room Only–Stewart Sterling | 2.00 | 4.00 | 6.00 | M |
| | The Body in the Bed–Stewart Sterling; c-Maguire (?) | | | | M |
| D464 | Tame the Wild Flesh–Wilene Shaw; 1st ed. 1960 | 1.50 | 3.00 | 4.50 | E |
| D465 | The Martian Missile–David Grinnell | 1.50 | 3.00 | 4.50 | SF |
| | The Atlantic Abomination–John Brunner; 1st ed. 1959 | | | | SF |
| D466 | Wild Bill Hickok–Richard O'Connor | 1.50 | 3.00 | 4.50 | W |
| D467 | Five, Four, Three, Two, One–Pfftt–William C. Anderson; 1st ed. 1960 | 2.50 | 5.00 | 7.50 | SF |
| D468 | Sentinels of Space–Eric Frank Russell; c-Schulz | 1.50 | 3.00 | 4.50 | SF |
| D469 | Running Scared–Bob McKnight; 1st ed. 1960 | 1.50 | 3.00 | 4.50 | M |
| | Man-Killer–Talmage Powell | | | | M |
| D470 | The Maverick–Ben Smith | 1.50 | 3.00 | 4.50 | W |
| | The Man Who Was Morgan–Gene Olson | | | | W |
| D471 | Sanctuary in the Sky–John Brunner | 1.50 | 3.00 | 4.50 | SF |
| | The Secret Martians–Jack Sharkey; 1st ed. 1960 | | | | SF |
| D472 | A Night for Screaming–Harry Whittington; c-Maguire (?) | 2.00 | 4.00 | 6.00 | M |
| D473 | The Greatest Adventure–John Taine | 2.50 | 5.00 | 7.50 | SF |
| G474 | Lost Mines and Hidden Treasure–Leland Lovelace | 1.50 | 3.00 | 4.50 | NF |
| D475 | The Marshall of Medicine Bend–Brad Ward | 1.25 | 2.50 | 3.75 | W |
| D476 | Double-Cross Dinero–Tom West | 1.50 | 3.00 | 4.50 | W |
| | Lost Valley–Edwin Booth | | | | W |
| D477 | The Duchess of Skid Row–Louis Trimble | 1.50 | 3.00 | 4.50 | W |
| | Love Me and Die–Louis Trimble | | | | M |
| D478 | Spacehive–Jeff Sutton; 1st ed. 1960 | 1.00 | 2.00 | 3.00 | SF |
| D479 | To the Tombaugh Station–Wilson Tucker; 1st ed. 1960 | 2.00 | 4.00 | 6.00 | SF |
| | Earthman Go Home!–Poul Anderson | | | | SF |
| G480 | The Strong Men–John Brick | 1.50 | 3.00 | 4.50 | A |
| D481 | The Biggest Holdup–Joseph F. Dinneen; aka The Alternate Case | 1.50 | 3.00 | 4.50 | NF |
| D482 | The Weapon Shops of Isher–A.E. Van Vogt | 1.50 | 3.00 | 4.50 | SF |
| D483 | The Corpse in the Picture Window–Bruce Cassidy | 1.50 | 3.00 | 4.50 | M |
| | If Wishes Were Hearses–J. Harvey Bond; 1st ed. 1961 | | | | M |
| D484 | Dead Man's Spurs–Al Cody; 1st ed. 1961 | 1.50 | 3.00 | 4.50 | W |
| | Ambush at Riflestock–Ray Hogan | | | | W |
| D485 | The Puzzle Planet–Robert A.W. Lowndes; 1st ed. 1961 | 1.50 | 3.00 | 4.50 | SF |
| | The Angry Espers–Lloyd Biggle, Jr | | | | SF |
| D486 | The Little Caesars–Edward DeRoo | 5.00 | 10.00 | 15.00 | JD |
| D487 | Four-Year Hitch–Leonard Sanders; 1st ed. 1961 | 1.00 | 2.00 | 3.00 | C |
| D488 | Third Time Down–Dan Brennan; 1st ed. 1961 | 1.50 | 3.00 | 4.50 | C |
| D489 | Somebody's Walking over My Grave–Robert Arthur; 1st ed. 1961; c-Maguire (?) | 1.50 | 3.00 | 4.50 | M |
| | Dally with a Deadly Doll–John Miles | | | | M |
| D490 | Adventures on Other Planets–ed. Donald A. Wollheim | 1.25 | 2.50 | 3.75 | SF |
| D491 | The Big Time–Fritz Leiber; 1st ed. 1961 | 3.00 | 6.00 | 9.00 | SF |
| | The Mind Spider and Other Stories–Fritz Leiber | | | | SF |
| D492 | Winter Drive–William Hopson | 1.50 | 3.00 | 4.50 | W |
| | The Wild Quarry–Giles A. Lutz | | | | W |
| D493 | The Queen's Awards/Fifth Series–ed. Ellery Queen; c-Maguire | 2.00 | 4.00 | 6.00 | M |
| D494 | Log Jam–Leslie Turner White | 1.50 | 3.00 | 4.50 | A |
| D495 | A Mania for Blondes–Samuel A. Krasney; 1st ed. 1961 | 1.50 | 3.00 | 4.50 | M |
| D496 | With Blood in Their Eyes–Steven Lawrence | 1.50 | 3.00 | 4.50 | W |
| | Killer's Canyon–Tom West | | | | W |
| D497 | Wandl the Invader–Ray Cummings; 1st ed. 1961 | 2.00 | 4.00 | 6.00 | SF |
| | I Speak for Earth–Keith Woodcott | | | | SF |
| D498 | Galactic Derelict–Andre Norton | 1.50 | 3.00 | 4.50 | SF |
| D499 | Night Drop–Frederick C. Davis | 1.50 | 3.00 | 4.50 | M |
| | High Heel Homicide–Frederick C. Davis | | | | M |
| G500 | The Bad Man of the West–George D. Hendricks | 1.50 | 3.00 | 4.50 | NF |
| D501 | Let Him Go Hang–Bud Clifton | 1.50 | 3.00 | 4.50 | M |
| D502 | Long Night at Lodgepole–Al Cody; 1st ed. 1961 | 1.50 | 3.00 | 4.50 | W |
| | Troubled Range–Paul Evan Lehman | | | | W |
| D503 | The Girl in the Death Seat–Fan Nichols | 1.50 | 3.00 | 4.50 | M |
| D504 | Master of the World–Jules Verne; movie tie-in | 1.00 | 2.00 | 3.00 | SF |
| D505 | The Surfside Caper–Louis Trimble | 1.50 | 3.00 | 4.50 | M |
| | In a Vanishing Room–Robert Colby; 1st ed. 1961 | | | | M |
| D506 | The Brazen Dream–Harry Harrison Kroll; 1st ed. 1961 | 1.50 | 3.00 | 4.50 | E |
| D507 | Meeting at Infinity–John Brunner; 1st ed. 1961 | 1.50 | 3.00 | 4.50 | SF |
| | Beyond the Silver Sky–Kenneth Bulmer; c-Emsh | | | | SF |
| D508 | More Macabre–ed. Donald A. Wollheim | 2.50 | 5.00 | 7.50 | HO |

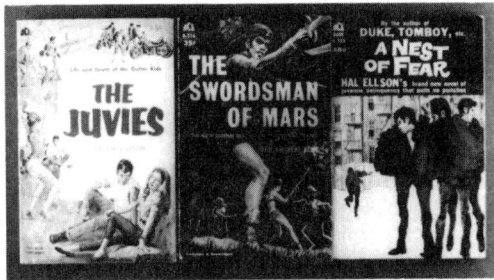

Ace D513, Ace D516, Ace D522.

Ace D523, Ace D574, Ace D579.

## ACE D/S/G-SERIES, *continued*

| | | V/Good | Fine | N/Mint | |
|---|---|---|---|---|---|
| D588 | Short-trigger Man–Merle Constiner; 1st ed. 1964 | 1.00 | 2.00 | 3.00 | W |
| D589 | The Nurse with the Silver Skates– Virginia B. McDonnell | .75 | 1.50 | 2.25 | R |
| D590 | Stampede at Hourglass–Lin Searles; 1st ed. 1964 | 1.00 | 2.00 | 3.00 | W |
| D591 | Northwest Nurse–Arlene Fitzgerald; 1st ed. 1964 | .75 | 1.50 | 2.25 | R |
| D592 | Gunslick Mountain–Nelson Nye | 1.00 | 2.00 | 3.00 | W |
| D593 | Sisters in White–Suzanne Roberts; 1st ed. 1965 | .75 | 1.50 | 2.25 | R |
| D594 | The Desperate Deputy of Cougar Hill– Louis Trimble; 1st ed. 1965 | 1.00 | 2.00 | 3.00 | W |
| D595 | Nurse Ann in Surgery–Ruth MacLeod; 1st ed. 1965 | .75 | 1.50 | 2.25 | R |
| D596 | Nurse on the Run–Arlene Hale; 1st ed. 1965 | .75 | 1.50 | 2.25 | R |
| D597 | The Hardest Man in the Sierras–L.P. Holmes; 1st ed. 1965 | 1.00 | 2.00 | 3.00 | W |
| D598 | Disaster Area Nurse–Arlene Hale; 1st ed. 1965 | .75 | 1.50 | 2.25 | R |
| D599 | Winged Victory for Nurse Kerry– Patricia Libby | .75 | 1.50 | 2.25 | R |

# ACE F-SERIES
# Ace Books, Inc./A.A. Wynn, Inc.

| | | V/Good | Fine | N/Mint | |
|---|---|---|---|---|---|
| F101 | Cruise Nurse–Joan Sargent; 1961 | .75 | 1.50 | 2.25 | R |
| | Calling Dr. Merryman–Margaret Howe | | | | R |
| F102 | Never Forget, Never Forgive–Clayton Fox | .75 | 1.50 | 2.25 | M |
| | The Flying Eye–Bob McKnight | | | | M |
| F103 | A Trap for Sam Dodge–Harry Whittington | 2.00 | 4.00 | 6.00 | W |
| | High Thunder–Lee Floren | | | | W |
| F104 | Mayday Orbit–Poul Anderson; 1961 | 1.25 | 2.50 | 3.75 | SF |
| | No Man's World–Kenneth Bulmer | | | | SF |
| F105 | The Best from Fantasy and Science Fiction, 5th Series–ed. Anthony Boucher | 1.25 | 2.50 | 3.75 | SF |
| F106 | The Gun from Nowhere–Tom West | 1.00 | 2.00 | 3.00 | W |
| | Justice at Spanish Flat–Brian Wynne | | | | W |
| F107 | Scratch a Thief–John Trinian | 1.00 | 2.00 | 3.00 | M |
| | My Pal, the Killer–Chester Warwick | | | | M |
| F108 | The Sun Saboteurs–Damon Knight | 1.25 | 2.50 | 3.75 | SF |
| | The Light of Lilith–G. McDonald Wallis | | | | SF |
| F109 | Storm over Warlock–Andre Norton; 1961 | 1.25 | 2.50 | 3.75 | SF |
| F110 | Track the Man Down–Ray Hogan | 1.00 | 2.00 | 3.00 | W |
| | Savage Range–Lee E. Wells | | | | W |
| F111 | To Have and to Kill–Robert Martin | 1.00 | 2.00 | 3.00 | M |
| | The Girl from Las Vegas–J.M. Flynn | | | | M |
| F112 | Barbara Ames, Private Secretary– Jeanne Judson | .75 | 1.50 | 2.25 | R |
| | Fashions for Carol–Nell Marr Dean | | | | R |
| F113 | Rebels of the Red Planet–Charles L. Fontenay | 1.50 | 3.00 | 4.50 | SF |
| | 200 Years to Christmas–J.T. McIntosh | | | | SF |
| F114 | The Bird of Time–Wallace West | 1.00 | 2.00 | 3.00 | SF |
| F115 | The Blonde Cried Murder–John Creighton; 1961 | 1.00 | 2.00 | 3.00 | M |
| | Killing Cousins–Fletcher Flora | | | | M |

| | | V/Good | Fine | N/Mint | |
|---|---|---|---|---|---|
| F116 | Deadman Canyon–Louis Trimble; 1961 | 1.00 | 2.00 | 3.00 | W |
| | The Lurking Gun–Clement Hardin | | | | W |
| F117 | The Door Through Space–Marion Zimmer Bradley | 2.00 | 4.00 | 6.00 | SF |
| | Rendezvous on a Lost World–A. Bertram Chandler; 1961 | | | | SF |
| F118 | Making Profits in the Stock Market– Jacob O. Kamm, PhD | .75 | 1.50 | 2.25 | NF |
| F119 | Delusion World–Gordon R. Dickson | 2.50 | 5.00 | 7.50 | SF |
| | Spacial Delivery–Gordon R. Dickson | | | | SF |
| F120 | Gunmen Can't Hide–Jack M. Bickham | 1.00 | 2.00 | 3.00 | W |
| | Come in Shooting–John Callahan | | | | W |
| F121 | Sing Me a Murder–Helen Nielsen | 1.00 | 2.00 | 3.00 | M |
| | Woman Missing and Other Stories– Helen Nielsen | | | | M |
| F122 | Dr. Kilbourne Comes Home–Dorothy Worley | .75 | 1.50 | 2.25 | R |
| | Calling Nurse Linda–Patti Stone; c-Maguire | | | | R |
| F123 | The Nemesis from Terra–Leigh Brackett; c-Emsh | 1.50 | 3.00 | 4.50 | SF |
| | Collision Course–Robert Silverberg | | | | SF |
| F124 | Slattery–Steven G. Lawrence | 1.00 | 2.00 | 3.00 | W |
| | Bullet Welcome for Slattery–Steven G. Lawrence | | | | W |
| F125 | The Widow Maker–Frank Diamond | 1.00 | 2.00 | 3.00 | M |
| | Deep Six–J.M. Flynn | | | | M |
| F126 | The Troublemaker–Edwin Booth | 1.00 | 2.00 | 3.00 | W |
| | A Marshal for Lawless–Ray Hogan | | | | W |
| F127 | Seven from the Stars–Marion Zimmer Bradley | 2.00 | 4.00 | 6.00 | SF |
| | Worlds of the Imperium–Keith Laumer | | | | SF |
| F128 | The Buzzard's Nest–Tom West | 1.00 | 2.00 | 3.00 | W |
| | Siege at High Meadow–Louis Trimble | | | | W |
| F129 | The Automated Goliath–William F. Temple | 1.00 | 2.00 | 3.00 | SF |
| | The Three Suns of Amara–William F. Temple | | | | SF |
| F130 | The Bullet-Proof Martyr–James A. Howard | 1.00 | 2.00 | 3.00 | M |
| | The Screaming Cargo–J.M. Flynn | | | | M |
| F131 | The Best from Fantasy and Science Fiction, 6th Series–ed. Anthony Boucher | 1.25 | 2.50 | 3.75 | SF |
| F132 | Scramble–Maj. Mario Cappelli, USAF | 1.00 | 2.00 | 3.00 | C |
| F133 | Secret Agent of Terra–John Brunner | 2.00 | 4.00 | 6.00 | SF |
| | The Rim of Space–A. Bertram Chandler | | | | SF |
| F134 | Tumbleweed Trigger–Gordon D. Shirreffs | 1.00 | 2.00 | 3.00 | W |
| | A Shooting at Sundust–Rod Patterson | | | | W |
| F135 | The Long Tomorrow–Leigh Brackett | 1.50 | 3.00 | 4.50 | SF |
| F136 | Childbirth: True Accounts of Unusual Experiences–ed. Dr. Myron Harkary | .75 | 1.50 | 2.25 | NF |
| F137 | Impossible–Yet It Happened!–R. Dewitt Miller; aka Forgotten Mysteries | .75 | 1.50 | 2.25 | NF |
| F138 | A Noose for Slattery–Steven G. Lawrence | 1.00 | 2.00 | 3.00 | W |
| | Walk a Narrow Trail–Steven G. Lawrence | | | | W |
| F139 | The Makeshift Rocket–Poul Anderson | 1.50 | 3.00 | 4.50 | SF |
| | Un-man–Poul Anderson | | | | SF |
| F140 | Love with a Harvard Accent–Leonie St. John; 1962 | 1.00 | 2.00 | 3.00 | |

*Ace F103, Ace F111, Ace F132.*

*Ace F138, Ace F151, Ace F166.*

ACE F-SERIES, *continued*

| | | V/Good | Fine | N/Mint | |
|---|---|---|---|---|---|
| F141 | The Darkness Before Tomorrow–Robert Moore Williams | 1.00 | 2.00 | 3.00 | SF |
| | The Ladder in the Sky–Keith Woodcott | | | | SF |
| F142 | Smoky Pass–L.P. Holmes; 1962 | 1.00 | 2.00 | 3.00 | W |
| | Wolf Brand–L.P. Holmes | | | | W |
| F143 | End of a Big Wheel–Clayton Fox | 1.00 | 2.00 | 3.00 | M |
| | A Stone Around Her Neck–Bob McKnight | | | | M |
| F144 | The Badge Shooters–Clement Hardin | 1.00 | 2.00 | 3.00 | W |
| | Massacre Basin–Frank Wynne | | | | W |
| F145 | Next Stop the Stars–Robert Silverberg | 2.00 | 4.00 | 6.00 | SF |
| | The Seed of Earth–Robert Silverberg | | | | SF |
| F146 | Sir Scoundrel–Jay Scotland (John Jakes) | 1.50 | 3.00 | 4.50 | A |
| F147 | Eye of the Monster–Andre Norton; 1962 | 1.50 | 3.00 | 4.50 | SF |
| | Sea Siege–Andre Norton | | | | SF |
| F148 | Wild Sky–Harry Whittington | 1.50 | 3.00 | 4.50 | W |
| | Dead Man's Double Cross–Tom West | | | | W |
| F149 | Cosmic Checkmate–Katherine MacLean & Charles V. deVet | 1.00 | 2.00 | 3.00 | SF |
| | King of the Fourth Planet–Robert Moore Williams | | | | SF |
| F150 | Rafe–Nelson Nye | 1.00 | 2.00 | 3.00 | W |
| | Hideout Mountain–Nelson Nye | | | | W |
| F151 | Reformatory Girls–Nedra Tyre | 3.50 | 7.00 | 10.50 | JD |
| F152 | Rio Desperado–Gordon D. Shirreffs | 1.00 | 2.00 | 3.00 | W |
| | Voice of the Gun–Gordon D. Shirreffs | | | | W |
| F153 | The Planet Savers–Marion Zimmer Bradley | 2.00 | 4.00 | 6.00 | SF |
| | The Sword of Aldones–Marion Zimmer Bradley | | | | SF |
| F154 | The Wizard of Linn–A.E. Van Vogt | 1.50 | 3.00 | 4.50 | SF |
| F155 | The Time of Terror–Lionel White | 1.50 | 3.00 | 4.50 | M |
| | A Death at Sea–Lionel White | | | | M |
| F156 | At the Earth's Core–Edgar Rice Burroughs; c-Krenkel | 2.00 | 4.00 | 6.00 | SF |
| F157 | The Moon Maid–Edgar Rice Burroughs; c-Krenkel | 2.00 | 4.00 | 6.00 | SF |
| F158 | Pellucidar–Edgar Rice Burroughs; c-Krenkel | 2.00 | 4.00 | 6.00 | SF |
| F159 | The Moon Men–Edgar Rice Burroughs; c-Emsh | 2.00 | 4.00 | 6.00 | SF |
| F160 | The Shotgunner–Ray Hogan | 1.00 | 2.00 | 3.00 | W |
| | New Gun for Kingdom City–Ray Hogan | | | | W |
| F161 | Times Without Number–John Brunner | 1.00 | 2.00 | 3.00 | SF |
| | Destiny's Orbit–David Grinnell | | | | SF |
| F162 | The Best from Fantasy and Science Fiction, 7th Series–ed. Anthony Boucher | 1.25 | 2.50 | 3.75 | SF |
| F163 | Doctor Ellen–Adele De Leeuw | .75 | 1.50 | 2.25 | R |
| F164 | Slattery's Gun Says No–Steven G. Lawrence | 1.00 | 2.00 | 3.00 | W |
| | Longhorns North–Steven G. Lawrence | | | | W |
| F165 | Cache from Outer Space–Philip Jose Farmer | 3.50 | 7.00 | 10.50 | SF |
| | The Celestial Blueprint–Philip Jose Farmer | | | | SF |
| F166 | Maigret and the Reluctant Witness–Georges Simenon | 1.50 | 3.00 | 4.50 | M |
| | Maigret Has Scruples–Georges Simenon | | | | M |
| F167 | Catseye–Andre Norton; 1962 | 1.50 | 3.00 | 4.50 | SF |
| F168 | Thuvia, Maid of Mars–Edgar Rice Burroughs; c-Krenkel | 2.50 | 5.00 | 7.50 | SF |
| F169 | Tarzan and the Lost Empire–Edgar Rice Burroughs; c-Frazetta | 2.50 | 5.00 | 7.50 | SF |
| F170 | The Chessmen of Mars–Edgar Rice Burroughs; c-Krenkel | 2.50 | 5.00 | 7.50 | SF |
| F171 | Tanar of Pellucidar–Edgar Rice Burroughs; c-Krenkel | 2.00 | 4.00 | 6.00 | SF |
| F172 | Gun Rich–Giles A. Lutz | 1.00 | 2.00 | 3.00 | W |
| | Battling Buckeroos–Tom West | | | | W |
| F173 | The Jewels of Aptor–Samuel R. Delany | 1.50 | 3.00 | 4.50 | SF |
| | Second Ending–James White | | | | SF |
| F174 | First Through Time–Rex Gordon | 1.00 | 2.00 | 3.00 | SF |
| F175 | Lament for Four Brides–Evelyn Berckman | 1.00 | 2.00 | 3.00 | R |
| F176 | The Outside Gun–Ray Hogan | 1.00 | 2.00 | 3.00 | W |
| | Gun Trap at Bright Water–Dan J. Stevens | | | | W |
| F177 | Warlord of Kor–Terry Carr | 1.50 | 3.00 | 4.50 | SF |
| | The Star Wasps–Robert Moore Williams | | | | SF |
| F178 | More Adventures on Other Planets–ed. Donald A. Wollheim | 1.00 | 2.00 | 3.00 | SF |
| F179 | Pirates of Venus–Edgar Rice Burroughs; c-Krenkel | 2.00 | 4.00 | 6.00 | SF |
| F180 | Tarzan at the Earth's Core–Edgar Rice Burroughs; c-Frazetta | 2.50 | 5.00 | 7.50 | SF |
| F181 | The Mastermind of Mars–Edgar Rice Burroughs; c-Krenkel | 2.50 | 5.00 | 7.50 | SF |
| F182 | The Monster Men–Edgar Rice Burroughs; c-Frazetta | 2.00 | 4.00 | 6.00 | SF |
| F183 | The Defiant Agents–Andre Norton | 1.50 | 3.00 | 4.50 | SF |
| F184 | The Kid from Lincoln County–Nelson Nye | 1.00 | 2.00 | 3.00 | W |
| | Death Valley Slim–Nelson Nye | | | | W |
| F185 | The Dragon Masters–Jack Vance | 2.50 | 5.00 | 7.50 | SF |
| | The Five Gold Bands–Jack Vance | | | | SF |
| F186 | The High Hander–William O. Turner | 1.00 | 2.00 | 3.00 | W |
| | Wild Horse Range–Louis Trimble | | | | W |
| F187 | Alpha Centauri–or Die!–Leigh Brackett | 1.00 | 2.00 | 3.00 | SF |
| | Legend of Lost Earth–G. McDonald Wallis | | | | SF |
| F188 | Armageddon 2419 A.D.–Philip Francis Nowlan | 1.50 | 3.00 | 4.50 | SF |
| F189 | Tarzan the Invincible–Edgar Rice Burroughs; c-Frazetta | 2.50 | 5.00 | 7.50 | SF |
| F190 | A Fighting Man of Mars–Edgar Rice Burroughs; c-Krenkel | 2.50 | 5.00 | 7.50 | SF |
| F191 | Journey to the Center of the Earth–Jules Verne | .75 | 1.50 | 2.25 | SF |
| F192 | Star Born–Andre Norton; 1963 | 1.50 | 3.00 | 4.50 | SF |
| F193 | The Son of Tarzan–Edgar Rice Burroughs; c-Frazetta | 2.50 | 5.00 | 7.50 | SF |
| F194 | Tarzan Triumphant–Edgar Rice Burroughs; c-Krenkel | 2.50 | 5.00 | 7.50 | SF |
| F195 | The Silent Invaders–Robert Silverberg | 1.00 | 2.00 | 3.00 | SF |
| | Battle on Venus–William F. Temple | | | | SF |
| F196 | Prairie Raiders–Harry Whittington | 2.00 | 4.00 | 6.00 | W |
| | Drygulch Town–Harry Whittington | | | | W |
| F197 | Witch World–Andre Norton; 1963 | 1.50 | 3.00 | 4.50 | SF |
| F198 | The Short Cases of Inspector Maigret–Georges Simenon | 1.50 | 3.00 | 4.50 | M |
| F199 | Captives of the Flame–Samuel R. Delany | 1.50 | 3.00 | 4.50 | SF |
| | The Psionic Menace–Samuel R. Delany | | | | SF |
| F200 | Triggering Texan–Tom West | 1.00 | 2.00 | 3.00 | W |
| | The Big Snow–Frank Wynne | | | | W |
| F201 | Doomsday, 1999–Paul MacTyre | .75 | 1.50 | 2.25 | SF |
| F202 | The Hovering Darkness–Evelyn Berckman | .75 | 1.50 | 2.25 | R |
| F203 | The Beasts of Tarzan–Edgar Rice Burroughs; c-Frazetta | 2.50 | 5.00 | 7.50 | SF |
| F204 | Tarzan and the Jewels of Opar–Edgar Rice Burroughs; c-Frazetta | 2.50 | 5.00 | 7.50 | SF |
| F205 | Tarzan and the City of Gold–Edgar Rice Burroughs; c-Frazetta | 2.50 | 5.00 | 7.50 | SF |
| F206 | Jungle Tales of Tarzan–Edgar Rice Burroughs; c-Frazetta | 2.50 | 5.00 | 7.50 | SF |
| F207 | The Stars Are Ours!–Andre Norton | 1.50 | 3.00 | 4.50 | SF |
| F208 | Side Me at Sundown–L.P. Holmes | 1.00 | 2.00 | 3.00 | W |
| | The Buzzards of Rocky Pass–L.P. Holmes | | | | W |
| F209 | Let the Spacemen Beware–Poul Anderson | 1.00 | 2.00 | 3.00 | SF |
| | The Wizard of Starship Poseidon–Kenneth Bulmer | | | | SF |
| F210 | Red Alert–Peter Bryant | .50 | 1.00 | 1.50 | SF |
| F211 | Planet of Peril–Otis Adelbert Kline; c-Krenkel | 2.00 | 4.00 | 6.00 | SF |
| F212 | Tarzan and the Lion Man–Edgar Rice Burroughs; c-Frazetta | 2.50 | 5.00 | 7.50 | SF |
| F213 | The Land That Time Forgot–Edgar Rice Burroughs; c-Krenkel | 2.00 | 4.00 | 6.00 | SF |
| F214 | The Wildcatters–Bill Burchardt | 1.00 | 2.00 | 3.00 | W |
| | The Man from Colorado–Louis Trimble | | | | W |
| F215 | Listen! the Stars!–John Brunner; c-Emsh | 1.00 | 2.00 | 3.00 | SF |
| | The Rebellers–Jane Roberts | | | | SF |
| F216 | The Man Who Upset the Universe–Isaac Asimov | 1.50 | 3.00 | 4.50 | SF |

## ACE F-SERIES, *continued*

| No. | Title | V/Good | Fine | N/Mint | |
|---|---|---|---|---|---|
| F217 | The Best from Fantasy and Science Fiction, 8th Series–ed. Anthony Boucher | 1.25 | 2.50 | 3.75 | SF |
| F218 | They Never Came Back–Churchill | .75 | 1.50 | 2.25 | NF |
| F219 | Ask Henry–Henry Makow | .75 | 1.50 | 2.25 | H |
| F220 | The People That Time Forgot–Edgar Rice Burroughs; c-Krenkel | 1.50 | 3.00 | 4.50 | SF |
| F221 | Lost on Venus–Edgar Rice Burroughs; c-Frazetta | 2.00 | 4.00 | 6.00 | SF |
| F222 | First on the Moon–Jeff Sutton | .75 | 1.50 | 2.25 | SF |
| F223 | Envoy to New Worlds–Keith Laumer | 1.50 | 3.00 | 4.50 | SF |
| | Flight from Yesterday–Robert Moore Williams | | | | SF |
| F224 | The Seven Six-Gunners–Nelson Nye | 1.00 | 2.00 | 3.00 | W |
| | Bancroft's Banco–Nelson Nye | | | | W |
| F225 | Space Viking–H. Beam Piper | 2.50 | 5.00 | 7.50 | SF |
| F226 | Huon of the Horn–Andre Norton; 1963 | 1.50 | 3.00 | 4.50 | F |
| F227 | The Astronauts Must Not Land–John Brunner | 1.00 | 2.00 | 3.00 | SF |
| | The Space-Time Juggler–John Brunner | | | | SF |
| F228 | We Die Alone–David Howarth | .75 | 1.50 | 2.25 | C |
| F229 | The Dead and the Deadly–Louis Trimble; 1963 | 1.00 | 2.00 | 3.00 | M |
| | Homicide Handicap–Bob McKnight | | | | M |
| F230 | Lobo Lawman–Tom West | 1.00 | 2.00 | 3.00 | W |
| | Trail of the Fresno Kid–Ray Hogan | | | | W |
| F231 | Star Gate–Andre Norton | 1.50 | 3.00 | 4.50 | SF |
| F232 | The Land of Hidden Men–Edgar Rice Burroughs; c-Krenkel | 2.00 | 4.00 | 6.00 | SF |
| F233 | Out of Time's Abyss–Edgar Rice Burroughs; c-Krenkel | 2.00 | 4.00 | 6.00 | SF |
| F234 | The Eternal Savage–Edgar Rice Burroughs; c-Krenkel | 2.00 | 4.00 | 6.00 | SF |
| F235 | The Lost Continent–Edgar Rice Burroughs; c-Frazetta | 2.00 | 4.00 | 6.00 | SF |
| F236 | The Time Traders–Andre Norton | 1.50 | 3.00 | 4.50 | SF |
| F237 | Beyond the Galactic Rim–A. Bertram Chandler | 2.00 | 4.00 | 6.00 | SF |
| | The Ship from Outside–A. Bertram Chandler | | | | SF |
| F238 | Brand Him Outlaw–Stephen Payne; 1963 | 1.00 | 2.00 | 3.00 | W |
| | Quicktrigger–Gordon D. Shirreffs | | | | W |
| F239 | Time and Again–Clifford D. Simak | .75 | 1.50 | 2.25 | SF |
| F240 | When the Sleeper Wakes–H.G. Wells | 1.00 | 2.00 | 3.00 | SF |
| F241 | Star Bridge–James E. Gunn & Jack Williamson | 1.50 | 3.00 | 4.50 | SF |
| F242 | Castaways' World–John Brunner | 1.50 | 3.00 | 4.50 | SF |
| | The Rites of Ohe–John Brunner | | | | SF |
| F243 | Lord of Thunder–Andre Norton; 1963; c-Schomburg | 1.50 | 3.00 | 4.50 | SF |
| F244 | Last Gun at Cabresto–Ray Hogan | 1.00 | 2.00 | 3.00 | W |
| | Valley of Violence–Edwin Booth | | | | W |
| F245 | Back to the Stone Age–Edgar Rice Burroughs; c-Krenkel | 2.00 | 4.00 | 6.00 | SF |
| F246 | Metropolis–Thea von Harbou | 1.50 | 3.00 | 4.50 | SF |
| F247 | Carson of Venus–Edgar Rice Burroughs; c-Frazetta | 2.00 | 4.00 | 6.00 | SF |
| F248 | Beyond the Stars–Ray Cummings | 1.50 | 3.00 | 4.50 | SF |
| F249 | The Hand of Zei–L. Sprague de Camp | 2.00 | 4.00 | 6.00 | SF |
| | The Search for Zei–L. Sprague de Camp | | | | SF |
| F250 | Gallows Gulch–Tom West | 1.00 | 2.00 | 3.00 | W |
| | The Masked Gun–Barry Cord | | | | W |
| F251 | The Game-Players of Titan–Philip K. Dick | 2.50 | 5.00 | 7.50 | SF |
| F252 | The Shooting of Storey James–John Clifford | 1.00 | 2.00 | 3.00 | W |
| F253 | One of Our Asteroids Is Missing–Calvin M. Knox | 1.00 | 2.00 | 3.00 | SF |
| | The Twisted Men–A.E. Van Vogt | | | | SF |
| F254 | Hardcase Halloran–William Heuman | 1.00 | 2.00 | 3.00 | W |
| | The Ghost Riders–Philip Ketchum | | | | W |
| F255 | The Prodigal Sun–Philip E. High | .75 | 1.50 | 2.25 | SF |
| F256 | Land of Terror–Edgar Rice Burroughs; c-Frazetta | 2.00 | 4.00 | 6.00 | SF |
| F257 | Alien Planet–Fletcher Pratt | 1.00 | 2.00 | 3.00 | SF |
| F258 | The Cave Girl–Edgar Rice Burroughs; c-Krenkel | 2.00 | 4.00 | 6.00 | SF |
| F259 | Prince of Peril–Otis Adelbert Kline; c-Krenkel | 2.00 | 4.00 | 6.00 | SF |
| F260 | Trail Drive–Brian Garfield; 1964 | 1.00 | 2.00 | 3.00 | W |
| | Trouble at Gunsight–Louis Trimble | | | | W |
| F261 | The Towers of Toron–Samuel R. Delany | 1.00 | 2.00 | 3.00 | SF |
| | The Lunar Eye–Robert Moore Williams | | | | SF |
| F262 | Reckless Men–Clifton Adams | 1.00 | 2.00 | 3.00 | W |
| F263 | Web of the Witch World–Andre Norton; 1964 | 1.50 | 3.00 | 4.50 | SF |
| F264 | Don't Cross My Line–Tom West; 1964 | 1.00 | 2.00 | 3.00 | W |
| | Contract in Cartridges–Ben Elliott | | | | W |
| F265 | The Houses of Iszm–Jack Vance | | | | SF |
| | Son of the Tree–Jack Vance | 2.50 | 5.00 | 7.50 | SF |
| F266 | Roundup on the Yellowstone–Allan Vaughan Elston | 1.00 | 2.00 | 3.00 | W |
| F267 | The Best from Fantasy and Science Fiction, 9th Series–ed. Robert P. Mills | 1.25 | 2.50 | 3.75 | SF |
| F268 | Escape on Venus–Edgar Rice Burroughs; c-Frazetta | 2.00 | 4.00 | 6.00 | SF |
| F269 | Quest of the Dawn Man–J.H. Rosny | 1.50 | 3.00 | 4.50 | SF |
| F270 | The Mad King–Edgar Rice Burroughs; c-Frazetta | 2.00 | 4.00 | 6.00 | SF |
| F271 | Outside the Universe–Edmond Hamilton | 1.50 | 3.00 | 4.50 | SF |
| F272 | No Job for a Cowboy–Stephen Payne | 1.00 | 2.00 | 3.00 | W |
| | The Man from Barranca Negra–Ray Hogan | | | | W |
| F273 | The Dark Intruder–Marion Zimmer Bradley | 2.00 | 4.00 | 6.00 | SF |
| | Falcons of Narabedla–Marion Zimmer Bradley | | | | SF |
| F274 | The Cosmic Computer–H. Beam Piper | 2.00 | 4.00 | 6.00 | SF |
| F275 | No Truce with Terra–Philip E. High | 1.00 | 2.00 | 3.00 | SF |
| | The Duplicators–Murray Leinster | | | | SF |
| F276 | The Wolf Slayer–William E. Vance | 1.00 | 2.00 | 3.00 | W |
| | Mr. Sixgun–Brian Wynne | | | | W |
| F277 | To Conquer Chaos–John Brunner | 1.50 | 3.00 | 4.50 | SF |
| F278 | Patty Goes to Washington–Frances Spatz Leighton; TV tie-in | 1.00 | 2.00 | 3.00 | |
| F279 | Sargasso of Space–Andre Norton; 1964 | 1.50 | 3.00 | 4.50 | SF |
| F280 | Savage Pellucidar–Edgar Rice Burroughs; c-Frazetta | 2.00 | 4.00 | 6.00 | SF |
| F281 | Atlantida–Pierre Benoit | 2.00 | 4.00 | 6.00 | F |
| F282 | Beyond the Farthest Star–Edgar Rice Burroughs; c-Frazetta | 2.00 | 4.00 | 6.00 | SF |
| F283 | The Day the World Ended–Sax Rohmer | 2.00 | 4.00 | 6.00 | SF |
| F284 | Border Passage–Lin Searles | 1.00 | 2.00 | 3.00 | W |
| | The Homesteader–Ben Smith | | | | W |
| F285 | The Million Year Hunt–Kenneth Bulmer | 1.00 | 2.00 | 3.00 | SF |
| | Ships to the Stars–Fritz Leiber | | | | SF |
| F286 | The Long Way North–Jim Bosworth | 1.00 | 2.00 | 3.00 | W |
| F287 | Key Out of Time–Andre Norton | 1.50 | 3.00 | 4.50 | SF |
| F288 | Fishing for Laughs–Hal Sherman | 1.00 | 2.00 | 3.00 | H |
| F289 | Demons' World–Kenneth Bulmer | 1.50 | 3.00 | 4.50 | SF |
| | I Want the Stars–Tom Purdom | | | | SF |
| F290 | The Night of the Bowstring–D.B. Olsen | 1.00 | 2.00 | 3.00 | W |
| F291 | Plague Ship–Andre Norton; 1964 | 1.50 | 3.00 | 4.50 | SF |
| F292 | The Man at Rope's End–Tom West | 1.00 | 2.00 | 3.00 | W |
| | The Hidden Rider of Dark Mountain–Gordon D. Shirreffs | | | | W |
| F293 | Moon Base–E.C. Tubb | 1.50 | 3.00 | 4.50 | SF |
| F294 | The Port of Peril–Otis Adelbert Kline; c-Frazetta | 2.00 | 4.00 | 6.00 | SF |
| F295 | The World of Null-A–A.E. Van Vogt | 1.50 | 3.00 | 4.50 | SF |
| F296 | Gulliver of Mars–Edwin L. Arnold; c-Frazetta | 1.50 | 3.00 | 4.50 | SF |
| F297 | Valley of the Flame–Henry Kuttner | 3.00 | 6.00 | 9.00 | SF |
| F298 | Treasure Trail from Tucson–Nelson Nye | 1.00 | 2.00 | 3.00 | W |
| | Sudden Country–Nelson Nye | | | | W |
| F299 | Endless Shadow–John Brunner | 1.50 | 3.00 | 4.50 | SF |
| | The Arsenal of Miracles–Gardner F. Fox | | | | SF |
| F300 | Vultures in the Sun–Brian Garfield | 1.00 | 2.00 | 3.00 | W |
| F301 | The Simulacra–Philip K. Dick | 2.00 | 4.00 | 6.00 | SF |
| F302 | Dragoon Pass–Frank Wynne | 1.00 | 2.00 | 3.00 | W |
| F303 | The Bloody Sun–Marion Zimmer Bradley | 1.50 | 3.00 | 4.50 | SF |
| F304 | The Radio Beasts–Ralph Milne Farley | 1.50 | 3.00 | 4.50 | SF |
| F305 | Almuric–Robert E. Howard; 1st ed. 1964 | 4.00 | 8.00 | 12.00 | SF |

| | V/Good | Fine | N/Mint | |
|---|---|---|---|---|

ACE F-SERIES, *continued*

| No. | Title | V/Good | Fine | N/Mint | |
|---|---|---|---|---|---|
| F306 | Earth's Last Citadel—C.L. Moore & Henry Kuttner; c-Schomburg | 2.00 | 4.00 | 6.00 | SF |
| F307 | Warrior of Llarn—Gardner F. Fox; c-Frazetta | 2.00 | 4.00 | 6.00 | SF |
| F308 | Judgement on Janus—Andre Norton; 1964; c-Schomburg | 1.50 | 3.00 | 4.50 | SF |
| F309 | Clans of the Alphane Moon—Philip K. Dick | 2.00 | 4.00 | 6.00 | SF |
| F310 | Galactic Derelict—Andre Norton | 1.50 | 3.00 | 4.50 | SF |
| F311 | Swordsmen in the Sky—Donald A. Wollheim; c-Frazetta | 2.00 | 4.00 | 6.00 | SF |
| F312 | The Radio Planet—Ralph Milne Farley | 1.50 | 3.00 | 4.50 | SF |
| F313 | A Brand New World—Ray Cummings | 1.50 | 3.00 | 4.50 | SF |
| F314 | The Universe Against Her—James H. Schmitz | 1.50 | 3.00 | 4.50 | SF |
| F315 | The Beast Master—Andre Norton; 1964 | 1.50 | 3.00 | 4.50 | SF |
| F316 | The Burntwood Men—Robert McCaig | 1.00 | 2.00 | 3.00 | W |
| F317 | The Escape Orbit—James White | 1.50 | 3.00 | 4.50 | SF |
| F318 | The Spot of Life—Austin Hall & Homer Eon Flint | 1.50 | 3.00 | 4.50 | SF |
| F319 | Crashing Suns—Edmond Hamilton | 1.50 | 3.00 | 4.50 | SF |
| F320 | The Martian Sphinx—Keith Woodcott | 1.50 | 3.00 | 4.50 | SF |
| F321 | Maza of the Moon—Otis Adelbert Kline; c-Frazetta | 2.00 | 4.00 | 6.00 | SF |
| F322 | City of a Thousand Suns—Samuel R. Delany | 1.50 | 3.00 | 4.50 | SF |
| F323 | Daybreak 2250 A.D.—Andre Norton; 1965 | 1.00 | 2.00 | 3.00 | SF |
| F324 | Apache Canyon—Brian Garfield | 1.00 | 2.00 | 3.00 | W |
| F325 | Ordeal in Otherwhere—Andre Norton; 1965 | 1.50 | 3.00 | 4.50 | SF |
| F326 | The Wizard of Lemuria—Lin Carter; c-Morrow | 1.50 | 3.00 | 4.50 | SF |
| F327 | The Dark World—Henry Kuttner | 3.50 | 7.00 | 10.50 | SF |
| F328 | The Galaxy Primes—Edward E. "Doc" Smith | 1.50 | 3.00 | 4.50 | SF |
| F329 | Storm over Warlock—Andre Norton | 1.50 | 3.00 | 4.50 | SF |
| F330 | What Strange Stars and Skies—Avram Davidson | .75 | 1.50 | 2.25 | SF |
| F331 | Gravestone Manor—Gahan Wilson | 1.50 | 3.00 | 4.50 | |
| F332 | Three Against the Witch World—Andre Norton; 1965 | 1.50 | 3.00 | 4.50 | SF |
| F333 | Rogue Queen—L. Sprague de Camp | 1.50 | 3.00 | 4.50 | SF |
| F334 | The Insect Warriors—Rex Dean Levie | 1.50 | 3.00 | 4.50 | SF |
| F335 | The Second Atlantis—Robert Moore Williams | 1.00 | 2.00 | 3.00 | SF |
| F337 | Dr. Bloodmoney, or, How We Got Along After the Bomb—Philip K. Dick | 1.50 | 3.00 | 4.50 | SF |
| F338 | Ace Crossword Puzzle Book No. 1 | 7.50 | 15.00 | 22.50 | NF |
| F339 | Private Duty for Nurse Scott—Arlene Hale | .50 | 1.00 | 1.50 | R |
| F340 | The Relentless Rider—John Shelley & David Shelley | 1.00 | 2.00 | 3.00 | W |
| F341 | A Prize for Nurse Darci—Suzanne Roberts | .50 | 1.00 | 1.50 | R |
| F342 | Lord Kalvan of Otherwhen—H. Beam Piper | 2.00 | 4.00 | 6.00 | SF |
| F343 | The Exile of Time—Ray Cummings; c-Schomburg | .75 | 1.50 | 2.25 | SF |
| F344 | The Well of the Worlds—Henry Kuttner; c-Schomburg | 2.50 | 5.00 | 7.50 | SF |
| F345 | The Lord of Death and the Queen of Life—Homer Eon Flint | 1.50 | 3.00 | 4.50 | SF |
| F346 | The Black Star Passes—John W. Campbell | 1.50 | 3.00 | 4.50 | SF |
| F347 | The Last Hope of Earth—Lan Wright | 1.00 | 2.00 | 3.00 | SF |
| F348 | Guns of Horse Prairie—Nelson Nye | 1.00 | 2.00 | 3.00 | W |
| F349 | Celebrity Suite Nurse—Suzanne Roberts | .50 | 1.00 | 1.50 | R |
| F350 | Star of Danger—Marion Zimmer Bradley | 1.50 | 3.00 | 4.50 | SF |
| F351 | The Holdout in the Diablos—Louis Trimble | 1.00 | 2.00 | 3.00 | W |
| F352 | Nurse on Leave—Arlene Hale | .50 | 1.00 | 1.50 | R |
| F353 | Rogue Dragon—Avram Davidson | 1.50 | 3.00 | 4.50 | SF |
| F354 | Hunter out of Time—Gardner F. Fox; frontis by Frazetta | 1.50 | 3.00 | 4.50 | SF |
| F355 | The Devolutionist and the Emancipatrix—Homer Eon Flint | 1.50 | 3.00 | 4.50 | SF |
| F356 | The Time Axis—Henry Kuttner; c-Schomburg | 1.50 | 3.00 | 4.50 | SF |
| F357 | Year of the Unicorn—Andre Norton; 1965 | 1.50 | 3.00 | 4.50 | SF |
| F358 | Wild Riders of Savage Valley—William Vance | 1.00 | 2.00 | 3.00 | W |
| F359 | Jungle Nurse—Sharon Heath | .50 | 1.00 | 1.50 | R |
| F360 | Rawhiders of the Brasada—L.L. Foreman | 1.00 | 2.00 | 3.00 | W |
| F361 | The Day of the Star Cities—John Brunner | 1.00 | 2.00 | 3.00 | SF |
| F362 | The Two Dr. Barlowes—Suzanne Roberts | .50 | 1.00 | 1.50 | R |
| F363 | Tama of the Light Country—Ray Cummings | 1.50 | 3.00 | 4.50 | SF |
| F364 | The Mightiest Machine—John W. Campbell | 1.50 | 3.00 | 4.50 | SF |
| F365 | Night of Masks—Andre Norton | 1.50 | 3.00 | 4.50 | SF |
| F366 | The Last Planet—Andre Norton; 1965 | 1.00 | 2.00 | 3.00 | SF |
| F367 | Maker of Universes—Philip Jose Farmer | 2.00 | 4.00 | 6.00 | SF |
| F368 | Chicago Nurse—Arlene Hale | .50 | 1.00 | 1.50 | R |
| F369 | The Lobo Horseman—Samuel Anthony Peeples | 1.00 | 2.00 | 3.00 | W |
| F370 | The Man from Andersonville—Brad Ward | 1.00 | 2.00 | 3.00 | W |
| F371 | Camp Nurse—Arlene Hale | .50 | 1.00 | 1.50 | R |
| F372 | Spacehounds of IPC—Edward E. "Doc" Smith | 1.25 | 2.50 | 3.75 | SF |
| F373 | The Sword of Lankor—Howard L. Cory | 1.50 | 3.00 | 4.50 | SF |
| F374 | The Atom Conspiracy—Jeff Sutton | 1.00 | 2.00 | 3.00 | SF |
| F375 | The Worlds of Robert A. Heinlein—Robert A. Heinlein | 1.50 | 3.00 | 4.50 | SF |
| F376 | The Odds Against Circle L—Lewis B. Patten | 1.00 | 2.00 | 3.00 | W |
| F377 | The Crack in Space—Philip K. Dick | 1.50 | 3.00 | 4.50 | SF |
| F378 | Danger—Nurse at Work—Mary Mann Fletcher | .50 | 1.00 | 1.50 | R |
| F379 | The Green Brain—Frank Herbert | 1.50 | 3.00 | 4.50 | SF |
| F380 | The Legend of Blackjack Sam—Lee Hoffman | 1.00 | 2.00 | 3.00 | W |
| F381 | Nurse at Shadow Manor—Sharon Heath | .50 | 1.00 | 1.50 | R |
| F382 | Bow Down to Null—Brian W. Aldiss | 1.25 | 2.50 | 3.75 | SF |
| F383 | Thongor of Lemuria—Lin Carter; c-Morrow | 2.00 | 4.00 | 6.00 | SF |
| F384 | The Savage Hours—L.P. Holmes | 1.00 | 2.00 | 3.00 | W |
| F385 | Emergency for Nurse Selena—Arlene Hale | .50 | 1.00 | 1.50 | R |
| F386 | The Time Traders—Andre Norton | 1.50 | 3.00 | 4.50 | SF |
| F387 | Mountain Nurse—Arlene Hale | .50 | 1.00 | 1.50 | R |
| F388 | Babel-17—Samuel R. Delany | 1.25 | 2.50 | 3.75 | SF |
| F389 | Shoot Him on Sight!—William Colt MacDonald | 1.00 | 2.00 | 3.00 | W |
| F390 | The Languages of Pao—Jack Vance | 2.00 | 4.00 | 6.00 | SF |
| F391 | Crossroads of Time—Andre Norton | 1.50 | 3.00 | 4.50 | SF |
| F392 | Saga of Lost Earths—Emil Petaja | 1.50 | 3.00 | 4.50 | SF |
| F393 | This Immortal—Roger Zelazny | 1.50 | 3.00 | 4.50 | SF |
| F394 | Journey for a Nurse—Gail Everett | .50 | 1.00 | 1.50 | R |
| F395 | Iron Hand—Nelson Nye | 1.00 | 2.00 | 3.00 | W |
| F396 | Worlds for the Taking—Kenneth Bulmer | 1.50 | 3.00 | 4.50 | SF |
| F397 | Nurse Kay's Conquest—Willo Davis Roberts | .50 | 1.00 | 1.50 | R |
| F398 | Somewhere a Voice—Eric Frank Russell | 1.50 | 3.00 | 4.50 | SF |
| F399 | Thief of Llarn—Gardner F. Fox; c-Morrow | 1.50 | 3.00 | 4.50 | SF |
| F400 | Jan of the Jungle—Otis Adelbert Kline | 2.00 | 4.00 | 6.00 | A |
| F401 | Outrage at Bearskin Forks—Merle Constiner | 1.00 | 2.00 | 3.00 | W |
| F402 | Quest of the Three Worlds—Cordwainer Smith | 1.50 | 3.00 | 4.50 | SF |
| F403 | The Dream Master—Roger Zelazny | 1.50 | 3.00 | 4.50 | SF |
| F404 | The Grabhorn Bounty—Clifton Adams | 1.00 | 2.00 | 3.00 | W |
| F405 | Vietnam Nurse—Suzanne Roberts | .50 | 1.00 | 1.50 | R |
| F406 | Tama, Princess of Mercury—Ray Cummings | 1.50 | 3.00 | 4.50 | SF |
| F407 | Day of the Minotaur—Thomas Burnett Swann | 2.00 | 4.00 | 6.00 | SF |
| F408 | The Sioux Spaceman—Andre Norton; 1966 | 1.50 | 3.00 | 4.50 | SF |
| F409 | Cliff Rider—Lin Searles | 1.00 | 2.00 | 3.00 | W |
| F410 | Lake Resort Nurse—Arlene Hale | .50 | 1.00 | 1.50 | R |
| F411 | The Mustang Trail—L.L. Foreman | 1.00 | 2.00 | 3.00 | W |
| F412 | The Gates of Creation—Philip Jose Farmer | 2.00 | 4.00 | 6.00 | SF |
| F413 | A Vacation for Nurse Dean—Sharon Heath | .50 | 1.00 | 1.50 | R |
| F414 | The Star Mill—Emil Petaja; 1966 | 1.50 | 3.00 | 4.50 | SF |

| | | V/Good | Fine | N/Mint | |
|---|---|---|---|---|---|

**ACE F-SERIES,** *continued*

| | | V/Good | Fine | N/Mint | |
|---|---|---|---|---|---|
| F415 | The Bravos–Brian Wynne | 1.00 | 2.00 | 3.00 | W |
| F416 | Utopia Minus X–Rex Gordon | .50 | 1.00 | 1.50 | SF |
| F417 | Once a Nurse–Willo Davis Roberts | .50 | 1.00 | 1.50 | R |
| F418 | Single Action–Nelson Nye | 1.00 | 2.00 | 3.00 | W |
| F419 | Rangeland Nurse–Suzanne Roberts | .50 | 1.00 | 1.50 | R |
| F420 | Planet of the Double Sun–Neil R. Jones | 1.00 | 2.00 | 3.00 | SF |
| F421 | Anarchaos–Curt Clark (Donald Westlake) | 1.50 | 3.00 | 4.50 | SF |
| F422 | The Sword of Rhiannon–Leigh Brackett | 1.50 | 3.00 | 4.50 | SF |
| F423 | Giant on Horseback–Lewis B. Patten | 1.00 | 2.00 | 3.00 | W |
| F424 | Community Nurse–Arlene Hale | .50 | 1.00 | 1.50 | R |
| F425 | World Without Stars–Poul Anderson | 1.50 | 3.00 | 4.50 | SF |
| F426 | The Genetic General–Gordon R. Dickson | 1.50 | 3.00 | 4.50 | SF |
| F427 | The Einstein Intersection–Samuel R. Delany | 1.25 | 2.50 | 3.75 | SF |
| F428 | Mascarada Pass–William Colt MacDonald | 1.00 | 2.00 | 3.00 | W |
| F429 | The World Jones Made–Philip K. Dick; 1967 | 2.00 | 4.00 | 6.00 | SF |
| F430 | Nurse on the Beach–Arlene Hale; 1967 | .50 | 1.00 | 1.50 | R |

# ACE G-SERIES
## Ace Books, Inc.

**Note: This 50-cent series branched off of Ace's initial D/S/G series, where earlier G numbers exist.**

| | | V/Good | Fine | N/Mint | |
|---|---|---|---|---|---|
| G500 | The Bad Man of the West–George D. Hendricks | 1.50 | 3.00 | 4.50 | NF |
| G501 | Incident at a Corner–Charlotte Armstrong | .75 | 1.50 | 2.25 | M |
| | The Unsuspected–Charlotte Armstrong | | | | M |
| G502 | Pat Garrett–Richard O'Connor | 1.50 | 3.00 | 4.50 | NF |
| G503 | The Stairway–Ursula Curtiss | .50 | 1.00 | 1.50 | M |
| | The Face of the Tiger–Ursula Curtiss | | | | M |
| G504 | Moscow–Theodor Plievier | .50 | 1.00 | 1.50 | C |
| G506 | Black Mail–Doris Miles Disney | .50 | 1.00 | 1.50 | M |
| | Did She Fall or Was She Pushed?– Doris Miles Disney | | | | M |
| G507 | Hell in the Heavens–Cpt. John M. Foster, USMCR | .50 | 1.00 | 1.50 | C |
| G508 | But Not Forgotten–Ruth Fenisong | .50 | 1.00 | 1.50 | M |
| | The Schemers–Ruth Fenisong | | | | M |
| G509 | The Virgin Huntress–Elisabeth Sanxay Holding | .50 | 1.00 | 1.50 | M |
| | The Innocent Mrs. Duff–Elisabeth Sanxay Holding | | | | M |
| G510 | The Case of the Weird Sisters– Charlotte Armstrong | 1.00 | 2.00 | 3.00 | M |
| | The Chocolate Cobweb–Charlotte Armstrong | | | | M |
| G511 | Who's Been Sitting in My Chair?– Charlotte Armstrong | .50 | 1.00 | 1.50 | M |
| | The Blank Wall–Elisabeth Sanxay Holding | | | | M |
| G512 | The Girl Who Had to Die–Elisabeth Sanxay Holding | .50 | 1.00 | 1.50 | M |

*Ace F278, Ace G510, Ace G507.*

| | | V/Good | Fine | N/Mint | |
|---|---|---|---|---|---|
| | Catch-as-Catch-Can–Charlotte Armstrong | | | | M |
| G513 | Then Came Two Women–Charlotte Armstrong | .50 | 1.00 | 1.50 | M |
| G514 | Something Blue–Charlotte Armstrong | .50 | 1.00 | 1.50 | M |
| G515 | The Long Walk–Slavomir Rawicz | .50 | 1.00 | 1.50 | A |
| G518 | The Opening Door–Helen Reilly | .50 | 1.00 | 1.50 | M |
| | Follow Me–Helen Reilly | | | | M |
| G519 | The Old Battle Axe–Elisabeth Sanxay Holding | .50 | 1.00 | 1.50 | M |
| | The Obstinate Murderer–Elisabeth Sanxay Holding | | | | M |
| G520 | Arena–Jay Scotland (John Jakes); 1963; c-Maguire | 1.50 | 3.00 | 4.50 | A |
| G521 | Mischief–Charlotte Armstrong | .50 | 1.00 | 1.50 | M |
| | The Better to Eat You–Charlotte Armstrong | | | | M |
| G522 | The Firebrand–George Challis | 1.25 | 2.50 | 3.75 | A |
| G523 | Hours to Kill–Ursula Curtiss | .50 | 1.00 | 1.50 | M |
| | The Forbidden Garden–Ursula Curtiss | | | | M |
| G524 | Widow's Mite–Elisabeth Sanxay Holding | .50 | 1.00 | 1.50 | M |
| | Who's Afraid–Elisabeth Sanxay Holding | | | | M |
| G525 | Spin the Web Tight–Dana Lyon | .50 | 1.00 | 1.50 | M |
| | The Tentacles–Dana Lyon | | | | M |
| G526 | The Dream Walker–Charlotte Armstrong | .50 | 1.00 | 1.50 | M |
| | The Mark of the Hand–Charlotte Armstrong | | | | M |
| G527 | The Bait and the Trap–George Challis | 1.25 | 2.50 | 3.75 | A |
| G528 | Certain Sleep–Helen Reilly | .50 | 1.00 | 1.50 | M |
| | Ding Dong Bell–Helen Reilly | | | | M |
| G529 | Mrs. Meeker's Money–Doris Miles Disney | .50 | 1.00 | 1.50 | M |
| | Unappointed Rounds–Doris Miles Disney | | | | M |
| G530 | The Unfinished Crime–Elisabeth Sanxay Holding; 1963 | .50 | 1.00 | 1.50 | M |
| | Net of Cobwebs–Elisabeth Sanxay Holding | | | | M |
| G531 | Not Me, Inspector–Helen Reilly | .50 | 1.00 | 1.50 | M |
| | The Canvas Dagger–Helen Reilly | | | | M |
| G532 | Traitors' Legion–Jay Scotland (John Jakes) | 1.50 | 3.00 | 4.50 | A |
| G533 | The Black-Eyed Stranger–Charlotte Armstrong | .50 | 1.00 | 1.50 | M |
| | The One-Faced Girl–Charlotte Armstrong | | | | M |
| G534 | Kill Joy–Elisabeth Sanxay Holding | .50 | 1.00 | 1.50 | M |
| | Speak of the Devil–Elisabeth Sanxay Holding | | | | M |
| G535 | The Frightened Child–Dana Lyon | .50 | 1.00 | 1.50 | M |
| | The Lost One–Dana Lyon | | | | M |
| G536 | The Day She Died–Helen Reilly | .50 | 1.00 | 1.50 | M |
| G537 | The Report on Unidentified Flying Objects–Edward J. Ruppelt | .50 | 1.00 | 1.50 | UF |
| G538 | Shadow Hawk–Andre Norton; 1964 | 1.25 | 2.50 | 3.75 | A |
| G539 | The House–Hilda Lawrence | .50 | 1.00 | 1.50 | M |
| | Composition for Four Hands–Hilda Lawrence | | | | M |
| G540 | A Little Less Than Kind–Charlotte Armstrong | .50 | 1.00 | 1.50 | M |
| G541 | The Evil Wish–Jean Potts | .50 | 1.00 | 1.50 | M |
| G542 | Meet Me Tonight–Martha Albrand | .50 | 1.00 | 1.50 | M |
| G543 | The Dark Place–Mildred Davis | .50 | 1.00 | 1.50 | M |
| | They Buried a Man–Mildred Davis | | | | M |
| G544 | The Wench Is Dead–Ruth Fenisong | .50 | 1.00 | 1.50 | M |
| G545 | The Trusting Victim–Dana Lyon | .50 | 1.00 | 1.50 | M |
| G546 | Compartment K–Helen Reilly | .50 | 1.00 | 1.50 | M |
| G547 | The Blind Spot–Homer Eon Flint & Austin Hall | 1.00 | 2.00 | 3.00 | SF |
| G548 | Let's Kill Uncle–Rohan O'Grady | .75 | 1.50 | 2.25 | M |
| G549 | The Iron Cobweb–Ursula Curtiss | .50 | 1.00 | 1.50 | M |
| G550 | The Listener–Theodora duBois | .50 | 1.00 | 1.50 | M |
| G551 | World's Best SF: 1965–eds. Terry Carr & Donald A. Wollheim | 1.00 | 2.00 | 3.00 | SF |
| G552 | Shannon Terror–Theodora DuBois; 1964 | .50 | 1.00 | 1.50 | M |
| G553 | The Thousand Coffins Affair–Michael Avallone; TV tie-in | 1.00 | 2.00 | 3.00 | M |
| G554 | The Velvet Target–Genevieve Holden | .50 | 1.00 | 1.50 | M |
| G555 | The Wasp–Ursula Curtiss | .50 | 1.00 | 1.50 | M |

ACE G-SERIES, *continued*

| | V/Good | Fine | N/Mint | |
|---|---|---|---|---|
| G556 Love with a Harvard Accent–Leonie St. John; 1965 | .50 | 1.00 | 1.50 | |
| G557 Out of the Dark–Ursula Curtiss | .50 | 1.00 | 1.50 | M |
| G558 Something's Happened to Kate–Genevieve Holden | .50 | 1.00 | 1.50 | M |
| G559 After Midnight–Martha Albrand | .50 | 1.00 | 1.50 | M |
| G560 The Doomsday Affair–Harry Whittington; TV tie-in | 1.00 | 2.00 | 3.00 | M |
| G561 Widow's Web–Ursula Curtiss | .50 | 1.00 | 1.50 | M |
| G562 The Long Body–Helen McCloy | .50 | 1.00 | 1.50 | M |
| G563 A Day in Monte Carlo–Martha Albrand | .50 | 1.00 | 1.50 | R |
| G564 The Copenhagen Affair–John Oram; TV tie-in | 1.00 | 2.00 | 3.00 | M |
| G565 The Deadly Climate–Ursula Curtiss | .50 | 1.00 | 1.50 | M |
| G566 Lady in the Mist–Theresa Charles; aka Nurse Alice in Love | .50 | 1.00 | 1.50 | |
| G567 The Shrouded Tower–Theresa Charles; aka The Man for Me | .50 | 1.00 | 1.50 | |
| G568 Escape While I Can–Melba Marlett | .50 | 1.00 | 1.50 | |
| G569 We Die Alone–David Howarth | .50 | 1.00 | 1.50 | NF |
| G570 The Weirdstone of Brisingamen–Alan Garner | 1.00 | 2.00 | 3.00 | SF |
| G571 The Dagger Affair–David McDaniel; TV tie-in | 1.00 | 2.00 | 3.00 | M |
| G572 The Man in the Mews–Joy Packer | .50 | 1.00 | 1.50 | |
| G573 Rattlesnake Range–Tom West | 1.00 | 2.00 | 3.00 | W |
| Top Gun from the Dakotas–Merle Constiner | | | | W |
| G574 The Kar-chee Reign–Avram Davidson | 1.25 | 2.50 | 3.75 | SF |
| Rocannon's World–Ursula K. LeGuin; 1966 | | | | SF |
| G575 Quin's Hide–Margaret Summerton | .50 | 1.00 | 1.50 | |
| G576 Clash of Star Kings–Avram Davidson | 1.25 | 2.50 | 3.75 | SF |
| Danger from Vega–John Rackham | | | | SF |
| G577 Killer's Gun–Ray Hogan | 1.00 | 2.00 | 3.00 | W |
| Big Man from the Brazos–Roger Spellman | | | | W |
| G578 Shadow of a Witch–Mary Paradise | .50 | 1.00 | 1.50 | |
| G579 Ride a Dim Trail–Lee E. Wells | 1.00 | 2.00 | 3.00 | W |
| Showdown in the Cayose–Louis Trimble | | | | W |
| G580 Inherit the Earth–Claude Nunes | 1.25 | 2.50 | 3.75 | SF |
| Dawnman Planet–Mack Reynolds | | | | SF |
| G581 The Mad Scientist Affair–John T. Phillifent; TV tie-in | 1.00 | 2.00 | 3.00 | M |
| G582 Journey to the Center of the Earth–Jules Verne | .50 | 1.00 | 1.50 | SF |
| G583 Festival of Darkness–Marie Garratt | .50 | 1.00 | 1.50 | |
| G584 The Ruthless Breed–Clement Hardin | 1.00 | 2.00 | 3.00 | W |
| Son of a Desperado–William E. Vance | | | | W |
| G585 The Planeteers–John W. Campbell | 1.50 | 3.00 | 4.50 | SF |
| The Ultimate Weapon–John W. Campbell | | | | SF |
| G586 Hawk of the Wilderness–William L. Chester | 1.25 | 2.50 | 3.75 | F |
| G587 The Wolf Pack–Frank Wynne | 1.00 | 2.00 | 3.00 | W |
| Gunfight at Laramie–Lee Hoffman | | | | W |
| G588 The Off-Worlders–John Baxter | 1.25 | 2.50 | 3.75 | SF |
| The Star Magicians–Lin Carter | | | | SF |
| G589 Ring of Mischief–Margaret Summerton | .50 | 1.00 | 1.50 | |
| G590 The Vampire Affair–David McDaniel; TV tie-in | 1.50 | 3.00 | 4.50 | M |
| G591 Hangrope Heritage–Tom West | 1.00 | 2.00 | 3.00 | W |
| Stage to Durango–Dan J. Stevens | | | | W |
| G592 A Planet of Your Own–John Brunner | 1.25 | 2.50 | 3.75 | SF |
| The Beasts of Kohl–John Rackham | | | | SF |
| G593 Face of an Angel–Mary Paradise | .50 | 1.00 | 1.50 | |
| G594 The Bloody Jungle–Charles W. Runyon | .75 | 1.50 | 2.25 | NF |
| G595 Quest Crosstime–Andre Norton; 1966 | 1.00 | 2.00 | 3.00 | SF |
| G596 The Demanding Land–Reese Sullivan | 1.00 | 2.00 | 3.00 | W |
| Hackett's Feud–John Callahan | | | | W |
| G597 Mankind Under the Leash–Thomas M. Disch | 1.25 | 2.50 | 3.75 | SF |
| Planet of Exile–Ursula K. LeGuin | | | | SF |
| G598 Bright Deadly Summer–Barbara James | .50 | 1.00 | 1.50 | |
| G599 Star Guard–Andre Norton; 1966 | .75 | 1.50 | 2.25 | SF |
| G600 The Radioactive Camel Affair–David McDaniel; TV tie-in | 1.50 | 3.00 | 4.50 | M |
| G601 The Return of Bullet Benton–John L. Shelley | 1.00 | 2.00 | 3.00 | W |
| The Hellsfire Lawman–Ray Hogan | | | | W |

| | V/Good | Fine | N/Mint | |
|---|---|---|---|---|
| G602 The Mind Monsters–Howard L. Cory | 2.00 | 4.00 | 6.00 | SF |
| The Unteleported Man–Philip K. Dick | | | | SF |
| G603 The Scent of Lilacs–Carolyn S. Wilson | .50 | 1.00 | 1.50 | |
| G604 Daktari–Jess Shelton; TV tie-in | 1.25 | 2.50 | 3.75 | A |
| G605 The Flying Saucer Gambit–Larry Maddock | .50 | 1.00 | 1.50 | SF |
| G606 The Man without a Planet–Lin Carter | 1.25 | 2.50 | 3.75 | SF |
| Time to Live–John Rackham | | | | SF |
| G607 Bitter Brand–Tom West | 1.00 | 2.00 | 3.00 | W |
| Rain of Fire–Merle Constiner | | | | W |
| G608 The Only Good Secretary–Jean Potts | .75 | 1.50 | 2.25 | W |
| G609 Contraband from Otherspace–A. Bertram Chandler | 2.00 | 4.00 | 6.00 | SF |
| Reality Forbidden–Philip E. High | | | | SF |
| G610 The Siege at Gunhammer–John L. Shelley | 1.00 | 2.00 | 3.00 | W |
| The Lusty Breed–Frank Wynne | | | | W |
| G611 The Best from Fantasy and Science Fiction, 12th Series–ed. Avram Davidson | 1.00 | 2.00 | 3.00 | SF |
| G612 Harlequin House–Leal Hayes | .50 | 1.00 | 1.50 | |
| G613 The Monster Wheel Affair–David McDaniel; TV tie-in | 1.50 | 3.00 | 4.50 | M |
| G614 Shock Wave–Walt Richmond & Leigh Richmond | 1.25 | 2.50 | 3.75 | SF |
| Envoy to the Dog Star–Frederick L. Shaw | | | | SF |
| G615 Legacy of the Slash M–Ray Hogan | 1.00 | 2.00 | 3.00 | W |
| Tracker–William E. Vance | | | | W |
| G616 Souvenir of Monique–Marion Zimmer Bradley; 1967 | 1.00 | 2.00 | 3.00 | |
| G617 The Diving Dames Affair–Peter Leslie; TV tie-in | 1.50 | 3.00 | 4.50 | M |
| G618 The Ship from Atlantis–H. Warner Munn | 1.25 | 2.50 | 3.75 | SF |
| The Stolen Sun–Emil Petaja | | | | SF |
| G619 Room to Swing a Loop–Stephen Payne | 1.00 | 2.00 | 3.00 | W |
| Gallows Ghost–Barry Cord | | | | W |
| G620 The Golden Goddess Gambit–Larry Maddock | .75 | 1.50 | 2.25 | SF |
| G621 Matravers Hall–Elizabeth Kellier | .50 | 1.00 | 1.50 | |
| G622 The Paxman Feud–Clement Hardin | 1.00 | 2.00 | 3.00 | W |
| Showdown at Serano–Tom West | | | | W |
| G623 These Savage Futurians–Philip E. High | 1.25 | 2.50 | 3.75 | SF |
| The Double Invaders–John Rackham | | | | SF |
| G624 The Secret of the Bayou–Francine Davenport | .50 | 1.00 | 1.50 | |
| G625 To Outrun Doomsday–Kenneth Bulmer | .75 | 1.50 | 2.25 | SF |
| G626 City of Illusions–Ursula K. LeGuin | .75 | 1.50 | 2.25 | SF |
| G627 The Big Time–Fritz Leiber | .75 | 1.50 | 2.25 | SF |
| G628 Shorty–Clifton Adams | .75 | 1.50 | 2.25 | W |
| G629 Nurse Missing–Elizabeth Kellier; aka Nurse to a Stranger | .50 | 1.00 | 1.50 | R |
| G630 Warlock of the Witch World–Andre Norton; 1967 | 1.25 | 2.50 | 3.75 | SF |
| G631 The Sunless World–Neil R. Jones | .75 | 1.50 | 2.25 | SF |
| G632 Nebula Alert–A. Bertram Chandler 1967 | 2.00 | 4.00 | 6.00 | SF |
| The Rival Rigellians–Mack Reynolds 1967 | | | | SF |
| G633 Return to Gunpoint–Wayne C. Lee | 1.00 | 2.00 | 3.00 | W |
| The Killers from Owl Creek–Dan J. Stevens | | | | W |
| G634 War of the Wing-men–Poul Anderson | .75 | 1.50 | 2.25 | SF |
| G635 Pilgrim's End–Lena Brooke McNamara | .50 | 1.00 | 1.50 | |
| G636 The Assassination Affair–J. Hunter Holly; TV tie-in | 1.50 | 3.00 | 4.50 | M |
| G637 The Ganymede Takeover–Philip K. Dick & Ray Nelson | 2.00 | 4.00 | 6.00 | SF |
| G638 The Action at Redstone Creek–Merle Constiner | 1.00 | 2.00 | 3.00 | W |
| A Time to Shoot It Out–Edwin Booth | | | | W |
| G639 The Weapon from Beyond–Edmond Hamilton | .75 | 1.50 | 2.25 | SF |
| G640 The Weirwoods–Thomas Burnett Swann; c-Morrow | 1.25 | 2.50 | 3.75 | SF |
| G641 Bright New Universe–Jack Williamson | .75 | 1.50 | 2.25 | SF |
| G642 Echo of a Texas Rifle–Kyle Hollingshead | 1.00 | 2.00 | 3.00 | W |
| Standoff at Massacre Buttes–Louis Trimble | | | | W |
| G643 Saverstall–Jean Vicary | .50 | 1.00 | 1.50 | |

## ACE G-SERIES, continued

| | Title | V/Good | Fine | N/Mint | |
|---|---|---|---|---|---|
| G644 | The Emerald Elephant Gambit–Larry Maddock | .75 | 1.50 | 2.25 | SF |
| G645 | The Invisibility Affair–Thomas Stratton; TV tie-in | 1.50 | 3.00 | 4.50 | M |
| G646 | The X Factor–Andre Norton | .75 | 1.50 | 2.25 | SF |
| G647 | S.O.S. from Three Worlds–Murray Leinster | .75 | 1.50 | 2.25 | SF |
| G648 | Crossfire at Barbed M–Tom West | 1.00 | 2.00 | 3.00 | W |
| | The Raid at Crazyhorse–William Vance | | | | W |
| G649 | The World Swappers–John Brunner | .75 | 1.50 | 2.25 | SF |
| G650 | Space War–Neil R. Jones | .75 | 1.50 | 2.25 | SF |
| G652 | The Disturbing Death of Jenkin Delaney–Michael Bonner | .75 | 1.50 | 2.25 | W |
| G653 | Doctor's Daughter–Arlene Hale | .50 | 1.00 | 1.50 | R |
| G654 | Catseye–Andre Norton; 1967 | .50 | 1.00 | 1.50 | SF |
| G655 | Witch World–Andre Norton; 1967 | .50 | 1.00 | 1.50 | SF |
| G656 | When the Star Kings Die–John Jakes | .75 | 1.50 | 2.25 | SF |
| G657 | Rider on the Roan–Nelson Nye | .75 | 1.50 | 2.25 | W |
| G658 | Leap in the Dark–Rona Randall | .50 | 1.00 | 1.50 | R |
| G659 | The Oxbow Deed–Clement Hardin | 1.00 | 2.00 | 3.00 | W |
| | Kincaid–John Callahan | | | | W |
| G660 | The Universe Maker–A.E. Van Vogt | .50 | 1.00 | 1.50 | SF |
| G661 | Big Planet–Jack Vance | .75 | 1.50 | 2.25 | SF |
| G662 | The Second Mally Lee–Elisabeth Kyle; aka Mally Lee | .50 | 1.00 | 1.50 | |
| G663 | The Mind Twisters Affair–Thomas Stratton; TV tie-in | 1.50 | 3.00 | 4.50 | M |
| G664 | Born Under Mars–John Brunner | .75 | 1.50 | 2.25 | SF |
| G665 | The Silver Flame–L.L. Foreman | .75 | 1.50 | 2.25 | W |
| G666 | Wayneston Hospital–Elizabeth Kellier | .50 | 1.00 | 1.50 | R |
| G667 | The Arsenal out of Time–David McDaniel | .50 | 1.00 | 1.50 | SF |
| G668 | A Badge for a Badman–Brian Wynne | 1.00 | 2.00 | 3.00 | W |
| | Devil's Butte–Ray Hogan | | | | W |
| G669 | The Coming of the Terrans–Leigh Brackett | .75 | 1.50 | 2.25 | SF |
| G670 | The Rainbow Affair–David McDaniel; TV tie-in | 1.50 | 3.00 | 4.50 | M |
| G671 | The Star and the Gun–Lewis B. Patten | .75 | 1.50 | 2.25 | W |
| G672 | University Nurse–Arlene Hale | .50 | 1.00 | 1.50 | R |
| G673 | Lords of the Starship–Mark S. Geston | .75 | 1.50 | 2.25 | SF |
| G674 | Two Pistols South of Deadwood–Merle Constiner | 1.00 | 2.00 | 3.00 | W |
| | No Man's Brand–William Vance | | | | W |
| G675 | The Secret Visitors–James White | .75 | 1.50 | 2.25 | SF |
| G676 | Storm in the Mountains–Nancy Buckingham | .50 | 1.00 | 1.50 | |
| G677 | Turning On–Damon Knight | .75 | 1.50 | 2.25 | SF |
| G678 | The Plundering Gun–L.L. Foreman | .75 | 1.50 | 2.25 | W |
| G679 | Nurse at Mystery Villa–Willo Davis Roberts | .50 | 1.00 | 1.50 | R |
| G680 | Cycle of Nemesis–Kenneth Bulmer | .75 | 1.50 | 2.25 | SF |
| G681 | Twin Worlds–Neil R. Jones | .75 | 1.50 | 2.25 | SF |
| G682 | Bandit Brand–Tom West | 1.00 | 2.00 | 3.00 | W |
| | Ride for Vengeance–John Callahan | | | | W |
| G683 | The Big Jump–Leigh Brackett | .50 | 1.00 | 1.50 | SF |
| G684 | Beauty that Must Die–Barbara James | .50 | 1.00 | 1.50 | |
| G685 | My Brother John–Herbert R. Purdum | .50 | 1.00 | 1.50 | W |
| G686 | The Odds Against Nurse Pat–Ray Dorien; aka Red Head Nurse | .50 | 1.00 | 1.50 | R |
| G687 | Stranger in Rampart–Dan J. Stevens | 1.00 | 2.00 | 3.00 | W |
| | The Hanging at Whiskey Smith–Eric Allen | | | | W |
| G688 | City of the Chasch–Jack Vance | .75 | 1.50 | 2.25 | SF |
| G689 | The Cross of Gold Affair–Fredric Davies; TV tie-in | 1.50 | 3.00 | 4.50 | M |
| G690 | The Beast Master–Andre Norton; 1967 | .50 | 1.00 | 1.50 | SF |
| G691 | Lord of Thunder–Andre Norton | .50 | 1.00 | 1.50 | SF |
| G692 | The Swordsman of Mars–Otis Adelbert Kline | 1.00 | 2.00 | 3.00 | F |
| G693 | Outlaws of Mars–Otis Adelbert Kline | 1.00 | 2.00 | 3.00 | F |
| G694 | The Dolphin and the Deep–Thomas Burnett Swann | 1.25 | 2.50 | 3.75 | SF |
| G695 | Bitter Grass–Theodore V. Olsen | .75 | 1.50 | 2.25 | W |
| G696 | Emergency Call–Arlene Hale | .50 | 1.00 | 1.50 | R |
| G697 | We Claim These Stars–Poul Anderson | .75 | 1.50 | 2.25 | SF |
| G698 | The Franklin Raid–Kyle Hollingshead | 1.00 | 2.00 | 3.00 | W |
| | Trouble at Tenkiller–Ray Hogan | | | | W |
| G699 | The Bride Wore Black–Cornell Woolrich | .75 | 1.50 | 2.25 | M |
| G700 | Will to Survive–Elizabeth Salter | .50 | 1.00 | 1.50 | R |
| G701 | The Closed Worlds–Edmond Hamilton | .75 | 1.50 | 2.25 | SF |
| G702 | Miracle at San Tanco–William Johnston; TV tie-in | 1.25 | 2.50 | 3.75 | F |
| G703 | Victory on Janus–Andre Norton; 1968 | .50 | 1.00 | 1.50 | SF |
| G704 | Navarro–Carse Boyd | .75 | 1.50 | 2.25 | W |
| G705 | Killers' Corral–Merle Constiner | 1.00 | 2.00 | 3.00 | |
| | The Long Wire–Barry Cord | | | | |
| G706 | The Jewels of Aptor–Samuel R. Delany | .50 | 1.00 | 1.50 | SF |
| G707 | The Master of Phoenix Hall–Edwina Marlow | .50 | 1.00 | 1.50 | |
| G708 | A Partnership with Death–Clifton Adams | .75 | 1.50 | 2.25 | W |
| G709 | Bedlam Planet–John Brunner | .75 | 1.50 | 2.25 | SF |
| G710 | The Face Behind the Mask–Tom West | 1.00 | 2.00 | 3.00 | W |
| | Marshal of Sangaree–Louis Trimble | | | | W |
| G711 | Nurse Stacey Comes Aboard–Rona Randall | .50 | 1.00 | 1.50 | R |
| G712 | The Best from Fantasy and Science Fiction, 3rd Series–eds. Anthony Boucher & J. Francis McComas | .75 | 1.50 | 2.25 | SF |
| G713 | The Best from Fantasy and Science Fiction, 4th Series–ed. Anthony Boucher | .75 | 1.50 | 2.25 | SF |
| G714 | The Best from Fantasy and Science Fiction, 5th Series–ed. Anthony Boucher | .75 | 1.50 | 2.25 | SF |
| G715 | The Best from Fantasy and Science Fiction, 6th Series–ed. Anthony Boucher | .75 | 1.50 | 2.25 | SF |
| G716 | Web of the Witch World–Andre Norton; 1968 | .75 | 1.50 | 2.25 | SF |
| G717 | Daybreak-2250 A.D.–Andre Norton | .50 | 1.00 | 1.50 | SF |
| G718 | Solar Lottery–Philip K. Dick | .75 | 1.50 | 2.25 | SF |
| G719 | Doomsday on Ajiat–Neil R. Jones | .75 | 1.50 | 2.25 | SF |
| G720 | Brand of the Gun–Brian Wynne | .75 | 1.50 | 2.25 | W |
| G721 | Dead Man's Gold–Lee Hoffman | 1.00 | 2.00 | 3.00 | W |
| | The Silver Concho–Dan P. Jenison | | | | W |
| G722 | My Favorite Nurse–Gail Everett | .50 | 1.00 | 1.50 | R |
| G723 | Star Hunter–Andre Norton | 1.00 | 2.00 | 3.00 | SF |
| | Voodoo Planet–Andre Norton | | | | SF |
| G724 | A Private Cosmos–Philip Jose Farmer | .75 | 1.50 | 2.25 | SF |
| G725 | The Littlest Rebels–William Johnston; TV tie-in | 1.25 | 2.50 | 3.75 | F |
| G726 | The Valdez Horses–Lee Hoffman | .75 | 1.50 | 2.25 | W |
| G727 | Return to Rio Fuego–Clay Ringold | 1.00 | 2.00 | 3.00 | W |
| | Tracks of the Hunter–John Callahan | | | | W |
| G728 | Across Time–David Grinnell | .50 | 1.00 | 1.50 | SF |
| G729 | The Utopia Affair–David McDaniel; TV tie-in | 1.50 | 3.00 | 4.50 | M |
| G730 | Psi High–Alan E. Nourse | .75 | 1.50 | 2.25 | SF |
| G731 | A Lost Mine Named Salvation–Nelson Nye | .75 | 1.50 | 2.25 | W |
| G732 | Ambush Reckoning–Clement Hardin | 1.00 | 2.00 | 3.00 | W |
| | The Trouble Borrower–Reese Sullivan | | | | W |
| G733 | At the Earth's Core–Edgar Rice Burroughs; c-Krenkel | 1.00 | 2.00 | 3.00 | SF |
| G734 | Pellucidar–Edgar Rice Burroughs; c-Krenkel | 1.00 | 2.00 | 3.00 | SF |
| G735 | Tanar of Pellucidar–Edgar Rice Burroughs; c-Krenkel | 1.00 | 2.00 | 3.00 | SF |
| G736 | Tarzan at the Earth's Core–Edgar Rice Burroughs; c-Frazetta | 1.00 | 2.00 | 3.00 | SF |
| G737 | Back to the Stone Age–Edgar Rice Burroughs; c-Krenkel | 1.00 | 2.00 | 3.00 | SF |
| G738 | Land of Terror–Edgar Rice Burroughs; c-Frazetta | 1.00 | 2.00 | 3.00 | SF |
| G739 | Savage Pellucidar–Edgar Rice Burroughs; c-Frazetta | 1.00 | 2.00 | 3.00 | SF |
| G740 | The Broken Lands–Fred Saberhagen | .75 | 1.50 | 2.25 | SF |
| G741 | Red Is the Valley–Joseph Wayne | .75 | 1.50 | 2.25 | W |
| G742 | Lone Star Roundup–Dean Owen | 1.00 | 2.00 | 3.00 | W |
| | Write His Name in Gunsmoke–Tom West | | | | W |
| G744 | Chateau Chaumand–Andrea Delmonico | .50 | 1.00 | 1.50 | |
| G745 | The Moon Maid–Edgar Rice Burroughs; c-Krenkel | 1.00 | 2.00 | 3.00 | SF |
| G746 | Marked Deck at Topango Wells–William Colt MacDonald | .75 | 1.50 | 2.25 | W |
| G747 | Killer on the Warbucket–Ray Hogan | 1.00 | 2.00 | 3.00 | W |
| | Sage Tower–Dean Owen | | | | W |
| G748 | The Moon Men–Edgar Rice Burroughs; c-Emsh | 1.00 | 2.00 | 3.00 | SF |
| G750 | Dr. Barry's Nurse–Arlene Hale | .50 | 1.00 | 1.50 | R |
| G751 | The Dark Place–Mildred Davis | .50 | 1.00 | 1.50 | R |

| | | V/Good | Fine | N/Mint | |
|---|---|---|---|---|---|

ACE G-SERIES, *continued*

| | | V/Good | Fine | N/Mint | |
|---|---|---|---|---|---|
| G752 | The Splintered Sunglasses Affair–Peter Leslie; TV tie-in | 1.50 | 3.00 | 4.50 | M |
| G753 | Moon of Gomrath–Alan Garner | .75 | 1.50 | 2.25 | SF |
| G754 | The War on Charity Ross–John M. Bickham | .75 | 1.50 | 2.25 | W |
| G755 | Trail of the Skulls–Wayne L. Lee | 1.00 | 2.00 | 3.00 | W |
| | The Four from Gila Bend–Merle Constiner | | | | W |
| G756 | Star Well–Alexei Panshin | .75 | 1.50 | 2.25 | SF |
| G757 | Remember with Tears–Helen Arvonen | .50 | 1.00 | 1.50 | R |
| G758 | Moondust–Thomas Burnett Swann | 1.25 | 2.50 | 3.75 | SF |
| G759 | Wenatchee Bend–Giff Cheshire | .75 | 1.50 | 2.25 | W |
| G760 | Bronc–X.X. Jones | 1.00 | 2.00 | 3.00 | |
| | The Vengeance Ghost–Reese Sullivan | | | | |
| G761 | Catch a Falling Star–John Brunner | .75 | 1.50 | 2.25 | SF |
| G762 | The Thurb Revolution–Alexei Panshin | .75 | 1.50 | 2.25 | SF |
| G763 | Hell-for-Leather Jones–John Shelley & David Shelley | .75 | 1.50 | 2.25 | W |
| G764 | West to the Pecos–Louis Trimble | 1.00 | 2.00 | 3.00 | W |
| | Jernigan–John Callahan; 1968 | | | | W |
| G766 | World of the Starwolves–Edmond Hamilton; 1968 | .75 | 1.50 | 2.25 | SF |

# ACE H-SERIES

## Ace Books, Inc.

| | | V/Good | Fine | N/Mint | |
|---|---|---|---|---|---|
| H1 | The Family Legal Adviser–Theodore R. Kupferman, LLB | .50 | 1.00 | 1.50 | NF |
| H2 | Curious Customs of Sex and Marriage–George Ryley Scott | .50 | 1.00 | 1.50 | NF |
| H3 | Dara the Cypriot–Louis Paul | .50 | 1.00 | 1.50 | A |
| H4 | My Lord Essex–Olive Eckerson | .50 | 1.00 | 1.50 | A |
| H5 | Born of the Sun–John H. Culp | .50 | 1.00 | 1.50 | W |
| H6 | Gold for the Caesars–Florence A. Seward | .50 | 1.00 | 1.50 | A |
| H7 | The Restless Land–John H. Culp | .50 | 1.00 | 1.50 | W |
| H8 | The Sword of Il Grande–Will Creed | .50 | 1.00 | 1.50 | A |
| H9 | Captive of Rome–Theodora DuBois | .50 | 1.00 | 1.50 | A |
| H10 | Berlin–Theodor Plievier | .50 | 1.00 | 1.50 | C |
| H11 | Moscow–Theodor Plievier | .50 | 1.00 | 1.50 | C |
| H12 | Strange Mysteries of Time and Space– Harold T. Wilkins | .50 | 1.00 | 1.50 | NF |
| H13 | The Mystery Monsters–Gardner Soule; 1965 | .50 | 1.00 | 1.50 | NF |
| H14 | Invisible Horizons–Vincent Gaddis | .50 | 1.00 | 1.50 | NF |
| H15 | World's Best SF: 1966–eds. Terry Carr & Donald A. Wollheim | .75 | 1.50 | 2.25 | SF |
| H16 | Ghosts I've Met–Hans Holzer | .50 | 1.00 | 1.50 | NF |
| H17 | Anatomy of a Phenomenon–Jacques Vallee | .50 | 1.00 | 1.50 | UF |
| H18 | H-Bomb over America–Jeff Sutton; 1967 | 1.00 | 2.00 | 3.00 | SF |
| H19 | The IF Reader of Science Fiction–ed. Frederik Pohl | .75 | 1.50 | 2.25 | SF |
| H20 | The Key to Irunium–Kenneth Bulmer; 1967 | 1.00 | 2.00 | 3.00 | SF |
| | The Wandering Tellurian–Alan Schwartz | | | | SF |
| H21 | The Last Castle–Jack Vance | 1.00 | 2.00 | 3.00 | SF |
| | World of the Sleeper–Tony Russell Wayman | | | | SF |
| H22 | Lord of the Green Planet–Emil Petaja | 1.00 | 2.00 | 3.00 | SF |
| | Five Against Arlane–Tom Purdom; 1967 | | | | SF |
| H23 | Arabella–Georgette Heyer | .50 | 1.00 | 1.50 | R |
| H24 | The Book of the Damned–Charles Fort | .50 | 1.00 | 1.50 | NF |
| H25 | House of the Pines–Jan Tempest | .50 | 1.00 | 1.50 | |
| H26 | The Best from Fantasy and Science Fiction, 13th Series–ed. Avram Davidson | .75 | 1.50 | 2.25 | SF |
| H27 | Crisis on Cheiron–Juanita Coulson | 1.00 | 2.00 | 3.00 | SF |
| | The Winds of Gath–E.C. Tubb | | | | SF |
| H28 | Challenge to Science–Jacques Vallee & Janine Vallee | .50 | 1.00 | 1.50 | UF |
| H29 | The Road to the Rim–A. Bertram Chandler | 1.50 | 3.00 | 4.50 | SF |
| | The Lost Millenium–Walt Richmond & Leigh Richmond | | | | SF |
| H30 | City–Clifford D. Simak | .75 | 1.50 | 2.25 | SF |
| H31 | Sleep in the Woods–Dorothy Eden | .50 | 1.00 | 1.50 | R |

| | | V/Good | Fine | N/Mint | |
|---|---|---|---|---|---|
| H32 | Games–Hal Ellson; movie tie-in | 1.50 | 3.00 | 4.50 | |
| H33 | Moon of Three Rings–Andre Norton | .75 | 1.50 | 2.25 | SF |
| H34 | Computer War–Mack Reynolds | 1.00 | 2.00 | 3.00 | SF |
| | Death Is a Dream–E.C. Tubb | | | | SF |
| H35 | The Daughters of Ardmore Hall– Dorothy Eden; aka The Schoolmaster's Daughter | .50 | 1.00 | 1.50 | |
| H36 | The Wrecks of Time–Michael Moorcock | 1.00 | 2.00 | 3.00 | SF |
| | Tramontane–Emil Petaja; 1967 | | | | SF |
| H37 | The Gilded Sarcophagus–Charlotte Hunt | .50 | 1.00 | 1.50 | |
| H38 | The Swords of Lankhmar–Fritz Leiber | 1.50 | 3.00 | 4.50 | F |
| H39 | Eye in the Sky–Philip K. Dick | 1.00 | 2.00 | 3.00 | SF |
| H40 | Alien Sea–John Rackham | 1.00 | 2.00 | 3.00 | SF |
| | C.O.D. Mars–E.C. Tubb | | | | SF |
| H41 | Into the Niger Bend–Jules Verne | 1.00 | 2.00 | 3.00 | SF |
| H42 | Why Call Them Back from Heaven?– Clifford D. Simak | 1.00 | 2.00 | 3.00 | SF |
| H43 | The City in the Sahara–Jules Verne | 1.00 | 2.00 | 3.00 | SF |
| H44 | The Quiet Gentleman–Georgette Heyer | .50 | 1.00 | 1.50 | R |
| H45 | Venetia–Georgette Heyer | .50 | 1.00 | 1.50 | R |
| H46 | Look of the Eagle–Robert L. Scott, Jr | .50 | 1.00 | 1.50 | NF |
| H47 | The Lively Ghosts of Ireland–Hans Holzer | .50 | 1.00 | 1.50 | NF |
| H48 | The Youth Monopoly–Ellen Wobig | 1.00 | 2.00 | 3.00 | SF |
| | The Pictures of Pavanne–Lan Wright | | | | SF |
| H49 | The Begum's Fortune–Jules Verne | 1.00 | 2.00 | 3.00 | SF |
| H50 | In a Glass Darkly–Janet Caird | .50 | 1.00 | 1.50 | SF |
| H51 | The Prism–Emil Petaja | 1.00 | 2.00 | 3.00 | SF |
| | Crown of Infinity–John Faucette | | | | SF |
| H52 | Yesterday and Tomorrow–Jules Verne | 1.00 | 2.00 | 3.00 | SF |
| H53 | The Progeny of the Adder–Leslie Whitten | 1.00 | 2.00 | 3.00 | HO |
| H54 | Past Master–R.A. Lafferty | 2.50 | 5.00 | 7.50 | SF |
| H55 | On Earth and in the Sky–Willy Ley | .50 | 1.00 | 1.50 | NF |
| H56 | Space Chantey–R.A. Lafferty; c-Bodé | 2.00 | 4.00 | 6.00 | SF |
| | A Pity about Earth–Ernest Hill | | | | SF |
| H57 | Rendezvous in Black–Cornell Woolrich | 1.00 | 2.00 | 3.00 | M |
| H58 | The Revolving Boy–Gertrude Friedberg | .50 | 1.00 | 1.50 | SF |
| H59 | The Time Mercenaries–Philip E. High | 1.00 | 2.00 | 3.00 | SF |
| | Anthropol–Louis Trimble | | | | SF |
| H60 | Carpathian Castle–Jules Verne | 1.00 | 2.00 | 3.00 | SF |
| H61 | Death in a Mist–Elizabeth Salter | .50 | 1.00 | 1.50 | |
| H62 | The Lincoln Hunters–Wilson Tucker | 1.00 | 2.00 | 3.00 | SF |
| H63 | The Real Bonnie and Clyde–Miriam Allen deFord | 1.00 | 2.00 | 3.00 | NF |
| H64 | The Flying Saucer Story–Brinsley Le Poer Trench | .50 | 1.00 | 1.50 | UF |
| H65 | The Key to Venudine–Kenneth Bulmer | 1.00 | 2.00 | 3.00 | SF |
| | Mercenary from Tomorrow–Mack Reynolds | | | | SF |
| H66 | The Black Path of Fear–Cornell Woolrich | 1.00 | 2.00 | 3.00 | M |
| H67 | The Village in the Treetops–Jules Verne | 1.00 | 2.00 | 3.00 | A |
| H68 | The Enigma of the Poltergeist– Raymond Bayliss | .50 | 1.00 | 1.50 | NF |
| H69 | Knight's Keep–Rona Randall | .50 | 1.00 | 1.50 | |
| H70 | Star Quest–Dean R. Koontz | 2.00 | 4.00 | 6.00 | SF |
| | Doom of the Green Planet–Emil Petaja | | | | SF |
| H71 | Isle for a Stranger–Dorothy Mackie Low | .50 | 1.00 | 1.50 | |

*Ace H9, Ace H16, Ace K109.*

### ACE H-SERIES, *continued*

| | | V/Good | Fine | N/Mint | |
|---|---|---|---|---|---|
| H72 | Picnic on Paradise–Joanna Russ | 1.50 | 3.00 | 4.50 | SF |
| H73 | Swords Against Wizardry–Fritz Leiber | 1.50 | 3.00 | 4.50 | F |
| H74 | New Lands–Charles Fort | .50 | 1.00 | 1.50 | NF |
| H75 | Cotillion–Georgette Heyer | .50 | 1.00 | 1.50 | R |
| H76 | April Lady–Georgette Heyer | .50 | 1.00 | 1.50 | R |
| H77 | The Singing Stone–Juanita Coulson | 1.00 | 2.00 | 3.00 | SF |
| | Derai–E.C. Tubb | | | | SF |
| H78 | The Hunt for the Meteor–Jules Verne | 1.00 | 2.00 | 3.00 | SF |
| H79 | The Two-Timers–Bob Shaw | 1.00 | 2.00 | 3.00 | SF |
| H80 | With Murder in Mind–Jan Roffman | .50 | 1.00 | 1.50 | M |
| H81 | Passport to the Unknown–John Macklin | .50 | 1.00 | 1.50 | NF |
| H83 | Vampires, Werewolves and Ghouls–Bernardt J. Hurwood | 1.50 | 3.00 | 4.50 | HO |
| H84 | Sorceress of the Witch World–Andre Norton | 1.50 | 3.00 | 4.50 | SF |
| H85 | Destination: Saturn–Lin Carter & David Grinnell | 1.00 | 2.00 | 3.00 | SF |
| | Invader on My Back–Philip E. High | | | | SF |
| H86 | Synthajoy–D.G. Compton | .50 | 1.00 | 1.50 | SF |
| H88 | Wild Talents–Charles Fort | .50 | 1.00 | 1.50 | NF |
| H89 | Dimensions Beyond the Known–John Macklin | .50 | 1.00 | 1.50 | NF |
| H90 | Swords in the Mist–Fritz Leiber | 1.50 | 3.00 | 4.50 | F |
| H91 | Target: Terra–Laurence Janifer & S.J. Treibich | 1.00 | 2.00 | 3.00 | SF |
| | The Proxima Project–John Rackham | | | | SF |
| H92 | The Far-out Worlds of A.E. Van Vogt–A.E. Van Vogt | 1.00 | 2.00 | 3.00 | SF |
| H93 | The Man in the Tricorn Hat–Delano Ames | .75 | 1.50 | 2.25 | M |
| H94 | Dwellers in Darkness–John Macklin | .50 | 1.00 | 1.50 | NF |
| H95 | So Bright the Vision–Clifford D. Simak | 1.00 | 2.00 | 3.00 | SF |
| | The Man Who Saw Tomorrow–Jeff Sutton | | | | SF |
| H96 | The Sundial–Shirley Jackson | .50 | 1.00 | 1.50 | |
| H97 | The Man with Three Jaguars–Delano Ames | .50 | 1.00 | 1.50 | M |
| H98 | The Cup of Thanatos–Charlotte Hunt; 1968 | .50 | 1.00 | 1.50 | |
| H99 | Prophecies on World Events by Nostradamus–Stewart Robb | .50 | 1.00 | 1.50 | NF |
| H100 | E.S.P. and You–Hans Holzer | .50 | 1.00 | 1.50 | NF |
| H101 | Spring Muslin–Georgette Heyer | .50 | 1.00 | 1.50 | R |
| H102 | Subspace Explorers–Edward E. "Doc" Smith | 1.00 | 2.00 | 3.00 | SF |
| H103 | The Age of Ruin–John Faucette | 1.00 | 2.00 | 3.00 | SF |
| | Code Duello–Mack Reynolds; 1968 | | | | SF |
| H104 | The Black Curtain–Cornell Woolrich | 1.00 | 2.00 | 3.00 | M |
| H105 | The Demon Breed–James H. Schmitz | 1.50 | 3.00 | 4.50 | SF |
| H106 | Perturbing Spirit–Janet Caird | .50 | 1.00 | 1.50 | |
| H107 | The Dark Gondola–Virginia Coffman | .50 | 1.00 | 1.50 | |
| H108 | Challenge to Reality–John Macklin | .50 | 1.00 | 1.50 | NF |
| H109 | The Man with Three Chins–Delano Ames | .50 | 1.00 | 1.50 | M |

# ACE K-SERIES/STAR SERIES

## Ace Books, Inc.

| | | V/Good | Fine | N/Mint | |
|---|---|---|---|---|---|
| K100 | The Long Dream–Richard Wright | .50 | 1.00 | 1.50 | |
| K101 | The Faiths Men Live By–Charles Francis Potter | .50 | 1.00 | 1.50 | NF |
| K102T | Alone–Richard E. Byrd | .50 | 1.00 | 1.50 | NF |
| K103 | Fiesta–Prudencio De Pereda | .50 | 1.00 | 1.50 | |
| K104 | Sickles the Incredible–W.A. Swanberg | .75 | 1.50 | 2.25 | NF |
| K105 | Winter Quarters–Alfred Duggan | .75 | 1.50 | 2.25 | A |
| K106 | The Improper Bohemians–Allen Churchill | .50 | 1.00 | 1.50 | NF |
| K107 | The Cross on the Drum–Hugh B. Cave | .75 | 1.50 | 2.25 | |
| K108 | The Three Days–Don Robertson | .50 | 1.00 | 1.50 | A |
| K109 | Johnny Got His Gun–Dalton Trumbo | 2.00 | 4.00 | 6.00 | C |
| K110 | The Seventh Day–Hans Hellmut Kirst | .75 | 1.50 | 2.25 | SF |
| K111T | The Cracked Reader–ed. Cracked Magazine; 1960 | 1.50 | 3.00 | 4.50 | H |
| K112 | The Royal City–Les Savage, Jr | .50 | 1.00 | 1.50 | A |
| K113 | Tall Short Stories–ed. Eric Duthie | .50 | 1.00 | 1.50 | H |
| K114 | Peril in Paradise–O.A. Bushnell; aka The Return of Lono | .50 | 1.00 | 1.50 | A |
| K115 | They Sailed into Oblivion–A.A. Hoehling | .50 | 1.00 | 1.50 | NF |
| K116 | Man Running–Elliot West; movie tie-in | .50 | 1.00 | 1.50 | M |

| | | V/Good | Fine | N/Mint | |
|---|---|---|---|---|---|
| K117 | Stranger than Science–Frank Edwards | .50 | 1.00 | 1.50 | NF |
| K118 | Children of the Wolf–Alfred Duggan | .75 | 1.50 | 2.25 | A |
| K119 | An Unhurried View of Erotica–Ralph Ginzburg | .50 | 1.00 | 1.50 | E |
| K120 | Lucrezia Borgia–Joan Haslip | .50 | 1.00 | 1.50 | A |
| K121 | Grenadine Etching–Robert C. Ruark | .50 | 1.00 | 1.50 | H |
| K122 | Spies Who Changed History–ed. Kurt Singer | .50 | 1.00 | 1.50 | NF |
| K123T | The Hunt–Richard B. Erno | .50 | 1.00 | 1.50 | A |
| K124 | Eskimo–Peter Freuchen | .50 | 1.00 | 1.50 | A |
| K125T | The Scandalous Scamps–Harold Mehling | .50 | 1.00 | 1.50 | NF |
| K126 | Breakdown–R. Dahl | .50 | 1.00 | 1.50 | NF |
| K127 | Fire–George R. Stewart | .50 | 1.00 | 1.50 | |
| K128S | Patterns of Sexual Behavior–Drs. Ford & Beach | .50 | 1.00 | 1.50 | NF |
| K129 | Conscience of the King–Alfred Duggan | .75 | 1.50 | 2.25 | A |
| A130 | The Hundred Stories–trans. Robert B. Douglas. Note: Although this book has an A prefix, it was created as part of the K series. | .50 | 1.00 | 1.50 | |
| K131 | The Importance of Feeling Inferior–Marie Beynon Ray | .50 | 1.00 | 1.50 | NF |
| K132 | Spies for the Blue and Gray–Harnett T. Kane | .50 | 1.00 | 1.50 | NF |
| K133 | Trask–Don Berry | .50 | 1.00 | 1.50 | |
| K134 | Operation Sea Lion–Peter Fleming | .50 | 1.00 | 1.50 | C |
| T135 | See Ace T-Series | | | | |
| K136 | Hoaxes–Curtis D. MacDougall | .75 | 1.50 | 2.25 | NF |
| K137 | The Private World of Cully Powers–George Bluestone | .50 | 1.00 | 1.50 | H |
| K138 | Ordeal by Hunger: The Story of the Donner Party Wagon Train–George R. Stewart | .50 | 1.00 | 1.50 | NF |
| K139 | Three's Company–Alfred Duggan | .75 | 1.50 | 2.25 | A |
| K140 | Your Child's Care–Harry R. Litchfield, MD & Leon H. Dembo, MD | .50 | 1.00 | 1.50 | NF |
| K141 | Michelangelo and Rembrandt–Emil Ludwig | .50 | 1.00 | 1.50 | B |
| K142 | Crimes That Shocked America–ed. Brant House | .50 | 1.00 | 1.50 | NF |
| K143 | The Twelfth Physician–Willa Gibbs | .50 | 1.00 | 1.50 | |
| K144 | Strangest of All–Frank Edwards | .50 | 1.00 | 1.50 | NF |
| K145 | The Marriage Bed–Dr. Harry F. Trashman | .50 | 1.00 | 1.50 | NF |
| K146 | Seal Morning–Rowena Farre (illus.) | .50 | 1.00 | 1.50 | |
| K147 | Baton Sinister–Carl J. Spinatelli | .50 | 1.00 | 1.50 | |
| K148 | The Chicago Underworld–Herbert Asbury; aka Gem of the Prairie | .75 | 1.50 | 2.25 | NF |
| K149 | Queen Cleopatra–Talbot Mundy | 1.25 | 2.50 | 3.75 | F |
| K150 | Lady Chatterley's Daughter–Patricia Robins | .50 | 1.00 | 1.50 | E |
| K151 | The Great Adventure: America in the First World War–Pierce G. Frederick | .50 | 1.00 | 1.50 | NF |
| K152 | Great Trials of Famous Lawyers–ed. Brant House | .50 | 1.00 | 1.50 | NF |
| K153 | A Marriage Doctor Speaks Her Mind about Sex–Rebecca Linswood | .50 | 1.00 | 1.50 | NF |
| K154 | Earth Abides–George R. Stewart | 1.00 | 2.00 | 3.00 | SF |
| K155 | The Strangest Things in the World–Thomas R. Henry | .50 | 1.00 | 1.50 | NF |
| K156 | The Book of the Damned–Charles Fort | .50 | 1.00 | 1.50 | NF |
| K157 | Miracles of Modern Surgery–E.H.G. Lutz | .50 | 1.00 | 1.50 | NF |
| K158 | Thunder Heights–Phyllis A. Whitney | .50 | 1.00 | 1.50 | |
| K159 | The Executioners–Robert Christophe | .50 | 1.00 | 1.50 | NF |
| K160 | The Werewolf of Paris–Guy Endore | 1.50 | 3.00 | 4.50 | HO |
| K161 | The FBI in Peace and War–Frederick L. Collins | .50 | 1.00 | 1.50 | NF |
| K162 | Gould's Millions–Richard O'Connor; 1962 | .50 | 1.00 | 1.50 | NF |
| K163 | The World's Strangest Mysteries–Rupert Furneaux | .50 | 1.00 | 1.50 | NF |
| K164 | The Trembling Hills–Phyllis Whitney | .50 | 1.00 | 1.50 | |
| K165 | The Lute and the Glove–Katherine Wigmore Eyre | .50 | 1.00 | 1.50 | |
| K166 | The Sundial–Shirley Jackson | .50 | 1.00 | 1.50 | |
| K167 | The Angelic Avengers–Pierre Andrezel (Isak Dinesen) | .50 | 1.00 | 1.50 | |
| K168 | Stranger Than Life–R. DeWitt Miller; aka You Do Take It with You | .50 | 1.00 | 1.50 | NF |
| K169 | The Shortest Gladding Years–Scott Sullivan; 1963 | .50 | 1.00 | 1.50 | |
| K170 | High Carnival–John J. Pugh | .50 | 1.00 | 1.50 | |

| | V/Good | Fine | N/Mint | |
|---|---|---|---|---|

ACE K-SERIES/STAR SERIES, *continued*

| | | V/Good | Fine | N/Mint | |
|---|---|---|---|---|---|
| K171 | Lady of Mallow–Dorothy Eden | .50 | 1.00 | 1.50 | |
| K172 | The Golden Pagans–Peter Bourne | .50 | 1.00 | 1.50 | A |
| K173 | To the Castle–Dorothea Malm | .50 | 1.00 | 1.50 | |
| K174 | The Grand Sophy–Georgette Heyer | .75 | 1.50 | 2.25 | R |
| K175 | Moura–Virginia Coffman | .50 | 1.00 | 1.50 | |
| K176 | Strange Powers of Unusual People–ed. Brant House | .50 | 1.00 | 1.50 | NF |
| K177 | My Theodosia–Anya Seton | .50 | 1.00 | 1.50 | R |
| K178 | The Quicksilver Pool–Phyllis A. Whitney | .50 | 1.00 | 1.50 | |
| K179 | Venetia–Georgette Heyer | .75 | 1.50 | 2.25 | R |
| K180 | To See a Stranger–Margaret Lynn | .50 | 1.00 | 1.50 | |
| K181 | The Sea House–Margaret Summerton | .50 | 1.00 | 1.50 | |
| K182 | Instant Self Analysis–Doris Webster & Mary A. Hopkins | .50 | 1.00 | 1.50 | NF |
| K183 | The House of Moreys–Phyllis Bentley | .50 | 1.00 | 1.50 | |
| K184 | Whistle for the Crows–Dorothy Eden | .50 | 1.00 | 1.50 | |
| K185 | Hangsaman–Shirley Jackson | .75 | 1.50 | 2.25 | |
| K186 | The Magic Power of Emotional Appeal–Roy Garn | .50 | 1.00 | 1.50 | NF |
| K187 | Victoria Grandolet–Henry Bellamann | .50 | 1.00 | 1.50 | |
| K188 | Alone–Richard E. Byrd | .50 | 1.00 | 1.50 | NF |
| K189 | The Hangman's Tree–Dorothy Cameron Disney | .50 | 1.00 | 1.50 | |
| K190 | Parents without Partners–Jim Egelson & Janet Frank Egelson | .50 | 1.00 | 1.50 | NF |
| K191 | The Brides of Bellenmore–Anne Maybury | .50 | 1.00 | 1.50 | |
| K192 | The House with Two Faces–Sheila Bishop | .50 | 1.00 | 1.50 | |
| K193 | A Psychiatrist Looks at Erotica– Franklin S. Klaf, MD & Bernhardt J. Hurwood | .50 | 1.00 | 1.50 | NF |
| K194 | Nightingale at Noon–Margaret Summerton | .50 | 1.00 | 1.50 | |
| K195 | How to Avoid Marriage–Dr. F.J. Schaukowitsch | .50 | 1.00 | 1.50 | NF |
| K196 | Navy Diver–Joseph Sidney Karneke & Victor Boesen | .50 | 1.00 | 1.50 | NF |
| K197 | Who Rides a Tiger–Doris Miles Disney | .50 | 1.00 | 1.50 | M |
| K198 | Stranger on a Cliff–Josephine Bell; aka To Let: Furnished | .50 | 1.00 | 1.50 | |
| K199 | Operators and Things–Barbara O'Brien | .50 | 1.00 | 1.50 | NF |
| K200 | The Whisper of Shadows–J.L.H. Whitney | .50 | 1.00 | 1.50 | |
| K201 | April Lady–Georgette Heyer | .75 | 1.50 | 2.25 | R |
| K202 | Junkie–William Burroughs | 1.50 | 3.00 | 4.50 | JD |
| K203 | Morgan's Castle–Jan Hilliard | .50 | 1.00 | 1.50 | |
| K204 | Charlie Chaplin–Robert Payne; aka The Great God Pan | 1.00 | 2.00 | 3.00 | B |
| K205 | Night of the Visitor–Ruth Willock | .50 | 1.00 | 1.50 | |
| K206 | Strange World–Frank Edwards; 1964 | .50 | 1.00 | 1.50 | NF |
| K207 | A Dark and Splendid Passion–Lady Eleanor Smith; aka The Man in Grey | .50 | 1.00 | 1.50 | |
| K208 | The Jungle Search for Nature's Cures– Nicole Maxwell; aka Witch Doctor's Apprentice | .50 | 1.00 | 1.50 | NF |
| K209 | The Veil of Silence–Aileen Seilaz; 1965 | .50 | 1.00 | 1.50 | |
| K210 | Ghost Hunter–Hans Holzer | .50 | 1.00 | 1.50 | NF |
| K211 | The Pavilion at Monkshood–Anne Maybury | .50 | 1.00 | 1.50 | |
| K212 | The Durable Fire–Sheila Bishop | .50 | 1.00 | 1.50 | R |

*Ace K132, Ace K160, Ace K180.*

| | | V/Good | Fine | N/Mint | |
|---|---|---|---|---|---|
| K213 | Dark Cypress–Edwina Noone (Michael Avallone) | 1.00 | 2.00 | 3.00 | |
| K214 | 100 Ways to Popularity–Jean O'Sullivan | .50 | 1.00 | 1.50 | NF |
| K215 | The Master of Montrolfe Hall–Rohan O'Grady; aka Pippin's Journal | .50 | 1.00 | 1.50 | |
| K216 | The Reflection of Evil–Jan Roffman; aka Death of a Fox | .50 | 1.00 | 1.50 | |
| K217 | Lo!–Charles Fort | .50 | 1.00 | 1.50 | NF |
| K218 | Cowboy–Ross Santee | .50 | 1.00 | 1.50 | W |
| K219 | The Silence of Herondale–Joan Aiken | .50 | 1.00 | 1.50 | |
| K220 | The Dark Shore–Susan Howatch; 1965 | .50 | 1.00 | 1.50 | |
| K221 | The Beckoning–Virginia Coffman | .50 | 1.00 | 1.50 | |
| K222 | Strange Destinies–John Macklin | .50 | 1.00 | 1.50 | NF |
| K223 | Corridor of Whispers–Edwina Noone (Michael Avallone) | 1.00 | 2.00 | 3.00 | |
| K224 | Strange Powers of Unusual People–ed. Brant House | .50 | 1.00 | 1.50 | NF |
| K225 | The Summer of Evil–Helen Arvonen; 1965 | .50 | 1.00 | 1.50 | |
| K226 | Sylvester, or, The Wicked Uncle– Georgette Heyer | .50 | 1.00 | 1.50 | |
| K227 | Green Fire–Anne Maybury | .50 | 1.00 | 1.50 | |
| K228 | Griffin Towers–Joan Winslow; 1966 | .50 | 1.00 | 1.50 | |
| K229 | Impossible–Yet It Happened!–R. DeWitt Miller | .50 | 1.00 | 1.50 | NF |
| K230 | The Pretty Ones–Dorothy Eden | .50 | 1.00 | 1.50 | |
| K231 | Promise Him Anything . . .–Lane Peters | .50 | 1.00 | 1.50 | H |
| K232 | The House of Fand–Anne Maybury | .50 | 1.00 | 1.50 | |
| K233 | Lady Chatterley's Daughter–Patricia Robins | .50 | 1.00 | 1.50 | E |
| K234 | The Devil Vicar–Virginia Coffman | .50 | 1.00 | 1.50 | |
| K235 | Sprig Muslin–Georgette Heyer | .75 | 1.50 | 2.25 | |
| K236 | Bridge of Fear–Dorothy Eden | .50 | 1.00 | 1.50 | |
| K237 | Beyond Human Understanding–S. Robert Tralins | .50 | 1.00 | 1.50 | NF |
| K238 | Someone Waiting–Anne Maybury | .50 | 1.00 | 1.50 | |
| K239 | The Sleeping Bride–Dorothy Eden | .50 | 1.00 | 1.50 | |
| K240 | The Waiting Sands–Susan Howatch | .50 | 1.00 | 1.50 | |
| K241 | Strange Guests–Brad Steiger | .50 | 1.00 | 1.50 | NF |
| K242 | The Legend of Susan Dane–Ruth Comfort Mitchell | .50 | 1.00 | 1.50 | R |
| K243 | The Deadly Travellers–Dorothy Eden | .50 | 1.00 | 1.50 | |
| K244 | The Gothic Reader–ed. Kurt Singer | 1.00 | 2.00 | 3.00 | |
| K246 | Castle Cloud–Joan Grant; aka The Laird and the Lady | .50 | 1.00 | 1.50 | |
| K247 | That Callahan Spunk!–Francis Ames | .50 | 1.00 | 1.50 | W |
| K248 | Whisper in the Dark–Anne Maybury | .50 | 1.00 | 1.50 | |
| K249 | The Brooding Lake–Dorothy Eden; aka Lamb to the Slaughter | .50 | 1.00 | 1.50 | |
| K250 | Strange Bonds between Animals and Men–Dr. Webb B. Garrison; aka Codfish, Cats and Civilization–Gary Webster | .50 | 1.00 | 1.50 | NF |
| K251 | Shadow of a Stranger–Anne Maybury | .50 | 1.00 | 1.50 | |
| K252 | The Trembling Hills–Phyllis A. Whitney | .50 | 1.00 | 1.50 | |
| K255 | Impossible–Yet It Happened– R. DeWitt Miller; aka Forgotten Mysteries | .50 | 1.00 | 1.50 | NF |
| K257 | I Am Gabriella!–Anne Maybury | .50 | 1.00 | 1.50 | |
| K258 | City of Forever–Barbara Blackburn | .50 | 1.00 | 1.50 | R |
| K259 | Strange Happenings–Michael Hervey; 1966 | .50 | 1.00 | 1.50 | NF |
| K260 | Dating and Mating by Computer–Joan Rich & Leslie Rich | .50 | 1.00 | 1.50 | NF |
| K261 | Night of the Letter–Dorothy Eden; aka Darling Clementine | .50 | 1.00 | 1.50 | |
| K262 | Walk into My Parlor–Rona Randall | .50 | 1.00 | 1.50 | |
| K263 | The Night My Enemy–Anne Maybury | .50 | 1.00 | 1.50 | |
| K264 | The Dark between the Stars–Jane Blackmore | .50 | 1.00 | 1.50 | |
| K265 | The Reluctant Widow–Georgette Heyer | .75 | 1.50 | 2.25 | |
| K267 | Listen to Danger–Dorothy Eden | .50 | 1.00 | 1.50 | |
| K268 | Treasure Hunting–Brad Steiger; 1967 | .75 | 1.50 | 2.25 | NF |
| K269 | Seven Days from Midnight–Rona Randall | .50 | 1.00 | 1.50 | |
| K270 | The Silver Cadies–Margaret Erskine | .50 | 1.00 | 1.50 | M |
| K271 | Falcon's Shadow–Anne Maybury | .50 | 1.00 | 1.50 | |
| K272 | Yankee Ghosts–Hans Holzer | .50 | 1.00 | 1.50 | NF |
| K273 | The Willow Herb–Rona Randall | .50 | 1.00 | 1.50 | |
| K275 | Crow Hollow–Dorothy Eden | .50 | 1.00 | 1.50 | |
| K276 | Strange Talents–Bernhardt J. Hurwood | .50 | 1.00 | 1.50 | NF |
| K277 | Stay until Tomorrow–Anne Maybury | .50 | 1.00 | 1.50 | |

| | V/Good | Fine | N/Mint | |
|---|---|---|---|---|

**ACE K-SERIES/STAR SERIES,** *continued*

| | | V/Good | Fine | N/Mint | |
|---|---|---|---|---|---|
| K278 | Circle of Death–Helen Arvonen | .50 | 1.00 | 1.50 | |
| K279 | The Strange and Uncanny–John Macklin | .50 | 1.00 | 1.50 | NF |
| K280 | Call in the Night–Susan Howatch | .50 | 1.00 | 1.50 | |
| K281 | No. 9 Belmont Square–Margaret Erskine | .50 | 1.00 | 1.50 | |
| K283 | Cloud over Malverton–Nancy Buckingham | .50 | 1.00 | 1.50 | |
| K285 | Hotel De Luxe–Rona Randall | .50 | 1.00 | 1.50 | R |
| K287 | Old Mrs. Ommanney Is Dead–Margaret Erskine | .50 | 1.00 | 1.50 | M |
| K288 | Strange Prophecies That Came True– Stewart Robb | .50 | 1.00 | 1.50 | NF |
| K289 | Night of the Stranger–Jane Blackmore | .50 | 1.00 | 1.50 | |
| K291 | We Have Lived Before: The Enigma of Reincarnation–Brad Steiger | .50 | 1.00 | 1.50 | NF |
| K292 | The Enigma of the Unknown–John Macklin | .50 | 1.00 | 1.50 | NF |
| K294 | Beware of the Bouquet–Joan Aiken | .50 | 1.00 | 1.50 | |
| K295 | The Woman at Belguardo–Margaret Erskine | .50 | 1.00 | 1.50 | |
| K296 | Strange Powers of the Mind–Warren Smith | .50 | 1.00 | 1.50 | NF |
| K297 | The Strange and Uncanny–John Macklin | .50 | 1.00 | 1.50 | NF |
| K298 | The Silver Cord–Rona Randall | .50 | 1.00 | 1.50 | |
| K299 | Fear of a Stranger–Rae Foley | .50 | 1.00 | 1.50 | |
| K300 | They Walk by Night–Michael Hervey | .50 | 1.00 | 1.50 | NF |
| K301 | The Laughing Ghost–Dorothy Eden | .50 | 1.00 | 1.50 | |
| K302 | The Legend of Baverstock Manor– Nancy Buckingham; 1968 | .50 | 1.00 | 1.50 | |
| K303 | Beware the Night–Jane Blackmore | .50 | 1.00 | 1.50 | |
| K304 | The Family at Tammerton–Margaret Erskine | .50 | 1.00 | 1.50 | |
| K305 | Strange Encounters–John Macklin; 1968 | .50 | 1.00 | 1.50 | NF |
| K307 | The Occult World of John Pendragon– ed. Brad Steiger; 1968 | .50 | 1.00 | 1.50 | NF |

# ACE M-SERIES

# Ace Books, Inc.

| | | V/Good | Fine | N/Mint | |
|---|---|---|---|---|---|
| M100 | Gun Junction–Barry Cord | 1.00 | 2.00 | 3.00 | W |
| | A Man Named Raglan–John Callahan | | | | W |
| M101 | People of the Talisman–Leigh Brackett; 1964 | 1.50 | 3.00 | 4.50 | SF |
| | The Secret of Sinharat–Leigh Brackett | | | | SF |
| M102 | Trouble at Hangdog Flats–Rod Patterson | 1.00 | 2.00 | 3.00 | W |
| | Hoodoo Guns–Ray Hogan | | | | W |
| M103 | The Golden People–Fred Saberhagen | 1.25 | 2.50 | 3.75 | SF |
| | Exile from Xanadu–Lan Wright | | | | SF |
| M104 | Sidewinder Showdown–Tom West | 1.00 | 2.00 | 3.00 | W |
| | Land Beyond the Law–Dan J. Stevens | | | | W |
| M105 | Message from the Eocene–Margaret St. Clair | 1.25 | 2.50 | 3.75 | SF |
| | Three Worlds of Futurity–Margaret St. Clair | | | | SF |
| M106 | The Blind Trail–Reese Sullivan | 1.00 | 2.00 | 3.00 | W |
| | Ride of Fury–Tim Kelly | | | | W |
| M107 | The Coils of Time–A. Bertram Chandler | 1.50 | 3.00 | 4.50 | SF |
| | Into the Alternate Universe–A. Bertram Chandler | | | | SF |
| M108 | Warpath West–Wayne C. Lee | 1.00 | 2.00 | 3.00 | W |
| | Gunfire Heritage–Rod Patterson | | | | W |
| M109 | The Ship That Sailed the Time Stream– G.C. Edmondson | 1.25 | 2.50 | 3.75 | SF |
| | Stranger Than You Think–G.C. Edmondson | | | | SF |
| M110 | Wolf on Horseback–Merle Constiner | 1.00 | 2.00 | 3.00 | W |
| | Bushwhack Brand–Tom West | | | | W |
| M111 | Land Beyond the Map–Kenneth Bulmer | 1.25 | 2.50 | 3.75 | SF |
| | Fugitive of the Stars–Edmond Hamilton | | | | SF |
| M112 | Rogue's Rendezvous–Nelson Nye | 1.00 | 2.00 | 3.00 | W |
| | Gunfeud at Tiedown–Nelson Nye | | | | W |
| M113 | Off Center–Damon Knight | 1.25 | 2.50 | 3.75 | SF |
| | The Rithian Terror–Damon Knight | | | | SF |
| M114 | Lynch Law Canyon–Frank Wynne | 1.00 | 2.00 | 3.00 | W |
| | Stampede at Farway Pass–Stephen Payne | | | | W |
| M115 | Enigma from Tantalus–John Brunner | 1.25 | 2.50 | 3.75 | SF |
| | The Repairmen of Cyclops–John Brunner | | | | SF |
| M116 | The Best from Fantasy and Science Fiction, 10th Series–ed. Robert P. Mills | 1.00 | 2.00 | 3.00 | SF |
| M117 | Our Man in Space–Bruce Ronald | 1.25 | 2.50 | 3.75 | SF |
| | Ultimatum in 2050 A.D.–Jack Sharkey | | | | SF |
| M118 | The Toughest Town in the Territory– Tom West | 1.00 | 2.00 | 3.00 | W |
| | Guns at Q Cross–Merle Constiner | | | | W |
| M119 | Journey to the Center of the Earth– Jules Verne | .75 | 1.50 | 2.25 | SF |
| M120 | Ambush at Yuma's Chimney–Nelson Nye | 1.00 | 2.00 | 3.00 | W |
| | Ride the Wild Land–John Callahan | | | | W |
| M121 | The Ballad of Beta-2–Samuel R. Delany; 1965 | 1.25 | 2.50 | 3.75 | SF |
| | Alpha Yes, Terra No–Emil Petaja | | | | SF |
| M122 | Tall for a Texan–Roger G. Spellman | 1.00 | 2.00 | 3.00 | W |
| | Outlaw Brand–William E. Vance | | | | W |
| M123 | The Altar on Ascanel–John Brunner | 1.25 | 2.50 | 3.75 | SF |
| | Android Avenger–Ted White | | | | SF |
| M124 | Battle at Rattlesnake Pass–Tom West | 1.00 | 2.00 | 3.00 | W |
| | Trail of Vanishing Ranchers–Stephen Payne | | | | W |
| M125 | Monsters in Orbit–Jack Vance | 1.50 | 3.00 | 4.50 | SF |
| | The World Between–Jack Vance | | | | SF |
| M126 | Valley of Savage Men–Harry Whittington | 1.50 | 3.00 | 4.50 | W |
| | Brother Badman–Ben Elliott | | | | W |
| M127 | We, The Venusians–John Rackham | 1.25 | 2.50 | 3.75 | SF |
| | The Water of Thought–Fred Saberhagen | | | | SF |
| M128 | The Night It Rained Bullets–Brian Wynne | 1.00 | 2.00 | 3.00 | W |
| | Nemesis of Circle A–Reese Sullivan | | | | W |
| M129 | The Alternate Martians–A. Bertram Chandler | 1.50 | 3.00 | 4.50 | SF |
| | The Empress of Outer Space– A. Bertram Chandler | | | | SF |
| M130 | Half Injun, Half Wildcat–John Callahan | 1.00 | 2.00 | 3.00 | W |
| | Outcast of Ute Bend–Clement Hardin | | | | W |
| M131 | Behold the Stars–Kenneth Bulmer | 1.25 | 2.50 | 3.75 | SF |
| | Planetary Agent X–Mack Reynolds | | | | SF |
| M132 | The King in Yellow–Robert W. Chambers | 1.25 | 2.50 | 3.75 | HO |
| M133 | Space Mercenaries–A. Bertram Chandler | 1.50 | 3.00 | 4.50 | SF |
| | The Caves of Mars–Emil Petaja | | | | SF |
| M134 | Lost Loot of Kittycat Ranch–Tom West | 1.00 | 2.00 | 3.00 | W |
| | Saddle the Wind–Lin Searles | | | | W |
| M135 | The Mad Metropolis–Philip E. High | 1.25 | 2.50 | 3.75 | SF |
| | Space Captain–Murray Leinster | | | | SF |
| M136 | Marshal of Pioche–Nelson Nye | 1.00 | 2.00 | 3.00 | W |
| | Panhandle Pistolero–Ray Hogan | | | | W |
| M137 | The Best from Fantasy and Science Fiction, 11th Series–ed. Robert P. Mills | 1.00 | 2.00 | 3.00 | SF |
| M138 | Call Me Hazard–Frank Wynne | 1.00 | 2.00 | 3.00 | W |
| | The Rincon Trap–Dean Owen | | | | W |
| M139 | Empire Star–Samuel R. Delany | 1.25 | 2.50 | 3.75 | SF |
| | The Tree Lord of Imeten–Tom Purdom | | | | SF |
| M140 | Deadly Like a .45–Reese Sullivan | 1.00 | 2.00 | 3.00 | W |
| | Last Stage to Gomorrah–Barry Cord | | | | W |
| M141 | The Brains of Earth–Jack Vance | 1.75 | 3.50 | 5.25 | SF |
| | The Many Worlds of Magnus Ridolph– Jack Vance | | | | SF |
| M142 | The Doppelgangers–H.F. Heard | .75 | 1.50 | 2.25 | SF |
| M143 | Islands of Space–John W. Campbell | 1.00 | 2.00 | 3.00 | SF |
| M144 | Trigger Trio–Ernest Haycox | .75 | 1.50 | 2.25 | W |
| M145 | The Patient at Tonesbury Manor– Elizabeth Kellier | .50 | 1.00 | 1.50 | |
| M146 | Cracked Again–ed. Cracked Magazine | 2.00 | 4.00 | 6.00 | H |
| M147 | The Stars Are Ours!–Andre Norton; 1966 | .75 | 1.50 | 2.25 | SF |
| M148 | Star Born–Andre Norton | .75 | 1.50 | 2.25 | SF |
| M149 | The Eyes of the Overworld–Jack Vance; 1966 | 1.25 | 2.50 | 3.75 | SF |
| M150 | The Defiant Agents–Andre Norton | .75 | 1.50 | 2.25 | SF |
| M151 | The Last Planet–Andre Norton; 1967 | .75 | 1.50 | 2.25 | SF |
| M152 | King of the World's Edge–H. Warner Munn | 1.25 | 2.50 | 3.75 | SF |

| | V/Good | Fine | N/Mint |
|---|---|---|---|

**ACE M-SERIES,** *continued*

| | | V/Good | Fine | N/Mint | |
|---|---|---|---|---|---|
| M153 | The Weapon Makers—A.E. Van Vogt; aka One Against Eternity | .75 | 1.50 | 2.25 | SF |
| M154 | Invaders from the Infinite—John W. Campbell | 1.00 | 2.00 | 3.00 | SF |
| M155 | Four for Tomorrow—Roger Zelazny | 1.25 | 2.50 | 3.75 | SF |
| M156 | Key Out of Time—Andre Norton; 1967 | .75 | 1.50 | 2.25 | SF |
| M157 | Star Gate—Andre Norton | .75 | 1.50 | 2.25 | SF |
| M158 | The Proud Riders—Brian Wynne | .75 | 1.50 | 2.25 | W |
| M159 | Down East Nurse—Sylvia Lloyd | .50 | 1.00 | 1.50 | R |
| M160 | Trail of Lost Skulls—Nelson Nye | .75 | 1.50 | 2.25 | W |
| M161 | Nurse at Moorcroft Manor—Sharon Heath | .50 | 1.00 | 1.50 | R |
| M162 | Edge of Time—David Grinnell | .75 | 1.50 | 2.25 | SF |
| M163 | The Wolver—Ray Hogan | .75 | 1.50 | 2.25 | W |
| M164 | Cross Country Nurse—Suzanne Roberts | .50 | 1.00 | 1.50 | R |
| M165 | Worlds of the Imperium—Keith Laumer; 1967 | .75 | 1.50 | 2.25 | SF |

Ace M139, Ace M160, Ace T136.

## ACE N-SERIES
### Ace Books, Inc.

| | | V/Good | Fine | N/Mint | |
|---|---|---|---|---|---|
| N1 | Retrospect 1964, U.P.I. Pictorial History of 1963; 1964 | .50 | 1.00 | 1.50 | NF |
| N2 | Retrospect 1965, U.P.I. Pictorial History of 1964; 1965 | .50 | 1.00 | 1.50 | NF |
| N3 | Dune—Frank Herbert; 1967 | 2.50 | 5.00 | 7.50 | SF |
| N4 | Is Anyone There?—Isaac Asimov | 1.00 | 2.00 | 3.00 | NF |
| N5 | The Betrayal—William R. Corson; 1968 | .75 | 1.50 | 2.25 | C |
| N6 | Edgar Rice Burroughs: Master of Adventure—Richard Lupoff; 1st rev. ed. 1968; c-Frazetta; interior illus. by Frazetta and Crandall | 2.50 | 5.00 | 7.50 | NF |

## ACE STAR SERIES—see ACE K-SERIES/ STAR SERIES

## ACE T-SERIES
### Ace Books, Inc.

| | | V/Good | Fine | N/Mint | |
|---|---|---|---|---|---|
| T135 | More Cracked—ed. Cracked Magazine; 1962 | 2.00 | 4.00 | 6.00 | H |
| T136 | Completely Cracked—ed. Cracked Magazine; 1962 | 2.00 | 4.00 | 6.00 | H |
| T137 | Basketball for Everyone—Clair Bee | .50 | 1.00 | 1.50 | S |

## ADVENTURE NOVEL CLASSIC
### Hillman Periodicals, Inc./Novel Selections, Inc.
**Digest Size**

| | | V/Good | Fine | N/Mint | |
|---|---|---|---|---|---|
| 1 | The Blanket of the Dark—John Buchan | 2.50 | 5.00 | 7.50 | A |
| 2 | Bardelys the Magnificent—Rafael Sabatini | 2.50 | 5.00 | 7.50 | A |
| 3 | Code of the North—Harold Titus | 2.50 | 5.00 | 7.50 | A |
| 4 | House of the Four Winds—John Buchan | 2.50 | 5.00 | 7.50 | A |
| 5 | The Queen's Messenger—Rafael Sabatini | 2.50 | 5.00 | 7.50 | A |
| 6 | Big Timber—Robert Ormond Case | 2.50 | 5.00 | 7.50 | A |
| 7 | Hands Up!—Albert M. Traynor | 2.50 | 5.00 | 7.50 | A |
| 8 | Wings over Panama—Granville Church | 2.50 | 5.00 | 7.50 | A |
| 9 | Below Zero—Harold Titus | 2.50 | 5.00 | 7.50 | A |
| 10 | Connie Morgan Hits the Trail—James Hendryx | 2.50 | 5.00 | 7.50 | A |
| 11 | The Vengeance of Hurricane Williams— Gordon Young | 2.50 | 5.00 | 7.50 | A |
| 12 | The Trampling of the Lilies—Rafael Sabatini | 2.50 | 5.00 | 7.50 | A |
| 13 | Gone North—Charles Alden Seltzer | 2.50 | 5.00 | 7.50 | W |
| 14 | Rivermen Die Broke—Alan Le May | 2.50 | 5.00 | 7.50 | A |
| 15 | The Courage of Marge O'Doone—James Oliver Curwood | 2.50 | 5.00 | 7.50 | A |
| 16 | Out from Shanghai—Sydney Parkman | 2.50 | 5.00 | 7.50 | A |

| | | V/Good | Fine | N/Mint | |
|---|---|---|---|---|---|
| 17 | Death Heads North—James Hendryx | 2.50 | 5.00 | 7.50 | A |
| 18 | River of Fear—Leslie Turner White | 2.50 | 5.00 | 7.50 | A |
| 19 | The Unknown Ranger—Tom Gill | 2.50 | 5.00 | 7.50 | A |
| 20 | Flight to Glory—L.L. Foreman | 2.50 | 5.00 | 7.50 | A |
| 21 | Hawk of the Desert—Albert M. Treynor | 2.50 | 5.00 | 7.50 | A |
| 22 | Secret Command—John Hawkins & Ward Hawkins | 2.50 | 5.00 | 7.50 | A |
| 23 | Hard Money—Luke Short | 2.50 | 5.00 | 7.50 | A |
| 24 | Jungle Murder—Alan Amos; aka Pray for a Miracle | 2.50 | 5.00 | 7.50 | A |
| 25 | Valley of the Sun—Clarence Buddington Kelland | 2.50 | 5.00 | 7.50 | W |
| 26 | Montana Rides—Evan Evans (Max Brand) | 2.50 | 5.00 | 7.50 | W |
| 27 | North to Danger—Tom Gill | 2.50 | 5.00 | 7.50 | A |
| 28 | Riot at Red Water—Frederick R. Bechdolt | 2.50 | 5.00 | 7.50 | W |
| 29 | Broken River—John Hawkins & Ward Hawkins | 2.50 | 5.00 | 7.50 | A |
| 30 | Arizona—Clarence Budington Kelland | 2.50 | 5.00 | 7.50 | W |
| 31 | Death Charter—Eustace L. Adams | 2.50 | 5.00 | 7.50 | A |
| 32 | Montana Rides Again—Evan Evans (Max Brand) | 2.50 | 5.00 | 7.50 | W |
| 33 | Stagecoach Kingdom—Harry Sinclair Drago | 2.50 | 5.00 | 7.50 | W |
| 34 | Journey to Murder—Robert Portner Koehler | 2.50 | 5.00 | 7.50 | M |
| 35 | Devil on His Trail—John Hawkins & Ward Hawkins | 2.50 | 5.00 | 7.50 | A |
| 36 | The Song of the Whip—Evan Evans (Max Brand) | 2.50 | 5.00 | 7.50 | W |
| 37 | Jungle Harvest—Tom Gill | 2.50 | 5.00 | 7.50 | A |
| 38 | Death over Moccasin Valley—E.E. Halleran | 2.50 | 5.00 | 7.50 | W |
| 39 | Flame in the Forest—Harold Titus | 2.50 | 5.00 | 7.50 | A |
| 40 | Ship Ashore—Sydney Parkman | 2.50 | 5.00 | 7.50 | A |
| 41 | Hard Rock Man—James Hendryx | 2.50 | 5.00 | 7.50 | A |
| 42 | Vanishing Ships—Philip M. Fisher | 2.50 | 5.00 | 7.50 | A |

## ALL-PICTURE MYSTERY
### St. John Publishing Company
**Digest Size**

| | | V/Good | Fine | N/Mint | |
|---|---|---|---|---|---|
| nn | The Case of the Winking Buddha— Manning Lee Stokes; orig. 1950; comic book style | 15.00 | 30.00 | 45.00 | M |
| nn | It Rhymes with Lust; orig. 1951; comic book style with Matt Baker art | 20.00 | 40.00 | 60.00 | M |

## AMAZING STORIES SCIENCE FICTION NOVEL
### Ziff-Davis Publishing Company
**Digest Size**

| | | V/Good | Fine | N/Mint | |
|---|---|---|---|---|---|
| nn | 20 Million Miles to Earth—Henry Slesar; 1957; movie tie-in | 15.00 | 30.00 | 45.00 | SF |

## AMERICAN FOLK-LORE AND HUMOR
## Atomic Books, Inc.

### Digest Size

| | | V/Good | Fine | N/Mint | |
|---|---|---|---|---|---|
| nn(1) | The True Story of Billy the Kid: The Outlaw | 4.00 | 8.00 | 12.00 | B |
| nn(2) | The True Story of "Wild Bill" Hickok: Gun Fighter–J.W. Buel; 1946 | 4.00 | 8.00 | 12.00 | B |
| nn(3) | The True Story of Jesse James: King of Robbers | 4.00 | 8.00 | 12.00 | B |

## AMERICAN LIBRARY
## David McKay Company

### Digest Size

| 1 | Silent Witness–John Stephen Strange | 2.50 | 5.00 | 7.50 | M |
|---|---|---|---|---|---|
| 2 | Acts of Black Night–Kathleen Moore Knight | 2.50 | 5.00 | 7.50 | M |
| 3 | Dead Man Control–Helen Reilly | 2.50 | 5.00 | 7.50 | M |
| 4 | The Case of the Constant God–Rufus King | 2.50 | 5.00 | 7.50 | M |
| nn | Death in Fancy Dress–Jeffrey Farjeon | 2.50 | 5.00 | 7.50 | M |
| nn | Murder Day By Day–Irvin S. Cobb | 2.50 | 5.00 | 7.50 | M |

## THE AMERICAN READER'S LIBRARY
## The American Crayon Company

### Digest Size

| 1 | A Treasury of Famous Old Favorites; 1943 | 2.00 | 4.00 | 6.00 | |
|---|---|---|---|---|---|
| 2 | The Valor of Ignorance–Gen. Homer Lea | 2.00 | 4.00 | 6.00 | NF |
| 3 | The Day of the Saxon–Gen. Homer Lea | 2.00 | 4.00 | 6.00 | NF |
| 4 | The Spell of the Yukon and The Ballads of a Cheechako–Robert W. Service; The Terrible Solomons–Jack London | 3.00 | 6.00 | 9.00 | |

## (ANGLO-AMERICAN PUBLISHING)
## Anglo-American Publishing Co., Ltd.

### Canadian

| nn | God's Little Acre–Erskine Caldwell; 1948. Note: Same cover as Penguin 581 | 1.50 | 3.00 | 4.50 | |
|---|---|---|---|---|---|

## ARCHER BOOKS
## Kaywin Publishers, Inc./Archer Press Ltd.

**Note: Some titles and editions have been seen without numbers indicated here.**

| 2 | Dames Are No Dice–Slim Vincent | 5.00 | 10.00 | 15.00 | E |
|---|---|---|---|---|---|
| 3 | Take It, and Like It–Spike Morelli (William Simpson Newton); 1951; c-Heade | 7.50 | 15.00 | 22.50 | E |
| 4 | This Thing Called "Sin"–Roland Vane (Ernest L. McKeag) | 5.00 | 10.00 | 15.00 | E |
| 5 | Dame in My Bed–Michael Storme; 1951; c-Heade | 7.50 | 15.00 | 22.50 | E |
| 6 | Satan's Sister–Tony Angelo; c-Heade | 9.00 | 18.00 | 27.00 | M |
| 8 | You'll Never Get Me–Spike Morelli (William Simpson Newton); 1952; c-Heade | 7.50 | 15.00 | 22.50 | E |
| 10 | The Body Ran Home–M. Perelli | 4.00 | 8.00 | 12.00 | M |
| 11 | Coffin for a Cutie–Spike Morelli (William Simpson Newton); c-Heade | 7.50 | 15.00 | 22.50 | M |
| 12 | Sinner's Shroud–Tony Angelo | 7.50 | 15.00 | 22.50 | E |

| 13 | The Worms Have Eaten Them–William James Elliott | 7.50 | 15.00 | 22.50 | E |
|---|---|---|---|---|---|
| 14 | Shipwreck Passion–William James Elliott | 7.50 | 15.00 | 22.50 | E |
| 15 | Lost Souls of Bohemia–William James Elliott | 10.00 | 20.00 | 30.00 | E |
| 28 | Girl from Tiger Bay–Roland Vane (Ernest L. McKeag) | 9.00 | 18.00 | 27.00 | E |
| 31 | Two Smart Dames–Gene Ross | 6.00 | 12.00 | 18.00 | E |
| 33 | Come into My Parlor–Jules-Jean Morac | 6.00 | 12.00 | 18.00 | E |
| 35 | Vice Rackets of Soho–Roland Vane (Ernest L. McKeag) | 20.00 | 40.00 | 60.00 | E |
| 36 | Flame–Paul Renin (Richard Goyne) | 7.50 | 15.00 | 22.50 | E |
| 37 | Willing Sinner–Roland Vane; c-Heade | 6.00 | 12.00 | 18.00 | E |
| 38 | Where They Breed–Louis-Charles Royer | 5.00 | 10.00 | 15.00 | E |
| 39 | Black Mistress–Louis-Charles Royer | 7.50 | 15.00 | 22.50 | E |
| 40 | Sin Stained–Roland Vane (Ernest L. McKeag) | 5.00 | 10.00 | 15.00 | E |
| 42 | Eternal Conflict–George Goodchild | 5.00 | 10.00 | 15.00 | E |
| 44 | Pleasure's Price–Paul Renin (Richard Goyne) | 5.00 | 10.00 | 15.00 | E |
| 45 | When Passion Rules–Pierre Flammeche | 6.00 | 12.00 | 18.00 | E |
| 47 | Double Life–Paul Renin (Richard Goyne) | 5.00 | 10.00 | 15.00 | E |
| 48 | Passionate Puritan–Ruy Du Montesse | 5.00 | 10.00 | 15.00 | E |
| 49 | Sultry Love–Louis Arthur Cunningham | 5.00 | 10.00 | 15.00 | E |
| 50 | Sex–Paul Renin (Richard Goyne); 1951 | 4.00 | 8.00 | 12.00 | E |
| 51 | Night Haunts of Paris–Roland Vane (Ernest L. McKeag); 1951 | 4.00 | 8.00 | 12.00 | E |
| 52 | Sinful Sisters–Roland Vane (Ernest L. McKeag); 1951; c-Heade | 12.00 | 24.00 | 36.00 | E |
| 53 | Love–Paul Renin (Richard Goyne) | 4.00 | 8.00 | 12.00 | E |
| 54 | Fortnight's Folly–Paul Renin (Richard Goyne) | 5.00 | 10.00 | 15.00 | E |
| 57 | Plaything of Passion–Jeanette Revere; 1951; c-Heade | 9.00 | 18.00 | 27.00 | E |
| 68 | White Slaves of New Orleans–Roland Vane (Ernest L. McKeag); c-Heade | 12.00 | 24.00 | 36.00 | E |
| 69 | Ladies of the Red Lamp–Roland Vane (Ernest L. McKeag); c-Heade | 7.50 | 15.00 | 22.50 | E |
| 70 | The Silken Lure–Pierre Flammeche; c-Heade | 7.50 | 15.00 | 22.50 | E |
| 71 | Unlucky Virgin–Michael Storme | 5.00 | 10.00 | 15.00 | E |
| 72 | Ladies Sleep Alone–Lew Della; 1951 | 4.00 | 8.00 | 12.00 | E |
| 81 | Outrage–Paul Renin (Richard Goyne) | 4.00 | 8.00 | 12.00 | E |
| 82 | Virtue–Paul Renin (Richard Goyne) | 5.00 | 10.00 | 15.00 | E |
| 83 | Men Women Love–Paul Renin (Richard Goyne) | 4.00 | 8.00 | 12.00 | E |
| 84 | Make Mine a Harlot–Michael Storme | 5.00 | 10.00 | 15.00 | E |
| 96 | Spoiled Lives–Pierre Flammeche; 1952; c-Heade | 9.00 | 18.00 | 27.00 | E |

## (ARGYLE)
## Argyle Press

### Digest Size

| nn | Germany Must Perish!–Theodore N. Kaufman; anti-Nazi war propaganda | 3.00 | 6.00 | 9.00 | |
|---|---|---|---|---|---|

## ARMED SERVICES EDITION
## Editions for the Armed Services, Inc.

| A1 | The Education of Hyman Kaplan–Leonard Q. Ross; 1943 | 2.00 | 4.00 | 6.00 | |
|---|---|---|---|---|---|
| A2 | Report from Tokyo–Joseph C. Grew | 2.00 | 4.00 | 6.00 | |
| A3 | Good Intentions–Ogden Nash | 2.00 | 4.00 | 6.00 | |
| A4 | Mama's Bank Account–Kathryn Forbes | 2.00 | 4.00 | 6.00 | |
| A5 | There Go the Ships–Robert Carse | 2.00 | 4.00 | 6.00 | |
| A6 | Sophie Halenczik, American–Rose C. Field | 2.00 | 4.00 | 6.00 | |
| A7 | Mr. Winkle Goes to War–Theodore Pratt | 2.00 | 4.00 | 6.00 | |
| A8 | Oliver Twist–Charles Dickens | 3.00 | 6.00 | 9.00 | |
| A9 | Tortilla Flat–John Steinbeck | 3.00 | 6.00 | 9.00 | |

**ARMED SERVICES EDITION,** *continued*

| ID | Title | V/Good | Fine | N/Mint | Note |
|---|---|---|---|---|---|
| A10 | World Series–John R. Tunis | 2.00 | 4.00 | 6.00 | B |
| A11 | My World and Welcome to It–James Thurber | 3.00 | 6.00 | 9.00 | H |
| A12 | Peace Marshal–Frank Gruber | 2.00 | 4.00 | 6.00 | W |
| A13 | Heathen Days–H.L. Mencken | 2.00 | 4.00 | 6.00 | |
| A14 | The Ship–C.S. Forester | 2.00 | 4.00 | 6.00 | A |
| A15 | The Human Comedy–William Saroyan | 2.00 | 4.00 | 6.00 | |
| A16 | Wind, Sand and Stars–Antoine De Saint-Exupery | 2.50 | 5.00 | 7.50 | |
| A17 | The Making of Modern Britain–J.B. Brebner & Allan Nevins | 2.00 | 4.00 | 6.00 | NF |
| A18 | The Arabs–Phillip K. Hitti | 2.00 | 4.00 | 6.00 | |
| A19 | The Unvanquished–Howard Fast | 2.00 | 4.00 | 6.00 | |
| A20 | Miracles of Military Medicine–Albert Q. Maisel | 2.00 | 4.00 | 6.00 | NF |
| A21 | A Time for Greatness–Herbert Agar | 2.00 | 4.00 | 6.00 | |
| A22 | The Ministry of Fear–Graham Greene | 2.00 | 4.00 | 6.00 | M |
| A23 | Happy Landings–eds. Max J. Herzberg, Merrill P. Paine, & Austin M. Works | 2.00 | 4.00 | 6.00 | |
| A24 | Typee–Herman Melville | 2.50 | 5.00 | 7.50 | A |
| A25 | George Washington Carver–Rackham Holt | 2.00 | 4.00 | 6.00 | B |
| A26 | Lord Jim–Joseph Conrad | 2.50 | 5.00 | 7.50 | A |
| A27 | Storm over the Land–Carl Sandburg | 2.50 | 5.00 | 7.50 | |
| A28 | Action at Aquila–Hervey Allen | 2.00 | 4.00 | 6.00 | |
| A29 | Reprisal–Grace Zaring Stone | 2.00 | 4.00 | 6.00 | |
| A30 | The Fireside Book of Dog Stories–ed. Jack Goodman | 2.00 | 4.00 | 6.00 | A |
| B31 | Let the Hurricane Roar–Rose Wilder Lane; 1943 | 2.00 | 4.00 | 6.00 | |
| B32 | Dynamite Cargo–Fred Herman | 2.00 | 4.00 | 6.00 | A |
| B33 | Come In–Robert Frost | 2.50 | 5.00 | 7.50 | |
| B34 | Ethan Frome–Edith Wharton | 2.50 | 5.00 | 7.50 | |
| B35 | Suds in Your Eye–Mary Lasswell | 2.00 | 4.00 | 6.00 | |
| B36 | Fight for Powder Valley!–Peter Field | 2.00 | 4.00 | 6.00 | W |
| B37 | Our Hearts Were Young and Gay–Cornelia Otis Skinner & Emily Kimbrough | 2.00 | 4.00 | 6.00 | |
| B38 | Gentle Annie–MacKinlay Kantor | 2.00 | 4.00 | 6.00 | |
| B39 | Benchley Beside Himself–Robert Benchley | 2.50 | 5.00 | 7.50 | H |
| B40 | To Walk the Night–William Sloane | 2.00 | 4.00 | 6.00 | |
| B41 | The Gaunt Woman–Edmund Gilligan | 2.00 | 4.00 | 6.00 | |
| B42 | Winter Range–Alan LeMay | 2.00 | 4.00 | 6.00 | W |
| B43 | Painted Buttes–Arthur Henry Gooden | 2.50 | 5.00 | 7.50 | W |
| B44 | Chicken Every Sunday–Rosemary Taylor | 2.00 | 4.00 | 6.00 | |
| B45 | Father and Glorious Descendant–Pardee Lowe | 2.00 | 4.00 | 6.00 | |
| B46 | Life in a Putty Knife Factory–H. Allen Smith | 2.00 | 4.00 | 6.00 | H |
| B47 | Lightship–Archie Binns | 2.00 | 4.00 | 6.00 | |
| B48 | Get Thee Behind Me–Hartzell Spence | 2.00 | 4.00 | 6.00 | |
| B49 | My Friend Flicka–Mary O'Hara | 2.00 | 4.00 | 6.00 | A |
| B50 | Moscow Dateline–Henry C. Cassidy | 2.00 | 4.00 | 6.00 | |
| B51 | The Uninvited–Dorothy Macardle | 2.50 | 5.00 | 7.50 | |
| B52 | Rome Haul–Walter D. Edmonds | 2.00 | 4.00 | 6.00 | |
| B53 | Powder River–Struthers Burt | 2.00 | 4.00 | 6.00 | W |
| B54 | The Natives Return–Louis Adamic | 2.00 | 4.00 | 6.00 | |
| B55 | The Yearling–Marjorie Kinnan Rawlings | 2.50 | 5.00 | 7.50 | |
| B56 | Hostages–Stefan Heym | 2.00 | 4.00 | 6.00 | |
| B57 | Good Neighbors–Hubert Herring | 2.00 | 4.00 | 6.00 | |
| B58 | Klondike Mike–Merrill Denison | 2.00 | 4.00 | 6.00 | |
| B59 | Delilah–Marcus Goodrich | 2.00 | 4.00 | 6.00 | |
| B60 | Arctic Adventure–Peter Freuchen | 2.50 | 5.00 | 7.50 | A |
| C61 | North Africa–Alan H. Brodrick; 1944 | 2.00 | 4.00 | 6.00 | |
| C62 | The Sea of Grass–Conrad Richter | 2.50 | 5.00 | 7.50 | A |
| C63 | The Mind in the Making–James Harvey Robinson | 2.00 | 4.00 | 6.00 | |
| C64 | Candide–Voltaire | 2.50 | 5.00 | 7.50 | |
| C65 | The Forest–Stewart Edward White | 2.00 | 4.00 | 6.00 | |
| C66 | Pistols for Hire–Nelson E. Nye | 2.00 | 4.00 | 6.00 | W |
| C67 | Seven Men–Max Beerbohm | 2.00 | 4.00 | 6.00 | |
| C68 | Swamp Water–Vereen Bell | 2.00 | 4.00 | 6.00 | |
| C69 | Unlocking Adventure–Charles Courtney | 2.00 | 4.00 | 6.00 | A |
| C70 | Penrod–Booth Tarkington | 2.50 | 5.00 | 7.50 | |
| C71 | Green Mansions–W.H. Hudson | 5.00 | 10.00 | 15.00 | F |
| D72 | Hopalong Cassidy Serves a Writ–Clarence E. Mulford | 2.50 | 5.00 | 7.50 | W |
| C73 | U.S. Foreign Policy–Walter Lippman | 2.00 | 4.00 | 6.00 | NF |
| C74 | Star Spangled Virgin–DuBose Heyward | 2.00 | 4.00 | 6.00 | |
| C75 | Black-out in Gretley–J.B. Priestley | 2.50 | 5.00 | 7.50 | |
| C76 | The Adventures of Tom Sawyer–Mark Twain | 3.00 | 6.00 | 9.00 | A |
| C77 | The Short Stories of Stephen Vincent Benet–Stephen Vincent Benet; 1st ed. 1944 | 2.50 | 5.00 | 7.50 | F |
| C78 | Miracle in Hellas–Betty Watson | 2.00 | 4.00 | 6.00 | |
| C79 | Fathoms–Frank Meier | 2.00 | 4.00 | 6.00 | A |
| C80 | Australian Frontier–Ernestine Hill | 2.00 | 4.00 | 6.00 | |
| C81 | Storm–George R. Stewart | 2.00 | 4.00 | 6.00 | A |
| C82 | Kabloona–Gontran de Poncins | 2.00 | 4.00 | 6.00 | |
| C83 | The Forest and the Fort–Hervey Allen | 2.00 | 4.00 | 6.00 | A |
| C84 | The Hawkeye–Herbert Quick | 2.00 | 4.00 | 6.00 | |
| C85 | . . . and a Few Marines–Col. John W. Thomason, Jr | 2.00 | 4.00 | 6.00 | |
| C86 | Starbuck–John Selby | 2.00 | 4.00 | 6.00 | |
| C87 | Great Smith–Edison Marshall | 2.00 | 4.00 | 6.00 | A |
| C88 | Paul Revere–Edith Forbes | 2.00 | 4.00 | 6.00 | A |
| C89 | Coronet–Manuel Komroff | 2.00 | 4.00 | 6.00 | |
| C90 | The Grapes of Wrath–John Steinbeck | 3.00 | 6.00 | 9.00 | |
| D91 | The Story of Dr. Wassell–James Hilton; 1944 | 2.00 | 4.00 | 6.00 | |
| D92 | Love at First Flight–Charles Spalding & Otis Carney | 2.00 | 4.00 | 6.00 | |
| D93 | Blazed Trail Stories–Stewart Edward White | 2.00 | 4.00 | 6.00 | A |
| D94 | Tumbling River Range–W.C. Tuttle | 2.00 | 4.00 | 6.00 | W |
| D95 | Colonel Effingham's Raid–Berry Fleming | 2.00 | 4.00 | 6.00 | A |
| D96 | Without Orders–Martha Albrand | 2.00 | 4.00 | 6.00 | |
| D97 | Death Comes for the Archbishop–Willa Cather | 2.50 | 5.00 | 7.50 | M |
| D98 | The Trees–Conrad Richter | 2.00 | 4.00 | 6.00 | A |
| D99 | The Night of the Summer Solstice–ed. Mark Van Doren | 2.00 | 4.00 | 6.00 | |
| D100 | Valley of the Sun–Clarence Buddington Kelland | 2.00 | 4.00 | 6.00 | W |
| D101 | Evidence of Things Seen–Elizabeth Daly | 2.50 | 5.00 | 7.50 | M |
| D102 | Java Head–Joseph Hergesheimer | 2.00 | 4.00 | 6.00 | |
| D103 | Mystery Ship–George S. Bryan | 2.00 | 4.00 | 6.00 | |
| D104 | Burma Surgeon–Gordon S. Seagrave | 2.00 | 4.00 | 6.00 | |
| D105 | On Being a Real Person–Harry Emerson Fosdick | 2.00 | 4.00 | 6.00 | |
| D106 | Rats, Lice and History–Hans Zinsser | 2.00 | 4.00 | 6.00 | NF |
| D107 | R.F.D.–Charles Allen Smart | 2.00 | 4.00 | 6.00 | |
| D108 | McSorley's Wonderful Saloon–Joseph Mitchell | 2.00 | 4.00 | 6.00 | |
| D109 | Country Lawyer–Bellamy Partridge | 2.00 | 4.00 | 6.00 | |
| D110 | The Adventures of Huckleberry Finn–Mark Twain | 3.00 | 6.00 | 9.00 | A |
| D111 | Blanche Fury–Joseph Shearing | 2.00 | 4.00 | 6.00 | |
| D112 | Cross Creek–Marjorie Kinnan Rawlings | 2.00 | 4.00 | 6.00 | |
| D113 | The Keys of the Kingdom–A.J. Cronin | 2.00 | 4.00 | 6.00 | |
| D114 | We Cannot Escape History–John T. Whitaker | 2.00 | 4.00 | 6.00 | NF |
| D115 | Slim–William Wister Haines | 2.00 | 4.00 | 6.00 | |
| D116 | The Best American Short Stories of 1942–ed. Martha Foley | 2.00 | 4.00 | 6.00 | |
| D117 | A Tree Grows in Brooklyn–Betty Smith | 2.00 | 4.00 | 6.00 | |
| D118 | The Robe–Lloyd C. Douglas | 2.50 | 5.00 | 7.50 | |
| D119 | Rivers of Glory–F. VanWyck Mason | 2.00 | 4.00 | 6.00 | |
| D120 | So Little Time–John P. Marquand | 2.00 | 4.00 | 6.00 | |
| E121 | State Fair–Phil Strong; 1944 | 2.00 | 4.00 | 6.00 | |
| E122 | Seven Essays–Ralph Waldo Emerson; 1st ed. 1944 | 2.00 | 4.00 | 6.00 | |
| E123 | Ghost Trails–W.C. Tuttle | 2.00 | 4.00 | 6.00 | W |
| E124 | The Range Hawk–Arthur Henry Gooden | 2.50 | 5.00 | 7.50 | W |
| E125 | The Mountain Divide–Frank H. Spearman | 2.00 | 4.00 | 6.00 | |
| E126 | A Sense of Humus–Bertha Damon | 2.00 | 4.00 | 6.00 | |
| E127 | Bushido–Alexandre Pernikoff | 2.50 | 5.00 | 7.50 | E |
| E128 | The Moon and Sixpence–W. Somerset Maugham | 2.50 | 5.00 | 7.50 | |
| E129 | Saddle and Ride–Ernest Haycox | 2.50 | 5.00 | 7.50 | W |
| E130 | Seven Keys to Baldpate–Earl Derr Biggers | 3.00 | 6.00 | 9.00 | M |
| E131 | Science Year Book of 1943–ed. John D. Ratcliff | 2.00 | 4.00 | 6.00 | NF |
| E132 | Green Hell–Duguid Duguid | 2.50 | 5.00 | 7.50 | |
| E133 | Ship of the Line–C.S. Forester | 2.00 | 4.00 | 6.00 | A |

**ARMED SERVICES EDITION,** *continued*

| No. | Title | V/Good | Fine | N/Mint | |
|---|---|---|---|---|---|
| E134 | Ordeal by Hunger–George R. Stewart | 2.00 | 4.00 | 6.00 | |
| E135 | The Gambler Takes a Wife–Myron Brinig | 2.00 | 4.00 | 6.00 | |
| E136 | Stories for Men–ed. Charles Grayson; 1st ed. 1944 | 2.00 | 4.00 | 6.00 | |
| E137 | Jamaica Inn–Daphne DuMaurier | 2.00 | 4.00 | 6.00 | |
| E138 | Random Harvest–James Hilton | 2.50 | 5.00 | 7.50 | |
| E139 | A Connecticut Yankee in King Arthur's Court–Mark Twain | 3.00 | 6.00 | 9.00 | F |
| E140 | Cimarron–Edna Ferber | 3.00 | 6.00 | 9.00 | W |
| E141 | I Married Adventure–Osa Johnson | 2.00 | 4.00 | 6.00 | |
| E142 | Windswept–Mary Ellen Chase | 2.00 | 4.00 | 6.00 | |
| E143 | Roughly Speaking–Louise Randall Pierson | 2.00 | 4.00 | 6.00 | |
| E144 | Hell on Ice–Comm. Edward Ellsberg | 2.00 | 4.00 | 6.00 | |
| E145 | Doctors on Horseback–James Thomas Flexner | 2.00 | 4.00 | 6.00 | |
| E146 | The Late George Apley–John P. Marquand | 2.00 | 4.00 | 6.00 | |
| E147 | Selected Short Stories–Stephen Crane; 1st ed. 1944 | 2.50 | 5.00 | 7.50 | |
| E148 | One Man's West–David Lavender | 2.00 | 4.00 | 6.00 | |
| E149 | Drums Along the Mohawk–Walter D. Edmonds | 2.50 | 5.00 | 7.50 | A |
| E150 | King's Row–Henry Bellaman | 2.00 | 4.00 | 6.00 | |
| F151 | Messer Marco Polo–Donn Byrne; 1944 | 2.00 | 4.00 | 6.00 | |
| F152 | Night Flight–Antoine de Saint-Exupéry | 2.00 | 4.00 | 6.00 | |
| F153 | The Selected Writings of Abraham Lincoln–Abraham Lincoln; 1st ed. 1944 | 2.50 | 5.00 | 7.50 | |
| F154 | Black Majesty–John W. Vandercook | 2.00 | 4.00 | 6.00 | A |
| F155 | Going Fishing–Negley Farson | 2.00 | 4.00 | 6.00 | |
| F156 | Lassie Come Home–Eric Knight | 2.00 | 4.00 | 6.00 | |
| F157 | Flying Colours–C.S. Forester | 2.00 | 4.00 | 6.00 | A |
| F158 | Clear the Tracks–Joseph Bromley | 2.00 | 4.00 | 6.00 | |
| F159 | Happy Days–H.L. Mencken | 2.00 | 4.00 | 6.00 | |
| F160 | Border Breed–William MacLeod Raine | 2.00 | 4.00 | 6.00 | W |
| F161 | Jungle Peace–William Beebe | 2.00 | 4.00 | 6.00 | |
| F162 | Selected Short Stories–Bret Harte; 1st ed. 1944 | 2.00 | 4.00 | 6.00 | |
| F163 | The Bar 20 Rides Again–Clarence E. Mulford | 2.50 | 5.00 | 7.50 | W |
| F164 | The Border Trumpet–Ernest Haycox | 2.00 | 4.00 | 6.00 | W |
| F165 | So Big–Edna Ferber | 2.00 | 4.00 | 6.00 | |
| F166 | West with the Night–Beryl Markham | 2.00 | 4.00 | 6.00 | |
| F167 | Land Below the Wind–Agnes Newton Keith | 2.00 | 4.00 | 6.00 | |
| F168 | Under a Lucky Star–Roy Chapman Andrews | 2.00 | 4.00 | 6.00 | |
| F169 | The Horse and Buggy Doctor–Arthur E. Hertzler | 2.00 | 4.00 | 6.00 | |
| F170 | Here is Your War–Ernie Pyle | 2.00 | 4.00 | 6.00 | NF |
| F171 | The Blazed Trail–Stewart Edward White | 2.00 | 4.00 | 6.00 | W |
| F172 | Round Up–Ring Lardner | 2.00 | 4.00 | 6.00 | |
| F173 | Old Jules–Mari Sandoz | 2.00 | 4.00 | 6.00 | W |
| F174 | Life on the Mississippi–Mark Twain | 3.00 | 6.00 | 9.00 | |
| F175 | The Essays of Charles Lamb–Charles Lamb; 1st ed. 1944 | 2.00 | 4.00 | 6.00 | |
| F176 | A Subtreasury of American Humor–eds. E.B. White & Katharine S. White | 2.00 | 4.00 | 6.00 | |
| F177 | Wellington–Phillip Guedalla | 2.00 | 4.00 | 6.00 | |
| F178 | Casuals of the Sea–William McFee | 2.00 | 4.00 | 6.00 | |
| F179 | Dr. Dogbody's Leg–James Norman Hall | 2.50 | 5.00 | 7.50 | |
| F180 | The Sea-Wolf–Jack London | 3.00 | 6.00 | 9.00 | A |
| G181 | The Glorious Pool–Thorne Smith; 1944 | 2.50 | 5.00 | 7.50 | H |
| G182 | White Fang–Jack London | 3.00 | 6.00 | 9.00 | A |
| G183 | Low Man on a Totem Pole–H. Allen Smith | 2.00 | 4.00 | 6.00 | A |
| G184 | Trail's End–William MacLeod Raine | 2.00 | 4.00 | 6.00 | W |
| G185 | My Antonia–Willa Cather | 2.00 | 4.00 | 6.00 | |
| G186 | Long, Long Ago–Alexander Woolcott | 2.00 | 4.00 | 6.00 | |
| G187 | Sam Small Flies Again–Eric Knight | 2.00 | 4.00 | 6.00 | |
| G188 | Taps for Private Tussie–Jesse Stuart | 2.00 | 4.00 | 6.00 | |
| G189 | Kamongo–Homer W. Smith | 2.00 | 4.00 | 6.00 | |
| G190 | The Trusty Knaves–Eugene Manlove Rhodes | 2.00 | 4.00 | 6.00 | W |
| G191 | Little Caesar–W.R. Burnett | 3.00 | 6.00 | 9.00 | M |
| G192 | Inside Benchley–Robert Benchley | 2.00 | 4.00 | 6.00 | H |
| G193 | How to Think Straight–Robert H. Thouless | 2.00 | 4.00 | 6.00 | |
| G194 | The Mirror of the Sea–Joseph Conrad | 2.50 | 5.00 | 7.50 | |
| G195 | Raiders of the Rimrock–Luke Short | 2.00 | 4.00 | 6.00 | W |
| G196 | A Crystal Age–W.H. Hudson | 2.00 | 4.00 | 6.00 | |
| G197 | Laugh with Leacock–Stephen Leacock | 2.00 | 4.00 | 6.00 | H |
| G198 | Kim–Rudyard Kipling | 2.50 | 5.00 | 7.50 | A |
| G199 | Journey into America–Donald Culross Peattie | 2.00 | 4.00 | 6.00 | |
| G200 | As the Earth Turns–Gladys Hasty Carroll | 2.00 | 4.00 | 6.00 | |
| G201 | Young Man of Caracas–T.R. Ybarra | 2.00 | 4.00 | 6.00 | |
| G202 | Arouse and Beware–MacKinlay Kantor | 2.00 | 4.00 | 6.00 | A |
| G203 | This Chemical Age–William Haynes | 2.00 | 4.00 | 6.00 | NF |
| G204 | Thunderhead–Mary O'Hara | 2.00 | 4.00 | 6.00 | A |
| G205 | The Fleet in the Forest–Carl D. Lane | 2.00 | 4.00 | 6.00 | |
| G206 | The Best American Short Stories of 1943–ed. Martha Foley | 2.00 | 4.00 | 6.00 | |
| G207 | Rogues' Company–Harry Harrison Kroll | 2.00 | 4.00 | 6.00 | |
| G208 | H.M. Pulham, Esq.–John P. Marquand | 2.00 | 4.00 | 6.00 | |
| G209 | Moby Dick–Herman Melville | 3.00 | 6.00 | 9.00 | |
| G210 | East of the Giants–George R. Stewart | 2.00 | 4.00 | 6.00 | |
| H211 | C/O Postmaster–Corp. Thomas R. St. George; 1944 | 2.00 | 4.00 | 6.00 | |
| H212 | Beyond the Desert–Eugene Manlove Rhodes | 2.00 | 4.00 | 6.00 | W |
| H213 | Payment Deferred–C.S. Forester | 2.00 | 4.00 | 6.00 | A |
| H214 | Buried Alive–Arnold Bennett | 2.00 | 4.00 | 6.00 | |
| H215 | Western Star–Stephen Vincent Benet | 2.00 | 4.00 | 6.00 | |
| H216 | Laughing Boy–Oliver LaFarge | 2.00 | 4.00 | 6.00 | |
| H217 | The Republic of Plato–ed. I.A. Richards | 2.00 | 4.00 | 6.00 | |
| H218 | Forward the Nation–Donald Culross Peattie | 2.00 | 4.00 | 6.00 | |
| H219 | Three Times I Bow–Carl Glick | 2.00 | 4.00 | 6.00 | |
| H220 | Night Over Fitch's Pond–Cora Jarrett | 2.00 | 4.00 | 6.00 | |
| H221 | The Cruise of the Snark–Jack London | 2.50 | 5.00 | 7.50 | |
| H222 | Riders of the Night–Eugene Cunningham | 2.00 | 4.00 | 6.00 | W |
| H223 | Danger in the Cards–Michael MacDougall | 2.00 | 4.00 | 6.00 | |
| H224 | Burning an Empire–Stewart H. Holbrook | 2.00 | 4.00 | 6.00 | |
| H225 | Animal Reveille–Richard Dempewolff | 2.00 | 4.00 | 6.00 | |
| H226 | Red Raskall–Clark McMeekin | 2.00 | 4.00 | 6.00 | |
| H227 | Corson of the J C–Clarence E. Mulford | 2.00 | 4.00 | 6.00 | W |
| H228 | Captain Caution–Kenneth Roberts | 2.00 | 4.00 | 6.00 | |
| H229 | The Cold Journey–Grace Zaring Stone (Ethel Vance) | 2.00 | 4.00 | 6.00 | |
| H230 | The Bishop's Jaegers–Thorne Smith | 2.50 | 5.00 | 7.50 | H |
| H231 | Innocent Merriment–Franklin P. Adams | 2.00 | 4.00 | 6.00 | |
| H232 | Carmen of the Rancho–Frank H. Spearman | 2.00 | 4.00 | 6.00 | |
| H233 | Cardigan–Robert W. Chambers | 2.00 | 4.00 | 6.00 | |
| H234 | Box Office–eds. Marjorie Barrows & George Eaton | 2.00 | 4.00 | 6.00 | |
| H235 | The Pacific Ocean–Felix Riesenberg | 2.00 | 4.00 | 6.00 | |
| H236 | The Travels of Marco Polo–ed. Manuel Komroff | 2.00 | 4.00 | 6.00 | A |
| H237 | The Ringed Horizon–Edmund Gilligan | 2.00 | 4.00 | 6.00 | |
| H238 | Botany Bay–Charles Nordhoff & James Norman Hall | 2.50 | 5.00 | 7.50 | A |
| H239 | How Green Was My Valley–Richard Llewellyn | 2.00 | 4.00 | 6.00 | |
| H240 | Chad Hanna–Walter D. Edmonds | 2.00 | 4.00 | 6.00 | |
| I241 | Avalanche–Kay Boyle; 1944 | 2.00 | 4.00 | 6.00 | |
| I242 | Semper Fidelis–Keith Ayling | 2.00 | 4.00 | 6.00 | |
| I243 | Mr. and Mrs. Cugat–Isabel Scott Rorick | 2.00 | 4.00 | 6.00 | |
| I244 | Ol' Man Adam an' His Chillun–Roark Bradford | 2.00 | 4.00 | 6.00 | |
| I245 | The Mystery of the Red Triangle–W.C. Tuttle | 2.00 | 4.00 | 6.00 | |
| I246 | We Followed Our Hearts to Hollywood–Emily Kimbrough | 2.00 | 4.00 | 6.00 | |
| I247 | Deserts on the March–Paul B. Sears | 2.00 | 4.00 | 6.00 | |
| I248 | Rogue Male–Geoffrey Household | 2.50 | 5.00 | 7.50 | M |
| I249 | High Tension–William Wister Haines | 2.50 | 5.00 | 7.50 | |
| I250 | The Book Nobody Knows–Bruce Barton | 2.50 | 5.00 | 7.50 | |
| I251 | Stage Coach Kingdom–Harry Sinclair Drago | 2.50 | 5.00 | 7.50 | W |
| I252 | Selected Short Stories–Katharine Mansfield; 1st ed. 1944 | 2.50 | 5.00 | 7.50 | |
| I253 | The Middle-aged Man on the Flying Trapeze–James Thurber | 2.50 | 5.00 | 7.50 | |

## ARMED SERVICES EDITION, *continued*

| No. | Title | V/Good | Fine | N/Mint | |
|---|---|---|---|---|---|
| I254 | Deep West–Ernest Haycox | 2.50 | 5.00 | 7.50 | W |
| I255 | Arizona–Clarence Buddington Kelland | 2.50 | 5.00 | 7.50 | W |
| I256 | Cow by the Tail–Jesse James Benton | 2.50 | 5.00 | 7.50 | |
| I257 | Hopalong Cassidy's Protege–Clarence E. Mulford | 2.50 | 5.00 | 7.50 | W |
| I258 | Coast Guard to the Rescue–Karl Baarslag | 2.00 | 4.00 | 6.00 | |
| I259 | On the Bottom–Comm. Edward Ellsberg | 2.00 | 4.00 | 6.00 | |
| I260 | Ashenden–W. Somerset Maugham. Note: Queen's Quorum No. 76 | 2.00 | 4.00 | 6.00 | M |
| I261 | Queen Victoria–Lytton Strachey | 2.00 | 4.00 | 6.00 | |
| I262 | The Tides of Malvern–Francis Griswold | 2.00 | 4.00 | 6.00 | |
| I263 | Ten . . . and Out–Alexander Johnston | 2.00 | 4.00 | 6.00 | |
| I264 | Victory–Joseph Conrad | 2.50 | 5.00 | 7.50 | |
| I265 | Mrs. Parkington–Louis Bromfield | 2.00 | 4.00 | 6.00 | |
| I266 | The Sea-Hawk–Rafael Sabatini | 2.50 | 5.00 | 7.50 | A |
| I267 | Honey in the Horn–H.L. Davis | 2.00 | 4.00 | 6.00 | |
| I268 | Jane Eyre–Charlotte Bronte | 2.00 | 4.00 | 6.00 | |
| I269 | Paradise–Esther Forbes | 2.00 | 4.00 | 6.00 | |
| I270 | My Son, My Son!–Howard Spring | 2.00 | 4.00 | 6.00 | |
| J271 | The Proud Sheriff–Eugene Manlove Rhodes; 1944 | 2.00 | 4.00 | 6.00 | W |
| J272 | My Name Is Aram–William Saroyan | 2.00 | 4.00 | 6.00 | |
| J273 | The Shadow Line–Joseph Conrad | 2.50 | 5.00 | 7.50 | |
| J274 | Tree Toad–Bob Davis | 2.00 | 4.00 | 6.00 | |
| J275 | Riot at Red Water–Frederick R. Bechdolt | 2.00 | 4.00 | 6.00 | W |
| J276 | Past the End of the Pavement–Charles J. Finney | 2.00 | 4.00 | 6.00 | |
| J277 | Lou Gehrig–Frank Graham | 2.00 | 4.00 | 6.00 | B |
| J278 | You Know Me, Al–Ring Lardner | 2.00 | 4.00 | 6.00 | |
| J279 | The Phantom Filly–George Agnew Chamberlain | 2.00 | 4.00 | 6.00 | |
| J280 | Sheriff of Yavisa–Charles H. Snow | 2.00 | 4.00 | 6.00 | |
| J281 | Davy Crockett–Constance Rourke | 2.00 | 4.00 | 6.00 | B |
| J282 | A High Wind in Jamaica–Richard Hughes | 2.00 | 4.00 | 6.00 | |
| J283 | The Gang's All Here–Harvey Smith | 2.00 | 4.00 | 6.00 | |
| J284 | Skin and Bones–Thorne Smith | 2.50 | 5.00 | 7.50 | H |
| J285 | The Last Adam–James Gould Cozzens | 2.00 | 4.00 | 6.00 | |
| J286 | South of Rio Grande–Max Brand | 2.00 | 4.00 | 6.00 | W |
| J287 | George M. Cohan–Ward Morehouse | 2.00 | 4.00 | 6.00 | B |
| J288 | The Golden Fleece–Norah Lofts | 2.00 | 4.00 | 6.00 | |
| J289 | End of Track–Ward Weaver (Van Wyck Mason) | 2.00 | 4.00 | 6.00 | |
| J290 | Selected Stories–Paul Gallico | 2.00 | 4.00 | 6.00 | |
| J291 | February Hill–Victoria Lincoln | 2.00 | 4.00 | 6.00 | |
| J292 | The Sea and the Jungle–H.M. Tomlinson | 2.00 | 4.00 | 6.00 | A |
| J293 | No Life for a Lady–Agnes Morley Cleaveland | 2.00 | 4.00 | 6.00 | |
| J294 | The Bayous of Louisiana–Harnett T. Kane | 2.00 | 4.00 | 6.00 | |
| J295 | The Wake of the Prairie Schooner–Irene D. Paden | 2.00 | 4.00 | 6.00 | |
| J296 | Vanity Fair–William M. Thackeray | 2.00 | 4.00 | 6.00 | |
| J297 | Selected Stories–Edgar Allan Poe; 1st ed. 1944 | 3.00 | 6.00 | 9.00 | |
| J298 | Young Ames–Walter D. Edmonds | 2.00 | 4.00 | 6.00 | A |
| J299 | The Apostle–Sholem Asch | 2.00 | 4.00 | 6.00 | |
| J300 | Good Night, Sweet Prince–Gene Fowler | 2.00 | 4.00 | 6.00 | |
| J301 | Forty-niners–Archer Butler Hulbert | 2.00 | 4.00 | 6.00 | |
| J302 | Indians Abroad–Carolyn Thomas Foreman | 2.00 | 4.00 | 6.00 | |
| K1 | This Simian World–Clarence Day; 1944 | 2.00 | 4.00 | 6.00 | |
| K2 | The Old Soak–Don Marquis | 2.00 | 4.00 | 6.00 | |
| K3 | The Call of the Wild–Jack London | 3.00 | 6.00 | 9.00 | A |
| K4 | The Dark Gentleman–G.B. Stern | 2.00 | 4.00 | 6.00 | |
| K5 | The Secret of Dr. Kildare–Max Brand | 2.00 | 4.00 | 6.00 | |
| K6 | The Noise of Their Wings–MacKinlay Kantor | 2.00 | 4.00 | 6.00 | |
| K7 | Bounty of the Wayside–William Beebe Wilder | 2.00 | 4.00 | 6.00 | |
| K8 | Stepsons of Light–Eugene Manlove Rhodes | 2.00 | 4.00 | 6.00 | W |
| K9 | Selected Short Stories–Ernest Hemingway; 1st ed. 1944 | 3.00 | 6.00 | 9.00 | |
| K10 | The Life and Death of Little Jo–Robert Bright | 2.00 | 4.00 | 6.00 | |
| K11 | Rebel of Ronde Valley–Charles H. Snow | 2.00 | 4.00 | 6.00 | |
| K12 | The St. Lawrence–Henry Beston | 2.00 | 4.00 | 6.00 | |
| K13 | Ethan Allen–Stewart H. Holbrook | 2.00 | 4.00 | 6.00 | A |
| K14 | The Wild Bunch–Ernest Haycox | 2.00 | 4.00 | 6.00 | W |
| K15 | The Stray Lamb–Thorne Smith | 2.50 | 5.00 | 7.50 | H |
| K16 | Selected Short Stories–O. Henry; 1st ed. 1944 | 2.50 | 5.00 | 7.50 | |
| K17 | The Eight Million–Meyer Berger | 2.00 | 4.00 | 6.00 | |
| K18 | Moon Tide–Willard Robertson | 2.00 | 4.00 | 6.00 | |
| K19 | The Journey of the Flame–Antonio de Fierro Blanco | 2.00 | 4.00 | 6.00 | |
| K20 | Young Man of the World–T.R. Ybarra | 2.00 | 4.00 | 6.00 | |
| K21 | Winter Wheat–Mildred Walker | 2.00 | 4.00 | 6.00 | |
| K22 | Walt Whitman–Henry Seidel Canby | 2.00 | 4.00 | 6.00 | B |
| K23 | Andrew Jackson: The Border Captain–Marquis James | 2.00 | 4.00 | 6.00 | B |
| K24 | Babbitt–Sinclair Lewis | 3.00 | 6.00 | 9.00 | |
| K25 | Yankee Lawyer, The Autobiography of Ephraim Tutt–Ephraim Tutt | 2.00 | 4.00 | 6.00 | |
| K26 | Suckers Progress–Herbert Asbury | 2.00 | 4.00 | 6.00 | |
| K27 | The Robe–Lloyd C. Douglas | 2.00 | 4.00 | 6.00 | |
| K28 | A Tree Grows in Brooklyn–Betty Smith | 2.00 | 4.00 | 6.00 | |
| K29 | AP: The Story of News–Oliver Gramling | 2.00 | 4.00 | 6.00 | NF |
| K30 | Benjamin Franklin–Carl Van Doren | 2.00 | 4.00 | 6.00 | B |
| K31 | Tristram Shandy–Laurence Sterne | 2.00 | 4.00 | 6.00 | |
| K32 | Rise to Follow–Albert Spalding | 2.00 | 4.00 | 6.00 | |
| L1 | A Book of Americans–Rosemary Benét & Stephen Vincent Benét; 1944 | 2.00 | 4.00 | 6.00 | B |
| L2 | My Life and Hard Times–James Thurber | 2.50 | 5.00 | 7.50 | H |
| L3 | Kilgour's Mare–Henry G. Lamond | 2.00 | 4.00 | 6.00 | |
| L4 | Etched in Moonlight–James Stephens | 2.00 | 4.00 | 6.00 | |
| L5 | Porgy–DuBose Heyward | 2.00 | 4.00 | 6.00 | |
| L6 | Great Poems from Chaucer to Whitman–ed. Louis Untermeyer; 1st ed. 1944 | 2.00 | 4.00 | 6.00 | |
| L7 | What Became of Anna Bolton–Louis Bromfield | 2.00 | 4.00 | 6.00 | |
| L8 | Montana Rides Again–Evan Evans (Max Brand) | 2.00 | 4.00 | 6.00 | W |
| L9 | The Sheriff's Son–William MacLeod Raine | 2.00 | 4.00 | 6.00 | W |
| L10 | Happy Stories Just to Laugh At–Stephen Leacock | 2.00 | 4.00 | 6.00 | H |
| L11 | Roaring River Range–Arthur Henry Gooden | 2.50 | 5.00 | 7.50 | W |
| L12 | There's One in Every Family–Frances Eisenberg | 2.00 | 4.00 | 6.00 | |
| L13 | The King Bird Rides–Max Brand | 2.00 | 4.00 | 6.00 | W |
| L14 | The Sea Is So Wide–Evelyn Eaton | 2.00 | 4.00 | 6.00 | |
| L15 | Omoo–Hermen Melville | 2.50 | 5.00 | 7.50 | A |
| L16 | Hackberry Cavalier–George Sessions Perry | 2.00 | 4.00 | 6.00 | |
| L17 | Turnabout–Thorne Smith | 2.50 | 5.00 | 7.50 | |
| L18 | 400 Million Customers–Carl Crow | 2.00 | 4.00 | 6.00 | |
| L19 | Fish and Tin Fish–Philip Wylie | 2.00 | 4.00 | 6.00 | |
| L20 | Eminent Victorians–Lytton Strachey | 2.00 | 4.00 | 6.00 | |
| L21 | Country Cured–Homer Croy | 2.00 | 4.00 | 6.00 | |
| L22 | Science at War–George W. Gray | 2.00 | 4.00 | 6.00 | NF |
| L23 | Bedford Village–Hervey Allen | 2.00 | 4.00 | 6.00 | |
| L24 | The Lady and the Arsenic–Joseph Shearing | 2.00 | 4.00 | 6.00 | |
| L25 | Dracula–Bram Stoker | 11.00 | 22.00 | 33.00 | HO |
| L26 | Wickford Point–John P. Marquand | 2.00 | 4.00 | 6.00 | |
| L27 | I, Claudius–Robert Graves | 2.00 | 4.00 | 6.00 | B |
| L28 | Selected Short Stories–Thomas Mann; 1st ed. 1944 | 2.00 | 4.00 | 6.00 | |
| L29 | Lust for Life–Irving Stone | 2.00 | 4.00 | 6.00 | B |
| L30 | Of Human Bondage–W. Somerset Maugham | 2.50 | 5.00 | 7.50 | |
| L31 | The Land Is Bright–Archie Binns | 2.00 | 4.00 | 6.00 | |
| L32 | Four Years in Paradise–Osa Johnson | 2.00 | 4.00 | 6.00 | |
| M1 | Selected Poems–A.E. Housman; 1st ed. 1944 | 2.00 | 4.00 | 6.00 | |
| M2 | Is Sex Necessary–James Thurber & E.B. White | 2.50 | 5.00 | 7.50 | H |
| M3 | Selected Short Stories of "Saki"–H.H. Munro; 1st ed. 1944 | 2.50 | 5.00 | 7.50 | |
| M4 | 20,000 Leagues under the Sea or David Copperfield–Robert Benchley | 2.50 | 5.00 | 7.50 | H |
| M5 | Pere Marquette–Agnes Repplier | 2.00 | 4.00 | 6.00 | |
| M6 | Copper Streak Trail–Eugene Manlove Rhodes | 2.00 | 4.00 | 6.00 | W |
| M7 | Dune Boy–Edwin Way Teale | 2.00 | 4.00 | 6.00 | |

|  |  | V/Good | Fine | N/Mint |  |
|---|---|---|---|---|---|

ARMED SERVICES EDITION, *continued*

| | | V/Good | Fine | N/Mint | |
|---|---|---|---|---|---|
| M8 | Paul Bunyon–James Stevens | 2.00 | 4.00 | 6.00 | |
| M9 | Science Yearbook of 1944–ed. John D. Ratcliff | 2.00 | 4.00 | 6.00 | NF |
| M10 | The Chicken-wagon Family–Barry Benefield | 2.00 | 4.00 | 6.00 | |
| M11 | The Big Ones Get Away–Philip Wylie | 2.00 | 4.00 | 6.00 | |
| M12 | Old McDonald Had a Farm–Angus McDonald | 2.00 | 4.00 | 6.00 | |
| M13 | Action by Night–Ernest Haycox | 2.00 | 4.00 | 6.00 | W |
| M14 | The Border Kid–Max Brand | 2.00 | 4.00 | 6.00 | W |
| M15 | Fighting Men of the West–Dane Coolidge | 2.00 | 4.00 | 6.00 | W |
| M16 | Tarzan of the Apes–Edgar Rice Burroughs | 60.00 | 120.00 | 180.00 | A |
| M17 | The Boomer–Harry Bedwell | 2.00 | 4.00 | 6.00 | |
| M18 | Such Interesting People–Robert J. Casey | 2.00 | 4.00 | 6.00 | |
| M19 | Call Her Rosie–Eva Bruce | 2.00 | 4.00 | 6.00 | |
| M20 | Larrish Hundred–A.R. Beverley-Giddings | 2.00 | 4.00 | 6.00 | |
| M21 | Country Editor–Henry Beetle Hough | 2.00 | 4.00 | 6.00 | |
| M22 | With a Dutch Accent–David Cornel de Jong | 2.00 | 4.00 | 6.00 | |
| M23 | Four Modern American Plays–Hellman, Thurber & Nugent, Chodorov & Fields, Kingsley; 1st ed. 1944 | 2.00 | 4.00 | 6.00 | |
| M24 | A Treasury of the World's Great Letters–ed. M. Lincoln Schuster | 2.00 | 4.00 | 6.00 | |
| M25 | Indigo–Christine Weston | 2.00 | 4.00 | 6.00 | |
| M26 | Barnum–M.R. Werner | 2.00 | 4.00 | 6.00 | |
| M27 | Show Me a Land–Clark McMeekin | 2.00 | 4.00 | 6.00 | |
| M28 | New Stories for Men–ed. Capt. Charles Grayson | 2.00 | 4.00 | 6.00 | |
| M29 | The Moonstone–Wilkie Collins | 2.50 | 5.00 | 7.50 | M |
| M30 | Der Fuehrer–Konrad Heiden | 2.00 | 4.00 | 6.00 | |
| M31 | Stars on the Sea–F. Van Wyck Mason | 2.00 | 4.00 | 6.00 | |
| M32 | While Still We Live–Helen MacInnes | 2.00 | 4.00 | 6.00 | |
| N1 | The Mysterious Stranger–Mark Twain; 1944 | 3.00 | 6.00 | 9.00 | |
| N2 | The Dream Department–S.J. Perelman | 2.00 | 4.00 | 6.00 | H |
| N3 | America–Stephen Vincent Benet | 2.00 | 4.00 | 6.00 | |
| N4 | The Man Nobody Knows–Bruce Barton | 2.00 | 4.00 | 6.00 | |
| N5 | The Crock of Gold–James Stephens | 2.00 | 4.00 | 6.00 | |
| N6 | Selected Poems–Carl Sandburg; 1st ed. 1944 | 2.50 | 5.00 | 7.50 | |
| N7 | Let Your Mind Alone–James Thurber | 2.50 | 5.00 | 7.50 | |
| N8 | We Pointed Them North–E.C. Abbott & Helena Huntington Smith | 2.00 | 4.00 | 6.00 | |
| N9 | Rim of the Desert–Ernest Haycox | 2.00 | 4.00 | 6.00 | W |
| N10 | Useless Cowboy–Alan Lemay | 2.00 | 4.00 | 6.00 | W |
| N11 | The Fallen Sparrow–Dorothy B. Hughes | 2.50 | 5.00 | 7.50 | M |
| N12 | Snow above Town–Donald Hough | 2.00 | 4.00 | 6.00 | |
| N13 | Kidnapped–Robert Louis Stevenson | 3.00 | 6.00 | 9.00 | A |
| N14 | The Summing Up–W. Somerset Maugham | 2.00 | 4.00 | 6.00 | |
| N15 | The Iron Trail–Max Brand | 2.00 | 4.00 | 6.00 | W |
| N16 | Riata and Spurs–Charles A. Siringo | 2.00 | 4.00 | 6.00 | W |
| N17 | Duel in the Sun–Niven Busch | 2.00 | 4.00 | 6.00 | W |
| N18 | Thunder Mountain–Theodore Pratt | 2.00 | 4.00 | 6.00 | |
| N19 | I Dive for Treasure–Lt. H.E. Riesenberg | 2.00 | 4.00 | 6.00 | |
| N20 | Prophet by Experience–Jack Iams | 2.00 | 4.00 | 6.00 | |
| N21 | Hangman's House–Donn Byrne | 2.00 | 4.00 | 6.00 | |
| N22 | The Great American Novel–Claude Brian Davis | 2.00 | 4.00 | 6.00 | |
| N23 | Fire Bell in the Night–Constance Robertson | 2.00 | 4.00 | 6.00 | |
| N24 | Bonin–Robert Standish | 2.00 | 4.00 | 6.00 | |
| N25 | Mathematics and the Imagination–James Newman & Edward Kasner | 2.00 | 4.00 | 6.00 | |
| N26 | Magnus Merriman–Eric Linklater | 2.00 | 4.00 | 6.00 | |
| N27 | Look Away, Look Away–Leslie Turner White | 2.00 | 4.00 | 6.00 | |
| N28 | Martin Eden–Jack London | 2.50 | 5.00 | 7.50 | A |
| N29 | The Turning Wheels–Stuart Cloete | 2.00 | 4.00 | 6.00 | |
| N30 | Perilous Journey–C.M. Sublette & Harry Harrison Kroll | 2.00 | 4.00 | 6.00 | |
| N31 | David Copperfield–Charles Dickens | 3.00 | 6.00 | 9.00 | |
| N32 | The Big Rock Candy Mountain–Wallace Stegner | 2.00 | 4.00 | 6.00 | |

| | | V/Good | Fine | N/Mint | |
|---|---|---|---|---|---|
| O1 | Selected Poems–Percy Bysshe Shelley; 1st ed. 1945 | 2.00 | 4.00 | 6.00 | |
| O2 | The Prophet–Kahlil Gibran | 2.50 | 5.00 | 7.50 | |
| O3 | The Art of Illusion–John Mulholland | 2.00 | 4.00 | 6.00 | |
| O4 | They Played the Game–Harry Grayson | 2.00 | 4.00 | 6.00 | |
| O5 | Tales of the Pampas–W.H. Hudson | 2.00 | 4.00 | 6.00 | A |
| O6 | Plowman's Folly–Edward H. Faulkner | 2.00 | 4.00 | 6.00 | |
| O7 | Mr. Glencannon Ignores the War–Guy Gilpatric | 2.00 | 4.00 | 6.00 | |
| O8 | My Dear Bella–Arthur Kober | 2.00 | 4.00 | 6.00 | |
| O9 | Donovan's Brain–Curt Siodmak | 6.00 | 12.00 | 18.00 | SF |
| O10 | Wild Horse Shorty–Nelson C. Nye | 2.00 | 4.00 | 6.00 | W |
| O11 | Journey into the Fog–Cornelia Goodhue | 2.00 | 4.00 | 6.00 | |
| O12 | The African Queen–C.S. Forester | 2.00 | 4.00 | 6.00 | A |
| O13 | Lost Worlds–Anne Terry White | 2.00 | 4.00 | 6.00 | |
| O14 | I Never Left Home–Bob Hope | 2.00 | 4.00 | 6.00 | |
| O15 | Island in the Sky–Ernest K. Gann | 2.50 | 5.00 | 7.50 | A |
| O16 | Crazy Weather–Charles L. McNichols | 2.00 | 4.00 | 6.00 | |
| O17 | Nobody Lives Forever–W.R. Burnett | 3.00 | 6.00 | 9.00 | M |
| O18 | Runyon A La Carte–Damon Runyon | 2.50 | 5.00 | 7.50 | |
| O19 | The Lost Weekend–Charles Jackson | 2.50 | 5.00 | 7.50 | |
| O20 | Selected Short Stories–John Russell; 1st ed. 1945 | 2.50 | 5.00 | 7.50 | |
| O21 | On the Danger Line–Georges Simenon | 2.50 | 5.00 | 7.50 | M |
| O22 | The Return of Tarzan–Edgar Rice Burroughs | 70.00 | 140.00 | 210.00 | A |
| O23 | Men like Gods–Robert Sturgis | 2.00 | 4.00 | 6.00 | |
| O24 | The Three Black Pennies–Joseph Hergesheimer | 2.00 | 4.00 | 6.00 | |
| O25 | Selwood of Sleepy Cat–Frank Spearman | 2.00 | 4.00 | 6.00 | W |
| O26 | We Live in Alaska–Constance Helmericks | 2.00 | 4.00 | 6.00 | |
| O27 | The Red Cock Crows–Frances Gaither | 2.00 | 4.00 | 6.00 | |
| O28 | Selected Short Stories of M.R. James–M.R. James; 1st ed. 1945 | 2.50 | 5.00 | 7.50 | |
| O29 | Leave Her to Heaven–Ben Ames Williams | 2.00 | 4.00 | 6.00 | |
| O30 | Blessed Are the Meek–Zofia Kossak | 2.00 | 4.00 | 6.00 | |
| O31 | Look Homeward Angel–Thomas Wolfe | 2.50 | 5.00 | 7.50 | |
| O32 | Look to the Mountain–LeGrand Cannon, Jr | 2.00 | 4.00 | 6.00 | |
| P1 | Lady into Fox–David Garnett; 1945 | 2.00 | 4.00 | 6.00 | |
| P2 | Boomerang–Comm. William Chambliss | 2.00 | 4.00 | 6.00 | C |
| P3 | Rookie of the Year–John R. Tunis | 2.00 | 4.00 | 6.00 | S |
| P4 | Hotel Splendide–Ludwig Bemelmans | 2.00 | 4.00 | 6.00 | |
| P5 | Lost Island–James Norman Hall | 2.50 | 5.00 | 7.50 | A |
| P6 | Not Quite Dead Enough–Rex Stout | 3.00 | 6.00 | 9.00 | M |
| P7 | The Great Bustard and Other People–Will Cuppy | 2.00 | 4.00 | 6.00 | |
| P8 | The Fighting Four–Max Brand | 2.00 | 4.00 | 6.00 | W |
| P9 | Valley of the Sky–Hubert D. Skidmore | 2.00 | 4.00 | 6.00 | |
| P10 | The Kingdom of Swing–Benny Goodman & Irving Kolodin | 2.00 | 4.00 | 6.00 | NF |
| P11 | Lie Down in Darkness–H.R. Hays | 2.00 | 4.00 | 6.00 | |
| P12 | The Valley of Silent Men–James Oliver Curwood | 2.00 | 4.00 | 6.00 | A |
| P13 | Mother Wore Tights–Miriam Young | 2.00 | 4.00 | 6.00 | |
| P14 | Pilotin' Come Natural–Frederick Way, Jr | 2.00 | 4.00 | 6.00 | |
| P15 | Starlight Pass–Tom Gill | 2.00 | 4.00 | 6.00 | W |
| P16 | Trail Town–Ernest Haycox | 2.00 | 4.00 | 6.00 | W |
| P17 | Blood upon the Snow–Hilda Lawrence | 2.50 | 5.00 | 7.50 | M |
| P18 | Many Happy Days I've Squandered–Arthur Loveridge | 2.00 | 4.00 | 6.00 | |
| P19 | Stories by Erskine Caldwell–Erskine Caldwell | 2.00 | 4.00 | 6.00 | |
| P20 | Danger Is My Business–Capt. John D. Craig | 2.00 | 4.00 | 6.00 | |
| P21 | Botts in War, Botts in Peace–William Hazlett Upson | 2.00 | 4.00 | 6.00 | |
| P22 | World's Great Humorous Stories–ed. Irvin S. Cobb | 2.00 | 4.00 | 6.00 | |
| P23 | Aunt Beardie–Joseph Shearing | 2.00 | 4.00 | 6.00 | |
| P24 | Rebellion of Leo McGuire–Clyde Brion Davis | 2.00 | 4.00 | 6.00 | |
| P25 | O. Henry Prize Stories of 1943–ed. Herschel Brickell | 2.00 | 4.00 | 6.00 | |
| P26 | One Man's Meat–E.B. White | 2.00 | 4.00 | 6.00 | |
| P27 | Dragonwyck–Anna Seton | 2.00 | 4.00 | 6.00 | |
| P28 | Slogum House–Mari Sandoz | 2.00 | 4.00 | 6.00 | |

ARMED SERVICES EDITION, *continued*

| No. | Title | V/Good | Fine | N/Mint | |
|---|---|---|---|---|---|
| P29 | The Republic–Charles A. Beard | 2.00 | 4.00 | 6.00 | |
| P30 | Brave Men–Ernie Pyle | 2.00 | 4.00 | 6.00 | NF |
| P31 | A Treasury of Science–Harlow Shapley | 2.00 | 4.00 | 6.00 | NF |
| P32 | Yankee from Olympus–Catharine Drinker Bowen | 2.00 | 4.00 | 6.00 | |
| Q1 | Excuse It, Please!–Cornelia Otis Skinner; 1945 | 2.00 | 4.00 | 6.00 | |
| Q2 | The Postman Always Rings Twice–James M. Cain | 2.50 | 5.00 | 7.50 | M |
| Q3 | The Story of George Gershwin–David Ewen | 2.00 | 4.00 | 6.00 | B |
| Q4 | The Education of T.C. Mitls–Hugh Gray & Lillian R. Leiber | 2.00 | 4.00 | 6.00 | |
| Q5 | The Feather Merchants–Max Shulman | 2.00 | 4.00 | 6.00 | |
| Q6 | The World Ends at Hoboken–Mel Heimer | 2.00 | 4.00 | 6.00 | |
| Q7 | High Time–Mary Lasswell | 2.00 | 4.00 | 6.00 | |
| Q8 | Keystone Kids–John R. Tunis | 2.00 | 4.00 | 6.00 | S |
| Q9 | Selected Short Stories–Sherwood Anderson; 1st ed. 1945 | 2.00 | 4.00 | 6.00 | |
| Q10 | Give 'Em the Ax–A.A. Fair | 2.50 | 5.00 | 7.50 | M |
| Q11 | Prairie Guns–E.E. Halleran | 2.00 | 4.00 | 6.00 | W |
| Q12 | Watch Out for Willie Carter–Theodore Naidish | 2.00 | 4.00 | 6.00 | |
| Q13 | The Passionate Witch–Thorne Smith | 2.50 | 5.00 | 7.50 | H |
| Q14 | Guerrilla–Lord Dunsany | 4.50 | 9.00 | 13.50 | |
| Q15 | The Corpse without a Clue–R.A.J. Walling | 2.50 | 5.00 | 7.50 | M |
| Q16 | Man in the Saddle–Ernest Haycox | 2.00 | 4.00 | 6.00 | W |
| Q17 | The Amethyst Spectacles–Frances Crane | 2.50 | 5.00 | 7.50 | M |
| Q18 | Beat to Quarters–C.S. Forester | 2.00 | 4.00 | 6.00 | A |
| Q19 | The Heritage of the Desert–Zane Grey | 2.00 | 4.00 | 6.00 | W |
| Q20 | Devil on His Trail–John Hawkins & Ward Hawkins | 2.00 | 4.00 | 6.00 | W |
| Q21 | Salt Water Daffy–Philip Wylie | 2.00 | 4.00 | 6.00 | |
| Q22 | The House of Cobwebs–Mary Reisner | 2.00 | 4.00 | 6.00 | |
| Q23 | Luck in All Weather–Donal Hamilton Haines | 2.00 | 4.00 | 6.00 | |
| Q24 | Happy Jack–Max Brand | 2.00 | 4.00 | 6.00 | W |
| Q25 | Mom Counted Six–Mac Gardner | 2.00 | 4.00 | 6.00 | |
| Q26 | Take Them Up Tenderly–Margaret Case Harriman | 2.00 | 4.00 | 6.00 | |
| Q27 | The Green Years–A.J. Cronin | 2.00 | 4.00 | 6.00 | |
| Q28 | The Saddle and the Plow–Ross McLaury Taylor | 2.00 | 4.00 | 6.00 | |
| Q29 | The Lively Lady–Kenneth Roberts | 2.00 | 4.00 | 6.00 | |
| Q30 | Reckon with the River–Clark McMeekin | 2.00 | 4.00 | 6.00 | |
| Q31 | The Razor's Edge–W. Somerset Maugham | 2.50 | 5.00 | 7.50 | |
| Q32 | Strange Fruit–Lillian Smith | 2.00 | 4.00 | 6.00 | |
| Q33 | The Seventh Cross–Anna Seghers | 2.00 | 4.00 | 6.00 | |
| Q34 | Wild Is the River–Louis Bromfield | 2.00 | 4.00 | 6.00 | |
| Q35 | Selected Plays–Eugene O'Neill; 1st ed. 1945 | 2.00 | 4.00 | 6.00 | |
| Q36 | The Shadow and the Glory–John Jennings | 2.50 | 5.00 | 7.50 | |
| Q37 | Time Out of Mind–Rachel Field | 2.00 | 4.00 | 6.00 | |
| Q38 | The Sea Witch–Alexander Laing | 2.00 | 4.00 | 6.00 | |
| Q39 | The Strange Woman–Ben Ames Williams | 2.00 | 4.00 | 6.00 | |
| Q40 | The Education of Henry Adams–Henry Adams | 2.00 | 4.00 | 6.00 | |
| R1 | The Ugly Dachshund–G.B. Stern; 1945 | 2.00 | 4.00 | 6.00 | |
| R2 | Selected Poems–John Keats; 1st ed. 1945 | 2.00 | 4.00 | 6.00 | |
| R3 | One More Spring–Robert Nathan | 2.00 | 4.00 | 6.00 | |
| R4 | Selected Short Stories–Dorothy Parker; 1st ed. 1945 | 2.00 | 4.00 | 6.00 | |
| R5 | After 1903–What?–Robert Benchley | 2.00 | 4.00 | 6.00 | |
| R6 | Psychology You Can Use–William H. Roberts | 2.00 | 4.00 | 6.00 | NF |
| R7 | Selected Radio Plays–Norman Corwin | 2.00 | 4.00 | 6.00 | |
| R8 | You Wouldn't Know Me from Adam–Col. Stoopnagle | 2.00 | 4.00 | 6.00 | |
| R9 | Sea Duty–Jacland Marmur | 2.00 | 4.00 | 6.00 | |
| R10 | The Dark Page–Samuel Michael Fuller | 2.00 | 4.00 | 6.00 | |
| R11 | War on the Cimarron–Luke Short | 2.00 | 4.00 | 6.00 | W |
| R12 | Geography in Human Destiny–Roderick Peattie | 2.00 | 4.00 | 6.00 | NF |
| R13 | Bermuda Calling–David Garth | 2.00 | 4.00 | 6.00 | |
| R14 | A Shorter History of Science–Sir William Cecil Dampier | 2.00 | 4.00 | 6.00 | NF |
| R15 | Crime on My Hands–George Sanders | 2.50 | 5.00 | 7.50 | |
| R16 | The American Character–D.W. Brogan | 2.00 | 4.00 | 6.00 | |
| R17 | Our Hearts Were Young and Gay–Emily Kimbrough & Cornelia Otis Skinner | 2.00 | 4.00 | 6.00 | |
| R18 | Winter Range–Alan LeMay | 2.00 | 4.00 | 6.00 | W |
| R19 | The Gaunt Woman–Edmund Gilligan | 2.00 | 4.00 | 6.00 | |
| R20 | Painted Buttes–Arthur Henry Gooden | 2.50 | 5.00 | 7.50 | W |
| R21 | Selected Short Stories–Katharine Anne Porter; 1st ed. 1945 | 2.00 | 4.00 | 6.00 | |
| R22 | Cluny Brown–Margery Sharp | 2.00 | 4.00 | 6.00 | |
| R23 | Of Men and Music–Deems Taylor | 2.00 | 4.00 | 6.00 | NF |
| R24 | The Long Chance–Max Brand | 2.00 | 4.00 | 6.00 | W |
| R25 | Kitty Foyle–Christopher Morley | 2.00 | 4.00 | 6.00 | |
| R26 | Combustion on Wheels–David L. Cohn | 2.00 | 4.00 | 6.00 | |
| R27 | Earth and High Heaven–Gwethalyn Graham | 2.00 | 4.00 | 6.00 | |
| R28 | Young 'Un–Herbert Best | 2.00 | 4.00 | 6.00 | |
| R29 | Gamble's Hundred–Clifford Dowdey | 2.00 | 4.00 | 6.00 | |
| R30 | The Bridal Wreath–Sigrid Undset | 2.00 | 4.00 | 6.00 | |
| R31 | Try and Stop Me–Bennett Cerf | 2.00 | 4.00 | 6.00 | |
| R32 | Captain Blood–Rafael Sabatini | 2.50 | 5.00 | 7.50 | A |
| R33 | Sleep No More–August Derleth | 4.50 | 9.00 | 13.50 | |
| R34 | Of Smiling Peace–Stefan Heym | 2.00 | 4.00 | 6.00 | |
| R35 | The Time for Decision–Sumner Welles | 2.00 | 4.00 | 6.00 | |
| R36 | For My Great Folly–Thomas B. Costain | 2.00 | 4.00 | 6.00 | |
| R37 | Disputed Passage–Lloyd C. Douglas | 2.00 | 4.00 | 6.00 | |
| R38 | The Way Our People Lived–W.E. Woodward | 2.00 | 4.00 | 6.00 | |
| R39 | Deep River–Henrietta Buckmaster | 2.00 | 4.00 | 6.00 | |
| R40 | Canal Town–Samuel Hopkins Adams | 2.00 | 4.00 | 6.00 | |
| S1 | A Wartime Whitman–ed. Maj. W.A. Aiken; 1945 | 2.00 | 4.00 | 6.00 | |
| S2 | Dear Baby–William Saroyan | 2.00 | 4.00 | 6.00 | |
| S3 | I Love You, I Love You, I Love You–Ludwig Bemelmans | 2.00 | 4.00 | 6.00 | |
| S4 | Castaway–James Gould Cozzens | 2.00 | 4.00 | 6.00 | |
| S5 | My World and Welcome to It–James Thurber | 2.50 | 5.00 | 7.50 | H |
| S6 | Peace Marshal–Frank Gruber | 2.00 | 4.00 | 6.00 | W |
| S7 | Not Too Narrow, Not Too Deep–Richard Sale | 2.50 | 5.00 | 7.50 | M |
| S8 | Selected Short Stories–Philip Wylie | 2.00 | 4.00 | 6.00 | |
| S9 | Selected Short Stories–Mark Twain | 3.00 | 6.00 | 9.00 | |
| S10 | Young Man with a Horn–Dorothy Baker | 2.00 | 4.00 | 6.00 | |
| S11 | A Pearl in Every Oyster–Frank Sullivan | 2.00 | 4.00 | 6.00 | |
| S12 | Unexpected Uncle–Eric Hatch | 2.00 | 4.00 | 6.00 | |
| S13 | The Mauve Decade–Thomas Beer | 2.00 | 4.00 | 6.00 | |
| S14 | In What Torn Ship–Evelyn Eaton | 2.00 | 4.00 | 6.00 | |
| S15 | Clipper Ship Men–Alexander Laing | 2.00 | 4.00 | 6.00 | |
| S16 | Alarum and Excursion–Virginia Perdue | 2.00 | 4.00 | 6.00 | |
| S17 | Captain Retread–Donald Hough | 2.00 | 4.00 | 6.00 | |
| S18 | Guns of the Frontier–William MacLeod Raine | 2.00 | 4.00 | 6.00 | W |
| S19 | Your Kids and Mine–Joe E. Brown | 2.00 | 4.00 | 6.00 | |
| S20 | After-Dinner Story–William Irish | 3.00 | 6.00 | 9.00 | M |
| S21 | The Case of the Black-eyed Blonde–Erle Stanley Gardner | 2.50 | 5.00 | 7.50 | M |
| S22 | Lost in the Horse Latitudes–H. Allen Smith | 2.00 | 4.00 | 6.00 | H |
| S23 | Hunted Riders–Max Brand | 2.00 | 4.00 | 6.00 | W |
| S24 | The Ox-bow Incident–W. Van Tillburg Clark | 3.00 | 6.00 | 9.00 | |
| S25 | The St. Louis Cardinals–Frederick G. Lieb | 2.00 | 4.00 | 6.00 | S |
| S26 | Selected Short Stories–Algernon Blackwood; 1st ed. 1945 | 3.00 | 6.00 | 9.00 | |
| S27 | An Almanac for Moderns–Donald Culross Peattie | 2.00 | 4.00 | 6.00 | |
| S28 | The Night Life of the Gods–Thorne Smith | 2.50 | 5.00 | 7.50 | H |
| S29 | People on Our Side–Edgar Snow | 2.00 | 4.00 | 6.00 | |
| S30 | The Great Lakes–Harlan Hatcher | 2.00 | 4.00 | 6.00 | |
| S31 | The Farm–Louis Bromfield | 2.00 | 4.00 | 6.00 | |
| S32 | The Bolinvars–Marguerite F. Bayliss | 2.00 | 4.00 | 6.00 | |
| S33 | The Yearling–Marjorie Kinnan Rawlings | 2.00 | 4.00 | 6.00 | |
| S34 | Klondike Mike–Merrill Denison | 2.00 | 4.00 | 6.00 | |
| S35 | Henry Esmond–William M. Thackeray | 2.00 | 4.00 | 6.00 | |

| | | V/Good | Fine | N/Mint | |
|---|---|---|---|---|---|
| S36 | The History of Rome Hanks–Joseph Stanley Pennell | 2.00 | 4.00 | 6.00 | |
| S37 | Henry the Eighth–Francis Hackett | 2.00 | 4.00 | 6.00 | |
| S38 | Arundel–Kenneth Roberts | 2.00 | 4.00 | 6.00 | |
| S39 | Green Dolphin Street–Elizabeth Goudge | 2.00 | 4.00 | 6.00 | |
| S40 | Boston Adventure–Jean Stafford | 2.00 | 4.00 | 6.00 | |
| T1 | Dithers and Jitters–Cornelia Otis Skinner; 1945 | 2.00 | 4.00 | 6.00 | |
| T2 | The Time Machine–H.G. Wells | 7.50 | 15.00 | 22.50 | SF |
| T3 | Anything Can Happen–George Papashvily & Helen Papashvily | 2.00 | 4.00 | 6.00 | |
| T4 | Men of Popular Music–David Ewen | 2.00 | 4.00 | 6.00 | NF |
| T5 | Cannery Row–John Steinbeck | 3.00 | 6.00 | 9.00 | |
| T6 | This Is Murder–Timothy Fuller | 2.00 | 4.00 | 6.00 | M |
| T7 | A Smattering of Ignorance–Oscar Levant | 2.00 | 4.00 | 6.00 | H |
| T8 | The Fireside Book of Verse–Louis Untermeyer | 2.00 | 4.00 | 6.00 | |
| T9 | Coming, Major!–Ezra Stone & Weldon Melick | 2.00 | 4.00 | 6.00 | |
| T10 | Men Against the Sea–Charles Nordhoff & James Norman Hall | 3.00 | 6.00 | 9.00 | A |
| T11 | We Farm for a Hobby and Make It Pay–Henry Tetlow | 2.00 | 4.00 | 6.00 | |
| T12 | The Stone of Chastity–Margery Sharp | 2.00 | 4.00 | 6.00 | |
| T13 | Benchley Beside Himself–Robert Benchley | 2.50 | 5.00 | 7.50 | H |
| T14 | Gentle Annie–MacKinlay Kantor | 2.00 | 4.00 | 6.00 | |
| T15 | The Outlaw Years–Robert M. Coates | 2.00 | 4.00 | 6.00 | |
| T16 | The Range Boss–Charles Alden Seltzer | 2.00 | 4.00 | 6.00 | W |
| T17 | Puzzle for Puppets–Patrick Quentin | 2.50 | 5.00 | 7.50 | M |
| T18 | Daisy Miller and Other Stories–Henry James | 2.00 | 4.00 | 6.00 | |
| T19 | Ridin' the Rainbow–Rosemary Taylor | 2.00 | 4.00 | 6.00 | |
| T20 | Pistol Passport–Eugene Cunningham | 2.00 | 4.00 | 6.00 | W |
| T21 | Riders of the Plains–Max Brand | 2.00 | 4.00 | 6.00 | W |
| T22 | Tunnel from Calais–David Rame | 2.00 | 4.00 | 6.00 | |
| T23 | The Edge of Running Water–William Sloane | 2.00 | 4.00 | 6.00 | |
| T24 | The New York Yankees–Frank Graham | 2.00 | 4.00 | 6.00 | S |
| T25 | The Best Plays of 1943–44–ed. Burns Mantle | 2.00 | 4.00 | 6.00 | |
| T26 | Freedom Road–Howard Fast | 2.00 | 4.00 | 6.00 | |
| T27 | Blow for a Landing–Ben Lucien Burman | 2.00 | 4.00 | 6.00 | |
| T28 | Wolf Law and Three Other Stories of the West–Foster, Nafziger, Shaw & Ranger; 1st ed. 1945 | 2.00 | 4.00 | 6.00 | W |
| T29 | The General's Lady–Esther Forbes | 2.00 | 4.00 | 6.00 | |
| T30 | Genesee Fever–Carl Carmer | 2.00 | 4.00 | 6.00 | |
| T31 | Battle Report–Comm. Walter Karig & Lt. Welbourne Kelley | 2.00 | 4.00 | 6.00 | C |
| T32 | The World We Live In–Louis Bromfield | 2.00 | 4.00 | 6.00 | |
| T33 | The Citadel–A.J. Cronin | 2.00 | 4.00 | 6.00 | |
| T34 | Whistle Stop–Maritta Wolff | 2.00 | 4.00 | 6.00 | |
| T35 | The Loon Feather–Iola Fuller | 2.00 | 4.00 | 6.00 | |
| T36 | Rebecca–Daphne DuMaurier | 2.00 | 4.00 | 6.00 | |
| T37 | Delilah–Marcus Goodrich | 2.00 | 4.00 | 6.00 | |
| T38 | Arctic Adventure–Peter Freuchen | 2.00 | 4.00 | 6.00 | A |
| T39 | Forever Amber–Kathleen Winsor | 2.50 | 5.00 | 7.50 | |
| T40 | Anna and the King of Siam–Margaret Landon | 2.50 | 5.00 | 7.50 | |
| 655 | Portrait of Jenny–Robert Nathan; 1945 | 2.00 | 4.00 | 6.00 | |
| 656 | Adventures of Superman–George Lowther | 100.00 | 200.00 | 300.00 | A |
| 657 | Barefoot Boy with Cheek–Max Shulman | 2.00 | 4.00 | 6.00 | H |
| 658 | The Charge of the Light Brigade–Alfred Lord Tennyson | 2.50 | 5.00 | 7.50 | |
| 659 | What's on Your Mind?–Joseph Dunninger | 2.00 | 4.00 | 6.00 | |
| 660 | The Outermost House–Henry Beston | 2.00 | 4.00 | 6.00 | |
| 661 | Look to the Frontiers–Roderick Peattie | 2.00 | 4.00 | 6.00 | |
| 662 | My Family, Right or Wrong–John P. Sousa, III | 2.00 | 4.00 | 6.00 | |
| 663 | Murder and the Married Virgin–Brett Halliday | 2.50 | 5.00 | 7.50 | M |
| 664 | Where Away–George Sessions Perry & Isabel Leighton | 2.00 | 4.00 | 6.00 | |
| 665 | The Old Dark House–J.B. Priestley | 2.50 | 5.00 | 7.50 | |
| 666 | Laura–Vera Caspary | 2.00 | 4.00 | 6.00 | |
| 667 | To Have and Have Not–Ernest Hemingway | 2.50 | 5.00 | 7.50 | |
| 668 | Mrs. Egg and Other Barbarians–Thomas Beer | 2.00 | 4.00 | 6.00 | |
| 669 | Mademoiselle Fifi and Other Stories–Guy de Maupassant; 1st ed. 1945 | 2.00 | 4.00 | 6.00 | |
| 670 | Gunman's Chance–Luke Short | 2.00 | 4.00 | 6.00 | W |
| 671 | The Glorious Pool–Thorne Smith | 2.50 | 5.00 | 7.50 | F |
| 672 | White Fang–Jack London | 3.00 | 6.00 | 9.00 | A |
| 673 | Low Man on a Totem Pole–H. Allen Smith | 2.00 | 4.00 | 6.00 | |
| 674 | Trail's End–William MacLeod Raine | 2.00 | 4.00 | 6.00 | W |
| 675 | The 17th Letter–Dorothy Cameron Disney | 2.00 | 4.00 | 6.00 | |
| 676 | Esquire's Jazz Book 1944–ed. Paul Eduard Miller | 2.00 | 4.00 | 6.00 | |
| 677 | Selected Short Stories–Walter D. Edmonds; 1st ed. 1945 | 2.00 | 4.00 | 6.00 | |
| 678 | Western Union–Zane Grey | 2.00 | 4.00 | 6.00 | W |
| 679 | The Captain from Connecticut–C.S. Forester | 2.00 | 4.00 | 6.00 | A |
| 680 | Calamity Town–Ellery Queen | 2.50 | 5.00 | 7.50 | M |
| 681 | Tomorrow Will Sing–Elliott Arnold | 2.00 | 4.00 | 6.00 | |
| 682 | Science Remakes the World–James Stokley | 2.00 | 4.00 | 6.00 | |
| 683 | Bugles in the Afternoon–Ernest Haycox | 2.50 | 5.00 | 7.50 | W |
| 684 | Prodigal Genius–John J. O'Neill | 2.00 | 4.00 | 6.00 | |
| 685 | The Cadavar of Gideon Wyck–ed. Alexander Laing | 2.00 | 4.00 | 6.00 | |
| 686 | Western Story Omnibus–ed. William Targ | 2.00 | 4.00 | 6.00 | W |
| 687 | Seven Gothic Tales–Isak Dinesen | 2.00 | 4.00 | 6.00 | |
| 688 | Barren Ground–Ellen Glasgow | 2.00 | 4.00 | 6.00 | |
| 689 | Great Smith–Edison Marshall | 2.00 | 4.00 | 6.00 | A |
| 690 | The Grapes of Wrath–John Steinbeck | 3.00 | 6.00 | 9.00 | |
| 691 | Pickwick Papers–Charles Dickens | 3.00 | 6.00 | 9.00 | |
| 692 | Lock, Stock and Barrel–Douglas Rigby & Elizabeth Rigby | 2.00 | 4.00 | 6.00 | |
| 693 | Immortal Wife–Irving Stone | 2.00 | 4.00 | 6.00 | |
| 694 | Journey in the Dark–Martin Flavin | 2.00 | 4.00 | 6.00 | |
| 695 | The McKenneys Carry On–Ruth McKenney; 1945 | 2.00 | 4.00 | 6.00 | |
| 696 | Quo Vadimus?–E.B. White | 2.00 | 4.00 | 6.00 | |
| 697 | Thunder over the Bronx–Arthur Kober | 2.00 | 4.00 | 6.00 | |
| 698 | The Island of Dr. Moreau–H.G. Wells | 9.00 | 18.00 | 27.00 | HO |
| 699 | Meet Me in St. Louis–Sally Benson | 2.00 | 4.00 | 6.00 | |
| 700 | A Home in the Century–Frederic F. Van de Water | 2.00 | 4.00 | 6.00 | |
| 701 | Another Claudia–Rose Franken | 2.00 | 4.00 | 6.00 | |
| 702 | I Am Gazing into My 8-Ball–Earl Wilson | 2.00 | 4.00 | 6.00 | |
| 703 | The Pastures of Heaven–John Steinbeck | 3.00 | 6.00 | 9.00 | |
| 704 | Paul Revere's Ride and Other Poems–Henry Wadsworth Longfellow; 1st ed. 1945 | 2.00 | 4.00 | 6.00 | |
| 705 | The Middle-Aged Man on the Flying Trapeze–James Thurber | 2.50 | 5.00 | 7.50 | |
| 706 | Deep West–Ernest Haycox | 2.00 | 4.00 | 6.00 | W |
| 707 | Arizona–Clarence Buddington Kelland | 2.00 | 4.00 | 6.00 | W |
| 708 | Cow by the Tail–Jesse James Benton | 2.00 | 4.00 | 6.00 | |
| 709 | To the Indies–C.S. Forester | 2.00 | 4.00 | 6.00 | A |
| 710 | Eddie and the Archangel Mike–Barry Benefield | 2.00 | 4.00 | 6.00 | |
| 711 | Wings of Fear–Mignon G. Eberhart | 2.50 | 5.00 | 7.50 | M |
| 712 | The Three Mesquiteers–William Colt MacDonald | 2.50 | 5.00 | 7.50 | W |
| 713 | The Golden Rooms–Vardis Fisher | 2.00 | 4.00 | 6.00 | |
| 714 | Lad: A Dog–Albert Payson Terhune | .50 | 1.00 | 1.50 | |
| 715 | Gunman's Gold–Max Brand | 2.00 | 4.00 | 6.00 | W |
| 716 | Tall Tale America–Walter Blair | 2.00 | 4.00 | 6.00 | |
| 717 | Webster's New Handy Dictionary–Merriam-Webster | 2.00 | 4.00 | 6.00 | NF |
| 718 | Webster's New Handy Dictionary–Merriam-Webster | 2.00 | 4.00 | 6.00 | NF |
| 719 | The Sad Sack–Sgt. George Baker | 10.00 | 20.00 | 30.00 | H |
| 720 | Voyage of the Golden Hind–Edmund Gilligan | 2.00 | 4.00 | 6.00 | |
| 721 | The Purple Land–W.H. Hudson | 2.00 | 4.00 | 6.00 | |
| 722 | Sunset Pass–Zane Grey | 2.00 | 4.00 | 6.00 | W |
| 723 | The Woman in the Window–J.H. Wallis; aka Once Off Guard | 2.50 | 5.00 | 7.50 | |

ARMED SERVICES EDITION, *continued*

| No. | Title | V/Good | Fine | N/Mint | |
|---|---|---|---|---|---|
| 724 | South Moon Under–Marjorie Kinnan Rawlings | 2.00 | 4.00 | 6.00 | |
| 725 | Pitcairn's Island–Charles Nordhoff & James Norman Hall | 3.00 | 6.00 | 9.00 | A |
| 726 | Jazzmen–eds. Frederic Ramsey, Jr & Charles Edward Smith | 2.00 | 4.00 | 6.00 | NF |
| 727 | Death and the Dancing Footman–Ngaio Marsh | 2.50 | 5.00 | 7.50 | M |
| 728 | Farewell to Sport–Paul Gallico | 2.00 | 4.00 | 6.00 | |
| 729 | Mankind So Far–William Howells | 2.00 | 4.00 | 6.00 | |
| 730 | The Dunwich Horror and Other Weird Tales–H.P. Lovecraft; 1st ed. 1945 | 20.00 | 40.00 | 60.00 | SF |
| 731 | . . . and a Few Marines–Col. John W. Thomason, Jr | 2.00 | 4.00 | 6.00 | |
| 732 | Starbuck–John Selby | 2.00 | 4.00 | 6.00 | |
| 733 | The Cross and the Arrow–Albert Maltz | 2.00 | 4.00 | 6.00 | |
| 734 | Lower Than the Angels–Walter Karig | 2.00 | 4.00 | 6.00 | |
| 735 | A Little Night Music–Gerald W. Johnson; 1945 | 2.00 | 4.00 | 6.00 | |
| 736 | My Heart Leaps Up and Other Poems–William Wordsworth; 1st ed. 1945 | 2.00 | 4.00 | 6.00 | |
| 737 | The Enchanted Voyage–Robert Nathan | 2.00 | 4.00 | 6.00 | F |
| 738 | Lives–Gustav Eckstein | 2.00 | 4.00 | 6.00 | |
| 739 | Soldier Art–Prize Winners in Special Services Art Contest | 2.00 | 4.00 | 6.00 | |
| 740 | Cartoons for Fighters–Sgt. Frank Brandt | 2.50 | 5.00 | 7.50 | H |
| 741 | Pipe Night–John O'Hara | 2.00 | 4.00 | 6.00 | |
| 742 | Joe, the Wounded Tennis Player–Morton Thompson | 2.00 | 4.00 | 6.00 | |
| 743 | Brag Dog and Other Stories–Vereen Bell; 1st ed. 1945 | 2.00 | 4.00 | 6.00 | |
| 744 | Harvard Has a Homicide–Timothy Fuller | 2.00 | 4.00 | 6.00 | M |
| 745 | The War of the Worlds–H.G. Wells | 9.00 | 18.00 | 27.00 | SF |
| 746 | Kid Galahad–Francis Wallace | 2.00 | 4.00 | 6.00 | S |
| 747 | Death on the Aisle–Frances Lockridge & Richard Lockridge | 2.50 | 5.00 | 7.50 | M |
| 748 | Starlight Rider–Ernest Haycox | 2.00 | 4.00 | 6.00 | W |
| 749 | Looking for a Bluebird–Joseph Wechsberg | 2.00 | 4.00 | 6.00 | |
| 750 | Cup of Gold–John Steinbeck | 3.00 | 6.00 | 9.00 | A |
| 751 | The Big Sleep–Raymond Chandler | 15.00 | 30.00 | 45.00 | M |
| 752 | The Valley of Dry Bones–Arthur Henry Gooden | 2.50 | 5.00 | 7.50 | W |
| 753 | Diamond River Man–Eugene Cunningham | 2.00 | 4.00 | 6.00 | W |
| 754 | Adventures of Hiram Holliday–Paul Gallico | 2.00 | 4.00 | 6.00 | |
| 755 | Let Your Mind Alone–James Thurber | 2.00 | 4.00 | 6.00 | H |
| 756 | We Pointed Them North–Helena Huntington Smith & E.C. Abbott | 2.00 | 4.00 | 6.00 | |
| 757 | The Eight Million–Meyer Berger | 2.00 | 4.00 | 6.00 | |
| 758 | Moon Tide–Willard Robertson | 2.00 | 4.00 | 6.00 | |
| 759 | Buck Peters, Ranchman–Clarence E. Mulford | 2.00 | 4.00 | 6.00 | W |
| 760 | Died in the Wool–Ngaio Marsh | 2.50 | 5.00 | 7.50 | M |
| 761 | Keep 'Em Crawling–William Hazlett Upson | 2.00 | 4.00 | 6.00 | |
| 762 | Joseph Lister–Rhoda Truax | 2.00 | 4.00 | 6.00 | |
| 763 | Listen for a Lonesome Drum–Carl Carmer | 2.00 | 4.00 | 6.00 | |
| 764 | The Asiatics–Frederick Prokosch | 2.00 | 4.00 | 6.00 | |
| 765 | World's Great Tales of the Sea–William McFee | 2.00 | 4.00 | 6.00 | A |
| 766 | Double Indemnity and Two Other Stories–James M. Cain; aka Three of a Kind | 2.50 | 5.00 | 7.50 | M |
| 767 | Selected Stories–Edgar Allan Poe | 2.50 | 5.00 | 7.50 | |
| 768 | Young Ames–Walter D. Edmonds | 2.00 | 4.00 | 6.00 | A |
| 769 | Life with Father and Mother–Clarence Day | 2.50 | 5.00 | 7.50 | |
| 770 | Quietly My Captain Waits–Evelyn Eaton | 2.00 | 4.00 | 6.00 | |
| 771 | Myths after Lincoln–Lloyd Lewis | 2.00 | 4.00 | 6.00 | |
| 772 | The Years–Virginia Woolf | 2.00 | 4.00 | 6.00 | |
| 773 | Timber Line–Gene Fowler | 2.00 | 4.00 | 6.00 | |
| 774 | Night unto Night–Philip Wylie | 2.00 | 4.00 | 6.00 | |
| 775 | Some Like Them Short–William March; 1945 | 2.00 | 4.00 | 6.00 | |
| 776 | The Collected Poems of Rupert Brooke–Rupert Brooke | 2.00 | 4.00 | 6.00 | |
| 777 | Canary–Gustav Eckstein | 2.00 | 4.00 | 6.00 | |
| 778 | A Genius in the Family–Hiram Percy Maxim | 2.00 | 4.00 | 6.00 | |
| 779 | On Borrowed Time–Lawrence Edward Watkin | 2.00 | 4.00 | 6.00 | |
| 780 | Horsethief Creek–Bliss Lomax (H.S. Drago) | 2.00 | 4.00 | 6.00 | W |
| 781 | Lou Gehrig–Frank Graham | 2.00 | 4.00 | 6.00 | B |
| 782 | You Know Me Al–Ring Lardner | 2.00 | 4.00 | 6.00 | |
| 783 | The Phantom Filly–George Chamberlain | 2.00 | 4.00 | 6.00 | |
| 784 | Sheriff of Yavisa–Charles H. Snow | 2.00 | 4.00 | 6.00 | W |
| 785 | The So Blue Marble–Dorothy B. Hughes | 2.00 | 4.00 | 6.00 | M |
| 786 | Blind Man's Bluff–Baynard Kendrick | 2.50 | 5.00 | 7.50 | M |
| 787 | Patrick Henry and the Frigate's Keel–Howard Fast | 2.00 | 4.00 | 6.00 | |
| 788 | The Bruiser–Edward L. McKenna | 2.00 | 4.00 | 6.00 | |
| 789 | Payoff for the Banker–Frances Lockridge & Richard Lockridge | 2.50 | 5.00 | 7.50 | M |
| 790 | This Is Our World–Paul B. Sears | 2.00 | 4.00 | 6.00 | |
| 791 | Trail Smoke–Ernest Haycox | 2.00 | 4.00 | 6.00 | W |
| 792 | Apartment in Athens–Glenway Wescott | 2.00 | 4.00 | 6.00 | |
| 793 | The Barefoot Mailman–Theodore Pratt | 2.00 | 4.00 | 6.00 | |
| 794 | The Long Valley–John Steinbeck | 3.00 | 6.00 | 9.00 | |
| 795 | King Solomon's Mines–H. Rider Haggard | 7.50 | 15.00 | 22.50 | A |
| 796 | Mr. Tutt Finds a Way–Arthur Train | 2.00 | 4.00 | 6.00 | |
| 797 | Forlorn River–Zane Grey | 2.00 | 4.00 | 6.00 | W |
| 798 | Pattern for Murder–Ione Sandberg Shriber | 2.00 | 4.00 | 6.00 | M |
| 799 | Butterfield 8–John O'Hara | 2.50 | 5.00 | 7.50 | |
| 800 | The Bishop's Wife and Two Other Novels–Robert Nathan; 1st ed. 1945 | 2.00 | 4.00 | 6.00 | |
| 801 | When Worlds Collide–Edwin Balmer & Philip Wylie | 6.00 | 12.00 | 18.00 | SF |
| 802 | Winter's Tales–Isak Dinesen | 2.00 | 4.00 | 6.00 | |
| 803 | Five Western Stories–Coburn, Foster, Ranger, McCulley, & Wilson; 1st ed. 1945 | 2.00 | 4.00 | 6.00 | W |
| 804 | Commodore Hornblower–C.S. Forester | 2.00 | 4.00 | 6.00 | A |
| 805 | Yankee Woman–Eric Baume | 2.00 | 4.00 | 6.00 | |
| 806 | The Hudson–Carl Carmer | 2.00 | 4.00 | 6.00 | |
| 807 | Sun in Their Eyes–Monte Barrett | 2.00 | 4.00 | 6.00 | W |
| 808 | Men Against Death–Paul de Kruif | 2.00 | 4.00 | 6.00 | NF |
| 809 | Men of Science in America–Bernard Jaffe | 2.00 | 4.00 | 6.00 | NF |
| 810 | Great Stories from Great Lives–Herbert V. Prochnow | 2.00 | 4.00 | 6.00 | |
| 811 | Mrs. Parkington–Louis Bromfield | 2.00 | 4.00 | 6.00 | |
| 812 | The Sea Hawk–Rafael Sabatini | 2.00 | 4.00 | 6.00 | A |
| 813 | Author's Choice–MacKinlay Kantor | 2.00 | 4.00 | 6.00 | |
| 814 | Ride with Me–Thomas B. Costain | 2.00 | 4.00 | 6.00 | |
| 815 | The Voice of the Turtle–John Van Druten; 1945 | 2.00 | 4.00 | 6.00 | |
| 816 | In the Fog–Richard Harding Davis | 2.00 | 4.00 | 6.00 | |
| 817 | Pal Joey–John O'Hara | 2.00 | 4.00 | 6.00 | |
| 818 | Rackety Rax–Joel Sayre | 2.00 | 4.00 | 6.00 | |
| 819 | The New Yorker's Baedeker; 1st ed. 1945 | 2.00 | 4.00 | 6.00 | |
| 820 | Selected Poems–John Masefield; 1st ed. 1945 | 2.00 | 4.00 | 6.00 | |
| 821 | The Half-Haunted Saloon–Richard Shattuck | 2.00 | 4.00 | 6.00 | |
| 822 | Up Front–Bill Mauldin | 2.00 | 4.00 | 6.00 | H |
| 823 | O Pioneers!–Willa Cather | 2.00 | 4.00 | 6.00 | |
| 824 | Electronics Today and Tomorrow–John Mills | 2.00 | 4.00 | 6.00 | NF |
| 825 | A Rose for Emily and Other Stories–William Faulkner; 1st ed. 1945 | 2.00 | 4.00 | 6.00 | |
| 826 | Coming of Age in Samoa–Margaret Mead | 2.00 | 4.00 | 6.00 | NF |
| 827 | The Indigo Necklace–Frances Crane | 2.50 | 5.00 | 7.50 | M |
| 828 | The Delicate Ape–Dorothy B. Hughes | 2.50 | 5.00 | 7.50 | M |
| 829 | Payment Deferred–C.S. Forester | 2.00 | 4.00 | 6.00 | A |
| 830 | Buried Alive–Arnold Bennett | 2.00 | 4.00 | 6.00 | |
| 831 | Virgin with Butterflies–Tom Powers | 2.00 | 4.00 | 6.00 | |
| 832 | The Sporting Gesture–Thomas L. Stix | 2.00 | 4.00 | 6.00 | |
| 833 | Square Deal Sanderson–Charles Alden Seltzer | 2.00 | 4.00 | 6.00 | W |
| 834 | Bar 20 Days–Clarence E. Mulford | 2.00 | 4.00 | 6.00 | W |
| 835 | American Guerilla in the Philippines–Ira Wolfert | 2.00 | 4.00 | 6.00 | C |

ARMED SERVICES EDITION, *continued*

| No. | Title | V/Good | Fine | N/Mint | |
|---|---|---|---|---|---|
| 836 | Claudia and David–Rose Franken | 2.00 | 4.00 | 6.00 | |
| 837 | Sundown Jim–Ernest Haycox | 2.00 | 4.00 | 6.00 | W |
| 838 | The Lady in the Lake–Raymond Chandler | 15.00 | 30.00 | 45.00 | M |
| 839 | River Song–Harry Hamilton | 2.00 | 4.00 | 6.00 | |
| 840 | The Biscuit Eater and Other Stories–James Street; 1st ed. 1945 | 2.00 | 4.00 | 6.00 | |
| 841 | The Upstart–Edison Marshall | 2.00 | 4.00 | 6.00 | A |
| 842 | Twin Sombreros–Zane Grey | 2.00 | 4.00 | 6.00 | W |
| 843 | Young Bess–Margaret Irwin | 2.00 | 4.00 | 6.00 | |
| 844 | Little Orvie–Booth Tarkington | 2.00 | 4.00 | 6.00 | |
| 845 | Pleasant Valley–Louis Bromfield | 2.00 | 4.00 | 6.00 | |
| 846 | McGraw of the Giants–Frank Graham | 2.00 | 4.00 | 6.00 | S |
| 847 | Cuckoo Time–Ralph Temple | 2.00 | 4.00 | 6.00 | |
| 848 | Time to Be Young–ed. Whit Burnett | 2.00 | 4.00 | 6.00 | |
| 849 | Bedford Village–Hervey Allen | 2.00 | 4.00 | 6.00 | |
| 850 | The Lady and the Arsenic–Joseph Shearing | 2.00 | 4.00 | 6.00 | |
| 851 | Dracula–Bram Stoker | 9.00 | 18.00 | 27.00 | HO |
| 852 | Wickford Point–John P. Marquand | 2.00 | 4.00 | 6.00 | |
| 853 | A Lion Is in the Streets–Adria Locke Langley | 2.00 | 4.00 | 6.00 | |
| 854 | Captain from Castile–Samuel Shellabarger | 2.00 | 4.00 | 6.00 | A |
| 855 | A Book of Americans–Stephen Vincent Benét | 2.00 | 4.00 | 6.00 | |
| 856 | My Life and Hard Times–James Thurber | 2.50 | 5.00 | 7.50 | H |
| 857 | Lyrics and Sonnets–Edna St. Vincent Millay; 1st ed. 1945 | 2.00 | 4.00 | 6.00 | |
| 858 | The Rumelhearts of Rampler Ave.– Maude Smith Delavan | 2.00 | 4.00 | 6.00 | |
| 859 | Tacey Cromwell–Conrad Richter | 2.00 | 4.00 | 6.00 | |
| 860 | The Royal Game–Stefan Zweig | 2.00 | 4.00 | 6.00 | |
| 861 | The Pearl Lagoon–Charles Nordhoff | 2.50 | 5.00 | 7.50 | A |
| 862 | The Great Gatsby–F. Scott Fitzgerald | 3.00 | 6.00 | 9.00 | |
| 863 | The Gray Champion and Other Tales– Nathaniel Hawthorne; 1st ed. 1945 | 2.50 | 5.00 | 7.50 | |
| 864 | Ariel: The Life of Shelley–Andrée Maurois | 2.00 | 4.00 | 6.00 | |
| 865 | My Ten Years in a Quandry–Robert Benchley | 2.50 | 5.00 | 7.50 | H |
| 866 | Tragic Ground–Erskine Caldwell | 2.00 | 4.00 | 6.00 | |
| 867 | Rim of the Desert–Ernest Haycox | 2.00 | 4.00 | 6.00 | W |
| 868 | Useless Cowboy–Alan LeMay | 2.00 | 4.00 | 6.00 | W |
| 869 | The Fallen Sparrow–Dorothy B. Hughes | 2.00 | 4.00 | 6.00 | M |
| 870 | Snow above Town–Donald Hough | 2.00 | 4.00 | 6.00 | |
| 871 | Green Thoughts and Other Strange Tales–John Collier; 1st ed. 1945 | 4.50 | 9.00 | 13.50 | F |
| 872 | Crazy like a Fox–S.J. Perelman | 2.00 | 4.00 | 6.00 | H |
| 873 | The Confidential Agent–Graham Greene | 2.00 | 4.00 | 6.00 | M |
| 874 | Ramrod–Luke Short | 2.00 | 4.00 | 6.00 | W |
| 875 | Mostly Canallers–Walter D. Edmonds | 2.00 | 4.00 | 6.00 | |
| 876 | The Countess to Boot–Jack Iams | 2.00 | 4.00 | 6.00 | M |
| 877 | Danger Trail–Max Brand | 2.00 | 4.00 | 6.00 | W |
| 878 | Deadline at Dawn–William Irish | 3.00 | 6.00 | 9.00 | M |
| 879 | Wind before Rain–John D. Weaver | 2.00 | 4.00 | 6.00 | |
| 880 | Walden–H. David Thoreau | 2.50 | 5.00 | 7.50 | |
| 881 | She–H. Rider Haggard | 7.50 | 15.00 | 22.50 | A |
| 882 | Colour Scheme–Ngaio Marsh | 2.50 | 5.00 | 7.50 | M |
| 883 | Desert Gold–Zane Grey | 2.00 | 4.00 | 6.00 | W |
| 884 | Ruggles of Red Gap–Harry Leon Wilson | 2.00 | 4.00 | 6.00 | |
| 885 | The Strange Case of Dr. Jekyll and Mr. Hyde–Robert Louis Stevenson; 1st ed. 1945 | 9.00 | 18.00 | 27.00 | HO |
| 886 | White Sales Crowding–Edmund Gilligan | 2.00 | 4.00 | 6.00 | |
| 887 | The Virginian–Owen Wister | 3.00 | 6.00 | 9.00 | W |
| 888 | Head O'W-Hollow–Jesse Stuart | 2.00 | 4.00 | 6.00 | |
| 889 | Five Acres and Independence–M.G. Kains | 2.00 | 4.00 | 6.00 | |
| 890 | Busman's Honeymoon–Dorothy L. Sayers | 2.50 | 5.00 | 7.50 | M |
| 891 | Hatter's Castle–A.J. Cronin | 2.00 | 4.00 | 6.00 | |
| 892 | The Sky's the Limit–ed. B.A. Botkin; 1st ed. 1945 | 2.00 | 4.00 | 6.00 | |
| 893 | The Loom of Language–Frederick Bodmer | 2.00 | 4.00 | 6.00 | |
| 894 | Reveille in Washington–Margaret Leach | 2.00 | 4.00 | 6.00 | |
| 895 | Dear Sir and Dumb-belles Letters– Juliet Lowell; 1946 | 2.00 | 4.00 | 6.00 | H |
| 896 | How to Do Practically Anything–Jack Goodman & Alan Green | 2.00 | 4.00 | 6.00 | |
| 897 | Bowleg Bill–Jeremiah Digges | 2.00 | 4.00 | 6.00 | |
| 898 | Walls Rise Up–George Sessions Perry | 2.00 | 4.00 | 6.00 | |
| 899 | Mr. Wilmer–Robert Lawson | 2.00 | 4.00 | 6.00 | |
| 900 | The Full Life and Other Stories–D.D. Beauchamp; 1st ed. 1946 | 2.00 | 4.00 | 6.00 | |
| 901 | The Daniel Jazz and Other Poems– Vachel Lindsay; 1st ed. 1946 | 2.00 | 4.00 | 6.00 | |
| 902 | My Bitter Half and Other Stories–John Weaver; 1st ed. 1946 | 2.00 | 4.00 | 6.00 | |
| 903 | Keep Your Head Down–Walter Bernstein | 2.00 | 4.00 | 6.00 | |
| 904 | The Story of Penicillin–Boris Sokoloff, MD | 2.00 | 4.00 | 6.00 | |
| 905 | Lost Island–James Norman Hall | 2.50 | 5.00 | 7.50 | A |
| 906 | Not Quite Dead Enough–Rex Stout | 2.50 | 5.00 | 7.50 | M |
| 907 | The Great Bustard and Other People– Will Cuppy | 2.00 | 4.00 | 6.00 | |
| 908 | The Fighting Four–Max Brand | 2.00 | 4.00 | 6.00 | W |
| 909 | Frankenstein–Mary Wollstonecraft Shelley | 10.50 | 21.00 | 31.50 | HO |
| 910 | The Happy Time–R. Fontaine | 2.00 | 4.00 | 6.00 | |
| 911 | Mantrap–Sinclair Lewis | 2.00 | 4.00 | 6.00 | |
| 912 | Ironies–Richard Connell | 2.00 | 4.00 | 6.00 | |
| 913 | Best Sport Stories of 1944–ed. Irving T. Marsh & Edward Ehre | 2.00 | 4.00 | 6.00 | S |
| 914 | The Lucky Stiff–Craig Rice | 2.50 | 5.00 | 7.50 | M |
| 915 | The Case of the Golddigger's Purse– Erle Stanley Gardner | 2.50 | 5.00 | 7.50 | M |
| 916 | Canyon Passage–Ernest Haycox | 2.00 | 4.00 | 6.00 | W |
| 917 | The Trail Horde–Charles Alden Seltzer | 2.00 | 4.00 | 6.00 | W |
| 918 | "Tex"–Clarence E. Mulford | 2.00 | 4.00 | 6.00 | W |
| 919 | The Folded Leaf–William Maxwell | 2.00 | 4.00 | 6.00 | |
| 920 | Jazz–Robert Goffin | 2.00 | 4.00 | 6.00 | NF |
| 921 | Concerning a Woman of Sin and Other Stories–Ben Hecht; 1st ed. 1946 | 2.00 | 4.00 | 6.00 | |
| 922 | Rain in the Doorway–Thorne Smith | 2.50 | 5.00 | 7.50 | H |
| 923 | Aunt Beardie–Joseph Shearing | 2.00 | 4.00 | 6.00 | |
| 924 | Rebellion of Leo McGuire–Clyde Brion Davis | 2.00 | 4.00 | 6.00 | |
| 925 | The Odyssey of Homer–translated by T.E. Shaw | 2.50 | 5.00 | 7.50 | |
| 926 | The Giaconda Smile and Other Stories–Aldous Huxley | 2.00 | 4.00 | 6.00 | |
| 927 | The Last Time I Saw Paris–Elliot Paul | 2.00 | 4.00 | 6.00 | |
| 928 | Fortitude–Hugh Walpole | 2.00 | 4.00 | 6.00 | |
| 929 | Names on the Land–George R. Stewart | 2.00 | 4.00 | 6.00 | |
| 930 | God's Angry Man–Leonard Ehrlich | 2.00 | 4.00 | 6.00 | |
| 931 | A. Woollcott–Samuel Hopkins Adams | 2.00 | 4.00 | 6.00 | B |
| 932 | Two Solitudes–Hugh MacLennan | 2.00 | 4.00 | 6.00 | |
| 933 | The Bedside Tables | 2.00 | 4.00 | 6.00 | H |
| 934 | The Best from Yank–Editors of Yank | 2.00 | 4.00 | 6.00 | |
| 935 | Dear Ruth–Norman Krasna; 1946 | 2.00 | 4.00 | 6.00 | |
| 936 | Set 'Em Up–Joe (The Markee) Madden | 2.00 | 4.00 | 6.00 | |
| 937 | The Deadly Dove–Rufus King | 2.50 | 5.00 | 7.50 | M |
| 938 | Admirals of the Caribbean–Francis Russell Hart | 2.00 | 4.00 | 6.00 | |
| 939 | Love Poems–Robert Browning & Elizabeth Barrett Browning; 1st ed. 1946 | 2.00 | 4.00 | 6.00 | |
| 940 | The Great God Pan and Other Weird Stories–Arthur Machen; 1st ed. 1946 | 4.50 | 9.00 | 13.50 | HO |
| 941 | Artie Greengroin, Pfc.–Harry Brown | 2.00 | 4.00 | 6.00 | |
| 942 | The World, the Flesh and Father Smith–Bruce Marshall | 2.00 | 4.00 | 6.00 | |
| 943 | Bedelia–Vera Caspary | 2.00 | 4.00 | 6.00 | |
| 944 | The Ransom of Red Chief and Other Stories–O. Henry; 1st ed. 1946 | 2.50 | 5.00 | 7.50 | |
| 945 | God's Little Acre–Erskine Caldwell | 2.00 | 4.00 | 6.00 | |
| 946 | Deadlier Than the Male–James Gunn | 2.00 | 4.00 | 6.00 | |
| 947 | Comanche Kid–E.B. Mann | 2.00 | 4.00 | 6.00 | W |
| 948 | Laugh It Off–Marione E. Derrickson | 2.00 | 4.00 | 6.00 | |
| 949 | The Boss of the Lazy Y–Charles Alden Seltzer | 2.00 | 4.00 | 6.00 | W |
| 950 | Killing the Goose–Frances Lockridge & Richard Lockridge | 2.50 | 5.00 | 7.50 | M |
| 951 | Prairie Guns–E.E. Halleran | 2.00 | 4.00 | 6.00 | W |
| 952 | Watch Out for Willie Carter–Theodore Naidish | 2.00 | 4.00 | 6.00 | |

ARMED SERVICES EDITION, *continued*

| # | Title | V/Good | Fine | N/Mint | |
|---|-------|--------|------|--------|---|
| 953 | The Passionate Witch–Thorne Smith | 2.50 | 5.00 | 7.50 | H |
| 954 | Guerrilla–Lord Dunsany | 3.00 | 6.00 | 9.00 | |
| 955 | The New Yorker Profiles; 1st ed. 1946 | 2.00 | 4.00 | 6.00 | |
| 956 | Cartridge Carnival–William Colt MacDonald | 2.00 | 4.00 | 6.00 | W |
| 957 | Winds, Blow Gently–Ronald Kirkbride | 2.00 | 4.00 | 6.00 | |
| 958 | The Food of the Gods–H.G. Wells | 9.00 | 18.00 | 27.00 | SF |
| 959 | Great Son–Edna Ferber | 2.00 | 4.00 | 6.00 | |
| 960 | Rockets and Jets–Herbert S. Zim | 2.00 | 4.00 | 6.00 | NF |
| 961 | Marta of Moscovy–Phil Strong | 2.00 | 4.00 | 6.00 | |
| 962 | Science Yearbook of 1945–ed. John D. Ratcliff | 2.00 | 4.00 | 6.00 | NF |
| 963 | The Brooklyn Dodgers–Frank Graham | 2.00 | 4.00 | 6.00 | S |
| 964 | Trail of the Money Bird–Dillon Ripley | 2.00 | 4.00 | 6.00 | |
| 965 | Esquire's First Sports Reader–ed. Herb Graffis | 2.00 | 4.00 | 6.00 | S |
| 966 | So Well Remembered–James Hilton | 2.00 | 4.00 | 6.00 | |
| 967 | There's Laughter in the Air!–Jack Gaver & Dave Stanley | 2.00 | 4.00 | 6.00 | H |
| 968 | Rickshaw Boy–Lau Shaw | 2.00 | 4.00 | 6.00 | |
| 969 | Cass Timberlane–Sinclair Lewis | 2.50 | 5.00 | 7.50 | |
| 970 | The Thurber Carnival–James Thurber | 2.50 | 5.00 | 7.50 | H |
| 971 | The Razor's Edge–W. Somerset Maugham | 2.50 | 5.00 | 7.50 | |
| 972 | Strange Fruit–Lillian Smith | 2.00 | 4.00 | 6.00 | |
| 973 | Against These Three–Stuart Cloete | 2.00 | 4.00 | 6.00 | |
| 974 | The City of Trembling Leaves–W. Van Tillburg Clark | 2.00 | 4.00 | 6.00 | |
| 975 | Gentlemen Overboard–Herbert Clyde Lewis; 1946 | 2.00 | 4.00 | 6.00 | |
| 976 | My Remarkable Uncle and Other Sketches–Stephen Leacock | 2.00 | 4.00 | 6.00 | |
| 977 | Buy and Acre–Paul Corey | 2.00 | 4.00 | 6.00 | |
| 978 | The Helicopters Are Coming–C.B.F. Macauley | 2.00 | 4.00 | 6.00 | |
| 979 | The Doctor's Son and Other Stories–John O'Hara | 2.00 | 4.00 | 6.00 | |
| 980 | Silversides–Robert Trumbull | 2.00 | 4.00 | 6.00 | |
| 981 | I'm a Stranger Here Myself–Ogden Nash | 2.00 | 4.00 | 6.00 | |
| 982 | Silvertip's Search–Max Brand | 2.00 | 4.00 | 6.00 | W |
| 983 | An Eye for an Eye–Oliver Weld Bayer | 2.00 | 4.00 | 6.00 | |
| 984 | The Man Who Was Thursday–G.K. Chesterton | 7.50 | 15.00 | 22.50 | F |
| 985 | Slow Train to Yesterday–Archie Robertson | 2.00 | 4.00 | 6.00 | |
| 986 | Our United States Secret Service–Irving Crump | 2.00 | 4.00 | 6.00 | |
| 987 | "Beau" Rand–Charles Alden Seltzer | 2.00 | 4.00 | 6.00 | W |
| 988 | Lay That Pistol Down–Richard Powell | 2.00 | 4.00 | 6.00 | M |
| 989 | Who Wants to Live Forever?–William MacLeod Raine | 2.00 | 4.00 | 6.00 | W |
| 990 | Louis Beretti–Donald Henderson Clarke | 2.50 | 5.00 | 7.50 | M |
| 991 | The Curse of the Bronze Lamp–Carter Dickson | 3.00 | 6.00 | 9.00 | M |
| 992 | Chicago Murders–ed. Sewell Peaslee Wright | 2.00 | 4.00 | 6.00 | |
| 993 | Sports Extra–ed. Stanley Frank | 2.00 | 4.00 | 6.00 | |
| 994 | The Private Life of Helen of Troy–John Erskine | 2.00 | 4.00 | 6.00 | A |
| 995 | The Amethyst Spectacles–Frances Crane | 2.50 | 5.00 | 7.50 | M |
| 996 | Beat to Quarters–C.S. Forester | 2.00 | 4.00 | 6.00 | A |
| 997 | The Heritage of the Desert–Zane Grey | 2.00 | 4.00 | 6.00 | W |
| 998 | Devil on His Trail–John Hawkins & Ward Hawkins | 2.00 | 4.00 | 6.00 | W |
| 999 | Rooster Crows for a Day–Ben Lucien Burman | 2.00 | 4.00 | 6.00 | |
| 1000 | Esquire's 1945 Jazz Book–ed. Paul Eduard Miller | 2.00 | 4.00 | 6.00 | NF |
| 1001 | Black Moon–Clark McMeekin | 2.00 | 4.00 | 6.00 | |
| 1002 | Twenty Careers of Tomorrow–Darrell Huff & Frances Huff | 2.00 | 4.00 | 6.00 | |
| 1003 | Dan Sickles–Edgcomb Pinchon | 2.00 | 4.00 | 6.00 | |
| 1004 | January Thaw–Bellamy Partridge | 2.00 | 4.00 | 6.00 | |
| 1005 | Arms and the Man and Two Other Plays–George Bernard Shaw; 1st ed. 1946 | 2.00 | 4.00 | 6.00 | |
| 1006 | The Birth of Mischief–Rafael Sabatini | 2.00 | 4.00 | 6.00 | |
| 1007 | All Brides Are Beautiful–Thomas Bell | 2.00 | 4.00 | 6.00 | |
| 1008 | Atoms in Action–George Russell Harrison | 2.00 | 4.00 | 6.00 | NF |
| 1009 | The Green Years–A.J. Cronin | 2.00 | 4.00 | 6.00 | |
| 1010 | The Saddle and the Plow–Ross McLaury Taylor | 2.00 | 4.00 | 6.00 | |
| 1011 | Best Short Stories of Jack London–Jack London | 2.50 | 5.00 | 7.50 | |
| 1012 | Some of These Days–Sophie Tucker | 2.00 | 4.00 | 6.00 | |
| 1013 | Of Time and the River–Thomas Wolfe | 2.50 | 5.00 | 7.50 | |
| 1014 | Northwest Passage–Kenneth Roberts | 2.00 | 4.00 | 6.00 | |
| 1015 | Selected Poems–A.E. Housman; 1946 | 2.00 | 4.00 | 6.00 | |
| 1016 | Is Sex Necessary–James Thurber & E.B. White | 2.50 | 5.00 | 7.50 | H |
| 1017 | I'll Try Anything Twice–Fred Russell | 2.00 | 4.00 | 6.00 | |
| 1018 | Your Personal Plane–John Paul Andrews | 2.00 | 4.00 | 6.00 | |
| 1019 | Parlor, Bedlam and Bath–S.J. Perelman & Q.J. Reynolds | 2.00 | 4.00 | 6.00 | H |
| 1020 | Till I Come Back to You–Thomas Bell | 2.00 | 4.00 | 6.00 | |
| 1021 | The Wolf Pack of Lobo Butte–W.C. Tuttle | 2.00 | 4.00 | 6.00 | W |
| 1022 | Rusty Guns–Bliss Lomax (H.S. Drago) | 2.00 | 4.00 | 6.00 | W |
| 1023 | The State of Music–Virgil Thomson | 2.00 | 4.00 | 6.00 | NF |
| 1024 | Liberal Education–Mark Van Doren | 2.00 | 4.00 | 6.00 | NF |
| 1025 | Dreamland–Clarence Buddington Kelland | 2.00 | 4.00 | 6.00 | |
| 1026 | The King Is Dead on Queen Street–Francis Bonnamy | 2.00 | 4.00 | 6.00 | |
| 1027 | Big Ben–Earl Schenck Miers | 2.00 | 4.00 | 6.00 | |
| 1028 | Red Sand–T.S. Stribling | 2.00 | 4.00 | 6.00 | |
| 1029 | Is It Anyone We Know?–George Price | 2.00 | 4.00 | 6.00 | |
| 1030 | "Drag" Harlan–Charles Alden Seltzer | 2.00 | 4.00 | 6.00 | W |
| 1031 | The Corpse in the Snowman–Nicholas Blake | 2.00 | 4.00 | 6.00 | M |
| 1032 | Make the Most of Your Life–Douglas E. Lurton | 2.00 | 4.00 | 6.00 | |
| 1033 | O Genteel Lady!–Esther Forbes | 2.00 | 4.00 | 6.00 | |
| 1034 | Panic–Helen McCloy | 2.00 | 4.00 | 6.00 | M |
| 1035 | Mahogany–Alfredo Segre | 2.00 | 4.00 | 6.00 | |
| 1036 | Buckaroo–Eugene Cunningham | 2.00 | 4.00 | 6.00 | W |
| 1037 | Frank Leahy and the Fighting Irish–Arch Ward | 2.00 | 4.00 | 6.00 | S |
| 1038 | They Tell No Tales–Manning Coles | 2.50 | 5.00 | 7.50 | M |
| 1039 | The Case of the Half-Wakened Wife–Erle Stanley Gardner | 2.50 | 5.00 | 7.50 | M |
| 1040 | The Japanese Nation–John F. Embree | 2.00 | 4.00 | 6.00 | NF |
| 1041 | The Lost Weekend–Charles Jackson | 3.00 | 6.00 | 9.00 | |
| 1042 | Selected Short Stories–John Russell | 2.00 | 4.00 | 6.00 | |
| 1043 | The Diamond As Big As the Ritz and Others–F. Scott Fitzgerald; 1st ed. 1946 | 2.00 | 4.00 | 6.00 | |
| 1044 | New World of Machines–Harland Manchester | 2.00 | 4.00 | 6.00 | NF |
| 1045 | Storm–George Stewart | 2.00 | 4.00 | 6.00 | |
| 1046 | Kabloona–Gontran de Poncins | 2.00 | 4.00 | 6.00 | |
| 1047 | Three O'Clock Dinner–Josephine Pinckney | 2.00 | 4.00 | 6.00 | |
| 1048 | Trelawny–Margaret Armstrong | 2.00 | 4.00 | 6.00 | |
| 1049 | Oil for the Lamps of China–Alice Tisdale Hobart | 2.00 | 4.00 | 6.00 | |
| 1050 | Modern American Short Stories–ed. Bennett Cerf | 2.00 | 4.00 | 6.00 | |
| 1051 | The Builders of the Bridge–D.B. Steinman | 2.00 | 4.00 | 6.00 | |
| 1052 | Saints and Strangers–George F. Willison | 2.00 | 4.00 | 6.00 | |
| 1053 | The White Tower–James Ramsey Ullman | 2.00 | 4.00 | 6.00 | |
| 1054 | The Stars Look Down–A.J. Cronin | 2.00 | 4.00 | 6.00 | |
| 1055 | Hunter's Moon and Other Stories–Edmund Gilligan; 1st ed. 1946 | 2.00 | 4.00 | 6.00 | |
| 1056 | The Love Poems of Robert Herrick–ed. Louis Untermeyer; 1st ed. 1946 | 2.00 | 4.00 | 6.00 | |
| 1057 | Excuse It, Please!–Cornelia Otis Skinner | 2.00 | 4.00 | 6.00 | |
| 1058 | The Postman Always Rings Twice–James M. Cain | 2.50 | 5.00 | 7.50 | M |
| 1059 | The Story of George Gershwin–David Ewen | 2.00 | 4.00 | 6.00 | |
| 1060 | The Education of T.C. Mits–Hugh Gray & Lillian R. Lieber | 2.00 | 4.00 | 6.00 | |
| 1061 | One Day on Beetle Rock–Sally Carrighar | 2.00 | 4.00 | 6.00 | |
| 1062 | Jumper–Nicholas Kalashnikoff | 2.00 | 4.00 | 6.00 | |

ARMED SERVICES EDITION, *continued*

| No. | Title | V/Good | Fine | N/Mint | |
|---|---|---|---|---|---|
| 1063 | Atomic Energy in the Coming Era–David Dietz | 2.00 | 4.00 | 6.00 | NF |
| 1064 | Block That Bride and Other Stories–George S. Brooks; 1st ed. 1946 | 2.00 | 4.00 | 6.00 | |
| 1065 | Kazan–James Oliver Curwood | 2.00 | 4.00 | 6.00 | A |
| 1066 | The New Yorker Reporter at Large; 1st ed. 1946 | 2.00 | 4.00 | 6.00 | |
| 1067 | Hold Autumn in Your Hand–George Sessions Perry | 2.00 | 4.00 | 6.00 | |
| 1068 | Inside the F.B.I.–John J. Floherty | 2.00 | 4.00 | 6.00 | NF |
| 1069 | The Department of Queer Complaints–Carter Dickson. Note: Queen's Quorum No. 92 | 4.50 | 9.00 | 13.50 | M |
| 1070 | Enrico Caruso–Dorothy Caruso | 2.00 | 4.00 | 6.00 | B |
| 1071 | The Vengeance of Jefferson Gawne–Charles Alden Seltzer | 2.00 | 4.00 | 6.00 | W |
| 1072 | The Man from Bar-20–Clarence E. Mulford | 2.00 | 4.00 | 6.00 | W |
| 1073 | Gold and Guns on Halfaday Creek–James B. Hendryx | 2.00 | 4.00 | 6.00 | W |
| 1074 | The Sunday Pigeon Murders–Craig Rice | 2.50 | 5.00 | 7.50 | M |
| 1075 | The Murder That Had Everything–Hulbert Footner | 2.50 | 5.00 | 7.50 | M |
| 1076 | Comic Relief–ed. R.N. Linscott | 2.00 | 4.00 | 6.00 | H |
| 1077 | We Took to the Woods–Louise Dickinson Rich | 2.00 | 4.00 | 6.00 | |
| 1078 | My True Love–Darwin L. Teilhet | 2.00 | 4.00 | 6.00 | |
| 1079 | The Story of the Great Geologists–Carroll Lane Fenton & Mildred Adams Fenton | 2.00 | 4.00 | 6.00 | NF |
| 1080 | Tales by Tolstoy–Leo Tolstoy; 1st ed. 1946 | 2.50 | 5.00 | 7.50 | |
| 1081 | You and Your Future Job–William G. Campbell & James H. Bedford | 2.00 | 4.00 | 6.00 | NF |
| 1082 | The Black Rose–Thomas B. Costain | 2.00 | 4.00 | 6.00 | A |
| 1083 | Walt Tully's Baseball Recorder–Walt Tulley; 1946 | 2.00 | 4.00 | 6.00 | S |
| 1084 | Repent in Haste–John P. Marquand | 2.00 | 4.00 | 6.00 | |
| 1085 | Best Cartoons of the Year 1945–ed. Lawrence Lariar | 2.00 | 4.00 | 6.00 | H |
| 1086 | The Lunatic at Large–J. Storer Clouston | 2.00 | 4.00 | 6.00 | |
| 1087 | Biography of the Earth–George Gamow | 2.00 | 4.00 | 6.00 | |
| 1088 | The Double Take–Roy Huggins | 2.50 | 5.00 | 7.50 | M |
| 1089 | If the Prospect Pleases–Ladd Haystead | 2.00 | 4.00 | 6.00 | |
| 1090 | Straight, Place and Show–Robert S. Dowst | 2.00 | 4.00 | 6.00 | |
| 1091 | The War of the Worlds–H.G. Wells | 6.00 | 12.00 | 18.00 | SF |
| 1092 | Kid Galahad–Francis Wallace | 2.00 | 4.00 | 6.00 | S |
| 1093 | Death on the Aisle–Frances Lockridge & Richard Lockridge | 2.50 | 5.00 | 7.50 | M |
| 1094 | Starlight Rider–Ernest Haycox | 2.00 | 4.00 | 6.00 | W |
| 1095 | A Small Store and Independence–David B. Greenberg & Henry Schindall | 2.00 | 4.00 | 6.00 | |
| 1096 | Steamboat Round the Bend–Ben Lucien Burman | 2.00 | 4.00 | 6.00 | |
| 1097 | Out of Control–Baynard Kendrick | 2.50 | 5.00 | 7.50 | M |
| 1098 | V as in Victim–Lawrence Treat | 2.50 | 5.00 | 7.50 | M |
| 1099 | Typhoon and the End of the Tether–Joseph Conrad; 1st ed. 1946 | 2.50 | 5.00 | 7.50 | |
| 1100 | The Egg and I–Betty MacDonald | 2.00 | 4.00 | 6.00 | H |
| 1101 | The Ranchman–Charles Alden Seltzer | 2.00 | 4.00 | 6.00 | W |
| 1102 | My Three Years with Eisenhower–Capt. Harry C. Butcher | 2.00 | 4.00 | 6.00 | NF |
| 1103 | The Well-Tempered Listener–Deems Taylor | 2.00 | 4.00 | 6.00 | NF |
| 1104 | The Manatee–Nancy Bruff | 2.00 | 4.00 | 6.00 | |
| 1105 | The Theory and Practice of Earning a Living–John F. Wharton | 2.00 | 4.00 | 6.00 | |
| 1106 | The Big Midget Murders–Craig Rice | 2.50 | 5.00 | 7.50 | M |
| 1107 | The Border Legion–Zane Grey | 2.00 | 4.00 | 6.00 | W |
| 1108 | The Saga of Billy the Kid–Walter Noble Burns | 2.00 | 4.00 | 6.00 | B |
| 1109 | Mr. Digby–Douglass Welch | 2.00 | 4.00 | 6.00 | |
| 1110 | White Water and Black Magic–Richard C. Gill | 2.00 | 4.00 | 6.00 | |
| 1111 | Saratoga Trunk–Edna Ferber | 2.00 | 4.00 | 6.00 | |
| 1112 | Radio's 100 Men of Science–Orrin E. Dunlap, Jr | 2.00 | 4.00 | 6.00 | NF |
| 1113 | Days and Nights–Konstantine Simonov | 2.00 | 4.00 | 6.00 | |
| 1114 | John Brown's Body–Stephen Vincent Benet | 2.50 | 5.00 | 7.50 | |
| 1115 | Prater Violet–Christopher Isherwood; 1946 | 2.00 | 4.00 | 6.00 | |
| 1116 | The Wolf–Sgt. Leonard Sansone | 2.00 | 4.00 | 6.00 | |
| 1117 | Come in like a Yankee and Other Stories–H. Vernor Dixon; 1st ed. 1946 | 2.00 | 4.00 | 6.00 | |
| 1118 | Joe Louis: American–Margery Miller | 2.00 | 4.00 | 6.00 | B |
| 1119 | The Zebra Derby–Max Shulman | 2.00 | 4.00 | 6.00 | |
| 1120 | Dingo–Henry G. Lamond | 2.00 | 4.00 | 6.00 | |
| 1121 | The Crock of Gold–James Stephens | 2.00 | 4.00 | 6.00 | |
| 1122 | Selected Poems of Carl Sandburg–Carl Sandburg | 2.50 | 5.00 | 7.50 | |
| 1123 | Port of Seven Strangers–Kathleen Moore Knight | 2.50 | 5.00 | 7.50 | |
| 1124 | Safari–Martin Johnson | 2.00 | 4.00 | 6.00 | |
| 1125 | The Bitter Tea of General Yen–Grace Zaring Stone | 2.00 | 4.00 | 6.00 | |
| 1126 | The Great American Customer–Carl Crow | 2.00 | 4.00 | 6.00 | |
| 1127 | Valiant Is the Word for Carrie–Barry Benefield | 2.00 | 4.00 | 6.00 | |
| 1128 | My Greatest Day in Baseball–ed. John P. Carmichael | 2.00 | 4.00 | 6.00 | S |
| 1129 | Courage Stout–William MacLeod Raine | 2.00 | 4.00 | 6.00 | W |
| 1130 | The Noose Is Drawn–Barber & Schabelitz | 2.00 | 4.00 | 6.00 | |
| 1131 | The Case of the Black-eyed Blonde–Erle Stanley Gardner | 2.50 | 5.00 | 7.50 | M |
| 1132 | Lost in the Horse Latitudes–H. Allen Smith | 2.00 | 4.00 | 6.00 | H |
| 1133 | Hunted Riders–Max Brand | 2.00 | 4.00 | 6.00 | W |
| 1134 | The Ox-bow Incident–Van Tillburg Clark | 2.50 | 5.00 | 7.50 | W |
| 1135 | Troopers West–Forbes Parkhill | 2.00 | 4.00 | 6.00 | W |
| 1136 | Woman at Bay–George Harmon Coxe | 2.50 | 5.00 | 7.50 | M |
| 1137 | Tales for Males–ed. Ed Fitzgerald | 2.00 | 4.00 | 6.00 | |
| 1138 | The Small General–Robert Standish | 2.00 | 4.00 | 6.00 | |
| 1139 | Caribbean Treasure–Ivan T. Sanderson | 2.00 | 4.00 | 6.00 | |
| 1140 | Miracles Ahead–Norman V. Carlisle & Frank B. Latham | 2.00 | 4.00 | 6.00 | |
| 1141 | The Bar-20 Three–Clarence E. Mulford | 2.00 | 4.00 | 6.00 | W |
| 1142 | Shakespeare–Mark Van Doren | 2.00 | 4.00 | 6.00 | B |
| 1143 | Where Do People Take Their Troubles?–Lee R. Steiner | 2.00 | 4.00 | 6.00 | |
| 1144 | The Cherokee Strip–Marquis James | 2.00 | 4.00 | 6.00 | |
| 1145 | Modern Woman in Love–ed. Christina Stead & William Blake | 2.00 | 4.00 | 6.00 | |
| 1146 | That Girl from Memphis–Wilbur Daniel Steele | 2.00 | 4.00 | 6.00 | |
| 1147 | Pal Joey–John O'Hara; 1946 | 2.00 | 4.00 | 6.00 | |
| 1148 | Rackety Rax–Joel Sayre | 2.00 | 4.00 | 6.00 | |
| 1149 | Anything Can Happen–George Papashvily & Helen Papashvily | 2.00 | 4.00 | 6.00 | |
| 1150 | Men of Popular Music–David Ewen | 2.00 | 4.00 | 6.00 | NF |
| 1151 | Many Long Years Ago–Ogden Nash | 2.00 | 4.00 | 6.00 | |
| 1152 | Winter Meeting–Grace Zaring Stone | 2.00 | 4.00 | 6.00 | |
| 1153 | Wheels in His Head–M.M. Musselman | 2.00 | 4.00 | 6.00 | |
| 1154 | The End of the Trail–Peter Field | 2.00 | 4.00 | 6.00 | W |
| 1155 | The Owl in the Cellar–Margaret Scherf | 2.50 | 5.00 | 7.50 | |
| 1156 | The Dark Ship and Other Selections from the New Yorker; 1st ed. 1946 | 2.00 | 4.00 | 6.00 | |
| 1157 | The Story of the Moon–Clyde Fisher | 2.00 | 4.00 | 6.00 | |
| 1158 | The Tenderfoot–W.H.B. Kent | 2.00 | 4.00 | 6.00 | W |
| 1159 | It's Still Maloney–Russell Maloney | 2.00 | 4.00 | 6.00 | |
| 1160 | Meet Your Ancestors–Roy Chapman Andrews | 2.00 | 4.00 | 6.00 | |
| 1161 | Tomorrow's Another Day–W.R. Burnett | 2.50 | 5.00 | 7.50 | M |
| 1162 | Murder within Murder–Frances Lockridge & Richard Lockridge | 2.50 | 5.00 | 7.50 | M |
| 1163 | Starlight Pass–Tom Gill | 2.00 | 4.00 | 6.00 | W |
| 1164 | Trail Town–Ernest Haycox | 2.00 | 4.00 | 6.00 | W |
| 1165 | The Salvation of Pisco Gabar and Other Stories–Geoffrey Household | 2.50 | 5.00 | 7.50 | |
| 1166 | She Came Back–Patricia Wentworth | 2.00 | 4.00 | 6.00 | |
| 1167 | Your Servant the Molecule–Walter S. Landis | 2.00 | 4.00 | 6.00 | NF |
| 1168 | Treasure Below–Comm. Edward Ellsberg | 2.00 | 4.00 | 6.00 | |
| 1169 | The Edge of Running Water–William Sloane | 2.00 | 4.00 | 6.00 | |

ARMED SERVICES EDITION, *continued*

| # | Title | V/Good | Fine | N/Mint | |
|---|---|---|---|---|---|
| 1170 | The New York Yankees–Frank Graham | 2.00 | 4.00 | 6.00 | S |
| 1171 | Top Stuff–ed. Harold Hart | 2.00 | 4.00 | 6.00 | |
| 1172 | The Gashouse Gang–J. Roy Stockton | 2.00 | 4.00 | 6.00 | S |
| 1173 | I Wouldn't Be in Your Shoes–William Irish | 3.00 | 6.00 | 9.00 | M |
| 1174 | Green Fire–Peter W. Ranier | 2.50 | 5.00 | 7.50 | |
| 1175 | Cobb's Cavalcade–ed. B.D. Zevin | 2.00 | 4.00 | 6.00 | |
| 1176 | The King's General–Daphne du Maurier | 2.00 | 4.00 | 6.00 | |
| 1177 | Arch of Triumph–Erich Marie Remarque | 2.00 | 4.00 | 6.00 | C |
| 1178 | While You Were Gone–ed. Jack Goodman | 2.00 | 4.00 | 6.00 | |
| 1179 | Last Chapter–Ernie Pyle; 1946 | 2.00 | 4.00 | 6.00 | C |
| 1180 | Third Avenue, New York–J. McNulty | 2.00 | 4.00 | 6.00 | |
| 1181 | Ravaged Range–Peter Field | 2.00 | 4.00 | 6.00 | W |
| 1182 | Williwaw–Gore Vidal | 2.00 | 4.00 | 6.00 | |
| 1183 | Outlaw on Horseback–Will Ermine | 2.00 | 4.00 | 6.00 | W |
| 1184 | Coroner Creek–Luke Short | 2.00 | 4.00 | 6.00 | W |
| 1185 | The Unforeseen–Dorothy Macardle | 3.00 | 6.00 | 9.00 | F |
| 1186 | Let's Kill George–Lucy Cores | 2.00 | 4.00 | 6.00 | |
| 1187 | Lord Hornblower–C.S. Forester | 2.00 | 4.00 | 6.00 | A |
| 1188 | With Bated Breath–Alice Campbell | 2.00 | 4.00 | 6.00 | |
| 1189 | A Solo in Tom-Toms–Gene Fowler | 2.00 | 4.00 | 6.00 | |
| 1190 | The Saturday Evening Post Stories 1942–1945 | 2.00 | 4.00 | 6.00 | |
| 1191 | Denver Murders–ed. Lee Casey; 1946 | 2.00 | 4.00 | 6.00 | M |
| 1192 | By Way of Wyoming–Curtis Bishop | 2.00 | 4.00 | 6.00 | |
| 1193 | A Rock in Every Snowball–Frank Sullivan | 2.00 | 4.00 | 6.00 | |
| 1194 | Death's Old Sweet Song–Jonathan Stagge | 3.00 | 6.00 | 9.00 | M |
| 1195 | The World in His Arms–Rex Beach | 2.00 | 4.00 | 6.00 | A |
| 1196 | Clattering Hoofs–William MacLeod Raine | 2.00 | 4.00 | 6.00 | W |
| 1197 | The Chicago Cubs–Warren Brown | 2.00 | 4.00 | 6.00 | S |
| 1198 | Man-eaters of Kumaon–James Corbett | 2.00 | 4.00 | 6.00 | A |
| 1199 | Jim Bridger, Mountain Man–Stanley Vestal | 2.00 | 4.00 | 6.00 | B |
| 1200 | Blaze of Noon–Ernest K. Gann | 2.00 | 4.00 | 6.00 | |
| 1201 | All the King's Men–Robert Penn Warren | 2.50 | 5.00 | 7.50 | |
| 1202 | Tell Your Sons–Willa Gibbs | 2.00 | 4.00 | 6.00 | |
| 1203 | Mister Roberts–Thomas Heggen; 1946 | 2.00 | 4.00 | 6.00 | |
| 1204 | Football Coach–Arthur Sampson | 2.00 | 4.00 | 6.00 | |
| 1205 | Benefit Performance–Richard Sale | 2.50 | 5.00 | 7.50 | M |
| 1206 | Double Cross Trail–E.E. Halleran | 2.00 | 4.00 | 6.00 | W |
| 1207 | Pikes Peek or Bust–Earl Wilson | 2.00 | 4.00 | 6.00 | |
| 1208 | Thunderbird Trail–William Colt MacDonald | 2.00 | 4.00 | 6.00 | W |
| 1209 | Stranger Than Truth–Vera Caspary | 2.00 | 4.00 | 6.00 | |
| 1210 | Companions of the Left Hand–George Tabori | 2.00 | 4.00 | 6.00 | |
| 1211 | Green Grass of Wyoming–Mary O'Hara | 2.00 | 4.00 | 6.00 | |
| 1212 | Driftwood Valley–Theodora C. Stanwell-Fletcher | 2.00 | 4.00 | 6.00 | |
| 1213 | The Best Stories of W.D. Steele–Wilbur Daniel Steele | 2.00 | 4.00 | 6.00 | |
| 1214 | Under the Red Sea Sun–Comm. Edward Ellsberg | 2.00 | 4.00 | 6.00 | |
| 1215 | The Big Clock–Kenneth Fearing; 1947 | 2.50 | 5.00 | 7.50 | M |
| 1216 | Mountain Riders–Max Brand | 2.00 | 4.00 | 6.00 | W |
| 1217 | Mr. Adam–Pat Frank | 2.50 | 5.00 | 7.50 | SF |
| 1218 | The Case of the Borrowed Brunette–Erle Stanley Gardner | 2.50 | 5.00 | 7.50 | M |
| 1219 | The Sudden Guest–Christopher LaFarge | 2.00 | 4.00 | 6.00 | |
| 1220 | White Man–Peter Freuchen | 2.00 | 4.00 | 6.00 | |
| 1221 | Frontier on the Potomac–Jonathan Daniels | 2.00 | 4.00 | 6.00 | |
| 1222 | The Silent Speaker–Rex Stout | 2.50 | 5.00 | 7.50 | M |
| 1223 | Strange and Fantastic Stories–ed. Joseph A. Margolies | 2.50 | 5.00 | 7.50 | |
| 1224 | Holdfast Gaines–Odell Shepard & Willard Shepard | 2.00 | 4.00 | 6.00 | |
| 1225 | B.F.'s Daughter–John P. Marquand | 2.00 | 4.00 | 6.00 | |
| 1226 | The Salem Frigate–John Jennings | 2.50 | 5.00 | 7.50 | A |
| 1227 | Boy from Nebraska–Ralph G. Martin; 1947 | 2.00 | 4.00 | 6.00 | |
| 1228 | Francis–David Stern | 2.00 | 4.00 | 6.00 | H |
| 1229 | Surreptitious Entry–Willis George | 2.00 | 4.00 | 6.00 | |

*Armed Services Edition 885, Armed Services Edition 1217, Armed Services Edition 1271.*

| # | Title | V/Good | Fine | N/Mint | |
|---|---|---|---|---|---|
| 1230 | Courage of the North–James B. Hendryx | 2.00 | 4.00 | 6.00 | W |
| 1231 | Death of a Tall Man–Frances Lockridge & Richard Lockridge | 2.50 | 5.00 | 7.50 | M |
| 1232 | The Wayward Bus–John Steinbeck | 3.00 | 6.00 | 9.00 | |
| 1233 | But Look, the Morn–MacKinlay Kantor | 2.00 | 4.00 | 6.00 | |
| 1234 | Saigon Singer–Van Wyck Mason | 2.00 | 4.00 | 6.00 | |
| 1235 | Fabulous Empire–Fred Gipson | 2.00 | 4.00 | 6.00 | |
| 1236 | The Colorado–Frank Waters | 2.00 | 4.00 | 6.00 | |
| 1237 | Eagles Fly West–Ed Ainsworth | 2.00 | 4.00 | 6.00 | |
| 1238 | Toil of the Brave–Inglis Fletcher | 2.00 | 4.00 | 6.00 | A |
| 1239 | Treasure of the Brasada–Les Savage, Jr; 1947 | 2.00 | 4.00 | 6.00 | W |
| 1240 | Six Gun Showdown–Tom West | 2.00 | 4.00 | 6.00 | W |
| 1241 | The Silver Leopard–Helen Reilly | 2.50 | 5.00 | 7.50 | M |
| 1242 | The Face of the Clam–Luther Whiteman | 2.00 | 4.00 | 6.00 | |
| 1243 | Command Decision–William Wister Haines | 2.00 | 4.00 | 6.00 | C |
| 1244 | The Shadowed Trail–Arthur Henry Gooden | 2.50 | 5.00 | 7.50 | W |
| 1245 | The Natural History of Nonsense–Bergen Evans | 2.00 | 4.00 | 6.00 | H |
| 1246 | My Late Wives–Carter Dickson | 3.00 | 6.00 | 9.00 | M |
| 1247 | The Quarry–Mildred Walker | 2.00 | 4.00 | 6.00 | |
| 1248 | Tales of the South Pacific–James A. Michener | 3.00 | 6.00 | 9.00 | |
| 1249 | Look South to the Polar Star–Holger Cahill | 2.00 | 4.00 | 6.00 | |
| 1250 | Not So Wild a Dream–Eric Sevareid | 2.00 | 4.00 | 6.00 | |
| 1251 | The Barber of Tubac–Nelson C. Nye; 1947 | 2.00 | 4.00 | 6.00 | W |
| 1252 | The Magnificent Barb–Dana Faralla | 2.00 | 4.00 | 6.00 | |
| 1253 | Mixture for Men–ed. Fred Feldkamp | 2.00 | 4.00 | 6.00 | |
| 1254 | Buckaroo's Code–Wayne D. Overholser | 2.00 | 4.00 | 6.00 | W |
| 1255 | Pick Your Victim–Pat McGerr | 2.50 | 5.00 | 7.50 | M |
| 1256 | The Widow-Makers–Michael Blankfort | 2.00 | 4.00 | 6.00 | |
| 1257 | The Border Bandit–Evan Evans (Max Brand) | 2.00 | 4.00 | 6.00 | W |
| 1258 | The Middle of Midnight–William Gilmore Beymer | 2.00 | 4.00 | 6.00 | |
| 1259 | Jeremy Bell–Clyde Brion Davis | 2.00 | 4.00 | 6.00 | |
| 1260 | The Detroit Tigers–Frederick G. Lieb | 2.00 | 4.00 | 6.00 | B |
| 1261 | Wake of the Red Witch–Garland Roark | 2.00 | 4.00 | 6.00 | A |
| 1262 | The Walls of Jericho–Paul I. Wellman | 2.00 | 4.00 | 6.00 | |
| 1263 | Valley of Vanishing Men–Max Brand; 1947 | 2.00 | 4.00 | 6.00 | W |
| 1264 | Gambler's Gold–Peter Field | 2.00 | 4.00 | 6.00 | W |
| 1265 | Aurora Dawn–Herman Wouk | 2.00 | 4.00 | 6.00 | |
| 1266 | The Strumpet Wind–Gordon Merrick | 2.00 | 4.00 | 6.00 | |
| 1267 | Long Storm–Ernest Haycox | 2.00 | 4.00 | 6.00 | W |
| 1268 | Gentleman's Agreement–Laura Z. Hobson | 2.00 | 4.00 | 6.00 | |
| 1269 | Final Curtain–Ngaio Marsh | 2.50 | 5.00 | 7.50 | M |
| 1270 | Death of a Doll–Hilda Lawrence | 2.50 | 5.00 | 7.50 | M |
| 1271 | The Boston Red Sox–Frederick G. Lieb | 2.00 | 4.00 | 6.00 | S |
| 1272 | 9 Lives before Thirty–Max Manus | 2.00 | 4.00 | 6.00 | |
| 1273 | Blood Brother–Elliott Arnold | 2.00 | 4.00 | 6.00 | W |
| 1274 | This Is the Story–David L. Cohn | 2.00 | 4.00 | 6.00 | |
| 1275 | Shadow Range–Curtis Bishop; 1947 | 2.00 | 4.00 | 6.00 | |
| 1276 | So Long at the Fair–Anthony Thorne | 2.00 | 4.00 | 6.00 | |

ARMED SERVICES EDITION, *continued*

| # | Title | V/Good | Fine | N/Mint | |
|---|---|---|---|---|---|
| 1277 | Silver Spurs–Mark Layton | 2.00 | 4.00 | 6.00 | |
| 1278 | Alaska: Land of Tomorrow–Edward A. Herron | 2.00 | 4.00 | 6.00 | NF |
| 1279 | With Intent to Deceive–Manning Coles | 2.50 | 5.00 | 7.50 | M |
| 1280 | The Sleeping Sphinx–John Dickson Carr | 2.50 | 5.00 | 7.50 | M |
| 1281 | Mr. On Loong–Robert Standish | 2.00 | 4.00 | 6.00 | |
| 1282 | Go-devil–Marguerite Eyssen | 2.00 | 4.00 | 6.00 | |
| 1283 | There Was Once a Slave–Shirley Graham | 2.00 | 4.00 | 6.00 | |
| 1284 | My Name Is Christopher Nagel–C.W. Grafton | 2.00 | 4.00 | 6.00 | |
| 1285 | The Wild Yazoo–John Myers Myers | 2.00 | 4.00 | 6.00 | W |
| 1286 | Jed Blaine's Woman–Evelyn Wells | 2.00 | 4.00 | 6.00 | |
| 1287 | Within the Ropes–Harold Rice; 1947 | 2.00 | 4.00 | 6.00 | |
| 1288 | Trail Dust–Bliss Lomax (H.S. Drago) | 2.00 | 4.00 | 6.00 | W |
| 1289 | How Green Was My Father–David Dodge | 2.50 | 5.00 | 7.50 | |
| 1290 | The Drifting Kid–Will Ermine | 2.00 | 4.00 | 6.00 | W |
| 1291 | Puzzle for Pilgrims–Patrick Quentin | 2.50 | 5.00 | 7.50 | M |
| 1292 | Ghost of a Chance–Kelley Roos | 2.00 | 4.00 | 6.00 | M |
| 1293 | Think of Death–Richard Lockridge & Frances Lockridge | 2.50 | 5.00 | 7.50 | M |
| 1294 | Valley of Wild Horses–Zane Grey | 2.00 | 4.00 | 6.00 | W |
| 1295 | Mrs. Mike–Benedict Freedman & Nancy Freedman | 2.00 | 4.00 | 6.00 | |
| 1296 | Little Gate–Annemarie Ewing | 2.00 | 4.00 | 6.00 | |
| 1297 | The Big Sky–A.B. Guthrie, Jr | 2.50 | 5.00 | 7.50 | W |
| 1298 | Famous Stories of Code and Cipher–ed. Raymond T. Bond | 2.00 | 4.00 | 6.00 | |
| 1299 | Hang and Rattle–Allan R. Bosworth | 2.00 | 4.00 | 6.00 | W |
| 1300 | Trail from Needle Rock–Peter Field | 2.00 | 4.00 | 6.00 | W |
| 1301 | Flannigan's Folly–George Milburn | 2.00 | 4.00 | 6.00 | |
| 1302 | The Case of the Fan-Dancer's Horse–Erle Stanley Gardner | 2.50 | 5.00 | 7.50 | M |
| 1303 | Blood Money–Francis Rufus Bellamy | 2.00 | 4.00 | 6.00 | M |
| 1304 | Master of the Mesa–William Colt MacDonald | 2.00 | 4.00 | 6.00 | W |
| 1305 | Tomorrow's a Holiday–Arthur Loveridge | 2.00 | 4.00 | 6.00 | |
| 1306 | Boston: Cradle of Liberty–John Jennings | 2.00 | 4.00 | 6.00 | |
| 1307 | Comrade Forest–Michael Leigh | 2.00 | 4.00 | 6.00 | |
| 1308 | The Side of the Angels–Robert McLaughlin | 2.00 | 4.00 | 6.00 | |
| 1309 | The Thresher–Herbert Krause | 2.00 | 4.00 | 6.00 | |
| 1310 | Vermilion–Idwal Jones | 2.00 | 4.00 | 6.00 | |
| 1311 | The False Rider–Max Brand; 1947 | 2.00 | 4.00 | 6.00 | W |
| 1312 | The Blue Horse of Taxco–Kathleen Moore Knight | 2.00 | 4.00 | 6.00 | M |
| 1313 | Los Angeles Murders–Craig Rice | 2.50 | 5.00 | 7.50 | M |
| 1314 | Passing By–Elliott Merrick | 2.00 | 4.00 | 6.00 | |
| 1315 | On My Way Home–Richard Phenix | 2.00 | 4.00 | 6.00 | |
| 1316 | Strikeout Story–Bob Feller | 2.00 | 4.00 | 6.00 | S |
| 1317 | The Harder They Fall–Budd Schulberg | 2.00 | 4.00 | 6.00 | |
| 1318 | Raw North–Charles E. Gillham | 2.00 | 4.00 | 6.00 | |
| 1319 | The Story of Mrs. Murphy–Natalie Anderson Scott | 2.00 | 4.00 | 6.00 | |
| 1320 | The Moneyman–Thomas B. Costain | 2.00 | 4.00 | 6.00 | |
| 1321 | Prince of Foxes–Samuel Shellabarger | 2.00 | 4.00 | 6.00 | A |
| 1322 | Home Country–Ernie Pyle | 2.00 | 4.00 | 6.00 | |

# ARMED SERVICES EDITION
## Readers League of America
### Special wartime releases of Pocket Book titles

| | Title | V/Good | Fine | N/Mint | |
|---|---|---|---|---|---|
| nn | The Good Earth–Pearl S. Buck | .75 | 1.50 | 2.25 | |
| nn | Magnificent Obsession–Lloyd C. Douglas | .75 | 1.50 | 2.25 | |
| nn | The Maltese Falcon–Dashiell Hammett | 1.00 | 2.00 | 3.00 | M |
| nn | Mutiny on the Bounty–Charles Nordhoff & James Hall | .75 | 1.50 | 2.25 | A |
| nn | The Pocket Book of Modern American Short Stories–ed. Philip Van Doren Stern | .75 | 1.50 | 2.25 | |
| nn | The Red Badge of Courage–Stephen Crane | .75 | 1.50 | 2.25 | |
| nn | Beat to Quarters–C.S. Forester | .75 | 1.50 | 2.25 | A |

# ARROW MYSTERY
## Arrow Publishers
### Digest Size

| # | Title | V/Good | Fine | N/Mint | |
|---|---|---|---|---|---|
| 5 | Murder on High Heels–Richard Burke | 2.50 | 5.00 | 7.50 | M |
| 6 | Murder on Friday–Harriette Ashbrook; aka The Purple Onion Mystery | 2.50 | 5.00 | 7.50 | M |
| 7 | Death Takes a Redhead–Anthony Gilbert; 1944, aka Dear Dead Woman | 2.50 | 5.00 | 7.50 | M |
| 8 | The Kissed Corpse–Asa Baker (Brett Halliday) | 2.50 | 5.00 | 7.50 | M |
| 9 | Invitation to Murder–Manning Long; aka False Alarm | 2.50 | 5.00 | 7.50 | M |
| 10 | Death Hides a Mask–M.E. Corne | 2.50 | 5.00 | 7.50 | M |
| 11 | Design for Murder–Frederic Arnold Kummer | 2.50 | 5.00 | 7.50 | M |

# ASTRO
## Astro Distributing Corporation
### Digest Size

**Note: Series continues as Quarter Books.**

| # | Title | V/Good | Fine | N/Mint | |
|---|---|---|---|---|---|
| 1 | Part-Time Virgin–James Clayford | 2.50 | 5.00 | 7.50 | E |
| 2 | Week-end Girl–James Clayford; c-Rodewald | 2.50 | 5.00 | 7.50 | E |
| 4 | Any Man's Girl–Luther Gordon | 2.50 | 5.00 | 7.50 | E |
| 5 | Divorce Bait | 2.50 | 5.00 | 7.50 | E |
| 9 | Unwilling Bride–Ethel Owen; aka Romance in the Rain | 2.50 | 5.00 | 7.50 | E |
| 10 | Confessions of a Good-Time Girl–Ethel Owen | 2.50 | 5.00 | 7.50 | E |
| 11 | Confessions of a Party Wife–Helen Ahern | 2.50 | 5.00 | 7.50 | E |
| 12 | Shakedown Dame–Dorothy Herzog; 1948; aka Undercover Woman | 2.50 | 5.00 | 7.50 | E |
| 14 | Shameless Virgin–Peggy Gaddis; 1948; aka One More Woman | 2.50 | 5.00 | 7.50 | E |
| 15 | Illicit Wife–James Clayford; aka Respectable? Note: Same cover as Quarter Book 69 | 4.00 | 8.00 | 12.00 | E |
| 16 | Wedding Night Confession–James Clayford; aka Wedding Night | 4.00 | 8.00 | 12.00 | E |
| 17 | Careless Virgin–James Clayford; c-Rodewald | 4.00 | 8.00 | 12.00 | E |
| 18 | Strange Mistress–James Clayford | 4.00 | 8.00 | 12.00 | E |
| 31 | Overnight Girl–Joan Sherman (Peggy Gaddis); aka Overnight Cabins | 4.00 | 8.00 | 12.00 | E |

# ATLAS MYSTERY
## Bard Publishing Corporation
### Digest Size

| | Title | V/Good | Fine | N/Mint | |
|---|---|---|---|---|---|
| nn | The Corpse and the Three Ex-Husbands–Sue McVeigh | 4.00 | 8.00 | 12.00 | M |
| nn | The Singing Widow–Veronica Parker Johns; 1945 | 4.00 | 8.00 | 12.00 | M |

# ATLAS MYSTERY
## Cornell Publishing Corporation
### Digest Size

| | Title | V/Good | Fine | N/Mint | |
|---|---|---|---|---|---|
| nn | H As in Hangman–Lawrence Treat | 4.00 | 8.00 | 12.00 | M |
| nn | Murder Goes to College–Kurt Steel; 1944 | 4.00 | 8.00 | 12.00 | M |

## ATLAS MYSTERY
### Euclid Publishing Company
**Digest Size**

| | | V/Good | Fine | N/Mint | |
|---|---|---|---|---|---|
| nn | Murder RFD–Herman Peterson | 4.00 | 8.00 | 12.00 | M |
| nn | Hush Gabriel–Veronica Parker Johns; 1944 | 4.00 | 8.00 | 12.00 | M |

## ATLAS MYSTERY
### Gem Publishing Company
**Digest Size**

| | | V/Good | Fine | N/Mint | |
|---|---|---|---|---|---|
| nn | Murder Will In–Carolyn Wells | 4.00 | 8.00 | 12.00 | M |
| nn | Death Goes Native–Max Long; 1944 | 4.00 | 8.00 | 12.00 | M |

## ATLAS MYSTERY
### Hercules Publishing Corporation
**Digest Size**

| | | V/Good | Fine | N/Mint | |
|---|---|---|---|---|---|
| nn | The Lisping Man–Frank Rawlings; 1944 | 5.00 | 10.00 | 15.00 | M |

## ATLAS MYSTERY
### London Publishing Corporation
**Digest Size**

| | | V/Good | Fine | N/Mint | |
|---|---|---|---|---|---|
| nn | Rattle His Bones–Julian Shore; 1944 | 4.00 | 8.00 | 12.00 | M |

## ATLAS MYSTERY
### Margood Publishing Company
**Digest Size**

| | | V/Good | Fine | N/Mint | |
|---|---|---|---|---|---|
| nn | Murder in the House with the Blue Eyes–J.N. Darby; 1944 | 4.00 | 8.00 | 12.00 | M |

## ATLAS MYSTERY
### Mohawk Publishing Corporation
**Digest Size**

| | | V/Good | Fine | N/Mint | |
|---|---|---|---|---|---|
| nn | Kill One, Kill Two–W.W. Anderson; 1944 | 4.00 | 8.00 | 12.00 | M |

## ATLAS MYSTERY
### Select Publications, Inc.
**Digest Size**

| | | V/Good | Fine | N/Mint | |
|---|---|---|---|---|---|
| nn | The Golden Dress–Ione Montgomery; 1944 | 4.00 | 8.00 | 12.00 | M |
| nn | Midsummer Night's Murder–Lee Crosby | 4.00 | 8.00 | 12.00 | M |
| nn | Shady Doings–Veronica Parker Johns | 4.00 | 8.00 | 12.00 | M |

## ATLAS MYSTERY
### Sphere Publishing Company
**Digest Size**

| | | V/Good | Fine | N/Mint | |
|---|---|---|---|---|---|
| nn | Final Appearance–Jeannette Covert Nolan | 4.00 | 8.00 | 12.00 | M |

## ATLAS MYSTERY
### Vital Publications, Inc./Current Detective Stories, Inc.
**Digest Size**

| | | V/Good | Fine | N/Mint | |
|---|---|---|---|---|---|
| 1 | Rendezvous with Dead Men–Nick Carter (John Chambliss); 1948; aka Murder on Skull Island | 5.00 | 10.00 | 15.00 | M |
| 2 | A Blonde for Murder–Walter B. Gibson; orig. 1948 | 9.00 | 18.00 | 27.00 | M |
| 3 | The Yellow Disk Murder–Nick Carter (T.C. McClary); 1948; aka Power | 5.00 | 10.00 | 15.00 | M |
| 4 | May not exist. It is strongly suspected that this missing number corresponds to the only seen Western Thriller, also published by Vital in 1948 as No. 4. | | | | |
| 5 | Looks That Kill–Walter B. Gibson; orig. 1948 | 9.00 | 18.00 | 27.00 | M |

## ATLAS MYSTERY
### Zenith Publishing Corporation
**Digest Size**

| | | V/Good | Fine | N/Mint | |
|---|---|---|---|---|---|
| nn | Murder with Long Hair–H. Donald Spatz; 1944 | 4.00 | 8.00 | 12.00 | M |
| nn | The Corpse Comes Ashore–John Merserau; 1945 | 4.00 | 8.00 | 12.00 | M |

## ATOMIC BOOKS
### Atomic Books, Inc.
**Digest Size**

| | | V/Good | Fine | N/Mint | |
|---|---|---|---|---|---|
| nn | The Case of the Golden Blond–Maurice LeBlanc; 1946, Sherlock Holmes pastiche | 9.00 | 18.00 | 27.00 | M |

## AURORA
### Dell Publishing Co., Inc.

| | | V/Good | Fine | N/Mint | |
|---|---|---|---|---|---|
| nn | The Complete Book of Plastic Model Kits–The Advisory Board of the Aurora Plastics Corporation; 1961; illus. | 1.00 | 2.00 | 3.00 | NF |

## AVON
### Avon Book Company/New Avon Library/ Avon Publishing Co., Inc./Avon Publications, Inc./Avon Book Division– Hearst Corporation

| | | V/Good | Fine | N/Mint | |
|---|---|---|---|---|---|
| nn(1) | Elmer Gantry–Sinclair Lewis; 1941 | 17.50 | 35.00 | 52.50 | |
| nn(2) | The Rubaiyat of Omar Khayyam– Edward Fitzgerald | 7.50 | 15.00 | 22.50 | |
| nn(3) | The Big Four–Agatha Christie | 12.50 | 25.00 | 37.50 | M |
| nn(4) | Ill Wind–James Hilton | 6.00 | 12.00 | 18.00 | |
| nn(5) | Dr. Priestly Investigates–John Rhode | 9.00 | 18.00 | 27.00 | M |
| nn(6) | The Haunted Hotel and 25 Other Ghost Stories–Wilkie Collins (ed. W. Bob Holland) | 7.50 | 15.00 | 22.50 | HO |
| nn(7) | The Plague Court Murders–Carter Dickson | 6.00 | 12.00 | 18.00 | M |
| nn(8) | The Corpse in the Green Pajamas– R.A.J. Walling | 6.00 | 12.00 | 18.00 | M |
| nn(9) | Willful and Premeditated–Freeman Wills Crofts | 4.50 | 9.00 | 13.50 | M |
| nn(10) | Dr. Thorndyke's Discovery–R. Austin Freeman | 7.50 | 15.00 | 22.50 | M |
| nn(11) | Count Bruga–Ben Hecht | 4.50 | 9.00 | 13.50 | M |

Avon 2, Avon 7, Avon 14.

| | | V/Good | Fine | N/Mint | |
|---|---|---|---|---|---|

AVON, *continued*

| | | V/Good | Fine | N/Mint | |
|---|---|---|---|---|---|
| nn(12) | Mosquitoes–William Faulkner | 6.00 | 12.00 | 18.00 | |
| nn(13) | Mystery at Spanish Hacienda–Jackson Gregory; 1942 | 4.50 | 9.00 | 13.50 | M |
| nn(14) | Call Her Savage–Tiffany Thayer | 7.50 | 15.00 | 22.50 | E |
| nn(15) | The Avon Book of Modern Short Stories; aka My Best Story | 4.50 | 9.00 | 13.50 | |
| nn(16) | Murder at Midnight–R.A.J. Walling | 6.00 | 12.00 | 18.00 | M |
| nn(17) | The Agony Column–Earl Derr Biggers. Note: Same cover as Avon No. 112 | 6.00 | 12.00 | 18.00 | M |
| nn(18) | The Man Who Murdered Himself–Geoffrey Holmes | 6.00 | 12.00 | 18.00 | M |
| nn(19) | 48 Saroyan Stories–William Saroyan | 4.50 | 9.00 | 13.50 | |
| nn(20) | The League of Frightened Men–Rex Stout | 7.50 | 15.00 | 22.50 | M |
| nn(21) | The Avon Book of Modern Crime Stories–John Rhode; aka Line Up; aka Detection Medley. Note: Reprinted as The Avon Book of Crime and Detective Stories. Still later an abridged edition was released as The Avon Book of Detective and Crime Stories. | 9.00 | 18.00 | 27.00 | M |
| nn(22) | The Red-Headed Woman–Katharine Brush | 4.50 | 9.00 | 13.50 | |
| nn(23) | Suspicious Characters–Dorothy L. Sayers; 1943 | 7.50 | 15.00 | 22.50 | M |
| nn(24) | Ashenden, or the British Agent–W. Somerset Maugham. Note: Queen's Quorum No. 76 | 4.50 | 9.00 | 13.50 | M |
| nn(25) | Trumpet in the Dust–Gene Fowler | 4.50 | 9.00 | 13.50 | |
| nn(26) | Seven Footprints to Satan–A.A. Merritt | 12.00 | 24.00 | 36.00 | SF |
| nn(27) | The Avon Book of Puzzles | 62.50 | 125.00 | 187.50 | NF |
| nn(28) | Tonight at 8:30–Noel Coward | 6.00 | 12.00 | 18.00 | |
| nn(29) | The Sabotage Murder Mystery–Margery Allingham | 6.00 | 12.00 | 18.00 | M |
| nn(30) | Gorgeous Ghoul Murder Case–Dwight V. Babcock | 6.00 | 12.00 | 18.00 | M |
| nn(31) | Doctor's Son–John O'Hara | 2.50 | 5.00 | 7.50 | |
| nn(32) | Stage Door Canteen–Delmer Daves; movie tie-in | 4.50 | 9.00 | 13.50 | C |
| nn(33) | Corpse in the Waxworks–John Dickson Carr | 6.00 | 12.00 | 18.00 | M |
| nn(34) | The Saint Goes On–Leslie Charteris | 6.00 | 12.00 | 18.00 | M |
| nn(35) | Poison for One–John Rhode | 9.00 | 18.00 | 27.00 | M |
| nn(36) | The Avon Book of Great Mystery Stories. Note: Apparently does not exist; later released as No. 86 in series | | | | |
| nn(37) | Coffin for One–Francis Beeding | 6.00 | 12.00 | 18.00 | M |
| nn(38) | The Big Sleep–Raymond Chandler | 25.00 | 50.00 | 75.00 | M |
| nn(39) | Rage in Heaven–James Hilton | 2.50 | 5.00 | 7.50 | |
| nn(40) | In the Teeth of the Evidence–Dorothy L. Sayers | 4.50 | 9.00 | 13.50 | M |
| 41 | The Narrow Corner–W. Somerset Maugham; 1944 | 3.00 | 6.00 | 9.00 | |
| 42 | The Passionate Year–James Hilton | 2.50 | 5.00 | 7.50 | |
| 43 | Burn Witch Burn–A.A. Merritt | 12.00 | 24.00 | 36.00 | SF |
| 44 | The Saint in New York–Leslie Charteris | 6.00 | 12.00 | 18.00 | M |
| 45 | Germany–Past, Present and Future–Lord Vansittart | 4.50 | 9.00 | 13.50 | NF |
| 46 | Death on the Nile–Agatha Christie | 6.00 | 12.00 | 18.00 | M |
| 47 | Shoe the Wild Mare–Gene Fowler | 2.50 | 5.00 | 7.50 | |
| 48 | The Road to Victory–Archbishop Francis J. Spellman | 2.50 | 5.00 | 7.50 | |
| 49 | The London Spy Murders–Peter Cheyney; aka The Stars Are Dark | 6.00 | 12.00 | 18.00 | M |

| | | V/Good | Fine | N/Mint | |
|---|---|---|---|---|---|
| 50 | Cakes and Ale–W. Somerset Maugham | 2.50 | 5.00 | 7.50 | |
| 51 | Nobody's in Town–Edna Ferber | 2.50 | 5.00 | 7.50 | |
| 52 | The Man Who Had Everything–Louis Bromfield | 2.50 | 5.00 | 7.50 | |
| 53 | Mystery of the Red Triangle–W.C. Tuttle | 3.00 | 6.00 | 9.00 | W |
| 54 | See What I Mean?–Lewis Browne | 4.50 | 9.00 | 13.50 | C |
| 55 | Presenting Lily Mars–Booth Tarkington | 2.50 | 5.00 | 7.50 | |
| 56 | Theatre–W. Somerset Maugham | 2.50 | 5.00 | 7.50 | |
| 57 | The Hills Beyond–Thomas Wolfe | 2.50 | 5.00 | 7.50 | |
| 58 | Winged Victory–Moss Hart | 2.50 | 5.00 | 7.50 | C |
| 59 | Heaven's My Destination–Thornton Wilder; 1945 | 2.50 | 5.00 | 7.50 | |
| 60 | Double Indemnity–James M. Cain | 3.00 | 6.00 | 9.00 | M |
| 61 | Murder in Three Acts–Agatha Christie | 4.50 | 9.00 | 13.50 | M |
| 62 | Over My Dead Body–Rex Stout | 4.50 | 9.00 | 13.50 | M |
| 63 | Five Murderers–Raymond Chandler. Note: Queen's Quorum No. 97 | 22.50 | 45.00 | 67.50 | M |
| 64 | Back Stage–Vicki Baum | 2.50 | 5.00 | 7.50 | |
| 65 | Now I'll Tell One–Harry Hershfield | 3.00 | 6.00 | 9.00 | H |
| 66 | Little Caesar–W.R. Burnett. Note: Same cover as the comic Famous Gangsters No. 3 | 7.50 | 15.00 | 22.50 | M |
| 67 | Action This Day–Bishop Francis J. Spellman | 2.50 | 5.00 | 7.50 | |
| 68 | A Homicide for Hannah–Dwight V. Babcock | 3.00 | 6.00 | 9.00 | M |
| 69 | The Stray Lamb–Thorne Smith | 2.50 | 5.00 | 7.50 | H |
| 70 | Poirot Loses a Client–Agatha Christie | 4.50 | 9.00 | 13.50 | M |
| 71 | The Saint Intervenes–Leslie Charteris | 3.00 | 6.00 | 9.00 | M |
| 72 | The Avon Story Teller; orig. 1945. Note: Includes Merritt, Chandler, others | 2.50 | 5.00 | 7.50 | |
| 73 | A Goodly Heritage–Mary Ellen Chase | 2.50 | 5.00 | 7.50 | |
| 74 | The Ghost Patrol and Other Stories–Sinclair Lewis | 2.50 | 5.00 | 7.50 | |
| 75 | The Mysterious Affair at Styles–Agatha Christie | 4.50 | 9.00 | 13.50 | M |
| 76 | Atomic Energy in the Coming Era–David Dietz | 2.50 | 5.00 | 7.50 | NF |
| 77 | The Long Valley–John Steinbeck | 3.00 | 6.00 | 9.00 | |
| 78 | To Step Aside–Noel Coward; 1946. Note: Same cover as Avon No. 105 | 2.50 | 5.00 | 7.50 | |
| 79 | Catherine Herself–James Hilton | 2.50 | 5.00 | 7.50 | |
| 80 | You Can't Keep the Change–Peter Cheyney. Note: Same cover as Avon Murder Mystery Monthly No. 15 | 4.50 | 9.00 | 13.50 | M |
| 81 | Bad Girl–Vina Delmar. Note: Same cover as Avon Romance Novel Monthly No. 2 | 2.50 | 5.00 | 7.50 | E |
| 82 | The Red Box–Rex Stout | 4.50 | 9.00 | 13.50 | M |
| 83 | Sight Unseen and the Confession–Mary Roberts Rinehart | 3.00 | 6.00 | 9.00 | |
| 84 | Mistress Wilding–Rafael Sabatini. Note: Same cover as Modern Short Story Monthly No. 36 | 2.50 | 5.00 | 7.50 | A |
| 85 | The Regatta Mystery–Agatha Christie | 4.50 | 9.00 | 13.50 | M |
| 86 | Avon Mystery Story Teller–anthology. Note: Includes Irish, Wallace, Carr, Christie | 4.50 | 9.00 | 13.50 | M |
| 87 | The Private Affairs of Bel Ami–Guy de Maupassant; movie tie-in | 2.50 | 5.00 | 7.50 | |
| 88 | Five Sinister Characters–Raymond Chandler | 22.50 | 45.00 | 67.50 | M |
| 89 | Death in the Air–Agatha Christie | 4.50 | 9.00 | 13.50 | M |
| 90 | Avon Ghost Reader–ed. Herbert | 12.00 | 24.00 | 36.00 | SF |

Avon 43, Avon 54, Avon 66.

Avon 109, Avon 117, Avon 133.

AVON, *continued*

|  |  | V/Good | Fine | N/Mint | |
|---|---|---|---|---|---|
|  | Williams. Note: Includes Merritt, Lovecraft, Derleth, Stoker |  |  |  |  |
| 91 | The French Key Mystery–Frank Gruber | 3.00 | 6.00 | 9.00 | M |
| 92 | Loose Ladies–Vina Delmar | 2.50 | 5.00 | 7.50 | E |
| 93 | The Dark Street Murders–Peter Cheyney | 4.50 | 9.00 | 13.50 | M |
| 94 | Butterfly 8–John O'Hara | 2.50 | 5.00 | 7.50 | |
| 95 | Black Orchids–Rex Stout | 4.50 | 9.00 | 13.50 | M |
| 96 | Black Angel–Cornell Woolrich | 6.00 | 12.00 | 18.00 | M |
| 97 | Wedding Ring–Beth Brown | 2.50 | 5.00 | 7.50 | R |
| 98 | The Virgin and the Gypsy–D.H. Lawrence | 2.50 | 5.00 | 7.50 | E |
| 99 | The Embezzler–James M. Cain | 2.50 | 5.00 | 7.50 | |
| 100 | The Secret Adversary–Agatha Christie. Note: Same cover as Avon Murder Mystery Monthly No. 8 | 4.50 | 9.00 | 13.50 | M |
| 101 | Avon Improved Cook Book–Pearl V. Metzelthin | 7.50 | 15.00 | 22.50 | |
| 102 | The Three Wise Guys and Other Stories–Damon Runyon | 2.50 | 5.00 | 7.50 | |
| 103 | Where There's a Will–Rex Stout | 4.50 | 9.00 | 13.50 | M |
| 104 | If I Should Die before I Wake–William Irish. Note: Same cover as Murder Mystery Monthly No. 13 and Avon Detective Mystery No. 2 | 12.00 | 24.00 | 36.00 | M |
| 105 | Lady Ann–Donald Henderson Clarke. Note: Same cover as Avon No. 78 | 2.00 | 4.00 | 6.00 | E |
| 106 | The Black Path of Fear–Cornell Woolrich | 4.50 | 9.00 | 13.50 | M |
| 107 | The Marriage Racket–Vina Delmar | 2.50 | 5.00 | 7.50 | |
| 108 | A Taste for Honey–H.F. Heard | 7.50 | 15.00 | 22.50 | M |
| 109 | Avon Bedside Companion; 1947 | 2.50 | 5.00 | 7.50 | |
| 110 | Terror at Night | 10.50 | 21.00 | 31.50 | SF |
| 111 | The Imperial Orgy–Edgar Saltus | 3.00 | 6.00 | 9.00 | E |
| 112 | The Squealer–Edgar Wallace. Note: Same cover as Avon No. 17 | 3.00 | 6.00 | 9.00 | M |
| 113 | Aphrodite–Pierre Louys | 3.00 | 6.00 | 9.00 | E |
| 114 | Sinister Errand–Peter Cheyney. Note: Same cover as the comic Parole Breakers No. 2 | 4.50 | 9.00 | 13.50 | M |
| 115 | The Avon Book of W. Somerset Maugham | 2.50 | 5.00 | 7.50 | |
| 116 | Kelly–Donald Henderson Clarke | 2.00 | 4.00 | 6.00 | E |
| 117 | Creep Shadow Creep–A.A. Merritt | 12.00 | 24.00 | 36.00 | SF |
| 118 | The Saint in Action–Leslie Charteris; aka The Ace of Knaves. Note: Same cover as the comic Saint No. 7 | 3.00 | 6.00 | 9.00 | M |
| 119 | The Better Taylors–Richard Taylor | 7.50 | 15.00 | 22.50 | |
| 120 | Alabam–Donald Henderson Clarke | 2.00 | 4.00 | 6.00 | E |
| 121 | Kept Woman–Vina Delmar. Note: Same cover as the comic Intimate Confessions No. 6 | 2.50 | 5.00 | 7.50 | R |
| 122 | Unconscious Witness–R. Austin Freeman. Note: Same cover as pulp magazine Private Detective Stories October, 1944, and Avon Detective Mysteries No. 3 | 3.00 | 6.00 | 9.00 | M |
| 123 | The Case of the Dark Hero–Peter Cheyney. Note: Same cover as the comic Saint No. 12 | 3.00 | 6.00 | 9.00 | A |
| 124 | Holiday for Murder–Agatha Christie. Note: Very similar to cover of The Shadow Magazine, June 1944 | 4.50 | 9.00 | 13.50 | M |
| 125 | The Door with Seven Locks–Edgar Wallace | 4.00 | 8.00 | 12.00 | M |
| 126 | Cold Blooded Murder–Freeman Wills Crofts | 7.50 | 15.00 | 22.50 | M |
| 127 | Eastern Shame Girl | 7.50 | 15.00 | 22.50 | E |
| 128 | Ten Nights of Love | 2.00 | 4.00 | 6.00 | E |
| 129 | The Gentleman in the Parlour–W. Somerset Maugham | 2.00 | 4.00 | 6.00 | |
| 130 | The Saint Goes West–Leslie Charteris; 1948 | 4.00 | 8.00 | 12.00 | M |
| 131 | Death Takes a Bow–Frances Lockridge & Richard Lockridge | 4.00 | 8.00 | 12.00 | M |
| 132 | 14 Great Short Stories from the Long Valley–John Steinbeck | 2.50 | 5.00 | 7.50 | |
| 133 | Naughty 90's Joke Book–Harold Meyers | 4.50 | 9.00 | 13.50 | H |
| 134 | Georgia Boy–Erskine Caldwell | 2.00 | 4.00 | 6.00 | E |
| 135 | The Woman and the Puppet–Pierre Louys | 2.00 | 4.00 | 6.00 | E |
| 136 | The Lurking Fear–H.P. Lovecraft | 15.00 | 30.00 | 45.00 | SF |

|  |  | V/Good | Fine | N/Mint | |
|---|---|---|---|---|---|
| 137 | Double Indemnity–James M. Cain | 3.50 | 7.00 | 10.50 | M |
| 138 | The Hard-Boiled Virgin–Jack Woodford; aka Lady Killer. Note: Same cover as Avon Romance Novel Monthly No. 1 | 2.00 | 4.00 | 6.00 | E |
| 139 | Liza of Lambeth–W. Somerset Maugham | 2.00 | 4.00 | 6.00 | E |
| 140 | In Bed We Cry–Ilka Chase | 2.00 | 4.00 | 6.00 | |
| 141 | Career in C Major–James M. Cain | 3.00 | 6.00 | 9.00 | |
| 142 | Killing the Goose–Frances Lockridge & Richard Lockridge | 3.00 | 6.00 | 9.00 | M |
| 143 | Casey–Hard-Boiled Detective–George Harmon Coxe | 6.00 | 12.00 | 18.00 | M |
| 144 | Hope of Heaven–John O'Hara | 2.00 | 4.00 | 6.00 | E |
| 145 | The Restless Passion–Vina Delmar; aka Women Live Too Long | 2.00 | 4.00 | 6.00 | E |
| 146 | The Abortive Hussy–Jack Woodford | 2.00 | 4.00 | 6.00 | E |
| 147 | The Avenging Saint–Leslie Charteris | 3.00 | 6.00 | 9.00 | M |
| 148 | Love, Health, and Marriage–John Cowan & Arthur Rose Guerard | 5.00 | 10.00 | 15.00 | NF |
| 149 | John Bartel Jr–Donald Henderson Clarke | 2.00 | 4.00 | 6.00 | E |
| 150 | A Love Episode–Emile Zola | 2.00 | 4.00 | 6.00 | E |
| 151 | Where the Girls Were Different–Erskine Caldwell. Note: Same cover as the comic Campus Romances No. 2 | 2.00 | 4.00 | 6.00 | E |
| 152 | Georgie May–Maxwell Bodenheim | 2.00 | 4.00 | 6.00 | E |
| 153 | Valley Vixen–Ben Ames Williams; aka Hostile Valley | 2.00 | 4.00 | 6.00 | E |
| 154 | When She Was Bad . . .–Katherine Brush; aka You Go Your Way | 2.00 | 4.00 | 6.00 | E |
| 155 | The Unfaithful Lady–Charles Pettit | 3.00 | 6.00 | 9.00 | E |
| 156 | Pardners of the Badlands–Bliss Lomax. Note: Same cover as the comic Jesse James No. 6 | 2.50 | 5.00 | 7.50 | W |
| 157 | Yesterday's Love–James T. Farrell | 2.00 | 4.00 | 6.00 | |
| 158 | Now I'll Tell One–Harry Hershfield | 3.00 | 6.00 | 9.00 | H |
| 159 | This Is Murder, Mr. Herbert–Day Keene; 1st ed. 1948 | 5.00 | 10.00 | 15.00 | M |
| 160 | Casanova's Homecoming–Arthur Schnitzler | 2.00 | 4.00 | 6.00 | E |
| 161 | Love's Lovely Counterfeit–James M. Cain | 3.50 | 7.00 | 10.50 | |
| 162 | The Avon Book of Complete Crosswords and Cryptograms–Clark Kinnaird | 57.50 | 115.00 | 172.50 | NF |
| 163 | Love in the Latin Quarter–Henri Murger | 2.50 | 5.00 | 7.50 | E |
| 164 | The Moving Finger–Agatha Christie | 4.00 | 8.00 | 12.00 | M |
| 165 | The Stone of Chastity–Margery Sharp | 2.00 | 4.00 | 6.00 | F |
| 166 | Psyche–Pierre Louys | 2.00 | 4.00 | 6.00 | E |
| 167 | Piping Hot–Emile Zola | 2.50 | 5.00 | 7.50 | E |
| 168 | A Virtuous Girl–Maxwell Bodenheim | 2.50 | 5.00 | 7.50 | E |
| 169 | The Amboy Dukes–Irving Shulman. Note: Three cover variations exist on this number, one of which is a movie tie-in | 3.00 | 6.00 | 9.00 | E |
| 170 | Bronc Buckaroo–J. Edward Leithead | 2.50 | 5.00 | 7.50 | W |
| 171 | Amorous Philandre–Jean-Galli De Bibiena. Note: Same cover as the comic For a Night of Love, unnumbered | 3.00 | 6.00 | 9.00 | F |
| 172 | Bubu of Montparnasse–Charles-Louis Philippe | 3.00 | 6.00 | 9.00 | E |
| 173 | On the Spot–Edgar Wallace. Note: Same cover as the comic Women to Love, unnumbered | 2.50 | 5.00 | 7.50 | |

Avon 165, Avon 174, Avon 178.

| | | V/Good | Fine | N/Mint | |
|---|---|---|---|---|---|

AVON, *continued*

| No. | Title | V/Good | Fine | N/Mint | |
|---|---|---|---|---|---|
| 174 | Sinful Woman–James M. Cain | 3.50 | 7.00 | 10.50 | |
| 175 | A Woman's Heart–Guy De Maupassant | 2.00 | 4.00 | 6.00 | E |
| 176 | Whose Body?–Dorothy L. Sayers | 4.50 | 9.00 | 13.50 | M |
| 177 | Midsummer Passion–Erskine Caldwell | 2.50 | 5.00 | 7.50 | E |
| 178 | Fast One–Paul Cain | 6.00 | 12.00 | 18.00 | M |
| 179 | Blondie Iscariot–Edgar Lustgarten. Note: Same cover as the comic Prison Break No. 3 | 4.50 | 9.00 | 13.50 | E |
| 180 | French Summer–Guy Gilpatric | 2.50 | 5.00 | 7.50 | E |
| 181 | Her Private Passions–Marty Holland; aka The Glass Heart | 2.50 | 5.00 | 7.50 | E |
| 182 | New Avon Bedside Companion; 1949 | 2.50 | 5.00 | 7.50 | |
| 183 | Burial of the Fruit–David Dortort | 3.00 | 6.00 | 9.00 | E |
| 184 | The Girl with the Hungry Eyes–ed. Don Wollheim; 1st ed. 1949 | 15.00 | 30.00 | 45.00 | SF |
| 185 | Never Come Morning–Nelson Algren | 3.00 | 6.00 | 9.00 | E |
| 186 | Night Cry–William L. Stuart | 4.50 | 9.00 | 13.50 | M |
| 187 | Love Trap–Vina Delmar | 6.00 | 12.00 | 18.00 | E |
| 188 | Fools and Their Folly–W. Somerset Maugham; aka Then and Now | 2.50 | 5.00 | 7.50 | |
| 189 | The Daughter of Fu Manchu–Sax Rohmer | 15.00 | 30.00 | 45.00 | M |
| 190 | The Life and Loves of a Modern Mr. Bluebeard–Ward Greene; aka Ride the Nightmare | 4.50 | 9.00 | 13.50 | E |
| 191 | Replenishing Jessica–Maxwell Bodenheim | 2.50 | 5.00 | 7.50 | E |
| 192 | Young Man of Manhattan–Katharine Brush | 2.50 | 5.00 | 7.50 | |
| 193 | The Impatient Virgin–Donald Henderson Clarke | 2.50 | 5.00 | 7.50 | E |
| 194 | Avon Book of New Stories of the Great Wild West–ed. Don Wollheim | 6.00 | 12.00 | 18.00 | W |
| 195 | Out of the Silent Planet–C.S. Lewis | 12.50 | 25.00 | 37.50 | SF |
| 196 | Memory of Love–Bessie Breuer | 2.50 | 5.00 | 7.50 | |
| 197 | The Son of the Grand Eunuch–Charles Pettit | 3.00 | 6.00 | 9.00 | E |
| 198 | Yvette and Other Stories–Guy de Maupassant | 2.50 | 5.00 | 7.50 | |
| 199 | The Miller and the Mayor's Wife–Pedro DeAlarcon | 2.50 | 5.00 | 7.50 | E |
| 200 | Your Most Intimate Problems–Lawrence Gould | 6.00 | 12.00 | 18.00 | NF |
| 201 | Strange Desires–Len Zinberg; aka What D'ya Know for Sure. Note: Same cover as the comic Campus Romances No. 3 | 2.50 | 5.00 | 7.50 | E |
| 202 | From Gags to Riches–Joey Adams | 4.50 | 9.00 | 13.50 | H |
| 203 | Quartet–W. Somerset Maugham | 2.50 | 5.00 | 7.50 | |
| 204 | Portrait of a Man with Red Hair–Hugh Walpole | 3.00 | 6.00 | 9.00 | HO |
| 205 | The Last Frontier–Howard Fast | 2.50 | 5.00 | 7.50 | W |
| 206 | The Palace of Pleasure–Jacques-Rochette de la Morliere | 2.50 | 5.00 | 7.50 | E |
| 207 | Virgie, Goodbye–Nathan Rothman. Note: Same cover as the comic Romantic Love No. 6 and Avon Monthly Novel No. 8 | 4.50 | 9.00 | 13.50 | E |
| 208 | The Devil Thumbs a Ride–Robert C. Du Soe | 4.50 | 9.00 | 13.50 | E |
| 209 | New Orleans Lady–Vina Delmar | 2.50 | 5.00 | 7.50 | |
| 210 | Wicked Sister–Helen Topping Miller | 2.50 | 5.00 | 7.50 | E |
| 211 | Scarf of Passion–Robert Bloch. Note: Same cover as Avon Monthly Novel No. 9 and the comic book Realistic Romances No. 1 | 10.00 | 20.00 | 30.00 | HO |

| | | V/Good | Fine | N/Mint | |
|---|---|---|---|---|---|
| 212 | Iron Man–W.R. Burnett. Note: Same cover as the comic Romantic Love No. 10 | 6.00 | 12.00 | 18.00 | |
| 213 | Nina–Donald Henderson Clarke | 2.50 | 5.00 | 7.50 | E |
| 214 | The Fox Woman and Other Stories–A.A. Merritt; 1st ed. 1949 | 12.50 | 25.00 | 37.50 | SF |
| 215 | All the Brothers Were Valiant–Ben Ames Williams | 2.50 | 5.00 | 7.50 | |
| 216 | Gladiator–Philip Wylie | 12.50 | 25.00 | 37.50 | SF |
| 217 | Miss Jill from Shanghai–Emily Hahn | 2.50 | 5.00 | 7.50 | E |
| 218 | Anyone Can Win at Gin Rummy and Canasta–Alfred Drake | 2.00 | 4.00 | 6.00 | NF |
| 219 | Finger Man–Raymond Chandler | 13.50 | 27.00 | 40.50 | M |
| 220 | I Married a Dead Man–Wiliam Irish | 13.50 | 27.00 | 40.50 | M |
| 221 | Don Juan–Ludwig Lewisohn | 2.50 | 5.00 | 7.50 | E |
| 222 | Neon Wilderness–Nelson Algren. Note: Same cover as the comic Intimate Confessions No. 1 | 10.50 | 21.00 | 31.50 | |
| 223 | Three Loves Had Margaret–James Hilton | 2.50 | 5.00 | 7.50 | |
| 224 | Port Afrique–Bernard Victor Dryer | 2.50 | 5.00 | 7.50 | E |
| 225 | Anyone Can Have a Great Vocabulary–J.L. Stephenson | 2.50 | 5.00 | 7.50 | NF |
| 226 | I Can Get It for You Wholesale!–Jerome Weidman | 3.00 | 6.00 | 9.00 | |
| 227 | Just What the Doctor Ordered–Dr. Anthony Bassler | 5.00 | 10.00 | 15.00 | H |
| 228 | Gilbert and Sullivan Operas–William Schwenck Gilbert & Arthur Sullivan; 1950 | 2.50 | 5.00 | 7.50 | |
| 229 | All About Girls | 5.00 | 10.00 | 15.00 | H |
| 230 | The Big Fights–Harold Meyers; orig. 1950 | 4.50 | 9.00 | 13.50 | S |
| 231 | Butterfield 8–John O'Hara | 2.50 | 5.00 | 7.50 | |
| 232 | Alabam–Donald Henderson Clarke | 1.50 | 3.00 | 4.50 | E |
| 233 | The Servant–Robin Maugham | 2.50 | 5.00 | 7.50 | E |
| 234 | The Old Goat–Tiffany Thayer | 2.00 | 4.00 | 6.00 | E |
| 235 | Seven Footprints to Satan–A.A. Merritt | 12.50 | 25.00 | 37.50 | SF |
| 236 | Venus of the Counting House–Emile Zola; c-Bergey | 4.50 | 9.00 | 13.50 | E |
| 237 | Tawny–Donald Henderson Clarke | 2.50 | 5.00 | 7.50 | E |
| 238 | The First Lady Chatterley–D.H. Lawrence | 2.50 | 5.00 | 7.50 | E |
| 239 | Bad Girl from Maine–Katharine Brush | 2.50 | 5.00 | 7.50 | |
| 240 | End as a Man–Calder Willingham | 2.50 | 5.00 | 7.50 | |
| 241 | What's in It for Me?–Jerome Weidman | 1.50 | 3.00 | 4.50 | E |
| 242 | The Case of the Untidy Murder–Frances Lockridge & Richard Lockridge | 4.50 | 9.00 | 13.50 | M |
| 243 | Mysterious Mickey Finn–Elliot Paul | 4.50 | 9.00 | 13.50 | M |
| 244 | Cry Tough!–Irving Shulman | 2.50 | 5.00 | 7.50 | E |
| 245 | The Big Four–Agatha Christie | 6.00 | 12.00 | 18.00 | M |
| 246 | A Shropshire Lad–Housman | 2.50 | 5.00 | 7.50 | |
| 247 | The Midsummer Fires–James Aswell | 2.50 | 5.00 | 7.50 | E |
| 248 | Love among the Haystacks–D.H. Lawrence | 2.50 | 5.00 | 7.50 | E |
| 249 | It Happens Every Spring–Valentine Davies | 2.50 | 5.00 | 7.50 | F |
| 250 | Carlotta–Robert Briffault; aka Fandango. Note: Same cover as the comic Intimate Confessions No. 3 and Avon Monthly Novel No. 13 | 4.50 | 9.00 | 13.50 | E |
| 251 | Sonnets from the Portuguese–Elizabeth Barrett Browning | 2.00 | 4.00 | 6.00 | |
| 252 | A Hell of a Good Time–James T. Farrell. Note: Same cover as the comic Romantic Love No. 1 | 2.50 | 5.00 | 7.50 | |
| 253 | Confidential–Donald Henderson Clarke; Note: Same cover as the comic book Realistic Romances No. 4 | 3.00 | 6.00 | 9.00 | E |
| 254 | Flame Vine–Helen Topping Miller | 3.00 | 6.00 | 9.00 | E |
| 255 | Tropical Passions–anthology. Note: Same cover as Avon Book Dividend No. 7 and basically the same as Avon Modern Short Story Monthly No. 44 | 3.00 | 6.00 | 9.00 | E |
| 256 | The Case of the Black Orchids–Rex Stout | 6.00 | 12.00 | 18.00 | M |
| 257 | Aphrodite–Pierre Louys | 4.50 | 9.00 | 13.50 | E |
| 258 | Hope of Heaven–John O'Hara | 2.50 | 5.00 | 7.50 | E |
| 259 | For a Night of Love–Emile Zola | 2.50 | 5.00 | 7.50 | E |
| 260 | Yesterday's Love–James T. Farrell | 2.50 | 5.00 | 7.50 | E |
| 261 | Avon Improved Cook Book–P.V. Metzelthin | 9.00 | 18.00 | 27.00 | NF |

Avon 338, Avon 343, Avon 353.

| | V/Good | Fine | N/Mint | |
|---|---|---|---|---|

AVON, *continued*

| # | | V/Good | Fine | N/Mint | |
|---|---|---|---|---|---|
| 262 | The Rubaiyat of Omar Khayyam—trans. Edward Fitzgerald | 2.50 | 5.00 | 7.50 | |
| 263 | The Gangs of New York—Herbert Asbury | 5.00 | 10.00 | 15.00 | NF |
| 264 | Six Deadly Dames—Frederick Nebel; 1st ed. 1950 | 10.00 | 20.00 | 30.00 | M |
| 265 | Mortgage on Life—Vicki Baum | 3.00 | 6.00 | 9.00 | E |
| 266 | Death in the Deep South—Ward Greene | 7.50 | 15.00 | 22.50 | E |
| 267 | A Bullet for Billy the Kid—Nelson Nye | 3.00 | 6.00 | 9.00 | W |
| 268 | Seven Slayers—Paul Cain | 10.00 | 20.00 | 30.00 | M |
| 269 | Jadie Greenway—I.S. Young | 2.50 | 5.00 | 7.50 | E |
| 270 | The Chastity of Gloria Boyd—Donald Henderson Clarke | 3.00 | 6.00 | 9.00 | E |
| 271 | Nana's Mother—Emile Zola | 2.50 | 5.00 | 7.50 | E |
| 272 | Europa—Robert Briffault. Note: Two cover variants: | | | | |
| | Girl by map | 3.00 | 6.00 | 9.00 | |
| | Girl in bondage | 15.00 | 30.00 | 45.00 | |
| 273 | Imperial City—Elmer Rice | 2.50 | 5.00 | 7.50 | E |
| 274 | T as in Trapped—Lawrence Treat | 3.00 | 6.00 | 9.00 | M |
| 275 | My Bride in the Storm—Theodore Pratt | 3.00 | 6.00 | 9.00 | E |
| 276 | Madwoman?—Emily Harvin | 6.00 | 12.00 | 18.00 | |
| 277 | Perelandra—C.S. Lewis | 10.00 | 20.00 | 30.00 | SF |
| 278 | A Killer Is Loose Among Us—Robert Terrall | 3.00 | 6.00 | 9.00 | M |
| 279 | The Price Is Right—Jerome Weidman | 2.50 | 5.00 | 7.50 | E |
| 280 | Dangerous Love—Jack Woodford; aka Temptress | 4.50 | 9.00 | 13.50 | E |
| 281 | Into Plutonian Depths—Stanton A. Coblentz | 15.00 | 30.00 | 45.00 | SF |
| 282 | Lovely Lady, Pity Me—Roy Huggins | 5.00 | 10.00 | 15.00 | M |
| 283 | She Posed for Death—Russell Gordon; aka Dead Level. Note: Same cover as the comic Parole Breakers No. 1 | 4.00 | 8.00 | 12.00 | M |
| 284 | Madam Is Dead—Robert Terrell; 1951 | 4.00 | 8.00 | 12.00 | M |
| 285 | An Earthman on Venus—Ralph Milne Farley; aka The Radio Man | 20.00 | 40.00 | 60.00 | SF |
| 286 | Kept Woman—Vina Delmar | 2.50 | 5.00 | 7.50 | E |
| 287 | How to Play Samba Canasta—Richard L. Frey; 1951 | 1.50 | 3.00 | 4.50 | NF |
| 288 | Front for Murder—Guy Emery | 4.50 | 9.00 | 13.50 | M |
| 289 | Friday for Death—Lawrence Lariar. Note: Same cover as the comic The Saint No. 10 | 3.00 | 6.00 | 9.00 | M |
| 290 | Gas-House McGinty—James T. Farrell | 3.00 | 6.00 | 9.00 | |
| 291 | Call Her Savage—Tiffany Thayer | 3.00 | 6.00 | 9.00 | E |
| 292 | Four Boys, a Girl and a Gun—Willard Wiener; aka Four Boys and a Gun. Note: Same cover as the comic Gangsters and Gun Molls No. 1 | 3.00 | 6.00 | 9.00 | JD |
| 293 | Hellbox—John O'Hara | 3.00 | 6.00 | 9.00 | |
| 294 | Sappho—Alphonse Daudet | 3.00 | 6.00 | 9.00 | |
| 295 | Avon Book of Puzzles for Everybody—John Paul Adams | 57.50 | 115.00 | 172.50 | NF |
| 296 | A Modern Lover—D.H. Lawrence | 3.00 | 6.00 | 9.00 | E |
| 297 | Untamed Darling—Jack Woodford; aka Iris | 4.50 | 9.00 | 13.50 | IE |
| 298 | House of Fury—Felice Swados. Note: Later titled Reform School Girl and adapted into a very rare and popular comic book of the same name | 12.50 | 25.00 | 37.50 | E |
| 299 | The Round-Up—Oscar J. Friend | 3.00 | 6.00 | 9.00 | W |
| 300 | The Amboy Dukes—Irving Shulman. Note: Two cover variants of this number | 3.00 | 6.00 | 9.00 | E |

Avon 264, Avon 266, Avon 280.

| # | | V/Good | Fine | N/Mint | |
|---|---|---|---|---|---|
| 301 | We Are Not Alone—James Hilton | 2.50 | 5.00 | 7.50 | |
| 302 | Perversity—Francis Carco | 3.00 | 6.00 | 9.00 | E |
| 303 | Dream Street—Robert Sylvester | 2.50 | 5.00 | 7.50 | E |
| 304 | Song Without Sermon—James Woolf. Note: Same cover as the comic Intimate Confessions No. 4 | 3.00 | 6.00 | 9.00 | |
| 305 | God Wears a Bow Tie—Lyle Stuart | 4.50 | 9.00 | 13.50 | E |
| 306 | Gone to Texas—John W. Thomason, Jr. Note: Same cover as the comic Bad Men of the West No. 1 | 3.00 | 6.00 | 9.00 | W |
| 307 | Big League Baseball | 4.50 | 9.00 | 13.50 | S |
| 308 | Musk, Hashish, and Blood—Hector France | 12.00 | 24.00 | 36.00 | E |
| 309 | Midsummer Passion—Erskine Caldwell | 3.00 | 6.00 | 9.00 | E |
| 310 | Bubu of Montparnasse—Charles-Louis Phillippe | 3.00 | 6.00 | 9.00 | E |
| 311 | The Saturday Evening Post Western Stories—ed. Barthold Fles | 4.50 | 9.00 | 13.50 | W |
| 312 | The Mysterious Affair at Styles—Agatha Christie | 4.50 | 9.00 | 13.50 | M |
| 313 | The Ugly Duchess—Lion Feuchtwanger | 3.00 | 6.00 | 9.00 | E |
| 314 | Nigger Heaven—Carl Van Vechten | 12.00 | 24.00 | 36.00 | E |
| 315 | The Metal Monster—A.A. Merritt | 12.00 | 24.00 | 36.00 | SF |
| 316 | Murder in Three Acts—Agatha Christie | 4.50 | 9.00 | 13.50 | M |
| 317 | Death on the Nile—Agatha Christie | 4.50 | 9.00 | 13.50 | M |
| 318 | Dear Sir—Juliet Lowell | 2.50 | 5.00 | 7.50 | H |
| 319 | Along the Broadway Beat—Louis Sobol | 3.00 | 6.00 | 9.00 | E |
| 320 | Gorgeous Ghoul Murder Case—Dwight V. Babcock | 6.00 | 12.00 | 18.00 | M |
| 321 | The Saint in New York—Leslie Charteris | 3.00 | 6.00 | 9.00 | M |
| 322 | Slipping Beauty—Jerome Weidman; aka The Horse That Could Whistle "Dixie" | 3.00 | 6.00 | 9.00 | E |
| 323 | The Furies in Her Body—Guy Endore; aka Methinks the Lady | 3.00 | 6.00 | 9.00 | F |
| 324 | The Ship of Ishtar—A.A. Merritt | 13.50 | 27.00 | 40.50 | SF |
| 325 | Ill Wind—James Hilton | 2.50 | 5.00 | 7.50 | |
| 326 | Burial of the Fruit—David Dortort | 3.00 | 6.00 | 9.00 | E |
| 327 | One Man Show—Tiffany Thayer | 3.00 | 6.00 | 9.00 | F |
| 328 | Strong Poison—Dorothy L. Sayers | 4.50 | 9.00 | 13.50 | M |
| 329 | Little Caesar—W.R. Burnett. Note: Same cover as the comic Police Line-Up No. 2 | 6.00 | 12.00 | 18.00 | M |
| 330 | Desperate Men—James D. Horan | 4.50 | 9.00 | 13.50 | NF |
| 331 | Trio—W. Somerset Maugham | 2.50 | 5.00 | 7.50 | |
| 332 | A Homicide for Hannah—Dwight V. Babcock | 3.00 | 6.00 | 9.00 | M |
| 333 | Line on Ginger—Robin Maugham | 3.00 | 6.00 | 9.00 | E |
| 334 | Red Bone Woman—Carlyle Tillery | 2.50 | 5.00 | 7.50 | E |
| 335 | In the Teeth of the Evidence—Dorothy L. Sayers | 4.50 | 9.00 | 13.50 | M |
| 336 | The Housekeeper's Daughter—Donald Henderson Clarke | 2.50 | 5.00 | 7.50 | E |
| 337 | The Agony Column—Earl Derr Biggers | 3.00 | 6.00 | 9.00 | M |
| 338 | Hollywood Bedside Reader | 4.50 | 9.00 | 13.50 | |
| 339 | The Terror of the Leopard Men—Juba Kennerley; 1st American ed. 1951 | 12.00 | 24.00 | 36.00 | NF |
| 340 | Midsummer Passion—Erskine Caldwell | 3.00 | 6.00 | 9.00 | E |
| 341 | The Saint Sees It Through—Leslie Charteris | 3.00 | 6.00 | 9.00 | M |
| 342 | The Woman Aroused—Ed Lacy | 7.50 | 15.00 | 22.50 | E |
| 343 | Six-Gun Melody—William Colt MacDonald. Note: Same cover as Avon Western Novel Monthly No. 3 | 3.00 | 6.00 | 9.00 | W |
| 344 | The Chinese Parrot—Earl Derr Biggers | 12.00 | 24.00 | 36.00 | M |
| 345 | I Lost My Girlish Laughter—Jane Allen | 3.00 | 6.00 | 9.00 | E |
| 346 | Possess Me Not—Fan Nichols | 4.50 | 9.00 | 13.50 | E |

| # | Title | V/Good | Fine | N/Mint | |
|---|---|---|---|---|---|
| | **AVON**, *continued* | | | | |
| 347 | The Saint at the Thieves' Picnic–Leslie Charteris | 3.00 | 6.00 | 9.00 | M |
| 348 | Jealous Woman–James M. Cain. Note: Same cover as the comic Campus Romance No. 1 | 3.00 | 6.00 | 9.00 | M |
| 349 | Mistress Murder–Peter Cheyney | 4.50 | 9.00 | 13.50 | M |
| 350 | Charlie Chan Carries On–Earl Derr Biggers | 12.00 | 24.00 | 36.00 | M |
| 351 | Millie's Daughter–Donald Henderson Clarke | 2.50 | 5.00 | 7.50 | E |
| 352 | Ninth Avenue–Maxwell Bodenheim | 2.50 | 5.00 | 7.50 | E |
| 353 | Poirot Loses a Client–Agatha Christie | 3.00 | 6.00 | 9.00 | M |
| 354 | The Werewolf of Paris–Guy Endore | 7.50 | 15.00 | 22.50 | HO |
| 355 | No Orchids for Miss Blandish–James Hadley Chase | 6.00 | 12.00 | 18.00 | M |
| 356 | I Can Get It for You Wholesale!– Jerome Weidman; movie tie-in | 3.00 | 6.00 | 9.00 | E |
| 357 | All about Girls | 3.00 | 6.00 | 9.00 | H |
| 358 | Woman and the Puppet–Pierre Louys | 2.50 | 5.00 | 7.50 | E |
| 359 | Can Can Americana–Harold Meyers; 1st ed. 1951 | 4.50 | 9.00 | 13.50 | NF |
| 360 | As They Reveled–Philip Wylie. Note: Same cover as the comic Realistic Romance No. 7 | 3.00 | 6.00 | 9.00 | E |
| 361 | Does not exist | | | | |
| 362 | Calamity Jane of Deadwood Gulch– Ethel Hueston | 6.00 | 12.00 | 18.00 | W |
| 363 | Murder Is Served–Frances Lockridge & Richard Lockridge | 3.00 | 6.00 | 9.00 | M |
| 364 | The Point of Honour–W. Somerset Maugham | 2.50 | 5.00 | 7.50 | |
| 365 | The Impatient Virgin–Donald Henderson Clarke | 3.00 | 6.00 | 9.00 | E |
| 366 | They'll Do It Every Time–Jimmy Hatlo | 3.50 | 7.00 | 10.50 | H |
| 367 | Outlaw Guns–E.E. Halleran | 3.00 | 6.00 | 9.00 | W |
| 368 | All the Girls He Wanted–John O'Hara | 3.00 | 6.00 | 9.00 | |
| 369 | The Dishonest Murderer–Francis Lockridge & Richard Lockridge | 3.00 | 6.00 | 9.00 | M |
| 370 | The Moon Pool–A.A. Merritt | 12.00 | 24.00 | 36.00 | SF |
| 371 | The Regatta Mystery–Agatha Christie | 4.50 | 9.00 | 13.50 | M |
| 372 | Cry Tough!–Irving Shulman | 2.50 | 5.00 | 7.50 | E |
| 373 | The Blue Negro–Robert Payne | 10.50 | 21.00 | 31.50 | E |
| 374 | Gun Fight at Horsethief Range–B.M. Bower; c-Bergey | 2.50 | 5.00 | 7.50 | W |
| 375 | Babes and Sucklings–Philip Wylie. Note: Same cover as the comic Intimate Confessions No. 8 | 3.00 | 6.00 | 9.00 | E |
| 376 | Home to Harlem–Claude McKay | 15.00 | 30.00 | 45.00 | E |
| 377 | Taffy–Philip B. Kaye | 9.00 | 18.00 | 27.00 | E |
| 378 | Marshal of Deer Creek–Al Cody | 2.50 | 5.00 | 7.50 | W |
| 379 | Death in the Air–Agatha Christie | 4.50 | 9.00 | 13.50 | M |
| 380 | If This Be Sin–Loren Wahl | 2.50 | 5.00 | 7.50 | E |
| 381 | Nothing So Strange–James Hilton | 2.50 | 5.00 | 7.50 | M |
| 382 | Tough Kid from Brooklyn–Robert Mende | 3.00 | 6.00 | 9.00 | |
| 383 | The Untamed Wife of Louis Scott–W. Carroll Munro; aka The Gift of Glory | 2.50 | 5.00 | 7.50 | E |
| 384 | Louis Beretti–Donald Henderson Clarke | 3.00 | 6.00 | 9.00 | M |
| 385 | Cat and Mouse–Christianna Brand; 1952 | 3.00 | 6.00 | 9.00 | M |
| 386 | Does not exist. Note: Announced as The Face in the Abyss by A. Merritt but instead released as Murder Mystery Monthly No. 29 | | | | |
| 387 | Maniac Rendezvous–Marc Brandel; aka Rain Before Seven | 6.00 | 12.00 | 18.00 | M |
| 388 | Does not exist. Note: Announced as After Many a Summer Dies the Swan–Aldous Huxley and later released as Avon AT435 | | | | |
| 389 | The Saturday Evening Post Fantasy Stories | 4.50 | 9.00 | 13.50 | SF |
| 390 | The Savage Gentleman–Philip Wylie | 6.00 | 12.00 | 18.00 | F |
| 391 | Maidens in the Midden–Oliver Anderson; aka In for a Penny | 3.00 | 6.00 | 9.00 | E |
| 392 | Burn, Witch, Burn–A.A. Merritt | 12.00 | 24.00 | 36.00 | SF |
| 393 | The Moron–Marc Brandel; aka The Choice | 6.00 | 12.00 | 18.00 | M |
| 394 | Murderer's Holiday–Donald Henderson Clarke | 3.00 | 6.00 | 9.00 | M |
| 395 | The Drunk, the Damned, and the | 3.00 | 6.00 | 9.00 | E |
| | Bedeviled–Terence Ford; aka He Feeds the Birds | | | | |
| 396 | His First Million Women–George Weston | 4.50 | 9.00 | 13.50 | SF |
| 397 | Nina–Donald Henderson Clarke. Note: Same cover as the comic Realistic Romances No. 8 | 3.00 | 6.00 | 9.00 | |
| 398 | Element of Shame–Cicely Schiller | 4.50 | 9.00 | 13.50 | E |
| 399 | . . .Plus Blood in Their Veins–Robert Paul Smith; 1952; aka So It Doesn't Whistle | 4.50 | 9.00 | 13.50 | E |
| 400 | Jule: Alabama Boy in Harlem–George Wylie Henderson | 4.50 | 9.00 | 13.50 | E |
| 401 | Perversity–Francis Carco | 3.00 | 6.00 | 9.00 | E |
| 402 | Dangerous Love–Jack Woodford | 4.50 | 9.00 | 13.50 | E |
| 403 | Untamed Darling–Jack Woodford; aka Iris | 4.50 | 9.00 | 13.50 | E |
| 404 | The Blackmailer–Ernst Klein; orig. 1952 | 2.50 | 5.00 | 7.50 | |
| 405 | How Brave We Live–Paul Monash | 2.50 | 5.00 | 7.50 | E |
| 406 | Two Beds for Roxane–Stephen Longstreet; aka The Sound of an American | 2.50 | 5.00 | 7.50 | E |
| 407 | Strange Brother–Blair Niles | 2.50 | 5.00 | 7.50 | |
| 408 | Tawny–Donald Henderson Clarke | 2.50 | 5.00 | 7.50 | E |
| 409 | Does not exist. Note: Announced as The Rites of Love by Jack Woodford | | | | |
| 410 | The Secret Adversary–Agatha Christie | 3.00 | 6.00 | 9.00 | M |
| 411 | Hospital Happy–Bob Dunn | 3.00 | 6.00 | 9.00 | H |
| 412 | Waiting for Willy–Jack Houston | 2.50 | 5.00 | 7.50 | |
| 413 | Dwellers in the Mirage–A.A. Merritt | 12.00 | 24.00 | 36.00 | SF |
| 414 | The Gringo Bandit–William Hopson | 3.00 | 6.00 | 9.00 | W |
| 415 | Musk, Hashish, and Blood–Hector France | 10.50 | 21.00 | 31.50 | E |
| 416 | The Frenchman in Mohammed's Harem–Mario Uchard | 6.00 | 12.00 | 18.00 | E |
| 417 | Star Lust–Jack Hanley | 3.00 | 6.00 | 9.00 | E |
| 418 | Call Her Savage–Tiffany Thayer | 3.00 | 6.00 | 9.00 | E |
| 419 | Never Come Morning–Nelson Algren | 2.50 | 5.00 | 7.50 | E |
| 420 | The Saint Goes West–Leslie Charteris | 2.50 | 5.00 | 7.50 | M |
| 421 | Love's Lovely Counterfeit–James M. Cain | 3.00 | 6.00 | 9.00 | |
| 422 | Butterfield 8–John O'Hara | 2.50 | 5.00 | 7.50 | |
| 423 | Love among the Haystacks–D.H. Lawrence | 2.50 | 5.00 | 7.50 | E |
| 424 | The Neon Wilderness–Nelson Algren. Note: Same cover as the comic Intimate Confessions No. 1 | 7.50 | 15.00 | 22.50 | E |
| 425 | The Tragedy of X–Ellery Queen | 2.50 | 5.00 | 7.50 | M |
| 426 | Guns Blaze at Sundown–Al Cody | 2.50 | 5.00 | 7.50 | W |
| 427 | Georgie May–Maxwell Bodenheim | 2.00 | 4.00 | 6.00 | E |
| 428 | The Servant–Robin Maugham | 2.00 | 4.00 | 6.00 | E |
| 429 | The Price Is Right–Jerome Weidman | 2.00 | 4.00 | 6.00 | E |
| 430 | House of Fury–Felice Swados | 6.00 | 12.00 | 18.00 | E |
| 431 | That Mrs. Renney–Donald Henderson Clarke | 2.00 | 4.00 | 6.00 | E |
| 432 | Saint Overboard–Leslie Charteris | 2.50 | 5.00 | 7.50 | M |
| 433 | Juvenile Delinquents–Leonard Kaufman; aka The Lower Part of the Sky | 2.50 | 5.00 | 7.50 | E |
| 434 | Murder Comes First–Frances Lockridge & Richard Lockridge | 2.50 | 5.00 | 7.50 | M |
| AT435 | After Many a Summer Dies the Swan– Aldous Huxley | 2.50 | 5.00 | 7.50 | SF |
| A436 | Too Dangerous to Be Free–James Hadley Chase | 2.50 | 5.00 | 7.50 | M |
| 437 | The Battle at Apache Pass–Harold Conrad; orig. 1952; movie tie-in | 2.00 | 4.00 | 6.00 | W |
| 438 | Confidential–Donald Henderson Clarke. Note: Same cover as the comic Realistic Romances No. 4 | 2.00 | 4.00 | 6.00 | E |
| 439 | Diplomatic Corpse–Phoebe Atwood Taylor | 2.00 | 4.00 | 6.00 | M |
| 440 | The Saint at the Thieves' Picnic–Leslie Charteris | 2.00 | 4.00 | 6.00 | M |
| 441 | A Mouse Is Born–Anita Loos | 2.00 | 4.00 | 6.00 | H |
| 442 | Slipping Beauty–Jerome Weidman; aka The Horse That Could Whistle ''Dixie'' | 2.50 | 5.00 | 7.50 | E |
| 443 | A Holiday for Murder–Agatha Christie | 2.50 | 5.00 | 7.50 | M |
| 444 | Four Boys, a Girl and a Gun–Willard | 2.00 | 4.00 | 6.00 | E |

**AVON,** *continued*

Wiener; aka Four Boys and a Gun. Note: Same cover as the comic Gangsters and Gun Molls No. 1

| | | V/Good | Fine | N/Mint | |
|---|---|---|---|---|---|
| AT445 | End As a Man–Calder Willingham | 2.00 | 4.00 | 6.00 | E |
| 446 | The Outcasts of Poker Flat–Bret Harte; movie tie-in | 2.00 | 4.00 | 6.00 | W |
| AT447 | Red Canvas–Marcel Wallenstein | 2.00 | 4.00 | 6.00 | E |
| 448 | The Last of Mr. Norris–Christopher Isherwood | 2.50 | 5.00 | 7.50 | E |
| 449 | The Virgin and the Gypsy–D.H. Lawrence | 2.00 | 4.00 | 6.00 | E |
| 450 | The Tragedy of Y–Ellery Queen | 2.00 | 4.00 | 6.00 | M |
| 451 | Gone to Texas–John W. Thomason, Jr | 2.00 | 4.00 | 6.00 | W |
| 452 | Red Bone Woman–Carlyle Tillery | 2.00 | 4.00 | 6.00 | E |
| 453 | Glamor Girls–Don Flowers | 2.50 | 5.00 | 7.50 | H |
| 454 | The Challenge of Smoke Wade–Robert J. Hogan | 2.00 | 4.00 | 6.00 | W |
| 455 | The Root of His Evil–James M. Cain | 2.00 | 4.00 | 6.00 | |
| 456 | The Chastity of Gloria Boyd–Donald Henderson Clarke | 2.00 | 4.00 | 6.00 | E |
| 457 | Bimini Run–Howard Hunt | 2.00 | 4.00 | 6.00 | |
| 458 | Because of My Love–Robert Paul Smith | 2.00 | 4.00 | 6.00 | E |
| 459 | Mademoiselle Fifi and Other Stories–Guy de Maupassant | 2.00 | 4.00 | 6.00 | |
| 460 | Outlaw Justice at Hangman's Coulee–Al Cody | 2.00 | 4.00 | 6.00 | W |
| 461 | Lady, Don't Die on My Doorstep–Joseph Shallit | 2.50 | 5.00 | 7.50 | M |
| 462 | Pardners of the Badlands–Bliss Lomax (H.S. Drago). Note: Same cover as the comic Jesse James No. 6 | 2.00 | 4.00 | 6.00 | W |
| 463 | The Saint in Action–Leslie Charteris; aka The Ace of Knaves. Note: Same cover as the comic The Saint No. 7 | 2.00 | 4.00 | 6.00 | M |
| 464 | The Rough and the Smooth–Robin Maugham | 2.00 | 4.00 | 6.00 | E |
| 465 | The Tragedy of Z–Ellery Queen | 2.00 | 4.00 | 6.00 | M |
| 466 | Gas-House McGinty–James T. Farrell | 2.00 | 4.00 | 6.00 | |
| 467 | Hell-Bent with Jake–Russell LaDue; aka No More with Me | 2.00 | 4.00 | 6.00 | E |
| 468 | A Hell of a Good Time–James T. Farrell | 2.00 | 4.00 | 6.00 | |
| 469 | Roaring Guns at Apache Landing–Robert J. Hogan | 2.00 | 4.00 | 6.00 | W |
| 470 | Low Company–Mark Benney | 2.00 | 4.00 | 6.00 | |
| 471 | Mr. and Mrs. North Meet Murder–Frances Lockridge & Richard Lockridge | 2.00 | 4.00 | 6.00 | M |
| 472 | The Headstrong Young Man–Donald Henderson Clarke; aka Regards to Broadway | 2.00 | 4.00 | 6.00 | E |
| 473 | The Saint's Getaway–Leslie Charteris | 2.00 | 4.00 | 6.00 | M |
| 474 | Outlaw Ambush on the Drumfire Trail–Tom J. Hopkins | 2.00 | 4.00 | 6.00 | W |
| 475 | Yesterday's Love–James T. Farrell | 1.50 | 3.00 | 4.50 | E |
| 476 | The Bride of Newgate–John Dickson Carr | 2.00 | 4.00 | 6.00 | M |
| 477 | The Saint Meets the Tiger–Leslie Charteris | 2.00 | 4.00 | 6.00 | M |
| 478 | A Bullet for Billy the Kid–Nelson C. Nye; aka Pistols for Hire | 1.50 | 3.00 | 4.50 | W |

*Avon 456, Avon 519, Avon 531.*

| | | V/Good | Fine | N/Mint | |
|---|---|---|---|---|---|
| 479 | Jealous Woman–James M. Cain. Note: Same cover as the comic Campus Romances No. 1 | 1.50 | 3.00 | 4.50 | |
| 480 | Millie–Donald Henderson Clarke | 1.50 | 3.00 | 4.50 | |
| 481 | The Hucksters–Frederic Wakeman | 1.50 | 3.00 | 4.50 | E |
| 482 | Avon Bedside Companion | 1.50 | 3.00 | 4.50 | |
| 483 | A Lady Named Lou–Donald Henderson Clarke | 2.00 | 4.00 | 6.00 | E |
| 484 | Murder in a Hurry–Frances Lockridge & Richard Lockridge | 1.50 | 3.00 | 4.50 | M |
| 485 | 12 Chinks and a Woman–James Hadley Chase | 4.50 | 9.00 | 13.50 | E |
| 486 | Bronc Buckaroo–J. Edward Leithead | 1.50 | 3.00 | 4.50 | W |
| 487 | Feud at Sundown–Robert Jasper; 1953 | 1.50 | 3.00 | 4.50 | W |
| 488 | Drury Lane's Last Case–Ellery Queen | 1.50 | 3.00 | 4.50 | M |
| 489 | The Saint Meets His Match–Leslie Charteris | 1.50 | 3.00 | 4.50 | M |
| 490 | Yell Bloody Murder–Joseph Shallit | 2.00 | 4.00 | 6.00 | M |
| 491 | Mesquiteer Mavericks–William Colt MacDonald | 1.50 | 3.00 | 4.50 | W |
| 492 | Waiting for Willy–Jack Houston | 1.50 | 3.00 | 4.50 | |
| 493 | Strange Brother–Blair Niles | 1.50 | 3.00 | 4.50 | |
| 494 | The Scarf–Robert Bloch | 5.00 | 10.00 | 15.00 | |
| 495 | Rebel's Roundup–W. Edmunds Claussen | 1.50 | 3.00 | 4.50 | W |
| 496 | Fast One–Paul Cain | 3.00 | 6.00 | 9.00 | M |
| 497 | A Night with Mr. Primrose–Whitfield Cook | 1.50 | 3.00 | 4.50 | |
| 498 | Six-Gun Melody–William Colt MacDonald | 1.50 | 3.00 | 4.50 | W |
| 499 | Chorus of Cuties–E. Simms Campbell | 2.50 | 5.00 | 7.50 | H |
| 500 | Colorado–William MacLeod Raine | 1.50 | 3.00 | 4.50 | W |
| 501 | The Untamed Wife of Louis Scott–W. Carroll Munro; aka The Gift of Glory | 1.50 | 3.00 | 4.50 | E |
| 502 | Mr. and Mrs. North and a Pinch of Poison–Frances Lockridge & Richard Lockridge | 1.50 | 3.00 | 4.50 | M |
| 503 | The Housekeeper's Daughter–Donald Henderson Clarke | 1.25 | 2.50 | 3.75 | E |
| 504 | The Chase–Richard G. Huber | 1.25 | 2.50 | 3.75 | E |
| 505 | Gun Fight at Horsethief Range–B.M. Bower; aka Five Furies of Leaning Ladder; c-Bergey | 1.25 | 2.50 | 3.75 | W |
| 506 | Nonce–Michael Brandon. Note: Same cover as Avon 781 | 1.50 | 3.00 | 4.50 | E |
| 507 | Straw Boss–E.E. Halleran | 1.25 | 2.50 | 3.75 | W |
| 508 | He Swung and He Missed–Eugene O'Brien | 1.25 | 2.50 | 3.75 | |
| 509 | The Four of Hearts–Ellery Queen | 2.00 | 4.00 | 6.00 | M |
| 510 | The Thin Line–Edward Atiyah | 1.25 | 2.50 | 3.75 | |
| 511 | Marshal of Deer Creek–Al Cody | 1.25 | 2.50 | 3.75 | W |
| 512 | The Gifted–Roswell G. Ham, Jr | 1.25 | 2.50 | 3.75 | |
| 513 | Bachelor's Joke Book–Leo Guild | 1.50 | 3.00 | 4.50 | H |
| 514 | The Vanishing Gun Slinger–William Colt MacDonald | 1.25 | 2.50 | 3.75 | W |
| 515 | Murder Out of Turn–Frances Lockridge & Richard Lockridge | 1.50 | 3.00 | 4.50 | M |
| 516 | The Gringo Bandit–William Hopson | 1.25 | 2.50 | 3.75 | W |
| 517 | The Fat Boy's Book–Elmer Wheeler | 1.50 | 3.00 | 4.50 | NF |
| 518 | The Avenging Saint–Leslie Charteris | 1.25 | 2.50 | 3.75 | M |
| 519 | Dennis the Menace–Hank Ketcham | 3.00 | 6.00 | 9.00 | H |
| 520 | Scratch the Surface–Edmund Schiddel | 1.25 | 2.50 | 3.75 | E |
| 521 | The Prisoner Ate a Hearty Breakfast–Jerome Ellison | 1.00 | 2.00 | 3.00 | E |
| 522 | Outlaw Guns–E.E. Halleran | 1.25 | 2.50 | 3.75 | W |
| 523 | The American Gun Mystery–Ellery Queen | 1.25 | 2.50 | 3.75 | M |
| 524 | The New Jimmy Hatlo Book–Jimmy Hatlo; 1st ed. 1953 | 2.50 | 5.00 | 7.50 | H |
| 525 | Guns Blaze at Sundown–Al Cody | 1.25 | 2.50 | 3.75 | W |
| 526 | Call for the Saint–Leslie Charteris | 1.25 | 2.50 | 3.75 | M |
| 527 | All about Girls | 2.00 | 4.00 | 6.00 | |
| 528 | Kiss the Killer–Joseph Shallit | 1.25 | 2.50 | 3.75 | M |
| 529 | Gunshot Empire–Lee E. Wells | 1.25 | 2.50 | 3.75 | W |
| 530 | Impatient Virgin–Donald Henderson Clarke | 1.50 | 3.00 | 4.50 | E |
| 531 | The Wages of Fear–Georges Arnaud | 1.25 | 2.50 | 3.75 | |
| 532 | Trouble in the Saddle–Arthur Henry Gooden | 1.25 | 2.50 | 3.75 | W |
| 533 | Follow the Saint–Leslie Charteris | 1.25 | 2.50 | 3.75 | M |
| 534 | The Time and the Place–Robert Paul Smith | 1.25 | 2.50 | 3.75 | E |

AVON, *continued*

| # | Title | V/Good | Fine | N/Mint | |
|---|---|---|---|---|---|
| 535 | Dead as a Dinosaur–Frances Lockridge & Richard Lockridge | 1.25 | 2.50 | 3.75 | M |
| 536 | Three-Notch Cameron–William Colt MacDonald | 1.25 | 2.50 | 3.75 | W |
| 537 | The Innocent Villa–Barnaby Conrad | 1.25 | 2.50 | 3.75 | |
| 538 | Dope, Inc.–Joachim Joesten; orig. 1953 | 6.00 | 12.00 | 18.00 | |
| 539 | Hardcase–Matt Kinkaid | 1.25 | 2.50 | 3.75 | |
| 540 | Pistols on the Pecos–Paul Evan Lehman | 1.25 | 2.50 | 3.75 | W |
| 541 | Burial of the Fruit–David Dortort | 2.50 | 5.00 | 7.50 | E |
| 542 | Call Me Killer–Max Carter | 1.50 | 3.00 | 4.50 | |
| 543 | Millie's Daughter–Donald Henderson Clarke | 1.25 | 2.50 | 3.75 | |
| 544 | The Saint and the Last Hero–Leslie Charteris | 1.25 | 2.50 | 3.75 | M |
| 545 | Circle of Desire–Robert Paul Smith; aka The Journey | 1.00 | 2.00 | 3.00 | E |
| 546 | The Hoodlums–John Eagle; orig. 1953 | 1.25 | 2.50 | 3.75 | E |
| 547 | Southern Daughter–Daniel White | 1.25 | 2.50 | 3.75 | |
| 548 | Away and Beyond–A.E. Van Vogt | 1.50 | 3.00 | 4.50 | |
| A549 | Tales of Love and Fury–anthology; 1st ed. 1953 | 1.50 | 3.00 | 4.50 | E |
| 550 | Renegade Guns–Robert J. Hogan | 1.25 | 2.50 | 3.75 | W |
| 551 | Stool Pigeon–Louis Malley | 1.25 | 2.50 | 3.75 | M |
| 552 | Man on the Tightrope–Neil Paterson | 1.25 | 2.50 | 3.75 | E |
| 553 | Rusty Desmond–Steve January; 1954 | 1.25 | 2.50 | 3.75 | E |
| 554 | I'll Call Every Monday–Orrie Hitt | 1.25 | 2.50 | 3.75 | |
| 555 | Rue Pigalle–Francis Carco | 1.25 | 2.50 | 3.75 | E |
| 556 | Guns of Circle 8–Jeff Cochran | 1.25 | 2.50 | 3.75 | W |
| 557 | Glamor Girls–Don Flowers | 2.00 | 4.00 | 6.00 | H |
| 558 | Case of the Billion Dollar Body–Joseph Shallit | 1.25 | 2.50 | 3.75 | M |
| 559 | A Cartoon Guide to the Kinsey Report–Charles Preston | 2.00 | 4.00 | 6.00 | H |
| 560 | Gang Girl–Wenzell Brown | 5.00 | 10.00 | 15.00 | JD |
| 561 | Enter without Desire–Ed Lacy | 1.25 | 2.50 | 3.75 | |
| 562 | Call of the Range–Arthur Henry Gooden | 1.25 | 2.50 | 3.75 | W |
| 563 | The Creepers–John Creasey | 1.25 | 2.50 | 3.75 | M |
| 564 | Every Bet's a Sure Thing–Thomas B. Dewey | 1.25 | 2.50 | 3.75 | M |
| 565 | Thunder Below–Thomas Rourke | 1.25 | 2.50 | 3.75 | E |
| 566 | Go for the Body–Ed Lacy | 1.25 | 2.50 | 3.75 | |
| 567 | Ship Ahoy | 2.00 | 4.00 | 6.00 | H |
| 568 | I Worked for Lucky Luciano–anon. | 1.50 | 3.00 | 4.50 | NF |
| 569 | Gunhand from Texas–William Heuman | 1.25 | 2.50 | 3.75 | W |
| 570 | Devil's Daughter–Floyd Shaw | 1.25 | 2.50 | 3.75 | |
| 571 | As They Reveled–Philip Wylie | 1.25 | 2.50 | 3.75 | E |
| 572 | Laughter Came Screaming–Henry Kane | 1.25 | 2.50 | 3.75 | M |
| 573 | The Long Noose–Lee E. Wells | 1.25 | 2.50 | 3.75 | W |
| 574 | Make My Bed in Hell–John B. Sanford; aka Seventy Times Seven | 1.25 | 2.50 | 3.75 | E |
| 575 | Louis Beretti–New York Hoodlum–Donald Henderson Clarke | 1.25 | 2.50 | 3.75 | M |
| 576 | Forbidden–Leo Brattes | 1.25 | 2.50 | 3.75 | |
| 577 | Jule: Alabama Boy in Harlem–George Wylie Henderson | 1.50 | 3.00 | 4.50 | |
| 578 | The Girl on the Left Bank–Joan Shepherd | 1.25 | 2.50 | 3.75 | |
| 579 | Rebel Ranger–William Colt MacDonald | 1.25 | 2.50 | 3.75 | W |
| 580 | The Guy from Coney Island–Jack Hanley | 1.25 | 2.50 | 3.75 | E |
| 581 | Love's Lovely Counterfeit–James M. Cain | 1.25 | 2.50 | 3.75 | |
| 582 | How Rough Can It Get?–Joe Weiss | 1.25 | 2.50 | 3.75 | |
| 583 | Death Has a Small Voice–Frances Lockridge & Richard Lockridge | 1.25 | 2.50 | 3.75 | M |
| 584 | Few Die Well–Sterling Noel | 1.25 | 2.50 | 3.75 | |
| 585 | Keeping Women in Line–Mischa Richter | 1.25 | 2.50 | 3.75 | |
| 586 | The Riddle of Ramrod Ridge–William Colt MacDonald | 1.25 | 2.50 | 3.75 | W |
| 587 | The Virgin and the Gypsy–D.H. Lawrence | 1.25 | 2.50 | 3.75 | E |
| 588 | Saint Errant–Leslie Charteris | 1.25 | 2.50 | 3.75 | M |
| 589 | The Other Side of the Night–Edmund Schiddel | 1.25 | 2.50 | 3.75 | |
| 590 | The Figure in the Dusk–John Creasey | .75 | 1.50 | 2.25 | M |
| 591 | The Wrong Turn–Daniel Harper | 1.25 | 2.50 | 3.75 | |
| 592 | The Phantom Pass–William Colt MacDonald | 1.25 | 2.50 | 3.75 | W |
| 593 | Nina–Donald Henderson Clarke | .75 | 1.50 | 2.25 | |
| 594 | The Pennycross Murders–Maurice Proctor | 1.25 | 2.50 | 3.75 | M |
| 595 | How Brave We Live–Paul Monash | .75 | 1.50 | 2.25 | |
| 596 | Gun Feud at Stampede Valley–Samuel A. Peeples | 1.25 | 2.50 | 3.75 | W |
| 597 | Night Cry–William L. Stuart | 1.50 | 3.00 | 4.50 | M |
| 598 | More All About Girls | 2.00 | 4.00 | 6.00 | H |
| 599 | Sinful Woman–James M. Cain | 1.25 | 2.50 | 3.75 | |
| 600 | More Dennis the Menace–Hank Ketcham | 2.50 | 5.00 | 7.50 | H |
| 601 | Love for a Stranger–John Pleasant McCoy | 1.25 | 2.50 | 3.75 | |
| 602 | My Business Is Murder–Henry Kane | 1.25 | 2.50 | 3.75 | M |
| 603 | Avon Bedside Companion–ed. Don Wollheim | 1.25 | 2.50 | 3.75 | |
| 604 | The Case of the Burning Bride–Alan Hynd; aka Alan Hynd's Murder | .75 | 1.50 | 2.25 | M |
| 605 | Death Hits the Jackpot–John Tiger | 1.25 | 2.50 | 3.75 | M |
| 606 | The Kansan–Richard Brister | 1.25 | 2.50 | 3.75 | W |
| 607 | Bubu of Montparnasse–Charles-Louis Philippe | 1.25 | 2.50 | 3.75 | E |
| 608 | Curtain for a Jester–Frances Lockridge & Richard Lockridge | 1.25 | 2.50 | 3.75 | M |
| 609 | French Postcards | 2.00 | 4.00 | 6.00 | H |
| 610 | The Saint Steps In–Leslie Charteris | 1.25 | 2.50 | 3.75 | M |
| 611 | The Saint in Europe–Leslie Charteris | 1.25 | 2.50 | 3.75 | M |
| 612 | The New Jimmy Hatlo Book–Jimmy Hatlo | 2.00 | 4.00 | 6.00 | H |
| 613 | Break-Up–Edmund Schiddel | 1.25 | 2.50 | 3.75 | E |
| 614 | And Dream of Evil–Tedd Thomey | 1.25 | 2.50 | 3.75 | |
| 615 | Tawny–Donald Henderson Clarke | 1.25 | 2.50 | 3.75 | |
| 616 | A Holiday for Murder–Agatha Christie | 1.25 | 2.50 | 3.75 | M |
| 617 | Battle of the Sexes–Charles Preston | 2.00 | 4.00 | 6.00 | H |
| 618 | Trinity in Violence–Henry Kane | 1.25 | 2.50 | 3.75 | M |
| 619 | The Saint Sees It Through–Leslie Charteris | 1.25 | 2.50 | 3.75 | M |
| 620 | Death in the Desert–Lee E. Wells | 1.25 | 2.50 | 3.75 | W |
| 621 | It Walks by Night–John Dickson Carr | 1.25 | 2.50 | 3.75 | M |
| 622 | Hellbound–Paul Monash | 1.25 | 2.50 | 3.75 | E |
| 623 | Beat Not the Bones–Charlotte Jay | 1.25 | 2.50 | 3.75 | M |
| 624 | The Stone of Chastity–Margery Sharp | 1.25 | 2.50 | 3.75 | F |
| 625 | A Taste for Murder–H.F. Heard | 1.25 | 2.50 | 3.75 | M |
| 626 | The Case of the Murdered Model–Thomas B. Dewey | 1.25 | 2.50 | 3.75 | M |
| 627 | Caveman Cartoons–Harold Meyers | 2.00 | 4.00 | 6.00 | H |
| 628 | The Monk and the Hangman's Daughter–Ambrose Bierce | 1.50 | 3.00 | 4.50 | |
| 629 | The Saint and Mr. Teal–Leslie Charteris | 1.25 | 2.50 | 3.75 | M |
| 630 | 20 Great Ghost Stories | 2.50 | 5.00 | 7.50 | HO |
| 631 | Murderer's Holiday–Donald Henderson Clarke | 1.25 | 2.50 | 3.75 | M |
| 632 | Jet Pilot–Tedd Thomey | 1.25 | 2.50 | 3.75 | |
| 633 | Klever Kid Kartoons–Harold Meyers | 1.50 | 3.00 | 4.50 | H |
| 634 | Miss Lonelyhearts–Nathanel West | 1.25 | 2.50 | 3.75 | |
| 635 | The Saint Goes West–Leslie Charteris | 1.25 | 2.50 | 3.75 | M |
| 636 | The Moving Finger–Agatha Christie | 1.25 | 2.50 | 3.75 | M |
| 637 | Animals Are Funnier Than People–Harold Meyers | 2.00 | 4.00 | 6.00 | H |
| 638 | Tropical Passions–anthology | 1.50 | 3.00 | 4.50 | E |
| 639 | Cartoons by Jimmy Hatlo; 1st ed. 1955 | 2.00 | 4.00 | 6.00 | H |
| 640 | The Man Who Never Was–Ewen Montague | 1.25 | 2.50 | 3.75 | |
| 641 | The Case of the Acid Throwers–John Creasey | .75 | 1.50 | 2.25 | M |
| 642 | The Fighting Texan–Paul Evan Lehman | 1.25 | 2.50 | 3.75 | W |
| 643 | South Sea Cartoons–Harold Meyers; c-Ward | 2.00 | 4.00 | 6.00 | H |
| 644 | Stories for Tonight–anthology; 1st ed. 1955 | 1.50 | 3.00 | 4.50 | |
| 645 | Puzzles for Everybody–John Paul Adams | 7.50 | 15.00 | 22.50 | NF |
| 646 | The Case of the Murdered Madam–Henry Kane | 1.25 | 2.50 | 3.75 | M |
| 647 | Unfaithful–John Baxter | 1.25 | 2.50 | 3.75 | |
| 648 | Murder in Three Acts–Agatha Christie | 1.25 | 2.50 | 3.75 | M |
| 649 | Nudist Cartoons–Harold Meyers | 2.00 | 4.00 | 6.00 | H |
| 650 | Confidential–Donald Henderson Clarke | 1.25 | 2.50 | 3.75 | |
| 651 | Murder in Las Vegas–Jack Waer | 1.25 | 2.50 | 3.75 | M |
| 652 | Hatlo's Inferno–Jimmy Hatlo; 1st ed. 1955 | 5.00 | 10.00 | 15.00 | H |
| 653 | The Saint Goes On–Leslie Charteris | 1.25 | 2.50 | 3.75 | M |

| | V/Good | Fine | N/Mint | |
|---|---|---|---|---|

AVON, *continued*

| # | Title | V/Good | Fine | N/Mint | |
|---|---|---|---|---|---|
| 654 | Bloody Kansas–Chuck Martin; 1st ed. 1955 | 1.25 | 2.50 | 3.75 | W |
| 655 | Seven Who Were Hanged–Leonid Andreyev | 1.25 | 2.50 | 3.75 | |
| 656 | Impatient Virgin–Donald Henderson Clarke | 2.00 | 4.00 | 6.00 | |
| 657 | The Doctor's Woman–H.P. Koenig | 1.25 | 2.50 | 3.75 | |
| 658 | Death in the Air–Agatha Christie | 1.25 | 2.50 | 3.75 | M |
| 659 | Hell-town in Texas–Leslie Ernenwein | 1.25 | 2.50 | 3.75 | W |
| 660 | Wake Up to Murder–Day Keene | 1.25 | 2.50 | 3.75 | M |
| 661 | Stories of Venial Sin–John O'Hara | 1.25 | 2.50 | 3.75 | |
| 662 | Teen-age Cartoons and Jokes–Harold Meyers | 2.00 | 4.00 | 6.00 | H |
| 663 | The Ace of Knaves–Leslie Charteris | 1.25 | 2.50 | 3.75 | M |
| 664 | Desire in the Deep South–Ward Greene | 2.00 | 4.00 | 6.00 | E |
| 665 | Dennis the Menace–Hank Ketcham | 2.50 | 5.00 | 7.50 | H |
| 666 | A Key to Death–Frances Lockridge & Richard Lockridge | 1.25 | 2.50 | 3.75 | M |
| 667 | The Range Bum–Kenneth Fowler | 1.25 | 2.50 | 3.75 | W |
| 668 | Woman and the Puppet–Pierre Louys | 1.25 | 2.50 | 3.75 | E |
| 669 | Sensualite–Georges de La Fouchardiere | 1.25 | 2.50 | 3.75 | E |
| 670 | The Fugitive Eye–Charlotte Jay | 1.25 | 2.50 | 3.75 | |
| 671 | A Lady Named Lou–Donald Henderson Clarke | 1.25 | 2.50 | 3.75 | E |
| 672 | Too French and Too Deadly–Henry Kane | 1.25 | 2.50 | 3.75 | |
| 673 | Henry Morgan's Joke Book–Henry Morgan | 1.50 | 3.00 | 4.50 | H |
| 674 | The Challenge of Smoke Wade–Robert J. Hogan | 1.25 | 2.50 | 3.75 | W |
| 675 | A Room in Berlin–Gunther Birkenfeld | 1.25 | 2.50 | 3.75 | |
| 676 | White Barrier–Noel Clad | 1.25 | 2.50 | 3.75 | |
| 677 | Case of the Black, Black Hearse–Frederic Freyer | 1.25 | 2.50 | 3.75 | M |
| 678 | The Fighting Kid from Eldorado–William Colt MacDonald | 1.25 | 2.50 | 3.75 | W |
| 679 | Hellbox–John O'Hara | 1.25 | 2.50 | 3.75 | |
| 680 | The Saint–The Happy Highwayman–Leslie Charteris | 1.25 | 2.50 | 3.75 | M |
| 681 | Showgirl Cartoons, Photographs, Stories–Harold Meyers | 2.00 | 4.00 | 6.00 | H |
| 682 | Chinese Love Tales–Edward Powys Mathers | 2.50 | 5.00 | 7.50 | |
| 683 | Coming, Aphrodite! | 1.50 | 3.00 | 4.50 | |
| 684 | The Passion Murders–Day Keene | 1.50 | 3.00 | 4.50 | M |
| 685 | Alibi Baby–Stewart Sterling | 1.25 | 2.50 | 3.75 | M |
| 686 | The Hungering Shame–R.V. Cassill; orig. 1956 | 1.25 | 2.50 | 3.75 | E |
| 687 | Vegas, Gunman Marshal–William Hopson | 1.25 | 2.50 | 3.75 | W |
| 688 | The Art Studio Murders–Edward Ronns | 1.25 | 2.50 | 3.75 | M |
| 689 | Riders of the Whistling Skull–William Colt MacDonald | 1.25 | 2.50 | 3.75 | W |
| 690 | The Big Four–Agatha Christie; c-Kinstler | 2.50 | 5.00 | 7.50 | M |
| 691 | Sappho–Alphonse Daudet | 1.25 | 2.50 | 3.75 | E |
| 692 | The Counterfeit General Montgomery–M.E. Clifton James | 1.25 | 2.50 | 3.75 | |
| 693 | The Hotshot–Fletcher Flora | 1.25 | 2.50 | 3.75 | |
| 694 | The Saint–Wanted for Murder–Leslie Charteris; aka Wanted for Murder | 1.25 | 2.50 | 3.75 | M |
| 695 | The Jungle of Love–Robin Maugham; aka Behind the Mirror; c-Kinstler (?) | 1.25 | 2.50 | 3.75 | |
| 696 | Murder Somewhere in This City–Maurice Procter; aka Hell in a City | 1.25 | 2.50 | 3.75 | M |
| 697 | The Girl with the Golden Eyes–Honore De Balzac | 1.25 | 2.50 | 3.75 | E |
| 698 | Smoking-Room Jokebook–Harold Meyers | 1.50 | 3.00 | 4.50 | H |
| 699 | Counterspy Murders–Peter Cheyney | 1.25 | 2.50 | 3.75 | M |
| 700 | Mirror of Your Mind–Joseph Whitney; orig. 1956 | 1.25 | 2.50 | 3.75 | NF |
| 701 | The Anatomy of a Crime–Joseph F. Dinneen | 1.25 | 2.50 | 3.75 | |
| 702 | The Room in the Dragon Inn–Joseph Sheridan LeFanu; aka The Room in the Dragon Volant | 1.25 | 2.50 | 3.75 | A |
| 703 | Armchair in Hell–Henry Kane | 1.25 | 2.50 | 3.75 | M |
| 704 | Whiplash War–Al Cody | 1.25 | 2.50 | 3.75 | W |
| 705 | Hunt the Killer–Day Keene | 1.50 | 3.00 | 4.50 | M |
| 706 | Operation Intrigue–Walter Hermann | 1.25 | 2.50 | 3.75 | |
| 707 | Hatlo Cartoons of 1956–Jimmy Hatlo; 1st ed. 1956 | 2.00 | 4.00 | 6.00 | H |
| 708 | Arrest the Saint!–Leslie Charteris | 1.25 | 2.50 | 3.75 | M |
| 709 | Montana Gunslinger–William Hopson | 1.25 | 2.50 | 3.75 | W |
| 710 | The Wound of Love–R.V. Cassill | 1.25 | 2.50 | 3.75 | |
| 711 | Experiment in Crime–Philip Wylie | 1.25 | 2.50 | 3.75 | |
| 712 | The Man Nobody Saw–Peter Cheyney; c-Kinstler | 1.50 | 3.00 | 4.50 | M |
| 713 | The Outraged Sect–Jada M. Davis; orig. 1956 | 1.25 | 2.50 | 3.75 | E |
| 714 | The Case of the Black Orchids–Rex Stout | 1.50 | 3.00 | 4.50 | M |
| 715 | The Vengeance Trail–Paul Evan Lehman | 1.25 | 2.50 | 3.75 | W |
| 716 | Poirot Investigates–Agatha Christie. Note: Queen's Quorum No. 70 | 1.25 | 2.50 | 3.75 | M |
| 717 | How Rough Can It Get?–Joe Weiss | 1.25 | 2.50 | 3.75 | |
| 718 | Enter the Saint–Leslie Charteris | 1.25 | 2.50 | 3.75 | M |
| 719 | Few Die Well–Sterling Noel | 1.25 | 2.50 | 3.75 | |
| 720 | Give a Man a Gun–John Creasey; aka A Gun for Inspector West | .75 | 1.50 | 2.25 | M |
| 721 | Lilly's Story–Ethel Wilson | 1.25 | 2.50 | 3.75 | |
| 722 | Gang Girl–Wenzell Brown | 4.00 | 8.00 | 12.00 | JD |
| 723 | Yucca City Outlaw–William Hopson; interior illus. by Jack Davis | 2.50 | 5.00 | 7.50 | W |
| 724 | Empty Saddles–Al Cody | 1.25 | 2.50 | 3.75 | W |
| 725 | The Case of the Bludgeoned Teacher–Jim Hollis | 1.25 | 2.50 | 3.75 | M |
| 726 | The Tragedy of Z–Ellery Queen | 1.25 | 2.50 | 3.75 | M |
| 727 | The Smuggled Atom Bomb–Philip Wylie | 1.50 | 3.00 | 4.50 | |
| 728 | Safari to Dishonor–Edmund Schiddel | 1.25 | 2.50 | 3.75 | |
| 729 | The Battle at Apache Pass–Harold Conrad; c-Kinstler | 1.25 | 2.50 | 3.75 | W |
| 730 | The Case of the Hypnotized Virgin–John Roeburt | 1.25 | 2.50 | 3.75 | M |
| 731 | Operation Tokyo–Ted Middleton; c-Kinstler | 1.25 | 2.50 | 3.75 | |
| 732 | The Kansan–Richard Brister | 1.25 | 2.50 | 3.75 | W |
| 733 | Who Killed Sweet Sue?–Henry Kane | 1.50 | 3.00 | 4.50 | M |
| 734 | The Case of the Dark Hero–Peter Cheyney | 1.50 | 3.00 | 4.50 | M |
| 735 | The Hoodlums–John Eagle | 1.25 | 2.50 | 3.75 | |
| 736 | The Yellow Turban–Charlotte Jay | 1.25 | 2.50 | 3.75 | M |
| 737 | And Dream of Evil–Tedd Thomey | 1.25 | 2.50 | 3.75 | |
| 738 | Invitation to Murder–Rex Stout | 1.50 | 3.00 | 4.50 | M |
| 739 | Hired Gun–Archie Joscelyn | 1.25 | 2.50 | 3.75 | W |
| 740 | Park Avenue Girl–Floyd Shaw | 1.25 | 2.50 | 3.75 | |
| 741 | Outlaw Loot–Paul Evan Lehman | 1.25 | 2.50 | 3.75 | W |
| 742 | KKK–Paul E. Walsh; orig. 1956 | 2.50 | 5.00 | 7.50 | |
| 743 | Love Affair–William Russell | 1.25 | 2.50 | 3.75 | |
| 744 | The Saint and the Sizzling Saboteur–Leslie Charteris | 1.25 | 2.50 | 3.75 | M |
| 745 | Martinis and Murder–Henry Kane | 1.25 | 2.50 | 3.75 | M |
| 746 | The Girl with the Frightened Eyes–Lawrence Lariar | 1.25 | 2.50 | 3.75 | |
| 747 | Tawny–Donald Henderson Clarke | 1.25 | 2.50 | 3.75 | E |
| 748 | Gunsight Showdown–Johnston McCulley | 1.25 | 2.50 | 3.75 | W |
| 749 | Violent Maverick–Walt Coburn | 1.25 | 2.50 | 3.75 | W |
| 750 | Southern Daughter–Daniel White | 1.25 | 2.50 | 3.75 | |
| 751 | Murder of the Park Avenue Playgirl–Henry Kane; 1957 | 1.25 | 2.50 | 3.75 | M |

*Avon 540, Avon 666, Avon 707.*

| | | V/Good | Fine | N/Mint | |
|---|---|---|---|---|---|

AVON, *continued*

| | | V/Good | Fine | N/Mint | |
|---|---|---|---|---|---|
| 752 | Death by Moonlight–Michael Innes; aka The Man from the Sea | 1.25 | 2.50 | 3.75 | M |
| 753 | The Passionate Seekers–Peter Matthiessen | 1.25 | 2.50 | 3.75 | |
| 754 | The Long Noose–Lee E. Wells | 1.25 | 2.50 | 3.75 | W |
| 755 | A Spy in the House of Love–Anais Nin | 1.25 | 2.50 | 3.75 | |
| 756 | The Saint–The Brighter Buccaneer– Leslie Charteris. Note: Abridged version of Queen's Quorum No. 84 | 1.25 | 2.50 | 3.75 | M |
| 757 | Inspector Maigret and the Dead Girl– Georges Simenon; c-Kinstler | 2.00 | 4.00 | 6.00 | M |
| 758 | Arizona Dead-shot–Nelson Nye | 1.25 | 2.50 | 3.75 | W |
| 759 | Fighting Buckaroo–Paul Evan Lehman | 1.25 | 2.50 | 3.75 | W |
| 760 | Love of Seven Dolls–Paul Gallico | 1.25 | 2.50 | 3.75 | |
| 761 | Death on the Double–Henry Kane | 1.25 | 2.50 | 3.75 | M |
| 762 | The Hotel Murders–Stewart Sterling | 1.25 | 2.50 | 3.75 | M |
| 763 | Vice Squad Cop–Michael Carey | 1.25 | 2.50 | 3.75 | M |
| 764 | The Dark Street Murders–Peter Cheyney | 1.50 | 3.00 | 4.50 | M |
| 765 | California Gunman–William Colt MacDonald | 1.25 | 2.50 | 3.75 | W |
| 766 | Mr. and Mrs. North and the Poisoned Playboy–Frances Lockridge & Richard Lockridge; aka Death of an Angel | 1.25 | 2.50 | 3.75 | M |
| 767 | The Murder Room–Paul Walsh | 1.25 | 2.50 | 3.75 | M |
| 768 | Sinful Woman–James M. Cain | 1.25 | 2.50 | 3.75 | |
| 769 | The Phantom Pass–William Colt MacDonald | 1.25 | 2.50 | 3.75 | W |
| 770 | Outlaw Fury–Burt Arthur | 1.25 | 2.50 | 3.75 | W |
| 771 | The Saint on the Spanish Main–Leslie Charteris | 1.25 | 2.50 | 3.75 | M |
| 772 | Murder in Manhattan–John Roeburt | 1.25 | 2.50 | 3.75 | M |
| 773 | The Woman and the Prowler–Stuart Friedman | 1.25 | 2.50 | 3.75 | |
| 774 | Gunfight at the O.K. Corral; movie tie-in | 2.00 | 4.00 | 6.00 | W |
| 775 | The Tall T–Elmore Leonard; movie tie-in | 7.50 | 15.00 | 22.50 | W |
| 776 | Sinister Murders–Peter Cheyney | 1.50 | 3.00 | 4.50 | M |
| 777 | Kiss and Kill–Reed McCary; aka Sleep with the Devil | 3.50 | 7.00 | 10.50 | |
| 778 | Tales of Midsummer Passion– anthology | 1.50 | 3.00 | 4.50 | |
| 779 | Gunsmoke Vengeance–Johnston McCulley; aka South of the Pass; c-Kinstler | 1.50 | 3.00 | 4.50 | W |
| 780 | The Lonely Man–Robert Turner; movie tie-in | 2.00 | 4.00 | 6.00 | W |
| 781 | The Calypso Murders–P.J. Mulholland. Note: Same cover as Avon No. 506 | 1.50 | 3.00 | 4.50 | M |
| 782 | Gun Feud at Stampede Valley–Samuel A. Peeples | 1.25 | 2.50 | 3.75 | W |
| 783 | Hot Rod Gang Rumble–Meyer Dolinsky | 5.00 | 10.00 | 15.00 | JD |
| 784 | Murder in Las Vegas–Jack Waer | 1.25 | 2.50 | 3.75 | M |
| 785 | Gun Play at the X-Bar-X–Burt Arthur | 1.25 | 2.50 | 3.75 | W |
| 786 | Murder, My Love–Edward Atiyah | 1.25 | 2.50 | 3.75 | M |
| 787 | The Case of the Murdered Model– Thomas B. Dewey | .75 | 1.50 | 2.25 | M |
| 788 | Six-gun Sawbones–Archie Joscelyn | 1.25 | 2.50 | 3.75 | W |
| 789 | More They'll Do It Every Time–Jimmy Hatlo; 1st ed. 1957 | 2.00 | 4.00 | 6.00 | H |
| 790 | My Business Is Murder–Henry Kane; c-Maguire | 1.25 | 2.50 | 3.75 | M |
| 791 | Texas Revenge–Archie Joscelyn; c-Kinstler | 1.25 | 2.50 | 3.75 | W |
| 792 | Murder in Lima–Robert A. Levey | 1.25 | 2.50 | 3.75 | M |
| 793 | The Moving Finger–Agatha Christie | 1.25 | 2.50 | 3.75 | M |
| 794 | The Ripper Murders–Maurice Proctor | 1.25 | 2.50 | 3.75 | M |
| 795 | Blood on the Saddle–Johnston McCulley | 1.25 | 2.50 | 3.75 | W |
| 796 | A Mask for Murder–Henry Kane | 1.25 | 2.50 | 3.75 | M |
| 797 | Cocktails and the Killer–Peter Cheyney | 1.25 | 2.50 | 3.75 | M |
| 798 | Outlaw–Archie Joscelyn; 1958 | 1.25 | 2.50 | 3.75 | W |
| 799 | Powdersmoke Range–William Colt MacDonald | 1.25 | 2.50 | 3.75 | W |
| 800 | Case of the Murdered Redhead– Frances Lockridge & Richard Lockridge | 1.25 | 2.50 | 3.75 | M |
| 801 | Night Cry–William L. Stuart | 1.25 | 2.50 | 3.75 | M |

Avon 775, Avon 783, Avon 830.

| | | V/Good | Fine | N/Mint | |
|---|---|---|---|---|---|
| 802 | Murder in Baracoa–Paul Walsh | 1.25 | 2.50 | 3.75 | M |
| 803 | Featuring the Saint–Leslie Charteris | 1.25 | 2.50 | 3.75 | M |
| 804 | Flesh and Fire–Georges Arnaud | 1.25 | 2.50 | 3.75 | |
| 805 | The Tough Texan–Paul Evan Lehman | 1.25 | 2.50 | 3.75 | W |
| 806 | Bandit in Black–Paul Evan Lehman | 1.25 | 2.50 | 3.75 | W |
| 807 | Wine, Women and Murder–John Roeburt | 1.25 | 2.50 | 3.75 | M |
| 808 | A Taste for Murder–H.F. Heard | 1.25 | 2.50 | 3.75 | M |
| 809 | The Vice Net–Michael Carey | 1.25 | 2.50 | 3.75 | M |
| 810 | Montana Helltown–Al Cody | 1.25 | 2.50 | 3.75 | W |
| 811 | Let Me Kill You, Sweetheart–Fletcher Flora | 1.25 | 2.50 | 3.75 | M |
| 812 | Bloody Wyoming–Al Cody | 1.25 | 2.50 | 3.75 | W |
| 813 | Fighting Kid from Texas–Archie Joscelyn | 1.25 | 2.50 | 3.75 | W |
| 814 | It's a Sin to Kill–Day Keene; orig. 1958 | 1.50 | 3.00 | 4.50 | M |
| 815 | Bachelor's Guide to the Opposite Sex– Max Lieg & Georges Pichard | 1.50 | 3.00 | 4.50 | H |
| 816 | Thunderbolt Range–Paul Evan Lehman; aka The Sheep Killers | 1.25 | 2.50 | 3.75 | W |
| 817 | The Doctor's Woman–H.P. Koenig | 1.25 | 2.50 | 3.75 | |
| 818 | Alias the Saint–Leslie Charteris | .75 | 1.50 | 2.25 | W |
| 819 | Cheyenne Kid–Archie Joscelyn | 1.25 | 2.50 | 3.75 | W |
| 820 | Stampede Canyon–Robert J. Hogan | 1.25 | 2.50 | 3.75 | W |
| 821 | Guns Blaze on Spiderweb Range–Walt Coburn | 1.25 | 2.50 | 3.75 | W |
| 822 | Montana Dead-Shot–Chuck Martin | 1.25 | 2.50 | 3.75 | W |
| 823 | Cry Killer!–Kenneth Fearing | .75 | 1.50 | 2.25 | M |
| 824 | Notched Guns–William Hopson | 1.25 | 2.50 | 3.75 | W |
| 825 | Gun-Whipped!–Paul Evan Lehman; orig. 1958 | 1.25 | 2.50 | 3.75 | W |
| 826 | Another New Jimmy Hatlo Book– Jimmy Hatlo; 1st ed. 1958 | 2.00 | 4.00 | 6.00 | H |
| 827 | The Saint on Guard–Leslie Charteris | .75 | 1.50 | 2.25 | M |
| 828 | Tall in the Saddle–Chuck Martin; c-Abbett | 1.25 | 2.50 | 3.75 | W |
| 829 | Hell Range in Texas–J.E. Grinstead | 1.25 | 2.50 | 3.75 | W |
| 830 | The Bitch–Gil Brewer | 1.25 | 2.50 | 3.75 | |
| 831 | Renegade Marshal–Paul Evan Lehman; aka Devil's Doorstep; c-Abbett | 1.25 | 2.50 | 3.75 | W |
| 832 | Disaster Trail–Al Cody | 1.25 | 2.50 | 3.75 | W |
| 833 | The Wolf Streak–Richard Brister | 1.25 | 2.50 | 3.75 | W |
| 834 | Concerning the Saint–Leslie Charteris | .75 | 1.50 | 2.25 | M |
| 835 | Too Hot to Kill–Stewart Sterling | 1.25 | 2.50 | 3.75 | M |
| 836 | Unfaithful–John Baxter. Note: Basically the same cover as Avon 114 | 1.25 | 2.50 | 3.75 | |
| 837 | Long Ride to Abilene–William Hopson | 1.25 | 2.50 | 3.75 | W |
| 838 | The Dead Ride Hard–Lynn Westland | 1.25 | 2.50 | 3.75 | W |
| 839 | Leave Her to Hell!–Fletcher Flora | .75 | 1.50 | 2.25 | |
| 841 | Day of Vengeance–Chuck Martin | .75 | 1.50 | 2.25 | W |
| 842 | Wyoming Ambush–Al Cody | .75 | 1.50 | 2.25 | W |
| 843 | Gunsmoke at Buffalo Basin–Paul Evan Lehman; c-Kinstler | 1.25 | 2.50 | 3.75 | W |
| 844 | Deadly Draw–Lee Floren | .75 | 1.50 | 2.25 | W |
| 845 | The Man from the Badlands–Paul Evan Lehman | 1.25 | 2.50 | 3.75 | W |
| 846 | Born Reckless–Milton Rogers | .75 | 1.50 | 2.25 | |
| 847 | My Name Is Violence–John D. Matthews & Jeffrey Roche | .75 | 1.50 | 2.25 | |
| 848 | The Saint Cleans Up–Leslie Charteris | .75 | 1.50 | 2.25 | M |
| 849 | It Happened at Thunder River–Bliss Lomax (H.S. Drago) | 1.25 | 2.50 | 3.75 | W |

**AVON,** *continued*

| | | V/Good | Fine | N/Mint | |
|---|---|---|---|---|---|
| 850 | The Manhunter–Paul Evan Lehman; aka Law of the Forty-five | .75 | 1.50 | 2.25 | W |
| 851 | Ship Ahoy | 1.50 | 3.00 | 4.50 | H |
| 852 | Fast Gun–Walt Coburn | .75 | 1.50 | 2.25 | W |
| 853 | French Postcards | 1.50 | 3.00 | 4.50 | H |
| 854 | Make Mine Vengeance–Robert Colby | .75 | 1.50 | 2.25 | |
| 855 | Then Came Mulvane–William Heuman | .75 | 1.50 | 2.25 | W |
| 856 | Bullet Law–Johnston McCulley | 1.25 | 2.50 | 3.75 | W |
| 857 | The Newest Jimmy Hatlo Cartoon Book–Jimmy Hatlo; 1st ed. 1959 | 2.00 | 4.00 | 6.00 | H |
| 858 | Branded–Walt Coburn | .75 | 1.50 | 2.25 | W |
| 859 | More All about Girls | 1.50 | 3.00 | 4.50 | H |
| 860 | Caveman Cartoons–Harold Meyers | 1.50 | 3.00 | 4.50 | H |
| 861 | Six Bullets Left–Barry Cord | .75 | 1.50 | 2.25 | W |
| 862 | Renegade Lawman–Gordon D. Shirreffs | .75 | 1.50 | 2.25 | W |
| 863 | Bloody Kansas–Chuck Martin | .75 | 1.50 | 2.25 | W |
| 864 | The Deadly Game–Norman Daniels; c-Abbett | 1.25 | 2.50 | 3.75 | M |
| 865 | The Fighting Kid from Eldorado– William Colt MacDonald; 1960 | 1.25 | 2.50 | 3.75 | W |
| 866 | Angel–Gil Brewer | 1.50 | 3.00 | 4.50 | M |
| 867 | Killer Behind a Badge–Will Cook | 1.25 | 2.50 | 3.75 | W |
| 868 | Lady for Sale–Norman A. Daniels; c-Abbett | 1.25 | 2.50 | 3.75 | M |
| 870 | Southern Daughter–Daniel White | 1.25 | 2.50 | 3.75 | E |
| 872 | Long Run–Nelson Nye; c-Abbett | 1.25 | 2.50 | 3.75 | W |
| 874 | Sinners Wild–Mark Reed | 1.25 | 2.50 | 3.75 | |
| 875 | Vegas, Gunman Marshall–William Hopson; aka Silver Gulch | 1.25 | 2.50 | 3.75 | W |
| 876 | Some Die Running–Norman A. Daniels | 1.25 | 2.50 | 3.75 | M |
| 878 | Guns to the Sunset–Dean Owen, 1960 | 1.25 | 2.50 | 3.75 | W |
| 1001 | Jew Suss–Lion Feuchtwanger; 1951; interior illus-Kinstler | 5.00 | 10.00 | 15.00 | E |
| 1002 | The Avon All-American Fiction Reader; 1951. Note: This volume includes 1st ed. publication of James M. Cain's Root of His Evil | 7.50 | 15.00 | 22.50 | |

# AVON ANNUAL
## Avon Book Company
### Digest Size

| | | V/Good | Fine | N/Mint |
|---|---|---|---|---|
| nn(1) | 18 Great Stories of Today–ed. Whit Burnett; 1944 | 2.50 | 5.00 | 7.50 |
| nn(2) | 18 Great Modern Stories–anthology; 1945 | 3.00 | 6.00 | 9.00 |
| nn(3) | 15 Great Stories of Today–anthology; 1946 | 3.00 | 6.00 | 9.00 |
| nn(4) | 11 Great Modern Stories–anthology; 1947 | 2.50 | 5.00 | 7.50 |

# AVON BARD
## Avon Publications, Inc./Avon Book Division–Hearst Corporation

| | | V/Good | Fine | N/Mint | |
|---|---|---|---|---|---|
| Bard 1 | (HI) The Rubaiyat of Omar Khayyam; 1955 | .50 | 1.00 | 1.50 | |
| Bard 2 | The Meaning and Psychology of Dreams–Wilheim Stekel | .50 | 1.00 | 1.50 | NF |
| Bard 3 | Anyone Can Have a Great Vocabulary– S.L. Stephenson | .50 | 1.00 | 1.50 | NF |
| Bard 4 | Favorite Stories–W. Somerset Maugham | .50 | 1.00 | 1.50 | |
| Bard 5 | (T05) My Lord What a Morning– Marian Anderson; 1958 | .50 | 1.00 | 1.50 | |
| Bard 6 | (T06) You and the Atom–Gerald Wendt | .50 | 1.00 | 1.50 | NF |
| Bard 7 | (T07) My Religion–Helen Keller | .50 | 1.00 | 1.50 | NF |
| Bard 8 | (T8) A Shropshire Lad–A.E. Housman | .50 | 1.00 | 1.50 | |
| Bard 9 | (T09) Albert Einstein–Arthur Beckhard | .50 | 1.00 | 1.50 | B |
| Bard 10 | Tchaikovsky–Edwin Evans | .50 | 1.00 | 1.50 | B |
| Bard 11 | (T11) Sonnets from the Portuguese– Elizabeth Barrett Browning | .50 | 1.00 | 1.50 | |

| | | V/Good | Fine | N/Mint | |
|---|---|---|---|---|---|
| Bard 12 | (T012) America Challenged–Justice William O. Douglas | .50 | 1.00 | 1.50 | NF |
| Bard 13 | (G13) Bertrand Russell Speaks His Mind–Bertrand Russell | .50 | 1.00 | 1.50 | |

# AVON BEDSIDE NOVELS
## Avon Publishing Company, Inc.
### Digest Size

| | | V/Good | Fine | N/Mint | |
|---|---|---|---|---|---|
| 1 | The Rites of Love–Jack Woodford | 10.00 | 20.00 | 30.00 | E |
| 2 | The Hard-boiled Virgin–Jack Woodford; 1950 | 10.00 | 20.00 | 30.00 | E |
| 3 | Queer Patterns–Lilyan Brock | 10.00 | 20.00 | 30.00 | E |
| 4 | Bedroom Eyes–Maurice Dekobra | 10.00 | 20.00 | 30.00 | E |
| 5 | Male and Female–Jack Woodford | 10.00 | 20.00 | 30.00 | E |
| 6 | The Passionate Princess–Jack Woodford; aka Proxy Princess | 10.00 | 20.00 | 30.00 | E |
| 7 | Millie–Donald Henderson Clarke | 10.00 | 20.00 | 30.00 | E |

# AVON BOOK DIVIDEND
## Avon Publishing Company, Inc.
### Digest Size

| | | V/Good | Fine | N/Mint | |
|---|---|---|---|---|---|
| 1 | The Abortive Hussy–Jack Woodford | 10.00 | 20.00 | 30.00 | E |
| 2 | Star Lust–Jack Hanley | 10.00 | 20.00 | 30.00 | E |
| 3 | New York Madness–Maxwell Bodenheim | 10.00 | 20.00 | 30.00 | E |
| 4 | Grounds for Divorce–Jack Woodford | 10.00 | 20.00 | 30.00 | E |
| 5 | Her Private Passions–Marty Holland | 10.00 | 20.00 | 30.00 | E |
| 6 | Teach Me to Love–Jack Woodford | 10.00 | 20.00 | 30.00 | E |
| 7 | Tropical Passions–anthology. Note: Same cover as Avon No. 255 and basically the same as Avon Modern Short Story Monthly No. 44 | 10.00 | 20.00 | 30.00 | E |

# AVON CS-SERIES
## Avon Book Company

| | | V/Good | Fine | N/Mint | |
|---|---|---|---|---|---|
| CS-2 | On Contemporary Literature–R. Kostelanetz; 1964 | .50 | 1.00 | 1.50 | NF |
| CS-3 | The Incas–Garcilaso de la Vega; 1964 | .50 | 1.00 | 1.50 | NF |

# AVON DETECTIVE MYSTERIES
## Avon Detective–Mysteries, Inc.
### Digest Size

| | | V/Good | Fine | N/Mint | |
|---|---|---|---|---|---|
| 1 | Includes Woolrich, Starrett, Christie, others; 1947 | 7.50 | 15.00 | 22.50 | M |
| 2 | Includes Carter Dickson, Eberhart, others; 1947. Note: Same cover as Avon No. 104 and Murder Mystery Monthly No. 13 | 7.50 | 15.00 | 22.50 | M |

*Avon (unlisted), Avon Bard 7, Avon F143.*

**AVON DETECTIVE MYSTERIES,** *continued*

| | | V/Good | Fine | N/Mint | |
|---|---|---|---|---|---|
| 3 | Includes Gruber, Rohmer, Brown, others; 1947. Note: Partially the same cover as Avon No. 122 and the pulp Private Detective Stories, October 1944 | 7.50 | 15.00 | 22.50 | M |

## AVON D/YD-SERIES
### Avon Book Company

| | | V/Good | Fine | N/Mint | |
|---|---|---|---|---|---|
| D1 | Russia at War–Alexander Werth | .50 | 1.00 | 1.50 | NF |
| D2 | The Rise and Fall of Stalin–Robert Payne; 1966 | .50 | 1.00 | 1.50 | NF |
| D3 | The Life and Death of Lenin–Robert Payne; 1967 | .50 | 1.00 | 1.50 | NF |
| D4 | The Interpretation of Dreams–Sigmund Freud; 1967 | .50 | 1.00 | 1.50 | NF |
| D5 | Mussolini: A Study in Power– I. Kirkpatrick; 1968 | .50 | 1.00 | 1.50 | NF |
| D6 | The Conservative Mind–Russell Kirk; 1968 | .50 | 1.00 | 1.50 | NF |
| D7 | Writers on the Left–Daniel Aaron | .50 | 1.00 | 1.50 | |
| D8 | Human Use of Human Beings: Cybernetics and Society–Norbert Wiener | .50 | 1.00 | 1.50 | NF |
| D9 | Great Scenes from the World Theater– ed. James L. Steffenson, Jr | .50 | 1.00 | 1.50 | |
| D10 | Interviews with Film Directors–ed. Andrew Sarris; 1969 | .50 | 1.00 | 1.50 | NF |
| D11 | The Empty Space–Peter Brook; 1969 | .50 | 1.00 | 1.50 | |
| YD13 | New Black Playwrights–ed. William Couch, Jr; 1970 | .50 | 1.00 | 1.50 | |

## AVON FANTASY NOVELS
### Avon Publishing Company

**Note: Coblentz's Into Plutonian Depths and Farley's Earthman on Venus were planned as No. 3 and No. 4 of the series but instead became No. 281 and No. 285 of the regular Avon series.**

| | | V/Good | Fine | N/Mint | |
|---|---|---|---|---|---|
| 1 | Princess of the Atom–Ray Cummings; 1950 | 7.50 | 15.00 | 22.50 | SF |
| 2 | The Green Girl–Jack Williamson; 1950 | 15.00 | 30.00 | 45.00 | SF |

## AVON F-SERIES
### Avon Book Company

| | | V/Good | Fine | N/Mint | |
|---|---|---|---|---|---|
| F100 | The Absence of a Cello–Ira Wallach; 1961 | .50 | 1.00 | 1.50 | H |
| F101 | This Demi-paradise, a Westchester Diary–Margaret Halsey | .50 | 1.00 | 1.50 | |
| F102 | By the Sea, By the Sea–George Sumner Albee | .50 | 1.00 | 1.50 | |
| F103 | Poirot Loses a Client–Agatha Christie | .75 | 1.50 | 2.25 | M |
| F104 | Cocktail Time–P.G. Wodehouse | .75 | 1.50 | 2.25 | H |
| F105 | The Self-starting Wheel–William Murry | .50 | 1.00 | 1.50 | |
| F106 | Yours Truly, Hugh Downs–Hugh Downs | .50 | 1.00 | 1.50 | B |
| F107 | Be Not Angry–William Michelfelder | .50 | 1.00 | 1.50 | |
| F108 | Man High– Lt. David G. Simons & Don A. Schanache | .50 | 1.00 | 1.50 | NF |
| F109 | Gentlemen Prefer Blondes–Anita Loos | .50 | 1.00 | 1.50 | |
| F110 | Claudine Married–Sidonie Colette | .50 | 1.00 | 1.50 | |
| F111 | Whose Body?–Dorothy L. Sayers | .75 | 1.50 | 2.25 | M |
| F112 | Empire of Evil–Sterling Noel; 1961 | .50 | 1.00 | 1.50 | |
| F113 | Scientists behind the Inventors–Roger Burlingame | .50 | 1.00 | 1.50 | NF |
| F114 | Deadly Duo–Margery Allingham; 1961 | .50 | 1.00 | 1.50 | M |
| F115 | The Little Friar–Hal Sherman | .50 | 1.00 | 1.50 | H |
| F116 | Nevada–Burt Arthur; 1962 | .75 | 1.50 | 2.25 | W |
| F117 | Crossword Carnival–anon. | 1.50 | 3.00 | 4.50 | NF |
| F118 | Little Fuzzy–H. Beam Piper | 2.00 | 4.00 | 6.00 | SF |
| F119 | Ferguson's Ferry–Noel Loomis | .75 | 1.50 | 2.25 | W |
| F120 | Boot Hill Silver–E.E. Halleran | .75 | 1.50 | 2.25 | W |

| | | V/Good | Fine | N/Mint | |
|---|---|---|---|---|---|
| F121 | A Crime for Mothers and Others–ed. Alfred Hitchcock | 1.00 | 2.00 | 3.00 | M |
| F122 | The Star Dwellers–James Blish; 1962 | 1.00 | 2.00 | 3.00 | SF |
| F123 | The Veils of Salome–Jay Scotland (John Jakes) | 1.50 | 3.00 | 4.50 | A |
| F124 | Thief River–Nelson Nye | .75 | 1.50 | 2.25 | W |
| F125 | The Overbury Affair–Miriam Allen de Ford | .50 | 1.00 | 1.50 | |
| F126 | Traitor Guns–Philip Ketchum | .75 | 1.50 | 2.25 | W |
| F127 | Red River Road–Allan K. Echols | .75 | 1.50 | 2.25 | W |
| F128 | The Scaffold at Hangman's Creek– Lewis B. Patten | .75 | 1.50 | 2.25 | W |
| F129 | Nurse March–William Neubauer | .50 | 1.00 | 1.50 | R |
| F130 | Crossword Puzzle Parade– anon. | 1.50 | 3.00 | 4.50 | NF |
| F131 | Rebel in Yankee Blue–Ray Hogan | .75 | 1.50 | 2.25 | W |
| F132 | Return of the Texan–Burt Arthur | .75 | 1.50 | 2.25 | W |
| F133 | Young Doctor Kildare–Max Brand | .50 | 1.00 | 1.50 | R |
| F134 | Untimely Death–Cyril Hare; aka He Should Have Died Hereafter | .50 | 1.00 | 1.50 | M |
| F135 | Ride with the Wild Wind–C. William Harrison | .75 | 1.50 | 2.25 | W |
| F137 | Longrider–L.L. Foreman | .75 | 1.50 | 2.25 | W |
| F138 | Ride with a Dark Moon–Kenneth Fowler | .50 | 1.00 | 1.50 | M |
| F139 | The Solid Gold Madonna–James Stark | .50 | 1.00 | 1.50 | M |
| F140 | The Echoing Wave–Dorothy Giberson | .50 | 1.00 | 1.50 | |
| F141 | Watching Out for Dulie–David Westheimer | .50 | 1.00 | 1.50 | |
| F142 | The Miracle of Doctor MacLennon– Maxwell Maltz, MD | .50 | 1.00 | 1.50 | R |
| F143 | Crossword Puzzle Cornucopia–ed. C. Maynard Nichols | 1.50 | 3.00 | 4.50 | NF |
| F144 | Mulvane on the Prod–William Heuman | .50 | 1.00 | 1.50 | W |
| F145 | Paula Wayne, Wasteland Doctor–Isabel Stewart Way | .50 | 1.00 | 1.50 | R |
| F146 | 69 Babylon Park–Harry Whittington | 1.50 | 3.00 | 4.50 | |
| F147 | Incurably Sick–anon. | 1.50 | 3.00 | 4.50 | H |
| F148 | The Bad Man–Joseph Wayne | .50 | 1.00 | 1.50 | W |
| F149 | Three-cornered War–Richard Wormser | .50 | 1.00 | 1.50 | W |
| F150 | No Mother to Guide Her–Anita Loos | .50 | 1.00 | 1.50 | |
| F151 | The Way of a Texan–Walt Coburn | .75 | 1.50 | 2.25 | W |
| F152 | Nurse Greer–Joan Harrison | .50 | 1.00 | 1.50 | R |
| F153 | Strangers–Albert Memmi; c-Abbett | .75 | 1.50 | 2.25 | E |
| F154 | They Won Their Spurs–ed. Nelson Nye | 1.00 | 2.00 | 3.00 | W |
| F155 | Meredith Blake, MD–Peggy Gaddis | .50 | 1.00 | 1.50 | R |
| F156 | The Five Faces of Murder–Jay Flynn | .50 | 1.00 | 1.50 | M |
| F157 | Prairie Teacher–Marion Marsh Brown | .50 | 1.00 | 1.50 | R |
| F158 | Alley Whoops!–Hal Sherman | .75 | 1.50 | 2.25 | H |
| F159 | Gunsmoke Vengeance–Johnston McCulley; aka South of the Pass | .75 | 1.50 | 2.25 | W |
| F160 | Nurse with Wings–Georgia Craig | .50 | 1.00 | 1.50 | R |
| F161 | Straight from Boothill–William Hopson | .75 | 1.50 | 2.25 | W |
| F162 | No Land Is Free–Joseph Chadwick | .50 | 1.00 | 1.50 | W |
| F163 | The Gun-shy Kid–Barry Cord; 1963 | .75 | 1.50 | 2.25 | W |
| F164 | Reach for Tomorrow–Georgia Craig; 1962 | .50 | 1.00 | 1.50 | R |
| F165 | Death of a Hooker–Henry Kane; 1963 | .50 | 1.00 | 1.50 | M |
| F166 | Happiness Hill–Florence Stuart; 1963 | .50 | 1.00 | 1.50 | R |
| F167 | Boothill Gospel–Chuck Martin | .50 | 1.00 | 1.50 | W |
| F168 | Nurse in Love–Isabel Stewart Way | .50 | 1.00 | 1.50 | R |
| F169 | Gunnison's Empire–James Keene | .50 | 1.00 | 1.50 | W |
| F170 | Ever Happen to You?–Bud Blake | .75 | 1.50 | 2.25 | H |
| F171 | Throw Back the Little Ones–Pat Colombo | .50 | 1.00 | 1.50 | M |
| F172 | New England Nurse–Adelaide Humphries | .50 | 1.00 | 1.50 | R |
| F173 | Gunsmoke in Nevada–Burt Arthur | .75 | 1.50 | 2.25 | W |
| F174 | Killer's Trail–Giles A. Lutz | .75 | 1.50 | 2.25 | W |
| F175 | Prison Nurse–William Neubauer | .50 | 1.00 | 1.50 | R |
| F176 | Vice-Squad Cop–Michael Carey | .50 | 1.00 | 1.50 | |
| F177 | Badman's Roost–Robert E. Trevathan | .75 | 1.50 | 2.25 | W |
| F178 | Stranger in Apache Basin–Ray Hogan | .75 | 1.50 | 2.25 | W |
| F179 | Las Vegas Nurse–Jane L. Sears | .50 | 1.00 | 1.50 | R |
| F180 | Television Nurse–Jane L. Sears | .50 | 1.00 | 1.50 | R |
| F181 | Invitation to a Hanging–Walt Coburn | .75 | 1.50 | 2.25 | W |
| F182 | Small Town Nurse–Emily Thorne; aka Enter Nurse Marian | .50 | 1.00 | 1.50 | R |
| F183 | A Career for Lynn–Nina Wilcox Putnam; aka Lynn, Cover Girl | .50 | 1.00 | 1.50 | R |
| F184 | Kennedy's Gold–Michael Bonner | .50 | 1.00 | 1.50 | |
| F185 | The Slaughter at Broken Bow–Gordon D. Shirreffs | .75 | 1.50 | 2.25 | W |

### AVON F-SERIES, *continued*

| | | V/Good | Fine | N/Mint | |
|---|---|---|---|---|---|
| F186 | Night Nurse–Fern Shepard | .50 | 1.00 | 1.50 | R |
| F187 | Requiem for a Gun–Burt Arthur | .75 | 1.50 | 2.25 | W |
| F188 | Two Guns North–Lee Floren | .75 | 1.50 | 2.25 | W |
| F189 | The Hard Homesteader–Clayton Fox | .75 | 1.50 | 2.25 | W |
| F190 | Washington Nurse–Tracy Adams | .50 | 1.00 | 1.50 | R |
| F191 | Buffalo River–John Raymond | .75 | 1.50 | 2.25 | W |
| F192 | Where There's A Will–Rex Stout; 1963 | .75 | 1.50 | 2.25 | M |
| F194 | The Girl Next Door–Peggy Gaddis | .50 | 1.00 | 1.50 | R |
| F197 | West Coast Nurse–Della Field | .50 | 1.00 | 1.50 | R |
| F198 | The Wild One–Bonnie Golightly | 1.50 | 3.00 | 4.50 | |
| F199 | Reach for the Sky–George Byram | .50 | 1.00 | 1.50 | |
| F200 | The Man behind the Star–Archie Joscelyn | .75 | 1.50 | 2.25 | W |
| F201 | The Pick of the Roundup–ed. Stephen Payne | 1.00 | 2.00 | 3.00 | W |
| F202 | Return to Deadman's–Al Cody | .75 | 1.50 | 2.25 | W |
| F203 | My Son the Medicine Man–Dana Fradon | .75 | 1.50 | 2.25 | H |
| F204 | Land of Promises–Joseph Wayne | .75 | 1.50 | 2.25 | W |
| F205 | Night Raider–Ray Hogan | .75 | 1.50 | 2.25 | W |
| F206 | Rodeo Clown–Stanley Noyes; aka No Flowers for a Clown | .50 | 1.00 | 1.50 | |
| F207 | Dr. Jenny of Timberland–Isabel Stewart Way | .50 | 1.00 | 1.50 | R |
| F208 | The Kansan–Richard Brister | .75 | 1.50 | 2.25 | W |
| F209 | The Long Cold Winter–Giles A. Lutz | .75 | 1.50 | 2.25 | W |
| F210 | The Hunter–Richard Ferber | .50 | 1.00 | 1.50 | |
| F211 | The Servant–Robin Maugham | | | | |
| F212 | Publicity Girl–Robin McKown | .50 | 1.00 | 1.50 | R |
| F213 | Ride A Crooked Mile–Burt Arthur & Budd Arthur | .50 | 1.00 | 1.50 | W |
| F216 | Harbor Nurse–Arlene J. Fitzgerald | .50 | 1.00 | 1.50 | R |
| F217 | Ride for Vengeance–Lewis Patten | .75 | 1.50 | 2.25 | W |
| F219 | Cross the Red Creek–Harry Whittington; 1964 | 1.50 | 3.00 | 4.50 | W |
| F220 | Deadman Junction–Joseph Wayne | .75 | 1.50 | 2.25 | W |
| F222 | Renegade Brand–Richard Brister | .75 | 1.50 | 2.25 | W |
| F223 | The Latchy Gun–Dean Owen | .75 | 1.50 | 2.25 | W |
| F225 | Dear President Johnson–Bill Adler & Charles Schulz; 1965 | 1.50 | 3.00 | 4.50 | H |
| F226 | An Avon Triple Western–Walt Coburn | 1.00 | 2.00 | 3.00 | W |
| F227 | Lead Reckoning–Ray Hogan | .75 | 1.50 | 2.25 | W |
| F228 | Red Rock Rifle–Dean Owen | .75 | 1.50 | 2.25 | W |
| F229 | Action at Truxton–Burt Arthur & Budd Arthur; 1966 | .75 | 1.50 | 2.25 | W |
| F230 | The Stranger–Burt Arthur & Budd Arthur | .75 | 1.50 | 2.25 | W |
| F231 | Powder Smoke–Ernest Haycox | 1.00 | 2.00 | 3.00 | W |
| F232 | Hollywood Nurse–Alice Brennan | .50 | 1.00 | 1.50 | R |
| F233 | Farewell to Texas–L.L. Foreman | .75 | 1.50 | 2.25 | W |
| F234 | The Dangerous Days of Kiowa Jones–Clifton Adams | .75 | 1.50 | 2.25 | W |
| F235 | Law Killer–Richard Brister | .75 | 1.50 | 2.25 | W |
| F236 | Gun Feud at Stampede Valley–Samuel A. Peeples | 1.00 | 2.00 | 3.00 | W |
| F237 | The Gunslinger–Burt Arthur | .75 | 1.50 | 2.25 | W |
| F238 | The Golden Land–Giles A. Lutz | .75 | 1.50 | 2.25 | W |
| F239 | Gunsmoke in Nevada–Burt Arthur | .75 | 1.50 | 2.25 | W |
| F240 | Vietnam Nurse–Della Field | .50 | 1.00 | 1.50 | R |
| F241 | Stir Up the Dust–William Colt MacDonald; 1966 | .75 | 1.50 | 2.25 | W |
| F242 | Action at Arcanum–William Colt MacDonald; 1966 | .75 | 1.50 | 2.25 | W |
| F244 | The Iron Marshall–Steven Lawrence; 1967 | .75 | 1.50 | 2.25 | W |
| F245 | Nevada–Burt Arthur; 1967 | .75 | 1.50 | 2.25 | W |

# AVON FANTASY READER

## Avon Book Company/Avon Novels, Inc.

### Digest Size

| | | V/Good | Fine | N/Mint | |
|---|---|---|---|---|---|
| 1 | Includes Leinster, Derleth, Merritt, Smith, others; 1947 | 5.00 | 10.00 | 15.00 | SF |
| 2 | Includes Pratt, Howard, Endore, Keller; 1947 | 3.00 | 6.00 | 9.00 | SF |
| 3 | Includes Merritt, Lovecraft, Moore, Bradbury, others; 1947 | 4.50 | 9.00 | 13.50 | SF |

| | | V/Good | Fine | N/Mint | |
|---|---|---|---|---|---|
| 4 | Includes Miller, Bradbury, Smith, Van Vogt, others; 1947 | 3.00 | 6.00 | 9.00 | SF |
| 5 | Includes Moore, Bloch, Jacobi, Kornbluth; 1947 | 3.00 | 6.00 | 9.00 | SF |
| 6 | Includes Lovecraft, Merritt, Hamilton, McClusky, others; 1948 | 4.50 | 9.00 | 13.50 | SF |
| 7 | Includes Moore, Rohmer, Howard, Merritt, others; 1948 | 4.50 | 9.00 | 13.50 | SF |
| 8 | Includes Howard, Bradbury, Lovecraft, Bierce, others; 1948 | 4.50 | 9.00 | 13.50 | SF |
| 9 | Includes Smith, Leiber, Kline, Bloch, others; 1949 | 3.00 | 6.00 | 9.00 | SF |
| 10 | Includes Howard, Lovecraft, Breuer, Wollheim, others; 1949 | 3.00 | 6.00 | 9.00 | SF |
| 11 | Includes Quinn, Bond, Stribling, Bradbury, others; 1949 | 3.00 | 6.00 | 9.00 | SF |
| 12 | Includes Howard, Smith, Rohmer, Wellman, others; 1949 | 3.00 | 6.00 | 9.00 | SF |
| 13 | Includes Long, Cummings, Derleth, Wandrel, others; 1950 | 3.00 | 6.00 | 9.00 | SF |
| 14 | Includes Howard, Bradbury, Cummings, Keller, others; 1950; c-Wood | 4.50 | 9.00 | 13.50 | SF |
| 15 | Includes Weinbaum, Smith, Kornbluth, Miller, others; 1951 | 3.00 | 6.00 | 9.00 | SF |
| 16 | Includes Bloch, Shiel, Wandrei, Long, others; 1951 | 3.00 | 6.00 | 9.00 | SF |
| 17 | Includes Bradbury, Lovecraft, Price, Chesterton, others; 1951 | 4.50 | 9.00 | 13.50 | SF |
| 18 | Includes Howard, Hodgson, Blackwood, Clark, others; 1952 | 6.00 | 12.00 | 18.00 | SF |

# AVON G-SERIES

## Avon Publishing Company, Inc.

**Note: The first two books of this series do not have the "G" prefix.**

| | | V/Good | Fine | N/Mint | |
|---|---|---|---|---|---|
| (G)1001 | Jew Suss–Lion Feuchtwanger; 1951; interior illus. by Kinstler | 5.00 | 10.00 | 15.00 | E |
| (G)1002 | The Avon All-American Fiction Reader; 1951. Note: This volume includes 1st ed. publication of James M. Cain's Root of His Evil | 7.50 | 15.00 | 22.50 | |
| G1003 | The Collected Works of Pierre Louys; 1951 | 6.00 | 12.00 | 18.00 | E |
| G1004 | Giant Mystery Reader | 7.50 | 15.00 | 22.50 | M |
| G1005 | Geraldine Bradshaw–Calder Willingham | 4.50 | 9.00 | 13.50 | E |
| G1006 | Men at War–Ernest Hemingway; 1952 | 4.50 | 9.00 | 13.50 | A |
| G1007 | Avon Webster English Dictionary | 4.50 | 9.00 | 13.50 | NF |
| G1008 | Temptation–John Pen | 7.50 | 15.00 | 22.50 | E |
| G1009 | The Big Brokers–Irving Shulman; 1953 | 4.50 | 9.00 | 13.50 | |
| G1010 | Out of This World to Forbidden Tibet–Lowell Thomas; 1954 | 1.00 | 2.00 | 3.00 | NF |
| G1011 | Master of the World–Cothburn O'Neal | 1.00 | 2.00 | 3.00 | A |
| G1012 | Send Me Down–Henry Steig | 1.00 | 2.00 | 3.00 | |
| G1013 | The Human Beast–Emile Zola | 1.00 | 2.00 | 3.00 | |
| G1014 | Journey to the End of the Night–Louis-Ferdinand Celine | 1.00 | 2.00 | 3.00 | |
| G1015 | Queen's Caprice–George Preedy | 1.00 | 2.00 | 3.00 | A |
| G1016 | Avon Book of Modern Writing No. 2–William Phillips & Philip Rahr | .75 | 1.50 | 2.25 | |
| G1017 | The Third Angel–Jerome Weldman; 1955 | 1.00 | 2.00 | 3.00 | E |
| G1018 | The Collected Works of Pierre Louys; 1955 | 1.50 | 3.00 | 4.50 | E |
| G1019 | Temptation–John Pen | 1.50 | 3.00 | 4.50 | E |
| G1020 | Point Counter Point–Aldous Huxley | 1.50 | 3.00 | 4.50 | |
| G1021 | Women in Love–D.H. Lawrence | 1.50 | 3.00 | 4.50 | E |
| G1022 | Death on the Installment Plan–Louis-Ferdinand Celine | 1.00 | 2.00 | 3.00 | |
| G1023 | The Big Brokers–Irving Shulman | 1.00 | 2.00 | 3.00 | |
| G1024 | Crime and Punishment–Fyodor Dostoyevsky; 1956 | 1.00 | 2.00 | 3.00 | |
| G1025 | Aaron's Rod–D.H. Lawrence | 1.00 | 2.00 | 3.00 | E |
| G1026 | Your Daughter Iris–Jerome Weidman | .75 | 1.50 | 2.25 | |
| G1027 | Those Barren Leaves–Aldous Huxley | 1.00 | 2.00 | 3.00 | |
| G1028 | The Rainbow–D.H. Lawrence | 1.00 | 2.00 | 3.00 | E |
| G1029 | Dishonored Flesh–Joseph Pennell | .75 | 1.50 | 2.25 | IE |

AVON G-SERIES, *continued*

| No. | Title | V/Good | Fine | N/Mint | |
|---|---|---|---|---|---|
| G1030 | Conquests of Tamerlane–Cothburn O'Neal; 1957 | .75 | 1.50 | 2.25 | A |
| G1031 | Point Counter Point–Aldous Huxley | 1.00 | 2.00 | 3.00 | |
| G1032 | The Third Angel–Jerome Weidman; 1958 | .75 | 1.50 | 2.25 | |
| G1033 | Temptation–John Penn; 1959 | 1.00 | 2.00 | 3.00 | E |
| G1034 | A Death in the Family–James Agee | .75 | 1.50 | 2.25 | |
| G1035 | Maggie Cassidy–Jack Kerouac; 1st ed. 1959 | 5.00 | 10.00 | 15.00 | |
| G1036 | The Last Summer–Boris Pasternak; 1st English lang. ed. 1959 | 2.50 | 5.00 | 7.50 | |
| G1037 | They Hanged My Saintly Billy–Robert Graves | .75 | 1.50 | 2.25 | |
| G1038 | The Rainbow–D.H. Lawrence | 1.00 | 2.00 | 3.00 | E |
| G1039 | Aaron's Rod–D.H. Lawrence | .75 | 1.50 | 2.25 | E |
| G1040 | 14 Great Short Stories by Soviet Authors–ed. George Reavey | .50 | 1.00 | 1.50 | |
| G1041 | Daughter of Eve–Noel B. Gerson; 1960 | .75 | 1.50 | 2.25 | A |
| G1042 | The Magnificent Ambersons–Booth Tarkington | .50 | 1.00 | 1.50 | A |
| G1043 | A Bell for Adano–John Hersey | .50 | 1.00 | 1.50 | A |
| G1044 | Guide to Intelligent Reducing–Gaylord Hauser | .50 | 1.00 | 1.50 | NF |
| G1045 | So Big–Edna Ferber | .50 | 1.00 | 1.50 | NF |
| G1046 | A Fever in the Blood–William Pearson | .50 | 1.00 | 1.50 | NF |
| G1047 | Goodness Had Nothing to Do with It–Mae West | .50 | 1.00 | 1.50 | B |
| G1048 | Damned Shall Be Desire–Stephen Coulter | .50 | 1.00 | 1.50 | B |
| G1049 | The Third Angel–Jerome Weidman | .50 | 1.00 | 1.50 | B |
| G1050 | Endurance–Alfred Lansing; 1960 | .50 | 1.00 | 1.50 | B |
| G1051 | In This Our Life–Ellen Glasgow | .50 | 1.00 | 1.50 | B |
| G1052 | A Twist of Sand–Geoffrey Jenkins | .50 | 1.00 | 1.50 | B |
| G1053 | Any Number Can Play–Clifton Fadiman | .50 | 1.00 | 1.50 | B |
| G1054 | Station Wagon in Spain–Frances Parkinson Keyes | .50 | 1.00 | 1.50 | B |
| G1056 | The Hiding Place–Robert Shaw | .50 | 1.00 | 1.50 | B |
| G1057 | Search for Love–Lucy Freeman | .50 | 1.00 | 1.50 | B |
| G1058 | Life of Jesus–Francois Mauriac | .75 | 1.50 | 2.25 | B |
| G1059 | Those Barren Leaves–Aldous Huxley | .50 | 1.00 | 1.50 | B |
| G1060 | Khrushchev and the Russian Challenge–Hearst, Considine, Conniff | .50 | 1.00 | 1.50 | NF |
| G1061 | Something of an Achievement–Gwyn Griffin; 1961 | .50 | 1.00 | 1.50 | NF |
| G1062 | History of Orgies–Bruno Partridge | .50 | 1.00 | 1.50 | NF |
| G1063 | John Kennedy: A Political Profile–James MacGreger Burns | .75 | 1.50 | 2.25 | NF |
| G1064 | Memoirs of a Professional Cad–George Sanders | .50 | 1.00 | 1.50 | B |
| G1065 | Babies by Choice or by Chance–Alan F. Guttmacher, MD | .50 | 1.00 | 1.50 | NF |
| G1066 | Perle, My Story–Perle Mesta & Robert Cahn | .50 | 1.00 | 1.50 | B |
| G1067 | A Departure from the Rules–Anthony Robinson | .50 | 1.00 | 1.50 | |
| G1068 | Dempsey–Considine & Slocum | .50 | 1.00 | 1.50 | B |
| G1069 | The Fire Escape–Susan Kale | .50 | 1.00 | 1.50 | |
| G1070 | Journey in the Dark–Martin Flavin; 1961 | .50 | 1.00 | 1.50 | |
| G1071 | A Clergyman's Daughter–George Orwell | 1.50 | 3.00 | 4.50 | |
| G1072 | The Secrets of Long Life–Dr. George Gallup & Evan Hill | .50 | 1.00 | 1.50 | NF |
| G1073 | The Master of Badger's Hall–Henry Treece | .50 | 1.00 | 1.50 | A |
| G1074 | Walk Egypt–Vinnie Williams | .50 | 1.00 | 1.50 | A |
| G1075 | Man into Orbit; aka Seven into Space–Joseph N. Bell | .75 | 1.50 | 2.25 | NF |
| G1076 | American Beauty–Edna Ferber | .50 | 1.00 | 1.50 | NF |
| G1077 | Belle out of Order–Belle Livingstone | .50 | 1.00 | 1.50 | NF |
| G1078 | He and She–Edward Le Comte | .50 | 1.00 | 1.50 | NF |
| G1079 | Iron Cavalier–Donald Barr Chidsey | .75 | 1.50 | 2.25 | A |
| G1081 | Fielding's Folly–Frances Parkinson Keyes | .50 | 1.00 | 1.50 | A |
| G1082 | A Peak in Darien–Roswell G. Ham, Jr | .50 | 1.00 | 1.50 | A |
| G1083 | Listen, America!–Daniel James | .50 | 1.00 | 1.50 | NF |
| G1084 | Pachanga–John A. Lucchese | .50 | 1.00 | 1.50 | NF |
| G1085 | The Big Smear–William R. Reardon; 1961 | .50 | 1.00 | 1.50 | NF |
| G1086 | Barry Goldwater: The Biography of a Conservative–Wood & Smith | .50 | 1.00 | 1.50 | B |
| G1087 | Eight Men–Richard Wright | 1.50 | 3.00 | 4.50 | B |
| G1088 | Lamb in His Bosom–Caroline Miller; 1961 | .50 | 1.00 | 1.50 | B |
| G1089 | Never Leave Me–Harold Robbins; 1961 | .50 | 1.00 | 1.50 | B |
| G1090 | The Saragossa Manuscript–Jan Potocki | .50 | 1.00 | 1.50 | F |
| G1091 | Love Is Where You Find It–Paula Christian | 1.50 | 3.00 | 4.50 | F |
| G1092 | 21st Century Sub–Frank Herbert; 1961 | .75 | 1.50 | 2.25 | SF |
| G1093 | John XXIII–The Story of the Pope–Francis X. Murphy | .50 | 1.00 | 1.50 | B |
| G1094 | The Able McLaughlins–Margaret Wilson | .50 | 1.00 | 1.50 | B |
| G1095 | Conquest of Happiness–Bertrand Russell | .50 | 1.00 | 1.50 | B |
| G1096 | The World of Clifford Simak–Clifford Simak | 1.00 | 2.00 | 3.00 | SF |
| G1097 | Death of Anger–Allan Seager; 1961 | .50 | 1.00 | 1.50 | SF |
| G1098 | Web of Hate–Frederik Mayer; 1962 | .50 | 1.00 | 1.50 | SF |
| G1099 | The Long Sword–Hunter D'Allard | .50 | 1.00 | 1.50 | A |
| G1100 | Women without Morals–Richard F. Gallagher | .50 | 1.00 | 1.50 | |
| G1101 | "My Lovely Adele"–Adrian Bennett | .50 | 1.00 | 1.50 | |
| G1102 | Some Other Times–Hollis Alpert | .50 | 1.00 | 1.50 | |
| G1103 | The Crooked Road–Thomas Curley; aka It's a Wise Child | .50 | 1.00 | 1.50 | |
| G1104 | The Checquer Board–Nevil Shute | .50 | 1.00 | 1.50 | |
| G1105 | Guide to Success in the Stock Market–ed. Ira V. Cobleigh | .50 | 1.00 | 1.50 | NF |
| G1106 | Garden Graphs | .50 | 1.00 | 1.50 | NF |
| G1107 | You Can Survive the Bomb–Col. Mel Mawrence | .50 | 1.00 | 1.50 | NF |
| G1108 | First Family–Christopher Davis | .50 | 1.00 | 1.50 | NF |
| G1109 | Now in November–Josephine Johnson | .50 | 1.00 | 1.50 | NF |
| G1110 | Libido Beach–Alain Abby | .50 | 1.00 | 1.50 | NF |
| G1111 | I Love You Honey, But the Season's Over–Connie Clausen | .50 | 1.00 | 1.50 | NF |
| G1112 | Stories of Scarlet Women–anon.; anthology | .50 | 1.00 | 1.50 | NF |
| G1113 | Verboten–Virginia Kellogg; 1962 | .50 | 1.00 | 1.50 | NF |
| G1114 | Heir Apparent–E.L. Withers | .50 | 1.00 | 1.50 | NF |
| G1115 | Escape from Red China–John Romanbello; aka Bird of Sorrow | .50 | 1.00 | 1.50 | NF |
| G1116 | Four Window Girl–Shepherd Mead | .75 | 1.50 | 2.25 | NF |
| G1117 | Eighteen Holes in My Head–Milton Gross | .50 | 1.00 | 1.50 | NF |
| G1118 | Trio–Dorothy Baker | .50 | 1.00 | 1.50 | NF |
| G1119 | Elegy in Manhattan–George Jessel | .50 | 1.00 | 1.50 | NF |
| G1120 | Talents Incorporated–Murray Leinster; 1962 | .75 | 1.50 | 2.25 | SF |
| G1121 | A Kind of Justice–Benjamin Siegel | .50 | 1.00 | 1.50 | SF |
| G1122 | His Family–Ernest Poole | .50 | 1.00 | 1.50 | SF |
| G1123 | Let the Crabgrass Grow–H. Allen Smith | .50 | 1.00 | 1.50 | H |
| G1124 | Other Worlds of Clifford Simak–Clifford Simak | 1.00 | 2.00 | 3.00 | SF |
| G1125 | Tom Blood, Highwayman–Gardner F. Fox; 1962 | 1.00 | 2.00 | 3.00 | A |
| G1126 | Bum Voyage–David Greer & F. Spatz Leighton | .50 | 1.00 | 1.50 | A |
| G1127 | Three Hearts and Three Lions–Paul Anderson | 1.00 | 2.00 | 3.00 | F |
| G1128 | Lesbian Love in Literature–ed. Stella Fox | 1.50 | 3.00 | 4.50 | E |
| G1129 | The Big Ball of Wax–Shepherd Mead | .75 | 1.50 | 2.25 | E |
| G1130 | The Wide Sea–ed. Arthur Kaplan | .50 | 1.00 | 1.50 | E |
| G1131 | A Walk with Love and Death–Hans Koningsberger; movie tie-in | .75 | 1.50 | 2.25 | A |
| G1132 | Adrift in a Boneyard–Robert Lewis Taylor | .50 | 1.00 | 1.50 | SF |
| G1133 | You're Better Off Naked–Wayne Healy | .50 | 1.00 | 1.50 | SF |
| G1134 | Old House of Fear–Russell Kirk | .50 | 1.00 | 1.50 | M |
| G1135 | A Seal Flies By–R.H. Pearson | .50 | 1.00 | 1.50 | M |
| G1136 | A Kind of Loving–Stan Barstow; movie tie-in | .50 | 1.00 | 1.50 | M |
| G1137 | My Life as a Small Boy–Wally Cox; 1962 | .75 | 1.50 | 2.25 | H |
| G1138 | George Washington September, Sir–Ronald Harwood | .50 | 1.00 | 1.50 | H |
| G1139 | Stephen Crane Anthology | 1.00 | 2.00 | 3.00 | H |
| G1140 | Crusade–Donn Byrne | .50 | 1.00 | 1.50 | A |
| G1141 | Harriet–Tom Karsell | .50 | 1.00 | 1.50 | |
| G1142 | Scarlet Sister Mary–Julia Peterkin | .50 | 1.00 | 1.50 | |
| G1143 | The Diploids–Katherine MacLean | .75 | 1.50 | 2.25 | SF |

**AVON G-SERIES,** *continued*

| | V/Good | Fine | N/Mint | |
|---|---|---|---|---|
| G1144 The Private World of William Faulkner–Robert Caughlin | .50 | 1.00 | 1.50 | NF |
| G1145 The Challenge of Freedom–Sen. Eugene J. McCarthy | .50 | 1.00 | 1.50 | NF |
| G1146 What Ever Happened to Baby Jane?–Henry Farrell; 1963; movie tie-in | 1.50 | 3.00 | 4.50 | |
| G1147 The Nephew–James Purdy | .50 | 1.00 | 1.50 | |
| G1148 Cry Slaughter–E.K. Tiempo | .50 | 1.00 | 1.50 | |
| G1149 Balboa–Robert Farrington | .50 | 1.00 | 1.50 | A |
| G1150 But Not Next Door–Harry Rosen & David Rosen | .50 | 1.00 | 1.50 | |
| G1151 Queer Patterns–Lilyan Brock | .75 | 1.50 | 2.25 | E |
| G1152 The Spinoza of Market Street–Isaac B. Singer | .50 | 1.00 | 1.50 | |
| G1153 The Whole Heart–Helen Howe | .50 | 1.00 | 1.50 | |
| G1154 The Space Plague–George O. Smith; aka Highways in Hiding | .75 | 1.50 | 2.25 | SF |
| G1155 Gibral-taric–John Simms | .50 | 1.00 | 1.50 | A |
| G1156 The U.N. in Action–Peter Lyon | .50 | 1.00 | 1.50 | NF |
| G1157 Death on the Sixth Day–Henry Farrell | .50 | 1.00 | 1.50 | |
| G1158 How Come A Nice Girl Like You Isn't Married?–Gwenna Packard | .50 | 1.00 | 1.50 | |
| G1159 The Quintessence of Queen–ed. Anthony Boucher | 1.50 | 3.00 | 4.50 | M |
| G1160 Anybody Who Owns His Own Home Deserves It–Alan King | .50 | 1.00 | 1.50 | H |
| G1162 Imaginary Lives–Marcel Schwob | .50 | 1.00 | 1.50 | |
| G1163 This Side of Love–Paula Christian | 1.50 | 3.00 | 4.50 | |
| G1164 Woman in Armor–Philip Ketcham | 1.00 | 2.00 | 3.00 | A |
| G1165 The Iron Ring–Ronald Bostwick | .50 | 1.00 | 1.50 | C |
| G1166 Fee, Fei, Fo, Fum–John Aylesworth | .50 | 1.00 | 1.50 | SF |
| G1167 Slim Down, Shape Up Diets for Teenagers–Gaynor Maddox | .50 | 1.00 | 1.50 | NF |
| G1168 From Outer Space–Hal Clement; aka Needle | .50 | 1.00 | 1.50 | SF |
| G1169 What about Teen-age Marriage?–Jeanne Sakol | .50 | 1.00 | 1.50 | NF |
| G1170 Doctors Wear Scarlet–Simon Raven | .50 | 1.00 | 1.50 | HO |
| G1171 Satan in Goray–Isaac B. Singer; 1963 | .50 | 1.00 | 1.50 | |
| G1172 It Always Rains in Rome–John F. Leeming | .50 | 1.00 | 1.50 | |
| G1173 Marlene Dietrich's ABC–Marlene Dietrich | 1.00 | 2.00 | 3.00 | |
| G1174 Break of Day–Sidonie Colette | .50 | 1.00 | 1.50 | |
| G1175 Hot Red Money–Baynard Kendrick; 1963 | .75 | 1.50 | 2.25 | M |
| G1176 Blood and Thunder–Dwight Taylor | .50 | 1.00 | 1.50 | |
| G1177 The Chinese Bell Murders–Robert van Gulik | 1.00 | 2.00 | 3.00 | M |
| G1178 Fright–ed. Charles Collins | 1.00 | 2.00 | 3.00 | HO |
| G1179 The White Voyage–John Christopher | 1.00 | 2.00 | 3.00 | SF |
| G1180 Death and the Joyful Woman–Ellis Peters | .50 | 1.00 | 1.50 | M |
| G1181 Suburbia's Coddled Kids–Peter Wyden | .50 | 1.00 | 1.50 | NF |
| G1182 The Monkeys–G.K. Wilkinson | .50 | 1.00 | 1.50 | |
| G1183 The Fugitive–Robert L. Fish | .75 | 1.50 | 2.25 | M |
| G1184 The Unpleasantness at the Bellona Club–Dorothy L. Sayers | .50 | 1.00 | 1.50 | M |
| G1185 Pilgrimage: The Book of the People–Zenna Henderson | .75 | 1.50 | 2.25 | SF |
| G1186 The Journal of Kitty Adair–R.T. Lawrence | .50 | 1.00 | 1.50 | |
| G1187 The Quintessence of Queen II–ed. Anthony Boucher | 1.50 | 3.00 | 4.50 | M |
| G1188 Poirot Loses a Client–Agatha Christie | .50 | 1.00 | 1.50 | M |
| G1189 The Hostage–Henry Farrell; 1963 | .50 | 1.00 | 1.50 | |
| G1190 Women Without Morals–Richard F. Gallagher | .50 | 1.00 | 1.50 | |
| G1191 Pan Satyrus–Richard Wormser | .50 | 1.00 | 1.50 | SF |
| G1192 Seven Footprints to Satan–A. Merritt; 1963 | 1.00 | 2.00 | 3.00 | F |
| G1193 The Devil in the Bush–Matthew Hood | .50 | 1.00 | 1.50 | M |
| G1194 The Big Money–Harold A. Masur; 1964 | .50 | 1.00 | 1.50 | |
| G1195 The Chinese Lake Murders–Robert van Gulik | 1.00 | 2.00 | 3.00 | M |
| G1197 The Unquiet Sleep–William Haggard | .50 | 1.00 | 1.50 | |
| G1198 Too Many Doctors–Holly Roth; 1964 | .50 | 1.00 | 1.50 | M |
| G1199 The Panama Portrait–Stanley Ellin | .50 | 1.00 | 1.50 | |
| G1200 Man's Favorite Sport–Morton Cooper | .50 | 1.00 | 1.50 | |
| G1201 The Metropolitan Opera Murders–Helen Traubel | .50 | 1.00 | 1.50 | |

| | V/Good | Fine | N/Mint | |
|---|---|---|---|---|
| G1202 Unnatural Death–Dorothy L. Sayers | .50 | 1.00 | 1.50 | M |
| G1203 The Clampetts of Beverly Hills–Jerry Fay | .75 | 1.50 | 2.25 | H |
| G1204 Rebel–John Clagett | .50 | 1.00 | 1.50 | A |
| G1205 The Tender Killer–S.B. Hough | .50 | 1.00 | 1.50 | |
| G1206 Can't Anybody Here Play This Game?–Jimmy Breslin; 1964 | .50 | 1.00 | 1.50 | S |
| G1207 How to Write a Song–Henry Kane | .50 | 1.00 | 1.50 | |
| G1208 The 1964 Olympics Guide–John V. Grombach | .50 | 1.00 | 1.50 | S |
| G1209 From High School to a Job–Adrian A. Paradis | .50 | 1.00 | 1.50 | NF |
| G1210 Banking on Death–Emma Lathen | .50 | 1.00 | 1.50 | M |
| G1211 Podkayne of Mars–Robert A. Heinlein; 1964 | .75 | 1.50 | 2.25 | SF |
| G1212 The Late Mrs. D.–Hillary Waugh | .50 | 1.00 | 1.50 | |
| G1214 I, Spy–Donald MacKenzie | .50 | 1.00 | 1.50 | |
| G1215 The Trial of Marie Besnard–Marie Besnard | .50 | 1.00 | 1.50 | |
| G1217 Man on a Nylon String–Whit Masterson | .50 | 1.00 | 1.50 | |
| G1219 The Chinese Nail Murders–Robert van Gulik | 1.00 | 2.00 | 3.00 | M |
| G1221 The Lone Wolf–Louis Joseph Vance | .75 | 1.50 | 2.25 | M |
| G1222 The World of Henry Orient–Nora Johnson | .75 | 1.50 | 2.25 | |
| G1223 The Big Four–Agatha Christie | .50 | 1.00 | 1.50 | M |
| G1224 Ashenden–W. Somerset Maugham. Note: Queen's Quorum No. 76 | .50 | 1.00 | 1.50 | M |
| G1225 The First Body–Laurence Payne | .50 | 1.00 | 1.50 | |
| G1226 Blue Sapphire–D.E. Stevenson | .50 | 1.00 | 1.50 | |
| G1227 The Day They Invaded New York–Irwin Lewis | 1.00 | 2.00 | 3.00 | SF |
| G1228 How Much?–Burt Blechman | .50 | 1.00 | 1.50 | |
| G1229 The Smell of Money–Matthew Head | .50 | 1.00 | 1.50 | |
| G1230 The Richer They Are–George Ellis | .50 | 1.00 | 1.50 | |
| G1231 The Time Twisters–J. Hunter Holly | .75 | 1.50 | 2.25 | SF |
| G1233 Tall, Dark and Deadly–Harold Q. Masur | .50 | 1.00 | 1.50 | M |
| G1234 The Adventurous Life of Winston Churchill–Geoffrey Bocca | .50 | 1.00 | 1.50 | B |
| G1236 New Crossword Puzzle Book No. 1–Jack Luzzato | 1.00 | 2.00 | 3.00 | NF |
| G1237 The Munsters–Morton Cooper; TV tie-in | 1.50 | 3.00 | 4.50 | H |
| G1238 Deadly Duo–Marjory Atlingham | .50 | 1.00 | 1.50 | M |
| G1239 Born Victim–Hillary Waugh | .50 | 1.00 | 1.50 | |
| G1240 Florentine Finish–Cornelius Hirschberg | .50 | 1.00 | 1.50 | |
| G1241 Isle of Snakes–Robert L. Fish; 1964 | .75 | 1.50 | 2.25 | M |
| G1243 The Perfectionist–Lane Kauffmann; 1965 | .50 | 1.00 | 1.50 | |
| G1244 A Rage in Harlem–Chester Himes | 1.50 | 3.00 | 4.50 | |
| G1245 Anna and Her Daughters–D.E. Stevenson | .50 | 1.00 | 1.50 | |
| G1246 The Make Believe Man–Elizabeth Fenwick | .50 | 1.00 | 1.50 | |
| G1247 Man from the Sea–Michael Innes | .50 | 1.00 | 1.50 | |
| G1248 Second Foundation–Isaac Asimov | .75 | 1.50 | 2.25 | SF |
| G1249 Death of a Painted Lady–Brian Cleeve | .50 | 1.00 | 1.50 | M |
| G1250 The Beverly Hillbillies Live It Up–Jerry Fay; 1965; TV tie-in | 1.50 | 3.00 | 4.50 | H |
| G1251 How the FBI Gets Its Man | .50 | 1.00 | 1.50 | NF |
| G1252 The Accomplice–Matthew Head | .50 | 1.00 | 1.50 | |
| G1253 Still Glides the Stream–D.E. Stevenson | .50 | 1.00 | 1.50 | |
| G1254 Boris Karloff's Favourite Horror Stories–ed. Boris Karloff | 1.25 | 2.50 | 3.75 | HO |
| G1255 Dead Calm–Charles Williams; 1965 | 1.25 | 2.50 | 3.75 | M |
| G1256 Murder Gone Mad–Philip MacDonald | .75 | 1.50 | 2.25 | M |
| G1257 The Rasp–Philip MacDonald | .75 | 1.50 | 2.25 | M |
| G1258 The Last Gamble–Harold Q. Masur | .50 | 1.00 | 1.50 | M |
| G1259 Make a Killing–Harold Q. Masur | .50 | 1.00 | 1.50 | M |
| G1260 Bel Lamington–D.E. Stevenson | .50 | 1.00 | 1.50 | |
| G1261 Congo Venus–Matthew Head | .50 | 1.00 | 1.50 | |
| G1262 Old House of Fear–Russell Kirk | .50 | 1.00 | 1.50 | M |
| G1263 The Will and the Deed–Ellis Peters | .50 | 1.00 | 1.50 | M |
| G1264 Rynox Murder–Philip MacDonald | .75 | 1.50 | 2.25 | M |
| G1265 Fletcher's End–D.L. Stevenson | .50 | 1.00 | 1.50 | |
| G1266 The Shrunken Head–Robert L. Fish | .75 | 1.50 | 2.25 | M |
| G1267 My Son the Murderer–Patrick Quentin | .75 | 1.50 | 2.25 | M |
| G1268 The Star Dwellers–James Blish | .50 | 1.00 | 1.50 | SF |
| G1269 A Pennant for the Kremlin–Paul Malloy | .50 | 1.00 | 1.50 | |
| G1271 Amberwell–D.E. Stevenson | .50 | 1.00 | 1.50 | |

| | V/Good | Fine | N/Mint |
|---|---|---|---|

| | | V/Good | Fine | N/Mint | |
|---|---|---|---|---|---|
| G1273 | One Man Show–Michael Innes | .50 | 1.00 | 1.50 | M |
| G1274 | Scientists Behind the Inventors–Roger Burlingame | .50 | 1.00 | 1.50 | NF |
| G1275 | How Awful about Allan–Henry Farrell | .50 | 1.00 | 1.50 | |
| G1276 | The Tarnished Angel–Hugh Pentecost | .50 | 1.00 | 1.50 | |
| G1277 | Make My Bed Soon–Jack Webb | .50 | 1.00 | 1.50 | |
| G1278 | Man Against Tomorrow–ed. William F. Nolan | .50 | 1.00 | 1.50 | SF |
| G1279 | It's Different Abroad–Henry Calvin | .50 | 1.00 | 1.50 | |
| G1280 | A Life for the Stars–James Blish | .75 | 1.50 | 2.25 | SF |
| G1281 | Beat Not the Bones–Charlotte Jay | .50 | 1.00 | 1.50 | M |
| G1282 | The Grave Maker's House–Rubin Weber | .50 | 1.00 | 1.50 | |
| G1283 | Is There a Traitor in the House?– Patricia McGerr | .50 | 1.00 | 1.50 | |
| G1284 | In the Last Analysis–Amanda Cross | .50 | 1.00 | 1.50 | M |
| G1285 | Where There's A Will–Rex Stout | .50 | 1.00 | 1.50 | M |
| G1286 | Grieve for the Past–Stanton Forbes | .50 | 1.00 | 1.50 | |
| G1287 | A Place for Murder–Emma Lathen | .50 | 1.00 | 1.50 | M |
| G1288 | Death and Circumstance–Hillary Waugh | .50 | 1.00 | 1.50 | |
| G1289 | Passage by Night–Hugh Marlowe | .50 | 1.00 | 1.50 | |
| G1290 | Blood Red–John Creasey; 1966 | .50 | 1.00 | 1.50 | M |
| G1291 | Deaf, Dumb and Blonde–John Creasey | .50 | 1.00 | 1.50 | M |
| G1292 | Accounting for Murder–Emma Lathen | .50 | 1.00 | 1.50 | M |
| G1293 | Mute Witness–Robert L. Pike | .75 | 1.50 | 2.25 | M |
| G1294 | The Golden Land–Giles A. Lutz | .50 | 1.00 | 1.50 | W |
| G1295 | Virgin Luck–Laurence Meynell | .50 | 1.00 | 1.50 | |
| G1296 | If Anything Happens to Hester–John Creasey | .50 | 1.00 | 1.50 | M |
| G1297 | Double Frame–John Creasey | .50 | 1.00 | 1.50 | M |
| G1298 | A Cage for Lovers–Dawn Powell | .50 | 1.00 | 1.50 | M |
| G1299 | The Fifteenth Pelican–Teré Rios | .75 | 1.50 | 2.25 | F |
| G1300 | The Hustler–Henry Williamson | .50 | 1.00 | 1.50 | |
| G1301 | The Professionals–Frank O'Rourke; 1966 | .75 | 1.50 | 2.25 | W |
| G1302 | No Orchids for Miss Blandish–James Hadley Chase | .50 | 1.00 | 1.50 | M |
| G1303 | Summerhill–D.E. Stevenson; 1967 | .50 | 1.00 | 1.50 | |
| G1304 | The Baron and the Chinese Puzzle– John Creasey | .50 | 1.00 | 1.50 | M |
| G1305 | Log Camp Nurse–Arlene Fitzgerald | .50 | 1.00 | 1.50 | R |
| G1306 | The Wailing Asteroid–Murray Leinster | .50 | 1.00 | 1.50 | SF |
| G1307 | The Man from Avon–Michael Avallone | .75 | 1.50 | 2.25 | H |
| G1308 | Challenge at Le Mans–Larry Kenyon | .50 | 1.00 | 1.50 | S |
| G1309 | The Stalking Moon–Theodore V. Olsen | .75 | 1.50 | 2.25 | W |
| G1310 | Miners in the Sky–Murray Leinster | .50 | 1.00 | 1.50 | SF |
| G1311 | The Mouth of the Pearl–Philip Jones | .50 | 1.00 | 1.50 | |
| G1312 | The Red Fathom–Robert Edmond Alter | .50 | 1.00 | 1.50 | M |
| G1313 | The Pledge–Friedrich Duerrenmatt | .50 | 1.00 | 1.50 | |
| G1314 | Traitor Guns–Philip Ketchum; 1967 | .75 | 1.50 | 2.25 | W |
| G1314 | The Day New York Trembled–Irwin Lewis; 1967 | .75 | 1.50 | 2.25 | SF |
| G1316 | Countdown at Monaco–Larry Kenyon | .50 | 1.00 | 1.50 | |
| G1317 | Cry Slaughter–E.K. Tiempo | .50 | 1.00 | 1.50 | |
| G1318 | The Space Gypsies–Murray Leinster | 1.00 | 2.00 | 3.00 | SF |
| G1319 | Volunteer Nurse–Arlene J. Fitzgerald | .50 | 1.00 | 1.50 | R |
| G1320 | Prairie Teacher–Marion Marsh Brown | .50 | 1.00 | 1.50 | |
| G1321 | Revenge at Indy–Larry Kenyon | .50 | 1.00 | 1.50 | S |
| G1322 | Doctor Who in an Exciting Adventure with the Daleks–David Whitaker; 1st ed., 1967; movie tie-in | 2.50 | 5.00 | 7.50 | SF |
| G1323 | Sixgun Wild–James Keene | .50 | 1.00 | 1.50 | W |
| G1324 | The Devil's Ring–Larry Kenyon | .50 | 1.00 | 1.50 | |
| G1325 | La Jornada | .50 | 1.00 | 1.50 | |
| G1326 | The Battlehorns–Alan Sillitoe | .50 | 1.00 | 1.50 | |
| G1328 | Cheyenne War Cry–Noel Loomis; 1967 | .75 | 1.50 | 2.25 | W |
| G1329 | The Miracle of Dr. MacLennon– Maxwell Maltz | .50 | 1.00 | 1.50 | R |
| G1331 | Lynn, Cover Girl–Nina Putnam | .50 | 1.00 | 1.50 | R |
| G1346 | The Cage–Talmage Powell | .50 | 1.00 | 1.50 | W |
| G2001 | After Many a Summer Dies the Swan– Alfdous Huxley; 1959 | .75 | 1.50 | 2.25 | SF |
| G2002 | Butterfield 8–John O'Hara; 1959 | .75 | 1.50 | 2.25 | |

## AVON GC-SERIES
## Avon Book Company

| | | V/Good | Fine | N/Mint |
|---|---|---|---|---|
| GC465 | Malcolm–James Purdy | .50 | 1.00 | 1.50 |

## AVON GO-SERIES
## Avon Book Company

| | | V/Good | Fine | N/Mint | |
|---|---|---|---|---|---|
| GO151 | Hannibal–Mary Dolan; aka Hannibal of Carthage; 1963 | .75 | 1.50 | 2.25 | A |

## AVON GS-SERIES
## Avon Book Company

| | | V/Good | Fine | N/Mint |
|---|---|---|---|---|
| GS1 | Miss Lonelyhearts–Nathanael West; 1964 | .50 | 1.00 | 1.50 |
| GS2 | End of the Road–John Barth; 1964 | .50 | 1.00 | 1.50 |
| GS3 | The Wild Duck–Henrik Ibsen; 1965 | .50 | 1.00 | 1.50 |
| GS4 | The Importance of Being Earnest– Oscar Wilde | .50 | 1.00 | 1.50 |
| GS5 | The Three Sisters–Anton Chekhov; 1965 | .50 | 1.00 | 1.50 |
| GS6 | Rose and the Ring–W.M.Thackeray | .50 | 1.00 | 1.50 |
| GS7 | A Shropshire Lad–A.E. Houseman | .50 | 1.00 | 1.50 |
| GS8 | Ghosts–Henrik Ibsen | .50 | 1.00 | 1.50 |
| GS9 | Miss Julie–August Strindberg | .50 | 1.00 | 1.50 |
| GS10 | The Cherry Orchard–Anton Chekov; 1965 | .50 | 1.00 | 1.50 |
| GS11 | Sonnets from the Portuguese–Elizabeth Barrett Browning | .50 | 1.00 | 1.50 |
| GS12 | The Playboy of the Western World– John M. Synge; 1967 | .50 | 1.00 | 1.50 |
| GS13 | Arms and the Man–George B. Shaw; 1967 | .50 | 1.00 | 1.50 |
| GS14 | The Rubaiyat of Omar Khayyam–trans. E. Fitzgerald | .50 | 1.00 | 1.50 |
| GS15 | Rime of the Ancient Mariner–Samuel Taylor Coleridge; 1967 | .50 | 1.00 | 1.50 |
| GS16 | Leaves of Grass–Walt Whitman; 1969 | .50 | 1.00 | 1.50 |

## AVON H-SERIES
## Avon Books, Inc.

| | | V/Good | Fine | N/Mint | |
|---|---|---|---|---|---|
| H100 | The Honyocker–Giles A. Lutz; 1962 | .75 | 1.50 | 2.25 | W |
| H101 | Night of Wenceslas–Lionel Davidson; 1962 | .50 | 1.00 | 1.50 | M |
| H102 | A Dog's Head–Jean Dutourd; 1963 | 1.00 | 2.00 | 3.00 | F |
| H103 | The Cannibal Who Overate–Hugh Pentecost; 1963 | .50 | 1.00 | 1.50 | |
| H104 | Bijoux–Francoise Des Ligneris (trans. Lowell Blair); 1963 | .50 | 1.00 | 1.50 | |
| H105 | One Thing I Know–Pati Hill | .50 | 1.00 | 1.50 | |
| H106 | Roll Your Tent Flaps, Girls!–K.P. Whittaker | .50 | 1.00 | 1.50 | H |
| H108 | It Walks By Night–John Dickson Carr; 1963 | .50 | 1.00 | 1.50 | M |

## AVON LOVE BOOK MONTHLY
## Avon Publishing Company, Inc.
**Digest Size**

| | | V/Good | Fine | N/Mint | |
|---|---|---|---|---|---|
| 1 | Blonde Baggage–Marty Holland | 10.00 | 20.00 | 30.00 | E |
| 2 | Chorus Girl–Thyra Samter Winslow | 10.00 | 20.00 | 30.00 | E |

## AVON M-SERIES
## Avon Book Company

| | | V/Good | Fine | N/Mint |
|---|---|---|---|---|
| M100 | On Contemporary Literature–ed. Richard Kostelanetz; 1970 (?) | .50 | 1.00 | 1.50 |

# AVON MODERN SHORT STORY MONTHLY

## Avon Publishing Company, Inc.

### Digest Size

| | | V/Good | Fine | N/Mint | |
|---|---|---|---|---|---|
| 1 | Cosmopolitans: 29 Short Stories– W. Somerset Maugham | 2.50 | 5.00 | 7.50 | |
| 2 | Files on Parade–John O'Hara | 2.50 | 5.00 | 7.50 | |
| 3 | To Step Aside–Noel Coward | 2.50 | 5.00 | 7.50 | |
| 4 | Selected Stories–William Saroyan | 2.50 | 5.00 | 7.50 | |
| 5 | Ill Wind–James Hilton | 2.50 | 5.00 | 7.50 | |
| 6 | Selected Short Stories–Sinclair Lewis | 2.50 | 5.00 | 7.50 | |
| 7 | 14 Great Stories–anthology | 2.50 | 5.00 | 7.50 | |
| 8 | First Person Singular–W.S. Maugham | 2.50 | 5.00 | 7.50 | |
| 9 | 13 Great Stories–John Steinbeck; 1943 | 2.50 | 5.00 | 7.50 | |
| 10 | 15 Selected Stories–James T. Farrell | 2.50 | 5.00 | 7.50 | |
| 11 | Selected Great Stories–Ben Hecht | 2.50 | 5.00 | 7.50 | |
| 12 | 34 More Great Stories–William Saroyan | 2.50 | 5.00 | 7.50 | |
| 13 | Three Short Novels–Louis Bromfield | 2.50 | 5.00 | 7.50 | |
| 14 | 22 Modern Stories–Erskine Caldwell | 2.50 | 5.00 | 7.50 | |
| 15 | 13 Great Modern Stories–anthology | 2.50 | 5.00 | 7.50 | |
| 16 | Eight Long Short Stories–Fannie Hurst | 2.50 | 5.00 | 7.50 | |
| 17 | Selected Stories–Thomas Wolfe | 2.50 | 5.00 | 7.50 | |
| 18 | Ah King–W.S. Maugham | 2.50 | 5.00 | 7.50 | |
| 19 | They Brought Their Women–Edna Ferber | 2.50 | 5.00 | 7.50 | |
| 20 | Twelve Selected Modern Stories– anthology | 2.50 | 5.00 | 7.50 | |
| 21 | Great Stories by James T. Farrell– James T. Farrell | 2.50 | 5.00 | 7.50 | |
| 22 | Career in C Major and Other Stories– James M. Cain; 1st ed. 1943 | 10.00 | 20.00 | 30.00 | |
| 23 | Great Stories of China–Pearl S. Buck | 2.50 | 5.00 | 7.50 | |
| 24 | Five Long Short Stories–Louis Bromfield | 2.50 | 5.00 | 7.50 | |
| 25 | Ten Great Stories–anthology | 2.50 | 5.00 | 7.50 | |
| 26 | A Thousand and One Afternoons in New York–Ben Hecht | 2.50 | 5.00 | 7.50 | |
| 27 | Ten Stories by Damon Runyon–Damon Runyon | 2.50 | 5.00 | 7.50 | |
| 28 | Twelve Great Stories–anthology | 2.50 | 5.00 | 7.50 | |
| 29 | Hope of Heaven and Other Stories– John O'Hara | 2.50 | 5.00 | 7.50 | |
| 30 | Georgia Boy and Other Stories–Erskine Caldwell | 2.50 | 5.00 | 7.50 | |
| 31 | Twelve Great Stories–anthology | 2.50 | 5.00 | 7.50 | |
| 32 | Welcome to the City and Other Stories–Irwin Shaw | 2.50 | 5.00 | 7.50 | |
| 33 | A New Collection of Short Stories– anthology | 2.50 | 5.00 | 7.50 | |
| 34 | Great Stories by Louis Bromfield | 2.50 | 5.00 | 7.50 | |
| 35 | The Trembling of a Leaf/Maugham's Tropical Love Stories–W. Somerset Maugham | 2.50 | 5.00 | 7.50 | |
| 36 | Stories of Love and Adventure–Rafael Sabatini. Note: Same cover as Avon No. 84. | 2.50 | 5.00 | 7.50 | A |
| 37 | Concerning a Woman of Sin and Other Stories–Ben Hecht. Note: Same cover as Avon Monthly Novel 17 | 2.50 | 5.00 | 7.50 | |
| 38 | Great Stories of Love and Intrigue–W. Somerset Maugham | 2.50 | 5.00 | 7.50 | |
| 39 | Stories of Venial Sin–John O'Hara | 2.50 | 5.00 | 7.50 | |
| 40 | Marianne in India–Lion Feuchtwanger | 2.50 | 5.00 | 7.50 | |
| 41 | Ten Selected Stories–James T. Farrell | 2.50 | 5.00 | 7.50 | |
| 42 | Hollywood Love Clinic–anthology | 2.50 | 5.00 | 7.50 | |
| 43 | East of Suez/Great Stories of the Tropics–W. Somerset Maugham | 2.50 | 5.00 | 7.50 | |
| 44 | Tropical Passions–anthology. Note: Basically the same cover as Avon No. 255 and Avon Book Dividend No. 7 | 2.50 | 5.00 | 7.50 | |
| 45 | Hellbox–John O'Hara | 2.50 | 5.00 | 7.50 | |
| 46 | Love among the Haystacks–D.H. Lawrence | 3.00 | 6.00 | 9.00 | |
| 47 | Love in Greenwich Village–Floyd Dell | 3.00 | 6.00 | 9.00 | |
| 48 | Night Club–Katharine Brush | 3.00 | 6.00 | 9.00 | |
| 49 | A Modern Lover–D.H. Lawrence | 3.00 | 6.00 | 9.00 | |
| 50 | All the Girls He Wanted–John O'Hara | 3.00 | 6.00 | 9.00 | |
| 51 | Romantic Young Lady–W. Somerset Maugham | 3.00 | 6.00 | 9.00 | |

# AVON MONTHLY NOVEL

## Avon Publishing Co., Inc.

### Digest Size

| | | V/Good | Fine | N/Mint | |
|---|---|---|---|---|---|
| 1 | Sinful Woman–James M. Cain; orig. 1947 | 20.00 | 40.00 | 60.00 | E |
| 2 | Her Private Passions–Marty Holland | 5.00 | 10.00 | 15.00 | E |
| 3 | The Regenerate Lover–D.H. Clarke | 5.00 | 10.00 | 15.00 | E |
| 4 | The Villain and the Virgin–J.H. Chase | 5.00 | 10.00 | 15.00 | E |
| 5 | Uneasy Virtue–Dana Wilson; 1948; aka Make with the Brains, Pierre | 5.00 | 10.00 | 15.00 | E |
| 6 | Strange Desires–Len Zinberg; aka What D'ya Know for Sure | 5.00 | 10.00 | 15.00 | E |
| 7 | 12 Chinks and a Woman–J.H. Chase | 10.00 | 20.00 | 30.00 | E |
| 8 | Virgie, Goodbye–Nathan Rothman. Note: Same cover as the comic Romantic Love No. 7 and Novel Library No. 33 | 5.00 | 10.00 | 15.00 | E |
| 9 | The Scarf of Passion–Robert Bloch; aka The Scarf. Note: Same cover as Avon No. 211, an unnumbered Avon Special of the same name, and the comic Realistic Romances No. 1 | 30.00 | 60.00 | 90.00 | E |
| 10 | The Lady Said Yes–G.V. Martin | 5.00 | 10.00 | 15.00 | E |
| 11 | The Devil Is Loneliness–Elma K. Lobaugh | 5.00 | 10.00 | 15.00 | E |
| 12 | Little Sins–Katharine Brush | 5.00 | 10.00 | 15.00 | E |
| 13 | Carlotta–Robert Briffault | 7.50 | 15.00 | 22.50 | E |
| 14 | The Man Who Drove Girls Wild–M.H. Hanline | 5.00 | 10.00 | 15.00 | E |
| 15 | The Darling of Paris–Marty Holland; orig. 1949 | 5.00 | 10.00 | 15.00 | E |
| 16 | Millie's Daughter–D.H. Clarke | 6.00 | 12.00 | 18.00 | E |
| 17 | Jealous Woman–J.M. Cain; 1st ed. 1949. Note: Same cover as Avon Short Story Monthly No. 37 | 20.00 | 40.00 | 60.00 | E |
| 18 | I'll Get You for This–J.H. Chase | 12.50 | 25.00 | 37.50 | E |
| 19 | One Night with Nancy–Wilson Collison | 6.00 | 12.00 | 18.00 | E |
| 20 | Ecstasy Girl–Jack Woodford | 5.00 | 10.00 | 15.00 | E |
| 21 | Tomcat in Tights–Jack Hanley | 5.00 | 10.00 | 15.00 | E |

# AVON MURDER MYSTERY MONTHLY

## Avon Book Company/Avon Publishing Company, Inc.

### Digest Size
### (Continuation of Avon Murder of the Month)

| | | V/Good | Fine | N/Mint | |
|---|---|---|---|---|---|
| 3 | Silinski–Master Criminal–Edgar Wallace | 7.50 | 15.00 | 22.50 | M |
| 4 | The French Key Mystery–Frank Gruber | 9.00 | 18.00 | 27.00 | M |
| 5 | Burn, Witch, Burn–A.A. Merritt | 7.50 | 15.00 | 22.50 | SF |
| 6 | The Postman Always Rings Twice– James M. Cain | 6.00 | 12.00 | 18.00 | M |
| 7 | The Big Sleep–Raymond Chandler | 20.00 | 40.00 | 60.00 | M |
| 8 | Maigret Aboard–Georges Simenon; 1943 | 7.50 | 15.00 | 22.50 | M |
| 9 | The Red Box–Rex Stout | 13.50 | 27.00 | 40.50 | M |
| 10 | Homicide for Hannah–Dwight V. Babcock | 7.50 | 15.00 | 22.50 | M |
| 11 | Creep Shadow Creep–A.A. Merritt | 7.50 | 15.00 | 22.50 | SF |
| 12 | Hungry Dog Murders–Frank Gruber | 10.00 | 20.00 | 30.00 | M |
| 13 | If the Shroud Fits–Kelley Roos. Note: Same cover as Avon No. 104 and Avon Detective Mystery No. 2 | 5.00 | 10.00 | 15.00 | M |
| 14 | Whose Body?–Dorothy L. Sayers | 6.00 | 12.00 | 18.00 | M |
| 15 | Premeditated Murder–Peter Cheyney; aka A Trap for Bellamy | 7.50 | 15.00 | 22.50 | M |
| 16 | Double Indemnity–James M. Cain; 1st ed. 1943 | 20.00 | 40.00 | 60.00 | M |

## AVON MURDER MYSTERY MONTHLY continued

| | | V/Good | Fine | N/Mint | |
|---|---|---|---|---|---|
| 17 | Who Killed Chloe?–Margery Allingham; aka Dancers in Mourning | 6.00 | 12.00 | 18.00 | M |
| 18 | The Moon Pool–A.A. Merritt; 1944 | 6.00 | 12.00 | 18.00 | SF |
| 19 | 5 Murderers–Raymond Chandler; 1st ed. 1944. Note: Queen's Quorum No. 97 | 62.50 | 125.00 | 187.50 | M |
| 20 | The Embezzler–James M. Cain; 1st ed. 1944 | 20.00 | 40.00 | 60.00 | M |
| 21 | Counter Spy Murders–Peter Cheyney; aka Dark Duet | 6.00 | 12.00 | 18.00 | M |
| 22 | Ace of Knaves–Leslie Charteris; aka The Saint Goes into Action | 7.50 | 15.00 | 22.50 | M |
| 23 | Simon Lash, Private Detective–Frank Gruber | 10.00 | 20.00 | 30.00 | M |
| 24 | Dwellers in the Mirage–A.A. Merritt | 6.00 | 12.00 | 18.00 | SF |
| 25 | About the Murder of a Startled Lady–Anthony Abbot | 7.50 | 15.00 | 22.50 | M |
| 26 | The Mysterious Affair at Styles–Agatha Christie | 7.50 | 15.00 | 22.50 | M |
| 27 | The Black Angel–Cornell Woolrich | 15.00 | 30.00 | 45.00 | M |
| 28 | Five Sinister Characters–Raymond Chandler; 1st ed. 1945 | 62.50 | 125.00 | 187.50 | M |
| 29 | The Face in the Abyss–A.A. Merritt | 6.00 | 12.00 | 18.00 | SF |
| 30 | Farewell to the Admiral–Peter Cheyney | 6.00 | 12.00 | 18.00 | M |
| 31 | If I Should Die Before I Wake–William Irish; 1st ed. 1945 | 22.50 | 45.00 | 67.50 | M |
| 32 | The Saint vs. Scotland Yard–Leslie Charteris | 7.50 | 15.00 | 22.50 | M |
| 33 | Nobody Lives Forever–W.R. Burnett | 7.50 | 15.00 | 22.50 | M |
| 34 | The Ship of Ishtar–A.A. Merritt. Note: Uses retouched cover from the pulp magazine Argosy, May 10, 1930 | 5.00 | 10.00 | 15.00 | SF |
| 35 | Flowers for the Judge–Margery Allingham; 1946 | 5.00 | 10.00 | 15.00 | M |
| 36 | They Never Say When–Peter Cheyney | 6.00 | 12.00 | 18.00 | M |
| 37 | Orchids to Murder–Hulbert Footner | 7.50 | 15.00 | 22.50 | M |
| 38 | Hannah Says Foul Play–Dwight V. Babcock; 1st ed. 1946 | 7.50 | 15.00 | 22.50 | M |
| 39 | Flash Casey–Detective–George Harmon Coxe; 1st ed. 1946 | 12.00 | 24.00 | 36.00 | M |
| 40 | High Sierra–W.R. Burnett | 9.00 | 18.00 | 27.00 | M |
| 41 | The Metal Monster–A.A. Merritt | 5.00 | 10.00 | 15.00 | SF |
| 42 | Borrowed Crime–William Irish; 1st ed. 1946 | 40.00 | 80.00 | 120.00 | M |
| 43 | Finger Man–Raymond Chandler; 1st ed. 1946 | 40.00 | 80.00 | 120.00 | M |
| 44 | Love's Lovely Counterfeit–James M. Cain; 1947 | 9.00 | 18.00 | 27.00 | M |
| 45 | On the Spot–Edgar Wallace | 7.50 | 15.00 | 22.50 | M |
| 46 | Green Ice Murders–Raoul Whitfield; 1947. Note: Same cover as the comic Police Line-Up No. 1 | 15.00 | 30.00 | 45.00 | M |
| 47 | The Blonde, the Gangster and the Private Eye–Dale Clark; 1950; aka The Red Rods | 17.50 | 35.00 | 52.50 | M |
| 48 | Murder in Her Big Blue Eyes–Julius Long; aka Keep the Coffins Coming. Note: Same cover as the comic Murderous Gangsters No. 3 | 17.50 | 35.00 | 52.50 | M |
| 49 | Lady, the Guy is Dead–Edward Ronns; 1950; aka No Place to Live. Note: Same cover as the comic The Saint No. 11 | 17.50 | 35.00 | 52.50 | M |

# AVON MURDER OF THE MONTH
## Avon Book Company
### Digest Size

**(Continued as Avon Murder Mystery Monthly)**

| | | V/Good | Fine | N/Mint | |
|---|---|---|---|---|---|
| 1 | Seven Footprints to Satan–A.A. Merritt; 1942 | 7.50 | 15.00 | 22.50 | SF |
| 2 | Mysterious Mickey Finn–Elliot Paul; 1942 | 7.50 | 15.00 | 22.50 | M |

# AVON N/YN-SERIES
## Avon Book Company

| | | V/Good | Fine | N/Mint | |
|---|---|---|---|---|---|
| N101 | A Journey to Matecumbe–Robert Lewis Taylor; 1962 | .50 | 1.00 | 1.50 | |
| N102 | Clem Anderson–R.V. Cassill | .50 | 1.00 | 1.50 | |
| N103 | Your Complete Home Medical Reference Book–Harold Hyman, MD | .50 | 1.00 | 1.50 | NF |
| N104 | The Centurions–Jean Larteguy; 1963 | .50 | 1.00 | 1.50 | |
| N105 | The Treasures of Time–ed. Leo C. Devel | .50 | 1.00 | 1.50 | |
| N106 | The River and the Wilderness–Don Robertson | .50 | 1.00 | 1.50 | |
| N107 | Sow Not in Anger–Jack Hoffenberg; 1964 | .50 | 1.00 | 1.50 | |
| N108 | The Saga of Flight–eds. Neville Duke & Edward Lenchbery | .50 | 1.00 | 1.50 | NF |
| N109 | Mrs. Seton–Joseph I. Dirvin, M.C. | .50 | 1.00 | 1.50 | |
| N110 | Harper's Bazaar Great Views to Dine By–Jerome Klein & Norman Reader | .50 | 1.00 | 1.50 | NF |
| N111 | Cheyenne Autumn–Marie Sandoz | 1.00 | 2.00 | 3.00 | W |
| N112 | Rags of Glory–Stuart Cloete | .50 | 1.00 | 1.50 | |
| N113 | The Quiet Crisis–Stewart Udall | .50 | 1.00 | 1.50 | |
| N114 | A Hero for Regis–Jack Hoffenberg | .50 | 1.00 | 1.50 | |
| N115 | The Sun Is My Undoing–Marguerite Steen; 1964 | .50 | 1.00 | 1.50 | |
| N116 | But Not for Love–Edwin Shrake; 1965 | .50 | 1.00 | 1.50 | |
| N117 | The Skin–Curzio Malaparte | .50 | 1.00 | 1.50 | |
| N118 | Radcliffe–David Storey | .50 | 1.00 | 1.50 | |
| N119 | Prodigal Women–Nancy Hale | .50 | 1.00 | 1.50 | |
| N120 | An Honorable State–Lane Kauffman | .50 | 1.00 | 1.50 | |
| N121 | Sir William–David Stacton | .50 | 1.00 | 1.50 | |
| N122 | The Praetorians–Jean Larteguy | .50 | 1.00 | 1.50 | |
| N123 | A Thunder at Dawn–Jack Hoffenberg | .50 | 1.00 | 1.50 | |
| N124 | Dylan Thomas in America–John Malcolm Brinnin | .75 | 1.50 | 2.25 | NF |
| N125 | Burton–Byron Farwell | .50 | 1.00 | 1.50 | |
| N126 | The Patriot–Harold Bienvenue | .50 | 1.00 | 1.50 | |
| N127 | Eric Mattson–Norman Katkov | .50 | 1.00 | 1.50 | |
| N128 | The Green Berets–Robin Moore | .75 | 1.50 | 2.25 | C |
| N129 | A Shadow of Eagles–Jane Barry; 1966 | .50 | 1.00 | 1.50 | |
| N130 | Up the Down Staircase–Bel Kaufman | .50 | 1.00 | 1.50 | |
| N131 | Napoleon and Josephine–Frances Massiker | .50 | 1.00 | 1.50 | |
| N132 | The Lost Command–Jean Larteguy; movie tie-in | .75 | 1.50 | 2.25 | C |
| N133 | The Hardwinners–John Quirk | .50 | 1.00 | 1.50 | |
| N134 | The Devil to Pay–Robin Moore; 1966 | .50 | 1.00 | 1.50 | C |
| N135 | Kaputt–Curzio Malaparte | .50 | 1.00 | 1.50 | |
| N136 | The Devil's Agent–Hans Habe | .50 | 1.00 | 1.50 | |
| N137 | The Penkovskiy Papers–Oleg Penkovskiy | .50 | 1.00 | 1.50 | |
| N138 | The High White Forest–Ralph Allen; 1966 | .50 | 1.00 | 1.50 | |
| N139 | The Fires of Brimstone–Patricia Gallagher; 1967 | .50 | 1.00 | 1.50 | |
| N140 | Sow Not in Anger–Jack Hoffenberg | .50 | 1.00 | 1.50 | |
| N141 | A Little Girl Is Dead–Harry Goldan | .50 | 1.00 | 1.50 | |
| N142 | A Journey to Matecumbe–Robert Lewis Taylor | .50 | 1.00 | 1.50 | |
| N143 | But Not for Love–Edwin Shrake | .50 | 1.00 | 1.50 | |
| N144 | Chaos Below Heaven–Eugene Vale | .50 | 1.00 | 1.50 | |
| N145 | The Skin–Curzio Malaparte | .50 | 1.00 | 1.50 | |
| N146 | A Hero for Regis–Jack Hoffenberg | .50 | 1.00 | 1.50 | |
| N147 | Flee the Angry Strangers–George Mandel | .50 | 1.00 | 1.50 | |
| N148 | Yellow Fever–Jean Larteguy | .50 | 1.00 | 1.50 | |
| N149 | The Rebellion of Yale Marratt–Robert Rimmer | .50 | 1.00 | 1.50 | |
| N150 | Czar–Thomas Wiseman; 1967 | .50 | 1.00 | 1.50 | |
| N151 | The Sun Is My Undoing–Marguerite Steen | .50 | 1.00 | 1.50 | |
| N155 | The Hounds of Hell–Jean Larteguy | .50 | 1.00 | 1.50 | |
| N156 | The Detective–Roderick Thorp | .50 | 1.00 | 1.50 | |
| N157 | The Whistling Zone–Herbert Kubly | .50 | 1.00 | 1.50 | |
| N159 | Nowhere City–Alison Lurie | .50 | 1.00 | 1.50 | |
| N160 | Confrontation–Norman Garbo & Howard Goodkind | .50 | 1.00 | 1.50 | |
| N161 | Court of Honor–Geoff Taylor | .50 | 1.00 | 1.50 | |
| N162 | The Ninety and Nine–William Brinkley | .50 | 1.00 | 1.50 | C |

| | | V/Good | Fine | N/Mint |
|---|---|---|---|---|

AVON N/YN-SERIES, *continued*

| # | Title | V/Good | Fine | N/Mint | |
|---|---|---|---|---|---|
| N163 | Hirohito–Leonard Mosley; 1967 | .75 | 1.50 | 2.25 | NF |
| N164 | With Kennedy–Pierre Salinger | .50 | 1.00 | 1.50 | NF |
| N171 | The Great Imposter & the Rascal and the Road–Robert Crichton | .50 | 1.00 | 1.50 | B |
| N174 | Dinner at Antoine's–Frances Parkinson Keyes | .50 | 1.00 | 1.50 | |
| N176 | All That Glitters–Frances Parkinson Keyes | .50 | 1.00 | 1.50 | |
| N177 | Blue Camellia–Frances Parkinson Keyes | .50 | 1.00 | 1.50 | |
| N178 | Steamboat Gothic–Frances Parkinson Keyes | .50 | 1.00 | 1.50 | |
| N182 | Joy Street–Frances Parkinson Keyes | .50 | 1.00 | 1.50 | |
| N185 | At Ease–Dwight D. Eisenhower; 1968 | .50 | 1.00 | 1.50 | NF |
| N189 | If All the Rebels Die–Samuel B. Southwell; 1968 | .50 | 1.00 | 1.50 | |
| N201 | The Dillinger Days–John Toland | .75 | 1.50 | 2.25 | |
| N202 | Onassis–Willi Frischauer; 1968 | .50 | 1.00 | 1.50 | B |
| N204 | Yankee Pasha–Edison Marshall; 1969 | .50 | 1.00 | 1.50 | A |
| N214 | Gypsy Sixpence–Edison Marshall; 1969 | .50 | 1.00 | 1.50 | A |
| N215 | The Landlord–Kristin Hunter | .50 | 1.00 | 1.50 | |
| N233 | The Sterile Cuckoo–John Treadwell Nichols; movie tie-in | .50 | 1.00 | 1.50 | |
| YN235 | Player Piano–Kurt Vonnegut, Jr | 1.00 | 2.00 | 3.00 | SF |

# AVON NS-SERIES
## Avon Publishing Co., Inc.

| # | Title | V/Good | Fine | N/Mint | |
|---|---|---|---|---|---|
| NS1 | Avon American Shakespeare Festival Edition: Hamlet, Much Ado About Nothing, Richard III–ed. Norman Holland | .50 | 1.00 | 1.50 | |
| NS2 | Call It Sleep–Henry Roth; 1964 | .50 | 1.00 | 1.50 | |
| NS3 | Thinking About the Unthinkable–Herman Kahn | .50 | 1.00 | 1.50 | |
| NS4 | Uncommon Reader–ed. Alice Morris | .50 | 1.00 | 1.50 | |
| NS5 | Johnson's Lives of the Poets–ed. Edmund Fuller; 1965 | .50 | 1.00 | 1.50 | NF |
| NS6 | The Unpossessed–Tess Slesinger; 1966 | .50 | 1.00 | 1.50 | |
| NS7 | The Middle of the Journey–Lionel Trilling | .50 | 1.00 | 1.50 | |
| NS8 | Encounter–Crawford Power | .50 | 1.00 | 1.50 | |
| NS9 | The Man Who Loved Children–Christina Stead | .50 | 1.00 | 1.50 | |
| NS10 | Animal Life and Lore–Osmond P. Breland | .50 | 1.00 | 1.50 | |
| NS11 | Disinherited–Dale van Every | .50 | 1.00 | 1.50 | |
| NS13 | The Second Oswald–Richard Popkin | 1.50 | 3.00 | 4.50 | |
| NS14 | Presidential Government–James MacGregor Burns | .50 | 1.00 | 1.50 | NF |
| NS15 | Khrushchev: A Career–Edward Crankshaw | .50 | 1.00 | 1.50 | NF |
| NS16 | Player Piano–Kurt Vonnegut, Jr | 1.50 | 3.00 | 4.50 | SF |
| NS17 | Act of Darkness–John Peale Bishop | .50 | 1.00 | 1.50 | |
| NS18 | A Death in the Family–James Agee | .50 | 1.00 | 1.50 | |
| NS19 | The Gates of the Forest–Elie Wiesel; 1967 | .50 | 1.00 | 1.50 | |
| NS20 | Life in the Crystal Palace–Alan Harrington | .50 | 1.00 | 1.50 | |
| NS21 | The Great Political Theories–Vol. 1–ed. Michael Curtis | .50 | 1.00 | 1.50 | NF |
| NS22 | The Great Political Theories–Vol. 2–ed. Michael Curtis | .50 | 1.00 | 1.50 | NF |
| NS23 | The War Game–Peter Watkins; 1967 | .50 | 1.00 | 1.50 | |
| NS25 | The Universe: From Flat Earth to Quasar–Isaac Asimov | .50 | 1.00 | 1.50 | NF |
| NS26 | Call It Sleep–Henry Roth; 1968 | .50 | 1.00 | 1.50 | |
| NS27 | The New Genetics–Leonard Engle | .50 | 1.00 | 1.50 | |
| NS28 | I Thought of Daisy–Edmund Wilson | .50 | 1.00 | 1.50 | |
| NS29 | The Me Nobody Knows: Children's Voices from the Ghetto–ed. Stephen M. Joseph | .50 | 1.00 | 1.50 | |
| NS30 | Are You Running With Me, Jesus?–Malcolm Boyd | .50 | 1.00 | 1.50 | |
| NS31 | The Slave–Isaac B. Singer | .50 | 1.00 | 1.50 | |

| # | Title | V/Good | Fine | N/Mint | |
|---|---|---|---|---|---|
| NS34 | The Writer in America–Van Wyck Brooks | .50 | 1.00 | 1.50 | |
| NS35 | Jean-Christophe. Vol. 1–Romain Rolland; 1969 | .50 | 1.00 | 1.50 | |
| NS36 | Jean-Christophe. Vol. 2–Romain Rolland | .50 | 1.00 | 1.50 | |
| NS37 | Jean-Christophe. Vol. 3–Romain Rolland | .50 | 1.00 | 1.50 | |
| NS38 | The Mind of the Dolphin–John Cunningham Lilly, MD | .50 | 1.00 | 1.50 | |
| NS39 | Dream Life of Balso Snell And A Cool Million–Nathanael West | .50 | 1.00 | 1.50 | |
| NS40 | The Floating Opera–John Barth | .50 | 1.00 | 1.50 | |
| NS41 | Pain–Vladimir Nabokov | .50 | 1.00 | 1.50 | |
| NS42 | The Town beyond the Wall–Elie Wiesel; 1969 | .50 | 1.00 | 1.50 | |

# AVON QS-SERIES
## Avon Book Company

| # | Title | V/Good | Fine | N/Mint | |
|---|---|---|---|---|---|
| QS1 | The Interpretation of Dreams–Sigmund Freud; 1965 | .50 | 1.00 | 1.50 | NF |
| QS2 | Four Centuries of Shakespearean Criticism–ed. Frank Kermode | .50 | 1.00 | 1.50 | NF |
| QS3 | The Nature of Politics–Michael Curtis | .50 | 1.00 | 1.50 | NF |
| QS4 | Prometheus–Andre Maurois; 1967 | .50 | 1.00 | 1.50 | |
| QS5 | Great Scenes from the World Theater–ed. James L. Steffensen, Jr | .50 | 1.00 | 1.50 | |
| QS6 | DeGaulle–Jean Lacouture; 1969 | .50 | 1.00 | 1.50 | NF |
| QS9 | Goodbye Jehovah–William Robert Miller; 1969 | .50 | 1.00 | 1.50 | |
| QS16 | Drug Awareness–Key Documents on LSD, Marijuana and the Drug Culture–ed. Richard E. Horman & Allan M. Fox; 1970 | .50 | 1.00 | 1.50 | NF |

# AVON ROMANCE NOVEL MONTHLY
## Avon Publishing Co., Inc.

### Digest Size

| # | Title | V/Good | Fine | N/Mint | |
|---|---|---|---|---|---|
| 1 | The Little Sinner–Ruby M. Ayers; 1949 | 6.00 | 12.00 | 18.00 | E |
| 2 | Love Should Be Laughter–Frances S. Moore | 6.00 | 12.00 | 18.00 | E |
| 3 | Help Yourself to Love–Peggy Dern; 1950 | 6.00 | 12.00 | 18.00 | E |

# AVON S-SERIES
## Avon Book Company

| # | Title | V/Good | Fine | N/Mint | |
|---|---|---|---|---|---|
| S101 | The Art of Keeping Fit–ed. Esquire; 1961 | .50 | 1.00 | 1.50 | NF |
| S102 | The Night They Raided Minsky's–Rowland Barber | .75 | 1.50 | 2.25 | |
| S103 | The President's Lady–Irving Stone | .50 | 1.00 | 1.50 | |
| S104 | Casserole Magic–Lousene Rousseau Brunner | .50 | 1.00 | 1.50 | NF |
| S105 | Nuremberg: The Third Reich on Trial–R. Gallagher | .75 | 1.50 | 2.25 | NF |
| S106 | I Walked with Heroes–Carlos P. Romulo; 1961 | .50 | 1.00 | 1.50 | NF |
| S107 | The Goddam White Man–David Lytton; 1962 | 1.00 | 2.00 | 3.00 | |
| S108 | By Antietam Creek–Don Robertson | .75 | 1.50 | 2.25 | |
| S109 | From Pagan to Christian–Lin Yu-tang | .50 | 1.00 | 1.50 | |
| S110 | Farewell to Fear–Toni Keitlin | .50 | 1.00 | 1.50 | |
| S111 | Special for Women–George Lefferts | .50 | 1.00 | 1.50 | |
| S112 | The Parthian–Vic Hurley | .50 | 1.00 | 1.50 | |
| S113 | The Safe Bridge–Frances Parkinson Keyes | .50 | 1.00 | 1.50 | |
| S114 | The Middle Mist–Mary Renault | .50 | 1.00 | 1.50 | |
| S115 | Education and the Good Life–Bertrand Russell | .50 | 1.00 | 1.50 | NF |

AVON S-SERIES, *continued*

| | | V/Good | Fine | N/Mint | |
|---|---|---|---|---|---|
| S116 | The Plague and the Fire–James Leasor; 1962 | .50 | 1.00 | 1.50 | NF |
| S117 | Battalion of Saints–Richard Wormser; 1963 | .50 | 1.00 | 1.50 | |
| S118 | It's the Irish–Bob Considine | .50 | 1.00 | 1.50 | |
| S119 | A Long and Happy Life–Reynolds Price | .50 | 1.00 | 1.50 | |
| S120 | Death and the Supreme Court–Barret E. Prettyman | .50 | 1.00 | 1.50 | NF |
| S121 | Conservatism–Dean Smith | .50 | 1.00 | 1.50 | NF |
| S122 | Liberalism–Milton Viorst | .50 | 1.00 | 1.50 | NF |
| S123 | The Case Against Natural Childbirth–Waldo L. Fielding, MD & Lois Benjamin | .50 | 1.00 | 1.50 | NF |
| S124 | The Country of Marriage–Jon Cleary | .50 | 1.00 | 1.50 | |
| S125 | The Rose of Tibet–Lionel Davidson | .50 | 1.00 | 1.50 | M |
| S126 | Lawd Today–Richard Wright | 1.00 | 2.00 | 3.00 | |
| S127 | Hugo Winners–ed. Isaac Asimov | .75 | 1.50 | 2.25 | SF |
| S128 | Genius–Patrick Dennis | .50 | 1.00 | 1.50 | |
| S129 | From the Back of the Bus–Dick Gregory | .75 | 1.50 | 2.25 | |
| S130 | Concord Rebel–August Derleth | 1.00 | 2.00 | 3.00 | NF |
| S131 | The Golden Wreck–A. McKee | .50 | 1.00 | 1.50 | |
| S132 | Never Leave Me–Harold Robbins | .50 | 1.00 | 1.50 | |
| S133 | A Death in the Family–James Agee | .50 | 1.00 | 1.50 | |
| S134 | A Bell for Adano–John Hersey | .50 | 1.00 | 1.50 | |
| S135 | Purple-6–Henry Brinton | .50 | 1.00 | 1.50 | SF |
| S136 | Once There Was a Nun–Ruth Montgomery; 1963 | .50 | 1.00 | 1.50 | |
| S137 | The 24-Hour Drink Book–Ralph Maloney; 1964 | .50 | 1.00 | 1.50 | NF |
| S138 | The Glory Circuit–Jess Gregg | .50 | 1.00 | 1.50 | |
| S139 | The Violent Man–A.E. Van Vogt | .75 | 1.50 | 2.25 | |
| S140 | The Slave–Isaac B. Singer | .50 | 1.00 | 1.50 | |
| S141 | The Six-Eleven–Al Morgan | .50 | 1.00 | 1.50 | |
| S142 | Add Life to Your Years–Ernest Boas, MD & Norman Boas, MD | .50 | 1.00 | 1.50 | NF |
| S143 | So Big–Edna Ferber; 1964 | .75 | 1.50 | 2.25 | |
| S144 | Border Guard–Don Whitehead | .50 | 1.00 | 1.50 | |
| S145 | That Kid: The Story of Jerry Lewis–Richard Gehman | 1.00 | 2.00 | 3.00 | B |
| S146 | Answer to Heaven–Patricia Gallagher | .50 | 1.00 | 1.50 | |
| S147 | The Pasang Run–Elleston Trevor | .50 | 1.00 | 1.50 | |
| S148 | Lyndon Johnson Story–Booth Mooney | .75 | 1.50 | 2.25 | NF |
| S149 | Italian Women Confess–ed. Gabriella Parca | .75 | 1.50 | 2.25 | |
| S150 | Red in the Morning–Edith Bergner | .50 | 1.00 | 1.50 | |
| S151 | Of Streets and Stars–Alan Marcus | .50 | 1.00 | 1.50 | |
| S152 | American Beauty–Edna Ferber | .75 | 1.50 | 2.25 | |
| S153 | Harry, the Rat with Women–Jules Feiffer | 1.00 | 2.00 | 3.00 | H |
| S154 | Station Wagon in Spain–Frances Parkinson Keyes | .50 | 1.00 | 1.50 | |
| S155 | Mrs. LBJ–Ruth Montgomery | .50 | 1.00 | 1.50 | NF |
| S156 | The Road Back–Erich Maria Remarque | .75 | 1.50 | 2.25 | |
| S157 | The Ruling Family–Mary N. Dolim | .50 | 1.00 | 1.50 | |
| S158 | The Disappearing Island–Geoffrey Jenkins | .50 | 1.00 | 1.50 | |
| S159 | Apostle for Our Time–John Clancy | .50 | 1.00 | 1.50 | |
| S160 | Great Son–Edna Ferber; 1964 | .75 | 1.50 | 2.25 | |
| S161 | Expendable Man–Dorothy Hughes | .50 | 1.00 | 1.50 | |
| S163 | Rascal–Sterling North; 1965 | .50 | 1.00 | 1.50 | |
| S164 | Dallas Public and Private–Warren Leslie | .50 | 1.00 | 1.50 | |
| S165 | My Lord What a Morning–Marian Anderson | .50 | 1.00 | 1.50 | B |
| S167 | The Film of Memory–Maurice Druon | .50 | 1.00 | 1.50 | |
| S168 | Quick before It Melts–Philip Benjamin | .50 | 1.00 | 1.50 | |
| S170 | A Significant Experience–Gwyn Griffin | .50 | 1.00 | 1.50 | |
| S171 | Legacy of a Spy–Henry S. Maxfield | .50 | 1.00 | 1.50 | |
| S172 | The Favorite Game–Leonard Cohen | .50 | 1.00 | 1.50 | |
| S173 | Trio–Dorothy Baker | .50 | 1.00 | 1.50 | |
| S174 | The Pond–Robert Murphy | .50 | 1.00 | 1.50 | |
| S175 | Dead Cert–Dick Francis | .75 | 1.50 | 2.25 | M |
| S176 | The Bunnies–John Quirk | .50 | 1.00 | 1.50 | |
| S177 | The Survivor–John Quirk | .50 | 1.00 | 1.50 | |
| S178 | Aspects of Love–David Garnett | .50 | 1.00 | 1.50 | |
| S180 | The Egg and I–Betty MacDonald | .50 | 1.00 | 1.50 | H |
| S181 | So Dear to My Heart–Sterling North | .50 | 1.00 | 1.50 | |
| S182 | Beat Not the Bones–Charlotte Jay | .50 | 1.00 | 1.50 | M |
| S183 | A Twist of Sand–Geoffrey Jenkins | .50 | 1.00 | 1.50 | |
| S185 | Focus–Arthur Miller | .50 | 1.00 | 1.50 | |
| S186 | Beautiful Joe–Marshall Saunders | .50 | 1.00 | 1.50 | |
| S187 | Men of Iron–Howard Pyle; 1965 | .50 | 1.00 | 1.50 | A |
| S188 | Anyone Who Owns His Own Home Deserves It–Alan King | .50 | 1.00 | 1.50 | H |
| S189 | Whose Body?–Dorothy Sayers | .50 | 1.00 | 1.50 | M |
| S190 | Kit Carson–Noel B. Gerson | .75 | 1.50 | 2.25 | B |
| S192 | Old Acquaintance–David Stacton | .50 | 1.00 | 1.50 | |
| S193 | The Italian Girl–Iris Murdoch | .50 | 1.00 | 1.50 | |
| S194 | Kilo–Miles Tripp | .50 | 1.00 | 1.50 | |
| S195 | Help! I'm a Prisoner in a Chinese Bakery–Alan King | .50 | 1.00 | 1.50 | H |
| S196 | The River of Diamonds–Geoffrey Jenkins | .50 | 1.00 | 1.50 | |
| S197 | The Lottery–Shirley Jackson | .75 | 1.50 | 2.25 | |
| S198 | Clouds of Witness–Dorothy Sayers | .50 | 1.00 | 1.50 | M |
| S199 | Which the Justice, Which the Thief–William Harrington | .50 | 1.00 | 1.50 | |
| S200 | Wild Voice of the North–Sally Carrighar | .50 | 1.00 | 1.50 | |
| S201 | The Guarded Palace–Jeffrey Bowen | .50 | 1.00 | 1.50 | |
| S202 | Cool Sleeps Balaban–Donald MacKenzie | .50 | 1.00 | 1.50 | |
| S203 | Virgo Descending | .50 | 1.00 | 1.50 | |
| S204 | The Scorpio Letters–Victor Canning | .50 | 1.00 | 1.50 | |
| S205 | Sixth Column–Peter Fleming | .50 | 1.00 | 1.50 | |
| S206 | The Tragedy of X–Ellery Queen | .50 | 1.00 | 1.50 | M |
| S207 | The Tragedy of Y–Ellery Queen | .50 | 1.00 | 1.50 | M |
| S208 | The Trap–John Knowler | .50 | 1.00 | 1.50 | |
| S210 | They Shall Have Stars–James Blish | 1.00 | 2.00 | 3.00 | SF |
| S211 | The Tragedy of Z–Ellery Queen | .50 | 1.00 | 1.50 | M |
| S212 | The Dark Fantastic–Whit Masterson | .50 | 1.00 | 1.50 | HO |
| S213 | Mama Made Minks–Sara Sandberg | .50 | 1.00 | 1.50 | H |
| S214 | Now in November–Josephine Johnson | .50 | 1.00 | 1.50 | |
| S215 | The French Doll–Vincent McConnor | .50 | 1.00 | 1.50 | |
| S216 | Ashenden–W. Somerset Maugham; 1966 | .50 | 1.00 | 1.50 | |
| S217 | Oona O'–Thomas Gallagher | .50 | 1.00 | 1.50 | |
| S218 | Earthman Come Home–James Blish | .75 | 1.50 | 2.25 | SF |
| S219 | The Voluptuaries–Melton Davis | .50 | 1.00 | 1.50 | |
| S220 | Prisoner of Tordesillas–Lawrence Schoonover | .50 | 1.00 | 1.50 | A |
| S221 | The Triumph of Time–James Blish | .50 | 1.00 | 1.50 | SF |
| S222 | Little Caesar–W.R. Burnett | .75 | 1.50 | 2.25 | M |
| S223 | Handwriting Analyzer–Jerome S. Meyer | .50 | 1.00 | 1.50 | NF |
| S224 | Foundation–Isaac Asimov | 1.00 | 2.00 | 3.00 | SF |
| S225 | Names and Faces of Heroes–Reynolds Price | .50 | 1.00 | 1.50 | |
| S226 | Safety Last–O'Connell & Myers | .50 | 1.00 | 1.50 | |
| S227 | Outpost of Freedom–Roger Donlon | .50 | 1.00 | 1.50 | |
| S228 | Never Leave Me–Harold Robbins | .50 | 1.00 | 1.50 | |
| S229 | The Ship of Ishtar–A. Merritt | 1.00 | 2.00 | 3.00 | F |
| S230 | The Possessors–John Christopher | .50 | 1.00 | 1.50 | |
| S231 | The Metal Monster–A. Merritt | 1.00 | 2.00 | 3.00 | F |
| S232 | A Cage for Lovers–Dawn Powell | .50 | 1.00 | 1.50 | |
| S233 | Dead Heat on a Merry-Go-Round–Evan Lee Heyman; movie tie-in; 1st ed. 1966 | .75 | 1.50 | 2.25 | |
| S234 | Foundation and Empire–Isaac Asimov | 1.00 | 2.00 | 3.00 | SF |
| S235 | The Hustler–Henry Williamson | .50 | 1.00 | 1.50 | |
| S236 | The Professionals–Frank O'Rourke; movie tie-in | .75 | 1.50 | 2.25 | W |
| S237 | Second Foundation–Isaac Asimov | 1.00 | 2.00 | 3.00 | SF |
| S238 | Murderers Sane and Mad–Miriam Allen de Ford | .50 | 1.00 | 1.50 | NF |
| S239 | The Room Upstairs–Mildred B. Davis | .50 | 1.00 | 1.50 | |
| S240 | Doctor, You've Got to Be Kidding!–Patte W. Mahan | .50 | 1.00 | 1.50 | |
| S241 | The Jealous One–Celia Fremlin | .50 | 1.00 | 1.50 | |
| S242 | A Grue of Ice–Geoffrey Jenkins | .50 | 1.00 | 1.50 | M |
| S243 | Pilgrimage: The Book of the People–Zenna Henderson | .75 | 1.50 | 2.25 | SF |
| S244 | Wait for the Wedding–Celia Fremlin | .50 | 1.00 | 1.50 | |
| S245 | I Saw Red China–Lisa Hobbs | .50 | 1.00 | 1.50 | NF |
| S246 | Threshold–Stephen Coulter | .50 | 1.00 | 1.50 | |
| S247 | Week with No Friday–Willard Marsh | .50 | 1.00 | 1.50 | |
| S248 | Answer to Heaven–Patricia Gallagher | .50 | 1.00 | 1.50 | |
| S250 | The President I Almost Was–Yetta Bronstein | .50 | 1.00 | 1.50 | |
| S251 | Monkeys, Go Home–G.K. Wilkinson; 1967 | 1.50 | 3.00 | 4.50 | H |
| S252 | The Comforts of the Damned–Wingate Froscher | .50 | 1.00 | 1.50 | |

AVON S-SERIES, *continued*

| | | V/Good | Fine | N/Mint | |
|---|---|---|---|---|---|
| S253 | Casserole Magic–Lousene Rousseau Brunner | .50 | 1.00 | 1.50 | NF |
| S254 | Jenny Abroad–Sandy Lesberg | .50 | 1.00 | 1.50 | |
| S255 | Needle–Hal Clement | .50 | 1.00 | 1.50 | SF |
| S256 | The Unpleasantness at the Bellona Club–Dorothy L. Sayers | .50 | 1.00 | 1.50 | M |
| S257 | A Circle in the Water–James McKinney | .50 | 1.00 | 1.50 | |
| S259 | Night of Wenceslas–Lionel Davidson | .50 | 1.00 | 1.50 | M |
| S260 | The Pulse of Danger–Jon Cleary | .50 | 1.00 | 1.50 | |
| S262 | Reason for Gladness–Mary Wallace | .50 | 1.00 | 1.50 | |
| S263 | Bullwhip Griffin–Sid Fleischman; movie tie-in | 1.00 | 2.00 | 3.00 | W |
| S264 | The Inner Room–Vera Randel | .50 | 1.00 | 1.50 | |
| S265 | Jenny–Sandy Lesberg; 1967 | .50 | 1.00 | 1.50 | |
| S266 | The Instant Saint–John Sherlock | .50 | 1.00 | 1.50 | |
| S268 | Snake Water–Alan Williams | .50 | 1.00 | 1.50 | |
| S269 | A Long Way to Go–Borden Deal | .75 | 1.50 | 2.25 | |
| S270 | Ring Around the Sun–Clifford D. Simate | 1.00 | 2.00 | 3.00 | SF |
| S271 | Dwellers in the Mirage–A. Merritt | 1.00 | 2.00 | 3.00 | F |
| S273 | A Kind of Treason–Robert Elegant | .50 | 1.00 | 1.50 | |
| S274 | Grand Prix–Manning Lee Stokes; movie tie-in | .75 | 1.50 | 2.25 | S |
| S275 | The Troublemakers–Celia Fremlin | .50 | 1.00 | 1.50 | |
| S277 | A Feast of Blood–ed. Charles Collins | 1.50 | 3.00 | 4.50 | HO |
| S278 | Six Weeks in March | .50 | 1.00 | 1.50 | |
| S279 | A Journey to Orassia–Alan Caillou | .50 | 1.00 | 1.50 | |
| S281 | Shooting Script–Gavia Lyall | .50 | 1.00 | 1.50 | |
| S282 | Natural Beauty Secrets–Deborah Rutledge | .50 | 1.00 | 1.50 | NF |
| S283 | The Naked Sword–Donald Barr Chidsey | .75 | 1.50 | 2.25 | A |
| S284 | Long Run South–Alan Williams; 1967 | .50 | 1.00 | 1.50 | |
| S285 | The Borscht Belt–Joey Adams | .50 | 1.00 | 1.50 | |
| S286 | Plant Poppies on My Grave–Arthur Kent | .50 | 1.00 | 1.50 | |
| S287 | A Girl Named Tamiko–Ronald Kirkbride | .50 | 1.00 | 1.50 | |
| S288 | No Blade of Grass–John Christopher; 1967 | 1.50 | 3.00 | 4.50 | SF |
| S289 | A Lesser Lion–Lane Kauffman | .50 | 1.00 | 1.50 | |
| S290 | The Dragon in the Sea–Frank Herbert | .50 | 1.00 | 1.50 | SF |
| S291 | American Guerrilla in the Philippines– Ira Wolfert | .50 | 1.00 | 1.50 | C |
| S292 | Mr. Zip–H. Allen Smith | .50 | 1.00 | 1.50 | |
| S293 | The Fire of Love–Barbara Cartland | .50 | 1.00 | 1.50 | R |
| S294 | The Golden Eagle–Robert Murphy | .50 | 1.00 | 1.50 | |
| S295 | Screen Test for Laurel–Dorothy Daniels | .50 | 1.00 | 1.50 | R |
| S296 | Raccoons are the Brightest People– Sterling North | .50 | 1.00 | 1.50 | |
| S297 | The Beard–Max Wilk; 1967 | .50 | 1.00 | 1.50 | |
| S298 | Living Way Out–Wyman Guin | .50 | 1.00 | 1.50 | |
| S299 | Fancy Man–Donald Barr Chidsey | .75 | 1.50 | 2.25 | A |
| S300 | The Money Hunters–Cothburn O'Neal | .50 | 1.00 | 1.50 | |
| S301 | The Shoot–Elleston Trevor | .50 | 1.00 | 1.50 | |
| S302 | Cold War Swap–Ross Thomas | .50 | 1.00 | 1.50 | |
| S303 | Tros–Talbot Mundy; 1967 | 1.00 | 2.00 | 3.00 | F |
| S304 | Privilege–John Burke; movie tie-in | .50 | 1.00 | 1.50 | |
| S305 | Promise Morning–Charles Mercer | .50 | 1.00 | 1.50 | |
| S306 | Kit Larkin–Ramona Stewart | .50 | 1.00 | 1.50 | |
| S307 | So This Is What Happened to Charlie Moe–Douglas Wallopp | .50 | 1.00 | 1.50 | H |
| S308 | Rescue Mission–John Ball | .50 | 1.00 | 1.50 | |
| S309 | Helma–Talbot Mundy; 1967 | 1.00 | 2.00 | 3.00 | F |
| S310 | Girl with the Golden Yo-Yo–Edmund Schiddel | .50 | 1.00 | 1.50 | |
| S311 | Danger by the Nile–Barbara Cartland | .50 | 1.00 | 1.50 | R |
| S312 | The Peregrine Falcon–Robert Murphy | .50 | 1.00 | 1.50 | |
| S313 | Vor–James Blish | .50 | 1.00 | 1.50 | SF |
| S314 | Lying-in–Paddy Kitchen | .50 | 1.00 | 1.50 | |
| S315 | Scratch the Surface–Edmund Schiddel | .50 | 1.00 | 1.50 | |
| S316 | Liafail–Talbot Mundy; 1967 | 1.00 | 2.00 | 3.00 | F |
| S318 | Helene–Talbot Mundy; 1967 | 1.00 | 2.00 | 3.00 | F |
| S319 | The Heaven Makers–Frank Herbert | .75 | 1.50 | 2.25 | SF |
| S322 | Ridin' the Rainbow–Rosemary Taylor | .50 | 1.00 | 1.50 | |
| S323 | Now Then!–John Brunner | .75 | 1.50 | 2.25 | SF |
| S325 | Thieves Like Us–Robert Edmond Alter; 1968 | .50 | 1.00 | 1.50 | M |
| S328 | The People: No Different Flesh–Zenna Henderson | .75 | 1.50 | 2.25 | SF |
| S329 | Master of Life and Death–Robert Silverberg | .75 | 1.50 | 2.25 | SF |
| S331 | Be Prepared!–Rice E. Cochran | .50 | 1.00 | 1.50 | H |
| S335 | Podkayne of Mars–Robert A. Heinlein | .75 | 1.50 | 2.25 | SF |
| S336 | 3 To the Highest Power–ed. William F. Nolan | .50 | 1.00 | 1.50 | SF |
| S337 | Jack of Eagles–James Blish | 1.00 | 2.00 | 3.00 | SF |
| S341 | The Double Man–Henry S. Maxfield | .50 | 1.00 | 1.50 | |
| S344 | Counterpoint–Alan Sillitoe; movie tie-in | .50 | 1.00 | 1.50 | |
| S345 | Weird Shadows from Beyond–ed. John Carnell; c-Kirby | 1.00 | 2.00 | 3.00 | HO |
| S346 | One Summer in Between–Melissa Mather | .50 | 1.00 | 1.50 | |
| S347 | Snow White and the Giants–J.T. McIntosh | 1.00 | 2.00 | 3.00 | SF |
| S349 | Costigan's Needle–Jerry Sohl | .50 | 1.00 | 1.50 | SF |
| S351 | The Final Programme–Michael Moorcock | .75 | 1.50 | 2.25 | SF |
| S354 | The Thomas Crown Affair–Evan Lee Heyman; 1st ed. 1968; movie tie-in | .50 | 1.00 | 1.50 | |
| S355 | The Expert Dreamers–Frederik Pohl | .75 | 1.50 | 2.25 | SF |
| S357 | The Stalking Moon–Theodore V. Olsen; movie tie-in | .50 | 1.00 | 1.50 | W |
| S361 | Night of the Vampire–Raymond Giles | 1.00 | 2.00 | 3.00 | |
| S363 | Brak the Barbarian–John Jakes; c-Frazetta | 1.50 | 3.00 | 4.50 | F |
| S365 | Invaders from Earth–Robert Silverberg | .75 | 1.50 | 2.25 | SF |
| S368 | Something Evil–Arthur Hoffe | .50 | 1.00 | 1.50 | |
| S372 | The Time Hoppers–Robert Silverberg | .75 | 1.50 | 2.25 | SF |
| S373 | The Castle Captive–Susan Ratcliffe | .50 | 1.00 | 1.50 | |
| S374 | Bullitt–Robert L. Pike | .75 | 1.50 | 2.25 | |
| S376 | The Pedestal–George Lanning | .50 | 1.00 | 1.50 | |
| S377 | Witch Bane–Robert Neill | .50 | 1.00 | 1.50 | |
| S378 | Doomsday Morning–C.L. Moore | .75 | 1.50 | 2.25 | SF |
| S386 | Heart of Juliet Jones–Stan Drake; 1969; comic strip reprints | 1.50 | 3.00 | 4.50 | R |
| S387 | Mary Worth–Saunders & Ernst; 1969; comic strip reprints | 1.50 | 3.00 | 4.50 | R |
| S389 | The Devil His Due–ed. Douglas Hill | 1.00 | 2.00 | 3.00 | HO |
| S395 | The Lonely Gun–Gordon D. Shirreffs | .75 | 1.50 | 2.25 | W |
| S396 | New Avon Crossword Puzzle Book 1 | 1.00 | 2.00 | 3.00 | NF |
| S398 | Shadow of Heaven–Bob Shaw | .75 | 1.50 | 2.25 | SF |
| S417 | Always the Black Knight–Lee Hoffman; 1970 | .50 | 1.00 | 1.50 | SF |
| YS418 | The Wild Duck–Henrik Ibsen | .50 | 1.00 | 1.50 | |
| YS419 | The Importance of Being Earnest– Oscar Wilde | .50 | 1.00 | 1.50 | |
| YS420 | The Three Sisters–Anton Chekhov | .50 | 1.00 | 1.50 | |
| YS421 | Ghosts–Henrik Ibsen | .50 | 1.00 | 1.50 | |
| YS422 | Miss Julie–August Strindberg | .50 | 1.00 | 1.50 | |
| YS423 | The Cherry Orchard–Anton Chekov | .50 | 1.00 | 1.50 | |
| S425 | By Gun and Spur–Joseph Wayne | .75 | 1.50 | 2.25 | W |
| YS426 | Arms and the Man–George B. Shaw | .50 | 1.00 | 1.50 | |

# AVON SS-SERIES

## Avon Publishing Co., Inc.

| | | V/Good | Fine | N/Mint | |
|---|---|---|---|---|---|
| SS1 | Those Barren Leaves–Aldous Huxley | .50 | 1.00 | 1.50 | |
| SS2 | Borstal Boy–Brendan Behan | .50 | 1.00 | 1.50 | |
| SS3 | Portrait of Hemingway–Lillian Ross; 1964 | .50 | 1.00 | 1.50 | B |
| SS4 | The Wind in the Willows–Kenneth Grahame | .50 | 1.00 | 1.50 | |
| SS5 | Roar Lion Roar–Irwin Faust | .50 | 1.00 | 1.50 | |
| SS6 | Dream Life of Balso Snell and A Cool Million–Nathaniel West | .50 | 1.00 | 1.50 | |
| SS7 | Gimpel the Fool–Isaac B. Singer | .50 | 1.00 | 1.50 | |
| SS8 | A Long and Happy Life–Reynolds Price | .50 | 1.00 | 1.50 | |
| SS9 | Tales of the Alhambra–Washington Irving | .50 | 1.00 | 1.50 | |
| SS10 | They Shoot Horses, Don't They?– Horace McCoy; 1966 | 1.00 | 2.00 | 3.00 | |
| SS11 | The Family of Pascual Duarte–Camilio José Cela | .50 | 1.00 | 1.50 | |
| SS12 | The Nephew–James Purdy | .50 | 1.00 | 1.50 | |
| SS13 | Miss Lonelyhearts–Nathanael West | .50 | 1.00 | 1.50 | |
| SS14 | Satan in Goray–Isaac B. Singer | .50 | 1.00 | 1.50 | |
| SS15 | Spinoza of Market Street–Isaac B. Singer | .50 | 1.00 | 1.50 | |
| SS16 | Two Blocks Apart–ed. Charlotte Meyerson | .50 | 1.00 | 1.50 | |
| SS17 | Mother Night–Kurt Vonnegut, Jr; 1967 | 1.50 | 3.00 | 4.50 | SF |
| SS18 | Portrait of Hemingway–Lillian Ross | 1.00 | 2.00 | 3.00 | B |
| SS22 | Borstal Boy–Brendan Behan | .50 | 1.00 | 1.50 | |

# AVON SCIENCE FICTION AND FANTASY READER

## Avon Novels, Inc./Stratford Novels, Inc.

### Digest Size

| | | V/Good | Fine | N/Mint | |
|---|---|---|---|---|---|
| 1 | Includes Clarke, Christopher, Jakes, others; 1953 | 3.00 | 6.00 | 9.00 | SF |
| 2 | Includes Vance, Clarke, Jakes, others; 1953 | 3.00 | 6.00 | 9.00 | SF |

# AVON SCIENCE FICTION READER

## Avon Novels, Inc.

### Digest Size

| | | V/Good | Fine | N/Mint | |
|---|---|---|---|---|---|
| 1 | Includes Hamilton, Merritt, Williamson, Smith, others; 1951 | 6.00 | 12.00 | 18.00 | SF |
| 2 | Includes Wandrel, Smith, Cummings, Dunsany, others; 1951 | 6.00 | 12.00 | 18.00 | SF |
| 3 | Includes Long, Wright, Lovecraft, Bok, others; 1952 | 6.00 | 12.00 | 18.00 | SF |

# AVON SPECIALS

## Avon Publishing Company, Inc.

### Digest Size

| | | V/Good | Fine | N/Mint | |
|---|---|---|---|---|---|
| nn | Seduction–Leo Guild | 7.50 | 15.00 | 22.50 | E |
| nn | A Lady Named Lou–D.H. Clarke | 7.50 | 15.00 | 22.50 | E |
| nn | Peeping Tom–Jack Woodford | 7.50 | 15.00 | 22.50 | E |
| nn | Night Club Girl–John Wilstach; 1951; aka Fiddler's Fee | 7.50 | 15.00 | 22.50 | E |
| nn | Three Gorgeous Hussies–Jack Woodford | 7.50 | 15.00 | 22.50 | E |
| nn | Free Lovers–Jack Woodford | 7.50 | 15.00 | 22.50 | E |
| nn | Scarf of Passion–Robert Bloch. Note: Same cover as Avon No. 211, Avon Monthly Novel No. 9, and the comic Realistic Romances No. 1. | 10.00 | 20.00 | 30.00 | E |
| nn | Venial Sin–John O'Hara | 7.50 | 15.00 | 22.50 | E |

# AVON T/AT-SERIES

## Avon Book Company/Avon Publishing Co., Inc.

| | | V/Good | Fine | N/Mint | |
|---|---|---|---|---|---|
| T2 | Aaron's Rod–D.H. Lawrence | .75 | 1.50 | 2.25 | E |
| AT51 | Bad Girl–Vina Delmar; 1953 | .75 | 1.50 | 2.25 | E |
| AT52 | The Night Air–Harrison Dowd | .75 | 1.50 | 2.25 | E |
| AT53 | The Second Oldest Profession–Robert Sylvester | .75 | 1.50 | 2.25 | E |
| AT54 | Madame Serpent–Jean Plaidy | .75 | 1.50 | 2.25 | A |
| AT55 | The Rake's Progress–Philip Lindsay | .75 | 1.50 | 2.25 | A |
| AT57 | Jessamy John–Phil Stong | .75 | 1.50 | 2.25 | |
| AT58 | The Scorpion–Anna Elisabet Weirauch | .75 | 1.50 | 2.25 | E |
| AT59 | The Rose and the Flame–Jonreed Lauritzen | .75 | 1.50 | 2.25 | |
| AT60 | Kings Mountain–Florette Henri | .75 | 1.50 | 2.25 | |
| AT61 | Stories in the Modern Manner | .50 | 1.00 | 1.50 | |
| AT62 | Powder Mission–Herbert E. Stover | .75 | 1.50 | 2.25 | |
| AT63 | The Hand of the Hunter–Jerome Weidman | .75 | 1.50 | 2.25 | E |
| AT64 | Son of Egypt–James Busbee, Jr | .75 | 1.50 | 2.25 | A |
| AT65 | Sex Habits of American Women–Dr. Fritz Wittels | .75 | 1.50 | 2.25 | NF |
| AT66 | The Avon Book of Modern Writing– eds. William Phillips & Philip Rahr | .50 | 1.00 | 1.50 | |
| AT67 | Dark Passions Subdue–Douglas Sanderson | .75 | 1.50 | 2.25 | |
| AT68 | I, Claudius–Robert Graves | .75 | 1.50 | 2.25 | A |
| AT69 | Intimacy–Jean-Paul Sartre | .75 | 1.50 | 2.25 | |
| AT70 | Turn Back the River–W.G. Hardy | .75 | 1.50 | 2.25 | |
| T71 | Painted Veils–James Huneker | .75 | 1.50 | 2.25 | E |
| T72 | Tide of Empire–Bates Baldwin | .75 | 1.50 | 2.25 | A |

| | | V/Good | Fine | N/Mint | |
|---|---|---|---|---|---|
| T73 | Yankee Mariner–James Busbee, Jr; 1954 | .75 | 1.50 | 2.25 | |
| T74 | Never Leave Me–Harold Robbins | .75 | 1.50 | 2.25 | E |
| T75 | After Many a Summer Dies the Swan– Aldous Huxley | .75 | 1.50 | 2.25 | SF |
| T76 | Blade of Conquest–Jonreed Lauritzen | .75 | 1.50 | 2.25 | A |
| T77 | More Stories in the Modern Manner | .50 | 1.00 | 1.50 | |
| T78 | A Foreign Affair–John Baxter | .75 | 1.50 | 2.25 | |
| T79 | The Scarlet Petticoat–Nard Jones | .75 | 1.50 | 2.25 | A |
| T80 | No Time like the Future–Nelson Bond | .75 | 1.50 | 2.25 | SF |
| T81 | Captain Adam–Donald Barr Chidsey | .75 | 1.50 | 2.25 | A |
| T82 | I'll Never Go There Any More–Jerome Weidman | .75 | 1.50 | 2.25 | |
| T83 | The Bitterweed Path–Thomas Hal Phillips | .75 | 1.50 | 2.25 | |
| T84 | Naked Acre–Francis Mitchell; aka The Wing and the Yoke | .75 | 1.50 | 2.25 | E |
| T85 | Gone to Texas–John W. Thomason, Jr | .75 | 1.50 | 2.25 | W |
| T86 | Savage Holiday–Richard Wright | 1.50 | 3.00 | 4.50 | |
| T87 | Dawn on Our Darkness–Emmanuel Robles | .75 | 1.50 | 2.25 | |
| T88 | Send Them Summer–Hansford Martin | .75 | 1.50 | 2.25 | |
| T89 | The Merry Mistress–Philip Lindsay | .75 | 1.50 | 2.25 | |
| T90 | Nine Days to Mukalla–Frederic Prokosch | .75 | 1.50 | 2.25 | A |
| T91 | The Dark Journey–Julian Green | .75 | 1.50 | 2.25 | |
| T92 | Belly Laughs Annual–Harold Meyers | .75 | 1.50 | 2.25 | H |
| T93 | What D'ya Know for Sure?–Len Zinberg | .75 | 1.50 | 2.25 | |
| T94 | Diary of a Chambermaid–Octave Mirbeau | 1.25 | 2.50 | 3.75 | E |
| T95 | Honeymoon Guide–Harold Meyers | 1.50 | 3.00 | 4.50 | H |
| T96 | Lord of the Isles–Donald Barr Chidsey | .75 | 1.50 | 2.25 | A |
| T97 | I Can Get It for You Wholesale!– Jerome Weidman | .75 | 1.50 | 2.25 | |
| T98 | Chattels of Eldorado–Edgar Jean Bracco; c-Kinstler | 1.50 | 3.00 | 4.50 | A |
| T99 | Tough Kid from Brooklyn–Robert Mende | .75 | 1.50 | 2.25 | |
| T100 | The Flesh and the Sea–John Dobbin | .75 | 1.50 | 2.25 | |
| T101 | Life and Death of a Tough Guy– Benjamin Appel; 1st ed. 1955 | .75 | 1.50 | 2.25 | JD |
| T102 | Droll Stories–Honore de Balzac | .75 | 1.50 | 2.25 | |
| T103 | What's in It for Me?–Jerome Weidman | .75 | 1.50 | 2.25 | E |
| T104 | Love in the Shadows–John Evans | .75 | 1.50 | 2.25 | E |
| T105 | Juvenile Delinquents–Lenard Kaufman | 4.00 | 8.00 | 12.00 | JD |
| T106 | Confessions of a Princess–H.R.H. | .75 | 1.50 | 2.25 | A |
| T107 | Butterfield 8–John O'Hara | .75 | 1.50 | 2.25 | |
| T108 | Never Come Morning–Nelson Algren | .75 | 1.50 | 2.25 | E |
| T109 | Various Temptations–anthology | 1.50 | 3.00 | 4.50 | |
| T110 | Royal Scandal–Philip Lindsay; c-Kinstler | 1.50 | 3.00 | 4.50 | A |
| T111 | Dishonor–Gerald Kersh; aka Night and the City | .75 | 1.50 | 2.25 | |
| T112 | An Artist in Love–Philip Lindsay; c-Kinstler | 1.50 | 3.00 | 4.50 | |
| T113 | Stories of Scarlet Women | .75 | 1.50 | 2.25 | E |
| T114 | The First Lady Chatterley–D.H. Lawrence | .75 | 1.50 | 2.25 | E |
| T115 | Seven Footprints to Satan–A.A. Merritt; 1956. Note: Same cover as Avon No. 272 (bondage variant) | 2.00 | 4.00 | 6.00 | SF |
| T116 | Suzanne, Savage Vixen–Jonreed Lauritzen | .75 | 1.50 | 2.25 | |
| T117 | Typee: A Peep at Polynesian Life– Herman Melville; c-Gauguin | 1.25 | 2.50 | 3.75 | E |
| T118 | The Loves of Liberace–Leo Guild | 3.50 | 7.00 | 10.50 | NF |
| T119 | Ashenden, or the British Agent–W. Somerset Maugham; c-Kinstler. Note: Queen's Quorum, No. 76 | 1.50 | 3.00 | 4.50 | M |
| T120 | The Kiss and the Duel–Anton Chekhov | .75 | 1.50 | 2.25 | |
| T121 | Down and Out in Paris and London– George Orwell | .75 | 1.50 | 2.25 | |
| T122 | To Love by Candlelight–Philip Lindsay; aka A Piece for Candlelight | .75 | 1.50 | 2.25 | E |
| T123 | Girls–for Men Only–John Paul Adams | 1.50 | 3.00 | 4.50 | H |
| T124 | Cry Tough!–Irving Shulman | .75 | 1.50 | 2.25 | |
| T125 | The Neon Wilderness–Nelson Algren | .75 | 1.50 | 2.25 | E |
| T126 | Gold for the Gay Masters–Harriet Gray | .75 | 1.50 | 2.25 | |
| T127 | Out of the Silent Planet–C.S. Lewis; c-Kinstler | 1.50 | 3.00 | 4.50 | SF |
| T128 | Emma: My Lord Admiral's Mistress– F.W. Kenyon | .75 | 1.50 | 2.25 | |

**AVON T/AT-SERIES**, *continued*

| ID | Title | V/Good | Fine | N/Mint | |
|---|---|---|---|---|---|
| T129 | The Gin Palace–Emile Zola | .75 | 1.50 | 2.25 | |
| T130 | The Savage Soldiers–Harold Waters & Aubrey Wisberg | .75 | 1.50 | 2.25 | |
| T131 | Slipping Beauty–Jerome Weidman | .75 | 1.50 | 2.25 | E |
| T132 | Naked Acre–Francis Mitchell | .75 | 1.50 | 2.25 | E |
| T133 | Polikushka and Two Hussars–Leo Tolstoy | .75 | 1.50 | 2.25 | |
| T134 | Captain Adam–Donald Barr Chidsey | .75 | 1.50 | 2.25 | A |
| T135 | The Moon Pool–A.A. Merritt | 1.25 | 2.50 | 3.75 | SF |
| T136 | Sir Naked Blade–Philip Lindsay | .75 | 1.50 | 2.25 | A |
| T137 | The Bride Comes to Yellow Sky–Stephen Crane | .75 | 1.50 | 2.25 | W |
| T138 | The Amboy Dukes–Irving Shulman | .75 | 1.50 | 2.25 | |
| T139 | The Gifted Sinners–Roswell G. Ham, Jr | .75 | 1.50 | 2.25 | E |
| T140 | Temptation in Paris–Honore De Balzac; aka Illusions Perdues | .75 | 1.50 | 2.25 | E |
| T141 | The Tragedy of X–Ellery Queen | .75 | 1.50 | 2.25 | |
| T142 | Murder in Port Afrique–Bernard Dryer | .75 | 1.50 | 2.25 | |
| T143 | Burial of the Fruit–David Dortort | .75 | 1.50 | 2.25 | E |
| T144 | Coming Up for Air–George Orwell | .75 | 1.50 | 2.25 | |
| T145 | Diary of a Chambermaid–Octave Mirbeau | .75 | 1.50 | 2.25 | E |
| T146 | 21st Century Sub–Frank Herbert; aka The Dragon in the Sea | .75 | 1.50 | 2.25 | SF |
| T147 | Money, Money, Money–David Wagoner | .75 | 1.50 | 2.25 | |
| T148 | Around the World in 80 Days–Jules Verne; movie tie-in | 1.50 | 3.00 | 4.50 | SF |
| T149 | Death on the Nile–Agatha Christie | .75 | 1.50 | 2.25 | M |
| T150 | Zarak–A.J. Beran; movie tie-in | 1.50 | 3.00 | 4.50 | A |
| T151 | Hannibal: Scourge of Imperial Rome–Mary Dolan; 1957; aka Hannibal of Carthage | .75 | 1.50 | 2.25 | A |
| T152 | The Ship of Ishtar–A.A. Merritt | 1.25 | 2.50 | 3.75 | SF |
| T153 | I'll Never Go There Any More–Jerome Weidman | .75 | 1.50 | 2.25 | |
| T154 | 26 Men and a Girl–Maxim Gorky | 1.25 | 2.50 | 3.75 | |
| T155 | Gladiator–Philip Wylie | 1.00 | 2.00 | 3.00 | SF |
| T156 | Bride of Violence–Harriet Gray | .75 | 1.50 | 2.25 | E |
| T157 | Perelandra–C.S. Lewis | 1.25 | 2.50 | 3.75 | SF |
| T158 | A Man Can Love Twice–Robert Paul Smith | .75 | 1.50 | 2.25 | |
| T159 | Intrigue in Paris–Sterling Noel | .75 | 1.50 | 2.25 | |
| T160 | After the Fireworks and Other Stories–Aldous Huxley; aka Brief Candles | .75 | 1.50 | 2.25 | E |
| T161 | Face in the Abyss–A.A. Merritt | 1.25 | 2.50 | 3.75 | SF |
| T162 | Teen-age Mobster–Benjamin Appel; aka Life and Death of a Tough Guy | 3.00 | 6.00 | 9.00 | JD |
| T163 | Love among the Haystacks–D.H. Lawrence | .75 | 1.50 | 2.25 | E |
| T164 | The Scarlet Petticoat–Nard Jones | .75 | 1.50 | 2.25 | |
| T165 | Boy on a Dolphin–David Divine; movie tie-in | 3.00 | 6.00 | 9.00 | A |
| T166 | Josephine, the Great Lover–N.P. Nezelof | .75 | 1.50 | 2.25 | E |
| T167 | 7 Dials Mystery–Agatha Christie | .75 | 1.50 | 2.25 | M |
| T168 | Tomorrow Plus X–Wilson Tucker; aka Time Bomb | .75 | 1.50 | 2.25 | SF |
| T169 | The Unholy Wife–John Roeburt; movie tie-in | 3.00 | 6.00 | 9.00 | E |
| T170 | Juvenile Hoods–Joseph Shallit | 3.00 | 6.00 | 9.00 | JD |
| T171 | The Duke's Temptation–Paula Batchelor | .75 | 1.50 | 2.25 | |
| T172 | The Metal Monster–A.A. Merritt | 1.25 | 2.50 | 3.75 | SF |
| T173 | Naked Morning–R.V. Cassill | .75 | 1.50 | 2.25 | |
| T174 | The Young Killers–Willard Wiener | 3.00 | 6.00 | 9.00 | JD |
| T175 | From Outer Space–Hal Clement | .75 | 1.50 | 2.25 | SF |
| T176 | A Holiday for Murder–Agatha Christie | .75 | 1.50 | 2.25 | M |
| T177 | Man on Fire–Owen Aherne; movie tie-in | 1.25 | 2.50 | 3.75 | |
| T178 | Beyond Mombasa–Joseph Hilton; movie tie-in | 1.50 | 3.00 | 4.50 | A |
| T179 | Cry Slaughter!–E.K. Tiempo | .75 | 1.50 | 2.25 | |
| T180 | The Space Plague–George O. Smith | .75 | 1.50 | 2.25 | SF |
| T181 | Pickup Alley–Edward Ronns; movie tie-in | 1.50 | 3.00 | 4.50 | E |
| T182 | An Affair to Remember–Owen Aherne; movie tie-in | 1.25 | 2.50 | 3.75 | |
| T183 | Butterfield 8–John O'Hara | .75 | 1.50 | 2.25 | |
| T184 | Drury Lane's Last Case–Ellery Queen | .75 | 1.50 | 2.25 | M |
| T185 | The Jungle–Nelson Algren | .75 | 1.50 | 2.25 | JD |
| T186 | The Time Dissolver–Jerry Sohl | .75 | 1.50 | 2.25 | SF |
| T187 | Temptations of Valerie–Harry Whittington; movie tie-in | 3.00 | 6.00 | 9.00 | E |
| T188 | Action of the Tiger–James Wellard; movie tie-in | 1.25 | 2.50 | 3.75 | A |
| T189 | Make My Bed in Hell–John B. Sanford | .75 | 1.50 | 2.25 | |
| T190 | The Hunchback of Notre Dame–Victor Hugo; movie tie-in | 3.50 | 7.00 | 10.50 | HO |
| T191 | Bomber Crew–Joseph Landon | .75 | 1.50 | 2.25 | C |
| T192 | Poirot Loses a Client–Agatha Christie | .75 | 1.50 | 2.25 | M |
| T193 | Year 2018!–James Blish | .75 | 1.50 | 2.25 | M |
| T194 | The Wild One–Bonnie Golightly | 1.50 | 3.00 | 4.50 | |
| T195 | The Flesh Agents–Jean Bosquet | .75 | 1.50 | 2.25 | |
| T196 | Man in the Shadow–Harry Whittington; movie tie-in | 3.00 | 6.00 | 9.00 | |
| T197 | Panzer Ghost Division–Thomas Goethals | .75 | 1.50 | 2.25 | C |
| T198 | Ride Out for Revenge–Burt Arthur; movie tie-in | .75 | 1.50 | 2.25 | W |
| T199 | The Saint vs. Scotland Yard–Leslie Charteris | .75 | 1.50 | 2.25 | M |
| T200 | Diary of a 16-Year Old French Girl–Sidonie Colette | .75 | 1.50 | 2.25 | |
| T201 | The Long Haul–Mervyn Mills; movie tie-in | 1.25 | 2.50 | 3.75 | |
| T202 | The Planet Explorer–Murray Leinster | .75 | 1.50 | 2.25 | SF |
| T203 | Les Girls–Constance Tomkinson; movie tie-in | 1.25 | 2.50 | 3.75 | |
| T204 | The Mysterious Affair at Styles–Agatha Christie | .75 | 1.50 | 2.25 | M |
| T205 | U-Boat Killer–Donald MacIntyre | .75 | 1.50 | 2.25 | NF |
| T206 | Soldier's Weekend–Hansford Martin | .75 | 1.50 | 2.25 | |
| T207 | The Price Is Right–Jerome Weidman | .75 | 1.50 | 2.25 | E |
| T208 | Seven Footprints to Satan–A.A. Merritt | .75 | 1.50 | 2.25 | SF |
| T209 | Don Gastone and the Women–Geoffredo Parise; aka Don Gastone and the Ladies | .75 | 1.50 | 2.25 | E |
| T210 | The Secret Adversary–Agatha Christie; 1958 | .75 | 1.50 | 2.25 | M |
| T211 | The Tortured Planet–C.S. Lewis | .75 | 1.50 | 2.25 | SF |
| T212 | Case of the Dark Wanton–Peter Cheyney | .75 | 1.50 | 2.25 | M |
| T213 | I Survived Hitler's Ovens–Olga Lengyel | .75 | 1.50 | 2.25 | NF |
| T214 | Hot Spell–Lonnie Coleman; movie tie-in | 1.50 | 3.00 | 4.50 | E |
| T215 | Tobruk Commando–Gordon Landsborough | .75 | 1.50 | 2.25 | C |

*Avon T117, Avon T150, Avon T185.*

*Avon T196, Avon T261, Avon T299.*

**AVON T/AT-SERIES,** *continued*

| | | V/Good | Fine | N/Mint | |
|---|---|---|---|---|---|
| T216 | Case of the Red Box–Rex Stout | .75 | 1.50 | 2.25 | M |
| T217 | Juvenile Delinquents–Lenard Kaufman; aka The Lower Part of the Sky | 2.50 | 5.00 | 7.50 | JD |
| T218 | A Modern Lover–D.H. Lawrence | .75 | 1.50 | 2.25 | E |
| T219 | Juvenile Jungle–Firth Counsel; movie tie-in | 5.00 | 10.00 | 15.00 | JD |
| T220 | The Regatta Mystery–Agatha Christie | .75 | 1.50 | 2.25 | M |
| T221 | Children of the Atom–Wilmar H. Shiras | .75 | 1.50 | 2.25 | SF |
| T222 | Officers' Plot to Kill Hitler–Constantine Fitzgibbon | .75 | 1.50 | 2.25 | NF |
| T223 | Never Come Morning–Nelson Algren | .75 | 1.50 | 2.25 | |
| T224 | Passiontide–Wirt Williams | .75 | 1.50 | 2.25 | |
| T225 | Earthman, Come Home–James Blish | .75 | 1.50 | 2.25 | SF |
| T226 | Raid at Dieppe–Quentin Reynolds | .75 | 1.50 | 2.25 | C |
| T227 | Belly Laughs Annual–Harold Meyers | 1.00 | 2.00 | 3.00 | H |
| T228 | The Lady Takes a Flyer–Edward Ronns; movie tie-in | 1.25 | 2.50 | 3.75 | M |
| T229 | Young and Wild–Morton Cooper; movie tie-in | 5.00 | 10.00 | 15.00 | JD |
| T230 | Cry Baby Killer–Joseph Hilton; movie tie-in | 5.00 | 10.00 | 15.00 | JD |
| T231 | Rogue's March–Maristan Chapman | .75 | 1.50 | 2.25 | A |
| T232 | 2nd Foundation: Galactic Empire–Isaac Asimov | .75 | 1.50 | 2.25 | SF |
| T233 | Impatient Virgin–Donald Henderson Clarke | .75 | 1.50 | 2.25 | |
| T234 | The Saint in Miami–Leslie Charteris | .75 | 1.50 | 2.25 | M |
| T235 | Gang Girl–Wenzell Brown | 4.00 | 8.00 | 12.00 | JD |
| T236 | The Secret Raiders–David Woodward | .75 | 1.50 | 2.25 | |
| T237 | High Cost of Loving–Bonnie Golightly; movie tie-in | 2.00 | 4.00 | 6.00 | |
| T238 | VOR–James Blish | .75 | 1.50 | 2.25 | SF |
| T239 | D-Day–John Gunther | .75 | 1.50 | 2.25 | C |
| T240 | I Can Get It for You Wholesale!–Jerome Weidman | .75 | 1.50 | 2.25 | |
| T241 | Teen-age Jungle–Harry Whittington | 5.00 | 10.00 | 15.00 | JD |
| T242 | The Four of Hearts–Ellery Queen | .75 | 1.50 | 2.25 | M |
| T243 | Murder in Three Acts–Agatha Christie | .75 | 1.50 | 2.25 | M |
| T244 | Naked Sin–Gordon Clark; orig. 1958 | .75 | 1.50 | 2.25 | E |
| T245 | The Tuesday Club Murders–Agatha Christie | .75 | 1.50 | 2.25 | M |
| T246 | Sunk!–Mochitsura Hashimoto | .75 | 1.50 | 2.25 | C |
| T247 | Delinquent!–Morton Cooper; orig. 1958 | 5.00 | 10.00 | 15.00 | JD |
| T248 | Chattels of Eldorado–Edgar Jean Bracco | .75 | 1.50 | 2.25 | A |
| T249 | Worlds Apart–J.T. McIntosh | .75 | 1.50 | 2.25 | SF |
| T250 | The Saint in England–Leslie Charteris | .75 | 1.50 | 2.25 | M |
| T251 | The Young Who Sin–John Haase | .75 | 1.50 | 2.25 | |
| T252 | The Mind Cage–A.E. Van Vogt | .75 | 1.50 | 2.25 | SF |
| T253 | Breathe No More, My Lady–Ed Lacy | .75 | 1.50 | 2.25 | M |
| T254 | Death of a Fool–Ngaio Marsh | .75 | 1.50 | 2.25 | M |
| T255 | Of All My Sins–Thomas Rourke | .60 | 1.20 | 1.80 | |
| T256 | Jet Ace–Tedd Thomey | .75 | 1.50 | 2.25 | C |
| T257 | High School Confidential–Morton Cooper; movie tie-in | 5.00 | 10.00 | 15.00 | JD |
| T258 | The G-String Murders–Gypsy Rose Lee. Note: Actually written by Craig Rice | .75 | 1.50 | 2.25 | M |
| T259 | Hiroshima Diary–Michihiko Hachlya | .75 | 1.50 | 2.25 | C |
| T260 | Painted Veils–James Huneker | .75 | 1.50 | 2.25 | |
| T261 | Waldo: Genius in Orbit–Robert A. Heinlein | .75 | 1.50 | 2.25 | SF |
| T262 | Gang Rumble–Edward Ronns | 4.00 | 8.00 | 12.00 | JD |
| T263 | Love in the Shadows–John Evans; aka Shadows Flying | .75 | 1.50 | 2.25 | E |
| T264 | Trinity in Violence–Henry Kane | .75 | 1.50 | 2.25 | M |
| T265 | Cry Attack!–John Burgan | .75 | 1.50 | 2.25 | C |
| T266 | The Vice Trap–Elliott Gilbert | .75 | 1.50 | 2.25 | |
| T267 | Naked Tide–Roderic Hastings | .75 | 1.50 | 2.25 | |
| T268 | ESPer–James Blish | .75 | 1.50 | 2.25 | SF |
| T269 | Mitsou–Sidonie Colette; movie tie-in | .75 | 1.50 | 2.25 | |
| T270 | Run for Your Life!–Sterling Noel; orig. 1958 | .75 | 1.50 | 2.25 | M |
| T271 | Raw Wind in Eden–Ed Robinson; movie tie-in | 2.00 | 4.00 | 6.00 | E |
| T272 | I Am a Marked Woman–anon. | .75 | 1.50 | 2.25 | E |
| T273 | The Bitterweed Path–Thomas Hal Phillips | .75 | 1.50 | 2.25 | |
| T274 | West of the Law–Al Cody | .75 | 1.50 | 2.25 | W |
| T275 | Destination: Infinity–Henry Kuttner | .75 | 1.50 | 2.25 | SF |
| T276 | Fistful of Death–Henry Kane | .75 | 1.50 | 2.25 | M |
| T277 | Sinful–Bart Frame | .75 | 1.50 | 2.25 | |
| T278 | Out for a Killing–John W. Vandercook | .75 | 1.50 | 2.25 | M |
| T279 | The Triumph of Time–James Blish | .75 | 1.50 | 2.25 | SF |
| T280 | Death Hits the Jackpot–Walter Wager | .75 | 1.50 | 2.25 | M |
| T281 | Lustful Summer–R.V. Cassill; orig. 1958 | .75 | 1.50 | 2.25 | E |
| T282 | Honeymoon Guide–Harold Meyers | 1.25 | 2.50 | 3.75 | H |
| T283 | A Hell of a Murder–Warren Carrier | .75 | 1.50 | 2.25 | M |
| T284 | Horror!–H.P. Lovecraft | 1.25 | 2.50 | 3.75 | HO |
| T285 | Shameless–James M. Cain | .75 | 1.50 | 2.25 | |
| T286 | The Merry Mistress–Philip Lindsay | .75 | 1.50 | 2.25 | |
| T287 | The Death Dealers–Isaac Asimov; 1st ed. 1958 | 1.25 | 2.50 | 3.75 | M |
| T288 | Shakedown for Murder–Ed Lacy | .75 | 1.50 | 2.25 | |
| T289 | BR-R-R!–ed. Groff Conklin; 1959 | .75 | 1.50 | 2.25 | HO |
| T290 | Prelude to Murder–Sterling Noel | .75 | 1.50 | 2.25 | M |
| T291 | Death Is the Last Lover–Henry Kane | .75 | 1.50 | 2.25 | M |
| T292 | The American Gun Mystery–Ellery Queen | .75 | 1.50 | 2.25 | M |
| T293 | The Buccaneer–R.V. Cassill; movie tie-in | 1.25 | 2.50 | 3.75 | A |
| T294 | Waiting for Willy–Jack Houston | .75 | 1.50 | 2.25 | |
| T295 | The Hot Half Hour–Robert L. Foreman | .75 | 1.50 | 2.25 | |
| T296 | Over My Dead Body–Rex Stout | .75 | 1.50 | 2.25 | M |
| T297 | Doomsday Morning–C.L. Moore | .75 | 1.50 | 2.25 | SF |
| T298 | Break-up–Edmund Schiddel | .75 | 1.50 | 2.25 | |
| T299 | Halfway to Hell–Harry Whittington | 3.00 | 6.00 | 9.00 | JD |
| T300 | Confidential–Donald Henderson Clarke | .75 | 1.50 | 2.25 | |
| T301 | Claudine–Sidonie Colette | .75 | 1.50 | 2.25 | |
| T302 | The Subterraneans–Jack Kerouac. Note: Original preface by Henry Miller | 2.50 | 5.00 | 7.50 | |
| T303 | Cry Tough!–Irving Shulman; movie tie-in | 4.00 | 8.00 | 12.00 | JD |
| T304 | Aliens 4–Theodore Sturgeon | .75 | 1.50 | 2.25 | SF |
| T305 | The Naked Sword–Donald Barr Chidsey | .75 | 1.50 | 2.25 | A |
| T306 | The Night Was Made for Murder–Will Cotton | .75 | 1.50 | 2.25 | M |
| T307 | Doorway to Death–Dan Marlowe | 1.00 | 2.00 | 3.00 | M |
| T308 | And Sin No More–H.P. Koenig | .75 | 1.50 | 2.25 | |
| T309 | Mark It for Murder–Douglas Sanderson | .75 | 1.50 | 2.25 | M |
| T310 | Beat Girl–Bonnie Golightly | 2.00 | 4.00 | 6.00 | |
| T311 | Anything for Kicks–Morton Cooper | 4.00 | 8.00 | 12.00 | JD |
| T312 | The Lonely Gun–Gordon D. Shirreffs | .75 | 1.50 | 2.25 | W |
| T313 | Diary of a Geisha Girl–Kimiko Omura & William Vaneer | .75 | 1.50 | 2.25 | E |
| T314 | Undressed to Kill–Peter Cheyney | .75 | 1.50 | 2.25 | M |
| T315 | Death in the Desert–Lee E. Wells | .75 | 1.50 | 2.25 | W |
| T316 | Ginny–Morton Cooper | .75 | 1.50 | 2.25 | |
| T317 | The Saint in New York–Leslie Charteris | .75 | 1.50 | 2.25 | M |
| T318 | Lord of the Isles–Donald Barr Chidsey | .75 | 1.50 | 2.25 | A |
| T319 | Too Innocent to Kill–Doris Miles Disney | .75 | 1.50 | 2.25 | M |
| T320 | The Blonde in Suite 14–Stewart Sterling | .75 | 1.50 | 2.25 | M |
| T321 | They Who Sin–John Roeburt | .75 | 1.50 | 2.25 | E |
| T322 | The Hard Man–Philip Ketchum | .75 | 1.50 | 2.25 | W |
| T323 | Pnin–Vladimir Nabokov | .75 | 1.50 | 2.25 | |
| T324 | The Jungle–Nelson Algren | 4.00 | 8.00 | 12.00 | JD |
| T325 | The Savage Warriors–Henry Treece; aka The Dark Island | .75 | 1.50 | 2.25 | A |
| T326 | Never Leave Me–Harold Robbins | .75 | 1.50 | 2.25 | E |
| T327 | Gun for Sale–Lee E. Wells | .75 | 1.50 | 2.25 | W |
| T328 | The Real Cool Killers–Chester Himes | 2.00 | 4.00 | 6.00 | |
| T329 | The Shame–Richard Himmel | .75 | 1.50 | 2.25 | |
| T330 | Blonde Bait–Stephen Marlowe | .75 | 1.50 | 2.25 | M |
| T331 | Savage Star–Lewis B. Patten | .75 | 1.50 | 2.25 | W |
| T332 | How Rough Can It Get?–Joe Weiss | .75 | 1.50 | 2.25 | |
| T333 | The Devil's Bride–Carter A. Vaughan | .75 | 1.50 | 2.25 | A |
| T334 | The Amboy Dukes–Irving Shulman | 2.50 | 5.00 | 7.50 | JD |
| T335 | Sugar–Gil Brewer; orig. 1959 | 1.50 | 3.00 | 4.50 | E |
| T336 | The Strange Co-ed–Bart Frame | .75 | 1.50 | 2.25 | |
| T337 | The Tragedy of Y–Ellery Queen | .75 | 1.50 | 2.25 | M |
| T338 | Nadia–Assia Djebar | .75 | 1.50 | 2.25 | |
| T339 | The Man Who Rode Alone–Lewis B. Patten | .75 | 1.50 | 2.25 | W |
| T340 | The Subterraneans–Jack Kerouac | 1.00 | 2.00 | 3.00 | |
| T341 | Iron Lover–Gardner F. Fox | 1.25 | 2.50 | 3.75 | A |
| T342 | The Unholy Lovers–Paul Monash | .75 | 1.50 | 2.25 | E |
| T343 | Find Eileen Hardin–Alive!–Andrew Frazer | .75 | 1.50 | 2.25 | |
| T344 | Three Loves Had She–Mark Schorer | .75 | 1.50 | 2.25 | |
| T345 | Monsters and Such–Murray Leinster | .75 | 1.50 | 2.25 | SF |

AVON T/AT-SERIES, *continued*

| | | V/Good | Fine | N/Mint | |
|---|---|---|---|---|---|
| T346 | Bachelor's Joke Book—Leo Guild | .75 | 1.50 | 2.25 | H |
| T347 | Strange Bargain—Harry Whittington | 1.50 | 3.00 | 4.50 | |
| T348 | This Range Is Mine—Dean Owen | .75 | 1.50 | 2.25 | W |
| T349 | Killer with a Key—Dan Marlowe | 1.00 | 2.00 | 3.00 | M |
| T350 | Love for a Stranger—John Pleasant McCoy | .75 | 1.50 | 2.25 | |
| T351 | Murder Is an Art—Michael Innes; aka One Man Show | .75 | 1.50 | 2.25 | M |
| T352 | Fort Suicide—Gordon D. Shirreffs | .75 | 1.50 | 2.25 | W |
| T353 | The Town That God Forgot—William Colt MacDonald | .75 | 1.50 | 2.25 | W |
| T354 | Beyond the Night—Cornell Woolrich; orig. 1959 | 3.00 | 6.00 | 9.00 | M |
| T355 | Bachelor Summer—Herbert D. Kastle | .75 | 1.50 | 2.25 | |
| T356 | Girl in a Jam—James Savage | .75 | 1.50 | 2.25 | |
| T357 | The Crazy Kill—Chester Himes | 2.00 | 4.00 | 6.00 | |
| T358 | The Mistress—Theodora Keogh | 1.25 | 2.50 | 3.75 | |
| T359 | Rusty Desmond—Steve January | 2.00 | 4.00 | 6.00 | JD |
| T360 | We Who Survived . . . the Fifth Ice Age—Sterling Noel | 2.50 | 5.00 | 7.50 | SF |
| T361 | Run, Killer, Run!—Lionel White; orig. 1959 | 1.50 | 3.00 | 4.50 | |
| T362 | The Man Who Could Cheat Death—Barre Lyndon & Jimmy Sangster; movie tie-in | 2.00 | 4.00 | 6.00 | SF |
| T363 | The Pagan Queen—Henry Treece; aka Red Queen, White Queen | 1.25 | 2.50 | 3.75 | A |
| T364 | Young Awakening—Robert Fontaine | .75 | 1.50 | 2.25 | |
| T365 | The Terrible Night—Peter Cheyney | .75 | 1.50 | 2.25 | M |
| T366 | The Figure in the Dusk—John Creasey | .75 | 1.50 | 2.25 | M |
| T367 | Avon Bedside Companion | .75 | 1.50 | 2.25 | |
| T368 | Cheyenne War Cry—Noel M. Loomis | .75 | 1.50 | 2.25 | W |
| T369 | Ambush at Scorpion Valley—William Colt MacDonald | .75 | 1.50 | 2.25 | W |
| T370 | The Captive—Norman Daniels; orig. 1959 | 1.00 | 2.00 | 3.00 | E |
| T371 | Planet in Peril—John Christopher | .75 | 1.50 | 2.25 | SF |
| T372 | The Long Night—Ovid Demaris | .75 | 1.50 | 2.25 | |
| T373 | Law Killer—Richard Brister | .75 | 1.50 | 2.25 | W |
| T374 | Where There's a Will—Rex Stout | .75 | 1.50 | 2.25 | M |
| T375 | I, Barbarian—Jay Scotland (John Jakes); orig. 1959 | 2.00 | 4.00 | 6.00 | A |
| T376 | Beat Not the Bones—Charlotte Jay | .50 | 1.00 | 1.50 | |
| T377 | McHugh—Jay Flynn | .50 | 1.00 | 1.50 | M |
| T378 | The Naked Land—Lee E. Wells | .75 | 1.50 | 2.25 | W |
| T379 | The Blockhouse—Jean-Paul Clebert; 1960 | .75 | 1.50 | 2.25 | NF |
| T380 | The Bastard of Orleans—Gardner F. Fox | 1.00 | 2.00 | 3.00 | A |
| T381 | Drury Lane's Last Case—Ellery Queen | .50 | 1.00 | 1.50 | M |
| T382 | Short Cut to Red River—Noel Loomis | .75 | 1.50 | 2.25 | W |
| T383 | Addicted to Murder—Theodore S. Drachman; aka Something for the Birds | .50 | 1.00 | 1.50 | M |
| T384 | The Big Gold Dream—Chester Himes | 2.00 | 4.00 | 6.00 | |
| T385 | Various Temptations—ed. anon. | 1.00 | 2.00 | 3.00 | |
| T386 | Mulvane's War—William Heuman | .75 | 1.50 | 2.25 | W |
| T387 | Swamp Tease—Edward Kempton | .75 | 1.50 | 2.25 | E |
| T388 | The Golden Slave—Poul Anderson; 1st ed. 1960 | 2.50 | 5.00 | 7.50 | A |
| T389 | Twists in Time—Murray Leinster | 1.00 | 2.00 | 3.00 | SF |
| T390 | The Subterraneans—Jack Kerouac | 1.00 | 2.00 | 3.00 | |
| T391 | The Bride of Newgate—John Dickson Carr | 1.25 | 2.50 | 3.75 | A |
| T392 | Doom Service—Dan Marlowe | .75 | 1.50 | 2.25 | M |
| T393 | Naked Morning—R.V. Cassill | .75 | 1.50 | 2.25 | E |
| T394 | Shakedown Strip—Louis Malley; aka Stool Pigeon | .50 | 1.00 | 1.50 | |
| T395 | The Cougar Kid—Johnston McCulley | .75 | 1.50 | 2.25 | W |
| T396 | Rebel Ranger—William Colt MacDonald | .75 | 1.50 | 2.25 | W |
| T397 | Voyage from Lesbos—Richard C. Robertiello, MD | .75 | 1.50 | 2.25 | E |
| T398 | Great Train Robberies of the West—Eugene B. Block | .75 | 1.50 | 2.25 | NF |
| T399 | The Iron Marshal—Steven C. Lawrence | .50 | 1.00 | 1.50 | W |
| T400 | The Invaders—Henry Treece; aka The Golden Strangers | 1.00 | 2.00 | 3.00 | A |
| T401 | Death on the Nile—Agatha Christie | .75 | 1.50 | 2.25 | M |
| T402 | West of the Wolverine—Paul Evan Lehman | .75 | 1.50 | 2.25 | W |
| T403 | Rebel Woman—Harry Whittington | 1.50 | 3.00 | 4.50 | A |
| T404 | Chance Meeting—Leigh Howard; aka Blind Date; movie tie-in | 1.00 | 2.00 | 3.00 | |
| T405 | Stop-Over—Morton Cooper | .50 | 1.00 | 1.50 | |
| T406 | It's Murder, McHugh—Jay Flynn | .50 | 1.00 | 1.50 | M |
| T407 | Power Play—William M. Goeney; aka The Moment of Truth | .50 | 1.00 | 1.50 | |
| T408 | The Doomstone—Cornell Woolrich; 1st ed. 1960 | 2.50 | 5.00 | 7.50 | M |
| T409 | Action at Arcanum—William Colt MacDonald | .75 | 1.50 | 2.25 | W |
| T410 | Out of the Silent Planet—C.S. Lewis | .75 | 1.50 | 2.25 | SF |
| T411 | The Shotgunner—Ray Hogan | .75 | 1.50 | 2.25 | W |
| T412 | Favorite Stories of W. Somerset Maugham—W. Somerset Maugham | .50 | 1.00 | 1.50 | |
| T413 | Cargo-Trouble—Paul Thomas | .50 | 1.00 | 1.50 | |
| T414 | Suzanne, Savage Vixen—Jonreed Lauritzen; aka Suzanne | .75 | 1.50 | 2.25 | A |
| T415 | The Homecoming Game—Howard Nemerov | .50 | 1.00 | 1.50 | |
| T416 | Richard Nixon—Earl Mazo | .75 | 1.50 | 2.25 | B |
| T417 | Reformatory Girls—Ray Morrison; 1960 | 1.50 | 3.00 | 4.50 | JD |
| T418 | The Buzzard Guns—Philip Ketchum | .75 | 1.50 | 2.25 | W |
| T419 | The Fall of Marty Moon—Andrew Frazer (Milton Lesser) | .50 | 1.00 | 1.50 | |
| T420 | Ashenden—W. Somerset Maugham. Note: Queen's Quorum No. 76 | .50 | 1.00 | 1.50 | |
| T421 | Roaring Lead—William Colt MacDonald | .75 | 1.50 | 2.25 | W |
| T422 | Death Has a Small Voice—Frances Lockridge & Richard Lockridge | .75 | 1.50 | 2.25 | M |
| T423 | Passport to Terror—Max Daniels | .50 | 1.00 | 1.50 | |
| T424 | Doctor in Love—Richard Gordon (Gordon Ostlere) | .50 | 1.00 | 1.50 | R |
| T425 | What's in It for Me?—Jerome Weidman | .50 | 1.00 | 1.50 | |
| T426 | Catch a Fallen Starlet—Douglas Sanderson | .50 | 1.00 | 1.50 | M |
| T427 | We Are Not Alone—James Hilton | .50 | 1.00 | 1.50 | |
| T428 | Sunrise Guns—William Colt MacDonald; aka Law of the Forty-Fives | .75 | 1.50 | 2.25 | W |
| T429 | Tristessa—Jack Kerouac; 1st ed. 1960 | 7.50 | 15.00 | 22.50 | E |
| T430 | Run for the Money—Robert Colby | .50 | 1.00 | 1.50 | |
| T431 | Bitter Creek—Al Cody (Archie Joscelyn) | .50 | 1.00 | 1.50 | W |
| T432 | Fancy-man—Donald Barr Chidsey | .75 | 1.50 | 2.25 | A |
| T433 | Gunhand from Texas—William Heuman | .50 | 1.00 | 1.50 | W |
| T434 | All Shot Up—Chester Himes | 2.00 | 4.00 | 6.00 | M |
| T436 | Hitler's Ovens—Olga Lengyel; aka Five Chimneys | .75 | 1.50 | 2.25 | NF |
| T437 | The Beast in Me and Other Animals—James Thurber | .75 | 1.50 | 2.25 | H |
| T438 | Life with Fiorello—Ernest Cuneo | .50 | 1.00 | 1.50 | NF |
| T439 | Beyond—Theodore Sturgeon | .50 | 1.00 | 1.50 | SF |
| T440 | Oh Careless Love—Maurice Zolotow | .50 | 1.00 | 1.50 | |
| T441 | My Sister's Keeper—Ronald Verlin Cassill | .50 | 1.00 | 1.50 | |
| T442 | The Shattered Affair—Bruce Palmer; aka Blind Man's Mark | .50 | 1.00 | 1.50 | |
| T443 | Spanish Pesos—William Colt MacDonald | .75 | 1.50 | 2.25 | W |
| T444 | A Body for McHugh—Jay Flynn | .50 | 1.00 | 1.50 | M |
| T446 | The Alamo—Steve Frazee; 1960; movie tie-in | 1.00 | 2.00 | 3.00 | A |
| T448 | The Golden Cage—Tereska Torres | .50 | 1.00 | 1.50 | |
| T449 | The Lottery—Shirley Jackson | 1.00 | 2.00 | 3.00 | |
| T450 | Die, Lover—Harry Whittington; aka Vengeful Sinner | 1.00 | 2.00 | 3.00 | |
| T451 | Savage Town—Lewis B. Patten | .50 | 1.00 | 1.50 | W |

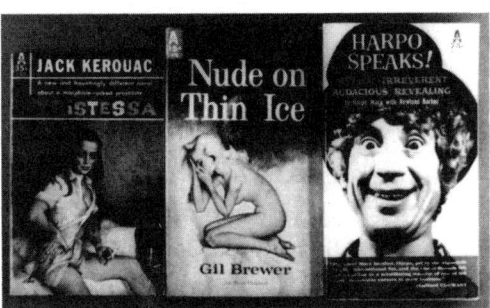

*Avon T429, Avon T470, Avon V2050.*

| V/Good | Fine | N/Mint |
| --- | --- | --- |

| Code | Title | V/Good | Fine | N/Mint | |
| --- | --- | --- | --- | --- | --- |
| T452 | The Fatal Frails–Dan Marlowe | .75 | 1.50 | 2.25 | M |
| T453 | Guns Against the Sun–Ray Hogan | .75 | 1.50 | 2.25 | W |
| T454 | The Young Who Sin–John Haase | .50 | 1.00 | 1.50 | E |
| T455 | Face of a Hero–Pierre Boulle | .50 | 1.00 | 1.50 | |
| T456 | Fort Frederick–Francoise des Ligneris | 1.50 | 3.00 | 4.50 | A |
| T457 | Tarnished Star–Lee E. Wells | .50 | 1.00 | 1.50 | W |
| T458 | A Day to Die–Steve Frazee | 1.00 | 2.00 | 3.00 | W |
| T459 | The Brimstone Bed–Day Keene | 1.50 | 3.00 | 4.50 | M |
| T460 | Martinis and Murder–Henry Kane; aka A Halo for Nobody | .75 | 1.50 | 2.25 | M |
| T461 | Night of the Gunmen–Steven C. Lawrence | .50 | 1.00 | 1.50 | W |
| T462 | The Gold-Plated Sewer–Ovid Demaris | .50 | 1.00 | 1.50 | |
| T463 | A Scent of White Poppies–John Christopher | 1.50 | 3.00 | 4.50 | |
| T464 | Eichmann, Man of Slaughter–John Donovan | 1.25 | 2.50 | 3.75 | NF |
| T465 | Malcolm–James Purdy | .50 | 1.00 | 1.50 | |
| T466 | Viva McHugh–Jay Flynn; 1960 | .50 | 1.00 | 1.50 | |
| T468 | Teen-Age Mobster–Benjamin Appel; aka Life and Death of a Tough Guy | 1.50 | 3.00 | 4.50 | JD |
| T469 | Girl on a Slay Ride–Louis Trimble | .50 | 1.00 | 1.50 | M |
| T470 | Nude on Thin Ice–Gil Brewer | 1.25 | 2.50 | 3.75 | M |
| T471 | Splinters of Fear–Nancy Watson Erikson | .50 | 1.00 | 1.50 | |
| T472 | Rogue Sword–Poul Anderson; 1st ed. 1960 | 1.50 | 3.00 | 4.50 | A |
| T473 | Lead Reckoning–Ray Hogan | .75 | 1.50 | 2.25 | W |
| T474 | A Breath of Scandal–Bonnie Golightly; 1960; movie tie-in | 1.50 | 3.00 | 4.50 | R |
| T475 | Magic Scapel–Maxwell Maltz, MD | .50 | 1.00 | 1.50 | R |
| T476 | Sixgun Wild–James Keene | .50 | 1.00 | 1.50 | W |
| T477 | Intrigue in Paris–Sterling Noel | .75 | 1.50 | 2.25 | M |
| T478 | Warrior Basin–Leslie Ernenwein | .75 | 1.50 | 2.25 | W |
| T479 | Lover, Let Me Live!–Norman Daniels | .75 | 1.50 | 2.25 | M |
| T480 | Prisoner of Tordesillas–Lawrence Schoonover | .75 | 1.50 | 2.25 | A |
| T481 | End of the Road–John Barth | .50 | 1.00 | 1.50 | |
| T482 | Psyche 59–Francoise de Ligneris | .50 | 1.00 | 1.50 | |
| T483 | The Wailing Asteroid–Murray Leinster | .75 | 1.50 | 2.25 | SF |
| T484 | Puzzle It Out–anon; 1960 | 1.00 | 2.00 | 3.00 | NF |
| T485 | Clean Crimes and Neat Murders–Alfred Hitchcock (Henry Slesar); 1961 | 1.25 | 2.50 | 3.75 | M |
| T486 | Bullets for Mulvane–William Heuman | .50 | 1.00 | 1.50 | W |
| T487 | Cheers!–Jim Collier | .50 | 1.00 | 1.50 | NF |
| T488 | Guide to Success in the Stock Market–Ira U. Cobleigh | .50 | 1.00 | 1.50 | NF |
| T489 | Beatville U.S.A.–George Mandel; 1961 | .75 | 1.50 | 2.25 | H |
| T490 | Doctor in Clover–Richard Gordon (Gordon Ostlere) | .50 | 1.00 | 1.50 | R |
| T491 | Shake A Crooked Town–Dan Marlowe | .75 | 1.50 | 2.25 | M |
| T492 | Bitter Water–Thomas Thompson | .75 | 1.50 | 2.25 | W |
| T493 | Flowers for the Judge–Margery Allingham | .50 | 1.00 | 1.50 | M |
| T494 | Trouble on the Tonto Rim–Nelson Nye; aka Killer of Cibecue | .75 | 1.50 | 2.25 | W |
| T495 | Suburban Wife–Kay Martin | .50 | 1.00 | 1.50 | |
| T496 | Look to Your Geese–Jacquin Sanders | .50 | 1.00 | 1.50 | |
| T497 | The Fiery Furnace–Lawrence Williams | .50 | 1.00 | 1.50 | |
| T498 | Ivan the Terrible–Gardner F. Fox; 1961 | 1.00 | 2.00 | 3.00 | A |
| T500 | The Action Man–Jay Flynn | .50 | 1.00 | 1.50 | M |
| T501 | Office Hi-Jinks–Jimmy Hatlo | 1.50 | 3.00 | 4.50 | H |
| T502 | Little Mistress–Arthur Orrmont | .50 | 1.00 | 1.50 | E |
| T503 | Girl Singer–Deborah Ishloan | .50 | 1.00 | 1.50 | |
| T504 | Enter, Sleeping–David Karp | .50 | 1.00 | 1.50 | M |
| T505 | Its Ugly Head–Derek Monsey; 1961 | .50 | 1.00 | 1.50 | |
| T506 | Hell Hath No Fury–Warren Griffen | .50 | 1.00 | 1.50 | |
| T507 | Gone to Texas–John W. Thomason, Jr; 1961 | 1.00 | 2.00 | 3.00 | W |
| T508 | Killers Five–William Hopson; aka Sunset Ranch | .75 | 1.50 | 2.25 | W |
| T509 | Gun Fury–Steven C. Lawrence | .50 | 1.00 | 1.50 | W |
| T510 | My Husband Arthur Murray–Betty Hannah Hoffman & Katherine Murray; 1961 | .50 | 1.00 | 1.50 | NF |
| T511 | The Doctor's Son–John O'Hara | .50 | 1.00 | 1.50 | |
| T512 | Blue and Grey–ed. Donald Honig | 1.00 | 2.00 | 3.00 | A |
| T513 | The Babe and I–Mrs. Babe Ruth | 1.00 | 2.00 | 3.00 | S |
| T514 | Portrait of a Sadist–Paull Hill | .50 | 1.00 | 1.50 | |
| T515 | The Proud Gun–Gordon D. Shirreffs | .75 | 1.50 | 2.25 | W |
| T516 | The Tragedy of Z–Ellery Queen | .50 | 1.00 | 1.50 | M |
| T517 | Texas Red–Al Cody (Archie Joscelyn) | .50 | 1.00 | 1.50 | W |
| T518 | The Avenging Saint–Leslie Charteris | .50 | 1.00 | 1.50 | M |
| T519 | Graduate Nurse–Ann Rush; aka Florida Nurse | .50 | 1.00 | 1.50 | R |
| T520 | The Devil's Whisper–Lee Borden | .50 | 1.00 | 1.50 | |
| T521 | Nero–Frank Castle | .75 | 1.50 | 2.25 | A |
| T522 | The Riddle of Ramrod Ridge–William Colt MacDonald | .75 | 1.50 | 2.25 | W |
| T523 | Ride to the Gun–Ray Hogan | .75 | 1.50 | 2.25 | W |
| T524 | He Owned the World–Charles Eric Maine | 1.25 | 2.50 | 3.75 | SF |
| T525 | Nurse Judy–Elizabeth Wesley | .50 | 1.00 | 1.50 | R |
| T526 | The Big Four–Agatha Christie | .50 | 1.00 | 1.50 | M |
| T527 | Tunes of Glory–James Kennaway; movie tie-in | .75 | 1.50 | 2.25 | |
| T528 | An American Romance–Hans Koningsberger; c-McGinnis | .50 | 1.00 | 1.50 | |
| T529 | The Fighting Texan–Paul Evan Lehman | .75 | 1.50 | 2.25 | W |
| T530 | The Tiger in the Smoke–Margery Allingham | .50 | 1.00 | 1.50 | M |
| T531 | Survive!–Evan Lee Heyman | .50 | 1.00 | 1.50 | NF |
| T532 | The Bridge–Manfred Gregor; movie tie-in | .75 | 1.50 | 2.25 | C |
| T533 | Apache Kill–William Hopson; 1961 | .75 | 1.50 | 2.25 | W |
| T534 | The Avon Crossword Puzzler–ed. Maynard Nichols | 2.00 | 4.00 | 6.00 | NF |
| T535 | The Love Survey–Morton Cooper | .50 | 1.00 | 1.50 | E |
| T536 | Renegade Gun–Lewis B. Patten | .75 | 1.50 | 2.25 | W |
| T537 | A Doctor for Barbara–Margaret Howe | .50 | 1.00 | 1.50 | R |
| T538 | Bugged for Murder–Ed Lacy | .75 | 1.50 | 2.25 | M |
| T538 | The Saint Errant–Leslie Charteris | .50 | 1.00 | 1.50 | M |
| T539 | The Snatchers–Lionel White; 1961 | 1.00 | 2.00 | 3.00 | M |
| T540 | Night Riders' Moon–Robert J. Hogan | .75 | 1.50 | 2.25 | W |
| T541 | The Dark of Summer–E.M. Parsons; 1961 | .50 | 1.00 | 1.50 | |
| T542 | Wanted: Smoke Wade–Robert J. Hogan; aka Savage Rebel | .75 | 1.50 | 2.25 | W |
| T543 | Settlement Nurse–Peggy Gaddis | .50 | 1.00 | 1.50 | R |
| T544 | Gunsmoke–Nelson C. Nye | .75 | 1.50 | 2.25 | W |
| T545 | Trail Boss from Texas–Barry Cord; 1961 | .50 | 1.00 | 1.50 | W |
| T546 | Renegade Ramrod–Leslie Ernenwein; 1961 | .75 | 1.50 | 2.25 | W |
| T547 | Poverty Range–Paul Evan Lehman; 1962 | .75 | 1.50 | 2.25 | W |
| T548 | The Wolf Streak–Richard Brister | .75 | 1.50 | 2.25 | W |
| T549 | Posse–George C. Appell; 1962 | .75 | 1.50 | 2.25 | W |
| T550 | Dead Man's Range–Allan K. Echols | .75 | 1.50 | 2.25 | W |
| T551 | Rio Renegade–Leslie Ernenwein; 1962 | .75 | 1.50 | 2.25 | W |
| T552 | Guilty Guns–Lewis B. Patten; 1963 | .75 | 1.50 | 2.25 | W |
| T553 | Hangtree Range–William Hopson; 1963 | .75 | 1.50 | 2.25 | W |
| T554 | The Third Rider–Barry Cord | .50 | 1.00 | 1.50 | W |
| T556 | The Shoot Out at Sentinel Peak–Richard Brister | .75 | 1.50 | 2.25 | W |
| T610 | The Saint Steps in–Leslie Charteris | .50 | 1.00 | 1.50 | M |
| T611 | The Saint in Europe–Leslie Charteris | .50 | 1.00 | 1.50 | M |
| T619 | The Saint Sees It Through–Leslie Charteris | .50 | 1.00 | 1.50 | M |
| T629 | The Saint and Mr. Teal–Leslie Charteris | .50 | 1.00 | 1.50 | M |
| T634 | Miss Lonelyhearts–Nathaniel West; 1959 | .50 | 1.00 | 1.50 | M |
| T658 | Death in the Air–Agatha Christie | .50 | 1.00 | 1.50 | M |
| T690 | The Big Four–Agatha Christie | .50 | 1.00 | 1.50 | M |
| T716 | Poirot Investigates–Agatha Christie | .50 | 1.00 | 1.50 | M |
| T771 | The Saint on the Spanish Main–Leslie Charteris | .50 | 1.00 | 1.50 | M |
| T793 | The Case of the Moving Finger–Agatha Christie | .50 | 1.00 | 1.50 | M |

# (AVON UNNUMBERED)

## Avon Publishing Company, Inc.

### Digest Size

| Code | Title | V/Good | Fine | N/Mint | |
| --- | --- | --- | --- | --- | --- |
| nn | Book of Jokes–Harry Hershfield | 5.00 | 10.00 | 15.00 | H |
| nn | Cuties–E. Simms Campbell; 1945 | 7.50 | 15.00 | 22.50 | H |
| nn | Cartoons from Colliers | 5.00 | 10.00 | 15.00 | H |

|  | | V/Good | Fine | N/Mint |
|---|---|---|---|---|

**(AVON UNNUMBERED),** *continued*

| | | V/Good | Fine | N/Mint |
|---|---|---|---|---|
| nn | Avon Home Gardener–Dean Halliday; 1952 | 1.00 | 2.00 | 3.00 NF |
| nn | Special for Women–George Lefferts; 1962; TV tie-in; printed for Purex | 1.50 | 3.00 | 4.50 |

# AVON V-SERIES
## Avon Book Company

| | | V/Good | Fine | N/Mint |
|---|---|---|---|---|
| V2031 | Point Counter Point–Aldous Huxley | .75 | 1.50 | 2.25 |
| V2032 | Affectionately, FDR–James Roosevelt & Sidney Shalett; 1961 | .50 | 1.00 | 1.50 NF |
| V2033 | Borstal Boy–Brendan Behan | .50 | 1.00 | 1.50 |
| V2034 | The Lifetime Reading Plan–Clifton Fadiman | .50 | 1.00 | 1.50 NF |
| V2035 | Stranger Come Home–William Shirer | .50 | 1.00 | 1.50 |
| V2036 | Great Themes in Political Theory. Vol. 1–Michael Curtis | .50 | 1.00 | 1.50 NF |
| V2037 | The Best from Cosmopolitan–ed. Richard Gehman | .50 | 1.00 | 1.50 |
| V2038 | The Air-Conditioned Nightmare–Henry Miller | 1.50 | 3.00 | 4.50 |
| V2039 | Cuba–First Soviet Satellite in the Americas–D. James | .50 | 1.00 | 1.50 NF |
| V2040 | The Life and Times of Rembrandt–Hendrik W. Van Loon | .50 | 1.00 | 1.50 B |
| V2041 | Ernest Hemingway: The Man and His Work–J.K.M. McCaffery | 1.50 | 3.00 | 4.50 B |
| V2042 | My Thirty Years Backstairs at the White House–Parks & Leighton | .50 | 1.00 | 1.50 NF |
| V2043 | Senator Marlowe's Daughter–Frances Parkinson Keyes; 1962 | .50 | 1.00 | 1.50 |
| V2044 | The Smut Peddlers–James Jackson Kilpatrick | .50 | 1.00 | 1.50 |
| V2045 | William Randolph Hearst–John K. Winkler | .50 | 1.00 | 1.50 B |
| V2046 | The Store–T.S. Stribling | .50 | 1.00 | 1.50 |
| V2047 | Everyone's Legal Adviser–William Capitman | .50 | 1.00 | 1.50 NF |
| V2048 | Great Themes in Political Theory. Vol. 2–Michael Curtis | .50 | 1.00 | 1.50 NF |
| V2049 | A Gay and Melancholy Sound–Merle Miller | .50 | 1.00 | 1.50 |
| V2050 | Harpo Speaks!–Harpo Marx & Rowland Barber | 1.25 | 2.50 | 3.75 B |
| V2051 | The Great Tradition–Frances Parkinson Keyes | .50 | 1.00 | 1.50 |
| V2052 | With Gall and Honey–R. Leslie Gourse | .50 | 1.00 | 1.50 |
| V2053 | Master of this Vessel–Gwyn Griffin; 1962 | .50 | 1.00 | 1.50 |
| V2054 | The Innocent Infidels–Al Hine; aka Lord Love a Duck | .50 | 1.00 | 1.50 |
| V2055 | Honey in the Horn–H.L. Davis | .50 | 1.00 | 1.50 |
| V2056 | Stranger in a Strange Land–Robert A. Heinlein | .50 | 1.00 | 1.50 SF |
| V2057 | Avon Webster English Dictionary; 1962 | .50 | 1.00 | 1.50 NF |
| V2058 | The House at Old Vine–Norah Lofts; 1963 | .50 | 1.00 | 1.50 |
| V2059 | White House Menus and Recipes–Francois Rysavy & Frances S. Leighton | .50 | 1.00 | 1.50 NF |
| V2060 | Decisions of Destiny–Richard Tobin | .50 | 1.00 | 1.50 NF |
| V2061 | Parts Unknown–Frances Parkinson Keyes | .50 | 1.00 | 1.50 |
| V2062 | The Islands of Unwisdom–Robert Graves | .50 | 1.00 | 1.50 |
| V2063 | Florence Nightingale–Cecil Woodham-Smith | .50 | 1.00 | 1.50 B |
| V2064 | The Murderers–Harry J. Anslinger & Will Oursler | .75 | 1.50 | 2.25 |
| V2065 | Winston Churchill–The Valiant Years–Jack LeVien & John Lord | .50 | 1.00 | 1.50 B |
| V2066 | The Young Reader's Treasury of British and American Verse | .50 | 1.00 | 1.50 |
| V2067 | Years of Grace–Margaret Ayer Barnes | .50 | 1.00 | 1.50 |
| V2068 | A Spy in Rome–Peter Tompkins | .50 | 1.00 | 1.50 |
| V2069 | Damned If You Do, Damned If You Don't–Marjorie K. Osterman | .50 | 1.00 | 1.50 |

| | | V/Good | Fine | N/Mint |
|---|---|---|---|---|
| V2070 | Actors Talk about Acting. Vol. 1–eds. Funke & Booth | .50 | 1.00 | 1.50 NF |
| V2071 | Actors Talk about Acting. Vol. 2–eds. Funke & Booth | .50 | 1.00 | 1.50 NF |
| V2072 | Japanese Short Stories–Ryvnosuke Akutagawa | 1.00 | 2.00 | 3.00 |
| V2073 | Conflict–Robert Leckie | .50 | 1.00 | 1.50 |
| V2074 | All the Way Home–Tad Mosel & Philip Reisman, Jr | .50 | 1.00 | 1.50 |
| V2075 | Watch the Northwind Rise–Robert Graves | .50 | 1.00 | 1.50 |
| V2076 | Mainside–Paul Mandel | .50 | 1.00 | 1.50 |
| V2077 | Dictionary of Cuisine–Alexander Duman | .50 | 1.00 | 1.50 NF |
| V2078 | The Temple of the Golden Pavilion–Yukio Mishima | .50 | 1.00 | 1.50 |
| V2079 | The Second Stone–Leslie A. Fiedler; 1964 | .50 | 1.00 | 1.50 |
| V2080 | The Conversion of Chaplain Cohen–Herbert Tarr | .50 | 1.00 | 1.50 |
| V2081 | The Time Has Come–John Rock, MD | .50 | 1.00 | 1.50 |
| V2082 | Trial at Bannock–Jesse Bier; 1964 | .50 | 1.00 | 1.50 |
| V2083 | Robinson–Muriel Spark | .50 | 1.00 | 1.50 |
| V2084 | Honey in the Horn–H.L. Davis | .50 | 1.00 | 1.50 |
| V2085 | The House at Sunset–Norah Lofts | .50 | 1.00 | 1.50 |
| V2086 | My Darling Clementine–Jack Fishman; 1964 | .50 | 1.00 | 1.50 |
| V2087 | The Speculators–John Gerstine | .50 | 1.00 | 1.50 |
| V2088 | The Dillinger Days–John Toland; 1964 | .75 | 1.50 | 2.25 NF |
| V2089 | The Far Side of Home–Maggie Davis | .50 | 1.00 | 1.50 |
| V2090 | Path for Our Valor–Thomas Dovlis | .50 | 1.00 | 1.50 |
| V2091 | Daughters and Rebels–Jessica Mitford | .50 | 1.00 | 1.50 |
| V2092 | The Unicorn–Iris Murdoch | .50 | 1.00 | 1.50 |
| V2093 | The Road Back–Erich Maria Remarque | .50 | 1.00 | 1.50 C |
| V2094 | The Deed–Gerold Frank | .50 | 1.00 | 1.50 |
| V2095 | The Girls of Slender Means–Muriel Spark | .50 | 1.00 | 1.50 |
| V2096 | Shakespeare–Peter Quenell | .50 | 1.00 | 1.50 B |
| V2097 | Home from the Hill–William Humphrey | .50 | 1.00 | 1.50 |
| V2098 | Vertical and Horizontal–Lillian Ross | .50 | 1.00 | 1.50 |
| V2099 | The Secret–James Drought | .50 | 1.00 | 1.50 |
| V2100 | Second Wife–Lewis Meyer | .50 | 1.00 | 1.50 |
| V2101 | Pacific War Diary–James Fahey | .75 | 1.50 | 2.25 NF |
| V2102 | The Glory Road–Robert A. Heinlein | 1.00 | 2.00 | 3.00 SF |
| V2103 | The Way It Is Under Twenty–Dr. Rose Franzblau | .50 | 1.00 | 1.50 NF |
| V2104 | The Third Angel–Jerome Weidman | .50 | 1.00 | 1.50 |
| V2105 | The Great Tradition–Frances Parkinson Keyes | .50 | 1.00 | 1.50 |
| V2106 | Behind the Burma Road–W.R. Peers & D. Brelis | .50 | 1.00 | 1.50 NF |
| V2107 | Admen–Shepherd Mead | .50 | 1.00 | 1.50 |
| V2108 | Wicked Pavilion–Dawn Powell; 1964 | .50 | 1.00 | 1.50 |
| V2109 | Mover–James Drought; 1965 | .50 | 1.00 | 1.50 |
| V2110 | The World Is a Wedding–Bernard Kops | .50 | 1.00 | 1.50 |
| V2111 | Planning for College–Sidney Margolius | .50 | 1.00 | 1.50 NF |
| V2112 | Annie Jordan–Mary Brinker Post | .50 | 1.00 | 1.50 |
| V2113 | Chicken Every Sunday–Rosemary Taylor | .50 | 1.00 | 1.50 H |
| V2114 | The Benefactor–Susan Sontag | .50 | 1.00 | 1.50 |
| V2115 | Fielding's Folly–Frances Parkinson Keyes | .50 | 1.00 | 1.50 |
| V2116 | The Safe Bridge–Frances Parkinson Keyes | .50 | 1.00 | 1.50 |
| V2117 | The Complete Guide to House Hunting–Tyler Stewart Rogers | .50 | 1.00 | 1.50 NF |
| V2118 | The Complete Coin Collector's Guide–Robert Svensson | .75 | 1.50 | 2.25 NF |
| V2119 | The Bishop's Mantle–Agnes Sligh Turnbull | .50 | 1.00 | 1.50 |
| V2120 | A Spy in Rome–Peter Tompkins | .50 | 1.00 | 1.50 |
| V2121 | The Lifetime Reading Plan–Clifton Fadiman | .50 | 1.00 | 1.50 NF |
| V2122 | Mangrove Town–Yael Lotan | .50 | 1.00 | 1.50 |
| V2123 | The Tightrope–Sidney Kauffmann | .50 | 1.00 | 1.50 |
| V2124 | The Magnificent Ambersons–Booth Tarkington | .50 | 1.00 | 1.50 |
| V2125 | A Hospital near Paris–Conrad Mahler | .50 | 1.00 | 1.50 |
| V2126 | Rose of Tibet–Lionel Davidson | .50 | 1.00 | 1.50 M |
| V2127 | Kiss Tomorrow Goodbye–Horace McCoy | 1.00 | 2.00 | 3.00 |

| | | V/Good | Fine | N/Mint |
|---|---|---|---|---|

| | | V/Good | Fine | N/Mint | |
|---|---|---|---|---|---|
| V2128 | The Chequer Board–Nevil Shute | .50 | 1.00 | 1.50 | |
| V2129 | Displaced Doctor–Richard Berczeller | .50 | 1.00 | 1.50 | |
| V2130 | Scandals of Clochmerle–Gabriel Chevallier | .50 | 1.00 | 1.50 | |
| V2131 | Lamb in His Bosom–Caroline Miller | .50 | 1.00 | 1.50 | |
| V2132 | Journey in the Dark–Martin Flavin | .50 | 1.00 | 1.50 | |
| V2133 | Freedom Observed–Gwyn Griffin; 1966 | .50 | 1.00 | 1.50 | |
| V2134 | The Comforters–Muriel Spark | .50 | 1.00 | 1.50 | |
| V2135 | The Parthian–Victor Hurley | .50 | 1.00 | 1.50 | |
| V2136 | Cabot Wright Begins–James Purdy | .50 | 1.00 | 1.50 | |
| V2137 | Roses in December–Frances Parkinson Keyes | .50 | 1.00 | 1.50 | |
| V2138 | The Catherine Wheel–Jean Stafford | .50 | 1.00 | 1.50 | |
| V2139 | Vonda Rosegood–Richard Dohrmann | .50 | 1.00 | 1.50 | |
| V2140 | The Joyous Season–Patrick Dennis | .50 | 1.00 | 1.50 | |
| V2141 | The Rolling Years–Agnes Sligh Turnbull | .50 | 1.00 | 1.50 | |
| V2142 | On Valor's Side–T. Grady Gallant | .50 | 1.00 | 1.50 | |
| V2143 | The Sterile Cuckoo–John Nichols; 1966 | .75 | 1.50 | 2.25 | |
| V2144 | The Flight of the Phoenix–Elleston Trevor; movie tie-in | 1.50 | 3.00 | 4.50 | |
| V2145 | A Severed Head–Iris Murdoch | .50 | 1.00 | 1.50 | |
| V2146 | The Pedlocks–Stephen Longstreet | .50 | 1.00 | 1.50 | |
| V2147 | Outrageous Opinions–Helen Gurley Brown | .50 | 1.00 | 1.50 | |
| V2148 | The Power–William Harrington | .50 | 1.00 | 1.50 | |
| V2149 | Left Hand Is the Dreamer–Nancy Wilson Ross | .50 | 1.00 | 1.50 | |
| V2150 | Lion of Lucca–Gardner F. Fox; 1966 | 1.00 | 2.00 | 3.00 | A |
| V2151 | The President's Lady–Irving Stone | .50 | 1.00 | 1.50 | |
| V2152 | Masterpieces of Murder–ed. Gerald Gross | .50 | 1.00 | 1.50 | NF |
| V2153 | There Goes What's Her Name–Virginia Graham | .50 | 1.00 | 1.50 | |
| V2154 | The Bell–Iris Murdoch | .50 | 1.00 | 1.50 | |
| V2155 | Now Comes Theodora–Daniel Ford | .50 | 1.00 | 1.50 | |
| V2156 | The Nightingale–Agnes Sligh Turnbull | .50 | 1.00 | 1.50 | |
| V2157 | Frederica–Georgette Heyer; 1966 | .75 | 1.50 | 2.25 | |
| V2158 | Waldorf–James Goldman | .50 | 1.00 | 1.50 | |
| V2159 | The Red and the Green–Iris Murdoch | .50 | 1.00 | 1.50 | |
| V2160 | The Conversion of Chaplain Cohen–Herbert Tarr | .50 | 1.00 | 1.50 | |
| V2161 | Parts Unknown–Frances Parkinson Keyes | .50 | 1.00 | 1.50 | |
| V2162 | The Violent Man–A.E. Van Vogt | .75 | 1.50 | 2.25 | SF |
| V2163 | Mover–James Drought; 1966 | .50 | 1.00 | 1.50 | |
| V2164 | Elizabeth Taylor–Elizabeth Taylor; 1967 | 1.50 | 3.00 | 4.50 | B |
| V2165 | The Beloved Invader–Eugenia Price | .50 | 1.00 | 1.50 | |
| V2166 | The Last of Lazarus–Robert Goldston | .50 | 1.00 | 1.50 | |
| V2167 | Burn, Baby, Burn | .50 | 1.00 | 1.50 | |
| V2168 | Fielding's Folly–Frances Parkinson Keyes | .50 | 1.00 | 1.50 | |
| V2169 | Shadow of My Brother–Davis Grubb | .50 | 1.00 | 1.50 | |
| V2170 | Under the Net–Iris Murdoch | .50 | 1.00 | 1.50 | |
| V2171 | The Wind at My Back–Pat O'Brien | .50 | 1.00 | 1.50 | |
| V2173 | The Strangler–Harold Banks | .50 | 1.00 | 1.50 | |
| V2174 | Remember the End–Agnes Sligh Turnbull | .50 | 1.00 | 1.50 | |
| V2175 | Sinews of Love–Alexander Cordell | .50 | 1.00 | 1.50 | |
| V2176 | Belle Catherine–Juliette Benzoni | .50 | 1.00 | 1.50 | |
| V2178 | Second Wife–Lewis Meyer; 1967 | .50 | 1.00 | 1.50 | |
| V2179 | Tony–Patrick Dennis | .50 | 1.00 | 1.50 | |
| V2180 | The Golden Journey–Agnes Sligh Turnbull | .50 | 1.00 | 1.50 | |
| V2181 | Time and Time Again–James Hilton | .50 | 1.00 | 1.50 | |
| V2182 | Red in the Morning–Edith Begner | .50 | 1.00 | 1.50 | |
| V2183 | Forge of Fury–Jack Hoffenberg | .50 | 1.00 | 1.50 | |
| V2184 | Who Shall Live, Who Shall Die?–Daniel Stern | .50 | 1.00 | 1.50 | |
| V2185 | The Tall Woman–Wilma Dykeman | .50 | 1.00 | 1.50 | |
| V2186 | Gown of Glory–Agnes Sligh Turnbull | .50 | 1.00 | 1.50 | |
| V2187 | The Sweet Dream–James Wakefield | .50 | 1.00 | 1.50 | |
| V2188 | Maggie Cassidy–Jack Kerouac; 1967 | 1.00 | 2.00 | 3.00 | |
| V2189 | Haven's End–John P. Marquand | .50 | 1.00 | 1.50 | |
| V2190 | The Gourmet in the Low-Calorie Kitchen–Helen Belinkie | .50 | 1.00 | 1.50 | NF |
| V2191 | Stranger in a Strange Land–Robert A. Heinlein | .75 | 1.50 | 2.25 | SF |
| V2192 | Murder Must Advertise–Dorothy L. Sayers | .75 | 1.50 | 2.25 | M |
| V2193 | Eagle Day–Richard Collier | .50 | 1.00 | 1.50 | |

| | | V/Good | Fine | N/Mint | |
|---|---|---|---|---|---|
| V2194 | The Far Family–Wilma Dykeman | .50 | 1.00 | 1.50 | |
| V2195 | The Day Must Dawn–Agnes Sligh Turnbull | .50 | 1.00 | 1.50 | |
| V2196 | Shannon–Patricia Gallagher | .50 | 1.00 | 1.50 | |
| V2197 | Sex Kick–Tristan Coffin | .50 | 1.00 | 1.50 | E |
| V2198 | The Last Bridge–Brian Garfield | .50 | 1.00 | 1.50 | C |
| V2199 | Morning Journey–James Hilton | .50 | 1.00 | 1.50 | |
| V2200 | The Favorite Game–Leonard Cohen | .50 | 1.00 | 1.50 | |
| V2201 | The Big Pick-up–Elleston Trevor | .50 | 1.00 | 1.50 | |
| V2203 | Five Women I Love–Bob Hope | .50 | 1.00 | 1.50 | NF |
| V2204 | The Great Tradition–Frances Parkinson Keyes | .50 | 1.00 | 1.50 | |
| V2209 | So Big–Edna Ferber; 1967 | .50 | 1.00 | 1.50 | |
| V2213 | Senator Marlowe's Daughter–Frances Parkinson Keyes | .50 | 1.00 | 1.50 | |
| V2215 | The Joyous Season–Patrick Dennis | .50 | 1.00 | 1.50 | |
| V2239 | For Love of Ivy–Carol Sturm Smith; movie tie-in | .75 | 1.50 | 2.25 | R |

## AVON VS-SERIES

## Avon Book Company

| | | V/Good | Fine | N/Mint | |
|---|---|---|---|---|---|
| VS1 | After Many a Summer Dies the Swan–Aldous Huxley; 1964 | .75 | 1.50 | 2.25 | |
| VS2 | The Writer in America–Van Wyck Brooks | .50 | 1.00 | 1.50 | NF |
| VS3 | De Profundis–Oscar Wilde | .50 | 1.00 | 1.50 | |
| VS4 | The Great English and American Essays–ed. Edmund Fuller | .50 | 1.00 | 1.50 | NF |
| VS5 | The Floating Opera–John Barth; 1965 | .50 | 1.00 | 1.50 | |
| VS6 | Malcolm–James Purdy | .50 | 1.00 | 1.50 | |
| VS7 | Jurgen–James Branch Cabell; 1965 | 1.00 | 2.00 | 3.00 | F |
| VS9 | Treasures of Time–ed. Leo Devel | .50 | 1.00 | 1.50 | |
| VS10 | Three Essays on Sexuality–Sigmund Freud | .50 | 1.00 | 1.50 | NF |
| VS11 | Jews without Money–Michael Gold; 1966 | 1.00 | 2.00 | 3.00 | |
| VS12 | A Death in the Family–James Ayee | .50 | 1.00 | 1.50 | |
| VS13 | Acrobat Admits–Alfred Grossman | .50 | 1.00 | 1.50 | |
| VS14 | Memento Mori–Muriel Spark 1966 | .50 | 1.00 | 1.50 | |
| VS15 | The Slave–Isaac B. Singer | .50 | 1.00 | 1.50 | |
| VS16 | Beetlecreek–William Demby; 1967 | .50 | 1.00 | 1.50 | |
| VS17 | Are You Running with Me, Jesus?–Malcolm Boyd | .50 | 1.00 | 1.50 | |
| VS18 | The end of the Road–John Barth; 1967 | .50 | 1.00 | 1.50 | |
| VS20 | Jules and Jim–Henri-Pierre Roch; 1967 | .50 | 1.00 | 1.50 | |
| VS21 | The Man Who Was Not with It–Herbert Gold; 1968 | .50 | 1.00 | 1.50 | |
| VS27 | Mother Night–Kurt Vonnegut, Jr | 1.00 | 2.00 | 3.00 | SF |
| VS29 | The Lottery–Shirley Jackson | 1.00 | 2.00 | 3.00 | |

## AVON WESTERN NOVEL MONTHLY

## Avon Publishing Co., Inc.

### Digest Size

| | | V/Good | Fine | N/Mint | |
|---|---|---|---|---|---|
| 1 | The Gun-Wolf of Tubac–Nelson C. Nye; 1949; aka The Barber of Tubac. Note: Partially same cover as the comic Western Bandits No. 1 | 6.00 | 12.00 | 18.00 | W |
| 2 | Cattle War Buckaroo–William Hopson; 1950; aka The Laughing Vaquero | 6.00 | 12.00 | 18.00 | W |
| 3 | Arizona Roundup–William Hopson | 6.00 | 12.00 | 18.00 | W |
| 4 | Great Stories of the Golden West–anthology | 6.00 | 12.00 | 18.00 | W |

## AVON WESTERN READER

## Avon Book Company

### Digest Size

| | | V/Good | Fine | N/Mint | |
|---|---|---|---|---|---|
| 1 | Includes Coburn, Raine, Haycox, others. Note: Same cover as pulp magazine Western Ace High Stories, October 1953 | 6.00 | 12.00 | 18.00 | W |
| 2 | Includes White, Drago, Haycox, others | 6.00 | 12.00 | 18.00 | W |

## AVON WESTERN READER, *continued*

| | | V/Good | Fine | N/Mint | |
|---|---|---|---|---|---|
| 3 | Includes Woolrich, Gruber, Haycox, Raine, others | 6.00 | 12.00 | 18.00 | W |
| 4 | Includes Gruber, Raine, Tuttle, others | 6.00 | 12.00 | 18.00 | W |

# AVON W/YW-SERIES
## Avon Book Company

| | | V/Good | Fine | N/Mint | |
|---|---|---|---|---|---|
| W100 | The Nature of Politics–Prof. Michael Curtis; 1962 | .50 | 1.00 | 1.50 | NF |
| W101 | Great Scenes from the World Theatre– ed. James L. Steffensen, Jr; 1965 | .50 | 1.00 | 1.50 | |
| W102 | Three Negro Classics: Up from Slavery–ed. John Hope Franklin; 1965 | 1.50 | 3.00 | 4.50 | |
| W103 | Writers on the Left–Daniel Aaron | .50 | 1.00 | 1.50 | |
| W105 | Escape from Freedom–Erich Fromm; 1965 | .50 | 1.00 | 1.50 | |
| W106 | The Complete Home Medical Encyclopedia–Dr. Harold T. Hyman | .50 | 1.00 | 1.50 | NF |
| W107 | Gene Parker's Complete Book of Skindiving; 1965 | .75 | 1.50 | 2.25 | NF |
| W108 | Color of Darkness–James Purdy | .50 | 1.00 | 1.50 | |
| W109 | The Horizon History of Christianity– Roland H. Bainton; 1966 | .50 | 1.00 | 1.50 | NF |
| W110 | Studies on Hysteria–J. Breuer & Sigmund Freud | .50 | 1.00 | 1.50 | NF |
| W111 | Prometheus: The Life of Balzac–Andre Maurois; 1967 | .50 | 1.00 | 1.50 | |
| W113 | Actors Talk about Acting–eds. Lewis Funke & John E. Booth | .50 | 1.00 | 1.50 | NF |
| W114 | Human Use of Human Beings: Cybernetics & Society–Norbert Wiener | .50 | 1.00 | 1.50 | NF |
| W117 | Battles Lost and Won–Hanson W. Baldwin | 1.00 | 2.00 | 3.00 | NF |
| W118 | Division Street: America–Studs Terkel; 1968 | 1.00 | 2.00 | 3.00 | |
| W119 | Thomas Woodrow Wilson–Sigmund Freud & William Bullitt | .50 | 1.00 | 1.50 | |
| W120 | Mussolini: A Study in Power–Ivone Kirkpatrick | .50 | 1.00 | 1.50 | NF |
| W121 | The Fantasticks–Tom Jones & Harvey Schmidt; 1968 | .50 | 1.00 | 1.50 | |
| W124 | Came a Cavalier–Frances Parkinson Keyes | .50 | 1.00 | 1.50 | |
| W125 | Crusade in Europe–Dwight D. Eisenhower | .75 | 1.50 | 2.25 | NF |
| W127 | Psychoanalytic Revolution–Martha Roberts; 1968 | .50 | 1.00 | 1.50 | |
| W130 | The Nature of Human Nature–Alex Comfort | .50 | 1.00 | 1.50 | |
| W134 | Picture–Lilian Ross; 1969 | .50 | 1.00 | 1.50 | |
| W135 | Thinking the Unthinkable–Herman Kahn | .50 | 1.00 | 1.50 | |
| W136 | The Secret of Gonen–Gertrude Samuels | .50 | 1.00 | 1.50 | |
| W142 | Shakespeare's Sonnets–ed. Barbara Herrnstein | .50 | 1.00 | 1.50 | |
| W144 | Classics Revisited–Kenneth Rexroth | .75 | 1.50 | 2.25 | |
| W145 | Building the Earth–Pierre Teilhard de Chardin | .50 | 1.00 | 1.50 | |
| W148 | The Disney Version–Richard Schickel; 1969 | .75 | 1.50 | 2.25 | |
| W155 | Czech Black Book–ed. Robert Littell; 1969 | .50 | 1.00 | 1.50 | |
| W166 | Macroscope–Piers Anthony | 1.00 | 2.00 | 3.00 | SF |
| YW170 | The Man Who Loved Children– Christina Stead | .50 | 1.00 | 1.50 | |
| YW172 | Woyzeck–Georg Büchner, Jr & Henry J. Schmidt | .50 | 1.00 | 1.50 | |
| W174 | How Old Will You Be in 1984?–ed. Diane Divoky; 1969 | .50 | 1.00 | 1.50 | NF |
| YW177 | Call It Sleep–Henry Roth | .50 | 1.00 | 1.50 | |
| W178 | Black History: Lost, Stolen or Strayed– Otto Lindenmeyer; 1970 | 1.00 | 2.00 | 3.00 | |
| W181 | The Strawberry Statement: Notes of a College Revolutionary–James Simon Kunen | 1.00 | 2.00 | 3.00 | NF |
| W182 | Borstal Boy–Brendan Behan; 1970 | .50 | 1.00 | 1.50 | |

| | | V/Good | Fine | N/Mint | |
|---|---|---|---|---|---|
| W186 | The Intimate Enemy–George R. Bach | .50 | 1.00 | 1.50 | |
| W187 | Cities in Flight–James Blish | .75 | 1.50 | 2.25 | SF |

# AVON XX-SERIES
## Avon Book Company

| | | V/Good | Fine | N/Mint | |
|---|---|---|---|---|---|
| XX1 | Camp Followers' Guide–ed. Niles Chignon; 1965 | .75 | 1.50 | 2.25 | H |

# AVON YQ-SERIES
## Avon Book Company

| | | V/Good | Fine | N/Mint | |
|---|---|---|---|---|---|
| YQ13 | All Hallow's Eve–Charles Williams | .50 | 1.00 | 1.50 | |

# AVON ZS-SERIES
## Avon Publishing Co., Inc.

| | | V/Good | Fine | N/Mint | |
|---|---|---|---|---|---|
| ZS101 | Wind in the Willows–Kenneth Graham; 1966 | .50 | 1.00 | 1.50 | |
| ZS102 | The Egg and I–Betty MacDonald | .50 | 1.00 | 1.50 | H |
| ZS103 | Once in a Time–A.A. Milne; 1966 | 1.00 | 2.00 | 3.00 | |
| ZS104 | White Eagles over Serbia–Lawrence Durrell | .50 | 1.00 | 1.50 | |
| ZS105 | Just So Stories–Rudyard Kipling | 1.00 | 2.00 | 3.00 | A |
| ZS106 | Rascal–Sterling North | .50 | 1.00 | 1.50 | |
| ZS107 | The Pond–Robert Murphy; 1966 | .50 | 1.00 | 1.50 | |
| ZS108 | So Dear to My Heart–Sterling North | .50 | 1.00 | 1.50 | |
| ZS110 | Tarka the Otter–Henry Williamson | .50 | 1.00 | 1.50 | |
| ZS111 | The Hundred and One Dalmations– Dodie Smith | 1.00 | 2.00 | 3.00 | |
| ZS112 | Endurance–Alfred Lansing | .50 | 1.00 | 1.50 | |
| ZS113 | Kit Carson–Noel B. Gerson | .50 | 1.00 | 1.50 | B |
| ZS114 | Lions in the Way–Bella Rodman | .50 | 1.00 | 1.50 | |
| ZS115 | Menagerie Manor–Gerald Durrell | .50 | 1.00 | 1.50 | |
| ZS116 | Splintered Sword–Henry Treece; 1967 | 1.00 | 2.00 | 3.00 | A |
| ZS117 | Maya the Bee–Waldemar Bonsels | .50 | 1.00 | 1.50 | |
| ZS118 | The Master–T.H. White | 1.00 | 2.00 | 3.00 | SF |
| ZS122 | The Wizard of Oz–L. Frank Baum | 1.00 | 2.00 | 3.00 | F |
| ZS129 | My Lord, What a Morning–Marian Anderson | .50 | 1.00 | 1.50 | B |
| ZS166 | Earthman's Burden–Paul Anderson & Gordon Dickson; 1970; c-Bodé | 4.00 | 8.00 | 12.00 | C |

# BALLANTINE BOOKS
## Ballantine Books, Inc.

| | | V/Good | Fine | N/Mint | |
|---|---|---|---|---|---|
| 1 | Executive Suite–Cameron Hawley; 1952 | 2.00 | 4.00 | 6.00 | |
| 2 | The Golden Spike–Hal Ellson; orig. 1952 | 3.50 | 7.00 | 10.50 | E |
| 3 | All My Enemies–Stanley Baron | 2.00 | 4.00 | 6.00 | |
| 4 | Saddle by Starlight–Luke Short; c-Saunders | 2.50 | 5.00 | 7.50 | W |
| 5 | The Witch's Thorn–Ruth Park | 2.00 | 4.00 | 6.00 | |
| 6 | Tides of Time–Emile Danoen; 1st ed. 1952; aka Dust in the Wind | 2.00 | 4.00 | 6.00 | E |
| 7 | Blood on the Land–Frank Bonham | 2.00 | 4.00 | 6.00 | W |
| 8 | The World of Li'l Abner–Al Capp | 6.00 | 12.00 | 18.00 | H |
| 9 | The Red Gate–LaSelle Gilman | 1.50 | 3.00 | 4.50 | |
| 10 | Concannon–Frank O'Rourke; c-Saunders | 2.50 | 5.00 | 7.50 | W |
| | With dust jacket | 35.00 | 70.00 | 105.00 | |
| 11 | War Bonnet–Clay Fisher | 2.00 | 4.00 | 6.00 | W |
| 12 | Heyday–W.M. Spackman; orig. 1953 | 1.50 | 3.00 | 4.50 | |
| 13 | First Blood–Jack Schaefer; orig. 1953 | 3.00 | 6.00 | 9.00 | W |
| 14 | Why Did They Kill?–John Bartlow Martin | 1.50 | 3.00 | 4.50 | NF |
| 15 | The Wheel and the Hearth–Lucia B. Moore | 1.50 | 3.00 | 4.50 | |
| 16 | Star Science Fiction Stories–ed. Frederik Pohl | 4.50 | 9.00 | 13.50 | SF |
| 17 | The Racer–Hans Ruesch | 1.50 | 3.00 | 4.50 | |
| 18 | Kingdom of the Spur–Gene Markey | 2.00 | 4.00 | 6.00 | W |

*Ballantine 8, Ballantine 27, Ballantine 29.*

*Ballantine 54, Ballantine 63, Ballantine 88.*

|  |  | V/Good | Fine | N/Mint | |
|---|---|---|---|---|---|
| | **BALLANTINE BOOKS,** *continued* | | | | |
| 19 | Stories of Sudden Truth—Elizabeth Abell & Joseph I. Green | 2.00 | 4.00 | 6.00 | |
| 20 | I Thought of Daisy—Edmund Wilson | 1.50 | 3.00 | 4.50 | |
| 21 | The Space Merchants—F. Pohl & C.M. Kornbluth; orig. 1953; c-Powers | 5.00 | 10.00 | 15.00 | SF |
| 22 | The Big Range—Jack Schaefer | 3.00 | 6.00 | 9.00 | W |
| 23 | Patrol—Fred Majdalany | 2.00 | 4.00 | 6.00 | |
| 24 | Desert Passage—Richard Poole | 2.00 | 4.00 | 6.00 | W |
| 25 | The Undying Fire—Fletcher Pratt; orig. 1953; c-Powers | 3.00 | 6.00 | 9.00 | SF |
| 26 | The City of Anger—William Manchester; orig. 1953 | 2.00 | 4.00 | 6.00 | |
| 27 | Summer Street—Hal Ellson; orig. 1953; c-Maguire | 3.00 | 6.00 | 9.00 | JD |
| 28 | The Secret Masters—Gerald Kersh; orig. 1953; aka The Great Wash; c-Powers | 3.00 | 6.00 | 9.00 | SF |
| 29 | Indian Country—Dorothy M. Johnson | 3.50 | 7.00 | 10.50 | |
| 30 | Ahead of Time—Henry Kuttner | 3.00 | 6.00 | 9.00 | SF |
| 31 | A Gradual Joy—Alma Routsong | 1.50 | 3.00 | 4.50 | |
| 32 | The Far Command—Elinor Chamberlain | 2.00 | 4.00 | 6.00 | |
| 33 | Childhood's End—Arthur C. Clarke; c-Powers | 3.00 | 6.00 | 9.00 | SF |
| 34 | The Best Short Stories of 1953 | 1.50 | 3.00 | 4.50 | |
| 35 | Gun Hand—Frank O'Rourke | 2.00 | 4.00 | 6.00 | |
| 36 | Earthly Creatures—Charles Jackson | 3.00 | 6.00 | 9.00 | |
| 37 | Silent Army—Chin Kee Onn | 2.00 | 4.00 | 6.00 | C |
| 38 | Bring the Jubilee—Ward Moore | 1.50 | 3.00 | 4.50 | SF |
| 39 | New Poems by American Poets—Rolfe Humphries | 1.50 | 3.00 | 4.50 | |
| 40 | Yellow Hair—Clay Fisher | 2.00 | 4.00 | 6.00 | W |
| 41 | Fahrenheit 451—Ray Bradbury; c-Powers | 7.50 | 15.00 | 22.50 | SF |
| 42 | Ratoons—Daphne Rooke | 1.50 | 3.00 | 4.50 | A |
| 43 | Silver Rock—Luke Short | 2.00 | 4.00 | 6.00 | W |
| 44 | The Valiant Virginians—James Warner Bellah | 2.00 | 4.00 | 6.00 | W |
| 45 | The Canyon—Jack Schaefer | 3.00 | 6.00 | 9.00 | W |
| 46 | More Than Human—Theodore Sturgeon; c-Powers | 3.00 | 6.00 | 9.00 | SF |
| 47 | King of Abilene—Thomas Thompson | 2.00 | 4.00 | 6.00 | W |
| 48 | The Burl Ives Song Book—Burl Ives | 2.00 | 4.00 | 6.00 | NF |
| 49 | Ride West—Frank O'Rourke | 2.00 | 4.00 | 6.00 | W |
| 50 | Out of the Deeps—John Wyndham; orig. 1953; aka The Kraken Wakes | 3.00 | 6.00 | 9.00 | SF |
| 51 | Law Man—Lee Leighton | 3.00 | 6.00 | 9.00 | W |
| 52 | Expedition to Earth—Arthur C. Clarke | 3.00 | 6.00 | 9.00 | SF |
| 53 | Edge of the World—Vincent McHugh | 1.50 | 3.00 | 4.50 | |
| 54 | The Bounty Hunters—Elmore Leonard; 1st ed. 1953 | 12.50 | 25.00 | 37.50 | W |
| 55 | Star Science Fiction Stories No. 2—ed. Frederik Pohl | 3.00 | 6.00 | 9.00 | SF |
| 56 | Dark Dominion—David Duncan; orig. 1954 | 3.00 | 6.00 | 9.00 | SF |
| 57 | Brandon's Empire—Dave Hardin | 1.50 | 3.00 | 4.50 | W |
| 58 | Riders to the Stars—Curt Siodmak | 2.00 | 4.00 | 6.00 | SF |
| 59 | The Tall Men—Clay Fisher | 2.00 | 4.00 | 6.00 | W |
| 60 | The Peacemaker—Richard Poole; orig. 1954 | 1.50 | 3.00 | 4.50 | W |
| 61 | Search the Sky—Frederik Pohl & C.M. Kornbluth; orig. 1954; c-Powers | 3.00 | 6.00 | 9.00 | SF |
| 62 | The Night Winds—Brian Talbot Cleeve | 1.50 | 3.00 | 4.50 | |
| 63 | New Short Novels—ed. Mary Louise Aswell; orig. 1954 | 2.00 | 4.00 | 6.00 | |
| 64 | Night Raid—Frank Bonham | 2.00 | 4.00 | 6.00 | W |
| 65 | West of Justice—John Hunter; orig. 1954 | 1.50 | 3.00 | 4.50 | W |
| 66 | The Coasts of the Earth—Harold E. Livingston; orig. 1954 | 1.00 | 2.00 | 3.00 | |
| 67 | Aircraft Carrier—Joseph Bryan III | 1.50 | 3.00 | 4.50 | NF |
| 68 | Prelude to Space—Arthur C. Clarke | 2.50 | 5.00 | 7.50 | SF |
| 69 | Thunder in the Sun—Frank O'Rourke | 1.50 | 3.00 | 4.50 | W |
| 70 | Broken Wagon—Norman A. Fox | 1.50 | 3.00 | 4.50 | W |
| 71 | Hero's Walk—Robert Crane; orig. 1954 | 3.00 | 6.00 | 9.00 | SF |
| 72 | Prize Articles 1954—ed. Llewellyn Miller; orig. 1954. Note: Contains first book appearance of a Ray Bradbury story | 2.00 | 4.00 | 6.00 | |
| 73 | Untouched by Human Hands—Robert Sheckley; orig. 1954 | 3.00 | 6.00 | 9.00 | SF |
| 74 | Trouble Rider—Thomas Thompson; orig. 1954 | 1.50 | 3.00 | 4.50 | W |
| 75 | American Accent—Elizabeth Abell | 1.00 | 2.00 | 3.00 | |
| 76 | Trumpets of Company K—William Chamberlain; orig. 1954 | 1.50 | 3.00 | 4.50 | W |
| F77 | Break Down the Walls—John Barlow Martin | 1.00 | 2.00 | 3.00 | NF |
| 78 | The Real Story of Lucille Ball—Eleanor Harris | 6.00 | 12.00 | 18.00 | B |
| 80 | Brain Wave—Poul Anderson; c-Powers | 2.50 | 5.00 | 7.50 | SF |
| 82 | High Vengeance—Frank O'Rourke | 1.50 | 3.00 | 4.50 | W |
| 84 | They Brought Their Guns—Thomas Thompson | 1.50 | 3.00 | 4.50 | W |
| 85 | The Feud at Spanish Ford—Frank Bonham | 1.50 | 3.00 | 4.50 | W |
| 86 | The Explorers—C.M. Kornbluth; orig. 1954 | 2.50 | 5.00 | 7.50 | SF |
| 87 | Fire in the Desert—Ford Logan | 2.00 | 4.00 | 6.00 | |
| 88 | Strange Conquest—Alfred Neumann | 1.50 | 3.00 | 4.50 | |
| 89 | Star Short Novels—ed. Frederik Pohl | 2.50 | 5.00 | 7.50 | SF |
| 90 | Security and the Middle East | 1.00 | 2.00 | 3.00 | NF |
| 91 | Shadows in the Sun—Chad Oliver; orig. 1954 | 2.50 | 5.00 | 7.50 | SF |
| 92 | A Life for a Life—Horst Fanyer; c-Maguire | 1.00 | 2.00 | 3.00 | |
| 93 | The Mad Reader—ed. Mad Magazine | 3.00 | 6.00 | 9.00 | H |
| 94 | Messiah—Gore Vidal; 1954; c-Powers | 3.00 | 6.00 | 9.00 | SF |
| 95 | Brave Harvest—Richard Cargoe; orig. 1954 | 1.50 | 3.00 | 4.50 | W |
| 96 | Star Science Fiction Stories No. 3—ed. Frederik Pohl | 2.00 | 4.00 | 6.00 | SF |
| 97 | Earthlight—Arthur C. Clarke; c-Powers | 2.00 | 4.00 | 6.00 | SF |
| 98 | Violence at Sundown—Frank O'Rourke | 1.50 | 3.00 | 4.50 | W |
| 99 | Of All Possible Worlds—William Tenn; orig. 1955; c-Powers | 3.00 | 6.00 | 9.00 | SF |
| 100 | Young—Miriam Colwell | 3.00 | 6.00 | 9.00 | JD |
| 101 | The Dam Busters—Paul Brickhill | 1.50 | 3.00 | 4.50 | NF |
| 102 | Beyond Eden—David Duncan; orig. 1955; c-Powers | 2.50 | 5.00 | 7.50 | SF |
| 103 | Rock—Hal Ellson | 3.50 | 7.00 | 10.50 | JD |
| 104 | Re-Birth—John Wyndham; orig. 1955; c-Powers | 2.50 | 5.00 | 7.50 | SF |
| 105 | How to Play with Your Child—A.F. Arnold | 1.50 | 3.00 | 4.50 | NF |
| 106 | Mad Strikes Back—ed. Mad Magazine | 3.00 | 6.00 | 9.00 | H |
| 107 | Gladiator-at-Law—Frederik Pohl & C.M. Kornbluth; c-Powers | 3.00 | 6.00 | 9.00 | SF |
| 108 | Marilyn Monroe As the Girl—Sam Shaw; movie tie-in | 15.00 | 30.00 | 45.00 | |

*Ballantine 100, Ballantine 111, Ballantine 117.*

| | | V/Good | Fine | N/Mint |
|---|---|---|---|---|

**BALLANTINE BOOKS,** *continued*

| | | V/Good | Fine | N/Mint | |
|---|---|---|---|---|---|
| 109 | Far and Away–Anthony Boucher; orig. 1955 | 3.00 | 6.00 | 9.00 | SF |
| 110 | The Mackenzie Raid–Red Reeder | 1.50 | 3.00 | 4.50 | W |
| 111 | Car Deal!–Frank O'Rourke; orig. 1955 | 1.50 | 3.00 | 4.50 | |
| 112 | My Lady Greensleeves–Constance Beresford-Howe | 1.50 | 3.00 | 4.50 | A |
| 113 | Another Kind–Chad Oliver; orig. 1955; c-Powers | 2.50 | 5.00 | 7.50 | SF |
| 114 | The Guests of Fame–Daniel Stern | 1.50 | 3.00 | 4.50 | |
| 115 | The Power of Negative Thinking– Charles Preston | 1.50 | 3.00 | 4.50 | H |
| 116 | Jet–Frank Harvey | 1.50 | 3.00 | 4.50 | C |
| 117 | The Girls from Planet 5–Richard Wilson; orig. 1955; c-Powers | 2.50 | 5.00 | 7.50 | SF |
| 118 | Great Dog Stories–ed. Stanley Kaufman | 2.00 | 4.00 | 6.00 | |
| 119 | Caviar–Theodore Sturgeon; orig. 1955 | 3.00 | 6.00 | 9.00 | |
| 120 | U-Boats at War–Harald Busch | 2.00 | 4.00 | 6.00 | NF |
| 121 | Lone Gun–Clark Brooker | 1.50 | 3.00 | 4.50 | W |
| 122 | No Boundaries–Henry Kuttner & C.L. Moore; orig. 1955 | 3.00 | 6.00 | 9.00 | |
| 123 | A Town Is Drowning–C.M. Kornbluth & Frederik Pohl | 5.00 | 10.00 | 15.00 | |
| 124 | Inside Mad– ed. Mad Magazine | 3.00 | 6.00 | 9.00 | H |
| 125 | North to Texas–Noel M. Loomis | 1.50 | 3.00 | 4.50 | W |
| 126 | Citizen in Space–Robert Sheckley; orig. 1955 | 2.50 | 5.00 | 7.50 | SF |
| 127 | How to Succeed in Business Without Really Trying–Shepherd Mead; 1956 | 1.50 | 3.00 | 4.50 | H |
| 128 | Hot Iron–Elmer Kelton | 2.50 | 5.00 | 7.50 | W |
| 129 | Tell Them Nothing–Hal Ellson | 4.00 | 8.00 | 12.00 | JD |
| 130 | Alternating Currents–Frederik Pohl; c-Powers | 2.50 | 5.00 | 7.50 | SF |
| F131 | A Woman of Bangkok–Jack Reynolds | 2.00 | 4.00 | 6.00 | |
| 132 | In One Head and Out the Other–Roger Price | 1.50 | 3.00 | 4.50 | H |
| F133 | The Best Short Stories of 1955–ed. Martha Foley | 1.50 | 3.00 | 4.50 | |
| 134 | Beyond Courage–Clay Blair, Jr | 1.50 | 3.00 | 4.50 | NF |
| 135 | Reach for Tomorrow–Arthur C. Clarke | 2.00 | 4.00 | 6.00 | SF |
| 136 | The Pioneers–Jack Schaefer | 2.00 | 4.00 | 6.00 | W |
| 137 | The God of Channel 1–Donald Stacy with Frederik Pohl | 4.00 | 8.00 | 12.00 | |
| 138 | My First 10,000,000 Sponsors–Frank Edwards | 1.50 | 3.00 | 4.50 | |
| F139 | The October Country–Ray Bradbury | 12.50 | 25.00 | 37.50 | SF |
| 140 | New Short Novels II; orig. 1956; c-Powers. Note: Contains Norman Mailer | 1.50 | 3.00 | 4.50 | |
| 141 | Never Plead Guilty–Bernard Averbuch & John Wesley Noble | 1.50 | 3.00 | 4.50 | NF |
| 142 | Devil's Canyon–E.E. Halleran | 1.50 | 3.00 | 4.50 | W |
| 143 | Flood–David Dempsey | 1.50 | 3.00 | 4.50 | |
| 144 | Presidential Year–C.M. Kornbluth & Frederik Pohl | 5.00 | 10.00 | 15.00 | |
| 145 | God Is My Co-Pilot–Gen. Robert L. Scott, Jr | 1.00 | 2.00 | 3.00 | C |
| 146 | Sea Songs of Sailing, Whaling and Fishing–Burl Ives | 2.00 | 4.00 | 6.00 | |
| 147 | Bright Phoenix–Harold Mead | 2.50 | 5.00 | 7.50 | SF |
| 148 | Beyond the Pass–Lee Leighton | 1.50 | 3.00 | 4.50 | W |
| 149 | Hard Men–Frank O'Rourke | 2.50 | 5.00 | 7.50 | W |
| F150 | The Power and the Prize–Howard Swiggett | 1.00 | 2.00 | 3.00 | |

| | | V/Good | Fine | N/Mint | |
|---|---|---|---|---|---|
| 151 | Nerves–Lester del Ray | 2.50 | 5.00 | 7.50 | SF |
| 152 | I'm for Me First–Roger Price; orig. 1956 | 1.00 | 2.00 | 3.00 | H |
| 153 | Blazing Border–E.E. Halleran | 1.50 | 3.00 | 4.50 | W |
| 155 | The Wright Brothers–Fred C. Kelly | 1.25 | 2.50 | 3.75 | |
| 157 | Fight for Control–David Karr | 1.50 | 3.00 | 4.50 | |
| 158 | The Night of the Coyotes–Philip Ketchum | 2.00 | 4.00 | 6.00 | W |
| 159 | The Human Angle–William Tenn | 3.00 | 6.00 | 9.00 | SF |
| 160 | Best Television Plays–ed. Gore Vidal | 1.50 | 3.00 | 4.50 | |
| 161 | Olympic Cavalcade of Sports–John V. Grombach; orig. 1956 | 1.00 | 2.00 | 3.00 | NF |
| F162 | The Cruiser–Warren Tute | 1.00 | 2.00 | 3.00 | |
| 163 | Grab Your Socks–Shel Silverstein | 3.50 | 7.00 | 10.50 | |
| 164 | Frontier–Marvin De Vries | 1.50 | 3.00 | 4.50 | W |
| 165 | I, Libertine–Frederick R. Ewing (Theodore Sturgeon & Jean Shepherd); orig. 1956; c-Freas | 6.00 | 12.00 | 18.00 | H |
| 166 | Scout–R.M. Roberts; orig. 1956 | 1.50 | 3.00 | 4.50 | W |
| 167 | To Live Forever–Jack Vance; c-Powers | 5.00 | 10.00 | 15.00 | SF |
| 168 | The Road to Stalingrad–Benno Zeiser | 1.00 | 2.00 | 3.00 | NF |
| F169 | The Scourge of the Swastika–Lord Russell of Liverpool | 2.00 | 4.00 | 6.00 | NF |
| 170 | Wagon Captain–E.E. Halleran | 1.50 | 3.00 | 4.50 | W |
| 171 | The Wild Reader–Bernard W. Shir-Cliff | 2.00 | 4.00 | 6.00 | |
| 172 | The World of Li'l Abner–Al Capp | 2.00 | 4.00 | 6.00 | H |
| 173 | Turn the Tigers Loose–Col. Walt Lasly with Frederik Pohl | 4.00 | 8.00 | 12.00 | W |
| 174 | The Big Ball of Wax–Shepherd Mead | 1.50 | 3.00 | 4.50 | H |
| 175 | Fish the Strong Waters–N.C. McDonald; orig. 1956 | 1.50 | 3.00 | 4.50 | A |
| 176 | Kansas Trail–Hascal Giles | 1.50 | 3.00 | 4.50 | W |
| 177 | I Drive the Turnpikes–and Survive– Paul Kearney | 1.50 | 3.00 | 4.50 | NF |
| 178 | Utterly Mad–ed. Mad Magazine | 3.00 | 6.00 | 9.00 | H |
| 179 | E Pluribus Unicorn–Theodore Sturgeon | 3.00 | 6.00 | 9.00 | SF |
| 180 | James Dean: A Biography–William Bast | 4.00 | 8.00 | 12.00 | B |
| 181 | Hangtown–Les Savage, Jr | 1.50 | 3.00 | 4.50 | W |
| 182 | Tales of Gooseflesh & Laughter–John Wyndham; orig. 1956; c-Powers | 3.00 | 6.00 | 9.00 | SF |
| 183 | Defeat at Sea–C.D. Bekker | 1.50 | 3.00 | 4.50 | NF |
| 184 | The German Raider Atlantis–Wolfgang Frank & Bernhard Rogge; 1957 | 1.50 | 3.00 | 4.50 | NF |
| 185 | Shadow on the Border–George C. Appell | 1.50 | 3.00 | 4.50 | W |
| 186 | Tales from the White Hart–Arthur C. Clarke | 2.50 | 5.00 | 7.50 | SF |
| 187 | Buffalo Wagons–Elmer Kelton | 2.00 | 4.00 | 6.00 | W |
| 188 | Cavalry Raid–Sydney E. Whitman | 1.50 | 3.00 | 4.50 | W |
| 189 | Fire Mission–William P. Mulvihill | 1.50 | 3.00 | 4.50 | |
| 190 | The Battle of the Bulge–Robert E. Merriam | 1.50 | 3.00 | 4.50 | NF |
| 191 | Halfway to Heaven–Terrance Flair | 1.50 | 3.00 | 4.50 | |
| 192 | Slave Ship–Frederik Pohl | 2.50 | 5.00 | 7.50 | SF |
| F193 | The First and the Last–Adolf Galland | 1.50 | 3.00 | 4.50 | |
| 194 | The Spotted Horse–Jack Dillon | 1.50 | 3.00 | 4.50 | |
| F195 | Wing Leader–Capt. J.E. Johnson | 1.00 | 2.00 | 3.00 | NF |
| 196 | The Lonely Women–Gerda Rhoads | 1.50 | 3.00 | 4.50 | |
| 197 | The Frozen Year–James Blish | 2.50 | 5.00 | 7.50 | SF |
| 198 | Fight at Sun Mountain–Clark Brooker | 1.50 | 3.00 | 4.50 | W |
| 199 | Edge of the City–Frederik Pohl | 5.00 | 10.00 | 15.00 | |
| 200 | Cycle of Fire–Hal Clement | 1.00 | 2.00 | 3.00 | SF |
| F201 | Zero–Okumiya Horikoshi & Martin Caidin | 1.50 | 3.00 | 4.50 | NF |
| 202 | Yellowhorse–Dee Brown | 1.50 | 3.00 | 4.50 | W |
| 203 | Paris Blues–Harold Flender | 1.50 | 3.00 | 4.50 | |
| F204 | The Best American Short Stories of 1956–ed. Martha Foley | 1.00 | 2.00 | 3.00 | |
| 205 | The Hostile Hills–E.E. Halleran | 1.50 | 3.00 | 4.50 | W |
| 206 | The Case against Tomorrow–Frederik Pohl | 2.50 | 5.00 | 7.50 | SF |
| 207 | U-Boat 977–Heinz Schaeffer | 1.50 | 3.00 | 4.50 | NF |
| 208 | Lawman's Pay–Frank C. Robertson | 1.50 | 3.00 | 4.50 | W |
| 209 | Commando Extraordinary–Charles Foley | .75 | 1.50 | 2.25 | |
| 210 | The Green Odyssey–Philip Jose Farmer; orig. 1957 | 7.50 | 15.00 | 22.50 | SF |
| 211 | Legend in the Dust–Frank O'Rourke | 1.50 | 3.00 | 4.50 | W |
| 212 | Gun Hand–Frank O'Rourke | 1.50 | 3.00 | 4.50 | W |
| 213 | Violence at Sundown–Frank O'Rourke | 1.50 | 3.00 | 4.50 | W |
| 214 | High Vengeance–Frank O'Rourke | 1.50 | 3.00 | 4.50 | W |
| 215 | Sometime, Never–John Wyndham, William Golding, Mervyn Peake | 1.50 | 3.00 | 4.50 | SF |

Ballantine 242, Ballantine F277K, Ballantine 301K.

| | | V/Good | Fine | N/Mint |
|---|---|---|---|---|

BALLANTINE BOOKS, *continued*

| | | V/Good | Fine | N/Mint | |
|---|---|---|---|---|---|
| 216 | Serenade to the Big Bird–Bert Stiles | 1.00 | 2.00 | 3.00 | |
| 217 | Between the Elephant's Eyes–Robert L. Scott, Jr | 1.00 | 2.00 | 3.00 | A |
| 218 | High Vacuum–Charles Eric Maine | 1.00 | 2.00 | 3.00 | SF |
| 219 | Spanish Ridge–E.E. Halleran | 1.25 | 2.50 | 3.75 | W |
| 220 | The Deep South Says Never–John Bartlow Martin | 1.50 | 3.00 | 4.50 | NF |
| 221 | The Password Is Courage–John Castle | .75 | 1.50 | 2.25 | NF |
| 222 | One Minute to Ditch–Cornelius Ryan | 1.25 | 2.50 | 3.75 | |
| 223 | A Woman in Berlin | 1.50 | 3.00 | 4.50 | |
| F224 | Midway–Mitsuo Fuchida & Masatake Okumiya | 1.50 | 3.00 | 4.50 | NF |
| F225 | Panzer Leader–Heinz Guderian | 1.50 | 3.00 | 4.50 | NF |
| 226 | New Poems by American Poets No. 2– ed. Rolfe Humphries | 1.00 | 2.00 | 3.00 | |
| 227 | The Battle for Leyte Gulf–C. Vann Woodward | 1.50 | 3.00 | 4.50 | NF |
| 228 | Aircraft Carrier–Joseph Bryan III | 1.00 | 2.00 | 3.00 | NF |
| 229 | Sergeant Bilko–Nat Hiken; TV tie-in. Note: Two cover variants exist for this edition. | 2.50 | 5.00 | 7.50 | H |
| 230 | Occam's Razor–David Duncan | .75 | 1.50 | 2.25 | SF |
| F231 | The 85 Days–R.W. Thompson | 1.50 | 3.00 | 4.50 | NF |
| 232 | Disaster Valley–Frank C. Robertson | 1.50 | 3.00 | 4.50 | W |
| 233 | The Crack in the Picture Window–John Keats | .75 | 1.50 | 2.25 | |
| F234 | The Bridge at Remagen–Ken Hechler | 1.25 | 2.50 | 3.75 | |
| 235 | Best TV Humor of 1957–ed. Irving Settel | 1.00 | 2.00 | 3.00 | H |
| 236 | Gunsmoke–Don Ward; orig. 1957; TV tie-in | 2.00 | 4.00 | 6.00 | W |
| 237 | Those Idiots from Earth–Richard Wilson | 2.00 | 4.00 | 6.00 | SF |
| 238 | Best TV Plays: 1957–ed. Florence Britton | .75 | 1.50 | 2.25 | |
| 239 | The Wild Sweet Wine–Don Congdon; orig. 1958 | 1.50 | 3.00 | 4.50 | |
| 240 | Chain Link–Owen Evens | 1.50 | 3.00 | 4.50 | |
| 241 | Indian Country–Dorothy M. Johnson | 1.25 | 2.50 | 3.75 | W |
| 242 | The Humbug Digest–Harvey Kurtzman | 2.50 | 5.00 | 7.50 | H |
| 243 | Man of Earth–Algis Budrys | 1.50 | 3.00 | 4.50 | SF |
| 244 | Kamikaze–Gordon T. Allred & Yasuo Kuwahara | 1.25 | 2.50 | 3.75 | NF |
| 245 | The Dam Busters–Paul Brickhill | 1.25 | 2.50 | 3.75 | NF |
| 246 | Robots and Changelings–Lester del Rey | 2.00 | 4.00 | 6.00 | SF |
| 247 | Barbed Wire–Elmer Kelton | 2.00 | 4.00 | 6.00 | W |
| F248 | Samurai!–Martin Caidin, Saburo Sakai, Fred Saito | 1.25 | 2.50 | 3.75 | |
| 249 | Earthlight–Arthur C. Clarke | 2.00 | 4.00 | 6.00 | SF |
| 250 | The Big Boxcar–Alfred Maund | 1.50 | 3.00 | 4.50 | |
| 251 | Sun Dance–Fred Grove | 1.50 | 3.00 | 4.50 | W |
| F252 | The Battle of Cassino–Fred Majdalany | 1.00 | 2.00 | 3.00 | NF |
| 253 | Patrol–Fred Majdalany | 1.00 | 2.00 | 3.00 | |
| 254 | Blood on the Land–Frank Bonham | 1.25 | 2.50 | 3.75 | W |
| 255 | Tomahawk–Lee Leighton | 1.25 | 2.50 | 3.75 | W |
| 256 | A Case of Conscience–James Blish | 1.50 | 3.00 | 4.50 | SF |
| 257 | The Graveyard Reader–Groff Conklin | 2.00 | 4.00 | 6.00 | HO |
| F258 | The Sea Wolves–Wolfgang Frank | 1.00 | 2.00 | 3.00 | |
| 259 | The Return of the Texan–L.L. Foreman; orig. 1958 | 1.25 | 2.50 | 3.75 | W |
| 260 | Deadly Image–Edmund Cooper | 1.00 | 2.00 | 3.00 | SF |
| F261 | The Big Show–Pierre Clostermann | 1.00 | 2.00 | 3.00 | |
| F262 | The One That Got Away–Kendal Burt & James Leasor | 1.00 | 2.00 | 3.00 | |
| 263 | The Mad Reader–ed. Mad Magazine | 2.00 | 4.00 | 6.00 | H |
| 264 | Mad Strikes Back–ed. Mad Magazine | 2.00 | 4.00 | 6.00 | H |
| 265 | Inside Mad–ed. Mad Magazine | 2.00 | 4.00 | 6.00 | H |
| 266 | Utterly Mad–ed. Mad Magazine | 2.00 | 4.00 | 6.00 | H |
| 267K | The Brothers Mad–ed. Mad Magazine | 2.00 | 4.00 | 6.00 | H |
| 268 | On an Odd Note–Gerald Kersh | 1.50 | 3.00 | 4.50 | SF |
| 269K | Hardrock–Frank Bonham | 1.50 | 3.00 | 4.50 | W |
| 272K | Star Science Fiction Stories No. 4– Frederik Pohl | 1.50 | 3.00 | 4.50 | SF |
| F273K | V-2: The Nazi Rocket–Walter Dornberger | 2.00 | 4.00 | 6.00 | NF |
| 274K | The Hanging Tree–Dorothy M. Johnson | 2.00 | 4.00 | 6.00 | W |
| 275K | Those About to Die–Daniel P. Mannix | 1.50 | 3.00 | 4.50 | NF |
| F276K | Stuka Pilot–Hans Ulrich Rudel | 1.00 | 2.00 | 3.00 | NF |
| F277K | This Woman–Pietro di Donato | 2.00 | 4.00 | 6.00 | |
| 278K | Count Five and Die–Barry Wynne | .75 | 1.50 | 2.25 | |

| | | V/Good | Fine | N/Mint | |
|---|---|---|---|---|---|
| 279K | Tomorrow's Gift–Edmund Cooper | 1.00 | 2.00 | 3.00 | SF |
| F280K | The Call Girl–Harold Greenwald | .75 | 1.50 | 2.25 | NF |
| 281K | The Old Copper Collar–Dan Cushman | 1.50 | 3.00 | 4.50 | |
| 282K | Colorado Gold–Lee Leighton & Chad Merriman | 1.50 | 3.00 | 4.50 | W |
| 283K | The Sledge Patrol–David Howarth | 1.00 | 2.00 | 3.00 | |
| 284K | After the Rain–John Bowen | 1.00 | 2.00 | 3.00 | SF |
| 285K | Rebel Ranger–S.E. Whitman | 1.25 | 2.50 | 3.75 | W |
| 286K | Ingenue–Millicent Brower | 1.50 | 3.00 | 4.50 | |
| 287K | How to Succeed with Women without Really Trying–Shepherd Mead | 1.50 | 3.00 | 4.50 | H |
| 288K | The Bright Road to Fear–Richard Martin Stern | 1.00 | 2.00 | 3.00 | M |
| 289K | Sergeant Bilko Joke Book; TV tie-in | 2.50 | 5.00 | 7.50 | H |
| 289K | The Avengers–Chad Merriman. Note: Apparently 298K misnumbered (actual 298K of this title as yet unseen) | 1.25 | 2.50 | 3.75 | W |
| 290K | The Tide Went Out–Charles Eric Maine | 1.00 | 2.00 | 3.00 | SF |
| F291K | Battle for the Rhine–R.W. Thompson | 1.00 | 2.00 | 3.00 | NF |
| 292K | Brain Surgeon–William Sharpe | 1.00 | 2.00 | 3.00 | |
| 293K | Heat Wave–Caesar Smith | 1.00 | 2.00 | 3.00 | |
| 294K | Apache Wells–Robert Steelman | 1.50 | 3.00 | 4.50 | |
| F295K | The Burl Ives Song Book–Burl Ives | 1.25 | 2.50 | 3.75 | NF |
| 296K | The Mad Reader–Harvey Kurtzman | 2.00 | 4.00 | 6.00 | H |
| 297K | Mad Strikes Back–Harvey Kurtzman | 2.00 | 4.00 | 6.00 | H |
| 298K | May not exist. See 289K. | | | | |
| 299K | The Midwich Cuckoos–John Wyndham | 2.50 | 5.00 | 7.50 | SF |
| 300K | End of a War–Edward Loomis | 1.00 | 2.00 | 3.00 | |
| 301K | Ride the Nightmare–Richard Matheson | 10.00 | 20.00 | 30.00 | M |
| 302K | The Beast–Daniel P. Mannix | 2.50 | 5.00 | 7.50 | NF |
| 303K | The Marching Morons–C.M. Kornbluth | 2.00 | 4.00 | 6.00 | SF |
| 304K | Shadow of a Star–Elmer Kelton | 2.00 | 4.00 | 6.00 | W |
| 305K | Sensual Love–ed. Don Congdon | 1.25 | 2.50 | 3.75 | |
| 306K | Tiger in the Sky–Robert L. Scott, Jr | .75 | 1.50 | 2.25 | |
| F307K | Air Spy–Constance Babington-Smith | .75 | 1.50 | 2.25 | NF |
| 308K | Star Science Fiction Stories No. 5–ed. Frederik Pohl | 1.50 | 3.00 | 4.50 | SF |
| 309K | Fort Starke–Wade Everett | 1.50 | 3.00 | 4.50 | |
| 310K | False Witness–Helen Nielsen | .75 | 1.50 | 2.25 | |
| 311K | Sex, Vice and Business–Monroe Fry | .75 | 1.50 | 2.25 | NF |
| 312K | Witch Doctor–N.C. McDonald | 1.25 | 2.50 | 3.75 | |
| F313K | Who Dares, Wins–Virginia Cowles | 1.00 | 2.00 | 3.00 | |
| 314K | God Is My Co-Pilot–Gen. Robert L. Scott, Jr | .75 | 1.50 | 2.25 | |
| 315K | Bunch Quitter–Chad Merriman | 1.00 | 2.00 | 3.00 | W |
| 316K | The Fourth "R"–George O. Smith | .75 | 1.50 | 2.25 | SF |
| 317K | Kamikaze–Gordon T. Alfred & Yasuo Kuwahara | .75 | 1.50 | 2.25 | NF |
| F318K | The Coast Watchers–Eric D. Feldt | .75 | 1.50 | 2.25 | |
| 319K | Stairway to Nowhere–Hal Ellson | 2.50 | 5.00 | 7.50 | JD |
| 320K | The Chemical Elements–Helen Miles Davis | .75 | 1.50 | 2.25 | NF |
| F322K | Boeing 707–Martin Caidin | .75 | 1.50 | 2.25 | NF |
| F323K | Thunderbolt!–Martin Caidin & Robert S. Johnson | .75 | 1.50 | 2.25 | NF |
| 324K | No Bugles, No Glory–Fred Grove | 1.00 | 2.00 | 3.00 | W |
| 325K | Tomorrow Times Seven–Frederik Pohl | 1.00 | 2.00 | 3.00 | SF |
| 326K | Deals with the Devil–ed. Basil Davenport; c-Powers | 2.00 | 4.00 | 6.00 | HO |
| 327K | Seed of Light–Edmund Cooper | 1.00 | 2.00 | 3.00 | SF |
| 328K | Black Rock Valley–S.E. Whitman | 1.50 | 3.00 | 4.50 | W |
| 329K | Air Force!–Frank Harvey | 1.00 | 2.00 | 3.00 | C |

BALLANTINE BOOKS, continued

| | | V/Good | Fine | N/Mint | |
|---|---|---|---|---|---|
| 331K | Suspense–Richard Martin Stern | 1.00 | 2.00 | 3.00 | M |
| F332K | Zeebrugge–Barrie Pitt | 1.00 | 2.00 | 3.00 | NF |
| F333K | Great Cases in Psychoanalysis–Harold Greenwald | .75 | 1.50 | 2.25 | |
| 334K | Winter of the Sioux–Robert Steelman | 1.50 | 3.00 | 4.50 | W |
| 335K | Wolfbane–Frederik Pohl & C.M. Kornbluth; orig. 1959; c-Powers | 2.00 | 4.00 | 6.00 | SF |
| F336K | Defeat in the East–Jurgen Thorwald | 1.00 | 2.00 | 3.00 | NF |
| 337K | Life among the Savages–Shirley Jackson | .75 | 1.50 | 2.25 | H |
| 338K | Harvey Kurtzman's Jungle Book–Harvey Kurtzman | 3.00 | 6.00 | 9.00 | H |
| F339K | To Live and Kill–Stefan Gazel | .75 | 1.50 | 2.25 | |
| 340K | Cartoon Countdown–Bernard Wiseman | 3.00 | 6.00 | 9.00 | H |
| 341K | The Outward Urge–John Wyndham & Lucas Parkes | .75 | 1.50 | 2.25 | SF |
| 342K | Raising Demons–Shirley Jackson | .75 | 1.50 | 2.25 | H |
| 343K | Stampede–Chad Merriman | 1.00 | 2.00 | 3.00 | W |
| 344K | First Command–Wade Everett | 1.50 | 3.00 | 4.50 | |
| 345K | The Funhouse–Benjamin Appel | 1.50 | 3.00 | 4.50 | SF |
| S346K | Pornography and the Law–Drs. Eberhard Kronhausen & Phyllis Kronhausen | .75 | 1.50 | 2.25 | NF |
| 347K | Rumor, Fear and the Madness of Crowds–J.P. Chaplin | 1.50 | 3.00 | 4.50 | NF |
| 348K | Eagle in the Bathtub–Jule Mannix | .75 | 1.50 | 2.25 | NF |
| F349K | American Aces–Edward H. Sims | .75 | 1.50 | 2.25 | NF |
| 350K | The World of Li'l Abner–Al Capp; movie tie-in | 1.50 | 3.00 | 4.50 | H |
| S351K | Rocket Manual for Amateurs–Bertrand R. Brinley | .75 | 1.50 | 2.25 | NF |
| 352K | Ordeal at Blood River–James Warner Bellah | 1.00 | 2.00 | 3.00 | W |
| 353K | Star Science Fiction Stories No. 6–ed. Frederik Pohl | 1.00 | 2.00 | 3.00 | SF |
| 354K | The Hell-Fire Club–Daniel P. Mannix | 1.50 | 3.00 | 4.50 | NF |
| 355K | Those About to Die–Daniel P. Mannix | 1.00 | 2.00 | 3.00 | NF |
| F356K | The Plague and I–Betty MacDonald | .75 | 1.50 | 2.25 | H |
| 357K | Feud at Spanish Ford–Frank Bonham | .75 | 1.50 | 2.25 | W |
| F358K | The Scourge of the Swastika–Lord Russell of Liverpool | .75 | 1.50 | 2.25 | NF |
| F359K | The Night Hamburg Died–Martin Caidin | 1.00 | 2.00 | 3.00 | NF |
| 360K | Fire Past the Future–Charles Eric Maine | 1.00 | 2.00 | 3.00 | SF |
| 361K | Tiberius–Ernst Mason | 1.00 | 2.00 | 3.00 | NF |
| 362K | Study in SISU–Austin Goodrich | 1.00 | 2.00 | 3.00 | NF |
| F363K | The Jazz Word–eds. Dom Cerulli, Burt Korall, Mort Nasatir | 1.00 | 2.00 | 3.00 | NF |
| 364K | Gunsmoke–ed. Don Ward; 1960; TV tie-in | 1.50 | 3.00 | 4.50 | W |
| 365K | Unearthly Neighbors–Chad Oliver | 1.00 | 2.00 | 3.00 | SF |
| 366K | Cavalry Sergeant–John L. Shelley | 1.00 | 2.00 | 3.00 | W |
| S367K | Sex in History–G. Rattray Taylor | 1.00 | 2.00 | 3.00 | NF |
| F368K | The Nine Days of Dunkirk–David Divine | 1.00 | 2.00 | 3.00 | NF |
| 370K | Zacherley's Midnight Snacks–ed. Zacherley; c-Powers | 2.00 | 4.00 | 6.00 | HO |
| 371K | Gold Is the Color of Blood–Robert Patterson | 1.00 | 2.00 | 3.00 | M |
| 372K | Grand Deception–ed. Alexander Klein | .75 | 1.50 | 2.25 | NF |
| 373K | Night Raid–Frank Bonham | 1.00 | 2.00 | 3.00 | W |
| F374K | The Life of a Burma Surgeon–Dr. Gordon Seagrave | .75 | 1.50 | 2.25 | NF |
| F375K | How Wide We Stray–Harold Mansfield | .75 | 1.50 | 2.25 | |
| S376K | Break Down the Walls–John Bartlow Martin | .75 | 1.50 | 2.25 | NF |
| 377K | The Sound of His Horn–Sarban | 2.00 | 4.00 | 6.00 | HO |
| F378K | This Woman–Pietro diDonato | 1.00 | 2.00 | 3.00 | |
| 379K | The Black Death–Johannes Nohl | 1.50 | 3.00 | 4.50 | NF |
| 380K | Tales to Be Told in the Dark–ed. Basil Davenport; c-Powers | 1.00 | 2.00 | 3.00 | HO |
| 381K | The Space Merchants–Frederik Pohl | .75 | 1.50 | 2.25 | SF |
| 382K | Fahrenheit 451–Ray Bradbury | 1.00 | 2.00 | 3.00 | SF |
| S383K | The Best American Short Stories 1959–eds. Martha Foley & David Burnett | 1.00 | 2.00 | 3.00 | |
| F384K | Stalingrad–Heinz Schroeter | 1.00 | 2.00 | 3.00 | NF |
| 385K | The Texas Rifles–Elmer Kelton | 1.25 | 2.50 | 3.75 | W |
| F386K | The Olympics, 1960 Edition–John V. Grombach | .75 | 1.50 | 2.25 | S |
| F387K | The Grey Seas Under–Farley Mowat | 1.00 | 2.00 | 3.00 | NF |
| 388K | The Unexpected Dimension–Algis Budrys | 1.50 | 3.00 | 4.50 | SF |

Ballantine 364K, Ballantine S383K, Ballantine 453K.

| | | V/Good | Fine | N/Mint | |
|---|---|---|---|---|---|
| S389K | Sex Histories of American College Men–E. Krenhausen & P. Krenhausen | 1.00 | 2.00 | 3.00 | NF |
| F390K | In Flanders Field–Leon Wolff | 1.00 | 2.00 | 3.00 | NF |
| 391K | Strange Relations–Philip José Farmer | 3.00 | 6.00 | 9.00 | SF |
| 392K | The American Slave Trade–John R. Spears | 1.50 | 3.00 | 4.50 | NF |
| 393K | Brain Wave–Poul Anderson | 1.00 | 2.00 | 3.00 | SF |
| 394K | Outlaw of the Natchez Trace–C. William Harrison | 1.25 | 2.50 | 3.75 | NF |
| 395K | Under Ten Flags–Wolfgang Frank & B. Rogge; movie tie-in | 1.00 | 2.00 | 3.00 | NF |
| 396K | Shadow of the Big Horn–E.E. Halleran | 1.25 | 2.50 | 3.75 | W |
| 397K | The Man Who Ate the World–Frederik Pohl | 1.50 | 3.00 | 4.50 | SF |
| 398K | Childhood's End–Arthur C. Clarke | .75 | 1.50 | 2.25 | SF |
| F399K | The Prostitute in Literature–eds. Harold Greenwald & Aron Krich | 1.25 | 2.50 | 3.75 | |
| 401K | Invisible Men–ed. Basil Davenport; c-Powers | 1.50 | 3.00 | 4.50 | SF |
| 402K | The Hanging Tree–Dorothy Johnson | 1.25 | 2.50 | 3.75 | W |
| F403K | The Shocking History of Advertising–E.S. Turner | 1.25 | 2.50 | 3.75 | NF |
| F404K | Samurai!–Saburo Sakai, Martin Caidin, Fred Saito | 1.00 | 2.00 | 3.00 | NF |
| 405K | Day of the Hunter–Ann Ahlswede | 1.25 | 2.50 | 3.75 | W |
| 406K | The Climacticon–Harold Livingston; c-Powers | 1.25 | 2.50 | 3.75 | SF |
| 407K | Of All Possible Worlds–William Tenn | 1.00 | 2.00 | 3.00 | SF |
| 408K | The Fabulous Rogues–ed. Alexander Klein | 1.00 | 2.00 | 3.00 | NF |
| F409K | The Rise and Fall of Hermann Goering–Willi Frischauer | 1.00 | 2.00 | 3.00 | NF |
| 410K | The Hurricane–Terrence Robertson | 1.00 | 2.00 | 3.00 | |
| F411K | Stride toward Freedom–Martin Luther King, Jr | 1.25 | 2.50 | 3.75 | NF |
| S412K | Days and Nights–Konstantine Simonov | 1.00 | 2.00 | 3.00 | C |
| 413K | Fight for the Valley–Lee Leighton | 1.25 | 2.50 | 3.75 | W |
| S414K | Stories of H.G. Wells–H.G. Wells | 1.50 | 3.00 | 4.50 | SF |
| F415K | A History of Courting–E.S. Turner | 1.00 | 2.00 | 3.00 | NF |
| S416K | Gallipoli–Alan Moorehead | 1.00 | 2.00 | 3.00 | NF |
| 417K | Zacherley's Vulture Stew–ed. Zacherley; c-Powers | 2.00 | 4.00 | 6.00 | HO |
| 418K | The Password Is Courage–John Castle | .75 | 1.50 | 2.25 | C |
| F419K | The First and the Last–Adolf Galland | .75 | 1.50 | 2.25 | NF |
| F420K | The Causes of World War Three–C. Wright Mills | .75 | 1.50 | 2.25 | NF |
| 421K | Legend in the Dust–Frank O'Rourke | 1.25 | 2.50 | 3.75 | W |
| 422K | Guardians of Time–Poul Anderson | 1.50 | 3.00 | 4.50 | SF |
| 423K | Re-Birth–John Wyndham | 1.00 | 2.00 | 3.00 | SF |
| F424K | Eichmann–The Man and His Crimes–Comer Clarke | 1.00 | 2.00 | 3.00 | NF |
| F425K | A Torch to the Enemy–Martin Caidin | 1.00 | 2.00 | 3.00 | NF |
| S426K | The People That Walk in Darkness–J.W. Scholte Nordholt | 1.00 | 2.00 | 3.00 | NF |
| 427K | The Magnificent Scoundrels–ed. Alexander Klein | 1.00 | 2.00 | 3.00 | NF |
| F428K | The Call Girl–Dr. Harold Greenwald; movie tie-in | 1.50 | 3.00 | 4.50 | NF |
| 429K | Last Scout–Wade Everett; 1960 | 1.25 | 2.50 | 3.75 | W |
| F430K | The Coming Political Breakthrough–Chester Bowles | .75 | 1.50 | 2.25 | NF |
| 431K | The Doll Maker–Sarban | 2.00 | 4.00 | 6.00 | HO |
| F432K | Folksong Jamboree–Miranda Marais | .75 | 1.50 | 2.25 | NF |

| | V/Good | Fine | N/Mint |
|---|---|---|---|

**BALLANTINE BOOKS,** *continued*

| Code | Title | V/Good | Fine | N/Mint | |
|---|---|---|---|---|---|
| F433K | The Danish Resistance–David Lampe | 1.00 | 2.00 | 3.00 | NF |
| 434K | 30 Day Wonder–Richard Wilson | 1.25 | 2.50 | 3.75 | SF |
| F435K | Money of Their Own–Murray Teigh Bloom | 1.00 | 2.00 | 3.00 | NF |
| S436K | A Piece of the Action–Herb Gardner | 1.00 | 2.00 | 3.00 | |
| 437K | Untouched by Human Hands–Robert Sheckley | 1.00 | 2.00 | 3.00 | SF |
| 438K | Night Killer–Chad Merriman | 1.25 | 2.50 | 3.75 | W |
| 439K | Drunkard's Walk–Frederik Pohl | 1.50 | 3.00 | 4.50 | SF |
| F440K | Most Dangerous Sea–Arnold S. Lott | 1.00 | 2.00 | 3.00 | |
| 441K | The Victorian Chaise Longue–Margharita Laski | 1.25 | 2.50 | 3.75 | HO |
| S442K | Joseph Goebbels–Curt Riess | 1.50 | 3.00 | 4.50 | NF |
| F443K | The Unconscious–Prof. J.P. Chaplin | 1.00 | 2.00 | 3.00 | NF |
| F444K | The Virgin Spring–Ulla Isaksson; movie tie-in | 1.00 | 2.00 | 3.00 | |
| 445 | Science Projects Handbook–ed. Science Service Assoc. | .75 | 1.50 | 2.25 | NF |
| F446K | Fads and Fallacies in the Name of Science–Martin Gardner | 1.00 | 2.00 | 3.00 | NF |
| F447K | Submarine Commander–Rear Adm. Ben Bryant | 1.00 | 2.00 | 3.00 | NF |
| 448K | Hunting Wolf–Ann Ahlswede | 1.25 | 2.50 | 3.75 | W |
| 449K | Trouble with Lichen–John Wyndham | 1.50 | 3.00 | 4.50 | SF |
| F450K | The Shocking History of Drugs–Richard Mathison; aka The Eternal Search | 1.50 | 3.00 | 4.50 | NF |
| 451K | The Fleet That Had to Die–Richard B. Hough | 1.25 | 2.50 | 3.75 | NF |
| 452K | Those About to Die–Daniel P. Mannix | 1.00 | 2.00 | 3.00 | NF |
| 453K | Village of the Damned–John Wyndham; movie tie-in; aka The Midwich Cuckoos | 1.50 | 3.00 | 4.50 | SF |
| F454K | Listen, Yankee–C. Wright Mills | .50 | 1.00 | 1.50 | NF |
| 455K | The Rimlanders–John L. Shelley; 1961 | 1.25 | 2.50 | 3.75 | W |
| F456K | Love Cults and Faith Healers–Arthur Orrmont | 1.00 | 2.00 | 3.00 | NF |
| S457K | Japanese Destroyer Captain–Capt. Hara, Fred Saito, Roger Pineau | 1.00 | 2.00 | 3.00 | NF |
| 458K | Some of Your Blood–Theodore Sturgeon | 1.50 | 3.00 | 4.50 | M |
| F459K | Stuka Pilot–Hans Ulrich Rudel | 1.00 | 2.00 | 3.00 | NF |
| 460K | The Mackenzie Raid–Col. Red Reeder; TV tie-in | 1.00 | 2.00 | 3.00 | W |
| 461K | Great Dog Stories–ed. Stanley Kaufmann | 1.00 | 2.00 | 3.00 | |
| 462K | More Than Human–Theodore Sturgeon | 1.00 | 2.00 | 3.00 | SF |
| F463K | Three Circles of Light–Pietro di Donato | 1.50 | 3.00 | 4.50 | |
| 464K | Smoke Wagon Road–R.M. Roberts | 1.25 | 2.50 | 3.75 | W |
| 465K | So Close to Home–James Blish | 1.50 | 3.00 | 4.50 | SF |
| 466K | Things with Claws–ed. Whitt Hallie Burnett; c-Powers | 1.50 | 3.00 | 4.50 | HO |
| S467K | Zero!–Martin Caidin, Masatako Okumiya, Jiro Horikoshi | 1.00 | 2.00 | 3.00 | NF |
| F468K | Brazen Chariots–Maj. Robert Crisp | 1.00 | 2.00 | 3.00 | NF |
| F469K | The Astonishing History of the Medical Profession–E.S. Turner | 1.00 | 2.00 | 3.00 | NF |
| F470K | Stride toward Freedom–Martin Luther King, Jr | 1.00 | 2.00 | 3.00 | NF |
| 471K | Warbonnet Creek–E.E. Halleran | 1.25 | 2.50 | 3.75 | W |
| 472K | Expedition to Earth–Arthur C. Clarke | 1.00 | 2.00 | 3.00 | SF |
| S473K | The Best American Short Stories: 1960–eds. David Burnett & Martha Foley | 1.00 | 2.00 | 3.00 | |
| F474K | Scourge of the Swastika–Lord Russell of Liverpool | 1.00 | 2.00 | 3.00 | NF |
| S475K | Love and the French–Nina Epton | 1.00 | 2.00 | 3.00 | NF |
| 476K | Turn Left at Thursday–Frederik Pohl | 1.50 | 3.00 | 4.50 | SF |
| 477K | God Is My Co-Pilot–Robert L. Scott | .75 | 1.50 | 2.25 | NF |
| 478K | Rebels, Rogues and Rascals–ed. Alexander Klein | 1.00 | 2.00 | 3.00 | NF |
| 479K | New Maps of Hell–Kingsley Amis; c-Powers. Note: History of science fiction | 2.00 | 4.00 | 6.00 | NF |
| 480K | The Other Passenger–John Keir Cross | 1.50 | 3.00 | 4.50 | SF |
| 481K | Gunlaw Hill–Frank O'Rourke | 1.25 | 2.50 | 3.75 | W |
| 482K | Reluctant Lawman–Edwin Booth | 1.25 | 2.50 | 3.75 | W |
| 483K | Strangers from Earth–Poul Anderson | 1.50 | 3.00 | 4.50 | SF |
| 484K | Messiah–Gore Vidal | .75 | 1.50 | 2.25 | SF |
| S485K | Panzer Leader–Heinz Guderian | 1.00 | 2.00 | 3.00 | NF |
| 486K | The Canyon–Jack Schaefer | 1.00 | 2.00 | 3.00 | W |
| F487K | Sartre on Cuba–Jean-Paul Sartre | 1.00 | 2.00 | 3.00 | NF |
| F488K | Five Down and Glory–Gene Gurney | 1.00 | 2.00 | 3.00 | NF |
| 492K | Inside Mad–ed. Mad Magazine | 1.00 | 2.00 | 3.00 | H |
| 493K | Utterly Mad–ed. Mad Magazine | 1.00 | 2.00 | 3.00 | H |
| 494K | The Brothers Mad–ed. Mad Magazine | 1.00 | 2.00 | 3.00 | H |
| 496K | Bandoleer Crossing–Frank O'Rourke | 1.25 | 2.50 | 3.75 | W |
| 497K | Bypass to Otherness–Henry Kuttner | 2.00 | 4.00 | 6.00 | SF |
| 498K | Ringstones–Sarban | 2.00 | 4.00 | 6.00 | HO |
| 499K | Song of the Axe–M.C. McDonald | 1.00 | 2.00 | 3.00 | A |
| 502K | Spanish Ridge–E.E. Halleran | 1.25 | 2.50 | 3.75 | W |
| 505K | Big Man, Big Mountain–Wade Everett | 1.25 | 2.50 | 3.75 | W |
| 506K | Not without Sorcery–Theodore Sturgeon | 2.00 | 4.00 | 6.00 | SF |
| 507K | The Lovers–Philip José Farmer | 5.00 | 10.00 | 15.00 | SF |
| 508K | Night's Black Agents–Fritz Leiber | 2.00 | 4.00 | 6.00 | F |
| S509K | Grand Inquest–Telford Taylor | 1.00 | 2.00 | 3.00 | |
| X510K | The Un-Americans–Frank J. Donner | .50 | 1.00 | 1.50 | NF |
| 511K | Slan–A.E. Van Vogt; c-Powers | 1.00 | 2.00 | 3.00 | SF |
| 512K | England under Hitler–Comer Clarke | .75 | 1.50 | 2.25 | NF |
| 513K | Admirals in Collision–Richard B. Hough | 1.00 | 2.00 | 3.00 | NF |
| F514K | Thunderbolt–Robert S. Johnson & Martin Caidin | 1.00 | 2.00 | 3.00 | NF |
| F515K | The Case of Barbara Graham–Bill Walker; movie tie-in | 1.50 | 3.00 | 4.50 | NF |
| X516K | Executive Suite–Cameron Hawley | .50 | 1.00 | 1.50 | |
| S517K | La Dolce Vita–Federico Fellini; movie tie-in | 2.00 | 4.00 | 6.00 | E |
| 518K | Outlaw Town–Edwin Booth | 1.25 | 2.50 | 3.75 | W |
| 519K | A Cupful of Space–Mildred Clingerman | 1.50 | 3.00 | 4.50 | SF |
| 520K | The Hospital–Kenneth Fearing | 1.50 | 3.00 | 4.50 | |
| 521K | Star Science Fiction Stories No. 1–ed. Frederik Pohl | .75 | 1.50 | 2.25 | SF |
| 522K | Tales of Love and Horror–ed. Don Congdon | 1.50 | 3.00 | 4.50 | HO |
| 523K | Glory Gamblers–Lesley Forden | 1.00 | 2.00 | 3.00 | NF |
| F524K | How to Raise Your Child's IQ–David Engler | .75 | 1.50 | 2.25 | NF |
| X525K | Burl Ives Song Book–Burl Ives | .75 | 1.50 | 2.25 | NF |
| 526K | Hombre–Elmore Leonard; 1st ed.; 1961 | 10.00 | 20.00 | 30.00 | W |
| 527 | Greener Than You Think–Ward Moore | 1.00 | 2.00 | 3.00 | SF |
| F528 | The Challenge of the Spaceship–Arthur C. Clarke | 1.00 | 2.00 | 3.00 | NF |
| S529 | Company Commander–Charles B. MacDonald | 1.00 | 2.00 | 3.00 | NF |
| S530 | The Press–A.J. Liebling | .50 | 1.00 | 1.50 | NF |
| 531 | The Clock Strikes 12–H.R. Wakefield | 1.25 | 2.50 | 3.75 | HO |
| F532 | The Complete Book of Birth Control–Alan F. Guttmacher, Winfield Best, Frederick S. Jaffe | .75 | 1.50 | | |
| F533 | Mutiny–Frank Tilsley | 1.25 | 2.50 | 3.75 | A |
| 534 | Donovan–Elmer Kelton | 1.25 | 2.50 | 3.75 | W |
| 535 | Buffalo Wagons–Elmer Kelton | 1.25 | 2.50 | 3.75 | W |
| X536 | The Defeat of John Hawkins–Rayner Unwin | 1.00 | 2.00 | 3.00 | NF |
| F537 | Kennedy in Power–Prof. James T. Crown, George P. Penty | .75 | 1.50 | 2.25 | NF |
| F538 | Science Projects Handbook–ed. Science Service Assoc. | .75 | 1.50 | 2.25 | NF |
| 539 | Tales from the White Hart–Arthur C. Clarke | 1.00 | 2.00 | 3.00 | SF |
| 540 | Sardonicus and Other Stories–Ray Russell; movie tie-in | 2.00 | 4.00 | 6.00 | HO |
| S541 | College Parodies–Will Lieberson & Martin Lieberson | 2.00 | 4.00 | 6.00 | H |
| 542 | Not Long for this World–August Derleth | 2.00 | 4.00 | 6.00 | HO |
| F543 | Moment of No Return–Stephen King-Hall | 1.50 | 3.00 | 4.50 | |
| 544 | Ride West for War–Chad Merriman | 1.25 | 2.50 | 3.75 | W |
| 545 | Out of the Deeps–John Wyndham | .75 | 1.50 | 2.25 | SF |
| 546 | The Infinite Moment–John Wyndham | 1.50 | 3.00 | 4.50 | SF |
| S547K | The Court of St. James's–E.S. Turner | 1.00 | 2.00 | 3.00 | NF |
| F548 | The Nuts among the Berries–Ronald Deutsch | 1.00 | 2.00 | 3.00 | NF |
| F549 | Samurai!–Saburo Sakai, Martin Caidin, Fred Saito | .75 | 1.50 | 2.25 | NF |
| 550 | Best Television Plays–ed. Gore Vidal | .75 | 1.50 | 2.25 | |
| 551 | Paris Blues–Harold Flender; movie tie-in | 1.50 | 3.00 | 4.50 | |
| 552 | . . . And Some Were Human–Lester del Rey | 2.00 | 4.00 | 6.00 | SF |
| X553 | War Underground–Alexander Barrie | 1.00 | 2.00 | 3.00 | NF |

BALLANTINE BOOKS, *continued*

| No. | Title | V/Good | Fine | N/Mint |
|---|---|---|---|---|
| 554 | Temporary Duty–Wade Everett | 1.25 | 2.50 | 3.75 W |
| F555 | The Primal Urge–Brian Aldiss | 1.50 | 3.00 | 4.50 SF |
| 556 | Zacherley's Midnight Snacks–ed. Zacherley | 1.25 | 2.50 | 3.75 HO |
| X557 | The Judgement of Paris–Gore Vidal | 1.00 | 2.00 | 3.00 |
| F558 | How to Succeed in Business without Really Trying–Shepherd Mead | 1.50 | 3.00 | 4.50 H |
| | With dust jacket | 10.00 | 20.00 | 30.00 |
| F559 | The Great Contest–Isaac Deutscher | 1.00 | 2.00 | 3.00 |
| 560 | Comanche Captives–Fred Grove | 1.25 | 2.50 | 3.75 W |
| F561 | The Silver Eggheads–Fritz Leiber | 2.00 | 4.00 | 6.00 SF |
| F562 | Caviar–Theodore Sturgeon | 1.00 | 2.00 | 3.00 SF |
| 563 | Alone by Night–eds. Don Congdon & Michael Congdon. Note: Includes scarce short story by Richard Matheson under his Logan Swanson pseudonym | 2.00 | 4.00 | 6.00 HO |
| F564 | The Peace Race–Seymour Melman | .50 | 1.00 | 1.50 NF |
| F565 | The Gods Were Neutral–Maj. Robert Crisp | .75 | 1.50 | 2.25 NF |
| 566 | The Mad Reader–ed. Mad Magazine | 1.00 | 2.00 | 3.00 H |
| F567 | The Nonconformers–David Evanier, Stanley Silverzweig | 1.00 | 2.00 | 3.00 NF |
| F568 | The Causes of World War III–C. Wright Mills | .50 | 1.00 | 1.50 NF |
| 569 | Day of the Gun–Clifton Adams | 1.25 | 2.50 | 3.75 W |
| F570 | Gladiator-at-Law–Frederik Pohl & C.M. Kornbluth | 1.00 | 2.00 | 3.00 SF |
| F571 | The Unsleep–Diana & Meir Gillon | 1.75 | 3.50 | 5.25 SF |
| S572 | Best American Short Stories 1961–ed. Martha Foley & David Burnett | 1.00 | 2.00 | 3.00 |
| F573 | The Crusades–Richard Suskind | 1.00 | 2.00 | 3.00 NF |
| 574 | Zacherley's Vulture Stew–ed. Zacherley | 1.25 | 2.50 | 3.75 HO |
| F575 | Ju-Ju and Justice in Nigeria–Frank Hives & Gascoine Lomley | 2.50 | 5.00 | 7.50 NF |
| F576 | How to Succeed with Women without Really Trying–Shepherd Mead | 1.25 | 2.50 | 3.75 H |
| 577 | Shadows with Eyes–Fritz Leiber | 2.50 | 5.00 | 7.50 HO |
| 578 | Gut Shot–Lee Leighton | 1.25 | 2.50 | 3.75 W |
| 579 | After Doomsday–Poul Anderson | 1.50 | 3.00 | 4.50 SF |
| F580 | The October Country–Ray Bradbury | 1.00 | 2.00 | 3.00 SF |
| F581 | Satan's Disciples–Robert C. Goldston | 1.00 | 2.00 | 3.00 NF |
| X582 | The Jollity Building–A.J. Liebling | .75 | 1.50 | 2.25 |
| F583 | The Night Hamburg Died–Martin Caidin | .50 | 1.00 | 1.50 NF |
| F584 | How to Bring Up Your Child to Enjoy Music–Howard Taubman | .50 | 1.00 | 1.50 NF |
| 585 | Harsh Reckoning–Phil Ketchum | 1.25 | 2.50 | 3.75 W |
| S586 | Les Liaisons Dangereuses–Roger Vadim; movie tie-in | 2.00 | 4.00 | 6.00 E |
| 587 | Nine Horrors and a Dream–Joseph Payne Brennan | 2.00 | 4.00 | 6.00 HO |
| F588 | The Alley God–Philip José Farmer | 2.50 | 5.00 | 7.50 SF |
| F589 | In the Life–Theodore Isaac Rubin, MD | .50 | 1.00 | 1.50 |
| 590 | Mad Strikes Back–ed. Mad Magazine | 1.00 | 2.00 | 3.00 H |
| F591 | Squadron Airborne–Elleston Trevor | 1.00 | 2.00 | 3.00 NF |
| F592 | Three Corvettes–Nicholas Monsarrat | 1.00 | 2.00 | 3.00 NF |
| F593 | The Cuban Invasion–Karl E. Meyer, Tad Szulc | 1.00 | 2.00 | 3.00 NF |
| 594 | Bitter Trail–Elmer Kelton | 1.25 | 2.50 | 3.75 W |
| F595 | Hospital Station–James White | 2.00 | 4.00 | 6.00 SF |
| F596 | H.M.S. Defiant–Frank Tilsey | 1.00 | 2.00 | 3.00 NF |
| 597 | The Man Who Ate the World–Frederik Pohl | 1.00 | 2.00 | 3.00 SF |
| F598 | Firsts of the Famous–ed. Whit Burnett | .75 | 1.50 | 2.25 |
| F599 | A Place to Sleep–Gerda Rhoads | .75 | 1.50 | 2.25 |
| S600 | The Kaiten Weapon–Yutaka Yok-ta, Joseph D. Harrington | 1.50 | 3.00 | 4.50 NF |
| S601 | Each Man Kills–Sanford Bayer | .75 | 1.50 | 2.25 |
| F602 | The Day the Earth Caught Fire–Barry Wells | 1.25 | 2.50 | 3.75 SF |
| F603 | Student–David Horowitz | 1.00 | 2.00 | 3.00 NF |
| 604 | Killer–Wade Everett | 1.25 | 2.50 | 3.75 W |
| F605 | Bruce Tegner Method of Self Defense–Bruce Tegner | 1.00 | 2.00 | 3.00 NF |
| F606 | The Big Clock–Kenneth Fearing | 1.00 | 2.00 | 3.00 M |
| F609 | Telepath–Arthur Sellings | 1.50 | 3.00 | 4.50 SF |
| 610 | Indian Country–Dorothy Johnson | 1.25 | 2.50 | 3.75 W |
| 612 | Star Science Fiction Stories No. 2–ed. Frederik Pohl | 1.00 | 2.00 | 3.00 SF |
| F613 | The Call Girl–Harold Greenwald | 1.00 | 2.00 | 3.00 NF |
| F614 | Gale Warning–Hammond Innes | 1.00 | 2.00 | 3.00 A |
| F615 | The Blue Ice–Hammond Innes | 1.00 | 2.00 | 3.00 A |
| 617 | Sidewinder–Edwin Booth | 1.25 | 2.50 | 3.75 W |
| 618 | Inside Mad–ed. Mad Magazine | 1.00 | 2.00 | 3.00 H |
| F619 | Return to Otherness–Henry Kuttner | 2.00 | 4.00 | 6.00 SF |
| F620 | The Savage Land–Ann Ahlswede | 2.00 | 4.00 | 6.00 W |
| F621 | The Overloaded Ark–Gerald Durrell | .75 | 1.50 | 2.25 NF |
| S622 | TV in America: The Morality of Hard Cash–Meyer Weinberg | .75 | 1.50 | 2.25 NF |
| F623 | The Probable Cause–Robert J. Serling | .75 | 1.50 | 2.25 NF |
| F624 | Hugger-Mugger in the Louvre–Elliot Paul | 1.25 | 2.50 | 3.75 M |
| F626 | Conditionally Human–Walter M. Miller, Jr | 1.25 | 2.50 | 3.75 SF |
| N628 | China: The Country Americans Are Not Allowed to Know–Felix Greene | .75 | 1.50 | 2.25 NF |
| 629 | The Survivor and Others–H.P. Lovecraft & August Derleth | 1.75 | 3.50 | 5.25 HO |
| 630 | Note: Stickers with this number appear on some copies of 449K (Trouble with Lichen–John Wyndham). | | | SF |
| 632 | Note: Stickers with this number appear on some copies of 465K (So Close to Home–James Blish). | | | SF |
| 635 | Crimson Desert–E.E. Halleran | 1.25 | 2.50 | 3.75 W |
| F636 | The Impossible–Richard Gardner | .75 | 1.50 | 2.25 NF |
| F637 | The Reign of Terror in the French Revolution–Cleveland Amory | 1.00 | 2.00 | 3.00 NF |
| F638 | The Wonder Effect–Frederik Pohl & C.M. Kornbluth | 1.50 | 3.00 | 4.50 SF |
| F639 | Eight Keys to Eden–Mark Clifton | 1.25 | 2.50 | 3.75 SF |
| 640 | Rogue River–Chad Merriman | 1.25 | 2.50 | 3.75 W |
| F641 | The Fiend in You–ed. Charles Beaumont | 2.50 | 5.00 | 7.50 HO |
| F642 | The Angry Mountain–Hammond Innes | 1.00 | 2.00 | 3.00 A |
| F643 | Jordi/Lisa and David–Theodore Isaac Rubin, MD | 1.00 | 2.00 | 3.00 |
| S644 | The Earl of Louisiana–A.J. Liebling | 1.00 | 2.00 | 3.00 |
| F645 | Courage in Both Hands–Allan B. Hunter | 1.00 | 2.00 | 3.00 |
| F646 | Concrete Crime–Manning Coles | 1.00 | 2.00 | 3.00 M |
| F647 | The Night Shapes–James Blish | 1.50 | 3.00 | 4.50 HO |
| F648 | Citizen in Space–Robert Sheckley | .75 | 1.50 | 2.25 SF |
| 649 | Hanging at Comanche Wells–Benjamin Capps | 1.25 | 2.50 | 3.75 W |
| S650 | The Hungry Eye–Eugene Paul | .75 | 1.50 | 2.25 |
| F651 | Dagger of the Mind–Kenneth Fearing | .75 | 1.50 | 2.25 M |
| F652 | Stalingrad–Heinz Schroeter | .75 | 1.50 | 2.25 NF |
| S653 | The Curse of the Misbegotten–Croswell Bowen | .75 | 1.50 | 2.25 |
| 654 | Utterly Mad–ed. Mad Magazine | 1.00 | 2.00 | 3.00 H |
| X655 | America in Hiding–Arthur I. Waskow, Stanley Newman | .50 | 1.00 | 1.50 NF |
| F656 | The Dam Busters–Paul Brickhill | .75 | 1.50 | 2.25 NF |
| F657 | Sometime, Never–William Golding, John Wyndham, Mervyn Peake | .75 | 1.50 | 2.25 F |
| F658 | Time Out for Tomorrow–Richard Wilson | 1.00 | 2.00 | 3.00 SF |
| 659 | The Big Drive–Wade Everett | 1.25 | 2.50 | 3.75 W |
| F660 | The Crossing–Will Cook | 1.25 | 2.50 | 3.75 W |
| F661 | The Killer Mine–Hammond Innes | 1.00 | 2.00 | 3.00 A |
| S662 | Zen Combat–Jay Gluck | 1.25 | 2.50 | 3.75 NF |
| S663 | Stories of the East–Somerset Maugham | 1.00 | 2.00 | 3.00 |
| F664 | Science Projects Handbook–ed. Science Service Assoc. | .50 | 1.00 | 1.50 NF |
| F665 | Crack in the Picture Window–John Keats | .50 | 1.00 | 1.50 H |
| 666 | Fire in the Desert–Ford Logan | 1.25 | 2.50 | 3.75 W |
| 667 | Hangtown–Les Savage, Jr | 1.25 | 2.50 | 3.75 W |
| 668 | The Night of the Coyotes–Phil Ketchum | 1.25 | 2.50 | 3.75 W |
| 669 | Lawman's Pay–Frank C. Robertson | 1.25 | 2.50 | 3.75 W |
| 670 | Chainlink–Owen Evens; c-Crair | 1.25 | 2.50 | 3.75 W |
| 671 | Sun Dance–Fred Grove | 1.25 | 2.50 | 3.75 W |
| 672 | Tomahawk–Lee Leighton | 1.25 | 2.50 | 3.75 W |
| 673 | The Return of the Texan–L.L. Foreman | 1.00 | 2.00 | 3.00 W |
| F674 | A Big Man in Saludas–Francis Rosenwald | 1.25 | 2.50 | 3.75 W |
| F675 | Star Science Fiction Stories No. 3–ed. Frederik Pohl | 1.00 | 2.00 | 3.00 SF |
| F676 | Fahrenheit 451–Ray Bradbury | .75 | 1.50 | 2.25 SF |
| 677 | Beyond the Pass–Lee Leighton | 1.00 | 2.00 | 3.00 W |
| F678 | U-Boats at War–Harald Busch | .75 | 1.50 | 2.25 NF |
| F679 | Traps–Friedrich Duerrenmatt | .75 | 1.50 | 2.25 |

| | V/Good | Fine | N/Mint |
|---|---|---|---|

**BALLANTINE BOOKS,** *continued*

| | | V/Good | Fine | N/Mint |
|---|---|---|---|---|
| F680 | The Frankenstein Reader–ed. Calvin T. Beck | 2.00 | 4.00 | 6.00 HO |
| S681 | Famous Tales of India–Rudyard Kipling | 1.50 | 3.00 | 4.50 A |
| 682 | The Hostile Hills–E.E. Halleran; 1963; c-Crair | .75 | 1.50 | 2.25 W |
| S683 | Pornography and the Law–Drs. E. Kronhausen & P. Kronhausen | .50 | 1.00 | 1.50 NF |
| F684 | Commando Extraordinary–Charles Foley | .50 | 1.00 | 1.50 NF |
| F685 | The Abominable Earthman–Frederik Pohl | 2.00 | 4.00 | 6.00 SF |
| F686 | The Bafut Beagles–Gerald Durrell | .75 | 1.50 | 2.25 NF |
| F687 | The First Men in the Moon–H.G. Wells | 1.50 | 3.00 | 4.50 SF |
| X688 | The Legacy–Nevil Shute | 1.00 | 2.00 | 3.00 |
| X689 | Most Secret–Nevil Shute | 1.00 | 2.00 | 3.00 |
| F690 | Trent's Last Case–E.C. Bentley | 1.00 | 2.00 | 3.00 M |
| 691 | Jet–Frank Harvey | 1.00 | 2.00 | 3.00 NF |
| 692 | Aircraft Carrier–J. Bryan III | 1.00 | 2.00 | 3.00 NF |
| 693 | Kamikaze–Yasuo Kuwahara & Gordon T. Allred | 1.00 | 2.00 | 3.00 NF |
| 694 | God Is My Co-Pilot–Robert L. Scott | .50 | 1.00 | 1.50 NF |
| S695 | Best American Short Stories 1962–ed. Martha Foley & David Burnett | 1.00 | 2.00 | 3.00 |
| F696 | The Naked Land–Hammond Innes | 1.00 | 2.00 | 3.00 A |
| F697 | The Battle of the Bulge–Robert E. Merriam | 1.00 | 2.00 | 3.00 NF |
| F698 | Earthlight–Arthur C. Clarke | .75 | 1.50 | 2.25 SF |
| 699 | Violence at Sundown–Frank O'Rourke | 1.25 | 2.50 | 3.75 W |
| DF700 | Power, Politics and People: The Collected Essays of C. Wright Mills | .50 | 1.00 | 1.50 NF |
| F701 | A Princess of Mars–Edgar Rice Burroughs; c-Abbett | 2.00 | 4.00 | 6.00 SF |
| F702 | The Gods of Mars–Edgar Rice Burroughs; c-Abbett | 2.00 | 4.00 | 6.00 SF |
| F703 | A Handful of Time–Rosel George Brown | 1.50 | 3.00 | 4.50 SF |
| F704 | Sweet Daddy–Theodore Isaac Rubin, MD | 1.00 | 2.00 | 3.00 |
| S705 | The War Game–Irving Louis Horowitz | .50 | 1.00 | 1.50 NF |
| F706 | Bones in the Barrow–Josephine Bell | 1.00 | 2.00 | 3.00 M |
| F707 | The Bright Road to Fear–Richard Martin Stern | 1.00 | 2.00 | 3.00 M |
| F708 | The Explorers–C.M. Kornbluth | .75 | 1.50 | 2.25 SF |
| F709 | Star Surgeon–James White | 1.50 | 3.00 | 4.50 SF |
| 710 | The Far Land–E.E. Halleran | 1.00 | 2.00 | 3.00 W |
| F711 | The Warlord of Mars–Edgar Rice Burroughs; c-Abbett | 2.00 | 4.00 | 6.00 SF |
| F712 | All the Way Down–Vincent Riccio & Bill Slocum | .75 | 1.50 | 2.25 |
| F713 | The Sea Lord–Showell Styles; aka The Frigate Captain | 1.00 | 2.00 | 3.00 A |
| 714 | Hardrock–Frank Bonham | .75 | 1.50 | 2.25 W |
| 715 | The Brothers Mad–ed. Mad Magazine | 1.00 | 2.00 | 3.00 H |
| X720 | No Highway–Nevil Shute | 1.00 | 2.00 | 3.00 |
| F721 | The Double Door–Theodora Keogh | 1.25 | 2.50 | 3.75 |
| F722 | The Grindle Nightmare–Q. Patrick | 1.00 | 2.00 | 3.00 M |
| F723 | American Aces–Edward H. Sims | .75 | 1.50 | 2.25 NF |
| F724 | Mutant–Henry Kuttner | 1.50 | 3.00 | 4.50 SF |
| F725 | Food of the Gods–H.G. Wells | 1.50 | 3.00 | 4.50 SF |
| X726 | A Dancer in Darkness–David Stacton | 1.50 | 3.00 | 4.50 |
| F727 | Fall over Cliff–Josephine Bell | 1.00 | 2.00 | 3.00 M |

| | | V/Good | Fine | N/Mint |
|---|---|---|---|---|
| F728 | Swords of Mars–Edgar Rice Burroughs; c-Abbett | 2.00 | 4.00 | 6.00 SF |
| Y729 | Barbed Wire–Elmer Kelton | 1.25 | 2.50 | 3.75 W |
| F730 | Star Short Novels–ed. Frederik Pohl | .75 | 1.50 | 2.25 SF |
| F731 | The First and the Last–Adolf Galland | .75 | 1.50 | 2.25 |
| X732 | Elephant Walk–Robert Standish | 1.00 | 2.00 | 3.00 |
| X733 | King Solomon's Mines–H. Rider Haggard | 1.50 | 3.00 | 4.50 A |
| F734 | Campbell's Kingdom–Hammond Innes | 1.00 | 2.00 | 3.00 A |
| Y735 | Horsehead Crossing–Elmer Kelton | 1.25 | 2.50 | 3.75 W |
| F737 | Samurai!–Saburo Sakai, Fred Saito, Martin Caidin | .75 | 1.50 | 2.25 NF |
| F738 | Search the Sky–Frederik Pohl & C.M. Kornbluth | 1.00 | 2.00 | 3.00 SF |
| F739 | Synthetic Men of Mars–Edgar Rice Burroughs | 2.00 | 4.00 | 6.00 SF |
| F740 | Memory of Love–Bessie Breuer | .75 | 1.50 | 2.25 |
| F741 | A Puzzle for Fools–Q. Patrick | 1.00 | 2.00 | 3.00 M |
| S742 | Best Stories of H.G. Wells–H.G. Wells; 1963 | 1.00 | 2.00 | 3.00 SF |
| X743 | Allan Quatermain–H. Rider Haggard | 1.50 | 3.00 | 4.50 A |
| X744 | Greatest Fighter Missions–Edward H. Sims | .75 | 1.50 | 2.25 NF |
| F745 | Tarzan of the Apes–Edgar Rice Burroughs; c-Powers | 2.00 | 4.00 | 6.00 A |
| F746 | The Return of Tarzan–Edgar Rice Burroughs; c-Powers | 2.00 | 4.00 | 6.00 A |
| F747 | The Beasts of Tarzan–Edgar Rice Burroughs; c-Powers | 2.00 | 4.00 | 6.00 A |
| F748 | The Son of Tarzan–Edgar Rice Burroughs; c-Powers | 2.00 | 4.00 | 6.00 A |
| F749 | Tarzan and the Jewels of Opar–Edgar Rice Burroughs; c-Powers | 2.00 | 4.00 | 6.00 A |
| F750 | Jungle Tales of Tarzan–Edgar Rice Burroughs; c-Powers | 2.00 | 4.00 | 6.00 A |
| F751 | Tarzan the Untamed–Edgar Rice Burroughs; c-Powers | 2.00 | 4.00 | 6.00 A |
| F752 | Tarzan the Terrible–Edgar Rice Burroughs; c-Powers | 2.00 | 4.00 | 6.00 A |
| F753 | Tarzan and the Golden Lion–Edgar Rice Burroughs; c-Powers | 2.00 | 4.00 | 6.00 A |
| F754 | Tarzan and the Ant-Men–Edgar Rice Burroughs; c-Powers | 2.00 | 4.00 | 6.00 A |
| F755 | The Pillars of Midnight–Elleston Trevor | .75 | 1.50 | 2.25 |
| F756 | Street Music–Theodora Keogh | 1.25 | 2.50 | 3.75 |
| X757 | Pastoral–Nevil Shute | 1.00 | 2.00 | 3.00 |
| Y759 | Devil's Canyon–E.E. Halleran | 1.00 | 2.00 | 3.00 W |
| F760 | The Marching Morons–C.M. Kornbluth | 1.00 | 2.00 | 3.00 SF |
| F761 | The Island of Dr. Moreau–H.G. Wells | 1.50 | 3.00 | 4.50 HO |
| F762 | Llana of Gathol–Edgar Rice Burroughs; c-Abbett | 2.00 | 4.00 | 6.00 SF |
| F764 | Thunderbolt–Robert S. Johnson & Martin Caidin | .75 | 1.50 | 2.25 NF |
| F765 | Those About to Die–Daniel P. Mannix | .75 | 1.50 | 2.25 NF |
| F766 | The Hell-Fire Club–Daniel P. Mannix | 1.00 | 2.00 | 3.00 NF |
| F767 | Death in Retirement–Josephine Bell | .75 | 1.50 | 2.25 M |
| F768 | Trapped–Hammond Innes; aka Wreckers Must Breathe | .75 | 1.50 | 2.25 A |
| Y769 | The Land Seekers–Fred Grove | 1.00 | 2.00 | 3.00 W |
| F770 | Thuvia, Maid of Mars–Edgar Rice Burroughs; c-Abbett | 2.00 | 4.00 | 6.00 SF |
| F772 | Tarzan, Lord of the Jungle–Edgar Rice Burroughs; c-Powers | 2.00 | 4.00 | 6.00 A |
| F773 | H.M.S. Marlborough Will Enter Harbor–Nicholas Monsarrat | .75 | 1.50 | 2.25 NF |
| X774 | Burl Ives Song Book–Burl Ives | .75 | 1.50 | 2.25 NF |
| F776 | The Chessmen of Mars–Edgar Rice Burroughs; c-Abbett | 2.00 | 4.00 | 6.00 SF |
| F777 | Tarzan and the Lost Empire–Edgar Rice Burroughs; c-Powers | 2.00 | 4.00 | 6.00 A |
| F778 | A Puzzle for Fiends–Q. Patrick | 1.00 | 2.00 | 3.00 M |

## BALLANTINE ADULT FANTASY
### Ballantine Books, Inc.

| | | V/Good | Fine | N/Mint |
|---|---|---|---|---|
| 01503 | The Last Unicorn–Peter S. Beagle | 2.00 | 4.00 | 6.00 F |
| 01602 | The Blue Star–Fletcher Pratt; 1969 | 3.00 | 6.00 | 9.00 SF |
| 01628 | The King of Elfland's Daughter–Lord Dunsany | 3.00 | 6.00 | 9.00 F |

*Ballantine F575, Ballantine S681, Ballantine F741.*

**BALLANTINE ADULT FANTASY,** *continued*

| No. | Title | V/Good | Fine | N/Mint | |
|---|---|---|---|---|---|
| 01652 | The Wood Beyond the World–William Morris | 3.00 | 6.00 | 9.00 | F |
| 01678 | The Silver Stallion–James Branch Cabell | 3.00 | 6.00 | 9.00 | F |
| 01711 | Lilith–George MacDonald | 3.00 | 6.00 | 9.00 | F |
| 01730 | The Young Magicians–ed. Lin Carter | 3.00 | 6.00 | 9.00 | F |
| 01731 | Dragons, Elves and Heroes–ed. Lin Carter | 3.00 | 6.00 | 9.00 | F |
| 01763 | Figures of Earth–James Branch Cabell | 3.00 | 6.00 | 9.00 | F |
| 01795 | The Sorceror's Ship–Hannes Bok | 3.00 | 6.00 | 9.00 | F |
| 01814 | Land of Unreason–L. Sprague de Camp; 1970 | 3.00 | 6.00 | 9.00 | SF |
| 01855 | The High Place–James Branch Cabell | 3.00 | 6.00 | 9.00 | F |
| 01879 | At the Edge of the World–Lord Dunsany | 3.00 | 6.00 | 9.00 | F |
| 01880 | Lud-in-the-Mist–Hope Mirrlees | 3.00 | 6.00 | 9.00 | F |
| 01902 | Phantastes–George MacDonald | 3.00 | 6.00 | 9.00 | F |
| 01923 | The Dream Quest of Unknown Kadath–H.P. Lovecraft | 3.00 | 6.00 | 9.00 | F |
| 01938 | Zothique–Clark Ashton Smith | 3.00 | 6.00 | 9.00 | SF |
| 01958 | The Shaving of Shagpat–George Meredith | 3.00 | 6.00 | 9.00 | F |
| 01959 | The Island of the Mighty–Evangeline Walton | 3.00 | 6.00 | 9.00 | F |
| 01981 | Deryni Rising–Katharine Kurtz | 3.00 | 6.00 | 9.00 | F |
| 01982 | The Well at World's End, Vol. 1–William Morris | 3.00 | 6.00 | 9.00 | F |
| 02015 | The Well at World's End, Vol. 2–William Morris | 3.00 | 6.00 | 9.00 | F |
| 02045 | Golden Cities, Far–ed. Lin Carter | 3.00 | 6.00 | 9.00 | F |
| 02067 | Something about Eve–James Branch Cabell | 3.00 | 6.00 | 9.00 | F |
| 02093 | Beyond the Golden Stair–Hannes Bok | 3.00 | 6.00 | 9.00 | F |
| 02107 | The Broken Sword–Poul Anderson; 1971 | 3.00 | 6.00 | 9.00 | F |
| 02145 | The Boats of the "Glen Carrig"–William Hope Hodgson | 3.00 | 6.00 | 9.00 | F |
| 02146 | The Doom That Came to Sarnath–H.P. Lovecraft | 3.00 | 6.00 | 9.00 | HO |
| 02178 | Red Moon and Black Mountain–Joy Chant | 3.00 | 6.00 | 9.00 | F |
| 02206 | Hyperborea–Clark Ashton Smith | 3.00 | 6.00 | 9.00 | SF |
| 02244 | Don Rodriguez: Chronicles of Shadow Valley–Lord Dunsany | 3.00 | 6.00 | 9.00 | F |
| 02279 | Vathek–William Beckford | 3.00 | 6.00 | 9.00 | F |
| 02305 | The Man Who Was Thursday–G.K. Chesterton | 15.00 | 30.00 | 45.00 | F |
| 02332 | The Children of Llyr–Evangeline Walton | 3.00 | 6.00 | 9.00 | F |
| 02364 | The Cream of the Jest–James Branch Cabell | 3.00 | 6.00 | 9.00 | F |
| 02365 | New Worlds for Old–ed. Lin Carter | 3.00 | 6.00 | 9.00 | F |
| 02394 | The Spawn of Cthulhu–ed. Lin Carter | 3.00 | 6.00 | 9.00 | HO |
| 02420 | Double Phoenix–Edmund Cooper & Roger L. Green | 3.00 | 6.00 | 9.00 | SF |
| 02421 | The Water of the Wondrous Isles–William Morris | 3.00 | 6.00 | 9.00 | F |
| 02446 | Khaled–F. Marion Crawford | 3.00 | 6.00 | 9.00 | F |
| 02467 | The World's Desire–H. Rider Haggard; 1972 | 3.00 | 6.00 | 9.00 | F |
| 02501 | Xiccarph–Clark Ashton Smith | 3.00 | 6.00 | 9.00 | SF |
| 02502 | The Lost Continent–C.J. Cutliffe-Hyne | 2.50 | 5.00 | 7.50 | F |
| 02545 | Domnei–James Branch Cabell | 3.00 | 6.00 | 9.00 | F |
| 02546 | Discoveries in Fantasy–ed. Lin Carter | 3.00 | 6.00 | 9.00 | F |
| 02574 | Kai Lung's Golden Hours–Ernest Bramah | 3.00 | 6.00 | 9.00 | F |
| 02598 | Deryni Checkmate–Katharine Kurtz | 3.00 | 6.00 | 9.00 | F |
| 02599 | Beyond the Fields We Know–Lord Dunsany | 3.00 | 6.00 | 9.00 | F |
| 02643 | The Three Imposters–Arthur Machen | 3.00 | 6.00 | 9.00 | SF |
| 02669 | The Night Land, Vol. 1–William Hope Hodgson | 3.00 | 6.00 | 9.00 | HO |
| 02670 | The Night Land, Vol. 2–William Hope Hodgson | 3.00 | 6.00 | 9.00 | HO |
| 02773 | The Song of Rhiannon–Evangeline Walton | 3.00 | 6.00 | 9.00 | F |
| 02789 | Great Short Novels of Adult Fantasy, Vol. 1–ed. Lin Carter | 3.00 | 6.00 | 9.00 | F |
| 02874 | Evenor–George MacDonald | 3.00 | 6.00 | 9.00 | F |
| 02892 | The Last Unicorn–Peter Beagle | .75 | 1.50 | 2.25 | F |
| 02995 | The Well at World's End, Vol. 1–William Morris | 2.50 | 5.00 | 7.50 | F |
| 02996 | The Well at World's End, Vol. 2–William Morris | 2.50 | 5.00 | 7.50 | F |
| 03057 | Orlando Furioso–Ludovico Ariosto; 1973 | 3.00 | 6.00 | 9.00 | SF |
| 03085 | The Charwoman's Shadow–Lord Dunsany | 3.00 | 6.00 | 9.00 | F |
| 03162 | Great Short Novels of Adult Fantasy, Vol. 2–ed. Lin Carter | 3.00 | 6.00 | 9.00 | F |
| 03261 | The Sundering Flood–William Morris | 2.50 | 5.00 | 7.50 | F |
| 03309 | Imaginary Worlds–ed. Lin Carter. Note: History of fantasy and science fiction | 3.00 | 6.00 | 9.00 | NF |
| 03353 | Poseidonis–Clark Ashton Smith | 3.00 | 6.00 | 9.00 | SF |
| 23416 | Excalibur–Sanders Anne Laubenthal | 3.00 | 6.00 | 9.00 | F |
| 23485 | High Deryni–Katharine Kurtz | 3.00 | 6.00 | 9.00 | F |
| 23515 | The Well at World's End, Vol. 1–William Morris | 1.50 | 3.00 | 4.50 | F |
| 23516 | The Well at World's End, Vol. 2–William Morris | 1.50 | 3.00 | 4.50 | F |
| 23517 | The King of Elfland's Daughter–Lord Dunsany | 3.00 | 6.00 | 9.00 | F |
| 23518 | Titus Groan–Mervyn Peake | 3.00 | 6.00 | 9.00 | F |
| 23519 | Gormenghast–Mervyn Peake | 3.00 | 6.00 | 9.00 | F |
| 23520 | Titus Alone–Mervyn Peake | 3.00 | 6.00 | 9.00 | F |
| 23526 | The Broken Sword–Poul Anderson | 1.50 | 3.00 | 4.50 | F |
| 23527 | The Dream Quest of Unknown Kadath–H.P. Lovecraft | 3.00 | 6.00 | 9.00 | F |
| 23528 | Lilith–George MacDonald | 3.00 | 6.00 | 9.00 | F |
| 23562 | Hrolf Kraki's Saga–Poul Anderson | 3.00 | 6.00 | 9.00 | F |
| 23611 | Red Moon and Black Mountain–Joy Chant | 1.50 | 3.00 | 4.50 | F |
| 23660 | The People of the Mist–H. Rider Haggard | 3.00 | 6.00 | 9.00 | F |
| 23730 | The Wood Beyond the World–William Morris; 1974 | 3.00 | 6.00 | 9.00 | F |
| 23787 | Kai Lung Unrolls His Mat–Ernest Bramah | 3.00 | 6.00 | 9.00 | F |
| 23886 | Over the Hills and Far Away–Lord Dunsany | 3.00 | 6.00 | 9.00 | F |
| 23927 | The People of the Mist–H. Rider Haggard | 1.50 | 3.00 | 4.50 | F |
| 24010 | Merlin's Ring–H. Warner Munn | 3.00 | 6.00 | 9.00 | F |
| 24209 | The Song of Rhiannon–Evangeline Walton | 3.00 | 6.00 | 9.00 | F |
| 24233 | Prince of Annwn–Evangeline Walton | 3.00 | 6.00 | 9.00 | F |

# BALLANTINE LADDER EDITION

## Ballantine Books, Inc.

| No. | Title | V/Good | Fine | N/Mint | |
|---|---|---|---|---|---|
| L1 | The Far Command–Elinor Chamberlain | 1.00 | 2.00 | 3.00 | A |
| L2 | The Red Gate–LaSelle Gilman | 1.00 | 2.00 | 3.00 | |
| L3 | The Pioneers–Jack Schaefer | 1.50 | 3.00 | 4.50 | W |
| L4 | The Umbrella Garden–Maria Yen | 1.00 | 2.00 | 3.00 | NF |
| L5 | As the Earth Turns–Gladys Hasty Carroll | 1.00 | 2.00 | 3.00 | |
| L6 | Made in America–John Kouwenhoven | 1.00 | 2.00 | 3.00 | NF |
| L7 | Horse and Buggy Doctor–Arthur E. Hertzler | 1.00 | 2.00 | 3.00 | NF |
| L8 | Washington Irving Selections | 1.00 | 2.00 | 3.00 | |
| L9 | Fifth Chinese Daughter–Jade Snow Wong | 1.50 | 3.00 | 4.50 | |
| L10 | Six Stories by Edgar Allen Poe | 1.50 | 3.00 | 4.50 | |

# BALLANTINE SPECIAL STUDENT EDITION

## Ballantine Books, Inc.

| No. | Title | V/Good | Fine | N/Mint | |
|---|---|---|---|---|---|
| S1 | The Great American Heritage–Bela Kornitzer | 1.00 | 2.00 | 3.00 | B |
| S2 | Executive Suite–Cameron Hawley | 1.00 | 2.00 | 3.00 | |
| S3 | The Far Command–Eleanor Chamberlain | 1.00 | 2.00 | 3.00 | A |
| S4 | The Red Gate–LaSelle Gilman | 1.00 | 2.00 | 3.00 | C |
| S5 | The Wright Brothers–Fred C. Kelly | 1.00 | 2.00 | 3.00 | B |
| S6 | Washington Irving–Anya Seton | 1.00 | 2.00 | 3.00 | B |
| S7 | Berlin: Pivot of German Destiny–ed. Charles B. Robson | 1.00 | 2.00 | 3.00 | NF |

BALLANTINE SPECIAL STUDENT EDITION, *continued*

| | | V/Good | Fine | N/Mint |
|---|---|---|---|---|
| S8 | The Dalai Lama–Lowell Thomas, Jr | 1.00 | 2.00 | 3.00 B |
| S9 | The Challenge of Coexistence–Milton Kovner | 1.00 | 2.00 | 3.00 NF |
| S10 | Arms Control: Issues for the Public–ed. Prof. Louis Henkin | 1.00 | 2.00 | 3.00 NF |
| S11 | To Turn the Tide–John F. Kennedy (ed. John W. Gardner) | 1.00 | 2.00 | 3.00 NF |
| S12 | Key to Economic Progress–G.D. Kousoulas | 1.00 | 2.00 | 3.00 NF |
| S13 | John H. Glenn: Astronaut–Lt. Col. Philip N. Pierce, USMC & Karl Schuon | 1.00 | 2.00 | 3.00 B |
| S14 | Cowboy Artist: The Life of Charles Marion Russell–Lola Shelton | 1.00 | 2.00 | 3.00 B |
| S15 | Century of Struggle: The Women's Rights Movement in the United States–Eleanor Flexner | 1.00 | 2.00 | 3.00 NF |
| S16 | The Spirit of Liberty: Papers and Addresses of Judge Learned Hand–ed. Irving Dilliard | 1.00 | 2.00 | 3.00 NF |

# BALLANTINE U-SERIES

## Ballantine Books, Inc.

| | | V/Good | Fine | N/Mint |
|---|---|---|---|---|
| U0001 | God Is My Co-Pilot–Robert L. Scott | .50 | 1.00 | 1.50 |
| U1001 | The Harsh Range–Chad Merriman | .75 | 1.50 | 2.25 W |
| U1002 | The Avengers–Chad Merriman | .75 | 1.50 | 2.25 W |
| U1003 | Snakehead–Chad Merriman | .75 | 1.50 | 2.25 W |
| U1010 | Comanche Captives–Fred Grove | .75 | 1.50 | 2.25 W |
| U1020 | High Fury–Harry Whittington; 1964 | 1.25 | 2.50 | 3.75 W |
| U1021 | Hangrope Town–Harry Whittington; 1964 | 1.25 | 2.50 | 3.75 W |
| U1022 | Wild Lonesome–Harry Whittington | 1.25 | 2.50 | 3.75 W |
| U1026 | Shotgun Marshall–Wade Everett; 1964 | 1.00 | 2.00 | 3.00 W |
| U1027 | Fort Starke–Wade Everett | 1.00 | 2.00 | 3.00 W |
| U1028 | Texas Ranger–Wade Everett | 1.00 | 2.00 | 3.00 W |
| U1029 | Tophand–Wade Everett; 1964 | 1.00 | 2.00 | 3.00 W |
| U1030 | Cavalry Recruit–Wade Everett | 1.00 | 2.00 | 3.00 W |
| U1031 | High Iron–E.E. Halleran; 1965 | .75 | 1.50 | 2.25 W |
| U1032 | Bullets for the Doctor–Wade Everett; 1965 | 1.00 | 2.00 | 3.00 W |
| U1035 | Indian Fighter–E.E. Halleran | 1.00 | 2.00 | 3.00 W |
| U1040 | Law Man–Lee Leighton | .75 | 1.50 | 2.25 W |
| U1041 | Fight for the Valley–Lee Leighton | .75 | 1.50 | 2.25 W |
| U1045 | The Hanging Tree–Dorothy Johnson | .75 | 1.50 | 2.25 W |
| U1046 | Ambush at Three Rivers–Robert Steelman | 1.25 | 2.50 | 3.75 W |
| U1047 | Forced March to Loon Creek–William Chamberlain | .75 | 1.50 | 2.25 W |
| U1048 | Trumpets of Company K–William Chamberlain | .75 | 1.50 | 2.25 W |
| U1049 | Winter of the Sioux–Robert Steelman | 1.25 | 2.50 | 3.75 W |
| U1050 | Destination Doubtful–William O. Turner | 1.00 | 2.00 | 3.00 W |
| U1051 | Massacre at Goliad–Elmer Kelton; 1965 | 1.25 | 2.50 | 3.75 W |
| U1052 | Apache Wells–Robert Steelman | 1.25 | 2.50 | 3.75 W |
| U1053 | The Trespassers–Giles Lutz | .75 | 1.50 | 2.25 W |
| U1054 | Ordeal at Blood River–James Warner Bellah; 1965 | .75 | 1.50 | 2.25 W |
| U2001 | Tarzan of the Apes–Edgar Rice Burroughs. Note: Third printing is TV tie-in | 1.50 | 3.00 | 4.50 A |
| U2002 | The Return of Tarzan–Edgar Rice Burroughs. Note: Third printing is TV tie-in | 1.50 | 3.00 | 4.50 A |
| U2003 | The Beasts of Tarzan–Edgar Rice Burroughs | 1.50 | 3.00 | 4.50 A |
| U2004 | The Son of Tarzan–Edgar Rice Burroughs | 1.50 | 3.00 | 4.50 A |
| U2005 | Tarzan and the Jewels of Opar–Edgar Rice Burroughs | 1.50 | 3.00 | 4.50 A |
| U2006 | Jungle Tales of Tarzan–Edgar Rice Burroughs | 1.50 | 3.00 | 4.50 A |
| U2007 | Tarzan the Untamed–Edgar Rice Burroughs | 1.50 | 3.00 | 4.50 A |
| U2008 | Tarzan the Terrible–Edgar Rice Burroughs | 1.50 | 3.00 | 4.50 A |

| | | V/Good | Fine | N/Mint |
|---|---|---|---|---|
| U2009 | Tarzan and the Golden Lion–Edgar Rice Burroughs | 1.50 | 3.00 | 4.50 A |
| U2010 | Tarzan and the Ant-Man–Edgar Rice Burroughs | 1.50 | 3.00 | 4.50 A |
| U2011 | Tarzan, Lord of the Jungle–Edgar Rice Burroughs | 1.50 | 3.00 | 4.50 A |
| U2012 | Tarzan and the Lost Empire–Edgar Rice Burroughs. Note: Although announced, this number apparently does not exist. | | | A |
| U2013 | Tarzan at the Earth's Core–Edgar Rice Burroughs; 1964, c-Powers | 2.00 | 4.00 | 6.00 A |
| U2014 | Tarzan the Invincible–Edgar Rice Burroughs; c-Powers | 2.00 | 4.00 | 6.00 A |
| U2015 | Tarzan Triumphant–Edgar Rice Burroughs; c-Powers | 2.00 | 4.00 | 6.00 A |
| U2016 | Tarzan and the City of Gold–Edgar Rice Burroughs; c-Powers | 2.00 | 4.00 | 6.00 A |
| U2017 | Tarzan and the Lion Man–Edgar Rice Burroughs; c-Powers | 2.00 | 4.00 | 6.00 A |
| U2018 | Tarzan and the Leopard Men–Edgar Rice Burroughs; c-Powers | 2.00 | 4.00 | 6.00 A |
| U2019 | Tarzan's Quest–Edgar Rice Burroughs; c-Powers | 2.00 | 4.00 | 6.00 A |
| U2020 | Tarzan and the Forbidden City–Edgar Rice Burroughs; c-Powers | 2.00 | 4.00 | 6.00 A |
| U2021 | Tarzan the Magnificent–Edgar Rice Burroughs; c-Powers | 2.00 | 4.00 | 6.00 A |
| U2022 | Tarzan and the "Foreign Legion"–Edgar Rice Burroughs; c-Powers | 2.00 | 4.00 | 6.00 A |
| U2023 | Tarzan and the Madman–Edgar Rice Burroughs; 1965, c-Abbett | 2.00 | 4.00 | 6.00 A |
| U2024 | Tarzan and the Castaways–Edgar Rice Burroughs; c-Abbett | 2.00 | 4.00 | 6.00 A |
| U2031 | A Princess of Mars–Edgar Rice Burroughs | 1.50 | 3.00 | 4.50 SF |
| U2032 | The Gods of Mars–Edgar Rice Burroughs | 1.50 | 3.00 | 4.50 SF |
| U2033 | The Warlord of Mars–Edgar Rice Burroughs | 1.50 | 3.00 | 4.50 SF |
| U2034 | Thuvia, Maid of Mars–Edgar Rice Burroughs | 1.50 | 3.00 | 4.50 SF |
| U2036 | The Mastermind of Mars–Edgar Rice Burroughs | 1.50 | 3.00 | 4.50 SF |
| U2037 | A Fighting Man of Mars–Edgar Rice Burroughs | 1.50 | 3.00 | 4.50 SF |
| U2038 | Swords of Mars–Edgar Rice Burroughs | 1.50 | 3.00 | 4.50 SF |
| U2039 | Synthetic Men of Mars–Edgar Rice Burroughs | 1.50 | 3.00 | 4.50 SF |
| U2040 | Llana of Gathol–Edgar Rice Burroughs | 1.50 | 3.00 | 4.50 SF |
| U2041 | John Carter of Mars–Edgar Rice Burroughs; c-Abbett | 2.00 | 4.00 | 6.00 SF |
| U2045 | The War Chief–Edgar Rice Burroughs | 2.50 | 5.00 | 7.50 W |
| U2046 | Apache Devil–Edgar Rice Burroughs | 3.50 | 7.00 | 10.50 W |
| U2048 | The Lad and the Lion–Edgar Rice Burroughs; c-Abbett | 2.00 | 4.00 | 6.00 A |
| U2101 | Mad Reader–ed. Mad Magazine; comic book reprints | .75 | 1.50 | 2.25 H |
| U2102 | Mad Strikes Back–ed. Mad Magazine; comic book reprints | .75 | 1.50 | 2.25 H |
| U2103 | Inside Mad–ed. Mad Magazine; comic book reprints | .75 | 1.50 | 2.25 H |
| U2104 | Utterly Mad–ed. Mad Magazine; comic book reprints | .75 | 1.50 | 2.25 H |
| U2105 | Brothers Mad–ed. Mad Magazine; comic book reprints | .75 | 1.50 | 2.25 H |
| U2106 | Tales from the Crypt; c-Frazetta. Note: Contains EC comic reprints | 6.00 | 12.00 | 18.00 HO |
| U2107 | The Vault of Horror; 1965, c-Frazetta. Note: Contains EC comic reprints | 5.00 | 10.00 | 15.00 HO |
| U2110 | Reach for Tomorrow–Arthur C. Clarke | .75 | 1.50 | 2.25 SF |
| U2111 | Childhood's End–Arthur C. Clarke | .75 | 1.50 | 2.25 SF |
| U2112 | Expedition to Earth–Arthur C. Clarke | .75 | 1.50 | 2.25 SF |
| U2113 | Tales from the White Hart–Arthur C. Clarke | .75 | 1.50 | 2.25 SF |
| U2120 | The Tattooed Heart–Theodora Keogh | 1.00 | 2.00 | 3.00 |
| U2121 | The Fascinator–Theodora Keogh | 1.00 | 2.00 | 3.00 |
| U2123 | The Gallant–Charity Blackstock | .75 | 1.50 | 2.25 M |
| U2124 | A House Possessed–Charity Blackstock | .75 | 1.50 | 2.25 M |
| U2125 | Dewey Death–Charity Blackstock | .75 | 1.50 | 2.25 M |
| U2126 | Foggy, Foggy Dew–Charity Blackstock | .75 | 1.50 | 2.25 M |

## BALLANTINE U-SERIES, continued

| | V/Good | Fine | N/Mint | |
|---|---|---|---|---|
| U2127 | The Shadow of Murder–Charity Blackstock | .75 | 1.50 | 2.25 M |
| U2128 | The Woman in the Woods–Charity Blackstock | .75 | 1.50 | 2.25 M |
| U2129 | Mr. Christopoulos–Charity Blackstock | .75 | 1.50 | 2.25 M |
| U2130 | Death in Amsterdam–Nicolas Freeling | .75 | 1.50 | 2.25 M |
| U2131 | Because of the Cats–Nicolas Freeling | .75 | 1.50 | 2.25 M |
| U2132 | Question of Loyalty–Nicolas Freeling | .75 | 1.50 | 2.25 M |
| U2133 | Double Barrel–Nicolas Freeling | .75 | 1.50 | 2.25 M |
| U2136 | The Complete Book of Birth Control– Winifred Best, Frederick S. Jaffe, Alan F. Guttmacher | .50 | 1.00 | 1.50 |
| U2137 | Stuka Pilot–Hans Ulrich Rudel | .50 | 1.00 | 1.50 NF |
| U2138 | Fahrenheit 451–Ray Bradbury | .50 | 1.00 | 1.50 SF |
| U2139 | October Country–Ray Bradbury | .75 | 1.50 | 2.25 SF |
| U2140 | Tales of the Incredible; c-Frazetta. Note: Contains EC comic reprints | 5.00 | 10.00 | 15.00 SF |
| U2141 | The Autumn People–Ray Bradbury; c-Frazetta. Note: Contains EC comic adaptation reprints | 5.00 | 10.00 | 15.00 SF |
| U2142 | Tomorrow Midnight–Ray Bradbury; 1966; c-Frazetta. Note: Contains EC comic adaptation reprints | 5.00 | 10.00 | 15.00 SF |
| U2144 | Jordi/Lisa and David–Theodore Isaac Rubin | .50 | 1.00 | 1.50 |
| U2150 | False Witness–Helen Nielsen; 1966 | .75 | 1.50 | 2.25 M |
| U2154 | The Upfold Witch–Josephine Bell | .75 | 1.50 | 2.25 M |
| U2155 | Double Doom–Josephine Bell | .75 | 1.50 | 2.25 M |
| U2156 | Easy Prey–Josephine Bell | .75 | 1.50 | 2.25 M |
| U2157 | Room for a Body–Josephine Bell | .75 | 1.50 | 2.25 M |
| U2158 | Death at the Medical Board–Josephine Bell | .75 | 1.50 | 2.25 M |
| U2159 | Murder on the Merry-Go-Round– Josephine Bell | .75 | 1.50 | 2.25 M |
| U2165 | The Call Girl–Harold Greenwald | .50 | 1.00 | 1.50 NF |
| U2166 | Great Cases in Psychoanalysis–Harold Greenwald | .50 | 1.00 | 1.50 NF |
| U2169 | The Blue World–Jack Vance | 2.00 | 4.00 | 6.00 SF |
| U2170 | Heat Wave–Caesar Smith | .75 | 1.50 | 2.25 M |
| U2171 | Star of Stars–ed. Frederik Pohl | 1.25 | 2.50 | 3.75 SF |
| U2172 | The Reefs of Space–Jack Williamson & Frederik Pohl | 1.25 | 2.50 | 3.75 SF |
| U2173 | The Space Merchants–Frederik Pohl & C.M. Kornbluth | .50 | 1.00 | 1.50 SF |
| U2174 | A Plague of Pythons–Frederik Pohl | 1.25 | 2.50 | 3.75 SF |
| U2175 | The Case Against Tomorrow–Frederik Pohl | .50 | 1.00 | 1.50 SF |
| U2176 | Starchild–Frederik Pohl & Jack Williamson | 1.50 | 3.00 | 4.50 SF |
| U2177 | Slave Ship–Frederik Pohl | .50 | 1.00 | 1.50 SF |
| U2178 | Digits and Dastards–Frederik Pohl | 1.25 | 2.50 | 3.75 SF |
| U2190 | The Human Angle–William Tenn | .75 | 1.50 | 2.25 SF |
| U2191 | Martian Time-Slip–Philip K. Dick; 1st ed. 1964 | 2.50 | 5.00 | 7.50 SF |
| U2192 | Inside Outside–Philip José Farmer; 1st ed. 1964 | 2.00 | 4.00 | 6.00 SF |
| U2193 | Dare–Philip José Farmer; 1st ed. 1965 | 3.50 | 7.00 | 10.50 SF |
| U2200 | Harry Hershfield Joke Book–Harry Hershfield | 1.00 | 2.00 | 3.00 H |
| U2202 | The Sea Wolves–Wolfgang Frank | .75 | 1.50 | 2.25 C |
| U2203 | Space by the Tale–Jerome Bixby | 1.00 | 2.00 | 3.00 SF |
| U2204 | Folksong Jamboree–Mirandat Marais | .50 | 1.00 | 1.50 NF |
| U2205 | The Chemical Elements–Helen Miles Davis | .75 | 1.50 | 2.25 NF |
| U2206 | Science Projects Handbook–ed. Science Service Assoc. | .50 | 1.00 | 1.50 NF |
| U2207 | U-Boat 977–Heinz Schaeffer | .75 | 1.50 | 2.25 NF |
| U2208 | Stride toward Freedom–Martin Luther King, Jr | .75 | 1.50 | 2.25 NF |
| U2210 | Defeat at Sea–C.D. Bekker | .75 | 1.50 | 2.25 C |
| U2212 | The View from the Stars–Walter M. Miller, Jr | 1.00 | 2.00 | 3.00 SF |
| U2213 | A World of Difference–Robert Conquest | 1.00 | 2.00 | 3.00 SF |
| U2214 | Future Tense–Jack Vance | 1.50 | 3.00 | 4.50 SF |
| U2215 | Close to Critical–Hal Clement | 1.00 | 2.00 | 3.00 SF |
| U2216 | A Pail of Air–Fritz Leiber | 1.50 | 3.00 | 4.50 SF |
| U2217 | Flush as May–P.M. Hubbard | .75 | 1.50 | 2.25 M |
| U2218 | Parkinson's Law–C. Northcote Parkinson | .50 | 1.00 | 1.50 H |

| | V/Good | Fine | N/Mint | |
|---|---|---|---|---|
| U2219 | The Whole Man–John Brunner | 1.00 | 2.00 | 3.00 SF |
| U2220 | No Limits–ed. J.W. Ferman | .75 | 1.50 | 2.25 SF |
| U2222 | Who Fears the Devil?–Manly Wade Wellman | 1.00 | 2.00 | 3.00 SF |
| U2223 | Squadron Airborne–Elleston Trevor | .75 | 1.50 | 2.25 NF |
| U2224 | Deadly Litter–James White | 1.75 | 3.50 | 5.25 SF |
| U2225 | Memoirs of a Sword Swallower–Daniel P. Mannix | 1.00 | 2.00 | 3.00 NF |
| U2226 | A Medal from Pamplona–Cameron Rougvie | .50 | 1.00 | 1.50 |
| U2227 | The Hunter and the Horns–W.H. Canaway | .75 | 1.50 | 2.25 |
| U2229 | Alice–E.V. Cunningham | .75 | 1.50 | 2.25 |
| U2230 | Traps–Friedrich Duerrenmatt | .50 | 1.00 | 1.50 |
| U2231 | More Than Human–Theodore Sturgeon | .75 | 1.50 | 2.25 SF |
| U2232 | The First Men in the Moon–H.G. Wells; movie tie-in | 1.00 | 2.00 | 3.00 SF |
| U2233 | The Loafers of Refuge–Joseph L. Green | 1.50 | 3.00 | 4.50 SF |
| U2234 | A Boy Ten Feet Tall–W.H. Canaway; movie tie-in | 1.50 | 3.00 | 4.50 A |
| U2235 | Natives of Space–Hal Clement | 1.00 | 2.00 | 3.00 SF |
| U2236 | Mortals and Monsters–Lester Del Rey | 1.25 | 2.50 | 3.75 SF |
| U2237 | Outlaw Mountain–Ray Hogan | .75 | 1.50 | 2.25 W |
| U2239 | Blue Mascara Tears–James McKimmey | .75 | 1.50 | 2.25 |
| U2240 | Down among the Dead Men–Patricia Moyes | .75 | 1.50 | 2.25 M |
| U2241 | Death on the Agenda–Patricia Moyes | .75 | 1.50 | 2.25 M |
| U2242 | Dead Men Don't Ski–Patricia Moyes | .75 | 1.50 | 2.25 M |
| U2243 | Murder A La Mode–Patricia Moyes | .75 | 1.50 | 2.25 M |
| U2244 | Falling Star–Patricia Moyes | .75 | 1.50 | 2.25 M |
| U2247 | E Pluribus Unicorn–Theodore Sturgeon | .75 | 1.50 | 2.25 SF |
| U2248 | After the Rain–John Bower | .75 | 1.50 | 2.25 |
| U2249 | World of Li'l Abner–Al Capp | .75 | 1.50 | 2.25 H |
| U2250 | Tangier Assignment–Cameron Rougvie | .75 | 1.50 | 2.25 |
| U2251 | A Case of Conscience–James Blish | .75 | 1.50 | 2.25 SF |
| U2252 | Five Days to Salt Lake–William O. Turner | 1.00 | 2.00 | 3.00 W |
| U2253 | Some of Your Blood–Theodore Sturgeon | 1.00 | 2.00 | 3.00 |
| U2254 | The Night of the Wolf–Fritz Leiber; 1966 | 1.50 | 3.00 | 4.50 HO |
| U2256 | Red River Country–E.E. Halleran; 1966 | 1.00 | 2.00 | 3.00 W |
| U2257 | Shadow of the Big Horn–E.E. Halleran | .75 | 1.50 | 2.25 W |
| U2260 | Vengeance–Wade Everett | 1.00 | 2.00 | 3.00 W |
| U2262 | Texas Yankee–Wade Everett | 1.00 | 2.00 | 3.00 W |
| U2263 | The Warrior–Wade Everett | 1.00 | 2.00 | 3.00 W |
| U2264 | Killer–Wade Everett | 1.00 | 2.00 | 3.00 W |
| U2265 | The Whiskey Traders–Wade Everett | 1.00 | 2.00 | 3.00 W |
| U2271 | Dracula–Bram Stoker, adapted by Otto Binder and Craig Tennis. Note: Comic book style; art by Al McWilliams | 3.00 | 6.00 | 9.00 HO |
| U2281 | From Doon with Death–Ruth Rendell | .75 | 1.50 | 2.25 M |
| U2285 | The Watch Below–James White | 1.50 | 3.00 | 4.50 SF |
| U2296 | A Gun for Braggs' Woman–Steve Frazee; 1966 | 1.25 | 2.50 | 3.75 W |
| U2301 | Big Ugly–Lee Leighton | .75 | 1.50 | 2.25 W |
| U2302 | Hanging at Pulpit Rock–Lee Leighton | .75 | 1.50 | 2.25 W |
| U2306 | Llano River–Elmer Kelton | 1.25 | 2.50 | 3.75 W |
| U2307 | After the Bugles–Elmer Kelton | 1.25 | 2.50 | 3.75 W |
| U2314 | Mighty Big River–Chad Merriman | .75 | 1.50 | 2.25 W |
| U2321 | Bugle and Spur–Frank O'Brian | .75 | 1.50 | 2.25 W |
| U2327 | I Had to Kill Her–Edwin Connell | .75 | 1.50 | 2.25 |
| U2328 | World of Ptavvs–Larry Niven; 1966 | 2.00 | 4.00 | 6.00 SF |
| U2329 | The Long Result–John Brunner | 1.00 | 2.00 | 3.00 SF |
| U2330 | Needle in a Timestack–Robert Silverberg | 1.25 | 2.50 | 3.75 SF |
| U2331 | New Dreams This Morning–ed. James Blish | 1.25 | 2.50 | 3.75 SF |
| U2332 | Man Hunt–Hunter Ingram; 1967 | 1.00 | 2.00 | 3.00 |
| U2333 | Bred to Kill–Lee Hoffman; 1967 | .75 | 1.50 | 2.25 W |
| U2334 | The Man from Granite–Philip Ketchum | 1.00 | 2.00 | 3.00 W |
| U2335 | Wyoming–Philip Ketchum; 1967 | 1.00 | 2.00 | 3.00 W |
| U2341 | Ahead of Time–Henry Kuttner | .75 | 1.50 | 2.25 SF |
| U2342 | Brain Wave–Poul Anderson | .50 | 1.00 | 1.50 SF |
| U2343 | Gladiator-at-Law–Frederik Pohl & C.M. Kornbluth | .50 | 1.00 | 1.50 SF |
| U2344 | Nerves–Lester del Rey | .50 | 1.00 | 1.50 SF |
| U2345 | The Green Odyssey–Philip José Farmer | .75 | 1.50 | 2.25 SF |
| U2346 | To Live Forever–Jack Vance; 1966 | .75 | 1.50 | 2.25 SF |

| | | V/Good | Fine | N/Mint | |
|---|---|---|---|---|---|

**BALLANTINE U-SERIES,** *continued*

| | | V/Good | Fine | N/Mint | |
|---|---|---|---|---|---|
| U2350 | Contested Valley–Hunter Ingram; 1968 | 1.00 | 2.00 | 3.00 | |
| U6039 | The Mucker–Edgar Rice Burroughs;<br>c-Abbett | 2.50 | 5.00 | 7.50 | A |
| U6035 | Treasure of the Black Falcon–John<br>Coleman Burroughs; orig. 1967 | 2.00 | 4.00 | 6.00 | SF |
| U6125 | Tarzan and the Valley of Gold–Fritz<br>Lieber; orig. 1966; movie tie-in;<br>c-Abbett | 3.00 | 6.00 | 9.00 | A |

## BANNER BOOKS
### The Hearst Corporation

| | | V/Good | Fine | N/Mint | |
|---|---|---|---|---|---|
| B40-101 | Gun Down in Quintana–Dean Owen;<br>1967 | .75 | 1.50 | 2.25 | W |
| B40-102 | Ride West to Pueblo–Kingsley West | .75 | 1.50 | 2.25 | W |
| B40-103 | Apache Lance–Kingsley West | .75 | 1.50 | 2.25 | W |
| B40-104 | The Iron Noose–Michael Bonner; 1967 | .75 | 1.50 | 2.25 | W |
| B40-105 | Superstition Range–Todhunter Ballard | .75 | 1.50 | 2.25 | W |
| B40-106 | Guns of Spring–Dean Owen | .75 | 1.50 | 2.25 | W |
| B40-107 | Outlaw Frenzy–J.L. Bouma | .75 | 1.50 | 2.25 | W |
| B50-101 | Way Out–Louis Charbonneau; 1967 | .75 | 1.50 | 2.25 | |
| B50-102 | The Tease–Gil Brewer | 1.50 | 3.00 | 4.50 | M |
| B50-103 | Get Dumm!–Jordan Brewer | .75 | 1.50 | 2.25 | H |
| B50-104 | Way to Go, Doll Baby!–William R. Cox | 1.00 | 2.00 | 3.00 | |
| B50-105 | The Girl on Crown Street–David Karp;<br>aka Cry Flesh | .75 | 1.50 | 2.25 | R |
| B50-106 | The House of Happy Mayhem–Walt<br>Sheldon | .75 | 1.50 | 2.25 | |
| B50-107 | Platoon–David Karp; 1967 | .75 | 1.50 | 2.25 | C |
| B50-108 | Sin for Me–Gil Brewer | 1.50 | 3.00 | 4.50 | E |
| B50-109 | Stay with Me, Love–Arlene Hale | .75 | 1.50 | 2.25 | R |
| B50-110 | The Big Feeling–David Karp | .75 | 1.50 | 2.25 | M |
| B50-111 | Hardman–David Karp | .75 | 1.50 | 2.25 | M |
| B50-112 | Six Graves to Munich–Mario Cleri | .75 | 1.50 | 2.25 | |
| B50-113 | The Brotherhood of Velvet–David Karp | .75 | 1.50 | 2.25 | |
| B50-114 | Province of Darkness–Patricia Morton | .75 | 1.50 | 2.25 | |
| B50-115 | Plunder Canyon–Parker Bonner; 1967 | .75 | 1.50 | 2.25 | W |
| B50-116 | Incident at Butler's Station–Richard<br>Wyler | .75 | 1.50 | 2.25 | W |
| B50-118 | The Savage Journey–Richard Wyler | .75 | 1.50 | 2.25 | W |
| B50-120 | The Men of Moncada–Philip Ketchum | .75 | 1.50 | 2.25 | W |
| B50-121 | Bend of the River–Arlene Hale | .75 | 1.50 | 2.25 | R |
| B60-101 | The Old Trade of Killing–John Harris;<br>1967 | .75 | 1.50 | 2.25 | M |
| B60-102 | A Dragon for Christmas–Gavin Black | .75 | 1.50 | 2.25 | M |
| B60-103 | Kalihari Kill–Samuel Dembo | .75 | 1.50 | 2.25 | M |
| B60-104 | Day of the Shark–Sam Ross | .75 | 1.50 | 2.25 | A |
| B60-105 | The President Is Missing–Henry A.<br>Milton | .75 | 1.50 | 2.25 | |
| B60-106 | Doomsday Mission–Harry Whittington | 1.50 | 3.00 | 4.50 | C |
| B60-107 | Sex Is a Private Affair–Kay Jarrett | .75 | 1.50 | 2.25 | NF |
| B60-108 | The Devious Defector–W.J. Saber; 1st<br>ed. 1967 | .75 | 1.50 | 2.25 | |
| B60-109 | Bella on the Roof–Hilary Ford | .75 | 1.50 | 2.25 | R |
| B60-111 | Somebody's Done For–David Goodis;<br>orig. 1967 | 6.00 | 12.00 | 18.00 | M |
| B60-112 | Face in the Pond–Clarissa Ross | .75 | 1.50 | 2.25 | |
| B75-101 | The Chicago Nurse Murders–George<br>Carpozi; 1967 | .75 | 1.50 | 2.25 | NF |

## BANNER MYSTERIES
### Fact and Fiction Publications
**Digest Size**

| | | V/Good | Fine | N/Mint | |
|---|---|---|---|---|---|
| 1 | The Sunday Pigeon Murders–Craig<br>Rice; 1945; c-Raboy | 7.50 | 15.00 | 22.50 | M |
| 2 | Death Goes to School–Q. Patrick;<br>1945; c-Raboy | 10.00 | 20.00 | 30.00 | M |

## BANTAM A-SERIES
### Bantam Books, Inc.
**(See Bantam Books for other A volumes)**

| | | V/Good | Fine | N/Mint | |
|---|---|---|---|---|---|
| A1 | Men and Volts at War–John A. Miller;<br>1948 | .75 | 1.50 | 2.25 | NF |

Banner Book B60-111, Banner Mystery 2, Bantam 2.

| | | V/Good | Fine | N/Mint | |
|---|---|---|---|---|---|
| A2 | Model Railroading; 1950 | .75 | 1.50 | 2.25 | NF |
| A3 | Main Street Merchant–Norman<br>Beasley; 1950 | .75 | 1.50 | 2.25 | B |
| A4 | How to Use Premiums in Your<br>Business to Increase Your Sales and<br>Profits; 1950 | 3.00 | 6.00 | 9.00 | NF |
| A5 | The Power of People–Charles P.<br>McCormick; 1952 | .75 | 1.50 | 2.25 | NF |

## BANTAM BIOGRAPHIES
### Bantam Books, Inc.

| | | V/Good | Fine | N/Mint | |
|---|---|---|---|---|---|
| FB400 | Cleopatra–Emil Ludwig; 1956 | .75 | 1.50 | 2.25 | B |
| FB401 | Henry the Eighth–Francis Hackett | .75 | 1.50 | 2.25 | B |
| FB402 | The Great Pierpont Morgan–Frederick<br>Lewis Allen | .75 | 1.50 | 2.25 | B |
| FB403 | Venetian Adventurer: Marco Polo–<br>Henry Hart | 1.00 | 2.00 | 3.00 | B |
| FB404 | Autobiography of Benvenuto Cellini | .75 | 1.50 | 2.25 | B |
| FB405 | The Last Billionaire, Henry Ford–<br>William C. Richards | .75 | 1.50 | 2.25 | B |
| FB406 | Up from Slavery–Booker T.<br>Washington | .75 | 1.50 | 2.25 | B |
| FB407 | The Borgias–J. Lucas-Dubreton | 1.00 | 2.00 | 3.00 | B |
| FB408 | Andrew Jackson–Gerald Johnson | .75 | 1.50 | 2.25 | B |
| FB409 | Madame de Pompadour–Nancy<br>Mitford; 1957 | .75 | 1.50 | 2.25 | B |
| FB410 | The Memoirs of Catherine the Great;<br>1957 | .75 | 1.50 | 2.25 | B |
| FB411 | Yankee from Olympus–Catherine<br>Drinker Bowen | .75 | 1.50 | 2.25 | B |
| FB412 | Genghis Khan–Harold Lamb | 1.00 | 2.00 | 3.00 | B |
| FB413 | The Life and Time of Rembrandt–<br>Hendrik Willem Van Loon | 1.00 | 2.00 | 3.00 | B |
| FB414 | Five and Ten–John K. Winkler | .75 | 1.50 | 2.25 | B |
| FB415 | The Memoirs of Casanova–Giacomo<br>Casanova; 1958 | 1.00 | 2.00 | 3.00 | B |
| FB416 | Charlemagne–Harold Lamb; 1958 | 1.00 | 2.00 | 3.00 | B |
| FB417 | Ashurbanipal–Washington Young | 1.00 | 2.00 | 3.00 | B |
| FB418 | Clarence Darrow for the Defense–<br>Irving Stone | .75 | 1.50 | 2.25 | B |

## BANTAM BOOKS
### Bantam Books, Inc.

| | | V/Good | Fine | N/Mint | |
|---|---|---|---|---|---|
| 1 | Life on the Mississippi–Mark Twain;<br>1945 | 2.50 | 5.00 | 7.50 | |
| 2 | The Gift Horse–Frank Gruber | 2.00 | 4.00 | 6.00 | M |
| 3 | Nevada–Zane Grey | 1.50 | 3.00 | 4.50 | W |
| 4 | Evidence of Things Seen–Elizabeth<br>Daly | 1.50 | 3.00 | 4.50 | M |
| 5 | Scaramouche–Rafael Sabatini | 1.50 | 3.00 | 4.50 | A |
| 6 | A Murder by Marriage–Robert George<br>Dean | 1.50 | 3.00 | 4.50 | M |
| 7 | The Grapes of Wrath–John Steinbeck<br>With dust jacket | 3.50<br>35.00 | 7.00<br>70.00 | 10.50<br>105.00 | |
| 8 | The Great Gatsby–F. Scott Fitzgerald<br>With dust jacket | 2.50<br>35.00 | 5.00<br>70.00 | 7.50<br>105.00 | |
| 9 | Rogue Male–Geoffrey Household<br>With dust jacket | 1.50<br>30.00 | 3.00<br>60.00 | 4.50<br>90.00 | A |

|  |  | V/Good | Fine | N/Mint |  |
|---|---|---|---|---|---|

BANTAM BOOKS, *continued*

| No. | Title | V/Good | Fine | N/Mint | |
|---|---|---|---|---|---|
| 10 | South Moon Under–Marjorie Kinnan Rawlings | 1.50 | 3.00 | 4.50 | E |
| 11 | Mr. and Mrs. Cugat–Isabel Scott Rorick | 1.50 | 3.00 | 4.50 | B |
| 12 | Then There Were Three–Geoffrey Homes | 1.50 | 3.00 | 4.50 | |
| 13 | The Last Time I Saw Paris–Elliot Paul | 2.00 | 4.00 | 6.00 | |
| 14 | Wind, Sand, and Stars–Antoine de Saint-Exupery | 1.50 | 3.00 | 4.50 | A |
| 15 | Meet Me in St. Louis–Sally Benson | 1.50 | 3.00 | 4.50 | H |
| 16 | The Town Cried Murder–Leslie Ford | 1.50 | 3.00 | 4.50 | M |
| 17 | Seventeen–Booth Tarkington | 1.50 | 3.00 | 4.50 | H |
| 18 | What Makes Sammy Run?–Budd Schulberg | 1.50 | 3.00 | 4.50 | |
| 19 | One More Spring–Robert Nathan | 1.50 | 3.00 | 4.50 | |
| | With dust jacket | 25.00 | 50.00 | 75.00 | |
| 20 | Oil for the Lamps of China–Alice Tisdale Hobart | 1.50 | 3.00 | 4.50 | |
| 21 | Men, Women, and Dogs–James Thurber; 1946 | 2.00 | 4.00 | 6.00 | H |
| 22 | Babbitt–Sinclair Lewis | 2.50 | 5.00 | 7.50 | |
| | With dust jacket | 22.50 | 45.00 | 67.50 | |
| 23 | The Fog Comes–Mary Collins | 1.50 | 3.00 | 4.50 | M |
| 24 | Valiant Is the Word for Carrie–Barry Benefield | 1.50 | 3.00 | 4.50 | |
| | With dust jacket | 20.00 | 40.00 | 60.00 | |
| 25 | Bugles in the Afternoon–Ernest Haycox; 1946 | 2.00 | 4.00 | 6.00 | W |
| 26 | Net of Cobwebs–Elisabeth Sanxay Holding | 1.50 | 3.00 | 4.50 | M |
| | With dust jacket | 25.00 | 50.00 | 75.00 | |
| 27 | Only Yesterday–Frederick Lewis Allan | 1.00 | 2.00 | 3.00 | |
| 28 | Night in Bombay–Louis Bromfield | 1.50 | 3.00 | 4.50 | |
| 29 | Was It Murder?–James Hilton | 1.50 | 3.00 | 4.50 | M |
| 30 | Citizen Tom Paine–Howard Fast | 1.50 | 3.00 | 4.50 | B |
| 31 | The Three Hostages–John Buchan | 1.50 | 3.00 | 4.50 | A |
| 32 | The Great Mouthpiece–Gene Fowler | 1.50 | 3.00 | 4.50 | B |
| 33 | The Prisoner of Zenda–Anthony Hope | 1.50 | 3.00 | 4.50 | A |
| 34 | First Come, First Kill–Francis Allen | 1.50 | 3.00 | 4.50 | M |
| 35 | My Dear Bella–Arthur Kober | 1.50 | 3.00 | 4.50 | H |
| 36 | Trail Boss–Peter Dawson (Frank Gruber) | 2.00 | 4.00 | 6.00 | W |
| 37 | Drawn and Quartered–Charles Addams | 4.50 | 9.00 | 13.50 | H |
| 38 | Anything for a Quiet Life–A.A. Avery | 1.00 | 2.00 | 3.00 | M |
| 39 | Long, Long Ago–Alexander Woollcott | 1.00 | 2.00 | 3.00 | |
| 40 | Captain from Connecticut–C.S. Forester | 1.50 | 3.00 | 4.50 | A |
| 41 | David Harum–Edward Noyes Westcott | 1.50 | 3.00 | 4.50 | |
| 42 | Road to Folly–Leslie Ford | 1.00 | 2.00 | 3.00 | M |
| 43 | The Lives of a Bengal Lancer–Francis Yeats-Brown | 1.50 | 3.00 | 4.50 | A |
| 44 | The Cold Journey–Grace Zaring Stone | 1.50 | 3.00 | 4.50 | |
| | With dust jacket | 30.00 | 60.00 | 90.00 | |
| 45 | A Bell for Adano–John Hersey | 1.00 | 2.00 | 3.00 | |
| 46 | Escape the Night–Mignon G. Eberhart | 1.00 | 2.00 | 3.00 | M |
| 47 | Home Ranch–Will James | 1.50 | 3.00 | 4.50 | NF |
| 48 | The Laughter of My Father–Carlos Bulosan | 1.50 | 3.00 | 4.50 | H |
| 49 | The Amethyst Spectacles–Frances Crane | 1.00 | 2.00 | 3.00 | M |
| 50 | The Buffalo Box–Frank Gruber | 2.00 | 4.00 | 6.00 | M |
| 51 | Death in the Blackout–Anthony Gilbert | 1.50 | 3.00 | 4.50 | M |
| 52 | No Hands on the Clock–Geoffrey Homes | 1.50 | 3.00 | 4.50 | M |
| 53 | Nothing Can Rescue Me–Elizabeth Daly | 1.50 | 3.00 | 4.50 | M |
| 54 | The Love Letters–Chris Massie | 1.00 | 2.00 | 3.00 | R |
| 55 | Tutt and Mr. Tutt–Arthur Train. Note: Queen's Quorum No. 66 | 2.50 | 5.00 | 7.50 | H |
| 56 | The Tonto Kid–Henry Herbert Knibbs | 1.50 | 3.00 | 4.50 | W |
| 57 | Anything for a Laugh–Bennett Cerf | 1.00 | 2.00 | 3.00 | H |
| 58 | ''Captains Courageous''–Rudyard Kipling | 2.50 | 5.00 | 7.50 | A |
| 59 | Wild Animals I Have Known– E. Thompson Seton | 1.50 | 3.00 | 4.50 | NF |
| 60 | The Kennel Murder Case–S.S. Van Dine | 1.50 | 3.00 | 4.50 | M |
| 61 | The Bantam Concise Dictionary | 1.00 | 2.00 | 3.00 | |
| 62 | Dead Center–Mary Collins | 1.00 | 2.00 | 3.00 | M |
| 63 | Green Mansions–W.H. Hudson | 2.00 | 4.00 | 6.00 | F |
| 64 | Harriet–Elizabeth Jenkins | 1.00 | 2.00 | 3.00 | |
| 65 | South Wind–Norman Douglas | 1.00 | 2.00 | 3.00 | A |
| 66 | She Loves Me Not–Edward Hope | 1.00 | 2.00 | 3.00 | H |
| 67 | The Bruiser–Jim Tully | 1.00 | 2.00 | 3.00 | S |
| | With dust jacket | 35.00 | 70.00 | 105.00 | |
| 68 | Guns from Powder Valley–Peter Field | 2.00 | 4.00 | 6.00 | W |
| 69 | The Grandmothers–Glenway Wescott | 1.00 | 2.00 | 3.00 | |
| 70 | Lay That Pistol Down–Richard Powell | 1.50 | 3.00 | 4.50 | M |
| 71 | Mountain Meadow–John Buchan | 1.50 | 3.00 | 4.50 | A |
| 72 | No Bones about It–Ruth Sawtell Wallis | 1.50 | 3.00 | 4.50 | |
| 73 | The Last of the Plainsman–Zane Grey | 2.00 | 4.00 | 6.00 | W |
| 74 | Halo in Blood–John Evans | 2.00 | 4.00 | 6.00 | M |
| 75 | Cannery Row–John Steinbeck; 1947 | 2.50 | 5.00 | 7.50 | |
| | With dust jacket | 35.00 | 70.00 | 105.00 | |
| 76 | Drink to Yesterday–Manning Coles | 1.25 | 2.50 | 3.75 | |
| 77 | Pistol Passport–Eugene Cunningham | 1.50 | 3.00 | 4.50 | W |
| 78 | Deadly Nightshade–Elizabeth Daly | 1.25 | 2.50 | 3.75 | M |
| 79 | A Tree Grows in Brooklyn–Betty Smith | 1.25 | 2.50 | 3.75 | |
| 80 | False to Any Man–Leslie Ford | 1.25 | 2.50 | 3.75 | M |
| 81 | Puzzles, Quizzes, and Games–Phyllis Fraser & Edith Young | 2.00 | 4.00 | 6.00 | NF |
| 82 | Ride the Man Down–Luke Short | 1.50 | 3.00 | 4.50 | W |
| 83 | Up Front–Bill Mauldin | 1.25 | 2.50 | 3.75 | H |
| 84 | The World, the Flesh and Father Smith–Bruce Marshall | 1.25 | 2.50 | 3.75 | |
| 85 | Death at the Door–Anthony Gilbert; aka He Came by Night | 1.25 | 2.50 | 3.75 | M |
| 86 | Border Roundup–Allan R. Bosworth | 1.50 | 3.00 | 4.50 | W |
| 87 | Apartment in Athens–Glenway Wescott | 1.50 | 3.00 | 4.50 | |
| 88 | Trigger Kid–Bennett Foster; aka The Maverick | 1.50 | 3.00 | 4.50 | W |
| 89 | Finders Keepers–Geoffrey Homes | 1.25 | 2.50 | 3.75 | M |
| 90 | The Uninvited–Dorothy Macardle | 1.50 | 3.00 | 4.50 | F |
| 91 | The 17th Letter–Dorothy Cameron Disney | 1.25 | 2.50 | 3.75 | M |
| 92 | My Life and Hard Times–James Thurber | 2.00 | 4.00 | 6.00 | H |
| 93 | Dagger of the Mind–Kenneth Fearing | 1.25 | 2.50 | 3.75 | M |
| 94 | The Crimson Horseshoe–Peter Dawson (Frank Gruber) | 2.00 | 4.00 | 6.00 | W |
| 95 | Assignment without Glory–Marcos Spinelli | 1.25 | 2.50 | 3.75 | M |
| 96 | The Scarab Murder Case–S.S. Van Dine | 1.50 | 3.00 | 4.50 | M |
| 97 | Swamp Water–Vereen Bell | 1.25 | 2.50 | 3.75 | |
| 98 | Cry Wolf–Marjorie Carleton | 1.25 | 2.50 | 3.75 | |
| 99 | Comanche Chaser–Dane Coolidge | 1.50 | 3.00 | 4.50 | W |
| 100 | The Cautious Amorist–Norman Lindsay; 1947 | 1.25 | 2.50 | 3.75 | |
| 101 | The Problem of the Green Capsule– J.D. Carr | 2.50 | 5.00 | 7.50 | M |
| 102 | Range Rider–W.H.B. Kent | 1.50 | 3.00 | 4.50 | W |

*Bantam 19 with dust jacket, Bantam 39, Bantam 47.*

*Bantam 55, Bantam 67, Bantam 68.*

**BANTAM BOOKS,** *continued*

| # | Title | V/Good | Fine | N/Mint | |
|---|---|---|---|---|---|
| 103 | The Bells of St. Mary's–George Victor Martin; movie tie-in | 2.00 | 4.00 | 6.00 | |
| 104 | Powder Valley Pay-Off–Peter Field | 1.50 | 3.00 | 4.50 | W |
| 105 | Our Hearts Were Young and Gay–Cornelia Otis Skinner & Emily Kimbrough | 1.25 | 2.50 | 3.75 | |
| 106 | Asylum–William Seabrook | 1.25 | 2.50 | 3.75 | |
| 107 | Murder in Brass–Lewis Padgett | 3.00 | 6.00 | 9.00 | M |
| 108 | Quick Draw–Curtis Bishop | 1.50 | 3.00 | 4.50 | |
| 109 | Blood from a Stone–Ruth Sawtell Wallis | 1.25 | 2.50 | 3.75 | M |
| 110 | Romance for Sale–Maysie Greig | 1.25 | 2.50 | 3.75 | R |
| 111 | Trouble Shooter–Robert Travor | 1.25 | 2.50 | 3.75 | |
| 112 | Hardcase–Luke Short | 1.25 | 2.50 | 3.75 | W |
| 113 | Riders of the Night–Eugene Cunningham | 1.25 | 2.50 | 3.75 | W |
| 114 | Old Lover's Ghost–Leslie Ford | 1.25 | 2.50 | 3.75 | M |
| 115 | Women Will Be Doctors–Hannah Lees | 1.25 | 2.50 | 3.75 | R |
| 116 | Great Stories from the Saturday Evening Post | 1.50 | 3.00 | 4.50 | |
| 117 | Stiffs Don't Vote–Geoffrey Homes; aka Forty Whacks | 1.25 | 2.50 | 3.75 | M |
| 118 | A Toast to Tomorrow–Manning Coles | 1.25 | 2.50 | 3.75 | |
| 119 | Double Deal–Allan R. Bosworth; aka Hang and Rattle | 1.50 | 3.00 | 4.50 | W |
| 120 | Secret beyond the Door–Rufus King; movie tie-in | 1.50 | 3.00 | 4.50 | |
| 121 | My Man Godfrey–Eric Hatch; aka Irene, the Stubborn Girl | 1.25 | 2.50 | 3.75 | E |
| 122 | A Certain Doctor French–Elizabeth Seifert | 1.25 | 2.50 | 3.75 | R |
| 123 | A Treasury of Folk Songs–Sylvia Kolb & John Kolb | 2.00 | 4.00 | 6.00 | NF |
| 124 | To Mary with Love–Richard Sherman | 1.25 | 2.50 | 3.75 | |
| 125 | February Hill–Victoria Lincoln; 1947 | 1.25 | 2.50 | 3.75 | E |
| 126 | Quality–Cid Ricketts Sumner | 1.25 | 2.50 | 3.75 | E |
| 127 | Chicago Murders–Sewell Peaslee Wright | 1.50 | 3.00 | 4.50 | NF |
| 128 | Six-Gun Outcast–Charles N. Heckelmann | 1.50 | 3.00 | 4.50 | W |
| 129 | "Whip" Ryder's Way–Grant Taylor | 1.50 | 3.00 | 4.50 | W |
| 130 | The Cinnamon Murder–Frances Crane | 1.50 | 3.00 | 4.50 | M |
| 131 | The Pearl–John Steinbeck; 2nd printing is movie tie-in | 2.50 | 5.00 | 7.50 | |
| 132 | Date with Death–Eaton K. Goldthwaite | 1.50 | 3.00 | 4.50 | M |
| 133 | Kid Galahad–Francis Wallace | 1.25 | 2.50 | 3.75 | |
| 134 | Hell for Breakfast–Alan LeMay | 1.50 | 3.00 | 4.50 | W |
| 135 | Mama's Bank Account–Kathryn Forbes; movie tie-in | 1.50 | 3.00 | 4.50 | |
| 136 | Up at the Villa–W. Somerset Maugham | 1.50 | 3.00 | 4.50 | |
| 137 | Wings of Fear–Mignon G. Eberhart; 1948 | 1.25 | 2.50 | 3.75 | M |
| 138 | Murder Cheats the Bride–Anthony Gilbert | 1.25 | 2.50 | 3.75 | M |
| 139 | Station West–Luke Short; movie tie-in | 1.50 | 3.00 | 4.50 | W |
| 140 | Coroner Creek–Luke Short | 1.50 | 3.00 | 4.50 | W |
| 141 | Scandals of Clochemerie–Gabriel Chevallier | 1.25 | 2.50 | 3.75 | |
| 142 | Treasure Island–Robert Louis Stevenson | 2.50 | 5.00 | 7.50 | A |
| 143 | The She-Wolf–H.H. Munro; aka A Saki Sampler. Note: Exists only as a Bantam dust jacket on Superior M656 | 30.00 | 60.00 | 90.00 | F |
| 144 | The Mighty Blockhead–Frank Gruber. Note: Exists only as a Bantam dust jacket on Superior M655 | 30.00 | 60.00 | 90.00 | |
| 145 | The Love Nest–Ring Lardner. Note: Exists only as a Bantam dust jacket on Superior M646 | 35.00 | 70.00 | 105.00 | H |
| 146 | The Rynox Murder Mystery–Philip MacDonald. Note: Exists only as a Bantam dust jacket on Superior M642 | 30.00 | 60.00 | 90.00 | M |
| 147 | Only the Good–Mary Collins | 1.25 | 2.50 | 3.75 | |
| 148 | On Ice–Robert George Dean. Note: Exists only as a Bantam dust jacket on Superior M654 | 30.00 | 60.00 | 90.00 | M |
| 149 | Good Night, Sheriff–Harrison R. Steeves. Note: Exists only as a Bantam dust jacket on Superior M657 | 30.00 | 60.00 | 90.00 | |
| 150 | The Informer–Liam O'Flaherty; 1948. | 25.00 | 50.00 | 75.00 | |

| # | Title | V/Good | Fine | N/Mint | |
|---|---|---|---|---|---|
| | Note: Exists only as a Bantam dust jacket on Superior M650 | | | | |
| 151 | The Navy Colt–Frank Gruber. Note: Exists only as a Bantam dust jacket on Superior M649 | 25.00 | 50.00 | 75.00 | |
| 152 | Mrs. Mike–Benedict Freedman & Nancy Freedman | 1.25 | 2.50 | 3.75 | |
| 154 | Twenty Grand Short Stories–Ernest Taggard | 1.25 | 2.50 | 3.75 | |
| 155 | Storm–George R. Stewart. Note: Exists only as a Bantam dust jacket on Penguin Special s238 | 25.00 | 50.00 | 75.00 | |
| 156 | Boomerang!–William C. Chambliss. Note: Exists only as a Bantam dust jacket on Infantry Journal J101 | 25.00 | 50.00 | 75.00 | |
| 158 | The Sign of the Ram–Margaret Ferguson; movie tie-in | 1.25 | 2.50 | 3.75 | E |
| 200 | Western Triggers–ed. Arnold Hano; 1948 | 1.50 | 3.00 | 4.50 | W |
| 201 | Trail South from Powder Valley–Peter Field | 1.50 | 3.00 | 4.50 | W |
| 202 | The Tenderfoot–W.H.B. Kent | 1.50 | 3.00 | 4.50 | W |
| 203 | Sugarfoot!–Clarence Budington Kelland | 1.25 | 2.50 | 3.75 | W |
| 204 | Blood on the Moon–Luke Short; aka Gunman's Chance | 1.50 | 3.00 | 4.50 | W |
| 205 | Red River–Borden Chase; aka Blazing Guns on the Chisholm Trail; movie tie-in | 2.00 | 4.00 | 6.00 | W |
| 206 | Deputy Marshal–Charles N. Heckelmann; c-Saunders | 1.50 | 3.00 | 4.50 | W |
| 207 | Short Grass–Thomas W. Blackburn; c-Saunders | 1.50 | 3.00 | 4.50 | W |
| 208 | Dead Man's Range–Tom J. Hopkins; aka Bullets over Broken Leg | 1.50 | 3.00 | 4.50 | W |
| 209 | Hard Money–Luke Short; 1949; c-Saunders | 1.50 | 3.00 | 4.50 | W |
| 210 | The Land Grabber–Peter Field; aka Fight for Powder Valley | 1.50 | 3.00 | 4.50 | W |
| 211 | The Rescue of Broken Arrow–Evan Evans | 1.50 | 3.00 | 4.50 | W |
| 212 | Fighting Man–Frank Gruber | 2.00 | 4.00 | 6.00 | W |
| 213 | Hell or High Water–Dick Pearce; aka Desert Steel | 1.50 | 3.00 | 4.50 | W |
| 214 | Rio Grande Kid–R.M. Hankins; aka Lonesome River Justice; c-Saunders | 1.50 | 3.00 | 4.50 | W |
| S221 | 30 Seconds over Tokyo–Ted W. Lawson. Note: Not part of regular series–reissue of Penguin Special, identified as 6th printing of March 1945, has unillustrated, plain blue cover | 2.00 | 4.00 | 6.00 | C |
| 227 | American Sexual Behaviour and the Kinsey Report–Morris L. Ernst & David Loth | 1.50 | 3.00 | 4.50 | NF |
| 250 | The Stagline Feud–Peter Dawson (Frank Gruber); 1948 | 1.50 | 3.00 | 4.50 | W |
| 251 | Relentless–Kenneth Perkins; aka Three Were Thoroughbreds | 1.50 | 3.00 | 4.50 | W |
| 252 | Barbed Wire–Bennett Foster; aka Powdersmoke Fence | 1.50 | 3.00 | 4.50 | W |
| | With dust jacket | 25.00 | 50.00 | 75.00 | |
| 253 | Wild Justice–Alan LeMay; aka The Smoky Years | 1.50 | 3.00 | 4.50 | W |
| 254 | Border Bandit–Evan Evans (Max Brand); c-Saunders | 1.50 | 3.00 | 4.50 | W |
| 255 | Badlands–Bennett Foster; c-Saunders | 1.50 | 3.00 | 4.50 | W |

*Bantam 209, Bantam 258, Bantam 311.*

BANTAM BOOKS, *continued*

| No. | Title | V/Good | Fine | N/Mint | |
|---|---|---|---|---|---|
| 256 | Western Roundup–ed. Arnold Hano | 1.50 | 3.00 | 4.50 | W |
| 257 | Arizona–Clarence Budington Kelland | 1.50 | 3.00 | 4.50 | W |
| 258 | Raiders of the Rimrock–Luke Short; 1949 | 1.50 | 3.00 | 4.50 | W |
| 259 | The Man from Wyoming–R.M. Hankins | 1.50 | 3.00 | 4.50 | W |
| 260 | Pay-off at Ladron–Bennett Foster | 1.50 | 3.00 | 4.50 | |
| 261 | The Wild Bunch–Ernest Haycox; c-Saunders | 1.50 | 3.00 | 4.50 | W |
| 262 | A Ghost Town on the Yellowstone– Elliot Paul | 1.50 | 3.00 | 4.50 | W |
| 300 | The Kidnap Murder Case–S.S. Van Dine | 1.50 | 3.00 | 4.50 | M |
| 301 | Headlined for Murder–Edwin Lanham | 1.25 | 2.50 | 3.75 | M |
| 302 | The Fabulous Clipjoint–Fredric Brown | 6.00 | 12.00 | 18.00 | M |
| | With dust jacket | 35.00 | 70.00 | 105.00 | |
| 303 | Siren in the Night–Leslie Ford | 1.25 | 2.50 | 3.75 | M |
| 304 | The Problem of the Wire Cage–John Dickson Carr | 2.00 | 4.00 | 6.00 | M |
| 305 | Hanged for a Sheep–Richard Lockridge & Francis Lockridge | 2.00 | 4.00 | 6.00 | M |
| 306 | The Day He Died–Lewis Padgett | 3.00 | 6.00 | 9.00 | M |
| 307 | The Bride Saw Red–Robert Carson | 1.25 | 2.50 | 3.75 | |
| 308 | The Silent Speaker–Rex Stout | 1.50 | 3.00 | 4.50 | M |
| 309 | The Case of the Mexican Knife– Geoffrey Homes; aka Street of the Crying Woman | 1.25 | 2.50 | 3.75 | M |
| 310 | Murder in the Glass Room–Edwin Rolfe & Lester Fuller | 1.25 | 2.50 | 3.75 | M |
| 311 | Saigon Singer–F. Van Wyck Mason | 1.25 | 2.50 | 3.75 | |
| 312 | The Indigo Necklace Murders–Frances Crane | 1.25 | 2.50 | 3.75 | M |
| 313 | The Chasm–Victor Canning | 1.25 | 2.50 | 3.75 | |
| | With dust jacket | 25.00 | 50.00 | 75.00 | |
| 314 | The Yellow Room–Mary Roberts Rinehart | 1.25 | 2.50 | 3.75 | M |
| 315 | Brighton Rock–Graham Greene | 1.25 | 2.50 | 3.75 | M |
| | With dust jacket | 25.00 | 50.00 | 75.00 | |
| 317 | Murder Is Cheap–Anthony Gilbert | 1.25 | 2.50 | 3.75 | M |
| 320 | As Long As I Live–Ione Sandberg Shriber | 1.25 | 2.50 | 3.75 | |
| 350 | Your Red Wagon–Edward Anderson; movie tie-in | 1.50 | 3.00 | 4.50 | |
| | With dust jacket | 30.00 | 60.00 | 90.00 | |
| 351 | The Lying Ladies–Robert Finnegan | 1.50 | 3.00 | 4.50 | |
| 352 | Miss Agatha Doubles for Death–H.L.V. Fletcher | 1.25 | 2.50 | 3.75 | M |
| 353 | The Book of the Dead–Elizabeth Daly | 1.50 | 3.00 | 4.50 | M |
| 354 | San Francisco Murders–Joseph Henry Jackson | 1.25 | 2.50 | 3.75 | NF |
| 355 | The Man Within–Graham Greene | 1.25 | 2.50 | 3.75 | M |
| | With dust jacket | 25.00 | 50.00 | 75.00 | |
| 356 | Sorry, Wrong Number–Lucille Fletcher & Allan Ullman; movie tie-in | 1.50 | 3.00 | 4.50 | |
| 357 | The Sealed Verdict–Lionel Shapiro; movie tie-in | 1.25 | 2.50 | 3.75 | |
| 358 | The Voice of the Corpse–Max Murray | 1.50 | 3.00 | 4.50 | M |
| 359 | All for the Love of a Lady–Leslie Ford; 1949 | 1.25 | 2.50 | 3.75 | M |
| 360 | One More Unfortunate–Edgar Lustgarten | 1.25 | 2.50 | 3.75 | M |
| | With dust jacket | 25.00 | 50.00 | 75.00 | |
| 361 | The Dead Ringer–Fredric Brown | 6.00 | 12.00 | 18.00 | M |
| 362 | The Dragon Murder Case–S.S. Van Dine | 1.50 | 3.00 | 4.50 | M |
| 363 | Many a Monster–Robert Finnegan | 1.25 | 2.50 | 3.75 | |
| 364 | Fire in the Snow–Hammond Innes | 1.50 | 3.00 | 4.50 | |
| 365 | The Man Who Could Not Shudder– John Dickson Carr | 1.50 | 3.00 | 4.50 | M |
| 366 | The Hound of the Baskervilles–Sir Arthur Conan Doyle | 4.00 | 8.00 | 12.00 | M |
| 400 | Winter Meeting–Ethel Vance; movie tie-in | 1.50 | 3.00 | 4.50 | |
| 401 | Yesterday's Madness–Marian Cockrell; movie tie-in | 1.25 | 2.50 | 3.75 | |
| 402 | The Red Pony–John Steinbeck; movie tie-in | 2.50 | 5.00 | 7.50 | |
| 403 | Beggar's Choice–George Axelrod | 1.25 | 2.50 | 3.75 | |
| 404 | Hiroshima–John Hersey | 2.00 | 4.00 | 6.00 | |
| 405 | The Hucksters–Frederic Wakeman | .75 | 1.50 | 2.25 | |
| 406 | Mickey–Peggy Goodin; aka Clementine; movie tie-in | 1.50 | 3.00 | 4.50 | |
| 407 | Behold This Woman–David Goodis | 5.00 | 10.00 | 15.00 | |
| 408 | Doctor Kim–Lucy Agnes Hancock | 1.25 | 2.50 | 3.75 | E |
| 409 | Low Man on a Totem Pole–H. Allen Smith | .75 | 1.50 | 2.25 | |
| 410 | The Grass Is Always Greener–George Malcolm-Smith | 1.25 | 2.50 | 3.75 | F |
| 411 | Hotel Hostess–Faith Baldwin | 1.25 | 2.50 | 3.75 | R |
| 412 | Encore for Love–Katharine Dunlop | 1.25 | 2.50 | 3.75 | R |
| 413 | Family Honeymoon–Homer Croy; movie tie-in | 1.50 | 3.00 | 4.50 | |
| 414 | Spendthrift–Eric Hatch | 1.25 | 2.50 | 3.75 | E |
| 415 | Something Wonderful to Happen– Darwin L. Teilhet | 1.25 | 2.50 | 3.75 | |
| 416 | Miss Dilly Says No–Theodore Pratt | 1.25 | 2.50 | 3.75 | |
| 417 | Confession–Dorothy Les Tina | 1.25 | 2.50 | 3.75 | |
| 418 | Someone Called Maggie Lane–Frances Shelley Wees | 1.25 | 2.50 | 3.75 | |
| 419 | My Flag Is Down–James Maresca | .75 | 1.50 | 2.25 | |
| 420 | Illusion–Allane Corliss; aka Marry for Love | 1.25 | 2.50 | 3.75 | E |
| 421 | No Place to Hide–David Bradley | 2.00 | 4.00 | 6.00 | |
| | With dust jacket | 20.00 | 40.00 | 60.00 | |
| 422 | Office Nurse–Adelaide Humphries | 1.25 | 2.50 | 3.75 | R |
| 423 | Stranger in Paris–W. Somerset Maugham | 1.25 | 2.50 | 3.75 | |
| 425 | My Sister, My Bride–Merriam Modell | 1.25 | 2.50 | 3.75 | |
| 426 | The Stranger–Lillian Bos Ross | 1.25 | 2.50 | 3.75 | W |
| 427 | Prison Nurse–Louis Berg | 1.50 | 3.00 | 4.50 | |
| 450 | Moonlit Voyage–Elizabeth Dunn; 1948 | 1.25 | 2.50 | 3.75 | |
| 451 | Love Is the Winner–Natalie Shipman; aka Who Wins His Love | 1.25 | 2.50 | 3.75 | |
| 452 | Cabbage Holiday–Anthony Thorne | 1.25 | 2.50 | 3.75 | E |
| 453 | Five Nights–Eric Hatch; aka Five Days | 1.25 | 2.50 | 3.75 | |
| 454 | The Chinese Room–Vivian Connell | .75 | 1.50 | 2.25 | |
| 455 | Love Is a Surprise!–Faith Baldwin | 1.25 | 2.50 | 3.75 | R |
| 456 | Yankee Storekeeper–R.E. Gould | 1.25 | 2.50 | 3.75 | |
| 458 | Dr. Woodward's Ambition–Elizabeth Seifert | 1.25 | 2.50 | 3.75 | E |
| 459 | Joan of Arc–Frances Winwar; movie tie-in | 1.50 | 3.00 | 4.50 | A |
| 460 | Earth and High Heaven–Gwethalyn Graham | 1.25 | 2.50 | 3.75 | E |
| 461 | Back Home–Bill Mauldin | 1.25 | 2.50 | 3.75 | |
| 462 | What Became of Anna Bolton?–Louis Bromfield | 1.25 | 2.50 | 3.75 | |
| | With dust jacket | 25.00 | 50.00 | 75.00 | |
| 463 | The Other Room–Worth Tuttle Hedden | 1.25 | 2.50 | 3.75 | E |
| 464 | Nurse into Woman–Marguerite Mooers Marshall | 1.25 | 2.50 | 3.75 | R |
| 465 | Bitter Forfeit–Mabel Louise Robinson | 1.25 | 2.50 | 3.75 | E |
| 466 | The Big Town–Ring Lardner | 1.25 | 2.50 | 3.75 | H |
| 467 | A Farewell to Arms–Ernest Hemingway | 2.50 | 5.00 | 7.50 | |
| 469 | Lady Godiva and Master Tom–Raoul C. Faure | 3.00 | 6.00 | 9.00 | E |
| 470 | The Men in Her Life–Edith Roberts | 1.25 | 2.50 | 3.75 | |
| 471 | Marry for Money–Faith Baldwin | 1.25 | 2.50 | 3.75 | R |
| 473 | Danger Trail–Theodore Pratt | 1.50 | 3.00 | 4.50 | |
| 474 | Hazard–Roy Chanslor | 1.25 | 2.50 | 3.75 | E |
| 476 | Road Show–Eric Hatch | .75 | 1.50 | 2.25 | |
| 477 | The Fascination–Jean Pedrick | 1.25 | 2.50 | 3.75 | E |
| 500 | My Greatest Day in Baseball–J.P. Carmichael | 1.50 | 3.00 | 4.50 | S |
| 501 | Strikeout Story–Bob Feller | 1.50 | 3.00 | 4.50 | S |
| 502 | The Unexpected–Bennett Cerf | 1.50 | 3.00 | 4.50 | SF |
| 503 | First Love–Elizabeth Abell & Joseph I. Greene | 1.25 | 2.50 | 3.75 | R |
| 504 | Kick-Off–Ed Fitzgerald | 1.50 | 3.00 | 4.50 | S |

Bantam 413, Bantam 467, Bantam 551.

Bantam 722, Bantam 728, Bantam 790.

| | | V/Good | Fine | N/Mint | |
|---|---|---|---|---|---|
| | **BANTAM BOOKS,** *continued* | | | | |
| 505 | Babe Ruth–Tom Meany | 1.50 | 3.00 | 4.50 | B |
| 506 | Lucky to Be a Yankee–Joe DiMaggio; 1949 | 2.00 | 4.00 | 6.00 | S |
| 507 | Clowning through Baseball–Al Schacht | 2.00 | 4.00 | 6.00 | S |
| 550 | Out of My Trunk–Milton Berle | 1.25 | 2.50 | 3.75 | H |
| 551 | The ABC of Horseracing–Dan Parker | 1.50 | 3.00 | 4.50 | NF |
| 552 | The Gashouse Gang–J. Roy Stockton | 1.50 | 3.00 | 4.50 | S |
| 553 | The Big Bet–Edward Harris Heth | 1.25 | 2.50 | 3.75 | E |
| 554 | Hot Leather–Beulah Marie Dix & Bertram Millhauser | 1.25 | 2.50 | 3.75 | |
| 555 | Great Stories from the Saturday Evening Post, 1947–ed. Ben Hibbs | 1.50 | 3.00 | 4.50 | |
| 556 | The Story of the Brooklyn Dodgers–Ed Fitzgerald | 1.50 | 3.00 | 4.50 | S |
| 557 | Jack Dempsey–Nat Fleischer | 1.50 | 3.00 | 4.50 | B |
| 700 | Blackjack–Joseph E. Kelleam; 1949 | 1.50 | 3.00 | 4.50 | W |
| 701 | Dead as a Dummy–Geoffrey Homes | 1.50 | 3.00 | 4.50 | M |
| 702 | The Rustlers–Luke Short | 1.50 | 3.00 | 4.50 | W |
| 703 | Hands Off!–Luke Short | 1.50 | 3.00 | 4.50 | W |
| 704 | The Memoirs of Sherlock Holmes–Sir Arthur Conan Doyle | 3.00 | 6.00 | 9.00 | M |
| 705 | Kingsblood Royal–Sinclair Lewis | 1.25 | 2.50 | 3.75 | |
| 706 | The Other Woman–Isabel Moore | 1.00 | 2.00 | 3.00 | |
| 707 | The Harder They Fall–Budd Schulberg | 1.25 | 2.50 | 3.75 | |
| 708 | The Captive Women–Walter D. Edmonds; aka In the Hands of the Senecas | 1.50 | 3.00 | 4.50 | A |
| 709 | The Web of Days–Edna Lee | .75 | 1.50 | 2.25 | E |
| 710 | The Pitfall–Jay J. Dratler | 1.25 | 2.50 | 3.75 | E |
| 711 | Summer Lightning–Allene Corliss | 1.25 | 2.50 | 3.75 | E |
| 712 | The African Queen–C.S. Forester | 2.50 | 5.00 | 7.50 | |
| 713 | Murder Listens In–Elizabeth Daly; aka Arrow Pointing Nowhere | 1.25 | 2.50 | 3.75 | M |
| 714 | The Gilded Rooster–Richard Emery Roberts | 1.25 | 2.50 | 3.75 | |
| 715 | My Greatest Day in Football–Murray Goodman & Leonard Lewin; c-Saunders | 1.50 | 3.00 | 4.50 | S |
| 716 | High Pressure–Ahmad Kamal; aka Full Fathom Five | 1.50 | 3.00 | 4.50 | E |
| | With dust jacket | 30.00 | 60.00 | 90.00 | |
| 717 | The Sun Also Rises–Ernest Hemingway | 2.50 | 5.00 | 7.50 | |
| 718 | Death Warmed Over–Mary Collins | 1.25 | 2.50 | 3.75 | M |
| 720 | Action at Three Peaks–Frank O'Rourke | 1.50 | 3.00 | 4.50 | W |
| 721 | Hollywood without Makeup–Pete Martin | 1.50 | 3.00 | 4.50 | NF |
| 722 | Too Many Women–Rex Stout | 1.50 | 3.00 | 4.50 | M |
| 723 | The Dark Wood–Christine Weston | 1.25 | 2.50 | 3.75 | E |
| 724 | The Heller–William E. Henning | 1.25 | 2.50 | 3.75 | E |
| 725 | Blackleg Range–Bennett Foster | 1.50 | 3.00 | 4.50 | W |
| 726 | Desert Law–Clarence Budington Kelland; c-Saunders | 1.50 | 3.00 | 4.50 | W |
| 727 | City Limits–Hollis Summers | 1.25 | 2.50 | 3.75 | JD |
| 728 | I Escaped from Devil's Island–Rene Belbenoit; aka Dry Guillotine | 1.50 | 3.00 | 4.50 | NF |
| 729 | Belvedere–Gwen Davenport | 1.25 | 2.50 | 3.75 | H |
| 730 | Dark Interlude–Peter Cheyney | 1.50 | 3.00 | 4.50 | M |
| 731 | Sheriff's Revenge–Peter Field; c-Saunders | 1.50 | 3.00 | 4.50 | W |
| 732 | Valley of the Shadow–Charles M. Warren | 1.50 | 3.00 | 4.50 | |
| 733 | The Valley of Fear–Sir Arthur Conan Doyle | 3.00 | 6.00 | 9.00 | M |

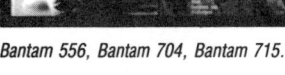

Bantam 556, Bantam 704, Bantam 715.

| | | V/Good | Fine | N/Mint | |
|---|---|---|---|---|---|
| 734 | Panther's Moon–Victor Canning; movie tie-in | .75 | 1.50 | 2.25 | M |
| 735 | A Plot for Murder–Fredric Brown | 6.00 | 12.00 | 18.00 | M |
| 736 | The Wine of Astonishment–Martha Gellhorn | 1.25 | 2.50 | 3.75 | |
| 737 | The Darker Brother–Bucklin Moon | 2.00 | 4.00 | 6.00 | |
| 738 | The Big Clock–Kenneth Fearing | 1.50 | 3.00 | 4.50 | M |
| 739 | The White Dress–Mignon G. Eberhart | 1.25 | 2.50 | 3.75 | M |
| 740 | Bullet Breed–Leslie Ernenwein; c-Saunders | 1.50 | 3.00 | 4.50 | W |
| 741 | Gale Warning–Hammond Innes | 1.50 | 3.00 | 4.50 | |
| 742 | Husbands and Lovers–Joseph I. Greene & Elizabeth Abell | 1.25 | 2.50 | 3.75 | E |
| 743 | Twelve O'Clock High–Sy Bartlett & Beirne Lay, Jr; movie tie-in | 2.00 | 4.00 | 6.00 | C |
| 744 | The Spring Begins–Helen Rich | 1.25 | 2.50 | 3.75 | E |
| 745 | Camille–Alexandre Dumas | 1.25 | 2.50 | 3.75 | E |
| 746 | Politics Is Murder–Edwin Lanham; 1950 | 1.25 | 2.50 | 3.75 | M |
| 747 | Bull-Whip–Luke Short | 1.25 | 2.50 | 3.75 | W |
| 748 | And the Wind Blows Free–Luke Short | 1.25 | 2.50 | 3.75 | W |
| 749 | The Angry Woman–James Ronald | 1.25 | 2.50 | 3.75 | |
| 750 | Thieves' Market–A.I. Bezzerides | .75 | 1.50 | 2.25 | |
| 751 | Shot in the Dark–Judith Merril | 4.50 | 9.00 | 13.50 | SF |
| 752 | The Wayward Bus–John Steinbeck | 2.50 | 5.00 | 7.50 | |
| 753 | Midnight Lace–MacKinlay Kantor | 1.25 | 2.50 | 3.75 | E |
| 754 | The Hour of Truth–David Davidson | 1.25 | 2.50 | 3.75 | |
| 755 | Wayward Angel–Verne Chute | 1.25 | 2.50 | 3.75 | M |
| 756 | The Smell of Murder–S.S. Van Dine | 1.50 | 3.00 | 4.50 | M |
| 757 | Ace-in-the-Hole Haggarty–R.M. Hankins | 1.25 | 2.50 | 3.75 | W |
| 758 | Desperate Choice–Dorothy Speare | 1.25 | 2.50 | 3.75 | |
| 759 | Tacey Cromwell–Conrad Richter | 1.25 | 2.50 | 3.75 | W |
| A760 | This Side of Innocence–Taylor Caldwell | 1.50 | 3.00 | 4.50 | |
| 761 | Explosion–Dorothy Cameron Disney | 1.25 | 2.50 | 3.75 | M |
| 762 | Seven Slash Range–Bennett Foster | 1.50 | 3.00 | 4.50 | W |
| 763 | Baseball's Greatest Teams–Tom Meany | 1.50 | 3.00 | 4.50 | S |
| 764 | Range Drifter–Thomas Thompson | 1.25 | 2.50 | 3.75 | W |
| 765 | Border City–Hart Stilwell | 2.50 | 5.00 | 7.50 | |
| 766 | Jassy–Norah Lofts | .75 | 1.50 | 2.25 | E |
| 767 | No Marriage in Paradise–Myron Brinig | 1.25 | 2.50 | 3.75 | E |
| 768 | Death Lifts the Latch–Anthony Gilbert | 1.25 | 2.50 | 3.75 | M |
| 769 | Valley of Violence–Louis Trimble | 1.25 | 2.50 | 3.75 | |
| 770 | The Whip–Sara Elizabeth Mason | 1.25 | 2.50 | 3.75 | |
| A771 | Leave Her to Heaven–Ben Ames Williams | 1.25 | 2.50 | 3.75 | |
| 772 | Flying Colors–C.S. Forester | 1.25 | 2.50 | 3.75 | A |
| 773 | Come Clean, My Love–Rosemary Taylor | 1.25 | 2.50 | 3.75 | |
| 774 | Heritage of the River–Muriel Elwood | 1.25 | 2.50 | 3.75 | |
| 775 | Hell's Corner–Peter Field | 1.25 | 2.50 | 3.75 | W |
| 776 | Only the Valient–Charles M. Warren | 1.25 | 2.50 | 3.75 | |
| 777 | The Furies–Niven Busch; movie tie-in | .75 | 1.50 | 2.25 | |
| 778 | Irene–Ronald Marsh | .75 | 1.50 | 2.25 | |
| 779 | The Case of the Unhappy Angels–Geoffrey Homes | 1.25 | 2.50 | 3.75 | M |
| 780 | Walk the Dark Streets–William Krasner | 1.25 | 2.50 | 3.75 | |
| 781 | The Enchanted Heart–Marjorie Worthington | 1.25 | 2.50 | 3.75 | |
| 782 | The Keys of the Kingdom–A.J. Cronin | 1.00 | 2.00 | 3.00 | |
| 783 | The Bloody Moonlight–Fredric Brown | 7.50 | 15.00 | 22.50 | M |
| 784 | Gunman's Legacy–Evan Evans | 1.25 | 2.50 | 3.75 | W |
| 785 | Pleasure Island–William Maier | 1.25 | 2.50 | 3.75 | E |

**BANTAM BOOKS,** *continued*

| No. | Title | V/Good | Fine | N/Mint | |
|---|---|---|---|---|---|
| 786 | Sins of New York–Milton Crane | 1.25 | 2.50 | 3.75 | |
| 787 | The Sister of Cain–Mary Collins | 1.25 | 2.50 | 3.75 | M |
| 788 | Long Storm–Ernest Haycox | 1.25 | 2.50 | 3.75 | W |
| 789 | Mary Hallam–Susan Ertz | 1.00 | 2.00 | 3.00 | |
| 790 | The Blazing Land–Norman Collins; aka Flames Coming Out of the Top | 1.25 | 2.50 | 3.75 | |
| 791 | The Feud at Single Shot–Luke Short | 1.25 | 2.50 | 3.75 | W |
| 792 | War on the Cimarron–Luke Short | 1.25 | 2.50 | 3.75 | W |
| 793 | Till Death Do Us Part–John Dickson Carr | 1.50 | 3.00 | 4.50 | M |
| 794 | Angels Camp–Kay Morrison | 1.50 | 3.00 | 4.50 | JD |
| 795 | My Sister, Goodnight–Gordon McDonell | 1.00 | 2.00 | 3.00 | |
| 796 | Lord and Master–Robert Standish; aka Elephant Walk | 1.25 | 2.50 | 3.75 | |
| 797 | The 3rd Man–Graham Greene | 1.50 | 3.00 | 4.50 | |
| A798 | The Underworld–Ira Wolfert; aka Tucker's People | .75 | 1.50 | 2.25 | E |
| 799 | Thunder on the Buckhorn–Frank O'Rourke; c-Saunders | 1.50 | 3.00 | 4.50 | |
| 800 | Halo for Satan–John Evans | 2.00 | 4.00 | 6.00 | M |
| 801 | The Steeper Cliff–David Davidson | 1.25 | 2.50 | 3.75 | |
| 802 | Fire–George R. Stewart | 1.25 | 2.50 | 3.75 | |
| 803 | Killer by Proxy–Selwyn Jepson | 1.25 | 2.50 | 3.75 | |
| A804 | Drums Along the Mohawk–Walter D. Edmonds | 1.50 | 3.00 | 4.50 | A |
| A805 | H.M. Pulham Esquire–John P. Marquand | 1.00 | 2.00 | 3.00 | |
| A806 | Woman of Property–Mabel Seeley | 1.00 | 2.00 | 3.00 | E |
| A807 | The Gallery–John Horne Burns | 1.25 | 2.50 | 3.75 | |
| 808 | The Owl Hoot Trail–Bennett Foster | 1.25 | 2.50 | 3.75 | W |
| 809 | Wicked Water–MacKinlay Kantor | 1.25 | 2.50 | 3.75 | |
| 810 | The Moon and Sixpence–W. Somerset Maugham | 1.50 | 3.00 | 4.50 | E |
| 811 | Any Shape or Form–Elizabeth Daly | 1.00 | 2.00 | 3.00 | M |
| 812 | Cotton Country–Hubert Creekmore; aka The Fingers of Night | 1.25 | 2.50 | 3.75 | E |
| 813 | Sailor Town–Paul Fox | .75 | 1.50 | 2.25 | |
| A814 | Never Love a Stranger–Harold Robbins | 1.25 | 2.50 | 3.75 | |
| A815 | A Lion Is in the Street–Adria Locke Langley | .75 | 1.50 | 2.25 | |
| 816 | Payment Deferred–C.S. Forester | 1.25 | 2.50 | 3.75 | M |
| 817 | The Whipping–Roy Flannagan | 3.00 | 6.00 | 9.00 | E |
| A818 | The Black Rose–Thomas B. Costain; movie tie-in | 2.50 | 5.00 | 7.50 | A |
| 819 | Donovan's Brain–Curt Siodmak | 3.00 | 6.00 | 9.00 | SF |
| 820 | The Purple Plain–H.E. Bates | 1.25 | 2.50 | 3.75 | |
| 821 | Reflections in a Golden Eye–Carson McCullers | .75 | 1.50 | 2.25 | |
| 822 | The Member of the Wedding–Carson McCullers | 1.25 | 2.50 | 3.75 | |
| 823 | Range Pirate–L.P. Holmes | 1.25 | 2.50 | 3.75 | W |
| 824 | And Be a Villain–Rex Stout | 1.50 | 3.00 | 4.50 | M |
| 825 | A Private Killing–James Benet | 1.25 | 2.50 | 3.75 | M |
| 826 | High Sierra–W.R. Burnett | 2.00 | 4.00 | 6.00 | |
| 827 | Thunder on the River–Charlton Laird | 1.25 | 2.50 | 3.75 | |
| 828 | American Guerrilla in the Philippines–Ira Wolfert | 1.25 | 2.50 | 3.75 | |
| 829 | An Affair of State–Pat Frank | .75 | 1.50 | 2.25 | |
| 830 | Anna Becker–Max White | 1.25 | 2.50 | 3.75 | E |
| 831 | The Screaming Mimi–Fredric Brown | 4.00 | 8.00 | 12.00 | M |
| 832 | Six-gun Doctor–Paul S. Powers | 1.25 | 2.50 | 3.75 | W |
| 833 | Shane–Jack Schaefer | 2.50 | 5.00 | 7.50 | W |
| 834 | The Golden Salamander–Victor Canning | .75 | 1.50 | 2.25 | |
| 835 | What Mad Universe–Fredric Brown | 3.00 | 6.00 | 9.00 | SF |
| 836 | Long Hunt–James Boyd | 1.25 | 2.50 | 3.75 | |
| 837 | The Green Flames–Marcos Spinelli; aka From Jungle Roots | 1.50 | 3.00 | 4.50 | |
| 838 | The Rebellion of Leo McGuire–Clyde Brion Davis | .75 | 1.50 | 2.25 | |
| 839 | Mission: Danger–Dod Orsborne; aka Master of the Girl Pat | .75 | 1.50 | 2.25 | |
| 840 | Bold New Program–Willard R. Espy | .75 | 1.50 | 2.25 | |
| 841 | Rider of the Rifle Rock–Bennett Foster | 1.25 | 2.50 | 3.75 | W |
| 842 | The Wooden Horse–Eric Williams; movie tie-in | .75 | 1.50 | 2.25 | |
| 843 | Ordeal by Slander–Owen Lattimore | .75 | 1.50 | 2.25 | |
| 844 | Brazos–Ross McLaury Taylor | .75 | 1.50 | 2.25 | |
| 845 | How to Survive an Atomic Bomb–Richard Gerstell | 2.00 | 4.00 | 6.00 | NF |
| 846 | This Is My Story–Eleanor Roosevelt | 1.00 | 2.00 | 3.00 | B |
| A847 | The Strange Woman–Ben Ames Williams | .75 | 1.50 | 2.25 | |
| 848 | The Queen Bee–Edna Lee | .75 | 1.50 | 2.25 | E |
| 849 | Another Woman's House–Mignon Eberhart | .75 | 1.50 | 2.25 | |
| 850 | Mayhem in B-Flat–Elliot Paul | 1.50 | 3.00 | 4.50 | |
| 851 | The Innocent Bottle–Anthony Gilbert | .75 | 1.50 | 2.25 | M |
| 852 | Catalina–W. Somerset Maugham | 1.25 | 2.50 | 3.75 | |
| 853 | Ambush–Luke Short | 1.25 | 2.50 | 3.75 | W |
| 854 | Fiddlefoot–Luke Short | 1.25 | 2.50 | 3.75 | W |
| 855 | A Sort of a Saga–Bill Mauldin | 1.25 | 2.50 | 3.75 | |
| 856 | The Rim of Terror–Hildegarde Tolman Teilhet | 1.25 | 2.50 | 3.75 | |
| 857 | The Haters–Theodore Strauss | 1.25 | 2.50 | 3.75 | |
| 858 | With Naked Foot–Emily Hahn | .75 | 1.50 | 2.25 | |
| 859 | Cyrano de Bergerac–Edmond Rostand; movie tie-in | 2.00 | 4.00 | 6.00 | |
| A860 | Captain from Castile–Samuel Shellabarger | 1.50 | 3.00 | 4.50 | |
| 861 | Verdict in Dispute–Edgar Lustgarten | 1.25 | 2.50 | 3.75 | M |
| 862 | The Mesh–Lucie Marchal | .75 | 1.50 | 2.25 | E |
| 863 | The Hangman's Tree–Dorothy Cameron Disney | .75 | 1.50 | 2.25 | M |
| 864 | Broken Valley–Thomas Thompson | 1.25 | 2.50 | 3.75 | W |
| 865 | The Hunter–Hugh Fosburgh | .75 | 1.50 | 2.25 | |
| A866 | Bright Feather–Robert Wilder; 1950 | .75 | 1.50 | 2.25 | A |
| A867 | Tender Is the Night–F. Scott Fitzgerald; 1951 | 2.00 | 4.00 | 6.00 | |
| A868 | The Grapes of Wrath–John Steinbeck | 1.50 | 3.00 | 4.50 | |
| A869 | Night in Bombay–Louis Bromfield | .75 | 1.50 | 2.25 | |
| 870 | Evered–Ben Ames Williams | .75 | 1.50 | 2.25 | |
| A871 | Bridal Journey–Dale Van Every | .75 | 1.50 | 2.25 | |
| 872 | The Passionate Pilgrim–Charles Terrot | .75 | 1.50 | 2.25 | |
| 873 | The Cow Thief Trail–Bennett Foster | 1.25 | 2.50 | 3.75 | W |
| 874 | Murder on the Purple Water–Frances Crane | 1.25 | 2.50 | 3.75 | M |
| 875 | Something for Nothing–H. Vernor Dixon | 2.00 | 4.00 | 6.00 | E |
| 876 | Compliments of a Fiend–Fredric Brown | 7.50 | 15.00 | 22.50 | M |
| 877 | Dog Eat Dog–Mary Collins | .75 | 1.50 | 2.25 | M |
| 878 | Ticket to Oblivion–Robert Parker | .75 | 1.50 | 2.25 | |
| 879 | Low Down–Reynolds Packard; aka The Kansas City Milkman | .75 | 1.50 | 2.25 | E |
| 880 | Tasker Martin–Diana Gaines | .75 | 1.50 | 2.25 | |
| 881 | Repent in Haste–John P. Marquand | .75 | 1.50 | 2.25 | E |
| 882 | Lone Hand–Evan Evans (Max Brand) | 1.25 | 2.50 | 3.75 | W |
| A883 | For Whom the Bell Tolls–Ernest Hemingway | 2.50 | 5.00 | 7.50 | |
| A884 | The Fires of Spring–James A. Michener | 1.50 | 3.00 | 4.50 | |
| 885 | House of Storm–Mignon G. Eberhart | .75 | 1.50 | 2.25 | M |
| 886 | The Martian Chronicles–Ray Bradbury | 3.00 | 6.00 | 9.00 | SF |
| 887 | The Husband Who Ran Away–Hildegarde Dolson | 1.25 | 2.50 | 3.75 | |
| 888 | Nobody Lives Forever–W.R. Burnett | 2.50 | 5.00 | 7.50 | |
| 889 | Dark Hunger–Theodore Strauss | .75 | 1.50 | 2.25 | |
| 890 | Run by Night–Hammond Innes | .75 | 1.50 | 2.25 | |
| 891 | Wolf Song–Harvey Fergusson | 1.25 | 2.50 | 3.75 | |
| 892 | Gunsmoke Justice–Louis Trimble | 1.25 | 2.50 | 3.75 | W |
| A893 | Cass Timberlane–Sinclair Lewis | 1.50 | 3.00 | 4.50 | |
| A894 | The Courts of the Lion–Robert W. Krepps | 1.25 | 2.50 | 3.75 | A |
| 895 | Nightmare in Manhattan–Thomas Walsh | .75 | 1.50 | 2.25 | |
| 896 | He Who Whispers–John Dickson Carr | 1.50 | 3.00 | 4.50 | M |
| 897 | Death Has a Past–Anita Boutell | 1.25 | 2.50 | 3.75 | M |
| 898 | Black Sage–L.P. Holmes | 1.25 | 2.50 | 3.75 | W |
| 899 | The Pastures of Heaven–John Steinbeck | 2.50 | 5.00 | 7.50 | |
| 900 | Arouse and Beware–MacKinlay Kantor | 1.50 | 3.00 | 4.50 | C |
| 901 | Shake Well before Using–Bennett Cerf | .75 | 1.50 | 2.25 | H |
| A902 | The Flames of Time–Baynard Kendrick | 2.00 | 4.00 | 6.00 | E |
| A903 | The Burnished Blade–Lawrence Schoonover | 1.50 | 3.00 | 4.50 | A |
| A904 | The Great Mouthpiece–Gene Fowler | .75 | 1.50 | 2.25 | B |
| 905 | Strangers on a Train–Patricia Highsmith | 2.50 | 5.00 | 7.50 | M |
| 906 | Bend of the Snake–Bill Gulick | 1.25 | 2.50 | 3.75 | W |
| 907 | The Case Against Myself–Gregory Tree | 1.25 | 2.50 | 3.75 | M |
| 908 | So Many Doors–Oakley Hall | .75 | 1.50 | 2.25 | E |

BANTAM BOOKS, *continued*

| | | V/Good | Fine | N/Mint | |
|---|---|---|---|---|---|
| 909 | The Narrow Corner–W. Somerset Maugham | .75 | 1.50 | 2.25 | |
| A910 | Wild Is the River–Louis Bromfield | .75 | 1.50 | 2.25 | C |
| 911 | Vengeance Valley–Luke Short | .75 | 1.50 | 2.25 | W |
| A912 | Captain Horatio Hornblower–C.S. Forester; movie tie-in | 2.50 | 5.00 | 7.50 | A |
| 913 | The Saturday Review Reader | .75 | 1.50 | 2.25 | |
| A914 | Stories for Here and Now–Elizabeth Abell & Joseph I. Green. Note: Two cover variants exist for first printing | | | | |
| | Illustrated cover | 1.50 | 3.00 | 4.50 | |
| | Lettered cover | 1.00 | 2.00 | 3.00 | |
| 915 | The Unforseen–Dorothy Macardle | .75 | 1.50 | 2.25 | F |
| 916 | Blackwater–Frank O'Rourke | .75 | 1.50 | 2.25 | W |
| 917 | To the Indies–C.S. Forester | .75 | 1.50 | 2.25 | A |
| A918 | Blood Brother–Elliott Arnold | 2.00 | 4.00 | 6.00 | W |
| A919 | B.F.'s Daughter–John P. Marquand | .75 | 1.50 | 2.25 | |
| 920 | Scottsboro Boy–Earl Conrad & Haywood Patterson | 1.00 | 2.00 | 3.00 | NF |
| 921 | 12 Against Crime–Edward D. Radin | .75 | 1.50 | 2.25 | |
| 922 | Apache–Will Levington Comfort | 1.50 | 3.00 | 4.50 | W |
| 923 | Hot Rod–Henry Gregor Felsen | 3.00 | 6.00 | 9.00 | |
| 924 | Saddle-man–Matt Stuart | 1.25 | 2.50 | 3.75 | W |
| 925 | Trouble in Triplicate–Rex Stout | 1.50 | 3.00 | 4.50 | M |
| 926 | Night without Sleep–Elick Moll | 1.25 | 2.50 | 3.75 | |
| 927 | The Judas Cat–Dorothy Salisbury Davis. Note: Two cover variants exist for first printing | | | | M |
| | Man with cat | 1.50 | 3.00 | 4.50 | |
| | Man with flashlight | 1.50 | 3.00 | 4.50 | |
| A928 | Flamingo Road–Robert Wilder | 1.25 | 2.50 | 3.75 | |
| 929 | Steel to the Sunset–Allan R. Bosworth | 1.25 | 2.50 | 3.75 | W |
| A930 | The Citadel–A.J. Cronin | .75 | 1.50 | 2.25 | |
| 931 | Louisville Saturday–Margaret Lohg | .75 | 1.50 | 2.25 | E |
| 932 | Torch for a Long Journey–Lionel Shapiro | .75 | 1.50 | 2.25 | |
| A933 | Look to the Mountain–Le Grand Cannon, Jr | .75 | 1.50 | 2.25 | |
| 934 | Blues for the Prince–Bart Spicer | .75 | 1.50 | 2.25 | |
| F935 | A Rage to Live–John O'Hara | .75 | 1.50 | 2.25 | |
| 936 | Previews of Entertainment–Gilbert Seldes | .75 | 1.50 | 2.25 | NF |
| 937 | Bright Victory–Baynard Kendrick; movie tie-in | 1.50 | 3.00 | 4.50 | |
| A938 | W.C. Fields: His Follies and His Fortunes–Robert Lewis Taylor | 2.00 | 4.00 | 6.00 | B |
| A939 | All the King's Men–Robert Penn Warren | 1.50 | 3.00 | 4.50 | |
| 940 | Apache Gold and Yaqui Silver–J. Frank Dobie | 1.50 | 3.00 | 4.50 | NF |
| 941 | Sundown Riders–Thomas Thompson | 1.25 | 2.50 | 3.75 | W |
| 942 | Romelle–W.R. Burnett | 2.00 | 4.00 | 6.00 | |
| 943 | Here Comes a Candle–Fredric Brown | 7.50 | 15.00 | 22.50 | M |
| A944 | Timeless Stories for Today and Tomorrow–Ray Bradbury | 3.00 | 6.00 | 9.00 | SF |
| 945 | Tomboy–Hal Ellson; intro. by F. Wertham | 4.00 | 8.00 | 12.00 | JD |
| 946 | No Survivors–Will Henry | 1.25 | 2.50 | 3.75 | W |
| 947 | A Room on the Route–Godfrey Blunder | 1.00 | 2.00 | 3.00 | |
| 948 | A Forest of Eyes–Victor Canning | .75 | 1.50 | 2.25 | |
| 949 | Woman of the World–W. Somerset Maugham | .75 | 1.50 | 2.25 | |
| 950 | Fifty Great Short Stories–ed. Milton Crane | .50 | 1.00 | 1.50 | |

| | | V/Good | Fine | N/Mint | |
|---|---|---|---|---|---|
| A951 | For My Great Folly–Thomas B. Costain | .75 | 1.50 | 2.25 | A |
| 952 | Death of a Salesman–Arthur Miller | 2.50 | 5.00 | 7.50 | |
| 953 | Burning Bright–John Steinbeck | 2.50 | 5.00 | 7.50 | |
| A954 | Grant of Land–Lucile Finlay | .75 | 1.50 | 2.25 | |
| A955 | The Dream Merchants–Harold Robbins | 1.25 | 2.50 | 3.75 | |
| A956 | The Earth Is the Lord's–Taylor Caldwell; 1952 | .75 | 1.50 | 2.25 | A |
| 957 | Colorado–Louis Bromfield | .75 | 1.50 | 2.25 | |
| 958 | Raton Pass–Thomas W. Blackburn | 1.00 | 2.00 | 3.00 | W |
| 959 | The Best Go First–Frank O'Malley | .75 | 1.50 | 2.25 | M |
| 960 | Cheaper by the Dozen–Ernestine Carey & Frank B. Gilbreth, Jr | 1.00 | 2.00 | 3.00 | |
| 961 | What a Man Wants–Harvey Fergusson; aka The Life of Riley | 1.00 | 2.00 | 3.00 | E |
| 962 | The Trees–Conrad Richter | .75 | 1.50 | 2.25 | |
| 963 | The God That Failed–Richard Crossman | .60 | 1.20 | 1.80 | |
| A964 | Terror in the Streets–Howard Whitman; c-Maguire | 1.50 | 3.00 | 4.50 | |
| A965 | Signal Thirty-two–MacKinlay Kantor | .60 | 1.20 | 1.80 | |
| 966 | Sawdust and Sixguns–Evan Evans | 1.00 | 2.00 | 3.00 | W |
| 967 | A Man without Friends–Margaret Echard | .75 | 1.50 | 2.25 | |
| 968 | Dig Me a Grave–John Spain | .75 | 1.50 | 2.25 | M |
| 969 | The Little Princesses–Marion Crawford | .75 | 1.50 | 2.25 | B |
| 970 | Jackson Mahaffey–Fred Ross | .75 | 1.50 | 2.25 | |
| 971 | The Confidential Agent–Graham Greene | 1.00 | 2.00 | 3.00 | |
| 972 | Dollar Cotton–John Faulkner | .75 | 1.50 | 2.25 | |
| A973 | The Prince of Foxes–Samuel Shellabarger | 1.00 | 2.00 | 3.00 | A |
| 974 | The Outlaw of Longbow–Peter Dawson (Frank Gruber) | 1.50 | 3.00 | 4.50 | W |
| 975 | The Golden Door–Bart Spicer | .75 | 1.50 | 2.25 | |
| 976 | The Gambler–William Krasner | .75 | 1.50 | 2.25 | |
| 977 | The Silver Hook–John Mortimer | .75 | 1.50 | 2.25 | E |
| 978 | Mima–Tom Hanlin; aka Yesterday Will Return | .75 | 1.50 | 2.25 | E |
| A979 | Model Railroading | 1.25 | 2.50 | 3.75 | NF |
| A980 | Bugles in the Afternoon–Ernest Haycox | 1.50 | 3.00 | 4.50 | W |
| A981 | The Shining Mountains–Dale Van Every | .75 | 1.50 | 2.25 | |
| 982 | Operation Cicero–L.C. Moyzisch | .75 | 1.50 | 2.25 | C |
| A983 | God Has a Long Face–Robert Wilder | .75 | 1.50 | 2.25 | |
| A984 | Ride with Me–Thomas B. Costain | .75 | 1.50 | 2.25 | A |
| A985 | His Eye Is on the Sparrow–Ethel Waters with Charles Samuels | .75 | 1.50 | 2.25 | B |
| A986 | Wyatt Earp, Frontier Marshal–Stuart N. Lake. Note: This alleged "true" biography contains controversial fictionalized stories presented as fact. | .75 | 1.50 | 2.25 | NF |
| A987 | Point of No Return–John P. Marquand | .75 | 1.50 | 2.25 | |
| 988 | Dead Man's Saddle–L.P. Holmes | .75 | 1.50 | 2.25 | W |
| 989 | Johnny Christmas–Forrester Blake | .75 | 1.50 | 2.25 | |
| 990 | Night of the Jabberwock–Fredric Brown | 7.50 | 15.00 | 22.50 | M |
| 991 | The Illustrated Man–Ray Bradbury | 3.00 | 6.00 | 9.00 | SF |
| 992 | Circus Doctor–J.Y. Henderson & Richard Taplinger | 1.00 | 2.00 | 3.00 | NF |
| 993 | The Gun–C.S. Forester | 1.00 | 2.00 | 3.00 | A |
| A994 | The Gentle Infidel–Lawrence Schoonover | .75 | 1.50 | 2.25 | A |
| A995 | The Witch Diggers–Jessamyn West | .75 | 1.50 | 2.25 | |
| 996 | The Sleeping Sphinx–John Dickson Carr | 1.50 | 3.00 | 4.50 | M |
| 997 | 12 Against the Law–Edward D. Radin | .75 | 1.50 | 2.25 | |
| 998 | Tomorrow's Another Day–W.R. Burnett | 2.50 | 5.00 | 7.50 | |
| A999 | Return to Paradise–James A. Michener | 1.50 | 3.00 | 4.50 | |
| A1000 | The Voice of Asia–James A. Michener | .75 | 1.50 | 2.25 | NF |
| 1001 | Stormy Range–Dwight Bennett | .75 | 1.50 | 2.25 | W |
| A1002 | Web of Destiny–Muriel Elwood | .75 | 1.50 | 2.25 | |
| A1003 | Far from Home–Richard Mason | .75 | 1.50 | 2.25 | |
| 1004 | High Prairie–E.E. Halleran | .75 | 1.50 | 2.25 | W |
| 1005 | Warbonnet Law–Frank O'Rourke | .75 | 1.50 | 2.25 | W |
| 1006 | Step Right Up!–Daniel P. Mannix | 1.50 | 3.00 | 4.50 | NF |
| 1007 | Castaway–James Gould Cozzens | .75 | 1.50 | 2.25 | |
| A1008 | Long Remember–MacKinlay Kantor | .75 | 1.50 | 2.25 | |
| A1009 | The Devil in Velvet–John Dickson Carr | 3.00 | 6.00 | 9.00 | M |
| 1010 | Laughter, Incorporated–Bennett Cerf | .75 | 1.50 | 2.25 | H |
| 1011 | Rifleman Dodd–C.S. Forester | 1.00 | 2.00 | 3.00 | A |
| 1012 | Murder on the West Bank–Elliot Paul | 1.50 | 3.00 | 4.50 | M |
| 1013 | The Clay Hand–Dorothy Salisbury Davis | .75 | 1.50 | 2.25 | M |
| 1014 | Alibi at Dusk–Ben Benson | .75 | 1.50 | 2.25 | M |

*Bantam 905, Bantam A912, Bantam A980.*

**BANTAM BOOKS, continued**

| No. | Title–Author | V/Good | Fine | N/Mint | |
|---|---|---|---|---|---|
| A1016 | The Judas Tree–Neil H. Swanson | .75 | 1.50 | 2.25 | |
| A1017 | Ann Carmeny–Hoffman Birney | .75 | 1.50 | 2.25 | |
| 1018 | Gun Law at Vermillion–Matt Stuart | .75 | 1.50 | 2.25 | W |
| 1019 | A Rough Shoot–Geoffrey Household | .75 | 1.50 | 2.25 | |
| 1020 | Theresa–Emile Zola | .75 | 1.50 | 2.25 | |
| F1021 | Soldier of Democracy–Kenneth S. Davis | .75 | 1.50 | 2.25 | |
| A1022 | Scaramouche–Rafael Sabatini | 1.25 | 2.50 | 3.75 | A |
| 1023 | Men Working–John Faulkner | 1.25 | 2.50 | 3.75 | |
| 1024 | The Survivors–Hammond Innes | 1.25 | 2.50 | 3.75 | |
| 1025 | Dark Madonna–Richard Summers | .75 | 1.50 | 2.25 | E |
| 1026 | Big Shot–Lawrence Treat | .75 | 1.50 | 2.25 | M |
| A1027 | High Towers–Thomas B. Costain | .75 | 1.50 | 2.25 | A |
| A1028 | Written on the Wind–Robert Wilder | .75 | 1.50 | 2.25 | |
| 1029 | Angel of Gaiety–Joseph Hitrec | .75 | 1.50 | 2.25 | |
| 1030 | The Frightened Dove–Peter Hardin | .75 | 1.50 | 2.25 | M |
| 1031 | West of Abilene–Vingie Roe | .75 | 1.50 | 2.25 | W |
| 1032 | The Second Confession–Rex Stout | 1.50 | 3.00 | 4.50 | M |
| A1033 | Inside U.S.A., Volume 1–John Gunther | .75 | 1.50 | 2.25 | NF |
| A1034 | Inside U.S.A., Volume 2–John Gunther | .75 | 1.50 | 2.25 | NF |
| A1035 | Live with Lightning–Mitchell Wilson | .75 | 1.50 | 2.25 | |
| A1036 | The Grand Portage–Walter O'Meara | .75 | 1.50 | 2.25 | |
| A1037 | Harper's Magazine Reader | .75 | 1.50 | 2.25 | |
| 1038 | Don't Touch Me–MacKinlay Kantor | .75 | 1.50 | 2.25 | E |
| 1039 | The Desert of Love–Francois Muriac | .75 | 1.50 | 2.25 | |
| 1040 | Death Has Many Doors–Fredric Brown | 6.00 | 12.00 | 18.00 | M |
| F1041 | The Silent Drum–Neil H. Swanson | .75 | 1.50 | 2.25 | |
| F1042 | The Stars Look Down–A.J. Cronin | .75 | 1.50 | 2.25 | |
| A1043 | Fighting Men of the West–Dane Coolidge | 1.50 | 3.00 | 4.50 | NF |
| A1044 | The Affairs of Flavie–Gabriel Chevallier | .75 | 1.50 | 2.25 | E |
| 1045 | The Grass Is Singing–Doris Lessing | 1.00 | 2.00 | 3.00 | |
| 1046 | The Farmers Hotel–John O'Hara | 1.00 | 2.00 | 3.00 | |
| 1047 | The End of My Life–Vance Bourjaily | .75 | 1.50 | 2.25 | E |
| 1048 | Summer Range–L.P. Holmes | .75 | 1.50 | 2.25 | W |
| 1049 | Black Sheep, Run–Bart Spicer | .75 | 1.50 | 2.25 | |
| A1050 | Grand Canary–A.J. Cronin | .75 | 1.50 | 2.25 | |
| A1051 | The Disenchanted–Budd Schulberg | .75 | 1.50 | 2.25 | |
| A1052 | The Last Englishman–Hebe Weenolsen | 1.25 | 2.50 | 3.75 | A |
| A1053 | No People like Show People–Maurice Zolotow | .75 | 1.50 | 2.25 | NF |
| 1054 | Cage of Darkness–Rene Masson | 1.00 | 2.00 | 3.00 | |
| 1055 | Pagoda–James Atlee Phillips | .75 | 1.50 | 2.25 | |
| 1056 | The Lonesome Quarter–Richard Wormser | .75 | 1.50 | 2.25 | W |
| 1057 | Cimarron Crossing–Michael Carder | .75 | 1.50 | 2.25 | W |
| 1058 | The Angry Mountain–Hammond Innes | .75 | 1.50 | 2.25 | |
| 1059 | The 31st of February–Julian Symons | .75 | 1.50 | 2.25 | M |
| A1060 | The Keys of the Kingdom–A.J. Cronin | .75 | 1.50 | 2.25 | |
| 1061 | Arizona–Clarence Budington Kelland | .75 | 1.50 | 2.25 | W |
| 1062 | The Tonto Kid–Henry Herbert Knibbs | 1.00 | 2.00 | 3.00 | W |
| 1063 | Ride the Man Down–Luke Short | 1.00 | 2.00 | 3.00 | W |
| 1064 | Trail Boss–Peter Dawson (Frank Gruber) | 1.25 | 2.50 | 3.75 | W |
| 1065 | Cannery Row–John Steinbeck | 1.25 | 2.50 | 3.75 | |
| 1066 | The Pastures of Heaven–John Steinbeck | 1.25 | 2.50 | 3.75 | |
| 1067 | Nevada–Zane Grey | .75 | 1.50 | 2.25 | W |
| 1068 | Valley of the Shadow–Charles M. Warren | .75 | 1.50 | 2.25 | |
| A1069 | Only Yesterday–Frederick Lewis Allen; 1953 | .75 | 1.50 | 2.25 | |
| 1070 | Beware the Pale Horse–Ben Benson | 1.00 | 2.00 | 3.00 | M |
| A1071 | Brave New World–Aldous Huxley | 3.50 | 7.00 | 10.50 | SF |
| A1072 | Nightrunners of Bengal–John Masters | .75 | 1.50 | 2.25 | |
| A1073 | An Unfound Door–Al Hine | .75 | 1.50 | 2.25 | |
| 1074 | Berenstain's Baby Book–Janice Berenstain & Stanley Berenstain | 1.00 | 2.00 | 3.00 | |
| 1075 | Play a Lone Hand–Luke Short | 1.00 | 2.00 | 3.00 | W |
| 1076 | Final Copy–Jay Barbette | .75 | 1.50 | 2.25 | M |
| 1077 | Space on My Hands–Fredric Brown | 3.50 | 7.00 | 10.50 | SF |
| 1078 | Hold Back the Night–Pat Frank | .75 | 1.50 | 2.25 | |
| 1079 | Is Another World Watching?–H.F. Heard | 2.50 | 5.00 | 7.50 | UF |
| 1080 | Single-handed–C.S. Forester | 1.00 | 2.00 | 3.00 | A |
| 1081 | Harbin's Ridge–Henry Giles | .75 | 1.50 | 2.25 | E |
| 1082 | Gunman Brand–Thomas Thompson | 1.00 | 2.00 | 3.00 | W |
| 1083 | A Gentle Murderer–Dorothy Salisbury Davis | .75 | 1.50 | 2.25 | M |
| A1084 | The Looking Glass–William March | .75 | 1.50 | 2.25 | E |
| A1085 | Storm Centre–Robert Standish | .75 | 1.50 | 2.25 | E |
| A1086 | Green Fire–Peter Rainier | 1.00 | 2.00 | 3.00 | |
| F1087 | So Little Time–John P. Marquand | .75 | 1.50 | 2.25 | |
| A1088 | Delilah–Marcus Goodrich | .75 | 1.50 | 2.25 | |
| A1089 | Coronado's Children–J. Frank Dobie | 2.00 | 4.00 | 6.00 | NF |
| A1090 | The Captive Witch–Dale Van Every | .75 | 1.50 | 2.25 | |
| A1091 | The Heart Is a Lonely Hunter–Carson McCullers | .75 | 1.50 | 2.25 | |
| 1092 | Parole Chief–David Dressler | .75 | 1.50 | 2.25 | |
| 1093 | The Day of the Locust–Nathanael West | .75 | 1.50 | 2.25 | |
| 1094 | A Drum Calls West–Bill Gulick | .75 | 1.50 | 2.25 | W |
| 1095 | The Smoky Trail–Matt Stuart | .75 | 1.50 | 2.25 | W |
| 1096 | Spin the Glass Web–Max Ehrlich | .75 | 1.50 | 2.25 | |
| A1097 | Come Fill the Cup–Harlan Ware | .75 | 1.50 | 2.25 | |
| A1098 | The Story of Ernie Pyle–Lee Miller | .75 | 1.50 | 2.25 | B |
| A1099 | Rome Haul–Walter D. Edmonds | .75 | 1.50 | 2.25 | |
| A1100 | Roger Sudden–Thomas H. Raddall | 1.25 | 2.50 | 3.75 | |
| 1101 | The Mountains Have No Shadow–Owen Cameron | .75 | 1.50 | 2.25 | |
| 1102 | Strange Courage–Evan Evans (Max Brand) | .75 | 1.50 | 2.25 | W |
| 1103 | Black Sage–L.P. Holmes | 1.25 | 2.50 | 3.75 | W |
| 1104 | Ambush–Luke Short | .75 | 1.50 | 2.25 | W |
| 1105 | Fiddlefoot–Luke Short | .75 | 1.50 | 2.25 | W |
| A1106 | Fancies and Goodnights–John Collier | 4.50 | 9.00 | 13.50 | SF |
| A1107 | Sunrise to Sunset–Samuel Hopkins Adams | .75 | 1.50 | 2.25 | A |
| 1108 | Full of Life–John Fante | .75 | 1.50 | 2.25 | |
| 1109 | Clara–Lonnie Coleman | .75 | 1.50 | 2.25 | |
| 1110 | Road Kid–Howard Pease | 1.25 | 2.50 | 3.75 | |
| 1111 | Brazos–Ross McLaury Taylor | .75 | 1.50 | 2.25 | W |
| 1112 | Badlands–Bennett Foster | .75 | 1.50 | 2.25 | W |
| 1113 | The Crimson Horseshoe–Peter Dawson (Frank Gruber) | 1.25 | 2.50 | 3.75 | W |
| 1114 | | | | | |
| 1115 | The Wild Bunch–Ernest Haycox | 1.00 | 2.00 | 3.00 | W |
| 1116 | Trigger Kid–Bennett Foster | .75 | 1.50 | 2.25 | W |
| 1117 | The Last Apaches–William Hopson | 1.00 | 2.00 | 3.00 | W |
| 1118 | Saturday Review Reader No. 2 | .75 | 1.50 | 2.25 | |
| 1119 | Below Suspicion–John Dickson Carr | 1.50 | 3.00 | 4.50 | M |
| 1120 | Gaptown Law–Louis Trimble | .75 | 1.50 | 2.25 | W |
| A1121 | The Golden Exile–Lawrence Schoonover | 1.50 | 3.00 | 4.50 | A |
| A1123 | Of Former Love–Emma Laird | .75 | 1.50 | 2.25 | E |
| 1124 | Little Men, Big World–W.R. Burnett | 2.50 | 5.00 | 7.50 | |
| 1125 | Air Bridge–Hammond Innes | .75 | 1.50 | 2.25 | |
| 1126 | The Long Green–Bart Spicer | .75 | 1.50 | 2.25 | |
| 1127 | Genghis Khan–Harold Lamb | 1.25 | 2.50 | 3.75 | B |
| 1128 | Thin Edge of Violence–William O'Farrell | .75 | 1.50 | 2.25 | |
| F1130 | Green Centuries–Caroline Gordon | .75 | 1.50 | 2.25 | |
| A1131 | The King's Cavalier–Samuel Shellabarger | 1.50 | 3.00 | 4.50 | A |
| 1132 | Rim of the Caprock–Noel M. Loomis | .75 | 1.50 | 2.25 | W |
| 1133 | The Far Cry–Fredric Brown | 7.50 | 15.00 | 22.50 | M |
| 1134 | The Fabulous Clipjoint–Fredric Brown | 2.50 | 5.00 | 7.50 | M |
| 1135 | Rock Bottom–Earl Conrad | .75 | 1.50 | 2.25 | |
| A1136 | Lament for Four Virgins–Lael Tucker | .75 | 1.50 | 2.25 | |
| A1137 | The Lute Player–Norah Lofts | .75 | 1.50 | 2.25 | |
| A1138 | Hill of the Hawk–Scott O'Dell | 1.50 | 3.00 | 4.50 | |
| A1139 | Melissa–Taylor Caldwell | .75 | 1.50 | 2.25 | |
| 1140 | Night Man–Lucille Fletcher & Allan Ullman | .75 | 1.50 | 2.25 | |
| 1141 | Lost Wolf River–Dwight Bennett | 1.00 | 2.00 | 3.00 | W |
| 1142 | Antic Hay–Aldous Huxley | 1.50 | 3.00 | 4.50 | |
| 1143 | Mountain Meadow–John Buchan | .75 | 1.50 | 2.25 | A |
| A1144 | Westward the River–Dale Van Every | 1.25 | 2.50 | 3.75 | |
| A1145 | The Great Rascal–Jay Monaghan | 1.50 | 3.00 | 4.50 | |
| A1146 | The Gallery–John Horne Burns | .75 | 1.50 | 2.25 | |
| 1147 | A Cry of Children–John Horne Burns | .75 | 1.50 | 2.25 | |
| 1148 | The Price of Salt–Claire Morgan | 1.00 | 2.00 | 3.00 | |
| 1149 | Gold under Skull Peak–Frank O'Rourke | .75 | 1.50 | 2.25 | |
| 1150 | The Night Watch–Thomas Walsh | .75 | 1.50 | 2.25 | |
| A1151 | Paradise–Esther Forbes | .75 | 1.50 | 2.25 | |
| F1152 | Model Railroading | 1.25 | 2.50 | 3.75 | NF |
| 1153 | A Worthy Man–Robert Standish | .75 | 1.50 | 2.25 | |
| 1154 | Man Drowning–Henry Kuttner | 5.00 | 10.00 | 15.00 | |
| A1156 | Reflections in a Golden Eye–Carson McCullers | .75 | 1.50 | 2.25 | |
| A1157 | Empress of Byzantium–Helen A. Mahler | 1.50 | 3.00 | 4.50 | A |
| A1158 | Argosy Book of Adventure Stories–Rogers Terrill | 1.50 | 3.00 | 4.50 | A |

## BANTAM BOOKS, *continued*

| | | V/Good | Fine | N/Mint | |
|---|---|---|---|---|---|
| A1159 | The Forbidden Ground–Neil H. Swanson | .75 | 1.50 | 2.25 | |
| A1160 | Juan Belmonte: Killer of Bulls–Juan Belmonte with Garcia & Manuel Chaves Nogales (ed. Leslie Charteris); 1953; aka The Making of a Bull Fighter | 1.50 | 3.00 | 4.50 | B |
| 1161 | Missing–Egon Hostovsky | .75 | 1.50 | 2.25 | |
| A1162 | And Ride a Tiger–Robert Wilder | .75 | 1.50 | 2.25 | |
| F1163 | What to Wear Where | 1.00 | 2.00 | 3.00 | NF |
| 1164 | Short Grass–Thomas W. Blackburn | 1.25 | 2.50 | 3.75 | W |
| F1165 | Flee the Angry Strangers–George Mandel | .75 | 1.50 | 2.25 | |
| 1166 | Laughter, Incorporated–Bennett Cerf | .75 | 1.50 | 2.25 | H |
| 1167 | Southwest–John Houghton Allen | .75 | 1.50 | 2.25 | |
| 1168 | No Survivors–Will Henry | 1.25 | 2.50 | 3.75 | W |
| 1169 | The Paradise below the Stairs–Andre Brincourt | .75 | 1.50 | 2.25 | |
| 1170 | The General–C.S. Forester | 1.00 | 2.00 | 3.00 | A |
| 1171 | 50 Great Artists–Bernard Myers | 1.25 | 2.50 | 3.75 | NF |
| 1172 | Bright Feather–Robert Wilder | 1.25 | 2.50 | 3.75 | |
| 1173 | In the Best Families–Rex Stout | 2.00 | 4.00 | 6.00 | M |
| 1174 | My Brother, My Enemy–Mitchell Wilson | .75 | 1.50 | 2.25 | |
| 1175 | Warwhoop–MacKinlay Kantor | 1.25 | 2.50 | 3.75 | |
| 1176 | We All Killed Grandma–Fredric Brown | 7.50 | 15.00 | 22.50 | M |
| 1177 | Bird of Prey–Victor Canning | .75 | 1.50 | 2.25 | |
| 1178 | The Quick Brown Fox–Lawrence Schoonover | 1.50 | 3.00 | 4.50 | |
| 1179 | Four Steps to the Wall–Jon Edgar Webb | .75 | 1.50 | 2.25 | |
| 1180 | Gunfighters Pay–William Hopson | 1.00 | 2.00 | 3.00 | W |
| 1181 | Wait for Tomorrow–Robert Wilder | .75 | 1.50 | 2.25 | E |
| 1182 | The Bizarre Sisters–Jay Walz & Audrey Walz | 1.00 | 2.00 | 3.00 | |
| 1183 | The Weight of the Cross–Robert O. Bowen | 1.25 | 2.50 | 3.75 | |
| 1184 | Cup of Gold–John Steinbeck | 1.25 | 2.50 | 3.75 | |
| 1185 | Dance to the Piper–Agnes deMille; 1954 | .75 | 1.50 | 2.25 | |
| 1186 | The Moneyman–Thomas B. Costain | .75 | 1.50 | 2.25 | |
| 1187 | The Deceivers–John Masters | 1.25 | 2.50 | 3.75 | |
| 1188 | Dead Pigeon–Robert P. Hanson | .75 | 1.50 | 2.25 | M |
| 1189 | Gunflame–John S. Daniels | .75 | 1.50 | 2.25 | W |
| 1190 | The Wonderful Country–Tom Lea | .75 | 1.50 | 2.25 | |
| 1191 | Son of Haman–Louis Cochran | .75 | 1.50 | 2.25 | |
| 1192 | The Other Room–Worth Tuttle Hedden | .75 | 1.50 | 2.25 | E |
| 1193 | Here Comes Joe Mungin–Chalmers S. Murray | .75 | 1.50 | 2.25 | |
| 1194 | Ask the Dust–John Fante | .75 | 1.50 | 2.25 | |
| 1195 | Catch a Tiger–Owen Cameron | .75 | 1.50 | 2.25 | |
| 1196 | The Ship–C.S. Forester | 1.00 | 2.00 | 3.00 | A |
| 1197 | Dead on Arrival–George Bagby | .75 | 1.50 | 2.25 | M |
| 1198 | Broken Lance–Frank Gruber | 1.25 | 2.50 | 3.75 | W |
| 1200 | Melville Goodwin, USA–John P. Marquand | .75 | 1.50 | 2.25 | |
| 1201 | Manhattan–Seymour Krim | .75 | 1.50 | 2.25 | |
| 1203 | The Kings of the Road–Ken W. Purdy | 3.00 | 6.00 | 9.00 | NF |
| 1204 | The Hate Merchant–Niven Busch | .75 | 1.50 | 2.25 | |
| 1205 | The Man from Brazil–E.B. Garside | .75 | 1.50 | 2.25 | |
| 1206 | Royal Gorge–Peter Dawson (Frank Gruber) | 1.25 | 2.50 | 3.75 | W |
| 1207 | The Burning Court–John Dickson Carr | 2.50 | 5.00 | 7.50 | M |
| 1208 | The Sea of Grass–Conrad Richter | .75 | 1.50 | 2.25 | A |
| 1209 | Gal Young 'Un–Marjorie Kinnan Rawlings | 1.00 | 2.00 | 3.00 | |
| 1210 | Our American Government–Wright Patman | .75 | 1.50 | 2.25 | NF |
| 1211 | The Wild Ohio–Bart Spicer | .75 | 1.50 | 2.25 | |
| 1212 | The Mustangs–J. Frank Dobie | 1.25 | 2.50 | 3.75 | NF |
| 1213 | Some Faces in the Crowd–Budd Schulberg | .75 | 1.50 | 2.25 | |
| 1214 | Someday, Boy–Sam Ross | .75 | 1.50 | 2.25 | |
| 1215 | The Deep End–Fredric Brown | 6.00 | 12.00 | 18.00 | M |
| 1216 | The Dead Ringer–Fredric Brown | 5.00 | 10.00 | 15.00 | M |
| 1217 | The Power and the Glory–Graham Greene | .75 | 1.50 | 2.25 | |
| 1219 | Hiroshima–John Hersey | .75 | 1.50 | 2.25 | |
| 1220 | Picaroon–Ernest Dudley | 1.00 | 2.00 | 3.00 | |
| 1221 | Troubling of a Star–Walt Sheldon | 1.25 | 2.50 | 3.75 | |
| 1225 | Swamp Water–Vereen Bell | .75 | 1.50 | 2.25 | |
| 1226 | Blood Will Tell–George Bagby | .75 | 1.50 | 2.25 | M |
| A1227 | A Treasury of Folk Songs–Sylvia Kolb & John Kolb | 1.25 | 2.50 | 3.75 | NF |
| A1228 | The Great Gatsby–F. Scott Fitzgerald | 1.25 | 2.50 | 3.75 | |
| A1229 | The God That Failed–Richard Crossman | .75 | 1.50 | 2.25 | |
| A1230 | Cyrano de Bergerac–Edmond Rostand | 1.25 | 2.50 | 3.75 | A |
| A1231 | Good for a Laugh–Bennett Cerf | .75 | 1.50 | 2.25 | H |
| 1232 | A Man Gets Around–John McNulty | .75 | 1.50 | 2.25 | |
| F1233 | Eyeless in Gaza–Aldous Huxley | 1.50 | 3.00 | 4.50 | |
| A1234 | Suleiman the Magnificent–Harold Lamb | 1.25 | 2.50 | 3.75 | A |
| A1235 | Seven–Carson McCullers | .75 | 1.50 | 2.25 | |
| A1236 | Wait, Son, October Is Near–John Bell Clayton | .75 | 1.50 | 2.25 | |
| 1237 | The Daughter of Bugle Ann–MacKinlay Kantor | .75 | 1.50 | 2.25 | |
| 1238 | Wicked Water–MacKinlay Kantor | .75 | 1.50 | 2.25 | |
| A1239 | The Restless Border–Dick Pearce | .75 | 1.50 | 2.25 | W |
| A1240 | A Farewell to Arms–Ernest Hemingway | 1.50 | 3.00 | 4.50 | |
| A1241 | The Golden Apples of the Sun–Ray Bradbury | 2.00 | 4.00 | 6.00 | SF |
| A1242 | The Saturday Review Reader No. 3 | .75 | 1.50 | 2.25 | |
| 1243 | Sword and Candle–Sidney Herschel Small | 1.25 | 2.50 | 3.75 | A |
| A1244 | Restless House–Emile Zola | .75 | 1.50 | 2.25 | |
| A1245 | A Good Man–Jefferson Young | .75 | 1.50 | 2.25 | |
| A1246 | Billy the Kid–Edwin Corle | 1.25 | 2.50 | 3.75 | |
| 1247 | Man Alone–William Doyle & Scott O'Dell | .75 | 1.50 | 2.25 | |
| A1249 | The Sun Also Rises–Ernest Hemingway | 1.50 | 3.00 | 4.50 | |
| A1250 | The Trembling Earth–Dale Van Every | .75 | 1.50 | 2.25 | |
| 1251 | Line to Tomorrow–Lewis Padgett | 2.00 | 4.00 | 6.00 | SF |
| 1252 | Murder by the Book–Rex Stout | 1.50 | 3.00 | 4.50 | M |
| 1253 | What Mad Universe–Fredric Brown | 2.50 | 5.00 | 7.50 | SF |
| A1254 | The Boyds of Black River–Walter D. Edmonds | 1.25 | 2.50 | 3.75 | |
| A1255 | The Woods Colt–Thames Williamson | .75 | 1.50 | 2.25 | |
| A1257 | Sea Struck–Bennett Stanley | .75 | 1.50 | 2.25 | |
| A1258 | Autumn Thunder–Robert Wilder | .75 | 1.50 | 2.25 | |
| A1260 | Crome Yellow–Aldous Huxley | 1.25 | 2.50 | 3.75 | |

*Bantam A1160, Bantam 1167, Bantam 1176.*

*Bantam 1203, Bantam 1295, Bantam A1443.*

BANTAM BOOKS, *continued*

| | | V/Good | Fine | N/Mint | |
|---|---|---|---|---|---|
| 1261 | The Martian Chronicles–Ray Bradbury | 1.50 | 3.00 | 4.50 | SF |
| A1262 | Utopia 14–Kurt Vonnegut, Jr | 3.50 | 7.00 | 10.50 | SF |
| 1264 | The Light in the Forest–Conrad Richter | .75 | 1.50 | 2.25 | |
| 1266 | Cannery Row–John Steinbeck | 1.25 | 2.50 | 3.75 | |
| F1267 | East of Eden–John Steinbeck | 3.00 | 6.00 | 9.00 | |
| A1268 | The Chinese Room–Vivian Connell | .75 | 1.50 | 2.25 | E |
| 1269 | The Bridges of Toko-ri–James A. Michener | 1.50 | 3.00 | 4.50 | C |
| 1271 | The Venus Death–Ben Benson | 1.25 | 2.50 | 3.75 | M |
| 1272 | Crazy Weather–Charles L. McNichols | .75 | 1.50 | 2.25 | |
| 1273 | Case File: FBI–The Gordons | .75 | 1.50 | 2.25 | M |
| F1274 | Best of the Bedside Esquire–Arnold Gingrich | 1.25 | 2.50 | 3.75 | |
| A1275 | In the Years of Our Lord–Manuel Komroff | .75 | 1.50 | 2.25 | |
| A1276 | The Streak–Paul Darcy Boles | .75 | 1.50 | 2.25 | |
| 1277 | The Stagline Feud–Peter Dawson (Frank Gruber) | 1.25 | 2.50 | 3.75 | W |
| 1278 | Costigan's Needle–Jerry Sohl | 1.25 | 2.50 | 3.75 | SF |
| F1279 | Battle Cry–Leon Uris | 1.00 | 2.00 | 3.00 | C |
| A1281 | White Hunter, Black Heart–Peter Viertel | 1.00 | 2.00 | 3.00 | |
| 1282 | The Illustrated Man–Ray Bradbury | 1.50 | 3.00 | 4.50 | SF |
| 1283 | Sailor Town–Paul Fox | .75 | 1.50 | 2.25 | |
| F1284 | Lord Vanity–Samuel Shellabarger; 1955 | 1.50 | 3.00 | 4.50 | A |
| 1285 | The Lights in the Sky Are Stars–Fredric Brown | 2.50 | 5.00 | 7.50 | SF |
| 1286 | Shakedown–Richard Ellington | .75 | 1.50 | 2.25 | M |
| 1287 | Bitter Sage–Frank Gruber; c-Gross | 1.25 | 2.50 | 3.75 | W |
| 1288 | The Cautious Amorist–Norman Lindsay | .75 | 1.50 | 2.25 | |
| A1289 | The Undaunted–John Harris | .75 | 1.50 | 2.25 | |
| A1290 | The Kill–Emile Zola | .75 | 1.50 | 2.25 | |
| A1291 | Tamerlane–Harold Lamb | 1.25 | 2.50 | 3.75 | A |
| A1292 | War with the Newts–Karel Capek | 1.50 | 3.00 | 4.50 | SF |
| 1293 | And the Wind Blows Free–Luke Short | 1.00 | 2.00 | 3.00 | W |
| 1294 | Third from the Sun–Richard Matheson | 5.00 | 10.00 | 15.00 | SF |
| 1295 | The Name Is Archer–John Ross MacDonald; 1st ed. 1955 | 6.00 | 12.00 | 18.00 | M |
| A1296 | How to Buy Stocks–Louis Engel | .50 | 1.00 | 1.50 | NF |
| 1297 | Shane–Jack Schaefer | 1.25 | 2.50 | 3.75 | W |
| 1298 | Nevada–Zane Grey | .75 | 1.50 | 2.25 | W |
| F1299 | The Thorndike-Barnhart Handy Pocket Dictionary–Clarence Barnhart | 1.25 | 2.50 | 3.75 | NF |
| A1300 | Never Love a Stranger–Harold Robbins | 1.00 | 2.00 | 3.00 | |
| F1301 | The Grapes of Wrath–John Steinbeck | 1.25 | 2.50 | 3.75 | |
| F1302 | Fifty Great Short Stories–Milton Crane | .75 | 1.50 | 2.25 | |
| A1303 | Twenty Grand Short Stories–Ernestine Taggard | .75 | 1.50 | 2.25 | |
| A1304 | Far from Customary Skies–Warren Eyster | .75 | 1.50 | 2.25 | |
| A1305 | Mr. Midshipman Hornblower–C.S. Forester | 1.00 | 2.00 | 3.00 | A |
| A1306 | The End of the Affair–Graham Greene | .75 | 1.50 | 2.25 | |
| A1307 | Man without a Star–Dee Linford | 1.25 | 2.50 | 3.75 | |
| 1308 | Drop Dead–George Bagby | .75 | 1.50 | 2.25 | M |
| 1309 | 1001 Valuable Things You Can Get Free–Mort Weisinger | .75 | 1.50 | 2.25 | NF |
| 1310 | More Adventures in Time and Space–Raymond J. Healy & J. Francis McComas | .75 | 1.50 | 2.25 | SF |
| 1311 | The Natural Way to Better Golf–Jack Burke | .75 | 1.50 | 2.25 | NF |
| 1312 | The Screaming Mimi–Fredric Brown | 2.50 | 5.00 | 7.50 | M |
| 1313 | High Gear–Evan Jones | .75 | 1.50 | 2.25 | |
| A1314 | To the Indies–C.S. Forester | 1.00 | 2.00 | 3.00 | A |
| 1315 | Murder Points a Finger–David Alexander | .75 | 1.50 | 2.25 | M |
| 1316 | This Gun for Hire–Graham Greene | 1.00 | 2.00 | 3.00 | |
| 1317 | The Syndic–C.M. Kornbluth | 1.25 | 2.50 | 3.75 | SF |
| A1318 | Sayonara–James A. Michener | 1.50 | 3.00 | 4.50 | |
| A1319 | The Enchanted Cup–Dorothy James Roberts | .75 | 1.50 | 2.25 | |
| A1320 | Peace of Mind–Joshua Loth Liebman | .75 | 1.50 | 2.25 | |
| F1321 | Beyond This Place–A.J. Cronin | .75 | 1.50 | 2.25 | |
| A1322 | Death of a Salesman–Arthur Miller | 1.25 | 2.50 | 3.75 | |
| 1323 | Target in Taffeta–Ben Benson | 1.25 | 2.50 | 3.75 | M |
| A1324 | To a God Unknown–John Steinbeck | 1.50 | 3.00 | 4.50 | |
| 1325 | The Nine Wrong Answers–John Dickson Carr | 1.25 | 2.50 | 3.75 | |
| 1326 | Prisoner's Base–Rex Stout | 1.50 | 3.00 | 4.50 | |
| 1327 | The Schirmer Inheritance–Eric Ambler; mentioned in Parade of Pleasure, pg. 174 | 1.50 | 3.00 | 4.50 | M |
| 1328 | Frontiers in Space–Everett F. Bleiler & T.E. Dikty | | | | SF |
| A1329 | Of Mice and Men–John Steinbeck | 2.00 | 4.00 | 6.00 | |
| 1330 | But That's Unprintable–Dave Breger | .75 | 1.50 | 2.25 | |
| A1331 | Captain Lightfoot–W.R. Burnett | 1.50 | 3.00 | 4.50 | A |
| A1332 | The Time of the Fire–Marc Brandel | 1.25 | 2.50 | 3.75 | |
| 1333 | Orient Express–Graham Greene | .75 | 1.50 | 2.25 | M |
| 1334 | Strange As It Seems–Elsie Hix | .75 | 1.50 | 2.25 | |
| A1335 | The Lotus and the Wind–John Masters | 1.25 | 2.50 | 3.75 | |
| A1336 | The Kentuckians–Janice Holt Giles | 1.25 | 2.50 | 3.75 | |
| F1337 | The Cobweb–William Gibson | .75 | 1.50 | 2.25 | |
| F1338 | All the King's Men–Robert Penn Warren | 1.25 | 2.50 | 3.75 | |
| A1339 | The Moon and Sixpence–W. Somerset Maugham | 1.25 | 2.50 | 3.75 | |
| A1340 | Don't Tread on Me–Horace V. Bird & Walter Karig | 1.00 | 2.00 | 3.00 | |
| A1342 | Laughter, Incorporated–Bennett Cerf | .75 | 1.50 | 2.25 | H |
| 1343 | The Man from Tomorrow–Wilson Tucker | 1.50 | 3.00 | 4.50 | SF |
| 1344 | High Dive–Frank O'Rourke | 1.00 | 2.00 | 3.00 | |
| 1345 | The Far Shore–Gordon Webber | .75 | 1.50 | 2.25 | |
| 1346 | Cattle, Guns and Men–Luke Short | 1.50 | 3.00 | 4.50 | W |
| 1347 | Johnny Vengeance–Frank Gruber | 1.25 | 2.50 | 3.75 | W |
| 1348 | F.B.I. Story–The Gordons | .75 | 1.50 | 2.25 | M |
| 1349 | Death's Long Shadow–Jay Barbette | .75 | 1.50 | 2.25 | M |
| F1350 | The Fires of Spring–James A. Michener | 1.00 | 2.00 | 3.00 | |
| 1351 | God and My Country–MacKinlay Kantor | .75 | 1.50 | 2.25 | |
| 1352 | Science Fiction Thinking Machines–ed. Groff Conklin | 1.50 | 3.00 | 4.50 | SF |
| A1353 | Alexander of Macedon–Harold Lamb | 1.25 | 2.50 | 3.75 | A |
| A1355 | View from the Air–Hugh Fosburgh | .75 | 1.50 | 2.25 | |
| 1356 | Station West–Luke Short | .75 | 1.50 | 2.25 | W |
| A1357 | The Informer–Liam O'Flaherty | .75 | 1.50 | 2.25 | |
| A1358 | Women and Children First–Paul Steiner | .75 | 1.50 | 2.25 | H |
| 1359 | The Girl in the Cage–Ben Benson | 1.25 | 2.50 | 3.75 | M |
| 1360 | Find a Victim–John Ross MacDonald | 1.50 | 3.00 | 4.50 | |
| 1361 | The Big Outfit–Peter Dawson (Frank Gruber) | 1.25 | 2.50 | 3.75 | W |
| 1362 | Deep Space–Eric Frank Russell | 1.25 | 2.50 | 3.75 | SF |
| 1363 | The Killers–Peter Dawson (Frank Gruber) | 2.00 | 4.00 | 6.00 | W |
| 1364 | Honey, I'm Home–Marione R. Nickles | .75 | 1.50 | 2.25 | |
| F1365 | The Complete Book of First Aid–John Henderson | .75 | 1.50 | 2.25 | NF |
| F1366 | The Spider King–Lawrence Schoonover | 1.25 | 2.50 | 3.75 | A |
| F1367 | New Campus Writing–Nolan Miller | .75 | 1.50 | 2.25 | |
| F1368 | The Second Happiest Day–John Philips | .75 | 1.50 | 2.25 | |
| A1369 | Brave New World–Aldous Huxley | 1.25 | 2.50 | 3.75 | SF |
| A1370 | Port Royal–Noel B. Gerson | 1.25 | 2.50 | 3.75 | A |
| 1371 | The Seven Year Itch–George Axelrod; movie tie-in | 2.50 | 5.00 | 7.50 | |
| 1372 | Tears for the Bride–Robert Martin | .75 | 1.50 | 2.25 | |
| 1373 | Hardcase–Luke Short | 1.25 | 2.50 | 3.75 | W |
| A1374 | The Case for the UFO–M.K. Jessup | 1.00 | 2.00 | 3.00 | UF |
| A1375 | They Went Wrong–Croswell Bowen | .75 | 1.50 | 2.25 | |
| 1376 | Giveaway–Steve Fisher | 1.50 | 3.00 | 4.50 | |
| 1377 | Scandals of Clochemerle–Gabriel Chevallier | .75 | 1.50 | 2.25 | |
| A1378 | The Art of Italian Cooking–Maria Lo Pinto & Milo Miloradovich | 1.00 | 2.00 | 3.00 | NF |
| F1379 | The Time of the Gringo–Elliott Arnold | 1.25 | 2.50 | 3.75 | |
| F1381 | Bhowani Junction–John Masters | 1.00 | 2.00 | 3.00 | |
| A1382 | Genghis Khan–Harold Lamb | 1.00 | 2.00 | 3.00 | A |
| 1383 | The Sands of Karakorum–James Ramsey Ullman | .75 | 1.50 | 2.25 | |
| 1384 | Delta Deputy–L.P. Holmes | 1.00 | 2.00 | 3.00 | W |
| 1385 | Winter Ambush–E.E. Halleran | 1.00 | 2.00 | 3.00 | W |
| 1386 | The Black Mountain–Rex Stout | 1.00 | 2.00 | 3.00 | M |
| 1387 | The Golden Spiders–Rex Stout | 1.00 | 2.00 | 3.00 | M |
| 1388 | Three Men Out–Rex Stout | 1.00 | 2.00 | 3.00 | M |
| 1389 | The Howls of Ivy–Henry Boltinoff | .60 | 1.20 | 1.80 | H |
| 1390 | Guns of the Timberlands–Louis L'Amour | 2.00 | 4.00 | 6.00 | W |
| A1391 | Hunter–J.A. Hunter | .75 | 1.50 | 2.25 | A |

| | V/Good | Fine | N/Mint |
|---|---|---|---|

BANTAM BOOKS, *continued*

| No. | Title | V/Good | Fine | N/Mint | |
|---|---|---|---|---|---|
| A1392 | The Do-It-Yourself Gadget Hunter's Guide–William Manners | .75 | 1.50 | 2.25 | NF |
| F1393 | The Alaskan–Robert Lund | 1.00 | 2.00 | 3.00 | |
| 1394 | Trouble in Triplicate–Rex Stout | 1.00 | 2.00 | 3.00 | M |
| 1395 | Too Many Women–Rex Stout | 1.00 | 2.00 | 3.00 | M |
| 1396 | Dead Man Pass–Peter Dawson (Frank Gruber) | 1.25 | 2.50 | 3.75 | W |
| 1397 | The Widow and the Web–Robert Martin | .75 | 1.50 | 2.25 | |
| 1398 | Pagan in Paradise–Susanne McConnaughey | .75 | 1.50 | 2.25 | |
| A1399 | Stranger in Paris–W. Somerset Maugham | .75 | 1.50 | 2.25 | |
| 1400 | Time: X–Wilson Tucker | 1.00 | 2.00 | 3.00 | SF |
| A1401 | Frontier: 150 Years of the West–Luke Short | 1.50 | 3.00 | 4.50 | NF |
| 1402 | King's Rebel–James D. Horan | 1.25 | 2.50 | 3.75 | |
| A1403 | Best Loved Books of the Twentieth Century–Vincent Starrett | 1.50 | 3.00 | 4.50 | NF |
| 1404 | Hazel–Ted Key | 1.50 | 3.00 | 4.50 | H |
| A1405 | Hotel Tallegrand–Paul Hyde Donner | .75 | 1.50 | 2.25 | |
| 1406 | The Red Pony–John Steinbeck | 1.00 | 2.00 | 3.00 | |
| 1407 | The Steel Web–Thomas Thompson; 1956 | .75 | 1.50 | 2.25 | W |
| 1408 | Terror on Broadway–David Alexander | .75 | 1.50 | 2.25 | M |
| 1409 | The Taming of Carney Wilde–Bart Spicer | .75 | 1.50 | 2.25 | |
| A1410 | The Courts of the Lion–Robert W. Krepps | .75 | 1.50 | 2.25 | A |
| A1411 | Who Rides with Wyatt–Will Henry | 1.25 | 2.50 | 3.75 | W |
| A1412 | Sweet Thursday–John Steinbeck | 1.25 | 2.50 | 3.75 | |
| A1413 | The Fifty-Minute Hour–Robert Lindner | .75 | 1.50 | 2.25 | |
| A1414 | 3 Weeks to a Better Memory–Brendan Byrne | .75 | 1.50 | 2.25 | NF |
| F1415 | Away All Boats–Kenneth Dodson | .75 | 1.50 | 2.25 | C |
| F1416 | Coromandel!–John Masters | 1.00 | 2.00 | 3.00 | |
| F1417 | Three Complete Western Novels–Luke Short | 2.00 | 4.00 | 6.00 | W |
| A1418 | The Complete Book of Roses–Dorothy H. Jenkins | .75 | 1.50 | 2.25 | NF |
| 1419 | Deep Hills–Matt Stuart | .75 | 1.50 | 2.25 | W |
| 1420 | Dead Fall–Dale Wilmer | .75 | 1.50 | 2.25 | |
| 1421 | The Burning Fuse–Ben Benson | 1.00 | 2.00 | 3.00 | M |
| 1422 | Hope of Heaven–John O'Hara | .75 | 1.50 | 2.25 | |
| 1423 | Star Shine–Fredric Brown | 2.50 | 5.00 | 7.50 | SF |
| A1424 | The Heart of the Matter–Graham Greene | .75 | 1.50 | 2.25 | |
| A1425 | The Long Swords–Edward Franklin | 1.00 | 2.00 | 3.00 | A |
| A1426 | Last Frontier–Richard Emery Roberts | 1.00 | 2.00 | 3.00 | |
| A1427 | The Round-the-World Cookbook–Myra Waldo | 1.00 | 2.00 | 3.00 | NF |
| F1428 | The Day Lincoln Was Shot–Jim Bishop. Note: "Special Tab Club Edition" exists of this title | .75 | 1.50 | 2.25 | |
| F1429 | The Citadel–A.J. Cronin | .75 | 1.50 | 2.25 | |
| F1430 | Model Railroading | .75 | 1.50 | 2.25 | NF |
| F1431 | The Dream Merchants–Harold Robbins | .75 | 1.50 | 2.25 | |
| 1432 | Woman Doctor–Hannah Lees | .75 | 1.50 | 2.25 | R |
| 1433 | Graduate Nurse–Lucy Agnes Hancock | .75 | 1.50 | 2.25 | R |
| 1434 | Ward Nurse–Marguerite Mooers Marshall | .75 | 1.50 | 2.25 | R |
| 1435 | Haywire Town–Robert McCaig | .75 | 1.50 | 2.25 | W |
| 1436 | His Name Was Death–Fredric Brown | 4.00 | 8.00 | 12.00 | M |
| 1437 | Street Rod–Henry Gregor Felsen | 2.00 | 4.00 | 6.00 | |
| 1438 | Violent Saturday–William L. Heath | 1.00 | 2.00 | 3.00 | |
| A1439 | The Four Lives of Mundy Tolliver–Ben Lucien Burman | .75 | 1.50 | 2.25 | |
| A1440 | Rap Sheet–My Forty Years outside the Law–Blackie Audett | 1.00 | 2.00 | 3.00 | |
| F1441 | The Golden Argosy–Van H. Cartmell & Charles Grayson | 1.00 | 2.00 | 3.00 | |
| F1442 | The Inspirational Reader–William Oliver Stevens | 1.00 | 2.00 | 3.00 | |
| A1443 | Forbidden Planet–W.J. Stuart; movie tie-in | 7.50 | 15.00 | 22.50 | SF |
| F1444 | For My Great Folly–Thomas B. Costain | .75 | 1.50 | 2.25 | A |
| F1445 | Life on the Mississippi–Mark Twain | 1.00 | 2.00 | 3.00 | |
| 1446 | High Vermilion–Luke Short | .75 | 1.50 | 2.25 | W |
| 1447 | The Third Bullet–John Dickson Carr | .75 | 1.50 | 2.25 | M |
| 1448 | Million Dollar Murder–Thomas Black | .75 | 1.50 | 2.25 | |
| A1450 | Ben-Hur–Lew Wallace | 1.00 | 2.00 | 3.00 | |
| 1451 | Crossfire–Louis Trimble | .75 | 1.50 | 2.25 | W |
| A1452 | Man against Nature–Charles Neider | .75 | 1.50 | 2.25 | |
| F1453 | Sincerely, Willis Wayde–John P. Marquand | .75 | 1.50 | 2.25 | |
| F1454 | Point of No Return–John P. Marquand | .75 | 1.50 | 2.25 | |
| 1455 | The Case of the Talking Bug–The Gordons | .75 | 1.50 | 2.25 | M |
| F1456 | The Burnished Blade–Lawrence Schoonover | .75 | 1.50 | 2.25 | A |
| 1457 | Picnic–William Inge; movie tie-in | 1.50 | 3.00 | 4.50 | |
| A1458 | Cyrano de Bergerac–Edmund Rostand | 1.00 | 2.00 | 3.00 | A |
| F1459 | The Sixth of June–Lionel Shapiro | .75 | 1.50 | 2.25 | |
| 1460 | Why the Long Puss?–Reamer Keller | .75 | 1.50 | 2.25 | |
| 1461 | Cry Viva!–William Hopson | .75 | 1.50 | 2.25 | W |
| A1462 | So Help Me God–Felix Jackson | .75 | 1.50 | 2.25 | |
| 1463 | The Harder They Fall–Budd Schulberg | .75 | 1.50 | 2.25 | |
| A1464 | A Wonderful World for Children–Peter Cardozo | .75 | 1.50 | 2.25 | NF |
| A1465 | Tiger of the Snows–Tenzing Norgay & James Ramsey Ullman | .75 | 1.50 | 2.25 | |
| 1466 | Rimrock–Luke Short | .75 | 1.50 | 2.25 | W |
| 1467 | The Renegade–John Prescott | .75 | 1.50 | 2.25 | W |
| 1468 | The Silver Cobweb–Ben Benson | 1.00 | 2.00 | 3.00 | M |
| 1469 | Trouble Comes Double–Robert P. Hansen | .75 | 1.50 | 2.25 | M |
| A1470 | Timeliner–Charles Eric Maine | 2.00 | 4.00 | 6.00 | SF |
| 1471 | My Flag Is Down–James Maresca | .50 | 1.00 | 1.50 | |
| A1472 | Captain Cut-Throat–John Dickson Carr | 1.00 | 2.00 | 3.00 | M |
| F1473 | The Wine of Youth–Robert Wilder | .50 | 1.00 | 1.50 | |
| F1474 | The Keys of the Kingdom–A.J. Cronin | .50 | 1.00 | 1.50 | |
| 1475 | Campaign Train–The Gordons | .75 | 1.50 | 2.25 | M |
| 1476 | Some Die Slow–William E. Heber | .50 | 1.00 | 1.50 | |
| 1477 | Here's Hazel–Ted Key | 1.50 | 3.00 | 4.50 | H |
| A1478 | The Pastures of Heaven–John Steinbeck | .75 | 1.50 | 2.25 | |
| 1479 | With Naked Foot–Emily Hahn | .50 | 1.00 | 1.50 | |
| A1480 | The Shipwrecked–Graham Greene | .75 | 1.50 | 2.25 | |
| A1481 | The Raiders–Will Henry | .75 | 1.50 | 2.25 | W |
| A1482 | The Fourth Horseman–Will Henry | .75 | 1.50 | 2.25 | |
| A1483 | Pillars of the Sky–Will Henry | .75 | 1.50 | 2.25 | |
| A1484 | The Great Short Stories of John O'Hara | .50 | 1.00 | 1.50 | |
| 1485 | Vengeance Valley–Luke Short | .75 | 1.50 | 2.25 | W |
| 1486 | The Burning Hills–Louis L'Amour | 2.00 | 4.00 | 6.00 | W |
| 1487 | A Cry in the Night–Whit Masterson | .75 | 1.50 | 2.25 | M |
| 1488 | The Limping Goose–Frank Gruber | 1.50 | 3.00 | 4.50 | |
| 1489 | Up at the Villa–W. Somerset Maugham | .50 | 1.00 | 1.50 | |
| A1490 | The Genius and the Goddess–Aldous Huxley | .75 | 1.50 | 2.25 | |
| A1491 | Guns of Chickamauga–Richard O'Connor | .75 | 1.50 | 2.25 | C |
| A1492 | Not This August–C.M. Kornbluth | 2.00 | 4.00 | 6.00 | SF |
| A1493 | Analyze Yourself–William Gerhardi & Leopold Loewenstein | 3.00 | 6.00 | 9.00 | NF |
| F1494 | Lost Pony Tracks–Ross Santee | 1.00 | 2.00 | 3.00 | W |
| F1495 | Apache Land–Ross Santee | 1.00 | 2.00 | 3.00 | W |
| 1496 | Nurse Landon's Challenge–Adelaide Humphries | .50 | 1.00 | 1.50 | R |
| S1497 | War and Peace–Leo Tolstoy | 1.00 | 2.00 | 3.00 | C |
| 1498 | Doctor Jane–Adeline McElfresh | .50 | 1.00 | 1.50 | R |
| A1499 | Dining Out in Any Language–Myra Waldo | .50 | 1.00 | 1.50 | NF |
| F1500 | Blood Brother–Elliott Arnold | 1.00 | 2.00 | 3.00 | W |
| 1502 | Follow the New Grass–Cliff Farrell | .75 | 1.50 | 2.25 | |
| 1503 | The Problem of the Wire Cage–John Dickson Carr | .75 | 1.50 | 2.25 | M |
| 1504 | The Man Who Could Not Shudder–John Dickson Carr | .75 | 1.50 | 2.25 | M |
| 1505 | The Problem of the Green Capsule–John Dickson Carr | .75 | 1.50 | 2.25 | M |
| 1506 | Hammer Me Home–Richard R. Werry | .75 | 1.50 | 2.25 | |
| 1507 | Reincarnation–The Whole Startling Story–R. DeWitt Miller | .75 | 1.50 | 2.25 | NF |
| A1508 | The Green Cockade–Frederic F. Van de Water | .75 | 1.50 | 2.25 | A |
| A1509 | "Captains Courageous"–Rudyard Kipling | .75 | 1.50 | 2.25 | A |
| F1510 | Waterfront–Budd Schulberg | .75 | 1.50 | 2.25 | |
| 1511 | Hold Back the Night–Pat Frank | .75 | 1.50 | 2.25 | |
| 1513 | Mama's Bank Account–Kathryn Forbes | .75 | 1.50 | 2.25 | |
| 1514 | Somewhere They Die–L.P. Holmes | .75 | 1.50 | 2.25 | W |
| 1515 | The Buscadero–Noel M. Loomis | .75 | 1.50 | 2.25 | W |
| 1516 | Campbell's Kingdom–Hammond Innes | .75 | 1.50 | 2.25 | |
| 1517 | Satan's Rock–Carl D. Burton | .75 | 1.50 | 2.25 | |
| 1518 | Bus Stop–William Inge; movie tie-in | 3.00 | 6.00 | 9.00 | |

Bantam 1486, Bantam F1597, Bantam 1697.

| | | V/Good | Fine | N/Mint | |
|---|---|---|---|---|---|
| | **BANTAM BOOKS,** *continued* | | | | |
| A1519 | The Circus of Dr. Lao and Other Improbable Stories–Ray Bradbury | 3.00 | 6.00 | 9.00 | SF |
| F1520 | The Count of Monte Cristo–Alexandre Dumas | 1.00 | 2.00 | 3.00 | A |
| 1523 | Sex Rears Its Lovely Head–Jerome Beatty, Jr | .75 | 1.50 | 2.25 | |
| A1525 | Royalist–Edward Grierson | .75 | 1.50 | 2.25 | |
| F1526 | The Hunchback of Notre Dame–Victor Hugo | 1.00 | 2.00 | 3.00 | A |
| 1527 | Bitter Sage–Frank Gruber. Note: 1956 3rd printing is movie tie-in for Tension at Table Rock; c-Gross | 1.00 | 2.00 | 3.00 | |
| A1528 | Common Sense Book of Puppy and Dog Care–Harry Miller | 1.00 | 2.00 | 3.00 | NF |
| 1529 | Hiroshima–John Hershey | .75 | 1.50 | 2.25 | |
| 1531 | Sunset Graze–Luke Short | .75 | 1.50 | 2.25 | W |
| 1532 | Gunman's Chance–Luke Short | .75 | 1.50 | 2.25 | W |
| 1533 | Coroner Creek–Luke Short | .75 | 1.50 | 2.25 | W |
| 1534 | Paint the Town Black–David Alexander | .75 | 1.50 | 2.25 | M |
| 1535 | The Pale Door–Lee Roberts | .75 | 1.50 | 2.25 | |
| F1536 | The Green Years–A.J. Cronin | .50 | 1.00 | 1.50 | |
| F1537 | Shannon's Way–A.J. Cronin | .50 | 1.00 | 1.50 | |
| 1538 | Rag Top–Henry Gregor Felsen | .75 | 1.50 | 2.25 | |
| 1539 | A Night to Remember–Walter Lord | .75 | 1.50 | 2.25 | NF |
| A1540 | Written on the Wind–Robert Wilder | .50 | 1.00 | 1.50 | |
| 1541 | The Age of the Tail–H. Allen Smith | .50 | 1.00 | 1.50 | H |
| 1542 | Beast in View–Margaret Millar | .75 | 1.50 | 2.25 | M |
| 1543 | Dead, She Was Beautiful–Whit Masterson | .75 | 1.50 | 2.25 | M |
| 1544 | The Pearl–John Steinbeck | .75 | 1.50 | 2.25 | |
| A1545 | Omar Khayyam–Harold Lamb | 1.00 | 2.00 | 3.00 | A |
| A1546 | Martians, Go Home–Fredric Brown | 2.00 | 4.00 | 6.00 | SF |
| 1547 | Adobe Walls–W.R. Burnett | 2.50 | 5.00 | 7.50 | W |
| 1549 | Latigo–Frank O'Rourke | .75 | 1.50 | 2.25 | W |
| A1550 | 19 Tales of Terror–Whit Burnett & Hallie Burnett | .75 | 1.50 | 2.25 | HO |
| 1551 | The Boss of Broken Spur–Nick Sumner | .75 | 1.50 | 2.25 | W |
| 1552 | Broken Shield–Ben Benson | 1.00 | 2.00 | 3.00 | M |
| A1553 | Forbidden Area–Pat Frank | .75 | 1.50 | 2.25 | SF |
| F1554 | Ten North Frederick–John O'Hara | .50 | 1.00 | 1.50 | |
| A1555 | The Wayward Bus–John Steinbeck | 1.25 | 2.50 | 3.75 | |
| F1556 | A New Southern Harvest–Albert Erskine & Robert Penn Warren | 1.50 | 3.00 | 4.50 | |
| A1557 | The Siege–Jay Williams | .75 | 1.50 | 2.25 | A |
| F1558 | Cartoon Treasury–Lucy Black & Pyke Johnson, Jr | 1.50 | 3.00 | 4.50 | H |
| 1559 | The Rainmaker–N. Richard Nash; movie tie-in | 1.50 | 3.00 | 4.50 | |
| A1560 | Antic Hay–Aldous Huxley | .75 | 1.50 | 2.25 | |
| 1561 | Tomboy–Hal Ellson | 2.00 | 4.00 | 6.00 | JD |
| 1562 | Nurse Fairchild's Decision–Zillah K. MacDonald | .50 | 1.00 | 1.50 | R |
| 1564 | Dead Freight for Piute–Luke Short | .75 | 1.50 | 2.25 | W |
| 1565 | The Wench Is Dead–Fredric Brown | 4.00 | 8.00 | 12.00 | M |
| 1566 | The Fabulous Clipjoint–Fredric Brown | 2.00 | 4.00 | 6.00 | M |
| 1567 | Death Has Many Doors–Fredric Brown | 3.50 | 7.00 | 10.50 | M |
| F1568 | Island in the Sun–Alec Waugh | .75 | 1.50 | 2.25 | |
| A1569 | Dragoon–Nelson & Shirley Wolford | .75 | 1.50 | 2.25 | |
| A1570 | Your Own Beloved Sons–Thomas Anderson | .50 | 1.00 | 1.50 | |
| A1571 | The Shores of Space–Richard Matheson | 4.00 | 8.00 | 12.00 | |

| | | V/Good | Fine | N/Mint | |
|---|---|---|---|---|---|
| F1572 | Cass Timberlane–Sinclair Lewis | .75 | 1.50 | 2.25 | |
| 1574 | Full of Life–John Fante | .50 | 1.00 | 1.50 | |
| 1575 | Nurse with Wings–Marguerite Mooers Marshall | .50 | 1.00 | 1.50 | R |
| 1576 | Tejas Country–Frank Miller | .75 | 1.50 | 2.25 | |
| 1577 | The Tough Die Hard–Robert Martin | .75 | 1.50 | 2.25 | |
| A1578 | The Year of the Tempest–Peter Matthiessen | .75 | 1.50 | 2.25 | |
| F1579 | Bitter Creek–James Boyd | .75 | 1.50 | 2.25 | |
| F1580 | Native Stone–Edwin Gilbert | .50 | 1.00 | 1.50 | |
| S1581 | The Boston Cooking School Cook Book–Fannie Farmer | .75 | 1.50 | 2.25 | NF |
| A1582 | Fear Strikes Out–Al Hirshberg & Jim Piersall | .75 | 1.50 | 2.25 | B |
| F1583 | A Rage to Live–John O'Hara | .75 | 1.50 | 2.25 | |
| 1584 | Captain McRae–William Herman | .75 | 1.50 | 2.25 | |
| 1585 | Dr. Woodward's Ambition–Elizabeth Seifert | .50 | 1.00 | 1.50 | E |
| A1586 | Seventeen–Booth Tarkington | .75 | 1.50 | 2.25 | H |
| A1587 | The Good Shepherd–C.S. Forester | 1.00 | 2.00 | 3.00 | |
| 1588 | The Feud at Single Shot–Luke Short | .75 | 1.50 | 2.25 | W |
| 1589 | Live Bait for Murder–William E. Herber | .75 | 1.50 | 2.25 | |
| 1590 | The Sound of White Water–Hugh Fosburgh | .75 | 1.50 | 2.25 | |
| F1591 | A Crossbowman's Story–George Millar | .75 | 1.50 | 2.25 | A |
| 1592 | Stop Dieting! Start Losing!–Ruth West | .50 | 1.00 | 1.50 | NF |
| A1593 | The Power–Frank M. Robinson | .75 | 1.50 | 2.25 | SF |
| 1594 | The Farmers Hotel–John O'Hara | .50 | 1.00 | 1.50 | |
| 1595 | The Bells of St. Mary's–George Victor Martin | .75 | 1.50 | 2.25 | |
| 1596 | The Baron of Boot Hill–Brad Ward | .75 | 1.50 | 2.25 | W |
| F1597 | Lord Jim–Joseph Conrad | 1.00 | 2.00 | 3.00 | A |
| A1598 | The Big Land–Frank Gruber | 1.25 | 2.50 | 3.75 | W |
| F1599 | The Cross of Iron–Willi Heinrich | .75 | 1.50 | 2.25 | C |
| A1600 | The Package Deal–W.T. Ballard | 1.50 | 3.00 | 4.50 | |
| 1601 | Shoot a Sitting Duck–David Alexander | .75 | 1.50 | 2.25 | M |
| 1602 | Square in the Middle–William Campbell Gault | 2.00 | 4.00 | 6.00 | M |
| A1603 | West of the River–Charlton Laird | .75 | 1.50 | 2.25 | |
| F1604 | Harry of Monmouth–A.M. Maughan | .75 | 1.50 | 2.25 | A |
| 1606 | 1001 Valuable Things You Can Get Free, No. 2–Mort Weisinger | .50 | 1.00 | 1.50 | NF |
| 1607 | Nora Meade, M.D.–Elizabeth Weslery | .50 | 1.00 | 1.50 | |
| A1608 | The Pass–Thomas Savage | .75 | 1.50 | 2.25 | |
| S1609 | A Treasury of Short Stories–Rudyard Kipling | .75 | 1.50 | 2.25 | |
| 1610 | The Gun–C.S. Forester | .75 | 1.50 | 2.25 | A |
| A1611 | Randall and the River of Time–C.S. Forester | .75 | 1.50 | 2.25 | A |
| 1612 | Starlight Basin–Giff Cheshire | .75 | 1.50 | 2.25 | W |
| 1613 | The Barbarous Coast–John Ross MacDonald | 1.50 | 3.00 | 4.50 | |
| 1614 | Visiting Nurse–Jeanne Judson | .50 | 1.00 | 1.50 | R |
| A1615 | Science Fiction Carnival–Fredric Brown & Mack Reynolds | 2.50 | 5.00 | 7.50 | SF |
| F1616 | Amy Vanderbilt's Everyday Etiquette–Amy Vanderbilt | .50 | 1.00 | 1.50 | NF |
| A1617 | What Makes Sammy Run?–Budd Schulberg | .75 | 1.50 | 2.25 | |
| 1618 | For All Your Life–Emilie Loring | .50 | 1.00 | 1.50 | |
| A1619 | The Ship–C.S. Forester | .50 | 1.00 | 1.50 | A |
| F1620 | Only Yesterday–Frederick Lewis Allen | .50 | 1.00 | 1.50 | |
| A1621 | The Chinese Room–Vivian Connell | .50 | 1.00 | 1.50 | E |
| F1622 | Eyeless in Gaza–Aldous Huxley | .50 | 1.00 | 1.50 | |
| 1623 | Mating Manual–Reamer Keller | .50 | 1.00 | 1.50 | |
| F1624 | A Thing of Beauty–A.J. Cronin | .50 | 1.00 | 1.50 | |
| A1625 | Arouse and Beware–MacKinlay Kantor | .50 | 1.00 | 1.50 | C |
| A1626 | Beau James–Gene Fowler | .75 | 1.50 | 2.25 | |
| A1627 | Long Storm–Ernest Haycox | .75 | 1.50 | 2.25 | W |
| 1628 | The Wild Bunch–Ernest Haycox | .75 | 1.50 | 2.25 | W |
| A1630 | Chocolates for Breakfast–Pamela Moore | .50 | 1.00 | 1.50 | |
| A1631 | Triple Jeopardy–Rex Stout | .75 | 1.50 | 2.25 | M |
| A1632 | Before Midnight–Rex Stout | .75 | 1.50 | 2.25 | M |
| A1633 | Three Witnesses–Rex Stout | .75 | 1.50 | 2.25 | M |
| A1634 | The Golden Princess–Alexander Baron | .75 | 1.50 | 2.25 | A |
| A1635 | A Face in the Crowd–Bud Schulberg | .50 | 1.00 | 1.50 | |
| A1636 | Goodbye, Mr. Chips–James Hilton | .75 | 1.50 | 2.25 | |
| F1637 | God Has a Long Face–Robert Wilder | .50 | 1.00 | 1.50 | |
| 1638 | Day of the Ram–William Campbell Gault | 2.00 | 4.00 | 6.00 | M |
| 1639 | Return of the Outlaw–Michael Carder | .75 | 1.50 | 2.25 | W |
| 1640 | A Family Party–John O'Hara | .50 | 1.00 | 1.50 | |

**BANTAM BOOKS,** *continued*

| No. | Title | V/Good | Fine | N/Mint | |
|---|---|---|---|---|---|
| A1641 | Sayonara–James A. Michener; movie tie-in | .75 | 1.50 | 2.25 | |
| 1642 | Man on the Buckskin–Peter Dawson (Frank Gruber) | 1.25 | 2.50 | 3.75 | W |
| F1643 | Jonathan Eagle–Alexander Laing | .75 | 1.50 | 2.25 | |
| 1645 | Her Soul to Keep–Marguerite Mooers Marshall | .50 | 1.00 | 1.50 | R |
| A1646 | Pebble in the Sky–Isaac Asimov | .75 | 1.50 | 2.25 | SF |
| F1647 | The Joker Is Wild–Art Cohn | .50 | 1.00 | 1.50 | |
| F1648 | Drums Along the Mohawk–Walter D. Edmonds | .75 | 1.50 | 2.25 | A |
| F1649 | New Campus Writing, No. 2–Nolan Miller | .75 | 1.50 | 2.25 | |
| A1650 | The Bridge at Andau–James A. Michener | .75 | 1.50 | 2.25 | C |
| A1651 | How to Buy Stocks–Louis Engel | .50 | 1.00 | 1.50 | NF |
| 1652 | Raiders of the Rimrock–Luke Short | .75 | 1.50 | 2.25 | W |
| A1653 | Will Success Spoil Rock Hunter?–George Axelrod; movie tie-in | 2.50 | 5.00 | 7.50 | |
| 1654 | Wagon Train–John Prescott | 1.00 | 2.00 | 3.00 | W |
| 1655 | Die, Little Goose–David Alexander | .75 | 1.50 | 2.25 | M |
| A1656 | The Man Who Paid His Way–Walt Sheldon | .50 | 1.00 | 1.50 | |
| A1657 | The Scimitar–Samuel Edwards | .75 | 1.50 | 2.25 | A |
| A1658 | 100 Stories of Business Success | .50 | 1.00 | 1.50 | |
| F1659 | The Last Hurrah–Edwin O'Connor | .75 | 1.50 | 2.25 | |
| F1660 | The Strange Woman–Ben Ames Williams | .75 | 1.50 | 2.25 | |
| F1661 | Indian-Fighting Army–Fairfax Downey | .75 | 1.50 | 2.25 | NF |
| F1662 | The Old Santa Fe Trail–Stanley Vestal | 1.50 | 3.00 | 4.50 | NF |
| S1663 | Model Railroading | .75 | 1.50 | 2.25 | NF |
| A1664 | Flamingo Road–Robert Wilder | .75 | 1.50 | 2.25 | |
| F1665 | A Parent's Guide to Children's Illnesses–John Henderson | .50 | 1.00 | 1.50 | NF |
| 1666 | Bugles West–Frank Gruber | 1.00 | 2.00 | 3.00 | W |
| 1667 | Carol Trent, Air Stewardess–Jeanne Judson | .50 | 1.00 | 1.50 | R |
| 1668 | The Whip–Luke Short | .75 | 1.50 | 2.25 | W |
| A1669 | The Quiet American–Graham Greene | .75 | 1.50 | 2.25 | |
| A1670 | The Frozen Jungle–Lawrence Earl | .75 | 1.50 | 2.25 | |
| A1671 | State of Siege–Eric Ambler | .75 | 1.50 | 2.25 | |
| A1672 | Pilgrimage to Earth–Robert Sheckley | 1.25 | 2.50 | 3.75 | SF |
| F1673 | The Queen's Cross–Lawrence Schoonover | .75 | 1.50 | 2.25 | A |
| F1674 | Return to Paradise–James A. Michener | .75 | 1.50 | 2.25 | |
| F1675 | H.M. Pulham, Esq.–John P. Marquand | .50 | 1.00 | 1.50 | |
| A1676 | Wild Animals I Have Known–Ernest Thompson Seton | .75 | 1.50 | 2.25 | NF |
| A1677 | The Bridge over the River Kwai–Pierre Boulle | 1.00 | 2.00 | 3.00 | C |
| F1678 | The Hunchback of Notre Dame–Victor Hugo | .75 | 1.50 | 2.25 | HO |
| 1679 | Pal Joey–John O'Hara; movie tie-in | 1.50 | 3.00 | 4.50 | |
| 1680 | Colt's Law–Luke Short | .75 | 1.50 | 2.25 | W |
| 1681 | Silver Canyon–Louis L'Amour | 2.00 | 4.00 | 6.00 | W |
| 1682 | Patrick Butler for the Defense–John Dickson Carr | .75 | 1.50 | 2.25 | M |
| 1683 | Till Death Do Us Part–John Dickson Carr | .75 | 1.50 | 2.25 | M |
| 1684 | He Who Whispers–John Dickson Carr | .75 | 1.50 | 2.25 | M |
| A1685 | Wagons to Tucson–Ed Newsom | .75 | 1.50 | 2.25 | W |
| F1687 | Dodge City: Queen of Cowtowns–Stanley Vestal | 1.50 | 3.00 | 4.50 | NF |
| F1688 | The Art of Mixing Drinks–Frederic A. Birmingham | .50 | 1.00 | 1.50 | |
| A1689 | Porgy–Du Bose Heyward | .75 | 1.50 | 2.25 | |
| A1690 | Stopover: Tokyo–John P. Marquand | .75 | 1.50 | 2.25 | |
| A1691 | Thank You, Mr. Moto–John P. Marquand | .75 | 1.50 | 2.25 | M |
| S1692 | 50 Great Artists–Bernard Myers | .75 | 1.50 | 2.25 | NF |
| A1693 | Death of a Man–Lael Tucker Wertenbaker | .75 | 1.50 | 2.25 | |
| 1694 | My Man Godfrey–Eric Hatch | .50 | 1.00 | 1.50 | E |
| 1695 | Trail Boss–Peter Dawson (Frank Gruber) | 1.00 | 2.00 | 3.00 | W |
| 1696 | Gun Smoke Showdown–Matt Stuart | .75 | 1.50 | 2.25 | W |
| 1697 | The Secret World of Roy Williams–Roy Williams | 2.50 | 5.00 | 7.50 | H |
| A1698 | The Ninth Hour–Ben Benson | 1.00 | 2.00 | 3.00 | M |
| A1699 | Touch of Evil–Whit Masterson | .75 | 1.50 | 2.25 | M |
| A1700 | The Hunters–James Salter | .75 | 1.50 | 2.25 | |
| A1701 | Rogue in Space–Fredric Brown | 2.50 | 5.00 | 7.50 | SF |
| F1702 | The Earth Is the Lord's–Taylor Caldwell | .75 | 1.50 | 2.25 | A |
| F1703 | Fancies and Goodnights–John Collier | 1.25 | 2.50 | 3.75 | SF |
| A1704 | The Day of the Locust–Nathanael West | .75 | 1.50 | 2.25 | |
| F1705 | The Fires of Spring–James A. Michener | .75 | 1.50 | 2.25 | |
| A1706 | Knock and Wait Awhile–William Rawle Weeks; 1958 | .75 | 1.50 | 2.25 | |
| A1707 | The Big War–Anton Myrer | .75 | 1.50 | 2.25 | C |
| A1708 | The Heller–William E. Henning | .75 | 1.50 | 2.25 | |
| 1709 | Outlaw's Code–Evan Evans (Max Brand) | .75 | 1.50 | 2.25 | W |
| 1710 | Ambush–Luke Short | .75 | 1.50 | 2.25 | W |
| 1711 | Special Nurse–Margaret Howe | .50 | 1.00 | 1.50 | R |
| 1712 | The Lenient Beast–Fredric Brown | 4.00 | 8.00 | 12.00 | M |
| A1713 | Sitka–Louis L'Amour | 2.00 | 4.00 | 6.00 | W |
| F1714 | Bugles and a Tiger–John Masters | .75 | 1.50 | 2.25 | |
| F1715 | Day of Infamy–Walter Lord | .75 | 1.50 | 2.25 | NF |
| A1717 | Nevada–Zane Grey | .75 | 1.50 | 2.25 | W |
| A1718 | The Last of the Plainsmen–Zane Grey | .75 | 1.50 | 2.25 | W |
| A1719 | The Spanish Gardener–A.J. Cronin | .50 | 1.00 | 1.50 | |
| F1720 | Tolbecken–Samuel Shellabarger | .75 | 1.50 | 2.25 | |
| A1721 | The Big Nickelodeon–Maritta Wolff | .75 | 1.50 | 2.25 | |
| F1722 | The Great World and Timothy Colt–Louis Auchincloss | .50 | 1.00 | 1.50 | |
| F1723 | Rachel Cade–Charles Mercer | .50 | 1.00 | 1.50 | |
| A1724 | Captain Ironhand–Rosamond Marshall | .75 | 1.50 | 2.25 | A |
| 1725 | Red River–Borden Chase | 1.00 | 2.00 | 3.00 | W |
| 1726 | Tales of Wells Fargo–Frank Gruber; TV tie-in | 1.50 | 3.00 | 4.50 | W |
| 1727 | Halo in Brass–John Evans | 1.50 | 3.00 | 4.50 | M |
| 1728 | Halo in Blood–John Evans | 1.50 | 3.00 | 4.50 | M |
| 1729 | Halo for Satan–John Evans | 1.50 | 3.00 | 4.50 | M |
| A1730 | Reprieve–John Resko | .75 | 1.50 | 2.25 | |
| A1731 | The Naked Sun–Isaac Asimov | 1.00 | 2.00 | 3.00 | SF |
| A1732 | The Life of the Party–Bennett Cerf | .50 | 1.00 | 1.50 | H |
| S1734 | The Red and the Black–Stendahl | .75 | 1.50 | 2.25 | |
| F1735 | Crime and Punishment–Fyodor Dostoyevsky | .75 | 1.50 | 2.25 | |
| 1736 | The Murder of Whistler's Brother–David Alexander | .75 | 1.50 | 2.25 | M |
| 1737 | The Light in the Forest–Conrad Richter | .75 | 1.50 | 2.25 | A |
| F1738 | Lancet–Garet Rogers | .50 | 1.00 | 1.50 | |
| A1739 | An End to Dying–Sam Astrachan | .75 | 1.50 | 2.25 | |
| F1740 | Say, Darling–Richard Bissell | .50 | 1.00 | 1.50 | |
| 1741 | Peace Marshal–Frank Gruber | 1.00 | 2.00 | 3.00 | W |
| 1742 | Lonesome River–Frank Gruber | 1.00 | 2.00 | 3.00 | W |
| 1743 | Fighting Man–Frank Gruber | 1.00 | 2.00 | 3.00 | W |
| F1744 | Our Valiant Few–F. Van Wyck Mason | .50 | 1.00 | 1.50 | |
| A1746 | Miracle Gardening–Samm Sinclair Baker | .50 | 1.00 | 1.50 | NF |
| F1747 | The Bantam Book of Correct Letter Writing–Lilian E. Watson | .50 | 1.00 | 1.50 | NF |
| A1748 | The Lives of a Bengal Lancer–Francis Yeats-Brown | .75 | 1.50 | 2.25 | A |
| F1749 | Cowhand: The Story of a Working Cowboy–Fred Gipson | 1.00 | 2.00 | 3.00 | NF |
| 1751 | Nancy Ross, Private Secretary–Jeanne Judson | .50 | 1.00 | 1.50 | R |
| A1752 | Never Love a Stranger–Harold Robbins | .50 | 1.00 | 1.50 | |
| A1753 | The Short Reign of Pippin IV–John Steinbeck | 2.50 | 5.00 | 7.50 | |
| A1754 | Cimarron–Edna Ferber | 1.00 | 2.00 | 3.00 | W |
| 1755 | Fiddlefoot–Luke Short | .75 | 1.50 | 2.25 | W |
| 1756 | Mr. Taxicab–James Maresca | .50 | 1.00 | 1.50 | |
| 1757 | The Screaming Mimi–Fredric Brown; movie tie-in | 2.50 | 5.00 | 7.50 | M |
| 1758 | Riddle of a Lady–Anthony Gilbert | .75 | 1.50 | 2.25 | M |
| A1759 | Yonder–Charles Beaumont | 2.50 | 5.00 | 7.50 | Sf |
| A1760 | The Invisible Curtain–Joseph Anthony | .50 | 1.00 | 1.50 | SF |
| F1761 | The Member of the Wedding–Carson McCullers | .50 | 1.00 | 1.50 | |
| F1762 | The Heart Is a Lonely Hunter–Carson McCullers | .50 | 1.00 | 1.50 | |
| F1763 | Reflections in a Golden Eye–Carson McCullers | .50 | 1.00 | 1.50 | |
| F1764 | Ballad of the Sad Cafe–Carson McCullers | 1.00 | 2.00 | 3.00 | |
| A1765 | Satellite!–William Beller & Erik Bergaust | .75 | 1.50 | 2.25 | NF |
| A1766 | Satellite E One–Jeffrey Lloyd Castle | .75 | 1.50 | 2.25 | SF |

**BANTAM BOOKS,** *continued*

| | | V/Good | Fine | N/Mint | |
|---|---|---|---|---|---|
| F1767 | Silver Spoon–Edwin Gilbert | .50 | 1.00 | 1.50 | |
| A1768 | Thieves' Market–A.I. Bezzerides | .50 | 1.00 | 1.50 | |
| 1769 | The Land Grabbers–John S. Daniels | .75 | 1.50 | 2.25 | W |
| A1770 | Rescue!–Elliott Arnold | .75 | 1.50 | 2.25 | |
| 1771 | Sorry, Wrong Number–Lucille Fletcher & Allan Ullman | .75 | 1.50 | 2.25 | |
| A1772 | Epitaph for a Spy–Eric Ambler | .75 | 1.50 | 2.25 | |
| A1773 | The Confidential Agent–Graham Greene | .75 | 1.50 | 2.25 | |
| A1774 | The Tyrant of Bagdad–Glenn Pierce | .75 | 1.50 | 2.25 | A |
| F1775 | The Art of Barbecue and Outdoor Cooking | .75 | 1.50 | 2.25 | NF |
| 1776 | Calling Doctor Jane–Adeline McElfresh | .50 | 1.00 | 1.50 | R |
| F1777 | South Wind–Norman Douglas | .50 | 1.00 | 1.50 | A |
| F1778 | The Mustangs–J. Frank Dobie | 1.00 | 2.00 | 3.00 | W |
| A1779 | The Wind Cannot Read–Richard Mason | .75 | 1.50 | 2.25 | |
| 1780 | Teacher's Pet–Michael Kanin & Fay Kanin | 1.00 | 2.00 | 3.00 | |
| A1781 | Life at Happy Knoll–John P. Marquand | .50 | 1.00 | 1.50 | |
| 1782 | The Big Frame–The Gordons | .75 | 1.50 | 2.25 | M |
| F1783 | Alabama Empire–Welbaurn Kelley | .75 | 1.50 | 2.25 | |
| A1784 | The Teen-age Diet Book–Ruth West | .75 | 1.50 | 2.25 | NF |
| A1785 | They Fought for the Sky–Quentin Reynolds | .75 | 1.50 | 2.25 | C |
| A1786 | Time in Advance–William Tenn | 1.00 | 2.00 | 3.00 | SF |
| 1787 | What, Then, Is Love–Emilie Loring | .50 | 1.00 | 1.50 | R |
| F1788 | Folk Songs of the Caribbean–James Morse | 1.00 | 2.00 | 3.00 | NF |
| F1789 | Three Plays–Thornton Wilder | .75 | 1.50 | 2.25 | |
| A1790 | A Wonderful World for Children, 2nd Revised Edition–Peter Cardozo | .50 | 1.00 | 1.50 | NF |
| F1791 | Rally Round the Flag, Boys!–Max Shulman | .50 | 1.00 | 1.50 | H |
| A1792 | The Lady–Conrad Richter | .50 | 1.00 | 1.50 | |
| A1793 | Ape and Essence–Aldous Huxley | .75 | 1.50 | 2.25 | |
| 1794 | The Lawbringers–William Porter | .75 | 1.50 | 2.25 | |
| A1795 | Might As Well Be Dead–Rex Stout | .75 | 1.50 | 2.25 | M |
| A1796 | Three for the Chair–Rex Stout | .75 | 1.50 | 2.25 | M |
| A1797 | The Silent Speaker–Rex Stout | .75 | 1.50 | 2.25 | M |
| A1798 | Sierra Baron–Thomas W. Blackburn | .75 | 1.50 | 2.25 | W |
| 1799 | Eve Cameron, M.D.–Ann Rush | .50 | 1.00 | 1.50 | R |
| A1800 | The Inn of the Sixth Happiness–Alan Burgess; movie tie-in | .75 | 1.50 | 2.25 | |
| A1801 | Getting Along in French–John Fisher & Mario Pei | .75 | 1.50 | 2.25 | NF |
| A1802 | Getting Along in Italian–Mario Pei | .75 | 1.50 | 2.25 | NF |
| F1803 | Typee–Herman Melville | 1.00 | 2.00 | 3.00 | A |
| F1804 | Tales of Fair and Gallant Ladies–Abbe de Brantome | .75 | 1.50 | 2.25 | |
| F1805 | Far, Far the Mountain Peak–John Masters | .75 | 1.50 | 2.25 | |
| 1806 | Gidget–Frederick Kohner; movie tie-in | .75 | 1.50 | 2.25 | R |
| F1807 | Home before Dark–Eileen Bassing | .50 | 1.00 | 1.50 | |
| A1808 | Wilderness Passage–Forrester Blake | .75 | 1.50 | 2.25 | |
| A1809 | Johnny Christmas–Forrester Blake | .75 | 1.50 | 2.25 | |
| 1810 | Think Fast, Mr. Moto–John P. Marquand | .75 | 1.50 | 2.25 | M |
| A1811 | Lieutenant Hornblower–C.S. Forester | .75 | 1.50 | 2.25 | A |
| A1812 | Honeymoon in Hell–Fredric Brown | 2.50 | 5.00 | 7.50 | SF |
| 1813 | If You Like Hazel–Ted Key | 1.50 | 3.00 | 4.50 | H |
| F1814 | The New Art of Selling–Elmer G. Leterman | .50 | 1.00 | 1.50 | NF |
| A1815 | Mr. Midshipman Hornblower–C.S. Forester | 1.00 | 2.00 | 3.00 | A |
| A1816 | Beat to Quarters–C.S. Forester | .75 | 1.50 | 2.25 | A |
| F1817 | The Philadelphian–Richard Powell | .50 | 1.00 | 1.50 | |
| F1818 | The Drummond Tradition–Charles Mercer | .50 | 1.00 | 1.50 | |
| A1819 | Underdog–W.R. Burnett | 2.00 | 4.00 | 6.00 | |
| A1820 | Great Circle–Robert Carse | .75 | 1.50 | 2.25 | |
| 1821 | Play a Lone Hand–Luke Short | .75 | 1.50 | 2.25 | W |
| 1822 | The Plunders–L.P. Holmes | .75 | 1.50 | 2.25 | W |
| 1823 | The Stag Party–William Krasner | .75 | 1.50 | 2.25 | |
| A1824 | Echo of a Bomb–Mark Derby | .75 | 1.50 | 2.25 | |
| A1825 | Station in Space–James E. Gunn | 1.00 | 2.00 | 3.00 | SF |
| A1826 | Helmet for My Pillow–Robert Leckie | .50 | 1.00 | 1.50 | |
| A1827 | The Art of French Cooking–Fernande Silve Garvin | .75 | 1.50 | 2.25 | NF |
| A1828 | Harry Black–David Walker | .75 | 1.50 | 2.25 | |
| A1831 | The Price of Salt–Claire Morgan | .75 | 1.50 | 2.25 | |
| F1832 | Patterns–Rod Serling | 1.00 | 2.00 | 3.00 | |
| F1833 | The Wapshot Chronicle–John Cheever | .75 | 1.50 | 2.25 | |

| | | V/Good | Fine | N/Mint | |
|---|---|---|---|---|---|
| A1834 | The Temple of Gold–William Goldman | .75 | 1.50 | 2.25 | |
| A1835 | The Killing Ground–Elleston Trevor | .50 | 1.00 | 1.50 | |
| A1836 | Tubie's Monument–Peter Keveson | .50 | 1.00 | 1.50 | |
| 1837 | Outlaw Valley–Evan Evans (Max Brand) | .75 | 1.50 | 2.25 | W |
| 1838 | The Trail from Texas–Dale Homer | .75 | 1.50 | 2.25 | W |
| 1839 | Blue City–John Ross MacDonald | 1.50 | 3.00 | 4.50 | |
| 1840 | The Dark Window–Thomas Walsh | .50 | 1.00 | 1.50 | |
| 1841 | A Nurse for Galleon Key–Ethel Hamill | .50 | 1.00 | 1.50 | R |
| A1842 | Bell, Book and Candle–John van Druten; movie tie-in | .50 | 1.00 | 1.50 | |
| S1843 | One Basket–Edna Ferber | .75 | 1.50 | 2.25 | |
| F1844 | Rascals in Paradise–James A. Michener & A. Grove Day | .75 | 1.50 | 2.25 | |
| A1845 | The Blue Chips–Jay Deiss | .50 | 1.00 | 1.50 | |
| A1846 | The Spiral Road–Jan de Hartog | .75 | 1.50 | 2.25 | |
| A1847 | Fire, Burn!–John Dickson Carr | .75 | 1.50 | 2.25 | M |
| A1848 | Louisville Saturday–Margaret Long | .75 | 1.50 | 2.25 | E |
| A1849 | The Sleeping Sphinx–John Dickson Carr | .75 | 1.50 | 2.25 | M |
| A1850 | The Fields–Conrad Richter | .50 | 1.00 | 1.50 | |
| A1851 | The Town–Conrad Richter | .50 | 1.00 | 1.50 | |
| A1852 | The Trees–Conrad Richter | .50 | 1.00 | 1.50 | |
| 1853 | Radigan–Louis L'Amour; 1st ed. 1958 | 2.50 | 5.00 | 7.50 | W |
| F1854 | 1000 Ways to Make $1,000–Helen Hoke | .50 | 1.00 | 1.50 | NF |
| 1855 | The North Star–Will Henry | .75 | 1.50 | 2.25 | |
| 1856 | The Outlaw of Longbow–Peter Dawson (Frank Gruber) | 1.25 | 2.50 | 3.75 | W |
| A1857 | Proud Land–Logan Forster | .75 | 1.50 | 2.25 | |
| 1858 | The Canvas Dagger–Helen Reilly | .75 | 1.50 | 2.25 | M |
| A1859 | First Train to Batylon–Max Ehrlich | .75 | 1.50 | 2.25 | |
| A1860 | The Big Eye–Max Ehrlich | .75 | 1.50 | 2.25 | SF |
| 1861 | Write Me a Poem, Baby–H. Allen Smith | .50 | 1.00 | 1.50 | H |
| F1862 | Pig Boats–Theodore Roscoe; 1960; abridged ed. of U.S. Submarine Operations in WWII | 1.50 | 3.00 | 4.50 | NF |
| A1864 | Jalna–Mazo de la Roche | .50 | 1.00 | 1.50 | |
| 1865 | Rawhide and Bob-wire–ed. Luke Short | 1.25 | 2.50 | 3.75 | W |
| 1866 | Summer of the Smoke–Luke Short | 1.00 | 2.00 | 3.00 | W |
| A1867 | A Stranger in My Arms–Robert Wilder | .50 | 1.00 | 1.50 | |
| A1868 | The Journey–George Tabori | .50 | 1.00 | 1.50 | |
| F1869 | Zoomar–Ernie Kovacs | .50 | 1.00 | 1.50 | |
| F1870 | The Prisoners of Combine D–Len Giovannitti | .75 | 1.50 | 2.25 | |
| A1871 | Little Caesar–W.R. Burnett | 1.00 | 2.00 | 3.00 | |
| F1872 | The Earthbreakers–Ernest Haycox | 1.00 | 2.00 | 3.00 | W |
| 1873 | Modoc, the Last Sundown–L.P. Holmes | .75 | 1.50 | 2.25 | W |
| 1875 | No Vacation for Maigret–Georges Simenon | .75 | 1.50 | 2.25 | M |
| 1876 | Rival to My Heart–Ann Pinchot | .50 | 1.00 | 1.50 | |
| F1877 | TV Movie Almanac and Ratings, 1958–1959–Steven H. Schever | 2.00 | 4.00 | 6.00 | NF |
| F1878 | Green Mansions–W.H. Hudson | 1.00 | 2.00 | 3.00 | F |
| S1879 | The Sound of Thunder–Taylor Caldwell | .50 | 1.00 | 1.50 | |
| A1880 | My Face for the World to See–Alfred Hayes | .50 | 1.00 | 1.50 | |
| 1883 | Death of a Postman–John Creasey | .75 | 1.50 | 2.25 | M |
| 1884 | The Gelignite Gang–John Creasey | .75 | 1.50 | 2.25 | M |
| A1885 | The Martian Chronicles–Ray Bradbury | 1.00 | 2.00 | 3.00 | SF |
| F1886 | The Tall Captains–Bart Spicer | .75 | 1.50 | 2.25 | |
| A1888 | Bat Masterson–Richard O'Connor; TV tie-in | 1.50 | 3.00 | 4.50 | W |
| A1890 | Across the Everglades–Budd Schulberg | .50 | 1.00 | 1.50 | |
| A1891 | Meet Me in St. Louis–Sally Benson | .50 | 1.00 | 1.50 | H |
| A1892 | Hot Rod–Henry Gregor Felsen | 1.00 | 2.00 | 3.00 | |
| 1893 | Rio Bravo–Leigh Brackett; movie tie-in | 5.00 | 10.00 | 15.00 | W |
| A1894 | Our Hearts Were Young and Gay–Cornelia Otis Skinner & Emily Kimbrough | .50 | 1.00 | 1.50 | |
| F1895 | East of Eden–John Steinbeck | 1.00 | 2.00 | 3.00 | |
| F1896 | Hitler, a Study in Tyranny–Alan Bullock | 1.00 | 2.00 | 3.00 | B |
| A1897 | The Betty Bissell Book of Home Cleaning–Betty Bissell; 1959 | .50 | 1.00 | 1.50 | NF |
| A1898 | So Many Doors–Oakley Hall | .50 | 1.00 | 1.50 | E |
| A1899 | Cry for Happy–George Campbell | .50 | 1.00 | 1.50 | |
| F1900 | Maggie Now–Betty Smith | .50 | 1.00 | 1.50 | |
| A1901 | The Hon. Rocky Slade–William Wister Haines | .75 | 1.50 | 2.25 | |
| F1902 | Slim–William Wister Haines | .75 | 1.50 | 2.25 | |
| F1903 | Ben-Hur–Lew Wallace | .75 | 1.50 | 2.25 | |

**BANTAM BOOKS,** *continued*

| No. | Title | V/Good | Fine | N/Mint | |
|---|---|---|---|---|---|
| A1904 | Mrs. Mike—Benedict Freedman & Nancy Freedman | .75 | 1.50 | 2.25 | |
| 1905 | The First Fast Draw—Louis L'Amour | 2.50 | 5.00 | 7.50 | W |
| 1907 | Nurse Howard's Assignment—Virginia Roberts | .50 | 1.00 | 1.50 | R |
| A1908 | The Price of Courage—Curt Anders | .50 | 1.00 | 1.50 | |
| 1909 | The Black Mirror—Ben Benson | .75 | 1.50 | 2.25 | M |
| 1910 | The Running Man—Ben Benson | .75 | 1.50 | 2.25 | M |
| 1911 | I Take This Man—Emilie Loring | .50 | 1.00 | 1.50 | |
| F1912 | Ice Palace—Edna Ferber | .75 | 1.50 | 2.25 | |
| F1913 | Crack of Doom—Willis Heinrich | .75 | 1.50 | 2.25 | |
| A1914 | Love Me Little—Amanda Vail | .50 | 1.00 | 1.50 | |
| F1915 | Ride the Red Earth—Paul I. Wellman | 1.00 | 2.00 | 3.00 | |
| 1916 | And the Wind Blows Free—Luke Short | .75 | 1.50 | 2.25 | W |
| A1917 | The Hunger and Other Stories—Charles Beaumont | 3.00 | 6.00 | 9.00 | SF |
| A1919 | The Red Knight of Germany—Floyd Gibbons | 1.50 | 3.00 | 4.50 | B |
| G1920 | And Save Them for Pallbearers—James Garrett | 1.00 | 2.00 | 3.00 | |
| A1921 | The Hard Sell—David Delman | .75 | 1.50 | 2.25 | |
| A1922 | Dandelion Wine—Ray Bradbury | 2.00 | 4.00 | 6.00 | |
| 1923 | The Mesh—Lucie Marchal | .50 | 1.00 | 1.50 | E |
| A1924 | The Teen-age Diet Book—Ruth West | .75 | 1.50 | 2.25 | NF |
| 1925 | Silent River—Wayne Roberts | .50 | 1.00 | 1.50 | |
| 1926 | Barbed Wire Kingdom—C. William Harrison | 1.00 | 2.00 | 3.00 | W |
| 1927 | The Convertible Hearse—William Campbell Gault | 2.00 | 4.00 | 6.00 | M |
| 1929 | Young Doctor Randall—Adeline McElfresh | .50 | 1.00 | 1.50 | R |
| A1930 | Theatre—W. Somerset Maugham | .50 | 1.00 | 1.50 | |
| A1931 | The Narrow Corner—W. Somerset Maugham | .50 | 1.00 | 1.50 | |
| F1932 | The Disenchanted—Bud Schulberg | .75 | 1.50 | 2.25 | |
| A1933 | The Daybreakers—Louis L'Amour; 1st ed. 1960 | 2.50 | 5.00 | 7.50 | W |
| 1934 | Outlaw—Frank Gruber | 1.25 | 2.50 | 3.75 | W |
| A1935 | Reckoning at Yankee Flat—Will Henry | 1.00 | 2.00 | 3.00 | W |
| 1936 | The Doctor Is a Lady—Beth Myers | .50 | 1.00 | 1.50 | |
| A1937 | The Witches—Jay Williams | 1.00 | 2.00 | 3.00 | |
| 1938 | My Dearest Love—Emilie Loring | .50 | 1.00 | 1.50 | |
| A1939 | Barefoot Boy with Cheek—Max Shulman | .50 | 1.00 | 1.50 | H |
| A1940 | The Feather Merchants—Max Shulman | .50 | 1.00 | 1.50 | H |
| A1941 | The Naked Maja—Samuel Edwards; movie tie-in | 1.00 | 2.00 | 3.00 | |
| A1942 | Night of the Quarter Moon—Franklin Coen | .75 | 1.50 | 2.25 | |
| A1943 | Getting Along in Spanish—Mario Pei & Eloy Vaquero | .75 | 1.50 | 2.25 | NF |
| A1944 | Getting Along in German—Mario Pei & Robert Politzer | .75 | 1.50 | 2.25 | NF |
| 1945 | A Night to Remember—Walter Lord | .75 | 1.50 | 2.25 | NF |
| F1946 | The Image Makers—Bernard Dryer | .50 | 1.00 | 1.50 | |
| F1947 | The Northern Light—A.J. Cronin | .50 | 1.00 | 1.50 | |
| 1948 | The Hours after Midnight—Joseph Hayes | .50 | 1.00 | 1.50 | |
| 1949 | Gunfighter's Return—Ben Smith | .75 | 1.50 | 2.25 | W |
| 1951 | Hill Country Nurse—Adeline McElfresh | .50 | 1.00 | 1.50 | R |
| A1952 | Point Ultimate—Jerry Sohl | 1.00 | 2.00 | 3.00 | SF |
| A1953 | Goren Presents the Italian Bridge System—Charles H. Goren | .75 | 1.50 | 2.25 | NF |
| A1954 | The Summer Lovers—Hollis Alpert | .75 | 1.50 | 2.25 | |
| F1955 | The Violated—Vance Bourjaily | .50 | 1.00 | 1.50 | |
| F1956 | The Wonderful Country—Tom Lea | .75 | 1.50 | 2.25 | A |
| A1957 | Blue Denim—James Leo Herlihy & William Noble | .75 | 1.50 | 2.25 | |
| A1958 | Solomon and Sheba—Jay Williams; movie tie-in | 1.25 | 2.50 | 3.75 | A |
| A1959 | Hard Money—Luke Short | .75 | 1.50 | 2.25 | W |
| A1961 | If Death Ever Slept—Rex Stout | .75 | 1.50 | 2.25 | M |
| A1962 | Doctor Barbara—Elizabeth Wesley (Adeline McElfresh); 1960 | .50 | 1.00 | 1.50 | R |
| F1963 | A Rage to Live—John O'Hara | .75 | 1.50 | 2.25 | |
| A1964 | Command Decision—William Wister Haines | .75 | 1.50 | 2.25 | |
| 1965 | The Beat Generation—Albert Zugsmith; orig. 1959; movie tie-in | 3.00 | 6.00 | 9.00 | JD |
| A1966 | Middle of the Night—Paddy Chayefsky | 1.00 | 2.00 | 3.00 | |
| F1968 | The Bramble Bush—Charles Mergendahl | .75 | 1.50 | 2.25 | |
| F1969 | Tomorrow to Live—William Herber | .50 | 1.00 | 1.50 | |
| A1970 | Nothing but the Night—James Yaffe | .75 | 1.50 | 2.25 | |
| A1971 | The Transcendent Man—Jerry Sohl | .75 | 1.50 | 2.25 | SF |
| F1972 | Hoof Trails and Wagon Tracks—ed. Don Ward | 1.50 | 3.00 | 4.50 | |
| 1973 | Bitter Ground—W.R. Burnett | 1.50 | 3.00 | 4.50 | |
| 1974 | The Blonde in Black—Ben Benson | 1.00 | 2.00 | 3.00 | M |
| 1975 | Nurse on Location—Virginia Roberts | .50 | 1.00 | 1.50 | R |
| F1976 | His Eye Is on the Sparrow—Ethel Waters & Charles Samuels | .50 | 1.00 | 1.50 | B |
| 1977 | Taggart—Louis L'Amour; 1st ed. 1959 | 2.50 | 5.00 | 7.50 | W |
| A1978 | Earth Is Room Enough—Isaac Asimov | 1.00 | 2.00 | 3.00 | SF |
| A1979 | An Air That Kills—Margaret Millar | 1.00 | 2.00 | 3.00 | M |
| F1980 | Warlock—Oakley Hall | 1.00 | 2.00 | 3.00 | W |
| A1981 | Sports Shorts—Mac Davis | 1.00 | 2.00 | 3.00 | S |
| A1982 | The Mouse That Roared—Leonard Wibberley | 1.50 | 3.00 | 4.50 | H |
| A1983 | Ask Any Girl—Winifred Wolfe | .50 | 1.00 | 1.50 | |
| 1984 | The Savages—Peter Dawson (Frank Gruber) | 1.25 | 2.50 | 3.75 | W |
| H1985 | Spartacus—Howard Fast; movie tie-in | 1.00 | 2.00 | 3.00 | A |
| A1986 | The Fume of Poppies—Jonathan Kozol | .75 | 1.50 | 2.25 | |
| F1987 | The Detroiters—Harold Livingston | .50 | 1.00 | 1.50 | |
| F1988 | The Voyagers—Dale Van Every | .50 | 1.00 | 1.50 | |
| A1989 | War on the Cimarron—Luke Short | .75 | 1.50 | 2.25 | W |
| 1990 | One for the Road—Fredric Brown | 4.00 | 8.00 | 12.00 | M |
| A1991 | Immortality, Inc.—Robert Sheckley | 1.00 | 2.00 | 3.00 | SF |
| A1992 | Dr. John's Decision—Dorothy Worley | .50 | 1.00 | 1.50 | |
| S1993 | French Stories—ed. Wallace Fowlie | .75 | 1.50 | 2.25 | |
| S1994 | Spanish Stories/Cuentos Españoles—ed. Angel Flores | 1.00 | 2.00 | 3.00 | |
| S1995 | Exodus—Leon Uris | 1.00 | 2.00 | 3.00 | C |
| F1996 | Battle Cry—Leon Uris | .50 | 1.00 | 1.50 | C |
| A1998 | Town Tamer—Frank Gruber | 1.25 | 2.50 | 3.75 | W |
| A1999 | The Crimson Horseshoe—Peter Dawson (Frank Gruber) | 1.25 | 2.50 | 3.75 | W |
| A2000 | Fear Is the Same—Carter Dickson | 3.50 | 7.00 | 10.50 | M |
| 2001 | The Affair of the Exotic Dancer—Ben Benson | 1.00 | 2.00 | 3.00 | M |
| 2002 | Debutante Nurse—Margaret Howe | .50 | 1.00 | 1.50 | R |
| A2003 | Notions Unlimited—Robert Scheckley | 1.00 | 2.00 | 3.00 | SF |
| F2004 | The End of the Affair—Graham Greene | .50 | 1.00 | 1.50 | |
| A2006 | Silver Rock—Luke Short | .75 | 1.50 | 2.25 | W |
| F2007 | The Shining Mountains—Dale Van Every | .50 | 1.00 | 1.50 | |
| A2008 | Prison Nurse—Louis Berg | .75 | 1.50 | 2.25 | R |
| A2009 | Irene—Ronald Marsh | .50 | 1.00 | 1.50 | |
| A2010 | The Forest Lord—Noel B. Gerson | 1.00 | 2.00 | 3.00 | |
| F2011 | The God That Failed—Richard Crossman | .75 | 1.50 | 2.25 | |
| A2012 | Sleep Till Noon—Max Shulman | .50 | 1.00 | 1.50 | H |
| S2013 | Women and Thomas Harrow—John P. Marquand | .50 | 1.00 | 1.50 | |
| F2014 | The Law—Roger Vailland; movie tie-in | .75 | 1.50 | 2.25 | |
| F2015 | Wyatt Earp, Frontier Marshal—Stuart N. Lake. Note: This alleged "true" biography contains controversial fictionalized stories presented as fact. | .75 | 1.50 | 2.25 | NF |
| A2016 | And Four to Go—Rex Stout | .75 | 1.50 | 2.25 | M |
| A2017 | 1001 Valuable Things You Can Get Free, No. 3—Mort Weisinger | .50 | 1.00 | 1.50 | NF |
| A2018 | Our Man in Havana—Graham Greene | .75 | 1.50 | 2.25 | |
| F2019 | The Actress—Bessie Breuer | .50 | 1.00 | 1.50 | R |
| A2020 | Rock—David Wagoner | 1.50 | 3.00 | 4.50 | |
| A2021 | The Marshal—Frank Gruber | 1.25 | 2.50 | 3.75 | W |
| A2022 | Guns of the Timberlands—Louis L'Amour; movie tie-in | 1.50 | 3.00 | 4.50 | W |
| A2023 | Champagne for One—Rex Stout | .75 | 1.50 | 2.25 | M |
| A2024 | The Doomsters—John Ross MacDonald | 1.50 | 3.00 | 4.50 | |
| N2026 | From the Terrace—John O'Hara | .75 | 1.50 | 2.25 | |
| A2028 | Rafferty—Lionel White | 1.25 | 2.50 | 3.75 | |
| F2029 | Signal Thirty-Two—MacKinlay Kantor | .75 | 1.50 | 2.25 | |
| 2030 | The Late Lamented—Fredric Brown | 4.00 | 8.00 | 12.00 | M |
| 2031 | Hill Smoke—L.P. Holmes | .60 | 1.20 | 1.80 | W |
| 2032 | War in Sandoval County—Wayne D. Overholser | 1.00 | 2.00 | 3.00 | W |
| F2033 | Beloved Infidel—Gerold Frank & Sheilah Graham | .75 | 1.50 | 2.25 | |
| A2034 | Look Back in Anger—John Osborne | .75 | 1.50 | 2.25 | |
| F2035 | The Day Lincoln Was Shot—Jim Bishop | .50 | 1.00 | 1.50 | NF |
| A2036 | Saddle by Starlight—Luke Short | .75 | 1.50 | 2.25 | W |
| F2038 | Tin Cans—Theodore Roscoe; 1960, abridged ed. of U.S. Destroyer Operations in WWII | 1.50 | 3.00 | 4.50 | |
| F2039 | Nineteen Stories—Graham Greene | .50 | 1.00 | 1.50 | |

| | | V/Good | Fine | N/Mint | |
|---|---|---|---|---|---|

**BANTAM BOOKS,** *continued*

| No. | Title | V/Good | Fine | N/Mint | |
|---|---|---|---|---|---|
| F2040 | Fandango Rock–John Masters | .75 | 1.50 | 2.25 | |
| F2041 | The Many Loves of Dobie Gillis–Max Shulman | 2.00 | 4.00 | 6.00 | H |
| A2042 | On the Line–Harvey Swados | .75 | 1.50 | 2.25 | |
| A2046 | Stories from the Twilight Zone–Rod Serling; TV tie-in | 1.50 | 3.00 | 4.50 | |
| A2055 | The Private Lives of Adam and Eve–Albert Zugsmith; movie tie-in | 2.00 | 4.00 | 6.00 | |
| F2058 | The Best Western Stories of Ernest Haycox–Ernest Haycox | 1.50 | 3.00 | 4.50 | W |
| A2060 | Sink the Bismarck!–C.S. Forester | 1.00 | 2.00 | 3.00 | C |
| A2063 | The Methods of Maigret–Georges Simenon | .75 | 1.50 | 2.25 | M |
| F2070 | The Russian Revolution–Alan Moorehead | .50 | 1.00 | 1.50 | |
| A2073 | Cheaper by the Dozen–Ernestine Carey & Frank B. Gilbreth, Jr | .75 | 1.50 | 2.25 | H |
| A2087 | Night Ride and Other Journies–Charles Beaumont | 3.00 | 6.00 | 9.00 | HO |
| A2135 | Knock Three-One-Two–Fredric Brown | 4.00 | 8.00 | 12.00 | M |
| A2153 | Flint–Louis L'Amour; 1st ed. 1961 | 2.50 | 5.00 | 7.50 | W |
| A2187 | The Mind Thing–Fredric Brown | 3.00 | 6.00 | 9.00 | |
| A2227 | More Stories from the Twilight Zone–Rod Serling; TV tie-in | 1.50 | 3.00 | 4.50 | |
| A2236 | Sackett–Louis L'Amour; 1st ed. 1961 | 2.50 | 5.00 | 7.50 | W |
| F2281 | The Beardless Warriors–Richard Matheson | 2.50 | 5.00 | 7.50 | C |
| A2308 | An Eye for an Eye–Leigh Brackett | 3.00 | 6.00 | 9.00 | M |
| A2325 | Shalako–Louis L'Amour; 1st ed. 1962 | 2.50 | 5.00 | 7.50 | W |
| A2386 | Killoe–Louis L'Amour; 1st ed. 1962 | 2.50 | 5.00 | 7.50 | W |
| A2412 | New Stories from the Twilight Zone–Rod Serling; TV tie-in | 1.50 | 3.00 | 4.50 | |
| A2449 | High Lonesome–Louis L'Amour; 1st ed. 1962 | 2.50 | 5.00 | 7.50 | W |
| J2467 | Third from the Sun–Richard Matheson; aka Born of Man and Woman | 3.00 | 6.00 | 9.00 | SF |
| A2494 | Lando–Louis L'Amour; 1st ed. 1962 | 2.50 | 5.00 | 7.50 | W |
| A2512 | Fallon–Louis L'Amour; 1st ed. 1963 | 2.50 | 5.00 | 7.50 | W |
| F2548 | How the West Was Won–Louis L'Amour; 1st ed. 1963; movie tie-in | 2.50 | 5.00 | 7.50 | W |
| J2579 | Catlow–Louis L'Amour; 1st ed. 1963 | 2.50 | 5.00 | 7.50 | W |
| J2587 | The Murderers–Fredric Brown | 5.00 | 10.00 | 15.00 | M |
| J2684 | Dark Canyon–Louis L'Amour; 1st ed. 1963 | 2.50 | 5.00 | 7.50 | W |
| J2712 | Mojave Crossing–Louis L'Amour; 1st ed. 1964 | 2.50 | 5.00 | 7.50 | W |
| J2766 | Kiowa Trail–Louis L'Amour; 1st ed. 1964 | 2.50 | 5.00 | 7.50 | W |
| J2796 | Hanging Woman Creek–Louis L'Amour; 1st ed. 1964 | 2.50 | 5.00 | 7.50 | W |
| E2853 | The Man of Bronze–Kenneth Robeson; 1964 | 1.50 | 3.00 | 4.50 | A |
| E2854 | The Thousand-Headed Man–Kenneth Robeson. Note: Same cover as Gold Key comic Doc Savage No. 1 | 1.50 | 3.00 | 4.50 | A |
| E2855 | Meteor Menace–Kenneth Robeson | 1.50 | 3.00 | 4.50 | A |
| J2902 | The High Graders–Louis L'Amour; 1st ed. 1965 | 2.00 | 4.00 | 6.00 | W |
| E3015 | The Polar Treasure–Kenneth Robeson; 1965 | 1.50 | 3.00 | 4.50 | A |
| E3016 | Brand of the Werewolf–Kenneth Robeson | 1.50 | 3.00 | 4.50 | A |
| E3017 | The Lost Oasis–Kenneth Robeson | 1.50 | 3.00 | 4.50 | A |
| E3033 | The Monsters–Kenneth Robeson | 1.50 | 3.00 | 4.50 | A |
| E3042 | The Land of Terror–Kenneth Robeson | 1.50 | 3.00 | 4.50 | A |
| E3047 | The Phantom City–Kenneth Robeson | 1.50 | 3.00 | 4.50 | A |
| E3055 | Mustang Man–Louis L'Amour; 1st ed. 1966 | 2.00 | 4.00 | 6.00 | W |
| F3093 | King Kong–Edgar Wallace, Merian C. Cooper, Delos W. Lovelace | 1.50 | 3.00 | 4.50 | HO |
| J3098 | The Broken Gun–Louis L'Amour; 1st ed. 1966 | 2.00 | 4.00 | 6.00 | W |
| E3110 | Quest of Qui–Kenneth Robeson; 1966 | 1.50 | 3.00 | 4.50 | A |
| E3115 | The Mystic Mullah–Kenneth Robeson | 1.50 | 3.00 | 4.50 | A |
| E3146 | Fear Cay–Kenneth Robeson | 1.50 | 3.00 | 4.50 | A |
| E3202 | Land of Always-Night–Kenneth Robeson | 1.50 | 3.00 | 4.50 | A |
| E3244 | Kid Rodelo–Louis L'Amour; 1st ed. 1966, movie tie-in | 2.00 | 4.00 | 6.00 | W |
| F3252 | Kilrone–Louis L'Amour; 1st ed. 1966 | 2.00 | 4.00 | 6.00 | W |
| E3269 | The Fantastic Island–Kenneth Robeson | 1.50 | 3.00 | 4.50 | A |
| E3296 | Murder Melody–Kenneth Robeson; 1967 | 1.50 | 3.00 | 4.50 | A |

| No. | Title | V/Good | Fine | N/Mint | |
|---|---|---|---|---|---|
| F3340 | The Spook Legion–Kenneth Robeson | 1.50 | 3.00 | 4.50 | A |
| F3356 | The Sky-Liners–Louis L'Amour; 1st ed. 1967 | 2.00 | 4.00 | 6.00 | W |
| F3387 | The Red Skull–Kenneth Robeson | 1.50 | 3.00 | 4.50 | A |
| F3441 | The Sargasso Ogre–Kenneth Robeson | 1.50 | 3.00 | 4.50 | A |
| F3486 | Pirate of the Pacific–Kenneth Robeson | 1.50 | 3.00 | 4.50 | A |
| F3533 | The Secret in the Sky–Kenneth Robeson | 1.50 | 3.00 | 4.50 | A |
| F3534 | Matagorda–Louis L'Amour; 1st ed. 1967 | 2.00 | 4.00 | 6.00 | W |
| F3569 | The Avengers Battle the Earth-Wrecker–Otto Binder; 1st ed. 1967 | 2.00 | 4.00 | 6.00 | A |
| F3580 | Down the Long Hills–Louis L'Amour; 1st ed. 1968 | 2.00 | 4.00 | 6.00 | W |
| F3584 | Cold Death–Kenneth Robeson | 1.50 | 3.00 | 4.50 | A |
| F3667 | The Czar of Fear–Kenneth Robeson | 1.50 | 3.00 | 4.50 | A |
| F3692 | Chancy–Louis L'Amour; 1st ed. 1968 | 2.00 | 4.00 | 6.00 | W |
| F3716 | Fortress of Solitude–Kenneth Robeson | 1.50 | 3.00 | 4.50 | A |
| F3755 | Mystery under the Sea–Kenneth Robeson | 1.50 | 3.00 | 4.50 | A |
| F3780 | The Great Gold Steal–Ted White; 1st ed. 1968; Captain America novel | 2.00 | 4.00 | 6.00 | A |
| F3782 | The Green Eagle–Kenneth Robeson | 1.50 | 3.00 | 4.50 | A |
| F3805 | Death in Silver–Kenneth Robeson | 1.50 | 3.00 | 4.50 | A |
| F3807 | Brionne–Louis L'Amour; 1st ed. 1968 | 2.00 | 4.00 | 6.00 | W |
| F3839 | The Deadly Dwarf–Kenneth Robeson | 1.50 | 3.00 | 4.50 | A |
| F3841 | The Devil's Playground–Kenneth Robeson | 1.50 | 3.00 | 4.50 | A |
| F3877 | The Other World–Kenneth Robeson | 2.00 | 4.00 | 6.00 | A |
| F3885 | The Annihilist–Kenneth Robeson | 2.00 | 4.00 | 6.00 | A |
| F3897 | The Flaming Falcons–Kenneth Robeson | 2.00 | 4.00 | 6.00 | A |
| H3916 | Shalako–Louis L'Amour; movie tie-in | 1.50 | 3.00 | 4.50 | W |
| H3935 | The Empty Land–Louis L'Amour; 1st ed. 1969 | 2.00 | 4.00 | 6.00 | W |
| F3937 | Dust of Death–Kenneth Robeson; 1969 | 2.00 | 4.00 | 6.00 | A |
| F3969 | The Terror in the Navy–Kenneth Robeson | 2.00 | 4.00 | 6.00 | A |
| F3986 | Mad Eyes–Kenneth Robeson | 2.00 | 4.00 | 6.00 | A |
| H4056 | Eyes of the Shadow–Maxwell Grant | 2.00 | 4.00 | 6.00 | M |
| H4065 | Red Snow–Kenneth Robeson | 2.00 | 4.00 | 6.00 | A |
| F4362 | The Squeaking Goblin–Kenneth Robeson | 2.00 | 4.00 | 6.00 | A |
| H4402 | The Lonely Men–Louis L'Amour; 1st ed. 1969 | 2.00 | 4.00 | 6.00 | W |
| F4403 | Resurrection Day–Kenneth Robeson | 2.00 | 4.00 | 6.00 | A |
| H4463 | The Living Shadow–Maxwell Grant | 2.00 | 4.00 | 6.00 | M |
| H4624 | The Dagger in the Sky–Kenneth Robeson | 2.00 | 4.00 | 6.00 | A |
| H4628 | Conagher–Louis L'Amour; 1st ed. 1969 | 2.00 | 4.00 | 6.00 | W |
| H4688 | The Shadow Laughs!–Maxwell Grant | 2.00 | 4.00 | 6.00 | M |
| H4689 | Merchants of Disaster–Kenneth Robeson | 2.00 | 4.00 | 6.00 | A |
| H4707 | Hex–Kenneth Robeson | 2.00 | 4.00 | 6.00 | A |
| H4721 | World's Fair Goblin–Kenneth Robeson | 2.00 | 4.00 | 6.00 | A |
| H4730 | The Gold Ogre–Kenneth Robeson | 2.00 | 4.00 | 6.00 | A |
| H4761 | The Man Who Shook the Earth–Kenneth Robeson | 2.00 | 4.00 | 6.00 | A |
| H4770 | The Death Tower–Maxwell Grant | 2.00 | 4.00 | 6.00 | M |
| H4810 | The Sea Magician–Kenneth Robeson | 2.00 | 4.00 | 6.00 | A |
| H4813 | The Man Called Noon–Louis L'Amour; 1st ed. 1970 | 2.00 | 4.00 | 6.00 | W |
| H4875 | The Men Who Smiled No More–Kenneth Robeson | 2.00 | 4.00 | 6.00 | A |
| H4884 | Hidden Death–Maxwell Grant | 2.00 | 4.00 | 6.00 | M |
| H5217 | The Midas Man–Kenneth Robeson; 1970 | 2.00 | 4.00 | 6.00 | A |
| H5309 | Land of Long Ju Ju–Kenneth Robeson | 2.00 | 4.00 | 6.00 | A |
| H5366 | Mad Eyes–Kenneth Robeson | 2.00 | 4.00 | 6.00 | A |
| H5367 | The Feathered Octopus–Kenneth Robeson | 2.00 | 4.00 | 6.00 | A |
| H5368 | Galloway–Louis L'Amour; 1st ed. 1970 | 2.00 | 4.00 | 6.00 | W |
| H5406 | The Sea Angel–Kenneth Robeson | 2.00 | 4.00 | 6.00 | A |
| H5413 | Gangdom's Doom–Maxwell Grant | 2.00 | 4.00 | 6.00 | M |
| H5422 | The Squeaking Goblins–Kenneth Robeson; 1971 | 2.00 | 4.00 | 6.00 | A |
| H5450 | Devil on the Moon–Kenneth Robeson | 1.50 | 3.00 | 4.50 | A |
| H5482 | Haunted Ocean–Kenneth Robeson | 2.00 | 4.00 | 6.00 | A |
| H5485 | Reilly's Luck–Louis L'Amour; 1st ed. 1970 | 2.00 | 4.00 | 6.00 | W |
| H5536 | The Vanisher–Kenneth Robeson | 1.50 | 3.00 | 4.50 | A |
| H5556 | The Mental Wizard–Kenneth Robeson | 2.00 | 4.00 | 6.00 | A |
| H5617 | He Could Stop the World–Kenneth Robeson | 1.50 | 3.00 | 4.50 | A |

**BANTAM BOOKS,** *continued*

| No. | Title | V/Good | Fine | N/Mint | |
|---|---|---|---|---|---|
| H5662 | The Golden Peril–Kenneth Robeson | 1.50 | 3.00 | 4.50 | A |
| H5705 | The Giggling Ghost–Kenneth Robeson | 1.50 | 3.00 | 4.50 | A |
| H5743 | Poison Island–Kenneth Robeson | 2.00 | 4.00 | 6.00 | A |
| S5747 | North to the Rails–Louis L'Amour; 1st ed. 1971 | 2.00 | 4.00 | 6.00 | W |
| S5788 | The Munitions Master–Kenneth Robeson | 2.00 | 4.00 | 6.00 | A |
| S5838 | The Yellow Cloud–Kenneth Robeson | 1.50 | 3.00 | 4.50 | A |
| Y5869 | Deadbone Erotica–Vaughn Bode; 1st ed. 1971. Note: Oversize $5\frac{1}{8}''$ x $8\frac{1}{4}''$ volume of collected comic strip reprints from Cavalier | 10.00 | 20.00 | 30.00 | F |
| S5871 | Blackmark–Gil Kane; orig. 1971. Note: Comic art novel | 2.00 | 4.00 | 6.00 | F |
| S5909 | The Majii–Kenneth Robeson | 1.50 | 3.00 | 4.50 | A |
| S5911 | Under the Sweetwater Rim–Louis L'Amour; 1st ed. 1971 | 2.00 | 4.00 | 6.00 | W |
| S6728 | Tucker–Louis L'Amour; 1st ed. 1971 | 2.00 | 4.00 | 6.00 | W |
| S7039 | Callaghen–Louis L'Amour; 1st ed. 1972 | 2.00 | 4.00 | 6.00 | W |
| S7280 | Treasure Mountain–Louis L'Amour; 1st ed. 1972 | 2.00 | 4.00 | 6.00 | W |
| S7282 | Ride the Dark Trail–Louis L'Amour; 1st ed. 1972 | 2.00 | 4.00 | 6.00 | W |

## BANTAM BOOKS (LOS ANGELES)

## Bantam Publications

**Note: Later printings of 21, 22, 23, 25, 26, 27, and 28 (and possibly others) have pictorial covers whereas first printings do not. Later pictorial cover variants are greater in desirability with first printings and are valued at 50% extra.**

| No. | Title | V/Good | Fine | N/Mint | |
|---|---|---|---|---|---|
| A1 | The Red Threads–Rex Stout | 60.00 | 120.00 | 180.00 | M |
| 1 | The Spanish Cape Mystery–Ellery Queen | 30.00 | 60.00 | 90.00 | M |
| 2 | Little Known Facts about Famous People–Dale Carnegie | 25.00 | 50.00 | 75.00 | NF |
| 3 | Your Health Questions–M.M.D. Fishbein | 25.00 | 50.00 | 75.00 | NF |
| 4 | Everybody's Dream Book, Your Dreams Explained | 25.00 | 50.00 | 75.00 | NF |
| 5 | How to Make Friends Easily–S. Currie | 25.00 | 50.00 | 75.00 | NF |
| 6 | Everybody's Book of Jokes and Wisecracks–J. Gregory | 25.00 | 50.00 | 75.00 | H |
| 7 | The Voice of Experience | 25.00 | 50.00 | 75.00 | |
| 8 | Favorite Poems: Popular Selections from the World's Literature | 25.00 | 50.00 | 75.00 | |
| 9 | Enter the G-Men–William Engle | 30.00 | 60.00 | 90.00 | M |
| 10 | 1000 Facts Worth Knowing | 25.00 | 50.00 | 75.00 | NF |
| 11 | How to Win and Hold a Husband–L. Martin | 25.00 | 50.00 | 75.00 | NF |
| 12 | The World's Great Love Affairs–Hendrik Willem Van Loon | 25.00 | 50.00 | 75.00 | |
| 13 | Poems of Passion–Ella Wheeler Wilcox | 25.00 | 50.00 | 75.00 | |
| 14 | The Lone Ranger and the Secret of Thunder Mountain–Fran Striker; aka Heigh-Yo Silver: A Story of the Lone Ranger | 40.00 | 80.00 | 120.00 | W |
| 15 | Children's Favorite Stories | 27.50 | 55.00 | 82.50 | |
| 16 | Grimm's Fairy Tales | 27.50 | 55.00 | 82.50 | |

*Bantam (Los Angeles) 9, Bantam (Los Angeles) 27, Bart House 12.*

| No. | Title | V/Good | Fine | N/Mint | |
|---|---|---|---|---|---|
| 17 | Private Lives of the Movie Stars–Eleanor Packer | 27.50 | 55.00 | 82.50 | NF |
| 18 | Love on the Run–Fred Macisaac | 27.50 | 55.00 | 82.50 | |
| 19 | The Tower of Flame/Jaragu of the Lost Islands–Rex Beach | 27.50 | 55.00 | 82.50 | A |
| 20 | The Story of Rabelais and Voltaire–Hendrik Willem Van Loon | 25.00 | 50.00 | 75.00 | |
| 21 | The Shadow and the Voice of Murder–Maxwell Grant | 100.00 | 200.00 | 300.00 | M |
| 22 | The Green Death–Brett Hutton | 30.00 | 60.00 | 90.00 | M |
| 23 | Tarzan in the Forbidden City–Edgar Rice Burroughs; 1940 | 150.00 | 300.00 | 450.00 | A |
| 24 | Humorous Anecdotes and Funny Stories | 25.00 | 50.00 | 75.00 | H |
| 25 | Nobody Heard the Shot–Donald Barr Chidsey | 27.50 | 55.00 | 82.50 | M |
| 26 | Mystery of the Blue Geranium and Other Tuesday Club Murders–Agatha Christie | 30.00 | 60.00 | 90.00 | M |
| 27 | Danger Mansion–Philip Wylie | 25.00 | 50.00 | 75.00 | M |
| 28 | Strangers in Flight–Mignon G. Eberhart | 25.00 | 50.00 | 75.00 | M |

## BANTAM CLASSICS

## Bantam Books, Inc.

| No. | Title | V/Good | Fine | N/Mint | |
|---|---|---|---|---|---|
| AC1 | Brave New World–Aldous Huxley | 1.25 | 2.50 | 3.75 | SF |
| FC2 | Four Great Comedies of the Restoration and Eighteenth Century | .75 | 1.50 | 2.25 | |
| SC3 | The Complete Short Stories of Mark Twain | 1.25 | 2.50 | 3.75 | |
| SC4 | The Idiot–Fyodor Dostoyevsky | .75 | 1.50 | 2.25 | |
| FC5 | Four Great Plays–Anton Chekhov | .75 | 1.50 | 2.25 | |
| FC6 | Sister Carrie–Theodore Dreiser | .75 | 1.50 | 2.25 | |
| FC7 | Lord Jim–Joseph Conrad | 1.25 | 2.50 | 3.75 | |
| FC8 | The Octopus–Frank Norris | .75 | 1.50 | 2.25 | |
| FC9 | Henry the Eighth–Francis Hackett | .75 | 1.50 | 2.25 | B |
| FC10 | Emma–Jane Austen | .75 | 1.50 | 2.25 | |
| FC11 | The Voyage of the Beagle–Charles Darwin | .75 | 1.50 | 2.25 | NF |
| AC12 | Of Mice and Men–John Steinbeck | .75 | 1.50 | 2.25 | |
| FC13 | Penguin Island–Anatole France | .75 | 1.50 | 2.25 | |
| AC14 | The Day of the Locust–Nathanael West | .75 | 1.50 | 2.25 | |
| FC15 | Only Yesterday–Frederick Lewis Allen | .75 | 1.50 | 2.25 | |
| FC16 | Four Short Novels–Herman Melville | .75 | 1.50 | 2.25 | |
| AC17 | Eugenie Grandet–Honore de Balzac | .75 | 1.50 | 2.25 | |
| AC18 | Cannery Row–John Steinbeck | .75 | 1.50 | 2.25 | |
| AC19 | Cyrano de Bergerac–Edmond Rostand | .75 | 1.50 | 2.25 | |
| FC20 | Two Years before the Mast–Richard Henry Dana | .75 | 1.50 | 2.25 | A |
| FC21 | Barchester Towers–Anthony Trollope | .75 | 1.50 | 2.25 | |
| AC22 | Crome Yellow–Aldous Huxley | .75 | 1.50 | 2.25 | |
| FC23 | Four Great Plays by Ibsen–Henrik Ibsen | .75 | 1.50 | 2.25 | |
| FC24 | Canterbury Tales–Geoffrey Chaucer | .75 | 1.50 | 2.25 | |
| AC25 | The Moon and Sixpence–W. Somerset Maugham; 1959 | .75 | 1.50 | 2.25 | |
| AC26 | Hiroshima–John Hersey | .75 | 1.50 | 2.25 | |
| FC27 | Cleopatra–Emil Ludwig | .75 | 1.50 | 2.25 | B |
| FC28 | Manhattan Transfer–John Dos Passos | .75 | 1.50 | 2.25 | |
| FC29 | Fifty Great Short Stories–Milton Crane | .75 | 1.50 | 2.25 | |
| FC30 | Crime and Punishment–Fyodor Dostoyevsky | .75 | 1.50 | 2.25 | |
| AC31 | The Crucible–Arthur Miller | .75 | 1.50 | 2.25 | |
| FC32 | Marriage and Morals–Bertrand Russell | .75 | 1.50 | 2.25 | |
| NC33 | 50 Great Artists–Bernard Myers | .75 | 1.50 | 2.25 | |
| FC34 | All the King's Men–Robert Penn Warren | .75 | 1.50 | 2.25 | |
| AC35 | Madame Bovary–Gustave Flaubert | .75 | 1.50 | 2.25 | |
| FC37 | Up from Slavery–Booker T. Washington | .75 | 1.50 | 2.25 | B |
| AC38 | Washington Square–Henry James | .75 | 1.50 | 2.25 | |
| FC39 | Life on the Mississippi–Mark Twain | 1.00 | 2.00 | 3.00 | |
| SC40 | The Red and the Black–Stendhal | .75 | 1.50 | 2.25 | |
| FC41 | Fathers and Sons–Ivan Turgenev | .75 | 1.50 | 2.25 | |
| AC42 | Rashomon and Other Stories–Ryunosuke Akutagawa | .75 | 1.50 | 2.25 | |
| SC43 | The Age of Reason–Jean-Paul Sartre | .75 | 1.50 | 2.25 | |
| FC44 | Citizen Tom Paine–Howard Fast | .75 | 1.50 | 2.25 | B |
| FC46 | War with the Newts–Karel Capek | .75 | 1.50 | 2.25 | SF |
| FC47 | The Finest Stories of Sean O'Faolain–Sean O'Faolain | .75 | 1.50 | 2.25 | |

| | V/Good | Fine | N/Mint | |
|---|---|---|---|---|

**BANTAM CLASSICS,** *continued*

| | | V/Good | Fine | N/Mint | |
|---|---|---|---|---|---|
| AC48 | Seventeen–Booth Tarkington | .75 | 1.50 | 2.25 | H |
| FC49 | Beyond the Pleasure Principle–Sigmund Freud | .75 | 1.50 | 2.25 | |
| AC50 | Pudd'nhead Wilson–Mark Twain; 1959 | 1.00 | 2.00 | 3.00 | |
| AC51 | Candide–Voltaire | .75 | 1.50 | 2.25 | |
| FC52 | Man and Superman–George Bernard Shaw | .75 | 1.50 | 2.25 | |

# BANTAM SPECIAL EDITION
## Bantam Books, Inc.
### Special Edition for Merrill Lynch, Pierce, Fenner and Smith

| | | V/Good | Fine | N/Mint |
|---|---|---|---|---|
| nn | How to Buy Stocks–Louis Engel; 1957 | .50 | 1.00 | 1.50 |

# BANTAM UNNUMBERED
## Bantam Books, Inc.

| | | V/Good | Fine | N/Mint | |
|---|---|---|---|---|---|
| nn | Roosevelt and Hopkins, Vol. 1–Robert E. Sherwood; 1950 | .75 | 1.50 | 2.25 | NF |
| nn | Roosevelt and Hopkins, Vol. 2–Robert E. Sherwood; 1950 | .75 | 1.50 | 2.25 | NF |
| nn | The Common Sense Book of Puppy and Dog Care–Harry Miller; 1956; Special Bantam Edition of Bantam A1528 | .75 | 1.50 | 2.25 | NF |

# (BARD)
## Bard Publishing Corporation
### Digest Size

| | | V/Good | Fine | N/Mint | |
|---|---|---|---|---|---|
| nn | Dead Giveaway–Dorothy Wheelock; 1944 | 3.50 | 7.00 | 10.50 | M |

# (BARNES)
## A.S. Barnes Company

| | | V/Good | Fine | N/Mint | |
|---|---|---|---|---|---|
| nn | The Encyclopedia of Sports–Frank G. Menke; 1955 | .50 | 1.00 | 1.50 | S |
| nn | Official 1957–58 Automobile Handbook– ed. Charles N. Barnard; 1957 | 1.00 | 2.00 | 3.00 | NF |

# BART HOUSE
## Bartholomew House, Inc.

| | | V/Good | Fine | N/Mint | |
|---|---|---|---|---|---|
| nn(1) | The Hand in the Cobbler's Safe–Seth Bailey; 1944 | 3.50 | 7.00 | 10.50 | M |
| nn(2) | The Delinquent Ghost–Eric Hatch | 3.00 | 6.00 | 9.00 | M |
| 3 | The Spy Trap–William Gilman | 3.00 | 6.00 | 9.00 | |
| 4 | Weird Shadow over Innsmouth–H.P. Lovecraft | 25.00 | 50.00 | 75.00 | SF |
| 5 | John Smith Hears Death Walking–Wyatt Blassingame | 4.00 | 8.00 | 12.00 | M |
| 6 | Rebirth–Thomas Calvert McClary | 10.00 | 20.00 | 30.00 | SF |
| 7 | The Shivering Bough–Noel Burke | 3.00 | 6.00 | 9.00 | M |
| 8 | The Blue Geranium–Dolan Birkley | 3.00 | 6.00 | 9.00 | M |
| 9 | The Waltz of Death–P.B. Maxon | 4.50 | 9.00 | 13.50 | M |
| 10 | The Devil Drives–Virgil Markham | 3.00 | 6.00 | 9.00 | M |
| 11 | Murder Meets Mephisto–Queena Mario; 1945 | 2.50 | 5.00 | 7.50 | M |
| 12 | The Dunwich Horror–H.P. Lovecraft | 22.50 | 45.00 | 67.50 | SF |
| 13 | 4 Feet in the Grave–Amelia Reynolds Long | 2.50 | 5.00 | 7.50 | M |
| 14 | The Wheelchair Corpse–Will Levinrew; aka Murder on the Palisades | 2.50 | 5.00 | 7.50 | M |
| 15 | Three Short Biers–Jimmy Starr | 2.50 | 5.00 | 7.50 | M |
| 16 | Murder Is Out–Lee Thayer | 2.50 | 5.00 | 7.50 | M |

| | | V/Good | Fine | N/Mint | |
|---|---|---|---|---|---|
| 17 | The Deaths of Lora Karen–Roman McDougald | 2.50 | 5.00 | 7.50 | M |
| 18 | Terry–Harriet T. Comstock | 2.50 | 5.00 | 7.50 | E |
| 19 | Said with Flowers–Anne Nash | 2.50 | 5.00 | 7.50 | M |
| 20 | Motionless Shadows–Kathleen Norris; aka Come Back to Me, Beloved | 2.00 | 4.00 | 6.00 | R |
| 21 | The Promise–Pearl S. Buck; 1946 | 2.00 | 4.00 | 6.00 | |
| 22 | Checkmate to Murder–E.C.R. Lorac | 2.50 | 5.00 | 7.50 | M |
| 23 | Roughly Speaking–Louise Randall Pierson | 2.00 | 4.00 | 6.00 | H |
| 24 | Murder Secretary–William Beyer; aka Eenie, Meenie, Minie–Murder! | 2.50 | 5.00 | 7.50 | M |
| 25 | Hollywood Mystery–Ben Hecht; aka I Hate Actors | 2.50 | 5.00 | 7.50 | M |
| 26 | Bury the Hatchet–Manning Long | 2.00 | 4.00 | 6.00 | M |
| 27 | Design for Dying–Louis Trimble | 2.00 | 4.00 | 6.00 | M |
| 28 | Grand Hotel–Vicki Baum | 2.00 | 4.00 | 6.00 | R |
| 29 | Puzzle in Porcelain–Robin Grey | 2.00 | 4.00 | 6.00 | M |
| 30 | The Lion's Skin–Rafael Sabatini | 2.50 | 5.00 | 7.50 | A |
| 31 | The Blue Cloak–Temple Bailey | 2.00 | 4.00 | 6.00 | R |
| 32 | Hangman's Tie–Christopher Hale | 2.50 | 5.00 | 7.50 | M |
| 33 | A Smattering of Ignorance–Oscar Levant | 2.00 | 4.00 | 6.00 | H |
| 34 | Death in the Cards–Ann T. Smith | 2.50 | 5.00 | 7.50 | M |
| 35 | The Clue in the Clay–D.B. Olsen | 2.00 | 4.00 | 6.00 | M |
| 36 | Murder among Friends–Lange Lewis | 2.00 | 4.00 | 6.00 | M |
| 39 | Can You Top This?–Senator Ed Ford, Harry Hershfield, Joe Laurie, Jr | 2.00 | 4.00 | 6.00 | H |
| 101 | Mr. Ace–Helen Christy; 1946; movie tie-in | 2.00 | 4.00 | 6.00 | M |
| 102 | The Sin of Harold Diddlebock–Harry Hershfield (ghostwritten by Walter B. Gibson); 1947; movie tie-in | 3.50 | 7.00 | 10.50 | H |
| 103 | Honeymoon–Elizabeth Ogilvie; movie tie-in | 2.50 | 5.00 | 7.50 | R |
| nn | The Defendant in the Case–ed. Henry Lieferant; 1946 | 3.00 | 6.00 | 9.00 | NF |

# BEACON
## Universal Publishing and Distributing Corporation

| | | V/Good | Fine | N/Mint | |
|---|---|---|---|---|---|
| B101 | She Got What She Wanted–Orrie Hitt; orig. 1954 | 3.00 | 6.00 | 9.00 | E |
| B102 | Pawn–Fan Nichols | 3.00 | 6.00 | 9.00 | E |
| B103 | Rooming House–Fred Malloy; orig. 1954 | 3.00 | 6.00 | 9.00 | E |
| B104 | Shabby Street–Orrie Hitt; orig. 1954 | 3.00 | 6.00 | 9.00 | E |
| B105 | King of the Khyber Rifles–Talbot Mundy. Note: Partially same cover as Beacon B154 | 5.00 | 10.00 | 15.00 | A |
| B106 | Walk in Darkness–Hans Habe | 3.00 | 6.00 | 9.00 | E |
| B107 | Stable Boy–Adam Rebel | 3.00 | 6.00 | 9.00 | E |
| B108 | Gutter Gang–Jay de Bekker | 7.50 | 15.00 | 22.50 | JD |
| B109 | Pick-up–Charles Willeford; 1st ed. 1955. Note: Same cover as Royal Giant No. 21 | 25.00 | 50.00 | 75.00 | E |
| B110 | Keyhole Peeper–Jay de Bekker | 3.00 | 6.00 | 9.00 | E |
| B111 | Liz–Frank Kane. Note: Same cover as Uni-Book 41 | 3.00 | 6.00 | 9.00 | E |

*Bart House 102, Beacon B103, Beacon B107.*

*Beacon B108, Beacon B113, Beacon B115.*

| | | V/Good | Fine | N/Mint | |
|---|---|---|---|---|---|
| BEACON, *continued* | | | | | |
| B112 | Lady Cop–J.T. Pritchard. Note: Virtually same cover as Uni-Book 32 | 3.00 | 6.00 | 9.00 | E |
| B113 | Highlights from Yank–The Army Weekly. Note: Same cover as Royal Giant 15 | 3.00 | 6.00 | 9.00 | C |
| B114 | Scandalous Lady–Fan Nichols | 3.00 | 6.00 | 9.00 | E |
| B115 | Gonzagas Woman–John Jakes | 3.50 | 7.00 | 10.50 | E |
| B116 | Hired Girl–Valerie Taylor | 3.50 | 7.00 | 10.50 | E |
| B117 | The Hussy–Idabel Williams. Note: Same cover as Universal Giant 1 | 3.00 | 6.00 | 9.00 | E |
| B118 | The Woman He Wanted–Daoma Winston. Note: Same cover as Royal Giant 27 | 3.00 | 6.00 | 9.00 | E |
| B119 | Forbidden Fruit–Curtis Lucas | 3.00 | 6.00 | 9.00 | E |
| B120 | Confessions of a Psychiatrist–Henry Lewis Nixon | 4.00 | 8.00 | 12.00 | E |
| B121 | Warped Women–Janet Pritchard | 3.00 | 6.00 | 9.00 | E |
| B122 | Dolly–Fan Nichols | 3.00 | 6.00 | 9.00 | E |
| B123 | Passion in the Pines–Jack Woodford & John B. Thompson. Note: Same cover as Uni-Book 63 | 3.00 | 6.00 | 9.00 | E |
| B124 | Honey–Jack Woodford & John B. Thompson. Note: Same cover as Uni-Book 64 | 3.00 | 6.00 | 9.00 | E |
| B125 | Swamp Hoyden–Jack Woodford & John B. Thompson. Note: Same cover as Uni-Books 36 and 71 | 3.00 | 6.00 | 9.00 | E |
| B126 | Unfaithful Wives–Orrie Hitt | 3.00 | 6.00 | 9.00 | E |
| B127 | Savage Eve–Jack Woodford & John B. Thompson. Note: Same cover as Uni-Book 60 | 3.00 | 6.00 | 9.00 | E |
| B128 | Witch on Wheels–William Boltin | 3.00 | 6.00 | 9.00 | E |
| B129 | Bayou Girl–John Thompson. Note: Same cover as Uni-Book 77 | 3.00 | 6.00 | 9.00 | E |
| B130 | High Priest of California–Charles Williford (Charles Willeford); 1st ed. (due to 1st publication of *Wild Wives*), 1956; aka Until I Am Dead | 20.00 | 40.00 | 60.00 | E |
| B131 | Rock'N Roll Gal–Ernie Weatherall. Note: Same cover as Uni-Book 38 | 10.00 | 20.00 | 30.00 | E |
| B132 | The Sucker–Orrie Hitt | 3.00 | 6.00 | 9.00 | E |
| B133 | French Model–Cecil Barr | 3.00 | 6.00 | 9.00 | E |
| B134 | Twisted–George Jones; c-Gross. Note: Same cover as Intimate No. 19 | 3.00 | 6.00 | 9.00 | E |
| B135 | Queer Affair–Carol Emery. Note: Same cover as Beacon B377, Intimate 52, and Stallion 210 | 3.00 | 6.00 | 9.00 | E |
| B136 | Shack Baby–Lon Williams | 3.00 | 6.00 | 9.00 | E |
| B137 | Nudist Camp–Orrie Hitt | 3.00 | 6.00 | 9.00 | E |
| B138 | Hitch-Hike Hussy–John B. Thompson & Jack Woodford | 3.00 | 6.00 | 9.00 | E |
| B139 | Pushover–Orrie Hitt. Note: Same cover as Beacon B380 and Uni-Book 44 | 3.00 | 6.00 | 9.00 | E |
| B140 | Sugar Doll–Jack Woodford & John B. Thompson | 3.00 | 6.00 | 9.00 | E |
| B141 | Love Peddler–Joe Weiss | 3.00 | 6.00 | 9.00 | E |
| B142 | The Promoter–Orrie Hitt | 3.00 | 6.00 | 9.00 | E |
| B143 | Shock Treatment–Wright Williams | 3.00 | 6.00 | 9.00 | E |
| B144 | Girls of the French Quarter–John B. Thompson | 3.00 | 6.00 | 9.00 | E |
| B145 | Passion Blues–Joe Weiss | 3.00 | 6.00 | 9.00 | E |

| | | V/Good | Fine | N/Mint | |
|---|---|---|---|---|---|
| B146 | Ladies Man–Orrie Hitt. Note: Same cover as Uni-Book 45 | 3.00 | 6.00 | 9.00 | E |
| B147 | Footloose Fraulein–Hans Habe | 3.00 | 6.00 | 9.00 | E |
| B148 | Love Fraud–Joe Weiss | 3.00 | 6.00 | 9.00 | E |
| B149 | Call Her Wanton–Lon Williams | 3.00 | 6.00 | 9.00 | E |
| B150 | Blonde Trap–Ernie Weatherall | 3.00 | 6.00 | 9.00 | E |
| B151 | Dolls and Dues–Orrie Hitt. Note: Same cover as Intimate 49 and Stallion 208 | 3.00 | 6.00 | 9.00 | E |
| B152 | Adam and Two Eves–anon. | 3.00 | 6.00 | 9.00 | E |
| B153 | Trailer Tramp–Orrie Hitt | 3.00 | 6.00 | 9.00 | E |
| B154 | Sinful Virgin–John B. Thompson. Note: Partially same cover as Beacon B105 | 3.00 | 6.00 | 9.00 | E |
| B155 | Gang Girl–Joe Weiss | 10.00 | 20.00 | 30.00 | E |
| B156 | Twilight Women–Les Scott. Note: Same cover as Universal Giant No. 9 | 3.00 | 6.00 | 9.00 | E |
| B157 | Paprika–Eric Von Stroheim. Note: Same cover as Universal Giant No. 2 | 3.00 | 6.00 | 9.00 | E |
| B158 | Teaser–Orrie Hitt | 3.00 | 6.00 | 9.00 | E |
| B159 | Ellie's Shack–Orrie Hitt. Note: Same cover as Intimate 11 | 3.00 | 6.00 | 9.00 | E |
| B160 | Honey Gal–Charles Willeford; 1st ed. 1958 | 25.00 | 50.00 | 75.00 | E |
| B161 | Back of Town–Herbert Pruett | 3.00 | 6.00 | 9.00 | E |
| B162 | Hill Hoyden–Lon Williams. Note: Same cover as Uni-Book 71 | 3.00 | 6.00 | 9.00 | E |
| B163 | Hell Bent–H.P. Ames | 3.00 | 6.00 | 9.00 | E |
| B164 | Suburban Wife–Orrie Hitt | 3.00 | 6.00 | 9.00 | E |
| B165 | Gutter Gang–Jay de Bekker | 4.00 | 8.00 | 12.00 | E |
| B166 | The Private Pleasures of Mary Linton–William Arthur | 3.00 | 6.00 | 9.00 | E |
| B167 | Play for Pay–Wright Williams | 3.00 | 6.00 | 9.00 | E |
| B168 | Summer Hotel–Orrie Hitt. Note: Same cover as Uni-Book 34 | 3.00 | 6.00 | 9.00 | E |
| B169 | Wild Oats–Orrie Hitt | 3.00 | 6.00 | 9.00 | E |
| B170 | Side Street–Wright Williams | 3.00 | 6.00 | 9.00 | E |
| B171 | Wild Hunger–Fred Malloy | 3.00 | 6.00 | 9.00 | E |
| B172 | Woman He Wanted–Daoma Winston | 3.00 | 6.00 | 9.00 | E |
| B173 | Forbidden Fruit–Curtis Lucas | 3.00 | 6.00 | 9.00 | E |
| B174 | Affairs of a Beauty Queen–Orrie Hitt | 3.00 | 6.00 | 9.00 | E |
| B175 | Lust Is a Woman–Charles Williford (Charles Willeford); 1st ed. 1958 | 25.00 | 50.00 | 75.00 | E |
| B176 | Call South 3300: Ask for Molly!–Orrie Hitt | 3.00 | 6.00 | 9.00 | E |
| B177 | Hill Hellion!–Lon Williams. Note: Same cover as Uni-Book 29 | 3.00 | 6.00 | 9.00 | E |
| B178 | Fair Game–Clement Wood | 3.00 | 6.00 | 9.00 | E |
| B179 | The Girl in the Black Chemise–Les Scott | 3.00 | 6.00 | 9.00 | E |
| B180 | Burlesque Girl–Orrie Hitt | 3.00 | 6.00 | 9.00 | E |
| B181 | Back Alley–Frank Smith. Note: Same cover as Falcon 43 and Intimate 20 | 3.00 | 6.00 | 9.00 | E |
| B182 | Fast Girl–Token West | 3.00 | 6.00 | 9.00 | E |
| B183 | The Naked and the Fair–Hal Moore | 3.00 | 6.00 | 9.00 | E |
| B184 | Confessions of a Psychiatrist–Henry Lewis Nixon. Note: Same cover as Uni-Book 31 | 3.00 | 6.00 | 9.00 | E |
| B185 | Rooming House–Fred Malloy | 3.00 | 6.00 | 9.00 | E |
| B186 | Trapped–Orrie Hitt | 3.00 | 6.00 | 9.00 | E |
| B187 | The Lusting Breed–Mary S. Gooch | 3.00 | 6.00 | 9.00 | E |
| B188 | I Made My Bed–Celia Hye | 3.00 | 6.00 | 9.00 | E |
| B189 | Studio Affair–Clement Wood | 3.00 | 6.00 | 9.00 | E |

*Beacon B160, Beacon B175, Beacon B180.*

| | | V/Good | Fine | N/Mint | |
|---|---|---|---|---|---|

BEACON, *continued*

| | | V/Good | Fine | N/Mint | |
|---|---|---|---|---|---|
| B190 | Three Women–March Hastings | 3.00 | 6.00 | 9.00 | E |
| B191 | Girl's Dormitory–Orrie Hitt | 3.00 | 6.00 | 9.00 | E |
| B192 | Forbidden–J.C. Priest | 3.00 | 6.00 | 9.00 | E |
| B193 | The Other Stranger–Daoma Winston | 3.00 | 6.00 | 9.00 | E |
| B194 | Shabby Street–Orrie Hitt | 3.00 | 6.00 | 9.00 | E |
| B195 | She Got What She Wanted–Orrie Hitt | 3.00 | 6.00 | 9.00 | E |
| B196 | The Mistress–Colin Ross | 3.00 | 6.00 | 9.00 | E |
| B197 | Woman Hunt–Orrie Hitt | 3.00 | 6.00 | 9.00 | E |
| B198 | Shame–March Hastings | 3.00 | 6.00 | 9.00 | E |
| B199 | Combat–The Best from Yank | 3.00 | 6.00 | 9.00 | C |
| B200 | Pick-up–Charles Willeford. Note: Same cover as Royal Giant 21 | 15.00 | 30.00 | 45.00 | E |
| B201 | Keyhole Peeper–Jay de Bekker | 3.00 | 6.00 | 9.00 | E |
| B202 | School for Girls–George Kramer | 3.00 | 6.00 | 9.00 | E |
| B203 | Hot Cargo–Orrie Hitt; 1958 | 3.00 | 6.00 | 9.00 | E |
| B204 | Surabaya–James Fox | 3.00 | 6.00 | 9.00 | A |
| B205 | Red Curtain–Duncan Taylor; 1959 | 3.00 | 6.00 | 9.00 | E |
| B206 | The Cheat–Orrie Hitt | 3.00 | 6.00 | 9.00 | E |
| B207 | Circle of Sin–March Hastings | 3.00 | 6.00 | 9.00 | E |
| B208 | Spawn of the Bayou–John B. Thompson | 3.00 | 6.00 | 9.00 | E |
| B209 | Rotten to the Core–Orrie Hitt | 3.00 | 6.00 | 9.00 | E |
| B210 | The Dispossessed–Geoffrey Wagner | 3.00 | 6.00 | 9.00 | E |
| B211 | Sheba–Orrie Hitt | 3.00 | 6.00 | 9.00 | E |
| B212 | Nudist Camp–Orrie Hitt | 3.00 | 6.00 | 9.00 | E |
| B213 | Hitch-Hike Hussy–John B. Thompson & Jack Woodford | 3.00 | 6.00 | 9.00 | E |
| B214 | Adulteress–Lon Williams | 3.00 | 6.00 | 9.00 | E |
| B215 | Passionate Land–Geoffrey Wagner | 3.00 | 6.00 | 9.00 | E |
| B216 | Steffi–Eunice Gray | 3.00 | 6.00 | 9.00 | E |
| B217 | Slave Ship–H.B. Drake | 3.00 | 6.00 | 9.00 | E |
| B218 | Strumpet's Seed–Fred Malloy | 3.00 | 6.00 | 9.00 | E |
| B219 | Tabasco–John B. Thompson | 3.00 | 6.00 | 9.00 | E |
| B220 | Scandalous Lady–Fan Nichols | 3.00 | 6.00 | 9.00 | E |
| B221 | The Hussy–Idabel Williams | 3.00 | 6.00 | 9.00 | E |
| B222 | The Widow–Orrie Hitt | 3.00 | 6.00 | 9.00 | E |
| B223 | Chris–Randy Salem | 3.00 | 6.00 | 9.00 | E |
| B224 | Half-caste–John B. Thompson | 3.00 | 6.00 | 9.00 | E |
| B225 | Kate–Chet Kinsey | 3.00 | 6.00 | 9.00 | E |
| B226 | The Strange Ones–Ben Travis | 3.00 | 6.00 | 9.00 | E |
| B227 | Add Flesh to the Fire–Orrie Hitt | 3.00 | 6.00 | 9.00 | E |
| B228 | Nude in the Mirror–George Viereck | 3.00 | 6.00 | 9.00 | E |
| B229 | Alcoholic Woman–Ruth M. Walsh | 3.00 | 6.00 | 9.00 | E |
| B230 | Odd Girl–Artemis Smith | 3.00 | 6.00 | 9.00 | E |
| B231 | Tap Softly on My Bedroom Door–Roswell Lewis | 3.00 | 6.00 | 9.00 | E |
| B232 | Private Club–Orrie Hitt. Note: Same cover as Ecstasy 16 | 3.00 | 6.00 | 9.00 | E |
| B233 | Turncoat–Richard Fox. Note: Same cover as Falcon 41 | 3.00 | 6.00 | 9.00 | E |
| B234 | Night of Shame–Lewis Lester | 3.00 | 6.00 | 9.00 | E |
| B235 | Lita–Fred Malloy | 3.00 | 6.00 | 9.00 | E |
| 236 | Odd John–Olaf Stapledon; 1959 | 7.50 | 15.00 | 22.50 | SF |
| B237 | The Needle–Sloane M. Britain | 7.50 | 15.00 | 22.50 | E |
| B238 | Carnival Girl–Orrie Hitt. Note: Same cover as Intimate 30 | 3.00 | 6.00 | 9.00 | E |
| B239 | The Peeper–Orrie Hitt | 3.00 | 6.00 | 9.00 | E |
| B240 | Temple of Lust–John Burton Thompson | 3.00 | 6.00 | 9.00 | E |
| B241 | Street Walker–E.S. Seeley | 3.00 | 6.00 | 9.00 | E |
| 242 | The Deviates–Raymond F. Jones | 6.00 | 12.00 | 18.00 | SF |
| B243 | Hellcat–Dorine Clark | 3.00 | 6.00 | 9.00 | E |
| B244 | The Virgin–Don Morro | 3.00 | 6.00 | 9.00 | E |
| B245 | The Young Hoods–Joe Castro | 7.50 | 15.00 | 22.50 | JD |
| B246 | The Divorcees–Scott Stone | 3.00 | 6.00 | 9.00 | E |
| B247 | Too Many Women–Barry Devlin | 3.00 | 6.00 | 9.00 | E |
| B248 | Margo–Scott Stone | 3.00 | 6.00 | 9.00 | E |
| 249 | Thirty One Short Stories from Colliers–anthology. Note: Includes some fantasy | 4.00 | 8.00 | 12.00 | |
| B250 | Too Hot to Handle–Orrie Hitt | 3.00 | 6.00 | 9.00 | E |
| B251 | One-Kind of Woman–Ralph Dean | 3.00 | 6.00 | 9.00 | E |
| B252 | Cheating Wives–Barry Devlin | 3.00 | 6.00 | 9.00 | E |
| B253 | Nude in the Sand–John Burton Thompson | 3.00 | 6.00 | 9.00 | E |
| B254 | Sin Doll–Orrie Hitt | 3.00 | 6.00 | 9.00 | E |
| B255 | Make Sure I Win–Barry Devlin | 3.00 | 6.00 | 9.00 | E |
| 256 | Troubled Star–George O. Smith; 1959 | 5.00 | 10.00 | 15.00 | SF |
| B257 | Shack Woman–Kathie Reed | 3.00 | 6.00 | 9.00 | E |
| B258 | Wild Blonde–Jack Kelly | 3.00 | 6.00 | 9.00 | E |
| B259 | Queer Patterns–Kay Addams | 3.00 | 6.00 | 9.00 | E |

| | | V/Good | Fine | N/Mint | |
|---|---|---|---|---|---|
| B260 | Basement Gang–David Williams; 1959. Note: Virtually same cover as Intimate 32 and Stallion 213 | 10.00 | 20.00 | 30.00 | JD |
| B261 | Tawny–Orrie Hill | 3.00 | 6.00 | 9.00 | E |
| B262 | Danielle–Joseph Foster | 3.00 | 6.00 | 9.00 | E |
| 263 | Pagan Passions–Randall Garrett & Larry M. Harris; 1st ed. 1959 | 6.00 | 12.00 | 18.00 | SF |
| B264 | Strange Thirsts–Michael Norday | 3.00 | 6.00 | 9.00 | E |
| B265 | Hot Blood–John B. Thompson | 3.00 | 6.00 | 9.00 | E |
| B266 | Strip-Tease Girl–Cal Anton | 3.00 | 6.00 | 9.00 | E |
| B267 | Ex-Virgin–Orrie Hitt | 3.00 | 6.00 | 9.00 | E |
| B268 | The Third Sex–Artemis Smith | 3.00 | 6.00 | 9.00 | E |
| B269 | Private School–J.C. Priest | 3.00 | 6.00 | 9.00 | E |
| 270 | Virgin Planet–Poul Anderson; 1960 | 6.00 | 12.00 | 18.00 | SF |
| B271 | Naked Desire–Henry Louis Nixon | 3.00 | 6.00 | 9.00 | E |
| B272 | Golden Tramp–Daoma Winston | 3.00 | 6.00 | 9.00 | E |
| B273 | Of G-Strings and Strippers–Mark Tryon | 3.00 | 6.00 | 9.00 | E |
| B274 | Suburban Sin–Orrie Hitt | 3.00 | 6.00 | 9.00 | E |
| B275 | Mimi–Lee Morell | 3.00 | 6.00 | 9.00 | E |
| B276 | Triangle of Sin–Manning | 3.00 | 6.00 | 9.00 | E |
| 277 | Flesh–Philip Jose Farmer; 1st ed. 1960 | 25.00 | 50.00 | 75.00 | SF |
| B278 | Sorority Sin–E.S. Seeley | 3.00 | 6.00 | 9.00 | E |
| B279 | Convention Girl–Rick Lucas | 3.00 | 6.00 | 9.00 | E |
| B280 | Warped–Michael Norday | 3.00 | 6.00 | 9.00 | E |
| B281 | Strange Circle–Gale Sydney | 3.00 | 6.00 | 9.00 | E |
| B282 | Mavis–Justin Kent | 3.00 | 6.00 | 9.00 | E |
| B283 | Night of the Lash–Barry Devlin | 3.00 | 6.00 | 9.00 | E |
| 284 | The Sex War–Sam Merwin; 1960; aka The White Widows | 6.00 | 12.00 | 18.00 | SF |
| B285 | Ex-Mistress–Thomas Stone | 3.00 | 6.00 | 9.00 | E |
| B286 | Helena's House–Kim Savage | 3.00 | 6.00 | 9.00 | E |
| B287 | Pound of Flesh–Simms Albert | 3.00 | 6.00 | 9.00 | E |
| B288 | Wayward Girl–Orrie Hitt | 3.00 | 6.00 | 9.00 | E |
| B289 | Warped Desire–Kay Addams | 3.00 | 6.00 | 9.00 | E |
| B290 | Scarlet City–Winchell Barry | 3.00 | 6.00 | 9.00 | E |
| 291 | A Woman a Day–Philip Jose Farmer; 1st ed. 1960 | 25.00 | 50.00 | 75.00 | SF |
| B292 | Male Virgin–Jack Woodford & John Burton Thompson | 3.00 | 6.00 | 9.00 | E |
| B293 | Station Wagon Wives–Janet Pritchard | 3.00 | 6.00 | 9.00 | E |
| B294 | The Torrid Teens–Orrie Hitt | 3.00 | 6.00 | 9.00 | E |
| B295 | Song of the Whip–Barry Devlin | 3.00 | 6.00 | 9.00 | E |
| B296 | Very Private Secretary–Jack Hanley | 3.00 | 6.00 | 9.00 | E |
| B297 | Summer Resort Women–Gordon Semple | 3.00 | 6.00 | 9.00 | E |
| 298 | The Mating Cry–A.E. Van Vogt; 1960; aka The House That Stood Still | 12.50 | 25.00 | 37.50 | SF |
| B299 | Ask for Therese–Evans Wall | 3.00 | 6.00 | 9.00 | E |
| B300 | Lingerie Limited–Ralph Dean | 3.00 | 6.00 | 9.00 | E |
| B301 | One More for the Road–John Burton Thompson | 3.00 | 6.00 | 9.00 | E |
| B302 | Doctor Prescott's Secret–Peggy Gaddis | 3.00 | 6.00 | 9.00 | E |
| B303 | Restless Women–Rick Lucas | 3.00 | 6.00 | 9.00 | E |
| B304 | From Door to Door–Orrie Hitt; 1960 | 3.00 | 6.00 | 9.00 | E |
| 305 | The Male Response–Brian Aldiss; 1st ed. 1961 | 6.00 | 12.00 | 18.00 | SF |
| B306 | Gutter Girl–Leo Rifkin & Tony Norman | 3.00 | 6.00 | 9.00 | JD |
| B307 | Pleasure Alley–Ralph Carter. Note: Same cover as Intimate 20 and Falcon 43 | 3.00 | 6.00 | 9.00 | E |
| B308 | Lucy–Kay Addams | 3.00 | 6.00 | 9.00 | E |
| B309 | Hucksters' Women–Rick Lucas | 3.00 | 6.00 | 9.00 | E |
| B310 | Infidelity–Fred Malloy | 3.00 | 6.00 | 9.00 | E |

*Beacon B260, Beacon 263, Beacon 270.*

**BEACON,** *continued*

| # | Title | V/Good | Fine | N/Mint | |
|---|---|---|---|---|---|
| B311 | Different–Dorene Clark | 3.00 | 6.00 | 9.00 | E |
| 312 | Sin in Space–Cyril Judd (Judith Merril & C.M. Kornbluth); 1961; aka Outpost Mars | 6.00 | 12.00 | 18.00 | SF |
| B313 | Private Chauffeur–N.R. DeMexico | 3.00 | 6.00 | 9.00 | E |
| B314 | Motel Girls–Orrie Hitt | 3.00 | 6.00 | 9.00 | E |
| B315 | She Learned the Hard Way–Scott Stone | 3.00 | 6.00 | 9.00 | E |
| B316 | Nurse's Quarters–Lee Morell | 3.00 | 6.00 | 9.00 | E |
| B317 | Trailer Camp Women–Doug Duperrault | 3.00 | 6.00 | 9.00 | E |
| B318 | Philanderer's Women–Lewis Lester | 3.00 | 6.00 | 9.00 | E |
| B320 | The Hayloft–Gregory Swanson | 3.00 | 6.00 | 9.00 | E |
| B321 | Lust for Love–Florence Stonebreaker | 3.00 | 6.00 | 9.00 | E |
| B322 | Intimate Physician–Florenz Branch | 3.00 | 6.00 | 9.00 | E |
| B323 | Wanton–Ben Smith | 3.00 | 6.00 | 9.00 | E |
| B324 | She Made Her Bed–Evans McKnight | 3.00 | 6.00 | 9.00 | E |
| B325 | Tell Them Anything–Orrie Hitt | 3.00 | 6.00 | 9.00 | E |
| B327 | Play Girl–Barney DeForest | 3.00 | 6.00 | 9.00 | E |
| B328 | Marijuana Girl–N.R. DeMexico | 15.00 | 30.00 | 45.00 | E |
| B329 | The Eager Ones–John Burton Thompson | 3.00 | 6.00 | 9.00 | E |
| B330 | Alcoholic Wife–G.G. Revelle | 3.00 | 6.00 | 9.00 | E |
| B337 | Prime Sucker–Harry Whittington | 3.00 | 6.00 | 9.00 | E |
| B350 | Strip the Town Naked–Whit Harrison (Harry Whittington) | 3.00 | 6.00 | 9.00 | E |
| B392 | Any Woman He Wanted–Whit Harrison (Harry Whittington) | 3.00 | 6.00 | 9.00 | E |

## (BEARMAN)
## Samuel Bearman
### Digest Size

| # | Title | V/Good | Fine | N/Mint | |
|---|---|---|---|---|---|
| nn | Past Sin–Eliot Brewster | 3.00 | 6.00 | 9.00 | E |

## BELMONT BOOKS
## Belmont Productions, Inc.

**Note: Later numbers in this series add a two-digit prefix, with the later stock number continuing the numbering sequence.**

| # | Title | V/Good | Fine | N/Mint | |
|---|---|---|---|---|---|
| 201 | Temptress–Andre Maurois; 1960; aka September Roses | 1.50 | 3.00 | 4.50 | E |
| 202 | The Question–Henri Alleg | 1.50 | 3.00 | 4.50 | NF |
| 203 | Payola Woman–Carson Bingham | 1.50 | 3.00 | 4.50 | E |
| 204 | Johnny Havoc–John Jakes | 2.50 | 5.00 | 7.50 | M |
| 205 | Who Live in Shadow–Judge John Murtagh & Sara Harris | 1.50 | 3.00 | 4.50 | NF |
| 206 | Bloody Precinct–Bill Douglas | 1.50 | 3.00 | 4.50 | M |
| 207 | The Cruel City–Joe Mackey | 1.50 | 3.00 | 4.50 | E |
| 208 | The Slave–Micheline Maurel; aka An Ordinary Camp | 1.50 | 3.00 | 4.50 | NF |
| 209 | Hong Kong Kill–Bryan Peters | 1.50 | 3.00 | 4.50 | E |
| 210 | The Oldest Profession–Jean Campbell | 1.50 | 3.00 | 4.50 | E |
| 211 | Cage of Passion–Isa Mari; movie tie-in | 1.50 | 3.00 | 4.50 | E |
| 212 | Something Wild–Alex Karmel; aka Mary Ann; movie tie-in | 2.00 | 4.00 | 6.00 | E |
| 213 | The Blanket–A.A. Murray | 1.50 | 3.00 | 4.50 | |
| 214 | Come-on Girl–Stuart Friedman | 1.50 | 3.00 | 4.50 | E |
| 215 | Lights, Camera, Murder–John Shepherd | 2.50 | 5.00 | 7.50 | M |
| 216 | Concha–Philippe Sollers; aka A Strange Solitude; c-Maguire | 2.50 | 5.00 | 7.50 | E |
| 217 | Sugar Shannon–Adam Knight | 1.50 | 3.00 | 4.50 | M |
| 218 | Sex-Clusive–Jack Heller | 3.00 | 6.00 | 9.00 | H |
| 219 | Hitler's Woman–Antoni Gronowicz; aka Hitler's Wife | 1.50 | 3.00 | 4.50 | B |
| 220 | South Pacific Affair–Ed Lacy; 1961 | 2.00 | 4.00 | 6.00 | E |
| 221 | Vice Cop–Richard Deming | 1.50 | 3.00 | 4.50 | M |
| 222 | A Wind Is Rising–William Russell | 1.50 | 3.00 | 4.50 | E |
| 223 | Skid Row U.S.A.–Sara Harris | 1.50 | 3.00 | 4.50 | NF |
| 224 | Lonely Boy Blues–Alan Kapelner | 1.50 | 3.00 | 4.50 | |
| 225 | Foxhole in Cairo–Leonard Mosley | 1.50 | 3.00 | 4.50 | |
| 226 | Neither Sin nor Shame–Ann Marie Burgess & Michael Burgess | 1.50 | 3.00 | 4.50 | |
| 227 | The Borgia Blade–Gardner F. Fox | 2.00 | 4.00 | 6.00 | A |

| # | Title | V/Good | Fine | N/Mint | |
|---|---|---|---|---|---|
| 228 | The Ladies Man–Carl Winston; movie tie-in | 1.50 | 3.00 | 4.50 | |
| 229 | Ten Against the Third Reich–Stan Smith | 1.50 | 3.00 | 4.50 | NF |
| 230 | Creeps by Night–ed. Dashiell Hammett | 2.50 | 5.00 | 7.50 | HO |
| 231 | My Life and Loves in Greenwich Village–Maxwell Bodenheim | 1.50 | 3.00 | 4.50 | B |
| 232 | The Day the War Ends–Irwin Shaw | 1.50 | 3.00 | 4.50 | NF |
| 233 | Nightmares–Robert Bloch | 3.50 | 7.00 | 10.50 | HO |
| 234 | Love Doctor–Florence Stonebraker | 1.50 | 3.00 | 4.50 | E |
| 235 | A Gun for Cantrell–Harry Sinclair Drago | 1.50 | 3.00 | 4.50 | W |
| 236 | Markham–Lawrence Block; TV tie-in | 3.00 | 6.00 | 9.00 | M |
| 237 | Stronger Than Fear–Richard Tregaskis | 1.50 | 3.00 | 4.50 | C |
| 238 | 13 Against the Rising Sun–Stanley E. Smith | 1.50 | 3.00 | 4.50 | NF |
| 239 | The Red Brain–ed. Dashiell Hammett | 2.50 | 5.00 | 7.50 | HO |
| 240 | Lover Boy–John B. Flint | 1.50 | 3.00 | 4.50 | E |
| 241 | The Trail of Johnny Dice–Harry Sinclair Drago | 1.50 | 3.00 | 4.50 | W |
| 242 | The Back of the Tiger–Richard Cargoe | 1.50 | 3.00 | 4.50 | E |
| 243 | The Love Mill–Louis Malley | 1.50 | 3.00 | 4.50 | E |
| 244 | Nurse Durand's Affair–Peggy Gaddis | 1.25 | 2.50 | 3.75 | R |
| 245 | Hotel Doctor–Frank Haskell | 1.25 | 2.50 | 3.75 | E |
| 246 | The Horror Expert–Frank B. Long | 3.00 | 6.00 | 9.00 | HO |
| 91-252 | Naughty but Dead–G.G. Fickling | 2.00 | 4.00 | 6.00 | M |
| 91-254 | M-Squad–David Saunders; TV tie-in | 2.50 | 5.00 | 7.50 | M |
| 90-261 | Johnny Havoc Meets Zelda–John Jakes | 2.50 | 5.00 | 7.50 | M |
| 90-265 | Jailbait Jungle–Wenzell Brown | 4.00 | 8.00 | 12.00 | JD |
| 90-269 | Hot as Fire, Cold as Ice–Harry Whittington | 2.50 | 5.00 | 7.50 | M |
| 90-275 | Horror 7–Robert Bloch; 1st ed. 1962 | 4.00 | 8.00 | 12.00 | HO |
| 90-276 | The Bedroom Bolero–Michael Avallone | 2.50 | 5.00 | 7.50 | M |
| 90-277 | It Was the Day of the Robot–Frank Belknap Long | 2.50 | 5.00 | 7.50 | SF |
| 90-281 | The Case of the Radioactive Redhead–G.G. Fickling | 2.00 | 4.00 | 6.00 | M |
| 90-286 | The Machine in Ward Eleven–Charles Willeford | 6.00 | 12.00 | 18.00 | SF |
| 90-289 | Johnny Havoc and the Girl Who Had "It"–John Jakes | 3.00 | 6.00 | 9.00 | M |
| 90-293 | There *Is* Something about a Dame–Michael Avallone | 2.00 | 4.00 | 6.00 | M |
| 90-297 | Tales of the Frightened–Michael Avallone | 2.50 | 5.00 | 7.50 | HO |
| 90-298 | Return of the Shadow–Walter Gibson; orig. 1963 | 5.00 | 10.00 | 15.00 | M |
| 90-316 | Nightmare Street–Hal Ellson | 4.00 | 8.00 | 12.00 | JD |
| 90-318 | Lust Is No Lady–Michael Avallone | 2.00 | 4.00 | 6.00 | E |

## BELMONT BOOKS L/B-SERIES
## Belmont Productions, Inc.

**Note: Later numbers in this series add a three-character pricing prefix, with the later stock numbers continuing the numbering sequence.**

| # | Title | V/Good | Fine | N/Mint | |
|---|---|---|---|---|---|
| L501 | Varieties of Love–Herbert Kubly | 1.25 | 2.50 | 3.75 | |
| L502 | The Incorrigibles–William Wiegand; aka The Treatment Man | 1.25 | 2.50 | 3.75 | |
| L503 | Sex Life of the Modern Adult–Dr. Leland E. Glover | 1.25 | 2.50 | 3.75 | NF |
| L504 | The Brigitte Bardot Story–George Carpozi, Jr | 5.00 | 10.00 | 15.00 | B |
| L505 | The Cheat–Charles Jackson; aka Earthly Creatures | 1.25 | 2.50 | 3.75 | |
| L506 | The Secret Agent's Badge of Courage–ed. Ernest Hemingway | 1.50 | 3.00 | 4.50 | |
| L507 | Meet the Mob–Detective Mullady & Bill Kofoed | 1.25 | 2.50 | 3.75 | NF |
| L508 | Marilyn Monroe: "Her Own Story"–George Carpori, Jr | 10.00 | 20.00 | 30.00 | B |
| L509 | The Battle of Leyte Gulf–Stan Smith | 1.25 | 2.50 | 3.75 | NF |
| L510 | Most Likely to Succeed–John Dos Passos | 1.25 | 2.50 | 3.75 | |
| L511 | The Traitor–W. Somerset Maugham | 1.25 | 2.50 | 3.75 | |
| L512 | The Shadow in the Rose Garden–D.H. Lawrence | 1.50 | 3.00 | 4.50 | E |
| L513 | How to Get Rich Buying Stocks–Ira U. Cobleigh | 1.00 | 2.00 | 3.00 | NF |

| | | V/Good | Fine | N/Mint |
|---|---|---|---|---|

BELMONT BOOKS L/B-SERIES, *continued*

| | | V/Good | Fine | N/Mint |
|---|---|---|---|---|
| L514 | Sinatra and His Rat Pack–Richard Gehman | 2.50 | 5.00 | 7.50 B |
| L515 | Memoirs–Admiral Karl Doenitz | 1.25 | 2.50 | 3.75 NF |
| L516 | The Ambassador–Aldous Huxley | 1.25 | 2.50 | 3.75 |
| L517 | Eat Your Troubles Away–Dr. Lelord Kordel | 1.00 | 2.00 | 3.00 NF |
| L518 | Come into My Parlor–Charles Washburn | 1.25 | 2.50 | 3.75 E |
| L519 | Khrushchev's "Mein Kampf"–Harrison E. Salisbury | 1.25 | 2.50 | 3.75 NF |
| L520 | Black-Shirt–Graham Fisher & Michael McNair-Wilson | 1.50 | 3.00 | 4.50 NF |
| L521 | The Integration of Maybelle Brown– Bonnie Golightly; 1961 | 1.25 | 2.50 | 3.75 E |
| L522 | Behind Every Door–Julius Horwitz | 1.25 | 2.50 | 3.75 |
| L523 | Sex Life of the Modern Teen-ager–Dr. Leland E. Glover | 1.00 | 2.00 | 3.00 NF |
| L524 | Berlin Betrayal–Willi Frischaver | 1.00 | 2.00 | 3.00 NF |
| 92-602 | The Shadow Strikes–Maxwell Grant (Dennis Lynds); orig. 1964 | 4.00 | 8.00 | 12.00 M |
| 92-603 | The Penultimate Truth–Philip K. Dick | 2.00 | 4.00 | 6.00 SF |
| 92-605 | The Lust Seekers–Peggy Gaddis; aka Man-Hungry Widow | 1.50 | 3.00 | 4.50 E |
| 92-606 | Masters of Science Fiction–anthology | 1.50 | 3.00 | 4.50 SF |
| 92-607 | The Corpse Moved Upstairs–Frank Gruber; aka The Mighty Blockhead | 1.50 | 3.00 | 4.50 M |
| 92-609 | The Crazy Mixed-Up Nude–G.G. Fickling | 1.50 | 3.00 | 4.50 M |
| 92-611 | The Unearth People–Kris Neville | 1.25 | 2.50 | 3.75 SF |
| 92-612 | Giants in the Earth–James Blish | 1.25 | 2.50 | 3.75 SF |
| | We, the Marauders–Robert Silverberg | | | SF |
| 92-615 | Shadow Beware–Maxwell Grant (Dennis Lynds); orig. 1965 | 4.00 | 8.00 | 12.00 M |
| 92-617 | The Case of Charles Dexter Ward–H.P. Lovecraft | 1.50 | 3.00 | 4.50 HO |
| 92-618 | Time Out of Joint–Philip K. Dick | 2.00 | 4.00 | 6.00 SF |
| 92-623 | Dirty Gertie–Henry Kane | 1.50 | 3.00 | 4.50 M |
| 92-624 | Cry Shadow–Maxwell Grant (Dennis Lynds); orig. 1965 | 4.00 | 8.00 | 12.00 M |
| 92-636 | Young Dillinger–Sidney Stuart (Michael Avallone) | 2.00 | 4.00 | 6.00 M |
| L92-526 | Himmler–Willi Frischauer; 1962 | 1.50 | 3.00 | 4.50 NF |
| L92-527 | Yours Truly, Jack the Ripper–Robert Bloch; 1st ed. 1962 | 4.00 | 8.00 | 12.00 HO |
| L92-528 | Heroic Battles of World War II–Maj. H. Oleck | 1.00 | 2.00 | 3.00 NF |
| L92-529 | A Psychiatrist Talks about Sex–F.S. Caprio, MD | 1.00 | 2.00 | 3.00 NF |
| L92-530 | More Nightmares–Robert Bloch; 1st ed. 1962 | 4.00 | 8.00 | 12.00 HO |
| L92-531 | The Amazing Hypno-Diet–Jack Heise | 1.00 | 2.00 | 3.00 NF |
| L92-532 | Zone of Violence–Donald Dunham | 1.00 | 2.00 | 3.00 |
| L92-533 | Eat Your Way to Happiness–Dr. Lelord Kordel | 1.00 | 2.00 | 3.00 NF |
| L92-534 | Diary of a French Doctor–Charles F. Bove, MD | 1.50 | 3.00 | 4.50 NF |
| L92-535 | Twisted–ed. Groff Conklin | 1.50 | 3.00 | 4.50 SF |
| L92-536 | Get Me Giesler–John Roeburt | 1.50 | 3.00 | 4.50 NF |
| L92-537 | Terror–Robert Bloch; 1st ed. 1962; aka Kill for Kali | 4.00 | 8.00 | 12.00 HO |
| L94-538 | Citizens–Meyer Levin | 1.00 | 2.00 | 3.00 |
| L92-539 | How to Get Along with Your Child– Shirley Camper | 1.00 | 2.00 | 3.00 NF |
| L92-540 | Private Case-Book of an M.D.–C.S. Wachtel | 1.00 | 2.00 | 3.00 NF |
| L92-541 | The Weird Ones–ed. H.L. Gold | 2.00 | 4.00 | 6.00 SF |
| L92-542 | The Lonely Sex–Estelle H. Ries | 1.00 | 2.00 | 3.00 SF |
| L92-543 | A Doctor's Personal Files–C.S. Wachtel | 1.00 | 2.00 | 3.00 SF |
| L92-544 | A Professional Gambler Tells How to Win–Mike "Pitcher" Barron | 1.00 | 2.00 | 3.00 SF |
| L92-545 | For Men Only–Beth Brown | 1.50 | 3.00 | 4.50 SF |
| L92-546 | My Friend Henry Miller–Alfred Perles | 2.50 | 5.00 | 7.50 SF |
| L92-547 | The X Report–from Sexology Magazine | 1.00 | 2.00 | 3.00 NF |
| L92-548 | Fathers Are Parents Too–Foster & English | 1.00 | 2.00 | 3.00 NF |
| L92-549 | Calories, Vitamins and Common Sense–H. Curtis Wood, Jr, MD | 1.00 | 2.00 | 3.00 NF |
| L92-550 | Lulie–Peggy Gaddis | 1.50 | 3.00 | 4.50 R |
| L92-551 | My Name Is Violence–John L. Matthews | 1.50 | 3.00 | 4.50 |

| | | V/Good | Fine | N/Mint |
|---|---|---|---|---|
| L92-552 | Normal and Abnormal Sex-Ways–Dr. Leo Klein | 1.00 | 2.00 | 3.00 NF |
| L92-553 | How to Get Rich with Security–E.S. Grant | 1.00 | 2.00 | 3.00 NF |
| L92-554 | The Profession of Marie Simone–Beth Brown | 1.50 | 3.00 | 4.50 R |
| L92-555 | Union Square–Albert Halper | 1.00 | 2.00 | 3.00 |
| L92-556 | A Biography of Vince Edwards–Geo. Carpozi, Jr | 1.50 | 3.00 | 4.50 B |
| L92-557 | Rare Science Fiction–ed. Ivan Howard | 1.50 | 3.00 | 4.50 SF |
| L92-558 | Eye Witness World War II Battles– H. Oleck | 1.50 | 3.00 | 4.50 NF |
| L92-559 | Your Happiness Is in the Stars– "Constella" | 1.00 | 2.00 | 3.00 NF |
| L92-560 | Sex-Life & the Criminal Law–John Roeburt | 1.50 | 3.00 | 4.50 NF |
| L92-561 | How to Be Lovelier–Laurel Goodwin | 1.00 | 2.00 | 3.00 NF |
| L92-562 | I Am Desire–Anon. | 1.50 | 3.00 | 4.50 E |
| L92-563 | Sex, Love, and Marriage–Dr. Paul Popenoe | 1.00 | 2.00 | 3.00 NF |
| L92-564 | 6 and the Silent Scream–ed. Ivan Howard | 1.50 | 3.00 | 4.50 SF |
| L92-565 | The Main Attraction–John Patrick & Steve Michaels (Michael Avallone); movie tie-in | 2.50 | 5.00 | 7.50 E |
| L92-566 | In a Word–James Thurber | 2.00 | 4.00 | 6.00 H |
| L92-567 | Novelets of Science Fiction–ed. Ivan Howard | 1.50 | 3.00 | 4.50 SF |
| L92-568 | Erotica Exotica–Garon & Wilson | 1.50 | 3.00 | 4.50 |
| L92-569 | The Hounds of Tindalos–Frank Belknap Long | 3.00 | 6.00 | 9.00 SF |
| L92-570 | Shock Corridor–Michael Avallone | 2.00 | 4.00 | 6.00 |
| L92-571 | Escape to Earth–ed. Ivan Howard | 1.50 | 3.00 | 4.50 SF |
| L92-572 | Satan in High-Heels–Noel Candler; movie tie-in | 5.00 | 10.00 | 15.00 E |
| L92-573 | Casanova Confidential–Jacques Casanova | 1.50 | 3.00 | 4.50 |
| L92-574 | Nudeniks–H. Kandel & D. Safran | 1.50 | 3.00 | 4.50 |
| L92-575 | Way Out–ed. Ivan Howard | 1.50 | 3.00 | 4.50 SF |
| L92-576 | The Wild Girls–Peggy Gaddis | 2.00 | 4.00 | 6.00 |
| L92-577 | Only an Inch from Glory–Albert Halper | 1.50 | 3.00 | 4.50 |
| L92-578 | Loves of the Orient–Gionanni Camisso; 1964 | 1.50 | 3.00 | 4.50 |
| L92-579 | The Dark Beasts–Frank Belknap Long | 2.50 | 5.00 | 7.50 SF |
| L92-580 | The Greatest Lover in the World–Alex Austin | 1.50 | 3.00 | 4.50 |
| L92-581 | Bed of an Empress–Leopold Sacher-Masoch | 1.50 | 3.00 | 4.50 |
| L92-582 | Things–ed. Ivan Howard | 2.00 | 4.00 | 6.00 HO |
| L92-583 | Claudine in Paris–Colette | 1.50 | 3.00 | 4.50 E |
| L92-584 | Worlds without End–Clifford D. Simak | 1.50 | 3.00 | 4.50 SF |
| L92-585 | Andrea Holland–Bart Frame | 1.50 | 3.00 | 4.50 |
| L92-586 | Swing Low, Swing Dead–Frank Gruber | 1.50 | 3.00 | 4.50 M |
| L92-587 | The Lusts of Casanova–Jacques Casanova | 2.00 | 4.00 | 6.00 E |
| L92-588 | The Non-Statistical Man–Raymond F. Jones | 1.50 | 3.00 | 4.50 SF |
| L92-589 | Bizarre Loves–Denys Val Baker | 1.50 | 3.00 | 4.50 E |
| L92-590 | Born To Be Bad–Mitchell Coleman | 1.50 | 3.00 | 4.50 E |
| L92-591 | Godling Go Home–Robert Silverberg | 1.50 | 3.00 | 4.50 SF |
| L92-592 | The French Key–Frank Gruber | 1.50 | 3.00 | 4.50 M |
| L92-593 | Not For a Day–Helga Moray | 1.00 | 2.00 | 3.00 |

*Belmont L92-574, Belmont L92-596, Belmont B50-737.*

| | V/Good | Fine | N/Mint | |
|---|---|---|---|---|

V/Good  Fine  N/Mint

**BELMONT BOOKS L/B-SERIES,** *continued*

| | | V/Good | Fine | N/Mint | |
|---|---|---|---|---|---|
| L92-594 | Mr. George and Other Odd Persons–August Derleth | 1.50 | 3.00 | 4.50 | SF |
| L92-595 | My Strangest Case–ed. Kurt Singer | 1.00 | 2.00 | 3.00 | |
| L92-596 | The Naked Kiss–Samuel Fuller; movie tie-in | 7.50 | 15.00 | 22.50 | E |
| L92-597 | The Spy Who Loved America–Jack Laflin | 1.00 | 2.00 | 3.00 | |
| L92-598 | Marie Arnaud, Spy–Fielding Hope | 1.00 | 2.00 | 3.00 | |
| L92-599 | Felicia–Mark Dane (Michael Avallone) | 2.00 | 4.00 | 6.00 | E |
| L92-600 | Odd Science Fiction–Frank Belknap Long | 2.00 | 4.00 | 6.00 | SF |
| B50-633 | Basil Rathbone Selects Strange Tales–ed. Lyle Kenyon Engel | 1.50 | 3.00 | 4.50 | HO |
| B50-640 | Amanda–Paula Christian | 2.00 | 4.00 | 6.00 | |
| B50-647 | The Shadow's Revenge–Maxwell Grant (Dennis Lynds); orig. 1965 | 4.00 | 8.00 | 12.00 | M |
| B50-651 | Squaresville Jag–Robert Tralins | 1.50 | 3.00 | 4.50 | |
| B50-663 | This Strange Tomorrow–Frank Belknap Long | 2.00 | 4.00 | 6.00 | SF |
| B50-675 | The Victorian Crown–Edwina Noone (Michael Avallone) | 1.50 | 3.00 | 4.50 | |
| B50-683 | Mark of the Shadow–Maxwell Grant (Dennis Lynds); orig. 1966 | 4.00 | 8.00 | 12.00 | M |
| B50-686 | The Second Secret–Edwina Noone (Michael Avallone) | 1.50 | 3.00 | 4.50 | |
| B50-695 | High Camp Superheroes–Jerry Siegel; 1st ed. 1966. Note: Contains comic book reprints | 3.00 | 6.00 | 9.00 | A |
| B50-704 | The Miss from S.I.S.–Bob Tralins | 2.50 | 5.00 | 7.50 | E |
| B50-709 | Shadow–Go Mad!–Maxwell Grant (Dennis Lynds); orig. 1966 | 4.00 | 8.00 | 12.00 | M |
| B50-717 | The Gate of Time–Philip Jose Farmer | 2.00 | 4.00 | 6.00 | SF |
| B50-718 | The Chic Chick Spy–Bob Tralins | 2.00 | 4.00 | 6.00 | |
| B50-725 | The Night of the Shadow–Maxwell Grant (Dennis Lynds); orig. 1966 | 4.00 | 8.00 | 12.00 | M |
| B50-726 | Lest Earth Be Conquered–Frank Belknap Long | 2.00 | 4.00 | 6.00 | SF |
| B50-727 | World of the Weird–Brad Steiger | 1.50 | 3.00 | 4.50 | |
| B50-735 | Monsters and Nightmares–Bernhardt J. Hurwood | 2.00 | 4.00 | 6.00 | HO |
| B50-736 | Tales of the Frightened–ed. Michael Avallone | 1.50 | 3.00 | 4.50 | HO |
| B50-737 | The Shadow: Destination Moon–Maxwell Grant (Dennis Lynds); orig. 1967 | 4.00 | 8.00 | 12.00 | M |
| B50-741 | Hawk–Richard Hardwick; TV tie-in | 1.50 | 3.00 | 4.50 | M |
| B50-743 | Search and Kill–Harold Calin | 1.50 | 3.00 | 4.50 | C |
| B50-745 | The Ring-a-Ding UFOs–Bob Tralins | 1.50 | 3.00 | 4.50 | |
| B50-754 | Masked Outlaw/The Gun–E.B. Mann | 1.50 | 3.00 | 4.50 | W |
| B50-762 | Making It Big–John Jakes | 1.50 | 3.00 | 4.50 | |
| B50-768 | A Few Fiends to Tea–Virginia Coffman | 4.00 | 8.00 | 12.00 | M |
| B50-779 | Doomsman–Harlan Ellison / Telepower–Lee Hoffman | 4.00 | 8.00 | 12.00 | SF / SF |
| B50-784 | El Hombre–Walt Coburn / Rustler's Warning–E.B. Mann | 1.50 | 3.00 | 4.50 | W / W |
| B50-787 | The Living Demons–Robert Bloch | 3.50 | 7.00 | 10.50 | HO |
| B50-800 | Pawn of Love–Florence Stonebraker; aka Raging Passions | 1.50 | 3.00 | 4.50 | E |
| B50-804 | Tower at the Edge of Time–Lin Carter | 2.00 | 4.00 | 6.00 | F |
| B50-809 | The Thief of Thoth–Lin Carter / And Others Shall Be Born–Frank B. Long | 2.00 | 4.00 | 6.00 | F / SF |
| B50-826 | Earth Unaware–Mack Reynolds; c-Jeff Jones | 2.00 | 4.00 | 6.00 | SF |
| B50-835 | A Talent for Loving–Bonnie Golightly | 2.00 | 4.00 | 6.00 | |
| B50-849 | Whom the Gods Would Slay–Ivan Jorgensen (Paul Fairman); c-Jeff Jones | 2.00 | 4.00 | 6.00 | F |
| B50-852 | Lords of Creation–Eando Binder; c-Jeff Jones | 2.00 | 4.00 | 6.00 | F |
| B50-853 | Giant of World's End–Lin Carter; c-Jeff Jones | 2.00 | 4.00 | 6.00 | SF |

# BELMONT BOOKS X-SERIES
## Belmont Productions, Inc.

| | | V/Good | Fine | N/Mint | |
|---|---|---|---|---|---|
| X201 | The Family Survival Handbook–Martin A. Smith & William E. Eliason | 1.50 | 3.00 | 4.50 | NF |

# BERKLEY
## Berkley Publishing Corporation

| | | V/Good | Fine | N/Mint | |
|---|---|---|---|---|---|
| 101 | The Pleasures of the Jazz Age–William Hodapp; 1955 | 1.50 | 3.00 | 4.50 | NF |
| 102 | Loveliest of Friends–G. Sheila Donisthorpe | 1.50 | 3.00 | 4.50 | |
| 103 | S.S. San Pedro–James Gould Cozzens | 1.25 | 2.50 | 3.75 | |
| 104 | Fever Pitch–Frank Waters | 1.25 | 2.50 | 3.75 | |
| 105 | Death of an Ad Man–Alfred Eichler | 1.25 | 2.50 | 3.75 | |
| 106 | Three Day Pass–to kill–James Wakefield Burke & Edward Grace | 1.50 | 3.00 | 4.50 | |
| 107 | Border Raider–William Hopson | 1.25 | 2.50 | 3.75 | W |
| 108 | They Shoot Horses, Don't They?–Horace McCoy | 2.50 | 5.00 | 7.50 | |
| 109 | So It Doesn't Whistle–Robert Paul Smith | 1.50 | 3.00 | 4.50 | |
| 110 | All the Girls We Loved–Prudencio DePereda | 1.50 | 3.00 | 4.50 | |
| 111 | Torture Garden–Octave Mirbeav | 6.00 | 12.00 | 18.00 | |
| 112 | Mask of Glass–Holly Roth | 1.00 | 2.00 | 3.00 | |
| 313 | Saddle Hawks–Bliss Lomax (H.S. Drago) | 1.50 | 3.00 | 4.50 | W |
| 314 | Andrew's Harvest–John Evans | 1.25 | 2.50 | 3.75 | |
| 315 | Eleven Blue Men–Berton Roueche | .50 | 1.00 | 1.50 | |
| 316 | Pattern for Panic–Richard S. Prather | 2.00 | 4.00 | 6.00 | M |
| 317 | Roadside Motel–Arthur Herbert Bryant | 1.25 | 2.50 | 3.75 | |
| 318 | White Hell–Don Tracy | 2.50 | 5.00 | 7.50 | |
| 319 | Portrait of a Woman–John Hyde Preston | 1.25 | 2.50 | 3.75 | |
| 320 | Sweetie Pie–Nadine Seltzer | 1.50 | 3.00 | 4.50 | H |
| 321 | Gunfighter Breed–Nelson Nye | 1.50 | 3.00 | 4.50 | W |
| 322 | Danger at Sea–Georges Simenon | 1.50 | 3.00 | 4.50 | M |
| 323 | The Temptation of Roger Heriott–Edward Newhouse | 1.25 | 2.50 | 3.75 | |
| 324 | Cowpoke Justice–William Hopson | 1.50 | 3.00 | 4.50 | W |
| 325 | Oh, Doctor!–Charles Preston; 1955 | 1.25 | 2.50 | 3.75 | H |
| 326 | The Velvet Whip–Leonard Snyder | 1.50 | 3.00 | 4.50 | |
| 327 | We Too Are Drifting–Gale Wilhelm | 2.00 | 4.00 | 6.00 | |
| 328 | I Should Have Stayed Home–Horace McCoy | 2.50 | 5.00 | 7.50 | |
| 329 | Who's in Charge Here?–George Price | 1.25 | 2.50 | 3.75 | H |
| 330 | Cartridge–Case Law–Nelson Nye | 1.25 | 2.50 | 3.75 | W |
| 331 | Joe and Jennie–Donald Henderson Clarke | 1.25 | 2.50 | 3.75 | |
| 332 | The Twisted Trail–Paul Evan Lehman | 1.25 | 2.50 | 3.75 | W |
| 333 | Cue for Murder–Matt Bryant | 1.25 | 2.50 | 3.75 | M |
| 334 | Manhunt–Philip Van Doren Stern | 1.25 | 2.50 | 3.75 | |
| 335 | Powder Burns–Al Cody | 1.25 | 2.50 | 3.75 | W |
| 336 | Mopsy–Gladys Parker | 1.25 | 2.50 | 3.75 | H |
| 337 | Only a Woman–Francis Carco | 1.50 | 3.00 | 4.50 | |
| 338 | The Man with My Face–Samuel W. Taylor | 1.25 | 2.50 | 3.75 | M |
| 339 | The Girl with the Golden Yo-Yo–Edmund Schiddel | 1.25 | 2.50 | 3.75 | |
| 340 | Danger Ashore–Georges Simenon | 1.50 | 3.00 | 4.50 | M |
| 341 | Outlaw of Hidden Valley–William Hopson | 1.25 | 2.50 | 3.75 | W |
| 342 | The Postman–Roger Martin du Gard | 1.25 | 2.50 | 3.75 | |
| 343 | Gunshot Trail–Nelson Nye | 1.25 | 2.50 | 3.75 | W |
| 344 | Mission to the Stars–A.E. Van Vogt | 1.50 | 3.00 | 4.50 | SF |

*Berkley 324, Berkley 345, Berkley Diamond D2003.*

**BERKLEY,** *continued*

| No. | Title | V/Good | Fine | N/Mint | |
|---|---|---|---|---|---|
| 345 | Cruel Is the Night–Howard Hunt | 2.00 | 4.00 | 6.00 | |
| 346 | The $64,000,000 Answer–Charles Preston | 2.50 | 5.00 | 7.50 | H |
| 347 | Tombstone Stage–William Hopson; 1956 | 1.25 | 2.50 | 3.75 | W |
| 348 | Dupree Blues–Dale Curran | 1.25 | 2.50 | 3.75 | |
| 349 | Strictly Business–Dale McFeatters | 1.25 | 2.50 | 3.75 | |
| 350 | Saddle Bow Slim–Nelson Nye; 1956 | 1.25 | 2.50 | 3.75 | W |
| 351 | The Magician–Georges Simenon | 1.50 | 3.00 | 4.50 | W |
| 353 | Forbidden River–Al Cody | 1.25 | 2.50 | 3.75 | W |
| 354 | The Narrowing Circle–Julian Symons | 1.25 | 2.50 | 3.75 | M |
| 356 | Outlaws of Lost River–Paul Evan Lehman | 1.25 | 2.50 | 3.75 | W |
| 358 | Bailey's Daughters–John De Meyer | 1.25 | 2.50 | 3.75 | |
| 359 | Loveliest of Friends–G. Sheila Donisthorpe | 1.50 | 3.00 | 4.50 | |
| 360 | Sweetie Pie–Nadine Seltzer | 1.50 | 3.00 | 4.50 | H |
| 361 | Seven Men from Now–Burt Kennedy; movie tie-in | 2.00 | 4.00 | 6.00 | W |
| 362 | Pattern for Panic–Richard S. Prather | 1.50 | 3.00 | 4.50 | M |
| 363 | Ranger's Revenge–Nelson Nye | 1.25 | 2.50 | 3.75 | W |
| 364 | Pistol Law–Paul Evan Lehman; aka Vengeance Valley | 1.25 | 2.50 | 3.75 | W |
| 365 | No Money Down–36 Months to Pay!–Charles Preston; 1957 | 1.25 | 2.50 | 3.75 | H |
| 366 | Ramrod Vengeance–William Hopson | 1.25 | 2.50 | 3.75 | W |
| 367 | We Too Are Drifting–Gale Wilhelm | 2.00 | 4.00 | 6.00 | |
| 368 | Kinkaid of Red Butte–Leslie Ernenwein | 1.25 | 2.50 | 3.75 | W |
| 369 | Only a Woman–Francis Carco | 1.50 | 3.00 | 4.50 | |
| 370 | Texas Vengeance–Paul Evan Lehman | 1.25 | 2.50 | 3.75 | W |
| 371 | Bubu of Montparnasse–Charles-Louis Philippe | 1.25 | 2.50 | 3.75 | E |
| 372 | Rustlers of the Rio Grande–Paul Evan Lehman | 1.25 | 2.50 | 3.75 | W |
| 373 | The Devil His Due–William O'Farrell | 1.25 | 2.50 | 3.75 | |
| 374 | Red Man's Range–Al Cody | 1.25 | 2.50 | 3.75 | W |
| 375 | The Lost and the Damned–Warren Carrier; 1957 | 1.25 | 2.50 | 3.75 | |
| 376 | We Dare You to Solve This!–John Paul Adams | 1.00 | 2.00 | 3.00 | NF |
| 377 | Twist of the Knife–Victor Canning | 1.25 | 2.50 | 3.75 | M |
| 378 | Brand of Iron–Al Cody | 1.25 | 2.50 | 3.75 | W |
| 379 | The Burial of Monsieur Bouvet–Georges Simenon | 1.50 | 3.00 | 4.50 | M |
| 380 | The Time Machine–H.G. Wells | 1.50 | 3.00 | 4.50 | SF |
| 381 | More Sweetie Pie–Nadine Seltzer | 1.50 | 3.00 | 4.50 | H |
| 382 | Tizzy–Kate Osann; 1958 | 1.50 | 3.00 | 4.50 | |
| 383 | Will-Yum–Fred Neher | 1.50 | 3.00 | 4.50 | H |
| 384 | Baby Sitter's Guide–Mary Furlong Moore; 1959 | 1.50 | 3.00 | 4.50 | NF |
| 385 | Hi-teens–Fred Neher | 1.50 | 3.00 | 4.50 | H |
| 386 | Phyllis–Ted Key | 1.50 | 3.00 | 4.50 | H |

# BERKLEY DIAMOND
## Berkley Publishing Corporation

| No. | Title | V/Good | Fine | N/Mint | |
|---|---|---|---|---|---|
| D2001 | Cruel Is the Night–Howard Hunt; 1959; c-Maguire | 1.25 | 2.50 | 3.75 | |
| D2002 | Guns Along the Arrowhead–Lee Floren | 1.25 | 2.50 | 3.75 | W |
| D2003 | The Big Kiss-off–Day Keene | 2.00 | 4.00 | 6.00 | M |
| D2004 | Shack Road Girl–Harry Whittington | 2.00 | 4.00 | 6.00 | E |
| D2005 | Descent to Darkness–Fritz Peters; c-Maguire | 1.25 | 2.50 | 3.75 | |
| D2006 | Wildcats of Tonto Basin–Nelson Nye | 1.25 | 2.50 | 3.75 | W |
| D2007 | Dressed to Kill–Milton K. Ozaki | 1.25 | 2.50 | 3.75 | M |
| D2008 | Hideaway–Fan Nichols | 1.25 | 2.50 | 3.75 | |
| D2009 | Rifle Law–Lee Floren | 1.25 | 2.50 | 3.75 | W |
| D2010 | Kill Me in Shimbashi–Earl Norman; c-Maguire | 2.00 | 4.00 | 6.00 | M |
| D2011 | Vengeance Trail–Charles M. Martin | 1.25 | 2.50 | 3.75 | W |
| D2012 | Messalina–Vivian Crockett; c-Maguire | 2.50 | 5.00 | 7.50 | E |
| D2013 | Drift Fence–Walt Coburn | 1.25 | 2.50 | 3.75 | W |
| D2014 | Twin Mavericks–William Hopson; aka Horse Thief Masquerade | 1.25 | 2.50 | 3.75 | W |
| D2015 | Renegade Cop–Jonathan Craig | 1.25 | 2.50 | 3.75 | |
| D2016 | Murder Doll–Milton K. Ozaki | 1.25 | 2.50 | 3.75 | M |
| D2017 | Guns Along the Pecos–Lee Floren | 1.25 | 2.50 | 3.75 | W |
| D2018 | Desert Desperados–Nelson Nye | 1.25 | 2.50 | 3.75 | W |

| No. | Title | V/Good | Fine | N/Mint | |
|---|---|---|---|---|---|
| D2019 | Married to Murder–Harry Whittington | 2.00 | 4.00 | 6.00 | M |
| D2020 | Naked Fury–Day Keene | 2.00 | 4.00 | 6.00 | E |
| D2021 | The Killer–Burt Arthur (Herbert Arthur) | 1.25 | 2.50 | 3.75 | W |
| D2022 | Martha Crane–Charles Gorham | 1.25 | 2.50 | 3.75 | E |
| D2023 | Model for Murder–Stephen Marlowe | 1.25 | 2.50 | 3.75 | M |
| D2024 | Sleep with the Devil–Day Keene | 2.00 | 4.00 | 6.00 | M |
| D2025 | Saddle Wolves–Allan K. Echols | 1.25 | 2.50 | 3.75 | W |
| D2026 | Only a Woman–Francis Carco | 1.50 | 3.00 | 4.50 | E |
| D2027 | The Assassin–E.M. Harper | 1.25 | 2.50 | 3.75 | |
| D2028 | Walk the Evil Street–David Wade | 1.25 | 2.50 | 3.75 | |
| D2030 | Outpost Trail–Al Cody | 1.25 | 2.50 | 3.75 | W |
| D2031 | Street of the Lost–Francis Carco | 2.50 | 5.00 | 7.50 | E |
| D2032 | The Naked Hunter–William Woolfolk | 1.25 | 2.50 | 3.75 | |
| D2033 | Thunder Valley–Burt Arthur | 1.25 | 2.50 | 3.75 | W |
| D2034 | Nude Croquet–ed. anon.; c-Maguire | 2.50 | 5.00 | 7.50 | |
| D2035 | Three for the Money–Barry Lake; c-Maguire | 2.00 | 4.00 | 6.00 | |
| D2036 | Hell Cop–P.J. Wolfson; aka Bodies Are Dust | 1.25 | 2.50 | 3.75 | M |
| D2037 | You'll Get Yours–William Ard; c-Maguire | 2.00 | 4.00 | 6.00 | M |
| D2038 | The Deadly Pick-up–Milton K. Ozaki | 1.25 | 2.50 | 3.75 | M |
| D2039 | Two-Gun Texan–Burt Arthur | 1.25 | 2.50 | 3.75 | W |
| D2040 | Evil Is My Love–Philip Van Doren Stern; aka Love Is the One with Wings | 1.25 | 2.50 | 3.75 | |
| D2041 | Say It with Murder–Edward Ronns | 1.25 | 2.50 | 3.75 | M |
| D2042 | Song of Penang–John Carlova | 1.25 | 2.50 | 3.75 | |
| D2043 | Slay Ride for a Lady–Harry Whittington | 1.50 | 3.00 | 4.50 | M |

# BERKLEY G/BG-SERIES
## Berkley Publishing Corporation

| No. | Title | V/Good | Fine | N/Mint | |
|---|---|---|---|---|---|
| G1 | The Lost Weekend–Charles Jackson; 1955 | 1.50 | 3.00 | 4.50 | |
| G2 | Sexual Conduct of the Teen-ager–Jules Archer & S.V. Lawton | 1.25 | 2.50 | 3.75 | NF |
| G3 | Possible Worlds of Science Fiction–ed. Groff Conklin | 1.25 | 2.50 | 3.75 | SF |
| G4 | South Street–William Gardner Smith | 1.25 | 2.50 | 3.75 | |
| G5 | Salambo–Gustave Flaubert | 2.50 | 5.00 | 7.50 | |
| G6 | If He Hollers Let Him Go–Chester Himes | 1.50 | 3.00 | 4.50 | |
| G7 | A Seed upon the Wind–William Michelfelder | .75 | 1.50 | 2.25 | |
| G8 | The Devil's Brigadier–Don Ryan | .75 | 1.50 | 2.25 | |
| G9 | Naked Hollywood–Mel Harris, Weegee | 1.50 | 3.00 | 4.50 | H |
| G10 | Lone Star Preacher–J.W. Thomason, Jr | 2.00 | 4.00 | 6.00 | W |
| G11 | Diana–Diana Fredericks | 2.00 | 4.00 | 6.00 | |
| G12 | Crazy Mixed-Up Kids–William Hodapp | 2.50 | 5.00 | 7.50 | |
| G13 | The Sign of Eros–Paul Bodin | 1.00 | 2.00 | 3.00 | |
| G14 | Messalina–Vivian Crockett | 1.50 | 3.00 | 4.50 | |
| G15 | A Lust to Live–E.B. Garside; 1956, aka Whirligig | 1.00 | 2.00 | 3.00 | |
| G16 | Jungle Fury–Robb White | 3.00 | 6.00 | 9.00 | E |
| G17 | The Thorn in the Flesh–D.H. Lawrence | 1.50 | 3.00 | 4.50 | |
| BG18 | Modern Writing No. 3–William Phillips & Philip Rahv | .75 | 1.50 | 2.25 | |
| G19 | The Rat Race–Alfred Bester | 2.00 | 4.00 | 6.00 | |
| G20 | Paris, My Love–Henry Calet | 1.00 | 2.00 | 3.00 | |
| G21 | Bessie Cotter–Wallace Smith | 1.00 | 2.00 | 3.00 | |
| G22 | Renee–H.R. Lenormand | 1.00 | 2.00 | 3.00 | |
| G23 | The Place of Jackals–Ronald Hardy | 1.00 | 2.00 | 3.00 | |
| G24 | Adios, O'Shaughnessy–Robert Tallman | 1.50 | 3.00 | 4.50 | |
| G25 | A Girl in Every Port–Donald R. Morris; 1956 | 1.50 | 3.00 | 4.50 | |
| G26 | Love on the Rocks–Elliott Chaze; aka The Golden Tag | 1.00 | 2.00 | 3.00 | |
| G27 | The Blaze of Noon–Rayner Heppenstall | 1.00 | 2.00 | 3.00 | |
| G28 | Young Man of Paris–Henri Calet | 1.50 | 3.00 | 4.50 | |
| G29 | Hypnotism Comes of Age–Raymond Rosenthal & Bernard Wolfe | 1.00 | 2.00 | 3.00 | |
| G30 | Intimacy–Jean-Paul Sartre | 1.50 | 3.00 | 4.50 | |
| G31 | Science Fiction Omnibus–ed. Groff Conklin | 1.50 | 3.00 | 4.50 | SF |
| G32 | Six Days in Marapore–Paul Scott | 1.50 | 3.00 | 4.50 | |
| G33 | Perversity–Francis Carco | 1.50 | 3.00 | 4.50 | E |
| G34 | Alabam–Donald Henderson Clarke | 1.00 | 2.00 | 3.00 | |

BERKLEY G/BG-SERIES, *continued*

| | | V/Good | Fine | N/Mint | |
|---|---|---|---|---|---|
| BG35 | Night Rider–Robert Penn Warren | 1.00 | 2.00 | 3.00 | |
| G36 | The Strange Case of Miss Annie Spragg–Louis Bromfield | 1.00 | 2.00 | 3.00 | SF |
| G37 | Virgie, Goodbye–Nathan Rothman | 1.00 | 2.00 | 3.00 | |
| G38 | Escape from Colditz–P.R. Reid | .75 | 1.50 | 2.25 | NF |
| G39 | Torture Garden–Octave Mirbeau | 5.00 | 10.00 | 15.00 | E |
| G40 | Daughters of Eve; c-Maguire | 2.00 | 4.00 | 6.00 | |
| G41 | Astounding Science Fiction Anthology–ed. John W. Campbell, Jr | 1.50 | 3.00 | 4.50 | SF |
| G42 | To Wake the Dead–John Dickson Carr | 1.50 | 3.00 | 4.50 | M |
| G43 | The Captain's Doll–D.H. Lawrence; c-Maguire | 2.00 | 4.00 | 6.00 | |
| G44 | My Sister, My Beloved–Edwina Mark; 1957 | 1.00 | 2.00 | 3.00 | |
| G45 | Scratch the Surface–Edmund Schiddel | 1.00 | 2.00 | 3.00 | |
| G46 | Aphrodite–Pierre Louys; c-Maguire | 2.00 | 4.00 | 6.00 | |
| G47 | Astounding Tales of Space and Time–John W. Campbell, Jr | 1.50 | 3.00 | 4.50 | SF |
| G48 | The Eight of Swords–John Dickson Carr; c-Maguire | 2.00 | 4.00 | 6.00 | M |
| G49 | A Dime a Throw–Jerome Weidman | 1.00 | 2.00 | 3.00 | |
| G50 | Diana–Diana Fredericks; 1957 | 1.50 | 3.00 | 4.50 | |
| G51 | The Body of Love–Charles Keats; c-Maguire | 2.00 | 4.00 | 6.00 | |
| G52 | The Virgin and the Gypsy–D.H. Lawrence; c-Maguire | 2.00 | 4.00 | 6.00 | E |
| G53 | The Big Book of Science Fiction–ed. Groff Conklin | 1.50 | 3.00 | 4.50 | SF |
| G54 | The Sign of Eros–Paul Bodin | 1.00 | 2.00 | 3.00 | |
| G55 | Love in a Hot Climate–Edmund Schiddel | 1.50 | 3.00 | 4.50 | |
| G56 | Jungle Fury–Robb White | 3.00 | 6.00 | 9.00 | |
| G57 | Take Me As I Am–Loren Wahl | 1.25 | 2.50 | 3.75 | |
| G58 | How Cheap Can You Get?–Martin Abzug; aka Seventh Avenue Story | 1.25 | 2.50 | 3.75 | E |
| G59 | The Woman Who Rode Away–D.H. Lawrence; c-Maguire | 2.00 | 4.00 | 6.00 | |
| G60 | The Case of the Constant Suicides–John Dickson Carr; c-Maguire | 2.00 | 4.00 | 6.00 | M |
| G61 | Andrew's Harvest–John Evans | 2.00 | 4.00 | 6.00 | |
| G62 | The Most Dangerous Game | 1.50 | 3.00 | 4.50 | |
| G63 | A Treasury of Science Fiction–ed. Groff Conklin | 1.25 | 2.50 | 3.75 | SF |
| G64 | The Tirpitz–David Woodward | 1.00 | 2.00 | 3.00 | NF |
| G65 | A Seed upon the Wind–William Michelfelder | 1.00 | 2.00 | 3.00 | |
| BG66 | Time Must Have a Stop–Aldous Huxley; c-Maguire | 2.00 | 4.00 | 6.00 | |
| G67 | Spy Catcher–Oreste Pinto | 1.00 | 2.00 | 3.00 | |
| G68 | This Is My Body; c-Maguire | 2.00 | 4.00 | 6.00 | |
| G69 | Affair in Capri–Mario Soldati | .75 | 1.50 | 2.25 | |
| BG70 | The Last Days of Hitler–H.R. Trevor-Roper | 1.00 | 2.00 | 3.00 | NF |
| G71 | Strangers in the Universe–Clifford D. Simak | 1.25 | 2.50 | 3.75 | SF |
| G72 | Poison in Jest–John Dickson Carr; c-Maguire | 2.00 | 4.00 | 6.00 | |
| BG73 | Salambo–Gustave Flaubert; c-Maguire | 7.50 | 15.00 | 22.50 | E |
| G74 | Olivia–Olivia; c-Maguire | 2.00 | 4.00 | 6.00 | |
| G75 | The Case of the Lady Who Took a Bath–Alan Hynd; 1957 | 1.00 | 2.00 | 3.00 | |
| G76 | The Chastity of Gloria Boyd–Donald Henderson Clarke; c-Maguire | 2.00 | 4.00 | 6.00 | |
| G77 | Beachheads in Space–August Derleth | 1.50 | 3.00 | 4.50 | SF |

| | | V/Good | Fine | N/Mint | |
|---|---|---|---|---|---|
| G78 | Harlem Is My Heaven–Ian Gordon | 2.50 | 5.00 | 7.50 | |
| G79 | Gun-Quick–Nelson Nye | 1.00 | 2.00 | 3.00 | W |
| G80 | The Blind Barber–John Dickson Carr | 2.00 | 4.00 | 6.00 | M |
| G81 | Depravity–Francis Carco | 1.50 | 3.00 | 4.50 | |
| BG82 | Graf Spee–Dudley Pope | 1.00 | 2.00 | 3.00 | NF |
| G83 | Martha Crane–Charles Gorham | 1.00 | 2.00 | 3.00 | |
| G84 | The Corpse with Sticky Fingers–George Bagby | 1.00 | 2.00 | 3.00 | M |
| G85 | Three of a Kind–P.J. Wolfson | 1.00 | 2.00 | 3.00 | |
| G86 | Juvenile Jungle | 4.00 | 8.00 | 12.00 | |
| G87 | Gunthrower–William Hopson | 1.25 | 2.50 | 3.75 | W |
| G88 | Trish–Margaret Maze Craig | 1.25 | 2.50 | 3.75 | |
| G89 | Great Sports Stories–Herman L. Masin | 1.25 | 2.50 | 3.75 | S |
| BG90 | Drive to Victory–Robert S. Allen | 1.00 | 2.00 | 3.00 | |
| G91 | The Four False Weapons–John Dickson Carr; c-Maguire | 2.00 | 4.00 | 6.00 | M |
| G92 | Legend of the Lost–Bonnie Golightly; movie tie-in | 3.00 | 6.00 | 9.00 | |
| G93 | All Woman's Flesh–Paul Bodin | 1.50 | 3.00 | 4.50 | |
| G94 | The Tunnel Escape–Eric Williams; 1958 | 1.00 | 2.00 | 3.00 | |
| G95 | Such Is My Beloved–Carol Hales | 1.00 | 2.00 | 3.00 | |
| BG96 | Rommel, the Desert Fox–Desmond Young | 1.00 | 2.00 | 3.00 | NF |
| G97 | Nude Croquet; c-Maguire | 2.00 | 4.00 | 6.00 | |
| G98 | Pattern for Panic–Richard S. Prather | 1.50 | 3.00 | 4.50 | M |
| G99 | G Stands for Gun–Nelson Nye | 1.25 | 2.50 | 3.75 | W |
| BG100 | Finnley Wren–Philip Wylie; 1958 | 1.00 | 2.00 | 3.00 | |
| G101 | Death Watch–John Dickson Carr; c-Maguire | 2.00 | 4.00 | 6.00 | M |
| BG102 | Stalingrad–Theodor Plievier | 1.00 | 2.00 | 3.00 | NF |
| G103 | Forbid Me Not–Blair Fuller | 1.00 | 2.00 | 3.00 | |
| G104 | Beyond Time and Space–August Derleth | 1.25 | 2.50 | 3.75 | SF |
| G105 | Intimacy–Jean-Paul Sartre | 1.25 | 2.50 | 3.75 | |
| G106 | S.S. San Pedro–James Gould Cozzens | .75 | 1.50 | 2.25 | |
| G107 | Escape from Colditz–P.R. Reid | .75 | 1.50 | 2.25 | NF |
| BG108 | The Exurbanites–A.C. Spectorsky | .75 | 1.50 | 2.25 | H |
| G109 | Marsha–Margaret Maze Craig | 1.00 | 2.00 | 3.00 | |
| BG110 | The Theory and Practice of Hell–Eugen Kogon | 1.50 | 3.00 | 4.50 | NF |
| G111 | The Strange Path–Gale Wilhelm; c-Maguire | 2.00 | 4.00 | 6.00 | |
| G112 | Bessie Cotter–Wallace Smith | 2.00 | 4.00 | 6.00 | |
| G113 | The Girl of the Roman Night–Dante Arfelli; aka The Unwanted | 1.00 | 2.00 | 3.00 | |
| G114 | The End of the Track–Andrew Garve | 1.25 | 2.50 | 3.75 | |
| G115 | Holocaust at Sea; the Drama of the Scharnhorst–Fritz-Otto Busch | 1.00 | 2.00 | 3.00 | NF |
| G116 | The Outer Reaches–August Derleth | 1.25 | 2.50 | 3.75 | SF |
| G117 | The Mad Hatter Mystery–John Dickson Carr | 2.00 | 4.00 | 6.00 | M |
| G118 | Guns of Arizona–Nelson Nye | 1.25 | 2.50 | 3.75 | W |
| G119 | The Enormous Radio and Other Stories–John Cheever | 4.50 | 9.00 | 13.50 | SF |
| G120 | Black Opium–Claude Farrere; c-Maguire | 25.00 | 50.00 | 75.00 | E |
| BG121 | The Fatal Decisions–Seymour Freidin & William Richardson | 1.00 | 2.00 | 3.00 | |
| G122 | Gideon of Scotland Yard–J.J. Marric; movie tie-in | 1.50 | 3.00 | 4.50 | M |
| G123 | To Whom It May Concern–Juliet Lowell | 1.00 | 2.00 | 3.00 | |
| G124 | Joe and Jennie–Donald Henderson Clarke | 1.00 | 2.00 | 3.00 | |

Berkley G42, Berkley G50, Berkley G68.

Berkley G86, Berkley G97, Berkley G186.

| | V/Good | Fine | N/Mint |
|---|---|---|---|

| | | V/Good | Fine | N/Mint | |
|---|---|---|---|---|---|
| G125 | So It Doesn't Whistle–Robert Paul Smith; 1958; c-Maguire | 2.00 | 4.00 | 6.00 | |
| G126 | Naomi Martin–Clarkson Crane | 1.00 | 2.00 | 3.00 | |
| S127 | Men at War–Ernest Hemingway | 1.50 | 3.00 | 4.50 | |
| BG128 | Sex in Our Changing World–John McPartland | 1.00 | 2.00 | 3.00 | NF |
| G129 | Hag's Nook–John Dickson Clarke; c-Maguire | 2.00 | 4.00 | 6.00 | |
| G130 | Thieves like Us–Edward Anderson | 1.00 | 2.00 | 3.00 | |
| G131 | Strange Ports of Call–August Derleth | 1.50 | 3.00 | 4.50 | SF |
| G132 | Tormented–Carolyn Weston | 1.50 | 3.00 | 4.50 | |
| G133 | Tropic Moon–Georges Simenon | 1.50 | 3.00 | 4.50 | M |
| G134 | I Should Have Stayed Home–Horace McCoy | 2.50 | 5.00 | 7.50 | |
| BG135 | The German Generals Talk–B.H. Liddell Hart | 1.50 | 3.00 | 4.50 | NF |
| G136 | China Doll–Edgar Jean Bracco; movie tie-in | 1.50 | 3.00 | 4.50 | |
| G137 | The 31st of February–Julian Symons; c-Maguire | 2.00 | 4.00 | 6.00 | M |
| G138 | Gunfighter Brand–Nelson Nye | 1.25 | 2.50 | 3.75 | W |
| G139 | If He Hollers Let Him Go–Chester Himes | 1.50 | 3.00 | 4.50 | |
| G140 | Infamy–Frances Carco | 1.50 | 3.00 | 4.50 | |
| G141 | My Sister, My Beloved–Edwina Mark | 1.50 | 3.00 | 4.50 | |
| G142 | Low Level Mission–Leon Wolff | 1.00 | 2.00 | 3.00 | |
| G143 | The Corpse in the Waxworks–John Dickson Carr; c-Maguire | 2.00 | 4.00 | 6.00 | M |
| G144 | Proud Youth–Alexander Eliot | 1.50 | 3.00 | 4.50 | |
| G145 | The Man Who Watched the Trains Go By–Georges Simenon | 1.50 | 3.00 | 4.50 | M |
| G146 | The Man Within–Graham Greene | 1.00 | 2.00 | 3.00 | |
| G147 | Bailey's Daughters–John DeMeyer | 1.00 | 2.00 | 3.00 | |
| G148 | Men, Martians and Machines–Eric Frank Russell | 1.00 | 2.00 | 3.00 | SF |
| BG149 | Ah King–W. Somerset Maugham; c-Maguire | 2.00 | 4.00 | 6.00 | |
| BG150 | The First Lady Chatterley–D.H. Lawrence; 1958 | 1.50 | 3.00 | 4.50 | |
| G151 | The Golden Jungle–William Howard Harris | 1.50 | 3.00 | 4.50 | |
| G152 | Hell's Kitchen–Benjamin Appel | 2.50 | 5.00 | 7.50 | |
| G153 | The Last of Mr. Norris–Christopher Isherwood; c-Maguire | 2.00 | 4.00 | 6.00 | |
| G154 | Gunshot Trail–Nelson Nye | 1.25 | 2.50 | 3.75 | W |
| G155 | Perversity–Francis Carco | 1.50 | 3.00 | 4.50 | E |
| G156 | Laughter in the Dark–Vladimir Nabokov; c-Maguire | 2.00 | 4.00 | 6.00 | |
| G157 | The Crooked Hinge–John Dickson Carr | 1.50 | 3.00 | 4.50 | M |
| G158 | Mystery Walks the Campus–Annette Turngren | 1.00 | 2.00 | 3.00 | M |
| G159 | Marcia, Private Secretary–Zillah K. MacDonald | 1.00 | 2.00 | 3.00 | R |
| G160 | Desire and Other Stories–Clement Wood | 1.50 | 3.00 | 4.50 | |
| G161 | The Wicked and the Warped–Max Alth | 1.00 | 2.00 | 3.00 | |
| G162 | The Evil That Men Do–George Victor Martin | 1.50 | 3.00 | 4.50 | |
| G163 | Worlds of Tomorrow–August Derleth | 1.50 | 3.00 | 4.50 | SF |
| G164 | Three Day Pass–to Kill–James Wakefield Burke & Edward Grace | 1.00 | 2.00 | 3.00 | M |
| G165 | The Pub Crawler–Maurice Procter; c-Maguire | 2.00 | 4.00 | 6.00 | M |
| G166 | Morning, Winter and Night–John Nairne Michaelson | 1.00 | 2.00 | 3.00 | |
| G167 | Adam and Evil–John Carlova | 1.50 | 3.00 | 4.50 | |
| G168 | Renee–H.R. Lenormand | 1.50 | 3.00 | 4.50 | |
| G169 | The Terrible Game–Dan Tyler Moore | 2.00 | 4.00 | 6.00 | A |
| G170 | Devil's Holiday–Fred Malloy | 1.50 | 3.00 | 4.50 | |
| G171 | Stag Stripper–Jack Hanley | 2.00 | 4.00 | 6.00 | |
| G172 | Loveliest of Friends–G. Sheila Donisthorpe | 2.00 | 4.00 | 6.00 | |
| G173 | We Too Are Drifting–Gale Wilhelm | 2.00 | 4.00 | 6.00 | |
| G174 | Only a Woman–Francis Carco | 1.50 | 3.00 | 4.50 | |
| G175 | Olivia–Olivia; 1958; c-Maguire | 2.00 | 4.00 | 6.00 | |
| G176 | Mystery on Graveyard Head–Edith Dorian | 1.00 | 2.00 | 3.00 | M |
| BG177 | Pocket Battleship–H.J. Brennecke & Theodor Krancke | 1.50 | 3.00 | 4.50 | NF |
| BG178 | The Hucksters–Frederic Wakeman | 1.00 | 2.00 | 3.00 | |
| G179 | No Bed of Her Own–Cicely Schiller; c-Maguire | 2.00 | 4.00 | 6.00 | |

| | | V/Good | Fine | N/Mint | |
|---|---|---|---|---|---|
| G180 | Boots and Saddles–Edgar Jean Braco; TV tie-in | 2.00 | 4.00 | 6.00 | W |
| G181 | Is My Flesh of Brass?–P.J. Wolfson | 1.50 | 3.00 | 4.50 | |
| G182 | Too Many Girls–Don Tracy | 2.00 | 4.00 | 6.00 | |
| G183 | Virgie, Goodbye–Nathan Rothman | 1.50 | 3.00 | 4.50 | |
| G184 | The Shameless Ones–Uberto Quintavalle | 1.50 | 3.00 | 4.50 | |
| G185 | Wicked Woman–Fred Malloy | 1.50 | 3.00 | 4.50 | |
| G186 | Scarlet Angel–Dorene Clark | 1.50 | 3.00 | 4.50 | |
| G187 | The Big Wheel–John Brooks | 1.00 | 2.00 | 3.00 | |
| G188 | The Incurable Wound–Berton Roueche | .50 | 1.00 | 1.50 | |
| G189 | Time to Come–August Derleth | 1.50 | 3.00 | 4.50 | SF |
| G190 | The Judge and His Hangman–Friedrich Durrenmatt | 1.00 | 2.00 | 3.00 | |
| G191 | Awakening–Jean-Baptiste Rossi | 1.00 | 2.00 | 3.00 | |
| G192 | Kill Me in Tokyo–Earl Norman; c-Maguire | 2.00 | 4.00 | 6.00 | |
| G193 | South Street–William Gardner Smith | 1.50 | 3.00 | 4.50 | |
| G194 | The Postman–Roger Martin duGard | 1.00 | 2.00 | 3.00 | |
| G195 | Hot Money Girl–Arlo Wayne | 1.50 | 3.00 | 4.50 | |
| G196 | Passion in Panama–Richard Marshe | 1.50 | 3.00 | 4.50 | |
| BG197 | The Professional–W.C. Heinz | 1.00 | 2.00 | 3.00 | |
| G198 | Early to Rise–Arnold E. Grisman; c-Maguire | 2.00 | 4.00 | 6.00 | |
| G199 | Make Me an Offer–Charles Gorham | 1.00 | 2.00 | 3.00 | |
| G200 | Sexual Conduct of the Teen-ager–Jules Archer & S.V. Lawton; 1954 | 1.50 | 3.00 | 4.50 | NF |
| G201 | Smoke Wagon Kid–Clem Colt | 1.25 | 2.50 | 3.75 | W |
| BG202 | Last in Convoy–James Pattinson | 1.00 | 2.00 | 3.00 | |
| G203 | Love around the World; c-Maguire | 2.00 | 4.00 | 6.00 | |
| G204 | The Blaze of Noon–Rayner Heppenstall | 1.00 | 2.00 | 3.00 | |
| G205 | Forbidden Pleasures–B. Devlin | 1.50 | 3.00 | 4.50 | |
| G206 | The Sinning Lens–Mark Tryon | 1.00 | 2.00 | 3.00 | |
| G207 | The Home Encyclopedia of Moving Your Family–Margaret Randall | 1.00 | 2.00 | 3.00 | NF |
| G208 | Mystery in Blue–Gertrude E. Mallette | 1.00 | 2.00 | 3.00 | M |
| G209 | The Singing Heart–Elizabeth Cadell; 1959 | 1.00 | 2.00 | 3.00 | |
| G210 | How to Make Your Emotions Work for You–Dorothy C. Finkelhor | 1.00 | 2.00 | 3.00 | NF |
| BG211 | 73 North–Dudley Pope | 1.00 | 2.00 | 3.00 | |
| BG212 | Prettiest Girl in Town–Thomas Fall | 1.50 | 3.00 | 4.50 | |
| BG213 | First Person Singular–W. Somerset Maugham; c-Maguire | 2.00 | 4.00 | 6.00 | |
| G214 | The Bowstring Murders–Carter Dickson; c-Maguire | 2.00 | 4.00 | 6.00 | M |
| G215 | Away and Beyond–A.E. Van Vogt | | | | SF |
| G216 | The Sign of Eros–Paul Bodin | 1.25 | 2.50 | 3.75 | |
| G217 | Love on the Rocks–Elliott Chaze; aka The Golden Tag | 1.50 | 3.00 | 4.50 | E |
| G218 | Jule–George Wylie Henderson | 1.50 | 3.00 | 4.50 | E |
| G219 | Sandy–John B. Thompson | 1.50 | 3.00 | 4.50 | |
| G220 | The Fire That Burns–Mark Tryon | 1.50 | 3.00 | 4.50 | |
| G221 | I'll Find My Love–Joan Dirksen | 1.00 | 2.00 | 3.00 | |
| G222 | The Big Book of Horse Stories–Page Cooper | 1.00 | 2.00 | 3.00 | |
| G223 | Beany Malone–Lenora Mattingly Weber | 1.00 | 2.00 | 3.00 | |
| G224 | I Flew for the Fuhrer–Heinz Knoke | 2.00 | 4.00 | 6.00 | NF |
| G225 | What D'ya Know for Sure?–Len Zinberg; 1959; c-Maguire | 2.00 | 4.00 | 6.00 | |
| G226 | All Woman's Flesh–Paul Bodin | 1.25 | 2.50 | 3.75 | |
| G227 | Blaze–Scott Stone | 1.00 | 2.00 | 3.00 | |
| G228 | Dreamboat–Rick Lucas | 1.00 | 2.00 | 3.00 | |
| G229 | Easy Living–Terence Ford | 1.00 | 2.00 | 3.00 | |
| G230 | Rambling Top Hand–William Hopson | 1.25 | 2.50 | 3.75 | W |
| BG231 | Dateline: Paris–Reynolds Packard; c-Maguire | 2.00 | 4.00 | 6.00 | |
| G232 | Deadlier Than the Male–James E. Gunn | 2.00 | 4.00 | 6.00 | M |
| G233 | Imagination Unlimited–T.E. Dikty & Everett F. Bleiler | 1.25 | 2.50 | 3.75 | SF |
| G234 | Guns of Horse Prairie–Nelson Nye | 1.25 | 2.50 | 3.75 | W |
| G235 | Channel Dash–Terence Robertson | 1.00 | 2.00 | 3.00 | |
| G236 | A Woman Called Desire–Richard Marshe | 1.50 | 3.00 | 4.50 | |
| G237 | Showroom Girls–Token West | 1.50 | 3.00 | 4.50 | |
| BG238 | The Lessons of Love–W. Carroll Munro | 1.50 | 3.00 | 4.50 | |
| BG239 | The Wooden Horse–Eric Williams | 1.00 | 2.00 | 3.00 | |
| G240 | House of Fury–Felice Swados; c-Maguire | 6.00 | 12.00 | 18.00 | JD |
| G241 | Pattern for Panic–Richard S. Prather | 1.50 | 3.00 | 4.50 | M |
| G242 | Duel on the Range–Burt Arthur | 1.25 | 2.50 | 3.75 | W |

|  | V/Good | Fine | N/Mint |  |
|---|---|---|---|---|

**BERKLEY G/BG-SERIES**, *continued*

| No. | Title | V/Good | Fine | N/Mint |  |
|---|---|---|---|---|---|
| G243 | Count Me In–Fan Nichols | 1.00 | 2.00 | 3.00 |  |
| G244 | Vice Girl–Sim Albert | 1.50 | 3.00 | 4.50 |  |
| G245 | The Odd Ones–Edwina Mark | 2.00 | 4.00 | 6.00 | E |
| G246 | The Frogmen–James Gleeson & T.J. Waldron | 1.50 | 3.00 | 4.50 |  |
| G247 | Box Star Buckaroo–Charles M. Martin | 1.25 | 2.50 | 3.75 | W |
| G248 | Three of a Kind–P.J. Wolfson | 1.00 | 2.00 | 3.00 |  |
| G249 | The Other Side of the Moon–August Derleth | 1.25 | 2.50 | 3.75 | SF |
| G250 | Native Girl–Harry Whittington; 1959 | 2.00 | 4.00 | 6.00 |  |
| G251 | Affairs of Marie-Odette–Cecil Saint-Laurent | 1.00 | 2.00 | 3.00 |  |
| G252 | Immoral Woman–Jack Hanley | 1.50 | 3.00 | 4.50 |  |
| G253 | Devil Take Her–Fan Nichols | 1.50 | 3.00 | 4.50 |  |
| BG254 | A Man Escaped–Andre Devigny | 1.00 | 2.00 | 3.00 |  |
| G255 | Hangman's Range–Lee Floren | 1.00 | 2.00 | 3.00 | W |
| G256 | The Incredible Truth–Chris Massie | 1.00 | 2.00 | 3.00 |  |
| G257 | Woman of the Night–Robert Carse | 1.50 | 3.00 | 4.50 |  |
| G258 | Wake Up to Murder–Day Keene; c-Maguire | 2.00 | 4.00 | 6.00 | M |
| G259 | Harlem Is My Heaven–Ian Gordon | 2.50 | 5.00 | 7.50 |  |
| G260 | Shanty Boat Girl–Kirk Westley | 1.50 | 3.00 | 4.50 |  |
| G261 | Strip Street–Jack Hanley | 1.50 | 3.00 | 4.50 |  |
| G262 | Down and Out in Paris and London–George Orwell | 2.00 | 4.00 | 6.00 |  |
| BG263 | The Knights of Bushido–Lord Russell | 1.50 | 3.00 | 4.50 | NF |
| BG264 | The Ginger Man–J.P. Donleavy | .75 | 1.50 | 2.25 |  |
| G265 | The Daughter of Time–Josephine Tey | .75 | 1.50 | 2.25 | M |
| G266 | The Girl Beneath the Lion–Andre Pieyre de Mandiargues | .75 | 1.50 | 2.25 |  |
| G267 | The Plague Court Murders–Carter Dickson | 1.50 | 3.00 | 4.50 | M |
| G268 | Cosmopolitans–W. Somerset Maugham; c-Maguire | 1.00 | 2.00 | 3.00 |  |
| G269 | Money, Marbles and Chalk–Douglas Fairbairn | 1.00 | 2.00 | 3.00 |  |
| G270 | Thomas Alva Edison–G. Glenwood Clark | 1.00 | 2.00 | 3.00 | B |
| G271 | Deliver Us from Evil–Thomas A. Dooley | 1.50 | 3.00 | 4.50 |  |
| G272 | The Edge of Tomorrow–Thomas A. Dooley | 1.50 | 3.00 | 4.50 |  |
| G273 | Something Foolish, Something Gay–Jane Sire & Glen Sire | 1.50 | 3.00 | 4.50 |  |
| G274 | Francie Comes Home–Emily Hahn | 1.00 | 2.00 | 3.00 |  |
| G275 | Comanche of the 7th–Margaret Leighton; 1959 | 1.50 | 3.00 | 4.50 | W |
| G276 | Sharon–Harriett H. Carr | 1.00 | 2.00 | 3.00 |  |
| G277 | Desert Love–Henry de Montheriant | 1.00 | 2.00 | 3.00 |  |
| G278 | Gideon's Month–J.J. Marric | 1.00 | 2.00 | 3.00 | M |
| G279 | Altars of the Heart–Richard Lebherz | 1.00 | 2.00 | 3.00 |  |
| G280 | A Touch of Strange–Theodore Sturgeon | 1.25 | 2.50 | 3.75 | SF |
| G281 | Death Turns the Tables–John Dickson Carr | 1.50 | 3.00 | 4.50 | M |
| G282 | The Other Side of the Night–Edmund Schiddel | 1.00 | 2.00 | 3.00 |  |
| G283 | Aphrodite–Pierre Louys | 1.50 | 3.00 | 4.50 | E |
| G284 | My Sister Eileen–Ruth McKenney | 1.00 | 2.00 | 3.00 |  |
| G285 | Blue Ribbon Romance–Jane S. McIlvaine; c-Maguire | 1.00 | 2.00 | 3.00 | R |
| G286 | Mystery of Hidden Village–Annette Turngren | 1.00 | 2.00 | 3.00 | M |
| G287 | The Emperor's Snuff Box–John Dickson Carr | 1.50 | 3.00 | 4.50 | M |
| G288 | Flight Nurse–Adelaide Humphries | .75 | 1.50 | 2.25 | R |
| G289 | The Enemy Stars–Poul Anderson | 1.00 | 2.00 | 3.00 | SF |
| G290 | The Thorn in the Flesh–D.H. Lawrence | 1.50 | 3.00 | 4.50 |  |
| G291 | Flight–Edgar Jean Bracco; TV-tie in | .75 | 1.50 | 2.25 |  |
| G292 | Laughs around the World | 1.00 | 2.00 | 3.00 | H |
| G293 | Meet the Malones–Lenora Mattingly Weber | 1.00 | 2.00 | 3.00 |  |
| G294 | Step to the Music–Phyllis A. Whitney | .75 | 1.50 | 2.25 |  |

## BERKLEY MEDALLION
### Berkley Publishing Corporation

| No. | Title | V/Good | Fine | N/Mint |  |
|---|---|---|---|---|---|
| X1734 | The Bat Staffel–Robert J. Hogan; 1969; c-Steranko | 2.50 | 5.00 | 7.50 | C |
| X1735 | The Spider Strikes–R.T.M. Scott | 2.50 | 5.00 | 7.50 | M |

| No. | Title | V/Good | Fine | N/Mint |  |
|---|---|---|---|---|---|
| X1746 | Purple Aces–Robert J. Hogan; c-Steranko | 2.50 | 5.00 | 7.50 | C |
| X1764 | Ace of the White Death–Robert J. Hogan; 1970; c-Steranko | 2.50 | 5.00 | 7.50 | C |
| nn(1774) | The Wheel of Death–R.T.M. Scott. Note: Was distributed as a free bonus with X1735 | 2.50 | 5.00 | 7.50 | M |
| X1782 | Wings of the Black Death–Grant Stockbridge | 2.50 | 5.00 | 7.50 | M |
| X2002 | Bombs from the Murder Wolves–Robert J. Hogan; 1971 | 2.50 | 5.00 | 7.50 | C |
| X2004 | Vultures of the White Death–Robert J. Hogan | 2.50 | 5.00 | 7.50 | C |
| X2023 | Flight from the Grave–Robert J. Hogan | 2.50 | 5.00 | 7.50 | C |
| X2043 | Fangs of the Sky Leopard–Robert J. Hogan | 3.50 | 7.00 | 10.50 | C |
| X2058 | The Mark of the Vulture–Robert J. Hogan | 2.50 | 5.00 | 7.50 | C |

## BEST BOOKS
### Consolidated Book Publishers
**Oversize–6″ x 8¾″**

| No. | Title | V/Good | Fine | N/Mint |  |
|---|---|---|---|---|---|
| 592 | Suspense Stories–ed. R.M. Barrows; nd; includes A. Christie, D. Runyon, and others; interior illus. by J. Allen St. John. | 7.50 | 15.00 | 22.50 | M |

## BEST DETECTIVE NOVEL OF THE MONTH
### Select Publications, Inc.
**Digest Size**
**(See also Best Detective Selection of the Month)**

| No. | Title | V/Good | Fine | N/Mint |  |
|---|---|---|---|---|---|
| 1 | Come and Be Killed–Dorothy Bennett | 7.50 | 15.00 | 22.50 | M |
| 2 | $1,000,000 in Corpses–Edward Ronns; 1942 | 7.50 | 15.00 | 22.50 | M |

## BEST DETECTIVE SELECTION OF THE MONTH
### Select Publications, Inc.
**Digest Size**
**(See also Best Detective Novel of the Month)**

| No. | Title | V/Good | Fine | N/Mint |  |
|---|---|---|---|---|---|
| 3 | Death Goes to a Party–Michael Jaffe | 7.50 | 15.00 | 22.50 | M |
| 4 | The Bloody Wig Murders–George Bagby | 7.50 | 15.00 | 22.50 | M |
| 5 | Pool of Death–Keats Patrick; aka Death Is a Tory | 7.50 | 15.00 | 22.50 | M |
| 6 | Wail for the Corpse–Lawrence Treat; aka B as in Banshee | 7.50 | 15.00 | 22.50 | M |
| 7 | The Corpse Hangs High–Edward Ronns | 7.50 | 15.00 | 22.50 | M |

*Berkley X2043, Best Detective Selection 4, Best Detective Selection 9.*

BEST DETECTIVE SELECTION OF THE MONTH, *continued*

| | | V/Good | Fine | N/Mint | |
|---|---|---|---|---|---|
| 8 | Modeled in Murder–Manning Long; 1943 | 7.50 | 15.00 | 22.50 | M |
| 9 | Say Yes to Murder–W.T. Ballard | 7.50 | 15.00 | 22.50 | M |
| nn | The Corpse Hangs High–Edward Ronns; 1943 | 7.50 | 15.00 | 22.50 | M |
| nn | Murder RFD–Herman Petersen | 7.50 | 15.00 | 22.50 | M |

# BESTSELLER LIBRARY/MYSTERY

## The American Mercury, Inc./Mercury Publications

### Digest Size

Bestseller Library 1, Bestseller Mystery B34, Bestseller Mystery B40.

| | | V/Good | Fine | N/Mint | |
|---|---|---|---|---|---|
| nn(1) | The Adventures of Ellery Queen–Ellery Queen | 2.00 | 4.00 | 6.00 | M |
| B2 | One More Spring–Robert Nathan | .75 | 1.50 | 2.25 | |
| B3 | More Adventures of Ellery Queen–Ellery Queen | 1.50 | 3.00 | 4.50 | M |
| B4 | Life Begins at Forty–Walter B. Pitkin | .75 | 1.50 | 2.25 | |
| B5 | Tobacco Road–Jack Kirkland (Erskine Caldwell) | 1.00 | 2.00 | 3.00 | E |
| B6 | Twenty-Four Hours–Louis Bromfield | .75 | 1.50 | 2.25 | |
| B7 | The Bellamy Trial–Frances Noyes Hart | .75 | 1.50 | 2.25 | M |
| B8 | The Devil to Pay–Ellery Queen | .75 | 1.50 | 2.25 | M |
| B9 | The Mysterious Mr. Quin–Agatha Christie | .75 | 1.50 | 2.25 | M |
| B10 | The Case of the Curious Bride–Erle Stanley Gardner | .75 | 1.50 | 2.25 | M |
| B11 | The Spanish Cape Mystery–Ellery Queen | .75 | 1.50 | 2.25 | M |
| B12 | Thank You, Mr. Moto–John P. Marquand | .75 | 1.50 | 2.25 | M |
| B13 | Lord Peter Views the Body–Dorothy L. Sayers | .75 | 1.50 | 2.25 | M |
| B14 | The Greek Coffin Mystery–Ellery Queen | .75 | 1.50 | 2.25 | M |
| B15 | Inquest–Percival Wilde | .75 | 1.50 | 2.25 | M |
| B16 | Murder in Stained Glass–Margaret Armstrong | .75 | 1.50 | 2.25 | M |
| B17 | The Egyptian Cross Mystery–Ellery Queen | .75 | 1.50 | 2.25 | M |
| B18 | Dead Man's Mirror–Agatha Christie | .75 | 1.50 | 2.25 | M |
| B19 | The Case of the Sleepwalker's Niece–Erle Stanley Gardner | .75 | 1.50 | 2.25 | M |
| B20 | In the Teeth of the Evidence–Dorothy L. Sayers | .75 | 1.50 | 2.25 | M |
| B21 | Murder in Three Acts–Agatha Christie | .75 | 1.50 | 2.25 | M |
| B22 | The D.A. Holds a Candle–Erle Stanley Gardner | .75 | 1.50 | 2.25 | M |
| B23 | Death in Ecstacy–Ngaio Marsh | .75 | 1.50 | 2.25 | M |
| B24 | A Face for a Clue–Georges Simenon | .75 | 1.50 | 2.25 | M |
| B25 | Partners in Crime–Agatha Christie | .75 | 1.50 | 2.25 | M |
| B26 | Does not exist | | | | |
| B27 | The Cairo Garter Murders–Van Wyck Mason | .75 | 1.50 | 2.25 | M |
| B28 | The Tragedy of Y–Ellery Queen | .75 | 1.50 | 2.25 | M |
| B29 | Murder up My Sleeve–Erle Stanley Gardner | .75 | 1.50 | 2.25 | M |
| B30 | The Man with No Face–Margaret Armstrong | .75 | 1.50 | 2.25 | M |
| B31 | Some Buried Caesar–Rex Stout | .75 | 1.50 | 2.25 | M |
| B32 | The Seven Dials Mystery–Agatha Christie | .75 | 1.50 | 2.25 | M |
| B33 | Black Plumes–Margery Allingham | .75 | 1.50 | 2.25 | M |
| B34 | The Department of Queer Complaints–Carter Dickson. Note: Queen's Quorum No. 92 | 2.50 | 5.00 | 7.50 | M |
| B35 | This Is Murder–Erle Stanley Gardner | .75 | 1.50 | 2.25 | M |
| B36 | The Regatta Mystery–Agatha Christie | .75 | 1.50 | 2.25 | M |
| B37 | The Whispering Cup–Mabel Seeley | .75 | 1.50 | 2.25 | M |
| B38 | Hangman's Holiday–Dorothy L. Sayers | .75 | 1.50 | 2.25 | M |
| B39 | The Boomerang Clue–Agatha Christie | .75 | 1.50 | 2.25 | M |
| B40 | $106,000 Blood Money–Dashiell Hammett; 1st ed. 1943 | 20.00 | 40.00 | 60.00 | M |
| B41 | The Flemish Shop–Georges Simenon | .75 | 1.50 | 2.25 | M |
| B42 | The G-String Murders–Gypsy Rose Lee. Note: Actually written by Craig Rice | .75 | 1.50 | 2.25 | M |
| B43 | Poirot Investigates–Agatha Christie | .75 | 1.50 | 2.25 | M |
| B44 | Where There's a Will–Rex Stout | .75 | 1.50 | 2.25 | M |

| | | V/Good | Fine | N/Mint | |
|---|---|---|---|---|---|
| B45 | Death in Five Boxes–Carter Dickson | .75 | 1.50 | 2.25 | M |
| B46 | Death in the Doll's House–Hannah Lees & Lawrence Bachmann | .75 | 1.50 | 2.25 | M |
| B47 | The Three Coffins–John Dickson Carr | .75 | 1.50 | 2.25 | M |
| B48 | The Secret Adversary–Agatha Christie | .75 | 1.50 | 2.25 | M |
| B49 | Dark Garden–Mignon G. Eberhart | .75 | 1.50 | 2.25 | M |
| B50 | The Adventures of Sam Spade–Dashiell Hammett; 1st ed. 1944 | 25.00 | 50.00 | 75.00 | M |
| B51 | Police at the Funeral–Margery Allingham | .75 | 1.50 | 2.25 | M |
| B52 | The Man in the Brown Suit–Agatha Christie | .75 | 1.50 | 2.25 | M |
| B53 | Thirty Days Hath September–Dorothy Cameron Disney & George Sessions Perry | .75 | 1.50 | 2.25 | M |
| B54 | Sad Cypress–Agatha Christie | .75 | 1.50 | 2.25 | M |
| B55 | The Pattern–Mignon G. Eberhart | .75 | 1.50 | 2.25 | M |
| B56 | Kingdom of Death–Margery Allingham | .75 | 1.50 | 2.25 | M |
| B57 | The Washington Legation Murders–Van Wyck Mason | .75 | 1.50 | 2.25 | M |
| B58 | Appointment with Death–Agatha Christie | .75 | 1.50 | 2.25 | M |
| B59 | The Case Book of Ellery Queen–Ellery Queen; orig. 1945 | 20.00 | 40.00 | 60.00 | M |
| B60 | Hangman's Whip–Mignon G. Eberhart | .75 | 1.50 | 2.25 | M |
| B61 | Murder at Hazelmoor–Agatha Christie | .75 | 1.50 | 2.25 | M |
| B62 | The Continental Op–Dashiell Hammett; 1st ed. 1945 | 15.00 | 30.00 | 45.00 | M |
| B63 | The Budapest Parade Murders–Van Wyck Mason | .75 | 1.50 | 2.25 | M |
| B64 | Artists in Crime–Ngaio Marsh | .75 | 1.50 | 2.25 | M |
| B65 | Compound for Death–Doris Miles Disney | .75 | 1.50 | 2.25 | M |
| B66 | Alarm of the Black Cat–D.B. Olsen | .75 | 1.50 | 2.25 | M |
| B67 | Dagger of the Mind–Kenneth Fearing | .75 | 1.50 | 2.25 | M |
| B68 | Vintage Murder–Ngaio Marsh | .75 | 1.50 | 2.25 | M |
| B69 | The Patience of Maigret–Georges Simenon; aka Battle of Nerves | .75 | 1.50 | 2.25 | M |
| B70 | Deadly Nightshade–Elizabeth Daly | .75 | 1.50 | 2.25 | M |
| B71 | The Crimson Circle–Edgar Wallace | .75 | 1.50 | 2.25 | M |
| B72 | The Parchment Key–Stanley Hopkins | .75 | 1.50 | 2.25 | M |
| B73 | The Affair of the Crimson Gull–Clifford Knight | .75 | 1.50 | 2.25 | M |
| B74 | Laura–Vera Caspary | .75 | 1.50 | 2.25 | M |
| B75 | Miss Silver Deals with Death–Patricia Wentworth | .75 | 1.50 | 2.25 | M |
| B76 | The Pricking Thumb–H.C. Branson | .75 | 1.50 | 2.25 | M |
| B77 | While She Sleeps–Ethel Lina White | .75 | 1.50 | 2.25 | M |
| B78 | Death Watch–John Dickson Carr | .75 | 1.50 | 2.25 | M |
| B79 | Mr. Parker Pyne, Detective–Agatha Christie | .75 | 1.50 | 2.25 | M |
| B80 | The Chuckling Fingers–Mabel Seeley | .75 | 1.50 | 2.25 | M |
| B81 | Hammett Homicides–Dashiell Hammett; 1st ed. 1946 | 20.00 | 40.00 | 60.00 | M |
| B82 | Quoth the Raven–Bruno Fischer | .75 | 1.50 | 2.25 | M |
| B83 | She Fell among Actors–James Warren | .75 | 1.50 | 2.25 | M |
| B84 | Sinners Never Die–A.E. Martin | .75 | 1.50 | 2.25 | M |
| B85 | The Black Honeymoon–Constance Little & Gwenyth Little | .75 | 1.50 | 2.25 | M |
| B86 | Murder in the Calais Coach–Agatha Christie | .75 | 1.50 | 2.25 | M |
| B87 | The Corpse with Purple Thighs–George Bagby | .75 | 1.50 | 2.25 | M |
| B88 | Whisper Murder–Vera Kelsey | .75 | 1.50 | 2.25 | M |
| B89 | The Blonde Died First–Dana Chambers | .75 | 1.50 | 2.25 | M |

| | V/Good | Fine | N/Mint |
|---|---|---|---|

BESTSELLER LIBRARY/MYSTERY, *continued*

| | | V/Good | Fine | N/Mint | |
|---|---|---|---|---|---|
| B90 | Deadline at Dawn–William Irish | .75 | 1.50 | 2.25 | M |
| B91 | The Department of Dead Ends–Roy Vickers; 1st ed. 1947. Note: Queen's Quorum No. 101 | 5.00 | 10.00 | 15.00 | M |
| B92 | The Book of the Dead–Elizabeth Daly | .75 | 1.50 | 2.25 | M |
| B93 | One Alone–Van Siller | .75 | 1.50 | 2.25 | M |
| B94 | Cops and Robbers–O. Henry | .75 | 1.50 | 2.25 | M |
| B95 | The Yellow Room–Mary Roberts Rinehart | .50 | 1.00 | 1.50 | M |
| B96 | Dead at the Take-Off–Lester Dent | 2.00 | 4.00 | 6.00 | M |
| B97 | The Man Who Slept All Day–Michael Venning | .75 | 1.50 | 2.25 | M |
| B98 | Stranger at Home–George Sanders | .75 | 1.50 | 2.25 | M |
| B99 | Cats Don't Need Coffins–D.B. Olsen | .75 | 1.50 | 2.25 | M |
| B100 | The Hawk–Roy Vickers | .75 | 1.50 | 2.25 | M |
| B101 | Lady to Kill–Lester Dent | 2.00 | 4.00 | 6.00 | M |
| B102 | Kiss the Blonde Goodbye–Finlay McDermid; aka Ghost Wanted | .75 | 1.50 | 2.25 | M |
| B103 | Rope for an Ape–Dana Chambers | .75 | 1.50 | 2.25 | M |
| B104 | Fear No More–Leslie Edgley | .75 | 1.50 | 2.25 | M |
| B105 | So Deadly Fair–Gertrude Walker | .75 | 1.50 | 2.25 | M |
| B106 | The Bleeding Scissors–Bruno Fischer | .75 | 1.50 | 2.25 | M |
| B107 | Make My Bed Soon–John Stephen Strange | .75 | 1.50 | 2.25 | M |
| 108 | Murder Picks the Jury–Harrison Hunt | .75 | 1.50 | 2.25 | M |
| B109 | The Angry Heart–Leslie Edgley | .75 | 1.50 | 2.25 | M |
| B110 | Bullets for a Blonde–Will Oursler; aka Departure Delayed | .75 | 1.50 | 2.25 | M |
| B111 | Death for My Beloved–Doris Miles Disney; aka Enduring Old Charms | .75 | 1.50 | 2.25 | M |
| B112 | The Book of the Lion–Elizabeth Daly | .75 | 1.50 | 2.25 | M |
| B113 | In Cold Blood–George Bagby | .75 | 1.50 | 2.25 | M |
| B114 | The Blue Horse of Taxco–Kathleen Moore Knight | .75 | 1.50 | 2.25 | M |
| B115 | Lady Afraid–Lester Dent | 2.00 | 4.00 | 6.00 | M |
| B116 | Fountain of Death–Hugh Lawrence Nelson | .75 | 1.50 | 2.25 | M |
| B117 | Death Has Four Hands–Hilda Lawrence; aka Composition for Four Hands | .75 | 1.50 | 2.25 | M |
| B118 | Short Shrift–Manning Long | .75 | 1.50 | 2.25 | M |
| B119 | The Dark River–Philip Clark | .75 | 1.50 | 2.25 | M |
| B120 | Devious Design–D.B. Olsen | .75 | 1.50 | 2.25 | M • |
| B121 | Nightfall–David Goodis | 3.00 | 6.00 | 12.00 | M |
| B122 | The Bleeding House–Hilda Lawrence; aka The House | .75 | 1.50 | 2.25 | M |
| B123 | Bait for Murder–Kathleen Moore Knight | .75 | 1.50 | 2.25 | M |
| B124 | Think Fast, Mr. Moto–John P. Marquand | .75 | 1.50 | 2.25 | M |
| B125 | Shark River–Richard Powell | .75 | 1.50 | 2.25 | M |
| B126 | For the Love of Murder–Margaret Scherf; aka Gilbert's Last Toothache | .75 | 1.50 | 2.25 | M |
| B127 | The Dark Light–Bart Spicer | .75 | 1.50 | 2.25 | M |
| B128 | The Monkey Murder–Stuart Palmer; 1st ed. 1950 | 3.00 | 6.00 | 12.00 | M |
| B129 | Place for a Poisoner–E.C.R. Lorac | .75 | 1.50 | 2.25 | M |
| B130 | Kill to Fit–Bruno Fischer | .75 | 1.50 | 2.25 | M |
| B131 | Kill 'Em with Kindness–Fred Dickenson | .75 | 1.50 | 2.25 | M |
| B132 | Days of Misfortune–Aaron Marc Stein | .75 | 1.50 | 2.25 | M |
| B133 | Too like the Dead–Dana Chambers; aka Too like the Lightning | .75 | 1.50 | 2.25 | M |
| B134 | A Lonely Way to Die–Hal Debrett | .75 | 1.50 | 2.25 | M |
| B135 | Murder for Millions–Nancy Rutledge; aka Emily Will Know | .75 | 1.50 | 2.25 | M |
| B136 | Blood on My Shoes–Jean Leslie; aka Shoes for My Love | .75 | 1.50 | 2.25 | M |
| B137 | He Didn't Mind Danger–Michael Gilbert | .75 | 1.50 | 2.25 | M |
| B138 | The Whitebird Murders–Thomas B. Black | .75 | 1.50 | 2.25 | M |
| B139 | Death of a Big Shot–Clifford Knight | .75 | 1.50 | 2.25 | M |
| B140 | Rather Cool for Mayhem–Lawrence G. Blochman • | .75 | 1.50 | 2.25 | M |
| B141 | Sinister Shelter–Charles L. Leonard | .75 | 1.50 | 2.25 | M |
| B142 | Hot Tip–Jack Dolph | .75 | 1.50 | 2.25 | M |
| B143 | Murder Makes a Deadline–Samuel M. Fuller; aka The Dark Page | .75 | 1.50 | 2.25 | M |
| B144 | Mr. Blessington's Imperialist Plot–John Sherwood | .75 | 1.50 | 2.25 | M |
| B145 | Half-Past Mortem–John Saxon | .75 | 1.50 | 2.25 | M |
| B146 | The Knife behind You–James Benet | .75 | 1.50 | 2.25 | M |
| B147 | The Man in the Mist–Francis Bonnamy | .75 | 1.50 | 2.25 | M |
| B148 | Smallbone Deceased–Michael Gilbert | .75 | 1.50 | 2.25 | M |
| B149 | These Arrows Point to Death–William O'Farrell | .75 | 1.50 | 2.25 | M |
| B150 | The Kahuna Killer–Juanita Sheridan | .75 | 1.50 | 2.25 | M |
| B151 | The 3-13 Murders–Thomas B. Black | .75 | 1.50 | 2.25 | M |
| B152 | Alias Basil Willing–Helen McCloy | .75 | 1.50 | 2.25 | M |
| B153 | FBI Story–The Gordons | .75 | 1.50 | 2.25 | M |
| B154 | Fatal Lover–Van Siller; aka The Last Resort | .75 | 1.50 | 2.25 | M |
| B155 | The Mamo Murders–Juanita Sheridan | .75 | 1.50 | 2.25 | M |
| B156 | Don't Kill, My Love–Rae Foley; aka Wake the Sleeping Wolf | .75 | 1.50 | 2.25 | M |
| B157 | F As in Flight–Lawrence Treat | .75 | 1.50 | 2.25 | M |
| B158 | Mask for Murder–Aaron Marc Stein | .75 | 1.50 | 2.25 | M |
| B159 | Divine and Deadly–Margaret Scherf; aka The Curious Custard Pie | .75 | 1.50 | 2.25 | M |
| B160 | Dead Ringer–Ferguson Findley; aka The Man in the Middle | .75 | 1.50 | 2.25 | M |
| B161 | The Fair and the Dead–John Stephen Strange; aka Reasonable Doubt | .75 | 1.50 | 2.25 | M |
| B162 | Murder Is a Gamble–Glenn Barns | .75 | 1.50 | 2.25 | M |
| B163 | Lust for Vengeance–Robert Bloomfield; aka Vengeance Streets | .75 | 1.50 | 2.25 | M |
| B164 | Death My Darling Daughters–Jonathan Stagge | 1.50 | 3.00 | 4.50 | M |
| B165 | Vice Squad–Leslie T. White; aka Harness Bull; movie tie-in | 2.50 | 5.00 | 7.50 | M |
| B166 | Dance of Death–Veronica Parker | .75 | 1.50 | 2.25 | M |
| B167 | The Virgin Huntress–Elizabeth Sanxay Holding | .75 | 1.50 | 2.25 | M |
| B168 | Dead Yesterday–Ruth Fenisong | .75 | 1.50 | 2.25 | M |
| B169 | One Murder Too Many–Edwin Lanham | .75 | 1.50 | 2.25 | M |
| B170 | Make Haste to Live–The Gordons | .75 | 1.50 | 2.25 | M |
| B171 | One Blonde Died–Leslie Edgley; aka The Runaway Pigeon | .75 | 1.50 | 2.25 | M |
| B172 | Killer Loose!–Genevieve Holden | .75 | 1.50 | 2.25 | M |
| B173 | The Corpse Who Had Too Many Friends–Hampton Stone | .75 | 1.50 | 2.25 | M |
| B174 | This Year's Death–John Godey | .75 | 1.50 | 2.25 | M |
| B175 | Lawyers Don't Hang–Glenn Barns | .75 | 1.50 | 2.25 | M |
| B176 | The Passionate Victims–Lange Lewis | .75 | 1.50 | 2.25 | M |
| B177 | Terror Lurks in Darkness–Dolores Hitchens | .75 | 1.50 | 2.25 | M |
| B178 | V As in Victim–Lawrence Treat | .75 | 1.50 | 2.25 | M |
| B179 | Lovely in Death–William O'Farrell; aka The Snakes of St. Cyr | .75 | 1.50 | 2.25 | M |
| B180 | Killer at His Back–John Godey; aka The Blue Hour | .75 | 1.50 | 2.25 | M |
| B181 | You'll Fry Tomorrow–M.V. Heberden; aka Exit This Way | .75 | 1.50 | 2.25 | M |
| B182 | The Case of the Missing Corpse–Edwin Lanham; aka Death of a Corinthian | .75 | 1.50 | 2.25 | M |
| B183 | Embrace of Death–Carroll Cox Estes; aka The Moon Gate | .75 | 1.50 | 2.25 | M |
| B184 | The Fatal Flirt–Dolores Hitchens; aka Beat Back the Tide | .75 | 1.50 | 2.25 | M |
| B185 | Too Lovely Too Live–Ruth Fenisong; aka Miscast for Murder | .75 | 1.50 | 2.25 | M |
| B186 | They All Bleed Red–Richard Sted | .75 | 1.50 | 2.25 | M |
| B187 | Buried for Pleasure–Edmund Crispin | .75 | 1.50 | 2.25 | M |
| B188 | The Blonde Betrayer–John Godey; aka The Man in Question | .75 | 1.50 | 2.25 | M |
| B189 | Trap for a Redhead–Stuart Palmer; aka Nipped in the Bud | 1.25 | 2.50 | 3.75 | M |

*Bestseller Mystery B165, Big Green 3, Big Green 4.*

| | | V/Good | Fine | N/Mint |
|---|---|---|---|---|

| | | V/Good | Fine | N/Mint | |
|---|---|---|---|---|---|
| B190 | Trial and Terror–Lawrence Treat | .75 | 1.50 | 2.25 | M |
| B191 | Shroud for a Lady–Elizabeth Daly; aka The Wrong Way Down | .75 | 1.50 | 2.25 | M |
| B192 | Another Morgue Heard From–Frederick C. Davis | .75 | 1.50 | 2.25 | M |
| B193 | Catch and Kill–Nicholas Blake; aka The Whisper in the Gloom | .75 | 1.50 | 2.25 | M |
| B194 | Network of Fear–Alvin Yudkoff; aka Circumstances Beyond Control | .75 | 1.50 | 2.25 | M |
| B195 | No Time for Terror–Philip MacDonald; aka Guest in the House | .75 | 1.50 | 2.25 | M |
| B196 | Murder Muscles In–Max Franklin; aka Justice Has No Sword | .75 | 1.50 | 2.25 | M |
| B197 | Murder Makes an Entrance–Clarence Budington Kelland | .75 | 1.50 | 2.25 | M |
| B198 | Black Alibi–Cornell Woolrich | 2.00 | 4.00 | 6.00 | M |
| B199 | The Book of the Crime–Elizabeth Daly | .75 | 1.50 | 2.25 | M |
| B200 | A Dirty Way to Die–George Bagby | .75 | 1.50 | 2.25 | M |
| B201 | Tell Her It's Murder–Helen Reilly | .75 | 1.50 | 2.25 | M |
| B202 | Take One for Murder–M.E. Chaber; aka As Old As Cain; 1955 | .75 | 1.50 | 2.25 | M |
| B203 | The Long Body–Helen McCloy | .75 | 1.50 | 2.25 | M |
| B204 | I Wake Up Screaming–Steve Fisher | .75 | 1.50 | 2.25 | M |
| B205 | Don't Look Back–Miriam Borgenicht | .75 | 1.50 | 2.25 | M |
| B206 | The Black Angel–Cornell Woolrich | 2.00 | 4.00 | 6.00 | M |
| B207 | Hang the Man High–Geoffrey Household; aka Fellow Passenger | .75 | 1.50 | 2.25 | M |
| B208 | The Deadly Truth–Helen McCloy | .75 | 1.50 | 2.25 | M |
| B209 | Bridge to Vengeance–Winston Graham; aka The Little Walls. Note: After No. 209, series became Bestseller Mystery Magazine | | | | |

# BIG GREEN DETECTIVE NOVEL
## Green Publishing Company
### Digest Size

| | | V/Good | Fine | N/Mint | |
|---|---|---|---|---|---|
| 2 | Hot Bullets for Love–Gentry Nyland; aka Mr. South Burned His Mouth. Note: Same cover as Double Action Detective No. 2 and Superior Detective Novel unnumbered | 5.00 | 10.00 | 15.00 | M |
| 3 | Run Corpse Run–Guy Pember-Hiller. Note: Same cover as Double Action Detective No. 3 | 4.00 | 8.00 | 12.00 | M |
| 4 | Murder with Love–Garland Lord | 4.00 | 8.00 | 12.00 | M |
| 5 | Target for Murder–Guy Elwyn Giles | 4.00 | 8.00 | 12.00 | M |

# BIG GREEN PUBLICATION
## Green Publishing Company
### Digest Size

| | | V/Good | Fine | N/Mint | |
|---|---|---|---|---|---|
| 5 | The Little Dog Barked–Anne Rowe | 3.00 | 6.00 | 9.00 | M |

# BLACK CAT DETECTIVE
## Crestwood Publishing Co., Inc.
### Digest Size

| | | V/Good | Fine | N/Mint | |
|---|---|---|---|---|---|
| 1 | 3 Died Variously–Guy Elwyn Giles | 2.50 | 5.00 | 7.50 | M |
| 2 | Bait for a Tiger–Bayard Veiller | 2.50 | 5.00 | 7.50 | M |
| 3 | Curtains for the Judge–Thomas Polsky | 2.50 | 5.00 | 7.50 | M |
| 3(4) | Dig Me a Grave–John Spain. Note: Incorrectly numbered No. 3, actually No. 4 | 2.50 | 5.00 | 7.50 | M |
| 5 | The Case of the Cheating Bride–Milton Propper; 1943 | 2.50 | 5.00 | 7.50 | M |
| 6 | Death Thumbs a Ride–Jean Lilly | 2.50 | 5.00 | 7.50 | M |
| 7 | The Beast Must Die–Nicholas Blake | 3.00 | 6.00 | 9.00 | M |
| 8 | The Body in the Road–Moray Dalton; 1944 | 2.50 | 5.00 | 7.50 | M |
| 9 | It Takes a Thief–Dan Billany | 2.50 | 5.00 | 7.50 | M |
| 10 | Crazy to Kill–Ann Cardwell | 2.50 | 5.00 | 7.50 | M |

*Black Cat Detective 8, Black Cat Detective 24, Black Cat Western 36.*

| | | V/Good | Fine | N/Mint | |
|---|---|---|---|---|---|
| 11 | John Doe–Murderer–William Dale | 2.50 | 5.00 | 7.50 | M |
| 12 | 6 Were to Die–Kirk Wales | 2.50 | 5.00 | 7.50 | M |
| 13 | Murder As Usual–Owen Fox Jerome | 2.50 | 5.00 | 7.50 | M |
| 14 | Dark Power–Elizabeth Sanxay Holding | 2.50 | 5.00 | 7.50 | M |
| 15 | Head Long for Murder–Merlda Mace; 1945 | 2.50 | 5.00 | 7.50 | M |
| 16 | The Crooked Circle–Gerald Verner | 2.50 | 5.00 | 7.50 | M |
| 17 | Motto for Murder–Merlda Mace | 2.50 | 5.00 | 7.50 | M |
| 18 | Murder Trouble–Louis Trimble | 2.50 | 5.00 | 7.50 | M |
| 19 | Murder in Miniatures–Sam Merwin, Jr | 2.50 | 5.00 | 7.50 | M |
| 20 | Murder in Plain Sight–Gerald Brown; 1946 | 2.50 | 5.00 | 7.50 | M |
| 21 | The Voodoo Goat–Audrey Gaines | 2.50 | 5.00 | 7.50 | M |
| 22 | And So He Had to Die–Donald Clough Cameron; 1946 | 2.50 | 5.00 | 7.50 | M |
| 23 | Judge Robinson Murdered!–R.L. Goldman | 2.50 | 5.00 | 7.50 | M |
| 24 | Death in the State House–Timothy Knox | 2.50 | 5.00 | 7.50 | M |
| 25 | Dear Dead Professor–K. Alison LaRoche | 2.50 | 5.00 | 7.50 | M |
| 26 | Murder in Haste–E.P. Fenwick | 2.50 | 5.00 | 7.50 | M |
| 27 | The Bright Face of Danger–Julius Fast; 1947 | 2.50 | 5.00 | 7.50 | M |
| 28 | Blondes Don't Cry–Merlda Mace | 2.50 | 5.00 | 7.50 | M |

# BLACK CAT WESTERN
## Crestwood Publishing Co., Inc.
### Digest Size

| | | V/Good | Fine | N/Mint | |
|---|---|---|---|---|---|
| 29 | The Outlaw of Antler–Frank C. Robertson | 2.00 | 4.00 | 6.00 | W |
| 30 | Prairie Pioneers–Lynn Westland | 2.00 | 4.00 | 6.00 | W |
| 31 | Blue River Riders–Archie Joscelyn | 2.00 | 4.00 | 6.00 | W |
| 32 | The Flying Y Brand–J.E. Grinstead | 2.00 | 4.00 | 6.00 | W |
| 33 | Gunsmoke in Paradise–Bert Arthur; 1948 | 2.00 | 4.00 | 6.00 | W |
| 34 | The Silver Cayuse–Lynn Westland | 2.00 | 4.00 | 6.00 | W |
| 35 | Bullet Justice–Tex Riley | 2.00 | 4.00 | 6.00 | W |
| 36 | Trail Trouble–Will Ermine; 1949 | 2.00 | 4.00 | 6.00 | W |
| 37 | Painted Post Range–Tom Gunn | 2.00 | 4.00 | 6.00 | W |
| 38 | Saddle River Spread–Lynn Westland | 2.00 | 4.00 | 6.00 | W |
| 39 | Nighthawk's Gold–Kim Knight | 2.00 | 4.00 | 6.00 | W |
| 40 | The Faceless Riders–Archie Joscelyn | 2.00 | 4.00 | 6.00 | W |
| 41 | Smoke in the West–Archie Joscelyn | 2.00 | 4.00 | 6.00 | W |
| 42 | Gunslammer–Lee Floren | 2.00 | 4.00 | 6.00 | W |
| 43 | Renegade Guns–James L. Rubel | 2.00 | 4.00 | 6.00 | W |
| 44 | Mad River Guns–Lee Floren | 2.00 | 4.00 | 6.00 | W |
| 45 | Outcast Law–Archie Joscelyn | 2.00 | 4.00 | 6.00 | W |

# BLACK KNIGHT
## Ideal Distributing Company
### Some Digest Size

| | | V/Good | Fine | N/Mint | |
|---|---|---|---|---|---|
| 15 | Corpse in the Wind–Robert Portner Koehler; digest size | 3.00 | 6.00 | 9.00 | M |
| 16 | Last Year's Snow–Don Tracey; digest size | 3.00 | 6.00 | 9.00 | M |

*Black Knight 15, Black Knight 28, Bleak House 12.*

*Bleak House 22, Bobley B4, Boblin unnumbered.*

| | | V/Good | Fine | N/Mint | |
|---|---|---|---|---|---|
| **BLACK KNIGHT,** *continued* | | | | | |
| 17 | Death to Drumbeat–Jeremy Lane; digest size | 3.00 | 6.00 | 9.00 | M |
| 18 | Murder behind the Mike–R.L. Goldman; digest size | 3.00 | 6.00 | 9.00 | M |
| 19 | Death by Dynamite–Joseph L. Bonney; digest size | 3.00 | 6.00 | 9.00 | M |
| 22 | Murder's Coming–Donald Clough Cameron | 3.00 | 6.00 | 9.00 | M |
| 24 | Murder for Real–Minna Barton | 4.00 | 8.00 | 12.00 | M |
| 25 | Come Dwell with Death–M.W. Glidden; digest size | 3.00 | 6.00 | 9.00 | M |
| 26 | Death Is No Lady–M.E. Corne; aka Death Is a Masquerade | 4.00 | 8.00 | 12.00 | M |
| 27 | The Psychiatric Murders–M. Scott Michel | 4.00 | 8.00 | 12.00 | M |
| 28 | The Kidnappers–Albert E. Ullman | 4.00 | 8.00 | 12.00 | M |
| 29 | Green for a Grave–Manning Lee Stokes | 4.00 | 8.00 | 12.00 | M |
| 30 | Make Mine Murder–R. Sidney Bowen | 4.00 | 8.00 | 12.00 | M |
| 31 | Dead Weight–Addison Simmons | 4.00 | 8.00 | 12.00 | M |
| 32 | Kill Him Tonight–Jeremy Lane | 4.00 | 8.00 | 12.00 | M |
| 33 | Stop Press–Murder!–Peter Stirling | 4.00 | 8.00 | 12.00 | M |
| 34 | Puzzle in Petticoats–Kootz | 4.00 | 8.00 | 12.00 | M |

## BLEAK HOUSE
## Parsee Publications
### Some Digest Size

| | | V/Good | Fine | N/Mint | |
|---|---|---|---|---|---|
| 12 | Design for Dying–Albert Jeffers; aka Screen for Murder; digest size | 3.00 | 6.00 | 9.00 | M |
| 13 | Murder Wore Green–Robert Portner Koehler; digest size | 3.00 | 6.00 | 9.00 | M |
| 14 | The Case of the Blood-stained Dime–Minna Barton; aka Murder Does Light Housekeeping | 4.00 | 8.00 | 12.00 | M |
| 15 | The Case of the Missing Corpse–Joan Langar | 4.00 | 8.00 | 12.00 | M |
| 16 | The Corpse in the Guest Room–Clement Wood | 4.00 | 8.00 | 12.00 | M |
| 17 | The Skyscraper Murder–Samuel Spewack | 4.00 | 8.00 | 12.00 | M |
| 18 | Murder Menagerie–Jeremy Lane | 4.00 | 8.00 | 12.00 | M |
| 19 | If I Should Murder–Patrick Laing | 4.00 | 8.00 | 12.00 | M |
| 20 | The Terror of the Headless Corpse–William Dale | 4.00 | 8.00 | 12.00 | M |
| 21 | Here Come the Dead–Robert Portner Koehler | 4.00 | 8.00 | 12.00 | M |
| 22 | White for a Shroud–Donald Clough Cameron | 4.00 | 8.00 | 12.00 | M |

## BOBLEY BOOKS
## Robert Edwards Publishing Co.
### Digest Size

| | | V/Good | Fine | N/Mint |
|---|---|---|---|---|
| B4 | Best Read Short Stories–anthology; 1946 | 2.50 | 5.00 | 7.50 |

## BOBLIN BOOK
## Boblin Sales Company
### Digest Size

| | | V/Good | Fine | N/Mint | |
|---|---|---|---|---|---|
| nn | The Adventures of Buffalo Bill–William F. Cody; movie tie-in | 7.50 | 15.00 | 22.50 | W |
| nn | The Jumping Frog and Sixteen Other Stories–Mark Twain | 4.00 | 8.00 | 12.00 | H |
| nn | Was It Murder?–James Hilton | 3.50 | 7.00 | 10.50 | W |
| nn | Judge Priest Turns Detective–Irvin S. Cobb | 4.00 | 8.00 | 12.00 | M |

## BONDED
## Bond-Charteris/Black/Jacobs/Shaw
### Digest Size

| | | V/Good | Fine | N/Mint | |
|---|---|---|---|---|---|
| 1 | The Saint Meets the Tiger–Leslie Charteris | 3.00 | 6.00 | 9.00 | M |
| 2 | Featuring the Saint–Leslie Charteris; 1945 | 3.00 | 6.00 | 9.00 | M |
| 3 | The Saint's Getaway–Leslie Charteris | 3.00 | 6.00 | 9.00 | M |
| 4 | The Saint's Choice of English Crime–ed. Leslie Charteris | 3.00 | 6.00 | 9.00 | M |
| 5 | Alias the Saint–Leslie Charteris | 3.00 | 6.00 | 9.00 | M |
| 6 | The Saint's Choice of American Crime–ed. Leslie Charteris | 3.00 | 6.00 | 9.00 | M |
| 7 | Paging the Saint–Leslie Charteris; aka Wanted for Murder | 3.00 | 6.00 | 9.00 | M |
| 8 | The Saint's Choice of True Crimes–ed. Leslie Charteris | 3.00 | 6.00 | 9.00 | M |
| 9 | The Saint's Choice of Humorous Crime Stories–ed. Leslie Charteris | 3.00 | 6.00 | 9.00 | M |
| 10 | Fast One–Paul Cain | 8.00 | 16.00 | 24.00 | M |
| 10A | Atomic Bomb–Malcolm Jameson | 7.50 | 15.00 | 22.50 | SF |
| 10B | Guns of Powder River–Oscar J. Friend | 6.00 | 12.00 | 18.00 | W |
| 11 | The Saint's Choice of Impossible Crime–ed. Leslie Charteris; 1st ed. 1945 | 8.00 | 16.00 | 24.00 | SF |
| 12 | The Craig Rice Mystery Digest–ed. Craig Rice | 5.00 | 10.00 | 15.00 | M |
| 13 | 8 Faces at 3–Craig Rice | 4.00 | 8.00 | 12.00 | M |

*Bonded 10, Bonded unnumbered, Bonded Mystery 1.*

| | | V/Good | Fine | N/Mint |
|---|---|---|---|---|

**BONDED,** *continued*

| | | V/Good | Fine | N/Mint | |
|---|---|---|---|---|---|
| 14 | The Saint Meets His Match–Leslie Charteris | 3.50 | 7.00 | 10.50 | M |
| 15 | Crime on My Hands–George Sanders | 4.00 | 8.00 | 12.00 | M |
| 16 | I'll Hate Myself in the Morning–Elliot Paul | 3.00 | 6.00 | 9.00 | M |
| nn | Lady on a Train–Leslie Charteris; movie tie-in | 10.00 | 20.00 | 30.00 | M |

## BONDED MYSTERY
### Anson Bond Publications, Inc.
**Some Digest Size**

| | | V/Good | Fine | N/Mint | |
|---|---|---|---|---|---|
| 1 | The Goose Is Cooked–Emnett Hogarth; digest size | 3.00 | 6.00 | 9.00 | M |
| 2 | Murder of a Novelist–Sally Wood; digest size | 3.00 | 6.00 | 9.00 | M |
| 3 | The Hungry House–Lilian Lauferty; digest size | 3.00 | 6.00 | 9.00 | M |
| 4 | Murder Strikes Thrice–Charles G. Booth; digest size | 3.00 | 6.00 | 9.00 | M |
| 5 | I'll Eat You Last–H.C. Branson | 4.00 | 8.00 | 12.00 | M |
| 6 | The Thing in the Brook–Peter Storme | 4.00 | 8.00 | 12.00 | M |
| 7 | Death Blew Out the Match–Kathleen Moore Knight | 4.00 | 8.00 | 12.00 | M |
| 8 | Twittering Bird Mystery–H.C. Bailey | 4.00 | 8.00 | 12.00 | M |
| 9 | Murder Needs a Name–Ruth Fenisong | 4.00 | 8.00 | 12.00 | M |
| 10 | "B" as in Banshee–Lawrence Treat | 4.00 | 8.00 | 12.00 | M |
| 11 | Johnnie–Dorothy B. Hughes | 4.00 | 8.00 | 12.00 | M |
| 12 | Kingdom of Death–Margery Allingham | 4.00 | 8.00 | 12.00 | M |
| 13 | Harbour–Philip MacDonald | 4.00 | 8.00 | 12.00 | M |
| 14 | Who's Afraid?–Elisabeth Sanxay Holding | 4.00 | 8.00 | 12.00 | M |
| 15 | Footsteps in the Air–Susan Wells | 4.00 | 8.00 | 12.00 | M |
| 16 | This Is Mr. Fortune–H.C. Bailey | 4.00 | 8.00 | 12.00 | M |

## BOOKS INC.
### Books Inc.
**Special wartime edition for the American Red Cross**

| | | V/Good | Fine | N/Mint | |
|---|---|---|---|---|---|
| nn | The Four of Hearts–Ellery Queen | 1.00 | 2.00 | 3.00 | M |

## (BOOKS INC.)
### Books, Inc.

| | | V/Good | Fine | N/Mint | |
|---|---|---|---|---|---|
| 102 | Giant Quiz Book–Fred Garrigus | 2.00 | 4.00 | 6.00 | |
| 107 | Webster's New Handy Pocket Dictionary–ed. Noah Webster & Edward N. Teall; 1952 | 1.00 | 2.00 | 3.00 | NF |

## (BOWKER)
### R.R. Bowker Company

| | | V/Good | Fine | N/Mint | |
|---|---|---|---|---|---|
| nn | Banned Books–Anne Lyon Haight; 1955. Note: Contains interesting information on the banning of some paperback books either as pornography or because of lurid covers | 6.00 | 12.00 | 18.00 | NF |

## BOYS AND GIRLS FICTION
### Samuel Lowe
**Digest Size**

| | | V/Good | Fine | N/Mint | |
|---|---|---|---|---|---|
| nn | The Cordova Treasure–anon.; 1948 | 1.50 | 3.00 | 4.50 | M |
| nn | Stories from Scott–retold by Russell Thorndike; 1st ed. 1948 | 2.50 | 5.00 | 7.50 | |

*Bonded Mystery 5, Broadway 7, Broadway 8.*

## BROADWAY NOVEL MONTHLY
### Diversey Periodicals, Inc.
**Digest Size**

| | | V/Good | Fine | N/Mint | |
|---|---|---|---|---|---|
| 1 | Infidelity–Arthur Weigal. Note: Same cover as comic Intimate Confessions No. 7 | 10.00 | 20.00 | 30.00 | E |
| 2 | Venus on Wheels–Maurice Dekobra | 10.00 | 20.00 | 30.00 | E |
| 3 | Ladies of the Evening–Milton Herbert Gropper; 1949 | 9.00 | 18.00 | 27.00 | E |
| 4 | Tom's Temptations–Don Prince | 10.00 | 20.00 | 30.00 | E |
| 5 | Night Boat–Timothy Trent | 10.00 | 20.00 | 30.00 | E |
| 6 | Three Loose Ladies–M.H. Gropper | 10.00 | 20.00 | 30.00 | E |
| 7 | Fleshpots of Malibu–Carroll Graham & Garrett Graham; aka Queer People | 10.00 | 20.00 | 30.00 | E |
| 8 | Blonde Baby–Wilson Collison | 10.00 | 20.00 | 30.00 | E |
| 9 | Dangerous Love–Jack Woodford | 10.00 | 20.00 | 30.00 | E |
| 10 | Untamed Darling–Jack Woodford | 10.00 | 20.00 | 30.00 | E |

## BRONZE BOOKS
### Designs Publishing Company
**Digest Size**

| | | V/Good | Fine | N/Mint | |
|---|---|---|---|---|---|
| 1 | Harlem Model–Luke Roberts; orig. 1952 | 30.00 | 60.00 | 90.00 | E |
| 2 | Hot Chocolate–Jesse Lee Carter; orig. 1952 | 35.00 | 70.00 | 105.00 | E |

## (BRUSSEL)
### J. Brussel
**Digest Size**

| | | V/Good | Fine | N/Mint | |
|---|---|---|---|---|---|
| nn | Murder in the Bedroom–Gaston Leroux; 1945 | 3.50 | 7.00 | 10.50 | M |
| nn | One Hundred Years of American Humor–ed. J. Brussel; 1945 | 2.50 | 5.00 | 7.50 | H |

*Bronze Book 2, Bull's-Eye Detective Novel 1, Cameo 309.*

| | | V/Good | Fine | N/Mint |
|---|---|---|---|---|

# BULL'S-EYE DETECTIVE NOVELS

## Duchess Printing and Publishing Co., Ltd.

### Digest Size
### (Canadian)

| | | V/Good | Fine | N/Mint | |
|---|---|---|---|---|---|
| 1 | Silent Terror—T.C.H. Jacobs; 1944 | 3.00 | 6.00 | 9.00 | M |
| 2 | Death by Desire—Richard Goyne | 3.00 | 6.00 | 9.00 | M |

# (CAMBRIDGE HOUSE)

## Cambridge House

### Digest Size

| | | V/Good | Fine | N/Mint | |
|---|---|---|---|---|---|
| nn | How to Make Money Writing for Comics Magazines—Robert Kanigher; 1943; contains scripts and art from Capt. Marvel and Steel Sterling comics | 10.00 | 20.00 | 30.00 | NF |
| nn | How to Make Money Writing for Newspapers and Magazines—Robert Kanigher; 1943 | 10.00 | 20.00 | 30.00 | NF |

# CAMEO

## Detective House, Inc.

### Digest Size

| | | V/Good | Fine | N/Mint | |
|---|---|---|---|---|---|
| 300 | No Man of Her Own—Florence Stonebraker | 4.00 | 8.00 | 12.00 | E |
| 301 | The Loves of Alice Brandt—Gene Harvey; orig. 1951 | 4.00 | 8.00 | 12.00 | E |
| 302 | Night of Ecstasy—William Arnold | 4.00 | 8.00 | 12.00 | E |
| 303 | Conquest of Margie—Norman Bligh | 4.00 | 8.00 | 12.00 | E |
| 304 | Naughty Blonde—Florence Stonebraker | 4.00 | 8.00 | 12.00 | E |
| 305 | Pick-Up at Midnight—Gene Harvey | 4.00 | 8.00 | 12.00 | E |
| 306 | Passion C.O.D.—Albert L. Quandt | 4.00 | 8.00 | 12.00 | E |
| 307 | Sin Preferred—Kermit Welles | 4.00 | 8.00 | 12.00 | E |
| 308 | Secret Affair—Amos Hatter; orig. 1951 | 4.00 | 8.00 | 12.00 | E |
| 309 | A Girl Called Joy—Gene Harvey | 4.00 | 8.00 | 12.00 | E |
| 310 | Pleasure Bound—Kermit Welles | 4.00 | 8.00 | 12.00 | E |
| 311 | The Affairs of a Country Girl—Gail Jordan & Peggy Gaddis | 4.00 | 8.00 | 12.00 | E |
| 312 | Crossroads of Desire—Amos Hatter | 4.00 | 8.00 | 12.00 | E |
| 313 | Three-Time Sinner—Norman Bligh | 4.00 | 8.00 | 12.00 | E |
| 314 | The Big Tease—William Arnold; orig. 1952 | 4.00 | 8.00 | 12.00 | E |
| 315 | Passion's Harvest—Florence Stonebraker; c-Gross | 4.00 | 8.00 | 12.00 | E |
| 316 | Soft Shoulders—Norman Bligh | 4.00 | 8.00 | 12.00 | E |
| 317 | Woman of Fire—Peggy Gaddis | 4.00 | 8.00 | 12.00 | E |
| 318 | Island Ecstasy—Amos Hatter | 4.00 | 8.00 | 12.00 | E |
| 319 | Beach Party—Ralph Douglas | 4.00 | 8.00 | 12.00 | E |
| 320 | Girl of the Midway—Amos Hatter | 4.00 | 8.00 | 12.00 | E |
| 321 | Tight Skirt—Frederic Spencer; c-Belarski | 4.00 | 8.00 | 12.00 | E |
| 322 | Loose Women—Robert E. Reynolds; orig. 1952 | 4.00 | 8.00 | 12.00 | E |
| 323 | Wild Girl—L. Dixon; c-Belarski | 4.00 | 8.00 | 12.00 | E |
| 324 | Young Nurse—Sylvia Erskine | 4.00 | 8.00 | 12.00 | E |
| 325 | Mountain Girl—Peggy Gaddis | 4.00 | 8.00 | 12.00 | E |
| 326 | At Ruby's Place—Jean Tucker | 4.00 | 8.00 | 12.00 | E |
| 327 | Cleo—Frederic Spencer; orig. 1953 | 4.00 | 8.00 | 12.00 | E |
| 328 | Country Girl—Gail Jordan & Peggy Gaddis | 4.00 | 8.00 | 12.00 | E |
| 329 | Backwoods Bride—Robert E. Reynolds; c-Gross | 4.00 | 8.00 | 12.00 | E |
| 330 | Reefer Girl—Jane Manning; orig. 1953; c-Nappi | 7.50 | 15.00 | 22.50 | E |
| 331 | House of Lost Women—Frank Haskell | 4.00 | 8.00 | 12.00 | E |
| 332 | Nurse's Quarters—Sylvia Erskine; c-Belarski | 4.00 | 8.00 | 12.00 | E |
| 333 | Young Sinner—Elisabeth Gill; orig. 1953 | 4.00 | 8.00 | 12.00 | E |
| 334 | Office Sinner—Gene Harvey; aka The Loves of Alice Brandt | 4.00 | 8.00 | 12.00 | E |
| 335 | Wild Girl—Lewis Dixon; c-Belarski | 4.00 | 8.00 | 12.00 | E |
| 336 | Doctor's Nurse—Gene Harvey; aka A Girl Called Joy | 4.00 | 8.00 | 12.00 | E |
| 337 | Mountain Bride—Peggy Gaddis | 4.00 | 8.00 | 12.00 | E |
| 338 | Shanty Boat Girl—Kermit Welles | 4.00 | 8.00 | 12.00 | E |
| 339 | French Maid—Morton Cooper | 4.00 | 8.00 | 12.00 | E |
| 340 | Young Nurse—Sylvia Erskine | 4.00 | 8.00 | 12.00 | E |
| 341 | Country Girl—Gail Jordan (Peggy Gaddis); aka The Affairs of a Country Girl; c-Gross | 4.00 | 8.00 | 12.00 | E |
| 342 | Shanty Girl—Jean Tucker; c-Belarski | 4.00 | 8.00 | 12.00 | E |
| 343 | Slum Doctor—Matthew Clay | 4.00 | 8.00 | 12.00 | E |
| 344 | Woman of Passion—Norman Bligh | 4.00 | 8.00 | 12.00 | E |
| 345 | Lost Women—Robert E. Reynolds | 4.00 | 8.00 | 12.00 | E |
| 346 | Backwoods Bride—Robert E. Reynolds | 4.00 | 8.00 | 12.00 | E |
| 347 | Nurse's Quarters—Sylvia Erskine | 4.00 | 8.00 | 12.00 | E |
| 348 | Boarding House—Frank Haskell; 1st ed. 1953; aka House of Lost Women | 4.00 | 8.00 | 12.00 | E |
| 349 | Waterfront Club—Joan Tucker | 4.00 | 8.00 | 12.00 | E |
| 350 | Island Girl—Amos Hatter | 4.00 | 8.00 | 12.00 | E |
| 351 | French Maid—Morton Cooper | 4.00 | 8.00 | 12.00 | E |
| 352 | Slum Doctor—Matthew Clay | 4.00 | 8.00 | 12.00 | E |
| 353 | Doctor's Nurse—Gene Harvey | 4.00 | 8.00 | 12.00 | E |
| 354 | Shanty Girl—Joan Tucker; c-Belarski | 4.00 | 8.00 | 12.00 | E |
| 355 | Runaway Girl—William Arnold | 4.00 | 8.00 | 12.00 | E |
| 356 | Nurse's Quarters—Sylvia Erskine | 4.00 | 8.00 | 12.00 | E |
| 357 | Woman of Passion—Norman Bligh; aka 3-Time Sinner | 4.00 | 8.00 | 12.00 | E |
| 359 | Boy-Chaser—Kate Nickerson | 4.00 | 8.00 | 12.00 | E |
| 360 | Hotel Waitress—Tom Manning | 4.00 | 8.00 | 12.00 | E |
| 361 | Shanty Boat Girl—Kirk Westley | 4.00 | 8.00 | 12.00 | E |
| 362 | Mountain Bride—Peggy Gaddis | 4.00 | 8.00 | 12.00 | E |
| 364 | Island Girl | 4.00 | 8.00 | 12.00 | E |
| 365 | Boarding House—Frank Haskell; aka House of Lost Women; c-Gross | 4.00 | 8.00 | 12.00 | E |
| 367 | Lost Women—Robert E. Reynolds | 4.00 | 8.00 | 12.00 | E |
| 368 | Blonde Hellcat—Arthur Marin | 4.00 | 8.00 | 12.00 | E |
| 369 | Wild Girl—Lewis Dixon; c-Belarski | 4.00 | 8.00 | 12.00 | E |

# CANDID LOVE NOVELS

## Crestwood Publishing Co., Inc.

### Digest Size

| | | V/Good | Fine | N/Mint | |
|---|---|---|---|---|---|
| 20 | Love for Sale—Gladys Sloan; aka Single Bed | 3.50 | 7.00 | 10.50 | E |
| 21 | Wild Weekend—Gene Harvey; 1949; aka Pack Up Your Sins; c-Wenzel | 3.50 | 7.00 | 10.50 | E |
| 22 | Notorious Woman—James Harlow | 3.50 | 7.00 | 10.50 | E |
| 23 | Lessons in Love—Florence Stonebraker; aka The Analyst; c-Wenzel | 3.50 | 7.00 | 10.50 | E |
| 24 | Hired Husband—Wright Williams | 3.50 | 7.00 | 10.50 | E |
| 25 | Disorderly Conduct—Charles Strong | 3.50 | 7.00 | 10.50 | E |
| 26 | For Men Only—Beth Brown | 3.50 | 7.00 | 10.50 | E |

# CARDINAL EDITIONS

## Pocket Books, Inc.

| | | V/Good | Fine | N/Mint | |
|---|---|---|---|---|---|
| C1 | Four Great Historical Plays—William Shakespeare | .75 | 1.50 | 2.25 | |
| C2 | Kings Row—Henry Bellamann | .75 | 1.50 | 2.25 | |
| C3 | In Tragic Life—Vardis Fisher | .75 | 1.50 | 2.25 | |
| C4 | Cutlass Empire—F. Van Wyck Mason | .75 | 1.50 | 2.25 | A |
| C5 | The Merriam—Webster Pocket Dictionary | .75 | 1.50 | 2.25 | NF |
| C6 | Hungry Hill—Daphne du Maurier | .75 | 1.50 | 2.25 | |
| C7 | A Short History of the Civil War—Fletcher Pratt | .75 | 1.50 | 2.25 | NF |
| C8 | Prince of Egypt—Dorothy Clarke Wilson | .75 | 1.50 | 2.25 | A |
| C9 | The Pocket Bible | 1.50 | 3.00 | 4.50 | NF |
| C10 | Lust for Life—Irving Stone; later printing (11th seen) is movie tie-in | .75 | 1.50 | 2.25 | |
| C11 | The Pocket Book of Verse—M.E. Speare | .75 | 1.50 | 2.25 | |

| | | V/Good | Fine | N/Mint | |
|---|---|---|---|---|---|

**CARDINAL EDITIONS,** *continued*

| | | V/Good | Fine | N/Mint | |
|---|---|---|---|---|---|
| C12 | The Pocket Book of Short Stories–M.E. Speare | .75 | 1.50 | 2.25 | |
| C13 | Roget's Pocket Thesaurus–Christopher Mawson & Katharine Whiting | .75 | 1.50 | 2.25 | NF |
| C14 | Four Great Tragedies–William Shakespeare | .75 | 1.50 | 2.25 | |
| C15 | Four Great Comedies–William Shakespeare | .75 | 1.50 | 2.25 | |
| C16 | The Pocket Book of Quotations–Henry Davidoff | .75 | 1.50 | 2.25 | |
| C17 | Tales from the Arabian Nights | 2.00 | 4.00 | 6.00 | |
| C18 | Honey in the Horn–H.L. Davis | .75 | 1.50 | 2.25 | |
| C19 | Cakes and Ale and Other Favorites–W. Somerset Maugham | .75 | 1.50 | 2.25 | |
| C20 | Rand McNally–Pocket World Atlas; 1952 | .75 | 1.50 | 2.25 | NF |
| C21 | Pride's Castle–Frank Yerby | .75 | 1.50 | 2.25 | A |
| C22 | The Pepper Tree–John Jennings | 1.50 | 3.00 | 4.50 | |
| C23 | Rivers of Glory–F. Van Wyck Mason | .75 | 1.50 | 2.25 | |
| C24 | The 100 Most Important People in the World Today–Donald Robinson | .75 | 1.50 | 2.25 | NF |
| C25 | A Short History of the American Revolution–John Hyde Preston; 1952 | .75 | 1.50 | 2.25 | NF |
| C26 | Tap Roots–James Street | .75 | 1.50 | 2.25 | |
| C27 | The Confessions of St. Augustine–Aurelius Augustinus | .75 | 1.50 | 2.25 | |
| C28 | Lives of Famous French Painters–Herman J. Wechsler | .75 | 1.50 | 2.25 | NF |
| C29 | The Pocket Book of Baby and Child Care–Benjamin Spock | .75 | 1.50 | 3.00 | NF |
| C30 | The Way West–A.B. Guthrie, Jr | 1.50 | 3.00 | 4.50 | W |
| C31 | The Man with the Golden Arm–Nelson Algren; later printing (2nd seen) is movie tie-in | 25.00 | 50.00 | 75.00 | |
| | With dust jacket | 20.00 | 40.00 | 60.00 | |
| C32 | The Loyalty of Free Men–Alan Barth | .75 | 1.50 | 2.25 | |
| C33 | Wuthering Heights–Emily Bronte | .75 | 1.50 | 2.25 | |
| C34 | Mutiny on the Bounty–James Norman Hall & Charles Nordhoff | 1.00 | 2.00 | 3.00 | A |
| C35 | A Tale of Two Cities–Charles Dickens; later printing (7th seen) is movie tie-in | .75 | 1.50 | 2.25 | |
| C36 | Famous Chinese Short Stories–Lin Yutang | 1.00 | 2.00 | 3.00 | |
| C37 | Pride and Prejudice–Jane Austen | .75 | 1.50 | 2.25 | |
| C38 | The Witching Pool–Robert Presnell, Jr | .75 | 1.50 | 2.25 | |
| C39 | Hour of Glory–Robert Lund | .75 | 1.50 | 2.25 | |
| C40 | The Disappearance–Philip Wylie | .75 | 1.50 | 2.25 | |
| C41 | The Conqueror–John Tebbel | 1.00 | 2.00 | 3.00 | A |
| C42 | The Return of the Native–Thomas Hardy | .75 | 1.50 | 2.25 | |
| C43 | Dawn's Early Light–Elswyth Thane | .75 | 1.50 | 2.25 | |
| C44 | Moll Flanders–Daniel Defoe | .75 | 1.50 | 2.25 | |
| C45 | Great Tales and Poems–Edgar Allan Poe | 1.25 | 2.50 | 3.75 | |
| C46 | Kinfolk–Pearl S. Buck | .75 | 1.50 | 2.25 | |
| C47 | Tess of the D'Urbervilles–Thomas Hardy | .75 | 1.50 | 2.25 | |
| C48 | The Great Short Stories of Robert Louis Stevenson–Robert Louis Stevenson | .75 | 1.50 | 2.25 | |
| C49 | Jubilee Trail–Gwen Bristow | .75 | 1.50 | 2.25 | |
| C50 | Immortal Poems of the English Language–Oscar Williams; 1952 | .75 | 1.50 | 2.25 | |
| C51 | Abraham Lincoln–Lord Charnwood | .75 | 1.50 | 2.25 | NF |
| C52 | The Big Sky–A.B. Guthrie, Jr | 1.00 | 2.00 | 3.00 | W |
| C53 | Rebecca–Daphne du Maurier | .75 | 1.50 | 2.25 | |
| C54 | The Golden Hawk–Frank Yerby | 1.00 | 2.00 | 3.00 | A |
| C55 | The Complete Sonnets, Songs and Poems of Shakespeare–William Shakespeare | .75 | 1.50 | 2.25 | |
| C56 | Caroline Hicks–Walter Karig | .75 | 1.50 | 2.25 | |
| C57 | Three Harbours–F. Van Wyck Mason | .75 | 1.50 | 2.25 | |
| C58 | River of the Sun–James Ramsey Ullman | .75 | 1.50 | 2.25 | |
| C59 | Madame Bovary–Gustave Flaubert | .75 | 1.50 | 2.25 | |
| C60 | Buddenbrooks–Thomas Mann | .75 | 1.50 | 2.25 | |
| C61 | Questions and Answers from the Book of Knowledge–E.U. McLoughlin | .75 | 1.50 | 2.25 | NF |
| C62 | The Golden Ass of Apuleius–Madaurensis Apuleius | .75 | 1.50 | 2.25 | |
| C63 | Of Human Bondage–W. Somerset Maugham | .75 | 1.50 | 2.25 | |
| C64 | The Turquoise–Anya Seton | .75 | 1.50 | 2.25 | |
| C65 | The Scarlet Letter–Nathaniel Hawthorne | .75 | 1.50 | 2.25 | |
| C66 | Dialogues of Plato | .75 | 1.50 | 2.25 | |
| C67 | The Song of Bernadette–Franz Werfel | .75 | 1.50 | 2.25 | |
| C68 | The Parasites–Daphne du Maurier | .75 | 1.50 | 2.25 | |
| C69 | The Foundling–Francis J. Spellman | .75 | 1.50 | 2.25 | |
| C70 | Morning Journey–James Hilton | .75 | 1.50 | 2.25 | |
| C71 | The Cardinal–Henry Morton Robinson | .75 | 1.50 | 2.25 | |
| C72 | The 42nd Parallel–John Dos Passos | .75 | 1.50 | 2.25 | |
| C73 | Passions Spin the Plot–Vardis Fisher; 1953 | .75 | 1.50 | 2.25 | |
| C74 | Tomorrow We Reap–James Childers & James Street | .75 | 1.50 | 2.25 | |
| C75 | English through Pictures–Book 1–Christine Gibson & I.A. Richards; 1953 | .75 | 1.50 | 2.25 | NF |
| C76 | The White Tower–James Ramsey Ullman | .75 | 1.50 | 2.25 | |
| C77 | My Six Convicts–Donald Powell Wilson | 1.50 | 3.00 | 4.50 | |
| C78 | French through Pictures–I.A. Richards & others | .75 | 1.50 | 2.25 | NF |
| C79 | Ivanhoe–Sir Walter Scott; later printing is movie tie-in | 1.00 | 2.00 | 3.00 | A |
| C80 | Discovery No. 1–John W. Aldridge & Vance Bourjaily | .75 | 1.50 | 2.25 | |
| C81 | Dinner at Belmont–Alfred Leland Crabb | .75 | 1.50 | 2.25 | |
| C82 | Fight against Fears–Lucy Freeman | .75 | 1.50 | 2.25 | |
| C83 | Spanish through Pictures–I.A. Richards, others | .75 | 1.50 | 2.25 | NF |
| C84 | The Producer–Richard Brooks | .75 | 1.50 | 2.25 | |
| C85 | The Southern Cook Book–Marion Brown | .75 | 1.50 | 2.25 | NF |
| C86 | The 100 Most Important People of 1953–Donald Robinson | .75 | 1.50 | 2.25 | NF |
| C87 | Floodtide–Frank Yerby | .75 | 1.50 | 2.25 | A |
| C88 | Jane Eyre–Charlotte Bronte | .75 | 1.50 | 2.25 | |
| C89 | The Ragged Ones–Burke Davis | 1.50 | 3.00 | 4.50 | |
| C90 | The Pocket Household Encyclopedia–N.H. Mager & S.K. Mager | .75 | 1.50 | 2.25 | NF |
| C91 | A Stone for Danny Fisher–Harold Robbins | .75 | 1.50 | 2.25 | |
| C92 | Look Away, Look Away–Leslie Turner White | 1.00 | 2.00 | 3.00 | |
| C93 | A Pocket Guide to the Trees–Rutherford Platt | .75 | 1.50 | 2.25 | NF |
| C94 | The Pocket Book of Robert Frost's Poems | .75 | 1.50 | 2.25 | |
| C95 | German through Pictures–I.A. Richards, others | .75 | 1.50 | 2.25 | NF |
| C96 | The Iron Mistress–Paul I. Wellman | 1.00 | 2.00 | 3.00 | A |
| C97 | The Earthbreakers–Ernest Haycox | 1.00 | 2.00 | 3.00 | W |
| C98 | The Pedlocks–Stephen Longstreet | .75 | 1.50 | 2.25 | |
| C99 | The King's General–Daphne du Maurier | .75 | 1.50 | 2.25 | |
| C100 | Flesh and the Dream–George Williams; 1953 | .75 | 1.50 | 2.25 | |
| C101 | Devils, Drugs and Doctors–Howard H. Haggard | 1.50 | 3.00 | 4.50 | NF |
| C102 | A Woman Called Fancy–Frank Yerby | .75 | 1.50 | 2.25 | |
| C103 | Yankee Stranger–Elswyth Thane | .75 | 1.50 | 2.25 | |
| C104 | The Imitation of Christ–Thomas A. Kempis | .75 | 1.50 | 2.25 | |
| C105 | Pavilion of Women–Pearl S. Buck | .75 | 1.50 | 2.25 | |
| C106 | Tales from the Decameron–Giovanni Boccaccio | .75 | 1.50 | 2.25 | |
| C107 | A Connecticut Yankee in King Arthur's Court–Mark Twain; 1954 | .75 | 1.50 | 2.25 | |
| C108 | Come, My Beloved–Pearl S. Buck | .75 | 1.50 | 2.25 | |
| C109 | The Pocket Book of American Poems–Louis Untermeyer | .75 | 1.50 | 2.25 | |
| C110 | Lincoln McKeever–Eleazar Lipsky | .75 | 1.50 | 2.25 | |
| C111 | The Good Earth–Pearl S. Buck | .75 | 1.50 | 2.25 | |
| C112 | How to Stop Worrying and Start Living–Dale Carnegie | .75 | 1.50 | 2.25 | NF |
| C113 | Great Essays–Houston Peterson | .75 | 1.50 | 2.25 | |
| C114 | God's Men–Pearl S. Buck | 1.00 | 2.00 | 3.00 | |
| C115 | Discovery No. 2–Vance Bourjaily | .75 | 1.50 | 2.25 | |

**CARDINAL EDITIONS,** *continued*

| No. | Title | V/Good | Fine | N/Mint | |
|---|---|---|---|---|---|
| C116 | Matthew Steel–Mildred Masterson McNeilly | .75 | 1.50 | 2.25 | |
| C117 | Captain Marooner–Louis B. Davidson & Eddie Doherty | 1.00 | 2.00 | 3.00 | A |
| C118 | Great Escapes–Basil Davenport | 1.00 | 2.00 | 3.00 | |
| C119 | We Are Betrayed–Vardis Fisher | 1.00 | 2.00 | 3.00 | |
| C120 | Giant–Edna Ferber; later printing (2nd seen) is movie tie-in | 1.50 | 3.00 | 4.50 | |
| C121 | Young Ames–Walter D. Edmonds | .75 | 1.50 | 2.25 | |
| C122 | The University of Chicago Spanish-English, English-Spanish Dictionary–Carlos Castillo | .75 | 1.50 | 2.25 | NF |
| C123 | Yorktown–Burke Davis | 1.00 | 2.00 | 3.00 | |
| C124 | The Saracen Blade–Frank Yerby | 1.00 | 2.00 | 3.00 | A |
| C125 | Carol Curtis' Complete Book of Knitting and Crocheting–Carol Curtis; 1954 | .75 | 1.50 | 2.25 | NF |
| C126 | The Court of Last Resort–Erle Stanley Gardner | .75 | 1.50 | 2.25 | M |
| C127 | Crimson Is the Eastern Shore–Don Tracy | 1.50 | 3.00 | 4.50 | |
| C128 | God's Angry Man–Leonard Ehrlich | .75 | 1.50 | 2.25 | |
| C129 | Marye Dahnke's Salad Book–Marye Dahnke | .75 | 1.50 | 2.25 | NF |
| C130 | Discovery No. 3–Vance Bourjaily | .75 | 1.50 | 2.25 | |
| C131 | 1919–John Dos Passos | .75 | 1.50 | 2.25 | |
| C132 | The Science Book of Wonder Drugs–Donald G. Cooley | .75 | 1.50 | 2.25 | NF |
| C133 | Winston Churchill–Robert Lewis Taylor | .75 | 1.50 | 2.25 | NF |
| C134 | Nana–Emile Zola | .75 | 1.50 | 2.25 | |
| C135 | The Exploration of Space–Arthur C. Clarke | .75 | 1.50 | 2.25 | NF |
| C136 | The Border Lord–Jan Westcott | 1.00 | 2.00 | 3.00 | |
| C137 | The Strange Brigade–John Jennings | 1.50 | 3.00 | 4.50 | A |
| C138 | Pleasant Valley–Louis Bromfield | .75 | 1.50 | 2.25 | |
| C139 | The Adventures of Huckleberry Finn–Mark Twain | 1.50 | 3.00 | 4.50 | |
| C140 | The Smoldering Sea–U.S. Anderson | .75 | 1.50 | 2.25 | |
| C141 | Jubal Troop–Paul I. Wellman | 1.00 | 2.00 | 3.00 | W |
| C142 | The Devil's Laughter–Frank Yerby | 1.00 | 2.00 | 3.00 | A |
| C143 | Discovery No. 4–Vance Bourjaily | .75 | 1.50 | 2.25 | |
| C144 | Night Light–Douglass Wallop | .75 | 1.50 | 2.25 | |
| C145 | Six Minutes a Day to Perfect Spelling–Harry Shefter | .75 | 1.50 | 2.25 | NF |
| C146 | Call Me Lucky–Bing Crosby | 1.50 | 3.00 | 4.50 | NF |
| C147 | Hope for the Troubled–Lucy Freeman | .75 | 1.50 | 2.25 | |
| C148 | Drawing Self-Taught–Arthur Zaidenberg | .75 | 1.50 | 2.25 | NF |
| C149 | The Bandit and the Priest–Audrey Erskine Lindop | .75 | 1.50 | 2.25 | |
| C150 | Freud: His Dream and Sex Theories; 1954 | .75 | 1.50 | 2.25 | NF |
| C151 | The Chieftain–Robert Payne | .75 | 1.50 | 2.25 | A |
| C152 | The Pocket Book Magazine–Franklin Watts | .75 | 1.50 | 2.25 | |
| C153 | My Cousin Rachel–Daphne du Maurier | .75 | 1.50 | 2.25 | |
| C154 | The Story of the World–John van Duyn Southworth | .75 | 1.50 | 2.25 | NF |
| C155 | A Minute of Prayer–Christopher Cross | .75 | 1.50 | 2.25 | |
| C156 | Great Tales of Fantasy and Imagination–Philip Van Doren Stern | 1.50 | 3.00 | 4.50 | SF |
| C157 | The Walsingham Woman–Jan Westcott; 1955 | .75 | 1.50 | 2.25 | |
| C158 | The Pocket Book of Ogden Nash–Ogden Nash | .75 | 1.50 | 2.25 | |
| C159 | Discovery No. 5–Vance Bourjaily | .75 | 1.50 | 2.25 | |
| C160 | The Pocket Book Magazine No. 2–Franklin Watts | .75 | 1.50 | 2.25 | |
| C161 | The Razor's Edge–W. Somerset Maugham | .75 | 1.50 | 2.25 | |
| C162 | The Kingpin–Tom Wickes | .75 | 1.50 | 2.25 | |
| C163 | The Silent World–Jacques-Yves Cousteau & Frederic Dumas | .75 | 1.50 | 2.25 | NF |
| C164 | Ever After–Elswyth Thane | .75 | 1.50 | 2.25 | |
| C165 | Golden Admiral–F. Van Wyck Mason | .75 | 1.50 | 2.25 | A |
| C166 | Six Weeks to Words of Power–Wilfred Funk | .75 | 1.50 | 2.25 | NF |
| C167 | The 1955 Baseball Almanac–Hy Turkin | 1.50 | 3.00 | 4.50 | S |
| C168 | Kiss Me Again, Stranger–Daphne du Maurier | .75 | 1.50 | 2.25 | |
| C169 | Sex and the Nature of Things–N.J. Berrill | .75 | 1.50 | 2.25 | NF |
| C170 | Hebrew through Pictures–I.A. Richards | 1.50 | 3.00 | 4.50 | NF |
| C171 | Hebrew Reader–I.A. Richards, others | 1.50 | 3.00 | 4.50 | NF |
| C172 | Silver Street Woman–Les Savage, Jr | .75 | 1.50 | 2.25 | |
| C173 | N.Y., N.Y.–Will Oursler | .75 | 1.50 | 2.25 | |
| C174 | The Science Book of the Human Body–Edith E. Sproul | .75 | 1.50 | 2.25 | NF |
| C175 | The Vixens–Frank Yerby; 1955 | 1.00 | 2.00 | 3.00 | |
| C176 | Disputed Passage–Lloyd C. Douglas | .75 | 1.50 | 2.25 | |
| C177 | No Villain Need Be–Vardis Fisher | 1.00 | 2.00 | 3.00 | |
| C178 | Sir Rogue–Leslie Turner White | 1.50 | 3.00 | 4.50 | A |
| C179 | A Marriage Manual–Hannah Stone & Abraham Stone | .75 | 1.50 | 2.25 | NF |
| C180 | Your Own Book of Camp Craft–Catherine T. Hammett | .75 | 1.50 | 2.25 | NF |
| C181 | The Pocket Cook Book–Elizabeth Woody | .75 | 1.50 | 2.25 | NF |
| C182 | Sign of the Pagan–Roger Fuller; movie tie-in | 1.25 | 2.50 | 3.75 | A |
| C183 | A Subtreasury of American Humor–ed. E.B. White & Katherine S. White | 1.00 | 2.00 | 3.00 | |
| C184 | Diane–Herbert Best | .75 | 1.50 | 2.25 | |
| C185 | Discovery No. 6–Vance Bourjaily | .75 | 1.50 | 2.25 | |
| C186 | How to Make More Money–Marvin Small | .75 | 1.50 | 2.25 | NF |
| C187 | The Blackboard Jungle–Evan Hunter | 4.00 | 8.00 | 12.00 | JD |
| C188 | The Duncan Hines Dessert Book–Duncan Hines | 1.00 | 2.00 | 3.00 | NF |
| C189 | Roanoke Renegade–Don Tracy | 1.50 | 3.00 | 4.50 | |
| C190 | Short Cuts to Effective English–Harry Shefter | .75 | 1.50 | 2.25 | NF |
| C191 | Aboard the Flying Swan–Stanley Wolpert | .75 | 1.50 | 2.25 | |
| C192 | Lord Grizzly–Frederick Manfred | 2.50 | 5.00 | 7.50 | W |
| C193 | Best-Seller Digest No. 1 | .75 | 1.50 | 2.25 | |
| C194 | American Captain–Edison Marshall | .75 | 1.50 | 2.25 | A |
| C195 | The French Quarter–Herbert Asbury | 2.00 | 4.00 | 6.00 | |
| C196 | The Compact Treasury of Inspiration–Kenneth S. Giniger | .75 | 1.50 | 2.25 | |
| C197 | Buccaneer Surgeon–C.V. Terry | 1.50 | 3.00 | 4.50 | A |
| C198 | The Gown of Glory–Agnes Sligh Turnball | .75 | 1.50 | 2.25 | |
| C199 | The Toastmaster's and Speaker's Handbook–Herbert V. Prochnow | .75 | 1.50 | 2.25 | NF |
| C200 | The Pocket Book Magazine No. 3–Franklin Watts; 1955 | .75 | 1.50 | 2.25 | |
| C201 | Italian through Pictures–I.A. Richards; 1956 | .75 | 1.50 | 2.25 | NF |
| C202 | Never Victorious, Never Defeated–Taylor Caldwell | .75 | 1.50 | 2.25 | |
| C203 | The Last Hunt–Milton Lott | 1.50 | 3.00 | 4.50 | W |
| C204 | The Adventurers–Ernest Haycox | .75 | 1.50 | 2.25 | W |
| C205 | Have Tux, Will Travel–Bob Hope | 1.00 | 2.00 | 3.00 | H |
| C206 | Ann Pillsbury's Baking Book–Ann Pillsbury | .75 | 1.50 | 2.25 | NF |
| C207 | The Science Book of Space Travel–Harold Leland Goodwin | .75 | 1.50 | 2.25 | NF |
| C208 | Benton's Row–Frank Yerby | 1.00 | 2.00 | 3.00 | A |
| C209 | The Virginian–Owen Wister | 1.50 | 3.00 | 4.50 | W |
| C210 | Somebody Up There Likes Me–Rowland Barber & Rocky Graziano | 1.50 | 3.00 | 4.50 | |
| C211 | Blue Hurricane–F. Van Wyck Mason | .75 | 1.50 | 2.25 | |
| C212 | The 1956 Baseball Almanac–Don Schiffer | 1.50 | 3.00 | 4.50 | S |
| C213 | The Long Goodbye–Raymond Chandler | 1.50 | 3.00 | 4.50 | M |
| C214 | Bless This House–Norah Lofts | .75 | 1.50 | 2.25 | |
| C215 | The Gadget Maker–Maxwell Griffith | 1.00 | 2.00 | 3.00 | |
| C216 | Mary Anne–Daphne du Maurier | .75 | 1.50 | 2.25 | |
| C217 | Big Business: A New Era–David E. Lilienthal | .75 | 1.50 | 2.25 | NF |
| C218 | The Man from Mesabi–Sarah Lockwood | .75 | 1.50 | 2.25 | |
| C219 | 79 Park Avenue–Harold Robbins | .75 | 1.50 | 2.25 | |
| C220 | Katrina–Jeramie Price | .75 | 1.50 | 2.25 | |
| C221 | "Before I Kill More . . ."–Lucy Freeman | .75 | 1.50 | 2.25 | |
| C222 | Anna and the King of Siam–Margaret Landon; movie tie-in | 1.50 | 3.00 | 4.50 | |
| C223 | The Great Man–Al Morgan | .75 | 1.50 | 2.25 | |
| C224 | My Brother's Keeper–Marcia Davenport | .75 | 1.50 | 2.25 | |
| C225 | The Lost Eagles–Ralph Graves; 1956 | .75 | 1.50 | 2.25 | |
| C226 | Tales of the South Pacific–James A. Michener; movie tie-in (1st and 2nd seen) | 2.00 | 4.00 | 6.00 | |
| C227 | Roxana–Marian Castle | .75 | 1.50 | 2.25 | |

CARDINAL EDITIONS, *continued*

| Code | Title | V/Good | Fine | N/Mint | Note |
|---|---|---|---|---|---|
| C228 | Carolina Corsair–Don Tracy | 1.50 | 3.00 | 4.50 | A |
| C229 | The View from Pompey's Head–Hamilton Basso | .75 | 1.50 | 2.25 | |
| C230 | The Man in the Gray Flannel Suit–Sloan Wilson; movie tie-in | .75 | 1.50 | 2.25 | |
| C231 | The U.P. Trail–Zane Grey | 2.50 | 5.00 | 7.50 | W |
| C232 | The Complete Guide to Home Sewing–S.K. Mager; 1957 | 1.00 | 2.00 | 3.00 | NF |
| C233 | The Gentleman–Edison Marshall | 1.00 | 2.00 | 3.00 | A |
| C234 | The Last Temptation–Joseph Viertel | .75 | 1.50 | 2.25 | |
| C235 | Heritage–Anthony West | .75 | 1.50 | 2.25 | |
| C236 | Quartet in ''H''–Evan Hunter | 3.00 | 6.00 | 9.00 | |
| C237 | How to Develop Self-Confidence–Dale Carnegie | .75 | 1.50 | 2.25 | NF |
| C238 | Profiles in Courage–John F. Kennedy | .75 | 1.50 | 2.25 | NF |
| C239 | The Border Legion–Zane Grey | 2.50 | 5.00 | 7.50 | W |
| C240 | Forgive Us Our Trespasses–Lloyd C. Douglas | .75 | 1.50 | 2.25 | |
| C241 | The Golden Journey–Agnes Sligh Turnbull | .75 | 1.50 | 2.25 | |
| C242 | Silver Leopard–F. Van Wyck Mason | .75 | 1.50 | 2.25 | A |
| C243 | The Quick Cook Book–Lois S. Kellogg | .75 | 1.50 | 2.25 | NF |
| C244 | The Wanderer–Mika Waltari | .75 | 1.50 | 2.25 | |
| C245 | Tender Victory–Taylor Caldwell | .75 | 1.50 | 2.25 | |
| C246 | The Winged Sword–Leslie Turner White | 1.50 | 3.00 | 4.50 | A |
| C247 | The Sudden Strangers–William E. Barrett | .75 | 1.50 | 2.25 | |
| C248 | Will Acting Spoil Marilyn Monroe?–Pete Martin | 10.00 | 20.00 | 30.00 | NF |
| C249 | Captain Rebel–Frank Yerby | 1.00 | 2.00 | 3.00 | A |
| C250 | Hilda Manning–Allan Seager; 1957 | .75 | 1.50 | 2.25 | |
| C251 | The Barbary Coast–Herbert Asbury | 1.50 | 3.00 | 4.50 | NF |
| C252 | Dynasty of Death–Taylor Caldwell | .75 | 1.50 | 2.25 | |
| C253 | Pemmican–Vardis Fisher | 2.00 | 4.00 | 6.00 | A |
| C254 | Deluxe Tour–Frederic Wakeman | .75 | 1.50 | 2.25 | |
| C255 | Mary–Sholem Asch | .75 | 1.50 | 2.25 | |
| C256 | First Steps in Reading English–Christine Gibson & I.A. Richards | .75 | 1.50 | 2.25 | NF |
| C257 | Magnificent Obsession–Lloyd C. Douglas | .75 | 1.50 | 2.25 | |
| C258 | English through Pictures–Book 2–Christine Gibson & I.A. Richards | .75 | 1.50 | 2.25 | NF |
| C259 | A First Workbook of French–I.A. Richards | .75 | 1.50 | 2.25 | NF |
| C260 | How to Work with Tools & Wood–Fred Gross | 1.00 | 2.00 | 3.00 | NF |
| C261 | The Painted Veil–W. Somerset Maugham; movie tie-in (of The Seventh Sin) | .75 | 1.50 | 2.25 | |
| C262 | The Swordsman–Jefferson Cooper (Gardner Fox) | 2.00 | 4.00 | 6.00 | A |
| C263 | The Dark Angel–Mika Waltari | .75 | 1.50 | 2.25 | |
| C264 | The Drift Fence–Zane Grey | 2.50 | 5.00 | 7.50 | W |
| C265 | The World's Best Recipes–Marvin Small | .75 | 1.50 | 2.25 | NF |
| C266 | Jenny–Ada Cook Lewis | .75 | 1.50 | 2.25 | |
| C267 | These Thousand Hills–A.B. Guthrie, Jr; movie tie-in | 1.50 | 3.00 | 4.50 | |
| C268 | The Case of the Sun-Bather's Diary–Erle Stanley Gardner | .75 | 1.50 | 2.25 | M |
| C269 | Green Light–Lloyd C. Douglas | .75 | 1.50 | 2.25 | |
| C270 | The Pocket Book of Erskine Caldwell Stories–E. Caldwell | .75 | 1.50 | 2.25 | |
| C271 | Canton Barrier–Andrew Geer; 1958 | .75 | 1.50 | 2.25 | |
| C272 | The Voice at the Back Door–Elizabeth Spencer | .75 | 1.50 | 2.25 | |
| C273 | The Magician–W. Somerset Maugham | .75 | 1.50 | 2.25 | |
| C274 | The Strong City–Taylor Caldwell | .75 | 1.50 | 2.25 | |
| C275 | The Case of the Terrified Typist–Erle Stanley Gardner; 1958 | .75 | 1.50 | 2.25 | M |
| C276 | The Scapegoat–Daphne du Maurier | .75 | 1.50 | 2.25 | |
| C277 | Chance Elson–W.T. Ballard | .75 | 1.50 | 2.25 | |
| C278 | Jericho's Daughters–Paul I. Wellman | .75 | 1.50 | 2.25 | |
| C279 | The Prosecuter–Bernard Botein | .75 | 1.50 | 2.25 | |
| C280 | The Innocent Ambassadors–Philip Wylie | .75 | 1.50 | 2.25 | |
| C281 | The Case of the Runaway Corpse–Erle Stanley Gardner | .75 | 1.50 | 2.25 | M |
| C282 | The Case of the Glamorous Ghost–Erle Stanley Gardner | .75 | 1.50 | 2.25 | M |
| C283 | The Case of the Half-Wakened Wife–Erle Stanley Gardner | .75 | 1.50 | 2.25 | M |
| C284 | The Case of the Empty Tin–Erle Stanley Gardner | .75 | 1.50 | 2.25 | M |
| C285 | The Case of the Lazy Lover–Erle Stanley Gardner | .75 | 1.50 | 2.25 | M |
| C286 | Cast the First Stone–Sara Harris & John M. Murtagh | .75 | 1.50 | 2.25 | |
| C287 | The Etruscan–Mika Waltari | .75 | 1.50 | 2.25 | A |
| C288 | The Hidden Persuaders–Vance Packard | .75 | 1.50 | 2.25 | |
| C289 | Basketball–Arnold ''Red'' Auerbach | 1.00 | 2.00 | 3.00 | S |
| C290 | The Promoters–Stephen Longstreet | .75 | 1.50 | 2.25 | |
| C291 | The D.A. Calls a Turn–Erle Stanley Gardner | .75 | 1.50 | 2.25 | M |
| C292 | The D.A. Breaks a Seal–Erle Stanley Gardner | .75 | 1.50 | 2.25 | M |
| C293 | The D.A. Takes a Chance–Erle Stanley Gardner | .75 | 1.50 | 2.25 | M |
| C294 | The D.A. Breaks an Egg–Erle Stanley Gardner | .75 | 1.50 | 2.25 | M |
| C295 | The D.A. Calls It Murder–Erle Stanley Gardner | .75 | 1.50 | 2.25 | M |
| C296 | Halfway Down the Stairs–Charles Thompson | .75 | 1.50 | 2.25 | |
| C297 | The Case of the Nervous Accomplice–Erle Stanley Gardner | .75 | 1.50 | 2.25 | M |
| C298 | No Down Payment–John McPartland; movie tie-in | .75 | 1.50 | 2.25 | |
| C299 | The Case of the Careless Kitten–Erle Stanley Gardner | .75 | 1.50 | 2.25 | M |
| C300 | Cherokee–Don Tracy; 1958 | 2.00 | 4.00 | 6.00 | |
| C301 | Riders of Judgement–Frederick Manfred | 2.00 | 4.00 | 6.00 | |
| C302 | The Case of the Crooked Candle–Erle Stanley Gardner | .75 | 1.50 | 2.25 | M |
| C303 | How to Win Friends and Influence People–Dale Carnegie | .75 | 1.50 | 2.25 | NF |
| C304 | Care and Training of Dogs–Arthur Frederick Jones | .75 | 1.50 | 2.25 | NF |
| C305 | Monsieur Yankee–Leslie Turner White | 1.50 | 3.00 | 4.50 | A |
| C306 | Cast of Characters–Al Morgan | .75 | 1.50 | 2.25 | |
| C307 | The Clue of the Forgotten Murder–Erle Stanley Gardner | .75 | 1.50 | 2.25 | M |
| C308 | Letter from Peking–Pearl S. Buck | .75 | 1.50 | 2.25 | |
| C309 | The Case of the Sulky Girl–Erle Stanley Gardner | .75 | 1.50 | 2.25 | M |
| C310 | Fairoaks–Frank Yerby | 1.00 | 2.00 | 3.00 | |
| C311 | The Final Hour–Taylor Caldwell | .75 | 1.50 | 2.25 | |
| C312 | Remembered Death–Agatha Christie | .75 | 1.50 | 2.25 | M |
| C313 | Cash McCall–Cameron Hawley | .75 | 1.50 | 2.25 | |
| C314 | A Parent's Guide to Children's Reading–Nancy Larrick | .75 | 1.50 | 2.25 | NF |
| C315 | Kings Go Forth–Joe David Brown | .75 | 1.50 | 2.25 | |
| C316 | Odds Against Tomorrow–William P. McGivern; some printings (2nd seen) are movie tie-in | 1.00 | 2.00 | 3.00 | M |
| C317 | The Diary of a Young Girl–Anne Frank; later printing is movie tie-in | 2.50 | 5.00 | 7.50 | NF |
| C318 | What Mrs. McGillicuddy Saw!–Agatha Christie; some printings are movie tie-in | .75 | 1.50 | 2.25 | M |
| C319 | New Tales of Space and Time–Raymond J. Healy; 1959 | .75 | 1.50 | 2.25 | SF |
| C320 | The Case of the One-Eyed Witness–Erle Stanley Gardner | .75 | 1.50 | 2.25 | M |
| C321 | On the Midnight Tide–Don Tracy | 1.50 | 3.00 | 4.50 | |
| C322 | To Have and to Hold–Mary Johnston | .75 | 1.50 | 2.25 | |
| C323 | The Case of the Demure Defendant–Erle Stanley Gardner | .75 | 1.50 | 2.25 | M |
| C324 | The Case of the Curious Bride–Erle Stanley Gardner | .75 | 1.50 | 2.25 | M |
| C325 | The Case of the Haunted Husband–Erle Stanley Gardner; 1959 | .75 | 1.50 | 2.25 | M |
| C326 | Jamaica Inn–Daphne du Maurier | .75 | 1.50 | 2.25 | |
| C327 | ''Where Did You Do?'' ''Out'' ''What Did You Do?'' ''Nothing''–Robert Paul Smith | .75 | 1.50 | 2.25 | |
| C328 | The Year the Yankees Lost the Pennant–Douglass Wallop; later printing is movie tie-in (for Damn Yankees) | 1.50 | 3.00 | 4.50 | |
| C329 | Case of the Lucky Legs–Erle Stanley Gardner | .75 | 1.50 | 2.25 | M |
| C330 | Kids Say the Darndest Things!–Art Linkletter; TV tie-in (for House Party) | .75 | 1.50 | 2.25 | H |
| C331 | The Pocket Book of Esquire Cartoons | 3.00 | 6.00 | 9.00 | H |

*Cardinal C331, Cardinal GC18, Carnival 906.*

| | | V/Good | Fine | N/Mint | |
|---|---|---|---|---|---|
| **CARDINAL EDITIONS,** *continued* | | | | | |
| C332 | The Case of the Cautious Coquette–Erle Stanley Gardner | .75 | 1.50 | 2.25 | M |
| C333 | The Trail Driver–Zane Grey | 2.50 | 5.00 | 7.50 | W |
| C334 | The Angry Wife–Pearl S. Buck | .75 | 1.50 | 2.25 | |
| C335 | Death Comes As the End–Agatha Christie | .75 | 1.50 | 2.25 | M |
| C336 | White Banners–Lloyd C. Douglas | .75 | 1.50 | 2.25 | |
| C337 | The Case of the Gilded Lily–Erle Stanley Gardner; TV tie-in (for Perry Mason) | .75 | 1.50 | 2.25 | M |
| C338 | The Immortal–Walter Ross | .75 | 1.50 | 2.25 | |
| C339 | Dragonwyck–Anya Seton | .75 | 1.50 | 2.25 | |
| C340 | The Man Who Broke Things–John Brooks | .75 | 1.50 | 2.25 | |
| C341 | The Case of the Lucky Loser–Erle Stanley Gardner | .75 | 1.50 | 2.25 | M |
| C342 | Young Mr. Keefe–Stephen Birmingham | .75 | 1.50 | 2.25 | |
| C343 | The Finishing Stroke–Ellery Queen | .75 | 1.50 | 2.25 | M |
| C344 | The Lady in the Lake–Raymond Chandler | 2.00 | 4.00 | 6.00 | M |
| C345 | The D.A. Cooks a Goose–Erle Stanley Gardner | .75 | 1.50 | 2.25 | M |
| C346 | The D.A. Draws a Circle–Erle Stanley Gardner | .75 | 1.50 | 2.25 | M |
| C347 | The D.A. Goes to Trial–Erle Stanley Gardner | .75 | 1.50 | 2.25 | M |
| C348 | The D.A. Holds a Candle–Erle Stanley Gardner | .75 | 1.50 | 2.25 | M |
| C349 | Peril at End House–Agatha Christie | .75 | 1.50 | 2.25 | M |
| C350 | A Gift from the Boys–Art Buchwald; 1959; later printing (2nd seen) is movie tie-in (for Surprise Package) | .75 | 1.50 | 2.25 | |
| C351 | Valley of Wild Horses–Zane Grey | 2.50 | 5.00 | 7.50 | W |
| C352 | The Serpent and the Staff–Frank Yerby | .75 | 1.50 | 2.25 | A |
| C353 | The Nine Lives of Michael Todd–Art Cohn | .75 | 1.50 | 2.25 | NF |
| C354 | 11th Pocket Book of Crossword Puzzles–ed. Margaret P. Farrar | 2.50 | 5.00 | 7.50 | NF |
| C355 | The Case of the Vagabond Virgin–Erle Stanley Gardner | .75 | 1.50 | 2.25 | M |
| C356 | Dear Abby–Abigail Van Buren | .75 | 1.50 | 2.25 | NF |
| C357 | Cat of Many Tails–Ellery Queen | .75 | 1.50 | 2.25 | M |
| C358 | Power Golf–Ben Hogan | 1.00 | 2.00 | 3.00 | S |
| C359 | The Low Calorie Diet–Marvin Small | .75 | 1.50 | 2.25 | NF |
| C360 | And Then There Were None–Agatha Christie | .75 | 1.50 | 2.25 | M |
| C361 | Towards Zero–Agatha Christie | .75 | 1.50 | 2.25 | M |
| C362 | A Murder Is Announced–Agatha Christie | .75 | 1.50 | 2.25 | M |
| C363 | Lady Chatterley's Lover–D.H. Lawrence | 1.00 | 2.00 | 3.00 | |
| C364 | The 1959 Pro Football Handbook–Don Schiffer | 1.25 | 2.50 | 3.75 | S |
| C365 | Return of the Eagles–F. Van Wyck Mason | .75 | 1.50 | 2.25 | |
| C366 | Frenchman's Creek–Daphne du Maurier | .75 | 1.50 | 2.25 | |
| C367 | The Foxes of Harrow–Frank Yerby | .75 | 1.50 | 2.25 | |
| C368 | Lucky Larribee–Max Brand | 1.00 | 2.00 | 3.00 | W |
| C369 | Lady L–Romain Gary | .75 | 1.50 | 2.25 | |
| C370 | Action by Night–Ernest Haycox | 1.00 | 2.00 | 3.00 | W |
| C371 | Gazella–Stuart Cloete | .75 | 1.50 | 2.25 | |
| C372 | The Long Love–Pearl S. Buck | .75 | 1.50 | 2.25 | |

| | | V/Good | Fine | N/Mint | |
|---|---|---|---|---|---|
| C373 | The Crossing–Clay Fisher | 1.00 | 2.00 | 3.00 | W |
| C374 | The Scientists–Eleazar Lipsky | .75 | 1.50 | 2.25 | NF |
| C375 | Playback–Raymond Chandler | 2.00 | 4.00 | 6.00 | M |
| C376 | The Case of the Dubious Bridegroom–Erle Stanley Gardner; TV tie-in (for Perry Mason) | .75 | 1.50 | 2.25 | M |
| C377 | The Case of the Screaming Women–Erle Stanley Gardner; TV tie-in (for Perry Mason) | .75 | 1.50 | 2.25 | M |
| C378 | The Case of the Substitute Face–Erle Stanley Gardner | .75 | 1.50 | 2.25 | M |
| C379 | The Case of the Perjured Parrot–Erle Stanley Gardner | .75 | 1.50 | 2.25 | M |
| C380 | The Case of the Borrowed Brunette–Erle Stanley Gardner | .75 | 1.50 | 2.25 | M |
| C381 | The Case of the Hesitant Hostess–Erle Stanley Gardner; TV tie-in (for Perry Mason) | .75 | 1.50 | 2.25 | M |
| C382 | The Seventh Man–Max Brand | .75 | 1.50 | 2.25 | W |
| C383 | Age of Consent–Norman Lindsay | .75 | 1.50 | 2.25 | |
| C384 | People Are Funny–Art Linkletter; TV tie-in | 1.00 | 2.00 | 3.00 | H |
| C385 | Raiders of Spanish Peaks–Zane Grey | 2.50 | 5.00 | 7.50 | W |
| C386 | Ordeal by Innocence–Agatha Christie | .75 | 1.50 | 2.25 | M |
| C389 | All the Young Men–Marvin H. Alpert; 1960; movie tie-in | 1.25 | 2.50 | 3.75 | |
| C391 | Third Man on the Mountain–James R. Ullman; 1959; movie tie-in | 1.25 | 2.50 | 3.75 | A |
| C401 | The Rat Race–Garson Kanin; 1960; movie tie-in | 1.25 | 2.50 | 3.75 | |
| C412 | Oceans "Eleven"–George Clayton Johnson & Jack Russell; 1960; movie tie-in | 1.50 | 3.00 | 3.75 | |
| C424 | The Fiercest Heart–Stuart Cloete; 1961; movie tie-in | 1.25 | 2.50 | 3.75 | |
| C437 | Hatari!–Michael Milner; 1962; movie tie-in | 1.50 | 3.00 | 4.50 | A |

# CARDINAL EDITIONS GC-SERIES
## Pocket Books, Inc.

| | | V/Good | Fine | N/Mint | |
|---|---|---|---|---|---|
| GC1 | The Cardinal–Henry Morton Robinson; 1953 | .75 | 1.50 | 2.25 | |
| GC2 | Three Harbours–F. Van Wyck Mason | .75 | 1.50 | 2.25 | |
| GC3 | Buddenbrooks–Thomas Mann | .75 | 1.50 | 2.25 | |
| GC4 | The Story of Philosophy–Will Durant | .75 | 1.50 | 2.25 | NF |
| GC5 | The Story of Mankind–Hendrik Willem Van Loon | .75 | 1.50 | 2.25 | NF |
| GC6 | Stars on the Sea–F. Van Wyck Mason | .75 | 1.50 | 2.25 | |
| GC7 | Langenscheidt's German-English, English-German Dictionary | .75 | 1.50 | 2.25 | NF |
| GC8 | Oh, Promised Land–James Street | .75 | 1.50 | 2.25 | |
| GC9 | Eagle in the Sky–F. Van Wyck Mason | .75 | 1.50 | 2.25 | |
| GC10 | The Cruel Sea–Nicholas Monsarrat | .75 | 1.50 | 2.25 | |
| GC11 | Napoleon–Emil Ludwig; 1954 | .75 | 1.50 | 2.25 | NF |
| GC12 | The Wall–John Hersey | .75 | 1.50 | 2.25 | |
| GC13 | The Office Encyclopedia–N.H. Mager & S.K. Mager | .75 | 1.50 | 2.25 | NF |
| GC14 | The Devil Rides Outside–John Howard Griffin | .75 | 1.50 | 2.25 | |
| GC15 | Immortal Poems of the English Language–Oscar Williams | .75 | 1.50 | 2.25 | |
| GC16 | The Pocket Book of Modern Verse–Oscar Williams | .75 | 1.50 | 2.25 | |
| GC17 | Proud New Flags–F. Van Wyck Mason | .75 | 1.50 | 2.25 | |
| GC18 | The Pocket Guide to Birds–Allen D. Cruickshank | 1.50 | 3.00 | 4.50 | NF |
| GC19 | The Pocket Household Encyclopedia–N.H. Mager & S.K. Mager | 1.00 | 2.00 | 3.00 | NF |
| GC20 | The Female–Paul I. Wellman | .75 | 1.50 | 2.25 | |
| GC21 | Marie Antoinette–Stefan Zweig | .75 | 1.50 | 2.25 | |
| GC22 | Desiree–Annemarie Selinko | .75 | 1.50 | 2.25 | |
| GC23 | The Lincoln Reader–Abraham Lincoln; 1955 | 1.50 | 3.00 | 4.50 | |
| GC24 | Larousse's French-English, English-French Dictionary | .75 | 1.50 | 2.25 | NF |
| GC25 | The Whitman Reader–Walt Whitman; 1955 | .75 | 1.50 | 2.25 | |
| GC26 | The Big Money–John Dos Passos | .75 | 1.50 | 2.25 | |
| GC27 | Understanding Surgery–Robert E. Rothenberg | .75 | 1.50 | 2.25 | NF |

| | | V/Good | Fine | N/Mint |
|---|---|---|---|---|

**CARDINAL EDITIONS GC-SERIES,** *continued*

| | | V/Good | Fine | N/Mint | |
|---|---|---|---|---|---|
| GC28 | Youngblood–John O. Killens | .75 | 1.50 | 2.25 | |
| GC29 | An Act of Love–Ira Wolfert | .75 | 1.50 | 2.25 | |
| GC30 | The Doctors Mayo–Helen Clapesattle; 1956 | .75 | 1.50 | 2.25 | NF |
| GC31 | The Egyptian–Mika Waltari | .75 | 1.50 | 2.25 | A |
| GC32 | Love Is Eternal–Irving Stone | .75 | 1.50 | 2.25 | |
| GC33 | A Baby's First Year–Benjamin Spock | .75 | 1.50 | 2.25 | NF |
| GC34 | The Adventurer–Mika Waltari | .75 | 1.50 | 2.25 | |
| GC35 | My Several Worlds–Pearl S. Buck | .75 | 1.50 | 2.25 | |
| GC36 | The Nazarene–Sholem Asch | .75 | 1.50 | 2.25 | |
| GC37 | The Search for Bridey Murphy–Morey Bernstein | .75 | 1.50 | 2.25 | |
| GC38 | The Apostle–Sholem Asch | .75 | 1.50 | 2.25 | |
| GC39 | Masters of Deceit–J. Edgar Hoover | .75 | 1.50 | 2.25 | |
| GC40 | Baby and Child Care–Benjamin Spock | 4.00 | 8.00 | 12.00 | NF |
| GC41 | Imperial Woman–Pearl S. Buck; 1958 | .75 | 1.50 | 2.25 | |
| GC42 | King of Paris–Guy Endore | 1.25 | 2.50 | 3.75 | A |
| GC43 | Moses–Sholem Asch | 1.25 | 2.50 | 3.75 | |
| GC44 | Language for Everybody–Mario Pei | 1.25 | 2.50 | 3.75 | NF |
| GC45 | The FBI Story–Don Whitehead; movie tie-in | 1.25 | 2.50 | 3.75 | |
| GC46 | The Townsman–Pearl S. Buck | 1.25 | 2.50 | 3.75 | |
| GC47 | Mondadori's Pocket Italian-English, English-Italian Dictionary–Alberto Tedeschi | 1.25 | 2.50 | 3.75 | NF |
| GC48 | A Stillness at Appomattox–Bruce Catton | 1.00 | 2.00 | 3.00 | NF |
| GC49 | The Prophet–Sholem Asch | .75 | 1.50 | 2.25 | |
| GC50 | Faster Reading Self-Taught–Harry Shefter; 1958 | .75 | 1.50 | 2.25 | NF |
| GC51 | The Family of Man–Edward Steichen | .75 | 1.50 | 2.25 | |
| GC52 | Baruch: My Own Story–Bernard Baruch | .75 | 1.50 | 2.25 | NF |
| GC53 | The Robe–Lloyd C. Douglas | .75 | 1.50 | 2.25 | |
| GC54 | The Nun's Story–Kathryn Hulme; movie tie-in | .75 | 1.50 | 2.25 | |
| GC55 | Kings Row–Henry Bellamann | .75 | 1.50 | 2.25 | |
| GC56 | Strangers When We Meet–Evan Hunter; 1959; later printing (3rd seen) is movie tie-in | .75 | 1.50 | 2.25 | |
| GC57 | Madame Curie–Eve Curie | .75 | 1.50 | 2.25 | NF |
| GC58 | The Kodak Camera Guide | 1.25 | 2.50 | 3.75 | NF |
| GC59 | The Big Fisherman–Lloyd C. Douglas; some later printings (2nd & 3rd seen) are movie tie-in | .75 | 1.50 | 2.25 | |
| GC60 | Diccionario del Idiona Espanol–Edwin B. Williams | 1.50 | 3.00 | 4.50 | NF |
| GC61 | The Roots of Heaven–Romain Gary; movie tie-in | .75 | 1.50 | 2.25 | |
| GC62 | Generation of Vipers–Philip Wylie | .75 | 1.50 | 2.25 | |
| GC63 | Justine–Lawrence Durrell | .75 | 1.50 | 2.25 | |
| GC64 | Sailor on Horseback–Jack London | 1.25 | 2.50 | 3.75 | A |
| GC65 | A Summer Place–Sloan Wilson; later printing (2nd seen) is movie tie-in | .75 | 1.50 | 2.25 | |
| GC66 | Madison Avenue, U.S.A.–Martin Mayer | .75 | 1.50 | 2.25 | |
| GC67 | High-Speed Math Self-Taught–Lester Meyers | .75 | 1.50 | 2.25 | NF |
| GC68 | The Best of Everything–Rona Jaffe; movie tie-in | .75 | 1.50 | 2.25 | |
| GC69 | The Stars in the Making–Cecilia Payne-Gaposchkin | .75 | 1.50 | 2.25 | |
| GC70 | Devils, Drugs and Doctors–Howard W. Haggard | 1.25 | 2.50 | 3.75 | NF |
| GC72 | Parrish–Mildred Savage; movie tie-in | .75 | 1.50 | 2.25 | |
| GC73 | The Day Christ Died–Jim Bishop | .75 | 1.50 | 2.25 | |
| GC74 | Compulsion–Meyer Levin; movie tie-in | .75 | 1.50 | 2.25 | |
| GC75 | Ben-Hur–Lew Wallace; 1959; movie tie-in | 1.00 | 2.00 | 3.00 | A |
| GC76 | Microbe Hunters–Paul De Kruif | 1.50 | 3.00 | 4.50 | NF |
| GC77 | The Winthrop Woman–Anya Seton; 1953 | .75 | 1.50 | 2.25 | |
| GC78 | The King Must Die–Mary Renault | .75 | 1.50 | 2.25 | |
| GC79 | The Enemy Camp–Jerome Weidman; 1959 | .75 | 1.50 | 2.25 | |
| GC81 | Tale of Valor–Vardis Fisher | .75 | 1.50 | 2.25 | A |
| GC84 | The Last Angry Man–Gerald Green; movie tie-in | 1.00 | 2.00 | 3.00 | |
| GC94 | The Young Savages–Evan Hunter; 1961, movie tie-in | 2.00 | 4.00 | 6.00 | JD |
| GC99 | Balthazar–Lawrence Durrell | .75 | 1.50 | 2.25 | |
| GC122 | West Side Story–Max Shulman; 1961, movie tie-in | 2.50 | 5.00 | 7.50 | JD |

| | | V/Good | Fine | N/Mint | |
|---|---|---|---|---|---|
| GC750 | The English-Portuguese Pocket Dictionary–Hygino Aliandro | .75 | 1.50 | 2.25 | NF |
| GC751 | Cash McCall–Cameron Hawley; 1957 | .75 | 1.50 | 2.25 | |
| GC752 | Katherine–Anya Seton | .75 | 1.50 | 2.25 | |
| GC753 | Something of Value–Robert Ruark; 1958; movie tie-in | .75 | 1.50 | 2.25 | |
| GC755 | The Tribe That Lost Its Head–Nicholas Monsarrat | .75 | 1.50 | 2.25 | |
| GC756 | Compulsion–Meyer Levin; 1959 | .75 | 1.50 | 2.25 | |
| GC757 | The Last Angry Man–Gerald Green | .75 | 1.50 | 2.25 | |
| GC758 | Aku-Aku–Thor Heyerdahl | .75 | 1.50 | 2.25 | |
| GC760 | Wild in the Country–J.R. Salamanca; 1961; movie tie-in | .75 | 1.50 | 2.25 | |
| nn | The 1954 Pocket Almanac; 1954 | .75 | 1.50 | 2.25 | NF |
| GC1955 | The 1955 Pocket Almanac; 1955 | .75 | 1.50 | 2.25 | NF |
| GC1956 | The 1956 Pocket Almanac; 1956 | .75 | 1.50 | 2.25 | NF |

# CARNIVAL
## Hanro Corporation
### Digest Size

| | | V/Good | Fine | N/Mint | |
|---|---|---|---|---|---|
| 901 | A Body to Own–Robert W. Harmon; 1952; aka Pickup; aka Sacrifice | 4.00 | 8.00 | 12.00 | E |
| 902 | Midnight Sinners–John Caldwall | 4.00 | 8.00 | 12.00 | E |
| 903 | Lovers Bewitched–William E. Gordon; aka Frenchy | 4.00 | 8.00 | 12.00 | E |
| 904 | Borrowed Ecstasy–Watkins E. Wright; aka Wild Passion | 4.00 | 8.00 | 12.00 | E |
| 905 | Strangers in the Dark–Peggy Gaddis; aka Pushover; c-Gross | 4.00 | 8.00 | 12.00 | E |
| 906 | A Lover for Anne–Sylvia Erskine; aka Men Call Her "Tramp"; c-Gross | 4.00 | 8.00 | 12.00 | E |
| 907 | Tempting Tigress–John Underwood; aka Bedtime Blonde | 4.00 | 8.00 | 12.00 | E |
| 908 | Girl-Hungry–William E. Gordon; aka The Transgressor | 4.00 | 8.00 | 12.00 | E |
| 909 | The Girl from Mimi's–Joan Tucker; aka Girl on the Make | 4.00 | 8.00 | 12.00 | E |
| 910 | Pick-Up–Albert L. Quandt; aka Ticket to Passion | 4.00 | 8.00 | 12.00 | E |
| 911 | Affairs of a Ward Nurse–Mitchell Coleman; aka Born to Be Bad | 4.00 | 8.00 | 12.00 | E |
| 912 | Wild Party–Frederic Spencer | 4.00 | 8.00 | 12.00 | E |
| 913 | Affairs of a Career Girl–Mitchell Coleman; 1953; aka Fast, Loose, and Lovely; c-Gross | 4.00 | 8.00 | 12.00 | E |
| 914 | Girl of the Slums–Raymond Blair | 5.00 | 10.00 | 15.00 | E |
| 915 | Lost to Desire–Peggy Gaddis | 4.00 | 8.00 | 12.00 | E |
| 916 | Passion's Harvest–Peggy Gaddis; aka Woman of Fire, c-Gross | 4.00 | 8.00 | 12.00 | E |
| 917 | Frenchie–David Charlson | 4.00 | 8.00 | 12.00 | E |
| 918 | Rapture Alley–Whit Harrison (Harry Whittington); 1953; c-Belarski | 9.00 | 18.00 | 27.00 | E |
| 919 | City Hotel–Jane Manning | 4.00 | 8.00 | 12.00 | E |
| 920 | Hotel Waitress–Gene Harvey | 4.00 | 8.00 | 12.00 | E |
| 921 | Girl Hungry–William Gordon | 4.00 | 8.00 | 12.00 | E |
| 922 | City of Sin–Robert O. Saber | 4.00 | 8.00 | 12.00 | E |
| 923 | Sinners Club–Harry Whittington; aka Teenage Jungle; c-Belarski | 6.00 | 12.00 | 18.00 | E |
| 924 | Pick-Up–Albert L. Quandt; 1954, aka Ticket to Passion | 4.00 | 8.00 | 12.00 | E |
| 925 | Reckless!–Kermit Welles; aka Pleasure Bound | 4.00 | 8.00 | 12.00 | E |
| 926 | Hotel Doctor–Frank Haskell | 4.00 | 8.00 | 12.00 | E |
| 927 | Boy Hungry–Kate Nickerson | 4.00 | 8.00 | 12.00 | E |
| 928 | Frenchie–David Charlson | 4.00 | 8.00 | 12.00 | E |
| 929 | Farm Hussy–Sylvia Erskine | 4.00 | 8.00 | 12.00 | E |
| 930 | Social Club–Albert L. Quandt | 4.00 | 8.00 | 12.00 | E |
| 931 | Backwoods Shack–Hallam Whitney (Harry Whittington) | 6.00 | 12.00 | 18.00 | E |
| 932 | Boy Madness–Ralph Douglas; c-Gross, aka Beach Party | 4.00 | 8.00 | 12.00 | E |
| 933 | City Hotel–Jane Manning; c-Pease | 4.00 | 8.00 | 12.00 | E |
| 934 | Farmer's Wife–Peggy Gaddis | 4.00 | 8.00 | 12.00 | E |
| 935 | Girl-Hungry–William E. Gordon; aka The Transgressor | 4.00 | 8.00 | 12.00 | E |
| 936 | Midnight Sinners–John Caldwall | 4.00 | 8.00 | 12.00 | E |
| 937 | Boy Chaser–Kate Nickerson | 4.00 | 8.00 | 12.00 | E |
| 938 | Farm Hussy–Sylvia Erskine | 4.00 | 8.00 | 12.00 | E |
| 939 | City Hotel–Jane Manning | 4.00 | 8.00 | 12.00 | E |

| | | V/Good | Fine | N/Mint | |
|---|---|---|---|---|---|

CARNIVAL, *continued*

| 940 | Farmer's Wife–Peggy Gaddis | 4.00 | 8.00 | 12.00 | E |
| 941 | Boy Madness–Ralph Douglas | 4.00 | 8.00 | 12.00 | E |
| 942 | City of Sin–Robert O. Saber | 4.00 | 8.00 | 12.00 | E |
| 943 | Backwoods Shack–Hallam Whitney (Harry Whittington) | 5.00 | 10.00 | 15.00 | E |
| 945 | Midnight Sinners–John Caldwall; aka Struggle | 4.00 | 8.00 | 12.00 | E |
| 948 | Big City Hellcat–Raymond Blair | 5.00 | 10.00 | 15.00 | E |
| 949 | Man-Chaser–Kirk Westley | 4.00 | 8.00 | 12.00 | E |
| 950 | Rapture Alley–Whit Harrison (Harry Whittington) | 7.50 | 15.00 | 22.50 | E |
| 951 | Boy Hungry–Kate Nickerson | 4.00 | 8.00 | 12.00 | E |
| 952 | Lost to Desire–Peggy Gaddis; 1953 | 4.00 | 8.00 | 12.00 | E |
| 953 | Strangers in the Dark–Peggy Gaddis | 4.00 | 8.00 | 12.00 | E |
| 954 | Man-Hungry–Mitchell Coleman | 4.00 | 8.00 | 12.00 | E |
| 955 | Young Passion–Watkins E. Wright | 4.00 | 8.00 | 12.00 | E |
| 956 | Big-Town Hellcat–Amos Hatter; aka On Borrowed Love | 5.00 | 10.00 | 15.00 | E |
| 957 | Boy Chaser–Kate Nickerson | 4.00 | 8.00 | 12.00 | E |

# CARROLL & GRAF
## Carroll & Graf

| 0-88184-061-0 | Law of the Desert Born–Louis L'amour; 1st ed. 1983 | 2.00 | 4.00 | 6.00 | W |
| 0-88184-062-9 | The Hills of Homicide–Louis L'amour; 1st ed. 1983 | 2.00 | 4.00 | 6.00 | M |
| 0-88184-132-3 | Vampire's Honeymoon–Cornell Woolrich; 1st ed. 1985 | 2.00 | 4.00 | 6.00 | HO |
| 0-88184-133-1 | Blind Date with Death–Cornell Woolrich; 1st ed. 1985 | 2.00 | 4.00 | 6.00 | M |
| 0-88184-250-8 | Riding for the Brand–Louis L'amour; 1st ed. 1986 | 2.00 | 4.00 | 6.00 | W |
| 0-88184-251-6 | Man Riding West–Louis L'amour; 1st ed. 1986 | 2.00 | 4.00 | 6.00 | W |

# CAVALCADE
## Delta Library, Inc.
### Digest Size

| nn | Madman on a Drum | 3.00 | 6.00 | 9.00 | M |
| 1 | Men Are Molehills–Ruth S. Livingston; 1946 | 2.50 | 5.00 | 7.50 | R |
| 2 | Magic for Murder–Armstrong Livingston | 3.00 | 6.00 | 9.00 | M |

# CENTURY
## Century Publications
### Some Digest Size

| 10 | The Man Who Murdered Himself– Geoffrey Homes; digest size | 3.00 | 6.00 | 9.00 | M |
| 11 | Outlaws Three | 3.00 | 6.00 | 9.00 | W |
| 12 | Murder without Makeup–Elda Benjamin; digest size | 3.00 | 6.00 | 9.00 | M |
| 13 | Here Comes the Corpse–George Bagby; digest size | 3.00 | 6.00 | 9.00 | M |
| 14 | Diagnosis: Murder–Rufus King; digest size | 3.00 | 6.00 | 9.00 | M |
| 15 | Ghost Trails–W.C. Tuttle; digest size | 3.00 | 6.00 | 9.00 | W |
| 16 | Renegade Roundup–William Colt MacDonald; digest size | 3.00 | 6.00 | 9.00 | W |
| 17 | As Good As Murdered–James O'Hanlon; digest size | 3.00 | 6.00 | 9.00 | M |
| 18 | Stab in the Back–Philip Wylie | 3.00 | 6.00 | 9.00 | M |
| | Bottom Deal–Judson Philips; digest size | | | | M |
| 19 | Fair Warning–Mignon G. Eberhart; digest size | 3.00 | 6.00 | 9.00 | M |
| 20 | Gun Bulldogger–Eugene Cunningham; digest size | 3.00 | 6.00 | 9.00 | M |
| 21 | The Sulu Sea Murders–Van Wyck Mason; digest size | 4.00 | 8.00 | 12.00 | M |

| 22 | Trigger Vengeance–John Trace; digest size | 3.00 | 6.00 | 9.00 | W |
| 23 | Death Came Dancing–Kathleen Moore Knight; digest size | 3.00 | 6.00 | 9.00 | M |
| 24 | The Trail of Gold–Dane Coolidge; digest size | 3.00 | 6.00 | 9.00 | W |
| 25 | Time Off for Murder–Zelda Popkin; digest size | 3.00 | 6.00 | 9.00 | M |
| 26 | Fallen Angel–Marty Holland; movie tie-in; digest size | 6.00 | 12.00 | 18.00 | E |
| 27 | Picture of the Victim–John S. Strange; digest size | 3.00 | 6.00 | 9.00 | M |
| 28 | Bad for Business–Rex Stout; digest size | 4.00 | 8.00 | 12.00 | M |
| 29 | All Concerned Notified–Helen Reilly; digest size | 3.00 | 6.00 | 9.00 | M |
| 30 | Weekend to Kill–Frederick Nebel | 3.00 | 6.00 | 9.00 | M |
| | Secret Corridors–Hugh Pentecost; digest size | | | | M |
| 31 | The Dark Corner–Leonard Q. Ross; movie tie-in; digest size | 6.00 | 12.00 | 18.00 | M |
| 32 | The Shanghai Bund Murders–Van Wyck Mason; digest size. Note: Cover variants | | | | |
| | Buddha cover | 6.00 | 12.00 | 18.00 | M |
| | Oriental menace cover | 15.00 | 30.00 | 45.00 | M |
| 33 | Corpses at Indian Stone–Philip Wylie; digest size | 3.00 | 6.00 | 9.00 | M |
| 34 | Red Gardenias–Jonathan Latimer; digest size | 3.00 | 6.00 | 9.00 | M |
| 35 | The Glass Slipper–Mignon Eberhardt | 3.00 | 6.00 | 9.00 | M |
| 37 | Singapore–William Bogert; movie tie-in; digest size | 10.00 | 20.00 | 30.00 | M |
| 50 | Dead Freight for Piute–Luke Short | 3.00 | 6.00 | 9.00 | W |
| 51 | Dust of the Trail–Bennett Foster | 3.00 | 6.00 | 9.00 | W |
| 52 | Danger on the Border–Frederick R. Bechdolt | 3.00 | 6.00 | 9.00 | W |
| 53 | Death Rides the Mesa–Tom Gill; digest size | 3.00 | 6.00 | 9.00 | W |
| 54 | The Leather Burners–Bliss Lomax; digest size | 3.00 | 6.00 | 9.00 | W |
| 55 | Don Desperado–L.L. Foreman; digest size | 3.00 | 6.00 | 9.00 | W |
| 56 | The Phantom Pass–William Colt MacDonald | 3.00 | 6.00 | 9.00 | W |
| 57 | Buckskin Empire–H.S. Drago; digest size | 3.00 | 6.00 | 9.00 | W |
| 58 | Gringo Gunfire–Bliss Lomax (H.S. Drago); digest size | 3.00 | 6.00 | 9.00 | W |
| 59 | Secret of the Wasteland–Bliss Lomax; digest size | 3.00 | 6.00 | 9.00 | W |
| nn(60) | Peace Marshal–Frank Gruber | 4.00 | 8.00 | 12.00 | W |
| 61 | Roaring Lead–William Colt MacDonald | 3.00 | 6.00 | 9.00 | W |
| 62 | Colt Comrades–Bliss Lomax (H.S. Drago) | 3.00 | 6.00 | 9.00 | W |
| nn(63) | Body and Soul–Sam Merwin, Jr; movie tie-in; digest size | 6.00 | 12.00 | 18.00 | |
| 64 | Outlaw–Frank Gruber; digest size | 4.00 | 8.00 | 12.00 | W |
| 65 | California Caballero–William Colt MacDonald | 3.00 | 6.00 | 9.00 | W |
| 66 | Sleep My Love–Leonard Q. Ross; movie tie-in | 6.00 | 12.00 | 18.00 | |
| 67 | No Nice Girl–Perry Lindsay (Peggy Gaddis) | 3.00 | 6.00 | 9.00 | E |
| 68 | A Double Life–Manly Wade Wellman; movie tie-in | 9.00 | 18.00 | 27.00 | |
| 69 | California Caballero–William Colt MacDonald; digest size | 3.00 | 6.00 | 9.00 | W |
| nn(70) | Cairo Garter Murders–Van Wyck Mason | 3.00 | 6.00 | 9.00 | M |
| 71 | Sign of the Gun–Archie Joscelyn | 3.00 | 6.00 | 9.00 | W |
| 72 | Gunsight–Frank Gruber | 3.00 | 6.00 | 9.00 | W |
| 73 | Saddles West–H.B. Hickey | 3.00 | 6.00 | 9.00 | W |
| 74 | Notched Guns–William Hopson | 3.00 | 6.00 | 9.00 | W |
| 75 | Scarlet Sin–John Saxon | 3.00 | 6.00 | 9.00 | E |
| 76 | Powdersmoke Range–W.C. MacDonald | 3.00 | 6.00 | 9.00 | W |
| 77 | Blonde Trouble–Perry Lindsay (Peggy Gaddis) | 3.00 | 6.00 | 9.00 | E |
| 78 | Gunsmoke–Lee Floren | 3.00 | 6.00 | 9.00 | W |
| 79 | Love Business–William Arthur | 3.00 | 6.00 | 9.00 | E |
| 80 | Cue for Passion–Gordon Semple | 3.00 | 6.00 | 9.00 | E |
| 81 | Drygulch Canyon–F.M. Bechdolt; digest size | 3.00 | 6.00 | 9.00 | W |

**CENTURY,** *continued*

| | | V/Good | Fine | N/Mint | |
|---|---|---|---|---|---|
| 82 | Ranger Justice–J.E. Grinstead | 3.00 | 6.00 | 9.00 | W |
| 83 | Ripe for Love–Carmen Snow | 3.00 | 6.00 | 9.00 | E |
| 84 | Marriage Is for Two–Phyllis Arthur | 3.00 | 6.00 | 9.00 | E |
| 85 | Unashamed–Perry Lindsay (Peggy Gaddis) | 3.00 | 6.00 | 9.00 | E |
| 86 | Bad Company–Gordon Semple | 3.00 | 6.00 | 9.00 | E |
| 87 | One More Lover–Thomas Stone | 3.00 | 6.00 | 9.00 | E |
| 88 | Hell's Horseman–William Hopson; may not exist, as this does exist as Prize 88 | 3.00 | 6.00 | 9.00 | W |
| 89 | Common Passion–John Saxon | 3.00 | 6.00 | 9.00 | E |
| 90 | Too Loose–Carlotta Baker | 3.00 | 6.00 | 9.00 | E |
| 91 | Scandalous–Ralph Carter | 3.00 | 6.00 | 9.00 | E |
| 92 | Outlaw Justice–Leigh Carder | 3.00 | 6.00 | 9.00 | W |
| 93 | Fleshpots–Florenz Branch | 3.00 | 6.00 | 9.00 | E |
| 94 | Passion's Way–Gordon Semple | 3.00 | 6.00 | 9.00 | E |
| 95 | Teaser–Craig Shepard | 3.00 | 6.00 | 9.00 | E |
| 96 | Body for Sale–Eliot Brewster | 3.00 | 6.00 | 9.00 | E |
| 97 | Call It Love–Hall Bennett | 3.00 | 6.00 | 9.00 | E |
| 98 | Quick Passion–Ralph Carter | 3.00 | 6.00 | 9.00 | E |
| 99 | Nice and Naughty–Gordon Semple | 3.00 | 6.00 | 9.00 | E |
| 99 | Trigger Vengeance–John Trace | 3.00 | 6.00 | 9.00 | W |
| 100 | Dark Memory–Jonathan Latimer; digest size | 3.50 | 7.00 | 10.50 | E |
| 101 | Bright Star of Danger–W.C. Chambers; digest size | 3.00 | 6.00 | 9.00 | |
| 102 | Hot Gold–Frederick R. Bechdolt; digest size | 3.50 | 7.00 | 10.50 | W |
| 103 | Without Reservations–Jane Allen & Mae Livingston; movie tie-in; digest size | 6.00 | 12.00 | 18.00 | E |
| 104 | The Green Man–Harold Sherman; digest size | 5.00 | 10.00 | 15.00 | SF |
| 105 | Man-Handled–Eliot Brewster | 3.00 | 6.00 | 9.00 | E |
| 106 | Marriage Later–William Arthur | 3.00 | 6.00 | 9.00 | E |
| 107 | Inherited Husband–Cecile Gilmore | 3.00 | 6.00 | 9.00 | E |
| 108 | Kept Woman–John Saxon | 3.00 | 6.00 | 9.00 | E |
| 109 | Passion's Lesson–Gordon Semple | 3.00 | 6.00 | 9.00 | E |
| 110 | Three Time Lover–Thomas Stone | 3.00 | 6.00 | 9.00 | E |
| 111 | Sinner Take All–William Arthur | 3.00 | 6.00 | 9.00 | E |
| 112 | Profane–Ralph Carter | 3.00 | 6.00 | 9.00 | E |
| 113 | Sinful Lady–Gordon Semple | 3.00 | 6.00 | 9.00 | E |
| 114 | Passion's Program–Florenz Branch | 3.00 | 6.00 | 9.00 | E |
| 115 | Two Time Lover–William Arthur | 3.00 | 6.00 | 9.00 | E |
| 116 | Time Trap–Rog Phillips; 1949 | 15.00 | 30.00 | 45.00 | SF |
| 117 | Red for Passion–Thomas Stone | 3.00 | 6.00 | 9.00 | E |
| 118 | Desperado–William Hopson | 3.00 | 6.00 | 9.00 | W |
| 119 | Love Slave–Gail Jordan | 3.00 | 6.00 | 9.00 | E |
| 120 | Forbidden Sin–William Arthur; aka Burlesque Girl | 3.00 | 6.00 | 9.00 | E |
| 121 | Voluptueous–Charles Thornton | 3.00 | 6.00 | 9.00 | E |
| 122 | Passion's Sin–Ralph Carter; aka The Quiet Passion | 3.00 | 6.00 | 9.00 | E |
| 123 | Past Folly–Florenz Branch | 3.00 | 6.00 | 9.00 | E |
| 124 | Worlds Within–Rog Phillips | 4.00 | 8.00 | 12.00 | SF |
| 125 | Trigger Trails–Hamilton Craigie | 3.00 | 6.00 | 9.00 | W |
| 126 | Street Girl–Eliot Brewster | 3.00 | 6.00 | 9.00 | E |
| 127 | Charming Sinner–Barry DeForest; aka Partners in Sin | 3.00 | 6.00 | 9.00 | E |
| 128 | Bullet Trail–Burt Arthur | 3.00 | 6.00 | 9.00 | W |
| 129 | Tombstone Stage–William Hopson | 3.00 | 6.00 | 9.00 | W |
| 130 | Sinful Love–William Arthur; aka Redhead | 3.00 | 6.00 | 9.00 | E |
| 131 | Reckless Range–Johnston McCulley | 3.00 | 6.00 | 9.00 | W |

| | | V/Good | Fine | N/Mint | |
|---|---|---|---|---|---|
| 132 | Six Gun Stampede–Jackson Cole | 4.00 | 8.00 | 12.00 | W |
| 133 | California Trail–H. Bedford Jones | 4.00 | 8.00 | 12.00 | W |
| 134 | Renegade Range–Archie Joscelyn | 3.00 | 6.00 | 9.00 | W |
| 135 | Saddle Wolves–Allan K. Echols | 3.00 | 6.00 | 9.00 | W |
| 136 | Headed for a Hearse–Jonathan Latimer | 3.00 | 6.00 | 9.00 | M |

# CHARIOT BOOKS–1ST SERIES

## Chariot Books

| | | V/Good | Fine | N/Mint | |
|---|---|---|---|---|---|
| CB101 | Convention Girl–Donald M. Wright; 1959 | 1.00 | 2.00 | 3.00 | X |
| CB102 | Mr. Madam–Mel Dumont | 1.00 | 2.00 | 3.00 | X |
| CB103 | The Naked Lovers–Chuck Little | 1.00 | 2.00 | 3.00 | X |
| CB104 | The Private Life of Eleanor–Rollin Cross | 1.00 | 2.00 | 3.00 | X |
| CB105 | Sex on Tap–Boris Noderheim | 1.00 | 2.00 | 3.00 | X |
| CB106 | The Last Virgin and Other True Stories of Lesbian Love in Greenwich Village–Noel O'Hara | 3.00 | 6.00 | 9.00 | X |
| CB107 | ''I Live to Love''–Hilary Hilton; 1959 | 1.00 | 2.00 | 3.00 | X |
| CB108 | The New Bathroom Reader–Donald H. Lawrence | 1.50 | 3.00 | 4.50 | X |
| CB109 | You Are Not Alone–Leon Klein & Uhlan | 1.00 | 2.00 | 3.00 | X |
| CB111 | Broadway Bait–Ray Damon | 1.00 | 2.00 | 3.00 | X |
| CB112 | Queen of Sheba–Victor Sardoux | 2.50 | 5.00 | 7.50 | X |
| CB113 | Carnival Girl–Max Gareth; 1960 | 2.50 | 5.00 | 7.50 | X |
| CB114 | The Deadly Passion–Ronald Bernard | 1.00 | 2.00 | 3.00 | X |
| CB115 | Bed Bait–Robert Devlin | 1.00 | 2.00 | 3.00 | X |
| CB116 | Blue Denim Doll–Arthur Adlon | 1.00 | 2.00 | 3.00 | X |
| CB117 | Boulevard Girl–Robert Chessman | 1.00 | 2.00 | 3.00 | X |
| CB118 | The Thrill-Seekers–Ray Damon; 1960 | 1.00 | 2.00 | 3.00 | X |
| CB119 | A Time to Love–Noel O'Hara | 1.00 | 2.00 | 3.00 | X |
| CB120 | Bad Girl Abroad–Arthur Adlon | 1.00 | 2.00 | 3.00 | X |
| CB121 | Jessica–Ray Damon | 1.00 | 2.00 | 3.00 | X |
| CB122 | Driven Desire–Robert Chessman | 1.00 | 2.00 | 3.00 | X |
| CB123 | Woman from Another Planet–Frank Belknap Long; 1960 | 4.00 | 8.00 | 12.00 | SF |
| CB124 | Your Sex Problems in Marriage–Edward Podolsky, MD | 1.00 | 2.00 | 3.00 | NF |
| CB125 | Lover Girl–Robert Devlin | 1.00 | 2.00 | 3.00 | X |
| CB126 | Hideaway Love–Robert Chessman | 1.00 | 2.00 | 3.00 | X |
| CB127 | Crazy Street, U.S.A.–Arthur Adlon | 1.00 | 2.00 | 3.00 | X |
| CB128 | The Invisible Man–H.G. Wells; 1960 | 2.50 | 5.00 | 7.50 | SF |
| CB129 | Untamed–Rick Wentworth | 1.00 | 2.00 | 3.00 | X |
| CB130 | Dangerous Affairs–Louis Roland | 1.00 | 2.00 | 3.00 | X |
| CB131 | Backstage Girl–Hyman Lindsay | 1.00 | 2.00 | 3.00 | X |
| CB132 | The Park Jungle–Robert Chessman | 1.00 | 2.00 | 3.00 | JD |
| CB133 | Jamestown Mistress–Carlson Wade | 2.50 | 5.00 | 7.50 | X |
| CB134 | The Prince of Poisoners–Arthur Adlon | 1.50 | 3.00 | 4.50 | B |
| CB135 | Virgie–Phil Brandon | 1.00 | 2.00 | 3.00 | X |
| CB136 | The Wild Party–Winslow Tandy | 1.00 | 2.00 | 3.00 | X |
| CB137 | Continental Tramp–Lee M. Vernon | 1.00 | 2.00 | 3.00 | X |
| CB138 | Sex Behavior of the American Secretary–W.H. Sprague | 1.00 | 2.00 | 3.00 | NF |
| CB139 | Black Is a Man–Harry Roskolenko | 1.00 | 2.00 | 3.00 | X |
| CB140 | Parlor Girl–Robert Devlin | 1.00 | 2.00 | 3.00 | X |
| CB141 | The King's Lust–Victorien Sardoux | 2.50 | 5.00 | 7.50 | X |
| CB142 | Butchers in Waiting–Carlson Wade | 1.00 | 2.00 | 3.00 | X |
| CB143 | Man Mad–David Challon | 1.00 | 2.00 | 3.00 | X |
| CB144 | Lady Darton's Sin–Arthur Adlon | 1.00 | 2.00 | 3.00 | X |
| CB145 | The Mercenary Lover–Lee Richards | 1.00 | 2.00 | 3.00 | X |
| CB146 | The Crest Inn Rape–G.G. Ravelle | 1.00 | 2.00 | 3.00 | X |
| CB147 | Prize Girl–Charles Thorne | 1.00 | 2.00 | 3.00 | X |

*Century 74, Century 104, Century 126.*

*Century 133, Chartered 18, Chartered 25.*

CHARIOT BOOKS–1ST SERIES, *continued*

| | | V/Good | Fine | N/Mint | |
|---|---|---|---|---|---|
| CB148 | Creole Desire–Margaret K. Demetre | 1.00 | 2.00 | 3.00 | X |
| CB149 | Passion Slave–Wilson MacDonald | 1.00 | 2.00 | 3.00 | X |
| CB150 | The Last 14–Tyrone C. Barr; aka Split Worlds; 1960 | 2.50 | 5.00 | 7.50 | SF |
| CB151 | Dungaree Sin–Frederick Lorenz | 1.00 | 2.00 | 3.00 | JD |
| CB152 | Butchers of Berlin–B. VonBluck | 1.50 | 3.00 | 4.50 | NF |
| CB153 | Tramp Wife–Orrie Hitt | 1.00 | 2.00 | 3.00 | X |
| CB154 | Driven Virgin–Arthur Adlon | 1.00 | 2.00 | 3.00 | X |
| CB155 | Virgin Nurse–Arthur Adlon | 1.00 | 2.00 | 3.00 | X |
| CB156 | Bitch on Wheels–Robert Devlin | 1.00 | 2.00 | 3.00 | X |
| CB157 | Sex Peddler–Arthur Adlon | 1.00 | 2.00 | 3.00 | X |
| CB158 | Hotel Girl–Orrie Hitt | 1.00 | 2.00 | 3.00 | X |
| CB159 | Video Virgin–Arthur Adlon | 1.00 | 2.00 | 3.00 | X |
| CB160 | Sex Cruise–Arthur Bliss | 1.00 | 2.00 | 3.00 | X |
| CB161 | Wild Model–Donald Wright | 1.00 | 2.00 | 3.00 | X |
| CB162 | The Mating Center–Frank Belknap Long; 1961 | 4.00 | 8.00 | 12.00 | SF |
| CB163 | Lonely Flesh–Orrie Hitt | 1.00 | 2.00 | 3.00 | X |
| CB164 | One Hell of a Dame–E.S. Seeley, Jr | 1.00 | 2.00 | 3.00 | X |
| CB165 | Vacation Sin–George Simon | 1.00 | 2.00 | 3.00 | X |
| CB167 | Party Doll–Orrie Hitt | 1.00 | 2.00 | 3.00 | X |
| CB168 | Loril Was a Tramp–C.E. Davis | 1.00 | 2.00 | 3.00 | X |
| CB169 | Sex Mad–Larry Hornes | 1.00 | 2.00 | 3.00 | X |
| CB172 | Sinful Wife–Ray Damon | 1.00 | 2.00 | 3.00 | X |
| CB173 | Love Plan–Robert Chessman | 1.00 | 2.00 | 3.00 | X |
| CB174 | Pillow Girl–E.S. Seeley, Jr | 1.00 | 2.00 | 3.00 | X |
| CB177 | Passion Club–E.S. Seeley, Jr | 1.00 | 2.00 | 3.00 | X |
| CB178 | Wild Oats–Ben Anderson | 1.00 | 2.00 | 3.00 | X |
| CB179 | Key Club Girl–Arthur Adlon | 1.00 | 2.00 | 3.00 | X |
| CB180 | Texas Tramp–John B. Thompson | 1.00 | 2.00 | 3.00 | X |
| CB181 | Affairs of Clio–Matt Gleason | 1.00 | 2.00 | 3.00 | X |
| CB182 | The Private Life of Eleanor–Rollin Coss | 1.00 | 2.00 | 3.00 | X |
| CB184 | Sex Behavior of the American Secretary–W.H. Sprague, PhD | 1.00 | 2.00 | 3.00 | NF |
| CB185 | Carnival Girl–Max Gareth | 1.00 | 2.00 | 3.00 | X |
| CB186 | Gay Wanton–John B. Thompson | 1.00 | 2.00 | 3.00 | X |
| CB187 | Man's Nurse–Orrie Hitt | 1.00 | 2.00 | 3.00 | X |
| CB189 | Vicky–Mel Dumont; 1961 | 1.00 | 2.00 | 3.00 | X |
| CB190 | Wild Bride–George Simon | 1.00 | 2.00 | 3.00 | X |
| CB193 | Wild Flesh–John Calley | 1.00 | 2.00 | 3.00 | X |
| CB194 | Suburban Sexpot–E.S. Seeley, Jr | 1.00 | 2.00 | 3.00 | X |
| CB195 | Hot Blood–Orrie Hitt | 1.00 | 2.00 | 3.00 | X |
| CB197 | Swamp Girl–D.W. Craig | 2.00 | 4.00 | 6.00 | X |
| CB198 | Arlette–A.E. Oliver | 1.00 | 2.00 | 3.00 | X |
| CB199 | Len's Girl–E.S. Seeley, Jr | 1.00 | 2.00 | 3.00 | X |
| CB200 | Pick-Up–N.M. Newland | 1.00 | 2.00 | 3.00 | X |
| CB201 | Naked Party–D.W. Craig | 1.00 | 2.00 | 3.00 | X |
| CB203 | Love Cult–Wayne Thurman | 1.00 | 2.00 | 3.00 | X |
| CB204 | Tramp Nurse–Arthur Adlon | 1.00 | 2.00 | 3.00 | X |
| CB205 | Nite-Flight Girl–Lee Shepard | 1.00 | 2.00 | 3.00 | X |
| CB207 | Hobo Girl–A.L. Roget | 1.50 | 3.00 | 4.50 | X |
| CB210 | Sex Peddler–Arthur Adlon | 1.00 | 2.00 | 3.00 | X |
| CB215 | Bareskin–George Simon | 1.00 | 2.00 | 3.00 | X |
| CB216 | Naked Nurse–Arthur Adlon; c-Maguire | 1.00 | 2.00 | 3.00 | X |
| CB218 | Campus Tramp–John Calley | 1.00 | 2.00 | 3.00 | X |
| CB220 | Willing Flesh–Powers | 1.00 | 2.00 | 3.00 | X |
| CB222 | The Sheer Affair–George Simon; aka Video Virgin; 1962 | 1.00 | 2.00 | 3.00 | X |

## CHARIOT BOOKS–2ND SERIES

### Chariot Books

| | | V/Good | Fine | N/Mint | |
|---|---|---|---|---|---|
| CB1601 | Love for Sale–D.W. Craig; 1962 | 1.00 | 2.00 | 3.00 | X |
| CB1602 | Cold Wife–Arthur Adlon | 1.00 | 2.00 | 3.00 | X |
| CB1603 | Hired Girl–George Simon | 1.00 | 2.00 | 3.00 | X |
| CB1604 | Honey–Orrie Hitt | 1.00 | 2.00 | 3.00 | X |
| CB1605 | Torrid Tramp–John Calley | 1.00 | 2.00 | 3.00 | X |
| CB1606 | Heat Wave–Jeffrey Powers | 1.00 | 2.00 | 3.00 | X |
| CB1607 | Female Fire–Arthur Adlon | 1.00 | 2.00 | 3.00 | X |
| CB1608 | Sin Sister–D.W. Craig | 1.00 | 2.00 | 3.00 | X |
| CB1609 | Sin Gym–George Simon | 1.00 | 2.00 | 3.00 | X |
| CB1610 | Twin Beds–Orrie Hitt; 1962 | 1.00 | 2.00 | 3.00 | X |
| CB1611 | Sex Market–W.R. MacDonald; 1962 | 1.00 | 2.00 | 3.00 | X |
| CB1612 | Lonely Wife–D.W. Craig; 1962 | 1.00 | 2.00 | 3.00 | X |
| CB1616 | Hungry Thighs–Sheldon March | 1.00 | 2.00 | 3.00 | X |
| CB1619 | Passion Street–Orrie Hitt | 1.00 | 2.00 | 3.00 | X |
| CB1620 | Bad Wife–Orrie Hitt; 1962 | 1.00 | 2.00 | 3.00 | X |
| CB1622 | I Am a Lesbian–Laverne P–––; 1962 | 2.00 | 4.00 | 6.00 | X |
| CB1624 | Born Bad–F.L. Naylor; 1962 | 1.00 | 2.00 | 3.00 | X |

## CHARTER BOOKS

### Charter Communications Inc.

| | | V/Good | Fine | N/Mint |
|---|---|---|---|---|
| 18900 | The Efficiency Expert–Edgar Rice Burroughs | 2.50 | 5.00 | 7.50 |
| 28903 | The Girl from Farris'–Edgar Rice Burroughs | 2.50 | 5.00 | 7.50 |

## CHARTERED

### Bond-Charteris Pub./Saint Enterprises, Inc.

**Digest Size**

| | | V/Good | Fine | N/Mint | |
|---|---|---|---|---|---|
| 17 | The Saint's Choice of Hollywood Crime Stories–ed. Leslie Charteris | 5.00 | 10.00 | 15.00 | M |
| 18 | Deadlier Than the Male–James Gunn | 3.50 | 7.00 | 10.50 | M |
| 19 | May not exist | | | | |
| 20 | May not exist | | | | |
| 21 | Seven Slayers–Paul Cain; 1st ed. 1946 | 25.00 | 50.00 | 75.00 | M |
| 22 | The Man Who Limped–Otis Adelbert Kline; 1st ed. 1946 | 20.00 | 40.00 | 60.00 | SF |
| 23 | May not exist | | | | |
| 24 | May not exist | | | | |
| 25 | The Last Door Bell–Frank Gruber | 5.00 | 10.00 | 15.00 | M |
| 26 | The Brighter Buccaneer–Leslie Charteris. Note: Queen's Quorum No. 84 | 3.00 | 6.00 | 9.00 | M |
| 27 | The Saint's Choice of Radio Thrillers–ed. Leslie Charteris | 5.00 | 10.00 | 15.00 | M |
| 28 | A Pocketful of Clues–James R. Langham | 3.00 | 6.00 | 9.00 | M |

## CHECKER BOOKS

### Checker Books, Inc.

| | | V/Good | Fine | N/Mint | |
|---|---|---|---|---|---|
| 1 | Terry and the Pirates: The Jewels of Jade–Edward J. Boylan, Jr; 1949; c-Wenzel | 9.00 | 18.00 | 27.00 | A |
| 2 | The Broadway Butterfly Murders–Tip Bliss | 6.00 | 12.00 | 18.00 | M |
| 3 | Make Mine Murder–Robert Bowen | 6.00 | 12.00 | 18.00 | M |
| 4 | Lost River Buckaroos–Charles M. Martin | 5.00 | 10.00 | 15.00 | W |
| 5 | Horror and Homicide–anthology; 1949 | 7.50 | 15.00 | 22.50 | M |
| 6 | Duke Herring–Maxwell Bodenheim; 1949; c-Wenzell | 6.00 | 12.00 | 18.00 | M |
| 7 | Master-at-Arms–Rafael Sabatini; 1949 | 5.00 | 10.00 | 15.00 | A |
| 8 | Taxi–Abraham Bernstein | 5.00 | 10.00 | 15.00 | |
| 9 | The Florentine Dagger–Ben Hecht; 1949 | 5.00 | 10.00 | 15.00 | M |
| 10 | Lady, Mind That Corpse–Hank Janson; 1949; c-Heade | 12.50 | 25.00 | 37.50 | M |
| 11 | The Practical Party Guide and Cook Book–Dorothy Bannett & Fifi Bannett | 5.00 | 10.00 | 15.00 | NF |
| 12 | Over 100 Best Cartoons–Patricia Fulford; 1949 | 7.50 | 15.00 | 22.50 | NF |

*Checkerbook 1, Checkerbook 4, Crest 139.*

# CHICAGO PAPERBACK HOUSE
## Chicago Paperback House, Inc.

| | | V/Good | Fine | N/Mint | |
|---|---|---|---|---|---|
| A101 | Murder, Absolutely Murder–Helen Cloutier; 1962 | 1.00 | 2.00 | 3.00 | M |
| A102 | The Big Squeeze–Christopher Athens | .75 | 1.50 | 2.25 | |
| A103 | Room at the Bottom–J.L. Potter | 1.00 | 2.00 | 3.00 | M |
| A104 | or Murder for Free–J.L. Potter | 1.00 | 2.00 | 3.00 | M |
| A105 | Keep Running–Keith Vining | 1.50 | 3.00 | 4.50 | M |
| A106 | Power's Pool–Zora Hansen | 1.00 | 2.00 | 3.00 | |
| A107 | House of the Hunter–Frank Taylor; 1962 | 2.00 | 4.00 | 6.00 | SF |
| A108 | Another Man's Hell–William C. Kemper, Jr | 2.00 | 4.00 | 6.00 | SF |
| A109 | Kill, Sweet Charity, Kill–J.L. Potter | 1.00 | 2.00 | 3.00 | M |
| A110 | Nothing But Blood–Pauline Smith | 1.00 | 2.00 | 3.00 | M |
| A111 | Wail of the Lonely Wench–A.J. Collins | 1.00 | 2.00 | 3.00 | |
| B100 | Eyewitness to Exodus–Beatrice Levin; 1962 | 1.00 | 2.00 | 3.00 | NF |
| B110 | The Paths Are Three–Vic Marina | .75 | 1.50 | 2.25 | |
| B120 | Cockfighter–Charles Willeford; 1st ed. 1962 | 15.00 | 30.00 | 45.00 | |
| B130 | Home Away from Home–Jack Woodford | .75 | 1.50 | 2.25 | |
| B140 | Postmark of America–R.T. Glenn | .75 | 1.50 | 2.25 | H |
| B150 | The Velvet Rut–Dan Brennan; 1962 | 1.25 | 2.50 | 3.75 | M |

# COLLINS WHITE CIRCLE
## Wm. Collins Sons & Co.
### (Canadian)

| | | V/Good | Fine | N/Mint | |
|---|---|---|---|---|---|
| nn | The Stoat–Lynn Brock; 1942 | 1.75 | 3.50 | 5.25 | M |
| nn | Death Leaves No Card–Miles Burton | 1.75 | 3.50 | 5.25 | M |
| nn | Mr. Babbacombe Dies–Miles Burton | 1.75 | 3.50 | 5.25 | M |
| nn | Death on Sunday–John Rhode; aka The Elm Tree Murder | 1.75 | 3.50 | 5.25 | M |
| nn | Death Pays a Dividend–John Rhode | 1.75 | 3.50 | 5.25 | M |
| nn | Dames Don't Care–Peter Cheyney | 1.75 | 3.50 | 5.25 | M |
| nn | This Man Is Dangerous–Peter Cheyney | 1.75 | 3.50 | 5.25 | M |
| nn | Mr. Mortimer Gets the Jitters–Berkeley Gray | 1.75 | 3.50 | 5.25 | M |
| nn | Conquest Takes All–Berkeley Gray | 1.75 | 3.50 | 5.25 | M |
| nn | Ironsides of the Yard–Victor Gunn | 1.75 | 3.50 | 5.25 | M |
| nn | Wanted for Murder–Henry Holt | 1.75 | 3.50 | 5.25 | M |
| nn | Mystery of the Smiling Doll–Henry Holt | 1.75 | 3.50 | 5.25 | M |
| nn | Death before Honour–David Hume | 1.75 | 3.50 | 5.25 | M |
| nn | Make Way for the Mourners–David Hume | 1.75 | 3.50 | 5.25 | M |
| nn | Overture to Death–Ngaio Marsh | 1.75 | 3.50 | 5.25 | M |
| nn | Death at the Bar–Ngaio Marsh | 1.75 | 3.50 | 5.25 | M |
| nn | Death of a Peer–Ngaio Marsh; aka Surfeit of Lampreys | 1.75 | 3.50 | 5.25 | M |
| nn | Verdict of Twelve–Raymond Postgate | 1.75 | 3.50 | 5.25 | M |
| nn | The Calendar–Edgar Wallace | 1.75 | 3.50 | 5.25 | M |
| nn | Doorway to Danger–Stephen Maddock | 1.75 | 3.50 | 5.25 | M |
| nn | Spades at Midnight–Stephen Maddock | 1.75 | 3.50 | 5.25 | M |
| nn | Seven Dead–J. Jefferson Farjeon | 1.75 | 3.50 | 5.25 | M |
| nn | The Bell of Death–Anthony Gilbert | 1.75 | 3.50 | 5.25 | M |
| nn | Wreckers Must Breathe–Hammond Innes; aka Trapped | 1.75 | 3.50 | 5.25 | M |
| nn | Jewel Thief–Arthur Mills | 1.75 | 3.50 | 5.25 | M |
| nn | Sweet Poison–Rupert Penny | 1.75 | 3.50 | 5.25 | M |
| nn | King's Enemies–J.M. Walsh | 1.75 | 3.50 | 5.25 | |
| nn | The Fighting Buckaroo–Tex Curran | 1.75 | 3.50 | 5.25 | W |
| nn | Man from Peace River–Wallace Q. Reid | 1.75 | 3.50 | 5.25 | W |
| nn | He Packed a Gun–C.W. Sanders | 1.75 | 3.50 | 5.25 | W |
| nn | The Turquoise Trail–W.C. Tuttle | 1.75 | 3.50 | 5.25 | W |
| nn | Death at Dykes Corner–E.C.R. Lorac | 1.75 | 3.50 | 5.25 | M |
| nn | Thou Shell of Death–Nicholas Blake | 1.75 | 3.50 | 5.25 | M |
| nn | My Own Murderer–Richard Hull | 1.75 | 3.50 | 5.25 | M |
| nn | The Sky Pilot–Ralph Connors | 1.75 | 3.50 | 5.25 | A |
| nn | The Flying Years–Frederick Niven | 1.75 | 3.50 | 5.25 | A |
| nn | Sunshine Sketches of a Little Town–Stephen Leacock | 1.75 | 3.50 | 5.25 | H |
| nn | Goose Feathers–George Digby | 1.75 | 3.50 | 5.25 | B |
| nn | Harvest Triumphant–Merrill Denison | 1.75 | 3.50 | 5.25 | NF |
| nn | The Nutmeg Tree–Margery Sharp | 1.75 | 3.50 | 5.25 | |
| nn | Attack Alarm–Hammond Innes | 1.75 | 3.50 | 5.25 | |
| nn | Belt of Suspicion–H.R. Wakefield | 1.75 | 3.50 | 5.25 | |
| nn | U-Boat in the Hebrides–A.D. Divine | 1.75 | 3.50 | 5.25 | C |
| nn | A Maid and a Million Men–James G. Dunton | 1.75 | 3.50 | 5.25 | |
| nn | Aunt Sunday Sees It Through–J. Jefferson Farjeon; aka Aunt Sunday Takes Command | 1.75 | 3.50 | 5.25 | M |
| nn | Vultures, Ltd.–Berkeley Gray | 1.75 | 3.50 | 5.25 | |
| nn | Literary Lapses–Stephen Leacock | 1.75 | 3.50 | 5.25 | H |
| nn | Barometer Rising–Hugh MacLennan | 1.75 | 3.50 | 5.25 | |
| nn | The Creaking Chair–Laurence Meynell | 1.75 | 3.50 | 5.25 | |
| nn | The King's English Dictionary–ed. A. Parrish | 1.75 | 3.50 | 5.25 | NF |
| nn | Death on the Boat Train–John Rhode | 1.75 | 3.50 | 5.25 | M |
| nn | Treasure Island–Robert Louis Stevenson | 1.75 | 3.50 | 5.25 | A |
| nn | Secret Weapons–J.M. Walsh | 1.75 | 3.50 | 5.25 | |
| nn | Death Takes a Flat–Miles Burton; aka Vacancy With Corpse | 1.75 | 3.50 | 5.25 | M |
| nn | Five Aces–David Hume | 1.75 | 3.50 | 5.25 | |
| 51 | Immortal Sergeant–John Brophy | 1.75 | 3.50 | 5.25 | C |
| 52 | Steady As You Go–Bartimeus | 1.75 | 3.50 | 5.25 | NF |
| 53 | Crime Unlimited–David Hume | 1.75 | 3.50 | 5.25 | M |
| 54 | No Sleep at All–James Warren | 1.75 | 3.50 | 5.25 | M |
| 55 | Death Takes a Flat–Miles Burton | 1.75 | 3.50 | 5.25 | M |
| 56 | The Unfortunate Murderer–Richard Hull | 1.75 | 3.50 | 5.25 | M |
| 57 | Policeman's Holiday–Rupert Penny | 1.75 | 3.50 | 5.25 | M |
| 58 | The Bloody Tower–John Rhode | 1.75 | 3.50 | 5.25 | M |
| 59 | Dangerous Curves–Peter Cheyney; aka Tower of Evil aka Callaghan | 1.75 | 3.50 | 5.25 | M |
| 60 | Six Feet of Dynamite–Berkeley Gray | 1.75 | 3.50 | 5.25 | A |
| 61 | Footsteps of Death–Victor Gunn | 1.75 | 3.50 | 5.25 | M |
| 62 | The Black Cripple–Richard Keverne | 1.75 | 3.50 | 5.25 | M |
| 63 | Date with a Spy–Stephan Maddock | 1.75 | 3.50 | 5.25 | M |
| 64 | Danger Zone–J.M. Walsh; 1943 | 1.75 | 3.50 | 5.25 | M |
| 65 | The Knife–Herbert Adams; aka The Strange Murder of Hatton, K.C. | 1.75 | 3.50 | 5.25 | M |
| 66 | The Beast Must Die–Nicholas Blake; 1943 | 1.75 | 3.50 | 5.25 | M |
| 67 | No Murder of Mine–Alice Campbell | 1.75 | 3.50 | 5.25 | M |
| 68 | Dark Lady–J. Jefferson Farjeon | 1.75 | 3.50 | 5.25 | M |
| 69 | Vanishing Corpse–Anthony Gilbert; aka She Vanished in the Dawn | 1.75 | 3.50 | 5.25 | M |
| 70 | The Whispering Man–Henry Holt | 1.75 | 3.50 | 5.25 | M |
| 71 | Slippery Staircase–E.C.R. Lorac | 1.75 | 3.50 | 5.25 | M |
| 72 | Night Exercise–John Rhode; aka Dead of the Night | 1.75 | 3.50 | 5.25 | M |
| 74 | Tunnel from Calais–David Rame | 1.75 | 3.50 | 5.25 | C |
| 75 | Barometer Rising–Hugh MacLennan | 1.75 | 3.50 | 5.25 | |
| 76 | Death and the Dancing Footman–Ngaio Marsh | 1.75 | 3.50 | 5.25 | M |
| 77 | Rehearsal for Marriage–Helena Grose | 1.75 | 3.50 | 5.25 | R |
| 78 | Wife in Uniform–Carol Gaye | 1.75 | 3.50 | 5.25 | R |
| 79 | The Commandos–Elliott Arnold | 1.75 | 3.50 | 5.25 | NF |
| 80 | The Ridin' Fool–Tex Curran | 1.75 | 3.50 | 5.25 | W |
| 81 | Ironside's Lone Hand–Victor Gunn | 1.75 | 3.50 | 5.25 | M |
| 82 | She Faded into Air–Ethel Lina White | 1.75 | 3.50 | 5.25 | M |
| 83 | Gentlemen of the Night–Stephen Maddock | 1.75 | 3.50 | 5.25 | M |
| 84 | O'Malley in the Saddle–Clem Yore | 1.75 | 3.50 | 5.25 | W |
| 85 | Miss Dynamite–Berkeley Gray | 1.75 | 3.50 | 5.25 | M |
| 86 | The Dark Duet–Peter Cheyney; aka Counter Spy Murders | 1.75 | 3.50 | 5.25 | M |
| 87 | The Judge Sums Up–J. Jefferson Farjeon | 1.75 | 3.50 | 5.25 | M |
| 88 | The Last Bullet–Tex Curran | 1.75 | 3.50 | 5.25 | W |
| 89 | Death at His Elbow–J.M. Walsh | 1.75 | 3.50 | 5.25 | M |
| 90 | The Fourth Bomb–John Rhode | 1.75 | 3.50 | 5.25 | M |
| 91 | Spearhead–John Brophy | 1.75 | 3.50 | 5.25 | C |
| 92 | Something Nasty in the Woodshed–Anthony Gilbert; aka Mystery in the Woodshed | 1.75 | 3.50 | 5.25 | M |
| 93 | The Nineteenth Hole Mystery–Herbert Adams | 1.75 | 3.50 | 5.25 | M |
| 94 | Heads You Live–David Hume | 1.75 | 3.50 | 5.25 | M |
| 95 | Wandering Cowboy–C.W. Sanders | 1.75 | 3.50 | 5.25 | W |
| 96 | Colour Scheme–Ngaio Marsh | 1.75 | 3.50 | 5.25 | M |
| 97 | You'd Be Surprised–Peter Cheyney | 1.75 | 3.50 | 5.25 | M |
| 98 | Calling All Cars–Henry Holt | 1.75 | 3.50 | 5.25 | M |
| 99 | Kitty–Rosamond Marshall | 1.75 | 3.50 | 5.25 | R |

COLLINS WHITE CIRCLE, *continued*

| | | V/Good | Fine | N/Mint | |
|---|---|---|---|---|---|
| 102 | Death Leaves No Card–Miles Burton | 1.75 | 3.50 | 5.25 | M |
| 104 | The Bell of Death–Anthony Gilbert | 1.75 | 3.50 | 5.25 | M |
| 105 | Mr. Mortimer Gets the Jitters–Berkeley Gray | 1.75 | 3.50 | 5.25 | M |
| 106 | Wanted for Murder–Henry Holt | 1.75 | 3.50 | 5.25 | M |
| 107 | Death before Honour–David Hume | 1.75 | 3.50 | 5.25 | M |
| 108 | Doorway to Danger–Stephen Maddock | 1.75 | 3.50 | 5.25 | M |
| 109 | Spades at Midnight–Stephen Maddock | 1.75 | 3.50 | 5.25 | M |
| 110 | Belt of Suspicion–H.R. Wakefield | 1.75 | 3.50 | 5.25 | M |
| 111 | A Maid and a Million Men–James G. Dunton | 1.75 | 3.50 | 5.25 | |
| 112 | Man from Peace River–Wallace Q. Reid | 1.75 | 3.50 | 5.25 | W |
| 113 | Overture to Death–Ngaio Marsh | 1.75 | 3.50 | 5.25 | M |
| 114 | Death at the Bar–Ngaio Marsh | 1.75 | 3.50 | 5.25 | M |
| 115 | The Fighting Buckaroo–Tex Curran | 1.75 | 3.50 | 5.25 | W |
| 116 | The Fying Years–Frederick Niven | 1.75 | 3.50 | 5.25 | A |
| 117 | Death of a Peer–Ngaio Marsh | 1.75 | 3.50 | 5.25 | M |
| 118 | Goose Feathers–George Digby | 1.75 | 3.50 | 5.25 | A |
| 119–199 | Apparently do not exist | | | | |
| 200 | Murder M.D.–Miles Burton | 1.75 | 3.50 | 5.25 | M |
| 201 | The Dark Square–Laurence Meynell | 1.75 | 3.50 | 5.25 | M |
| 202 | The Case of the Abdominal Snowman–Nicholas Blake | 1.75 | 3.50 | 5.25 | M |
| 203 | Case of the Tea Cosy's Aunt–Anthony Gilbert | 1.75 | 3.50 | 5.25 | M |
| 204 | Case in the Clinic–E.C.R. Lorac | 1.75 | 3.50 | 5.25 | M |
| 205 | Ironsides Smashes Through–Victor Gunn | 1.75 | 3.50 | 5.25 | M |
| 206 | Darkness Falls from the Air–Nigel Balchin | 1.75 | 3.50 | 5.25 | |
| 207 | Murder Gone Mad–Philip MacDonald | 1.75 | 3.50 | 5.25 | M |
| 208 | McSorley's Wonderful Saloon–Joseph Mitchell | 1.75 | 3.50 | 5.25 | F |
| 210 | Congo Song–Stuart Cloete | 3.00 | 6.00 | 9.00 | A |
| 211 | The Stars Are Dark–Peter Cheyney; aka London Spy Murders | 1.75 | 3.50 | 5.25 | M |
| 213 | Literary Lapses–Stephen Leacock | 1.75 | 3.50 | 5.25 | H |
| 214 | 24 Hours Leave–Renee Shann | 1.75 | 3.50 | 5.25 | R |
| 215 | Stone of Chastity–Margery Sharp | 1.75 | 3.50 | 5.25 | R |
| 216 | You Can't Keep the Change–Peter Cheyney | 1.75 | 3.50 | 5.25 | M |
| 217 | Woman in Red–Anthony Gilbert | 1.75 | 3.50 | 5.25 | M |
| 218 | Bluewater Landing–Wallace Q. Reid | 1.75 | 3.50 | 5.25 | W |
| 219 | Dangerous Curves–Peter Cheyney; aka Callaghan | 1.75 | 3.50 | 5.25 | M |
| 220 | From This Day Forward–Elswyth Thane | 1.75 | 3.50 | 5.25 | R |
| 221 | All Fall Down–L.A.G. Strong | 1.75 | 3.50 | 5.25 | M |
| 222 | The Sixteenth Stair–E.C.R. Lorac | 1.75 | 3.50 | 5.25 | M |
| 223 | Sunshine Sketches of a Little Town–Stephen Leacock | 1.75 | 3.50 | 5.25 | H |
| 224 | The Nutmeg Tree–Margery Sharp | 1.75 | 3.50 | 5.25 | |
| 225 | The Commandos–Elliott Arnold | 1.75 | 3.50 | 5.25 | C |
| 226 | The New Sin–Helena Grose | 1.75 | 3.50 | 5.25 | R |
| 227 | Blonde for Danger–Berkeley Gray | 1.75 | 3.50 | 5.25 | M |
| 228 | The Noose–Philip MacDonald | 1.75 | 3.50 | 5.25 | M |
| 229 | 30 Days to Live–Anthony Gilbert | 1.75 | 3.50 | 5.25 | M |
| 230 | Shabby Tiger–Howard Spring; 1945 | 1.75 | 3.50 | 5.25 | |
| 231 | The Small Back Room–Nigel Balchin | 1.75 | 3.50 | 5.25 | |
| 232 | No Light Came On–Alice Campbell | 1.75 | 3.50 | 5.25 | M |
| 233 | Prowl No More Lady–James Warren | 1.75 | 3.50 | 5.25 | M |
| 234 | The Morning After–Helena Grose | 1.75 | 3.50 | 5.25 | R |
| 235 | Sealed Room Murder–Rupert Penny | 1.75 | 3.50 | 5.25 | M |
| 236 | Dead on the Track–John Rhode | 1.75 | 3.50 | 5.25 | M |
| 237 | And Death Came Too–Richard Hull | 1.75 | 3.50 | 5.25 | M |
| 238 | She Fell among Actors–James Warren | 1.75 | 3.50 | 5.25 | M |
| 239 | Room Number Six–J. Jefferson Farjeon | 1.75 | 3.50 | 5.25 | M |
| 240 | Farewell to the Admiral–Peter Cheyney | 1.75 | 3.50 | 5.25 | M |
| 241 | Dark Sunlight–Jennifer Ames | 1.75 | 3.50 | 5.25 | M |
| 242 | Death Came Softly–E.C.R. Lorac | 1.75 | 3.50 | 5.25 | M |
| 243 | Dishonour among Thieves–David Hume | 1.75 | 3.50 | 5.25 | M |
| 244 | The Gay Desperado–Berkeley Gray | 1.75 | 3.50 | 5.25 | M |
| 245 | Dames Don't Care–Peter Cheyney | 1.75 | 3.50 | 5.25 | M |
| 246 | Yeoman's Hospital–Helen Ashton | 1.75 | 3.50 | 5.25 | |
| 247 | Live Dangerously–Axel Kielland | 1.75 | 3.50 | 5.25 | M |
| 248 | Hard Facts–Howard Spring; 1946 | 1.75 | 3.50 | 5.25 | A |
| 249 | Adventures of Huckleberry Finn–Mark Twain; 1946 | 1.75 | 3.50 | 5.25 | |
| 250 | Green Mask–J. Jefferson Farjeon | 1.75 | 3.50 | 5.25 | M |

| | | V/Good | Fine | N/Mint | |
|---|---|---|---|---|---|
| 251 | Rachel Rosing–Howard Spring | 1.75 | 3.50 | 5.25 | |
| 252 | The Three Corpse Trick–Miles Burton | 1.75 | 3.50 | 5.25 | M |
| 253 | Another Little Drink–Peter Cheyney | 1.75 | 3.50 | 5.25 | M |
| 254 | Family Orchestra–Mary Howard | 1.75 | 3.50 | 5.25 | R |
| 255 | The Devil Man–Edgar Wallace | 1.75 | 3.50 | 5.25 | M |
| 256 | Night of Flame–Dyson Carter | 1.75 | 3.50 | 5.25 | R |
| 257 | Tobacco Road–Erskine Caldwell | 2.50 | 5.00 | 7.50 | |
| 258 | Check Mate to Murder–E.C.R. Lorac | 1.75 | 3.50 | 5.25 | M |
| 259 | Man Who Was Not There–Ethel Lina White | 1.75 | 3.50 | 5.25 | M |
| 260 | Reluctant Millionaire–Maysie Greig | 1.75 | 3.50 | 5.25 | R |
| 261 | This Is the House–Shelley Smith | 1.75 | 3.50 | 5.25 | M |
| 262 | Death at the Door–Anthony Gilbert | 1.75 | 3.50 | 5.25 | M |
| 263 | Restless Beauty–Jenifer Ames | 1.75 | 3.50 | 5.25 | R |
| 264 | Turning Wheels–Stuart Cloete | 1.75 | 3.50 | 5.25 | A |
| 265 | Timber–Roderick Haig-Brown | 1.75 | 3.50 | 5.25 | |
| 266 | The Tall Man–John Ross | 1.75 | 3.50 | 5.25 | M |
| 267 | Cavalier Conquest–Berkely Gray | 1.75 | 3.50 | 5.25 | M |
| 268 | The Smiler with the Knife–Nicholas Blake | 1.75 | 3.50 | 5.25 | M |
| 269 | Girl about Town–Renee Shann | 1.75 | 3.50 | 5.25 | R |
| 270 | Man Killer–Evelyn Winch | 1.75 | 3.50 | 5.25 | |
| 271 | The Dead Man Laughs–Victor Gunn (Berkeley Gray) | 1.75 | 3.50 | 5.25 | M |
| 272 | Too Dangerous to Live–David Hume | 1.75 | 3.50 | 5.25 | M |
| 273 | Miss Dilly Says No–Theodore Pratt | 1.75 | 3.50 | 5.25 | |
| 274 | Men Die at Cyprus Lodge–John Rhode | 1.75 | 3.50 | 5.25 | M |
| 275 | They See in Darkness–Ethel Lina White | 1.75 | 3.50 | 5.25 | M |
| 276 | The Doctor of the North–Wallace Q. Reid | 1.75 | 3.50 | 5.25 | A |
| 277 | They Never Say When–Peter Cheyney | 1.75 | 3.50 | 5.25 | M |
| 278 | A Lady Fell in Love–Anne Maybury | 1.75 | 3.50 | 5.25 | R |
| 279 | Case of the Stolen Bridegroom–Herbert Adams | 1.75 | 3.50 | 5.25 | |
| 280 | The Girl with a Million–Maysie Greig | 1.75 | 3.50 | 5.25 | R |
| 281 | The Writing on the Wall–Herbert Adams | 1.75 | 3.50 | 5.25 | M |
| 282 | The Scarlet Button–Anthony Gilbert | 1.75 | 3.50 | 5.25 | M |
| 283 | Murder by Matchlight–E.C.R. Lorac | 1.75 | 3.50 | 5.25 | M |
| 284 | The House of Shadows–J. Jefferson Farjeon | 1.75 | 3.50 | 5.25 | M |
| 285 | Cross Roads–Renee Shann | 1.75 | 3.50 | 5.25 | R |
| 286 | Meet the Dragon–David Hume | 1.75 | 3.50 | 5.25 | M |
| 287 | Cowboy Say Your Prayers–Will Ermine | 1.75 | 3.50 | 5.25 | W |
| 288 | Step in the Dark–Ethel Lina White | 1.75 | 3.50 | 5.25 | M |
| 289 | Early Morning Murder–Miles Burton | 1.75 | 3.50 | 5.25 | M |
| 290 | Favorite Wife–May Edginton | 1.75 | 3.50 | 5.25 | |
| 291 | Convict 1066–Berkeley Gray | 1.75 | 3.50 | 5.25 | M |
| 292 | Queen's Folly–Elswyth Thane | 1.75 | 3.50 | 5.25 | A |
| 293 | Poison Ivy–Peter Cheyney | 1.75 | 3.50 | 5.25 | M |
| 294 | Island Alert–J.N. Walsh | 1.75 | 3.50 | 5.25 | M |
| 295 | Nurse's Aide–Lucy Agnes Hancock | 1.75 | 3.50 | 5.25 | R |
| 296 | Born in Paradise–Armine Von Tempski | 1.75 | 3.50 | 5.25 | B |
| 297 | Nine to Five–Harvey Smith | 1.75 | 3.50 | 5.25 | |
| 298 | Left Handed Death–Richard Hull | 1.75 | 3.50 | 5.25 | M |
| 299 | Short Grass Range–Ranger Lee | 1.75 | 3.50 | 5.25 | W |
| 300 | Died in the Wool–Ngaio Marsh | 1.75 | 3.50 | 5.25 | M |
| 301 | With Bated Breath–Alice Campbell | 1.75 | 3.50 | 5.25 | M |
| 302 | Experiment in Love–May Edington | 1.75 | 3.50 | 5.25 | R |
| 303 | Dangerous Honeymoon–Axel Kielland | 1.75 | 3.50 | 5.25 | M |
| 304 | The Flowering Thorn–Margery Sharp | 1.75 | 3.50 | 5.25 | R |
| 305 | Lady Incognito–J.M. Walsh | 1.75 | 3.50 | 5.25 | M |
| 306 | Rattlesnake–Wade Smith | 1.75 | 3.50 | 5.25 | W |
| 307 | Cottonwood Creek–Gary Marshall | 1.75 | 3.50 | 5.25 | W |
| 308 | Her Heart in Her Throat–Ethel Lina White | 1.75 | 3.50 | 5.25 | M |
| 309 | Valley before Me–Ranger Lee | 1.75 | 3.50 | 5.25 | W |
| 310 | Thorn-Apple Tree–Grace Campbell | 1.75 | 3.50 | 5.25 | A |
| 311 | The Third Victim–J. Jefferson Farjeon | 1.75 | 3.50 | 5.25 | M |
| 312 | Table for Two–Maysie Greig | 1.75 | 3.50 | 5.25 | R |
| 313 | Dutchess Hotspur–Rosamond Marshall | 1.75 | 3.50 | 5.25 | |
| 314 | A Dream Come True–Pamela A. Wynne; 1947 | 1.75 | 3.50 | 5.25 | R |
| 315 | The Safebridge–Frances Parkinson Keyes | 1.75 | 3.50 | 5.25 | A |
| 316 | Dark Hero–Peter Cheyney | 1.75 | 3.50 | 5.25 | M |
| 317 | Guns of Arizona–Gary Marshall | 1.75 | 3.50 | 5.25 | W |
| 318 | Battle at Black Mesa–Wade Smith | 1.75 | 3.50 | 5.25 | W |
| 319 | True By the Sun–Lida Larrimore | 1.75 | 3.50 | 5.25 | R |
| 320 | Overture to Trouble–Stephen Maddock | 1.75 | 3.50 | 5.25 | M |
| 321 | The Dangerous Age–Maysie Greig | 1.75 | 3.50 | 5.25 | R |
| 322 | Heading for A Wreath–David Hume | 1.75 | 3.50 | 5.25 | M |

| | V/Good | Fine | N/Mint | |
|---|---|---|---|---|

| | | V/Good | Fine | N/Mint |
|---|---|---|---|---|

COLLINS WHITE CIRCLE, *continued*

| No. | Title | V/Good | Fine | N/Mint | |
|---|---|---|---|---|---|
| 482 | Cabbagetown–Hugh Garner | 2.50 | 5.00 | 7.50 | |
| 483 | If I Live to Dine–Hillary Waugh; aka Madam Will Not Dine Tonight | 1.75 | 3.50 | 5.25 | M |
| 484 | City Doctor–Thomas Stone | 1.75 | 3.50 | 5.25 | R |
| 485 | Spot the Lady–Lester Powell | 1.75 | 3.50 | 5.25 | M |
| 486 | Dare-devil Conquest–Berkeley Gray | 1.75 | 3.50 | 5.25 | M |
| 487 | Moving Ahead on Your Job–Richard P. Calhoon | 1.75 | 3.50 | 5.25 | NF |
| 488 | Lady Behave–Peter Cheyney | 1.75 | 3.50 | 5.25 | M |
| 489 | Always Elizabeth–Carol Gaye | 1.75 | 3.50 | 5.25 | R |
| 490 | Flash-Hold for Murder–Paul Whelton | 1.75 | 3.50 | 5.25 | M |
| 492 | Private Line–Stephen Maddock | 1.75 | 3.50 | 5.25 | M |
| 494 | She'll Love You Dead–Charles Franklin | 1.75 | 3.50 | 5.25 | M |
| 496 | Murder Can't Stop–W.T. Ballard | 1.75 | 3.50 | 5.25 | M |
| 497 | Danger by my Side–Allan MacKinnon | 1.75 | 3.50 | 5.25 | M |
| 498 | No Tears for Hilda–Andrew Garve | 1.75 | 3.50 | 5.25 | M |
| 499 | Die in the Dark–Anthony Gilbert; aka The Missing Widow | 1.75 | 3.50 | 5.25 | M |
| 500 | Delayed Harvest–Rona Randall | 1.75 | 3.50 | 5.25 | M |
| 501 | Special Delivery–Val Gielgud | 1.75 | 3.50 | 5.25 | M |
| 502 | Bow to the Storm–Mary Howard | 1.75 | 3.50 | 5.25 | R |
| 503 | Time to Kill–J.M. Walsh | 1.75 | 3.50 | 5.25 | M |
| 505 | Dead Lion–John & Emery Bonnett | 1.75 | 3.50 | 5.25 | M |
| 506 | No Duty on a Corpse–Max Murray | 1.75 | 3.50 | 5.25 | M |
| 507 | Young Doctor Kenway–Rona Randall | 1.75 | 3.50 | 5.25 | R |
| 508 | No Mask for Murder–Andrew Garve; 1951 | 1.75 | 3.50 | 5.25 | M |
| 509 | The Ranch in the Canyon–Ranger Lee | 1.75 | 3.50 | 5.25 | W |
| 510 | Dark Bahama–Peter Cheyney | 1.75 | 3.50 | 5.25 | M |
| 511 | The Sharon Women–Anne Maybury | 1.75 | 3.50 | 5.25 | R |
| 512 | Seven Dawns to Death–Berkeley Gray | 1.75 | 3.50 | 5.25 | M |
| 513 | Party of Eight–Laurence Meynell | 1.75 | 3.50 | 5.25 | M |
| 514 | The White South–Hammond Innes | 1.75 | 3.50 | 5.25 | A |
| 515 | Cat and Mouse–Christina Brand | 1.75 | 3.50 | 5.25 | M |
| 516 | Crime on Cote Des Neiges–David Montrose | 1.75 | 3.50 | 5.25 | M |
| 517 | Present Reconning–Hugh Garner | 1.75 | 3.50 | 5.25 | M |
| 518 | Shoot-Up at Two Rivers–Chester Wills | 1.75 | 3.50 | 5.25 | W |
| 519 | Man with a Calico Face–Shelley Smith | 1.75 | 3.50 | 5.25 | M |
| 520 | Golden Future–Lyndon Snow | 1.75 | 3.50 | 5.25 | |
| 521 | One Night to Kill–Charles Franklin | 1.75 | 3.50 | 5.25 | M |
| 522 | Uninvited Corpse–Paul Whelton | 1.75 | 3.50 | 5.25 | M |
| 523 | A Murder Is Announced–Agatha Christie | 1.75 | 3.50 | 5.25 | M |
| 524 | Which I Never–L.A.G. Strong | 1.75 | 3.50 | 5.25 | M |
| 525 | Murder in Hollywood–W.T. Ballard | 1.75 | 3.50 | 5.25 | M |
| 526 | Accident by Design–E.C.R. Lorac; 1951 | 1.75 | 3.50 | 5.25 | M |
| 527 | Operation Conquest–Berkeley Gray; 1952 | 1.75 | 3.50 | 5.25 | M |
| 528 | Lovely You–Kate Aitken | 1.75 | 3.50 | 5.25 | |
| 529 | Barometer Rising–Hugh MacLennan | 1.75 | 3.50 | 5.25 | |
| 530 | The Last Appointment–Hartley Howard | 1.75 | 3.50 | 5.25 | M |
| 531 | Pocketful of Canada–ed. John D. Robins | 1.75 | 3.50 | 5.25 | |
| 533 | The Sleeping Bacchus–Hillary St. George Saunders | 1.75 | 3.50 | 5.25 | M |
| 534 | Turvey: A Picaresque Novel–Earle Birney | 1.75 | 3.50 | 5.25 | |
| 535 | Ladies Won't Wait–Peter Cheyney; aka Cocktails and the Killer | 1.75 | 3.50 | 5.25 | M |
| 536 | Below the Border–Wade Smith | 1.75 | 3.50 | 5.25 | W |
| 537 | Goose Feathers–George Digby | 1.75 | 3.50 | 5.25 | |
| 539 | Murder over Dorval–David Montrose | 1.75 | 3.50 | 5.25 | M |
| 540 | Two Solitudes–Hugh MacLennan | 1.75 | 3.50 | 5.25 | |
| 541 | They Came to Bagdad–Agatha Christie | 1.75 | 3.50 | 5.25 | M |
| 542 | Maid for Murder–Charles Franklin | 1.75 | 3.50 | 5.25 | M |
| 543 | The Yellow Sweater and Other Stories–Hugh Garner | 3.00 | 6.00 | 9.00 | |
| 544 | The Angry Mountain–Hammond Innes | 1.75 | 3.50 | 5.25 | A |
| 545 | Devilman–Edgar Wallace | 1.75 | 3.50 | 5.25 | M |

## (COLUMBIA BROADCASTING SYSTEM)
## Columbia Broadcasting System

| | | V/Good | Fine | N/Mint | |
|---|---|---|---|---|---|
| nn | From Pearl Harbor into Tokyo–orig. 1945 | 2.00 | 4.00 | 6.00 | NF |
| nn | From D-Day through Victory in Europe–eds. Paul Hollister & Robert Strunsky; orig. 1945 | 2.00 | 4.00 | 6.00 | NF |

# COMET BOOKS
## Pocket Books, Inc.
### Most digest size (See also Pocket Book Jr.)

| | | V/Good | Fine | N/Mint | |
|---|---|---|---|---|---|
| 1 | Wagons Westward–Armstrong Sperry; 1948 | 1.00 | 2.00 | 3.00 | W |
| 2 | Batter Up–Jackson Scholz | 1.00 | 2.00 | 3.00 | S |
| 3 | Star Spangled Summer–Janet Lambert | 1.00 | 2.00 | 3.00 | R |
| 4 | Tawny–Thomas C. Hinkle; standard paperback size | 1.50 | 3.00 | 4.50 | A |
| 5 | 300 Tricks You Can Do–Howard Thurston | 1.00 | 2.00 | 3.00 | NF |
| 6 | Peggy Covers the News–Emma Bugbee | 1.00 | 2.00 | 3.00 | |
| 7 | Winged Mystery–Alan Gregg | 1.00 | 2.00 | 3.00 | M |
| 8 | Your Own Joke Book–Gertrude Crampton | 1.00 | 2.00 | 3.00 | H |
| 9 | Sue Barton, Student Nurse–Helen Boylston; standard paperback size | 1.00 | 2.00 | 3.00 | |
| 10 | The Tatooed Man–Howard Pease | 1.00 | 2.00 | 3.00 | A |
| 11 | Skycruiser–Howard M. Brier | 1.00 | 2.00 | 3.00 | |
| 12 | The Spanish Cave–Geoffrey Household | 1.00 | 2.00 | 3.00 | M |
| 13 | The Green Turtle Mystery–Ellery Queen Jr; 1949; c-Powers | 1.50 | 3.00 | 4.50 | M |
| 14 | Silver–Thomas C. Hinkle; c-Powers | 1.50 | 3.00 | 4.50 | W |
| 15 | Strangers in the Desert–Alice Russell | 1.00 | 2.00 | 3.00 | |
| 16 | The Southpaw–Donal Hamilton Haines | 1.00 | 2.00 | 3.00 | S |
| 17 | Bat Boy of the Giants–Garth Garreau | 1.00 | 2.00 | 3.00 | S |
| 18 | Big Red–Jim Kjelgaard | 1.50 | 3.00 | 4.50 | |
| 19 | The Mystery of the Empty Room–Augusta Seaman | 1.00 | 2.00 | 3.00 | M |
| 20 | Husky: Co-Pilot of the Pilgrim–Rutherford Montgomery | 1.00 | 2.00 | 3.00 | |
| 21 | Starbuck Valley Winter–Roderick Haig-Brown | 1.00 | 2.00 | 3.00 | |
| 22 | Hobby Horse Hill–Lavinia R. Davis | 1.00 | 2.00 | 3.00 | |
| 23 | Your Own Party Book–Gertrude Crampton | 1.00 | 2.00 | 3.00 | NF |
| 24 | Gray Wolf–Rutherford Montgomery | 1.00 | 2.00 | 3.00 | |
| 25 | Fighting Coach–Jackson Scholz; 1949; c-Powers | 1.50 | 3.00 | 4.50 | |
| 26 | Midnight–Rutherford Montgomery | 1.00 | 2.00 | 3.00 | |
| 27 | Forest Patrol–Jim Kjelgaard | 1.00 | 2.00 | 3.00 | |
| 28 | Scarface–Andre Norton | 3.50 | 7.00 | 10.50 | A |
| 29 | Lightning on Ice–Philip Harkins | 1.00 | 2.00 | 3.00 | S |
| 30 | No Other White Men–Julia Davis; interior illus. by Powers | 1.50 | 3.00 | 4.50 | |
| 31 | Indian Paint–Glen Balch | 1.00 | 2.00 | 3.00 | |
| 32 | Puppy Stakes–Betty Cavanna | 1.00 | 2.00 | 3.00 | |
| 33 | Long Wharf–Howard Pease | 1.00 | 2.00 | 3.00 | A |
| 34 | Fun With Puzzles–Joseph Leeming | 1.50 | 3.00 | 4.50 | NF |

# CORINTH (REGENCY) SUSPENSE
## Corinth Publications, Inc.

| | | V/Good | Fine | N/Mint | |
|---|---|---|---|---|---|
| CR101 | Phantom Detective/The Vampire Murders–Robert Wallace; 1965 | 4.00 | 8.00 | 12.00 | M |
| CR102 | Phantom Detective/The Dancing Doll Murders–Robert Wallace | 4.00 | 8.00 | 12.00 | M |
| CR103 | Phantom Detective/The Beast-King Murders–Robert Wallace | 4.00 | 8.00 | 12.00 | M |
| CR104 | Phantom Detective/Tycoon of Crime–Robert Wallace | 4.00 | 8.00 | 12.00 | M |
| CR105 | Phantom Detective/The Broadway Murders–Robert Wallace | 4.00 | 8.00 | 12.00 | M |
| CR106 | Phantom Detective/The Daggers of Kali–Robert Wallace | 4.00 | 8.00 | 12.00 | M |
| CR107 | Phantom Detective/Murder under the Big Top–Robert Wallace | 4.00 | 8.00 | 12.00 | M |
| CR108 | Phantom Detective/The Trail of Death–Robert Wallace | 4.00 | 8.00 | 12.00 | M |
| CR109 | Phantom Detective/Yellow Shadows of Death–Robert Wallace | 4.00 | 8.00 | 12.00 | M |
| CR110 | Phantom Detective/Murder Trail–Robert Wallace | 4.00 | 8.00 | 12.00 | M |
| CR111 | Phantom Detective/The Green Glare Murders–Robert Wallace | 4.00 | 8.00 | 12.00 | M |
| CR112 | Phantom Detective/Fangs of Murder–Robert Wallace | 4.00 | 8.00 | 12.00 | M |

## CORINTH (REGENCY) SUSPENSE, *continued*

| No. | Title | V/Good | Fine | N/Mint | |
|---|---|---|---|---|---|
| CR113 | Phantom Detective/The Curio Murders–Robert Wallace | 4.00 | 8.00 | 12.00 | M |
| CR114 | Phantom Detective/Murder Stalks a Billion–Robert Wallace | 4.00 | 8.00 | 12.00 | M |
| CR115 | Phantom Detective/Murder Money–Robert Wallace | 4.00 | 8.00 | 12.00 | M |
| CR116 | Operator No. 5/Legions of the Death Master–Curtis Steele | 5.00 | 10.00 | 15.00 | A |
| CR117 | Phantom Detective/Death Glow–Robert Wallace | 4.00 | 8.00 | 12.00 | M |
| CR118 | Doctor Death/12 Must Die–Zorro | 6.00 | 12.00 | 18.00 | HO |
| CR119 | Phantom Detective/Stones of Satan–Robert Wallace | 4.00 | 8.00 | 12.00 | M |
| CR120 | Operator No. 5/The Army of the Dead–Curtis Steele | 5.00 | 10.00 | 15.00 | A |
| CR121 | Doctor Death/The Gray Creatures–Zorro | 6.00 | 12.00 | 18.00 | HO |
| CR122 | Secret Agent X/The Torture Trust–Brant House | 5.00 | 10.00 | 15.00 | A |
| CR123 | Phantom Detective/The Melody Murders–Robert Wallace | 4.00 | 8.00 | 12.00 | M |
| CR124 | Operator No. 5/The Invisible Empire–Curtis Steele | 5.00 | 10.00 | 15.00 | A |
| CR125 | Doctor Death/The Shriveling Murders–Zorro | 6.00 | 12.00 | 18.00 | HO |
| CR126 | Secret Agent X/Servants of the Skull–Brant House | 5.00 | 10.00 | 15.00 | A |
| CR127 | Phantom Detective/The Uniformed Killers–Robert Wallace | 4.00 | 8.00 | 12.00 | M |
| CR128 | Operator No. 5/Master of Broken Men–Curtis Steele | 5.00 | 10.00 | 15.00 | A |
| CR129 | Doctor Death/Doctor Death and Other Terror Tales–Zorro | 6.00 | 12.00 | 18.00 | HO |
| CR130 | Secret Agent X/Curse of the Mandarin's Fan–Brant House | 5.00 | 10.00 | 15.00 | A |
| CR131 | Phantom Detective/The Forty Thieves–Robert Wallace | 4.00 | 8.00 | 12.00 | M |
| CR132 | Operator No. 5/Hosts of the Flaming Death–Curtis Steele | 5.00 | 10.00 | 15.00 | A |
| CR133 | Dusty Ayres/Black Lightning–Robert Sidney Bowen | 4.00 | 8.00 | 12.00 | C |
| CR134 | Secret Agent X/City of the Living Dead–Brant House | 5.00 | 10.00 | 15.00 | A |
| CR135 | Phantom Detective/Death under Contract–Robert Wallace | 4.00 | 8.00 | 12.00 | M |
| CR136 | Operator No. 5/Blood Reign of the Dictator–Curtis Steele | 5.00 | 10.00 | 15.00 | A |
| CR137 | Dusty Ayres/Crimson Doom–Robert Sidney Bowen | 4.00 | 8.00 | 12.00 | C |
| CR138 | Secret Agent X/The Death-Torch Terror–Brant House | 5.00 | 10.00 | 15.00 | A |
| CR139 | Phantom Detective/The Corpse Parade–Robert Wallace | 4.00 | 8.00 | 12.00 | M |
| CR140 | Operator No. 5/March of the Flame Marauders–Curtis Steele | 5.00 | 10.00 | 15.00 | A |
| CR141 | Dusty Ayres/Purple Tornado–Robert Sidney Bowen | 4.00 | 8.00 | 12.00 | C |
| CR142 | Secret Agent X/Octopus of Crime–Brant House | 5.00 | 10.00 | 15.00 | A |
| CR143 | The House of Living Death and Other Terror Tales–anthology | 6.00 | 12.00 | 18.00 | HO |
| CR144 | Operator No. 5/Invasion of the Yellow Warlords–Curtis Steele | 5.00 | 10.00 | 15.00 | A |
| CR145 | Dusty Ayres/The Telsa Raiders–Robert Sidney Bowen | 4.00 | 8.00 | 12.00 | C |
| CR146 | Secret Agent X/The Sinister Scourge–Brant House | 5.00 | 10.00 | 15.00 | A |
| CR147 | Death's Loving Arms and Other Terror Tales–anthology | 6.00 | 12.00 | 18.00 | HO |
| CR148 | Dusty Ayres/Black Invaders vs. the Battle Birds–Robert Sidney Bowen | 4.00 | 8.00 | 12.00 | C |

# CREST BOOKS
## Fawcett Publications, Inc.

| No. | Title | V/Good | Fine | N/Mint | |
|---|---|---|---|---|---|
| 114 | Best Cartoons from True; 1955 | 2.50 | 5.00 | 7.50 | H |
| 115 | Run, Thief, Run–Frank Gruber | 1.50 | 3.00 | 4.50 | M |
| 116 | Top Hand with a Gun–Harry Sinclair Drago | 1.00 | 2.00 | 3.00 | W |
| 117 | Stranger at the Door–Gil Meynier | 1.00 | 2.00 | 3.00 | |

| No. | Title | V/Good | Fine | N/Mint | |
|---|---|---|---|---|---|
| 118 | The Best from Captain Billy's Whiz Bang–Lester Grady | 4.00 | 8.00 | 12.00 | H |
| 119 | Love in Dishevelment–David Greenhood | 1.00 | 2.00 | 3.00 | |
| 120 | Avenger from Texas–Will Ermine | 1.00 | 2.00 | 3.00 | W |
| 121 | Affair–Emily Hahn | 1.00 | 2.00 | 3.00 | |
| 122 | A Journey with Love–Denys Val Baker; 1956 | 1.00 | 2.00 | 3.00 | |
| 123 | Riders by Night–Nelson Nye | 1.00 | 2.00 | 3.00 | W |
| s124 | The Golden Hussy–Octavus Roy Cohen | 1.00 | 2.00 | 3.00 | |
| 125 | So Sweet, So Cruel–Julian Farren | 1.00 | 2.00 | 3.00 | |
| 126 | Captive in the Night–Donald Stokes | 1.00 | 2.00 | 3.00 | |
| 127 | The Education of a French Model–Kiki | 1.00 | 2.00 | 3.00 | E |
| 128 | The Thundering Trail–Norman A. Fox; c-Gross | 1.00 | 2.00 | 3.00 | W |
| s129 | Son of the Giant–Stuart Engstrand | 1.00 | 2.00 | 3.00 | |
| 130 | Jadie–I.S. Young; aka Jadie Greenway | 1.00 | 2.00 | 3.00 | E |
| 131 | Gunsmoke on the Mesa–Davis Dresser | 1.00 | 2.00 | 3.00 | W |
| 132 | Lie Down, Killer–Richard S. Prather | 1.00 | 2.00 | 3.00 | M |
| s133 | All My Sins–Norbert Estey | 1.00 | 2.00 | 3.00 | E |
| 134 | Destination, Danger–William Colt MacDonald | 1.00 | 2.00 | 3.00 | W |
| 135 | A Man's Affair–Dawn Powell | 1.00 | 2.00 | 3.00 | |
| 136 | Down through the Night–Julius Fast | 1.00 | 2.00 | 3.00 | |
| 137 | War on the Range–Norman A. Fox | 1.00 | 2.00 | 3.00 | W |
| 138 | The Memoirs of Maisie–Maude Hutchins; 1956 | 1.00 | 2.00 | 3.00 | |
| 139 | So Nude, So Dead–Richard Marsten | 2.00 | 4.00 | 6.00 | M |
| s140 | Of Sin and the Flesh–Robert De Vries | 1.00 | 2.00 | 3.00 | |
| 141 | Sex without Tears–Norman Lockridge & Virgil Partch | 1.00 | 2.00 | 3.00 | H |
| 142 | Dagger of Flesh–Richard S. Prather | 1.00 | 2.00 | 3.00 | M |
| s143 | Hypnotism and the Power Within–S.J. VanPelt | 1.00 | 2.00 | 3.00 | NF |
| s144 | Come Desire Me–Anton Fereva | 1.00 | 2.00 | 3.00 | |
| s145 | You Can Live after Death–Harold Sherman | 1.00 | 2.00 | 3.00 | |
| 146 | Code of the Gun–Gordon D. Shirreffs | 1.00 | 2.00 | 3.00 | W |
| 147 | And the Girl Screamed–Gil Brewer | 2.00 | 4.00 | 6.00 | E |
| s148 | My First Two Thousand Years–Paul Eldridge & George Sylvester Viereck | 1.50 | 3.00 | 4.50 | F |
| 149 | The Comanche Scalp–William Colt MacDonald | 1.00 | 2.00 | 3.00 | W |
| 150 | The Rule of the Pagbeasts–J.T. McIntosh; aka The Fittest | 2.00 | 4.00 | 6.00 | SF |
| 151 | Saturday Night Town–Harry Whittington | 2.00 | 4.00 | 6.00 | |
| 152 | Ambush at Buffalo Wallow–T.D. Allen | 1.00 | 2.00 | 3.00 | W |
| 153 | The Golden Lure–Michael Barrett | 1.00 | 2.00 | 3.00 | |
| 154 | Six-gun Vengeance–Dudley Dean | 1.00 | 2.00 | 3.00 | W |
| 155 | Crazy Cartoons by VIP–Virgil Partch | 1.50 | 3.00 | 4.50 | H |
| s156 | The Trumpet Unblown–William Hoffman; 1957 | 1.00 | 2.00 | 3.00 | W |
| d157 | A Walk on the Wild Side–Nelson Algren | 2.50 | 5.00 | 7.50 | JD |
| 158 | Badge for a Gunfighter–Clair Huffaker | 1.50 | 3.00 | 4.50 | W |
| 159 | Office Laffs–Charles Preston | 1.50 | 3.00 | 4.50 | H |
| d160 | A Dream of Kings–Davis Grubb | 1.00 | 2.00 | 3.00 | |
| 161 | Last Stand at Anvil Pass–Merle Constiner | 1.00 | 2.00 | 3.00 | W |
| 162 | Seawife–J.M. Scott; movie tie-in | 1.00 | 2.00 | 3.00 | |
| s163 | The Empire–and Martin Brill–George deMare; 1957 | 1.00 | 2.00 | 3.00 | |
| 164 | Gunswift–Stewart Gordon | 1.00 | 2.00 | 3.00 | |

*Crest 151, Crest 187, Crest 248.*

**CREST BOOKS,** *continued*

| | | V/Good | Fine | N/Mint | |
| --- | --- | --- | --- | --- | --- |
| 165 | The Right to Love–Markoosha Fischer | 1.00 | 2.00 | 3.00 | |
| 166 | The Conquering Prince–Gardner F. Fox | 1.50 | 3.00 | 4.50 | A |
| 167 | Badman–Clair Huffaker; movie tie-in | 1.50 | 3.00 | 4.50 | W |
| s168 | Way to Happiness–Fulton J. Sheen | 1.00 | 2.00 | 3.00 | |
| 169 | Evil in the Night–Erico Verissimo | 1.00 | 2.00 | 3.00 | |
| 170 | Fury Trail–Giles A. Lutz | 1.00 | 2.00 | 3.00 | W |
| s171 | Strangers in Paradise–Howard Otway | 1.00 | 2.00 | 3.00 | |
| 172 | Case of the Brunette Bombshell–Hillary Waugh | 1.00 | 2.00 | 3.00 | M |
| 173 | Little Tramp–Gil Brewer | 2.00 | 4.00 | 6.00 | E |
| 174 | Valley of Violent Men–Lewis B. Patten | 1.00 | 2.00 | 3.00 | W |
| s175 | The Loving and the Lost–James Lord | 1.00 | 2.00 | 3.00 | |
| d176 | Tom Jones–Henry Fielding | 1.00 | 2.00 | 3.00 | |
| 177 | Border Renegade–Dudley Dean | 1.00 | 2.00 | 3.00 | W |
| s178 | The Spiked Heel–Richard Marsten | 2.00 | 4.00 | 6.00 | |
| 179 | Walk with Evil–Robert Wilder | 1.00 | 2.00 | 3.00 | |
| d180 | According to Hoyle–Richard Frey | 1.00 | 2.00 | 3.00 | NF |
| 181 | Gun the Man Down–Giles A. Lutz | 1.00 | 2.00 | 3.00 | W |
| s182 | Seed of Violence–Williams Forrest | 1.00 | 2.00 | 3.00 | |
| s183 | The Home Book of Italian Cooking–Angela Catanzaro | 1.00 | 2.00 | 3.00 | NF |
| s184 | City at World's End–Edmond Hamilton | 1.50 | 3.00 | 4.50 | SF |
| 185 | Top Gun–Gordon Donalds | 1.00 | 2.00 | 3.00 | W |
| t186 | The Heart Has Its Reasons–Duchess of Windsor | 1.00 | 2.00 | 3.00 | |
| 187 | Whisper Their Love–Valerie Taylor | 2.50 | 5.00 | 7.50 | E |
| s188 | Beyond Defeat–Hans Werner Richter; 1957 | 1.00 | 2.00 | 3.00 | |
| 189 | The Hell-Fire Kid–Steve Shannon | 1.00 | 2.00 | 3.00 | W |
| s190 | Sweepings–Lester Cohen | 1.00 | 2.00 | 3.00 | |
| 191 | A Dram of Poison–Charlotte Armstrong | 1.00 | 2.00 | 3.00 | M |
| 192 | Mantrap–Duane Yarnell | 1.00 | 2.00 | 3.00 | E |
| 193 | Rider from Thunder Mountain–Clair Huffaker | 1.50 | 3.00 | 4.50 | W |
| s194 | And Come Back a Man–John Bell Clayton | 1.00 | 2.00 | 3.00 | |
| 195 | Meet Morocco Jones–Jack Baynes | 1.50 | 3.00 | 4.50 | M |
| 196 | The New Crest Crossword Puzzle Book–James Freeman | 2.50 | 5.00 | 7.50 | NF |
| s197 | Five Tales from Tomorrow–T.E. Dikty | 1.00 | 2.00 | 3.00 | SF |
| 198 | West of Devil's Canyon–Richard Poole; 1958 | 1.00 | 2.00 | 3.00 | |
| d199 | Eastern Love–Edward Powys Mathers | 1.50 | 3.00 | 4.50 | |
| s200 | Gas-House McGinty–James T. Farrell | 1.00 | 2.00 | 3.00 | |
| s201 | The Hungry Years–Annabel Johnson | 1.00 | 2.00 | 3.00 | |
| t202 | Mandingo–Kyle Onstott | 1.00 | 2.00 | 3.00 | E |
| s203 | House in Shanghai–Emily Hahn | 1.00 | 2.00 | 3.00 | |
| s204 | The Home Book of French Cooking–Anita Abbott & Lisa Andors | 1.00 | 2.00 | 3.00 | NF |
| 205 | Texas Fury–John Callahan | 1.00 | 2.00 | 3.00 | W |
| 206 | Baby Moll–Steve Brackeen | 1.00 | 2.00 | 3.00 | |
| s207 | Off Limits–Hans Habe | 1.00 | 2.00 | 3.00 | |
| s208 | The Magnificent Rascal–Thomas Sancton | 1.00 | 2.00 | 3.00 | |
| s209 | The 27th Day–John Mantley | 1.50 | 3.00 | 4.50 | SF |
| 210 | Swamp Babe–Robert Faherty | 1.50 | 3.00 | 4.50 | E |
| 211 | High Hell–Steve Frazee | 1.50 | 3.00 | 4.50 | W |
| s212 | Night of Fire and Snow–Alfred Coppel; 1958 | 1.00 | 2.00 | 3.00 | |
| 213 | Did You Kill Mona Leeds?–John Roeburt; aka The Lunatic Time | 1.00 | 2.00 | 3.00 | M |
| s214 | Of Love Forbidden–Anna Elisabet Weirauch | 1.00 | 2.00 | 3.00 | |
| s215 | All Quiet on the Western Front–Erich Maria Remarque | 1.00 | 2.00 | 3.00 | |
| s216 | From the Earth to the Moon and Round the Moon–Jules Verne | 1.50 | 3.00 | 4.50 | SF |
| s217 | The Legion of the Damned–Sven Hassel | 1.00 | 2.00 | 3.00 | |
| s218 | A Fool There Was–John Manson | 1.00 | 2.00 | 3.00 | |
| 219 | Dr. Anders' Dilemma–Henry Lieferaut & Sylvia Lieferaut | 1.00 | 2.00 | 3.00 | |
| s220 | The Best of Balzac–Honore de Balzac | 1.00 | 2.00 | 3.00 | |
| s221 | Yanqui's Woman–George McKenna | 1.00 | 2.00 | 3.00 | |
| 222 | Posse from Hell–Clair Huffaker | 1.50 | 3.00 | 4.50 | W |
| s223 | How You Can Take Better Photos–Simon Nathan | 1.00 | 2.00 | 3.00 | NF |
| 224 | Hand of the Mafia–Jack Baynes | 1.00 | 2.00 | 3.00 | M |
| 225 | Root of Evil–James Cross | 1.00 | 2.00 | 3.00 | |
| s226 | Ralph 124C41 + –Hugo Gernsback | 2.00 | 4.00 | 6.00 | SF |
| s227 | The Pink Hotel–Patrick Dennis & Dorothy Erskine | 1.00 | 2.00 | 3.00 | |

| | | V/Good | Fine | N/Mint | |
| --- | --- | --- | --- | --- | --- |
| d228 | The Durable Fire–Howard Swiggett | 1.00 | 2.00 | 3.00 | |
| 229 | Wild–Gil Brewer | 2.00 | 4.00 | 6.00 | E |
| 230 | The Widow Wore Red–Richard Wormser | 1.00 | 2.00 | 3.00 | M |
| s231 | Awake Monique–Astrid Van Royen | 1.00 | 2.00 | 3.00 | |
| d232 | Blue Camellia–Frances Parkinson Keyes | 1.00 | 2.00 | 3.00 | |
| s233 | Small Town D.A.–Robert Traver | 1.00 | 2.00 | 3.00 | |
| 234 | The Peeping Tom Murders–Jack Baynes | 1.50 | 3.00 | 4.50 | M |
| 235 | The Red Sombrero–Nelson Nye | 1.00 | 2.00 | 3.00 | W |
| s236 | Stigma for Valor–Williams Forest | 1.00 | 2.00 | 3.00 | |
| s237 | Ten Seconds to Hell–Lawrence Bachmann; movie tie-in | 1.00 | 2.00 | 3.00 | |
| 238 | The Vengeful Virgin–Gil Brewer; 1958 | 2.00 | 4.00 | 6.00 | E |
| 239 | Cartoon Laffs from True–Bill McIntyre | 1.00 | 2.00 | 3.00 | H |
| s240 | The Best of Crunch and Des–Philip Wylie; TV tie-in | 1.00 | 2.00 | 3.00 | |
| s241 | The Power of Positive Living–Douglas Lurton | 1.00 | 2.00 | 3.00 | NF |
| 242 | The Wind River Kid–Will Cook | 1.00 | 2.00 | 3.00 | W |
| s243 | The Dangerous Games–Tereska Torres | 1.00 | 2.00 | 3.00 | |
| s244 | The Unforgiven–J. Edward Leithead; movie tie-in | 2.00 | 4.00 | 6.00 | W |
| s245 | Race to the Stars–Oscar J. Friend & Leo Margulies | 1.00 | 2.00 | 3.00 | SF |
| 246 | The Long Nightmare–John Roeburt | 1.00 | 2.00 | 3.00 | |
| 247 | Mask of Evil–Charlotte Armstrong | 1.00 | 2.00 | 3.00 | M |
| 248 | End of a Call Girl–William Campbell Gault | 2.50 | 5.00 | 7.50 | M |
| d249 | The Black Obelisk–Erich Maria Remarque | 1.00 | 2.00 | 3.00 | |
| s250 | The Grand Seduction–Marcel Ayme | 1.00 | 2.00 | 3.00 | |
| s251 | The Doctor's Husband–Elizabeth Seifert | 1.00 | 2.00 | 3.00 | R |
| s252 | The House on the Beach–E.L. Withers; c-Powers | 1.50 | 3.00 | 4.50 | |
| 253 | Murder Bait–Duane Yarnell | 1.00 | 2.00 | 3.00 | M |
| s254 | Bad Girls–ed. Leo Margulies | 4.00 | 8.00 | 12.00 | JD |
| 255 | Lie Down, Killer–Richard S. Prather | 1.00 | 2.00 | 3.00 | M |
| d256 | A Treasury of True–Charles N. Barnard | 1.00 | 2.00 | 3.00 | |
| s257 | Pappy's Women–Jack Gotshall | 1.00 | 2.00 | 3.00 | E |
| s258 | Six from Worlds Beyond–T.E. Dikty | 1.00 | 2.00 | 3.00 | SF |
| s259 | Devil's Prize–Samuel Edwards | 1.00 | 2.00 | 3.00 | |
| 260 | Night Lady–William Campbell Gault | 2.50 | 5.00 | 7.50 | |
| 261 | Gold at Kansas Gulch–Steve Frazee | 1.50 | 3.00 | 4.50 | W |
| d262 | Fun with Mathematics–Jerome S. Meyer | 1.00 | 2.00 | 3.00 | NF |
| s263 | Please Don't Eat the Daisies–Jean Kerr; 1959; 4th printing is movie tie-in | 1.00 | 2.00 | 3.00 | |
| d264 | The Silver Mountain–Dan Cushman | 1.50 | 3.00 | 4.50 | |
| s265 | The Great Captains–Henry Treece | 1.00 | 2.00 | 3.00 | A |
| 266 | Clementine Cherie–Jean Bellus | 1.00 | 2.00 | 3.00 | |
| s267 | Edge of Twilight–Paula Christian; 1st ed. 1959 | 3.00 | 6.00 | 9.00 | |
| 268 | The Vanishing Vixen–Roy B. Sparkia | 1.00 | 2.00 | 3.00 | |
| s269 | The Great Religions by Which Men Live–Tynette Hills & Floyd H. Ross | 1.00 | 2.00 | 3.00 | |
| s270 | The Devil's Agent–Hans Habe | 1.00 | 2.00 | 3.00 | |
| d271 | Seven Keys to Koptic Court–Herbert D. Kastle | 1.00 | 2.00 | 3.00 | |
| s272 | Young and Deadly–ed. Leo Margulies | 4.00 | 8.00 | 12.00 | JD |
| s273 | The Caves of Night–John Christopher | 2.00 | 4.00 | 6.00 | |
| 274 | Fighting Rawhide–Lewis B. Patten | 1.00 | 2.00 | 3.00 | W |
| s275 | How to Retire and Enjoy It–Ray Giles | 1.00 | 2.00 | 3.00 | NF |
| d276 | The World's Ten Greatest Novels–W. Somerset Maugham | 1.00 | 2.00 | 3.00 | |
| 277 | Dagger of Flesh–Richard S. Prather | 1.00 | 2.00 | 3.00 | M |
| d278 | Days in the Yellow Leaf–William Hoffman | 1.00 | 2.00 | 3.00 | |
| s279 | Enter Laughing–Carl Reiner | 1.00 | 2.00 | 3.00 | B |
| s280 | The Damned Wear Wings–David Camerer | 1.00 | 2.00 | 3.00 | |
| 281 | The Wayward Widow–William Campbell Gault | 2.50 | 5.00 | 7.50 | E |
| s282 | Three from Out There–ed. Leo Margulies | 1.50 | 3.00 | 4.50 | SF |
| s283 | The Way to Inner Peace–Bishop Fulton J. Sheen | 1.00 | 2.00 | 3.00 | |
| s284 | How to Write and Speak Effective English–Edward Frank Allen | 1.00 | 2.00 | 3.00 | NF |
| d285 | Wine of Life–Charles Gorham | 1.00 | 2.00 | 3.00 | |

| | | V/Good | Fine | N/Mint | |
|---|---|---|---|---|---|

**CREST BOOKS,** *continued*

| # | Title | V/Good | Fine | N/Mint | |
|---|---|---|---|---|---|
| 286 | Dead Dolls Don't Talk–Day Keene; orig. 1959 | 2.50 | 5.00 | 7.50 | M |
| 287 | The Cautious Bachelor–Sarel Eimerl | 1.00 | 2.00 | 3.00 | |
| s288 | Legacy of a Spy–Henry S. Maxfield | 1.00 | 2.00 | 3.00 | |
| s289 | Handsome's Seven Women–Theodore Pratt | 1.00 | 2.00 | 3.00 | |
| s290 | The Girls in 3-B–Valerie Taylor | 2.50 | 5.00 | 7.50 | |
| s291 | The Sergeant–Dennis Murphy | 1.00 | 2.00 | 3.00 | |
| 292 | The Eighth Mrs. Bluebeard–Hillary Waugh | 1.00 | 2.00 | 3.00 | M |
| d293 | Steamboat Gothic–Frances Parkinson Keyes | 1.00 | 2.00 | 3.00 | |
| 294 | Pardon My Blooper–Kermit Schafer | 1.00 | 2.00 | 3.00 | H |
| s295 | The Executioners–John D. MacDonald | 1.00 | 2.00 | 3.00 | M |
| 296 | Passport to Peril–Stephen Marlowe | 1.00 | 2.00 | 3.00 | M |
| 297 | Doctor's Temptation–Henry Lieferant & Sylvia Lieferant | 1.00 | 2.00 | 3.00 | |
| 298 | In This Corner–Dennis the Menace–Hank Ketcham | 1.50 | 3.00 | 4.50 | H |
| s299 | The Way We Live Now–Warren Miller | 1.00 | 2.00 | 3.00 | |
| d300 | North from Rome–Helen MacInnes | 1.00 | 2.00 | 3.00 | |
| s301 | Shake Hands with the Devil–Rearden Conner | 1.00 | 2.00 | 3.00 | |
| s302 | The Girl Cage–Charles Mergendahl | 1.00 | 2.00 | 3.00 | |
| 303 | Night of Violence–Louis Charbonneau | 1.00 | 2.00 | 3.00 | |
| 304 | Creole Woman–Gardner F. Fox | 1.50 | 3.00 | 4.50 | E |
| d305 | The Old Blood–Edgar Mittelholzer | 1.00 | 2.00 | 3.00 | |
| s306 | Sun in the Hunter's Eyes–Mark Derby | 1.00 | 2.00 | 3.00 | |
| s307 | The Horn–Clellon Holmes | 3.00 | 6.00 | 9.00 | |
| s308 | A Stir of Echoes–Richard Matheson | 3.00 | 6.00 | 9.00 | SF |
| 309 | Sweet Wild Wench–William Campbell Gault | 2.50 | 5.00 | 7.50 | E |
| 310 | The Red Scarf–Gil Brewer | 2.00 | 4.00 | 6.00 | |
| 311 | Crazy Cartoons by VIP–Virgil Partch | 2.00 | 4.00 | 6.00 | H |
| d312 | Showcase–Martin Dibner | 1.00 | 2.00 | 3.00 | |
| 313 | The Mark–Charles E. Israel | 1.00 | 2.00 | 3.00 | |
| d314 | Joy Street–Frances Parkinson Keyes | 1.00 | 2.00 | 3.00 | |
| 315 | Rendezvous–Steve Frazee | 1.50 | 3.00 | 4.50 | W |
| 316 | Danger in My Blood–Steve Brackeen | 1.00 | 2.00 | 3.00 | |
| s317 | The Insolent Chariots–John Keats | 1.00 | 2.00 | 3.00 | H |
| s318 | The Enjoyment of Love in Marriage–LeMon Clark | 1.00 | 2.00 | 3.00 | NF |
| d319 | Lost Summer–Christopher Davis | 1.00 | 2.00 | 3.00 | |
| s320 | Venus in Sparta–Louis Auchircloss | 1.00 | 2.00 | 3.00 | |
| s321 | The Shook-up Generation–Harrison S. Salisbury | 2.50 | 5.00 | 7.50 | JD |
| s322 | The Passionate City–Ian Stuart Black | 1.00 | 2.00 | 3.00 | |
| 323 | You've Got Him Cold–Thomas B. Dewey | 2.00 | 4.00 | 6.00 | |
| s324 | Treasure Book of Fairy Tales–Ann McGovern | 2.00 | 4.00 | 6.00 | |
| 325 | Morocco Jones in the Case of the Golden Angel–Jack Baynes | 1.50 | 3.00 | 4.50 | M |
| t326 | By Love Possessed–James Gould Cozzens; later printing (2nd seen) is movie tie-in | 1.00 | 2.00 | 3.00 | |
| s327 | Murder on the Mistral–Vincent Gaspard Malo | 1.00 | 2.00 | 3.00 | M |
| s328 | The Bystander–Albert Guerard | 1.00 | 2.00 | 3.00 | |
| s329 | The Star of Life–Edmond Hamilton | 1.00 | 2.00 | 3.00 | SF |
| d330 | Tom Jones–Henry Fielding | 1.00 | 2.00 | 3.00 | |
| s331 | Drink and Be Merry–Lester Grady | 1.00 | 2.00 | 3.00 | H |
| s332 | Someone from the Past–Margot Bennett | 1.00 | 2.00 | 3.00 | |
| d333 | Victorine–Frances Parkinson Keyes | 1.00 | 2.00 | 3.00 | |
| 334 | Kill My Love–Kyle Hunt | 1.00 | 2.00 | 3.00 | M |
| s335 | A Little Revolution–Paul Edmondson | 1.00 | 2.00 | 3.00 | |
| s336 | Strange Are the Ways of Love–Lesley Evans | 1.00 | 2.00 | 3.00 | |
| s337 | All Quiet on the Western Front–Erich Maria Remarque | 1.00 | 2.00 | 3.00 | |
| d338 | Lolita–Vladimir Nabokov; 1959 | 1.00 | 2.00 | 3.00 | E |
| 339 | Lyn Darling, M.D.–Ray Dorien | 1.00 | 2.00 | 3.00 | |
| 340 | Jimmy Hoffa's Hot–John Bartlow Martin | 1.50 | 3.00 | 4.50 | |
| s341 | The Badge–Jack Webb | 1.00 | 2.00 | 3.00 | M |
| s342 | No Place on Earth–Louis Charbonneau | 1.00 | 2.00 | 3.00 | SF |
| s343 | The Ruling Passion–George deMare | 1.00 | 2.00 | 3.00 | |
| 344 | Meet Morocco Jones–Jack Baynes | 1.50 | 3.00 | 4.50 | M |
| S345 | Young Love–Johannes Allen; 1960 | .50 | 1.00 | 1.50 | |
| S347 | The Steel Cocoon–Bentz Plagemann | .75 | 1.50 | 2.25 | C |
| S348 | Trail of Tears–Williams Forrest | .75 | 1.50 | 2.25 | W |
| 349 | Devil in Dungarees–Albert Conroy | .75 | 1.50 | 2.25 | |
| D350 | Home Medical Encyclopedia–Paul Kuhne | .50 | 1.00 | 1.50 | NF |
| D351 | Nine Coaches Waiting–Mary Stewart | .50 | 1.00 | 1.50 | |
| S352 | They Sell Sex–Sara Harris | .50 | 1.00 | 1.50 | NF |
| S353 | The Bright Young Things–Amanda Vail (Warren Miller) | .50 | 1.00 | 1.50 | |
| 354 | Frenzy–James O. Causey | .50 | 1.00 | 1.50 | |
| D356 | 25 Magic Steps to Word Power–Wilfred Funk | .50 | 1.00 | 1.50 | NF |
| 357 | Trouble Rides Tall–Harry Whittington | 1.50 | 3.00 | 4.50 | W |
| D358 | Clotilde–Cécil Saint Laurent | .50 | 1.00 | 1.50 | E |
| S359 | Please Write for Details–John D. MacDonald | 1.00 | 2.00 | 3.00 | M |
| 360 | The Case of the Chased and the Unchaste–Thomas B. Dewey | 2.00 | 4.00 | 6.00 | M |
| 361 | Million Dollar Tramp–William Campbell Gault | 2.50 | 5.00 | 7.50 | M |
| S362 | Get Out of My Sky–ed. Leo Margulies | .75 | 1.50 | 2.25 | SF |
| 363 | So You Think You Know Baseball!–Harry Simmons | .75 | 1.50 | 2.25 | S |
| S364 | Off Limits–Hans Habe | .50 | 1.00 | 1.50 | |
| D365 | The Ugly American–William J. Lederer & Eugene Burdick; movie tie-in | .50 | 1.00 | 1.50 | |
| 366 | The Dark Road–James Cross | .50 | 1.00 | 1.50 | |
| S367 | The Fugitives–Robert Gutwillig | .50 | 1.00 | 1.50 | |
| 368 | The Authentic Death of Hendry Jones–Charles Neider | .50 | 1.00 | 1.50 | |
| 369 | What Are the Odds?–Leo Guild | .50 | 1.00 | 1.50 | NF |
| 370 | Swamp Babe–Robert Faherty; aka Big Old Sun | 1.50 | 3.00 | 4.50 | NF |
| D371 | Modern Manners: Etiquette for all Occasions–Carolyn Hagner Shaw | .50 | 1.00 | 1.50 | |
| D372 | This Fiery Night–Joan Vatsek | .50 | 1.00 | 1.50 | |
| S373 | Carlotta McBride–Charles Gorham | .50 | 1.00 | 1.50 | |
| S374 | Cricket Smith–Monte Linkletter | .50 | 1.00 | 1.50 | |
| 375 | A Dream of Falling–Mary O. Rank | .50 | 1.00 | 1.50 | |
| D376 | How to Invest Safely and for Profit–Adolph Suehsdorf | .50 | 1.00 | 1.50 | NF |
| D377 | A Walk on the Wild Side–Nelson Algren | .75 | 1.50 | 2.25 | JD |
| 378 | Dennis the Menace . . . Teacher's Threat–Hank Ketcham | 1.00 | 2.00 | 3.00 | H |
| D379 | The Violators–Francis Irby Gwaltney; aka The Numbers of Our Days | .50 | 1.00 | 1.50 | |
| S380 | The Notion of Sin–Robert McLaughlin | .50 | 1.00 | 1.50 | |
| S381 | The Con Man–Dan Cushman; aka Goodbye, Old Dry | 1.00 | 2.00 | 3.00 | M |
| 382 | The Girl with a Secret–Charlotte Armstrong | .50 | 1.00 | 1.50 | M |
| 383 | A Dram of Poison–Charlotte Armstrong | .50 | 1.00 | 1.50 | M |
| D384 | The Trumpet Unblown–William Hoffman | .50 | 1.00 | 1.50 | |
| S385 | Psycho–Robert Bloch; movie tie-in | 5.00 | 10.00 | 15.00 | HO |
| S386 | The Cool World–Warren Miller | .75 | 1.50 | 2.25 | JD |
| S387 | The Story of Andrea Fields: Woman and Doctor–Elizabeth Seifert | .50 | 1.00 | 1.50 | |
| S388 | Penknife in My Heart–Nicholas Blake | .75 | 1.50 | 2.25 | M |
| D389 | Think and Grow Rich–Napoleon Hill | .50 | 1.00 | 1.50 | |
| 390 | Best Cartoons from True–ed. True Mag. | 1.00 | 2.00 | 3.00 | H |
| D391 | According to Hoyle–Richard L. Frey | .50 | 1.00 | 1.50 | NF |
| S392 | Of Love Forbidden–Anna Elisabet Weirauch | .50 | 1.00 | 1.50 | |
| S393 | Kings Will Be Tyrants–Ward Hawkins | .50 | 1.00 | 1.50 | A |
| 394 | VIP Tosses a Party–William McIntyre & Virgil Partch | 1.00 | 2.00 | 3.00 | H |
| S395 | The Wizard of Oz–L. Frank Baum; 1960 | 1.00 | 2.00 | 3.00 | F |
| S396 | A Handful of Men–Robert Wilder | .50 | 1.00 | 1.50 | W |
| S397 | Walk with Evil–Robert Wilder | .50 | 1.00 | 1.50 | |
| 398 | Seven Ways from Sundown–Clair Huffaker; movie tie-in | 1.25 | 2.50 | 3.75 | W |
| D399 | The Marauders–Charlton Ogburn, Jr | .50 | 1.00 | 1.50 | |
| S400 | The Crossroads–John D. MacDonald | 1.00 | 2.00 | 3.00 | M |
| S401 | The Breeze from Camelot–Viña Delmar | .50 | 1.00 | 1.50 | |
| 402 | Dennis the Menace Rides Again–Hank Ketcham | 1.00 | 2.00 | 3.00 | H |
| 403 | Clash of Shadows–Howard Rigsby | .50 | 1.00 | 1.50 | |
| D404 | Night of Fire and Snow–Alfred Coppel | .50 | 1.00 | 1.50 | |
| S405 | The Pink Hotel–Dorothy Erskine & Patrick Dennis | .50 | 1.00 | 1.50 | |
| T406 | Poor No More–Robert C. Ruark | .50 | 1.00 | 1.50 | |

Crest S395, Crest S429, Crest S487.

| | | V/Good | Fine | N/Mint | |
|---|---|---|---|---|---|
| **CREST BOOKS,** *continued* | | | | | |
| S407 | Warrior's Rest–Christiana Rochefort | .50 | 1.00 | 1.50 | C |
| 408 | The Pyx–John Buell | .50 | 1.00 | 1.50 | |
| D409 | My Fight for Sanity–Judith Kruger | .50 | 1.00 | 1.50 | |
| S410 | Concerning a Woman of Sin and Others–ed. Dan Talbot | .50 | 1.00 | 1.50 | |
| D411 | The Longest Day–Cornelius Ryan | .75 | 1.50 | 2.25 | C |
| S412 | Invitation to a Beheading–Vladimir Nabokov | .50 | 1.00 | 1.50 | |
| S413 | The Lion House–Marjorie Lee | .50 | 1.00 | 1.50 | |
| S414 | Earthquake–Milton Berle & John Roeburt | .75 | 1.50 | 2.25 | |
| 415 | If the Shoe Fits–Lee Roberts | .50 | 1.00 | 1.50 | |
| D416 | Town Burning–Thomas Williams | .50 | 1.00 | 1.50 | |
| D417 | The Affair in Arcady–James Wellard | .50 | 1.00 | 1.50 | |
| 418 | Little Tramp–Gil Brewer | 2.00 | 4.00 | 6.00 | |
| 419 | Back Alley Jungle–ed. Leo Margulies; 1960 | 4.00 | 8.00 | 12.00 | JD |
| S420 | Back of Sunset–John Cleary | .50 | 1.00 | 1.50 | |
| S421 | Flaming Star–Clair Huffaker; movie tie-in | 2.50 | 5.00 | 7.50 | W |
| D422 | The Tatooed Rood–Kyle Onstott & Lance Horner | .50 | 1.00 | 1.50 | |
| S423 | The Crime–Stephen Longstreet | .75 | 1.50 | 2.25 | |
| S424 | That French Girl–Joseph Hilton | .50 | 1.00 | 1.50 | |
| D425 | How to Win at Contract Bridge–Richard L. Frey | .50 | 1.00 | 1.50 | NF |
| D426 | My First 2000 Years–George S. Viereck & Paul Eldridge | 1.00 | 2.00 | 3.00 | F |
| D427 | The Ivy Trap–Douglas Angus | .50 | 1.00 | 1.50 | |
| D428 | Gemini–William Kelley | .50 | 1.00 | 1.50 | |
| S429 | True Spy Stories–ed. Robert Deindorfer | 1.00 | 2.00 | 3.00 | NF |
| S430 | Welcome Honorable Visitors–Jean Raspail | .50 | 1.00 | 1.50 | |
| S431 | The Looters–Albert Conroy; 1961 | .50 | 1.00 | 1.50 | |
| D432 | Cure Your Nerves Yourself–Dr. Louis E. Bisch | .50 | 1.00 | 1.50 | NF |
| T433 | Webster's New School and Office Dictionary | .50 | 1.00 | 1.50 | NF |
| D434 | Brood of Fury–Jess Shelton | .50 | 1.00 | 1.50 | |
| D435 | Love or Whatever It Is–Warren Leslie | .50 | 1.00 | 1.50 | |
| S436 | The Great Escape–Paul Brickhill; later printing is movie tie-in | .75 | 1.50 | 2.25 | C |
| D437 | 1,001 Selections from the Big Fun Book–Jerome S. Meyer | .75 | 1.50 | 2.25 | NF |
| D438 | Folk Medicine–D.C. Jarvis, MD | .50 | 1.00 | 1.50 | NF |
| S439 | Auschwitz: A Doctor's Eyewitness Account–Dr. Miklos Nyiszli | .75 | 1.50 | 2.25 | NF |
| D440 | The Deathmakers–Glen Sire | .50 | 1.00 | 1.50 | |
| D441 | The Thirteenth Apostle–Eugene Vale | .50 | 1.00 | 1.50 | |
| S442 | The Dangerous Games–Tereska Torrès | .75 | 1.50 | 2.25 | |
| S443 | The Gods of Our Time–Cothburn O'Neal | .50 | 1.00 | 1.50 | |
| S444 | You Be the Judge–ed. Ashley Halsey, Jr | .75 | 1.50 | 2.25 | NF |
| D445 | The Happy Medium–Lissa Charell | .50 | 1.00 | 1.50 | |
| D446 | My Brother Michael–Mary Stewart | .50 | 1.00 | 1.50 | |
| S447 | Road Show–John Haase; 1961 | .75 | 1.50 | 2.25 | |
| S448 | Sail a Crooked Ship–Nathaniel Benchley; movie tie-in | .50 | 1.00 | 1.50 | H |
| D449 | Unfaithful–Dr. Frank S. Caprioi; aka Marital Infidelity | .50 | 1.00 | 1.50 | NF |

| | | V/Good | Fine | N/Mint | |
|---|---|---|---|---|---|
| S450 | Dennis the Menace, A.M.* (*Ambassador of Mischief)–Hank Ketcham | 1.00 | 2.00 | 3.00 | H |
| S451 | Some Angry Angel–Richard Condon | .50 | 1.00 | 1.50 | |
| S452 | False Scent–Ngaio Marsh | .50 | 1.00 | 1.50 | M |
| D453 | The Scene–Clarence L. Cooper, Jr | .50 | 1.00 | 1.50 | |
| D454 | Teach Yourself French–Sir John Adams & N. Scarlyn Wilson | .50 | 1.00 | 1.50 | NF |
| D455 | Zsa Zsa Gabor: My Story Written for Me–Gerald Frank | 3.00 | 6.00 | 9.00 | B |
| R456 | South of the Angels–Jessamyn West | .50 | 1.00 | 1.50 | |
| D457 | The Sands of Kalahari–William Mulvihill; later printing is movie tie-in | .75 | 1.50 | 2.25 | A |
| D458 | True Civil War Stories–ed. Joseph Millard | 1.00 | 2.00 | 3.00 | NF |
| D459 | Handbook of Everyday Law–Martin J. Ross | .50 | 1.00 | 1.50 | NF |
| D460 | The Home Book of Italian Cooking–Angela Catanzaro (aka Mama Mia Italian Cookbook) | .50 | 1.00 | 1.50 | NF |
| D461 | All Quiet on the Western Front–Erich Maria Remarque | .50 | 1.00 | 1.50 | C |
| R462 | Away from Home–Rona Jaffe | .50 | 1.00 | 1.50 | |
| D463 | 90 Miles from Home–Warren Miller | .50 | 1.00 | 1.50 | |
| S464 | The End of the Night–John D. MacDonald | 1.00 | 2.00 | 3.00 | M |
| S465 | Wanted, Dennis the Menace–Hank Ketcham | .75 | 1.50 | 2.25 | H |
| S466 | The Crime of Giovanni Venturi–Howard Shaw | | | | |
| S467 | Dennis the Menace Rides Again–Hank Ketcham | .75 | 1.50 | 2.25 | H |
| D468 | Mistress of Mellyn–Victoria Holt | .50 | 1.00 | 1.50 | |
| S469 | Young Man Willing–Roy Doliner | .50 | 1.00 | 1.50 | |
| D470 | Hangman's Song–Jess Shelton | .50 | 1.00 | 1.50 | |
| S471 | Aground–Charles Williams | 2.00 | 4.00 | 6.00 | M |
| D472 | Madam, Will You Talk?–Mary Stewart | .50 | 1.00 | 1.50 | M |
| D473 | Way to Happiness–Bishop Fulton J. Sheen | .50 | 1.00 | 1.50 | NF |
| D474 | Way to Inner Peace–Bishop Fulton J. Sheen | .50 | 1.00 | 1.50 | NF |
| M475 | A Distant Trumpet–Paul Horgan | .50 | 1.00 | 1.50 | |
| R476 | Decision at Delphi–Helen MacInnes | .50 | 1.00 | 1.50 | M |
| D477 | Sylvia–E.V. Cunningham | .50 | 1.00 | 1.50 | |
| S478 | Hey! B.C.–Johnny Hart; 1961 | .75 | 1.50 | 2.25 | H |
| S479 | Vengeance Is the Spur–Harry Whittington | 1.50 | 3.00 | 4.50 | W |
| D480 | True War Stories–ed. Bob Considine | .75 | 1.50 | 2.25 | NF |
| S481 | Handsome's Seven Women–Theodore Pratt | .50 | 1.00 | 1.50 | |
| M482 | The Side of the Angels–Alexander Fedoroff | .50 | 1.00 | 1.50 | |
| D483 | Son and Heir–Edith Begner | .50 | 1.00 | 1.50 | |
| S484 | The Burning Eye–Victor Cunning | .50 | 1.00 | 1.50 | |
| S485 | Daily Bread–Ralph Maloney | .50 | 1.00 | 1.50 | |
| D486 | Small Town D.A.–Robert Traver | .50 | 1.00 | 1.50 | |
| S487 | Another Kind of Love–Paula Christian; 1st ed. 1961 | 3.00 | 6.00 | 9.00 | |
| S488 | Cartoon Laffs from True–ed. Bill McIntyre | .75 | 1.50 | 2.25 | H |
| D489 | Execution–Colin McDougall | .50 | 1.00 | 1.50 | |
| T490 | The Trend Is Up–Anthony West | .50 | 1.00 | 1.50 | |
| S491 | Countdown to Murder–Herbert Kastle | .50 | 1.00 | 1.50 | M |
| D492 | My 21 Years in the White House–Alonzo Fields | .50 | 1.00 | 1.50 | NF |
| S493 | Baby Sitter's Guide by Dennis the Menace–Hank Ketcham | .75 | 1.50 | 2.25 | H |
| S494 | City at World's End–Edmond Hamilton | .50 | 1.00 | 1.50 | SF |
| S495 | Edge of Twilight–Paula Christian | 2.00 | 4.00 | 6.00 | |
| D496 | A Walk on the Wild Side–Nelson Algren; some later printings (4th and 5th seen) are movie tie-in | .50 | 1.00 | 1.50 | JD |
| D497 | I Swear and Vow–Stefan Olivier | .50 | 1.00 | 1.50 | |
| S498 | The True Album of Cartoons–ed. True Mag. | .75 | 1.50 | 2.25 | H |
| S499 | Seven Lies South–William P. McGivern | .50 | 1.00 | 1.50 | |
| D500 | Marnie–Winston Graham; 1962; movie tie-in | .75 | 1.50 | 2.25 | |
| S501 | Dennis the Menace vs. Everybody–Hank Ketcham | .75 | 1.50 | 2.25 | H |
| R502 | Fate Is the Hunter–Ernest K. Gann | .50 | 1.00 | 1.50 | |
| D503 | Citizen of New Salem–Paul Horgan | .50 | 1.00 | 1.50 | |

**CREST BOOKS,** *continued*

| | | V/Good | Fine | N/Mint | |
|---|---|---|---|---|---|
| D504 | A Question of Innocence–Donald Winks | .50 | 1.00 | 1.50 | |
| D505 | How to Play Your Best Golf all the Time–Tommy Armour | .50 | 1.00 | 1.50 | NF |
| S506 | The Power of Positive Living–Douglas Lurton | .50 | 1.00 | 1.50 | NF |
| R507 | Home Medical Encyclopedia–Paul Kuhne; aka Medicine for the Layman | .50 | 1.00 | 1.50 | NF |
| D508 | Thunder on the Right–Mary Stewart | .50 | 1.00 | 1.50 | |
| R509 | My Hero–Robert Carson | .50 | 1.00 | 1.50 | |
| T510 | The Gay Place–William Brammer | .50 | 1.00 | 1.50 | |
| S511 | Call Dr. Margaret–Ray Dorien | .50 | 1.00 | 1.50 | |
| S512 | In This Corner . . . Dennis the Menace–Hank Ketcham | .75 | 1.50 | 2.25 | H |
| S513 | Party Fun and Games–Alexander Van Rensselaer | .50 | 1.00 | 1.50 | NF |
| S514 | The Snake Has All the Lines–Jean Kerr | .50 | 1.00 | 1.50 | H |
| D515 | Heaven Has No Favorites–Erich Maria Remarque | .50 | 1.00 | 1.50 | |
| R516 | Arch of Triumph–Erich Maria Remarque | .50 | 1.00 | 1.50 | |
| T517 | Rizpah–Charles E. Israel | .50 | 1.00 | 1.50 | |
| S518 | Nightmare–Ann Blaisdell | .50 | 1.00 | 1.50 | |
| D519 | Just Off Fifth–Edith Begner | .50 | 1.00 | 1.50 | |
| S520 | Cape Fear–John D. MacDonald; aka The Executioners | 1.00 | 2.00 | 3.00 | M |
| D521 | How to Write & Speak Effective English–Edward Frank Allen | .50 | 1.00 | 1.50 | NF |
| A522 | The Rise and Fall of the Third Reich–William L. Shirer | .75 | 1.50 | 2.25 | NF |
| D523 | P.T. 109–Robert J. Donovan; 1962; movie tie-in | .75 | 1.50 | 2.25 | NF |
| S524 | Murder Money–Jay Bennett | .50 | 1.00 | 1.50 | M |
| M525 | Came a Cavalier–Frances Parkinson Keyes | .50 | 1.00 | 1.50 | |
| T526 | A Place in My Head–William Hoffman | .50 | 1.00 | 1.50 | |
| S527 | Pardon My Blooper–Kermit Schafer | .75 | 1.50 | 2.25 | H |
| R528 | Blue Camellia–Frances Parkinson Keyes | .50 | 1.00 | 1.50 | |
| D529 | The Purveyor–John Starr | .50 | 1.00 | 1.50 | |
| R530 | The Golden Youth of Lee Prince–Aubrey Goodman | .50 | 1.00 | 1.50 | |
| D531 | The Day of the Triffids–John Wyndham | 1.50 | 3.00 | 4.50 | |
| D532 | These Unlucky Deeds–Richard Martin Stern | .50 | 1.00 | 1.50 | |
| D533 | Talking Your Way Around the World–Mario Pei | .50 | 1.00 | 1.50 | |
| D534 | Awake Monique–Astrid Van Royen | .50 | 1.00 | 1.50 | |
| D535 | American Ballads–Charles O'Brien Kennedy | .50 | 1.00 | 1.50 | NF |
| R536 | Think and Grow Rich–Napoleon Hill | .50 | 1.00 | 1.50 | NF |
| D537 | Arthritis and Folk Medicine–D.C. Jarvis, MD | .50 | 1.00 | 1.50 | NF |
| D538 | Rabbit, Run–John Updike | .50 | 1.00 | 1.50 | |
| R539 | A Talent for Loving–Richard Condon | .50 | 1.00 | 1.50 | |
| T540 | Russia under Khrushchev–Alexander Werth | .50 | 1.00 | 1.50 | NF |
| D541 | The New Way to Eat and Get Slim–Donald G. Cooley | .50 | 1.00 | 1.50 | NF |
| D542 | The Way We Live Now–Warren Miller | .50 | 1.00 | 1.50 | |
| D543 | Beyond Defeat–Hans Werner Richter | .50 | 1.00 | 1.50 | |
| D544 | How to Use the Power of Prayer–Harold Sherman | .50 | 1.00 | 1.50 | NF |
| D545 | A Nation of Sheep–William J. Lederer | .50 | 1.00 | 1.50 | |
| R546 | The Blue of Capricorn–Eugene Burdick | .50 | 1.00 | 1.50 | |
| D547 | Time Is the Simplest Thing–Clifford D. Simak | .50 | 1.00 | 1.50 | SF |
| S548 | New Faces on the Barroom Floor–VIP | .75 | 1.50 | 2.25 | H |
| D549 | The Judgement–Tom Wicker | .50 | 1.00 | 1.50 | |
| D550 | Nine Coaches Waiting–Mary Stewart | .50 | 1.00 | 1.50 | |
| D551 | Becoming a Mother–Dr. Theodore R. Seidman & Marvin H. Albert | .50 | 1.00 | 1.50 | NF |
| T552 | Do Not Go Gentle–David MacCuish | .50 | 1.00 | 1.50 | |
| M553 | The Chess Players–Frances Parkinson Keyes | .50 | 1.00 | 1.50 | |
| D554 | JFK: Boyhood to White House–Bruce Lee; aka Boy's Life of John F. Kennedy | 1.00 | 2.00 | 3.00 | B |
| D555 | The Old Man and the Boy–Robert Ruark | .50 | 1.00 | 1.50 | |
| S556 | How to Become a Successful Student–Otis D. Froe & Maurice A. Lee | .50 | 1.00 | 1.50 | NF |
| D557 | Tales for a Rainy Night–ed. David Alexander | 1.00 | 2.00 | 3.00 | |
| R558 | Joy Street–Frances Parkinson Keyes | .50 | 1.00 | 1.50 | |
| M559 | A Distant Trumpet–Paul Horgan | .50 | 1.00 | 1.50 | |
| R560 | Look Younger, Live Longer–Gayelord Hauser | .50 | 1.00 | 1.50 | NF |
| S561 | Dennis the Menace, Happy Half-pint–Hank Ketcham | .75 | 1.50 | 2.25 | H |
| D562 | The Young Marrieds–Judith Heiman | .50 | 1.00 | 1.50 | |
| D563 | Wildfire at Midnight–Mary Stewart | .50 | 1.00 | 1.50 | |
| S564 | The Wonderful World of Peanuts–Charles Schulz | .75 | 1.50 | 2.25 | H |
| D565 | The Lost Years of Jesus Revealed–Dr. Charles Francis Potter | .50 | 1.00 | 1.50 | |
| R566 | The Old Blood–Edgar Mittelholzer | .50 | 1.00 | 1.50 | |
| R567 | Ring of Bright Water–Gavin Maxwell | .50 | 1.00 | 1.50 | |
| R568 | North from Rome–Helen MacInnes | .50 | 1.00 | 1.50 | |
| D569 | Modern Manners: Etiquette for All Occasions–Carolyn Hagner Shaw | .50 | 1.00 | 1.50 | |
| T570 | Little Me–Patrick Dennis | .50 | 1.00 | 1.50 | |
| D571 | How Much Is That In Dollars?–Art Buchwald | .50 | 1.00 | 1.50 | H |
| S572 | Who's Got the Action–Alexander Rose; movie tie-in | .50 | 1.00 | 1.50 | |
| S573 | Hey Peanuts!–Charles Schulz | .75 | 1.50 | 2.25 | H |
| S574 | Work This One Out–L.H. Longley-Cook | .50 | 1.00 | 1.50 | NF |
| R575 | The Longest Day–Cornelius Ryan | .75 | 1.50 | 2.25 | NF |
| D576 | Carl Sandburg–Harry Golden | .75 | 1.50 | 2.25 | B |
| M577 | Crescent Carnival–Frances Parkinson Keyes | .50 | 1.00 | 1.50 | |
| D578 | The Watchman–Davis Grubb | .50 | 1.00 | 1.50 | |
| D579 | True Tales of Hitler's Reich–Richard Hanser | 1.00 | 2.00 | 3.00 | NF |
| R580 | Is *That* in the Bible?–Dr. Charles Francis Potter | .75 | 1.50 | 2.25 | NF |
| D581 | The Spiked Heel–Richard Marsten | 1.25 | 2.50 | 3.75 | |
| R582 | Victorine–Frances Parkinson Keyes | .50 | 1.00 | 1.50 | |
| D583 | 25 Magic Steps to Word Power–Wilfred Funk | .50 | 1.00 | 1.50 | |
| D584 | CIA–The Inside Story–Andrew Tully | .50 | 1.00 | 1.50 | NF |
| T585 | Honor Bright–Frances Parkinson Keyes | .50 | 1.00 | 1.50 | |
| D586 | Sylvia–E.V. Cunningham. Note: Movie tie-in of Sylvia apparently does not exist, as all copies of this book seen contain horror novel Sylva by Vercors (Jean Bruller) | .50 | 1.00 | 1.50 | E |
| D587 | McCaffery–Charles Gorham | .50 | 1.00 | 1.50 | |
| S588 | Please Don't Eat the Daisies–Jean Kerr | .50 | 1.00 | 1.50 | H |
| S589 | The Girls in 3-B–Valerie Taylor | 1.50 | 3.00 | 4.50 | |
| R590 | The Ivy Tree–Mary Stewart | .50 | 1.00 | 1.50 | |
| T591 | The Rothschilds–Frederic Morton | .50 | 1.00 | 1.50 | B |
| T592 | The Long Summer of George Adams–Weldon Hill | .50 | 1.00 | 1.50 | |
| T593 | My Brother Ernest Hemingway–Leicester Hemingway | 1.50 | 3.00 | 4.50 | NF |
| R594 | Prize Stories 1962: The O'Henry Awards–ed. Richard Poirier | .50 | 1.00 | 1.50 | |
| S595 | Phyllis–E.V. Cunningham | .50 | 1.00 | 1.50 | |
| K596 | Warrior's Rest–Christiana Rochefort; movie tie-in | 1.50 | 3.00 | 4.50 | C |
| D597 | Five Tales from Tomorrow–ed. T.E. Dikty | .50 | 1.00 | 1.50 | SF |
| T598 | Mirror, Mirror on the Wall–Gayelord Hauser | .50 | 1.00 | 1.50 | NF |
| T599 | Fia, Fia–James Ramsey Ullman | .50 | 1.00 | 1.50 | |
| T600 | The Royal Box–Frances Parkinson Keyes | .50 | 1.00 | 1.50 | |
| D601 | Why So Tired?–Marguerite Clark | .50 | 1.00 | 1.50 | |
| D602 | Million Dollar Puzzle Book–; 1963 | 1.00 | 2.00 | 3.00 | NF |
| R603 | Town Burning–Thomas Williams | .50 | 1.00 | 1.50 | |
| R604 | Captain Newman, M.D.–Leo Rosten; movie tie-in | .50 | 1.00 | 1.50 | |
| D605 | Pigeon Feathers and Other Stories–John Updike | .50 | 1.00 | 1.50 | |
| D606 | The Simple Honorable Man–Conrad Richter | .50 | 1.00 | 1.50 | |
| D607 | Way to Happy Living–Bishop Fulton J. Sheen | .50 | 1.00 | 1.50 | NF |
| R608 | The Power of Positive Thinking–Norman Vincent Peale | .50 | 1.00 | 1.50 | |
| D609 | Thunder on the Right–Mary Stewart | .50 | 1.00 | 1.50 | |
| M610 | Northwest Passage–Kenneth Roberts | .50 | 1.00 | 1.50 | A |
| M611 | Lydia Bailey–Kenneth Roberts | .50 | 1.00 | 1.50 | A |

**CREST BOOKS,** *continued*

| Code | Title | V/Good | Fine | N/Mint | |
|------|-------|--------|------|--------|--|
| D612 | The Long Winter–John Christopher | 1.00 | 2.00 | 3.00 | SF |
| D613 | How to Live 365 Days a Year–John A. Schindler, MD | .50 | 1.00 | 1.50 | NF |
| T614 | World-Wide French Dictionary–Richard Switzer & Herbert S. Gochberg | .50 | 1.00 | 1.50 | NF |
| K615 | Psycho–Robert Bloch | .75 | 1.50 | 2.25 | HO |
| K616 | The Unforgiven–Alan LeMay | .75 | 1.50 | 2.25 | W |
| R617 | According to Hoyle–Richard L. Frey | .50 | 1.00 | 1.50 | NF |
| R618 | Kirkland Revels–Victoria Holt | .50 | 1.00 | 1.50 | R |
| S619 | Good Grief, Charlie Brown–Charles Schulz | .75 | 1.50 | 2.25 | H |
| D620 | The Home Book of Barbecue Cooking–Myra Waldo | .50 | 1.00 | 1.50 | NF |
| D621 | Man and Sex–Joseph J. Kaufman, MD & Griffith Borgeson | .50 | 1.00 | 1.50 | NF |
| D622 | The Deathmakers–Glen Sire | .50 | 1.00 | 1.50 | |
| D623 | The Great Escape–Paul Brickhill; later printing (3rd seen) is movie tie-in | .50 | 1.00 | 1.50 | C |
| M624 | Uhuru–Robert Ruark | .75 | 1.50 | 2.25 | A |
| T625 | Welcome to Thebes–Glendon Swarthout | .50 | 1.00 | 1.50 | |
| S626 | For the Love of Peanuts–Charles Schulz | .75 | 1.50 | 2.25 | H |
| R627 | You're Entitle'–Harry Golden | .50 | 1.00 | 1.50 | H |
| D628 | Invitation to Double-Crostics–Elizabeth S. Kingsley | .50 | 1.00 | 1.50 | NF |
| D629 | Mistress of Mellyn–Victoria Holt | .50 | 1.00 | 1.50 | R |
| M630 | Mandingo–Kyle Onstott | .50 | 1.00 | 1.50 | E |
| T631 | Decision at Delphi–Helen MacInnes | .50 | 1.00 | 1.50 | |
| D632 | One Day in the Life of Ivan Denisovich–Alexander Solzhenitsyn | 2.00 | 4.00 | 6.00 | |
| M633 | The Sound of Bow Bells–Jerome Weidman | .50 | 1.00 | 1.50 | |
| R634 | How to Win at Contract Bridge–Richard L. Frey | .50 | 1.00 | 1.50 | NF |
| D635 | Window on the Square–Phyllis A. Whitney | .50 | 1.00 | 1.50 | |
| S636 | Dennis the Menace, Household Hurricane–Hank Ketcham | .75 | 1.50 | 2.25 | H |
| K637 | Dear Abby on Marriage–Abigail Van Buren | .50 | 1.00 | 1.50 | NF |
| D638 | Gilligan's Last Elephant–Gerald Hanley | .50 | 1.00 | 1.50 | A |
| T639 | King Rat–James Clavell | .75 | 1.50 | 2.25 | C |
| S640 | Top Hand with a Gun–Harry Sinclair Drago; aka Guardians of the Sage | .75 | 1.50 | 2.25 | W |
| T641 | Steamboat Gothic–Frances Parkinson Keyes | .50 | 1.00 | 1.50 | |
| D642 | Cure Your Nerves Yourself–Dr. Louis E. Bisch | .50 | 1.00 | 1.50 | NF |
| S643 | Top Gun–Gordon Daniels | .50 | 1.00 | 1.50 | W |
| R644 | Be Happier, Be Healthier–Gayelord Hauser | .50 | 1.00 | 1.50 | NF |
| D645 | The Enjoyment of Love in Marriage–Dr. LeMon Clark; aka Sex and You | .50 | 1.00 | 1.50 | NF |
| K646 | Kids Sure Rite Funny–Art Linkletter | .50 | 1.00 | 1.50 | H |
| R647 | Letters from the Earth–Mark Twain (ed. Bernard DeVoto) | .75 | 1.50 | 2.25 | |
| M648 | Oliver Wiswell–Kenneth Roberts | .50 | 1.00 | 1.50 | |
| T649 | Joy Street–Frances Parkinson Keyes | .50 | 1.00 | 1.50 | |
| M650 | Arundel–Kenneth Roberts | .50 | 1.00 | 1.50 | A |
| S651 | Dennis the Menace-Who Me?–Hank Ketcham | .75 | 1.50 | 2.25 | H |
| K652 | Mr. Seidman and the Geisha–Elick Moll | .50 | 1.00 | 1.50 | |
| R653 | Flush Times–Warren Miller | .50 | 1.00 | 1.50 | |
| D654 | The New Webster's Crossword Puzzle Dictionary–Bettye F. Melnicove | .50 | 1.00 | 1.50 | NF |
| R655 | The Tattooed Rood–Kyle Onstott & Lance Horner | .50 | 1.00 | 1.50 | |
| R656 | Blue Camellia–Frances Parkinson Keyes | .50 | 1.00 | 1.50 | |
| S657 | Dennis the Menace . . . Teacher's Threat–Hank Ketcham | .75 | 1.50 | 2.25 | H |
| M658 | Drum–Kyle Onstott | .50 | 1.00 | 1.50 | E |
| M659 | Madame Castel's Lodger–Frances Parkinson Keyes | .50 | 1.00 | 1.50 | |
| M660 | King's Row–Henry Bellamann | .50 | 1.00 | 1.50 | |
| R661 | A Flash of Green–John D. MacDonald | 1.00 | 2.00 | 3.00 | M |
| D662 | Is It Safe to Drink the Water?–Art Buchwald | .50 | 1.00 | 1.50 | H |
| S663 | Top Sacred–Hugh Burnett | .50 | 1.00 | 1.50 | |
| K664 | Auschwitz: A Doctor's Eyewitness Account–Dr. Miklos Nyiszli | .50 | 1.00 | 1.50 | NF |
| T665 | South of the Angels–Jessamyn West | .50 | 1.00 | 1.50 | |
| D666 | See Without Glasses–Ralph MacFadyen | .50 | 1.00 | 1.50 | NF |
| R667 | Guide to Confident Living–Norman Vincent Peale | .50 | 1.00 | 1.50 | NF |
| S668 | Fun with Peanuts–Charles M. Schulz | .75 | 1.50 | 2.25 | H |
| M669 | Also the Hills–Frances Parkinson Keyes | .50 | 1.00 | 1.50 | |
| D670 | Amorous Tales of the Decameron–Giovanni Boccaccio | .50 | 1.00 | 1.50 | |
| D671 | Who Fired the First Shot?–Ashley Halsey, Jr | .50 | 1.00 | 1.50 | |
| M672 | Poor No More–Robert C. Ruark | .50 | 1.00 | 1.50 | |
| R673 | My First 2000 Years–George S. Viereck & Paul Eldridge | .75 | 1.50 | 2.25 | F |
| K674 | The Wizard of Oz–L. Frank Baum; 1964 | 1.00 | 2.00 | 3.00 | F |
| R675 | Triumph–Philip Wylie | .50 | 1.00 | 1.50 | |
| D676 | The Same Door–John Updike | .50 | 1.00 | 1.50 | |
| D677 | The Poorhouse Fair–John Updike | .50 | 1.00 | 1.50 | |
| R678 | Double Your Reading Speed–Reading Laboratory, Inc. | .50 | 1.00 | 1.50 | NF |
| K679 | A Dram of Poison–Charlotte Armstrong | .50 | 1.00 | 1.50 | M |
| S680 | Avenger from Texas–Will Ermine | .75 | 1.50 | 2.25 | W |
| T681 | Silent Spring–Rachel Carson | .50 | 1.00 | 1.50 | NF |
| R682 | The Centaur–John Updike | .50 | 1.00 | 1.50 | |
| M683 | The River Road–Frances Parkinson Keyes | .50 | 1.00 | 1.50 | |
| S684 | Back to B.C.–Johnny Hart | .75 | 1.50 | 2.25 | H |
| D685 | A Catholic Parent's Guide to Sex Education–Dr. Audrey Kelly | .75 | 1.50 | 2.25 | NF |
| D686 | The Insolent Chariots–John Keats | .50 | 1.00 | 1.50 | H |
| S687 | Pardon My Blooper–ed. Kermit Schafer | .75 | 1.50 | 2.25 | H |
| D688 | My Brother Michael–Mary Stewart | .50 | 1.00 | 1.50 | |
| M689 | The Sand Pebbles–Richard McKenna | .50 | 1.00 | 1.50 | A |
| T690 | The Moonflower Vine–Jetta Carleton | .50 | 1.00 | 1.50 | |
| M691 | The Tin Drum–Günter Grass | .50 | 1.00 | 1.50 | |
| R692 | The Surgeon–W.C. Heinz | .50 | 1.00 | 1.50 | |
| T693 | Teach Yourself Russian–Maximilian Fourman | .50 | 1.00 | 1.50 | NF |
| K695 | So You Think You Know Baseball?–Harry Simmons | .50 | 1.00 | 1.50 | S |
| S696 | Gunsmoke on the Mesa–Davis Dresser | .50 | 1.00 | 1.50 | W |
| R697 | Handbook of Everyday Law–Martin J. Ross | .50 | 1.00 | 1.50 | NF |
| T698 | World-Wide German Dictionary–Paul H. Glucksman | .50 | 1.00 | 1.50 | NF |
| R699 | Souls of Black Folk–W.E.B. DuBois | 3.00 | 6.00 | 9.00 | |
| K700 | The Cool World–Warren Miller; later printing (4th seen) is movie tie-in | .50 | 1.00 | 1.50 | JD |
| D701 | The Sands of Kalahari–William Mulvihill | .50 | 1.00 | 1.50 | A |
| D702 | Madam, Will You Talk?–Mary Stewart | .50 | 1.00 | 1.50 | |
| T703 | The Pyramid Climbers–Vance Packard | .50 | 1.00 | 1.50 | |
| T704 | Gabriela, Clove and Cinnamon–Jorge Amado | .50 | 1.00 | 1.50 | |
| D705 | Teenage Tyranny–Grace Hechinger & Fred M. Hechinger | 1.00 | 2.00 | 3.00 | |
| K706 | Maggie-Her Marriage–Taylor Caldwell | .50 | 1.00 | 1.50 | |
| K707 | The Doctor's Husband–Elizabeth Seifert | .50 | 1.00 | 1.50 | |
| S708 | Pogo for President–Walt Kelly; 1964 | 6.00 | 12.00 | 18.00 | H |
| D709 | The Education of a Golfer–Sam Snead & Al Stump | .50 | 1.00 | 1.50 | S |
| K710 | Of Love Forbidden–Anna Elisabet Weirauch; aka The Scorpion | .50 | 1.00 | 1.50 | |
| R711 | One Man's Way–Arthur Gordon | .50 | 1.00 | 1.50 | B |
| R712 | Stay Alive All Your Life–Norman Vincent Peale | .50 | 1.00 | 1.50 | NF |
| M713 | Sword at Sunset–Rosemary Sutcliff | 1.00 | 2.00 | 3.00 | A |
| K714 | Best Cartoons–from True Mag. | .75 | 1.50 | 2.25 | H |
| D715 | The Painless Way to Stop Smoking–Jack G. Heise | .50 | 1.00 | 1.50 | NF |
| D716 | The Messenger–Charles Wright | .50 | 1.00 | 1.50 | |
| R717 | The Moon-Spinners–Mary Stewart; movie tie-in | .75 | 1.50 | 2.25 | M |
| K718 | Shock Treatment–Winfred Van Atta; movie tie-in | .75 | 1.50 | 2.25 | |
| R719 | The Home Book of Italian Cooking–Angela Catanzaro; aka Mama Mia Italian Cookbook | .50 | 1.00 | 1.50 | NF |

CREST BOOKS, *continued*

| | | V/Good | Fine | N/Mint | |
|---|---|---|---|---|---|
| M720 | A Distant Trumpet—Paul Horgan | .50 | 1.00 | 1.50 | |
| D721 | Seven Tears for Apollo—Phyllis A. Whitney | .50 | 1.00 | 1.50 | |
| S722 | Here Comes Charlie Brown—Charles M. Schulz | .75 | 1.50 | 2.25 | H |
| R723 | The Marauders—Charlton Ogburn, Jr | .50 | 1.00 | 1.50 | |
| M724 | The Gay Place—William Brammer | .50 | 1.00 | 1.50 | |
| T725 | The Trend Is Up—Anthony West | .50 | 1.00 | 1.50 | |
| D726 | Mary, Mary and Other Plays—Jean Kerr | .50 | 1.00 | 1.50 | |
| T727 | The Man with the Golden Arm—Nelson Algren | .75 | 1.50 | 2.25 | |
| L728 | Get Out of My Sky—Leo Margulies | .50 | 1.00 | 1.50 | SF |
| T729 | A Man Called Peter—Catherine Marshall | .50 | 1.00 | 1.50 | |
| M730 | Rabble in Arms—Kenneth Roberts | .50 | 1.00 | 1.50 | A |
| T731 | John F. Kennedy, President—Hugh Sidey | 1.00 | 2.00 | 3.00 | B |
| R732 | Heaven Has No Favorites—Erich Maria Remarque | .50 | 1.00 | 1.50 | |
| R733 | The Trumpet Unblown—William Hoffman | .50 | 1.00 | 1.50 | |
| D734 | Doctor Golf—William Price Fox | .50 | 1.00 | 1.50 | |
| T735 | The American Way of Death—Jessica Mitford | .50 | 1.00 | 1.50 | NF |
| R736 | Marnie—Winston Graham; later printing (3rd seen) is movie tie-in | .50 | 1.00 | 1.50 | |
| D737 | The Late Clara Beame—Taylor Caldwell | .50 | 1.00 | 1.50 | |
| R738 | The Professional: Lyndon B. Johnson—William S. White | .50 | 1.00 | 1.50 | B |
| R739 | Mr. Kennedy and the Negroes—Harry Golden | 1.50 | 3.00 | 4.50 | NF |
| R740 | The Official Rules of Card Games—Albert H. Morehead | .50 | 1.00 | 1.50 | NF |
| D741 | The Day of the Triffids—John Wyndham | .75 | 1.50 | 2.25 | SF |
| K742 | Hanno's Doll—Evelyn Piper | .50 | 1.00 | 1.50 | |
| T743 | Fate Is the Hunter—Ernest K. Gann; later printing (4th seen) is movie tie-in | .50 | 1.00 | 1.50 | |
| D744 | Modern Rules of Order—Luther S. Cushing | .50 | 1.00 | 1.50 | |
| M745 | Grandmother and the Priests—Taylor Caldwell | .50 | 1.00 | 1.50 | |
| T746 | The Venetian Affair—Helen MacInnes | .50 | 1.00 | 1.50 | |
| R747 | The Learning Tree—Gordon Parks | .50 | 1.00 | 1.50 | |
| T748 | While Still We Live—Helen MacInnes | .50 | 1.00 | 1.50 | |
| D749 | The Way We Live Now—Warren Miller | .50 | 1.00 | 1.50 | |
| D750 | Powers of Attorney—Louis Auchincloss | .50 | 1.00 | 1.50 | |
| T751 | Do Not Go Gentle—David MacCuish | .50 | 1.00 | 1.50 | |
| D752 | Time Is the Simplest Thing—Clifford D. Simak | .75 | 1.50 | 2.25 | SF |
| R753 | How to Study—Harry Maddox | .50 | 1.00 | 1.50 | NF |
| K754 | Woman's Day Magazine Presents Treasure Book of Fairy Tales—ed. Ann McGovern | 1.50 | 3.00 | 4.50 | F |
| S755 | Dennis the Menace, Make-Believe Angel—Hank Ketcham | .75 | 1.50 | 2.25 | H |
| R756 | The Scent of Water—Elizabeth Goudge | .50 | 1.00 | 1.50 | |
| D757 | Tales for a Rainy Night—ed. David Alexander | .75 | 1.50 | 2.25 | HO |
| L758 | City at World's End—Edmond Hamilton | .50 | 1.00 | 1.50 | SF |
| R759 | Dr. Spock Talks with Mothers—Benjamin Spock, MD | .50 | 1.00 | 1.50 | NF |
| T760 | The Golden Hammer—Sonya Arcone | .50 | 1.00 | 1.50 | |
| R761 | Ice Station Zebra—Alistair Maclean | 1.50 | 3.00 | 4.50 | |
| D762 | I Chose Capitol Punishment—Art Buchwald | .50 | 1.00 | 1.50 | H |
| D763 | John Goldfarb, Please Come Home—William Peter Blatty; movie tie-in | .50 | 1.00 | 1.50 | |
| T764 | The Black Obelisk—Erich Maria Remarque | .50 | 1.00 | 1.50 | |
| R765 | The Privacy Invaders—Myron Brenton | .50 | 1.00 | 1.50 | |
| T766 | The Complete Chessplayer—Fred Reinfeld | .50 | 1.00 | 1.50 | NF |
| K767 | Hey!, B.C.—Johnny Hart | .75 | 1.50 | 2.25 | H |
| T768 | Of Good and Evil—Ernest K. Gann | .50 | 1.00 | 1.50 | |
| T769 | To Live Again—Catherine Marshall | .50 | 1.00 | 1.50 | |
| T770 | Away from Home—Rona Jaffe | .50 | 1.00 | 1.50 | |
| T771 | Horn of the Hunter—Robert Ruark | .50 | 1.00 | 1.50 | |
| T772 | Captain Caution—Kenneth Roberts | .50 | 1.00 | 1.50 | A |
| D773 | A for Andromeda—Fred Hoyle & John Elliot | .50 | 1.00 | 1.50 | |
| R774 | Wine Coaches Waiting—Mary Stewart | .50 | 1.00 | 1.50 | |
| D775 | The Shook-Up Generation—Harrison E. Salisbury | 1.50 | 3.00 | 4.50 | JD |
| T776 | Dorothy and Red—Vincent Sheean | .50 | 1.00 | 1.50 | |
| D777 | The I Hate to Cook Book—Peg Bracken | .50 | 1.00 | 1.50 | H |
| R778 | Bride of Pendorric—Victoria Holt | .50 | 1.00 | 1.50 | R |
| S779 | Very Funny, Charlie Brown!—Charles M. Schulz | .75 | 1.50 | 2.25 | H |
| M780 | The Adventures of Augie March—Saul Bellow | .50 | 1.00 | 1.50 | |
| K781 | Seance on a Wet Afternoon—Mark McShane; movie tie-in | .50 | 1.00 | 1.50 | |
| D782 | Awake Monique—Astrid Van Royen | .50 | 1.00 | 1.50 | |
| T783 | The New Way to Better Hearing—Victor L. Browd | .50 | 1.00 | 1.50 | NF |
| R784 | Understanding the New Mathematics—Evelyn B. Rosenthal | .50 | 1.00 | 1.50 | NF |
| K785 | Ann Landers Talks to Teen-agers About Sex—Ann Landers | .50 | 1.00 | 1.50 | NF |
| D786 | Black Amber—Phyllis A. Whitney | .50 | 1.00 | 1.50 | |
| T787 | Verse (The Carpenter's Hen & Telephone Poles)—John Updike | .50 | 1.00 | 1.50 | |
| K788 | Cape Fear—John D. MacDonald; aka The Executioners | .75 | 1.50 | 2.25 | M |
| D789 | Sylvia—E.V. Cunningham. Note: Movie tie-in of Sylvia apparently does not exist, as all copies of this book seen contain horror novel Sylva by Vercors (Jean Bruller) | .50 | 1.00 | 1.50 | E |
| D790 | Assassination!—Ben Abro | .50 | 1.00 | 1.50 | |
| R791 | Is *That* in the Bible?—Dr. Charles Francis Potter | .75 | 1.50 | 2.25 | NF |
| R792 | The Amazing Results of Positive Thinking—Norman Vincent Peale | .50 | 1.00 | 1.50 | NF |
| R793 | Looking for the General—Warren Miller | .50 | 1.00 | 1.50 | SF |
| R794 | The Night in Lisbon—Erich Maria Remarque | .50 | 1.00 | 1.50 | |
| K795 | The Last Quarter Hour—Jean Bruce | .50 | 1.00 | 1.50 | |
| R796 | Careful, He Might Hear You—Sumner Locke Elliott | .50 | 1.00 | 1.50 | |
| D797 | The Young Marrieds—Judith Heiman | .50 | 1.00 | 1.50 | |
| R798 | The Pilgrim Project—Hank Searls; 1965 | .50 | 1.00 | 1.50 | |
| R799 | The Keepers of the House—Shirley Ann Grau | .50 | 1.00 | 1.50 | |
| R800 | The Rocks Remain—Gavin Maxwell | .50 | 1.00 | 1.50 | |
| R801 | I and My True Love—Helen MacInnes | .50 | 1.00 | 1.50 | |
| K802 | Under the Skin—Dorothea Bennett | .50 | 1.00 | 1.50 | |
| D803 | How to Play Your Best Golf All the Time—Tommy Armour | .50 | 1.00 | 1.50 | NF |
| T804 | Victorine—Frances Parkinson Keyes | .50 | 1.00 | 1.50 | |
| M805 | Master of Falconhurst—Kyle Onstott | .50 | 1.00 | 1.50 | |
| K806 | Trouble in Tokyo—Jean Bruce | .50 | 1.00 | 1.50 | |
| R807 | The Ipcress File—Len Deighton | .75 | 1.50 | 2.25 | |
| D808 | Mirage—Howard Fast; aka Fallen Angel | .50 | 1.00 | 1.50 | |
| T809 | The Tattooed Rood—Kyle Onstott & Lance Horner | .50 | 1.00 | 1.50 | E |
| M810 | Steamboat Gothic—Frances Parkinson Keyes | .50 | 1.00 | 1.50 | |
| D811 | The New Webster's Crossword Puzzle Dictionary—Bettye F. Melnicove | .50 | 1.00 | 1.50 | NF |
| D812 | Fifth Planet—Fred & Geoffrey Hoyle | .50 | 1.00 | 1.50 | SF |
| D813 | Small Town D.A.—Robert Traver | .50 | 1.00 | 1.50 | |
| D814 | Twelve Tales of Suspense and the Supernatural—ed. Davis Grubb | .75 | 1.50 | 2.25 | HO |
| R815 | You Are Not the Target—Laura Archera Huxley | .50 | 1.00 | 1.50 | |
| T816 | The Third Day—Joseph Hayes; movie tie-in | .50 | 1.00 | 1.50 | |
| R817 | Venus in Sparta—Louis Auchincloss | .50 | 1.00 | 1.50 | |
| K818 | What Next, Charlie Brown?—Charles M. Schulz | .75 | 1.50 | 2.25 | H |
| R819 | The Gypsy Moths—James Drought | .50 | 1.00 | 1.50 | A |
| D820 | The Lost Years of Jesus Revealed—Dr. Charles Francis Potter | .50 | 1.00 | 1.50 | NF |
| T821 | Home Medical Encyclopedia—Paul Kuhne, MD | .50 | 1.00 | 1.50 | NF |
| M822 | The Side of the Angels—Alexander Fedoroff | .50 | 1.00 | 1.50 | |
| T823 | The Ivy Tree—Mary Stewart | .50 | 1.00 | 1.50 | |
| M824 | In Vivo—Mildred Savage | .50 | 1.00 | 1.50 | |
| R825 | The Great World and Timothy Colt—Louis Auchincloss | .50 | 1.00 | 1.50 | |

| | V/Good | Fine | N/Mint | |
|---|---|---|---|---|

CREST BOOKS, *continued*

| | | V/Good | Fine | N/Mint | |
|---|---|---|---|---|---|
| K826 | The Snake Has All the Lines–Jean Kerr | .50 | 1.00 | 1.50 | H |
| K827 | To Goof or Not to Goof–Dick Clark | 1.50 | 3.00 | 4.50 | |
| D828 | It's All in the Stars–''Zolar'' | .50 | 1.00 | 1.50 | |
| R829 | Window on the Square–Phyllis A. Whitney | .50 | 1.00 | 1.50 | |
| D830 | The I Hate to Housekeep Book–Peg Bracken | .50 | 1.00 | 1.50 | H |
| K831 | For the Love of Peanuts–Charles M. Schulz | .75 | 1.50 | 2.25 | H |
| R832 | Love or Perish–Smiley Blanton, MD | .50 | 1.00 | 1.50 | |
| R833 | The Siege of Harlem–Warren Miller | .50 | 1.00 | 1.50 | |
| D834 | Please Don't Eat the Daisies–Jean Kerr; 1965; TV tie-in | .50 | 1.00 | 1.50 | H |
| M835 | By Love Possessed–James Gould Cozzens | .50 | 1.00 | 1.50 | |
| R836 | Owls' Watch–ed. George Brandon Saul; 1965 | 1.00 | 2.00 | 3.00 | HO |
| T837 | This Rough Magic–Mary Stewart | .50 | 1.00 | 1.50 | |
| M838 | A Flag Full of Stars–Don Robertson | .50 | 1.00 | 1.50 | |
| R839 | Look Younger, Live Longer–Gayelord Hauser | .50 | 1.00 | 1.50 | |
| R840 | Modern Manners: Etiquette for All Occasions–Carolyn Hagner Shaw | .50 | 1.00 | 1.50 | NF |
| M841 | The Man–Irving Wallace | .50 | 1.00 | 1.50 | |
| T842 | An Infinity of Mirrors–Richard Condon | .50 | 1.00 | 1.50 | |
| R843 | The Enemy–James Drought | .50 | 1.00 | 1.50 | |
| R844 | Teach Yourself German–Sir John Adams | .50 | 1.00 | 1.50 | NF |
| T845 | The Old Blood–Edgar Mittelholzer | .50 | 1.00 | 1.50 | |
| K846 | Untimely Ripped–Mark McShane | .50 | 1.00 | 1.50 | M |
| M847 | Joy Street–Frances Parkinson Keyes | .50 | 1.00 | 1.50 | |
| R848 | Wicked Angel–Taylor Caldwell | .50 | 1.00 | 1.50 | |
| T849 | King Rat–James Clavell; 1965 | .50 | 1.00 | 1.50 | C |
| M850 | Reminiscences–Douglas MacArthur | .50 | 1.00 | 1.50 | B |
| M851 | Little Big Man–Thomas Berger; 1965 | 1.50 | 3.00 | 4.50 | W |
| R852 | Problems of Parents–Benjamin Spock, MD | .50 | 1.00 | 1.50 | NF |
| R853 | My Brother Michael–Mary Stewart | .50 | 1.00 | 1.50 | |
| K854 | Hey, Peanuts!–Charles M. Schulz | .75 | 1.50 | 2.25 | H |
| R855 | Mistress of Mellyn–Victoria Holt | .50 | 1.00 | 1.50 | R |
| D856 | The Liquidator–John Gardner | .50 | 1.00 | 1.50 | |
| R857 | Seize the Day–Saul Bellow | .50 | 1.00 | 1.50 | |
| K858 | Good Grief, Charlie Brown!–Charles M. Schulz | .75 | 1.50 | 2.25 | H |
| R859 | Teach Yourself Spanish–N. Scarlyn Wilson | .50 | 1.00 | 1.50 | NF |
| M860 | Dennis the Menace, Happy Half-Pint–Hank Ketcham | .75 | 1.50 | 2.25 | H |
| D861 | Sands of the Kalahari–William Mulvihill | .50 | 1.00 | 1.50 | A |
| R862 | Madam, Will You Talk?–Mary Stewart | .50 | 1.00 | 1.50 | |
| D863 | Friday the Rabbi Slept Late–Harry Kemelman | .50 | 1.00 | 1.50 | M |
| T864 | The Master-Key to Riches–Napoleon Hill | .50 | 1.00 | 1.50 | NF |
| D865 | The Nanny–Evelyn Piper; movie tie-in | .50 | 1.00 | 1.50 | |
| M866 | Book of the Eskimos–Peter Freuchen | .50 | 1.00 | 1.50 | A |
| K867 | Dennis the Menace, A.M.* (*Ambassador of Mischief)–Hank Ketcham | .75 | 1.50 | 2.25 | H |
| M868 | Herzog–Saul Bellow | .50 | 1.00 | 1.50 | |
| K869 | Dennis the Menace–Household Hurricane–Hank Ketcham | .75 | 1.50 | 2.25 | H |
| K870 | Here Comes Charlie Brown–Charles M. Schulz | .75 | 1.50 | 2.25 | H |
| K871 | Fun with Peanuts–Charles M. Schulz | .75 | 1.50 | 2.25 | H |
| T872 | Think and Grow Rich–Napoleon Hill | .50 | 1.00 | 1.50 | NF |
| R873 | Mathematics for Pleasure–Oswald Jacoby | .50 | 1.00 | 1.50 | NF |
| K874 | Dennis the Menace–Teacher's Threat–Hank Ketcham | .75 | 1.50 | 2.25 | H |
| K875 | The Wonderful World of Peanuts–Charles M. Schulz | .75 | 1.50 | 2.25 | H |
| K876 | B.C. Strikes Back–Johnny Hart; 1965 | .75 | 1.50 | 2.25 | H |
| R877 | The Q Document–James Hall Roberts | .50 | 1.00 | 1.50 | M |
| T878 | Those Harper Women–Stephen Birmingham | .50 | 1.00 | 1.50 | |
| M879 | Henderson the Rain King–Saul Bellow | .50 | 1.00 | 1.50 | |
| M880 | Nina's Book–Eugene Burdick | .50 | 1.00 | 1.50 | |
| T881 | Crest Colorprint World Atlas–Gwen M. Schultz | .50 | 1.00 | 1.50 | NF |
| T883 | The Words–Jean-Paul Sartre; 1966 | .50 | 1.00 | 1.50 | |
| K884 | We're On Your Side, Charlie Brown–Charles M. Schulz | .75 | 1.50 | 2.25 | H |

| | | V/Good | Fine | N/Mint | |
|---|---|---|---|---|---|
| T885 | Bride of Pendorric–Victoria Holt | .50 | 1.00 | 1.50 | R |
| M886 | Decision at Delphi–Helen MacInnes | .50 | 1.00 | 1.50 | |
| K887 | Dennis the Menace Rides Again–Hank Ketcham | .75 | 1.50 | 2.25 | H |
| K888 | Wanted, Dennis the Menace–Hank Ketcham | .75 | 1.50 | 2.25 | H |
| T889 | The Blue of Capricorn–Eugene Burdick | .50 | 1.00 | 1.50 | |
| T890 | A Walk on the Wild Side–Nelson Algren | .50 | 1.00 | 1.50 | JD |
| T891 | P.S. Wilkinson–C.D.B. Bryan | .50 | 1.00 | 1.50 | |
| R892 | Darkwater–Dorothy Eden | .50 | 1.00 | 1.50 | |
| R893 | Wildfire at Midnight–Mary Stewart | .50 | 1.00 | 1.50 | |
| R894 | Thunder on the Right–Mary Stewart | .50 | 1.00 | 1.50 | |
| T895 | Blue Camellia–Frances Parkinson Keyes | .50 | 1.00 | 1.50 | |
| R899 | Modesty Blaise–Peter O'Donnell; 1960; movie tie-in | 1.50 | 3.00 | 4.50 | M |

## CRIME-ADVENTURE SERIES
## Brentwood Publications

| | | V/Good | Fine | N/Mint | |
|---|---|---|---|---|---|
| FB1007 | Sex Demon of Jangal–Lynton Wright Brent; 1964 | 3.00 | 6.00 | 9.00 | F |
| FB1008 | Flaming Lust–Lynton Wright Brent; 1964 | 3.00 | 6.00 | 9.00 | F |
| FB1010 | Double Trouble–Rosqua Wassam | 1.50 | 3.00 | 4.50 | E |
| FB1011 | Sins of Cheryl–Rodger Blake | 1.50 | 3.00 | 4.50 | E |
| FB1012 | Squaw Trail–Lynton Wright Brent | 2.00 | 4.00 | 6.00 | W |
| FB1013 | Lavender Love Rumble–Lynton Wright Brent | 2.00 | 4.00 | 6.00 | E |
| FB1014 | The Desert Is a Woman–Lynton Wright Brent | 2.00 | 4.00 | 6.00 | W |
| FB1015 | Silent Sex Trail–Lynton Wright Brent; 1965 | 2.00 | 4.00 | 6.00 | W |
| FB1016 | The Furious Passion of the Laughing Gun–Lynton Wright Brent | 2.00 | 4.00 | 6.00 | W |
| FB1017 | The Passion Tree–Lynton Wright Brent | 2.00 | 4.00 | 6.00 | W |
| FB1018 | Sex and the Hospital–Lynton Wright Brent | 1.50 | 3.00 | 4.50 | E |
| FB1019 | Violent Love Stalks the Plains–Lynton Wright Brent | 2.00 | 4.00 | 6.00 | W |
| FB1020 | Passionate Peril at Fort Tomahawk–Lynton Wright Brent | 2.00 | 4.00 | 6.00 | W |
| FB1021 | Lust Gallops into the Desert–Lynton Wright Brent; 1965 | 2.50 | 5.00 | 7.50 | W |

## CRIME NOVEL SELECTION
## Red Circle Magazines, Inc.

### Digest Size

| | | V/Good | Fine | N/Mint | |
|---|---|---|---|---|---|
| 1 | Strangler's Holiday–Kurt Steel; 1942; aka Murder in G-Sharp; c-Saunders | 7.50 | 15.00 | 22.50 | M |
| 2 | The Traveling Corpses–Kurt Steel | 7.50 | 15.00 | 22.50 | M |
| 3 | The Submarine Signaled . . . Murder–Allan R. Bosworth | 7.50 | 15.00 | 22.50 | M |
| 4 | Murder for What?–Kurt Steel | 7.50 | 15.00 | 22.50 | M |
| 5 | 3 Girls and a Killer–H. Donald Spatz | 7.50 | 15.00 | 22.50 | M |
| nn | Death Is the Host–Lawrence Lariar; 1943; aka Death Paints the Picture | 7.50 | 15.00 | 22.50 | M |

*Crime Novel Selection 2, Crime Novel Selection 5, Crimes of Love & Passion 2.*

# CRIMES OF LOVE AND PASSION
## Louellen Publishing Company
### Digest Size

| | | V/Good | Fine | N/Mint | |
|---|---|---|---|---|---|
| 1 | The Secret Lover of Madeleine Smith–ed. Paul Renin; 1945 | 5.00 | 10.00 | 15.00 | E |
| 2 | The Crimes of Belle Gunness–ed. Paul Renin | 5.00 | 10.00 | 15.00 | E |
| 3 | Dorothy Jordan, the Siren of Old Drury–ed. Paul Renin | 5.00 | 10.00 | 15.00 | E |
| 4 | Bela Kiss–ed. Paul Renin | 5.00 | 10.00 | 15.00 | E |

# (CROSSWORD PLEASURE)
## Crossword Pleasure, Inc.

| | | V/Good | Fine | N/Mint | |
|---|---|---|---|---|---|
| nn | Today's New, Enlarged Crossword Dictionary–Davis Shulman; 1960 | .75 | 1.50 | 2.25 | NF |
| nn | Collector's Crosswords–With a Medical Twist–Jesse Jacobs; 1st ed. 1961 | 2.00 | 4.00 | 6.00 | NF |

# CROW EDITIONS
## Alval Publishers of Canada, Ltd.
### (Canadian)

| | | V/Good | Fine | N/Mint | |
|---|---|---|---|---|---|
| 21 | Sister of the Damned–Lara Jefferson | 2.00 | 4.00 | 6.00 | E |
| 22 | Red Moon of Desire–Darryl X. Dexter | 2.00 | 4.00 | 6.00 | E |
| 23 | Careless Virgin–James Clayford (Peggy Gaddis) | 2.00 | 4.00 | 6.00 | E |
| 24 | Overnight Girl–Joan Sherman (Peggy Gaddis); aka Overnight Cabins | 2.00 | 4.00 | 6.00 | E |
| 25 | Reckless Maiden–Peggy Gaddis | 2.00 | 4.00 | 6.00 | E |
| 26 | Weekend Girl–James Clayford (Peggy Gaddis ) | 2.00 | 4.00 | 6.00 | E |
| 27 | Impatient Temptress–James Clayford | 2.00 | 4.00 | 6.00 | E |
| 28 | Party-wife–Helen Ahern | 2.00 | 4.00 | 6.00 | E |
| 29 | Wedding Night Confession–Luther Gordon | 2.00 | 4.00 | 6.00 | E |
| 30 | Frenchy–Harmon Bellamy | 2.00 | 4.00 | 6.00 | E |
| 31 | Good Girl–By Day–James Clayford (Peggy Gaddis) | 2.00 | 4.00 | 6.00 | E |
| 32 | Illicit Honeymoon–James Clayford (Peggy Gaddis) | 2.00 | 4.00 | 6.00 | E |
| 33 | Pick-up–Harmon Bellamy | 2.00 | 4.00 | 6.00 | E |
| 34 | Night of Passion–Luther Gordon | 2.00 | 4.00 | 6.00 | E |
| 35 | Hot Number–Roy Langdale | 2.00 | 4.00 | 6.00 | E |
| 36 | Midnight Sinners–John Caldwall | 2.00 | 4.00 | 6.00 | E |
| 37 | Desirable–Luther Gordon | 2.00 | 4.00 | 6.00 | E |
| 38 | Paid in Full–Harmon Bellamy | 2.00 | 4.00 | 6.00 | E |
| 39 | Lady in a Hurry–Norman Bligh | 2.00 | 4.00 | 6.00 | E |
| 40 | Side Show Girl–James Clayford (Peggy Gaddis) | 3.00 | 6.00 | 9.00 | E |
| 41 | Lady in Waiting–James Clayford (Peggy Gaddis) | 2.00 | 4.00 | 6.00 | E |
| 42 | Too Many Sweethearts–Norman Bligh | 2.00 | 4.00 | 6.00 | E |
| 43 | Easy Come–Easy Go–Roy Langdale | 2.00 | 4.00 | 6.00 | E |
| 44 | Lovely to Look At–Harmon Bellamy | 2.00 | 4.00 | 6.00 | E |

*Crow 40, Croydon 13, Croydon 15.*

# CROYDON
## Croydon Publishing Co./Star Publications, Inc.
### Digest Size unless noted

| | | V/Good | Fine | N/Mint | |
|---|---|---|---|---|---|
| nn | Vicious Circle–Manning Long; 1945; c-Cole | 4.00 | 8.00 | 12.00 | M |
| nn | Many a Murder–Delia Van Deusen; 1945; aka Murder Bicarb; c-Cole | 4.00 | 8.00 | 12.00 | M |
| nn | Murders I've Seen–Philip Mechem; 1945; aka And Not for Love | 3.50 | 7.00 | 10.50 | M |
| nn | Here Lies Blood–M.M. Mannon; c-Cole | 4.00 | 8.00 | 12.00 | M |
| nn | Have You Seen This Man?–Gene Hurley; c-Cole | 4.00 | 8.00 | 12.00 | M |
| nn | Dogwatch–Carlyn Coffin | 3.50 | 7.00 | 10.50 | M |
| nn | Murder at Belle Camille–Monte Barrett | 3.50 | 7.00 | 10.50 | M |
| 6 | Murder Makes a Villain–Dennis Scott; c-Cole | 4.00 | 8.00 | 12.00 | M |
| 8 | Murder on the Mountain–Christine Noble Govan; c-Cole | 4.00 | 8.00 | 12.00 | M |
| 9 | The Dead Take No Bows–Richard Burke; c-Cole | 4.00 | 8.00 | 12.00 | M |
| 11 | Cheaters at Love–Wright Williams; c-Cole | 4.00 | 8.00 | 12.00 | E |
| 12 | Love Hungry–E.J. Jerome; aka Cute Kid; c-Cole | 4.00 | 8.00 | 12.00 | M |
| 13 | Reckless Virgin–Glen Watkins; c-Cole; small size | 5.00 | 10.00 | 15.00 | E |
| 14 | Shadows of Lust–Ralph Carter; c-Cole; small size | 5.00 | 10.00 | 15.00 | E |
| 15 | Fool for Love–Wright Williams; c-Cole; small size | 5.00 | 10.00 | 15.00 | E |
| 16 | Sinner–Gordon Semple; 1950; aka Life of Passion; c-Cole; small size | 5.00 | 10.00 | 15.00 | E |
| 17 | Street of Sin–Wright Williams | 3.50 | 7.00 | 10.50 | E |
| 18 | Slave of Desire–Gordon Semple | 3.50 | 7.00 | 10.50 | E |
| 19 | Restless Wife–Gail Jordan (Peggy Gaddis); aka Passionate Lover | 3.50 | 7.00 | 10.50 | E |
| 20 | The Shame at Vanna Gilbert–Glenn Watkins; aka Sinful Life | 3.50 | 7.00 | 10.50 | E |
| 21 | Shameless Sue–Gordon Semple | 3.50 | 7.00 | 10.50 | E |
| 22 | Strange Desires–Richard Himmel | 3.50 | 7.00 | 10.50 | E |
| 23 | Sins of a Private Secretary–Gail Jordan (Peggy Gaddis) | 3.50 | 7.00 | 10.50 | E |
| 24 | Love-Hungry Doctor–Florence Stonebraker; 1953 | 3.50 | 7.00 | 10.50 | E |
| 25 | Spotlight on Sin–Doug Duperrault | 3.50 | 7.00 | 10.50 | E |
| 26 | Immoral Models–Joan Sherman (Peggy Gaddis); orig. 1952 | 3.50 | 7.00 | 10.50 | E |
| 27 | Career of Sin–Gordon Semple | 3.50 | 7.00 | 10.50 | E |
| 28 | Mountain Sinner–Delmar Kingsland | 3.50 | 7.00 | 10.50 | E |
| 30 | Intimate Affairs of a French Nurse–Florence Stonebraker | 3.50 | 7.00 | 10.50 | E |
| 31 | Army Mistress–David Williams; orig. 1953 | 3.50 | 7.00 | 10.50 | E |
| 32 | Two Timing Wife–Joan Sherman (Peggy Gaddis) | 3.50 | 7.00 | 10.50 | E |
| 33 | High Priced Party Girl–Bart Frame | 3.50 | 7.00 | 10.50 | E |
| 34 | Gang Mistress–Doug Duperault | 7.50 | 15.00 | 22.50 | E |
| 35 | Vengeful Sinner–Harry Whittington; aka Die Lover | 3.50 | 7.00 | 10.50 | E |
| 36 | Blonde Temptress–Gordon Semple; orig. 1953 | 3.50 | 7.00 | 10.50 | E |
| 37 | Strange Passions–Florence Stonebraker | 3.50 | 7.00 | 10.50 | E |
| 38 | Part-time Wife–Gerald Foster | 3.50 | 7.00 | 10.50 | E |
| 39 | Indiscretions of a French Model | 3.50 | 7.00 | 10.50 | E |
| 40 | Cellar Club Girl–Alan Bennett | 6.00 | 12.00 | 18.00 | E |
| 41 | Secrets of a Paris Night–Denise Marcelle | 3.50 | 7.00 | 10.50 | E |
| 42 | Scandals at a Nudist Colony–William Vaneer | 3.50 | 7.00 | 10.50 | E |
| 43 | Love Hungry Boss–Peggy Gaddis | 3.50 | 7.00 | 10.50 | E |
| 44 | Confessions of a B-Girl–Sim Albert; orig. 1953 | 3.50 | 7.00 | 10.50 | E |
| 45 | Man-Hungry Widow–Peggy Gaddis | 3.50 | 7.00 | 10.50 | E |
| 46 | Girl Crazy Professor–Florence Stonebraker | 3.50 | 7.00 | 10.50 | E |
| 47 | Red-Headed Sinners–Jonathan Craig | 3.50 | 7.00 | 10.50 | E |
| 48 | Co-ed Sinners–Bart Frame | 3.50 | 7.00 | 10.50 | E |
| 49 | Sinful Island Vacation–William Vaneer | 3.50 | 7.00 | 10.50 | E |

CROYDON, *continued*

| # | Title | V/Good | Fine | N/Mint | |
|---|---|---|---|---|---|
| 50 | Soldier's Sinner–Doug Dupperault | 3.50 | 7.00 | 10.50 | E |
| 51 | Love-Starved Woman–Peggy Gaddis | 3.50 | 7.00 | 10.50 | E |
| 52 | Love Cult–William Vaneer | 5.00 | 10.00 | 15.00 | E |
| 53 | Warped Desires–Gordon Semple; aka Slave of Desire | 3.50 | 7.00 | 10.50 | E |
| 54 | Scandalous French Doctor–Jean Calvert; orig. 1954 | 3.50 | 7.00 | 10.50 | E |
| 55 | Shameless Play-Girl–Florence Stonebraker | 3.50 | 7.00 | 10.50 | E |
| 56 | Confessions of a Pick-up Girl–Sim Albert; orig. 1954 | 3.50 | 7.00 | 10.50 | E |
| 57 | Love-Crazy Millionaire–Gordon Semple | 3.50 | 7.00 | 10.50 | E |
| 58 | Back Road Motel–William Vaneer | 3.50 | 7.00 | 10.50 | E |
| 59 | Scandals at a Country Club–Bart Frame; orig. 1954 | 3.50 | 7.00 | 10.50 | E |
| 60 | Forbidden Passions–Wright Williams; aka Lust for Love | 3.00 | 6.00 | 9.00 | E |
| 61 | Sinner–Gordon Semple | 3.50 | 7.00 | 10.50 | E |
| 62 | Night Club Sinner–Harry Whittington; aka Vengeful Sinner | 4.00 | 8.00 | 12.00 | E |
| 63 | Man-Crazy Hussy–Gordon Semple | 3.50 | 7.00 | 10.50 | E |
| 64 | Sin Cruise–Florence Stonebraker | 3.50 | 7.00 | 10.50 | E |
| 65 | Indiscretions of a TV Sinner–Gordon Semple; orig. 1954 | 3.50 | 7.00 | 10.50 | E |
| 66 | Joy Girl–Delmar Kingsland; orig. 1954 | 3.50 | 7.00 | 10.50 | E |
| 67 | House of Sinners–Peggy Gaddis | 3.50 | 7.00 | 10.50 | E |
| 68 | Lady of Many Sins–Gerald Foster | 3.50 | 7.00 | 10.50 | E |
| 69 | Scandalous Nurse–Peggy Gaddis; orig. 1954 | 3.50 | 7.00 | 10.50 | E |
| 70 | Confessions of a Ladie's Chauffeur–Florence Stonebraker | 3.50 | 7.00 | 10.50 | E |
| 71 | Bad Girls' Club–William Davids | 5.00 | 10.00 | 15.00 | E |
| 72 | Hoyden of the Mountains–Delmar Kingsland | 3.50 | 7.00 | 10.50 | E |
| 73 | Woman-Crazy Doctor–Sim Albert | 3.50 | 7.00 | 10.50 | E |
| 74 | Playboy's Nurse–Gordon Semple | 3.50 | 7.00 | 10.50 | E |
| 75 | Strange Desires–Ralph Himmel | 4.00 | 8.00 | 12.00 | E |
| 76 | Story of a Slum Girl's Career of Sin–Gordon Semple | 3.50 | 7.00 | 10.50 | E |
| 77 | French Sinner–Sim Albert | 3.50 | 7.00 | 10.50 | E |
| 78 | Stag-Party Girl–Bart Frame | 3.50 | 7.00 | 10.50 | E |
| 80 | Lonely Soldiers–William David; aka Army Mistress | 3.50 | 7.00 | 10.50 | E |
| 81 | Rooming House Girl–Sim Albert | 3.50 | 7.00 | 10.50 | E |
| 82 | Thrill-Hungry Girl–Peggy Gaddis | 3.50 | 7.00 | 10.50 | E |
| 83 | Affairs of a Party Girl–Bart Frame | 3.50 | 7.00 | 10.50 | E |
| 85 | Indiscretions of a French Model–Bart Frame | 3.50 | 7.00 | 10.50 | E |
| 86 | Soldier's Girl–Joan Sherman (Peggy Gaddis) | 3.50 | 7.00 | 10.50 | E |
| 87 | Wild Bride–Sim Albert; orig. 1954 | 3.50 | 7.00 | 10.50 | E |
| 88 | Maybelle–Georgia Girl in Harlem–Bart Frame; orig. 1954 | 4.00 | 8.00 | 12.00 | E |
| 89 | Shanty-Town Tease–Florence Stonebraker | 3.50 | 7.00 | 10.50 | E |
| 90 | Man-Crazy Nurse–Peggy Gaddis | 3.50 | 7.00 | 10.50 | E |
| 91 | Waterfront Girl–Gordon Semple | 3.50 | 7.00 | 10.50 | E |
| 92 | Warped Desires–Gordon Semple | 3.50 | 7.00 | 10.50 | E |
| 93 | Confessions of a B-Girl–Sim Albert | 3.50 | 7.00 | 10.50 | E |
| 94 | Tenement Girl–Alan Bennett; 1955, aka Cellar Club Girl | 4.00 | 8.00 | 12.00 | E |
| 95 | Confessions of a Wild Co-ed–Florence Stonebraker | 3.50 | 7.00 | 10.50 | E |
| 96 | French Pick-Up–Denise Marcelle | 3.50 | 7.00 | 10.50 | E |
| 97 | Man-Hungry Widow–Peggy Gaddis | 3.50 | 7.00 | 10.50 | E |
| 101 | She Lived in Sin–Ralph Carter | 3.50 | 7.00 | 10.50 | E |
| 102 | Shameful Love–Thomas Stone | 3.50 | 7.00 | 10.50 | E |
| 103 | Sinner–Gordon Semple; aka Life of Passion | 3.50 | 7.00 | 10.50 | E |
| 104 | Life of Lust–Wright Williams | 3.50 | 7.00 | 10.50 | E |
| 105 | Sin Island–Ralph Carter; aka Passion's Folly | 3.50 | 7.00 | 10.50 | E |
| 106 | Immoral Woman–Lee Jacquin | 3.50 | 7.00 | 10.50 | E |
| 107 | Intimate Affairs of a Sinful Model–Joan Sherman (Peggy Gaddis) | 3.50 | 7.00 | 10.50 | E |
| 108 | Sins of an Aspiring Actress | 3.50 | 7.00 | 10.50 | E |
| 109 | Back-Country Wench–Gail Jordan (Peggy Gaddis) | 3.50 | 7.00 | 10.50 | E |
| 110 | Scandalous Career Girl–Gordon Semple | 3.50 | 7.00 | 10.50 | E |

# CROYDON HOW-TO BOOKS
## Croydon Publishing Company
### Digest Size

| # | Title | V/Good | Fine | N/Mint | |
|---|---|---|---|---|---|
| 11 | The Giant Hobby Handbook; 1953; c-Cole | 2.50 | 5.00 | 7.50 | NF |

# DAGGER HOUSE MYSTERY
## Dagger House, Inc.
### Digest Size

| # | Title | V/Good | Fine | N/Mint | |
|---|---|---|---|---|---|
| 20 | Murder at Lover's Lake–Margaretta Brucker | 3.00 | 6.00 | 9.00 | M |
| 22 | Good Night for Murder–Philip Ketchum | 3.00 | 6.00 | 9.00 | M |
| 24 | If a Body Kill a Body–Peter Mortimer | 3.00 | 6.00 | 9.00 | M |
| 26 | You Can't Kill a Corpse–Louis Trimble; 1947 | 3.00 | 6.00 | 9.00 | M |
| 28 | Murder Makes a Marriage–Schuyler Broocks; 1947 | 3.00 | 6.00 | 9.00 | M |

# DEATH HOUSE
## William H. Wise & Co., Inc.
### Digest Size

| # | Title | V/Good | Fine | N/Mint | |
|---|---|---|---|---|---|
| nn | Vengeance Pulls the Trigger–Sturges Mason Schley; aka Who'd Shoot a Genius? | 5.00 | 10.00 | 15.00 | M |
| nn | Death Springs the Trap–Eaton K. Goldthwaite; aka You Did It | 5.00 | 10.00 | 15.00 | M |
| 3 | Murder on the Downbeat–Robert Avery | 5.00 | 10.00 | 15.00 | M |
| 4 | The Case of the Nameless Corpse–Eaton K. Goldthwaite | 5.00 | 10.00 | 15.00 | M |
| 5 | Dead Reckoning–Francis Bonnamy | 5.00 | 10.00 | 15.00 | M |
| 6 | Full Crash Dive–Allan R. Bosworth; aka Murder Goes to Sea | 5.00 | 10.00 | 15.00 | M |

# DELL
## Dell Publishing Company, Inc.

| # | Title | V/Good | Fine | N/Mint | |
|---|---|---|---|---|---|
| 1 | Death in the Library–Philip Ketchum; 1943 | 30.00 | 60.00 | 90.00 | M |
| 2 | Dead or Alive–Patricia Wentworth | 4.00 | 8.00 | 12.00 | M |
| 3 | Murder-on-Hudson–Jennifer Jones | 6.00 | 12.00 | 18.00 | M |
| 4 | The American Gun Mystery–Ellery Queen; aka Death at the Rodeo | 4.00 | 8.00 | 12.00 | M |
| 5 | Four Frightened Women–George Harmon Coxe | 5.00 | 10.00 | 15.00 | M |
| 6 | Ill Met by Moonlight–Leslie Ford | 3.50 | 7.00 | 10.50 | M |
| 7 | See You at the Morgue–Lawrence G. Blochman | 5.00 | 10.00 | 15.00 | M |
| 8 | The Tuesday Club Murders–Agatha Christie | 8.00 | 16.00 | 24.00 | M |
| 9 | Double for Death–Rex Stout | 6.00 | 12.00 | 18.00 | M |
| 10 | The Lone Wolf–Louis Joseph Vance | 5.00 | 10.00 | 15.00 | M |
| 11 | Hearses Don't Hurry–Stephen Ransome | 5.00 | 10.00 | 15.00 | M |
| 12 | Wife vs. Secretary–Faith Baldwin | 6.00 | 12.00 | 18.00 | R |
| 13 | Death Wears a White Gardenia–Zelda Popkin | 4.00 | 8.00 | 12.00 | M |
| 14 | The Doctor Died at Dusk–Geoffrey Homes | 5.00 | 10.00 | 15.00 | M |
| 15 | The Golden Swan Murder–Dorothy Cameron Disney | 5.00 | 10.00 | 15.00 | M |
| 16 | The Unicorn Murders–Carter Dickson | 7.00 | 14.00 | 21.00 | M |
| 17 | The Dead Can Tell–Helen Reilly | 5.00 | 10.00 | 15.00 | M |
| 18 | The Puzzle of the Silver Persian–Stuart Palmer | 6.00 | 12.00 | 18.00 | M |
| 19 | Death over Sunday–James Francis Bonnell | 4.00 | 8.00 | 12.00 | M |
| 20 | Tambay Gold–Samuel Hopkins Adams | 4.50 | 9.00 | 13.50 | R |

| | | V/Good | Fine | N/Mint | |
|---|---|---|---|---|---|
| DELL, *continued* | | | | | |
| 21 | I Was a Nazi Flyer–Gottfried Leske | 15.00 | 30.00 | 45.00 | C |
| 22 | Holiday Homicide–Rufus King | 4.00 | 8.00 | 12.00 | M |
| 23 | The Private Practice of Michael Shayne–Brett Halliday | 6.00 | 12.00 | 18.00 | M |
| 24 | The Phantom of the Opera–Gaston Leroux | 12.00 | 24.00 | 36.00 | M |
| 25 | Speak No Evil–Mignon G. Eberhart | 3.00 | 6.00 | 9.00 | M |
| 26 | The Raft–Robert Trumbull | 3.00 | 6.00 | 9.00 | A |
| 27 | The Camera Clue–George Harmon Coxe | 4.50 | 9.00 | 13.50 | M |
| 28 | The Mountain Cat Murders–Rex Stout | 4.00 | 8.00 | 12.00 | M |
| 29 | Curtains for the Copper–Thomas Polsky | 5.00 | 10.00 | 15.00 | M |
| 30 | Memo to a Firing Squad–Frederick Hazlitt Brennan | 5.00 | 10.00 | 15.00 | C |
| 31 | The Fallen Sparrow–Dorothy B. Hughes | 4.00 | 8.00 | 12.00 | M |
| 32 | This Time for Keeps–John MacCormac | 4.00 | 8.00 | 12.00 | NF |
| 33 | Dance of Death–Helen McCloy; 1944 | 4.00 | 8.00 | 12.00 | M |
| 34 | Crime Hound–Mary Semple Scott | 4.00 | 8.00 | 12.00 | M |
| 35 | The Cat Saw Murder–D.B. Olsen | 4.00 | 8.00 | 12.00 | M |
| 36 | The Hammersmith Murders–David Frome | 4.00 | 8.00 | 12.00 | M |
| 37 | Queen of the Flat-tops–Stanley Johnston | 3.50 | 7.00 | 10.50 | C |
| 38 | Liberty Laughs–Frances Cavanah & Ruth Weir | 15.00 | 30.00 | 45.00 | H |
| 39 | Murder Challenges Valcour–Rufus King | 4.00 | 8.00 | 12.00 | M |
| 40 | The Case of Jennie Brice–Mary Roberts Rinehart | 3.00 | 6.00 | 9.00 | M |
| 41 | The Man Who Didn't Exist–Geoffrey Homes | 4.00 | 8.00 | 12.00 | M |
| 42 | Murder at Scandal House–Peter Hunt | 4.00 | 8.00 | 12.00 | M |
| 43 | Midnight Sailing–Lawrence G. Blochman | 4.00 | 8.00 | 12.00 | M |
| 44 | Reply Paid–H.F. Heard | 3.50 | 7.00 | 10.50 | M |
| 45 | Too Many Cooks–Rex Stout | 5.00 | 10.00 | 15.00 | M |
| 46 | The Boomerang Clue–Agatha Christie | 4.00 | 8.00 | 12.00 | M |
| 47 | Keeper of the Keys–Earl Derr Biggers | 7.50 | 15.00 | 22.50 | M |
| 48 | The Cross-Eyed Bear Murders–Dorothy B. Hughes | 4.00 | 8.00 | 12.00 | M |
| 49 | The Feathered Serpent–Edgar Wallace | 4.00 | 8.00 | 12.00 | M |
| 50 | The Iron Spiders–Baynard Kendrick; 1944 | 4.00 | 8.00 | 12.00 | M |
| 51 | While the Wind Howled–Audrey Gaines | 4.00 | 8.00 | 12.00 | M |
| 52 | The Body That Wasn't Uncle–George Worthing Yates | 4.00 | 8.00 | 12.00 | M |
| 53 | Blood Money–Dashiell Hammett | 15.00 | 30.00 | 45.00 | M |
| 54 | Harvard Has a Homicide–Timothy Fuller | 3.00 | 6.00 | 9.00 | M |
| 55 | The D.A.'s Daughter–Herman Petersen | 4.00 | 8.00 | 12.00 | M |
| 56 | The Frightened Stiff–Kelley Roos | 3.00 | 6.00 | 9.00 | M |
| 57 | Murder at the White Cat–Mary Roberts Rinehart | 3.00 | 6.00 | 9.00 | M |
| 58 | Murder for the Asking–George Harmon Coxe | 4.00 | 8.00 | 12.00 | M |
| 59 | Turn on the Heat–A.A. Fair | 4.00 | 8.00 | 12.00 | M |
| 60 | Thirteen at Dinner–Agatha Christie | 4.00 | 8.00 | 12.00 | M |
| 61 | The Clue of the Judas Tree–Leslie Ford | 3.00 | 6.00 | 9.00 | M |
| 62 | The Strawstack Murder–Dorothy Cameron Disney | 4.00 | 8.00 | 12.00 | M |
| 63 | Mourned on Sunday–Helen Reilly | 4.00 | 8.00 | 12.00 | M |
| 64 | Blood on the Black Market–Brett Halliday | 6.00 | 12.00 | 18.00 | M |
| 65 | Scotland Yard Department of Queer Complaints–Carter Dickson. Note: Queen's Quorum No. 92 | 7.50 | 15.00 | 22.50 | M |
| 66 | A Talent for Murder–Anna Mary Wells | 3.50 | 7.00 | 10.50 | M |
| 67 | Hidden Ways–Frederic F. Van de Water | 3.50 | 7.00 | 10.50 | M |
| 68 | Juliet Dies Twice–Lange Lewis | 3.50 | 7.00 | 10.50 | M |
| 69 | Death from a Top Hat–Clayton Rawson; 1945 | 5.00 | 10.00 | 15.00 | M |
| 70 | The Red Bull–Rex Stout; aka Some Buried Caesar | 3.50 | 7.00 | 10.50 | M |
| 71 | Murder in the Mist–Zelda Popkin | 3.50 | 7.00 | 10.50 | M |
| 72 | The Man in the Moonlight–Helen McCloy | 3.50 | 7.00 | 10.50 | M |
| 73 | Week-end Marriage–Faith Baldwin | 3.00 | 6.00 | 9.00 | R |
| 74 | The Murder That Had Everything–Hulbert Footner | 3.50 | 7.00 | 10.50 | M |
| 75 | The Affair of the Scarlet Crab–Clifford Knight; 1945 | 3.50 | 7.00 | 10.50 | M |
| 76 | Death in the Back Seat–Dorothy Cameron Disney | 3.00 | 6.00 | 9.00 | M |
| 77 | G. I. Jokes–Lou Nielsen | 15.00 | 30.00 | 45.00 | H |
| 78 | Murder Wears a Mummer's Mask–Brett Halliday | 4.00 | 8.00 | 12.00 | M |
| 79 | The Hornet's Nest–Bruno Fischer | 4.00 | 8.00 | 12.00 | M |
| 80 | Prescription for Murder–Hannah Lees | 3.00 | 6.00 | 9.00 | M |
| 81 | The Glass Triangle–George Harmon Coxe | 4.00 | 8.00 | 12.00 | M |
| 82 | Curtains for the Editor–Thomas Polsky | 4.00 | 8.00 | 12.00 | M |
| 83 | With This Ring–Mignon G. Eberhart | 3.00 | 6.00 | 9.00 | M |
| 84 | Gold Comes in Brick–A.A. Fair | 3.00 | 6.00 | 9.00 | M |
| 85 | The Savage Gentleman–Philip Wylie | 5.00 | 10.00 | 15.00 | A |
| 86 | The Man Who Murdered Goliath–Geoffrey Homes | 3.50 | 7.00 | 10.50 | M |
| 87 | Painted for the Kill–Lucy Cores | 3.50 | 7.00 | 10.50 | M |
| 88 | The Creeps–Anthony Abbot | 5.00 | 10.00 | 15.00 | M |
| 89 | Dell Book of Jokes–Frances Cavanah & Ruth Weir | 10.50 | 21.00 | 31.50 | H |
| 90 | A Man Called Spade–Dashiell Hammett | 15.00 | 30.00 | 45.00 | M |
| 91 | The Case of the Constant Suicides–John Dickson Carr | 4.50 | 9.00 | 13.50 | M |
| 92 | Suspense Stories–ed. Alfred Hitchcock | 9.00 | 18.00 | 27.00 | M |
| 93 | Beyond the Dark–Kieran Abbey | 3.50 | 7.00 | 10.50 | M |
| 94 | No Crime for a Lady–Zelda Popkin | 3.00 | 6.00 | 9.00 | M |
| 95 | The Last Express–Baynard Kendrick | 3.00 | 6.00 | 9.00 | M |
| 96 | Skeleton Key–Lenore Glen Offord | 3.00 | 6.00 | 9.00 | M |
| 97 | Trail Boss of Indian Beef–Harold Channing Wire; 1946; aka Indian Beef | 3.00 | 6.00 | 9.00 | W |
| 98 | Spring Harrowing–Phoebe Atwood Taylor | 2.00 | 4.00 | 6.00 | M |
| 99 | Now, Voyager–Olive Higgins Prouty | 2.00 | 4.00 | 6.00 | R |
| 100 | The So Blue Marble–Dorothy B. Hughes; 1946 | 2.00 | 4.00 | 6.00 | M |
| 101 | Murder with Pictures–George Harmon Coxe | 2.50 | 5.00 | 7.50 | M |
| 102 | You Only Hang Once–H.W. Roden | 3.50 | 7.00 | 10.50 | M |
| 103 | Murder Is a Kill-Joy–Elisabeth Sanxay Holding | 3.00 | 6.00 | 9.00 | M |
| 104 | The Crooking Finger–Cleve F. Adams | 3.50 | 7.00 | 10.50 | M |

Dell 36, Dell 38, Dell 45.

Dell 86, Dell 89, Dell 90.

**DELL, continued**

| # | Title | V/Good | Fine | N/Mint | |
|---|---|---|---|---|---|
| 105 | Appointment with Death–Agatha Christie | 3.50 | 7.00 | 10.50 | M |
| 106 | Made Up to Kill–Kelley Roos | 3.00 | 6.00 | 9.00 | M |
| 107 | The Deadly Truth–Helen McCloy | 3.00 | 6.00 | 9.00 | M |
| 108 | Death in Five Boxes–Carter Dickson | 3.50 | 7.00 | 10.50 | M |
| 109 | Spill the Jackpot–A.A. Fair | 3.00 | 6.00 | 9.00 | M |
| 110 | Wall of Eyes–Margaret Millar | 3.00 | 6.00 | 9.00 | M |
| 111 | Greenmask–Jefferson Farjeon | 3.00 | 6.00 | 9.00 | M |
| 112 | Michael Shayne's Long Chance–Brett Halliday | 3.00 | 6.00 | 9.00 | M |
| 113 | The Whistling Hangman–Baynard Kendrick | 3.00 | 6.00 | 9.00 | M |
| 114 | Three Women in Black–Helen Reilly | 3.00 | 6.00 | 9.00 | M |
| 115 | The Broken Vase–Rex Stout | 3.50 | 7.00 | 10.50 | M |
| 116 | Honor Bound–Faith Baldwin | 3.00 | 6.00 | 9.00 | R |
| 117 | Women Are Like That–Alice Elinor Lambert | 3.00 | 6.00 | 9.00 | R |
| 118 | Half Angel–Fanny Heaslip Lea | 3.00 | 6.00 | 9.00 | R |
| 119 | Robin Hill–Lida Larrimore | 3.00 | 6.00 | 9.00 | R |
| 120 | Man in the Saddle–Ernest Haycox | 2.50 | 5.00 | 7.50 | W |
| 121 | Footprints on the Ceiling–Clayton Rawson | 3.50 | 7.00 | 10.50 | M |
| 122 | Death in the Doll's House–Lawrence Bachmann & Hannah Lees | 2.50 | 5.00 | 7.50 | M |
| 123 | Too Many Bones–Ruth Sawtell Wallace | 3.00 | 6.00 | 9.00 | M |
| 124 | The Man in Lower Ten–Mary Roberts Rinehart | 2.50 | 5.00 | 7.50 | M |
| 125 | Dreadful Hollow–Irina Karlova; 1946 | 3.00 | 6.00 | 9.00 | M |
| 126 | Murderer's Choice–Anna Mary Wells | 3.00 | 6.00 | 9.00 | M |
| 127 | Old Bones–Herman Petersen | 3.00 | 6.00 | 9.00 | M |
| 128 | Murder and the Married Virgin–Brett Halliday | 3.00 | 6.00 | 9.00 | M |
| 129 | The Continental Op–Dashiell Hammett | 12.00 | 24.00 | 36.00 | M |
| 130 | The Harvey Girls–Samuel Hopkins Adams | 3.00 | 6.00 | 9.00 | R |
| 131 | The Red Lamp–Mary Roberts Rinehart | 3.00 | 6.00 | 9.00 | M |
| 132 | The Visitor–Carl Randau & Leane Zugsmith | 3.00 | 6.00 | 9.00 | M |
| 133 | Cobweb House–Elizabeth Holloway | 3.00 | 6.00 | 9.00 | M |
| 134 | Wives to Burn–Lawrence G. Blochman | 3.00 | 6.00 | 9.00 | M |
| 135 | Meat for Murder–Lange Lewis | 3.00 | 6.00 | 9.00 | M |
| 136 | Wolf in Man's Clothing–Mignon G. Eberhart | 3.00 | 6.00 | 9.00 | M |
| 137 | Crimson Friday–Dorothy Cameron Disney | 3.50 | 7.00 | 10.50 | M |
| 138 | Men Are Such Fools–Faith Baldwin | 3.00 | 6.00 | 9.00 | R |
| 139 | Love–and the Countess to Boot–Jack Iams | 3.00 | 6.00 | 9.00 | R |
| 140 | Footprint of Cinderella–Philip Wylie | 2.50 | 5.00 | 7.50 | R |
| 141 | The Swift Hour–Harriett Thurman | 2.50 | 5.00 | 7.50 | R |
| 142 | Cold Steal–Alice Tilton | 3.00 | 6.00 | 9.00 | M |
| 143 | Bar the Doors!–ed. Alfred Hitchcock | 7.50 | 15.00 | 22.50 | M |
| 144 | The White Brigand–Edison Marshall; 1947 | 2.50 | 5.00 | 7.50 | A |
| 145 | Murder in Mesopotamia–Agatha Christie | 3.00 | 6.00 | 9.00 | M |
| 146 | Alphabet Hicks–Rex Stout | 3.50 | 7.00 | 10.50 | M |
| 147 | The Lady Is Afraid–George Harmon Coxe | 3.00 | 6.00 | 9.00 | M |
| 148 | Name Your Poison–Helen Reilly | 3.00 | 6.00 | 9.00 | M |
| 149 | The Blackbirder–Dorothy B. Hughes | 3.00 | 6.00 | 9.00 | M |
| 150 | Midsummer Nightmare–Christopher Hale; 1947 | 3.00 | 6.00 | 9.00 | M |

*Dell 116, Dell 153, Dell 198.*

| # | Title | V/Good | Fine | N/Mint | |
|---|---|---|---|---|---|
| 151 | Who's Calling?–Helen McCloy | 3.00 | 6.00 | 9.00 | M |
| 152 | Jokes, Gags and Wisecracks–Ted Shane | 12.00 | 24.00 | 36.00 | H |
| 153 | Western Stories–Gene Autry | 4.00 | 8.00 | 12.00 | W |
| 154 | Return of the Continental Op–Dashiell Hammett | 13.50 | 27.00 | 40.50 | M |
| 155 | Sailor, Take Warning!–Kelley Roos | 2.50 | 5.00 | 7.50 | M |
| 156 | Blow-down–Lawrence G. Blochman | 2.50 | 5.00 | 7.50 | M |
| 157 | Fire Will Freeze–Margaret Millar | 3.00 | 6.00 | 9.00 | M |
| 158 | The Devil in the Bush–Matthew Head | 3.00 | 6.00 | 9.00 | M |
| 159 | If a Body–George Worthing Yates | 3.00 | 6.00 | 9.00 | M |
| 160 | Double or Quits–A.A. Fair | 3.00 | 6.00 | 9.00 | M |
| 161 | The Man Next Door–Mignon G. Eberhart | 3.00 | 6.00 | 9.00 | M |
| 162 | Odor of Violets–Baynard Kendrick | 3.00 | 6.00 | 9.00 | M |
| 163 | Self-made Woman–Faith Baldwin | 2.50 | 5.00 | 7.50 | R |
| 164 | The Left Leg–Alice Tilton | 2.50 | 5.00 | 7.50 | M |
| 165 | Wiped Out–John D. Newsom | 3.00 | 6.00 | 9.00 | A |
| 166 | The Wall–Mary Roberts Rinehart | 2.50 | 5.00 | 7.50 | M |
| 167 | White Fawn–Olive Higgins Prouty | 2.50 | 5.00 | 7.50 | R |
| 168 | The Corpse Came Calling–Brett Halliday | 2.50 | 5.00 | 7.50 | M |
| 169 | Murdock's Acid Test–George Harmon Coxe; aka The Barotique Mystery | 2.50 | 5.00 | 7.50 | M |
| 170 | Reluctant Millionaire–Maysie Greig | 2.50 | 5.00 | 7.50 | R |
| 171 | Octagon House–Phoebe Atwood Taylor | 2.50 | 5.00 | 7.50 | M |
| 172 | Sad Cypress–Agatha Christie | 3.50 | 7.00 | 10.50 | M |
| 173 | Rim of the Pit–Hake Talbot | 3.00 | 6.00 | 9.00 | M |
| 174 | The Sheik–E.M. Hull | 3.50 | 7.00 | 10.50 | A |
| 175 | And So to Murder–Carter Dickson; 1947 | 3.50 | 7.00 | 10.50 | M |
| 176 | The Headless Lady–Clayton Rawson | 5.00 | 10.00 | 15.00 | M |
| 177 | The Hand in the Glove–Rex Stout | 3.50 | 7.00 | 10.50 | M |
| 178 | The Pink Camellia–Temple Bailey | 3.00 | 6.00 | 9.00 | R |
| 179 | Trail's End–William MacLeod Raine | 3.00 | 6.00 | 9.00 | W |
| 180 | The Rat Began to Gnaw the Rope–C.W. Grafton | 2.00 | 4.00 | 6.00 | M |
| 181 | Great Black Kanba–Gwenyth & Constance Little | 2.50 | 5.00 | 7.50 | M |
| 182 | No Time to Kill–George Harmon Coxe | 2.50 | 5.00 | 7.50 | M |
| 183 | American Acres–Louise Redfield Peattie | 2.50 | 5.00 | 7.50 | R |
| 184 | Murder Is My Business–Brett Halliday | 3.00 | 6.00 | 9.00 | M |
| 185 | Too Busy to Die–H.W. Roden | 3.50 | 7.00 | 10.50 | M |
| 186 | She Ate Her Cake–Blair Treynor | 2.50 | 5.00 | 7.50 | M |
| 187 | N or M?–Agatha Christie | 2.50 | 5.00 | 7.50 | M |
| 188 | Splendid Quest–Edison Marshall | 2.50 | 5.00 | 7.50 | R |
| 189 | Kind Are Her Answers–Mary Renault | 2.50 | 5.00 | 7.50 | R |
| 190 | Dead Man's Gift–Zelda Popkin | 2.50 | 5.00 | 7.50 | M |
| 191 | The Lady in the Tower–Katherine Newlin Burt | 2.50 | 5.00 | 7.50 | |
| 192 | Tugboat Annie–Norman Reilly Raine | 3.00 | 6.00 | 9.00 | |
| 193 | Scarecrow–Eaton K. Goldthwaite | 3.00 | 6.00 | 9.00 | M |
| 194 | The Innocent Mrs. Duff–Elisabeth Sanxay Holding | 2.50 | 5.00 | 7.50 | M |
| 195 | Beam Ends–Errol Flynn | 2.50 | 5.00 | 7.50 | A |
| 196 | Rich Girl, Poor Girl–Faith Baldwin | 2.50 | 5.00 | 7.50 | R |
| 197 | Kiss the Blood Off My Hands–Gerald Butler; aka The Unafraid | 2.50 | 5.00 | 7.50 | M |
| 198 | The Glass Mask–Lenore Glen Offord | 2.50 | 5.00 | 7.50 | M |
| 199 | The Secret of Chimneys–Agatha Christie | 2.50 | 5.00 | 7.50 | M |
| 200 | The Opening Door–Helen Reilly; 1947 | 2.50 | 5.00 | 7.50 | M |
| 201 | The First Men in the Moon–H.G. Wells | 9.00 | 18.00 | 27.00 | SF |
| 202 | Mrs. Murdock Takes a Case–George Harmon Coxe | 2.50 | 5.00 | 7.50 | M |
| 203 | The State vs. Elinor Norton–Mary Roberts Rinehart | 2.50 | 5.00 | 7.50 | M |
| 204 | The Frightened Pigeon–Richard Burke | 2.50 | 5.00 | 7.50 | M |
| 205 | Dell Book of Crossword Puzzles–Kathleen Rafferty | 50.00 | 100.00 | 150.00 | NF |
| 206 | Hold Your Breath–ed. Alfred Hitchcock | 7.50 | 15.00 | 22.50 | M |
| 207 | The Crimson Feather–Sara Elizabeth Mason | 3.00 | 6.00 | 9.00 | M |
| 208 | The Black Curtain–Cornell Woolrich | 4.00 | 8.00 | 12.00 | M |
| 209 | The Iron Gates–Margaret Millar | 3.00 | 6.00 | 9.00 | M |
| 210 | Ride the Pink Horse–Dorothy B. Hughes; 1948 | 2.50 | 5.00 | 7.50 | M |
| 211 | Owls Don't Blink–A.A. Fair | 3.00 | 6.00 | 9.00 | M |
| 212 | Cue for Murder–Helen McCloy | 3.00 | 6.00 | 9.00 | M |
| 213 | Unidentified Woman–Mignon G. Eberhart | 2.50 | 5.00 | 7.50 | M |

Dell 207, Dell 221, Dell 232.

| | | V/Good | Fine | N/Mint | |
|---|---|---|---|---|---|
| DELL, *continued* | | | | | |
| 214 | The Birthday Murder–Lange Lewis | 2.50 | 5.00 | 7.50 | M |
| 215 | Dr. Parrish, Resident–Sydney Thompson | 2.50 | 5.00 | 7.50 | R |
| 216 | Golden Earrings–Yolanda Foldes | 2.50 | 5.00 | 7.50 | R |
| 217 | Gun Smoke Yarns–Gene Autry | 3.00 | 6.00 | 9.00 | W |
| 218 | H As in Hunted–Lawrence Treat | 2.50 | 5.00 | 7.50 | M |
| 219 | The Smell of Money–Matthew Head | 2.50 | 5.00 | 7.50 | M |
| 220 | Hospital Nocturne–Alice Elinor Lambert | 2.50 | 5.00 | 7.50 | M |
| 221 | Dark Passage–David Goodis | 9.00 | 18.00 | 27.00 | M |
| 222 | Marked for Murder–Brett Halliday | 2.50 | 5.00 | 7.50 | M |
| 223 | Hammett Homicides–Dashiell Hammett | 12.00 | 24.00 | 36.00 | M |
| 224 | How to Pick a Mate–Clifford Adams & Vance Packard | 2.50 | 5.00 | 7.50 | NF |
| 225 | Silent Are the Dead–George Harmon Coxe; 1948 | 2.50 | 5.00 | 7.50 | M |
| 226 | Murder at the Vicarage–Agatha Christie | 2.50 | 5.00 | 7.50 | M |
| 227 | Trail Town–Ernest Haycox | 2.50 | 5.00 | 7.50 | W |
| 228 | Murder on Angler's Island–Helen Reilly | 2.00 | 4.00 | 6.00 | M |
| 229 | Murder within Murder–Richard Lockridge & Frances Lockridge | 2.50 | 5.00 | 7.50 | M |
| 230 | Blind Man's Bluff–Baynard Kendrick | 2.50 | 5.00 | 7.50 | M |
| 231 | A Halo for Nobody–Henry Kane | 2.50 | 5.00 | 7.50 | M |
| 232 | The Rope Began to Hang the Butcher–C.W. Grafton | 2.50 | 5.00 | 7.50 | M |
| 233 | The Upstart–Edison Marshall | 2.00 | 4.00 | 6.00 | A |
| 234 | Student Nurse–Renee Shann | 2.00 | 4.00 | 6.00 | R |
| 235 | Red Threads–Rex Stout | 2.50 | 5.00 | 7.50 | M |
| 236 | Skyscraper–Faith Baldwin | 2.00 | 4.00 | 6.00 | R |
| 237 | House of Darkness–Allan MacKinnon | 2.50 | 5.00 | 7.50 | M |
| 238 | Gunsight Pass–William MacLeod Raine | 2.50 | 5.00 | 7.50 | W |
| 239 | Candidate for Love–Maysie Greig | 2.00 | 4.00 | 6.00 | R |
| 240 | The Charred Witness–George Harmon Coxe | 2.00 | 4.00 | 6.00 | M |
| 241 | The Bat–Mary Roberts Rinehart | 2.00 | 4.00 | 6.00 | M |
| 242 | The Unafraid–Gerald Butler; movie tie-in; aka Kiss the Blood Off My Hands | 2.00 | 4.00 | 6.00 | M |
| 243 | Owls Don't Blink–A.A. Fair | 2.00 | 4.00 | 6.00 | M |
| 244 | Judas, Incorporated–Kurt Steel | 2.50 | 5.00 | 7.50 | M |
| 245 | Wallflowers–Temple Bailey | 2.00 | 4.00 | 6.00 | R |
| 246 | Bar-20 Days–Clarence E. Mulford | 2.50 | 5.00 | 7.50 | W |
| 247 | One Angel Less–H.W. Roden | 2.00 | 4.00 | 6.00 | M |
| 248 | Dangerous Ground–Francis Wickware | 2.00 | 4.00 | 6.00 | M |
| 249 | Stars Still Shine–Lida Larrimore | 2.00 | 4.00 | 6.00 | R |
| 250 | Skyline Riders–Francis W. Hilton; 1948 | 2.00 | 4.00 | 6.00 | W |
| 251 | Banbury Bog–Phoebe Atwood Taylor | 2.00 | 4.00 | 6.00 | M |
| 252 | Benefit Performance–Richard Sale | 2.50 | 5.00 | 7.50 | M |
| 253 | Treasure of the Brasada–Les Savage, Jr | 2.50 | 5.00 | 7.50 | W |
| 254 | Bats Fly at Dusk–A.A. Fair | 2.50 | 5.00 | 7.50 | M |
| 255 | Enchanted Oasis–Faith Baldwin | 2.00 | 4.00 | 6.00 | R |
| 256 | Madonna of the Sleeping Cars–Maurice Dekobra | 2.00 | 4.00 | 6.00 | R |
| 257 | Murder in Retrospect–Agatha Christie | 2.50 | 5.00 | 7.50 | M |
| 258 | No Coffin for the Corpse–Clayton Rawson | 4.00 | 8.00 | 12.00 | M |
| 259 | Murder Wears Mukluks–Eunice Mays Boyd | 2.50 | 5.00 | 7.50 | M |
| 260 | Chinese Red–Richard Burke | 2.50 | 5.00 | 7.50 | M |
| 261 | Do Not Disturb–Helen McCloy | 2.50 | 5.00 | 7.50 | M |
| 262 | Rope–Alfred Hitchcock; movie tie-in. Note: Actually written by Don Ward | 9.00 | 18.00 | 27.00 | M |
| 263 | The Panic-Stricken–Mitchell Wilson | 2.00 | 4.00 | 6.00 | M |

| | | V/Good | Fine | N/Mint | |
|---|---|---|---|---|---|
| 264 | Fear and Trembling–ed. Alfred Hitchcock | 7.50 | 15.00 | 22.50 | M |
| 265 | Men under the Sea–Frank Meier | 2.50 | 5.00 | 7.50 | A |
| 266 | Ghost of a Chance–Kelley Roos | 2.50 | 5.00 | 7.50 | M |
| 267 | Not Quite Dead Enough–Rex Stout | 3.00 | 6.00 | 9.00 | M |
| 268 | Blood on Biscayne Bay–Brett Halliday | 3.00 | 6.00 | 9.00 | M |
| 269 | The Invisible Man–H.G. Wells | 9.00 | 18.00 | 27.00 | SF |
| 270 | It Ain't Hay–David Dodge; 1949 | 7.50 | 15.00 | 22.50 | M |
| 271 | Gunsmoke and Trail Dust–Bliss Lomax (Harry Sinclair Drago); aka Trail Dust | 2.00 | 4.00 | 6.00 | W |
| 272 | The Velvet Fleece–Lois Eby & John C. Fleming | 2.50 | 5.00 | 7.50 | M |
| 273 | Death Knell–Baynard Kendrick | 2.00 | 4.00 | 6.00 | M |
| 274 | The Body Missed the Boat–Jack Iams | 2.50 | 5.00 | 7.50 | M |
| 275 | Where There's Smoke–Stewart Sterling; 1949 | 2.50 | 5.00 | 7.50 | M |
| 276 | Murder for Two–George Harmon Coxe | 2.50 | 5.00 | 7.50 | M |
| 277 | Ex-Wife–Ursula Parott | 3.00 | 6.00 | 9.00 | R |
| 278 | Second Dell Book of Crossword Puzzles–Kathleen Rafferty | 62.50 | 125.00 | 187.50 | NF |
| 279 | Sons of the Shiek–E.M. Hull | 2.50 | 5.00 | 7.50 | A |
| 280 | Counterfeit Wife–Brett Halliday | 3.00 | 6.00 | 9.00 | M |
| 281 | Anthony Adverse in Italy–Hervey Allen | 2.00 | 4.00 | 6.00 | A |
| 282 | Western Stories–William MacLeod Raine | 4.50 | 9.00 | 13.50 | W |
| 283 | Anthony Adverse in Africa–Hervey Allen | 2.00 | 4.00 | 6.00 | A |
| 284 | Outlaw on Horseback–Will Ermine | 2.00 | 4.00 | 6.00 | W |
| 285 | Anthony Adverse in America–Hervey Allen | 2.00 | 4.00 | 6.00 | A |
| 286 | Eisenhower Was My Boss–Kay Summersby | 3.00 | 6.00 | 9.00 | NF |
| 287 | The Silver Leopard–Helen Reilly | 5.00 | 10.00 | 15.00 | M |
| 288 | The Heart Remembers–Faith Baldwin | 3.00 | 6.00 | 9.00 | R |
| 289 | Bitter Ending–Alexander Irving | 2.50 | 5.00 | 7.50 | M |
| 290 | The Pioneers–Courtney Ryley Cooper | 2.00 | 4.00 | 6.00 | A |
| 291 | So Dear to My Heart–Sterling North; movie tie-in | 3.50 | 7.00 | 10.50 | |
| 292 | Hits, Runs, & Errors–Robert Smith | 2.50 | 5.00 | 7.50 | S |
| 293 | Cards on the Table–Agatha Christie | 2.50 | 5.00 | 7.50 | M |
| 294 | Jim the Conqueror–Peter B. Kyne | 2.00 | 4.00 | 6.00 | W |
| 295 | The Goblin Market–Helen McCloy | 2.50 | 5.00 | 7.50 | M |
| 296 | Little Women–Louisa May Alcott; movie tie-in. Note: Actually written by Jean Webb | 2.50 | 5.00 | 7.50 | R |
| 297 | The Great Mistake–Mary Roberts Rinehart | 2.00 | 4.00 | 6.00 | M |
| 298 | Promise of Love–Mary Renault | 2.00 | 4.00 | 6.00 | R |
| 299 | Bad for Business–Rex Stout | 3.00 | 6.00 | 9.00 | M |
| 300 | The Paintin' Pistoleer–Walker A. Thompkins; 1949 | 2.50 | 5.00 | 7.50 | W |
| 301 | "Q" as in Quicksand–Lawrence Treat | 2.50 | 5.00 | 7.50 | M |
| 302 | The Dark Device–Hannah Lees | 2.50 | 5.00 | 7.50 | M |
| 303 | The Mirabilis Diamond–Jerome Odlum | 2.50 | 5.00 | 7.50 | M |
| 304 | Doctor Hudson's Secret Journal–Lloyd C. Douglas | 2.00 | 4.00 | 6.00 | R |
| 305 | Invasion from Mars–Orson Welles. Note: Actually edited by Don Ward | 6.00 | 12.00 | 18.00 | SF |
| 306 | Brandy for a Hero–William O'Farrell | 2.50 | 5.00 | 7.50 | M |
| 307 | Pick Your Victim–Pat McGerr | 3.00 | 6.00 | 9.00 | M |
| 308 | Dead Yellow Women–Dashiell Hammett | 13.50 | 27.00 | 40.50 | M |
| 309 | Satin Straps–Maysie Greig | 2.00 | 4.00 | 6.00 | R |

Dell 287, Dell 307, Dell 320.

**DELL,** *continued*

| # | Title | V/Good | Fine | N/Mint | |
|---|---|---|---|---|---|
| 310 | West of Texas Law–Walker A. Tompkins | 2.00 | 4.00 | 6.00 | W |
| 311 | Bengal Fire–Lawrence G. Blochman | 2.50 | 5.00 | 7.50 | A |
| 312 | The Gaunt Woman–Edmund Gilligan | 2.00 | 4.00 | 6.00 | A |
| 313 | Death of a Bullionaire–A.B. Cunningham | 2.00 | 4.00 | 6.00 | M |
| 314 | Dead Wrong–Stewart Sterling | 2.50 | 5.00 | 7.50 | M |
| 315 | Cats Prowl at Night–A.A. Fair | 2.50 | 5.00 | 7.50 | M |
| 316 | Armchair in Hell–Henry Kane | 2.50 | 5.00 | 7.50 | M |
| 317 | Alder Gulch–Ernest Haycox | 2.00 | 4.00 | 6.00 | W |
| 318 | Alimony–Faith Baldwin | 2.50 | 5.00 | 7.50 | R |
| 319 | The Man in the Brown Suit–Agatha Christie | 2.50 | 5.00 | 7.50 | M |
| 320 | The Cave Girl–Edgar Rice Burroughs | 8.00 | 16.00 | 24.00 | A |
| 321 | Assignment in Guiana–George Harmon Coxe | 2.00 | 4.00 | 6.00 | M |
| 322 | Death of a Tall Man–Richard Lockridge & Frances Lockridge | 2.50 | 5.00 | 7.50 | M |
| 323 | Murder and the Married Virgin–Brett Halliday | 2.00 | 4.00 | 6.00 | M |
| 324 | The Corpse Came Calling–Brett Halliday | 2.00 | 4.00 | 6.00 | M |
| 325 | Michael Shayne's Long Chance–Brett Halliday; 1949 | 2.00 | 4.00 | 6.00 | M |
| 326 | Murder Is My Business–Brett Halliday | 2.00 | 4.00 | 6.00 | M |
| 327 | Leave Cancelled–Nicholas Monsarrat | 2.00 | 4.00 | 6.00 | R |
| 328 | Cream of the Crop–Ed Fort | 2.00 | 4.00 | 6.00 | |
| 329 | Young Doctor Kildare–Max Brand | 2.00 | 4.00 | 6.00 | R |
| 330 | Report for a Corpse–Henry Kane | 2.00 | 4.00 | 6.00 | M |
| 331 | Anna Lucasta–Jean Francis Webb; movie tie-in | 2.50 | 5.00 | 7.50 | |
| 332 | Fact Detective Mysteries–W.A. Swanberg; 1st ed. 1949 | 2.50 | 5.00 | 7.50 | NF |
| 333 | Stampede–E.B. Mann | 2.00 | 4.00 | 6.00 | W |
| 334 | The Case of the Seven Sneezes–Anthony Boucher | 3.00 | 6.00 | 9.00 | M |
| 335 | Double Treasure–Clarence Budington Kelland | 2.00 | 4.00 | 6.00 | W |
| 336 | Afterglow–Ruby M. Ayers | 2.00 | 4.00 | 6.00 | R |
| 337 | Just Around the Corner–Stuart Brock | 2.00 | 4.00 | 6.00 | M |
| 338 | The Lady Regrets–James M. Fox | 2.00 | 4.00 | 6.00 | M |
| 339 | She–H. Rider Haggard. Note: Retold by Don Ward | 7.50 | 15.00 | 22.50 | F |
| 340 | The Care of Your Child from Infancy to Six–William Rosenson & Bela Schick | 2.50 | 5.00 | 7.50 | NF |
| 341 | The Upstart–Edison Marshall | 2.00 | 4.00 | 6.00 | |
| 342 | Sons of the Sheik–E.M. Hull | 2.50 | 5.00 | 7.50 | R |
| 343 | The Chinese Doll–Wilson Tucker | 3.00 | 6.00 | 9.00 | M |
| 344 | Bedeviled–Libbie Block | 2.00 | 4.00 | 6.00 | M |
| 345 | Wake for a Lady–H.W. Roden | 2.50 | 5.00 | 7.50 | M |
| 346 | The Accomplice–Matthew Head | 2.00 | 4.00 | 6.00 | |
| 347 | Trail Town–Ernest Haycox | 2.00 | 4.00 | 6.00 | W |
| 348 | A Halo for Nobody–Henry Kane | 2.00 | 4.00 | 6.00 | M |
| 349 | Too Busy to Die–H.W. Roden | 2.50 | 5.00 | 7.50 | M |
| 350 | It Ain't Hay–David Dodge; 1949 | 6.00 | 12.00 | 18.00 | M |
| 351 | Showdown–Errol Flynn | 2.50 | 5.00 | 7.50 | A |
| 352 | Gunsmoke Graze–Peter Dawson (Frank Gruber) | 2.00 | 4.00 | 6.00 | W |
| 353 | Yankee Pasha–Edison Marshall | 3.50 | 7.00 | 10.50 | A |
| 354 | The Philadelphia Murder Story–Leslie Ford | 2.00 | 4.00 | 6.00 | M |
| 355 | The One That Got Away–Helen McCloy | 2.00 | 4.00 | 6.00 | M |
| 356 | Death in the Doll's House–Lawrence Bachmann & Hannah Lees | 2.00 | 4.00 | 6.00 | M |
| 357 | Leave It to Psmith–P.G. Wodehouse | 2.50 | 5.00 | 7.50 | H |
| 358 | To a God Unknown–John Steinbeck | 3.00 | 6.00 | 9.00 | |
| 359 | Trail's End–William MacLeod Raine | 2.00 | 4.00 | 6.00 | W |
| 360 | Don Lorenzo's Bride–Juanita Savage | 2.00 | 4.00 | 6.00 | |
| 361 | Haunted Lady–Mary Roberts Rinehart | 2.00 | 4.00 | 6.00 | M |
| 362 | Silent in the Saddle–Norman A. Fox | 2.00 | 4.00 | 6.00 | W |
| 363 | Blue City–Kenneth Millar (Ross MacDonald) | 2.50 | 5.00 | 7.50 | M |
| 364 | Forlorn Island–Edison Marshall | 2.50 | 5.00 | 7.50 | A |
| 365 | The Death of a Worldly Woman–A.B. Cunningham | 2.00 | 4.00 | 6.00 | M |
| 366 | Unfinished Business–Cary Lucas | 2.00 | 4.00 | 6.00 | M |
| 367 | Suspense Stories–ed. Alfred Hitchcock | 4.50 | 9.00 | 13.50 | M |
| 368 | The Moon's Our Home–Faith Baldwin; 1950 | 2.00 | 4.00 | 6.00 | R |
| 369 | Panic–Helen McCloy | 2.00 | 4.00 | 6.00 | M |
| 370 | He Wouldn't Kill Patience–Carter Dickson | 2.50 | 5.00 | 7.50 | M |
| 371 | Wisteria Cottage–Robert M. Coates | 3.50 | 7.00 | 10.50 | |
| 372 | Buckaroo's Code–Wayne D. Overholser | 2.00 | 4.00 | 6.00 | W |
| 373 | The Heart Has April Too–Gladys Taber | 2.00 | 4.00 | 6.00 | R |
| 374 | Night and the City–Gerald Kersh; movie tie-in | 2.50 | 5.00 | 7.50 | M |
| 375 | Date with Darkness–Donald Hamilton; 1950 | 2.00 | 4.00 | 6.00 | M |
| 376 | Out of Control–Baynard Kendrick | 2.50 | 5.00 | 7.50 | M |
| 377 | Alias the Dead–George Harmon Coxe | 2.00 | 4.00 | 6.00 | M |
| 378 | Last of the Longhorns–Will Ermine | 2.00 | 4.00 | 6.00 | W |
| 379 | Nightmare Town–Dashiell Hammett | 7.50 | 15.00 | 22.50 | M |
| 380 | Invitation to Live–Lloyd C. Douglas | 2.00 | 4.00 | 6.00 | |
| 381 | The Clever Sister–Margaret Culkin Banning | 2.00 | 4.00 | 6.00 | R |
| 382 | Celeste . . . the Gold Coast Virgin–Rosamond Marshall | 5.00 | 10.00 | 15.00 | E |
| 383 | Rutledge Trails the Ace of Spades–William MacLeod Raine | 2.00 | 4.00 | 6.00 | W |
| 384 | Girl Meets Body–Jack Iams | 2.50 | 5.00 | 7.50 | M |
| 385 | Blood on the Stars–Brett Halliday | 2.00 | 4.00 | 6.00 | M |
| 386 | The Uncomplaining Corpses–Brett Halliday | 2.00 | 4.00 | 6.00 | M |
| 387 | Tickets for Death–Brett Halliday | 2.00 | 4.00 | 6.00 | M |
| 388 | Murder Wears a Mummer's Mask–Brett Halliday | 2.00 | 4.00 | 6.00 | M |
| 389 | Give 'Em the Ax–A.A. Fair | 2.50 | 5.00 | 7.50 | M |
| 390 | The Cabinda Affair–Matthew Head | 2.00 | 4.00 | 6.00 | M |
| 391 | Murder at Hazelmoor–Agatha Christie | 2.00 | 4.00 | 6.00 | M |
| 392 | Virgin with Butterflies–Tom Powers | 2.00 | 4.00 | 6.00 | |
| 393 | The Code of the Woosters–P.G. Wodehouse | 2.50 | 5.00 | 7.50 | H |
| 394 | Return to Night–Mary Renault | 2.00 | 4.00 | 6.00 | |
| 395 | Devil's Stronghold–Leslie Ford | 2.00 | 4.00 | 6.00 | M |
| 396 | After Midnight–Martha Albrand | 2.00 | 4.00 | 6.00 | |
| 397 | The Farmhouse–Helen Reilly | 2.00 | 4.00 | 6.00 | M |
| 398 | Murder in Any Language–Kelley Roos | 2.00 | 4.00 | 6.00 | M |
| 399 | The Ridin' Kid From Powder River–Henry Herbert Knibbs | 2.00 | 4.00 | 6.00 | W |
| 400 | Big City after Dark–Jack Lait & Lee Mortimer; 1950 | 2.00 | 4.00 | 6.00 | |
| 401 | They Can't All Be Guilty–M.V. Heberden | 2.00 | 4.00 | 6.00 | M |
| 402 | The Captive of the Sahara–E.M. Hull | 2.00 | 4.00 | 6.00 | R |
| 403 | The Man in Lower Ten–Mary Roberts Rinehart; interior illus. | 2.00 | 4.00 | 6.00 | M |
| 404 | The Case of Jennie Brice–Mary Roberts Rinehart | 2.00 | 4.00 | 6.00 | M |
| 405 | The Long Escape–David Dodge | 2.00 | 4.00 | 6.00 | |
| 406 | Cactus Cavalier–Norman A. Fox | 2.00 | 4.00 | 6.00 | W |
| 407 | To a God Unknown–John Steinbeck | 2.00 | 4.00 | 6.00 | |
| 408 | Blue City–Kenneth Millar (Ross MacDonald) | 2.00 | 4.00 | 6.00 | M |
| 409 | Strangers May Kiss–Ursula Parrott | 2.00 | 4.00 | 6.00 | R |
| 410 | The Affair at the Boat Landing–A.G. Cunningham | 2.00 | 4.00 | 6.00 | M |
| 411 | A Man Called Spade–Dashiell Hammett | 7.50 | 15.00 | 22.50 | M |
| 412 | Seven Deadly Sisters–Pat McGerr | 2.00 | 4.00 | 6.00 | M |
| 413 | Arizona Feud–Frank R. Adams | 2.00 | 4.00 | 6.00 | W |
| 414 | Cleopatra's Nights–ed. Allan Barnard | 4.50 | 9.00 | 13.50 | A |
| 415 | Ladies in Hades–Frederic Arnold Kummer | 3.00 | 6.00 | 9.00 | F |
| 416 | They Drive by Night–A.I. Bezzerides | 2.00 | 4.00 | 6.00 | |
| 417 | Tell Me about Women–Harry Reasoner | 2.00 | 4.00 | 6.00 | |
| 418 | Gunsmoke and Trail Dust–Bliss Lomax (Harry Sinclair Drago); aka Trail Dust | 2.00 | 4.00 | 6.00 | W |
| 419 | Murder Is Mutual–Jack Dolph | 2.00 | 4.00 | 6.00 | M |
| 420 | Dead Sure–Stewart Sterling | 2.00 | 4.00 | 6.00 | M |
| 421 | Dead Yellow Women–Dashiell Hammett | 12.00 | 24.00 | 36.00 | M |
| 422 | Yankee Pasha–Edison Marshall | 3.00 | 6.00 | 9.00 | A |
| 423 | Murder in Havana–George Harmon Coxe | 2.00 | 4.00 | 6.00 | M |
| 424 | The Bandit Trail–William MacLeod Raine | 2.00 | 4.00 | 6.00 | W |
| 425 | Breakdown–Louis Paul; 1950 | 2.00 | 4.00 | 6.00 | |
| 426 | A Taste for Violence–Brett Halliday | 1.50 | 3.00 | 4.50 | M |
| 427 | Dead Man's Diary and Dinner at Dupre's–Brett Halliday | 1.50 | 3.00 | 4.50 | M |

| | | V/Good | Fine | N/Mint | | | | V/Good | Fine | N/Mint | |
|---|---|---|---|---|---|---|---|---|---|---|---|
| **DELL**, *continued* | | | | | | 474 | The Miracle of the Bells–Russell | 1.50 | 3.00 | 4.50 | |
| 428 | Call for Michael Shayne–Brett Halliday | 1.50 | 3.00 | 4.50 | M | | Janney; movie tie-in | | | | |
| 429 | The Private Practice of Michael | 1.50 | 3.00 | 4.50 | M | 475 | Manhattan Nights–Faith Baldwin; 1951 | 1.50 | 3.00 | 4.50 | R |
| | Shayne–Brett Halliday | | | | | 476 | My True Love Lies–Lenore Glen Offord | 1.50 | 3.00 | 4.50 | |
| 430 | She Walks Alone–Helen McCloy | 2.00 | 4.00 | 6.00 | M | 477 | Crosstown–John Held, Jr | 1.50 | 3.00 | 4.50 | |
| 431 | Benjamin Blake, Son of Fury–Edison | 1.50 | 3.00 | 4.50 | A | 478 | Plunder of the Sun–David Dodge | 1.50 | 3.00 | 4.50 | A |
| | Marshall | | | | | 479 | The Web of Evil–Lucille Emerick | 1.50 | 3.00 | 4.50 | |
| 432 | Stag Night–Phillips Rogers | 3.00 | 6.00 | 9.00 | E | 480 | The Thirsty Land–Norman A. Fox | 1.50 | 3.00 | 4.50 | W |
| 433 | King Solomon's Mines–H. Rider | 3.50 | 7.00 | 10.50 | A | 481 | The Skeleton in the Clock–Carter | 2.00 | 4.00 | 6.00 | M |
| | Haggard; movie tie-in. Note: Actually | | | | | | Dickson | | | | |
| | written by Jean Francis Webb | | | | | 482 | Women Must Weep–Ruth Adams | 1.50 | 3.00 | 4.50 | R |
| 434 | Dell Crossword Puzzle Dictionary– | 2.00 | 4.00 | 6.00 | NF | | Knight | | | | |
| | Kathleen Rafferty | | | | | 483 | What a Body!–Alan Green | 2.50 | 5.00 | 7.50 | |
| 435 | Their Ancient Grudge–Harry Harrison | 2.50 | 5.00 | 7.50 | E | 484 | Untamed–Helga Moray | 2.50 | 5.00 | 7.50 | |
| | Kroll | | | | | 485 | The Queen and the Corpse–Max | 1.50 | 3.00 | 4.50 | M |
| 436 | Gone to Earth–Mary Webb; movie | 2.00 | 4.00 | 6.00 | | | Murray | | | | |
| | tie-in | | | | | 486 | Blood Money–Dashiell Hammett | 7.50 | 15.00 | 22.50 | M |
| 437 | Gunpowder Lightning–Bertrand W. | 2.00 | 4.00 | 6.00 | W | 487 | Castle in the Swamp–Edison Marshall | 1.50 | 3.00 | 4.50 | |
| | Sinclair | | | | | 488 | Bombay Mail–Lawrence C. Blochman | 2.00 | 4.00 | 6.00 | A |
| 438 | All Men Are Liars–John Stephen | 2.00 | 4.00 | 6.00 | | 489 | My Chinese Wife–Karl Eskelund | 1.50 | 3.00 | 4.50 | |
| | Strange | | | | | 490 | The Stirrup Boss–Peter Dawson (Frank | 1.50 | 3.00 | 4.50 | W |
| 439 | The Border Lord–Jan Westcott | 2.00 | 4.00 | 6.00 | A | | Gruber) | | | | |
| 440 | New York Confidential–Jack Lait & Lee | 1.50 | 3.00 | 4.50 | NF | 491 | The Labors of Hercules–Agatha | 2.00 | 4.00 | 6.00 | M |
| | Mortimer | | | | | | Christie | | | | |
| 441 | Murder with Pictures–George Harmon | 2.00 | 4.00 | 6.00 | M | 492 | Blood of the Lamb–Charles Baker, Jr | 1.50 | 3.00 | 4.50 | |
| | Coxe | | | | | 493 | She Shall Have Murder–Delano Ames | 1.50 | 3.00 | 4.50 | M |
| 442 | Root of Evil–Eaton K. Goldthwaite | 2.00 | 4.00 | 6.00 | M | 494 | Miss Pinkerton–Mary Roberts Rinehart | 1.50 | 3.00 | 4.50 | M |
| 443 | Dinner at Antoine's–Frances Parkinson | 1.50 | 3.00 | 4.50 | | 495 | Double for Death–Rex Stout | 2.00 | 4.00 | 6.00 | M |
| | Keyes | | | | | 496 | Whispers in the Sun–Maysie Greig | 1.50 | 3.00 | 4.50 | R |
| 444 | Tender Mercy–Lenard Kaufman | 2.00 | 4.00 | 6.00 | E | 497 | The Three Roads–Kenneth Millar (Ross | 1.50 | 3.00 | 4.50 | |
| 445 | The High Road–Faith Baldwin | 2.00 | 4.00 | 6.00 | R | | MacDonald) | | | | |
| 446 | Yours Ever–Maysie Greig | 1.50 | 3.00 | 4.50 | R | 498 | Staircase 4–Helen Reilly | 1.50 | 3.00 | 4.50 | M |
| 447 | The Woman in Black–Leslie Ford | 2.00 | 4.00 | 6.00 | M | 499 | West of the Rimrock–Wayne D. | 1.50 | 3.00 | 4.50 | W |
| 448 | Flaming Canyon–Walker A. Tompkins | 2.00 | 4.00 | 6.00 | W | | Overholser | | | | |
| 449 | West of Texas Law–Walker A. | 2.00 | 4.00 | 6.00 | W | 500 | Blood and Sand–Vincente Blasco | 2.00 | 4.00 | 6.00 | |
| | Tompkins; aka Hang-Rope Harvest | | | | | | Ibanez; 1951 | | | | |
| 450 | Alder Gulch–Ernest Haycox; 1950 | 2.00 | 4.00 | 6.00 | W | 501 | The Demon Caravan–Georges Surdez | 2.00 | 4.00 | 6.00 | A |
| 451 | The Long Rope–Francis W. Hilton | 2.00 | 4.00 | 6.00 | W | 502 | The Groom Lay Dead–George Harmon | 2.00 | 4.00 | 6.00 | M |
| 452 | A Man Called Spade–Dashiell Hammett | 6.00 | 12.00 | 18.00 | M | | Coxe | | | | |
| 453 | The Camera Clue–George Harmon | 2.00 | 4.00 | 6.00 | M | 503 | Marked for Murder–Brett Halliday | 1.50 | 3.00 | 4.50 | M |
| | Coxe | | | | | 504 | The Sunnier Side–Charles Jackson | 1.50 | 3.00 | 4.50 | |
| 454 | Murder on the Links–Agatha Christie | 2.00 | 4.00 | 6.00 | M | 505 | Murder with Southern Hospitality– | 1.50 | 3.00 | 4.50 | M |
| 455 | Hang by Your Neck–Henry Kane | 2.00 | 4.00 | 6.00 | M | | Leslie Ford | | | | |
| 456 | Gentlemen of the Jungle–Tom Gill | 2.00 | 4.00 | 6.00 | A | 506 | The Window at the White Cat–Mary | 1.50 | 3.00 | 4.50 | M |
| 457 | Death Draws the Line–Jack Iams | 2.00 | 4.00 | 6.00 | M | | Roberts Rinehart | | | | |
| 458 | A Taste for Violence–Brett Halliday | 2.00 | 4.00 | 6.00 | M | 507 | Francis–David Stern; movie tie-in | 3.00 | 6.00 | 9.00 | H |
| 459 | Blood on Biscayne Bay–Brett Halliday | 1.50 | 3.00 | 4.50 | M | 508 | The Baited Blonde–Robinson MacLean | 2.00 | 4.00 | 6.00 | M |
| 460 | Give 'Em the Ax–A.A. Fair | 2.00 | 4.00 | 6.00 | M | 509 | Blazing Trails–Francis W. Hilton | 1.50 | 3.00 | 4.50 | W |
| 461 | Innocent Bystander–Craig Rice | 1.50 | 3.00 | 4.50 | M | 510 | You Play the Black and the Red Comes | 1.50 | 3.00 | 4.50 | M |
| 462 | Desperate Angel–Helen Topping Miller | 1.50 | 3.00 | 4.50 | | | Up–Richard Hallas | | | | |
| 463 | The Inconvenient Bride–James M. Fox | 1.50 | 3.00 | 4.50 | M | 511 | Slippery Hitch–Gerald Butler | 1.50 | 3.00 | 4.50 | M |
| 464 | The Corpse in the Corner Saloon– | 1.50 | 3.00 | 4.50 | M | 512 | The Robbed Heart–Clifton Cuthbert | 1.50 | 3.00 | 4.50 | |
| | Hampton Stone | | | | | 513 | Alarm in the Night–Stewart Sterling | 1.50 | 3.00 | 4.50 | M |
| 465 | Death Haunts the Dark Lane–A.B. | 1.50 | 3.00 | 4.50 | M | 514 | Do Not Murder before Christmas–Jack | 1.50 | 3.00 | 4.50 | M |
| | Cunningham | | | | | | Iams | | | | |
| 466 | Pirates of the Range–B.M. Bower | 1.50 | 3.00 | 4.50 | W | 515 | Message from a Stranger–Marya | 1.50 | 3.00 | 4.50 | |
| 467 | Money to Burn–Peter B. Kyne | 1.50 | 3.00 | 4.50 | | | Mannes | | | | |
| 468 | Jungle Hunting Thrills–Edison Marshall | 2.50 | 5.00 | 7.50 | A | 516 | No Highway–Nevil Shute; movie tie-in | 1.50 | 3.00 | 4.50 | |
| 469 | Uncle Dynamite–P.G. Wodehouse | 2.00 | 4.00 | 6.00 | H | 517 | The Sagebrush Bandit–Bliss Lomax | 1.50 | 3.00 | 4.50 | W |
| 470 | Flight of an Angel–Verne Chute; 1951 | 1.50 | 3.00 | 4.50 | | | (H.S. Drago) | | | | |
| 471 | Vigilante–Richard Summers | 1.50 | 3.00 | 4.50 | | 518 | Shell Game–Richard Powell | 1.50 | 3.00 | 4.50 | M |
| 472 | Crows Can't Count–A.A. Fair | 1.50 | 3.00 | 4.50 | M | 519 | Through a Glass, Darkly–Helen McCloy | 1.50 | 3.00 | 4.50 | M |
| 473 | The Steel Mirror–Donald Hamilton | 1.50 | 3.00 | 4.50 | | 520 | Dead Giveaway–Hugh Lawrence Nelson | 1.50 | 3.00 | 4.50 | |
| | | | | | | 521 | Hell Cat–Idabel Williams | 3.00 | 6.00 | 9.00 | |
| | | | | | | 522 | The Glass Triangle–George Harmon | 1.50 | 3.00 | 4.50 | M |
| | | | | | | | Coxe | | | | |
| | | | | | | 523 | Zane Grey Western Award Stories–ed. | 2.00 | 4.00 | 6.00 | W |
| | | | | | | | anon. | | | | |
| | | | | | | 524 | Once in Vienna–Vicki Baum | 1.50 | 3.00 | 4.50 | |
| | | | | | | 525 | Diamond Lil–Mae West; 1951 | 3.50 | 7.00 | 10.50 | E |
| | | | | | | 526 | The Gentle Hangman–James M. Fox | 3.00 | 6.00 | 9.00 | M |
| | | | | | | 527 | Trouble Valley–Ward West | 1.50 | 3.00 | 4.50 | W |
| | | | | | | 528 | Young Claudia–Rose Franken | 1.50 | 3.00 | 4.50 | R |
| | | | | | | 529 | Sad Cypress–Agatha Christie | 1.50 | 3.00 | 4.50 | M |
| | | | | | | 530 | Love Stories of India–Edison Marshall | 2.00 | 4.00 | 6.00 | A |
| | | | | | | 531 | Death in Four Colors–Brandon Bird | 1.50 | 3.00 | 4.50 | M |
| | | | | | | 532 | The Incredible Year–Faith Baldwin | 1.50 | 3.00 | 4.50 | R |
| | | | | | | 533 | This Is It, Michael Shayne–Brett | 1.50 | 3.00 | 4.50 | M |
| | | | | | | | Halliday | | | | |
| | | | | | | 534 | New York Confidential–Jack Lait & Lee | 1.50 | 3.00 | 4.50 | NF |
| | | | | | | | Mortimer | | | | |

*Dell 458, Dell 507, Dell 523.*

**DELL,** *continued*

| # | Title | V/Good | Fine | N/Mint | |
|---|---|---|---|---|---|
| 535 | Edge of Panic–Henry Kane | 1.50 | 3.00 | 4.50 | M |
| 536 | Tarzan and the Lost Empire–Edgar Rice Burroughs | 6.00 | 12.00 | 18.00 | A |
| 537 | Hag's Nook–John Dickson Carr | 2.00 | 4.00 | 6.00 | M |
| 538 | The Creeping Siamese–Dashiell Hammett | 9.00 | 18.00 | 27.00 | M |
| 539 | Shadow on the Range–Norman A. Fox | 1.50 | 3.00 | 4.50 | W |
| 540 | Too Many Cooks–Rex Stout | 2.00 | 4.00 | 6.00 | M |
| 541 | Episode of the Wandering Knife–Mary Roberts Rinehart | 1.50 | 3.00 | 4.50 | M |
| 542 | Fools Die on Friday–A.A. Fair | 1.50 | 3.00 | 4.50 | M |
| 543 | A Graveyard to Let–Carter Dickson | 1.50 | 3.00 | 4.50 | M |
| 544 | Wait for the Dawn–Martha Albrand | 1.50 | 3.00 | 4.50 | |
| 545 | The Sheriff of San Miguel–Allan Vaughan Elston | 1.50 | 3.00 | 4.50 | W |
| 546 | Hunt with the Hounds–Mignon G. Eberhart | 1.50 | 3.00 | 4.50 | M |
| 547 | Date with Death–Leslie Ford | 1.50 | 3.00 | 4.50 | M |
| 548 | That Girl from Memphis–Wilbur Daniel Steele | 1.50 | 3.00 | 4.50 | |
| 549 | The Jade Venus–George Harmon Coxe | 1.50 | 3.00 | 4.50 | M |
| 550 | Mr. Parker Pyne, Detective–Agatha Christie; 1951 | 1.50 | 3.00 | 4.50 | M |
| 551 | Manhunt West–Walker A. Tomkins | 1.50 | 3.00 | 4.50 | W |
| 552 | Murder Begins at Home–Delano Ames | 1.50 | 3.00 | 4.50 | M |
| 553 | The Mark of Zorro–Johnston McCulley | 3.00 | 6.00 | 9.00 | W |
| 554 | Letter to Five Wives–John Klempner | 2.00 | 4.00 | 6.00 | R |
| 555 | Causeway to the Past–William O'Farrell | 1.50 | 3.00 | 4.50 | |
| 556 | Draw of Drag–Wayne D. Overholser | 1.50 | 3.00 | 4.50 | W |
| 557 | Backwoods Woman–Jack Boone | 1.50 | 3.00 | 4.50 | E |
| 558 | Do Evil in Return–Margaret Millar | 1.50 | 3.00 | 4.50 | M |
| 559 | Renegade Canyon–Peter Dawson (Frank Gruber) | 1.50 | 3.00 | 4.50 | W |
| 560 | The Neat Little Corpse–Max Murray | 1.50 | 3.00 | 4.50 | M |
| 561 | Crescent Carnival–Frances Parkinson Keyes; 1952 | 1.50 | 3.00 | 4.50 | |
| 562 | Raw Land–Luke Short | 1.50 | 3.00 | 4.50 | W |
| 563 | The King's Choice–Margaret Campbell Barnes | 1.50 | 3.00 | 4.50 | A |
| 564 | Death-watch–John Dickson Carr | 1.50 | 3.00 | 4.50 | M |
| 565 | The Red Tassel–David Dodge | 1.50 | 3.00 | 4.50 | |
| 566 | The Happy Time–Robert Fontaine | 1.50 | 3.00 | 4.50 | |
| 567 | The Harem–Louis-Charles Royer | 2.00 | 4.00 | 6.00 | E |
| 568 | Passport to Peril–Robert Parker | 1.50 | 3.00 | 4.50 | |
| 569 | Stormy in the West–Norman A. Fox | 1.50 | 3.00 | 4.50 | W |
| 570 | The Mysterious Mr. Quin–Agatha Christie | 1.50 | 3.00 | 4.50 | M |
| 571 | No Mask for Murder–Andrew Garve | 1.50 | 3.00 | 4.50 | M |
| 572 | Dark Moon of March–Emmett Gowen | 1.50 | 3.00 | 4.50 | |
| 573 | The Wheel Is Fixed–James M. Fox | 1.50 | 3.00 | 4.50 | M |
| 574 | For Richer, for Poorer . . .–Faith Baldwin | 1.50 | 3.00 | 4.50 | R |
| 575 | Montana, Here I Be!–Dan Cushman; 1952 | 2.00 | 4.00 | 6.00 | W |
| 576 | Murder at Arroways–Helen Reilly | 1.50 | 3.00 | 4.50 | M |
| 577 | Murder Twice Told–Donald Hamilton | 1.50 | 3.00 | 4.50 | M |
| 578 | Framed in Blood–Brett Halliday | 1.50 | 3.00 | 4.50 | M |
| 579 | Nobody Wore Black–Delano Ames | 1.50 | 3.00 | 4.50 | |
| 580 | Until You Are Dead–Henry Kane | 1.50 | 3.00 | 4.50 | M |
| 581 | The Lost Buckaroo–Bliss Lomax (H.S. Drago) | 1.50 | 3.00 | 4.50 | W |
| 582 | Trial by Marriage–Vereen Bell | 1.50 | 3.00 | 4.50 | |
| 583 | Dead of Night–Stewart Sterling | 1.50 | 3.00 | 4.50 | M |
| 584 | Proceed at Will–Burke Wilkinson | 1.50 | 3.00 | 4.50 | |
| 585 | The Circular Staircase–Mary Roberts Rinehart | 1.50 | 3.00 | 4.50 | M |
| 586 | Dangerous Legacy–George Harmon Coxe | 1.50 | 3.00 | 4.50 | M |
| 587 | The Stampeders–James B. Hendryx | 1.50 | 3.00 | 4.50 | W |
| 588 | The Unknown Path–Anne Meredith | 1.50 | 3.00 | 4.50 | |
| 589 | The Cabin in the Cotton–Harry Harrison Kroll | 1.50 | 3.00 | 4.50 | E |
| 590 | Counterfeit Wife–Brett Halliday | 1.50 | 3.00 | 4.50 | M |
| 591 | Rocket to the Morgue–Anthony Boucher | 3.00 | 6.00 | 9.00 | M |
| 592 | Rustlers' Bend–Will Ermine | 1.50 | 3.00 | 4.50 | W |
| 593 | Too Hot to Handle–Frank G. Presnell | 1.50 | 3.00 | 4.50 | M |
| 594 | Keep Cool, Mr. Jones–Timothy Fuller | 1.50 | 3.00 | 4.50 | M |
| 595 | My Enemy, My Wife–Allen Haden | 1.50 | 3.00 | 4.50 | |
| 596 | A Taste of Murder–Joanna Cannan | 1.50 | 3.00 | 4.50 | M |
| 597 | Georgia Girl–Margaret Rebecca Lay; c-Gross | 1.50 | 3.00 | 4.50 | |
| 598 | Return of a Fighter–Ernest Haycox | 1.50 | 3.00 | 4.50 | W |
| 599 | Heaven Ran Last–William P. McGivern | 1.50 | 3.00 | 4.50 | |
| 600 | Rogue Queen–L. Sprague de Camp; 1952 | 6.00 | 12.00 | 18.00 | SF |
| 601 | Before It's Too Late–Stuart Palmer | 2.50 | 5.00 | 7.50 | M |
| 602 | Tequila–Margaret Page Hood | 1.50 | 3.00 | 4.50 | |
| 603 | Bedrooms Have Windows–A.A. Fair | 1.50 | 3.00 | 4.50 | M |
| 604 | Sudden Fear–Edna Sherry | 1.50 | 3.00 | 4.50 | M |
| 605 | The Congo Venus–Matthew Head | 1.50 | 3.00 | 4.50 | |
| 606 | Savage Range–Luke Short | 1.50 | 3.00 | 4.50 | W |
| 607 | Funny Side Up–ed. anon. Note: edited by James E. Gunn | 2.50 | 5.00 | 7.50 | H |
| 608 | The Human Beast–George Milburn & Emile Zola | 2.00 | 4.00 | 6.00 | E |
| 609 | Brother Death–John Lodwick | 1.50 | 3.00 | 4.50 | |
| 610 | Dr. Norton's Wife–Mildred Walker | 1.50 | 3.00 | 4.50 | |
| 611 | How to Get Rich in Washington–Blair Bolles | 1.50 | 3.00 | 4.50 | |
| 612 | Follow, as the Night–Pat McGerr | 1.50 | 3.00 | 4.50 | M |
| 613 | Saddlebum–William MacLeod Raine | 1.50 | 3.00 | 4.50 | W |
| 614 | Jewels for a Shroud–Walter de Steiguer | 1.50 | 3.00 | 4.50 | M |
| 615 | The Sea Is a Woman–Lonnie Coleman | 1.50 | 3.00 | 4.50 | |
| 616 | No Range Is Free–E.E. Halleran | 1.50 | 3.00 | 4.50 | W |
| 617 | Dividend on Death–Brett Halliday | 1.50 | 3.00 | 4.50 | M |
| 618 | Man in the Saddle–Ernest Haycox | 1.50 | 3.00 | 4.50 | W |
| 619 | Spill the Jackpot–A.A. Fair | 1.50 | 3.00 | 4.50 | M |
| 620 | Turn on the Heat–A.A. Fair | 1.50 | 3.00 | 4.50 | M |
| 621 | Lament for the Bride–Helen Reilly | 1.50 | 3.00 | 4.50 | M |
| 622 | Age of Consent–Clem Yore | 1.50 | 3.00 | 4.50 | |
| 623 | Fatal in Furs–James M. Fox | 1.50 | 3.00 | 4.50 | M |
| 624 | Steel to the South–Wayne D. Overholser | 1.50 | 3.00 | 4.50 | W |
| 625 | Border Town–Carroll Graham; 1952 | 1.50 | 3.00 | 4.50 | |
| 626 | Three Doors to Death–Rex Stout | 1.50 | 3.00 | 4.50 | M |
| 627 | When Worlds Collide–Philip Wylie & Edwin Balmer | 3.00 | 6.00 | 9.00 | SF |
| 628 | Speak No Evil–Mignon G. Eberhart | 1.50 | 3.00 | 4.50 | M |
| 629 | Gunsight Pass–William MacLeod Raine | 1.50 | 3.00 | 4.50 | W |
| 630 | Untamed–Helga Moray | 2.00 | 4.00 | 6.00 | |
| 631 | What Rhymes with Murder?–Jack Iams | 1.50 | 3.00 | 4.50 | M |
| 632 | Border Ambush–Walker A. Tompkins | 1.50 | 3.00 | 4.50 | W |
| 633 | Three Blind Mice–Agatha Christie | 1.50 | 3.00 | 4.50 | M |
| 634 | Two If by Sea–Roger Bax; c-McCarthy | 1.50 | 3.00 | 4.50 | |
| 635 | To Wake the Dead–John Dickson Carr | 1.50 | 3.00 | 4.50 | M |
| 636 | Triggerman–Frank Austin; aka The Sheriff Rides | 1.50 | 3.00 | 4.50 | W |
| 637 | Indian Beef–Harold Channing Wire; aka Trail Boss of Indian Beef | 1.50 | 3.00 | 4.50 | W |
| 638 | See You at the Morgue–Lawrence G. Blochman | 1.50 | 3.00 | 4.50 | M |
| 639 | Good Luck to the Corpse–Max Murray | 1.50 | 3.00 | 4.50 | M |
| 640 | The Life and Death of the Wicked Lady Skelton–Magdalen King-Hall | 2.00 | 4.00 | 6.00 | |
| 641 | Carry My Coffin Slowly–Lee Herrington | 1.50 | 3.00 | 4.50 | M |
| 642 | Tall Man Riding–Norman A. Fox | 1.50 | 3.00 | 4.50 | W |
| 643 | Deadline at Durango–Allan Vaughan Elston | 1.50 | 3.00 | 4.50 | W |
| 644 | The Fifth Key–George Harmon Coxe | 1.50 | 3.00 | 4.50 | M |
| 645 | The Body That Wasn't Uncle–George Worthing Yates | 1.50 | 3.00 | 4.50 | M |
| 646 | No Mourners Present–Frank G. Presnell | 1.50 | 3.00 | 4.50 | M |
| 647 | King Colt–Luke Short | 1.50 | 3.00 | 4.50 | W |
| 648 | Fabia–Olive Higgins Prouty | 1.50 | 3.00 | 4.50 | |
| 649 | The Kind Man–Helen Nielsen | 1.50 | 3.00 | 4.50 | |
| 650 | Night at the Mocking Widow–Carter Dickson; 1953 | 1.50 | 3.00 | 4.50 | M |
| 651 | Desperate Moment–Martha Albrand | 1.50 | 3.00 | 4.50 | |
| 652 | The Bat–Mary Roberts Rinehart | 1.00 | 2.00 | 3.00 | M |
| 653 | Outlaw on Horseback–Will Ermine | 1.50 | 3.00 | 4.50 | W |
| 654 | Dell Crossword Puzzles–Kathleen Rafferty | 20.00 | 40.00 | 60.00 | NF |
| 655 | No Tears for Hilda–Andrew Garve | 1.50 | 3.00 | 4.50 | M |
| 656 | Badlands Justice–Dan Cushman | 2.00 | 4.00 | 6.00 | W |
| 657 | The Hunter–James Aldridge | 1.50 | 3.00 | 4.50 | |
| 658 | To Catch a Thief–David Dodge | 1.50 | 3.00 | 4.50 | |
| 659 | Stairway to an Empty Room–Dolores Hitchens | 1.50 | 3.00 | 4.50 | M |
| 660 | Buckskin Empire–Harry Sinclair Drago | 1.50 | 3.00 | 4.50 | W |
| 661 | Stormy Present–Hope Field | 1.50 | 3.00 | 4.50 | |
| 662 | Murder Leaves a Ring–Fay Grissom Stanley | 1.50 | 3.00 | 4.50 | M |
| 663 | The Arms of Venus–John Appleby | 1.50 | 3.00 | 4.50 | |

| | | V/Good | Fine | N/Mint | |
|---|---|---|---|---|---|
| DELL, *continued* | | | | | |
| 664 | The Boomerang Clue–Agatha Christie | 1.50 | 3.00 | 4.50 | M |
| 665 | Dead Weight–Frank Kane | 2.50 | 5.00 | 7.50 | M |
| 666 | The Law Busters–Bliss Lomax (H.S. Drago) | 1.50 | 3.00 | 4.50 | W |
| 667 | Four Fallen Women–anthology | 2.00 | 4.00 | 6.00 | E |
| 668 | Bodies Are Where You Find Them–Brett Halliday | 1.50 | 3.00 | 4.50 | M |
| 669 | Never Look Back–Mignon G. Eberhart | 1.50 | 3.00 | 4.50 | M |
| 670 | The Witching Night–C.S. Cody | 3.00 | 6.00 | 9.00 | M |
| 671 | 1953 Racing Almanac–Rowland Barber & John I. Day | 1.50 | 3.00 | 4.50 | NF |
| 672 | Don't Cry for Me–William Campbell Gault | 2.50 | 5.00 | 7.50 | M |
| 673 | Treasure of the Brasada–Les Savage, Jr | 1.50 | 3.00 | 4.50 | W |
| 674 | The Broken Vase–Rex Stout | 1.50 | 3.00 | 4.50 | M |
| 675 | Hardly a Man Is Now Alive–Herbert Brean; 1953 | 1.50 | 3.00 | 4.50 | |
| 676 | All over Town–George Milburn | 1.50 | 3.00 | 4.50 | |
| 677 | Texas Fury–John Callahan | 1.50 | 3.00 | 4.50 | W |
| 678 | Fashioned for Murder–George Harmon Coxe | 1.50 | 3.00 | 4.50 | M |
| 679 | Night Has a Thousand Eyes–William Irish | 4.00 | 8.00 | 12.00 | M |
| 680 | First He Died–Clifford D. Simak | 2.00 | 4.00 | 6.00 | SF |
| 681 | The Picture of Dorian Grey–Oscar Wilde | 3.00 | 6.00 | 9.00 | HO |
| 682 | The Gallows in My Garden–Richard Deming | 1.50 | 3.00 | 4.50 | M |
| 683 | An Overdose of Death–Agatha Christie | 1.50 | 3.00 | 4.50 | M |
| 684 | The Silver Star–Will Ermine | 1.50 | 3.00 | 4.50 | W |
| 685 | The Scarlet Slippers–James M. Fox | 1.50 | 3.00 | 4.50 | M |
| 686 | The Juggler–Michael Blankfort | 1.50 | 3.00 | 4.50 | |
| 687 | The Frightened Stiff–Kelley Roos | 1.50 | 3.00 | 4.50 | M |
| 688 | The Proud Sheriff–Eugene Manlove Rhodes | 1.50 | 3.00 | 4.50 | W |
| 689 | The Bahamas Murder Case–Leslie Ford | 1.50 | 3.00 | 4.50 | M |
| 690 | Behind the Crimson Blind–Carter Dickson | 1.50 | 3.00 | 4.50 | M |
| 691 | Bats Fly at Dusk–A.A. Fair | 1.50 | 3.00 | 4.50 | M |
| 692 | The River Road–Frances Parkinson Keyes | 1.50 | 3.00 | 4.50 | |
| 693 | Nightmare at Noon–Stewart Sterling | 1.50 | 3.00 | 4.50 | M |
| 694 | Roughshod–Norman A. Fox | 1.50 | 3.00 | 4.50 | W |
| 695 | The Other One–Catherine Turney | 1.50 | 3.00 | 4.50 | M |
| 696 | Slan–A.E. Van Vogt | 3.00 | 6.00 | 9.00 | SF |
| 697 | At Last, Mr. Tolliver–William Wiegand; c-Powers | 1.50 | 3.00 | 4.50 | |
| 698 | The Big Fist–Clyde Ragsdale | 1.50 | 3.00 | 4.50 | |
| 699 | Buckaroo's Code–Wayne D. Overholser | 1.50 | 3.00 | 4.50 | W |
| 700 | Curtains for the Copper–Thomas Polsky; 1953 | 1.50 | 3.00 | 4.50 | M |
| 701 | They Died Laughing–Alan Green | 1.50 | 3.00 | 4.50 | |
| 702 | Bounty Guns–Luke Short | 1.50 | 3.00 | 4.50 | W |
| 703 | The Stockade–Kenneth Lamott | 1.50 | 3.00 | 4.50 | E |
| 704 | The Chill–E.C. Bentley | 1.50 | 3.00 | 4.50 | M |
| 705 | Brutally with Love–Edith Pope | 1.50 | 3.00 | 4.50 | |
| 706 | The Mad Hatter Mystery–John Dickson Carr | 1.50 | 3.00 | 4.50 | M |
| 707 | Gold Brick Range–Allan Vaughan Elston | 1.50 | 3.00 | 4.50 | W |
| 708 | Mosquitoes–William Faulkner | 1.50 | 3.00 | 4.50 | |
| 709 | Three Women in Black–Helen Reilly | 1.25 | 2.50 | 3.75 | M |
| 710 | The Follower–Patrick Quentin | 1.50 | 3.00 | 4.50 | M |

| | | V/Good | Fine | N/Mint | |
|---|---|---|---|---|---|
| 711 | Challenge to Danger–William MacLeod Raine | 1.50 | 3.00 | 4.50 | W |
| 712 | The Natural–Bernard Malamud | 2.50 | 5.00 | 7.50 | S |
| 713 | Strangle Hold–Mary McMullen | 1.50 | 3.00 | 4.50 | |
| 714 | Matador–Barnaby Conrad | 2.00 | 4.00 | 6.00 | A |
| 715 | Four Lost Ladies–Stuart Palmer | 2.50 | 5.00 | 7.50 | M |
| 716 | Gunsmoke Graze–Peter Dawson (Frank Gruber) | 1.25 | 2.50 | 3.75 | W |
| 717 | Trial by Terror–Paul Gallico | 1.00 | 2.00 | 3.00 | |
| 718 | Double or Quits–A.A. Fair | 1.00 | 2.00 | 3.00 | M |
| 719 | The Iron Virgin–James M. Fox | 1.50 | 3.00 | 4.50 | M |
| 720 | The Ripper from Rawhide–Dan Cushman | 1.50 | 3.00 | 4.50 | W |
| 721 | Mercy Island–Theodore Pratt | 1.50 | 3.00 | 4.50 | |
| 722 | A Shot of Murder–Jack Iams | 3.00 | 6.00 | 9.00 | M |
| 723 | When Dorinda Dances–Brett Halliday | 1.25 | 2.50 | 3.75 | M |
| 724 | Guns along the Yellowstone–Bliss Lomax (H.S. Drago) | 1.25 | 2.50 | 3.75 | W |
| 725 | Seeds of Contemplation–Thomas Merton; 1953 | 1.00 | 2.00 | 3.00 | |
| 726 | Blow Hot, Blow Cold–Gerald Butler | 1.25 | 2.50 | 3.75 | M |
| 727 | The Burden of Guilt–Ian Gordon | 1.00 | 2.00 | 3.00 | |
| 728 | The Dell Bowling Handbook–Joe Falcaro & Murray Goodman | 1.00 | 2.00 | 3.00 | NF |
| 729 | Fabulous Gunman–Wayne D. Overholser | 1.25 | 2.50 | 3.75 | W |
| 730 | Vanish in an Instant–Margaret Millar | 1.50 | 3.00 | 4.50 | M |
| 731 | Fetish–Christine Garnier | 2.00 | 4.00 | 6.00 | |
| 732 | The Double Man–Helen Reilly | 1.00 | 2.00 | 3.00 | M |
| 733 | The Fatal Caress–Richard Barker | 1.00 | 2.00 | 3.00 | M |
| 734 | The Lady Is Afraid–George Harmon Coxe | 1.25 | 2.50 | 3.75 | M |
| 735 | A Corpse for Christmas–Henry Kane | 1.25 | 2.50 | 3.75 | M |
| 736 | The Cumberland Rifles–Noel B. Gerson | 1.25 | 2.50 | 3.75 | A |
| 737 | Ghostly Hoofbeats–Norman A. Fox | 1.00 | 2.00 | 3.00 | W |
| 738 | Nothing More Than Murder–Jim Thompson | 6.00 | 12.00 | 18.00 | M |
| 739 | Hurry the Darkness–Maurice Procter | 1.00 | 2.00 | 3.00 | M |
| 740 | Blow-down–Lawrence B. Blochman | 1.50 | 3.00 | 4.50 | |
| 741 | Dr. Gatskill's Blue Shoes–Paul Conant | 1.00 | 2.00 | 3.00 | |
| 742 | Colorado Showdown–Allan Vaughan Elston | 1.00 | 2.00 | 3.00 | W |
| 743 | Mum's the Word for Murder–Brett Halliday | 1.00 | 2.00 | 3.00 | M |
| 744 | Death Has Deep Roots–Michael Gilbert | 1.00 | 2.00 | 3.00 | |
| 745 | Venturous Lady–George Harmon Coxe | 1.00 | 2.00 | 3.00 | M |
| 746 | The Bloody Bokhara–William Campbell Gault | 2.00 | 4.00 | 6.00 | M |
| 747 | Dead on the Level–Helen Nielsen; 1954 | 1.00 | 2.00 | 3.00 | M |
| 748 | Trail Town–Ernest Haycox | 1.00 | 2.00 | 3.00 | W |
| 749 | Bare Trap–Frank Kane | 1.00 | 2.00 | 3.00 | M |
| 750 | The Gabriel Horn–Felix Holt; 1954 | 1.00 | 2.00 | 3.00 | |
| 751 | Barbary Hoard–John Appleby | 1.50 | 3.00 | 4.50 | |
| 752 | The Spider Lily–Bruno Fischer | 1.50 | 3.00 | 4.50 | M |
| 753 | Murder after Hours–Agatha Christie | 1.50 | 3.00 | 4.50 | M |
| 754 | Laughing on the Inside–Bill Yates | 1.50 | 3.00 | 4.50 | H |
| 755 | Smoky Range–E.E. Halleran | 1.25 | 2.50 | 3.75 | W |
| 756 | Whomsoever I Shall Kiss–Curt Siodmak | 1.00 | 2.00 | 3.00 | |
| 757 | The Hollow Needle–George Harmon Coxe | 1.50 | 3.00 | 4.50 | M |
| 758 | The Clock Strikes 13–Herbert Brean | 1.00 | 2.00 | 3.00 | |
| 759 | Black Widow–Patrick Quentin | 1.50 | 3.00 | 4.50 | M |
| 760 | Outpost Mars–Cyril Judd | 1.50 | 3.00 | 4.50 | SF |
| 761 | Sex after Forty–John Gilmore & S.A. Lewin | 1.50 | 3.00 | 4.50 | NF |
| 762 | Silver Doll–Blair Treynor | 1.50 | 3.00 | 4.50 | M |
| 763 | The Key to Nicholas Street–Stanley Ellin | 1.00 | 2.00 | 3.00 | |
| 764 | Prairie Marshal–Walker A. Tompkins | 1.00 | 2.00 | 3.00 | W |
| 765 | By-line for Murder–Andrew Garve | 1.00 | 2.00 | 3.00 | M |
| 766 | Nell Gwyn: Royal Mistress–John H. Wilson | 1.00 | 2.00 | 3.00 | A |
| 767 | Dead Man's Plans–Mignon G. Eberhart; c-Powers | 1.00 | 2.00 | 3.00 | M |
| 768 | What Really Happened–Brett Halliday | 1.00 | 2.00 | 3.00 | M |
| 769 | Brand of Empire–Luke Short | 1.50 | 3.00 | 4.50 | W |
| 770 | Thirteen at Dinner–Agatha Christie | 1.00 | 2.00 | 3.00 | M |
| 771 | The Loved One–Evelyn Waugh | 1.00 | 2.00 | 3.00 | |
| 772 | Top of the Heap–A.A. Fair | 1.00 | 2.00 | 3.00 | M |
| 773 | Evil Became Them–Pat Root | 1.00 | 2.00 | 3.00 | |
| 774 | Sam Snead's Natural Golf–Sam Snead | 1.00 | 2.00 | 3.00 | S |
| 775 | The Corpse in the Waxworks–John Dickson Carr; 1954; c-Powers | 2.00 | 4.00 | 6.00 | M |

*Dell 696, Dell 712, Dell 835.*

**DELL,** *continued*

| No. | Title | V/Good | Fine | N/Mint | |
|---|---|---|---|---|---|
| 776 | Gun Bulldogger–Eugene Cunningham | 1.50 | 3.00 | 4.50 | W |
| 777 | The Tiger in the Smoke–Margery Allingham; c-Powers | 1.25 | 2.50 | 3.75 | M |
| 778 | Crows Can't Count–A.A. Fair | 1.00 | 2.00 | 3.00 | M |
| 779 | Widow's Won't Wait–Dolores Hitchens | 1.00 | 2.00 | 3.00 | M |
| 780 | Tall in the Saddle–Gordon Young | 1.00 | 2.00 | 3.00 | W |
| 781 | Beyond Infinity–Robert Spencer Carr | 1.50 | 3.00 | 4.50 | SF |
| 782 | The Red Lamp–Mary Roberts Rinehart | 1.00 | 2.00 | 3.00 | M |
| 783 | Long Lightning–Norman A. Fox | 1.00 | 2.00 | 3.00 | W |
| 784 | Dead Babes in the Woods–D.B. Olsen | 1.50 | 3.00 | 4.50 | M |
| 785 | Bullet Proof–Frank Kane | 1.50 | 3.00 | 4.50 | M |
| 786 | Hold It, Florence–Whitney Darrow, Jr | 1.00 | 2.00 | 3.00 | |
| 787 | The Long Memory–Howard Clewes | 1.00 | 2.00 | 3.00 | |
| 788 | Murder Is the Pay-off–Leslie Ford | 1.00 | 2.00 | 3.00 | M |
| 789 | Stagecoach Kingdom–Harry Sinclair Drago | 1.00 | 2.00 | 3.00 | W |
| 790 | The Corpse That Refused to Stay Dead–Hampton Stone | 1.50 | 3.00 | 4.50 | M |
| 791 | The Long Loud Silence–Wilson Tucker | 2.50 | 5.00 | 7.50 | SF |
| 792 | The Evil Men Do–Benedict Kiely; aka Honey Seems Bitter | 1.50 | 3.00 | 4.50 | |
| 793 | The Bandit Trail–William MacLeod Raine | 1.50 | 3.00 | 4.50 | W |
| 794 | Sleep, My Love–Robert Martin | 1.00 | 2.00 | 3.00 | |
| 795 | The Canvas Coffin–William Campbell Gault | 2.50 | 5.00 | 7.50 | M |
| 796 | West of the Rimrock–Wayne D. Overholser | 1.00 | 2.00 | 3.00 | W |
| 797 | The Harlot Killer–ed. Allan Barnard | 3.00 | 6.00 | 9.00 | |
| 798 | Cooking for Two–Janet McKenzie Hill | 1.00 | 2.00 | 3.00 | NF |
| 799 | Inland Passage–George Harmon Coxe | 1.00 | 2.00 | 3.00 | M |
| 800 | Daisy Miller and the Turn of the Screw–Henry James; 1954 | 1.00 | 2.00 | 3.00 | |
| 801 | Riders of the Buffalo Grass–Bliss Lomax (H.S. Drago) | 1.00 | 2.00 | 3.00 | W |
| 802 | Asylum–William Seabrook; c-Powers | 1.00 | 2.00 | 3.00 | |
| 803 | One Night with Nora–Brett Halliday | 1.00 | 2.00 | 3.00 | M |
| 804 | Wide Loop–Nelson Nye | 1.00 | 2.00 | 3.00 | W |
| 805 | Murder in Mesopotamia–Agatha Christie | 1.00 | 2.00 | 3.00 | M |
| 806 | Obit Delayed–Helen Nielsen | 1.00 | 2.00 | 3.00 | M |
| 807 | Vile Bodies–Evelyn Waugh | 1.00 | 2.00 | 3.00 | |
| 808 | Deadlock–Ruth Fenisong | 1.00 | 2.00 | 3.00 | M |
| 809 | Some Women Won't Wait–A.A. Fair | 1.00 | 2.00 | 3.00 | M |
| 810 | Roundup on the Picketwire–Allan Vaughan Elston | 1.00 | 2.00 | 3.00 | W |
| 811 | The Unknown Quantity–Mignon G. Eberhart | 1.00 | 2.00 | 3.00 | M |
| 812 | Deep Is the Night–James Wellard | 1.00 | 2.00 | 3.00 | |
| 813 | My Name Is Michael Sibley–John Bingham | 1.00 | 2.00 | 3.00 | M |
| 814 | Haunted Lady–Mary Roberts Rinehart | 1.00 | 2.00 | 3.00 | M |
| 815 | Valley of Guns–Wayne D. Overholser | 1.00 | 2.00 | 3.00 | W |
| 816 | Five Alarm Funeral–Stewart Sterling | 1.50 | 3.00 | 4.50 | M |
| 817 | The Pigskin Bag–Bruno Fischer; 1955 | 1.50 | 3.00 | 4.50 | |
| 818 | The Golden Violet–Joseph Shearing | 1.00 | 2.00 | 3.00 | |
| 819 | The Amazing Adventures of Father Brown–G.K. Chesterton | 1.50 | 3.00 | 4.50 | M |
| 820 | Is Sex Necessary?–James Thurber & E.B. White | 1.50 | 3.00 | 4.50 | H |
| 821 | Riders of Buck River–William MacLeod Raine | 1.00 | 2.00 | 3.00 | W |
| 822 | Poisons Unknown–Frank Kane | 1.50 | 3.00 | 4.50 | M |
| 823 | A Town of Masks–Dorothy Salisbury Davis | 1.00 | 2.00 | 3.00 | M |
| 824 | The Company She Keeps–Mary McCarthy | 1.00 | 2.00 | 3.00 | |
| 825 | Gunfire Men–L.L. Foreman; 1955 | 1.00 | 2.00 | 3.00 | W |
| 826 | Savage Range–Luke Short | 1.00 | 2.00 | 3.00 | W |
| 827 | Murder through the Looking Glass–Andrew Garve | 1.00 | 2.00 | 3.00 | M |
| 828 | Strawberry Roan–Clem Colt | 1.00 | 2.00 | 3.00 | W |
| 829 | Before I Wake–Brett Halliday | 1.00 | 2.00 | 3.00 | M |
| 830 | There Is a Tide–Agatha Christie | 1.00 | 2.00 | 3.00 | M |
| 831 | The Rawhide Years–Norman A. Fox | 1.00 | 2.00 | 3.00 | W |
| 832 | The Stirrup Boss–Peter Dawson (Frank Gruber) | 1.25 | 2.50 | 3.75 | W |
| 833 | Recipe for Homicide–Lawrence G. Blochman | 1.00 | 2.00 | 3.00 | M |
| 834 | The Strangers–William E. Wilson | 1.00 | 2.00 | 3.00 | |
| 835 | Blood on the Boards–William Campbell Gault | 2.50 | 5.00 | 7.50 | M |
| 836 | Gold Comes in Bricks–A.A. Fair | 1.00 | 2.00 | 3.00 | M |
| 837 | Detour to Death–Helen Nielsen | 1.00 | 2.00 | 3.00 | M |
| 838 | The Frightened Fiancee–George Harmon Coxe | 1.00 | 2.00 | 3.00 | M |
| 839 | Baseball's Greatest Players–Tom Meany | 1.00 | 2.00 | 3.00 | S |
| 840 | The Bridal Bed Murders–A.E. Martin | 1.00 | 2.00 | 3.00 | M |
| 841 | The Evil of Time–Evelyn Berckman | 1.00 | 2.00 | 3.00 | |
| 842 | The Corpse Came Calling–Brett Halliday | 1.00 | 2.00 | 3.00 | M |
| 843 | Man the Beast and the Wild, Wild Women–Virgil Partch | 2.00 | 4.00 | 6.00 | H |
| 844 | The Proud Diggers–William O. Turner | 1.00 | 2.00 | 3.00 | W |
| 845 | Death Commits Bigamy–James M. Fox | 1.00 | 2.00 | 3.00 | M |
| 846 | Tough Hand–Wayne D. Overholser | 1.00 | 2.00 | 3.00 | W |
| 847 | The Bad Seed–William March | 1.00 | 2.00 | 3.00 | |
| 848 | Give the Little Corpse a Great Big Hand–George Bagby | 1.00 | 2.00 | 3.00 | |
| 849 | Wyoming Gun–Tom Roan | 1.00 | 2.00 | 3.00 | W |
| 850 | The Shocking Secret–Holly Roth; 1955 | 1.00 | 2.00 | 3.00 | M |
| 851 | Run to Death–Patrick Quentin | 1.00 | 2.00 | 3.00 | M |
| 852 | The Affairs of Caroline Cherie–Cecil Saint-Laurent | 1.00 | 2.00 | 3.00 | |
| 853 | The Body on the Bench–Dorothy B. Hughes | 1.00 | 2.00 | 3.00 | M |
| 854 | Heather Mary–J.M. Scott | 2.00 | 4.00 | 6.00 | |
| 855 | The Witness for the Prosecution–Agatha Christie | 1.00 | 2.00 | 3.00 | M |
| 856 | To Walk the Night–William Sloane | 1.00 | 2.00 | 3.00 | M |
| 857 | Dead and Gone–Brandon Bird | 1.00 | 2.00 | 3.00 | M |
| 858 | Bury Me Not–Allan R. Bosworth | 1.00 | 2.00 | 3.00 | W |
| 859 | The Crooked Hinge–John Dickson Carr | 1.00 | 2.00 | 3.00 | M |
| 860 | Seeing Red–Theodora DuBois | 1.00 | 2.00 | 3.00 | |
| 861 | Saddle Up for Sunlight–Allan Vaughan Elston | 1.00 | 2.00 | 3.00 | W |
| 862 | My Favorite Football Stories–Red Grange | 1.00 | 2.00 | 3.00 | S |
| 863 | The Law at Randado–Elmore Leonard | 3.50 | 7.00 | 10.50 | W |
| 864 | The Thirsty Land–Norman A. Fox | 1.00 | 2.00 | 3.00 | W |
| 865 | Death Has Three Lives–Brett Halliday | 1.00 | 2.00 | 3.00 | M |
| 866 | Michael Shayne's Long Chance–Brett Halliday | 1.00 | 2.00 | 3.00 | M |
| 867 | She Woke to Darkness–Brett Halliday | 1.00 | 2.00 | 3.00 | M |
| 868 | Run, Killer, Run–William Campbell Gault | 2.50 | 5.00 | 7.50 | M |
| 869 | Bounty Guns–Luke Short | 1.50 | 3.00 | 4.50 | W |
| 870 | The Danger Within–Michael Gilbert | 1.00 | 2.00 | 3.00 | |
| 871 | Murder in Retrospect–Agatha Christie | 1.00 | 2.00 | 3.00 | M |
| 872 | Grin and Bear It–George Lichty | 1.00 | 2.00 | 3.00 | H |
| 873 | The Tender Poisoner–John Bingham | 1.50 | 3.00 | 4.50 | M |
| 874 | The Big Money–Harold Q. Masur | 1.00 | 2.00 | 3.00 | M |
| 875 | The Violent Land–Wayne D. Overholser; 1955 | 1.00 | 2.00 | 3.00 | W |
| 876 | The Long Chase–James B. Hendryx | 1.00 | 2.00 | 3.00 | W |
| 877 | Man Missing–Mignon G. Eberhart | 1.00 | 2.00 | 3.00 | M |
| 878 | The Border Jumpers–Will C. Brown | 1.00 | 2.00 | 3.00 | W |
| 879 | Gold on the Hoof–Walker A. Tompkins | 1.00 | 2.00 | 3.00 | W |
| 880 | The Silent Women–Margaret Page Hood | 1.00 | 2.00 | 3.00 | |
| 881 | Fog of Doubt–Christianna Brand; 1956 | 1.00 | 2.00 | 3.00 | |
| 882 | The High Passes–John Reese | 1.00 | 2.00 | 3.00 | |
| 883 | The Murder That Wouldn't Stay Solved–Hampton Stone | 1.00 | 2.00 | 3.00 | M |
| 884 | Danger West!–Robert McCaig | 1.00 | 2.00 | 3.00 | W |

*Dell 863, Dell 898, Dell D304.*

**DELL,** *continued*

| # | Title | V/Good | Fine | N/Mint | |
|---|-------|--------|------|--------|---|
| 885 | Straw Man–Doris Miles Disney | 1.00 | 2.00 | 3.00 | M |
| 886 | Grave Danger–Frank Kane | 1.00 | 2.00 | 3.00 | |
| 887 | The Ponder Heart–Eudora Welty | 1.00 | 2.00 | 3.00 | |
| 888 | Murder at the Vicarage–Agatha Christie | 1.00 | 2.00 | 3.00 | M |
| 889 | Trail's End–William MacLeod Raine | 1.00 | 2.00 | 3.00 | W |
| 890 | My Son, the Murderer–Patrick Quentin | 1.00 | 2.00 | 3.00 | M |
| 891 | Blood on the Stars–Brett Halliday | 1.00 | 2.00 | 3.00 | M |
| 892 | Quick on the Shoot–George C. Appell | 1.00 | 2.00 | 3.00 | |
| 893 | The Frightened Fingers–Spencer Dean | 1.00 | 2.00 | 3.00 | M |
| 894 | Thin Air–Howard Browne | 1.00 | 2.00 | 3.00 | |
| 895 | Raw Land–Luke Short | 1.00 | 2.00 | 3.00 | W |
| 896 | The Butcher's Wife–Owen Cameron | 1.00 | 2.00 | 3.00 | |
| 897 | The Twilighters–Noel M. Loomis | 1.00 | 2.00 | 3.00 | W |
| 898 | Gulf Coast Girl–Charles Williams; c-Maguire | 2.50 | 5.00 | 7.50 | |
| 899 | Cats Prowl at Night–A.A. Fair | 1.00 | 2.00 | 3.00 | M |
| 900 | The Woman on the Roof–Helen Nielsen; 1956 | 1.00 | 2.00 | 3.00 | M |
| 901 | Red Hot Ice–Frank Kane | 1.00 | 2.00 | 3.00 | M |
| 902 | Eye Witness–George Harmon Coxe | 1.00 | 2.00 | 3.00 | M |
| 903 | Draw or Drag–Wayne D. Overholser | 1.00 | 2.00 | 3.00 | W |
| 904 | The Body in the Basket–George Bagby | 1.00 | 2.00 | 3.00 | M |
| 905 | In a Deadly Vein–Brett Halliday | 1.00 | 2.00 | 3.00 | M |
| 906 | Day of the Outlaw–Lee E. Wells | 1.00 | 2.00 | 3.00 | W |
| 907 | Shadow on the Range–Norman A. Fox | 1.00 | 2.00 | 3.00 | W |
| 908 | Washington Whispers Murder–Leslie Ford | 1.00 | 2.00 | 3.00 | M |
| 909 | Day of the Dead–Bart Spicer | 1.00 | 2.00 | 3.00 | |
| 910 | The Restless Hands–Bruno Fischer | 1.00 | 2.00 | 3.00 | |
| 911 | Lazy H Feud–Ed LaVanway | 1.00 | 2.00 | 3.00 | W |
| 912 | Cards on the Table–Agatha Christie | 1.00 | 2.00 | 3.00 | M |
| 913 | Goodbye to Gunsmoke–Ralph Catlin | 1.00 | 2.00 | 3.00 | W |
| 914 | Stranger in Town–Brett Halliday | 1.00 | 2.00 | 3.00 | M |
| 915 | Masterpiece in Murder–Richard Powell | 1.00 | 2.00 | 3.00 | M |
| 916 | Last of the Longhorns–Will Ermine | 1.00 | 2.00 | 3.00 | W |
| 917 | The Opening Door–Helen Reilly | 1.00 | 2.00 | 3.00 | M |
| 918 | Green Light for Death–Frank Kane | 1.50 | 3.00 | 4.50 | M |
| 919 | Their Guns Were Fast–Harry Sinclair Drago | 1.00 | 2.00 | 3.00 | W |
| 920 | The Lively Corpse–Margaret Millar | 1.50 | 3.00 | 4.50 | M |
| 921 | The Cautious Maiden–Cecil Saint-Laurent | 1.00 | 2.00 | 3.00 | |
| 922 | The Hidden Grave–Peter Hardin | 1.00 | 2.00 | 3.00 | |
| 923 | Scout Commander–S.E. Whitman | 1.00 | 2.00 | 3.00 | |
| 924 | Cast a Long Shadow–Wayne D. Overholser | 1.00 | 2.00 | 3.00 | W |
| 925 | The Tall Dark Man–Anne Chamberlain; 1956 | 1.00 | 2.00 | 3.00 | |
| 926 | Murder in the Raw–William Campbell Gault | 2.50 | 5.00 | 7.50 | M |
| 927 | Stormy in the West–Norman A. Fox | 1.00 | 2.00 | 3.00 | W |
| 928 | The Unquiet Corpse–William Sloane | 1.00 | 2.00 | 3.00 | M |
| 929 | Dead Stop–Doris Miles Disney | 1.00 | 2.00 | 3.00 | M |
| 930 | The Texas Pistol–James Keene; 1957 | 1.00 | 2.00 | 3.00 | |
| 931 | Never Bet Your Life–George Harmon Coxe | 1.00 | 2.00 | 3.00 | M |
| 932 | Rustlers' Bend–Will Ermine | 1.00 | 2.00 | 3.00 | W |
| 933 | Murder at Nightfall–Edna Sherry | 1.00 | 2.00 | 3.00 | M |
| 934 | A Taste for Violence–Brett Halliday | 1.00 | 2.00 | 3.00 | M |
| 935 | Border Guns–Eugene Cunningham | 1.00 | 2.00 | 3.00 | W |
| 936 | Worse Than Murder–Evelyn Berckman | 1.00 | 2.00 | 3.00 | |
| 937 | Murder at Hazelmoor–Agatha Christie | 1.00 | 2.00 | 3.00 | M |
| 938 | Renegade Canyon–Peter Dawson (Frank Gruber) | 1.25 | 2.50 | 3.75 | W |
| 939 | Fools Die on Friday–A.A. Fair | 1.00 | 2.00 | 3.00 | M |
| 940 | Escape from Five Shadows–Elmore Leonard | 3.50 | 7.00 | 10.50 | W |
| 941 | Murder Is a Witch–John Bingham; c-Powers | 1.00 | 2.00 | 3.00 | M |
| 942 | The Sagebrush Bandit–Bliss Lomax (H.S. Drago) | 1.00 | 2.00 | 3.00 | W |
| 943 | The Man Who Had Too Much to Lose–Hampton Stone | 1.00 | 2.00 | 3.00 | M |
| 944 | Bury Me Deep–Harold Q. Masur | 1.00 | 2.00 | 3.00 | M |
| 945 | Alder Gulch–Ernest Haycox | 1.00 | 2.00 | 3.00 | W |
| 946 | The Blonde Cried Murder–Brett Halliday | 1.00 | 2.00 | 3.00 | M |
| 947 | The Settler–William O. Turner | 1.00 | 2.00 | 3.00 | W |
| 948 | Steel to the South–Wayne D. Overholser; c-Gross | 1.00 | 2.00 | 3.00 | W |
| 949 | Dead Storage–George Bagby | 1.00 | 2.00 | 3.00 | M |
| 950 | Night Passage–Norman A. Fox; 1957 | 1.00 | 2.00 | 3.00 | W |

| # | Title | V/Good | Fine | N/Mint | |
|---|-------|--------|------|--------|---|
| 951 | Murder in a Nunnery–Eric Shepherd | 1.00 | 2.00 | 3.00 | M |
| 952 | Man in the Saddle–Ernest Haycox | 1.00 | 2.00 | 3.00 | W |
| 953 | Dead of Summer–Dana Mosely | 1.00 | 2.00 | 3.00 | |
| 954 | To Ride the River With–William MacLeod Raine | 1.00 | 2.00 | 3.00 | W |
| 955 | Postmark Murder–Mignon G. Eberhart | 1.00 | 2.00 | 3.00 | M |
| 956 | Riding Gun–Eugene Cunningham | 1.00 | 2.00 | 3.00 | W |
| 957 | This Is It, Michael Shayne–Brett Halliday | 1.00 | 2.00 | 3.00 | M |
| 958 | Framed in Blood–Brett Halliday | 1.00 | 2.00 | 3.00 | M |
| 959 | The Brass and the Blue–James Keene | 1.00 | 2.00 | 3.00 | |
| 960 | Murder and the Married Virgin–Brett Halliday | 1.00 | 2.00 | 3.00 | M |
| 961 | Mr. Parker Pyne, Detective–Agatha Christie | 1.00 | 2.00 | 3.00 | M |
| 962 | King Colt–Luke Short | 1.00 | 2.00 | 3.00 | W |
| 963 | Savage Range–Luke Short | 1.00 | 2.00 | 3.00 | W |
| 964 | Inspector Maigret and the Burglar's Wife–Georges Simenon | 1.00 | 2.00 | 3.00 | M |
| 965 | Murder Is My Business–Brett Halliday; 1958 | 1.00 | 2.00 | 3.00 | M |
| 966 | The Diamond Hitch–Frank O'Rourke | 1.00 | 2.00 | 3.00 | |
| 967 | Secret of the Wastelands–Bliss Lomax (Harry Sinclair Drago) | 1.00 | 2.00 | 3.00 | W |
| 968 | The Blonde Died Dancing–Kelley Roos | 1.00 | 2.00 | 3.00 | M |
| 969 | Stranger from Arizona–Norman A. Fox | 1.00 | 2.00 | 3.00 | W |
| 970 | Focus on Murder–George Harmon Coxe | 1.00 | 2.00 | 3.00 | M |
| 971 | Seven Days before Dying–Helen Nielsen | 1.00 | 2.00 | 3.00 | M |
| 972 | Gunlock–Wayne D. Overholser | 1.00 | 2.00 | 3.00 | W |
| 973 | The Fatal Foursome–Frank Kane | 1.00 | 2.00 | 3.00 | |
| 974 | Stampede at Blue Springs–Gene Olson | 1.00 | 2.00 | 3.00 | |
| 975 | Return of a Fighter–Ernest Haycox; 1958 | 1.00 | 2.00 | 3.00 | W |
| 976 | Dear Doctor–Juliet Lowell | 1.00 | 2.00 | 3.00 | H |
| 977 | Vertigo–Pierre Boileau & Thomas Narcejac; movie tie-in | 2.50 | 5.00 | 7.50 | M |
| 978 | Weep for a Blonde–Brett Halliday | 1.00 | 2.00 | 3.00 | M |
| 979 | Bullet Brand–Nick Sumner | 1.00 | 2.00 | 3.00 | W |
| 980 | Tall Man Riding–Norman A. Fox | 1.00 | 2.00 | 3.00 | W |
| 981 | The Uncomplaining Corpses–Brett Halliday | 1.00 | 2.00 | 3.00 | M |
| 982 | The Diehard–Jean Potts | 1.00 | 2.00 | 3.00 | |
| 983 | The Demon Stirs–Owen Cameron | 1.50 | 3.00 | 4.50 | |
| 984 | Man on a Rope–George Harmon Coxe | 1.00 | 2.00 | 3.00 | M |
| 985 | So Young, So Cold, So Fair–John Creasey | 1.00 | 2.00 | 3.00 | M |
| 986 | Man of the West–Will C. Brown; movie tie-in; aka The Border Jumpers; c-Gross | 2.00 | 4.00 | 6.00 | W |
| 987 | Heads You Lose–Brett Halliday | 1.00 | 2.00 | 3.00 | M |
| 988 | Shoot the Works–Brett Halliday | 1.00 | 2.00 | 3.00 | M |
| 989 | Tickets for Death–Brett Halliday | 1.00 | 2.00 | 3.00 | M |
| 990 | Here We Go Again and Bottle Fatigue–Virgil Partch | 2.00 | 4.00 | 6.00 | H |
| 991 | Deadly Beloved–William Ard | 3.00 | 6.00 | 9.00 | M |
| 992 | Don't Count the Corpses–Christopher Monig | 1.00 | 2.00 | 3.00 | M |
| 993 | Desperate Man–Wayne D. Overholser | 1.00 | 2.00 | 3.00 | W |
| 994 | Grounds for Murder–John Appleby | 1.00 | 2.00 | 3.00 | W |
| 995 | Lady Killer–William M. Hardy | 1.00 | 2.00 | 3.00 | |
| 996 | Now, Will You Try for Murder?–Harry Olesker; 1959 | 1.00 | 2.00 | 3.00 | M |
| 997 | Cop Killer–George Bagby | 1.50 | 3.00 | 4.50 | M |
| 998 | Lover Boy–Janice Berenstain & Stanley Berenstain | 1.50 | 3.00 | 4.50 | M |
| 999 | The Trouble with Fidelity–George Malcolm-Smith | 1.00 | 2.00 | 3.00 | |
| 1000 | Justice, My Brother!–James Keene; 1959 | 1.00 | 2.00 | 3.00 | |
| 1001 | Dear Hollywood–Juliet Lowell | 1.00 | 2.00 | 3.00 | H |
| 1002 | The Badlands Beyond–Norman A. Fox | 1.00 | 2.00 | 3.00 | W |
| 1003 | Once a Widow–Lee Roberts | 1.00 | 2.00 | 3.00 | |
| 1004 | She Asked for Murder–Edna Sherry | 1.00 | 2.00 | 3.00 | M |
| 1005 | Stranger with a Gun–Bliss Lomax (H.S. Drago) | 1.00 | 2.00 | 3.00 | W |
| 1006 | Trapped!–Jean Hougron | 1.00 | 2.00 | 3.00 | |
| 1007 | A Gem of a Murder–Carleton Keith | 1.00 | 2.00 | 3.00 | |
| 1008 | The Lone Deputy–Wayne D. Overholser | 1.00 | 2.00 | 3.00 | W |
| 1009 | Last Night at Black Hammer–Gene Olson; 1960 | 1.00 | 2.00 | 3.00 | W |

**DELL,** *continued*

| | | V/Good | Fine | N/Mint | |
|---|---|---|---|---|---|
| 1010 | Last Call for a Gunfighter—Bliss Lomax (Harry Sinclair Drago); 1960 | 1.00 | 2.00 | 3.00 | W |
| 1012 | Death out of Focus—Bill Gault | 2.00 | 4.00 | 6.00 | M |
| 1013 | The Man Who Disappeared—Edgar Bohle | 1.00 | 2.00 | 3.00 | |
| 1014 | Roughshod—Norman A. Fox | 1.00 | 2.00 | 3.00 | W |
| 1019 | Dear Justice—Juliet Lowell | 1.00 | 2.00 | 3.00 | H |
| 1020 | Rope the Wind—Norman A. Fox; 1960 | 1.00 | 2.00 | 3.00 | W |

# DELL D-SERIES
## Dell Publishing Company, Inc.

| | | V/Good | Fine | N/Mint | |
|---|---|---|---|---|---|
| D101 | Chicago Confidential—Jack Lait & Lee Mortimer; 1952 | .50 | 1.00 | 1.50 | NF |
| D102 | The Great Smith—Edison Marshall | 1.50 | 3.00 | 4.50 | A |
| D103 | Gypsy Sixpence—Edison Marshall | 1.50 | 3.00 | 4.50 | |
| D104 | Tomorrow Will Be Better—Betty Smith | .75 | 1.50 | 2.25 | |
| D105 | The Natchez Woman—Alice Walworth Graham | .75 | 1.50 | 2.25 | |
| D106 | Mrs. Craddock—W. Somerset Maugham | .75 | 1.50 | 2.25 | |
| D107 | Rivers Parting—Shirley Barker | .75 | 1.50 | 2.25 | |
| D108 | Washington Confidential—Jack Lait & Lee Mortimer | .50 | 1.00 | 1.50 | NF |
| D109 | The Chequer Board—Nevil Shute | .75 | 1.50 | 2.25 | |
| D110 | The Forest and the Fort—Hervey Allen | .75 | 1.50 | 2.25 | |
| D111 | Gold for My Fair Lady—Sidney H. Courtier | .75 | 1.50 | 2.25 | A |
| D112 | Three Hundred Pillsbury Prize Recipes | .75 | 1.50 | 2.25 | NF |
| D113 | The Phantom Emperor—Neil H. Swanson | 1.00 | 2.00 | 3.00 | |
| D114 | Go Down to Glory—Richard Warren Hatch | 1.00 | 2.00 | 3.00 | |
| | With dust jacket | 30.00 | 60.00 | 90.00 | |
| D115 | The Circle of the Day—Helen Howe | .75 | 1.50 | 2.25 | |
| D116 | Slogum House—Mari Sandoz | .75 | 1.50 | 2.25 | |
| D117 | Across the River and Into the Trees—Ernest Hemingway; 1953 | 2.00 | 4.00 | 6.00 | |
| D118 | Really the Blues—Mezz Mezzrow & Bernard Wolfe | .75 | 1.50 | 2.25 | |
| D119 | Castle in the Swamp—Edison Marshall | .75 | 1.50 | 2.25 | |
| D120 | Snowslide—Carl Jonas | .75 | 1.50 | 2.25 | |
| D121 | Caroline Cherie—Cecil Saint-Laurent | .75 | 1.50 | 2.25 | |
| D122 | The Infinite Woman—Edison Marshall | .75 | 1.50 | 2.25 | |
| D123 | The Legacy—Nevil Shute | .75 | 1.50 | 2.25 | |
| D124 | Jefferson Selleck—Carl Jonas | .75 | 1.50 | 2.25 | |
| D125 | Captain Ebony—Hamilton Cochran; 1953 | 1.50 | 3.00 | 4.50 | A |
| D126 | The Swimming Pool—Mary Roberts Rinehart | .75 | 1.50 | 2.25 | M |
| D127 | Diamond Head—Houston Branch & Frank Waters | 1.50 | 3.00 | 4.50 | |
| D128 | Bedford Village—Hervey Allen | .75 | 1.50 | 2.25 | |
| D129 | Boom Town—Jack O'Connor | .75 | 1.50 | 2.25 | |
| D130 | Round the Bend—Nevil Shute | .75 | 1.50 | 2.25 | |
| D131 | Gina—George Albert Glay | .75 | 1.50 | 2.25 | |
| D132 | Tallulah—Tallulah Bankhead; 1954 | .75 | 1.50 | 2.25 | B |
| D133 | Caroline Coquette—Cecil Saint-Laurent | .75 | 1.50 | 2.25 | |
| D134 | Fresh Water Fishing—Arthur Carhart | .75 | 1.50 | 2.25 | NF |
| D135 | Reap the Whirlwind—Jean Hougron | .75 | 1.50 | 2.25 | |
| D136 | The Rogue from Padua—Jay Williams | .75 | 1.50 | 2.25 | A |
| D137 | The Bold Sabouteurs—Chandler Brossard | .75 | 1.50 | 2.25 | JD |
| D138 | Daughter of Strangers—Elizabeth Boatwright Coker | .75 | 1.50 | 2.25 | |
| D139 | The Viking—Edison Marshall | .75 | 1.50 | 2.25 | A |
| D140 | This Side of Paradise—F. Scott Fitzgerald | .75 | 1.50 | 2.25 | |
| D141 | Three to Get Married—Fulton J. Sheen | .75 | 1.50 | 2.25 | |
| D142 | The Story of America—Hendrik Willem Van Loon | .75 | 1.50 | 2.25 | NF |
| D143 | The Doctor of Bean Street—Simon Kent | 1.50 | 3.00 | 4.50 | |
| D144 | Rogue's Holiday—Hamilton Cochran | 1.00 | 2.00 | 3.00 | A |
| D145 | The Magnificent Bastards—Lucy Herndon Crockett; 1955 | .75 | 1.50 | 2.25 | |
| D146 | How to Help Your Doctor Help You—Walter C. Alvarez | .75 | 1.50 | 2.25 | NF |
| D147 | The Long Rifle—Steward Edward White | 1.50 | 3.00 | 4.50 | A |
| D148 | Fresh and Salt Water Spinning—Eugene Burns | .75 | 1.50 | 2.25 | NF |

| | | V/Good | Fine | N/Mint | |
|---|---|---|---|---|---|
| D149 | The Night of the Hunter—Davis Grubb | 1.00 | 2.00 | 3.00 | |
| D150 | Who Goes There?—John W. Campbell, Jr; 1955 | 2.00 | 4.00 | 6.00 | SF |
| D151 | Sylvia—Edgar Mittelholzer | .75 | 1.50 | 2.25 | |
| D152 | Sunset Land—Eugene Manlove Rhodes | 1.50 | 3.00 | 4.50 | W |
| D153 | Herself Surprised—Joyce Cary | .75 | 1.50 | 2.25 | |
| D154 | The Frightened Wife—Mary Roberts Rinehart | .75 | 1.50 | 2.25 | M |
| D155 | Guns and Hunting—Pete Brown | .75 | 1.50 | 2.25 | NF |
| D156 | Tell It on the Drums—Robert Krepps | 1.00 | 2.00 | 3.00 | A |
| D157 | Caravan to Xanadu—Edison Marshall; c-Gross | 1.00 | 2.00 | 3.00 | A |
| D158 | Indigo—Christine Weston | .75 | 1.50 | 2.25 | |
| D159 | The Man Who Killed Lincoln—Philip Van Doren Stern | .75 | 1.50 | 2.25 | |
| D160 | Trial—Don M. Mankiewicz; 1956 | .75 | 1.50 | 2.25 | |
| D161 | The Tumult and the Shouting—Grantland Rice | .75 | 1.50 | 2.25 | S |
| D162 | The Drinker—Hans Fallada | .75 | 1.50 | 2.25 | |
| D163 | Brideshead Revisited—Evelyn Waugh | .75 | 1.50 | 2.25 | |
| D164 | The Dark Arena—Mario Puzo | .75 | 1.50 | 2.25 | |
| D165 | The Wall—Mary Roberts Rinehart | .75 | 1.50 | 2.25 | M |
| D166 | Bonjour Tristesse—Francoise Sagan | .75 | 1.50 | 2.25 | |
| D167 | The Picture of Dorian Grey—Oscar Wilde | 1.00 | 2.00 | 3.00 | HO |
| D168 | Mosquitoes—William Faulkner | .75 | 1.50 | 2.25 | |
| D169 | Roads from the Fort—Arvid Shulenberger | .75 | 1.50 | 2.25 | |
| D170 | The Young Lovers—Julian Halevy | .75 | 1.50 | 2.25 | |
| D171 | The Steep Ascent—Anne Morrow Lindbergh | .75 | 1.50 | 2.25 | |
| D172 | Fourteen for Tonight—Steve Allen | .75 | 1.50 | 2.25 | |
| D173 | Benjamin Blake—Edison Marshall | .75 | 1.50 | 2.25 | A |
| D174 | An Affair of Dishonor—Louis A. Brennan | .75 | 1.50 | 2.25 | |
| D175 | The Far Country—Nevil Shute; 1956; movie tie-in | 1.00 | 2.00 | 3.00 | |
| D176 | Mrs. Craddock—W. Somerset Maugham | .75 | 1.50 | 2.25 | |
| D177 | Warhorse—John Cunningham | .75 | 1.50 | 2.25 | |
| D178 | The Golden Kazoo—John G. Schneider | .75 | 1.50 | 2.25 | F |
| D179 | The Yellow Room—Mary Roberts Rinehart | .75 | 1.50 | 2.25 | M |
| D180 | Child Behavior: Gesell Institute—Louis Bates Ames & Frances L. Ilg | .75 | 1.50 | 2.25 | NF |
| D181 | Daisy Miller and the Turn of the Screw—Henry James | .75 | 1.50 | 2.25 | |
| D182 | Listen! The Wind—Anne Morrow Lindbergh | .75 | 1.50 | 2.25 | |
| D183 | Nightmare—Guy Endore | 1.50 | 3.00 | 4.50 | |
| D184 | The Company She Keeps—Mary McCarthy | .75 | 1.50 | 2.25 | |
| D185 | Ship's Company—Lonnie Coleman; 1957 | .75 | 1.50 | 2.25 | |
| D186 | The Bride Wore Black—Cornell Woolrich | 1.50 | 3.00 | 4.50 | M |
| D187 | Trial by Fury—Craig Rice | .75 | 1.50 | 2.25 | M |
| D188 | Laura—Vera Caspary | .75 | 1.50 | 2.25 | M |
| D189 | No Man Is an Island—Thomas Merton | .75 | 1.50 | 2.25 | |
| D190 | Blaze of the Sun—Jean Hougren | .75 | 1.50 | 2.25 | |
| D191 | Winter's Tales—Isak Dinesen | .75 | 1.50 | 2.25 | F |
| D192 | A Puzzle for Fools—Patrick Quentin | .75 | 1.50 | 2.25 | M |
| D193 | Aspects of Love—David Garnett | .75 | 1.50 | 2.25 | |
| D194 | Warrant for X—Philip MacDonald | .75 | 1.50 | 2.25 | M |
| D195 | The Wicked Village—Gabriel Chevallier | .75 | 1.50 | 2.25 | |
| D196 | Headed for a Hearse—Jonathan Latimer | .75 | 1.50 | 2.25 | M |
| D197 | The Circular Staircase—Mary Roberts Rinehart | .75 | 1.50 | 2.25 | M |
| D198 | The Loved and the Unloved—Thomas Hal Phillips | .75 | 1.50 | 2.25 | |
| D199 | Love in the South Seas—Bengt Danielsson | 1.00 | 2.00 | 3.00 | |
| D200 | Dell Crossword Puzzle Dictionary—Kathleen Rafferty; 1957 | .75 | 1.50 | 2.25 | NF |
| D201 | A Coffin for Dimitrios—Eric Ambler | .75 | 1.50 | 2.25 | M |
| D202 | Mountain Boy—Felix Holt | .75 | 1.50 | 2.25 | |
| D203 | The Red Right Hand—Joel Townsley Rogers | .75 | 1.50 | 2.25 | M |
| D204 | The Mark of Zorro—Johnston McCulley; TV tie-in | 2.50 | 5.00 | 7.50 | A |
| D205 | The Lonely Passion of Judith Hearne—Brian Moore | 1.25 | 2.50 | 3.75 | |
| D206 | A Certain Smile—Francoise Sagan | .75 | 1.50 | 2.25 | |

**DELL D-SERIES,** *continued*

| | | V/Good | Fine | N/Mint | |
|---|---|---|---|---|---|
| D207 | Phantom Lady–William Irish | 1.25 | 2.50 | 3.75 | M |
| D208 | Seeds of Contemplation–Thomas Merton; 1958 | .75 | 1.50 | 2.25 | |
| D209 | Paths of Glory–Humphrey Cobb; movie tie-in | 1.50 | 3.00 | 4.50 | |
| D210 | Owls Don't Blink–A.A. Fair | .75 | 1.50 | 2.25 | M |
| D211 | Spill the Jackpot–A.A. Fair | .75 | 1.50 | 2.25 | M |
| D212 | Bedrooms Have Windows–A.A. Fair | .75 | 1.50 | 2.25 | M |
| D213 | Give 'Em the Ax–A.A. Fair | .75 | 1.50 | 2.25 | M |
| D214 | A Charmed Life–Mary McCarthy | .75 | 1.50 | 2.25 | |
| D215 | Before the Fact–Frances Iles | .75 | 1.50 | 2.25 | M |
| D216 | The Long Rifle–Stewart Edward White | 1.25 | 2.50 | 3.75 | A |
| D217 | Sad Cypress–Agatha Christie | .75 | 1.50 | 2.25 | M |
| D218 | The Witness for the Prosecution– Agatha Christie | .75 | 1.50 | 2.25 | M |
| D219 | House Party–Virginia Rowans | .75 | 1.50 | 2.25 | |
| D220 | The Door–Mary Roberts Rinehart | .75 | 1.50 | 2.25 | M |
| D221 | Dead Sure–Herbert Brean | .75 | 1.50 | 2.25 | M |
| D222 | The Loved One–Evelyn Waugh | .75 | 1.50 | 2.25 | |
| D223 | Fer-de-lance–Rex Stout | .75 | 1.50 | 2.25 | M |
| D224 | No Time at All–Charles Einstein | .75 | 1.50 | 2.25 | |
| D225 | Ride the Pink Horse–Dorothy B. Hughes; 1958 | .75 | 1.50 | 2.25 | M |
| D226 | A Real Gone Guy–Frank Kane | .75 | 1.50 | 2.25 | M |
| D227 | The Beast Must Die–Nicholas Blake | .75 | 1.50 | 2.25 | M |
| D228 | Two-thirds of a Ghost–Helen McCloy | .75 | 1.50 | 2.25 | M |
| D229 | A Houseful of Love–Marjorie Housepian | .75 | 1.50 | 2.25 | |
| D230 | The Amazing Adventures of Father Brown–G.K. Chesterton | .75 | 1.50 | 2.25 | M |
| D231 | 12 Stories They Wouldn't Let Me Do on TV–ed. Alfred Hitchcock | .75 | 1.50 | 2.25 | M |
| D232 | Tall, Dark and Deadly–Harold Q. Masur | .75 | 1.50 | 2.25 | M |
| D233 | The Bellamy Trial–Frances Noyes Hart | .75 | 1.50 | 2.25 | M |
| D234 | Death of a Ghost–Margery Allingham | .75 | 1.50 | 2.25 | M |
| D235 | Dead Man's Mirror–Agatha Christie | .75 | 1.50 | 2.25 | M |
| D236 | Appointment with Death–Agatha Christie | .75 | 1.50 | 2.25 | M |
| D237 | The Brain Pickers–Hallie Burnett | .75 | 1.50 | 2.25 | |
| D238 | Background to Danger–Eric Ambler | .75 | 1.50 | 2.25 | M |
| D239 | Grand Hotel–Vicki Baum | .75 | 1.50 | 2.25 | |
| D240 | Rage of Desire–Charles Mergendahl | .75 | 1.50 | 2.25 | |
| D241 | The Flower Drum Song–C.Y. Lee; movie tie-in | 1.00 | 2.00 | 3.00 | |
| D242 | Miss Pinkerton–Mary Roberts Rinehart | .75 | 1.50 | 2.25 | M |
| D243 | Secrets of Successful Selling–John D. Murphy | .75 | 1.50 | 2.25 | NF |
| D244 | Falling through Space–Richard Hillary | .75 | 1.50 | 2.25 | |
| D245 | Corner Boy–Herbert Simmons | .75 | 1.50 | 2.25 | JD |
| D246 | A Mirror for Observers–Edgar Pangborn | 1.00 | 2.00 | 3.00 | SF |
| D247 | The Mystery of the Dead Police–Philip MacDonald | .75 | 1.50 | 2.25 | M |
| D248 | The Private Practice of Michael Shayne–Brett Halliday | .75 | 1.50 | 2.25 | M |
| D249 | The Man in the Brown Suit–Agatha Christie | .75 | 1.50 | 2.25 | M |
| D250 | Suddenly a Corpse–Harold Q. Masur; 1958 | .75 | 1.50 | 2.25 | M |
| D251 | The Great Mistake–Mary Roberts Rinehart | .75 | 1.50 | 2.25 | M |
| D252 | The Mountain Cat Murders–Rex Stout | .75 | 1.50 | 2.25 | M |
| D253 | Turn on the Heat–A.A. Fair | .75 | 1.50 | 2.25 | M |
| D254 | The Secrets of Caroline Cherie–Cecil Saint-Laurent; 1959 | .75 | 1.50 | 2.25 | |
| D255 | The Main in the Queue–Josephine Tey | .75 | 1.50 | 2.25 | M |
| D256 | The Living Bread–Thomas Merton | .75 | 1.50 | 2.25 | |
| D257 | The Decline and Fall of Practically Everybody–Will Cuppy | .75 | 1.50 | 2.25 | H |
| D258 | The Camp Followers–Ugo Pirro | .75 | 1.50 | 2.25 | |
| D259 | Another Man's Murder–Mignon G. Eberhart | .75 | 1.50 | 2.25 | M |
| D260 | Student Nurse–Renee Shann | .75 | 1.50 | 2.25 | R |
| D261 | The Man in the Net–Patrick Quentin | .75 | 1.50 | 2.25 | M |
| D262 | The Secret of Chimneys–Agatha Christie | .75 | 1.50 | 2.25 | M |
| D263 | Into the Valley–John Hersey | .75 | 1.50 | 2.25 | |
| D264 | Slay Ride–Frank Kane | .75 | 1.50 | 2.25 | M |
| D265 | The Doctor's Secret–Hans Kades | .75 | 1.50 | 2.25 | |
| D266 | The Story of Walt Disney–Pete Martin & Diane Disney Miller | 2.50 | 5.00 | 7.50 | B |
| D267 | The Golden Eagle–John Jennings | 1.50 | 3.00 | 4.50 | A |
| D268 | The Strange Bedfellow–Evelyn Berckman | .75 | 1.50 | 2.25 | |
| D269 | Call for Michael Shayne–Brett Halliday | .75 | 1.50 | 2.25 | M |
| D270 | Murder in Venice–Thomas Sterling | .75 | 1.50 | 2.25 | M |
| D271 | Murder on Their Minds–George Harmon Coxe | .75 | 1.50 | 2.25 | M |
| D272 | Shadow of a Killer–William Mole | .75 | 1.50 | 2.25 | |
| D273 | Focus–Arthur Miller | .75 | 1.50 | 2.25 | |
| D274 | The Third Level–Jack Finney | 1.50 | 3.00 | 4.50 | |
| D275 | A Hole in the Ground–Andrew Garve; 1959 | .75 | 1.50 | 2.25 | M |
| D276 | The Man in Lower Ten–Mary Roberts Rinehart | .75 | 1.50 | 2.25 | M |
| D277 | Those without Shadows–Francoise Sagan | .75 | 1.50 | 2.25 | |
| D278 | The Girl Who Kept Knocking Them Dead–Hampton Stone | .75 | 1.50 | 2.25 | M |
| D279 | In Case of Emergency–Georges Simenon | .75 | 1.50 | 2.25 | M |
| D280 | Trigger Mortis–Frank Kane | .75 | 1.50 | 2.25 | M |
| D281 | 13 More Stories They Wouldn't Let Me Do on TV–Alfred Hitchcock | .75 | 1.50 | 2.25 | M |
| D282 | The Talented Mr. Ripley–Patricia Highsmith | 1.00 | 2.00 | 3.00 | |
| D283 | Murder and the Wanton Bride–Brett Halliday | .75 | 1.50 | 2.25 | M |
| D284 | Earthshaker–Robert W. Krepps | 1.50 | 3.00 | 4.50 | A |
| D285 | Lover's Point–C.Y. Lee | .75 | 1.50 | 2.25 | |
| D286 | The Gentle Murderer–Dorothy Salisbury Davis | .75 | 1.50 | 2.25 | M |
| D287 | The Meaning of Dreams–Calvin S. Hall | .75 | 1.50 | 2.25 | NF |
| D288 | Murder on the Links–Agatha Christie | .75 | 1.50 | 2.25 | M |
| D289 | Brand of Empire–Luke Short | .75 | 1.50 | 2.25 | W |
| D290 | Trail Town–Ernest Haycox | .75 | 1.50 | 2.25 | W |
| D291 | Marked for Murder–Brett Halliday | .75 | 1.50 | 2.25 | M |
| D292 | Dead Man's Diary and a Taste for Cognac–Brett Halliday | .75 | 1.50 | 2.25 | M |
| D293 | Dividend on Death–Brett Halliday | .75 | 1.50 | 2.25 | M |
| D294 | The Sensualists–Ben Hecht | .75 | 1.50 | 2.25 | |
| D295 | Jesse James Was My Neighbor–Homer Croy | 1.00 | 2.00 | 3.00 | NF |
| D296 | The Color of Murder–Julian Symons | .75 | 1.50 | 2.25 | M |
| D297 | Sophie–Geoffrey Wagner | .75 | 1.50 | 2.25 | |
| D298 | Murder on Broadway–Harold Q. Masur | .75 | 1.50 | 2.25 | M |
| D299 | One More Unfortunate–Edgar Lustgarten | .75 | 1.50 | 2.25 | M |
| D300 | Long Shot–David Mark; 1959 | .75 | 1.50 | 2.25 | |
| D301 | The Woman in the Woods–Lee Blackstock | .75 | 1.50 | 2.25 | |
| D302 | The Hound of the Baskervilles–Arthur Conan Doyle | 1.50 | 3.00 | 4.50 | M |
| D303 | Only Akiko–Duncan Thorp | .75 | 1.50 | 2.25 | |
| D304 | Angel's Ransom–David Dodge | .75 | 1.50 | 2.25 | |
| D305 | The Labors of Hercules–Agatha Christie | 1.00 | 2.00 | 3.00 | M |
| D306 | The April Robin Murders–Ed McBain & Craig Rice | .75 | 1.50 | 2.25 | M |
| D307 | Gypsy–Gypsy Rose Lee | .75 | 1.50 | 2.25 | B |
| D308 | Kind Are Her Answers–Mary Renault | .75 | 1.50 | 2.25 | R |
| D309 | Top of the Heap–A.A. Fair | .75 | 1.50 | 2.25 | M |
| D310 | Boulevard–Robert Sabatier | .75 | 1.50 | 2.25 | |
| D311 | The Eighth Circle–Stanley Ellin | .75 | 1.50 | 2.25 | |
| D312 | Twixt Twelve and Twenty–Pat Boone | .25 | .50 | .75 | |
| D313 | The Silent Life–Thomas Merton | .75 | 1.50 | 2.25 | |
| D314 | Fit to Kill–Brett Halliday | .75 | 1.50 | 2.25 | M |
| D315 | The Search–Myrick Land | .75 | 1.50 | 2.25 | |
| D316 | The Confession and Sight Unseen– Mary Roberts Rinehart | .75 | 1.50 | 2.25 | M |
| D317 | The Heart Remembers–Faith Baldwin | .75 | 1.50 | 2.25 | R |
| D318 | The Shrew Is Dead–Shelley Smith | .75 | 1.50 | 2.25 | |
| D319 | Child of Our Time–Michael del Castillo | .75 | 1.50 | 2.25 | |
| D320 | The Sunlit Ambush–Mark Derby | .75 | 1.50 | 2.25 | M |
| D321 | The Red House Mystery–A.A. Milne | .75 | 1.50 | 2.25 | M |
| D322 | The Man with Two Wives–Patrick Quentin | .75 | 1.50 | 2.25 | M |
| D323 | The Three Coffins–John Dickson Carr | .75 | 1.50 | 2.25 | M |
| D324 | Mrs. Bridge–Evan S. Connell, Jr | .75 | 1.50 | 2.25 | |
| D325 | Quiet Horror–Stanley Ellin | .75 | 1.50 | 2.25 | HO |
| D326 | The Mysterious Mr. Quinn–Agatha Christie | .75 | 1.50 | 2.25 | M |
| D327 | Bodies Are Where You Find Them– Brett Halliday | .75 | 1.50 | 2.25 | M |

**DELL D-SERIES,** *continued*

| | | V/Good | Fine | N/Mint | |
|---|---|---|---|---|---|
| D328 | Moment of Danger–Donald MacKenzie | .75 | 1.50 | 2.25 | |
| D329 | You Can't Live Forever–Harold Q. Masur | .75 | 1.50 | 2.25 | M |
| D330 | The Bat–Mary Roberts Rinehart | .75 | 1.50 | 2.25 | M |
| D331 | Murder in Miami–Brett Halliday | .75 | 1.50 | 2.25 | M |
| D333 | Bare Trap–Frank Kane | 1.00 | 2.00 | 3.00 | M |
| D336 | Scarface–Armitage Trail; 1959 | 1.50 | 3.00 | 4.50 | M |
| D337 | Gulf Coast Girl–Charles Williams; 1960; aka Scorpion Reef | 2.00 | 4.00 | 6.00 | M |
| D338 | The Girl Who Cried Wolf–Hillary Waugh | .75 | 1.50 | 2.25 | M |
| D339 | Death and Daisy Bland–Nicholas Blake | .75 | 1.50 | 2.25 | M |
| D340 | The Boomerang Clue–Agatha Christie | .75 | 1.50 | 2.25 | M |
| D341 | A Terrible Beauty–Arthur J. Roth; movie tie-in; c-Gross | 1.50 | 3.00 | 4.50 | C |
| D342 | Blood on Biscayne Bay–Brett Halliday | .75 | 1.50 | 2.25 | M |
| D343 | Journey into Fear–Eric Ambler | .75 | 1.50 | 2.25 | M |
| D344 | Home-Town Doctor–Elizabeth Seifert | .75 | 1.50 | 2.25 | R |
| D345 | House of Terror–Evelyn Berckman | .75 | 1.50 | 2.25 | M |
| D346 | One Minute Past Eight–George Harmon Coxe; c-Maguire | .75 | 1.50 | 2.25 | M |
| D347 | Charley Weaver's Letters from Mama– Cliff Arquette | .75 | 1.50 | 2.25 | H |
| D348 | Bats Fly at Dusk–Erle Stanley Gardner | .75 | 1.50 | 2.25 | M |
| D349 | The Very First Time–Richard Fisher | .75 | 1.50 | 2.25 | |
| D350 | Bounty Guns–Luke Short | 1.00 | 2.00 | 3.00 | W |
| D351 | Murder off the Record–John Bingham; c-Maguire | .75 | 1.50 | 2.25 | M |
| D352 | The After House–Mary Roberts Rinehart | .75 | 1.50 | 2.25 | M |
| D353 | The Way Up–Joseph Whitehill | .75 | 1.50 | 2.25 | |
| D354 | The Mousetrap–Agatha Christie | .75 | 1.50 | 2.25 | M |
| D355 | Target: Mike Shayne–Brett Halliday | .75 | 1.50 | 2.25 | M |
| D356 | Bedelia–Vera Caspary | .75 | 1.50 | 2.25 | |
| D357 | Muscle Beach–Ira Wallach | 1.50 | 3.00 | 4.50 | |
| D358 | Counterfeit Wife–Brett Halliday | .75 | 1.50 | 2.25 | M |
| D359 | When Dorinda Dances–Brett Halliday | .75 | 1.50 | 2.25 | M |
| D360 | The Case of the Missing Coed–William Hardy | .75 | 1.50 | 2.25 | M |
| D361 | Double or Quits–A.A. Fair | .75 | 1.50 | 2.25 | M |
| D362 | Dead, Man, Dead–David Alexander | .75 | 1.50 | 2.25 | M |
| D363 | No Place to Run–Philip Alston Stone | .75 | 1.50 | 2.25 | M |
| D364 | Wanted: Danny Fontaine–William Ard; aka As Bad As I Am | 2.50 | 5.00 | 7.50 | M |
| D365 | The Murders on Fox Island–Margaret Page Hood | .75 | 1.50 | 2.25 | M |
| D366 | The Case of Jennie Brice–Mary Roberts Rinehart | .75 | 1.50 | 2.25 | M |
| D367 | Rawhiders and Renegades–ed. Harry E. Maule | .75 | 1.50 | 2.25 | W |
| D368 | Strange Bondage–Donald Stewart; c-Maguire | 2.00 | 4.00 | 6.00 | |
| D369 | Murder Is No Accident–Jerome Barry | .75 | 1.50 | 2.25 | M |
| D370 | An Overdose of Death–Agatha Christie; aka The Patriotic Murders | .75 | 1.50 | 2.25 | M |
| D372 | Some Women Won't Wait–A.A. Fair | .75 | 1.50 | 2.25 | M |
| D373 | Crows Can't Count–A.A. Fair | .75 | 1.50 | 2.25 | M |
| D374 | Date with a Dead Man–Brett Halliday | .75 | 1.50 | 2.25 | M |
| D375 | The Obituary Club–Hugh Pentecost; c-Maguire | .75 | 1.50 | 2.25 | M |
| D376 | Exit Dying–Harry Olesker | .75 | 1.50 | 2.25 | M |
| D377 | Assault on a Queen–Jack Finney; 1960 | 2.00 | 4.00 | 6.00 | |
| D378 | Dear Mr. Congressman–Juliet Lowell | .75 | 1.50 | 2.25 | H |
| D379 | Murder Takes No Holiday–Brett Halliday | .75 | 1.50 | 2.25 | M |
| D380 | Hospital Nocturne–Alice Eleanor Lambert | .75 | 1.50 | 2.25 | R |
| D381 | What Really Happened–Brett Halliday | .75 | 1.50 | 2.25 | M |
| D382 | Ghostly Hoofbeats–Norman A. Fox; c-Gross | .75 | 1.50 | 2.25 | W |
| D383 | So Rich, So Lovely, and So Dead–Hal Q. Masur | .75 | 1.50 | 2.25 | M |
| D384 | Murder in Retrospect–Agatha Christie | .75 | 1.50 | 2.25 | M |
| D385 | Greenwillow–B.J. Chute | .75 | 1.50 | 2.25 | F |
| D386 | Requiem for a Blonde–Kelley Roos | .75 | 1.50 | 2.25 | M |
| D387 | One Night with Nora–Brett Halliday | .75 | 1.50 | 2.25 | M |
| D388 | Murder in Montmartre–Noel Vexin; 1st U.S. ed. 1960; trans. Jonas Berry & Lawrence G. Blochman | .75 | 1.50 | 2.25 | M |
| D390 | Murder after Hours–Agatha Christie; aka The Hollow | .75 | 1.50 | 2.25 | M |
| D391 | Die like A Dog–Brett Halliday | .75 | 1.50 | 2.25 | M |
| D392 | Dead Wrong–George Bagby | .75 | 1.50 | 2.25 | M |
| D393 | Three at the Wedding–Loula Grace Erdman | .75 | 1.50 | 2.25 | R |
| D394 | Suspicious Circumstances–Patrick Quentin; c-Maguire | .75 | 1.50 | 2.25 | M |
| D395 | Dear Doctor–Juliet Lowell | .75 | 1.50 | 2.25 | H |
| D396 | The Kiss of Death–Eleazar Lipsky; c-Abbett; 1961 | 1.25 | 2.50 | 3.75 | M |
| D397 | Teensville U.S.A.–ed. Lawrence Lariar; 1961 | 1.25 | 2.50 | 3.75 | H |
| D398 | The Promise of Muder–Mignon G. Eberhart | .75 | 1.50 | 2.25 | M |
| D399 | You Can't Escape–Faith Baldwin | .75 | 1.50 | 2.25 | R |
| D400 | Hearn's Valley–Wayne G. Overholser; 1961 | .75 | 1.50 | 2.25 | W |
| D401 | The Corpse Came Calling–Brett Halliday | .75 | 1.50 | 2.25 | M |
| D402 | Private Duty–Faith Baldwin | .75 | 1.50 | 2.25 | R |
| D403 | There Is a Tide–Agatha Christie | .75 | 1.50 | 2.25 | M |
| D404 | 13 at Dinner–Agatha Christie | .75 | 1.50 | 2.25 | M |
| D405 | Murder in Mesopotamia–Agatha Christie | .75 | 1.50 | 2.25 | M |
| D406 | Gold Comes in Bricks–A.A. Fair | .75 | 1.50 | 2.25 | M |
| D407 | The Bottletop Affair–Gordon Cotler; aka The Horizontal Lieutenant; movie tie-in | 1.00 | 2.00 | 3.00 | H |
| D408 | Rosemarie–Erich Kuby | .75 | 1.50 | 2.25 | |
| D409 | Reckoning at Rimbow–Norman A. Fox | .75 | 1.50 | 2.25 | W |
| D410 | The Sailcloth Shroud–Charles Williams; c-Abbett | 2.00 | 4.00 | 6.00 | M |
| D411 | The Window at the White Cat–Mary Roberts Rinehart; 1961 | .75 | 1.50 | 2.25 | M |
| D412 | Doctor on Trial–Elizabeth Seifert | .75 | 1.50 | 2.25 | R |
| D413 | Redheaded Nurse–Bennie C. Hall | 1.00 | 2.00 | 3.00 | R |
| D415 | Innocent Bystander–Faith Baldwin | .75 | 1.50 | 2.25 | R |
| D416 | Michael Shayne's Long Chance–Brett Halliday | .75 | 1.50 | 2.25 | M |
| D417 | The Deadlier Sex–Genevieve Manceron; 1st U.S. edition 1961; trans. Jonas Berry & Lawrence G. Blochman | .75 | 1.50 | 2.25 | M |
| D418 | Dust Devil–Walter S. James | .75 | 1.50 | 2.25 | W |
| D419 | Nurse Barclay's Dilemna–Adelaide Humphries; c-Abbett | .75 | 1.50 | 2.25 | R |
| D420 | The Grave's in the Meadow–Manning Lee Stokes | .75 | 1.50 | 2.25 | M |
| D421 | The Impetuous Mistress–George Harmon Coxe; c-Abbett | .75 | 1.50 | 2.25 | |
| D422 | The Hours before Dawn–Celia Fremlin | .75 | 1.50 | 2.25 | M |
| D423 | Death Has Three Lives–Brett Halliday | .75 | 1.50 | 2.25 | M |
| D424 | Dolls Are Deadly–Brett Halliday | .75 | 1.50 | 2.25 | M |
| D425 | Stranger in Town–Brett Halliday | .75 | 1.50 | 2.25 | M |
| D427 | Have a Baby, My Wife Just Had a Cigar–Stanley Berenstain & Janice Berenstain | 1.25 | 2.50 | 3.75 | H |
| D428 | When Doctors Marry–Elizabeth Seifert | .75 | 1.50 | 2.25 | R |
| D429 | Brand Rider–Ed LaVanway | .75 | 1.50 | 2.25 | W |
| D430 | Preposterous Papa–Lewis Meyer | .75 | 1.50 | 2.25 | B |
| D431 | Cats Prowl at Night–A.A. Fair | .75 | 1.50 | 2.25 | M |
| D432 | The Hard Pursued–Norman A. Fox | .75 | 1.50 | 2.25 | W |
| D433 | Episode of the Wandering Knife–Mary Roberts Rinehart | .75 | 1.50 | 2.25 | M |
| D434 | The Hustler–Walter Tevis; 1961; movie tie-in | 2.50 | 5.00 | 7.50 | |
| D436 | Doctor at the Crossroads–Elizabeth Seifert | .75 | 1.50 | 2.25 | R |
| D437 | The Homicidal Virgin–Brett Halliday | .75 | 1.50 | 2.25 | M |
| D442 | The Judas Gun–Wayne D. Overholser | .75 | 1.50 | 2.25 | W |
| D443 | The Doctor's Bride–Elizabeth Seifert; 1961 | .75 | 1.50 | 2.25 | R |
| D444 | 6th Book of Dell Cross Word Puzzles– ed. Kathleen Rafferty | 3.00 | 6.00 | 9.00 | |
| D446 | She Woke to Darkness–Brett Halliday; 1962 | .75 | 1.50 | 2.25 | M |
| D447 | Call Me Mrs.–Stanley Berenstain & Janice Berenstain; 1st ed. 1961 | 1.25 | 2.50 | 3.75 | H |
| D451 | Bullet Proof–Frank Kane; 1961 | .75 | 1.50 | 2.25 | M |
| D457 | Raw Land–Luke Short; aka Gunsmoke Graze | .75 | 1.50 | 2.25 | W |
| D463 | A Taste for Violence–Brett Halliday; 1962 | .75 | 1.50 | 2.25 | M |

# DELL F-SERIES
## Dell Publishing Company

| | | V/Good | Fine | N/Mint | |
|---|---|---|---|---|---|
| F50 | Gus the Great–Thomas W. Duncan; 1953 | .75 | 1.50 | 2.25 | |
| F51 | Canal Town–Samuel Hopkins Adams | .75 | 1.50 | 2.25 | |
| F52 | Wake of the Red Witch–Garland Roark | 1.00 | 2.00 | 3.00 | A |
| F53 | War and Peace–Leo Tolstoy; 1955 | 1.00 | 2.00 | 3.00 | |
| F55 | The Brothers Karamazov–Fyodor Dostoyevsky | .75 | 1.50 | 2.25 | |
| F56 | The Story of Edgar Cayce–Thomas Sugrue | .75 | 1.50 | 2.25 | B |
| F57 | Bedside Book of Famous French Stories–Belle Becker & Robert N. Linscott | .75 | 1.50 | 2.25 | |
| F58 | Raintree County–Ross Lockridge, Jr; 1957 | 2.00 | 4.00 | 6.00 | A |
| F59 | Life of Christ–Giovanni Papini | 1.00 | 2.00 | 3.00 | B |
| F60 | The Ninth Wave–Eugene Burdick | .75 | 1.50 | 2.25 | |
| F61 | Peyton Place–Grace Metalious | 1.50 | 3.00 | 4.50 | |
| F62 | How to Take Better Pictures–Joseph C. Keeley | .75 | 1.50 | 2.25 | NF |
| F63 | Dodsworth–Sinclair Lewis | .75 | 1.50 | 2.25 | |
| F64 | The Savage Place–Leon Arden; 1958 | .75 | 1.50 | 2.25 | |
| F65 | Make Each Day Count–James Keller | .75 | 1.50 | 2.25 | NF |
| F66 | Maybe I'm Dead–Joe Klaas | .75 | 1.50 | 2.25 | |
| F67 | The Viking–Edison Marshall; movie tie-in | 1.50 | 3.00 | 4.50 | A |
| F68 | Brideshead Revisited–Evelyn Waugh | .75 | 1.50 | 2.25 | |
| F69 | Beloved–Vina Delmar | .75 | 1.50 | 2.25 | |
| F70 | David Copperfield–Charles Dickens | .75 | 1.50 | 2.25 | |
| F71 | The Bounty Lands–William Ellis | .75 | 1.50 | 2.25 | |
| F72 | The Upstart–Edison Marshall; 1959 | 1.00 | 2.00 | 3.00 | A |
| F73 | Sharks and Little Fish–Wolfgang Ott | 1.00 | 2.00 | 3.00 | NF |
| F74 | A Handful of Dust and Decline and Fall–Evelyn Waugh | .75 | 1.50 | 2.25 | |
| F75 | Anatomy of a Murder–Robert Traver; 1959 | .75 | 1.50 | 2.25 | M |
| F76 | The Horse Soldiers–Harold Sinclair; movie tie-in | 2.50 | 5.00 | 7.50 | A |
| F77 | The Fiery Trial–Carl Sandburg | .75 | 1.50 | 2.25 | |
| F78 | Embezzled Heaven–Franz Werfel | .75 | 1.50 | 2.25 | |
| F79 | Ben-Hur–Lew Wallace | 1.00 | 2.00 | 3.00 | A |
| F80 | This Earth Is Mine–Alice Tisdale Hobart | .75 | 1.50 | 2.25 | |
| F81 | The Raw Edge–Benjamin Appel | .75 | 1.50 | 2.25 | |
| F82 | The Circus in the Attic–Robert Penn Warren | .75 | 1.50 | 2.25 | |
| F83 | Theme for Ballet–Vicki Baum | .75 | 1.50 | 2.25 | |
| F84 | The Beat Generation and the Angry Young Men–Gene Feldman & Max Gartenberg | 2.50 | 5.00 | 7.50 | |
| F85 | Ranchero–Stewart Edward White | 2.00 | 4.00 | 6.00 | W |
| F86 | On My Own–Eleanor Roosevelt | .75 | 1.50 | 2.25 | |
| F87 | Yankee Pasha–Edison Marshall | 1.00 | 2.00 | 3.00 | A |
| F88 | Baa Baa Black Sheep–Pappy Boyington | 1.00 | 2.00 | 3.00 | NF |
| F89 | Great True Adventures–Lowell Thomas | 1.00 | 2.00 | 3.00 | NF |
| F90 | Harrison High–John Farris | 2.00 | 4.00 | 6.00 | |
| F91 | Return to Peyton Place–Grace Metalious | 1.50 | 3.00 | 4.50 | R |
| F92 | My Story–Mary Astor | .75 | 1.50 | 2.25 | B |
| F93 | Elephant Hill–Robin White; 1960 | .75 | 1.50 | 2.25 | A |
| F94 | The Intruder–Charles Beaumont | 2.50 | 5.00 | 7.50 | |
| F95 | The Magnificent Bastards–Lucy Herndon Crockett | .75 | 1.50 | 2.25 | |
| F97 | Savage Destiny–Edgar Mittelholzer; 1960 | .75 | 1.50 | 2.25 | A |
| F98 | Gypsy Sixpence–Edison Marshall | .75 | 1.50 | 2.25 | A |
| F99 | My Ten Years as a Counter-spy–Boris Morros; c-Powers; movie tie-in | 1.00 | 2.00 | 3.00 | NF |
| F105 | Toward the Morning–Hervey Allen; c-Abbett | .75 | 1.50 | 2.25 | A |
| F112 | Groucho and Me–Groucho Marx; 1960 | 2.00 | 4.00 | 6.00 | B |
| F115 | The Misfits–Arthur Miller; 1960; movie tie-in | 2.50 | 5.00 | 7.50 | |
| F118 | The Year's Best S-F, 5th Annual Edition–ed. Judith Merrill; 1961, c-Powers | 2.00 | 4.00 | 6.00 | SF |
| F136 | The Golden Scalpel–Seymour Kern; c-Abbett | 1.50 | 3.00 | 4.50 | |

| | | V/Good | Fine | N/Mint | |
|---|---|---|---|---|---|
| F140 | Soldier in the Rain–William Goldman | .75 | 1.50 | 2.25 | |
| F150 | Love and Mrs. Sargent–Virginia Rowans; c-Abbett | 1.25 | 2.50 | 3.75 | |
| F155 | The Living Bread–Thomas Merton; c-Powers | 1.25 | 2.50 | 3.75 | |
| F174 | Diamond Fever–Robert W. Krepps; 1961, aka Baboon Rock | 1.50 | 3.00 | 4.50 | A |
| F178 | The Crooked Road–Morris L. West; c-Abbett | 1.25 | 2.50 | 3.75 | M |
| F181 | That Egyptian Woman–Noel B. Gerson; c-Abbett | 1.25 | 2.50 | 3.75 | A |

# DELL FIRST EDITIONS
## Dell Publishing Company, Inc.

| | | V/Good | Fine | N/Mint | |
|---|---|---|---|---|---|
| 1E | Down–Walt Grove; 1953 | 1.50 | 3.00 | 4.50 | |
| 2E | Madball–Frederic Brown; 1st ed., 1953 | 6.00 | 12.00 | 18.00 | |
| D3 | Women–A.M. Krich | 1.00 | 2.00 | 3.00 | |
| 4 | Girl on the Beach–George Sumner Albee | 1.25 | 2.50 | 3.75 | |
| 5 | The Bloody Spur–Charles Einstein | 1.25 | 2.50 | 3.75 | M |
| 6 | Next Time Is for Life–Paul Warren | 1.25 | 2.50 | 3.75 | |
| 7 | Bold Rider–Luke Short | 1.50 | 3.00 | 4.50 | W |
| 8 | Back Country–William Fuller; 1954 | 1.50 | 3.00 | 4.50 | |
| D9 | 6 Great Short Novels of Science Fiction–ed. Groff Conklin; c-Powers | 1.50 | 3.00 | 4.50 | SF |
| F10 | The Ribald Reader–ed. A.M. Krich | 1.50 | 3.00 | 4.50 | |
| 11 | Arrow in the Dust–L.L. Foreman | 1.25 | 2.50 | 3.75 | W |
| 12 | Area of Suspicion–John D. MacDonald; 1st ed. 1954 | 4.00 | 8.00 | 12.00 | M |
| 13 | Fever Heat–Angus Vicker | 1.25 | 2.50 | 3.75 | |
| 14 | The Man from Laramie–T.T. Flynn | 1.25 | 2.50 | 3.75 | W |
| D15 | Men–A.M. Krich | 1.50 | 3.00 | 4.50 | |
| F16 | Short Story Masterpieces–eds. Albert Erskine & Robert Penn Warren | 1.25 | 2.50 | 3.75 | |
| 17 | The Crooked City–Robert Kyle | 1.25 | 2.50 | 3.75 | |
| 18 | Smoky Valley–Donald Hamilton | 1.50 | 3.00 | 4.50 | W |
| 19 | Conduct Unbecoming–Charles Fenton | 1.25 | 2.50 | 3.75 | |
| D20 | I Detest All My Sins–Jack Weeks | 1.25 | 2.50 | 3.75 | |
| 21 | French Cartoons–William Cole & Douglas McKee | 1.50 | 3.00 | 4.50 | H |
| 22 | The Nothing Man–Jim Thompson; 1st ed. 1954 | 20.00 | 40.00 | 60.00 | |
| 23 | Teresa–Les Savage, Jr | 1.25 | 2.50 | 3.75 | W |
| 24 | The Joys She Chose–Matthew Peters | 1.25 | 2.50 | 3.75 | |
| 25 | Trouble on Big Cat–Glenn Corbin; 1954 | 1.25 | 2.50 | 3.75 | |
| 26 | The Deadly Mermaid–James Atlee Phillips | 1.50 | 3.00 | 4.50 | |
| 27 | Night Walker–Donald Hamilton | 1.25 | 2.50 | 3.75 | |
| 28 | Goat Island–William Fuller | 1.25 | 2.50 | 3.75 | |
| 29 | Sole Survivor–Louis Falstein | 1.25 | 2.50 | 3.75 | |
| 30 | Plain Murder–C.S. Forester | 1.25 | 2.50 | 3.75 | |
| 31 | The Man on the Blue–Luke Short | 1.25 | 2.50 | 3.75 | W |
| 32 | Year of Consent–Kendell Foster Crossen | 1.25 | 2.50 | 3.75 | SF |
| 33 | Two Faces West–T.T. Flynn | 1.25 | 2.50 | 3.75 | W |
| 34 | The Calm Man–David Cort | 1.25 | 2.50 | 3.75 | |
| F35 | Six Great Modern Short Novels | 1.25 | 2.50 | 3.75 | |
| 36 | The Golden Urge–Robert Kyle | 1.25 | 2.50 | 3.75 | |
| 37 | Last of the Breed–Les Savage, Jr | 1.25 | 2.50 | 3.75 | W |
| 38 | The Book of Prayers–Elfrieda McCauley & Leon McCauley | 1.25 | 2.50 | 3.75 | |
| 39 | Too Funny for Words–Bill Yates | 1.25 | 2.50 | 3.75 | H |
| D40 | The Handbook of Beauty–Constance Hart | 1.25 | 2.50 | 3.75 | NF |
| 41 | Dakota Rifle–Frank O'Rourke | 1.50 | 3.00 | 4.50 | W |
| 42 | The Body Snatchers–Jack Finney; 1st ed. 1955; aka Invasion of the Body Snatchers | 7.00 | 14.00 | 21.00 | SF |
| 43 | New Ways to Greater Word Power–Roger B. Goodman & David Lewin | 1.25 | 2.50 | 3.75 | NF |
| 44 | Now Is the Time–Lillian Smith | 1.25 | 2.50 | 3.75 | |
| 45 | City of Love–Daniel Talbot | 1.25 | 2.50 | 3.75 | |
| 46 | Line of Fire–Donald Hamilton | 1.25 | 2.50 | 3.75 | |
| 47 | The Only Game in Town–Charles Einstein | 1.25 | 2.50 | 3.75 | |
| F48 | The Complete Book of Gardening–W.W. Goodpasture | 1.25 | 2.50 | 3.75 | NF |

**DELL FIRST EDITIONS,** *continued*

| No. | Title | V/Good | Fine | N/Mint | |
|---|---|---|---|---|---|
| 49 | A Gun for Billy Reo–C. Hall Thompson; 1955 | 1.25 | 2.50 | 3.75 | W |
| 50 | Marital Blitz–Janice Berenstain & Stanley Berenstain | 1.50 | 3.00 | 4.50 | H |
| 51 | Nice Guys Finish Last–Robert Kyle | 1.25 | 2.50 | 3.75 | |
| 52 | Fort Sun Dance–Manly Wade Wellman | 2.50 | 5.00 | 7.50 | |
| D53 | Everybody's Book of Modern Diet and Nutrition–Henrietta Fleck & Elizabeth Munves | 1.25 | 2.50 | 3.75 | NF |
| FE54 | How to Draw and Paint–Henry Gasser | 1.25 | 2.50 | 3.75 | NF |
| 55 | What, When, Where and How to Drink–David Meyers & Richard L. Williams | 1.50 | 3.00 | 4.50 | NF |
| D56 | Too Near the Sun–Gordon Forbes | 1.25 | 2.50 | 3.75 | |
| 57 | Women of the Avalon–L.L. Foreman | 1.25 | 2.50 | 3.75 | W |
| 58 | After Innocence–Ian Gordon | 1.25 | 2.50 | 3.75 | |
| 59 | The Big Fifty–Frank O'Rourke | 2.00 | 4.00 | 6.00 | W |
| 60 | Dell Crossword Puzzles–Rosalind Moore & Kathleen Rafferty | 5.00 | 10.00 | 15.00 | NF |
| 61 | The Dirty Shame–John R. Humphries | 1.25 | 2.50 | 3.75 | |
| 62 | A Bullet for Cinderella–John D. MacDonald; 1st ed. 1955; aka On the Make | 3.50 | 7.00 | 10.50 | M |
| 63 | Hunger Mountain–William R. Scott | 1.25 | 2.50 | 3.75 | |
| 64 | More French Cartoons–William Cole & Douglas McKee | 1.50 | 3.00 | 4.50 | H |
| 65 | Return to Warbow–Les Savage, Jr | 1.25 | 2.50 | 3.75 | W |
| 66 | A Tiger in the Night–Robert Kyle | 1.25 | 2.50 | 3.75 | |
| 67 | The Fastest Gun–Dan Cushman | 1.50 | 3.00 | 4.50 | W |
| 68 | Bought with a Gun–Luke Short | 1.50 | 3.00 | 4.50 | W |
| FE69 | Six Centuries of Great Poetry–eds. Albert Erskine & Robert Penn Warren | 1.25 | 2.50 | 3.75 | |
| 70 | Marauder's Moon–Luke Short | 1.50 | 3.00 | 4.50 | W |
| 71 | Local Color–John Andrew Rice | 1.50 | 3.00 | 4.50 | |
| D72 | How to Build and Operate a Model Railroad–Marshall McClintock | 1.25 | 2.50 | 3.75 | NF |
| 73 | In His Blood–Harold R. Daniels | 1.25 | 2.50 | 3.75 | |
| 74 | Queen's Own–George C. Appell | 1.50 | 3.00 | 4.50 | A |
| FE75 | The Long Playing Record Guide–Warren de Motte; 1955 | 1.25 | 2.50 | 3.75 | NF |
| 76 | Wiretap!–Charles Einstein | 1.25 | 2.50 | 3.75 | |
| 77 | Dangerous Dames–Mike Shayne | 1.50 | 3.00 | 4.50 | M |
| 78 | Little Iodine–Jimmy Hatlo | 4.00 | 8.00 | 12.00 | H |
| 79 | The $64,000 Question Quiz Book; TV tie-in | 2.00 | 4.00 | 6.00 | NF |
| D80 | Short Stories, Short Plays and Songs by Noel Coward | 1.25 | 2.50 | 3.75 | |
| D81 | Down–Walt Grove | 1.25 | 2.50 | 3.75 | |
| 82 | Texas, Blood Red–Shepard Rifkin; 1956 | 1.25 | 2.50 | 3.75 | W |
| 83 | Night Fell on Georgia–Louise & Charles Samuels | 1.25 | 2.50 | 3.75 | |
| FE84 | The New Hammond-Dell World Atlas | 1.25 | 2.50 | 3.75 | NF |
| 85 | April Evil–John D. MacDonald; 1st ed. 1956 | 3.50 | 7.00 | 10.50 | M |
| D86 | While the City Sleeps–Charles Einstein | 1.25 | 2.50 | 3.75 | |
| 87 | The Loner–Bliss Lomax (H.S. Drago) | 1.25 | 2.50 | 3.75 | W |
| 88 | Intent to Kill–Michael Bryan | 1.25 | 2.50 | 3.75 | M |
| 89 | Battle Royal–Frank O'Rourke; c-Gross | 1.50 | 3.00 | 4.50 | A |
| D90 | The Last Enemy–Berton Roueche | 1.25 | 2.50 | 3.75 | |
| 91 | Mad River–Donald Hamilton | 1.25 | 2.50 | 3.75 | |
| 92 | Night Boat to Paris–Richard Jessup | 1.25 | 2.50 | 3.75 | |

*Dell First Edition 85, Dell First Edition A184, Dell First Edition A202.*

| No. | Title | V/Good | Fine | N/Mint | |
|---|---|---|---|---|---|
| 93 | Forever Funny–Bill Yates | 1.50 | 3.00 | 4.50 | H |
| 94 | Atlantic Avenue–Albert Halper | 1.50 | 3.00 | 4.50 | |
| 95 | The Devil's Spawn–Robert Carse | 1.50 | 3.00 | 4.50 | A |
| 96 | The Great Locomotive Chase–MacLennan Roberts; movie tie-in | 2.00 | 4.00 | 6.00 | A |
| 97 | Juvenile Delinquency–Charles Preston | 2.50 | 5.00 | 7.50 | NF |
| FE98 | Modern French Painting, 1855–1956–Samuel Hunter | 1.25 | 2.50 | 3.75 | NF |
| D99 | Thirteen Great Stories–Daniel Talbot | 1.25 | 2.50 | 3.75 | |
| FE100 | Six Great Modern Plays–ed. Edward Parone; 1956 | 1.25 | 2.50 | 3.75 | |
| 103 | The Angry Man–T.T. Flynn | 1.25 | 2.50 | 3.75 | W |
| 104 | The Last Chance–Frank O'Rourke | 1.50 | 3.00 | 4.50 | |
| 105 | The Pace That Kills–William Fuller | 1.25 | 2.50 | 3.75 | |
| 106 | Be My Victim–Robert Dietrich | 1.25 | 2.50 | 3.75 | M |
| 107 | Singapore Passage–Donald Barr Chidsey | 1.50 | 3.00 | 4.50 | A |
| 108 | Segundo–Frank O'Rourke | 1.50 | 3.00 | 4.50 | W |
| 109 | Cry Passion–Richard Jessup | 1.25 | 2.50 | 3.75 | |
| A110 | Riders West–anthology | 1.50 | 3.00 | 4.50 | W |
| A111 | The Big Success–Ian Gordon | 1.25 | 2.50 | 3.75 | |
| A112 | The Girl in 304–Harold R. Daniels | 1.25 | 2.50 | 3.75 | |
| A113 | Murder in the Wind–John D. MacDonald; 1st ed. 1956 | 3.50 | 7.00 | 10.50 | M |
| A114 | The Big Bite–Charles Williams | 3.50 | 7.00 | 10.50 | |
| A115 | Maverick–Verne Athanas | 1.25 | 2.50 | 3.75 | W |
| A116 | Kundu–Morris L. West | 1.25 | 2.50 | 3.75 | |
| A117 | Johnny Liddell's Morgue–Frank Kane | 1.25 | 2.50 | 3.75 | M |
| A118 | The Race of Giants–Matt Kinkaid | 1.25 | 2.50 | 3.75 | |
| A119 | Cimarron Trace–James Norman | 1.25 | 2.50 | 3.75 | W |
| A120 | Wetback–William O'Farrell | 1.25 | 2.50 | 3.75 | |
| A121 | The Last Laugh–Charles Einstein | 1.25 | 2.50 | 3.75 | |
| A122 | The Branded Man–Luke Short | 1.50 | 3.00 | 4.50 | W |
| A123 | Assignment: Murder–Donald Hamilton | 1.25 | 2.50 | 3.75 | M |
| A124 | Rebel Gun–Arthur Stever | 1.25 | 2.50 | 3.75 | W |
| A125 | This Is Little Lulu–Marge | 3.50 | 7.00 | 10.50 | H |
| A126 | Key Witness–Frank Kane | 1.25 | 2.50 | 3.75 | M |
| A127 | Lone Hand–L.L. Foreman | 1.25 | 2.50 | 3.75 | W |
| A128 | The King and Four Queens–Theodore Sturgeon; 1st ed. 1956 | 4.00 | 8.00 | 12.00 | W |
| A129 | Bottoms Up!–Charles Preston | 1.25 | 2.50 | 3.75 | H |
| A130 | Death Trap–John D. MacDonald; 1st ed. 1957 | 3.50 | 7.00 | 10.50 | M |
| A131 | The Bravados–Frank O'Rourke | 1.50 | 3.00 | 4.50 | |
| A132 | Under the Badge–C. Hall Thompson | 1.25 | 2.50 | 3.75 | W |
| A133 | The Girl in the Frame–William Fuller | 1.25 | 2.50 | 3.75 | |
| A134 | Bold Rider–Luke Short | 1.25 | 2.50 | 3.75 | W |
| A135 | Desert Guns–Steve Frazee | 1.50 | 3.00 | 4.50 | W |
| A136 | A Taste of Brass–Robert Donald Locke | 1.25 | 2.50 | 3.75 | |
| A137 | A Shady Place to Die–John Savage | 1.25 | 2.50 | 3.75 | |
| A138 | Showdown at Stony Crest–Joseph Wayne | 1.25 | 2.50 | 3.75 | W |
| A139 | The House of Numbers–Jack Finney | 1.50 | 3.00 | 4.50 | |
| A140 | Tall Wyoming–Dan Cushman | 1.50 | 3.00 | 4.50 | W |
| A141 | Murder on the Rocks–Robert Dietrich | 1.25 | 2.50 | 3.75 | M |
| A142 | The Living End–Frank Kane | 1.25 | 2.50 | 3.75 | M |
| A143 | The Outcast–Richard Ferber | 1.25 | 2.50 | 3.75 | |
| A144 | Death for Sale–Henry Kane | 1.25 | 2.50 | 3.75 | M |
| A145 | Murder in Majorca–Michael Bryan | 1.25 | 2.50 | 3.75 | M |
| A146 | The Dice Spelled Murder–Al Fray | 1.25 | 2.50 | 3.75 | M |
| A147 | Year of the Gun–Giff Cheshire | 1.25 | 2.50 | 3.75 | W |
| A148 | Treachery at Rock Point–Peter Dawson (Frank Gruber) | 2.00 | 4.00 | 6.00 | W |
| A149 | Death at Flood Tide–Louis A. Brennan | 1.25 | 2.50 | 3.75 | |
| A150 | Tough Country–Frank Bonham; 1958 | 1.25 | 2.50 | 3.75 | W |
| A151 | The Man on the Blue–Luke Short | 1.50 | 3.00 | 4.50 | W |
| A152 | The Price of Murder–John D. MacDonald; 1st ed. 1957 | 3.50 | 7.00 | 10.50 | M |
| A153 | Brad Dolan's Blonde Cargo–William Fuller | 1.25 | 2.50 | 3.75 | M |
| A154 | Bought with a Gun–Luke Short; 1958 | 1.50 | 3.00 | 4.50 | W |
| A155 | Blackmail, Inc.–Robert Kyle | 1.25 | 2.50 | 3.75 | |
| A156 | The Body Looks Familiar–Richard Wormser | 1.25 | 2.50 | 3.75 | M |
| A157 | The Bravados–Frank O'Rourke | 1.50 | 3.00 | 4.50 | W |
| A158 | Brad Dolan's Miami Manhunt–William Fuller | 1.25 | 2.50 | 3.75 | M |
| A159 | The Perfect Victim–James McKimmey | 1.25 | 2.50 | 3.75 | |
| A160 | A Bullet for a Blonde–Paul Kruger | 1.25 | 2.50 | 3.75 | M |
| A161 | Come Back for More–Al Fray | 1.25 | 2.50 | 3.75 | M |
| A162 | The Hostiles–Richard Ferber | 1.25 | 2.50 | 3.75 | |
| A163 | Under Cover of Night–Manning Lee Stokes | 1.25 | 2.50 | 3.75 | M |

## DELL FIRST EDITIONS, *continued*

| | | V/Good | Fine | N/Mint | |
|---|---|---|---|---|---|
| A164 | Talk of the Town–Charles Williams | 3.50 | 7.00 | 10.50 | |
| A165 | All the Way–Charles Williams | 3.50 | 7.00 | 10.50 | |
| A166 | Man from Nowhere–T.T. Flynn | 1.25 | 2.50 | 3.75 | W |
| A167 | Built for Trouble–Al Fray | 1.25 | 2.50 | 3.75 | M |
| A168 | Revenge–Jack Ehrlich | 1.25 | 2.50 | 3.75 | |
| A169 | The Concubine–Michael East | 1.25 | 2.50 | 3.75 | |
| A170 | The Snatch–Harold R. Daniels | 1.25 | 2.50 | 3.75 | |
| A171 | Buckskin Man–Thomas W. Blackburn | 1.25 | 2.50 | 3.75 | W |
| A172 | The Long Rope–Hal G. Evarts | 1.25 | 2.50 | 3.75 | W |
| A173 | Nellie the Nurse–Kaz | 1.50 | 3.00 | 4.50 | H |
| A174 | The Raiders–Richard Ferber; 1959 | 1.25 | 2.50 | 3.75 | |
| A175 | The House on Q Street–Robert Dietrich | 1.25 | 2.50 | 3.75 | M |
| A176 | 77 Sunset Strip–Roy Huggins; TV tie-in | 2.00 | 4.00 | 6.00 | M |
| A177 | Sound of Gunfire–Frank Bonham | 1.25 | 2.50 | 3.75 | W |
| A178 | The Other Woman–Bill Yates | 1.50 | 3.00 | 4.50 | H |
| A179 | On Becoming a Woman–Irene Kane & Mary McGee Williams | 1.25 | 2.50 | 3.75 | NF |
| A180 | The Naked City–Sterling Silliphant; TV tie-in | 2.00 | 4.00 | 6.00 | M |
| A181 | Darby O'Gill and the Little People–Lawrence Edward Watkin; movie tie-in | 2.50 | 5.00 | 7.50 | F |
| A182 | Sweet Cheat–Peter Duncan | 1.25 | 2.50 | 3.75 | |
| A183 | Laredo Road–Will C. Brown | 1.25 | 2.50 | 3.75 | W |
| A184 | Last Stand at Saber River–Elmore Leonard | 6.00 | 12.00 | 18.00 | W |
| A185 | Winner Take All–James McKimmey | 1.25 | 2.50 | 3.75 | |
| A186 | Last Stage West–Frank Bonham | 1.25 | 2.50 | 3.75 | W |
| A187 | Kay Manion, M.D.–Adeline McElfresh | 1.25 | 2.50 | 3.75 | R |
| A188 | Corruption City–Horace McCoy | 4.00 | 8.00 | 12.00 | M |
| A189 | Tight Squeeze–William Fuller | 1.25 | 2.50 | 3.75 | |
| A190 | McCracken in Command–James Keene | 1.25 | 2.50 | 3.75 | |
| A191 | Texas Heller–E.M. Parsons | 1.25 | 2.50 | 3.75 | W |
| A192 | Model for Murder–Robert Kyle | 1.25 | 2.50 | 3.75 | M |
| A193 | Epitaph for a Tramp–David Markson | 1.25 | 2.50 | 3.75 | |
| A194 | The Deadly Duo–Richard Jessup; 1959 | 1.25 | 2.50 | 3.75 | |
| A197 | End of a Stripper–Robert Dietrich; 1960 | 1.25 | 2.50 | 3.75 | M |
| A198 | Doctor with a Gun–Richard Ferber | 1.25 | 2.50 | 3.75 | W |
| A199 | Killer in Town–Clifton Adams | 1.25 | 2.50 | 3.75 | W |
| A200 | Cain's Woman–O.G. Benson | 2.00 | 4.00 | 6.00 | M |
| A201 | The Gun and the Law–Joseph Wayne | 1.25 | 2.50 | 3.75 | W |
| A202 | The Half-Caste–Dan Cushman | 1.50 | 3.00 | 4.50 | W |
| A205 | Gunman's Harvest–James Keene | 1.25 | 2.50 | 3.75 | W |
| A206 | Wings for Nurse Bennett–Adeline McElfresh | 1.25 | 2.50 | 3.75 | R |
| A207 | The Blazing Land–Hal G. Evarts | 1.25 | 2.50 | 3.75 | W |
| A209 | Nellie's Bedfellows–Kaz; 1960 | 1.50 | 3.00 | 4.50 | H |
| B101 | The Official American Medical Association Book of Health–W.W. Bauer; 1957 | 1.25 | 2.50 | 3.75 | NF |
| B102 | New Worlds of Modern Science–Leonard Engel | 1.25 | 2.50 | 3.75 | NF |
| B103 | SF: The Year's Greatest Science-Fiction and Fantasy–ed. Judith Merrill | 1.50 | 3.00 | 4.50 | SF |
| B104 | The Walt Disney Story of Our Friend the Atom–Heinz Haber | 1.50 | 3.00 | 4.50 | NF |
| B105 | Moses and the Ten Commandments–Paul Ilton & MacLennan Roberts | 1.50 | 3.00 | 4.50 | |
| B106 | A Treasury of Faith–Leon McCauley | 1.25 | 2.50 | 3.75 | |
| B107 | Stories for the Dead of Night–ed. Don Congdon | 1.50 | 3.00 | 4.50 | HO |
| B108 | More Than Flesh–Louis A. Brennan | 1.25 | 2.50 | 3.75 | |
| B109 | The Fabulous Buccaneer–Robert Carse | 1.50 | 3.00 | 4.50 | A |
| B110 | SF: The Year's Greatest Science-Fiction and Fantasy, 2nd Annual Volume–ed. Judith Merril | 1.50 | 3.00 | 4.50 | SF |
| B111 | By Appointment Only–Russell Boltar | 1.25 | 2.50 | 3.75 | |
| B112 | A Man of Affairs–John D. MacDonald; 1st ed. 1957 | 3.50 | 7.00 | 10.50 | M |
| B113 | Sea Avenger–Jack Beater & MacLennan Roberts | 1.50 | 3.00 | 4.50 | A |
| B114 | Girl Out Back–Charles Williams | 3.00 | 6.00 | 9.00 | |
| B115 | The Big Country–Donald Hamilton | 2.50 | 5.00 | 7.50 | W |
| B116 | The Accused–Harold R. Daniels | 2.50 | 5.00 | 7.50 | |
| B117 | The Deceivers–John D. MacDonald; 1st ed. 1958 | 3.50 | 7.00 | 10.50 | M |
| B118 | Lowdown–Richard Jessup | 2.50 | 5.00 | 7.50 | |
| B119 | SF: The Year's Greatest Science-Fiction and Fantasy, 3rd Annual Volume–ed. Judith Merril | 1.50 | 3.00 | 4.50 | SF |

| | | V/Good | Fine | N/Mint | |
|---|---|---|---|---|---|
| B120 | The Cosmic Rape–Theodore Sturgeon | 1.50 | 3.00 | 4.50 | SF |
| B121 | Soft Touch–John D. MacDonald; 1st ed. 1958, aka Man-Trap | 3.50 | 7.00 | 10.50 | M |
| B122 | Untamed–Warner Hall | 1.50 | 3.00 | 4.50 | |
| B123 | Syndicate Girl–Frank Kane; 1959 | 1.25 | 2.50 | 3.75 | M |
| B124 | The Two Lives of Dr. Stratton–Russell Boltar | 1.25 | 2.50 | 3.75 | |
| B125 | The Lineup–Frank Kane | 1.25 | 2.50 | 3.75 | M |
| B126 | The Strain–Kenneth E. Shiflet | 1.25 | 2.50 | 3.75 | |
| B127 | Deadly Welcome–John D. MacDonald; 1st ed. 1959 | 3.50 | 7.00 | 10.50 | M |
| B128 | The Five Pennies–Grady Johnson; movie tie-in | 1.50 | 3.00 | 4.50 | |
| B129 | SF: The Year's Greatest Science-Fiction and Fantasy, 4th Annual Volume–ed. Judith Merril | 1.50 | 3.00 | 4.50 | SF |
| B130 | Marauders' Moon–Luke Short | 1.50 | 3.00 | 4.50 | W |
| B131 | Girl on the Beach–George Sumner Albee | 1.25 | 2.50 | 3.75 | |
| B132 | Paula–Don Kingery | 1.25 | 2.50 | 3.75 | |
| B133 | The Flesh Merchants–Bob Thomas | 1.25 | 2.50 | 3.75 | |
| B134 | On the Make–John D. MacDonald; aka A Bullet for Cinderella | 1.50 | 3.00 | 4.50 | M |
| B135 | The Witch Finder–Thomas L. O'Brien | 2.00 | 4.00 | 6.00 | |
| B136 | The Joy Boys–Walt Grove | 2.00 | 4.00 | 6.00 | |
| B137 | Juke Box King–Frank Kane | 2.00 | 4.00 | 6.00 | |
| B138 | The Sirens of Titan–Kurt Vonnegut, Jr; orig. 1959 | 10.00 | 20.00 | 30.00 | SF |
| B139 | Sin Street–Bob Bristow | 1.50 | 3.00 | 4.50 | |
| B140 | Montana!–C. Hall Thompson | 1.25 | 2.50 | 3.75 | |
| B141 | The Lethal Sex–John D. MacDonald | 2.00 | 4.00 | 6.00 | M |
| B142 | Poker According to Maverick; TV tie-in. Note: Two premium variants also exist for Willys Motors and the Drackett Company | 1.50 | 3.00 | 4.50 | NF |
| B143 | Marital Blitz–Janice Berenstain & Stanley Berenstain | 1.50 | 3.00 | 4.50 | H |
| B144 | The Pace That Kills–William Fuller | 1.25 | 2.50 | 3.75 | M |
| B145 | When She Was Bad–William Ard; 1st ed. 1960 | 3.50 | 7.00 | 10.50 | |
| B146 | April Evil–John D. MacDonald; 1960 | 2.00 | 4.00 | 6.00 | M |
| B147 | Fire in the Flesh–Jack Sheridan | | | | |
| B148 | Career–Victor Chapin; movie tie-in | 1.25 | 2.50 | 3.75 | |
| B149 | Dell Crossword Puzzles–ed. Kathleen Rafferty | 4.00 | 8.00 | 12.00 | NF |
| B150 | A Short Bier–Frank Kane | 1.50 | 3.00 | 4.50 | M |
| B151 | The Long Knife–Louis A. Brennan | 1.25 | 2.50 | 3.75 | W |
| B152 | Scent of Mystery–Kelley Roos | 1.25 | 2.50 | 3.75 | M |
| B153 | Local Talent–William Fuller; aka Goat Island | 1.25 | 2.50 | 3.75 | M |
| B154 | Parole–Jack Ehrlich; c-Abbett | 1.25 | 2.50 | 3.75 | W |
| B155 | Peter Gunn–Henry Kane; TV tie-in | 2.00 | 4.00 | 6.00 | M |
| B156 | Have Gun, Will Travel–Noel Loomis; TV tie-in | 2.00 | 4.00 | 6.00 | W |
| B157 | Cornered!–James McKimmey | 1.25 | 2.50 | 3.75 | M |
| B158 | Man Bait–Jack Liston; c-Maguire | 2.00 | 4.00 | 6.00 | M |
| B159 | Time to Prey–Frank Kane | 1.25 | 2.50 | 3.75 | M |
| B160 | Crack in the Mirror–Marcel Haedrich | 1.25 | 2.50 | 3.75 | M |
| B161 | Just Married–Jerry Marcus | 1.25 | 2.50 | 3.75 | H |
| B162 | Mistress to Murder–Robert Dietrich (E. Howard Hunt) | 1.50 | 3.00 | 4.50 | M |
| B163 | Murder on Her Mind–Robert Dietrich (E. Howard Hunt) | 1.50 | 3.00 | 4.50 | M |

*Dell First Edition B122, Dell First Edition B142, Dell First Edition B156.*

**DELL FIRST EDITIONS,** *continued*

| | | V/Good | Fine | N/Mint | |
|---|---|---|---|---|---|
| B164 | Good Time Girl–Don Kingery | 1.25 | 2.50 | 3.75 | M |
| B165 | Mr. Lucky–Albert Conroy (Marvin H. Albert); TV tie-in | 2.00 | 4.00 | 6.00 | M |
| B166 | Bedside Lover Boy–Stanley Berenstain & Janice Berenstain | 1.50 | 3.00 | 4.50 | H |
| B167 | Murder in the Wind–John D. MacDonald; c-Abbett | 2.00 | 4.00 | 6.00 | M |
| B168 | Ann Kenyon, Surgeon–Adeline McElfresh; c-Abbett | 1.25 | 2.50 | 3.75 | R |
| B169 | 24 Hours to Kill–James McKimmey | 1.25 | 2.50 | 3.75 | M |
| B170 | The Man from Santa Clara–Donald Hamilton | 1.25 | 2.50 | 3.75 | W |
| B171 | A Time for Passion–Mark Howard | 1.25 | 2.50 | 3.75 | |
| B172 | The Deputy–Roe Richmond; TV tie-in | 2.00 | 4.00 | 6.00 | W |
| B173 | Key Witness–Frank Kane; movie tie-in | 1.50 | 3.00 | 4.50 | M |
| B174 | Due or Die–Frank Kane; 1961 | 1.25 | 2.50 | 3.75 | M |
| B175 | Boatniks–Bernard Wiseman | 1.50 | 3.00 | 4.50 | H |
| B176 | Bitter Valley–Richard Ferber | 1.25 | 2.50 | 3.75 | W |
| B177 | Night Call–Adeline McElfresh | 1.25 | 2.50 | 3.75 | R |
| B178 | Kill Now, Pay Later–Robert Kyle | 1.25 | 2.50 | 3.75 | M |
| B179 | Rx for Love–Elizabeth Stowe | 1.25 | 2.50 | 3.75 | R |
| B180 | A Cold Wind in August–Burton Wohl; c-Abbett | 1.25 | 2.50 | 3.75 | |
| B181 | The Great Bank Robbery–Frank O'Rourke | 1.50 | 3.00 | 4.50 | W |
| B182 | Steve Bentley's Calypso Caper–Robert Dietrich | 1.25 | 2.50 | 3.75 | M |
| B183 | Love of Life–Margaret Manners; TV tie-in | 1.25 | 2.50 | 3.75 | R |
| B184 | Touché–eds. Douglas McKee & William Cole | 1.25 | 2.50 | 3.75 | H |
| B185 | Kay Manion, M.D.–Adeline McElfresh | 1.25 | 2.50 | 3.75 | R |
| B186 | The Counterfeit Courier–James C. Sheers; c-Abbett | 1.25 | 2.50 | 3.75 | M |
| B187 | Dead Rite–Frank Kane | 1.25 | 2.50 | 3.75 | M |
| B188 | Champagne at Dawn–Robert Carroll; c-Abbett | 1.25 | 2.50 | 3.75 | R |
| B189 | Epitaph for a Beatnik–David Markson | 1.25 | 2.50 | 3.75 | |
| B190 | Calling Nurse Nellie–Kaz | 1.50 | 3.00 | 4.50 | H |
| B191 | Death Comes Early–William R. Cox | 1.25 | 2.50 | 3.75 | M |
| B192 | The Wrong Ones–James McKimmey | 1.25 | 2.50 | 3.75 | M |
| B193 | Marked–Robert Bristow | 1.25 | 2.50 | 3.75 | M |
| B194 | Think Fast, Ranger–Will C. Brown; 1961 | 1.25 | 2.50 | 3.75 | W |
| B195 | Shock!–Richard Matheson; c-Powers | 2.50 | 5.00 | 7.50 | SF |
| B197 | Stacked Deck–Frank Kane | 1.25 | 2.50 | 3.75 | M |
| B198 | My Darling Evangeline–Henry Kane | 1.25 | 2.50 | 3.75 | M |
| B199 | Yogi Bear Goes to College–William Hanna & Joe Barbera; comic book reprints; TV tie-in | 3.00 | 6.00 | 9.00 | H |
| B200 | On Becoming a Woman–Mary Williams & Irene Kane | 1.25 | 2.50 | 3.75 | NF |
| B201 | Hospital Hill–Adeline McElfresh; c-Abbett | 1.25 | 2.50 | 3.75 | R |
| B202 | Breaking through the Laugh Barrier–Dana Fradon | 1.25 | 2.50 | 3.75 | H |
| B203 | Angel Eyes–Robert Dietrich | 1.25 | 2.50 | 3.75 | M |
| B204 | The Body Snatchers–Jack Finney; c-Powers; aka Invasion of the Body Snatchers | 2.00 | 4.00 | 6.00 | SF |
| B206 | Never Take Candy from a Stranger–Roger Garis; movie tie-in | 1.50 | 3.00 | 4.50 | |
| B207 | The Golden Hooligan–Thomas B. Dewey | 2.00 | 4.00 | 6.00 | M |
| B209 | Riding High–T.T. Flynn | 1.25 | 2.50 | 3.75 | W |
| B210 | Willa–Gilbert Terrell | 1.25 | 2.50 | | |
| B211 | The Long Ride–James McKimmey; c-Abbett | 1.25 | 2.50 | 3.75 | M |
| B213 | Nellie's New Frontier–Kaz | 1.50 | 3.00 | 4.50 | H |
| B214 | Morgan the Pirate–Robert Carse; c-Gross, movie tie-in | 2.00 | 4.00 | 6.00 | A |
| B215 | Go, Honeylou–Thomas B. Dewey | 2.00 | 4.00 | 6.00 | M |
| B216 | Thief of Baghdad–Richard Wormser; c-Gross, movie tie-in | 2.50 | 5.00 | 7.50 | A |
| B218 | Clayburn–Al Conroy; c-Gross | 1.50 | 3.00 | 4.50 | W |
| B220 | Slow Burn–Jack Ehrlich; c-Abbett | 1.25 | 2.50 | 3.75 | M |
| B225 | Treasure of the Black Hills–John B. Prescott; c-Gross | 1.50 | 3.00 | 4.50 | W |
| B226 | The Mourning After–Frank Kane | 1.25 | 2.50 | 3.75 | M |
| B227 | Cry, Baby–Jack Ehrlich; c-Abbett | 1.25 | 2.50 | 3.75 | M |
| B230 | Squeeze Play–James McKimmey; c-Abbett | 1.25 | 2.50 | 3.75 | M |

Dell First Edition B165, Dell First Edition B214, Dell First Edition B216.

| | | V/Good | Fine | N/Mint | |
|---|---|---|---|---|---|
| B232 | My Kind of Game–Anthony Rome | 1.25 | 2.50 | 3.75 | M |
| C101 | The American Heritage Reader–ed. Stephen Becker | 1.25 | 2.50 | 3.75 | |
| C102 | A Popular History of Music–Carter Harman | 1.25 | 2.50 | 3.75 | NF |
| C103 | From Medicine Man to Freud–Jan Ehrenwald; 1956 | 1.25 | 2.50 | 3.75 | NF |
| C104 | The Second Ribald Reader–ed. A.M. Krich | 1.25 | 2.50 | 3.75 | |
| C105 | Great Scenes from Great Novels–ed. Robert Terrall | 1.25 | 2.50 | 3.75 | |
| C106 | The Handbook of Beauty–Constance Hart | 1.25 | 2.50 | 3.75 | NF |
| C107 | Combat: European Theater–World War II–Don Congdon | 1.00 | 2.00 | 3.00 | NF |
| C108 | Combat: Pacific Theater–World War II–Don Congdon | 1.00 | 2.00 | 3.00 | NF |
| C109 | Dell Crossword Dictionary–Kathleen Rafferty; 1960 | 1.25 | 2.50 | 3.75 | NF |
| C110 | Women–ed. A.M. Krich | 1.25 | 2.50 | 3.75 | |
| C111 | Six Great Short Science Fiction Novels–ed. Groff Conklin; c-Powers | 1.25 | 2.50 | 3.75 | SF |
| C112 | Call after Six–Charles Mergendahl | 1.25 | 2.50 | 3.75 | |
| C113 | Men–ed. A.M. Krich | 1.25 | 2.50 | 3.75 | |
| C115 | Stiletto–Harold Robbins; 1961, c-Abbett | 3.00 | 6.00 | 9.00 | |
| C117 | By Appointment Only–Russell Boltar | 1.25 | 2.50 | 3.75 | |
| C120 | A Cold Wind in August–Burton Wohl; c-Abbett | 1.25 | 2.50 | 3.75 | |
| C121 | Bachelor in Paradise–Vera Caspary; movie tie-in | 1.25 | 2.50 | 3.75 | |
| C127 | The Conspirators–Frank Kane | 1.25 | 2.50 | 3.75 | M |
| K101 | Come September–Marvin H. Albert; 1961, movie tie-in | 1.50 | 3.00 | 4.50 | |
| K102 | The Naked Country–Michael East | 1.50 | 3.00 | 4.50 | A |
| K103 | Night School–R.V. Cassill | 1.25 | 2.50 | 3.75 | |
| K104 | Susan Slade–Doris Hume; movie tie-in | 1.25 | 2.50 | 3.75 | R |
| K105 | Sing Out Sweet Homicide–John Roeburt; TV tie-in | 1.50 | 3.00 | 4.50 | M |
| K106 | My Geisha–Saul Cooper; movie tie-in | 1.50 | 3.00 | 4.50 | |
| K107 | Daisy–Sim Wenner | 1.25 | 2.50 | 3.75 | |
| K108 | Too Soon Tomorrow–Chris Pendleton | 1.25 | 2.50 | 3.75 | R |
| K109 | Mike Shayne's Torrid 12–ed. Leo Margulies | 1.50 | 3.00 | 4.50 | M |
| K110 | Jeff Benton, M.D.–Adeline McElfresh; 1962 | 1.50 | 3.00 | 4.50 | R |
| K111 | Target for Tonight–Richard Telfair; c-Abbett, TV tie-in | 2.00 | 4.00 | 6.00 | M |
| K112 | Hawaiian Eye–Frank Castle; TV tie-in | 2.00 | 4.00 | 6.00 | M |
| K113 | Cruise to the Sun–Robert Carroll | 1.25 | 2.50 | 3.75 | R |
| K115 | Jill Nolan, R.N.–Adeline McElfresh | 1.25 | 2.50 | 3.75 | R |
| K116 | Soft Touch–John D. MacDonald | 1.50 | 3.00 | 4.50 | M |
| K117 | Missy–Gilbert Terrell; 1962 | 1.25 | 2.50 | 3.75 | |

# DELL LAUREL EDITIONS

## Dell Publishing Company, Inc.

| | | V/Good | Fine | N/Mint | |
|---|---|---|---|---|---|
| LB110 | New Ways to Greater Word Power–Roger B. Goodman & David Lewin | .75 | 1.50 | 2.25 | NF |
| LB111 | The World in Space–Alexander Marshack | .75 | 1.50 | 2.25 | NF |
| LB112 | Hamlet–William Shakespeare | .75 | 1.50 | 2.25 | |

## DELL LAUREL EDITIONS, *continued*

| No. | Title | V/Good | Fine | N/Mint |
|---|---|---|---|---|
| LB113 | The Taming of the Shrew–William Shakespeare | .75 | 1.50 | 2.25 |
| LB114 | Romeo and Juliet–William Shakespeare | .75 | 1.50 | 2.25 |
| LB115 | Richard III–William Shakespeare | .75 | 1.50 | 2.25 |
| LB116 | Great Flying Stories–Frank W. Anderson, Jr | 1.00 | 2.00 | 3.00 |
| LB117 | The Walt Disney Story of Our Friend the Atom–Heinz Haber; c-Powers | 1.25 | 2.50 | 3.75 NF |
| LB118 | The Merchant of Venice–William Shakespeare | .75 | 1.50 | 2.25 |
| LB119 | Julius Caesar–William Shakespeare | .75 | 1.50 | 2.25 |
| LB120 | Poe–Edgar Allan Poe | .75 | 1.50 | 2.25 |
| LB121 | Whitman–Walt Whitman | .75 | 1.50 | 2.25 |
| LB122 | Coleridge–Samuel Taylor Coleridge | .75 | 1.50 | 2.25 |
| LB123 | Wordsworth–William Wordsworth | .75 | 1.50 | 2.25 |
| LB124 | Macbeth–William Shakespeare | .75 | 1.50 | 2.25 |
| LB125 | Twelfth Night–William Shakespeare | .75 | 1.50 | 2.25 |
| LB126 | Great Tales of Action and Adventure–George Bennett; c-Powers | .75 | 1.50 | 2.25 |
| LB127 | Great Sea Stories–Alan Villiers; c-Powers | .75 | 1.50 | 2.25 |
| LB128 | Kim–Rudyard Kipling; c-Powers | .75 | 1.50 | 2.25 A |
| LB129 | Othello–William Shakespeare | .75 | 1.50 | 2.25 |
| LB130 | As You Like It–William Shakespeare | .75 | 1.50 | 2.25 |
| LB131 | Keats–John Keats; c-Powers | .75 | 1.50 | 2.25 |
| LB132 | Longfellow–Henry Wadsworth Longfellow; c-Powers | .75 | 1.50 | 2.25 |
| LB133 | The Winter's Tale–William Shakespeare | .75 | 1.50 | 2.25 |
| LB134 | Henry IV, Part 1–William Shakespeare; 1959 | .75 | 1.50 | 2.25 |
| LB135 | Kidnapped–Robert Louis Stevenson; c-Powers | .75 | 1.50 | 2.25 A |
| LB136 | Blake–ed. Ruthven Todd; c-Powers | .75 | 1.50 | 2.25 |
| LB137 | A Midsummer Night's Dream–William Shakespeare | .75 | 1.50 | 2.25 |
| LB138 | Emily Dickinson–ed. John Malcolm Brinnin; c-Powers | .75 | 1.50 | 2.25 |
| LB139 | Much Ado about Nothing–William Shakespeare | .75 | 1.50 | 2.25 |
| LB140 | The Swiss Family Robinson–Johann Wyss; c-Powers; movie tie-in | .75 | 1.50 | 2.25 A |
| LB141 | King Lear–William Shakespeare | .75 | 1.50 | 2.25 |
| LB144 | The Sonnets–William Shakespeare | .75 | 1.50 | 2.25 |
| LB145 | The Picture of Dorian Gray–Oscar Wilde; 1960 | .75 | 1.50 | 2.25 HO |
| LB146 | The Loved One–Evelyn Waugh | .75 | 1.50 | 2.25 |
| LB147 | Browning–ed. Reed Whittemore | .75 | 1.50 | 2.25 |
| LB148 | Whittier–ed. Donald Hall; c-Powers | .75 | 1.50 | 2.25 |
| LB149 | The Tempest–William Shakespeare | .75 | 1.50 | 2.25 |
| LB150 | King Richard II–William Shakespeare | .75 | 1.50 | 2.25 |
| LB151 | Marvell–ed. Joseph H. Summers; c-Powers | .75 | 1.50 | 2.25 |
| LB152 | Ben Jonson–ed. John Hollander; c-Powers | .75 | 1.50 | 2.25 |
| LB153 | All's Well That Ends Well–William Shakespeare | .75 | 1.50 | 2.25 |
| LB154 | Antony and Cleopatra–William Shakespeare | .75 | 1.50 | 2.25 |
| LB155 | Silas Marner–George Eliot; c-Powers | .75 | 1.50 | 2.25 |
| LB156 | Shelley–ed. William Meredith; c-Powers | .75 | 1.50 | 2.25 |
| LB157 | Dryden–ed. Reuben A. Brower; c-Powers | .75 | 1.50 | 2.25 |
| LB158 | Henry V–William Shakespeare | .75 | 1.50 | 2.25 |
| LB159 | Measure for Measure–William Shakespeare | .75 | 1.50 | 2.25 |
| LC101 | Four Plays–George Bernard Shaw | .75 | 1.50 | 2.25 |
| LC102 | Great English Short Stories–ed. Christopher Isherwood | .75 | 1.50 | 2.25 |
| LC103 | Great American Short Stories–eds. Mary Stegner & Wallace Stegner | .75 | 1.50 | 2.25 |
| LC104 | The New Dell Modern American Dictionary–Jess Stein | .75 | 1.50 | 2.25 NF |
| LC105 | Common Wild Animals and Their Young–Rita Vandivert and William Vandivert | .75 | 1.50 | 2.25 NF |
| LC106 | The Modern Meat Cookbook–Jeannette Frank | .75 | 1.50 | 2.25 NF |
| LC107 | Panorama: The Laurel Reader No. 1–ed. R.F. Tannenbaum | .75 | 1.50 | 2.25 |
| LC108 | Lincoln and the Civil War–Courtlandt Canby | .75 | 1.50 | 2.25 NF |
| LC109 | Six Centuries of Great Poetry–Albert Erskine & Robert Penn Warren | .75 | 1.50 | 2.25 |
| LC110 | Great Russian Short Stories–ed. Norris Houghton | .75 | 1.50 | 2.25 |
| LC111 | Mark Twain–Mark Twain; c-Powers | .75 | 1.50 | 2.25 |
| LC112 | A Catholic Prayer Book–Dale Francis | .75 | 1.50 | 2.25 |
| LC113 | Jean-Christophe–Romain Rolland | .75 | 1.50 | 2.25 |
| LC114 | Martin Eden–Jack London; c-Powers | .75 | 1.50 | 2.25 |
| LC115 | How to Draw the Human Figure–John R. Grabach | .75 | 1.50 | 2.25 NF |
| LC116 | Emerson–Ralph Waldo Emerson | .75 | 1.50 | 2.25 |
| LC117 | The Wings of the Dove–Henry James | .75 | 1.50 | 2.25 |
| LC118 | Madame Bovary–Gustave Flaubert | .75 | 1.50 | 2.25 |
| LC119 | Elmer Gantry–Sinclair Lewis | .75 | 1.50 | 2.25 |
| LC120 | Child Behavior: Gesell Institute–Louise Bates Ames & Frances L. Ilg | .75 | 1.50 | 2.25 NF |
| LC121 | The Aspern Papers and the Spoils of Poynton–Henry James | .75 | 1.50 | 2.25 |
| LC122 | Pride and Prejudice–Jane Austen | .75 | 1.50 | 2.25 |
| LC123 | Three Plays by Ibsen–Henrik Ibsen | .75 | 1.50 | 2.25 |
| LC124 | Everybody's Book of Modern Diet and Nutrition–Henrietta Fleck & Elizabeth Munves | .75 | 1.50 | 2.25 NF |
| LC125 | How to Draw and Paint–Henry Gasser; 1959 | .75 | 1.50 | 2.25 NF |
| LC126 | Great Stories by Chekhov–Anton Chekhov; c-Powers | .75 | 1.50 | 2.25 |
| LC127 | Great Italian Short Stories–ed. Pier Pasinetti | .75 | 1.50 | 2.25 |
| LC128 | Sense and Sensibility–Jane Austen | .75 | 1.50 | 2.25 |
| LC129 | Pushkin–Alexander Pushkin | .75 | 1.50 | 2.25 NF |
| LC130 | Poetry: A Modern Guide to Its Understanding and Enjoyment–Elizabeth Drew | .75 | 1.50 | 2.25 |
| LC131 | The House of the Dead–Fyodor Dostoyevsky | .75 | 1.50 | 2.25 |
| LC132 | Six Great Modern Short Novels | .75 | 1.50 | 2.25 |
| LC133 | Four Great Russian Short Novels | .75 | 1.50 | 2.25 |
| LC134 | Voltaire–Voltaire | .75 | 1.50 | 2.25 |
| LC135 | Maupassant–Guy de Maupassant | .75 | 1.50 | 2.25 |
| LC136 | Washington Square and the Europeans–Henry James | .75 | 1.50 | 2.25 |
| LC137 | Freud: His Life and His Mind–Helen W. Puner | .75 | 1.50 | 2.25 B |
| LC138 | Lives of the Noble Greeks–Plutarch | .75 | 1.50 | 2.25 B |
| LC139 | Lives of the Noble Romans–Plutarch | .75 | 1.50 | 2.25 B |
| LC140 | Stevenson–Robert Louis Stevenson | .75 | 1.50 | 2.25 |
| LX101 | A History of the United States–William Miller | .75 | 1.50 | 2.25 NF |
| LX102 | Short Story Masterpieces–eds. Albert Erskine & Robert Penn Warren | .75 | 1.50 | 2.25 |
| LX103 | Six Great Modern Plays–ed. Edward Parone | .75 | 1.50 | 2.25 |
| LX104 | Brideshead Revisited–Evelyn Waugh | .75 | 1.50 | 2.25 |
| LX105 | Moby Dick–Herman Mellville | .75 | 1.50 | 2.25 A |
| LX106 | Crime and Punishment–Fyodor Dostoyevsky | .75 | 1.50 | 2.25 |
| LX107 | How to Draw and Paint–Henry Gasser | .75 | 1.50 | 2.25 NF |
| LX108 | Jude the Obscure–Thomas Hardy | .75 | 1.50 | 2.25 |
| LX109 | The Titan–Theodore Dreiser | .75 | 1.50 | 2.25 |
| LX110 | Six Centuries of Great Poetry–eds. Albert Erskine & Robert Penn Warren | .75 | 1.50 | 2.25 |
| LX111 | Bulfinch's Mythology–Thomas Bulfinch | .75 | 1.50 | 2.25 |
| LX112 | Ballet: A New Guide to the Liveliest Art–Walter Terry | .75 | 1.50 | 2.25 NF |
| LX113 | Abraham Lincoln: The Prairie Years–Carl Sandburg | .75 | 1.50 | 2.25 B |
| LX114 | Abraham Lincoln: The War Years, 1861–1864–Carl Sandburg | .75 | 1.50 | 2.25 B |
| LX115 | Abraham Lincoln: The War Years, 1864–1865–Carl Sandburg | .75 | 1.50 | 2.25 B |
| LX116 | Famous American Plays of the 20's–ed. Kenneth MacGowan | .75 | 1.50 | 2.25 |
| LX117 | Famous American Plays of the 30s–ed. Harold Clurman | .75 | 1.50 | 2.25 |
| LX118 | Sister Carrie–Theodore Dreiser | .75 | 1.50 | 2.25 |
| LX119 | Famous American Plays of the 40s–ed. Henry Hewes | .75 | 1.50 | 2.25 |
| LX120 | How to Draw the Human Figure–John R. Grabach | .75 | 1.50 | 2.25 NF |
| LY101 | An American Tragedy–Theodore Dreiser | .75 | 1.50 | 2.25 |

| | | V/Good | Fine | N/Mint |
|---|---|---|---|---|

DELL LAUREL EDITIONS, *continued*

| | | V/Good | Fine | N/Mint |
|---|---|---|---|---|
| LY102 | Modern American Painting and Sculpture–Samuel Hunter | .75 | 1.50 | 2.25 NF |
| LY111 | Seven Pillars of Wisdom–T.E. Lawrence; 1962; movie tie-in | 2.00 | 4.00 | 6.00 |

## DELL M-SERIES
### Dell Publishing Company, Inc.

| | | | | |
|---|---|---|---|---|
| M101 | The Complete Book of Plastic Model Kits–Advisory Board, Aurora Plastics Corporation; 1961 | 1.50 | 3.00 | 4.50 NF |
| M102 | Secrets of Successful Fishing–Henry Shakespeare; 1962; some copies have title page sticker noting this as TV tie-in | 1.25 | 2.50 | 3.75 NF |

## DELL MYSTERY NOVELS
### Dell Publishing Company, Inc.
**Digest Size**

| | | | | |
|---|---|---|---|---|
| 1 | Includes Brett Halliday, William Campbell Gault, Bruno Fischer; 1955 | 3.00 | 6.00 | 9.00 M |

## DELL SPECIAL STUDENT EDITIONS
### Dell Publishing Company, Inc.

| | | | | |
|---|---|---|---|---|
| nn | The American Heritage Reader–ed. Stephen Becker; 1958 | .75 | 1.50 | 2.25 NF |
| nn | Great American Short Stories–eds. Wallace and Mary Stegner; 1959 | .75 | 1.50 | 2.25 |
| nn | Mark Twain–ed. Edmund Fuller; 1959 | .75 | 1.50 | 2.25 |
| nn | Six Great Modern Short Novels–1961 | .75 | 1.50 | 2.25 |
| nn | The World in Space–Alexander Marshack; 1960 | .75 | 1.50 | 2.25 NF |
| nn | The Yellow Room–Mary Roberts Rinehart; 1956 | .75 | 1.50 | 2.25 M |

## DELL 10-CENT BOOKS
### Dell Publishing Company, Inc.

| | | | | |
|---|---|---|---|---|
| 1 | Trumpets West–Luke Short; 1951 | 4.00 | 8.00 | 12.00 W |
| 2 | Rain–W.S. Maugham | 4.00 | 8.00 | 12.00 R |
| 3 | Night Bus–Samuel H. Adams | 4.00 | 8.00 | 12.00 R |
| 4 | Locked Doors–Mary Roberts Rinehart | 4.00 | 8.00 | 12.00 M |
| 5 | Bride from Broadway–Faith Baldwin | 4.00 | 8.00 | 12.00 R |
| 6 | The Wedding Journey–Walter D. Edmonds | 3.00 | 6.00 | 9.00 R |
| 7 | Deadly Is the Diamond–Mignon G. Eberhart | 4.00 | 8.00 | 12.00 M |
| 8 | Journey for Life–Pearl S. Buck | 4.00 | 8.00 | 12.00 |
| 9 | Strangers in Love–Vina Delmar | 4.00 | 8.00 | 12.00 R |
| 10 | Trees Die at the Top–Edna Ferber | 3.00 | 6.00 | 9.00 |
| 11 | Marihuana–William Irish | 37.50 | 75.00 | 112.50 M |
| 12 | The Longhorn Legion–Norman A. Fox; 1st ed. 1951 | 4.00 | 8.00 | 12.00 W |
| 13 | Sun, Sea and Sand–John P. Marquand | 4.00 | 8.00 | 12.00 |
| 14 | The Name Is Mary–Fannie Hurst | 4.00 | 8.00 | 12.00 R |
| 15 | A Taste for Cognac–Brett Halliday | 6.00 | 12.00 | 18.00 M |
| 16 | The Beachcomber–W.S. Maugham | 4.00 | 8.00 | 12.00 |
| 17 | Remembering Laughter–Wallace Stegner | 3.00 | 6.00 | 9.00 |
| 18 | Free Woman–Katharine Brush | 4.00 | 8.00 | 12.00 R |
| 19 | Death Walks in Marble Halls–Lawrence Blochman; 1st ed. 1951 | 5.00 | 10.00 | 15.00 M |
| 20 | Broken Arrow Range–Thomas W. Blackburn; 1st ed. 1951 | 4.00 | 8.00 | 12.00 W |
| 21 | Door to Death–Rex Stout | 7.50 | 15.00 | 22.50 M |
| 22 | Alibi for Isabel–Mary Roberts Rinehart | 4.00 | 8.00 | 12.00 M |
| 23 | The Lamp of God–Ellery Queen | 7.50 | 15.00 | 22.50 M |
| 24 | Pal Joey–John O'Hara | 3.50 | 7.00 | 10.50 |
| 25 | South of Cancer–John Hersey | 4.00 | 8.00 | 12.00 |

*Dell 10¢ 21, Dell 10¢ 24, Dell 10¢ 30.*

| | | V/Good | Fine | N/Mint |
|---|---|---|---|---|
| 26 | You'll Never See Me Again–William Irish; 1st ed. 1951 | 25.00 | 50.00 | 75.00 M |
| 27 | Thief Is an Ugly Word–Paul Gallico | 5.00 | 10.00 | 15.00 |
| 28 | Beauty Marks the Spot–Kelley Roos | 5.00 | 10.00 | 15.00 M |
| 29 | Delilah of the Back Stairs–Geoffrey Household | 5.00 | 10.00 | 15.00 |
| 30 | Wife vs. Secretary–Faith Baldwin | 5.00 | 10.00 | 15.00 R |
| 31 | Chinese Nightmare–Hugh Pentecost; 1st ed. 1951 | 7.50 | 15.00 | 22.50 M |
| 32 | The Murderer Who Wanted More–Baynard Kendrick | 6.00 | 12.00 | 18.00 M |
| 33 | The Case of the Dancing Sandwiches–Fredric Brown; 1st ed. 1951 | 37.50 | 75.00 | 112.50 M |
| 34 | Better Off Dead–Helen McCloy; 1st ed. 1951 | 5.00 | 10.00 | 15.00 M |
| 35 | Superstition Farm–Perry Stowe | 7.50 | 15.00 | 22.50 |
| 36 | Universe–Robert Heinlein; 1st ed. 1951 | 20.00 | 40.00 | 60.00 SF |

## DELL TOLD IN PICTURES
### Dell Publishing Company, Inc.
**Digest Size, All Comic Book Style**

| | | | | |
|---|---|---|---|---|
| 1 | Twice Loved; 1950 | 13.50 | 27.00 | 40.50 R |
| 2 | Four Frightened Women–George Harmon Coxe; 1950 | 15.00 | 30.00 | 45.00 M |

## (DELL UNNUMBERED)
### Dell Publishing Company, Inc.
**Some Digest Size**

| | | | | |
|---|---|---|---|---|
| nn | Blondie and Dagwood in Footlight Folly–Chic Young; 1947 | 25.00 | 50.00 | 75.00 H |
| nn | Dick Tracy and the Woo-Woo Sisters–Chester Gould; 1947. Note: Actually written by Albert Stoffel | 30.00 | 60.00 | 90.00 M |
| nn | Hopalong Cassidy–Clarence E. Mulford; nd; movie tie-in; digest size | 10.00 | 20.00 | 30.00 W |

*Dell 10¢ 33, Dell Told in Pictures 2, Dell unnumbered.*

| | V/Good | Fine | N/Mint |
|---|---|---|---|

(DELL UNNUMBERED), *continued*

| | | V/Good | Fine | N/Mint |
|---|---|---|---|---|
| nn | Jungle Belles–animal photos with gag captions | 30.00 | 60.00 | 90.00 |
| nn | Gable's Secret Marriage–1951 | 10.00 | 20.00 | 30.00 NF |

## DELL X-SERIES
### Dell Publishing Company

| | | V/Good | Fine | N/Mint |
|---|---|---|---|---|
| X1 | The James Beard Cookbook–James A. Beard & Isabel E. Callvert; 1st ed. 1959 | 5.00 | 10.00 | 15.00 NF |
| X5 | Chautauqua–Day Keene and Dwight Vincent; 1961 | 2.00 | 4.00 | 6.00 |
| X6 | Trouble in the Flesh–Max Wylie; c-Abbett | 1.25 | 2.50 | 3.75 |
| X12 | A Decade of Fantasy and Science Fiction–ed. Robert P. Mills; 1962; c-Powers | 1.50 | 3.00 | 4.50 SF |
| X15 | The White Nile–Alan Moorehead; 1962 | 1.50 | 3.00 | 4.50 NF |

## (DEMOCRATIC NATIONAL COMMITTEE)
### Democratic National Committee

| | | V/Good | Fine | N/Mint |
|---|---|---|---|---|
| 886 | How to Win in 1952: The Facts About the Democratic Road to Prosperity, Peace and Freedom–1952 | 1.00 | 2.00 | 3.00 NF |

## DERBY BOOKS
### Derby Publishing Company
#### (Canadian)

| | | V/Good | Fine | N/Mint | |
|---|---|---|---|---|---|
| 1 | Profane–Ralph Carter | 2.00 | 4.00 | 6.00 | E |
| 2 | Sinner Take All–William Arthur | 2.00 | 4.00 | 6.00 | E |
| 3 | Passion or Kingdom–Claude Anet; 1949; aka Idyll's End | 2.00 | 4.00 | 6.00 | E |
| 4 | Burning Desire–Perry Lindsay | 2.00 | 4.00 | 6.00 | E |
| 6 | The Long Night–Joe Lederer | 2.00 | 4.00 | 6.00 | E |
| 7 | Men to Burn–William Arthur; 1950 | 2.00 | 4.00 | 6.00 | E |
| 8 | Bedroom for Three–Charles Thornton | 2.00 | 4.00 | 6.00 | E |
| 9 | The Body Betrays–Wayne Way | 2.00 | 4.00 | 6.00 | E |
| 10 | Lush Lady–Gail Jordan | 2.00 | 4.00 | 6.00 | E |
| 11 | Highway Jane–Gordon Semple | 2.00 | 4.00 | 6.00 | E |
| 12 | Borrowed Husband–Florenz Branch | 2.00 | 4.00 | 6.00 | E |

## DETECTIVE NOVEL CLASSIC
### Hillman Periodicals/Novel Selections, Inc.
#### Digest Size

| | | V/Good | Fine | N/Mint | |
|---|---|---|---|---|---|
| nn | Murder in the Bookshop–Caroline Wells | 3.50 | 7.00 | 10.50 | M |
| 2 | The Pedigreed Murder Case–J.S. Fletcher | 2.50 | 5.00 | 7.50 | M |
| 3 | Death by Remote Control–Emmett Hogarth | 3.00 | 6.00 | 9.00 | M |
| 4 | The Case Is Closed–Patricia Wentworth | 2.50 | 5.00 | 7.50 | M |
| 5 | The Radio Studio Murder–Caroline Wells | 2.50 | 5.00 | 7.50 | M |
| 6 | The Scarecrow Murders–Frederic Arnold Kummer | 2.50 | 5.00 | 7.50 | M |
| 7 | The Case of the Rusted Room–John Donavan | 2.50 | 5.00 | 7.50 | M |
| 8 | Murder Will Out–Jeanette Covert Nolan | 2.50 | 5.00 | 7.50 | M |
| 9 | Hong-Kong Airbase Murders–Van Wyck Mason | 2.50 | 5.00 | 7.50 | M |
| 10 | The Clue of the Twisted Face–Frederic Arnold Kummer | 2.50 | 5.00 | 7.50 | M |

*Derby 7, Detective Novel Classic (n/n), Detective Novel Classic 9.*

| | | V/Good | Fine | N/Mint | |
|---|---|---|---|---|---|
| 11 | The Bathtub Murder Case–E.R. Punshon | 2.50 | 5.00 | 7.50 | M |
| 12 | The Blue Santo Murder Mystery–Margaret Armstrong | 2.50 | 5.00 | 7.50 | M |
| 13 | Design for Murder–Percival Wilde | 2.50 | 5.00 | 7.50 | M |
| 14 | Murder in the Morning–Anthony Wynnes | 2.50 | 5.00 | 7.50 | M |
| 15 | The Strange Death of Manny Square–A.B. Cunningham | 2.50 | 5.00 | 7.50 | M |
| 16 | Death of a Greek–John Brandon | 2.50 | 5.00 | 7.50 | M |
| 17 | Murder on Stilts–Gregory Dean | 2.50 | 5.00 | 7.50 | M |
| 18 | The Penguin Pool Murder–Stuart Palmer | 3.00 | 6.00 | 9.00 | M |
| 19 | The Case of the Headless Corpse–Dennis Allan | 2.50 | 5.00 | 7.50 | M |
| 20 | Death at "the Bottoms"–A.B. Cunningham | 2.50 | 5.00 | 7.50 | M |
| 21 | Tickets for Death–Brett Halliday | 2.50 | 5.00 | 7.50 | M |
| 22 | Murder for a Wanton–Whitman Chambers | 2.50 | 5.00 | 7.50 | M |
| 23 | Murder in the Mews–Helen Reilly | 2.50 | 5.00 | 7.50 | M |
| 24 | Little Hercules–Francis Wallace | 2.50 | 5.00 | 7.50 | M |
| 25 | The Bancock Murder Case–A.B. Cunningham | 2.50 | 5.00 | 7.50 | M |
| 26 | The Uncomplaining Corpses–Brett Halliday | 2.50 | 5.00 | 7.50 | M |
| 27 | Steps to Murder–Robert Portner Koehler | 2.50 | 5.00 | 7.50 | M |
| 28 | Dead Men Leave No Fingerprints–Whitman Chambers | 2.50 | 5.00 | 7.50 | M |
| 29 | Death over Hollywood–Charles Saxby & Louis Molnar | 2.50 | 5.00 | 7.50 | M |
| 30 | The Affair at the Boat Landing–A.B. Cunningham | 2.50 | 5.00 | 7.50 | M |
| 31 | Bodies Are Where You Find Them–Brett Halliday | 2.50 | 5.00 | 7.50 | M |
| 32 | The Eight of Swords–John Dickson Carr | 3.00 | 6.00 | 9.00 | M |
| 33 | Murder by Latitude–Rufus King | 2.50 | 5.00 | 7.50 | M |
| 34 | Exit Screaming–Christopher Hale | 2.50 | 5.00 | 7.50 | M |
| 35 | Death Is Like That–John Spain | 2.50 | 5.00 | 7.50 | M |
| 36 | Death and Bitters–Kit Christian | 2.50 | 5.00 | 7.50 | M |
| 37 | The Great Yant Mystery–A.B. Cunningham | 2.50 | 5.00 | 7.50 | M |
| 38 | A Murderer in This House–Rufus King; aka Somewhere in This House | 2.50 | 5.00 | 7.50 | M |
| 39 | Dead of Winter–Christopher Hale | 2.50 | 5.00 | 7.50 | M |
| 40 | The 4 False Weapons–John Dickson Carr | 3.00 | 6.00 | 9.00 | M |
| 41 | The Gull Cove Murders–Eli Colter | 2.50 | 5.00 | 7.50 | M |
| 42 | The Cane-Patch Mystery–A.B. Cunningham | 2.50 | 5.00 | 7.50 | M |
| 43 | The Cat Wears a Noose–D.B. Olsen | 2.50 | 5.00 | 7.50 | M |
| 44 | The Evil Star–John Spain | 2.50 | 5.00 | 7.50 | M |
| 45 | Down among the Dead Men–Stewart Sterling | 2.50 | 5.00 | 7.50 | M |
| 46 | Death Visits the Apple Hole–A.B. Cunningham | 2.50 | 5.00 | 7.50 | M |
| 47 | Blood on Nassau's Moon–Walbridge McCully | 2.50 | 5.00 | 7.50 | M |
| 48 | Murder Makes a Racket–M.V. Heberden | 2.50 | 5.00 | 7.50 | M |

DETECTIVE NOVEL CLASSIC, *continued*

| | | V/Good | Fine | N/Mint | |
|---|---|---|---|---|---|
| 49 | I Can't Die Here–Jeannette Covert Nolan | 2.50 | 5.00 | 7.50 | M |
| 50 | The Body Fell on Berlin–Richard Lakin | 2.50 | 5.00 | 7.50 | M |
| 51 | Rumor Hath It–Christopher Hale | 2.50 | 5.00 | 7.50 | M |
| 52 | Murder before Midnight–A.B. Cunningham | 2.50 | 5.00 | 7.50 | M |
| 53 | Doctors Beware!–Walbridge McCully | 2.50 | 5.00 | 7.50 | M |
| 54 | Neck in a Noose–E.X. Ferrars | 2.50 | 5.00 | 7.50 | M |

# DIAMOND LIBRARY
## The Diamond Library
### Digest Size

| | | | | | |
|---|---|---|---|---|---|
| nn | Murder by Mandate–Elston & Beam; 1945 | 5.00 | 10.00 | 15.00 | M |
| nn | Murder Goes Fishing–Theodore Pratt | 5.00 | 10.00 | 15.00 | M |

# DIVERSEY LOVE BOOK MONTHLY
## Diversey Publishing Corporation
### Digest Size

| | | | | | |
|---|---|---|---|---|---|
| 1 | Bedroom Eyes–Maurice De Kobra | 9.00 | 18.00 | 27.00 | E |
| 2 | One Night with Nancy–Wilson Collison; 1948. Note: Same cover as Novel Library No. 20 | 9.00 | 18.00 | 27.00 | E |

# DIVERSEY POPULAR NOVELS
## Diversey Periodicals, Inc.
### Digest Size

| | | | | | |
|---|---|---|---|---|---|
| 1 | Broadway Virgin–Lois Bull; 1949 | 9.00 | 18.00 | 27.00 | E |
| 2 | Naked on Roller Skates–Maxwell Bodenheim. Note: Same cover as Novel Library No. 46 | 15.00 | 30.00 | 45.00 | E |

# DIVERSEY PRIZE NOVELS
## Diversey Periodicals, Inc.
### Digest Size

| | | | | | |
|---|---|---|---|---|---|
| 3 | The Passions of Linda Lane–Frances Marion; 1949; aka Minnie Flynn | 7.50 | 15.00 | 22.50 | E |
| 4 | Fast Woman–Marty Holland | 7.50 | 15.00 | 22.50 | E |
| 5 | Love for Sale–John Wilstach; 1949; aka The Fate of Fay Delroy. Note: Same cover as comic Romantic Love No. 4 | 7.50 | 15.00 | 22.50 | E |
| 6 | The Amorous Interne–Edward Reltid. Note: Same cover as comic Realistic Romances No. 6 | 7.50 | 15.00 | 22.50 | E |

*Diversey Love 1, Diversey Prize 6, Domino Mysteries 2.*

# DIVERSEY ROMANCE NOVELS
## Diversey Publishing Corporation
### Digest Size

| | | | | | |
|---|---|---|---|---|---|
| 1 | Reform School Girl–Felice Swados; 1948; aka House of Fury. Note: Same cover as Reform School Girl comic book. *Prices can vary widely on this book.* | 112.50 | 225.00 | 337.50 | E |

# DOCKET SERIES
## Oceana Publications

| | | | | |
|---|---|---|---|---|
| 1 | The Holmes Reader–ed. Julius J. Marke; 1955 | 1.25 | 2.50 | 3.75 |
| 2 | The Freedom Reader–ed. Edwin S. Newman | 1.25 | 2.50 | 3.75 |
| 3 | The Marshall Reader–ed. Erwin C. Surrency | 1.25 | 2.50 | 3.75 |
| 4 | The Wilson Reader–ed. Frances Farmer; 1956 | 1.25 | 2.50 | 3.75 |
| 5 | The Daniel Webster Reader–ed. Bertha Rothe | 1.25 | 2.50 | 3.75 |
| 6 | The Medico-Legal Reader–ed. Samuel Polsky | 1.25 | 2.50 | 3.75 |
| 7 | The Brandeis Reader–ed. Ervin Pollack | 1.25 | 2.50 | 3.75 |
| 8 | The American Jurisprudence Reader–ed. T.A. Cowan | 1.25 | 2.50 | 3.75 |

# DOMINO BOOKS
## Lancer Books, Inc.

**Note: The two-digit prefix is a price code; the last three digits are the stock number. Earlier Domino Books were part of the Lancer series and are listed there.**

| | | | | | |
|---|---|---|---|---|---|
| 82100 | Girl after Girl–A.L. Roget; 1965 | .75 | 1.50 | 2.25 | E |
| 82101 | Their Aching Hungers–Sylvia Sharon; aka No Barriers | .75 | 1.50 | 2.25 | E |
| 82102 | Trouble in Skirts–Vicki Spain | .75 | 1.50 | 2.25 | E |
| 82103 | Naked in the Night–Rea Michaels; 1965 | .75 | 1.50 | 2.25 | E |
| 82104 | Playgirl for Hire–Sylvia Sharon; 1966 | .75 | 1.50 | 2.25 | E |
| 82105 | The Constant Urge–Donna Richards | .75 | 1.50 | 2.25 | E |
| 82106 | The Path They Choose–Cathy Jordan | .75 | 1.50 | 2.25 | E |
| 82107 | This Wild Desire–Orrie Hitt; aka The Passion Hunters | .75 | 1.50 | 2.25 | E |
| 82108 | The Hours of Rapture–Sheldon Lord | .75 | 1.50 | 2.25 | E |
| 82109 | The Bait of Her Body–Vicki Spain | .75 | 1.50 | 2.25 | E |
| 82110 | 200 Miles to Sin–Craig Frome | .75 | 1.50 | 2.25 | E |
| 82111 | The Women He Had–Lisa Fanchon | .75 | 1.50 | 2.25 | E |
| 82112 | The Strangers Kiss–Eve Scott | .75 | 1.50 | 2.25 | E |
| 82113 | Sin and Sin Again–Dale Greggsen | .75 | 1.50 | 2.25 | E |
| 82114 | Lust Couples–Sheldon Lord | .75 | 1.50 | 2.25 | E |
| 84700 | Circle of Sin–Leslie Behan; 1965 | .75 | 1.50 | 2.25 | E |
| 84701 | Backdrop for Passion–Linda Whitmore; 1966 | .75 | 1.50 | 2.25 | E |
| 84702 | The Life She Wanted–Linda Whitmore | .75 | 1.50 | 2.25 | E |
| 84703 | Lust Man–Walt Lewis; 1966 | .75 | 1.50 | 2.25 | E |

# DOMINO MYSTERIES
## Duchess Printing and Publishing Co., Ltd.
### Digest Size

| | | | | | |
|---|---|---|---|---|---|
| 1 | The "Q" Squad–Gerald Verner; 1944 | 4.00 | 8.00 | 12.00 | M |
| 2 | Gentleman of Crime–Arthur Gask | 3.50 | 7.00 | 10.50 | M |

# DORENE
## Dorene Publishing Co., Inc.
**Digest Size**

| | | V/Good | Fine | N/Mint | |
|---|---|---|---|---|---|
| 1 | 30 Tales of Romance and Adventure–ed. Arnold Shaw; 1st ed. 1945 | 2.00 | 4.00 | 6.00 | |

# DOUBLE ACTION DETECTIVE
## Close-Up, Inc.
**Digest Size**

| 1 | Run, Corpse, Run–Guy Pember-Hiller | 7.50 | 15.00 | 22.50 | M |
|---|---|---|---|---|---|
| 2 | Hot Bullets for Love–Gentry Nyland; 1943; aka Mr. South Burned His Mouth. Note: Same cover as Big Green Detective Novel No. 2 and Superior Mystery Novel Unnumbered | 7.50 | 15.00 | 22.50 | M |
| 3 | Jealousy Pulls the Trigger–M.E. Corne; 1943; aka A Magnet for Murder. Note: Same cover as Big Green Detective Novel No. 3 | 7.50 | 15.00 | 22.50 | M |

# DOUBLE-ACTION POCKETBOOK
## Columbia Publications, Inc.
**Digest Size**

| nn | City of Glass–Noel Loomis; 1955 | 5.00 | 10.00 | 15.00 | SF |
|---|---|---|---|---|---|

# (DOUBLEDAY)
## Doubleday and Company, Inc.

| nn | The Farmer Takes a Hand–Marquis Childs; orig. 1952 | 1.00 | 2.00 | 3.00 | NF |
|---|---|---|---|---|---|
| nn | The Caine Mutiny–Herman Wouk; 1954; movie and theatrical tie-in | 3.00 | 6.00 | 9.00 | |
| nn | Worldwide Travel Regulations Made Easy–Richard Joseph & Muriel Richter; 1954 | .75 | 1.50 | 2.25 | NF |
| nn | 2001 Household Hints and Dollar Stretchers–Michael Gore; 1957 | .50 | 1.00 | 1.50 | NF |

# (DOUBLEDAY DORAN)
## Doubleday, Doran and Company, Inc.
**Digest Size**

| nn | Come Wind, Come Weather–Daphne Du Maurier; 1941 | 2.00 | 4.00 | 6.00 | |
|---|---|---|---|---|---|

# (DOUGLAS)
## Douglas Publishing, Inc.

| nn | Today's Business Market–John Garris; 1954 | 2.00 | 4.00 | 6.00 | NF |
|---|---|---|---|---|---|

# EAGLE BOOKS
## Eagle Books, Inc./New American Library

| nn(1) | Dear Sir–Juliet Lowell; 1943 | 2.50 | 5.00 | 7.50 | H |
|---|---|---|---|---|---|
| nn(2) | Kitty–Rosamond Marshall; 1945 | 1.50 | 3.00 | 4.50 | E |
| E3 | Duchess Hotspur–Rosamond Marshall; 1947 | 1.50 | 3.00 | 4.50 | E |

# ECSTASY NOVEL MAGAZINE/NOVEL
## Falcon Books, Inc./Publisher's Productions, Inc/Astro Publishing Co.
**Digest Size**

| nn(1) | A Body to Own–Trudy Hamilton; Vol. 1, No. 1 (Nov. 1949) | 6.00 | 12.00 | 18.00 | E |
|---|---|---|---|---|---|
| nn(2) | Paula Has a Price–Perry Lindsay; Vol. 1, No. 2 (Jan. 1949). Note: Error–actually Jan. 1950 | 6.00 | 12.00 | 18.00 | E |
| nn(3) | Harlot in Her Heart–Norman Bligh; Vol. 1, No. 3 (March 1950); c-Rodewald | 6.00 | 12.00 | 18.00 | E |
| nn(4) | (May 1950) | 6.00 | 12.00 | 18.00 | E |
| nn(5) | Intimate Confessions of an Artist's Model–Norman Bligh (July 1950) | 6.00 | 12.00 | 18.00 | E |
| nn(6) | (Sept. 1950) | 6.00 | 12.00 | 18.00 | E |
| nn(7) | Confessions of a Dime-a-Dance Queen–Doug Duperrault (Nov. 1950); c-Gross | 6.00 | 12.00 | 18.00 | E |
| nn(8) | Virgin or Harlot?–Peggy Gaddis (Jan. 1951) | 6.00 | 12.00 | 18.00 | E |
| nn(9) | Bed-Time Angel–Norman Bligh (March 1951) | 6.00 | 12.00 | 18.00 | E |
| 10 | Never Say "No!"–Luther Gordon | 6.00 | 12.00 | 18.00 | E |
| 11 | Free and Easy–Luther Gordon; aka After Passion; 1951 | 6.00 | 12.00 | 18.00 | E |
| 12 | Web of Sin–Anthony Scott; aka Virgin's Holiday | 6.00 | 12.00 | 18.00 | E |
| 14 | Doris–Broadway Virgin–Elizabeth Deane | 6.00 | 12.00 | 18.00 | E |
| 15 | Wanton by Night–James Clayford | 6.00 | 12.00 | 18.00 | E |
| 16 | They Call Her "Easy"–Gwen Lyons; 1951. Note: Same cover as Beacon B232 | 6.00 | 12.00 | 18.00 | E |
| 17 | Come Night, Come Desire–David Wade (Norman Daniels) | 6.00 | 12.00 | 18.00 | E |
| nn | The Private Life of a Street Girl–James Clayford; c-Gross | 6.00 | 12.00 | 18.00 | E |

# (EDELL)
## The Edell Company
**Digest Size**

| nn | The Case of the Deadly Drops–Gerald Benedict | 3.00 | 6.00 | 9.00 | M |
|---|---|---|---|---|---|

# EERIE SERIES
## Eerie Publishing Co./Spotlight Publishers
**Digest Size**

| 1 | The Case of the Curious Heel–Ken Crossen; nd | 5.00 | 10.00 | 15.00 | M |
|---|---|---|---|---|---|
| 2 | Murder in Mocking Valley–Will Crowell | 5.00 | 10.00 | 15.00 | M |
| 3 | The Corpse Wore No Shoes–Donald Thompson | 5.00 | 10.00 | 15.00 | M |
| 4 | Satan Comes Across–Bennett Barlay; 1945 | 5.00 | 10.00 | 15.00 | M |
| 5 | Murder in the Radio Department–Alfred Eichler | 5.00 | 10.00 | 15.00 | M |
| 6 | The Pleasure Primer–ed. anon. | 4.00 | 8.00 | 12.00 | |
| 7 | A Spy in the Room–Denison Clift | 5.00 | 10.00 | 15.00 | M |
| 8 | Homicide Johnny–Stephen Gould | 4.00 | 8.00 | 12.00 | M |
| 9 | Haunted Harbor–Dayle Douglas; 1945 | 5.00 | 10.00 | 15.00 | M |
| 10 | Adventures of the Great Crimebusters–ed. anon.; 1st ed. 1945; anthology | 4.00 | 8.00 | 12.00 | M |

| | | V/Good | Fine | N/Mint |
|---|---|---|---|---|

## (ENTERPRISE SPORTS)
### Enterprise Sports Publications

| nn | Horse Sense Catches Fish!–Johnny Dieckman; 1957 | .50 | 1.00 | 1.50 S |
|---|---|---|---|---|

## ESSEX HOUSE ORIGINAL
### Essex House

| 0101 | Blue Movie–Michael Perkins; orig. 1968 | 7.50 | 15.00 | 22.50 X |
|---|---|---|---|---|
| 0102 | The Agency–David Meltzer; orig. 1968 | 9.00 | 18.00 | 27.00 SF |
| 0103 | Binding with Briars–Paul V. Dallas; orig. 1968 | 7.50 | 15.00 | 22.50 X |
| 0104 | The Agent–David Meltzer; orig. 1968 | 9.00 | 18.00 | 27.00 SF |
| 0105 | Abducted–Michael MacPherson; orig. 1968 | 7.50 | 15.00 | 22.50 X |
| 0106 | Happiness Bastard–Kirby Doyle; orig. 1968 | 7.50 | 15.00 | 22.50 X |
| 0107 | How Many Blocks in the Pile?–David Meltzer; orig. 1968 | 9.00 | 18.00 | 27.00 SF |
| 0108 | The Image of the Beast–Philip Jose Farmer; orig. 1968 | 50.00 | 100.00 | 150.00 SF |
| 0109 | Evil Companions–Michael Perkins; orig. 1968 | 9.00 | 18.00 | 27.00 SF |
| 0110 | Coupled–Gil Porter | 7.50 | 15.00 | 22.50 X |
| 0111 | Orf–David Meltzer; orig. 1968 | 7.50 | 15.00 | 22.50 |
| 0112 | Season of the Witch–Hank Stine; orig. 1968 | 11.00 | 22.00 | 33.00 SF |
| 0113 | Ravished–Richard E. Geis; orig. 1968 | 7.50 | 15.00 | 22.50 X |
| 0114 | Queen of Heat–Michael Perkins; orig. 1968 | 7.50 | 15.00 | 22.50 X |
| 0115 | Notes of a Dirty Old Man–Charles Bukowski; orig. 1969 | 10.00 | 20.00 | 30.00 X |
| 0116 | The Martyr–David Meltzer; orig. 1969 | 7.50 | 15.00 | 22.50 X |
| 0117 | Lovely–David Meltzer; orig. 1969 | 9.00 | 18.00 | 27.00 SF |
| 0118 | The Tour–Michael Perkins; orig. 1969 | 7.50 | 15.00 | 22.50 X |
| 0119 | The Bitter Seed–Henry Toledano; orig. 1969 | 7.50 | 15.00 | 22.50 X |
| 0120 | Mindblower–Charles McNaughton, Jr; orig. 1969 | 7.50 | 15.00 | 22.50 X |
| 0121 | A Feast Unknown–Philip Jose Farmer; orig. 1969 | 50.00 | 100.00 | 150.00 SF |
| 0122 | Healer–David Meltzer; orig. 1969 | 9.00 | 18.00 | 27.00 SF |
| 0123 | Whacking Off–Michael Perkins; orig. 1969 | 7.50 | 15.00 | 22.50 X |
| 0124 | Biker–Jane Gallion; orig. 1969 | 9.00 | 18.00 | 27.00 SF |
| 0125 | Terminus–Michael Perkins; orig. 1969 | 9.00 | 18.00 | 27.00 SF |
| 0126 | Tender Buns–P.N. Dedeaux | 7.50 | 15.00 | 22.50 X |
| 0127 | Over Easy–Alan S. Marlowe; orig. 1969 | 7.50 | 15.00 | 22.50 X |
| 0128 | Stoned–Jane Gallion; orig. 1969 | 7.50 | 15.00 | 22.50 X |
| 0129 | Out–David Meltzer; orig. 1969 | 9.00 | 18.00 | 27.00 SF |
| 0130 | Trans–Jerry Anderson; orig. 1969 | 7.50 | 15.00 | 22.50 X |
| 0131 | Roach–Gil Lamont; orig. 1969 | 7.50 | 15.00 | 22.50 X |
| 0132 | Estelle–Michael Perkins; orig. 1969 | 7.50 | 15.00 | 22.50 X |
| 0133 | The Geek–Alice Louise Ramirez; orig. 1969 | 7.50 | 15.00 | 22.50 X |
| 0134 | Glue Factory–David Meltzer; orig. 1969 | 9.00 | 18.00 | 27.00 SF |
| 0135 | The Nothing Things–P.N. Dedeaux; orig. 1969 | 7.50 | 15.00 | 22.50 X |
| 0136 | Raw Meat–Richard E. Geis; orig. 1969 | 9.00 | 18.00 | 27.00 SF |
| 0137 | A Sort of Justice–Henry Toledano; orig. 1969 | 7.50 | 15.00 | 22.50 X |
| 0138 | Get It On–Gary Bradbrook; orig. 1969 | 7.50 | 15.00 | 22.50 X |
| 0139 | Blown–Philip Jose Farmer; orig. 1969 | 57.50 | 115.00 | 172.50 SF |
| 0140 | Down Here–Michael Perkins; orig. 1970 | 7.50 | 15.00 | 22.50 X |
| 0141 | Thrill City–Hank Stine; orig. 1969 | 7.50 | 15.00 | 22.50 X |
| 0142 | Gropie–Barry Luck; orig. 1970 | 7.50 | 15.00 | 22.50 X |

## ETON BOOKS
### Eton Books, Inc.

| ET51 | Sex Habits of American Women–Fritz Wittels, MD | 2.00 | 4.00 | 6.00 NF |
|---|---|---|---|---|
| 101 | United States Book of Baby & Child Care; 1951 | 2.00 | 4.00 | 6.00 NF |

| | | V/Good | Fine | N/Mint |
|---|---|---|---|---|
| 102 | Sex Habits of American Women–Fritz Wittels, MD | 2.00 | 4.00 | 6.00 NF |
| 103 | The Hygiene of Marriage–Millard Spencer Everett | 2.00 | 4.00 | 6.00 NF |
| ET104 | Control Blood Pressure–Herman Pomeranz, MD | 2.00 | 4.00 | 6.00 NF |
| ET105 | How to Understand Your Dreams–Wilhelm Stekel | 2.00 | 4.00 | 6.00 NF |
| ET106 | The Show of Violence–Fredric Wertham | 4.00 | 8.00 | 12.00 NF |
| ET107 | Authentic Librettos of the Grand Opera | 2.00 | 4.00 | 6.00 NF |
| ET108 | This Is Russia Un-Censored!–Edmund Stevens | 2.00 | 4.00 | 6.00 NF |
| E109 | Self-Mastery through Psycho-Analysis–William J. Fielding; 1952 | 2.00 | 4.00 | 6.00 NF |
| E110 | I Killed Stalin–Sterling Noel | 3.00 | 6.00 | 9.00 SF |
| E111 | Sin in Their Blood–Ed Lacy; orig. 1952 | 2.50 | 5.00 | 7.50 M |
| E112 | Kiss My Fist!–James Hadley Chase | 4.00 | 8.00 | 12.00 M |
| E113 | The Renegade Hills–Allan K. Echols; orig. 1952 | 3.00 | 6.00 | 9.00 W |
| E114 | Give Me Your Love–Jerome Weidman; orig. 1952 | 2.50 | 5.00 | 7.50 E |
| E115 | I'll Bring Her Back–Peter Cheyney; aka Dark Bahama | 2.50 | 5.00 | 7.50 |
| E116 | The Marijuana Mob–James Hadley Chase | 15.00 | 30.00 | 45.00 M |
| E117 | Invitation to Dishonor–Eric Arthur | 2.50 | 5.00 | 7.50 E |
| E118 | Gun-Play in Killer Canyon–Tevis Miller | 3.00 | 6.00 | 9.00 W |
| E119 | I Killed Stalin–Sterling Noel; illus. in Parade of Pleasure | 4.50 | 9.00 | 13.50 SF |
| E120 | Mark It with a Stone–George Victor Martin | 2.50 | 5.00 | 7.50 E |
| E121 | Queer Patterns–Lilyan Brock | 3.00 | 6.00 | 9.00 E |
| E122 | Paris Escort–Daniel Harper; orig. 1953 | 2.00 | 4.00 | 6.00 E |
| E123 | Strip for Violence–Ed Lacy; orig. 1953 | 2.50 | 5.00 | 7.50 M |
| E124 | Tuck's Girl–Marcel Wallenstein; orig. 1953 | 2.00 | 4.00 | 6.00 |
| E125 | Gunfighter–Paul Craig | 2.50 | 5.00 | 7.50 W |
| E126 | May not exist | | | |
| E127 | Stir Up the Dust–William Colt MacDonald; orig. 1953 | 2.50 | 5.00 | 7.50 W |
| E128 | Stagecoach to Hellfire Pass–Paul Evan Lehman | 2.00 | 4.00 | 6.00 W |
| E129 | Wit from Overseas–Roy Hoopes, Jr | 2.00 | 4.00 | 6.00 |
| E130 | May not exist | | | |
| E131 | Vengeance Valley–Allan K. Echols | 2.00 | 4.00 | 6.00 W |
| E132 | Hide-out–Larry Holden | 2.50 | 5.00 | 7.50 M |

## (EUGENICS)
### Eugenics Publishing Co., Inc.

| 100 | Married Love–Dr. Marie C. Stopes | .75 | 1.50 | 2.25 NF |
|---|---|---|---|---|
| K101 | The Torch of Life, a Key to Sex Harmony–Frederick M. Rossiter, MD; 1952. Note: Two cover variants seen | .75 | 1.50 | 2.25 NF |
| K102 | The Sex Life of the Single, the Engaged and the Married–Maurice Chideckel | .75 | 1.50 | 2.25 |
| K103 | Medical Sex Dictionary–William J. Robinson | .75 | 1.50 | 2.25 |

Eton 101, Eton E118, Eton E123.

# EUROPA BOOKS
## Comet Publications

**Note: Some have fold-out covers.**

| | | V/Good | Fine | N/Mint | |
|---|---|---|---|---|---|
| nn | Stripped for Murder–Mark Sade; 1st ed. 1963. Note: Author given as Roger Blake inside book | 3.00 | 6.00 | 9.00 | M |
| 801 | Red Light–W.W. Sanger | 3.00 | 6.00 | 9.00 | X |
| 804 | Sisters of Evil and Lust–X Miles | 3.00 | 6.00 | 9.00 | X |
| 1101 | Berlin Bed–Fritz Jantzen; 1963; fold-out cover | 5.00 | 10.00 | 15.00 | X |
| 1102 | Sin on the Continent–Art Romer; fold-out cover | 5.00 | 10.00 | 15.00 | X |
| 1103 | Sin Safari–H.T. Lord; fold-out cover | 5.00 | 10.00 | 15.00 | X |
| 1104 | Satan's Daughters–Jack Leech; fold-out cover | 5.00 | 10.00 | 15.00 | X |
| 1105 | Sexual Interlude–Frederick Dessiers; fold-out cover | 5.00 | 10.00 | 15.00 | X |
| 1106 | Sex after Seven–Mark Sade; 1963; fold-out cover | 5.00 | 10.00 | 15.00 | M |

# EXOTIC NOVEL MAGAZINE/NOVEL
## Falcon Books, Inc./Publisher's Productions, Inc./Astro Publishing Co.

### Digest Size

| | | V/Good | Fine | N/Mint | |
|---|---|---|---|---|---|
| nn(1) | Pay for My Kiss!–Luther Gordon; Vol. 1, No. 1 (April 1949); c-Rodewald | 6.00 | 12.00 | 18.00 | E |
| nn(2) | Any Man's Girl–Luther Gordon; Vol. 1, No. 2 (June 1949); c-Rodewald | 6.00 | 12.00 | 18.00 | E |
| nn(3) | Divorce Bait!–James Clayford; Vol. 1, No. 3 (Aug. 1949) | 6.00 | 12.00 | 18.00 | E |
| nn(4) | Her First Sin!–Jack Woodford; Vol. 1, No. 4 (Oct. 1949) | 6.00 | 12.00 | 18.00 | E |
| nn(5) | Buy My Love!–Perry Lindsay; Vol. 1, No. 5 (Dec. 1949); c-Rodewald | 6.00 | 12.00 | 18.00 | E |
| nn(6) | Passion's Slave–Gene Harvey; Vol. 1, No. 6 (Feb. 1950); c-Gross | 6.00 | 12.00 | 18.00 | E |
| nn(7) | (April 1950) | 6.00 | 12.00 | 18.00 | E |
| nn(8) | Three Men and a Mistress–Florence Stonebraker (June 1950) | 6.00 | 12.00 | 18.00 | E |
| nn(9) | (Aug. 1950) | 6.00 | 12.00 | 18.00 | E |
| nn(10) | Thrill Girl–Gene Harvey (Oct. 1950); c-Gross | 6.00 | 12.00 | 18.00 | E |
| nn(11) | Men Call Her "Tramp"–Joan Sherman (Dec. 1950). Note: Same cover as Phantom Books 502 | 6.00 | 12.00 | 18.00 | E |
| nn(12) | Bodies on Fire–Joan Sherman (Feb. 1951) | 6.00 | 12.00 | 18.00 | E |
| 14 | Tonight for Sure!–James Clayford; aka Strange Bedmates; c-Gross | 6.00 | 12.00 | 18.00 | E |
| 15 | Man Crazy–James Clayford | 6.00 | 12.00 | 18.00 | E |
| 16 | Bad as the Rest–Tom Stone | 6.00 | 12.00 | 18.00 | E |
| 17 | Ten Toes Up–Anthony Scott; 1951 | 6.00 | 12.00 | 18.00 | E |
| 18 | Give Me Ecstasy–Mark Reed (Norman Daniels) | 6.00 | 12.00 | 18.00 | E |
| 19 | Fever Hot–Jon Balmer | 6.00 | 12.00 | 18.00 | E |
| 20 | Lovers Don't Sleep–Laura Hale; 1951 | 6.00 | 12.00 | 18.00 | E |
| nn | Once There Was a Virgin–Norman Bligh | 6.00 | 12.00 | 18.00 | E |
| nn | Suzy Meets a Man–Joan Sherman (Peggy Gaddis) | 6.00 | 12.00 | 18.00 | E |

# FABIAN BOOKS
## Fabian Books Publications

| | | V/Good | Fine | N/Mint | |
|---|---|---|---|---|---|
| Z102 | Satan's Harvest–Sanford Aday; 1956 | 1.00 | 2.00 | 3.00 | X |
| Z103 | Sex Gauntlet to Murder–Mark Shane | 1.00 | 2.00 | 3.00 | X |
| Z107 | Incest for Rene–Kip Madigan | 1.00 | 2.00 | 3.00 | X |
| Z109 | A Road Divided–Reese Hayes | 1.00 | 2.00 | 3.00 | X |
| Z112 | The Black Night–Betty Short | 1.00 | 2.00 | 3.00 | X |
| Z113 | My Bed Has Echoes–Sydney Omarr; 1957 | 1.00 | 2.00 | 3.00 | X |
| Z114 | Stairways to Sin–Kip Madigan | 1.00 | 2.00 | 3.00 | X |

| | | V/Good | Fine | N/Mint | |
|---|---|---|---|---|---|
| Z115 | Long December–Reese Hayes | 1.00 | 2.00 | 3.00 | X |
| Z116 | The Rambling Maids–Betty Short | 1.00 | 2.00 | 3.00 | X |
| Z117 | Dark Quarters–Stella Hampton | 1.00 | 2.00 | 3.00 | X |
| Z118 | Tainted Wife–Willi Peters; 1957 | 1.00 | 2.00 | 3.00 | X |
| Z119 | Violent Surrender–Cherri Southern | 1.00 | 2.00 | 3.00 | X |
| Z120 | Taxi Dancers–Eve Linkletter | 1.00 | 2.00 | 3.00 | X |
| Z121 | Push-over–Lora Sela | 1.00 | 2.00 | 3.00 | X |
| Z122 | High Pillow–Betty Short; 1958 | 1.00 | 2.00 | 3.00 | X |
| Z123 | Beach Maverick–Floyd Haynes | 1.00 | 2.00 | 3.00 | X |
| Z124 | The Gay One–Eve Linkletter | 1.00 | 2.00 | 3.00 | X |
| Z125 | Man Is a Sexual Being–W. de Ortega Maxey | 1.00 | 2.00 | 3.00 | X |
| Z126 | Nor Fears of Hell–William Bennett | 1.00 | 2.00 | 3.00 | X |
| Z127 | Imposed Rebellion–James Williams | 1.00 | 2.00 | 3.00 | X |
| Z128 | Our Flesh Was Cheap–Eve Linkletter; 1959 | 1.00 | 2.00 | 3.00 | X |
| Z129 | One Violent Year–R. Brandon | 1.00 | 2.00 | 3.00 | X |
| Z130 | Tomorrow's Light–Dorothy Mencer | 1.00 | 2.00 | 3.00 | X |
| Z131 | Passionate Lovie–Dolores Dee | 1.00 | 2.00 | 3.00 | X |
| Z132 | Naked Return–G. McIntosh | 1.00 | 2.00 | 3.00 | X |
| Z133 | Rose of Sharon–L. Bradley | 1.00 | 2.00 | 3.00 | X |
| Z135 | Never to Belong–James Williams; 1960 | 1.00 | 2.00 | 3.00 | X |
| Z136 | The Third Bedroom–Brenda Baker | 1.00 | 2.00 | 3.00 | X |
| Z138 | Return to Vista–John Foster | 1.00 | 2.00 | 3.00 | X |
| Z139 | The Tainted Rosary–Mary S. Gooch | 1.00 | 2.00 | 3.00 | X |
| Z140 | Twice a Fool–Bunny Strand | 1.00 | 2.00 | 3.00 | X |
| Z141 | Beyond the Realm–Marie Turni | 1.00 | 2.00 | 3.00 | X |
| Z142 | Age of Insolence–Don Rowell; 1961 | 1.00 | 2.00 | 3.00 | X |
| Z143 | Emotional Jungle–Ann Freeman | 1.00 | 2.00 | 3.00 | X |
| Z144 | Cherita–Ann Freeman | 1.00 | 2.00 | 3.00 | X |
| Z145 | The Violent and the Fair–James Beely | 1.00 | 2.00 | 3.00 | X |
| Z146 | B-Girl Decoy–Eve Linkletter | 1.00 | 2.00 | 3.00 | X |
| Z147 | Dark Holiday–Ernest Dammann | 1.00 | 2.00 | 3.00 | X |
| Z148 | The Barefoot Blonde–Jay Vincent; 1961 | 1.00 | 2.00 | 3.00 | X |
| Z149 | Fancy House Lady–Derrick Fairman | 1.00 | 2.00 | 3.00 | X |
| Z150 | Clouded Passion–Arthur A. Howe | 1.00 | 2.00 | 3.00 | X |
| Z151 | Sex King–Roger Blake; 1962 | 1.00 | 2.00 | 3.00 | X |
| Z152 | High Beat–Arthur A. Howe | 1.00 | 2.00 | 3.00 | X |
| Z153 | Too Late to Cry–Jennie Joseph | 1.00 | 2.00 | 3.00 | X |
| Z154 | Circle of Lust–Jannet Anderson | 1.00 | 2.00 | 3.00 | X |
| Z155 | Girl in the Middle–Roger Blake; 1962 | 1.00 | 2.00 | 3.00 | X |
| Z156 | Wayward Mother–Von Hofman | 1.00 | 2.00 | 3.00 | X |
| Z157 | Sex Queen–Roger Blake; 1962 | 1.00 | 2.00 | 3.00 | X |
| Z158 | Rape of Eden–Adam Coulter | 1.00 | 2.00 | 3.00 | X |
| Z159 | The Last Retreat–Glenn Langdon | 1.00 | 2.00 | 3.00 | X |

# FABIAN FAVORITES
## Fabian Books Ltd.

| | | V/Good | Fine | N/Mint | |
|---|---|---|---|---|---|
| Z160 | Scarlet Sisters–Joseph Devon | 1.00 | 2.00 | 3.00 | X |
| Z161 | Honey Baby–Rex Nevins; 1964 | 1.00 | 2.00 | 3.00 | X |
| Z162 | Red Light–Guy Vance | 1.00 | 2.00 | 3.00 | X |
| Z163 | Our Flesh Was Cheap–Eve Linkletter | 1.00 | 2.00 | 3.00 | X |
| Z164 | The Third Bedroom–Brenda Baker | 1.00 | 2.00 | 3.00 | X |
| Z165 | Her Unholy Flame–Geraldine Brian; 1967 | 1.00 | 2.00 | 3.00 | X |
| Z166 | Hotel Stenographer–Maria Flecha | 1.00 | 2.00 | 3.00 | X |

# FABIAN READER
## Fabian Books Ltd.

| | | V/Good | Fine | N/Mint | |
|---|---|---|---|---|---|
| Z1 | Decisive Years–Marsha Bates | 1.00 | 2.00 | 3.00 | X |
| Z2 | Emotional Jungle–Ann Freeman | 1.00 | 2.00 | 3.00 | X |
| Z3 | Cherita–Ann Freeman | 1.00 | 2.00 | 3.00 | X |
| Z4 | Nor Fears of Hell–William Bennett | 1.00 | 2.00 | 3.00 | X |
| Z5 | Imposed Rebellion–James Williams | 1.00 | 2.00 | 3.00 | X |
| Z6 | Satan's Harvest–Sanford Aday | 1.00 | 2.00 | 3.00 | X |
| Z7 | A Road Divided–Reese Hayes | 1.00 | 2.00 | 3.00 | X |
| Z8 | Rene–Kip Madigan | 1.00 | 2.00 | 3.00 | X |
| Z9 | The Rambling Maids–Betty Short | 1.00 | 2.00 | 3.00 | X |
| Z10 | Passionate Lovie–Dolores Dee | 1.00 | 2.00 | 3.00 | X |
| nn | Fabian Reader | 1.50 | 3.00 | 4.50 | X |
| | Too Late to Cry–Jennie Joseph; 1962 | | | | |
| | Return to Vista–John Foster | | | | |

|  |  | V/Good | Fine | N/Mint |  |
|---|---|---|---|---|---|

## FALCON BOOKS
### Falcon Books, Inc.
#### Digest Size

| 21 | Season for Sin–Anthony Scott | 6.00 | 12.00 | 18.00 | E |
|---|---|---|---|---|---|
| 22 | The Scarlet Bride–Mark Reed (Norman Daniels) | 6.00 | 12.00 | 18.00 | E |
| 23 | Mabel and Men!–George Bottari; orig. 1952 | 6.00 | 12.00 | 18.00 | E |
| 24 | Three for Passion–Hodge Evens | 6.00 | 12.00 | 18.00 | E |
| 25 | Case of the Cancelled Redhead–Hamlin Daly (E. Hoffman Price); orig. 1952 | 9.00 | 18.00 | 27.00 | M |
| 26 | Lay Down and Die–Mark Reed (Norman Daniels) | 6.00 | 12.00 | 18.00 | E |
| 27 | Lida Lynn–Daughter of Passion–Norma Dann (Norman Daniels) | 6.00 | 12.00 | 18.00 | E |
| 28 | Girls Out of Hell!–Joe Weiss | 9.00 | 18.00 | 27.00 | E |
| 29 | Mistress on a Deathbed!–Norman A. Daniels; orig. 1952 | 6.00 | 12.00 | 18.00 | M |
| 30 | Dagger of Flesh–Richard Prather | 9.00 | 18.00 | 27.00 | E |
| 31 | Slave Girl–Tom Roan | 7.50 | 15.00 | 22.50 | E |
| 32 | Sins of the Flesh–Mark Reed (Norman Daniels) | 7.50 | 15.00 | 22.50 | E |
| 33 | Yellow-Head!–Hodge Evans; orig. 1952 | 7.50 | 15.00 | 22.50 | E |
| 34 | Shack Girl–Norma Dann (Norman Daniels) | 7.50 | 15.00 | 22.50 | E |
| 35 | Raise the Devil–David Wade (Norman Daniels) | 6.00 | 12.00 | 18.00 | E |
| 36 | Junkie–Johnathan Craig; orig. 1952 | 10.00 | 20.00 | 30.00 | E |
| 37 | Woman Hunter–Laura Hale | 7.50 | 15.00 | 22.50 | E |
| 38 | Sweet Savage–Norma Dann (Norman Daniels) | 6.00 | 12.00 | 18.00 | E |
| 39 | Joy Street– | 6.00 | 12.00 | 18.00 | E |
| 40 | Whip-Hand!–Hodge Evens; orig. 1952 | 7.50 | 15.00 | 22.50 | E |
| 41 | The Evil Sleep!–Evan Hunter; orig. 1952. Note: Same cover as Beacon B233 | 6.00 | 12.00 | 18.00 | M |
| 42 | The Long Night–Bryce Walton | 6.00 | 12.00 | 18.00 | E |
| 43 | House of 1,000 Desires–Mark Reed (Norman Daniels); orig. 1953. Note: Same cover as Intimate No. 20, Beacon B181, and B307 | 9.00 | 18.00 | 27.00 | E |
| 44 | Honky Tonk Girl–Charles Beckman, Jr | 7.50 | 15.00 | 22.50 | E |

## FAMOUS MYSTERY SERIES
### Howard Publications
#### Digest Size (Canadian)

| 1 | Murder Takes a Honeymoon–Edith Fleming; 1940 | 3.50 | 7.00 | 10.50 | M |
|---|---|---|---|---|---|
| 2 | The Pay-off–Joe Barry | 3.00 | 6.00 | 9.00 | M |

## FAWCETT PUBLICATIONS, FAWCETT-GOLD MEDAL–see GOLD MEDAL

## FEDERAL
### Federal Publishing Company
#### (Canadian)

| 1 | Marjorie–Tex Lane; 1950 | 2.00 | 4.00 | 6.00 | E |
|---|---|---|---|---|---|
| 2 | Room Girl–Beth Brown; 1951 | 2.00 | 4.00 | 6.00 | E |
| 3 | Variety's the Life–Frank E. Kane | 2.00 | 4.00 | 6.00 | E |
| 4 | Jetsam Journey–Frank E. Kane; 1952 | 2.00 | 4.00 | 6.00 | E |

## FEINER
### J.P. Feiner
#### Digest Size

| nn | The Greatest Adventure Stories Ever Told–Arnold Shaw; 1945 | 1.50 | 3.00 | 4.50 | A |
|---|---|---|---|---|---|

*Falcon 33, Fiesta 6, Fighting Forces unnumbered.*

|  |  | V/Good | Fine | N/Mint |  |
|---|---|---|---|---|---|

## FEMACK PUBLICATIONS
### The Femack Company
#### Digest Size

| nn | He Died Laughing–Lawrence Lariar | 3.00 | 6.00 | 9.00 | M |
|---|---|---|---|---|---|

## FIESTA BOOKS
### Rio Publishing Corporation
#### Digest Size

| 1 | The Lady Was a Tramp–Nick Baroni | 3.00 | 6.00 | 9.00 | E |
|---|---|---|---|---|---|
| 2 | Ask for Therese–Evans Wall (Peggy Gaddis); orig. 1952 | 3.00 | 6.00 | 9.00 | E |
| 3 | Love Fetish–Evans Wall (Peggy Gaddis) | 3.00 | 6.00 | 9.00 | E |
| 5 | Television Tramp– | 3.00 | 6.00 | 9.00 | E |
| 6 | Unwanted Wife–Ben Smith | 3.00 | 6.00 | 9.00 | E |

## FIGHTING FORCES SERIES
### The Infantry Journal
#### Some Are Digest Size

**Note: Some Fighting Forces Series titles are also Penguin Specials and are listed under that imprint.**

| F14 | Report on the Army, 1939–1943–George C. Marshall | 1.25 | 2.50 | 3.75 | NF |
|---|---|---|---|---|---|
| nn | World War II–Roger W. Shugg & H.A. DeWeerd | 1.25 | 2.50 | 3.75 | NF |
| nn | Selected Speeches and Statements–George C. Marshall | 1.25 | 2.50 | 3.75 | NF |
| nn | Fishes and Shells of the Pacific World | 1.25 | 2.50 | 3.75 | NF |
| nn | Plant Life of the Pacific World–Merrill | 1.25 | 2.50 | 3.75 | NF |
| nn | Native Peoples of the Pacific World–Felix M. Keesing | 1.50 | 3.00 | 4.50 | NF |
| nn | Japan and the Japanese | 1.50 | 3.00 | 4.50 | NF |
| nn | Japan's Military Masters–Hillis Lory | 1.50 | 3.00 | 4.50 | NF |

*Famous Mystery 2, Federal 4, Femack (unlisted).*

| | | V/Good | Fine | N/Mint |
|---|---|---|---|---|

**FIGHTING FORCES SERIES,** *continued*

| | | V/Good | Fine | N/Mint |
|---|---|---|---|---|
| nn | Survival | 2.00 | 4.00 | 6.00 NF |
| nn | We Cannot Escape History–John Whitaker | 1.25 | 2.50 | 3.75 NF |
| nn | America's Navy in World War II–Gilbert Cant | 1.25 | 2.50 | 3.75 NF |
| nn | Abraham Lincoln and the Fifth Column–George Fort Milton; 1943 | 1.25 | 2.50 | 3.75 NF |
| nn | America in Arms–John McA. Palmer | 1.25 | 2.50 | 3.75 NF |
| nn | Animals of the Pacific World–Hill, Carter & Tate | 1.50 | 3.00 | 4.50 NF |
| nn | The Battle Is the Pay-off–Major Ingersoll | 1.25 | 2.50 | 3.75 NF |
| nn | Blitzkrieg: Armies on Wheels–S.L.A. Marshall | 1.25 | 2.50 | 3.75 NF |
| nn | Burma Surgeon–Gordon Seagrave | 1.25 | 2.50 | 3.75 NF |
| nn | The Capture of Attu | 1.25 | 2.50 | 3.75 NF |
| nn | Combat First Aid: How to Save Lives in Battle | 1.50 | 3.00 | 4.50 NF |
| nn | Conflict: The American Civil War–George Fort Milton | 1.25 | 2.50 | 3.75 NF |
| nn | Defense Against Chemical War | 3.00 | 6.00 | 9.00 NF |
| nn | Fear in Battle–John Dollard | 1.25 | 2.50 | 3.75 |
| nn | Freedom Speaks: Ideals of Democracy in Poetry and Prose | 1.25 | 2.50 | 3.75 |
| nn | Fundamentals of Electricity–Mott-Smith | 1.25 | 2.50 | 3.75 NF |
| nn | Fundamentals of Mathematics–Mott-Smith & Van de Water | 1.25 | 2.50 | 3.75 NF |
| nn | Gas Warfare–Alden H. Waitt | 2.50 | 5.00 | 7.50 NF |
| nn | The German Soldier: How He Is Trained | 1.50 | 3.00 | 4.50 NF |
| nn | Great Soldiers of the First World War–H.A. DeWeerd | 1.25 | 2.50 | 3.75 NF |
| nn | The Gun–C.S. Forester | 1.25 | 2.50 | 3.75 A |
| nn | Hitler's Second Army–Alfred Vagts | 1.25 | 2.50 | 3.75 NF |
| nn | How to Abandon Ship–Richards & Banigan | 1.50 | 3.00 | 4.50 NF |
| nn | How to Shoot the U.S. Army Rifle | 1.25 | 2.50 | 3.75 NF |
| nn | Island Victory: How Kwajalein Was Won | 1.25 | 2.50 | 3.75 NF |
| nn | The Jap Soldier: How He Is Trained | 1.50 | 3.00 | 4.50 NF |
| nn | Leadership for American Army Leaders–E.L. Munson | 1.25 | 2.50 | 3.75 NF |
| nn | The Living Thoughts of Clausewitz | 1.25 | 2.50 | 3.75 |
| nn | The Lost Battalion–Thomas M. Johnson & Fletcher Pratt; 1943 | 1.25 | 2.50 | 3.75 NF |
| nn | Machine Warfare–J.F.C. Fuller | 1.25 | 2.50 | 3.75 NF |
| nn | The Making of Modern China–Owen & Eleanor Lattimore | 1.25 | 2.50 | 3.75 NF |
| nn | The Nazi State–William Ebenstein | 1.25 | 2.50 | 3.75 NF |
| nn | Our Enemy Japan–Wilfrid Fleisher | 1.25 | 2.50 | 3.75 NF |
| nn | Reptiles of the Pacific World–A. Loveridge | 1.50 | 3.00 | 4.50 NF |
| nn | Patriot Battles, 1775–1782–A.C.M. Azoy | 1.25 | 2.50 | 3.75 NF |
| nn | Report on India–T.A. Raman | 1.25 | 2.50 | 3.75 NF |
| nn | Rifleman Dodd–C.S. Forester | 1.25 | 2.50 | 3.75 A |
| nn | Rifles and Machine Guns of the World's Armies–Johnson | 1.25 | 2.50 | 3.75 NF |
| nn | The Russian Army–Walter Kerr | 1.25 | 2.50 | 3.75 NF |
| nn | Scouting and Patrolling | 1.25 | 2.50 | 3.75 NF |
| nn | Sergeant Terry Bull: His Ideas on War and Fighting–Terry Bull | 1.25 | 2.50 | 3.75 NF |
| nn | Short History of the Army and Navy–Fletcher Pratt | 1.25 | 2.50 | 3.75 NF |
| nn | So You're Going Overseas–R.S. Barker | 1.25 | 2.50 | 3.75 NF |
| nn | The Story of West Point, 1802–1943–R.E. Dupuy | 1.25 | 2.50 | 3.75 NF |
| nn | Studies on War | 1.25 | 2.50 | 3.75 NF |
| nn | Tank-Fighter Team–R.M. Gerard | 1.25 | 2.50 | 3.75 NF |
| nn | Thesaurus of Humor | 1.25 | 2.50 | 3.75 H |
| nn | Weapons for the Future–Johnson & Haven | 2.00 | 4.00 | 6.00 NF |
| nn | What to Do Aboard the Transport. Note: Co-publication with Science Service | 1.25 | 2.50 | 3.75 NF |
| nn | Modern Battle: Campaigns of 1939–1941–P.W. Thompson | 1.25 | 2.50 | 3.75 NF |
| nn | New Ways of War–Tom Wintringham | 1.25 | 2.50 | 3.75 NF |
| nn | Warships at Work–T.A. Hardy | 1.25 | 2.50 | 3.75 NF |
| nn | Pipeline to Battle: Campaigns in Africa–Major Rainier | 1.25 | 2.50 | 3.75 NF |
| nn | Engineer Training Notebook | 1.25 | 2.50 | 3.75 NF |

| | | V/Good | Fine | N/Mint |
|---|---|---|---|---|
| nn | Company Duties: A Checklist | 1.25 | 2.50 | 3.75 NF |
| nn | Machine Gunner's Handbook–C.H. Coates | 1.25 | 2.50 | 3.75 NF |
| nn | Driver Training: Handbook for Instructors | 1.25 | 2.50 | 3.75 NF |
| nn | Keep 'Em Rolling: Handbook for Drivers | 1.25 | 2.50 | 3.75 NF |
| nn | You Must Be Fit | 1.25 | 2.50 | 3.75 |
| nn | Platoon Record Book | 1.25 | 2.50 | 3.75 NF |
| nn | Squad Record Book | 1.25 | 2.50 | 3.75 NF |
| nn | Our Armed Forces: A Complete Description | 1.25 | 2.50 | 3.75 NF |
| nn | Spanish Dictionary for the Soldier–Frank Henius | 1.25 | 2.50 | 3.75 NF |
| nn | French Dictionary for the Soldier–Frank Henius | 1.25 | 2.50 | 3.75 NF |
| nn | German Dictionary for the Soldier–Frank Henius | 1.25 | 2.50 | 3.75 NF |
| nn | Italian Dictionary for the Soldier–Frank Henius | 1.25 | 2.50 | 3.75 NF |
| nn | Italian Sentence Book for the Soldier–Frank Henius | 1.25 | 2.50 | 3.75 NF |
| nn | Insects of the Pacific World–C.H. Curran | 1.50 | 3.00 | 4.50 NF |
| nn | Solution in Asia–Owen Lattimore | 1.25 | 2.50 | 3.75 NF |
| nn | The War in Outline, 1939–1943 | 1.25 | 2.50 | 3.75 NF |
| nn | The Pacific World–ed. Fairfield Osborn; digest size | 1.50 | 3.00 | 4.50 NF |

# FIGHTING WESTERN NOVEL

## Novel Selections, Inc./Hillman

### Digest Size

| | | V/Good | Fine | N/Mint |
|---|---|---|---|---|
| 1 | The Cougar Kid–Johnston McCulley | 2.00 | 4.00 | 6.00 W |
| 2 | Under the Mesa Rim–Chandler Whipple | 2.00 | 4.00 | 6.00 W |
| 3 | Two-Gun Texan–Herbert Shappiro | 2.00 | 4.00 | 6.00 W |
| 4 | Rope Neckties–John Wilstach | 2.00 | 4.00 | 6.00 W |
| 5 | Coyote Hunter–Denver Bardwell | 2.00 | 4.00 | 6.00 W |
| 6 | Silver Spurs–Charles Alden Seltzer | 2.00 | 4.00 | 6.00 W |
| 7 | Stranger at Storm Range–Dan James | 2.00 | 4.00 | 6.00 W |
| 8 | South of the Pass–Johnston McCulley | 2.00 | 4.00 | 6.00 W |
| 9 | Coyote Song–Clem Colt | 2.00 | 4.00 | 6.00 W |
| 10 | Gunthunder on the Rio–Dan James | 2.00 | 4.00 | 6.00 W |
| 11 | Six-Gun Showdown–Tom West | 2.00 | 4.00 | 6.00 W |
| 12 | Ghost Bullet Range–Johnson McCulley | 2.00 | 4.00 | 6.00 W |
| 14 | Law of the Trail–J.E. Grinstead | 2.00 | 4.00 | 6.00 W |
| 15 | Kincaid of Red Butte–Leslie Ernenwein | 2.00 | 4.00 | 6.00 W |
| 16 | Trigger Trail–Roy Manning | 2.00 | 4.00 | 6.00 W |
| 17 | Quarter Horse–Gordon Young | 2.00 | 4.00 | 6.00 W |
| 18 | Vengeance Valley–Roy Manning | 2.00 | 4.00 | 6.00 W |
| 19 | Miracle Range–William K. Reilly | 2.00 | 4.00 | 6.00 W |
| 20 | Spectre Spread–Tom West | 2.00 | 4.00 | 6.00 W |
| 21 | Prairie Smoke–Will Ermine | 2.00 | 4.00 | 6.00 W |
| 22 | The Cougar of Canyon Caballo–Paul Evan Lehman | 2.00 | 4.00 | 6.00 W |
| 23 | The Bar D Boss–Ranger Lee | 2.00 | 4.00 | 6.00 W |
| 24 | Painted Post Roundup–Tom Dunn | 2.00 | 4.00 | 6.00 W |
| 25 | The Drifting Kid–Will Ermine | 2.00 | 4.00 | 6.00 W |
| 26 | Prairie Pinto–Lynn Westland | 2.00 | 4.00 | 6.00 W |
| 27 | Wolves of the Chaperral–Paul Evan Lehman | 2.00 | 4.00 | 6.00 W |
| 28 | Prentiss of the Box 8–Lynn Westland | 2.00 | 4.00 | 6.00 W |
| 29 | Rustler's Odds–Glen Hanley | 2.00 | 4.00 | 6.00 W |
| 30 | Tall in the Saddle–Gordon Young | 2.00 | 4.00 | 6.00 W |
| 31 | Powdersmoke Pay-off–Tom West | 2.00 | 4.00 | 6.00 W |
| 32 | The Lost Range–Frank C. Robertson | 2.00 | 4.00 | 6.00 W |
| 33 | Black Creek Buckaroo–Anson Piper | 2.00 | 4.00 | 6.00 W |
| 34 | Rustlers of Table Butte–Ernie Phillips | 2.00 | 4.00 | 6.00 W |
| 35 | The Rio Kid–Tom Roan | 2.00 | 4.00 | 6.00 W |
| 36 | The Cowboy from Alamos–C.H. Snow | 2.00 | 4.00 | 6.00 W |
| 37 | Phantom Rustlers–Francis W. Hilton | 2.00 | 4.00 | 6.00 W |
| 38 | Wild Horse Shorty–Nelson Nye | 2.00 | 4.00 | 6.00 W |
| 39 | Brand of the Open Hand–Frank C. Robertson | 2.00 | 4.00 | 6.00 W |
| 40 | Return to the Range–Lynn Westland | 2.00 | 4.00 | 6.00 W |
| 41 | Blood of Kings–Nelson C. Nye | 2.00 | 4.00 | 6.00 W |
| 42 | Gun Lord of Silver River–Tom Roan | 2.00 | 4.00 | 6.00 W |
| 43 | Senor Avalanche–Johnston McCulley | 2.00 | 4.00 | 6.00 W |

# FINGERPRINT MYSTERY
## Readers Detective Book Service
### Digest Size

| | | V/Good | Fine | N/Mint | |
|---|---|---|---|---|---|
| nn | Murder Rings Twice–Helen Joan Hultman; aka Murder on Route 40 | 2.50 | 5.00 | 7.50 | M |
| nn | The Man Without a Head–Joseph Bowen | 2.50 | 5.00 | 7.50 | M |

# FIVE STAR MYSTERY
## Green Publishing Company
### Digest Size

| | | V/Good | Fine | N/Mint | |
|---|---|---|---|---|---|
| 1 | The Dress Circle Murders–Peter Yates; orig. 1945 | 3.00 | 6.00 | 9.00 | M |
| 2 | Murder out of Mind–Kendell Foster Crossen; orig. 1945 | 3.00 | 6.00 | 9.00 | M |
| 3 | You'll Die Laughing–Bruce Elliott; orig. 1945 | 3.00 | 6.00 | 9.00 | M |
| 4 | Death Comes to Dinner–Peter Yates; orig. 1945 | 3.00 | 6.00 | 9.00 | M |
| 5 | The Invisible Man Murders–Richard Foster; orig. 1945 | 3.00 | 6.00 | 9.00 | M |
| 6 | Murder Seeks an Agent–Wenzell Brown; orig. 1945 | 3.00 | 6.00 | 9.00 | M |
| 7 | Death in the Hands of Talent–Peter Yates | 2.50 | 5.00 | 7.50 | M |
| 13 | The Laughing Buddha Murders–Richard Foster (Kendell Foster Crossen) | 2.50 | 5.00 | 7.50 | M |
| 15 | The Case of the Phantom Fingerprints–Kendell Foster Crossen | 2.50 | 5.00 | 7.50 | M |
| 16 | Curtain Call for Murder–Peter Yates | 2.50 | 5.00 | 7.50 | M |
| 21 | The Dress Circle Murders–Peter Yates | 2.50 | 5.00 | 7.50 | M |
| 22 | Murder Out of Mind–Kendell Foster Crossen | 2.50 | 5.00 | 7.50 | M |
| 26 | You'll Die Laughing–Bruce Elliott | 2.50 | 5.00 | 7.50 | M |
| 28 | Death Comes to Dinner–Peter Yates | 2.50 | 5.00 | 7.50 | M |
| 35 | Curtain Call for Murder–Peter Yates | 2.50 | 5.00 | 7.50 | M |
| 36 | The Invisible Man Murders–Richard Foster (Kendell Foster Crossen) | 2.50 | 5.00 | 7.50 | M |
| 37 | Death in the Hands of Talent–Peter Yates; orig. 1945 | 2.50 | 5.00 | 7.50 | M |
| 38 | Murder Seeks an Agent–Wenzell Brown | 2.50 | 5.00 | 7.50 | M |
| 41 | Death's Long Shadow–Katharine Wolffe; orig. 1946 | 2.50 | 5.00 | 7.50 | M |
| 42 | Death Wears a Green Hat–Will Creed; orig. 1946 | 3.00 | 6.00 | 9.00 | M |
| 43 | Crime Is of the Essence–Joe Csida; orig. 1946 | 2.50 | 5.00 | 7.50 | M |
| 44 | The Corpse Is Indignant–Douglas Stapleton & Helen A. Carey; orig. 1946 | 2.50 | 5.00 | 7.50 | M |
| 45 | Murder in the Rough–Leslie Allen (Horace Brown); orig. 1946 | 3.00 | 6.00 | 9.00 | M |
| 46 | Kill to Fit–Bruno Fischer | 2.50 | 5.00 | 7.50 | M |
| 47 | Death Comes Grinning–Will Creed | 3.00 | 6.00 | 9.00 | M |

*Five Star Mystery 22, Galaxy Novel 29, Galaxy Novel 35.*

# FOTONOVELS
## Fotonovel Publications

**Note: All are movie tie-in's with 200 + color photographs. All books are numbered 89752, 089752, or 08972.**

| | V/Good | Fine | N/Mint | |
|---|---|---|---|---|
| Americathon 1998; orig. 8/79 | 1.50 | 3.00 | 4.50 | SF |
| Best of Rocky and The Complete Rocky II; orig. 6/79 | 1.50 | 3.00 | 4.50 | |
| Buck Rogers in the 25th Century; orig. 7/79 | 2.00 | 4.00 | 6.00 | SF |
| The Champ; orig. 3/79 | 1.50 | 3.00 | 4.50 | |
| Grease; orig. 6/78 | 1.50 | 3.00 | 4.50 | |
| Hair; orig. 3/79 | 1.50 | 3.00 | 4.50 | |
| Heaven Can Wait; orig. 7/78 | 2.00 | 4.00 | 6.00 | F |
| Ice Castles; orig. 12/78 | 1.50 | 3.00 | 4.50 | |
| Invasion of the Body Snatchers; orig. 1/79 | 2.50 | 5.00 | 7.50 | SF |
| Lord of the Rings; orig. 4/79 | 2.00 | 4.00 | 6.00 | F |
| Love at First Bite; orig. 3/79 | 2.00 | 4.00 | 6.00 | H |
| Nightwing; orig. 5/79 | 2.00 | 4.00 | 6.00 | HO |
| Revenge of the Pink Panther; orig. 5/79 | 1.50 | 3.00 | 4.50 | H |

# FRANCE BOOKS
## International Publishing

**Note: Some have fold-out covers.**

| | | V/Good | Fine | N/Mint | |
|---|---|---|---|---|---|
| F1 | Las Vegas Call Girl–Frank Meline; 1962; fold-out cover | 1.50 | 3.00 | 4.50 | X |
| F2 | Male Nympho–Duke Shannon | 1.00 | 2.00 | 3.00 | X |
| F3 | Ring-a-Ding Lover–Seth Ahriman | 1.00 | 2.00 | 3.00 | X |
| F4 | Time Out for Sex–Dirk Novak; fold-out cover | 1.50 | 3.00 | 4.50 | X |
| F5 | The Fare Sex, Life of a Las Vegas Cab Driver | 1.00 | 2.00 | 3.00 | X |
| F6 | The Violator–Bill Leslie; fold-out cover | 1.50 | 3.00 | 4.50 | X |
| F7 | Honeymoon Motel–Richard E. Geis; fold-out cover | 1.50 | 3.00 | 4.50 | X |
| F8 | Bedroom City–Richard E. Geis | 1.25 | 2.50 | 3.75 | X |
| F9 | Shook Up Sex–Tedd Black | 1.00 | 2.00 | 3.00 | X |
| F10 | Part Time Virgin–Bill Danger | 1.00 | 2.00 | 3.00 | X |
| F11 | Door to Door Rape!–Frank Melne; fold-out cover | 1.50 | 3.00 | 4.50 | X |
| F12 | Ding a Ling Broad–Duke Shannon | 1.00 | 2.00 | 3.00 | X |
| F13 | Broads Make the Odds–Steve Bartdorf | 1.00 | 2.00 | 3.00 | X |
| F14 | Lust Planet–Russ Olin | 2.00 | 4.00 | 6.00 | SF |
| F15 | Cleopatra's Blonde Sex Rival–Walt Vickery; fold-out cover | 1.50 | 3.00 | 4.50 | X |
| F16 | Carnal Women–John Rutherford; fold-out cover | 1.50 | 3.00 | 4.50 | X |
| F17 | Call Me Nympho–Peggy Swenson (Richard E. Geis); fold-out cover | 1.50 | 3.00 | 4.50 | X |
| F19 | Eros Laughed–Bart Meyers; fold-out cover | 1.50 | 3.00 | 4.50 | X |
| F20 | Desire!–T.J. Smith; fold-out cover | 1.50 | 3.00 | 4.50 | X |
| F21 | Silent Sex–Jim Harmon; 1962; fold-out cover | 1.50 | 3.00 | 4.50 | X |
| F22 | Sex Nut–Frank Richards; fold-out cover | 1.50 | 3.00 | 4.50 | X |
| F23 | Hot Load–Will Saxon; fold-out cover | 1.50 | 3.00 | 4.50 | X |
| F24 | Strange Harem–Jan Hudson (George H. Smith); fold-out cover | 1.50 | 3.00 | 4.50 | X |
| F25 | Sex Trap–Don Rico; fold-out cover | 1.50 | 3.00 | 4.50 | X |
| F26 | Golden Lust–Adam Coulter; fold-out cover | 1.50 | 3.00 | 4.50 | X |
| F27 | In the Nude for Love–Bill Danger; fold-out cover | 1.50 | 3.00 | 4.50 | X |
| F28 | Lion Lover–Gay Tom; fold-out cover | 1.50 | 3.00 | 4.50 | X |
| F29 | Jazz Me Baby–Karl Kelly; fold-out cover | 1.50 | 3.00 | 4.50 | X |
| F30 | Twist Session–Jim Harmon; fold-out cover | 1.50 | 3.00 | 4.50 | X |
| F31 | Carnival Sex–Gary Bolin; fold-out cover | 1.50 | 3.00 | 4.50 | X |
| F32 | Hollywood Lesbian–Donna Richards; fold-out cover | 1.50 | 3.00 | 4.50 | X |

| | V/Good | Fine | N/Mint | |
|---|---|---|---|---|
| **FRANCE BOOKS,** *continued* | | | | |
| F33 Orgy House–Frank Richards; fold-out cover | 1.50 | 3.00 | 4.50 | X |
| F34 Loverboy–anon.; fold-out cover | 1.50 | 3.00 | 4.50 | X |
| F35 Girlsville–Richard E. Geis; 1963; fold-out cover | 1.50 | 3.00 | 4.50 | X |
| F36 Female and Fatal–Kendall Hill; fold-out cover | 1.50 | 3.00 | 4.50 | X |
| F37 Prisoners of Lesbos–Donna Richards; fold-out cover | 1.50 | 3.00 | 4.50 | X |
| F38 Wanton Women–Will Saxon; fold-out cover | 1.50 | 3.00 | 4.50 | X |
| F39 My Foul Lady–Alan Roberts; fold-out cover | 1.50 | 3.00 | 4.50 | X |
| F40 Lesbian Torment–Bill Leslie; fold-out cover | 1.50 | 3.00 | 4.50 | X |
| F41 Half-way to Hell–Serg Ross; fold-out cover | 1.50 | 3.00 | 4.50 | X |
| F42 Big Mama–Adam Coulter; fold-out cover | 1.50 | 3.00 | 4.50 | X |
| F46 Bowling Bum–Gold | 1.00 | 2.00 | 3.00 | X |
| F47 Miss Brutal–Sol Tabor | 1.25 | 2.50 | 3.75 | M |
| F48 Dark Obsession–Gilliam | 1.00 | 2.00 | 3.00 | X |
| F49 Lesbos in Panama–Neil Egri; 1963 | 1.00 | 2.00 | 3.00 | X |
| F50 A Place Named Hell–M.J. Deer (George H. Smith & M.J. Deer); 1963 | 2.00 | 4.00 | 6.00 | SF |
| F54 Strange Fire–Neil Egri | 1.00 | 2.00 | 3.00 | X |
| F55 The Greeks Had a Sex for It–Novak | 1.00 | 2.00 | 3.00 | X |
| F56 Debauchee–Coulter | 1.00 | 2.00 | 3.00 | X |
| F57 Sins of Cheryl–Roger Blake | 1.00 | 2.00 | 3.00 | X |
| F58 Convict Lust– | 1.00 | 2.00 | 3.00 | X |
| F59 Sin Model–J.D. Ford; 1963 | 1.00 | 2.00 | 3.00 | X |
| F60 Hollywood Homo–Wagman | 1.00 | 2.00 | 3.00 | X |
| F61 Autosex–Michael E. Knerr; 1963 | 2.00 | 4.00 | 6.00 | SF |
| F62 Illicit Bed–MacDonald | 1.00 | 2.00 | 3.00 | X |
| F63 Terry–Dominic Plato | 1.00 | 2.00 | 3.00 | X |
| F64 Confessions of a Movie Star–Dominic Plato | 1.00 | 2.00 | 3.00 | X |
| F65 Sex in Nero's Rome–Victor Harris | 1.00 | 2.00 | 3.00 | X |
| F66 Flames of Desire–M.J. Deer (George H. Smith & M.J. Deer); 1963 | 2.00 | 4.00 | 6.00 | SF |
| F68 Vacation for Sex–anon. | 1.00 | 2.00 | 3.00 | X |

## FRANCE ELITE
### International Publishing

| | V/Good | Fine | N/Mint | |
|---|---|---|---|---|
| E1 ABC's of Sex–Jake Lee; 1962 | 1.00 | 2.00 | 3.00 | NF |
| E2 Sadism, Masochism–William Leslie | 1.00 | 2.00 | 3.00 | NF |
| E3 The Case for Sexual Freedom–René Guyon; 1963 | 1.00 | 2.00 | 3.00 | NF |
| E4 Resort Sport– | 1.00 | 2.00 | 3.00 | X |

## FREEWAY PRESS/VENUS FREEWAY PRESS
### Freeway Press

| | V/Good | Fine | N/Mint | |
|---|---|---|---|---|
| FP2001 Son of the Flying Tiger–Marshall Macao; 1973; c-Barry Smith | 1.50 | 3.00 | 4.50 | A |
| FP2002 Jailbirds in the Back Seat–Marcus Van Heller | 1.00 | 2.00 | 3.00 | E |
| FP2003 Soho Sheila–Sheila Foster | 1.00 | 2.00 | 3.00 | E |
| FP2004 Acid Temple Ball–Mary Sativa | 1.00 | 2.00 | 3.00 | E |
| FP2005 Sea of Thighs–Ray Kainen | 1.00 | 2.00 | 3.00 | E |
| FP2006 Frost–A Gay Thriller–Richard Amory | 1.00 | 2.00 | 3.00 | E |
| FP2007 Mama Liz Drinks Deep–Howard Rheingold | 1.00 | 2.00 | 3.00 | E |
| FP2008 Return of the Opium Wars–Marshall Macao; c-Barry Smith | 1.50 | 3.00 | 4.50 | A |
| FP2009 Mama Liz Tastes Flesh–Howard Rheingold | 1.00 | 2.00 | 3.00 | E |
| FP2010 Mayfair Mistress–Sheila Foster (Michael Bernet) | 1.00 | 2.00 | 3.00 | E |
| FP2011 Auburn–H.B. Randolph | 1.00 | 2.00 | 3.00 | E |
| FP2012 The Woman Thing–Harriet Daimler | 1.00 | 2.00 | 3.00 | E |
| FP2013 Innocence–Harriet Daimler | 1.00 | 2.00 | 3.00 | E |
| FP2014 Darling–Harriet Daimler | 1.00 | 2.00 | 3.00 | E |

| | V/Good | Fine | N/Mint | |
|---|---|---|---|---|
| FP2015 The Rape of Sun Lee Fong–Marshall Macao; 1973; c-Barry Smith | 1.50 | 3.00 | 4.50 | A |
| FP2016 Secret Sisterhood–Howard Rheingold | 1.00 | 2.00 | 3.00 | E |
| FP2017 Lay of the Land–Norman Singer | 1.00 | 2.00 | 3.00 | E |
| FP2018 Kid Stogie–Al Rosenzweig | 1.00 | 2.00 | 3.00 | E |
| FP2019 Neck of the Woods–Monroe C. Speer | 1.00 | 2.00 | 3.00 | |
| FP2020 Star–An Astrological Guide to Living in the Age of Aquarius–Alan C. Oken | 1.00 | 2.00 | 3.00 | NF |
| FP2021 The Office Workers' Manifesto–Lynn O'Connor, Pat Mialoca, Walter Russell | 1.00 | 2.00 | 3.00 | NF |
| FP2022 The Kak–Abdullah Conspiracy– Marshall Macao; 1973; c-Barry Smith | 1.50 | 3.00 | 4.50 | A |
| FP2023 Barbara–Frank Newman | 1.00 | 2.00 | 3.00 | E |
| FP2024 My Mother Taught Me–Tor Kung | 1.00 | 2.00 | 3.00 | E |
| FP2025 Big Woman–Mullin Garr (William David Boynton) | 1.00 | 2.00 | 3.00 | E |
| FP2026 The Land of Plenty–James Rusk, Jr | 1.00 | 2.00 | 3.00 | NF |
| FP2027 Lost Atlantis–James Bramwell | 1.00 | 2.00 | 3.00 | NF |
| FP2028 The Romance of Sorcery–Sax Rohmer | 1.25 | 2.50 | 3.75 | NF |
| FP2029 Red Plague in Bolivia–Marshall Macao; c-Barry Smith | 1.00 | 2.00 | 3.00 | A |
| FP2030 Mind Blower–Marco Vassi | 1.00 | 2.00 | 3.00 | |
| FP2031 The Gentle Degenerates–Marco Vassi | 1.00 | 2.00 | 3.00 | |
| FP2032 Willow Song–Richard Amory | 1.00 | 2.00 | 3.00 | |
| FP2033 1994: Jack Anderson Against Dr. Tek!–Howard Rheingold; 1974 | 1.00 | 2.00 | 3.00 | SF |
| FP2034 A Guide to the Golden Years–James Rusk, Jr | 1.00 | 2.00 | 3.00 | NF |
| FP2035 The Book of the Hand–Katharine St. Hill | 1.00 | 2.00 | 3.00 | NF |
| FP2036 True Ghost Stories–Cheiro (Louis Harmon) | 1.00 | 2.00 | 3.00 | NF |
| FP2037 New York Necromancy–Marshall Macao; 1974; c-Barry Smith | 1.00 | 2.00 | 3.00 | A |
| FP2038 House on the Borderland–William Hope Hodgson | 1.50 | 3.00 | 4.50 | HO |
| FP2039 The Texan–Victor Norwood | 1.00 | 2.00 | 3.00 | W |
| FP2040 Harpo Speaks– | 1.50 | 3.00 | 4.50 | B |
| FP2041 The Masked Invasion–Curtis Steele; Operator 5 No. 1 | 1.50 | 3.00 | 4.50 | A |
| FP2042 The Numbers of Life–Kevin Quinn Avery | 1.00 | 2.00 | 3.00 | NF |
| FP2043 Pyramid Power–Max Toth & Greg Nielsen | 1.00 | 2.00 | 3.00 | NF |
| FP2044 The Red Right Hand–Joel Townsley Rogers | 1.00 | 2.00 | 3.00 | M |
| FP2045 War of the Gurus–Howard Rheingold | 1.25 | 2.50 | 3.75 | SF |
| FP2046 Operator 5 No. 2: The Invisible Empire–Curtis Steele; 1974; Operator 5 No. 2 | 1.50 | 3.00 | 4.50 | A |
| FP2047 President Kissinger–Monroe Rosenthal & Donald Munson | 5.00 | 10.00 | 15.00 | F |
| FP2053 Alta in the Shadows–Honoria de Sackville | | | | |
| FP2055 Mark of the Vulture–Marshall Macao; 1974 | 1.50 | 3.00 | 4.50 | A |
| FP2056 The Yellow Scourge–Curtis Steele; Operator 5 No. 3 | 1.50 | 3.00 | 4.50 | A |
| FP2057 Lawman's Code–Victor Norwood | 1.00 | 2.00 | 3.00 | W |

## (FRIARS)
### Friars Publications

| | V/Good | Fine | N/Mint | |
|---|---|---|---|---|
| nn "So Help Me"–George Jessel; nd | .75 | 1.50 | 2.25 | B |
| nn You Too Can Make a Speech–George Jessel; nd | .75 | 1.50 | 2.25 | |

## GALAXY SCIENCE FICTION NOVELS
### Galaxy Publishing Corporation
#### 1–31 Are Digest Size

| | V/Good | Fine | N/Mint | |
|---|---|---|---|---|
| 1 Sinister Barrier–Eric Frank Russell | 2.00 | 4.00 | 6.00 | SF |
| 2 Legion of Space–Jack Williamson | 2.00 | 4.00 | 6.00 | SF |

*Gem 101, Gold Medal 101, Gold Medal 106.*

|  |  | V/Good | Fine | N/Mint |
|---|---|---|---|---|

GALAXY SCIENCE FICTION NOVELS, *continued*

| 3 | Prelude to Space–Arthur C. Clarke; 1st ed. 1951 | 2.50 | 5.00 | 7.50 SF |
| 4 | The Amphibians–S. Fowler Wright | 2.00 | 4.00 | 6.00 SF |
| 5 | The World Below–S. Fowler Wright | 2.00 | 4.00 | 6.00 SF |
| 6 | The Alien–Raymond F. Jones; 1st ed. 1951 | 2.00 | 4.00 | 6.00 SF |
| 7 | Empire–Clifford D. Simak; 1st ed. 1951 | 2.00 | 4.00 | 6.00 SF |
| 8 | Odd John–Olaf Stapledon | 2.00 | 4.00 | 6.00 SF |
| 9 | Four Sided Triangle–William F. Temple | 2.00 | 4.00 | 6.00 SF |
| 10 | Rat Race–Jay Franklin | 2.00 | 4.00 | 6.00 SF |
| 11 | City in the Sea–Wilson Tucker | 2.00 | 4.00 | 6.00 SF |
| 12 | The House of Many Worlds–Sam Merwin, Jr | 2.00 | 4.00 | 6.00 SF |
| 13 | Seeds of Life–John Taine | 2.00 | 4.00 | 6.00 SF |
| 14 | Pebble in the Sky–Isaac Asimov | 2.00 | 4.00 | 6.00 SF |
| 15 | Three Go Back–J. Leslie Mitchell | 2.00 | 4.00 | 6.00 SF |
| 16 | The Warriors of Day–James Blish; 1st ed. 1953 | 2.00 | 4.00 | 6.00 SF |
| 17 | Well of the Worlds–Lewis Padgett | 2.00 | 4.00 | 6.00 SF |
| 18 | City at World's End–Edmond Hamilton | 2.00 | 4.00 | 6.00 SF |
| 19 | Jack of Eagles–James Blish | 2.00 | 4.00 | 6.00 SF |
| 20 | The Black Galaxy–Murray Leinster | 2.00 | 4.00 | 6.00 SF |
| 21 | The Humanoids–Jack Williamson | 2.00 | 4.00 | 6.00 SF |
| 22 | Killer to Come–Sam Merwin, Jr | 2.00 | 4.00 | 6.00 SF |
| 23 | Murder in Space–David V. Reed | 2.00 | 4.00 | 6.00 SF |
| 24 | Lest Darkness Fall–L. Sprague de Camp | 2.50 | 5.00 | 7.50 SF |
| 25 | The Last Spaceship–Murray Leinster; 1955 | 2.50 | 5.00 | 7.50 SF |
| 26 | Chessboard Planet–Lewis Padgett (Henry Kuttner & C.L. Moore); aka The Fairy Chessman | 5.00 | 10.00 | 15.00 SF |
| 27 | Tarnished Utopia–Malcolm Jameson | 3.00 | 6.00 | 9.00 SF |
| 28 | Destiny Times Three–Fritz Leiber | 4.50 | 9.00 | 13.50 SF |
| 29 | Fear–L. Ron Hubbard | 12.50 | 25.00 | 37.50 SF |
| 30 | Double Jeopardy–Fletcher Pratt | 2.50 | 5.00 | 7.50 SF |
| 31 | Shambleau–C.L. Moore | 6.00 | 12.00 | 18.00 SF |
| 32 | Address: Centauri–F.L. Wallace; c-Wood | 2.50 | 5.00 | 7.50 SF |
| 33 | Mission of Gravity–Hal Clement; c-Wood | 2.50 | 5.00 | 7.50 SF |
| 34 | Twice in Time–Manly Wade Wellman; c-Wood | 2.50 | 5.00 | 7.50 SF |
| 35 | The Forever Machine–Mark Clifton & Frank Riley; c-Wood | 2.50 | 5.00 | 7.50 SF |

# GEM BOOKS
## Gem Books, Inc.
### Digest Size

| 101 | She Lived in Sin–Ralph Carter; 1952; aka The Sins of Donna Kenyon | 4.00 | 8.00 | 12.00 E |
| 102 | Shameful Love–Thomas Stone; aka Raging Passions | 4.00 | 8.00 | 12.00 E |

# GOLDEN WILLOW
## Golden Willow Press, Inc.
### Digest Size

| 51 | Rampage in the Rockies–Shoshone Green; 1945 | 2.50 | 5.00 | 7.50 W |
| 52 | So Much Blood–Bruno Fischer; 1946 | 3.00 | 6.00 | 9.00 M |
| 54 | Steel to the Sunset–Allan R. Bosworth | 2.50 | 5.00 | 7.50 W |
| 55 | Murder by Schedule–Julian Hinckley; 1946; aka The Letter in His Throat | 2.50 | 5.00 | 7.50 M |
| 56 | Its Love I'm After–F. Eberhard | 2.50 | 5.00 | 7.50 |

# GOLD MEDAL
## Fawcett Publications, Inc.

| nn(99) | The Best from True, the Man's Magazine; 1949 | 5.00 | 10.00 | 15.00 |

|  |  | V/Good | Fine | N/Mint |
|---|---|---|---|---|
| nn(100) | What Today's Woman Should Know about Marriage and Sex–ed. Today's Woman | 4.00 | 8.00 | 12.00 NF |
| 101 | We Are the Public Enemies–Alan Hynd; orig. 1950 | 4.00 | 8.00 | 12.00 NF |
| 102 | Man Story–anthology; 1st ed. 1950 | 2.50 | 5.00 | 7.50 A |
| 103 | The Persian Cat–John Flagg | 2.00 | 4.00 | 6.00 M |
| 104 | I'll Find You–Richard Himmel | 2.00 | 4.00 | 6.00 M |
| 105 | Nude in Mink–Sax Rohmer; orig. 1950 | 6.00 | 12.00 | 18.00 M |
| 106 | Stretch Dawson–W.R. Burnett | 4.50 | 9.00 | 13.50 W |
| 107 | The Flying Saucers Are Real–Donald Keyhoe | 1.50 | 3.00 | 4.50 UF |
| 108 | Devil May Care–Wade Miller | 2.00 | 4.00 | 6.00 M |
| 109 | The Awakening of Jenny–Lillian Colter | 1.50 | 3.00 | 4.50 E |
| 110 | Million Dollar Murder–Edward Ronns | 2.00 | 4.00 | 6.00 M |
| 111 | The Wild Horse–Les Savage, Jr; aka Black Horse Canyon | 2.50 | 5.00 | 7.50 W |
| 112 | Your Child and You–Sidonie Matsner Gruenberg (ed. Frances Ullman) | 2.00 | 4.00 | 6.00 NF |
| 113 | The Violent Ones–Howard Hunt | 2.00 | 4.00 | 6.00 M |
| 114 | No Business for a Lady–James Rubel | 2.00 | 4.00 | 6.00 M |
| 115 | Help Wanted–for Murder–William L. Rohde | 2.00 | 4.00 | 6.00 M |
| 116 | The Slaughtered Lovelies–Don Stanford | 2.50 | 5.00 | 7.50 M |
| 117 | State Department Murders–Edward Ronns | 2.00 | 4.00 | 6.00 M |
| 118 | The Goldfish Murders–Will Mitchell | 2.00 | 4.00 | 6.00 M |
| 119 | The Tormented–Theodore Pratt | 2.00 | 4.00 | 6.00 E |
| 120 | The Man Who Said No–Walt Grove | 2.00 | 4.00 | 6.00 |
| 121 | The Desperado–Clifton Adams | 2.00 | 4.00 | 6.00 W |
| 122 | One Wild Oat–MacKinlay Kantor | 2.00 | 4.00 | 6.00 E |
| 123 | House of Flesh–Bruno Fischer; orig. 1950 | 2.50 | 5.00 | 7.50 M |
| 124 | The Brass Cupcake–John D. MacDonald; orig. 1950 | 10.00 | 20.00 | 30.00 M |
| 125 | The Obsessed–Gertrude Schweitzer; 1950 | 1.50 | 3.00 | 4.50 |
| 126 | Dallas–Will F. Jenkins (Murray Leinster); orig. 1950; movie tie-in | 4.50 | 9.00 | 13.50 W |
| 127 | Case of the Vanishing Beauty–Richard S. Prather | 6.00 | 12.00 | 18.00 M |
| 128 | Three Secrets–Margaret Lee Runbeck; movie tie-in | 2.00 | 4.00 | 6.00 |
| 129 | Mansion of Evil–Joseph Millard; orig. 1950. Note: Comic book format | 30.00 | 60.00 | 90.00 M |

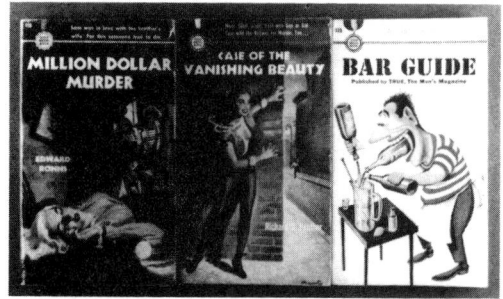

*Gold Medal 110, Gold Medal 127, Gold Medal 135.*

GOLD MEDAL, *continued*

| # | Title | V/Good | Fine | N/Mint | |
|---|---|---|---|---|---|
| 130 | A Man of Parts–Vivian Connell | 1.50 | 3.00 | 4.50 | |
| 131 | Guns at Broken Bow–William Heuman | 2.00 | 4.00 | 6.00 | W |
| 132 | Women's Barracks–Tereska Torres | 2.50 | 5.00 | 7.50 | E |
| 133 | Catspaw Ordeal–Edward Ronns | 1.50 | 3.00 | 4.50 | |
| 134 | Hell-bent for Danger–Walt Grove | 2.00 | 4.00 | 6.00 | W |
| 135 | Bar Guide–Virgil Partch & Ted Shane | 2.50 | 5.00 | 7.50 | H |
| 136 | Savage Bride–Cornell Woolrich; orig. 1951 | 6.00 | 12.00 | 18.00 | M |
| 137 | War Bonnet Pass–Logan Stewart | 2.00 | 4.00 | 6.00 | W |
| 138 | The Corpse That Walked–Octavus Roy Cohen; aka Masquerade in Miami | 2.00 | 4.00 | 6.00 | M |
| 139 | Stolen Woman–Wade Miller | 2.00 | 4.00 | 6.00 | E |
| 140 | Gunfighter's Return–Leslie Ernenwein | 2.00 | 4.00 | 6.00 | W |
| 141 | Hill Girl–Charles Williams; orig. 1951 | 3.00 | 6.00 | 9.00 | E |
| 142 | Jewel of the Java Sea–Dan Cushman | 2.00 | 4.00 | 6.00 | A |
| 143 | The Chinese Keyhole–Richard Himmel | 1.50 | 3.00 | 4.50 | M |
| 144 | Winchester Cut–Mark Sabin | 2.00 | 4.00 | 6.00 | W |
| 145 | High Red for Dead–William L. Rohde; orig. 1951 | 2.00 | 4.00 | 6.00 | M |
| 146 | Roll the Wagons–William Heuman | 2.00 | 4.00 | 6.00 | W |
| 147 | Bodies in Bedlam–Richard S. Prather | 2.50 | 5.00 | 7.50 | M |
| 148 | The Lady Kills–Bruno Fischer; orig. 1951 | 2.00 | 4.00 | 6.00 | E |
| 149 | Gunsmoke Reckoning–Joseph Chadwick | 2.00 | 4.00 | 6.00 | W |
| 150 | Come Murder Me–James Kieran; 1951 | 2.00 | 4.00 | 6.00 | M |
| 151 | Death and the Naked Lady–John Flagg | 2.00 | 4.00 | 6.00 | |
| 152 | The Killer–Wade Miller; orig. 1951 | 2.00 | 4.00 | 6.00 | M |
| 153 | Cocotte–Theodore Pratt | 2.00 | 4.00 | 6.00 | E |
| 154 | A Gun in His Hand–Victor Rosen | 2.00 | 4.00 | 6.00 | |
| 155 | The Apache–James Warner Bellah | 2.00 | 4.00 | 6.00 | W |
| 156 | The Texas Gun–Leslie Ernenwein | 2.00 | 4.00 | 6.00 | W |
| 157 | Westport Landing–Homer Hatten | 2.00 | 4.00 | 6.00 | |
| 158 | Naked Ebony–Dan Cushman | 2.00 | 4.00 | 6.00 | |
| 159 | Barren Land Murders–Luke Short | 2.50 | 5.00 | 7.50 | W |
| 160 | Catnips at Love and Marriage–Walter Chandoh & Rhar Dee | 5.00 | 10.00 | 15.00 | H |
| 161 | Son of the Flying Y–Will F. Jenkins (Murray Leinster); orig. 1951 | 2.50 | 5.00 | 7.50 | W |
| 162 | Bargain in Blood–Don Stanford; orig. 1951 | 2.00 | 4.00 | 6.00 | M |
| 163 | Big City Girl–Charles Williams; orig. 1951 | 3.50 | 7.00 | 10.50 | E |
| 164 | Murder for the Bride–John D. MacDonald; 1st ed. 1951 | 12.50 | 25.00 | 37.50 | M |
| 165 | Everybody Had a Gun–Richard S. Prather | 2.50 | 5.00 | 7.50 | M |
| 166 | I Can't Stop Running–Edward Ronns; orig. 1951 | 1.50 | 3.00 | 4.50 | M |
| 167 | The Judas Hour–Howard Hunt | 2.00 | 4.00 | 6.00 | M |
| 168 | A Noose for the Desperado–Clifton Adams | 2.00 | 4.00 | 6.00 | W |
| 169 | Satan Is a Woman–Gil Brewer | 2.50 | 5.00 | 7.50 | E |
| 170 | Death on a Ferris Wheel–Aylwin Lee Martin | 1.50 | 3.00 | 4.50 | M |
| 171 | I, Mobster–anon. | 2.00 | 4.00 | 6.00 | |
| 172 | Lost Lady–Octavus Roy Cohen | 2.00 | 4.00 | 6.00 | M |
| 173 | The Tiger's Wife–Wade Miller | 1.50 | 3.00 | 4.50 | |
| 174 | Rider from Nowhere–Joseph Chadwick | 2.00 | 4.00 | 6.00 | W |
| 175 | Gay Ghastly Holiday–Sebastian Blayne; 1951 | 2.00 | 4.00 | 6.00 | M |
| 176 | Crockett's Woman–Eric Hatch | 1.50 | 3.00 | 4.50 | |
| 177 | This Is Costello–Norton Mockridge & Robert H. Prall | 2.00 | 4.00 | 6.00 | NF |
| 178 | Cabin Road–John Faulkner | 2.00 | 4.00 | 6.00 | E |
| 179 | I Have Gloria Kirby–Richard Himmel; orig. 1951 | 1.50 | 3.00 | 4.50 | M |
| 180 | The Girl in the Stateroom–Charles Boswell & Lewis Thompson | 2.50 | 5.00 | 7.50 | NF |
| 181 | Shanghai Flame–A.S. Fleischman; orig. 1951 | 2.00 | 4.00 | 6.00 | E |
| 182 | They Died Healthy–Logan Stewart | 2.00 | 4.00 | 6.00 | W |
| 183 | . . . and Be My Love–Ledru Baker, Jr; orig. 1951 | 2.00 | 4.00 | 6.00 | E |
| 184 | Thunderclap–Jack Sheridan; orig. 1951 | 2.00 | 4.00 | 6.00 | E |
| 185 | We Never Called Him Henry–Harry Bennett & Paul Marcus | 1.50 | 3.00 | 4.50 | B |
| 186 | Judge Me Not–John D. MacDonald; orig. 1951 | 10.00 | 20.00 | 30.00 | M |
| 187 | Hunt the Man Down–William Heuman | 2.00 | 4.00 | 6.00 | W |
| 188 | Get Out of Town–Paul Connolly | 2.00 | 4.00 | 6.00 | |
| 189 | Cassidy's Girl–David Goodis; orig. 1951 | 4.00 | 8.00 | 12.00 | E |
| 190 | Fires That Destroy–Harry Whittington | 2.50 | 5.00 | 7.50 | M |
| 191 | It's Your Money–Come and Get It–Sidney Margolius | 2.00 | 4.00 | 6.00 | NF |
| 192 | The Devil's Mistress–Kenneth Thomas | 2.00 | 4.00 | 6.00 | |
| 193 | The Trail–Logan Stewart | 2.00 | 4.00 | 6.00 | W |
| 194 | The Decoy–Edward Ronns | 2.00 | 4.00 | 6.00 | M |
| 195 | Saratoga Mantrap–Dexter St. Clare | 2.00 | 4.00 | 6.00 | |
| 196 | So Rich, So Dead–Gil Brewer | 2.00 | 4.00 | 6.00 | M |
| 197 | The Lady and the Cheetah–John Flagg | 2.00 | 4.00 | 6.00 | |
| 198 | To Hell Together–H. Vernor Dixon | 2.00 | 4.00 | 6.00 | E |
| 199 | Sumuru–Sax Rohmer; orig. 1951 | 7.50 | 15.00 | 22.50 | A |
| 200 | Weep for Me–John D. MacDonald; orig. 1951 | 9.00 | 18.00 | 27.00 | M |
| 201 | Stampede–Yukon Miles | 2.00 | 4.00 | 6.00 | W |
| 202 | The Unpossessed–William H. Fielding | 1.50 | 3.00 | 4.50 | |
| 203 | Find This Woman–Richard S. Prather | 2.50 | 5.00 | 7.50 | M |
| 204 | Death for Mr. Big–John Gonzales | 1.50 | 3.00 | 4.50 | M |
| G205 | Handsome–Theodore Pratt | 1.50 | 3.00 | 4.50 | |
| 206 | To Kiss or Kill–Day Keene; orig. 1951 | 4.00 | 8.00 | 12.00 | E |
| G207 | River Girl–Charles Williams; orig. 1951 | 3.00 | 6.00 | 9.00 | E |
| 208 | Wild Blood–A.C. Abbott | 2.00 | 4.00 | 6.00 | W |
| 209 | Fools Walk In–Bruno Fischer | 2.00 | 4.00 | 6.00 | M |
| 210 | Don't Get Caught–Carter Cullen | 2.00 | 4.00 | 6.00 | M |
| 211 | 13 French Street–Gil Brewer; orig. 1951 | 2.00 | 4.00 | 6.00 | E |
| s212 | Deep Is the Pit–H. Vernor Dixon; orig. 1952 | 2.00 | 4.00 | 6.00 | E |
| 213 | The Golden Woman–Eric Hatch | 1.50 | 3.00 | 4.50 | |
| 214 | Fear Comes Calling–Aylwin Lee Martin | 2.00 | 4.00 | 6.00 | M |
| 215 | Conquest–Homer Hatten | 2.00 | 4.00 | 6.00 | |
| 216 | Red Runs the River–William Heuman | 2.00 | 4.00 | 6.00 | W |
| 217 | Passage to Terror–Edward Ronns; orig. 1952 | 2.00 | 4.00 | 6.00 | E |
| 218 | Here Is My Body–Booth Mooney | 2.00 | 4.00 | 6.00 | |
| 219 | The Sheltering Night–Steve Fisher; orig. 1952 | 2.50 | 5.00 | 7.50 | M |
| 220 | Give a Man a Gun–Leslie Ernenwein | 2.00 | 4.00 | 6.00 | W |
| 221 | The Forbidden Room–Jaclen Steele | 2.00 | 4.00 | 6.00 | |
| 222 | Spring Fire–Vin Packer; orig. 1952 | 2.00 | 4.00 | 6.00 | E |
| 223 | Look Behind You, Lady–A.S. Fleischman | 1.50 | 3.00 | 4.50 | |
| 224 | Tears Are for Angels–Paul Connolly; orig. 1952 | 2.00 | 4.00 | 6.00 | |
| 225 | Home Is the Sailor–Day Keene; orig. 1952 | 2.50 | 5.00 | 7.50 | M |
| 226 | Of Tender Sin–David Goodis; orig. 1952 | 10.00 | 20.00 | 30.00 | |
| 227 | The Creeping Shadow–Sam Merwin, Jr | 2.00 | 4.00 | 6.00 | M |
| 228 | Appointment in Paris–Fay Adams | 1.50 | 3.00 | 4.50 | M |
| 229 | Little Sister–Lee Roberts; orig. 1952 | 2.00 | 4.00 | 6.00 | E |
| 230 | The Colonel's Lady–Clifton Adams | 2.00 | 4.00 | 6.00 | W |
| 231 | The Road's End–Albert Conroy; orig. 1952 | 2.00 | 4.00 | 6.00 | E |
| 232 | Woman Soldier–Arnold Rodin; orig. 1952 | 2.50 | 5.00 | 7.50 | C |
| 233 | Way of a Wanton–Richard S. Prather | 2.00 | 4.00 | 6.00 | M |
| 234 | The Sharp Edge–Richard Himmel | 2.00 | 4.00 | 6.00 | |
| 235 | The Avenger–Matthew Blood | 1.50 | 3.00 | 4.50 | M |
| 236 | Lone Star–Borden Chase; movie tie-in | 2.00 | 4.00 | 6.00 | W |
| 237 | Terror in the Sun–Richard Glendinning; orig. 1952 | 2.00 | 4.00 | 6.00 | E |
| 238 | Uncle Good's Girls–John Faulkner | 1.50 | 3.00 | 4.50 | E |
| 239 | Don't Cry, Beloved–Edward Ronns | | | | M |
| 240 | The Damned–John D. MacDonald; orig. 1952 | 5.00 | 10.00 | 15.00 | M |
| 241 | Savage Interlude–Dan Cushman | 2.50 | 5.00 | 7.50 | A |
| 242 | Trapped–Richard Hayward; orig. 1952 | 2.00 | 4.00 | 6.00 | M |
| 243 | The Secret Rider–Logan Stewart | 2.00 | 4.00 | 6.00 | W |
| 244 | The Cheaters–Ledru Baker, Jr | 2.00 | 4.00 | 6.00 | M |
| 245 | Double Cross–Joseph Chadwick; orig. 1952 | 2.00 | 4.00 | 6.00 | W |
| 246 | The Scarlet Venus–Chalmers Green; orig. 1952 | 1.50 | 3.00 | 4.50 | E |
| 247 | Cry at Dusk–Lester Dent; orig. 1952 | 4.00 | 8.00 | 12.00 | M |
| 248 | Blackmailer–George Axelrod | 2.00 | 4.00 | 6.00 | |
| 249 | Cartoon Laffs from True–ed. Clyde Carley | 2.50 | 5.00 | 7.50 | H |
| 250 | Dark Intruder–Vin Packer; 1952 | 1.50 | 3.00 | 4.50 | |
| 251 | The Caged–Fan Nichols | 1.50 | 3.00 | 4.50 | |
| 252 | Satan Takes the Helm–Calvin Clements | 2.00 | 4.00 | 6.00 | |

| | | V/Good | Fine | N/Mint | |
|---|---|---|---|---|---|
| | **GOLD MEDAL**, *continued* | | | | |
| 253 | The Crimson Frame–Aylwin Lee Martin | 1.50 | 3.00 | 4.50 | M |
| 254 | About Doctor Ferrel–Day Keene; orig. 1952 | 2.50 | 5.00 | 7.50 | E |
| 255 | The White Squaw–Larabie Sutter | 3.00 | 6.00 | 9.00 | W |
| 256 | Street of the Lost–David Goodis; orig. 1952 | 10.00 | 20.00 | 30.00 | E |
| 257 | Branded Woman–Wade Miller | 2.00 | 4.00 | 6.00 | |
| 258 | Escape to Love–Edward S. Aarons | 1.50 | 3.00 | 4.50 | |
| 259 | Walk in Fear–W.T. Ballard; aka I Could Kill You | 2.50 | 5.00 | 7.50 | |
| 260 | Men into Beasts–George Sylvester Viereck | 1.50 | 3.00 | 4.50 | M |
| 261 | Devil's Legacy–Joseph Chadwick | 1.50 | 3.00 | 4.50 | W |
| 262 | Who Evil Thinks–Richard Glendinning | 1.50 | 3.00 | 4.50 | |
| 263 | Love Me Now–John McPartland; orig. 1952 | 1.50 | 3.00 | 4.50 | E |
| 264 | Brenda–Lehi Zane; orig. 1952 | 1.50 | 3.00 | 4.50 | E |
| 265 | Darling, It's Death–Richard S. Prather | 1.50 | 3.00 | 4.50 | M |
| 266 | Plunder–Benjamin Appel | 1.50 | 3.00 | 4.50 | C |
| 267 | Secret of Death Valley–William Heuman | 1.50 | 3.00 | 4.50 | W |
| 268 | Whisper Her Name–Howard Hunt | 1.50 | 3.00 | 4.50 | |
| 269 | The Devil Drives–Robert Ames | 1.50 | 3.00 | 4.50 | |
| 270 | The Fast Buck–Bruno Fischer; orig. 1952 | 2.00 | 4.00 | 6.00 | M |
| 271 | Blood on the Sun–Chad Merriman | 1.50 | 3.00 | 4.50 | |
| 272 | Take Me As I Am–William H. Fielding | 1.50 | 3.00 | 4.50 | |
| 273 | Unholy Flame–Olga Rosmanith; orig. 1952 | 2.00 | 4.00 | 6.00 | E |
| 274 | Beyond Desire–Richard Himmel | 1.50 | 3.00 | 4.50 | |
| 275 | Move Along, Stranger–Frank Castle; 1953 | 1.50 | 3.00 | 4.50 | |
| 276 | Mountain Girl–Cord Wainer (Thomas Dewey); orig. 1952 | 1.50 | 3.00 | 4.50 | E |
| 277 | Flight to Darkness–Gil Brewer | 2.00 | 4.00 | 6.00 | |
| 278 | That French Girl–Joseph Hilton | 1.50 | 3.00 | 4.50 | |
| 279 | The Big Guy–Wade Miller | 1.50 | 3.00 | 4.50 | |
| 280 | The Sinners–Edward S. Aarons | 1.50 | 3.00 | 4.50 | M |
| 281 | Swamp Brat–Allen O'Quinn | 2.00 | 4.00 | 6.00 | E |
| 282 | Woman of Cairo–John Flagg | 1.50 | 3.00 | 4.50 | |
| 283 | The Fire Goddess–Sax Rohmer; orig. 1952; aka Virgin in Flames | 7.50 | 15.00 | 22.50 | A |
| 284 | Whip Hand–Joseph Chadwick | 1.50 | 3.00 | 4.50 | W |
| 285 | Too Rich to Die–H. Vernor Dixon | 2.00 | 4.00 | 6.00 | |
| 286 | Hell Hath No Fury–Charles Williams; orig. 1953 | 3.00 | 6.00 | 9.00 | E |
| 287 | On to Santa Fe–William Heuman | 1.50 | 3.00 | 4.50 | W |
| 288 | Maggie–Her Marriage–Taylor Caldwell; orig. 1953 | 1.50 | 3.00 | 4.50 | E |
| 289 | The Chislers–Albert Conroy; orig. 1953 | 1.50 | 3.00 | 4.50 | E |
| 290 | Jungle She–Dan Cushman; orig. 1953 | 4.00 | 8.00 | 12.00 | |
| 291 | Whom Gods Destroy–Clifton Adams | 1.50 | 3.00 | 4.50 | |
| 292 | Run, Chico, Run–Wenzell Brown; orig. 1953 | 2.50 | 5.00 | 7.50 | JD |
| 293 | Mystery Raider–Leslie Ernenwein | 1.50 | 3.00 | 4.50 | W |
| 294 | The Girl in the Red Velvet Swing–Charles Samuels | 1.50 | 3.00 | 4.50 | NF |
| 295 | Danger in Paradise–A.S. Fleischman | 1.50 | 3.00 | 4.50 | |
| 296 | Black Wings Has My Angel–Elliott Chaze | 1.50 | 3.00 | 4.50 | M |
| 297 | Lovers Are Losers–Howard Hunt | 1.50 | 3.00 | 4.50 | |
| 298 | Dead Low Tide–John D. MacDonald; orig. 1953 | 6.00 | 12.00 | 18.00 | M |
| 299 | Six-gun Code–Perry Westwood | 1.50 | 3.00 | 4.50 | W |
| 300 | The Borgia Blade–Gardner F. Fox; 1953 | 2.00 | 4.00 | 6.00 | A |
| 301 | Leave Her to God–O.O. Osborne | 1.50 | 3.00 | 4.50 | |
| 302 | Masquerade into Madness–Russ Meservey | 1.50 | 3.00 | 4.50 | |
| 303 | Barge Girl–Calvin Clements | 1.50 | 3.00 | 4.50 | E |
| 304 | The Snatchers–Lionel White; orig. 1953 | 2.50 | 5.00 | 7.50 | M |
| 305 | Ridge Runner–Chad Merriman | 1.50 | 3.00 | 4.50 | W |
| 306 | The Girl in the Death Cell–Fred J. Cook | 1.50 | 3.00 | 4.50 | NF |
| 307 | Witch of Salem–Benjamin Siegel; orig. 1953 | 2.00 | 4.00 | 6.00 | E |
| 308 | Hideaway–Nikki Content | 1.50 | 3.00 | 4.50 | |
| 309 | Sword in His Hand–John Vail | 2.00 | 4.00 | 6.00 | A |
| 310 | Keelboats North–William Heuman | 1.50 | 3.00 | 4.50 | W |
| 311 | Thieves Fall Out–Cameron Kay | 1.50 | 3.00 | 4.50 | |
| s312 | Gold Medal Treasury of American Verse–ed. John Gilland Brunini | | | | |
| 313 | War Bonnet Pass–Logan Stewart | 1.50 | 3.00 | 4.50 | W |
| 314 | Gunsmoke Reckoning–Joseph Chadwick | 1.50 | 3.00 | 4.50 | W |
| 315 | Saturday's Harvest–Paul Shelley | 1.50 | 3.00 | 4.50 | |
| 316 | Up a Winding Stair–H. Vernor Dixon | 2.00 | 4.00 | 6.00 | |
| 317 | Come Feed on Me–Morton Cooper | 1.50 | 3.00 | 4.50 | M |
| 318 | Ambush at Rincon–Dudley Dean | 1.50 | 3.00 | 4.50 | W |
| 319 | The Crooked Mile–Norbert Fagan | 1.50 | 3.00 | 4.50 | |
| 320 | Escape from Morales–Virginia Myers | 1.50 | 3.00 | 4.50 | |
| 321 | Nude in Mink–Sax Rohmer | 2.00 | 4.00 | 6.00 | M |
| 322 | Guns at Broken Bow–William Heuman | 1.50 | 3.00 | 4.50 | W |
| 323 | The Neon Jungle–John D. MacDonald; orig. 1953 | 17.50 | 35.00 | 52.50 | M |
| 324 | Look Back to Love–Vin Packer | 1.50 | 3.00 | 4.50 | |
| 325 | Terror in the Night–Sebastian Blayne; 1953; aka Until Death Do Us | 1.50 | 3.00 | 4.50 | M |
| 326 | Moment of Truth–Arnold Rodin | 1.50 | 3.00 | 4.50 | |
| 327 | Savage Stronghold–Logan Stewart | 1.50 | 3.00 | 4.50 | W |
| 328 | Madame Buccaneer–Gardner F. Fox; orig. 1953 | 2.00 | 4.00 | 6.00 | A |
| 329 | Gunfighter's Return–Leslie Ernenwein | 1.50 | 3.00 | 4.50 | W |
| 330 | Roll the Wagons–William Heuman | 1.50 | 3.00 | 4.50 | W |
| 331 | South of the Sun–Wade Miller | 1.50 | 3.00 | 4.50 | |
| 332 | Timberjack–Dan Cushman | 2.00 | 4.00 | 6.00 | A |
| 333 | To Love to Hate–Fay Adams | 1.50 | 3.00 | 4.50 | |
| 334 | The Girl in Lover's Lane–Charles Boswell & Lewis Thompson | 1.50 | 3.00 | 4.50 | NF |
| 335 | Valley of Angry Men–Matthew Gant | 1.50 | 3.00 | 4.50 | |
| 336 | Tokyo Doll–John McPartland | 2.00 | 4.00 | 6.00 | |
| 337 | Bar Guide–Virgil Partch & Ted Shane | 1.50 | 3.00 | 4.50 | H |
| 338 | Rider from Nowhere–Joseph Chadwick | 1.50 | 3.00 | 4.50 | W |
| s339 | Escape to Eden–Theodore Pratt | | | | |
| 340 | Nothing in Her Way–Charles Williams | 3.00 | 6.00 | 9.00 | |
| 341 | Ride a High Horse–Richard S. Prather | 1.50 | 3.00 | 4.50 | M |
| 342 | Belle Bradley, Her Story–anon. | 1.50 | 3.00 | 4.50 | |
| 343 | Run for Your Life–Bruno Fischer | 1.50 | 3.00 | 4.50 | M |
| 344 | Wagon Train Woman–Alan Henry | 1.50 | 3.00 | 4.50 | W |
| 345 | Hell's Our Destination–Gil Brewer | 1.50 | 3.00 | 4.50 | M |
| 346 | Son of the Flying Y–Will F. Jenkins (Murray Leinster) | 1.50 | 3.00 | 4.50 | W |
| 347 | Hondo–Louis L'Amour; orig. 1953; movie tie-in | 4.00 | 8.00 | 12.00 | W |
| 348 | The Moon in the Gutter–David Goodis; orig. 1953 | 12.00 | 24.00 | 36.00 | |
| 349 | I Came to Kill–Gordon Davis | 1.50 | 3.00 | 4.50 | M |
| 350 | Rage in Texas–Howard Rigsby; 1953 | 1.50 | 3.00 | 4.50 | W |
| 351 | The Girl in Poison Cottage–Jim Bishop & H. Hoffmann | 1.50 | 3.00 | 4.50 | NF |
| 352 | Eagle on His Wrist–Homer Hatten | 1.50 | 3.00 | 4.50 | |
| 353 | The Fall of Suzanne Swift–V.A. McMillen | 1.50 | 3.00 | 4.50 | E |
| 354 | Big Red's Daughter–John McPartland | 1.50 | 3.00 | 4.50 | E |
| 355 | Big Stan–John Monahan (W.R. Burnett); 1st ed. 1954 | 2.50 | 5.00 | 7.50 | |
| 356 | Paradise Motel–Jack Sheridan | 1.50 | 3.00 | 4.50 | |
| 357 | Guns along the Wickiup–D.B. Newton | 1.50 | 3.00 | 4.50 | W |
| 358 | Pappy and the Promised Land–Jack Gotshall | 1.50 | 3.00 | 4.50 | |
| 359 | The Girl in the House of Hate–Charles Samuels & Louise Samuels | 1.50 | 3.00 | 4.50 | NF |
| 360 | One Sword for Love–Gardner F. Fox | 2.00 | 4.00 | 6.00 | A |
| 361 | Rampage–Leslie Ernenwein | 1.50 | 3.00 | 4.50 | W |
| 362 | Come Back, My Love–Edward S. Aarons; orig. 1954 | 1.50 | 3.00 | 4.50 | M |
| 363 | Come Destroy Me–Vin Packer | 1.50 | 3.00 | 4.50 | |
| 364 | Gold Brick Cassie–David Loth | 1.50 | 3.00 | 4.50 | NF |
| 365 | Monte Carlo Mission–Vivian Connell | 1.50 | 3.00 | 4.50 | |
| 366 | This Woman Is Mine–Harry Whittington | 2.50 | 5.00 | 7.50 | |
| 367 | Rails West–Logan Stewart | 1.50 | 3.00 | 4.50 | W |
| 368 | Malay Woman–A.S. Fleischman | 2.00 | 4.00 | 6.00 | A |
| 369 | Seminole–Theodore Pratt | 3.00 | 6.00 | 9.00 | A |
| 370 | A Lover for Cindy–H. Vernon Dixon | 2.00 | 4.00 | 6.00 | |
| 371 | Go Home, Stranger–Charles Williams | 4.00 | 8.00 | 12.00 | |
| 372 | Notorious–Day Keene; orig. 1954 | 4.00 | 8.00 | 12.00 | |
| 373 | Two Deaths Must Die–Richard Himmel | 1.50 | 3.00 | 4.50 | M |
| 374 | Come Out Shooting–Joseph Chadwick | 1.50 | 3.00 | 4.50 | W |
| 375 | As a Man Falls–Howard Rigsby; 1954 | 1.50 | 3.00 | 4.50 | M |
| 376 | Take Your Last Look–Matt Brady | 1.50 | 3.00 | 4.50 | M |
| 377 | The Range Grabbers–Sidney Stewart | 1.50 | 3.00 | 4.50 | W |
| 378 | Let Them Eat Bullets–Howard Schoenfeld | 1.50 | 3.00 | 4.50 | M |
| 379 | Women's Barracks–Tereska Torres | 1.50 | 3.00 | 4.50 | E |

## GOLD MEDAL, *continued*

| | | V/Good | Fine | N/Mint | |
|---|---|---|---|---|---|
| 380 | A Killer Is Loose–Gil Brewer | 2.50 | 5.00 | 7.50 | M |
| 381 | Fury on the Plains–Chad Merriman | 1.50 | 3.00 | 4.50 | W |
| 382 | One against the Odds–Norbert Fagan | 1.50 | 3.00 | 4.50 | |
| 383 | Cartoon Fun from True–ed. True Magazine | 1.50 | 3.00 | 4.50 | H |
| 384 | The Girl with the Scarlet Brand–Charles Boswell & Lewis Thompson | 1.50 | 3.00 | 4.50 | NF |
| 385 | Sweet Money Girl–Benjamin Appel | 1.50 | 3.00 | 4.50 | M |
| 386 | The Beautiful and Dead–Ross MacRoss | 1.50 | 3.00 | 4.50 | M |
| d387 | Driven–Richard Gehman | 1.50 | 3.00 | 4.50 | M |
| 388 | I'll Take What's Mine–Nard Jones | 1.50 | 3.00 | 4.50 | |
| 389 | Retreat into Night–Richard Glendinning | 1.50 | 3.00 | 4.50 | |
| 390 | Renegade Gun–Joseph Chadwick | 1.50 | 3.00 | 4.50 | W |
| 391 | Dear, Deadly Beloved–John Flagg | 1.50 | 3.00 | 4.50 | M |
| 392 | The Fabulous Finn–Don Cushman | 2.00 | 4.00 | 6.00 | |
| 393 | The Face of Evil–John McPartland | 2.00 | 4.00 | 6.00 | M |
| 394 | The Gentleman Rogue–Gardner F. Fox | 2.00 | 4.00 | 6.00 | A |
| 395 | And Two Shall Meet–Richard Mason | 1.50 | 3.00 | 4.50 | |
| 396 | The Dark Throne–John Vail | 1.50 | 3.00 | 4.50 | A |
| 397 | The Girl on the Gallows–Q. Patrick | 2.00 | 4.00 | 6.00 | M |
| 398 | Spring Fire–Vin Packer | 1.50 | 3.00 | 4.50 | E |
| 399 | A Woman for Henry–Allen O'Quinn | 1.50 | 3.00 | 4.50 | |
| 400 | Lucinda–Howard Rigsby; 1954 | 1.50 | 3.00 | 4.50 | |
| 401 | Saddle the Storm–Harry Whittington | 2.50 | 5.00 | 7.50 | |
| 402 | French for Murder–Bernard Mara | 2.00 | 4.00 | 6.00 | M |
| s403 | Portrait of Lisa–William Brothers | 1.50 | 3.00 | 4.50 | |
| 404 | The Wickedest Man–Joseph Millard | 2.00 | 4.00 | 6.00 | |
| 405 | There Was a Crooked Man–Day Keene; orig. 1954 | 4.00 | 8.00 | 12.00 | |
| 406 | Affair in Tokyo–John McPartland | 2.00 | 4.00 | 6.00 | |
| 407 | Man Divided–Dean Douglas | 1.50 | 3.00 | 4.50 | |
| 408 | Return of Sumuru–Sax Rohmer; orig. 1954 | 6.00 | 12.00 | 18.00 | A |
| 409 | Some Must Die–Gil Brewer | 2.00 | 4.00 | 6.00 | M |
| 410 | Uncle Good's Girls–John Faulkner | 2.50 | 5.00 | 7.50 | E |
| 411 | Black Horse Canyon–Les Savage, Jr; aka The Wild Horse; movie tie-in | 2.00 | 4.00 | 6.00 | W |
| 412 | Hell Ship to Kuma–Calvin Clements | 2.00 | 4.00 | 6.00 | |
| 413 | Always Leave 'Em Dying–Richard S. Prather | 1.50 | 3.00 | 4.50 | M |
| 414 | Ride for Texas–William Heuman | 1.50 | 3.00 | 4.50 | W |
| 415 | Runaway Black–Richard Marsten | 2.00 | 4.00 | 6.00 | |
| 416 | Jezebel in Crinoline–Homer Hatten | 1.50 | 3.00 | 4.50 | E |
| 417 | I Am Legend–Richard Matheson; orig. 1954 | 15.00 | 30.00 | 45.00 | SF |
| 418 | 13 French Street–Gil Brewer | 2.00 | 4.00 | 6.00 | |
| 419 | Come Murder Me–James Kieran | 1.50 | 3.00 | 4.50 | M |
| 420 | All These Condemned–John D. MacDonald | 4.00 | 8.00 | 12.00 | M |
| 421 | Smash-up–Theodore Pratt | 1.50 | 3.00 | 4.50 | |
| 422 | Two-Gun Law–Clifton Adams | 1.50 | 3.00 | 4.50 | W |
| 423 | Death Is a Lovely Dame–Matthew Blood | 1.50 | 3.00 | 4.50 | M |
| 424 | Girl on the Run–Edward S. Aarons | 1.50 | 3.00 | 4.50 | M |
| 425 | Case of the Vanishing Beauty–Richard S. Prather; 1954 | 1.50 | 3.00 | 4.50 | M |
| 426 | Whisper His Sin–Vin Packer | 1.50 | 3.00 | 4.50 | |
| 427 | Cry Down the Lonely Night–Milton White | 1.50 | 3.00 | 4.50 | |
| 428 | Street of No Return–David Goodis; orig. 1954 | 12.00 | 24.00 | 36.00 | |
| 429 | The Range Buster–William Heuman | 1.50 | 3.00 | 4.50 | W |

*Gold Medal 402, Gold Medal 451, Gold Medal 516.*

| | | V/Good | Fine | N/Mint | |
|---|---|---|---|---|---|
| 430 | Beautiful Humbug–William H. Fielding | 1.50 | 3.00 | 4.50 | |
| 431 | The Girl on the Lonely Beach–Fred J. Cook | 1.50 | 3.00 | 4.50 | NF |
| s432 | Handsome–Theodore Pratt | 1.50 | 3.00 | 4.50 | |
| 433 | Somebody Loves Me–Nancy Morgan | 1.50 | 3.00 | 4.50 | |
| 434 | A Touch of Death–Charles Williams; aka And Share Alike | 4.00 | 8.00 | 12.00 | |
| 435 | The Dangerous One–Robert Ames | 1.50 | 3.00 | 4.50 | |
| 436 | The Man from Riondo–Dudley Dean | 1.50 | 3.00 | 4.50 | W |
| 437 | So Wicked My Love–Bruno Fischer; aka Incident at Coney Island | 1.50 | 3.00 | 4.50 | M |
| 438 | Women of Kali–Gardner F. Fox | 3.00 | 6.00 | 9.00 | A |
| 439 | Cabin Road–John Faulkner | 2.00 | 4.00 | 6.00 | E |
| s440 | The Cunning and the Haunted–Richard Jessup | 1.50 | 3.00 | 4.50 | |
| 441 | Sow the Wild Wind–John Vail | 1.50 | 3.00 | 4.50 | A |
| 442 | Rebel Raider–Joseph Chadwick | 1.50 | 3.00 | 4.50 | W |
| 443 | Wild Breed–Ted Stratton | 1.50 | 3.00 | 4.50 | |
| 444 | Mission to Murder–Richard Glendinning | 1.50 | 3.00 | 4.50 | M |
| 445 | Funny Cartoons by VIP–Virgil Partch; 1955 | 1.50 | 3.00 | 4.50 | H |
| 446 | Hill Girl–Charles Williams | 2.00 | 4.00 | 6.00 | E |
| 447 | Make My Coffin Strong–William R. Cox | 1.50 | 3.00 | 4.50 | |
| 448 | 77 Rue Paradise–Gil Brewer | 2.00 | 4.00 | 6.00 | |
| 449 | The Mating Cry–Frank Daniels | 1.50 | 3.00 | 4.50 | |
| 450 | Strange But True–ed. Mee Morningside; 1955 | 1.50 | 3.00 | 4.50 | NF |
| 451 | Bad Day at Black Rock–Michael Niall; movie tie-in | 2.50 | 5.00 | 7.50 | M |
| 452 | Outcast of Murder Mesa–Kenneth Fowler | 1.50 | 3.00 | 4.50 | W |
| s453 | City of Women–Nancy Morgan | 1.50 | 3.00 | 4.50 | E |
| s454 | The Hunger and the Hate–H. Vernor Dixon | 2.00 | 4.00 | 6.00 | |
| 455 | The Sin Shouter of Cabin Road–John Faulkner | 1.50 | 3.00 | 4.50 | E |
| 456 | Shanghai Incident–Steve Dodge | 1.50 | 3.00 | 4.50 | |
| 457 | Many Rivers to Cross–Steve Frazee | 1.50 | 3.00 | 4.50 | W |
| 458 | The Girl in Murder Flat–Mel Heimer | 1.50 | 3.00 | 4.50 | NF |
| 459 | Lady in Dread–Ryerson Johnson | 1.50 | 3.00 | 4.50 | |
| 460 | I'll Find You–Richard Himmel | 1.50 | 3.00 | 4.50 | M |
| 461 | The Glitter and the Greed–Robert W. Taylor; c-Maguire | 1.50 | 3.00 | 4.50 | |
| 462 | Funny Business–Charlest Preston | 1.50 | 3.00 | 4.50 | H |
| 463 | Strangers in My Bed–Allen O'Quinn | 1.50 | 3.00 | 4.50 | |
| 464 | Bullet Barricade–Leslie Ernenwein | 1.50 | 3.00 | 4.50 | W |
| 465 | A New Way to Eat and Get Slim–Donald G. Cooley | 1.50 | 3.00 | 4.50 | NF |
| 466 | Death Was the Bridegroom–Charles Samuels | 1.50 | 3.00 | 4.50 | NF |
| s467 | River Girl–Charles Williams | 4.00 | 8.00 | 12.00 | E |
| 468 | Forever Is Today–Richard Mason | 1.50 | 3.00 | 4.50 | |
| 469 | Mad Baxter–Wade Miller | 1.50 | 3.00 | 4.50 | M |
| 470 | The Big Caper–Lionel White; orig. 1955 | 2.50 | 5.00 | 7.50 | M |
| 471 | Song of the Gun–Dudley Dean | 1.50 | 3.00 | 4.50 | W |
| 472 | A Bullet for My Lady–Bernard Mara | 1.50 | 3.00 | 4.50 | M |
| 473 | Violence in the Night–Alan Hynd | 1.50 | 3.00 | 4.50 | |
| s474 | The Tormented–Theodore Pratt | 1.50 | 3.00 | 4.50 | |
| 475 | Angels in the Gutter–Joseph Hilton; 1955 | 3.00 | 6.00 | 9.00 | JD |
| 476 | Blonde Savage–John Vail | 2.00 | 4.00 | 6.00 | A |
| 477 | Prey by Night–Malcolm Douglas | 1.50 | 3.00 | 4.50 | |
| 478 | Heller with a Gun–Louis L'Amour | 3.50 | 7.00 | 10.50 | W |
| 479 | The Soft Arms of Death–Richard Hayward | 1.50 | 3.00 | 4.50 | |
| 480 | The Girls in Nightmare House–Charles Boswell & Lewis Thompson | 1.50 | 3.00 | 4.50 | NF |
| 481 | The Damned–John D. MacDonald | 1.50 | 3.00 | 4.50 | M |
| 482 | The Brass Cupcake–John D. MacDonald | 1.50 | 3.00 | 4.50 | M |
| 483 | Death's Sweet Song–Clifton Adams | 1.50 | 3.00 | 4.50 | |
| 484 | Rebel Wench–Gardner F. Fox | 2.00 | 4.00 | 6.00 | A |
| 485 | West to the Sun–Noel M. Loomis | 1.50 | 3.00 | 4.50 | W |
| 486 | Dark Heritage–John Foster | 1.50 | 3.00 | 4.50 | |
| 487 | The Truth about Belle Gunness–Lillian de la Torre | 1.50 | 3.00 | 4.50 | |
| 488 | Cry of the Flesh–Richard Himmel | 1.50 | 3.00 | 4.50 | |
| 489 | Find This Woman–Richard S. Prather | 1.50 | 3.00 | 4.50 | M |
| 490 | Mine to Avenge–Thomas Wills (William Ard) | 4.00 | 8.00 | 12.00 | M |

## GOLD MEDAL, *continued*

| No. | Title | V/Good | Fine | N/Mint | |
|---|---|---|---|---|---|
| 491 | Assignment to Disaster–Edward S. Aarons | 1.50 | 3.00 | 4.50 | M |
| 492 | Plunder Range–Homer Hatten | 1.50 | 3.00 | 4.50 | W |
| 493 | The Golden Frame–Joseph Chadwick | 1.50 | 3.00 | 4.50 | |
| 494 | Who Has Wilma Lathrop?–Day Keene; orig. 1955 | 4.00 | 8.00 | 12.00 | M |
| 495 | Hell Strip–Lee Richards | 1.50 | 3.00 | 4.50 | |
| 496 | Bodies in Bedlam–Richard S. Prather | 1.50 | 3.00 | 4.50 | M |
| 497 | Way of a Wanton–Richard S. Prather | 1.50 | 3.00 | 4.50 | M |
| 498 | One of Our H-Bombs Is Missing–Frederick Hazlitt Brennan | 2.50 | 5.00 | 7.50 | M |
| 499 | Blood Alley–A.S. Fleischman; movie tie-in | 2.50 | 5.00 | 7.50 | A |
| 500 | So Fair, So Evil–Paul Connolly; 1955 | 1.50 | 3.00 | 4.50 | |
| 501 | Trouble Rides Tall–William Hopson | 1.50 | 3.00 | 4.50 | W |
| 502 | Homicide Hussy–Atha McGuire | 1.50 | 3.00 | 4.50 | M |
| 503 | Death Lies Deep–William Guinn | 1.50 | 3.00 | 4.50 | M |
| 504 | Everybody Had a Gun–Richard S. Prather | 1.50 | 3.00 | 4.50 | M |
| 505 | Darling, It's Death–Richard S. Prather | 1.50 | 3.00 | 4.50 | M |
| 506 | Stop This Man–Peter Rabe | 2.50 | 5.00 | 7.50 | M |
| 507 | Murder in the Navy–Richard Marsten | 2.00 | 4.00 | 6.00 | M |
| 508 | Strip for Murder–Richard S. Prather | 1.50 | 3.00 | 4.50 | M |
| 509 | We Walk Alone–Ann Aldrich; orig. 1955 | 2.50 | 5.00 | 7.50 | E |
| 510 | The Thrill Kids–Vin Packer | 2.50 | 5.00 | 7.50 | JD |
| 511 | The Broken Spur–Dudley Dean | 1.50 | 3.00 | 4.50 | W |
| 512 | Ride the Dark Storm–Nard Jones | 1.50 | 3.00 | 4.50 | |
| 513 | Stolen Woman–Wade Miller | 1.50 | 3.00 | 4.50 | |
| 514 | Shanghai Flame–A.S. Fleischman | 1.50 | 3.00 | 4.50 | |
| s515 | A Rage to Die–Richard Jessup | 1.50 | 3.00 | 4.50 | |
| 516 | To Tame a Land–Louis L'Amour | 3.50 | 7.00 | 10.50 | W |
| 517 | Journey into Death–Jack Johnson | 1.50 | 3.00 | 4.50 | |
| 518 | Awake and Die–Robert Ames | 1.50 | 3.00 | 4.50 | M |
| 519 | Lie Down with Lions–Marvin H. Albert | 1.50 | 3.00 | 4.50 | |
| 520 | Benny Muscles In–Peter Rabe | 2.50 | 5.00 | 7.50 | M |
| 521 | The Killer–Wade Miller | 1.50 | 3.00 | 4.50 | |
| s522 | Run, Chico, Run–Wenzell Brown | 1.50 | 3.00 | 4.50 | JD |
| 523 | The Second Longest Night–Stephen Marlowe | 2.00 | 4.00 | 6.00 | M |
| 524 | My Deadly Angel–John Chelton | 1.50 | 3.00 | 4.50 | |
| 525 | Your Sins and Mine–Taylor Caldwell | 1.50 | 3.00 | 4.50 | |
| 526 | Gunsmoke Empire–Lewis B. Patten | 1.50 | 3.00 | 4.50 | W |
| 527 | Renegade Brand–Richard Brister | 1.50 | 3.00 | 4.50 | W |
| 528 | A Shroud for Jesso–Peter Rabe | 2.50 | 5.00 | 7.50 | M |
| 529 | The Decoy–Edward Ronns | 1.50 | 3.00 | 4.50 | M |
| 530 | The Wounded and the Slain–David Goodis; orig. 1955 | 12.00 | 24.00 | 36.00 | |
| 531 | The Dead Darling–Jonathan Craig | 1.50 | 3.00 | 4.50 | M |
| 532 | The Neighbor's Kids–George Clark | 1.50 | 3.00 | 4.50 | |
| 533 | Gambling Man–Clifton Adams | 1.50 | 3.00 | 4.50 | |
| 534 | The Outlaw Breed–D.B. Newton | 1.50 | 3.00 | 4.50 | W |
| 535 | Port Orient–Dan Cushman | 2.50 | 5.00 | 7.50 | A |
| 536 | Cocotte–Theodore Pratt | 1.25 | 2.50 | 3.75 | |
| 537 | House of Flesh–Bruno Fischer | 1.50 | 3.00 | 4.50 | M |
| 538 | Flesh–and Mr. Rawlie–Morton Cooper | 1.50 | 3.00 | 4.50 | |
| 539 | Rain of Terror–Malcolm Douglas; 1955 | 1.50 | 3.00 | 4.50 | |
| 540 | Zowie! Girl Meets Boy–Charles Preston | 1.80 | 3.60 | 5.40 | H |
| 541 | Horsemen from Hell–Homer Hatten | 1.50 | 3.00 | 4.50 | W |
| 542 | The Lone Gun–Howard Rigsby | 1.50 | 3.00 | 4.50 | W |
| 543 | The Chinese Keyhole–Richard Himmel | 1.25 | 2.50 | 3.75 | M |
| 544 | Cassidy's Girl–David Goodis | 2.50 | 5.00 | 7.50 | E |

*Gold Medal 540, Gold Medal 555, Gold Medal s577.*

| No. | Title | V/Good | Fine | N/Mint | |
|---|---|---|---|---|---|
| 545 | Hell-bent for Danger–Walt Grove | 1.50 | 3.00 | 4.50 | |
| 546 | Killer in White–Tedd Thomey | 1.50 | 3.00 | 4.50 | M |
| 547 | A House in Naples–Peter Rabe | 2.50 | 5.00 | 7.50 | M |
| 548 | To Hell–and Texas–Giles A. Lutz | 1.50 | 3.00 | 4.50 | W |
| s549 | Queen of Sheba–Gardner F. Fox; orig. 1956 | 3.00 | 6.00 | 9.00 | A |
| s550 | Down to Eternity–Richard O'Connor; movie tie-in | 1.50 | 3.00 | 4.50 | |
| 551 | Too Many Crooks–Richard S. Prather; aka Ride a High Horse | 1.50 | 3.00 | 4.50 | M |
| 552 | Men into Beasts–George Sylvester Viereck | 2.00 | 4.00 | 6.00 | |
| 553 | The Law and Jake Wade–Marvin H. Albert | 2.00 | 4.00 | 6.00 | W |
| 554 | The Violent Hours–Frank Castle | 1.50 | 3.00 | 4.50 | |
| 555 | Sinister Madonna–Sax Rohmer; orig. 1956 | 6.00 | 12.00 | 18.00 | A |
| 556 | Hold Back the Sun–John Vail | 1.50 | 3.00 | 4.50 | A |
| 557 | Hot, Sweet and Blue–Jack Baird | 1.50 | 3.00 | 4.50 | |
| 558 | Trapped–Richard Hayward | 1.50 | 3.00 | 4.50 | |
| 559 | Woman Soldier–Arnold Rodin | 1.50 | 3.00 | 4.50 | C |
| 560 | The Guns of Fort Petticoat–C. William Harrison; movie tie-in | 2.50 | 5.00 | 7.50 | W |
| 561 | Death Must Wait–Don Kingery | 1.50 | 3.00 | 4.50 | |
| 562 | This Gun for Gloria–Bernard Mara | 2.00 | 4.00 | 6.00 | M |
| 563 | Build My Gallows High–Roy Benard Sparkla | 1.50 | 3.00 | 4.50 | |
| s564 | Cry Blood–H. Vernor Dixon | 2.00 | 4.00 | 6.00 | |
| 565 | Little Sister–Lee Roberts | 1.25 | 2.50 | 5.00 | E |
| 566 | I Have Gloria Kirby–Richard Himmel | 1.50 | 3.00 | 4.50 | |
| 567 | The Golden Bawd–Giles A. Lutz | 1.50 | 3.00 | 4.50 | |
| 568 | Assignment–Treason–Edward S. Aarons | 1.50 | 3.00 | 4.50 | M |
| 569 | Gunfire at Salt Fork–William Hopson | 1.50 | 3.00 | 4.50 | W |
| 570 | My Mistress, Death–Robert Spafford | 1.50 | 3.00 | 4.50 | |
| 571 | I'll See You in Hell–John McPartland | 2.00 | 4.00 | 6.00 | M |
| 572 | Look Behind You, Lady–A.S. Fleischman | 1.50 | 3.00 | 4.50 | |
| 573 | Rope Law–Lewis B. Patten | 1.50 | 3.00 | 4.50 | W |
| 574 | Danger for Breakfast–John McPartland | 1.50 | 3.00 | 4.50 | M |
| 575 | Mecca for Murder–Stephen Marlowe; 1956 | 2.00 | 4.00 | 6.00 | M |
| 576 | Catch a Falling Star–Reed Marr | 1.50 | 3.00 | 4.50 | |
| s577 | The Shrinking Man–Richard Matheson | 15.00 | 30.00 | 45.00 | SF |
| 578 | Dark Intruder–Vin Packer | 1.50 | 3.00 | 4.50 | |
| 579 | The Road's End–Albert Conroy | 1.50 | 3.00 | 4.50 | |
| 580 | Rio Bravo–Gordon D. Shirreffs | 1.50 | 3.00 | 4.50 | W |
| 581 | The Young and Violent–Vin Packer | 2.00 | 4.00 | 6.00 | JD |
| 582 | Morgue for Venus–Jonathan Craig | 1.50 | 3.00 | 4.50 | M |
| s583 | Hypnosis and You–Ben Benson & Howard D. Tawney | 1.50 | 3.00 | 4.50 | NF |
| 584 | The Diehards–Dudley Dean | 1.50 | 3.00 | 4.50 | W |
| 585 | Swamp Brat–Allen O'Quinn | 1.50 | 3.00 | 4.50 | |
| 586 | Let Them Eat Bullets–Howard Schoenfeld | 1.50 | 3.00 | 4.50 | M |
| s587 | Johnny Concho–Noel M. Loomis; movie tie-in | 2.00 | 4.00 | 6.00 | W |
| s588 | The Innocent and Willing–Morton Cooper | 1.50 | 3.00 | 4.50 | |
| 589 | Love after Five–Richard Mason | 1.50 | 3.00 | 4.50 | |
| s590 | Edgar Cayce–Mystery Man of Miracles–Joseph Millard | 1.50 | 3.00 | 4.50 | NF |
| 591 | Knee-deep in Death–Bruno Fischer | 1.50 | 3.00 | 4.50 | M |
| 592 | The Wailing Frail–Richard S. Prather | 1.50 | 3.00 | 4.50 | M |
| 593 | Law of the Trigger–Clifton Adams | 1.50 | 3.00 | 4.50 | W |
| 594 | Kill the Boss Good-bye–Peter Rabe | 2.50 | 5.00 | 7.50 | M |
| 595 | Brute in Brass–Harry Whittington | 2.00 | 4.00 | 6.00 | |
| 596 | The Wild Party–John McPartland; movie tie-in | 2.00 | 4.00 | 6.00 | |
| s597 | The Women with Claws–Williams Forrest | 1.50 | 3.00 | 4.50 | |
| 598 | Always Leave 'Em Dying–Richard S. Prather | 1.50 | 3.00 | 4.50 | M |
| 599 | Mountain Girl–Cord Wainer | 1.50 | 3.00 | 4.50 | E |
| 600 | Fools Walk In–Bruno Fischer; 1956 | 1.50 | 3.00 | 4.50 | M |
| 601 | Tough Hombre–Dudley Dean | 1.50 | 3.00 | 4.50 | W |
| 602 | White Warrior–Lewis B. Patten; c-McCarthy | 1.50 | 3.00 | 4.50 | W |
| 603 | Bring Him Back Dead–Day Keene; orig. 1956 | 4.00 | 8.00 | 12.00 | |
| 604 | The Name's Buchanan–Jonas Ward (William Ard) | 4.00 | 8.00 | 12.00 | W |
| 605 | Dead and Kicking–Frank Castle | 1.50 | 3.00 | 4.50 | |

GOLD MEDAL, *continued*

| No. | Title | V/Good | Fine | N/Mint | |
| --- | --- | --- | --- | --- | --- |
| 606 | Operation–Murder–Lionel White; orig. 1956 | 3.00 | 6.00 | 9.00 | |
| s607 | The Diamond Bikini–Charles Williams | 7.50 | 15.00 | 22.50 | |
| 608 | The Chiselers–Albert Conroy | 1.50 | 3.00 | 4.50 | E |
| 609 | The Borgia Blade–Gardner F. Fox | 2.00 | 4.00 | 6.00 | A |
| 610 | Don't Get Caught–Carter Cullen | 1.50 | 3.00 | 4.50 | |
| 611 | Desire in the Dust–Harry Whittington | 2.50 | 5.00 | 7.50 | |
| 612 | Dig My Grave Deep–Peter Rabe | 2.50 | 5.00 | 7.50 | M |
| 613 | He Rode Alone–Steve Frazee | 2.00 | 4.00 | 6.00 | W |
| 614 | The Deadly Dames–Malcolm Douglas | 1.50 | 3.00 | 4.50 | |
| 615 | Three Violent People–Leonard Praskins & Barney Slater; movie tie-in | 2.00 | 4.00 | 6.00 | W |
| s616 | Killer in Silk–H. Vernor Dixon | 2.00 | 4.00 | 6.00 | M |
| 617 | About Doctor Ferrel–Day Keene | 2.50 | 5.00 | 7.50 | |
| s618 | Handsome–Theodore Pratt | 1.50 | 3.00 | 4.50 | |
| 619 | Prairie Reckoning–Paul Durst | 1.50 | 3.00 | 4.50 | W |
| 620 | High Gun–Leslie Ernenwein; c-McCarthy | 1.50 | 3.00 | 4.50 | W |
| 621 | Assignment–Suicide–Edward S. Aarons | 1.50 | 3.00 | 4.50 | M |
| 622 | Murder on the Side–Day Keene; orig. 1956 | 4.00 | 8.00 | 12.00 | M |
| 623 | Down There–David Goodis; orig. 1956; aka Shoot the Piano Player | 12.00 | 24.00 | 36.00 | |
| s624 | Dark Don't Catch Me–Vin Packer | 1.50 | 3.00 | 4.50 | |
| 625 | Go Home Stranger–Charles Williams; 1956 | 4.00 | 8.00 | 12.00 | |
| 626 | Of Tender Sin–David Goodis | 2.50 | 5.00 | 7.50 | E |
| 627 | Trouble Is My Name–Stephen Marlowe | 1.50 | 3.00 | 4.50 | M |
| 628 | Murder in Monaco–John Flagg | 1.50 | 3.00 | 4.50 | M |
| 629 | The Deadly Chase–Carter Cullen | 1.50 | 3.00 | 4.50 | |
| 630 | The White Squaw–Larabie Sutter | 3.00 | 6.00 | 9.00 | W |
| 631 | Violence Valley–William Heuman | 1.50 | 3.00 | 4.50 | W |
| s632 | Search for Surrender–Borden Deal | 1.50 | 3.00 | 4.50 | |
| 633 | The Sin Shouter of Cabin Road–John Faulkner | 1.50 | 3.00 | 4.50 | E |
| 634 | State Department Murders–Edward Ronns | 1.50 | 3.00 | 4.50 | M |
| 635 | Seminole–Theodore Pratt; 1957 | 2.00 | 4.00 | 6.00 | A |
| 636 | Vengeance under Law–Frank Castle | 1.50 | 3.00 | 4.50 | |
| 637 | Running Target–Steve Frazee | 1.50 | 3.00 | 4.50 | |
| 638 | Women without Men–Reed Marr | 1.50 | 3.00 | 4.50 | |
| 639 | Bugles on the Prairie–Gordon D. Shirreffs; c-McCarthy | 1.50 | 3.00 | 4.50 | W |
| 640 | The Wicked Streets–Wenzell Brown | 2.50 | 5.00 | 7.50 | JD |
| s641 | The Golden Sorrow–Theodore Pratt | 1.50 | 3.00 | 4.50 | |
| s642 | Sweet Money Girl–Benjamin Appel | 1.50 | 3.00 | 4.50 | |
| 643 | I Am Legend–Richard Matheson | 3.00 | 6.00 | 9.00 | SF |
| 644 | Ride the Gold Mare–Ovid Demaris | 1.50 | 3.00 | 4.50 | |
| 645 | Case of the Cold Coquette–Jonathan Craig | 1.50 | 3.00 | 4.50 | M |
| 646 | The Reluctant Gun–Howard Rigsby | 1.50 | 3.00 | 4.50 | |
| 647 | Cheyenne Saturday–Richard Jessup | 1.50 | 3.00 | 4.50 | W |
| 648 | Terror over London–Gardner F. Fox | 2.00 | 4.00 | 6.00 | M |
| s649 | The Wings of Eagles–Walt Grove; movie tie-in | 3.00 | 6.00 | 9.00 | B |
| 650 | The Corpse That Walked–Octavus Roy Cohen; 1957 | 1.50 | 3.00 | 4.50 | M |
| 651 | Big City Girl–Charles Williams | 2.00 | 4.00 | 6.00 | E |
| 652 | Street of the Lost–David Goodis | 2.50 | 5.00 | 7.50 | |
| s653 | Odd Girl Out–Ann Bannon | 3.50 | 7.00 | 10.50 | |
| 654 | Pure Sweet Hell–Malcolm Douglas | 1.50 | 3.00 | 4.50 | |
| 655 | Gun in the Valley–Dudley Dean | 1.50 | 3.00 | 4.50 | W |
| 656 | Westward the Drums–L.A. Hearne | 1.50 | 3.00 | 4.50 | |
| 657 | The Cut Is Death–Peter Rabe | 2.50 | 5.00 | 7.50 | M |
| 658 | Murder Is My Dish–Stephen Marlowe | 1.50 | 3.00 | 4.50 | M |
| 659 | Hell Strip–Lee Richards | 1.50 | 3.00 | 4.50 | |
| s660 | The Young Don't Cry–Richard Jessup | 1.50 | 3.00 | 4.50 | |
| s661 | The Maricopa Trail–Noel M. Loomis | 1.50 | 3.00 | 4.50 | W |
| 662 | Buchanan Says No–Jonas Ward (William Ard) | 4.00 | 8.00 | 12.00 | W |
| 663 | Death Takes the Bus–Lionel White; orig. 1957 | 2.50 | 5.00 | 7.50 | M |
| 664 | So I'm a Heel–Mike Heller | 1.50 | 3.00 | 4.50 | |
| 665 | Three's a Shroud–Richard S. Prather | 1.50 | 3.00 | 4.50 | M |
| 666 | Assignment–Stella Marni–Edward S. Aarons | 1.50 | 3.00 | 4.50 | M |
| 667 | Saddle Justice–Steven C. Lawrence | 1.50 | 3.00 | 4.50 | W |
| 668 | Don't Let Her Die–Tarn Scott | 1.50 | 3.00 | 4.50 | |
| 669 | So Young, So Wicked–Jonathan Craig | 1.50 | 3.00 | 4.50 | M |
| 670 | Agreement to Kill–Peter Rabe | 2.50 | 5.00 | 7.50 | M |
| 671 | Lusty Conquest–Lee Richards | 1.50 | 3.00 | 4.50 | E |
| 672 | Long Ride West–Richard Jessup | 1.50 | 3.00 | 4.50 | W |
| s673 | Women's Barracks–Tereska Torres | 1.50 | 3.00 | 4.50 | |
| 674 | Outlaw's Son–Clifton Adams | 1.50 | 3.00 | 4.50 | W |
| 675 | One Wild Oat–MacKinlay Kantor; 1957 | 1.50 | 3.00 | 4.50 | |
| 676 | Nice Guys Finish Dead–Albert Conroy | 1.50 | 3.00 | 4.50 | |
| 677 | Have Gat–Will Travel–Richard S. Prather | 1.50 | 3.00 | 4.50 | M |
| 678 | It's My Funeral–Peter Rabe | 2.50 | 5.00 | 7.50 | M |
| 679 | Gun Talk at Yuma–Frank Castle | 1.50 | 3.00 | 4.50 | W |
| 680 | The Hoods Take Over–Ovid Demaris | 2.50 | 5.00 | 7.50 | JD |
| 681 | Heller from Texas–William Heuman | 1.50 | 3.00 | 4.50 | W |
| 682 | The Tiger's Wife–Wade Miller | 1.25 | 2.50 | 3.75 | M |
| 683 | A Noose for the Desperado–Clifton Adams | 1.50 | 3.00 | 4.50 | W |
| s684 | Re-enter Fu Manchu–Sax Rohmer; orig. 1957 | 4.50 | 9.00 | 13.50 | A |
| 685 | Sundown at Crazy Horse–Vechel Howard | 1.50 | 3.00 | 4.50 | W |
| 686 | Last Stand at Papago Wells–Louis L'Amour; orig. 1957; c-McCarthy | 3.50 | 7.00 | 10.50 | W |
| 687 | Hostage for a Hood–Lionel White | 2.50 | 5.00 | 7.50 | |
| s688 | The Girl in the Belfry–Joseph Henry Jackson & Lenore Glen Offord | 1.50 | 3.00 | 4.50 | NF |
| 689 | Three-Day Terror–Vin Packer | 1.50 | 3.00 | 4.50 | |
| 690 | Crockett's Woman–Eric Hatch | 1.50 | 3.00 | 4.50 | |
| 691 | Fire in the Flesh–David Goodis; orig. 1957 | 12.00 | 24.00 | 36.00 | |
| 692 | Harry the Men High–Noel M. Loomis & Paul Leslie Peil | 1.50 | 3.00 | 4.50 | |
| 693 | Killers Are My Meat–Stephen Marlowe | 1.50 | 3.00 | 4.50 | M |
| 694 | Murder in the Raw–Bruno Fischer | 1.50 | 3.00 | 4.50 | M |
| 695 | Lovely and Lethal–Frank Castle | 1.50 | 3.00 | 4.50 | |
| 696 | Apache Rising–Marvin H. Albert | 1.50 | 3.00 | 4.50 | W |
| 697 | Hill Girl–Charles Williams | 2.00 | 4.00 | 6.00 | |
| 698 | The Baby Doll Murders–James O. Causey | 1.50 | 3.00 | 4.50 | M |
| 699 | Comanche Vengeance–Richard Jessup | 1.50 | 3.00 | 4.50 | W |
| 700 | The Tall Stranger–Louis L'Amour; orig. 1957; movie tie-in | 3.50 | 7.00 | 10.50 | W |
| 701 | Run from the Hunter–Keith Grantland (Charles Beaumont) | 7.50 | 15.00 | 22.50 | |
| 702 | The Case of the Beautiful Body–Jonathan Craig | 1.50 | 3.00 | 4.50 | M |
| 703 | The Voodoo Murders–Michael Avallone | 2.50 | 5.00 | 7.50 | M |
| s704 | This Is Costello–Norton Mockridge & Robert Prall | 1.50 | 3.00 | 4.50 | NF |
| 705 | Stagecoach West–William Heuman | 1.50 | 3.00 | 4.50 | W |
| 706 | The Massacre at San Pablo–Lewis B. Patten | 1.50 | 3.00 | 4.50 | W |
| 707 | Assignment–Budapest–Edward S. Aarons | 1.50 | 3.00 | 4.50 | M |
| 708 | The Brat–Gil Brewer | 2.00 | 4.00 | 6.00 | E |
| 709 | Murder in Red–Frank Castle | 1.50 | 3.00 | 4.50 | M |
| 710 | Journey into Terror–Peter Rabe | 2.50 | 5.00 | 7.50 | M |
| 711 | A Man of Parts–Vivian Connell | 1.50 | 3.00 | 4.50 | |
| 712 | The Wailing Frail–Richard S. Prather | 1.50 | 3.00 | 4.50 | M |
| 713 | Summons to Silverhorn–Kenneth Fowler | 1.50 | 3.00 | 4.50 | |
| 714 | Ambush on the Mesa–Gordon D. Shirreffs | 1.50 | 3.00 | 4.50 | W |
| 715 | Case of the Deadly Kiss–Milton K. Ozaki | 1.50 | 3.00 | 4.50 | M |

*Gold Medal 703, Gold Medal s734, Gold Medal 775.*

GOLD MEDAL, *continued*

| # | Title | V/Good | Fine | N/Mint | |
|---|---|---|---|---|---|
| 716 | Come Night, Come Evil–Jonathan Craig | 1.50 | 3.00 | 4.50 | M |
| 717 | For Love of Imabelle–Chester Himes | 3.50 | 7.00 | 10.50 | |
| 718 | The Crazy Mixed-Up Corpse–Michael Avallone; orig. 1957 | 2.50 | 5.00 | 7.50 | M |
| 719 | Savage Bride–Cornell Woolrich | 2.00 | 4.00 | 6.00 | M |
| 720 | Barren Land Showdown–Luke Short; aka Barren Land Murders | 1.50 | 3.00 | 4.50 | W |
| 721 | Murder on the Line–William L. Rohde | 1.50 | 3.00 | 4.50 | M |
| 722 | A Town to Tame–Joseph Chadwick | 1.50 | 3.00 | 4.50 | W |
| 723 | Five Rode West–Lewis B. Patten | 1.50 | 3.00 | 4.50 | W |
| 724 | The Damned–John D. MacDonald | 1.50 | 3.00 | 4.50 | M |
| s725 | The Great Debauch–Williams Forrest; 1958 | 1.50 | 3.00 | 4.50 | E |
| s726 | Three Times Infinity–Leo Margulies | 1.00 | 2.00 | 3.00 | SF |
| s727 | We, Too, Must Love–Ann Aldrich; orig. 1958 | 2.50 | 5.00 | 7.50 | E |
| 728 | Heller with a Gun–Louis L'Amour | 2.00 | 4.00 | 6.00 | W |
| 729 | Uncle Good's Girls–John Faulkner | 1.50 | 3.00 | 4.50 | E |
| 730 | Cabin Road–John Faulkner | 1.50 | 3.00 | 4.50 | E |
| s731 | 5:45 to Suburbia–Vin Packer | 1.50 | 3.00 | 4.50 | |
| 732 | Ripe Fruit–John McPartland | 1.50 | 3.00 | 4.50 | |
| 733 | Guns of Rio Conchos–Clair Huffaker | 2.00 | 4.00 | 6.00 | W |
| s734 | Teen-age Terror–Wenzell Brown | 2.50 | 5.00 | 7.50 | JD |
| s735 | The Rich and the Damned–Richard Himmel | 1.50 | 3.00 | 4.50 | |
| 736 | Cowboy–Clair Huffaker; movie tie-in | 2.00 | 4.00 | 6.00 | W |
| 737 | Dead Low Tide–John D. MacDonald | 2.00 | 4.00 | 6.00 | M |
| 738 | The Violent Ones–Howard Hunt | 1.50 | 3.00 | 4.50 | M |
| 739 | I, Mobster | 1.50 | 3.00 | 4.50 | M |
| 740 | Web of Murder–Harry Whittington | 2.00 | 4.00 | 6.00 | M |
| 741 | Outcast Gun–Giles A. Lutz | 1.50 | 3.00 | 4.50 | W |
| 742 | One-Man Massacre–Jonas Ward (William Ard) | 4.00 | 8.00 | 12.00 | W |
| 743 | I Like 'Em Tough–Curt Cannon | 2.00 | 4.00 | 6.00 | |
| 744 | The Secret of Sylvia–Lee Borden | 1.50 | 3.00 | 4.50 | |
| 745 | Take a Murder, Darling–Richard S. Prather | 1.50 | 3.00 | 4.50 | M |
| s746 | River Girl–Charles Williams | 2.00 | 4.00 | 6.00 | E |
| 747 | The Hoods Come Calling–Nick Quarry (Marvin H. Albert) | 2.00 | 4.00 | 6.00 | M |
| 748 | Badman's Holiday–Will Cook | 1.50 | 3.00 | 4.50 | W |
| 749 | Assignment–Angelina–Edward S. Aarons | 1.50 | 3.00 | 4.50 | M |
| 750 | The Lusting Drive–Ovid Demaris; 1958 | 1.50 | 3.00 | 4.50 | |
| s751 | War with the Gizmos–Murray Leinster | 2.00 | 4.00 | 6.00 | SF |
| 752 | Dakota Boomtown–Frank Castle | 1.50 | 3.00 | 4.50 | W |
| 753 | So Wicked My Love–Bruno Fischer | 1.00 | 2.00 | 3.00 | M |
| 754 | The Obsessed–Gertrude Schweitzer | 1.00 | 2.00 | 3.00 | |
| 755 | The Lady Kills–Bruno Fischer | 1.00 | 2.00 | 3.00 | M |
| 756 | The Law and Jake Wade–Marvin H. Albert; movie tie-in | 2.50 | 5.00 | 7.50 | W |
| s757 | Sumuru–Sax Rohmer | 2.00 | 4.00 | 6.00 | A |
| 758 | Devil May Come–Wade Miller | 1.50 | 3.00 | 4.50 | |
| 759 | Wyoming Jones–Richard Telfair | 1.50 | 3.00 | 4.50 | |
| 760 | The Bounty Killer–Marvin H. Albert; movie tie-in | 2.00 | 4.00 | 6.00 | W |
| 761 | Park Avenue Tramp–Fletcher Flora | 1.50 | 3.00 | 4.50 | E |
| s762 | The Tycoon and the Tigress–William R. Cox | 1.00 | 2.00 | 3.00 | |
| 763 | Stop This Man–Peter Rabe | 2.50 | 5.00 | 7.50 | M |
| s764 | The Rise and Fall of Dr. Carey–O.O. Osborne | 1.00 | 2.00 | 3.00 | |
| 765 | No Business for a Lady–James Rubel | 1.00 | 2.00 | 3.00 | M |
| 766 | Catspaw Ordeal–Edward Ronns | 1.00 | 2.00 | 3.00 | M |
| 767 | Murder for the Bride–John D. MacDonald | 2.00 | 4.00 | 6.00 | M |
| d768 | The Lost Years of Jesus Revealed–Rev. Dr. Charles Francis Potter | 1.50 | 3.00 | 4.50 | NF |
| 769 | Violence Is My Business–Stephen Marlowe | 1.50 | 3.00 | 4.50 | M |
| 770 | The Scrambled Yeggs–Richard S. Prather | 2.50 | 5.00 | 7.50 | M |
| 771 | Texas Outlaw–Richard Jessup | 1.50 | 3.00 | 4.50 | W |
| 772 | Feud at Forked River–Philip Ketchum | 1.50 | 3.00 | 4.50 | W |
| s773 | Mission for Vengeance–Peter Rabe | 2.50 | 5.00 | 7.50 | M |
| s774 | We Walk Alone–Ann Aldrich | 2.00 | 4.00 | 6.00 | |
| 775 | Coffin for a Hood–Lionel White; orig. 1958 | 2.50 | 5.00 | 7.50 | M |
| 776 | Murder Comes Calling–Malcolm Douglas | 1.50 | 3.00 | 4.50 | M |
| s777 | Clemmie–John D. MacDonald | 2.00 | 4.00 | 6.00 | |
| 778 | Home Is the Outlaw–Lewis B. Patten | 1.50 | 3.00 | 4.50 | W |
| 779 | Tucson–Paul Leslie Peil; movie tie-in | 1.50 | 3.00 | 4.50 | |
| 780 | The Mob Says Murder–Albert Conroy | 1.50 | 3.00 | 4.50 | M |
| 781 | Here Is My Body–Booth Mooney | 1.50 | 3.00 | 4.50 | |
| 782 | Judge Me Not–John D. MacDonald | 1.50 | 3.00 | 4.50 | M |
| s783 | The Fast Buck–Bruno Fischer | 1.50 | 3.00 | 4.50 | M |
| 784 | Case of the Petticoat Murder–Jonathan Craig | 1.50 | 3.00 | 4.50 | M |
| 785 | The Forbidden Land–Dan Cushman | 2.00 | 4.00 | 6.00 | A |
| 786 | Too Young to Die–Lionel White; orig. 1958 | 2.50 | 5.00 | 7.50 | M |
| 787 | Death's Lovely Mask–John Flagg | 1.50 | 3.00 | 4.50 | M |
| 788 | Brand of a Texan–Steven C. Lawrence | 1.50 | 3.00 | 4.50 | W |
| 789 | Tall in the West–Vechel Howard; c-Abbett | 1.50 | 3.00 | 4.50 | W |
| s790 | The Neon Jungle–John D. MacDonald | 1.50 | 3.00 | 4.50 | M |
| s791 | Branded Woman–Wade Miller | 1.00 | 2.00 | 3.00 | |
| 792 | The Brass Cupcake–John D. MacDonald | 1.50 | 3.00 | 4.50 | M |
| s793 | Spring Fire–Vin Packer | 1.50 | 3.00 | 4.50 | |
| 794 | Trouble at Borrasca Rim–Mark Owen | 1.50 | 3.00 | 4.50 | |
| 795 | Case of the Cop's Wife–Milton K. Ozaki | 1.00 | 2.00 | 3.00 | M |
| s796 | Self-made Widow–Philip Race | 1.00 | 2.00 | 3.00 | M |
| s797 | The Evil Friendship–Vin Packer | 1.50 | 3.00 | 4.50 | |
| 798 | Guns of North Texas–Will Cook | 1.50 | 3.00 | 4.50 | W |
| 799 | Assignment–Madeline–Edward S. Aarons | 1.00 | 2.00 | 3.00 | M |
| 800 | Two Deaths Must Die–Richard Himmel | 1.00 | 2.00 | 3.00 | M |
| s801 | The Man Who Said No–Walt Grove; 1958 | 1.00 | 2.00 | 3.00 | |
| s802 | The Devil's Mistress–Kenneth Thomas; movie tie-in | 1.00 | 2.00 | 3.00 | |
| 803 | Buchanan Gets Mad–Jonas Ward (William Ard) | 4.00 | 8.00 | 12.00 | W |
| 804 | Relentless Gun–Giles A. Lutz | 1.00 | 2.00 | 3.00 | W |
| 805 | The Deadly Pay-off–William H. Duhart | 1.00 | 2.00 | 3.00 | |
| 806 | Murder in Room 13–Albert Conroy | 1.00 | 2.00 | 3.00 | M |
| 807 | Death Takes an Option–Neil MacNeil | 1.00 | 2.00 | 3.00 | M |
| 808 | Party Girl–Marvin H. Albert; movie tie-in | 1.50 | 3.00 | 4.50 | R |
| s809 | Plunder–Benjamin Appel | 1.00 | 2.00 | 3.00 | C |
| 810 | The Killer–Wade Miller | 1.00 | 2.00 | 3.00 | M |
| 811 | Take Your Last Look–Matt Brady | 1.00 | 2.00 | 3.00 | |
| s812 | The Ungilded Lily–Morton Cooper | 1.00 | 2.00 | 3.00 | |
| 813 | Terror Is My Trade–Stephen Marlowe | 1.50 | 3.00 | 4.50 | M |
| 814 | I'm Cannon–for Hire–Curt Cannon | 1.50 | 3.00 | 4.50 | M |
| 815 | Showdown at War Cloud–Lewis B. Patten | 1.00 | 2.00 | 3.00 | W |
| 816 | Fort Desperation–Frank Castle | 1.00 | 2.00 | 3.00 | W |
| s817 | Slab Happy–Richard S. Prather | 1.00 | 2.00 | 3.00 | M |
| 818 | Everybody Had a Gun–Richard S. Prather | 1.00 | 2.00 | 3.00 | M |
| 819 | Bodies in Bedlam–Richard S. Prather | 1.00 | 2.00 | 3.00 | M |
| 820 | Case of the Vanishing Beauty–Richard S. Prather | 1.00 | 2.00 | 3.00 | M |
| 821 | Find This Woman–Richard S. Prather | 1.00 | 2.00 | 3.00 | M |
| 822 | Man on the Run–Charles Williams | 5.00 | 10.00 | 15.00 | |
| 823 | Passage to Samoa–Day Keene; orig. 1958 | 4.00 | 8.00 | 12.00 | |
| 824 | Trail of a Tramp–Nick Quarry (Marvin H. Albert) | 1.50 | 3.00 | 4.50 | |
| s825 | Blood on the Desert–Peter Rabe; 1958; c-Powers | 2.50 | 5.00 | 7.50 | |
| 826 | Renegade Posse–Marvin H. Albert | 1.00 | 2.00 | 3.00 | W |
| 827 | Day of the Gun–Richard Telfair | 1.00 | 2.00 | 3.00 | W |
| s828 | Naked Ebony–Dan Cushman | 1.00 | 2.00 | 3.00 | A |
| s829 | The Awakening of Jenny–Lillian Colter | 1.00 | 2.00 | 3.00 | E |
| 830 | Way of a Wanton–Richard S. Prather | 1.00 | 2.00 | 3.00 | M |
| 831 | Fires That Destroy–Harry Whittington | 1.50 | 3.00 | 4.50 | |
| s832 | The Monster From World's End–Murray Leinster | 2.00 | 4.00 | 6.00 | SF |
| d833 | I Am a Woman–Ann Bannon | 3.50 | 7.00 | 10.50 | |
| 834 | Assignment–Carlotta Cortez–Edward S. Aarons | 1.50 | 3.00 | 4.50 | M |
| 835 | The Captain Must Die–Robert Colby | 1.00 | 2.00 | 3.00 | |
| s836 | Smoke in the Valley–Steve Frazee | 1.00 | 2.00 | 3.00 | W |
| 837 | Outcast of Cripple Creek–Will Cook | 1.00 | 2.00 | 3.00 | W |
| 838 | Darling, It's Death–Richard S. Prather | 1.00 | 2.00 | 3.00 | M |
| d839 | City of Women–Nancy Morgan | 1.00 | 2.00 | 3.00 | |
| s840 | Jewel of the Java Sea–Dan Cushman | 1.00 | 2.00 | 3.00 | |
| 841 | . . . And Be My Love–Ledru Baker, Jr | 1.00 | 2.00 | 3.00 | |
| 842 | Wagon Train West–William Heuman | 1.00 | 2.00 | 3.00 | W |

**GOLD MEDAL,** *continued*

| No. | Title | V/Good | Fine | N/Mint | |
|---|---|---|---|---|---|
| 843 | Outlaw Marshal–Ray Hogan | 1.00 | 2.00 | 3.00 | W |
| s844 | Third on a Seesaw–Neil MacNeil | 1.00 | 2.00 | 3.00 | |
| s845 | Kitten with a Whip–Wade Miller | 2.00 | 4.00 | 6.00 | |
| 846 | That Jane from Maine–Marvin H. Albert; 1959; movie tie-in | 1.50 | 3.00 | 4.50 | H |
| 847 | The Bloody Medallion–Richard Telfair | 1.00 | 2.00 | 3.00 | M |
| 848 | Strip for Murder–Richard S. Prather | 1.00 | 2.00 | 3.00 | M |
| 849 | Always Leave 'Em Dying–Richard S. Prather | 1.00 | 2.00 | 3.00 | M |
| 850 | Too Many Crooks–Richard S. Prather; 1959 | 1.00 | 2.00 | 3.00 | M |
| 851 | The Wailing Frail–Richard S. Prather | 1.00 | 2.00 | 3.00 | M |
| d852 | Tempest–R.V. Cassill; movie tie-in | 1.00 | 2.00 | 3.00 | A |
| s853 | The Rest Must Die–Richard Foster (K.F. Crossen); orig. 1959; c-Powers | 2.00 | 4.00 | 6.00 | SF |
| 854 | Murder with Love–Vechel Howard | 1.00 | 2.00 | 3.00 | M |
| 855 | Secret of the Second Door–Robert Colby | 1.00 | 2.00 | 3.00 | |
| 856 | The Reformed Gun–Marvin H. Albert | 1.00 | 2.00 | 3.00 | W |
| 857 | Savage Breed–Joseph Chadwick | 1.00 | 2.00 | 3.00 | W |
| 858 | 13 French Street–Gil Brewer | 1.00 | 2.00 | 3.00 | E |
| s859 | Beyond Desire–Richard Himmel | 1.00 | 2.00 | 3.00 | E |
| 860 | Have Gat–Will Travel–Richard S. Prather | 1.00 | 2.00 | 3.00 | M |
| s861 | The Twisted Ones–Vin Packer | 2.50 | 5.00 | 7.50 | JD |
| 862 | A Ticket to Hell–Harry Whittington | 1.50 | 3.00 | 4.50 | |
| 863 | Assignment–Helene–Edward S. Aarons | 1.00 | 2.00 | 3.00 | M |
| 864 | Bring Me Another Corpse–Peter Rabe | 2.50 | 5.00 | 7.50 | M |
| 865 | Above the Palo Duro–Noel M. Loomis | 1.00 | 2.00 | 3.00 | W |
| 866 | The Ruthless Men–Lewis B. Patten | 1.00 | 2.00 | 3.00 | W |
| 867 | Smash-up–Theodore Pratt | 1.00 | 2.00 | 3.00 | |
| 868 | Return of Sumuru–Sax Rohmer | 1.50 | 3.00 | 4.50 | A |
| s869 | The Judas Hour–Howard Hunt | 1.00 | 2.00 | 3.00 | M |
| 870 | Let Them Eat Bullets–Howard Schoenfeld | 1.00 | 2.00 | 3.00 | M |
| 871 | Strangers in My Bed–Allen O'Quinn | 1.00 | 2.00 | 3.00 | |
| 872 | Case of the Nervous Nude–Jonathan Craig | 1.00 | 2.00 | 3.00 | M |
| 873 | Prowler in the Night–Jack Matcha | 1.00 | 2.00 | 3.00 | M |
| 874 | Take a Step to Murder–Day Keene; orig. 1959 | 2.50 | 5.00 | 7.50 | M |
| 875 | Armande–Daniel May; 1959 | 1.00 | 2.00 | 3.00 | |
| 876 | The Brave Rifles–Gordon D. Shirreffs | 1.00 | 2.00 | 3.00 | W |
| 877 | The Homing Bullet–Giles A. Lutz | 1.00 | 2.00 | 3.00 | W |
| 878 | Murder on Her Mind–Vechel Howard | 1.00 | 2.00 | 3.00 | M |
| 879 | Wake Up and Scream–Milton K. Ozaki | 1.00 | 2.00 | 3.00 | M |
| 880 | Homicide Is My Game–Stephen Marlowe | 1.50 | 3.00 | 4.50 | M |
| 881 | The Kingdom of Johnny Cool–John McPartland | 1.50 | 3.00 | 4.50 | M |
| 882 | Lawless Guns–Dudley Dean | 1.00 | 2.00 | 3.00 | W |
| 883 | Wyoming Jones for Hire–Richard Telfair | 1.00 | 2.00 | 3.00 | W |
| 884 | Weep for Me–John D. MacDonald | 2.50 | 5.00 | 7.50 | M |
| 885 | The Mating Cry–Frank Daniels | 1.00 | 2.00 | 3.00 | M |
| 886 | House of Flesh–Bruno Fischer | 1.00 | 2.00 | 3.00 | M |
| s887 | Over Her Dead Body–Richard S. Prather | 1.00 | 2.00 | 3.00 | M |
| 888 | Killer Take All–Philip Race | 1.00 | 2.00 | 3.00 | M |
| 889 | Backwoods Tramp–Harry Whittington | 2.00 | 4.00 | 6.00 | E |
| 890 | The Corpse That Talked–Richard Telfair | 1.00 | 2.00 | 3.00 | M |
| 891 | A Hole in the Head–Arnold Schulman; movie tie-in | 2.50 | 5.00 | 7.50 | |
| 892 | Marshal without a Badge–Ray Hogan | 1.00 | 2.00 | 3.00 | W |
| 893 | To Tame a Land–Louis L'Amour | 1.50 | 3.00 | 4.50 | W |
| 894 | All These Condemned–John D. MacDonald | 1.00 | 2.00 | 3.00 | M |
| 895 | Assignment to Disaster–Edward S. Aarons | 1.00 | 2.00 | 3.00 | M |
| 896 | Three's a Shroud–Richard S. Prather | 1.00 | 2.00 | 3.00 | M |
| s897 | Cry Kill–Wenzell Brown | 2.50 | 5.00 | 7.50 | JD |
| 898 | Two Guns for Hire–Neil MacNeil | 1.00 | 2.00 | 3.00 | |
| 899 | Bier for a Chaser–Richard Foster (K.F. Crossen); orig. 1959 | 2.00 | 4.00 | 6.00 | M |
| 900 | Return to Vikki–John Tomerlin; 1959 | 1.00 | 2.00 | 3.00 | |
| 901 | The Lustful Ape–Bruno Fischer | 1.00 | 2.00 | 3.00 | M |
| 902 | Rider from Wind River–Marvin H. Albert | 1.00 | 2.00 | 3.00 | W |
| s903 | The Thrill Kids–Vin Packer | 2.50 | 5.00 | 7.50 | JD |
| 904 | Cartoon Fun from True | 1.50 | 3.00 | 4.50 | H |
| 905 | Hondo–Louis L'Amour | 1.50 | 3.00 | 4.50 | W |
| 906 | Assignment–Stella Marni–Edward S. Aarons | 1.00 | 2.00 | 3.00 | M |
| s907 | The Beach Girls–John D. MacDonald | 4.00 | 8.00 | 12.00 | M |
| s908 | Uncle Sagamore and His Girls–Charles Williams | 7.50 | 15.00 | 22.50 | E |
| 909 | The Last Night–John McPartland | 1.50 | 3.00 | 4.50 | |
| s910 | The Slasher–Ovid Demaris | 1.00 | 2.00 | 3.00 | M |
| s911 | Assignment–Lili Lamaris–Edward S. Aarons | 1.00 | 2.00 | 3.00 | M |
| 912 | Gun Shy–Dudley Dean & Les Savage, Jr | 1.00 | 2.00 | 3.00 | W |
| s913 | Angels in the Gutter–Joseph Hilton | 2.50 | 5.00 | 7.50 | JD |
| 914 | Trouble Is My Name–Stephen Marlowe | 1.00 | 2.00 | 3.00 | M |
| 915 | It's My Funeral–Peter Rabe | 2.50 | 5.00 | 7.50 | M |
| 916 | Bullet Barricade–Leslie Ernenwein | 1.00 | 2.00 | 3.00 | W |
| s917 | Teen-age Mafia–Wenzell Brown | 2.50 | 5.00 | 7.50 | JD |
| 918 | Pillow Talk–Marvin H. Albert; movie tie-in | 2.00 | 4.00 | 6.00 | R |
| s919 | Women in the Shadows–Ann Bannon | 3.50 | 7.00 | 10.50 | |
| 920 | Top Man with a Gun–Lewis B. Patten | 1.00 | 2.00 | 3.00 | W |
| 921 | The Wife Next Door–R.V. Cassill | 1.00 | 2.00 | 3.00 | |
| s922 | To Hell Together–H. Vernor Dixon | 1.00 | 2.00 | 3.00 | |
| 923 | Assignment–Suicide–Edward S. Aarons | 1.00 | 2.00 | 3.00 | M |
| 924 | The Avenger–Matthew Blood | 1.00 | 2.00 | 3.00 | M |
| 925 | Song of the Gun–Dudley Dean; 1959 | 1.00 | 2.00 | 3.00 | W |
| d926 | Double in Trouble–Stephen Marlowe & Richard S. Prather | 1.00 | 2.00 | 3.00 | M |
| 927 | Ain't Gonna Rain No More–John Faulkner | 1.50 | 3.00 | 4.50 | E |
| 928 | Second-hand Nude–Bruno Fischer | 1.00 | 2.00 | 3.00 | M |
| s929 | Emperor Fu Manchu–Sax Rohmer; orig. 1959 | 3.50 | 7.00 | 10.50 | A |
| 930 | Case of the Village Tramp–Jonathan Craig | 1.00 | 2.00 | 3.00 | M |
| 931 | Too Hot to Hold–Day Keene; orig. 1959 | 3.50 | 7.00 | 10.50 | |
| 932 | The Secret of Apache Canyon–Richard Telfair | 1.00 | 2.00 | 3.00 | W |
| s933 | The Tormented–Theodore Pratt | 1.00 | 2.00 | 3.00 | |
| 934 | Little Sister–Lee Roberts | 1.00 | 2.00 | 3.00 | E |
| 935 | Many Rivers to Cross–Steve Frazee | 1.00 | 2.00 | 3.00 | W |
| s936 | The Big Guy–Wade Miller | 1.00 | 2.00 | 3.00 | |
| s937 | Four from Planet 5–Murray Leinster; orig. 1959 | 2.00 | 4.00 | 6.00 | SF |
| 938 | The Girl with No Place to Hide–Nick Quarry | 1.00 | 2.00 | 3.00 | M |
| 939 | Time Enough to Die–Peter Rabe | 2.50 | 5.00 | 7.50 | M |
| 940 | The Deadly Desire–Robert Colby | 1.00 | 2.00 | 3.00 | |
| s941 | The Young and Violent–Vin Packer | 2.00 | 4.00 | 6.00 | JD |
| 942 | Witness This Woman–Gardner F. Fox | 1.50 | 3.00 | 4.50 | |
| 943 | Stage to Painted Creek–Vechel Howard | 1.00 | 2.00 | 3.00 | W |
| 944 | The Range Buster–William Heuman | 1.00 | 2.00 | 3.00 | W |
| 945 | The Tiger's Wife–Wade Miller | 1.00 | 2.00 | 3.00 | M |
| s946 | Thunderclap–Jack Sheridan | 1.00 | 2.00 | 3.00 | |
| 948 | Kiss Off the Dead–Garrity; 1960 | 1.00 | 2.00 | 3.00 | M |
| S949 | Lament for a Virgin–Lionel White | 2.00 | 4.00 | 6.00 | M |
| 950 | Backwoods Teaser–Gil Brewer | 2.00 | 4.00 | 6.00 | |
| 951 | Buchanan's Revenge–Jonas Ward (William Ard) | 4.00 | 8.00 | 12.00 | W |
| 952 | Nero's Mistress–John Tessitore; movie tie-in | 2.50 | 5.00 | 7.50 | E |
| S953 | This Woman–Albert Idell | 1.00 | 2.00 | 3.00 | |
| 955 | Heller with a Gun–Louis L'Amour; movie tie-in | 2.00 | 4.00 | 6.00 | W |
| 957 | Death of a Citizen–Donald Hamilton | 1.00 | 2.00 | 3.00 | |
| 958 | Yellowleg–A.S. Fleischman | 1.00 | 2.00 | 3.00 | W |
| 959 | Heat of Night–Harry Whittington | 2.00 | 4.00 | 6.00 | |
| 960 | The Extortioners–Ovid Demaris | 1.00 | 2.00 | 3.00 | |
| S961 | Slam the Big Door–John D. MacDonald | 5.00 | 10.00 | 15.00 | M |
| S962 | The Damned–John D. MacDonald | 1.00 | 2.00 | 3.00 | M |
| 963 | Dead Low Tide–John D. MacDonald | 1.00 | 2.00 | 3.00 | M |
| 964 | Hot Dam–Neil MacNeil | 1.00 | 2.00 | 3.00 | |
| S965 | Odd Girl Out–Ann Bannon; 1st ed. 1960 | 3.50 | 7.00 | 10.50 | |
| S966 | 5:45 to Suburbia–Vin Packer | 1.00 | 2.00 | 3.00 | |
| 967 | My Lovely Executioner–Peter Rabe | 2.50 | 5.00 | 7.50 | M |
| 968 | Death of a Ladies' Man–Lee Roberts (Robert Lee Martin) | 1.00 | 2.00 | 3.00 | M |
| 969 | Thimk Cartoon Collection | 1.50 | 3.00 | 4.50 | H |
| 970 | Blood Moon–Frank Castle | 1.50 | 3.00 | 4.50 | W |

GOLD MEDAL, *continued*

| # | Title | V/Good | Fine | N/Mint | |
|---|---|---|---|---|---|
| 971 | Assignment–Budapest–Edward S. Aarons | 1.00 | 2.00 | 3.00 | M |
| 972 | Pure Sweet Hell–Malcolm Douglas | 1.00 | 2.00 | 3.00 | |
| D973 | Driven–Richard Gehman | 1.00 | 2.00 | 3.00 | |
| 974 | Outcast of Murder Mesa–Kenneth Fowler | 1.00 | 2.00 | 3.00 | W |
| S975 | World without Women–Day Keene & Leonard Pruyn | 2.50 | 5.00 | 7.50 | SF |
| S976 | The Girl on the Best Seller List–Vin Packer | 1.00 | 2.00 | 3.00 | |
| S977 | Journey to a Woman–Ann Bannon; 1st ed. 1960 | 3.50 | 7.00 | 10.50 | |
| 978 | The Wranglers–Will Cook | 1.00 | 2.00 | 3.00 | W |
| 979 | Assignment–Zoraya–Edward S. Aarons | 1.00 | 2.00 | 3.00 | M |
| 980 | Johnny Staccato–Frank Boyd; TV tie-in | 1.00 | 2.00 | 3.00 | M |
| 981 | Inquest–Milton K. Ozaki | 1.00 | 2.00 | 3.00 | M |
| S982 | The Beats–ed. Seymour Krim | 2.50 | 5.00 | 7.50 | |
| 984 | Rebel Raider–Joseph Chadwick | 1.00 | 2.00 | 3.00 | W |
| 986 | Death Is My Comrade–Stephen Marlowe (Milton Lesser) | 1.00 | 2.00 | 3.00 | |
| 987 | The Three-Way Split–Gil Brewer | 1.50 | 3.00 | 4.50 | |
| 988 | One for Sleep–Frank Bonham | 1.00 | 2.00 | 3.00 | M |
| S989 | Dark December–Alfred Coppel | 1.00 | 2.00 | 3.00 | SF |
| S990 | Dance with the Dead–Richard S. Prather | 1.00 | 2.00 | 3.00 | M |
| S991 | Starfall–John Cunningham | 1.00 | 2.00 | 3.00 | |
| 992 | Ride for Texas–William Heuman | 1.00 | 2.00 | 3.00 | W |
| 993 | Funny Cartoons by VIP–Virgil Partch | 1.50 | 3.00 | 4.50 | H |
| 994 | Shanghai Incident–Stephen Becker | 1.00 | 2.00 | 3.00 | |
| 995 | Too Late for Mourning–Richard Foster | 2.00 | 4.00 | 6.00 | M |
| 996 | Murder Me for Kicks–Peter Rabe | 2.50 | 5.00 | 7.50 | M |
| S997 | 13 Great Stories of Science Fiction–ed. Groff Conklin | 1.00 | 2.00 | 3.00 | SF |
| 998 | Steal Big–Lionel White | 2.00 | 4.00 | 6.00 | M |
| 999 | Sundance–Richard Telfair; TV tie-in | 2.00 | 4.00 | 6.00 | W |
| S1000 | North Beach Girl–John Trinian | 1.00 | 2.00 | 3.00 | E |
| 1001 | South of the Sun–Wade Miller | 1.00 | 2.00 | 3.00 | M |
| S1002 | The Kid Was a Killer–Caryl Chessman | 1.50 | 3.00 | 4.50 | |
| 1003 | The Second Longest Night–Stephen Marlowe | 1.00 | 2.00 | 3.00 | M |
| 1004 | Funny Business–ed. Charles Preston | 1.00 | 2.00 | 3.00 | H |
| S1005 | College Confidential–Irving Shulman; movie tie-in | 2.00 | 4.00 | 6.00 | E |
| 1006 | Scream Bloody Murder–Richard Telfair | 1.00 | 2.00 | 3.00 | M |
| 1007 | The Enforcer–Ovid Demaris | 1.00 | 2.00 | 3.00 | M |
| S1008 | Pieces of the Game–Lee Gifford | 1.00 | 2.00 | 3.00 | C |
| D1009 | Carol in a Thousand Cities–ed. Ann Aldrich | 2.50 | 5.00 | 7.50 | |
| 1010 | McGivern–T.V. Olsen | 1.50 | 3.00 | 4.50 | W |
| 1011 | Murder in the Raw–Bruno Fischer | 1.00 | 2.00 | 3.00 | M |
| S1012 | Hell Hath No Fury–Charles Williams | 2.00 | 4.00 | 6.00 | M |
| S1013 | The Murder Kick–Wenzell Brown | 1.50 | 3.00 | 4.50 | M |
| 1014 | Lila My Lovely–Dudley Dean | 1.00 | 2.00 | 3.00 | |
| S1015 | The Only Girl in the Game–John D. MacDonald | 5.00 | 10.00 | 15.00 | M |
| 1016 | High Lawless–T.V. Olsen | 1.50 | 3.00 | 4.50 | W |
| 1017 | It Started in Naples–Saul Cooper; movie tie-in | 1.50 | 3.00 | 4.50 | H |
| 1018 | Peril Is My Pay–Stephen Marlowe | 1.50 | 3.00 | 4.50 | M |
| 1019 | Mountain Girl–Cord Wainer (Thomas Dewey) | 1.50 | 3.00 | 4.50 | |
| 1020 | Hostage for a Hood–Lionel White | 1.00 | 2.00 | 3.00 | M |
| 1021 | The Name's Buchanan–Jonas Ward (William Ard) | 1.50 | 3.00 | 4.50 | W |
| 1023 | Hell to Eternity–Edward S. Aarons; movie tie-in | 1.50 | 3.00 | 4.50 | C |
| 1024 | Meanwhile Back at the Morgue–Michael Avallone | 2.00 | 4.00 | 6.00 | M |
| 1025 | The Wrecking Crew–Donald Hamilton | 1.50 | 3.00 | 4.50 | M |
| 1026 | Buchanan on the Prod–Jonas Ward (William Ard) | 4.00 | 8.00 | 12.00 | W |
| 1027 | Sinner Take All–Wade Miller | 1.00 | 2.00 | 3.00 | M |
| S1028 | Seminole–Theodore Pratt | 1.00 | 2.00 | 3.00 | A |
| S1029 | Strip for Murder–Richard S. Prather | 1.00 | 2.00 | 3.00 | M |
| 1030 | He Rode Alone–Steve Frazee | 1.00 | 2.00 | 3.00 | W |
| 1031 | Uncle Good's Week-end Party–John Faulkner | 1.50 | 3.00 | 4.50 | |
| S1032 | Way of a Wanton–Richard S. Prather | 1.00 | 2.00 | 3.00 | M |
| 1033 | No Chance in Hell–Nick Quarry (Marvin H. Albert) | 1.00 | 2.00 | 3.00 | M |
| 1034 | Hot Saturday–P.J. Reed-Marr; 1960 | 1.00 | 2.00 | 3.00 | |
| 1035 | Texas Fever–Donald Hamilton | 1.00 | 2.00 | 3.00 | W |
| S1036 | Assignment–Mara Tirana–Edward S. Aarons | 1.00 | 2.00 | 3.00 | M |
| 1037 | The Trouble with Love–Basil Heatter | 1.00 | 2.00 | 3.00 | |
| S1038 | Vip's All New Bar Guide–John Armstrong & Virgil Partch | 1.50 | 3.00 | 4.50 | H |
| S1039 | Darling, It's Death–Richard S. Prather | 1.00 | 2.00 | 3.00 | M |
| S1040 | Always Leave 'Em Dying–Richard S. Prather | 1.00 | 2.00 | 3.00 | M |
| 1041 | The Tall Stranger–Louis L'Amour | 1.50 | 3.00 | 4.50 | W |
| S1042 | Run, Chico, Run–Wenzell Brown | 1.50 | 3.00 | 4.50 | JD |
| 1043 | The Star Trap–Robert Colby | 1.00 | 2.00 | 3.00 | |
| 1044 | Hell Can Wait–Harry Whittington | 2.00 | 4.00 | 6.00 | |
| 1045 | The Turncoat–Hal G. Evarts | 1.00 | 2.00 | 3.00 | |
| S1046 | The Comfortable Coffin–ed. Richard S. Prather; 1960 | 2.00 | 4.00 | 6.00 | M |
| S1047 | Angel's Flight–Lou Cameron | 1.00 | 2.00 | 3.00 | |
| S1049 | Have Gat–Will Travel–Richard S. Prather | 1.00 | 2.00 | 3.00 | M |
| 1050 | Desire in the Dust–Harry Whittington; movie tie-in | 1.00 | 2.00 | 3.00 | |
| S1051 | The Wailing Frail–Richard S. Prather | 1.00 | 2.00 | 3.00 | M |
| 1053 | Till It Hurts–Nick Quarry (Marvin Albert) | 1.00 | 2.00 | 3.00 | M |
| 1054 | The Girl Between–Bruno Fischer | 1.00 | 2.00 | 3.00 | M |
| 1055 | The Death Ride–Neil MacNeil | 1.00 | 2.00 | 3.00 | M |
| 1056 | The Dark Raiders–E.E. Halleran | 1.00 | 2.00 | 3.00 | W |
| S1057 | Rogue Moon–Algis Budrys | 1.50 | 3.00 | 4.50 | SF |
| 1058 | Connolly's Woman–Harry Whittington | 1.50 | 3.00 | 4.50 | |
| S1059 | Too Many Crooks–Richard S. Prather; aka Ride a High Horse | 1.00 | 2.00 | 3.00 | M |
| S1060 | Three's a Shroud–Richard S. Prather | 1.00 | 2.00 | 3.00 | M |
| S1061 | The Neon Jungle–John D. MacDonald | 1.50 | 3.00 | 4.50 | M |
| 1062 | Run from the Hunter–Keith Grantland (Charles Beaumont) | 3.50 | 7.00 | 10.50 | M |
| 1063 | The Late Mrs. Five–Richard Wormser | 1.00 | 2.00 | 3.00 | |
| S1064 | End of a J.D.–John Gonzales | 2.00 | 4.00 | 6.00 | JD |
| S1065 | Case of the Laughing Virgin–Jonathan Craig | 1.00 | 2.00 | 3.00 | M |
| S1066 | The Marriage–Ann Bannon; 1st ed. 1960 | 3.50 | 7.00 | 10.50 | |
| 1067 | Gunswift–T.V. Olsen | 1.50 | 3.00 | 4.50 | W |
| S1068 | Wild Harvest–Stephen Longstreet | 1.50 | 3.00 | 4.50 | |
| S1069 | Judge Me Not–John D. MacDonald; 1960 | 1.50 | 3.00 | 4.50 | M |
| S1070 | The Sin Shouter of Cabin Road–John Faulkner | 1.50 | 3.00 | 4.50 | |
| 1071 | Ambush on the Mesa–Gordon D. Shirreffs | 1.00 | 2.00 | 3.00 | W |
| S1072 | Shell Scott's Seven Slaughters–Richard S. Prather; 1961 | 2.00 | 4.00 | 6.00 | M |
| S1073 | Assignment–Lowlands–Edward S. Aarons | 1.00 | 2.00 | 3.00 | M |
| S1074 | The Damnation of Adam Blessing–Vin Packer | 1.00 | 2.00 | 3.00 | |
| S1075 | Felony Tank–Malcolm Braly | 1.00 | 2.00 | 3.00 | |
| S1076 | Where Is Janice Gantry?–John D. MacDonald | 5.00 | 10.00 | 15.00 | M |
| S1077 | The Slavers–Richard Telfair | 1.50 | 3.00 | 4.50 | |
| S1078 | Murder Is My Dish–Stephen Marlowe | 1.00 | 2.00 | 3.00 | M |
| S1079 | Nice Guys Finish Dead–Albert Conroy | 1.00 | 2.00 | 3.00 | M |
| S1080 | Barren Land Showdown–Luke Short; aka Barren Land Murders | 1.00 | 2.00 | 3.00 | W |
| S1081 | High Gun–Leslie Ernenwein | 1.00 | 2.00 | 3.00 | W |
| S1082 | The Removers–Donald Hamilton | 1.00 | 2.00 | 3.00 | |
| S1083 | Night Squad–David Goodis; 1st ed. 1961 | 10.00 | 20.00 | 30.00 | M |
| S1084 | Badman's Holiday–Will Cook | 1.00 | 2.00 | 3.00 | W |
| S1085 | Mona–Lawrence Block | 2.50 | 5.00 | 7.50 | M |
| S1086 | Shadow of a Gun–Carter Travis Young | 1.00 | 2.00 | 3.00 | W |
| S1087 | Whip Hand–W. Franklin Sanders; c-Abbett | 2.50 | 5.00 | 7.50 | |
| S1088 | The Hoods Take Over–Ovid Demaris | 2.00 | 4.00 | 6.00 | JD |
| S1089 | Murder on the Line–William L. Rohde; aka High Red for Dead | 1.00 | 2.00 | 3.00 | M |
| S1090 | Ripe Fruit–John McPartland | 1.50 | 3.00 | 4.50 | |
| S1091 | Assignment–Burma Girl–Edward S. Aarons | 1.00 | 2.00 | 3.00 | M |
| S1092 | Pattern for Panic–Richard S. Prather | 1.00 | 2.00 | 3.00 | M |
| S1093 | Season of Assassins–Geoffrey Wagner | 1.00 | 2.00 | 3.00 | |
| S1094 | Good Luck, Sucker–Richard Telfair | 1.00 | 2.00 | 3.00 | M |
| S1095 | Swamp Sister–Robert Edmond Alter | 1.50 | 3.00 | 4.50 | |

GOLD MEDAL, *continued*

| | | V/Good | Fine | N/Mint | |
|---|---|---|---|---|---|
| S1098 | Killers Are My Meat–Stephen Marlowe | 1.00 | 2.00 | 3.00 | M |
| S1099 | The Great Debauch–William Forrest | 1.00 | 2.00 | 3.00 | C |
| S1100 | Death for Mr. Big–John Gonzales | 1.00 | 2.00 | 3.00 | |
| S1101 | The Big Gamble–Robert W. Krepps; movie tie-in | 1.50 | 3.00 | 4.50 | |
| S1102 | Nurses' Quarters–R.V. Cassill | 1.00 | 2.00 | 3.00 | |
| S1103 | House Dick–Gordon Davis | 1.00 | 2.00 | 3.00 | M |
| S1104 | The Savage Breast–John Trinian | 1.00 | 2.00 | 3.00 | |
| S1105 | Chuka–Richard Jessup | 1.50 | 3.00 | 4.50 | W |
| S1106 | The Snow Leopard–Sigmund Miller | 1.00 | 2.00 | 3.00 | M |
| S1107 | Short Ribs–Frank O'Neal | 1.00 | 2.00 | 3.00 | H |
| S1108 | Street of No Return–David Goodis | 2.00 | 4.00 | 6.00 | |
| S1109 | Park Avenue Tramp–Fletcher Flora | 1.50 | 3.00 | 4.50 | E |
| S1110 | So Wicked My Love–Bruno Fischer | 1.00 | 2.00 | 3.00 | M |
| S1112 | Area of Suspicion–John D. MacDonald | 1.00 | 2.00 | 3.00 | M |
| S1113 | Suddenly by Shotgun–Norman Daniels | 1.00 | 2.00 | 3.00 | M |
| S1114 | The Big Red Ball–Lou Cameron | 1.00 | 2.00 | 3.00 | C |
| S1115 | Isolation Booth–Bob Kaufman & Lou Morheim | 1.00 | 2.00 | 3.00 | |
| S1116 | Manhunt Is My Mission–Stephen Marlowe | 1.50 | 3.00 | 4.50 | M |
| S1117 | Ramrod Rider–T.V. Olsen; 1961 | 1.50 | 3.00 | 4.50 | W |
| S1118 | Assignment–Angelina–Edward S. Aarons | 1.00 | 2.00 | 3.00 | M |
| S1121 | The Last Sunset–Vechel Howard; movie tie-in | 1.50 | 3.00 | 4.50 | W |
| S1122 | Fever Heat–Angus Vicker | 1.00 | 2.00 | 3.00 | |
| S1123 | Desert Stake-Out–Harry Whittington | 2.00 | 4.00 | 6.00 | W |
| S1124 | Shadow of a Doubt–Harrison Judd | 1.00 | 2.00 | 3.00 | |
| D1125 | Make My Bed in Hell–Leonard Bishop; 1961 | 1.00 | 2.00 | 3.00 | M |
| S1126 | Any Man's Girl–Basil Heatter | 1.00 | 2.00 | 3.00 | |
| S1127 | The Telltale Tart–Peter Duncan | 1.00 | 2.00 | 3.00 | |
| S1129 | Take a Murder, Darling–Richard S. Prather | 1.00 | 2.00 | 3.00 | M |
| S1131 | Valley of Wrath–John Prescott | 1.00 | 2.00 | 3.00 | W |
| S1132 | Madball–Fredric Brown | 3.00 | 6.00 | 9.00 | M |
| S1133 | Drive East on 66–Richard Wormser | 1.00 | 2.00 | 3.00 | |
| S1134 | God's Back Was Turned–Harry Whittington | 2.00 | 4.00 | 6.00 | E |
| S1135 | The Paradise Gun–John Flagg | 1.00 | 2.00 | 3.00 | |
| S1136 | "Candyleg"–Ovid Demaris | 1.00 | 2.00 | 3.00 | |
| S1138 | Hill Girl–Charles Williams | 1.50 | 3.00 | 4.50 | |
| S1139 | The Scrambled Yeggs–Richard S. Prather | 1.50 | 3.00 | 4.50 | M |
| S1140 | 3-Day Terror–Vin Packer | 1.00 | 2.00 | 3.00 | M |
| D1141 | Inside the John Birch Society–Gene Grove | 1.00 | 2.00 | 3.00 | NF |
| S1142 | Angel with Dirty Wings–John Eugene Hasty | 1.50 | 3.00 | 4.50 | |
| S1143 | Tropical Disturbance–Theodore Pratt | 1.50 | 3.00 | 4.50 | |
| S1144 | Dig That Crazy Grave–Richard S. Prather | 1.00 | 2.00 | 3.00 | M |
| S1145 | Round the Clock at Volari's–W.R. Burnett | 2.50 | 5.00 | 7.50 | M |
| S1146 | Something in the Shadows–Vin Packer | 1.00 | 2.00 | 3.00 | M |
| S1147 | Come Night, Come Evil–Jonathan Craig | 1.00 | 2.00 | 3.00 | |
| S1148 | To Hell–and Texas–Giles A. Lutz | 1.00 | 2.00 | 3.00 | W |
| S1149 | The Magnolia Murder–Wyatt Bell | 1.00 | 2.00 | 3.00 | M |
| S1150 | Some Die Hard–Nick Quarry (Marvin Albert) | 1.50 | 3.00 | 4.50 | M |
| S1151 | Frantic–Noël Calef | 1.00 | 2.00 | 3.00 | M |
| S1152 | Assignment–Ankara–Edward S. Aarons | 1.00 | 2.00 | 3.00 | M |
| S1153 | Canary in a Cat House–Kurt Vonnegut, Jr; 1st ed. 1961 | 10.00 | 20.00 | 30.00 | SF |
| S1154 | The Warring Breed–Dale Michaels | 1.00 | 2.00 | 3.00 | W |
| S1155 | Devil May Care–Wade Miller | 1.00 | 2.00 | 3.00 | M |
| S1156 | Savage Bride–Cornell Woolrich | 1.50 | 3.00 | 4.50 | M |
| S1157 | Dagger of Flesh–Richard S. Prather | 1.00 | 2.00 | 3.00 | M |
| D1158 | The Grave of Heroes–James Cross | 1.00 | 2.00 | 3.00 | |
| S1159 | Port Angelique–Richard Jessup | 1.00 | 2.00 | 3.00 | |
| S1160 | Girls on the Rampage–Wenzell Brown | 2.50 | 5.00 | 7.50 | JD |
| S1161 | Rockabilly–Harlan Ellison | 15.00 | 30.00 | 45.00 | |
| S1162 | Death Pulls a Doublecross–Lawrence Block | 2.50 | 5.00 | 7.50 | M |
| S1163 | Harvey Kurtzman's Fast-Acting Help!–Harvey Kurtzman | 2.00 | 4.00 | 6.00 | H |
| S1164 | The Defenders–Edward S. Aarons; TV tie-in | 1.50 | 3.00 | 4.50 | |
| S1165 | Clemmie–John D. MacDonald | 1.50 | 3.00 | 4.50 | |

| | | V/Good | Fine | N/Mint | |
|---|---|---|---|---|---|
| S1166 | Lie Down Killer–Richard S. Prather | 1.00 | 2.00 | 3.00 | M |
| S1167 | Apache Rising–Marvin H. Albert | 1.50 | 3.00 | 4.50 | W |
| S1168 | Brand of the Star–T.V. Olsen | 1.50 | 3.00 | 4.50 | W |
| D1169 | El Cid–Robert W. Krepps; movie tie-in | 1.00 | 2.00 | 3.00 | A |
| S1170 | Cry Me a Killer–Garrity | 1.00 | 2.00 | 3.00 | M |
| S1171 | Women's Barracks–Tereska Torres | 1.00 | 2.00 | 3.00 | |
| S1172 | Wolf Cop–Richard Jessup | 1.50 | 3.00 | 4.50 | M |
| S1173 | Carla–Joseph R. Marshall | 1.00 | 2.00 | 3.00 | |
| D1174 | The Rise and Fall of Dr. Carey–O.O. Osborne | 1.00 | 2.00 | 3.00 | |
| S1175 | Gypsy, Go Home–William O'Farrell | 1.00 | 2.00 | 3.00 | |
| D1176 | Wheels of Terror–Sven Hassel; aka Døden Pa Larve Fødder | 1.50 | 3.00 | 4.50 | C |
| S1177 | One Monday We Killed Them All–John D. MacDonald; 1961 | 3.50 | 7.00 | 10.50 | M |
| S1178 | The Skin Game–Frank Bonham | 1.50 | 3.00 | 4.50 | W |
| S1179 | Jennifer James, R.N.–Norman Daniels | 1.00 | 2.00 | 3.00 | |
| S1180 | Heller from Texas–William Heuman | 1.00 | 2.00 | 3.00 | W |
| S1181 | One Wild Oat–Mackinlay Kantor; 1961 | 1.00 | 2.00 | 3.00 | |
| S1182 | Mexican Slay Ride–Neil MacNeil | 1.00 | 2.00 | 3.00 | M |
| S1183 | The Sky Divers–Lou Cameron; 1962 | 1.00 | 2.00 | 3.00 | |
| S1184 | The Name of the Game Is Death–Dan J. Marlowe | 2.00 | 4.00 | 6.00 | M |
| S1185 | The Perfect Squelch–ed. Ashley Halsey, Jr | 1.00 | 2.00 | 3.00 | H |
| S1186 | The New Breed–Lee Costigan; TV tie-in | 1.50 | 3.00 | 4.50 | M |
| D1187 | The Girl in Lover's Lane–Charles Boswell & Lewis Thompson | 1.00 | 2.00 | 3.00 | NF |
| D1188 | The Girl in the House of Hate–Charles Boswell & Louise Samuels | 1.00 | 2.00 | 3.00 | NF |
| S1189 | Assignment–Madeleine–Edward S. Aarons | 1.00 | 2.00 | 3.00 | M |
| S1190 | A Haven for the Damned–Harry Whittington | 2.00 | 4.00 | 6.00 | E |
| S1191 | Mother Night–Kurt Vonnegut, Jr; 1st ed. 1962 | 7.50 | 15.00 | 22.50 | |
| S1192 | The Couch–Robert Bloch | 3.00 | 6.00 | 9.00 | |
| S1193 | Lover Come Back–Marvin H. Albert; movie tie-in | 1.50 | 3.00 | 4.50 | |
| S1194 | The Silencers–Donald Hamilton | 1.00 | 2.00 | 3.00 | |
| S1195 | I Am a Woman–Ann Bannon | 2.00 | 4.00 | 6.00 | |
| D1196 | We Walk Alone–Ann Aldrich | 1.50 | 3.00 | 4.50 | |
| S1197 | The Notorious Landlady–Irving Shulman; movie tie-in | 1.50 | 3.00 | 4.50 | |
| S1198 | A Key to the Suite–John D. MacDonald | 5.00 | 10.00 | 15.00 | |
| D1199 | Songs for Pickin' and Singin'–ed. James F. Leisy | 1.00 | 2.00 | 3.00 | NF |
| S1200 | The Long Saturday Night–Charles Williams | 4.00 | 8.00 | 12.00 | |
| S1201 | Perfect Pigeon–Richard Wormser | 1.00 | 2.00 | 3.00 | M |
| D1202 | The Devil's Mistress–Kenneth Thomas; aka The Dark Rose | 1.00 | 2.00 | 3.00 | |
| D1203 | The Shrinking Man–Richard Matheson | 3.00 | 6.00 | 9.00 | SF |
| D1204 | Because You Are A Woman–ed. Frank J. McGowan, MD | 1.00 | 2.00 | 3.00 | NF |
| S1205 | Living High–Stephen Longstreet | 2.50 | 5.00 | 7.50 | |
| S1206 | Escape from Zahrain–Michael Barrett; aka Appointment in Zahrain; movie tie-in | 1.50 | 3.00 | 4.50 | |
| S1207 | Wait Till Dark–John Cunningham | 1.00 | 2.00 | 3.00 | M |
| S1208 | Kill the Clown–Richard S. Prather | 1.00 | 2.00 | 3.00 | M |
| S1209 | Cartoon Fun–ed. True magazine | 1.50 | 3.00 | 4.50 | H |
| S1211 | Boys' Night Out–Robert W. Krepps; movie tie-in | 1.00 | 2.00 | 3.00 | |
| S1212 | No French Leave–Webb Beech | 1.00 | 2.00 | 3.00 | |
| S1213 | That Touch of Mink–John Tessitore; movie tie-in | 1.50 | 3.00 | 4.50 | R |
| S1214 | Jeopardy Is My Job–Stephen Marlowe | 1.00 | 2.00 | 3.00 | M |
| S1215 | Abortion, Murder or Mercy–as told to Margaret Witte | 1.00 | 2.00 | 3.00 | |
| S1216 | The Man from Riondo–Dudley Dean | 1.00 | 2.00 | 3.00 | W |
| S1217 | Find This Woman–Richard S. Prather | 1.00 | 2.00 | 3.00 | M |
| S1218 | Reveille–James Warner Bellah | 1.00 | 2.00 | 3.00 | W |
| D1219 | Fun with Double Crostics–Elizabeth S. Kingsley & Doris Nash Wortman | 1.00 | 2.00 | 3.00 | NF |
| S1220 | The Open Square–Ford Clarke | 1.00 | 2.00 | 3.00 | |
| S1221 | The Girl from Midnight–Wade Miller | 1.00 | 2.00 | 3.00 | M |
| D1222 | My Life with Princess Margaret–David John Payne | 1.50 | 3.00 | 4.50 | B |
| S1223 | Crazy Cartoons by VIP–Virgil Partch | 1.50 | 3.00 | 4.50 | H |
| D1224 | Beebo Brinker–Ann Bannon; 1st ed. 1962 | 4.00 | 8.00 | 12.00 | |

| | | V/Good | Fine | N/Mint | |
|---|---|---|---|---|---|

GOLD MEDAL, *continued*

| Code | Title | V/Good | Fine | N/Mint | |
|---|---|---|---|---|---|
| S1225 | Harvey Kurtzman's Second Helping–Harvey Kurtzman | 2.00 | 4.00 | 6.00 | H |
| S1226 | For the Asking–Harold R. Daniels | 1.00 | 2.00 | 3.00 | |
| R1227 | World War II: A Photographic Record of the War in Europe from D-Day to V-E Day–Ralph G. Martin & Richard Harrity | 2.00 | 4.00 | 6.00 | NF |
| S1228 | Someone's Sleeping in My Bed–John Gonzales | 1.00 | 2.00 | 3.00 | |
| S1229 | Relentless Gun–Giles A. Lutz | 1.00 | 2.00 | 3.00 | W |
| S1230 | Creative Hairdo Ideas–Hope Johnson | 1.00 | 2.00 | 3.00 | NF |
| S1231 | Atoms and Evil–Robert Bloch | 3.00 | 6.00 | 9.00 | HO |
| K1232 | Southern Fried–William Price Fox; 1962 | 2.50 | 5.00 | 7.50 | H |
| S1233 | Massacre Creek–Hal G. Evarts | 1.00 | 2.00 | 3.00 | W |
| D1234 | Two Souls, One Body–Jason Marks & Howard Philips | 1.00 | 2.00 | 3.00 | |
| S1235 | Everybody Had a Gun–Richard S. Prather | 1.00 | 2.00 | 3.00 | M |
| S1236 | Five Rode West–Lewis B. Patten | 1.00 | 2.00 | 3.00 | W |
| S1237 | Assignment–Karachi–Edward S. Aarons | 1.00 | 2.00 | 3.00 | M |
| S1238 | The Mutilators–Basil Heatter | 1.00 | 2.00 | 3.00 | |
| S1239 | Savage Sierra–T.V. Olsen | 1.00 | 2.00 | 3.00 | W |
| S1240 | Four-Time Loser–Dan Lynch (actually written by Robert Silverberg) | 3.00 | 6.00 | 9.00 | |
| S1241 | Intimate Victims–Vin Packer | 1.00 | 2.00 | 3.00 | |
| S1242 | Bodies in Bedlam–Richard S. Prather | 1.00 | 2.00 | 3.00 | M |
| D1243 | 13 Great Stories of Science Fiction–ed. Groff Conklin | 1.00 | 2.00 | 3.00 | SF |
| S1244 | The First Gold Medal Crossword Puzzle Book–ed. Charles Preston | 4.00 | 8.00 | 12.00 | NF |
| K1245 | The Last Days of Sodom and Gomorrah–Richard Wormser; movie tie-in | 1.50 | 3.00 | 4.50 | A |
| S1246 | Murderer's Row–Donald Hamilton | 1.00 | 2.00 | 3.00 | |
| K1247 | The Desire Years–Leonard Bishop | 1.00 | 2.00 | 3.00 | JD |
| S1248 | Someone and Felicia Warwick–Raymond Mason | 1.00 | 2.00 | 3.00 | M |
| S1249 | Case of the Vanishing Beauty–Richard S. Prather | 1.00 | 2.00 | 3.00 | M |
| S1250 | Day of the Gun–Richard Telfair | 1.00 | 2.00 | 3.00 | M |
| K1251 | Dance with the Dead–Richard S. Prather | 1.00 | 2.00 | 3.00 | M |
| S1252 | Without Consent–Theodore Pratt; 1962 | 1.00 | 2.00 | 3.00 | |
| S1253 | Taras Bulba–Robert W. Krepps; movie tie-in | 1.50 | 3.00 | 4.50 | A |
| S1254 | You Damn Men Are All Alike–William Cole & Douglas McKee | 2.50 | 5.00 | 7.50 | H |
| S1255 | Delfina–Steve Brackeen | 1.00 | 2.00 | 3.00 | M |
| S1256 | The Empty Quarter–Lou Cameron | 1.50 | 3.00 | 4.50 | |
| S1258 | The Brat–Gil Brewer | 1.00 | 2.00 | 3.00 | |
| S1259 | The Girl, the Gold Watch and Everything–John D. MacDonald | 5.00 | 10.00 | 15.00 | F |
| S1260 | One Wife's Ways–Gardner F. Fox; 1962 | 2.00 | 4.00 | 6.00 | M |
| K1261 | The Savage Kick–Neil Pritchie | 1.50 | 3.00 | 4.50 | |
| S1262 | The Box–Peter Rabe; 1962 | 2.50 | 5.00 | 7.50 | M |
| S1263 | The Real Jack Parr–George Johnson | 1.50 | 3.00 | 4.50 | B |
| K1264 | Slab Happy–Richard S. Prather | 1.50 | 3.00 | 4.50 | M |
| S1265 | Gunfire at Salt Fork–William Hopson | 1.00 | 2.00 | 3.00 | W |
| 1266 | We Too Must Love–Ann Aldrich | 2.00 | 4.00 | 6.00 | |
| S1267 | Miss Caroline–Gerald Gardner & Frank Johnson | 1.50 | 3.00 | 4.50 | H |
| S1268 | The Death Cycle–Charles Runyon | 1.00 | 2.00 | 3.00 | |
| S1269 | Some Mischief Still–John Eugene Hasty | 1.00 | 2.00 | 3.00 | M |
| S1270 | Assignment–Sorrento Siren–Edward S. Aarons | 1.00 | 2.00 | 3.00 | M |
| S1271 | A Nice Girl Like You . . .–Richard Wormser; 1963 | 1.00 | 2.00 | 3.00 | M |
| K1272 | Over Her Dead Body–Richard S. Prather | 1.00 | 2.00 | 3.00 | M |
| S1273 | Texas Outlaw–Richard Jessup | 1.00 | 2.00 | 3.00 | W |
| S1274 | The Moonlight War–Clifton Adams | 1.00 | 2.00 | 3.00 | W |
| S1275 | Strange But True–ed. True magazine | 1.00 | 2.00 | 3.00 | NF |
| K1276 | The Man Who Fell to Earth–Walter Tevis | 3.00 | 6.00 | 9.00 | SF |
| K1277 | The Peddler–Richard S. Prather | 1.00 | 2.00 | 3.00 | M |
| S1278 | County Hospital–Norman Daniels | 1.50 | 3.00 | 4.50 | |
| K1279 | Darling, It's Death–Richard S. Prather | 1.00 | 2.00 | 3.00 | M |
| K1280 | Pattern for Panic–Richard S. Prather | 1.00 | 2.00 | 3.00 | M |
| S1281 | Tall in the West–Vechel Howard | 1.00 | 2.00 | 3.00 | W |
| K1282 | Too Many Crooks–Richard S. Prather; aka Ride a High Horse | 1.00 | 2.00 | 3.00 | M |
| K1283 | Something Burning–Norman Daniels | 1.50 | 3.00 | 4.50 | M |
| K1284 | Another Time, Another Woman–Walter Kaylin | 1.00 | 2.00 | 3.00 | M |
| K1285 | Francesca–Stephen Marlowe | 1.00 | 2.00 | 3.00 | M |
| K1286 | The Black Camp–Lou Cameron | 1.00 | 2.00 | 3.00 | C |
| K1287 | Shell Scott's Seven Slaughters–Richard S. Prather | 1.00 | 2.00 | 3.00 | M |
| D1288 | Double in Trouble–Richard S. Prather & Stephen Marlowe | 1.50 | 3.00 | 4.50 | M |
| K1289 | Nothing in Her Way–Charles Williams; 1963 | 2.00 | 4.00 | 6.00 | |
| K1290 | Spring Fire–Vin Packer | 1.00 | 2.00 | 3.00 | |
| K1291 | I Could Go on Singing–John D. MacDonald; 1963; movie tie-in | 5.00 | 10.00 | 15.00 | |
| K1292 | On the Run–John D. MacDonald | 5.00 | 10.00 | 15.00 | M |
| K1293 | Follow That Hearse!–John Gonzales | 1.00 | 2.00 | 3.00 | |
| K1294 | Alone at Night–Vin Packer | 1.00 | 2.00 | 3.00 | M |
| S1295 | Bigger Than Texas–William R. Cox | 1.00 | 2.00 | 3.00 | W |
| D1296 | 1963 Official Baseball Almanac–ed. Bill Wise | 1.50 | 3.00 | 4.50 | S |
| K1297 | The Comfortable Coffin–Richard S. Prather | 1.00 | 2.00 | 3.00 | M |
| K1298 | Dig That Crazy Grave–Richard S. Prather | 1.00 | 2.00 | 3.00 | M |
| K1299 | Whisper Their Love–Valerie Taylor; 1963 | 3.00 | 6.00 | 9.00 | |
| S1300 | Saddle Justice–Steven C. Lawrence | 1.00 | 2.00 | 3.00 | W |
| K1301 | Island of Love–Herb Edwards | 1.00 | 2.00 | 3.00 | |
| K1302 | The Drowner–John D. MacDonald | 5.00 | 10.00 | 15.00 | M |
| K1303 | Don't Speak to Strange Girls–Harry Whittington | 2.00 | 4.00 | 6.00 | |
| K1304 | Assignment–Manchurian Doll–Edward S. Aarons | 1.00 | 2.00 | 3.00 | M |
| S1305 | King Fisher's Road–Shepard Rifkin | 1.00 | 2.00 | 3.00 | W |
| K1306 | Women without Men–P.J. Reed-Marr | 1.00 | 2.00 | 3.00 | |
| K1307 | Assignment–Mara Tirana–Edward S. Aarons | 1.00 | 2.00 | 3.00 | M |
| K1308 | Secret of Sylvia–Lee Borden | 1.00 | 2.00 | 3.00 | |
| S1309 | Brand of a Texan–Steven C. Lawrence | 1.00 | 2.00 | 3.00 | W |
| K1310 | Virgin Cay–Basil Heatter | 1.00 | 2.00 | 3.00 | |
| K1311 | Shake Him 'Till He Rattles–Malcolm Braly | 1.00 | 2.00 | 3.00 | |
| K1312 | The Lady's Not for Living–Dexter St. Clair | 1.00 | 2.00 | 3.00 | M |
| K1313 | We Two Won't Last–Ann Aldrich | 3.00 | 6.00 | 9.00 | |
| S1314 | Halfway to Hell–Giles A. Lutz | 1.00 | 2.00 | 3.00 | W |
| S1315 | Killer in White–Tedd Thomey | 1.00 | 2.00 | 3.00 | M |
| K1316 | The Scrambled Yeggs–Richard S. Prather; aka Pattern for Murder | 1.50 | 3.00 | 4.50 | M |
| S1317 | Top Man with a Gun–Lewis B. Patten | 1.00 | 2.00 | 3.00 | W |
| K1318 | The Beach Girls–John D. MacDonald | 1.00 | 2.00 | 3.00 | M |
| K1319 | "K"–Leslie Waller | 1.00 | 2.00 | 3.00 | |
| K1320 | Color Him Dead–Charles Runyon | 1.00 | 2.00 | 3.00 | M |
| K1321 | The Green Wound–Philip Atlee | 1.00 | 2.00 | 3.00 | |
| S1322 | My Son, the Doctor–ed. Medical Times & Resident Physician | 1.00 | 2.00 | 3.00 | H |
| K1323 | Message from Marise–Paul Kruger | 1.00 | 2.00 | 3.00 | |
| D1324 | Three Times Infinity–ed. Leo Margulies | 1.00 | 2.00 | 3.00 | SF |
| K1325 | I'm Cannon–for Hire–Curt Cannon | 1.00 | 2.00 | 3.00 | M |
| K1326 | 13 French Street–Gil Brewer | 1.00 | 2.00 | 3.00 | M |
| S1327 | The Wind River Kid–Will Cook | 1.00 | 2.00 | 3.00 | W |
| D1328 | The Beats–ed. Seymour Krim | 2.00 | 4.00 | 6.00 | |
| R1329 | 1963 Official Pro Football Almanac–ed. Bill Wise | 1.50 | 3.00 | 4.50 | S |
| S1330 | The Appaloosa–Robert MacLeod | 1.50 | 3.00 | 4.50 | W |
| S1331 | Super Bloopers–ed. Kermit Schafer | 1.50 | 3.00 | 4.50 | H |
| D1332 | The Addict–ed. Dan Wakefield | 2.00 | 4.00 | 6.00 | NF |
| K1333 | The Ambushers–Donald Hamilton | 1.00 | 2.00 | 3.00 | |
| K1334 | Death of a Citizen–Donald Hamilton | 1.00 | 2.00 | 3.00 | |
| K1335 | The Wrecking Crew–Donald Hamilton | 1.00 | 2.00 | 3.00 | |
| K1336 | The Removers–Donald Hamilton | 1.00 | 2.00 | 3.00 | |
| K1337 | A House in Naples–Peter Rabe | 1.50 | 3.00 | 4.50 | M |
| K1338 | The Golden Urge–Robert Kyle | 1.00 | 2.00 | 3.00 | |
| K1339 | The Second Gold Medal Crossword Puzzle Book–ed. Charles Preston | 4.00 | 8.00 | 12.00 | NF |
| K1340 | Strongarm–Dan J. Marlowe | 1.50 | 3.00 | 4.50 | M |
| K1341 | For Love or Money–John Tessitore | 1.00 | 2.00 | 3.00 | H |
| S1342 | The Oceola Kill–Clay Randall | 1.00 | 2.00 | 3.00 | |
| K1343 | The Kingdom of Johnny Cool–John McPartland; movie tie-in | 1.50 | 3.00 | 4.50 | |

GOLD MEDAL, *continued*

| Item | Title | V/Good | Fine | N/Mint | |
|---|---|---|---|---|---|
| K1344 | Go Home, Stranger–Charles Williams; 1963 | 2.00 | 4.00 | 6.00 | |
| S1345 | The Bounty Killer–Marvin H. Albert | 1.00 | 2.00 | 3.00 | W |
| K1346 | The Evil Friendship–Vin Packer | 1.00 | 2.00 | 3.00 | |
| K1347 | The Bastard's Name Is War–Lou Cameron | 1.00 | 2.00 | 3.00 | C |
| K1348 | Counterfeit Kill–Gordon Davis | 1.00 | 2.00 | 3.00 | M |
| K1349 | The Right People–Robert Kaufman & Peter Barry | 1.00 | 2.00 | 3.00 | H |
| K1350 | McLintock–Richard Wormser; movie tie-in | 2.00 | 4.00 | 6.00 | W |
| S1351 | Gun Shy–Les Savage, Jr & Dudley Dean | 1.00 | 2.00 | 3.00 | W |
| D1352 | Age of the Junkman–P.D. Ballard | 1.00 | 2.00 | 3.00 | |
| K1353 | A Touch of Death–Charles Williams | 2.00 | 4.00 | 6.00 | M |
| S1354 | Slam the Big Door–John D. MacDonald | 1.00 | 2.00 | 3.00 | M |
| K1355 | Mad Baxter–Wade Miller | 1.00 | 2.00 | 3.00 | M |
| D1356 | Songs for Pickin' and Singin'–ed. James F. Leisy | 1.00 | 2.00 | 3.00 | NF |
| S1357 | Hardcase for Hire–Clay Randall | 1.00 | 2.00 | 3.00 | W |
| K1358 | Charade–Peter Stone; movie tie-in | 1.50 | 3.00 | 4.50 | R |
| D1359 | Amazing But True Animals–Doug Storer | 1.00 | 2.00 | 3.00 | NF |
| K1360 | Diecast–Michael Brett | 1.00 | 2.00 | 3.00 | |
| K1361 | Adam Clayton Powell–Claude Lewis | 1.00 | 2.00 | 3.00 | B |
| K1362 | The Wife Next Door–R.V. Cassill | 1.00 | 2.00 | 3.00 | E |
| K1363 | Kitten with a Whip–Wade Miller; 1963 | 1.50 | 3.00 | 4.50 | M |
| K1364 | Look Behind You, Lady–A.S. Fleischman | 1.00 | 2.00 | 3.00 | |
| S1365 | Hang the Men High–Noel Loomis & Paul Leslie Piel | 1.00 | 2.00 | 3.00 | W |
| D1366 | 12 Great Classics of Science Fiction–ed. Groff Conklin | 1.00 | 2.00 | 3.00 | SF |
| K1367 | The Venetian Blonde–A.S. Fleischman | 1.00 | 2.00 | 3.00 | |
| R1368 | Comrades of War–Sven Hassel | 1.50 | 3.00 | 4.50 | C |
| S1369 | The Lone Gun–Howard Rigsby | 1.00 | 2.00 | 3.00 | W |
| K1370 | Assignment–Helene–Edward S. Aarons | 1.00 | 2.00 | 3.00 | M |
| S1371 | Many Rivers to Cross–Steve Frazee; 1963 | 1.00 | 2.00 | 3.00 | W |
| K1372 | Assignment–Lili Lamaris–Edward S. Aarons | 1.00 | 2.00 | 3.00 | M |
| K1373 | Assignment–Carlotta Cortez–Edward S. Aarons | 1.00 | 2.00 | 3.00 | M |
| K1374 | The Pink Palace–Chester Anderson | 1.00 | 2.00 | 3.00 | |
| S1375 | A Noose for the Desperado–Clifton Adams | 1.00 | 2.00 | 3.00 | W |
| K1376 | Joker in the Deck–Richard S. Prather | 1.00 | 2.00 | 3.00 | M |
| K1377 | Dead Ringer–Bob Thomas; movie tie-in | 1.50 | 3.00 | 4.50 | |
| S1378 | Gunslingers Can't Quit–William R. Scott | 1.00 | 2.00 | 3.00 | W |
| K1379 | Strictly Personal–Leo Guild & Charles Rodrigues | 1.00 | 2.00 | 3.00 | H |
| K1380 | Ring Around Rosy–Gordon Davis | 1.00 | 2.00 | 3.00 | M |
| K1381 | Strip for Murder–Richard S. Prather | 1.00 | 2.00 | 3.00 | M |
| K1382 | Way of a Wanton–Richard S. Prather | 1.00 | 2.00 | 3.00 | M |
| K1383 | Find This Woman–Richard S. Prather | 1.00 | 2.00 | 3.00 | M |
| K1384 | No Way to Treat a Lady–Harry Longbaugh | 1.00 | 2.00 | 3.00 | M |
| D1385 | The Fall of the Roman Empire–Harry Whitthurst; 1964; movie tie-in | 1.50 | 3.00 | 4.50 | A |
| K1386 | The Shadowers–Donald Hamilton | 1.00 | 2.00 | 3.00 | |
| S1387 | Posse at High Pass–Marvin H. Albert | 1.00 | 2.00 | 3.00 | W |
| K1388 | Mail Order Bride–Van Cort; movie tie-in | 1.50 | 3.00 | 4.50 | |
| D1389 | The Only Girl in the Game–John D. MacDonald | 2.00 | 4.00 | 6.00 | M |
| S1390 | The Hell-fire Kid–Steve Shannon | 1.00 | 2.00 | 3.00 | W |
| K1391 | Murderers' Row–Donald Hamilton | 1.00 | 2.00 | 3.00 | |
| K1392 | The Silencers–Donald Hamilton | 1.00 | 2.00 | 3.00 | |
| S1393 | The Ruthless Gun–T.C. Lewellen | 1.00 | 2.00 | 3.00 | W |
| K1394 | Judge Me Not–John D. MacDonald | 1.00 | 2.00 | 3.00 | M |
| D1395 | Merchants of Venus–Bernard Evslin | 1.00 | 2.00 | 3.00 | |
| K1396 | Case of the Silent Stranger–Jonathan Craig | 1.00 | 2.00 | 3.00 | M |
| K1397 | Four from Planet 5–Murray Leinster | 1.00 | 2.00 | 3.00 | SF |
| K1398 | Assignment–The Girl in the Gondola–Edward S. Aarons | 1.00 | 2.00 | 3.00 | M |
| K1399 | Little Sister–Lee Roberts | 1.00 | 2.00 | 3.00 | |
| K1401 | Gun Talk at Yuma–Frank Castle | 1.00 | 2.00 | 3.00 | W |
| K1402 | Everybody Had a Gun–Richard S. Prather | 1.00 | 2.00 | 3.00 | M |

| Item | Title | V/Good | Fine | N/Mint | |
|---|---|---|---|---|---|
| K1403 | Stop this Man–Peter Rabe | 1.50 | 3.00 | 4.50 | M |
| S1404 | Comanche Vengeance–Richard Jessup | 1.00 | 2.00 | 3.00 | W |
| K1405 | The Deep Blue Goodby–John D. MacDonald | 5.00 | 10.00 | 15.00 | M |
| K1406 | Nightmare in Pink–John D. MacDonald. Note: First Travis McGee novel | 5.00 | 10.00 | 15.00 | M |
| K1407 | Take a Murder, Darling–Richard S. Prather | 1.00 | 2.00 | 3.00 | M |
| D1408 | General Douglas MacArthur–Bob Considine | 1.00 | 2.00 | 3.00 | B |
| K1409 | Cartoons out of My Own Head–Virgil Partch | 1.50 | 3.00 | 4.50 | H |
| K1410 | Pillow Talk–Marvin H. Albert; movie tie-in | 1.50 | 3.00 | 4.50 | R |
| D1411 | Odd Girl Out–Ann Bannon | 2.00 | 4.00 | 6.00 | |
| S1412 | Funny Cartoons by VIP–Virgil Partch | 1.50 | 3.00 | 4.50 | H |
| K1413 | Violence Is My Business–Stephen Marlowe | 1.00 | 2.00 | 3.00 | M |
| S1414 | North Fork to Hell–Dan Cushman | 1.50 | 3.00 | 4.50 | W |
| D1415 | The Nylon Island–Stephen Longstreet | 1.50 | 3.00 | 4.50 | |
| S1416 | Logan's Choice–Frank Bonham | 1.00 | 2.00 | 3.00 | W |
| K1417 | A Purple Place for Dying–John D. MacDonald | 5.00 | 10.00 | 15.00 | M |
| K1418 | Seven Votes for Death–Pat Bannister | 1.00 | 2.00 | 3.00 | M |
| S1419 | Summons to Silverhorn–Kenneth Fowler | 1.00 | 2.00 | 3.00 | W |
| K1420 | Drum Beat–Berlin–Stephen Marlowe | 1.00 | 2.00 | 3.00 | M |
| K1421 | Clemmie–John D. MacDonald | 1.00 | 2.00 | 3.00 | M |
| K1422 | The Wailing Frail–Richard S. Prather | 1.00 | 2.00 | 3.00 | M |
| K1423 | Assignment–Burma Girl–Edward S. Aarons | 1.00 | 2.00 | 3.00 | M |
| S1424 | Funny Business–ed. Charles Preston | 1.50 | 3.00 | 4.50 | H |
| K1425 | Dagger of Flesh–Richard S. Prather | 1.00 | 2.00 | 3.00 | M |
| K1426 | Journey into Terror–Peter Rabe | 2.50 | 5.00 | 7.50 | M |
| K1427 | Bedtime Story–Richard Wormser; movie tie-in | 1.50 | 3.00 | 4.50 | |
| D1428 | Tomorrow X 4–ed. Damon Knight | 1.00 | 2.00 | 3.00 | SF |
| S1429 | Gringo–L.L. Foreman | 1.00 | 2.00 | 3.00 | W |
| S1430 | The Tall Stranger–Louis L'Amour | 1.00 | 2.00 | 3.00 | W |
| K1431 | Article 92: Murder-Rape–Webb Beech | 1.00 | 2.00 | 3.00 | M |
| K1432 | Bodies in Bedlam–Richard S. Prather | 1.00 | 2.00 | 3.00 | M |
| K1433 | The Unsinkable Molly Brown–Al Hine; movie tie-in | 1.50 | 3.00 | 4.50 | |
| D1434 | Women in the Shadows–Ann Bannon | 2.00 | 4.00 | 6.00 | |
| K1435 | The Armored Dove–Nord Riley | 1.00 | 2.00 | 3.00 | H |
| K1436 | Gunswift–T.V. Olsen; 1964 | 1.00 | 2.00 | 3.00 | W |
| K1437 | Lie Down, Killer–Richard S. Prather | 1.00 | 2.00 | 3.00 | M |
| K1438 | Pop. 1280–Jim Thompson; 1st ed. 1964 | 15.00 | 30.00 | 45.00 | M |
| K1439 | Kill the Clown–Richard S. Prather | 1.00 | 2.00 | 3.00 | M |
| S1440 | Last Command–Will Cook | 1.00 | 2.00 | 3.00 | W |
| K1441 | Never Live Twice–Dan J. Marlowe | 1.00 | 2.00 | 3.00 | M |
| K1442 | Assignment–Ankara–Edward S. Aarons | 1.00 | 2.00 | 3.00 | M |
| D1443 | How Do You Feel About Sex?–Dr. Leland E. Glover | 1.00 | 2.00 | 3.00 | NF |
| D1444 | 13 Great Stories of Science Fiction–ed. Groff Conklin | 1.00 | 2.00 | 3.00 | SF |
| K1445 | Case of the Vanishing Beauty–Richard S. Prather | 1.00 | 2.00 | 3.00 | M |
| K1446 | The Day New York Went Dry–Charles Einstein | 2.00 | 4.00 | 6.00 | SF |
| S1447 | A Man Called Brazos–T.V. Olsen | 1.00 | 2.00 | 3.00 | W |
| K1448 | Always Leave 'Em Dying–Richard S. Prather | 1.00 | 2.00 | 3.00 | M |
| K1449 | Scandal on the Sand–John Trinian | 1.00 | 2.00 | 3.00 | |
| K1450 | Women's Barracks–Tereska Torres | 1.00 | 2.00 | 3.00 | E |
| K1451 | One Monday We Killed Them All–John D. MacDonald | 1.00 | 2.00 | 3.00 | M |
| K1452 | The Ravagers–Donald Hamilton | 1.00 | 2.00 | 3.00 | |
| K1453 | He Rode Alone–Steve Frazee | 1.00 | 2.00 | 3.00 | W |
| D1454 | 1964 Official Pro Football Almanac–ed. Bill Wise | 1.50 | 3.00 | 4.50 | NF |
| K1455 | Hell to Eternity–Edward S. Aarons | 1.00 | 2.00 | 3.00 | C |
| K1456 | Assignment–Zoraya–Edward S. Aarons | 1.00 | 2.00 | 3.00 | M |
| D1457 | Hootenanny Tonight!–ed. James F. Leisy | 1.00 | 2.00 | 3.00 | NF |
| K1458 | Re-enter Fu Manchu–Sax Rohmer; 1964 | 1.00 | 2.00 | 3.00 | A |
| S1459 | Guns of Rio Conchos–Clair Huffaker; movie tie-in | 1.50 | 3.00 | 4.50 | W |
| S1460 | Last Ride to Los Lobos–William Chamberlain | 1.00 | 2.00 | 3.00 | W |

GOLD MEDAL, *continued*

| | | V/Good | Fine | N/Mint | |
|---|---|---|---|---|---|
| K1461 | The Damned–John D. MacDonald | 1.00 | 2.00 | 3.00 | M |
| K1462 | The Cockeyed Corpse–Richard S. Prather | 1.00 | 2.00 | 3.00 | M |
| K1463 | Three's a Shroud–Richard S. Prather | 1.00 | 2.00 | 3.00 | M |
| K1464 | The Quick Red Fox–John D. MacDonald | 5.00 | 10.00 | 15.00 | M |
| K1465 | Send Me No Flowers–Robert W. Krepps; movie tie-in | 1.50 | 3.00 | 4.50 | R |
| K1466 | Wild–Gil Brewer | 1.50 | 3.00 | 4.50 | |
| K1467 | Warrior's Way–Webb Beech | 1.00 | 2.00 | 3.00 | C |
| S1468 | Wyoming Jones–Richard Telfair | 1.00 | 2.00 | 3.00 | W |
| K1469 | Where Is Janice Gantry?–John D. MacDonald | 1.00 | 2.00 | 3.00 | M |
| K1470 | The Huntress–Williams Forrest | 1.00 | 2.00 | 3.00 | |
| K1471 | Have Gat–Will Travel–Richard S. Prather | 1.00 | 2.00 | 3.00 | M |
| K1472 | Night Walker–Donald Hamilton | 1.00 | 2.00 | 3.00 | M |
| K1473 | A Certain French Girl–Nathaniel Tanchuck; aka The French Bathtub | 1.00 | 2.00 | 3.00 | |
| L1474 | Rogue Moon–Algis Budrys | 1.50 | 3.00 | 4.50 | SF |
| S1475 | Thimk–ed. Charles Preston | 1.50 | 3.00 | 4.50 | H |
| S1476 | Judas Gun–Gordon D. Shirreffs | 1.00 | 2.00 | 3.00 | W |
| K1477 | Meet Andy Capp–Smythe | 1.50 | 3.00 | 4.50 | H |
| K1478 | Home Is the Outlaw–Lewis B. Patten | 1.00 | 2.00 | 3.00 | W |
| D1479 | This Woman–Albert Idell | 1.00 | 2.00 | 3.00 | |
| K1480 | Line of Fire–Donald Hamilton | 1.00 | 2.00 | 3.00 | |
| K1481 | Assignment–Madeleine–Edward S. Aarons | 1.00 | 2.00 | 3.00 | M |
| K1482 | Amos Flagg–Lawman–Clay Randall | 1.00 | 2.00 | 3.00 | W |
| K1483 | Trouble–Texas Style–John Bramlett | 1.00 | 2.00 | 3.00 | W |
| K1484 | Two Guns for Hire–Neil MacNeil | 1.00 | 2.00 | 3.00 | W |
| K1485 | Harvey Kurtzman's Fast Acting Help!–Harvey Kurtzman | 2.00 | 4.00 | 6.00 | H |
| D1486 | End of a Millionaire–P.D. Ballard | 1.00 | 2.00 | 3.00 | M |
| K1487 | Mission for Vengeance–Peter Rabe | 1.50 | 3.00 | 4.50 | M |
| K1488 | Sunburst–Phyllis Gotlieb | 1.00 | 2.00 | 3.00 | |
| K1489 | The Silken Baroness–Philip Atlee | 1.00 | 2.00 | 3.00 | |
| K1490 | Kitten with a Whip–Wade Miller; movie tie-in | 2.50 | 5.00 | 7.50 | M |
| K1491 | Assassins Have Starry Eyes–Donald Hamilton; aka Assignment–Murder | 1.00 | 2.00 | 3.00 | |
| K1492 | Hondo–Louis L'Amour | 1.50 | 3.00 | 4.50 | W |
| K1493 | The Green Fields of Hell–Lou Cameron | 1.00 | 2.00 | 3.00 | C |
| L1494 | The Reassembled Man–Herbert D. Kastle; c-Frazetta | 2.50 | 5.00 | 7.50 | SF |
| K1495 | Assignment–Lowlands–Edward S. Aarons | 1.00 | 2.00 | 3.00 | M |
| K1496 | A Key to the Suite–John D. MacDonald | 1.00 | 2.00 | 3.00 | M |
| K1497 | Assignment–Sulu Sea–Edward S. Aarons | 1.00 | 2.00 | 3.00 | M |
| S1498 | Cartoon Fun–ed. True magazine | 1.50 | 3.00 | 4.50 | H |
| D1499 | A Deadly Shade of Gold–John D. MacDonald | 5.00 | 10.00 | 15.00 | M |
| K1500 | Mad River–Donald Hamilton | 1.00 | 2.00 | 3.00 | W |
| K1501 | To Tame a Land–Louis L'Amour | 1.50 | 3.00 | 4.50 | W |
| K1502 | Texas by the Tail–Jim Thompson; 1st ed. 1965 | 12.50 | 25.00 | 37.50 | |
| K1503 | The Company Girls–Mona Williams | 2.00 | 4.00 | 6.00 | E |
| L1504 | World without Women–Day Keene & Leonard Pruyn | 1.00 | 2.00 | 3.00 | SF |
| K1505 | Assignment–Karachi–Edward S. Aarons | 1.00 | 2.00 | 3.00 | M |
| D1506 | Harvey Kurtzman's Fun and Games–Harvey Kurtzman | 2.00 | 4.00 | 6.00 | H |
| K1507 | The Prettiest Girl I Ever Killed–Charles Runyon | 1.00 | 2.00 | 3.00 | M |
| K1508 | Drum Beat–Dominique–Stephen Marlowe | 1.00 | 2.00 | 3.00 | M |
| K1509 | Sex and the Man Who Used to Be Single–ed. Charles Preston | 1.00 | 2.00 | 3.00 | H |
| K1510 | Dakota Boomtown–Frank Castle | 1.00 | 2.00 | 3.00 | W |
| K1511 | None But the Brave–Lou Cameron; movie tie-in | 1.50 | 3.00 | 4.50 | C |
| K1512 | Now He Is Legend–Gordon D. Shirreffs | 1.00 | 2.00 | 3.00 | W |
| K1513 | The Girl, the Gold Watch and Everything–John D. MacDonald | 1.00 | 2.00 | 3.00 | F |
| D1514 | The Humor of JFK–Booton Herndon | 1.50 | 3.00 | 4.50 | H |
| K1515 | Assignment–Stella Marni–Edward S. Aarons | 1.00 | 2.00 | 3.00 | M |
| R1516 | 1965 Official Baseball Almanac–ed. Bill Wise | 1.50 | 3.00 | 4.50 | S |
| K1517 | West to the Sun–Noel Loomis | 1.00 | 2.00 | 3.00 | W |

| | | V/Good | Fine | N/Mint | |
|---|---|---|---|---|---|
| D1518 | Handsome–Theodore Pratt | 1.00 | 2.00 | 3.00 | |
| K1519 | Major Dundee–Richard Wormser; 1965; movie tie-in | 1.00 | 2.00 | 3.00 | W |
| K1520 | No Business for a Lady–James L. Rubel | 1.00 | 2.00 | 3.00 | M |
| K1521 | The Bedroom Derby–Nord Riley | 1.00 | 2.00 | 3.00 | |
| K1522 | The Killer Inside Me–Jim Thompson | 6.00 | 12.00 | 18.00 | M |
| K1523 | Harvey Kurtzman's Second Helping–Harvey Kurtzman | 2.00 | 4.00 | 6.00 | H |
| K1524 | Death Deep Down–Dan J. Marlowe | 1.00 | 2.00 | 3.00 | M |
| K1525 | Assignment–Budapest–Edward S. Aarons | 1.00 | 2.00 | 3.00 | M |
| K1526 | The Branded Man–Hal G. Evarts | 1.00 | 2.00 | 3.00 | W |
| K1527 | Danger Is My Line–Stephen Marlowe | 1.00 | 2.00 | 3.00 | M |
| D1528 | Area of Suspicion–John D. MacDonald | 1.00 | 2.00 | 3.00 | M |
| K1529 | Not I, Said the Vixen–Bill S. Ballinger | 1.00 | 2.00 | 3.00 | M |
| K1530 | Texas Outlaw–Richard Jessup | 1.00 | 2.00 | 3.00 | W |
| K1531 | Where Murder Waits–Gordon Davis | 1.00 | 2.00 | 3.00 | M |
| K1532 | The Wicked Walk on Every Side–Ford Clark | 1.00 | 2.00 | 3.00 | |
| K1533 | Prize Bloopers–ed. Kermit Schafer | 1.50 | 3.00 | 4.50 | H |
| K1534 | Assignment to Disaster–Edward S. Aarons | 1.00 | 2.00 | 3.00 | M |
| K1535 | Assignment–Angelina–Edward S. Aarons | 1.00 | 2.00 | 3.00 | M |
| K1536 | Heller from Texas–William Heuman | 1.00 | 2.00 | 3.00 | W |
| K1537 | Murder for the Bride–John D. MacDonald | 1.00 | 2.00 | 3.00 | M |
| K1538 | Relentless Gun–Giles A. Lutz; 1965 | 1.00 | 2.00 | 3.00 | W |
| K1539 | Assignment–Suicide–Edward S. Aarons | 1.00 | 2.00 | 3.00 | M |
| K1540 | Girl in a Big Brass Bed–Peter Rabe | 2.00 | 4.00 | 6.00 | M |
| K1541 | The Art of Love–John Gonzales; movie tie-in | 1.50 | 3.00 | 4.50 | NF |
| K1542 | To Hell–and Texas–Giles A. Lutz | 1.00 | 2.00 | 3.00 | W |
| D1543 | Murder in the Wind–John D. MacDonald; 1965 | 1.00 | 2.00 | 3.00 | M |
| D1544 | Monsters Galore–ed. Bernhardt J. Hurwood | 2.50 | 5.00 | 7.50 | HO |
| K1545 | The Girls in 3-B–Valerie Taylor; 1965 | 3.00 | 6.00 | 9.00 | |
| K1546 | The Blue Kimono Kill–Walt Sheldon | 1.00 | 2.00 | 3.00 | M |
| K1547 | All These Condemned–John D. MacDonald | 1.00 | 2.00 | 3.00 | M |
| D1548 | Make War in Madness–Webb Beech | 1.00 | 2.00 | 3.00 | |
| D1549 | Five Unearthly Visions–ed. Groff Conklin | 1.00 | 2.00 | 3.00 | SF |
| R1550 | My Years with Churchill–Norman MacGowan | 1.00 | 2.00 | 3.00 | B |
| K1551 | Texas Fever–Donald Hamilton | 1.00 | 2.00 | 3.00 | W |
| D1552 | A Man of Affairs–John D. MacDonald | 1.00 | 2.00 | 3.00 | M |
| D1553 | We, Too, Must Love–Ann Aldrich | 1.50 | 3.00 | 4.50 | |
| D1554 | What You Should Know about Coins and Coin Collecting–Burton Hobson | 1.50 | 3.00 | 4.50 | NF |
| K1555 | The Girl with the Long Green Heart–Lawrence Block | 2.50 | 5.00 | 7.50 | M |
| K1556 | Assignment–Sorrento Siren–Edward S. Aarons | 1.00 | 2.00 | 3.00 | M |
| K1557 | Massacre Creek–Hal G. Evarts | 1.00 | 2.00 | 3.00 | W |
| D1558 | Pattern for Panic–Richard S. Prather | 1.00 | 2.00 | 3.00 | M |
| K1559 | Assignment–Manchurian Doll–Edward S. Aarons | 1.00 | 2.00 | 3.00 | M |
| R1560 | Double in Trouble–Richard S. Prather & Stephen Marlowe | 1.00 | 2.00 | 3.00 | M |
| D1561 | Night Slaves–Jerry Sohl | 1.50 | 3.00 | 4.50 | SF |
| D1562 | Morituri–W.J. Lueddecke; movie tie-in | 1.00 | 2.00 | 3.00 | |
| K1563 | The Deceivers–John D. MacDonald | 1.00 | 2.00 | 3.00 | M |
| R1564 | World War II: A Photographic Record of the War in the Pacific from Pearl Harbor to V-J Day–Ralph G. Martin | 2.00 | 4.00 | 6.00 | C |
| R1565 | World War II: A Photographic Record of the War in Europe from D-Day to V-E Day–Ralph G. Martin & Richard Harrity | 2.00 | 4.00 | 6.00 | C |
| K1566 | The Brass Cupcake–John D. MacDonald | 1.00 | 2.00 | 3.00 | M |
| K1567 | Five Rode West–Lewis B. Patten | 1.00 | 2.00 | 3.00 | W |
| K1568 | Canyon of the Gun–T.V. Olsen | 1.00 | 2.00 | 3.00 | W |
| K1569 | Once a Thief–Zekial Marko; aka Scratch a Thief; movie tie-in | 1.00 | 2.00 | 3.00 | |
| K1570 | Assignment–Mara Tirana–Edward S. Aarons | 1.00 | 2.00 | 3.00 | M |
| D1571 | Over Her Dead Body–Richard S. Prather | 1.00 | 2.00 | 3.00 | M |
| D1572 | Bogart–Richard Gehman | 1.00 | 2.00 | 3.00 | B |

GOLD MEDAL, *continued*

| Code | Title | V/Good | Fine | N/Mint | |
|---|---|---|---|---|---|
| D1573 | Bright Orange for the Shroud–John D. MacDonald; 1st ed. 1965 | 6.00 | 12.00 | 18.00 | M |
| K1574 | Buchanan Gets Mad–Jonas Ward (William Ard) | 1.50 | 3.00 | 4.50 | W |
| K1575 | Buchanan's Revenge–Jonas Ward (William Ard) | 1.50 | 3.00 | 4.50 | W |
| K1576 | Buchanan on the Prod–Jonas Ward (William Ard); 1965 | 1.50 | 3.00 | 4.50 | W |
| K1577 | The Reward–Michael Barrett; movie tie-in | 1.50 | 3.00 | 4.50 | |
| R1578 | 1965 Official Pro Football Almanac–ed. Bill Wise | 1.00 | 2.00 | 3.00 | S |
| D1579 | April Evil–John D. MacDonald | 1.00 | 2.00 | 3.00 | M |
| K1580 | Judge Me Not–John D. MacDonald | 1.00 | 2.00 | 3.00 | M |
| D1581 | Slab Happy–Richard S. Prather | 1.00 | 2.00 | 3.00 | M |
| D1582 | Generation X–Charles Hamblett & Jane Deverson | 2.00 | 4.00 | 6.00 | JD |
| D1583 | Assignment–The Cairo Dancers–Edward S. Aarons | 1.00 | 2.00 | 3.00 | M |
| D1584 | Poor H. Allen Smith's Almanack–H. Allen Smith | 1.00 | 2.00 | 3.00 | H |
| K1585 | Day of the Gun–Richard Telfair | 1.00 | 2.00 | 3.00 | W |
| D1586 | The Magic Man and Other Science-Fantasy Stories–ed. Charles Beaumont | 4.00 | 8.00 | 12.00 | SF |
| K1587 | On the Run–John D. MacDonald | 1.50 | 3.00 | 4.50 | M |
| D1588 | Death Trap–John D. MacDonald | 1.50 | 3.00 | 4.50 | M |
| K1589 | What Next, Andy Capp?–Smythe | 1.00 | 2.00 | 3.00 | H |
| D1590 | The Beach Girls–John D. MacDonald | 1.00 | 2.00 | 3.00 | M |
| D1591 | Hot Prowl–Herbert D. Kastle | 1.00 | 2.00 | 3.00 | M |
| D1592 | Darling, It's Death–Richard S. Prather | 1.00 | 2.00 | 3.00 | M |
| D1593 | Spring Fire–Vin Packer | 1.00 | 2.00 | 3.00 | |
| D1594 | Man-to-Man Answers–ed. True magazine | 1.00 | 2.00 | 3.00 | NF |
| D1595 | The Scrambled Yeggs–Richard S. Prather; aka Pattern for Murder | 1.00 | 2.00 | 3.00 | M |
| K1596 | Amos Flagg–High Gun–Clay Randall | 1.00 | 2.00 | 3.00 | W |
| K1597 | Ramrod Rider–T.V. Olsen; 1965 | 1.00 | 2.00 | 3.00 | W |
| D1598 | Dig That Crazy Grave–Richard S. Prather | 1.00 | 2.00 | 3.00 | M |
| D1599 | The Drowner–John D. MacDonald | 1.00 | 2.00 | 3.00 | M |
| D1600 | Too Many Crooks–Richard S. Prather; aka Ride a High Horse | 1.00 | 2.00 | 3.00 | M |
| D1601 | Fun with Brain Puzzlers–L.H. Longley-Cook | 2.00 | 4.00 | 6.00 | NF |
| D1602 | The Shadowers–Donald Hamilton | 1.00 | 2.00 | 3.00 | |
| K1603 | Desert Stakeout–Harry Whittington | 1.50 | 3.00 | 4.50 | W |
| D1604 | Strip for Murder–Richard S. Prather | 1.00 | 2.00 | 3.00 | M |
| D1605 | Cockeyed Crosswords–Ted Shane | 2.50 | 5.00 | 7.50 | NF |
| D1606 | Slam the Big Door–John D. MacDonald | 1.00 | 2.00 | 3.00 | M |
| D1607 | Way of a Wanton–Richard S. Prather | 1.00 | 2.00 | 3.00 | M |
| D1608 | The Devastators–Donald Hamilton; 1965 | 1.00 | 2.00 | 3.00 | |
| D1609 | The Price of Murder–John D. MacDonald | 1.00 | 2.00 | 3.00 | M |
| D1610 | The Quick Red Fox–John D. MacDonald | 1.00 | 2.00 | 3.00 | M |
| D1611 | Carny Kill–Robert Edmond Alter; 1966 | 1.00 | 2.00 | 3.00 | M |
| D1612 | Assignment–Burma Girl–Edward S. Aarons | 1.00 | 2.00 | 3.00 | M |
| D1613 | Assignment–Madeleine–Edward S. Aarons | 1.00 | 2.00 | 3.00 | M |
| D1614 | Stretch and Discover Tension in Repose–Millicent Linden | 1.00 | 2.00 | 3.00 | NF |
| K1615 | Outcast Gun–Giles A. Lutz; 1966 | 1.00 | 2.00 | 3.00 | W |
| D1616 | Moment to Moment–Alec Coppel; movie tie-in | 1.00 | 2.00 | 3.00 | |
| D1617 | The Steel Mirror–Donald Hamilton | 1.00 | 2.00 | 3.00 | |
| D1619 | Songs for Pickin' and Singin'–ed. James F. Leisy | 1.00 | 2.00 | 3.00 | NF |
| D1620 | Find This Woman–Richard S. Prather | 1.00 | 2.00 | 3.00 | M |
| D1621 | Soft Touch–John D. MacDonald | 1.00 | 2.00 | 3.00 | M |
| K1622 | The Name's Buchanan–Jonas Ward (William Ard) | 1.50 | 3.00 | 4.50 | W |
| D1623 | Murder Twice Told–Donald Hamilton | 1.00 | 2.00 | 3.00 | M |
| K1624 | A Town to Tame–Joseph Chadwick | 1.00 | 2.00 | 3.00 | W |
| K1625 | Crazy Cartoons by VIP–Virgil Partch | 1.50 | 3.00 | 4.50 | H |
| D1626 | The Rare Breed–Theodore Sturgeon; movie tie-in | 4.00 | 8.00 | 12.00 | W |
| K1627 | Tall in the West–Vechel Howard | 1.00 | 2.00 | 3.00 | W |
| D1628 | Another Part of the Galaxy–ed. Groff Conklin | 1.00 | 2.00 | 3.00 | SF |
| D1629 | The Peddler–Richard S. Prather | 1.00 | 2.00 | 3.00 | M |
| D1630 | Assignment–Ankara–Edward S. Aarons | 1.00 | 2.00 | 3.00 | M |
| D1631 | Assignment–Zornya–Edward S. Aarons | 1.00 | 2.00 | 3.00 | M |
| D1632 | The Death Bird Contract–Philip Atlee | 1.00 | 2.00 | 3.00 | |
| D1633 | The End of the Night–John D. MacDonald | 1.50 | 3.00 | 4.50 | M |
| D1634 | The Paper Pistol Contract–Philip Atlee | 1.00 | 2.00 | 3.00 | |
| D1635 | A Bullet for Cinderella–John D. MacDonald | 1.50 | 3.00 | 4.50 | M |
| D1636 | The Only Girl in the Game–John D. MacDonald | 1.50 | 3.00 | 4.50 | M |
| K1637 | Spitting on the Sheriff and other Diversions–Charles Rodrigues | 2.00 | 4.00 | 6.00 | H |
| D1638 | Lie Down, Killer–Richard S. Prather | 1.00 | 2.00 | 3.00 | M |
| D1639 | The Girl from Midnight–Wade Miller | 1.00 | 2.00 | 3.00 | M |
| D1640 | Assignment–School for Spies–Edward S. Aarons | 1.00 | 2.00 | 3.00 | M |
| D1641 | The Silencers–Donald Hamilton | 1.00 | 2.00 | 3.00 | |
| K1642 | Chuka–Richard Jessup | 1.00 | 2.00 | 3.00 | W |
| K1643 | A Texan Comes Riding–Steven C. Lawrence | 1.00 | 2.00 | 3.00 | W |
| R1644 | Comrades of War–Sven Hassel | 1.50 | 3.00 | 4.50 | C |
| D1645 | The Vengeance Man–Dan J. Marlowe | 1.00 | 2.00 | 3.00 | M |
| D1646 | The Wrecking Crew–Donald Hamilton | 1.00 | 2.00 | 3.00 | |
| D1648 | Case of the Vanishing Beauty–Richard S. Prather | 1.00 | 2.00 | 3.00 | M |
| R1649 | Please Write for Details–John D. MacDonald | 1.50 | 3.00 | 4.50 | M |
| D1650 | The Sexually Adequate Female–Frank S. Caprio, MD | 1.00 | 2.00 | 3.00 | NF |
| K1651 | One-Man Massacre–Jonas Ward (William Ard); 1966 | 1.50 | 3.00 | 4.50 | W |
| D1652 | The Sexually Adequate Male–Frank S. Caprio, MD | 1.00 | 2.00 | 3.00 | NF |
| D1653 | Assignment–Budapest–Edward S. Aarons | 1.00 | 2.00 | 3.00 | M |
| D1654 | Assignment–Sulu Sea–Edward S. Aarons | 1.00 | 2.00 | 3.00 | M |
| D1655 | The Most Amazing But True–Doug Storer | 1.00 | 2.00 | 3.00 | NF |
| D1656 | Assignment–Treason–Edward S. Aarons | 1.00 | 2.00 | 3.00 | M |
| K1657 | Brand of a Texan–Steven C. Lawrence | 1.00 | 2.00 | 3.00 | W |
| D1658 | The Spy Catchers–Neil MacNeil | 1.00 | 2.00 | 3.00 | |
| D1659 | Deadly Welcome–John D. MacDonald | 1.50 | 3.00 | 4.50 | M |
| D1660 | Assignment–Helene–Edward S. Aarons | 1.00 | 2.00 | 3.00 | M |
| D1661 | Assignment–The Girl in the Gondola–Edward S. Aarons | 1.00 | 2.00 | 3.00 | M |
| D1662 | A Funny Thing Happened . . .–Norton Mockridge | 1.00 | 2.00 | 3.00 | H |
| D1663 | Kill the Clown–Richard S. Prather | 1.00 | 2.00 | 3.00 | M |
| D1664 | The Dirty War of Sergeant Slade–Lou Cameron | 1.00 | 2.00 | 3.00 | C |
| D1665 | The Bloody Medallion–Richard Telfair | 1.00 | 2.00 | 3.00 | M |
| K1666 | Duel at Diablo–Marvin H. Albert; movie tie-in | 1.50 | 3.00 | 4.50 | W |
| K1667 | Stagecoach–Robert W. Krepps; movie tie-in | 1.50 | 3.00 | 4.50 | W |
| K1668 | Sundown at Crazy Horse–Vechel Howard | 1.00 | 2.00 | 3.00 | W |
| D1669 | 12 Great Classics of Science Fiction–ed. Groff Conklin | 1.00 | 2.00 | 3.00 | SF |
| D1670 | A Man for All Women–Chandler Brossard | 1.00 | 2.00 | 3.00 | |
| R1671 | Brooks Wilson Ltd.–J.M. Ryan | 1.00 | 2.00 | 3.00 | |
| D1672 | Assignment–Suicide–Edward S. Aarons | 1.00 | 2.00 | 3.00 | M |
| D1673 | The Ravagers–Donald Hamilton | 1.00 | 2.00 | 3.00 | |
| D1674 | Darker Than Amber–John D. MacDonald | 1.00 | 2.00 | 3.00 | M |
| K1675 | The Man from Riondo–Dudley Dean | 1.00 | 2.00 | 3.00 | W |
| D1676 | A Season for Violence–Thomas B. Dewey | 2.00 | 4.00 | 6.00 | M |
| K1677 | Amos Flagg Rides Out–Clay Randall | 1.00 | 2.00 | 3.00 | W |
| K1678 | Bigger Than Texas–William R. Cox | 1.00 | 2.00 | 3.00 | W |
| D1679 | VIP's Illustrated Woman Driver's Manual–Alan Riefe & Virgil Partch | 2.00 | 4.00 | 6.00 | H |
| D1680 | Three Times Infinity–ed. Leo Margulies | 1.00 | 2.00 | 3.00 | SF |
| D1681 | Joker in the Deck–Richard S. Prather | 1.00 | 2.00 | 3.00 | M |
| D1682 | Nightmare in Pink–John D. MacDonald | 1.00 | 2.00 | 3.00 | M |
| D1683 | It's Cold Out There–Malcolm Braly | 1.00 | 2.00 | 3.00 | |
| T1684 | A Flash of Green–John D. MacDonald | 1.00 | 2.00 | 3.00 | M |
| D1685 | The Comfortable Coffin–ed. Richard S. Prather | 1.00 | 2.00 | 3.00 | M |
| D1686 | Drum Beat–Madrid–Stephen Marlowe | 1.00 | 2.00 | 3.00 | M |

GOLD MEDAL, *continued*

| | | V/Good | Fine | N/Mint | |
|---|---|---|---|---|---|
| D1687 | Murderers' Row—Donald Hamilton | 1.00 | 2.00 | 3.00 | |
| K1688 | White Apache—William Forrest | 1.00 | 2.00 | 3.00 | W |
| K1689 | Buchanan Says No—Jonas Ward (William Ard); 1966 | 1.50 | 3.00 | 4.50 | W |
| D1690 | End of the Tiger and Other Stories—John D. MacDonald | 1.00 | 2.00 | 3.00 | M |
| D1691 | The Map on the Ceiling—John Pierce | 1.00 | 2.00 | 3.00 | |
| D1692 | Assignment—Carlotta Cortez—Edward S. Aarons | 1.00 | 2.00 | 3.00 | M |
| D1693 | The Pan Book of Horror Stories—ed. Herbert van Thal | 2.00 | 4.00 | 6.00 | HO |
| D1694 | The Irish Beauty Contract—Philip Atlee | 1.00 | 2.00 | 3.00 | |
| D1695 | Assignment—Cong Hai Kill—Edward S. Aarons | 1.00 | 2.00 | 3.00 | M |
| D1696 | The Removers—Donald Hamilton | 1.00 | 2.00 | 3.00 | |
| D1697 | Death of a Citizen—Donald Hamilton | 1.00 | 2.00 | 3.00 | |
| M1698 | Falconhurst Fancy—Lance Horner & Kyle Onstott | 1.00 | 2.00 | 3.00 | |
| D1699 | The Neon Jungle—John D. MacDonald | 1.00 | 2.00 | 3.00 | M |
| K1700 | Gunswift—T.V. Olsen | 1.00 | 2.00 | 3.00 | W |
| D1701 | A Party to Murder—Lionel White | 1.50 | 3.00 | 4.50 | M |
| D1702 | The Silken Baroness Contract—Philip Atlee | 1.00 | 2.00 | 3.00 | |
| D1703 | Assignment to Disaster—Edward S. Aarons | 1.00 | 2.00 | 3.00 | M |
| D1704 | Venice in October—Jose André Lacour | 1.00 | 2.00 | 3.00 | |
| K1705 | The Moonlight War—Clifton Adams | 1.00 | 2.00 | 3.00 | W |
| D1706 | Case of the Brazen Beauty—Jonathan Craig | 1.00 | 2.00 | 3.00 | M |
| D1707 | Assignment—Lili Lamaris—Edward S. Aarons | 1.00 | 2.00 | 3.00 | M |
| K1708 | The True Album of Cartoons—ed. True magazine | 1.50 | 3.00 | 4.50 | H |
| D1709 | Secret of Canfield House—Florence Hurd | 1.00 | 2.00 | 3.00 | |
| D1710 | Three's a Shroud—Richard S. Prather | 1.00 | 2.00 | 3.00 | M |
| K1711 | Andy Capp Sounds Off—Smythe | 1.00 | 2.00 | 3.00 | H |
| D1712 | Murder for the Bride—John D. MacDonald | 1.00 | 2.00 | 3.00 | M |
| D1713 | Bar Guide—Ted Shane & VIP (Virgil Partch) | 1.50 | 3.00 | 4.50 | H |
| D1714 | The Spy Who Was 3 Feet Tall—Peter Rabe | 2.00 | 4.00 | 6.00 | |
| K1715 | Gunfire at Salt Fork—William Hopson | 1.00 | 2.00 | 3.00 | W |
| D1716 | The L.S.D. Story—John Cashman | 2.00 | 4.00 | 6.00 | NF |
| D1717 | Everybody Had a Gun—Richard S. Prather | 1.00 | 2.00 | 3.00 | M |
| D1718 | Bodies in Bedlam—Richard S. Prather | 1.00 | 2.00 | 3.00 | M |
| D1719 | The Fickle Finger of Fate—John A. Keel | 1.00 | 2.00 | 3.00 | H |
| D1720 | The Appaloosa—Richard MacLeod; 1966; movie tie-in | 1.50 | 3.00 | 4.50 | W |
| D1722 | The Thief Who Couldn't Sleep—Lawrence Block; orig. 1966. Note: First Tanner novel | 4.00 | 8.00 | 12.00 | M |

## GOLD MEDAL (BRITISH)
### Fawcett Publications, Inc.

| | | V/Good | Fine | N/Mint | |
|---|---|---|---|---|---|
| 1 | No Business for a Lady—James L. Rubel | 1.25 | 2.50 | 3.75 | M |
| 2 | Million Dollar Murder—Edward Ronns | 1.25 | 2.50 | 3.75 | M |
| 3 | Stretch Dawson—W.R. Burnett | 1.50 | 3.00 | 4.50 | W |
| 4 | Dallas—Will F. Jenkins (Murray Leinster); movie tie-in | 2.00 | 4.00 | 6.00 | W |
| 5 | The Desperado—Clifton Adams | 1.25 | 2.50 | 3.75 | W |
| 6 | High Red for Dead—William L. Rohde | 1.25 | 2.50 | 3.75 | M |
| 7 | To Kiss or Kill—Day Keene | 1.25 | 2.50 | 3.75 | M |
| 8 | Lost Lady—Octavus Roy Cohen | 1.25 | 2.50 | 3.75 | M |
| 12 | Help Wanted—for Murder—William L. Rohde | 1.25 | 2.50 | 3.75 | M |
| 13 | Crockett's Woman—Eric Hatch | 1.00 | 2.00 | 3.00 | |
| 15 | Look Behind You Lady—A.S. Fleischman | 1.00 | 2.00 | 3.00 | |
| 16 | A Noose for the Desperado—Clifton Adams | 1.25 | 2.50 | 3.75 | W |
| 17 | Stampede—Yukon Miles | 1.25 | 2.50 | 3.75 | W |
| 18 | Everybody Had a Gun—Richard S. Prather | 1.25 | 2.50 | 3.75 | M |
| 19 | Death and the Naked Lady—John Flagg | 1.25 | 2.50 | 3.75 | M |
| 20 | The Secret Rider—Logan Stewart | 1.25 | 2.50 | 3.75 | W |

| | | V/Good | Fine | N/Mint | |
|---|---|---|---|---|---|
| 21 | Give a Man a Gun—Leslie Ernenwein | 1.25 | 2.50 | 3.75 | W |
| 22 | I Have Gloria Kirby—Richard Himmel | 1.25 | 2.50 | 3.75 | M |
| 23 | The Judas Hour—Howard Hunt | 1.25 | 2.50 | 3.75 | |
| 24 | Naked Ebony—Dan Cushman | 1.25 | 2.50 | 3.75 | |
| 25 | Maggie—Her Marriage—Taylor Caldwell | 1.25 | 2.50 | 3.75 | E |
| 26 | Woman of Cairo—John Flagg | 1.25 | 2.50 | 3.75 | |
| 27 | Hunt the Man Down—William Heumann | 1.25 | 2.50 | 3.75 | W |
| 28 | Death on a Ferris Wheel—Alwin Lee Martin | 1.25 | 2.50 | 3.75 | M |
| 29 | The Texas Gun—Leslie Ernenwein | 1.25 | 2.50 | 3.75 | W |
| 30 | The Man Who Said No—Walt Grove | 1.25 | 2.50 | 3.75 | M |
| 31 | Red Runs the River—William Heumann | 1.25 | 2.50 | 3.75 | W |
| 32 | Wild Blood—A.C. Abbott | 1.25 | 2.50 | 3.75 | W |
| 33 | Jungle She—Dan Cushman | 2.00 | 4.00 | 6.00 | A |
| 34 | Take Me As I Am—William Fielding | 1.25 | 2.50 | 3.75 | M |
| 35 | The Trail—Logan Stewart | 1.25 | 2.50 | 3.75 | W |
| 36 | The Sinners—Edward S. Aarons | 1.25 | 2.50 | 3.75 | M |
| 37 | Hondo—Louis L'Amour | 2.00 | 4.00 | 6.00 | W |
| 38 | Witch of Salem—Benjamin Siegal | 1.50 | 3.00 | 4.50 | |
| 39 | Barren Land Murders—Luke Short | 1.25 | 2.50 | 3.75 | W |
| 40 | Rider from Nowhere—Joseph Chadwick | 1.25 | 2.50 | 3.75 | W |
| 41 | Murder for the Bride—John D. MacDonald | 1.50 | 3.00 | 4.50 | M |
| 42 | Run for Your Life—Bruno Fischer | 1.25 | 2.50 | 3.75 | M |
| 43 | Mystery Raider—Leslie Ernenwein | 1.25 | 2.50 | 3.75 | W |
| 44 | Madame Buccaneer—Gardner F. Fox | 1.50 | 3.00 | 4.50 | A |
| 45 | Come Feed on Me—Morton Cooper | 1.25 | 2.50 | 3.75 | |
| 46 | Terror in the Night—Sebastian Blayne | 1.25 | 2.50 | 3.75 | M |
| 47 | Up a Winding Stair—H. Vernor Dixon | 1.50 | 3.00 | 4.50 | |
| 48 | Move Along, Stranger—Frank Castle | 1.25 | 2.50 | 3.75 | W |
| 49 | Double Cross—Joseph Chadwick | 1.25 | 2.50 | 3.75 | W |
| 50 | Gunsmoke Reckoning—Joseph Chadwick | 1.25 | 2.50 | 3.75 | W |
| 51 | The Lady and the Cheetah—John Flagg | 1.25 | 2.50 | 3.75 | |
| 52 | Come Back My Love—Edward S. Aaron | 1.25 | 2.50 | 3.75 | M |
| 53 | The White Squaw—Larabie Sutter | 2.00 | 4.00 | 6.00 | W |
| 54 | Nothing in Her Way—Charles Williams | 2.50 | 5.00 | 7.50 | M |
| 55 | Branded Woman—Wade Miller | 1.25 | 2.50 | 3.75 | |
| 56 | Whip Hand—Joseph Chadwick | 1.25 | 2.50 | 3.75 | W |
| 57 | The Neon Jungle—John D. MacDonald | 1.25 | 2.50 | 3.75 | M |
| 58 | Hideaway—Nikki Content | 1.25 | 2.50 | 3.75 | M |
| 59 | Keelboats North—William Heumann | 1.25 | 2.50 | 3.75 | W |
| 60 | Tokyo Doll—John McPartland | 1.50 | 3.00 | 4.50 | |
| 61 | Secret of Death Valley—William Heumann | 1.25 | 2.50 | 3.75 | W |
| 62 | Devil's Legacy—Joseph Chadwick | 1.25 | 2.50 | 3.75 | |
| 63 | Danger in Paradise—A.S. Fleischman | 1.25 | 2.50 | 3.75 | A |
| 64 | Moment of Truth—Arnold Rodin | 1.25 | 2.50 | 3.75 | |
| 65 | Barge Girl—Calvin Clements | 1.25 | 2.50 | 3.75 | E |
| 66 | Savage Stronghold—Logan Stewart | 1.25 | 2.50 | 3.75 | W |
| 67 | The Borgia Blade—Gardner F. Fox | 1.50 | 3.00 | 4.50 | A |
| 68 | The Girl in the Death Cell—Fred J. Cook | 1.25 | 2.50 | 3.75 | M |
| 69 | Big Red's Daughter—John McPartland | 1.25 | 2.50 | 3.75 | M |
| 70 | Gunfighter's Return—Leslie Ernenwein | 1.25 | 2.50 | 3.75 | W |
| 71 | Saturday's Harvest—Paul Shelley | 1.25 | 2.50 | 3.75 | |
| 72 | The Brass Cupcake—John D. MacDonald | 1.50 | 3.00 | 4.50 | M |
| 81 | The Crooked Mile—Norbert Fagan | 1.25 | 2.50 | 3.75 | |

## GOLD MEDAL BOOKS
### Gold Medal Books, Inc.
Digest size

| | | V/Good | Fine | N/Mint |
|---|---|---|---|---|
| nn | The Desert of Love—Francois Mauriac | 2.00 | 4.00 | 6.00 |
| nn | Five Sisters—Violet Kazarine | 2.00 | 4.00 | 6.00 |
| nn | Georgie May—Maxwell Bodenheim | 2.00 | 4.00 | 6.00 |
| nn | Show Girl—J.P. McEvoy | 2.00 | 4.00 | 6.00 |

## GOLD STAR BOOKS
### New International Library, Inc.

| | | V/Good | Fine | N/Mint | |
|---|---|---|---|---|---|
| IL7-11 | Kill Her with Passion—Hank Janson | 1.50 | 3.00 | 4.50 | M |
| IL7-12 | Lover—Hank Janson; c-Maguire | 2.00 | 4.00 | 6.00 | M |
| IL7-13 | Brazen Seductress—Hank Janson; c-Maguire | 2.00 | 4.00 | 6.00 | M |
| IL7-14 | A Nice Way to Die—Hank Janson | 1.50 | 3.00 | 4.50 | M |
| IL7-15 | It's Bedtime Baby—Hank Janson | 1.50 | 3.00 | 4.50 | M |
| IL7-16 | Hell's Angels—Hank Janson; c-Maguire | 2.00 | 4.00 | 6.00 | M |

GOLD STAR BOOKS, *continued*

| | | V/Good | Fine | N/Mint | |
|---|---|---|---|---|---|
| IL7-17 | Hot House–Hank Janson | 1.50 | 3.00 | 4.50 | M |
| IL7-18 | Passionate Playmates–Hank Janson; c-Maguire | 2.00 | 4.00 | 6.00 | M |
| IL7-19 | Demented–Donald Jordon Young; c-Maguire | 2.00 | 4.00 | 6.00 | E |
| IL7-20 | Her Weapon Is Passion–Hank Janson | 1.50 | 3.00 | 4.50 | M |
| IL7-21 | Sanitarium of Tears–Steve Thurman | 1.50 | 3.00 | 4.50 | E |
| IL7-22 | Cold Dead Coed–Hank Janson | 1.50 | 3.00 | 4.50 | M |
| IL7-23 | Psycho-Sexual Problems–Alex M. Szedenik | 1.00 | 2.00 | 3.00 | NF |
| IL7-24 | Lay Down Dead–Matthew Bradley | 1.50 | 3.00 | 4.50 | M |
| IL7-25 | Shocking Tales of Perversion–ed. Chester W. Krone, Jr | 1.00 | 2.00 | 3.00 | NF |
| IL7-26 | All the Gay Girls–Margurite Frame | 1.50 | 3.00 | 4.50 | E |
| IL7-27 | One Helluva Blow–George Werner | 1.50 | 3.00 | 4.50 | SF |
| IL7-28 | Fanny–Hank Janson | 1.50 | 3.00 | 4.50 | M |
| IL7-29 | Adultery in Suburbia–Matthew Bradley | 1.00 | 2.00 | 3.00 | E |
| IL7-30 | The Hackamore Feud–Matt Stuart | 1.00 | 2.00 | 3.00 | W |
| IL7-31 | Whiplash–R.W. Taylor | 1.00 | 2.00 | 3.00 | |
| IL7-32 | Expectant Nymph–Hank Janson; c-Maguire | 2.00 | 4.00 | 6.00 | M |
| IL7-33 | Buffalo Bill's Leap For Life; or, The White Death of Beaver Wash–By the Author of "Buffalo Bill" (ed. Edward T. LeBlanc) | 2.00 | 4.00 | 6.00 | W |
| IL7-34 | Buffalo Bill's Spy Shadower; or, The Hermit of Grand Canyon–By the Author of "Buffalo Bill" (ed. Edward T. LeBlanc) | 2.00 | 4.00 | 6.00 | W |
| IL7-35 | Campus Call Girl–Scott O'Neill | 1.50 | 3.00 | 4.50 | E |
| IL7-36 | Anatomy of a Psycho–Alex M. Szedenik | 1.00 | 2.00 | 3.00 | E |
| IL7-37 | Running the Gauntlet; or, The Pawnee Chief's Last Stand–By an Old Scout (ed. Edward T. LeBlanc) | 2.00 | 4.00 | 6.00 | W |
| IL7-38 | Green Corn Dance; or, A Lively Time with the Pawnees–By an Old Scout (ed. Edward T. LeBlanc) | 2.00 | 4.00 | 6.00 | W |
| IL7-39 | Love Is for Everybody–Angela Gilbert | 1.50 | 3.00 | 4.50 | E |
| IL7-40 | Sex and the Coed–James B. Fairly | 1.50 | 3.00 | 4.50 | E |
| IL7-41 | Girl Possessed–Dean Owen | 1.50 | 3.00 | 4.50 | E |
| IL7-42 | Tarzan & the Silver Globe–Barton Werper; orig. 1964. Note: The unauthorized New Tarzan Series was written by Peter and Peggy O'Neill Scott and was stopped by legal action in early 1965 with unsold copies being destroyed. | 7.50 | 15.00 | 22.50 | SF |
| IL7-43 | Buffalo Bill's Raid of Death; or, The Border Robin Hood–By the Author of "Buffalo Bill" (ed. Edward T. LeBlanc) | 2.00 | 4.00 | 6.00 | W |
| IL7-44 | Buffalo Bill's Feather-Weight; or, Apache Charley, the Indian Athlete–By the Author of "Buffalo Bill" (ed. Edward T. LeBlanc) | 2.00 | 4.00 | 6.00 | W |
| IL7-45 | Puzzle Lovers Dictionary–ed. Orville Pfieffer | 1.50 | 3.00 | 4.50 | NF |
| IL7-46 | Young Wild West's Prairie Pioneers; or, Fighting the Way to the Golden Loop–By an Old Scout (ed. Edward T. LeBlanc) | 2.00 | 4.00 | 6.00 | W |

*Gold Star IL7-32, Gold Star IL7-42, Gold Star IL7-43.*

| | | V/Good | Fine | N/Mint | |
|---|---|---|---|---|---|
| IL7-47 | The Renegade Rustlers; or, Saved by the Sorrel Stallion–By an Old Scout (ed. Edward T. LeBlanc) | 2.00 | 4.00 | 6.00 | W |
| IL7-48 | The Exotic Seductress–Hank Janson | 1.50 | 3.00 | 4.50 | M |
| IL7-49 | Tarzan & the Cave City–Barton Werper; orig., 1964. Note: The unauthorized New Tarzan Series was written by Peter and Peggy O'Neill Scott and was stopped by legal action in early 1965 with unsold copies being destroyed. | 7.50 | 15.00 | 22.50 | A |
| IL7-50 | Sex and the Starlets–Scott O'Neill | 1.50 | 3.00 | 4.50 | E |
| IL7-51 | Vicki–Matty Edmund | 1.50 | 3.00 | 4.50 | E |
| IL7-52 | Buffalo Bill's Tomahawk Duel; or, Playing Redskins at Their Own Game–By the Author of "Buffalo Bill" (ed. Edward T. LeBlanc) | 2.00 | 4.00 | 6.00 | W |
| IL7-53 | Buffalo Bill's Double; or, The False Guide–By the Author of "Buffalo Bill" (ed. Edward T. LeBlanc) | 2.00 | 4.00 | 6.00 | W |
| IL7-54 | Tarzan & the Snake People–Barton Werper; orig. 1964. Note: The unauthorized New Tarzan Series was written by Peter and Peggy O'Neill Scott and was stopped by legal action in early 1965 with unsold copies being destroyed. | 7.50 | 15.00 | 22.50 | SF |
| IL7-55 | Sex and the Jet Set–Scott O'Neill | 1.50 | 3.00 | 4.50 | E |
| IL7-56 | What Makes You Tick? Vol. 1–Aries/Taurus–Margot Mason | 1.00 | 2.00 | 3.00 | NF |
| IL7-57 | The Sexy Vixen–Hank Janson | 1.50 | 3.00 | 4.50 | M |
| IL7-58 | Wild West and the "Salted" Mine; or, The Double Game for a Million–By an Old Scout (ed. Edward T. LeBlanc) | 2.00 | 4.00 | 6.00 | W |
| IL7-59 | Wild West's Whirlwind Riders; or, Chasing the Border Thugs–By an Old Scout (ed. Edward T. LeBlanc) | 2.00 | 4.00 | 6.00 | W |
| IL7-60 | Tarzan & the Abominable Snowman–Barton Werper; orig. 1965. Note: The unauthorized New Tarzan Series was written by Peter and Peggy O'Neill Scott and was stopped by legal action in early 1965 with unsold copies being destroyed. | 9.00 | 18.00 | 27.00 | SF |
| IL7-61 | Sex and the Divorcee–Scott O'Neill | 1.50 | 3.00 | 4.50 | E |
| IL7-62 | What Makes You Tick? Vol. II–Gemini/Cancer–Margot Mason | 1.00 | 2.00 | 3.00 | NF |
| IL7-63 | The Affairs of Paula–Hank Janson | 1.50 | 3.00 | 4.50 | M |
| IL7-64 | Part-Time Call Girl–A Wife Who Was One | 1.50 | 3.00 | 4.50 | E |
| IL7-65 | Tarzan & the Winged Invaders–Barton Werper; orig. 1965. Note: The unauthorized New Tarzan Series was written by Peter and Peggy O'Neill Scott and was stopped by legal action in early 1965 with unsold copies being destroyed. | 10.00 | 20.00 | 30.00 | SF |
| IL7-66 | Sex in the Service–Scott O'Neill | 1.50 | 3.00 | 4.50 | E |
| IL7-67 | Sex and the Oriental–Peter Howard | 1.50 | 3.00 | 4.50 | E |
| IL7-68 | A Nympho Named Sylvia–Hank Janson | 1.50 | 3.00 | 4.50 | M |
| IL7-69 | What Makes You Tick? Vol. III–Margot Mason | 1.00 | 2.00 | 3.00 | NF |
| IL7-70 | Becky–Hank Janson | 1.50 | 3.00 | 4.50 | M |
| IL7-71 | Sex and the Alcoholic–Scott O'Neill | 1.50 | 3.00 | 4.50 | E |
| IL7-72 | What Makes You Tick? Vol. IV–Margot Mason | 1.00 | 2.00 | 3.00 | NF |
| IL7-73 | Twilight Girls–Sherry Dale | 1.50 | 3.00 | 4.50 | E |
| IL7-74 | Buffalo Bill's Fair Square Deal; or, The Duke of the Dagger's Dead Lock–By the Author of "Buffalo Bill" (ed. Edward T. LeBlanc) | 2.00 | 4.00 | 6.00 | W |
| IL7-75 | Nympho Nurse–Jerry James | 1.50 | 3.00 | 4.50 | E |
| IL7-76 | Woman Hating Surgeon–Jerry James | 1.50 | 3.00 | 4.50 | E |

# GRAPHIC

## Graphic Publishing Company, Inc.

| | | V/Good | Fine | N/Mint | |
|---|---|---|---|---|---|
| 11 | Murder–Queen High–Bill Miller & Bob Wade; 1949 | 2.00 | 4.00 | 6.00 | M |
| 12 | If I Live to Dine–Hillary Waugh | 1.50 | 3.00 | 4.50 | M |

*Graphic 20, Graphic 43, Graphic 45.*

| | | V/Good | Fine | N/Mint | |
|---|---|---|---|---|---|
| GRAPHIC, *continued* | | | | | |
| 13 | Flash–Hold for Murder–Paul Whelton | 1.50 | 3.00 | 4.50 | M |
| 14 | Death Commits Bigamy–James M. Fox | 1.50 | 3.00 | 4.50 | M |
| 15 | Tex–Clarence E. Mulford | 1.50 | 3.00 | 4.50 | W |
| 16 | Deadline at Dawn–William Irish | 3.50 | 7.00 | 10.50 | M |
| 17 | Call the Lady Indiscreet–Paul Whelton | 1.50 | 3.00 | 4.50 | M |
| 18 | Dealing Out Death–W.T. Ballard | 2.00 | 4.00 | 6.00 | M |
| 19 | Lures of Death–Paul Whelton; 1950 | 2.00 | 4.00 | 6.00 | M |
| 20 | Dilemma of the Dead Lady–William Irish | 5.00 | 10.00 | 15.00 | M |
| 21 | The Widow Gay–A.A. Marcus | 1.50 | 3.00 | 4.50 | M |
| 22 | Tough Cop–John Roeburt | 1.50 | 3.00 | 4.50 | M |
| 23 | The Man from Bar 20–Clarence E. Mulford | 2.00 | 4.00 | 6.00 | W |
| 24 | Uninvited Corpse–Paul Whelton | 1.50 | 3.00 | 4.50 | M |
| 25 | The Singing Scorpion–William Colt MacDonald | 1.50 | 3.00 | 4.50 | W |
| 26 | Murder Can't Stop–W.T. Ballard | 2.00 | 4.00 | 6.00 | M |
| 27 | Corpse on the Town–John Roeburt | 1.50 | 3.00 | 4.50 | M |
| 28 | Tex–Clarence E. Mulford; 1951 | 1.50 | 3.00 | 4.50 | W |
| 29 | Memo for Murder–Dal Wilmer; orig. 1951 | 1.50 | 3.00 | 4.50 | M |
| 30 | Runyon First and Last–Damon Runyon | 2.00 | 4.00 | 6.00 | H |
| 31 | Deadly Night Call–William Irish | 2.50 | 5.00 | 7.50 | M |
| 32 | Hangover House–Sax Rohmer | 2.00 | 4.00 | 6.00 | M |
| 33 | The Dummy Murder Case–Milton K. Ozaki; orig. 1951 | 1.50 | 3.00 | 4.50 | M |
| 34 | Texas Men–Paul Evan Lehman | 1.50 | 3.00 | 4.50 | W |
| 35 | Walk the Bloody Boulevard–A.A. Marcus | 1.50 | 3.00 | 4.50 | M |
| 36 | Call Me Killer–Harry Whittington; orig. 1951 | 2.50 | 5.00 | 7.50 | M |
| 37 | Pardon My Blood–Paul Whelton | 1.50 | 3.00 | 4.50 | M |
| 38 | Tough Cop–John Roeburt | 1.50 | 3.00 | 4.50 | M |
| 39 | Vultures of Paradise Valley–Paul Evan Lehman | 1.50 | 3.00 | 4.50 | W |
| 40 | The Crooked Circle–Manning Lee Stokes | 1.50 | 3.00 | 4.50 | M |
| 41 | Murder Is My Mistress–Harry Whittington; orig. 1951 | 2.50 | 5.00 | 7.50 | M |
| 42 | There Are Dead Men in Manhattan–John Roeburt | 1.50 | 3.00 | 4.50 | M |
| 43 | If the Coffin Fits–Day Keene; 1952 | 3.50 | 7.00 | 10.50 | M |
| 44 | Gun Hawk–Leslie Ernenwein | 1.50 | 3.00 | 4.50 | W |
| 45 | Death for a Hussy–Aylwin Lee Martin | 1.50 | 3.00 | 4.50 | M |
| 46 | Mourn the Hangman–Harry Whittington; orig. 1952 | 2.50 | 5.00 | 7.50 | M |
| 47 | Faces in the Dust–Paul Evan Lehman | 1.50 | 3.00 | 4.50 | W |
| 48 | Pattern for Murder–David Knight | 1.50 | 3.00 | 4.50 | M |
| 49 | In Comes Death–Paul Whelton | 1.50 | 3.00 | 4.50 | M |
| 50 | The Singing Scorpion–William Colt MacDonald | 1.50 | 3.00 | 4.50 | W |
| 51 | Framed in Guilt–Day Keene | 2.50 | 5.00 | 7.50 | M |
| 52 | There Oughta Be a Law!–Al Fagaly & Harry Shorten | 2.00 | 4.00 | 6.00 | H |
| 53 | Tex–Clarence E. Mulford | 1.50 | 3.00 | 4.50 | W |
| 54 | Murder–Queen High–Bill Miller & Bob Wade | 1.50 | 3.00 | 4.50 | M |
| 55 | A Shot in the Dark–Richard Powell | 1.50 | 3.00 | 4.50 | M |
| 56 | Texas Men–Paul Evan Lehman | 1.50 | 3.00 | 4.50 | M |
| 57 | The Deadly Pick-up–Milton K. Ozaki; 1953 | 1.50 | 3.00 | 4.50 | M |
| 58 | Strange Witness–Day Keene; orig. 1953 | 2.50 | 5.00 | 7.50 | M |

| | | V/Good | Fine | N/Mint | |
|---|---|---|---|---|---|
| 59 | Dark Destiny–Edward Ronns | 1.50 | 3.00 | 4.50 | M |
| 60 | Dead Man's Tide–William Richards; orig. 1953 | 1.50 | 3.00 | 4.50 | M |
| 61 | There Oughta Be a Law!–Al Fagaly & Harry Shorten | 2.00 | 4.00 | 6.00 | H |
| 62 | Gun Hawk–Leslie Ernenwein | 1.50 | 3.00 | 4.50 | W |
| 63 | Tough Cop–John Roeburt | 1.50 | 3.00 | 4.50 | M |
| 64 | Walk the Bloody Boulevard–A.A. Marcus | 1.50 | 3.00 | 4.50 | M |
| 65 | Murder Can't Stop–W.T. Ballard | 2.00 | 4.00 | 6.00 | M |
| 66 | Vultures of Paradise Valley–Paul Evan Lehman | 1.50 | 3.00 | 4.50 | W |
| 67 | Post-mark Homicide–A.A. Marcus; aka The Widow Gay. Note: Same cover as Harlequin 90 | 1.50 | 3.00 | 4.50 | M |
| 68 | The Net–Edward Ronns | 1.50 | 3.00 | 4.50 | M |
| 69 | Runyon First and Last–Damon Runyon | 1.50 | 3.00 | 4.50 | H |
| 70 | Late Last Night–James Reach | 1.50 | 3.00 | 4.50 | M |
| 71 | Pardon My Blood–Paul Whelton; 1954 | 1.50 | 3.00 | 4.50 | M |
| 72 | Dealing Out Death–W.T. Ballard | 2.00 | 4.00 | 6.00 | M |
| 73 | Handle with Fear–Thomas B. Dewey | 2.00 | 4.00 | 6.00 | M |
| 74 | Two-gun Fury–Charles M. Martin | 1.50 | 3.00 | 4.50 | W |
| 75 | The Big Kiss-off–Day Keene; orig. 1954 | 2.50 | 5.00 | 7.50 | M |
| 76 | Say It with Murder–Edward Ronns | 1.50 | 3.00 | 4.50 | M |
| 77 | Gunman's Creed–L.P. Holmes | 1.50 | 3.00 | 4.50 | W |
| 78 | Hangover House–Sax Rohmer | 2.00 | 4.00 | 6.00 | M |
| 79 | Dressed to Kill–Milton Ozaki | 1.50 | 3.00 | 4.50 | M |
| 80 | Blood on the Range–Eli Colter | 1.50 | 3.00 | 4.50 | W |
| 81 | Deadly Night Call–William Irish | 2.00 | 4.00 | 6.00 | M |
| 82 | Stand Up and Die–Frances Lockridge & Richard Lockridge | 2.00 | 4.00 | 6.00 | M |
| 83 | The Fatal Cast–Curtiss T. Gardner | 1.50 | 3.00 | 4.50 | M |
| 84 | Your Shot, Darling–Lillian Bergquist & Irving Moore | 1.50 | 3.00 | 4.50 | M |
| 85 | More There Oughta Be a Law!–Al Fagaly & Harry Shorten | 2.00 | 4.00 | 6.00 | H |
| 86 | Texas Pride–Charles M. Martin | 1.50 | 3.00 | 4.50 | W |
| 87 | Homicidal Lady–Day Keene; orig. 1954 | 2.50 | 5.00 | 7.50 | M |
| 88 | Outlaw Justice–Ford Pendleton | 1.50 | 3.00 | 4.50 | M |
| 89 | The Scarab Murder Case–S.S. Van Dine | 2.50 | 5.00 | 7.50 | M |
| 90 | Too Young to Die–Robert O. Saber | 1.50 | 3.00 | 4.50 | M |
| 91 | Tex–Clarence E. Mulford | 1.50 | 3.00 | 4.50 | W |
| 92 | The Deadly Pick-up–Milton K. Ozaki | 1.50 | 3.00 | 4.50 | M |
| 93 | Say It with Bullets–Richard Powell | 1.50 | 3.00 | 4.50 | M |
| 94 | Model for Murder–Stephen Marlowe; 1955 | 1.50 | 3.00 | 4.50 | M |
| 95 | Call the Lady Indiscreet–Paul Whelton | 1.50 | 3.00 | 4.50 | M |
| 96 | Gun Lightning!–Steve Thurman | 1.50 | 3.00 | 4.50 | W |
| 97 | One Touch of Blood–Samm Sinclair Baker | 1.50 | 3.00 | 4.50 | M |
| 98 | Too Many Murderers–Manning Lee Stokes | 1.50 | 3.00 | 4.50 | M |
| 99 | Sucker Bait–Robert O. Saber | 1.50 | 3.00 | 4.50 | M |
| 100 | Faces in the Dust–Paul Evan Lehman | 1.50 | 3.00 | 4.50 | W |
| 101 | Cry Torment–Victor H. Johnson | 1.50 | 3.00 | 4.50 | M |
| 102 | Die by Night–M.S. Marbie | 1.50 | 3.00 | 4.50 | M |
| 103 | Girl in the Red Dress–Richard Cargoe | 1.50 | 3.00 | 4.50 | M |
| 104 | Mugs, Molls and Dr. Harvey–George Malcolm-Smith | 1.50 | 3.00 | 4.50 | H |
| 105 | Murder Has Many Faces–William Grew | 1.50 | 3.00 | 4.50 | M |
| 106 | Trap–George E. Jones | 1.50 | 3.00 | 4.50 | M |
| 107 | The Adventures of Ferd'nand–Mik | 1.50 | 3.00 | 4.50 | H |
| 108 | Phantom Lady–William Irish | 3.00 | 6.00 | 9.00 | M |

*Graphic 69, Graphic 86, Graphic G203.*

| | | V/Good | Fine | N/Mint | |
|---|---|---|---|---|---|

GRAPHIC, *continued*

| # | Title | V/Good | Fine | N/Mint | |
|---|---|---|---|---|---|
| 109 | More There Oughta Be a Law!–Al Fagaly & Harry Shorten | 2.00 | 4.00 | 6.00 | H |
| 110 | The Hollow Man–John Roeburt | 2.00 | 4.00 | 6.00 | M |
| 111 | A Dame Called Murder–Robert O. Saber | 2.00 | 4.00 | 6.00 | M |
| 112 | Gun Hawk–Leslie Ernenwein | 1.50 | 3.00 | 4.50 | W |
| 113 | Unfinished Crime–Helen McCloy | 1.50 | 3.00 | 4.50 | M |
| 114 | They All Ran Away–Edward Ronns | 1.50 | 3.00 | 4.50 | M |
| 115 | Make Way for Murder–A.A. Marcus | 1.50 | 3.00 | 4.50 | M |
| 116 | Hell Rider–Ford Pendleton | 1.50 | 3.00 | 4.50 | W |
| 117 | Murder Can't Wait–Manning Lee Stokes | 1.50 | 3.00 | 4.50 | M |
| 118 | And Kill Once More–Al Fray | 1.50 | 3.00 | 4.50 | M |
| 119 | Mood for Murder–Frank Gruber; 1956 | 2.00 | 4.00 | 6.00 | M |
| 120 | Texas Guns–Leslie Ernenwein | 1.50 | 3.00 | 4.50 | W |
| 121 | Tough Cop–John Roeburt | 1.50 | 3.00 | 4.50 | M |
| 122 | Homicide Lost–William E. Vance | 1.50 | 3.00 | 4.50 | M |
| 123 | A Time for Murder–Robert O. Saber | 1.50 | 3.00 | 4.50 | M |
| 124 | Gunpoint!–John L. Shelley | 1.50 | 3.00 | 4.50 | W |
| 125 | The Intruder–Octavus Roy Cohen | 1.50 | 3.00 | 4.50 | M |
| 126 | Murder's End–Robert Kelston; c-Maguire | 2.00 | 4.00 | 6.00 | M |
| 127 | So Lovely to Kill–Harrison Wade | 1.50 | 3.00 | 4.50 | M |
| 128 | Two-gun Fury–Charles M. Martin | 1.50 | 3.00 | 4.50 | W |
| 129 | Six-gun Heritage–Brad Ward | 1.50 | 3.00 | 4.50 | W |
| 130 | Late Last Night–James Reach | 1.50 | 3.00 | 4.50 | M |
| 131 | This Kill Is Mine–Dean Evans | 1.50 | 3.00 | 4.50 | M |
| 132 | I Prefer Murder–Charles A. Landolf & Browning Norton | 1.50 | 3.00 | 4.50 | M |
| 133 | Gunmaster–Ford Pendleton | 1.50 | 3.00 | 4.50 | W |
| 134 | Who Dies There?–James Duff; orig. 1956 | 1.50 | 3.00 | 4.50 | M |
| 135 | Murder–Very Dry–Samm Sinclair Baker | 1.50 | 3.00 | 4.50 | M |
| 136 | Killer's Choice–Stuart Brock | 1.50 | 3.00 | 4.50 | M |
| 137 | Blood on the Range–Eli Colter | 1.50 | 3.00 | 4.50 | W |
| 138 | The Corpse Next Door–John Farris; orig. 1956 | 1.50 | 3.00 | 4.50 | M |
| 139 | Some Die Young–James Duff | 1.50 | 3.00 | 4.50 | M |
| 140 | Gun Trail–Mack Saunders | 1.50 | 3.00 | 4.50 | W |
| 141 | Dressed to Kill–Milton Ozaki | 1.25 | 2.50 | 3.75 | M |
| 142 | Fair Prey–Will Duke | 1.50 | 3.00 | 4.50 | M |
| 143 | Three Must Die!–Dan Gregory | 1.50 | 3.00 | 4.50 | M |
| 144 | Gunman's Creed–L.P. Holmes; 1957 | 1.50 | 3.00 | 4.50 | W |
| 145 | While Murder Waits–Bruce Cassiday | 1.50 | 3.00 | 4.50 | M |
| 146 | Six-guns Wild–Gene Thompson | 1.50 | 3.00 | 4.50 | W |
| 147 | Killer, Take All!–James O. Causey | 1.50 | 3.00 | 4.50 | M |
| 148 | Say It with Bullets–Richard Powell | 1.50 | 3.00 | 4.50 | M |
| 149 | Murder without Tears–Leonard Lupton | 1.50 | 3.00 | 4.50 | M |
| 150 | Too Young to Die–Robert O. Saber | 1.50 | 3.00 | 4.50 | M |
| 151 | Gun Proud–Lewis B. Patten | 1.50 | 3.00 | 4.50 | W |
| 152 | Call Me Deadly–Hal Braham | 1.50 | 3.00 | 4.50 | M |
| 153 | Gun Lightning!–Steve Thurman | 1.50 | 3.00 | 4.50 | W |
| 154 | Outlaw Justice–Ford Pendleton | 1.50 | 3.00 | 4.50 | W |
| 155 | Gun Chance–Ford Pendleton | 1.50 | 3.00 | 4.50 | W |
| 156 | Sucker Bait–Robert O. Saber | 1.50 | 3.00 | 4.50 | M |
| 157 | Hell Rider–Ford Pendleton | 1.50 | 3.00 | 4.50 | W |

# GRAPHIC G-SERIES

## Graphic Publishing Company, Inc.

| # | Title | V/Good | Fine | N/Mint | |
|---|---|---|---|---|---|
| G101 | Captain for Elizabeth–Jan Westcott; 1952 | 1.50 | 3.00 | 4.50 | A |
| G201 | Captain for Elizabeth–Jan Westcott; 1953 | 1.25 | 2.50 | 3.75 | A |
| G202 | River Queen–Charles N. Heckelmann | 2.00 | 4.00 | 6.00 | A |
| G203 | 45 Murderers–Craig Rice | 2.50 | 5.00 | 7.50 | M |
| G204 | How to Live with Your Heart–Peter J. Steincrohn; 1954 | 1.50 | 3.00 | 4.50 | NF |
| G205 | King's Rogue–Max Peacock | 1.50 | 3.00 | 4.50 | A |
| G206 | The Gladiators–Arthur Koestler | 1.50 | 3.00 | 4.50 | A |
| G207 | Great Sea Stories of Modern Times–William McFee | 1.50 | 3.00 | 4.50 | A |
| G208 | Swords for Charlemagne–Mario Pei; 1955 | 1.25 | 2.50 | 3.75 | A |
| G209 | The Golden Blade–John Clou | 1.50 | 3.00 | 4.50 | A |
| G210 | Gunman's Spawn–Ben Thompson | 1.50 | 3.00 | 4.50 | W |
| G211 | Captain for Elizabeth–Jan Westcott | 1.25 | 2.50 | 3.75 | A |
| G212 | Rogue Royal–Donn O'Hara; 1956; c-Maguire | 2.00 | 4.00 | 6.00 | A |
| G213 | The Gladiators–Arthur Koestler | 1.50 | 3.00 | 4.50 | A |

| # | Title | V/Good | Fine | N/Mint | |
|---|---|---|---|---|---|
| G214 | Captain Bashful–Donald Barr Chidsey | 1.50 | 3.00 | 4.50 | A |
| G215 | Call Me Duke–Harry Grey | 1.50 | 3.00 | 4.50 | M |
| G216 | The Private Life of Helen of Troy–John Erskine | 2.50 | 5.00 | 7.50 | A |
| G217 | Eve's Daughters–Laurette Pizer; 1957 | 1.50 | 3.00 | 4.50 | E |
| G218 | Guns of Hell Valley–John Prescott | 1.50 | 3.00 | 4.50 | W |
| G219 | Swords for Charlemagne–Mario Pei | 1.25 | 2.50 | 3.75 | A |
| G220 | The Golden Blade–John Clou; c-Maguire | 1.50 | 3.00 | 4.50 | A |
| G221 | River Queen–Charles N. Heckelmann | 1.25 | 2.50 | 3.75 | A |
| G222 | The Fair and the Bold–Donn O'Hara | 1.25 | 2.50 | 3.75 | A |
| G223 | Gunman's Spawn–Ben Thompson | 1.25 | 2.50 | 3.75 | W |

# (GREAT AMERICAN PUBLICATIONS, INC.)

## Great American Publications, Inc.

| # | Title | V/Good | Fine | N/Mint | |
|---|---|---|---|---|---|
| nn | Economy Driving–ed. Peter Bowman; orig. 1956 | 1.25 | 2.50 | 3.75 | NF |
| nn | How to Psycho Analyze Yourself–Joseph Ralph; 1956; aka Self-Analysis Made Simple | 1.00 | 2.00 | 3.00 | |

# (GREEN)

## Green Publishing Company

### Digest Size

| # | Title | V/Good | Fine | N/Mint | |
|---|---|---|---|---|---|
| 6 | Some Like It Hot–Sidney Marshall | 3.00 | 6.00 | 9.00 | M |
| 7 | 11 True Crimes–Joseph Gollomb | 3.00 | 6.00 | 9.00 | NF |
| 8 | The Laughing Loon–Josiah E. Greene | 3.00 | 6.00 | 9.00 | M |
| 9 | The Owl's Warning–Herman Landon | 3.00 | 6.00 | 9.00 | M |
| 10 | Death in the Sun–Charles Saxby. Note: Incorrectly says "1st edition" | 3.00 | 6.00 | 9.00 | M |
| 11 | A Dagger in the Dark–Walter E. Eberhardt | 3.00 | 6.00 | 9.00 | M |
| 12 | Kill or Cure–William Francis | 3.00 | 6.00 | 9.00 | M |
| 13 | Murder Stalks the Mayor–R.T.M. Scott | 3.00 | 6.00 | 9.00 | M |
| 14 | The Backstage Mystery–Octavus Roy Cohen | 3.00 | 6.00 | 9.00 | M |

# (GREEN)

## Larkin, Roosevelt, and Larkin, Ltd.

### Digest Size

| # | Title | V/Good | Fine | N/Mint | |
|---|---|---|---|---|---|
| 1 | Rough on Rats–William Francis | 3.00 | 6.00 | 9.00 | M |

# (GREEN)

## R.W. Voigt

### Digest Size

| # | Title | V/Good | Fine | N/Mint | |
|---|---|---|---|---|---|
| 2 | The Back Seat Murder–Herman Landon | 3.00 | 6.00 | 9.00 | M |

# (GREEN)

## The Spotlight

### Digest Size

| # | Title | V/Good | Fine | N/Mint | |
|---|---|---|---|---|---|
| 3 | Murder on Shark Island–Jack DeWitt | 3.00 | 6.00 | 9.00 | M |
| 4 | Bury Me Not–William Francis | 3.00 | 6.00 | 9.00 | M |

# GREEN DRAGON

## Ideal Distributing Company/W.H. Wise & Company

### Some Digest Size

| # | Title | V/Good | Fine | N/Mint | |
|---|---|---|---|---|---|
| 1 | Murder Makes By-Lines–Kelliher Secrist; digest size | 3.00 | 6.00 | 9.00 | M |
| 2 | The Mausoleum Key–Norman A. Daniels; digest size | 3.00 | 6.00 | 9.00 | M |

Green 3, Green 4, Green Dragon 19.

| | | V/Good | Fine | N/Mint | |
|---|---|---|---|---|---|
| | **GREEN DRAGON,** *continued* | | | | |
| 3 | Johnny on the Spot–Amen Dell; digest size | 3.00 | 6.00 | 9.00 | M |
| 4 | A Murder a Day–Robert Avery; digest size | 3.00 | 6.00 | 9.00 | M |
| 5 | The Moscow Mystery–Iry Litrinoff; digest size | 3.00 | 6.00 | 9.00 | M |
| 6 | The Snatch–R.L. Goldman; digest size | 3.00 | 6.00 | 9.00 | M |
| 8 | A Most Immoral Murder–H. Ashbrook; digest size | 3.00 | 6.00 | 9.00 | M |
| 9 | Murder Moves On–Jack Dall; digest size | 3.00 | 6.00 | 9.00 | M |
| 10 | Death Plays Solitaire–R.L. Goldman; digest size | 3.00 | 6.00 | 9.00 | M |
| 11 | Too Many Murderers–George Childerness; digest size | 3.00 | 6.00 | 9.00 | M |
| 12 | Grave without Grass–Donald Clough Cameron; digest size | 3.00 | 6.00 | 9.00 | M |
| 13 | Ten Words of Poison–Barry Perowne; digest size | 3.00 | 6.00 | 9.00 | M |
| 14 | Talent for Murder–John L. Benton; digest size | 3.00 | 6.00 | 9.00 | M |
| 16 | Murder without Clues–Joseph L. Bonney; digest size | 3.00 | 6.00 | 9.00 | M |
| 17 | . . . and Death Drove On–Robert Fleming; digest size | 3.00 | 6.00 | 9.00 | M |
| 18 | Murder Comes Back–H. Ashbrook; digest size | 3.00 | 6.00 | 9.00 | M |
| 19 | Death Defies the Doctor–Denis Muir; digest size | 3.00 | 6.00 | 9.00 | M |
| 20 | Death at Her Elbow–Donald Clough Cameron; digest size | 3.00 | 6.00 | 9.00 | M |
| 21 | The Man Who Was Murdered Twice–Robert H. Leitfred; digest size | 3.00 | 6.00 | 9.00 | M |
| 23 | I Thought I'd Die–David V. Reed; 1st ed.; aka The Metal Monster Murders; digest size | 3.00 | 6.00 | 9.00 | M |
| 24 | If I Die, It's Murder–Mari Ervin; digest size | 3.00 | 6.00 | 9.00 | M |
| 25 | She Screamed Blue Murder–Kelliher Secrist | 4.00 | 8.00 | 12.00 | M |
| 26 | Stone Dead–Patrick Laing | 4.00 | 8.00 | 12.00 | M |
| 27 | About the Murder of the Night Club Lady–Anthony Abbot | 4.00 | 8.00 | 12.00 | M |
| 28 | Headsman's Holiday–Dean Hawkins | 4.00 | 8.00 | 12.00 | M |
| 29 | The Late Lamented Lady–Marie Blizard | 4.00 | 8.00 | 12.00 | M |

Green Dragon 27, Griffin unnumbered, Gunfire Western Novel 22.

| | | V/Good | Fine | N/Mint | |
|---|---|---|---|---|---|
| 30 | A Matter of Policy–Sam Merwin, Jr | 4.00 | 8.00 | 12.00 | M |
| 31 | Murder by Magic–Amelia Reynolds Long | 4.00 | 8.00 | 12.00 | M |
| 32 | The Men in Her Death–Marie Blizard | 4.00 | 8.00 | 12.00 | M |
| 33 | Death Is Thy Neighbor–Laurence Dwight Smith | 4.00 | 8.00 | 12.00 | M |
| nn | The Corpse with the Listening Ear–Laurence Dwight Smith | 3.00 | 6.00 | 9.00 | M |

# GRIFFIN BOOKS
## Griffin Books
### Digest Size

| | | V/Good | Fine | N/Mint | |
|---|---|---|---|---|---|
| nn | Love on Call–John Saxon | 3.00 | 6.00 | 9.00 | E |
| nn | Confessions of a Hat Check Girl–Carl Sturdy | 3.00 | 6.00 | 9.00 | E |
| nn | Hotel Love–W. McClellan | 3.00 | 6.00 | 9.00 | E |
| nn | Stolen Love–Thomas Stone; aka Too Much Love | 3.00 | 6.00 | 9.00 | E |
| nn | Easy Virtue–Carl Sturdy; aka Professional Model | 3.00 | 6.00 | 9.00 | E |
| nn | Wronged Virgin–Gladys Sloan; aka Professional Passion | 3.00 | 6.00 | 9.00 | E |
| nn | Office Playgirl–Eliot Brewster; aka Hard Love | 3.00 | 6.00 | 9.00 | E |
| nn | Love Siren–Florenz Branch | 3.00 | 6.00 | 9.00 | E |

# GUNFIRE WESTERN NOVEL
## Novel Selections, Inc./Hillman
### Digest Size

| | | V/Good | Fine | N/Mint | |
|---|---|---|---|---|---|
| 6 | The Morgan Trail–W.C. Tuttle | 2.00 | 4.00 | 6.00 | W |
| 7 | The Deputy Sheriff–Clarence E. Mulford | 2.00 | 4.00 | 6.00 | W |
| 8 | Boomtown Buccaneers–William Colt MacDonald | | | | W |
| 9 | Vigilante War in Buena Vista–Frank C. Robertson | 2.00 | 4.00 | 6.00 | W |
| 10 | Prairie Fire–D. Bardwell | 2.00 | 4.00 | 6.00 | W |
| 11 | Rebel Ranger–William Colt MacDonald | 2.00 | 4.00 | 6.00 | W |
| 12 | Cowman's Jack-Pot–Frank C. Robertson | 2.00 | 4.00 | 6.00 | W |
| 13 | Devlin's Day Off–Amos Moore | 2.00 | 4.00 | 6.00 | W |
| 14 | Six-Gun Melody–William Colt MacDonald | 2.00 | 4.00 | 6.00 | W |
| 15 | Getley's Gold–Frank C. Robertson; c-Saunders | 2.00 | 4.00 | 6.00 | W |
| 16 | Smoke Tree Range–Arthur Henry Gooden | 2.00 | 4.00 | 6.00 | W |
| 17 | Thunderbird Trail–William Colt MacDonald | 2.00 | 4.00 | 6.00 | W |
| 18 | Dangerous Dust–Kim Knight | 2.00 | 4.00 | 6.00 | W |
| 19 | The Vanishing Gunslinger–William Colt MacDonald | 2.00 | 4.00 | 6.00 | W |
| 20 | Grizzly Meadows–Frank C. Robertson | 2.00 | 4.00 | 6.00 | W |
| 21 | The Phantom Corral–Bliss Lomax (H.S. Drago) | 2.00 | 4.00 | 6.00 | W |
| 22 | The Three Mesquiteers–William Colt MacDonald | 2.00 | 4.00 | 6.00 | W |
| 23 | Dunn of the Double D–N.M. Newland | 2.00 | 4.00 | 6.00 | W |
| 24 | The Range Rebellion–W.D. Hoffman | 2.00 | 4.00 | 6.00 | W |
| 25 | Boss of the OK–Brett Rider | 2.00 | 4.00 | 6.00 | W |
| 26 | Master of the Mesa–William Colt MacDonald | 2.00 | 4.00 | 6.00 | W |
| 27 | Painted Post Law–Tom Gunn | 2.00 | 4.00 | 6.00 | W |
| 28 | Outlaw Guns–E.E. Halleran | 2.00 | 4.00 | 6.00 | W |
| 30 | Miracle at Gopher Creek–Stuart Hardy | 2.00 | 4.00 | 6.00 | W |
| 31 | Tangled Trail–Roy Manning | | | | W |
| 32 | Desert Water–Harry Sinclair Drago | 2.00 | 4.00 | 6.00 | W |
| 33 | Rope Crazy–Frank C. Robertson | 2.00 | 4.00 | 6.00 | W |
| 34 | Outlaw of Hidden Valley–John Sims | 2.00 | 4.00 | 6.00 | W |
| 35 | Botched Brand–Tom West | 2.00 | 4.00 | 6.00 | W |
| 36 | Feud at Silver Bend–J.E. Grinstead | 2.00 | 4.00 | 6.00 | W |
| 37 | The Man from Nowhere–Stuart Hardy | 2.00 | 4.00 | 6.00 | W |
| 38 | Grass Means Fight–Kirk Deming | 2.00 | 4.00 | 6.00 | W |
| 39 | Ranch of the Two Thumbs–Archie Joscelyn | 2.00 | 4.00 | 6.00 | W |
| 41 | Milk River Range–Lee Floren | 2.00 | 4.00 | 6.00 | W |

GUNFIRE WESTERN NOVEL, *continued*

| # | Title | V/Good | Fine | N/Mint | |
|---|---|---|---|---|---|
| 42 | Guns along the Border–Charles H. Snow | 2.00 | 4.00 | 6.00 | W |
| 43 | The Long S–Lee Floren | 2.00 | 4.00 | 6.00 | W |
| 44 | Long Loop Raiders–Lynn Westland | 2.00 | 4.00 | 6.00 | W |
| 45 | Rebel on the Range–Ranger Lee | 2.00 | 4.00 | 6.00 | W |
| 46 | The Pride of Pine Creek–Frank C. Robertson | 2.00 | 4.00 | 6.00 | W |
| 47 | Boss of Northern Star–Archie Joscelyn | 2.00 | 4.00 | 6.00 | W |
| 48 | Montana Outlaw–Tom Roan | 2.00 | 4.00 | 6.00 | W |
| 49 | Range Lawyer–Johnston McCulley | 2.00 | 4.00 | 6.00 | W |
| 50 | Silver Gulch–William Hopson | 2.00 | 4.00 | 6.00 | W |
| 51 | Smuggler's Range–Lee Floren | 2.00 | 4.00 | 6.00 | W |
| 52 | Outlaws of Sugar Loaf–Charles H. Snow | 2.00 | 4.00 | 6.00 | W |
| 53 | Dusty Boots–Lee Thomas | 2.00 | 4.00 | 6.00 | W |

# HANDI-BOOKS

## Quinn Publishing Co., Inc.

| # | Title | V/Good | Fine | N/Mint | |
|---|---|---|---|---|---|
| nn(1) | Odds on the Hot Seat–Judson Phillips; 1941 | 7.50 | 15.00 | 22.50 | M |
| nn(2) | Decoy–Cleve F. Adams | 6.00 | 12.00 | 18.00 | M |
| nn(3) | 12 Chinks and a Woman–James Hadley Chase; 1942 | 9.00 | 18.00 | 27.00 | M |
| nn(4) | Seven Men–Theodore Roscoe | 7.50 | 15.00 | 22.50 | M |
| nn(5) | Curtains for the Copper–Thomas Polsky | 6.00 | 12.00 | 18.00 | M |
| nn(6) | A Bullet in His Cap–Robert Fleming | 6.00 | 12.00 | 18.00 | M |
| nn(7) | The Black Door–Cleve Adams | 5.00 | 10.00 | 15.00 | M |
| 8 | She Got What She Asked For–James Ronald | 6.00 | 12.00 | 18.00 | M |
| 9 | Vicious Circle–Manning Long | 5.00 | 10.00 | 15.00 | M |
| 10 | The Case of the Vanishing Women–Robert Archer | 6.00 | 12.00 | 18.00 | M |
| 11 | The Nine Dark Hours–Lenore Glen Offord | 6.00 | 12.00 | 18.00 | M |
| 12 | The Big Frame–Sam Merwin, Jr; 1943 | 6.00 | 12.00 | 18.00 | M |
| 13 | Lazarus No. 7–Richard Sale | 9.00 | 18.00 | 27.00 | SF |
| 14 | Black Alibi–Cornell Woolrich | 15.00 | 30.00 | 45.00 | M |
| 15 | The Case of the Walking Corpse–Brett Halliday | 7.50 | 15.00 | 22.50 | M |
| 16 | The 14th Trump–Judson Phillips | 6.00 | 12.00 | 18.00 | M |
| 17 | Footsteps behind Her–Mitchell Wilson | 6.00 | 12.00 | 18.00 | M |
| 18 | The Unscrupulous Mr. Callaghan–Peter Cheyney | 6.00 | 12.00 | 18.00 | M |
| 19 | Passing Strange–Richard Sale | 6.00 | 12.00 | 18.00 | M |
| 20 | To a Blindfold Lady–Joseph Purtell | 6.00 | 12.00 | 18.00 | M |
| 21 | The Case of the Shivering Chorus Girls–James Atlee Phillips | 6.00 | 12.00 | 18.00 | M |
| 22 | The Blonde Died First–Dana Chambers; 1944 | 6.00 | 12.00 | 18.00 | M |
| 23 | Five Alarm Funeral–Stewart Sterling | 6.00 | 12.00 | 18.00 | M |
| 24 | Murder in Marble–Judson Phillips | 6.00 | 12.00 | 18.00 | M |
| 25 | Court of Shadows–Giles Jackson | 6.00 | 12.00 | 18.00 | M |
| 26 | To Catch a Thief–Daphne Sanders | 4.00 | 8.00 | 12.00 | M |
| 27 | I Wake Up Screaming–Steve Fisher | 8.00 | 12.00 | 18.00 | M |
| 28 | The Frightened Man–Dana Chambers | 5.00 | 10.00 | 15.00 | M |
| 29 | The Woman in Red–Anthony Gilbert | 6.00 | 12.00 | 18.00 | M |
| 30 | The X-Ray Murders–M. Scott Michel | 6.00 | 12.00 | 18.00 | M |
| 31 | The Case of the Curious Chair–Richard Power | 5.00 | 10.00 | 15.00 | M |
| 32 | No Good from a Corpse–Leigh Brackett | 9.00 | 18.00 | 27.00 | M |
| 33 | Up Jumped the Devil–Cleve Adams | 6.00 | 12.00 | 18.00 | M |
| 34 | The Last Secret–Dana Chambers; 1945 | 5.00 | 10.00 | 15.00 | SF |
| 35 | The Snake in the Grass–James Howard Wellard | 3.50 | 7.00 | 10.50 | M |
| 36 | The Walls Came Tumbling Down–Jo Eisinger | 3.50 | 7.00 | 10.50 | M |
| 37 | The Dark Voyage–Hugh Addis | 4.00 | 8.00 | 12.00 | M |
| 38 | The Man with the Lumpy Nose–Lawrence Lariar | 4.00 | 8.00 | 12.00 | M |
| 39 | Send Another Coffin–F.G. Presnell | 4.00 | 8.00 | 12.00 | M |
| 40 | Dead Little Rich Girl–Norbert Davis | 6.00 | 12.00 | 18.00 | M |
| 41 | If I Kill Him–John & Ward Hawkins | 3.50 | 7.00 | 10.50 | M |
| 42 | The Fall Guy–Joe Barry | 3.50 | 7.00 | 10.50 | M |
| 43 | The Body on the Pavement–Gordon Meyrick | 3.50 | 7.00 | 10.50 | M |
| 44 | Knife in My Back–Sam Merwin, Jr | 3.50 | 7.00 | 10.50 | M |
| 45 | The Blonde Is Dead–John Dow; aka The Little Boy Laughed | 4.00 | 8.00 | 12.00 | M |
| 46 | The Case of the Tearless Widow–John Roeburt; 1946 | 3.50 | 7.00 | 10.50 | M |
| 47 | Sweet Murder–M. Scott Michel | 3.50 | 7.00 | 10.50 | M |
| 48 | The Body Next Door–Eaton K. Goldthwaite | 3.50 | 7.00 | 10.50 | M |
| 49 | The Corpse Who Wouldn't Die–Ed Doherty | 3.50 | 7.00 | 10.50 | M |
| 50 | The Dangerous Dead–William Brandon | 3.50 | 7.00 | 10.50 | M |
| 51 | Darling, This Is Death–Dana Chambers | 3.50 | 7.00 | 10.50 | M |
| 52 | The Triple Cross–Joe Barry | 3.50 | 7.00 | 10.50 | M |
| 53 | Puzzle for Players–Patrick Quentin | 3.50 | 7.00 | 10.50 | M |
| 54 | Oh, Murderer Mine–Norbert Davis | 6.00 | 12.00 | 18.00 | M |
| 55 | Blood on the Cat–Nancy Rutledge | 3.50 | 7.00 | 10.50 | M |
| 56 | Lady with the Dice–Joel Townsley Rogers | 3.50 | 7.00 | 10.50 | M |
| 57 | Death against Venus–Dana Chambers | 3.50 | 7.00 | 10.50 | M |
| 58 | The Corpse Awaits–Owen Fox Jerome; 1947 | 3.50 | 7.00 | 10.50 | M |
| 59 | One of These Seven–Carolynne & Malcolm Logan | 3.50 | 7.00 | 10.50 | M |
| 60 | The Gloved Hand–Leigh Bryson | 3.50 | 7.00 | 10.50 | M |
| 61 | The Black Key–M. Scott Michel | 3.50 | 7.00 | 10.50 | M |
| 62 | The Murder of the U.S.A.–Will F. Jenkins (Murray Leinster) | 9.00 | 18.00 | 27.00 | SF |
| 63 | The Clean-Up–Joe Barry | 2.50 | 5.00 | 7.50 | M |
| 64 | The Fourth Star–Richard Burke | 2.50 | 5.00 | 7.50 | M |
| 65 | Guilty Bystander–Wade Miller | 3.00 | 6.00 | 9.00 | M |
| 66 | Probably does not exist | | | | |
| 67 | Probably does not exist | | | | |
| 68 | Killers Play Rough–Adam Ring | 3.00 | 6.00 | 9.00 | M |
| 69 | Bullet Breed–Leslie Ernenwein | 2.50 | 5.00 | 7.50 | W |
| 70 | Run for Your Life–Michael Stark; 1948 | 2.50 | 5.00 | 7.50 | M |
| 71 | The Range Maverick–Oscar J. Friend | 2.50 | 5.00 | 7.50 | W |
| 72 | Death About Face–Frank Kane | 2.50 | 5.00 | 7.50 | M |
| 73 | Only the Brave–Paul Evan Lehman | 2.50 | 5.00 | 7.50 | W |
| 74 | If You Have Tears–John Evans | 2.50 | 5.00 | 7.50 | M |
| 75 | Boss of Panamint–Leslie Ernenwein | 2.50 | 5.00 | 7.50 | W |
| 76 | Cargo of Fear–Jay L. Currier | 2.50 | 5.00 | 7.50 | M |
| 77 | Calamity Range–Paul Evan Lehman | 2.50 | 5.00 | 7.50 | W |
| 78 | This Deadly Dark–Lee Wilson | 2.50 | 5.00 | 7.50 | M |
| 79 | Gun Harvest–Oscar J. Friend | 2.50 | 5.00 | 7.50 | W |
| 80 | Not with My Neck–Tom Van Dycke & Ben Kerner | 2.50 | 5.00 | 7.50 | M |
| 81 | Empty Saddles–Al Cody | 2.50 | 5.00 | 7.50 | W |
| 82 | Witch's Moon–Giles Jackson; 1949 | 2.50 | 5.00 | 7.50 | M |
| 83 | The Faro Kid–Leslie Ernenwein. Note: Same cover as Harlequin 89 | 2.50 | 5.00 | 7.50 | W |
| 84 | Yaller Gal–Carolina Lee | 2.50 | 5.00 | 7.50 | E |
| 85 | The Great I Am–Lewis Graham | 2.50 | 5.00 | 7.50 | E |
| 86 | Dig Another Grave–Don Cameron | 2.50 | 5.00 | 7.50 | M |
| 87 | Idaho–Paul Evan Lehman | 2.50 | 5.00 | 7.50 | W |
| 88 | Hope to Die–Hillary Waugh | 2.50 | 5.00 | 7.50 | M |
| 89 | The King of Thunder Valley–Archie Joscelyn | 2.50 | 5.00 | 7.50 | W |
| 90 | Love to Burn–Peggy Gaddis | 2.50 | 5.00 | 7.50 | E |
| 91 | Lulie–Joan Sherman; aka Courtesan Street | 2.50 | 5.00 | 7.50 | E |
| 92 | The Girl with the Frightened Eyes–Lawrence Lariar | 2.50 | 5.00 | 7.50 | M |
| 93 | Rebel Yell–Leslie Ernenwein | 2.50 | 5.00 | 7.50 | W |
| 94 | They All Died Young–Charles Boswell; orig. 1949 | 2.50 | 5.00 | 7.50 | M |
| 95 | The Outcast of Lazy S–Eli Colter | 2.50 | 5.00 | 7.50 | W |
| 96 | The Black Dark Murders–Robert O. Saber | 2.50 | 5.00 | 7.50 | M |
| 97 | A Lover Would Be Nice–Hugh Herbert | 2.50 | 5.00 | 7.50 | E |
| 98 | Spider House–Van Wyck Mason | 2.50 | 5.00 | 7.50 | M |
| 99 | The Cold Trail–Paul Evan Lehman | 2.50 | 5.00 | 7.50 | W |
| 100 | Too Many Women–Milton K. Ozaki; 1950 | 2.50 | 5.00 | 7.50 | M |
| 101 | The Range Doctor–Oscar J. Friend | 2.50 | 5.00 | 7.50 | W |
| 102 | Satan's Gal–Carolina Lee | 2.50 | 5.00 | 7.50 | E |
| 103 | Maverick Guns–J.E. Grinstead | 2.50 | 5.00 | 7.50 | W |
| 104 | The Restless Corpse–Alan Pruitt | 3.00 | 6.00 | 9.00 | M |
| 105 | The Rider from Yonder–Norman A. Fox | 2.50 | 5.00 | 7.50 | W |
| 106 | Three for the Money–Joe Barry | 3.00 | 6.00 | 9.00 | M |
| 107 | The Siren of Silver Valley–Paul Evan Lehman | 2.50 | 5.00 | 7.50 | W |
| 108 | The Affair of the Frigid Blonde–Robert O. Saber | 3.50 | 7.00 | 10.50 | M |

*Handi-Books 116, Handi-Books 120, Handi-Books Western 2.*

| | | V/Good | Fine | N/Mint | |
|---|---|---|---|---|---|

## HANDI-BOOKS, *continued*

| | | V/Good | Fine | N/Mint | |
|---|---|---|---|---|---|
| 109 | Shannahan's Feud–Archie Joscelyn | 2.50 | 5.00 | 7.50 | W |
| 110 | The Glass Ladder–Paul W. Fairman | 2.50 | 5.00 | 7.50 | M |
| 111 | Renegade Ramrod–Leslie Ernenwein | 2.50 | 5.00 | 7.50 | W |
| 112 | No Wings on a Cop–Cleve Adams | 2.50 | 5.00 | 7.50 | M |
| 113 | Barricade–Oscar J. Friend | 2.50 | 5.00 | 7.50 | W |
| 114 | False Face–Leslie Edgley | 2.50 | 5.00 | 7.50 | M |
| 115 | Range King–J.E. Grinstead | 2.50 | 5.00 | 7.50 | W |
| 116 | A Fiend in Need–Milton K. Ozaki | 2.50 | 5.00 | 7.50 | M |
| 117 | Thunder of Hoofs–Tex Holt | 2.50 | 5.00 | 7.50 | W |
| 118 | Window with the Sleeping Nude–Robert Leslie Bellem | 9.00 | 18.00 | 27.00 | M |
| 119 | Vengeance Valley–Paul Evan Lehman | 2.50 | 5.00 | 7.50 | W |
| 120 | Slay Ride for a Lady–Harry Whittington; orig. 1950 | 3.00 | 6.00 | 9.00 | W |
| 121 | Rawhide Summons–Brett Austin | 2.50 | 5.00 | 7.50 | W |
| 122 | Dark Memory–Edward Ronns | 2.50 | 5.00 | 7.50 | M |
| 123 | When Texans Rode–J.E. Grinstead | 2.50 | 5.00 | 7.50 | W |
| 124 | The Scented Flesh–Robert O. Saber; 1951 | 2.50 | 5.00 | 7.50 | M |
| 125 | Valley of the Tyrant–Dick Pearce | 2.50 | 5.00 | 7.50 | W |
| 126 | Yaller Gal–Carolina Lee | 2.50 | 5.00 | 7.50 | E |
| 127 | The Faro Kid–Leslie Ernenwein | 2.50 | 5.00 | 7.50 | W |
| 128 | Pursuit–Lawrence G. Blochman; orig. 1951 | 3.00 | 6.00 | 9.00 | M |
| 129 | The Heiress of Copper Butte–Paul W. Fairman; aka The Montana Vixen | 3.00 | 6.00 | 9.00 | W |
| 130 | The Dove–Robert O. Saber; orig. 1951. Note: Same cover as digest magazine Strange, July 1952 | 3.00 | 6.00 | 9.00 | M |
| 131 | The Lady Was a Tramp–Harry Whittington; orig. 1951 | 3.00 | 6.00 | 9.00 | M |
| 132 | Trail Rider–Lynn Westland | 2.50 | 5.00 | 7.50 | W |
| 133 | Boot Hill–Clay Weston | 2.50 | 5.00 | 7.50 | W |
| 134 | Murder Is Dangerous–Saul Levinson; c-Saunders | 2.50 | 5.00 | 7.50 | M |
| 135 | Typed for a Corpse–Alan Pruitt; c-Saunders | 2.50 | 5.00 | 7.50 | M |
| 136 | Dark Canyon–Tex Holt; c-Saunders | 2.50 | 5.00 | 7.50 | W |
| 137 | Yucca City Outlaw–William Hopson; c-Saunders. Note: Same cover as Harlequin 158 | 2.50 | 5.00 | 7.50 | W |
| 138 | The Brass Monkey–Harry Whittington; orig. 1951 | 3.50 | 7.00 | 10.50 | M |
| 139 | The Lady Killers–William T. Brannon; 1951 | 2.50 | 5.00 | 7.50 | M |

## HANDI-BOOKS WESTERN

## Quinn Publishing Co., Inc.

| | | | | | |
|---|---|---|---|---|---|
| 1 | The Cow Kingdom–Paul Evan Lehman; 1947 | 3.50 | 7.00 | 10.50 | W |
| 2 | Rio Renegade–Leslie Ernenwein | 3.50 | 7.00 | 10.50 | W |
| 3 | The Long Noose–Oscar J. Friend | 3.50 | 7.00 | 10.50 | W |
| 4 | West of the Wolverine–Paul Evan Lehman | 3.50 | 7.00 | 10.50 | W |

## HANDY BOOKS

## Adam Publishing Co.

### (Canadian)

| | | | | | |
|---|---|---|---|---|---|
| 1 | The Face That Launched a Thousand Ships–Thomas P. Kelley; 1st ed. 1941 | 12.50 | 25.00 | 37.50 | |
| 2 | Red Ally–Major E. Cecil-Smith. Note: Existence of this title not verified | 8.00? | 16.00? | 24.00? | |

## HANGMAN'S HOUSE

## Parsee Publications

### Some Digest Size

| | | | | | |
|---|---|---|---|---|---|
| 1 | Murder on the Pike–Arville Nonweiler; digest size | 3.00 | 6.00 | 9.00 | M |
| 2 | Puzzle in Paint–Kootz (Samuel Melvin); digest size | 3.00 | 6.00 | 9.00 | M |

| | | V/Good | Fine | N/Mint | |
|---|---|---|---|---|---|
| 3 | Murder in False Face–George Childerness; digest size | 3.00 | 6.00 | 9.00 | M |
| 4 | The Man Who Feared–Will F. Jenkins (Murray Leinster); digest size | 4.00 | 8.00 | 12.00 | M |
| 5 | Death Gets a Head–A.R. McKenzie; digest size | 3.00 | 6.00 | 9.00 | M |
| 6 | Fit to Kill–Hans C. Owen; digest size | 3.00 | 6.00 | 9.00 | M |
| 7 | Murder on Beacon Hill–Gerald Brown; digest size | 3.00 | 6.00 | 9.00 | M |
| 8 | Death like Thunder–Hugh Holman; digest size | 3.00 | 6.00 | 9.00 | M |
| 9 | The Corpse in the Cab–Aldin Vinton; aka Mystery in Green; digest size | 3.00 | 6.00 | 9.00 | M |
| 10 | Murder in Odd Sizes–Helen Joan Hultman; digest size | 3.00 | 6.00 | 9.00 | M |
| 11 | Murder Wore Green–Robert Portner Koehler; digest size | 3.00 | 6.00 | 9.00 | M |
| 12 | May not exist | | | | |
| 13 | The Cowl of Doom–Edward Ronns; aka Death in a Lighthouse | 4.00 | 8.00 | 12.00 | M |
| 14 | The Corpse That Spoke–Robert H. Leitfred | 4.00 | 8.00 | 12.00 | M |
| 15 | The Cipher of Death–F.L. Gregory | 3.50 | 7.00 | 10.50 | M |
| 16 | Thereby Hangs a Corpse–Clarence Mullen | 4.00 | 8.00 | 12.00 | M |
| 17 | The Road House Murders–Robert Portner Koehler | 4.00 | 8.00 | 12.00 | M |
| 18 | Memory of a Scream–David X. Manners | 4.00 | 8.00 | 12.00 | M |
| 19 | Death in 1-2-3–Robert D. Abrahams | 4.00 | 8.00 | 12.00 | M |
| 20 | Murder Steals the Show–Lee Hirsch | 4.00 | 8.00 | 12.00 | M |
| 21 | Lady That's My Skull–Carl Shannon | 4.00 | 8.00 | 12.00 | M |

## HANRO

## Hanro Corporation

### Digest Size

| | | | | | |
|---|---|---|---|---|---|
| 1 | Careless Hussy–Thomas Stone | 3.00 | 6.00 | 9.00 | E |
| 2 | Shady Lady–Perry Lindsay (Peggy Gaddis) | 3.00 | 6.00 | 9.00 | E |
| 3 | Illegal Wife–Wright Williams | 3.00 | 6.00 | 9.00 | E |
| 4 | Confessions of a Part-Time Bride–Hall Bennett; aka Make the Man Pay | 3.00 | 6.00 | 9.00 | E |

*Hangman's House 11, Hangman's House 17, Harlequin 3.*

# HARLEQUIN
## Harlequin Books, Ltd.
### (Canadian)

**Note: This publisher has more fragile covers and binding than most. Upper grades are particularly scarce.**

| # | Title | V/Good | Fine | N/Mint | |
|---|-------|--------|------|--------|--|
| 1 | The Manatee–Nancy Bruff; 1949 | 6.00 | 12.00 | 18.00 | A |
| 2 | Lost House–Frances Shelly Wees | 6.00 | 12.00 | 18.00 | |
| 3 | Maelstrom–Howard Hunt | 6.00 | 12.00 | 18.00 | |
| 4 | Double Image–Arthur Herbert Bryant | 6.00 | 12.00 | 18.00 | |
| 5 | Close to My Heart–Margaret Nichols | 6.00 | 12.00 | 18.00 | |
| 6 | Wolf of the Mesas–Charles H. Snow | 6.00 | 12.00 | 18.00 | W |
| 7 | The House on Craig Street–Ronald J. Cooke | 6.00 | 12.00 | 18.00 | |
| 8 | Honeymoon Mountain–Frances Shelley Wees | 6.00 | 12.00 | 18.00 | R |
| 9 | The Dark Page–Samuel Michael Fuller | 6.00 | 12.00 | 18.00 | |
| 10 | Here's Blood in Your Eye–Manning Long | 6.00 | 12.00 | 18.00 | M |
| 11 | The Wicked Lady Skelton–Magdalen King-Hall | 6.00 | 12.00 | 18.00 | |
| 12 | A Killer Is Loose Among Us–Robert Terrall | 5.00 | 10.00 | 15.00 | M |
| 13 | His Wife the Doctor–Joseph McCord | 6.00 | 12.00 | 18.00 | |
| 14 | Six-Guns of Sandoval–Charles H. Snow | 6.00 | 12.00 | 18.00 | W |
| 15 | Virgin With Butterflies–Tom Powers | 6.00 | 12.00 | 18.00 | E |
| 16 | No Nice Girl–Perry Lindsay (Peggy Gaddis) | 6.00 | 12.00 | 18.00 | E |
| 17 | The D.A.'s Daughter–Herman Petersen | 6.00 | 12.00 | 18.00 | |
| 18 | Rebel of Ronde Valley–Charles H. Snow | 6.00 | 12.00 | 18.00 | W |
| 19 | Gina–George Albert Glay | 6.00 | 12.00 | 18.00 | E |
| 20 | Flame Vine–Helen Topping Miller | 6.00 | 12.00 | 18.00 | E |
| 21 | Renegade Ranger–Charles H. Snow | 6.00 | 12.00 | 18.00 | W |
| 22 | Crazy to Kill–Ann Cardwell | 6.00 | 12.00 | 18.00 | M |
| 23 | City for Conquest–Aben Kandel | 6.00 | 12.00 | 18.00 | |
| 24 | Painted Post Outlaws–Tom Gunn | 6.00 | 12.00 | 18.00 | W |
| 25 | Blondes Don't Cry–Merlda Mace | 6.00 | 12.00 | 18.00 | |
| 26 | Gambling on Love–Gail Jordan (Peggy Gaddis); 1950 | 6.00 | 12.00 | 18.00 | R |
| 27 | Kiss Your Elbow–Alan Handley | 6.00 | 12.00 | 18.00 | |
| 28 | One Year with Grace–Martin Mooney | 6.00 | 12.00 | 18.00 | |
| 29 | Gunfighter Breed–Nelson C. Nye | 6.00 | 12.00 | 18.00 | W |
| 30 | Portrait of Love–Margaret Nichols | 6.00 | 12.00 | 18.00 | R |
| 31 | The Golden Feather–Theda Kenyon | 6.00 | 12.00 | 18.00 | |
| 32 | The Hollywood Mystery–Ben Hecht | 6.00 | 12.00 | 18.00 | M |
| 33 | Candle in the Morning–Helen Topping Miller | 6.00 | 12.00 | 18.00 | |
| 34 | Mobtown Clipper–S.S. Rabl | 6.00 | 12.00 | 18.00 | |
| 35 | Lush Valley–Patricia Campbell | 6.00 | 12.00 | 18.00 | |
| 36 | Murder over Broadway–Fred Malina | 6.00 | 12.00 | 18.00 | M |
| 37 | Amaru–R.D. Frisbie | 6.00 | 12.00 | 18.00 | |
| 38 | Sheriff of Yavisa–Charles H. Snow | 6.00 | 12.00 | 18.00 | W |
| 39 | Be Still My Love–June Truesdell | 6.00 | 12.00 | 18.00 | R |
| 40 | Pass Key to Murder–Blair Reed | 6.00 | 12.00 | 18.00 | M |
| 41 | Panthers' Moon–Victor Canning | 6.00 | 12.00 | 18.00 | |
| 42 | House in Harlem–M. Scott Michel | 7.50 | 15.00 | 22.50 | E |
| 43 | The Clean-Up–Joe Barry | 6.00 | 12.00 | 18.00 | M |
| 44 | The So Blue Marble–Dorothy B. Hughes | 6.00 | 12.00 | 18.00 | M |

*Harlequin 11, Harlequin 43, Harlequin 79.*

| # | Title | V/Good | Fine | N/Mint | |
|---|-------|--------|------|--------|--|
| 45 | Night and the City–Gerald Kersh | 6.00 | 12.00 | 18.00 | M |
| 46 | Fair Stranger–Cecile Gilmore | 6.00 | 12.00 | 18.00 | |
| 47 | Registered Nurse–Carl Sturdy | 6.00 | 12.00 | 18.00 | R |
| 48 | Poldrate Street–Garnett Weston | 6.00 | 12.00 | 18.00 | |
| 49 | Weep Not Fair Lady–John Evans | 6.00 | 12.00 | 18.00 | |
| 50 | One Way Street–Joseph McCord; 1950 | 6.00 | 12.00 | 18.00 | |
| 51 | The Pocket Purity Cook Book | 10.00 | 20.00 | 30.00 | NF |
| 52 | Livre de Cuisine Purity, Petit Format | 12.50 | 25.00 | 37.50 | NF |
| 53 | Pale Blonde of Sands Street–William C. White | 6.00 | 12.00 | 18.00 | |
| 54 | Speak of the Devil–Elizabeth Sanxay Holding | 6.00 | 12.00 | 18.00 | M |
| 55 | Mr. Sandeman Loses His Life–Eugene Healy | 6.00 | 12.00 | 18.00 | |
| 56 | The Mayor of Cote St. Paul–Ronald J. Cooke | 6.00 | 12.00 | 18.00 | |
| 57 | Murder Man–William Bogart | 6.00 | 12.00 | 18.00 | M |
| 58 | Outposts of Vengeance–E.E. Halleran | 6.00 | 12.00 | 18.00 | W |
| 59 | Cardinal Rock–Richard Sale | 6.00 | 12.00 | 18.00 | |
| 60 | Lady Killer–Elizabeth Sanxay Holding | 6.00 | 12.00 | 18.00 | M |
| 61 | Shadow of the Badlands–E.E. Halleran | 6.00 | 12.00 | 18.00 | W |
| 62 | Message from a Corpse–Sam Merwin, Jr | 6.00 | 12.00 | 18.00 | M |
| 63 | The Dangerous Dead–William Brandon | 6.00 | 12.00 | 18.00 | M |
| 64 | Sinister Warning–M. Scott Michel | 6.00 | 12.00 | 18.00 | |
| 65 | Bridewell Beauty–H.M.E. Clamp | 6.00 | 12.00 | 18.00 | R |
| 66 | Royce of the Royal Mounted–Ames Moore | 6.00 | 12.00 | 18.00 | A |
| 67 | Criss Cross–Don Tracy | 6.00 | 12.00 | 18.00 | M |
| 68 | The Queen City Murder Case–William G. Bogart | 6.00 | 12.00 | 18.00 | M |
| 69 | Payoff in Black–William G. Schofield | 6.00 | 12.00 | 18.00 | M |
| 70 | Knife in My Back–Sam Merwin, Jr | 6.00 | 12.00 | 18.00 | M |
| 71 | Bouquet Knitter's Guide | 6.00 | 12.00 | 18.00 | NF |
| 72 | Night of Terror–Joy Brown | 6.00 | 12.00 | 18.00 | M |
| 73 | The King of Thunder Valley–Archie Joscelyn | 6.00 | 12.00 | 18.00 | W |
| 74 | Spider House–Van Wyck Mason | 6.00 | 12.00 | 18.00 | |
| 75 | Maverick Guns–J.E. Grinstead; 1950 | 6.00 | 12.00 | 18.00 | W |
| 76 | The Corpse Came Back–Amelia Reynolds Long | 6.00 | 12.00 | 18.00 | M |
| 77 | A Night at Club Bagdad–Owen Fox Jerome | 6.00 | 12.00 | 18.00 | |
| 78 | Rink Rat–Don MacMillan | 6.00 | 12.00 | 18.00 | |
| 79 | Lazarus #7–Richard Sale | 20.00 | 40.00 | 60.00 | SF |
| 80 | The Case of the Six Bullets–R.M. Laurenson | 6.00 | 12.00 | 18.00 | M |
| 81 | Idaho–Paul E. Lehman | 6.00 | 12.00 | 18.00 | W |
| 82 | The Cold Trail–Paul E. Lehman | 6.00 | 12.00 | 18.00 | W |
| 83 | The Fall Guy–Joe Barry | 6.00 | 12.00 | 18.00 | M |
| 84 | The Triple Cross–Joe Barry | 6.00 | 12.00 | 18.00 | M |
| 85 | She Died on the Stairway–Knight Rhoades | 6.00 | 12.00 | 18.00 | M |
| 86 | Double Life–Owen Fox Jerome | 6.00 | 12.00 | 18.00 | |
| 87 | Murder in Miniatures–Sam Merwin, Jr | 6.00 | 12.00 | 18.00 | M |
| 88 | Renegade Ramrod–Leslie Ernenwein | 6.00 | 12.00 | 18.00 | W |
| 89 | The Faro Kid–Leslie Ernenwein. Note: Same cover as Handi-Book 83 | 6.00 | 12.00 | 18.00 | W |
| 90 | The Widow Gay–A.A. Marcus; aka Post-Mark Homicide. Note: Same cover as Graphic 67 | 6.00 | 12.00 | 18.00 | M |
| 91 | Lady, That's My Skull–Carl Shannon; 1951 | 6.00 | 12.00 | 18.00 | M |
| 92 | Dig Another Grave–Don Cameron | 6.00 | 12.00 | 18.00 | M |
| 93 | Empty Saddles–Al Cody | 6.00 | 12.00 | 18.00 | W |
| 94 | The Range Doctor–Oscar J. Friend | 6.00 | 12.00 | 18.00 | |
| 95 | You're Lonely When You're Dead–James Hadley Chase | 6.00 | 12.00 | 18.00 | M |
| 96 | The Rider from Yonder–Norman A. Fox | 6.00 | 12.00 | 18.00 | W |
| 97 | My Old Man's Badge–Ferguson Findley | 6.00 | 12.00 | 18.00 | |
| 98 | Jigger Moran–John Roeburt | 6.00 | 12.00 | 18.00 | M |
| 99 | Murder-Queen High–Bob Wade & Bill Miller | 6.00 | 12.00 | 18.00 | M |
| 100 | Black Rider–Jackson Cole; 1951 | 6.00 | 12.00 | 18.00 | W |
| 101 | Three for the Money–Joe Barry | 6.00 | 12.00 | 18.00 | M |
| 102 | Wreath for a Redhead–Brian Moore | 8.00 | 16.00 | 24.00 | M |
| 103 | Wanton City–O.M. Hall | 6.00 | 12.00 | 18.00 | E |
| 104 | Tough Cop–John Roeburt | 6.00 | 12.00 | 18.00 | M |
| 105 | Vengeance Valley–Paul Evan Lehman | 6.00 | 12.00 | 18.00 | W |
| 106 | The Window with the Sleeping Nude–Robert Leslie Bellem | 8.00 | 16.00 | 24.00 | M |
| 107 | The Man from Bar-20–Clarence E. Mulford | 6.00 | 12.00 | 18.00 | W |

HARLEQUIN, *continued*

| No. | Title | V/Good | Fine | N/Mint | |
|---|---|---|---|---|---|
| 108 | No Orchids for Miss Blandish–James Hadley Chase | 8.00 | 16.00 | 24.00 | M |
| 109 | Corpse on the Town–John Roeburt | 6.00 | 12.00 | 18.00 | M |
| 110 | Tombstone Stage–William Hopson | 6.00 | 12.00 | 18.00 | W |
| 111 | The Flesh of the Orchid–James Hadley Chase | 6.00 | 12.00 | 18.00 | M |
| 112 | Gina–George Albert Glay | 6.00 | 12.00 | 18.00 | E |
| 113 | Beyond the Blue Mountains–Jean Plaidy (Victoria Holt) | 5.00 | 10.00 | 15.00 | R |
| 114 | Johnny Saxon–William G. Bogart | 6.00 | 12.00 | 18.00 | M |
| 115 | Manhattan Underworld–John Roeburt | 6.00 | 12.00 | 18.00 | M |
| 116 | Kill the Toff–John Creasey | 6.00 | 12.00 | 18.00 | M |
| 117 | The Executioners–Brian Moore | 8.00 | 16.00 | 24.00 | |
| 118 | Range Justice–Paul Evan Lehman | 6.00 | 12.00 | 18.00 | W |
| 119 | When Texans Ride–J.E. Grinstead | 6.00 | 12.00 | 18.00 | W |
| 120 | Slay Ride for a Lady–Harry Whittington | 7.50 | 15.00 | 22.50 | M |
| 121 | Run for Your Life–Michael Stark | 6.00 | 12.00 | 18.00 | M |
| 122 | A Matter of Policy–Sam Merwin, Jr | 6.00 | 12.00 | 18.00 | M |
| 123 | Saddle Wolves–Allan K. Echols | 6.00 | 12.00 | 18.00 | W |
| 124 | The Dead Stay Dumb–James Hadley Chase | 6.00 | 12.00 | 18.00 | M |
| 125 | The Hidden Portal–Garnett Weston; 1951 | 6.00 | 12.00 | 18.00 | |
| 126 | Death About Face–Frank Kane | 6.00 | 12.00 | 18.00 | M |
| 127 | Dark Memory–Edward Ronns | 6.00 | 12.00 | 18.00 | M |
| 128 | Law of the '45–Paul Evan Lehman | 6.00 | 12.00 | 18.00 | W |
| 129 | Hire This Killer–Ferguson Findley | 6.00 | 12.00 | 18.00 | M |
| 130 | Figure It Out for Yourself–James Hadley Chase | 6.00 | 12.00 | 18.00 | M |
| 131 | Tex–Clarence E. Mulford | 6.00 | 12.00 | 18.00 | W |
| 132 | False Face–Leslie Edgley | 6.00 | 12.00 | 18.00 | |
| 133 | Frontier Doctor–Bradford Scott | 6.00 | 12.00 | 18.00 | W |
| 134 | The Killers–George C. Henderson | 6.00 | 12.00 | 18.00 | |
| 135 | Lay Her among the Lilies–James Hadley Chase | 6.00 | 12.00 | 18.00 | M |
| 136 | Boot Hill–Weston Clay | 6.00 | 12.00 | 18.00 | W |
| 137 | Berlin of Midnight–Robert Joseph | 6.00 | 12.00 | 18.00 | |
| 138 | Emma Hart–Lozania Prole | 5.00 | 10.00 | 15.00 | |
| 139 | The Glass Ladder–Paul W. Fairman | 6.00 | 12.00 | 18.00 | |
| 140 | The Lady Was a Tramp–Harry Whittington | 7.50 | 15.00 | 22.50 | M |
| 141 | Roger Sudden–Thomas H. Raddall | 6.00 | 12.00 | 18.00 | A |
| 142 | Doctor by Day–Thomas Stone | 6.00 | 12.00 | 18.00 | |
| 143 | Rebel Yell–Leslie Ernenwein | 6.00 | 12.00 | 18.00 | W |
| 144 | City for Conquest–Aben Kandel | 6.00 | 12.00 | 18.00 | |
| 145 | Rio Renegade–Leslie Ernenwein | 6.00 | 12.00 | 18.00 | W |
| 146 | Trail Rider–Lynn Westland | 6.00 | 12.00 | 18.00 | W |
| 147 | Pardon My Body–Dale Bogard | 7.50 | 15.00 | 22.50 | M |
| 148 | Wagon Train Westward–Lynn Westland; 1952 | 6.00 | 12.00 | 18.00 | W |
| 149 | Remembering Laughter–Wallace Stegner | 6.00 | 12.00 | 18.00 | |
| 150 | Paprika–Erich Von Stroheim; 1952 | 6.00 | 12.00 | 18.00 | E |
| 151 | The Great I Am–Lewis Graham | 6.00 | 12.00 | 18.00 | |
| 152 | Great Oaks–Ben Ames Williams | 6.00 | 12.00 | 18.00 | |
| 153 | Outlaw Valley–Al Cody | 6.00 | 12.00 | 18.00 | W |
| 154 | Rasputin and Crimes That Shook the World–Richard Hirsch | 6.00 | 12.00 | 18.00 | NF |
| 155 | Canyon of the Damned–Tex Holt | 6.00 | 12.00 | 18.00 | W |
| 156 | Blood of the North–James B. Hendryx | 6.00 | 12.00 | 18.00 | A |
| 157 | The Bizarre Sisters–Jay & Audrey Walz | 6.00 | 12.00 | 18.00 | E |
| 158 | Yucca City Outlaw–William Hopson; c-Saunders. Note: Same cover as Handi-Book 137 | 6.00 | 12.00 | 18.00 | W |
| 159 | The Smiling Tiger–Glen Offord | 6.00 | 12.00 | 18.00 | |
| 160 | Twelve Chinks and a Woman–James Hadley Chase | 30.00 | 60.00 | 90.00 | E |
| 161 | Health, Sex and Birth Control–Percy E. Ryberg, MD | 5.00 | 10.00 | 15.00 | NF |
| 162 | The River's End–James Oliver Curwood | 6.00 | 12.00 | 18.00 | |
| 163 | Guntown–Dan Carew | 6.00 | 12.00 | 18.00 | W |
| 164 | Captain for Elizabeth–Jan Westcott | 5.00 | 10.00 | 15.00 | A |
| 165 | Bats with Baby Faces–W. Stanley Moss | 6.00 | 12.00 | 18.00 | M |
| 166 | The Big Fist–Clyde B. Ragsdale | 6.00 | 12.00 | 18.00 | |
| 167 | Love Me–and Die!–Day Keene | 8.00 | 16.00 | 24.00 | M |
| 168 | Hunt the Killer–Day Keene | 8.00 | 16.00 | 24.00 | M |
| 169 | Lady of Cleves–Margaret Campbell Barnes | 6.00 | 12.00 | 18.00 | |
| 170 | The Sea Is So Wide–Evelyn Eaton | 6.00 | 12.00 | 18.00 | A |
| 171 | Savage Justice–Leslie Ernenwein | 6.00 | 12.00 | 18.00 | W |
| 172 | Gun Law–Paul Evan Lehman | 6.00 | 12.00 | 18.00 | W |
| 173 | Anna–Anneke de Lange | 5.00 | 10.00 | 15.00 | |
| 174 | Murder Is My Racket–Robert H. Leitfred | 6.00 | 12.00 | 18.00 | M |
| 175 | The Commandos–Elliot Arnold; 1952 | 6.00 | 12.00 | 18.00 | C |
| 176 | The Valley of Silent Men–James Oliver Curwood | 6.00 | 12.00 | 18.00 | A |
| 177 | The House That Stood Still–A.E. van Vogt | 30.00 | 60.00 | 90.00 | SF |
| 178 | The Goldsmith's Wife–Jean Plaidy (Victoria Holt) | 6.00 | 12.00 | 18.00 | R |
| 179 | Madame Serpent–Jean Plaidy (Victoria Holt) | 6.00 | 12.00 | 18.00 | R |
| 180 | If the Coffin Fits–Day Keene | 8.00 | 16.00 | 24.00 | M |
| 181 | The Wicked Lady Skelton–Magdalen King-Hall | 6.00 | 12.00 | 18.00 | |
| 182 | Crime on My Hands–Carl G. Hodges. Note: Same cover as Phantom Books No. 506 | 9.00 | 18.00 | 27.00 | M |
| 183 | Evening Street–Katrina Johnson | 6.00 | 12.00 | 18.00 | |
| 184 | Black Jade–Angeline Taylor | 8.00 | 16.00 | 24.00 | |
| 185 | Naked Fury–Day Keene | 8.00 | 16.00 | 24.00 | |
| 186 | Why Be a Sucker?–D.M. LeBourdais | 6.00 | 12.00 | 18.00 | NF |
| 187 | Shanghai Jezebel–Mark Corrigan | 8.00 | 16.00 | 24.00 | E |
| 188 | Beggars Might Ride–George Albert Glay | 6.00 | 12.00 | 18.00 | |
| 189 | The Nymph and the Lamp–Thomas H. Raddall | 6.00 | 12.00 | 18.00 | E |
| 190 | Slave Ship–H.B. Drake | 6.00 | 12.00 | 18.00 | A |
| 191 | Prison Doctor–Louis Berg, MD | 6.00 | 12.00 | 18.00 | |
| 192 | Swamp Willow–Edwina Elroy | 6.00 | 12.00 | 18.00 | E |
| 193 | The Firebrand–George Challis | 6.00 | 12.00 | 18.00 | A |
| 194 | Triggerman–Abel Shott | 6.00 | 12.00 | 18.00 | |
| 195 | Nine to Five–Harvey Smith | 6.00 | 12.00 | 18.00 | |
| 196 | His Majesty's Yankees–Thomas H. Raddall | 6.00 | 12.00 | 18.00 | A |
| 197 | Strictly for Cash–James Hadley Chase | 6.00 | 12.00 | 18.00 | M |
| 198 | The Rawhider–Charles N. Heckelmann | 6.00 | 12.00 | 18.00 | W |
| 199 | The Double Shuffle–James Hadley Chase | 6.00 | 12.00 | 18.00 | M |
| 200 | Doctor of Lonesome River–Edison Marshall; 1952 | 6.00 | 12.00 | 18.00 | A |
| 201 | The Unfulfilled–W.G. Hardy | 6.00 | 12.00 | 18.00 | |
| 202 | Copper Town–Paul W. Fairman | 6.00 | 12.00 | 18.00 | W |
| 203 | Daughter of Satan–Jean Plaidy (Victoria Holt) | 7.50 | 15.00 | 22.50 | E |
| 204 | Gun Hawk–Leslie Ernenwein; 1953 | 6.00 | 12.00 | 18.00 | W |
| 205 | The Black Flame–Stanley G. Weinbaum | 25.00 | 50.00 | 75.00 | SF |
| 206 | You Never Know with Women–James Hadley Chase | 6.00 | 12.00 | 18.00 | E |
| 207 | Three Ships West–Harry Symons | 6.00 | 12.00 | 18.00 | |
| 208 | Pillar of Fire–George Borodin | 6.00 | 12.00 | 18.00 | |
| 209 | The Rock Cried Out–Edward Stanley | 6.00 | 12.00 | 18.00 | |
| 210 | McSorley's Wonderful Saloon–Joseph Mitchell | 6.00 | 12.00 | 18.00 | |
| 211 | The Cautious Amorist–Norman Lindsay | 5.00 | 10.00 | 15.00 | |
| 212 | Shooting Valley–Lynn Westland | 6.00 | 12.00 | 18.00 | W |
| 213 | The Royal Story–Richard J. Doyle | 5.00 | 10.00 | 15.00 | NF |
| 214 | Paprika–Erich von Stroheim | 5.00 | 10.00 | 15.00 | E |
| 215 | Turn Back the River–W.G. Hardy | 6.00 | 12.00 | 18.00 | |
| 216 | No Mean City–A. McArthur & H. Kingsley Long | 6.00 | 12.00 | 18.00 | |
| 217 | The Sea Hawk–Rafael Sabatini | 6.00 | 12.00 | 18.00 | A |
| 218 | The Golden Amazon–John Russell Fearn | 37.50 | 75.00 | 112.50 | SF |
| 219 | Girls in White–Rona Randall | 6.00 | 12.00 | 18.00 | |
| 220 | Masked Rider–Will Garth | 6.00 | 12.00 | 18.00 | W |
| 221 | The Great Impersonation–E. Phillips Oppenheim | 5.00 | 10.00 | 15.00 | A |
| 222 | Mad Mike–George Goodchild | 6.00 | 12.00 | 18.00 | |
| 223 | The Wages of Virtue–P.C. Wren | 6.00 | 12.00 | 18.00 | A |
| 224 | Lady Hobo–Beth Brown | 6.00 | 12.00 | 18.00 | E |
| 225 | Sir Rusty Sword–Phillip Lindsay; 1953 | 6.00 | 12.00 | 18.00 | A |
| 226 | The Owlhoot Trail–Buck Billings | 6.00 | 12.00 | 18.00 | W |
| 227 | We Too Can Die–Paul Le Butt | 6.00 | 12.00 | 18.00 | |
| 228 | Drums of Dambala–H. Bedford Jones | 7.50 | 15.00 | 22.50 | A |
| 229 | Framed in Guilt–Day Keene | 8.00 | 16.00 | 24.00 | M |
| 230 | Women Spies–Kurt Singer | 7.50 | 15.00 | 22.50 | E |
| 231 | Legionnaire–John Robb | 6.00 | 12.00 | 18.00 | A |
| 232 | Malay Gold–H. Bedford Jones | 7.50 | 15.00 | 22.50 | A |
| 233 | Die with Me Lady–Ronald Cocking | 6.00 | 12.00 | 18.00 | M |
| 234 | Rebound–Dick Diespecker | 6.00 | 12.00 | 18.00 | |
| 235 | General Duty Nurse–Lucy Agnes Hancock | 5.00 | 10.00 | 15.00 | R |
| 236 | Gun Thrower–William L. Hopson | 6.00 | 12.00 | 18.00 | W |

|  | | | **V/Good** | **Fine** | **N/Mint** | |
|---|---|---|---|---|---|---|

**HARLEQUIN,** *continued*

| # | Title | V/Good | Fine | N/Mint | |
|---|---|---|---|---|---|
| 375 | Miss Doctor–Elizabeth Seifert | 2.50 | 5.00 | 7.50 | R |
| 376 | Blake Hospital–Dorothy Worley; 1957 | 2.50 | 5.00 | 7.50 | R |
| 377 | The Secret of Chimneys–Agatha Christie | 6.00 | 12.00 | 18.00 | M |
| 378 | The Ringer–Edgar Wallace | 6.00 | 12.00 | 18.00 | M |
| 379 | The Doctor Takes a Wife–Elizabeth Seifert | 2.50 | 5.00 | 7.50 | R |
| 380 | The River's End–James Oliver Curwood | 6.00 | 12.00 | 18.00 | A |
| 381 | Doctor Joel–Watkins E. Wright | 2.50 | 5.00 | 7.50 | R |
| 382 | Never Trust a Woman–Raymond Marshall | 2.50 | 5.00 | 7.50 | |
| 383 | Valley of Silent Men–James Oliver Curwood | 6.00 | 12.00 | 18.00 | A |
| 384 | Nurse Ellen–Peggy Dern | 2.50 | 5.00 | 7.50 | R |
| 385 | Eve–James Hadley Chase | 6.00 | 12.00 | 18.00 | |
| 386 | The Faro Kid–Leslie Ernenwein | 6.00 | 12.00 | 18.00 | W |
| 387 | White Face–Edgar Wallace | 6.00 | 12.00 | 18.00 | M |
| 388 | Doctor Scott–Peggy Dern | 2.50 | 5.00 | 7.50 | R |
| 389 | Circle F Cowboy–Chuck Martin | 6.00 | 12.00 | 18.00 | W |
| 390 | Adopted Derelicts–Bluebell S. Phillips | 6.00 | 12.00 | 18.00 | |
| 391 | How to Get More from Your Car–W.J. Young & E.R. McCrea | 5.00 | 10.00 | 15.00 | NF |
| 392 | Doctor of Mercy–Elizabeth Seifert | 2.50 | 5.00 | 7.50 | R |
| 393 | A Forest of Eyes–Victor Canning | 4.00 | 8.00 | 10.00 | |
| 394 | Lady Doctor–Peggy Gaddis | 2.50 | 5.00 | 7.50 | R |
| 395 | The Angel of Terror–Edgar Wallace | 6.00 | 12.00 | 18.00 | M |
| 396 | Double Cross Ranch–Will Watson | 5.00 | 10.00 | 15.00 | W |
| 397 | The Shorn Lamb–Lucy Agnes Hancock | 2.50 | 5.00 | 7.50 | R |
| 398 | Sagebrush–Wade Hamilton | 5.00 | 10.00 | 15.00 | W |
| 399 | Royce of the Royal Mounted–Amos Moore | 6.00 | 12.00 | 18.00 | W |
| 400 | The Cage–Sydney Horter; 1957 | 6.00 | 12.00 | 18.00 | M |
| 401 | The Doctor Disagrees–Elizabeth Seifert | 2.50 | 5.00 | 7.50 | R |
| 402 | The Football Gravy Train–Frank O'Rourke | 5.00 | 10.00 | 15.00 | S |
| 403 | Next of Kin–George Goodchild | 2.50 | 5.00 | 7.50 | R |
| 404 | Law in the Saddle–Paul Evan Lehman | 6.00 | 12.00 | 18.00 | W |
| 405 | City Nurse–Peggy Gaddis | 2.50 | 5.00 | 7.50 | R |
| 406 | The Flaming Forest–James Oliver Curwood | 5.00 | 10.00 | 15.00 | A |
| 407 | The Hospital in Buwambo–Anne Vinton | 2.50 | 5.00 | 7.50 | R |
| 408 | Rink Rat–Don MacMillan | 6.00 | 12.00 | 18.00 | |
| 409 | Hospital Corridors–Mary Burchell; 1958; Harlequin's 1st Mills & Boon romance | 2.50 | 5.00 | 7.50 | R |
| 410 | Dark Journey–Sydney Horler | 6.00 | 12.00 | 18.00 | |
| 411 | Range King–J.E. Grinstead | 6.00 | 12.00 | 18.00 | W |
| 412 | Nurse Trenton–Caroline Trench | 2.50 | 5.00 | 7.50 | R |
| 413 | I'll Get You for This–James Hadley Chase | 6.00 | 12.00 | 18.00 | M |
| 414 | Devil's Portage–Charles Stoddard | 6.00 | 12.00 | 18.00 | |
| 415 | The Normal Child–Alan Brown, MD | 2.50 | 5.00 | 7.50 | NF |
| 416 | Doctor Lucy–Barbara Allen | 2.50 | 5.00 | 7.50 | R |
| 417 | Maverick Guns–J.E. Grinstead | 6.00 | 12.00 | 18.00 | W |
| 418 | The Feathered Serpent–Edgar Wallace | 6.00 | 12.00 | 18.00 | M |
| 419 | Nurse Warding Takes Charge–Caroline Trench | 2.50 | 5.00 | 7.50 | R |
| 420 | The Squeaker–Edgar Wallace | 6.00 | 12.00 | 18.00 | M |
| 421 | The Golden Amazon's Triumph–John Russell Fearn | 40.00 | 80.00 | 120.00 | SF |
| 422 | Then Come Kiss Me–Mary Burchell | 2.50 | 5.00 | 7.50 | R |
| 423 | Nurse Greve–Jane Arbor | 2.50 | 5.00 | 7.50 | R |
| 424 | Flashing Spikes–Frank O'Rourke | 5.00 | 10.00 | 15.00 | S |
| 425 | The Return of the Nighthawk–Sydney Horler; 1958 | 6.00 | 12.00 | 18.00 | |
| 426 | The World's Greatest Spy Stories–ed. Kurt Singer | 5.00 | 10.00 | 15.00 | |
| 427 | Nurse Brookes–Kate Norway | 2.50 | 5.00 | 7.50 | R |
| 428 | The Strange Countess–Edgar Wallace | 6.00 | 12.00 | 18.00 | M |
| 429 | Steele of the Royal Mounted–James Oliver Curwood | 6.00 | 12.00 | 18.00 | A |
| 430 | Ship's Nurse–Alex Stuart | 2.50 | 5.00 | 7.50 | R |
| 431 | The Silent Valley–Jean S. MacLeod | 5.00 | 10.00 | 15.00 | |
| 432 | The Lady Lost Her Head–Manning Lee Stokes | 6.00 | 12.00 | 18.00 | M |
| 433 | Because of Doctor Danville–Elizabeth Hoy | 2.50 | 5.00 | 7.50 | R |
| 434 | Dear Doctor Everett–Jean S. MacLeod | 2.50 | 5.00 | 7.50 | R |
| 435 | Canada's Greatest Crimes–Thomas P. Kelley | 6.00 | 12.00 | 18.00 | NF |
| 436 | Garrison Hospital–Alex Stuart | 2.50 | 5.00 | 7.50 | R |
| 437 | Saddlebag Surgeon–Robert Tyre | 2.50 | 5.00 | 7.50 | |
| 438 | Master of Surgery–Alex Stuart | 2.50 | 5.00 | 7.50 | |
| 439 | Hospital in Sudan–Anne Vinton | 2.50 | 5.00 | 7.50 | R |
| 440 | Pardon My Parka–Joan Walker | 2.50 | 5.00 | 7.50 | R |
| 441 | Murder on the Links–Agatha Christie | 6.00 | 12.00 | 18.00 | M |
| 442 | Curling with Ken Watson–Ken Watson | 5.00 | 10.00 | 15.00 | NF |
| 443 | Nurse on Call–Elizabeth Gilzean | 2.50 | 5.00 | 7.50 | R |
| 444 | Double Dan–Edgar Wallace | 6.00 | 12.00 | 18.00 | M |
| 445 | Nurse in the Tropics–Peggy Dern | 2.50 | 5.00 | 7.50 | R |
| 446 | To Please the Doctor–Marjorie Moore | 2.50 | 5.00 | 7.50 | R |
| 447 | The Crimson Circle–Edgar Wallace; 1959 | 6.00 | 12.00 | 18.00 | M |
| 448 | Bridal Array–Elizabeth Cadell | 2.50 | 5.00 | 7.50 | R |
| 449 | Nurse in Training–Elizabeth Hoy | 2.50 | 5.00 | 7.50 | R |
| 450 | Gay Canadian Rogues–Frank Rasky; 1959 | 6.00 | 12.00 | 18.00 | NF |
| 451 | Air Ambulance–Jean S. MacLeod | 2.50 | 5.00 | 7.50 | R |
| 452 | Crescent Dream Book and Fortune Teller | 6.00 | 12.00 | 18.00 | NF |
| 453 | Corner Cupboard–Carlyle Allison | 2.50 | 5.00 | 7.50 | R |
| 454 | Nurse in Love–Jane Arbor | 2.50 | 5.00 | 7.50 | R |
| 455 | Smoke over Sikanaska–J.S. Gowland | 5.00 | 10.00 | 15.00 | A |
| 456 | The Yellow Snake–Edgar Wallace | 6.00 | 12.00 | 18.00 | M |
| 457 | Physical Fitness for All the Family–Lloyd Percival | 4.00 | 8.00 | 12.00 | NF |
| 458 | Next Patient, Doctor Anne–Elizabeth Gilzean | 2.50 | 5.00 | 7.50 | R |
| 459 | Ring for the Nurse–Marjorie Moore | 2.50 | 5.00 | 7.50 | R |
| 460 | At the Villa Rose–A.E.W. Mason | 2.50 | 5.00 | 7.50 | R |
| 461 | For Ever and Ever–Mary Burchell | 2.50 | 5.00 | 7.50 | R |
| 462 | Love from a Surgeon–Elizabeth Gilzean | 2.50 | 5.00 | 7.50 | R |
| 463 | Nurse Brodie–Kate Norway | 2.50 | 5.00 | 7.50 | R |
| 464 | The Captain's Table–Alex Stuart | 2.50 | 5.00 | 7.50 | |
| 465 | My Greatest Crime Story–ed. Kurt Singer | 6.00 | 12.00 | 18.00 | |
| 466 | The Traitor's Gate–Edgar Wallace | 6.00 | 12.00 | 18.00 | M |
| 467 | Nurse to the Island–Caroline Trench | 2.50 | 5.00 | 7.50 | R |
| 468 | Surgeon of Distinction–Mary Burchell | 2.50 | 5.00 | 7.50 | R |
| 469 | Maggy–Sara Seale | 2.50 | 5.00 | 7.50 | R |
| 470 | The Cat in the Convoy–William G. Schofield | 5.00 | 10.00 | 15.00 | |
| 471 | Nurse Hilary–Peggy Gaddis | 2.50 | 5.00 | 7.50 | R |
| 472 | Young Doctor Kirkdene–Elizabeth Hoy | 2.50 | 5.00 | 7.50 | R |
| 473 | The Cockoo in Spring–Elizabeth Cadell | 2.50 | 5.00 | 7.50 | R |
| 474 | Towards the Dawn–Jane Arbor | 2.50 | 5.00 | 7.50 | R |
| 475 | The Mind of Mr. J. G. Reeder–Edgar Wallace; 1959 | 6.00 | 12.00 | 18.00 | M |
| 476 | Nurse Jess–Joyce Dingwell | 2.50 | 5.00 | 7.50 | R |
| 477 | Hospital Blue–Anne Vinton | 2.50 | 5.00 | 7.50 | R |
| 478 | Dear Trustee–Mary Burchell | 2.50 | 5.00 | 7.50 | R |
| 479 | The Case of the Ebony Queen–Cleo Adkins | 6.00 | 12.00 | 18.00 | |
| 480 | Grey Cup Cavalcade–Tony Allan | 6.00 | 12.00 | 18.00 | |
| 481 | Bachelor of Medicine–Alex Stuart | 2.50 | 5.00 | 7.50 | R |
| 482 | Nurse Harlowe–Jane Arbor | 2.50 | 5.00 | 7.50 | R |
| 483 | My Heart Has Wings–Elizabeth Hoy | 2.50 | 5.00 | 7.50 | R |
| 484 | The Northing Tramp–Edgar Wallace | 6.00 | 12.00 | 18.00 | M |
| 485 | Island Hospital–Elizabeth Houghton | 2.50 | 5.00 | 7.50 | R |
| 486 | Nurse Caril's New Post–Caroline Trench | 2.50 | 5.00 | 7.50 | R |
| 487 | The Happy Enterprise–Eleanor Farnes | 2.50 | 5.00 | 7.50 | |
| 488 | The Man Who Died Twice–Sydney Horler | 6.00 | 12.00 | 18.00 | |
| 489 | Consulting Surgeon–Jane Arbor | 2.50 | 5.00 | 7.50 | R |

*Harlequin 421, Harlequin 475, Harlequin 635.*

HARLEQUIN, *continued*

| No. | Title | V/Good | Fine | N/Mint | |
|---|---|---|---|---|---|
| 490 | Nurse MacLean Goes West–Elizabeth Gilzean | 2.50 | 5.00 | 7.50 | R |
| 491 | Nurse Tennant–Elizabeth Hoy | 2.00 | 4.00 | 6.00 | R |
| 492 | Hospital Pro–Marjorie Moore | 2.00 | 4.00 | 6.00 | R |
| 493 | The Man at the Carlton–Edgar Wallace | 6.00 | 12.00 | 18.00 | M |
| 494 | Love Is My Reason–Mary Burchell | 2.00 | 6.00 | 6.00 | R |
| 495 | Nurse with a Dream–Norrey Ford | 2.00 | 4.00 | 6.00 | R |
| 496 | Nurse in White–Lucy Agnes Hancock | 2.00 | 4.00 | 6.00 | R |
| 497 | Doctor Garth–Elizabeth Hoy | 2.00 | 4.00 | 6.00 | R |
| 498 | Nurse Atholl Returns–Jane Arbor | 2.00 | 4.00 | 6.00 | R |
| 499 | Junior Pro–Kate Norway | 2.00 | 4.00 | 6.00 | R |
| 500 | Honorary Surgeon–Marjorie Moore; 1959 | 2.00 | 4.00 | 6.00 | R |
| 501 | Do Something Dangerous–Elizabeth Hoy | 2.00 | 4.00 | 6.00 | R |
| 502 | Blood of Her Ancestors–Lucy Agnes Hancock; 1960 | 2.00 | 4.00 | 6.00 | R |
| 503 | Nurse in Charge–Elizabeth Gilzean | 2.00 | 4.00 | 6.00 | R |
| 504 | Peter Raynal, Surgeon–Marjorie Moore | 2.00 | 4.00 | 6.00 | R |
| 505 | Meet Doctor Kettering–Marguerite Lees | 2.00 | 4.00 | 6.00 | R |
| 506 | Queen's Counsel–Alex Stuart | 2.00 | 4.00 | 6.00 | R |
| 507 | It's Wise to Forget–Elizabeth Hoy | 2.00 | 4.00 | 6.00 | R |
| 508 | Senior Surgeon–Marjorie Moore | 2.00 | 4.00 | 6.00 | R |
| 509 | Nurse Secretary–Marjorie Moore | 2.00 | 4.00 | 6.00 | R |
| 510 | Doctor Halcott–Marguerite Lees | 2.00 | 4.00 | 6.00 | R |
| 511 | Strange Recompense–Catherine Airlie | 2.00 | 4.00 | 6.00 | R |
| 512 | Australian Hospital–Joyce Dingwell | 2.00 | 4.00 | 6.00 | R |
| 513 | Far Sanctuary–Jane Arbor | 2.00 | 4.00 | 6.00 | R |
| 514 | Twin Nurse–Bess Norton | 2.00 | 4.00 | 6.00 | R |
| 515 | A Case for Nurse Clare–Marguerite Lees | 2.00 | 4.00 | 6.00 | R |
| 516 | Prisoner of Love–Jean S. MacLeod | 2.00 | 4.00 | 6.00 | R |
| 517 | Doctors Together–Jean S. MacLeod | 2.00 | 4.00 | 6.00 | R |
| 518 | Hospital in Paradise–Juliet Shore | 2.00 | 4.00 | 6.00 | R |
| 519 | Doctor Pamela–Anne Vinton | 2.00 | 4.00 | 6.00 | R |
| 520 | Doctor Derrington–Marjorie Moore | 2.00 | 4.00 | 6.00 | R |
| 521 | On the Air–Mary Burchell | 2.00 | 4.00 | 6.00 | R |
| 522 | The Living Legend–Alan Phillips | 2.50 | 5.00 | 7.50 | |
| 523 | Doctor Reid–Peggy Gaddis | 2.00 | 4.00 | 6.00 | R |
| 524 | Queen's Nurse–Jane Arbor | 2.00 | 4.00 | 6.00 | |
| 525 | Nurse Elliot's Diary–Kate Norway | 2.00 | 4.00 | 6.00 | R |
| 526 | When You Have Found Me–Elizabeth Hoy | 2.00 | 4.00 | 6.00 | R |
| 527 | Return to Love–Alex Stuart | 2.00 | 4.00 | 6.00 | R |
| 528 | Wife by Arrangement–Mary Burchell | 2.00 | 4.00 | 6.00 | R |
| 529 | Theatre Nurse–Hilda Pressley | 2.00 | 4.00 | 6.00 | R |
| 530 | Dr. Daring's Love Affair–Anne Vinton | 2.00 | 4.00 | 6.00 | R |
| 531 | Doctor Memsahib–Juliet Shore | 2.00 | 4.00 | 6.00 | R |
| 532 | To Win a Paradise–Elizabeth Hoy | 2.00 | 4.00 | 6.00 | R |
| 533 | Over the Blue Mountains–Mary Burchell | 2.00 | 4.00 | 6.00 | R |
| 534 | Doctor's Wife–In Secret–Anne Vinton | 2.00 | 4.00 | 6.00 | R |
| 535 | Under the Red Cross–Juliet Shore | 2.00 | 4.00 | 6.00 | R |
| 536 | Hospital at Night–Marguerite Lees | 2.00 | 4.00 | 6.00 | R |
| 537 | Castle in Corsica–Anne Weale | 2.00 | 4.00 | 6.00 | R |
| 538 | Strange Request–Marjorie Bassett | 2.00 | 4.00 | 6.00 | R |
| 539 | Hospital on Wheels–Anne Lorraine | 2.00 | 4.00 | 6.00 | R |
| 540 | Village Nurse–Marguerite Lees | 2.00 | 4.00 | 6.00 | R |
| 541 | The Way in the Dark–Jean S. MacLeod | 2.00 | 4.00 | 6.00 | R |
| 542 | City of Dreams–Elizabeth Hoy | 2.00 | 4.00 | 6.00 | R |
| 543 | The Little Doctor–Jean S. MacLeod | 2.00 | 4.00 | 6.00 | R |
| 544 | Doctor Sara–Peggy Gaddis | 2.00 | 4.00 | 6.00 | R |
| 545 | Nurse Lang–Jean S. MacLeod | 2.00 | 4.00 | 6.00 | R |
| 546 | Choose the One You'll Marry–Mary Burchell | 2.00 | 4.00 | 6.00 | R |
| 547 | The Gated Road–Jean S. MacLeod | 2.00 | 4.00 | 6.00 | R |
| 548 | Psychiatric Nurse–Elizabeth Gilzean | 2.00 | 4.00 | 6.00 | R |
| 549 | Doctor Mary's Mission–Juliet Shore | 2.00 | 4.00 | 6.00 | R |
| 550 | Canadian Etiquette Dictionary–Claire Wallace; 1960 | 3.00 | 6.00 | 9.00 | NF |
| 551 | Grass Roots Nurse–Georgia Craig | 2.00 | 4.00 | 6.00 | R |
| 552 | Caribbean Melody–Peggy Dern | 2.00 | 4.00 | 6.00 | R |
| 553 | The House of Seven Fountains–Anne Weale | 2.00 | 4.00 | 6.00 | R |
| 554 | My Dear Doctor–Anne Lorraine | 2.00 | 4.00 | 6.00 | R |
| 555 | Love thy Physician–Hilda Nickson | 2.00 | 4.00 | 6.00 | R |
| 556 | Staff Nurse in the Tyrol–Elizabeth Houghton | 2.00 | 4.00 | 6.00 | R |
| 557 | Nurse Carol's Secret–Nerina Hilliard | 2.00 | 4.00 | 6.00 | R |
| 558 | Nurse in Malaya–Vivian Stuart | 2.00 | 4.00 | 6.00 | R |
| 559 | Nurse Wayne in the Tropics–Anne Vinton | 2.00 | 4.00 | 6.00 | R |
| 560 | Wintersbride–Sara Seale | 2.00 | 4.00 | 6.00 | R |
| 561 | The Girl Who Kept Faith–Marguerite Lees | 2.00 | 4.00 | 6.00 | R |
| 562 | Christmas Gift–Lucy Agnes Hancock; 1960 | 2.00 | 4.00 | 6.00 | R |
| 563 | Hospital in the Highlands–Anne Vinton; 1961 | 2.00 | 4.00 | 6.00 | R |
| 564 | Doctor to the Isles–Juliet Shore | 2.00 | 4.00 | 6.00 | R |
| 565 | Paris–And My Love–Mary Burchell | 2.00 | 4.00 | 6.00 | R |
| 566 | Jungle Doctor–Vivian Stuart | 2.00 | 4.00 | 6.00 | R |
| 567 | Harley Street Surgeon–Dorothy Rivers | 2.00 | 4.00 | 6.00 | R |
| 568 | Nurse at Sea–Juliet Shore | 2.00 | 4.00 | 6.00 | R |
| 569 | Wife to Doctor Dan–Hilary Darke | 2.00 | 4.00 | 6.00 | R |
| 570 | Night Nurse–Hilda Pressley | 2.00 | 4.00 | 6.00 | R |
| 571 | Children's Hospital–Elizabeth Gilzean | 2.00 | 4.00 | 6.00 | R |
| 572 | So Dear to My Heart–Susan Barrie | 2.00 | 4.00 | 6.00 | R |
| 573 | Dear Fugitive–Elizabeth Hoy | 2.00 | 4.00 | 6.00 | R |
| 574 | Along Came Doctor Ann–Vivian Stuart | 2.00 | 4.00 | 6.00 | R |
| 575 | Doctor Standing–Jane Beech | 2.00 | 4.00 | 6.00 | R |
| 576 | Sandflower–Jane Arbor | 2.00 | 4.00 | 6.00 | R |
| 577 | White Hunter–Elizabeth Hoy | 2.00 | 4.00 | 6.00 | R |
| 578 | Nurse Templar–Anne Weale | 2.00 | 4.00 | 6.00 | R |
| 579 | Nurse Angela–Hilary Preston | 2.00 | 4.00 | 6.00 | R |
| 580 | Nursey Nolan–Juliet Shore | 2.00 | 4.00 | 6.00 | R |
| 581 | Yankee Surgeon–Elizabeth Gilzean | 2.00 | 4.00 | 6.00 | R |
| 582 | Winter Is Past–Anne Weale | 2.00 | 4.00 | 6.00 | R |
| 583 | This Merry Bond–Sara Seale | 2.00 | 4.00 | 6.00 | R |
| 584 | Village Hospital–Margaret Malcolm | 2.00 | 4.00 | 6.00 | R |
| 585 | Nurse to the Cruise–Anne Vinton | 2.00 | 4.00 | 6.00 | R |
| 586 | Cameron of Gare–Jean S. MacLeod | 2.00 | 4.00 | 6.00 | R |
| 587 | Heart Specialist–Susan Barrie | 2.00 | 4.00 | 6.00 | R |
| 588 | Island Nurse–Georgia Craig | 2.00 | 4.00 | 6.00 | R |
| 589 | The Doctor's Challenge–Marjorie Moore | 2.00 | 4.00 | 6.00 | R |
| 590 | First, the Doctor–Anne Lorraine | 2.00 | 4.00 | 6.00 | R |
| 591 | Hotel Nurse–Anne Lorraine | 2.00 | 4.00 | 6.00 | R |
| 592 | Marriage Compromise–Margaret Malcolm | 2.00 | 4.00 | 6.00 | R |
| 593 | Lucifer's Angel–Violet Winspear | 1.50 | 3.00 | 4.50 | R |
| 594 | Doctor Sara Comes Home–Elizabeth Houghton | 1.50 | 3.00 | 4.50 | R |
| 595 | Emergency Nurse–Anne Lorraine | 1.50 | 3.00 | 4.50 | R |
| 596 | Hope for the Doctor–Margaret Malcolm | 1.50 | 3.00 | 4.50 | R |
| 597 | Special Nurse–Jean S. MacLeod | 1.50 | 3.00 | 4.50 | R |
| 598 | Doctor Mary Courage–Alex Stuart | 1.50 | 3.00 | 4.50 | R |
| 599 | Nurse Companion–Jean S. MacLeod | 1.50 | 3.00 | 4.50 | R |
| 600 | Hospital Librarian–Margaret Malcolm | 1.50 | 3.00 | 4.50 | R |
| 601 | Nurse Nicky–Lilian Chisholm | 1.50 | 3.00 | 4.50 | R |
| 602 | Repent at Leisure–Joan Walker | 1.50 | 3.00 | 4.50 | |
| 603 | Across the Counter–Mary Burchell | 1.50 | 3.00 | 4.50 | R |
| 604 | Flight to the Stars–Pamela Kent | 1.50 | 3.00 | 4.50 | R |
| 605 | Dear Sir–Mary Burchell | 1.50 | 3.00 | 4.50 | R |
| 606 | Doctor in Bondage–Jean S. MacLeod | 1.50 | 3.00 | 4.50 | R |
| 607 | Doctor's Prejudice–Joyce Dingwell | 1.50 | 3.00 | 4.50 | R |
| 608 | White-Coated Girl–Anne Lorraine | 1.50 | 3.00 | 4.50 | R |
| 609 | Doctor's Secretary–Marjorie Moore | 1.50 | 3.00 | 4.50 | R |
| 610 | Doctor at Hilltops–Lilian Chisholm | 1.50 | 3.00 | 4.50 | R |
| 611 | Nurse Blade's First Week–Mary Hunton | 1.50 | 3.00 | 4.50 | R |
| 612 | Patient for Doctor Gaird–Anne Lorraine | 1.50 | 3.00 | 4.50 | R |
| 613 | Nurse in the House–Margaret Malcolm | 1.50 | 3.00 | 4.50 | R |
| 614 | Island for Sale–Alex Stuart | 1.50 | 3.00 | 4.50 | R |
| 615 | Summer Lightning–Jill Tahourdin | 1.50 | 3.00 | 4.50 | R |
| 616 | Love Him or Leave Him–Mary Burchell | 1.50 | 3.00 | 4.50 | R |
| 617 | And Be Thy Love–Rose Burghley | 1.50 | 3.00 | 4.50 | R |
| 618 | Doctor Di at the Crossroads–Anne Vinton | 1.50 | 3.00 | 4.50 | R |
| 619 | Staff Nurse on Gynae–Hilda Pressley | 1.50 | 3.00 | 4.50 | R |
| 620 | White Doctor–Celine Conway | 1.50 | 3.00 | 4.50 | R |
| 621 | Nurse to Captain Andy–Jill Christian | 1.50 | 3.00 | 4.50 | R |
| 622 | Football Flashbacks–Tony Allan; 1961 | 2.50 | 5.00 | 7.50 | S |
| 623 | Thursday Clinic–Anne Lorraine | 1.50 | 3.00 | 4.50 | R |
| 624 | Nurse Linnet's Release–Averil Ives | 1.50 | 3.00 | 4.50 | R |
| 625 | Nurse Abroad–Essie Summers | 1.50 | 3.00 | 4.50 | R |
| 626 | Nurse Trent's Children–Joyce Dingwell | 1.50 | 3.00 | 4.50 | R |
| 627 | With all My Worldly Goods–Mary Burchell | 1.50 | 3.00 | 4.50 | R |
| 628 | The House of the Laird–Susan Barrie | 1.50 | 3.00 | 4.50 | R |
| 629 | To Love Again–Denise Robins | 1.50 | 3.00 | 4.50 | R |
| 630 | Stranger in Their Midst–Jean S. MacLeod | 1.50 | 3.00 | 4.50 | R |
| 631 | Doctor's House–Dorothy Rivers | 1.50 | 3.00 | 4.50 | R |
| 632 | Nurse for the Doctor–Averil Ives | 1.50 | 3.00 | 4.50 | R |
| 633 | Children's Nurse–Kathryn Blair | 1.50 | 3.00 | 4.50 | R |

HARLEQUIN, *continued*

| | | V/Good | Fine | N/Mint | |
|---|---|---|---|---|---|
| 634 | Surgeon's Wife—Margaret Malcolm | 1.50 | 3.00 | 4.50 | R |
| 635 | Curling Today—Ken Watson; 1961 | 2.00 | 4.00 | 6.00 | S |
| 636 | Nurse Candida—Caroline Trench; 1962 | 1.50 | 3.00 | 4.50 | R |
| 637 | Career Nurse—Anne Lorraine | 1.50 | 3.00 | 4.50 | R |
| 638 | Mountain Clinic—Jean S. MacLeod | 1.50 | 3.00 | 4.50 | R |
| 639 | Nurse in Spain—Alex Stuart | 1.50 | 3.00 | 4.50 | R |
| 640 | Spencer's Hospital—Alex Stuart | 1.50 | 3.00 | 4.50 | R |
| 641 | Hospital Secretary—Margaret Baumann | 1.50 | 3.00 | 4.50 | R |
| 642 | The White Jacket—Kate Norway | 1.50 | 3.00 | 4.50 | R |
| 643 | Nurse Jane & Dr. John—Hilary Preston | 1.50 | 3.00 | 4.50 | R |
| 644 | Never to Love—Anne Weale | 1.50 | 3.00 | 4.50 | R |
| 645 | The Gentle Prisoner—Sara Seale | 1.50 | 3.00 | 4.50 | R |
| 646 | Nurse in Waiting—Jane Arbor | 1.50 | 3.00 | 4.50 | R |
| 647 | Jungle Hospital—Juliet Shore | 1.50 | 3.00 | 4.50 | R |
| 648 | Gray's Hospital—Joan Blair | 1.50 | 3.00 | 4.50 | R |
| 649 | Kate of Outpatients—Elizabeth Gilzean | 1.50 | 3.00 | 4.50 | R |
| 650 | The Golden Rose—Kathryn Blair | 1.50 | 3.00 | 4.50 | R |
| 651 | Dangerous Obsession—Jean S. MacLeod | 1.50 | 3.00 | 4.50 | R |
| 652 | Diana Drake, M.D.—Lilian Chisholm | 1.50 | 3.00 | 4.50 | R |
| 653 | The Waiting Room—Bess Norton | 1.50 | 3.00 | 4.50 | R |
| 654 | Cherry Blossom Clinic—Elizabeth Hunter | 1.50 | 3.00 | 4.50 | R |
| 655 | Outpost Hospital—Sheila Ridley | 1.50 | 3.00 | 4.50 | R |
| 656 | Stormy Haven—Rosalind Brett | 1.50 | 3.00 | 4.50 | R |
| 657 | Orphan Bride—Sara Seale | 1.50 | 3.00 | 4.50 | R |
| 658 | Reluctant Relation—Mary Burchell | 1.50 | 3.00 | 4.50 | R |
| 659 | Gone Away—Marjorie Moore | 1.50 | 3.00 | 4.50 | R |
| 660 | Doctor Raoul's Romance—Penelope Butler | 1.50 | 3.00 | 4.50 | R |
| 661 | Doctor's Ward—Sara Seale | 1.50 | 3.00 | 4.50 | R |
| 662 | Tread Softley, Nurse—Hilary Neal | 1.50 | 3.00 | 4.50 | R |
| 663 | In Care of the Doctor—Barbara Rowan | 1.50 | 3.00 | 4.50 | R |
| 664 | Love for the Matron—Elizabeth Houghton | 1.50 | 3.00 | 4.50 | R |
| 665 | A Problem for Dr. Brett—Marjorie Norrell | 1.50 | 3.00 | 4.50 | R |
| 666 | Love, the Surgeon—Hilda Pressley | 1.50 | 3.00 | 4.50 | R |
| 667 | Nurse Laurie—Kathryn Blair | 1.50 | 3.00 | 4.50 | R |
| 668 | No Roses in June—Essie Summers | 1.50 | 3.00 | 4.50 | R |
| 669 | A Cruise for Cinderella—Alex Stuart | 1.50 | 3.00 | 4.50 | R |
| 670 | Operation Love—Hilda Nickson | 1.50 | 3.00 | 4.50 | R |
| 671 | Doctor's Choice—Margaret Baumann | 1.50 | 3.00 | 4.50 | R |
| 672 | Gregor Lothian, Surgeon—Joan Blair | 1.50 | 3.00 | 4.50 | R |
| 673 | Village Clinic—Ann Cameron | 1.50 | 3.00 | 4.50 | R |
| 674 | The Silver Dragon—Jean S. MacLeod | 1.50 | 3.00 | 4.50 | R |
| 675 | Wide Pastures—Celine Conway | 1.50 | 3.00 | 4.50 | R |
| 676 | Doctor Venables' Practice—Anne Vinton | 1.50 | 3.00 | 4.50 | R |
| 677 | The Doctor Next Door—Lilian Chisholm | 1.50 | 3.00 | 4.50 | R |
| 678 | Doctor in the Tropics—Vivian Stuart; 1962 | 1.50 | 3.00 | 4.50 | R |
| 679 | The Nurse Most Likely—Kate Starr | 1.50 | 3.00 | 4.50 | R |
| 680 | Black Charles—Esther Wyndham | 1.50 | 3.00 | 4.50 | R |
| 681 | I'll Never Marry—Juliet Armstrong | 1.50 | 3.00 | 4.50 | R |
| 682 | Plantation Doctor—Kathryn Blair | 1.50 | 3.00 | 4.50 | R |
| 683 | Doctor's Desire—Averil Ives | 1.50 | 3.00 | 4.50 | R |
| 684 | Doctor on Horseback—Alex Stuart | 1.50 | 3.00 | 4.50 | R |
| 685 | Doctor Mark Temple—Elizabeth Gilzean | 1.50 | 3.00 | 4.50 | R |
| 686 | Stolen Heart—Mary Burchell | 1.50 | 3.00 | 4.50 | R |
| 687 | Four Roads to Windrush—Susan Barrie | 1.50 | 3.00 | 4.50 | R |
| 688 | Stevie, Student Nurse—Marguerite Lees | 1.50 | 3.00 | 4.50 | R |
| 689 | Nurse in India—Juliet Armstrong | 1.50 | 3.00 | 4.50 | R |
| 690 | Nurse of All Work—Jane Arbor | 1.50 | 3.00 | 4.50 | R |
| 691 | Doctor Benedict—Joyce Dingwell | 1.50 | 3.00 | 4.50 | R |
| 692 | The Only Charity—Sara Seale | 1.50 | 3.00 | 4.50 | R |
| 693 | Towards the Sun—Rosalind Brett | 1.50 | 3.00 | 4.50 | R |
| 694 | Football Today and Yesterday—Tony Allan; 1962 | 2.50 | 5.00 | 7.50 | S |
| 695 | Vengeance of the Black Donnellys—Thomas P. Kelley | 2.50 | 5.00 | 7.50 | NF |
| 696 | Staff Nurse in Love—Hilda Pressley | 1.50 | 3.00 | 4.50 | R |
| 697 | Patient in Love—Bethea Creese | 1.50 | 3.00 | 4.50 | R |
| 698 | Good Night Nurse—Anne Lorraine | 1.50 | 3.00 | 4.50 | R |
| 699 | The Doctor Is Engaged—Nan Asquith | 1.50 | 3.00 | 4.50 | R |
| 700 | Tamarisk Bay—Kathryn Blair | 1.50 | 3.00 | 4.50 | R |
| 701 | Doctor's Love—Jane Arbor | 1.50 | 3.00 | 4.50 | R |
| 702 | Surgeons in Love—Hilda Nickson | 1.50 | 3.00 | 4.50 | R |
| 703 | Doctor Grant of Bonnybraes—Joan Blair | 1.50 | 3.00 | 4.50 | R |
| 704 | Private Case—Marguerite Lees | 1.50 | 3.00 | 4.50 | R |
| 705 | The Last of the Logans—Alex Stuart | 1.50 | 3.00 | 4.50 | R |
| 706 | Peace River Country—Ralph Allen; 1962 | 1.50 | 3.00 | 4.50 | |
| 707 | Holiday Hospital—Juliet Shore; 1963 | 1.50 | 3.00 | 4.50 | R |
| 708 | Calling Nurse Grant—Lilian Chisholm | 1.50 | 3.00 | 4.50 | R |
| 709 | Senior Surgeon At St. David's—Elizabeth Gilzean | 1.50 | 3.00 | 4.50 | R |
| 710 | A Nurse Is Born—Bess Norton | 1.50 | 3.00 | 4.50 | R |
| 711 | My Heart's in the Highlands—Jean S. MacLeod | 1.50 | 3.00 | 4.50 | R |
| 712 | House of Conflict—Mary Burchell | 1.50 | 3.00 | 4.50 | R |
| 713 | Nurse of My Heart—Jill Christian | 1.50 | 3.00 | 4.50 | R |
| 714 | Young Nurse Payne—Valerie K. Nelson | 1.50 | 3.00 | 4.50 | R |
| 715 | The Heat of a Hospital—Anne Vinton | 1.50 | 3.00 | 4.50 | R |
| 716 | The Doctor's Daughters—Anne Weale | 1.50 | 3.00 | 4.50 | R |
| 717 | The House at Tegwani—Kathryn Blair | 1.50 | 3.00 | 4.50 | R |
| 718 | All This Difference—Dorothy Dumbrille | 1.50 | 3.00 | 4.50 | R |
| 719 | Forbidden Island—Sara Seale | 1.50 | 3.00 | 4.50 | R |
| 720 | General Hospital—Marguerite Lees | 1.50 | 3.00 | 4.50 | R |
| 721 | Ship's Surgeon—Celine Conway | 1.50 | 3.00 | 4.50 | R |
| 722 | Doctor's Orders—Eleanor Farnes | 1.50 | 3.00 | 4.50 | R |
| 723 | Nurse Langridge, Heiress—Margaret Malcolm | 1.50 | 3.00 | 4.50 | R |
| 724 | House of the Shining Tide—Essie Summers | 1.50 | 3.00 | 4.50 | R |
| 725 | The Song and the Sea—Isobel Chace | 1.50 | 3.00 | 4.50 | R |
| 726 | Surgeon for Tonight—Elizabeth Houghton | 1.50 | 3.00 | 4.50 | R |
| 727 | Nurses of the Tourist Service—Gladys Fullbrooke; 1963 | 1.50 | 3.00 | 4.50 | R |
| 728 | Reluctant Nurse—Anne Lorraine | 1.50 | 3.00 | 4.50 | R |
| 729 | Surgeons at Arms—Mary Hunton | 1.50 | 3.00 | 4.50 | R |
| 730 | The Stars of San Cecilio—Susan Barrie | 1.50 | 3.00 | 4.50 | R |
| 731 | Whispering Palms—Rosalind Brett | 1.50 | 3.00 | 4.50 | R |
| 732 | River Nurse—Joyce Dingwell | 1.50 | 3.00 | 4.50 | R |
| 733 | Stevie, Staff Nurse—Marguerite Lees | 1.50 | 3.00 | 4.50 | R |
| 734 | Doctor Andrew, Guardian—Olga Gillman | 1.50 | 3.00 | 4.50 | R |
| 735 | Quayside Hospital—Hilda Nickson | 1.50 | 3.00 | 4.50 | R |
| 736 | The Tall Pines—Celine Conway | 1.50 | 3.00 | 4.50 | R |
| 737 | Maiden Flight—Betty Beaty | 1.50 | 3.00 | 4.50 | R |
| 738 | Send for Doctor—Anne Lorraine | 1.50 | 3.00 | 4.50 | R |
| 739 | When a Nurse Is Young—Lilian Chisholm | 1.50 | 3.00 | 4.50 | R |
| 740 | Nurse on Holiday—Rosalind Brett | 1.50 | 3.00 | 4.50 | R |
| 741 | Nurse at Hand—Marjorie Ellison | 1.50 | 3.00 | 4.50 | R |
| 742 | Come Blossom-Time, My Love—Essie Summers | 1.50 | 3.00 | 4.50 | R |
| 743 | The House on Flamingo Cay—Anne Weale | 1.50 | 3.00 | 4.50 | R |
| 744 | Verena Fayre, Probationer—Valerie K. Nelson | 1.50 | 3.00 | 4.50 | R |
| 745 | Tender Nurse—Hilda Nickson | 1.50 | 3.00 | 4.50 | R |
| 746 | Nurse Marika, Loyal in All—Mary Burchell | 1.50 | 3.00 | 4.50 | R |
| 747 | Lucy Lamb, Doctor's Wife—Sara Seale | 1.50 | 3.00 | 4.50 | R |
| 748 | The Valley of Palms—Jean S. MacLeod | 1.50 | 3.00 | 4.50 | R |
| 749 | Wild Crocus—Kathryn Blair | 1.50 | 3.00 | 4.50 | R |
| 750 | A Nurse about the Place—Anne Lorraine | 1.50 | 3.00 | 4.50 | R |
| 751 | Night Superintendent—Hilda Pressley; 1963 | 1.50 | 3.00 | 4.50 | R |
| 752 | The Ordeal of Nurse Thompson—Nora Sanderson | 1.50 | 3.00 | 4.50 | R |
| 753 | Doctor May—Eleanor Farnes | 1.50 | 3.00 | 4.50 | R |
| 754 | The Rancher Needs a Wife—Celine Conway | 1.50 | 3.00 | 4.50 | R |
| 755 | September in Paris—Andrea Blake | 1.50 | 3.00 | 4.50 | R |
| 756 | Ward Hostess—Marguerite Lees | 1.50 | 3.00 | 4.50 | R |
| 757 | The Palm-Thatched Hospital—Juliet Shore | 1.50 | 3.00 | 4.50 | R |
| 758 | Helping Doctor Medway—Jan Haye | 1.50 | 3.00 | 4.50 | R |
| 759 | Young Doctor Ashley—Marjorie Norrell | 1.50 | 3.00 | 4.50 | R |
| 760 | Fair Horizon—Rosalind Brett | 1.50 | 3.00 | 4.50 | R |
| 761 | The House in the Timberwoods—Joyce Dingwell | 1.50 | 3.00 | 4.50 | R |
| 762 | Hospital in New Zealand—Nora Sanderson | 1.50 | 3.00 | 4.50 | R |
| 763 | A Surgical Affair—Shirley Summerskill | 1.50 | 3.00 | 4.50 | R |
| 764 | Nurse Ann Wood—Valerie K. Nelson | 1.50 | 3.00 | 4.50 | R |
| 765 | A Case of Heart Trouble—Susan Barrie | 1.50 | 3.00 | 4.50 | R |
| 766 | The Enchanting Island—Kathryn Blair | 1.50 | 3.00 | 4.50 | R |
| 767 | The Silver Dolphin—Anne Weale | 1.50 | 3.00 | 4.50 | R |
| 768 | Never a Day So Bright—Kate Aitken | 1.50 | 3.00 | 4.50 | |
| 769 | Nursing Auxiliary—Marguerite Lees | 1.50 | 3.00 | 4.50 | R |
| 770 | Nurse Margaret's Big Mistake—Anne Vinton | 1.50 | 3.00 | 4.50 | R |
| 771 | Nurse Prue in Ceylon—Gladys Fullbrook | 1.50 | 3.00 | 4.50 | R |

HARLEQUIN, *continued*

| | | V/Good | Fine | N/Mint | |
|---|---|---|---|---|---|
| 772 | Chloe Wilde, Student Nurse–Joan Turner | 1.50 | 3.00 | 4.50 | R |
| 773 | Winds in the Wilderness–Rosalind Brett | 1.50 | 3.00 | 4.50 | R |
| 774 | Heatherleigh–Essie Summers | 1.50 | 3.00 | 4.50 | R |
| 775 | That Nice Nurse Nevin–Jan Tempest | 1.50 | 3.00 | 4.50 | R |
| 776 | Nurse Foster's Foolish Heart–Hilda Nickson | 1.50 | 3.00 | 4.50 | R |
| 777 | Scatterbrains–Student Nurse–Margaret Malcolm | 1.50 | 3.00 | 4.50 | R |
| 778 | A Case in the Alps–Margaret Baumann | 1.50 | 3.00 | 4.50 | R |
| 779 | Mistress of Brown Furrows–Susan Barrie | 1.50 | 3.00 | 4.50 | R |
| 780 | Jasmine Harvest–Jane Arbor | 1.50 | 3.00 | 4.50 | R |
| 781 | Then She Fled Me–Sara Seale | 1.50 | 3.00 | 4.50 | R |
| 782 | Inherit My Heart–Mary Burchell | 1.50 | 3.00 | 4.50 | R |
| 783 | Portrait of Susan–Rosalind Brett | 1.50 | 3.00 | 4.50 | R |
| 784 | Where No Roads Go–Essie Summers; 1963 | 1.50 | 3.00 | 4.50 | R |
| 785 | The Surgeon's Marriage–Kathryn Blair; 1964 | 1.50 | 3.00 | 4.50 | R |
| 786 | A Ring for the Doctor–Anne Lorraine | 1.50 | 3.00 | 4.50 | R |
| 787 | The Two Faces of Nurse Roberts–Nora Sanderson | 1.50 | 3.00 | 4.50 | R |
| 788 | The Gentle Surgeon–Hilda Pressley | 1.50 | 3.00 | 4.50 | R |
| 789 | Country of the Heart–Catherine Airlie | 1.50 | 3.00 | 4.50 | R |
| 790 | South to the Sun–Betty Beaty | 1.50 | 3.00 | 4.50 | R |
| 791 | City of Palms–Pamela Kent | 1.50 | 3.00 | 4.50 | R |
| 792 | Gates of Dawn–Susan Barrie | 1.50 | 3.00 | 4.50 | R |
| 793 | The Starched Cap–Valerie K. Nelson | 1.50 | 3.00 | 4.50 | R |
| 794 | Surgeon's Return–Hilda Nickson | 1.50 | 3.00 | 4.50 | R |
| 795 | Hospital Technician–Marguerite Lees | 1.50 | 3.00 | 4.50 | R |
| 796 | Nurse Incognito–Fay Chandos | 1.50 | 3.00 | 4.50 | R |
| 797 | The Black Cameron–Jean S. MacLeod | 1.50 | 3.00 | 4.50 | R |
| 798 | If This Is Love–Anne Weale | 1.50 | 3.00 | 4.50 | R |
| 799 | Love Is For Ever–Barbara Rowan | 1.50 | 3.00 | 4.50 | R |
| 800 | Sweet Waters–Rosalind Brett | 1.50 | 3.00 | 4.50 | R |
| 801 | Desert Nurse–Jane Arbor· | 1.50 | 3.00 | 4.50 | R |
| 802 | Nurse Mary's Engagement–Essie Summers | 1.50 | 3.00 | 4.50 | R |
| 803 | Model Nurse–Ivy Ferrari | 1.50 | 3.00 | 4.50 | R |
| 804 | Bladons Rock–Pamela Kent | 1.50 | 3.00 | 4.50 | R |
| 805 | Love This Enemy–Kathryn Blair | 1.50 | 3.00 | 4.50 | R |
| 806 | The Golden Peaks–Eleanor Farnes | 1.50 | 3.00 | 4.50 | R |
| 807 | Full Tide–Celine Conway | 1.50 | 3.00 | 4.50 | R |
| 808 | The Girl at Snowy River–Joyce Dingwell | 1.50 | 3.00 | 4.50 | R |
| 809 | Send for Nurse Vincent–Margaret Malcolm | 1.50 | 3.00 | 4.50 | R |
| 810 | Doctor of Rhua–Alex Stuart | 1.50 | 3.00 | 4.50 | R |
| 811 | Nurse Harriet Come Home–Joan Blair | 1.50 | 3.00 | 4.50 | R |
| 812 | Factory Nurse–Hilary Neal | 1.50 | 3.00 | 4.50 | R |
| 813 | The Wedding Dress–Mary Burchell | 1.50 | 3.00 | 4.50 | R |
| 814 | A Long Way from Home–Jane Fraser | 1.50 | 3.00 | 4.50 | R |
| 815 | Young Tracy–Rosalind Brett | 1.50 | 3.00 | 4.50 | R |
| 816 | The Youngest Bridesmaid–Sara Seale | 1.50 | 3.00 | 4.50 | R |
| 817 | Doctor Pilgrim's Progress–Anne Vinton | 1.50 | 3.00 | 4.50 | R |
| 818 | Second Year Nurse–Valerie K. Nelson | 1.50 | 3.00 | 4.50 | R |
| 819 | Nurse Saxon's Patient–Marjorie Norrell | 1.50 | 3.00 | 4.50 | R |
| 820 | The World of Nurse Mitchell–Hilda Nickson | 1.50 | 3.00 | 4.50 | R |
| 821 | The Wild Land–Isobel Chace | 1.50 | 3.00 | 4.50 | R |
| 822 | The Time and the Place–Essie Summers | 1.50 | 3.00 | 4.50 | R |
| 823 | Dear Adversary–Kathryn Blair | 1.50 | 3.00 | 4.50 | R |
| 824 | Amber Five–Betty Beaty | 1.50 | 3.00 | 4.50 | R |
| 825 | Make Up Your Mind Nurse–Phyllis Matthewman | 1.50 | 3.00 | 4.50 | R |
| 826 | Doctor's Assistant–Celine Conway | 1.50 | 3.00 | 4.50 | R |
| 827 | Sheila of Children's Ward–Margaret Baumann | 1.50 | 3.00 | 4.50 | R |
| 828 | Ship's Doctor–Kate Starr | 1.50 | 3.00 | 4.50 | R |
| 829 | Sweet Barbary–Pamela Kent | 1.50 | 3.00 | 4.50 | R |
| 830 | All I Ask–Anne Weale | 1.50 | 3.00 | 4.50 | R |
| 831 | Hotel at Treloan–Susan Barrie | 1.50 | 3.00 | 4.50 | R |
| 832 | No Silver Spoon–Jane Arbor | 1.50 | 3.00 | 4.50 | R |
| 833 | Seaside Hospital–Pauline Ash | 1.50 | 3.00 | 4.50 | R |
| 834 | Nurse Annabel–Valerie K. Nelson | 1.50 | 3.00 | 4.50 | R |
| 835 | Part-Time Nurse–Elizabeth Houghton | 1.50 | 3.00 | 4.50 | R |
| 836 | Doctor Phillip–Hilda Nickson | 1.50 | 3.00 | 4.50 | R |
| 837 | Away Went Love–Mary Burchell | 1.50 | 3.00 | 4.50 | R |
| 838 | Dear Dragon–Sara Seale; 1964 | 1.50 | 3.00 | 4.50 | R |
| 839 | Tangle in Sunshine–Rosalind Brett | 1.50 | 3.00 | 4.50 | R |
| 840 | The House of Adriano–Nerina Hilliard | 1.50 | 3.00 | 4.50 | R |
| 841 | Doctor in Brazil–Patricia Fenwick | 1.50 | 3.00 | 4.50 | R |
| 842 | Nurse Barby's Secret Love–Margaret Baumann | 1.50 | 3.00 | 4.50 | R |
| 843 | A Nurse at Barbazon–Kathryn Blair | 1.50 | 3.00 | 4.50 | R |
| 844 | Nurse Alison's Trust–Mary Burchell | 1.50 | 3.00 | 4.50 | R |
| 845 | Flower for a Bride–Barbara Rowan | 1.50 | 3.00 | 4.50 | R |
| 846 | Above the Clouds–Esther Wyndham | 1.50 | 3.00 | 4.50 | R |
| 847 | The Smoke and the Fire–Essie Summers | 1.50 | 3.00 | 4.50 | R |
| 848 | The Keeper's House–Jane Fraser | 1.50 | 3.00 | 4.50 | R |
| 849 | A Nurse for Mr. Henderson–Anne Lorraine | 1.50 | 3.00 | 4.50 | R |
| 850 | Nurse Anne's Impersonation–Caroline Trench | 1.50 | 3.00 | 4.50 | R |
| 851 | Nurse Carol's Decision–Lilian Chisholm | 1.50 | 3.00 | 4.50 | R |
| 852 | Nurse Julia of Queen Frida's–Valerie K. Nelson | 1.50 | 3.00 | 4.50 | R |
| 853 | Sugar Island–Jean S. MacLeod | 1.50 | 3.00 | 4.50 | R |
| 854 | Tender Conquest–Joyce Dingwell | 1.50 | 3.00 | 4.50 | R |
| 855 | Until We Met–Anne Weale | 1.50 | 3.00 | 4.50 | R |
| 856 | Too Young to Marry–Rosalind Brett | 1.50 | 3.00 | 4.50 | R |
| 857 | Island Doctor–Olga Gillman | 1.50 | 3.00 | 4.50 | R |
| 858 | My Surgeon Neighbour–Jane Arbor | 1.50 | 3.00 | 4.50 | R |
| 859 | Nurse in Ireland–Bethea Creese | 1.50 | 3.00 | 4.50 | R |
| 860 | Nurse at the Top–Marion Collin | 1.50 | 3.00 | 4.50 | R |
| 861 | Bewildered Heart–Kathryn Blair | 1.50 | 3.00 | 4.50 | R |
| 862 | Moon over the Alps–Essie Summers | 1.50 | 3.00 | 4.50 | R |
| 863 | The Blue Caribbean–Celine Conway | 1.50 | 3.00 | 4.50 | R |
| 864 | Now and Always–Andrea Blake | 1.50 | 3.00 | 4.50 | R |
| 865 | A Partner for Doctor Phillip–Nora Sanderson | 1.50 | 3.00 | 4.50 | R |
| 866 | Doctor Luke–Lilian Chisholm | 1.50 | 3.00 | 4.50 | R |
| 867 | Dr. Colin's Obsession–Anne Lorraine | 1.50 | 3.00 | 4.50 | R |
| 868 | Emergency for Doctor Bill–Reta Cameron | 1.50 | 3.00 | 4.50 | R |
| 869 | The Reluctant Guest–Rosalind Brett | 1.50 | 3.00 | 4.50 | R |
| 870 | The Dark Stranger–Sara Seale; 1964 | 1.50 | 3.00 | 4.50 | R |
| 871 | Yours To Command–Mary Burchell | 1.50 | 3.00 | 4.50 | R |
| 872 | Haven of the Heart–Averil Ives | 1.50 | 3.00 | 4.50 | R |
| 873 | Nurse Julie of Ward Three–Joan Callender | 1.50 | 3.00 | 4.50 | R |
| 874 | Nurse at Ryeminster–Ivy Ferrari | 1.50 | 3.00 | 4.50 | R |
| 875 | Doctor David Advises–Hilary Wilde | 1.50 | 3.00 | 4.50 | R |
| 876 | Serenade for Doctor Bray–Juliet Shore | 1.50 | 3.00 | 4.50 | R |
| 877 | Dangerous Waters–Rosalind Brett | 1.50 | 3.00 | 4.50 | R |
| 878 | This Kind of Love–Kathryn Blair | 1.50 | 3.00 | 4.50 | R |
| 870 | Sweet to Remember–Anne Weale | 1.50 | 3.00 | 4.50 | R |
| 880 | Once You Have Found Him–Esther Wyndham; 1964 | 1.50 | 3.00 | 4.50 | R |
| 881 | Don't Marry a Doctor–Marguerite Lees; 1965 | 1.50 | 3.00 | 4.50 | R |
| 882 | For Love of a Surgeon–Hilda Nickson | 1.50 | 3.00 | 4.50 | R |
| 883 | Nurse Trudie Is Engaged–Marjorie Norrell | 1.50 | 3.00 | 4.50 | R |
| 884 | Nurse at Cap Flamingo–Violet Winspear | 1.50 | 3.00 | 4.50 | R |
| 885 | At the Villa Massina–Celine Conway | 1.50 | 3.00 | 4.50 | R |
| 886 | Bachelors Galore–Essie Summers | 1.50 | 3.00 | 4.50 | R |
| 887 | Lake of Shadows–Jane Arbor | 1.50 | 3.00 | 4.50 | R |
| 888 | Heart of a Rose–Rachel Lindsay | 1.50 | 3.00 | 4.50 | R |
| 889 | For Love of Doctor David–Lilian Chisholm | 1.00 | 2.00 | 3.00 | R |
| 890 | Two Sisters–Valerie K. Nelson | 1.00 | 2.00 | 3.00 | R |
| 891 | The Hospital World of Susan Wray–Anne Lorraine | 1.00 | 2.00 | 3.00 | R |
| 892 | The Local Doctor–Juliet Armstrong | 1.00 | 2.00 | 3.00 | R |
| 893 | Sweet Deceiver–Kathryn Blair | 1.00 | 2.00 | 3.00 | R |
| 894 | The Third in the House–Joyce Dingwell | 1.00 | 2.00 | 3.00 | R |
| 895 | And Falsely Pledge My Love–Mary Burchell | 1.00 | 2.00 | 3.00 | R |
| 896 | Child Friday–Sara Seale; 1965 | 1.00 | 2.00 | 3.00 | R |
| 897 | Nurse Hilary's Holiday Task–Jan Haye | 1.00 | 2.00 | 3.00 | R |
| 898 | Doctor Robert Comes Around–Nan Asquith | 1.00 | 2.00 | 3.00 | R |
| 899 | Ann Bell, Nursing Aide–Gladys Fullbrook | 1.00 | 2.00 | 3.00 | R |
| 900 | Then Came a Surgeon–Hilda Pressley | 1.00 | 2.00 | 3.00 | R |
| 901 | Hope for Tomorrow–Anne Weale | 1.00 | 2.00 | 3.00 | R |
| 902 | Mountain of Dreams–Barbara Rowan | 1.00 | 2.00 | 3.00 | R |
| 903 | So Loved and So Far–Elizabeth Hoy | 1.00 | 2.00 | 3.00 | R |
| 904 | Moon at the Full–Susan Barrie | 1.00 | 2.00 | 3.00 | R |

HARLEQUIN, *continued*

| 905 | Doctor Down Under–Anne Vinton | 1.00 | 2.00 | 3.00 | R |
|---|---|---|---|---|---|
| 906 | Nurse Molly–Marjorie Norrell | 1.00 | 2.00 | 3.00 | R |
| 907 | Two for the Doctor–Joan Blair | 1.00 | 2.00 | 3.00 | R |
| 908 | Elizabeth Brown, Children's Nurse–Rosalind Brett | 1.00 | 2.00 | 3.00 | R |
| 909 | Desert Doorway–Pamela Kent | 1.00 | 2.00 | 3.00 | R |
| 910 | The Master of Tawhai–Essie Summers | 1.00 | 2.00 | 3.00 | R |
| 911 | Return of Simon–Celine Conway | 1.00 | 2.00 | 3.00 | R |
| 912 | The Dream and the Dancer–Eleanor Farnes | 1.00 | 2.00 | 3.00 | R |
| 913 | Doctors Three–Marion Collin | 1.00 | 2.00 | 3.00 | R |
| 914 | Doctor in Malaya–Anne Weale | 1.00 | 2.00 | 3.00 | R |
| 915 | The Strange Quest of Nurse Anne–Mary Burchell | 1.00 | 2.00 | 3.00 | R |
| 916 | Doctor Vannard's Patients–Pauline Ash | 1.00 | 2.00 | 3.00 | R |
| 917 | The Timber Man–Joyce Dingwell | 1.00 | 2.00 | 3.00 | R |
| 918 | These Delights–Sara Seale | 1.00 | 2.00 | 3.00 | R |
| 919 | Dear Intruder–Jane Arbor | 1.00 | 2.00 | 3.00 | R |
| 920 | The Man at Mulera–Kathryn Blair | 1.00 | 2.00 | 3.00 | R |
| 921 | Desert Doctor–Violet Winspear | 1.00 | 2.00 | 3.00 | R |
| 922 | The Taming of Nurse Conway–Nora Sanderson | 1.00 | 2.00 | 3.00 | R |
| 923 | Kit Cavendish–Private Nurse–Margaret Malcolm | 1.00 | 2.00 | 3.00 | R |
| 924 | Doctor Jonathan–Jan Alan | 1.00 | 2.00 | 3.00 | R |
| 925 | Homeward the Heart–Elizabeth Hoy | 1.00 | 2.00 | 3.00 | R |
| 926 | Mountain Magic–Susan Barrie; 1965 | 1.00 | 2.00 | 3.00 | R |
| 927 | The Scars Shall Fade–Nerina Hilliard | 1.00 | 2.00 | 3.00 | R |
| 928 | The Garden of Don Jose–Rose Burghley | 1.00 | 2.00 | 3.00 | R |
| 929 | Hospital of Bamboo–Juliet Shore | 1.00 | 2.00 | 3.00 | R |
| 930 | Staff Nurse Sally–Marjorie Norrell | 1.00 | 2.00 | 3.00 | R |
| 931 | Charge Nurse–Hilary Neal | 1.00 | 2.00 | 3.00 | R |
| 932 | Nurse's Dilemma–Hilda Pressley | 1.00 | 2.00 | 3.00 | R |
| 933 | Bride in Flight–Essie Summers | 1.00 | 2.00 | 3.00 | R |
| 934 | My Dear Cousin–Celine Conway | 1.00 | 2.00 | 3.00 | R |
| 935 | A House for Sharing–Isobel Chace | 1.00 | 2.00 | 3.00 | R |
| 936 | Tiger Hall–Esther Wyndham | 1.00 | 2.00 | 3.00 | R |
| 937 | The Case for Nurse Sheridan–Nora Sanderson | 1.00 | 2.00 | 3.00 | R |
| 938 | The Doctor Is Indifferent–Juliet Armstrong | 1.00 | 2.00 | 3.00 | R |
| 939 | Doctor's Daughter–Jean S. MacLeod | 1.00 | 2.00 | 3.00 | R |
| 940 | Substitute Nurse–Valerie K. Nelson | 1.00 | 2.00 | 3.00 | R |
| 941 | Mayenga Farm–Kathryn Blair | 1.00 | 2.00 | 3.00 | R |
| 942 | The House by the Lake–Eleanor Farnes | 1.00 | 2.00 | 3.00 | R |
| 943 | Enemy Lover–Pamela Kent | 1.00 | 2.00 | 3.00 | R |
| 944 | Whisper of Doubt–Andrea Blake | 1.00 | 2.00 | 3.00 | R |
| 945 | Doctor Sandy–Margaret Malcolm | 1.00 | 2.00 | 3.00 | R |
| 946 | Nurse Judith's Engagement–Marjorie Norrell | 1.00 | 2.00 | 3.00 | R |
| 947 | Nurse Jane at Sea–Margaret Baumann | 1.00 | 2.00 | 3.00 | R |
| 948 | Islands of Summer–Anne Weale | 1.00 | 2.00 | 3.00 | R |
| 949 | The Third Uncle–Sara Seale | 1.00 | 2.00 | 3.00 | R |
| 950 | Kingfisher Tide–Jane Arbor | 1.00 | 2.00 | 3.00 | R |
| 951 | The Enchanted Trap–Kate Starr | 1.00 | 2.00 | 3.00 | R |
| 952 | A Cottage in Spain–Rosalind Brett | 1.00 | 2.00 | 3.00 | R |
| 953 | Alex Rayner, Dental Nurse–Marjorie Lewty | 1.00 | 2.00 | 3.00 | R |
| 954 | Doctor Westland–Kathryn Blair | 1.00 | 2.00 | 3.00 | R |
| 955 | Nurse with a Problem–Jane Marney | 1.00 | 2.00 | 3.00 | R |
| 956 | Take Me with You–Mary Burchell | 1.00 | 2.00 | 3.00 | R |
| 957 | No Legacy for Lindsay–Essie Summers | 1.00 | 2.00 | 3.00 | R |
| 958 | Young Bar–Jane Fraser; 1965 | 1.00 | 2.00 | 3.00 | R |
| 959 | Who Loves Believes–Elizabeth Hoy | 1.00 | 2.00 | 3.00 | R |
| 960 | Man of Destiny–Rose Burghley | 1.00 | 2.00 | 3.00 | R |
| 961 | Nurse Jane and Cousin Paul–Valerie K. Nelson | 1.00 | 2.00 | 3.00 | R |
| 962 | Nurse Madeline of Eden Grove–Marjorie Norrell | 1.00 | 2.00 | 3.00 | R |
| 963 | Nurse Willow's Ward–Jan Tempest | 1.00 | 2.00 | 3.00 | R |
| 964 | Project Sweetheart–Joyce Dingwell | 1.00 | 2.00 | 3.00 | R |
| 965 | Came a Stranger–Celine Conway | 1.00 | 2.00 | 3.00 | R |
| 966 | Crane Castle–Jean S. MacLeod | 1.00 | 2.00 | 3.00 | R |
| 967 | The Wings of the Morning–Susan Barrie | 1.00 | 2.00 | 3.00 | R |
| 968 | Sweet Brenda–Penelope Walsh | 1.00 | 2.00 | 3.00 | R |
| 969 | Nurse Afloat–Jane Marnay | 1.00 | 2.00 | 3.00 | R |
| 970 | A Challenge to Nurse Honor–Pauline Ash | 1.00 | 2.00 | 3.00 | R |
| 971 | Nurse Rivers' Secret–Anne Durham | 1.00 | 2.00 | 3.00 | R |
| 972 | Barbary Moon–Kathryn Blair | 1.00 | 2.00 | 3.00 | R |
| 973 | Time of Grace–Sara Seale | 1.00 | 2.00 | 3.00 | R |

| 974 | Night of the Hurricane–Andrea Blake | 1.00 | 2.00 | 3.00 | R |
|---|---|---|---|---|---|
| 975 | Sister of the Housemaster–Eleanor Farnes | 1.00 | 2.00 | 3.00 | R |
| 976 | Flamingoes on the Lake–Isobel Chace; 1965 | 1.00 | 2.00 | 3.00 | R |

# HART BOOKS
## Horace Hart, Inc.

### Digest Size

| K1 | The House of Creeping Horror–George F. Worts | 2.00 | 4.00 | 6.00 | M |
|---|---|---|---|---|---|
| K2 | The Diamonds of Death–Borden Chase; aka Blue, White and Perfect | 1.50 | 3.00 | 4.50 | M |

# (HERCULES)
## Hercules Publishing Corporation

### Digest Size

| nn | D–As in Dead–Lawrence Treat; 1943 | 4.00 | 8.00 | 12.00 | M |
|---|---|---|---|---|---|

# HILLMAN BOOKS
## Hillman Periodicals, Inc.

| nn(1) | Let's Make Mary–Jack Hanley; 1948 | 2.00 | 4.00 | 6.00 | E |
|---|---|---|---|---|---|
| 2 | Tumbling River Range–W.C. Tuttle | 2.50 | 5.00 | 7.50 | W |
| 3 | Casanova's Memoirs–Giacomo Casanova | 2.00 | 4.00 | 6.00 | E |
| 4 | Ironheart–William MacLeod Raine | 2.50 | 5.00 | 7.50 | W |
| 5 | Bluffer's Luck–W.C. Tuttle | 2.50 | 5.00 | 7.50 | W |
| 6 | Riders of Buck River–William MacLeod Raine | 2.50 | 5.00 | 7.50 | W |
| 7 | Sex and Marriage Problems–E.B. Taylor | 2.50 | 5.00 | 7.50 | NF |
| 8 | I Chose Freedom–Victor Kravchenko | 2.50 | 5.00 | 7.50 | NF |
| 9 | Guns on the High Mesa–Arthur Henry Gooden | 2.50 | 5.00 | 7.50 | W |
| 10 | Murder under Construction–Sue MacVeigh | 2.50 | 5.00 | 7.50 | M |
| 11 | Steve Yeager–William MacLeod Raine | 2.50 | 5.00 | 7.50 | W |
| 12 | Ten Droll Tales–Honore de Balzac; includes some science fiction/fantasy | 2.50 | 5.00 | 7.50 | |
| 13 | Hell in the Saddle–Ed Earl Repp | 2.50 | 5.00 | 7.50 | W |
| 14 | The Physiology of Love–Remy de Gourmont; 1949 | 2.50 | 5.00 | 7.50 | NF |
| 15 | Hanging Judge–Bruce Hamilton | 2.50 | 5.00 | 7.50 | M |
| 16 | Gold–Clarence Budington Kelland | 2.00 | 4.00 | 6.00 | W |
| 17 | Gun Hawk–Ed Earl Repp | 2.50 | 5.00 | 7.50 | W |
| 18 | Collusion–Theodore D. Irwin | 2.50 | 5.00 | 7.50 | NF |
| 19 | The Red Rider of Smoky Range–William Colt MacDonald | 3.00 | 6.00 | 9.00 | W |
| 20 | Dark Hazard–W.R. Burnett | 3.00 | 6.00 | 9.00 | M |
| 21 | Marriage, Sex, and Family Problems and How to Solve Them–John J. Anthony | 2.50 | 5.00 | 7.50 | NF |
| 22 | The Shadowed Trail–Arthur Henry Gooden | 2.50 | 5.00 | 7.50 | W |

*Hillman 5, Hillman 38, Hillman 130.*

| | | V/Good | Fine | N/Mint |
|---|---|---|---|---|

**HILLMAN BOOKS**, *continued*

| # | Title | V/Good | Fine | N/Mint | |
|---|---|---|---|---|---|
| 23 | 42 Days for Murder–Roger Torrey | 2.00 | 4.00 | 6.00 | M |
| 24 | The Trail of Danger–William MacLeod Raine | 2.50 | 5.00 | 7.50 | W |
| 25 | The Deputy of Carabina–William Colt MacDonald | 2.50 | 5.00 | 7.50 | W |
| 26 | Straws in the Wind–W.C. Tuttle | 2.50 | 5.00 | 7.50 | W |
| 27 | Dead on Arrival | 2.00 | 4.00 | 6.00 | |
| 28 | The Redhead from Sun Dog–W.C. Tuttle. Note: Same cover as Western Novel Classic 89 | 2.50 | 5.00 | 7.50 | W |
| 29 | Big-Town Round Up–William MacLeod Raine | 2.50 | 5.00 | 7.50 | W |
| 30 | Buzzard Tracks–Tom J. Hopkins | 2.50 | 5.00 | 7.50 | W |
| 31 | Wheels in the Dust–William Colt MacDonald | 2.50 | 5.00 | 7.50 | W |
| 32 | Bear Paw–Dane Coolidge | 2.50 | 5.00 | 7.50 | W |
| 33 | Rusty Guns–Bliss Lomax | 2.50 | 5.00 | 7.50 | W |
| 34 | King of Crazy River–William Colt MacDonald | 2.50 | 5.00 | 7.50 | W |
| 35 | Smoky River–Tom Roan | 2.50 | 5.00 | 7.50 | W |
| 36 | King of the Bush–William MacLeod Raine | 2.50 | 5.00 | 7.50 | W |
| 37 | Hashknife of Stormy River–W.C. Tuttle | 2.50 | 5.00 | 7.50 | W |
| 38 | Nothing More Than Murder–Jim Thompson | 30.00 | 60.00 | 90.00 | M |
| 39 | Meet Mr. Mulliner–P.G. Wodehouse | 2.50 | 5.00 | 7.50 | H |
| 40 | Trouble at the JHC–W.C. Tuttle | 2.50 | 5.00 | 7.50 | W |
| 41 | The Dying Earth–Jack Vance; 1st ed. 1950 | 75.00 | 150.00 | 225.00 | SF |
| 42 | Roaring River–William MacLeod Raine | 2.50 | 5.00 | 7.50 | W |
| 43 | Arizona Nights–Stewart Edward White | 2.50 | 5.00 | 7.50 | W |
| 44 | The Trusty Knaves–Eugene Manlove Rhodes | 2.50 | 5.00 | 7.50 | W |
| 45 | Story of a Russian Spy–Alexander Foote; aka Handbook for Spies | 2.50 | 5.00 | 7.50 | B |
| 46 | Copper Streak Trail–Eugene Manlove Rhodes | 2.50 | 5.00 | 7.50 | W |
| 47 | Scattergun Ranch–Tom J. Hopkins | 2.50 | 5.00 | 7.50 | W |
| 48 | Father of the Bride–Edward Streeter; movie tie-in | 3.50 | 7.00 | 10.50 | |
| 100 | The Witnesses–Georges Simenon | 1.50 | 3.00 | 4.50 | M |
| 101 | Texas Man–William MacLeod Raine; 1957 | 1.50 | 3.00 | 4.50 | W |
| 102 | Lightning Swift–William Colt MacDonald | 1.50 | 3.00 | 4.50 | W |
| 103 | The Short Night–Russell Turner; 1957 | 1.50 | 3.00 | 4.50 | |
| 104 | Rimrock Town–William Heuman | 1.50 | 3.00 | 4.50 | W |
| 105 | The Watchmaker–Georges Simenon | 1.50 | 3.00 | 4.50 | M |
| 106 | Sex without Guilt–Albert Ellis; 1959 | 1.50 | 3.00 | 4.50 | NF |
| 107 | The Tormentors–Robert Payne | 1.50 | 3.00 | 4.50 | |
| 108 | Roy Bean: Law West of the Pecos–C.L. Sonnichsen | 1.50 | 3.00 | 4.50 | NF |
| 109 | Horses, Women and Guns–Nelson Nye | 1.50 | 3.00 | 4.50 | W |
| 110 | The Greatest Lover in the World–Alex Austin | 1.50 | 3.00 | 4.50 | |
| 111 | Morocco Episode–William Brothers; c-Maguire | 2.00 | 4.00 | 6.00 | M |
| 112 | The Sins of Skid Row–John White | 1.50 | 3.00 | 4.50 | E |
| 113 | Soldier's Women–Stan Smith | 1.50 | 3.00 | 4.50 | |
| 114 | Temptation in a Southern Town–William L. Heath | 2.00 | 4.00 | 6.00 | E |
| 115 | Dead Warrior–John Myers Myers | 2.00 | 4.00 | 6.00 | W |
| 116 | A Strange Innocence–Charles Mergendahl | 1.50 | 3.00 | 4.50 | |
| 117 | Cassandra–Frances Clippinger | 1.50 | 3.00 | 4.50 | E |
| 118 | The Jayhawkers–Saul Cooper; movie tie-in | 1.50 | 3.00 | 4.50 | W |
| 119 | A Killer's Kiss–Hal Ellson | 1.50 | 3.00 | 4.50 | JD |
| 120 | Let's Make Mary–Jack Hanley | 1.50 | 3.00 | 4.50 | |
| 121 | The Sinful One–Edwina Mark | 1.50 | 3.00 | 4.50 | |
| 122 | Sixgun Helltown–Charles M. Martin; aka Sixgun Town | 1.50 | 3.00 | 4.50 | W |
| 123 | Savage Conqueror–Davenport Steward | 1.50 | 3.00 | 4.50 | A |
| 124 | The Sinful Love–Calvin Turner | 1.50 | 3.00 | 4.50 | |
| 125 | Death Is Confidential–Lawrence Larlar | 1.50 | 3.00 | 4.50 | M |
| 126 | And Then Murder–Julius Fast | 1.50 | 3.00 | 4.50 | M |
| 127 | Maverick Gun–Barry Cord; aka Gun-Proddy Hombre | 1.50 | 3.00 | 4.50 | W |
| 128 | Elisa–Edmond de Goncourt | 1.50 | 3.00 | 4.50 | |
| 129 | The Moments Between–Robert C. Ackworth; 1959 | 1.50 | 3.00 | 4.50 | E |
| 130 | The Elvis Presley Story–James Gregory; 1st ed. 1960 | 12.50 | 25.00 | 37.50 | B |
| 131 | An Acre of Love–Alice Brennan | 1.50 | 3.00 | 4.50 | |
| 132 | The Last Bullet–Nelson C. Nye | 1.50 | 3.00 | 4.50 | W |
| 133 | Dillinger–Saul Cooper; movie tie-in | 1.50 | 3.00 | 4.50 | NF |
| 134 | Warrior's Mistress–Evelyn Anthony | 1.50 | 3.00 | 4.50 | A |
| 135 | The Intimate Ones–Bonnie Golightly | 2.00 | 4.00 | 6.00 | E |
| 136 | To Kill Again–Rex Stout; aka The Rubber Band | 1.50 | 3.00 | 4.50 | M |
| 137 | Gunsmoke Territory–Philip Ketchum | 1.50 | 3.00 | 4.50 | W |
| 138 | Whispered Sex | 1.50 | 3.00 | 4.50 | E |
| 139 | A Killer's Bargain–Dean Owen | 1.50 | 3.00 | 4.50 | W |
| 140 | The Devil Sword–Kevin Matthews (Gardner F. Fox) | 1.50 | 3.00 | 4.50 | A |
| 141 | Sextasy–ed. Ed Lowe | 1.50 | 3.00 | 4.50 | H |
| 142 | The Agony of Love–Claude Roy | 1.50 | 3.00 | 4.50 | E |
| 143 | You Killed Elizabeth–Brett Halliday | 2.00 | 4.00 | 6.00 | M |
| 144 | The Angry Horsemen–Lewis B. Patten | 1.50 | 3.00 | 4.50 | W |
| 145 | A Lover's Blade–James M. Fox | 1.50 | 3.00 | 4.50 | A |
| 146 | A Deadly Affair–Ed Lacy | 1.50 | 3.00 | 4.50 | M |
| 147 | Shield for a Killer–Al Cody | 1.50 | 3.00 | 4.50 | W |
| 148 | The Forbidden–Livia de Stefani; aka Black Grapes | 1.50 | 3.00 | 4.50 | |
| 149 | The Strange Diagnosis–Maxence Van der Meersch; aka Bodies and Souls | 1.00 | 2.00 | 3.00 | E |
| 150 | Smoke of the Texan–Paul Evan Lehman | 1.50 | 3.00 | 4.50 | W |
| 151 | Ruby MacLaine–John Roeburt | 1.50 | 3.00 | 4.50 | E |
| 153 | The Bitter Passion–John W. Wadleigh | 1.00 | 2.00 | 3.00 | |
| 154 | Scandal in Suburbia–Gardner F. Fox | 1.50 | 3.00 | 4.50 | E |
| 155 | The Outlaw Breed–Lee Floren | 1.50 | 3.00 | 4.50 | W |
| 156 | The Awakening–John Cantwell | 1.00 | 2.00 | 3.00 | E |
| 157 | The Violent Years–Melvin H. Purvis | 1.50 | 3.00 | 4.50 | NF |
| 158 | A Taste of Passion–Kay Martin | 1.00 | 2.00 | 3.00 | E |
| 159 | The Lawless Guns–Bliss Lomax | 1.50 | 3.00 | 4.50 | W |
| 160 | Love among the Damned–James McGovern; aka No Ruined Castles | 1.00 | 2.00 | 3.00 | E |
| 162 | The Shades of Evil–Bonnie Golightly; 1960 | 2.00 | 4.00 | 6.00 | E |
| 163 | Blood and Roses–Robin Carlisle | 1.00 | 2.00 | 3.00 | |
| 164 | Gunfight at the O.K. Corral–Nelson C. Nye | 1.50 | 3.00 | 4.50 | W |
| 165 | Kriegle Prisoner of War–Kenneth W. Simmons | 1.50 | 3.00 | 4.50 | C |
| 166 | Hangman's Country–Lewis B. Patten | 1.25 | 2.50 | 3.75 | W |
| 167 | An End to Passion–Hervée Bazin | 1.00 | 2.00 | 3.00 | |
| 170 | Auschwitz–Otto Kurst | 1.00 | 2.00 | 3.00 | NF |
| 171 | The Low Calory Cookbook–Bernard Koten | 1.25 | 2.50 | 3.75 | NF |
| 172 | The Gifts of Love–Andrina Iverson | 1.00 | 2.00 | 3.00 | |
| 173 | Candy Frost, Emergency Nurse–Ethel Hamill | .75 | 1.50 | 2.25 | R |
| 174 | The Return–Herbert Mitgang | 1.00 | 2.00 | 3.00 | |
| 175 | Bedeviled–Raymond Mason | 1.00 | 2.00 | 3.00 | E |
| 176 | Edge of the Badlands–Joseph Chadwick | 1.00 | 2.00 | 3.00 | W |
| 177 | Sex and Love–Frank S. Caprio, MD | 1.00 | 2.00 | 3.00 | E |
| 178 | Rebel Ramrod–Dean Owen | 1.25 | 2.50 | 3.75 | W |
| 181 | Isabelle–Jean Forton; 1960 | 1.00 | 2.00 | 3.00 | E |
| 182 | None So Blind–Mitchell Wilson | 1.00 | 2.00 | 3.00 | |
| 183 | The Long Rope–William O. Turner | 1.25 | 2.50 | 3.75 | W |
| 184 | City of Vice–John Gosling & Douglas Warner; aka The Shame of a City | 1.25 | 2.50 | 3.75 | |
| 185 | Nina Grant, Pediatric Nurse–Patti Stone | .75 | 1.50 | 2.25 | R |
| 186 | The Captives–Michael Wells; 1961 | 1.00 | 2.00 | 3.00 | E |

Hillman 135, Hillman Detective Novel 1, Holloway House HH103.

**HILLMAN BOOKS,** *continued*

| | | V/Good | Fine | N/Mint | |
|---|---|---|---|---|---|
| S188 | How to Buy Real Estate for Spectacular Profits–Clyde T. Cadwallader | .75 | 1.50 | 2.25 | NF |
| 189 | Colt '60–Paul Evan Lehman | 1.25 | 2.50 | 3.75 | W |
| 190 | Payment in Sin–Kay Martin | 1.25 | 2.50 | 3.75 | E |
| 191 | The Dedicated–Willa Gibbs | 1.00 | 2.00 | 3.00 | |
| 193 | Murder, Murder, Murder–ed. Helen McCloy & Brett Halliday | 1.50 | 3.00 | 4.50 | M |
| 194 | The Taste of Ashes–Bill Stern & Oscar Fraley | 1.25 | 2.50 | 3.75 | |
| 195 | Bachelor's Guide to Women–Pierre du Milieu | 1.25 | 2.50 | 3.75 | |
| 196 | Always Love a Stranger–Roger Davis | 1.00 | 2.00 | 3.00 | E |
| 197 | Montana Gun–Louis Trimble | 1.25 | 2.50 | 3.75 | W |
| F198 | Stephen Greene–William Kendall Clarke | 1.25 | 2.50 | 3.75 | |
| F199 | Year the World Went Mad–Allen Churchill | .75 | 1.50 | 2.25 | NF |
| 200 | Slade–Barry Cords; aka Starlight Range | 1.00 | 2.00 | 3.00 | W |
| 201 | The Comforts of the Damned–Wingate Froscher | .75 | 1.50 | 2.25 | E |
| F202 | The Flute of Love–John Berry | 1.25 | 2.50 | 3.75 | |
| 203 | Street of Brass–Fielden Farrington | .75 | 1.50 | 2.25 | |
| 204 | The Golden Image–Ethel Hamill | .75 | 1.50 | 2.25 | R |
| 205 | Cardboard Lover–Kevin Matthews (Gardner F. Fox); 1961 | 1.25 | 2.50 | 3.75 | E |

## HILLMAN DETECTIVE NOVEL

### Hillman Periodicals, Inc.

| | | V/Good | Fine | N/Mint | |
|---|---|---|---|---|---|
| 1 | The Arabian Nights Murder–John Dickson Carr; 1943 | 6.00 | 12.00 | 18.00 | M |

## HIP BOOKS

### Hip Books, Inc.

| | | V/Good | Fine | N/Mint | |
|---|---|---|---|---|---|
| 1 | The Mystery of the Red Suitcase–Lula M. Day; 1946 | 7.50 | 15.00 | 22.50 | M |

## HOLLOWAY HOUSE

### Holloway House Publishing Company

| | | V/Good | Fine | N/Mint | |
|---|---|---|---|---|---|
| HH101 | The Trial of Adolf Eichmann–Dewey W. Linze; 1961 | 1.00 | 2.00 | 3.00 | NF |
| HH102 | Hemingway: Life and Death of a Giant–Kurt Singer | 1.50 | 3.00 | 4.50 | B |
| HH103 | The Many Loves of Casanova, Volume 1–Giacomo Casanova | 1.50 | 3.00 | 4.50 | E |
| HH104 | The Many Loves of Casanova, Volume 2–Giacomo Casanova | 1.50 | 3.00 | 4.50 | E |
| | Note: HH103 and 104 were issued as an illustrated boxed set | | | | |
| | Complete set, boxed | 15.00 | 30.00 | 45.00 | E |
| HH105 | Hollywood Screwballs–Leo Guild; 1962 | 1.50 | 3.00 | 4.50 | NF |
| HH106 | The Best of Adam–ed. Luthar Ashley; 1962 | 1.50 | 3.00 | 4.50 | |
| HH107 | How to Win at Cards, Dice, Races, Roulette–Mike Goodman; 1963 | 1.00 | 2.00 | 3.00 | NF |
| HH108 | I Am Not Ashamed–Barbara Payton | 3.00 | 6.00 | 9.00 | NF |
| HH109 | Adult View of Love and Sex | 1.00 | 2.00 | 3.00 | |
| HH110 | Jayne Mansfield's Wild, Wild World–Jayne Mansfield & Mickey Hargitay | 7.50 | 15.00 | 22.50 | B |
| HH112 | Ladies on Call–Lee Francis | 1.00 | 2.00 | 3.00 | B |
| HH113 | The Tortured Sex–John S. Yankowski & Herman K. Wolff | 1.00 | 2.00 | 3.00 | NF |
| HH114 | The Yankowski Report on Premarital Sex–John S. Yankowski | 1.00 | 2.00 | 3.00 | NF |
| HH115 | Only When I Laugh–Jim Backus | 1.50 | 3.00 | 4.50 | H |
| HH116 | Satyricon: Memoirs of a Lusty Roman–trans. Paul J. Gillette | 1.00 | 2.00 | 3.00 | E |
| HH117 | Prostitution, U.S.A.–Mike Bruno & David B. Weiss | 1.00 | 2.00 | 3.00 | NF |
| HH118 | An Uncensored History of Pornography–Paul J. Gillette, PhD | 1.00 | 2.00 | 3.00 | NF |
| HH119 | My Name Is Leona Gage, Will Somebody Please Help Me?–Leona Gage | 4.00 | 8.00 | 12.00 | B |

| | | V/Good | Fine | N/Mint | |
|---|---|---|---|---|---|
| HH120 | Inside the Dodgers | 1.50 | 3.00 | 4.50 | S |
| HH121 | Point Your Tail in the Right Direction–Jeri Emmett | 2.00 | 4.00 | 6.00 | B |
| HH122 | Some Like it Dark–Kipp Washington as told to Leo Guild | 1.00 | 2.00 | 3.00 | E |
| HH123 | The Complete Marquis de Sade, Volume 1–Marquis de Sade | 1.00 | 2.00 | 3.00 | E |
| HH124 | The Complete Marquis de Sade, Volume 2–Marquis de Sade | 1.00 | 2.00 | 3.00 | E |
| | Note: HH123 and 124 were issued as an illustrated boxed set | | | | |
| | Complete set, boxed | 4.00 | 8.00 | 12.00 | E |
| HH125 | My Life in Crime | 1.00 | 2.00 | 3.00 | NF |
| HH126 | Role of the Dominant Female in American Society–Dr. Hermann K. Wolff | 1.00 | 2.00 | 3.00 | |
| HH127 | Get Me Gladys!–Cy Rice; 1966 | 1.00 | 2.00 | 3.00 | B |
| HH128 | Compulsive Desire–Dr. Hermann K. Wolff | 1.00 | 2.00 | 3.00 | NF |
| HH129 | Adam's Best Fiction–ed. Thomas H. Schulz | 1.50 | 3.00 | 4.50 | |
| HH130 | Psychodynamics of Unconventional Sex Behavior–Paul J. Gillette, PhD | 1.00 | 2.00 | 3.00 | NF |
| HH131 | Ribald Russian Classics | 1.00 | 2.00 | 3.00 | E |
| HH132 | Adam's Swinging Party Humor | 1.50 | 3.00 | 4.50 | H |
| HH133 | Memoirs of Dolly Morton | 1.00 | 2.00 | 3.00 | B |
| HH134 | Grushenka: Three Times a Woman–anon. | 1.00 | 2.00 | 3.00 | E |
| HH135 | Francon Duclos: Memoirs of a Paris Madam–Marquis de Sade | 1.00 | 2.00 | 3.00 | E |
| HH136 | Children in Danger: The Molesters–Cy Rice | 1.00 | 2.00 | 3.00 | NF |
| HH137 | De Figuris Veneris–Friedrich Karl Forberg | 1.00 | 2.00 | 3.00 | NF |
| HH138 | Venus in India–Captain Charles Devereaux | 1.00 | 2.00 | 3.00 | E |
| HH139 | Pimp: Story of My Life–Iceberg Slim | 1.00 | 2.00 | 3.00 | B |
| HH140 | The Lopinson Case–Paul J. Gillette | 1.00 | 2.00 | 3.00 | NF |
| HH141 | Skouras: King of Fox Studios–Carlo Curti | 1.50 | 3.00 | 4.50 | B |
| HH142 | Art and Science of Lovemaking–Paul J. Gillette, PhD | 1.00 | 2.00 | 3.00 | NF |
| HH143 | Nine Holes of Jade–Su-Ling | 1.00 | 2.00 | 3.00 | B |
| HH144 | The Harem Omnibus–anon. (Lustful Turk & A Night in a Moorish Harem) | 1.00 | 2.00 | 3.00 | E |
| HH145 | Debauched Hospodar–Guillaume Apollinaire | 1.00 | 2.00 | 3.00 | E |
| HH146 | Pauline: Memoirs of a Singer–anon. | 1.00 | 2.00 | 3.00 | B |
| HH147 | Memoirs of a Russian Princess–anon. | 1.00 | 2.00 | 3.00 | B |
| HH148 | The Adventures of Father Silas & Flesh and Bone–Beauregard de Farniente & Henry Crannach | 1.00 | 2.00 | 3.00 | E |
| HH149 | 1600 Floogle Street–Don McGuire | 1.00 | 2.00 | 3.00 | H |
| HH150 | The Nigger Bible–Robert H. deCoy | 1.00 | 2.00 | 3.00 | |
| HH151 | Trick Baby–Iceberg Slim | 1.00 | 2.00 | 3.00 | B |
| HH152 | Mistress of Cuba–Rita Benuto | 1.00 | 2.00 | 3.00 | B |
| HH153 | A Place in Hell–H.R. Kaye | 1.00 | 2.00 | 3.00 | B |
| HH154 | The Hellcats–Robert F. Slatzer | 1.00 | 2.00 | 3.00 | B |
| HH155 | Robert Francis Kennedy–Lawrence J. Quirk | 1.00 | 2.00 | 3.00 | NF |
| HH156 | Swingers Guide for the Single Girl–Marie & Hector Roget | 1.00 | 2.00 | 3.00 | NF |
| HH157 | The Nun–Denis Diderot | 1.00 | 2.00 | 3.00 | E |
| HH158 | Honey Man–Mike Panos | 1.00 | 2.00 | 3.00 | E |
| HH159 | Freak Show Man–Jerry Holtman | 1.00 | 2.00 | 3.00 | B |
| HH160 | To Kill a Black Man–Louis E. Lomax | 1.00 | 2.00 | 3.00 | B |
| HH161 | Legion of Outcasts–Hurk Davis | 1.00 | 2.00 | 3.00 | NF |
| HH162 | Divorcee a Go-Go–Elaine Stanton | 1.00 | 2.00 | 3.00 | B |
| HH163 | Honolulu Madam–Iolana Mitsuko | 1.00 | 2.00 | 3.00 | B |
| HH164 | The Cherry Dance–Tami Miyoshi | 1.00 | 2.00 | 3.00 | B |
| HH165 | The Day Television Died–Don McGuire | 1.00 | 2.00 | 3.00 | H |
| HH166 | The Big Black Fire–Robert H. deCoy | 1.00 | 2.00 | 3.00 | B |
| HH167 | Alcatraz: Number 1172–Steve Ellis | 1.00 | 2.00 | 3.00 | NF |
| HH168 | The Studio–Leo Guild | 1.00 | 2.00 | 3.00 | B |
| HH169 | Nights of Malta–Gina Zammit | 1.00 | 2.00 | 3.00 | NF |
| HH170 | The Devil's Brand–Paul Gillette | 1.00 | 2.00 | 3.00 | E |
| HH171 | Blood on the Rhine–Nick Hurk | 1.00 | 2.00 | 3.00 | NF |
| HH172 | Damned Spot–Barry Cuff | 1.00 | 2.00 | 3.00 | |
| HH173 | The Girl Who Loved Black–Leo Guild | 1.00 | 2.00 | 3.00 | |
| HH174 | The Goddess Stick–Aaron Flood | 1.00 | 2.00 | 3.00 | E |
| HH175 | All the Loving Couples–Leo Gordon; movie tie-in | 3.00 | 6.00 | 9.00 | E |
| HH176 | Mama Black Widow–Iceberg Slim | 1.00 | 2.00 | 3.00 | |
| HH177 | A Memory without Pain–Scott Flohr | 1.00 | 2.00 | 3.00 | E |

| | V/Good | Fine | N/Mint | |
|---|---|---|---|---|

| | | V/Good | Fine | N/Mint | |
|---|---|---|---|---|---|
| HH178 | Three Sisters and Their Mother–anon. | 1.00 | 2.00 | 3.00 | E |
| HH179 | The Right Fuse–Barry Cuff; 1969 | 1.00 | 2.00 | 3.00 | E |
| HH180 | The Starlet–Leo Guild; movie tie-in | 2.00 | 4.00 | 6.00 | E |
| HH181 | Tacuara!–Olga Rich | 1.00 | 2.00 | 3.00 | |
| HH182 | Day and Night–Pierre Berg | 1.00 | 2.00 | 3.00 | E |

# (HOWARD)
## F.E. Howard Publications
### Digest Size
### (Canadian)

| | | V/Good | Fine | N/Mint | |
|---|---|---|---|---|---|
| nn | I Hate You to Death–Keith Edgar; 1944 | 3.50 | 7.00 | 10.50 | M |
| nn | True Mysteries and Murders–anthology | 3.50 | 7.00 | 10.50 | NF |
| nn | Honduras Double Cross–Keith Edgar | 3.50 | 7.00 | 10.50 | M |
| nn | The Incendiary Blonde–Keith Edgar | 3.50 | 7.00 | 10.50 | M |

# THE INFANTRY JOURNAL
## The Infantry Journal

| | | V/Good | Fine | N/Mint | |
|---|---|---|---|---|---|
| J101 | Boomerang–William C. Shambliss; 1945 | 1.50 | 3.00 | 4.50 | A |
| J102 | The U.S. Marines on Iwo Jima; 1945 | 1.50 | 3.00 | 4.50 | NF |

# INTIMATE NOVELS
## Design Publishing Company
### Digest Size

| | | V/Good | Fine | N/Mint | |
|---|---|---|---|---|---|
| 1 | Wayward Bride–Paul Gaillard; 1950; aka One Unfaithful Year | 3.00 | 6.00 | 9.00 | E |
| 2 | French Model–Cecil Barr; aka Daffodil | 3.00 | 6.00 | 9.00 | E |
| 3 | Cheap Hotel–Gerald Foster; aka Night Clerk | 3.00 | 6.00 | 9.00 | E |
| 4 | Plaything–Gordon Semple | 3.00 | 6.00 | 9.00 | E |
| 5 | Secrets of a Society Doctor–Jerry Cole | 3.00 | 6.00 | 9.00 | E |
| 6 | Divorce Racket Girls–Jed Anthony | 3.00 | 6.00 | 9.00 | E |
| 7 | Greenwich Village Girl–Robert Norcross | 6.00 | 12.00 | 18.00 | E |
| 8 | Gin Wedding–Ann Lawrence | 3.00 | 6.00 | 9.00 | E |
| 9 | Temptress–Elliot Brewster | 3.00 | 6.00 | 9.00 | E |
| 10 | Dangerous Trade–Charles Thornton | 3.00 | 6.00 | 9.00 | E |
| 11 | Swamp Girl–Perry Lindsay (Peggy Gaddis). Note: Same cover as Beacon B159 | 4.00 | 8.00 | 12.00 | E |
| 12 | Seventh Wife–Barry de Forest | 3.00 | 6.00 | 9.00 | E |
| 13 | Local Talent–Florence Stonebraker | 3.00 | 6.00 | 9.00 | E |
| 14 | Off Limits–Bruce Manning | 3.00 | 6.00 | 9.00 | E |
| 15 | Private Chauffeur–N.R. De Mexico | 3.00 | 6.00 | 9.00 | E |
| 16 | Lust for Love–Florence Stonebraker | 3.00 | 6.00 | 9.00 | E |
| 17 | The Sins of Janet Benson, Showgirl–Ben West | 3.00 | 6.00 | 9.00 | E |
| 18 | Hot Lips–Jack Hanley | 2.50 | 5.00 | 7.50 | E |
| 19 | Mail-Order Passion–Hall Bennett; c-Gross. Note: Same cover as Beacon B134 | 3.00 | 6.00 | 9.00 | E |
| 20 | Pleasure Alley–Ralph Carter; orig. 1952. Note: Same cover as Falcon 43 and Beacon B181 and B307 | 2.50 | 5.00 | 7.50 | E |

*Howard unnumbered, Intimate 18, Intimate 34.*

| | | V/Good | Fine | N/Mint | |
|---|---|---|---|---|---|
| 21 | Dr. Randolph's Women–Thomas Stone | 3.00 | 6.00 | 9.00 | E |
| 22 | Office Wife–Richard Grant; aka Teaser | 3.00 | 6.00 | 9.00 | E |
| 23 | Ex-Mistress–Thomas Stone | 3.00 | 6.00 | 9.00 | E |
| 24 | The Whipping Room–Florenz Branch | 4.00 | 8.00 | 12.00 | E |
| 25 | Triangle of Sin–Bruce Manning | 3.00 | 6.00 | 9.00 | E |
| 26 | Very Private Secretary–Jack Hanley | 3.00 | 6.00 | 9.00 | E |
| 27 | Tramp Girl–Thomas Stone | 3.00 | 6.00 | 9.00 | E |
| 28 | Back Country Woman–Evans Wall; aka A Time to Sow | 3.00 | 6.00 | 9.00 | E |
| 29 | Shameless Wife–Wayne Way | 3.00 | 6.00 | 9.00 | E |
| 30 | Tent-Show Bride–Jack Hanley. Note: Same cover as Beacon B238 | 3.00 | 6.00 | 9.00 | E |
| 31 | Naked Desire–Henry Lewis Nixon; orig. 1953 | 3.00 | 6.00 | 9.00 | E |
| 32 | Basement Gang–David Williams; orig. 1953. Note: Same cover as Stallion 213 and virtually identical to Beacon B260 | 10.00 | 20.00 | 30.00 | E |
| 33 | Scarlet City–Winchell Barry | 3.00 | 6.00 | 9.00 | E |
| 34 | Shack Woman–Kathie Reed | 3.00 | 6.00 | 9.00 | E |
| 35 | Private Practice–Thomas Stone | 3.00 | 6.00 | 9.00 | E |
| 36 | Waterfront Blonde–Gordon Semple | 3.00 | 6.00 | 9.00 | E |
| 37 | New York Model–Jack Hanley | 3.00 | 6.00 | 9.00 | E |
| 38 | Lily of New Orleans–Beth Brown; aka For Men Only | 3.00 | 6.00 | 9.00 | E |
| 39 | Dr. Breyton's Wife–Florenz Branch | 3.00 | 6.00 | 9.00 | E |
| 40 | Crusher's Girl–Gordon Semple | 3.00 | 6.00 | 9.00 | E |
| 41 | Forbidden Desire–Kathie Reed | 3.00 | 6.00 | 9.00 | E |
| 42 | Village Girl–Kathie Reed | 3.00 | 6.00 | 9.00 | E |
| 43 | The Marriage Rite–Evans Wall | 3.00 | 6.00 | 9.00 | E |
| 44 | Miami Widow–Gene Harvey | 3.00 | 6.00 | 9.00 | E |
| 45 | Pound of Flesh–Simms Albert | 3.00 | 6.00 | 9.00 | E |
| 46 | Trailer Camp Girl–Doug Dupperault | 3.00 | 6.00 | 9.00 | E |
| 47 | Red-Headed Nurse–Thomas Stone | 3.00 | 6.00 | 9.00 | E |
| 48 | Cafe Society Sinner–Bruce Manning; orig. 1953 | 3.00 | 6.00 | 9.00 | E |
| 49 | Strange Circle–Gale Sydney; orig. 1953. Note: Same cover as Stallion 208 and Beacon B151 | 3.00 | 6.00 | 9.00 | E |
| 51 | Ship's Doctor–Henry Lewis Nixon; orig. 1954 | 3.00 | 6.00 | 9.00 | E |
| 52 | Gutter Star–Dorine B. Clark. Note: Same cover as Stallion 210 and Beacon B135 and B377 | 3.00 | 6.00 | 9.00 | E |
| 53 | Girl Stowaway–Roy Booth | 3.00 | 6.00 | 9.00 | E |
| 54 | Bachelor Girl–Dorine Clark | 3.00 | 6.00 | 9.00 | E |
| 55 | Secret's of a Doctor's Bride–Henry Lewis Nixon | 3.00 | 6.00 | 9.00 | E |
| 56 | Odd Girl–Hal R. Moore | 3.00 | 6.00 | 9.00 | E |

# JACKET LIBRARY
## National Home Library Foundation

| | | V/Good | Fine | N/Mint | |
|---|---|---|---|---|---|
| nn(1) | Treasure Island–R.L. Stevenson; 1932 | 2.50 | 5.00 | 7.50 | A |
| nn(2) | The New Testament | 2.50 | 5.00 | 7.50 | |
| nn(3) | Green Mansions–W.H. Hudson | 3.00 | 6.00 | 9.00 | F |
| nn(4) | The Way of All Flesh–Samuel Butler | 2.00 | 4.00 | 6.00 | |
| nn(5) | The Merchant of Venice–William Shakespeare | 2.00 | 4.00 | 6.00 | |
| nn(6) | Emerson's Essays–Ralph Waldo Emerson | 2.00 | 4.00 | 6.00 | |
| nn(7) | Pierre Goriot–Honore de Balzac | 2.00 | 4.00 | 6.00 | |
| nn(8) | Alice in Wonderland, Through the Looking Glass, Hunting of the Shark–Lewis Carroll | 3.00 | 6.00 | 9.00 | F |
| nn(9) | The Adventures of Tom Sawyer–Mark Twain | 3.00 | 6.00 | 9.00 | A |
| nn(10) | Tales of Sherlock Holmes–Arthur Conan Doyle | 5.00 | 10.00 | 15.00 | M |
| nn(11) | Under the Greenwood Tree–Thomas Hardy | 2.00 | 4.00 | 6.00 | |
| nn(12) | The Golden Treasury of Song and Verse | 2.00 | 4.00 | 6.00 | |
| nn(13) | Cyrano de Bergerac–Edmond Rostand; 1933 | 2.00 | 4.00 | 6.00 | A |
| nn(14) | Other People's Money–Louis D. Brandeis | 2.00 | 4.00 | 6.00 | NF |
| nn | The Art of Love–a Parisian Casanova. Note: Ironically retitled reprint of Cyrano de Bergerac (No. 13) | 2.50 | 5.00 | 7.50 | A |

## (JAMES)

## C.L.R. James

| | | V/Good | Fine | N/Mint | |
|---|---|---|---|---|---|
| nn | Mariners, Renegades and Castaways– C.L.R. James; orig. 1953 | 3.00 | 6.00 | 9.00 | B |

## JOE MOSS MYSTERY

### Publisher unknown

#### Digest Size

| | | | | | |
|---|---|---|---|---|---|
| nn | Murder on Both Sides–Abner Sideman; 1945 | 3.50 | 7.00 | 10.50 | M |

## JONATHAN MYSTERY

### The Jonathan Press, Inc.

#### Digest Size

| | | V/Good | Fine | N/Mint | |
|---|---|---|---|---|---|
| J1 | The Chinese Orange Mystery–Ellery Queen | .75 | 1.50 | 2.25 | M |
| J2 | Too Many Cooks–Rex Stout | .75 | 1.50 | 2.25 | M |
| J3 | A Man Lay Dead–Ngaio Marsh | .75 | 1.50 | 2.25 | M |
| J4 | The Bowstring Murders–Carter Dickson | .75 | 1.50 | 2.25 | M |
| J5 | The French Powder Mystery–Ellery Queen | .75 | 1.50 | 2.25 | M |
| J6 | Over My Dead Body–Rex Stout | .75 | 1.50 | 2.25 | M |
| J7 | Murder for Christmas–Agatha Christie | .75 | 1.50 | 2.25 | M |
| J8 | Maigret Sits It Out–Georges Simenon | .75 | 1.50 | 2.25 | M |
| J9 | The Broken Vase–Rex Stout | .75 | 1.50 | 2.25 | M |
| J10 | Death in the Air–Agatha Christie | .75 | 1.50 | 2.25 | M |
| J11 | The Red Widow Murders–Carter Dickson | .75 | 1.50 | 2.25 | M |
| J12 | The Roman Hat Mystery–Ellery Queen | .75 | 1.50 | 2.25 | M |
| J13 | N or M?–Agatha Christie | .75 | 1.50 | 2.25 | M |
| J14 | The White Priory Murders–Carter Dickson | .75 | 1.50 | 2.25 | M |
| J15 | Cordially Invited to Meet Death–Rex Stout | .75 | 1.50 | 2.25 | M |
| J16 | Murder in Restrospect–Agatha Christie | .75 | 1.50 | 2.25 | M |
| J17 | The Return of the Continental Op– Dashiell Hammett; 1st ed. 1945 | 20.00 | 40.00 | 60.00 | M |
| J18 | Maigret Returns–Georges Simenon | .75 | 1.50 | 2.25 | M |
| J19 | The Plague Court Murders–Carter Dickson | .75 | 1.50 | 2.25 | M |
| J20 | Passing Strange–Richard Sale | .75 | 1.50 | 2.25 | M |
| J21 | Arrow Pointing Nowhere–Elizabeth Daly | .75 | 1.50 | 2.25 | M |
| J22 | Design for Murder–Percival Wilde | .75 | 1.50 | 2.25 | M |
| J23 | Black Alibi–Cornell Woolrich | 2.00 | 4.00 | 6.00 | M |
| J24 | Lazarus #7–Richard Sale | 2.00 | 4.00 | 6.00 | SF |
| J25 | It Walks by Night–John Dickson Carr | .75 | 1.50 | 2.25 | M |
| J26 | The Riddles of Hildegarde Withers– Stuart Palmer; 1st ed. 1947. Note: Queen's Quorum No. 100 | 1.25 | 2.50 | 3.75 | M |
| J27 | Not Quite Dead Enough–Rex Stout | .75 | 1.50 | 2.25 | M |
| J28 | Jethro Hammer–Michael Venning | .75 | 1.50 | 2.25 | M |
| J29 | Dead Yellow Women–Dashiell Hammett; 1st ed. 1947 | 20.00 | 40.00 | 60.00 | M |

*Joe Moss Mystery unnumbered, Jonathan Press J24, Jonathan Press J48.*

| | | V/Good | Fine | N/Mint | |
|---|---|---|---|---|---|
| J30 | The Glass Triangle–George Harmon Coxe | | | | M |
| J31 | And So to Death–William Irish | 2.00 | 4.00 | 6.00 | M |
| J32 | Dancers in Mourning–Margery Allingham | .75 | 1.50 | 2.25 | M |
| J33 | The League of Frightened Men–Rex Stout | .75 | 1.50 | 2.25 | M |
| J34 | Dead, Dead Women–Dana Chambers; aka The Case of Caroline Animus | .75 | 1.50 | 2.25 | M |
| J35 | Build My Gallows High–Geoffrey Homes | .75 | 1.50 | 2.25 | M |
| J36 | The Big Knockover–Dashiell Hammett; 1948; aka $106,000 Blood Money | 3.50 | 7.00 | 10.50 | M |
| J37 | The Pinball Murders–Thomas B. Black | .75 | 1.50 | 2.25 | M |
| J38 | The Frightened Man–Dana Chambers | .75 | 1.50 | 2.25 | M |
| J39 | With Intent to Deceive–Manning Coles | .75 | 1.50 | 2.25 | M |
| J40 | The Continental Op–Dashiell Hammett | 3.50 | 7.00 | 10.50 | M |
| J41 | The 3-13 Murders–Thomas B. Black | .75 | 1.50 | 2.25 | M |
| J42 | The Billion Dollar Body–Joseph Shallit | .75 | 1.50 | 2.25 | M |
| J43 | Darling, This Is Death–Dana Chambers | .75 | 1.50 | 2.25 | M |
| J44 | Dead Level–Russell Gordon | .75 | 1.50 | 2.25 | M |
| J45 | The Spider Lily–Bruno Fischer | .75 | 1.50 | 2.25 | M |
| J46 | The Last Secret–Dana Chambers | .75 | 1.50 | 2.25 | M |
| J47 | Deadhead–Charles Marquis Warren | .75 | 1.50 | 2.25 | M |
| J48 | The Creeping Siamese–Dashiell Hammett; 1st ed. 1950 | 20.00 | 40.00 | 60.00 | M |
| J49 | Mr. Moto Is So Sorry–John P. Marquand | .75 | 1.50 | 2.25 | M |
| J50 | Death against Venus–Dana Chambers | .75 | 1.50 | 2.25 | M |
| J51 | The Black Angel–Cornell Woolrich | 2.00 | 4.00 | 6.00 | M |
| J52 | No Hero–John P. Marquand | .75 | 1.50 | 2.25 | M |
| J53 | Dangerous Blondes–Kelley Roos; aka If the Shroud Fits | .75 | 1.50 | 2.25 | M |
| J54 | Ming Yellow–John P. Marquand | .75 | 1.50 | 2.25 | M |
| J55 | Blood on the Blonde–Dana Chambers; aka Witch's Moon | .75 | 1.50 | 2.25 | M |
| J56 | Dead Weight–Frank Kane | .75 | 1.50 | 2.25 | M |
| J57 | Dangerous by Nature–Manning Coles | .75 | 1.50 | 2.25 | M |
| J58 | The Blonde Died First–Dana Chambers | .75 | 1.50 | 2.25 | M |
| J59 | Woman in the Dark–Dashiell Hammett; 1st ed. 1951 | 20.00 | 40.00 | 60.00 | M |
| J60 | The Blue Ice–Hammond Innes | .75 | 1.50 | 2.25 | M |
| J61 | The Black Path of Fear–Cornell Woolrich | 2.00 | 4.00 | 6.00 | M |
| J62 | Now or Never–Manning Coles | .75 | 1.50 | 2.25 | M |
| J63 | Rope for an Ape–Dana Chambers | 1.00 | 2.00 | 3.00 | M |
| J64 | Bullet Proof–Frank Kane | .75 | 1.50 | 2.25 | M |
| J65 | The Fifth Grave–Jonathan Latimer | .75 | 1.50 | 2.25 | M |
| J66 | Die like a Dog–Frank Gruber; aka The Hungry Dog | 1.00 | 2.00 | 3.00 | M |
| J67 | Scared to Death–George Bagby | .75 | 1.50 | 2.25 | M |
| J68 | Operation Manhunt–Manning Coles; aka Alias Uncle Hugo | .75 | 1.50 | 2.25 | M |
| J69 | Murder in the Madhouse–Jonathan Latimer | .75 | 1.50 | 2.25 | M |
| J70 | Kiss for a Killer–Dorothy B. Hughes; aka The Scarlet Imperial | .75 | 1.50 | 2.25 | M |
| J71 | A Body for the Bride–George Bagby; aka The Original Carcase | .75 | 1.50 | 2.25 | M |
| J72 | Too Tough to Die–Frank Gruber; aka The Lock and the Key | 1.00 | 2.00 | 3.00 | M |
| J73 | Dead Drunk–George Bagby | .75 | 1.50 | 2.25 | M |
| J74 | All That Glitters–Manning Coles | .75 | 1.50 | 2.25 | M |
| J75 | Layout for a Corpse–Gene Goldsmith | .75 | 1.50 | 2.25 | M |
| J76 | Fall Guy for a Killer–Frank Gruber; aka The Yellow Overcoat | 1.00 | 2.00 | 3.00 | M |
| J77 | Some Dames Are Deadly–Jonathan Latimer; aka Red Gardenias | .75 | 1.50 | 2.25 | M |
| J78 | Payoff in Blood–Hal Calin; aka Rocks and Ruin | .75 | 1.50 | 2.25 | M |
| J79 | Deadly Lure–Whitman Chambers | .75 | 1.50 | 2.25 | M |
| J80 | Death Rides a Painted Horse–Robert Patrick Wilmot | .75 | 1.50 | 2.25 | M |
| J81 | Lust to Kill–Edward Lee | .75 | 1.50 | 2.25 | M |
| J82 | Naked Fear–John Farr; aka Don't Feed the Animals | .75 | 1.50 | 2.25 | M |
| J83 | Give the Girl a Gun–Richard Deming; aka Whistle Past the Graveyard | .75 | 1.50 | 2.25 | M |
| J84 | Headed for a Hearse–Jonathan Latimer | .75 | 1.50 | 2.25 | M |
| J85 | The Long Arm of Murder–Frank Gruber; aka Murder '97 | 1.00 | 2.00 | 3.00 | M |
| J86 | Hell Street–Max Franklin | .75 | 1.50 | 2.25 | M |
| J87 | Death Ain't Commercial–George Bagby | .75 | 1.50 | 2.25 | M |

*Keep-Worthy 4, Knickerbocker (unlisted), Knickerbocker unnumbered.*

| | | V/Good | Fine | N/Mint |
|---|---|---|---|---|

**LADDER EDITION,** *continued*

| | | V/Good | Fine | N/Mint |
|---|---|---|---|---|
| L7 | Horse and Buggy Doctor–Arthur E. Hertzler | 1.00 | 2.00 | 3.00 |
| L8 | Washington Irving Selections– Washington Irving | 1.00 | 2.00 | 3.00 |
| L9 | Fifth Chinese Daughter–Jade Snow Wong | 1.00 | 2.00 | 3.00 |
| L10 | Six Stories by Edgar Allan Poe–Edgar Allan Poe | 1.00 | 2.00 | 3.00 HO |

# LADDER EDITION
## Pocket Books, Inc.
### Special Abridged Edition

| | | V/Good | Fine | N/Mint |
|---|---|---|---|---|
| SP10 | My Nine Lives in the Red Army– Mikhael Soloviev; 1957 | 1.00 | 2.00 | 3.00 NF |

# LADDER EDITION
## Pyramid Books
### Special Abridged Edition

| | | V/Good | Fine | N/Mint |
|---|---|---|---|---|
| E15 | Thomas Jefferson–Gene Lisitzky; 1959 | .50 | 1.00 | 1.50 B |
| E36 | Doctors to the World–Murray Morgan; 1960 | .50 | 1.00 | 1.50 NF |

# LADDER EDITION
## Washington Square Press, Inc.
### Special Abridged Edition

| | | V/Good | Fine | N/Mint |
|---|---|---|---|---|
| WS78 | King of Jazz: Louis Armstrong– Jeanette Eaton; 1964; aka Trumpeter's Tale | .75 | 1.50 | 2.25 B |

# LANCER BOOKS
## Lancer Books, Inc.

| | | V/Good | Fine | N/Mint |
|---|---|---|---|---|
| 70-001 | Which Way to Mecca, Jack?–William Peter Blatty | 1.00 | 2.00 | 3.00 H |
| 70-002 | Therefore Be Bold–Herbert Gold; 1962 | .50 | 1.00 | 1.50 |
| 70-003 | What Became of Anna Bolton–Louis Broomfield | 1.00 | 2.00 | 3.00 |
| 70-004 | Natural Child–Calder Willingham | .50 | 1.00 | 1.50 |
| 70-005 | What Is Jack Parr Really Like?–William H.A. Carr | 1.00 | 2.00 | 3.00 B |
| 70-006 | Ben Casey–William Johnston; 1962; TV tie-in | 1.50 | 3.00 | 4.50 |
| 70-007 | Dr. Kildare's Secret Romance–Norman Daniels; 1962; TV tie-in | 1.50 | 3.00 | 4.50 |
| 70-008 | Memory of Passion–Gil Brewer | 1.00 | 2.00 | 3.00 |
| 70-009 | Naked in Hollywood–Bob Lucas; 1962 | 1.50 | 3.00 | 4.50 |
| 70-010 | My Body–Robert Dietrich | .50 | 1.00 | 1.50 M |
| 70-011 | Ben Casey–A Rage for Justice– Norman Daniels; TV tie-in; fold-out interior photo | 1.50 | 3.00 | 4.50 |
| 70-012 | Two Surgeons–Richard Meade | .50 | 1.00 | 1.50 R |
| 70-013 | Frenzy–Jonathan Craig | 1.00 | 2.00 | 3.00 M |
| 70-015 | White Slave Ship–Eunice Sudak; 1962; movie tie-in | 2.00 | 4.00 | 6.00 A |
| 70-016 | Lone Gun–Eric Allen | .75 | 1.50 | 2.25 W |
| 70-029 | The Golden Key–William O'Farrell | .50 | 1.00 | 1.50 M |
| 70-030 | The Creepers–John Creasey | .50 | 1.00 | 1.50 M |
| 70-031 | Dr. Reade's Decision–Bruce Cassiday; 1962 | .50 | 1.00 | 1.50 R |
| 70-032 | Dr. Kildare's Finest Hour–Norman Daniels; 1963; TV tie-in | 1.50 | 3.00 | 4.50 |
| 70-033 | Empty Saddles–Al Cody | .75 | 1.50 | 2.25 W |
| 70-034 | The Raven–Eunice Sudak; 1963; movie tie-in | 2.00 | 4.00 | 6.00 HO |
| 70-035 | Sam Benedict: Cast the First Stone– Norman Daniels & Elsie Lee; TV tie-in | 1.50 | 3.00 | 4.50 |

| | | V/Good | Fine | N/Mint |
|---|---|---|---|---|
| 70-037 | Ben Casey: The Strength of His Hands–Sam Elkin; 1963; TV tie-in | 1.50 | 3.00 | 4.50 |
| 70-041 | The Man from the Diners' Club–Sam Beal; movie tie-in | 1.00 | 2.00 | 3.00 |
| 70-042 | Combat!–Harold Calin; 1963; TV tie-in | 1.50 | 3.00 | 4.50 C |
| 70-043 | Dr. Kildare: The Heart Has an Answer– William Johnston; 1963; TV tie-in | 1.50 | 3.00 | 4.50 |
| 70-044 | Border Raider–William Hopson | .75 | 1.50 | 2.25 W |
| 70-045 | Ben Casey: The Fire Within–Norman Daniels; TV tie-in | 1.50 | 3.00 | 4.50 |
| 70-047 | Tombstone Stage–William Hopson | .75 | 1.50 | 2.25 W |
| 70-048 | Never Give a Millionaire an Even Break–Henry Kane | .50 | 1.00 | 1.50 M |
| 70-049 | Dr. Kildare: The Faces of Love–William Johnston; TV tie-in | 1.50 | 3.00 | 4.50 |
| 70-050 | President's Agent–Joseph Hilton | .50 | 1.00 | 1.50 |
| 70-051 | High Saddle–William Hopson | .75 | 1.50 | 2.25 W |
| 70-052 | X–Eunice Sudak; 1963; movie tie-in | 2.00 | 4.00 | 6.00 HO |
| 70-055 | General Hospital–B. Hirschfeld; TV tie-in | 1.50 | 3.00 | 4.50 |
| 70-059 | Wives and Lovers–Michael Milner; movie tie-in | 1.00 | 2.00 | 3.00 |
| 70-060 | Combat: Men, Not Heroes–Harold Calin; 1963; TV tie-in | 2.00 | 4.00 | 6.00 C |
| 70-062 | Kings of the Sun–Harold Calin; 1963; movie tie-in | 1.50 | 3.00 | 4.50 A |
| 70-067 | Comedy of Terrors–Elsie Lee; 1964; movie tie-in | 2.50 | 5.00 | 7.50 H |
| 70-068 | Woman's Doctor–Dan Endersby | .75 | 1.50 | 2.25 E |
| 70-073 | Muscle Beach Party–Elsie Lee; 1964; movie tie-in | 3.00 | 6.00 | 9.00 |
| 70-075 | Stormy Range–Dwight Bennett; 1964 | .75 | 1.50 | 2.25 W |
| 70-080 | The New Nurse–Florence Stuart; 1965 | .50 | 1.00 | 1.50 R |
| 71-301 | The Knife–Hal Ellson; 1961 | 2.50 | 5.00 | 7.50 JD |
| 71-302 | Lust of Private Cooper–James Gordon | .50 | 1.00 | 1.50 |
| 71-303 | The Pit and the Pendulum–Lee Sheridan; 1961; movie tie-in | 2.00 | 4.00 | 6.00 HO |
| 71-304 | Dead in Bed–Henry Kane | .75 | 1.50 | 2.25 M |
| 71-306 | Country Nurse–Maude McCurdy Welch | .50 | 1.00 | 1.50 R |
| 71-307 | Dark Hazard–W.R. Burnett | 1.00 | 2.00 | 3.00 M |
| 71-308 | Doctor Kildare–Robert C. Ackworth; 1962; TV tie-in | 1.50 | 3.00 | 4.50 |
| 71-309 | Too Late Blues–Stuart James; movie tie-in | 1.50 | 3.00 | 4.50 |
| 71-311 | Curtains for a Lover–Robert Dietrich | .75 | 1.50 | 2.25 M |
| 71-312 | The Blood Red Oscar–Elsie Lee | .75 | 1.50 | 2.25 M |
| 71-313 | Premature Burial–Max Hallan Danne; 1962; movie tie-in | 2.00 | 4.00 | 6.00 HO |
| 71-315 | Love Cult–Harry Whittington | 1.50 | 3.00 | 4.50 E |
| 71-316 | Robert Taylor Starring in The Detectives–Norman Daniels; TV tie-in | 1.50 | 3.00 | 4.50 M |
| 71-317 | Red-Headed Sinners–Jonathan Craig | .75 | 1.50 | 2.25 M |
| 71-319 | Hitler–Michael Sheridan; movie tie-in | 1.50 | 3.00 | 4.50 NF |
| 71-320 | Escape from Hell–Stan Smith | .75 | 1.50 | 2.25 NF |
| 71-321 | Gringo Gun–E.E. Halleran | .75 | 1.50 | 2.25 W |
| 71-324 | Taras Bulba–Nicolai Gogol | .75 | 1.50 | 2.25 A |
| 71-325 | Poe's Tales of Terror–Eunice Sudak; movie tie-in | 2.50 | 5.00 | 7.50 HO |
| 71-326 | Nurse's Dormitory–Alice Brennan; 1962 | .50 | 1.00 | 1.50 R |

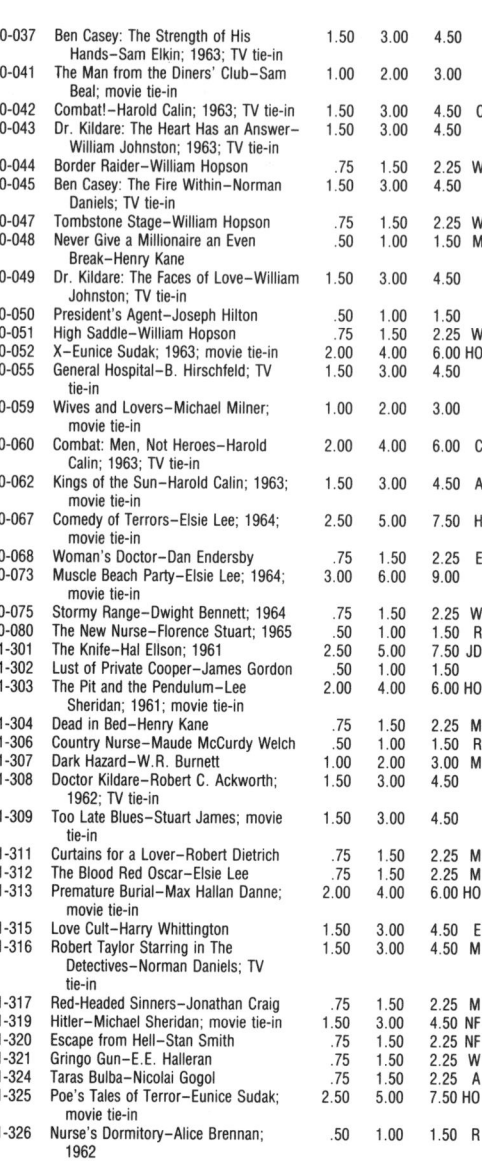

*Lancer 70-042, Lancer 77-701 (unlisted).*

**LANCER BOOKS,** *continued*

| No. | Title | V/Good | Fine | N/Mint | |
|---|---|---|---|---|---|
| 72-717 | Primitive Passions–Joe McDow | .75 | 1.50 | 2.25 | E |
| 72-718 | Sweet Torment–Sylvia Sharon | .75 | 1.50 | 2.25 | E |
| 72-719 | Weekend Wanton–Ian Gordon | .75 | 1.50 | 2.25 | E |
| 72-721 | The Valley of Creation–Edmond Hamilton; 1964 | 1.50 | 3.00 | 4.50 | SF |
| 72-723 | The Missing Witness–Norman Daniels; TV tie-in | 1.50 | 3.00 | 4.50 | |
| 72-726 | Lust Prowl–Orrie Hitt | 1.00 | 2.00 | 3.00 | E |
| 72-727 | Just Your Body, Baby–Rea Michaels | .75 | 1.50 | 2.25 | E |
| 72-728 | Las Vegas Madam–Matt Harding | .75 | 1.50 | 2.25 | E |
| 72-729 | The Sins of Tonia–Sylvia Sharon | .75 | 1.50 | 2.25 | E |
| 72-730 | A Hole in the Ground–Andrew Garve | .75 | 1.50 | 2.25 | M |
| 72-732 | The Beatle Book; 1964 | 3.00 | 6.00 | 9.00 | NF |
| 72-734 | Madam Kozik's Girls–A.L. Roget; 1964 | .75 | 1.50 | 2.25 | E |
| 72-735 | How Dark My Love–Rea Michaels | .75 | 1.50 | 2.25 | E |
| 72-736 | Fear to Tread–Michael Gilbert | .75 | 1.50 | 2.25 | M |
| 72-737 | Smallbone Deceased–Michael Gilbert | .75 | 1.50 | 2.25 | M |
| 72-738 | Death Has Deep Roots–Michael Gilbert | .75 | 1.50 | 2.25 | M |
| 72-739 | No Tears for Hilda–Andrew Garve | .75 | 1.50 | 2.25 | M |
| 72-740 | Golden Blood–Jack Williamson | 1.00 | 2.00 | 3.00 | SF |
| 72-741 | Two-Way Street–Rea Michaels | .75 | 1.50 | 2.25 | E |
| 72-742 | The Sad Gay Life–Donna Richards | .75 | 1.50 | 2.25 | E |
| 72-743 | Teen Temptations–Bart Michaels | .75 | 1.50 | 2.25 | E |
| 72-744 | Where the Sin Is–A.L. Roget | .75 | 1.50 | 2.25 | E |
| 72-745 | Sex and the Secretary–Sprague | .50 | 1.00 | 1.50 | E |
| 72-748 | Pumpkin Eater–Penelope Mortimer; movie tie-in | 1.00 | 2.00 | 3.00 | |
| 72-749 | A World Divided–Jill Monte | .75 | 1.50 | 2.25 | E |
| 72-750 | Where Lovers Fear to Tread–Rea Michaels | .75 | 1.50 | 2.25 | |
| 72-751 | Sky High–Michael Gilbert | .75 | 1.50 | 2.25 | M |
| 72-752 | A Taste for Honey–H.F. Heard | .75 | 1.50 | 2.25 | M |
| 72-753 | The Naked Sun–Isaac Asimov | 1.00 | 2.00 | 3.00 | SF |
| 72-754 | Reply Paid–H.F. Heard | .75 | 1.50 | 2.25 | M |
| 72-755 | When Love Must Hide–Jessica Bayne | .75 | 1.50 | 2.25 | E |
| 72-756 | The Perfumed Flesh–Donna Richards | .75 | 1.50 | 2.25 | E |
| 72-757 | For Sin's Sake–Arthur Adlon | .75 | 1.50 | 2.25 | E |
| 72-758 | Transit–Edmund Cooper; 1964 | .75 | 1.50 | 2.25 | SF |
| 72-761 | The Reign of Wizardry–Jack Williamson; c-Frazetta | 1.50 | 3.00 | 4.50 | F |
| 72-762 | Diary of a Nymph–X | .75 | 1.50 | 2.25 | E |
| 72-764 | The Midway at Midnight–Leslie Behan | .75 | 1.50 | 2.25 | E |
| 72-765 | Deliver Her to Evil–Sylvia Sharon | .75 | 1.50 | 2.25 | E |
| 72-766 | The Sweet Smell of Sin–Rea Michaels | .75 | 1.50 | 2.25 | E |
| 72-768 | Divide and Rule–L. Sprague de Camp | 1.00 | 2.00 | 3.00 | SF |
| 72-769 | The Kept Man–Wenzell Brown | 1.00 | 2.00 | 3.00 | NF |
| 72-770 | Teen-age Party & Fun Quiz Book–Neil Farber | .75 | 1.50 | 2.25 | NF |
| 72-771 | After the Fine Weather–Michael Gilbert | .75 | 1.50 | 2.25 | M |
| 72-772 | The Million-Dollar Night–Lewis Poole | .75 | 1.50 | 2.25 | E |
| 72-773 | A Kind of Marriage–Leone Matthews | .75 | 1.50 | 2.25 | E |
| 72-774 | The Pleasures We Know–Barbara Wilson | .75 | 1.50 | 2.25 | E |
| 72-779 | The Moonflower–Phyllis Whitney | .50 | 1.00 | 1.50 | |
| 72-780 | Secret Melody–Paula Minton | .50 | 1.00 | 1.50 | |
| 72-781 | Woman's Darling–A.L. Roget | .75 | 1.50 | 2.25 | E |
| 72-782 | We Love in Shadow–Sylvia Sharon | .75 | 1.50 | 2.25 | E |
| 72-784 | Season of Evil–Elsie Lee | .50 | 1.00 | 1.50 | |
| 72-785 | Libby–Rea Michaels; 1965 | .75 | 1.50 | 2.25 | E |
| 72-786 | The Secret Places–A.L. Roget | .75 | 1.50 | 2.25 | E |
| 72-787 | The Odd World–Donna Richards | .75 | 1.50 | 2.25 | E |
| 72-788 | All Night Long–Sandra Sterling | .75 | 1.50 | 2.25 | E |
| 72-789 | You Sane Men–Laurence M. Janifer | 1.00 | 2.00 | 3.00 | SF |
| 72-790 | Blood and Judgment–Michael Gilbert | .75 | 1.50 | 2.25 | M |
| 72-791 | Mistress of Mount Fair–Jane Gordon | .50 | 1.00 | 1.50 | |
| 72-792 | No Barriers–Sylvia Sharon | .75 | 1.50 | 2.25 | E |
| 72-793 | The Needs We Share–Rea Michaels | .75 | 1.50 | 2.25 | E |
| 72-794 | Dark Triangle–Dale Greggson | .75 | 1.50 | 2.25 | E |
| 72-795 | World without Men–Trudy Starling | .75 | 1.50 | 2.25 | E |
| 72-796 | Heritage of Folly–Catherine Marchant | .50 | 1.00 | 1.50 | |
| 72-797 | Mostly by Moonlight–Dorothy Daniels | .50 | 1.00 | 1.50 | |
| 72-799 | Angela, Be Bad–Oscar Bessie | .75 | 1.50 | 2.25 | E |
| 72-900 | Cloak of Evil–Rea Michaels | .75 | 1.50 | 2.25 | E |
| 72-901 | Brand of Shame–Donna Richards | .75 | 1.50 | 2.25 | E |
| 72-902 | The Off-Limits World–Carla Josephs | .75 | 1.50 | 2.25 | E |
| 72-903 | The Deeds of Dr. Deadcert–Joan Fleming | .50 | 1.00 | 1.50 | M |
| 72-904 | Strike Force–Norman Daniels | .75 | 1.50 | 2.25 | C |
| 72-905 | Speak It in Whispers–Arthur Adlon | .75 | 1.50 | 2.25 | E |
| 72-906 | She Devil–Vin Fields | .75 | 1.50 | 2.25 | E |
| 72-907 | Who Calls It Sin?–Vicki Spain | .75 | 1.50 | 2.25 | E |
| 72-908 | Evil in the House–Evelyn Bond | .50 | 1.00 | 1.50 | |
| 72-909 | Day of the Arrow–Philip Loraine | .50 | 1.00 | 1.50 | R |
| 72-910 | Combat! No Rest for Heroes–Harold Calin; TV tie-in | 2.50 | 5.00 | 7.50 | C |
| 72-911 | Nightmare in July–Clara Coleman | .50 | 1.00 | 1.50 | |
| 72-912 | The Burning Flesh–Sylvia Sharon | .75 | 1.50 | 2.25 | E |
| 72-913 | Duet in Darkness–Rea Michaels | .75 | 1.50 | 2.25 | E |
| 72-914 | To Drown Our Lusts–Vicki Spain | .75 | 1.50 | 2.25 | E |
| 72-915 | Women like Me–Donna Richards | .75 | 1.50 | 2.25 | E |
| 72-916 | The Smuggled Atom Bomb–Philip Wylie | 1.00 | 2.00 | 3.00 | SF |
| 72-917 | General Hospital: Emergency Entrance–Burt Hirschfeld; 1965; TV tie-in | 2.00 | 4.00 | 6.00 | |
| 72-918 | The Man from O.R.G.Y.–Ted Mark | 1.00 | 2.00 | 3.00 | |
| 72-919 | Clouds over Vellanti–Elsie Lee | .50 | 1.00 | 1.50 | |
| 72-920 | The Brooding House–Alice Brennan | .50 | 1.00 | 1.50 | |
| 72-921 | Too Good for Men–Arthur Adlon | .75 | 1.50 | 2.25 | E |
| 72-922 | Sisterhood of the Flesh–Dale Greggson | .75 | 1.50 | 2.25 | E |
| 72-923 | Obey Me, My Love–Sylvia Sharon | .75 | 1.50 | 2.25 | E |
| 72-924 | Honeymoon Hotel–Malcolm Maxwell | .75 | 1.50 | 2.25 | E |
| 72-925 | She–H. Rider Haggard | 1.00 | 2.00 | 3.00 | A |
| 72-926 | Engraved in Evil–Paula Minton | .50 | 1.00 | 1.50 | |
| 72-927 | Tryst with Terror–Wilma Winthrop | .50 | 1.00 | 1.50 | |
| 72-928 | Curse of the Island Pool–Virginia Coffman | .50 | 1.00 | 1.50 | |
| 72-929 | Take Me in Passion–Donna Richards | .75 | 1.50 | 2.25 | E |
| 72-930 | In Love's Dark Corners–Leslie Behan | .75 | 1.50 | 2.25 | E |
| 72-931 | Rapture for Three–Sylvia Sharon | .75 | 1.50 | 2.25 | E |
| 72-932 | House of Four Windows–Delphine C. Lyons | .50 | 1.00 | 1.50 | |
| 72-933 | The Unguarded–Dorothy Daniels | .50 | 1.00 | 1.50 | |
| 72-934 | Dark Moon, Lost Lady–Elsie Lee | .50 | 1.00 | 1.50 | |
| 72-935 | Experiment in Crime–Philip Wylie | .50 | 1.00 | 1.50 | |
| 72-936 | The Smashers–Hugo Paul | .50 | 1.00 | 1.50 | |
| 72-937 | Gladiator–Philip Wylie | 1.00 | 2.00 | 3.00 | SF |
| 72-938 | Who Seek in Shadow–Vin Fields | .75 | 1.50 | 2.25 | E |
| 72-939 | The Flesh Surrenders–Dale Greggson | .75 | 1.50 | 2.25 | E |
| 72-940 | Passionate Tigress–John Saxon | .75 | 1.50 | 2.25 | E |
| 72-941 | The Love Trap–Ian Gordon | .75 | 1.50 | 2.25 | E |
| 72-942 | The Mindwarpers–Eric Frank Russell | 1.00 | 2.00 | 3.00 | SF |
| 72-943 | The Tower Room–Dorothy Daniels | .50 | 1.00 | 1.50 | |
| 72-944 | Evil at Roger's Cross–Catherine Marchant | .50 | 1.00 | 1.50 | |
| 72-945 | Ravenkill–Paulette Warren | .50 | 1.00 | 1.50 | |
| 72-946 | House of Shadows–Evelyn Bond | .50 | 1.00 | 1.50 | |
| 72-948 | The Sins of Tonia–Sylvia Sharon | .75 | 1.50 | 2.25 | E |
| 72-949 | The Velvet Embrace–Barbara Wilson | .75 | 1.50 | 2.25 | E |
| 72-950 | Don't Stop My Love–Donna Richards | .75 | 1.50 | 2.25 | E |
| 72-951 | The Agony of Desire–Sylvia Sharon | .75 | 1.50 | 2.25 | E |
| 72-952 | The Silken Underground–Vicki Spain | .75 | 1.50 | 2.25 | E |
| 72-953 | Too Many Men–Ian Gordon | .75 | 1.50 | 2.25 | E |
| 72-954 | Lady of Storm House–Evelyn Bond | .50 | 1.00 | 1.50 | |
| 72-955 | Heiress of Bayou Vache–Harriet Stone | .50 | 1.00 | 1.50 | |
| 72-956 | Hand of the Imposter–Paula Minton | .50 | 1.00 | 1.50 | |
| 72-957 | The Tuscany Madonna–Miriam Canfield | .50 | 1.00 | 1.50 | |
| 72-958 | The 9-Month Caper–Ted Mark | 1.00 | 2.00 | 3.00 | |
| 72-960 | Bonnie–Oscar Bessie | .75 | 1.50 | 2.25 | E |
| 72-961 | The Swappers–Rea Michaels | .75 | 1.50 | 2.25 | E |
| 72-962 | A Special Passion–Arthur Adlon | .75 | 1.50 | 2.25 | E |
| 72-963 | Passion Pool–Orrie Hitt | .75 | 1.50 | 2.25 | E |
| 72-964 | Island of the Accursed–Wilma Winthrop | .50 | 1.00 | 1.50 | |
| 72-965 | The Secret of Cromwell Crossing–Daoma Winston | .50 | 1.00 | 1.50 | |
| 72-966 | Dance in Darkness–Dorothy Daniels | .50 | 1.00 | 1.50 | |
| 72-967 | Greenwood–Jean Phillips | .50 | 1.00 | 1.50 | |
| 72-968 | Do Evil in Return–Margaret Millar | .50 | 1.00 | 1.50 | |
| 72-970 | Heirloom of Tragedy–Edwina Noone (Michael Avallone) | 1.00 | 2.00 | 3.00 | |
| 72-971 | Teen Temptress–Bart Michaels | 1.50 | 3.00 | 4.50 | E |
| 72-972 | Lust Queen–Rea Michaels | .75 | 1.50 | 2.25 | E |
| 72-973 | Fulfill Me, Darling–Vin Fields | .75 | 1.50 | 2.25 | E |
| 72-974 | Our Furtive Love–Donna Richards | .75 | 1.50 | 2.25 | E |
| 72-975 | All-Girl Office–Arthur Adlon | .75 | 1.50 | 2.25 | E |
| 72-976 | Rose's Last Summer–Margaret Millar | .50 | 1.00 | 1.50 | |
| 72-977 | A Gathering of Moondust–Patricia Morton | .50 | 1.00 | 1.50 | |
| 72-978 | Orphan of the Shadows–Paula Minton | .50 | 1.00 | 1.50 | |
| 72-979 | House of Strangers–Meg Padget | .50 | 1.00 | 1.50 | |
| 72-980 | Cliffside Castle–Dorothy Daniels | .50 | 1.00 | 1.50 | |
| 72-981 | Autumn Romance–Philip Wylie | .50 | 1.00 | 1.50 | R |
| 72-982 | Lady in Darkness–Evelyn Bond | .50 | 1.00 | 1.50 | |
| 72-983 | Castle Terror–Marion Zimmer Bradley | 1.50 | 3.00 | 4.50 | |

| | V/Good | Fine | N/Mint |
|---|---|---|---|

LANCER BOOKS, *continued*

| No. | Title | V/Good | Fine | N/Mint | |
|---|---|---|---|---|---|
| 72-984 | The Mists of Memory–Catherine Marchant | .50 | 1.00 | 1.50 | |
| 72-985 | Some Beckoning Wraith–Paulette Warren | .50 | 1.00 | 1.50 | |
| 72-986 | Vanish in an Instant–Margaret Millar | .50 | 1.00 | 1.50 | |
| 72-987 | Murder through the Looking Glass–Andrew Garve | .75 | 1.50 | 2.25 | M |
| 72-988 | A Dream to Share–Lisa Roberts | .50 | 1.00 | 1.50 | R |
| 72-989 | The Nude Who Never–Ted Mark | 1.00 | 2.00 | 3.00 | |
| 72-990 | Mansion of the Green Windows–Elsie Lee | .50 | 1.00 | 1.50 | |
| 72-991 | A Scent of Sandalwood–Clara Coleman | .50 | 1.00 | 1.50 | |
| 72-992 | The Secret of Shower Tree–Virginia Coffman | .50 | 1.00 | 1.50 | |
| 72-993 | The Templeton Memoirs–Dorothy Daniels | .50 | 1.00 | 1.50 | |
| 72-994 | Wall of Eyes–Margaret Millar | .50 | 1.00 | 1.50 | |
| 72-996 | The Real Gone Girls–Ted Mark | 1.00 | 2.00 | 3.00 | |
| 73-200 | The Corpse in the Castle–Ed Friend; 1970; TV tie-in | 1.50 | 3.00 | 4.50 | |
| 73-205 | The Bloop Box–William Johnston; TV tie-in | 1.50 | 3.00 | 4.50 | |
| 73-206 | The Quarterback Who Came to Dinner–William Johnston; 1970; TV tie-in | 1.50 | 3.00 | 4.50 | |
| 73-216 | The One-Armed Murder–Richard Gallagher; 1971; TV tie-in | 1.50 | 3.00 | 4.50 | |
| 73-217 | Broom Hilda–Russell Myers | 1.00 | 2.00 | 3.00 | H |
| 73-219 | Strange Report; TV tie-in | 1.00 | 2.00 | 3.00 | |
| 73-401 | A Peculiar Treasure–Edna Ferber | .75 | 1.50 | 2.25 | |
| 73-402 | Paris Mitchell of Kings Row–H. Bellaman & K. Bellaman | .50 | 1.00 | 1.50 | |
| 73-403 | Tomorrow Will Be Better–Betty Smith | .50 | 1.00 | 1.50 | |
| 73-405 | The Hearth and Eagle–Anya Seton | .50 | 1.00 | 1.50 | |
| 73-406 | The Sixth of June–Lionel Shapiro | .50 | 1.00 | 1.50 | |
| 73-408 | Up Front–Bill Mauldin | .75 | 1.50 | 2.25 | H |
| 73-409 | Nelson Algren's Own Book of Lonesome Monsters–ed. Nelson Algren; orig. 1962 | 3.00 | 6.00 | 9.00 | |
| 73-410 | Prince Bart–Jay Richard Kennedy | .50 | 1.00 | 1.50 | |
| 73-411 | Teaser–Orrie Hitt | 1.00 | 2.00 | 3.00 | E |
| 73-417 | The Frustrated American–B.W. Von Block | .50 | 1.00 | 1.50 | |
| 73-419 | The Lonely Life–Bette Davis | 1.50 | 3.00 | 4.50 | B |
| 73-420 | Sexual Behavior of American Nurses–W.D. Sprague, PhD | .50 | 1.00 | 1.50 | NF |
| 73-421 | Darker Than You Think–Jack Williamson | 1.00 | 2.00 | 3.00 | SF |
| 73-425 | The Colour out of Space–H.P. Lovecraft; 1964 | 1.50 | 3.00 | 4.50 | HO |
| 73-427 | Kindling–Nevil Shute | .75 | 1.50 | 2.25 | |
| 73-432 | An Old Captivity–Nevil Shute | .75 | 1.50 | 2.25 | |
| 73-433 | Upbeat–Irving Shulman | .50 | 1.00 | 1.50 | |
| 73-434 | Sybil–Louis Auchincloss | .50 | 1.00 | 1.50 | |
| 73-436 | House of Men–Catherine Marchant | .50 | 1.00 | 1.50 | |
| 73-437 | A Law for the Lion–Louis Auchincloss | .50 | 1.00 | 1.50 | |
| 73-439 | Star-raker–Donald Gordon | .75 | 1.50 | 2.25 | A |
| 73-440 | Sexual Rebellion in the Sixties–W.D. Sprague, MD | .50 | 1.00 | 1.50 | NF |
| 73-441 | The Man Who Wanted Stars–Dean McLaughlin | 1.00 | 2.00 | 3.00 | SF |
| 73-442 | Flight of the Bat–Donald Gordon | .50 | 1.00 | 1.50 | R |
| 73-443 | House on the Fens–Catherine Marchant | .50 | 1.00 | 1.50 | |
| 73-445 | Sex and the Divorced Woman–L.T. Woodward (Robert Silverberg) | .50 | 1.00 | 1.50 | E |
| 73-446 | The Girl from Pussycat–Ted Mark | 1.00 | 2.00 | 3.00 | |
| 73-449 | Sea Jewel–Linden Grierson | .50 | 1.00 | 1.50 | R |
| 73-450 | Vacation Romance–Linden Grierson | .50 | 1.00 | 1.50 | R |
| 73-461 | Pussycat, Pussycat!–Ted Mark; 1966 | 1.00 | 2.00 | 3.00 | |
| 73-468 | Siege Perilous–Lester del Rey; aka Man without A Planet | 1.00 | 2.00 | 3.00 | SF |
| 73-469 | A Study in Terror–Ellery Queen; movie tie-in; 1st ed. 1966 | 3.00 | 6.00 | 9.00 | M |
| 73-472 | Royal Street–Francis Swann | .50 | 1.00 | 1.50 | |
| 73-476 | Phoenix Prime–Ted White; c-Frazetta; 1st ed. 1966 | 1.50 | 3.00 | 4.50 | SF |
| 73-477 | Dr. Nyet–Ted Mark | 1.00 | 2.00 | 3.00 | |
| 73-479 | The Devil's Church–F. Draco | 1.00 | 2.00 | 3.00 | HO |
| 73-485 | My Son, the Double Agent–Ted Mark | 1.00 | 2.00 | 3.00 | |
| 73-486 | Gordon of Khartoum–Paul Charrier | 1.00 | 2.00 | 3.00 | A |
| 73-487 | The Man from O.R.G.Y. No. 1–Ted Mark | 1.00 | 2.00 | 3.00 | |
| 73-488 | The 9-Month Caper–Ted Mark | 1.00 | 2.00 | 3.00 | |
| 73-489 | The Nude Who Never–Ted Mark | 1.00 | 2.00 | 3.00 | |
| 73-490 | The Real Gone Girls–Ted Mark | 1.00 | 2.00 | 3.00 | |
| 73-500 | Ian Fleming: The Fantastic 007 Man–Richard Gant; 1966 | 2.50 | 5.00 | 7.50 | B |
| 73-504 | Building Blocks of the Universe–Isaac Asimov | 1.00 | 2.00 | 3.00 | NF |
| 73-505 | The Corridors of Time–Poul Anderson; 1966 | 1.00 | 2.00 | 3.00 | SF |
| 73-508 | A Hard Day's Knight–Ted Mark | 1.00 | 2.00 | 3.00 | |
| 73-515 | Ted Mark Reader–Ted Mark | 1.00 | 2.00 | 3.00 | |
| 73-516 | Hell's Brigade–ed. Charles Goodman | 1.00 | 2.00 | 3.00 | NF |
| 73-517 | Z for Zaborra–Eva-Lis Wuorio | .50 | 1.00 | 1.50 | R |
| 73-518 | Waiting for a Tiger–Ben Healey | .50 | 1.00 | 1.50 | R |
| 73-522 | Helen All Alone–William Buchan | .50 | 1.00 | 1.50 | R |
| 73-524 | The Woman with the Portuguese Basket–Eva-lis Wuorio | .50 | 1.00 | 1.50 | R |
| 73-526 | Conan the Adventurer–Robert E. Howard & L. Sprague de Camp; 1966; c-Frazetta | 1.50 | 3.00 | 4.50 | A |
| 73-527 | The Unhatched Egghead–Ted Mark | 1.00 | 2.00 | 3.00 | |
| 73-528 | The Sorceress of Qar–Ted White; 1st ed. 1966 | 1.00 | 2.00 | 3.00 | F |
| 73-531 | Do Evil in Return–Margaret Millar | .50 | 1.00 | 1.50 | |
| 73-536 | The Lady in the Lightning–Katherine Tobias | .50 | 1.00 | 1.50 | R |
| 73-540 | 13–Philip Loraine; 1966; aka Day of the Arrow; aka Eye of the Devil | 1.00 | 2.00 | 3.00 | |
| 73-541 | The Head of Medusa–Alicia Grace (Irving Greenfield); 1967 | .50 | 1.00 | 1.50 | |
| 73-545 | The Stealer of Souls–Michael Moorcock; 1967 | 1.50 | 3.00 | 4.50 | F |
| 73-546 | The Nude Wore Black–Ted Mark | 1.00 | 2.00 | 3.00 | |
| 73-548 | Wait for the Dawn–Martha Albrand | .50 | 1.00 | 1.50 | R |
| 73-549 | Conan the Warrior–Robert E. Howard; 1967; c-Frazetta | 1.50 | 3.00 | 4.50 | F |
| 73-550 | The Girls from Planet 5–Richard Wilson | 1.00 | 2.00 | 3.00 | SF |
| 73-556 | Desperate Moment–Martha Albrand | .50 | 1.00 | 1.50 | R |
| 73-562 | Gladiator–Philip Wylie | 1.00 | 2.00 | 3.00 | SF |
| 73-563 | Room at the Topless–Ted Mark | 1.00 | 2.00 | 3.00 | |
| 73-564 | You'll Hang, My Love–Swann & Emerick | .50 | 1.00 | 1.50 | R |
| 73-566 | Ship of Spies–Gerald Sinstadt | .50 | 1.00 | 1.50 | |
| 73-568 | Strike from the Sky–Alexander McKee | .75 | 1.50 | 2.25 | NF |
| 73-571 | Nightmare of Eyes–Don Rico | .50 | 1.00 | 1.50 | R |
| 73-572 | Conan the Conqueror–Robert E. Howard; 1967; c-Frazetta | 1.50 | 3.00 | 4.50 | F |
| 73-573 | Slaves of Sleep–L. Ron Hubbard | 2.50 | 5.00 | 7.50 | SF |
| 73-575 | Clouds over Vellanti–Elsie Lee | .50 | 1.00 | 1.50 | R |
| 73-576 | Nightmare in July–Clara Coleman | .50 | 1.00 | 1.50 | |
| 73-577 | The Valley of Creation–Edmond Hamilton | 1.00 | 2.00 | 3.00 | SF |
| 73-579 | Stormbringer–Michael Moorcock | 1.50 | 3.00 | 4.50 | F |
| 73-580 | The Warriors of Day–James Blish | .75 | 1.50 | 2.25 | SF |
| 73-581 | I Hide, We Seek–Richard Martin Stern | .50 | 1.00 | 1.50 | R |
| 73-582 | The Assassins–Frederic Mullally | .50 | 1.00 | 1.50 | R |
| 73-583 | The Gaunt Woman–John Blackburn | .50 | 1.00 | 1.50 | |
| 73-586 | Bride of the Shadows–Laura Mae Jansen | .50 | 1.00 | 1.50 | R |
| 73-588 | Doobie Doo–Ivan C. Karp | .50 | 1.00 | 1.50 | H |
| 73-589 | Burwyck's Wander–S.J. Treibich | .50 | 1.00 | 1.50 | |
| 73-591 | The Busy Body–Donald E. Westlake; movie tie-in; c-Frazetta | 2.00 | 4.00 | 6.00 | H |
| 73-598 | Shadow of an Unknown Woman–Daoma Winston | .50 | 1.00 | 1.50 | R |
| 73-599 | Conan the Usurper–Robert E. Howard, L. Sprague de Camp; 1967; c-Frazetta | 1.50 | 3.00 | 4.50 | F |
| 73-600 | The Mind Brothers–Peter Heath | .75 | 1.50 | 2.25 | SF |
| 73-602 | The Golden Deed–Andrew Garve | .75 | 1.50 | 2.25 | M |
| 73-603 | The Moonflower–Phyllis A. Whitney | .50 | 1.00 | 1.50 | |
| 73-604 | Nurse in Nassau–Rose Williams | .50 | 1.00 | 1.50 | R |
| 73-605 | Engraved in Evil–Paula Minton | .50 | 1.00 | 1.50 | |
| 73-606 | The Last of the Breed–Don Rico | .50 | 1.00 | 1.50 | |
| 73-607 | Gorgonzola, Won't You Please Come Home?–Clyde Ames | .75 | 1.50 | 2.25 | |
| 73-608 | The Colour out of Space–H.P. Lovecraft | 1.00 | 2.00 | 3.00 | HO |
| 73-609 | The Russian Interpreter–Michael Frayn | .50 | 1.00 | 1.50 | |
| 73-611 | You Can't Escape–Laurence M. Janifer | .50 | 1.00 | 1.50 | R |
| 73-612 | The Spy at the Villa Miranda–Elsie Lee | .50 | 1.00 | 1.50 | R |
| 73-613 | A Fear in Borzano–Willa Jay | .50 | 1.00 | 1.50 | |
| 73-614 | The Spy with the Blue Kazoo–Dagmar | .50 | 1.00 | 1.50 | H |

**LANCER BOOKS,** *continued*

| | V/Good | Fine | N/Mint | |
|---|---|---|---|---|
| 73-615 Firebug–Robert Bloch | 2.00 | 4.00 | 6.00 | M |
| 73-616 A Study in Terror–Ellery Queen | 1.50 | 3.00 | 4.50 | M |
| 73-617 Operation Axe-Handle–Jacob McCroskey | .50 | 1.00 | 1.50 | C |
| 73-619 The Dragon's Lair–Isabel D'Este Wenzell | .50 | 1.00 | 1.50 | |
| 73-621 Vice Isn't Private–Brian Cleeve | .50 | 1.00 | 1.50 | |
| 73-622 Psychiatric Nurse–Fern Shepard | .50 | 1.00 | 1.50 | R |
| 73-623 The Shrewsbury Horror–T.A. Waters; aka In the Halls of Evil | .75 | 1.50 | 2.25 | |
| 73-624 The UFO Report–Irving A. Greenfield | .50 | 1.00 | 1.50 | UF |
| 73-625 In the Absence of Mrs. Peterson–Nigel Balchin | .50 | 1.00 | 1.50 | R |
| 73-627 Death of a Pornographer–Anthony Lejeune | .50 | 1.00 | 1.50 | |
| 73-628 The Rape of Berlin–W. Howard Baker | .50 | 1.00 | 1.50 | |
| 73-629 In Black and Whitey–Ed Lacy | 1.00 | 2.00 | 3.00 | M |
| 73-630 Golden Blood–Jack Williamson | 1.00 | 2.00 | 3.00 | SF |
| 73-631 Assassins from Tomorrow–Peter Heath | .75 | 1.50 | 2.25 | SF |
| 73-632 Opal Street–June Wetherell | .50 | 1.00 | 1.50 | |
| 73-633 House of Hate–Dorothy Fletcher | .50 | 1.00 | 1.50 | |
| 73-634 Make Love, Not Waves–Jay Martin | .50 | 1.00 | 1.50 | M |
| 73-635 Lady of Battle Mountain–Matt Stuart | .50 | 1.00 | 1.50 | |
| 73-636 Space Plague–George O. Smith; aka Highways in Hiding | 1.00 | 2.00 | 3.00 | SF |
| 73-637 The Eagle's Nest–Dorothy Daniels | .50 | 1.00 | 1.50 | |
| 73-639 The Daisy Dilemma–Don Rico | .50 | 1.00 | 1.50 | |
| 73-640 Hangman's Country–Lewis B. Patten | .75 | 1.50 | 2.25 | W |
| 73-643 The House of Two Wives–William D. Frissell | .50 | 1.00 | 1.50 | R |
| 73-644 Vigilante–21st Century–Robert Moore Williams | 1.00 | 2.00 | 3.00 | SF |
| 73-645 Nurse in the Tropics–Ann Gilmer | .50 | 1.00 | 1.50 | R |
| 73-646 Traitor!–W. Howard Baker | .50 | 1.00 | 1.50 | |
| 73-647 A Taste for Honey–H.F. Heard | .75 | 1.50 | 2.25 | M |
| 73-648 The Piper on the Mountain–Ellis Peters | .50 | 1.00 | 1.50 | R |
| 73-649 Nurse of Brooding Mansion–Paulette Warren | .50 | 1.00 | 1.50 | |
| 73-650 King Kull–Robert E. Howard & Lin Carter; 1967; c-Krenkel | 1.50 | 3.00 | 4.50 | F |
| 73-651 Wyoming Gun Law–Lee Floren | .75 | 1.50 | 2.25 | W |
| 73-652 Yes from No Man's Land–Bernard Kops | .50 | 1.00 | 1.50 | |
| 73-653 Nightmare–Anne Blaisdell | .50 | 1.00 | 1.50 | |
| 73-656 Psychedelic Spy–T.A. Waters | 1.50 | 3.00 | 4.50 | |
| 73-659 Night of the Wolf–W. Howard Baker | 1.00 | 2.00 | 3.00 | |
| 73-660 The Hand of Cain–Martin Thomas | .75 | 1.50 | 2.25 | |
| 73-662 The Carnelian Cube–L. Sprague de Camp & Fletcher Pratt | 1.00 | 2.00 | 3.00 | F |
| 73-663 Eye of the Devil–Philip Loraine; aka Day of the Arrow; aka 13 | .50 | 1.00 | 1.50 | R |
| 73-665 Gun Grudge–Walt Coburn | .75 | 1.50 | 2.25 | W |
| 73-666 Riders by Night–Nelson Nye | .75 | 1.50 | 2.25 | W |
| 73-668 Ring and Walk In–Miriam Borgenicht | .50 | 1.00 | 1.50 | M |
| 73-669 Women's Battalion–W.A. Ballinger | 1.00 | 2.00 | 3.00 | C |
| 73-671 The Dirty Game–W. Howard Baker | .75 | 1.50 | 2.25 | |
| 73-672 Waters of Death–Irving A. Greenfield | .75 | 1.50 | 2.25 | SF |
| 73-674 House Malign–Julie Wellsley | .50 | 1.00 | 1.50 | |
| 73-675 Experiment in Crime–Philip Wylie | .50 | 1.00 | 1.50 | |
| 73-677 Ensign Flandry–Poul Anderson | .75 | 1.50 | 2.25 | SF |
| 73-680 Seed of Evil–Petrina Crawford | .50 | 1.00 | 1.50 | |
| 73-683 The Spy Who Came in from the Copa–Dagmar | .50 | 1.00 | 1.50 | |
| 73-685 Conan–Robert E. Howard, L. Sprague de Camp & Lin Carter; 1967; c-Frazetta | 1.50 | 3.00 | 4.50 | F |
| 73-687 Lobo Law–Will Ermine | .75 | 1.50 | 2.25 | W |
| 73-688 The Jewel in the Skull–Michael Moorcock | 1.50 | 3.00 | 4.50 | F |
| 73-690 Transit–Edmund Cooper | .75 | 1.50 | 2.25 | SF |
| 73-691 Science Fiction Inventions–ed. Damon Knight | .75 | 1.50 | 2.25 | SF |
| 73-693 The Other Side of Hate–Richard Pierce | .50 | 1.00 | 1.50 | |
| 73-694 Zanthar of the Many Worlds–Robert Moore Williams; c-Jeff Jones | 1.00 | 2.00 | 3.00 | F |
| 73-701 The End of Eternity–Isaac Asimov | .75 | 1.50 | 2.25 | SF |
| 73-702 The Naked Sun–Isaac Asimov | .75 | 1.50 | 2.25 | SF |
| 73-703 The Currents of Space–Isaac Asimov | .75 | 1.50 | 2.25 | SF |
| 73-704 The Stars like Dust–Isaac Asimov; 1968 | .75 | 1.50 | 2.25 | SF |
| 73-706 The Vampire Cameo–Dorothea Nile (Michael Avallone) | 1.50 | 3.00 | 4.50 | |

| | V/Good | Fine | N/Mint | |
|---|---|---|---|---|
| 73-707 The Sorcerer's Amulet–Michael Moorcock; 1968 | 1.50 | 3.00 | 4.50 | F |
| 73-712 The Silent Hostage–Sarah Gainham | .50 | 1.00 | 1.50 | R |
| 73-713 Love That Spy!–T.A. Waters | 1.50 | 3.00 | 4.50 | |
| 73-714 Through the Dark Curtain–Peter Saxon | .50 | 1.00 | 1.50 | |
| 73-715 The Day of Timestop–Philip José Farmer; aka A Woman a Day | 1.00 | 2.00 | 3.00 | SF |
| 73-718 Dirge for a Lady–Alice N. White | .50 | 1.00 | 1.50 | |
| 73-719 A Girl Called Boots–Don Sted | .50 | 1.00 | 1.50 | E |
| 73-720 The Witching Night–C.S. Cody (Leslie Waller) | .75 | 1.50 | 2.25 | |
| 73-721 Wolfshead–Robert E. Howard; 1968; c-Frazetta | 1.50 | 3.00 | 4.50 | F |
| 73-724 Return to the Ardennes–Harold Calin | .75 | 1.50 | 2.25 | C |
| 73-727 Daymares–Fredric Brown; 1968 | 5.00 | 10.00 | 15.00 | M |
| 73-732 Seetee Ship–Jack Williamson | 1.00 | 2.00 | 3.00 | SF |
| 73-733 Seetee Shock–Jack Williamson | 1.00 | 2.00 | 3.00 | SF |
| 73-734 Lost Wolf River–Dwight Bennett | .75 | 1.50 | 2.25 | W |
| 73-735 I, the Machine–Paul W. Fairman | 1.00 | 2.00 | 3.00 | SF |
| 73-737 Gringo Gun–E.E. Halleran | .75 | 1.50 | 2.25 | W |
| 73-739 Bluebeard's Daughter–Marion Zimmer Bradley | 1.50 | 3.00 | 4.50 | |
| 73-740 Great Science Fiction Adventures–ed. Larry T. Shaw | .75 | 1.50 | 2.25 | SF |
| 73-746 Master of the Undead–Hugo Paul (Gardner F. Fox) | 1.50 | 3.00 | 4.50 | HO |
| 73-748 The Reign of Wizardry–Jack Williamson; c-Frazetta | 1.50 | 3.00 | 4.50 | F |
| 73-750 The Curse of Rathlaw–Peter Saxon | .75 | 1.50 | 2.25 | |
| 73-752 Bloodworld–Laurence M. Janifer; aka You Sane Men | .75 | 1.50 | 2.25 | SF |
| 73-753 The Erotica Caper–Jay Martin | .50 | 1.00 | 1.50 | E |
| 73-754 The Orgy at Madame Dracula's–F.W. Paul (Paul Fairman) | 2.00 | 4.00 | 6.00 | |
| 73-756 Deep in a Dark Country–Patricia Drew | .50 | 1.00 | 1.50 | |
| 73-757 Lone Gun–Eric Allen | .75 | 1.50 | 2.25 | W |
| 73-758 Enchanted Circle–Alicia Grace | .50 | 1.00 | 1.50 | |
| 73-761 The Sword of the Dawn–Michael Moorcock; 1968 | 1.50 | 3.00 | 4.50 | F |
| 73-764 Stormy Range–Dwight Bennett | .75 | 1.50 | 2.25 | W |
| 73-765 Barb Wire–Walt Coburn | .75 | 1.50 | 2.25 | W |
| 73-766 The Bell from Infinity–Robert Moore Williams | .75 | 1.50 | 2.25 | SF |
| 73-767 Autumn Romance–Philip Wylie | .50 | 1.00 | 1.50 | |
| 73-769 The Blackwood Cult–T.A. Waters | .50 | 1.00 | 1.50 | |
| 73-770 Dropout–Martin Yoseloff | .50 | 1.00 | 1.50 | |
| 73-774 Night Riders' Moon–Robert J. Hogan | .75 | 1.50 | 2.25 | W |
| 73-777 The Brass Key–Francis Swann | .50 | 1.00 | 1.50 | |
| 73-778 The Bank with the Bamboo Door–Dolores Hitchens | .50 | 1.00 | 1.50 | |
| 73-779 I Passed as a Teenager–Lyn Tornabene | .50 | 1.00 | 1.50 | NF |
| 73-780 Conan the Avenger–Robert E. Howard, Bjorn Nyberg & L. Sprague de Camp; c-Frazetta | 1.50 | 3.00 | 4.50 | F |
| 73-781 The Limbo Affair–Anthony Firth | .50 | 1.00 | 1.50 | M |
| 73-783 Men Who Die Twice–Peter Heath | .75 | 1.50 | 2.25 | SF |
| 73-784 Satan's Child–Peter Saxon | .75 | 1.50 | 2.25 | |
| 73-785 A Warm Bed in Reno–Jason Morgan | .50 | 1.00 | 1.50 | |
| 73-788 The Kill Squad–Walter Bond | .75 | 1.50 | 2.25 | M |
| 73-789 The Challenge of Smoke Wade–Robert J. Hogan | .75 | 1.50 | 2.25 | W |
| 73-793 The Passion Flower Puzzle–Don Rico | .50 | 1.00 | 1.50 | |
| 73-794 Lady in Shadows–Antonia Lamb | .50 | 1.00 | 1.50 | |
| 73-796 Feud at Sundown–Robert J. Hogan | .75 | 1.50 | 2.25 | W |
| 73-797 Into the Slave Nebula–John Brunner; aka Slavers of Space | 1.00 | 2.00 | 3.00 | SF |
| 73-798 Little Often Fanny–Norman Jackson | .50 | 1.00 | 1.50 | |
| 73-799 Mask of Silence–Sheila McErlean | .75 | 1.50 | 2.25 | M |
| 73-800 Conan of the Isles–Robert E. Howard, L. Sprague de Camp & Lin Carter | 1.50 | 3.00 | 4.50 | F |
| 73-801 Killer's Brand–H.A. DeRosso | .75 | 1.50 | 2.25 | W |
| 73-802 Guess Who's Coming to Kill You–Ellery Queen | .75 | 1.50 | 2.25 | M |
| 73-803 Fondle with Care–Jay Martin | .75 | 1.50 | 2.25 | H |
| 73-804 Fulfillment–Elsie Lee | .50 | 1.00 | 1.50 | |
| 73-805 Zanthar at Moon's Madness–Robert Moore Williams; c-Jeff Jones | 1.00 | 2.00 | 3.00 | F |
| 73-806 The Texas Breed–James D. Sayers | .75 | 1.50 | 2.25 | W |
| 73-807 Two-Gun Law–Robert J. Hogan | .75 | 1.50 | 2.25 | W |
| 73-808 Call of the Flesh–Virginia Coffman | .50 | 1.00 | 1.50 | |
| 73-809 Captain Sex–Norman Jackson | .75 | 1.50 | 2.25 | |
| 73-810 Who?–Algis Budrys; 1968 | 1.00 | 2.00 | 3.00 | SF |
| 73-812 Boss Gun–Nelson Nye | .75 | 1.50 | 2.25 | W |

**LANCER BOOKS,** *continued*

| Code | Title | V/Good | Fine | N/Mint | |
|---|---|---|---|---|---|
| 73-813 | Ramrod Vengeance–Nelson Nye | .75 | 1.50 | 2.25 | W |
| 73-814 | A Study in Terror–Ellery Queen | 1.00 | 2.00 | 3.00 | M |
| 73-815 | Cabot–Philip Ketchum | .75 | 1.50 | 2.25 | W |
| 73-816 | Loco!–Nelson Nye | .75 | 1.50 | 2.25 | W |
| 73-817 | Dead in Bed–Henry Kane | .75 | 1.50 | 2.25 | M |
| 73-818 | Bloody Range–James D. Sayers | .75 | 1.50 | 2.25 | W |
| 73-819 | Dingo–J.M. Scott | .75 | 1.50 | 2.25 | |
| 73-820 | Arizona Renegade–Nelson Nye | .75 | 1.50 | 2.25 | W |
| 73-822 | Brandy on the Rocks–Maryl James | .50 | 1.00 | 1.50 | |
| 73-823 | Don't Just Die There–Henry Kane | .75 | 1.50 | 2.25 | M |
| 73-824 | The Secret of the Runestaff–Michael Moorcock; 1969 | 1.50 | 3.00 | 4.50 | F |
| 73-825 | Stanton Bishop, M.D.–Norman Daniels | .50 | 1.00 | 1.50 | R |
| 73-826 | Bang the Doll Slowly–Clyde Ames | .75 | 1.50 | 2.25 | E |
| 73-827 | Gun-Hawk Valley–Philip Ketchum | .75 | 1.50 | 2.25 | W |
| 73-828 | Fanny for Free–Norman Jackson | .75 | 1.50 | 2.25 | |
| 73-829 | Hannibal Brooks–Lou Cameron; movie tie-in | 1.00 | 2.00 | 3.00 | |
| 73-830 | The Day of the Arrow–Philip Loraine; aka 13; aka Eye of the Devil | .50 | 1.00 | 1.50 | R |
| 73-831 | Haelstrom Manor–S.J. Treibich | .50 | 1.00 | 1.50 | |
| 73-832 | The Last of the Breed–Don Rico | .50 | 1.00 | 1.50 | |
| 73-833 | Edge of the Desert–Matt Stuart | .75 | 1.50 | 2.25 | W |
| 73-834 | Ghost at Ravenkill Manor–Paulette Warren | .50 | 1.00 | 1.50 | |
| 73-835 | The Death of a Hooker–Henry Kane | .75 | 1.50 | 2.25 | M |
| 73-836 | Zanthar at Trip's End–Robert Moore William | 1.00 | 2.00 | 3.00 | F |
| 73-837 | Fanny's Double Feature–Norman Jackson | .75 | 1.50 | 2.25 | |
| 73-838 | My Friend Tony–William Johnston; TV tie-in | 1.00 | 2.00 | 3.00 | |
| 73-839 | The Schack Job–Henry Kane | .75 | 1.50 | 2.25 | M |
| 73-840 | To the Dark Tower–Lyda Belknap Long | 1.00 | 2.00 | 3.00 | |
| 73-841 | The Wine of Vengeance–Julie Wellsley | .50 | 1.00 | 1.50 | |
| 73-842 | Some Beckoning Wraith–Paulette Warren | .50 | 1.00 | 1.50 | |
| 73-843 | The Devil's Church–F. Draco | .50 | 1.00 | 1.50 | |
| 73-845 | Texas Guns–Ray Hogan | .75 | 1.50 | 2.25 | W |
| 73-846 | The Man Who Tamed Dodge–Philip Ketchum | .75 | 1.50 | 2.25 | W |
| 73-847 | Border Bandit–Ray Hogan | .75 | 1.50 | 2.25 | W |
| 73-849 | The Brady Bunch–William Johnston; 1969; TV tie-in | 1.50 | 3.00 | 4.50 | |
| 73-850 | Scalpel of Honor–Dolores Craig | .50 | 1.00 | 1.50 | R |
| 73-851 | Outlaw Vengeance–James D. Sayers | .75 | 1.50 | 2.25 | W |
| 73-852 | A Tycoon for Ann–Glenna Finley | .50 | 1.00 | 1.50 | R |
| 73-853 | The Lancer Book of Puns and Anagrams–Mel Taub | 1.50 | 3.00 | 4.50 | NF |
| 73-854 | Summer Season–Jane Rossiter | .50 | 1.00 | 1.50 | R |
| 73-855 | Airport Nurse–Rose Williams | .50 | 1.00 | 1.50 | R |
| 73-856 | Rustlers' Trail–James D. Sayers | .75 | 1.50 | 2.25 | W |
| 73-858 | Don't Call Me Madame–Henry Kane | .75 | 1.50 | 2.25 | M |
| 73-859 | The Man Who Turned Outlaw–Philip Ketchum | .75 | 1.50 | 2.25 | W |
| 73-860 | Nurse on Call–Ann Gilmer | .50 | 1.00 | 1.50 | R |
| 73-861 | Detour to Romance–Katherine McComb | .50 | 1.00 | 1.50 | R |
| 73-862 | The Darkest Room–Grace Corren | .50 | 1.00 | 1.50 | |
| 73-863 | Bloody Crossing–Robert J. Hogan | .75 | 1.50 | 2.25 | W |
| 73-864 | Showdown at the P.T.A. Corral–William Johnston; TV tie-in | 1.50 | 3.00 | 4.50 | |
| 73-865 | Riverwood–Jane Corby | .50 | 1.00 | 1.50 | |
| 73-866 | The Shadow and the Fear–Jane Corby | .50 | 1.00 | 1.50 | |
| 73-867 | Guns of Arizona–Charles N. Heckelmann | .75 | 1.50 | 2.25 | W |
| 73-869 | Quick Crosswords–Boris Randolph | 1.00 | 2.00 | 3.00 | NF |
| 73-870 | Bullet Valley–James D. Sayers | .75 | 1.50 | 2.25 | W |
| 73-871 | The Man Who Sold Leadville–Philip Ketchum | .75 | 1.50 | 2.25 | W |
| 73-872 | Count Up to Blast-Down–William Johnston; TV tie-in | 1.50 | 3.00 | 4.50 | |
| 73-873 | Three Loves for Cecily–Frances Dean Hancock | .50 | 1.00 | 1.50 | R |
| 73-874 | Montana Crossing–Giles A. Lutz | .75 | 1.50 | 2.25 | W |
| 73-875 | Homecoming Nurse–Rose Dana | .50 | 1.00 | 1.50 | R |
| 73-876 | Nanny and the Professor–William Johnston; TV tie-in | 1.50 | 3.00 | 4.50 | |
| 73-877 | Nurse of Brooding Mansion–Paulette Warren | .50 | 1.00 | 1.50 | |
| 73-878 | Resort Nurse–Rose Dana | .50 | 1.00 | 1.50 | R |
| 73-879 | Herbert Ettenson's Best Crossword Puzzles–Herbert Ettenson | 1.50 | 3.00 | 4.50 | NF |
| 73-880 | Pistols for Hire–Nelson Nye | .75 | 1.50 | 2.25 | W |
| 73-881 | Wyoming Gun Law–Lee Floren | .75 | 1.50 | 2.25 | W |
| 73-882 | Climb the Dark Mountain–Julie Wellsley | .50 | 1.00 | 1.50 | |
| 73-883 | The Searching Heart–Virginia C. Holmgren | .50 | 1.00 | 1.50 | |
| 73-884 | The Mercenary–Burt Hirschfeld; TV tie-in | 1.00 | 2.00 | 3.00 | |
| 73-885 | Cruise Ship Nurse–Rose Dana | .50 | 1.00 | 1.50 | R |
| 73-886 | Gunslammer–Lee Floren | .75 | 1.50 | 2.25 | W |
| 73-887 | Bullets for Badwater–Al P. Nelson | .75 | 1.50 | 2.25 | W |
| 73-888 | Kelly's Heroes–Burt Hirschfeld; movie tie-in | 1.50 | 3.00 | 4.50 | |
| 73-889 | What Hath Nanny Wrought–William Johnston; TV tie-in (for Nanny and the Professor) | 1.50 | 3.00 | 4.50 | |
| 73-890 | Herbert Ettenson's 2nd Book of Best Crossword Puzzles | 1.00 | 2.00 | 3.00 | NF |
| 73-891 | The Bumbler Strikes Again–William Johnston; TV tie-in (for The Brady Bunch) | 1.50 | 3.00 | 4.50 | |
| 73-892 | Gunsmoke Holiday–Lee Floren | .75 | 1.50 | 2.25 | W |
| 73-893 | Bullets West–James D. Sayers | .75 | 1.50 | 2.25 | W |
| 73-894 | Soul Nurse–Rose Dana | .50 | 1.00 | 1.50 | R |
| 73-895 | Smoky River–Lee Floren | .75 | 1.50 | 2.25 | W |
| 73-896 | Killers of the Diamond A–James D. Sayers | .75 | 1.50 | 2.25 | W |
| 73-897 | Seven Brave Men–Brian Garfield; 1970 | .75 | 1.50 | 2.25 | W |
| 73-898 | Winchester Wages–Lee Floren | .75 | 1.50 | 2.25 | W |
| 73-899 | The Cherished Heart–Nancy MacDougall Kennedy | .50 | 1.00 | 1.50 | R |
| 74-501 | The Colour out of Space–H.P. Lovecraft | 1.00 | 2.00 | 3.00 | HO |
| 74-502 | The Dunwich Horror–H.P. Lovecraft | 1.50 | 3.00 | 4.50 | HO |
| 74-503 | Killer Tank–Norman Daniels | .75 | 1.50 | 2.25 | C |
| 74-504 | View from a Height–Isaac Asimov | 1.00 | 2.00 | 3.00 | NF |
| 74-505 | I Was the Cat–Mathilde-Lily Carré | .50 | 1.00 | 1.50 | NF |
| 74-506 | Castle at Witches' Coven–Virginia Coffman | .50 | 1.00 | 1.50 | |
| 74-507 | Secret of the Ghostly Shroud–Nancy Buckingham | .50 | 1.00 | 1.50 | R |
| 74-508 | Season of Evil–Jane Gordon | .50 | 1.00 | 1.50 | |
| 74-509 | Star Barbarian–Dave van Arnam | 1.00 | 2.00 | 3.00 | SF |
| 74-510 | Signal Red–Harold Calin | .75 | 1.50 | 2.25 | C |
| 74-511 | The Judas Diary–W. Howard Baker | .75 | 1.50 | 2.25 | |
| 74-512 | Travels with a Duchess–Menna Gallie | .50 | 1.00 | 1.50 | |
| 74-513 | Women's Battalion–W.A. Ballinger | .75 | 1.50 | 2.25 | C |
| 74-514 | Black Gold–William H.A. Carr | .75 | 1.50 | 2.25 | |
| 74-515 | Evil in the House–Evelyn Bond | .50 | 1.00 | 1.50 | |
| 74-516 | Death Lives in the Mansion–Douglas Locke | .50 | 1.00 | 1.50 | |
| 74-517 | Blood River–James D. Sayers | .75 | 1.50 | 2.25 | W |
| 74-518 | Rustlers' Ranch–James D. Sayers | .75 | 1.50 | 2.25 | W |
| 74-519 | The Humanoids–Jack Williamson | 1.00 | 2.00 | 3.00 | SF |
| 74-520 | Mistress of Ghosthaven–Jean Bellamy | .50 | 1.00 | 1.50 | |
| 74-521 | In Black and Whitey–Ed Lacy | .75 | 1.50 | 2.25 | |
| 74-522 | The Sexy Egg Love-In–Jay Martin | .50 | 1.00 | 1.50 | E |
| 74-523 | Dirty Son of a Witch–Sid Jacobson | .75 | 1.50 | 2.25 | E |
| 74-524 | The Space Dreamers–Arthur C. Clarke | .75 | 1.50 | 2.25 | SF |
| 74-525 | The Shattered Raven–Edward D. Hoch | 1.50 | 3.00 | 4.50 | M |
| 74-526 | The Tunnel War–Lou Cameron | .75 | 1.50 | 2.25 | C |
| 74-527 | The Campus Murders–Ellery Queen | 1.00 | 2.00 | 3.00 | M |
| 74-528 | That Night–Jane Blackmore | .50 | 1.00 | 1.50 | |
| 74-529 | The Brooding House–Alice Brennan | .50 | 1.00 | 1.50 | |
| 74-530 | Night Falls at Bitterhill–Paulette Warren | .50 | 1.00 | 1.50 | |
| 74-531 | The Planned Parenthood Caper–F.W. Paul (Paul Fairman) | .50 | 1.00 | 1.50 | |
| 74-532 | Anything You Can Do . . .–Randall Garrett | .75 | 1.50 | 2.25 | SF |
| 74-533 | Catch the Starwinds–A. Bertram Chandler | 1.25 | 2.50 | 3.75 | SF |
| 74-534 | Castle Terror–Marion Zimmer Bradley | 1.25 | 2.50 | 3.75 | |
| 74-535 | Island of the Accursed–Wilma Winthrop | .50 | 1.00 | 1.50 | |
| 74-536 | The Corridors of Time–Poul Anderson | .75 | 1.50 | 2.25 | SF |
| 74-537 | Time Gladiator–Mack Reynolds; 1969 | 1.00 | 2.00 | 3.00 | SF |
| 74-538 | Siege Perilous–Lester del Rey; aka Man without A Planet | .75 | 1.50 | 2.25 | SF |
| 74-539 | The UFO Report: New Revised 1969 Edition–Irving Greenfield | .50 | 1.00 | 1.50 | UF |

**LANCER BOOKS,** *continued*

| | | V/Good | Fine | N/Mint | |
|---|---|---|---|---|---|
| 74-540 | Number One–David Moessinger; movie tie-in | .75 | 1.50 | 2.25 | |
| 74-541 | The 9-Month Caper–Ted Mark | 1.00 | 2.00 | 3.00 | |
| 74-542 | Pussycat, Pussycat!–Ted Mark | 1.00 | 2.00 | 3.00 | |
| 74-543 | The Man from O.R.G.Y.–Ted Mark | 1.00 | 2.00 | 3.00 | |
| 74-544 | Dr. Nyet–Ted Mark | 1.00 | 2.00 | 3.00 | |
| 74-545 | A Whiff of Death–Isaac Asimov; aka The Death Dealers | 1.00 | 2.00 | 3.00 | M |
| 74-546 | The Empty People–K.M. O'Donnell (Barry N. Malzberg) | 1.50 | 3.00 | 4.50 | SF |
| 74-547 | The Dying Earth–Jack Vance | 1.50 | 3.00 | 4.50 | SF |
| 74-548 | Satan's Coast–Elsie Lee | .50 | 1.00 | 1.50 | |
| 74-549 | Return to Darkness–Willo Davis Roberts | .50 | 1.00 | 1.50 | |
| 74-550 | Stranger in a Dark Land–Julie Wellsley | .50 | 1.00 | 1.50 | |
| 74-551 | The Moonflower–Phyllis A. Whitney | .50 | 1.00 | 1.50 | |
| 74-552 | Devil by the Sea–Nina Bawden | .50 | 1.00 | 1.50 | |
| 74-553 | The Lay of the Land–F.W. Paul (Paul Fairman) | .75 | 1.50 | 2.25 | |
| 74-554 | Letters to a Black Boy–Bob Teague | .50 | 1.00 | 1.50 | |
| 74-556 | The Mighty Barbarians–ed. Hans Stefan Santesson; 1969 | 1.50 | 3.00 | 4.50 | F |
| 74-557 | Needle–Hal Clement; aka From Outer Space | 1.00 | 2.00 | 3.00 | SF |
| 74-558 | Curse of Still Valley–Sharon Wagner | .50 | 1.00 | 1.50 | |
| 74-559 | Who Dies There?–Henry Kane | .75 | 1.50 | 2.25 | M |
| 74-560 | The Liquid Man–C.B. Gilford | 1.00 | 2.00 | 3.00 | SF |
| 74-561 | King Kull–Robert E. Howard & Lin Carter; c-Krenkel | 1.25 | 2.50 | 3.75 | F |
| 74-562 | Snatch an Eye–Henry Kane | .75 | 1.50 | 2.25 | M |
| 74-563 | In the Halls of Evil–T.A. Waters; aka The Shrewsbury Horror | 1.00 | 2.00 | 3.00 | |
| 74-564 | Kavin's World–David Mason; c-Frazetta | 1.50 | 3.00 | 4.50 | F |
| 74-565 | Wharf Sinister–Alicia Grace | .50 | 1.00 | 1.50 | |
| 74-566 | My Son the Double Agent–Ted Mark | 1.00 | 2.00 | 3.00 | |
| 74-567 | The Nude Who Never–Ted Mark | 1.00 | 2.00 | 3.00 | |
| 74-569 | Ted Mark Reader–Ted Mark | 1.00 | 2.00 | 3.00 | |
| 74-570 | A Hard Day's Knight–Ted Mark | 1.00 | 2.00 | 3.00 | |
| 74-571 | The Girl from Pussycat–Ted Mark | 1.00 | 2.00 | 3.00 | |
| 74-572 | The Unhatched Egghead–Ted Mark | 1.00 | 2.00 | 3.00 | |
| 74-573 | Agent of Entropy–Martin Siegel | .75 | 1.50 | 2.25 | SF |
| 74-574 | Survivor of Darkness–Dorothy Daniels | .50 | 1.00 | 1.50 | |
| 74-575 | House of Stolen Memories–Dorothy Daniels; aka Mansion of Lost Memories | .50 | 1.00 | 1.50 | |
| 74-576 | A Touch of the Witch–June Wetherell | .50 | 1.00 | 1.50 | |
| 74-577 | Dark Love, Dark Magic–O.T. Jackson | .50 | 1.00 | 1.50 | |
| 74-578 | The Green Stone–Suzanne Blanc | .50 | 1.00 | 1.50 | |
| 74-579 | Redbeard–Michael Resnick | 1.00 | 2.00 | 3.00 | SF |
| 74-580 | Litany of Evil–Alice Brennan | .50 | 1.00 | 1.50 | |
| 74-581 | Garden of Satan–Claire Vincent | .50 | 1.00 | 1.50 | |
| 74-582 | Angel, Angel, Down We Go–William Johnston; movie tie-in | 1.50 | 3.00 | 4.50 | |
| 74-583 | Isle of the Undead–Virginia Coffman | 1.00 | 2.00 | 3.00 | |
| 74-584 | The Cavalier's Corpse–Theodora DuBois | .50 | 1.00 | 1.50 | |
| 74-585 | Now Begins Tomorrow–ed. Damon Knight; aka First Flight | .50 | 1.00 | 1.50 | SF |
| 74-586 | Let the Fire Fall–Kate Wilhelm | 1.50 | 3.00 | 4.50 | SF |
| 74-587 | Prisoners of the Sky–Carroll M. Capps | .75 | 1.50 | 2.25 | SF |
| 74-588 | Money, Murder and the McNeills–Theodora DuBois | .50 | 1.00 | 1.50 | |
| 74-590 | The Name of the Game–Eric Wilkins | .50 | 1.00 | 1.50 | |
| 74-591 | The Girl with the Polka-dot Box–F.W. Paul (Paul Fairman) | .75 | 1.50 | 2.25 | |
| 74-592 | The Sorceress of Qar–Ted White | 1.00 | 2.00 | 3.00 | F |
| 74-593 | Phoenix Prime–Ted White; c-Frazetta | 1.50 | 3.00 | 4.50 | F |
| 74-594 | On a Fated Night–Dorothea Malm | .50 | 1.00 | 1.50 | R |
| 74-595 | Don't Go Away Dead–Henry Kane | .75 | 1.50 | 2.25 | M |
| 74-596 | The Girl from Aquarius–Dani Lawrence | .50 | 1.00 | 1.50 | |
| 74-597 | Ghost of Coquina Key–Jean Bellamy | .50 | 1.00 | 1.50 | |
| 74-598 | Gemini in Darkness–Clarissa Ross | .50 | 1.00 | 1.50 | |
| 74-599 | The Waiting Darkness–Willo Davis Roberts | .50 | 1.00 | 1.50 | |
| 74-600 | The Long Loud Silence–Wilson Tucker | 1.00 | 2.00 | 3.00 | SF |
| 74-601 | World without Children/The Earth Quarter–Damon Knight | 1.00 | 2.00 | 3.00 | SF |
| 74-602 | The Plague of Silence–John Creasey | 1.00 | 2.00 | 3.00 | |
| 74-603 | The Devil and Destiny–Theodora DuBois | .50 | 1.00 | 1.50 | |
| 74-604 | East of Desolation–Jack Higgins | .50 | 1.00 | 1.50 | |
| 74-605 | A Taste for Honey–H.F. Heard | .50 | 1.00 | 1.50 | M |

| | | V/Good | Fine | N/Mint | |
|---|---|---|---|---|---|
| 74-606 | Stars for the Toff–John Creasey | .50 | 1.00 | 1.50 | M |
| 74-607 | The Toff and the Deep Blue Sea–John Creasey | .50 | 1.00 | 1.50 | M |
| 74-608 | Sport for the Baron–John Creasey | .50 | 1.00 | 1.50 | M |
| 74-609 | The Brides of Lucifer–Miriam Lynch | 1.00 | 2.00 | 3.00 | |
| 74-610 | Private Eyeful–Henry Kane | .75 | 1.50 | 2.25 | M |
| 74-611 | The Small Tawny Cat–Virginia Coffman | .50 | 1.00 | 1.50 | |
| 74-612 | Return to the Stars–Edmond Hamilton | 1.00 | 2.00 | 3.00 | SF |
| 74-613 | Curse of the Island Pool–Virginia Coffman | .50 | 1.00 | 1.50 | |
| 74-614 | A Boy Named Cash–Albert Govoni | 1.00 | 2.00 | 3.00 | B |
| 74-615 | The Templeton Memoirs–Dorothy Daniels | .50 | 1.00 | 1.50 | |
| 74-616 | Timestop!–Philip José Farmer; aka A Woman a Day; aka The Day of Timestop | .75 | 1.50 | 2.25 | SF |
| 74-617 | The Footsteps–Theodora DuBois | .50 | 1.00 | 1.50 | |
| 74-618 | The Blackwood Cult–T.A. Waters | 1.50 | 3.00 | 4.50 | |
| 74-619 | The Sevier Secrets–Dorothy Daniels | .50 | 1.00 | 1.50 | |
| 74-620 | Shadow of a Past Love–Willo Davis Roberts | .50 | 1.00 | 1.50 | |
| 74-621 | The Dark Symphony–Dean R. Koontz | 2.50 | 5.00 | 7.50 | SF |
| 74-622 | Call the Toff–John Creasey | .50 | 1.00 | 1.50 | M |
| 74-623 | The Blight–John Creasey | .50 | 1.00 | 1.50 | M |
| 74-624 | The Midnight Riders–James D. Sayers; aka Beyond Midnight Chasm | .75 | 1.50 | 2.25 | W |
| 74-625 | Hangman's Valley–Joseph Chadwick | .75 | 1.50 | 2.25 | W |
| 74-626 | Break the Toff–John Creasey | .50 | 1.00 | 1.50 | M |
| 74-627 | Time Rogue–Leo P. Kelley | 1.00 | 2.00 | 3.00 | SF |
| 74-628 | The Sorcerer's Skull–David Mason | 1.25 | 2.50 | 3.75 | F |
| 74-629 | The Bow Street Terror–T.A. Waters | .50 | 1.00 | 1.50 | |
| 74-630 | Dark Shadows at Bitterhill–Paulette Warren | .50 | 1.00 | 1.50 | |
| 74-631 | The House at Fern Canyon–Willo Davis Roberts | .50 | 1.00 | 1.50 | |
| 74-632 | Mrs. Barrenger's Dirty Book–Daoma Winston | .50 | 1.00 | 1.50 | |
| 74-633 | Kindling–Nevil Shute | .50 | 1.00 | 1.50 | |
| 74-634 | Ordeal–Nevil Shute | .50 | 1.00 | 1.50 | |
| 74-635 | "Mumsy, Nanny, Sonny and Girly"–Brian Comport; movie tie-in | 1.00 | 2.00 | 3.00 | |
| 74-636 | The Coffin Things–Michael Avallone | 2.00 | 4.00 | 6.00 | HO |
| 74-637 | Cavanaugh Keep–Miriam Leslie | .50 | 1.00 | 1.50 | |
| 74-638 | Brand of the Outlaw–Al P. Nelson | .75 | 1.50 | 2.25 | W |
| 74-639 | The High Terrace–Virginia Coffman | .50 | 1.00 | 1.50 | |
| 74-640 | The Black Hearts Murders–Ellery Queen | 1.50 | 3.00 | 4.50 | |
| 74-641 | Out of the Fog–Clarissa Ross | .50 | 1.00 | 1.50 | |
| 74-642 | Follow the Toff–John Creasey | .50 | 1.00 | 1.50 | M |
| 74-643 | Kiss! Kiss! Kill!–Henry Kane | .75 | 1.50 | 2.25 | M |
| 74-644 | The Naked Sun–Isaac Asimov | .50 | 1.00 | 1.50 | SF |
| 74-645 | The Devil's Mistress–Virginia Coffman | .50 | 1.00 | 1.50 | |
| 74-646 | Better Wed Than Dead–Henry Kane; aka Unholy Trio | 1.50 | 3.00 | 4.50 | M |
| 74-647 | Day of Dark Memory–Jean Philips | .50 | 1.00 | 1.50 | |
| 74-648 | Blood Moon–Jan Alexander | .50 | 1.00 | 1.50 | |
| 74-649 | Star Rogue–Lin Carter | 1.00 | 2.00 | 3.00 | SF |
| 74-650 | The Man Who Fell to Earth–Walter Tevis | 1.00 | 2.00 | 3.00 | SF |
| 74-651 | The Savage Heart–Norman Daniels | .75 | 1.50 | 2.25 | |
| 74-652 | The Famine–John Creasey | .50 | 1.00 | 1.50 | |
| 74-653 | The Toff on Fire–John Creasey | .50 | 1.00 | 1.50 | M |
| 74-654 | Phantom at Lost Lake–Delphine C. Lyons | .50 | 1.00 | 1.50 | |
| 74-655 | Waters of Death–Irving A. Greenfield | .50 | 1.00 | 1.50 | SF |
| 74-656 | Hell's Gate–Dean R. Koontz | 2.50 | 5.00 | 7.50 | SF |
| 74-657 | Essay on the Duty of Civil Disobedience and Walden–Henry David Thoreau | .50 | 1.00 | 1.50 | NF |
| 74-658 | Hunt the Toff–John Creasey | .50 | 1.00 | 1.50 | M |
| 74-659 | Affair for the Baron–John Creasey | .50 | 1.00 | 1.50 | M |
| 74-660 | Fear No Evil–Alice Brennan | .50 | 1.00 | 1.50 | |
| 74-661 | Daughters of Cain–Miriam Lynch | .50 | 1.00 | 1.50 | |
| 74-662 | Beware the Kindly Stranger–Clarisa Ross | .50 | 1.00 | 1.50 | |
| 74-663 | The Attic Rope–Dorothy Daniels | .50 | 1.00 | 1.50 | |
| 74-664 | The Bomb Job–Henry Kane | .75 | 1.50 | 2.25 | M |
| 74-665 | The Toff and the Great Illusion–John Creasey | .50 | 1.00 | 1.50 | M |
| 74-666 | Kill the Toff–John Creasey | .50 | 1.00 | 1.50 | M |
| 74-667 | Naked to the Stars–Gordon R. Dickson | 1.00 | 2.00 | 3.00 | SF |
| 74-668 | The City of the Beast–Michael Moorcock; aka Warriors of Mars | .75 | 1.50 | 2.25 | F |

LANCER BOOKS, *continued*

| | | V/Good | Fine | N/Mint | |
|---|---|---|---|---|---|
| 74-669 | Farewell to Vienna–Dorothy Fletcher | .50 | 1.00 | 1.50 | |
| 74-670 | Shadows–Jan Alexander | .50 | 1.00 | 1.50 | |
| 74-671 | Tree of Evil–June Wetherell | .50 | 1.00 | 1.50 | |
| 74-672 | House of Mirror Images–Daoma Winston | .50 | 1.00 | 1.50 | |
| 74-673 | Rake's Junction–Peter Kanto | .50 | 1.00 | 1.50 | |
| 74-674 | The Toff and the Deadly Parson–John Creasey | .50 | 1.00 | 1.50 | M |
| 74-675 | The Flood–John Creasey | .50 | 1.00 | 1.50 | |
| 74-676 | The Carnelian Cube–L. Sprague de Camp & Fletcher Pratt | 1.00 | 2.00 | 3.00 | F |
| 74-677 | Report on Probability A–Brian W. Aldiss | .75 | 1.50 | 2.25 | SF |
| 74-678 | The Marble Angel–Dorothy Daniels | .50 | 1.00 | 1.50 | |
| 74-679 | Night of the Black Tower–Olga Sinclair | .50 | 1.00 | 1.50 | |
| 74-680 | Dark Cedars–Ann Fenton | .50 | 1.00 | 1.50 | |
| 74-681 | Country of the Wolf–Sharon Wagner | .50 | 1.00 | 1.50 | |
| 74-682 | Mass for a Dead Witch–Alicia Grace | 1.00 | 2.00 | 3.00 | |
| 74-683 | Burn!–Norman Gant; movie tie-in | .50 | 1.00 | 1.50 | |
| 74-684 | The Woman with the Portuguese Basket–Eva-lis Wuorio | .50 | 1.00 | 1.50 | |
| 74-685 | Here Comes the Toff–John Creasey | .50 | 1.00 | 1.50 | M |
| 74-686 | The Toff at the Fair–John Creasey | .50 | 1.00 | 1.50 | M |
| 74-687 | Barrier World–Louis Charbonneau | 1.00 | 2.00 | 3.00 | SF |
| 74-688 | Lord of Blood–Dave Van Arnam; 1970; c–Jim Steranko | 1.25 | 2.50 | 3.75 | SF |
| 74-689 | Journey into Twilight–Miriam Lynch | .50 | 1.00 | 1.50 | |
| 74-690 | Legacy of the Lost–June Wetherell | .50 | 1.00 | 1.50 | |
| 74-691 | The Tarot Spell–Willo Davis Roberts | .50 | 1.00 | 1.50 | |
| 74-692 | Legend of the Loch–Alanna Knight | .50 | 1.00 | 1.50 | |
| 74-693 | Panzer!–Harold Calin | .75 | 1.50 | 2.25 | C |
| 74-694 | Sleep without Dreams–Henry Kane | .75 | 1.50 | 2.25 | M |
| 74-695 | Girley–Brian Comport; movie tie-in | 1.00 | 2.00 | 3.00 | |
| 74-696 | Explosion–Eva-lis Wuorio | .50 | 1.00 | 1.50 | |
| 74-697 | Priestess of the Damned–Virginia Coffman | .50 | 1.00 | 1.50 | |
| 74-698 | Satan's World–Poul Anderson | 1.00 | 2.00 | 3.00 | SF |
| 74-699 | The Magic of Atlantis–ed. Lin Carter | 1.00 | 2.00 | 3.00 | F |
| 74-700 | Kiss the Toff–John Creasey | .50 | 1.00 | 1.50 | M |
| 74-705 | Shadowland–Elaine Evans (Gil Brewer) | 1.00 | 2.00 | 3.00 | |
| 74-706 | Alex in Wonderland–Burt Hirschfeld; movie tie-in | 1.00 | 2.00 | 3.00 | F |
| 74-707 | The Mighty Swordsmen–ed. Hans Stefan Santesson; 1970; c–Jim Steranko | 1.50 | 3.00 | 4.50 | A |
| 74-708 | The Last Valley–J.B. Pick; movie tie-in | 1.00 | 2.00 | 3.00 | A |
| 74-709 | Inspector West Regrets–John Creasey | .50 | 1.00 | 1.50 | M |
| 74-710 | Terror Factor–Eva-lis Wuorio | .50 | 1.00 | 1.50 | |
| 74-712 | The Creepers–John Creasey | .50 | 1.00 | 1.50 | M |
| 74-713 | Meeting in Madrid–Dorothy Fletcher | .50 | 1.00 | 1.50 | R |
| 74-714 | Greenwood–Jean Phillips | .50 | 1.00 | 1.50 | |
| 74-715 | Maridu–Sharon Wagner | .50 | 1.00 | 1.50 | |
| 74-716 | Evil at Roger's Cross–Catherine Marchant | .50 | 1.00 | 1.50 | |
| 74-717 | Invitation to Evil–Willo Davis Roberts | .50 | 1.00 | 1.50 | |
| 74-719 | Beastchild–Dean R. Koontz | 2.50 | 5.00 | 7.50 | SF |
| 74-720 | Holiday for Inspector West–John Creasey | .50 | 1.00 | 1.50 | M |
| 74-721 | The Leaves of Time–Neal Barrett, Jr | 1.00 | 2.00 | 3.00 | SF |
| 74-722 | Outworlder–Lin Carter; 1971 | 1.00 | 2.00 | 3.00 | SF |
| 74-723 | The Unearthly–Dorothy Daniels | .50 | 1.00 | 1.50 | |
| 74-724 | Flight of a Fallen Angel–Daoma Winston | .50 | 1.00 | 1.50 | |
| 74-725 | Beyond Recall–Dorothy Fletcher | .50 | 1.00 | 1.50 | R |
| 74-726 | Witches' Holiday–Miriam Lynch | .50 | 1.00 | 1.50 | |
| 74-727 | Dark Memories–Jane Morella | .50 | 1.00 | 1.50 | |
| 74-728 | Fengriffen–David Case | .50 | 1.00 | 1.50 | |
| 74-729 | The Devil's Virgin–Virginia Coffman | .50 | 1.00 | 1.50 | |
| 74-730 | In the Hour before Midnight–Jack Higgins | .50 | 1.00 | 1.50 | |
| 74-731 | A Procession of the Damned–Wilson Tucker | 1.00 | 2.00 | 3.00 | M |
| 74-733 | October Witch–Alanna Knight | .50 | 1.00 | 1.50 | |
| 74-734 | King's Pawn–Willo Davis Roberts | .50 | 1.00 | 1.50 | |
| 74-735 | Glimpse into Terror–Clarissa Ross | .50 | 1.00 | 1.50 | |
| 74-736 | Lord of the Spiders–Michael Moorcock; aka Blades of Mars | .75 | 1.50 | 2.25 | F |
| 74-737 | The Toff Goes to Market–John Creasey | .50 | 1.00 | 1.50 | M |
| 74-738 | Death in Cold Print–John Creasey | .50 | 1.00 | 1.50 | M |
| 74-739 | Dark Love, Dark Magic–O.T. Jackson | .50 | 1.00 | 1.50 | |
| 74-741 | Ten Million Years to Friday–John Lymington | 1.00 | 2.00 | 3.00 | SF |
| 74-742 | The Corridors of Time–Poul Anderson | .75 | 1.50 | 2.25 | SF |
| 74-744 | Lattimore Arch–Angela Gray | .50 | 1.00 | 1.50 | |
| 74-745 | House of Fools–Jan Alexander | .50 | 1.00 | 1.50 | |
| 74-746 | Lonely Toys–Miriam Lynch | .50 | 1.00 | 1.50 | |
| 74-747 | Riverwood–Miriam Lynch | .50 | 1.00 | 1.50 | |
| 74-748 | The Priest's Wife–; movie tie-in | 1.00 | 2.00 | 3.00 | |
| 74-749 | Battle for Inspector West–John Creasey | .50 | 1.00 | 1.50 | M |
| 74-750 | Survival World–Frank Belknap Long | 1.00 | 2.00 | 3.00 | SF |
| 74-752 | Devil's Dreamer–Alice Brennan | .50 | 1.00 | 1.50 | |
| 74-753 | Nor Spell Nor Charm–Alice N. West | .50 | 1.00 | 1.50 | |
| 74-754 | Voice from the Grave–Clarissa Ross | .50 | 1.00 | 1.50 | |
| 74-757 | The Beauty Queen Killer–John Creasey | .50 | 1.00 | 1.50 | M |
| 74-758 | Two Faces of Fear–Julie Wellsley | .50 | 1.00 | 1.50 | |
| 74-759 | The Sleep–John Creasey | .75 | 1.50 | 2.25 | |
| 74-760 | Trail's End at 'Dobie Town–K.R.G. Granger | .75 | 1.50 | 2.25 | W |
| 74-761 | Terror Trap–Willo Davis Roberts | .50 | 1.00 | 1.50 | |
| 74-762 | Place on Dark Island–Grace Corren | .50 | 1.00 | 1.50 | |
| 74-765 | Wharf Sinister–Alicia Grace | .50 | 1.00 | 1.50 | |
| 74-767 | Death of a Racehorse–John Creasey | .50 | 1.00 | 1.50 | M |
| 74-769 | Circle of Evil–Sharon Wagner | .50 | 1.00 | 1.50 | |
| 74-770 | The Haunting of Villa Gabriel–Clarissa Ross | .50 | 1.00 | 1.50 | |
| 74-772 | The Witch Tree–Lyda Belknap Long (Frank Belknap Long); 1971 | 1.50 | 3.00 | 4.50 | |
| 74-773 | Chalet Diabolique–Virginia Coffman | .50 | 1.00 | 1.50 | |
| 74-775 | Lone Trail for the Virginian–Dean Owen; TV tie-in | 1.00 | 2.00 | 3.00 | W |
| 74-776 | The Time Shifters–Sam Merwin, Jr | 1.00 | 2.00 | 3.00 | SF |
| 74-777 | Showdown–Norman Daniels | .75 | 1.50 | 2.25 | W |
| 74-778 | Space for Hire–William F. Nolan | .75 | 1.50 | 2.25 | SF |
| 74-779 | The Last Express–Baynard Kendrick | .75 | 1.50 | 2.25 | M |
| 74-782 | The Doomsday Exhibit–Paul W. Fairman | .50 | 1.00 | 1.50 | SF |
| 74-783 | Murder by Gemini–Richard Gallagher; TV tie-in | .75 | 1.50 | 2.25 | M |
| 74-784 | Reservations for Death–Baynard Kendrick | .75 | 1.50 | 2.25 | M |
| 74-788 | Blind Man's Bluff–Baynard Kendrick | .75 | 1.50 | 2.25 | M |
| 74-789 | Ride into Gunsmoke–L.P. Holmes | .75 | 1.50 | 2.25 | W |
| 74-790 | Nevada Rampage–L.P. Holmes | .75 | 1.50 | 2.25 | W |
| 74-791 | Thunder Trail–Norman Daniels; 1972 | .75 | 1.50 | 2.25 | W |
| 74-793 | Savage Guns–Matt Stuart | .75 | 1.50 | 2.25 | W |
| 74-794 | Blood Trail to Bannack–Norman Daniels; 1973 | .75 | 1.50 | 2.25 | W |
| 74-795 | Bridget Loves Bernie–Paul Fairman; TV tie-in | 1.50 | 3.00 | 4.50 | R |
| 74-796 | Lone Gun–Eric Allen; 1973 | .75 | 1.50 | 2.25 | W |
| 74-800 | Hangman's Valley–Joseph Chadwick | .75 | 1.50 | 2.25 | W |
| 74-802 | Outlaw Vengeance–James D. Sayers; 1973 | .75 | 1.50 | 2.25 | W |
| (74-)801 | Super Karate Made Easy–Moja Rone (no prefix) | .50 | 1.00 | 1.50 | NF |
| 74-802 | Martyrs and Fighters–Paul Friedman | .75 | 1.50 | 2.25 | NF |
| 74-803 | Selected Writings of the Marquis de Sade–; 1962 | .50 | 1.00 | 1.50 | E |
| 74-804 | Modern Sex Techniques–Robert Street | .50 | 1.00 | 1.50 | NF |
| 74-805 | 100 Years of Lynchings–Ralph Ginzberg | 2.00 | 4.00 | 6.00 | NF |
| 74-806 | Green Dolphin Street–Elizabeth Goudge | .50 | 1.00 | 1.50 | R |
| 74-807 | The Dying Earth–Jack Vance | 2.00 | 4.00 | 6.00 | F |
| 74-808 | A Martian Odyssey–Stanley G. Weinbaum | 1.00 | 2.00 | 3.00 | SF |
| 74-809 | The Diner's Club Drink Book–Matty Simmons | .50 | 1.00 | 1.50 | NF |
| 74-810 | Recalled to Life–Robert Silverberg | 1.00 | 2.00 | 3.00 | SF |
| 74-811 | The Twenty-Second Century–John Christopher | 1.50 | 3.00 | 4.50 | SF |
| 74-812 | The Humanoids–Jack Williamson | 1.00 | 2.00 | 3.00 | SF |
| 74-813 | The Sexual Deviate–Benjamin Morse, MD | .50 | 1.00 | 1.50 | NF |
| 74-814 | The Autobiography of Will Rogers–ed. Donald Day | 1.00 | 2.00 | 3.00 | B |
| 74-815 | The Stars like Dust–Isaac Asimov; 1963 | 1.00 | 2.00 | 3.00 | SF |
| 74-816 | The Currents of Space–Isaac Asimov | 1.00 | 2.00 | 3.00 | SF |
| 74-817 | A Modern Marriage Manual–Benjamin Morse, MD | .50 | 1.00 | 1.50 | NF |
| 74-818 | The End of Eternity–Isaac Asimov | 1.00 | 2.00 | 3.00 | SF |
| 74-819 | Dreadful Sanctuary–Eric Frank Russell (rev.) | 1.00 | 2.00 | 3.00 | SF |
| 74-820 | Combat Judo Made Easy–Claude St. Denise | .75 | 1.50 | 2.25 | NF |

LANCER BOOKS, *continued*

| | | V/Good | Fine | N/Mint | |
|---|---|---|---|---|---|
| 74-821 | Twilight Women–L.T. Woodward, MD (Robert Silverberg) | 1.00 | 2.00 | 3.00 | NF |
| 74-822 | The Sexual Behavior of the American College Girl–Benjamin Morse, MD | .50 | 1.00 | 1.50 | NF |
| 74-823 | Nymphomania–Dr. Franklin Klaf, MD | .50 | 1.00 | 1.50 | NF |
| 74-824 | The Natural Superiority of Women–Ashley Montagu | .50 | 1.00 | 1.50 | NF |
| 74-825 | Super Karate Made Easy–Moja Rone | .50 | 1.00 | 1.50 | NF |
| 74-826 | Memoirs of a Coxcomb–John Cleland | .50 | 1.00 | 1.50 | E |
| 74-827 | The Kennedy Women–Robert Curran | .75 | 1.50 | 2.25 | B |
| 74-828 | Burlesque–Martin Collyer; has one fold-out insert | 5.00 | 10.00 | 15.00 | NF |
| 74-831 | From Torment to Rapture–Sylvia Sharon | .75 | 1.50 | 2.25 | E |
| 74-832 | The Medici Fountain–Joseph Kessel | .50 | 1.00 | 1.50 | |
| 74-833 | Patterns of Adultery–W.D. Sprague, PhD | .50 | 1.00 | 1.50 | NF |
| 74-834 | Tower in the West–Frank Norris | .50 | 1.00 | 1.50 | |
| 74-835 | Sadism–L.T. Woodward, MD (Robert Silverberg) | 1.00 | 2.00 | 3.00 | E |
| 74-836 | Another Way of Love–Joe Weiss | .75 | 1.50 | 2.25 | E |
| 74-837 | Blood of a Lion–Alfred Maund | .50 | 1.00 | 1.50 | |
| 74-838 | The Scalpel's Edge–Alfred A. Weinstein, MD | .50 | 1.00 | 1.50 | |
| 74-839 | Lady Sings the Blues–Billie Holiday & William Dufty | 1.00 | 2.00 | 3.00 | B |
| 74-840 | Torture Garden–Octave Mirbeau; c-Frazetta | 7.50 | 15.00 | 22.50 | F |
| 74-841 | Candy–Maxwell Kenton | 1.00 | 2.00 | 3.00 | E |
| 74-842 | The Procurer–Hugo Paul (Gardner F. Fox) | 2.00 | 4.00 | 6.00 | NF |
| 74-843 | Punishment for Passion–Sylvia Sharon | .75 | 1.50 | 2.25 | E |
| 74-844 | Pursuit of the Prodigal–Louis Auchincloss | .50 | 1.00 | 1.50 | |
| 74-845 | Another Woman's Bed–Linda Whitmore | .75 | 1.50 | 2.25 | E |
| 74-846 | The Gay Year–M de F | .50 | 1.00 | 1.50 | E |
| 74-848 | The Golden Nymph–Linda Whitmore | .75 | 1.50 | 2.25 | E |
| 74-850 | The Bedroom Philosophers–Marquis de Sade | .50 | 1.00 | 1.50 | E |
| 74-851 | The Hourglass–Edwin Gilbert | .50 | 1.00 | 1.50 | |
| 74-852 | Confessions of a Married Man–Burgess | .50 | 1.00 | 1.50 | E |
| 74-853 | Modern Sex Techniques–Robert Street | .50 | 1.00 | 1.50 | NF |
| 74-854 | The Tenant of Wildfell Hall–Anne Bronte | .50 | 1.00 | 1.50 | |
| 74-858 | On a Fated Night–Dorothea Malm | .50 | 1.00 | 1.50 | R |
| 74-859 | Test Yourself–William Bernard & Leopold | .75 | 1.50 | 2.25 | NF |
| 74-864 | The Breakwater–George Mandel | .50 | 1.00 | 1.50 | |
| 74-865 | Satyriasis: A Study of Male Nympho-mania–Franklin S. Klaf, MD | .50 | 1.00 | 1.50 | NF |
| 74-868 | The House on the Hill–Jane Whitehead | .50 | 1.00 | 1.50 | |
| 74-872 | Don't Look Behind You!–Samuel Rogers | .50 | 1.00 | 1.50 | |
| 74-873 | Suffer a Witch–Rae Foley | .50 | 1.00 | 1.50 | |
| 74-874 | Sleep–Gay Gaer Luce & Julius Segal | .50 | 1.00 | 1.50 | NF |
| 74-876 | Ambulance Call–Nathan D. Shiff, MD | .50 | 1.00 | 1.50 | |
| 74-877 | Season of Evil–Jane Gordon; 1967 | .50 | 1.00 | 1.50 | |
| 74-878 | The Devil of the Stairs–Pat Root | .50 | 1.00 | 1.50 | |
| 74-879 | The Templeton Memoirs–Dorothy Daniels | .50 | 1.00 | 1.50 | |
| 74-880 | Secret Melody–Paula Minton | .50 | 1.00 | 1.50 | |
| 74-881 | The Running Spy–Joseph Milton | .50 | 1.00 | 1.50 | |
| 74-882 | Fog Hides the Fury–Paula Minton | .50 | 1.00 | 1.50 | |
| 74-883 | That Winter–Merle Miller | .50 | 1.00 | 1.50 | |
| 74-884 | Kindling–Nevil Shute | .50 | 1.00 | 1.50 | |
| 74-885 | Sybil–Louis Auchincloss | .50 | 1.00 | 1.50 | |
| 74-886 | Cloak of Folly–Burke Boyce | .50 | 1.00 | 1.50 | R |
| 74-887 | Upbeat–Irving Shulman | .50 | 1.00 | 1.50 | |
| 74-888 | The Career of David Noble–Frances Parkinson Keyes | .50 | 1.00 | 1.50 | |
| 74-889 | Catalina–W. Somerset Maugham | .75 | 1.50 | 2.25 | |
| 74-890 | Rose's Last Summer–Margaret Millar | .50 | 1.00 | 1.50 | |
| 74-891 | Restless Are the Sails–Evelyn Eaton | .50 | 1.00 | 1.50 | R |
| 74-892 | One Million Centuries–Richard A. Lupoff | 1.00 | 2.00 | 3.00 | SF |
| 74-894 | The Clouded Mirror–Evelyn Bond | .50 | 1.00 | 1.50 | |
| 74-895 | Norman's Letter–Gavin Lambert | .50 | 1.00 | 1.50 | E |
| 74-897 | The Kept Woman–Wenzell Brown | .75 | 1.50 | 2.25 | NF |
| 74-898 | Landfall–Nevil Shute | .50 | 1.00 | 1.50 | |

| | | V/Good | Fine | N/Mint | |
|---|---|---|---|---|---|
| 74-899 | Ayesha, the Return of She–H. Rider Haggard; 1967 | 1.50 | 3.00 | 4.50 | F |
| 74-900 | Frame-up–Andrew Garve | .75 | 1.50 | 2.25 | |
| 74-904 | House on the Fens–Catherine Marchant | .50 | 1.00 | 1.50 | |
| 74-905 | Rest in Agony–Paul W. Fairman | 1.00 | 2.00 | 3.00 | SF |
| 74-908 | Curse of the Island Pool–Virginia Coffman | .50 | 1.00 | 1.50 | |
| 74-909 | One Man Too Many–Virginia Coffman | .50 | 1.00 | 1.50 | |
| 74-910 | The Naked Blade–Frederick Faust | 1.00 | 2.00 | 3.00 | A |
| 74-911 | The Well of the Unicorn–Fletcher Pratt | 1.00 | 2.00 | 3.00 | SF |
| 74-912 | Bride of Terror–Evelyn Bond | .75 | 1.50 | 2.25 | |
| 74-915 | Black Heather–Virginia Coffman | .50 | 1.00 | 1.50 | |
| 74-916 | The Moonflower–Phyllis A. Whitney | .50 | 1.00 | 1.50 | |
| 74-921 | Death in Captivity–Michael Gilbert; 1968 | .75 | 1.50 | 2.25 | |
| 74-922 | They Never Looked Inside–Michael Gilbert | .75 | 1.50 | 2.25 | |
| 74-923 | Ordeal–Nevil Shute | .50 | 1.00 | 1.50 | |
| 74-925 | Pursuit of the Prodigal–Louis Auchincloss | .50 | 1.00 | 1.50 | |
| 74-927 | The Dissent of Dominick Shapiro–Bernard Kops | .50 | 1.00 | 1.50 | |
| 74-928 | Doctor's Office–Elsie Lee | .50 | 1.00 | 1.50 | R |
| 74-929 | Valley of Shadows–Delphine C. Lyons | .50 | 1.00 | 1.50 | |
| 74-930 | Of Time and Space and Other Things–Isaac Asimov | 1.00 | 2.00 | 3.00 | NF |
| 74-932 | Inside the F.B.I.–Norman Ollestad | .75 | 1.50 | 2.25 | NF |
| 74-933 | The Creepers–John Creasey | .50 | 1.00 | 1.50 | M |
| 74-934 | The Case against Paul Raeburn–John Creasey | .50 | 1.00 | 1.50 | M |
| 74-935 | Tarnished Scalpel–Norman Daniels | .75 | 1.50 | 2.25 | |
| 74-936 | The Brain Machine–George O. Smith; aka The Fourth "R" | .75 | 1.50 | 2.25 | SF |
| 74-937 | Rapture for Three–Vivian Elmore | .50 | 1.00 | 1.50 | E |
| 74-938 | Nurse at Danger Mansion–Dorothy Daniels | .50 | 1.00 | 1.50 | |
| 74-939 | A Secret Understanding–Merle Miller | .50 | 1.00 | 1.50 | |
| 74-941 | Zanthar at the Edge of Never–Robert Moore Williams | 1.00 | 2.00 | 3.00 | F |
| 74-942 | The Coffin Things–Michael Avallone | 1.50 | 3.00 | 4.50 | HO |
| 74-943 | A Meeting by the River–Christopher Isherwood | 1.00 | 2.00 | 3.00 | |
| 74-944 | Great Science Fiction Adventures–ed. Larry T. Shaw | .75 | 1.50 | 2.25 | SF |
| 74-945 | Explosion!–Eva-Lis Wuorio; aka Mid-summer Lokki | .50 | 1.00 | 1.50 | |
| 74-947 | Finistere–Fritz Peters | .50 | 1.00 | 1.50 | E |
| 74-949 | The Man Who Wanted Stars–Dean McLaughlin | .50 | 1.00 | 1.50 | SF |
| 74-950 | The Loom of Terror–Paula Minton | .50 | 1.00 | 1.50 | |
| 74-951 | Golden Nymph–Roger Conway | .50 | 1.00 | 1.50 | |
| 74-952 | In My Soul I Am Free–Brad Steiger | .75 | 1.50 | 2.25 | |
| 74-953 | Flying Saucers in Fact and Fiction–ed. Hans Stefan Santesson | .50 | 1.00 | 1.50 | UF |
| 74-954 | The Richest Girl in the World–Virginia Coffman | .50 | 1.00 | 1.50 | |
| 74-956 | The Case for an Afterlife–Roy Ald | .50 | 1.00 | 1.50 | |
| 74-957 | A Year among the Girls–Darrell G. Raynor | .50 | 1.00 | 1.50 | NF |
| 74-958 | Conan–Robert E. Howard, L. Sprague de Camp & Lin Carter; c-Frazetta | 1.50 | 3.00 | 4.50 | F |
| 74-960 | The Good Guy–Lou Cameron | .50 | 1.00 | 1.50 | |
| 74-963 | Conan the Freebooter–Robert E. Howard, L. Sprague de Camp & Lin Carter | 1.50 | 3.00 | 4.50 | F |
| 74-964 | The Savage Scalpel–Alain Rothstein | .50 | 1.00 | 1.50 | R |
| 74-965 | Waiting for a Tiger–Nelson Nye | .75 | 1.50 | 2.25 | W |
| 74-966 | An Air That Kills–Margaret Millar | 1.00 | 2.00 | 3.00 | |
| 74-967 | Death Is a Swinger–Jason Morgan | .75 | 1.50 | 2.25 | M |
| 74-968 | The Life She Wanted–Roger Conway | .50 | 1.00 | 1.50 | |
| 74-969 | Wall of Eyes–Margaret Millar | .75 | 1.50 | 2.25 | R |
| 74-970 | The Eagle's Nest–Dorothy Daniels | .50 | 1.00 | 1.50 | |
| 74-971 | This Ancient Evil–Dorothy Daniels | .50 | 1.00 | 1.50 | |
| 74-972 | Cliffside Castle–Dorothy Daniels | .50 | 1.00 | 1.50 | |
| 74-973 | The Rest Is Silence–Virginia Coffman | .50 | 1.00 | 1.50 | |
| 74-974 | The Shadow Box–Virginia Coffman | .50 | 1.00 | 1.50 | |
| 74-975 | The Hypnotic I–Cybelle Barnet | .50 | 1.00 | 1.50 | NF |
| 74-976 | Conan the Wanderer–Robert E. Howard, L. Sprague de Camp & Lin Carter | 1.50 | 3.00 | 4.50 | F |
| 74-977 | The Moonlit Door–Anne Maybury | .50 | 1.00 | 1.50 | |
| 74-978 | Vatican Roulette–David Lodge | .50 | 1.00 | 1.50 | H |

**LANCER BOOKS,** *continued*

| No. | Title | V/Good | Fine | N/Mint | |
|---|---|---|---|---|---|
| 74-979 | The Co-ordinator–Andrew York | .50 | 1.00 | 1.50 | |
| 74-980 | Mansion of Golden Windows–Elsie Lee | .50 | 1.00 | 1.50 | |
| 74-981 | House of Shadows–Evelyn Bond | .50 | 1.00 | 1.50 | |
| 74-982 | Dance in Darkness–Dorothy Daniels | .50 | 1.00 | 1.50 | |
| 74-983 | The Lonely Steeple–Victor Wolfson | .50 | 1.00 | 1.50 | |
| 74-984 | Lady in Darkness–Evelyn Bond | .50 | 1.00 | 1.50 | |
| 74-985 | Jackie and Ari–for Love or Money?–George Carpozi | 1.00 | 2.00 | 3.00 | NF |
| 74-986 | The Naked Sun–Isaac Asimov | .50 | 1.00 | 1.50 | SF |
| 74-987 | The Devil's Instrument–Mary Fletcher | .50 | 1.00 | 1.50 | |
| 74-988 | The Nature of Witches–Joan Sanders | .50 | 1.00 | 1.50 | |
| 74-989 | Fanny Comes Across!–Norman Jackson | .75 | 1.50 | 2.25 | |
| 74-991 | The Secret of the Villa Como–Susan Marvin | .50 | 1.00 | 1.50 | |
| 74-992 | The Mists of Memory–Catherine Marchant | .50 | 1.00 | 1.50 | |
| 74-993 | Tremble of a Hand–Richard Pierce | .50 | 1.00 | 1.50 | R |
| 74-994 | The Others–Irving A. Greenfield | 1.00 | 2.00 | 3.00 | SF |
| 74-995 | House of Men–Catherine Marchant | .50 | 1.00 | 1.50 | |
| 74-996 | Adding a Dimension–Isaac Asimov | 1.00 | 2.00 | 3.00 | NF |
| 74-998 | Texas Outlaws–K.R.G. Granger; aka Tejanos! | .75 | 1.50 | 2.25 | W |
| 74-999 | Enchanted Island–Anne Mather | .50 | 1.00 | 1.50 | R |
| 75-001 | Kama Sutra of Vatsyayana | .75 | 1.50 | 2.25 | NF |
| 75-002 | The Perfumed Garden of the Sheikh Nefzaoui | .75 | 1.50 | 2.25 | NF |
| 75-003 | Justine–Marquis de Sade | .50 | 1.00 | 1.50 | E |
| 75-004 | The Ananga Ranga of Kalyana Malla or, The Hindu Art of Love | .75 | 1.50 | 2.25 | E |
| 75-005 | Juliette–Marquis de Sade; 1965 | .50 | 1.00 | 1.50 | E |
| 75-006 | The Power of Aikido–Claude St. Denise | .50 | 1.00 | 1.50 | NF |
| 75-007 | The Jewel in the Lotus–Allen Edwardes | .75 | 1.50 | 2.25 | NF |
| 75-008 | Women–John Philip Lundin, PhD | .75 | 1.50 | 2.25 | NF |
| 75-009 | Pale Fire–Vladimir Nabokov | .50 | 1.00 | 1.50 | |
| 75-010 | The Alcoholic Woman–Benjamin Karpman MD | .50 | 1.00 | 1.50 | NF |
| 75-014 | Men–Gloria Barrett; 1967 | .75 | 1.50 | 2.25 | |
| 75-016 | The Jewel in the Lotus–Allen Edwardes | .50 | 1.00 | 1.50 | E |
| 75-017 | The Perfumed Garden of the Sheikh Nefzaoui | .50 | 1.00 | 1.50 | NF |
| 75-019 | Sophisticated Sex Techniques in Marriage–L.T. Woodward, MD | .50 | 1.00 | 1.50 | NF |
| 75-020 | The Jasper Gate–Jonathan Quayne | .50 | 1.00 | 1.50 | E |
| 75-021 | Low Carbohydrate Diet Cookbook–Roy Ald | .50 | 1.00 | 1.50 | NF |
| 75-022 | The Sea Is So Wide–Evelyn Eaton | .75 | 1.50 | 2.25 | R |
| 75-023 | The Notebooks of Captain Georges–Jean Renoir | .50 | 1.00 | 1.50 | E |
| 75-024 | After Work Cookbook–Roy Ald | .50 | 1.00 | 1.50 | NF |
| 75-025 | Mistresses–John Philip Lundin, PhD | .50 | 1.00 | 1.50 | NF |
| 75-026 | The Promiscuous Woman–Wenzell Brown | .75 | 1.50 | 2.25 | NF |
| 75-028 | Groovy Chick!–Patricia Bentley; 1967 | .75 | 1.50 | 2.25 | E |
| 75-029 | Eros and Capricorn–John Warren Wells | .50 | 1.00 | 1.50 | NF |
| 75-030 | The 2nd Easy Gourmet Cookbook–Elsie Lee | .50 | 1.00 | 1.50 | NF |
| 75-031 | The Bedroom Game–A.L. Bristoe; 1968 | .50 | 1.00 | 1.50 | E |
| 75-035 | Sexual Deviations in the Female–Louis S. London | .50 | 1.00 | 1.50 | NF |
| 75-036 | Test Yourself–Bernard & Leopold | .50 | 1.00 | 1.50 | NF |
| 75-038 | The Magic Island–William Seabrook | .50 | 1.00 | 1.50 | NF |
| 75-039 | Eros Pursued–Kathleen Price | .50 | 1.00 | 1.50 | NF |
| 75-040 | Modern Sex Techniques–Robert Street | .50 | 1.00 | 1.50 | NF |
| 75-041 | The Taboo Breakers–John Warren Wells | .50 | 1.00 | 1.50 | NF |
| 75-042 | The Search for Bridey Murphy–Morey Bernstein | .50 | 1.00 | 1.50 | NF |
| 75-043 | Candy–Maxwell Kenton | .50 | 1.00 | 1.50 | E |
| 75-045 | The Dragon of the Ishtar Gate–L. Sprague de Camp; 1968; c-Krenkel | 1.50 | 3.00 | 4.50 | F |
| 75-047 | Chane–Norman Gant | .50 | 1.00 | 1.50 | |
| 75-048 | The Male Nymphomaniac–Franklin S. Klaf, MD | .50 | 1.00 | 1.50 | NF |
| 75-049 | Modern Marriage Manual–Benjamin Morse, MD | .50 | 1.00 | 1.50 | NF |
| 75-050 | Night Falls on the City–Sarah Gainham | .50 | 1.00 | 1.50 | |
| 75-051 | Slaver–Leslie Gladson | .75 | 1.50 | 2.25 | |
| 75-052 | Sparhawk–Lionel Webb | .75 | 1.50 | 2.25 | |
| 75-053 | Black Vengeance–Norman Gant | .75 | 1.50 | 2.25 | |
| 75-054 | H.M.S. Leviathan–John Winton | .75 | 1.50 | 2.25 | C |
| 75-055 | Mistress of Bayou Labelle–Lou Cameron | .75 | 1.50 | 2.25 | |
| 75-056 | Song of Africa–Leland Tracy | .75 | 1.50 | 2.25 | |
| 75-057 | Bestseller–Toni Freedman | .50 | 1.00 | 1.50 | |
| 75-058 | The Lust Club–Sylvia Sharon | .50 | 1.00 | 1.50 | E |
| 75-060 | Sex and the Supernatural–Brad Steiger | .50 | 1.00 | 1.50 | |
| 75-061 | Rogue Slave–Lionel Webb | .75 | 1.50 | 2.25 | |
| 75-063 | Law of the Lash–Norman Daniels | .75 | 1.50 | 2.25 | |
| 75-064 | A Woman of My Age–Nina Bawden | .50 | 1.00 | 1.50 | |
| 75-065 | My Search for Manhood–Marc Weston | .50 | 1.00 | 1.50 | NF |
| 75-066 | Black Ivory–S.J. Treibich; 1969 | 1.00 | 2.00 | 3.00 | |
| 75-067 | Strike from the Sky–Alexander McKee | .50 | 1.00 | 1.50 | C |
| 75-068 | The Sex Cheats–W.D. Sprague, MD | .50 | 1.00 | 1.50 | NF |
| 75-069 | The Tiger's Fang–Paul Twitchell | .50 | 1.00 | 1.50 | |
| 75-070 | Slave Empire–Norman Gant | .75 | 1.50 | 2.25 | |
| 75-071 | Master of Wyndward–Norman Daniels | .75 | 1.50 | 2.25 | |
| 75-072 | Conan of Cimmeria–Robert E. Howard, L. Sprague de Camp & Lin Carter; 1969; c-Frazetta | 1.50 | 3.00 | 4.50 | F |
| 75-073 | Children of the Supernatural–Robert Tralins | .75 | 1.50 | 2.25 | |
| 75-074 | Plantation Breed–Hugo Paul (Gardner F. Fox) | 2.00 | 4.00 | 6.00 | |
| 75-075 | Black Brute–Robert Tralins | 1.50 | 3.00 | 4.50 | |
| 75-076 | Dark Frenzy–Buford Griffen | .75 | 1.50 | 2.25 | |
| 75-077 | The Fortunate Pilgrim–Mario Puzo | .50 | 1.00 | 1.50 | |
| 75-078 | King's Blacks–Leslie Gladson | .75 | 1.50 | 2.25 | |
| 75-079 | The Black and the Damned–Harold Calin | .75 | 1.50 | 2.25 | |
| 75-080 | Pendulum–John Christopher | 1.00 | 2.00 | 3.00 | SF |
| 75-081 | Lady Sings the Blues–Billie Holiday & William Duffy; movie tie-in | 1.00 | 2.00 | 3.00 | |
| 75-082 | The Nymph Syndrome–Jean Francis | .50 | 1.00 | 1.50 | R |
| 75-083 | Runaway Slave–Robert Tralins | 1.50 | 3.00 | 4.50 | |
| 75-084 | The Best of Sexplosion– | .50 | 1.00 | 1.50 | NF |
| 75-085 | The Monstrous Undead–Bernhardt J. Hurwood | 1.50 | 3.00 | 4.50 | |
| 75-086 | Ashanti–Lou Cameron | .50 | 1.00 | 1.50 | |
| 75-087 | Combat Judo–Claude St. Denise | .50 | 1.00 | 1.50 | NF |
| 75-089 | Beast–Leslie Gladson | .75 | 1.50 | 2.25 | |
| 75-090 | The Advance Man–Norman Jackson | .50 | 1.00 | 1.50 | E |
| 75-091 | The Frog Pond–Joyce MacIver | .50 | 1.00 | 1.50 | |
| 75-092 | The Sharpshooter–Norman Jackson | .50 | 1.00 | 1.50 | |
| 75-093 | The Candidate's Wife–Virginia Coffman | .50 | 1.00 | 1.50 | |
| 75-094 | Slave's Revenge–Robert Tralins | 1.50 | 3.00 | 4.50 | |
| 75-095 | Black Hercules–Stuart Jason (Oscar Wilson) | 1.00 | 2.00 | 3.00 | |
| 75-096 | Black Cargo–Harold Calin | .75 | 1.50 | 2.25 | |
| 75-097 | Young Man on the Make–William Hurley | .50 | 1.00 | 1.50 | NF |
| 75-098 | Slave's Blood–Robert R. Vaugh, Jr | .75 | 1.50 | 2.25 | |
| 75-099 | Fanny Hill Meets Captain Sex–Norman Jackson | 1.50 | 3.00 | 4.50 | |
| 75-100 | Black Love–Stuart Jason (Oscar Wilson) | 1.00 | 2.00 | 3.00 | |
| 75-101 | The Real Gone Girls–Ted Mark | .75 | 1.50 | 2.25 | |
| 75-102 | Conan the Adventurer–Robert E. Howard & L. Sprague de Camp; c-Frazetta | 1.00 | 2.00 | 3.00 | F |
| 75-103 | Conan the Usurper–Robert E. Howard & L.S. de Camp; c-Frazetta | 1.00 | 2.00 | 3.00 | F |
| 75-104 | Conan–Robert E. Howard, L. Sprague de Camp & Lin Carter; c-Frazetta | 1.00 | 2.00 | 3.00 | F |
| 75-105 | Black Hell–Harold Calin | .75 | 1.50 | 2.25 | |
| 75-106 | Six Days to Suez–Harold Calin | .50 | 1.00 | 1.50 | C |
| 75-107 | The Objector–E.R. Stuart | .50 | 1.00 | 1.50 | |
| 75-108 | Infinity One–ed. Robert Hoskins | .50 | 1.00 | 1.50 | SF |
| 75-109 | Yoga for You–Claude Bragdon | .50 | 1.00 | 1.50 | NF |
| 75-110 | Crazy October–James Leo Herlihy | .50 | 1.00 | 1.50 | |
| 75-111 | Black Lord–Stuart Jason (Oscar Wilson) | 1.00 | 2.00 | 3.00 | |
| 75-112 | Rock Bottom–Earl Conrad | .75 | 1.50 | 2.25 | |
| 75-113 | Master of the Dark Gate–John Jakes; 1970; c-Jim Steranko | 2.00 | 4.00 | 6.00 | F |
| 75-114 | Quadroon–Jonathan Craig | .75 | 1.50 | 2.25 | |
| 75-115 | Ghosts and Other Strangers–Pauline Saltzman | .50 | 1.00 | 1.50 | |
| 75-116 | Panther John–Robert Tralins | 1.50 | 3.00 | 4.50 | |
| 75-117 | Wheels of Terror–Sven Hassel | .75 | 1.50 | 2.25 | C |

LANCER BOOKS, *continued*

| No. | Title | V/Good | Fine | N/Mint |  |
|---|---|---|---|---|---|
| 75-118 | Run! Nigger, Run!–Zach Carver | .75 | 1.50 | 2.25 |  |
| 75-119 | Conan the Freebooter–Robert E. Howard | 1.00 | 2.00 | 3.00 | F |
| 75-120 | The Legion of the Damned–Sven Hassel | .75 | 1.50 | 2.25 | C |
| 75-121 | Dining Out at Home–Sophie Leavitt | .50 | 1.00 | 1.50 | NF |
| 75-122 | Inside the F.B.I.–Norman Ollestad | .50 | 1.00 | 1.50 | NF |
| 75-123 | The Abolitionist–Leslie Gladson | .75 | 1.50 | 2.25 |  |
| 75-124 | Black Drums–Robert J. Scott | 1.00 | 2.00 | 3.00 |  |
| 75-125 | That Summer in Connecticut–Isabel Moore | .50 | 1.00 | 1.50 |  |
| 75-126 | An Old Captivity–Nevil Shute | .50 | 1.00 | 1.50 |  |
| 75-127 | A Meeting by the River–Christopher Isherwood | 1.00 | 2.00 | 3.00 |  |
| 75-128 | Iceworld–Hal Clement | .75 | 1.50 | 2.25 | SF |
| 75-129 | The Premier–Earl Conrad | .50 | 1.00 | 1.50 |  |
| 75-130 | Clairvoyance in Women–Robert Tralins | .75 | 1.50 | 2.25 |  |
| 75-131 | How to Meet (and Keep) Your Man Through Astrology–Ilya Chambertin | .50 | 1.00 | 1.50 | NF |
| 75-132 | I, B.I.T.C.H.–Caroline Hennessey | .75 | 1.50 | 2.25 | NF |
| 75-133 | Kelwin–Neal Barrett, Jr | 1.00 | 2.00 | 3.00 | F |
| 75-134 | The Beach Generation–Daoma Winston | .50 | 1.00 | 1.50 |  |
| 75-135 | Mistress of the Lash–Robert Vaughan | 1.50 | 3.00 | 4.50 |  |
| 75-136 | Conan of the Isles–Robert E. Howard, L. Sprague de Camp & Lin Carter | 1.00 | 2.00 | 3.00 | F |
| 75-137 | Conan the Conqueror–Robert E. Howard; c-Frazetta | 1.00 | 2.00 | 3.00 | F |
| 75-139 | Rafferty and Co.–Betty Wahl | .50 | 1.00 | 1.50 |  |
| 75-140 | A Peculiar Treasure–Edna Ferber | .75 | 1.50 | 2.25 | NF |
| 75-141 | Hey, White Girl–Susan Gregory | .75 | 1.50 | 2.25 |  |
| 75-142 | Ratman's Notebooks–Stephen Gilbert; aka Willard | 1.50 | 3.00 | 4.50 | HO |
| 75-143 | Ambulance Call–Nathan A. Schiff, MD | .50 | 1.00 | 1.50 |  |
| 75-144 | Coming Together–Alice Denham | .50 | 1.00 | 1.50 |  |
| 75-145 | The Third Policeman–Flann O'Brien | .50 | 1.00 | 1.50 |  |
| 75-146 | Black Master–Stuart Jason (Oscar Wilson) | 1.00 | 2.00 | 3.00 |  |
| 75-147 | The Scalpel's Edge–Alfred A. Weinstein, MD | .50 | 1.00 | 1.50 |  |
| 75-148 | Conan the Warrior–Robert E. Howard; c-Frazetta | 1.00 | 2.00 | 3.00 | F |
| 75-149 | Conan the Avenger–Robert E. Howard, Bjorn Nyberg & L. Sprague de Camp; c-Frazetta | 1.00 | 2.00 | 3.00 | F |
| 75-154 | Wastrels–Leslie Gladson | .50 | 1.00 | 1.50 |  |
| 75-156 | Up Your Banners–Donald E. Westlake | 2.50 | 5.00 | 7.50 |  |
| 75-157 | Machismo–Gramm Hall | .75 | 1.50 | 2.25 |  |
| 75-158 | The Glove Job–Henry Kane; 1971 | .75 | 1.50 | 2.25 | M |
| 75-160 | Bestseller–Toni Freedman | .50 | 1.00 | 1.50 |  |
| 75-162 | Herbs: The Magic Healers–Paul Twitchell | .50 | 1.00 | 1.50 | NF |
| 75-165 | Black Emperor–Stuart Jason (Oscar Wilson); 1971; c-Frazetta | 15.00 | 30.00 | 45.00 |  |
| 75-166 | Infinity Two–ed. Robert Hoskins | .50 | 1.00 | 1.50 | SF |
| 75-167 | Bio-Organics: Your Food and Your Health–James Rorty & N. Philip Norman, MD | .50 | 1.00 | 1.50 | NF |
| 75-168 | King on Queen–F.W. Paul (Paul Fairman) | .75 | 1.50 | 2.25 |  |
| 75-169 | Tipping Point–Lou Cameron | .50 | 1.00 | 1.50 |  |
| 75-170 | I Paid My Dues–Babs Gonzales | .50 | 1.00 | 1.50 | NF |
| 75-171 | Kronski–McSmash–Timothy Harris | 2.50 | 5.00 | 7.50 | H |
| 75-172 | Prelude to Space–Arthur C. Clarke | .50 | 1.00 | 1.50 | SF |
| 75-174 | Mud War–Lou Cameron | .75 | 1.50 | 2.25 | C |
| 75-177 | Alcindor and the Big O–John Devaney | .50 | 1.00 | 1.50 | S |
| 75-180 | The Tail Job–Henry Kane | .75 | 1.50 | 2.25 | M |
| 75-181 | Conan the Buccaneer–L. Sprague de Camp & Lin Carter; c-Frazetta | 1.50 | 3.00 | 4.50 | F |
| 75-183 | Get Your Health Together–Joan Weiner | .50 | 1.00 | 1.50 | NF |
| 75-184 | The Young Surgeons–Edith P. Begner | .50 | 1.00 | 1.50 | R |
| 75-185 | Tau Zero–Poul Anderson | 1.00 | 2.00 | 3.00 | SF |
| 75-186 | Masque of Satan–Virginia Coffman | .75 | 1.50 | 2.25 |  |
| 75-188 | Baneful Sorceries, or; the Countess Bewitched–Joan Sanders | .75 | 1.50 | 2.25 |  |
| 75-189 | Willard–Stephen Gilbert; aka Ratman's Notebooks; movie tie-in | 1.50 | 3.00 | 4.50 | HO |
| 75-190 | The Toff Proceeds–John Creasey | .50 | 1.00 | 1.50 | M |
| 75-197 | The Ashes of Falconwyck–Angela Gray | .50 | 1.00 | 1.50 |  |
| 75-199 | Masters of the Pit–Michael Moorcock; aka Barbarians of Mars | .75 | 1.50 | 2.25 | F |
| 75-200 | The Shrewsbury Horror–T.A. Waters | 1.50 | 3.00 | 4.50 |  |
| 75-204 | Transit–Edmund Cooper | .50 | 1.00 | 1.50 | SF |
| 75-205 | The Nude Who Never–Ted Mark | .50 | 1.00 | 1.50 |  |
| 75-210 | The Man from O.R.G.Y.–Ted Mark | .50 | 1.00 | 1.50 |  |
| 75-214 | The Girl from Pussycat–Ted Mark | .50 | 1.00 | 1.50 |  |
| 75-215 | The Toff and the Golden Boy–John Creasey | .50 | 1.00 | 1.50 | M |
| 75-216 | Falling Up–Miles Donis | .50 | 1.00 | 1.50 |  |
| 75-217 | The Shores of Tomorrow–David Mason | 1.00 | 2.00 | 3.00 | SF |
| 75-223 | Murder Makes Haste–John Creasey | .50 | 1.00 | 1.50 | M |
| 75-224 | The Templeton Memoirs–Dorothy Daniels | .50 | 1.00 | 1.50 |  |
| 75-225 | The Rest Is Silence–Virginia Coffman | .50 | 1.00 | 1.50 |  |
| 75-226 | Shadow Box–Virginia Coffman | .50 | 1.00 | 1.50 |  |
| 75-228 | Attic Rope–Dorothy Daniels | .50 | 1.00 | 1.50 |  |
| 75-230 | Survivor of Darkness–Virginia Coffman | .50 | 1.00 | 1.50 |  |
| 75-234 | Cliffside Castle–Dorothy Daniels | .50 | 1.00 | 1.50 |  |
| 75-237 | The Touch of Death–John Creasey | .50 | 1.00 | 1.50 |  |
| 75-238 | Vintage Evil–Jane Peart | .50 | 1.00 | 1.50 |  |
| 75-239 | The Ghost Dancers– | .50 | 1.00 | 1.50 |  |
| 75-246 | Sport for Inspector West–John Creasey | .50 | 1.00 | 1.50 | M |
| 75-247 | The Dunwich Horror–H.P. Lovecraft | .75 | 1.50 | 2.25 | HO |
| 75-248 | The Colour out of Space–H.P. Lovecraft | .50 | 1.00 | 1.50 | HO |
| 75-252 | Starwolf!–Ted White; 1971 | 1.00 | 2.00 | 3.00 | F |
| 75-254 | From Satan, with Love–Virginia Coffman | .75 | 1.50 | 2.25 |  |
| 75-257 | Suffer a Witch–Rae Foley; aka Gilt Edge | .50 | 1.00 | 1.50 |  |
| 75-260 | The Stewardess Strangler–Richard Gallagher; TV tie-in (for Cannon) | .50 | 1.00 | 1.50 | M |
| 75-261 | A Corpse for Christmas–Henry Kane | .75 | 1.50 | 2.25 | M |
| 75-265 | The Dark Man and Others–Robert E. Howard; 1972 | 1.50 | 3.00 | 4.50 | F |
| 75-267 | The Mayeroni Myth–Daoma Winston | .50 | 1.00 | 1.50 |  |
| 75-271 | House Malign–Julie Wellsley | .50 | 1.00 | 1.50 |  |
| 75-274 | The Savage Scalpel–Alain Rothstein | .50 | 1.00 | 1.50 | R |
| 75-276 | The Doctor in Ward B–Jean Francis | .50 | 1.00 | 1.50 | R |
| 75-277 | The Blue Movie Murders–Ellery Queen | 1.00 | 2.00 | 3.00 | M |
| 75-278 | The Waters of Centaurus–Rosel George Brown | .75 | 1.50 | 2.25 | SF |
| 75-281 | The Moorwood Legacy–Iris Foster | .50 | 1.00 | 1.50 |  |
| 75-282 | The Devil's Dress–Mary Fletcher | .50 | 1.00 | 1.50 |  |
| 75-286 | A Piece of Something Big–Harry Reed | .50 | 1.00 | 1.50 |  |
| 75-287 | Out of Control–Baynard Kendrick | .75 | 1.50 | 2.25 | M |
| 75-288 | Death of an Assassin–John Creasey | .50 | 1.00 | 1.50 | M |
| 75-289 | The First Blood–Lou Cameron; 1972 | .50 | 1.00 | 1.50 | C |
| 75-290 | The Time Masters–Wilson Tucker | .75 | 1.50 | 2.25 | SF |
| 75-293 | Becca's Child–Willo Davis Roberts | .50 | 1.00 | 1.50 |  |
| 75-294 | A Darker Heritage–Gerda Ann Cerra (Dean R. Koontz) | 2.50 | 5.00 | 7.50 |  |
| 75-295 | The House at Swansea–Alicia Grace (Irving Greenfield) | .50 | 1.00 | 1.50 |  |
| 75-296 | The Love of Lucifer–Daoma Winston | .50 | 1.00 | 1.50 |  |
| 75-297 | Legend of the Loch–Alanna Knight | .50 | 1.00 | 1.50 |  |
| 75-299 | Wolfbane–Robert E. Howard; c-Frazetta | 1.00 | 2.00 | 3.00 | F |
| 75-303 | Thank You for the Giant Tortoise–Mary Ann Madden | .50 | 1.00 | 1.50 | H |
| 75-304 | Give a Man a Gun–John Creasey | .50 | 1.00 | 1.50 | M |
| 75-305 | You Die Today!–Baynard Kendrick; TV tie-in | .75 | 1.50 | 2.25 |  |
| 75-306 | Starblood–Dean R. Koontz | 2.50 | 5.00 | 7.50 | SF |
| 75-309 | Dance with the Devil–Deanna Dwyer (reported to be Dean R. Koontz, but not authenticated) | 2.50 | 5.00 | 7.50 |  |
| 75-312 | Fengriffen–David Case | .50 | 1.00 | 1.50 |  |
| 75-315 | A Whiff of Death–Isaac Asimov; aka The Death Dealers | .50 | 1.00 | 1.50 | M |
| 75-317 | Go Away to Murder–John Creasey | .50 | 1.00 | 1.50 | M |
| 75-319 | Operation Chaos–Paul Anderson | 1.00 | 2.00 | 3.00 | SF |
| 75-320 | Infinity Three–ed. Robert Hoskins | .50 | 1.00 | 1.50 | SF |
| 75-329 | A November Wind–Paul Geddes | .50 | 1.00 | 1.50 |  |
| 75-331 | A Score for the Toff–John Creasey | .50 | 1.00 | 1.50 | M |
| 75-332 | Strange Disappearances–Brad Steiger | .50 | 1.00 | 1.50 | NF |
| 75-333 | Cloak of Aesir–John W. Campbell, Jr | 1.00 | 2.00 | 3.00 | SF |
| 75-334 | Stormy Range–Dwight Bennett | .75 | 1.50 | 2.25 | W |
| 75-335 | Sing a Dark Song–Willo Davis Roberts | .50 | 1.00 | 1.50 |  |
| 75-336 | Tarot Spell–Willo Davis Roberts | .50 | 1.00 | 1.50 |  |
| 75-342 | Child of Rage–Jim Thompson; 1st ed. 1972 | 30.00 | 60.00 | 90.00 | M |
| 75-343 | Singles City–John Brodman | .50 | 1.00 | 1.50 |  |
| 75-344 | Doorway to Death–John Creasey | .50 | 1.00 | 1.50 | M |
| 75-345 | Overlay–Barry N. Malzberg | 1.00 | 2.00 | 3.00 | SF |

**LANCER BOOKS,** *continued*

| | | V/Good | Fine | N/Mint | |
|---|---|---|---|---|---|
| 75-346 | Into the Slave Nebula–John Brunner; aka Slavers of Space | .75 | 1.50 | 2.25 | SF |
| 75-347 | Gun Law at Vermillion–L.P. Holmes | .75 | 1.50 | 2.25 | W |
| 75-348 | The Spectral Mist–Clarissa Ross | .50 | 1.00 | 1.50 | |
| 75-349 | Phantom of Glencourt–Clarissa Ross | .50 | 1.00 | 1.50 | |
| 75-350 | Secret of the Pale Lover–Clarissa Ross | .50 | 1.00 | 1.50 | |
| 75-351 | Gemini in Darkness–Clarissa Ross | .50 | 1.00 | 1.50 | |
| 75-352 | Out of the Fog–Clarissa Ross | .50 | 1.00 | 1.50 | |
| 75-353 | Beware the Kindly Stranger–Clarissa Ross | .50 | 1.00 | 1.50 | |
| 75-354 | House of Four Widows–Delphine C. Lyons | .50 | 1.00 | 1.50 | |
| 75-355 | Depths of Yesterday–Delphine C. Lyons | .50 | 1.00 | 1.50 | |
| 75-356 | Junior Bonner–Paul W. Fairman | .50 | 1.00 | 1.50 | |
| 75-358 | Valley of Shadows–Delphine C. Lyons | .50 | 1.00 | 1.50 | |
| 75-359 | This Outward Angel–Alanna Knight | .50 | 1.00 | 1.50 | |
| 75-360 | Surgeon's Ordeal–Edith P. Begner | .50 | 1.00 | 1.50 | R |
| 75-361 | The Return of Kavin–David Mason | 1.50 | 3.00 | 4.50 | F |
| 75-362 | The Humanoids–Jack Williamson | .75 | 1.50 | 2.25 | SF |
| 75-363 | Hang the Little Man–John Creasey | .50 | 1.00 | 1.50 | M |
| 75-364 | Dark Music–Charlotte Russell | .50 | 1.00 | 1.50 | |
| 75-365 | Children of the Storm–Deanna Dwyer (reported to be Dean R. Koontz, but not authenticated) | 2.50 | 5.00 | 7.50 | |
| 75-366 | The Warlock's Daughter–Angela Gray | .50 | 1.00 | 1.50 | |
| 75-367 | Her Stepfather's House–June Wetherell | .50 | 1.00 | 1.50 | |
| 75-368 | Satan's Coast–Elsie Lee | .50 | 1.00 | 1.50 | |
| 75-369 | Stranger in a Dark Land–Julie Wellsley | .50 | 1.00 | 1.50 | |
| 75-370 | Soldato!–Al Conroy | .75 | 1.50 | 2.25 | M |
| 75-371 | King Kull–Robert E. Howard & Lin Carter; c-Krenkel | .75 | 1.50 | 2.25 | F |
| 75-372 | Kavin's World–David Mason | 1.00 | 2.00 | 3.00 | F |
| 75-373 | The Dying Earth–Jack Vance | 1.00 | 2.00 | 3.00 | SF |
| 75-374 | Ensign Flandry–Poul Anderson | .75 | 1.50 | 2.25 | SF |
| 75-375 | The Sleeping Sorceress–Michael Moorcock | 1.50 | 3.00 | 4.50 | F |
| 75-376 | The Dreaming City–Michael Moorcock | 1.50 | 3.00 | 4.50 | F |
| 75-377 | Blackwell's Ghost–Angela Gray | .50 | 1.00 | 1.50 | |
| 75-379 | Dangerous Legacy–Willo Davis Roberts | .50 | 1.00 | 1.50 | |
| 75-382 | Death Grip–Al Conroy | .75 | 1.50 | 2.25 | |
| 75-384 | The Oasis–John Creasey | .50 | 1.00 | 1.50 | |
| 75-385 | Needle–Hal Clement; aka From Outer Space | .50 | 1.00 | 1.50 | SF |
| 75-386 | Warlock–Dean R. Koontz | 2.50 | 5.00 | 7.50 | SF |
| 75-387 | Infinity Four–ed. Robert Hoskins | .50 | 1.00 | 1.50 | SF |
| 75-388 | Satan's World–Poul Anderson | .75 | 1.50 | 2.25 | SF |
| 75-389 | Tryst with Terror–Wilma Winthrop | .50 | 1.00 | 1.50 | |
| 75-392 | Seminar in Evil–Daoma Winston | .50 | 1.00 | 1.50 | |
| 75-393 | The Dark of Summer–Deanna Dwyer (reported to be Dean R. Koontz, but not authenticated) | 2.50 | 5.00 | 7.50 | |
| 75-394 | Deadly Sea, Deadly Sand–Iris Foster | .50 | 1.00 | 1.50 | |
| 75-396 | The Sicilian Heritage–Jack Higgins | .50 | 1.00 | 1.50 | |
| 75-398 | Ship of the Damned–Joseph Hilton | .50 | 1.00 | 1.50 | |
| 75-399 | A Martian Odyssey–Stanley G. Weinbaum | .50 | 1.00 | 1.50 | SF |
| 75-400 | The House on the Moat–Virginia Coffman | .50 | 1.00 | 1.50 | |
| 75-401 | To Kill a Witch–Alice Brennan | .50 | 1.00 | 1.50 | |
| 75-402 | Evil in the Family–Grace Corren | .50 | 1.00 | 1.50 | |
| 75-403 | A Dark and Deadly Love–Elaine Evans (Gil Brewer) | 1.00 | 2.00 | 3.00 | |
| 75-404 | Burwyck's Wander–S.J. Treibich | .50 | 1.00 | 1.50 | |
| 75-405 | Sinister Gardens–Willo Davis Roberts | .50 | 1.00 | 1.50 | |
| 75-406 | The Fabulous Lakers–Merv Harris | .50 | 1.00 | 1.50 | S |
| 75-407 | The Schack Job–Henry Kane | .75 | 1.50 | 2.25 | M |
| 75-408 | Don't Call Me Madam–Henry Kane | .75 | 1.50 | 2.25 | M |
| 75-409 | Don't Go Away Dead–Henry Kane | .75 | 1.50 | 2.25 | M |
| 75-410 | Come Kill with Me–Henry Kane | .75 | 1.50 | 2.25 | M |
| 75-411 | The Diabolist–Paul W. Fairman; aka Rest in Agony | .75 | 1.50 | 2.25 | SF |
| 75-412 | Kill for the Millions–Henry Kane | .75 | 1.50 | 2.25 | M |
| 75-413 | Destination Infinity–Henry Kuttner; aka Fury | 1.00 | 2.00 | 3.00 | SF |
| 75-414 | The Mindwarpers–Eric Frank Russell | .75 | 1.50 | 2.25 | SF |
| 75-415 | Witch of the Dark Gate–John Jakes; c-Frazetta | 2.50 | 5.00 | 7.50 | F |
| 75-416 | Moonwind–Sharon Wagner | .50 | 1.00 | 1.50 | |
| 75-417 | The Secret of Benjamin Square–Jennifer Plum | .50 | 1.00 | 1.50 | |
| 75-418 | It Comes by Night–Clarissa Ross | .50 | 1.00 | 1.50 | |

| | | V/Good | Fine | N/Mint | |
|---|---|---|---|---|---|
| 75-419 | Shamus–Raymond Giles; movie tie-in | 1.00 | 2.00 | 3.00 | M |
| 75-420 | Shaggy Planet–Ron Goulart | 2.00 | 4.00 | 6.00 | SF |
| 75-421 | Bumsider–Carroll M. Capps (C.C. MacApp) | 1.00 | 2.00 | 3.00 | SF |
| 75-422 | Iceworld–Hal Clement | .50 | 1.00 | 1.50 | SF |
| 75-424 | The Evil at Queen's Priory–Virginia Coffman | .50 | 1.00 | 1.50 | |
| 75-425 | Nightshade–Iris Foster | .50 | 1.00 | 1.50 | |
| 75-426 | Dark Masquerade–Elna Stone | .50 | 1.00 | 1.50 | |
| 75-427 | Horror House–Paulette Warren | .50 | 1.00 | 1.50 | |
| 75-428 | Night of the Darkest Moon–Jane Peart | .50 | 1.00 | 1.50 | |
| 75-430 | Devil by the Sea–Nina Bawden | .50 | 1.00 | 1.50 | |
| 75-431 | The Reign of Wizardry–Jack Williamson; c-Frazetta | 1.00 | 2.00 | 3.00 | F |
| 75-433 | Stranglehold!–Al Conroy | .50 | 1.00 | 1.50 | |
| 75-434 | Invitation to Evil–Willo Davis Roberts | .50 | 1.00 | 1.50 | |
| 75-438 | A Fear of Heights–Virginia Coffman | .50 | 1.00 | 1.50 | |
| 75-439 | The Brand Inheritance–Dorothy Fletcher | .50 | 1.00 | 1.50 | |
| 75-442 | Dracula–Bram Stoker; movie tie-in | 4.00 | 8.00 | 12.00 | HO |
| 75-443 | The Enforcer–Andrew Sugar | .75 | 1.50 | 2.25 | |
| 75-444 | Deep in a Dark Country–Patricia Drew | .50 | 1.00 | 1.50 | |
| 75-445 | The Haunted Earth–Dean R. Koontz; 1973 | 2.50 | 5.00 | 7.50 | SF |
| 75-446 | Pig World–Charles W. Runyon | 1.00 | 2.00 | 3.00 | SF |
| 75-448 | Shadow on the Sun–Sharon Wagner | .50 | 1.00 | 1.50 | |
| 75-449 | Evil Children–Willo Davis Roberts | .50 | 1.00 | 1.50 | |
| 75-450 | The Brooding House–Alice Brennan | .50 | 1.00 | 1.50 | |
| 75-452 | A Haunted Place–Virginia Coffman | .50 | 1.00 | 1.50 | |
| 75-453 | The Eagle's Nest–Dorothy Daniels | .50 | 1.00 | 1.50 | |
| 75-455 | To Kill a House–Suzanne Roberts | .50 | 1.00 | 1.50 | |
| 75-456 | Ravenswood Hall–Angela Gray | .50 | 1.00 | 1.50 | |
| 75-457 | The Darkest Room–Grace Corren | .50 | 1.00 | 1.50 | |
| 75-458 | Seed of Evil–Petrina Crawford | .50 | 1.00 | 1.50 | |
| 75-459 | Murder Mission!–Al Conroy | .50 | 1.00 | 1.50 | |
| 75-461 | Calling Doctor Kill!–Andrew Sugar | .75 | 1.50 | 2.25 | |
| 75-462 | Blaster No. 1: The Girl with the Dynamite Bangs–Lou Cameron | .75 | 1.50 | 2.25 | A |
| 75-463 | Surgeon's Oath–William Johnston | .50 | 1.00 | 1.50 | R |
| 75-464 | Robots Have No Tails–Henry Kuttner | 1.00 | 2.00 | 3.00 | SF |
| 75-465 | The Devil's Generation–ed. Vic Ghidalia; 1973; c-Frazetta | 2.50 | 5.00 | 7.50 | SF |
| 75-466 | Farewell to Vienna–Dorothy Fletcher | .50 | 1.00 | 1.50 | R |
| 75-467 | Fear No Evil–Alice Brennan | .50 | 1.00 | 1.50 | |
| 75-469 | Nightmare at Riverview–Angela Gray | .50 | 1.00 | 1.50 | |
| 75-470 | Brooding Mansion–Paulette Warren | .50 | 1.00 | 1.50 | |
| 75-471 | Cavanaugh Keep–Miriam Leslie | .50 | 1.00 | 1.50 | |
| 75-472 | The Golden Evenings of Summer–Will Stanton; movie tie-in | 1.00 | 2.00 | 3.00 | |
| 75-473 | Kill City–Andrew Sugar | .75 | 1.50 | 2.25 | |
| 75-476 | Garden of Shadows–Virginia Coffman | .50 | 1.00 | 1.50 | |
| 75-477 | Infinity Five–ed. Robert Hoskins | .75 | 1.50 | 2.25 | SF |
| 75-478 | To the Dark Tower–Lyda Belknap Long | 1.50 | 3.00 | 4.50 | |
| 75-479 | That Night–Jane Blackmore | .50 | 1.00 | 1.50 | |
| 75-480 | Litany of Evil–Alice Brennan | .50 | 1.00 | 1.50 | |
| 75-481 | The Wine of Vengeance–Julie Wellsley | .50 | 1.00 | 1.50 | |
| 75-482 | Garden of Satan–Claire Vincent | .50 | 1.00 | 1.50 | |
| 75-486 | The Men Inside–Barry N. Malzberg | 1.00 | 2.00 | 3.00 | SF |
| 75-487 | Coffy–Paul W. Fairman; movie tie-in | 1.00 | 2.00 | 3.00 | |
| 75-490 | Blood Run!–Al Conroy | .75 | 1.50 | 2.25 | |
| 75-491 | The Girl with Something Extra–Paul W. Fairman; 1973; TV tie-in | 1.50 | 3.00 | 4.50 | SF |
| 75-498 | Demon Child–Deanna Dwyer (reported to be Dean R. Koontz, but not authenticated) | 2.00 | 4.00 | 6.00 | |
| 75-509 | Haelstrom Manor–S.J. Treibich | .50 | 1.00 | 1.50 | |
| 75-516 | Secret Melody–Paula Minton | .50 | 1.00 | 1.50 | |
| 75-521 | The Dark of Memory–Paula Minton | .50 | 1.00 | 1.50 | |
| 75-525 | My Body–Robert Dietrich (E. Howard Hunt); 1973 | 1.00 | 2.00 | 3.00 | |
| 78-726 | Master of the Undead–Hugo Paul (Gardner F. Fox) | 2.00 | 4.00 | 6.00 | |

# (LARCH)
# Larch Publications

| | | V/Good | Fine | N/Mint | |
|---|---|---|---|---|---|
| 1 | Gag and Cartoon Book | 2.00 | 4.00 | 6.00 | H |
| 2 | Joke and Cartoon Book; 1944 | 2.00 | 4.00 | 6.00 | H |

# LASER BOOKS

## Laser Books

**Note: All have covers by Kelly Freas.**

| | | V/Good | Fine | N/Mint | |
|---|---|---|---|---|---|
| nn | Seeds of Change–Thomas F. Monteleone; orig. 1975 | 1.25 | 2.50 | 3.75 | SF |
| 1 | Renegades of Time–Raymond F. Jones; orig. 1975 | 1.25 | 2.50 | 3.75 | SF |
| 2 | Herds–Stephen Goldin; orig. 1975 | 1.25 | 2.50 | 3.75 | SF |
| 3 | Crash Landing on Iduna–Arthur Tofte; orig. 1975 | 1.25 | 2.50 | 3.75 | SF |
| 4 | Gates of the Universe–Robert Coulson & Gene Deweese; orig. 1975 | 1.25 | 2.50 | 3.75 | SF |
| 5 | Walls within Walls–Arthur Tofte; orig. 1975 | 1.25 | 2.50 | 3.75 | SF |
| 6 | Serving in Time–Gordon Eklund; orig. 1975 | 1.25 | 2.50 | 3.75 | SF |
| 7 | Seeklight–K.W. Jeter; orig. 1975 | 2.50 | 5.00 | 7.50 | SF |
| 8 | Caravan–Stephen Goldin; orig. 1975 | 1.25 | 2.50 | 3.75 | SF |
| 9 | Invasion–Aaron Wolfe (Dean R. Koontz); orig. 1975 | 7.50 | 15.00 | 22.50 | HO |
| 10 | Falling toward Forever–Gordon Eklund; orig. 1975 | 1.25 | 2.50 | 3.75 | SF |
| 11 | Unto the Last Generation–Juanita Coulson; orig. 1975 | 1.25 | 2.50 | 3.75 | SF |
| 12 | The King of Eolim–Raymond F. Jones; orig. 1975 | 1.25 | 2.50 | 3.75 | SF |
| 13 | Blake's Progress–R.F. Nelson; orig. 1975 | 1.25 | 2.50 | 3.75 | SF |
| 14 | Birthright–Kathleen Sky; orig. 1975 | 1.25 | 2.50 | 3.75 | SF |
| 15 | The Star Web–George Zebrowski; orig. 1975 | 1.25 | 2.50 | 3.75 | SF |
| 16 | Kane's Odyssey–Jeff Clinton; orig. 1976 | 1.25 | 2.50 | 3.75 | SF |
| 17 | The Black Roads–Joe L. Hensley; orig. 1976 | 2.00 | 4.00 | 6.00 | SF |
| 18 | Legacy–J.F. Bone; orig. 1976 | 1.25 | 2.50 | 3.75 | SF |
| 19 | The Unknown Shore–Donald Malcolm; orig. 1976 | 1.25 | 2.50 | 3.75 | SF |
| 20 | Space Trap–Juanita Coulson; orig. 1976 | 1.25 | 2.50 | 3.75 | SF |
| 21 | A Law for the Stars–John Morressy; orig. 1976 | 1.25 | 2.50 | 3.75 | SF |
| 22 | Keeper–Joan Hunter Holly; orig. 1976 | 1.25 | 2.50 | 3.75 | SF |
| 23 | Birth of Fire–Jerry Pournelle; orig. 1976 | 1.25 | 2.50 | 3.75 | SF |
| 24 | Ruler of the World–J.T. McIntosh; orig. 1976 | 1.25 | 2.50 | 3.75 | SF |
| 25 | Scavenger Hunt–Stephen Goldin; orig. 1976 | 1.25 | 2.50 | 3.75 | SF |
| 26 | To Renew the Ages–Robert Coulson; orig. 1976 | 1.25 | 2.50 | 3.75 | SF |
| 27 | The Horde–Joseph Green; orig. 1976 | 1.25 | 2.50 | 3.75 | SF |
| 28 | The Skies Discrowned–Timothy Powers; orig. 1976 | 2.50 | 5.00 | 7.50 | SF |
| 29 | The Iron Rain–Donald Malcolm; orig. 1976 | 1.25 | 2.50 | 3.75 | SF |
| 30 | The Seeker–David Bischoff & Christopher Lampton; orig. 1976 | 1.25 | 2.50 | 3.75 | SF |
| 31 | The Galactic Invaders–James R. Berry; orig. 1976 | 1.25 | 2.50 | 3.75 | SF |
| 32 | Then Beggars Could Ride–R.F. Nelson; orig. 1976 | 1.25 | 2.50 | 3.75 | SF |
| 33 | The Dreamfields–K.W. Jeter; orig. 1976 | 2.50 | 5.00 | 7.50 | SF |
| 34 | Seas of Ernathe–Jeffrey Carver; orig. 1976 | 1.25 | 2.50 | 3.75 | SF |
| 35 | I, Aleppo–Jerry Sohl; orig. 1976 | 1.25 | 2.50 | 3.75 | SF |
| 36 | Jeremy Case–Gene DeWeese; orig. 1976 | 1.25 | 2.50 | 3.75 | SF |
| 37 | The Meddlers–J.F. Bone; orig. 1976 | 1.25 | 2.50 | 3.75 | SF |
| 38 | Ice Prison–Kathleen Sky; orig. 1976 | 1.25 | 2.50 | 3.75 | SF |
| 39 | Brandyjack–Augustine Funnell; orig. 1976 | 1.25 | 2.50 | 3.75 | SF |
| 40 | Master of the Stars–Robert Hoskins; orig. 1976 | 1.25 | 2.50 | 3.75 | SF |
| 41 | Future Sanctuary–Lee Harding; orig. 1976 | 1.25 | 2.50 | 3.75 | SF |
| 42 | Cross of Empire–Christopher Lampton; orig. 1976 | 1.25 | 2.50 | 3.75 | SF |
| 43 | Spawn–Donald F. Glut; orig. 1976 | 1.25 | 2.50 | 3.75 | SF |
| 44 | But What of Earth?–Piers Anthony & Robert Coulson; orig. 1976 | 1.25 | 2.50 | 3.75 | SF |
| 45 | Finish Line–Stephen Goldin; orig. 1976 | 1.25 | 2.50 | 3.75 | SF |
| 46 | Dance of the Apocalypse–Gordon Eklund; orig. 1976 | 1.25 | 2.50 | 3.75 | SF |
| 47 | Epitaph in Rust–Timothy Powers; orig. 1976 | 2.50 | 5.00 | 7.50 | SF |
| 48 | Rebels of Merka–Augustine Funnell; orig. 1976 | 1.25 | 2.50 | 3.75 | SF |
| 49 | Tiger in the Stars–Zach Hughes; orig. 1976 | 1.25 | 2.50 | 3.75 | SF |
| 50 | West of Honor–Jerry Pournelle; orig. 1976 | 1.25 | 2.50 | 3.75 | SF |
| 51 | Mindwipe!–Steve Hahn; orig. 1976 | 1.25 | 2.50 | 3.75 | SF |
| 52 | The Extraterritorial–John Morressy; orig. 1977 | 1.25 | 2.50 | 3.75 | SF |
| 53 | The Ecolog–R. Faraday Nelson; orig. 1977 | 1.25 | 2.50 | 3.75 | SF |
| 54 | The River and the Dream–Raymond F. Jones; orig. 1977 | 1.25 | 2.50 | 3.75 | SF |
| 55 | Shepherd–Joan Hunter Holly; orig. 1977 | 4.00 | 8.00 | 12.00 | SF |
| 56 | Gift of the Manti–J.F. Bone & Roy Myers; orig. 1977 | 4.00 | 8.00 | 12.00 | SF |
| 57 | Shadow on the Stars–Robert B. Marcus; orig. 1977 | 4.00 | 8.00 | 12.00 | SF |

# LEISURE LIBRARY

## Leisure Library, Inc.

### Digest Size

| | | V/Good | Fine | N/Mint | |
|---|---|---|---|---|---|
| 1 | My Life Is My Own–Jules-Jean Morac | 6.00 | 12.00 | 18.00 | E |
| 2 | Death for a Doll–Spike Morelli; c-Heade | 7.50 | 15.00 | 22.50 | M |
| 3 | Pick-Up Girl–Roland Vance; c-Heade | 6.00 | 12.00 | 18.00 | E |
| 4 | Make Mine a Shroud–Michael Storme; c-Heade | 7.50 | 15.00 | 22.50 | M |
| 5 | Hot Dames on Cold Slabs–Michael Storme; c-Heade | 12.50 | 25.00 | 37.50 | M |
| 6 | No Prude–Jules-Jean Morac | 5.00 | 10.00 | 15.00 | E |
| 7 | This Way for Hell–Spike Morelli; 1952, c-Heade | 10.00 | 20.00 | 30.00 | M |
| 8 | White Slave Racket–Roland Vane; c-Heade | 17.50 | 35.00 | 52.50 | E |
| 9 | Two Smart Dames–Gene Ross; c-Heade | 6.00 | 12.00 | 18.00 | E |
| 10 | Midnight Sinner–Paul Renin; c-Heade | 6.00 | 12.00 | 18.00 | E |
| 11 | Curtains for Carla–Michael Storme | 5.00 | 10.00 | 15.00 | M |
| 12 | Bertrand and the Blondes–Jules-Jean Morac; 1952; c-Heade | 6.00 | 12.00 | 18.00 | E |
| 13 | Sorry for You, Beautiful–Gene Ross; 1952; c-Heade | 6.00 | 12.00 | 18.00 | E |
| 14 | Wedding Night–Paul Renin; 1952; c-Heade | 6.00 | 12.00 | 18.00 | E |
| 15 | Carmen Was a Virgin–Michael Storme; c-Heade | 6.00 | 12.00 | 18.00 | E |
| 16 | Amorous Adventuress–Roland Vane; 1952; c-Heade | 6.00 | 12.00 | 18.00 | E |
| 17 | Honey, Hold That Scream!–Tony Angelo; c-Heade | 7.50 | 15.00 | 22.50 | M |
| 18 | She Who Hesitates–Paul Renin; c-Heade | 6.00 | 12.00 | 18.00 | E |
| 19 | A Corpse Spells Danger–Michael Storme; 1953 | 5.00 | 10.00 | 15.00 | M |
| 20 | Pagan Interlude–Rosalind Brett | 5.00 | 10.00 | 15.00 | E |
| 21 | Curves Cause Trouble–Gene Ross; 1953; c-Heade | 6.00 | 12.00 | 18.00 | E |
| 22 | Thou Shalt Not–Paul Renin | 6.00 | 12.00 | 18.00 | E |
| 23 | This Woman Is Death–Michael Storme; c-Heade | 6.00 | 12.00 | 18.00 | M |
| 24 | White Man's Slave–Mary Clare; c-Heade | 10.00 | 20.00 | 30.00 | E |

# LEV GLEASON LIBRARY

## Lev Gleason Publications, Inc.

### Digest Size

| | | V/Good | Fine | N/Mint | |
|---|---|---|---|---|---|
| 101 | Hotel Wife–Ruth Lyons | 3.00 | 6.00 | 9.00 | E |
| 102 | Devil-May-Care Girl–John Saxon; aka Something like Passion | 3.00 | 6.00 | 9.00 | E |

| | V/Good | Fine | N/Mint |
|---|---|---|---|

| # | Title | V/Good | Fine | N/Mint | |
|---|---|---|---|---|---|
| 103 | The Wench is Willing–Griffith James; 1949 | 3.00 | 6.00 | 9.00 | E |
| 104 | Passion's Darling–Thomas Stone | 3.00 | 6.00 | 9.00 | E |
| 105 | Scandal Girl–Doris Knight; aka Infamous Woman | 3.00 | 6.00 | 9.00 | E |
| 106 | Dishonorable Lady–Richard Lee | 3.00 | 6.00 | 9.00 | E |

# LION

## Lion Books, Inc.

### (See also Red Circle)

| # | Title | V/Good | Fine | N/Mint | |
|---|---|---|---|---|---|
| 8 | Hungry Men–Edward Anderson; 1949 | 4.00 | 8.00 | 12.00 | |
| 9 | Anniversary–Ludwig Lewisohn | 4.00 | 8.00 | 12.00 | E |
| 10 | Canyon Hell–Peter Dawson; aka High Country | 4.00 | 8.00 | 12.00 | W |
| 11 | The Blonde Body–Michael Morgan | 4.00 | 8.00 | 12.00 | M |
| 14 | The Lottery–Shirley Jackson | 7.50 | 15.00 | 22.50 | SF |
| 15 | Soft Shoulders–Peter Shelley | 3.00 | 6.00 | 9.00 | E |
| 16 | The Devil's Daughter–Peter Marsh | 4.00 | 8.00 | 12.00 | E |
| 17 | Dust of the Trail–Bennett Foster; 1950 | 3.00 | 6.00 | 9.00 | W |
| 18 | Christ in Concrete–Pietro di Donato; movie tie-in | 2.50 | 5.00 | 7.50 | |
| 19 | He Ran All the Way–Sam Ross | 3.00 | 6.00 | 9.00 | M |
| 20 | Gambler's Gun Luck–Brett Austin | 3.00 | 6.00 | 9.00 | W |
| 21 | To Keep or Kill–Wilson Tucker | 4.50 | 9.00 | 13.50 | M |
| 22 | The French Touch–Jack Iams | 3.00 | 6.00 | 9.00 | |
| 23 | Baseball Stars of 1950–Bruce Jacobs; orig. 1950 | 6.00 | 12.00 | 18.00 | S |
| 24 | Twilight Men–Andre Tellier | 3.00 | 6.00 | 9.00 | |
| 25 | The Intimate Stranger–William Lynch; 1950 | 3.00 | 6.00 | 9.00 | E |
| 26 | The Outward Room–Millen Brand | 3.00 | 6.00 | 9.00 | |
| 27 | Dead Man's Gorge–E.B. Mann | 3.00 | 6.00 | 9.00 | W |
| 28 | Gun Devil!–W. Edmunds Claussen | 3.00 | 6.00 | 9.00 | W |
| 29 | Walk Hard–Talk Loud–Len Zinberg | 3.00 | 6.00 | 9.00 | |
| 30 | The Indiscreet Confessions of a Nice Girl–anon. | 3.00 | 6.00 | 9.00 | E |
| 31 | The Small Back Room–Nigel Balchin | 3.00 | 6.00 | 9.00 | E |
| 32 | Ceylon–Margaret Rebecca Lay | 3.00 | 6.00 | 9.00 | E |
| 33 | The Continental Touch–Josef Wechsberg | 3.00 | 6.00 | 9.00 | |
| 34 | Guns of Arizona–Charles N. Heckelmann | 3.00 | 6.00 | 9.00 | W |
| 35 | Man Tracks–Bennett Foster | 3.00 | 6.00 | 9.00 | W |
| 36 | The Road through the Wall–Shirley Jackson | 4.00 | 8.00 | 12.00 | M |
| 37 | Guns on the Santa Fe–Peter Dawson (Frank Gruber) | 3.50 | 7.00 | 10.50 | W |
| 38 | The Lustful Ape–Russell Gray (Bruno Fischer); orig. 1950 | 4.50 | 9.00 | 13.50 | |
| 39 | Brain Guy–Benjamin Appel | 4.00 | 8.00 | 12.00 | M |
| 40 | All Thy Conquests–Alfred Hayes | 3.00 | 6.00 | 9.00 | |
| 41 | The Big Night–Stanley Ellin; aka Dreadful Summit | 3.00 | 6.00 | 9.00 | E |
| 42 | Spring Riot–Jay Presson | 3.00 | 6.00 | 9.00 | E |
| 43 | Massacre–James Warner Bellah | 3.00 | 6.00 | 9.00 | W |
| 44 | His Dead Wife–Elizabeth Eastman | 4.00 | 8.00 | 12.00 | |
| 45 | Now Sleeps the Beast–Don Tracy | 4.00 | 8.00 | 12.00 | |
| 46 | A Slight Case of Scandal–Jack Iams; aka Prematurely Gay | 3.00 | 6.00 | 9.00 | E |

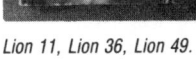

*Lion 11, Lion 36, Lion 49.*

| # | Title | V/Good | Fine | N/Mint | |
|---|---|---|---|---|---|
| 47 | Trouble Follows Me–Kenneth Millar (Ross MacDonald) | 4.00 | 8.00 | 12.00 | M |
| 48 | The Dark Tunnel–Kenneth Millar (Ross MacDonald) | 4.00 | 8.00 | 12.00 | M |
| 49 | All Quiet on the Western Front–Erich Maria Remarque | 3.50 | 7.00 | 10.50 | C |
| 50 | Oregon Trunk–Dan J. Stevens; 1951 | 3.00 | 6.00 | 9.00 | W |
| 51 | Tall, Dark and Dead–Kermit Jaediker | 3.00 | 6.00 | 9.00 | |
| 52 | No Letters for the Dead–Gale Wilhelm | 3.50 | 7.00 | 10.50 | E |
| 53 | Arena of Love–Helene Eliat | 3.00 | 6.00 | 9.00 | E |
| 54 | Joy Street–Clifton Cuthbert | 3.00 | 6.00 | 9.00 | |
| 55 | El Paso–W. Edmunds Claussen | 3.00 | 6.00 | 9.00 | W |
| 56 | The Glass Lady–Asa Bordages | 3.00 | 6.00 | 9.00 | E |
| 57 | Affair–Emily Hahn | 3.00 | 6.00 | 9.00 | |
| 58 | Art Colony–Clifton Cuthbert | 3.00 | 6.00 | 9.00 | E |
| 59 | Border Woman–Richard Carroll & Gregory Mason; aka Mexican Gallop | 3.00 | 6.00 | 9.00 | W |
| 60 | Murders in Silk–Mike Teagle | 3.00 | 6.00 | 9.00 | M |
| 61 | Wolf Dog Range–Will Watson | 3.00 | 6.00 | 9.00 | W |
| 62 | Blondes Are Skin Deep–Louis Trimble | 3.00 | 6.00 | 9.00 | M |
| 63 | Cage Me a Peacock–Noel Langley | 3.00 | 6.00 | 9.00 | E |
| 64 | The Savage–Mikhail Artzybasheff | 3.00 | 6.00 | 9.00 | E |
| 65 | Killers Five–William Hopson; aka Sunset Ranch | 3.00 | 6.00 | 9.00 | W |
| 66 | The Ranch Cat–William Hopson; aka Straight from Boot Hill | 3.00 | 6.00 | 9.00 | E |
| 67 | MacArthur–Man of Action–Frank Kelley & Cornelius Ryan | 3.00 | 6.00 | 9.00 | B |
| 68 | My Flesh Is Sweet–Day Keene; orig. 1951 | 6.00 | 12.00 | 18.00 | E |
| 69 | The Cheat–Don Tracy; aka Criss-Cross | 5.00 | 10.00 | 15.00 | E |
| 70 | We Too Are Drifting–Gale Wilhelm | 3.50 | 7.00 | 10.50 | E |
| 71 | America's Cities of Sin–ed. Noah Sarlat | 3.00 | 6.00 | 9.00 | NF |
| 72 | The Tigress–Jeff Bogar; aka Payoff for Paula | 3.00 | 6.00 | 9.00 | E |
| 73 | Innocent Madame–Eleanore Browne; 1952 | 3.00 | 6.00 | 9.00 | E |
| 74 | Either Is Love–Elisabeth Craigin | 3.00 | 6.00 | 9.00 | E |
| 75 | Die, Damn You!–Paul Durst | 3.00 | 6.00 | 9.00 | W |
| 76 | A Walk in the Sun–Harry Brown | 3.00 | 6.00 | 9.00 | C |
| 77 | The Lust of Private Cooper–James Gordon | 3.00 | 6.00 | 9.00 | E |
| 78 | Nevada Killing–Duke Montana; aka Lynch Law in Perdition | 3.00 | 6.00 | 9.00 | W |
| 79 | My Gun, Her Body–Jeff Bogar; aka Dinah for Danger | 3.00 | 6.00 | 9.00 | E |
| 80 | Third Ward–Newark–Curtis Lucas | 3.00 | 6.00 | 9.00 | |
| 81 | The Lurking Man–Gerald Butler; aka Mad with Much Heart | 3.00 | 6.00 | 9.00 | E |
| 82 | War in Korea–Marguerite Higgins | 3.00 | 6.00 | 9.00 | C |
| 83 | Bodies Are Dust–P.J. Wolfson | 3.00 | 6.00 | 9.00 | |
| 84 | Earth Woman–Edwin J. Becker; aka Coble Hill | 3.00 | 6.00 | 9.00 | E |
| 85 | Lie Down, Killer–Richard S. Prather; orig. 1952 | 3.50 | 7.00 | 10.50 | M |
| 86 | Tough Kid–William Attaway; aka Let Me Breathe Thunder | 3.00 | 6.00 | 9.00 | E |
| 87 | You'll Get Yours–Thomas Wills (William Ard) | 4.00 | 8.00 | 12.00 | |
| 88 | The Missouri Maiden–C. William Harrison; orig. 1952 | 3.00 | 6.00 | 9.00 | |
| 89 | Route 28–Ward Greene | 3.00 | 6.00 | 9.00 | E |
| 90 | Pistolman–Steve Frazee | 3.00 | 6.00 | 9.00 | W |
| 91 | So Low, So Lovely–Curtis Lucas | 3.00 | 6.00 | 9.00 | |
| 92 | South Sea Tales–Jack London | 3.00 | 6.00 | 9.00 | A |
| 93 | The Big Feeling–Daniel Karp; orig. 1952 | 3.00 | 6.00 | 9.00 | E |
| 94 | Lona–John Evans; aka If You Have Tears; c-Bergey | 3.50 | 7.00 | 10.50 | E |
| 95 | Hell's Kitchen–Benjamin Appel | 3.50 | 7.00 | 10.50 | M |
| 96 | Utah Hell Guns–Steve Frazee | 3.00 | 6.00 | 9.00 | W |
| 97 | America's Cities of Sin–ed. Noah Sarlat | 3.00 | 6.00 | 9.00 | NF |
| 98 | Prelude to a Certain Midnight–Gerald Kersh; c-Belarski | 4.00 | 8.00 | 12.00 | |
| 99 | The Killer Inside Me–Jim Thompson; orig. 1952 | 35.00 | 70.00 | 105.00 | |
| 100 | One Is a Lonely Number–Bruce Elliot; c-Bergey | 3.00 | 6.00 | 9.00 | E |
| 101 | Joy Street–Clifton Cuthbert | 3.00 | 6.00 | 9.00 | E |
| 102 | Bailey's Daughters–John DeMeyer | 3.00 | 6.00 | 9.00 | E |
| 103 | Eat Dog or Die!–C. William Harrison | 3.00 | 6.00 | 9.00 | W |
| 104 | Little Killer–Gene Paul; orig. 1952 | 3.50 | 7.00 | 10.50 | |

*Lion 95, Lion 99, Lion 127.*

|  | | V/Good | Fine | N/Mint | |
|---|---|---|---|---|---|

LION, *continued*

| # | Title | V/Good | Fine | N/Mint | |
|---|---|---|---|---|---|
| 105 | The Brotherhood of Velvet–David Karp | 3.50 | 7.00 | 10.50 | E |
| 106 | Sintown, U.S.A.–Noah Sarlat | 3.00 | 6.00 | 9.00 | E |
| 107 | Candide–Voltaire | 3.00 | 6.00 | 9.00 | |
| 108 | Cropper's Cabin–Jim Thompson; orig. 1952 | 35.00 | 70.00 | 105.00 | E |
| 109 | The Naked Storm–Simon Eisner (C.M. Kornbluth) | 9.00 | 18.00 | 27.00 | E |
| 110 | The Peddlers–Douglas Ring | 3.00 | 6.00 | 9.00 | |
| 111 | Company K–William March | 3.00 | 6.00 | 9.00 | C |
| 112 | The Man I Killed–Shel Walker | 3.00 | 6.00 | 9.00 | E |
| 113 | The Montana Vixen–Paul W. Fairman; aka The Heiress of Copper Butte | 3.00 | 6.00 | 9.00 | W |
| 114 | Luther–Roy Flannagan | 3.00 | 6.00 | 9.00 | E |
| 115 | Cora Potts–Ward Greene | 3.00 | 6.00 | 9.00 | E |
| 116 | Saskia–Claude Marais | 3.00 | 6.00 | 9.00 | E |
| 117 | Run the Wild River–D.L. Champion; 1953 | 3.00 | 6.00 | 9.00 | |
| 118 | The Haploids–Jerry Sohl | 3.00 | 6.00 | 9.00 | SF |
| 119 | Hardman–David Karp; orig. 1953 | 3.00 | 6.00 | 9.00 | |
| 120 | Recoil–Jim Thompson; orig. 1953 | 35.00 | 70.00 | 105.00 | |
| 121 | The Strange Path–Gale Wilhelm | 3.50 | 7.00 | 10.50 | E |
| 122 | Life and Death in Soviet Russia–El Campesino (Valentin Gonzalez & Julian Gorkin) | 3.00 | 6.00 | 9.00 | NF |
| 123 | Don't Dig Deeper–William Francis | 3.00 | 6.00 | 9.00 | : |
| 124 | The Burglar–David Goodis; orig. 1953 | 25.00 | 50.00 | 75.00 | M |
| 125 | Baseball Stars of 1953–Bruce Jacobs; orig. 1953 | 6.00 | 12.00 | 18.00 | S |
| 126 | Mojave Guns–Roe Richmond | 3.00 | 6.00 | 9.00 | W |
| 127 | The Alcoholics–Jim Thompson; orig. 1953 | 35.00 | 70.00 | 105.00 | |
| 128 | His Great Journey–Manuel Komroff | 2.50 | 5.00 | 7.50 | |
| 129 | .44–J.A. DeRosso | 2.50 | 5.00 | 7.50 | W |
| 130 | Sharp the Bugle Calls–Steve Frazee; orig. 1953 | 3.00 | 6.00 | 9.00 | W |
| 131 | Bourbon Street–G.H. Otis; orig. 1953 | 3.00 | 6.00 | 9.00 | M |
| 132 | Cry, Flesh–David Karp | 3.00 | 6.00 | 9.00 | |
| 133 | The Dark Chase–David Goodis; aka Nightfall | 22.50 | 45.00 | 67.50 | M |
| 134 | Colorado Creek–E.E. Halleran | 2.50 | 5.00 | 7.50 | W |
| 135 | Half–Jordan Park (C.M. Kornbluth); orig. 1953 | 9.00 | 18.00 | 27.00 | E |
| 136 | Fighting Man–Mark Morgan | 2.50 | 5.00 | 7.50 | |
| 137 | Someone Is Bleeding–Richard Matheson; orig. 1953 | 25.00 | 50.00 | 75.00 | M |
| 138 | Dark the Summer Dies–Walter Untermeyer, Jr; orig. 1953 | 2.50 | 5.00 | 7.50 | E |
| 139 | Gunman's Grudge–George C. Appell | 2.50 | 5.00 | 7.50 | W |
| 140 | Cockpit–Warwick Scott | 3.00 | 6.00 | 9.00 | |
| 141 | Rooming House–Berton Roueche; aka Black Weather | 3.00 | 6.00 | 9.00 | E |
| 142 | "I Was There"–Ken Jones; orig. 1953 | 2.50 | 5.00 | 7.50 | NF |
| 143 | The Wild Bunch–Peter Dawson (Frank Gruber) | 3.00 | 6.00 | 9.00 | W |
| 144 | A Tent on Corsica–Martin Quigley | 2.50 | 5.00 | 7.50 | |
| 145 | Malenkov–Robert Frazier; orig. 1953 | 2.50 | 5.00 | 7.50 | NF |
| 146 | Frankenstein–Mary Wollstonecraft Shelley | 7.50 | 15.00 | 22.50 | SF |
| 147 | The Wench and the Flame–Robert L. Timnell | 2.50 | 5.00 | 7.50 | |
| 148 | Doomsday–Warwick Scott; orig. 1953 | 3.00 | 6.00 | 9.00 | SF |
| 149 | Bad Boy–Jim Thompson; orig. 1953 | 35.00 | 70.00 | 105.00 | |
| 150 | Lawman's Feud–Steve Frazee | 2.50 | 5.00 | 7.50 | W |
| 151 | Slaughter Street–Louis Falstein; orig. 1953 | 2.50 | 5.00 | 7.50 | E |
| 152 | A Rage at Sea–Frederick Lorenz; orig. 1953 | 2.00 | 4.00 | 6.00 | E |
| 153 | Tough Guy–A.I. Bezzerides; aka Long Haul | 2.50 | 5.00 | 7.50 | |
| 154 | Naked in the Dark–Gene Paul | 2.00 | 4.00 | 6.00 | E |
| 155 | Savage Night–Jim Thompson; orig. 1953 | 35.00 | 70.00 | 105.00 | |
| 156 | Hero's Lust–Kermit Jaedicker | 2.50 | 5.00 | 7.50 | |
| 157 | The Lone Gunhawk–Frank Gruber | 2.50 | 5.00 | 7.50 | W |
| 158 | The Utah Kid–Roe Richmond | 2.00 | 4.00 | 6.00 | W |
| 159 | Sin People–George Milburn; aka Oklahoma Town | 2.50 | 5.00 | 7.50 | E |
| 160 | Sexual Practices of American Women–Christopher Gerould; orig. 1953 | 3.00 | 6.00 | 9.00 | NF |
| 161 | The Hoodlum–Eleazar Lipsky | 3.00 | 6.00 | 9.00 | |
| 162 | Angel–Curtis Lucas | 3.00 | 6.00 | 9.00 | |
| 163 | Gunsight–Frank Gruber | 2.50 | 5.00 | 7.50 | W |
| 164 | Platoon–Adam Singer | 3.00 | 6.00 | 9.00 | |
| 165 | The Big Lure–William Manners | 2.50 | 5.00 | 7.50 | |
| 166 | Dock Walloper–Benjamin Appel | 3.00 | 6.00 | 9.00 | M |
| 167 | Every Man's Bible–Manuel Komroff | 3.00 | 6.00 | 9.00 | |
| 168 | Killer's Crossing–Burt Arthur | 2.50 | 5.00 | 7.50 | W |
| 169 | The Gunslammer–Lee Floren | 2.50 | 5.00 | 7.50 | W |
| 170 | Sailor's Luck–Basil Heatter | 2.50 | 5.00 | 7.50 | |
| 171 | Hot Cargo–G.H. Otis | 3.00 | 6.00 | 9.00 | |
| 172 | Korea's Heroes–Bruce Jacobs | 2.50 | 5.00 | 7.50 | NF |
| 173 | The Dream and the Flesh–Vivian Connell; aka The Peacock Is a Gentleman | 2.00 | 4.00 | 6.00 | |
| 174 | The Corrupters–William Francis; 1953 | 2.50 | 5.00 | 7.50 | E |
| 175 | The Gun Trail–H.A. DeRosso | 2.50 | 5.00 | 7.50 | W |
| 176 | Valerie–Jordan Park (C.M. Kornbluth); orig. 1953; c-Maguire | 10.00 | 20.00 | 30.00 | E |
| 177 | Men and Women–William Kozlenko; orig. 1953 | 2.50 | 5.00 | 7.50 | |
| 178 | Bloody River–Paul Durst | 2.50 | 5.00 | 7.50 | W |
| 179 | Conjure Wife–Fritz Leiber; c-Maguire | 10.00 | 20.00 | 30.00 | F |
| 180 | Fury on Sunday–Richard Matheson; orig. 1953 | 30.00 | 60.00 | 90.00 | |
| 181 | The Oxbow Kill–C. William Harrison | 2.00 | 4.00 | 6.00 | |
| 182 | O'Mara–Laurence Greene | 2.00 | 4.00 | 6.00 | |
| 183 | Trouble on Crazyman–Sam Allison | 2.50 | 5.00 | 7.50 | W |
| 184 | The Criminal–Jim Thompson; orig. 1953 | 35.00 | 70.00 | 105.00 | M |
| 185 | The Kidnapper–Robert Bloch; orig. 1954 | 25.00 | 50.00 | 75.00 | |
| 186 | The Blonde on the Street Corner–David Goodis; orig. 1954 | 25.00 | 50.00 | 75.00 | |
| 187 | The Dakota Deal–Riley Ryan | 2.00 | 4.00 | 6.00 | W |
| 188 | The Naked Year–Philip Atlee; aka The Inheritors | 2.00 | 4.00 | 6.00 | E |
| 189 | Two-Gun Texan–Burt Arthur | 2.00 | 4.00 | 6.00 | W |
| 190 | The Joy Wheel–Paul W. Fairman | 2.00 | 4.00 | 6.00 | |
| 191 | Strange Desires–ed. J. Vernon Shea | 2.00 | 4.00 | 6.00 | |
| 192 | The Golden Gizmo–Jim Thompson; orig. 1954 | 35.00 | 70.00 | 105.00 | |
| 193 | Night Never Ends–Frederick Lorenz | 2.00 | 4.00 | 6.00 | |
| 194 | Baseball Stars of 1954–Bruce Jacobs; orig. 1954 | 6.00 | 12.00 | 18.00 | S |
| 195 | Apache Greed–William Hopson | 3.00 | 6.00 | 9.00 | W |
| 196 | A Dog's Head–Jean Dutourd | 5.00 | 10.00 | 15.00 | F |
| 197 | The Naked Night–Dan Brennan | 2.50 | 5.00 | 7.50 | |
| 198 | Sin Pit–Paul Meskil | 2.50 | 5.00 | 7.50 | |
| 199 | Ambush Hell–George C. Appell | 2.50 | 5.00 | 7.50 | W |
| 200 | The Long Thrill–Olga Rosmanith; orig. 1954 | 2.00 | 4.00 | 6.00 | |
| 201 | Roughneck–Jim Thompson; orig. 1954 | 35.00 | 70.00 | 105.00 | E |
| 202 | Hoboes and Harlots–George Milburn; orig. 1954 | 3.00 | 6.00 | 9.00 | E |
| 203 | Whip Hand–Rod Patterson | 2.50 | 5.00 | 7.50 | W |
| 204 | Sleep with the Devil–Day Keene; orig. 1954 | 6.00 | 12.00 | 18.00 | E |
| 205 | Human?–Judith Merril | 3.00 | 6.00 | 9.00 | SF |
| 206 | Alley Girl–Jonathan Craig; orig. 1954 | 3.00 | 6.00 | 9.00 | M |
| 207 | Tiger Street–Elleston Treror | 2.50 | 5.00 | 7.50 | |
| 208 | Win–or Else!–D.J. Michael; orig. 1954 | 2.50 | 5.00 | 7.50 | S |
| 209 | A Way with Women–William Gwinn | 2.50 | 5.00 | 7.50 | |
| 210 | Joy House–Day Keene; orig. 1954 | 7.50 | 15.00 | 22.50 | |
| 211 | Boss Man–Roy B. Sparkia | 2.50 | 5.00 | 7.50 | E |

LION, *continued*

| No. | Title | V/Good | Fine | N/Mint | |
|---|---|---|---|---|---|
| 212 | A Swell-Looking Babe–Jim Thompson; orig. 1954 | 35.00 | 70.00 | 105.00 | |
| 213 | Stag Gag–Sandy Nelkin & Pat Untermeyer | 2.50 | 5.00 | 7.50 | H |
| 214 | Fully Dressed and in His Right Mind–Michael Fessier | 4.00 | 8.00 | 12.00 | SF |
| 215 | Strange Sisters–Fletcher Flora | 3.00 | 6.00 | 9.00 | |
| 216 | Dormitory Women–R.V. Cassill | 2.50 | 5.00 | 7.50 | E |
| 217 | The Gunthrowers–Steve Frazee | 2.50 | 5.00 | 7.50 | W |
| 218 | A Hell of a Woman–Jim Thompson; orig. 1954 | 35.00 | 70.00 | 105.00 | |
| 219 | Wharf Girl–William Manners | 3.00 | 6.00 | 9.00 | |
| 220 | Me an' You–Jay Thomas Caldwell | 2.50 | 5.00 | 7.50 | |
| 221 | The Naked and the Lost–Franklin M. Davis, Jr | 2.50 | 5.00 | 7.50 | |
| 222 | Evil Roots–Walter Untermeyer, Jr; orig. 1954 | 2.50 | 5.00 | 7.50 | E |
| 223 | The Savage Chase–Frederick Lorenz; orig. 1954 | 2.50 | 5.00 | 7.50 | |
| 224 | Black Friday–David Goodis; orig. 1954 | 25.00 | 50.00 | 75.00 | M |
| 225 | Jazz Bum–William Gwinn | 2.50 | 5.00 | 7.50 | |
| 226 | Tina–Robert Bruce | 2.00 | 4.00 | 6.00 | E |
| 227 | Sinner's Game–Linton Baldwin | 2.00 | 4.00 | 6.00 | E |
| 228 | Act of Violence–Basil Heatter | 2.00 | 4.00 | 6.00 | |
| 229 | Champs and Bums–Bucklin Moon | 2.00 | 4.00 | 6.00 | |
| 230 | False Night–Algis Budrys | 3.00 | 6.00 | 9.00 | SF |
| 231 | House of Evil–Clayre Lipman & Michel Lipman | 2.00 | 4.00 | 6.00 | E |
| 232 | Room for a Stranger–Constantine Fitzgibbon; 1955 | 2.00 | 4.00 | 6.00 | |
| 233 | The Deluge–Leonardo da Vinci (ed. Robert Payne) | 3.00 | 6.00 | 9.00 | SF |

# LION LIBRARY/LION BOOK
## Lion Books, Inc.

| No. | Title | V/Good | Fine | N/Mint | |
|---|---|---|---|---|---|
| LL1 | Number One–John Dos Passos; 1954 | 1.50 | 3.00 | 4.50 | |
| LL2 | A Woman's Life–Guy de Maupassant | 1.50 | 3.00 | 4.50 | |
| LL3 | The Sky Block–Steve Frazee | 2.00 | 4.00 | 6.00 | SF |
| LL4 | The Flesh Baron–P.J. Wolfson; aka Is My Flesh of Brass | 1.50 | 3.00 | 4.50 | |
| LL5 | The Sin and the Flesh–Lloyd S. Thompson | 1.50 | 3.00 | 4.50 | |
| LL6 | The Damned–Daniel Talbot | 2.50 | 5.00 | 7.50 | |
| LL7 | The Green Millenium–Fritz Leiber | 3.00 | 6.00 | 9.00 | SF |
| LL8 | Gods and Demons–Manuel Komroff | 1.50 | 3.00 | 4.50 | |
| LL9 | Passage to Violence–Stetson Kennedy; orig. 1954 | 1.50 | 3.00 | 4.50 | |
| LL10 | Escape to Nowhere–David Karp; 1955 | 1.50 | 3.00 | 4.50 | SF |
| LL11 | Dark Plunder–Victor Rosen | 1.50 | 3.00 | 4.50 | E |
| LL12 | Baseball Stars of 1955–Bruce Jacobs; orig. 1955 | 3.50 | 7.00 | 10.50 | S |
| LL13 | Hell's Pavement–Damon Knight | 2.50 | 5.00 | 7.50 | SF |
| LL14 | Lila–Curtis Lucas; orig. 1955 | 2.50 | 5.00 | 7.50 | E |
| LL15 | The Unleashed Will–Christopher Clark | 1.50 | 3.00 | 4.50 | E |
| LL16 | The Passionate Season–Victor Wolfson | 1.50 | 3.00 | 4.50 | |
| LL17 | The Best Cartoons from France–Edna Bennett | 2.00 | 4.00 | 6.00 | H |

*Lion 224, Lion LL10, Lion LL24.*

| No. | Title | V/Good | Fine | N/Mint | |
|---|---|---|---|---|---|
| LL18 | The Lost Men–Benedict Thielen | 1.50 | 3.00 | 4.50 | |
| LL19 | The Hills Beyond–Thomas Wolfe | 1.50 | 3.00 | 4.50 | |
| LL20 | Net of Outrage–William Derby | 1.50 | 3.00 | 4.50 | |
| LL21 | How I Made a Million–Noah Sarlat | 1.50 | 3.00 | 4.50 | |
| LL22 | The Wild Place–Bogart Carlaw | 1.50 | 3.00 | 4.50 | |
| LL23 | How like a God–Rex Stout | 3.00 | 6.00 | 9.00 | |
| LL24 | For Stags Only–Sandy Nelkin & Pat Untermeyer, Jr | 2.00 | 4.00 | 6.00 | H |
| LL25 | Galaxy of Ghouls–Judith Merril | 3.00 | 6.00 | 9.00 | SF |
| LL26 | The Stork Didn't Bring You–Louis Pemberton | 1.50 | 3.00 | 4.50 | NF |
| LL27 | A Mask of Guilt–Sigrid de Lima | 1.50 | 3.00 | 4.50 | |
| LL28 | Don't You Weep, Don't You Moan–Richard Coleman | 1.50 | 3.00 | 4.50 | |
| LL29 | Curve Ball Laughs–Herman L. Masin; orig. 1955 | 1.50 | 3.00 | 4.50 | SH |
| LL30 | Great Tales of the Deep South | 2.00 | 4.00 | 6.00 | |
| LL31 | Nineteen Stories–Graham Green | 1.50 | 3.00 | 4.50 | |
| LL32 | Whipsaw–William MacLeod Raine | 1.50 | 3.00 | 4.50 | W |
| LL33 | The Storm and the Silence–David Walker | 1.50 | 3.00 | 4.50 | |
| LL34 | The Tunnel of Love–Peter DeVries | 1.50 | 3.00 | 4.50 | |
| LL35 | The Fall of Valor–Charles Jackson | 1.50 | 3.00 | 4.50 | |
| LL36 | Oregon Trunk–Dan J. Stevens | 1.50 | 3.00 | 4.50 | |
| LL37 | Fruit of Desire–Willa Gibbs | 1.50 | 3.00 | 4.50 | |
| LL38 | Cartoons the French Way–Rene Goscinny | 2.00 | 4.00 | 6.00 | H |
| LL39 | Parent's Magazine Book of Baby Care–Eleanor S. Duncan | 1.25 | 2.50 | 3.75 | NF |
| LL40 | Trouble Follows Me–Kenneth Millar (Ross MacDonald) | 2.00 | 4.00 | 6.00 | E |
| LL41 | Collision–James Gordon | 1.50 | 3.00 | 4.50 | |
| LL42 | Adventures of a Young Man–John Dos Passos | 1.50 | 3.00 | 4.50 | |
| LL43 | The Kid from Dodge City–Bennett Foster | 1.50 | 3.00 | 4.50 | W |
| LL44 | Desperate Asylum–Fletcher Flora | 1.50 | 3.00 | 4.50 | |
| LL45 | The Night before Dying–Robert M. Coates | 1.50 | 3.00 | 4.50 | |
| LL46 | The Flesh Painter–Ad Gordon; orig. 1955; c-Gauguin | 2.00 | 4.00 | 6.00 | B |
| LL47 | Strange Barriers–J. Vernon Shea | 2.00 | 4.00 | 6.00 | |
| LL48 | The Naked and the Guilty–Ralph Ingersoll | 1.50 | 3.00 | 4.50 | |
| LL49 | The Outward Room–Miller Brand | 1.50 | 3.00 | 4.50 | |
| LL50 | Roberta Cowell's Story–Roberta Cowell | 3.00 | 6.00 | 9.00 | |
| LL51 | Hungry Men–Edward Anderson | 1.50 | 3.00 | 4.50 | |
| LL52 | I Die Slowly–Kenneth Millar (Ross MacDonald) | 2.00 | 4.00 | 6.00 | |
| LL53 | Great Tales of City Dwellers–Alex Austin; c-Maguire | 2.00 | 4.00 | 6.00 | |
| LL54 | The Wild Breed–Frank Bonham | 1.50 | 3.00 | 4.50 | |
| LL55 | Cora Potts–Ward Green | 1.50 | 3.00 | 4.50 | |
| LL56 | Love–William Saroyan | 1.50 | 3.00 | 4.50 | |
| LL57 | Ramrod–George C. Appell | 1.50 | 3.00 | 4.50 | W |
| LL58 | The Saturday Evening Post Cartoons–John Bailey | 2.00 | 4.00 | 6.00 | H |
| LL59 | He Ran All the Way–Sam Ross | 1.50 | 3.00 | 4.50 | |
| LL60 | The Sins of Joy Monson–Ludwig Lewisohn | 1.50 | 3.00 | 4.50 | |
| LB61 | Leashed Guns–Peter Dawson (Frank Gruber) | 2.00 | 4.00 | 6.00 | W |
| LB62 | Company K–William March | 1.50 | 3.00 | 4.50 | |
| LL63 | A Party Everynight–Frederick Lorenz; 1956 | 1.50 | 3.00 | 4.50 | |
| LL64 | Kill the Beloved–Lane Kauffmann; aka The Perfectionist | 1.50 | 3.00 | 4.50 | M |
| LL65 | Two Thieves–Manuel Komroff | 1.50 | 3.00 | 4.50 | |
| LL66 | The Naked Year–Philip Atlee | 1.50 | 3.00 | 4.50 | |
| LL67 | Pius XII: Eugenio Pacelli, Pope of Peace–Oscar Haleck & James F. Murray, Jr. | 1.50 | 3.00 | 4.50 | B |
| LL68 | All Thy Conquests–Alfred Hayes | 1.50 | 3.00 | 4.50 | |
| LB69 | Utah Hell Guns–Steve Frazee | 1.50 | 3.00 | 4.50 | W |
| LB70 | Fighting Man–Mark Morgan | 1.50 | 3.00 | 4.50 | E |
| LL71 | Cage Me a Peacock–Noel Langley | 1.50 | 3.00 | 4.50 | |
| LL72 | Gunman's Land–from the Western Writers of America; c-Gross | 1.50 | 3.00 | 4.50 | W |
| LL73 | A Handful of Hell–ed. Noah Sarlat | 1.50 | 3.00 | 4.50 | |
| LL74 | Baseball Stars of 1956–Bruce Jacobs; orig. 1956 | 3.00 | 6.00 | 9.00 | S |
| LL75 | Joy Street–Clifton Cuthbert | 1.50 | 3.00 | 4.50 | E |
| LL76 | The Heart in Exile–Rodney Garland | 1.50 | 3.00 | 4.50 | |

Lion LL74, Lion LL89, Lion LL142.

| | | V/Good | Fine | N/Mint |
|---|---|---|---|---|
| LL125 | The Naked Storm–Simon Eisner (C.M. Kornbluth) | 4.50 | 9.00 | 13.50 |
| LL126 | Gil Paust's Gun Book–Gil Paust | 1.50 | 3.00 | 4.50 NF |
| LL127 | Combat!–Noah Sarlat | 1.50 | 3.00 | 4.50 C |
| LL128 | The Troubled Midnight–Rodney Garland | 1.50 | 3.00 | 4.50 |
| LB129 | You'll Get Yours–Thomas Wills (William Ard) | 3.00 | 6.00 | 9.00 |
| LB130 | The Hardboiled Lineup–ed. Harry Widmer | 3.00 | 6.00 | 9.00 |
| LB131 | Nightfall–David Goodis; aka The Dark Chase | 3.00 | 6.00 | 9.00 M |
| LB132 | Logan–Evan Hall; aka Colorado Creek | 1.50 | 3.00 | 4.50 |
| LL133 | Rooming House–Berton Roueche | 1.50 | 3.00 | 4.50 |
| LL134 | Raft of Despair–Ensio Tiira | 1.50 | 3.00 | 4.50 A |
| LL135 | The Big Rape–James Wakefield Burke | 1.50 | 3.00 | 4.50 |
| LL136 | Leave Her to Heaven–Ben Ames Williams | 1.50 | 3.00 | 4.50 |
| LB137 | Killer's Game–Edward Hudiburg | 1.50 | 3.00 | 4.50 |
| LB138 | A Hell of a Woman–Jim Thompson | 5.00 | 10.00 | 15.00 |
| LB139 | Bloody River–Paul Durst | 1.50 | 3.00 | 4.50 W |
| LB140 | Bachelor's Anonymous–Vivian Connell | 1.50 | 3.00 | 4.50 |
| LL141 | Women without Men–Alex Austin | 1.50 | 3.00 | 4.50 |
| LL142 | The Kill-Off–Jim Thompson; orig. 1957 | 15.00 | 30.00 | 45.00 |
| LB143 | Thread of Evil–Charles Jackson | 1.50 | 3.00 | 4.50 |
| LB144 | Hot–Frederick Lorenz | 1.50 | 3.00 | 4.50 |
| LB145 | .44–H.A. DeRosso | 1.50 | 3.00 | 4.50 W |
| LB147 | The Naked Night–Dan Brenman; 1957 | 1.50 | 3.00 | 4.50 |
| LL148 | The Bedside Corpse–Stuart Friedman; aka The Gray Eyes | 1.25 | 2.50 | 3.75 M |
| LL149 | A Killer among Us–Ben Ames Williams | 1.50 | 3.00 | 4.50 M |
| LL150 | Baseball Stars of 1957–Bruce Jacobs; orig. 1957 | 2.50 | 5.00 | 7.50 S |
| LL151 | Brain Guy–Benjamin Appel | 2.50 | 5.00 | 7.50 |
| LB152 | Dolls Are Murder–Harold Q. Masur | 2.50 | 5.00 | 7.50 M |
| LB153 | Valerie–Jordan Park (C.M. Kornbluth) | 1.50 | 3.00 | 4.50 E |
| LB154 | The Man from Texas–H.A. DeRosso; aka The Gun Trail | 1.50 | 3.00 | 4.50 W |
| LB155 | The Gun-Hung Men–Leslie Ernenwein; aka Rio Renegade | 1.50 | 3.00 | 4.50 W |
| LB156 | Hangtree Range–William Hopson | 1.50 | 3.00 | 4.50 W |
| LB157 | Wyoming War–Sam Allison; aka Trouble on Crazyman | 1.50 | 3.00 | 4.50 W |
| LL158 | The Big Make–Gene Paul; c-Maguire | 1.50 | 3.00 | 4.50 |
| LL160 | Hoboes and Harlots–George Milburn | 1.50 | 3.00 | 4.50 |
| LL161 | Gunman's Grudge–George C. Appell | 1.50 | 3.00 | 4.50 W |
| LL162 | | | | |
| LB163 | LaSignora–Elio Bartolini | 1.50 | 3.00 | 4.50 E |
| LB164 | Whip Hand–Rod Patterson | 1.50 | 3.00 | 4.50 W |
| LB165 | A Rage at Sea–Frederick Lorenz | 1.50 | 3.00 | 4.50 |
| LL167 | This Is It!–Noah Sarlat; c-Maguire | 1.50 | 3.00 | 4.50 |
| LL168 | The Bedside Bachelor–Paul Steiner | 1.50 | 3.00 | 4.50 H |
| LL170 | The Red Lily–Anatole France | 1.50 | 3.00 | 4.50 |
| LB171 | The Sleeper–Holly Roth | 1.50 | 3.00 | 4.50 |
| LB172 | Slaughter Street–Louis Falstein; c-Maguire | 1.50 | 3.00 | 4.50 |
| LB173 | The Gunthrowers–Steve Frazee | 1.50 | 3.00 | 4.50 W |
| LB174 | The Seventh Trumpet–Peter Julian | 1.50 | 3.00 | 4.50 |
| LL175 | Five Who Vanished–Robert Levin | 1.50 | 3.00 | 4.50 |

| | | V/Good | Fine | N/Mint |
|---|---|---|---|---|
| | LION LIBRARY/LION BOOK, *continued* | | | |
| LB77 | Tough Kid–William Attaway; aka Let Me Breathe Thunder | 1.50 | 3.00 | 4.50 E |
| LB78 | Pistolman–Steve Frazee | 1.50 | 3.00 | 4.50 W |
| LL79 | Slade–Ad Gordon | 1.50 | 3.00 | 4.50 |
| LL80 | Art Buchwald's Paris–Art Buchwald | 1.50 | 3.00 | 4.50 |
| LL81 | All Quiet on the Western Front–Erich Maria Remarque | 1.50 | 3.00 | 4.50 C |
| LL82 | Julie–George Milburn | 1.50 | 3.00 | 4.50 |
| LL83 | Rogues and Lovers–Noah Sarlat | 1.50 | 3.00 | 4.50 E |
| LL84 | To Keep or Kill–Wilson Tucker; c-Maguire | 2.00 | 4.00 | 6.00 M |
| LB85 | Two-Gun Texan–Burt Arthur | 1.50 | 3.00 | 4.50 W |
| LL86 | The Girl on Crown Street–David Karp | 1.50 | 3.00 | 4.50 |
| LL87 | The Brass Bed–Fletcher Flora | 1.50 | 3.00 | 4.50 |
| LL88 | Great Tales of the Far West–ed. Alex Austin | 1.50 | 3.00 | 4.50 |
| LL89 | The Gunslingers–Harry Widmer | 1.50 | 3.00 | 4.50 W |
| LL90 | Around the World in 80 Days–Jules Verne | 1.50 | 3.00 | 4.50 A |
| LL91 | A Knife Is Silent–David Kent | 1.50 | 3.00 | 4.50 M |
| LB92 | Lonely Boy Blues–Allan Kapelner | 1.50 | 3.00 | 4.50 |
| LB93 | Gunsight–Frank Gruber | 1.50 | 3.00 | 4.50 W |
| LB94 | Luther–Roy Flannagan | 2.00 | 4.00 | 6.00 |
| LL95 | Stories for Stags–Eddie Davis | 1.50 | 3.00 | 4.50 H |
| LL96 | Kiss Her Goodbye–Wade Miller | 1.50 | 3.00 | 4.50 M |
| LL97 | Sorority House–Jordan Park (C.M. Kornbluth & Frederick Pohl) | 6.00 | 12.00 | 18.00 E |
| LL98 | Art Colony–Clifton Cuthbert | 1.50 | 3.00 | 4.50 E |
| LB99 | French and Frisky–Rene Goscinny | 2.00 | 4.00 | 6.00 H |
| LB100 | Gun Hell–Riley Ryan | 1.50 | 3.00 | 4.50 W |
| LB101 | The Utah Kid–Roe Richmond; aka Conestoga Cowboy | 1.50 | 3.00 | 4.50 W |
| LL102 | The Oracle–Edwin O'Connor | 1.50 | 3.00 | 4.50 |
| LL103 | Sports Laughs–Herman Le Masin; orig. 1956; c-Powers | 1.50 | 3.00 | 4.50 SH |
| LL104 | Ruby–Frederick Lorenz | 1.50 | 3.00 | 4.50 |
| LL105 | Bedtime Laughs–Paul Steiner | 1.50 | 3.00 | 4.50 H |
| LL106 | House of Dolls–Ka-tzetnik 135633 | 1.50 | 3.00 | 4.50 NF |
| LB107 | Candide–Voltaire | 1.50 | 3.00 | 4.50 |
| LB108 | Lawman's Feud–Steve Frazee | 1.50 | 3.00 | 4.50 W |
| LB109 | Platoon–Adam Singer | 1.50 | 3.00 | 4.50 |
| LL110 | His Great Journey–Manuel Komroff | 1.50 | 3.00 | 4.50 |
| LL111 | Wives and Lovers–Alex Austin | 1.50 | 3.00 | 4.50 |
| LL112 | The Dream and the Flesh–Vivian Connell | 1.50 | 3.00 | 4.50 |
| LL113 | World So Wide–Sinclair Lewis | 1.50 | 3.00 | 4.50 |
| LL114 | Quintet–ed. anon.; includes A. Huxley, R. Wright, W. Saroyan, L. Tolstoi & G. de Maupassant | 1.50 | 3.00 | 4.50 |
| LB115 | Paula–Gale Wilhelm; aka No Letters for the Dead | 2.00 | 4.00 | 6.00 |
| LB116 | Alley Kids–Benjamin Appel; aka Hell's Kitchen | 1.50 | 3.00 | 4.50 JD |
| LB117 | The Lone Gunhawk–Frank Gruber; aka Smoky Road | 1.50 | 3.00 | 4.50 W |
| LL118 | The Cheat–Don Tracy; aka Criss-Cross | 2.00 | 4.00 | 6.00 |
| LL119 | College Humor–Sandy Nelkin | 1.50 | 3.00 | 4.50 H |
| LL120 | My Old Man–Richard B. Erno | 1.50 | 3.00 | 4.50 |
| LL121 | Desire and Damnation–William March; aka Come in at the Door | 1.50 | 3.00 | 4.50 |
| LB122 | Either Is Love–Elisabeth Craigin | 1.50 | 3.00 | 4.50 |
| LB123 | The Oxbow Kill–C. William Harrison | 1.50 | 3.00 | 4.50 |
| LB124 | Recoil–Jim Thompson; c-Maguire | 5.00 | 10.00 | 15.00 |

# LOVE ROMANCE SERIES

## Palace Promotions

### Digest Size

| | | V/Good | Fine | N/Mint |
|---|---|---|---|---|
| 1 | Nice and Naughty–Gordon Semple | 3.50 | 7.00 | 10.50 E |
| 2 | Faithfully Yours–Eliot Brewster; c-Cole. Note: Although No. 2 is on cover, No. 11 is on spine. | 3.50 | 7.00 | 10.50 E |
| 3 | Love Above All–Eliot Brewster; c-Cole. Note: Although No. 3 is on cover, No. 12 is on spine. | 3.50 | 7.00 | 10.50 E |

# (LUCOM)

## David Lucom, Publishers

### Digest Size

| | | V/Good | Fine | N/Mint |
|---|---|---|---|---|
| nn | The Case of the Walking Corpse–Armstrong Livingston; 1945 | 3.50 | 7.00 | 10.50 M |

Lucom unnumbered, Magazine Village 6, Magabooks 3.

| | | V/Good | Fine | N/Mint |
|---|---|---|---|---|

## (MACFADDEN)
### MacFadden Publications, Inc.

| | | V/Good | Fine | N/Mint |
|---|---|---|---|---|
| nn | Unpublished True Stories–from the private files of True Story Magazine; 1952 | 2.00 | 4.00 | 6.00 |

## MACFADDEN BOOKS
### MacFadden-Bartell Corporation

| | | V/Good | Fine | N/Mint | |
|---|---|---|---|---|---|
| 50-114 | Tops in Pops Plus a Rock 'n' Roll Roundup–Steve Kahn; orig. 1961 | 2.50 | 5.00 | 7.50 | NF |
| 50-159 | The Executives Comic Book–Harvey Kurtzman & Wili Elder; 1st ed. 1962. Note: Comic story reprints from Help magazine including T*rz*n | 4.00 | 8.00 | 12.00 | H |
| 50-210 | All about the Beatles–Edward De Blasio; 1st ed. 1964 | 5.00 | 10.00 | 15.00 | NF |

## MAGABOOKS
### Galaxy Publishing Corporation
**Digest Size**

| | | V/Good | Fine | N/Mint | |
|---|---|---|---|---|---|
| 1 | Badge of Infamy–Lester del Rey | 1.50 | 3.00 | 4.50 | SF |
| | The Sky Is Falling–Lester del Rey | | | | SF |
| 2 | After Worlds End–Jack Williamson | 1.50 | 3.00 | 4.50 | SF |
| | The Legion of Time–Jack Williamson | | | | SF |
| 3 | Baby Is Three–Theodore Sturgeon | 1.50 | 3.00 | 4.50 | SF |
| | . . . and My Fear Is Great–Theodore Sturgeon | | | | SF |

## (MAGAZINE VILLAGE)
### Magazine Village, Inc.
**Digest Size**

| | | V/Good | Fine | N/Mint | |
|---|---|---|---|---|---|
| 5 | Confessions of a Park Avenue Playgirl–Carl Sturdy; aka Society Doctor | 3.00 | 6.00 | 9.00 | E |
| 6 | Illicit Honeymoon–Lois Bull; 1948; aka Seven Make a Honeymoon | 4.00 | 8.00 | 12.00 | E |
| 7 | Hard Boiled Mistress–Lois Bull; 1948; aka Mating Woman. Note: Cover gives E.T. Keating as author | 3.00 | 6.00 | 9.00 | E |

## (MANHATTAN)
### Manhattan Fiction Publishing
**Digest Size**

| | | V/Good | Fine | N/Mint | |
|---|---|---|---|---|---|
| nn | Harem Nights–B.J. Vaswani; 1947 | 3.50 | 7.00 | 10.50 | E |

| | | V/Good | Fine | N/Mint | |
|---|---|---|---|---|---|

## (MASTHEAD)
### The Masthead Corporation

| | | V/Good | Fine | N/Mint | |
|---|---|---|---|---|---|
| nn | Seagram's Sports Almanac–; 1955 | .50 | 1.00 | 1.50 | S |

## MENTOR BOOKS
### New American Library
**(See also Pelican; reprinted by Mentor after Pelican/Mentor name change.)**

| | | V/Good | Fine | N/Mint | |
|---|---|---|---|---|---|
| M26 | American Essays–Charles B. Shaw; 1948 | .50 | 1.00 | 1.50 | |
| M27 | Biography of the Earth–George Gamow | .75 | 1.50 | 2.25 | NF |
| M28 | Science and the Modern World–Alfred North Whitehead | .50 | 1.00 | 1.50 | NF |
| M29 | The Autobiography of an Ex-Coloured Man–James Weldon Johnson | 1.50 | 3.00 | 4.50 | |
| M30 | American in Perspective–Henry Steele Commager | .50 | 1.00 | 1.50 | |
| M31 | Man in the Modern World–Julian Huxley | .50 | 1.00 | 1.50 | |
| M32 | The Greek Way to Western Civilization–Edith Hamilton | .75 | 1.50 | 2.25 | NF |
| M33 | Indians of the Americas–John Collier | .75 | 1.50 | 2.25 | NF |
| M34 | The Law and You–Max Radin | .50 | 1.00 | 1.50 | NF |
| M35 | The Limitations of Science–J.W.N. Sullivan; 1949 | .50 | 1.00 | 1.50 | NF |
| M36 | How to Know the Birds–Roger Tory Peterson | 1.50 | 3.00 | 4.50 | NF |
| M37 | Russia–Bernard Pares | .75 | 1.50 | 2.25 | NF |
| | With dust jacket | 9.00 | 18.00 | 27.00 | |
| M38 | The Age of Jackson–Arthur M. Schlesinger, Jr | .75 | 1.50 | 2.25 | NF |
| M39 | Life on Other Worlds–H. Spencer Jones | .75 | 1.50 | 2.25 | |
| M40 | Arts and the Man–Irwin Edman | .50 | 1.00 | 1.50 | NF |
| M41 | The Aims of Education–Alfred North Whitehead | .50 | 1.00 | 1.50 | NF |
| M42 | Ballet–George Amberg; aka Ballet in America | .50 | 1.00 | 1.50 | NF |
| M43 | Science and the Moral Life–Max Otto | .50 | 1.00 | 1.50 | NF |
| M44 | The Coming of Age in Samoa–Margaret Mead | .75 | 1.50 | 2.25 | NF |
| M45 | Beethoven–J.W.N. Sullivan | .75 | 1.50 | 2.25 | B |
| M46 | The Iliad–Homerus; 1950 | .75 | 1.50 | 2.25 | |
| M47 | Music for the Millions–David Ewen | .50 | 1.00 | 1.50 | NF |
| M48 | How to Know the Wild Flowers–Alfred Stefferud | 1.50 | 3.00 | 4.50 | NF |
| M49 | The Revolt of the Masses–Jose Ortega y Gasset | .75 | 1.50 | 2.25 | |
| M50 | The Next Development in Man–Lancelot Law White; 1950 | .50 | 1.00 | 1.50 | |
| M51 | The Oregon Trail–Francis Parkman | .75 | 1.50 | 2.25 | W |
| M52 | New Handbook of the Heavens–Hubert J. Bernhard | .50 | 1.00 | 1.50 | NF |
| M53 | Reconstruction in Philosophy–John Dewey | .50 | 1.00 | 1.50 | NF |
| M54 | 100 Modern Poems–Selden Rodman | .50 | 1.00 | 1.50 | |
| M55 | Life Stories of Men Who Shaped History–Plutarchus | .75 | 1.50 | 2.25 | B |
| M56 | Sex and Temperament in Three Primitive Societies–Margaret Mead | .75 | 1.50 | 2.25 | NF |
| M57 | Lenin–David Shub | .75 | 1.50 | 2.25 | B |
| M58 | Introduction to Economic Science–George Soule; 1951 | .50 | 1.00 | 1.50 | NF |
| M59 | The Democratic Way of Life–Eduard C. Lindeman & T.V. Smith | .50 | 1.00 | 1.50 | NF |
| M60 | The Summing Up–W. Somerset Maugham | .50 | 1.00 | 1.50 | |
| M61 | A Gallery of Americans–Frank Luther Mott | .50 | 1.00 | 1.50 | B |
| M62 | How to Know American Antiques–Alice Winchester | .75 | 1.50 | 2.25 | NF |
| M63 | How to Know the American Mammals–Ivan T. Sanderson | 1.00 | 2.00 | 3.00 | NF |
| M64 | Man Makes Himself–V. Gordon Childe | .50 | 1.00 | 1.50 | |
| M65 | The World of Copernicus–Angus Armitage | .75 | 1.50 | 2.25 | NF |

MENTOR BOOKS, *continued*

| | | V/Good | Fine | N/Mint |
|---|---|---|---|---|
| M66 | The Meaning of Evolution–George Gaylord Simpson | .50 | 1.00 | 1.50 NF |
| M67 | Psychopathology in Everyday Life–Sigmund Freud | .50 | 1.00 | 1.50 NF |
| M68 | On Understanding Science–James B. Conant | .50 | 1.00 | 1.50 NF |
| M69 | The Prince–Niccolo Machiavelli; 1952 | .75 | 1.50 | 2.25 |
| M70 | Jefferson–Saul K. Padover | .50 | 1.00 | 1.50 B |
| M71 | The Universe and Dr. Einstein–Lincoln Barnett | .50 | 1.00 | 1.50 NF |
| M72 | Greek Historical Thought–Arnold J. Toynbee | .75 | 1.50 | 2.25 NF |
| Ms73 | New World Writing No. 1 | .50 | 1.00 | 1.50 |
| M74 | Heredity, Race and Society–Th. Dobzhansky & L.C. Dunn | .50 | 1.00 | 1.50 NF |
| M75 | A World Apart–Gustaw Herling; 1952 | .50 | 1.00 | 1.50 |
| M76 | Good Reading | .50 | 1.00 | 1.50 |
| M77 | The Birth and Death of the Sun–George Gamow | .75 | 1.50 | 2.25 NF |
| M78 | A Documentary History of the United States–Richard D. Heffner | .50 | 1.00 | 1.50 NF |
| Ms79 | New World Writing No. 2 | .50 | 1.00 | 1.50 |
| M80 | American Diplomacy: 1900-1950–George F. Kennan | .50 | 1.00 | 1.50 NF |
| M81 | What to Listen for in Music–Aaron Copeland; 1953 | .75 | 1.50 | 2.25 NF |
| M82 | The Wonderful World of Books–Alfred Stefferud | .50 | 1.00 | 1.50 NF |
| M83 | Out of My Life and Thought–Albert Schweitzer & Everett Skillings | .75 | 1.50 | 2.25 NF |
| M84 | How to Know and Predict the Weather–Robert Moore Fisher | 1.00 | 2.00 | 3.00 NF |
| Ms85 | New World Writing No. 3 | .50 | 1.00 | 1.50 |
| Ms86 | Mythology–Edith Hamilton | .75 | 1.50 | 2.25 |
| M87 | Walden and Civil Disobedience–Henry David Thoreau | .75 | 1.50 | 2.25 |
| M88 | A History of the World in 240 Pages–Rene Sedillot | .50 | 1.00 | 1.50 NF |
| M89 | Patterns of Culture–Ruth Benedict | .50 | 1.00 | 1.50 NF |
| Ms90 | The Golden Treasury–F.T. Palgrave & Oscar Williams | .75 | 1.50 | 2.25 |
| M91 | Growing Up in New Guinea–Margaret Mead | .75 | 1.50 | 2.25 NF |
| M92 | The Odyssey–Homerus | .75 | 1.50 | 2.25 |
| M93 | The Theory of the Leisure Class | .50 | 1.00 | 1.50 NF |
| Ms94 | The Meaning of the Glorious Koran–Mohammed Marmaduke Pickthall | .75 | 1.50 | 2.25 NF |
| M95 | The Living U. S. Constitution–Saul K. Padover | .75 | 1.50 | 2.25 NF |
| Ms96 | New World Writing No. 4 | .50 | 1.00 | 1.50 |
| Ms97 | One Two Three . . . Infinity–George Gamow | .75 | 1.50 | 2.25 |
| M98 | The Shaping of the Modern Mind–Crane Brinton | .50 | 1.00 | 1.50 NF |
| M99 | Greek Civilization and Character–Arnold J. Toynbee | .50 | 1.00 | 1.50 NF |
| M100 | The Sea Around Us–Rachel L. Carson; 1954 | .50 | 1.00 | 1.50 NF |
| MD101 | Philosophy in a New Key–Susanne K. Langer | .50 | 1.00 | 1.50 NF |
| M102 | Basic Selections from Emerson–Ralph Waldo Emerson | .50 | 1.00 | 1.50 |
| M103 | The Song of God: Bhagavad-gita | .75 | 1.50 | 2.25 |
| M104 | Highlights of Modern Literature–Francis Brown | .50 | 1.00 | 1.50 |
| M105 | The Life of the Spider–John Crompton | .50 | 1.00 | 1.50 NF |
| Ms106 | New World Writing No. 5 | .50 | 1.00 | 1.50 |
| M107 | Ethics in a Business Society–Douglass Cater & Marquis W. Childs | .50 | 1.00 | 1.50 |
| Ms108 | An Analysis of the Kinsey Reports on Sexual Behavior in the Human Male and Female–Donald Porter Geddes | .50 | 1.00 | 1.50 NF |
| M109 | The World of History–Courtlands Canby & Nancy E. Gross | .50 | 1.00 | 1.50 |
| Ms110 | The Iliad–Homerus | .75 | 1.50 | 2.25 |
| M111 | The Life of the Bee–Maurice Maeterlinck | .50 | 1.00 | 1.50 NF |
| Ms112 | The Uses of the Past–Herbert J. Muller | .75 | 1.50 | 2.25 |
| Ms113 | The Inferno–Dante Alighieri | .75 | 1.50 | 2.25 |
| Ms114 | New Handbook of the Heavens–Hubert J. Bernhard & others | .50 | 1.00 | 1.50 NF |
| M115 | Men, Wages and Employment in the Modern U. S. Economy–George Soule | .50 | 1.00 | 1.50 |
| Ms116 | The Holy Bible in Brief–James Reeves | .75 | 1.50 | 2.25 NF |
| Ms117 | Leaves of Grass–Walt Whitman | .75 | 1.50 | 2.25 |
| Ms118 | New World Writing No. 6 | .50 | 1.00 | 1.50 |
| Ms119 | Psychology of Sex–Havelock Ellis | .50 | 1.00 | 1.50 NF |
| Ms120 | The Birth and Death of the Sun–George Gamow | .75 | 1.50 | 2.25 NF |
| Ms121 | The Dynamics of Soviet Society–W.W. Rostow | .50 | 1.00 | 1.50 NF |
| MD122 | Good Listening–R.D. Darrell | .50 | 1.00 | 1.50 NF |
| Ms123 | Ballet in America–George Amberg | .50 | 1.00 | 1.50 NF |
| Ms124 | Good Reading | .50 | 1.00 | 1.50 |
| M125 | The Nature of the Universe–Fred Hoyle; 1955 | .50 | 1.00 | 1.50 NF |
| Ms126 | The Age of Belief–Anne Fremantle | .50 | 1.00 | 1.50 NF |
| MD127 | Here I Stand–Roland H. Bainton | .50 | 1.00 | 1.50 |
| M128 | Under the Sea Wind–Rachel L. Carson | .50 | 1.00 | 1.50 NF |
| M129 | The Way of Life–Lao-Tzu | .75 | 1.50 | 2.25 |
| MD130 | New World Writing No. 7 | .50 | 1.00 | 1.50 |
| MD131 | The Teachings of the Compassionate Buddha–Edwin A. Burtt | .75 | 1.50 | 2.25 |
| MD132 | The Creative Process–Brewster Ghiselin | .50 | 1.00 | 1.50 |
| MD133 | Sex and Temperament in Three Primitive Societies–Margaret Mead | .50 | 1.00 | 1.50 NF |
| MD134 | Cultural Patters and Technical Change–Margaret Mead | .50 | 1.00 | 1.50 NF |
| M135 | The Law and You–Max Radin | .50 | 1.00 | 1.50 NF |
| M136 | Mohammedanism–H.A.R. Gibb | .50 | 1.00 | 1.50 NF |
| MD137 | American Essays–Charles B. Shaw | .50 | 1.00 | 1.50 |
| MD138 | Biography of the Earth–George Gamow | .50 | 1.00 | 1.50 NF |
| MD139 | Science and the Moral Life–Max Otto | .50 | 1.00 | 1.50 NF |
| MD140 | Lenin–David Shub | .50 | 1.00 | 1.50 B |
| MD141 | Adventures of Ideas–Alfred North Whitehead | .50 | 1.00 | 1.50 |
| MD142 | The Age of Analysis–Morton White | .50 | 1.00 | 1.50 NF |
| M143 | Ideas of the Great Economists–George Soule | .50 | 1.00 | 1.50 NF |
| MD144 | Life on Other Worlds–H. Spencer Jones | .50 | 1.00 | 1.50 |
| MD145 | The Age of Jackson–Arthur M. Schlesinger, Jr | .50 | 1.00 | 1.50 NF |
| MD146 | New World Writing No. 8 | .50 | 1.00 | 1.50 |
| M147 | A Primer of Freudian Psychology–Calvin S. Hall | .50 | 1.00 | 1.50 NF |
| MD148 | Man in the Modern World–Julian Huxley | .50 | 1.00 | 1.50 |
| MD149 | The Oregon Trail–Francis Parkman | .50 | 1.00 | 1.50 W |
| MD150 | Male and Female–Margaret Mead; 1955 | .50 | 1.00 | 1.50 |
| M151 | The Sayings of Confucius–Confucius | .50 | 1.00 | 1.50 |
| MD152 | The Aims of Education–Alfred North Whitehead | .50 | 1.00 | 1.50 NF |
| MD153 | The Coming of Age in Samoa–Margaret Mead | .50 | 1.00 | 1.50 NF |
| MD154 | Man Makes Himself–V. Gordon Childe | .50 | 1.00 | 1.50 |
| M155 | Scheherezade: Tales from the 1001 Nights | .75 | 1.50 | 2.25 |
| M156 | Company Manners–Louis Kronenberger | .50 | 1.00 | 1.50 |
| MD157 | The Wonderful World of Books–Alfred Stefferud | .50 | 1.00 | 1.50 NF |
| MD158 | The Age of Reason–Stuart Hampshire | .50 | 1.00 | 1.50 NF |
| M159 | The Painter's Eye–Maurice Grosser | .50 | 1.00 | 1.50 NF |
| MD160 | Jefferson–Saul K. Padover | .50 | 1.00 | 1.50 B |
| MD161 | Democracy in America–Alexis de Tocqueville | .50 | 1.00 | 1.50 NF |
| MD162 | Science and the Modern World–Alfred North Whitehead | .50 | 1.00 | 1.50 NF |
| MD163 | Religion and the Rise of Capitalism–R.H. Tawney | .50 | 1.00 | 1.50 NF |
| MD164 | Greek Historical Thought–Arnold J. Toynbee | .50 | 1.00 | 1.50 NF |
| MD165 | Human Destiny–Pierre Lecomte du Nouy | .50 | 1.00 | 1.50 |
| MD166 | Life Stories of Men Who Shaped History–Plutarchus | .50 | 1.00 | 1.50 B |
| MD167 | Great Dialogues of Plato | .50 | 1.00 | 1.50 |
| M168 | Books That Changed the World–Robert B. Downs | .50 | 1.00 | 1.50 |

MENTOR BOOKS, *continued*

| | | V/Good | Fine | N/Mint |
|---|---|---|---|---|
| MD169 | America in Perspective–Henry Steele Commager | .50 | 1.00 | 1.50 |
| MD170 | New World Writing No. 9 | .50 | 1.00 | 1.50 |
| MD171 | Indians of the Americas–John Collier | .50 | 1.00 | 1.50 NF |
| MD172 | The Age of Enlightenment–Isaiah Berlin | .50 | 1.00 | 1.50 NF |
| MD173 | The Shaping of the Modern Mind–Crane Brinton | .50 | 1.00 | 1.50 |
| M174 | The Public Philosophy–Walter Lippmann | .50 | 1.00 | 1.50 |
| MD175 | American Skyline–Henry Hope Reed & Christopher Tunnard | .50 | 1.00 | 1.50 |
| MD176 | Walden and Civil Disobedience–Henry David Thoreau | .50 | 1.00 | 1.50 |
| MD177 | The Papal Encyclicals in Their Historical Context–Anne Fremantle | .50 | 1.00 | 1.50 NF |
| MD178 | Good Reading | .50 | 1.00 | 1.50 |
| MD179 | The Reader's Companion to World Literature–Lillian Herlands Hornstein | .50 | 1.00 | 1.50 |
| MD180 | Dialogues of Alfred North Whitehead | .50 | 1.00 | 1.50 |
| M181 | Christopher Columbus, Mariner–Samuel Eliot Morison | .50 | 1.00 | 1.50 B |
| MD182 | Russia and America: Dangers and Prospects–Henry L. Roberts | .50 | 1.00 | 1.50 |
| MD183 | New World Writing No. 10 | .50 | 1.00 | 1.50 |
| MD184 | The Age of Adventure–Giorgio deSantillana | .50 | 1.00 | 1.50 NF |
| MD185 | The Age of Ideaology–Henry O. Aiken | .50 | 1.00 | 1.50 NF |
| MD186 | 100 American Poems–Selden Rodman | .50 | 1.00 | 1.50 |
| MD187 | 100 Modern Poems–Selden Rodman | .50 | 1.00 | 1.50 |
| MD188 | The Cycle of American Literature–Robert E. Spiller; 1957 | .50 | 1.00 | 1.50 |
| MD189 | The Mentor Book of Religious Verse–Horace Gregory & Marya Zaturenska | .75 | 1.50 | 2.25 |
| MD190 | The Nature of the Non-Western World–Vera Micheles Dean | .50 | 1.00 | 1.50 NF |
| MD191 | On Life and Sex–Havelock Ellis | .50 | 1.00 | 1.50 NF |
| MD192 | Realm of the Incas–Victor W. Von Hagen | .50 | 1.00 | 1.50 NF |
| MD193 | Of the Imitation of Christ–Thomas a Kempis | .50 | 1.00 | 1.50 NF |
| M194 | The Upanishads | .50 | 1.00 | 1.50 |
| MD195 | Eight Great Tragedies–Sylvan Barnet & others | .50 | 1.00 | 1.50 |
| MD196 | New World Writing No. 11 | .50 | 1.00 | 1.50 |
| MD197 | The Anvil of Civilization–Leonard Cottrell | .50 | 1.00 | 1.50 NF |
| M198 | The Hedgehog and the Fox–Isaiah Berlin | .50 | 1.00 | 1.50 |
| MD199 | The Living Talmud: The Wisdom of the Fathers | .50 | 1.00 | 1.50 |
| MD200 | The Frontiers of Astronomy–Fred Hoyle | .50 | 1.00 | 1.50 NF |
| MD201 | The Silver Treasury of Light Verse–Oscar Williams | .50 | 1.00 | 1.50 |
| MD202 | On Love, Family and the Good Life–Plutarchus | .50 | 1.00 | 1.50 |
| MD203 | The Summing Up–W. Somerset Maugham | .50 | 1.00 | 1.50 |
| MD204 | Evolution in Action–Julian Huxley | .50 | 1.00 | 1.50 |
| MD205 | Three Great Irishmen–Arland Ussher | .50 | 1.00 | 1.50 |
| MD206 | The Negro in American Culture–Margaret Just Butcher | 1.50 | 3.00 | 4.50 NF |
| MD207 | Don Quixote–Miguel de Cervantes | .50 | 1.00 | 1.50 |
| MD208 | Arms and Men–Walter Millis | .50 | 1.00 | 1.50 |
| MD209 | Language–Joshua Whatmough | .50 | 1.00 | 1.50 NF |
| MD210 | New World Writing No. 12 | .50 | 1.00 | 1.50 |
| MD211 | Enjoying Modern Art–Sarah Newmeyer | .50 | 1.00 | 1.50 NF |
| MD212 | Modern Music–John Tasker Howard & James Lyons | .50 | 1.00 | 1.50 NF |
| MD213 | The Roman Way to Western Civilization–Edith Hamilton | .50 | 1.00 | 1.50 NF |
| MD214 | The Creation of the Universe–George Gamow | .50 | 1.00 | 1.50 NF |
| MD215 | The Authentic New Testament; 1958 | .50 | 1.00 | 1.50 |
| MD216 | Eight Great Comedies–Sylvan Barnet & others | .50 | 1.00 | 1.50 |
| MD217 | Medicine and Man–Ritchie Calder | .50 | 1.00 | 1.50 NF |
| MD218 | The Theory of Business Enterprise–Thorstein Veblen | .50 | 1.00 | 1.50 NF |
| MD219 | The Meaning of the Dead Sea Scrolls–A. Powell Davies | .75 | 1.50 | 2.25 NF |
| MD220 | The United Nations and How It Works–David Cushman Coyle | .50 | 1.00 | 1.50 NF |
| MD221 | The Varieties of Religious Experience–William James | .50 | 1.00 | 1.50 NF |
| MD222 | The Origin of the Species–Charles Darwin | .50 | 1.00 | 1.50 NF |
| MT223 | The Meaning of the Glorious Koran–Mohammed Marmaduke Pickthall | .50 | 1.00 | 1.50 |
| MD224 | A Short History of India and Pakistan–T. Walter Wallbank | .50 | 1.00 | 1.50 NF |
| MD225 | The Dark Ages–W.P. Ker; 1958 | .50 | 1.00 | 1.50 NF |
| MD226 | The Greek Philosophers–Rex Warner | .50 | 1.00 | 1.50 NF |
| MD227 | Human Types–Raymond Firth | .50 | 1.00 | 1.50 |
| MD228 | The True Believer–Eric Hoffer | .50 | 1.00 | 1.50 |
| MD229 | Books That Changed the World–Robert B. Downs | .50 | 1.00 | 1.50 NF |
| MD230 | Russia–Bernard Pares | .50 | 1.00 | 1.50 |
| MD231 | The Universe and Dr. Einstein–Lincoln Barnett | .50 | 1.00 | 1.50 NF |
| MT232 | The Reader's Companion to World Literature–Lillian Herlands Horstein & others | .50 | 1.00 | 1.50 |
| MT233 | New World Writing No. 13 | .50 | 1.00 | 1.50 |
| MD234 | Relativity for the Layman–James A. Coleman | .50 | 1.00 | 1.50 |
| MT235 | Great Writings of Goethe–Johann Wolfgang von Goethe | .50 | 1.00 | 1.50 |
| MD236 | The Aztec: Man and Tribe–Victor W. Von Hagen | .75 | 1.50 | 2.25 NF |
| MD237 | Bertrand Russell's Best–Bertrand Russell | .50 | 1.00 | 1.50 |
| MT238 | The Oedipus Plays of Sophocles | .50 | 1.00 | 1.50 |
| MD239 | Man: His First Million Years–Ashley Montagu | .50 | 1.00 | 1.50 NF |
| MD240 | The Story of Jazz–Marshall Stearns | .50 | 1.00 | 1.50 NF |
| MT241 | Three Great Plays of Euripides | .50 | 1.00 | 1.50 |
| MD242 | The Edge of the Sea–Rachel L. Carson | .50 | 1.00 | 1.50 NF |
| MD243 | A Treasury of Asian Literature–John D. Yohannan | .50 | 1.00 | 1.50 |
| MD244 | Religion without Revelation–Julian Huxley | .50 | 1.00 | 1.50 |
| MT245 | The Golden Treasury–F.T. Palgrave & Oscar Williams | .50 | 1.00 | 1.50 |
| MT246 | New World Writing No. 14 | .50 | 1.00 | 1.50 |
| MD247 | Stories from Shakespeare–Marchette Chute; 1959 | .50 | 1.00 | 1.50 |
| MT248 | Mainsprings of Civilization–Ellsworth Huntington | .50 | 1.00 | 1.50 |
| MT249 | Rebels and Redcoats–Hugh F. Rankin & George Scheer | .50 | 1.00 | 1.50 NF |
| MD250 | The Statesman–Henry Taylor | .50 | 1.00 | 1.50 |
| MD251 | The Origins of Oriental Civilization–Walter A. Fairservis, Jr | .50 | 1.00 | 1.50 NF |
| MD252 | The First Christian–A. Powell Davies | .50 | 1.00 | 1.50 |
| MD253 | The Religions of Man–Huston Smith | .50 | 1.00 | 1.50 |
| MD254 | The Young Caesar–Rex Warner | .50 | 1.00 | 1.50 B |
| MD255 | Growing Up in New Guinea–Margaret Mead | .50 | 1.00 | 1.50 NF |
| MT256 | The Papal Encyclicals in Their Historical Context–Anne Fremantle | .50 | 1.00 | 1.50 |
| MT257 | Stores from Shakespeare–Marchette Chute | .50 | 1.00 | 1.50 |
| MD258 | The ABC of Relativity–Bertrand Russell | .50 | 1.00 | 1.50 |
| MD259 | The Undiscovered Self–C.G. Jung | .50 | 1.00 | 1.50 NF |
| MT260 | New World Writing No. 15 | .50 | 1.00 | 1.50 |
| MD261 | Music and Imagination–Aaron Copeland | .50 | 1.00 | 1.50 NF |
| MT262 | The History of Western Art–Erwin O. Christenson | .50 | 1.00 | 1.50 NF |
| MD263 | The Liveliest Art–Arthur Knight | .50 | 1.00 | 1.50 |
| MD264 | The Crust of the Earth–Samuel Rapport & Helen Wright | .50 | 1.00 | 1.50 NF |
| MD265 | The Renaissance–Walter Pater | .50 | 1.00 | 1.50 NF |
| M266 | This Little Band of Prophets–Anne Fremantle | .50 | 1.00 | 1.50 |
| MD267 | The American Presidency–Clinton Rossiter | .50 | 1.00 | 1.50 |
| MD268 | Islam in Modern History–Wilfred Cantwell Smith | .50 | 1.00 | 1.50 NF |
| MD269 | Chinese Thought, from Confucius to Mao Tse-Tung–Herrlee G. Creel | .75 | 1.50 | 2.25 |
| M270 | Outline of Russian Literature | .50 | 1.00 | 1.50 |

| | | V/Good | Fine | N/Mint |
|---|---|---|---|---|

| No. | Title | V/Good | Fine | N/Mint | |
|---|---|---|---|---|---|
| MD271 | A Primer of Freudian Psychology–Calvin S. Hall | .50 | 1.00 | 1.50 | NF |
| MD272 | The Sea Around Us–Rachel L. Carson | .50 | 1.00 | 1.50 | NF |
| MD273 | The Way of Zen–Alan W. Watts | .75 | 1.50 | 2.25 | |
| MD274 | A History of the Western World–L.J. Cheney | .50 | 1.00 | 1.50 | |
| MD275 | The Greek Experience–C.M. Bowra; 1959 | .50 | 1.00 | 1.50 | |
| MD276 | Understanding Chemistry–Lawrence P. Lessing | .50 | 1.00 | 1.50 | NF |
| MD277 | The Song of Songs | .50 | 1.00 | 1.50 | |
| MD278 | The March Up Country: Xenophon's Anabasis | .50 | 1.00 | 1.50 | |
| MD279 | Gestalt Psychology–Wolfgang Kohler | .50 | 1.00 | 1.50 | NF |
| MD280 | War Commentaries of Caesar–ed. Rex Warner | .75 | 1.50 | 2.25 | NF |
| MD281 | The New Mathematics–Irving Adler | .50 | 1.00 | 1.50 | NF |
| MD283 | The Satyricon–Petronius | .75 | 1.50 | 2.25 | |
| MT287 | Eight Great Comedies–Sylvan Barnet & others | .50 | 1.00 | 1.50 | |

## MENTOR GUIDES

### New American Library of World Literature, Inc.

| No. | Title | V/Good | Fine | N/Mint | |
|---|---|---|---|---|---|
| G2 | How to Know and Enjoy New York–Carl Maas; 1949 | .75 | 1.50 | 2.25 | NF |

## MERCURY LIBRARY

### The American Mercury, Inc.

#### Digest Size

| No. | Title | V/Good | Fine | N/Mint | |
|---|---|---|---|---|---|
| L1 | Archie and Mehitabel–Don Marquis | 2.50 | 5.00 | 7.50 | H |

## MERCURY MYSTERY

### The American Mercury, Inc./Mercury Publications

#### Digest Size

**Note: After No. 209, the series became Mercury Mystery Book–Magazine.**

| No. | Title | V/Good | Fine | N/Mint | |
|---|---|---|---|---|---|
| 1 | The Postman Always Rings Twice–James M. Cain | .75 | 1.50 | 2.25 | M |
| 2 | Everything Is Thunder–J.L. Hardy | .75 | 1.50 | 2.25 | |
| 3 | Thirteen Steps–Whitman Chambers | .75 | 1.50 | 2.25 | M |
| 4 | Company K–William March | .75 | 1.50 | 2.25 | |
| 5 | Thieves like Us–Edward Anderson | .75 | 1.50 | 2.25 | M |
| 6 | Weeping Is for Women–Donald Barr Chidsey | 1.00 | 2.00 | 3.00 | |
| 7 | Diamond Jim Brady–Parker Morell | .75 | 1.50 | 2.25 | |
| 8 | Hot Saturday–Harvey Fergusson | .75 | 1.50 | 2.25 | |
| 9 | Criss-Cross–Don Tracy | 1.00 | 2.00 | 3.00 | M |
| 10 | The General–C.S. Forester | .75 | 1.50 | 2.25 | A |
| 11 | Mantrap–Sinclair Lewis | .75 | 1.50 | 2.25 | |
| 12 | I Cover the Waterfront–Max Miller | .75 | 1.50 | 2.25 | NF |
| 13 | To the Vanquished–I.A.R. Wylie | .75 | 1.50 | 2.25 | |
| 14 | Death in the Deep South–Ward Greene | 1.00 | 2.00 | 3.00 | M |
| 15 | Indelible–Elliot H. Paul | 1.00 | 2.00 | 3.00 | |
| 16 | Once Too Often–Whitman Chambers | .75 | 1.50 | 2.25 | M |
| 17 | The Prodigal Parents–Sinclair Lewis | .75 | 1.50 | 2.25 | |
| 18 | The Loving Spirit–Daphne du Maurier | .75 | 1.50 | 2.25 | |
| 19 | East Wind; West Wind–Pearl S. Buck | .75 | 1.50 | 2.25 | |
| 20 | Cup of Gold–John Steinbeck | 1.00 | 2.00 | 3.00 | A |
| 21 | The Missing Miniature–Erich Kastner | .75 | 1.50 | 2.25 | |
| 22 | County Court–Roy Flannagan | .75 | 1.50 | 2.25 | |
| 23 | The Devil in Satin–Dornford Yates | .75 | 1.50 | 2.25 | |
| 24 | Divide by Two–Mildred Gilman | .75 | 1.50 | 2.25 | |
| 25 | The Light That Failed–Rudyard Kipling | 1.00 | 2.00 | 3.00 | A |
| 26 | Never in Vain–J.L. Hardy | .75 | 1.50 | 2.25 | |
| 27 | The Dutch Shoe Mystery–Ellery Queen | .75 | 1.50 | 2.25 | M |
| 28 | Jamaica Inn–Daphne du Maurier | .75 | 1.50 | 2.25 | |
| 29 | Class Reunion–Franz Werfel | .75 | 1.50 | 2.25 | |
| 30 | Dr. Norton's Wife–Mildred Walker | .75 | 1.50 | 2.25 | |
| 31 | The Death of M. Gallet–Georges Simenon | .75 | 1.50 | 2.25 | M |
| 32 | The Door Between–Ellery Queen | .75 | 1.50 | 2.25 | M |
| 33 | Fifty Roads to Town–Frederick Nebel | 1.50 | 3.00 | 4.50 | M |
| 34 | Strawstack–Dorothy Cameron Disney | .75 | 1.50 | 2.25 | M |
| 35 | Death of Lord Haw Haw–Brett Rutledge | .75 | 1.50 | 2.25 | M |
| 36 | The Siamese Twin Mystery–Ellery Queen | .75 | 1.50 | 2.25 | M |
| 37 | Meet Nero Wolfe–Rex Stout | 1.00 | 2.00 | 3.00 | M |
| 38 | Headed for a Hearse–Jonathan Latimer | .75 | 1.50 | 2.25 | M |
| 39 | Halfway House–Ellery Queen | .75 | 1.50 | 2.25 | M |
| 40 | The D.A. Calls It Murder–Erle Stanley Gardner | .75 | 1.50 | 2.25 | M |
| 41 | Poirot Loses a Client–Agatha Christie | .75 | 1.50 | 2.25 | M |
| 42 | The American Gun Mystery–Ellery Queen | .75 | 1.50 | 2.25 | M |
| 43 | Murder at the Vicarage–Agatha Christie | .75 | 1.50 | 2.25 | M |
| 44 | The Norths Meet Murder–Richard Lockridge & Frances Lockridge | .75 | 1.50 | 2.25 | M |
| 45 | The Listening House–Mabel Seeley | .75 | 1.50 | 2.25 | M |
| 46 | The Incredible Theft–Agatha Christie | .75 | 1.50 | 2.25 | M |
| 47 | The Four of Hearts–Ellery Queen | .75 | 1.50 | 2.25 | M |
| 48 | The League of Frightened Men–Rex Stout | .75 | 1.50 | 2.25 | M |
| 49 | Mystery Mile–Margery Allingham | .75 | 1.50 | 2.25 | M |
| 50 | Murder in Mesopotamia–Agatha Christie | .75 | 1.50 | 2.25 | M |
| 51 | Hasty Wedding–Mignon G. Eberhart | .75 | 1.50 | 2.25 | M |
| 52 | The Unicorn Murders–Carter Dickson | .75 | 1.50 | 2.25 | M |
| 53 | Cards on the Table–Agatha Christie | .75 | 1.50 | 2.25 | M |
| 54 | The Golden Swan Murder–Dorothy Cameron Disney | .75 | 1.50 | 2.25 | M |
| 55 | Red Gardenias–Jonathan Latimer | .75 | 1.50 | 2.25 | M |
| 56 | The D.A. Draws a Circle–Erle Stanley Gardner | .75 | 1.50 | 2.25 | M |
| 57 | The Dragon's Teeth–Ellery Queen | .75 | 1.50 | 2.25 | M |
| 58 | The Case of the Dangerous Dowager–Erle Stanley Gardner | .75 | 1.50 | 2.25 | M |
| 59 | Thirteen at Dinner–Agatha Christie | .75 | 1.50 | 2.25 | M |
| 60 | Good Night, Sheriff–Harrison R. Steeves | .75 | 1.50 | 2.25 | M |
| 61 | The Singing Clock–Virginia Perdue | .75 | 1.50 | 2.25 | M |
| 62 | The Clew of the Forgotten Murder–Erle Stanley Gardner | .75 | 1.50 | 2.25 | M |
| 63 | A Toast to Tomorrow–Manning Coles | .75 | 1.50 | 2.25 | M |
| 64 | The Black Curtain–Cornell Woolrich | 1.50 | 3.00 | 4.50 | M |
| 65 | Verdict of Twelve–Raymond Postgate | .75 | 1.50 | 2.25 | M |
| 66 | Death on the Nile–Agatha Christie | .75 | 1.50 | 2.25 | M |
| 67 | Mystery in the Woodshed–Anthony Gilbert | .75 | 1.50 | 2.25 | M |
| 68 | Challenge to the Reader–Ellery Queen | .75 | 1.50 | 2.25 | M |
| 69 | The Secret of Chimneys–Agatha Christie | .75 | 1.50 | 2.25 | M |
| 70 | A Taste for Honey–H.F. Heard | .75 | 1.50 | 2.25 | M |
| 71 | Death in the Back Seat–Dorothy Cameron Disney | .75 | 1.50 | 2.25 | M |
| 72 | Black Orchids–Rex Stout | .75 | 1.50 | 2.25 | M |
| 73 | Keep It Quiet–Selwyn Jepson | .75 | 1.50 | 2.25 | M |
| 74 | The Crying Sisters–Mabel Seeley | .75 | 1.50 | 2.25 | M |
| 75 | The Case of the Haunted Brides–William DuBois | .75 | 1.50 | 2.25 | M |
| 76 | Mystery Week-End–Percival Wilde | .75 | 1.50 | 2.25 | M |
| 77 | Murder out of Turn–Frances Lockridge & Richard Lockridge | .75 | 1.50 | 2.25 | M |
| 78 | Folio on Florence White–Will Oursler | .75 | 1.50 | 2.25 | M |
| 79 | The Nursing Home Murder–Ngaio Marsh & Dr. Henry Jellett | .75 | 1.50 | 2.25 | M |
| 80 | He Fell Down Dead–Virginia Perdue | .75 | 1.50 | 2.25 | M |
| 81 | Once Off Guard–J.H. Wallis | .75 | 1.50 | 2.25 | M |
| 82 | I Wouldn't Be in Your Shoes–William Irish | 1.50 | 3.00 | 4.50 | M |
| 83 | Tinsley's Bones–Percival Wilde | .75 | 1.50 | 2.25 | M |
| 84 | The Moving Finger–Agatha Christie | .75 | 1.50 | 2.25 | M |
| 85 | The Case of the Weird Sisters–Charlotte Armstrong | .75 | 1.50 | 2.25 | M |
| 86 | The Trial of Vincent Doon–Will Oursler | .75 | 1.50 | 2.25 | M |
| 87 | Donovan's Brain–Curt Siodmak | 2.50 | 5.00 | 7.50 | SF |
| 88 | The White Cockatoo–Mignon G. Eberhart | .75 | 1.50 | 2.25 | M |
| 89 | Maigret to the Rescue–Georges Simenon | .75 | 1.50 | 2.25 | M |

MERCURY MYSTERY, *continued*

| # | Title | V/Good | Fine | N/Mint | |
|---|---|---|---|---|---|
| 90 | The Bach Festival Murders–Blanche Bloch | .75 | 1.50 | 2.25 | M |
| 91 | The Woman in Red–Anthony Gilbert | .75 | 1.50 | 2.25 | M |
| 92 | The Case of the Foster Father–Virginia Perdue | .75 | 1.50 | 2.25 | M |
| 93 | The Bride Dined Alone–Vera Kelsey | .75 | 1.50 | 2.25 | M |
| 94 | The Black Paw–Constance Little & Gwenyth Little | .75 | 1.50 | 2.25 | M |
| 95 | Look Your Last–John Stephen Strange | .75 | 1.50 | 2.25 | M |
| 96 | The Smell of Money–Matthew Head | .75 | 1.50 | 2.25 | M |
| 97 | The Rat Began to Gnaw the Rope–C.W. Grafton | .75 | 1.50 | 2.25 | M |
| 98 | Keep It Quiet–Richard Hull | .75 | 1.50 | 2.25 | M |
| 99 | The Spectral Bride–Joseph Shearing | .75 | 1.50 | 2.25 | M |
| 100 | Murder on the Links–Agatha Christie | .75 | 1.50 | 2.25 | M |
| 101 | Mr. Bowling Buys a Newspaper–Donald Henderson | .75 | 1.50 | 2.25 | M |
| 102 | Beware the Hoot Owl–Nancy Rutledge | .75 | 1.50 | 2.25 | M |
| 103 | Murder through the Looking Glass–Michael Venning | .75 | 1.50 | 2.25 | M |
| 104 | Footsteps behind Her–Mitchell Wilson | .75 | 1.50 | 2.25 | M |
| 105 | There Was a Crooked Man–Kelley Roos | .75 | 1.50 | 2.25 | M |
| 106 | The Undertaker Dies–Garnett Weston | .75 | 1.50 | 2.25 | M |
| 107 | The Black Rustle–Constance Little & Gwenyth Little | .75 | 1.50 | 2.25 | M |
| 108 | Thirty Days to Live–Anthony Gilbert | .75 | 1.50 | 2.25 | M |
| 109 | Clues to Christabel–Mary Fitt | .75 | 1.50 | 2.25 | M |
| 110 | Dr. Fell, Detective and Other Stories–John Dickson Carr; 1st ed. 1947 | 15.00 | 30.00 | 45.00 | M |
| 111 | Payment Deferred–C.S. Forester | .75 | 1.50 | 2.25 | M |
| 112 | The Case Book of Mr. Campion–Margery Allingham; 1st ed. 1947 | 3.00 | 6.00 | 9.00 | M |
| 113 | Pattern for Murder–Ione Sandberg Shriber | .75 | 1.50 | 2.25 | M |
| 114 | Dark Road–Doris Miles Disney | .75 | 1.50 | 2.25 | M |
| 115 | Too Many Suspects–John Rhode | .75 | 1.50 | 2.25 | M |
| 116 | The Outsiders–A.E. Martin | .75 | 1.50 | 2.25 | M |
| 117 | Case of the Giant Killer–H.S. Branson | .75 | 1.50 | 2.25 | M |
| 118 | The Hangover Murders–Adam Hobhouse | .75 | 1.50 | 2.25 | M |
| 119 | When Last I Died–Gladys Mitchell | .75 | 1.50 | 2.25 | M |
| 120 | Nightmare Town–Dashiell Hammett; 1st ed. 1948 | 20.00 | 40.00 | 60.00 | M |
| 121 | The Bandaged Nude–Robert Finnegan | .75 | 1.50 | 2.25 | M |
| 122 | And Hope to Die–Richard Powell | .75 | 1.50 | 2.25 | M |
| 123 | The Whitebird Murders–Thomas B. Black | .75 | 1.50 | 2.25 | M |
| 124 | The Dying Room–Manning Lee Stokes | .75 | 1.50 | 2.25 | M |
| 125 | Come and Be Killed–Shelley Smith | .75 | 1.50 | 2.25 | M |
| 126 | Let the Tiger Die–Manning Coles | .75 | 1.50 | 2.25 | M |
| 127 | The Pigskin Bag–Bruno Fischer | .75 | 1.50 | 2.25 | M |
| 128 | Fatal Bride–Van Siller; aka The Curtain Between | .75 | 1.50 | 2.25 | M |
| 129 | Death of a Tall Man–Frances Lockridge & Richard Lockridge | .75 | 1.50 | 2.25 | M |
| 130 | I Am the Cat–Rosemary Kutak | .75 | 1.50 | 2.25 | M |
| 131 | They Can Only Hang You Once–Dashiell Hammett; aka The Adventures of Sam Spade; Queen's Quorum No. 96 | 3.50 | 7.00 | 10.50 | M |
| 132 | Legacy in Blood–Margery Allingham; aka Flowers for the Judge | .75 | 1.50 | 2.25 | M |
| 133 | Untidy Murder–Frances Lockridge & Richard Lockridge | .75 | 1.50 | 2.25 | M |
| 134 | Sweet and Deadly–David Duncan; aka The Bramble Bush | .75 | 1.50 | 2.25 | M |
| 135 | Dead Man Blues–William Irish | 1.50 | 3.00 | 4.50 | M |
| 136 | Relative to Poison–E.C.R. Lorac | .75 | 1.50 | 2.25 | M |
| 137 | I Want to Go Home–Richard Lockridge & Frances Lockridge | .75 | 1.50 | 2.25 | M |
| 138 | The King and the Corpse–Max Murray | .75 | 1.50 | 2.25 | M |
| 139 | Last Laugh, Mr. Moto–John P. Marquand | .75 | 1.50 | 2.25 | M |
| 140 | Murder Makes Me Nervous–Margaret Scherf | .75 | 1.50 | 2.25 | M |
| 141 | Call for the Saint–Leslie Charteris | 1.00 | 2.00 | 3.00 | M |
| 142 | Too Good to Be True–J.F. Hutton | .75 | 1.50 | 2.25 | M |
| 143 | Nightmare–Edward S. Aarons | .75 | 1.50 | 2.25 | M |
| 144 | Not Negotiable–Manning Coles | .75 | 1.50 | 2.25 | M |
| 145 | Murder Is Served–Frances Lockridge & Richard Lockridge | .75 | 1.50 | 2.25 | M |
| 146 | Rogue's Coat–Theodora DuBois | .75 | 1.50 | 2.25 | M |
| 147 | The Beast Must Die–Nicholas Blake | .75 | 1.50 | 2.25 | M |
| 148 | The Bulldog Has the Key–F.W. Bronson | .75 | 1.50 | 2.25 | M |
| 149 | The Girl with the Hole in Her Head–Hampton Stone | .75 | 1.50 | 2.25 | M |
| 150 | The Stalking Man–Wilson Tucker | 1.50 | 3.00 | 4.50 | M |
| 151 | And Dangerous to Know–Elizabeth Daly | .75 | 1.50 | 2.25 | M |
| 152 | Terror in the Town–Edward Ronns | .75 | 1.50 | 2.25 | M |
| 153 | The Leaden Bubble–H.C. Branson | .75 | 1.50 | 2.25 | M |
| 154 | Spin Your Web, Lady!–Richard Lockridge & Frances Lockridge | .75 | 1.50 | 2.25 | M |
| 155 | Death from a Top Hat–Clayton Rawson | 1.50 | 3.00 | 4.50 | M |
| 156 | Drop Dead–George Bagby | .75 | 1.50 | 2.25 | M |
| 157 | Dig Me Later–Miriam-Ann Hagen | .75 | 1.50 | 2.25 | M |
| 158 | House on Telegraph Hill–Dana Lyon; aka The Frightened Child | .75 | 1.50 | 2.25 | M |
| 159 | Sudden Vengeance–Edmind Crispin | .75 | 1.50 | 2.25 | M |
| 160 | The Three Fears–Jonathan Stagge | 1.50 | 3.00 | 4.50 | M |
| 161 | Dr. Bruderstein Vanishes–John Sherwood | .75 | 1.50 | 2.25 | M |
| 162 | Death of a Nymph–Evelyn Piper; aka The Motive | .75 | 1.50 | 2.25 | M |
| 163 | Give Up the Ghost–Margaret Erskine | .75 | 1.50 | 2.25 | M |
| 164 | Death at the Rodeo–Ellery Queen; aka The American Gun Mystery | .75 | 1.50 | 2.25 | M |
| 165 | Death and Letters–Elizabeth Daly | .75 | 1.50 | 2.25 | M |
| 166 | Skeleton in the Closet–A.B. Cunningham | .75 | 1.50 | 2.25 | M |
| 167 | Ill Wind–Ruth Fenisong | .75 | 1.50 | 2.25 | M |
| 168 | Murder Comes Home–Anthony Gilbert | .75 | 1.50 | 2.25 | M |
| 169 | The House in the Forest–Marten Cumberland | .75 | 1.50 | 2.25 | M |
| 170 | Murder Goes to Press–Cicely Cairns | .75 | 1.50 | 2.25 | M |
| 171 | Never Fight a Lady–Seldon Truss | .75 | 1.50 | 2.25 | M |
| 172 | The Murder in Gay Ladies–James Ronald; aka Murder in the Family | .75 | 1.50 | 2.25 | M |
| 173 | The Sound of Murder–Kenneth Fearing; aka The Loneliest Girl in the World | .75 | 1.50 | 2.25 | M |
| 174 | A Noose for Her–Edmund Crispin; aka The Long Divorce | .75 | 1.50 | 2.25 | M |
| 175 | The Party Was a Payoff–Elizabeth Sanxay Holding; aka Too Many Bottles | .75 | 1.50 | 2.25 | M |
| 176 | A Grave Case of Murder–Roger Bax | .75 | 1.50 | 2.25 | M |
| 177 | Fish and Kill–MacDonald Hastings; aka Cork on the Water | .75 | 1.50 | 2.25 | M |
| 178 | D As in Dead–Lawrence Treat | .75 | 1.50 | 2.25 | M |
| 179 | Blood on Baker Street–Anthony Boucher; aka The Case of the Baker Street Irregulars | 2.50 | 5.00 | 7.50 | M |
| 180 | The Body in the Bridal Bed–Richard Shattuck; aka The Wedding Guest Sat on a Stone | .75 | 1.50 | 2.25 | M |
| 181 | Murder Gone Mad–Philip MacDonald | .75 | 1.50 | 2.25 | M |
| 182 | The Dead Don't Care–Jonathan Latimer | .75 | 1.50 | 2.25 | M |
| 183 | Lady Marked for Murder–Peggy Bacon; aka The Inward Eye | .75 | 1.50 | 2.25 | M |
| 184 | Come Out Killing–Robert Reeves; aka No Love Lost | .75 | 1.50 | 2.25 | M |
| 185 | The Widow-Makers–Michael Blankfort | .75 | 1.50 | 2.25 | M |
| 186 | Clues to Burn–Lenore Glen Offord | .75 | 1.50 | 2.25 | M |
| 187 | The Pinball Murders–Thomas B. Black | .75 | 1.50 | 2.25 | M |
| 188 | Death Is a Lover–Nedra Tyre; aka Mouse in Eternity | .75 | 1.50 | 2.25 | M |
| 189 | The Missing Heiress–Bernice Carey | .75 | 1.50 | 2.25 | M |
| 190 | The Christmas Murder–Cyril Hare; aka An English Murder | .75 | 1.50 | 2.25 | M |
| 191 | Kiss the Boss Goodbye–Frank Gruber; aka The Last Doorbell | 1.50 | 3.00 | 4.50 | M |
| 192 | Trial by Terror–Frances Lockridge & Richard Lockridge; aka Death by Association | .75 | 1.50 | 2.25 | M |
| 193 | The Wrong Body–Anthony Gilbert | .75 | 1.50 | 2.25 | M |
| 194 | With Blood and Kisses–Richard Shattuck; aka The Snark Was a Boojum | .75 | 1.50 | 2.25 | M |
| 195 | The Screaming Bride–H.T. Teilhet; aka A Private Undertaking | .75 | 1.50 | 2.25 | M |
| 196 | Baltimore Madame–Helen Knowland; aka Madame Baltimore | .75 | 1.50 | 2.25 | M |

## MERCURY MYSTERY, *continued*

| | | V/Good | Fine | N/Mint | |
|---|---|---|---|---|---|
| 197 | Murder by the Day–Veronica Parker Johns | .75 | 1.50 | 2.25 | M |
| 198 | Murder of a Mistress–John Sherwood; aka Ambush for Anatol | .75 | 1.50 | 2.25 | M |
| 199 | Blood Runs Cold–A.B. Cunningham; aka The Hunter Is the Hunted | .75 | 1.50 | 2.25 | M |
| 200 | Killer in the Crowd–Josephine Tey; aka The Man in the Queue | .75 | 1.50 | 2.25 | M |
| 201 | The Deadly Chase–John M. Eshelman; aka The Long Chase | .75 | 1.50 | 2.25 | M |
| 202 | The Frightened Widow–Bernice Carey; aka Their Nearest and Dearest | .75 | 1.50 | 2.25 | M |
| 203 | The Bride of Death–Ngaio Marsh; aka Spinsters in Jeopardy | .75 | 1.50 | 2.25 | M |
| 204 | They Buried a Man–Mildred Davis | .75 | 1.50 | 2.25 | M |
| 205 | You Die Today–Baynard Kendrick | 1.00 | 2.00 | 3.00 | M |
| 206 | Death of a Cheat–John M. Eshelman | .75 | 1.50 | 2.25 | M |
| 207 | Savage Breast–Manning Long | .75 | 1.50 | 2.25 | M |
| 208 | Killer in the Straw–Richard Lockridge & Frances Lockridge; aka Death at the Gentle Bull | .75 | 1.50 | 2.25 | M |
| 209 | The Blonde with the Deadly Past– Mabel Seeley; aka The Whistling Shadow | .75 | 1.50 | 2.25 | M |
| 233 | A Man Named Thin–Dashiell Hammett; 1st ed. 1962 | 7.50 | 15.00 | 22.50 | M |

# MERIT BOOKS–1st SERIES
## Camerarts Publications

| | | V/Good | Fine | N/Mint | |
|---|---|---|---|---|---|
| 351 | Boudoir Treachery–Arnold Marmor; 1960 | 1.50 | 3.00 | 4.50 | X |
| 352 | Untamed Passion–George L. Bottari | 1.50 | 3.00 | 4.50 | X |
| 353 | The 13 Sinners–Arnold Marmor | 1.50 | 3.00 | 4.50 | M |
| 354 | Sin Trail–Oren Arnold | 1.50 | 3.00 | 4.50 | X |
| 501 | Kiss of Death–Malcolm Knight; 1960 | 1.50 | 3.00 | 4.50 | X |
| 503 | The Love Machine–Auren Paul | 2.00 | 4.00 | 6.00 | SF |
| 504 | High Priced Blonde–Malcolm Knight | 1.50 | 3.00 | 4.50 | X |
| 505 | Seduction without Choice–Arnold Marmor | 1.50 | 3.00 | 4.50 | X |
| 506 | Damned!–James Glenn | 1.50 | 3.00 | 4.50 | X |
| 507 | Abnormal Lover–Clark Connor | 1.50 | 3.00 | 4.50 | X |
| 508 | Seduced!–Damon Drake; 1960 | 1.50 | 3.00 | 4.50 | X |
| 510 | The Flesh Market–George Cassidy; 1961 | 1.50 | 3.00 | 4.50 | X |
| 512 | Warped Desires–Les Hinshaw | 1.50 | 3.00 | 4.50 | X |
| 513 | Gang Mistress–Bill Lauren | 4.00 | 8.00 | 12.00 | X |
| 514 | House of Lust–Walter A. Coon | 1.50 | 3.00 | 4.50 | X |
| 517 | Forced Seduction–Richard J. Zott | 1.50 | 3.00 | 4.50 | X |
| 518 | Wild Pursuit–Bill Lauren | 1.50 | 3.00 | 4.50 | X |
| 519 | The Work of the Devil–Ennis Willie | 1.50 | 3.00 | 4.50 | X |
| 520 | Perverted Urge–Jay Fulton | 1.50 | 3.00 | 4.50 | X |
| 521 | Thwarted Passions–Allan Horn | 1.50 | 3.00 | 4.50 | X |
| 523 | Valley of Lust–Adam Coulter | 1.50 | 3.00 | 4.50 | X |
| 524 | Surrender to Passion–Victor Tremont | 1.50 | 3.00 | 4.50 | X |
| 526 | Rocco's Babe–Jerry M. Goff, Jr | 1.50 | 3.00 | 4.50 | X |
| 529 | Hot-Blooded Blonde–Neal Neitzel | 1.50 | 3.00 | 4.50 | X |
| 530 | Gal Bait–Bill Lauren | 1.50 | 3.00 | 4.50 | X |
| 531 | Hell Cat–Arnold Marmor | 1.50 | 3.00 | 4.50 | X |
| 534 | Everything But Love–Jerry M. Goff, Jr | 1.50 | 3.00 | 4.50 | X |
| 535 | Bribed Seduction–George Jade | 1.50 | 3.00 | 4.50 | X |
| 540 | Vegas Wenches–James L. Rubel | 1.50 | 3.00 | 4.50 | M |
| 544 | Abnormal Passion–John Nemec | 1.50 | 3.00 | 4.50 | X |
| 546 | Carnal Lust–Adam Walker; 1962 | 1.50 | 3.00 | 4.50 | X |
| 547 | $1,000 Nymph–Thomas Vail | 1.50 | 3.00 | 4.50 | X |
| 548 | Abnormal Assault–Jerry M. Goff, Jr | 1.50 | 3.00 | 4.50 | X |
| 550 | The Flesh Peddlers–Herb Montgomery | 1.50 | 3.00 | 4.50 | X |
| 557 | Modern Harem–Thomas Vail | 1.50 | 3.00 | 4.50 | X |
| 559 | Magnificent Teaser–Tina Powers & Jerry M. Goff, Jr | 1.50 | 3.00 | 4.50 | B |
| 602 | Autobiography of the Pervert!–Myles Neville (told to Jerry M. Goff, Jr); 1961 | 1.50 | 3.00 | 4.50 | X |
| 603 | Wanton Wench!–Jerry M. Goff, Jr; 1961 | 1.50 | 3.00 | 4.50 | X |
| 606 | Exchange Lovers–Jerry M. Goff, Jr; 1962 | 1.50 | 3.00 | 4.50 | X |
| 611 | Love Me Now!–Jerry M. Goff, Jr; 1962 | 1.50 | 3.00 | 4.50 | X |
| 624 | Sadistic Wench–Kevin North; 1962 | 1.50 | 3.00 | 4.50 | X |

| | | V/Good | Fine | N/Mint | |
|---|---|---|---|---|---|
| 626 | Abnormal Wench–Doug Harvey | 1.50 | 3.00 | 4.50 | X |
| 627 | Seduction without Choice–Arnold Marmor | 1.50 | 3.00 | 4.50 | X |
| 628 | Damned!–James Glenn | 1.50 | 3.00 | 4.50 | X |
| 629 | Wild Lovers–Herb Montgomery | 1.50 | 3.00 | 4.50 | X |
| 639 | Torrid Wenches–Arnold Marmor; aka Boudoir Treachery | 1.50 | 3.00 | 4.50 | X |
| 640 | Perverted Nymph–Malcolm Knight; aka Kiss of Death | 1.50 | 3.00 | 4.50 | X |
| 647 | Carnal Charmer–Lloyd Royce; 1962 | 1.50 | 3.00 | 4.50 | X |
| 648 | The Flesh Market–George Cassidy | 1.50 | 3.00 | 4.50 | M |
| 650 | Teasing Nymph–Bob McKnight | 1.50 | 3.00 | 4.50 | X |
| 652 | Forbidden Desire–Kevin North; 1963 | 1.50 | 3.00 | 4.50 | X |
| 654 | 3 Man-Hungry Women–Gene Cross | 1.50 | 3.00 | 4.50 | X |
| 656 | Fantastic Orgy–Aren Paul; aka The Love Machine | 1.50 | 3.00 | 4.50 | SF |
| 661 | Luscious, Teasing Body!–Ennis Willie; 1963 | 1.50 | 3.00 | 4.50 | X |
| 668 | Modern Gigolo–Ennis Willie | 1.50 | 3.00 | 4.50 | X |
| 669 | Unconventional Lovers–Walter A. Coon | 1.50 | 3.00 | 4.50 | X |
| 675 | Carnal Love Nest–Ennis Willie | 1.50 | 3.00 | 4.50 | X |
| 676 | Strange Seduction–Richard J. Zott | 1.50 | 3.00 | 4.50 | X |
| 677 | Thrill Hungry–Bill Lauren | 1.50 | 3.00 | 4.50 | X |
| 678 | Modern Love–Ennis Willie | 1.50 | 3.00 | 4.50 | X |
| 679 | Insatiable–Jay Fulton | 1.50 | 3.00 | 4.50 | X |
| 680 | Wanton Desire–Allan Horn | 1.50 | 3.00 | 4.50 | X |
| 681 | Seduction Campaign–Bruce Shelly; aka My Woman | 1.50 | 3.00 | 4.50 | X |
| 682 | Carnal Madness–Ennis Willie | 1.50 | 3.00 | 4.50 | X |
| 683 | Scarlet Goddess–Ennis Willie | 1.50 | 3.00 | 4.50 | X |
| 684 | Untamed Female–Jerry M. Goff, Jr; 1963 | 1.50 | 3.00 | 4.50 | X |
| 686 | Naked Greed–Adam Coulter | 1.50 | 3.00 | 4.50 | X |
| 688 | Possessed Woman–George Jade | 1.50 | 3.00 | 4.50 | X |
| 694 | Twisted Mistress–Ennis Willie | 1.50 | 3.00 | 4.50 | X |
| 695 | Street Girl–Robert Raczyk | 1.50 | 3.00 | 4.50 | X |
| 6100 | Cindy Honey–Jerry M. Goff, Jr | 1.50 | 3.00 | 4.50 | X |
| 6101 | Aura of Sensuality–Ennis Willie | 1.50 | 3.00 | 4.50 | X |
| 6102 | Overpassionate Blonde!–Neal Neitzel | 1.50 | 3.00 | 4.50 | X |

# MERIT BOOKS–2nd SERIES
## Camerarts Publications

| | | V/Good | Fine | N/Mint | |
|---|---|---|---|---|---|
| 6M408 | Politician's Playgirl–Ennis Willie | 1.50 | 3.00 | 4.50 | X |
| 6M410 | Irresistible!–George Jade | 1.50 | 3.00 | 4.50 | X |
| 6M412 | Passionate Plaything–Mark Randolf | 1.50 | 3.00 | 4.50 | X |
| 6M415 | So Naked! So Dead!–Ennis Willie | 1.50 | 3.00 | 4.50 | X |
| 6M417 | Fantastic Seducer–Jerry M. Goff, Jr | 1.50 | 3.00 | 4.50 | X |
| 6M421 | Beware: Woman on the Loose–Jerry M. Goff, Jr; 1963 | 1.50 | 3.00 | 4.50 | X |
| 6M422 | Haven for the Damned–Ennis Willie | 1.50 | 3.00 | 4.50 | X |
| 6M424 | Demon Lover–Damon Drake | 1.50 | 3.00 | 4.50 | X |
| 6M430 | Passion Contest–Jerry M. Goff, Jr | 1.50 | 3.00 | 4.50 | X |
| 6M434 | Game of Passion–Ennis Willie | 1.50 | 3.00 | 4.50 | X |
| 6M441 | A New Kind of Love–Ennis Willie | 1.50 | 3.00 | 4.50 | X |
| 6M443 | Fun Girl– | | | | |
| 6M445 | Shocking Desire!–Jerry M. Goff, Jr | 1.50 | 3.00 | 4.50 | X |
| 6M451 | Sensual Game–Ennis Willie | 1.50 | 3.00 | 4.50 | X |
| 6M461 | And Some Were Evil–Ennis Willie; 1964 | 1.50 | 3.00 | 4.50 | X |
| 6M463 | Modern Mistress– | 1.50 | 3.00 | 4.50 | X |
| 6M464 | High Priced Nymph–Thomas Vail | 1.50 | 3.00 | 4.50 | X |
| 6M467 | Woman of the Evening–Clark Conner | 1.50 | 3.00 | 4.50 | X |
| 6M480 | Warped Ambitions–Ennis Willie | 1.50 | 3.00 | 4.50 | X |
| 6M482 | Bizarre Love Nest–Gene Cross | 1.50 | 3.00 | 4.50 | X |
| 6M484 | The Case of the Loaded Garter Holster–Ennis Willie | 1.50 | 3.00 | 4.50 | M |
| 6M485 | Every Man's Dream–Win Blue | 1.50 | 3.00 | 4.50 | X |
| 6M486 | Bizarre Invitation–Thomas Vail | 1.50 | 3.00 | 4.50 | X |
| 6M487 | Passion Has No Rule Book–Ennis Willie | 1.50 | 3.00 | 4.50 | X |
| 6M488 | Bizarre Harem–Thomas Vail | 1.50 | 3.00 | 4.50 | X |
| 6M489 | Erotic Search–Ennis Willie | 1.50 | 3.00 | 4.50 | X |
| 6M490 | Monsters, Maidens & Mayhem–A Pictorial History of Hollywood Film Monsters–Brad Steiger; 1965 | 3.00 | 6.00 | 9.00 | NF |
| 6M493 | To Live Dangerously–Ennis Willie | 1.50 | 3.00 | 4.50 | X |
| 7M807 | Down Passion's Road–Bill Lauren | 1.50 | 3.00 | 4.50 | X |
| 7M808 | A Pictorial History of Hollywood Nudity–Ray Lee; 1964 | 4.00 | 8.00 | 12.00 | NF |

## MERIT BOOKS–2nd SERIES, continued

| | | V/Good | Fine | N/Mint | |
|---|---|---|---|---|---|
| 7M809 | Mine–All Mine!–Myles Neville & Jerry M. Goff, Jr | 1.50 | 3.00 | 4.50 | B |
| 7M810 | The Sexperts: Touched by Temptation–Steve Blake; 1965; movie tie-in | 3.00 | 6.00 | 9.00 | X |
| 7M811 | Sexual Taboos and You!–Joseph Burstela, PhD | 1.50 | 3.00 | 4.50 | NF |
| 7M812 | Sensual Imposter–Jerry M. Goff, Jr | 1.50 | 3.00 | 4.50 | X |
| 7M813 | Sex and the Starlet–Steve Blake; movie tie-in | 3.00 | 6.00 | 9.00 | NF |
| 7M814 | Bizarre Beauties–Brad Steiger; 1965 | 2.50 | 5.00 | 7.50 | NF |
| 7M816 | Ghosts, Ghouls and other Peculiar People–Brad Steiger | 2.50 | 5.00 | 7.50 | NF |
| 7M817 | Master Movie Monsters–Brad Steiger; 1965 | 3.00 | 6.00 | 9.00 | NF |
| 7M820 | Sensual Secret Agents–Brad Steiger; 1965 | 2.50 | 5.00 | 7.50 | NF |

# MERIT BOOKS
## Century Publications
### Digest Size

| | | V/Good | Fine | N/Mint | |
|---|---|---|---|---|---|
| B9 | Passion's Folly–Ralph Carter | 4.00 | 8.00 | 12.00 | E |
| B10 | Operation Interstellar–George O. Smith; 1950 | 4.50 | 9.00 | 13.50 | SF |
| B11 | Sin for Two–Perry Lindsay | 4.00 | 8.00 | 12.00 | E |
| B13 | World of IF–Rog Phillips; 1951 | 5.00 | 10.00 | 15.00 | SF |
| B14 | Model for Love–Gerald Seton | 4.00 | 8.00 | 12.00 | E |
| B16 | The Tin Ear–A.J. Collins | 4.00 | 8.00 | 12.00 | |

# (METRO)
## Metro Publications
### Digest Size

| | | V/Good | Fine | N/Mint | |
|---|---|---|---|---|---|
| nn | The Spy in the Room–Denison Clift | 2.50 | 5.00 | 7.50 | M |
| nn | Sabotage: The Secret War against America–Sayers & Kahn | 3.00 | 6.00 | 9.00 | NF |
| 7 | Homicide Johnny–Stephen Gould | 2.50 | 5.00 | 7.50 | M |

# MIDWOOD
## Midwood Enterprises, Inc.

| | | V/Good | Fine | N/Mint | |
|---|---|---|---|---|---|
| nn | There Oughta Be a Law–Al Fagaly & Harry Shorten; 1957 | 5.00 | 10.00 | 15.00 | H |
| 4 | There Oughta Be a Law–Al Fagaly & Harry Shorten; 1958 | 4.00 | 8.00 | 12.00 | H |
| nn(5) | I Take What I Want–Hal Ellson | 5.00 | 10.00 | 15.00 | JD |
| nn(6) | Call Me Mistress–Tomlin Rede | 3.50 | 7.00 | 10.50 | E |
| 7 | Love Nest–Loren Beauchamp (Robert Silverberg) | 3.50 | 7.00 | 10.50 | E |
| 8 | Carla–Sheldon Lord | 3.50 | 7.00 | 10.50 | E |
| 9 | A Strange Kind of Love–Sheldon Lord | 3.50 | 7.00 | 10.50 | E |
| 10 | Affair with Lucy–Orrie Hitt | 3.50 | 7.00 | 10.50 | E |
| 11 | Immoral Wife–Gordon Mitchell | 3.50 | 7.00 | 10.50 | E |
| 12 | Girl of the Streets–Orrie Hitt | 3.50 | 7.00 | 10.50 | E |
| 13 | Hired Lover–Fred Martin; orig. 1959 | 3.50 | 7.00 | 10.50 | E |
| 14 | Born to Be Bad–Sheldon Lord; orig. 1959 | 3.50 | 7.00 | 10.50 | E |
| 15 | All My Lovers–Alan Marshall | 3.50 | 7.00 | 10.50 | E |
| 16 | Summer Romance–Orrie Hitt; orig. 1959 | 3.50 | 7.00 | 10.50 | E |
| 17 | Backstage Love–Alan Marshall | 3.50 | 7.00 | 10.50 | E |
| 18 | Connie–Loren Beauchamp (Robert Silverberg); orig. 1959 | 3.50 | 7.00 | 10.50 | E |
| 20 | Man Hungry–Alan Marshall | 3.50 | 7.00 | 10.50 | E |
| 21 | Unwilling Sinner–Loren Beauchamp (Robert Silverberg) | 3.50 | 7.00 | 10.50 | E |
| 22 | Sally–Alan Marshall | 3.50 | 7.00 | 10.50 | E |
| 23 | As Bad As They Come–Orrie Hitt; orig. 1959 | 3.50 | 7.00 | 10.50 | E |
| 24 | 69 Barrow Street–Sheldon Lord; orig. 1959 | 3.50 | 7.00 | 10.50 | E |
| 25 | Sin School–Don Holliday; orig. 1959 | 3.50 | 7.00 | 10.50 | E |
| 26 | Just Ask for Margaret–W.B. Tasker; orig. 1959 | 3.50 | 7.00 | 10.50 | E |

| | | V/Good | Fine | N/Mint | |
|---|---|---|---|---|---|
| 28 | All the Girls Were Willing–Alan Marshall; orig. 1960 | 3.50 | 7.00 | 10.50 | E |
| 29 | Another Night, Another Love–Loren Beauchamp (Robert Silverberg); orig. 1959 | 3.50 | 7.00 | 10.50 | E |
| 29 | Of Shame and Joy–Sheldon Lord (Lawrence Block); orig. 1960. Note: Two No. 29s seen, one of which is missing No. 27, misnumbered. | 4.00 | 8.00 | 12.00 | |
| 30 | Meg–Loren Beauchamp (Robert Silverberg) | 3.50 | 7.00 | 10.50 | E |
| 31 | The Wife Next Door–Alan Marshall | 3.50 | 7.00 | 10.50 | E |
| 32 | Woman Hater–Dave Carson | 3.50 | 7.00 | 10.50 | E |
| 33 | A Woman Must Love–Sheldon Lord | 3.50 | 7.00 | 10.50 | E |
| 34 | The Cheaters–Orrie Hitt; orig. 1960 | 3.50 | 7.00 | 10.50 | E |
| 35 | Kept–Sheldon Lord | 3.50 | 7.00 | 10.50 | E |
| 36 | Virgin's Summer–Alan Marshall | 3.50 | 7.00 | 10.50 | E |
| 37 | Anybody's Girl–March Hastings | 3.50 | 7.00 | 10.50 | E |
| 38 | A Doctor and His Mistress–Orrie Hitt | 3.50 | 7.00 | 10.50 | E |
| 39 | Sins of Martha Leslie–Don Holliday | 3.50 | 7.00 | 10.50 | E |
| 40 | Candy–Sheldon Lord | 3.50 | 7.00 | 10.50 | E |
| 41 | A Girl Called Honey–Sheldon Lord & Alan Marshall | 3.50 | 7.00 | 10.50 | E |
| 42 | Stag Model–James Harvey | 3.50 | 7.00 | 10.50 | E |
| 43 | Chita–Max Gareth | 3.50 | 7.00 | 10.50 | E |
| 44 | Strange Breed–Aldo Lucchesi | 3.50 | 7.00 | 10.50 | E |
| 45 | Two of a Kind–Orrie Hitt | 3.50 | 7.00 | 10.50 | E |
| 46 | Glad to Be Bad–Adam Roberts | 3.50 | 7.00 | 10.50 | E |
| 47 | Unnatural–Sloane Britton | 3.50 | 7.00 | 10.50 | E |
| 48 | So Willing–Sheldon Lord & Alan Marshall (Lawrence Block & Donald Westlake) | 4.50 | 9.00 | 13.50 | E |
| 49 | Farm Girl–George Cassidy | 3.50 | 7.00 | 10.50 | E |
| 50 | Ladies Masseur–James Harvey | 3.50 | 7.00 | 10.50 | E |
| 51 | All about Annette–Alan Marshall | 3.50 | 7.00 | 10.50 | E |
| 52 | Meet Marilyn–Sloane Britain | 3.50 | 7.00 | 10.50 | E |
| 53 | The Unashamed–March Hastings– orig. 1960 | 3.50 | 7.00 | 10.50 | E |
| 54 | Lana–Joan Ellis | 3.50 | 7.00 | 10.50 | E |
| 55 | 21 Gay Street–Sheldon Lord | 3.50 | 7.00 | 10.50 | E |
| 56 | The Blonde–Peggy Swenson | 3.50 | 7.00 | 10.50 | E |
| 57 | Insatiable–Sloane Britain | 3.50 | 7.00 | 10.50 | E |
| 58 | Sabrina and the Senator–Nick Vendor | 3.50 | 7.00 | 10.50 | E |
| 59 | A Twilight Affair–James Harvey | 3.50 | 7.00 | 10.50 | E |
| 60 | All the Way–Michael Avallone | 3.50 | 7.00 | 10.50 | E |
| 61 | Flame–Joan Ellis | 3.50 | 7.00 | 10.50 | E |
| 62 | Sally–Alan Marshall | 3.50 | 7.00 | 10.50 | E |
| 63 | The Unfortunate Flesh–Randy Salem | 3.50 | 7.00 | 10.50 | E |
| 64 | Million Dollar Mistress–Clyde Allison | 3.50 | 7.00 | 10.50 | E |
| 65 | Nurse Carolyn–Loren Beauchamp (Robert Silverberg) | 3.50 | 7.00 | 10.50 | E |
| 66 | Sin School–Don Holliday | 3.50 | 7.00 | 10.50 | E |
| 67 | A Touch of Depravity–Paul Russo | 3.50 | 7.00 | 10.50 | E |
| 68 | There Oughta Be a Law–Al Fagaly & Harry Shorten | 6.00 | 12.00 | 18.00 | H |
| 69 | Liza's Apartment–Joan Ellis | 3.50 | 7.00 | 10.50 | E |
| 70 | Sin on Wheels–Loren Beauchamp (Robert Silverberg) | 3.50 | 7.00 | 10.50 | E |
| 71 | A Woman–Bruce Elliot | 3.50 | 7.00 | 10.50 | E |
| 72 | The Path Between–Jay Warren | 3.50 | 7.00 | 10.50 | E |
| 73 | The Sex Peddlers–Clyde Allison | 3.50 | 7.00 | 10.50 | E |
| 74 | Connie–Loren Beauchamp (Robert Silverberg) | 3.00 | 6.00 | 9.00 | E |
| 75 | Common Law Wife–Kramer | 3.50 | 7.00 | 10.50 | E |
| 76 | Pleasure Girl–Joan Ellis | 3.50 | 7.00 | 10.50 | E |
| F77 | Bucks County Report–Stuart James | 3.50 | 7.00 | 10.50 | E |
| 78 | Restless Virgin–Paul V. Russo | 3.50 | 7.00 | 10.50 | E |
| 79 | Your Sins and Mine–George Parksmith | 3.50 | 7.00 | 10.50 | E |
| 80 | The Jealous and the Free–March Hastings | 3.50 | 7.00 | 10.50 | E |
| 81 | School for Sex–Arnold English | 3.50 | 7.00 | 10.50 | E |
| F82 | These Curious Pleasures–Sloane Britton | 3.50 | 7.00 | 10.50 | E |
| 83 | One Flesh–Paul V. Russo | 3.50 | 7.00 | 10.50 | E |
| 84 | Lament for a Virgin–Art Serra | 3.50 | 7.00 | 10.50 | E |
| 85 | Silky–Dallas Mayo | 3.50 | 7.00 | 10.50 | E |
| 86 | The Fires Within–Loren Beauchamp (Robert Silverberg) | 3.50 | 7.00 | 10.50 | E |
| 87 | Drive-in-Girl–R.C. Gold | 3.50 | 7.00 | 10.50 | E |
| F88 | Stag Starlet–Paul V. Russo | 3.50 | 7.00 | 10.50 | E |
| 89 | Middle of Time–James Wycoff | 3.50 | 7.00 | 10.50 | E |
| F90 | Step Down to Darkness–David Highsmith | 3.50 | 7.00 | 10.50 | E |

| | | V/Good | Fine | N/Mint | |
|---|---|---|---|---|---|

**MIDWOOD,** *continued*

| | | V/Good | Fine | N/Mint | |
|---|---|---|---|---|---|
| F91 | Sex Behavior of the American Housewife–W.D. Sprague | 3.50 | 7.00 | 10.50 | E |
| 92 | The Weekend–Thomas Cox | 3.50 | 7.00 | 10.50 | E |
| 93 | A Moment's Pleasure–Clyde Merrick | 3.50 | 7.00 | 10.50 | E |
| 94 | This Yielding Flesh–Paul V. Russo | 3.50 | 7.00 | 10.50 | E |
| F95 | Gay Interlude–Carol Clanton | 3.50 | 7.00 | 10.50 | E |
| F96 | Jews without Money–Michael Gold | 3.50 | 7.00 | 10.50 | E |
| F97 | Desire under the Sun–George McGee | 3.50 | 7.00 | 10.50 | E |
| 98 | Kitten–Dallas Mayo | 3.50 | 7.00 | 10.50 | E |
| 99 | Redhead–Joan Ellis | 3.50 | 7.00 | 10.50 | E |
| 100 | A Need for Love–Dallas Mayo | 3.50 | 7.00 | 10.50 | E |
| F102 | And When She Was Bad–Loren Beauchamp (Robert Silverberg) | 3.50 | 7.00 | 10.50 | E |
| F103 | 69 Barrow Street–Sheldon Lord (some Sheldon Lord titles are by Lawrence Block but it is unclear which ones) | 3.50 | 7.00 | 10.50 | E |
| F109 | Torment–Don Holliday; c-Maguire | 4.00 | 8.00 | 12.00 | E |
| F110 | The Unloved–Peggy Swenson (Richard E. Geis) | 3.50 | 7.00 | 10.50 | E |
| 115 | Married Mistress–Orrie Hitt | 3.00 | 6.00 | 9.00 | E |
| 120 | Women in Prison–Mike Avallone | 4.00 | 8.00 | 12.00 | E |
| F130 | Norma–George Glennon; c-Maguire | 4.00 | 8.00 | 12.00 | E |
| 131 | Carla–Sheldon Lord (some Sheldon Lord titles are by Lawrence Block but it is unclear which ones) | 3.50 | 7.00 | 10.50 | E |
| F132 | Stag Stripper–Mike Avallone | 3.50 | 7.00 | 10.50 | E |
| Y135 | The Little Black Book–Mike Avallone | 3.50 | 7.00 | 10.50 | E |
| F145 | Strange Delights–Loren Beauchamp (Robert Silverberg) | 3.50 | 7.00 | 10.50 | E |
| F146 | Sinners in White–Mike Avallone | 3.50 | 7.00 | 10.50 | E |
| 150 | Mail Order Sex–Orrie Hitt | 3.00 | 6.00 | 9.00 | E |
| Y159 | 21 Gay Street–Sheldon Lord (some Sheldon Lord titles are by Lawrence Block but it is unclear which ones) | 3.50 | 7.00 | 10.50 | E |
| 160 | The Blonde–Peggy Swenson (Richard E. Geis) | 3.50 | 7.00 | 10.50 | E |
| 165 | Puta–Sheldon Lord (some Sheldon Lord titles are by Lawrence Block but it is unclear which ones) | 3.50 | 7.00 | 10.50 | E |
| Y168 | Flight Hostess Rogers–Michael Avallone | 3.50 | 7.00 | 10.50 | E |
| 170 | The Passer–Sam Merwin Jr | 3.00 | 6.00 | 9.00 | E |
| Y184 | All the Way–Mike Avallone | 3.50 | 7.00 | 10.50 | E |
| F189 | Sex Kitten–Mike Avallone | 3.50 | 7.00 | 10.50 | E |
| F202 | The Platinum Trap–Mike Avallone | 3.50 | 7.00 | 10.50 | E |
| F205 | Never Love a Call Girl–Mike Avallone | 3.50 | 7.00 | 10.50 | E |
| F206 | Campus Sex Club–Loren Beauchamp (Robert Silverberg) | 3.50 | 7.00 | 10.50 | E |
| F225 | Unnatural Urge–Orrie Hitt | 3.00 | 6.00 | 9.00 | E |
| D231 | The Wild Week–Jason Hytes Imitation Lovers–March Hastings; 1963; eight interior illustration plates by Frank Frazetta | 30.00 | 60.00 | 90.00 | E / E |
| F247 | Sea Nymph–Peggy Swenson (Richard E. Geis) | 3.50 | 7.00 | 10.50 | E |
| F259 | The Cruel Touch–Alan Marshall (Donald Westlake) | 4.00 | 8.00 | 12.00 | E |
| F274 | Pajama Party–Peggy Swenson (Richard E. Geis) | 3.50 | 7.00 | 10.50 | E |
| F275 | Irma La Douce–Billy Wilder & I.A.L. Diamond; movie tie-in | 4.00 | 8.00 | 12.00 | E |

*Midwood F132, Midwood D231, Midwood F275.*

| | | V/Good | Fine | N/Mint | |
|---|---|---|---|---|---|
| F276 | Sin on Wheels–Loren Beauchamp (Robert Silverberg) | 3.50 | 7.00 | 10.50 | E |
| S277 | Perfumed–Jason Hytes Pampered–Kimberly Kemp; 1963; ten interior illustration plates by Frank Frazetta | 35.00 | 70.00 | 105.00 | E / E |
| F292 | Nurse Carolyn–Loren Beauchamp (Robert Silverberg) | 3.50 | 7.00 | 10.50 | E |
| F322 | No Sense of Shame–Dan Brennan | 3.00 | 6.00 | 9.00 | E |
| F346 | A World without Men–Valerie Taylor | 3.50 | 7.00 | 10.50 | |
| 34-395 | The Dangerous Age–Joan Ellis Bad by Choice–Jason Hytes; 1964; eight interior illustration plates by Frank Frazetta | 35.00 | 70.00 | 105.00 | E / E |
| 32-424 | Gang Girl–Joan Ellis | 5.00 | 10.00 | 15.00 | JD |
| 32-427 | Journey to Fulfillment–Valerie Taylor | 3.50 | 7.00 | 10.50 | |
| 32-550 | Enough of Sorrow–Jill Emerson (Lawrence Block) | 4.00 | 8.00 | 12.00 | E |
| 34-612 | Perfumed–Jason Hytes The Wild Week–Jason Hytes; 1966; eight interior illustration plates by Frank Frazetta | 30.00 | 60.00 | 90.00 | E / E |
| 33-655 | No Sense of Shame–Dan Brennan | 3.00 | 6.00 | 9.00 | E |

## MIDWOOD-TOWER
### Tower Publications, Inc.

| | | V/Good | Fine | N/Mint | |
|---|---|---|---|---|---|
| X312 | Tear Gas and Hungry Dogs–William Sloan | 1.00 | 2.00 | 3.00 | |
| F329 | Return to Lesbos–Valerie Taylor | 2.00 | 4.00 | 6.00 | |
| F330 | Two Must Die–Henry Kane | 1.00 | 2.00 | 3.00 | M |
| X347 | Friends and Lovers–Oscar Pinkus | 1.00 | 2.00 | 3.00 | |
| F348 | The Pagan Empress–Kevin Matthews (Gardner F. Fox) | 1.50 | 3.00 | 4.50 | A |
| F370 | Cry into the Wind–Eugenie Gaffney | 1.00 | 2.00 | 3.00 | |

## MODERN LIVING COUNCIL
### Modern Living Council, Inc.
**Digest size**

| | | V/Good | Fine | N/Mint | |
|---|---|---|---|---|---|
| nn | Love, Emotions and Your Health–Norman Ober; 1952 | 1.25 | 2.50 | 3.75 | |
| nn | It Happened to Me; orig. 1953 | 1.25 | 2.50 | 3.75 | |

## MODERN SHORT STORY MONTHLY– see AVON

## MONARCH AMERICANA
### Monarch Books, Inc.

| | | V/Good | Fine | N/Mint | |
|---|---|---|---|---|---|
| MA300 | King of the Harem Heaven–Anthony Sterling; 1960; c-Maguire | 3.00 | 6.00 | 9.00 | E |
| MA301 | She Wouldn't Surrender–James Kendricks (Gardner F. Fox); c-Maguire | 2.50 | 5.00 | 7.50 | NF |
| MA302 | Lucky Luciano–Ovid Demaris | 1.50 | 3.00 | 4.50 | B |
| MA303 | Outlaw Queen–Glenn Shirley | 3.00 | 6.00 | 9.00 | B |
| MA304 | The Wicked, Wicked Women–James Kendricks (Gardner F. Fox); 1961 | 4.00 | 8.00 | 12.00 | |
| MA305 | Blood-and-Guts Patton–Jack Pearl | 1.50 | 3.00 | 4.50 | B |
| MA306 | Breakthrough–Franklin M. Davis, Jr | 1.50 | 3.00 | 4.50 | NF |
| MA307 | The Lindbergh Kidnaping Case–Ovid Demaris | 1.50 | 3.00 | 4.50 | NF |
| MA308 | The Sam Houston Story–Dean Owen | 1.50 | 3.00 | 4.50 | B |
| MA309 | The Apache Wars–John Conway | 1.50 | 3.00 | 4.50 | NF |
| MA310 | Harem Island–Anthony Sterling | 2.50 | 5.00 | 7.50 | E |
| MA311 | The Dillinger Story–Ovid Demaris | 1.50 | 3.00 | 4.50 | NF |
| MA312 | The Kennedy Cabinet–Deane Heller & David Heller | 1.50 | 3.00 | 4.50 | NF |
| MA313 | "Baby Face" Nelson–Steve Thurman | 1.50 | 3.00 | 4.50 | B |
| MA314 | America's War Heroes–Jay Scott | 1.50 | 3.00 | 4.50 | NF |
| MA315 | General Douglas MacArthur–Jack Pearl | 1.50 | 3.00 | 4.50 | B |
| MA316 | America's Major Air Disasters–D.S. Halacy, Jr | 1.50 | 3.00 | 4.50 | NF |

MONARCH AMERICANA, *continued*

| | | V/Good | Fine | N/Mint | |
|---|---|---|---|---|---|
| MA317 | The Battle of Anzio–T.R. Fehrenbach; 1962 | 1.50 | 3.00 | 4.50 | NF |
| MA318 | "Legs" Diamond–Sam Curzon | 1.50 | 3.00 | 4.50 | B |
| MA319 | U.S. Marines in Action–T.R. Fehrenbach | 1.50 | 3.00 | 4.50 | NF |
| MA320 | Anne Bonny, Pirate Queen–Douglas Brown (Walter Gibson); 1st ed. 1962 | 4.00 | 8.00 | 12.00 | B |
| MA321 | Tarawa–Tom Bailey | 1.50 | 3.00 | 4.50 | NF |
| MA322 | Aerial Dogfights of World War II–Jack Pearl | 1.50 | 3.00 | 4.50 | NF |
| MA323 | The "Dutch" Schultz Story–Ted Addy | 1.50 | 3.00 | 4.50 | B |
| MA324 | The Sioux Indian Wars–John Conway | 1.50 | 3.00 | 4.50 | NF |
| MA325 | King of the Free Lovers–Anson Hunter | 3.00 | 6.00 | 9.00 | NF |
| MA326 | The Frank Costello Story–Bill Brennan | 1.50 | 3.00 | 4.50 | B |
| MA327 | Woman-Breaker–John Conway | 2.00 | 4.00 | 6.00 | B |
| MA328 | Admiral "Bull" Halsey–Jack Pearl | 1.50 | 3.00 | 4.50 | B |
| MA329 | Marine War Heroes–Jay Scott | 1.50 | 3.00 | 4.50 | NF |
| MA333 | The Texas Rangers–John Conway; 1963 | 1.50 | 3.00 | 4.50 | NF |
| MA338 | Rifle for Rent–Gene Caesar | 1.50 | 3.00 | 4.50 | B |
| MA350 | The U.S. Navy in Action–John Clagett | 1.50 | 3.00 | 4.50 | NF |
| MA357 | The Comanche Wars–Tom Bailey; 1963 | 1.50 | 3.00 | 4.50 | NF |
| MA363 | Army War Heroes–Jay Scott | 1.50 | 3.00 | 4.50 | NF |
| MA384 | The Violent Americans–Irwin Porges | 1.00 | 2.00 | 3.00 | NF |
| MA393 | Born to Kill–Glenn Shirley | 2.50 | 5.00 | 7.50 | NF |
| MA402 | The Cheyenne Wars–Joseph Millard | 1.50 | 3.00 | 4.50 | NF |

# MONARCH BOOKS

## Monarch Books, Inc.

| | | V/Good | Fine | N/Mint | |
|---|---|---|---|---|---|
| 101 | Dark Hunger–Don James; 1958 | 1.50 | 3.00 | 4.50 | |
| 102 | Winter Range–Alan LeMay | 1.50 | 3.00 | 4.50 | W |
| 103 | Love Me Now–Fan Nichols; c-DeSoto | 1.50 | 3.00 | 4.50 | |
| 104 | Rawhider from Texas–Dean Owen | 1.50 | 3.00 | 4.50 | W |
| 105 | Shadow of the Mafia–Louis Malley | 1.50 | 3.00 | 4.50 | |
| 106 | Rogue Lover–Leon Phillips; 1959 | 1.50 | 3.00 | 4.50 | |
| 107 | Wild to Possess–Gil Brewer; c-Maguire | 4.00 | 8.00 | 12.00 | |
| 108 | Brand Fires on the Ridge–Ernest Haycox | 1.50 | 3.00 | 4.50 | W |
| 109 | Marmaduke Rides Again–Brad Anderson | 1.50 | 3.00 | 4.50 | H |
| 110 | Touch Me Not–Brian Harwin; c-Maguire | 2.00 | 4.00 | 6.00 | |
| 111 | Sword of Casanova–James Kendricks (Gardner F. Fox) | 3.00 | 6.00 | 9.00 | A |
| 112 | Spring of Desire–Louis Falstein | 1.50 | 3.00 | 4.50 | |
| 113 | Thunderhead Range–Sam Bowie | 1.50 | 3.00 | 4.50 | W |
| 114 | Killer Cop–Ferguson Findley | 1.50 | 3.00 | 4.50 | |
| 115 | Madigan's Women–John Conway | 1.50 | 3.00 | 4.50 | |
| 116 | Some Like It Tough–Jack Karney | 1.50 | 3.00 | 4.50 | |
| 117 | Stronger Than Passion–George Byram | 1.50 | 3.00 | 4.50 | |
| 118 | Way of the Wicked–William Woolfolk | 2.00 | 4.00 | 6.00 | E |
| 119 | Occasion of Sin–Robert William Taylor | 1.50 | 3.00 | 4.50 | E |
| 120 | Take Me Home–Fletcher Flora | 1.50 | 3.00 | 4.50 | E |
| 121 | Kiss Me Quick–Karl Kramer; c-Maguire | 2.00 | 4.00 | 6.00 | |
| 122 | Season for Love–Whitman Chambers | 1.50 | 3.00 | 4.50 | |
| 123 | Beyond Our Pleasure–James Kendricks | 1.50 | 3.00 | 4.50 | |
| 124 | All I Can Get–William Ard; 1st ed. 1959; c-Maguire | 3.00 | 6.00 | 9.00 | |
| 125 | Nikki–Stuart Friedman; 1959; c-Maguire | 2.00 | 4.00 | 6.00 | A |
| 126 | Law of the Gun–Max Brand; aka The Seven of Diamonds | 1.50 | 3.00 | 4.50 | W |
| 127 | Lust to Live–Peter W. Denzer | 1.50 | 3.00 | 4.50 | |
| 128 | Hell Is My Destination–John Conway | 1.50 | 3.00 | 4.50 | E |
| 129 | End to Innocence–Robert Carse | 1.50 | 3.00 | 4.50 | |
| 130 | We Burn like Fire–Will Cook | 1.50 | 3.00 | 4.50 | |
| 131 | The Darkness of Love–Harry Olive | 1.50 | 3.00 | 4.50 | |
| 132 | Save Them for Violence–James M. Fox | 1.50 | 3.00 | 4.50 | |
| 133 | The Flesh Peddlers–Frank Boyd; c-Maguire | 2.50 | 5.00 | 7.50 | E |
| 134 | Fury in the Heart–W.T. Ballard | 1.50 | 3.00 | 4.50 | |
| 135 | Hangman's Mesa–Dan J. Sterens | 1.50 | 3.00 | 4.50 | W |
| 136 | Not for a Curse–Karl Kramer | 1.50 | 3.00 | 4.50 | |
| 137 | Jailbait Street–Hal Ellson | 5.00 | 10.00 | 15.00 | JD |
| 138 | Stephana–Joseph Foster; c-Maguire | 2.50 | 5.00 | 7.50 | |
| 139 | In Savage Surrender–Whitman Chambers | 1.50 | 3.00 | 4.50 | |
| 140 | The Glory Jumpers–Delano Stagg | 1.50 | 3.00 | 4.50 | |

| | | V/Good | Fine | N/Mint | |
|---|---|---|---|---|---|
| 141 | Falcons of France–James Norman Hall & Charles Nordhoff | 1.50 | 3.00 | 4.50 | C |
| 142 | Night after Night–Steve Thurman | 1.50 | 3.00 | 4.50 | |
| 143 | Jack the Ripper–Stuart James; 1960, movie tie-in | 7.50 | 15.00 | 22.50 | HO |
| 144 | The Revolt of Jill Braddock–Stuart Friedman | 1.50 | 3.00 | 4.50 | |
| 146 | Tamiko–Ronald Kirkbride; aka A Girl Named Tamiko; c-Maguire | 2.00 | 4.00 | 6.00 | E |
| 147 | Like Ice She Was–William Ard; 1st ed. 1960 | 3.00 | 6.00 | 9.00 | M |
| 148 | This Dark Desire–John Conway; c-Maguire | 2.00 | 4.00 | 6.00 | E |
| 149 | The Flesh and the Flame–Robert Carse; c-DeSoto | 1.50 | 3.00 | 4.50 | E |
| 150 | Most Likely to Love–Fletcher Flora; c-DeSoto | 1.50 | 3.00 | 4.50 | E |
| 151 | Kill Me Sweet–Jess Wilcox | 1.50 | 3.00 | 4.50 | |
| 152 | The Sins of Billy Serene–William Ard; 1st ed. 1960; c-Maguire | 3.00 | 6.00 | 9.00 | M |
| 154 | Outlaw Rider–Max Brand; aka Happy Jack | 1.50 | 3.00 | 4.50 | W |
| 155 | The Practice of Passion–Peter W. Denzer; c-Maguire | 2.00 | 4.00 | 6.00 | E |
| 156 | Manhandled–Whitman Chambers | 1.50 | 3.00 | 4.50 | E |
| 157 | Yield to the Night–Jack Karney; c-DeSoto | 2.00 | 4.00 | 6.00 | JD |
| 158 | The Adulterers–James Kendricks (Gardner F. Fox) | 2.50 | 5.00 | 7.50 | E |
| 159 | The Deadly September–Karl Kramer; c-Maguire | 2.00 | 4.00 | 6.00 | |
| 160 | The Cage of Love–Robert Carse | 1.50 | 3.00 | 4.50 | |
| 161 | Naked Before My Captors–Berger F. Newell | 1.50 | 3.00 | 4.50 | |
| 162 | She'll Get Hers–John Plunkett | 1.50 | 3.00 | 4.50 | |
| 163 | This Violent Land–William H. Jacobs | 1.50 | 3.00 | 4.50 | W |
| 164 | A Rage of Desire–Clayton Matthews | 1.50 | 3.00 | 4.50 | |
| 165 | Young and Innocent–Edwin West | 1.50 | 3.00 | 4.50 | E |
| 166 | They Flew the Atlantic–Robert de la Croix | 1.50 | 3.00 | 4.50 | NF |
| 167 | One Touch of Ecstasy–Gwynne Wimberly | 1.50 | 3.00 | 4.50 | E |
| 168 | Play It Hard–Gil Brewer; 1960; c-DeSoto | 2.00 | 4.00 | 6.00 | |
| 169 | The Family Nobody Wanted–Helen Doss; c-Maguire | 2.00 | 4.00 | 6.00 | |
| 171 | Marilyn K.–Lionel White | 2.00 | 4.00 | 6.00 | |
| 172 | Babe in the Woods–William Ard; 1st ed. 1961. Note: Lawrence Block ghost-wrote last half of this novel following Ard's death. | 3.00 | 6.00 | 9.00 | M |
| 173 | The Satyr–James McKimmey, Jr | 1.50 | 3.00 | 4.50 | |
| 174 | Love in Suburbia–John Conway | 1.50 | 3.00 | 4.50 | E |
| 177 | Susan Latimer, Clinic Nurse–Maud McCurdy Welch | 1.50 | 3.00 | 4.50 | R |
| 178 | When the Lusting Began–Tedd Thomey | 1.50 | 3.00 | 4.50 | |
| 179 | Run Naked in the Night–Harry Olive | 1.50 | 3.00 | 4.50 | |
| 181 | The Trouble with Ava–Stuart Friedman | 1.50 | 3.00 | 4.50 | E |
| 182 | This Bed We Made–Artemis Smith; c-DeSoto | 1.50 | 3.00 | 4.50 | |
| 183 | $50 a Night–Don James; c-Maguire | 2.00 | 4.00 | 6.00 | E |

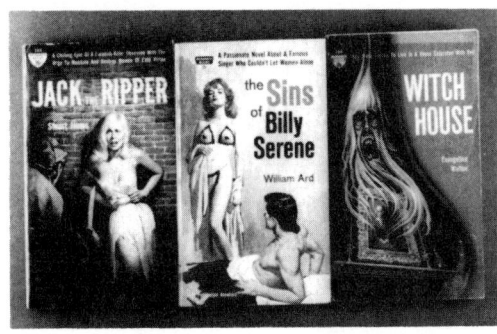

*Monarch 143, Monarch 152, Monarch 264.*

|  |  | V/Good | Fine | N/Mint |  |
|---|---|---|---|---|---|

MONARCH BOOKS, *continued*

| # | Title | V/Good | Fine | N/Mint |  |
|---|---|---|---|---|---|
| 184 | The Lovers of Pompeii—Theodore Pratt | 1.50 | 3.00 | 4.50 |  |
| 185 | Eve's Apple—Ronald Simpson | 1.50 | 3.00 | 4.50 | E |
| 186 | The Klaxon Girls—Tom Rowland; c-Maguire | 2.00 | 4.00 | 6.00 | E |
| 187 | Appointment in Hell—Gil Brewer; orig. 1961 | 2.00 | 4.00 | 6.00 |  |
| 188 | The Girl from Big Pine—Talmage Powell; c-DeSoto | 1.50 | 3.00 | 4.50 |  |
| 189 | Campus Doll—Edwin West | 1.50 | 3.00 | 4.50 |  |
| 191 | And Love So Wild—Charles Little; c-DeSoto | 1.50 | 3.00 | 4.50 |  |
| 192 | The Damned and the Innocent—Glenn Canary | 1.50 | 3.00 | 4.50 | E |
| 193 | All Her Vices—Steve Rand | 1.50 | 3.00 | 4.50 | E |
| 194 | Run Tough, Run Hard—Carson Bingham | 2.00 | 4.00 | 6.00 | JD |
| 195 | Have Love, Will Share—Brian Agar; c-DeSoto | 1.50 | 3.00 | 4.50 | E |
| 196 | Lament for Julie—Robert Colby | 1.50 | 3.00 | 4.50 |  |
| 197 | Day of Blood—William Vance | 1.50 | 3.00 | 4.50 |  |
| 198 | Cynthia Doyle, Nurse in Love—Adelaide Humphries | 1.50 | 3.00 | 4.50 | R |
| 199 | Brother and Sister—Edwin West | 1.50 | 3.00 | 4.50 | E |
| 200 | A Flame Too Hot—Karl Kramer | 1.50 | 3.00 | 4.50 |  |
| 201 | The Fly Girls—Stuart Friedman; c-Maguire | 2.00 | 4.00 | 6.00 | E |
| 202 | Debbie—Paul Daniels; c-DeSoto | 1.50 | 3.00 | 4.50 | E |
| 203 | This Is My Night—Richard Deming | 1.50 | 3.00 | 4.50 |  |
| 205 | Episode on the Riviera—Mack Reynolds | 2.00 | 4.00 | 6.00 | E |
| 206 | By Passion Obsessed—V.J. Coberly | 1.50 | 3.00 | 4.50 | E |
| 207 | The Strange Ways of Love—Clayton Matthews | 1.50 | 3.00 | 4.50 | E |
| 208 | Doctor's Choice—Susan Lennox; c-Maguire | 2.00 | 4.00 | 6.00 | R |
| 209 | The Reckless Lovers—Robert Donald Locke | 1.50 | 3.00 | 4.50 | E |
| 211 | So Sweet, So Wicked—Steve Rand | 1.50 | 3.00 | 4.50 |  |
| 212 | Beyond All Desire—Tom Phillips | 1.50 | 3.00 | 4.50 | E |
| 213 | The Green Planet—J. Hunter Holly | 1.50 | 3.00 | 4.50 | SF |
| 214 | A Kiss before Loving—Mack Reynolds | 2.00 | 4.00 | 6.00 | E |
| 215 | Make Mine Mavis—William Ard (John Jakes); 1st ed. 1961 | 2.50 | 5.00 | 7.50 | M |
| 217 | The Seducer—Fletcher Flora; c-DeSoto | 1.50 | 3.00 | 4.50 | E |
| 219 | Make Every Kiss Count—Ronald Simpson; c-Maguire | 2.00 | 4.00 | 6.00 | E |
| 220 | The Transistor Girls—Paul Daniels; c-Maguire | 2.00 | 4.00 | 6.00 | E |
| 221 | My Father's Wife—Jay Carr; c-DeSoto | 1.50 | 3.00 | 4.50 | E |
| 222 | A Sin in Time—John Conway | 1.50 | 3.00 | 4.50 | E |
| 223 | The Nurse Knows Best—Adelaide Humphries | 1.50 | 3.00 | 4.50 | R |
| 224 | Ladies of the Dark—Alexander Bolton; c-Maguire | 2.00 | 4.00 | 6.00 | E |
| 225 | Tropic Fury—Christopher Gale | 1.50 | 3.00 | 4.50 | C |
| 226 | Call Boy—Will Newbury | 1.50 | 3.00 | 4.50 | E |
| 227 | It Happened in Hawaii—Carson Bingham | 1.50 | 3.00 | 4.50 | E |
| 228 | The Bed Sheet Jungle—Tom Phillips; c-DeSoto | 1.50 | 3.00 | 4.50 | E |
| 229 | The Raper—Jack McCready; c-DeSoto | 1.50 | 3.00 | 4.50 | E |
| 230 | The Arizonans—Brian Garfield | 1.50 | 3.00 | 4.50 | W |
| 231 | And So to Bed—William Ard (John Jakes); 1st ed. 1962 | 2.50 | 5.00 | 7.50 | M |
| 232 | Strange Affair—Edwin West | 1.50 | 3.00 | 4.50 | E |
| 233 | Playboy—Paul Daniels | 1.50 | 3.00 | 4.50 | E |
| 234 | The Executive Suite Girls—Sam Webster | 1.50 | 3.00 | 4.50 | E |
| 235 | Summer Cruise—Frances Dean Hancock; c-Maguire | 2.50 | 5.00 | 7.50 | R |
| 236 | Bamboo Camp No. 10—Franklin M. Davis, Jr | 2.50 | 5.00 | 7.50 | C |
| 237 | The Key Game—Don James | 1.50 | 3.00 | 4.50 | E |
| 238 | Ask for Lois—John Barkley | 1.50 | 3.00 | 4.50 | E |
| 239 | The Faster We Live—Bill Brennan | 1.50 | 3.00 | 4.50 |  |
| 240 | Encounter—J. Hunter Holly | 1.50 | 3.00 | 4.50 | SF |
| 241 | Rasputin: The Mad Monk—Stuart Friedman; c-Maguire | 3.00 | 6.00 | 9.00 |  |
| 242 | Easy Come, Easy Love—Philip Tremont | 1.50 | 3.00 | 4.50 | E |
| 243 | Teen-age Tramp—William Johnston; c-DeSoto | 2.50 | 5.00 | 7.50 | E |
| 244 | Kim—Robert Colby | 1.50 | 3.00 | 4.50 | E |
| 245 | Cancel These Vows—Sam Webster | 1.50 | 3.00 | 4.50 | E |
| 246 | Lightning Gun—Steve Thurman | 1.50 | 3.00 | 4.50 | W |
| 248 | The Trailer Park Girls—Glenn Canary | 2.50 | 5.00 | 7.50 | E |
| 249 | The Strange Women—Miriam Gardner (Marion Zimmer Bradley) | 4.00 | 8.00 | 12.00 | E |
| 250 | The Lolita Lovers—John Clarke; c-DeSoto | 1.50 | 3.00 | 4.50 | E |
| 251 | Island Nurse—Marcia Ford | 1.50 | 3.00 | 4.50 | R |
| 252 | The Space Egg—Russ Winterbotham | 1.50 | 3.00 | 4.50 | SF |
| 253 | The Promiscuous Doll—Clayton Matthews | 1.50 | 3.00 | 4.50 | E |
| 254 | The Cover Girls—Paul Daniels | 1.50 | 3.00 | 4.50 | E |
| 255 | Frenzied—Vin Taylor | 1.50 | 3.00 | 4.50 | E |
| 256 | Renegade Range—Philip Ketchum | 1.50 | 3.00 | 4.50 | W |
| 257 | Ravaged—Stuart Friedman | 1.50 | 3.00 | 4.50 | E |
| 258 | Hollywood Starlet—Don James; c-DeSoto | 1.50 | 3.00 | 4.50 | E |
| 259 | This Time We Love—Mack Reynolds | 1.50 | 3.00 | 4.50 | E |
| 260 | The Flying Eyes—J. Hunter Holly | 1.50 | 3.00 | 4.50 | SF |
| 261 | That Girl Marian—H. Vernor Dixon | 1.50 | 3.00 | 4.50 | E |
| 262 | Tropic of Cleo—Rick Holmes | 1.50 | 3.00 | 4.50 | E |
| 263 | Tormented Lovers—Daoma Winston | 1.50 | 3.00 | 4.50 | E |
| 264 | Witch House—Evangeline Walton | 2.50 | 5.00 | 7.50 | HO |
| 265 | A Halo for Dr. Michael—Dorothy Worley | 1.50 | 3.00 | 4.50 | R |
| 267 | More about Marmaduke—Anderson & Leeming | 1.50 | 3.00 | 4.50 | H |
| 268 | The Wives of Friends—Sam Webster | 1.50 | 3.00 | 4.50 | E |
| 269 | Give Me This Woman—William Ard (John Jakes) | 2.50 | 5.00 | 7.50 | M |
| 270 | The Red Planet—Russ Winterbotham | 1.50 | 3.00 | 4.50 | SF |
| 271 | Maverick Brand—D.B. Newton | 1.50 | 3.00 | 4.50 | W |
| 272 | The Surgeons—Stuart Friedman | 1.50 | 3.00 | 4.50 |  |
| 273 | The Sorority Girls—Tom Phillips; c-DeSoto | 1.50 | 3.00 | 4.50 | E |
| 274 | Adulteress—Anderson Avery | 1.50 | 3.00 | 4.50 | E |
| 275 | Save Her for Loving—William Johnston | 1.50 | 3.00 | 4.50 | E |
| 276 | An Act of Passion—Wenzell Brown | 1.50 | 3.00 | 4.50 | E |
| 277 | Dixie Doctor—Marcia Ford; c-Maguire | 2.00 | 4.00 | 6.00 | E |
| 278 | The Party Lovers—Philip Hadrian (Philip Ketchum) | 1.50 | 3.00 | 4.50 | E |
| 279 | The Loved and the Lost—Walker E. Blake | 1.50 | 3.00 | 4.50 | E |
| 281 | The Bow and the Lance—Don Catlin | 1.50 | 3.00 | 4.50 | W |
| 282 | Beautiful But Bad—Robert Colby | 1.50 | 3.00 | 4.50 | E |
| 283 | The Loves of Dr. Devere—Carson Bingham | 1.50 | 3.00 | 4.50 | E |
| 284 | Girls on the Wing—William Johnston; c-Maguire | 2.00 | 4.00 | 6.00 | E |
| 285 | The Pleasure in Women—Ted Lee | 1.50 | 3.00 | 4.50 | E |
| 287 | Prelude to Love—Marcia Ford | 1.50 | 3.00 | 4.50 | E |
| 288 | Suburban Lovers—Jay Carr | 1.50 | 3.00 | 4.50 | E |
| 289 | Faithless—Clayton Matthews | 1.50 | 3.00 | 4.50 | E |
| 290 | Juice Town—Dean Owen | 1.50 | 3.00 | 4.50 | E |
| 291 | The Show Girls—Paul Daniels | 1.50 | 3.00 | 4.50 | E |
| 292 | Seven Brave Men—Bennett Garland (Brian W. Garfield) | 1.50 | 3.00 | 4.50 | W |
| 293 | Women of Evil—Wenzell Brown | 1.50 | 3.00 | 4.50 | E |
| 294 | Irina—Stuart Friedman | 1.50 | 3.00 | 4.50 | E |
| 296 | The Gates of Brass—F.J. Kelly; c-Maguire | 2.00 | 4.00 | 6.00 |  |
| 297 | Ten from Infinity—Ivar Jorgenson | 1.50 | 3.00 | 4.50 | SF |
| 298 | The Pleasure Seekers—H. Vernor Dixon | 2.00 | 4.00 | 6.00 | E |
| 299 | Ruby—Paul Daniels | 1.50 | 3.00 | 4.50 | E |
| 330 | The Go Girls—Will Laurence; 1963 | 2.50 | 5.00 | 7.50 | JD |
| 332 | The Trouble Shooter—Dan Catlin | 1.50 | 3.00 | 4.50 | W |
| 334 | Campus Lovers—Edwin West | 1.50 | 3.00 | 4.50 | E |
| 335 | Spare Her Heaven—Morgan Ives (Marion Zimmer Bradley) | 4.00 | 8.00 | 12.00 | E |
| 336 | Emergency for Dr. Starr—William Johnston | 1.50 | 3.00 | 4.50 | R |
| 339 | G.I. Girls—John Jakes | 3.00 | 6.00 | 9.00 | E |
| 340 | And Wake Up Loving—George G. Revelle | 1.50 | 3.00 | 4.50 | E |
| 342 | The Running Man—J. Hunter Holly | 1.50 | 3.00 | 4.50 | SF |
| 344 | The Rape of Lucia—Peter Denzer | 1.50 | 3.00 | 4.50 | E |
| 345 | Like Wild—Eric Allen | 1.50 | 3.00 | 4.50 | E |
| 346 | Love under Capricorn—Rick Holmes; c-Maguire | 2.00 | 4.00 | 6.00 | E |
| 347 | The Cruise Ship Girls—Will Newbury | 2.00 | 4.00 | 6.00 | E |
| 349 | The Valiant Breed—John Conway | 1.50 | 3.00 | 4.50 | W |
| 351 | Fathers and Daughters—Stuart Friedman | 1.50 | 3.00 | 4.50 | E |
| 352 | My Sister, My Love—Miriam Gardner (Marion Zimmer Bradley) | 4.00 | 8.00 | 12.00 | E |
| 354 | The Day the Earth Froze—Gerald Hatch | 1.50 | 3.00 | 4.50 | SF |

*Monarch MA320, Monarch 330, Monarch MM602.*

| | | V/Good | Fine | N/Mint | |
|---|---|---|---|---|---|
| 418 | Twilight Lovers–Miriam Gardner (Marion Zimmer Bradley) | 2.50 | 5.00 | 7.50 | E |
| 419 | Once More with Passion–Walker E. Blake | 1.50 | 3.00 | 4.50 | E |
| 420 | Louisa–Eric Allen; c-DeSoto | 1.50 | 3.00 | 4.50 | E |
| 421 | Run like a Thief–Michael Niall | 1.50 | 3.00 | 4.50 | M |
| 422 | Jealous–Paul Daniels | 1.50 | 3.00 | 4.50 | E |
| 423 | Gun and Star–Dan Temple | 1.50 | 3.00 | 4.50 | W |
| 424 | Nurse Dawn's Discovery–Iris Barry | 1.50 | 3.00 | 4.50 | R |
| 426 | Most Likely to Love–Fletcher Flora; c-DeSoto | 1.50 | 3.00 | 4.50 | E |
| 428 | Murder Is for Keeps–Peter Chambers | 1.50 | 3.00 | 4.50 | M |
| 429 | The Revolt of Abbe Lee–James MacBrian | 1.50 | 3.00 | 4.50 | E |
| 431 | Planet Big Zero–Franklin Hadley | 1.50 | 3.00 | 4.50 | SF |
| 432 | The Lone Gunhawk–Frank Gruber | 1.50 | 3.00 | 4.50 | W |
| 433 | Kiss Me Quick–Karl Kramer; c-Maguire | 2.00 | 4.00 | 6.00 | |
| 434 | Manhandled–Peter Chambers | 1.50 | 3.00 | 4.50 | |
| 435 | For Every Young Heart–Connie Francis | 1.50 | 3.00 | 4.50 | NF |
| 436 | Adolescent Sexual Behavior–Benjamin Morse, MD | 1.50 | 3.00 | 4.50 | NF |
| 437 | The Luscious Puritan–Stuart Friedman | 1.50 | 3.00 | 4.50 | E |
| 438 | I Am an Adulteress–Monica Haviland | 1.50 | 3.00 | 4.50 | E |
| 440 | Peril of the Peloncillos–Ben Smith | 1.50 | 3.00 | 4.50 | A |
| 441 | Cast a Long Shadow–Frank Bonham | 1.50 | 3.00 | 4.50 | W |
| 442 | Dr. Starr in Crisis–William Johnston | 1.50 | 3.00 | 4.50 | R |
| 443 | The Day the Oceans Overflowed–Charles Fontenay | 1.50 | 3.00 | 4.50 | SF |
| 444 | Play It Hard–Gil Brewer; c-DeSoto | 2.00 | 4.00 | 6.00 | M |
| 445 | The Way We Love–Stuart Friedman | 1.50 | 3.00 | 4.50 | E |
| 446 | Isometric and Isotonic Exercises for Men and Women–I.G. Edmonds | 1.50 | 3.00 | 4.50 | NF |
| 447 | Indian Wars of the U.S. Army–Fairfax Downey | 1.50 | 3.00 | 4.50 | NF |
| 448 | The Anatomy of Adultery–Gary Gordon | 1.50 | 3.00 | 4.50 | E |
| 451 | All about Amy–Tom Phillips | 1.50 | 3.00 | 4.50 | E |
| 454 | New Doctor at Tower General–John J. Miller | 1.50 | 3.00 | 4.50 | R |
| 455 | Love in Suburbia–John Conway | 1.50 | 3.00 | 4.50 | E |
| 456 | $50.00 a Night–Don James; c-Maguire | 2.00 | 4.00 | 6.00 | E |
| 457 | The Inside on L.B.J.–Frank L. Kluckhohm | 1.50 | 3.00 | 4.50 | NF |
| 458 | Encyclopedia of the World's Great Events: 1941–Deane Heller & David Heller | 1.50 | 3.00 | 4.50 | NF |
| 459 | The Fantastic Lodge–ed. Helen MacGill Hughes | 1.50 | 3.00 | 4.50 | JD |
| 460 | The Golden Witch–Wenzell Brown | 1.50 | 3.00 | 4.50 | E |
| 461 | The Corrupter–Clayton Matthews | 1.50 | 3.00 | 4.50 | E |
| 463 | Coeds Three–Carlton Joyce | 1.50 | 3.00 | 4.50 | E |
| 464 | The Unending Night–George H. Smith | 1.50 | 3.00 | 4.50 | SF |
| 465 | High Country Showdown–Ray Gaulden | 1.50 | 3.00 | 4.50 | W |
| 466 | Diagnosis Love–Frank Bonham | 1.50 | 3.00 | 4.50 | R |
| 467 | This Bed We Made–Artemis Smith; c-DeSoto | 1.50 | 3.00 | 4.50 | E |
| 469 | Monarch German Phonetic Dictionary–Dr. Bernard Rechtschaffen & Dr. Conrad P. Homberger | 1.50 | 3.00 | 4.50 | NF |
| 470 | Love of 7 Dolls–Paul Gallico; 1965 | 1.50 | 3.00 | 4.50 | |
| 471 | The World Grabbers–Paul W. Fairman; TV tie-in | 1.50 | 3.00 | 4.50 | SF |
| 472 | The Law and the Marriage Bed–Gary Gordon | 1.50 | 3.00 | 4.50 | NF |
| 473 | Invasion from 2500–Norman Edwards | 1.50 | 3.00 | 4.50 | SF |
| 474 | The Men in Her Life–Nicholas Gorham (Noel B. Gerson) | 1.50 | 3.00 | 4.50 | E |
| 477 | The Money Trap–Lionel White | 1.50 | 3.00 | 4.50 | |
| 478 | The Day the Machines Stopped–Christopher Anvil | 1.50 | 3.00 | 4.50 | SF |
| 479 | Encyclopedia of the World's Great Events: 1964–D.S. Halacy, Jr | 1.50 | 3.00 | 4.50 | NF |
| 480 | The Glory Jumpers–Delano Stagg | 1.50 | 3.00 | 4.50 | |
| 483 | Girl from Big Pine–Powell; c-DeSoto | 1.50 | 3.00 | 4.50 | |
| 484 | The Ramparts We Watch–Robert S. Horowitz | 1.50 | 3.00 | 4.50 | NF |
| 486 | The Damned and the Innocent–Glenn Canary | 1.50 | 3.00 | 4.50 | E |
| 487 | Run Tough, Run Hard–Carson Bingham | 1.50 | 3.00 | 4.50 | JD |
| 492 | End to Innocence–Robert Carse | 1.50 | 3.00 | 4.50 | NF |
| 493 | Monarch Spanish Phonetic Dictionary–Ferdinando D. Maurino, PhD | 1.50 | 3.00 | 4.50 | NF |
| 494 | Undertow–Helen Parkhurst | 1.50 | 3.00 | 4.50 | NF |
| 495 | Desert Crucible–Don Catlin | 1.50 | 3.00 | 4.50 | |

| | | V/Good | Fine | N/Mint | |
|---|---|---|---|---|---|
| MONARCH BOOKS, *continued* | | | | | |
| 355 | Love Comes to Dr. Starr–William Johnston | 1.50 | 3.00 | 4.50 | R |
| 356 | West of Quarantine–Todhunter Ballard | 1.50 | 3.00 | 4.50 | W |
| 358 | The Pitchmen–Don James | 1.50 | 3.00 | 4.50 | |
| 359 | Another Night, Another Love–Eric Allen; c-DeSoto | 1.50 | 3.00 | 4.50 | E |
| 360 | The Kept Woman–Mack Reynolds; c-DeSoto | 2.00 | 4.00 | 6.00 | E |
| 361 | By Her Own Hand–Frank Bonham | 1.50 | 3.00 | 4.50 | |
| 362 | Rest in Agony–Ivar Jorgenson | 1.50 | 3.00 | 4.50 | SF |
| 364 | Wild to Possess–Gil Brewer; c-Maguire | 2.00 | 4.00 | 6.00 | E |
| 365 | She'll Hate Me Tomorrow–Richard Deming | 1.50 | 3.00 | 4.50 | E |
| 366 | Fraternity Row–Carlton Joyce | 1.50 | 3.00 | 4.50 | E |
| 367 | This Climate of Love–Lowell Roberts (Robin Moore) | 1.50 | 3.00 | 4.50 | E |
| 368 | The Colors of Space–Marion Zimmer Bradley | 2.00 | 4.00 | 6.00 | SF |
| 369 | Town Marshal–Dan Catlin | 1.50 | 3.00 | 4.50 | W |
| 370 | The Chillingworth Murder Case–Ernie Hutter | 1.50 | 3.00 | 4.50 | M |
| 372 | The Gang Girls–Carson Bingham; 1963 | 3.50 | 7.00 | 10.50 | JD |
| 373 | Lana–Monica Haviland | 1.50 | 3.00 | 4.50 | E |
| 375 | Rampage West–Leslie Ernenwein | 1.50 | 3.00 | 4.50 | W |
| 376 | Walk Out of Darkness–Arlene Karson | 1.50 | 3.00 | 4.50 | R |
| 377 | Nikki Revisited–Stuart Friedman | 1.50 | 3.00 | 4.50 | E |
| 380 | Season for Love–Whitman Chambers | 1.50 | 3.00 | 4.50 | E |
| 381 | I Prefer Girls–Jessie Dumont; c-Maguire | 2.00 | 4.00 | 6.00 | E |
| 382 | Roz–James MacBrian | 1.50 | 3.00 | 4.50 | E |
| 383 | Hangman's Mesa–Dan Stevens | 1.50 | 3.00 | 4.50 | W |
| 385 | My Neighbor's Wife–Sam Webster | 1.50 | 3.00 | 4.50 | E |
| 386 | Obsession–Lionel White | 1.50 | 3.00 | 4.50 | M |
| 388 | Doomsday Wing–George H. Smith | 1.50 | 3.00 | 4.50 | SF |
| 389 | Occasion of Sin–Robert William Taylor | 1.50 | 3.00 | 4.50 | E |
| 390 | The Hamelin Plague–A. Bertram Chandler; c-Maguire | 2.00 | 4.00 | 6.00 | SF |
| 391 | High Storm–Bennett Garland (Brian W. Garfield & T.V. Olsen) | 1.50 | 3.00 | 4.50 | W |
| 392 | Beyond Our Pleasure–James Kendricks (Gardner F. Fox) | 2.00 | 4.00 | 6.00 | E |
| 395 | The Violent Lady–Michael E. Knerr | 1.50 | 3.00 | 4.50 | A |
| 396 | The Heisters–Robert Page Jones | 1.50 | 3.00 | 4.50 | M |
| 397 | 21 Sunset Drive–Henry Ellsworth | 1.50 | 3.00 | 4.50 | E |
| 399 | Jailbait Street–Hal Ellson | 2.50 | 5.00 | 7.50 | JD |
| 400 | Surgical Nurse–Florence Palmer; c-Maguire | 2.00 | 4.00 | 6.00 | R |
| 401 | Rawhider from Texas–Dean Owen | 1.50 | 3.00 | 4.50 | W |
| 403 | Sherry–Wenzell Brown | 1.50 | 3.00 | 4.50 | E |
| 404 | Society Doctor–Sam Webster | 1.50 | 3.00 | 4.50 | R |
| 405 | The Jet Set–Mack Reynolds; 1964 | 1.50 | 3.00 | 4.50 | E |
| 408 | Mary Adams, Student Nurse–Alice Brennan; c-Maguire | 2.00 | 4.00 | 6.00 | R |
| 410 | Young and Innocent–Edwin West; c-Maguire | 2.00 | 4.00 | 6.00 | E |
| 411 | The Power of Positive Loving–William Johnston | 1.50 | 3.00 | 4.50 | H |
| 412 | November Reef–Robin Maugham | 1.50 | 3.00 | 4.50 | A |
| 414 | The Gods Hate Kansas–Joseph Millard | 1.50 | 3.00 | 4.50 | SF |
| 415 | The Last Outlaw–Bennett Garland (Brian W. Garfield) | 1.50 | 3.00 | 4.50 | W |

MONARCH BOOKS, *continued*

| | | V/Good | Fine | N/Mint | |
|---|---|---|---|---|---|
| 496 | Riot Night in Cedarville–Warren Caryl; c-DeSoto | 1.50 | 3.00 | 4.50 | |
| 499 | Bloody Beaches, Marines Die Hard–Delano Stagg | 1.50 | 3.00 | 4.50 | C |
| 500 | The Sound of Trumpets–Charles Little | 1.50 | 3.00 | 4.50 | |
| 551 | The Strange Ways of Love–Clayton Matthews | 1.50 | 3.00 | 4.50 | E |
| 552 | The Troubles of Doctor Cortland–Stuart Friedman | 1.50 | 3.00 | 4.50 | E |
| 554 | Debbie–Paul Daniels; c-DeSoto | 1.50 | 3.00 | 4.50 | E |
| 556 | Doing What Comes Naturally–Walker E. Blake; c-DeSoto | 1.50 | 3.00 | 4.50 | E |
| 557 | Waterfront Girl–Rick Holmes | 1.50 | 3.00 | 4.50 | E |
| 558 | The Despoiler–Will Laurence | 1.50 | 3.00 | 4.50 | E |
| 559 | Rat Alley–Robison | 1.50 | 3.00 | 4.50 | |
| 560 | The Man from Gunsight–William Chamberlain | 1.50 | 3.00 | 4.50 | W |
| 561 | Octoroon–John Conway | 1.50 | 3.00 | 4.50 | |
| 563 | The Child-Woman–Rick Holmes; 1965; c-DeSoto | 1.50 | 3.00 | 4.50 | E |

## MONARCH HUMAN BEHAVIOR SERIES
## Monarch Books, Inc.

| | | V/Good | Fine | N/Mint | |
|---|---|---|---|---|---|
| MB501 | Women in Trouble–James Donner; 1959; c-Maguire | 3.00 | 6.00 | 9.00 | NF |
| MB502 | The Sexual Side of Love–Don James | 1.25 | 2.50 | 3.75 | NF |
| MB503 | Tormented Women–Edward J. McGoldrick, Jr; c-Maguire | 2.00 | 4.00 | 6.00 | NF |
| MB504 | Go with God–Jim Bishop | 1.25 | 2.50 | 3.75 | NF |
| MB505 | Crime and Passion–Eugene B. Mozes, MD | 1.25 | 2.50 | 3.75 | NF |
| MB506 | The Power of Marital Love–Don James; c-Maguire | 2.00 | 4.00 | 6.00 | NF |
| MB507 | Sex and the Armed Services–L.T. Woodward, MD (Robert Silverberg); c-Maguire | 2.00 | 4.00 | 6.00 | NF |
| MB508 | I Sell Love–Liz Crowley | 1.25 | 2.50 | 3.75 | NF |
| MB509 | The Book of Miracles–Zsolt Aradi; c-Maguire | 1.25 | 2.50 | 3.75 | NF |
| MB510 | Bedeviled–Wenzell Brown; c-Maguire | 2.00 | 4.00 | 6.00 | NF |
| MB511 | Sex Fiend–L.T. Woodward, MD (Robert Silverberg) | 1.25 | 2.50 | 3.75 | NF |
| MB512 | Folk and Modern Medicine–Don James | 1.25 | 2.50 | 3.75 | NF |
| MB513 | The Lesbian–Dr. Benjamin Morse | 1.25 | 2.50 | 3.75 | NF |
| MB514 | It's Cheaper to Die–William Michelfelder | 1.25 | 2.50 | 3.75 | NF |
| MB515 | The Single Girl–Dr. Walter C. Brown | 1.25 | 2.50 | 3.75 | NF |
| MB516 | Sex and Hypnosis–L.T. Woodward, MD (Robert Silverberg) | 1.25 | 2.50 | 3.75 | NF |
| MB517 | Teen-age Brides–Henry Galus; c-Maguire | 1.25 | 2.50 | 3.75 | NF |
| MB518 | Sexual Surrender in Women–Benjamin Morse, MD; c-Maguire | 2.00 | 4.00 | 6.00 | NF |
| MB519 | The Divorcée–Ralph C. O'Hara, MD | 1.25 | 2.50 | 3.75 | NF |
| MB520 | Registered Nurse–Joan Lawson, RN | 1.25 | 2.50 | 3.75 | NF |
| MB521 | Sex in Our Schools–L.T. Woodward, MD (Robert Silverberg) | 1.25 | 2.50 | 3.75 | NF |
| MB522 | Crack-up in Suburbia–Jay Carr | 1.25 | 2.50 | 3.75 | NF |
| MB523 | I Am a Nympho–Troy Alden | 1.25 | 2.50 | 3.75 | NF |
| MB524 | Unwed Mothers–Henry S. Galus; c-Maguire | 3.50 | 7.00 | 10.50 | NF |
| MB525 | Sins of Our Cities–Gary Gordon; c-DeSoto | 1.25 | 2.50 | 3.75 | NF |
| MB526 | I Am a Teen-age Dope Addict–Valerie Jordan | 4.00 | 8.00 | 12.00 | JD |
| MB527 | The Homosexual–Benjamin Morse, MD | 1.25 | 2.50 | 3.75 | NF |
| MB528 | Medical Problems of Women–Martin James, MD | 1.25 | 2.50 | 3.75 | NF |
| MB529 | I Am a Lesbian–Lee Chapman (Marion Zimmer Bradley) | 5.00 | 10.00 | 15.00 | NF |
| MB530 | Virgin Wives–L.T. Woodward, MD (Robert Silverberg) | 1.25 | 2.50 | 3.75 | NF |
| MB531 | The Sexual Revolution–Benjamin Morse, MD | 1.25 | 2.50 | 3.75 | NF |
| MB532 | Prostitution around the World–Stan Burnett & Alan Seeger | 1.25 | 2.50 | 3.75 | NF |
| MB533 | The Impotent Male–Dr. Leland E. Glover | 1.25 | 2.50 | 3.75 | NF |

| | | V/Good | Fine | N/Mint | |
|---|---|---|---|---|---|
| MB534 | Girls and Gangs–Don James; c-DeSoto | 3.00 | 6.00 | 9.00 | JD |
| MB535 | The Sexually Promiscuous Female–Benjamin Morse, MD | 1.25 | 2.50 | 3.75 | NF |
| MB536 | Cancer and You–Martin James, MD | 1.25 | 2.50 | 3.75 | NF |
| MB537 | The Sexually Promiscuous Male–Benjamin Morse, MD | 1.25 | 2.50 | 3.75 | NF |
| MB538 | You and Your Sex Life–L.T. Woodward, MD (Robert Silverberg) | 1.25 | 2.50 | 3.75 | NF |
| MB539 | The Girl Market–Ann Marie Burgess & Michael Burgess | 1.25 | 2.50 | 3.75 | NF |
| MB540 | The College Female–William E. Miles | 1.25 | 2.50 | 3.75 | NF |
| MB541 | Sex and the Armed Services–L.T. Woodward, MD (Robert Silverberg) | 1.25 | 2.50 | 3.75 | NF |
| MB542 | Let's Tell the Truth about Sex–Howard Whitman | 1.25 | 2.50 | 3.75 | NF |
| MB543 | The Lesbian–Benjamin Morse, MD | 1.25 | 2.50 | 3.75 | NF |
| MB544 | Sex Fiend–L.T. Woodward, MD (Robert Silverberg); c-Maguire | 2.00 | 4.00 | 6.00 | NF |
| MB545 | Virginity–Martin Magee | 1.25 | 2.50 | 3.75 | NF |
| MB546 | Men, Women and Marriage–Ernest Havemann | 1.25 | 2.50 | 3.75 | NF |
| MB547 | Masochism–L.T. Woodward, MD (Robert Silverberg) | 1.25 | 2.50 | 3.75 | NF |
| MB548 | The College Male–Henry Ellsworth | 1.25 | 2.50 | 3.75 | NF |
| MB549 | The Impact of Women–Henry S. Galus | 1.25 | 2.50 | 3.75 | NF |
| MB550 | Sex in Business–Gary Gordon | 1.25 | 2.50 | 3.75 | NF |

## MONARCH K-SERIES
## Monarch Books, Inc.

| | | V/Good | Fine | N/Mint | |
|---|---|---|---|---|---|
| K50 | Congo Song–Stuart Cloete; 1958 | 1.50 | 3.00 | 4.50 | E |
| K52 | This Naked Love–Helga Moray; aka Untamed; 1959 | 1.50 | 3.00 | 4.50 | E |
| K53 | The Angry Time–Leonard Bishop; c-Maguire; 1961 | 2.50 | 5.00 | 7.50 | JD |
| K54 | Jacqueline Kennedy–Deane Heller & David Heller | 1.50 | 3.00 | 4.50 | B |
| K55 | Elizabeth Taylor–John B. Allan (Donald Westlake); 1961 | 3.50 | 7.00 | 10.50 | B |
| K56 | Sir Winston Churchill–Edgar Black | 1.50 | 3.00 | 4.50 | B |
| K57 | Richard Nixon–George Johnson | 1.50 | 3.00 | 4.50 | B |
| K58 | The Loves of Errol Flynn–Tedd Thomey | 1.50 | 3.00 | 4.50 | B |
| K59 | Pope John XXIII: Pastoral Prince–Randall Garrett | 2.00 | 4.00 | 6.00 | B |
| K60 | Princess Grace Kelly–Robert Newman | 1.50 | 3.00 | 4.50 | B |
| K61 | Eleanor Roosevelt–George Johnson | 1.50 | 3.00 | 4.50 | B |
| K62 | Shirley Temple–Lois Eby | 3.00 | 6.00 | 9.00 | B |
| K63 | Kim Novak: Goddess of Love–Charles E. Fritch | 3.00 | 6.00 | 9.00 | B |
| K64 | Eisenhower–George Johnson | 1.50 | 3.00 | 4.50 | B |
| K65 | S.O.S.: The World's Great Sea Disasters–Keith Jameson | 1.50 | 3.00 | 4.50 | NF |
| K66 | Robert F. Kennedy: Assistant President–Gary Gordon; 1962 | 1.50 | 3.00 | 4.50 | B |
| K67 | Doris Day–Tedd Thomey | 3.00 | 6.00 | 9.00 | B |
| K68 | The Fabulous Rockefellers–Robert Silverberg | 1.50 | 3.00 | 4.50 | B |
| K69 | Encyclopedia of the World's Great Events: 1936–D.S. Halacy, Jr | 1.50 | 3.00 | 4.50 | NF |
| K70 | The Anatomy of Rape–Gary Gordon; 1963 | 1.50 | 3.00 | 4.50 | NF |
| K71 | Pope Paul VI–Andre Fabert | 1.50 | 3.00 | 4.50 | B |
| K72 | Mary, Mother of Jesus–Edward Jablonski | 1.50 | 3.00 | 4.50 | B |
| K73 | Encyclopedia of the World's Great Events: 1932–D.S. Halacy, Jr | 1.00 | 2.00 | 3.00 | NF |
| K74 | The Dangerous Assassins–Jack Pearl; 1964 | 1.50 | 3.00 | 4.50 | NF |

## MONARCH LANGUAGE SERIES
## Monarch Books, Inc.

| | | V/Good | Fine | N/Mint | |
|---|---|---|---|---|---|
| ML20 | Monarch Italian Phonetic Dictionary–Joseph Castelli | .50 | 1.00 | 1.50 | NF |

## MONARCH MOVIE SERIES
### Monarch Books, Inc.

**Note: All titles are movie tie-ins.**

| | | V/Good | Fine | N/Mint | |
|---|---|---|---|---|---|
| MM600 | The Enemy General–Dan Pepper & Max Gareth; 1960 | 2.50 | 5.00 | 7.50 | C |
| MM601 | The Stranglers of Bombay–Stuart James | 3.50 | 7.00 | 10.50 | A |
| MM602 | The Brides of Dracula–Dean Owen; c-Maguire | 15.00 | 30.00 | 45.00 | HO |
| MM603 | Gorgo–Carson Bingham | 5.00 | 10.00 | 15.00 | HO |
| MM604 | Konga–Dean Owen; 1960 | 5.00 | 10.00 | 15.00 | HO |
| MM605 | Reptilicus–Dean Owen; 1961 | 5.00 | 10.00 | 15.00 | HO |
| MM606 | The Street Is My Beat–Carson Bingham; c-DeSoto | 3.50 | 7.00 | 10.50 | E |
| MM607 | "Mad Dog" Coll–Steve Thurman | 3.00 | 6.00 | 9.00 | M |

## MONARCH SELECT
### Monarch Books, Inc.

| | | V/Good | Fine | N/Mint | |
|---|---|---|---|---|---|
| SP1 | First American Into Space–Robert Silverberg | 1.50 | 3.00 | 4.50 | NF |
| MS1 | Fidel Castro Assassinated–Lee Duncan; 1961 | 2.00 | 4.00 | 6.00 | F |
| MS2 | The Berlin Crisis: Prelude to World War III?–Deane & David Heller | 1.00 | 2.00 | 3.00 | NF |
| MS3 | America: Listen!–Frank L. Kluckhohn. Note: Later reprints add an A or B suffix to the book number. | .50 | 1.00 | 1.50 | NF |
| MS4 | The Rise and Fall of the Japanese Empire–Gary Gordon; 1962 | 1.00 | 2.00 | 3.00 | NF |
| MS5 | Planned Parenthood–Henry De Forrest, MD | .50 | 1.00 | 1.50 | NF |
| MS6 | The Naked Rise of Communism–Frank L. Kluckhohn | .50 | 1.00 | 1.50 | NF |
| MS7 | Forget about Calories–Leland H. O'Brian | .50 | 1.00 | 1.50 | NF |
| MS8 | The Cold War–Deane Heller & David Heller | .50 | 1.00 | 1.50 | NF |
| MS9 | A Gallery of the Saints–Randall Garrett; 1963 | 1.50 | 3.00 | 4.50 | NF |
| MS10 | The History of Surgery–L.T. Woodward, MD (Robert Silverberg) | .50 | 1.00 | 1.50 | NF |
| MS11 | The Red Carpet–Ezra Taft Benson | .50 | 1.00 | 1.50 | NF |
| MS12 | The Kennedy Recession–Merryle Stanley Rukeyser | .50 | 1.00 | 1.50 | NF |
| MS13 | How to Stay Young and Beautiful–Jan Michael; 1963 | .50 | 1.00 | 1.50 | NF |
| MS14 | The Real Story on Cuba–James Bayard | .50 | 1.00 | 1.50 | NF |
| MS15 | Thermonuclear Warfare–Poul Anderson | 2.50 | 5.00 | 7.50 | NF |
| MS16 | The Crisis in Cuba–Thomas Freeman | .50 | 1.00 | 1.50 | NF |
| MS17 | Skin and Scuba Diving–Richard Hardwick | .50 | 1.00 | 1.50 | NF |
| MS18 | What's Wrong with U.S. Foreign Policy?–Frank L. Kluckhohn | .50 | 1.00 | 1.50 | NF |
| MS19 | They Fought under the Sea–ed. of Navy Times | 1.50 | 3.00 | 4.50 | NF |
| MS20 | The Washington Waste-Makers–George Johnson | .50 | 1.00 | 1.50 | NF |
| MS21 | The Cool Book–Art Unger | 1.00 | 2.00 | 3.00 | NF |
| MS22 | The Attack on Our Free Choice–Merryle Stanley Rukeyser | .50 | 1.00 | 1.50 | NF |
| MS23 | Jacqueline Kennedy–Deane Heller & David Heller | 1.50 | 3.00 | 4.50 | B |
| MS24 | Battleground: World War I–Jack Pearl; 1964 | 1.00 | 2.00 | 3.00 | NF |
| MS25 | The Magnificent Kennedy Women–Stanley P. Friedman | 1.50 | 3.00 | 4.50 | B |

## MURDER MYSTERY MONTHLY–see
## AVON MURDER MYSTERY MONTHLY

## MYSTERY NOVEL CLASSIC
### Novel Selections, Inc.

**Digest Size**

**(Continuation of Mystery Novel of the Month)**

| | | V/Good | Fine | N/Mint | |
|---|---|---|---|---|---|
| 42 | The Case of the Advertised Murders–Minna Bardon | 2.50 | 5.00 | 7.50 | M |
| 43 | What Price Murder–Cleve F. Adams | 2.50 | 5.00 | 7.50 | M |
| 44 | Murder Is Not Mute–Audrey Newell; 1943 | 2.50 | 5.00 | 7.50 | M |
| 45 | Mystery of the Hushing Pool–J.S. Fletcher | 2.50 | 5.00 | 7.50 | M |
| 46 | The Jordans Murder–Sydney Fowler | 2.50 | 5.00 | 7.50 | M |
| 47 | Fair Warning–Mignon G. Eberhart; 1943 | 2.50 | 5.00 | 7.50 | M |
| 48 | Date for Murder–Louis Trimble | 2.50 | 5.00 | 7.50 | M |
| 49 | Streamlined Murder–Sue McVeigh | 2.50 | 5.00 | 7.50 | M |
| 50 | The Bride Brings Death–Darby St. John; 1943 | 2.50 | 5.00 | 7.50 | M |
| 51 | Murder on Ghost Tree Island–K.S. Daiger | 2.50 | 5.00 | 7.50 | M |
| 52 | The Death of a Celebrity–Hulbert Footner | 2.50 | 5.00 | 7.50 | M |
| 53 | The Ballot Box Murders–John Stephen Strange | 2.50 | 5.00 | 7.50 | M |
| 54 | Death Wears a Bridal Veil–Kathleen Moore Knight | 2.50 | 5.00 | 7.50 | M |
| 55 | Murder without Clues–Eleanor Pierson; aka The Defense Rests | 2.50 | 5.00 | 7.50 | M |
| 56 | The Glass Slipper–Mignon G. Eberhart | 2.50 | 5.00 | 7.50 | M |
| 57 | Death Writes an Ad–Marion Holbrook; aka Suitable for Framing | 2.50 | 5.00 | 7.50 | M |
| 58 | Hostess to Murder–Elizabeth Sanxay Holding | 2.50 | 5.00 | 7.50 | M |
| 59 | Murder at World's End–John Stephen Strange | 2.50 | 5.00 | 7.50 | M |
| 60 | The Case of the Tainted Token–Kathleen Moore Knight | 2.50 | 5.00 | 7.50 | M |
| 61 | Bring Me Another Murder–Whitman Chambers | 2.50 | 5.00 | 7.50 | M |
| 62 | The Girl Died Laughing–Viola Paradise | 2.50 | 5.00 | 7.50 | M |
| 63 | Wanted: A Murderess–Marion Holbrook | 2.50 | 5.00 | 7.50 | M |
| 64 | O As in Omen–Lawrence Treat | 2.50 | 5.00 | 7.50 | M |
| 65 | Echo of a Bomb–Van Siller | 2.50 | 5.00 | 7.50 | M |
| 66 | Shadows on the Wall–Mary Reisner | 2.50 | 5.00 | 7.50 | M |
| 67 | They Came to Kill–Margaret Scherf | 2.50 | 5.00 | 7.50 | M |
| 68 | The Leather Man Murders–Lawrence Treat | 2.50 | 5.00 | 7.50 | M |
| 69 | The Case of the Dowager's Etching–Rufus King | 2.50 | 5.00 | 7.50 | M |
| 70 | Terror by Twilight–Kathleen Moore Knight | 2.50 | 5.00 | 7.50 | M |
| 71 | The Corpse Grows a Beard–Margaret Scherf | 2.50 | 5.00 | 7.50 | M |
| 72 | Escape While I Can–Melba Marlot | 2.50 | 5.00 | 7.50 | M |
| 73 | The Case of the Copy-Hook Killing–Royce Howes | 2.50 | 5.00 | 7.50 | M |
| 74 | The Case of the Absent Corpse–Katharine Hill | 2.50 | 5.00 | 7.50 | M |
| 75 | The Case of the Kippered Corpse–Margaret Scherf | 2.50 | 5.00 | 7.50 | M |
| 76 | Acts of Black Night–Kathleen Moore Knight | 2.50 | 5.00 | 7.50 | M |
| 77 | Death Checks In–Stephen Ransome | 2.50 | 5.00 | 7.50 | M |
| 78 | Let the Skeletons Rattle–Frederick C. Davis | 2.50 | 5.00 | 7.50 | M |
| 79 | Clue of the Frightening Coin–Jessica Ryan | 2.50 | 5.00 | 7.50 | M |
| 80 | Murder Goes Astray–M.V. Heberden | 2.50 | 5.00 | 7.50 | M |
| 81 | Dead Man's Float–Amber Dean | 2.50 | 5.00 | 7.50 | M |
| 82 | The Case of the Absent-minded Professor–Aaron Mark Stein | 2.50 | 5.00 | 7.50 | M |
| 83 | The Cat's Cradle Murders–Jerome Barry; aka Leopard Cat's Cradle | 2.50 | 5.00 | 7.50 | M |
| 84 | Death Rides Tandem–Walbridge McCully | 2.50 | 5.00 | 7.50 | M |
| 86 | Lady of Night–Jerome Barry | 2.50 | 5.00 | 7.50 | M |
| 87 | Cat's Claw–D.B. Olsen | 2.50 | 5.00 | 7.50 | M |

MYSTERY NOVEL CLASSIC, *continued*

| | | V/Good | Fine | N/Mint | |
|---|---|---|---|---|---|
| 88 | The Case of the Wicked Twin–Lois Eby & John C. Fleming | 2.50 | 5.00 | 7.50 | M |
| 89 | The Blonde Is Dead–Amber Dean | 2.50 | 5.00 | 7.50 | M |
| 90 | One Man Must Die–A.B. Cunningham | 2.50 | 5.00 | 7.50 | M |
| 91 | Stream Sinister–Kathleen Moore Knight | 2.50 | 5.00 | 7.50 | M |
| 92 | Bells for the Dead–Kathleen Moore Knight | 2.50 | 5.00 | 7.50 | M |
| 94 | Death Rides a Sorrel Horse–A.B. Cunningham | 2.50 | 5.00 | 7.50 | M |
| 95 | Over the Line–Alec Coppel | 2.50 | 5.00 | 7.50 | M |
| 96 | Murder Strikes an Atomic Unit–Theodora DuBois | 2.50 | 5.00 | 7.50 | M |
| 97 | The Butler Died in Brooklyn–Ruth Fenisong | 2.50 | 5.00 | 7.50 | M |
| 98 | Family Skeleton–Doris Miles Disney | 2.50 | 5.00 | 7.50 | M |

# MYSTERY NOVEL OF THE MONTH
## Novel Selections, Inc.
### Digest Size
### (Continued as Mystery Novel Classic)

| | | V/Good | Fine | N/Mint | |
|---|---|---|---|---|---|
| nn | Murder by Proxy–Colver Harris; 1938 | 2.50 | 5.00 | 7.50 | M |
| nn | 42 Days for Murder–Roger Torrey; 1939 | 2.50 | 5.00 | 7.50 | M |
| nn | The Merry-Go-Round of Murder–Joseph F. Dinneen; 1939 | 2.50 | 5.00 | 7.50 | M |
| nn | Murder on the S-23–Steve Fisher | 3.00 | 6.00 | 9.00 | M |
| nn | Murders in Silk–Mike Teagle | 2.50 | 5.00 | 7.50 | M |
| nn | Death Is a Stowaway–Wesley Price | 2.50 | 5.00 | 7.50 | M |
| nn | Liar Dice–J.S. Mosher; 1941 | 2.50 | 5.00 | 7.50 | M |
| nn | The Mussolini Murder Case–Bernard Newman; 1939 | 2.50 | 5.00 | 7.50 | M |
| nn | The Clue of the Hungry Corpse–Inigo Jones | 2.50 | 5.00 | 7.50 | M |
| nn | If I Die Before I Wake–Sherwood King | 2.50 | 5.00 | 7.50 | M |
| nn | Death Takes a Dive–Eric Heath | 2.50 | 5.00 | 7.50 | M |
| nn | Murder in the Museum–Eric Heath | 2.50 | 5.00 | 7.50 | M |
| nn | The Case of the Crumpled Knave–Anthony Boucher | 3.00 | 6.00 | 9.00 | M |
| nn | Case of the Beckoning Dead–Nigel Morland (John Donavan) | 2.50 | 5.00 | 7.50 | M |
| nn | The Night Before Murder–Steve Fisher; 1938 | 3.00 | 6.00 | 9.00 | M |
| nn | The Case of the Severed Skull–Henri Weiner; 1940 | 2.50 | 5.00 | 7.50 | M |
| nn | Poison from a Wealthy Widow–Paul Haggard; 1940 | 2.50 | 5.00 | 7.50 | M |
| 18 | A Gentleman for the Gallows–Sydney Horler | 2.50 | 5.00 | 7.50 | M |
| 19 | Cradled in Murder!–Rudd Fleming; 1941 | 2.50 | 5.00 | 7.50 | M |
| 20 | Clue in Two Flats–R.L.F. McCombs | 2.50 | 5.00 | 7.50 | M |
| 21 | Murder Stops the Clock–Craig Rice | 2.50 | 5.00 | 7.50 | M |
| 22 | The Case of the Thing in the Brook–Peter Storme | 2.50 | 5.00 | 7.50 | M |
| 23 | Murder at Coney Island–James O'Hanlon | 2.50 | 5.00 | 7.50 | M |
| 24 | Death Comes Courting–Isabel Garland | 2.50 | 5.00 | 7.50 | M |
| 25 | Murder by Invitation–Richard Hull | 2.50 | 5.00 | 7.50 | M |
| 26 | Death in the Chalk Pits–E.R. Punshon | 2.50 | 5.00 | 7.50 | M |
| 27 | Grand Central Murder–Sue MacVeigh | 2.50 | 5.00 | 7.50 | M |
| 28 | Murder on Stage–Sutherland Scott; 1941 | 2.50 | 5.00 | 7.50 | M |
| 29 | The Case of the Rented Coffin–Laurence Dwight Smith | 2.50 | 5.00 | 7.50 | M |
| 30 | Death Took a Publisher–Norman Forrest; 1942 | 2.50 | 5.00 | 7.50 | M |
| 31 | Death before Breakfast–Cleve F. Adams | 2.50 | 5.00 | 7.50 | M |
| 32 | Murder at the Schoolhouse–A.B. Cunningham | 2.50 | 5.00 | 7.50 | M |
| 33 | The Albatross Murders–Inigo Jones | 2.50 | 5.00 | 7.50 | M |
| 34 | I'll Kill You Last–H.C. Branson | 2.50 | 5.00 | 7.50 | M |
| 35 | Murder at Deer Lick–A.B. Cunningham | 2.50 | 5.00 | 7.50 | M |
| 36 | And Sudden Death–Cleve F. Adams | 2.50 | 5.00 | 7.50 | M |
| 37 | The Corpse in Company K–Robert Avery | 2.50 | 5.00 | 7.50 | M |

| | | V/Good | Fine | N/Mint | |
|---|---|---|---|---|---|
| 38 | The Vice Czar Murders–Franklin Charles | 2.50 | 5.00 | 7.50 | M |
| 39 | Murder on Every Floor–Ann Demarest | 2.50 | 5.00 | 7.50 | M |
| 40 | The Clue of the Red Carnation–Burton Stevenson | 2.50 | 5.00 | 7.50 | M |
| 41 | The Case of the Blue Lacquer Box–George F. Worts. Note: Last in series, Mystery Novel Classic is on cover (title of continuation of series), but Mystery Novel of the Month is inside and on back cover. | 2.50 | 5.00 | 7.50 | M |

# MYSTERY PUZZLE OF THE MONTH
## Pearl Publishing Company

| | | V/Good | Fine | N/Mint | |
|---|---|---|---|---|---|
| 1 | Date-Line for Doom–Mike Shayne. Note: Boxed color crime puzzle and b&w book; price is for complete boxed set. | 15.00 | 30.00 | 45.00 | M |

# (NATIONAL DAIRY)
## National Dairy Products Corp.

| | | V/Good | Fine | N/Mint | |
|---|---|---|---|---|---|
| nn | 641 Tested Recipes from the Sealtest Kitchens–; 1964 | .50 | 1.00 | 1.50 | NF |

# NEW CLASSICS HOUSE
## Novel Books/Camerarts Publications

| | | V/Good | Fine | N/Mint | |
|---|---|---|---|---|---|
| 7N730 | Taboo–anthology; 1st ed. 1964; includes Robert Bloch, Harlan Ellison, Fritz Leiber, Nelson Algren, Charles Beaumont, Ray Russell, Paul Neimark | 25.00 | 50.00 | 75.00 | |
| 7N760 | Taboo 2–anthology; 1st ed. 1965; includes James T. Farrell, Jay Nash, Paul Neimark, Con Sellers | 7.50 | 15.00 | 22.50 | |

# NEWS STAND LIBRARY–1st SERIES
## Export Publishing Enterprises Limited
### (Canadian)

| | | V/Good | Fine | N/Mint | |
|---|---|---|---|---|---|
| nn | Artists Models and Murder–Tedd Steele; c. 1946 | 2.00 | 4.00 | 6.00 | M |
| nn | The Governor's Mistress–Warren Desmond | 2.00 | 4.00 | 6.00 | A |
| 1 | Mark It with a Stone–George Victor Martin; 1948 | 2.00 | 4.00 | 6.00 | E |
| 3 | The Ravager–David Lord | 2.00 | 4.00 | 6.00 | E |
| 4 | Possess Me Not–Fan Nichols | 2.00 | 4.00 | 6.00 | E |
| 5 | Comments on the Kinsey Report | 2.00 | 4.00 | 6.00 | NF |
| 6 | Broken Melody–Ronald Kirkbride | 2.00 | 4.00 | 6.00 | E |
| 7 | Marriage a-la Mode–Gustin Smith | 2.00 | 4.00 | 6.00 | E |
| 10 | Paradise in Montparnasse–Maurice Dekobra | 2.00 | 4.00 | 6.00 | E |
| 12 | Blood of the West–Paul Evan Lehman | 2.50 | 5.00 | 7.50 | E |
| 14 | Harlot–Cicely Schiller | 2.00 | 4.00 | 6.00 | E |
| 15 | The Long November–James Benson Nablo | 2.00 | 4.00 | 6.00 | E |
| 16 | Pay for Her Passion–Gladys Stone; aka The Sinful Sisters | 2.00 | 4.00 | 6.00 | E |
| 17 | Once a Sinner–Gail Jordan (Peggy Gaddis); 1948 | 2.00 | 4.00 | 6.00 | E |
| 18 | Hope of Heaven–John O'Hara | 2.00 | 4.00 | 6.00 | |
| 20 | Negligee–Gladys Sloan | 2.00 | 4.00 | 6.00 | E |
| 21 | Red Lights in the Village–Gladys Stone | 2.00 | 4.00 | 6.00 | E |
| 22 | The Lost Virgin–Gail Jordan (Peggy Gaddis); 1949 | 2.00 | 4.00 | 6.00 | E |
| 23 | Bed and the Blonde–Ian Peel | 2.00 | 4.00 | 6.00 | E |
| 24 | Queen of Tarts–Perry Lindsay (Peggy Gaddis) | 2.00 | 4.00 | 6.00 | E |

| | | V/Good | Fine | N/Mint | |
|---|---|---|---|---|---|

NEWS STAND LIBRARY—1st SERIES, *continued*

| # | Title | V/Good | Fine | N/Mint | |
|---|---|---|---|---|---|
| 25 | Call House Madam—Serge C. Wolsey | 2.00 | 4.00 | 6.00 | E |
| 26 | Eager Is the Flesh—Richard McMullen | 2.00 | 4.00 | 6.00 | E |
| 29 | Lady of Lust—Carlotta Baker | 2.00 | 4.00 | 6.00 | E |
| 30 | Room Service—Eliot Brewster; 1949 | 2.00 | 4.00 | 6.00 | E |
| 31 | Private Performance—Glen Watkins (on cover)/Eliot Brewster (on title page) | 2.00 | 4.00 | 6.00 | E |
| 32 | Each Night a Black Desire—Bentz Plagemann; aka Into the Labyrinth | 2.00 | 4.00 | 6.00 | E |
| 33 | Scream a Wanton Song—Wright Williams; aka Excess Wife | 2.00 | 4.00 | 6.00 | E |
| 34 | Street Girl—Eliot Brewster | 2.00 | 4.00 | 6.00 | E |
| 35 | The Flesh Is Willing—James Clayford (Peggy Gaddis) | 2.00 | 4.00 | 6.00 | E |
| 36 | Limbo City—Edwin B. Self | 2.00 | 4.00 | 6.00 | E |
| 37 | The Red Rods—Dale Clark; aka The Blonde, the Gangster, and the Private Eye | 3.00 | 6.00 | 9.00 | M |
| 38 | Two Time Doll—Gordon Semple | 2.00 | 4.00 | 6.00 | E |
| 39 | Nightfall—David Goodis; 1949 | 7.50 | 15.00 | 22.50 | M |
| 40 | Sligo—Brendon Wood | 2.00 | 4.00 | 6.00 | E |
| 42 | Gloria—Glen Watkins; aka Fall Girl | 2.00 | 4.00 | 6.00 | E |
| 44 | Bodies Are Dust—P.J. Wolfson | 2.00 | 4.00 | 6.00 | E |
| 47 | What Men Don't Like about Women—Horton | 2.00 | 4.00 | 6.00 | E |
| 48 | Shack-up Girl—Perry Lindsay (Peggy Gaddis) | 2.00 | 4.00 | 6.00 | E |
| 49 | Always Lock the Door—Ruth D'Agostino | 2.00 | 4.00 | 6.00 | E |
| 50 | Fever Heat—Robert Ravel | 2.00 | 4.00 | 6.00 | E |
| 52 | Sweet Serenade—George Willis; aka The Wild Faun. Note: 5A on cover | 2.00 | 4.00 | 6.00 | E |
| 53 | Sin for Your Supper—Milton Douglas. Note: 6A on cover | 2.00 | 4.00 | 6.00 | E |
| 54 | Heed the Thunder—Jim Thompson; 1949 | 37.50 | 75.00 | 112.50 | |
| 55 | Dangerous Escapade—J.A. Park | 2.00 | 4.00 | 6.00 | E |
| 56 | Love for Hire—Ralph Carter; aka The Quiet Passion | 2.00 | 4.00 | 6.00 | E |
| 59 | Pagan—Jack Romaine | 2.00 | 4.00 | 6.00 | E |
| 60 | He Dared Not Look Behind—Cledwyn Hughes | 2.50 | 5.00 | 7.50 | M |
| 65 | Love Goes Fast—Ursula Parrot | 2.00 | 4.00 | 6.00 | E |
| 66 | This Was Joanna—Neil H. Perrin; 1949 | 2.00 | 4.00 | 6.00 | E |
| 67 | Frustration—G.H. Henderson | 2.00 | 4.00 | 6.00 | E |
| 68 | Chinatown Baby—Thomas Burke | 3.50 | 7.00 | 10.50 | E |
| 71 | Marriage a la Mode—Gustin Smith | 2.00 | 4.00 | 6.00 | E |
| 72 | Sex Is Everybody's Business—Justus D. Wilbur | 2.00 | 4.00 | 6.00 | E |
| 81 | Office Girl—H.J. Krier | 2.00 | 4.00 | 6.00 | E |
| 83 | Trial before Marriage—Clark W. Dailey | 2.00 | 4.00 | 6.00 | E |
| 84 | Sugar-Puss on Dorchester Street—Al Palmer; 1949 | 2.50 | 5.00 | 7.50 | E |
| 88 | Lover Boy—Julian Swift | 2.00 | 4.00 | 6.00 | E |
| 89 | Death Be My Destiny—Neil H. Perrin | 2.50 | 5.00 | 7.50 | M |
| 90 | Tough Guy—Philip Clare | 2.50 | 5.00 | 7.50 | M |
| 91 | Round Moon—Genevieve Weinsott | 2.00 | 4.00 | 6.00 | E |
| 93 | Daughter of Desire—Fletcher Knight | 2.00 | 4.00 | 6.00 | E |
| 95 | Let Out the Beast—Leonard Fischer; 1950 | 5.00 | 10.00 | 15.00 | SF |
| 102 | Pick-up—Leslie Scott | 2.00 | 4.00 | 6.00 | E |
| 103 | Sin and Shackles—Gail Jordan (Peggy Gaddis) | 2.00 | 4.00 | 6.00 | E |
| 104 | Never See the Sun—Moll Bennett | 2.00 | 4.00 | 6.00 | E |
| 106 | Soft Shoulders—Peter Shelley | 2.00 | 4.00 | 6.00 | E |
| 108 | Time Trap—Rog Phillips; 1950 | 6.00 | 12.00 | 18.00 | SF |
| 109 | The Devil's Daughter—Peter Marsh | 2.00 | 4.00 | 6.00 | E |
| 110 | Strange Desires—Alan Malston | 2.00 | 4.00 | 6.00 | E |
| 111 | He Learned about Women—Ted Greenshade | 2.00 | 4.00 | 6.00 | E |
| 113 | The Intimate Stranger—William Lynch | 2.00 | 4.00 | 6.00 | E |
| 114 | Blonde Tigress—John Wilstach | 2.00 | 4.00 | 6.00 | E |
| 117 | Too Many Women—Gerry Martin | 2.00 | 4.00 | 6.00 | E |
| 121 | Outlaw Justice—Leigh Carder | 2.50 | 5.00 | 7.50 | W |
| 122 | The Gorilla's Daughter—Thomas P. Kelley; 1950 | 6.00 | 12.00 | 18.00 | SF |
| 128 | A Killer Back Stage—Joshua Willard | 2.00 | 4.00 | 6.00 | M |
| 129 | Dear Dead Harry—Scott Michel | 2.50 | 5.00 | 7.50 | M |
| 131 | The Pillar of Fire—Gordon Green | 2.00 | 4.00 | 6.00 | E |
| 133 | Outlaw Deputy—Murray Leinster | 5.00 | 10.00 | 15.00 | W |
| 135 | Design for Dying—Louis Trimble | 2.00 | 4.00 | 6.00 | M |
| 137 | Espionage Agent—Denison Clift | 2.00 | 4.00 | 6.00 | |
| 139 | Reno Tramp—Florence Stonebraker | 2.00 | 4.00 | 6.00 | E |
| 141 | Destroy the U.S.A.—Will F. Jenkins (Murray Leinster); aka Murder of the U.S.A. | 5.00 | 10.00 | 15.00 | SF |
| 142 | Worlds Within—Rog Phillips | 5.00 | 10.00 | 15.00 | SF |
| 148 | A Man to Play With—Gene Harvey | 2.00 | 4.00 | 6.00 | E |
| 151 | Soul of Passion—Richard Himmel | 2.00 | 4.00 | 6.00 | E |
| 153 | Suzie Needs a Man—Martha Knowles; 1951 | 2.00 | 4.00 | 6.00 | E |
| 155 | Harlot in Her Heart—Norman Bligh | 2.00 | 4.00 | 6.00 | E |

# NEWS STAND LIBRARY—2nd SERIES
## Export Publishing Enterprises Limited
### (Canadian)

| # | Title | V/Good | Fine | N/Mint | |
|---|---|---|---|---|---|
| 1A | Negligee—Gladys Sloan; 1949 | 2.00 | 4.00 | 6.00 | E |
| 2A | The Long November—James Benson Nablo | 2.00 | 4.00 | 6.00 | E |
| 3A | Pay for Her Passion—P.J. Wolfson; aka Is My Flesh of Brass | 2.00 | 4.00 | 6.00 | E |
| 4A | Each Night a Black Desire—Bentz Plagemann | 2.00 | 4.00 | 6.00 | E |
| 5A | Offer Any Price—George Willis | 2.00 | 4.00 | 6.00 | |
| | With dust jacket | 20.00 | 40.00 | 60.00 | E |
| 6A | Sin for Your Supper—Milton Douglas | 2.00 | 4.00 | 6.00 | E |
| 7A | The Pagans—Jack Benedict | 2.00 | 4.00 | 6.00 | E |
| | With dust jacket | 20.00 | 40.00 | 60.00 | E |
| 8A | Dirty City—Michael Young | 2.00 | 4.00 | 6.00 | E |
| | With dust jacket | 20.00 | 40.00 | 60.00 | E |
| 9A | Torch of Violence—David Forrest | 2.00 | 4.00 | 6.00 | M |
| | With dust jacket | 20.00 | 40.00 | 60.00 | M |
| 10A | This Was Joanna—Grant R. Brooks | 2.00 | 4.00 | 6.00 | E |
| 11A | The House on Craig Street—Ronald J. Cooke | 2.00 | 4.00 | 6.00 | E |
| 12A | Frustration—Henry C. Clayton | 2.00 | 4.00 | 6.00 | E |
| 13A | No Place in Heaven—Laura Warren | 2.00 | 4.00 | 6.00 | E |
| 14A | Death Be My Destiny—Neil H. Perrin | 2.50 | 5.00 | 7.50 | M |
| | With dust jacket | 20.00 | 40.00 | 60.00 | M |
| 15A | Jesse James—Thomas P. Kelley | 2.50 | 5.00 | 7.50 | NF |
| | With dust jacket | 20.00 | 40.00 | 60.00 | NF |
| 16A | Daughters of Desire—Fletcher Knight | 2.00 | 4.00 | 6.00 | E |
| 17A | Penthouse Killings—Brown | 2.00 | 4.00 | 6.00 | M |
| | With dust jacket | 20.00 | 40.00 | 60.00 | M |
| 18A | Let Out the Beast—Leonard Fischer; 1950 | 5.00 | 10.00 | 15.00 | SF |
| | With dust jacket | 20.00 | 40.00 | 60.00 | SF |
| 19A | In Passion's Fiery Pit—J. Brown | 2.00 | 4.00 | 6.00 | E |
| 20A | Sugar Puss on Dorchester Street—Al Palmer | 2.00 | 4.00 | 6.00 | E |
| | With dust jacket | 20.00 | 40.00 | 60.00 | E |
| 21A | The Door Between—Neil H. Perrin | 2.00 | 4.00 | 6.00 | E |
| | With dust jacket | 20.00 | 40.00 | 60.00 | E |
| 22A | Governor's Mistress—Warren Desmond | 2.50 | 5.00 | 7.50 | A |
| 23A | Pick-up—Leslie Scott | 2.00 | 4.00 | 6.00 | E |
| 24A | Overnight Escapade—Stephen Mark | 2.00 | 4.00 | 6.00 | E |
| 25A | Strange Desires—Alan Malston | 2.00 | 4.00 | 6.00 | E |
| 26A | He Learned about Women—Ted Greenshade | 2.00 | 4.00 | 6.00 | E |

News Stand Library 153, News Stand Library 17A, News Stand Library 27A.

NEWS STAND LIBRARY–2nd SERIES, *continued*

| | | V/Good | Fine | N/Mint | |
|---|---|---|---|---|---|
| 27A | Waste No Tears–Jarvis Warwick (Hugh Garner) | 7.50 | 15.00 | 22.50 | E |
| 28A | Too Many Women–Gerry Martin | 2.00 | 4.00 | 6.00 | E |

## NEWSSTAND LIBRARY–1st SERIES
### Newsstand Library, Inc.

| | | V/Good | Fine | N/Mint | |
|---|---|---|---|---|---|
| 501 | The Lewd Angel–Carl Marcus; 1959 | 1.00 | 2.00 | 3.00 | X |
| 503 | The Gorgeous Devil–George H. Smith; 1959 | 1.25 | 2.50 | 3.75 | X |
| U504 | Curiosities of Medicine–Richard Di Giacomo Dee; 1959 | 1.00 | 2.00 | 3.00 | NF |
| U505 | Savage Breed–William K. Douglas | 1.00 | 2.00 | 3.00 | X |
| 506 | The Devil's Lash–Louis Karney | 1.00 | 2.00 | 3.00 | X |
| 507 | Satan's Mate–George H. Smith; 1960 | 1.00 | 2.00 | 3.00 | X |
| 508 | Serenade to Seduction–Thom Martin; 1960 | .75 | 1.50 | 2.25 | X |
| 509 | The Beckoning Flame–Don Michaud; 1960 | .75 | 1.50 | 2.25 | X |
| 510 | Playhouse Passion–Edward Culver | .75 | 1.50 | 2.25 | X |
| 511 | Office Playgirl–B.J. Gillan, Jr | 1.00 | 2.00 | 3.00 | X |
| 512 | Only Her Body for Sale–Vince Del Rocco | 1.00 | 2.00 | 3.00 | X |
| 513 | The Syndicate–Robert Chestnut | 1.00 | 2.00 | 3.00 | X |
| 514 | Red House on Green Street–Wanda Lane; 1960 | 1.00 | 2.00 | 3.00 | X |
| 515 | Daughter of Joy–James Harvey | 1.00 | 2.00 | 3.00 | X |
| 516 | Bobby Sox Sinners–Jack Mertes | 1.00 | 2.00 | 3.00 | X |
| 517 | Sex Kitten–Richard E. Geis; 1960 | 1.25 | 2.50 | 3.75 | X |
| 518 | Vagabond Virgin–J.A. Flannigan | 1.00 | 2.00 | 3.00 | X |
| 519 | Lust for Youth–Warner Jackson | 1.00 | 2.00 | 3.00 | X |
| 521 | Gallery of Perversion–Paul Kingston | 1.00 | 2.00 | 3.00 | X |
| 522 | Blonde Danger–Bill Lauren; 1960 | 1.00 | 2.00 | 3.00 | X |
| 523 | Have Wife Will Trade–Gene D. Robinson | 1.00 | 2.00 | 3.00 | X |
| U524 | Too Hot for Hell–Andrew Laird; 1960 | 1.00 | 2.00 | 3.00 | X |

## NEWSSTAND LIBRARY–2nd SERIES
### Newsstand Library, Inc.

| | | V/Good | Fine | N/Mint | |
|---|---|---|---|---|---|
| U101 | Streets Paved with Gold–Friday Locke; 1958 | 1.00 | 2.00 | 3.00 | X |
| U102 | The Fraudulent Broad–James L. Rubel; 1958 | 1.00 | 2.00 | 3.00 | X |
| U103 | The Big Blues–Pat Bunyan | 1.00 | 2.00 | 3.00 | X |
| U104 | All the Natives Are Lovers–William Bradbury; 1958 | 1.00 | 2.00 | 3.00 | X |
| U105 | The Bawdy Mrs. Grey–Henry Lewis Nixon; 1959 | 1.00 | 2.00 | 3.00 | X |
| U106 | The Demands of the Flesh–March Hastings; 1959 | 1.00 | 2.00 | 3.00 | X |
| U107 | The Peddlers–G.A. Graeme | 1.00 | 2.00 | 3.00 | X |
| U109 | Obsessed–March Hastings | 1.00 | 2.00 | 3.00 | X |
| U110 | Riptide–James Harsh | 1.00 | 2.00 | 3.00 | X |
| U111 | Twenty Years behind Red Curtains–Nancy Dean | 1.00 | 2.00 | 3.00 | X |
| U112 | The Soft Whip of Passion–G.H. Smith; 1959 | 1.25 | 2.50 | 3.75 | X |
| U113 | Six for Flight 13–Henry Lewis Nixon | 1.00 | 2.00 | 3.00 | X |
| U114 | The Evil Ear–G.A. Graeme | 1.00 | 2.00 | 3.00 | X |
| U115 | Dark Desire–G.H. Smith; 1959 | 1.25 | 2.50 | 3.75 | X |
| U116 | Fear of Incest–March Hastings | 1.00 | 2.00 | 3.00 | X |
| U117 | She Had to Be Loved!–Edward Culver; 1959 | 1.00 | 2.00 | 3.00 | X |
| U118 | Veil of Torment–March Hastings | 1.00 | 2.00 | 3.00 | X |
| U119 | First Person Third Sex–Sloane Britain | 1.25 | 2.50 | 3.75 | X |
| U120 | Private World–Connie Sellers; 1959 | 1.00 | 2.00 | 3.00 | X |
| U121 | The Yellow Press–H.D. Spaulding | 1.00 | 2.00 | 3.00 | X |
| U122 | The Tenement Kid–Karl Edd; 1959 | 2.00 | 4.00 | 6.00 | JD |
| U123 | The Wife Traders–G.A. Graeme | 1.00 | 2.00 | 3.00 | X |
| U124 | Bitter Love–King | 1.00 | 2.00 | 3.00 | X |
| U125 | The Censored Screen–Brian Dunn; 1960 | 1.00 | 2.00 | 3.00 | X |
| U126 | Agreement to Love–Joseph Heron | 1.00 | 2.00 | 3.00 | X |
| U127 | Carnal Greed–Pauline C. Smith; 1960 | 1.00 | 2.00 | 3.00 | M |
| U128 | The Grip of Lust–Guy Corbett | 1.00 | 2.00 | 3.00 | X |
| U129 | Black Desire–Robert Hayes; 1960 | 1.00 | 2.00 | 3.00 | X |

| | | V/Good | Fine | N/Mint | |
|---|---|---|---|---|---|
| U130 | The Youngest Harlot–Jay Carpenter | 1.00 | 2.00 | 3.00 | JD |
| U131 | Swamp Bred–George H. Smith; 1960 | 1.50 | 3.00 | 4.50 | X |
| U132 | Arrividerci, Ava–Carl Marcus | 1.00 | 2.00 | 3.00 | X |
| U133 | The Wanton One–James Rubel; 1960 | 1.00 | 2.00 | 3.00 | X |
| U134 | Her Mother's Husband–M. Anderson | 1.00 | 2.00 | 3.00 | X |
| U135 | Shanty Girl–Hal R. Moore | 1.00 | 2.00 | 3.00 | X |
| U136 | Bogus Lover–Hy Silver | 1.00 | 2.00 | 3.00 | X |
| U137 | The Woman Chaser–Charles Willeford; 1st ed. 1960 | 10.00 | 20.00 | 30.00 | X |
| U138 | Come Sin with Me–George Toward | 1.00 | 2.00 | 3.00 | X |
| U139 | Torch of Desire–Edward Booth | 1.00 | 2.00 | 3.00 | X |
| U140 | Devil's Caress–Della Wand | 1.00 | 2.00 | 3.00 | X |
| U141 | The Wicked Wife–Robert K. Shedd | 1.00 | 2.00 | 3.00 | X |
| U142 | Diploma of Passion–Clayton Hickerson; 1961 | 1.00 | 2.00 | 3.00 | X |
| U143 | Cavern of Rage–W. Warner Jackson | 1.00 | 2.00 | 3.00 | X |
| U144 | Like Crazy, Man–Richard E. Geis | 1.50 | 3.00 | 4.50 | X |
| U145 | Creature of Sin–Alfred B. Glaser | 1.00 | 2.00 | 3.00 | X |
| U146 | Deadly Desire–Edward Booth; 1961 | 1.00 | 2.00 | 3.00 | X |
| U147 | Lesbos Hill–George P. Toward | 1.00 | 2.00 | 3.00 | X |
| U148 | Good Time Girl–Jack Allan | 1.00 | 2.00 | 3.00 | X |
| U149 | On the Make–Della Wand | 1.00 | 2.00 | 3.00 | X |
| U150 | Chains of Passion–Edward Booth | 1.00 | 2.00 | 3.00 | X |
| U151 | Mr. Madam–Hote Rock | 1.00 | 2.00 | 3.00 | X |
| U152 | Crack-up–March Hastings | 1.00 | 2.00 | 3.00 | X |
| U153 | Amorous Avenger–Roy Kelsey | 1.00 | 2.00 | 3.00 | M |
| U154 | Affair on Board–Roy Kelsey | 1.00 | 2.00 | 3.00 | X |
| U155 | Love Is a Gentle Whip–Jack Allan | 1.00 | 2.00 | 3.00 | X |
| U156 | A Matter of Adultery–Don Lee; 1961 | 1.00 | 2.00 | 3.00 | X |
| U157 | The 3rd Theme–March Hastings | .75 | 1.50 | 2.25 | X |
| U158 | One Day in Hell–Hugh Zachary | 1.00 | 2.00 | 3.00 | X |
| U159 | So Strange Our Love–Joseph Heron; 1961 | 1.00 | 2.00 | 3.00 | X |
| U160 | A Family Affair–Keith Vinning | 1.00 | 2.00 | 3.00 | X |
| U161 | Chasm of Lust–B.V. McLane, Jr | 1.00 | 2.00 | 3.00 | X |
| U162 | You Can't Escape Me–John Tyler | 1.00 | 2.00 | 3.00 | X |
| U163 | Portrait of Torment–Edgar A. Martin | 1.00 | 2.00 | 3.00 | X |
| U164 | Bedroom Alibi–Paul Kruger | 1.00 | 2.00 | 3.00 | X |
| U165 | Commit the Sins–William A. Austin; 1961 | 1.00 | 2.00 | 3.00 | X |
| U166 | Chained Sex–Paul Curtis | 1.00 | 2.00 | 3.00 | X |
| U167 | Sex Is Like Money–T.A. Maschke | 1.00 | 2.00 | 3.00 | X |
| U168 | Make It on Temple Street–Oral Leigh Berryman | .75 | 1.50 | 2.25 | X |
| U169 | Anything Goes–Robert Carney | 1.00 | 2.00 | 3.00 | X |
| U170 | Understudy for Love–Charles Willeford; 1st ed. 1961 | 12.50 | 25.00 | 37.50 | X |
| U171 | Amorous Dietitian–Mary Shomette Gooch; 1961 | 1.00 | 2.00 | 3.00 | X |
| U172 | Blackmail and Old Lace–Thomas Vail | 1.00 | 2.00 | 3.00 | X |
| U173 | Sinful Cowboy–Ted E. Abrams | 1.00 | 2.00 | 3.00 | X |
| U174 | Whirlpool of Thunder–Warren Caryl; 1961 | .75 | 1.50 | 2.25 | M |
| U175 | Jambalaya Lover Man–J.L. Potter; 1961 | 1.50 | 3.00 | 4.50 | X |
| U176 | Venus of Lesbos–Steve Bell | 1.00 | 2.00 | 3.00 | X |
| U177 | Four O'Clock on Friday–Philip Storey | 1.00 | 2.00 | 3.00 | X |
| U178 | Deadly Deceit–Paul Curtis | 1.00 | 2.00 | 3.00 | X |
| U179 | Drawn By Desire–William R. Wiseman | 1.00 | 2.00 | 3.00 | X |
| U180 | Doomed Sinner–Dan Brennan | 1.00 | 2.00 | 3.00 | X |
| U181 | The Insatiable Lisa–Dorothy Wind | 1.00 | 2.00 | 3.00 | X |
| U182 | No Experience Necessary–Charles Willeford; 1st ed. 1962 | 12.50 | 25.00 | 37.50 | X |
| U183 | Sexy Psycho–Lillan Dowling | 1.00 | 2.00 | 3.00 | X |
| U184 | Back Seat Lover–Bob Barksdale & Robert Hunter | 1.00 | 2.00 | 3.00 | X |

## NO IMPRINT
### Universal Publishing Company
#### Digest size

| | | V/Good | Fine | N/Mint | |
|---|---|---|---|---|---|
| nn | Red Hot–Ray Booth; reprinted as Universal Romance with same cover | 2.50 | 5.00 | 7.50 | E |

## NO IMPRINT
### Unknown publisher

| | | V/Good | Fine | N/Mint | |
|---|---|---|---|---|---|
| D1920 | How to Build and Operate a Model Railroad–Marshall McClintock; 1955 | .50 | 1.00 | 1.50 | NF |

# NO IMPRINT

## Unknown publisher

### Digest Size

| | | V/Good | Fine | N/Mint | |
|---|---|---|---|---|---|
| nn | War Birds–Diary of an Unknown Aviator; 1951 | 2.50 | 5.00 | 7.50 | C |

# NOVEL BOOKS–1st SERIES

## Camerarts Publications

| | | V/Good | Fine | N/Mint | |
|---|---|---|---|---|---|
| 3501 | Nympho Lodge–Jack Lynn; 1959 | 2.00 | 4.00 | 6.00 | M |
| 3502 | Torture Love-Cage–Jack Savage | 1.50 | 3.00 | 4.50 | X |
| 3503 | Virgin Bounty–Glenn Low | 1.50 | 3.00 | 4.50 | W |
| 3504 | Seduction on the Run!–Louis Fisher; 1959 | 2.00 | 4.00 | 6.00 | M |
| 3505 | Lucky Rape–Hank Walters; 1960 | 1.50 | 3.00 | 4.50 | X |
| 3506 | Chartered Love–Conrad Dawn | 1.50 | 3.00 | 4.50 | X |
| 3508 | Forbidden Love–Glenn Low | 1.50 | 3.00 | 4.50 | X |
| 5001 | Brute Passion–Ron Whelan | 1.50 | 3.00 | 4.50 | X |
| 5002 | Torrid Twins–Jack Lynn | 2.00 | 4.00 | 6.00 | M |
| 5003 | Makeout Charlie–Mike Orleans | 1.50 | 3.00 | 4.50 | H |
| 5004 | Backhill Sinners–Glenn Low | 1.50 | 3.00 | 4.50 | X |
| 5005 | Swamp Lust–George H. Smith | 2.00 | 4.00 | 6.00 | X |
| 5006 | Mad for Kicks–Jack Lynn | 2.00 | 4.00 | 6.00 | M |
| 5007 | Loverboy!–Jack Lynn | 1.50 | 3.00 | 4.50 | M |
| 5008 | Delta Doll–George H. Smith | 2.00 | 4.00 | 6.00 | X |
| 5009 | Sin Eater–Glenn Low | 1.50 | 3.00 | 4.50 | X |
| 5010 | Bayou Babe–George H. Smith; c-Bill Ward | 5.00 | 10.00 | 15.00 | X |
| 5011 | Wild Party!–Louis Fisher; c-Bill Ward | 5.00 | 10.00 | 15.00 | M |
| 5012 | Sadist on the Loose–George H. Smith; 1960 | 1.50 | 3.00 | 4.50 | X |
| 5013 | Playboy in Paris–Mike Skinner | 1.50 | 3.00 | 4.50 | M |
| 5014 | Broad Bait!–Jack Lynn | 1.50 | 3.00 | 4.50 | M |
| 5015 | Any Time-Any Place–Conrad Dawn | 1.50 | 3.00 | 4.50 | X |
| 5016 | Carnal Orgy–Con Sellers & Marcia Hall | 1.50 | 3.00 | 4.50 | X |
| 5017 | The Golden Hussy–George H. Smith | 2.00 | 4.00 | 6.00 | X |
| 5018 | Perverted Passions–Glenn Low | 1.50 | 3.00 | 4.50 | X |
| 5019 | Willing Women–Connie Sellers | 1.50 | 3.00 | 4.50 | X |
| 5020 | Brutal Ecstasy–George H. Smith; aka Tatan | 2.00 | 4.00 | 6.00 | X |
| 5021 | Forced Gigolos–Roe Richmond | 1.50 | 3.00 | 4.50 | X |
| 5022 | Pleasure House–Con Sellers; 1960 | 1.50 | 3.00 | 4.50 | X |
| 5023 | Hot Stuff–George H. Smith; 1960 | 2.00 | 4.00 | 6.00 | X |
| 5024 | Marks of Lust–Glenn Low | 1.50 | 3.00 | 4.50 | X |
| 5025 | Animal Broad–Con Sellers | 1.50 | 3.00 | 4.50 | X |
| 5026 | Huge Hunger–George H. Smith | 2.00 | 4.00 | 6.00 | X |
| 5027 | The Passion Pit–Jack Lynn | 2.00 | 4.00 | 6.00 | M |
| 5028 | Wench!–Con Sellers & Della Bannion | 1.50 | 3.00 | 4.50 | X |
| 5029 | Hot Jazz–George H. Smith; 1960 | 2.00 | 4.00 | 6.00 | X |
| 5030 | Honey Blood–Glenn Low; 1961 | 1.50 | 3.00 | 4.50 | X |
| 5031 | Brute–Con Sellers | 1.50 | 3.00 | 4.50 | X |
| 5032 | The Teaser–Allan Horn | 1.50 | 3.00 | 4.50 | X |
| 5033 | Brute Madness–Ledru Baker, Jr | 1.50 | 3.00 | 4.50 | X |
| 5034 | Wild Women–Jack Lynn | 2.00 | 4.00 | 6.00 | M |
| 5035 | Playground of Violence–Mike Skinner | 1.50 | 3.00 | 4.50 | X |
| 5036 | Taken!–Dan Brennan | 2.00 | 4.00 | 6.00 | X |
| 5037 | Oriental Orgy–Conrad Dawn | 1.50 | 3.00 | 4.50 | X |
| 5038 | Women on the Loose–Jack Lynn | 2.00 | 4.00 | 6.00 | M |
| 5039 | Vagabond Lover–Con Sellers; 1961 | 1.50 | 3.00 | 4.50 | X |
| 5040 | Insane Desire–Adam Coulter | 1.50 | 3.00 | 4.50 | X |
| 5041 | Anything for Money–V. Tremont | 1.50 | 3.00 | 4.50 | X |
| 5043 | Goddess of Trouble–Mike Skinner | 1.50 | 3.00 | 4.50 | X |
| 5044 | The Cheaters–Bob Hayes | 1.50 | 3.00 | 4.50 | X |
| 5045 | Big Man–Con Sellers | 1.50 | 3.00 | 4.50 | X |
| 5046 | Torrid Island–Bob Tralins | 1.50 | 3.00 | 4.50 | X |
| 5047 | Hood's Mistress–Hank Walters | 1.50 | 3.00 | 4.50 | X |
| 5048 | Potent Stuff–Al James | 1.50 | 3.00 | 4.50 | X |
| 5049 | Tall and Torrid–Jack Lynn | 2.00 | 4.00 | 6.00 | M |
| 5050 | Primitive Orgy–Bob Tralins; 1961 | 1.50 | 3.00 | 4.50 | X |
| 5053 | Frustrated!–Ed Storey | 1.50 | 3.00 | 4.50 | X |
| 5054 | Primitive Passion–Mike Hearst | 1.50 | 3.00 | 4.50 | X |
| 5055 | Too Much Broad–Conrad Dawn | 1.50 | 3.00 | 4.50 | X |
| 5056 | Double Seduction–Jack Lynn | 1.50 | 3.00 | 4.50 | M |
| 5057 | Top Madam–Con Sellers & Rani Lane | 1.50 | 3.00 | 4.50 | X |
| 5058 | Shocking Adultery–Frank W. Marshall | 1.50 | 3.00 | 4.50 | X |
| 5059 | 5 Wild Dames!–Big Bob Tralins | 1.50 | 3.00 | 4.50 | X |
| 5060 | Female Psycho Ward–Con Sellers | 1.50 | 3.00 | 4.50 | X |
| 5061 | Hot Bed–Matt Shipwreck | 1.50 | 3.00 | 4.50 | X |
| 5062 | Wild for Kicks–John Nemec | 1.50 | 3.00 | 4.50 | X |
| 5063 | Forced Females–Jack Lynn | 2.00 | 4.00 | 6.00 | M |
| 5064 | Giant Orgy–Alex Lord | 1.50 | 3.00 | 4.50 | X |
| 5065 | Easy Women–Orrie Hitt; 1961 | 1.50 | 3.00 | 4.50 | X |
| 5066 | Wholesale Seduction–Jack Lynn; 1961 | 2.00 | 4.00 | 6.00 | M |
| 5068 | Hungry for Men!–Lou Fisher | 1.50 | 3.00 | 4.50 | X |
| 5069 | Easy Sue–John Nemec | 1.50 | 3.00 | 4.50 | X |
| 5070 | Passion Potion!–Big Bob Tralins; 1961 | 1.50 | 3.00 | 4.50 | X |
| 5071 | Violent Orgy!–J.J. Jordan | 1.50 | 3.00 | 4.50 | X |
| 5072 | Sleep with Me!–Dan Brennan; 1962 | 2.00 | 4.00 | 6.00 | X |
| 5073 | Seduction Salon–Big Bob Tralins; 1962 | 1.50 | 3.00 | 4.50 | X |
| 5074 | Seduction on the Run!–Louis Fisher | 1.75 | 3.50 | 5.25 | M |
| 5075 | Brutal Ecstasy–George H. Smith; aka Tatan | 2.00 | 4.00 | 6.00 | X |
| 5077 | Hired Nympho–Big Bob Tralins; 1962 | 1.50 | 3.00 | 4.50 | X |
| 5082 | Frustrated Females!–Orrie Hitt | 1.50 | 3.00 | 4.50 | X |
| 5083 | Broad Bait!–Jack Lynn | 1.50 | 3.00 | 4.50 | M |
| 5084 | 3 Willing Females–Matt Sartone | 1.50 | 3.00 | 4.50 | X |
| 5085 | Raw Passions–Bill Anthony | 1.50 | 3.00 | 4.50 | X |
| 5088 | Loose Women–Bill Anthony | 1.50 | 3.00 | 4.50 | X |
| 5089 | Warped Woman–Orrie Hitt | 1.50 | 3.00 | 4.50 | X |
| 5090 | Shelih–Ralph Oliver | 1.50 | 3.00 | 4.50 | X |
| 5091 | Wildest Wench!–Bill Anthony | 1.50 | 3.00 | 4.50 | X |
| 5092 | Sadist on the Loose!–George H. Smith; 1962 | 2.00 | 4.00 | 6.00 | X |
| 6001 | Powerful Passion–John Jakes; 1961 | 3.00 | 6.00 | 9.00 | X |
| 6002 | French Quarter Wenches–Con Sellers | 1.50 | 3.00 | 4.50 | X |
| 6003 | Amazon Lover–Conrad Dawn | 1.50 | 3.00 | 4.50 | X |
| 6004 | Carnal Diary–Con Sellers | 1.50 | 3.00 | 4.50 | X |
| 6006 | Shocking Mistress!–Orrie Hitt; 1961 | 1.50 | 3.00 | 4.50 | X |
| 6007 | Fantastic Seduction–Con Sellers & Nora Heron; 1962 | 1.50 | 3.00 | 4.50 | X |
| 6008 | Abnormal Norma–Orrie Hitt | 1.50 | 3.00 | 4.50 | X |
| 6009 | Wild Body!–John Elliot | 1.50 | 3.00 | 4.50 | X |
| 6011 | The Backwoods Hussies–George H. Smith | 2.00 | 4.00 | 6.00 | X |
| 6014 | Bed Crazy–Orrie Hitt | 1.50 | 3.00 | 4.50 | X |
| 6017 | Gigantic Passions | 1.50 | 3.00 | 4.50 | X |
| 6019 | Loverboy!–Jack Lynn; 1962 | 1.50 | 3.00 | 4.50 | M |
| 6021 | The Farmer's Daughter–George H. Smith; 1962 | 2.00 | 4.00 | 6.00 | X |
| 6024 | Shocking Nymphs!–Moss Tadrack | 1.50 | 3.00 | 4.50 | M |
| 6026 | The Secret Perversions of Kay Addams–Orrie Hitt & Kay Addams | 1.50 | 3.00 | 4.50 | B |
| 6027 | Playboy in Paris–Mike Skinner | 1.50 | 3.00 | 4.50 | M |
| 6028 | Delta Doll–George H. Smith | 1.50 | 3.00 | 4.50 | X |
| 6029 | Torrid Tramps–George H. Smith; 1962 | 2.00 | 4.00 | 6.00 | X |
| 6033 | Immoral Motel–Howard O'Connor | 1.50 | 3.00 | 4.50 | X |
| 6034 | Animal Doll–Con Sellers & Pamela Dean | 1.50 | 3.00 | 4.50 | X |
| 6036 | Brute Passion–Ron Whelan | 1.50 | 3.00 | 4.50 | X |
| 6037 | Swamp Lust–George H. Smith; 1962 | 1.50 | 3.00 | 4.50 | X |
| 6038 | Freak Lover–Bob Tralins | 1.50 | 3.00 | 4.50 | X |
| 6040 | Fever Hot Woman!–George H. Smith | 2.00 | 4.00 | 6.00 | X |
| 6043 | Tabu Desires–Glenn Low | 1.50 | 3.00 | 4.50 | X |
| 6045 | Carnal Cage–George H. Smith | 2.00 | 4.00 | 6.00 | X |
| 6047 | Shocking She-Animal!–George H. Smith | 2.00 | 4.00 | 6.00 | X |
| 6048 | House of Pleasure–Con Sellers | 1.50 | 3.00 | 4.50 | X |
| 6049 | Mass Orgy–Glenn Low | 1.50 | 3.00 | 4.50 | W |
| 6050 | House of Perversion–Hank Walters | 1.50 | 3.00 | 4.50 | X |
| 6052 | Abnormal Cravings–King Gannett | 1.50 | 3.00 | 4.50 | X |
| 6053 | Slaves of Passion!–Moss Tadrack | 1.50 | 3.00 | 4.50 | X |
| 6054 | Man-Hungry Female–Orrie Hitt; 1962 | 1.50 | 3.00 | 4.50 | X |
| 6059 | Erotic Orgy!–George H. Smith | 2.00 | 4.00 | 6.00 | X |
| 6060 | Unstoppable Seducer!–Jack Lynn; 1962 | 2.00 | 4.00 | 6.00 | M |
| 6061 | Her Uncontrollable Hungers–Dan Brennan; 1962 | 2.00 | 4.00 | 6.00 | X |
| 6062 | Incredible Incredible Incredible Orgy Orgy Orgy–Bob Tralins | 1.50 | 3.00 | 4.50 | X |
| 6064 | Colossal Carnality–Robert Tralins | 1.50 | 3.00 | 4.50 | X |
| 6067 | 3 in a Bed!–George H. Smith; 1963 | 2.00 | 4.00 | 6.00 | X |
| 6068 | Unbelievable 3 and 1 Orgy!–Russell Trainer | 1.50 | 3.00 | 4.50 | X |
| 6069 | Overpassionate Love-Slaves!–Lou Fisher | 2.00 | 4.00 | 6.00 | X |
| 6070 | Unbearable Ecstasy–J.J. Jordan | 1.50 | 3.00 | 4.50 | X |
| 6071 | 10 Shockingest Seductions–Jack Lynn | 2.00 | 4.00 | 6.00 | M |
| 6072 | World's Wildest Seductions–Jack Lynn; 1963 | 2.00 | 4.00 | 6.00 | M |
| 6076 | Hottest Bedroom!–Matt Nake | 1.50 | 3.00 | 4.50 | X |
| 6077 | Overdeveloped Dolls!–Jack Nemec | 1.50 | 3.00 | 4.50 | X |

| | | V/Good | Fine | N/Mint | |
|---|---|---|---|---|---|

**NOVEL BOOKS–1st SERIES,** *continued*

| No. | Title | V/Good | Fine | N/Mint | |
|---|---|---|---|---|---|
| 6079 | Carnal College!–Moss Tadrack | | | | X |
| 6080 | Titine–George H. Smith | 2.00 | 4.00 | 6.00 | X |
| 6081 | F.S.C.–Con Sellers; aka Mr. Tomorrow | 2.50 | 5.00 | 7.50 | SF |
| 6082 | White Hot Woman!–Jack Lynn; aka Wild Woman | 2.00 | 4.00 | 6.00 | M |
| 6083 | Sensual Stenos!–Jack Lynn; aka Women on the Loose | 2.00 | 4.00 | 6.00 | M |
| 6084 | Erotic Room–Con Sellers; aka Brute | 1.50 | 3.00 | 4.50 | X |
| 6085 | My Wild Nights with Nine Nudists!– Orrie Hitt & Kay Addams | 1.50 | 3.00 | 4.50 | X |
| 6086 | Rita–Rex Weldon | 1.50 | 3.00 | 4.50 | X |
| 6087 | Goddess of Raw Passions–Robert Tralins | 1.50 | 3.00 | 4.50 | SF |
| 6088 | My Two Strangest Lovers–Orrie Hitt & Kay Addams | 1.50 | 3.00 | 4.50 | X |
| 6089 | Odd Orgy–Con Sellers | 1.50 | 3.00 | 4.50 | X |
| 6090 | Passion Parlor–Bob Tralins | 1.50 | 3.00 | 4.50 | X |
| 6091 | Taboo Thrills–Orrie Hitt; aka Warped Women | 1.50 | 3.00 | 4.50 | X |
| 6092 | Hot Harem–Con Sellers; aka Animal Broad | 1.50 | 3.00 | 4.50 | X |
| 6093 | Thrilling Tortures–Matt Sartone; aka 3 Willing Females | 1.50 | 3.00 | 4.50 | X |
| 6094 | A New Kind of Orgy–Con Sellers | 1.50 | 3.00 | 4.50 | X |
| 6095 | Carnal Clique!–Frank Cannon | 1.50 | 3.00 | 4.50 | X |
| 6096 | Inflamed Dames!–Orrie Hitt | 1.50 | 3.00 | 4.50 | X |
| 6097 | "I Need a Man!"–Orrie Hitt | 1.50 | 3.00 | 4.50 | X |
| 6098 | Incredible Seduction–Con Sellers & Nora Heron | 1.50 | 3.00 | 4.50 | X |
| 6099 | French Passion Goddess–Mike Skinner | 1.50 | 3.00 | 4.50 | M |
| 60100 | 4 Insatiable Nymphs!–Jack Lynn; 1963 | 1.50 | 3.00 | 4.50 | M |
| 60102 | Shores' Women–Richard Logan | 1.50 | 3.00 | 4.50 | X |
| 60103 | Cherry–Orrie Hitt & Kay Addams; 1963 | 1.50 | 3.00 | 4.50 | X |
| 60104 | Reunion in Eros–Harry Manis | 1.50 | 3.00 | 4.50 | M |
| 60105 | A Shocking Female–Bill Johnston | 1.50 | 3.00 | 4.50 | M |
| 60106 | A Modern Marriage–Bob Hayes | 1.50 | 3.00 | 4.50 | X |
| 60107 | "They All Touch Me"–Hank Walters | 1.50 | 3.00 | 4.50 | X |
| 60108 | Big Blondes–Ralph Oliver | 1.50 | 3.00 | 4.50 | X |
| 60109 | Oversensual–Harry Manis | 1.50 | 3.00 | 4.50 | X |
| 60110 | The Molester–Joe Lucas | 1.50 | 3.00 | 4.50 | X |
| 60111 | Madam Olga–Dallas Larrimore | 1.50 | 3.00 | 4.50 | X |
| 60112 | Unique Urge–J.J. Jordan | 1.50 | 3.00 | 4.50 | X |
| 60113 | "Play with Me!"–Ralph Oliver | 1.50 | 3.00 | 4.50 | X |
| 60114 | "Cora Is a Nympho . . ."–Harry Whittington | 3.00 | 6.00 | 9.00 | X |
| 60115 | Peculiarly Passionate Pair–Rex Weldon | 1.50 | 3.00 | 4.50 | X |
| 60116 | An American Sodom–Orrie Hitt | 1.50 | 3.00 | 4.50 | X |
| 60117 | Without Inhibitions–Frank Cannon | 1.50 | 3.00 | 4.50 | X |
| 7501 | "I Changed My Sex"–Hedy Jo Star; 1963 | 1.50 | 3.00 | 4.50 | X |
| 7502 | Imprisoned Passions–Con Sellers & Holly Jordan | 1.50 | 3.00 | 4.50 | B |
| 7504 | My Bisexual 3 Years–Con Sellers & Ann Vail | 1.50 | 3.00 | 4.50 | B |
| 7505 | The Farmer's Other Daughter–George H. Smith; 1963 | 2.00 | 4.00 | 6.00 | X |

## NOVEL BOOKS–2nd SERIES
## Camerarts Publications

| No. | Title | V/Good | Fine | N/Mint | |
|---|---|---|---|---|---|
| 6N222 | Carny Tease–Bill Anthony; 1963 | 1.50 | 3.00 | 4.50 | M |
| 6N223 | Perverse Triangle–Rex Weldon | 1.50 | 3.00 | 4.50 | X |
| 6N224 | Unclean Urges–Bill Anthony | 1.50 | 3.00 | 4.50 | X |
| 6N226 | Donna Is Different . . .–Big Bob Tralins | 1.50 | 3.00 | 4.50 | X |
| 6N227 | "Let Us Titillate You . . ."–George Jones | 1.50 | 3.00 | 4.50 | X |
| 6N228 | Her Odd Hungers–Don Bartell | 1.50 | 3.00 | 4.50 | X |
| 6N229 | The Playmate–Larry Payne | 1.50 | 3.00 | 4.50 | X |
| 6N230 | Desire in Duplicate!–Jack Lynn | 2.00 | 4.00 | 6.00 | M |
| 6N231 | "All Men Excite Me!"–Richard Logan | 1.50 | 3.00 | 4.50 | M |
| 6N232 | Only Half Pure!–Dirk Carson | 1.50 | 3.00 | 4.50 | X |
| 6N235 | String of White Girls–Martin Davidson | 1.50 | 3.00 | 4.50 | X |
| 6N236 | Tatan–George H. Smith | 2.00 | 4.00 | 6.00 | X |
| 6N237 | Dicey Mae–George H. Smith; 1963 | 2.00 | 4.00 | 6.00 | X |
| 6N239 | The Perverters–Larry McMullen | 1.50 | 3.00 | 4.50 | X |
| 6N240 | Love Experiment–Bob Tralins | 1.50 | 3.00 | 4.50 | X |
| 6N243 | Perversion in the Sand . . .–Rex Weldon; 1964 | 1.50 | 3.00 | 4.50 | X |

| No. | Title | V/Good | Fine | N/Mint | |
|---|---|---|---|---|---|
| 6N248 | Sweater Girl–George H. Smith | 2.00 | 4.00 | 6.00 | X |
| 6N250 | The Touch of Lust–Jack Kahler | 1.50 | 3.00 | 4.50 | X |
| 6N252 | More! More! More!–Orrie Hitt; aka Man-Hungry Female | 1.50 | 3.00 | 4.50 | X |
| 6N253 | Beyond Love–Orrie Hitt & Kay Addams | 1.50 | 3.00 | 4.50 | B |
| 6N255 | And Men My Food . . .–Marcia Hall & Con Sellers | 1.50 | 3.00 | 4.50 | B |
| 6N256 | The Love Seekers–Orrie Hitt; 1964 | 1.50 | 3.00 | 4.50 | X |
| 6N258 | Seduction Seminar–J.J. Proferes | 1.50 | 3.00 | 4.50 | M |
| 6N263 | The Tenth Bed–Jack Lynn; aka 10 Shockingest Seductions | 2.00 | 4.00 | 6.00 | M |
| 6N266 | Incredibly Excited–Riley Leeper; 1964 | 1.50 | 3.00 | 4.50 | X |
| 6N270 | Sensual Heat–Lou Fisher; aka Seduction on the Run | 1.50 | 3.00 | 4.50 | M |
| 6N273 | White and Wanton–Robert H. Badrig | 1.50 | 3.00 | 4.50 | X |
| 6N274 | One Hot Summer Night . . .–Russell S. Brown | 1.50 | 3.00 | 4.50 | X |
| 6N278 | Talent for Passion–Russell Trainer | 1.50 | 3.00 | 4.50 | X |
| 6N281 | Days of Passion, Nights of Love–E.B. Crowe | 1.50 | 3.00 | 4.50 | X |
| 6N282 | Den of Eroticism–Con Sellers | 1.50 | 3.00 | 4.50 | X |
| 6N285 | Nudist in My Office–Howard Joseph Boyle | 1.50 | 3.00 | 4.50 | M |
| 7N706 | The Abortionists–Russell Trainer | 1.50 | 3.00 | 4.50 | X |
| 7N707 | Nights in Aphrodisia–Duke Lardner | 1.50 | 3.00 | 4.50 | X |
| 7N708 | After-Midnight Girls–Al James; 1963 | 1.50 | 3.00 | 4.50 | X |
| 7N709 | The 5th Orgy–Duke Lardner | 1.50 | 3.00 | 4.50 | X |
| 7N710 | "The Blood Feast"–L.E. Murphy (H.G. Lewis); 1st ed. 1964; movie tie-in | 25.00 | 50.00 | 75.00 | HO |
| 7N712 | Narcissistic Sisters–Jack Lynn | 1.50 | 3.00 | 4.50 | M |
| 7N714 | Erotic Awakening–Arnold | 1.50 | 3.00 | 4.50 | X |
| 7N715 | My Life and Loves–Mandy Rice-Davies | 1.50 | 3.00 | 4.50 | B |
| 7N716 | Magnificently Sensuous–Moss Tadrack | 1.50 | 3.00 | 4.50 | |
| 7N718 | Unique Tease–Jody Lark & Con Sellers | 1.50 | 3.00 | 4.50 | X |
| 7N719 | Two Thousand Maniacs!–Herschell G. Lewis; 1st ed. 1964; movie tie-in | 25.00 | 50.00 | 75.00 | HO |
| 7N723 | Sequel to "I Changed My Sex"–Hedy Jo Star | 1.50 | 3.00 | 4.50 | B |
| 7N726 | Institute of Sensuality–Moss Tadrack | 1.50 | 3.00 | 4.50 | X |
| 7N728 | Crimes of Dr. K–Jack Savage | 2.00 | 4.00 | 6.00 | X |
| 7N729 | Color Me Blood Red–Herschell G. Lewis; 1st ed. 1964; movie tie-in | 25.00 | 50.00 | 75.00 | HO |
| 7N731 | Erotic Play–Bob Tralins; 1964 | 1.50 | 3.00 | 4.50 | X |
| 7N734 | The Third Seduction–Jack Lynn; 1964 | 2.00 | 4.00 | 6.00 | M |
| 7N737 | Christine–Gus Stevens | 1.50 | 3.00 | 4.50 | X |
| 7N741 | I Was a Negro Playboy "Bunny"–Anna English | 2.50 | 5.00 | 7.50 | B |
| 7N742 | Candi–Leon | 1.50 | 3.00 | 4.50 | X |
| 7N744 | The Love Worshippers–Bob Tralins; 1964; aka Goddess of Raw Passions | 1.50 | 3.00 | 4.50 | SF |
| 7N746 | 15 Sex Queens on Sex–by the World's Most Seductive Women | 1.50 | 3.00 | 4.50 | NF |
| 7N747 | Moonshine Mountain–Charles Glore; 1st ed. 1964; movie tie-in | 15.00 | 30.00 | 45.00 | X |
| 7N751 | Wilma's Wants–Orrie Hitt; 1964 | 1.50 | 3.00 | 4.50 | X |
| 7N752 | Lillit–George H. Smith; 1965 | 2.00 | 4.00 | 6.00 | X |
| 7N756 | The One and Only Jean–Bob Tralins | 1.50 | 3.00 | 4.50 | X |
| 7N758 | Jenkins' Lovers–Orrie Hitt; 1965 | 1.50 | 3.00 | 4.50 | X |

## NOVEL LIBRARY
## Diversey Publishing Corporation

| No. | Title | V/Good | Fine | N/Mint | |
|---|---|---|---|---|---|
| 1 | 3 Gorgeous Hussies–Jack Woodford; 1948 | 6.00 | 12.00 | 18.00 | E |
| 2 | Ecstasy Girl–Jack Woodford | 5.00 | 10.00 | 15.00 | E |
| 3 | Free Lovers–Jack Woodford; aka Fiddler's Fee | 5.00 | 10.00 | 15.00 | E |
| 4 | The Passionate Princess–Jack Woodford; aka Proxy Princess | 5.00 | 10.00 | 15.00 | E |
| 5 | Wanton Venus–Maurice LeBlanc | 4.50 | 9.00 | 13.50 | |
| 6 | Peeping Tom–Jack Woodford; aka Come into My Parlor | 6.00 | 12.00 | 18.00 | E |
| 7 | Grounds for Divorce–Jack Woodford; aka Love at Last | 5.00 | 10.00 | 15.00 | E |
| 8 | The Regenerate Lover–D.H. Clarke; aka Young and Healthy; 1949 | 5.00 | 10.00 | 15.00 | E |
| 9 | The Street of Painted Lips–Maurice DeKobra | 6.00 | 12.00 | 18.00 | E |
| 10 | Woman without Love?–Roswell Williams | 6.00 | 12.00 | 18.00 | E |

Novel Library 8, Novel Library 16, Novel Library 17.

Novel Library 27, Novel Library 37, Novel Library 42.

| | | V/Good | Fine | N/Mint | |
|---|---|---|---|---|---|

NOVEL LIBRARY, *continued*

| 11 | The Villain and the Virgin–J.H. Chase; aka No Orchids for Miss Blandish | 6.00 | 12.00 | 18.00 | E |
| 12 | Uneasy Virtue–Dana Wilson. Note: Same cover as comic Romantic Love No. 3 | 6.00 | 12.00 | 18.00 | E |
| 13 | A Good Time Man–E.P. Keating. Note: Same cover as comic Romantic Love No. 12 | 5.00 | 10.00 | 15.00 | E |
| 14 | Gold Diggers–Lois Bull | 6.00 | 12.00 | 18.00 | E |
| 15 | Playthings of Desire–J. Wesley Putnam | 5.00 | 10.00 | 15.00 | E |
| 16 | Women to Love–Sinclair Drago | 6.00 | 12.00 | 18.00 | E |
| 17 | Frisco Gal–Clarkson Crane; aka Naomi Martin. Note: Same cover as comic Romantic Love No. 11 | 6.00 | 12.00 | 18.00 | E |
| 18 | Bedroom Eyes–Maurice DeKobra | 6.00 | 12.00 | 18.00 | E |
| 19 | Louis Beretti–D.H. Clarke | 5.00 | 10.00 | 15.00 | E |
| 20 | One Night with Nancy–Wilson Collison. Note: Same cover as Diversey Love Book Monthly No. 2 | 6.00 | 12.00 | 18.00 | E |
| 21 | The Love Toy–anon. (H.S. Drago) | 6.00 | 12.00 | 18.00 | E |
| 22 | Mirabelle: Woman of Passion–Ellen Caren | 5.00 | 10.00 | 15.00 | E |
| 23 | Broadway Virgin–Lois Bull | 5.00 | 10.00 | 15.00 | E |
| 24 | Infidelity–Arthur Weigall. Note: Same cover as comic Intimate Confessions No. 7 and Broadway Novel No. 1 | 7.50 | 15.00 | 22.50 | E |
| 25 | Venus on Wheels–Maurice DeKobra; 1949 | 6.00 | 12.00 | 18.00 | E |
| 26 | The Immodest Maidens–Eleanore Browne; aka Make Me Yours | 6.00 | 12.00 | 18.00 | E |
| 27 | Ladies of Chance–Anthony Scott | 6.00 | 12.00 | 18.00 | E |
| 28 | The Love Clinic–Maurice DeKobra | 5.00 | 10.00 | 15.00 | E |
| 29 | All Dames Are Dynamite–Timothy Trent | 5.00 | 10.00 | 15.00 | E |
| 30 | Diary of Death–Wilson Collison | 5.00 | 10.00 | 15.00 | E |
| 31 | Millions for Love–Colette Roberts | 5.00 | 10.00 | 15.00 | E |
| 32 | Dishonorable Darling–Wilson Collison; 1950; aka Farewell to Women | 5.00 | 10.00 | 15.00 | E |
| 33 | The Women in His Life–Eleanor Nash; aka Bachelors Are Made. Note: Same cover as comic Romantic Love No. 6 | 5.00 | 10.00 | 15.00 | E |
| 34 | Crystal Girl–Stephen Longstreet. Note: Same cover as comic Romantic Love No. 5 | 5.00 | 10.00 | 15.00 | E |
| 35 | The Lady Said Yes–George Martin | 5.00 | 10.00 | 15.00 | E |
| 36 | Male and Female–Jack Woodford | 4.50 | 9.00 | 13.50 | E |
| 37 | 12 Chinamen and a Woman–J.H. Chase | 6.00 | 12.00 | 18.00 | E |
| 38 | Sixty Seconds–Maxwell Bodenheim | 5.00 | 10.00 | 15.00 | E |
| 39 | No Bed of Her Own–Val Lewton. Note: Same cover as comic Realistic Romances No. 3 | 6.00 | 12.00 | 18.00 | E |
| 40 | Wild Parties–Max Lief | 6.00 | 12.00 | 18.00 | E |
| 41 | Help Wanted–Male–Thomas Stone. Note: Same cover as Avon comic Romantic Love No. 9 | 5.00 | 10.00 | 15.00 | E |
| 42 | Lady for Love–Alan Brener Schultz | 5.00 | 10.00 | 15.00 | E |
| 43 | How to Play Canasta–Richard L. Frey | 1.50 | 3.00 | 4.50 | NF |
| 44 | Teach Me to Love–Jack Woodford | 5.00 | 10.00 | 15.00 | E |
| 45 | Blonde Baggage–Marty Holland | 9.00 | 18.00 | 27.00 | E |

| | | V/Good | Fine | N/Mint | |
|---|---|---|---|---|---|
| 46 | Naked on Roller Skates–Maxwell Bodenheim. Note: Same cover as Diversey Popular Novel No. 2 | 11.00 | 22.00 | 33.00 | E |

# NOVEL SELECTIONS
## Novel Selections, Inc.

| 51 | The Bastard–Erskine Caldwell | 1.50 | 3.00 | 4.50 | E |
| 52 | Poor Fool–Erskine Caldwell | 1.50 | 3.00 | 4.50 | E |

# (NOVELS INC.)
## Novels Inc.
### Digest Size

| nn | Come Sin with Me–Gail Jordan (Peggy Gaddis) | 2.50 | 5.00 | 7.50 | E |
| nn | Made for Loving–William Arthur; c-Rodewald | 2.50 | 5.00 | 7.50 | E |
| nn | Sinner in Gingham–Gail Jordan (Peggy Gaddis) | 2.50 | 5.00 | 7.50 | E |
| 9 | Stag Stripper–Gene Harvey | 2.50 | 5.00 | 7.50 | E |
| 10 | The Tigress–John Saxon | 2.50 | 5.00 | 7.50 | E |

# OLYMPIC FOTO-READERS
## Book Publishers

| F101 | The Love Rebellion–Charles Wyant; movie tie-in, 1967 | 3.50 | 7.00 | 10.50 | X |
| F102 | She-Master–Enid Walker | 2.50 | 5.00 | 7.50 | X |
| F103 | Deep Inside–Arnold Davidson; movie tie-in | 3.50 | 7.00 | 10.50 | X |
| F104 | Nymphs Anonymous–Rolf Kirby | 3.00 | 6.00 | 9.00 | X |
| F105 | Girls Together–Janice Taylor; 1968 | 2.50 | 5.00 | 7.50 | X |
| F106 | A Different Kind of Love–Sue Ferrante | 2.50 | 5.00 | 7.50 | X |
| F107 | For Love or Money–Arthur Windsor | 2.50 | 5.00 | 7.50 | X |
| F108 | The Acid Eaters–Rolf Kirby; movie tie-in | 5.00 | 10.00 | 15.00 | X |
| F109 | Come Play with Me–Nick Cosentino & Julie-Shirley Miles | 2.50 | 5.00 | 7.50 | X |
| F110 | The Red Whip–Clement Goodwood | 2.50 | 5.00 | 7.50 | X |
| F111 | The Deadly Organ–Walter Meiter | 3.00 | 6.00 | 9.00 | X |
| F112 | The Animal–Holly Nefesh | 3.00 | 6.00 | 9.00 | X |
| F113 | In Heat–Shirley Miles | 2.50 | 5.00 | 7.50 | X |
| F114 | College Girls–Kim Tahere; 1968 | 3.00 | 6.00 | 9.00 | X |

# OMNIBUS
## Omnibus Publishing Company
### Digest Size

| nn | Night of Crime–Armstrong Livingston | 6.00 | 12.00 | 18.00 | M |

# $1,000 PRIZE MYSTERY NOVELS
## Magna Publications, Inc.
### Oversized Digest Size

| | | V/Good | Fine | N/Mint | |
|---|---|---|---|---|---|
| nn(1) | The Laughing Buddha–Vincent Starrett; 1st ed. 1937 | 40.00 | 80.00 | 120.00 | M |

# ORIGINAL NOVELS
## Original Novels, Inc.
### Digest Size

| | | V/Good | Fine | N/Mint | |
|---|---|---|---|---|---|
| 700 | Women of the Night–Peggy Gaddis; orig. 1951; c-Gross | 4.00 | 8.00 | 12.00 | E |
| 701 | Backstage Affair–Amos Hatter | 4.00 | 8.00 | 12.00 | E |
| 702 | Strictly for Pleasure–Norman Bligh; orig. 1951 | 4.00 | 8.00 | 12.00 | E |
| 703 | Cellar Club–Albert Quandt | 6.00 | 12.00 | 18.00 | E |
| 704 | Gambler's Girl–Kermit Welles | 4.00 | 8.00 | 12.00 | E |
| 705 | On Borrowed Love–Amos Hatter | 4.00 | 8.00 | 12.00 | E |
| 706 | Scarlet Lil–Florence Stonebraker | 4.00 | 8.00 | 12.00 | E |
| 707 | Beyond Desire–Albert L. Quandt; orig. 1952 | 4.00 | 8.00 | 12.00 | E |
| 708 | Forever Evil–Harry Whittington | 4.00 | 8.00 | 12.00 | E |
| 709 | Gang Moll–Albert L. Quandt | 4.00 | 8.00 | 12.00 | E |
| 710 | See No Evil–Kermit Welles | 4.00 | 8.00 | 12.00 | E |
| 711 | Crime Boss–Albert Quandt | 4.00 | 8.00 | 12.00 | E |
| 712 | Farewell to Passion–Day Keene | 5.00 | 10.00 | 15.00 | E |
| 713 | Sleep with the Devil–Reed McCary | 4.00 | 8.00 | 12.00 | E |
| 714 | Body and Passion–Whit Harrison (Harry Whittington) | 4.00 | 8.00 | 12.00 | E |
| 715 | Wayward Nymph–Elisabeth Gill | 4.00 | 8.00 | 12.00 | E |
| 716 | Cellar Club–Albert L. Quandt | 4.00 | 8.00 | 12.00 | E |
| 717 | Sheila's Daughter–William Arnold | 4.00 | 8.00 | 12.00 | E |
| 718 | Savage Love–Whit Harrison (Harry Whittington); orig. 1952; c-Belarski | 4.00 | 8.00 | 12.00 | E |
| 719 | Harlem Woman–William Arnold | 5.00 | 10.00 | 15.00 | E |
| 720 | Baby Sitter–Albert L. Quandt; orig. 1952 | 4.00 | 8.00 | 12.00 | E |
| 721 | Zip-Gun Angels–Albert L. Quandt. Note: Same cover as Star 750 | 9.00 | 18.00 | 27.00 | JD |
| 722 | City of Sin–Robert O. Saber; orig. 1952 | 4.00 | 8.00 | 12.00 | E |
| 723 | Backwoods Hussy–Hallam Whitney (Harry Whittington) | 4.00 | 8.00 | 12.00 | E |
| 724 | Runaway Girl–William Arnold | 4.00 | 8.00 | 12.00 | E |
| 725 | Ringside Jezebel–Kate Nickerson; orig. 1953 | 3.50 | 7.00 | 10.50 | E |
| 726 | Dream Club–Albert L. Quandt; aka Beyond Desire | 5.00 | 10.00 | 15.00 | E |
| 727 | Visiting Nurse–Norman Bligh; orig. 1953 | 4.00 | 8.00 | 12.00 | E |
| 728 | Baby Peddler–Albert L. Quandt | 4.00 | 8.00 | 12.00 | E |
| 729 | Street of the Blues–Kate Nickerson | 4.00 | 8.00 | 12.00 | E |
| 730 | Waterfront Girl–Amos Hatter | 4.00 | 8.00 | 12.00 | E |
| 731 | Shack Road–Hallam Whitney (Harry Whittington); orig. 1953 | 4.00 | 8.00 | 12.00 | E |
| 732 | Streets of Paris–Robert E. Reynolds; c-Belarski | 4.00 | 8.00 | 12.00 | E |
| 733 | Backwoods Hussy–Hallam Whitney (Harry Whittington) | 4.00 | 8.00 | 12.00 | E |
| 734 | Runaway Girl–William Arnold | 4.00 | 8.00 | 12.00 | E |
| 735 | Boy Crazy–Albert L. Quandt; aka Zip Gun Angels | 5.00 | 10.00 | 15.00 | E |
| 737 | City Girl–Hallam Whitney (Harry Whittington) | 4.00 | 8.00 | 12.00 | E |
| 738 | Cellar Club–Albert L. Quandt | 4.50 | 9.00 | 13.50 | E |
| 739 | Ward Nurse–Mitchell Coleman; aka Born to be Bad; aka Affairs of a Ward Nurse | 4.00 | 8.00 | 12.00 | E |
| 740 | River Boat Girl–Norman Bligh; aka Strictly for Pleasure; c-Belarski | 4.00 | 8.00 | 12.00 | E |
| 741 | Motel Mistress–Norman Bligh; aka Remembered Moment | 4.00 | 8.00 | 12.00 | E |
| 742 | Shanty Road–Whit Harrison (Harry Whittington) | 4.00 | 8.00 | 12.00 | E |
| 743 | Big City Nurse–Albert L. Quandt; aka Baby Peddler | 4.00 | 8.00 | 12.00 | E |
| 744 | City Streets–Gene Harvey | 4.00 | 8.00 | 12.00 | E |

| | | V/Good | Fine | N/Mint | |
|---|---|---|---|---|---|
| 746 | French Alley–Matthew Clay; orig. 1954 | 4.00 | 8.00 | 12.00 | E |
| 749 | City Girl–Hallam Whitney (Harry Whittington) | 4.00 | 8.00 | 12.00 | E |

# PADELL
## Padell Book and Magazine Company
### Digest Size

| | | | | | |
|---|---|---|---|---|---|
| nn | Tales of French Love and Passion–Guy de Maupassant; 1943 | 2.00 | 4.00 | 6.00 | |
| nn | From Dance Hall to White Slavery–John Dillon | 6.00 | 12.00 | 18.00 | E |
| nn | The Tragedies of the White Slaves–H.M. Lytle; 1945 | 6.00 | 12.00 | 18.00 | E |
| nn | How to Be the Life of the Party–Jack Powelson; 1945 | 2.00 | 4.00 | 6.00 | H |
| nn | Joe Miller's Joke Book–Joe Miller; 1943 | 2.00 | 4.00 | 6.00 | H |
| nn | How to Be a Detective–A.H. Farrar | 2.00 | 4.00 | 6.00 | NF |

# PAPERBACK LIBRARY–1ST SERIES
## Paperback Library, Inc.

**Note: Two digit prefix is price code; last three numbers are stock number.**

| | | | | | |
|---|---|---|---|---|---|
| 52-127 | Men without Bones–Gerald Kersh; 1962 | 3.00 | 6.00 | 9.00 | HO |
| 52-128 | The Private Hell of Hemingway–Milt Machlin | 2.50 | 5.00 | 7.50 | B |
| 52-131 | Cleopatra in Mink–Cy Rice | 3.00 | 6.00 | 9.00 | |
| 52-149 | Ellison Wonderland–Harlan Ellison | 5.00 | 10.00 | 15.00 | SF |
| 52-156 | Love Me–And Die–Day Keene | 1.50 | 3.00 | 4.50 | |
| 52-165 | Delilah–Jefferson Cooper (Gardner F. Fox) | 3.00 | 6.00 | 9.00 | A |
| 53-269 | Sappho of Lesbos–Jefferson Cooper (Gardner F. Fox) | 3.00 | 6.00 | 9.00 | A |
| 52-290 | The Best from Famous Monsters of Filmland–ed. Forrest J. Ackerman; 1st ed. 1964 | 5.00 | 10.00 | 15.00 | NF |
| 52-363 | Ghostwind–Rachel Ann Payne (John Jakes) | 2.00 | 4.00 | 6.00 | R |
| 54-438 | Night Has a Thousand Eyes–George Hopley (Cornell Woolrich) | 2.00 | 4.00 | 6.00 | M |
| 52-504 | Son of Famous Monsters of Filmland–ed. Forrest J. Ackerman; 1st ed. 1964 | 5.00 | 10.00 | 15.00 | NF |
| 52-586 | Thongor against the Gods–Lin Carter; c-Frazetta | 2.00 | 4.00 | 6.00 | F |
| 53-618 | The Tritonian Ring–L. Sprague de Camp; c-Frazetta | 2.50 | 5.00 | 7.50 | SF |
| 53-665 | Thongor in the City of Magicians–Lin Carter; 1968; c-Frazetta | 2.00 | 4.00 | 6.00 | F |
| 52-687 | The Goddess of Ganymede–Michael Resnick; c-Jeff Jones | 1.50 | 3.00 | 4.50 | F |
| 55-693 | The Serpent–Jane Gaskell; c-Frazetta | 2.00 | 4.00 | 6.00 | F |
| 54-731 | Jezebel–Jefferson Cooper (Gardner F. Fox) | 2.50 | 5.00 | 7.50 | A |
| 55-738 | Atlan–Jane Gaskell; c-Frazetta | 2.00 | 4.00 | 6.00 | F |
| 54-748 | Who Is Ayn Rand?–Nathaniel Branden & Barbara Branden | 2.50 | 5.00 | 7.50 | B |
| 52-760 | Pursuit on Ganymede–Michael Resnick; 1st ed. 1968 | 1.50 | 3.00 | 4.50 | F |
| 53-780 | Thongor at the End of Time–Lin Carter; 1968; c-Frazetta | 1.50 | 3.00 | 4.50 | F |
| 54-800 | Slave of the Roman Sword–Jefferson Cooper (Gardner F. Fox) | 3.50 | 7.00 | 10.50 | A |
| 52-806 | The Swingers–Albert L. Quandt; aka Cellar Club; aka The Cool Crowd | 2.00 | 4.00 | 6.00 | JD |
| 52-813 | Famous Monsters of Filmland Strike Back–ed. Forrest J. Ackerman; 1st ed. 1965 | 5.00 | 10.00 | 15.00 | NF |
| 52-833 | The Other Side of Desire–Paula Christian | 2.00 | 4.00 | 6.00 | |
| 54-973 | This Sword for Hire–Jefferson Cooper (Gardner F. Fox) | 3.00 | 6.00 | 9.00 | A |
| 52-979 | The Sheik–E.M. Hull; movie tie-in | 1.50 | 3.00 | 4.50 | R |

## PAPERBACK LIBRARY–2ND SERIES
### Paperback Library, Inc.

**Note: Two digit prefix is price code; last three numbers are stock number.**

| | | V/Good | Fine | N/Mint | |
|---|---|---|---|---|---|
| 64-019 | The City–Jane Gaskell; c-Jeff Jones | 1.50 | 3.00 | 4.50 | F |
| 63-089 | Brak the Barbarian vs. The Sorceress–John Jakes; 1st ed. 1969; c-Frazetta | 2.00 | 4.00 | 6.00 | F |
| 63-166 | Jirel of Joiry–C.L. Moore | 2.00 | 4.00 | 6.00 | F |
| 63-184 | Brak the Barbarian vs. The Mark of the Demons–John Jakes; 1st ed. 1969 | 1.50 | 3.00 | 4.50 | F |
| 63-359 | The Druid Stone–Simon Majors (Gardner F. Fox) | 3.00 | 6.00 | 9.00 | |
| 64-624 | THX 1138–Ben Bova & George Lucas; movie tie-in | 1.50 | 3.00 | 4.50 | SF |
| 66-627 | Horror in the Cinema–Ivan Butler; 1971 | 2.00 | 4.00 | 6.00 | NF |
| 64-729 | Green Lantern and Green Arrow No. 1–Denny O'Neill; 1st ed. 1972. Note: Contains comic book reprints | 2.50 | 5.00 | 7.50 | A |
| 64-755 | Green Lantern and Green Arrow No. 2–Denny O'Neill; 1st ed. 1972. Note: Contains comic book reprints | 2.50 | 5.00 | 7.50 | A |

## PAPILLON BOOKS
### Aware Press, Inc.

| | | V/Good | Fine | N/Mint | |
|---|---|---|---|---|---|
| OSF-501 | The Last Breath–Eugene Carl Shaffer; 1974 | .75 | 1.50 | 2.25 | SF |
| OSF-502 | Mr. Tomorrow–Con Sellers; 1974 | 1.25 | 2.50 | 3.75 | SF |
| OSF-503 | Prison Planet–Victor D. Heywood; 1974 | 1.25 | 2.50 | 3.75 | SF |
| OSM-901 | Devils in Candy Houses–William Wall; 1974 | 1.25 | 2.50 | 3.75 | HO |
| OSM-902 | The Crestwood Traps–G.M. Snodgress; 1974 | .75 | 1.50 | 2.25 | M |
| OSM-903 | Time Running Out–Robert Crane; 1974 | .75 | 1.50 | 2.25 | |
| OSM-904 | Wake Up Dead–William Wall; 1974 | .75 | 1.50 | 2.25 | |

## (PARENTS INSTITUTE)
### The Parents Institute, Inc.

**Digest Size**

| | | V/Good | Fine | N/Mint |
|---|---|---|---|---|
| nn | Best Stories for Boys and Girls–anthology; 1938; includes Mickey Mouse and Pluto | 12.50 | 25.00 | 37.50 |

## PELICAN BOOKS
### New American Library

**(See also Mentor Books; Pelican reprints issued as Mentor Books)**

| | | V/Good | Fine | N/Mint | |
|---|---|---|---|---|---|
| P1 | Public Opinion–Walter Lippmann; 1946 | .50 | 1.00 | 1.50 | NF |
| P2 | Patterns of Culture–Ruth Benedict | .50 | 1.00 | 1.50 | NF |
| P3 | You and Music–Christian Darnton | .50 | 1.00 | 1.50 | NF |
| P4 | The Birth and Death of the Sun–George Gamow | .50 | 1.00 | 1.50 | NF |
| P5 | An Enemy of the People: Anti-Semitism–James Parkes | 1.00 | 2.00 | 3.00 | NF |
| P6 | What Happened in History–V. Gordon Childe | .50 | 1.00 | 1.50 | NF |
| P7 | The Physiology of Sex–Kenneth Walker | .50 | 1.00 | 1.50 | NF |
| P8 | Mathematician's Delight–W.W. Sawyer | .50 | 1.00 | 1.50 | NF |
| P9 | The Weather–Raymond Bush & George Kimble | .50 | 1.00 | 1.50 | NF |
| P10 | America's Role in the World Economy–Alvin H. Hansen | .50 | 1.00 | 1.50 | NF |
| P11 | Heredity, Race and Society–Th. Dobzhansky & L.C. Dunn | .50 | 1.00 | 1.50 | NF |
| P12 | The Story of Human Birth–Alan F. Guttmacher; 1947 | .50 | 1.00 | 1.50 | NF |
| P13 | Thomas Jefferson on Democracy | .50 | 1.00 | 1.50 | NF |
| P14 | Introducing Shakespeare–G.B. Harrison | .50 | 1.00 | 1.50 | NF |
| P15 | Emerson: The Basic Writings of America's Sage–Ralph Waldo Emerson | .50 | 1.00 | 1.50 | NF |
| P16 | The Personality of Animals–H. Munro Fox | .50 | 1.00 | 1.50 | NF |
| P17 | Human Breeding and Survival–Guy I. Burch & Elmer Pendell | .50 | 1.00 | 1.50 | NF |
| P18 | Is Marriage Necessary?–George H. Bartlett | .50 | 1.00 | 1.50 | NF |
| P19 | Good Reading | .50 | 1.00 | 1.50 | NF |
| P20 | An Introduction to Modern Architecture–Elizabeth B. Mock & J.M. Richards | .50 | 1.00 | 1.50 | NF |
| P21 | The Odyssey–Homerus | .50 | 1.00 | 1.50 | NF |
| P22 | Religion and the Rise of Capitalism–R.H. Tawney | .50 | 1.00 | 1.50 | NF |
| P23 | Heredity, Race and Society–Th. Dobzhansky & L.C. Dunn | .50 | 1.00 | 1.50 | NF |
| P24 | Sweden: The Middle Way–Marquis W. Childs; 1948 | .50 | 1.00 | 1.50 | NF |
| P25 | Philosophy in a New Key–Susanne K. Langer | .50 | 1.00 | 1.50 | NF |

## PENGUIN
### Penguin Books, Inc.

**(See also Signet; some issued as Penguin Signet)**

| | | V/Good | Fine | N/Mint | |
|---|---|---|---|---|---|
| 60 | The Dark Invader–Captain von Rintelen | 1.50 | 3.00 | 4.50 | |
| 79 | The Rasp–Philip MacDonald | 1.50 | 3.00 | 4.50 | M |
| | With dust jacket | 15.00 | 30.00 | 45.00 | |
| 239 | Stealthy Terror–John Ferguson | 1.50 | 3.00 | 4.50 | M |
| 276 | The Case of the Late Pig–Margery Allingham | 1.50 | 3.00 | 4.50 | M |
| 339 | High Rising–Angela Thirkell | 1.50 | 3.00 | 4.50 | |
| 501 | Murder by an Aristocrat–Mignon G. Eberhart; 1942 | 1.50 | 3.00 | 4.50 | M |
| 502 | Pygmalion–George Bernard Shaw | 1.50 | 3.00 | 4.50 | |
| 503 | Death of a Ghost–Margery Allingham | 1.50 | 3.00 | 4.50 | M |
| | With dust jacket | 25.00 | 50.00 | 75.00 | |
| 504 | All Concerned Notified–Helen Reilly | 1.50 | 3.00 | 4.50 | M |
| 505 | The Mother–Pearl S. Buck | 1.50 | 3.00 | 4.50 | |
| 506 | Two Survived–Guy Pearce Jones | 1.50 | 3.00 | 4.50 | |
| 507 | The Physiology of Sex–Kenneth Walker | 1.50 | 3.00 | 4.50 | |
| 508 | Walden–Henry David Thoreau | 1.50 | 3.00 | 4.50 | |
| 509 | The Pastures of Heaven–John Steinbeck | 2.00 | 4.00 | 6.00 | |
| 510 | Trent's Own Case–Warner H. Allen & E.C. Bentley | 1.50 | 3.00 | 4.50 | M |
| 511 | Cause for Alarm–Eric Ambler | 1.50 | 3.00 | 4.50 | M |
| 512 | The Strange Case of Miss Annie Spragg–Louis Bromfield | 1.50 | 3.00 | 4.50 | |
| 513 | The Catalyst Club–George Dyer | 1.50 | 3.00 | 4.50 | |
| 514 | Tombstone–Walter Noble Burns | 1.50 | 3.00 | 4.50 | NF |
| 515 | The Confidential Agent–Graham Greene; 1943 | 1.50 | 3.00 | 4.50 | |
| 516 | Genghis Khan–Harold Lamb | 1.50 | 3.00 | 4.50 | B |
| 517 | Philosopher's Holiday–Irwin Edman | 1.50 | 3.00 | 4.50 | |
| 518 | The Middle Temple Murder–J.S. Fletcher | 1.50 | 3.00 | 4.50 | M |
| 519 | A Blunt Instrument–Georgette Heyer | 1.50 | 3.00 | 4.50 | M |
| 520 | The Saga of Billy the Kid–Walter Noble Burns | 1.50 | 3.00 | 4.50 | B |
| 521 | The Ox-Box Incident–Walter Van Tilburg Clark | 1.50 | 3.00 | 4.50 | W |
| 522 | Sabotage–Cleve F. Adams | 1.50 | 3.00 | 4.50 | |
| 523 | Leaves of Grass–Walt Whitman | 1.50 | 3.00 | 4.50 | |
| 524 | Pencil Points to Murder–W.A. Barber & R.F. Schabelitz | 1.50 | 3.00 | 4.50 | M |
| 525 | The Penguin Book of Sonnets–Carl Withers | 1.50 | 3.00 | 4.50 | |
| 526 | My Own Murderer–Richard Hull | 1.50 | 3.00 | 4.50 | M |
| 527 | The Telephone Booth Indian–A.J. Liebling | 1.50 | 3.00 | 4.50 | |
| 528 | The Blind Barber–John Dickson Carr | 1.50 | 3.00 | 4.50 | M |
| 529 | Kitty Foyle–Christopher Morley; 1944 | 1.50 | 3.00 | 4.50 | |
| 530 | The Ministry of Fear–Graham Greene | 1.50 | 3.00 | 4.50 | |
| 531 | Drawn Conclusion–W.A. Barber & R.F. Schabelitz | 1.50 | 3.00 | 4.50 | M |

PENGUIN, *continued*

| | | V/Good | Fine | N/Mint | |
|---|---|---|---|---|---|
| 532 | Hag's Nook–John Dickson Carr | 1.50 | 3.00 | 4.50 | M |
| 533 | The Purple Sickle Murder–Freeman Wills Crofts | 1.50 | 3.00 | 4.50 | |
| 534 | Black Plumes–Margery Allingham | 2.50 | 5.00 | 7.50 | |
| 535 | The Old Dark House–J.B. Priestley | 1.50 | 3.00 | 4.50 | |
| 536 | In Hazard–Richard Hughes | 1.50 | 3.00 | 4.50 | |
| 537 | Out of This World–Julius Fast | 1.50 | 3.00 | 4.50 | SF |
| 538 | The Laughing Fox–Frank Gruber | 2.00 | 4.00 | 6.00 | |
| | With dust jacket | 25.00 | 50.00 | 75.00 | |
| 539 | Laughing Boy–Oliver LaFarge | 1.50 | 3.00 | 4.50 | |
| 540 | My Name Is Aram–William Saroyan | 1.50 | 3.00 | 4.50 | |
| 541 | Mr. Pinkerton Grows a Beard–David Frome | 1.50 | 3.00 | 4.50 | M |
| 542 | Murder Enters the Picture–W.A. Barber & R.F. Schabelitz | 1.50 | 3.00 | 4.50 | M |
| 543 | Shell of Death–Nicholas Blake | 1.50 | 3.00 | 4.50 | M |
| 544 | Ten Holy Horrors–Francis Beeding | 1.50 | 3.00 | 4.50 | M |
| 545 | The Talking Clock–Frank Gruber | 2.00 | 4.00 | 6.00 | |
| | With dust jacket | 25.00 | 50.00 | 75.00 | |
| 546 | O'Halloran's Luck–Stephen Vincent Benet | 1.50 | 3.00 | 4.50 | |
| 547 | Death of My Aunt–C.H.B. Kitchin | 1.50 | 3.00 | 4.50 | M |
| 548 | Black-Out in Gretley–J.B. Priestley | 1.50 | 3.00 | 4.50 | |
| 549 | Murders in Volume II–Elizabeth Daly | 1.50 | 3.00 | 4.50 | M |
| 550 | To Walk the Night–William Sloane | 1.50 | 3.00 | 4.50 | |
| 551 | Mr. Littlejohn–Martin Flavin | 1.50 | 3.00 | 4.50 | |
| 552 | Murder in Trinidad–John W. Vandercook | 1.50 | 3.00 | 4.50 | M |
| 553 | Nine Times Nine–H.H. Holmes (Anthony Boucher); 1945 | 4.50 | 9.00 | 13.50 | M |
| 554 | Tales of Piracy, Crime and Ghosts–Daniel Defoe | 2.00 | 4.00 | 6.00 | A |
| 555 | Dr. Toby Finds Murder–Sturges Mason Schley | 1.50 | 3.00 | 4.50 | M |
| 557 | McSorley's Wonderful Saloon–Joseph Mitchell | 1.50 | 3.00 | 4.50 | |
| 558 | Porgy–Du Bose Heyward | 1.50 | 3.00 | 4.50 | |
| 559 | Death of a Saboteur–Hulbert Footner | 1.50 | 3.00 | 4.50 | |
| 560 | Murder in Fiji–John W. Vandercook | 1.50 | 3.00 | 4.50 | M |
| 561 | Young Man with a Horn–Dorothy Baker | 1.50 | 3.00 | 4.50 | |
| 562 | Simon Lash, Private Detective–Frank Gruber | 2.00 | 4.00 | 6.00 | M |
| 563 | Appointment in Samarra–John O'Hara | 1.50 | 3.00 | 4.50 | |
| 564 | Maigret Travels South–Georges Simenon | 1.50 | 3.00 | 4.50 | M |
| 565 | Step in the Dark–Ethel Lina White | 1.50 | 3.00 | 4.50 | M |
| 566 | Say Yes to Murder–W.T. Ballard | 2.00 | 4.00 | 6.00 | M |
| 567 | Trouble in July–Erskine Caldwell | 1.50 | 3.00 | 4.50 | |
| 568 | Night Flight–Antoine de Saint Exupery | 1.50 | 3.00 | 4.50 | |
| 569 | Conceived in Liberty–Howard Fast | 1.50 | 3.00 | 4.50 | |
| 570 | And Berry Came Too–Dornford Yates | 1.50 | 3.00 | 4.50 | |
| 571 | Death Down East–Eleanor Blake | 1.50 | 3.00 | 4.50 | M |
| 572 | The Good Soldier Schweik–Jaroslav Hasek; 1946 | 1.50 | 3.00 | 4.50 | |
| 573 | The Turning Wheels–Stuart Cloete | 1.50 | 3.00 | 4.50 | |
| 574 | A Passage to India–E.M. Forster | 1.50 | 3.00 | 4.50 | |
| 575 | The Cask–Freeman Wills Crofts | 1.50 | 3.00 | 4.50 | M |
| | With dust jacket | 20.00 | 40.00 | 60.00 | |
| 576 | The Lovely Lady–D.H. Lawrence | 1.50 | 3.00 | 4.50 | |
| 577 | Manhattan Transfer–John Dos Passos | 1.50 | 3.00 | 4.50 | |
| 578 | Bread and Wine–Ignazio Silone | 1.50 | 3.00 | 4.50 | |
| 579 | Patience of Maigret–Georges Simenon | 1.50 | 3.00 | 4.50 | M |
| 580 | Pal Joey–John O'Hara | 1.50 | 3.00 | 4.50 | |
| 581 | God's Little Acre–Erskine Caldwell | 1.50 | 3.00 | 4.50 | |
| 582 | Thunder on the Left–Christopher Morley | 1.50 | 3.00 | 4.50 | |
| 583 | Vein of Iron–Ellen Glasgow | 1.50 | 3.00 | 4.50 | |
| 584 | Dead Reckoning–Francis Bonnamy | 1.50 | 3.00 | 4.50 | M |
| 585 | Winesburg, Ohio–Sherwood Anderson | 1.50 | 3.00 | 4.50 | |
| 586 | The Rasp–Philip MacDonald | 1.50 | 3.00 | 4.50 | M |
| | With dust jacket | 20.00 | 40.00 | 60.00 | |
| 587 | Martin Eden–Jack London | 1.50 | 3.00 | 4.50 | A |
| 588 | The Unvanquished–Howard Fast | 1.50 | 3.00 | 4.50 | |
| 589 | Back Street–Fannie Hurst | 1.50 | 3.00 | 4.50 | |
| 590 | Orlando–Virginia Woolf | 1.50 | 3.00 | 4.50 | |
| 591 | Mildred Pierce–James M. Cain | 1.50 | 3.00 | 4.50 | |
| 592 | Malice in Wonderland–Nicholas Blake | 1.50 | 3.00 | 4.50 | M |
| 593 | Handbook of Politics and Voters' Guide–Lowell Mellett | 1.50 | 3.00 | 4.50 | NF |
| 594 | Heavenly Discourse–Charles Erskine Scott Wood | 1.50 | 3.00 | 4.50 | |
| 595 | Cabbages and Kings–O. Henry | 1.50 | 3.00 | 4.50 | |
| 596 | The Heart Is a Lonely Hunter–Carson McCullers | 1.50 | 3.00 | 4.50 | |
| 597 | The Summing Up–W. Somerset Maugham | 1.50 | 3.00 | 4.50 | |
| 598 | Put Out the Light–Ethel Lina White | 1.50 | 3.00 | 4.50 | M |
| 599 | Tortilla Flat–John Steinbeck | 2.00 | 4.00 | 6.00 | |
| 600 | Montana Rides!–Evan Evans (Max Brand) | 1.50 | 3.00 | 4.50 | W |
| 601 | Jurgen–James Branch Cabell | 2.00 | 4.00 | 6.00 | F |
| 602 | The New Veteran–Charles G. Bolte | 1.50 | 3.00 | 4.50 | |
| 603 | Short Stories of James T. Farrell | 1.50 | 3.00 | 4.50 | |
| 604 | Trio–Dorothy Baker | 1.50 | 3.00 | 4.50 | |
| 605 | Cimarron–Edna Ferber | 2.00 | 4.00 | 6.00 | W |
| 606 | A Rope of Sand–Francis Bonnamy | 1.50 | 3.00 | 4.50 | M |
| 607 | Pygmalion–George Bernard Shaw | 1.50 | 3.00 | 4.50 | |
| 608 | Major Barbara–George Bernard Shaw | 1.50 | 3.00 | 4.50 | |
| 609 | Saint Joan–George Bernard Shaw | 1.50 | 3.00 | 4.50 | |
| 610 | Lady Chatterley's Lover–D.H. Lawrence | 2.00 | 4.00 | 6.00 | |
| 611 | Messer Marco Polo–Donn Byrne | 1.50 | 3.00 | 4.50 | |
| 612 | Christianity Takes a Stand–William Scarlett | 1.50 | 3.00 | 4.50 | NF |
| 613 | The Odyssey–Homerus | 1.50 | 3.00 | 4.50 | A |
| 614 | The Penguin Hoyle–Albert H. Morehead & Geoffrey Mott-Smith | 1.50 | 3.00 | 4.50 | NF |
| 615 | Lady into Fox and a Man in the Zoo–David Garnett | 1.50 | 3.00 | 4.50 | F |
| 616 | Eleven of Diamonds–Baynard Kendrick | 1.50 | 3.00 | 4.50 | M |
| 617 | Saratoga Trunk–Edna Ferber; 1947 | 1.50 | 3.00 | 4.50 | |
| 618 | The Perennial Boarder–Phoebe Atwood Taylor | 1.50 | 3.00 | 4.50 | |
| | With dust jacket | 25.00 | 50.00 | 75.00 | |
| 619 | Almayer's Folly–Joseph Conrad | 1.50 | 3.00 | 4.50 | |
| 620 | Montana Rides Again–Evan Evans (Max Brand) | 1.50 | 3.00 | 4.50 | W |
| 621 | Serenade–James M. Cain | 1.50 | 3.00 | 4.50 | |
| 622 | Looking for a Bluebird–Josef Wechsberg | 1.50 | 3.00 | 4.50 | |
| 623 | The Silver Jackass–Frank Gruber | 2.00 | 4.00 | 6.00 | |
| 624 | The Velvet Well–John Gearon | 1.50 | 3.00 | 4.50 | |
| 625 | Daisy Miller and an International Episode–Henry James | 1.50 | 3.00 | 4.50 | |
| 626 | The Purple Onion Mystery–Harriette Ashbrook | 1.50 | 3.00 | 4.50 | M |
| 627 | Tobacco Road–Erskine Caldwell | 1.50 | 3.00 | 4.50 | |
| 628 | The Innocent Voyage–Richard Hughes | 1.50 | 3.00 | 4.50 | |
| 629 | The King Is Dead on Queen Street–Francis Bonnamy | 1.50 | 3.00 | 4.50 | M |
| 630 | Mother Wore Tights–Miriam Young | 1.50 | 3.00 | 4.50 | |
| 631 | A Funeral in Eden–Paul McGuire | 1.50 | 3.00 | 4.50 | |
| 632 | Sanctuary–William Faulkner | 1.50 | 3.00 | 4.50 | |
| 633 | Great Son–Edna Ferber | 1.50 | 3.00 | 4.50 | |
| 634 | The Unbearable Bassington–Saki | 1.50 | 3.00 | 4.50 | |
| 635 | Blood on Lake Louisa–Baynard Kendrick | 1.50 | 3.00 | 4.50 | |
| 636 | The Voice of Bugle Ann and the Romance of Rosy Ridge–MacKinlay Kantor | 1.50 | 3.00 | 4.50 | |
| 637 | Hotel Splendide–Ludwig Bemelmans | 1.50 | 3.00 | 4.50 | |
| 638 | A Portrait of Jennie–Robert Nathan | 1.50 | 3.00 | 4.50 | |
| 639 | So Big–Edna Ferber | 1.50 | 3.00 | 4.50 | |
| 640 | Cartoons: All in Line–Saul Steinberg | 2.00 | 4.00 | 6.00 | H |

*Penguin 562, Penguin 575 with dust jacket, Penguin 592.*

Penguin 645, Penguin Special s229, Pennant P23.

| | | V/Good | Fine | N/Mint | |
|---|---|---|---|---|---|
| s211 | The Good Soldier Schweik–Jaroslav Hasek | 1.50 | 3.00 | 4.50 | |
| s212 | Psychology for the Fighting Man; 1943 | 1.50 | 3.00 | 4.50 | NF |
| s213 | Empire in the Changing World–W.K. Hancock | 1.50 | 3.00 | 4.50 | NF |
| s214 | Hitler's Second Army–Alfred Hancock; 1943 | 1.50 | 3.00 | 4.50 | NF |
| s215 | Handbook for Army Wives and Mothers–Catherine Redmond | 1.50 | 3.00 | 4.50 | NF |
| s216 | A History of the War–Rudolf Modley | 1.50 | 3.00 | 4.50 | NF |
| s217 | The Next Germany | 1.50 | 3.00 | 4.50 | NF |
| s218 | Shipyard Diary of a Woman Welder–Augusta H. Clawson | 2.00 | 4.00 | 6.00 | NF |
| s219 | The Moon Is Down–John Steinbeck; 1943 | 2.00 | 4.00 | 6.00 | |
| s220 | Guadalcanal Diary–Richard Tregaskis; 1943 | 1.50 | 3.00 | 4.50 | C |
| s221 | Thirty Seconds over Tokyo–Ted W. Lawson; 1944 | 1.50 | 3.00 | 4.50 | C |
| s222 | The British Navy's Air Arm–Owen Rutter | 1.50 | 3.00 | 4.50 | NF |
| s223 | They Were Expendable–W.L. White | 1.50 | 3.00 | 4.50 | |
| s224 | A Short History of the Army and Navy–Fletcher Pratt | 1.50 | 3.00 | 4.50 | NF |
| s225 | G. I. Sketch Book–Aimee Crane | 1.50 | 3.00 | 4.50 | |
| s226 | The Battle Is the Pay-off–Ralph Ingersoll; 1944 | 1.50 | 3.00 | 4.50 | |
| s227 | This Is the Navy–Gilbert Cant | 1.50 | 3.00 | 4.50 | NF |
| s229 | Psychology for the Returning Serviceman–Marjorie van de Water; 1945 | 1.50 | 3.00 | 4.50 | NF |
| s230 | I Knew Your Soldier–Eleanor Stevenson & Pete Martin | 1.50 | 3.00 | 4.50 | |
| s231 | Cartoons for Fighters–Frank Brandt; 1945 | 2.00 | 4.00 | 6.00 | |
| s233 | Soldier Art | 2.00 | 4.00 | 6.00 | |
| s237 | Pipeline to Battle–Peter W. Rainier | 1.50 | 3.00 | 4.50 | |
| s238 | Storm–George R. Stewart | 1.50 | 3.00 | 4.50 | |
| s239 | This Is the Navy–Gilbert Cant | 1.50 | 3.00 | 4.50 | NF |
| s240 | Island Victory–S.L.A. Marshall | 1.50 | 3.00 | 4.50 | |

| | | V/Good | Fine | N/Mint | |
|---|---|---|---|---|---|
| **PENGUIN,** *continued* | | | | | |
| 641 | Murder! Great True Crime Cases–ed. Alan Hynd | 1.50 | 3.00 | 4.50 | NF |
| 642 | The Kiss of Death–Eleazar Lipsky | 1.50 | 3.00 | 4.50 | |
| 643 | Young Lonigan–James T. Farrell | 1.50 | 3.00 | 4.50 | |
| 644 | Short Stories of Thomas Wolfe | 1.50 | 3.00 | 4.50 | |
| 645 | Song of the Whip–Evan Evans (Max Brand) | 1.50 | 3.00 | 4.50 | W |
| 646 | Journeyman–Erskine Caldwell | 1.50 | 3.00 | 4.50 | E |
| 647 | Uncle Tom's Children–Richard Wright | 2.50 | 5.00 | 7.50 | |
| 648 | Deadly Weapon–Wade Miller | 1.50 | 3.00 | 4.50 | M |
| 649 | The Tyranny of Sex–Ludwig Lewisohn | 1.50 | 3.00 | 4.50 | |
| 650 | American Beauty–Edna Ferber | 1.50 | 3.00 | 4.50 | |
| 651 | Market for Murder–Frank Gruber | 2.00 | 4.00 | 6.00 | M |
| 652 | The New Quiz Book–Albert H. Morehead & Geoffrey Mott-Smith | 2.00 | 4.00 | 6.00 | NF |
| 653 | Show Boat–Edna Ferber | 2.00 | 4.00 | 6.00 | |
| 654 | Great Western Stories–ed. William Targ | 2.00 | 4.00 | 6.00 | W |
| 655 | Great Murder Stories | 2.00 | 4.00 | 6.00 | M |
| 656 | Christ Stopped at Eboli–Carlo Levi | 1.50 | 3.00 | 4.50 | |
| 657 | Desire Me–Leonhard Frank | 1.50 | 3.00 | 4.50 | |
| 658 | Death of a Swagman–Arthur W. Upfield | 2.50 | 5.00 | 7.50 | M |
| 659 | The Wild Palms–William Faulkner | 1.50 | 3.00 | 4.50 | |

## PENGUIN GUIDES
### Penguin Books, Inc.

| | | V/Good | Fine | N/Mint | |
|---|---|---|---|---|---|
| G1 | The Penguin Guide to California–Carl Maas; 1947 | 1.00 | 2.00 | 3.00 | NF |

## PENGUIN SPECIALS
### Penguin Books, Inc./The Infantry Journal

| | | V/Good | Fine | N/Mint | |
|---|---|---|---|---|---|
| s75 | New Ways of War–Tom Wintringham; 1940 | 1.50 | 3.00 | 4.50 | NF |
| | With dust jacket | 3.00 | 6.00 | 9.00 | NF |
| s77 | The Psychology of Fear and Courage–Edward Glover; 1940 | 1.50 | 3.00 | 4.50 | |
| s81 | Russia–Bernard Pares; 1943 | 1.00 | 2.00 | 3.00 | |
| s82 | Aircraft Recognition–R.A. Saville-Sneath | 1.50 | 3.00 | 4.50 | NF |
| s169 | The Atom and the Energy Revolution–Norman Lansdell | 1.50 | 3.00 | 4.50 | |
| s201 | What's That Plane–Walter Pitkin, Jr; 1942 | 1.50 | 3.00 | 4.50 | NF |
| s202 | New Soldier's Handbook | 1.50 | 3.00 | 4.50 | NF |
| s203 | Guerrilla Warfare–"Yank" Levy | 1.50 | 3.00 | 4.50 | NF |
| s204 | How the Jap Army Fights–Paul W. Thompson & others; 1942 | 1.50 | 3.00 | 4.50 | NF |
| s206 | How Russia Prepared–Maurice Edelman | 1.50 | 3.00 | 4.50 | NF |
| s207 | Christianity and Social Order–William Temple | 1.50 | 3.00 | 4.50 | NF |
| s209 | Americans vs. Germans; 1942 | 1.50 | 3.00 | 4.50 | NF |
| s210 | Modern Battle–Paul W. Thompson | 1.50 | 3.00 | 4.50 | NF |

## PENNANT
### Pennant Books/Bantam Books, Inc.

| | | V/Good | Fine | N/Mint | |
|---|---|---|---|---|---|
| P1 | Navajo Canyon–Thomas W. Blackburn; 1953 | 1.25 | 2.50 | 3.75 | W |
| P2 | The Last of the Plainsmen–Zane Grey | 1.50 | 3.00 | 4.50 | W |
| P3 | Epitaph for a Spy–Eric Ambler | 1.25 | 2.50 | 3.75 | M |
| P4 | Stamped for Murder–Ben Benson | 1.25 | 2.50 | 3.75 | M |
| P5 | In Those Days–Harvey Fergusson | 1.25 | 2.50 | 3.75 | W |
| P6 | Mojave–Edwin Corle | 1.25 | 2.50 | 3.75 | W |
| P7 | Vanity Row–W.R. Burnett | 1.50 | 3.00 | 4.50 | |
| P8 | Sunset Rider–Matt Stuart | 1.25 | 2.50 | 3.75 | W |
| P9 | Ruler of the Range–Peter Dawson (Frank Gruber) | 1.50 | 3.00 | 4.50 | W |
| P10 | Six-Gun Boss–Clay Randall | 1.25 | 2.50 | 3.75 | W |
| P11 | A Time to Kill–Geoffrey Household | 1.25 | 2.50 | 3.75 | M |
| P12 | Warrant for a Wanton–Michael Gillian | 1.25 | 2.50 | 3.75 | |
| P13 | Apache Desert–L.P. Holmes | 1.25 | 2.50 | 3.75 | W |
| P14 | Action at War Bow Valley–Michael Carder | 1.25 | 2.50 | 3.75 | W |
| P15 | Takeoff–C.M. Kornbluth | 1.50 | 3.00 | 4.50 | SF |
| P16 | Lily in Her Coffin–Ben Benson | 1.25 | 2.50 | 3.75 | M |
| P17 | Gunsmoke over Big Muddy–Frank O'Rourke | 1.25 | 2.50 | 3.75 | M |
| P18 | Wire in the Wind–Matt Stuart | 1.25 | 2.50 | 3.75 | W |
| P19 | Reap the Wild Wind–Thelma Strabel | 1.25 | 2.50 | 3.75 | A |
| P20 | Two and the Town–Henry Gregor Felsen | 1.25 | 2.50 | 3.75 | |
| P21 | Border Graze–Dwight Bennett | 1.25 | 2.50 | 3.75 | W |
| P22 | Long Ride–Peter Dawson (Frank Gruber) | 1.50 | 3.00 | 4.50 | W |
| P23 | Man-Eaters of Kumaon–Jim Corbett | 1.25 | 2.50 | 3.75 | NF |
| P24 | Murder Won't Out–Russel Crouse | 1.25 | 2.50 | 3.75 | M |
| P25 | High Starlight–L.P. Holmes | 1.25 | 2.50 | 3.75 | W |
| P26 | Santa Fe Passage–Clay Fisher | 1.25 | 2.50 | 3.75 | W |
| P27 | Burro Alley–Edwin Corle | 1.25 | 2.50 | 3.75 | |
| P28 | Blackcock's Feather–Maurice Walsh | 1.25 | 2.50 | 3.75 | A |
| P29 | The Naked Spur–Rolfe Bloom & Allan Ullman; 1954 | 1.25 | 2.50 | 3.75 | W |

*Pennant P30, Pennant P59, Perma Books M3012.*

# PENNANT STUDENT EDITIONS
## Bantam Books, Inc.
### Note: Other titles exist in this series.

| | | V/Good | Fine | N/Mint |
|---|---|---|---|---|
| nn | Life on the Mississippi–Mark Twain | 1.00 | 2.00 | 3.00 |
| nn | God and My Country–MacKinlay Kantor; 1957 | .50 | 1.00 | 1.50 |

# PERMA BOOKS
## Pocket Books, Inc.

| | | V/Good | Fine | N/Mint | |
|---|---|---|---|---|---|
| M1000 | Peace of Soul–Fulton J. Sheen; 1954 | 1.00 | 2.00 | 3.00 | |
| M1600 | The Greatest Book Ever Written–Fulton Oursler | 1.00 | 2.00 | 3.00 | |
| M3001 | Texan-Killer–Gene Austin; 1955 | 1.50 | 3.00 | 4.50 | W |
| M3002 | Too Dead to Run–Jason Manor | 1.50 | 3.00 | 4.50 | M |
| M3003 | Spur to the Smoke–Steve Frazee | 1.50 | 3.00 | 4.50 | W |
| M3004 | Life among the Savages–Shirley Jackson | 1.50 | 3.00 | 4.50 | NF |
| M3005 | Tender to Danger–Eliot Reed | 1.50 | 3.00 | 4.50 | M |
| M3006 | Boy Gang–Mark Kennedy | 3.00 | 6.00 | 9.00 | JD |
| M3007 | The Desperate Hours–Joseph Hayes | 1.50 | 3.00 | 4.50 | E |
| M3008 | Horse Thief Crossing–Tom J. Hopkins | 1.50 | 3.00 | 4.50 | W |
| M3009 | Honky-tonk Woman–Bliss Lomax | 1.50 | 3.00 | 4.50 | W |
| M3010 | The Crimson Clue–George Harmon Coxe | 1.50 | 3.00 | 4.50 | M |
| M3011 | The Stainless Steel Kimono–Elliott Chaze | 1.50 | 3.00 | 4.50 | H |
| M3012 | Dead Game–Michael Avallone | 3.00 | 6.00 | 9.00 | M |
| M3013 | Massacre Trail–George C. Appell | 1.50 | 3.00 | 4.50 | W |
| M3014 | End of the Gun–H.A. DeRosso | 1.50 | 3.00 | 4.50 | W |
| M3015 | The Queen's Awards: Eighth Series–Ellery Queen | 1.50 | 3.00 | 4.50 | M |
| M3016 | The Secret Road–Bruce Lancaster | 1.50 | 3.00 | 4.50 | |
| M3017 | The Big Water–Mark Derby | 1.50 | 3.00 | 4.50 | |
| M3018 | Tejanos!–K.R.G. Granger | 1.50 | 3.00 | 4.50 | |
| M3019 | Doubles in Death–William Grew | 1.50 | 3.00 | 4.50 | M |
| M3020 | The Dreamers–J. Bigelow Clark | 1.50 | 3.00 | 4.50 | |
| M3021 | The Settling of the Sage–Hal G. Evarts | 1.50 | 3.00 | 4.50 | W |
| M3022 | The Big Boodle–Robert Sylvester | 1.50 | 3.00 | 4.50 | |
| M3023 | Top Hand–Dwight Bennett | 1.50 | 3.00 | 4.50 | W |
| M3024 | Frenchman's River–Will Ermine | 1.50 | 3.00 | 4.50 | W |
| M3025 | The Maras Affair–Eliot Reed | 1.50 | 3.00 | 4.50 | M |
| M3026 | Easy Money–Frank Peace; 1956 | 1.50 | 3.00 | 4.50 | |
| M3027 | World Out of Mind–J.T. McIntosh; c-Powers | 1.50 | 3.00 | 4.50 | SF |
| M3028 | The Bad Step–Mark Derby | 1.50 | 3.00 | 4.50 | |
| M3029 | Do It Yourself–Morris Brickman | 1.00 | 2.00 | 3.00 | NF |
| M3030 | Border Fever–C. William Harrison | 1.50 | 3.00 | 4.50 | W |
| M3031 | Fractured French–F.S. Pearson II & Richard Taylor | 1.00 | 2.00 | 3.00 | H |
| M3032 | The Mean Streets–Thomas B. Dewey | 2.00 | 4.00 | 6.00 | E |
| M3033 | Blood Money–Dan J. Stevens | 1.50 | 3.00 | 4.50 | |
| M3034 | Snow Fury–Richard Holden | 5.00 | 10.00 | 15.00 | SF |
| M3035 | Bar 4 Roundup of Best Western Stories–Scott Meredith | 1.50 | 3.00 | 4.50 | W |
| M3036 | Visa to Death–Ed Lacy; c-Maguire | 1.50 | 3.00 | 4.50 | |
| M3037 | Cop Hater–Ed McBain; 1st ed. 1956 | 4.00 | 8.00 | 12.00 | M |
| M3038 | Pay-off at Black Hawk–Harry Sinclair Drago | 1.50 | 3.00 | 4.50 | W |
| M3039 | The Perma Quiz Book–Joseph Nathan Kane | 2.00 | 4.00 | 6.00 | NF |
| M3040 | Sleep with Strangers–Dolores Hitchens | 1.50 | 3.00 | 4.50 | M |
| M3041 | To Have and Have Not–Ernest Hemingway | 2.50 | 5.00 | 7.50 | |
| M3042 | From Here to Shimbashi–John Sack | 1.00 | 2.00 | 3.00 | |
| M3043 | Red Harvest–Dashiell Hammett | 2.00 | 4.00 | 6.00 | |
| M3044 | Showdown Creek–Lucas Todd | 1.50 | 3.00 | 4.50 | W |
| M3045 | The Avenger–Dwight Bennett | 1.50 | 3.00 | 4.50 | W |
| M3046 | The Murder of Eleanor Pope–Henry Kuttner | 3.50 | 7.00 | 10.50 | M |
| M3047 | Blessed Event–Bill O'Malley | 1.00 | 2.00 | 3.00 | H |
| M3048 | Live and Let Die–Ian Fleming | 12.50 | 25.00 | 37.50 | M |
| M3049 | Tumbling Range Woman–Steve Frazee | 1.50 | 3.00 | 4.50 | W |
| M3050 | Droodles–Roger Price; 1956 | 1.00 | 2.00 | 3.00 | H |
| M3051 | F. O. B. Murder–Bert Hitchens & Dolores Hitchens | 1.00 | 2.00 | 3.00 | M |
| M3052 | The Brass Brigade–Frank Peace | 1.00 | 2.00 | 3.00 | |
| M3053 | Invasion of Privacy–Harry Kurnitz | 1.00 | 2.00 | 3.00 | M |

| | | V/Good | Fine | N/Mint | |
|---|---|---|---|---|---|
| **PENNANT,** *continued* | | | | | |
| P30 | Bold Raiders of the West–Frederick R. Bechdolt | 1.25 | 2.50 | 3.75 | W |
| P31 | The Outlaw Years–Robert M. Coates | 1.25 | 2.50 | 3.75 | NF |
| P32 | Walls Rise Up–George Sessions Perry | 1.25 | 2.50 | 3.75 | |
| P33 | Shadow of the Butte–Thomas Thompson | 1.25 | 2.50 | 3.75 | W |
| P34 | Dodge City: Queen of Cowtowns–Stanley Vestal | 1.25 | 2.50 | 3.75 | NF |
| P35 | Walk the Dark Bridge–William O'Farrell | 1.25 | 2.50 | 3.75 | |
| P36 | Elephant Bill–J.H. Williams | 1.25 | 2.50 | 3.75 | NF |
| P37 | Longhorn Empire–Will Ermine | 1.25 | 2.50 | 3.75 | W |
| P38 | Outlaw Valley–Evan Evans (Max Brand) | 1.25 | 2.50 | 3.75 | W |
| P39 | American Me–Beatrice Griffith | 1.25 | 2.50 | 3.75 | |
| P40 | Doubloons–Charles B. Driscoll | 1.25 | 2.50 | 3.75 | A |
| P41 | The Bronze Mermaid–Paul Ernst | 1.25 | 2.50 | 3.75 | |
| P42 | Saddle-Man–Matt Stuart | 1.25 | 2.50 | 3.75 | W |
| P43 | Fort Starvation–Frank Gruber | 1.50 | 3.00 | 4.50 | W |
| P44 | Adventures in Time and Space–Raymond J. Healy & J. Francis McComas | 1.25 | 2.50 | 3.75 | SF |
| P46 | Guaracha Trail–George Parker | 1.25 | 2.50 | .3.75 | |
| P47 | Tombstone–Clarence Budington Kelland | 1.25 | 2.50 | 3.75 | W |
| P48 | When Oil Ran Red–Clay Randall | 1.25 | 2.50 | 3.75 | W |
| P49 | The Sixpenny Dame–Eaton K. Goldthwaite | 1.25 | 2.50 | 3.75 | |
| P50 | One Way Ticket–Eugene O'Brien | 1.25 | 2.50 | 3.75 | |
| P51 | A Vaquero of the Brush Country–J. Frank Dobie | 1.25 | 2.50 | 3.75 | NF |
| P52 | The Border Queen–Nick Sumner | 1.25 | 2.50 | 3.75 | W |
| P53 | Toll Mountain–Robert McCaig | 1.25 | 2.50 | 3.75 | |
| P54 | To the Last Man–William E. Barrett | 1.25 | 2.50 | 3.75 | |
| P55 | Repeat Performance–William O'Farrell | 1.25 | 2.50 | 3.75 | |
| P56 | Beyond Human Ken–Judith Merril | 1.25 | 2.50 | 3.75 | SF |
| P57 | Horse Thief Trail–Frederick R. Bechdolt | 1.25 | 2.50 | 3.75 | W |
| P59 | Mostly Murder–Fredric Brown | 9.00 | 18.00 | 27.00 | M |
| P61 | The Argosy Book of Sports Stories–ed. Rogers Terrill | 1.25 | 2.50 | 3.75 | S |
| P64 | The Stakes are High–Brent Ashabranner | 1.25 | 2.50 | 3.75 | |
| P65 | In Winter Light–Edwin Corle | 1.25 | 2.50 | 3.75 | |
| P67 | Dry Bones in the Valley–William MacLeod Raine | 1.25 | 2.50 | 3.75 | W |
| P69 | The Nester–John S. Daniels | 1.25 | 2.50 | 3.75 | W |
| P75 | The Altered Ego–Jerry Sohl; 1955 | 1.25 | 2.50 | 3.75 | SF |
| P76 | Whiplash–Brad Ward | 1.25 | 2.50 | 3.75 | W |
| P77 | High Country–Peter Dawson (Frank Gruber) | 1.25 | 2.50 | 3.75 | W |
| P79 | Code Three–James M. Fox | 1.25 | 2.50 | 3.75 | |

# PENNANT MYSTERY
## Maco
### Digest Size

| | | V/Good | Fine | N/Mint | |
|---|---|---|---|---|---|
| 1 | Death Out of Thin Air–Stuart Towne (Clayton Rawson) | 12.50 | 25.00 | 37.50 | M |
| 2 | The Six Iron Spiders–Phoebe Atwood Taylor | 5.00 | 10.00 | 15.00 | M |
| 3 | So Much Blood–Bruno Fischer | 5.00 | 10.00 | 15.00 | M |
| 4 | The Purple Parrot–C.B. Clason | 5.00 | 10.00 | 15.00 | M |

**PERMA BOOKS,** *continued*

| No. | Title | V/Good | Fine | N/Mint | |
|---|---|---|---|---|---|
| M3054 | Play It Yourself–Jack Bassett & Norman Monath | 1.50 | 3.00 | 4.50 | |
| M3055 | The Con Man–Ed McBain; 1st ed. 1957 | 4.00 | 8.00 | 12.00 | M |
| M3056 | Green Hills of Africa–Ernest Hemingway | 2.50 | 5.00 | 7.50 | |
| M3057 | The Perma X-Word Puzzle Book– Alexander Field | 4.00 | 8.00 | 12.00 | NF |
| M3058 | The Murder of Ann Avery–Henry Kuttner | 3.50 | 7.00 | 10.50 | M |
| M3059 | Hot Town–Frank Malachy | 1.50 | 3.00 | 4.50 | |
| M3060 | Best Jokes for All Occasions–Jerry Lieberman & Powers Moulton | 1.00 | 2.00 | 3.00 | H |
| M3061 | The Mugger–Ed McBain; 1st ed. 1956 | 4.00 | 8.00 | 12.00 | M |
| M3062 | The Pusher–Ed McBain; 1st ed. 1956 | 5.00 | 10.00 | 15.00 | M |
| M3063 | Die in the Saddle–Lincoln Drew | 1.50 | 3.00 | 4.50 | W |
| M3064 | The Bloody Sevens–Jefferson Cooper; 1957 | 1.50 | 3.00 | 4.50 | |
| M3065 | Wilbert–Gill Fox | 1.00 | 2.00 | 3.00 | |
| M3066 | Murder Is Where You Find It–Robert P. Hansen | 1.50 | 3.00 | 4.50 | M |
| M3067 | Pets–Including Women–Charles Preston | 1.50 | 3.00 | 4.50 | H |
| M3068 | Decision at Broken Butte–Harry Sinclair Drago | 1.50 | 3.00 | 4.50 | W |
| M3069 | The Last Round–Frank O'Rourke | 1.50 | 3.00 | 4.50 | W |
| M3070 | Too Hot to Handle–Ian Fleming; aka Moonraker | 12.50 | 25.00 | 37.50 | M |
| M3071 | Chronicle of the Calypso Clipper–John Jennings | 1.50 | 3.00 | 4.50 | A |
| M3072 | Death in the Wind–Edwin Lanham | 1.50 | 3.00 | 4.50 | |
| M3073 | The Wild Life–Herbert Gold | 1.50 | 3.00 | 4.50 | |
| M3074 | The Maltese Falcon–Dashiell Hammett | 3.00 | 6.00 | 9.00 | M |
| M3075 | Oh, What a Wonderful Wedding– Virginia Rowans; 1957 | 1.50 | 3.00 | 4.50 | |
| M3076 | Ellery Queen's Awards: Tenth Series– Ellery Queen | 1.50 | 3.00 | 4.50 | M |
| M3077 | Boomer–Clay Randall | 1.50 | 3.00 | 4.50 | |
| M3078 | Feeling No Pain–Bill O'Malley | 1.50 | 3.00 | 4.50 | H |
| M3079 | Unhappy Hooligan–Stuart Palmer | 2.00 | 4.00 | 6.00 | M |
| M3080 | The Splintered Man–M.E. Chaber | 3.00 | 6.00 | 9.00 | M |
| M3081 | The Wild West Joke Book–Oren Arnold | 1.50 | 3.00 | 4.50 | H |
| M3082 | Bar 5 Roundup of Best Western Stories–Scott Meredith | 1.50 | 3.00 | 4.50 | W |
| M3083 | Choice Cartoons from Sports Illustrated–Charles Preston | 1.50 | 3.00 | 4.50 | H |
| M3084 | Diamonds Are Forever–Ian Fleming | 8.00 | 16.00 | 24.00 | M |
| M3085 | Wild Grass–Harry Sinclair Drago | 1.50 | 3.00 | 4.50 | W |
| M3086 | Montana Bad Man–Roe Richmond | 1.50 | 3.00 | 4.50 | W |
| M3087 | The Golden Widow–Floyd Mahannah | 1.50 | 3.00 | 4.50 | |
| M3088 | Pursuit–Lewis B. Patten | 1.50 | 3.00 | 4.50 | W |
| M3089 | The Brave, Bad Girls–Thomas B. Dewey | 2.00 | 4.00 | 6.00 | |
| M3090 | Don't Do It Yourself–Morris Brickman | 1.50 | 3.00 | 4.50 | NF |
| M3091 | The Men in Her Death–Stephen Ransome | 1.50 | 3.00 | 4.50 | |
| M3092 | Ride the Wind South–John Hunter | 1.50 | 3.00 | 4.50 | |
| M3093 | Unarmed Killer–William Harrison | 1.50 | 3.00 | 4.50 | W |
| M3094 | This Is My Funniest–Whit Burnett | 1.00 | 2.00 | 3.00 | H |
| M3095 | Shadow of the Rope–Ray Gaulden | 1.50 | 3.00 | 4.50 | |
| M3096 | Widow's Pique–Blair Treynor | 1.50 | 3.00 | 4.50 | M |
| M3097 | Vanishing Ladies–Richard Marsten | 2.00 | 4.00 | 6.00 | |
| M3098 | Red–Richard Vincent | 1.50 | 3.00 | 4.50 | |
| M3099 | Nurse Kathy–Adeline McElfresh; 1958 | 1.00 | 2.00 | 3.00 | R |

*Perma Books M3070, Perma Books M3097, Perma Books M4070.*

| No. | Title | V/Good | Fine | N/Mint | |
|---|---|---|---|---|---|
| M3100 | One-Way Ticket–Bert Hitchens & Dolores Hitchens | 1.50 | 3.00 | 4.50 | M |
| M3101 | Cavalry Scout–Dee Brown | 1.50 | 3.00 | 4.50 | W |
| M3102 | Marcia Blake, Publicity Girl–Nancy Webb | 1.00 | 2.00 | 3.00 | R |
| M3103 | The Saint around the World–Leslie Charteris | 1.50 | 3.00 | 4.50 | M |
| M3104 | Lash of Idaho–Roe Richmond | 1.50 | 3.00 | 4.50 | W |
| M3105 | O'Malley's Nuns–Bill O'Malley | 1.50 | 3.00 | 4.50 | H |
| M3106 | Lead with Your Left–Ed Lacy | 1.50 | 3.00 | 4.50 | |
| M3107 | Yellow Rope–Lincoln Drew | 1.50 | 3.00 | 4.50 | W |
| M3108 | Killer's Choice–Ed McBain; 1st ed. 1958 | 4.00 | 8.00 | 12.00 | M |
| M3109 | The Lonely Law–Matt Stuart | 1.50 | 3.00 | 4.50 | W |
| M3110 | The Vengeful Men–Ray Gaulden | 1.50 | 3.00 | 4.50 | W |
| M3111 | The Best from Manhunt–Scott Meredith & Sidney Meredith | 3.50 | 7.00 | 10.50 | M |
| M3112 | Three Trails–George C. Appell | 1.50 | 3.00 | 4.50 | W |
| M3113 | Killer's Payoff–Ed McBain; 1st ed. 1958 | 4.00 | 8.00 | 12.00 | M |
| M3114 | Deadly Summer–Glenn M. Barns | 1.50 | 3.00 | 4.50 | |
| M3115 | Showdown at Sunset–Harry Sinclair Drago | 1.50 | 3.00 | 4.50 | W |
| M3116 | Bar 6 Roundup of Best Western Stories–Scott Meredith | 1.50 | 3.00 | 4.50 | W |
| M3117 | Even the Wicked–Richard Marsten | 2.00 | 4.00 | 6.00 | |
| M3118 | Spearhead–Franklin M. Davis, Jr | 1.50 | 3.00 | 4.50 | C |
| M3119 | Lady Killer–Ed McBain; 1st ed. 1958 | 4.00 | 8.00 | 12.00 | M |
| M3120 | Rifle Ranch–Lincoln Drew | 1.50 | 3.00 | 4.50 | W |
| M3122 | The Velvet Ape–David C. Holmes | 2.50 | 5.00 | 7.50 | |
| M3123 | The Marshal from Deadwood–John Hunter; 1958 | 1.50 | 3.00 | 4.50 | |
| M4001 | Botany Bay–James Norman Hall & Charles Nordhoff; 1955 | 1.50 | 3.00 | 4.50 | |
| M4002 | The High and the Mighty–Ernest K. Gann | 1.50 | 3.00 | 4.50 | |
| M4003 | Peace with God–Billy Graham | 1.00 | 2.00 | 3.00 | |
| M4004 | Anyone's My Name–Seymour Shubin | 1.00 | 2.00 | 3.00 | |
| M4005 | The Velvet Doublet–James Street | 1.50 | 3.00 | 4.50 | A |
| M4006 | Corpus of Joe Bailey–Oakley Hall | 1.00 | 2.00 | 3.00 | |
| M4007 | The Time Is Noon–Hiram Haydn | 1.00 | 2.00 | 3.00 | |
| M4008 | Storm Haven–Frank G. Slaughter | 1.00 | 2.00 | 3.00 | |
| M4009 | The Art of Living–Norman Vincent Peale | 1.00 | 2.00 | 3.00 | |
| M4010 | The Girl with the Glass Heart–Daniel Stern | 1.00 | 2.00 | 3.00 | E |
| M4011 | Stories of the Foreign Legion–Percival C. Wren | 1.50 | 3.00 | 4.50 | A |
| M4012 | Sight without Glasses–Harold M. Peppard | 1.50 | 3.00 | 4.50 | NF |
| M4013 | Be Glad You're Neurotic–Louis E. Bisch | 1.00 | 2.00 | 3.00 | NF |
| M4014 | Best Jokes–Powers Moulton | 1.50 | 3.00 | 4.50 | H |
| M4015 | Eat and Reduce–Victor H. Lindlahr | .50 | 1.00 | 1.50 | NF |
| M4016 | The Fundamentals of Contract Bridge– Charles H. Goren | .50 | 1.00 | 1.50 | NF |
| M4017 | Modern Parables–Fulton Oursler | 1.00 | 2.00 | 3.00 | |
| M4018 | New Standard Book of Model Letters for All Occasions–Leo J. Henkin | 1.00 | 2.00 | 3.00 | |
| M4019 | Sex and the Love-Life–William J. Fielding | .50 | 1.00 | 1.50 | NF |
| M4020 | Word Power Made Easy–Norman Lewis | .50 | 1.00 | 1.50 | NF |
| M4021 | The Perma Cross Word Puzzle Dictionary–Frank Eaton Newman | .50 | 1.00 | 1.50 | NF |
| M4022 | Operation Future–Groff Conklin | 1.50 | 3.00 | 4.50 | SF |
| M4023 | Your Legal Advisor–Samuel G. Kling | 1.00 | 2.00 | 3.00 | NF |
| M4024 | The Well of Loneliness–Radclyffe Hall | 2.50 | 5.00 | 7.50 | |
| M4025 | Spencer Brade, M.D.–Frank G. Slaughter; 1955 | 1.00 | 2.00 | 3.00 | |
| M4026 | That None Should Die–Frank G. Slaughter | 1.00 | 2.00 | 3.00 | |
| M4027 | East Side General–Frank G. Slaughter | 1.00 | 2.00 | 3.00 | |
| M4028 | The Deep Six–Martin Dibner | 1.00 | 2.00 | 3.00 | |
| M4029 | To Hell and Back–Audie Murphy | 1.50 | 3.00 | 4.50 | B |
| M4030 | The Standard Bartender's Guide– Patrick Gavin Duffy & James A. Beard | 1.25 | 2.50 | 3.75 | NF |
| M4031 | The Song of Ruth–Frank G. Slaughter | 1.00 | 2.00 | 3.00 | |
| M4032 | Captain of the Medici–John J. Pugh | 1.50 | 3.00 | 4.50 | A |
| M4033 | Lift Up Your Heart–Fulton J. Sheen | 1.00 | 2.00 | 3.00 | |
| M4034 | Soldier of Fortune–Ernest K. Gann | 1.50 | 3.00 | 4.50 | |
| M4035 | Your Child from 2 to 5–Morton Edwards | 1.00 | 2.00 | 3.00 | NF |

PERMA BOOKS, *continued*

| | | V/Good | Fine | N/Mint | |
|---|---|---|---|---|---|
| M4036 | The Greatest Faith Ever Known–Fulton Oursler | 1.50 | 3.00 | 4.50 | |
| M4037 | The Cotton Road–Frank Feville | 1.00 | 2.00 | 3.00 | |
| M4038 | A Touch of Glory–Frank G. Slaughter; 1956 | 1.00 | 2.00 | 3.00 | |
| M4039 | Prisoner in Paradise–Garet Rogers | 1.00 | 2.00 | 3.00 | |
| M4040 | But We Were Born Free–Elmer Davis | 1.50 | 3.00 | 4.50 | |
| M4041 | Lights along the Shore–Fulton Oursler | 1.00 | 2.00 | 3.00 | |
| M4042 | Mardios Beach–Oakley Hall | 1.00 | 2.00 | 3.00 | |
| M4043 | The Silver Oar–Howard Breslin | 1.00 | 2.00 | 3.00 | |
| M4044 | Ceremony of Love–Thomas Williams | 1.00 | 2.00 | 3.00 | |
| M4045 | The Strongbox–Howard Swiggett | 1.00 | 2.00 | 3.00 | |
| M4046 | The Greatest Story Ever Told–Fulton Oursler | 1.00 | 2.00 | 3.00 | |
| M4047 | Divine Mistress–Frank G. Slaughter | 1.50 | 3.00 | 4.50 | |
| M4048 | Battle Surgeon–Frank G. Slaughter | 1.00 | 2.00 | 3.00 | C |
| M4049 | The Galileans–Frank G. Slaughter | 1.00 | 2.00 | 3.00 | |
| M4050 | Slattery's Hurricane–Herman Wouk; 1956 | 1.50 | 3.00 | 4.50 | |
| M4051 | The Healer–Frank G. Slaughter | 1.00 | 2.00 | 3.00 | |
| M4052 | The Hound of Earth–Vance Bourjaily | 1.00 | 2.00 | 3.00 | |
| M4053 | Air Surgeon–Frank G. Slaughter | 1.00 | 2.00 | 3.00 | C |
| M4054 | Fort Everglades–Frank G. Slaughter | 2.50 | 5.00 | 7.50 | A |
| M4055 | The Road to Bithynia–Frank G. Slaughter | 1.00 | 2.00 | 3.00 | |
| M4056 | South Sea Stories–W. Somerset Maugham | 1.50 | 3.00 | 4.50 | |
| M4057 | Darien Venture–C.V. Terry | 1.50 | 3.00 | 4.50 | |
| M4058 | Shad Run–Howard Breslin | 1.00 | 2.00 | 3.00 | |
| M4059 | The Will to Live–Arnold A. Hutschnecker. Note: Also exists in a printing without M prefix | 1.00 | 2.00 | 3.00 | |
| M4060 | Science and Surgery–Frank G. Slaughter | 1.00 | 2.00 | 3.00 | |
| M4061 | Run Silent, Run Deep–Edward L. Beach; movie tie-in. Note: Also exists in a printing without M prefix | 1.50 | 3.00 | 4.50 | C |
| M4062 | Kon-Tiki–Thor Heyerdahl | 1.50 | 3.00 | 4.50 | NF |
| M4063 | Cell 2455, Death Row–Caryl Chessman | 1.50 | 3.00 | 4.50 | B |
| M4064 | Flight from Natchez–Frank G. Slaughter. Note: Also exists in a printing without M prefix | 1.00 | 2.00 | 3.00 | |
| M4065 | How to Eat Better for Less Money–Sam W. Aaron | .25 | .50 | .75 | NF |
| M4066 | The Complete Letter Writer–N.H. Mayer & S.K. Mayer | .50 | 1.00 | 1.50 | NF |
| M4067 | H. M. S. Ulysses–Alistair MacLean | 1.00 | 2.00 | 3.00 | A |
| M4068 | Winter Harvest–Norah Lofts | 1.00 | 2.00 | 3.00 | |
| M4069 | The Scarlet Cord–Frank G. Slaughter | 1.00 | 2.00 | 3.00 | |
| M4070 | The Highwayman–Noel B. Gerson | 1.50 | 3.00 | 4.50 | A |
| M4071 | The Smiling Rebel–Harnett T. Kane | 1.50 | 3.00 | 4.50 | |
| M4072 | The Golden Isle–Frank G. Slaughter | 1.00 | 2.00 | 3.00 | |
| M4073 | The Dice of God–Hoffman Birney | 1.00 | 2.00 | 3.00 | |
| M4074 | How to Win and Hold a Mate–Samuel G. Kling | 1.00 | 2.00 | 3.00 | NF |
| M4075 | Christopher Humble–Charles B. Judah; 1957 | 1.00 | 2.00 | 3.00 | |
| M4076 | The Corsair–Madeleine Fabiola Kent | 1.50 | 3.00 | 4.50 | A |
| M4077 | The Loving Couple–Virginia Rowans | 1.00 | 2.00 | 3.00 | |
| M4078 | Kentucky Pride–Gene Markey | 1.00 | 2.00 | 3.00 | |
| M4079 | The Wreck of the Mary Deare–Hammond Innes | 1.00 | 2.00 | 3.00 | |
| M4080 | Breakaway–Wally Depew | 1.00 | 2.00 | 3.00 | |
| M4081 | Position Unknown–Ian Mackersey | 1.00 | 2.00 | 3.00 | |
| M4082 | Murder of a Mistress–Henry Kuttner | 4.50 | 9.00 | 13.50 | M |
| M4083 | Bellevue Is My Home–S.R. Cutolo & others | 1.00 | 2.00 | 3.00 | NF |
| M4084 | Rate Yourself–Pauline Arnold | 1.00 | 2.00 | 3.00 | NF |
| M4085 | Underworld U. S. A.–Joseph F. Dinneen | 1.00 | 2.00 | 3.00 | NF |
| M4086 | Diamond in the Sky–Mary Orr | 1.00 | 2.00 | 3.00 | |
| M4087 | The Warrior–Frank G. Slaughter | 1.00 | 2.00 | 3.00 | |
| M4088 | Dracula–Bram Stoker | 2.50 | 5.00 | 7.50 | HO |
| M4089 | The Guns of Navarone–Alistair MacLean | 1.00 | 2.00 | 3.00 | C |
| M4090 | The Calendar Epic–James Kubeck | 1.00 | 2.00 | 3.00 | |
| M4091 | Twilight for the Gods–Ernest K. Gann | 1.00 | 2.00 | 3.00 | |
| M4092 | Sword and Scalpel–Frank G. Slaughter | 1.00 | 2.00 | 3.00 | |
| M4093 | The Proving Flight–David Beaty | 1.00 | 2.00 | 3.00 | |
| M4094 | Star of Macedon–Karl V. Eiker | 1.00 | 2.00 | 3.00 | |
| M4095 | In the Wet–Nevil Shute | 1.00 | 2.00 | 3.00 | |
| M4096 | Murder of a Wife–Henry Kuttner | 4.50 | 9.00 | 13.50 | M |

*Perma Books M4088, Permabooks P41, Permabooks P96.*

| | | V/Good | Fine | N/Mint | |
|---|---|---|---|---|---|
| M4097 | The Midwife of Pont Clery–Flora Sandstrom | 1.00 | 2.00 | 3.00 | |
| M4098 | Till the Rafters Ring–Roswell G. Ham, Jr | 1.00 | 2.00 | 3.00 | |
| M4099 | The Tortured Path–Kendell Foster Crossen | 1.00 | 2.00 | 3.00 | |
| M4100 | The Golden Ones–C.V. Terry; 1958 | 1.50 | 3.00 | 4.50 | |
| M4101 | The Second Perma Quiz Book–Joseph Nathan Kane | 1.50 | 3.00 | 4.50 | |
| M4102 | The Mask–Stuart Cloete | 1.00 | 2.00 | 3.00 | |
| M4103 | The Royal Vultures–Hillel Black & Sam Kolman | 1.00 | 2.00 | 3.00 | |
| M4104 | The Success–Helen Howe | 1.00 | 2.00 | 3.00 | |
| M4105 | The Country Club Set–Otis Carney | 1.00 | 2.00 | 3.00 | |
| M4106 | What to Tell Your Children about Sex–Adie Suehsdorf | 1.00 | 2.00 | 3.00 | NF |
| M4107 | Doctor Pygmalion–Maxwell Maltz | 1.00 | 2.00 | 3.00 | |
| M4108 | Give Me Possession–Paul Horgan | 1.00 | 2.00 | 3.00 | |
| M4109 | Flight Hostess–Emily Thorne | .75 | 1.50 | 2.25 | |
| M4110 | Astrology and You–Carroll Righter | .75 | 1.50 | 2.25 | NF |
| M4111 | The Mapmaker–Frank G. Slaughter | .75 | 1.50 | 2.25 | |
| M4112 | No Hiding Place–Beth Day | .75 | 1.50 | 2.25 | |
| M4113 | The Questing Sword–Jefferson Cooper (Gardner F. Fox) | 3.00 | 6.00 | 9.00 | |
| M4114 | The Bixby Girls–Rosamond Marshall; 1959 | .75 | 1.50 | 2.25 | |
| M4115 | Pork Chop Hill–S.L.A. Marshall; movie tie-in | 1.50 | 3.00 | 4.50 | |
| M4116 | South by Java Head–Alistair MacLean | 1.00 | 2.00 | 3.00 | A |
| M4117 | Veronica's Veil–Jefferson Cooper (Gardner F. Fox) | 3.00 | 6.00 | 9.00 | |
| M4118 | The D. A.'s Man–Harold Danforth & James D. Horan | .75 | 1.50 | 2.25 | |
| M4119 | The Devil's Cross–Walter O'Meara | .75 | 1.50 | 2.25 | |
| M4120 | Wasp–Eric Frank Russell | .75 | 1.50 | 2.25 | SF |
| M4121 | The Forbidden Road–Victor Canning | .75 | 1.50 | 2.25 | |
| M4122 | The Counterfeit Traitor–Alexander Klein | .75 | 1.50 | 2.25 | |
| M4123 | Betty White's Teen-age Dance Book–Betty White | 1.00 | 2.00 | 3.00 | NF |
| M4124 | Imitation of Life–Fannie Hurst | .75 | 1.50 | 2.25 | |
| M4125 | 10 Days to a Successful Memory–Joyce Brothers & Edward P.F. Eagan; 1959 | .50 | 1.00 | 1.50 | NF |
| M4126 | A Family Affair–Roger Eddy | .75 | 1.50 | 2.25 | |
| M4127 | Scent of Cloves–Norah Lofts | .50 | 1.00 | 1.50 | |
| M4128 | Home from the Hill–William Humphrey | .50 | 1.00 | 1.50 | |
| M4129 | His Majesty's Highwayman–Donald Barr Chidsey | 1.50 | 3.00 | 4.50 | A |
| M4130 | Daybreak–Frank G. Slaughter | .50 | 1.00 | 1.50 | |
| M4131 | The Pocket Book of Household Hints–Holly Cantus | .50 | 1.00 | 1.50 | NF |
| M4132 | Warm Bodies–Donald R. Morris | .50 | 1.00 | 1.50 | |
| M4133 | A Man against Fate–Frank Canizio & Robert Markel | .50 | 1.00 | 1.50 | |
| M4134 | Freud: His Dream and Sex Theories–Joseph Jastrow | .50 | 1.00 | 1.50 | NF |
| M4135 | The Southern Cross–Peter French | .50 | 1.00 | 1.50 | |
| M4136 | The Fundamentals of Fishing and Hunting–Byron Dalrymple | .50 | 1.00 | 1.50 | |
| M4138 | Fun for the Family–Jerome S. Meyer | 1.00 | 2.00 | 3.00 | NF |
| M4139 | The Captives of Mora Island–Victor Canning | 1.00 | 2.00 | 3.00 | |
| M4140 | All about Men–Joseph H. Peck | .50 | 1.00 | 1.50 | |
| M4141 | The Cultured Man–Ashley Montagu | .50 | 1.00 | 1.50 | NF |
| M4142 | Top of the World–Hans Ruesch | .50 | 1.00 | 1.50 | |

| | V/Good | Fine | N/Mint |
|---|---|---|---|
| **PERMA BOOKS,** *continued* | | | |
| M4143 Abandon Ship (The Death of the USS Indianapolis)–Richard F. Newcomb | .75 | 1.50 | 2.25 NF |
| M4145 The Widow's Tale–John Coates | .50 | 1.00 | 1.50 |
| M4146 Woman Obsessed–John Mantley; movie tie-in | .75 | 1.50 | 2.25 |
| M4147 AMF Guide to Natural Bowling–Victor Kalman | .50 | 1.00 | 1.50 NF |
| M4148 A Guide to Better Living–N.H. Mayer & S.K. Mayer | .50 | 1.00 | 1.50 NF |
| M4149 Sands of Mars–Arthur C. Clarke | .75 | 1.50 | 2.25 |
| M4150 Killer's Wedge–Ed McBain; 1959 | 1.50 | 3.00 | 4.50 M |
| M4151 Tales Out of (Night) School–Hy Gardner | .50 | 1.00 | 1.50 H |
| M4152 The Savage–Noel Clad | 1.00 | 2.00 | 3.00 |
| M4153 Settlement Nurse–Rosie M. Banks | .50 | 1.00 | 1.50 R |
| M4154 Pax–Middleton Kieffer | .50 | 1.00 | 1.50 |
| M4155 Backlash–Morris L. West | .50 | 1.00 | 1.50 |
| M4156 Your Guide to a Higher Income– William Kiplinger & staff | .50 | 1.00 | 1.50 NF |
| M4158 Five Galaxy Short Novels–ed. H.L. Gold | 1.00 | 2.00 | 3.00 SF |
| M4161 Journey to the Center of the Earth– Jules Verne; movie tie-in | 2.00 | 4.00 | 6.00 SF |
| M4162 Three Minutes a Day–James Keller | .50 | 1.00 | 1.50 |
| M4165 Deadly Lady of Madagascar–C.V. Terry | 1.00 | 2.00 | 3.00 |
| M4168 Hound-dog Man–Fred Gipson; movie tie-in | 1.50 | 3.00 | 4.50 |
| M4182 Lorena–Frank G. Slaughter | .50 | 1.00 | 1.50 |
| M4185 Starfire–Robert Buckner | .50 | 1.00 | 1.50 SF |
| M4189 Adams Fall–Jason Ridgeway | .50 | 1.00 | 1.50 |
| M4197 The World That Couldn't Be–ed. H.L. Gold; 1961 | 1.00 | 2.00 | 3.00 SF |
| M4200 The Maltese Falcon–Dashiell Hammett; 1961 | 1.00 | 2.00 | 3.00 M |
| M4201 Red Harvest–Dashiell Hammett | .75 | 1.50 | 2.25 M |
| M4202 The Thin Man–Dashiell Hammett | .75 | 1.50 | 2.25 M |
| M4203 Diminishing Returns–E.L. Withers | .50 | 1.00 | 1.50 |
| M5000 Son of a Hundred Kings–Thomas B. Costain; 1955 | 1.00 | 2.00 | 3.00 A |
| M5001 A General Introduction to Psychoanalysis–Sigmund Freud | .50 | 1.00 | 1.50 NF |
| M5002 The Shorter Bartlett's Familiar Questions–John Bartlett | .50 | 1.00 | 1.50 NF |
| M5003 The Silver Chalice–Thomas B. Costain; 1956 | 1.00 | 2.00 | 3.00 A |
| M5004 Stories of the Great Operas–Milton Cross | .50 | 1.00 | 1.50 NF |
| M5005 The Story of the Bible–Hendrik Willem van Loon | .75 | 1.50 | 2.25 NF |
| M5006 A Complete Guide to Gardening– Montague Free; 1957 | .50 | 1.00 | 1.50 NF |
| M5007 The Concise Treasury of Great Poems– Louis Untermeyer; 1958 | .50 | 1.00 | 1.50 |
| M5008 When Your Child Is Ill–Samuel Karelitz | .50 | 1.00 | 1.50 NF |
| M5009 The Sexual Responsibility of Woman– Maxine Davis; 1959 | .50 | 1.00 | 1.50 |
| M5010 The Well of Loneliness–Radclyffe Hall | 1.50 | 3.00 | 4.50 |
| M5011 Only in America–Harry Golden | .50 | 1.00 | 1.50 |
| M5012 The Legal Encyclopedia for Home and Business–Samuel G. Kling | .50 | 1.00 | 1.50 NF |
| M5013 Schifferes' Family Medical Ency- clopedia–Justus J. Schifferes | .50 | 1.00 | 1.50 NF |
| M5014 The Greatest Book Ever Written–Fulton Oursler | 1.00 | 2.00 | 3.00 |
| M7500 Gone with the Wind–Margaret Mitchell; 1958 | 3.50 | 7.00 | 10.50 |

# PERMA BOOKS (Hardbound)
## Perma Books/Doubleday and Company, Inc.
### See also Perma Books (Softbound)

| | V/Good | Fine | N/Mint |
|---|---|---|---|
| P1 Best Loved Poems–ed. Richard Charlton MacKenzie | 1.00 | 2.00 | 3.00 |
| P2 How to Write Letters for All Occasions–Alexander L. Sheff & Edna Ingalls | 1.00 | 2.00 | 3.00 NF |

| | V/Good | Fine | N/Mint |
|---|---|---|---|
| P3 Best Quotations for All Occasions–ed. Lewis C. Henry | 1.00 | 2.00 | 3.00 |
| P4 Common Errors in English and How to Avoid Them–Alexander M. Witherspoon | 1.00 | 2.00 | 3.00 NF |
| P5 The Standard Bartender's Guide– Patrick Duffy | 1.00 | 2.00 | 3.00 NF |
| P6 Sex and the Love Life–William J. Fielding | 1.00 | 2.00 | 3.00 NF |
| P7 Eat and Reduce!–Victor H. Lindlahr | 1.00 | 2.00 | 3.00 |
| P8 Best Jokes for All Occasions–ed. Powers Moulton | 1.00 | 2.00 | 3.00 H |
| P9 Ida Bailey Allen's Cook Book | 1.00 | 2.00 | 3.00 NF |
| P10 The Conquest of Fear–Basil King | 1.00 | 2.00 | 3.00 |
| P11 How Shall I Tell My Child?–Belle S. Mooney | .75 | 1.50 | 2.25 |
| P12 The Male Hormone–Paul de Kruif | .75 | 1.50 | 2.25 NF |
| P13 Something to Live By–Dorothea Kopplin | .75 | 1.50 | 2.25 |
| P14 Sight without Glasses–Harold M. Peppard; 1948 | .50 | 1.00 | 1.50 NF |
| P15 Blackstone's Tricks Anyone Can Do– Harry Blackstone | 4.50 | 9.00 | 13.50 NF |
| P16 Fortune Telling for Fun and Popularity– Paul Showers | 1.50 | 3.00 | 4.50 NF |
| P17 Handy Encyclopedia of Useful Information–ed. Lewis Copeland | 1.00 | 2.00 | 3.00 NF |
| P18 Famous Sheriffs and Western Outlaws–William MacLeod Raine | 2.00 | 4.00 | 6.00 NF |
| P19 Good English Made Easy–J. Milnor Dorey | .75 | 1.50 | 2.25 NF |
| P20 Mathematics for Home and Business– William L. Schaaf, PHD | .75 | 1.50 | 2.25 NF |
| P21 Modern Sex Life–Edwin W. Hirsch | .75 | 1.50 | 2.25 NF |
| P22 Life with Mother–Clarence Day | .75 | 1.50 | 2.25 |
| P23 Strange Customs of Courtship and Marriage–William J. Fielding | .75 | 1.50 | 2.25 NF |
| P24 Brief Biographies of Famous Men and Women–W. Stuart Sewell | 1.00 | 2.00 | 3.00 NF |
| P25 Handy Legal Adviser for Home and Business–Samuel G. Kling | .50 | 1.00 | 1.50 NF |
| P26 What Your Dreams Mean–Herbert Hespro | 1.00 | 2.00 | 3.00 |
| P27 Handbook for House Repairs–Louis Gelders & Eugene O'Hare | .75 | 1.50 | 2.25 NF |
| P28 A Short History of the World–J. Milnor Dorey | .75 | 1.50 | 2.25 NF |
| P29 In His Steps–Charles M. Sheldon | .75 | 1.50 | 2.25 |
| P30 Stories for Men–Charles Grayson | 1.50 | 3.00 | 4.50 |
| P31 The Art of Enjoying Music–Sigmund Spaeth | .75 | 1.50 | 2.25 NF |
| P32 Photography As a Hobby–Fred B. Barton | .75 | 1.50 | 2.25 NF |
| P33 Winning Poker–Oswald Jacoby | .75 | 1.50 | 2.25 NF |
| P34 The Handy Book of Hobbies–Geoffrey Mott-Smith | .75 | 1.50 | 2.25 NF |
| P35 Dale Carnegie's Five Minute Biographies–Dale Carnegie | .75 | 1.50 | 2.25 NF |
| P36 Astrology for Everyone–Evangeline Adams | .75 | 1.50 | 2.25 |
| P37 Numerology–Morris C. Goodman | .75 | 1.50 | 2.25 NF |
| P38 Three Famous French Novels | .75 | 1.50 | 2.25 |
| P39 Character Reading Made Easy– Frederick Meier | .75 | 1.50 | 2.25 |
| P40 Stop Me If You've Heard This One–ed. Lew Lehr, Cal Tinney, & Roger Bower | .75 | 1.50 | 2.25 H |
| P41 Best Short Stories of Jack London | 2.00 | 4.00 | 6.00 |
| P42 The Art of Living–Norman Vincent Peale | 1.00 | 2.00 | 3.00 |
| P43 The Human Body and How It Works– Elbert Tokay, PHD | .75 | 1.50 | 2.25 NF |
| P44 A Handy Illustrated Guide to Football– ed. Sam Nisenson | .75 | 1.50 | 2.25 NF |
| P45 The Golden Book of Prayer–D.B. Aldrich | .75 | 1.50 | 2.25 |
| P46 How to Control Worry–Matthew N. Chappell | .75 | 1.50 | 2.25 |
| P47 A Handy Illustrated Guide to Basketball–ed. Sam Nisenson | .75 | 1.50 | 2.25 NF |
| P48 Better Speech for You–Daniel P. Eginton | .75 | 1.50 | 2.25 NF |
| P49 The Man Nobody Knows–Bruce Barton | 1.00 | 2.00 | 3.00 |

**PERMA BOOKS (Hardbound),** *continued*

| | V/Good | Fine | N/Mint |
|---|---|---|---|
| P50 | Psychoanalysis and Love–Andre Tridon | .75 | 1.50 | 2.25 | |
| P51 | The Key to Your Personality–Charles B. Roth | .75 | 1.50 | 2.25 | |
| P52 | A Handy Illustrated Guide to Bowling– ed. Sam Nisenson | .75 | 1.50 | 2.25 NF |
| P53 | A Handy Illustrated Guide to Boxing– ed. Sam Nisenson | .75 | 1.50 | 2.25 NF |
| P54 | Magic Explained–Walter B. Gibson | 10.00 | 20.00 | 30.00 NF |
| P55 | The Handy Book of Indoor Games– Geoffrey Mott-Smith | .75 | 1.50 | 2.25 NF |
| P57 | Understanding Human Nature–Alfred Adler | .75 | 1.50 | 2.25 |
| P58 | Bridge Quiz Book–Charles H. Goren; 1st ed. 1949 | .75 | 1.50 | 2.25 NF |
| P59 | Reading Handwriting for Fun and Popularity–Dorothy Sara | .75 | 1.50 | 2.25 NF |
| P60 | Be Glad You're Neurotic–Louis E. Bisch | .75 | 1.50 | 2.25 |
| P61 | Grammar Made Easy–Richard D. Mallery | .75 | 1.50 | 2.25 NF |
| P62 | Permabook of Art Masterpieces–Ray Brock | 1.00 | 2.00 | 3.00 NF |
| P63 | The Handy Book of Gardening–Albert E. Wilkinson & Victor A. Tiedjens | .75 | 1.50 | 2.25 NF |
| P64 | The Meaning of Psychoanalysis–Martin W. Peck | .75 | 1.50 | 2.25 NF |
| P65 | Know Your Real Abilities–C.V. & M.E. Broadley | .75 | 1.50 | 2.25 |
| P66 | Stories of Famous Operas–Harold V. Milligan | .75 | 1.50 | 2.25 |
| P67 | The Science Fiction Galaxy–Groff Conklin | 2.50 | 5.00 | 7.50 SF |
| P68 | How to Use Your Imagination to Make Money–C.B. Roth | .75 | 1.50 | 2.25 |
| P69 | Favorite Verse of Edgar A. Guest; 1950 | 1.00 | 2.00 | 3.00 |
| P70 | Perma Handy World Atlas–Geographia Map Co., Inc. | 1.00 | 2.00 | 3.00 NF |
| P71 | Goren's Canasta Up-to-Date–Charles H. Goren | .75 | 1.50 | 2.25 NF |
| P72 | Meditations and My Daily Strength– Preston Bradley | .75 | 1.50 | 2.25 |
| P73 | Personality Pointers–Jill Edwards | .75 | 1.50 | 2.25 |
| P74 | South Sea Stories–W. Somerset Maugham | 1.00 | 2.00 | 3.00 |
| P75 | Manners for Millions–Sophie C. Hadida | .75 | 1.50 | 2.25 |
| P76 | The Care and Handling of Dogs–Jack Baird | .75 | 1.50 | 2.25 NF |
| P77 | A Handy Illustrated Guide to Baseball– ed. Sam Nisenson | .75 | 1.50 | 2.25 NF |
| P78 | Buried Treasure–Ken Krippene | 1.00 | 2.00 | 3.00 NF |
| P79 | Everyday Speech–Bess Sondel | .75 | 1.50 | 2.25 NF |
| P80 | The New Standard Ready Reckoner | .75 | 1.50 | 2.25 |
| P81 | How to Read Palms–Litzka Raymond | 1.00 | 2.00 | 3.00 |
| P82 | The Perma Week-End Companion– Edwin Valentine Mitchell | .75 | 1.50 | 2.25 |
| P83 | How to Travel for Fun–Helen Eva Tates | .75 | 1.50 | 2.25 NF |
| P85 | Dictionary of First Aid for Emergencies–H. Pomeranz | .75 | 1.50 | 2.25 NF |
| P86 | The Perma Rhyming Dictionary– Langford Reed | .75 | 1.50 | 2.25 NF |
| P87 | Famous Scenes from Shakespeare–Van H. Cartmell; 1950 | 1.00 | 2.00 | 3.00 |
| P88 | Reading for Enjoyment–Donald MacCampbell | .75 | 1.50 | 2.25 NF |
| P89 | The Perma Crossword Puzzle Dictionary–Frank Eaton Newman | .75 | 1.50 | 2.25 NF |
| P90 | Essentials of Arithmetic–Henry Sticker | .50 | 1.00 | 1.50 NF |
| P91 | The Perma Treasury of Love Poems– ed. William Lord | .75 | 1.50 | 2.25 |
| P92 | Favorite Stories from the Bible–S.E. Frost, Jr | 1.00 | 2.00 | 3.00 |
| P94 | Perma Book of Ghost Stories–W. Bob Holland | 3.50 | 7.00 | 10.50 |
| P95 | Strange Tales of Famous Frauds–Henry Thomas & Dana Lee Thomas | 1.00 | 2.00 | 3.00 NF |
| P96 | Powdersmoke Justice–William Colt MacDonald | 1.50 | 3.00 | 4.50 W |
| P97 | You Can Win–Norman Vincent Peale | 1.00 | 2.00 | 3.00 |
| P99 | Married Love–Marie Stopes | .50 | 1.00 | 1.50 NF |
| P100 | Fundamentals of Contract Bridge– Charles H. Goren | .75 | 1.50 | 2.25 NF |
| P101 | Careers That Change Your World– James Keller | .50 | 1.00 | 1.50 |

## PERMA BOOKS (Softbound)
## Perma Books/Doubleday and Company, Inc.

### See also Perma Books (Hardbound)

| | V/Good | Fine | N/Mint |
|---|---|---|---|
| P5 | The Standard Bartender's Guide– Patrick Gavin Duffy; 1951 | .50 | 1.00 | 1.50 NF |
| P7 | Eat and Reduce–Victor H. Lindlahr; 1952 | .50 | 1.00 | 1.50 NF |
| P8 | Best Jokes for All Occasions–Moulton | .75 | 1.50 | 2.25 H |
| P21 | Modern Sex Life–Edwin W. Hirsch | .50 | 1.00 | 1.50 NF |
| P22 | Life with Mother–Clarence Day | .50 | 1.00 | 1.50 |
| P25 | Handy Legal Advisor for Home and Business–Samuel G. Kling; 1951 | .50 | 1.00 | 1.50 NF |
| P65 | Know Your Real Abilities–Charles V. Broadley & Margaret E. Broadley; 1953 | .50 | 1.00 | 1.50 NF |
| P89 | The Perma Cross-Word Puzzle Dictionary–Frank Eaton Newman; 1951 | .50 | 1.00 | 1.50 NF |
| P98 | New Standard Book of Model Letters for All Occasions–Leo J. Henkin; 1951 | .50 | 1.00 | 1.50 NF |
| P101 | Careers That Change Your World– James Keller | .50 | 1.00 | 1.50 |
| P105 | Three Minutes a Day–James Keller | .50 | 1.00 | 1.50 NF |
| P106 | How to Overcome Nervous Stomach Trouble–Joseph F. Montague | .50 | 1.00 | 1.50 NF |
| P107 | In a Dark Garden–Frank G. Slaughter | 1.00 | 2.00 | 3.00 |
| P108 | Unconquered–Neil H. Swanson | 1.50 | 3.00 | 4.50 |
| P109 | One Tropical Night–Vicki Baum | 1.00 | 2.00 | 3.00 |
| P110 | Bell Timson–Marguerite Steen | 1.00 | 2.00 | 3.00 |
| P111 | Castaway Island–William George Weekley | 1.50 | 3.00 | 4.50 |
| P112 | The Well of Loneliness–Radclyffe Hall | 3.00 | 6.00 | 9.00 |
| P113 | Poems for Men–Damon Runyon | 2.50 | 5.00 | 7.50 |
| P114 | The Mudlark–Theodore Bonnet | 1.00 | 2.00 | 3.00 |
| P115 | The Chain–Paul I. Wellman | 1.50 | 3.00 | 4.50 |
| P116 | Fear Is the Hunter–Hildegarde Tolman Teilhet | 1.50 | 3.00 | 4.50 |
| P117 | In the Grip of Terror–Groff Conklin | 3.50 | 7.00 | 10.50 HO |
| P118 | As Tough As They Come–ed. Will Oursler | 4.00 | 8.00 | 12.00 |
| P119 | To Hell and Back–Audie Murphy | 2.00 | 4.00 | 6.00 B |
| P120 | The Case of the Little Doctor–Hilda Lewis | 1.00 | 2.00 | 3.00 M |
| P121 | The Golden Isle–Frank G. Slaughter | 1.50 | 3.00 | 4.50 A |
| P122 | New Stories for Men–Charles Grayson | 1.50 | 3.00 | 4.50 |
| P123 | The Beautiful and the Damned–F. Scott Fitzgerald | 1.50 | 3.00 | 4.50 |
| P124 | Arrest the Saint!–Leslie Charteris | 3.00 | 6.00 | 9.00 M |
| P125 | The Salem Frigate–John Jennings; 1951 | 1.50 | 3.00 | 4.50 A |
| P126 | Spurs West!–Joseph T. Shaw | 2.00 | 4.00 | 6.00 W |
| P127 | Fair Wind to Java–Garland Roark | 1.50 | 3.00 | 4.50 |
| P128 | Night without Stars–Winston Graham | 1.50 | 3.00 | 4.50 |
| P129 | The Walls of Jericho–Paul I. Wellman | 1.50 | 3.00 | 4.50 |
| P130 | The Thorndike-Barnhart Handy Pocket Dictionary–Clarence Barnhart | 1.00 | 2.00 | 3.00 NF |
| P131 | You Can Change the World–James Keller | .75 | 1.50 | 2.25 NF |
| P132 | Chad Hanna–Walter D. Edmonds | 1.50 | 3.00 | 4.50 A |
| P133 | The Sea Eagles–John Jennings | 1.50 | 3.00 | 4.50 A |
| P134 | The Raging Tide–Ernest K. Gann | 1.50 | 3.00 | 4.50 |
| P135 | The Greatest Story Ever Told–Fulton Oursler | 1.50 | 3.00 | 4.50 |
| P136 | Quietly My Captain Waits–Evelyn Eaton | 1.50 | 3.00 | 4.50 E |
| P137 | Lusty Wind for Carolina–Inglis Fletcher | 2.00 | 4.00 | 6.00 A |
| P138 | Black Judas–Burke Wilkinson; aka Run Mongoose | 1.50 | 3.00 | 4.50 E |
| P139 | Rainbow in the Royals–Garland Roark | 1.50 | 3.00 | 4.50 E |
| P140 | Divine Mistress–Frank G. Slaughter | 1.50 | 3.00 | 4.50 A |
| P141 | Land of Vengeance–John Jennings; aka Call the New World | 1.50 | 3.00 | 4.50 |
| P142 | Angel with Spurs–Paul I. Wellman; 1952 | 1.50 | 3.00 | 4.50 W |
| P143 | Tidewater–Clifford Dowdey | 1.50 | 3.00 | 4.50 E |
| P144 | Scarlet Cockerel–Gerald Lagard | 1.50 | 3.00 | 4.50 A |
| P145 | Beyond the End of Time–Frederik Pohl | 3.00 | 6.00 | 9.00 SF |
| P146 | Tom Bone–Charles B. Judah | 1.50 | 3.00 | 4.50 E |
| P147 | The Turning Wheels–Stuart Cloete | 1.50 | 3.00 | 4.50 E |
| P148 | Guard of Honor–James Gould Cozzens | 1.50 | 3.00 | 4.50 |

**PERMA BOOKS (Softbound),** *continued*

| No. | Title | V/Good | Fine | N/Mint | |
|---|---|---|---|---|---|
| P149 | Phantom Fortress–Bruce Lancaster | 1.50 | 3.00 | 4.50 | |
| P150 | The Man with One Talent–Josiah E. Greene; 1952 | 1.50 | 3.00 | 4.50 | |
| P151 | Roanoke Hundred–Inglis Fletcher | 2.00 | 4.00 | 6.00 | A |
| P152 | The Color of Blood–E. Ralph Rundell | 1.50 | 3.00 | 4.50 | |
| P153 | Before the Sun Goes Down–Elizabeth Metzger Howard | 1.50 | 3.00 | 4.50 | |
| P154 | Gentleman's Agreement–Laura Z. Hobson | 1.50 | 3.00 | 4.50 | |
| P155 | Fort Everglades–Frank G. Slaughter | 1.50 | 3.00 | 4.50 | A |
| P156 | If a Man Be Mad–Harold Maine | 1.50 | 3.00 | 4.50 | |
| P157 | River to the West–John Jennings | 1.50 | 3.00 | 4.50 | A |
| P158S | Crusade in Europe–Dwight D. Eisenhower | 1.50 | 3.00 | 4.50 | NF |
| P159 | Bugles Blow No More–Clifford Dowdey | 1.50 | 3.00 | 4.50 | |
| P160 | The Mission of Jeffery Tomaly–Darwin L. Teilhet | 1.00 | 2.00 | 3.00 | |
| P161 | Woman in Love–Lucy Cores | 1.00 | 2.00 | 3.00 | |
| P162 | The Ironmaster–Anne Powers | 1.50 | 3.00 | 4.50 | |
| P163 | Morning Time–Charles O'Neill | 1.50 | 3.00 | 4.50 | |
| P164 | My Lord America–Alex Rackowe | 1.50 | 3.00 | 4.50 | |
| P165S | Lydia Bailey–Kenneth Roberts | 1.50 | 3.00 | 4.50 | |
| P166 | The Plymouth Adventure–Ernest Gebler | 1.50 | 3.00 | 4.50 | |
| P167 | Hear This Woman–Ann Pinchot & Ben Pinchot | 1.00 | 2.00 | 3.00 | |
| P168 | Sir Pagan–Henry John Colyton | 1.50 | 3.00 | 4.50 | A |
| P169 | Sing at My Wake–Jo Sinclair | 1.50 | 3.00 | 4.50 | |
| P170 | Be My Love–Harriet Hinsdale | 1.00 | 2.00 | 3.00 | E |
| P171 | Bennett's Welcome–Inglis Fletcher | 2.00 | 4.00 | 6.00 | A |
| P172 | Government Is Your Business–James Keller | .50 | 1.00 | 1.50 | NF |
| P173 | Rogue's Honor–Anne Powers; aka Ride East! Ride West! | 1.50 | 3.00 | 4.50 | A |
| P174 | Stronghold–Donald Barr Chidsey | 1.50 | 3.00 | 4.50 | A |
| P175 | Victory in the Dust–Arthur Phillips; 1952 | 1.50 | 3.00 | 4.50 | |
| P176 | Trumpet to Arms–Bruce Lancaster | 1.50 | 3.00 | 4.50 | |
| P177 | Modern Parables–Fulton Oursler | 1.00 | 2.00 | 3.00 | |
| P178S | Green Dolphin Street–Elizabeth Goudge | 1.00 | 2.00 | 3.00 | |
| P179 | Big Old Sun–Robert Faherty | 1.00 | 2.00 | 3.00 | |
| P180 | That None Should Die–Frank G. Slaughter | 1.00 | 2.00 | 3.00 | |
| P181 | They Had a Glory–Davenport Steward | 2.00 | 4.00 | 6.00 | A |
| P182 | King's Arrow–Joseph Patrick | 1.50 | 3.00 | 4.50 | A |
| P183 | Something to Live By–Dorothea S. Kopplin | .75 | 1.50 | 2.25 | |
| P184 | The Fundamentals of Contract Bridge–Charles H. Goren | .75 | 1.50 | 2.25 | NF |
| P185 | Journey to Nowhere–Martin Dibner; aka The Bachelor Seals | .75 | 1.50 | 2.25 | |
| P186 | Devil's Spawn–Wenzell Brown | 2.50 | 5.00 | 7.50 | A |
| P187S | Murder, Inc.–Sid Feder & Burton B. Turkus | 2.00 | 4.00 | 6.00 | NF |
| P188 | Restless Are the Sails–Evelyn Eaton | 1.50 | 3.00 | 4.50 | |
| P189 | Men of Albermarle–Inglis Fletcher | 2.00 | 4.00 | 6.00 | A |
| P190 | The Celebrity–Laura Z. Hobson | 1.00 | 2.00 | 3.00 | |
| P191 | Beau Geste–Percival C. Wren | 1.50 | 3.00 | 4.50 | A |
| P192 | Detour–Norma Ciraci | 2.00 | 4.00 | 6.00 | E |
| P193 | Silver Nutmeg–Norah Lofts; 1953 | 2.50 | 5.00 | 7.50 | E |
| P194 | Dark Memory–Jonathan Latimer | 1.50 | 3.00 | 4.50 | |
| P195 | Battle Surgeon–Frank G. Slaughter | 1.00 | 2.00 | 3.00 | C |
| P196 | The Scarlet Patch–Bruce Lancaster | 1.50 | 3.00 | 4.50 | |
| P197 | Port of Call–Maxwell Griffith | 1.50 | 3.00 | 4.50 | |
| P198 | Slant of the Wild Wind–Garland Roark | 1.50 | 3.00 | 4.50 | A |
| P199S | The Prodigal Women–Nancy Hale | 1.00 | 2.00 | 3.00 | |
| P200 | Rogue Errant–Michael Leigh; 1953 | 1.50 | 3.00 | 4.50 | A |
| P201S | The Story of the Bible–Hendrik Willem van Loon | .75 | 1.50 | 2.25 | NF |
| P202S | A General Introduction to Psychoanalysis–Sigmund Freud | .50 | 1.00 | 1.50 | NF |
| P203 | Music Out of Dixie–Harold Sinclair | 1.50 | 3.00 | 4.50 | |
| P204 | The Wire–David Walker | 1.00 | 2.00 | 3.00 | |
| P205S | The Shorter Bartlett's Familiar Quotations–John Bartlett | .75 | 1.50 | 2.25 | NF |
| P206S | The Concise Treasury of Great Poems–Louis Untermeyer | .75 | 1.50 | 2.25 | |
| P207 | Raleigh's Eden–Inglis Fletcher | 2.00 | 4.00 | 6.00 | A |
| P208 | Grand Hotel–Vicki Baum | 1.50 | 3.00 | 4.50 | |
| P209 | Word Power Made Easy–Norman Lewis | .50 | 1.00 | 1.50 | NF |
| P210 | Schnozzola–Gene Fowler | 2.00 | 4.00 | 6.00 | B |
| P211 | The Long Run–J. Bigelow Clark | 1.00 | 2.00 | 3.00 | |
| P212S | 7 Arts–ed. Fernando Puma | 1.00 | 2.00 | 3.00 | |
| P213S | New Voices: American Writing Today–Don M. Wolfe | 1.00 | 2.00 | 3.00 | |
| P214 | To Hell and Back–Audie Murphy | 1.50 | 3.00 | 4.50 | B |
| P215 | The Gladiator–Thames Williamson | 1.50 | 3.00 | 4.50 | A |
| P216 | Toil of the Brave–Inglis Fletcher | 2.00 | 4.00 | 6.00 | A |
| P217S | Show Biz–Abel Green & Joe Laurie, Jr | 1.50 | 3.00 | 4.50 | NF |
| P218 | East Side General–Frank G. Slaughter | 1.00 | 2.00 | 3.00 | |
| P219 | Venture in the East–Bruce Lancaster | 1.50 | 3.00 | 4.50 | |
| P220 | In a Dark Garden–Frank G. Slaughter | 1.00 | 2.00 | 3.00 | |
| P221 | The Golden Isle–Frank G. Slaughter | 1.00 | 2.00 | 3.00 | |
| P222 | Touched in Fire–John Tebbel | 1.50 | 3.00 | 4.50 | |
| P223 | The Bengal Tiger–Hall Hunter (Edison Marshall) | 1.50 | 3.00 | 4.50 | A |
| P224 | Summer in Rome–Paul Hyde Bonner | 1.00 | 2.00 | 3.00 | |
| P225 | Beyond the Blue Mountains–Jean Plaidy; 1953 (Victoria Holt) | 1.00 | 2.00 | 3.00 | |
| P226 | Spencer Brade, M.D.–Frank G. Slaughter | 1.00 | 2.00 | 3.00 | |
| P227 | Swing the Big-Eyed Rabbit–John Pleasant McCoy | 1.00 | 2.00 | 3.00 | E |
| P228 | Immortal Wife–Irving Stone | 1.00 | 2.00 | 3.00 | |
| P229 | Front Office–Herbert Lyons | 1.00 | 2.00 | 3.00 | |
| P230 | Indian Summer–Robert Sylvester | 1.00 | 2.00 | 3.00 | |
| P231 | The Golden Egg–James Pollak | 1.00 | 2.00 | 3.00 | |
| P232 | Beau Sabreur–Percival C. Wren | 1.50 | 3.00 | 4.50 | A |
| P233 | Divine Mistress–Frank G. Slaughter | 1.50 | 3.00 | 4.50 | |
| P234 | No Bugles Tonight–Bruce Lancaster | 1.50 | 3.00 | 4.50 | |
| P235 | Yankee Woman–Eric Baume | 1.50 | 3.00 | 4.50 | A |
| P236 | Shadow of Tomorrow–Frederik Pohl | 3.00 | 6.00 | 9.00 | SF |
| P237 | Salome, the Princess of Galilee–Henry Denker | 1.50 | 3.00 | 4.50 | A |
| 238 | Trail End–Tom J. Hopkins | 1.50 | 3.00 | 4.50 | W |
| 239 | Women in Prison–Joan Henry | 2.50 | 5.00 | 7.50 | |
| P240 | The Bowl of Brass–Paul I. Wellman | 1.50 | 3.00 | 4.50 | |
| P241 | The Road to Bithynia–Frank G. Slaughter | 1.50 | 3.00 | 4.50 | |
| P242 | The Handy Home Medical Adviser–Morris Fishbein | .75 | 1.50 | 2.25 | NF |
| P243 | Kon Tiki–Thor Heyerdahl | 1.00 | 2.00 | 3.00 | NF |
| 244 | The Tall Dolores–Michael Avallone | 2.00 | 4.00 | 6.00 | M |
| 245 | Memory of Love–Bessie Brever | 1.00 | 2.00 | 3.00 | |
| P246 | Coins in the Fountain–John H. Secondari | 1.00 | 2.00 | 3.00 | |
| P247 | My Love Must Wait–Ernestine Hill | 1.00 | 2.00 | 3.00 | |
| P248 | Panama Passage–Donald Barr Chidsey | 1.50 | 3.00 | 4.50 | |
| P249 | Big Beverage–William T. Campbell | 1.00 | 2.00 | 3.00 | |
| P250S | The Greatest Book Ever Written–Fulton Oursler; 1953 | 1.00 | 2.00 | 3.00 | |
| 251 | The Old Man's Place–John B. Sanford | 1.00 | 2.00 | 3.00 | |
| 252 | The Face in the Shadows–Peter Ordway | 1.00 | 2.00 | 3.00 | M |
| 253 | To Have and Have Not–Ernest Hemingway | 2.00 | 4.00 | 6.00 | |
| P254 | Crossroads in Time–Groff Conklin | 2.00 | 4.00 | 6.00 | SF |
| P255 | By Valour and Arms–James Street | 1.00 | 2.00 | 3.00 | |
| P256 | The Shadow and the Glory–John Jennings | 1.50 | 3.00 | 4.50 | A |
| 257 | The Secret Brand–Gene Austin | 1.00 | 2.00 | 3.00 | |
| 258 | The Assault–Allen R. Matthews | 1.00 | 2.00 | 3.00 | |
| P259 | Air Surgeon–Frank G. Slaughter | 1.00 | 2.00 | 3.00 | C |
| P260 | Thunder in the Wilderness–Harry Hamilton | 1.00 | 2.00 | 3.00 | |
| P261 | Baghdad-by-the-Bay–Herb Caen | 1.00 | 2.00 | 3.00 | |
| P262S | 7 Arts No. 2–ed. Fernando Puma; 1954 | 1.00 | 2.00 | 3.00 | |
| 263 | The Comancheros–Paul I. Wellman | 1.50 | 3.00 | 4.50 | W |
| 264 | City–Clifford D. Simak | 2.50 | 5.00 | 7.50 | SF |
| 265 | Element of Risk–Mark Derby | 1.00 | 2.00 | 3.00 | |
| P266 | Bright to the Wanderer–Bruce Lancaster | 1.00 | 2.00 | 3.00 | |
| P267 | Down and Out in Paris and London–George Orwell | 2.50 | 5.00 | 7.50 | |
| P268 | Queen's Gift–Inglis Fletcher | 2.00 | 4.00 | 6.00 | A |
| P269S | The Celluloid Jungle–Robert Carson | 1.00 | 2.00 | 3.00 | |
| 270 | Nine to Five–W.H. Prosser | 1.00 | 2.00 | 3.00 | |
| 271 | Range War–Tom J. Hopkins | 1.00 | 2.00 | 3.00 | W |
| 272 | Why I Know There Is a God–Fulton Oursler | 1.00 | 2.00 | 3.00 | |
| P273 | The Sinner of Saint Ambrose–Robert Raynolds | 1.00 | 2.00 | 3.00 | E |
| P274 | The Wreck of the Running Gale–Garland Roark | 2.00 | 4.00 | 6.00 | A |
| P275 | The White Rabbit–Bruce Marshall; 1954 | 3.50 | 7.00 | 10.50 | C |

*Permabooks P296, Permabooks P300, Permabooks 310.*

| | | V/Good | Fine | N/Mint | |
|---|---|---|---|---|---|
| **PERMA BOOKS (Softbound),** *continued* | | | | | |
| P276 | The Will to Live–Arnold A. Hutschenecker | 1.00 | 2.00 | 3.00 | |
| 277 | With Murder for Some–H.C. Huston | 1.00 | 2.00 | 3.00 | M |
| 278 | The Intruders–Robert Bright | 1.00 | 2.00 | 3.00 | |
| 279 | The Lost World–Arthur Conan Doyle | 2.00 | 4.00 | 6.00 | SF |
| P280 | Seed of Mischief–Willa Gibbs | 1.00 | 2.00 | 3.00 | |
| P281 | Killers in Africa–Alexander Lake | 1.00 | 2.00 | 3.00 | |
| P282 | The Proud Retreat–Clifford Dowdey | 1.00 | 2.00 | 3.00 | A |
| P283 | The Rifleman–John Brick | 1.00 | 2.00 | 3.00 | |
| P284S | The Silver Chalice–Thomas B. Costain | 1.00 | 2.00 | 3.00 | A |
| P285S | Gardening–Montague Free | 1.00 | 2.00 | 3.00 | NF |
| 286 | The Condemned–Jo Pagano | 1.00 | 2.00 | 3.00 | |
| 287 | The Crooked Man–Shelley Smith | 1.00 | 2.00 | 3.00 | |
| 288 | Destination Revenge–Jim Conroy | 1.00 | 2.00 | 3.00 | |
| 289 | The Spitting Image–Michael Avallone | 2.50 | 5.00 | 7.50 | |
| P290 | The Galileans–Frank G. Slaughter | 1.00 | 2.00 | 3.00 | |
| P291 | Outsiders: Children of Wonder–William Tenn | 3.00 | 6.00 | 9.00 | SF |
| P292 | Day of the Harvest–Helen Upshaw | 1.00 | 2.00 | 3.00 | |
| P293 | Gentleman Ranker–John Jennings | 1.50 | 3.00 | 4.50 | A |
| P294 | Gone with the Wind–Margaret Mitchell | 7.50 | 15.00 | 22.50 | |
| 295 | Escape the Thunder–Lonnie Coleman; c-Maguire | 1.50 | 3.00 | 4.50 | |
| P296 | Green Hills of Africa–Ernest Hemingway | 2.00 | 4.00 | 6.00 | |
| 297 | Flying Saucers from Outer Space–Donald Keyhoe | 1.00 | 2.00 | 3.00 | UF |
| P298 | The Golden Eagle–Noel B. Gerson | 1.50 | 3.00 | 4.50 | A |
| P299 | The Southpaw–Mark Harris | 1.00 | 2.00 | 3.00 | S |
| P300 | Father Divine: Holy Husband–Sara Harris; 1954 | 3.50 | 7.00 | 10.50 | B |
| P301 | The High and the Mighty–Ernest K. Gann | 1.50 | 3.00 | 4.50 | |
| P305 | The Babylonians–Nathaniel Norsen Weinreb | 1.00 | 2.00 | 3.00 | A |
| 308 | Tic-Polonga–Russ Anderton | 1.00 | 2.00 | 3.00 | |
| 310 | Against the Fall of Night–Arthur C. Clarke | 2.50 | 5.00 | 7.50 | SF |
| P311 | The Deep Six–Martin Dibner | 1.50 | 3.00 | 4.50 | |
| P313 | He Hanged Them High–Homer Croy | 1.50 | 3.00 | 4.50 | NF |

## (PETERS)
### Peters Publishing Company

| | | V/Good | Fine | N/Mint | |
|---|---|---|---|---|---|
| 4 | Danger Today–Willis Striker; 1952. Note: It is strongly suspected that this book corresponds to missing Wide World entry. | 1.50 | 3.00 | 4.50 | NF |

## PHANTOM BOOKS
### Hanro Corporation
#### Digest Size

| | | V/Good | Fine | N/Mint | |
|---|---|---|---|---|---|
| 500 | Homicide Hotel–Joe Barry; orig. 1951 | 6.00 | 12.00 | 18.00 | M |
| 501 | Kisses Can Kill–Donnell Carey; orig. 1951 | 5.00 | 10.00 | 15.00 | M |

| | | V/Good | Fine | N/Mint | |
|---|---|---|---|---|---|
| 502 | The Deadly Lover–Robert O. Saber; orig. 1951. Note: Same cover as an unnumbered Exotic Novel | 5.00 | 10.00 | 15.00 | M |
| 503 | Married to Murder–Harry Whittington; orig. 1951 | 5.00 | 10.00 | 15.00 | M |
| 504 | Love Me and Die!–Day Keene; orig. 1951 | 6.00 | 12.00 | 18.00 | M |
| 505 | Satan's Widow–Harry Whittington; orig. 1952 | 5.00 | 10.00 | 15.00 | M |
| 506 | Crime on My Hands–Carl G. Hoges; orig. 1952 c-Gross. Note: Same cover as Harlequin No. 182 | 6.00 | 12.00 | 18.00 | M |
| 507 | Hunt the Killer–Day Keene; orig. 1951 | 6.00 | 12.00 | 18.00 | M |
| 508 | Swamp Kill–Whit Harrison (Harry Whittington); orig. 1952 | 5.00 | 10.00 | 15.00 | M |
| 509 | Naked Fury–Day Keene; orig. 1952 | 6.00 | 12.00 | 18.00 | M |
| 510 | Murder Doll–Robert O. Saber; orig. 1952 | 5.00 | 10.00 | 15.00 | M |
| 511 | Violent Night–Whit Harrison (Harry Whittington); orig. 1952 | 5.00 | 10.00 | 15.00 | M |
| 512 | No Way Out–Robert O. Saber; orig. 1952 | 5.00 | 10.00 | 15.00 | M |
| 513 | Wake Up to Murder–Day Keene; orig. 1952 | 3.50 | 7.00 | 10.50 | M |

## PHANTOM MYSTERY
### Unknown Publisher

| | | | | | |
|---|---|---|---|---|---|
| 1 | Rocket to the Morgue–H.H. Holmes (Anthony Boucher); 1st ed. 1942 | 25.00 | 50.00 | 75.00 | M |

## PHOENIX
### Phoenix Books

| | | | | | |
|---|---|---|---|---|---|
| nn | Tokyo Escapade–Shel Walker; orig. 1955 | 20.00 | 40.00 | 60.00 | M |

## PITMAN EDITION
### Pitman Publishing Corporation

| | | | | | |
|---|---|---|---|---|---|
| nn | Franklin Delano Roosevelt: A Memorial–ed. Donald Porter Geddes. Note: Variant edition of Pocket Book No. 300 | .75 | 1.50 | 2.25 | B |

## POCKET BOOK
### Pocket Books, Inc.

| | | | | | |
|---|---|---|---|---|---|
| nn | The Good Earth–Pearl S. Buck; 1938; introductory book of series | 50.00 | 100.00 | 150.00 | |
| 1 | Lost Horizon–James Hilton; 1939 | 37.50 | 75.00 | 112.50 | |
| 2 | Wake Up and Live–Dorothea Brande | 12.50 | 25.00 | 37.50 | NF |
| 3 | Five Great Tragedies–William Shakespeare | 15.00 | 30.00 | 45.00 | |
| 4 | Topper–Thorne Smith | 25.00 | 50.00 | 75.00 | H |
| 5 | The Murder of Roger Ackroyd–Agatha Christie | 30.00 | 60.00 | 90.00 | M |
| 6 | Enough Rope–Dorothy Parker | 15.00 | 30.00 | 45.00 | |
| 7 | Wuthering Heights–Emily Bronte | 15.00 | 30.00 | 45.00 | |
| 8 | The Way of All Flesh–Samuel Butler | 15.00 | 30.00 | 45.00 | |
| 9 | The Bridge of San Luis Rey–Thornton Wilder | 12.50 | 25.00 | 37.50 | |
| 10 | Bambi–Felix Salten | 15.00 | 30.00 | 45.00 | |
| 11 | The Good Earth–Pearl S. Buck | 5.00 | 10.00 | 15.00 | |
| 12 | Great Short Stories–Guy de Maupassant | 3.50 | 7.00 | 10.50 | |
| 13 | Show Boat–Edna Ferber | 3.50 | 7.00 | 10.50 | |
| 14 | A Tale of Two Cities–Charles Dickens | 3.50 | 7.00 | 10.50 | |
| 15 | The Story of Mankind–Hendrik Willem Van Loon | 2.50 | 5.00 | 7.50 | NF |
| 16 | Green Mansions–W.H. Hudson | 6.00 | 12.00 | 18.00 | |
| 17 | The Chinese Orange Mystery–Ellery Queen | 3.50 | 7.00 | 10.50 | M |
| 18 | Pinocchio–Carlo Collodi | 4.50 | 9.00 | 13.50 | |

*Pocket Book 18, Pocket Book 35, Pocket Book 54.*

|  |  | V/Good | Fine | N/Mint |  |
|---|---|---|---|---|---|
| **POCKET BOOK,** *continued* |  |  |  |  |  |
| 19 | Abraham Lincoln–Lord Charnwood | 3.50 | 7.00 | 10.50 | NF |
| 20 | The Return of the Native–Thomas Hardy | 3.50 | 7.00 | 10.50 |  |
| 21 | Murder Must Advertise–Dorothy L. Sayers | 4.50 | 9.00 | 13.50 | M |
| 22 | The Swiss Family Robinson–Johann Wyss | 5.00 | 10.00 | 15.00 | A |
| 23 | The Autobiography of Benjamin Franklin–B. Franklin | 2.50 | 5.00 | 7.50 | NF |
| 24 | The Corpse with the Floating Foot–R.A.J. Walling | 3.50 | 7.00 | 10.50 | M |
| 25 | Treasure Island–Robert Louis Stevenson; 1939 | 4.50 | 9.00 | 13.50 | A |
| 26 | Elizabeth and Essex–Lytton Strachey | 2.50 | 5.00 | 7.50 |  |
| 27 | Appointment in Samarra–John O'Hara | 3.50 | 7.00 | 10.50 |  |
| 28 | Jeeves–P.G. Wodehouse | 3.50 | 7.00 | 10.50 |  |
| 29 | A Christmas Carol–Charles Dickens | 5.00 | 10.00 | 15.00 |  |
| 30 | The Little French Girl–Anne Douglas Sedgwick | 3.50 | 7.00 | 10.50 |  |
| 31 | The Hunchback of Notre Dame–Volume I–Victor Hugo | 4.50 | 9.00 | 13.50 | A |
| 32 | The Hunchback of Notre Dame–Volume II–Victor Hugo | 4.50 | 9.00 | 13.50 | A |
| 33 | The Watchman's Clock–Leslie Ford | 3.50 | 7.00 | 10.50 | M |
| 34 | Gulliver's Travels–Jonathan Swift; 1940; movie tie-in | 6.00 | 12.00 | 18.00 | A |
| 35 | Beau Geste–Percival C. Wren | 4.50 | 9.00 | 13.50 | A |
| 36 | The Three Musketeers–Volume I–Alexandre Dumas | 4.50 | 9.00 | 13.50 | A |
| 37 | The Three Musketeers–Volume II–Alexandre Dumas | 4.50 | 9.00 | 13.50 | A |
| 38 | The Mystery of the Blue Train–Agatha Christie | 4.50 | 9.00 | 13.50 | M |
| 39 | Great Tales and Poems–Edgar Allan Poe | 4.50 | 9.00 | 13.50 |  |
| 40 | The Man Nobody Knows–Bruce Barton | 3.50 | 7.00 | 10.50 |  |
| 41 | The Constant Nymph–Margaret Kennedy | 3.50 | 7.00 | 10.50 |  |
| 42 | Autobiography of Benvenuto Cellini–B. Cellini | 3.50 | 7.00 | 10.50 | NF |
| 43 | The Lodger–Marie Belloc Lowndes | 3.50 | 7.00 | 10.50 |  |
| 44 | Mother–Kathleen Norris | 3.50 | 7.00 | 10.50 |  |
| 45 | The Light That Failed–Rudyard Kipling | 3.50 | 7.00 | 10.50 |  |
| 46 | The Bowstring Murders–Carter Dickson | 4.50 | 9.00 | 13.50 | M |
| 47 | Bring 'Em Back Alive–Edward Anthony & Frank Buck | 2.50 | 5.00 | 7.50 | A |
| 48 | Scarlet Sister Mary–Julia Peterkin | 3.50 | 7.00 | 10.50 |  |
| 49 | Dr. Ehrlich's Magic Bullet–Paul deKruif (later editions retitled Microbe Hunters); movie tie-in | 2.50 | 5.00 | 7.50 | NF |
| 50 | The House without a Key–Earl Derr Biggers; 1940 | 4.50 | 9.00 | 13.50 | M |
| 51 | Thunder on the Left–Christopher Morley | 3.50 | 7.00 | 10.50 |  |
| 52 | The House of the Seven Gables–Nathaniel Hawthorne | 3.50 | 7.00 | 10.50 |  |
| 53 | The Best of Damon Runyon–Damon Runyon | 3.50 | 7.00 | 10.50 |  |
| 54 | The Great Prince Shan–E. Phillips Oppenheim | 3.00 | 6.00 | 9.00 |  |
| 55 | Our Town–Thornton Wilder; movie tie-in | 3.50 | 7.00 | 10.50 |  |

|  |  | V/Good | Fine | N/Mint |  |
|---|---|---|---|---|---|
| 56 | The Green Bay Tree–Louis Bromfield | 2.50 | 5.00 | 7.50 |  |
| 57 | After Such Pleasures–Dorothy Parker | 2.50 | 5.00 | 7.50 |  |
| 58 | Tom Brown's School Days–Thomas Hughes | 3.50 | 7.00 | 10.50 |  |
| 59 | Think Fast, Mr. Moto–John P. Marquand | 4.50 | 9.00 | 13.50 | M |
| 60 | The Scandal of Father Brown–G.K. Chesterton | 4.50 | 9.00 | 13.50 | M |
| 61 | Bob, Son of Battle–Alfred Ollivant | 4.50 | 9.00 | 13.50 | A |
| 62 | The Pocket Book of Verse–M.E. Speare | 2.50 | 5.00 | 7.50 |  |
| 63 | Pride and Prejudice–Jane Austin | 2.50 | 5.00 | 7.50 |  |
| 64 | While the Patient Slept–Mignon G. Eberhart | 2.50 | 5.00 | 7.50 | M |
| 65 | The Four Million–O. Henry | 2.50 | 5.00 | 7.50 |  |
| 66 | National Velvet–Enid Bagnold | 6.00 | 12.00 | 18.00 |  |
| 67 | Heidi–Johanna Spyri | 4.50 | 9.00 | 13.50 |  |
| 68 | How to Win Friends and Influence People–Dale Carnegie | 2.00 | 4.00 | 6.00 | NF |
| 69 | The Thirty-nine Steps–John Buchan | 3.50 | 7.00 | 10.50 |  |
| 70 | The Mystery of the Dead Police–Philip MacDonald | 3.50 | 7.00 | 10.50 | M |
| 71 | The French Powder Mystery–Ellery Queen | 3.50 | 7.00 | 10.50 | M |
| 72 | Anne of Windy Poplars–L.M. Montgomery | 2.50 | 5.00 | 7.50 |  |
| 73 | The Case of the Velvet Claws–Erle Stanley Gardner | 7.50 | 15.00 | 22.50 | M |
| 74 | The Unpleasantness at the Bellona Club–Dorothy L. Sayers | 3.50 | 7.00 | 10.50 | M |
| 75 | Little Men–Louisa May Alcott; 1940 | 6.00 | 12.00 | 18.00 |  |
| 76 | Sunset Gun–Dorothy Parker | 3.50 | 7.00 | 10.50 |  |
| 77 | The Roman Hat Mystery–Ellery Queen | 2.50 | 5.00 | 7.50 | M |
| 78 | Oh, You Tex!–William MacLeod Raine | 3.50 | 7.00 | 10.50 | W |
| 79 | Murder in the Calais Coach–Agatha Christie | 3.50 | 7.00 | 10.50 | M |
| 80 | Up from Slavery–Booker T. Washington | 3.50 | 7.00 | 10.50 |  |
| 81 | The Red House Mystery–A.A. Milne | 3.00 | 6.00 | 9.00 | M |
| 82 | Captain Blood–Rafael Sabatini | 3.50 | 7.00 | 10.50 | A |
| 83 | A Puzzle for Fools–Patrick Quentin | 3.50 | 7.00 | 10.50 | M |
| 84 | The Riddle of the Sands–Erskine Childers | 2.50 | 5.00 | 7.50 |  |
| 85 | Clouds of Witness–Dorothy L. Sayers | 3.50 | 7.00 | 10.50 | M |
| 86 | The Red Widow Murders–Carter Dickson | 3.50 | 7.00 | 10.50 | M |
| 87 | Mister Glencannon–Guy Gilpatric; 1941 | 2.50 | 5.00 | 7.50 |  |
| 88 | The ABC Murders–Agatha Christie | 2.50 | 5.00 | 7.50 | M |
| 89 | And Now Good-bye–James Hilton | 2.50 | 5.00 | 7.50 |  |
| 90 | The Case of the Sulky Girl–Erle Stanley Gardner | 2.50 | 5.00 | 7.50 | M |
| 91 | The Pocket Book of Short Stories–M.E. Speare | 2.50 | 5.00 | 7.50 |  |
| 92 | The Pocket Bible | 3.50 | 7.00 | 10.50 |  |
| 93 | Goodbye, Mr. Chips–James Hilton | 2.50 | 5.00 | 7.50 |  |
| 94 | Greenmantle–John Buchan | 2.50 | 5.00 | 7.50 |  |
| 95 | The Sherlock Holmes Pocket Book–Arthur Conan Doyle | 6.00 | 12.00 | 18.00 | M |
| 96 | Believe It or Not–Robert Ripley | 4.00 | 8.00 | 12.00 | NF |
| 97 | The Werewolf of Paris–Guy Endore | 15.00 | 30.00 | 45.00 | HO |
| 98 | The Circular Staircase–Mary Roberts Rinehart | 2.50 | 5.00 | 7.50 | M |
| 99 | The Adventures of Ellery Queen–Ellery Queen. Note: Queen's Quorum No. 88 | 3.50 | 7.00 | 10.50 | M |

*Pocket Book 66, Pocket Book 82, Pocket Book 97.*

POCKET BOOK, *continued*

| # | Title | V/Good | Fine | N/Mint | |
|---|---|---|---|---|---|
| 100 | The General Died at Dawn–Charles G. Booth; 1941 | 3.50 | 7.00 | 10.50 | |
| 101 | It Walks by Night–John Dickson Carr | 6.00 | 12.00 | 18.00 | M |
| 102 | The Philadelphia Story–Philip Barry; movie tie-in | 4.00 | 8.00 | 12.00 | |
| 103 | The Pocket Book of Great Detectives–ed. Lee Wright | 4.50 | 9.00 | 13.50 | M |
| 104 | Nana–Emile Zola | 3.00 | 6.00 | 9.00 | E |
| 105 | Sir John Magill's Last Journey–Freeman Wills Crofts | 4.50 | 9.00 | 13.50 | M |
| 106 | The Case of the Lucky Legs–Erle Stanley Gardner | 2.50 | 5.00 | 7.50 | M |
| 107 | The Pocket Book of Etiquette–Margery Wilson | 2.50 | 5.00 | 7.50 | NF |
| 108 | The Pocket Reader–ed. Philip Van Doren Stern | 2.50 | 5.00 | 7.50 | |
| 109 | The Siamese Twin Mystery–Ellery Queen | 3.50 | 7.00 | 10.50 | M |
| 110 | The Pocket Book of Boners; interior illus. by Dr. Suess | 3.00 | 6.00 | 9.00 | H |
| 111 | Mr. Pinkerton Finds a Body–David Frome | 3.00 | 6.00 | 9.00 | M |
| 112 | Fer-de-Lance–Rex Stout | 3.50 | 7.00 | 10.50 | M |
| 113 | Enter a Murderer–Ngaio Marsh | 3.50 | 7.00 | 10.50 | M |
| 114 | Five Great Comedies–William Shakespeare | 2.00 | 4.00 | 6.00 | |
| 115 | Dodsworth–Sinclair Lewis | 2.50 | 5.00 | 7.50 | |
| 116 | The Case of the Howling Dog–Erle Stanley Gardner | 2.50 | 5.00 | 7.50 | M |
| 117 | The Pocket Book of Mystery Stories–ed. Lee Wright | 3.50 | 7.00 | 10.50 | M |
| 118 | We Are Not Alone–James Hilton | 2.50 | 5.00 | 7.50 | |
| 119 | The Pocket History of the World–H.G. Wells | 2.50 | 5.00 | 7.50 | NF |
| 120 | Life Begins at Forty–Walter B. Pitkin | 2.50 | 5.00 | 7.50 | |
| 121 | The Album–Mary Roberts Rinehart | 2.50 | 5.00 | 7.50 | M |
| 122 | The Simple Way of Poison–Leslie Ford | 3.50 | 7.00 | 10.50 | M |
| 123 | Dr. Jekyll and Mr. Hyde–Robert Louis Stevenson; movie tie-in | 6.00 | 12.00 | 18.00 | SF |
| 124 | Mr. Pinkerton Goes to Scotland Yard–David Frome | 3.00 | 6.00 | 9.00 | M |
| 125 | The Tragedy of X–Ellery Queen; 1941 | 2.50 | 5.00 | 7.50 | M |
| 126 | Pocket Self-Pronouncing Dictionary and Vocabulary Builder–William J. Pelo | 2.50 | 5.00 | 7.50 | NF |
| 127 | The Pocket Book of the War–Quincy Howe | 2.50 | 5.00 | 7.50 | NF |
| 128 | The Rubaiyat of Omar Khayyam–Omar Khayyam | 2.50 | 5.00 | 7.50 | |
| 129 | The Singapore Exile Murders–F. van Wyck Mason | 2.50 | 5.00 | 7.50 | M |
| 130 | Strong Poison–Dorothy L. Sayers | 3.50 | 7.00 | 10.50 | M |
| 131 | While Rome Burns–Alexander Woollcott | 2.50 | 5.00 | 7.50 | |
| 132 | The Pocket Quiz Book–Louise Crittenden & Rosejeanne Slifer | 2.50 | 5.00 | 7.50 | NF |
| 133 | The Black Camel–Earl Derr Biggers | 4.50 | 9.00 | 13.50 | M |
| 134 | The New Adventures of Ellery Queen–Ellery Queen | 3.50 | 7.00 | 10.50 | M |
| 135 | Long Remember–MacKinlay Kantor | 2.00 | 4.00 | 6.00 | |
| 136 | Without Armor–James Hilton; 1942 | 2.00 | 4.00 | 6.00 | |
| 137 | Death in a White Tie–Ngaio Marsh | 2.50 | 5.00 | 7.50 | M |
| 138 | The Case of the Caretaker's Cat–Erle Stanley Gardner | 2.50 | 5.00 | 7.50 | M |
| 139 | You Can't Do Business with Hitler–Douglas Miller | 2.50 | 5.00 | 7.50 | NF |
| 140 | The Door–Mary Roberts Rinehart | 2.50 | 5.00 | 7.50 | M |
| 141 | The Saint-Fiacre Affair–Georges Simenon | 3.00 | 6.00 | 9.00 | M |
| 142 | The Pocket Companion–ed. Philip Van Doren Stern | 2.00 | 4.00 | 6.00 | |
| 143 | The Man Who Came to Dinner–Moss Hart & George S. Kaufman; movie tie-in | 2.00 | 4.00 | 6.00 | |
| 144 | Singing Guns–Max Brand | 2.50 | 5.00 | 7.50 | W |
| 145 | The Pocket Book of Modern American Plays–ed. Bennett Cerf | 2.50 | 5.00 | 7.50 | |
| 146 | The Spanish Cape Mystery–Ellery Queen | 3.00 | 6.00 | 9.00 | M |
| 147 | The Royal Road to Romance–Richard Halliburton | 3.00 | 6.00 | 9.00 | |
| 148 | The Pocket Book of Vegetable Gardening–Charles Nissley | 2.50 | 5.00 | 7.50 | NF |
| 149 | Escape–Ethel Vance | 2.00 | 4.00 | 6.00 | |
| 150 | The Office Wife–Faith Baldwin; 1942 | 2.50 | 5.00 | 7.50 | R |
| 151 | Hugger-Mugger in the Louvre–Elliot Paul | 3.50 | 7.00 | 10.50 | M |
| 152 | The Balcony–Dorothy Cameron Disney | 2.50 | 5.00 | 7.50 | M |
| 153 | The Man from Scotland Yard–David Frome | 3.50 | 7.00 | 10.50 | M |
| 154 | The Red Badge of Courage–Stephen Crane | 3.50 | 7.00 | 10.50 | |
| 155 | Hunger Fighters–Paul de Kruif | 1.50 | 3.00 | 4.50 | NF |
| 156 | The White Priory Murders–Carter Dickson | 3.00 | 6.00 | 9.00 | M |
| 157 | The Case of the Counterfeit Eye–Erle Stanley Gardner | 2.50 | 5.00 | 7.50 | M |
| 158 | Damon Runyon Favorites–Damon Runyon. Note: Two cover variants exist for first printing. | 2.50 | 5.00 | 7.50 | |
| 159 | Mrs. Miniver–Jan Struther | 2.00 | 4.00 | 6.00 | |
| 160 | The Art of Thinking–Ernest Dimnet | 2.50 | 5.00 | 7.50 | NF |
| 161 | The Spirit of the Border–Zane Grey | 3.50 | 7.00 | 10.50 | W |
| 162 | Arrowsmith–Sinclair Lewis | 2.50 | 5.00 | 7.50 | |
| 163 | Have His Carcase–Dorothy L. Sayers | 2.50 | 5.00 | 7.50 | M |
| 164 | A Puzzle for Players–Patrick Quentin | 3.00 | 6.00 | 9.00 | M |
| 165 | The Pocket Entertainer–Shirley Cunningham | 2.00 | 4.00 | 6.00 | NF |
| 166 | The Norths Meet Murder–Richard Lockridge & Frances Lockridge | 3.00 | 6.00 | 9.00 | M |
| 167 | Peril at End House–Agatha Christie | 3.00 | 6.00 | 9.00 | M |
| 168 | The Chinese Parrot–Earl Derr Biggers | 3.50 | 7.00 | 10.50 | M |
| 169 | The Nutmeg Tree–Margery Sharp; movie tie-in | 2.00 | 4.00 | 6.00 | |
| 170 | Defense Will Not Win the War–W.F. Kernan | 1.50 | 3.00 | 4.50 | NF |
| 171 | The Cape Cod Mystery–Phoebe Atwood Taylor | 2.50 | 5.00 | 7.50 | M |
| 172 | The Pocket Mystery Reader–ed. Lee Wright | 3.00 | 6.00 | 9.00 | M |
| 173 | The Strategy of Terror–Edmond Taylor | 3.00 | 6.00 | 9.00 | NF |
| 174 | Beat to Quarters–C.S. Forester | 2.50 | 5.00 | 7.50 | |
| 175 | Green Light–Lloyd C. Douglas; 1942 | 2.00 | 4.00 | 6.00 | |
| 176 | The Pocket Book of Quotations–ed. Henry Davidoff | 2.00 | 4.00 | 6.00 | NF |
| 177 | The Case of the Curious Bride–Erle Stanley Gardner | 2.50 | 5.00 | 7.50 | M |
| 178 | I Saw It Happen–Lewis Gannett | 2.50 | 5.00 | 7.50 | |
| 179 | The Greek Coffin Mystery–Ellery Queen | 2.50 | 5.00 | 7.50 | M |
| 180 | The Peacock Feather Murders–Carter Dickson | 3.00 | 6.00 | 9.00 | M |
| 181 | The Pocket Cook Book–Elizabeth Woody | 3.00 | 6.00 | 9.00 | NF |
| 182 | The Pocket Book of America–ed. Philip Van Doren Stern | 2.50 | 5.00 | 7.50 | |
| 183 | The Return to Religion–Henry C. Link | 2.00 | 4.00 | 6.00 | |
| 184 | A Silent Witness–R. Austin Freeman | 3.00 | 6.00 | 9.00 | M |
| 185 | The Nine Tailors–Dorothy L. Sayers | 3.00 | 6.00 | 9.00 | M |
| 186 | Above Suspicion–Helen MacInnes | 2.50 | 5.00 | 7.50 | |
| 187 | The Pocket Book of Dog Stories–ed. Harold Berman | 3.00 | 6.00 | 9.00 | |
| 188 | The Hurricane–James Norman Hall & Charles Nordhoff | 2.50 | 5.00 | 7.50 | A |
| 189 | My Sister Eileen–Ruth McKenney | 2.00 | 4.00 | 6.00 | |
| 190 | The Best of Mr. Fortune Stories–H.C. Bailey | 4.50 | 9.00 | 13.50 | M |
| 191 | Behind That Curtain–Earl Derr Biggers | 3.00 | 6.00 | 9.00 | M |
| 192 | Prelude to Victory–James B. Reston | 2.00 | 4.00 | 6.00 | |
| 193 | Journey Into Fear–Eric Ambler | 2.00 | 4.00 | 6.00 | |
| 194 | The Coming Battle of Germany–William B. Ziff | 2.50 | 5.00 | 7.50 | NF |
| 195 | The Pocket History of the United States–Henry Steele Commager & Alan Nevius | 2.00 | 4.00 | 6.00 | NF |
| 196 | The Thin Man–Dashiell Hammett; 1943 | 7.50 | 15.00 | 22.50 | M |
| 197 | The Pocket Book of War Humor–ed. Bennett Cerf | 2.50 | 5.00 | 7.50 | H |
| 198 | The Human Body–Logan Glendening | 2.00 | 4.00 | 6.00 | NF |
| 199 | Arsenic and Old Lace–Joseph Kesselring | 2.50 | 5.00 | 7.50 | H |
| 200 | The Pocket Book of Flower Gardening–Montague Free; 1943 | 2.00 | 4.00 | 6.00 | NF |
| 201 | The Case of the Stuttering Bishop–Erle Stanley Gardner | 2.00 | 4.00 | 6.00 | M |
| 202 | The Dutch Shoe Mystery–Ellery Queen | 2.00 | 4.00 | 6.00 | M |
| 203 | Mission to Moscow–Joseph E. Davies | 1.50 | 3.00 | 4.50 | NF |
| 204 | Death Lights a Candle–Phoebe Atwood Taylor | 2.50 | 5.00 | 7.50 | M |

POCKET BOOK, *continued*

| No. | Title | V/Good | Fine | N/Mint | |
|-----|-------|--------|------|--------|---|
| 205 | Rebecca–Daphne du Maurier | 2.00 | 4.00 | 6.00 | |
| 206 | See Here, Private Hargrove–Marion Hargrove | 1.00 | 2.00 | 3.00 | H |
| 207 | Charlie Chan Carries On–Earl Derr Biggers | 3.50 | 7.00 | 10.50 | M |
| 208 | The Rubber Band–Rex Stout | 3.50 | 7.00 | 10.50 | M |
| 209 | Topper Takes a Trip–Thorne Smith | 3.50 | 7.00 | 10.50 | H |
| 210 | The Pocket Book of Crossword Puzzles–Margaret Petherbridge | 10.00 | 20.00 | 30.00 | NF |
| 211 | The Glass Key–Dashiell Hammett; 1942 | 6.00 | 12.00 | 18.00 | M |
| 212 | Farewell My Lovely–Raymond Chandler | 7.50 | 15.00 | 22.50 | M |
| 213 | The Pocket Book of True Crime Stories–ed. Anthony Boucher; 1943 | 4.50 | 9.00 | 13.50 | NF |
| 214 | The Pocket Book of Science Fiction–ed. Donald A. Wollheim | 9.00 | 18.00 | 27.00 | SF |
| 215 | Magnificent Obsession–Lloyd C. Douglas | 1.50 | 3.00 | 4.50 | |
| 216 | Mutiny on the Bounty–James Norman Hall & Charles Nordhoff | 2.50 | 5.00 | 7.50 | A |
| 217 | The Pocket Book of Home Canning–Elizabeth Beveridge | 2.00 | 4.00 | 6.00 | NF |
| 218 | Claudia–Rose Franken | 2.00 | 4.00 | 6.00 | |
| 219 | The Punch and Judy Murders–Carter Dickson | 3.50 | 7.00 | 10.50 | M |
| 220 | What to Do Till the Doctor Comes–Donald Armstrong & Grace T. Hallock | 2.00 | 4.00 | 6.00 | NF |
| 221 | Overture to Death–Ngaio Marsh | 3.00 | 6.00 | 9.00 | M |
| 222 | Fast Company–Marco Page | 2.00 | 4.00 | 6.00 | M |
| 223 | The Case of the Lame Canary–Erle Stanley Gardner | 2.00 | 4.00 | 6.00 | M |
| 224 | The Great Impersonation–E. Phillips Oppenheim | 1.50 | 3.00 | 4.50 | |
| 225 | Into the Valley–John Hersey; 1943 | 1.50 | 3.00 | 4.50 | |
| 226 | The House of Exile–Nora Wain | 2.00 | 4.00 | 6.00 | |
| 227 | The Egyptian Cross Mystery–Ellery Queen | 2.50 | 5.00 | 7.50 | M |
| 228 | The Bigger They Come–A.A. Fair | 2.00 | 4.00 | 6.00 | M |
| 229 | One World–Wendell L. Willkie | 1.50 | 3.00 | 4.50 | |
| 230 | The Pocket Aviation Quiz Book–Milton Figen | 2.50 | 5.00 | 7.50 | NF |
| 231 | The Judas Window–Carter Dickson | 3.50 | 7.00 | 10.50 | M |
| 232 | A Coffin for Dimitrios–Eric Ambler | 2.00 | 4.00 | 6.00 | M |
| 233 | The Pocket Book of Cartoons–ed. Bennett Cerf | 2.50 | 5.00 | 7.50 | H |
| 234 | Vogue's Pocket Book of Home Dressmaking | 2.00 | 4.00 | 6.00 | NF |
| 235 | Assignment in Brittany–Helen MacInnes | 2.00 | 4.00 | 6.00 | |
| 236 | The Pocket Book of Father Brown–G.K. Chesterton | 4.00 | 8.00 | 12.00 | M |
| 237 | Trial by Fury–Craig Rice | 2.00 | 4.00 | 6.00 | M |
| 238 | The Pocket Book of Modern American Short Stories–ed. Philip Van Doren Stern | 1.50 | 3.00 | 4.50 | |
| 239 | How to Play Winning Checkers–Millard Hopper | 3.00 | 6.00 | 9.00 | NF |
| 240 | Madame Bovary–Gustave Flaubert; 1943 | 1.50 | 3.00 | 4.50 | |
| 241 | Red Harvest–Dashiell Hammett | 6.00 | 12.00 | 18.00 | M |
| 242 | The Case of the Substitute Face–Erle Stanley Gardner | 2.00 | 4.00 | 6.00 | M |
| 243 | The Steinbeck Pocket Book–John Steinbeck | 3.50 | 7.00 | 10.50 | |
| 244 | U.S. Foreign Policy–Walter Lippmann; 1944 | 1.50 | 3.00 | 4.50 | NF |
| 245 | The Four of Hearts–Ellery Queen | 2.50 | 5.00 | 7.50 | M |
| 246 | The Lady in the Morgue–Jonathan Latimer | 3.00 | 6.00 | 9.00 | M |
| 247 | No Surrender–Martha Albrand | 2.00 | 4.00 | 6.00 | |
| 248 | The Canary Murder Case–S.S. Van Dine | 2.00 | 4.00 | 6.00 | M |
| 249 | The Patriotic Murders–Agatha Christie | 2.50 | 5.00 | 7.50 | M |
| 250 | Destry Rides Again–Max Brand; 1944 | 2.00 | 4.00 | 6.00 | W |
| 251 | The Ogden Nash Pocket Book–Ogden Nash | 1.50 | 3.00 | 4.50 | |
| 252 | The Case of the Dangerous Dowager–Erle Stanley Gardner | 2.00 | 4.00 | 6.00 | M |
| 253 | Phantom Lady–William Irish | 3.00 | 6.00 | 9.00 | M |
| 254 | The New Testament | 2.50 | 5.00 | 7.50 | |
| 255 | The New Pocket Quiz Book–Louise Crittenden & Rosejeanne Slifer | 2.00 | 4.00 | 6.00 | NF |

| No. | Title | V/Good | Fine | N/Mint | |
|-----|-------|--------|------|--------|---|
| 256 | The Greene Murder Case–S.S. Van Dine | 2.00 | 4.00 | 6.00 | M |
| 257 | Enter the Saint–Leslie Charteris | 2.50 | 5.00 | 7.50 | M |
| 258 | The Late George Apley–John P. Marquand | 2.00 | 4.00 | 6.00 | |
| 259 | Halfway House–Ellery Queen. Note: 1st printing published in unique oblong format, with binding along top | 7.50 | 15.00 | 22.50 | M |
| 260 | The Pocket Book of Games–Albert H. Morehead | 2.50 | 5.00 | 7.50 | NF |
| 261 | And Then There Were None–Agatha Christie | 2.50 | 5.00 | 7.50 | M |
| 262 | The Somerset Maugham Pocket Book–W.S. Maugham | 2.50 | 5.00 | 7.50 | |
| 263 | The D.A. Calls It Murder–Erle Stanley Gardner | 2.00 | 4.00 | 6.00 | M |
| 264 | The Bellamy Trial–Frances Noyes Hart | 2.00 | 4.00 | 6.00 | |
| 265 | AAF: The Official Guide | 2.00 | 4.00 | 6.00 | NF |
| 266 | Lend-lease: Weapon for Victory–Edward R. Stettinius, Jr | 2.00 | 4.00 | 6.00 | NF |
| 267 | Land below the Wind–Agnes Newton Keith | 2.00 | 4.00 | 6.00 | |
| 268 | The Maltese Falcon–Dashiell Hammett | 6.00 | 12.00 | 18.00 | M |
| | With dust jacket | 30.00 | 60.00 | 90.00 | |
| 269 | Trent's Last Case–E.C. Bentley | 2.50 | 5.00 | 7.50 | M |
| 270 | The Devil to Pay–Ellery Queen | 2.50 | 5.00 | 7.50 | M |
| 271 | The Bride Wore Black–Cornell Woolrich | 3.00 | 6.00 | 9.00 | M |
| 272 | The Happy Highwayman–Leslie Charteris | 2.50 | 5.00 | 7.50 | M |
| 273 | Tarawa–Robert Sherrod | 2.00 | 4.00 | 6.00 | C |
| 274 | Here Is Your War–Ernie Pyle | 2.00 | 4.00 | 6.00 | NF |
| 275 | Random Harvest–James Hilton; 1944 | 2.00 | 4.00 | 6.00 | |
| 276 | The Story Pocket Book–ed. Whit Burnett | 2.00 | 4.00 | 6.00 | |
| 277 | The Case of the Sleepwalker's Niece–Erle Stanley Gardner | 2.00 | 4.00 | 6.00 | M |
| 278 | Experiment Perilous–Margaret Carpenter | 2.00 | 4.00 | 6.00 | |
| 279 | A Bell for Adano–John Hersey | 1.50 | 3.00 | 4.50 | |
| 280 | Life with Father–Clarence Day | 2.50 | 5.00 | 7.50 | H |
| 281 | Pastoral–Nevil Shute; 1945 | 1.50 | 3.00 | 4.50 | |
| 282 | The Human Comedy–William Saroyan | 1.50 | 3.00 | 4.50 | |
| 283 | Calamity Town–Ellery Queen | 2.00 | 4.00 | 6.00 | M |
| 284 | The Pocket Book of Adventure Stories–ed. Philip Van Doren Stern | 2.00 | 4.00 | 6.00 | A |
| 285 | Evil under the Sun–Agatha Christie | 2.50 | 5.00 | 7.50 | M |
| 286 | Background to Danger–Eric Ambler | 2.00 | 4.00 | 6.00 | M |
| 287 | The D.A. Holds a Candle–Erle Stanley Gardner | 2.00 | 4.00 | 6.00 | M |
| 288 | TVA: Democracy on the March–David E. Lilienthal | 1.50 | 3.00 | 4.50 | NF |
| 289 | Having a Wonderful Crime–Craig Rice | 2.50 | 5.00 | 7.50 | M |
| 290 | Jalna–Mazo de la Roche | 1.50 | 3.00 | 4.50 | |
| 291 | The Complete Sayings of Jesus–ed. Arthur Hinds | 3.00 | 6.00 | 9.00 | |
| 292 | Take It Easy–Damon Runyon | 2.50 | 5.00 | 7.50 | |
| 293 | The Pocket Book of Western Stories–ed. Harry E. Maule | 2.50 | 5.00 | 7.50 | W |
| 294 | The Pocket Book of Jokes–ed. Bennett Cerf | 2.00 | 4.00 | 6.00 | H |
| 295 | The Dain Curse–Dashiell Hammett | 6.00 | 12.00 | 18.00 | M |
| 296 | Claudia and David–Rose Franken | 1.50 | 3.00 | 4.50 | |
| 297 | Death at the Bar–Ngaio Marsh | 2.00 | 4.00 | 6.00 | M |
| 298 | They'll Do It Every Time–Jimmy Hatlo | 3.00 | 6.00 | 9.00 | H |
| 299 | The Pocket Book of Basic English–I.A. Richards | 1.50 | 3.00 | 4.50 | NF |
| 300 | Franklin Delano Roosevelt: A Memorial–Donald Porter Geddes; 1945 | 1.00 | 2.00 | 3.00 | B |
| 301 | The Border Trumpet–Ernest Haycox | 2.50 | 5.00 | 7.50 | W |
| 302 | Young Doctor Galahad–Elizabeth Selfert | 1.50 | 3.00 | 4.50 | |
| 303 | The Reader Is Warned–Carter Dickson | 2.50 | 5.00 | 7.50 | M |
| 304 | Alexander Botts: Earthworm Tractors–William Hazlett Upson | 3.00 | 6.00 | 9.00 | |
| 305 | The Bishop Murder Case–S.S. Van Dine | 2.00 | 4.00 | 6.00 | M |
| 306 | Small Beer–Ludwig Bemelmans | 2.00 | 4.00 | 6.00 | |
| 307 | Trial and Error–Anthony Berkeley | 1.50 | 3.00 | 4.50 | M |
| | With dust jacket | 17.50 | 35.00 | 52.50 | |
| 308 | The Pocket Book of Modern Verse–ed. Ted Malone | 1.50 | 3.00 | 4.50 | |
| 309 | Rats, Lice and History–Hans Zinsser | 2.50 | 5.00 | 7.50 | NF |

Pocket Book 280, Pocket Book 337, Pocket Book 366.

Pocket Book 373, Pocket Book 389, Pocket Book 407.

| | | V/Good | Fine | N/Mint | |
|---|---|---|---|---|---|

POCKET BOOK, *continued*

| No. | Title | V/Good | Fine | N/Mint | |
|---|---|---|---|---|---|
| 310 | The Whoop-up Trail–B.M. Bower | 2.50 | 5.00 | 7.50 | W |
| 311 | White Collar Girl–Faith Baldwin | 2.00 | 4.00 | 6.00 | R |
| 312 | The Case of the Shoplifter's Shoe–Erle Stanley Gardner | 2.00 | 4.00 | 6.00 | M |
| 313 | The Tragedy of Y–Ellery Queen | 2.00 | 4.00 | 6.00 | M |
| 314 | The Bishop's Jaegers–Thorne Smith | 2.50 | 5.00 | 7.50 | H |
| 315 | Stalk the Hunter–Mitchell Wilson | 2.50 | 5.00 | 7.50 | |
| 316 | Fightin' Fool–Max Brand | 2.50 | 5.00 | 7.50 | W |
| 317 | On Borrowed Time–Lawrence Edward Watkin | 2.50 | 5.00 | 7.50 | |
| 318 | Farewell to Sport–Paul Gallico | 2.00 | 4.00 | 6.00 | S |
| 319 | Easy to Kill–Agatha Christie | 2.50 | 5.00 | 7.50 | M |
| 320 | The High Window–Raymond Chandler | 5.00 | 10.00 | 15.00 | M |
| 321 | Chicken Every Sunday–Rosemary Taylor | 2.00 | 4.00 | 6.00 | |
| | With dust jacket; movie tie-in | 20.00 | 40.00 | 60.00 | |
| 322 | The Last Frontier–Howard Fast | 2.50 | 5.00 | 7.50 | W |
| 323 | 400 Million Customers–Carl Crow | 2.00 | 4.00 | 6.00 | |
| 324 | Busman's Honeymoon–Dorothy L. Sayers | 2.00 | 4.00 | 6.00 | M |
| | With dust jacket | 17.50 | 35.00 | 52.50 | |
| 325 | The Sea-Wolf–Jack London; 1946 | 2.50 | 5.00 | 7.50 | A |
| 326 | There Was an Old Woman–Ellery Queen | 2.50 | 5.00 | 7.50 | M |
| 327 | Country Lawyer–Bellamy Partridge | 2.00 | 4.00 | 6.00 | |
| 328 | Warrant for X–Philip MacDonald | 2.00 | 4.00 | 6.00 | M |
| 329 | The Fashion in Shrouds–Margery Allingham | 2.00 | 4.00 | 6.00 | M |
| 330 | You Must Relax–Edmund Jacobson | 2.00 | 4.00 | 6.00 | |
| 331 | Verdict of Twelve–Raymond Postgate | 3.00 | 6.00 | 9.00 | |
| 332 | Junior Miss–Sally Benson | 2.00 | 4.00 | 6.00 | |
| 333 | The Benson Murder Case–S.S. Van Dine | 2.00 | 4.00 | 6.00 | M |
| 334 | The D.A. Draws a Circle–Erle Stanley Gardner | 2.00 | 4.00 | 6.00 | M |
| 335 | Nine–and Death Makes Ten–Carter Dickson | 2.50 | 5.00 | 7.50 | M |
| 336 | Blood upon the Snow–Hilda Lawrence | 2.50 | 5.00 | 7.50 | M |
| 337 | Hopalong Cassidy Returns–Clarence E. Mulford | 2.50 | 5.00 | 7.50 | W |
| 338 | The Pocket History of the Second World War–Henry Steele Commager | 1.50 | 3.00 | 4.50 | NF |
| 339 | Young Widow–Clarissa Fairchild Cushman | 2.00 | 4.00 | 6.00 | |
| 340 | The Atomic Age Opens–Donald Porter Geddes | 2.00 | 4.00 | 6.00 | NF |
| 341 | The Body in the Library–Agatha Christie | 2.50 | 5.00 | 7.50 | M |
| 342 | The Pocket Book of Story Poems–ed. Louis Untermeyer | 2.00 | 4.00 | 6.00 | |
| 343 | First Aid for the Ailing House–Roger B. Whitman | 2.00 | 4.00 | 6.00 | NF |
| 344 | Lust for Life–Irving Stone | 2.00 | 4.00 | 6.00 | |
| 345 | Spiderweb Trail–Eugene Cunningham | 2.50 | 5.00 | 7.50 | W |
| 346 | A Pinch of Poison–Richard Lockridge & Frances Lockridge | 3.00 | 6.00 | 9.00 | M |
| 347 | The Phantom Filly–George Agnew Chamberlain | 2.50 | 5.00 | 7.50 | |
| 348 | Gringo Guns–Peter Field | 2.50 | 5.00 | 7.50 | W |
| 349 | Fielding's Folly–Frances Parkinson Keyes | 2.00 | 4.00 | 6.00 | |
| 350 | Death Turns the Tables–John Dickson Carr; 1946 | 3.00 | 6.00 | 9.00 | M |
| 351 | Color Scheme–Ngaio Marsh | 2.00 | 4.00 | 6.00 | M |
| 352 | Disputed Passage–Lloyd C. Douglas | 1.50 | 3.00 | 4.50 | |
| 353 | The Valley of Dry Bones–Arthur Henry Gooden | 2.50 | 5.00 | 7.50 | W |
| 354 | To Have and to Hold–Mary Johnston | 2.00 | 4.00 | 6.00 | |
| 355 | The Tragedy of Z–Ellery Queen | 2.00 | 4.00 | 6.00 | M |
| 356 | The Horse and Buggy Doctor–Arthur E. Hertzler | 2.00 | 4.00 | 6.00 | |
| 357 | Taps for Private Tussie–Jesse Stuart | 2.00 | 4.00 | 6.00 | |
| 358 | Men against the Sea–James Norman Hall & Charles Nordhoff | 2.00 | 4.00 | 6.00 | A |
| 359 | Dragon Seed–Pearl S. Buck | 2.00 | 4.00 | 6.00 | |
| 360 | The Stephen Vincent Benet Pocketbook–Stephen Vincent Benet | 2.00 | 4.00 | 6.00 | |
| 361 | Home Sweet Homicide–Craig Rice | 2.00 | 4.00 | 6.00 | M |
| 362 | Steele of the Royal Mounted–James Oliver Curwood | 2.00 | 4.00 | 6.00 | A |
| 363 | Steamboat Round the Bend–Ben Lucien Burman | 2.00 | 4.00 | 6.00 | |
| 364 | The Journey Home–Zelda Popkin | 1.50 | 3.00 | 4.50 | |
| 365 | Dragonwyck–Anya Seton | 1.50 | 3.00 | 4.50 | |
| 366 | Barnaby–Crockett Johnson | 1.50 | 3.00 | 4.50 | |
| 367 | The Best-Loved Poems and Ballads of James Whitcomb Riley–J.W. Riley | 1.50 | 3.00 | 4.50 | |
| 368 | Murder up My Sleeve–Erle Stanley Gardner | 2.00 | 4.00 | 6.00 | M |
| 369 | Silvertip–Max Brand | 2.00 | 4.00 | 6.00 | W |
| 370 | Action at Aquila–Hervey Allen | 2.00 | 4.00 | 6.00 | |
| 371 | The Last Trail–Zane Grey | 2.50 | 5.00 | 7.50 | W |
| 372 | The Emperor's Snuff Box–John Dickson Carr | 2.50 | 5.00 | 7.50 | M |
| 373 | Lad: A Dog–Albert Payson Terhune | 2.00 | 4.00 | 6.00 | |
| 374 | The Pocket Book of Robert Frost's Poems | 2.00 | 4.00 | 6.00 | |
| 375 | Whiteoaks of Jalna–Mazo de la Roche; 1947 | 1.50 | 3.00 | 4.50 | |
| 376 | Murder Out of Town–Richard Lockridge & Frances Lockridge | 2.50 | 5.00 | 7.50 | M |
| 377 | The Pocket Book of Baby & Child Care–Benjamin Spock | 4.00 | 8.00 | 12.00 | NF |
| 378 | The Case of the Perjured Parrot–Erle Stanley Gardner | 2.00 | 4.00 | 6.00 | M |
| 379 | Devils, Drugs and Doctors–Howard W. Haggard | 2.00 | 4.00 | 6.00 | |
| 380 | Medical Center–Faith Baldwin | 1.50 | 3.00 | 4.50 | R |
| 381 | The Murder of My Aunt–Richard Hull | 2.00 | 4.00 | 6.00 | M |
| 382 | Freedom Road–Howard Fast | 2.00 | 4.00 | 6.00 | |
| 383 | Roget's Pocket Thesaurus–Christopher Mawson & Katherine Whiting | 1.50 | 3.00 | 4.50 | NF |
| 384 | The Pocket Book of Ghost Stories–ed. Philip Van Doren Stern | 3.00 | 6.00 | 9.00 | |
| 385 | The Red Right Hand–Joel Townsley Rogers | 1.50 | 3.00 | 4.50 | M |
| 386 | Seeing Is Believing–Carter Dickson | 2.50 | 5.00 | 7.50 | M |
| 387 | White Banners–Lloyd C. Douglas | 1.50 | 3.00 | 4.50 | |
| 388 | The Pocket Book of Humerous Verse–ed. David McCord | 2.00 | 4.00 | 6.00 | H |
| 389 | The Lady in the Lake–Raymond Chandler | 3.50 | 7.00 | 10.50 | M |
| 390 | South of Rio Grande–Max Brand | 2.00 | 4.00 | 6.00 | W |

Pocket Book 450, Pocket Book 457, Pocket Book 516.

| | | V/Good | Fine | N/Mint | |
|---|---|---|---|---|---|

POCKET BOOK, *continued*

| No. | Title | V/Good | Fine | N/Mint | |
|---|---|---|---|---|---|
| 391 | The Lucky Stiff–Craig Rice | 2.00 | 4.00 | 6.00 | M |
| 392 | The Pocket Book of Erskine Caldwell Stories–Erskine Caldwell | 2.00 | 4.00 | 6.00 | |
| 393 | The Walsh Girls–Elizabeth Janeway | 2.00 | 4.00 | 6.00 | |
| 394 | The Bamboo Blonde–Dorothy B. Hughes | 2.00 | 4.00 | 6.00 | M |
| 395 | Cluny Brown–Margery Sharp | 1.50 | 3.00 | 4.50 | |
| 396 | Laugh with Leacock–Stephen Leacock | 1.50 | 3.00 | 4.50 | H |
| 397 | The Pocket Atlantic–Edward Weeks | 1.50 | 3.00 | 4.50 | |
| 398 | Towards Zero–Agatha Christie | 2.00 | 4.00 | 6.00 | M |
| 399 | The Fear Makers–Darwin L. Teilhet | 2.00 | 4.00 | 6.00 | |
| 400 | Madame Curie–Eve Curie; 1946 | 1.50 | 3.00 | 4.50 | B |
| 401 | The Passionate Witch–Thorne Smith | 2.50 | 5.00 | 7.50 | H |
| 402 | Darkness of Slumber–Rosemary Kutak | 2.00 | 4.00 | 6.00 | |
| 403 | Jamaica Inn–Daphne du Maurier | 1.50 | 3.00 | 4.50 | |
| 404 | Past Imperfect–Ilka Chase | 1.50 | 3.00 | 4.50 | |
| 405 | Forgive Us Our Trespasses–Lloyd C. Douglas | 1.50 | 3.00 | 4.50 | |
| 406 | Runyon a la Carte–Damon Runyon | 2.00 | 4.00 | 6.00 | |
| 407 | The D.A. Goes to Trial–Erle Stanley Gardner | 3.50 | 7.00 | 10.50 | M |
| 408 | The Lost God and Other Adventure Stories–John Russell | 4.50 | 9.00 | 13.50 | A |
| 409 | The Glorious Pool–Thorne Smith | 2.50 | 5.00 | 7.50 | H |
| 410 | The Covered Wagon–Emerson Hough | 2.50 | 5.00 | 7.50 | W |
| 411 | Death on the Aisle–Richard Lockridge & Frances Lockridge | 2.50 | 5.00 | 7.50 | M |
| 412 | Slim–William Wister Haines | 2.00 | 4.00 | 6.00 | |
| 413 | The Sea of Grass–Conrad Richter; movie tie-in | 1.50 | 3.00 | 4.50 | |
| 414 | The Case of the Baited Hook–Erle Stanley Gardner | 2.00 | 4.00 | 6.00 | M |
| 415 | Frenchman's Creek–Daphne du Maurier | 1.50 | 3.00 | 4.50 | |
| 416 | Bill Stern's Favorite Boxing Stories–B. Stern | 1.50 | 3.00 | 4.50 | S |
| 417 | The Peter Arno Pocket Book–Peter Arno | 1.50 | 3.00 | 4.50 | H |
| 418 | The Razor's Edge–W. Somerset Maugham; 1947 | 1.50 | 3.00 | 4.50 | |
| 419 | Before the Fact–Francis Iles | 2.00 | 4.00 | 6.00 | M |
| 420 | Puzzle for Puppets–Patrick Quentin | 2.50 | 5.00 | 7.50 | M |
| 421 | The Merriam Webster Pocket Dictionary | 1.50 | 3.00 | 4.50 | NF |
| 422 | The Delicate Ape–Dorothy B. Hughes | 2.00 | 4.00 | 6.00 | M |
| 423 | The Fighting Four–Max Brand | 2.00 | 4.00 | 6.00 | W |
| 424 | The Pocket Treasury–Louis Untermeyer | 1.50 | 3.00 | 4.50 | |
| 425 | The G-String Murders–Gypsy Rose Lee (actually written by Craig Rice); 1947 | 1.50 | 3.00 | 4.50 | M |
| 426 | The Second Believe It or Not–Robert Ripley | 2.50 | 5.00 | 7.50 | NF |
| 427 | The Innocent Flower–Charlotte Armstrong | 1.50 | 3.00 | 4.50 | M |
| 428 | The Night Life of the Gods–Thorne Smith | 2.00 | 4.00 | 6.00 | H |
| 429 | North of 36–Emerson Hough | 2.00 | 4.00 | 6.00 | W |
| 430 | Good Night, Sweet Prince–Gene Fowler | 1.50 | 3.00 | 4.50 | |
| 431 | The Pocket Book of Famous French Short Stories–ed. Eric Swenson | 1.50 | 3.00 | 4.50 | |
| 432 | Malice Aforethought–Francis Iles | 2.50 | 5.00 | 7.50 | M |
| 433 | The Song of Bernadette–Franz Werfel | 1.50 | 3.00 | 4.50 | |
| 434 | The Sunday Pigeon Murders–Craig Rice | 2.00 | 4.00 | 6.00 | M |
| 435 | Father Malachy's Miracle–Bruce Marshall | 1.50 | 3.00 | 4.50 | F |
| 436 | The Lost Gallows–John Dickson Carr | 2.50 | 5.00 | 7.50 | M |
| 437 | Death and the Dancing Footman–Ngaio Marsh | 2.00 | 4.00 | 6.00 | M |
| 438 | The Clue of the Forgotten Murder–Erle Stanley Gardner | 2.00 | 4.00 | 6.00 | M |
| 439 | A Time to Die–Hilda Lawrence | 2.00 | 4.00 | 6.00 | M |
| 440 | Wife for Sale–Kathleen Norris | 2.00 | 4.00 | 6.00 | |
| 441 | The Shepherd of the Hills–Harold Bell Wright | 2.00 | 4.00 | 6.00 | W |
| 442 | Daisy Kenyon–Elizabeth Joneway | 1.50 | 3.00 | 4.50 | |
| 443 | The Postman Always Rings Twice–James M. Cain; movie tie-in | 2.50 | 5.00 | 7.50 | M |
| 444 | The Unsuspected–Charlotte Armstrong; movie tie-in | 1.50 | 3.00 | 4.50 | M |

| No. | Title | V/Good | Fine | N/Mint | |
|---|---|---|---|---|---|
| 445 | Private Duty–Faith Baldwin | 1.50 | 3.00 | 4.50 | R |
| 446 | The Pocket Book of O. Henry Prize Stories–ed. Herschel Brickell | 1.50 | 3.00 | 4.50 | |
| 447 | Turnabout–Thorne Smith | 2.00 | 4.00 | 6.00 | H |
| 448 | Castle Skull–John Dickson Carr | 3.00 | 6.00 | 9.00 | M |
| 449 | My Ten Years in a Quandry–Robert Benchley | 2.00 | 4.00 | 6.00 | H |
| 450 | The 2nd Pocket Book of Crossword Puzzles–Margaret Petherbridge; 1947 | 7.50 | 15.00 | 22.50 | NF |
| 451 | Remembered Death–Agatha Christie | 2.00 | 4.00 | 6.00 | M |
| 452 | Dracula–Bram Stoker | 10.00 | 20.00 | 30.00 | HO |
| 453 | Mystery House–Kathleen Norris | 1.50 | 3.00 | 4.50 | |
| 454 | Dread Journey–Dorothy B. Hughes | 2.00 | 4.00 | 6.00 | M |
| 455 | The Treasure of the Sierra Madre–B. Traven; movie tie-in | 3.00 | 6.00 | 9.00 | A |
| 456 | District Nurse–Faith Baldwin | 1.50 | 3.00 | 4.50 | R |
| 457 | Pitcairn's Island–James Norman Hall & Charles Nordhoff | 2.00 | 4.00 | 6.00 | A |
| 458 | Win, Place and Show–Robert Dowst | 2.00 | 4.00 | 6.00 | |
| 459 | Dragon's Teeth–Ellery Queen; 1948 | 3.00 | 6.00 | 9.00 | M |
| 460 | Slay the Loose Ladies–Patrick Quentin | 2.50 | 5.00 | 7.50 | M |
| 461 | The Thursday Turkey Murders–Craig Rice | 2.50 | 5.00 | 7.50 | M |
| 462 | How Green Was My Valley–Richard Llewellyn | 2.00 | 4.00 | 6.00 | |
| 463 | Doctor's Wife–Maysie Greig | 1.50 | 3.00 | 4.50 | |
| 464 | The Case of the Rolling Bones–Erle Stanley Gardner | 2.00 | 4.00 | 6.00 | M |
| 465 | Death Comes as the End–Agatha Christie | 2.00 | 4.00 | 6.00 | M |
| 466 | Rim of the Desert–Ernest Haycox | 2.00 | 4.00 | 6.00 | W |
| 467 | Circle C Moves In–Brett Rider | 1.50 | 3.00 | 4.50 | W |
| 468 | The Case of the Silent Partner–Erle Stanley Gardner | 2.00 | 4.00 | 6.00 | M |
| 469 | Kitty–Rosamond Marshall | 1.50 | 3.00 | 4.50 | |
| 470 | A Lantern in Her Hand–Bess Streeter Aldrich | 1.50 | 3.00 | 4.50 | |
| 471 | The Door Between–Ellery Queen | 2.00 | 4.00 | 6.00 | M |
| 472 | Odd Man Out–F.L. Green; movie tie-in | 1.50 | 3.00 | 4.50 | |
| 473 | Under Northern Stars–William MacLeod Raine | 2.00 | 4.00 | 6.00 | W |
| 474 | The Barbary Coast–Herbert Asbury | 2.50 | 5.00 | 7.50 | NF |
| 475 | Death of a Peer–Ngaio Marsh; 1947 | 2.00 | 4.00 | 6.00 | M |
| 476 | The Corpse Steps Out–Craig Rice | 1.50 | 3.00 | 4.50 | M |
| 477 | Tales from the Decameron–Giovanni Boccaccio | 1.50 | 3.00 | 4.50 | |
| 478 | Death–and the Gilded Man–Carter Dickson | 2.50 | 5.00 | 7.50 | M |
| 479 | Did She Fall?–Thorne Smith | 2.00 | 4.00 | 6.00 | M |
| 480 | Passion Flower–Kathleen Norris | 1.50 | 3.00 | 4.50 | |
| 481 | The Emperor's Physician–J.R. Perkins | 1.50 | 3.00 | 4.50 | |
| 482 | Deep Summer–Gwen Bristow; 1948 | 1.50 | 3.00 | 4.50 | |
| 483 | The King's General–Daphne du Maurier | 1.50 | 3.00 | 4.50 | |
| 484 | The Chair for Martin Rome–Henry Edward Helseth; movie tie-in | 1.50 | 3.00 | 4.50 | |
| 485 | The Hollow–Agatha Christie | 1.50 | 3.00 | 4.50 | M |
| 486 | If Winter Comes–A.S.M. Hutchinson; movie tie-in | 1.50 | 3.00 | 4.50 | |
| 487 | The Yukon Trail–William MacLeod Raine | 2.00 | 4.00 | 6.00 | W |
| 488 | Walls of Gold–Kathleen Norris | 1.50 | 3.00 | 4.50 | |

POCKET BOOK, *continued*

| No. | Title | V/Good | Fine | N/Mint | |
|-----|-------|--------|------|--------|---|
| 489 | I Am Gazing Into My 8-Ball–Earl Wilson | 1.50 | 3.00 | 4.50 | H |
| 490 | Skin and Bones–Thorne Smith | 2.00 | 4.00 | 6.00 | H |
| 491 | The Border Kid–Max Brand | 2.00 | 4.00 | 6.00 | W |
| 492 | The Deadly Pavilion–Hilda Lawrence | 1.50 | 3.00 | 4.50 | M |
| 493 | The Flying Yorkshireman–Eric Knight | 2.00 | 4.00 | 6.00 | F |
| 494 | My Favorite Sports Stories–Bill Stern | 1.50 | 3.00 | 4.50 | S |
| 495 | Carry On, Jeeves!–P.G. Wodehouse | 2.50 | 5.00 | 7.50 | H |
| 496 | Farmer Takes a Wife–John Gould | 1.50 | 3.00 | 4.50 | |
| 497 | A Connecticut Yankee in King Arthur's Court–Mark Twain | 2.00 | 4.00 | 6.00 | F |
| 498 | Mr. Adam–Pat Frank | 1.50 | 3.00 | 4.50 | SF |
| 499 | Another Claudia–Rose Franken | 1.50 | 3.00 | 4.50 | |
| 500 | The Sexual Side of Marriage–M.J. Exner; 1948 | 1.50 | 3.00 | 4.50 | NF |
| 501 | Payoff for the Banker–Richard Lockridge & Frances Lockridge | 2.50 | 5.00 | 7.50 | M |
| 502 | High Tension–William Wister Haines | 2.00 | 4.00 | 6.00 | |
| 503 | Peabody's Mermaid–Guy Pearce & Constance Jones; movie tie-in | 1.50 | 3.00 | 4.50 | F |
| 504 | Fun in Bed–Frank Scully | 1.50 | 3.00 | 4.50 | H |
| 505 | Mr. Blandings Builds His Dream House–Eric Hodgins; movie tie-in | 1.50 | 3.00 | 4.50 | |
| 506 | The Pursuit of Love–Nancy Mitford | 1.50 | 3.00 | 4.50 | |
| 507 | She Died a Lady–Carter Dickson | 2.50 | 5.00 | 7.50 | M |
| 508 | Deep Waters–Ruth Moore; movie tie-in | 1.50 | 3.00 | 4.50 | |
| 509 | The Stolen Stallion–Max Brand | 2.00 | 4.00 | 6.00 | W |
| 510 | The Pocket Book of O. Henry Stories–O. Henry | 1.50 | 3.00 | 4.50 | |
| 511 | We Took to the Woods–Louise Dickinson Rich | 1.50 | 3.00 | 4.50 | |
| 512 | This Is Murder–Erle Stanley Gardner | 1.50 | 3.00 | 4.50 | M |
| 513 | Rehearsal for Love–Faith Baldwin | 1.50 | 3.00 | 4.50 | R |
| 514 | Flame of Sunset–L.P. Holmes | 1.50 | 3.00 | 4.50 | W |
| 515 | Anna Karenina–Leo Tolstoy; movie tie-in | 1.50 | 3.00 | 4.50 | |
| 516 | Tales of the South Pacific–James A. Michener | 2.00 | 4.00 | 6.00 | |
| 517 | The Murderer Is a Fox–Ellery Queen | 2.00 | 4.00 | 6.00 | M |
| 518 | The Stray Lamb–Thorne Smith | 2.00 | 4.00 | 6.00 | H |
| 519 | Oliver Twist–Charles Dickens | 2.00 | 4.00 | 6.00 | |
| 520 | Student Nurse–Lucy Agnes Hancock | 1.50 | 3.00 | 4.50 | |
| 521 | More Deaths Than One–Bruno Fischer | 2.00 | 4.00 | 6.00 | M |
| 522 | Freud: His Dream and Sex Theories–Joseph Jastrow | 1.50 | 3.00 | 4.50 | NF |
| 523 | The Longhorn Feud–Max Brand | 2.00 | 4.00 | 6.00 | W |
| 524 | The Double Take–Roy Huggins | 2.00 | 4.00 | 6.00 | M |
| 525 | The Foolish Virgin–Kathleen Norris; 1948 | 1.50 | 3.00 | 4.50 | |
| 526 | Desert Town–Ramona Stewart | 1.50 | 3.00 | 4.50 | |
| 527 | Final Curtain–Ngaio Marsh | 2.00 | 4.00 | 6.00 | M |
| 528 | The Big Midget Murders–Craig Rice | 2.50 | 5.00 | 7.50 | M |
| 529 | The Pocket Book of American Poems–ed. Louis Untermeyer | 1.50 | 3.00 | 4.50 | |
| 530 | Guns on the Cimarron–Allan Vaughan Elston | 1.50 | 3.00 | 4.50 | W |
| 531 | Saddle and Ride–Ernest Haycox | 1.50 | 3.00 | 4.50 | W |
| 532 | Four Great Tragedies–William Shakespeare | 1.50 | 3.00 | 4.50 | |
| 533 | Four Great Comedies–William Shakespeare | 1.50 | 3.00 | 4.50 | |
| 534 | The Turquoise–Anya Seton | 1.50 | 3.00 | 4.50 | |
| 535 | Precious Bane–Mary Webb | 1.50 | 3.00 | 4.50 | |
| 536 | The Ballad and the Source–Rosamond Lehmann | 1.50 | 3.00 | 4.50 | |
| 537 | The Shadowy Third–Marco Page | 1.50 | 3.00 | 4.50 | M |
| 538 | You Got to Stay Happy–Robert Carson | 1.00 | 2.00 | 3.00 | |
| 539 | Age of Consent–Norman Lindsay | 1.50 | 3.00 | 4.50 | E |
| 540 | Death of a Doll–Hilda Lawrence | 2.00 | 4.00 | 6.00 | M |
| 541 | Professional Lover–Maysie Greig | 1.50 | 3.00 | 4.50 | |
| 542 | Death Stalks the Range–Brett Rider | 1.50 | 3.00 | 4.50 | W |
| 543 | Five Acres and Independence–M.G. Kains | 1.00 | 2.00 | 3.00 | |
| 544 | The Case of the Turning Tide–Erle Stanley Gardner | 1.50 | 3.00 | 4.50 | M |
| 545 | The Pocket Book of True Stories–ed. Ernest Heyn | 2.50 | 5.00 | 7.50 | |
| 546 | Rain in the Doorway–Thorne Smith | 2.00 | 4.00 | 6.00 | H |
| 547 | Silvertips Strike–Max Brand | 2.00 | 4.00 | 6.00 | W |
| 548 | Minute for Murder–Nicholas Blake | 2.00 | 4.00 | 6.00 | M |
| 549 | Younger Sister–Kathleen Norris | 1.50 | 3.00 | 4.50 | R |
| 550 | Mister Roberts–Thomas Heggen; 1948 | 2.00 | 4.00 | 6.00 | |

Pocket Book 524, Pocket Book 551, Pocket Book 578.

| No. | Title | V/Good | Fine | N/Mint | |
|-----|-------|--------|------|--------|---|
| 551 | The Scarlet Letter–Nathaniel Hawthorne | 2.00 | 4.00 | 6.00 | |
| 552 | Silas Marner–George Eliot | 2.00 | 4.00 | 6.00 | |
| 553 | Economics in One Lesson–Henry Hazlitt | 1.00 | 2.00 | 3.00 | NF |
| 554 | Texas Triggers–Eugene Cunningham | 1.50 | 3.00 | 4.50 | W |
| 555 | Bill Stern's Favorite Football Stories–B. Stern | 1.00 | 2.00 | 3.00 | S |
| 556 | Anything Can Happen–George Papashvily & Helen Papashvily | 1.00 | 2.00 | 3.00 | |
| 557 | The Horizontal Man–Helen Eustis | 1.50 | 3.00 | 4.50 | |
| 558 | Bury Me Deep–Harold Q. Masur | 1.50 | 3.00 | 4.50 | M |
| 559 | Carmen and Other Stories–Prosper Merimee; movie tie-in | 1.50 | 3.00 | 4.50 | |
| 560 | So Evil My Love–Joseph Shearing; 1949 | 1.50 | 3.00 | 4.50 | |
| 561 | The D.A. Cooks a Goose–Erle Stanley Gardner | 1.50 | 3.00 | 4.50 | M |
| 562 | The Babe Ruth Story–Bob Considine & Babe Ruth | 2.50 | 5.00 | 7.50 | B |
| 563 | Range Boss–D.B. Newton | 1.50 | 3.00 | 4.50 | W |
| 564 | A City of Bells–Elizabeth Goudge | 1.50 | 3.00 | 4.50 | |
| 565 | The French Quarter–Herbert Asbury | 2.00 | 4.00 | 6.00 | NF |
| 566 | The Egg and I–Betty MacDonald | 1.50 | 3.00 | 4.50 | H |
| 567 | Outlaws Three–Peter Field | 2.00 | 4.00 | 6.00 | W |
| 568 | The Curse of the Bronze Lamp–Carter Dickson | 2.50 | 5.00 | 7.50 | M |
| 569 | 30 Days to a More Powerful Vocabulary–Wilfred Funk & Norman Lewis | 1.00 | 2.00 | 3.00 | NF |
| 570 | Rendezvous in Black–Cornell Woolrich | 2.50 | 5.00 | 7.50 | M |
| 571 | Command Decision–William Wister Haines | 1.50 | 3.00 | 4.50 | C |
| 572 | Favorite Baseball Stories–Bill Stern | 1.50 | 3.00 | 4.50 | S |
| 573 | Sundown Jim–Ernest Haycox | 1.50 | 3.00 | 4.50 | W |
| 574 | Unmarried Couple–Maysie Greig | 1.50 | 3.00 | 4.50 | |
| 575 | The Chocolate Cobweb–Charlotte Armstrong; 1949 | 1.50 | 3.00 | 4.50 | M |
| 576 | Anna and the King of Siam–Margaret Landon | 2.00 | 4.00 | 6.00 | |
| 577 | The Foxes of Harrow–Frank Yerby | 1.50 | 3.00 | 4.50 | |
| 578 | The Pocket Book of Old Masters–Herman J. Wechsler | 3.00 | 6.00 | 9.00 | NF |
| 579 | Famous Artists and Their Models–Thomas Craven | 3.00 | 6.00 | 9.00 | NF |
| 580 | Fun for the Family–Jerome S. Meyer | 1.50 | 3.00 | 4.50 | NF |
| 581 | The Painted Veil–W. Somerset Maugham | 1.00 | 2.00 | 3.00 | |
| 582 | Wilders Walk Away–Herbert Brean | 1.50 | 3.00 | 4.50 | |
| 583 | Dr. Whitney's Secretary–Dorothy Pierce Walker | 1.50 | 3.00 | 4.50 | |
| 584 | King of the Range–Max Brand | 1.50 | 3.00 | 4.50 | W |
| 585 | Hit the Saddle–Allan Vaughan Elston | 1.50 | 3.00 | 4.50 | W |
| 586 | The Pocket Weekend Book–ed. Philip Van Doren Stern | 1.50 | 3.00 | 4.50 | |
| 587 | In a Lonely Place–Dorothy B. Hughes; c-Frank McCarthy | 1.50 | 3.00 | 4.50 | M |
| 588 | Conspirator–Humphrey Slater | 1.50 | 3.00 | 4.50 | |
| 589 | The Handsome Road–Gwen Bristow | 1.50 | 3.00 | 4.50 | |
| 590 | The Case of the Haunted Husband–Erle Stanley Gardner | 1.50 | 3.00 | 4.50 | M |
| 591 | Alexandra–Gladys Schmitt | 1.50 | 3.00 | 4.50 | |
| 592 | The Strange Case of Lucile Clery–Joseph Shearing | 1.00 | 2.00 | 3.00 | |

Pocket Book 593, Pocket Book 601, Pocket Book 621.

Pocket Book 628, Pocket Book 642, Pocket Book 656.

| | | V/Good | Fine | N/Mint | |
|---|---|---|---|---|---|
| **POCKET BOOK,** *continued* | | | | | |
| 593 | The Call of the Wild–Jack London | 2.00 | 4.00 | 6.00 | A |
| 594 | Deep West–Ernest Haycox | 1.50 | 3.00 | 4.50 | W |
| 595 | The D.A. Calls a Turn–Erle Stanley Gardner | 1.50 | 3.00 | 4.50 | M |
| 596 | Try and Stop Me–Bennett Cerf | 1.00 | 2.00 | 3.00 | H |
| 597 | The Story of Mrs. Murphy–Natalie Anderson Scott | 1.50 | 3.00 | 4.50 | |
| 598 | Let's Explore Your Mind–Albert Edward Wiggam | 1.50 | 3.00 | 4.50 | |
| 599 | Secret Marriage–Kathleen Norris | 1.50 | 3.00 | 4.50 | |
| 600 | The Big Sky–A.B. Guthrie, Jr; 1949 | 2.00 | 4.00 | 6.00 | W |
| 601 | Lani–Margaret Widdemer | 1.50 | 3.00 | 4.50 | |
| 602 | Too Late for Tears–Roy Huggins | 2.00 | 4.00 | 6.00 | M |
| 603 | Woman in Her Way–Faith Baldwin | 1.00 | 2.00 | 3.00 | R |
| 604 | Lost Stage Valley–Frank Bonham | 1.50 | 3.00 | 4.50 | W |
| 605 | Burned Fingers–Kathleen Norris | 1.50 | 3.00 | 4.50 | |
| 606 | Disposing of Henry–Roger Bax | 1.50 | 3.00 | 4.50 | M |
| 607 | Seven Short Novels from the Woman's Home Companion–ed. Barthold Fles | 1.50 | 3.00 | 4.50 | |
| 608 | Action by Night–Ernest Haycox | 1.50 | 3.00 | 4.50 | W |
| 609 | Valley of Vanishing Men–Max Brand | 2.00 | 4.00 | 6.00 | W |
| 610 | West of the Law–Al Cody | 1.50 | 3.00 | 4.50 | W |
| 611 | Square Shooter–William MacLeod Raine | 1.50 | 3.00 | 4.50 | W |
| 612 | Moby Dick–Herman Melville | 2.50 | 5.00 | 7.50 | A |
| 613 | No Private Heaven–Faith Baldwin | 1.50 | 3.00 | 4.50 | R |
| 614 | Love Is a Deadly Weapon–Patrick Quentin; aka Puzzle for Friends; c-Frank McCarthy | 2.00 | 4.00 | 6.00 | M |
| 615 | Desert Island Decameron–H. Allen Smith | 1.00 | 2.00 | 3.00 | H |
| 616 | Kim–Rudyard Kipling | 1.50 | 3.00 | 4.50 | A |
| 617 | There Is a Tide–Agatha Christie | 1.50 | 3.00 | 4.50 | M |
| 618 | The Big Con–David W. Maurer | 1.25 | 2.50 | 3.75 | |
| 619 | The Case of the Empty Tin–Erle Stanley Gardner | 1.50 | 3.00 | 4.50 | M |
| 620 | Circle C Carries On–Brett Rider; c-Frank McCarthy | 1.50 | 3.00 | 4.50 | W |
| 621 | The Life and Times of the Shmoo–Al Capp | 6.00 | 12.00 | 18.00 | H |
| 622 | The Pocket Book of Great Operas–Henry Simon & Abraham Veinus | 1.50 | 3.00 | 4.50 | NF |
| 623 | Red Rust–Cornelia James Cannon | 1.50 | 3.00 | 4.50 | |
| 624 | Shoot the Works–Richard Ellington | 1.50 | 3.00 | 4.50 | M |
| 625 | Mink Coat–Kathleen Norris; 1949. Note: Same cover as Pocket Book (British) No. B4 | 1.25 | 2.50 | 3.75 | |
| 626 | Died in the Wool–Ngaio Marsh | 1.50 | 3.00 | 4.50 | M |
| 627 | The Renegade–L.L. Foreman | 1.50 | 3.00 | 4.50 | W |
| 628 | The Best of Wodehouse–P.G. Wodehouse; 1st ed. 1949 | 4.50 | 9.00 | 13.50 | H |
| 629 | Care and Training of Dogs–Arthur Frederick Jones | 1.50 | 3.00 | 4.50 | NF |
| 630 | So Well Remembered–James Hilton | 1.00 | 2.00 | 3.00 | |
| 631 | Jean-Christophe–Romain Rolland | 1.50 | 3.00 | 4.50 | |
| 632 | Black Ivory–Norman Collins | 2.00 | 4.00 | 6.00 | |
| 633 | My Late Wives–Carter Dickson | 2.50 | 5.00 | 7.50 | M |
| 634 | Silvertips Chase–Max Brand | 2.00 | 4.00 | 6.00 | W |
| 635 | Black Jade–Angeline Taylor | 1.50 | 3.00 | 4.50 | |
| 636 | What Are the Odds?–Leo Guild | 1.50 | 3.00 | 4.50 | NF |
| 637 | Jed Blaine's Woman–Evelyn Wells | 1.25 | 2.50 | 3.75 | |
| 638 | The Room Upstairs–Mildred Davis | 1.50 | 3.00 | 4.50 | |
| 639 | The Man with My Face–Samuel W. Taylor | 1.50 | 3.00 | 4.50 | M |
| 640 | Canyon Passage–Ernest Haycox | 1.50 | 3.00 | 4.50 | W |
| 641 | Minute Mysteries–Austin Ripley | 1.50 | 3.00 | 4.50 | M |
| 642 | Pavilion of Women–Pearl S. Buck | 1.50 | 3.00 | 4.50 | |
| 643 | The Case of the Drowning Duck–Erle Stanley Gardner | 1.50 | 3.00 | 4.50 | M |
| 644 | Sister Carrie–Theodore Dreiser | 1.25 | 2.50 | 3.75 | |
| 645 | Stars in My Crown–Joe David Brown | 1.25 | 2.50 | 3.75 | |
| 646 | They Died with Their Boots On–Thomas Ripley | 1.50 | 3.00 | 4.50 | W |
| 647 | The Trial of Mary Dugan–Bayard Veiller & William Almon Wolff; 1950 | 1.25 | 2.50 | 3.75 | |
| 648 | Disaster Trail–Al Cody | 1.50 | 3.00 | 4.50 | W |
| 649 | The Saturday Evening Post Sports Stories–Red Smith | 1.25 | 2.50 | 3.75 | S |
| 650 | French Taught with Pictures–I.A. Richards; 1950 | 1.25 | 2.50 | 3.75 | NF |
| 651 | The Fourth Postman–Craig Rice | 1.50 | 3.00 | 4.50 | M |
| 652 | The Sea Chase–Andrew Geer | 2.00 | 4.00 | 6.00 | |
| 653 | Spotlight–Helen Topping Miller | 1.25 | 2.50 | 3.75 | |
| 654 | Consultation Room–Frederic Loomis | 1.25 | 2.50 | 3.75 | |
| 655 | The Vixens–Frank Yerby | 1.25 | 2.50 | 3.75 | |
| 656 | Man-size–William MacLeod Raine | 1.50 | 3.00 | 4.50 | W |
| 657 | The Bishop's Mantle–Agnes Sligh Turnbull | 1.25 | 2.50 | 3.75 | |
| 658 | Give Love the Air–Faith Baldwin | 1.25 | 2.50 | 3.75 | R |
| 659 | Voice Out of Darkness–Ursula Curtiss | 1.50 | 3.00 | 4.50 | M |
| 660 | Return of the Rio Kid–Don Davis | 1.50 | 3.00 | 4.50 | W |
| 661 | Gods and Goddesses in Art and Legend–Herman J. Wechsler | 3.00 | 6.00 | 9.00 | NF |
| 662 | The Blank Wall–Elisabeth Sanxay Holding | 1.50 | 3.00 | 4.50 | M |
| 663 | Renegade Ranch–Roy Manning | 1.50 | 3.00 | 4.50 | W |
| 664 | No Trumpet before Him–Nelia Gardner White | 1.50 | 3.00 | 4.50 | |
| 665 | More Work for the Undertaker–Margery Allingham | 1.50 | 3.00 | 4.50 | M |
| 666 | The Girl on the Via Flaminia–Alfred Hayes | 1.50 | 3.00 | 4.50 | |
| 667 | The Case of the Smoking Chimney–Erle Stanley Gardner | 1.50 | 3.00 | 4.50 | M |
| 668 | Valley Thieves–Max Brand | 1.50 | 3.00 | 4.50 | W |
| 669 | Drury Lane's Last Case–Ellery Queen | 1.50 | 3.00 | 4.50 | M |
| 670 | The Casebook of Sherlock Holmes–Arthur Conan Doyle | 3.00 | 6.00 | 9.00 | M |
| 671 | The Franchise Affair–Josephine Tey | 1.50 | 3.00 | 4.50 | |
| 672 | Pilgrim's Inn–Elizabeth Goudge | 1.25 | 2.50 | 3.75 | |
| 673 | One Woman–Tiffany Thayer | 1.25 | 2.50 | 3.75 | |
| 674 | All You Need to Know about Fishing, Hunting and Camping–Byron Dalrymple | 1.50 | 3.00 | 4.50 | NF |
| 675 | Desert Rails–L.P. Holmes; 1950 | 1.50 | 3.00 | 4.50 | W |
| 676 | The Fate of the Immodest Blonde–Patrick Quentin | 1.50 | 3.00 | 4.50 | M |
| 677 | The Pocket Book of Greek Art–Thomas Craven | 3.00 | 6.00 | 9.00 | NF |
| 678 | The Case of the Buried Clock–Erle Stanley Gardner | 1.50 | 3.00 | 4.50 | M |
| 679 | Peony–Pearl S. Buck | 1.50 | 3.00 | 4.50 | |
| 680 | The Moving Target–John Ross MacDonald | 3.50 | 7.00 | 10.50 | M |

*Pocket Book 714, Pocket Book 753, Pocket Book 755.*

POCKET BOOK, *continued*

| | | V/Good | Fine | N/Mint | |
|---|---|---|---|---|---|
| 681 | Rampart Street–Everett Webber & Olga Webber | 2.00 | 4.00 | 6.00 | |
| 682 | Small Talk–Syms | 1.50 | 3.00 | 4.50 | H |
| 683 | The Boss of the Lazy 9–Peter Field | 1.50 | 3.00 | 4.50 | W |
| 684 | The Pocket Treasury of American Folklore–ed. B.A. Botkin | 1.50 | 3.00 | 4.50 | |
| 685 | Wine, Women and Words–Billy Rose | 1.25 | 2.50 | 3.75 | B |
| 686 | Five O'Clock Surgeon–Dorothy Pierce Walker | 1.25 | 2.50 | 3.75 | |
| 687 | Flaming Irons–Max Brand | 1.50 | 3.00 | 4.50 | W |
| 688 | Three Men and Diana–Kathleen Norris | 1.25 | 2.50 | 3.75 | |
| 689 | The Case of the Drowsy Mosquito–Erle Stanley Gardner | 1.50 | 3.00 | 4.50 | M |
| 690 | Annie Jordan–Mary Brinker Post | 1.25 | 2.50 | 3.75 | |
| 691 | The Fighting Edge–William MacLeod Raine | 1.50 | 3.00 | 4.50 | W |
| 692 | Special Nurse–Lucy Agnes Hancock | 1.25 | 2.50 | 3.75 | |
| 693 | The Whispering Corpse–William P. McGivern | 1.50 | 3.00 | 4.50 | M |
| 694 | Killer's Range–E.B. Mann | 1.50 | 3.00 | 4.50 | W |
| 695 | Rhubarb–H. Allen Smith | 3.00 | 6.00 | 9.00 | H |
| 696 | The Big Sleep–Raymond Chandler | 6.00 | 12.00 | 18.00 | M |
| 697 | Without Magnolias–Bucklin Moon | 1.25 | 2.50 | 3.75 | |
| 698 | The Darker the Night–Herbert Brean | 1.25 | 2.50 | 3.75 | |
| 699 | No Benefit of Law–Brett Rider | 1.50 | 3.00 | 4.50 | W |
| 700 | Of Human Bondage–W. Somerset Maugham; 1950 | 2.00 | 4.00 | 6.00 | |
| 701 | Big Sol–Henry Von Rhau | 1.25 | 2.50 | 3.75 | |
| 702 | Desperado's Gold–L.L. Foreman | 1.50 | 3.00 | 4.50 | W |
| 703 | Rustlers' Canyon–E.E. Halleran | 1.50 | 3.00 | 4.50 | W |
| 704 | Suddenly a Corpse–Harold Q. Masur | 1.50 | 3.00 | 4.50 | M |
| 705 | Hired Guns–Max Brand | 1.50 | 3.00 | 4.50 | W |
| 706 | Death Rides the Pecos–Davis Dresser | 1.50 | 3.00 | 4.50 | W |
| 707 | The Girl from Nowhere–Rae Foley | 1.50 | 3.00 | 4.50 | |
| 708 | The Pocket History of American Painting–James Thomas Flexner | 3.00 | 6.00 | 9.00 | NF |
| 709 | Halo in Brass–John Evans | 3.50 | 7.00 | 10.50 | |
| 710 | An Apple for Eye–Kathleen Norris | 1.25 | 2.50 | 3.75 | |
| 711 | Midnight Round-up–Peter Field | 2.00 | 4.00 | 6.00 | W |
| 712 | The Doctor at Coffin Gap–Les Savage, Jr | 1.50 | 3.00 | 4.50 | W |
| 713 | Hound-dog Man–Fred Gipson | 1.50 | 3.00 | 4.50 | |
| 714 | The Asphalt Jungle–W.R. Burnett | 3.00 | 6.00 | 9.00 | M |
| 715 | The University of Chicago Spanish-English, English-Spanish Dictionary–Carlos Castillo & others | 1.50 | 3.00 | 4.50 | NF |
| 716 | The Trouble with Murder–Roger Bax | 1.50 | 3.00 | 4.50 | M |
| 717 | The Bandit of the Black Hills–Max Brand | 1.50 | 3.00 | 4.50 | W |
| 718 | Great American Sports Humor–ed. Mac Davis | 1.50 | 3.00 | 4.50 | SH |
| 719 | Singing Lariat–Will Ermine | 1.50 | 3.00 | 4.50 | W |
| 720 | Spanish through Pictures–I.A. Richards | 1.50 | 3.00 | 4.50 | NF |
| 721 | Border Breed–William MacLeod Raine | 1.50 | 3.00 | 4.50 | W |
| 722 | Opus 21–Philip Wylie | 1.00 | 2.00 | 3.00 | |
| 723 | The Hearth and the Eagle–Anya Seton | 1.00 | 2.00 | 3.00 | |
| 724 | The Case of the Careless Kitten–Erle Stanley Gardner | 1.50 | 3.00 | 4.50 | M |
| 725 | Suitable for Framing–James Atlee Phillips; 1950 | 1.50 | 3.00 | 4.50 | M |
| 726 | Dusty Wagons–Matt Stuart | 1.50 | 3.00 | 4.50 | W |
| 727 | Perilous Passage–Arthur Mayse | 1.50 | 3.00 | 4.50 | |
| 728 | The Feather Merchants–Max Shulman | 1.00 | 2.00 | 3.00 | |
| 729 | Chesapeake Cavalier–Don Tracy | 1.50 | 3.00 | 4.50 | A |
| 730 | This Is America–Max Herzberg | 1.00 | 2.00 | 3.00 | |
| 731 | The 3rd Pocket Book of Crossword Puzzles–Margaret Petherbridge | 5.00 | 10.00 | 15.00 | NF |
| 732 | Cowboy–Ross Santee | 1.50 | 3.00 | 4.50 | W |
| 733 | Ghost Gold–Tom West | 1.00 | 2.00 | 3.00 | W |
| 734 | The Red Dress–John Watson | 1.50 | 3.00 | 4.50 | |
| 735 | The March Hare Murders–E.X. Ferrars | 1.50 | 3.00 | 4.50 | M |
| 736 | Coffin Corner–George Bagby | 1.50 | 3.00 | 4.50 | M |
| 737 | Murder One–Eleazar Lipsky | 1.50 | 3.00 | 4.50 | M |
| 738 | Dead Lion–Emery Bonett & John Bonett | 1.50 | 3.00 | 4.50 | |
| 739 | The Man Who Held Five Aces–Jean Leslie | 1.50 | 3.00 | 4.50 | |
| 740 | Ten Day's Wonder–Ellery Queen | 1.50 | 3.00 | 4.50 | M |
| 741 | The Case of the Journeying Boy–Michael Innes | 1.50 | 3.00 | 4.50 | M |
| 742 | Head of a Traveller–Nicholas Blake | 3.00 | 6.00 | 9.00 | M |
| 743 | On the Dodge–William MacLeod Raine | 1.50 | 3.00 | 4.50 | W |

| | | V/Good | Fine | N/Mint | |
|---|---|---|---|---|---|
| 744 | Hunted Riders–Max Brand | 1.50 | 3.00 | 4.50 | W |
| 745 | Lord Johnnie–Leslie Turner White | 1.50 | 3.00 | 4.50 | A |
| 746 | Wilderness Nurse–Marguerite Mooers Marshall | 1.25 | 2.50 | 3.75 | R |
| 747 | Combat–Van Van Praag | 1.25 | 2.50 | 3.75 | C |
| 748 | Call It Treason–George Howe; 1951; 3rd printing is movie tie-in retitled Decision before Dawn | 1.50 | 3.00 | 4.50 | |
| 749 | The Golden Hawk–Frank Yerby | 1.50 | 3.00 | 4.50 | A |
| 750 | The Little Sister–Raymond Chandler | 4.00 | 8.00 | 12.00 | M |
| 751 | The Perfect Hostess–Maureen Daly | 1.25 | 2.50 | 3.75 | |
| 752 | Beyond a Reasonable Doubt–C.W. Grafton | 1.25 | 2.50 | 3.75 | M |
| 753 | Crooked House–Agatha Christie | 1.50 | 3.00 | 4.50 | M |
| 754 | Riders by Night–Nelson Nye | 1.50 | 3.00 | 4.50 | W |
| 755 | The Human Side of Animals–Vance Packard | 1.50 | 3.00 | 4.50 | NF |
| 756 | It's a Crime–Richard Ellington | 1.50 | 3.00 | 4.50 | M |
| 757 | The Man with the Golden Arm–Nelson Algren | 2.00 | 4.00 | 6.00 | |
| 758 | The Case of the Crooked Candle–Erle Stanley Gardner. Note: Same cover as Pocket Book (British) No. B50 | 1.50 | 3.00 | 4.50 | M |
| 759 | The Tenderfoot Kid–Peter Field | 2.00 | 4.00 | 6.00 | W |
| 760 | Outlaw Vengeance–Samuel A. Peeples | 2.00 | 4.00 | 6.00 | W |
| 761 | Rustlers' Moon–Will Ermine | 1.50 | 3.00 | 4.50 | W |
| 762 | Swing, Brother, Swing–Ngaio Marsh | 1.50 | 3.00 | 4.50 | M |
| 763 | All the Ship's at Sea–William J. Lederer | 1.50 | 3.00 | 4.50 | |
| 764 | Laughing Boy–Oliver LaFarge | 1.50 | 3.00 | 4.50 | |
| 765 | The Pocket Book of Great Drawings–ed. Paul J. Sachs | 3.00 | 6.00 | 9.00 | NF |
| 766 | Law of the Gun–Brett Rider | 1.50 | 3.00 | 4.50 | W |
| 767 | The Big Wheel–John Brooks | 1.50 | 3.00 | 4.50 | |
| 768 | The Fight for the Sweetwater–Bliss Lomax (Harry Sinclair Drago) | 1.50 | 3.00 | 4.50 | W |
| 769 | Bitter Creek–Al Cody | 1.50 | 3.00 | 4.50 | W |
| 770 | The Naked Eye–Gita Lewis & Henriette Martin | 1.50 | 3.00 | 4.50 | |
| 771 | The Brave Bulls–Tom Lea | 1.50 | 3.00 | 4.50 | |
| 772 | Ruggles of Red Gap–Harry Leon Wilson | 1.25 | 2.50 | 3.75 | H |
| 773 | My Dead Wife–William Worley | 2.50 | 5.00 | 7.50 | M |
| 774 | The House without a Door–Thomas Sterling | 1.50 | 3.00 | 4.50 | |
| 775 | The 22 Brothers–Dana Sage; 1951. Note: Same cover as Pocket Book (British) No. B60 | 1.50 | 3.00 | 4.50 | |
| 776 | The End Is Known–Geoffrey Holiday Hall | 1.50 | 3.00 | 4.50 | |
| 777 | So Young a Body–Frank Bunce | 1.50 | 3.00 | 4.50 | |
| 778 | Top of the World–Hans Ruesch | 1.50 | 3.00 | 4.50 | |
| 779 | And When She Was Bad She Was Murdered–Richard Starnes | 2.00 | 4.00 | 6.00 | M |
| 780 | The Way West–A.B. Guthrie, Jr | 2.00 | 4.00 | 6.00 | W |
| 781 | Rustlers of Beacon Creek–Max Brand | 1.50 | 3.00 | 4.50 | W |
| 782 | Dialogues of Plato | 1.50 | 3.00 | 4.50 | |
| 783 | Outlaw Trail–E.E. Halleran | 1.50 | 3.00 | 4.50 | W |
| 784 | Come and Kill Me–Josephine Tey | 1.50 | 3.00 | 4.50 | |
| 785 | The Golden Fury–Marian Castle | 1.50 | 3.00 | 4.50 | |
| 786 | Very Cold for May–William P. McGivern | 1.50 | 3.00 | 4.50 | |
| 787 | Ranger's Luck–William MacLeod Raine | 1.50 | 3.00 | 4.50 | W |

**POCKET BOOK,** *continued*

| # | Title | V/Good | Fine | N/Mint | |
|---|---|---|---|---|---|
| 788 | The Pocket Guide to the Wildflowers–Samuel Gottscho | 2.00 | 4.00 | 6.00 | NF |
| 789 | Ann Pillsbury's Baking Book–Ann Pillsbury | 1.50 | 3.00 | 4.50 | NF |
| 790 | Rough Justice–Ernest Haycox | 1.50 | 3.00 | 4.50 | W |
| 791 | Red Range–Eugene Cunningham | 1.50 | 3.00 | 4.50 | W |
| 792 | The Case of the Black-eyed Blonde–Erle Stanley Gardner | 1.50 | 3.00 | 4.50 | M |
| 793 | Diagnosis: Homicide–Lawrence G. Blochman | 1.50 | 3.00 | 4.50 | M |
| 794 | Broncho Apache–Paul I. Wellman | 2.00 | 4.00 | 6.00 | W |
| 795 | Hold Autumn in Your Hand–George Sessions Perry | 1.25 | 2.50 | 3.75 | |
| 796 | For Doctors Only–Francis Leo Golden | 1.50 | 3.00 | 4.50 | H |
| 797 | The Outlaw–Max Brand | 1.50 | 3.00 | 4.50 | W |
| 798 | Under the Skin–Phyllis Bottome | 1.50 | 3.00 | 4.50 | |
| 799 | Dardanelles Derelict–F. Van Wyck Mason | 1.50 | 3.00 | 4.50 | |
| 800 | Conception, Pregnancy and Birth–J.D. Ratcliff; 1951 | 1.00 | 2.00 | 3.00 | NF |
| 801 | Reprisal–Arthur Gordon | 1.50 | 3.00 | 4.50 | |
| 802 | Big As Life–John Pleasant McCoy | 1.50 | 3.00 | 4.50 | |
| 803 | The Hide Rustlers–Les Savage, Jr | 1.50 | 3.00 | 4.50 | W |
| 804 | The Deadly Miss Ashley–Frederick C. Davis | 1.50 | 3.00 | 4.50 | M |
| 805 | Mischief–Charlotte Armstrong | 1.50 | 3.00 | 4.50 | M |
| 806 | Murder's Web–Dorothy Dunn | 1.50 | 3.00 | 4.50 | M |
| 807 | Bullets for a Badman–Bennett Foster | 1.50 | 3.00 | 4.50 | W |
| 808 | The Sheriff of Painted Post–Tom Gunn | 1.50 | 3.00 | 4.50 | W |
| 809 | Colt Comrades–Bliss Lomax (Harry Sinclair Drago) | 1.50 | 3.00 | 4.50 | W |
| 810 | The Freeholder–Joe David Brown | 1.50 | 3.00 | 4.50 | A |
| 811 | The Witch of Spring–William Shore | 2.00 | 4.00 | 6.00 | E |
| 812 | The Case of the Golddigger's Purse–Erle Stanley Gardner | 1.50 | 3.00 | 4.50 | M |
| 813 | Stone Cold Dead–Richard Ellington | 2.00 | 4.00 | 6.00 | M |
| 814 | The Poisoned Chocolates Case–Anthony Berkeley | 1.50 | 3.00 | 4.50 | M |
| 815 | The Sheriff's Son–William MacLeod Raine | 1.50 | 3.00 | 4.50 | W |
| 816 | Wall of Guns–Jim O'Mara | 1.50 | 3.00 | 4.50 | W |
| 817 | Something about Midnight–D.B. Olsen | 1.50 | 3.00 | 4.50 | M |
| 818 | High Valley–Charmian Clift & George Henry Johnston | 1.50 | 3.00 | 4.50 | |
| 819 | Mingo Dabney–James Street | 1.50 | 3.00 | 4.50 | A |
| 820 | A Murder Is Announced–Agatha Christie | 1.50 | 3.00 | 4.50 | M |
| 821 | The Drowning Pool–John Ross MacDonald | 3.50 | 7.00 | 10.50 | M |
| 822 | Cat of Many Tails–Ellery Queen | 1.50 | 3.00 | 4.50 | M |
| 823 | Trouble Is My Business–Raymond Chandler | 6.00 | 12.00 | 18.00 | M |
| 824 | The Road to San Jacinto–L.L. Foreman | 2.50 | 5.00 | 7.50 | W |
| 825 | Sexual Feeling in Married Men and Women–G. Lombard Kelly; 1951 | 1.25 | 2.50 | 3.75 | NF |
| 826 | Face of a Hero–Louis Falstein | 1.50 | 3.00 | 4.50 | |
| 827 | The Hepburn–Jan Westcott | 1.25 | 2.50 | 3.75 | |
| 828 | Murder City–Oakley Hall | 1.50 | 3.00 | 4.50 | M |
| 829 | Murder of a Nymph–Margot Neville | 1.50 | 3.00 | 4.50 | M |
| 830 | Homeward Borne–Ruth Chatterton | 1.50 | 3.00 | 4.50 | |
| 831 | The San Quentin–Clinton T. Duffy & Dean Jennings | 1.50 | 3.00 | 4.50 | NF |
| 832 | The Case of the Half-Wakened Wife–Erle Stanley Gardner | 1.50 | 3.00 | 4.50 | M |
| 833 | Of Missing Persons–David Goodis | 5.00 | 10.00 | 15.00 | M |
| 834 | Signal Guns at Sunup–John Jo Carpenter | 1.50 | 3.00 | 4.50 | |
| 835 | Alice in Wonderland and Other Favorites–Lewis Carroll | 3.00 | 6.00 | 9.00 | F |
| 836 | Attack–Perry Wolff; 1952 | 1.50 | 3.00 | 4.50 | C |
| 837 | The Golden Herd–Curt Carroll | 1.50 | 3.00 | 4.50 | |
| 838 | About Mrs. Leslie–Vina Delmar | 1.25 | 2.50 | 3.75 | E |
| 839 | Walk with the Devil–Elliott Arnold | 1.50 | 3.00 | 4.50 | |
| 840 | The Zebra Derby–Max Shulman | 1.25 | 2.50 | 3.75 | |
| 841 | Painted Post Law–Tom Gunn | 1.50 | 3.00 | 4.50 | W |
| 842 | Gun Showdown–William MacLeod Raine | 1.50 | 3.00 | 4.50 | W |
| 843 | The Great Snow–Henry Morton Robinson | 1.50 | 3.00 | 4.50 | |
| 844 | Each Bright River–Mildred Masterson McNeilly | 1.50 | 3.00 | 4.50 | |
| 845 | The Candy Kid–Dorothy B. Hughes | 1.50 | 3.00 | 4.50 | |
| 846 | Pick-up on Noon Street–Raymond Chandler | 4.00 | 8.00 | 12.00 | M |
| 847 | The Smoking Iron–Peter Field | 2.00 | 4.00 | 6.00 | W |
| 848 | Danger Trail–Max Brand | 1.50 | 3.00 | 4.50 | W |
| 849 | The Build-up Boys–Jeremy Kirk | 1.25 | 2.50 | 3.75 | |
| 850 | Foxfire–Anya Seton; 1952 | 1.25 | 2.50 | 3.75 | |
| 851 | White Witch Doctor–Louise A. Stinetorf | 1.50 | 3.00 | 4.50 | |
| 852 | Martha Logan's Meat Cook Book–Thora Campbell & Beth Bailey McLean | 1.00 | 2.00 | 3.00 | NF |
| 853 | Death on Treasure Trail–Don Davis | 1.50 | 3.00 | 4.50 | W |
| 854 | Why Slug a Postman?–Seldon Truss | 1.50 | 3.00 | 4.50 | |
| 855 | The Case of the Backward Mule–Erle Stanley Gardner | 1.50 | 3.00 | 4.50 | M |
| 856 | The Case of the Borrowed Brunette–Erle Stanley Gardner | 1.50 | 3.00 | 4.50 | M |
| 857 | Black Majesty–John W. Vandercook | 1.50 | 3.00 | 4.50 | A |
| 858 | Another Mug for the Bier–Richard Starnes | 1.50 | 3.00 | 4.50 | M |
| 859 | Bold Passage–Frank Bonham | 1.50 | 3.00 | 4.50 | W |
| 860 | You Can't Live Forever–Harold Q. Masur | 1.50 | 3.00 | 4.50 | M |
| 861 | Grant of Kingdom–Harvey Fergusson | 1.50 | 3.00 | 4.50 | |
| 862 | The Beckoning Door–Mabel Seeley | 1.50 | 3.00 | 4.50 | M |
| 863 | The People against O'Hara–Eleazar Lipsky | 1.50 | 3.00 | 4.50 | |
| 864 | By Rope and Lead–Ernest Haycox | 1.50 | 3.00 | 4.50 | W |
| 865 | Tonto Riley–Lee E. Wells | 1.50 | 3.00 | 4.50 | W |
| 866 | The Story of My Psychoanalysis–John Knight | 3.00 | 6.00 | 9.00 | NF |
| 867 | The Raid–John Brick | 1.50 | 3.00 | 4.50 | |
| 868 | Strumpet City–Don Tracy; aka Streets of Askelon | 1.50 | 3.00 | 4.50 | |
| 869 | The D.A. Breaks a Seal–Erle Stanley Gardner | 1.50 | 3.00 | 4.50 | M |
| 870 | Shield for Murder–William P. McGivern | 1.50 | 3.00 | 4.50 | M |
| 871 | The Hangman of Sleepy Valley–Davis Dresser; c-Frank McCarthy | 1.50 | 3.00 | 4.50 | W |
| 872 | What the Doctor Ordered–Francis Leo Golden | 1.50 | 3.00 | 4.50 | H |
| 873 | Magnus the Magnificent–Leslie Turner White | 1.50 | 3.00 | 4.50 | A |
| 874 | Double, Double–Ellery Queen | 1.50 | 3.00 | 4.50 | M |
| 875 | The Hard-Boiled Omnibus–ed. Joseph T. Shaw; 1952 | 5.00 | 10.00 | 15.00 | M |
| 876 | Double Cross Trail–E.E. Halleran | 1.50 | 3.00 | 4.50 | W |
| 877 | Gunman's Gold–Max Brand | 1.50 | 3.00 | 4.50 | W |
| 878 | Dark Laughter–Sherwood Anderson | 1.50 | 3.00 | 4.50 | |
| 879 | New York 22–Ilka Chase | 1.50 | 3.00 | 4.50 | |
| 880 | The Black-Eyed Stranger–Charlotte Armstrong | 1.50 | 3.00 | 4.50 | M |
| 881 | The Eleventh Hour–Robert B. Sinclair | 1.50 | 3.00 | 4.50 | |
| 882 | Death Rides the Night–Peter Field | 2.00 | 4.00 | 6.00 | W |
| 883 | The Captain–Russell Thacher | 1.50 | 3.00 | 4.50 | |
| 884 | The Sultan's Warrior–Bates Baldwin | 2.00 | 4.00 | 6.00 | A |
| 885 | Southern Territory–Robert Tallant | 1.50 | 3.00 | 4.50 | |
| 886 | The Case of the Fan-Dancer's Horse–Erle Stanley Gardner; c-Bergey. Note: Special Libby-Owens-Ford premium variant exists of this title and is a TV tie-in. | 2.00 | 4.00 | 6.00 | M |
| 887 | Judgement on Deltchev–Eric Ambler | 1.25 | 2.50 | 3.75 | |
| 888 | Shadow Riders of the Yellowstone–Les Savage, Jr | 1.50 | 3.00 | 4.50 | W |
| 889 | Beulah Land–H.L. Davis | 1.50 | 3.00 | 4.50 | |
| 890 | A Complete Guide to Home Sewing–Sylvia K. Mager | 1.25 | 2.50 | 3.75 | NF |
| 891 | The Unknown Lincoln–Dale Carnegie | 2.00 | 4.00 | 6.00 | NF |
| 892 | The Pocket Stamp Album–H.E. Harris | 6.00 | 12.00 | 18.00 | NF |
| 893 | Your Own Book of Campcraft–Catherine T. Hammett | 1.50 | 3.00 | 4.50 | NF |
| 894 | Horns for the Devil–Louis Malley | 1.50 | 3.00 | 4.50 | M |
| 895 | Mystery Ranch–Max Brand | 1.50 | 3.00 | 4.50 | W |
| 896 | Miami Murder-Go-Round–Marston LaFrance | 1.50 | 3.00 | 4.50 | M |
| 897 | They Come to Baghdad–Agatha Christie | 1.50 | 3.00 | 4.50 | M |
| 898 | Cop–Jack Karney | 1.50 | 3.00 | 4.50 | |
| 899 | Cobean's Naked Eye–Samuel E. Cobean | 1.50 | 3.00 | 4.50 | H |
| 900 | Scirocco–Romualdo Romano; 1952; c-Belarski | 1.50 | 3.00 | 4.50 | |

POCKET BOOK, *continued*

| | | V/Good | Fine | N/Mint | |
|---|---|---|---|---|---|
| 901 | Murder for the Holidays—Howard Rigsby | 1.50 | 3.00 | 4.50 | M |
| 902 | The End of the Trail—Peter Field | 2.00 | 4.00 | 6.00 | W |
| 903 | Miracle on 34th Street—Valentine Davies; movie tie-in | 6.00 | 12.00 | 18.00 | F |
| 904 | Fear in the Night—Irving Schwartz | 1.50 | 3.00 | 4.50 | |
| 905 | The Women of Champion City—Doris Davis | 2.00 | 4.00 | 6.00 | E |
| 906 | Lynch-Rope Law—Davis Dresser | 1.50 | 3.00 | 4.50 | W |
| 907 | The Way Some People Die—John Ross MacDonald | 3.50 | 7.00 | 10.50 | M |
| 908 | New Tales of Space and Time—Raymond J. Healy | 1.50 | 3.00 | 4.50 | SF |
| 909 | The Case of the Lazy Lover—Erle Stanley Gardner; 1953 | 1.50 | 3.00 | 4.50 | M |
| 910 | The Streak—Max Brand | 1.50 | 3.00 | 4.50 | W |
| 911 | My Gun Is My Law—Will Ermine | 1.50 | 3.00 | 4.50 | W |
| 912 | . . . And to My Beloved Husband—Philip Loraine | 1.50 | 3.00 | 4.50 | |
| 913 | Dark Dream—Robert Martin | 1.50 | 3.00 | 4.50 | |
| 914 | The Man from Thief River—Peter Field | 2.00 | 4.00 | 6.00 | W |
| 915 | Ruby—Vina Delmar; 1952 | 1.25 | 2.50 | 3.75 | |
| 916 | The Simple Art of Murder—Raymond Chandler | 4.00 | 8.00 | 12.00 | M |
| 917 | The Other Body in Grant's Tomb—Richard Starnes | 1.50 | 3.00 | 4.50 | M |
| 918 | Shadows Move among Them—Edgar Mittelholzer | 1.50 | 3.00 | 4.50 | |
| 919 | The Lord God of the Flesh—Jules Romains | 1.50 | 3.00 | 4.50 | |
| 920 | Space Platform—Murray Leinster; c-Bergey | 2.00 | 4.00 | 6.00 | SF |
| 921 | Rio Kid Justice—Don Davis | 1.50 | 3.00 | 4.50 | W |
| 922 | The Case of the Lonely Heiress—Erle Stanley Gardner | 1.50 | 3.00 | 4.50 | M |
| 923 | Hangman's Hat—Paul Ernst | 1.50 | 3.00 | 4.50 | |
| 924 | The Left Hand of God—William E. Barrett | 2.00 | 4.00 | 6.00 | |
| 925 | Favorite Hymns—ed. Albert H. Morehead & James Morehead; 1953 | 2.00 | 4.00 | 6.00 | NF |
| 926 | The Origin of Evil—Ellery Queen | 1.50 | 3.00 | 4.50 | M |
| 927 | Red Blizzard—Clay Fisher | 1.50 | 3.00 | 4.50 | W |
| 928 | Power Golf—Ben Hogan | 1.25 | 2.50 | 3.75 | NF |
| 929 | Himalayan Assignment—F. Van Wyck Mason | 1.50 | 3.00 | 4.50 | |
| 930 | The Hair-Trigger Kid—Max Brand | 1.50 | 3.00 | 4.50 | W |
| 931 | Reclining Figure—Marco Page | 1.50 | 3.00 | 4.50 | |
| 932 | Captain Barney—Jan Westcott | 1.50 | 3.00 | 4.50 | A |
| 933 | Basketball—Arnold "Red" Averbach | 1.25 | 2.50 | 3.75 | NF |
| 934 | Kill and Tell—Howard Rigsby | 1.50 | 3.00 | 4.50 | M |
| 935 | Out from Eden—Victoria Lincoln | 1.25 | 2.50 | 3.75 | |
| 936 | The Proud Ones—Verne Athanas | 1.25 | 2.50 | 3.75 | W |
| 937 | Sheriff on the Spot—Peter Field | 2.00 | 4.00 | 6.00 | W |
| 938 | Candlemas Bay—Ruth Moore | 1.25 | 2.50 | 3.75 | |
| 939 | The Sundowners—Jon Cleary | 1.50 | 3.00 | 4.50 | |
| 940 | Catch a Killer—Ursula Curtiss | 1.50 | 3.00 | 4.50 | M |
| 941 | Exit for a Dame—Richard Ellington | 1.50 | 3.00 | 4.50 | M |
| 942 | Painted Post Range—Tom Gunn | 1.50 | 3.00 | 4.50 | W |
| 943 | Planet of the Dreamers—John D. MacDonald | 3.00 | 6.00 | 9.00 | SF |
| 944 | Winds of Morning—H.L. Davis | 1.50 | 3.00 | 4.50 | |
| 945 | Floodtide—Frank Yerby | 1.50 | 3.00 | 4.50 | A |
| 946 | River of Rogues—A.R. Beverley Giddings | 2.00 | 4.00 | 6.00 | A |
| 947 | The War of the Worlds—H.G. Wells; movie tie-in | 3.00 | 6.00 | 9.00 | SF |
| 948 | Laughter Is Legal—Dr. Francis Leo Golden | 1.50 | 3.00 | 4.50 | H |
| 949 | Two Clues—Erle Stanley Gardner | 1.50 | 3.00 | 4.50 | M |
| 950 | Single Jack—Max Brand; 1953 | 1.50 | 3.00 | 4.50 | W |
| 951 | Portrait of a Marriage—Pearl S. Buck | 1.25 | 2.50 | 3.75 | |
| 952 | Stella—Jan de Hartog | 1.25 | 2.50 | 3.75 | |
| 953 | The Sea—Jan de Hartog | 1.25 | 2.50 | 3.75 | |
| 954 | Outlaw Thickets—Les Savage, Jr | 1.50 | 3.00 | 4.50 | W |
| 955 | 101 Best Loved Songs—Albert H. Morehead & James Morehead | 1.25 | 2.50 | 3.75 | NF |
| 956 | Mrs. McGinty's Dead—Agatha Christie | 1.50 | 3.00 | 4.50 | M |
| 957 | Woman's Medical Problems—Maxine Davis | 1.25 | 2.50 | 3.75 | NF |
| 958 | Outside the Law—Philip Loraine | 1.50 | 3.00 | 4.50 | M |
| 959 | The Man from Nazareth—Harry Emerson Fosdick | 1.50 | 3.00 | 4.50 | B |

*Pocket Book 959, Pocket Book 1098, Pocket Book 1106.*

| | | V/Good | Fine | N/Mint | |
|---|---|---|---|---|---|
| 960 | Calendar of Crime—Ellery Queen; c-Richard Powers | 1.50 | 3.00 | 4.50 | M |
| 961 | The Crooked Frame—William P. McGivern | 1.50 | 3.00 | 4.50 | M |
| 962 | Canyon of Death—Peter Field | 2.00 | 4.00 | 6.00 | W |
| 963 | Excuse It, Please!—Cornelia Otis Skinner | 1.50 | 3.00 | 4.50 | |
| 964 | Trespass—Eugene Brown | 1.50 | 3.00 | 4.50 | |
| 965 | The Case of the Vagabond Virgin—Erle Stanley Gardner | 1.50 | 3.00 | 4.50 | M |
| 966 | The 4th Pocket Book of Crossword Puzzles—Margaret Petherbridge Farrar | 5.00 | 10.00 | 15.00 | NF |
| 967 | Snaketrack—Frank Bonham | 1.50 | 3.00 | 4.50 | W |
| 968 | The Low Calorie Diet—Marvin Small | 1.00 | 2.00 | 3.00 | NF |
| 969 | The Tender Age—Russell Thacher | 1.00 | 2.00 | 3.00 | |
| 970 | The Diary of a Young Girl—Anne Frank | 1.50 | 3.00 | 4.50 | NF |
| 971 | Marked for Murder—John Ross MacDonald | 3.00 | 6.00 | 9.00 | M |
| 972 | Halfway to Timberline—Ward West | 1.50 | 3.00 | 4.50 | W |
| 973 | Tough Company—Clem Colt | 1.50 | 3.00 | 4.50 | W |
| 974 | The Highland Hawk—Leslie Turner White | 1.50 | 3.00 | 4.50 | |
| 975 | Blood in Your Eye—Robert Patrick Wilmot; 1954 | 1.50 | 3.00 | 4.50 | M |
| 976 | The Case of the Dubious Bridegroom—Erle Stanley Gardner | 1.50 | 3.00 | 4.50 | M |
| 977 | Wild Drum Beat—F. Van Wyck Mason | 1.50 | 3.00 | 4.50 | |
| 978 | Land of the Lawless—Les Savage, Jr | 1.50 | 3.00 | 4.50 | W |
| 979 | Vengeance Trail—Max Brand | 1.50 | 3.00 | 4.50 | W |
| 980 | A Great Time to Be Alive—Harry Emerson Fosdick | 1.25 | 2.50 | 3.75 | |
| 981 | The Big Heat—William P. McGivern | 1.50 | 3.00 | 4.50 | M |
| 982 | Doctor Two-Guns—Peter Field | 2.00 | 4.00 | 6.00 | W |
| 983 | Pioneer Loves—Ernest Haycox | 1.50 | 3.00 | 4.50 | W |
| 984 | The Shining Tides—Win Brooks | 1.50 | 3.00 | 4.50 | |
| 985 | Worse Than Murder—David Duncan | 1.50 | 3.00 | 4.50 | M |
| 986 | Watchdog of Thunder River—Will Ermine | 1.50 | 3.00 | 4.50 | W |
| 987 | The Whistler—E.B. Mann | 1.50 | 3.00 | 4.50 | W |
| 988 | Last Seen Wearing . . .—Hillary Waugh | 1.50 | 3.00 | 4.50 | W |
| 989 | Sands of Mars—Arthur C. Clarke | 2.00 | 4.00 | 6.00 | SF |
| 990 | Coyote Gulch—Peter Field | 2.00 | 4.00 | 6.00 | W |
| 991 | Border Guns—Max Brand | 1.50 | 3.00 | 4.50 | W |
| 992 | Ripley's New Believe It or Not!—Robert Ripley | 2.00 | 4.00 | 6.00 | NF |
| 993 | The Hidden Flower—Pearl S. Buck | 1.25 | 2.50 | 3.75 | |
| 994 | April Snow—Lillian Budd | 1.25 | 2.50 | 3.75 | |
| 995 | The Medicine Whip—John & Margaret Harris | 1.25 | 2.50 | 3.75 | |
| 996 | Lyle Brown's Sport Quiz—Lyle Brown | 1.25 | 2.50 | 3.75 | S |
| 997 | Murder on Monday—Robert Patrick Wilmont | 1.50 | 3.00 | 4.50 | M |
| 998 | So Rich, So Lovely, and So Dead—Harold Q. Masur | 1.50 | 3.00 | 4.50 | M |
| 999 | Rogue Valley—Verne Athanas | 1.50 | 3.00 | 4.50 | W |
| 1000 | The Little World of Don Camillo—Giovanni Guareschi; 1954 | 1.25 | 2.50 | 3.75 | |
| 1001 | Homer Crist—John Brick | 1.25 | 2.50 | 3.75 | |
| 1002 | Painted Post Gunplay—Tom Gunn | 1.50 | 3.00 | 4.50 | W |
| 1003 | Funerals Are Fatal—Agatha Christie | 1.50 | 3.00 | 4.50 | M |
| 1004 | The Big Deal—Selig Seligman | 1.50 | 3.00 | 4.50 | |
| 1005 | The King Is Dead—Ellery Queen | 1.50 | 3.00 | 4.50 | M |

POCKET BOOK, *continued*

| | | V/Good | Fine | N/Mint | |
|---|---|---|---|---|---|
| 1006 | The Amber Fire–Don Tracy | 1.50 | 3.00 | 4.50 | |
| 1007 | My Best Science Fiction Story–Leo Margulies & Oscar J. Friend | 2.00 | 4.00 | 6.00 | SF |
| 1008 | Windom's Way–James Ramsey Ullman | 1.50 | 3.00 | 4.50 | |
| 1009 | The Case of the Cautious Coquette–Erle Stanley Gardner | 1.50 | 3.00 | 4.50 | M |
| 1010 | The D.A. Takes a Chance–Erle Stanley Gardner | 1.50 | 3.00 | 4.50 | M |
| 1011 | Murder on the Frontier–Ernest Haycox | 1.50 | 3.00 | 4.50 | W |
| 1012 | Tale of Two Lovers–Henry Morton Robinson | 1.50 | 3.00 | 4.50 | |
| 1013 | Tales for Salesmen–Francis Leo Golden | 1.25 | 2.50 | 3.75 | H |
| 1014 | The Covered Wagon–Emerson Hope | 1.50 | 3.00 | 4.50 | W |
| 1015 | The Girls of Sanfrediano–Vasco Pratolini | 1.25 | 2.50 | 3.75 | |
| 1016 | Last Race–Jon Manchip White | 1.50 | 3.00 | 4.50 | |
| 1017 | Johnny Guitar–Roy Chanslor | 1.50 | 3.00 | 4.50 | |
| 1018 | The Gun Tamer–Max Brand | 1.50 | 3.00 | 4.50 | W |
| 1019 | In Love–Alfred Hayes | 1.25 | 2.50 | 3.75 | |
| 1020 | Meet Me at the Morgue–John Ross MacDonald | 3.00 | 6.00 | 9.00 | M |
| 1021 | Murder with Mirrors–Agatha Christie | 1.50 | 3.00 | 4.50 | M |
| 1022 | Troubled Range–E.B. Mann | 1.50 | 3.00 | 4.50 | W |
| 1023 | Two-Gun Rio Kid–Don Davis | 1.50 | 3.00 | 4.50 | W |
| 1024 | The Barbarians–F. Van Wyck Mason | 1.50 | 3.00 | 4.50 | A |
| 1025 | How to Stop Smoking–Herbert Brean; 1954 | 1.00 | 2.00 | 3.00 | NF |
| 1026 | The Intruder–Helen Fowler | 1.25 | 2.50 | 3.75 | |
| 1027 | Law Badge–Peter Field | 2.00 | 4.00 | 6.00 | W |
| 1028 | Outlaw–Ernest Haycox | 1.50 | 3.00 | 4.50 | W |
| 1029 | The Case of the Negligent Nymph–Erle Stanley Gardner | 1.50 | 3.00 | 4.50 | M |
| 1030 | Rogue Cop–William P. McGivern | 1.50 | 3.00 | 4.50 | M |
| 1031 | Busted Range–Will Ermine | 1.50 | 3.00 | 4.50 | W |
| 1032 | The Colors of the Day–Romain Gary | 1.50 | 3.00 | 4.50 | |
| 1033 | The Night Horseman–Max Brand | 1.50 | 3.00 | 4.50 | W |
| 1034 | Walk Out on Death–Charlotte Armstrong; 1955 | 1.50 | 3.00 | 4.50 | M |
| 1035 | The Outlaw of Eagle's Nest–Peter Field | 2.00 | 4.00 | 6.00 | W |
| 1036 | A Pocket Full of Rye–Agatha Christie | 1.50 | 3.00 | 4.50 | M |
| 1037 | Space Tug–Murray Leinster | 2.00 | 4.00 | 6.00 | SF |
| 1038 | You Shall Know Them–Vercors | 2.00 | 4.00 | 6.00 | SF |
| 1039 | The Beautiful Frame–William Pearson | 1.50 | 3.00 | 4.50 | M |
| 1040 | Boss of the Plains–Will Ermine | 1.50 | 3.00 | 4.50 | W |
| 1041 | The Case of the One-eyed Witness–Erle Stanley Gardner | 1.50 | 3.00 | 4.50 | M |
| 1042 | The Little Ark–Jan de Hartog | 1.25 | 2.50 | 3.75 | |
| 1043 | The Story of Esther Costello–Nicholas Monsarrat | 1.25 | 2.50 | 3.75 | |
| 1044 | The Long Goodbye–Raymond Chandler | 3.50 | 7.00 | 10.50 | M |
| 1045 | Science Fiction Terror Tales–Groff Conklin | 2.50 | 5.00 | 7.50 | SF |
| 1046 | Time and Time Again–James Hilton | 1.50 | 3.00 | 4.50 | |
| 1047 | Rogue's Yarn–John Jennings | 1.50 | 3.00 | 4.50 | A |
| 1048 | Ride the Dark Hills–W. Edmunds Claussen | 1.50 | 3.00 | 4.50 | W |
| 1049 | The Scarlet Letters–Ellery Queen | 1.50 | 3.00 | 4.50 | M |
| 1050 | Three for the Money–James McConnaughey; 1955 | 1.50 | 3.00 | 4.50 | |
| 1051 | A Fair Wind Home–Ruth Moore | 1.25 | 2.50 | 3.75 | |
| 1052 | The D.A. Breaks an Egg–Erle Stanley Gardner | 1.50 | 3.00 | 4.50 | M |
| 1053 | Crackers in Bed–Vic Fredericks | 1.25 | 2.50 | 3.75 | |
| 1054 | Gambler's Gold–Peter Field | 2.00 | 4.00 | 6.00 | W |
| 1055 | I Die Possessed–J.B. O'Sullivan | 1.25 | 2.50 | 3.75 | M |
| 1056 | Seven Trails–Max Brand | 1.50 | 3.00 | 4.50 | W |
| 1057 | How to Work with Tools and Wood–Fred Gross | 1.25 | 2.50 | 3.75 | NF |
| 1058 | Murder's Nest–Charlotte Armstrong | 1.50 | 3.00 | 4.50 | M |
| 1059 | Hero Driver–Alfred Coppel | 1.50 | 3.00 | 4.50 | |
| 1060 | Hired Hand–Nelson Nye | 1.50 | 3.00 | 4.50 | W |
| 1061 | Arrow in the Moon–John Harris & Margaret Harris | 1.50 | 3.00 | 4.50 | |
| 1062 | Margin of Terror–William P. McGivern | 1.50 | 3.00 | 4.50 | M |
| 1063 | The Case of the Musical Cow–Erle Stanley Gardner | 1.50 | 3.00 | 4.50 | M |
| 1064 | Stage Road to Denver–Allan Vaughan Elston | 1.50 | 3.00 | 4.50 | W |
| 1065 | The Tenderfoot–Max Brand | 1.50 | 3.00 | 4.50 | W |
| 1066 | The Conquest of Don Pedro–Harvey Fergusson | 1.25 | 2.50 | 3.75 | |

| | | V/Good | Fine | N/Mint | |
|---|---|---|---|---|---|
| 1067 | Don Camillo and His Flock–Giovanni Guareschi | 1.25 | 2.50 | 3.75 | |
| 1068 | Mustang Mesa–Peter Field | 2.00 | 4.00 | 6.00 | W |
| 1069 | Prairie Guns–Ernest Haycox | 1.50 | 3.00 | 4.50 | W |
| 1070 | The Victim Was Important–Joe Rayter | 1.50 | 3.00 | 4.50 | M |
| 1071 | Arrow in the Hill–Jefferson Cooper (Gardner F. Fox) | 1.50 | 3.00 | 4.50 | W |
| 1072 | The 5th Pocket Book of Crossword Puzzles–Margaret Petherbridge Farrar | 4.05 | 8.10 | 12.15 | NF |
| 1073 | Cress Delahanty–Jessamyn West | 1.25 | 2.50 | 3.75 | |
| 1074 | Invaders of Earth–Groff Conklin | 1.50 | 3.00 | 4.50 | SF |
| 1075 | A Ray and a Bone–Hillary Waugh; 1955 | 1.25 | 2.50 | 3.75 | |
| 1076 | Captain Judas–F. Van Wyck Mason | 1.50 | 3.00 | 4.50 | A |
| 1077 | The Deadly Climate–Ursula Curtiss | 1.50 | 3.00 | 4.50 | M |
| 1078 | Five against the House–Jack Finney | 3.00 | 6.00 | 9.00 | M |
| 1079 | The Fool Killer–Helen Eustis | 1.50 | 3.00 | 4.50 | |
| 1080 | Baby Sitter's Guide, by Dennis the Menace–Hank Ketcham & Bob Harmon | 2.00 | 4.00 | 6.00 | H |
| 1081 | Ravaged Range–Peter Field | 2.00 | 4.00 | 6.00 | W |
| 1082 | The Glass Village–Ellery Queen | 1.50 | 3.00 | 4.50 | M |
| 1083 | And Sometimes Death–Jo Valentine; aka The Trouble in Thor | 1.50 | 3.00 | 4.50 | M |
| 1084 | The Untamed–Max Brand | 1.50 | 3.00 | 4.50 | W |
| 1085 | The Under Dog and Other Mysteries–Agatha Christie | 1.50 | 3.00 | 4.50 | M |
| 1086 | Wagon Wheel Gap–Allan Vaughan Elston | 1.50 | 3.00 | 4.50 | W |
| 1087 | The New Peter Arno Pocket Book–Peter Arno; 1956 | 1.50 | 3.00 | 4.50 | H |
| 1088 | Guns in the Saddle–Peter Field | 2.00 | 4.00 | 6.00 | W |
| 1089 | The Case of the Fiery Fingers–Erle Stanley Gardner | 1.50 | 3.00 | 4.50 | M |
| 1090 | The Devil Threw Dice–Amber Dean | 1.50 | 3.00 | 4.50 | M |
| 1091 | Rider of the Midnight Range–Will Ermine | 1.50 | 3.00 | 4.50 | W |
| 1092 | The Case of the Angry Mourner–Erle Stanley Gardner | 1.50 | 3.00 | 4.50 | M |
| 1093 | The Compleat Practical Joker–H. Allen Smith | 1.25 | 2.50 | 3.75 | H |
| 1094 | Death Rides the Dondrino–Roe Richmond | 1.50 | 3.00 | 4.50 | W |
| 1095 | Alibi for Murder–Charlotte Armstrong | 1.50 | 3.00 | 4.50 | M |
| 1096 | Doctor Hudson's Secret Journal–Lloyd C. Douglas | 1.25 | 2.50 | 3.75 | |
| 1097 | Tragedy Trail–Max Brand | 1.50 | 3.00 | 4.50 | W |
| 1098 | Guys and Dolls–Damon Runyon. Note: Queen's Quorum No. 82 | 2.00 | 4.00 | 6.00 | |
| 1099 | Good Morning, Miss Dove–Frances Gray Patton | 1.00 | 2.00 | 3.00 | |
| 1100 | Off the Cuff–Jerry Lieberman; 1956 | 1.25 | 2.50 | 3.75 | H |
| 1101 | Cry, Coyote–Steve Frazee | 1.50 | 3.00 | 4.50 | W |
| 1102 | A Most Contagious Game–Samuel Grafton | 1.25 | 2.50 | 3.75 | |
| 1103 | Showdown–Allan Vaughan Elston | 1.25 | 2.50 | 3.75 | W |
| 1104 | Once a Fighter . . .–Les Savage, Jr | 1.25 | 2.50 | 3.75 | W |
| 1105 | Waterfront Cop–William P. McGivern | 1.25 | 2.50 | 3.75 | |
| 1106 | Feeding Your Baby and Child–Miriam E. Lowenberg & Benjamin Spock | 2.00 | 4.00 | 6.00 | NF |
| 1107 | The Case of the Moth-eaten Mink–Erle Stanley Gardner | 1.50 | 3.00 | 4.50 | M |
| 1108 | The Brass Command–Clay Fisher | 1.25 | 2.50 | 3.75 | W |
| 1109 | Don't Hang Me Too High–J.B. O'Sullivan | 1.25 | 2.50 | 3.75 | |
| 1110 | Governor's Choice–Martin Mayer | .75 | 1.50 | 2.25 | |
| 1111 | The Big Store–Oscar Schisgall | 1.25 | 2.50 | 3.75 | |
| 1112 | The Girl from Frisco–William Heuman | 1.25 | 2.50 | 3.75 | W |
| 1113 | Man of the West–Philip Yordan | 1.25 | 2.50 | 3.75 | |
| 1114 | So Many Steps to Death–Agatha Christie | 1.25 | 2.50 | 3.75 | M |
| 1115 | Two Tickets for Tangier–F. Van Wyck Mason | 1.25 | 2.50 | 3.75 | |
| 1116 | Forbidden Valley–Allan Vaughan Elston | 1.25 | 2.50 | 3.75 | W |
| 1117 | The River Witch–Marjorie McIntyre | 1.25 | 2.50 | 3.75 | |
| 1118 | Q.B.I.–Ellery Queen | 1.00 | 2.00 | 3.00 | M |
| 1119 | Onions in the Stew–Betty MacDonald | 1.25 | 2.50 | 3.75 | H |
| 1120 | Dragnet: Case No. 561–David Knight; TV tie-in | 2.00 | 4.00 | 6.00 | M |
| 1121 | The Case of the Grinning Gorilla–Erle Stanley Gardner | 1.50 | 3.00 | 4.50 | M |
| 1122 | The False Rider–Max Brand | 1.25 | 2.50 | 3.75 | W |

Pocket Book 1126, Pocket Book 1153, Pocket Book 1177.

| | | V/Good | Fine | N/Mint | |
|---|---|---|---|---|---|
| POCKET BOOK, *continued* | | | | | |
| 1123 | The Road to Laramie–Peter Field | 2.00 | 4.00 | 6.00 | W |
| 1124 | Cowboy, Say Your Prayers!–Will Ermine | 1.25 | 2.50 | 3.75 | W |
| 1125 | Dennis the Menace Rides Again–Hank Ketcham; 1956 | 1.50 | 3.00 | 4.50 | H |
| 1126 | The Jungle Kids–Evan Hunter | 4.00 | 8.00 | 12.00 | JD |
| 1127 | The Case of the Hesitant Hostess–Erle Stanley Gardner | 1.50 | 3.00 | 4.50 | M |
| 1128 | The Guns of Witchwater–Colby Wolford | 1.25 | 2.50 | 3.75 | |
| 1129 | The 6th Pocket Book of Crossword Puzzles–Margaret Petherbridge Farrar | 4.00 | 8.00 | 12.00 | NF |
| 1130 | Strictly for Laughs–Joey Adams | 1.25 | 2.50 | 3.75 | H |
| 1131 | The Treasure of Pleasant Valley–Frank Yerby | 1.25 | 2.50 | 3.75 | |
| 1132 | Asking for Trouble–Joe Rayter | 1.25 | 2.50 | 3.75 | |
| 1133 | Galloping Broncos–Max Brand | 1.25 | 2.50 | 3.75 | W |
| 1134 | The Iron Bronc–Will Ermine | 1.25 | 2.50 | 3.75 | W |
| 1135 | The Parson of Gunbarrel Basin–Nelson Nye | 1.25 | 2.50 | 3.75 | W |
| 1136 | Sinners and Shrouds–Jonathan Latimer | 1.50 | 3.00 | 4.50 | M |
| 1137 | The Big Pasture–Clay Fisher | 1.25 | 2.50 | 3.75 | W |
| 1138 | The Case of the Fugitive Nurse–Erle Stanley Gardner | 1.50 | 3.00 | 4.50 | M |
| 1139 | Castle Garac–Nicholas Monsarrat | 1.25 | 2.50 | 3.75 | |
| 1140 | The Invisible Man–H.G. Wells | 3.00 | 6.00 | 9.00 | HO |
| 1141 | Hunt the Man Down–William Pearson; 1957 | 1.25 | 2.50 | 3.75 | |
| 1142 | The Lonely Grass–Nelson Nye | 1.25 | 2.50 | 3.75 | W |
| 1143 | Lysander–F. Van Wyck Mason | 1.25 | 2.50 | 3.75 | |
| 1144 | The Laff Parade–Jerry Lieberman | 1.25 | 2.50 | 3.75 | H |
| 1145 | Stab in the Dark–Joe Rayter | 1.25 | 2.50 | 3.75 | |
| 1146 | The Dangerous Years–Douglass Wallop | 1.25 | 2.50 | 3.75 | |
| 1147 | Combat Nurse–Frieda K. Franklin | .75 | 1.50 | 2.25 | R |
| 1148 | The Last Rodeo–Ernest Haycox | 1.25 | 2.50 | 3.75 | W |
| 1149 | The Gambler–Max Brand | 1.25 | 2.50 | 3.75 | W |
| 1150 | The Man on the Couch–Mischa Richter; 1957 | .75 | 1.50 | 2.25 | |
| 1151 | Hickory Dickory Death–Agatha Christie | 1.25 | 2.50 | 3.75 | M |
| 1152 | The Men from the Boys–Ed Lacy | 1.25 | 2.50 | 3.75 | M |
| 1153 | Wanted: Dennis the Menace–Hank Ketcham | 1.50 | 3.00 | 4.50 | H |
| 1154 | The 7th Pocket Book of Crossword Puzzles–Margaret Petherbridge Farrar | 4.00 | 8.00 | 12.00 | NF |
| 1155 | The Case of the Green-eyed Sister–Erle Stanley Gardner | 1.50 | 3.00 | 4.50 | M |
| 1156 | The 7 File–William P. McGivern | 1.25 | 2.50 | 3.75 | M |
| 1157 | Widow's Web–Ursula Curtiss | .75 | 1.50 | 2.25 | M |
| 1158 | Cakes and Ale–W. Somerset Maugham | .75 | 1.50 | 2.25 | |
| 1159 | The Blue Mustang–Clay Fisher | 1.25 | 2.50 | 3.75 | W |
| 1160 | Double Entendre–Newton Wilson Hoke | 1.25 | 2.50 | 3.75 | |
| 1161 | Maverick's Return–Peter Field | 2.00 | 4.00 | 6.00 | W |
| 1162 | Combat Mission–Joe David Brown | .75 | 1.50 | 2.25 | C |
| 1163 | The Wyoming Bubble–Allan Vaughan Elston | 1.25 | 2.50 | 3.75 | W |
| 1164 | The Bulls and the Bees–Roger Eddy | 1.25 | 2.50 | 3.75 | |
| 1165 | Ripley's Believe It or Not! 4th Series–Robert Ripley | 2.00 | 4.00 | 6.00 | NF |
| 1166 | Lone Wolf–Bennett Foster | 1.25 | 2.50 | 3.75 | W |
| 1167 | Inspector Queen's Own Case–Ellery Queen | 1.25 | 2.50 | 3.75 | M |
| 1168 | Smiling Desperado–Max Brand | 1.25 | 2.50 | 3.75 | W |
| 1169 | War on the Saddle Rock–Will Ermine | 1.25 | 2.50 | 3.75 | W |
| 1170 | The Case of the Restless Redhead–Erle Stanley Gardner | 1.50 | 3.00 | 4.50 | M |
| 1171 | When Strangers Meet–Robert Bloomfield | 1.25 | 2.50 | 3.75 | |
| 1172 | The Seven Islands–Jon Godden | 1.25 | 2.50 | 3.75 | A |
| 1173 | Sheriff Wanted!–Peter Field | 2.00 | 4.00 | 6.00 | W |
| 1174 | Dead Man's Folly–Agatha Christie | 1.25 | 2.50 | 3.75 | M |
| 1175 | The 8th Pocket Book of Crossword Puzzles–Margaret Petherbridge Farrar; 1957 | 4.00 | 8.00 | 12.00 | NF |
| 1176 | Captain Nemesis–F. Van Wyck Mason | 1.25 | 2.50 | 3.75 | A |
| 1177 | Old Yeller–Fred Gipson | 1.25 | 2.50 | 3.75 | A |
| 1178 | Rebecca's Pride–Donald McNutt Douglass | 2.50 | 5.00 | 7.50 | E |
| 1179 | Dennis the Menace vs. Everybody–Hank Ketcham | 1.50 | 3.00 | 4.50 | H |
| 1180 | The Invisible Outlaw–Max Brand | 1.25 | 2.50 | 3.75 | W |
| 1181 | The Marked Men–Allan Vaughan Elston | 1.25 | 2.50 | 3.75 | W |
| 1182 | The 9th Pocket Book of Crossword Puzzles–Margaret Petherbridge Farrar | 4.00 | 8.00 | 12.00 | NF |
| 1183 | No Blade of Grass–John Christopher | 2.50 | 5.00 | 7.50 | SF |
| 1184 | The NBC Book of Stars–Earl Wilson | 2.50 | 5.00 | 7.50 | NF |
| 1185 | The Brave Cowboy–Edward Abbey | 1.25 | 2.50 | 3.75 | W |
| 1186 | Santa Fe Passage–Clay Fisher; 1958 | 1.25 | 2.50 | 3.75 | W |
| 1187 | Powder Valley Showdown–Peter Field | 2.00 | 4.00 | 6.00 | W |
| 1188 | The Abode of Love–AuGray Menen | .75 | 1.50 | 2.25 | |
| 1189 | My Kingdom for a Hearse–Craig Rice | 1.50 | 3.00 | 4.50 | M |
| 1190 | Outlaw Breed–Max Brand | 1.25 | 2.50 | 3.75 | W |
| 1191 | Last Stage to Aspen–Allan Vaughan Elston | 1.25 | 2.50 | 3.75 | W |
| 1192 | The Enemy Below–D.A. Rayner; movie tie-in | 1.25 | 2.50 | 3.75 | C |
| 1193 | Night Extra–William P. McGivern | 1.25 | 2.50 | 3.75 | M |
| 1194 | Shotting Melody–E.B. Mann | 1.25 | 2.50 | 3.75 | W |
| 1195 | Ripley's Believe It or Not! 5th Series–Robert Ripley | 2.00 | 4.00 | 6.00 | NF |
| 1196 | Wagonmaster–Robert Turner; TV tie-in | 3.50 | 7.00 | 10.50 | W |
| 1197 | Hard Man–Leo Katcher | 1.25 | 2.50 | 3.75 | |
| 1198 | Dragnet: The Case of the Courteous Killer–Richard Deming; TV tie-in | 3.00 | 6.00 | 9.00 | M |
| 1199 | The Day the Money Stopped–Brendan Gill | 1.25 | 2.50 | 3.75 | |
| 1200 | Too Humerous to Mention–Charles Preston; 1958 | 1.25 | 2.50 | 3.75 | H |
| 1201 | The Sulu Sea Murders–F. Van Wyck Mason | 1.25 | 2.50 | 3.75 | |
| 1202 | The Tank Destroyers–Lawrence H. Kahn | 1.25 | 2.50 | 3.75 | C |
| 1203 | Trail Partners–Max Brand | 1.25 | 2.50 | 3.75 | W |
| 1204 | The O.S.S. and I–William J. Morgan | 1.25 | 2.50 | 3.75 | |
| 1205 | Return to Powder Valley–Peter Field | 2.00 | 4.00 | 6.00 | W |
| 1206 | The Murder of the Missing Link–Vercors; aka You Shall Know Them | 2.00 | 4.00 | 6.00 | SF |
| 1207 | The Assault–Allen R. Matthews | 1.25 | 2.50 | 3.75 | C |
| 1208 | Ripley's Believe It or Not! 6th Series–Robert Ripley | 2.00 | 4.00 | 6.00 | NF |
| 1209 | Yellowstone Kelly–Clay Fisher; movie tie-in | 1.50 | 3.00 | 4.50 | W |
| 1210 | Betty Cornell's Glamour Guide for Teens–Betty Cornell | .75 | 1.50 | 2.25 | NF |
| 1211 | Grand Mesa–Allan Vaughan Elston | 1.25 | 2.50 | 3.75 | W |
| 1212 | Beyond the Call of Duty–Eugene Brown | 1.25 | 2.50 | 3.75 | |
| 1213 | Blacksnake Trail–Peter Field | 2.00 | 4.00 | 6.00 | W |
| 1214 | Dragnet: The Case of the Crime King–Richard Deming; TV tie-in | 3.00 | 6.00 | 9.00 | M |
| 1215 | Knocked a Loop–Craig Rice | 1.50 | 3.00 | 4.50 | M |
| 1216 | The Scout–Robert Turner; TV tie-in | 3.50 | 7.00 | 10.50 | W |
| 1217 | Dennis the Menace: Household Hurricane–Hank Ketcham | 1.50 | 3.00 | 4.50 | H |
| 1218 | Ensign O'Toole and Me–William J. Lederer | 1.25 | 2.50 | 3.75 | H |
| 1219 | The China Sea Murders–F. Van Wyck Mason | 1.25 | 2.50 | 3.75 | M |
| 1220 | Murder on Delivery–Spencer Dean | 1.25 | 2.50 | 3.75 | M |
| 1221 | Speedy–Max Brand | 1.25 | 2.50 | 3.75 | W |
| 1222 | The Winds of Time–Chad Oliver; c-Powers | 1.50 | 3.00 | 4.50 | SF |
| 1223 | The Gracious Lily Affair–F. Van Wyck Mason; 1959 | 1.25 | 2.50 | 3.75 | |

| | | V/Good | Fine | N/Mint | |
|---|---|---|---|---|---|

**POCKET BOOK,** *continued*

| No. | Title | V/Good | Fine | N/Mint | |
|---|---|---|---|---|---|
| 1224 | Brother Sebastian—Chon Day | 1.25 | 2.50 | 3.75 | H |
| 1225 | A Roman Affair—Ercole Patti | .75 | 1.50 | 2.25 | |
| 1226 | Wagons West!—Robert Turner; TV tie-in | 3.50 | 7.00 | 10.50 | W |
| 1227 | The 10th Pocket Book of Crossword Puzzles—Margaret Petherbridge Farrar | 4.00 | 8.00 | 12.00 | NF |
| 1228 | Blood on the Trail—Max Brand | 1.25 | 2.50 | 3.75 | W |
| 1229 | The Hit—Julian Mayfield | 1.25 | 2.50 | 3.75 | M |
| 1230 | End of the Line—Bert Hitchens & Dolores Hitchens | 1.25 | 2.50 | 3.75 | M |
| 1231 | The Broken Angel—Floyd Mahannah | 1.50 | 3.00 | 4.50 | M |
| 1232 | The Man Who Shot Quantrill—George Appell | 1.25 | 2.50 | 3.75 | W |
| 1233 | Thanks to the Saint—Leslie Charteris | 1.25 | 2.50 | 3.75 | M |
| 1234 | Stranger in the Land—Colby Wolford | 1.25 | 2.50 | 3.75 | |
| 1235 | Big Man—Richard Marsten | 1.50 | 3.00 | 4.50 | |
| 1236 | Visiting Nurse—Margaret Howe | .75 | 1.50 | 2.25 | R |
| 1237 | Captain Seadog—Jefferson Cooper (Gardner F. Fox) | 2.00 | 4.00 | 6.00 | A |
| 1238 | May not exist | | | | |
| 1239 | Fool's Gold—Delores Hitchens | 1.25 | 2.50 | 3.75 | |
| 1240 | The Lady Came to Kill—M.E. Chaber | 1.50 | 3.00 | 4.50 | M |
| 1241 | Outlaw Valley—Peter Field | 2.00 | 4.00 | 6.00 | W |
| 1242 | Brother Juniper—Justin McCarthy | 1.25 | 2.50 | 3.75 | H |
| 1243 | Surgical Nurse—Rosie M. Banks | .75 | 1.50 | 2.25 | R |
| 1244 | Fire Brain—Max Brand | 1.25 | 2.50 | 3.75 | W |
| 1245 | Substitute Doctor—Elizabeth Seifert | .75 | 1.50 | 2.25 | |
| 1246 | The Mission—Dean Brelis | 1.25 | 2.50 | 3.75 | |
| 1247 | The Angry Land—Frank Bass | 1.25 | 2.50 | 3.75 | |
| 1248 | Dishonor among Thieves—Spencer Dean | 1.25 | 2.50 | 3.75 | M |
| 1249 | Badlands Buccaneer—John Hunter | 1.25 | 2.50 | 3.75 | W |
| 1250 | The Killer Is Mine—Talmage Powell; 1959 | 1.25 | 2.50 | 3.75 | |
| 1251 | Beyond Wind River—Les Savage, Jr | 1.25 | 2.50 | 3.75 | W |
| 1252 | Cairo Intrigue—William Manchester | 1.25 | 2.50 | 3.75 | |
| 1253 | Seventeen—Bernard Lansky | .75 | 1.50 | 2.25 | H |
| 1254 | Rio Grande Deadline—Allan Vaughan Elston | 1.25 | 2.50 | 3.75 | W |
| 1255 | Murder Takes a Wife—James Howard | 1.25 | 2.50 | 3.75 | M |
| 1256 | Never Kill a Cop—Lee Costigan | 1.25 | 2.50 | 3.75 | |
| 1257 | Rebel Basin—Harry Sinclair Drago | 1.25 | 2.50 | 3.75 | W |
| 1258 | May not exist | | | | |
| 1259 | A Hearse of Another Color—M.E. Chaber | 1.25 | 2.50 | 3.75 | M |
| 1260 | Trail from Needle Rock—Peter Field | 1.25 | 2.50 | 3.75 | W |
| 1261 | Mark Kilby Solves a Murder—Robert Caine Frazer | 1.00 | 2.00 | 3.00 | M |
| 1262 | Reason for Murder—Jack Usher | 1.25 | 2.50 | 3.75 | M |
| 1263 | A Butcher's Dozen of Wicked Women—ed. Lee Wright | 2.00 | 4.00 | 6.00 | M |
| 1264 | Buckskin Affair—Harry Sinclair Drago | 1.25 | 2.50 | 3.75 | M |

# POCKET BOOK (BRITISH)
## Jarrold and Sons Limited

| No. | Title | V/Good | Fine | N/Mint | |
|---|---|---|---|---|---|
| B1 | Ming Yellow—John P. Marquand; 1950 | 2.00 | 4.00 | 6.00 | |
| B2 | Pro—Bruce Hamilton | 2.00 | 4.00 | 6.00 | |
| B3 | The Lost Weekend—Charles Jackson | 2.00 | 4.00 | 6.00 | |
| B4 | Mink Coat—Kathleen Norris. Note: Same cover as Pocket Book No. 625 | 2.00 | 4.00 | 6.00 | |
| B5 | The Anatomy of Murder—Dorothy L. Sayers | 2.00 | 4.00 | 6.00 | M |
| B6 | Farewell Campo 12—Brigadier James Hargest | 2.00 | 4.00 | 6.00 | |
| B7 | The Hound of the Baskervilles—Sir Arthur Conan Doyle | 3.50 | 7.00 | 10.50 | M |
| B8 | The Other Day—Dorothy Whipple | 2.00 | 4.00 | 6.00 | |
| B9 | Circle C Moves On—Arthur Henry Gooden | 2.00 | 4.00 | 6.00 | W |
| B10 | Outlaws Three—Peter Field | 2.00 | 4.00 | 6.00 | W |
| B11 | Double Indemnity—James M. Cain | 2.00 | 4.00 | 6.00 | M |
| B12 | Famous British Short Stories—ed. Lyle Blair | 2.00 | 4.00 | 6.00 | |
| B13 | Maiden's Trip—Emma Smith | 2.00 | 4.00 | 6.00 | |
| B14 | Lam to the Slaughter—A.A. Fair | 2.00 | 4.00 | 6.00 | M |
| B15 | Tell Death to Wait—Anita Boutell | 2.00 | 4.00 | 6.00 | M |
| B16 | Evensong—Beverly Nichols | 2.00 | 4.00 | 6.00 | |
| B17 | The Dippers—Ben Travers | 2.00 | 4.00 | 6.00 | |

| No. | Title | V/Good | Fine | N/Mint | |
|---|---|---|---|---|---|
| B18 | Pardners of the Badlands—Bliss Lomax (Harry Sinclair Drago) | 2.00 | 4.00 | 6.00 | W |
| B19 | The Wind That Blows—F.W. Lister | 2.00 | 4.00 | 6.00 | |
| B20 | Kid Galahad—Francis Wallace | 2.00 | 4.00 | 6.00 | S |
| B21 | The Selected Short Stories of H.E. Bates | 2.00 | 4.00 | 6.00 | |
| B22 | The Mountain Village—Chun-Chan Yeh | 2.50 | 5.00 | 7.50 | |
| B23 | The Whispering House—Margaret Erskine | 2.00 | 4.00 | 6.00 | |
| B24 | The Jury—Gerald Bullett; 1951 | 2.00 | 4.00 | 6.00 | |
| B25 | Great Dramas and Poems from the Bible—ed. C. Lloyd-Jones | 2.00 | 4.00 | 6.00 | |
| B26 | Give Up the Ghost—Margaret Erskine | 2.00 | 4.00 | 6.00 | |
| B27 | Tenderfoot Boss—Arthur Henry Gooden | 2.00 | 4.00 | 6.00 | W |
| B28 | Prairie Smoke—Will Ermine | 2.00 | 4.00 | 6.00 | W |
| B29 | Let Him Have Judgement—Bruce Hamilton | 2.00 | 4.00 | 6.00 | |
| B30 | Mildred Pierce—James M. Cain | 2.50 | 5.00 | 7.50 | |
| B31 | The Bachelor of Arts—R.K. Narayan | 2.00 | 4.00 | 6.00 | |
| B32 | The Pilgrim's Progress—John Bunyan | 2.00 | 4.00 | 6.00 | |
| B33 | Blonde Iscariot—Edgar Lustgarten | 2.50 | 5.00 | 7.50 | |
| B34 | "It's Loaded, Mr. Bauer"—John P. Marquand | 2.00 | 4.00 | 6.00 | |
| B35 | Gallows Parade—George Charles | 2.00 | 4.00 | 6.00 | |
| B36 | Stage Coach Kingdom—Harry Sinclair Drago | 2.00 | 4.00 | 6.00 | W |
| B37 | Death of a Salesman—Arthur Miller | 2.50 | 5.00 | 7.50 | |
| B38 | Pocket Book of Modern Cooking—Philip Harben | 2.00 | 4.00 | 6.00 | NF |
| B39 | Famous Sporting Stories—ed. John Arlot | 2.00 | 4.00 | 6.00 | S |
| B40 | Pocket Book of Popular Poetry—ed. John Pudney | 2.00 | 4.00 | 6.00 | |
| B41 | Rehearsal for Love—Faith Baldwin; c-Heade | 5.00 | 10.00 | 15.00 | R |
| B42 | Tropical Tales—Howard Jones | 2.00 | 4.00 | 6.00 | |
| B43 | You're Lonely When You're Dead—James Hadley Chase | 2.50 | 5.00 | 7.50 | M |
| B44 | The Concertgoer's Handbook—Hubert Ross | 2.00 | 4.00 | 6.00 | NF |
| B45 | No, Sir Jeremy—Anthony Weymouth | 2.00 | 4.00 | 6.00 | |
| B46 | Spill the Jackpot—A.A. Fair; 1952 | 2.00 | 4.00 | 6.00 | M |
| B47 | Tempt Me Not—Anthony Weymouth | 2.00 | 4.00 | 6.00 | |
| B48 | Before the Fact—Francis Iles | 2.00 | 4.00 | 6.00 | M |
| B49 | The Case of the Haunted Husband—Erle Stanley Gardner | 2.00 | 4.00 | 6.00 | M |
| B50 | The Case of the Crooked Candle—Erle Stanley Gardner. Note: Same cover as Pocket Book No. 758 | 2.00 | 4.00 | 6.00 | M |
| B51 | Age Cannot Wither—Ursula Bloom | 2.00 | 4.00 | 6.00 | |
| B52 | Turn on the Heat—A.A. Fair | 2.00 | 4.00 | 6.00 | M |
| B53 | So Young a Body—Frank Bunce | 2.00 | 4.00 | 6.00 | |
| B54 | High, Wild and Handsome—Lytle Shannon | 2.00 | 4.00 | 6.00 | |
| B55 | How Stalin Knows—Justin Atholl | 2.00 | 4.00 | 6.00 | |
| B56 | Black Jade—Angeline Taylor | 3.00 | 6.00 | 9.00 | |
| B57 | Keeper of the Keys—Earl Derr Biggers | 3.00 | 6.00 | 9.00 | M |
| B58 | Operation Cicero—L.C. Moyzisch | 2.00 | 4.00 | 6.00 | |
| B59 | The Glittering Serpent—Emmeline Morrison | 2.00 | 4.00 | 6.00 | |
| B60 | The 22 Brothers—Dana Sage. Note: Same cover as Pocket Book No. 775 | 2.00 | 4.00 | 6.00 | |
| B61 | Panama Is Burning—Philip Lindsay | 2.00 | 4.00 | 6.00 | |
| B62 | The Case of the Golddigger's Purse—Erle Stanley Gardner | 2.00 | 4.00 | 6.00 | M |
| B64 | One Dagger for Two—Philip Lindsay | 2.00 | 4.00 | 6.00 | |
| B65 | The D.A. Holds a Candle—Erle Stanley Gardner | 2.00 | 4.00 | 6.00 | M |
| B66 | The D.A. Goes to Trial—Erle Stanley Gardner | 2.00 | 4.00 | 6.00 | M |
| B67 | The Case of the Baited Hook—Erle Stanley Gardner | 2.00 | 4.00 | 6.00 | M |
| B68 | The Black Camel—Earl Derr Biggers; movie tie-in | 4.00 | 8.00 | 12.00 | M |
| B69 | Murder for Two—George Harmon Coxe | 2.00 | 4.00 | 6.00 | M |
| B70 | Quo Vadis/The Story of the MGM Technicolor Film | 4.00 | 8.00 | 12.00 | |
| B71 | Broncho Apache—Paul I. Wellman | 2.00 | 4.00 | 6.00 | W |
| B73 | Wayne of the Flying W—Arthur Henry Gooden | 2.00 | 4.00 | 6.00 | W |
| B74 | Here's Blood in Your Eye—Manning Long | 2.00 | 4.00 | 6.00 | M |
| B77 | The Lives of Harry Lime—Orson Welles | 4.00 | 8.00 | 12.00 | |

|  | V/Good | Fine | N/Mint |
|---|---|---|---|

**POCKET BOOK (BRITISH),** *continued*

| B78 | The Purple Plain–H.E. Bates | 2.00 | 4.00 | 6.00 | |
|---|---|---|---|---|---|
| B79 | Ivor Novello–Peter Noble | 3.00 | 6.00 | 9.00 | B |
| B80 | Vicious Circle–Manning Long | 2.00 | 4.00 | 6.00 | M |
| B82 | Rimrock Red–Lytle Shannon | 2.00 | 4.00 | 6.00 | W |
| B86 | The D.A. Cooks a Goose–Erle Stanley Gardner | 2.00 | 4.00 | 6.00 | M |
| B88 | Trailers of the Sage–J.K. Bassett | 2.00 | 4.00 | 6.00 | W |
| B89 | The Ghost Knows His Greengages–R.B. Saxe | 2.00 | 4.00 | 6.00 | |
| B90 | Murder in Havana–George Harmon Coxe | 2.00 | 4.00 | 6.00 | M |
| B92 | The Ink Street Murder–Francis Grierson | 2.00 | 4.00 | 6.00 | M |
| B94 | Short Shift–Manning Long | 2.00 | 4.00 | 6.00 | M |
| B100 | Pickwick Papers–Charles Dickens | 2.00 | 4.00 | 6.00 | |
| B106 | Arizona Justice–Stuart Hardy | 2.00 | 4.00 | 6.00 | W |

## POCKET BOOK COLLECTOR'S EDITION

### Pocket Books, Inc.

| nn(1) | The Autobiography of Benjamin Franklin–Benjamin Franklin | 1.00 | 2.00 | 3.00 |
|---|---|---|---|---|
| nn(2) | A Christmas Carol–Charles Dickens | 2.00 | 4.00 | 6.00 |
| nn(3) | The Dialogues of Plato | 1.00 | 2.00 | 3.00 |
| nn(4) | Four Comedies of William Shakespeare | 1.00 | 2.00 | 3.00 |
| nn(5) | Four Tragedies of William Shakespeare | 1.00 | 2.00 | 3.00 |
| nn(6) | Gods and Goddesses in Art and Legend–Herman J. Wechsler | 1.00 | 2.00 | 3.00 |
| nn(7) | Great Short Stories of Guy De Maupassant | 1.00 | 2.00 | 3.00 |
| nn(8) | The House of the Seven Gables–Nathaniel Hawthorne | 1.00 | 2.00 | 3.00 |
| nn(9) | Madame Bovary–Gustave Flaubert | 1.00 | 2.00 | 3.00 |
| nn(10) | The Merriam-Webster Pocket Dictionary | 1.00 | 2.00 | 3.00 |
| nn(11) | A Pocket Book of Greek Art–Thomas Craven | 1.00 | 2.00 | 3.00 |
| nn(12) | The Pocket Book of Quotations–ed. Henry Davidoff | 1.00 | 2.00 | 3.00 |
| nn(13) | The Pocket Thesaurus–Roget | 1.00 | 2.00 | 3.00 |
| nn(14) | Pride and Prejudice–Jane Austen | 1.00 | 2.00 | 3.00 |
| nn(15) | The Return of the Native–Thomas Hardy | 1.00 | 2.00 | 3.00 |
| nn(16) | The Scarlet Letter–Nathaniel Hawthorne | 1.50 | 3.00 | 4.50 |
| nn(17) | Stories of the Great Operas–Henry W. Simon & Abraham Veinus | 1.00 | 2.00 | 3.00 |
| nn(18) | A Tale of Two Cities–Charles Dickens | 1.50 | 3.00 | 4.50 |
| nn(19) | Tales from the Decameron–Giovanni Boccaccio | 1.00 | 2.00 | 3.00 |
| nn(20) | Wuthering Heights–Emily Bronte | 1.00 | 2.00 | 3.00 |

## POCKET BOOK JR.

### Pocket Books, Inc.

**(Continuation of Comet Books)**

| J35 | Ski Patrol–Montgomery Atwater | .75 | 1.50 | 2.25 | A |
|---|---|---|---|---|---|
| J36 | Long Lash–Bertrand Shurtleff | .75 | 1.50 | 2.25 | |
| J37 | Tom Sawyer–Mark Twain | 1.25 | 2.50 | 3.75 | A |
| J38 | Baldy of Nome–Esther Birdsall Darling | .75 | 1.50 | 2.25 | A |
| J39 | Sponger's Jinx–Bert Sackett | .75 | 1.50 | 2.25 | A |
| J40 | Mountain Pony–Henry V. Larom | .75 | 1.50 | 2.25 | A |
| J41 | Black Storm–Thomas C. Hinkle | .75 | 1.50 | 2.25 | W |
| J42 | Huckleberry Finn–Mark Twain | 1.25 | 2.50 | 3.75 | A |
| J43 | Black Beauty–Anna Sewell | 1.25 | 2.50 | 3.75 | |
| J44 | Popularity Plus–Sally S. Simpson | .75 | 1.50 | 2.25 | |
| J45 | Your Own Book of Funny Stories | .75 | 1.50 | 2.25 | H |
| J46 | Your Own Book of Campcraft–Catherine T. Hammett | .75 | 1.50 | 2.25 | NF |
| J47 | The Mystery of Batty Ridge–Allan Gregg | .75 | 1.50 | 2.25 | M |
| J48 | Buffalo Bill–Shannon Garst | .75 | 1.50 | 2.25 | B |
| J49 | Blue Treasure–Helen Girvan | .75 | 1.50 | 2.25 | |
| J50 | Tiger Roan–Glenn Balch | .75 | 1.50 | 2.25 | |
| J51 | Kingdom of Flying Men–Frederick Nelson Litten | .75 | 1.50 | 2.25 | |
| J52 | Gridiron Challenge–Jackson Scholz | .75 | 1.50 | 2.25 | S |

*Pocket Book 1209, Pocket Book Jr. J42, Pocket Book Jr. J57.*

|  | V/Good | Fine | N/Mint |
|---|---|---|---|

| J53 | Sue Barton, Senior Nurse–Helen Dore Boylston | .75 | 1.50 | 2.25 | R |
|---|---|---|---|---|---|
| J54 | Logging Chance–M.H. Lasher | .75 | 1.50 | 2.25 | |
| J55 | Touchdown Twins–Philip Harkins | .75 | 1.50 | 2.25 | S |
| J56 | Cowdog–Ned Andrews | .75 | 1.50 | 2.25 | |
| J57 | The Black Arrow–Robert Louis Stevenson | 1.00 | 2.00 | 3.00 | A |
| J58 | Mustang–Thomas C. Hinkle | .75 | 1.50 | 2.25 | W |
| J59 | Pivot Man–Dick Friendlich | .75 | 1.50 | 2.25 | S |
| J60 | Buckskin Brigade–Jim Kjelgaard; 1951 | .75 | 1.50 | 2.25 | A |
| J61 | Black Spaniel Mystery–Betty Cavanna | .75 | 1.50 | 2.25 | M |
| J62 | Yellowstone Scout–William Marshall Rush | .75 | 1.50 | 2.25 | W |
| J63 | The Great Houdini–Samuel Stein & Beryl Williams | .75 | 1.50 | 2.25 | B |
| J64 | Secret Sea–Robb White | .75 | 1.50 | 2.25 | |
| J65 | Mountain Pony and the Pinto Colt–Henry V. Larom | .75 | 1.50 | 2.25 | W |
| J66 | High, Inside!–Guy Emery | .75 | 1.50 | 2.25 | |
| J67 | The Kid Comes Back–John R. Tunis | .75 | 1.50 | 2.25 | S |
| J68 | The Teen-age Manual–Edith Heal | .75 | 1.50 | 2.25 | NF |
| J69 | Back to Treasure Island–H.A. Calahan | .75 | 1.50 | 2.25 | |
| J70 | Shag–Thomas C. Hinkle | .75 | 1.50 | 2.25 | |
| J71 | The Jinx Ship–Howard Pease | .75 | 1.50 | 2.25 | A |
| J72 | Beyond Rope and Fence–David Grew | .75 | 1.50 | 2.25 | |
| J73 | The Wind in the Rigging–Howard Pease | .75 | 1.50 | 2.25 | A |
| J74 | Riders of the Gabilans–Graham Dean | .75 | 1.50 | 2.25 | |
| J75 | Wolf Dogs of the North–Jack Hines | .75 | 1.50 | 2.25 | A |
| J76 | The Ship without a Crew–Howard Pease | .75 | 1.50 | 2.25 | A |
| J77 | Partners of Powder Hole–Robert Davis | .75 | 1.50 | 2.25 | |

## POCKET BOOK–SPECIAL EDITION

### Pocket Books, Inc.

| nn | Green Light–Lloyd C. Douglas; 1942. Note: Special edition of Pocket Book No. 175, issued for the American Red Cross | 1.00 | 2.00 | 3.00 | |
|---|---|---|---|---|---|
| nn | Official AAF Guide Book; 1944. Note: Special edition of Pocket Book No. 265, issued for the Army Air Forces | 1.00 | 2.00 | 3.00 | NF |

## POCKET BOOK SPECIAL

### Pocket Books, Inc.

**Note: All are in varying oversize and/or oblong sizes.**

| 10001 | Eggbert–LAF; 1962 | 1.00 | 2.00 | 3.00 | H |
|---|---|---|---|---|---|
| 10002 | The Dennison Complete Party Guide | 1.00 | 2.00 | 3.00 | NF |
| 10003 | My Name . . . Jose Jimenez–Bill Dana | 1.50 | 3.00 | 4.50 | H |
| 10004 | Repair Your Chevrolet Yourself–Grant | 1.50 | 3.00 | 4.50 | NF |
| 10005 | Repair Your Ford Yourself–Grant | 1.50 | 3.00 | 4.50 | NF |
| 10006 | Repair Your Plymouth Yourself–Grant | 1.50 | 3.00 | 4.50 | NF |
| 10007 | So This Is Matrimony!–Syd Hoff | 1.00 | 2.00 | 3.00 | H |
| 10008 | Calories Don't Count–Taller; 1963 | 1.00 | 2.00 | 3.00 | |
| 10009 | Royal Canadian Air Force Exercise Plans for Physical Fitness | .50 | 1.00 | 1.50 | NF |

| | V/Good | Fine | N/Mint | |
|---|---|---|---|---|

**POCKET BOOK SPECIAL,** *continued*

| No. | Title | V/Good | Fine | N/Mint | |
|---|---|---|---|---|---|
| 10010 | More Who's in Charge Here—Hy Gardner | 1.50 | 3.00 | 4.50 | H |
| 10011 | Inside Eggbert—LAF | 1.00 | 2.00 | 3.00 | H |
| 10012 | The World Is My Yo-Yo—Brown | .50 | 1.00 | 1.50 | |
| 10014 | Mad Libs—Price & Stern; 1965 | .50 | 1.00 | 1.50 | H |
| 10015 | Son of Mad Libs—Price & Stern | .50 | 1.00 | 1.50 | H |
| 10016 | Old Farmer's Almanac—Thomas | .50 | 1.00 | 1.50 | |
| 10023 | The Private World of Pablo Picasso—Duncan | 1.00 | 2.00 | 3.00 | |
| 10024 | Osborn on Leisure—Osborn | .50 | 1.00 | 1.50 | |
| 10025 | The Model | .50 | 1.00 | 1.50 | |
| 10026 | The Conformers | .50 | 1.00 | 1.50 | |
| 10027 | What Not to Name the Baby—Price & Stern | .50 | 1.00 | 1.50 | |
| 10028 | Non-Quotes | .50 | 1.00 | 1.50 | |
| 10032 | Eggbert's Diary for a ''Lady-in-Waiting''—LAF | 1.00 | 2.00 | 3.00 | H |
| 10035 | Buttercup—Teress | .50 | 1.00 | 1.50 | |
| 10036 | Art Afterpieces—Kimball | 1.00 | 2.00 | 3.00 | H |
| 10041 | The Automobile Annual; 1965 | 1.00 | 2.00 | 3.00 | NF |
| 10042 | The Gun Annual | 1.00 | 2.00 | 3.00 | NF |
| 10043 | Once upon a Dungeon—Don Edwing & John Severin | 1.50 | 3.00 | 4.50 | H |
| 10044 | Germs I Have Known—Jacobson | .50 | 1.00 | 1.50 | |
| 10045 | New News-Reals—Hy Gardner; 1965 | 2.00 | 4.00 | 6.00 | H |
| 10046 | 30 Ways to Stop Smoking—Gescheidt & Jacobs | .50 | 1.00 | 1.50 | |
| 10047 | The Power of Faith—Ishmael | .50 | 1.00 | 1.50 | |
| 10048 | That Was the Week That Was—Hy Gardner | 1.50 | 3.00 | 4.50 | H |
| 10050 | New News-Reals—Hy Gardner | 2.00 | 4.00 | 6.00 | H |
| 10051 | How to Exercise without Moving a Muscle | .50 | 1.00 | 1.50 | |
| 10052 | Happy New Baby | .50 | 1.00 | 1.50 | |
| 10053 | Self Defense & Physical Fitness | .50 | 1.00 | 1.50 | NF |
| 10054 | Michelangelo: The Pieta and Other Masterpieces | 1.00 | 2.00 | 3.00 | |
| 10055 | For Lovers Only Cook Book | .50 | 1.00 | 1.50 | |
| 10056 | Playboy's Females | 3.00 | 6.00 | 9.00 | |
| 10057 | How to Protect Yourself on the Streets and in the Home | .50 | 1.00 | 1.50 | NF |
| 10058 | The Power of Faith—Ishmael | .50 | 1.00 | 1.50 | |
| 10059 | More Playboy Teevee Jeebies | 1.50 | 3.00 | 4.50 | H |
| 10060 | Walter Jetton's LBJ Barbecue Cook Book | 1.00 | 2.00 | 3.00 | |
| 10061 | The United States Coast Guard Boating Guide | .50 | 1.00 | 1.50 | NF |
| 10062 | The Humor and Warmth of Pope John XXIII | 1.00 | 2.00 | 3.00 | |
| 10063 | Tales of Horror | 1.50 | 3.00 | 4.50 | HO |
| 10064 | Weight Control | .50 | 1.00 | 1.50 | |
| 10065 | Mine Son the Samurai | .50 | 1.00 | 1.50 | |
| 10066 | Eggbert's Advice to the Love-Born—LAF | 1.00 | 2.00 | 3.00 | H |
| 10067 | Make It Now—Bake It Later 1 | .50 | 1.00 | 1.50 | NF |
| 10068 | Make It Now—Bake It Later 2 | .50 | 1.00 | 1.50 | NF |
| 10069 | Make It Now—Bake It Later 3 | .50 | 1.00 | 1.50 | NF |
| 10070 | Wall Street Wisdom | .50 | 1.00 | 1.50 | |
| 10071 | Who's in Charge Here—1966—Hy Gardner | 1.50 | 3.00 | 4.50 | H |
| 10072 | The Child | .50 | 1.00 | 1.50 | |
| 10073 | U.S. Government Cookbook | .50 | 1.00 | 1.50 | |
| 10074 | The Rape of the Republican Party | 1.00 | 2.00 | 3.00 | |
| 10075 | The Farmer's Almanac Cook Book | .50 | 1.00 | 1.50 | |
| 10076 | Shed Pounds with Cocktails and Gourmet Fare | .50 | 1.00 | 1.50 | |
| 10078 | What Manner of Man | .50 | 1.00 | 1.50 | |
| 10079 | U.S. Deskbook of Facts and Statistics for 1966 | .50 | 1.00 | 1.50 | |
| 10080 | Here's Soupy Sales! | 1.00 | 2.00 | 3.00 | H |
| 10081 | Loxfinger—Sol Weinstein; 1st ed. 1965; 007 parody | 5.00 | 10.00 | 15.00 | H |
| 10082 | CBS Reports: Abortion and the Law | .50 | 1.00 | 1.50 | |
| 10084 | New York City in Crisis | .50 | 1.00 | 1.50 | |
| 10085 | Chet Huntley's News Analysis | 1.00 | 2.00 | 3.00 | |
| 10087 | It's a Riot to Diet | .50 | 1.00 | 1.50 | |
| 10094 | Matzohball—Sol Weinstein; 1st ed. 1966; 007 parody | 5.00 | 10.00 | 15.00 | H |
| 10139 | Illya: That Man from U.N.C.L.E.—Chandler Brossard; TV tie-in | 5.00 | 10.00 | 15.00 | NF |
| 10172 | On the Secret Service of His Majesty the Queen—Sol Weinstein; 1st ed. 1966; 007 parody | 5.00 | 10.00 | 15.00 | H |

| No. | Title | V/Good | Fine | N/Mint | |
|---|---|---|---|---|---|
| 10504 | Eggbert and Eggberta—LAF | 1.00 | 2.00 | 3.00 | H |
| 10505 | Who's in Charge Here?—Hy Gardner | 1.50 | 3.00 | 4.50 | H |
| 10506 | Sooper Mad Libs—Price & Stern | .50 | 1.00 | 1.50 | H |
| 10529 | Sing Along with Jack—Schwartz | .50 | 1.00 | 1.50 | |
| 10542 | The Bible in the Public Schools | .50 | 1.00 | 1.50 | |
| 10546 | The Elephant Book | 1.00 | 2.00 | 3.00 | H |
| 10556 | New York: A Practical Guide | .50 | 1.00 | 1.50 | NF |
| 10558 | What's for Dinner? Family Circle's Meal Planning Cookbook | .50 | 1.00 | 1.50 | |
| 10559 | You: Do-it-Yourself Analysis | .50 | 1.00 | 1.50 | |
| 10560 | Complete Droodles | .50 | 1.00 | 1.50 | |
| 10563 | Little Lessons from History | .50 | 1.00 | 1.50 | |
| 10564 | Elephants, Grapes and Pickles | 1.50 | 3.00 | 4.50 | H |
| 10567 | Picasso and Pie | 1.00 | 2.00 | 3.00 | |
| 10581 | The Racing Flag: The Story of Nascar | 1.50 | 3.00 | 4.50 | NF |
| 10582 | Living in Florida | .50 | 1.00 | 1.50 | NF |
| 10583 | Monster Mad Libs—Price & Stern | .50 | 1.00 | 1.50 | H |
| 10584 | The Language of Flowers | .50 | 1.00 | 1.50 | |
| 10585 | Far from the City of Class | .50 | 1.00 | 1.50 | |
| 10586 | Facial Isometrics | .50 | 1.00 | 1.50 | |
| 10587 | M Is for Monster | 1.00 | 2.00 | 3.00 | |
| 10588 | Designs to Color | .50 | 1.00 | 1.50 | |
| 10589 | The Very Important Person Note Book | 1.00 | 2.00 | 3.00 | |
| 10590 | Little Lessons from History Calendar—1966; 1965 | .50 | 1.00 | 1.50 | |
| 10591 | Fasten Your Seat Belt | .50 | 1.00 | 1.50 | |

# POCKET LIBRARY

## Pocket Books, Inc.

| No. | Title | V/Good | Fine | N/Mint | |
|---|---|---|---|---|---|
| PL1 | Man and State: The Political Philosophers—Saxe Commins & Robert N. Linscott; 1954 | .75 | 1.50 | 2.25 | NF |
| PL2 | Man and Man: The Social Philosophers—Saxe Commins & Robert N. Linscott | .75 | 1.50 | 2.25 | NF |
| PL3 | Man and the Universe: The Philosophers of Science—Saxe Commins & Robert N. Linscott | .75 | 1.50 | 2.25 | NF |
| PL4 | Man and Spirit: The Speculative Philosophers—Saxe Commins & Robert N. Linscott | .75 | 1.50 | 2.25 | NF |
| PL5 | The Imitation of Christ—Thomas A. Kempis | .75 | 1.50 | 2.25 | |
| PL6 | The Golden Ass of Apuleius—Apuleius Madaurensis | .75 | 1.50 | 2.25 | |
| PL7 | Dialogues of Plato | .75 | 1.50 | 2.25 | |
| PL8 | Famous Chinese Short Stories—Lin Yutang | .75 | 1.50 | 2.25 | |
| PL9 | Pride and Prejudice—Jane Austen | .75 | 1.50 | 2.25 | |
| PL10 | Wuthering Heights—Emily Bronte | .75 | 1.50 | 2.25 | |
| PL11 | The Story of Philosophy—Will Durant | .75 | 1.50 | 2.25 | NF |
| PL12 | The Story of Mankind—Hendrik Willem Van Loon | .75 | 1.50 | 2.25 | NF |
| PL13 | The Pocket Bible | .75 | 1.50 | 2.25 | |
| PL14 | The Great Short Stories of Robert Louis Stevenson | .75 | 1.50 | 2.25 | |
| PL15 | The House of the Seven Gables—Nathaniel Hawthorne | .75 | 1.50 | 2.25 | |
| PL16 | Tales from the Arabian Nights | .75 | 1.50 | 2.25 | |
| PL17 | The Way West—A.B. Guthrie, Jr | .75 | 1.50 | 2.25 | W |
| PL18 | The Autobiography of Benjamin Franklin—Benjamin Franklin | .75 | 1.50 | 2.25 | B |
| PL19 | Ivanhoe—Walter Scott | .75 | 1.50 | 2.25 | A |
| PL20 | The Red Badge of Courage—Stephen Crane | .75 | 1.50 | 2.25 | A |
| PL21 | The Pocket Book of Great Operas—Henry Simon & Abraham Veinus | .75 | 1.50 | 2.25 | |
| PL22 | A Tale of Two Cities—Charles Dickens | .75 | 1.50 | 2.25 | |
| PL23 | The Return of the Native—Thomas Hardy | .75 | 1.50 | 2.25 | |
| PL24 | The Pocket Book of Modern American Short Stories—ed. Philip van Doren Stern | .75 | 1.50 | 2.25 | |
| PL25 | Tess of the D'Urbervilles—Thomas Hardy | .75 | 1.50 | 2.25 | |
| PL26 | The Scarlet Letter—Nathaniel Hawthorne; 1955 | .75 | 1.50 | 2.25 | |
| PL27 | Silas Marner—George Eliot | .75 | 1.50 | 2.25 | |
| PL28 | Moby Dick—Herman Melville | .75 | 1.50 | 2.25 | |

POCKET LIBRARY, *continued*

| | | V/Good | Fine | N/Mint |
|---|---|---|---|---|
| PL29 | Great Short Stories–Guy de Maupassant | .75 | 1.50 | 2.25 |
| PL30 | Four Great Tragedies–William Shakespeare | .75 | 1.50 | 2.25 |
| PL31 | Four Great Comedies–William Shakespeare | .75 | 1.50 | 2.25 |
| PL32 | German Stories and Tales–Robert Pick | .75 | 1.50 | 2.25 |
| PL33 | The Basic Ideas of Alexander Hamilton | .75 | 1.50 | 2.25 |
| PL34 | Kidnapped–Robert Louis Stevenson | .75 | 1.50 | 2.25 |
| PL35 | The New Pocket Anthology of American Verse–Oscar Williams; 1955 | .75 | 1.50 | 2.25 |
| PL36 | The Bridge of San Luis Rey–Thornton Wilder | .75 | 1.50 | 2.25 |
| PL37 | French Stories and Tales–Stanley Geist; 1956 | .75 | 1.50 | 2.25 |
| PL38 | The Pocket Book of O. Henry Stories | .75 | 1.50 | 2.25 |
| PL39 | The Adventures of Tom Sawyer–Mark Twain | .75 | 1.50 | 2.25 |
| PL40 | Spanish Stories and Tales–ed. Harriet de Onis | .75 | 1.50 | 2.25 |
| PL41 | The Pocket Book of Verse–ed. M.E. Speare | .75 | 1.50 | 2.25 |
| PL42 | The Adventures of Huckleberry Finn–Mark Twain | .75 | 1.50 | 2.25 |
| PL43 | Tales from the Decameron–Giovanni Boccaccio | .75 | 1.50 | 2.25 |
| PL44 | Jane Eyre–Charlotte Bronte | .75 | 1.50 | 2.25 |
| PL45 | The Confessions of St. Augustine–Aurelius Augustinus | .75 | 1.50 | 2.25 |
| PL46 | Great Tales and Poems–Edgar Allan Poe | .75 | 1.50 | 2.25 |
| PL47 | The Pocket Book of Robert Frost's Poems | .75 | 1.50 | 2.25 |
| PL48 | Irish Stories and Tales–ed. Devin A. Garrity | .75 | 1.50 | 2.25 |
| PL49 | Treasure Island–Robert Louis Stevenson | .75 | 1.50 | 2.25 |
| PL50 | Great Expectations–Charles Dickens | .75 | 1.50 | 2.25 |
| PL51 | Gulliver's Travels–Jonathan Swift; 1957 | .75 | 1.50 | 2.25 |
| PL52 | The Mayor of Casterbridge–Thomas Hardy | .75 | 1.50 | 2.25 |
| PL53 | The Pilgrim's Progress–John Bunyan | .75 | 1.50 | 2.25 |
| PL54 | The Vicar of Wakefield–Oliver Goldsmith | .75 | 1.50 | 2.25 |
| PL55 | The Pocket Book of Short Stories–ed. M.E. Speare | .75 | 1.50 | 2.25 |
| PL56 | The Confessions of Jean–Jacques Rousseau | .75 | 1.50 | 2.25 |
| PL57 | The Tragedy of King Lear–William Shakespeare | .75 | 1.50 | 2.25 |
| PL58 | Great Essays in Science–ed. Martin Gardner | .75 | 1.50 | 2.25 |
| PL59 | The Marble Fawn–Nathaniel Hawthorne | .75 | 1.50 | 2.25 |
| PL60 | The Merchant of Venice–William Shakespeare | .75 | 1.50 | 2.25 |
| PL61 | The Tragedy of Othello, the Moor of Venice–William Shakespeare | .75 | 1.50 | 2.25 |
| PL62 | The Last of the Mohicans–James Fenimore Cooper | .75 | 1.50 | 2.25 |
| PL63 | Nana–Emile Zola; 1958 | .75 | 1.50 | 2.25 |
| PL64 | The Tragedy of Hamlet, Prince of Denmark–William Shakespeare | .75 | 1.50 | 2.25 |
| PL65 | Mid-century–Orville Prescott | .75 | 1.50 | 2.25 |
| PL66 | The Tragedy of Julius Caesar–William Shakespeare | .75 | 1.50 | 2.25 |
| PL67 | A Midsummer's Night's Dream–William Shakespeare | .75 | 1.50 | 2.25 |
| PL68 | A Christmas Carol–Charles Dickens | .75 | 1.50 | 2.25 |
| PL69 | Madame Bovary–Gustave Flaubert | .75 | 1.50 | 2.25 |
| PL70 | The Tragedy of Macbeth–William Shakespeare; 1959 | .75 | 1.50 | 2.25 |
| PL71 | Laughing Boy–Oliver La Farge | .75 | 1.50 | 2.25 |
| PL500 | The Story of Philosophy–Will Durant | .75 | 1.50 | 2.25 |
| PL501 | The Story of Mankind–Hendrik Willem Van Loon | .75 | 1.50 | 2.25 |
| PL502 | Ivanhoe–Walter Scott | .75 | 1.50 | 2.25 |
| PL503 | The New Pocket Anthology of American Verse–ed. Oscar Williams | .75 | 1.50 | 2.25 |
| PL504 | Immortal Poems of the English Language–ed. Oscar Williams | .75 | 1.50 | 2.25 |

| | | V/Good | Fine | N/Mint |
|---|---|---|---|---|
| PL505 | The Pocket Book of Modern Verse–ed. Oscar Williams | .75 | 1.50 | 2.25 |
| PL506 | Tales from the Arabian Nights | .75 | 1.50 | 2.25 |
| PL507 | Adam Bede–George Eliot; 1956 | .75 | 1.50 | 2.25 |
| PL508 | Lorna Doone–R.D. Blackmore | .75 | 1.50 | 2.25 |
| PL509 | The Mill on the Floss–George Eliot | .75 | 1.50 | 2.25 |
| PL510 | Robinson Crusoe–Daniel Defoe | .75 | 1.50 | 2.25 |
| PL511 | The Life and Opinions of Tristram Shandy, Gentleman–Laurence Sterne | .75 | 1.50 | 2.25 |
| PL512 | The Pocket History of the United States–Henry Steele Commager & Allan Nevins | .75 | 1.50 | 2.25 |
| PL513 | The Way West–A.B. Guthrie, Jr | .75 | 1.50 | 2.25 |
| PL514 | Oliver Twist–Charles Dickens; 1957 | .75 | 1.50 | 2.25 |
| PL515 | The Pocket History of American Painting–James Thomas Flexner | .75 | 1.50 | 2.25 |
| PL516 | Story Poems–Louis Untermeyer | .75 | 1.50 | 2.25 |
| PL517 | Don Quixote–Miguel de Cervantes | .75 | 1.50 | 2.25 |
| PL518 | Essays in Philosophy–James Bayley & Houston Peterson | .75 | 1.50 | 2.25 |
| PL519 | The Pocket Aristotle–Aristotle | .75 | 1.50 | 2.25 |
| PL520 | The Selected Essays of Montaigne–Michel de Montaigne | .75 | 1.50 | 2.25 |

# POCKET LIBRARY OF GREAT ART
## Pocket Books, Inc./N. Abrams, Inc.

| | | V/Good | Fine | N/Mint | |
|---|---|---|---|---|---|
| A1 | Degas–Daniel Catton Rich; 1953 | .75 | 1.50 | 2.25 | NF |
| A2 | El Greco–John F. Matthews | .75 | 1.50 | 2.25 | NF |
| A3 | Toulouse-Lautrec–Samuel Hunter | .75 | 1.50 | 2.25 | NF |
| A4 | Cezanne–Theodore Rousseau, Jr | .75 | 1.50 | 2.25 | NF |
| A5 | Dufy–Alfred Werner | .75 | 1.50 | 2.25 | NF |
| A6 | Van Gogh–Robert Goldwater | .75 | 1.50 | 2.25 | NF |
| A7 | The French Impressionists and Their Circle–Herman J. Wechsler | .75 | 1.50 | 2.25 | NF |
| A8 | Rembrandt–Wilhelm Koehler | .75 | 1.50 | 2.25 | NF |
| A9 | Botticelli–Frederick Hartt | .75 | 1.50 | 2.25 | NF |
| A10 | Matisse–Clement Greenberg | .75 | 1.50 | 2.25 | NF |
| A11 | Renoir–Milton S. Fox | .75 | 1.50 | 2.25 | NF |
| A12 | Utrillo–Alfred Werner | .75 | 1.50 | 2.25 | NF |
| A13 | Manet–S. Lane Faison, Jr; 1954 | .75 | 1.50 | 2.25 | NF |
| A14 | Rouault–Jacques Maritain | .75 | 1.50 | 2.25 | NF |
| A15 | Gauguin–John Rewald | .75 | 1.50 | 2.25 | NF |
| A16 | Modigliani–Jacques Lipchitz | .75 | 1.50 | 2.25 | NF |
| A17 | Rubens–Julius S. Held | .75 | 1.50 | 2.25 | NF |
| A18 | Pissarro–John Rewald | .75 | 1.50 | 2.25 | NF |
| A19 | Velazquez–Margaretta Salinger | .75 | 1.50 | 2.25 | NF |
| A20 | Picasso (Blue and Rose Periods)–William S. Lieberman | .75 | 1.50 | 2.25 | NF |
| A21 | Bruegel–Wolfgang Stechow; 1955 | .75 | 1.50 | 2.25 | NF |
| A22 | Goya–Frederick S. Wight | .75 | 1.50 | 2.25 | NF |
| A23 | Michelangelo–Margaretta Salinger | .75 | 1.50 | 2.25 | NF |
| A24 | Flower Painting by the Great Masters–Margaret Fairbanks Marcus | .75 | 1.50 | 2.25 | NF |

# PONY BOOKS
## Stamford House

| | | V/Good | Fine | N/Mint | |
|---|---|---|---|---|---|
| 45 | Your Life in the Atom World–John Houston Craige; 1946 | 3.00 | 6.00 | 9.00 | NF |
| 46 | The Singing Corpse–Bernard Dougall; 1945 | 3.00 | 6.00 | 9.00 | M |
| 47 | The Orange Divan–Valentine Williams | 3.00 | 6.00 | 9.00 | M |
| 48 | The Narrow Cell–Dale Clark | 3.00 | 6.00 | 9.00 | M |
| 49 | The Corpse with the Red-Headed Friend–R.A.J. Walling | 3.00 | 6.00 | 9.00 | M |
| 50 | The Wager and the House at Fernwood–Fulton Oursler; 1st ed. 1946 | 3.00 | 6.00 | 9.00 | |
| 51 | The Heart Has Wings–Faith Baldwin | 2.00 | 4.00 | 6.00 | R |
| 52 | A Clue for Mr. Fortune–H.C. Bailey | 3.00 | 6.00 | 9.00 | M |
| 53 | Unhurrying Chase–Morris Markey; 1st ed. 1946 | 4.00 | 8.00 | 12.00 | |
| 54 | Cellini Smith: Detective–Robert Reeves | 3.00 | 6.00 | 9.00 | M |
| 55 | Second Hand Wife–Kathleen Norris | 3.00 | 6.00 | 9.00 | |
| 56 | Wanted: Someone Innocent–Margery Allingham; 1st ed. 1946 | 3.50 | 7.00 | 10.50 | M |

| | V/Good | Fine | N/Mint |
|---|---|---|---|

PONY BOOKS, *continued*

| | | V/Good | Fine | N/Mint | |
|---|---|---|---|---|---|
| 57 | The Stolen Squadron–Charles L. Leonard | 2.00 | 4.00 | 6.00 | C |
| 58 | Salt River Ranny–Nelson C. Nye | 3.00 | 6.00 | 9.00 | W |
| 59 | One Small Candle–Cecil Roberts | 2.00 | 4.00 | 6.00 | |
| 60 | The Bishop's Crime–H.C. Bailey | 3.00 | 6.00 | 9.00 | M |
| 61 | Fifty Famous Sports Stories–Caswell Adams; 1st ed. 1946 | 2.50 | 5.00 | 7.50 | S |
| 62 | The Inconvenient Corpse–E.P. Fenwick | 3.00 | 6.00 | 9.00 | M |
| 63 | Death and the Devil–Paul Whelton | 3.00 | 6.00 | 9.00 | M |
| 64 | Mr. Fortune Wonders–H.C. Bailey | 3.00 | 6.00 | 9.00 | M |
| 65 | The Quiz Crossword Puzzle Book; orig. 1946 | 20.00 | 40.00 | 60.00 | NF |
| 66 | Blood of the North–James B. Hendryx | 2.50 | 5.00 | 7.50 | A |

Pony Book (Weldun) 126, Popular Library 14, Popular Library 32.

## PONY BOOKS
## Weldun
### (Canadian)

| | | V/Good | Fine | N/Mint | |
|---|---|---|---|---|---|
| 122 | The Corpse Is Indignant–Douglas Stapleton & Helen A. Carey | 3.00 | 6.00 | 9.00 | M |
| 123 | The Waltz of Death–P.B. Maxon | 3.00 | 6.00 | 9.00 | M |
| 124 | Hellcat–Isabel Williams | 3.00 | 6.00 | 9.00 | E |
| 125 | Monkeys in the Mirror–Donald Bayne Hobart | 3.00 | 6.00 | 9.00 | R |
| 126 | Orchids to You–Hank Janson | 3.00 | 6.00 | 9.00 | M |
| 127 | The Lion Murders–Elwood Brown | 3.00 | 6.00 | 9.00 | M |

## POPULAR LIBRARY
## Popular Library, Inc.

| | | V/Good | Fine | N/Mint | |
|---|---|---|---|---|---|
| nn(1) | Saint Overboard–Leslie Charteris; 1943 | 25.00 | 50.00 | 75.00 | M |
| nn(2) | Danger in the Dark–Mignon G. Eberhart | 7.00 | 14.00 | 21.00 | M |
| nn(3) | Crime of Violence–Rufus King | 7.00 | 14.00 | 21.00 | M |
| 4 | Murder in the Madhouse–Jonathan Latimer | 5.00 | 10.00 | 15.00 | M |
| 5 | Miss Pinkerton–Mary Roberts Rinehart | 5.00 | 10.00 | 15.00 | M |
| 6 | Three Bright Pebbles–Leslie Ford | 4.00 | 8.00 | 12.00 | M |
| 7 | Death Demands an Audience–Helen Reilly | 5.00 | 10.00 | 15.00 | M |
| 8 | Death for Dear Clara–Q. Patrick | 5.00 | 10.00 | 15.00 | M |
| 9 | The Eee Pie Murders–David Frome | 3.00 | 6.00 | 9.00 | M |
| 10 | To Wake the Dead–John Dickson Carr | 7.50 | 15.00 | 22.50 | M |
| 11 | The Stoneware Monkey–R. Austin Freeman | 5.00 | 10.00 | 15.00 | M |
| 12 | Death Sits on the Board–John Rhode | 5.00 | 10.00 | 15.00 | M |
| 13 | Valcour Meets Murder–Rufus King | 4.00 | 8.00 | 12.00 | M |
| 14 | The Criminal C.O.D.–Phoebe Atwood Taylor | 5.00 | 10.00 | 15.00 | M |
| 15 | The Third Eye–Ethel Lina White | 3.00 | 6.00 | 9.00 | M |
| 16 | The Dead Don't Care–Jonathan Latimer | 5.00 | 10.00 | 15.00 | M |
| 17 | The House on the Roof–Mignon G. Eberhart | 4.00 | 8.00 | 12.00 | M |
| 18 | Tragedy in the Hollow–Freeman Wills Crofts | 4.00 | 8.00 | 12.00 | M |
| 19 | The Crooked Hinge–John Dickson Carr | 5.00 | 10.00 | 15.00 | M |
| 20 | Murder in Shinbone Alley–Helen Reilly | 4.00 | 8.00 | 12.00 | M |

Pocket Library PL28, Pony Book (Stamford) 54, Pony Book (Stamford) 64.

| | | V/Good | Fine | N/Mint | |
|---|---|---|---|---|---|
| 21 | The After House–Mary Roberts Rinehart; 1944 | 3.00 | 6.00 | 9.00 | M |
| 22 | Murder Masks Miami–Rufus King | 3.00 | 6.00 | 9.00 | M |
| 23 | S.S. Murder–Q. Patrick | 5.00 | 10.00 | 15.00 | M |
| 24 | Reno Rendezvous–Leslie Ford | 4.00 | 8.00 | 12.00 | M |
| 25 | Out of Order–Phoebe Atwood Taylor; 1944 | 4.00 | 8.00 | 12.00 | M |
| 26 | Mr. Pinkerton Has the Clue–David Frome | 4.00 | 8.00 | 12.00 | M |
| 27 | From This Dark Stairway–Mignon G. Eberhart | 4.00 | 8.00 | 12.00 | M |
| 28 | The Burning Court–John Dickson Carr | 6.00 | 12.00 | 18.00 | M |
| 29 | Weekend with Death–Patricia Wentworth | 4.00 | 8.00 | 12.00 | M |
| 30 | There's Trouble Brewing–Nicholas Blake | 5.00 | 10.00 | 15.00 | M |
| 31 | Murder by the Clock–Rufus King | 4.00 | 8.00 | 12.00 | M |
| 32 | The Wheel Spins–Ethel Lina White; movie tie-in for The Lady Vanishes | 6.00 | 12.00 | 18.00 | M |
| 33 | McKee of Centre Street–Helen Reilly | 4.00 | 8.00 | 12.00 | M |
| 34 | Mr. Pinkerton at the Old Angel–David Frome; aka Visitor in the Night | 4.00 | 8.00 | 12.00 | M |
| 35 | The Mystery of Hunting's End–Mignon G. Eberhart | 4.00 | 8.00 | 12.00 | M |
| 36 | Death and the Maiden–Q. Patrick | 5.00 | 10.00 | 15.00 | M |
| 37 | Mother Finds a Body–Gypsy Rose Lee (Craig Rice) | 4.00 | 8.00 | 12.00 | M |
| 38 | The Dark Ships–Hulbert Footner | 4.00 | 8.00 | 12.00 | M |
| 39 | In the Balance–Patricia Wentworth | 4.00 | 8.00 | 12.00 | M |
| 40 | The Stars Spell Death–Jonathan Stagge | 6.00 | 12.00 | 18.00 | M |
| 41 | The Smiler with the Knife–Nicholas Blake | 5.00 | 10.00 | 15.00 | M |
| 42 | Murdered: One by One–Francis Beeding | 4.00 | 8.00 | 12.00 | M |
| 43 | The Fatal Kiss Mystery–Rufus King; 1945 | 4.00 | 8.00 | 12.00 | M |
| 44 | The Brass Chills–Hugh Pentecost | 4.00 | 8.00 | 12.00 | M |
| 45 | The Wrong Murder–Craig Rice | 6.00 | 12.00 | 18.00 | M |
| 46 | Sound of Revelry–Octavus Roy Cohen | 4.00 | 8.00 | 12.00 | M |
| 47 | Return to the Scene–Q. Patrick; aka The Green Diary | 5.00 | 10.00 | 15.00 | M |
| 48 | Mr. Smith's Hat–Helen Reilly | 4.00 | 8.00 | 12.00 | M |
| 49 | Tiger Milk–David Garth | 5.00 | 10.00 | 15.00 | M |
| 50 | Green Shiver–Clyde B. Clason; 1945 | 4.00 | 8.00 | 12.00 | M |
| 51 | The Whispering Cup–Mabel Seeley | 4.00 | 8.00 | 12.00 | M |
| 52 | Murder by Prescription–Jonathan Stagge | 6.00 | 12.00 | 18.00 | M |
| 53 | Cancelled in Red–Hugh Pentecost | 4.00 | 8.00 | 12.00 | M |
| 54 | Her Heart in Her Throat–Ethel Lina White | 4.00 | 8.00 | 12.00 | M |
| 55 | Murder in the Willett Family–Rufus King | 6.00 | 12.00 | 18.00 | M |
| 56 | Dead for a Ducat–Helen Reilly | 4.00 | 8.00 | 12.00 | M |
| 57 | The Twelve Disguises–Francis Beeding | 4.00 | 8.00 | 12.00 | M |
| 58 | The Turquoise Shop–Frances Crane | 4.00 | 8.00 | 12.00 | M |
| 59 | The Case of the Solid Key–Anthony Boucher | 5.00 | 10.00 | 15.00 | M |
| 60 | The Corpse in the Snowman–Nicholas Blake | 5.00 | 10.00 | 15.00 | M |
| 61 | The Mad Hatter Mystery–John Dickson Carr | 5.00 | 10.00 | 15.00 | M |

*Popular Library 60, Popular Library 88, Popular Library 108.*

POPULAR LIBRARY, *continued*

| # | Title | V/Good | Fine | N/Mint | |
|---|-------|--------|------|--------|---|
| 62 | The Yellow Taxi–Jonathan Stagge | 6.00 | 12.00 | 18.00 | M |
| 63 | Sing a Song of Homicide–James R. Langham | 3.00 | 6.00 | 9.00 | M |
| 64 | They Can't Hang Me–James Ronald | 3.00 | 6.00 | 9.00 | M |
| 65 | The Woman in the Picture–John August | 3.00 | 6.00 | 9.00 | M |
| 66 | The Blind Side–Patricia Wentworth | 3.00 | 6.00 | 9.00 | M |
| 67 | Murder on the Yacht–Rufus King | 6.00 | 12.00 | 18.00 | M |
| 68 | The Cat Screams–Todd Downing | 2.50 | 5.00 | 7.50 | M |
| 69 | The Listening House–Mabel Seeley; 1946 | 2.50 | 5.00 | 7.50 | M |
| 70 | Mr. Polton Explains–R. Austin Freeman | 4.00 | 8.00 | 12.00 | M |
| 71 | Hell Let Loose–Francis Beeding | 2.50 | 5.00 | 7.50 | M |
| 72 | Who Killed Aunt Maggie?–Medora Field | 3.00 | 6.00 | 9.00 | M |
| 73 | Hasty Wedding–Mignon G. Eberhart | 3.00 | 6.00 | 9.00 | M |
| 74 | Murder in Season–Octavus Roy Cohen; aka Romance in Crimson | 3.00 | 6.00 | 9.00 | M |
| 75 | She Faded into Air–Ethel Lina White; 1946 | 2.50 | 5.00 | 7.50 | M |
| 76 | Fog–Valentine Williams & Dorothy Rice Sims | 3.00 | 6.00 | 9.00 | M |
| 77 | Buckaroo–Eugene Cunningham | 2.50 | 5.00 | 7.50 | M |
| 78 | Timbal Gulch Trail–Max Brand | 2.50 | 5.00 | 7.50 | W |
| 79 | Rolling Stone–Patricia Wentworth | 2.50 | 5.00 | 7.50 | M |
| 80 | The Golden Box–Frances Crane | 2.50 | 5.00 | 7.50 | M |
| 81 | Three Thirds of a Ghost–Timothy Fuller | 2.50 | 5.00 | 7.50 | M |
| 82 | The 24th Horse–Hugh Pentecost | 2.50 | 5.00 | 7.50 | M |
| 83 | The Black-Headed Pins–Constance Little & Gwenyth Little | 2.50 | 5.00 | 7.50 | M |
| 84 | Challenge for Three–David Garth | 2.50 | 5.00 | 7.50 | M |
| 85 | Trouble Shooter–Ernest Haycox | 3.50 | 7.00 | 10.50 | W |
| 86 | Bucky Follows a Cold Trail–William MacLeod Raine | 3.50 | 7.00 | 10.50 | W |
| 87 | Fatal Descent–John Rhode & Carter Dickson | 6.00 | 12.00 | 18.00 | M |
| 88 | Romance in the First Degree–Octavus Roy Cohen | 3.50 | 7.00 | 10.50 | M |
| 89 | The Right Murder–Craig Rice | 5.00 | 10.00 | 15.00 | M |
| 90 | The Scarlet Circle–Jonathan Stagge | 5.00 | 10.00 | 15.00 | M |
| 91 | The Sea-Hawk–Rafael Sabatini | 5.00 | 10.00 | 15.00 | A |
| 92 | All Over But the Shooting–Richard Powell | 3.00 | 6.00 | 9.00 | M |
| 93 | The Blue Lacquer Box–George F. Worts | 3.00 | 6.00 | 9.00 | M |
| 94 | The Mortal Storm–Phyllis Bottome | 2.00 | 4.00 | 6.00 | M |
| 95 | The Red Law–Jackson Gregory | 3.00 | 6.00 | 9.00 | W |
| 96 | Singing River–W.C. Tuttle. Note: Spine mistakenly identifies this as "Library Popular [sic]" release. | 3.00 | 6.00 | 9.00 | W |
| 97 | A Variety of Weapons–Rufus King | 3.00 | 6.00 | 9.00 | M |
| 98 | Dividend on Death–Brett Halliday | 3.00 | 6.00 | 9.00 | M |
| 99 | Dead of the Night–John Rhode | 3.50 | 7.00 | 10.50 | M |
| 100 | The African Poison Murders–Elspeth Huxley; 1947 | 3.00 | 6.00 | 9.00 | M |
| 101 | Lummox–Fanny Hurst | 2.00 | 4.00 | 6.00 | |
| 102 | Duel in the Sun–Niven Busch; movie tie-in | 2.00 | 4.00 | 6.00 | W |
| 103 | The Phantom Canoe–William Byron Mowery; 1947 | 3.00 | 6.00 | 9.00 | |
| 104 | Mesquite Jenkins, Tumbleweed–Clarence E. Mulford | 3.00 | 6.00 | 9.00 | W |
| 105 | The Case Is Closed–Patricia Wentworth | 3.00 | 6.00 | 9.00 | M |
| 106 | The Corpse with the Eerie Eye–R.A.J. Walling | 3.00 | 6.00 | 9.00 | M |
| 107 | Crossword Puzzles | 37.50 | 75.00 | 112.50 | NF |
| 108 | The Yellow Violet–Frances Crane | 3.00 | 6.00 | 9.00 | M |
| 109 | I'll Sing at Your Funeral–Hugh Pentecost | 3.00 | 6.00 | 9.00 | M |
| 110 | Congo Song–Stuart Cloete | 3.50 | 7.00 | 10.50 | E |
| 111 | Bedelia–Vera Caspary; movie tie-in | 3.50 | 7.00 | 10.50 | E |
| 112 | The Black Shrouds–Constance Little & Gwenyth Little | 3.00 | 6.00 | 9.00 | M |
| 113 | Crucible–Ben Ames Williams | 3.00 | 6.00 | 9.00 | |
| 114 | Ramrod–Luke Short; movie tie-in | 3.00 | 6.00 | 9.00 | W |
| 115 | Popular Book of Cartoons–ed. Ned L. Pines | 15.00 | 30.00 | 45.00 | H |
| 116 | The Red House–George Agnew Chamberlain; movie tie-in | 3.50 | 7.00 | 10.50 | M |
| 117 | This Is Murder, Mr. Jones–Timothy Fuller | 3.50 | 7.00 | 10.50 | M |

| # | Title | V/Good | Fine | N/Mint | |
|---|-------|--------|------|--------|---|
| 118 | The Flying U's Last Stand–B.M. Bower | 3.00 | 6.00 | 9.00 | W |
| 119 | Firebrand–Tom Gill | 3.00 | 6.00 | 9.00 | W |
| 120 | The Spiral Staircase–Ethel Lina White | 3.50 | 7.00 | 10.50 | M |
| 121 | A Losing Game–Freeman Wills Crofts | 3.50 | 7.00 | 10.50 | M |
| 122 | The Adventures of Dr. Thorndyke–R. Austin Freeman; aka The Singing Bone | 3.50 | 7.00 | 10.50 | M |
| 123 | A Question of Proof–Nicholas Blake | 3.50 | 7.00 | 10.50 | M |
| 124 | Design in Evil–Rufus King | 3.00 | 6.00 | 9.00 | M |
| 125 | Said the Spider to the Fly–Richard Shattuck; 1947 | 3.00 | 6.00 | 9.00 | M |
| 126 | The Deadly Sunshade–Phoebe Atwood Taylor | 3.00 | 6.00 | 9.00 | M |
| 127 | Paradise Trail–William Byron Mowery | 3.00 | 6.00 | 9.00 | W |
| 128 | The Voice of the Pack–Edison Marshall | 3.00 | 6.00 | 9.00 | W |
| 129 | I Wake Up Screaming–Steve Fisher | 4.00 | 8.00 | 12.00 | M |
| 130 | The Mystery Companion–ed. A.L. Furman | 4.50 | 9.00 | 13.50 | M |
| 131 | The Clock Strikes Twelve–Patricia Wentworth | 3.00 | 6.00 | 9.00 | M |
| 132 | Seven Keys to Baldpate–Earl Derr Biggers | 4.00 | 8.00 | 12.00 | M |
| 133 | Advance Agent–John August | 3.00 | 6.00 | 9.00 | |
| 134 | Fighting Blood–Gordon Young | 3.00 | 6.00 | 9.00 | W |
| 135 | Law Rides the Range–Walt Coburn | 3.00 | 6.00 | 9.00 | W |
| 136 | Appointment with Danger–David Garth; aka Road to Glenfairlie | 3.00 | 6.00 | 9.00 | M |
| 137 | Six Time Death–William Irish; aka After-dinner Story. Note: Queen's Quorum No. 95 | 8.00 | 16.00 | 24.00 | M |
| 138 | The Case against Mrs. Ames–Arthur Somers Roche; c-Belarski. Note: Same cover as pulp magazine Popular Detective, November 1945 | 3.00 | 6.00 | 9.00 | M |
| 139 | The Corpse with the Grimy Glove–R.A.J. Walling; 1948 | 3.00 | 6.00 | 9.00 | M |
| 140 | Secret Valley–Jackson Gregory | 3.00 | 6.00 | 9.00 | W |
| 141 | Winter Range–Alan LeMay. Note: Same cover as pulp magazine Range Riders Western, March 1947 | 3.00 | 6.00 | 9.00 | W |
| 142 | Guardians of the Desert–Tom Gill | 3.00 | 6.00 | 9.00 | W |
| 143 | Free Grass–Ernest Haycox | 3.00 | 6.00 | 9.00 | W |
| 144 | Danger in Paradise–Octavus Roy Cohen | 4.00 | 8.00 | 12.00 | M |
| 145 | Gunsmoke Trail–William MacLeod Raine; aka Moran Beats Back | 3.00 | 6.00 | 9.00 | W |
| 146 | Hopalong Cassidy Takes Cards–C.E. Mulford | 4.00 | 8.00 | 12.00 | M |
| 147 | The Private Life of Helen of Troy–John Erskine; c-Belarski | 15.00 | 30.00 | 45.00 | E |
| 148 | The Ranger Way–Eugene Cunningham | 3.00 | 6.00 | 9.00 | W |
| 149 | Hidden Blood–W.C. Tuttle. Note: Same cover as pulp magazine Range Riders Western, Summer 1945 | 3.50 | 7.00 | 10.50 | W |
| 150 | Crossword Puzzles, Book Two; 1948 | 35.00 | 70.00 | 105.00 | NF |
| 151 | Double Cross Ranch–Charles Alden Seltzer | 3.00 | 6.00 | 9.00 | W |
| 152 | Rancher's Revenge–Max Brand | 3.00 | 6.00 | 9.00 | W |
| 153 | The Secret of Father Brown–G.K. Chesterton | 5.00 | 10.00 | 15.00 | M |
| 154 | The Case of the Crumpled Knave–Anthony Boucher; c-Belarski | 8.00 | 16.00 | 24.00 | M |

*Popular Library 150, Popular Library 155, Popular Library 181.*

POPULAR LIBRARY, *continued*

| | | V/Good | Fine | N/Mint | |
|---|---|---|---|---|---|
| 155 | The Dreadful Night–Ben Ames Williams | 5.00 | 10.00 | 15.00 | M |
| 156 | Popular Book of Western Stories–ed. Leo Margulies | 3.00 | 6.00 | 9.00 | W |
| 157 | The Flying U Strikes–B.M. Bower | 3.00 | 6.00 | 9.00 | W |
| 158 | The Strangled Witness–Leslie Ford | 5.00 | 10.00 | 15.00 | M |
| 159 | About the Murder of the Circus Queen–Anthony Abbot; c-Belarski | 4.00 | 8.00 | 12.00 | M |
| 160 | The Silver Star–Jackson Gregory | 3.00 | 6.00 | 9.00 | W |
| 161 | Thunder in the Dust–Alan LeMay | 3.00 | 6.00 | 9.00 | W |
| 162 | Love Has No Alibi–Octavus Roy Cohen; c-Belarski | 4.50 | 9.00 | 13.50 | M |
| 163 | Death at Sea–Richard Sale; aka Destination Unknown | 5.00 | 10.00 | 15.00 | M |
| 164 | Lady in Peril–Ben Ames Williams; aka Money Musk; c-Belarski | 4.00 | 8.00 | 12.00 | M |
| 165 | Valley of Vanishing Herds–W.C. Tuttle | 3.00 | 6.00 | 9.00 | W |
| 166 | Sky-Pilot Cowboy–Walt Coburn | 3.00 | 6.00 | 9.00 | W |
| 167 | Pattern of Murder–Mignon G. Eberhart; aka The Pattern; c-Belarski. Note: Same cover as pulp magazine Thrilling Detective, November 1945 | 4.00 | 8.00 | 12.00 | M |
| 168 | Death and Taxes–David Dodge; c-Belarski | 5.00 | 10.00 | 15.00 | M |
| 169 | The Bitter Tea of General Yen–Grace Zaring Stone; 1949 | 5.00 | 10.00 | 15.00 | E |
| 170 | Omnibus of American Humor–ed. Robert N. Linscott; aka Comic Relief | 2.50 | 5.00 | 7.50 | H |
| 171 | Chaffee of Roaring Horse–Ernest Haycox. Note: Same cover as pulp magazine Thrilling Western, November 1944 | 2.50 | 5.00 | 7.50 | W |
| 172 | Pistol Pardners–William MacLeod Raine; aka The Black Tolts | 3.00 | 6.00 | 9.00 | W |
| 173 | Death Is a Lovely Lady–Ruth Fenisong; aka Jenny Kissed Me | 3.00 | 6.00 | 9.00 | M |
| 174 | The Three Coffins–John Dickson Carr; c-Belarski | 3.00 | 6.00 | 9.00 | M |
| 175 | Roaring Guns–Gordon Young; 1949; aka Red Clark O'Tulluco | 3.00 | 6.00 | 9.00 | W |
| 176 | Diamond River Range–Eugene Cunningham; aka Diamond River Man. Note: Same cover as pulp magazine Range Riders Western, September 1947 | 2.50 | 5.00 | 7.50 | W |
| 177 | Some Day I'll Kill You–Dana Chambers | 3.00 | 6.00 | 9.00 | M |
| 178 | Death Is Like That–John Spain; c-Belarski | 4.00 | 8.00 | 12.00 | M |
| 179 | Outlaw Breed–William Byron Mowery; aka The Black Automatic | 3.00 | 6.00 | 9.00 | W |
| 180 | Wild West–Bertrand W. Sinclair | 3.00 | 6.00 | 9.00 | W |
| 181 | How I Pick Winners–Ken Kling | 6.00 | 12.00 | 18.00 | NF |
| 182 | Little Known Facts about Well Known People–Dale Carnegie | 2.50 | 5.00 | 7.50 | NF |
| 183 | Gentle Annie–MacKinlay Kantor; c-Belarski | 2.50 | 5.00 | 7.50 | |
| 184 | Marshal of Sundown–Jackson Gregory | 2.50 | 5.00 | 7.50 | W |
| 185 | Whispering Smith–Frank H. Spearman; movie tie-in | 3.00 | 6.00 | 9.00 | |
| 186 | Cartoon Fun–Ned L. Pines | 15.00 | 30.00 | 45.00 | H |
| 187 | Selected Western Stories–ed. Leo Margulies; 1st ed. 1949 | 3.00 | 6.00 | 9.00 | W |

| | | V/Good | Fine | N/Mint | |
|---|---|---|---|---|---|
| 188 | The Yellow Overcoat–Frank Gruber; c-Belarski. Note: Same cover as pulp magazine Thrilling Detective, August 1947 | 5.00 | 10.00 | 15.00 | M |
| 189 | The Death Wish–Elisabeth Sanxay Holding | 3.00 | 6.00 | 9.00 | M |
| 190 | The Gay Bandit of the Border–Tom Gill | 3.00 | 6.00 | 9.00 | W |
| 191 | Barb Wire–Walt Coburn | 2.50 | 5.00 | 7.50 | W |
| 192 | Bodies Are Where You Find Them–Brett Halliday; c-Belarski | 5.00 | 10.00 | 15.00 | M |
| 193 | The Case of the Constant God–Rufus King; c-Belarski | 4.00 | 8.00 | 12.00 | M |
| 194 | Death on Scurvy Street–Ben Ames Williams; c-Belarski | 4.00 | 8.00 | 12.00 | M |
| 195 | Ward 20–James Warner Bellah; c-Belarski | 3.00 | 6.00 | 9.00 | E |
| 196 | There's Always Time to Die–Octavus Roy Cohen; aka I Love You Again | 4.00 | 8.00 | 12.00 | M |
| 197 | Pursuit of a Parcel–Patricia Wentworth | 4.00 | 8.00 | 12.00 | M |
| 198 | Hopalong Cassidy's Saddle Mate–Clarence E. Mulford; aka Hopalong Cassidy's Protege | 3.00 | 6.00 | 9.00 | W |
| 199 | Whispering Range–Ernest Haycox | 3.00 | 6.00 | 9.00 | W |
| 200 | Bats in the Belfry–Norman Matson; 1949 | 3.00 | 6.00 | 9.00 | F |
| 201 | Blood on Her Shoe–Medora Field | 2.50 | 5.00 | 7.50 | M |
| 202 | Shear the Black Sheep–David Dodge | 3.00 | 6.00 | 9.00 | M |
| 203 | Wild Horse Valley–W.C. Tuttle | 2.50 | 5.00 | 7.50 | W |
| 204 | Arizona Jim–Charles Alden Seltzer | 3.00 | 6.00 | 9.00 | W |
| 205 | Home Is the Hangman–Richard Sale; c-Belarski | 4.00 | 8.00 | 12.00 | M |
| 206 | The Grindle Nightmare–Q. Patrick | 5.00 | 10.00 | 15.00 | M |
| 207 | Reunion with Murder–Timothy Fuller | 4.00 | 8.00 | 12.00 | M |
| 208 | The Deputy at Snow Mountain–Edison Marshall | 3.00 | 6.00 | 9.00 | W |
| 209 | Gunsight Trail–Alan LeMay | 3.00 | 6.00 | 9.00 | W |
| 210 | That Winter–Merle Miller | 2.50 | 5.00 | 7.50 | E |
| 211 | The Doll's Trunk Murder–Helen Reilly; c-Belarski | 20.00 | 40.00 | 60.00 | M |
| 212 | Awake to Darkness–Richard McMullen; c-Belarski | 2.50 | 5.00 | 7.50 | E |
| 213 | Rustlers' Gap–William MacLeod Raine | 3.00 | 6.00 | 9.00 | W |
| 214 | Guns in the Valley–William Byron Mowery; aka The Valley Beyond | 3.00 | 6.00 | 9.00 | W |
| 215 | The Silver Forest–Ben Ames Williams; c-Belarski | 5.00 | 10.00 | 15.00 | E |
| 216 | Cup of Gold–John Steinbeck; c-Belarski | 4.00 | 8.00 | 12.00 | A |
| 217 | Tales of Chinatown–Sax Rohmer; c-Belarski (?) | 20.00 | 40.00 | 60.00 | M |
| 218 | The Pink Umbrella Murder–Frances Crane; aka The Pink Umbrella; c-Belarski | 4.00 | 8.00 | 12.00 | M |
| 219 | Duke–Hal Ellson; c-Belarski | 7.50 | 15.00 | 22.50 | JD |
| 220 | The Damon Runyon Story–Ed Weiner; c-Belarski (?) | 5.00 | 10.00 | 15.00 | B |
| 221 | Gentlemen Prefer Blondes–Anita Loos; c-Bergey | 12.50 | 25.00 | 37.50 | E |
| 222 | Something's Got to Give–Marion Hargrove; c-Bergey (?) | 2.50 | 5.00 | 7.50 | H |
| 223 | Picture Quiz Book–ed. John Paul Adams; 1950; c-Schomburg | 20.00 | 40.00 | 60.00 | NF |
| 224 | Sun in Their Eyes–Monte Barrett; c-Belarski | 2.00 | 4.00 | 6.00 | W |
| 225 | Fast on the Draw–Gordon Young; aka Red Clark Rides Alone | 3.00 | 6.00 | 9.00 | W |
| 226 | Sudden Bill Dorn–Jackson Gregory | 2.00 | 4.00 | 6.00 | W |
| 227 | The Illustrious Corpse–Tiffany Thayer; c-Belarski. Note: Same cover as pulp magazine Popular Detective, September 1948 | 3.00 | 6.00 | 9.00 | M |
| 228 | The Sex Machine–Shepherd Mead; aka The Magnificent MacInnes; c-Schomburg | 4.00 | 8.00 | 12.00 | SF |
| 229 | Homicide Johnny–Steve Fisher; c-Belarski | 7.50 | 15.00 | 22.50 | M |
| 230 | Focus–Arthur Miller; c-Belarski | 2.50 | 5.00 | 7.50 | |
| 231 | The Chuckling Fingers–Mabel Seeley | 3.00 | 6.00 | 9.00 | M |
| 232 | The Key–Patricia Wentworth | 3.00 | 6.00 | 9.00 | M |
| 233 | Macamba–Lilla Van Saher; c-Belarski | 3.00 | 6.00 | 9.00 | E |
| 234 | Quick Triggers–Eugene Cunningham; 1950 | 3.00 | 6.00 | 9.00 | W |
| 235 | Starlight Rider–Ernest Haycox | 3.00 | 6.00 | 9.00 | W |

*Popular Library 221, Popular Library, 229, Popular Library 236.*

*Popular Library 267, Popular Library 281, Popular Library 287.*

| | V/Good | Fine | N/Mint | |
|---|---|---|---|---|
| **POPULAR LIBRARY,** *continued* | | | | |
| 236 Pikes Peek or Bust–Earl Wilson; c-Schomburg | 3.50 | 7.00 | 10.50 | H |
| 237 Drums of Destiny–Peter Bourne; c-Bergey (?) | 4.00 | 8.00 | 12.00 | A |
| 238 She'll Be Dead by Morning–Dana Chambers | 3.00 | 6.00 | 9.00 | M |
| 239 The Evil Star–John Spain | 4.00 | 8.00 | 12.00 | M |
| 240 Acres and Pains–S.J. Perelman | 3.00 | 6.00 | 9.00 | H |
| 241 Fortunes of Captain Blood–Rafael Sabatini; c-Belarski; movie tie-in | 3.50 | 7.00 | 10.50 | A |
| 242 Riders of the Smoky Land–Edison Marshall | 3.00 | 6.00 | 9.00 | W |
| 243 Texas Breed–William MacLeod Raine | 3.00 | 6.00 | 9.00 | W |
| 244 Find Me in Fire–Robert Lowry | 7.50 | 15.00 | 22.50 | E |
| 245 Death Is a Gold Coin–Ruth Fenisong | 3.00 | 6.00 | 9.00 | M |
| 246 Murder by Latitude–Rufus King | 3.00 | 6.00 | 9.00 | M |
| 247 Not Too Narrow–Not Too Deep– Richard Sale | 3.00 | 6.00 | 9.00 | |
| 248 The Great Ones–Ralph Ingersoll | 3.00 | 6.00 | 9.00 | E |
| 249 Twisted Trails–W.C. Tuttle; aka The Santa Dolores Stage | 3.00 | 6.00 | 9.00 | W |
| 250 Mavericks–Walt Coburn; 1950 | 3.00 | 6.00 | 9.00 | W |
| 251 Eagle at My Eyes–Norman Katkov | 2.50 | 5.00 | 7.50 | E |
| 252 Bullets for the Bridegroom–David Dodge | 3.00 | 6.00 | 9.00 | M |
| 253 Yesterday's Murder–Craig Rice; aka Telefair | 3.00 | 6.00 | 9.00 | M |
| 254 The Pale Blonde of Sands Street– William Chapman White; c-Bergey | 3.00 | 6.00 | 9.00 | E |
| 255 The Lone Rider–Jackson Gregory | 3.00 | 6.00 | 9.00 | W |
| 256 Drygulch Trail–William MacLeod Raine | 3.00 | 6.00 | 9.00 | W |
| 257 Whistle Stop–Maritta M. Wolff | 3.00 | 6.00 | 9.00 | E |
| 258 Six Nights of Mystery–William Irish; 1st ed. 1950 | 20.00 | 40.00 | 60.00 | M |
| 259 Murder in the Mews–Helen Reilly | 3.00 | 6.00 | 9.00 | M |
| 260 The Edge of Doom–Leo Brady; movie tie-in; c-Belarski | 2.50 | 5.00 | 7.50 | M |
| 261 Painted Ponies–Alan LeMay | 3.00 | 6.00 | 9.00 | W |
| 262 Guns of the Arrowhead–Gordon Young; aka Red Clark of the Arrowhead. Note: Same cover as pulp magazine Thrilling Western, November 1945 | 3.00 | 6.00 | 9.00 | W |
| 263 Murder at Cambridge–Q. Patrick | 4.00 | 8.00 | 12.00 | M |
| 264 Dangerous Lady–Octavus Roy Cohen; c-Belarski | 3.00 | 6.00 | 9.00 | M |
| 265 The Girl in the Spike-Heeled Shoes– Martin Yoseloff | 3.00 | 6.00 | 9.00 | |
| 266 The Captain's Lady–Basil Heatter | 3.00 | 6.00 | 9.00 | E |
| 267 Turn of the Table–Jonathan Stagge | 5.00 | 10.00 | 15.00 | M |
| 268 The Nine Waxed Faces–Francis Beeding; c-Belarski | 3.00 | 6.00 | 9.00 | M |
| 269 Mirror, Mirror on the Wall–Mona Kent | 3.00 | 6.00 | 9.00 | E |
| 270 Tempered Blade–Monte Barrett | 2.50 | 5.00 | 7.50 | A |
| 271 Riders West–Ernest Haycox | 3.00 | 6.00 | 9.00 | W |
| 272 Trail's End–Edison Marshall; aka The Strength of the Pines | 3.00 | 6.00 | 9.00 | W |
| 273 The Big Eye–Max Ehrlich; c-Bergey | 3.50 | 7.00 | 10.50 | SF |
| 274 They Move with the Sun–Daniel Taylor | 2.50 | 5.00 | 7.50 | E |
| 275 Murder at Midnight–Richard Sale; 1950 | 4.00 | 8.00 | 12.00 | M |
| 276 Somewhere in This House–Rufus King; c-Belarski | 3.00 | 6.00 | 9.00 | M |
| 277 The Sure Thing–Merle Miller | 2.50 | 5.00 | 7.50 | E |
| 278 The Hero–Millard Lampell; c-Bergey | 3.00 | 6.00 | 9.00 | |
| 279 Shortgrass–Hal G. Evarts | 3.00 | 6.00 | 9.00 | W |
| 280 The River Bend Feud–William MacLeod Raine | 3.00 | 6.00 | 9.00 | W |
| 281 That's My Baby–Josef A. Schneider | 3.00 | 6.00 | 9.00 | |
| 282 The Four False Weapons–John Dickson Carr; c-Belarski (?) | 4.00 | 8.00 | 12.00 | M |
| 283 Silence in Court–Patricia Wentworth. Note: Same cover as pulp magazine Detective Novel, August 1945 | 3.00 | 6.00 | 9.00 | M |
| 284 Laura–Vera Caspary | 2.50 | 5.00 | 7.50 | M |
| 285 The Curtain Never Falls–Joey Adams; c-Bergey | 3.00 | 6.00 | 9.00 | E |
| 286 Murder of the Clergyman's Mistress– Anthony Abbot | 4.00 | 8.00 | 12.00 | M |
| 287 Don't Look Behind You–Samuel Rogers; c-Belarski (?) | 3.00 | 6.00 | 9.00 | M |
| 288 The Leather Pushers–H.C. Witwer; c-Bergey | 3.00 | 6.00 | 9.00 | S |
| 289 Trail of the Macaw–Eugene Cunningham | 3.00 | 6.00 | 9.00 | W |
| 290 The Ringtailed Rannyhans–Walt Coburn | 3.00 | 6.00 | 9.00 | W |
| 291 The Wrath and the Wind–Alexander Key | 3.00 | 6.00 | 9.00 | A |
| 292 Overboard–George F. Worts; c-Belarski. Note: Same cover as pulp magazine G-Men Detective, March 1949 | 15.00 | 30.00 | 45.00 | E |
| 293 The Hangman's Whip–Mignon G. Eberhart; c-Belarski. Note: Same cover as pulp magazine Mystery Book, Summer 1949 | 7.50 | 15.00 | 22.50 | M |
| 294 The Two Worlds of Johnny Truro– George Sklar | 2.00 | 4.00 | 6.00 | E |
| 295 The Wolf That Fed Us–Robert Lowry | 2.50 | 5.00 | 7.50 | E |
| 296 The Dead Tree Gives No Shelter–Virgil Scott | 2.50 | 5.00 | 7.50 | E |
| 297 Shotgun Gold–W.C. Tuttle | 2.50 | 5.00 | 7.50 | W |
| 298 Guns of Mist River–Jackson Cole | 3.00 | 6.00 | 9.00 | W |
| 299 A Woman of Samaria–James Wesley Ingles; c-Belarski | 7.50 | 15.00 | 22.50 | E |
| 300 The Winds of Fear–Hodding Carter; c-Belarski | 7.50 | 15.00 | 22.50 | E |
| 301 The Fifth Grave–Jonathan Latimer; 1950; c-Belarski | 3.00 | 6.00 | 9.00 | M |
| 302 The Old Battle Ax–Elisabeth Sanxay Holding; c-Belarski. Note: Same cover as pulp magazine Detective Novel, Spring 1949 | 5.00 | 10.00 | 15.00 | M |
| 303 Bound Girl–Everett Webber & Olga Webber | 4.00 | 8.00 | 12.00 | E |
| 304 This Spring of Love–Charles Mergendahl; 1951 | 2.50 | 5.00 | 7.50 | |
| 305 The Desert Hawk–Harry Sinclair Drago | 3.00 | 6.00 | 9.00 | W |
| 306 The Haunted Hills–B.M. Bower | 3.00 | 6.00 | 9.00 | W |
| 307 Her Life to Live–Oriana Atkinson; aka Big Eyes; c-Bergey | 7.50 | 15.00 | 22.50 | E |
| 308 It's a Free Country–Ben Ames Williams | 2.50 | 5.00 | 7.50 | |
| 309 The Dancing Detective–William Irish | 10.00 | 20.00 | 30.00 | M |
| 310 Here Lies the Body–Richard Burke | 5.00 | 10.00 | 15.00 | M |
| 311 Smoke Up the Valley–Monte Barrett | 2.50 | 5.00 | 7.50 | W |
| 312 Mamie Brandon–Jack Sheridan; c-Belarski | 2.50 | 5.00 | 7.50 | E |
| 313 The Far Call–Jackson Gregory | 3.00 | 6.00 | 9.00 | W |

*Popular Library 292, Popular Library 298, Popular Library 309.*

POPULAR LIBRARY, *continued*

| | | V/Good | Fine | N/Mint | |
|---|---|---|---|---|---|
| 314 | Edge of Beyond–James B. Hendryx | 3.00 | 6.00 | 9.00 | |
| 315 | Check Your Wits–Jules Leopold | 12.00 | 24.00 | 36.00 | NF |
| 316 | Tuesday to Bed–Francis Sill Wickware | 3.00 | 6.00 | 9.00 | E |
| 317 | The Night before Murder–Steve Fisher; c-Belarski | 4.00 | 8.00 | 12.00 | M |
| 318 | The Deadly Dove–Rufus King | 4.00 | 8.00 | 12.00 | M |
| 319 | My Forbidden Past–Polan Banks; movie tie-in | 3.00 | 6.00 | 9.00 | E |
| 320 | Excuse My Dust–Bellamy Partridge | 3.00 | 6.00 | 9.00 | H |
| 321 | Trouble on the Border–Gordon Young | 3.00 | 6.00 | 9.00 | W |
| 322 | Hell and High Water–William MacLeod Raine | 3.00 | 6.00 | 9.00 | W |
| 323 | Home Guide to Repair, Upkeep and Remodeling–William H. Crouse | 4.50 | 9.00 | 13.50 | NF |
| 324 | My Old Man's Badge–Ferguson Findley | 3.00 | 6.00 | 9.00 | M |
| 325 | Murder by the Dozen–Hugh Wiley; 1951 | 3.00 | 6.00 | 9.00 | M |
| 326 | Behind the Flying Saucers–Frank Scully; c-Bergey | 3.50 | 7.00 | 10.50 | UF |
| 327 | Stranger and Alone–J. Saunders Redding | 3.00 | 6.00 | 9.00 | |
| 328 | Soldiers' Daughters Never Cry–Audrey Erskine Lindop; c-Belarski | 2.50 | 5.00 | 7.50 | E |
| 329 | Bullet Brand–Hal G. Evarts; aka Spanish Acres | 3.00 | 6.00 | 9.00 | W |
| 330 | The Trouble Trailer–W.C. Tuttle | 3.00 | 6.00 | 9.00 | W |
| 331 | Campus Town–Hart Stilwell | 20.00 | 40.00 | 60.00 | E |
| 332 | Don't Ever Love Me–Octavus Roy Cohen; c-Belarski. Note: Same cover as pulp magazine Mystery Book Magazine, Winter 1950 | 5.00 | 10.00 | 15.00 | M |
| 333 | Lonesome Road–Patricia Wentworth | 3.00 | 6.00 | 9.00 | M |
| 334 | The Magnificent Courtesan–Lozania Prole; c-Belarski | 5.00 | 10.00 | 15.00 | E |
| 335 | Shadow of a Hero–Allan Chase | 2.50 | 5.00 | 7.50 | |
| 336 | The Parents' Manual–Anna W.M. Wolfe | 4.50 | 9.00 | 13.50 | NF |
| 337 | Ace in the Hole–Jackson Gregory | 3.00 | 6.00 | 9.00 | W |
| 338 | Starlight Pass–Tom Gill | 3.00 | 6.00 | 9.00 | W |
| 339 | The Lion and the Lamb–E. Phillips Oppenheim; c-Belarski | 4.00 | 8.00 | 12.00 | |
| 340 | Smart Guy–William MacHaug; aka The Affairs of O'Malley. Note: Same cover as pulp magazine Phantom Detective, August 1945 | 4.00 | 8.00 | 12.00 | M |
| 341 | Season for Passion–Lee Manning; c-Belarski | 3.00 | 6.00 | 9.00 | C |
| 342 | End of Track–Ward Weaver (Van Wyck Mason) | 3.00 | 6.00 | 9.00 | W |
| 343 | While Murder Waits–John Esteven; c-Belarski | 4.00 | 8.00 | 12.00 | M |
| 344 | The Applegreen Cat–Frances Crane; c-Belarski | 6.00 | 12.00 | 18.00 | M |
| 345 | Bullets at Clearwater–Edison Marshall; aka The Snowshoe Trail | 2.50 | 5.00 | 7.50 | W |
| 346 | Ramrod–Luke Short | 2.50 | 5.00 | 7.50 | W |
| 347 | Hoodlum–Charley Robertson; aka Shadow of a Cloud | 2.50 | 5.00 | 7.50 | E |
| 348 | Adios, O'Shaughnessy–Robert Tallman | 2.50 | 5.00 | 7.50 | E |
| 349 | Poison in Jest–John Dickson Carr | 3.50 | 7.00 | 10.50 | M |
| 350 | The Dogs Do Bark–Jonathan Stagge; 1951 | 4.00 | 8.00 | 12.00 | M |
| 351 | Tonight Is Forever–Charles Mergendahl; aka Don't Wait Up for Spring; c-Bergey | 3.00 | 6.00 | 9.00 | |
| 352 | Cotton Moon–Catherine Tracy | 3.00 | 6.00 | 9.00 | E |
| 353 | The Big Corral–Al Cody | 3.00 | 6.00 | 9.00 | W |
| 354 | Gun Feud–W.C. Tuttle; aka Wandering Dogies | 3.00 | 6.00 | 9.00 | W |
| 355 | I'll Be Right Home, Ma–Henry Denker | 2.50 | 5.00 | 7.50 | E |
| 356 | This Woman Is Mine–P.J. Wolfson; aka All Women Die | 2.50 | 5.00 | 7.50 | E |
| 357 | How I Became a Girl Reporter–Hyman Goldberg | 2.50 | 5.00 | 7.50 | E |
| 358 | Mrs. Candy and Saturday Night– Robert Tallant; c-Bergey (?) | 2.50 | 5.00 | 7.50 | E |
| 359 | Beyond the Rio Grande–William MacLeod Raine | 2.50 | 5.00 | 7.50 | W |
| 360 | The Silver Desert–Ernest Haycox | 2.50 | 5.00 | 7.50 | W |
| 361 | Winter Kill–Steve Fisher; c-Belarski | 4.00 | 8.00 | 12.00 | M |
| 362 | Never Walk Alone–Rufus King; aka The Case of the Dowager's Etchings; c-Belarski. Note: Same cover as pulp magazine Phantom Detective, Summer 1950 | 4.00 | 8.00 | 12.00 | M |
| 363 | The Traitor–William L. Shirer | 2.50 | 5.00 | 7.50 | M |
| 364 | The Ringing of the Glass–Preston Schoyer; c-Belarski | 3.00 | 6.00 | 9.00 | |
| 365 | Copperbelt–Nigel Sligh | 2.50 | 5.00 | 7.50 | |
| 366 | Please Send Me Absolutely Free!– Arkady Leokum | 2.50 | 5.00 | 7.50 | E |
| 367 | Shotgun Guard–D.B. Newton | 3.00 | 6.00 | 9.00 | W |
| 368 | Apache Crossing–Will Ermine. Note: Same cover as pulp magazine Giant Western, August 1949 | 3.00 | 6.00 | 9.00 | W |
| 369 | My Love Wears Black–Octavus Roy Cohen | 4.00 | 8.00 | 12.00 | M |
| 370 | The Crying Sisters–Mabel Seeley | 3.00 | 6.00 | 9.00 | M |
| 371 | The Strumpet Sea–Ben Ames Williams; c-Belarski | 2.50 | 5.00 | 7.50 | A |
| 372 | Wintertime–Jan Valtin | 2.50 | 5.00 | 7.50 | E |
| 373 | The Weeping and the Laughter–Vera Caspary | 2.50 | 5.00 | 7.50 | E |
| 374 | Dark Drums–Wenzell Brown | 2.50 | 5.00 | 7.50 | E |
| 375 | Texas Sheriff–Eugene Cunningham; 1951 | 2.50 | 5.00 | 7.50 | W |
| 376 | Trouble at Moon Dance–A.B. Guthrie, Jr; aka Murders at Moon Dance | 2.50 | 5.00 | 7.50 | W |
| 377 | Shadow of Madness–Hugh Pentecost; c-Bergey (?) | 3.50 | 7.00 | 10.50 | M |
| 378 | You're Lonely When You're Dead– James Hadley Chase | 3.50 | 7.00 | 10.50 | M |
| 379 | No Narrow Path–Catharine Whitcomb; aka The Hill of Glass; c-Belarski | 3.50 | 7.00 | 10.50 | E |
| 380 | Rear Guard–James Warner Bellah; aka The White Invader | 2.50 | 5.00 | 7.50 | W |
| 381 | Heads Off at Midnight–Francis Beeding | 3.00 | 6.00 | 9.00 | M |
| 382 | Dark Threat–Patricia Wentworth; c-Belarski. Note: Same cover as pulp magazine Black Book Detective, Summer 1949 | 3.00 | 6.00 | 9.00 | M |
| 383 | The Man from Texas–Jackson Gregory | 2.50 | 5.00 | 7.50 | W |
| 384 | Range Boss–Gordon Young; aka Red Clark, Range Boss. Note: Same cover as pulp magazine Hopalong Cassidy, Fall 1950 (No. 1) | 2.50 | 5.00 | 7.50 | W |
| 385 | Once Off Guard–J.H. Wallace | 2.50 | 5.00 | 7.50 | E |
| 386 | Cottage Sinister–Q. Patrick | 3.00 | 6.00 | 9.00 | M |
| 387 | Casualty–Robert Lowry | 3.00 | 6.00 | 9.00 | E |
| 388 | Hang My Wreath–Ward Weaver (Van Wyck Mason) | 2.50 | 5.00 | 7.50 | |
| 389 | This Way Out–James Ronald | 2.50 | 5.00 | 7.50 | M |
| 390 | Trails by Night–Tom J. Hopkins | 2.50 | 5.00 | 7.50 | W |
| 391 | Mooney–William Brown Meloney | 2.50 | 5.00 | 7.50 | E |
| 392 | Jailbait–William Bernard; illus. in Parade of Pleasure; c-Belarski | 4.00 | 8.00 | 12.00 | JD |
| 393 | The Bed She Made–Leslie Waller; 1952 | 2.50 | 5.00 | 7.50 | E |
| 394 | Echo of Evil–Manuel Komroff | 2.50 | 5.00 | 7.50 | E |
| 395 | Day into Night–David Westheimer; aka The Magic Fallacy | 2.50 | 5.00 | 7.50 | E |
| 396 | Love Me Sailor–Robert S. Close | 2.50 | 5.00 | 7.50 | |
| 397 | Border Feud–Tom Gill; aka Red Earth | 2.50 | 5.00 | 7.50 | W |
| 398 | Trail Smoke–Ernest Haycox | 2.50 | 5.00 | 7.50 | W |
| 399 | Whirlpool–James Leal Henderson | 2.50 | 5.00 | 7.50 | E |
| 400 | Slay Ride–Frank Kane; 1952 | 2.50 | 5.00 | 7.50 | |
| 401 | Wine of Violence–Ralph Ingersoll | 2.00 | 4.00 | 6.00 | E |
| 402 | Main Line–Livingston Biddle, Jr | 2.00 | 4.00 | 6.00 | E |
| 403 | The Reef–Keith Wheeler | 2.00 | 4.00 | 6.00 | E |
| 404 | Divorce–James Warner Bellah | 2.00 | 4.00 | 6.00 | |

| POPULAR LIBRARY, *continued* | | | | |
|---|---|---|---|---|
| 405 | Troubled Spring–John Brick | 2.00 | 4.00 | 6.00 |
| 406 | Montana Road–Harry Sinclair Drago | 2.50 | 5.00 | 7.50 W |
| 407 | Bonanza Gulch–Matt Stuart | 2.00 | 4.00 | 6.00 |
| 408 | Waterfront–Ferguson Findley | 3.50 | 7.00 | 10.50 E |
| 409 | One by One–Fan Nichols | 2.00 | 4.00 | 6.00 E |
| 410 | The Marx Brothers–Kyle Crichton | 6.00 | 12.00 | 18.00 B |
| 411 | Revolt of the Triffids–John Wyndham; aka Day of the Triffids; c-Bergey | 6.00 | 12.00 | 18.00 SF |
| 412 | The Spell–Gustav Breuer | 2.00 | 4.00 | 6.00 E |
| 413 | A Woman of Forty–Desmond Hall | 2.00 | 4.00 | 6.00 |
| 414 | The Texas Kid–William MacLeod Raine; aka The Dam Yank | 2.00 | 4.00 | 6.00 W |
| 415 | Pardners of the Dim Trails–Walt Coburn | 2.00 | 4.00 | 6.00 W |
| 416 | The Perfect Frame–William Ard | 2.50 | 5.00 | 7.50 E |
| 417 | A Yank on Piccadilly–C.L. McDermott | 2.00 | 4.00 | 6.00 E |
| 418 | The Impudent Rifle–Dick Pearce; c-Belarski | 2.00 | 4.00 | 6.00 |
| 419 | Lower Than Angels–Walter Karig | 2.00 | 4.00 | 6.00 E |
| 420 | Trial by Gunsmoke–Jim O'Mara | 2.00 | 4.00 | 6.00 W |
| 421 | A Matter of Morals–Joseph Gies | 2.00 | 4.00 | 6.00 E |
| 422 | The Vanquished–Alan Marcus; aka Straw to Make Brick; c-Belarski | 2.50 | 5.00 | 7.50 C |
| 423 | Johnny Bogan–Leonora Baccante | 2.00 | 4.00 | 6.00 E |
| 424 | Fright–George Hopley (William Irish); c-Belarski | 20.00 | 40.00 | 60.00 M |
| 425 | Thunder Valley–Burt Arthur; 1952 | 2.00 | 4.00 | 6.00 W |
| 426 | The Black Door–Cleve F. Adams | 2.50 | 5.00 | 7.50 M |
| 427 | More Beautiful Than Murder–Octavus Roy Cohen; c-Belarski (?) | 3.00 | 6.00 | 9.00 M |
| 428 | The Train from Pittsburgh–Julian Farsen | 2.00 | 4.00 | 6.00 E |
| 429 | Two-Gun Man–Gordon Young; aka Red Clark, Two-Gun Man | 2.00 | 4.00 | 6.00 W |
| 430 | Guardians of the Trail–Jackson Gregory | 2.00 | 4.00 | 6.00 W |
| 431 | Strangler's Serenade–William Irish; c-Belarski | 10.00 | 20.00 | 30.00 M |
| 432 | The Great Mail Robbery–Clarence Budington Kelland; c-Bergey (?) | 2.50 | 5.00 | 7.50 E |
| 433 | Bitter Fruit–Peter Packer; aka White Crocus | 2.00 | 4.00 | 6.00 |
| 434 | So Deadly Fair–Gertrude Walker | 2.00 | 4.00 | 6.00 E |
| 435 | The Lost Ones–Stevan Javellana; aka Without Seeing the Dawn | 2.00 | 4.00 | 6.00 E |
| 436 | Arizona Guns–William MacLeod Raine | 2.00 | 4.00 | 6.00 W |
| 437 | Six-Gun Gamble–D.B. Newton | 2.00 | 4.00 | 6.00 W |
| 438 | At Sundown the Tiger–Ethel Mannin | 2.00 | 4.00 | 6.00 |
| 439 | Rip Tide–Lee Wichelns; aka Masterson | 2.00 | 4.00 | 6.00 |
| 440 | The Cruel Dawn–Alfred Viazzi | 2.50 | 5.00 | 7.50 E |
| 441 | Thief River–Nelson Nye | 2.00 | 4.00 | 6.00 W |
| 442 | Head of the Mountain–Ernest Haycox | 2.00 | 4.00 | 6.00 W |
| 443 | Sweet and Deadly–Verne Chute | 2.00 | 4.00 | 6.00 |
| 444 | Isle of the Damned–George John Seaton | 2.00 | 4.00 | 6.00 A |
| 445 | Timbal Gulch Trail–Max Brand | 2.00 | 4.00 | 6.00 W |
| 446 | The Night and the Naked–Gordon Merrick; aka The Strumpet Wind | 2.00 | 4.00 | 6.00 E |
| 447 | Dragon's Island–Jack Williamson; c-Bergey (?) | 4.50 | 9.00 | 13.50 SF |
| 448 | You Can't Catch Me–Lawrence Lariar | 2.00 | 4.00 | 6.00 E |
| 449 | Gunswift–Jack Byrne | 2.00 | 4.00 | 6.00 W |
| 450 | Trouble Shooter–Ernest Haycox; 1952 | 2.00 | 4.00 | 6.00 W |
| 451 | Maharajah–Richard Cargoe | 2.50 | 5.00 | 7.50 E |
| 452 | I'll Get Mine–Thurston Scott; aka Cure It with Honey | 6.00 | 12.00 | 18.00 E |
| 453 | Neither Five nor Three–Helen MacInnes | 2.00 | 4.00 | 6.00 E |
| 454 | Two-edged Vengeance–W.T. Ballard | 2.00 | 4.00 | 6.00 W |
| 455 | Hellgate Canyon–Fred Delano | 2.00 | 4.00 | 6.00 |
| 456 | What Price Murder–Cleve F. Adams | 2.50 | 5.00 | 7.50 M |
| 457 | The Boy Came Back–Charles H. Knickerbocker | 2.00 | 4.00 | 6.00 E |
| 458 | Pray Love, Remember–Stephen Wendt | 2.00 | 4.00 | 6.00 |
| 459 | Burmese Days–George Orwell | 3.00 | 6.00 | 9.00 E |
| 460 | Rawhide Range–Ernest Haycox | 2.00 | 4.00 | 6.00 W |
| 461 | Born to Trouble–Nelson Nye | 2.00 | 4.00 | 6.00 W |
| 462 | A Bullet for My Love–Octavus Roy Cohen | 2.50 | 5.00 | 7.50 M |
| 463 | The Big Bubble–Theodore Pratt | 2.00 | 4.00 | 6.00 E |
| 464 | The Unfulfilled–W.G. Hardy | 2.00 | 4.00 | 6.00 E |
| 465 | Guns of Vengeance–Jim O'Mara | 2.00 | 4.00 | 6.00 W |
| 466 | The Outriders–Irving Ravetch | 2.00 | 4.00 | 6.00 |

| 467 | Shakedown–Ben Kerr (William Ard) | 3.00 | 6.00 | 9.00 |
|---|---|---|---|---|
| 468 | Dark Surrender–Peter Packer | 2.00 | 4.00 | 6.00 |
| 469 | Hard to Get–Edwin Gilbert | 2.00 | 4.00 | 6.00 |
| 470 | Headline Crimes of the Year–Edward D. Radin | 2.50 | 5.00 | 7.50 NF |
| 471 | Range beyond the Law–William MacLeod Raine | 2.00 | 4.00 | 6.00 W |
| 472 | Texan on the Prod–Philip Ketchum | 2.00 | 4.00 | 6.00 W |
| 473 | Bluebeard's Seventh Wife–William Irish; 1st ed. 1952 | 15.00 | 30.00 | 45.00 M |
| 474 | The Night Thorn–Ian Gordon; 1953 | 2.50 | 5.00 | 7.50 E |
| 475 | Rancher's Revenge–Max Brand | 2.00 | 4.00 | 6.00 W |
| 476 | Showdown–W.T. Ballard & James C. Lynch | 2.00 | 4.00 | 6.00 W |
| 477 | The Diary–William Ard | 2.50 | 5.00 | 7.50 |
| 478 | Don't Crowd Me–Evan Hunter | 2.00 | 4.00 | 6.00 |
| 479 | Torment–Scott Graham Williamson | 2.00 | 4.00 | 6.00 E |
| 480 | Superstition Range–Parker Bonner | 2.00 | 4.00 | 6.00 W |
| 481 | Desert of the Damned–Nelson Nye | 2.00 | 4.00 | 6.00 W |
| 482 | Don't Get Caught–M.E. Chaber; aka Hangman's Harvest | 2.00 | 4.00 | 6.00 M |
| 483 | Ask for Linda–Fan Nichols | 2.00 | 4.00 | 6.00 E |
| 484 | The Girl Cage–Charles Mergendahl | 2.00 | 4.00 | 6.00 E |
| 485 | Glitter–A.B. Shiffrin | 2.00 | 4.00 | 6.00 E |
| 486 | Chaffee of Roaring Horse–Ernest Haycox | 2.00 | 4.00 | 6.00 W |
| 487 | Quick Trigger Law–Jim O'Mara; aka Death at War Dance | 2.00 | 4.00 | 6.00 W |
| 488 | Naked and Alone–Michael Lawrence | 2.00 | 4.00 | 6.00 |
| 489 | Duel in the Sun–Niven Busch | 2.00 | 4.00 | 6.00 W |
| 490 | Venables–Geoffrey Wagner | 2.00 | 4.00 | 6.00 E |
| 491 | Blood on the Forge–William Attaway | 2.00 | 4.00 | 6.00 |
| 492 | Incident at Sun Mountain–Todhunter Ballard | 2.00 | 4.00 | 6.00 W |
| 493 | High Mesa–Tex Grady | 2.00 | 4.00 | 6.00 W |
| 494 | Double Cross–Mike Moran | 2.00 | 4.00 | 6.00 |
| 495 | H Is for Heroin–David Hulburd | 5.00 | 10.00 | 15.00 E |
| 496 | Stranger in Our Midst–Robert Carson | 2.00 | 4.00 | 6.00 E |
| 497 | You Can't See around Corners–Jon Cleary | 2.00 | 4.00 | 6.00 |
| 498 | Texas Rawhider–Jack Barton | 2.00 | 4.00 | 6.00 W |
| 499 | Guns of the Barricade Bunch–Philip Ketchum | 2.00 | 4.00 | 6.00 W |
| 500 | Time to Kill–Terry Spain | 2.50 | 5.00 | 7.50 E |
| 501 | The Closest Kin There Is–Clara Winston | 2.00 | 4.00 | 6.00 E |
| 502 | A Girl for Danny–William Ard; 1st ed. 1953 | 3.50 | 7.00 | 10.50 |
| 503 | Rickey–Charles Calitri | 2.00 | 4.00 | 6.00 |
| 504 | Joey Adams' Joke Book–Joey Adams | 2.00 | 4.00 | 6.00 H |
| 505 | Ten against Caesar–K.R.G. Granger | 2.00 | 4.00 | 6.00 W |
| 506 | Fighting Cowman–Louis Trimble | 2.00 | 4.00 | 6.00 W |
| 507 | The Big Fear–Theo Durrant (Anthony Boucher); aka The Marble Forest | 6.00 | 12.00 | 18.00 M |
| 508 | The Loving and the Daring–Francoise Mallet; aka The Illusionist | 2.00 | 4.00 | 6.00 E |
| 509 | Rage in the Wind–Boyd Cochrell | 2.00 | 4.00 | 6.00 E |
| 510 | The Night Is Mine–David Davidson; aka In Another Country | 2.00 | 4.00 | 6.00 E |
| 511 | Renegade of Rainbow Basin–Hal G. Evarts | 2.00 | 4.00 | 6.00 W |
| 512 | Ramrod from Hell–Ernie Wayne | 2.00 | 4.00 | 6.00 |
| 513 | Beyond the Law–Edward D. Radin | 2.00 | 4.00 | 6.00 NF |
| 514 | Darling, I Hate You–T.S. Matthews | 2.00 | 4.00 | 6.00 |
| 515 | The Hard Way–Robert V. Williams | 2.00 | 4.00 | 6.00 |
| 516 | Island in the Sky–Ernest K. Gann | 2.00 | 4.00 | 6.00 A |
| 517 | Free Grass–Ernest Haycox | 2.00 | 4.00 | 6.00 W |
| 518 | Rustler of the Owlhorns–Jim O'Mara | 2.00 | 4.00 | 6.00 W |
| 519 | Blondes Die Young–Bill Peters | 2.00 | 4.00 | 6.00 |
| 520 | The Tightrope–Stanley Kauffmann | 2.00 | 4.00 | 6.00 E |
| 521 | Six Angels at My Back–John Bell Clayton | 2.00 | 4.00 | 6.00 E |
| 522 | China Coaster–Don Smith | 2.00 | 4.00 | 6.00 E |
| 523 | Facts of Life and Love for Teenagers–Evelyn Millis Duvall | 1.50 | 3.00 | 4.50 NF |
| 524 | West of Quarantine–W.T. Ballard | 2.00 | 4.00 | 6.00 W |
| 525 | Stranger from Texas–Ray Townsend; 1953 | 2.00 | 4.00 | 6.00 W |
| 526 | You Can't Stop Me–William Ard | 3.00 | 6.00 | 9.00 M |
| 527 | Bond of the Flesh–Rosamond Marshall | 2.00 | 4.00 | 6.00 E |
| 528 | Hooked–Will Oursler & Laurence D. Smith | 3.00 | 6.00 | 9.00 E |
| 529 | Liana–Martha Gellhorn | 1.50 | 3.00 | 4.50 E |

POPULAR LIBRARY, *continued*

| # | Title | V/Good | Fine | N/Mint | |
|---|-------|--------|------|--------|---|
| 530 | All the Way Down–M.E. Chaber | 2.00 | 4.00 | 6.00 | M |
| 531 | West of the Law–William MacLeod Raine | 1.50 | 3.00 | 4.50 | W |
| 532 | The Saddle Bum–Philip Ketchum | 1.50 | 3.00 | 4.50 | W |
| 533 | Smooth and Deadly–Quentin Reynolds; aka I, Willie Sutton | 1.50 | 3.00 | 4.50 | NF |
| 534 | Strange Lovers–Armando Meoni | 1.50 | 3.00 | 4.50 | E |
| 535 | Thunder in the Dust–Alan LeMay | 1.50 | 3.00 | 4.50 | W |
| 536 | Count Me In–Fan Nichols | 1.50 | 3.00 | 4.50 | E |
| 537 | The Grim Canyon–Ernest Haycox | 1.50 | 3.00 | 4.50 | W |
| 538 | Point of a Gun–Dean Owen | 1.50 | 3.00 | 4.50 | W |
| 539 | Kiss Me Hard–Tom Brandt | 1.50 | 3.00 | 4.50 | |
| 540 | My Enemy, the World–Guido D'Agostino | 1.50 | 3.00 | 4.50 | E |
| 541 | This Heart, This Hunter–Hallie Burnett | 1.50 | 3.00 | 4.50 | |
| 542 | The Ranger Way–Eugene Cunningham | 1.50 | 3.00 | 4.50 | W |
| 543 | The Flesh and the Spirit–Charles Shaw; aka Heaven Knows, Mr. Allison | 2.00 | 4.00 | 6.00 | E |
| 544 | The Mark of the Moon–Francis Gerard | 4.50 | 9.00 | 13.50 | E |
| 545 | The Silver Star–Jackson Gregory | 1.50 | 3.00 | 4.50 | W |
| 546 | Hard Rock Rancher–William E. Vance | 1.50 | 3.00 | 4.50 | W |
| 547 | Mother Finds a Body–Gypsy Rose Lee (Craig Rice) | 1.50 | 3.00 | 4.50 | M |
| 548 | Stay Away, Joe–Dan Cushman; 1954 | 2.00 | 4.00 | 6.00 | |
| 549 | Monkey on My Back–Wenzell Brown | 3.00 | 6.00 | 9.00 | JD |
| 550 | Love for Lydia–H.E. Bates | 1.50 | 3.00 | 4.50 | E |
| 551 | I Dive for Treasure–Lt. Harry E. Rieseberg | 1.50 | 3.00 | 4.50 | A |
| 552 | High Iron–Todhunter Ballard | 1.50 | 3.00 | 4.50 | W |
| 553 | Texas Breed–William MacLeod Raine | 1.50 | 3.00 | 4.50 | W |
| 554 | Some Day I'll Kill You–Dana Chambers | 1.50 | 3.00 | 4.50 | M |
| 555 | Martha Crane–Charles Gorham | 1.50 | 3.00 | 4.50 | |
| 556 | Wilderness Rogue–Henry Schindall; aka Let the Spring Come | 1.50 | 3.00 | 4.50 | A |
| 557 | Possessed–June Wetherell | 1.50 | 3.00 | 4.50 | |
| 558 | The Tiger in Summer–Michael Keon | 3.00 | 6.00 | 9.00 | E |
| 559 | Be Happier, Be Healthier–Gayelord Hauser | 1.50 | 3.00 | 4.50 | NF |
| 560 | Gunning for Trouble–L.L. Foreman | 1.50 | 3.00 | 4.50 | W |
| 561 | Gunsight Trail–Alan LeMay | 1.50 | 3.00 | 4.50 | W |
| 562 | I Take All–Robert Carson | 1.50 | 3.00 | 4.50 | |
| 563 | A Secret Story–William Saroyan | 1.50 | 3.00 | 4.50 | |
| 564 | The Sword of Satan–H.M. Mons | 1.50 | 3.00 | 4.50 | A |
| 565 | The Innocent at Large–Noel Langley | 1.50 | 3.00 | 4.50 | |
| 566 | Cradle of the Sun–John Claggett | 1.50 | 3.00 | 4.50 | A |
| 567 | Starlight Rider–Ernest Haycox | 1.50 | 3.00 | 4.50 | W |
| 568 | Shortgrass–Hal G. Evarts | 1.50 | 3.00 | 4.50 | W |
| 569 | A Private Party–William Ard | 2.50 | 5.00 | 7.50 | E |
| 570 | The Violent Wedding–Robert Lowry | 2.00 | 4.00 | 6.00 | |
| 571 | Isle of Demons–John Clarke Bowman | 1.50 | 3.00 | 4.50 | A |
| 572 | Country Girl–Richard McMullen | 1.50 | 3.00 | 4.50 | |
| 573 | The Girl in the Spike-Heeled Shoes–Martin Yoseloff | 1.50 | 3.00 | 4.50 | |
| 574 | Fighting Blood–Gordon Young | 1.50 | 3.00 | 4.50 | W |
| 575 | The Texas Gun–Philip Ketchum; 1954 | 1.50 | 3.00 | 4.50 | W |
| 576 | The Dead Tree Gives No Shelter–Virgil Scott | 1.00 | 2.00 | 3.00 | E |
| 577 | The Wire God–Jack Willard | 1.50 | 3.00 | 4.50 | |
| 578 | Rainbow Road–Davenport Steward | 1.50 | 3.00 | 4.50 | E |
| 579 | Are Your Troubles Psychosomatic?–J.A. Winter | 1.00 | 2.00 | 3.00 | NF |
| 580 | We Burn like Candles–Bernice Kevinoky; aka All the Young Summer Days | 1.50 | 3.00 | 4.50 | |
| 581 | Dark Drums–Wenzell Brown | 1.50 | 3.00 | 4.50 | E |
| 582 | Highgrader–Hal G. Evarts | 1.50 | 3.00 | 4.50 | W |
| 583 | Rifle Pass–Dean Owen | 1.50 | 3.00 | 4.50 | W |
| 584 | Run, Brother, Run!–Tom Brandt | 1.50 | 3.00 | 4.50 | E |
| 585 | Rogue Wind–Ugo Moretti | 1.50 | 3.00 | 4.50 | |
| 586 | Devil Take Her–Fan Nichols | 1.50 | 3.00 | 4.50 | |
| 587 | Dark Streets of Paris–Jean-Louis Curtis | 1.50 | 3.00 | 4.50 | |
| 588 | The Mountain–Henri Troyat | 1.50 | 3.00 | 4.50 | |
| 589 | Guns Up–Ernest Haycox; 1st ed. 1954 | 2.50 | 5.00 | 7.50 | W |
| 590 | Gold Town Gunman–Ray Townsend; c-Saunders | 2.50 | 5.00 | 7.50 | W |
| 591 | No Angels for Me–William Ard; 1st ed. 1954 | 3.50 | 7.00 | 10.50 | |
| 592 | Teen-age Gangs–Madeline Darr & Dale Kramer | 3.00 | 6.00 | 9.00 | JD |
| 593 | The Gilded Hearse–Charles Gorham | 2.00 | 4.00 | 6.00 | |
| 594 | The Brass God–Richard G. Hubler | 1.50 | 3.00 | 4.50 | |
| 595 | Why We Behave As We Do–Frank S. Caprio | 1.50 | 3.00 | 4.50 | NF |
| 596 | Frontier Feud–Will Cook | 1.50 | 3.00 | 4.50 | W |
| 597 | Marshal of Sundown–Jackson Gregory | 1.50 | 3.00 | 4.50 | W |
| 598 | The Innocent One–James Reach | 1.50 | 3.00 | 4.50 | |
| 599 | The Night Is My Undoing–Delmar Jackson | 1.50 | 3.00 | 4.50 | |
| 600 | The Feared and the Fearless–Guthrie Wilson | 1.50 | 3.00 | 4.50 | C |
| 601 | The Naked Sword–Arthea Mitchell | 1.50 | 3.00 | 4.50 | A |
| 602 | The Dim View–Basil Heatter | 1.50 | 3.00 | 4.50 | E |
| 603 | Outlaw Brand–Parker Bonner | 1.50 | 3.00 | 4.50 | W |
| 604 | Gun Law–Philip Ketchum | 1.50 | 3.00 | 4.50 | W |
| 605 | Crimes of Passion–Edward D. Radin | 1.50 | 3.00 | 4.50 | NF |
| 606 | The Departure–John Olden Sherry | 1.50 | 3.00 | 4.50 | |
| 607 | Too Fast We Live–Richard Glendinning | 1.50 | 3.00 | 4.50 | |
| 608 | The Wrath and the Wind–Alexander Key | 1.50 | 3.00 | 4.50 | A |
| 609 | The Survivors–Ronald McKie | 1.50 | 3.00 | 4.50 | |
| 610 | Bad Men and Good–ed. Western Writers of America | 1.50 | 3.00 | 4.50 | W |
| 611 | Trail of the Damned–Jack Barton | 1.50 | 3.00 | 4.50 | W |
| 612 | Hot Freeze–Martin Brett | 1.50 | 3.00 | 4.50 | |
| 613 | The Eternal Galilean–Fulton J. Sheen | 1.00 | 2.00 | 3.00 | NF |
| 614 | Mark of the Hunter–Gene Caesar | 1.50 | 3.00 | 4.50 | |
| 615 | Give and Take–Thomas H. Raddall | 1.50 | 3.00 | 4.50 | |
| 616 | Riders West–Ernest Haycox | 1.50 | 3.00 | 4.50 | W |
| 617 | Rawhide Gunman–W.T. Ballard | 1.50 | 3.00 | 4.50 | W |
| 618 | Ten Roads to Hell–Robert Travers | 1.50 | 3.00 | 4.50 | |
| 619 | Naked to My Past–Frederic Wakeman; aka Mandrake Root | 1.50 | 3.00 | 4.50 | |
| 620 | Everybody Slept Here–Elliott Arnold | 1.50 | 3.00 | 4.50 | |
| 621 | Episode–Peter W. Denzer | 1.50 | 3.00 | 4.50 | |
| 622 | The Last Princess–Charles O. Locke | 1.50 | 3.00 | 4.50 | A |
| 623 | Renegade River–Ray Townsend | 1.00 | 2.00 | 3.00 | W |
| 624 | Quick Triggers–Eugene Cunningham | 1.50 | 3.00 | 4.50 | W |
| 625 | Flee the Night in Anger–Dan Keller; 1954 | 1.50 | 3.00 | 4.50 | |
| 626 | All Passion Spent–Chandler Brossard | 1.00 | 2.00 | 3.00 | |
| 627 | The Naked Hunter–William Woolfolk | 1.00 | 2.00 | 3.00 | |
| 628 | Cry the Lonely Flesh–Jesse L. Lasky, Jr | 1.00 | 2.00 | 3.00 | E |
| 629 | Friend or Foe?–Oreste Pinto | 1.00 | 2.00 | 3.00 | |
| 630 | Smoke up the Valley–Monte Barrett | 1.00 | 2.00 | 3.00 | W |
| 631 | Prairie Guns–Will Cook | 1.50 | 3.00 | 4.50 | W |
| 632 | Now It's My Turn–M.E. Chaber | 1.50 | 3.00 | 4.50 | M |
| 633 | Hotel Room–Natalie Anderson Scott; 1955 | 1.00 | 2.00 | 3.00 | |
| 634 | Naked in the Night–Jon Cleary | 1.00 | 2.00 | 3.00 | |
| 635 | The Wild Years–Donn O'Hara | 1.00 | 2.00 | 3.00 | |
| 636 | Men and the Sea–Sterling Lord | 1.50 | 3.00 | 4.50 | |
| 637 | Six-Gun Ambush–Max Brand | 1.50 | 3.00 | 4.50 | W |
| 638 | Blizzard Range–W.T. Ballard | 1.50 | 3.00 | 4.50 | W |
| 639 | Don't Come Crying to Me–William Ard | 2.50 | 5.00 | 7.50 | |
| 640 | Kiss the Night Away–C.G. Lumbard; aka Senior Spring | 1.00 | 2.00 | 3.00 | |
| 641 | The Naked I–Roy Chanslor | 1.00 | 2.00 | 3.00 | |
| 642 | I'll Never Let You Go–Fan Nichols | 1.00 | 2.00 | 3.00 | E |
| 643 | Boldness Be My Friend–Richard Pape | 1.00 | 2.00 | 3.00 | |
| 644 | Vengeance Trail–Ernest Haycox; 1st ed. 1955 | 1.50 | 3.00 | 4.50 | W |
| 645 | Desperation Valley–Philip Ketchum | 1.50 | 3.00 | 4.50 | W |
| 646 | Up to Her Neck–John Newton Chance | 1.00 | 2.00 | 3.00 | |
| 647 | Wide-Open Town–Robert F. Mirvish | 1.00 | 2.00 | 3.00 | E |
| 648 | Naked Canvas–Warwick Scott | 1.00 | 2.00 | 3.00 | E |
| 649 | Down the Dark Street–Siegel Fleisher | 1.00 | 2.00 | 3.00 | |
| 650 | Fair Game–Karl Kramer; 1955 | 1.00 | 2.00 | 3.00 | |
| 651 | Apache Agent–Hal G. Evarts | 1.00 | 2.00 | 3.00 | W |
| 652 | Fury at Painted Rock–Will Cook | 1.50 | 3.00 | 4.50 | W |
| 653 | Down I Go–Ben Kerr (William Ard); 1st ed. 1955 | 3.50 | 7.00 | 10.50 | M |
| 654 | The Nature of Love–H.E. Bates | 1.00 | 2.00 | 3.00 | |
| 655 | Dream of Innocence–Turnley Walker | 1.00 | 2.00 | 3.00 | |
| 656 | Passion Road–Richard Glendinning | 1.00 | 2.00 | 3.00 | |
| 657 | You Belong to Me–Sam Ross | 1.00 | 2.00 | 3.00 | |
| 658 | Desire in the Streets–Renato Cannavale | 1.00 | 2.00 | 3.00 | |
| 659 | Brand of Fury–Jack Barton | 1.00 | 2.00 | 3.00 | W |
| 660 | You Asked for It–Ian Fleming; aka Casino Royale | 20.00 | 40.00 | 60.00 | M |
| 661 | Live and Let Live–Chesley Wilson | 1.00 | 2.00 | 3.00 | |
| 662 | Deep Is My Desire–Ian Gordon | 1.00 | 2.00 | 3.00 | |
| 663 | Fast and Loose–Speed Lamkin | 1.00 | 2.00 | 3.00 | |
| 664 | Night After Night–Leonard Nathan | 1.00 | 2.00 | 3.00 | |

*Popular Library 639, Popular Library 660, Popular Library 675.*

| | | V/Good | Fine | N/Mint | |
|---|---|---|---|---|---|

**POPULAR LIBRARY,** *continued*

| | | V/Good | Fine | N/Mint | |
|---|---|---|---|---|---|
| 665 | Farewell, My Young Lover–Glenn Scott | 1.00 | 2.00 | 3.00 | |
| 666 | Sundown Basin–Ray Townsend | 1.00 | 2.00 | 3.00 | W |
| 667 | Blonde and Beautiful–Richard Foster (K.F. Crossen); orig. 1955 | 1.50 | 3.00 | 4.50 | |
| 668 | Strip the Heart–Jacquin Sanders; aka Freakshow | 1.00 | 2.00 | 3.00 | E |
| 669 | Sail the Dark Tide–Davenport Steward | 1.50 | 3.00 | 4.50 | A |
| 670 | The Bad One–Lowell Barrington | 1.00 | 2.00 | 3.00 | |
| 671 | Drag Me Down–E.B. Stuart | 1.00 | 2.00 | 3.00 | |
| 672 | A Time for Pleasure–Phyllis Hastings | 1.00 | 2.00 | 3.00 | |
| 673 | Rider from Texas–Philip Ketchum | 1.00 | 2.00 | 3.00 | W |
| 674 | Web of Passion–Edward D. Radin | 1.00 | 2.00 | 3.00 | |
| 675 | Cry Hard, Cry Fast–John D. MacDonald; 1st ed. 1955 | 7.50 | 15.00 | 22.50 | M |
| 676 | This Is My Night–Robert Lowry | 1.50 | 3.00 | 4.50 | |
| 677 | Wicked We Love–Mordecai Richler | 1.00 | 2.00 | 3.00 | |
| 678 | Bobby Sox–Marty Links | 1.00 | 2.00 | 3.00 | H |
| 679 | Good-Time Girl–Conrad Maine | 1.00 | 2.00 | 3.00 | |
| 680 | Trigger Trail–W.T. Ballard | 1.00 | 2.00 | 3.00 | W |
| 681 | Don't Push Me Around–Elliott Gilbert | 1.00 | 2.00 | 3.00 | |
| 682 | The Divine Romance–Fulton J. Sheen | 1.00 | 2.00 | 3.00 | |
| 683 | The Valley of Love–H.E. Bates | 1.00 | 2.00 | 3.00 | |
| 684 | Only the Brave–Allan R. Bosworth | 1.00 | 2.00 | 3.00 | |
| 685 | The Big Rumble–Wenzell Brown | 2.50 | 5.00 | 7.50 | JD |
| 686 | The Naked and the Damned–Robert Shafer; aka The Conquered Place | 2.50 | 5.00 | 7.50 | |
| 687 | Bullet Range–Will Cook | 1.00 | 2.00 | 3.00 | W |
| 688 | Surrender to Love–Charles Boswell & Lewis Thompson | 1.00 | 2.00 | 3.00 | |
| 689 | The Lovers–Mitchell Wilson | 1.00 | 2.00 | 3.00 | |
| 690 | The Long Watch–Robert F. Mirvish | 1.00 | 2.00 | 3.00 | |
| 691 | All That Love Allows–Paul Darcy Boles | 1.00 | 2.00 | 3.00 | |
| 692 | If You Are a Woman–Lee Graham | 1.00 | 2.00 | 3.00 | |
| 693 | Desert Showdown–Max Brand; aka Trouble Trail | 1.00 | 2.00 | 3.00 | W |
| 694 | Forbidden Valley–Thomas Thompson | 1.00 | 2.00 | 3.00 | W |
| 695 | Blondes Are My Trouble–Martin Brett | 1.00 | 2.00 | 3.00 | |
| 696 | I'll Cry Tomorrow–Lillian Roth | 1.00 | 2.00 | 3.00 | |
| 697 | Contrary Pleasure–John D. MacDonald | 6.00 | 12.00 | 18.00 | |
| 698 | Oops! Wrong Party!–Syd Hoff | 1.50 | 3.00 | 4.50 | H |
| 699 | The Whole Town Knew–Francis Irby Gwaltney | 1.00 | 2.00 | 3.00 | |
| 700 | Secret River and the Trail of the Bare-foot Pony–Ernest Haycox; 1st ed. 1955 | 2.50 | 5.00 | 7.50 | W |
| 701 | Trail Drive–Bill Gulick; aka A Thousand for the Caribou | 1.00 | 2.00 | 3.00 | W |
| 702 | Sweet and Low-down–Jack Waer | 1.00 | 2.00 | 3.00 | |
| 703 | Lovers in Torment–Gordon Merrick | 1.00 | 2.00 | 3.00 | |
| 704 | The Judas Kiss–Jay J. Dratler | 1.00 | 2.00 | 3.00 | |
| 705 | A New Desire–Stanley Kauffmann | 1.00 | 2.00 | 3.00 | |
| 706 | Angel Face–Fan Nichols | 1.00 | 2.00 | 3.00 | |
| 707 | Rawhide Guns–Frank Bonham | 1.00 | 2.00 | 3.00 | W |
| 708 | Ambush Range–Jack Barton | 1.00 | 2.00 | 3.00 | W |
| 709 | Show No Mercy–Lindsay Hardy | 1.00 | 2.00 | 3.00 | |
| 710 | The World in the Evening–Christopher Isherwood | 1.50 | 3.00 | 4.50 | |
| 711 | Woman of Paris–Guy des Cars | 1.00 | 2.00 | 3.00 | |
| 712 | Sigmund Freud for Everybody–Rachel Baker | .75 | 1.50 | 2.25 | NF |
| 713 | The Fall of Night–Giose Rimanelli | 1.00 | 2.00 | 3.00 | |
| 714 | Saddlebow Rancher–Ray Townsend | 1.00 | 2.00 | 3.00 | W |

| | | V/Good | Fine | N/Mint | |
|---|---|---|---|---|---|
| 715 | Guns along the Chisholm–Will C. Brown | 1.00 | 2.00 | 3.00 | W |
| 716 | After Dark, My Sweet–Jim Thompson; 1st ed. 1955 | 30.00 | 60.00 | 90.00 | |
| 717 | Mistress of Rogues–Rosemond Marshall; 1956; aka The Dollmaster | 1.50 | 3.00 | 4.50 | A |
| 718 | Carnival Girl–Richard Glendinning | 1.00 | 2.00 | 3.00 | |
| 719 | These Women–Gregory d'Alessio | 1.00 | 2.00 | 3.00 | |
| 720 | Come and Get Me–Johnny Laredo | 1.00 | 2.00 | 3.00 | |
| 721 | Brothers on the Trail–Max Brand | 1.00 | 2.00 | 3.00 | W |
| 722 | The Fighting Texan–Will Cook | 1.00 | 2.00 | 3.00 | W |
| 723 | Mr. Trouble–William Ard | 2.50 | 5.00 | 7.50 | |
| 724 | The Widow–Georges Simenon | 1.00 | 2.00 | 3.00 | M |
| 725 | I'll Fix You–Hal Ellson; 1st ed. 1956 | 3.00 | 6.00 | 9.00 | JD |
| 726 | The Fugitive Romans–William Murray | 1.00 | 2.00 | 3.00 | |
| 727 | Revolt of the Sinners–Ugo Zatterin | 1.00 | 2.00 | 3.00 | |
| 728 | Gun Talk–Ernest Haycox | 1.00 | 2.00 | 3.00 | W |
| 729 | The Vengeance Riders–Jack Barton | 1.00 | 2.00 | 3.00 | W |
| 730 | My Love Is Violent–Thomas B. Dewey; 1st ed. 1956 | 2.50 | 5.00 | 7.50 | M |
| 731 | The Searchers–Alan LeMay; movie tie-in | 2.50 | 5.00 | 7.50 | W |
| 732 | The Naked Hours–Wenzell Brown | 1.00 | 2.00 | 3.00 | |
| 733 | The Double Life–Thomas Gallagher | 1.00 | 2.00 | 3.00 | |
| 734 | The Violators–Israel Beckhardt & Wenzell Brown | 1.00 | 2.00 | 3.00 | |
| 735 | Gunman from Texas–W.T. Ballard | 1.00 | 2.00 | 3.00 | W |
| 736 | The Drifters–Allan R. Bosworth | 1.00 | 2.00 | 3.00 | |
| 737 | You Live Once–John D. MacDonald; 1st ed. 1956 | 7.50 | 15.00 | 22.50 | M |
| 738 | The Persistant Image–Gladys Schmitt | 1.00 | 2.00 | 3.00 | |
| 739 | Wilderness Virgin–John Clagett | 1.00 | 2.00 | 3.00 | A |
| 740 | You've Got Me in Stitches–Lawrence Lariar | 1.00 | 2.00 | 3.00 | |
| 741 | Ambush Rider–Hal G. Evarts | 1.00 | 2.00 | 3.00 | W |
| 742 | Rawhide River–Cliff Farrell | 1.00 | 2.00 | 3.00 | W |
| 743 | Jailbait–William Bernard; c-Belarski | 2.00 | 4.00 | 6.00 | JD |
| 744 | I'm No Good–Peter W. Denzer | 1.00 | 2.00 | 3.00 | |
| 745 | The Pitfall–Jay J. Dratler | 1.00 | 2.00 | 3.00 | |
| 746 | The Savage Streets–Floyd Miller | 1.00 | 2.00 | 3.00 | |
| 747 | Wine of Desire–LaSelle Gilman | 1.00 | 2.00 | 3.00 | |
| 748 | Trumpets to the West–Will Cook | 1.00 | 2.00 | 3.00 | W |
| 749 | Death Cries in the Streets–Samuel A. Krasney | 1.00 | 2.00 | 3.00 | |
| 750 | Border Town Girl–John D. MacDonald; 1st ed. 1956 | 7.50 | 15.00 | 22.50 | M |
| 751 | Hotel Fever–Arnold Gifford | 1.00 | 2.00 | 3.00 | |
| 752 | Dark Night of Love–Calvin Clements | 1.00 | 2.00 | 3.00 | |
| 753 | To Love and to Hate–Frieda K. Franklin | 1.00 | 2.00 | 3.00 | |
| 754 | Let Me Alone–Donald Windham | 3.00 | 6.00 | 9.00 | JD |
| 755 | The Mountain Men–Bill Gulick | 1.00 | 2.00 | 3.00 | W |
| 756 | Hell Is a City–William Ard | 2.50 | 5.00 | 7.50 | |
| 757 | Duke–Hal Ellson; c-Belarski | 2.00 | 4.00 | 6.00 | JD |
| 758 | The Last Party–Robert Lowry | 1.50 | 3.00 | 4.50 | |
| 759 | Fair in Love and War–Denton Whitson | 1.00 | 2.00 | 3.00 | |
| 760 | I Get What I Want–Larry Heller | 1.00 | 2.00 | 3.00 | |
| 761 | The Man From Missouri–Frank Gruber | 1.50 | 3.00 | 4.50 | W |
| 762 | The Innocent and the Wicked–Phyllis Hastings | 1.00 | 2.00 | 3.00 | |
| 763 | I Fear You Not–Ben Kerr (William Ard); 1st ed. 1956 | 3.50 | 7.00 | 10.50 | M |
| 764 | Why Johnny Can't Read–Rudolf Flesch | 1.00 | 2.00 | 3.00 | |
| 765 | The Cruel Tower–William B. Hartley | 1.00 | 2.00 | 3.00 | |
| 766 | Fraulein Lili Marlene–James Wakefield Burke | 1.00 | 2.00 | 3.00 | E |
| 767 | A Rider of the High Mesa–Ernest Haycox | 1.00 | 2.00 | 3.00 | W |
| 768 | Gun in His Hand–Jack Barton | 1.00 | 2.00 | 3.00 | W |
| 769 | Run . . . Run . . . Run . . . –Frank Taubes | 1.00 | 2.00 | 3.00 | |
| 770 | The Actor–Niven Busch | 1.00 | 2.00 | 3.00 | |
| 771 | A Night Out–Basil Heatter | 1.00 | 2.00 | 3.00 | |
| 772 | Guns of the Lawless–W.T. Ballard | 1.00 | 2.00 | 3.00 | W |
| 773 | Apache Ambush–Will Cook | 1.00 | 2.00 | 3.00 | W |
| 774 | Walk a Wicked Mile–Robert P. Hansen | 1.00 | 2.00 | 3.00 | |
| 775 | Behold This Woman–David Goodis; 1956 | 5.00 | 10.00 | 15.00 | |
| 776 | This Is It!–Hal Ellson; 1st ed. 1956 | 3.00 | 6.00 | 9.00 | JD |
| 777 | Love from France–Edna Bennett & Brant House | 1.50 | 3.00 | 4.50 | H |
| 778 | The Night Raiders–Hal G. Evarts | 1.00 | 2.00 | 3.00 | W |
| 779 | Born to Gunsmoke–Thomas Thompson | 1.00 | 2.00 | 3.00 | W |

| | | V/Good | Fine | N/Mint |
|---|---|---|---|---|

POPULAR LIBRARY, *continued*

| | | V/Good | Fine | N/Mint | |
|---|---|---|---|---|---|
| 780 | Murder Makes Me Mad–Ferguson Findley | 1.50 | 3.00 | 4.50 | M |
| 781 | Take All You Can Get–Steve Fisher | 1.50 | 3.00 | 4.50 | M |
| 782 | The Hustlers–Sam Ross | 1.00 | 2.00 | 3.00 | |
| 783 | The Man from Idaho–Dan Temple | 1.00 | 2.00 | 3.00 | W |
| 784 | The Return of the Rancher–Frank Austin | 1.00 | 2.00 | 3.00 | W |
| 785 | Damned If He Does–Ben Kerr (William Ard); 1st ed. 1956 | 3.50 | 7.00 | 10.50 | M |
| 786 | Moods and Truths–Fulton J. Sheen | 1.00 | 2.00 | 3.00 | NF |
| 787 | The Dream Peddlers–Floyd Miller | 1.00 | 2.00 | 3.00 | |
| 788 | The Gunpointer–Dean Owen | 1.00 | 2.00 | 3.00 | W |
| 789 | Powder Smoke–Jackson Gregory | 1.00 | 2.00 | 3.00 | W |
| 790 | Run While You Can–William Woolfolk | 1.00 | 2.00 | 3.00 | |
| 791 | He Walks by Night–Fan Nichols; 1957 | 1.00 | 2.00 | 3.00 | |
| 792 | Ramrod–Luke Short | 1.00 | 2.00 | 3.00 | W |
| 793 | Day of the .44–Jack Barton | 1.00 | 2.00 | 3.00 | W |
| 794 | The Tramplers–Jason Manor | 1.00 | 2.00 | 3.00 | M |
| 795 | Marmaduke–Brad Anderson & Phil Leeming | 1.00 | 2.00 | 3.00 | H |
| 796 | The Silver Desert–Ernest Haycox | 1.00 | 2.00 | 3.00 | W |
| 797 | Six-Gun Maverick–Philip Ketchum | 1.00 | 2.00 | 3.00 | W |
| 798 | Spin the Glass Web–Max Ehrlich | 1.00 | 2.00 | 3.00 | M |
| 799 | Sabrina Kane–Will Cook | 1.00 | 2.00 | 3.00 | W |
| 800 | Island of the Pit–Vincent James; 1957 | 1.00 | 2.00 | 3.00 | |
| 801 | The Jackson Trail–Max Brand | 1.00 | 2.00 | 3.00 | W |
| 802 | Last-Chance Range–Dean Owen | 1.00 | 2.00 | 3.00 | W |
| 803 | Club 17–Ben Kerr (William Ard); 1st ed. 1957 | 3.50 | 7.00 | 10.50 | M |
| 804 | On the Prod–Ernest Haycox | 1.00 | 2.00 | 3.00 | W |
| 805 | Arizona Guns–William MacLeod Raine | 1.00 | 2.00 | 3.00 | W |
| 806 | The Deadly Finger–Henry Kane | 1.50 | 3.00 | 4.50 | M |
| 807 | The Girls from Goldfield–Jacquin Sanders | 1.00 | 2.00 | 3.00 | |
| 808 | Fort Vengeance–Gordon D. Shirreffs | 1.00 | 2.00 | 3.00 | W |
| 809 | My Brother's Wife–Harry Davis | 1.00 | 2.00 | 3.00 | |
| 810 | Maverick Empire–Lewis Ford | 1.00 | 2.00 | 3.00 | W |
| 811 | Flee from Terror–Martin Brett | 1.00 | 2.00 | 3.00 | |
| 812 | Laugh Yourself Well–Eddie Davis | 1.00 | 2.00 | 3.00 | H |
| 813 | Dead Man's Trail–Philip Ketchum | 1.00 | 2.00 | 3.00 | W |
| 814 | Silver Bullets–C.S. Park | 1.00 | 2.00 | 3.00 | W |
| 815 | Swamp Fire–Don Kingery | 1.00 | 2.00 | 3.00 | |
| 816 | And Where She Stops–Thomas B. Dewey; 1st ed. 1957 | 2.50 | 5.00 | 7.50 | M |
| 817 | Calibre–Irving Shulman | 1.00 | 2.00 | 3.00 | |
| 818 | Doctor Paradise–Jay J. Dratler | 1.00 | 2.00 | 3.00 | |
| 819 | Let the Sky Fall–Roger Dee | 1.00 | 2.00 | 3.00 | |
| 820 | Teen-age Gangs–Madeline Karr & Dale Kramer | 3.50 | 7.00 | 10.50 | JD |
| 821 | The Whipping Boy–S.E. Pfoutz | 1.00 | 2.00 | 3.00 | |
| 822 | Valley Vultures–Max Brand | 1.00 | 2.00 | 3.00 | W |
| 823 | One Thing on My Mind–Herbert D. Kastle | 1.00 | 2.00 | 3.00 | |
| 824 | A Girl, a Man and a River–John Hawkins & Ward Hawkins | 1.00 | 2.00 | 3.00 | |
| 825 | Scandal in Troy–Eva Hemmer Hansen; 1957 | 1.00 | 2.00 | 3.00 | |
| 826 | The Mustangers–Jack Barton | 1.00 | 2.00 | 3.00 | W |
| 827 | Lone Hand from Texas–Will Cook | 1.00 | 2.00 | 3.00 | W |
| 828 | Sunset Strip–James Reach | 1.00 | 2.00 | 3.00 | |
| 829 | Probably does not exist | | | | |
| 830 | The Empty Trap–John D. MacDonald; 1st ed. 1957 | 7.50 | 15.00 | 22.50 | M |
| 831 | Dead Man Range–Ernest Haycox | 1.00 | 2.00 | 3.00 | W |
| 832 | Massacre Creek–Gordon D. Shirreffs; 1958 | 1.00 | 2.00 | 3.00 | W |
| 833 | The Plundered Land–Coe Williams | 1.00 | 2.00 | 3.00 | W |
| 834 | Red Range–Eugene Cunningham | 1.00 | 2.00 | 3.00 | W |
| 835 | The Avenging Gun–J.L. Gouma | 1.00 | 2.00 | 3.00 | W |

# POPULAR LIBRARY EAGLE

## Popular Library, Inc.

**Note: After EB104, subsequent Eagle books were included in numbering sequence for Popular Library G-Series.**

| | | V/Good | Fine | N/Mint | |
|---|---|---|---|---|---|
| EB1 | The Captain's Lady–Basil Heatter; 1953 | 1.00 | 2.00 | 3.00 | E |
| EB2 | Rustlers' Gap–William MacLeod Raine; aka Courage Stout | 1.00 | 2.00 | 3.00 | W |
| EB3 | Ward 20–James Warner Bellah | 1.00 | 2.00 | 3.00 | E |
| EB4 | Whispering Range–Ernest Haycox | 1.00 | 2.00 | 3.00 | W |
| EB5 | She'll Be Dead by Morning–Dana Chambers | 1.00 | 2.00 | 3.00 | M |
| EB6 | The Loves of Lucrezia–Francesca Wright; 1954 | 1.00 | 2.00 | 3.00 | E |
| EB7 | Yellowstone Passage–Coe Williams | 1.00 | 2.00 | 3.00 | W |
| EB8 | The Pale Blonde of Sands Street– William Chapman White | 1.00 | 2.00 | 3.00 | |
| EB9 | Julia–Margot Bland | 1.00 | 2.00 | 3.00 | |
| EB10 | The Red Law–Jackson Gregory | 1.00 | 2.00 | 3.00 | W |
| EB11 | Macamba–Lilla van Saher | 1.00 | 2.00 | 3.00 | E |
| EB12 | Fight or Run–Giles A. Lutz | 1.00 | 2.00 | 3.00 | W |
| EB13 | Gentle Annie–MacKinlay Kantor | 1.00 | 2.00 | 3.00 | W |
| EB14 | Gunmen's Grass–Lewis Ford | 1.00 | 2.00 | 3.00 | W |
| EB15 | The G-String Murders–Gypsy Rose Lee (Craig Rice) | 1.00 | 2.00 | 3.00 | M |
| EB16 | Satan Was a Man–Edward Hale Bierstadt | 1.00 | 2.00 | 3.00 | |
| EB17 | Secret Valley–Jackson Gregory | 1.00 | 2.00 | 3.00 | W |
| EB18 | This Spring of Love–Charles Mergendahl | 1.00 | 2.00 | 3.00 | |
| EB19 | Desert Cache–Dave Barron | 1.00 | 2.00 | 3.00 | W |
| EB20 | The Boat–Walter Gibson | 1.00 | 2.00 | 3.00 | |
| EB21 | The River Bend Feud–William MacLeod Raine | 1.00 | 2.00 | 3.00 | W |
| EB22 | Born of the Sun–Geoffrey Wagner | 1.00 | 2.00 | 3.00 | |
| EB23 | Troopers West–Forbes Parkhill | 1.00 | 2.00 | 3.00 | W |
| EB24 | Passion Is the Gale–Jane Winton | 1.00 | 2.00 | 3.00 | |
| EB25 | Trouble Trail–Coe Williams; 1954 | 1.00 | 2.00 | 3.00 | W |
| EB26 | The Eagle and the Wind–Herbert E. Stover | 1.00 | 2.00 | 3.00 | |
| EB27 | Pistol Pardners–William MacLeod Raine; aka The Black Tolts | 1.00 | 2.00 | 3.00 | W |
| EB28 | The Tough Ones–Whit Burnett & Hallie Burnett | 2.00 | 4.00 | 6.00 | JD |
| EB29 | Danger Trail–J.L. Bouma | 1.00 | 2.00 | 3.00 | W |
| EB30 | I'll Get You Yet–James Howard | 1.00 | 2.00 | 3.00 | |
| EB31 | Six-Gun Buckaroo–Clem Colt; aka Smoke Talk | 1.00 | 2.00 | 3.00 | W |
| EB32 | The Girl from Easy Street–Richard Foster (K.F. Crossen); orig. 1955 | 1.50 | 3.00 | 4.50 | |
| EB33 | Brush Rider–Dean Owen | 1.00 | 2.00 | 3.00 | W |
| EB34 | Too Hard to Handle–Derrick Nabarro | 1.00 | 2.00 | 3.00 | |
| EB35 | Drygulch Trail–William MacLeod Raine | 1.00 | 2.00 | 3.00 | W |
| EB36 | Tombolo–Nicholas Fersen | 1.00 | 2.00 | 3.00 | |
| EB37 | Outlaw River–Dan Temple; aka Missouri Passage | 1.00 | 2.00 | 3.00 | W |
| EB38 | That Girl on the River–Ted Fox | 1.00 | 2.00 | 3.00 | E |
| EB39 | Go for Your Gun–Coe Williams | 1.00 | 2.00 | 3.00 | W |
| EB40 | Tonight and Forever–Simon Kent | 1.00 | 2.00 | 3.00 | |
| EB41 | Texas Spurs–J.L. Bouma | 1.00 | 2.00 | 3.00 | W |
| EB42 | The Girl in the Red Jaguar–Jason Manor | 1.00 | 2.00 | 3.00 | E |
| EB43 | Reluctant Gunman–William MacLeod Raine | 1.00 | 2.00 | 3.00 | W |
| EB44 | Leave It to Me–George Joseph | 1.00 | 2.00 | 3.00 | |
| EB45 | Apache War Cry–William E. Vance | 1.00 | 2.00 | 3.00 | W |
| EB46 | I Like It Tough–James Howard | 1.00 | 2.00 | 3.00 | |
| EB47 | Fugitive's Canyon–Hal G. Evarts | 1.00 | 2.00 | 3.00 | W |
| EB48 | River of Eyes–Lawrence Earl | 1.00 | 2.00 | 3.00 | |
| EB49 | Gunfighter from Montana– Lewis Ford | 1.00 | 2.00 | 3.00 | W |
| EB50 | Don't Get in My Way–Frances Clippinger; 1955 | 1.00 | 2.00 | 3.00 | |
| EB51 | Beyond the Rio Grande–William MacLeod Raine | 1.00 | 2.00 | 3.00 | W |
| EB52 | Time to Embrace–Joseph Foster | 1.00 | 2.00 | 3.00 | |
| EB53 | Fighting Indians of the West–David C. Cooke | 1.50 | 3.00 | 4.50 | NF |
| EB54 | Barbary Slave–Kevin Matthews (Gardner F. Fox) | 2.00 | 4.00 | 6.00 | A |
| EB55 | Mesquire Maverick–Eugene Cunningham | 1.00 | 2.00 | 3.00 | W |
| EB56 | No Halo for Me–Jason Manor; 1956 | 1.00 | 2.00 | 3.00 | |
| EB57 | Longhorn Stampede–Philip Ketchum | 1.00 | 2.00 | 3.00 | W |
| EB58 | Lament for a Lover–Patricia Highsmith | 1.50 | 3.00 | 4.50 | |
| EB59 | Six-Gun Feud–William MacLeod Raine | 1.00 | 2.00 | 3.00 | W |
| EB60 | Storm Fear–Clinton Seeley | 1.00 | 2.00 | 3.00 | |
| EB61 | Border Vengeance–J.L. Bouman | 1.00 | 2.00 | 3.00 | W |
| EB62 | Strange Customs of Courtship and Marriage–William J. Fielding | .75 | 1.50 | 2.25 | NF |
| EB63 | Apache Crossing–Will Ermine | 1.00 | 2.00 | 3.00 | W |

*Popular Library 830, Popular Library Eagle EB78, Popular Library G114.*

| | | V/Good | Fine | N/Mint |
|---|---|---|---|---|

**POPULAR LIBRARY EAGLE,** *continued*

| | | V/Good | Fine | N/Mint | |
|---|---|---|---|---|---|
| EB64 | The Battle Done–S. Leonard Rubinstein | 1.00 | 2.00 | 3.00 | |
| EB65 | The Elkhorn Feud–Philip Ketchum | 1.00 | 2.00 | 3.00 | W |
| EB66 | All or Nothing–Max Catto | 1.00 | 2.00 | 3.00 | |
| EB67 | Desert Feud–William MacLeod Raine | 1.00 | 2.00 | 3.00 | W |
| EB68 | Don't Say No–Olga Rosmanith | 1.00 | 2.00 | 3.00 | |
| EB69 | Hard Rock Town–Joseph Gage | 1.00 | 2.00 | 3.00 | |
| EB70 | Blow Out My Torch–James Howard | 1.00 | 2.00 | 3.00 | |
| EB71 | Montana Road–Harry Sinclair Drago | 1.00 | 2.00 | 3.00 | W |
| EB72 | Hard and Fast–U.S. Anderson | 1.00 | 2.00 | 3.00 | |
| EB73 | The Texas Kid–William MacLeod Raine | 1.00 | 2.00 | 3.00 | W |
| EB74 | Maracaibo–Sterling Silliphant | 1.00 | 2.00 | 3.00 | |
| EB75 | The Big Gun–Philip Ketchum; 1956 | 1.00 | 2.00 | 3.00 | |
| EB76 | The Bed She Made–Leslie Waller | 1.00 | 2.00 | 3.00 | E |
| EB77 | Defiance Mountain–Frank Bonham | 1.00 | 2.00 | 3.00 | W |
| EB78 | Tory Mistress–Kevin Matthews (Gardner F. Fox) | 2.00 | 4.00 | 6.00 | A |
| EB79 | Desert of the Damned–Nelson Nye | 1.00 | 2.00 | 3.00 | W |
| EB80 | Judas Journey–Lee Roberts; 1957 | 1.00 | 2.00 | 3.00 | |
| EB81 | High Grass Valley–Wayne D. Overholser & William MacLeod Raine | 1.00 | 2.00 | 3.00 | W |
| EB82 | Free Ride–James M. Fox | 1.00 | 2.00 | 3.00 | |
| EB83 | Roundup–W.T. Ballard | 1.00 | 2.00 | 3.00 | W |
| EB84 | The Loving and the Daring–Francoise Mallet | 1.00 | 2.00 | 3.00 | E |
| EB85 | Man Without a Gun–Hal G. Evarts | 1.00 | 2.00 | 3.00 | W |
| EB86 | The Spoiled Children–Philippe Heriat | 1.00 | 2.00 | 3.00 | |
| EB87 | Burning Valley–J.L. Bouma | 1.00 | 2.00 | 3.00 | W |
| EB88 | Heaven Knows, Mr. Allison–Charles Shaw | 1.00 | 2.00 | 3.00 | |
| EB89 | Rawhide Rider–Thomas Thompson | 1.00 | 2.00 | 3.00 | W |
| EB90 | Die on Easy Street–James Howard | 1.00 | 2.00 | 3.00 | |
| EB91 | Trouble on the Brazos–Will C. Brown | 1.00 | 2.00 | 3.00 | W |
| EB92 | In Search of Love–William Fain | 1.00 | 2.00 | 3.00 | |
| EB93 | Trail Town Marshal–W.T. Ballard | 1.00 | 2.00 | 3.00 | W |
| EB94 | Duel in the Sun–Niven Busch | 1.00 | 2.00 | 3.00 | W |
| EB95 | I Am Fifteen . . . and I Don't Want to Die–Christine Arnothy | 1.00 | 2.00 | 3.00 | |
| EB96 | Just So Far–Floyd Miller | 1.00 | 2.00 | 3.00 | |
| EB97 | More Bobby Sox–Marty Links | 1.00 | 2.00 | 3.00 | H |
| EB98 | California Passage–Cliff Farrell | 1.00 | 2.00 | 3.00 | W |
| EB99 | Bullet Lease–Dan Temple | 1.00 | 2.00 | 3.00 | W |
| EB100 | Portrait of Rene–Harry Davis; 1957 | 1.00 | 2.00 | 3.00 | |
| EB101 | Border Breed–William MacLeod Raine; 1958 | 1.00 | 2.00 | 3.00 | W |
| EB102 | Stay Away, Joe–Dan Cushman | 1.00 | 2.00 | 3.00 | |
| EB103 | Hardcase Range–Jackson Gregory | 1.00 | 2.00 | 3.00 | W |
| EB104 | The Blonde and Johnny Malloy–Ben Kerr (William Ard); 1st ed. 1958 | 3.00 | 6.00 | 9.00 | M |

# POPULAR LIBRARY G-SERIES

## Popular Library, Inc.

| | | V/Good | Fine | N/Mint | |
|---|---|---|---|---|---|
| G100 | Sangaree–Frank G. Slaughter; 1952 | 1.25 | 2.50 | 3.75 | A |
| G101 | The Nymph and the Lamp–Thomas H. Raddall | 1.25 | 2.50 | 3.75 | |
| G102 | From the Sea and the Jungle–Robert Carse; c-DeSoto | 2.00 | 4.00 | 6.00 | |

| | | V/Good | Fine | N/Mint | |
|---|---|---|---|---|---|
| G103 | Mask of Glory–Dan Levin | 1.25 | 2.50 | 3.75 | |
| G104 | Savage Cavalier–Noel B. Gerson; aka Savage Gentleman | 2.00 | 4.00 | 6.00 | A |
| G105 | The Big Cage–Robert Lowry | 2.00 | 4.00 | 6.00 | |
| G106 | Courtroom–Quentin Reynolds | 1.25 | 2.50 | 3.75 | |
| G107 | The Golden Road–Peter Bourne | 2.00 | 4.00 | 6.00 | A |
| G108 | Red Lion Inn–Robert Payne | 1.25 | 2.50 | 3.75 | |
| G109 | The Glorious Three–June Wetherell | 1.25 | 2.50 | 3.75 | |
| G110 | Congo Song–Stuart Cloete | 1.50 | 3.00 | 4.50 | E |
| G111 | The Forsaken–Ferenc Kormendi | 1.25 | 2.50 | 3.75 | |
| G112 | Point Venus–Susanne McConnaughey | 1.25 | 2.50 | 3.75 | E |
| G113 | Marianne–Rhys Davies | 1.25 | 2.50 | 3.75 | |
| G114 | Find Me in Fire–Robert Lowry | 2.00 | 4.00 | 6.00 | E |
| G115 | The Naked Rich–Vivian Connell | 1.25 | 2.50 | 3.75 | |
| G116 | Sword of Fortune–Noel B. Gerson; 1953 | 1.50 | 3.00 | 4.50 | A |
| G117 | Angle of Attack–Joseph Landon | 1.25 | 2.50 | 3.75 | |
| G118 | The Forest Cavalier–Roy Flannagan | 1.50 | 3.00 | 4.50 | A |
| G119 | Jasmine Street–Clifford Dowdey | 1.25 | 2.50 | 3.75 | |
| G120 | The City Beyond–Lucille Emerick | 1.25 | 2.50 | 3.75 | |
| G121 | Look Down in Mercy–Walter Baxter | 1.25 | 2.50 | 3.75 | |
| G122 | After the Big House–Fred Berson | 1.25 | 2.50 | 3.75 | |
| G123 | Charlie Dell–Anderson Wayne | 1.25 | 2.50 | 3.75 | |
| G124 | Afraid in the Dark–Mark Derby | 1.25 | 2.50 | 3.75 | |
| G125 | The Beach House–Stephen Longstreet | 1.50 | 3.00 | 4.50 | |
| G126 | The Big Rape–James Wakefield Burke | 1.25 | 2.50 | 3.75 | |
| G127 | The Scarlet Sword–H.E. Bates | 1.25 | 2.50 | 3.75 | |
| G128 | One Winter in Boston–Robert M. Smith | 1.25 | 2.50 | 3.75 | |
| G129 | Free and Easy–June Wetherell | 1.25 | 2.50 | 3.75 | |
| G130 | Tisa–Helga Moray | 2.50 | 5.00 | 7.50 | E |
| G131 | The Gathering Darkness–Thomas Gallagher | 1.25 | 2.50 | 3.75 | |
| G132 | Watch for the Dawn–Stuart Cloete | 1.25 | 2.50 | 3.75 | |
| G133 | Three Comrades–Erich Maria Remarque; illus. in Parade of Pleasure | 1.50 | 3.00 | 4.50 | |
| G134 | Whistle Stop–Maritta Wolff | 1.25 | 2.50 | 3.75 | E |
| G135 | When the Gods Are Silent–Mikhail Soloviev; B&W illus. in Parade of Pleasure | 1.50 | 3.00 | 4.50 | |
| G136 | Prince Bart–Jay Richard Kennedy | 1.25 | 2.50 | 3.75 | |
| G137 | Sun in Their Eyes–Monte Barrett | 1.25 | 2.50 | 3.75 | W |
| G138 | Blood Royal–Robert Payne | 2.00 | 4.00 | 6.00 | A |
| G139 | Marie of the Isles–Robert Gaillard | 1.25 | 2.50 | 3.75 | |
| G140 | A House Is Not a Home–Polly Adler | 1.25 | 2.50 | 3.75 | |
| G141 | These Items of Desire–Louis A. Brennan | 1.25 | 2.50 | 3.75 | |
| G142 | The Hot and the Cool–Edwin Gilbert | 1.25 | 2.50 | 3.75 | |
| G143 | Rage to Love–Frank Tilsley | 1.25 | 2.50 | 3.75 | |
| G144 | The Strong Don't Cry–Estelle Slater; 1955 | 1.25 | 2.50 | 3.75 | |
| G145 | The Flesh Is Real–Irving Shulman; aka The Square Trap | 1.25 | 2.50 | 3.75 | |
| G146 | Rumble on the Docks–Frank Paley | 2.50 | 5.00 | 7.50 | JD |
| G147 | This Is Temptation–James Ronald | 1.25 | 2.50 | 3.75 | |
| G148 | The Only Sin–Anne Powers | 1.25 | 2.50 | 3.75 | |
| G149 | Never Say Love–Pierre Sichel | 1.25 | 2.50 | 3.75 | |
| G150 | The Girl from Rome–Michel Durafour | 1.25 | 2.50 | 3.75 | |
| G151 | The Image and the Search–Walter Baxter | 1.25 | 2.50 | 3.75 | |
| G152 | The Golden Wildcat–Margaret Widdemer | 1.25 | 2.50 | 3.75 | |
| G153 | A Time to Love and a Time to Die–Erich Maria Remarque | 1.50 | 3.00 | 4.50 | |
| G154 | Many Loves Have I–William Brown Meloney | 1.25 | 2.50 | 3.75 | |
| G155 | The Luciano Story–Sid Feder & Joachim Joesten; 1956 | 1.50 | 3.00 | 4.50 | NF |
| G156 | Tomorrow!–Philip Wylie | 1.25 | 2.50 | 3.75 | SF |
| G157 | The Iron Maiden–Edwin Lanham | 1.25 | 2.50 | 3.75 | |
| G158 | Between Darkness and Day–Gordon Merrick | 1.25 | 2.50 | 3.75 | |
| G159 | Louisiana Cavalier–Everett Webber | 1.25 | 2.50 | 3.75 | |
| G160 | The Tormented–Audrey Erskine Lindop | 1.25 | 2.50 | 3.75 | |
| G161 | Diversey–MacKinlay Kantor | 1.25 | 2.50 | 3.75 | |
| G162 | The Reckless Years–Virginia Oakey | 1.25 | 2.50 | 3.75 | |
| G163 | Sangaree–Frank G. Slaughter | 1.25 | 2.50 | 3.75 | |
| G164 | Red Carpet for Mamie Eisenhower–Alden Hatch; aka Red Carpet for Mamie | 1.25 | 2.50 | 3.75 | NF |
| G165 | Never Too Young–Joseph Weeks | 1.25 | 2.50 | 3.75 | |
| G166 | Headquarters–Quentin Reynolds | 1.25 | 2.50 | 3.75 | |

| | V/Good | Fine | N/Mint | |
|---|---|---|---|---|

**POPULAR LIBRARY G-SERIES,** *continued*

| | | V/Good | Fine | N/Mint | |
|---|---|---|---|---|---|
| G167 | A Room in Paris–Peggy Mann | 1.25 | 2.50 | 3.75 | |
| G168 | The Four Winds–David Beaty | 1.25 | 2.50 | 3.75 | |
| G169 | Captain Whitecap–John Clagett | 1.25 | 2.50 | 3.75 | A |
| G170 | Folies–Bergere–Paul Derval | 1.25 | 2.50 | 3.75 | |
| G171 | A Tale for Midnight–Frederic Prokosch | 1.25 | 2.50 | 3.75 | |
| G172 | The Other Side of Paradise–Paul Hyde Bonner | 1.25 | 2.50 | 3.75 | |
| G173 | The Night Is So Dark–Robert M. Coates | 1.25 | 2.50 | 3.75 | |
| G174 | Red Sky at Midnight–Robert F. Mirvish | 1.25 | 2.50 | 3.75 | |
| G175 | Children of the Dark–Irving Shulman; 1957; movie tie-in (for *Rebel without a Cause*) | 7.50 | 15.00 | 22.50 | JD |
| G176 | Rogue Cavalier–Rosamond Marshall | 1.25 | 2.50 | 3.75 | A |
| G177 | Her French Husband–Phyllis Hastings | 1.00 | 2.00 | 3.00 | |
| G178 | Hot Winds of Summer–John H. Secondari | 1.00 | 2.00 | 3.00 | |
| G179 | The Wild Country–Louis Bromfield | 1.00 | 2.00 | 3.00 | |
| G180 | Hang My Wreath–Ward Weaver (Van Wyck Mason) | 1.00 | 2.00 | 3.00 | |
| G181 | Erika–James McGovern | 1.00 | 2.00 | 3.00 | |
| G182 | Girls on Parole–Katherine Sullivan | 2.50 | 5.00 | 7.50 | NF |
| G183 | Man of the World–Stanley Kauffmann | 1.00 | 2.00 | 3.00 | |
| G184 | The Last Voyage of the Lusitania–A.A. Hoehling & Mary Hoehling (cover supposedly by Kelly Freas) | 1.00 | 2.00 | 3.00 | NF |
| G185 | Honey from a Dark Hive–Bernice Kavinoky | 1.00 | 2.00 | 3.00 | |
| G186 | The Sultan's Warrior–Bates Baldwin | 1.00 | 2.00 | 3.00 | A |
| G187 | The Quick and the Loving–Clifford Irving | 1.00 | 2.00 | 3.00 | |
| G188 | Episode in the Sun–Curry Holden | 1.00 | 2.00 | 3.00 | |
| G189 | All the Trumpets Sounded–W.G. Hardy | 1.00 | 2.00 | 3.00 | |
| G190 | Happy Marriage–John A. O'Brien | 1.00 | 2.00 | 3.00 | |
| G191 | Savage Cavalier–Noel B. Gerson | 1.00 | 2.00 | 3.00 | A |
| G192 | The Sleepless Moon–H.E. Bates | 1.00 | 2.00 | 3.00 | |
| G193 | Keep the Aspidistra Flying–George Orwell | 1.00 | 2.00 | 3.00 | |
| G194 | A Cry of Children–John Horne Burns | 1.00 | 2.00 | 3.00 | |
| G195 | The Valley of God–Irene Patai | 1.00 | 2.00 | 3.00 | |
| G196 | Sisters of the Night–Jess Stearn | 1.00 | 2.00 | 3.00 | |
| G197 | On the Dodge–William MacLeod Raine | 1.00 | 2.00 | 3.00 | W |
| G198 | A House in Peking–Robert Payne | 1.00 | 2.00 | 3.00 | |
| G199 | The Miracle of Lourdes–Ruth Cranston | 1.50 | 3.00 | 4.50 | NF |
| G200 | Way of a Buccaneer–Davenport Steward | 1.50 | 3.00 | 4.50 | A |
| G201 | The Red Sands of Santa Maria–Bill Murphy | 1.00 | 2.00 | 3.00 | |
| G202 | Ten Days in August–Bernard Frizell | 1.00 | 2.00 | 3.00 | |
| G203 | Facts of Life and Love for Teenagers–Evelyn Millis Duvall | 1.00 | 2.00 | 3.00 | NF |
| G204 | Dust in the Sun–Jon Cleary | 1.00 | 2.00 | 3.00 | |
| G205 | Mamba–Stuart Cloete | 1.00 | 2.00 | 3.00 | |
| G206 | The Beach House–Stephen Longstreet | 1.50 | 3.00 | 4.50 | |
| G207 | Tempered Blade–Monte Barrett | 1.00 | 2.00 | 3.00 | A |
| G208 | Lady Sings the Blues–William Dufty & Billy Holliday; 1958 | 2.00 | 4.00 | 6.00 | B |
| G209 | Life Is Worth Living–Fulton J. Sheen | 1.00 | 2.00 | 3.00 | |
| G210 | Jubilee–John Brick | 1.00 | 2.00 | 3.00 | |
| G211 | Pitchman–Robin Moore | 1.00 | 2.00 | 3.00 | |
| G212 | Work of Darkness–Jack Karney | 1.00 | 2.00 | 3.00 | |
| G213 | So Far from Spring–Peggy Simpson Curry | 1.00 | 2.00 | 3.00 | |
| G214 | Burmese Days–George Orwell | 1.50 | 3.00 | 4.50 | E |
| G215 | The Red Room–Francoise Mallet | 1.00 | 2.00 | 3.00 | |
| G216 | Joey Adams' Joke Book–Joey Adams | 1.00 | 2.00 | 3.00 | H |
| G217 | The Silver Lion–Noel B. Gerson | 1.00 | 2.00 | 3.00 | A |
| G218 | Trouble Shooter–Ernest Haycox | 1.00 | 2.00 | 3.00 | W |
| G219 | Bond of the Flesh–Rosamond Marshall | 1.00 | 2.00 | 3.00 | |
| G220 | What's Left of April–Robert Lowry | 2.00 | 4.00 | 6.00 | |
| G221 | A House on the Rhine–Frances Faviell | 1.50 | 3.00 | 4.50 | |
| G222 | Walk through the Valley–Borden Deal | 1.50 | 3.00 | 4.50 | |
| G223 | The Sheriff's Son–William MacLeod Raine | 1.50 | 3.00 | 4.50 | W |
| G224 | Sex Attitudes in the Home–Ralph G. Eckert | 1.50 | 3.00 | 4.50 | NF |
| G225 | The Hell Bent Kid–Charles O. Locke | 1.50 | 3.00 | 4.50 | W |
| G226 | God Is Late–Christine Arnothy | 1.50 | 3.00 | 4.50 | |
| G227 | Pride of Innocence–David Buckley | 1.50 | 3.00 | 4.50 | |
| G228 | They Died in the Chair–Wenzell Brown | 1.50 | 3.00 | 4.50 | |
| G229 | Awake to Darkness–Richard McMullen | 1.50 | 3.00 | 4.50 | E |
| G230 | The Happy Valley–Max Brand | 1.50 | 3.00 | 4.50 | W |
| G231 | I Know My Love–Fan Nichols | 1.50 | 3.00 | 4.50 | |
| G232 | The Man from Yuma–Hal G. Evarts | 1.50 | 3.00 | 4.50 | W |
| G233 | Give Us This Day–Sidney Stewart | 1.50 | 3.00 | 4.50 | |
| G234 | The Priest–Joseph Caruso | 1.50 | 3.00 | 4.50 | |
| G235 | Six Angels at My Back–John Bell Clayton | 1.50 | 3.00 | 4.50 | E |
| G236 | Cry Scandal–William Ard | 3.00 | 6.00 | 9.00 | |
| G237 | Chaffee of Roaring Horse–Ernest Haycox | 1.00 | 2.00 | 3.00 | W |
| G238 | Texas Triggers–Eugene Cunningham | 1.00 | 2.00 | 3.00 | W |
| G239 | I Take the Rap–Gordon Shelly | 1.00 | 2.00 | 3.00 | |
| G240 | Gun Hand–Cliff Farrell | 1.00 | 2.00 | 3.00 | W |
| G241 | Don't Touch Me–MacKinlay Kantor | 1.00 | 2.00 | 3.00 | |
| G242 | Dream of a Woman–Jay J. Dratler | 1.00 | 2.00 | 3.00 | |
| G243 | Queen of the East–Alexander Baron | 1.00 | 2.00 | 3.00 | A |
| G244 | From the Sea and the Jungle–Robert Carse | 1.00 | 2.00 | 3.00 | A |
| G245 | Manhunt–Donald MacKenzie | 1.00 | 2.00 | 3.00 | |
| G246 | Man-Size–William MacLeod Raine | 1.00 | 2.00 | 3.00 | W |
| G247 | Showdown in the Sun–Bill Gulick | 1.00 | 2.00 | 3.00 | W |
| G248 | The Deadly Reasons–Edward D. Radin | 1.00 | 2.00 | 3.00 | |
| G249 | Saddle Tramp–W.T. Ballard | 1.00 | 2.00 | 3.00 | W |
| G250 | The Squirrel Cage–Edwin Gilbert | 1.00 | 2.00 | 3.00 | |
| G251 | Best Seller–William Murray | 1.00 | 2.00 | 3.00 | |
| G252 | The Kind of Guy I Am–Robert McAllister & Floyd Miller | 1.00 | 2.00 | 3.00 | |
| G253 | Liana–Martha Gellhorn | 1.00 | 2.00 | 3.00 | E |
| G254 | Trial by Fire–Charles Elliott | 1.00 | 2.00 | 3.00 | |
| G255 | Rawhide Gunman–W.T. Ballard | 1.00 | 2.00 | 3.00 | W |
| G256 | Caribbean Cavalier–Davenport Steward | 1.50 | 3.00 | 4.50 | A |
| G257 | The Silver Star–Jackson Gregory | 1.00 | 2.00 | 3.00 | W |
| G258 | The Rib of the Hawk–Rosamond Marshall | 1.00 | 2.00 | 3.00 | |
| G259 | The Violent Wedding–Robert Lowry | 2.00 | 4.00 | 6.00 | |
| G260 | Calendar Model–Gloria Gale | 1.00 | 2.00 | 3.00 | |
| G261 | Free Grass–Ernest Haycox | 1.00 | 2.00 | 3.00 | W |
| G262 | Take a Number–Armando T. Perretta | 1.00 | 2.00 | 3.00 | |
| G263 | Apache Agent–Hal G. Evarts | 1.00 | 2.00 | 3.00 | W |
| G264 | Square Shooter–William MacLeod Raine | 1.00 | 2.00 | 3.00 | W |
| G265 | This Is for Keeps–George Joseph | 1.00 | 2.00 | 3.00 | |
| G266 | Life without Father–Muriel Resnik | 1.00 | 2.00 | 3.00 | |
| G267 | Painted Ponies–Alan LeMay | 1.00 | 2.00 | 3.00 | W |
| G268 | The Big Bubble–Theodore Pratt; c-Maguire | 3.00 | 6.00 | 9.00 | E |
| G269 | All for a Woman–Jay J. Dratler | 1.00 | 2.00 | 3.00 | |
| G270 | Dead or Alive–Max Brand | 1.00 | 2.00 | 3.00 | W |
| G271 | Cry Hard, Cry Fast–John D. MacDonald | 2.00 | 4.00 | 6.00 | M |
| G272 | Spiderweb Trail–Eugene Cunningham | 1.00 | 2.00 | 3.00 | W |
| G273 | The Life of All Living–Fulton J. Sheen | 1.00 | 2.00 | 3.00 | |
| G274 | Trouble at Moon Dance–A.B. Guthrie, Jr | 1.00 | 2.00 | 3.00 | W |
| G275 | Tiger by the Tail–Charles Mergendahl | 1.00 | 2.00 | 3.00 | |
| G276 | Fury at Painted Rock–Will Cook | 1.00 | 2.00 | 3.00 | W |
| G277 | Don't Crowd Me–Evan Hunter | 1.00 | 2.00 | 3.00 | |
| G278 | Bullet Ambush–William MacLeod Raine | 1.00 | 2.00 | 3.00 | W |
| G279 | The Cut of the Ax–Delmar Jackson | 1.00 | 2.00 | 3.00 | |
| G280 | The Naked Rich–Vivian Connell | 1.00 | 2.00 | 3.00 | |
| G281 | A Strange Affair–Felix Jackson | 1.00 | 2.00 | 3.00 | |
| G282 | The Man Inside–M.E. Chaber (K.F. Crossen) | 1.50 | 3.00 | 4.50 | M |
| G283 | Trail Smoke–Ernest Haycox | 1.00 | 2.00 | 3.00 | W |
| G284 | The Wicked Blade–Robert Carse | 1.00 | 2.00 | 3.00 | A |
| G285 | Rage on the Bar–Geoffrey Wagner | 1.00 | 2.00 | 3.00 | |
| G286 | Showdown at Pistol Flat–C.S. Park | 1.00 | 2.00 | 3.00 | W |
| G287 | I'll Get Mine–Thurston Scott; aka Cure It with Honey | 3.00 | 6.00 | 9.00 | E |
| G288 | Shadow Valley–Gordon D. Shirreffs | 1.00 | 2.00 | 3.00 | W |
| G289 | Seize the Day–Saul Bellow | 1.00 | 2.00 | 3.00 | |
| G290 | Naked to My Pride–Howard Rigsby | 1.00 | 2.00 | 3.00 | |
| G291 | The Devil Must–Tom Wicker | 1.00 | 2.00 | 3.00 | |
| G292 | Ramrod from Hell–Leslie Ernenwein | 1.00 | 2.00 | 3.00 | W |
| G293 | Woman of Egypt–Kevin Matthews (Gardner F. Fox) | 2.00 | 4.00 | 6.00 | A |
| G294 | Buckaroo–Eugene Cunningham | 1.50 | 3.00 | 4.50 | W |
| G295 | The Tough Tenderfoot–William MacLeod Raine; aka Who Wants to Live Forever? | 1.50 | 3.00 | 4.50 | W |
| G296 | The Closest Kin There Is–Clara Winston | 1.50 | 3.00 | 4.50 | E |
| G297 | We Burn like Candles–Bernice Kavinoky; 1959 | 1.50 | 3.00 | 4.50 | E |

POPULAR LIBRARY G-SERIES, *continued*

| ID | Title | V/Good | Fine | N/Mint | |
|---|---|---|---|---|---|
| G298 | Love Is a Four-letter Word-Anita Rowe Block | 1.50 | 3.00 | 4.50 | |
| G299 | Gold in the Sky-Max Catto | 1.50 | 3.00 | 4.50 | |
| G300 | Lone Rider-Ernest Haycox; aka The Black Clan | 1.50 | 3.00 | 4.50 | W |
| G301 | Boy with a Gun-James Dean Sanderson | 1.50 | 3.00 | 4.50 | |
| G302 | Go to Sleep, Jeannie-Thomas B. Dewey; 1st ed. 1959 | 3.00 | 6.00 | 9.00 | M |
| G303 | End of Track-Ward Weaver (Van Wyck Mason) | 2.50 | 5.00 | 7.50 | W |
| G304 | Cry, Brother, Cry-Jack Karney | 2.50 | 5.00 | 7.50 | JD |
| G305 | The River Bend Feud-William MacLeod Raine | 2.50 | 5.00 | 7.50 | W |
| G306 | The Staked Plain-Frank X. Tolbert | 2.50 | 5.00 | 7.50 | W |
| G307 | The Boy Came Back-Charles H. Knickerbocker | 2.50 | 5.00 | 7.50 | E |
| G308 | The Last Hero-Peter W. Denzer | 2.50 | 5.00 | 7.50 | |
| G309 | Trouble on the Massacre-W.T. Ballard | 2.50 | 5.00 | 7.50 | W |
| G310 | Time to Remember-Anderson Wayne | 2.50 | 5.00 | 7.50 | |
| G311 | The Losers-Clifford Irving | 2.50 | 5.00 | 7.50 | |
| G312 | The Last Princess-Charles O. Locke | 2.50 | 5.00 | 7.50 | A |
| G313 | Double Agent-Gene Stackelberg | 2.50 | 5.00 | 7.50 | |
| G314 | Guns of Abilene-James B. Chaffin | 2.50 | 5.00 | 7.50 | W |
| G315 | The Time of the Panther-Wesley Ford Davis | 2.50 | 5.00 | 7.50 | |
| G316 | Face of a Hero-Louis Falstein | 2.50 | 5.00 | 7.50 | |
| G317 | Dark Drums-Wenzell Brown | 2.50 | 5.00 | 7.50 | E |
| G318 | Riders West-Ernest Haycox | 2.50 | 5.00 | 7.50 | W |
| G319 | The Savage Affair-Virgil Scott | 2.50 | 5.00 | 7.50 | |
| G320 | Two-edged Vengeance-W.T. Ballard | 2.50 | 5.00 | 7.50 | W |
| G321 | Jailbait-William Bernard | 2.50 | 5.00 | 7.50 | JD |
| G322 | The Untamed Breed-Jack Barton | 2.50 | 5.00 | 7.50 | W |
| G323 | Beyond My Worth-Lillian Roth | 2.50 | 5.00 | 7.50 | |
| G324 | Breaking Point-Jacob Presser | 2.50 | 5.00 | 7.50 | |
| G325 | Ask for Linda-Fan Nichols | 2.50 | 5.00 | 7.50 | E |
| G326 | Starlight Rider-Ernest Haycox | 2.50 | 5.00 | 7.50 | W |
| G327 | Timbal Gulch Trail-Max Brand | 2.50 | 5.00 | 7.50 | W |
| G328 | A Private Party-William Ard | 2.50 | 5.00 | 7.50 | E |
| G329 | New York Call Girl-Robert Lowry | 1.50 | 3.00 | 4.50 | E |
| G330 | After Long Silence-Robert Gutwillig | 1.50 | 3.00 | 4.50 | |
| G331 | Bitter Fruit-Peter Packer | 1.50 | 3.00 | 4.50 | |
| G332 | Texas Sheriff-Eugene Cunningham | 1.50 | 3.00 | 4.50 | W |
| G333 | That Randall Girl-Samuel Edwards | 1.50 | 3.00 | 4.50 | E |
| G334 | A Secret Story-William Saroyan | 1.50 | 3.00 | 4.50 | |
| G335 | Showdown-W.T. Ballard & James C. Lynch | 1.50 | 3.00 | 4.50 | W |
| G336 | Johnny Bogan-Leonora Baccante | 1.50 | 3.00 | 4.50 | E |
| G337 | Decision at Piute Wells-Philip Ketchum | 1.50 | 3.00 | 4.50 | W |
| G338 | Blondes Die Young-Bill Peters | 1.50 | 3.00 | 4.50 | |
| G339 | The Young Life-Leo Townsend | 1.50 | 3.00 | 4.50 | |
| G340 | See How They Burn-Edwin Gilbert | 1.50 | 3.00 | 4.50 | |
| G341 | Cradle of the Sun-John Clagett | 1.50 | 3.00 | 4.50 | A |
| G342 | Prodigal Shepherd-Al Hirshberg & Robert Pfau | 1.50 | 3.00 | 4.50 | |
| G343 | The Texas Kid-William MacLeod Raine | 1.50 | 3.00 | 4.50 | W |
| G344 | The Night and the Naked-Gordon Merrick | 1.50 | 3.00 | 4.50 | E |
| G345 | Thunder in the Dust-Alan LeMay | 1.50 | 3.00 | 4.50 | W |
| G346 | I'll Get You Yet-James Howard | 1.50 | 3.00 | 4.50 | |
| G347 | Guns of the Tom Dee and The Valley of the Rogue-Ernest Haycox; 1st ed. 1959 | 2.50 | 5.00 | 7.50 | W |
| G348 | Free and Easy-June Wetherell | 1.00 | 2.00 | 3.00 | |
| G349 | The Eagle and the Wind-Herbert E. Stover | 1.00 | 2.00 | 3.00 | |
| G350 | Ward 20-James Warner Bellah | 1.00 | 2.00 | 3.00 | E |
| G351 | Head of the Mountain-Ernest Haycox | 1.00 | 2.00 | 3.00 | W |
| G352 | The Tough Ones-Whit Burnett & Hallie Burnett | 1.00 | 2.00 | 3.00 | |
| G353 | Gold Town Gunman-Ray Townsend | 1.00 | 2.00 | 3.00 | W |
| G354 | Naked and Alone-Michael Lawrence | 1.00 | 2.00 | 3.00 | |
| G355 | Gun Law-Philip Ketchum | 1.00 | 2.00 | 3.00 | W |
| G356 | The Groves of Desire-Nathaniel Norsen Weinreb | 1.00 | 2.00 | 3.00 | |
| G357 | Drums of Empire-Robert Carse | 1.00 | 2.00 | 3.00 | |
| G358 | Duke-Hal Ellson | 2.00 | 4.00 | 6.00 | JD |
| G359 | Violent Valley-Wade Ashburn | 1.00 | 2.00 | 3.00 | |
| G360 | Love Is a Man's Affair-Fred Kerner | 1.00 | 2.00 | 3.00 | |
| G361 | Texas Breed-William MacLeod Raine | 1.00 | 2.00 | 3.00 | W |
| G362 | The Girl in the Red Jaguar-Jason Manor | 1.00 | 2.00 | 3.00 | E |
| G363 | Gunsight Trail-Alan LeMay | 1.00 | 2.00 | 3.00 | W |
| G364 | Good Housekeeping's the Better Way-the editiors of Good Housekeeping Magazine | .50 | 1.00 | 1.50 | NF |
| G365 | Spring in Fialta-Vladimir Nabokov | 1.00 | 2.00 | 3.00 | |
| G366 | Danny and the Boys-Robert Travor | 1.00 | 2.00 | 3.00 | |
| G367 | Rawhide Range-Ernest Haycox | 1.00 | 2.00 | 3.00 | W |
| G368 | Julia-Margot Bland | 1.00 | 2.00 | 3.00 | |
| G369 | Rancher's Revenge-Max Brand | 1.00 | 2.00 | 3.00 | W |
| G370 | Rifle Pass-Dean Owen | 1.00 | 2.00 | 3.00 | W |
| G371 | Cindy and I-Joey Adams | .75 | 1.50 | 2.25 | |
| G372 | This Spring of Love-Charles Mergendahl | 1.00 | 2.00 | 3.00 | |
| G373 | The Sins of Maria-Bruce Cameron | 1.00 | 2.00 | 3.00 | |
| G374 | Pistol Pardners-William MacLeod Raine | 1.00 | 2.00 | 3.00 | W |
| G375 | So Strong a Flame-Bernice Kavinoky | 1.00 | 2.00 | 3.00 | |
| G376 | Lily and the Sergeant-Martin Yoseloff | 1.00 | 2.00 | 3.00 | |
| G377 | The Girls on the 10th Floor-Steve Allen | 1.00 | 2.00 | 3.00 | |
| G378 | Outlaw River-Dan Temple | 1.00 | 2.00 | 3.00 | W |
| G379 | Gentle Annie-MacKinlay Kantor | 1.00 | 2.00 | 3.00 | W |
| G380 | Marshal of Sundown-Jackson Gregory | 1.00 | 2.00 | 3.00 | W |
| G381 | Seek Out and Destroy-James D. Horan | 1.00 | 2.00 | 3.00 | |
| G382 | Aimee-M.L. Law | 1.00 | 2.00 | 3.00 | E |
| G383 | The Dr. Lewis Affair-Lane Johnstone | 1.00 | 2.00 | 3.00 | |
| G384 | Guadalcanal Diary-Richard Tregaskis | 1.00 | 2.00 | 3.00 | C |
| G385 | Country Girl-Richard McMullen | 1.00 | 2.00 | 3.00 | E |
| G386 | A Matter of Morals-Joseph Gies | 1.00 | 2.00 | 3.00 | E |
| G387 | Texas Spurs-J.L. Bouma | 1.00 | 2.00 | 3.00 | W |
| G388 | Brush Rider-Dean Owen | 1.00 | 2.00 | 3.00 | W |
| G389 | Gunfire Man-Philip Ketchum | 1.00 | 2.00 | 3.00 | W |
| G390 | Desert Feud-William MacLeod Raine | 1.00 | 2.00 | 3.00 | W |
| G391 | The Scarlet Guidon-Ray Toepfer | 1.00 | 2.00 | 3.00 | |
| G392 | The Living Wood-Louis de Wohl | 1.00 | 2.00 | 3.00 | |
| G393 | The Loves of Lucrezia-Francesca Wright | 1.00 | 2.00 | 3.00 | |
| G394 | Beyond the Rio Grande-William MacLeod Raine | 1.00 | 2.00 | 3.00 | W |
| G395 | Find Me in Fire-Robert Lowry | 1.50 | 3.00 | 4.50 | E |
| G396 | The Man from Texas-Jackson Gregory | 1.00 | 2.00 | 3.00 | W |
| G397 | Trouble Trail-Coe Williams | 1.00 | 2.00 | 3.00 | W |
| G398 | Six-Gun Ambush-Max Brand | 1.00 | 2.00 | 3.00 | W |
| G399 | Unarmed in Paradise-Ellen Marsh; 1960 | .50 | 1.00 | 1.50 | |
| G400 | Her Life to Live-Oriana Atkinson; aka They Called Him Blue Blazes | .50 | 1.00 | 1.50 | |
| G401 | Drygulch Trail-William MacLeod Raine | .75 | 1.50 | 2.25 | W |
| G402 | Guns Up-Ernest Haycox | .75 | 1.50 | 2.25 | W |
| G403 | The Untouchables-Eliot Ness & Oscar Fraley; TV tie-in | 1.50 | 3.00 | 4.50 | NF |
| G405 | Veronica-Constance Lovelaud | .50 | 1.00 | 1.50 | |
| G407 | Trumpets to the West-Will Cook | .75 | 1.50 | 2.25 | W |
| G408 | The Tiger in Summer-Michael Keon | .75 | 1.50 | 2.25 | A |
| G409 | The Wrath and the Wind-Alexander Key | .75 | 1.50 | 2.25 | A |
| G410 | The Affairs of Nicholas Solon-Monroe Engel; aka The Visions of Nicholas Solon | .50 | 1.00 | 1.50 | |
| G411 | Blizzard Range-Todhunter Ballard | .75 | 1.50 | 2.25 | W |
| G412 | Danger Trail-J.L. Bouma | .75 | 1.50 | 2.25 | W |
| G413 | Fugitive's Canyon-Hal Evarts | .75 | 1.50 | 2.25 | W |
| G414 | West of the Law-William MacLeod Raine; aka Glory Hole | .75 | 1.50 | 2.25 | W |
| G415 | Panther Mountain-John Brick | .50 | 1.00 | 1.50 | |
| G416 | Woman Doctor-Alice Lent Covert; aka the Distant Drum | .50 | 1.00 | 1.50 | |
| G417 | The Luciano Story-S. Feder | .50 | 1.00 | 1.50 | NF |
| G418 | Whispering Range-Ernest Haycox | .75 | 1.50 | 2.25 | W |
| G419 | Town for Scandal-Ruth Tabrah; aka The Voices of Others | .50 | 1.00 | 1.50 | |
| G420 | Tell Me, Stranger-Charles Bracelen Flood | .50 | 1.00 | 1.50 | |
| G421 | Ramrod-Luke Short (Frederick Glidden) | .75 | 1.50 | 2.25 | W |
| G422 | Brothers on the Trail-Max Brand (Frederick Faust) | .75 | 1.50 | 2.25 | W |
| G423 | Rustler's Gap-William MacLeod Raine; aka Courage Stout | .75 | 1.50 | 2.25 | W |
| G424 | Tonight Is Forever-Charles Mergendahl | .50 | 1.00 | 1.50 | |
| G425 | The Burning Air-Eugene Mirabelli | .50 | 1.00 | 1.50 | |
| G426 | Epitaph for an Enemy-George Barr | .50 | 1.00 | 1.50 | |
| G427 | The Brass God-Richard G. Hubler | .50 | 1.00 | 1.50 | |

POPULAR LIBRARY G-SERIES, *continued*

| | | V/Good | Fine | N/Mint | |
|---|---|---|---|---|---|
| G428 | Someone to Love–Nina Farewell | .50 | 1.00 | 1.50 | |
| G429 | Trail Drive–Bill Gulick; aka A Thousand for the Caribou | .75 | 1.50 | 2.25 | W |
| G431 | The Dame's the Game–Al Fray | .50 | 1.00 | 1.50 | M |
| G432 | Desert Showdown–Max Brand; aka Trouble Trails | .75 | 1.50 | 2.25 | W |
| G433 | Brand of Fury--Jack Barton (Joseph Chadwick); 1960 | .50 | 1.00 | 1.50 | |
| G434 | Strange Lovers–Armando Meoni | .50 | 1.00 | 1.50 | |
| G435 | The Ways of Desire–David Garnett; aka A Shot in the Dark | .50 | 1.00 | 1.50 | |
| G436 | The Velvet Knife–Irving Shulman | 1.00 | 2.00 | 3.00 | |
| G437 | The Neighborhood–David Mark | .50 | 1.00 | 1.50 | |
| G438 | This Land Is Mine–Wyatt Blassingame; aka Live from the Devil | .50 | 1.00 | 1.50 | |
| G439 | Grim Canyon–Ernest Haycox; 1960 | .75 | 1.50 | 2.25 | W |
| G440 | Trigger Trail–Todhunter Ballard | .75 | 1.50 | 2.25 | W |
| G441 | Forbidden Valley–Thomas Thompson; 1960 | .75 | 1.50 | 2.25 | W |
| G442 | Bullet Range–Will Cook; 1960 | .75 | 1.50 | 2.25 | W |
| G443 | China Coaster–Don Smith | .50 | 1.00 | 1.50 | A |
| G444 | Dark Surrender–Peter Packer; aka The Inward Voyage | .50 | 1.00 | 1.50 | E |
| G445 | Smoke Up the Valley–Monte Barrett | .75 | 1.50 | 2.25 | W |
| G446 | Trail of the Damned–Jack Barton (Joseph Chadwick) | .50 | 1.00 | 1.50 | |
| G447 | That Girl on the River–Edward Fox; 1960 | .50 | 1.00 | 1.50 | |
| G448 | Go for Your Gun–Coe Williams (C. William Harrison) | .75 | 1.50 | 2.25 | W |
| G449 | Tangerine–Christine de Rivoyre | .50 | 1.00 | 1.50 | |
| G450 | The Face of Love–Lenore Coffee | .50 | 1.00 | 1.50 | |
| G451 | Ambush Rider–Hal G. Evarts | .75 | 1.50 | 2.25 | W |
| G452 | Too Hot for Hawaii–Thomas B. Dewey | 2.00 | 4.00 | 6.00 | M |
| G453 | Jane Arden, Registered Nurse–Kathleen Harris (Adelaide Humphries) | .50 | 1.00 | 1.50 | R |
| G454 | The Hot Summer Days–Eve Kaufman; aka The Happy Summer Days | .50 | 1.00 | 1.50 | |
| G455 | The Daughters of Necessity–Peter S. Feibleman | .50 | 1.00 | 1.50 | |
| G456 | Macamba–Lilla Van Saher | .75 | 1.50 | 2.25 | E |
| G457 | Walk into Hell–Richard Gibson Hubler; aka I've Got Mine | .50 | 1.00 | 1.50 | C |
| G458 | Rawhide River–Cliff Farrell; aka West with the Missouri | .75 | 1.50 | 2.25 | W |
| G459 | Arizona Guns–William MacLeod Raine; aka A Man Four-Square | .75 | 1.50 | 2.25 | W |
| G460 | Desert of the Damned–Nelson Nye; 1960 | .75 | 1.50 | 2.25 | W |
| G461 | Vengeance Trail–Ernest Haycox | .75 | 1.50 | 2.25 | W |
| G462 | Kitty, I Hardly Knew You–Edward McSorley | .50 | 1.00 | 1.50 | |
| G463 | The Wilderness–Carter A. Vaughan | .75 | 1.50 | 2.25 | A |
| G464 | Miss America–Daniel Stern | .50 | 1.00 | 1.50 | |
| G465 | By the North Gate–Gwyn Griffin | .50 | 1.00 | 1.50 | |
| G466 | Renegade of Rainbow Basin–Hal Evarts | .75 | 1.50 | 2.25 | W |
| G469 | Born to Gunsmoke–Thomas Thompson; 1960 | .75 | 1.50 | 2.25 | W |
| G470 | The Naked Sword–Anthea Mitchell | .75 | 1.50 | 2.25 | A |
| G471 | Passion Is the Gale–Jane Winton | .50 | 1.00 | 1.50 | R |
| G472 | Tresa–Benedict Freedman & Nancy Freedman | .50 | 1.00 | 1.50 | |
| G473 | Dark Sea Running–George Morrill | .50 | 1.00 | 1.50 | |
| G474 | Powder Smoke–Jackson Gregory | .75 | 1.50 | 2.25 | W |
| G475 | The Marmot Drive–John Hersey | .50 | 1.00 | 1.50 | |
| G476 | Gettysburg–John Brick | 1.00 | 2.00 | 3.00 | A |
| G477 | Rawhide Guns–Frank Bonham | .75 | 1.50 | 2.25 | W |
| G478 | Secret River–Ernest Haycox | .75 | 1.50 | 2.25 | W |
| G479 | The Girl from Easy Street–Richard Foster | .50 | 1.00 | 1.50 | E |
| G480 | The Mutiny of the Romaas–Jack London | 1.00 | 2.00 | 3.00 | A |
| G481 | One Fierce Hour and Sweet–Sophie Treadwell | .50 | 1.00 | 1.50 | |
| G483 | The Test–Pierre Boulle | .50 | 1.00 | 1.50 | |
| G485 | The Battle Done–S. Leonard Rubinstein | .50 | 1.00 | 1.50 | C |
| G486 | The Adventures of Sherlock Holmes–Sir Arthur Conan Doyle | 1.25 | 2.50 | 3.75 | M |
| G487 | Honey from a Dark Hive–Bernice Kavinoky | .50 | 1.00 | 1.50 | |
| G489 | Montana Road–Harry Sinclair Drago; 1960 | .75 | 1.50 | 2.25 | W |
| G493 | Low Man on the Totem Pole–H. Allen Smith | .50 | 1.00 | 1.50 | H |
| G494 | Apache Ambush–Will Cook | .75 | 1.50 | 2.25 | W |
| G495 | Meet Me in Darkness–Raymond Banks | .50 | 1.00 | 1.50 | |
| G497 | Jane Arden, Staff Nurse–Kathleen Harris | .50 | 1.00 | 1.50 | R |
| G501 | Geisha–Stephen Longstreet | .75 | 1.50 | 2.25 | |
| G502 | Try for Elegance–David Loomis; 1961 | .50 | 1.00 | 1.50 | |
| G503 | Berdoo's Woman–Eugene O'Donnell; aka Berdoo | .50 | 1.00 | 1.50 | |
| G504 | Day of the .44–Jack Barton (Joseph Chadwick) | .75 | 1.50 | 2.25 | W |
| G507 | You Kill Me–John D. MacDonald; aka You Live Once | 1.25 | 2.50 | 3.75 | M |
| G508 | "And God Created Woman"–Simone Colette; movie tie-in | 5.00 | 10.00 | 15.00 | E |
| G509 | Mrs. Sherman's Summer–Marjorie Fischer | .50 | 1.00 | 1.50 | |
| G510 | Nicchia–Geoffrey Wagner | .50 | 1.00 | 1.50 | A |
| G511 | Radius of Action–DeWitt Copp | .50 | 1.00 | 1.50 | |
| G512 | 4 Against the Mob–Oscar Fraley; TV tie-in (for The Untouchables) | 2.00 | 4.00 | 6.00 | NF |
| G513 | The Vengeance Riders–Joseph Chadwick | .75 | 1.50 | 2.25 | W |
| G514 | Shortgrass–Hal G. Evarts; 1961 | .75 | 1.50 | 2.25 | W |
| G515 | Return of the Rancher–Frank Austin | .75 | 1.50 | 2.25 | W |
| G516 | The Aquanauts–Daniel Bard; TV tie-in | 2.50 | 5.00 | 7.50 | A |
| G517 | A Race of Rebels–Andrew Tully | .50 | 1.00 | 1.50 | A |
| G518 | Tour of Duty–Walter J. Sheldon | .50 | 1.00 | 1.50 | |
| G519 | The Golden Wildcat–Margaret Widdemer | .50 | 1.00 | 1.50 | A |
| G522 | The Seventeen Book of Young Living–Enid A. Haupt | .50 | 1.00 | 1.50 | NF |
| G523 | Murder in Three Acts–Agatha Christie; 1961 | .75 | 1.50 | 2.25 | M |
| G524 | Guns along the Chisholm–Will C. Brown | .75 | 1.50 | 2.25 | W |
| G526 | The Mountain Men–Bill Gulick; aka White Men, Red Men and Mountain Men | 1.00 | 2.00 | 3.00 | W |
| G527 | All in a Night's Work–Saul Cooper; movie tie-in | 1.00 | 2.00 | 3.00 | |
| G529 | Doctor Paradise–Jay J. Dratler | .50 | 1.00 | 1.50 | |
| G531 | The 39 Steps–John Buchan | .50 | 1.00 | 1.50 | M |
| G532 | The Dead Beat–Robert Bloch | 2.50 | 5.00 | 7.50 | M |
| G535 | On the Prod–Ernest Haycox | .75 | 1.50 | 2.25 | W |
| G536 | Ecstasy–Simone Colette; movie tie-in | 2.50 | 5.00 | 7.50 | E |
| G538 | Conant–W.R. Burnett | 3.00 | 6.00 | 9.00 | M |
| G539 | The Wolf That Fed Us–Robert Lowry | .50 | 1.00 | 1.50 | |
| G540 | Don't Touch Me–MacKinlay Kantor | .50 | 1.00 | 1.50 | |
| G541 | Stay Away Joe–Dan Cushman; 1961 | .75 | 1.50 | 2.25 | |
| G542 | Julie–Bernard Frizell | .50 | 1.00 | 1.50 | |
| G543 | Death in the Air–Agatha Christie; 1961 | .75 | 1.50 | 2.25 | M |
| G545 | The Paratrooper of Mechanic Avenue–Lester Goran | .50 | 1.00 | 1.50 | |
| G546 | I Made My Bed–Kathy O'Farrell (as told to Rube Goldberg) | .50 | 1.00 | 1.50 | |
| G547 | The Computer Kill–Raymond Banks | | | | M |
| G550 | Fools Paradise–Bertrand Poirot-Delpech | .50 | 1.00 | 1.50 | |
| G551 | New York Call Girl–Robert Lowry | .50 | 1.00 | 1.50 | |
| G552 | TV Guide Roundup–ed. of TV Guide; 1961 | 2.50 | 5.00 | 7.50 | NF |
| G553 | Jury of One–Mignon G. Eberhart | .50 | 1.00 | 1.50 | M |
| G554 | Miami Undercover–Evan Lee Heyan; TV tie-in | 1.25 | 2.50 | 3.75 | M |
| G556 | Your Sins and Mine–Taylor Caldwell | .50 | 1.00 | 1.50 | |
| G557 | Life in a Putty Knife Factory–H. Allen Smith | .50 | 1.00 | 1.50 | H |
| G559 | The Cruise–Nicholas Gorham | .50 | 1.00 | 1.50 | |
| G560 | Donovan's Brain–Curt Siodmak; 1961 | 1.00 | 2.00 | 3.00 | SF |
| G562 | The Monitor Affair–Clarence Buddington Kelland | 1.00 | 2.00 | 3.00 | A |
| G563 | The Coming of Fabrizze–Raymond De Capite; 1961 | .50 | 1.00 | 1.50 | |
| G564 | A Tapping on the Wall–Helen Hull; 1962 | .50 | 1.00 | 1.50 | M |
| G565 | Hark, Hark, the Lark!–H.E. Bates | .50 | 1.00 | 1.50 | |
| G566 | Jane Arden, Student Nurse–Kathleen Harris | .50 | 1.00 | 1.50 | R |
| G567 | The Love Investigator–Ernest Gébler | .50 | 1.00 | 1.50 | |

POPULAR LIBRARY G-SERIES, *continued*

| G573 | It Had Been a Mild, Delicate Night–Tom Kaye; 1962 | .50 | 1.00 | 1.50 | |

## POPULAR LIBRARY PC-SERIES
### Popular Library, Inc.

| PC300 | Adventures of Captain David Grief–Jack London | .75 | 1.50 | 2.25 | A |
| PC400 | Be My Guest–Conrad Hilton | .50 | 1.00 | 1.50 | NF |

## POPULAR LIBRARY SP-SERIES
### Popular Library, Inc.

| SP 2 | The Adventures of Augie March–Saul Bellow; 1955 | .75 | 1.50 | 2.25 | |
| SP 3 | Crossword Puzzles; 1956 | 2.50 | 5.00 | 7.50 | NF |
| SP 4 | The Doctors–Andre Soubiran | .75 | 1.50 | 2.25 | |
| SP 5 | Between Heaven and Hell–Francis Irby Gwaltney; movie tie-in | 1.00 | 2.00 | 3.00 | |
| SP 6 | Auntie Mame–Patrick Dennis | .75 | 1.50 | 2.25 | |
| SP 7 | A Tree Grows in Brooklyn–Betty Smith | .75 | 1.50 | 2.25 | |
| SP 8 | Courtroom–Quentin Reynolds; 1957 | .75 | 1.50 | 2.25 | |
| SP 9 | Roll Back the Sky–Ward Taylor | .75 | 1.50 | 2.25 | |
| SP10 | The Spear–Louis de Wohl | .75 | 1.50 | 2.25 | |
| SP11 | The Butchers–Leonard Bishop | 1.50 | 3.00 | 4.50 | JD |
| SP12 | Big Fella–Henry W. Clune; 1958 | .75 | 1.50 | 2.25 | |
| SP13 | Onionhead–Weldon Hill | .75 | 1.50 | 2.25 | H |
| SP14 | Three Comrades–Erich Maria Remarque | .75 | 1.50 | 2.25 | C |
| SP15 | Webster's New World Dictionary of the American Language–David B. Guralnik | .75 | 1.50 | 2.25 | NF |
| SP16 | Guestward Ho!–Patrick Dennis & Barbara Hooton | .75 | 1.50 | 2.25 | |
| SP17 | The Nymph and the Lamp–Thomas H. Raddall | .75 | 1.50 | 2.25 | E |
| SP18 | Shadow of the Moon–M.M. Kaye | .75 | 1.50 | 2.25 | |
| SP19 | The Wind in His Fists–John Jennings | 1.00 | 2.00 | 3.00 | A |
| SP20 | The Forest Cavalier–Roy Flannagan | .75 | 1.50 | 2.25 | A |
| SP21 | A Time to Love and a Time to Die–Erich Maria Remarque | .75 | 1.50 | 2.25 | C |
| SP22 | If I Forget Thee–Robert S. de Ropp | .75 | 1.50 | 2.25 | |
| SP23 | Dream of Innocence–Turnley Walker | .75 | 1.50 | 2.25 | |
| SP24 | Lower than Angels–Walter Karig | .75 | 1.50 | 2.25 | E |
| SP25 | Tisa–Helga Moray; 1958 | .75 | 1.50 | 2.25 | A |
| SP26 | Woman Surgeon–Else K. LaRoe | .75 | 1.50 | 2.25 | |
| SP27 | A Moment of Warmth–Francis Irby Gwaltney | .75 | 1.50 | 2.25 | |
| SP28 | Drums of Destiny–Peter Bourne | .75 | 1.50 | 2.25 | A |
| SP29 | Good Deeds Must Be Punished–Irving Shulman | .75 | 1.50 | 2.25 | |
| SP30 | The Philanderer–Stanley Kauffmann | .75 | 1.50 | 2.25 | |
| SP31 | The City of Libertines–W.G. Hardy | .75 | 1.50 | 2.25 | |
| SP32 | My Father–My Son–William Duffy & Edward G. Robinson, Jr | 1.50 | 3.00 | 4.50 | |
| SP33 | Marie of the Isles–Robert Gaillard | .75 | 1.50 | 2.25 | |
| SP34 | Red Lion Inn–Robert Payne | .75 | 1.50 | 2.25 | A |
| SP35 | The Late Liz–Elizabeth Burns | .75 | 1.50 | 2.25 | |
| SP36 | A House Is Not a Home–Polly Adler | .75 | 1.50 | 2.25 | |
| SP37 | Love for Lydia–H.E. Bates | .75 | 1.50 | 2.25 | E |
| SP38 | A Tale for Midnight–Frederic Prokosch | .75 | 1.50 | 2.25 | |
| SP39 | Whistle Stop–Maritta Wolff | .75 | 1.50 | 2.25 | E |
| SP40 | Blood Royal–Robert Payne | .75 | 1.50 | 2.25 | A |
| SP41 | Look Down in Mercy–Walter Baxter | .75 | 1.50 | 2.25 | |
| SP42 | The Good Housekeeping Book of Baby and Child Care–L. Emmett Holt, Jr | .75 | 1.50 | 2.25 | NF |
| SP43 | Rage to Love–Frank Tilsley | .75 | 1.50 | 2.25 | |
| SP44 | Dark Fury–Helga Moray | .75 | 1.50 | 2.25 | |
| SP45 | These Items of Desire–Louis A. Brennan | .75 | 1.50 | 2.25 | |
| SP46 | The Big Cage–Robert Lowry | 1.00 | 2.00 | 3.00 | |
| SP47 | The Strong Don't Cry–Estelle Slater | .75 | 1.50 | 2.25 | |
| SP48 | The Insider–James Kelly | .75 | 1.50 | 2.25 | |
| SP49 | Love Affair–Herbert Carson | .75 | 1.50 | 2.25 | E |
| SP50 | Kingsblood Royal–Sinclair Lewis; 1959 | .75 | 1.50 | 2.25 | |
| SP51 | The Greater Glory–Lester Gorn | .75 | 1.50 | 2.25 | |
| SP52 | The Golden Touch–Al Dewlen | .75 | 1.50 | 2.25 | |

| | V/Good | Fine | N/Mint |

| SP53 | The Great Days–John Dos Passos | .75 | 1.50 | 2.25 | |
| SP54 | Roses from the South–Perceval Reniers; 1960 | .50 | 1.00 | 1.50 | |
| SP55 | Princess Sophia–Edison Marshall | .50 | 1.00 | 1.50 | |
| SP56 | Henderson, the Rain King–Saul Bellow | .50 | 1.00 | 1.50 | |
| SP57 | Profane Junction–Leslie Turner White; 1960 | .75 | 1.50 | 2.25 | A |
| SP59 | Save Me the Sun–Hassoldt Davis | .50 | 1.00 | 1.50 | |
| SP61 | The Forsaken–Ferenc Kormendi | .50 | 1.00 | 1.50 | |
| SP62 | Adams of the Bounty–Erle Wilson | 1.00 | 2.00 | 3.00 | A |
| SP63 | Anatomy of Eve–Leopold Stein, MD, aka Loathsome Women | .50 | 1.00 | 1.50 | |
| SP64 | The Glorious Three–June Pat Wetherell | .50 | 1.00 | 1.50 | |
| SP65 | View from the Top–Al Hine; aka the Birthday Boy | .50 | 1.00 | 1.50 | |
| SP67 | The Virginian–Owen Wister; 1960 | .75 | 1.50 | 2.25 | W |
| SP68 | The Passionate Journey–Irving Stone | .50 | 1.00 | 1.50 | A |
| SP69 | The Pagan King–Edison Marshall; 1960 | .75 | 1.50 | 2.25 | A/F |
| SP72 | The Wind in His Fists–John Jennings; 1960 | .75 | 1.50 | 2.25 | A |
| SP73 | The Bulwark–Theodore Dreiser | .50 | 1.00 | 1.50 | |
| SP75 | The Hour before the Dawn–W. Somerset Maugham | .50 | 1.00 | 1.50 | C |
| SP76 | A Time to Love and a Time to Die–Erich Maria Remarque | .50 | 1.00 | 1.50 | C |
| SP77 | Francis of Assisi–Louis de Wohl | .50 | 1.00 | 1.50 | B |
| SP78 | Black Spice–Davenport Stewart | 2.00 | 4.00 | 6.00 | A |
| SP80 | Diary of a D.A.–Martin M. Frank; 1961 | .50 | 1.00 | 1.50 | NF |
| SP82 | Ten Days in August–Bernard Frizell | .50 | 1.00 | 1.50 | |
| SP83 | Jubilee–John Brick | 1.00 | 2.00 | 3.00 | |
| SP85 | Ritual in the Dark–Colin Wilson; 1961 | .50 | 1.00 | 1.50 | M |
| SP89 | Sun in Capricorn–Hamilton Basso | .50 | 1.00 | 1.50 | |
| SP90 | Bride of Fortune–Harnett Thomas Kane | .50 | 1.00 | 1.50 | |
| SP91 | The Inn of Five Lovers–Cecil St. Laurent | .50 | 1.00 | 1.50 | |
| SP93 | The Yankee Brig–Carter A. Vaughan; 1961 | 1.00 | 2.00 | 3.00 | A |
| SP94 | Three Men on the Left Hand–Ilka Chase | .50 | 1.00 | 1.50 | |
| SP96 | That Far Paradise–Gene Markey | .50 | 1.00 | 1.50 | |
| SP97 | 22 Terrace Place–Charles Mergendahl | .50 | 1.00 | 1.50 | |
| SP98 | Charlie Chaplin–Charles Chaplin, Jr | 2.50 | 5.00 | 7.50 | B |
| SP99 | The Devil at 4 O'clock–Max Catto; movie tie-in | .75 | 1.50 | 2.25 | |
| SP100 | Man Into Woman–Niels Hoyer; 1953 | 1.50 | 3.00 | 4.50 | NF |
| SP100 | The King's Vixen–Pamela Hill; 1961 | .50 | 1.00 | 1.50 | |
| SP101 | The Beach House–Stephen Longstreet | .75 | 1.50 | 2.25 | |
| SP102 | Desert Island DeCameron–ed. H. Allen Smith | .50 | 1.00 | 1.50 | H |
| SP103 | U.S. Secret Service–W. Bowen | 1.00 | 2.00 | 3.00 | NF |
| SP104 | Kitty–Rosamond Marshall | .50 | 1.00 | 1.50 | R |
| SP106 | The Butchers–Leonard Bishop; 1961 | .50 | 1.00 | 1.50 | JD |
| SP107 | Between Heaven and Hell–Francis Gwaltney; aka The Day the Century Ended | .50 | 1.00 | 1.50 | |
| SP109 | The Sea Hawk–Rafael Sabatini; 1961 | .75 | 1.50 | 2.25 | A |
| SP110 | The Traitor–William L. Shirer | .50 | 1.00 | 1.50 | |
| SP111 | Waikiki Beachnik–H. Allen Smith | .50 | 1.00 | 1.50 | H |
| SP115 | Sangaree–Frank G. Slaughter | .50 | 1.00 | 1.50 | A |
| SP117 | The 3 Faces of Eve–Corbett H. Thigpen & Hervey M. Cleckley | 1.50 | 3.00 | 4.50 | |
| SP118 | Madame Goldenflower–C.Y. Lee | .50 | 1.00 | 1.50 | |
| SP119 | To Step Aside–Noel Coward | .50 | 1.00 | 1.50 | |
| SP120 | Adventures of a Young Man–John Dos Passos | .50 | 1.00 | 1.50 | |
| SP122 | This Sporting Life–David Storey | .50 | 1.00 | 1.50 | |
| SP125 | Reunion–Merle Miller | .50 | 1.00 | 1.50 | |
| SP126 | All the Naked Heroes–Alan Kapelner | .50 | 1.00 | 1.50 | |
| SP127 | Assignment Churchill–W. Thompson | .50 | 1.00 | 1.50 | |
| SP128 | The Seduction–Susan Yorke | .50 | 1.00 | 1.50 | |
| SP129 | The Esquire Reader–eds. Arnold Gingrich, L. Rust Hills, Gene Lichtenstein | .75 | 1.50 | 2.25 | |
| SP131 | The Charlatan–Carter A. Vaughan; 1961 | 1.00 | 2.00 | 3.00 | A |
| SP133 | The Compassionate Tiger–Hunton Downs | .50 | 1.00 | 1.50 | |
| SP134 | The Sultan's Warrior–Bates Baldwin; 1961 | .75 | 1.50 | 2.25 | A |
| SP135 | The Fountain of Arethusa–Maurice Zermatten | .50 | 1.00 | 1.50 | |
| SP136 | Island in the Sky–Ernest K. Gann; 1961 | .50 | 1.00 | 1.50 | A |

| | | V/Good | Fine | N/Mint | |
|---|---|---|---|---|---|

POPULAR LIBRARY SP-SERIES, *continued*

| No. | Title | V/Good | Fine | N/Mint | |
|---|---|---|---|---|---|
| SP138 | The Fleet in the Window–David Bergamini; 1962 | .50 | 1.00 | 1.50 | |
| SP140 | Lay Siege to Heaven–Louis de Wohl | .50 | 1.00 | 1.50 | |
| SP141 | The Silver Lion–Noel B. Gerson; 1962 | .75 | 1.50 | 2.25 | A |
| SP142 | Billy Budd, Foretopman–Herman Melville | .75 | 1.50 | 2.25 | |
| SP143 | The Saturday Evening Post Reader of Western Stories–ed. E.N. Brandt; 1962 | 1.00 | 2.00 | 3.00 | W |
| SP147 | The Bright Sands–Robert Lewis Taylor | .50 | 1.00 | 1.50 | |
| SP148 | Don't Tell Alfred–Nancy Mitford | .50 | 1.00 | 1.50 | |
| SP149 | The Melody of Sex–Max Catto; 1962 | .50 | 1.00 | 1.50 | |
| SP156 | The Burning Sea–Iain Crawford | .50 | 1.00 | 1.50 | |
| SP157 | The Vandal–Richard O'Connor | .75 | 1.50 | 2.25 | A |
| SP158 | Last Plane to Shanghai–Richard Treyaskis | .50 | 1.00 | 1.50 | |
| SP159 | Christ in Concrete–Pietro Di Donato | .75 | 1.50 | 2.25 | |
| SP160 | Streets of Night–John Dos Passos | .50 | 1.00 | 1.50 | |
| SP162 | Father of the Bride–Edward Streeter | .75 | 1.50 | 2.25 | |
| SP164 | Naked in a Cactus Garden–Jesse L. Lasky, Jr | .50 | 1.00 | 1.50 | |
| SP165 | The Troubled Midnight–John Gunther | .50 | 1.00 | 1.50 | |
| SP166 | The Flight of the Dancing Bear–Mark Rascovich | .50 | 1.00 | 1.50 | |
| SP169 | The Redhead–Alfred Andersch | .50 | 1.00 | 1.50 | |
| SP170 | The War of the Worlds–H.G. Wells; 1962 | .75 | 1.50 | 2.25 | SF |
| SP171 | Jimmy Riddle–Ian Brook | .50 | 1.00 | 1.50 | |
| SP172 | The Pursuit of Agent M–DeWitt Copp | .50 | 1.00 | 1.50 | |
| SP173 | Flight into Camden–David Storey | .50 | 1.00 | 1.50 | |
| SP174 | Mr. Blandings Builds His Dream House–Eric Hodgins | .50 | 1.00 | 1.50 | |
| SP176 | Gentle Annie–MacKinlay Kantor | .50 | 1.00 | 1.50 | |
| SP178 | The Off-Islanders–Nathaniel Benchley | .50 | 1.00 | 1.50 | |
| SP179 | The Passionate Journey–Irving Stone | .50 | 1.00 | 1.50 | |
| SP180 | The Searchers–Alan Le May | .75 | 1.50 | 2.25 | W |
| SP184 | The Sirens Let Him Go–David Lloyd | .50 | 1.00 | 1.50 | |
| SP185 | An Excess of Love–Seymour Epstein; aka Pillar of Salt | .50 | 1.00 | 1.50 | |
| SP187 | View from the Top–Al Hine; aka the Birthday Boy | .50 | 1.00 | 1.50 | |
| SP188 | Chant of the Hawk–John Harris & Margaret Harris | .50 | 1.00 | 1.50 | |
| SP190 | Mountains of Gilead–Jesse Hill Ford | .50 | 1.00 | 1.50 | |
| SP192 | The Virginian–Owen Wister | .50 | 1.00 | 1.50 | W |
| SP193 | Road to Sodom–Jean Rees | .50 | 1.00 | 1.50 | |
| SP195 | The Doomsday Men–J.B. Priestley | .75 | 1.50 | 2.25 | M |
| SP197 | They Came to Kill–E. Rachlis | .50 | 1.00 | 1.50 | |
| SP200 | Duel in the Sun–Niven Busch; 1962 | .50 | 1.00 | 1.50 | |
| SP201 | The Wandering of Desire–Marlon Montgomery; 1963 | .50 | 1.00 | 1.50 | |
| SP202 | Fausto's Keyhole–Jean Arnaldi | .50 | 1.00 | 1.50 | |
| SP204 | The Scarlet Sword–H.E. Bates; 1963 | .50 | 1.00 | 1.50 | A |
| SP205 | The Forgotten Smile–Margaret Kennedy | .50 | 1.00 | 1.50 | |
| SP206 | The Penitent–Pietro DiDonato | .50 | 1.00 | 1.50 | |
| SP207 | Captain Blood Returns–Rafael Sabatini | 1.50 | 3.00 | 4.50 | A |
| SP208 | The Black Shrike–Ian Stuart (Alistair MacLean) | 1.00 | 2.00 | 3.00 | A |
| SP209 | The Bright Nemesis–John Gunther | .50 | 1.00 | 1.50 | |
| SP212 | A Child Is Waiting–Abby Mann; movie tie-in | 1.00 | 2.00 | 3.00 | |
| SP214 | Double Exposure–Théo Fleischman | .50 | 1.00 | 1.50 | |
| SP215 | My Six Loves–Peter V.K. Funk; movie tie-in | 1.00 | 2.00 | 3.00 | |
| SP216 | By Dim and Flaring Lamps–Alan Le May | .50 | 1.00 | 1.50 | |
| SP217 | The Tattooed Countess–Carl Van Vechten | .50 | 1.00 | 1.50 | |
| SP218 | Hud–Larry McMurtry; aka Horseman, Pass By; movie tie-in | 2.00 | 4.00 | 6.00 | |
| SP219 | Love in a Cold Climate–Nancy Mitford | .50 | 1.00 | 1.50 | |
| SP221 | On the Make–Dan Cushman; aka Brothers in Kickapoo | 1.00 | 2.00 | 3.00 | |
| SP222 | Mistress Wilding–Rafael Sabatini | .75 | 1.50 | 2.25 | A |
| SP224 | Trilby–George Du Maurier | .50 | 1.00 | 1.50 | |
| SP227 | The Year of the Spaniard–Henry Castor | .50 | 1.00 | 1.50 | |
| SP228 | The Hounds of God–Rafael Sabatini | .75 | 1.50 | 2.25 | A |
| SP229 | Walk into Hell–Richard G. Hubler; aka I've Got Mine | .50 | 1.00 | 1.50 | |
| SP231 | The Satan Bug–Ian Stuart (Alistair MacLean) | 1.00 | 2.00 | 3.00 | |

| No. | Title | V/Good | Fine | N/Mint | |
|---|---|---|---|---|---|
| SP232 | The Shapes of Sleep–John B. Priestley | .50 | 1.00 | 1.50 | M |
| SP233 | Heaven Knows, Mr. Allison–Charles Shaw; aka The Flesh and the Spirit | .50 | 1.00 | 1.50 | |
| SP234 | Master-at-Arms–Rafael Sabatini | .75 | 1.50 | 2.25 | A |
| SP237 | To Be Read before Midnight–ed. Ellery Queen; 1963 | 1.00 | 2.00 | 3.00 | M |
| SP239 | The Hittite–Noel B. Gerson | .75 | 1.50 | 2.25 | A |
| SP240 | Sea Road to Yorktown–Harvey Haislip | .50 | 1.00 | 1.50 | A |
| SP241 | 22 Terrace Place–Charles Mergendahl | .50 | 1.00 | 1.50 | |
| SP242 | And the Boys–Robert Traver | .50 | 1.00 | 1.50 | |
| SP244 | The Daughter of the Hawk–Cecil S. Forester | .75 | 1.50 | 2.25 | A |
| SP245 | Goodby to Some–Gordon Forbes | .50 | 1.00 | 1.50 | |
| SP246 | Tiara Tahiti–Geoffrey Cotterell; 1963 | .50 | 1.00 | 1.50 | |
| SP247 | The 7th Mourner–Dorothy Gardiner; 1964 | .50 | 1.00 | 1.50 | |
| SP248 | Death and Chicanery–Philip MacDonald | .75 | 1.50 | 2.25 | M |
| SP249 | Dark Lady–Doris Miles Disney | .50 | 1.00 | 1.50 | M |
| SP250 | The Man in the High Castle–Philip K. Dick | 2.00 | 4.00 | 6.00 | SF |
| SP251 | Lord Fancy–Leslie Turner White | .75 | 1.50 | 2.25 | A |
| SP252 | Blade of Honor–John J. Pugh | .75 | 1.50 | 2.25 | A |
| SP253 | Ambush Range–Jack Barton | .50 | 1.00 | 1.50 | W |
| SP254 | Dead Man's Trail–Philip Ketchum | .75 | 1.50 | 2.25 | W |
| SP255 | Scoundrels' Brigade–Carter A. Vaughan; 1964 | .75 | 1.50 | 2.25 | A |
| SP256 | The Elkhorn Feud–Philip Ketchum | .50 | 1.00 | 1.50 | W |
| SP257 | The Great Impersonation–E. Phillips Oppenheim | .50 | 1.00 | 1.50 | A |
| SP258 | The Untouchables–Eliot Ness & Oscar Fraley; TV tie-in | 1.00 | 2.00 | 3.00 | NF |
| SP259 | Guns of the Lawless–Todhunter Ballard | .50 | 1.00 | 1.50 | W |
| SP260 | The Chancellor–Lawrence Schoonover | .50 | 1.00 | 1.50 | A |
| SP261 | The Fool Killer–Helen Eustis | .50 | 1.00 | 1.50 | M |
| SP262 | High Grass Valley–William MacLeod Raine | .50 | 1.00 | 1.50 | W |
| SP263 | The Prize Master–Harvey Haislip | .50 | 1.00 | 1.50 | A |
| SP264 | Find the Woman–Doris Miles Disney | .50 | 1.00 | 1.50 | M |
| SP265 | The Master of Ballantrae–Robert Louis Stevenson | .50 | 1.00 | 1.50 | A |
| SP266 | Send a Gunboat–Douglas Reeman | .50 | 1.00 | 1.50 | |
| SP267 | The Big Gun–Philip Ketchum; 1964 | .50 | 1.00 | 1.50 | W |

# POPULAR LIBRARY W-SERIES

## Popular Library, Inc.

| No. | Title | V/Good | Fine | N/Mint |
|---|---|---|---|---|
| W400 | I, James Dean–T.T. Thomas | 3.50 | 7.00 | 10.50 |
| W500 | Fire Down Below–Simon Kent; movie tie-in | 1.00 | 2.00 | 3.00 |
| W600 | The Treasury of Ribaldry–Volume 1– Louis Untermeyer | .75 | 1.50 | 2.25 |

# POWELL/TIGER

## Powell Publications, Inc.

| No. | Title | V/Good | Fine | N/Mint | |
|---|---|---|---|---|---|
| PP101 | The Sexual Adventurers–Allen Evans (T) | 1.00 | 2.00 | 3.00 | E |
| PP102 | Confessions of a Female Cabbie–Les James (T) | 1.00 | 2.00 | 3.00 | E |
| PP103 | The Sex Barbarians–John Slade (T) | 1.00 | 2.00 | 3.00 | NF |
| PP104 | Crime and Violence in the U.S.A.– Richard Fusilier & Lynton W. Brent (T) | 1.00 | 2.00 | 3.00 | NF |
| PP105 | Naked on the Strip–Pete Mausert (T) | 1.00 | 2.00 | 3.00 | E |
| PP106 | The Prostitutes–Spenser & West (T) | 1.00 | 2.00 | 3.00 | NF |
| PP107 | Nympho–Fred MacDonald (T) | 1.00 | 2.00 | 3.00 | E |
| PP108 | The Rebellion of Youth–Lynton Wright Brent; 1968 (T) | 1.00 | 2.00 | 3.00 | NF |
| PP109 | Scandal in Sex–Mark Willit (T) | 1.00 | 2.00 | 3.00 | E |
| PP110 | Mate Mixing–Rolf Fuchs (T) | 1.00 | 2.00 | 3.00 | E |
| PP111 | Blowout!–Donald Franklyn (T) | 1.00 | 2.00 | 3.00 | E |
| PP112 | The Body Merchants–David Johnson (T) | 1.00 | 2.00 | 3.00 | E |
| PP113 | Blood in the Street–Lynton Wright Brent | 1.00 | 2.00 | 3.00 | |
| PP114 | Outlaw Village–Lynton Wright Brent | 1.50 | 3.00 | 4.50 | W |
| PP115 | Accent on Sex–Lynn Brandt (T) | 1.00 | 2.00 | 3.00 | E |
| PP116 | Jean–Howard Jackson (T) | 1.00 | 2.00 | 3.00 | E |

| | V/Good | Fine | N/Mint |
|---|---|---|---|

| | | V/Good | Fine | N/Mint |
|---|---|---|---|---|
| PP117 | Good Girls Do Too–Kevin Alen (T) | 1.00 | 2.00 | 3.00 E |
| PP118 | Dear Liza–Stacey Lubell; 1969 (T) | 1.00 | 2.00 | 3.00 E |
| PP119 | Hollywood Crime and Scandal–Lynton Wright Brent | 1.00 | 2.00 | 3.00 NF |
| PP120 | Apache Killers–Lynton Wright Brent | 1.50 | 3.00 | 4.50 W |
| PP121 | Swordmen of Vistar–Charles Nuetzel; 1969 | 2.00 | 4.00 | 6.00 F |
| PP122 | On the Make–Fredric Blake (T) | 1.00 | 2.00 | 3.00 E |
| PP123 | Passion Island–Pete Mausert (T) | 1.00 | 2.00 | 3.00 E |
| PP124 | Room Service–Spenser & West (T) | 1.00 | 2.00 | 3.00 E |
| PP125 | Woman on Her Back–Ric Arana (T) | 1.00 | 2.00 | 3.00 E |
| PP126 | Murder Times 4–Charles Nuetzel | 1.50 | 3.00 | 4.50 M |
| PP127 | Apache Tomahawk–Lynton Wright Brent | 1.50 | 3.00 | 4.50 W |
| PP128 | Out of the Unknown–A.E. Van Vogt & E. Mayne Hull | 1.50 | 3.00 | 4.50 SF |
| PP129 | Mama's Diary–Edward D. Wood, Jr (T) | 2.00 | 4.00 | 6.00 E |
| PP130 | Sex Odyssey '69–Rolf Fuchs (T) | 1.00 | 2.00 | 3.00 E |
| PP131 | Bedtime Is Playtime–Steve Petrea (T) | 1.00 | 2.00 | 3.00 E |
| PP132 | Take Me, I'm Yours–Jack Belmont (T) | 1.00 | 2.00 | 3.00 E |
| PP133 | Hollywood Mysteries–Charles Nuetzel; 1969 | 1.50 | 3.00 | 4.50 NF |
| PP134 | Apache Massacre–Lynton Wright Brent | 1.50 | 3.00 | 4.50 W |
| PP135 | Images of Tomorrow–Charles Nuetzel | 1.00 | 2.00 | 3.00 SF |
| PP136 | Big Broad (T) | 1.00 | 2.00 | 3.00 E |
| PP137 | Family of Lust–Norton Hornay (T) | 1.00 | 2.00 | 3.00 E |
| PP138 | Potpourri (T) | 1.00 | 2.00 | 3.00 E |
| PP139 | Sex Kittens–Stu Rivers (T) | 1.00 | 2.00 | 3.00 E |
| PP140 | Softly As I Kill You–Charles Nuetzel; 1969 | 1.50 | 3.00 | 4.50 M |
| PP141 | Warpaint in the Desert–Lynton Wright Brent | 1.50 | 3.00 | 4.50 W |
| PP142 | Science Fiction World of Forrest J. Ackerman & Friends | 1.50 | 3.00 | 4.50 SF |
| PP143 | Marry Me Again Sometime (T) | 1.00 | 2.00 | 3.00 E |
| PP144 | Baby-faced Harlot–Frank Ewing (T) | 1.00 | 2.00 | 3.00 E |
| PP145 | Woman Ashamed (T) | 1.00 | 2.00 | 3.00 E |
| PP146 | Allison (T) | 1.00 | 2.00 | 3.00 |
| PP147 | One Man's Crime–Lynton Wright Brent | 1.50 | 3.00 | 4.50 M |
| PP148 | Thunder of the Arrows–Lynton Wright Brent | 1.50 | 3.00 | 4.50 W |
| PP149 | Warriors of Noomas–Charles Nuetzel; 1969 | 2.00 | 4.00 | 6.00 F |
| PP154 | Memos from Purgatory–Harlan Ellison; 1969 | 2.00 | 4.00 | 6.00 JD |
| PP155 | Detective on the Prowl–Lynton Wright Brent | 1.50 | 3.00 | 4.50 M |
| PP157 | Raiders of Noomas–Charles Nuetzel; 1969 | 2.00 | 4.00 | 6.00 F |
| PP158 | Sex-plosion–Miller (T) | 1.00 | 2.00 | 3.00 E |
| PP159 | Widow for Hire–Ladd E. Linsley (T) | 1.00 | 2.00 | 3.00 M |
| PP160 | Secret Ecstasy (T) | 1.00 | 2.00 | 3.00 E |
| PP161 | Sexual Fantasia–Spenser & West (T) | 1.00 | 2.00 | 3.00 NF |
| PP162 | Jungle, Jungle–Charles Nuetzel; 1969 | 2.00 | 4.00 | 6.00 A |
| PP163 | Consider Yourself Dead | 1.00 | 2.00 | 3.00 |
| PP165 | Star Man–Stuart J. Byrne; 1969 | 1.50 | 3.00 | 4.50 SF |
| PP166 | Assignment Sex (T) | 1.00 | 2.00 | 3.00 |
| PP167 | My Double Life (T) | 1.00 | 2.00 | 3.00 |
| PP168 | Computa-Nymph (T) | 1.00 | 2.00 | 3.00 |
| PP169 | Born to Be Loved (T) | 1.00 | 2.00 | 3.00 |
| PP170 | Death of a Detective–Lynton Wright Brent; 1969 | 1.50 | 3.00 | 4.50 M |
| PP171 | Operation Nightmare | 1.50 | 3.00 | 4.50 |
| PP172 | Land of No Return/Pinto Paradise | 1.50 | 3.00 | 4.50 W |
| PP173 | Invasion of Mars–Garrett P. Serviss | 1.00 | 2.00 | 3.00 SF |
| PP174 | Exposure (T) | 1.00 | 2.00 | 3.00 E |
| PP175 | The Swappers (T) | 1.00 | 2.00 | 3.00 E |
| PP176 | One Way Street–Grant Elliot (T) | 1.00 | 2.00 | 3.00 JD |
| PP177 | Sex Bash (T) | 1.00 | 2.00 | 3.00 E |
| PP178 | Burma–Lee O. Miller | 1.00 | 2.00 | 3.00 C |
| PP179 | Goldlust–Albert Augustus, Jr (Charles Nuetzel); 1969 | 2.00 | 4.00 | 6.00 A |
| PP180 | Trail-blazers West–Del Rayburn | 1.50 | 3.00 | 4.50 W |
| PP181 | Two Dozen Dragon Eggs–Donald A. Wollheim | 2.00 | 4.00 | 6.00 SF |
| PP182 | The Bisexuals (T) | 1.00 | 2.00 | 3.00 E |
| PP183 | The Widows (T) | 1.00 | 2.00 | 3.00 E |
| PP184 | Quest–Cort Martin (T) | 1.00 | 2.00 | 3.00 E |
| PP185 | Come to me Baby (T) | 1.00 | 2.00 | 3.00 E |
| PP186 | Death Deal–Ben E. Miller | 1.50 | 3.00 | 4.50 |
| PP187 | Big Dano–Ric Arana | 1.50 | 3.00 | 4.50 |

*Powell PP134, Powel PP149, Powell PP213.*

| | | V/Good | Fine | N/Mint |
|---|---|---|---|---|
| PP188 | The Color of Blood–William H. James | 1.50 | 3.00 | 4.50 W |
| PP189 | The Slaves of Lomooro–Albert Augustus, Jr (Charles Nuetzel) | 2.00 | 4.00 | 6.00 SF |
| PP190 | The Oralists–Jean Spenser & Roger West (T) | 1.00 | 2.00 | 3.00 E |
| PP194 | Hager's Castle–Clayton Matthews | 1.50 | 3.00 | 4.50 M |
| PP195 | The Set-up–Ben Miller | 1.50 | 3.00 | 4.50 M |
| PP196 | Gunman's Code | 1.50 | 3.00 | 4.50 W |
| PP197 | Crazy Mixed-up Planet–Charles E. Fritch | 1.50 | 3.00 | 4.50 SF |
| PP202 | The Mendoza File–Clayton Matthews | 1.50 | 3.00 | 4.50 M |
| PP203 | Shroud 9–Robert Turner | 2.00 | 4.00 | 6.00 HO |
| PP204 | Trackdown | 1.50 | 3.00 | 4.50 W |
| PP205 | Godman!–John Bloodstone (Stuart J. Byrne); 1970 | 1.50 | 3.00 | 4.50 SF |
| PP210 | Operation: Countdown | 1.50 | 3.00 | 4.50 |
| PP211 | The Other People–Pat A. Brisco | 1.50 | 3.00 | 4.50 HO |
| PP212 | Look Down, Look Down–Arthur Moore | 1.50 | 3.00 | 4.50 A |
| PP213 | Darkness Weaves–Karl Edward Wagner; 1970 | 2.00 | 4.00 | 6.00 F |
| 1001N | The Eagle Had Wax Wings–Edward A. Clapham | 1.50 | 3.00 | 4.50 C |
| 1002N | Weekend of Terror | 1.50 | 3.00 | 4.50 HO |
| 1003N | Leatherwood–Stack Sutton | 1.50 | 3.00 | 4.50 W |
| 1004N | Horses' Asteroid–Charles E. Fritch | 1.50 | 3.00 | 4.50 SF |
| 1005N | Nylon Nightmare–Clayton Matthews | 1.50 | 3.00 | 4.50 M |
| 1008N | Santana Morning–Mike Dolan | 1.50 | 3.00 | 4.50 SF |
| 1009N | Death Is a Drag–Don Hoyt & Art Moore; 1970 | 1.50 | 3.00 | 4.50 M |
| 1010N | The Outragers–Bruce Fowler | 1.50 | 3.00 | 4.50 M |
| 1011N | No Trumpets, No Drums–Jack Matcha | 1.50 | 3.00 | 4.50 |

# (PREFERRED BOOKS)

## Preferred Books Co.

### Digest Size

| | | V/Good | Fine | N/Mint |
|---|---|---|---|---|
| 1 | The Hallowed Hour–A.H. Parr; 1946 | 1.25 | 2.50 | 3.75 |
| 2 | The Mountains Moved–A.H. Parr | 1.25 | 2.50 | 3.75 |

# PREMIER BOOKS

## Fawcett Publications, Inc.

| | | V/Good | Fine | N/Mint |
|---|---|---|---|---|
| S12 | The Power of Positive Living–Douglas Lurton; 1955 | .50 | 1.00 | 1.50 NF |
| S13 | How to Write and Speak Effective English–Edward Frank Allen | .50 | 1.00 | 1.50 NF |
| S14 | The Enjoyment of Love in Marriage–LeMon Clark | .50 | 1.00 | 1.50 NF |
| S15 | Best Quotations for All Occasions–Lewis C. Henry | .50 | 1.00 | 1.50 NF |
| S16 | The Art of Thinking–Ernest Dimnet | .50 | 1.00 | 1.50 NF |
| S17 | Mademoiselle de Maupin–Theophile Gautier | .50 | 1.00 | 1.50 |
| S18 | Look Younger, Live Longer–Gayelord Hauser; 1956 | .50 | 1.00 | 1.50 NF |
| S19 | The Way of Woman–Johnson E. Fairchild | .50 | 1.00 | 1.50 NF |

| | V/Good | Fine | N/Mint |
|---|---|---|---|

**PREMIER BOOKS,** *continued*

| | V/Good | Fine | N/Mint |
|---|---|---|---|
| S20 | Philosophy for Pleasure–Hector Hawton | .50 | 1.00 | 1.50 NF |
| S21 | The Fascinating Insect World of J. Henri Fabre–Edwin Way Teale | .50 | 1.00 | 1.50 NF |
| S22 | Your Key to Happiness–Harold Sherman | .50 | 1.00 | 1.50 NF |
| d23 | The Sex Life of Wild Animals–Eugene Burns | 1.00 | 2.00 | 3.00 NF |
| S24 | The Strange Story of Our Earth– A. Hyatt Verrill | .50 | 1.00 | 1.50 NF |
| S25 | My Life As an Indian–J.W. Schultz | .50 | 1.00 | 1.50 NF |
| S26 | The Living Tide–N.S. Berrill | .50 | 1.00 | 1.50 NF |
| S27 | A Key to the Heavens–Leo Mattersdorf | .50 | 1.00 | 1.50 NF |
| S28 | The Wisdom and Ideas of Plato–David Appel & Eugene Freeman | .50 | 1.00 | 1.50 NF |
| S29 | A Book about American History– George Stimpson | .50 | 1.00 | 1.50 NF |
| S30 | The World's Ten Greatest Novels– W. Somerset Maugham | .50 | 1.00 | 1.50 |
| S31 | The Benjamin Franklin Sampler | .50 | 1.00 | 1.50 |
| S32 | American Ballads–David Jordan & Charles O'Brien Kennedy | .50 | 1.00 | 1.50 |
| S33 | The Origin of Things–Julius E. Lips | .50 | 1.00 | 1.50 NF |
| d34 | Abraham Lincoln–Emil Ludwig | .50 | 1.00 | 1.50 B |
| S35 | Understanding Other People–Stuart Palmer | .50 | 1.00 | 1.50 NF |
| S36 | Party Fun and Games–Alexander Van Rensselaer; 1956 | .50 | 1.00 | 1.50 NF |
| S37 | According to Hoyle–Richard Frey | .50 | 1.00 | 1.50 NF |
| S38 | Unfaithful–Frank S. Caprio | .50 | 1.00 | 1.50 |
| S39 | The Great Religions by Which Men Live–Tynette Hills & Floyd H. Ross | .50 | 1.00 | 1.50 NF |
| d40 | George Washington–W.E. Woodward | .50 | 1.00 | 1.50 B |
| S41 | The Home Book of Italian Cooking– Angela Catanzaro; 1957 | .50 | 1.00 | 1.50 NF |
| S42 | How You Can Forecast the Weather– Eric Sloane | .50 | 1.00 | 1.50 NF |
| S43 | Discover Your Self!–Stephen Lackner | .50 | 1.00 | 1.50 NF |
| S44 | Animal Wonder World–Frank Lane | .50 | 1.00 | 1.50 NF |
| d45 | Meet General Grant–W.E. Woodward | 1.00 | 2.00 | 3.00 B |
| S46 | What Your Dreams Mean–Emil A. Gutheil | .50 | 1.00 | 1.50 NF |
| S47 | Boswell's Johnson Sampler–James Boswell | .50 | 1.00 | 1.50 |
| S48 | How to Make Psychology Work for You–Abraham P. Sperling | .50 | 1.00 | 1.50 NF |
| S49 | Crucibles: the Story of Chemistry– Bernard Jaffe | .50 | 1.00 | 1.50 NF |
| d50 | Man's Emerging Mind–N.J. Berrill | .50 | 1.00 | 1.50 NF |
| d51 | The Miracle of Language–Charlton Laird | .50 | 1.00 | 1.50 NF |
| d52 | Understanding Human Nature–Alfred Adler | .50 | 1.00 | 1.50 NF |
| d53 | The Kipling Sampler–Rudyard Kipling | 1.00 | 2.00 | 3.00 |
| d54 | Shakespeare without Tears–Margaret Webster | .50 | 1.00 | 1.50 |
| d55 | The Son of Man–Emil Ludwig | .50 | 1.00 | 1.50 NF |
| d56 | Fun with Mathematics–Jerome S. Meyer | .50 | 1.00 | 1.50 NF |
| d57 | Cure Your Nerves Yourself–Louis E. Bisch | .50 | 1.00 | 1.50 NF |
| d58 | Mirror for Man–Clyde Kluckhohn | .50 | 1.00 | 1.50 NF |
| d59 | The Practical Way to a Better Memory–Bruno Furst | .50 | 1.00 | 1.50 NF |
| d60 | They Walked with God–Michael Williams | .50 | 1.00 | 1.50 NF |
| d61 | The Living Thoughts of Thomas Jefferson | .50 | 1.00 | 1.50 |
| d62 | Freedom from Money Worries–Martha Patton & Price A. Patton; 1958 | .50 | 1.00 | 1.50 NF |
| d63 | The Living Thoughts of Henry David Thoreau | .50 | 1.00 | 1.50 |
| d64 | How to Understand Music–Oscar Thompson | .50 | 1.00 | 1.50 NF |
| d65 | Riddles of Science–J. Arthur Thomson | .50 | 1.00 | 1.50 NF |
| d66 | Becoming a Mother–Marvin H. Albert & T.R. Seidman | 1.00 | 2.00 | 3.00 NF |
| d67 | The Living Thoughts of Ralph Waldo Emerson | .50 | 1.00 | 1.50 |
| d68 | See without Glasses–Ralph MacFadyen | .50 | 1.00 | 1.50 NF |
| d69 | Magic, Myth and Medicine–D.T. Atkinson | .50 | 1.00 | 1.50 NF |
| d70 | The Growth of Physical Science–James Jeans | .50 | 1.00 | 1.50 NF |
| d71 | How to Live with Yourself and Like It– Henry Clay Lindgren | .50 | 1.00 | 1.50 NF |
| d72 | The Living Thoughts of Machiavelli– Niccolo Machiavelli | .50 | 1.00 | 1.50 |
| d73 | How to Use the Power of Prayer– Harold Sherman | .50 | 1.00 | 1.50 NF |
| d74 | The Living Thoughts of Confucius– Confucius; 1959 | .50 | 1.00 | 1.50 |
| d75 | Philosophy for Pleasure–Hector Hawton | .50 | 1.00 | 1.50 NF |
| d76 | The Living Thoughts of Spinoza– Benedictus de Spinoza | .50 | 1.00 | 1.50 |
| d77 | Your Key to Happiness–Harold Sherman | .50 | 1.00 | 1.50 NF |
| d78 | Understanding Other People–Stuart Palmer | .50 | 1.00 | 1.50 NF |
| d79 | The Story of America–Hendrik Willem Van Loon | .50 | 1.00 | 1.50 NF |
| d80 | You and the Universe–N.J. Berrill | .50 | 1.00 | 1.50 NF |
| d81 | Much Loved Books, Volume 1–James O'Donnell Bennett | .50 | 1.00 | 1.50 |
| d82 | The Living Thoughts of Darwin– Charles Darwin | .50 | 1.00 | 1.50 |
| d83 | The Inhabited Universe–Derek D. Dempster & Kenneth W. Gatland | .50 | 1.00 | 1.50 NF |
| d84 | The Wisdom and Ideas of Plato–David Appel & Eugene Freeman | .50 | 1.00 | 1.50 |
| d85 | Readings from World Religions– Selwyn Gurney Champion & Dorothy Short | .50 | 1.00 | 1.50 NF |
| d86 | Discover Yourself–Stephen Lackner | .50 | 1.00 | 1.50 NF |

# PRIVATE EDITIONS
## Crescent Publishing Co.
### Digest Size

| | | V/Good | Fine | N/Mint |
|---|---|---|---|---|
| 1 | Nature Girl–Thomas Stone | 3.00 | 6.00 | 9.00 E |
| 2 | Playful Wife–Hall Bennett (on cover)/ Thomas Stone (on title page) | 3.00 | 6.00 | 9.00 E |

# PRIZE
## Century Publications

| | | V/Good | Fine | N/Mint |
|---|---|---|---|---|
| 52 | No Nice Girl–Perry Lindsay (Peggy Gaddis) | 3.00 | 6.00 | 9.00 E |
| 53 | Saddles West!–H.B. Hickey | 3.00 | 6.00 | 9.00 W |
| 54 | Scarlet Sin–John Saxon | 3.00 | 6.00 | 9.00 E |
| 55 | Love Business–William Arthur | 3.00 | 6.00 | 9.00 E |
| 56 | Cue for Passion–Gordon Semple | 3.00 | 6.00 | 9.00 E |
| 57 | Ripe for Love–Carmen Snow | 3.00 | 6.00 | 9.00 E |
| 58 | Marriage Is for Two–Phyllis Arthur | 3.00 | 6.00 | 9.00 E |
| 59 | Unashamed–Perry Lindsay (Peggy Gaddis) | 3.00 | 6.00 | 9.00 E |
| 60 | Bad Company–Gordon Semple | 3.00 | 6.00 | 9.00 E |
| 61 | One More Lover–Thomas Stone | 3.00 | 6.00 | 9.00 E |
| 63 | The Common Passion–John Saxon | 3.00 | 6.00 | 9.00 E |

*Prize Book 52, Prize Love Novel 20, Prize Love Novel 24.*

| | V/Good | Fine | N/Mint |
|---|---|---|---|

PRIZE, *continued*

| 64 | Too Loose–Carlotta Baker | 3.00 | 6.00 | 9.00 E |
|---|---|---|---|---|
| 65 | Scandalous–Ralph Carter | 3.00 | 6.00 | 9.00 E |
| 66 | Fleshpots–Florenz Branch | 3.00 | 6.00 | 9.00 E |
| 88 | Hell's Horseman–William Hopson | 3.00 | 6.00 | 9.00 W |

# PRIZE LOVE NOVELS
## Crestwood Publishing Co., Inc.
### Digest Size

| 20 | Thanks, Angel–Cynthia Millburn; 1946 | 3.00 | 6.00 | 9.00 E |
|---|---|---|---|---|
| 22 | Old Man's Darling–John Saxon | 3.00 | 6.00 | 9.00 R |
| 23 | Night Club Angel–Ralph Carter | 3.00 | 6.00 | 9.00 E |
| 24 | Time for Love–Lee Jacquin | 3.00 | 6.00 | 9.00 E |
| 25 | Passion's Prophecy–Thomas Stone | 3.00 | 6.00 | 9.00 E |
| 26 | Sisters in Sin–Eliot Brewster | 3.00 | 6.00 | 9.00 E |
| 27 | Skin Deep–Eliot Brewster | 3.00 | 6.00 | 9.00 E |
| 28 | Love Racket–Beth Brown | 3.00 | 6.00 | 9.00 E |

# PRIZE MYSTERY NOVELS
## Crestwood Publishing Co., Inc.
### Digest Size

| 1 | The Rose Petal Murders–Charles G. Givens; 1943 | 3.00 | 6.00 | 9.00 M |
|---|---|---|---|---|
| 2 | Murder at the Mike–Charles Saxby | 3.00 | 6.00 | 9.00 M |
| 4 | Hot Ice–Robert J. Casey | 3.00 | 6.00 | 9.00 M |
| 5 | And Sudden Death–Cleve F. Adams | 3.00 | 6.00 | 9.00 M |
| 6 | Fall Guy for Murder–Lawrence Goldman | 3.00 | 6.00 | 9.00 M |
| 7 | The Great Insurance Murders–Milton Propper | 3.00 | 6.00 | 9.00 M |
| 8 | The Station Wagon Murder–Milton Propper; 1944 | 3.00 | 6.00 | 9.00 M |
| 9 | The Third Owl–Robert J. Casey | 2.50 | 5.00 | 7.50 M |
| 10 | Murder on Safari–Elspeth Huxley | 3.00 | 6.00 | 9.00 M |
| 11 | The Frightened Girl–Michael Crombie | 3.00 | 6.00 | 9.00 M |
| 12 | The Third Degree–Joe Barry | 2.50 | 5.00 | 7.50 M |
| 13 | Sinner's Castle–S. Andrew Wood | 3.00 | 6.00 | 9.00 M |
| 14 | The Purple Pony Murders–Sidney E. Porcelain; 1945 | 3.00 | 6.00 | 9.00 M |
| 15 | The Camp-Meeting Murders–Vance Randolph & Nancy Clemens | 3.00 | 6.00 | 9.00 M |
| 16 | Murder without Motive–R.L. Goldman | 3.00 | 6.00 | 9.00 M |
| 17 | Invitation to Kill–Gardner Low | 3.00 | 6.00 | 9.00 M |
| 18 | Out on Bail–R.L. Goldman | 3.00 | 6.00 | 9.00 M |
| 19 | Murder for Breakfast–Peter Hunt | 3.00 | 6.00 | 9.00 M |
| 20 | Murder Is Forgetful–William G. Bogart | 3.00 | 6.00 | 9.00 M |
| 21 | The Wolf Howls Murder–Manning Lee Stokes; 1946 | 3.00 | 6.00 | 9.00 M |
| 22 | Message from a Corpse–Sam Merwin, Jr | 3.00 | 6.00 | 9.00 M |
| 23 | Never Say Die–McKnight Malmar | 3.00 | 6.00 | 9.00 M |
| 24 | The Walls Came Tumbling Down–Jo Eisinger | 3.00 | 6.00 | 9.00 M |
| 25 | The Thorne Theater Mystery–Joshua Willard | 3.00 | 6.00 | 9.00 M |
| 26 | Death Dines Out–Theodora DuBois | 3.00 | 6.00 | 9.00 M |
| 27 | It's My Own Funeral–Dana Lyon; 1947 | 3.00 | 6.00 | 9.00 M |
| 28 | Two Names for Death–E.P. Fenwick | 3.00 | 6.00 | 9.00 M |
| 29 | The Straw Donkey Case–A.S. Fleischman | 3.00 | 6.00 | 9.00 M |
| 30 | Major Crime–Oliver Keystone | 3.00 | 6.00 | 9.00 M |

# PRIZE SCIENCE FICTION NOVELS
## Crestwood Publishing Co., Inc.
### Digest Size

| 10 | Fight for Life–Murray Leinster | 5.00 | 10.00 | 15.00 SF |
|---|---|---|---|---|
| 11 | Sojarof of Titan–Manly Wade Wellman; 1st ed. nd | 5.00 | 10.00 | 15.00 SF |

*Prize Science Fiction 11, Prize Western 36, Prize Western 37.*

| | V/Good | Fine | N/Mint |
|---|---|---|---|

# PRIZE WESTERN NOVELS
## Crestwood Publishing Co., Inc.
### Digest Size

| 20 | Gunsmoke over Utah–Herbert Shappiro; 1946 | 2.00 | 4.00 | 6.00 W |
|---|---|---|---|---|
| 21 | Lawless Range–C.H. Heckelman | 2.00 | 4.00 | 6.00 W |
| 22 | Trail of Lost Men–Tex Holt | 2.00 | 4.00 | 6.00 W |
| 23 | Wolf's Candle–Dane Coolidge; 1947 | 2.00 | 4.00 | 6.00 W |
| 24 | Thunder of Hoofs–Tex Holt | 2.00 | 4.00 | 6.00 W |
| 25 | Trouble at Moon Pass–Herbert Shappiro | 2.00 | 4.00 | 6.00 W |
| 26 | Trouble from Texas–Stuart Hardy | 2.00 | 4.00 | 6.00 W |
| 27 | Silver City Rangers–Herbert Shappiro; 1948 | 2.00 | 4.00 | 6.00 W |
| 28 | Judge Colt–Archie Joscelyn | 2.00 | 4.00 | 6.00 W |
| 29 | Gunmaster of Saddleback–D.B. Newton | 2.00 | 4.00 | 6.00 W |
| 30 | Smoke of the .45–Harry S. Drago | 2.00 | 4.00 | 6.00 W |
| 32 | Powder Smoke Blood–Clav Star | 2.00 | 4.00 | 6.00 W |
| 33 | Point West–Tex Holt | 2.00 | 4.00 | 6.00 W |
| 34 | Ramrod Vengeance–John Sims | 2.00 | 4.00 | 6.00 W |
| 35 | Wyoming Trail–Walter A. Tompkins | 2.00 | 4.00 | 6.00 W |
| 36 | Bravo Trail–Leigh Carder | 2.00 | 4.00 | 6.00 W |
| 37 | Valley of Death–Burt Arthur | 2.00 | 4.00 | 6.00 W |
| 38 | Yellow Dust–V.J. Hanson | 2.00 | 4.00 | 6.00 W |
| 39 | Trouble Buster–Earl Sumner | 2.00 | 4.00 | 6.00 W |
| 40 | Guns of Powder River–Lee Floren | 2.00 | 4.00 | 6.00 W |

# (PUTNAM)
## G.P. Putnams Sons

| nn | This Is Nixon: The Man and His Work–James Keogh; 1956 | 2.50 | 5.00 | 7.50 NF |
|---|---|---|---|---|

# PYRAMID BOOKS
## Almat Publishing Corp./Pyramid Books

**Note: Nos. 1–10 do not exist, and No. 13 probably does not exist.**

| 11 | Passionate Virgin–Perry Lindsay; 1949; aka Brief Pleasure | 6.00 | 12.00 | 18.00 E |
|---|---|---|---|---|
| 12 | Reckless Passion–Gordon Sample | 5.00 | 10.00 | 15.00 E |
| 14 | Blonde Mistress–Hall Bennett | 5.00 | 10.00 | 15.00 E |
| 15 | Palm Beach Apartment–Gail Jordan (Peggy Gaddis) | 5.00 | 10.00 | 15.00 E |
| 16 | Set-up for Murder–Peter Cheyney; 1950 | 5.00 | 10.00 | 15.00 M |
| 17 | Tavern Girl–Glen Watkins | 4.00 | 8.00 | 12.00 E |
| 18 | Shameless Honeymoon–Thomas Stone | 4.00 | 8.00 | 12.00 E |
| 19 | The Moonstone–Wilkie Collins | 2.50 | 5.00 | 7.50 M |
| 20 | Terror in Times Square–Alan Handley | 5.00 | 10.00 | 15.00 M |
| 21 | Sin Street–Dorine Manners | 4.00 | 8.00 | 12.00 E |

Putnam unnumbered, Pyramid 12, Pyramid 21.

Pyramid 25, Pyramid 45, Pyramid 66.

PYRAMID BOOKS, *continued*

| | | V/Good | Fine | N/Mint | |
|---|---|---|---|---|---|
| 22 | The Dead Men Grin–Bruno Fischer | 4.00 | 8.00 | 12.00 | M |
| 23 | Cry Shame!–Katherine Everard | 4.00 | 8.00 | 12.00 | E |
| 24 | The Manatee–Nancy Bruff | 3.00 | 6.00 | 9.00 | E |
| 25 | The Orphan Outlaw–Clarence E. Mulford | 4.00 | 8.00 | 12.00 | W |
| 26 | Arizona Ranger–A. Scott Leslie | 4.00 | 8.00 | 12.00 | W |
| 27 | Sinful Cities of the Western World–Hendrik de Leeuw | 4.00 | 8.00 | 12.00 | E |
| 28 | The Shame of Mary Quinn–Clifton Cuthbert | 4.00 | 8.00 | 12.00 | E |
| 29 | Stairway to Death–Bruno Fischer | 5.00 | 10.00 | 15.00 | M |
| 30 | Madeleine–anon. | 3.00 | 6.00 | 9.00 | E |
| 31 | Tough Town–Jack Karney; 1951; aka The Ragged Edge | 3.50 | 7.00 | 10.50 | JD |
| 32 | The Divided Path–Nial Kent | 3.00 | 6.00 | 9.00 | E |
| 33 | Roadside Night–Erwin N. Nistler & Gerry P. Broderick | 3.00 | 6.00 | 9.00 | E |
| 34 | Rustlers' Range–Bradford Scott | 3.00 | 6.00 | 9.00 | W |
| 35 | French Doctor–Louis-Charles Royer | 3.00 | 6.00 | 9.00 | E |
| 36 | Tombstone Trail–A. Scott Leslie | 3.00 | 6.00 | 9.00 | W |
| 37 | Farm Girl–William Brown Meloney; aka Rusty to the Sun | 4.00 | 8.00 | 12.00 | E |
| 38 | The Raft–Robert Trumbull | 2.50 | 5.00 | 7.50 | A |
| 39 | Swamp Girl–Evans Wall | 15.00 | 30.00 | 45.00 | E |
| 40 | Texas Fury–Jackson Cole | 3.00 | 6.00 | 9.00 | W |
| 41 | The House of Madame Tellier–Guy de Maupassant; 1952 | 3.00 | 6.00 | 9.00 | E |
| G42 | The King's Mistress–Jean Plaidy; aka The Goldsmith's Wife | 3.00 | 6.00 | 9.00 | E |
| G43 | Teen-Age-Vice!–Courtney Ryley Cooper | 4.00 | 8.00 | 12.00 | JD |
| 44 | The Stranger in Boots–A. Scott Leslie | 3.00 | 6.00 | 9.00 | W |
| 45 | I Am a Fugitive from a Chain Gang–Robert E. Burns; movie tie-in | 7.50 | 15.00 | 22.50 | |
| 46 | 23 Women–anon. | 5.00 | 10.00 | 15.00 | E |
| 47 | Thunder Range–Jackson Cole | 3.00 | 6.00 | 9.00 | W |
| G48 | Cage of Lust–Allan Seager; aka Equinox | 3.00 | 6.00 | 9.00 | E |
| 49 | A Diary of Love–Maude Hutchins | 3.00 | 6.00 | 9.00 | E |
| G50 | Yama, the Hell-Hole–Alexandre Kuprin; 1952 | 3.00 | 6.00 | 9.00 | E |
| 51 | Border Hell–Jackson Cole | 3.00 | 6.00 | 9.00 | W |
| G52 | Tillie–David Westheimer; 1952; aka Summer on the Water | 2.50 | 5.00 | 7.50 | E |
| 53 | The Bruiser–Jim Tully | 2.50 | 5.00 | 7.50 | |
| G54 | Yankee Trader–Stanley Morton | 3.00 | 6.00 | 9.00 | E |
| 55 | Downfall–Bentz Plagemann | 2.50 | 5.00 | 7.50 | E |
| 56 | The Death Riders–Jackson Cole | 3.00 | 6.00 | 9.00 | W |
| G57 | The Wild Ones–Vardis Fisher | 2.50 | 5.00 | 7.50 | E |
| 58 | Female Convict–as told to Vincent E. Burns | 4.00 | 8.00 | 12.00 | NF |
| G59 | Sweet Man–Gilmore Millen | 3.00 | 6.00 | 9.00 | E |
| G60 | Bitter Love–Dyson Taylor | 2.50 | 5.00 | 7.50 | E |
| 61 | The Texan–A. Scott Leslie | 3.00 | 6.00 | 9.00 | W |
| 62 | Let's Go Naked–ed. Don Wollheim | 5.00 | 10.00 | 15.00 | E |
| 63 | Apache Devil–Edwin Corle | 3.00 | 6.00 | 9.00 | W |
| G64 | The Heavenly Sinner–Everett Harre | 2.50 | 5.00 | 7.50 | E |
| 65 | One Way Street–Nick Morino | 2.50 | 5.00 | 7.50 | |
| 66 | Trigger Law–Jackson Cole | 3.00 | 6.00 | 9.00 | W |
| G67 | Hospital Doctor–Edward Young | 2.50 | 5.00 | 7.50 | E |
| 68 | Georgia Hotel–Scott Laurence | 2.50 | 5.00 | 7.50 | E |
| G69 | The Brute–Guy des Cars | 2.50 | 5.00 | 7.50 | E |
| 70 | Massacre Canyon–Jackson Cole; 1953 | 3.00 | 6.00 | 9.00 | W |
| 71 | A Woman of Paris–Andre Tellier | 2.50 | 5.00 | 7.50 | E |
| G72 | The Dark Urge–Robert W. Taylor | 2.50 | 5.00 | 7.50 | E |
| 73 | Killer Country–Jackson Cole | 3.00 | 6.00 | 9.00 | E |
| 74 | The Come-On–Whitman Chambers | 2.50 | 5.00 | 7.50 | E |
| G75 | Pirate Wench–Frank Shay; 1953 | 3.00 | 6.00 | 9.00 | A |
| 76 | Two Years Before the Mast–Richard Henry Dana | 3.00 | 6.00 | 9.00 | A |
| G77 | Stella and Joe–Lester Cohen; 1953; aka Coming Home | 2.50 | 5.00 | 7.50 | E |
| 78 | Blood Feud–Dave Ricks | 2.50 | 5.00 | 7.50 | W |
| 79 | The Heel–William L. Rohde | 2.50 | 5.00 | 7.50 | E |
| 80 | Beware the Lady–Cornell Woolrich; 1953; aka The Bride Wore Black | 10.00 | 20.00 | 30.00 | E |
| 81 | Texas Fists–Jackson Cole | 3.00 | 6.00 | 9.00 | W |
| 82 | Loves of Goya–Marion Chapman | 2.50 | 5.00 | 7.50 | E |
| 83 | The Bohemian–Jules Koslow | 2.50 | 5.00 | 7.50 | E |
| 84 | Love Camp–Louis-Charles Royer | 6.00 | 12.00 | 18.00 | E |
| 85 | Chinese Lover–Charles Pettit | 3.50 | 7.00 | 10.50 | E |
| G86 | The Spitfires–Beril Becker; 1953; aka Whirlwind in Petticoats | 2.50 | 5.00 | 7.50 | E |
| 87 | Gun-Runners–Jackson Cole | 3.00 | 6.00 | 9.00 | W |
| G88 | The Moonstone–Wilkie Collins | 2.00 | 4.00 | 6.00 | M |
| 89 | She-Devil–Harry Hervey | 3.00 | 6.00 | 9.00 | E |
| 90 | Chicago Woman–Robert O. Saber; aka The Dove | 2.50 | 5.00 | 7.50 | E |
| 91 | Land Grab–Jackson Cole | 3.00 | 6.00 | 9.00 | W |
| 92 | Road Show–Jim Tully | 2.50 | 5.00 | 7.50 | E |
| 93 | Houseboy–Walton Fairbanks | 2.50 | 5.00 | 7.50 | E |
| 94 | Sailor's Leave–Brian Moore | 3.50 | 7.00 | 10.50 | E |
| 95 | Showdown Trail–William Colt MacDonald; aka The Red Rider of Smoky Range | 2.50 | 5.00 | 7.50 | W |
| 96 | Mimi–Robert W. Taylor; 1953 | 2.50 | 5.00 | 7.50 | E |
| 97 | The Big Fake–Murray Forbes; 1953; aka Hollow Triumph | 2.00 | 4.00 | 6.00 | E |
| 98 | The Sea Tyrant–Peter Freuchen | 2.00 | 4.00 | 6.00 | E |
| 99 | There Goes Shorty Higgins–Jack Karney | 2.00 | 4.00 | 6.00 | E |
| 100 | Cellini–Benvenuto Cellini; 1953 | 2.00 | 4.00 | 6.00 | A |
| 101 | Cow Thief–William Colt MacDonald | 2.00 | 4.00 | 6.00 | W |
| 102 | African Mistress–Louis-Charles Royer | 3.00 | 6.00 | 9.00 | E |
| 103 | Backstairs–L.K. Scott | 2.00 | 4.00 | 6.00 | E |
| 104 | Big Mike–Charles Givens; 1953; aka Anchor Money | 2.00 | 4.00 | 6.00 | M |
| 105 | Lesson in Love–Emile Zola; aka Pot-Bouille | 2.00 | 4.00 | 6.00 | E |
| 106 | The Ordeal of Pvt. Heath–Jeb Stuart | 2.00 | 4.00 | 6.00 | |
| 107 | Scandal–Robert W. Taylor; orig. 1954 | 2.00 | 4.00 | 6.00 | E |
| 108 | Texas Tornado–Jackson Cole | 3.00 | 6.00 | 9.00 | W |
| 109 | After Dark–Max White | 2.00 | 4.00 | 6.00 | E |
| 110 | The Redhead from Chicago–Louis-Charles Royer | 2.00 | 4.00 | 6.00 | E |
| 111 | Gun Town–Jackson Cole | 3.00 | 6.00 | 9.00 | W |
| 112 | Hill Man–John Garth | 2.00 | 4.00 | 6.00 | E |
| 113 | Sporting Lady–Gene Gauntier | 2.00 | 4.00 | 6.00 | E |
| 114 | The Harem–Louis-Charles Royer | 2.00 | 4.00 | 6.00 | E |
| 115 | Two-Gun Deputy–William Colt MacDonald | 2.00 | 4.00 | 6.00 | W |

**PYRAMID BOOKS,** *continued*

| # | Title | V/Good | Fine | N/Mint | |
|---|---|---|---|---|---|
| 116 | His Kind of Woman–Michael Morgan | 2.00 | 4.00 | 6.00 | E |
| 117 | Outlawed–Jackson Cole | 3.00 | 6.00 | 9.00 | W |
| 118 | Woman on the Wall–Marshall McClintock | 2.00 | 4.00 | 6.00 | E |
| 119 | The Great Balsamo–Maurice Zolotow | 2.00 | 4.00 | 6.00 | E |
| G120 | The Counsul at Sunset–Gerald Hanley | 2.00 | 4.00 | 6.00 | E |
| 121 | With Sirens Screaming–Ernest Booth | 2.00 | 4.00 | 6.00 | E |
| 122 | I Was a Drug Addict–Leroy Street & David Loth | 4.00 | 8.00 | 12.00 | |
| 123 | Blind Alley–Bant Singer | 2.00 | 4.00 | 6.00 | E |
| 124 | Bullets High–Jackson Cole | 2.50 | 5.00 | 7.50 | W |
| 125 | Bold Moment–Victor H. Johnson; 1954; aka The Horncasters | 2.50 | 5.00 | 7.50 | E |
| 126 | The Junk Pusher–Robert W. Taylor | 3.00 | 6.00 | 9.00 | E |
| G127 | Teen-Age Vice!–Courtney Ryley Cooper | 2.50 | 5.00 | 7.50 | JD |
| 128 | One for the Road–Robert Dietrich | 2.00 | 4.00 | 6.00 | E |
| G129 | Dark Brother–Gerald Gordon | 2.00 | 4.00 | 6.00 | E |
| 130 | A Diary of Love–Maude Hutchins | 2.00 | 4.00 | 6.00 | E |
| 131 | Ex-Con–Stuart Friedman | 2.00 | 4.00 | 6.00 | |
| 132 | Jungle Heat–Dale Wilmer; orig. 1954 | 2.00 | 4.00 | 6.00 | |
| 133 | Pierre's Woman–Jacques de Bout | 2.00 | 4.00 | 6.00 | E |
| 134 | Savage Triangle–Louis-Charles Royer | 2.00 | 4.00 | 6.00 | E |
| 135 | The Cheat–Robert Dietrich | 2.00 | 4.00 | 6.00 | E |
| 136 | Night in Manila–John Langdon | 2.00 | 4.00 | 6.00 | E |
| G137 | The King's Mistress–Jean Plaidy (Victoria Holt) | 2.00 | 4.00 | 6.00 | E |
| 138 | His Father's Wife–Day Keene; orig. 1954 | 5.00 | 10.00 | 15.00 | E |
| 139 | I Was a House Detective–Dev Collans & Stewart Sterling; 1955 | 2.00 | 4.00 | 6.00 | E |
| G140 | Yankee Trader–Stanley Morton | 2.00 | 4.00 | 6.00 | E |
| G141 | The Wild Ones–Vardis Fisher | 2.00 | 4.00 | 6.00 | E |
| G142 | Sweet Man–Gilmore Millen | 2.00 | 4.00 | 6.00 | E |
| 143 | Lovers in the Sun–Robert Payne; orig. 1955 | 2.00 | 4.00 | 6.00 | E |
| 144 | Texas Manhunt–Jackson Cole | 2.50 | 5.00 | 7.50 | W |
| G145 | Cage of Lust–Allan Seager | 2.00 | 4.00 | 6.00 | E |
| G146 | The Heavenly Sinner–Everett Harre | 2.00 | 4.00 | 6.00 | E |
| 147 | For I Have Sinned–Ruth Sachs | 2.00 | 4.00 | 6.00 | E |
| 148 | Roadside Night–Gerry P. Broderick & Erwin N. Nistler | 2.00 | 4.00 | 6.00 | E |
| 149 | The Texan–A. Scott Leslie | 2.50 | 5.00 | 7.50 | W |
| G150 | Devil's Cargo–Si Podolin; 1955 | 2.00 | 4.00 | 6.00 | E |
| 151 | The Proposition–Hunt Collins | 2.00 | 4.00 | 6.00 | E |
| 152 | Just Married | 2.00 | 4.00 | 6.00 | H |
| 153 | Gunsmoke Trail–Jackson Cole | 2.50 | 5.00 | 7.50 | W |
| G154 | Farm Girl–William Brown Meloney | 2.00 | 4.00 | 6.00 | E |
| 155 | Trouble Shooter–Jackson Cole | 2.50 | 5.00 | 7.50 | W |
| 156 | Dangerous Game–anthology. Note: Same cover as magazine Man's Adventure, June 1955 | 2.00 | 4.00 | 6.00 | A |
| G157 | Shriek with Pleasure–Toni Howard | 2.00 | 4.00 | 6.00 | E |
| 158 | Diary of a Nun–Oscar de Mejo | 2.00 | 4.00 | 6.00 | |
| 159 | One Way Street–Nick Marino | 2.00 | 4.00 | 6.00 | |
| G160 | Tell Me, Doctor–Dr. Henry B. Safford | 2.00 | 4.00 | 6.00 | NF |
| G161 | Mademoiselle De Maupin–Theophile Gautier | 2.00 | 4.00 | 6.00 | E |
| 162 | Gun-Blaze–Jackson Cole | 2.50 | 5.00 | 7.50 | W |
| 163 | Bed of Hate–Si Podolin | 2.00 | 4.00 | 6.00 | E |
| 164 | Of a Strange Woman–James Wakefield Burke | 2.00 | 4.00 | 6.00 | E |
| 165 | Town Quarry–Martin Manners | 2.00 | 4.00 | 6.00 | E |
| 166 | French Doctor–Louis-Charles Royer | 2.00 | 4.00 | 6.00 | E |
| 167 | Texas Fury–Jackson Cole | 2.50 | 5.00 | 7.50 | W |
| 168 | Swamp Girl–Evans Wall | 4.00 | 8.00 | 12.00 | E |
| 169 | Shadow at Noon–Harry White (Harry Whittington) | 2.50 | 5.00 | 7.50 | W |
| G170 | Strange Friends–Agnete Holk | 2.00 | 4.00 | 6.00 | E |
| 171 | Two-Gun Devil–Jackson Cole | 2.50 | 5.00 | 7.50 | W |
| 172 | The Range Kid–William Colt MacDonald | 2.00 | 4.00 | 6.00 | W |
| 173 | Brand of Cain–Wade B. Cantrell | 2.00 | 4.00 | 6.00 | W |
| 174 | The Wanton Hour–Lewis Clay | 2.00 | 4.00 | 6.00 | E |
| 175 | Madeleine–anon. | 1.50 | 3.00 | 4.50 | E |
| 176 | Love Off-Limits–Arthur Curtin; 1956 | 1.50 | 3.00 | 4.50 | E |
| G177 | Pere Goriot–Honore de Balzac | 1.50 | 3.00 | 4.50 | |
| 178 | The Texas Terror–Bradford Scott | 2.50 | 5.00 | 7.50 | W |
| 179 | The Shame of Mary Quinn–Clifton Cuthbert | 1.50 | 3.00 | 4.50 | E |
| G180 | The Seed of McCoy–Jack London | 2.00 | 4.00 | 6.00 | A |
| G181 | My Sister, My Bride–Merriam Modell | 1.50 | 3.00 | 4.50 | E |
| 182 | The Owlhoot Trail–Buck Billings | 2.00 | 4.00 | 6.00 | W |

| # | Title | V/Good | Fine | N/Mint | |
|---|---|---|---|---|---|
| 183 | The World's Worst Women–Bernard O'Donnell | 2.00 | 4.00 | 6.00 | E |
| G184 | A Way Home–Theodore Sturgeon (ed. by Groff Conklin) | 2.00 | 4.00 | 6.00 | SF |
| G185 | The Sin Underneath–Bentz Plagemann; aka Into the Labyrinth; aka Downfall | 1.50 | 3.00 | 4.50 | E |
| 186 | Trigger Talk–Bradford Scott | 2.50 | 5.00 | 7.50 | |
| 187 | Gunman's Gold–Johnston McCulley | 1.50 | 3.00 | 4.50 | W |
| R188 | It's Never Too Late to Leave–Anna K. Daniels | 1.50 | 3.00 | 4.50 | |
| G189 | Shadows of Shame–John Taylor | 1.50 | 3.00 | 4.50 | E |
| 190 | Badland's Boss–Bradford Scott | 2.50 | 5.00 | 7.50 | W |
| 191 | Female Convict–as told to Vincent G. Burns | 2.00 | 4.00 | 6.00 | NF |
| 192 | Range Rebel–Gordon D. Shirreffs | 1.50 | 3.00 | 4.50 | W |
| 193 | Taking a Turn for the Nurse–Kaz | 1.50 | 3.00 | 4.50 | H |
| 194 | The Gunhand–Paul Evan Lehman | 1.50 | 3.00 | 4.50 | W |
| 195 | The Six-Gun Syndicate–Norman A. Fox | 1.50 | 3.00 | 4.50 | W |
| 196 | Let's Go Naked–ed. Donald A. Wollheim | 2.50 | 5.00 | 7.50 | H |
| G197 | The Future Mr. Dolan–Charles Gorham | 2.00 | 4.00 | 6.00 | E |
| 198 | Hell and High Water–ed. Michael Dewell | 1.50 | 3.00 | 4.50 | A |
| 199 | Canyon Killers–Bradford Scott | 2.00 | 4.00 | 6.00 | W |
| 200 | The Girl on the Couch–Georgiana Hunter; 1956 | 1.50 | 3.00 | 4.50 | E |
| G201 | Celeste–Rosamond Marshall | 1.50 | 3.00 | 4.50 | E |
| R202 | The House of Madame Tellier–Guy de Maupassant | 1.50 | 3.00 | 4.50 | E |
| 203 | Lynch Law–Paul Evan | 1.50 | 3.00 | 4.50 | W |
| 204 | The Stranger in Boots–A. Scott Leslie | 2.00 | 4.00 | 6.00 | W |
| 205 | Playgirls, U.S.A.–Eddie Davis | 1.50 | 3.00 | 4.50 | |
| G206 | Creep into Thy Narrow Bed–Leonard Bishop | 1.50 | 3.00 | 4.50 | E |
| R207 | Yama, the Hell-Hole–Alexandre Kuprin | 1.50 | 3.00 | 4.50 | E |
| 208 | The Big Gun–James Cavanaugh | 1.50 | 3.00 | 4.50 | W |
| 209 | Gunsmoke over Texas–Bradford Scott | 2.00 | 4.00 | 6.00 | W |
| R210 | Women and Vodka–ed. Mark Merrill | 1.50 | 3.00 | 4.50 | E |
| R211 | Drinkers of Darkness–Gerald Hanley | 1.50 | 3.00 | 4.50 | E |
| G212 | The Other Side of the Street–Shirley Jackson; aka The Road Through the Wall | 2.50 | 5.00 | 7.50 | M |
| G213 | The Miracle of Growth–Arnold Sundgaard | 1.50 | 3.00 | 4.50 | NF |
| G214 | Tomorrow and Tomorrow–Hunt Collins | 1.50 | 3.00 | 4.50 | SF |
| 215 | Houseboy–Walton Fairbanks | 1.50 | 3.00 | 4.50 | E |
| 216 | Outlaw Brand–Tom West | 1.00 | 2.00 | 3.00 | W |
| G217 | The Man from Paris–Louis-Charles Royer | 1.50 | 3.00 | 4.50 | E |
| G218 | Wild Country–Noel M. Loomis | 1.50 | 3.00 | 4.50 | E |
| 219 | The Avenger–Bradford Scott | 2.00 | 4.00 | 6.00 | W |
| 220 | Border Blood–Bradford Scott | 2.00 | 4.00 | 6.00 | W |
| 221 | Pyramid Crossword Book–Jack Luzzatto | 4.00 | 8.00 | 12.00 | NF |
| G222 | The Jealous Mistress–Paul Elbogen | 1.50 | 3.00 | 4.50 | E |
| R223 | The Intimate Problems of Women–Henry B. Safford | 1.25 | 2.50 | 3.75 | NF |
| G224 | The Damned One–Guy des Cars | 1.25 | 2.50 | 3.75 | E |
| 225 | A Gunman Rode North–William Hopson; 1956 | 1.25 | 2.50 | 3.75 | W |
| G226 | Give Me a Little Something–William L. Rohde | 1.25 | 2.50 | 3.75 | E |
| G227 | The Love Makers–Mark Merrill | 1.25 | 2.50 | 3.75 | E |
| G228 | Handwriting Analysis–Dorothy Sara | 1.25 | 2.50 | 3.75 | NF |
| 229 | Bold Moment–Victor H. Johnson; aka The Horncasters | 1.25 | 2.50 | 3.75 | E |
| 230 | Reach for Your Guns–Curtis Bishop | 1.25 | 2.50 | 3.75 | W |
| 231 | Flaming Lead–William Colt MacDonald | 1.25 | 2.50 | 3.75 | W |
| R232 | Woman without Love–Andre Maurois | 1.25 | 2.50 | 3.75 | E |
| G233 | Tillie–David Westheimer | 1.25 | 2.50 | 3.75 | E |
| G234 | Men against the Stars–Martin Greenberg; 1957 | 1.25 | 2.50 | 3.75 | SF |
| 235 | One for the Road–Robert Dietrich | 1.25 | 2.50 | 3.75 | E |
| R236 | The Hearth and the Strangeness–N. Martin Kramer | 1.25 | 2.50 | 3.75 | E |
| R237 | How to Help Your Husband Get Ahead–Mrs. Dale Carnegie | 1.00 | 2.00 | 3.00 | |
| 238 | Dead Man's Trail–Bradford Scott | 1.50 | 3.00 | 4.50 | W |
| G239 | Feud at Five Rivers–Jack April | 1.25 | 2.50 | 3.75 | W |
| G240 | Sex Is Better in College–ed. Henry Boltinoff | 1.25 | 2.50 | 3.75 | H |
| G241 | The Night It Happened–Martin Manners | 1.25 | 2.50 | 3.75 | E |

| | | V/Good | Fine | N/Mint | |
|---|---|---|---|---|---|

| | | V/Good | Fine | N/Mint | |
|---|---|---|---|---|---|
| G242 | Come See Them Die–Harold Hadley | 1.25 | 2.50 | 3.75 | |
| R243 | Death Be Not Proud–John Gunther | 1.25 | 2.50 | 3.75 | |
| G244 | Gone to Texas–ed. Leo Margulies | 1.25 | 2.50 | 3.75 | W |
| 245 | Blood Brand–Larry Lawson | 1.25 | 2.50 | 3.75 | W |
| R246 | Sex and Marriage–Havelock Ellis | 1.25 | 2.50 | 3.75 | NF |
| G247 | The Synthetic Man–Theodore Sturgeon | 1.25 | 2.50 | 3.75 | SF |
| G248 | Tonight It's Me–Robert Schlick | 1.25 | 2.50 | 3.75 | |
| G249 | Sin Street–Dorine Manners | 1.25 | 2.50 | 3.75 | E |
| 250 | The Gun Crasher–William L. Rohde; 1957 | 1.25 | 2.50 | 3.75 | W |
| 251 | Rimrock Raiders–Leslie Scott | 1.50 | 3.00 | 4.50 | W |
| G252 | Teenage Vice!–Courtney Ryley Cooper | 2.00 | 4.00 | 6.00 | JD |
| G253 | Unrepentant Sinners–Louis-Charles Royer | 1.25 | 2.50 | 3.75 | |
| G254 | The Lusty Men–William R. Cox | 1.25 | 2.50 | 3.75 | |
| 255 | Double-Cross Ranch–Stuart Brock | 1.25 | 2.50 | 3.75 | W |
| R256 | Why Can't We Have a Baby?–James Henry Ferguson | 1.25 | 2.50 | 3.75 | |
| R257 | Crescent City–William E. Wilson | 1.25 | 2.50 | 3.75 | |
| 258 | Powder Burn–Bradford Scott | 1.50 | 3.00 | 4.50 | W |
| 259 | Gunhand's Play–Archie Joscelyn | 1.25 | 2.50 | 3.75 | W |
| G260 | The First Time–Chandler Brossard | 1.25 | 2.50 | 3.75 | |
| G261 | I Was a House Detective–Dev Collans & Stewart Sterling | 1.25 | 2.50 | 3.75 | E |
| G262 | Twilight Men–Andre Tellier | 1.25 | 2.50 | 3.75 | |
| G263 | Taboo–James Wakefield Burke | 1.25 | 2.50 | 3.75 | E |
| 264 | Curse of Texas Gold–Bradford Scott | 1.50 | 3.00 | 4.50 | W |
| 265 | Bravo Trail–Eugene Cunningham | 1.25 | 2.50 | 3.75 | W |
| G266 | His Father's Wife–Day Keene | 2.00 | 4.00 | 6.00 | E |
| G267 | The Fourth World–Daphne Athas | 1.25 | 2.50 | 3.75 | |
| G268 | Impossible Greeting Cards–Len Levinson | 1.25 | 2.50 | 3.75 | |
| 269 | Gunsmoke Mesa–Dan James | 1.25 | 2.50 | 3.75 | W |
| G270 | Stairway to Death–Bruno Fischer | 1.25 | 2.50 | 3.75 | M |
| G271 | The Young Punks–ed. Leo Margulies | 4.00 | 8.00 | 12.00 | JD |
| G272 | Georgia Hotel–Scott Laurence | 1.25 | 2.50 | 3.75 | E |
| R273 | Take Off Your Mask–Ludwig Eidelberg | 1.25 | 2.50 | 3.75 | |
| G274 | This Girl for Hire–G.G. Fickling | 3.00 | 6.00 | 9.00 | M |
| G275 | The Fuzzy Pink Nightgown–Sylvia Tate; 1957; movie tie-in | 2.50 | 5.00 | 7.50 | |
| G276 | Thunderbird Trail–William Colt MacDonald | 1.25 | 2.50 | 3.75 | W |
| G277 | The Law Bringers–Bliss Lomax (H.S. Drago) | 1.25 | 2.50 | 3.75 | W |
| G278 | Bitter Love–Dyson Taylor | 1.25 | 2.50 | 3.75 | E |
| R279 | Inherit the Night–Robert Christie | 1.25 | 2.50 | 3.75 | |
| G280 | Yellow Kid Weil–William T. Brannon | 1.25 | 2.50 | 3.75 | B |
| R281 | Gestapo–Edward Crankshaw | 1.25 | 2.50 | 3.75 | |
| 282 | The Texas Hawk–Bradford Scott | 1.50 | 3.00 | 4.50 | W |
| G283 | V.I.P.–William L. Rohde | 1.25 | 2.50 | 3.75 | |
| G284 | The Name Is Chambers–Henry Kane; 1st ed. 1957 | 3.50 | 7.00 | 10.50 | M |
| G285 | All His Women–Daniel Taylor | 1.25 | 2.50 | 3.75 | |
| 286 | Two-Gun Deputy–William Colt MacDonald | 1.25 | 2.50 | 3.75 | W |
| 287 | The Sheriff–Forrest Covington | 1.25 | 2.50 | 3.75 | W |
| G288 | Smoke among the Plains–Vingie Roe | 1.25 | 2.50 | 3.75 | W |
| R289 | I Am Adam–Maxine Kaufman | 1.25 | 2.50 | 3.75 | |
| R290 | Frankenstein–Mary Wollstonecraft Shelley | 1.25 | 2.50 | 3.75 | SF |
| G291 | Isle of the Damned–George John Seaton | 1.25 | 2.50 | 3.75 | |
| G292 | You're Wrong, Delaney–Charles Shaw | 1.25 | 2.50 | 3.75 | M |
| 293 | Death Canyon–Bradford Scott | 1.50 | 3.00 | 4.50 | W |
| 294 | The Range Kid–William Colt MacDonald | 1.00 | 2.00 | 3.00 | W |
| G295 | The Daughter–Arthur Markowitz | 1.00 | 2.00 | 3.00 | |
| G296 | Here's the Answer–Albert Mitchell | 1.00 | 2.00 | 3.00 | |
| G297 | Hospital Doctor–Edward Young | 1.00 | 2.00 | 3.00 | E |
| G298 | Hellflower–George O. Smith | 1.50 | 3.00 | 4.50 | SF |
| G299 | Perfect 36–Ed Spingarn | 1.50 | 3.00 | 4.50 | |
| R300 | Michael Strogoff–Jules Verne; 1957 | 1.00 | 2.00 | 3.00 | A |
| G301 | She-Devil–Harry Hervey | 1.00 | 2.00 | 3.00 | E |
| 302 | Tombstone Showdown–Leslie Scott | 1.50 | 3.00 | 4.50 | W |
| 303 | Blood-Moon Range–Bob Obets | 1.00 | 2.00 | 3.00 | W |
| G304 | The Case of the Attic Lover–Alan Hynd | 1.00 | 2.00 | 3.00 | |
| R305 | Mrs. Parkington–Louis Bromfield; c-Maguire | 1.00 | 2.00 | 3.00 | |
| G306 | Dead Wrong–Larry Holden | 1.00 | 2.00 | 3.00 | |
| 307 | The Hard Men–Roe Richmond; 1958; aka Riders of Red Butte | 1.00 | 2.00 | 3.00 | W |
| 308 | Shootin' Man–Bradford Scott | 1.50 | 3.00 | 4.50 | W |

| | | V/Good | Fine | N/Mint | |
|---|---|---|---|---|---|
| G309 | Yaller Gal–Carolina Lee | 1.50 | 3.00 | 4.50 | E |
| G310 | The Wild Ones–Vardis Fisher | 1.00 | 2.00 | 3.00 | E |
| G311 | Fury with Legs–Gil Lawrence | 1.00 | 2.00 | 3.00 | |
| G312 | Bedlam–Andre Soubiran; c-Maguire | 1.50 | 3.00 | 4.50 | |
| G313 | Flame of the Osage–Fred Grove | 1.00 | 2.00 | 3.00 | W |
| 314 | High Trail–R.D. Whitinger | 1.00 | 2.00 | 3.00 | W |
| G315 | City Limits–Nick Marino | 1.00 | 2.00 | 3.00 | |
| R316 | The Affairs of Casanova–Giacomo Casanova | 1.00 | 2.00 | 3.00 | E |
| G317 | French Doctor–Louis-Charles Royer | 1.00 | 2.00 | 3.00 | E |
| R318 | The Death of Hitler's Germany–Georges Blond | 1.50 | 3.00 | 4.50 | NF |
| 319 | The Blaze of Guns–Bradford Scott | 1.00 | 2.00 | 3.00 | W |
| G320 | Love Camp–Louis-Charles Royer | 1.50 | 3.00 | 4.50 | E |
| G321 | The Hills Beyond–Thomas Wolfe | 1.00 | 2.00 | 3.00 | |
| G322 | Twenty-One–Jack Barry | 1.00 | 2.00 | 3.00 | |
| G323 | Seven Days to Death–J.J. Marric | 1.00 | 2.00 | 3.00 | M |
| G324 | Baseball Stars of 1958–Ray Robinson | 1.50 | 3.00 | 4.50 | S |
| 325 | Naked Spurs–Larry Lawson; 1958 | 1.00 | 2.00 | 3.00 | W |
| G326 | House of Dolls–Ka-Tzetnik | 1.00 | 2.00 | 3.00 | NF |
| G327 | Take My Face–Peter Held (Jack Vance) | 25.00 | 50.00 | 75.00 | M |
| G328 | The Mustard Seed–Vicki Baum | 1.00 | 2.00 | 3.00 | |
| G329 | Hangtree Country–Eric Allen | 1.00 | 2.00 | 3.00 | W |
| R330 | Hitler's Secret Service–Walter Schellenberg | 1.50 | 3.00 | 4.50 | NF |
| G331 | Curve Ball Laughs–Herman L. Masin | 1.00 | 2.00 | 3.00 | H |
| G332 | The Skylark of Space–E.E. "Doc" Smith | 1.25 | 2.50 | 3.75 | SF |
| 333 | Railtown Sheriff–Stuart Brock | 1.00 | 2.00 | 3.00 | W |
| G334 | The Girl on the Couch–Georgiana Hunter | 1.00 | 2.00 | 3.00 | E |
| G335 | Gideon's Night–J.J. Marric | 1.00 | 2.00 | 3.00 | M |
| G336 | Cropper's Cabin–Jim Thompson | 12.50 | 25.00 | 37.50 | |
| G337 | Operation Cicero–L.C. Moyzisch | 1.00 | 2.00 | 3.00 | NF |
| G338 | The Sleeper–Holly Roth | 1.00 | 2.00 | 3.00 | |
| G339 | Who?–Algis Budrys | 1.25 | 2.50 | 3.75 | SF |
| R340 | Brainwashing–Edward Hunter | 1.00 | 2.00 | 3.00 | |
| G341 | Strange Fulfillment–Denys Val Baker | 1.00 | 2.00 | 3.00 | |
| G342 | Never the Same Again–Gerald Tesch | 1.00 | 2.00 | 3.00 | |
| G343 | Bed and Broad–ed. Henry Boltinoff | 1.00 | 2.00 | 3.00 | H |
| G344 | A Gun for Honey–G.G. Fickling | 3.00 | 6.00 | 9.00 | M |
| G345 | Prison Girl–Wenzell Brown; c-Maguire | 2.00 | 4.00 | 6.00 | E |
| G346 | Cartoons for Men Only–Sandy Nelkin | 1.50 | 3.00 | 4.50 | H |
| 347 | The Young Texan–Paul Evan Lehman | 1.00 | 2.00 | 3.00 | W |
| G348 | House of Hate–W. Craig Thomas | 1.00 | 2.00 | 3.00 | |
| G349 | The Lost Combat–Ralph Leveridge | 1.00 | 2.00 | 3.00 | |
| G350 | The Name is Malone–Craig Rice; 1st ed. 1958 | 4.00 | 8.00 | 12.00 | M |
| G351 | 70,000 to 1–Quentin Reynolds | 1.00 | 2.00 | 3.00 | C |
| G352 | Rumble–Harlan Ellison; orig. 1958 | 25.00 | 50.00 | 75.00 | JD |
| G353 | Room to Swing–Ed Lacy; c-Maguire | 1.50 | 3.00 | 4.50 | M |
| G354 | Night Man–Lucille Fletcher & Allan Ullman | 1.00 | 2.00 | 3.00 | E |
| G355 | The Case of the Nameless Corpse–Clarence Budington Kelland | 1.00 | 2.00 | 3.00 | M |
| G356 | Lincoln's Commando–Ralph J. Roske & Charles Van Doren | 1.00 | 2.00 | 3.00 | NF |
| G357 | Mr. Arkadin–Orson Welles; c-Maguire | 1.00 | 2.00 | 3.00 | |
| G358 | Killer Colt–James Woodruff Smith | 1.00 | 2.00 | 3.00 | W |
| G359 | Sidewalk Caesar–Donald Honig | 1.00 | 2.00 | 3.00 | M |
| G360 | The Megstone Plot–Andrew Garve | 1.00 | 2.00 | 3.00 | M |
| G361 | The Scarlet Treasury of Great Confessions–Whit Burnett | 1.00 | 2.00 | 3.00 | |
| G362 | Good Luck to the Corpse–Max Murray | 1.00 | 2.00 | 3.00 | M |
| G363 | The Mad Marshal–William Colt MacDonald | 1.00 | 2.00 | 3.00 | W |
| G364 | The Bad Girls–Bud Clifton | 4.00 | 8.00 | 12.00 | E |
| G365 | All Thy Conquests–Alfred Hayes | 1.00 | 2.00 | 3.00 | |
| G366 | Girl on the Loose–G.G. Fickling | 3.00 | 6.00 | 9.00 | M |
| R367 | My Brother's Bride–William March | 1.00 | 2.00 | 3.00 | |
| G368 | The Man of Cold Rages–Jordan Park (C.M. Kornbluth) | 9.00 | 18.00 | 27.00 | M |
| G369 | Summer Boy–Walter Lowrey | 1.00 | 2.00 | 3.00 | |
| 370 | Thunderbird Range–W.C. Tuttle | 1.00 | 2.00 | 3.00 | W |
| G371 | I Cried in the Dark–Ann Scott | 1.00 | 2.00 | 3.00 | |
| G372 | The Crimson in the Purple–Holly Roth; c-Maguire | 1.25 | 2.50 | 3.75 | |
| G373 | The Fastest Man Alive–Frank K. Everest, Jr & John Guenther | 1.00 | 2.00 | 3.00 | NF |
| G374 | Death Is My Dancing Partner–Cornell Woolrich; orig. 1958 | 10.00 | 20.00 | 30.00 | M |
| G375 | Platoon–Adam Singer; 1958 | 1.00 | 2.00 | 3.00 | C |
| G376 | West of the Pecos–Paul Evan | 1.00 | 2.00 | 3.00 | W |

PYRAMID BOOKS, *continued*

| | | V/Good | Fine | N/Mint | |
|---|---|---|---|---|---|
| G377 | Female Convict–as told to Vincent G. Burns | 1.00 | 2.00 | 3.00 | NF |
| G378 | An Outcast of the Islands–Joseph Conrad; orig. 1959 | 4.00 | 8.00 | 12.00 | |
| G379 | The Spy–Vincent Brome | 1.00 | 2.00 | 3.00 | |
| G380 | These Lonely, These Dead–Robert Colby | 1.00 | 2.00 | 3.00 | |
| G381 | The New Italian Cook Book–Rose L. Sorce | 1.00 | 2.00 | 3.00 | NF |
| G382 | So Soon to Die–Jeremy York | 1.00 | 2.00 | 3.00 | |
| G383 | The Silver Dark–Herbert Clyde Lewis | 1.00 | 2.00 | 3.00 | |
| G384 | Whisper of Love–Fletcher Flora | 1.00 | 2.00 | 3.00 | |
| G385 | The Survivor–John Ehle | 1.00 | 2.00 | 3.00 | |
| G386 | The Young Punks–ed. Leo Margulies | 4.00 | 8.00 | 12.00 | JD |
| G387 | The Dream and the Flesh–Vivian Connell; c-Maguire | 1.00 | 2.00 | 3.00 | |
| G388 | Never Smile at Children–E.T. French | 1.00 | 2.00 | 3.00 | |
| 389 | Gallows Trail–Garth Davis | 1.00 | 2.00 | 3.00 | W |
| G390 | Vera–Robert Scott Taylor | 1.00 | 2.00 | 3.00 | |
| G391 | The Black Orchid–Edward Ronns; movie tie-in | 1.00 | 2.00 | 3.00 | |
| G392 | Baseball Stars of 1959–Ray Robinson | 1.25 | 2.50 | 3.75 | S |
| G393 | The Lost One–Dana Lyon | 1.00 | 2.00 | 3.00 | |
| 394 | How Sharp the Point–P.J. Wolfson; orig. 1959 | 1.00 | 2.00 | 3.00 | W |
| G395 | So Dead, My Lovely–Day Keene; orig. 1959; c-Maguire | 4.00 | 8.00 | 12.00 | M |
| 396 | The Longhorn Brand–Wade Hamilton | 1.00 | 2.00 | 3.00 | W |
| G397 | Off the Beaten Orbit–Judith Merril | 1.25 | 2.50 | 3.75 | SF |
| G398 | Sins of Their Fathers–Marjorie Rittwagen | 1.00 | 2.00 | 3.00 | |
| G399 | The Beauty Makers–Nedda Lamont | 1.00 | 2.00 | 3.00 | |
| G400 | The Husband–Vera Caspary; 1959 | 1.00 | 2.00 | 3.00 | |
| G401 | Five Who Vanished–Robert Levin | 1.00 | 2.00 | 3.00 | |
| G402 | City of Chains–William E. Pettit | 1.00 | 2.00 | 3.00 | |
| 403 | Rimrock Renegade–Wade Hamilton | 1.00 | 2.00 | 3.00 | W |
| G404 | Take Off Your Mask–Ludwig Eidelberg | 1.00 | 2.00 | 3.00 | |
| G405 | Al Capone–John Roeburt | 1.25 | 2.50 | 3.75 | |
| G406 | War Fish–George Grider & Lydel Sims | 1.00 | 2.00 | 3.00 | C |
| G407 | The Affair–Hans Koningsberger | 1.00 | 2.00 | 3.00 | |
| G408 | Hilda, Take Heed–Jeremy York | 1.00 | 2.00 | 3.00 | |
| 409 | Dead in Texas–Bradford Scott | 1.25 | 2.50 | 3.75 | W |
| G410 | The Power Gods–Bud Clifton | 3.00 | 6.00 | 9.00 | JD |
| G411 | Honey in the Flesh–G.G. Fickling | 3.00 | 6.00 | 9.00 | M |
| G412 | The Oracle–Edwin O'Connor; c-Maguire | 1.25 | 2.50 | 3.75 | |
| G413 | The Shame of Mary Quinn–Clifton Cuthbert | 1.00 | 2.00 | 3.00 | E |
| G414 | Born Innocent–Creighton Brown-Burnham | 1.00 | 2.00 | 3.00 | |
| G415 | The Bride Is Much Too Beautiful–Odette Joyeux | 1.00 | 2.00 | 3.00 | |
| G416 | The Falling Torch–Algis Budrys | 1.25 | 2.50 | 3.75 | SF |
| G417 | The Red Lily–Anatole France | 1.00 | 2.00 | 3.00 | |
| R418 | Five Soldiers–Paul Vialar | 1.00 | 2.00 | 3.00 | C |
| R419 | The Divine Passion–Vardis Fisher; c-Maguire | 3.00 | 6.00 | 9.00 | E |
| 420 | Texas Badman–Bradford Scott | 1.25 | 2.50 | 3.75 | W |
| G421 | The Passionate Season–Victor Wolfson | 1.00 | 2.00 | 3.00 | |
| G422 | Mamma's Boarding House–John D. Fitzgerald | 1.00 | 2.00 | 3.00 | |
| G423 | Make Mine Love–Faber Birren | 1.00 | 2.00 | 3.00 | |
| G424 | The Banker's Daughter–Vladimir B. Grinioff | 1.00 | 2.00 | 3.00 | |
| G425 | Acts of Violence–William Kozlenko; 1959 | 1.00 | 2.00 | 3.00 | |
| 426 | The Range Terror–Bradford Scott; orig. 1959 | 1.25 | 2.50 | 3.75 | W |
| G427 | A Really Sincere Guy–Robert Van Riper | 1.00 | 2.00 | 3.00 | |
| G428 | Celeste–Rosamond Marshall | 1.00 | 2.00 | 3.00 | E |
| G429 | Crime Cop–Larry Holden | 1.00 | 2.00 | 3.00 | |
| G430 | That Kind of Woman–Robert Lowry | 1.50 | 3.00 | 4.50 | |
| G431 | One to Grow On–Nathaniel Benchley | 1.00 | 2.00 | 3.00 | |
| G432 | Private Eyeful–Henry Kane; c-Maguire | 1.50 | 3.00 | 4.50 | M |
| R433 | 10,000 Eyes–Richard Collier | 1.00 | 2.00 | 3.00 | |
| G434 | Four for the Future–ed. Groff Conklin | 1.00 | 2.00 | 3.00 | SF |
| 435 | Texas Vengeance–Bradford Scott | 1.25 | 2.50 | 3.75 | W |
| G436 | A Diary of Love–Maude Hutchins | 1.00 | 2.00 | 3.00 | E |
| G437 | Slaughter Street–Louis Falstein | 1.00 | 2.00 | 3.00 | |
| G438 | So Love Returns–Robert Nathan | 1.00 | 2.00 | 3.00 | |
| G439 | The Hoods Ride In–Wenzell Brown | 3.00 | 6.00 | 9.00 | JD |
| G440 | No Nice Girl–Gale Wilhelm | 1.50 | 3.00 | 4.50 | |
| G441 | Seeds of Murder–Jeremy York | 1.00 | 2.00 | 3.00 | |
| 442 | Gun Law–Bradford Scott | 1.25 | 2.50 | 3.75 | W |
| G443 | Dark Violence–Lee Bergman | 1.00 | 2.00 | 3.00 | |
| G444 | Cut Me In–Jack Karney | 1.00 | 2.00 | 3.00 | |
| G445 | But Not for Me–Edward Ronns | 1.00 | 2.00 | 3.00 | |
| G446 | The Magnificent Female–Cecil Saint-Laurent | 1.00 | 2.00 | 3.00 | |
| R447 | Leave Her to Heaven–Ben Ames Williams | 1.00 | 2.00 | 3.00 | |
| G448 | Dead in Bead–Day Keene; orig. 1959 | 4.00 | 8.00 | 12.00 | M |
| G449 | The Future Mr. Dolan–Charles Gorham | 1.00 | 2.00 | 3.00 | |
| G450 | Enemy in Sight–J.E. MacDonnell; 1959 | 1.00 | 2.00 | 3.00 | |
| G451 | Guns between Suns–William Colt MacDonald | 1.00 | 2.00 | 3.00 | W |
| G452 | The Divided Path–Nial Kent | 1.00 | 2.00 | 3.00 | E |
| G453 | Girl on the Prowl–G.G. Fickling | 3.00 | 6.00 | 9.00 | M |
| 454 | Possessed–Anne Chamberlain | 1.00 | 2.00 | 3.00 | |
| 455 | Holster Law–Bradford Scott; orig. 1959 | 1.25 | 2.50 | 3.75 | |
| G456 | Hungry Men–Edward Anderson | 1.00 | 2.00 | 3.00 | |
| G457 | The Big Bedroom–Edward Ronns | 1.00 | 2.00 | 3.00 | |
| G458 | Man of Many Minds–E. Everett Evans | 1.00 | 2.00 | 3.00 | SF |
| R459 | Cookbook of Fabulous Foods for People You Love–Carolyn Coggins | 1.00 | 2.00 | 3.00 | NF |
| G460 | Farm Girl–William Brown Meloney | 1.00 | 2.00 | 3.00 | E |
| G461 | The Long Night–Julian Mayfield | 1.00 | 2.00 | 3.00 | |
| G462 | Fire in My Blood–Lady Newborough; c-Maguire | 1.50 | 3.00 | 4.50 | E |
| G463 | Court Martial–Jack Ehrlich | 1.00 | 2.00 | 3.00 | |
| G464 | Tough Cop–John Roeburt | 1.00 | 2.00 | 3.00 | M |
| G465 | The Loner–James Woodruff Smith | 1.00 | 2.00 | 3.00 | |
| G466 | Rooming House–Berton Roueche | 1.00 | 2.00 | 3.00 | |
| G467 | Gestapo–Edward Crankshaw | 1.00 | 2.00 | 3.00 | |
| G468 | The Woman Racket–Gil Lawrence | 1.00 | 2.00 | 3.00 | |
| G469 | Once More with Feeling–Ann Pinchot; 1960; movie tie-in | 1.00 | 2.00 | 3.00 | |
| G470 | It's Never Too Late to Love–Anna K. Daniels, MD | 1.00 | 2.00 | 3.00 | NF |
| G471 | Dead End–Ed Lacy; aka Be Careful How You Live | 1.00 | 2.00 | 3.00 | M |
| R472 | The Golden Rooms–Vardis Fisher; c-Maguire | 3.00 | 6.00 | 9.00 | A |
| G473 | Frogman!–J.E. MacDonnell | 1.00 | 2.00 | 3.00 | C |
| G474 | Strange Sisters–Fletcher Flora | 1.25 | 2.50 | 3.75 | E |
| G475 | The Pecos Trail–Bradford Scott | 1.25 | 2.50 | 3.75 | W |
| R476 | The King's Mistress–Jean Plaidy (Eleanor Hibbert); aka The Goldsmith's Wife | 1.00 | 2.00 | 3.00 | R |
| R477 | The Wild Ones–Vardis Fisher; aka Dark Bridwell | 1.00 | 2.00 | 3.00 | A |
| G478 | I Always Wanted to Be Somebody–Althea Gibson | 1.00 | 2.00 | 3.00 | S |
| G479 | Sam–Lonnie Coleman | 1.00 | 2.00 | 3.00 | |
| G480 | Space Prison–Tom Godwin; aka The Survivors | 2.50 | 5.00 | 7.50 | SF |
| G481 | Roadside Night–Erwin N. Nistler & Gerry P. Broderick | 1.00 | 2.00 | 3.00 | |
| G482 | The Last Notch–Matthew Gant | 1.00 | 2.00 | 3.00 | W |
| G483 | Women on the Wall–ed. Marshall McClintock | 1.00 | 2.00 | 3.00 | E |
| G484 | The Big Fix–Ed Lacy | 1.00 | 2.00 | 3.00 | M |
| G485 | The New Pyramid Book of Crossword Puzzles–Jack Luzzatto | 2.50 | 5.00 | 7.50 | NF |
| R486 | D-Day–David Howarath | 1.00 | 2.00 | 3.00 | NF |
| G487 | Baseball Stars of 1960–Ray Robinson | 1.25 | 2.50 | 3.75 | S |
| G489 | The Night Is for Screaming–Robert Turner | 1.00 | 2.00 | 3.00 | M |
| G490 | Comanche Crossing–Paul Leslie Peil | 1.00 | 2.00 | 3.00 | W |
| G491 | Old John's Woman–George Milburn; aka Julie | 1.00 | 2.00 | 3.00 | |
| G492 | Gun Gamble–Bradford Scott; aka The Slick-Iron Trail | 1.25 | 2.50 | 3.75 | W |
| G493 | Night Nurse–David Holmes; c-Maguire | 1.50 | 3.00 | 4.50 | R |
| R494 | The Complete Book of Outdoor Cookery–James A. Beard & Helen Evans Brown | 1.50 | 3.00 | 4.50 | NF |
| G495 | Jungle Heat–Wade Miller | 1.00 | 2.00 | 3.00 | M |
| G496 | Fighting Generals–ed. Phil Hirsch | 1.00 | 2.00 | 3.00 | NF |
| G497 | Either Is Love–Elisabeth Craigin | 1.00 | 2.00 | 3.00 | R |
| G498 | Raider's Revenge–Ray Hogan | 1.00 | 2.00 | 3.00 | W |
| G499 | Out of Bounds–Judith Merril; 1960 | 1.25 | 2.50 | 3.75 | SF |
| R500 | Gershwin–Robert Payne | 1.00 | 2.00 | 3.00 | B |

Pyramid G487, Pyramid G529, Python 002-7.

| | | V/Good | Fine | N/Mint | |
|---|---|---|---|---|---|
| **PYRAMID BOOKS,** *continued* | | | | | |
| G501 | The Big Gun–James Cavanaugh | 1.00 | 2.00 | 3.00 | |
| G502 | The Tomorrow People–Judith Merril | 1.25 | 2.50 | 3.75 | SF |
| G503 | House of Dolls–Ka-tzetnik 135633 (Karol Cetynski) | 1.00 | 2.00 | 3.00 | |
| G504 | Dames, Danger, Death–ed. Leo Margulies; 1960 | 2.00 | 4.00 | 6.00 | M |
| G505 | The Faro Kid–Leslie Ernenwein | 1.00 | 2.00 | 3.00 | W |
| G506 | The Love Lush–Vivian Connell; aka Bachelors Anonymous | 1.00 | 2.00 | 3.00 | E |
| G507 | Lone Star Rider–Bradford Scott (Leslie Scott) | 1.25 | 2.50 | 3.75 | W |
| G508 | The Shame of Mary Quinn–Clifton Cuthbert; aka Thunder without Rain | 1.00 | 2.00 | 3.00 | E |
| G509 | The Time of Desire–Louis Charbonneau; aka Nor All Your Tears | 1.00 | 2.00 | 3.00 | |
| G510 | The Mothers–Vardis Fisher | 1.50 | 3.00 | 4.50 | A |
| G511 | Flesh of the Earth–Alexander Campbell | 1.00 | 2.00 | 3.00 | E |
| G512 | Range Justice–Paul Evan Lehman; 1960 | 1.00 | 2.00 | 3.00 | W |
| G513 | The Brass Bed–Fletcher Flora; c-Maguire | 1.25 | 2.50 | 3.75 | E |
| G514 | The Lost World–Sir Arthur Conan Doyle; 1960; movie tie-in | 1.50 | 3.00 | 4.50 | SF |
| G516 | Memoirs of an Assassin– Avner | 1.00 | 2.00 | 3.00 | NF |
| G517 | Pirate Wench–Frank Shay | 1.00 | 2.00 | 3.00 | A |
| R519 | Treasury Agent–The Inside Story–Andrew Tully | 1.00 | 2.00 | 3.00 | NF |
| G520 | Kiss for a Killer–G.G. Fickling; 1960 | 3.00 | 6.00 | 9.00 | M |
| G521 | Town Quarry–Martin Manners | 1.00 | 2.00 | 3.00 | E |
| R522 | The Passion Within–Vardis Fisher | 1.50 | 3.00 | 4.50 | A |
| G523 | Ambush Trail–Bradford Scott | 1.25 | 2.50 | 3.75 | W |
| G525 | Nita's Place–Harry Whittington | 1.25 | 2.50 | 3.75 | E |
| R527 | Darkness and the Deep–Vardis Fisher | 1.50 | 3.00 | 4.50 | A |
| G528 | The Bomb–Fernand Gigon | 1.00 | 2.00 | 3.00 | NF |
| G529 | Payola–Day Keene; 1st ed., 1960 | 4.00 | 8.00 | 12.00 | M |
| G530 | The Incomplete Enchanter–L. Sprague de Camp & Fletcher Pratt | 2.00 | 4.00 | 6.00 | SF |
| G531 | Gunpoint–ed. Leo Margulies; 1960 | 1.25 | 2.50 | 3.75 | W |
| G532 | The Long White Road–Marvin W. Albert | 1.00 | 2.00 | 3.00 | |
| G534 | Hill Man–John Garth | 1.00 | 2.00 | 3.00 | |
| G535 | The Texan–Scott Leslie | 1.25 | 2.50 | 3.75 | W |
| R537 | The Valley of Vision–Vardis Fisher | 1.50 | 3.00 | 4.50 | A |
| G538 | Lover Man–Alston Anderson | 1.00 | 2.00 | 3.00 | |
| G539 | The Big Corral–Al Cody (Archie Joscelyn) | 1.00 | 2.00 | 3.00 | W |
| G540 | The Ghost Raider–Ray Hogan | 1.00 | 2.00 | 3.00 | W |
| R541 | Yama, the Pit–Alexander Kuprin; aka Yama, the Hell Hole | 1.00 | 2.00 | 3.00 | |
| G542 | Guns of the Alamo–Bradford Scott | 1.25 | 2.50 | 3.75 | W |
| G544 | Venus Plus X–Theodore Sturgeon | 1.25 | 2.50 | 3.75 | SF |
| R545 | 70,000 to One–Quentin Reynolds; 1960 | 1.00 | 2.00 | 3.00 | C |
| R546 | My Holy Satan–Vardis Fisher | 1.50 | 3.00 | 4.50 | A |
| G547 | Fatal Journey–Vahé Katcha; aka The Hook; movie tie-in | 1.00 | 2.00 | 3.00 | |
| G548 | The Big Grab–John Trinian | 1.00 | 2.00 | 3.00 | M |
| G549 | Female Convict–as told to Vincent G. Burns; c-Maguire | 1.50 | 3.00 | 4.50 | NF |
| G550 | The Death Dealers–ed. Phil Hirsch | 1.25 | 2.50 | 3.75 | NF |
| G552 | A Woman's Life–Guy de Maupassant | 1.00 | 2.00 | 3.00 | |

| | | V/Good | Fine | N/Mint | |
|---|---|---|---|---|---|
| R553 | The House of Madame Tellier–Guy de Maupassant | 1.00 | 2.00 | 3.00 | |
| G554 | Against the Fall of Night–Arthur C. Clarke | 1.25 | 2.50 | 3.75 | SF |
| R556 | Belafonte–Arnold Shaw; 1960 | 1.25 | 2.50 | 3.75 | B |
| G557 | A Month among the Girls–Maryse Choisy (trans. Lawrence G. Blochman) | 1.00 | 2.00 | 3.00 | NF |
| G558 | Take Off Your Mask–Ludwig Eidelberg, MD | 1.00 | 2.00 | 3.00 | NF |
| G559 | The Lost Europeans–Emanuel Litvinoff | 1.00 | 2.00 | 3.00 | |
| G560 | Dig a Dead Doll–G.G. Fickling | 3.00 | 6.00 | 9.00 | M |
| G561 | Head Nurse–Kathleen Harris | 1.00 | 2.00 | 3.00 | R |
| G562 | French Doctor–Louis-Charles Royer; c-Maguire | 1.50 | 3.00 | 4.50 | E |
| G565 | Perfect 36–Ed Spingarn; c-Maguire | 1.50 | 3.00 | 4.50 | E |
| G566 | The Mobster–John Roeburt | 1.00 | 2.00 | 3.00 | M |
| G568 | Doctors and Lovers–Roy Sparkin | 1.00 | 2.00 | 3.00 | |
| G569 | The Name Is Chambers–Henry Kane | 1.25 | 2.50 | 3.75 | M |
| G570 | Basketball Stars of 1961–William G. Mokray | 1.00 | 2.00 | 3.00 | S |
| G571 | Spy Hunt–Norman Daniels; 1960 | 1.00 | 2.00 | 3.00 | M |
| G573 | Valley of Hunted Men–Bradford Scott | 1.25 | 2.50 | 3.75 | W |
| G574 | In His Steps–Charles M. Sheldon | 1.00 | 2.00 | 3.00 | |
| G575 | Texas Fists–Jackson Cole; 1961 | 1.25 | 2.50 | 3.75 | W |
| R576 | The World, the Flesh and Father Smith–Bruce Marshall | 1.00 | 2.00 | 3.00 | |
| G578 | Journey into Violence–Harry Whittington; 1961 | 1.25 | 2.50 | 3.75 | M |
| G579 | The Insidious Doctor Fu-Manchu–Sax Rohmer; 1961 | 1.25 | 2.50 | 3.75 | A |
| G580 | Diary of a Nun–Oscar DeMejo | 1.00 | 2.00 | 3.00 | |
| G581 | The Stranger from Texas–Allan K. Echols | 1.00 | 2.00 | 3.00 | W |
| G582 | Pyramid Crossword Puzzle Book No. 3–Jack Luzzatto | 2.50 | 5.00 | 7.50 | NF |
| G583 | The War between the Mates–ed. Phil Hirsch | 1.25 | 2.50 | 3.75 | H |
| G584 | The Picture of Dorian Gray–Oscar Wilde | 1.00 | 2.00 | 3.00 | HO |
| G585 | The Death Riders–Jackson Cole; 1961 | 1.25 | 2.50 | 3.75 | W |
| R586 | The Moonstone–Wilkie Collins | 1.00 | 2.00 | 3.00 | M |
| R587 | Dr. Goebbels–His Life and Death–Roger Manvell & Heinrich Fraenkel | 1.00 | 2.00 | 3.00 | NF |
| R588 | How Like a God–Rex Stout | 1.00 | 2.00 | 3.00 | M |
| G589 | Dollar Man–John Turner | 1.00 | 2.00 | 3.00 | M |
| G590 | The Unexpected–ed. Leo Margulies; 1961 | 1.25 | 2.50 | 3.75 | SF |
| G591 | Gunsmoke on the Rio Grande–Bradford Scott | 1.25 | 2.50 | 3.75 | W |
| G592 | The First Time–ed. Chandler Brossard | 1.00 | 2.00 | 3.00 | |
| G593 | All His Women–Daniel Taylor; aka They Move with the Sun | 1.00 | 2.00 | 3.00 | |
| G594 | Border Hell–Jackson Cole | 1.25 | 2.50 | 3.75 | W |
| G595 | The Prisoner of Zenda–Anthony Hope | 1.00 | 2.00 | 3.00 | A |
| G596 | World So Wide–Sinclair Lewis | 1.00 | 2.00 | 3.00 | |
| G597 | The Valley of Vision–Vardis Fisher | 1.50 | 3.00 | 4.50 | A |
| G598 | Medical Nightmares–ed. Phil Hirsch | 1.00 | 2.00 | 3.00 | NF |
| R599 | The Gadfly–Ethel L. Voynich | 1.00 | 2.00 | 3.00 | |
| G600 | Guerrilla Girls–Harry Whittington | 1.50 | 3.00 | 4.50 | E |
| G601 | Tillie–David Westheimer; aka Summer on the Water | 1.00 | 2.00 | 3.00 | |
| G602 | Rangers at Bay–Bradford Scott | 1.25 | 2.50 | 3.75 | W |
| G603 | The Daughter–Arthur Markowitz | 1.00 | 2.00 | 3.00 | |
| G604 | Texas Manhunt–Jackson Cole; 1961 | 1.25 | 2.50 | 3.75 | W |
| G605 | Baseball Stars of 1961–ed. Ray Robinson | 1.25 | 2.50 | 3.75 | S |
| R607 | The Dark Urge–Ludwig Eidelberg, MD | 1.00 | 2.00 | 3.00 | NF |
| R608 | His Great Journey–Manuel Komroff | 1.00 | 2.00 | 3.00 | |
| G609 | Prison Girl–Wenzell Brown | 1.25 | 2.50 | 3.75 | |
| G610 | Smugglers' Brand–Bradford Scott | 1.25 | 2.50 | 3.75 | W |
| G611 | Trigger Law–Jackson Cole | 1.25 | 2.50 | 3.75 | W |
| R612 | Brainwashing–Edward Hunter | 1.00 | 2.00 | 3.00 | NF |
| R613 | Captain Blood–Rafael Sabatini | 1.00 | 2.00 | 3.00 | A |
| R614 | Quintet: Stories by De Maupassant, A. Huxley, Saroyan, Tolstoi, R. Wright | 1.00 | 2.00 | 3.00 | |
| G615 | Orbit Unlimited–Poul Anderson | 1.00 | 2.00 | 3.00 | SF |
| R616 | The Spy–Vincent Brome; aka The Way Back | 1.00 | 2.00 | 3.00 | |
| G617 | The Bad Girls–Bud Clifton | 3.00 | 6.00 | 9.00 | JD |
| G618 | The King of Thunder Valley–Archie Joscelyn | 1.00 | 2.00 | 3.00 | W |

| | | V/Good | Fine | N/Mint | |
|---|---|---|---|---|---|
| **PYRAMID BOOKS,** *continued* | | | | | |
| R619 | It's Never Too Late to Love–Anna K. Daniels, MD | 1.00 | 2.00 | 3.00 | NF |
| R620 | Clark Gable–George Carpozi, Jr | 1.25 | 2.50 | 3.75 | B |
| R621 | The Street–Ann Petry | 1.00 | 2.00 | 3.00 | |
| G622 | Voyage to the Bottom of the Sea–Theodore Sturgeon; TV tie-in | 1.50 | 3.00 | 4.50 | SF |
| G623 | Blood and Honey–G.G. Fickling | 3.00 | 6.00 | 9.00 | M |
| G624 | The Green Rain–Paul Tabori | 1.00 | 2.00 | 3.00 | SF |
| R625 | Concentration Camp–Eugene Heimler; aka Night of the Mist | 1.00 | 2.00 | 3.00 | |
| R628 | The Divine Passion–Vardis Fisher | 1.50 | 3.00 | 4.50 | A |
| R629 | The Island of the Innocent–Vardis Fisher | 1.50 | 3.00 | 4.50 | A |
| R630 | The Night Life of the Gods–Thorne Smith | 1.00 | 2.00 | 3.00 | F |
| R631 | Five Soldiers–Paul Vialar | 1.00 | 2.00 | 3.00 | |
| R633 | The Curve and the Tusk–Stuart Cloete | 1.00 | 2.00 | 3.00 | A |
| R634 | Doctor's Nurse–Gene Harvey; aka A Girl Called Joy | 1.00 | 2.00 | 3.00 | R |
| R635 | Strange Barriers–ed. J. Vernon Shea | 1.00 | 2.00 | 3.00 | |
| G636 | The Synthetic Man–Theodore Sturgeon | 1.00 | 2.00 | 3.00 | SF |
| G637 | Skeleton Trail–Bradford Scott | 1.25 | 2.50 | 3.75 | W |
| G638 | Massacre Canyon–Jackson Cole | 1.00 | 2.00 | 3.00 | W |
| R639 | The Silver Bacchanal–Rene Fulop-Miller | 1.00 | 2.00 | 3.00 | |
| G641 | The Return of Dr. Fu-Manchu–Sax Rohmer | 1.25 | 2.50 | 3.75 | A |
| G642 | 6 x H–Robert A. Heinlein; aka The Unpleasant Profession of Jonathan Hoag | 2.00 | 4.00 | 6.00 | SF |
| G643 | Barbary Devil–Jeffrey Gardner | 1.00 | 2.00 | 3.00 | A |
| G644 | I Was a House Detective–Dev Collans & Stewart Sterling | 1.00 | 2.00 | 3.00 | NF |
| G645 | Border Jumper–Walt Coburn | 1.00 | 2.00 | 3.00 | W |
| R646 | South Sea Tales–Jack London | 1.00 | 2.00 | 3.00 | A |
| R647 | Dark Brother–Gerald Gordon | 1.00 | 2.00 | 3.00 | |
| G648 | Yaller Gal–Caroline Lee | 1.00 | 2.00 | 3.00 | E |
| R649 | 13 Famous Patients–Noah Fabricant, MD | 1.00 | 2.00 | 3.00 | NF |
| R650 | Lesson in Love–Emile Zola | 1.00 | 2.00 | 3.00 | |
| G651 | The Berlin Couriers–James McGovern | 1.00 | 2.00 | 3.00 | |
| R652 | The Endless Road–Roger Treat | 1.00 | 2.00 | 3.00 | |
| G653 | Starlet!–John Turner | 1.00 | 2.00 | 3.00 | E |
| G654 | Tomorrow and Tomorrow–Hunt Collins | 1.00 | 2.00 | 3.00 | SF |
| G655 | To Still the Guns–James Woodruff Smith | 1.00 | 2.00 | 3.00 | W |
| R657 | Intimations of Eve–Vardis Fisher | 1.50 | 3.00 | 4.50 | A |
| G658 | The Planet Strappers–Raymond Z. Gallun | 1.00 | 2.00 | 3.00 | SF |
| X659 | Yoga for Perfect Health–Alain | 1.00 | 2.00 | 3.00 | NF |
| R660 | The Man Who Rode the Thunder–Lt. Col. William H. Rankin | 1.00 | 2.00 | 3.00 | NF |
| R661 | The Grand Duke and Mr. Primm–Lindsay Hardy | 1.00 | 2.00 | 3.00 | |
| G662 | Fighting Eagles–ed. Phil Hirsch; 1961 | 1.00 | 2.00 | 3.00 | NF |
| G663 | Kiss the Tiger–Franklin M. Davis, Jr | 1.00 | 2.00 | 3.00 | |
| G664 | The Raft–Robert Trumbull | 1.00 | 2.00 | 3.00 | A |
| G665 | The Ghoul Keepers–ed. Leo Margulies | 1.25 | 2.50 | 3.75 | HO |
| R667 | Hitler's Heirs–Paul Meskil | 1.00 | 2.00 | 3.00 | NF |
| G670 | Doctors and Sinners–Roy Sparkia | 1.00 | 2.00 | 3.00 | |
| G671 | The Name Is Malone–Craig Rice | 1.25 | 2.50 | 3.75 | M |
| F672 | The Stainless Steel Rat–Harry Harrison | 1.50 | 3.00 | 4.50 | SF |
| F673 | A Way Home–Theodore Sturgeon | 1.00 | 2.00 | 3.00 | SF |
| G674 | Rangeland Guns–Bradford Scott | 1.25 | 2.50 | 3.75 | W |
| F675 | Basketball Stars of 1962–William Mokray | 1.00 | 2.00 | 3.00 | S |
| X676 | The Hills Beyond–Thomas Wolfe; 1961 | 1.00 | 2.00 | 3.00 | |
| R677 | Adam and the Serpent–Vardis Fisher | 1.50 | 3.00 | 4.50 | A |
| R678 | The Van Langeren Girl–Brian Cooper | 1.00 | 2.00 | 3.00 | |
| F680 | The Young Nurses–Harry Whittington | 1.25 | 2.50 | 3.75 | E |
| F681 | Strange Fulfillment–Denys Val Baker | 1.00 | 2.00 | 3.00 | |
| F682 | Naked to the Stars–Gordon R. Dickson | 1.25 | 2.50 | 3.75 | SF |
| G684 | The Desert Killers–Bradford Scott | 1.25 | 2.50 | 3.75 | W |
| R685 | Lawrence of Arabia–Robert Payne | 1.25 | 2.50 | 3.75 | A |
| R686 | A Month among the Men–Maryse Choisy; 1962 | 1.00 | 2.00 | 3.00 | NF |
| F688 | The Hand of Fu Manchu–Sax Rohmer; 1962 | 1.25 | 2.50 | 3.75 | A |
| F689 | Born of Battle–Robert Crane | 1.00 | 2.00 | 3.00 | C |
| F692 | The Glass Cage–Edward Ronns (Edward S. Aarons) | 1.00 | 2.00 | 3.00 | |
| F693 | The Falling Torch–Algis Budrys; 1962 | 1.00 | 2.00 | 3.00 | SF |

| | | V/Good | Fine | N/Mint | |
|---|---|---|---|---|---|
| G694 | Boss of Panamint–Leslie Ernenwein | 1.00 | 2.00 | 3.00 | W |
| F698 | The Haunted Stars–Edmond Hamilton | 1.00 | 2.00 | 3.00 | SF |
| F701 | Cry Shame!–K. Martin | 1.00 | 2.00 | 3.00 | |
| F703 | The Wall around the World–Theodore Cogswell | 1.00 | 2.00 | 3.00 | SF |
| G704 | The Masked Raiders–Bradford Scott | 1.25 | 2.50 | 3.75 | W |
| T706 | The Man in the Iron Mask–Alexandre Dumas | 1.00 | 2.00 | 3.00 | A |
| F709 | Room to Swing–Ed Lacy | 1.00 | 2.00 | 3.00 | M |
| F710 | Baseball Stars of 1962–ed. Ray Robinson | 1.25 | 2.50 | 3.75 | S |
| F711 | Sam–Lonnie Coleman | 1.00 | 2.00 | 3.00 | |
| F712 | House of Evil–John Trinian | 1.00 | 2.00 | 3.00 | |
| G714 | Guns of Bangtown–Bradford Scott | 1.25 | 2.50 | 3.75 | W |
| X716 | Jesus Came Again–Vardis Fisher | 1.25 | 2.50 | 3.75 | |
| F720 | The Name Is Jordan–Harold Q. Masur; 1st ed., 1962 | 3.50 | 7.00 | 10.50 | M |
| F721 | Something for the Boys . . . Girls–ed. Phil Hirsch | 1.25 | 2.50 | 3.75 | H |
| F722 | The Castle of Iron–L. Sprague de Camp & Fletcher Pratt | 1.25 | 2.50 | 3.75 | SF |
| R728 | Topper Takes a Trip–Thorne Smith | 1.25 | 2.50 | 3.75 | F |
| R730 | A Nearness of Evil–Carley Mills | 1.00 | 2.00 | 3.00 | |
| F731 | Steel Shivs–Bernard Sorkin | 4.00 | 8.00 | 12.00 | JD |
| F732 | Venus Plus X–Theodore Sturgeon | 1.00 | 2.00 | 3.00 | SF |
| F733 | Worlds of When–ed. Groff Conklin | 1.00 | 2.00 | 3.00 | SF |
| G734 | Texas Rider–Bradford Scott | 1.25 | 2.50 | 3.75 | W |
| R736 | The Music Man–Meredith Willson; movie tie-in | 1.00 | 2.00 | 3.00 | |
| R737 | The Mad World of Bridge–Jack Olsen | .75 | 1.50 | 2.25 | NF |
| F739 | A Hell of a Woman–Jim Thompson; 1962 | 12.50 | 25.00 | 37.50 | M |
| F740 | The Mask of Fu Manchu–Sax Rohmer | 1.25 | 2.50 | 3.75 | A |
| F742 | Mars Is My Destination–Frank Belknap Long | 1.25 | 2.50 | 3.75 | SF |
| F744 | The Magnificent Female–Cécil Saint-Laurent | 1.00 | 2.00 | 3.00 | |
| G745 | Doom Trail–Bradford Scott | 1.25 | 2.50 | 3.75 | W |
| T746 | Orphans in Gethsemane, Vol. 1–Vardis Fisher | 1.50 | 3.00 | 4.50 | |
| F749 | Just Married–ed. O.T. House | 1.00 | 2.00 | 3.00 | H |
| F750 | The Divorcees–Kay Martin | 1.00 | 2.00 | 3.00 | E |
| F751 | Body of the Crime–Larry Heller | 1.00 | 2.00 | 3.00 | M |
| F752 | The Flesh–Louis-Charles Royer (trans. Lawrence G. Blochman) | 1.00 | 2.00 | 3.00 | E |
| F753 | Five Weeks in a Balloon–Gardner F. Fox; movie tie-in | 2.00 | 4.00 | 6.00 | A |
| T756 | Orphans in Gethsemane, Vol. 2–Vardis Fisher | 1.50 | 3.00 | 4.50 | |
| X758 | Leave Her to Heaven–Ben Ames Williams | 1.00 | 2.00 | 3.00 | |
| F760 | Calling Dr. Dare–Kill–Bob Tupper | 1.25 | 2.50 | 3.75 | H |
| F761 | The Bride of Fu Manchu–Sax Rohmer; 1962 | 1.25 | 2.50 | 3.75 | A |
| F763 | Dome World–Dean McLaughlin | 1.00 | 2.00 | 3.00 | SF |
| F764 | The Skylark of Space–Edward E. "Doc" Smith | 1.00 | 2.00 | 3.00 | SF |
| G765 | Texas Devil–Bradford Scott | 1.25 | 2.50 | 3.75 | W |
| R767 | First Lady–Charlotte Curtis | 1.00 | 2.00 | 3.00 | B |
| X768 | My Brother's Bride–William March; aka The Tallons | 1.00 | 2.00 | 3.00 | |
| F770 | Secret: Hong Kong–Franklin M. Davis, Jr | 1.00 | 2.00 | 3.00 | |
| F771 | War with the Robots–Harry Harrison; 1962 | 2.00 | 4.00 | 6.00 | SF |
| R772 | So Love Returns–Robert Nathan | 1.00 | 2.00 | 3.00 | F |
| G773 | Death Rides the Rio Grande–Bradford Scott | 1.25 | 2.50 | 3.75 | W |
| F774 | Space Prison–Tom Godwin; aka The Survivors | 2.00 | 4.00 | 6.00 | SF |
| F775 | Feud at Five Rivers–Jack April; 1962 | 1.00 | 2.00 | 3.00 | W |
| X777 | Peace like a River–Vardis Fisher; aka The Passion Within | 1.25 | 2.50 | 3.75 | |
| R779 | The Rites of Spring–Soya; aka Seventeen | 1.00 | 2.00 | 3.00 | |
| F782 | The Hands of Love–Maude Hutchins; aka Victorine | 1.00 | 2.00 | 3.00 | R |
| F783 | Brain Twister–Mark Philips | 1.00 | 2.00 | 3.00 | SF |
| F784 | The Caves of Steel–Isaac Asimov | 1.00 | 2.00 | 3.00 | SF |
| F785 | Marked Man–James Woodruff Smith | 1.00 | 2.00 | 3.00 | |
| F786 | Mission of Gravity–Hal Clement | 1.00 | 2.00 | 3.00 | SF |
| R787 | Cleopatra–Jeffrey K. Gardner; 1962 | 1.00 | 2.00 | 3.00 | A |
| R788 | Return to Night–Mary Renault | 1.00 | 2.00 | 3.00 | |

| | | V/Good | Fine | N/Mint |
|---|---|---|---|---|

**PYRAMID BOOKS, continued**

| | | V/Good | Fine | N/Mint |
|---|---|---|---|---|
| F790 | The Naked Flame–Evelyn Cornell | 1.00 | 2.00 | 3.00 |
| F792 | Night Nurse–David Holmes | 1.00 | 2.00 | 3.00 R |
| F793 | A Diary of Love–Maude Hutchins | 1.00 | 2.00 | 3.00 |
| F794 | D-99–H.B. Fyfe | 1.00 | 2.00 | 3.00 SF |
| G796 | Gunsight Showdown–Bradford Scott; 1962 | 1.25 | 2.50 | 3.75 W |
| R798 | Claudia–Rose Franken | 1.00 | 2.00 | 3.00 |
| R800 | Combat Cameraman–Jerry J. Joswick & Lawrence A. Keating | 1.00 | 2.00 | 3.00 NF |
| F802 | Fury with Legs–Gil Lawrence | 1.00 | 2.00 | 3.00 |
| R803 | Crane Eden–Earl Conrad | 1.00 | 2.00 | 3.00 |
| F804 | The Drums of Fu Manchu–Sax Rohmer | 1.25 | 2.50 | 3.75 A |
| F805 | Joyleg–Ward Moore & Avram Davidson | 1.00 | 2.00 | 3.00 SF |
| F806 | The Tomorrow People–Judith Merril | 1.00 | 2.00 | 3.00 SF |
| G807 | Trail of Blood and Bones–Bradford Scott | 1.25 | 2.50 | 3.75 W |
| F808 | Swamp Girl–Evans Wall; aka No-Nation Girl | 1.50 | 3.00 | 4.50 E |
| T810 | The Turnbulls–Taylor Caldwell | 1.00 | 2.00 | 3.00 |
| T811 | The Eagles Gather–Taylor Caldwell | 1.00 | 2.00 | 3.00 |
| F812 | The Power of Positive Drinking–"Norman Lemon Peel" (ed. Phil Hirsch) | 1.00 | 2.00 | 3.00 H |
| R814 | The Art of Seduction–Corrado Pallenberg | 1.00 | 2.00 | 3.00 NF |
| F816 | Farm Girl–William Brown Meloney; aka Rush to the Sun | 1.00 | 2.00 | 3.00 |
| F817 | Lest Darkness Fall–L. Sprague de Camp | 1.25 | 2.50 | 3.75 SF |
| F818 | Orbit Unlimited–Paul Anderson | 1.00 | 2.00 | 3.00 SF |
| G819 | Outlaw Gold–Bradford Scott | 1.25 | 2.50 | 3.75 W |
| G820 | The Young Texan–Paul Evan Lehman | 1.00 | 2.00 | 3.00 W |
| F821 | Man-Crazy Nurse–Peggy Gaddis | 1.00 | 2.00 | 3.00 R |
| R822 | Not Quite Dead Enough–Rex Stout; 1963 (Green Door mystery) | 1.25 | 2.50 | 3.75 M |
| R823 | The Crying Sisters–Mabel Seeley (Green Door mystery) | 1.25 | 2.50 | 3.75 M |
| R824 | The Long Skeleton–Frances Lockridge & Richard Lockridge (Green Door mystery) | 1.25 | 2.50 | 3.75 M |
| R825 | Madam Maigret's Own Case–Georges Simenon (Green Door mystery) | 1.25 | 2.50 | 3.75 M |
| R827 | The Last Combat–Ralph Leveridge; aka Walk on the Water | 1.00 | 2.00 | 3.00 |
| F828 | Woman Doctor–Peter Baldwin | 1.00 | 2.00 | 3.00 R |
| F829 | The Dreaming Earth–John Brunner | 1.00 | 2.00 | 3.00 SF |
| F830 | Out of Bounds–ed. Judith Merril | 1.00 | 2.00 | 3.00 SF |
| G831 | Gundown!–Bradford Scott; 1963 | 1.25 | 2.50 | 3.75 W |
| X832 | My Holy Satan–Vardis Fisher | 1.50 | 3.00 | 4.50 A |
| T834 | The Strong City–Taylor Caldwell | 1.00 | 2.00 | 3.00 |
| X835 | The Valley of Vision–Vardis Fisher; 1963 | 1.50 | 3.00 | 4.50 A |
| F837 | Shadow of Fu Manchu–Sax Rohmer; 1963 | 1.25 | 2.50 | 3.75 A |
| F839 | Bogey Men–Robert Bloch | 3.00 | 6.00 | 9.00 HO |
| F840 | Slave Planet–Laurence M. Janifer | 1.25 | 2.50 | 3.75 SF |
| F841 | Either Is Love–Elisabeth Craigin | 1.00 | 2.00 | 3.00 R |
| G842 | The Hate Trail–Bradford Scott; 1963 | 1.25 | 2.50 | 3.75 W |
| F844 | John Dillinger–Dean Fredericks | 1.00 | 2.00 | 3.00 NF |
| X845 | The Divine Passion–Vardis Fisher; 1963 | 1.25 | 2.50 | 3.75 A |
| R846 | The White God–Theodore Pratt | 1.00 | 2.00 | 3.00 A |
| R847 | Night Train to Paris–Manning Coles (Green Door mystery) | 1.25 | 2.50 | 3.75 M |
| X848 | Oil for the Lamps of China–Alice Tisdale Hobart | 1.00 | 2.00 | 3.00 |
| F850 | Backstairs–L.K. Scott | 1.00 | 2.00 | 3.00 |
| R851 | The Unknown–ed. D.R. Bensen | 1.00 | 2.00 | 3.00 SF |
| F852 | 9 Stories from Men against the Stars–ed. Martin Greenberg | 1.00 | 2.00 | 3.00 SF |
| G853 | The Last Notch–Matthew Gant | 1.00 | 2.00 | 3.00 |
| G854 | Gun Justice–Bradford Scott | 1.25 | 2.50 | 3.75 W |
| R855 | Death on the Prairie: Vol. 1 of the Indian Wars of the West–Paul I. Wellman | 1.25 | 2.50 | 3.75 NF |
| X857 | The Island of the Innocent–Vardis Fisher | 1.50 | 3.00 | 4.50 A |
| F858 | The Island of Fu Manchu–Sax Rohmer | 1.25 | 2.50 | 3.75 A |
| F859 | Waldo and Magic, Inc.–Robert A. Heinlein | 1.00 | 2.00 | 3.00 SF |

| | | V/Good | Fine | N/Mint |
|---|---|---|---|---|
| R860 | Great Tales of Old Russia–ed. David Markson; aka Women and Vodka | 1.00 | 2.00 | 3.00 |
| F862 | The Great Explosion–Eric Frank Russell | 1.00 | 2.00 | 3.00 SF |
| R863 | Strange Friends–Agnele Holk | 1.00 | 2.00 | 3.00 |
| R864 | Summer Boy–Walter B. Lowery; aka Watch Night | 1.00 | 2.00 | 3.00 |
| G865 | Gunsmoke Talk–Bradford Scott | 1.25 | 2.50 | 3.75 W |
| F866 | Rumble–Harlan Ellison | 5.00 | 10.00 | 15.00 JD |
| R867 | Death in the Desert: Vol. 2 of the Indian Wars of the West–Paul I. Wellman | 2.00 | 4.00 | 6.00 NF |
| X868 | The Gentleman–Edison Marshall | 1.00 | 2.00 | 3.00 |
| R869 | The Wild Ones–Vardis Fisher; aka Dark Bridwell | 1.50 | 3.00 | 4.50 |
| R870 | How like a God–Rex Stout | 1.00 | 2.00 | 3.00 M |
| R872 | Gideon's Night–J.V. Marric (Green Door mystery) | 1.25 | 2.50 | 3.75 M |
| R873 | Ming Yellow–John P. Marquand (Green Door mystery) | 1.25 | 2.50 | 3.75 M |
| F874 | The Damned One–Guy Des Cars (trans. Lawrence G. Blochman) | 1.00 | 2.00 | 3.00 |
| F875 | The Impossibles–Mark Phillips | 1.00 | 2.00 | 3.00 SF |
| G876 | Bullets for a Ranger–Bradford Scott | 1.25 | 2.50 | 3.75 W |
| R877 | Two–Eric Jourdan | 1.00 | 2.00 | 3.00 |
| T878 | The Balance Wheel–Taylor Caldwell | 1.00 | 2.00 | 3.00 |
| T879 | Melissa–Taylor Caldwell | 1.00 | 2.00 | 3.00 |
| R881 | Husbands and Wives–Somerset Maugham | 1.00 | 2.00 | 3.00 |
| R883 | Intimations of Eve–Vardis Fisher | 1.50 | 3.00 | 4.50 A |
| R884 | Voyage into Violence–Frances Lockridge & Richard Lockridge (Green Door mystery) | 1.25 | 2.50 | 3.75 M |
| F886 | The Earth War–Mack Reynolds; 1963 | 1.00 | 2.00 | 3.00 SF |
| F887 | City Limits–Nick Marino | 1.00 | 2.00 | 3.00 |
| G888 | The Rattlesnake Bandit–Bradford Scott; aka Corpse and Cartridge | 1.25 | 2.50 | 3.75 W |
| G889 | The Texas Hawk–Bradford Scott; 1963 | 1.25 | 2.50 | 3.75 W |
| N891 | Dynasty of Death–Taylor Caldwell | 1.00 | 2.00 | 3.00 |
| R893 | The Sky and the Forest–Cecil S. Forester | 1.00 | 2.00 | 3.00 |
| R894 | Too Many Cooks–Rex Stout (Green Door mystery) | 1.25 | 2.50 | 3.75 M |
| R895 | The Fingerprint–Patricia Wentworth (Green Door mystery) | 1.25 | 2.50 | 3.75 M |
| R896 | Great Tales of City Dwellers–ed. Alex Austin | 1.00 | 2.00 | 3.00 |
| F897 | Roadside Night–Erwin N. Nistler & Gerry P. Broderick | 1.00 | 2.00 | 3.00 |
| F898 | The Million Cities–J.T. McIntosh | 1.00 | 2.00 | 3.00 SF |
| F899 | Three in One–ed. Leo Margulies | 1.00 | 2.00 | 3.00 SF |
| F900 | The Stranger in Boots–A. Scott Leslie | 1.25 | 2.50 | 3.75 W |
| G901 | Rustlers' Guns–Bradford Scott | 1.25 | 2.50 | 3.75 W |
| F902 | Fighting Generals–ed. W. Phil Hirsch | 1.00 | 2.00 | 3.00 NF |
| X903 | I Learned about Women from Them–Virgil G. Damon, MD & Isabella Taves | 1.00 | 2.00 | 3.00 NF |
| T904 | Three Loves–A.J. Cronin | 1.00 | 2.00 | 3.00 |
| T905 | The Wide House–Taylor Caldwell | 1.00 | 2.00 | 3.00 |
| R906 | Dark Death–Anthony Gilbert; aka Black Death (Green Door mystery) | 1.00 | 2.00 | 3.00 M |
| F908 | The Insidious Dr. Fu Manchu–Sax Rohmer | 1.25 | 2.50 | 3.75 A |
| F909 | Supermind–Mark Philips | 1.00 | 2.00 | 3.00 SF |
| F910 | 6 x H–Robert A. Heinlein; aka The Unpleasant Profession of Jonathan Hoag | 1.25 | 2.50 | 3.75 SF |
| G911 | Killer's Doom–Bradford Scott | 1.25 | 2.50 | 3.75 W |
| R912 | Behind Enemy Lines–James Dean Sanderson | 1.00 | 2.00 | 3.00 NF |
| F913 | Football Stars of 1963–Barry Gottehrer | 1.00 | 2.00 | 3.00 S |
| T916 | Hatter's Castle–A.J. Cronin | 1.00 | 2.00 | 3.00 |
| R917 | Black Orchids–Rex Stout (Green Door mystery) | 1.25 | 2.50 | 3.75 M |
| R918 | McCall's Guide to Teenage Beauty and Glamour–Betsy Keiffer | 1.00 | 2.00 | 3.00 NF |
| R919 | The League of Frightened Men–Rex Stout (Green Door mystery) | 1.00 | 2.00 | 3.00 M |
| R920 | Proof of the Pudding–Phoebe Atwood Taylor (Green Door mystery) | 1.00 | 2.00 | 3.00 M |
| R921 | The Young Punks–ed. Leo Margulies; 1963 | 3.00 | 6.00 | 9.00 JD |
| R922 | Celebration of Fools–Lawrence Hughes | 1.00 | 2.00 | 3.00 |
| F923 | The Fury of Earth–Dean McLaughlin | 1.00 | 2.00 | 3.00 SF |

## PYRAMID BOOKS, *continued*

| | | V/Good | Fine | N/Mint | |
|---|---|---|---|---|---|
| F924 | Skylark Three–Edward E. "Doc" Smith | 1.25 | 2.50 | 3.75 | SF |
| F925 | Any Number Can Win–John Trinian; aka The Big Grab | 1.00 | 2.00 | 3.00 | M |
| G926 | Death's Corral–Bradford Scott | 1.25 | 2.50 | 3.75 | W |
| F927 | Railtown Sheriff–Stuart Brock | 1.00 | 2.00 | 3.00 | W |
| R928 | The Hurricane–Charles Nordhoff & James Norman Hall | 1.00 | 2.00 | 3.00 | A |
| T929 | There Was a Time–Taylor Caldwell | 1.00 | 2.00 | 3.00 | |
| R930 | Rogue Male–Geoffrey Household | 1.00 | 2.00 | 3.00 | M |
| R931 | Some Buried Caesar–Rex Stout (Green Door mystery) | 1.25 | 2.50 | 3.75 | M |
| R932 | Death at Deep End–Patricia Wentworth; aka Anna, Where Are You? (Green Door mystery) | 1.25 | 2.50 | 3.75 | M |
| F933 | Raiders from the Rings–Alan E. Nourse | 1.00 | 2.00 | 3.00 | SF |
| T934 | The Whole Truth and Nothing But–Hedda Hopper & James Brough | 1.00 | 2.00 | 3.00 | NF |
| R936 | The General's Wench–Rosamond Marshall | 1.00 | 2.00 | 3.00 | |
| F938 | Town Quarry–Martin Manners | 1.00 | 2.00 | 3.00 | |
| G939 | Ranger's Revenge–Bradford Scott | 1.25 | 2.50 | 3.75 | W |
| F940 | Six-Gun Syndicate–Norman A. Fox | 1.00 | 2.00 | 3.00 | W |
| F941 | Man of Two Worlds–Raymond F. Jones; aka Renaissance | 1.00 | 2.00 | 3.00 | SF |
| R942 | Fifth Wife–Vincent Gowen; aka Sun and Moon | 1.00 | 2.00 | 3.00 | |
| R943 | Castle Garac–Nicholas Monsarrat | 1.00 | 2.00 | 3.00 | |
| R944 | Fellow Passenger–Geoffrey Household | 1.00 | 2.00 | 3.00 | M |
| F945 | Basketball Stars 1964–William G. Mokray | 1.00 | 2.00 | 3.00 | S |
| F946 | President Fu Manchu–Sax Rohmer | 1.25 | 2.50 | 3.75 | A |
| R947 | Gideon's Week–J.J. Marric; aka Seven Days to Death (Green Door mystery) | 1.25 | 2.50 | 3.75 | M |
| F948 | Skylark of Valeron–Edward E. "Doc" Smith; 1963 | 1.25 | 2.50 | 3.75 | SF |
| R949 | Sgt. Corbin's War–Robert Crane | 1.00 | 2.00 | 3.00 | C |
| R950 | Swords and Sorcery–ed. L. Sprague de Camp; c-Finlay | 2.50 | 5.00 | 7.50 | F |
| G951 | Outlaw Land–Bradford Scott | 1.25 | 2.50 | 3.75 | W |
| F952 | Sundown Jim–Ernest Haycox | 1.00 | 2.00 | 3.00 | W |
| G953 | Showdown at Skull Canyon–Bradford Scott | 1.25 | 2.50 | 3.75 | W |
| T954 | The Officer Factory–Hans Hellmut Kirst | 1.00 | 2.00 | 3.00 | C |
| R955 | The Strange and the Damned–Denys Val Baker | 1.00 | 2.00 | 3.00 | |
| R956 | Without Armor–James Hilton | 1.00 | 2.00 | 3.00 | |
| R957 | Arabesque–Geoffrey Household | 1.00 | 2.00 | 3.00 | M |
| R960 | Over My Dead Body–Rex Stout (Green Door mystery) | 1.25 | 2.50 | 3.75 | M |
| R961 | Experiment Perilous–Margaret Carpenter (Green Door mystery) | 1.25 | 2.50 | 3.75 | M |
| R962 | The Unknown Five–ed. D.R. Bensen | 1.00 | 2.00 | 3.00 | SF |
| F963 | The Wonder War–Laurence M. Janifer; 1964 | 1.00 | 2.00 | 3.00 | SF |
| F964 | West of the Pecos–Paul Evan (Paul Evan Lehman); 1964 | 1.00 | 2.00 | 3.00 | W |
| R966 | Duchess Hotspur–Rosamond Marshall | 1.00 | 2.00 | 3.00 | |
| R967 | A Rough Shoot–Geoffrey Household; 1964 | 1.00 | 2.00 | 3.00 | M |
| X968 | The Green Bay Tree–Louis Bromfield | 1.00 | 2.00 | 3.00 | |
| R969 | Octagon House–Phoebe Atwood Taylor (Green Door mystery) | 1.25 | 2.50 | 3.75 | M |
| R970 | Fer-de-lance–Rex Stout; 1964 (Green Door mystery) | 1.25 | 2.50 | 3.75 | M |
| F971 | The Secret War–Norman Daniels | 1.00 | 2.00 | 3.00 | |
| F972 | Nita's Place–Harry Whittington | 1.00 | 2.00 | 3.00 | E |
| F973 | Dimension 4–ed. Groff Conklin | 1.00 | 2.00 | 3.00 | SF |
| F974 | Sturgeon in Orbit–Theodore Sturgeon | 1.00 | 2.00 | 3.00 | SF |
| G975 | Guns for Hire–Bradford Scott | 1.25 | 2.50 | 3.75 | W |
| F976 | The Faro Kid–Leslie Ernenwein | 1.00 | 2.00 | 3.00 | W |
| R977 | The Street–Ann Petry | 1.00 | 2.00 | 3.00 | |
| R978 | The Great Snow–Henry Morton Robinson | 1.00 | 2.00 | 3.00 | |
| R979 | A Time to Kill–Geoffrey Household | 1.00 | 2.00 | 3.00 | M |
| R981 | Jane Hadden–Rosamond Marshall | 1.00 | 2.00 | 3.00 | |
| R982 | Celeste–Rosamond Marshall | 1.00 | 2.00 | 3.00 | |
| R983 | The Red Box–Rex Stout (Green Door mystery) | 1.25 | 2.50 | 3.75 | |
| R984 | A Case for Mr. Crook–Anthony Gilbert (Green Door mystery) | 1.00 | 2.00 | 3.00 | M |
| R985 | Lovers in the Sun–Robert Payne | 1.00 | 2.00 | 3.00 | |

| | | V/Good | Fine | N/Mint | |
|---|---|---|---|---|---|
| F986 | Regan's Planet–Robert Silverberg | 1.00 | 2.00 | 3.00 | SF |
| F987 | Doctor to the Stars–Murray Leinster | 1.00 | 2.00 | 3.00 | SF |
| F988 | The Ghost Trail–Bradford Scott | 1.25 | 2.50 | 3.75 | W |
| F989 | Boss of Panamint–Leslie Ernenwein; 1964 | 1.00 | 2.00 | 3.00 | W |
| R1200 | A Cellarful of Noise–Brian Epstein; 1965 | 5.00 | 10.00 | 15.00 | NF |

# PYRAMID ROYAL (PR/PG-SERIES)

## Pyramid Books

### (Some Pyramid Royal editions are part of regular Pyramid series.)

| | | V/Good | Fine | N/Mint | |
|---|---|---|---|---|---|
| PR10 | The Compact Bible; 1956 | 1.00 | 2.00 | 3.00 | |
| PR11 | The Moonstone–Wilkie Collins; 1958 | .75 | 1.50 | 2.25 | M |
| PR12 | Two Years Before the Mast–Richard Henry Dana | .75 | 1.50 | 2.25 | A |
| PG13 | The Sky Block–Steve Frazee | 1.50 | 3.00 | 4.50 | SF |
| PR14 | I Married a Hunter–Marjorie Michael | .75 | 1.50 | 2.25 | |
| PR15 | The Lost World–Arthur Conan Doyle | 1.25 | 2.50 | 3.75 | SF |
| PR16 | The Scarlet Pimpernel–Baroness Orczy | 1.25 | 2.50 | 3.75 | A |
| PG17 | Go, Man, Go–Edgar Williams & Dave Zinkoff | 1.00 | 2.00 | 3.00 | |
| PG18 | Sports Laughs–Herman L. Masin | .75 | 1.50 | 2.25 | H |
| PR19 | It's Never Too Late to Love–Anna K. Daniels; 1959 | .75 | 1.50 | 2.25 | |
| PR20 | The Dog Who Wouldn't Be–Farley Mowat | 1.00 | 2.00 | 3.00 | |
| PR21 | Pere Goriot–Honore de Balzac | .75 | 1.50 | 2.25 | |
| PR22 | The Miracle of Growth–Arnold Sundgaard | .50 | 1.00 | 1.50 | NF |
| PR23 | Handwriting Analysis–Dorothy Sara | .75 | 1.50 | 2.25 | NF |
| PG24 | Daughter of the Gold Rush–Corey Ford & Klondy Nelson | .75 | 1.50 | 2.25 | |
| PR25 | Lady Chatterley's Lover–D.H. Lawrence | .75 | 1.50 | 2.25 | |
| PG26 | At Home in India–Cynthia Bowles | .75 | 1.50 | 2.25 | |
| PG28 | Big Doc's Girl–Mary Medearis; 1960 | .50 | 1.00 | 1.50 | R |
| PG29 | Mutts, Mongrels, Mischief–eds. William B. Coates & Bernard Seeman | .75 | 1.50 | 2.25 | |
| PR30 | How to Live with Diabetes–Henry Dolger, MD | .50 | 1.00 | 1.50 | NF |
| PR31 | An Outcast of the Islands–Joseph Conrad | 1.00 | 2.00 | 3.00 | |
| SPR32 | The Three Musketeers–Alexandre Dumas; 1960 | .75 | 1.50 | 2.25 | A |
| PG33 | The Scarlet Pimpernel–Baroness Orczy | .75 | 1.50 | 2.25 | A |
| PG34 | Not Death, But Love–Constance Buel Burnett; 1960 | .75 | 1.50 | 2.25 | B |
| PR35 | Man into Space–Martin Caidin; 1961 | .75 | 1.50 | 2.25 | NF |
| PR36 | Selected Stories of Bret Harte | .75 | 1.50 | 2.25 | W |
| T37 | An Age of Kings–William Shakespeare; TV tie-in | .75 | 1.50 | 2.25 | |
| PR39 | Your Health and Chiropractic–Thorp McClusky | .75 | 1.50 | 2.25 | NF |
| PR41 | Let's Twist!–George Carpozi, Jr | .75 | 1.50 | 2.25 | NF |
| PF42 | Miss Peach–Mell; 1962 | 1.00 | 2.00 | 3.00 | H |
| PF43 | Baseball Stars of 1963–ed. Ray Robinson; 1963 | 1.00 | 2.00 | 3.00 | S |

# PYRAMID STUDENT EDITION

## Pyramid Books, Inc.

| | | V/Good | Fine | N/Mint | |
|---|---|---|---|---|---|
| nn | Battle Hymn–Dean E. Hess; 1959 | .75 | 1.50 | 2.25 | C |

# PYTHON

## Python Publishing Group

| | | V/Good | Fine | N/Mint | |
|---|---|---|---|---|---|
| 002-7 | Legend in Blue Steel–Spider Page (Norvell Page); 1st ed. 1979; c-Gross. Note: Unpublished Spider novel from 1943 that was published with character renamed Blue Steel | 2.50 | 5.00 | 7.50 | A |

## QUARTER BOOKS

## Magazine Village, Inc./Astro Distributing Corp.

### Digest Size
### (See also Astro)

| | | V/Good | Fine | N/Mint | |
|---|---|---|---|---|---|
| 14 | Pleasure Girl–Luther Gordon | 4.00 | 8.00 | 12.00 | E |
| 17 | Sinful–James Clayford (Peggy Gaddis) | 4.00 | 8.00 | 12.00 | E |
| 19 | Bed Time Girl–James Clayford (Peggy Gaddis) | 4.00 | 8.00 | 12.00 | E |
| 20 | Fighting Horse Valley–Murray Leinster; aka Texas Gun Slinger | 5.00 | 10.00 | 15.00 | W |
| 21 | Shamed–Luther Gordon; aka Made for Love; c-Rodewald | 4.00 | 8.00 | 12.00 | E |
| 22 | Unfaithful–Luther Gordon | 4.00 | 8.00 | 12.00 | E |
| 23 | Texas Gun Law–Murray Leinster; aka Black Sheep | 5.00 | 10.00 | 15.00 | W |
| 24 | Passion's Mistress–Luther Gordon; c-Rodewald | 4.00 | 8.00 | 12.00 | E |
| 25 | Wanted Dead or Alive–Murray Leinster; aka Outlaw Guns | 5.00 | 10.00 | 15.00 | W |
| 26 | Respectable Harlot–James Clayford (Peggy Gaddis); aka Unfaithful; c-Rodewald | 4.00 | 8.00 | 12.00 | E |
| 27 | Sinful!–James Clayford (Peggy Gaddis); aka Love Runs Away | 4.00 | 8.00 | 12.00 | E |
| 28 | Lure for Love–James Clayford (Peggy Gaddis); aka Nine O'Clock Parade; c-Gross | 4.00 | 8.00 | 12.00 | E |
| 29 | Immoral!–Luther Gordon; aka The Naked Escape; c-Gross | 4.00 | 8.00 | 12.00 | E |
| 30 | Marriage Can Wait | 4.00 | 8.00 | 12.00 | E |
| 31 | Wicked–Luther Gordon | 4.00 | 8.00 | 12.00 | E |
| 32 | Careless–James Clayford (Peggy Gaddis); c-Gross | 4.00 | 8.00 | 12.00 | E |
| 33 | Naughty Virgin–Luther Gordon; aka Women Are Freight | 4.00 | 8.00 | 12.00 | E |
| 34 | Pleasure Girl–Luther Gordon | 4.00 | 8.00 | 12.00 | E |
| 35 | Ecstasy–Luther Gordon | 4.00 | 8.00 | 12.00 | E |
| 36 | Tempted–Luther Gordon; aka Pleasure Girl; c-Rodewald | 4.00 | 8.00 | 12.00 | E |
| 37 | Love Cheat–Luther Gordon; aka Love Is No Sin; c-Gross | 6.00 | 12.00 | 18.00 | E |
| 38 | Wolf Trap Blonde–Luther Gordon; aka Marriage Agency; 1949; c-Gross | 4.00 | 8.00 | 12.00 | E |
| 39 | Frenchy–Harmon Bellamy | 5.00 | 10.00 | 15.00 | E |
| 40 | Night of Passion–John Caldwall; aka Bedmates | 4.00 | 8.00 | 12.00 | E |
| 41 | Pick-Up–Harmon Bellamy; aka Sacrifice; c-Gross | 5.00 | 10.00 | 15.00 | E |
| 42 | Midnight Sinner–John Caldwall | 4.00 | 8.00 | 12.00 | E |
| 43 | Vera Is a Tramp–Gerald Foster | 4.00 | 8.00 | 12.00 | E |
| 44 | Bad Woman–Russell Higgins; 1949 | 4.00 | 8.00 | 12.00 | E |
| 45 | Hot Number–Ross Sloane; aka Beach Brat | 4.00 | 8.00 | 12.00 | E |
| 46 | Call Girl–Gail Jordan (Perry Gaddis); aka Passion for Profit | 4.00 | 8.00 | 12.00 | E |
| 47 | Sin Child–Norman Bligh; 1949 | 4.00 | 8.00 | 12.00 | E |
| 48 | As Good As Married–Peggy Lindsay (Peggy Gaddis); c-Gross | 4.00 | 8.00 | 12.00 | E |
| 49 | The Intimate Affairs of a Burlesque Queen–R. Higgins; aka Burlesque Queen | 4.00 | 8.00 | 12.00 | E |
| 50 | Overnight Blonde–Charles E. Colohan; aka Big Blonde | 4.00 | 8.00 | 12.00 | E |
| 51 | Wild Passion–Watkins E. Wright | 4.00 | 8.00 | 12.00 | E |
| 52 | Everyone Loves Irene–Wright Williams | 4.00 | 8.00 | 12.00 | E |
| 52 | Three Naked Souls–Ron Sloane | 4.00 | 8.00 | 12.00 | E |
| 53 | Virgin No More–Charles E. Colohan | 4.00 | 8.00 | 12.00 | E |
| 54 | Illicit Desires–H.M. Appel; aka The Farmer's Daughter; c-Gross | 4.00 | 8.00 | 12.00 | E |
| 55 | Wedding Night Confession–James Clayford (Peggy Gaddis) | 4.00 | 8.00 | 12.00 | E |
| 56 | Bedtime Blonde–John Wilstach | 4.00 | 8.00 | 12.00 | E |
| 57 | The Virgin and the Barfly–Gerald Foster | 4.00 | 8.00 | 12.00 | E |
| 58 | Margie Is for Loving–Watkins E. Wright | 4.00 | 8.00 | 12.00 | E |
| 60 | Room and Dame–Gerald Foster | 4.00 | 8.00 | 12.00 | E |
| 61 | Careless Virgin–James Clayford (Peggy Gaddis); c-Rodewald | 4.00 | 8.00 | 12.00 | E |
| 62 | Everyone Loves Irene–Wright Williams; c-Gross | 4.00 | 8.00 | 12.00 | E |
| 63 | One Night with Diane–H. Jones | 4.00 | 8.00 | 12.00 | E |
| 64 | Bed Time Girl–James Clayford (Peggy Gaddis) | 4.00 | 8.00 | 12.00 | E |
| 65 | Passionate Pick-Up–Doug Duperault; c-Gross | 4.00 | 8.00 | 12.00 | E |
| 66 | Flesh and Females–Harmon Bellamy; aka The Transgressors | 4.00 | 8.00 | 12.00 | E |
| 67 | Shamed–Luther Gordon; aka Made For Love, c-Rodewald | 4.00 | 8.00 | 12.00 | E |
| 68 | Marriage Can Wait–James Clayford (Peggy Gaddis); aka Eve in the Garden | 4.00 | 8.00 | 12.00 | E |
| 69 | Illicit Wife–James Clayford (Peggy Gaddis); aka Respectable? Note: Same cover as Astro No. 15 | 4.00 | 8.00 | 12.00 | E |
| 70 | Naughty Virgin–Luther Gordon; aka Women Are Freight | 4.00 | 8.00 | 12.00 | E |
| 71 | Passion's Mistress–Luther Gordon; aka Pure Girl | 4.00 | 8.00 | 12.00 | E |
| 72 | Respectable Harlot–James Clayford (Peggy Gaddis); aka Unfaithful | 4.00 | 8.00 | 12.00 | E |
| 73 | Love Life of a Hollywood Mistress–Florence Stonebraker; orig. 1950 | 4.00 | 8.00 | 12.00 | E |
| 74 | "Leg Art" Virgin–Gene Harrey; orig. 1950 | 4.00 | 8.00 | 12.00 | E |
| 75 | Sins of Allie May–Albert L. Quandt | 4.00 | 8.00 | 12.00 | E |
| 76 | Quickie–Gerald Foster | 4.00 | 8.00 | 12.00 | E |
| 77 | Red-Light Babe–Doug Duperault; orig. 1950 | 4.00 | 8.00 | 12.00 | E |
| 78 | Waterfront Hotel–Norman Bligh | 4.00 | 8.00 | 12.00 | E |
| 79 | Bad Sue–Norman Bligh | 4.00 | 8.00 | 12.00 | E |
| 80 | Frisco Dame–Florence Stonebraker | 4.00 | 8.00 | 12.00 | E |
| 81 | Fast, Loose, and Lovely–Norman Bligh | 4.00 | 8.00 | 12.00 | E |
| 82 | Illicit Pleasure–Peggy Gaddis | 4.00 | 8.00 | 12.00 | E |
| 83 | Four Men and a Dame–Florence Stonebraker | 4.00 | 8.00 | 12.00 | E |
| 84 | Born to Be Bad–Norman Bligh | 4.00 | 8.00 | 12.00 | E |
| 85 | The Flesh Is Weak–Florence Stonebraker | 4.00 | 8.00 | 12.00 | E |
| 86 | Girl on the Make!–Joan Sherman (Peggy Gaddis) | 4.00 | 8.00 | 12.00 | E |
| 87 | Ticket to Passion–Albert L. Quandt | 4.00 | 8.00 | 12.00 | E |
| 88 | Untamed Woman–Amos Hatter | 4.00 | 8.00 | 12.00 | E |
| 89 | The Lady Is Taboo–Norman Bligh; orig. 1951; c-Gross | 4.00 | 8.00 | 12.00 | E |
| 90 | Flirting Eyes–Florence Stonebraker; orig. 1951 | 4.00 | 8.00 | 12.00 | E |
| 91 | Street Girl–Albert L. Quandt | 4.00 | 8.00 | 12.00 | E |
| 92 | Three Men and a Mistress–Florence Stonebraker | 4.00 | 8.00 | 12.00 | E |
| 93 | Thrill Me Suzy–Joan Sherman (Peggy Gaddis) | 4.00 | 8.00 | 12.00 | E |
| 94 | Confessions of an Artist's Model–Norman Bligh; c-Gross | 4.00 | 8.00 | 12.00 | E |
| 95 | Diary of a Pleasure Cruise–Anthony Scott; aka Stolen Sins | 4.00 | 8.00 | 12.00 | E |
| 96 | Confessions of a Dime a Dance Queen–Doug Dupperault | 4.00 | 8.00 | 12.00 | E |

## QUICK READER

## Royce Publishers

### Small Size–3″ x 4¾

| | | V/Good | Fine | N/Mint | |
|---|---|---|---|---|---|
| 101 | Stories of Guy de Maupassant–Guy de Maupassant; 1943 | 4.00 | 8.00 | 12.00 | |
| 102 | The Killer–Stewart Edward White | 4.00 | 8.00 | 12.00 | E |
| 103 | Nana–Emile Zola | 4.00 | 8.00 | 12.00 | E |
| 104 | The Chillers | 5.00 | 10.00 | 15.00 | |
| 105 | You'll Laugh Your Head Off | 4.00 | 8.00 | 12.00 | H |
| 106 | Great Short Stories–anthology | 4.00 | 8.00 | 12.00 | |
| 107 | The Florentine Dagger–Ben Hecht | 4.00 | 8.00 | 12.00 | A |
| 108 | Webster's Dictionary | 3.50 | 7.00 | 10.50 | NF |
| 109 | Bushido–Alexandre Pernikoff | 8.00 | 16.00 | 24.00 | C |
| 110 | Jane Eyre–Charlotte Bronte | 4.00 | 8.00 | 12.00 | |
| 111 | Here's Reading You'll Enjoy | 4.00 | 8.00 | 12.00 | |
| 112 | More Fun Than Looking through a Keyhole | 4.00 | 8.00 | 12.00 | H |
| 113 | Murder on Shark Island–Jack DeWitt | 5.00 | 10.00 | 15.00 | M |

*Quick Reader 124, Quick Reader 128, Quick Reader 107.*

| QUICK READER, *continued* | V/Good | Fine | N/Mint | |
|---|---|---|---|---|
| 114 | Crime and Punishment–Fyodor Dostoyevsky | 3.00 | 6.00 | 9.00 | |
| 115 | How to Safeguard Your Income, Children | 4.00 | 8.00 | 12.00 | NF |
| 116 | Try This for Size–anthology | 4.00 | 8.00 | 12.00 | |
| 117 | Count Bruga–Ben Hecht | 4.00 | 8.00 | 12.00 | |
| 118 | How to Tell Your Friends from the Apes–Will Cuppy | 4.00 | 8.00 | 12.00 | H |
| 119 | A Tale of Two Cities–Charles Dickens | 4.00 | 8.00 | 12.00 | |
| 120 | Time Out for Murder–Ellery Queen & others | 5.00 | 10.00 | 15.00 | M |
| 121 | The Curve of the Catenary–Mary Roberts Rinehart; 1st ed., 1944 | 4.00 | 8.00 | 12.00 | M |
| 122 | Wuthering Heights–Emily Bronte; 1944 | 4.00 | 8.00 | 12.00 | |
| 123 | True Murders Not Quite Solved–Alvin F. Harlow | 4.00 | 8.00 | 12.00 | NF |
| 124 | 15 Short Short Surprise Stories–anthology | 4.00 | 8.00 | 12.00 | |
| 125 | Strictly on the Funny Side; 1944 | 4.00 | 8.00 | 12.00 | H |
| 126 | Love Is a Funny Business–anthology | 4.00 | 8.00 | 12.00 | H |
| 127 | Celebrated Stories Made into Movies | 2.50 | 5.00 | 7.50 | |
| 128 | Cat and Mouse–Hugh Pentecost | 2.50 | 5.00 | 7.50 | M |
| 129 | The Way of All Flesh–Samuel Butler | 4.00 | 8.00 | 12.00 | |
| 130 | Treasure Island–Robert Louis Stevenson | 4.50 | 9.00 | 13.50 | A |
| 131 | Seven Keys to Baldpate–Earl Derr Biggers; 1945 | 4.50 | 9.00 | 13.50 | M |
| 132 | I'll Be Glad When You're Dead–Dana Lyon | 2.50 | 5.00 | 7.50 | M |
| 133 | Gentlemen Prefer Blondes–Anita Loos | 4.00 | 8.00 | 12.00 | |
| 134 | Mr. Pinkerton–Passage for One–David Frome | 3.00 | 6.00 | 9.00 | M |
| 135 | Humorous Ghost Stories | 4.00 | 8.00 | 12.00 | H |
| 136 | Gulliver's Travels–Jonathan Swift | 4.50 | 9.00 | 13.50 | A |
| 137 | Bedside Bedlam–anthology | 4.00 | 8.00 | 12.00 | H |
| 138 | Mademoiselle de Maupin–Theophile Gautier | 4.00 | 8.00 | 12.00 | |
| 139 | One Side Please–anthology | 4.00 | 8.00 | 12.00 | H |
| 140 | The Best of Edgar Allan Poe–Edgar Allan Poe | 4.00 | 8.00 | 12.00 | |
| 141 | Quick Reader Bible | 4.00 | 8.00 | 12.00 | |
| 142 | Dr. Jekyll and Mr. Hyde–Robert Louis Stevenson | 5.00 | 10.00 | 15.00 | SF |
| 143 | Great Comedies Made into Movies | 4.00 | 8.00 | 12.00 | |
| 144 | Unforgettable French Love Stories | 4.00 | 8.00 | 12.00 | |
| 145 | The Dead Man's Tale–Hugh Pentecost | 4.00 | 8.00 | 12.00 | M |
| 146 | Probably does not exist | | | | |
| 147 | Probably does not exist | | | | |
| 148 | Blind Trail at Sunrise–W.C. Tuttle | 4.00 | 8.00 | 12.00 | W |
| 149 | Camille–Alexandre Dumas | 4.00 | 8.00 | 12.00 | |

## (QUINN)
## Quinn Publishing Company
### Digest Size

| nn | The 1st World of IF–anthology | 1.50 | 3.00 | 4.50 | SF |
|---|---|---|---|---|---|
| nn | The 2nd World of IF–anthology | 1.50 | 3.00 | 4.50 | SF |

# RAINBOW
## Magazine Productions, Inc.
### Digest Size

| 101 | Thrill Girl–Gene Harvey; 1950 | 4.00 | 8.00 | 12.00 | E |
|---|---|---|---|---|---|
| 102 | Reno Tramp–Florence Stonebraker | 4.00 | 8.00 | 12.00 | E |
| 103 | Wild Is the Woman–Laura Hale; orig. 1951 | 4.00 | 8.00 | 12.00 | E |
| 104 | Moment of Rapture–Jon Balmer; c-Gross | 4.00 | 8.00 | 12.00 | E |
| 105 | Four Dames Named Sin–Mark Reed (Norman Daniels) | 4.00 | 8.00 | 12.00 | E |
| 106 | Nora's No Angel–Tom Stone; 1951; c-Gross | 4.00 | 8.00 | 12.00 | E |
| 107 | Street of Dark Desires–Mark Reed (Norman Daniels) | 4.00 | 8.00 | 12.00 | E |
| 108 | Passion Has Red Lips–R.R. McCollum | 4.00 | 8.00 | 12.00 | E |
| 109 | Her Candle Burns Hot!–Hodge Evens; 1951 | 4.00 | 8.00 | 12.00 | E |
| 110 | Sleepy Time Honey–Kathryn Culver | 4.00 | 8.00 | 12.00 | E |
| 111 | Walk the Evil Street–David Wade; orig. 1952 | 4.00 | 8.00 | 12.00 | E |
| 112 | Red Headed Wench–Tom Stone; orig. 1952 | 4.00 | 8.00 | 12.00 | E |
| 113 | Play Rough!–Rick Wayne | 4.00 | 8.00 | 12.00 | E |
| 114 | Tease the Wild Flame–Mark Reed (Norman Daniels) | 4.00 | 8.00 | 12.00 | E |
| 115 | Carnival of Passion–Val Munroe; c-Gross | 4.00 | 8.00 | 12.00 | E |
| 116 | She Walks by Night–David Wade (Norman Daniels) | 4.00 | 8.00 | 12.00 | E |
| 117 | Bedroom in Hell–Norman A. Daniels | 4.00 | 8.00 | 12.00 | E |
| 118 | Kiss of Fire–Laura Hale | 4.00 | 8.00 | 12.00 | E |
| 119 | Joy Ride!–Roger Treat; c-Gross | 4.00 | 8.00 | 12.00 | E |
| 120 | The Nude Stranger–Mark Reed (Norman Daniels); orig. 1952 | 4.00 | 8.00 | 12.00 | E |
| 121 | Seven Hungry Men–Lionel White; c-Gross | 4.00 | 8.00 | 12.00 | E |
| 122 | The Madam Who Blushed–Terry Burleson | 4.00 | 8.00 | 12.00 | E |
| 123 | Vice Cop–Mark Reed (Norman Daniels) | 4.00 | 8.00 | 12.00 | E |
| 124 | Bedroom with a View–David Wade (Norman Daniels); orig. 1952; c-Gross | 4.00 | 8.00 | 12.00 | E |
| 125 | Tender Hearted Harlot–Val Munroe | 4.00 | 8.00 | 12.00 | E |
| 126 | She Devil–Robert Turner | 4.00 | 8.00 | 12.00 | E |
| 127 | The Big Woman–Mel Colton; orig. 1953 | 4.00 | 8.00 | 12.00 | E |
| 128 | The Twist!–Norma Dann (Norman Daniels); orig. 1953 | 4.00 | 8.00 | 12.00 | E |
| 129 | Only Human–David Wade (Norman Daniels); orig. 1953 | 4.00 | 8.00 | 12.00 | E |
| 130 | Off Limits–George Bottari; 1953; c-Gross | 4.00 | 8.00 | 12.00 | E |

# RAINBOW BOOKS
## The Colonial Press, Inc./Stravon Publishers
### Digest Size

| 2 | The Complete Bedside Joke Book–Howard Stackman; 1955 | 2.00 | 4.00 | 6.00 | H |
|---|---|---|---|---|---|
| 102 | The Complete Golf Joke Book–Seymour Dunn; 1953 | 2.00 | 4.00 | 6.00 | H |
| 103 | Ten Perfect Crimes–Hank Sterling; 1954 | 2.00 | 4.00 | 6.00 | NF |

# READERS CHOICE LIBRARY
## St. John Publishing Company
### Some Digest Size

| 1 | Six-Gun Law in Wrango–Frank C. Robertson; digest size | 3.00 | 6.00 | 9.00 | W |
|---|---|---|---|---|---|

|  | | V/Good | Fine | N/Mint |  |
|--|--|--------|------|--------|--|

READERS CHOICE LIBRARY, *continued*

| No. | Title | V/Good | Fine | N/Mint | |
|-----|-------|--------|------|--------|--|
| 2 | Smoky Road–Frank Gruber; digest size | 3.00 | 6.00 | 9.00 | W |
| 3 | Gina–George Albert Glay | 2.50 | 5.00 | 7.50 | M |
| 4 | The Powder Burner–Frank C. Robertson; c-Saunders | 2.50 | 5.00 | 7.50 | W |
| 5 | The Stranger from Texas–Allan K. Echols; digest size | 2.50 | 5.00 | 7.50 | W |
| 6 | Texas Lightning–E.B. Mann; digest size | 2.50 | 5.00 | 7.50 | W |
| 7 | Shoe the Wild Mare–Gene Fowler | 2.50 | 5.00 | 7.50 | W |
| 8 | Green Light for Death–Frank Kane | 6.00 | 12.00 | 18.00 | W |
| 9 | Smoky Joe–W.F. Bragg; digest size | 2.50 | 5.00 | 7.50 | W |
| 10 | Barb Wire Showdown–Allan K. Echols; digest size | 2.50 | 5.00 | 7.50 | W |
| 11 | Stranger Than Truth–Vera Caspary | 2.50 | 5.00 | 7.50 | E |
| 12 | Nightmare–William Irish; aka I Wouldn't Be in Your Shoes | 3.50 | 7.00 | 10.50 | M |
| 13 | Western Outlaw–Frank Gruber; digest size | 3.00 | 6.00 | 9.00 | W |
| 14 | Trouble Shootin' Man–Frank C. Robertson; digest size | 2.50 | 5.00 | 7.50 | W |
| 15 | The Lock and the Key–Frank Gruber; digest size | 3.00 | 6.00 | 9.00 | M |
| 16 | Murder '97–Frank Gruber; digest size | 3.00 | 6.00 | 9.00 | M |
| 17 | Gun Crazy–Wayne D. Overholser; digest size | 2.50 | 5.00 | 7.50 | W |
| 18 | Bloody Saddles–L.P. Holmes; digest size | 2.50 | 5.00 | 7.50 | W |
| 19 | Broken Lance–Frank Gruber; digest size | 3.00 | 6.00 | 9.00 | W |
| 20 | Trumpet in the Dust–Gene Fowler; digest size | 2.00 | 4.00 | 6.00 | E |
| 21 | Don't Wait for Love–Maysie Grieg; digest size | 2.50 | 5.00 | 7.50 | E |
| 22 | The Hussy–Boine Grainger; digest size | 2.50 | 5.00 | 7.50 | E |
| 23 | Veiled Murder–Alice Campbell; digest size | 2.50 | 5.00 | 7.50 | M |
| 24 | Red Rustlers–Frank C. Robertson; digest size | 2.50 | 5.00 | 7.50 | W |
| 25 | Bonanza Queen–Zola Ross; digest size | 2.50 | 5.00 | 7.50 | E |
| 26 | The Killers–G.C. Henderson; digest size | 2.50 | 5.00 | 7.50 | W |
| 27 | Sinful Bargain–Michael Valbeck; aka Headlong for Heaven; digest size | 2.50 | 5.00 | 7.50 | E |
| 29 | Gunsmoke–Clem Colt; digest size | 2.50 | 5.00 | 7.50 | W |
| 30 | Scandalous Lovers–N.P. Nezelof; digest size | 2.50 | 5.00 | 7.50 | E |
| 31 | Farm Girl–de Lange; digest size | 2.50 | 5.00 | 7.50 | E |
| 32 | Secret Affair–Houston Branch & Frank Waters; digest size | 2.50 | 5.00 | 7.50 | E |
| 33 | Prairie Guns–E.E. Halleran; digest size | 2.50 | 5.00 | 7.50 | W |
| 35 | Wild Oats–Howard Rockey; digest size | 2.50 | 5.00 | 7.50 | E |
| 36 | Strange Love–Bernard Glemser | 2.50 | 5.00 | 7.50 | E |
| 37 | They Call It Sin–Alberta Stedman Eagan | 2.50 | 5.00 | 7.50 | E |
| 38 | Death Is My Lover–Stuart Brock | 2.00 | 4.00 | 6.00 | E |
| 39 | Lover Boy–Eric Rhodes Hayden | 2.00 | 4.00 | 6.00 | E |
| 40 | Tracks in the Sand–H.A. DeRosso | 2.50 | 5.00 | 7.50 | |

## (READER'S LEAGUE)
## Readers League of America

**NOTE: These were special reissues of Pocket Book titles, using same covers and slightly modified format.**

| No. | Title | V/Good | Fine | N/Mint | |
|-----|-------|--------|------|--------|--|
| nn | The Pocket Book of Crossword Puzzles–ed. Margaret Petherbridge | 1.00 | 2.00 | 3.00 | |
| nn | The Adventures of Ellery Queen–Ellery Queen | 1.00 | 2.00 | 3.00 | M |
| nn | The Pocket Book of Modern American Short Stories–ed. Philip Van Doren Stern | 1.00 | 2.00 | 3.00 | |
| nn | The Tragedy of X–Ellery Queen | 1.00 | 2.00 | 3.00 | M |
| nn | Ripley's Believe It or Not–Robert Ripley | 1.00 | 2.00 | 3.00 | |
| nn | Overture to Death–Ngaio Marsh; special edition for American Red Cross | 1.00 | 2.00 | 3.00 | M |

*Reader's Choice 8, Reader's Choice 12, Reader's League unnumbered.*

| No. | Title | V/Good | Fine | N/Mint | |
|-----|-------|--------|------|--------|--|
| nn | The Pocket Book of Cartoons–ed. Bennett A. Cerf | 1.00 | 2.00 | 3.00 | H |
| nn | A Tale of Two Cities–Charles Dickens; special edition for American Red Cross | 1.00 | 2.00 | 3.00 | |
| nn | The Thin Man–Dashiell Hammett; special edition for American Red Cross | 1.50 | 3.00 | 4.50 | M |
| nn | Fast Company–Marco Page; special edition for American Red Cross | 1.00 | 2.00 | 3.00 | M |
| nn | The Great Impersonation–E. Phillips Oppenheim; special edition for American Red Cross | 1.00 | 2.00 | 3.00 | |
| nn | Red Harvest–Dashiell Hammett; special edition for American Red Cross | 1.50 | 3.00 | 4.50 | M |
| nn | The Case of the Dangerous Dowager–Erle Stanley Gardner | 1.00 | 2.00 | 3.00 | M |
| nn | The Four of Hearts–Ellery Queen | 1.00 | 2.00 | 3.00 | M |
| nn | Jeeves–P.G. Wodehouse | 1.00 | 2.00 | 3.00 | H |
| nn | Enter the Saint–Leslie Charteris | 1.00 | 2.00 | 3.00 | M |
| nn | The Case of the Substitute Face–Erle Stanley Gardner | 1.00 | 2.00 | 3.00 | M |
| nn | The Pocket Entertainer; 1942 | 1.00 | 2.00 | 3.00 | NF |
| nn | Phantom Lady–William Irish | 2.00 | 4.00 | 6.00 | M |
| nn | The Egyptian Cross Mystery–Ellery Queen | 1.00 | 2.00 | 3.00 | M |
| nn | The Case of the Stuttering Bishop–Erle Stanley Gardner | 1.00 | 2.00 | 3.00 | M |
| nn | Halfway House–Ellery Queen; special edition for American Red Cross | 1.00 | 2.00 | 3.00 | M |
| nn | Topper Takes a Trip–Thorne Smith | 1.00 | 2.00 | 3.00 | |
| nn | The Chinese Parrot–Earl Derr Biggers | 1.50 | 3.00 | 4.50 | M |
| nn | The Circular Staircase–Mary Roberts Rinehart | 1.00 | 2.00 | 3.00 | M |
| nn | Abraham Lincoln–G.R. Benson | 1.00 | 2.00 | 3.00 | |
| nn | And Then There Were None–Agatha Christie; special edition for American Red Cross | 1.00 | 2.00 | 3.00 | M |
| nn | Lost Horizon–James Hilton | 1.00 | 2.00 | 3.00 | |
| nn | Here Is Your War–Ernie Pyle | 1.00 | 2.00 | 3.00 | |
| nn | Trial by Fury–Craig Rice | 1.00 | 2.00 | 3.00 | M |

## RED ARROW BOOKS
## Red Arrow Books

**Note: Pictorial and nonpictorial covers probably exist of each title, valued equally.**

| No. | Title | V/Good | Fine | N/Mint | |
|-----|-------|--------|------|--------|--|
| 1 | Thirteen at Dinner–Agatha Christie; 1939 | 15.00 | 30.00 | 45.00 | M |
| 2 | Murder-on-Hudson–Jennifer Jones | 10.00 | 20.00 | 30.00 | M |
| 3 | Murders in Praed Street–John Rhode | 12.50 | 25.00 | 37.50 | M |
| 4 | Death in the Library–Philip Ketchum | 10.00 | 20.00 | 30.00 | M |
| 5 | Death Wears a White Gardenia–Zelda Popkin | 7.50 | 15.00 | 22.50 | M |
| 6 | My South Sea Island–Eric Musprat | 10.00 | 20.00 | 30.00 | |
| 7 | Yankee Komisar–Comm. S.M. Riis | 7.50 | 15.00 | 22.50 | |
| 8 | Girl Hunt–Laurence D. Smith | 10.00 | 20.00 | 30.00 | |
| 9 | The Seven Sleepers–Francis Beeding | 7.50 | 15.00 | 22.50 | |
| 10 | Captain Nemesis–F. Van Wyck Mason | 7.50 | 15.00 | 22.50 | A |

| | | V/Good | Fine | N/Mint | |
|---|---|---|---|---|---|

RED ARROW BOOKS, *continued*

| | | V/Good | Fine | N/Mint | |
|---|---|---|---|---|---|
| 11 | Windswept–Olga Moore | 10.00 | 20.00 | 30.00 | |
| 12 | Pirate's Purchase–Ben Ames Williams | 7.50 | 15.00 | 22.50 | A |

# RED CIRCLE
## Select Publications, Inc.
### (See also Lion)

| | | V/Good | Fine | N/Mint | |
|---|---|---|---|---|---|
| 1 | Sex Life and You–Jules Archer & Maxine Sawyer; 1949 | 7.50 | 15.00 | 22.50 | NF |
| 2 | Passionate Fool–John Moroso; aka Poor Passionate Fool | 7.50 | 15.00 | 22.50 | E |
| 3 | Leg Artist–Gene Harvey | 7.50 | 15.00 | 22.50 | E |
| 4 | Blonde Menace–Don Martin; aka Shed No Tears; movie tie-in | 7.50 | 15.00 | 22.50 | E |
| 5 | Body or Soul–Royal Peters | 7.50 | 15.00 | 22.50 | E |
| 6 | Passion in the Dust–Paul Evan Lehman | 6.00 | 12.00 | 18.00 | W |
| 7 | Hot Date–Elliot Storm; aka Shame Girl | 6.00 | 12.00 | 18.00 | E |
| 12 | Why Get Married?–Token West | 7.50 | 15.00 | 22.50 | E |
| 13 | Carnival of Love–Anthony Scott; 1949; aka Mardi Gras Madness | 7.50 | 15.00 | 22.50 | E |

# RED DAGGER MYSTERY
## Dagger House, Inc.
### Digest Size

| | | V/Good | Fine | N/Mint | |
|---|---|---|---|---|---|
| 21 | Death for a Hussy–Allison Holt; 1946; aka Bier for a Hussy | 3.00 | 6.00 | 9.00 | M |
| 23 | Kill at Dusk–Philip Ketchum; 1946 | 3.00 | 6.00 | 9.00 | M |
| 25 | Murder from the Mind–Patrick Laing; 1947 | 3.00 | 6.00 | 9.00 | M |
| 27 | There Are Dead Men in Manhattan– John Roeburt; 1947 | 3.00 | 6.00 | 9.00 | M |
| 29 | Blood on the Beach–H. Holley; 1947 | 3.00 | 6.00 | 9.00 | M |

# RED SEAL BOOKS
## Fawcett Publications, Inc.

| | | V/Good | Fine | N/Mint | |
|---|---|---|---|---|---|
| 7 | The Sky Tramps–Dennison O'Hara; orig. 1952 | 1.50 | 3.00 | 4.50 | E |
| 8 | Each Life to Live–Richard Gehman; orig. 1952 | 1.50 | 3.00 | 4.50 | E |
| 9 | This Woman–Albert Idell; orig. 1952 | 1.50 | 3.00 | 4.50 | E |
| 10 | Naked in the Streets–Ryerson Johnson | 1.50 | 3.00 | 4.50 | E |
| 11 | Out of the Sea–Don Smith; orig. 1952 | 1.50 | 3.00 | 4.50 | A |
| 12 | City of Women–Nancy Morgan; orig. 1952 | 2.00 | 4.00 | 6.00 | E |
| 13 | The Sea Waifs–John Vail; orig. 1952 | 1.50 | 3.00 | 4.50 | E |
| 14 | Halo for a Heel–Mike Skelly; orig. 1952 | 1.50 | 3.00 | 4.50 | E |
| 15 | Bride of the Sword–Homer Hatten | 1.50 | 3.00 | 4.50 | A |
| 16 | The Golden Sorrow–Theodore Pratt | 1.50 | 3.00 | 4.50 | E |
| 17 | The Quest–O.O. Osborne; orig. 1952 | 1.50 | 3.00 | 4.50 | E |
| 18 | The Marriage Bed–H. Vernor Dixon | 2.00 | 4.00 | 6.00 | E |
| 19 | Lili of Paris–Fay Adams; orig. 1952 | 1.50 | 3.00 | 4.50 | E |

Red Arrow 3, Red Circle 4, Red Dagger 25.

Red Dagger 27, Red Seal 10, Regency RB107.

| | | V/Good | Fine | N/Mint | |
|---|---|---|---|---|---|
| 20 | Girl from Town–Jack Sheridan; orig. 1952 | 1.50 | 3.00 | 4.50 | E |
| 21 | Be Still My Heart–Steve Fisher | 2.00 | 4.00 | 6.00 | |
| 22 | American Ballads; orig. 1952 | 1.50 | 3.00 | 4.50 | NF |
| 23 | The Magnificent Moll–John Gonzales | 1.50 | 3.00 | 4.50 | E |
| 24 | One for Hell–Jada M. Davis | 1.50 | 3.00 | 4.50 | E |
| 25 | Thy Name Is Woman–Hilda Van Siller; orig. 1952 | 1.50 | 3.00 | 4.50 | E |
| 26 | This, Too, Is Love–Sam Ross | 1.50 | 3.00 | 4.50 | E |
| 27 | Love Isn't for Now–John Vail; orig. 1953 | 1.50 | 3.00 | 4.50 | E |
| 28 | Mississippi Flame–Ryerson Johnson | 1.50 | 3.00 | 4.50 | E |
| 29 | Fare Thee Well–Robert Spafford; orig. 1953 | 1.50 | 3.00 | 4.50 | E |

# REGENCY
## Regency Books

| | | V/Good | Fine | N/Mint | |
|---|---|---|---|---|---|
| RB101 | Firebug–Robert Bloch; orig. 1961 | 10.00 | 20.00 | 30.00 | |
| RB102 | Gentleman Junkie–Harlan Ellison; 1st ed. 1961 | 25.00 | 50.00 | 75.00 | JD |
| RB103 | Mr. Ballerina–Ronn Marvin; orig. 1961 | 2.50 | 5.00 | 7.50 | |
| RB104 | The Brain Buyers–James Sagebiel; orig. 1961 | 2.50 | 5.00 | 7.50 | |
| RB105 | Divide the Night–Donald Honig; orig. 1961 | 2.50 | 5.00 | 7.50 | |
| RB106 | Memos from Purgatory–Harlan Ellison; 1st ed. 1961 | 27.50 | 55.00 | 82.50 | JD |
| RB107 | Stories by the Man Nobody Knows– B. Traven; orig. 1961 | 7.50 | 15.00 | 22.50 | |
| RB108 | The Torment of the Kids–Hal Ellson; orig. 1961 | 6.00 | 12.00 | 18.00 | JD |
| RB109 | Weed–Clarence L. Cooper, Jr; orig. 1961 | 3.50 | 7.00 | 10.50 | |
| RB110 | Some Will Not Die–Algis Budrys; orig. 1961 | 6.00 | 12.00 | 18.00 | |
| RB111 | What Mad Oracle?–Thomas N. Scortia; orig. 1961 | 4.50 | 9.00 | 13.50 | |
| RB112 | The Man in the Water–Robert Sheckley; orig. 1961 | 6.00 | 12.00 | 18.00 | |
| RB113 | The Eleventh Commandment–Lester Del Rey; orig. 1962 | 6.00 | 12.00 | 18.00 | SF |
| RB114 | Panic!–David Alexander; orig. 1962 | 2.50 | 5.00 | 7.50 | NF |
| RB115 | The Crooked Cops–W.T. Brannon; orig. 1962 | 2.50 | 5.00 | 7.50 | NF |
| RB116 | The Dark Messenger–Clarence L. Cooper, Jr; orig. 1962 | 2.50 | 5.00 | 7.50 | |
| RB117 | Muscle on Broadway–Paul B. Weston; orig. 1962 | 2.50 | 5.00 | 7.50 | NF |
| RB118 | Fire and the Night–Philip Jose Farmer; orig. 1962 | 4.50 | 9.00 | 13.50 | |
| RB301 | Philosopher of Evil/The Life and Times of the Marquis de Sade–Walter Drummond (Robert Silverberg); orig. 1962 | 3.50 | 7.00 | 10.50 | NF |
| RB302 | The Pangs of Love–ed. Chandler Brossard; 1st ed. 1962 | 2.50 | 5.00 | 7.50 | |
| RB303 | The Hills of Creation–Neil Elliot Blum; orig. 1962 | 2.50 | 5.00 | 7.50 | |
| RB304 | A Hammer in the City–Paul B. Weston; orig. 1962 | 3.00 | 6.00 | 9.00 | NF |

|  | | V/Good | Fine | N/Mint |
|---|---|---|---|---|

REGENCY, *continued*

| RB305 | Bloody Grass–Hobe Gilmore; orig. 1962 | 3.00 | 6.00 | 9.00 |
| RB306 | White Man Go!–Roskolenko; orig. 1962 | 2.50 | 5.00 | 7.50 NF |
| RB307 | In the Line of Fire–Jackson M. Bowling; orig. 1962 | 2.50 | 5.00 | 7.50 |
| RB308 | Crimes and Chaos–Avram Davidson | 4.50 | 9.00 | 13.50 NF |
| RB309 | You Will Never Be the Same– Cordwainer Smith | 6.00 | 12.00 | 18.00 SF |
| RB310 | Damn It!–William E. Miles; orig. 1963 | 2.50 | 5.00 | 7.50 NF |
| RB311 | The Gilded Witch–Jack Webb; orig. 1963 | 3.00 | 6.00 | 9.00 |
| RB312 | Women of the Swastika–Hal Vetter; orig. 1963 | 3.00 | 6.00 | 9.00 NF |
| RB313 | Black!–Clarence L. Cooper, Jr; orig. 1963 | 3.50 | 7.00 | 10.50 |
| RB314 | Truman and the Pendergasts–Frank Mason (Algis Budrys); orig. 1963 | 4.00 | 8.00 | 12.00 NF |
| RB315 | Queen Street–Matthew Gant; orig. 1963 | 3.50 | 7.00 | 10.50 |
| RB316 | Hack No. 777–Ed Bunin; orig. 1963 | 2.50 | 5.00 | 7.50 NF |
| RB317 | The Rabble Rousers–Eric Frank Russell; orig. 1963 | 3.50 | 7.00 | 10.50 NF |
| RB318 | How to Spend Money–Walter Drummond (Robert Silverberg); orig. 1963 | 3.00 | 6.00 | 9.00 NF |
| RB319 | KKK–Ben Haas; orig. 1963 | 3.00 | 6.00 | 9.00 NF |
| RB320 | Hollywood, R.I.P.–I.G. Edmonds; orig. 1963 | 3.00 | 6.00 | 9.00 NF |
| RB321 | The Expatriates–Mack Reynolds; orig. 1963 | 3.50 | 7.00 | 10.50 NF |
| RB322 | The Grifters–Jim Thompson; orig. 1963 | 35.00 | 70.00 | 105.00 NF |
| RB323 | Fighting Men, U.S.A.–James Warner Bellah; 1st ed. 1963 | 2.50 | 5.00 | 7.50 NF |
| RB324 | No Law But Their Own–Joe Millard; orig. 1963 | 3.00 | 6.00 | 9.00 NF |

## REGENCY SUSPENSE–see CORINTH SUSPENSE

## (RETAIL DISTRIBUTORS)
### Retail Distributors, Inc.

| nn | World's Champs–Lester Bromberg; 1958 | 1.00 | 2.00 | 3.00 S |
| 101 | Hoodlums Los Angeles–Ted Prager & Larry Craft; 1959 | 1.00 | 2.00 | 3.00 NF |
| 102 | Hoodlums New York–Ted Prager & Leeds Moberley; 1959 | 1.00 | 2.00 | 3.00 NF |

## REX STOUT MYSTERY
### Avon Book Company/Avon Detective-Mysteries, Inc.
#### Digest Size

| 1 | Includes Hammett, Stout, Christie, Steinbeck, others; 1945 | 5.00 | 10.00 | 15.00 M |
| 2 | Includes Hammett, Chandler, Dickson, Cain, others | 4.50 | 9.00 | 13.50 M |
| 3 | Includes Hammett, Lovecraft, Irish, Carr, others; 1946 | 4.50 | 9.00 | 13.50 M |
| 4 | Includes Dickson, Starrett, Freeman, Blackwood, others | 4.50 | 9.00 | 13.50 M |
| 5 | Includes Stout, Woolrich, Dickson, Sayers, others | 4.50 | 9.00 | 13.50 M |
| 6 | Includes Bradbury, Charteris, Sayers, Ambler, others | 4.50 | 9.00 | 13.50 M |
| 7 | Includes Irish, Cain, Fitzgerald, Collier, others; 1947 | 4.50 | 9.00 | 13.50 M |
| 8 | Includes Woolrich, Crofts, Collier, Starrett, others | 4.50 | 9.00 | 13.50 M |
| 9 | Includes Boucher, Crofts, Collier, Forester, others | 4.50 | 9.00 | 13.50 M |

Regency RB315, Regency RB322, Retail Distributors 101.

|  | | V/Good | Fine | N/Mint |
|---|---|---|---|---|

## ROMANTIC NOVELS
### Romantic Reprints
#### Digest Size

| nn | Dance Hall Girl–Ann Lawrence; c-Rodewald | 2.50 | 5.00 | 7.50 E |
| nn | Reckless Girl–John Saxon | 2.50 | 5.00 | 7.50 E |
| nn | Affairs of a Mistress–Gordon Semple; aka Time for Passion | 2.50 | 5.00 | 7.50 E |
| nn | The Loves of a Harlot–Beth Brown; aka For Men Only; c-Rodewald | 2.50 | 5.00 | 7.50 E |

## ROYAL GIANT EDITION
### Royal Books/Universal Publishing and Distributing Corp.
#### Digest Size
#### (See also Universal Giant Edition)

| 12 | Jimgrim Sahib–Talbot Mundy; aka Jimgrim | 4.50 | 9.00 | 13.50 A |
| 13 | Note: May not exist | | | |
| 14 | Matador–Marguerite Steen | 3.00 | 6.00 | 9.00 A |
| 15 | Highlights from Yank. Note: Same cover as Beacon B113 | 3.00 | 6.00 | 9.00 |
| 16 | Stalingrad–Theodor Plievier | 3.00 | 6.00 | 9.00 C |
| 17 | The Other Stranger–Daoma Winston; orig. 1953 | 3.00 | 6.00 | 9.00 E |
|  | Adam and Two Eves–anon. | | | E |
| 18 | Allan Quatermain–H. Rider Haggard | 4.50 | 9.00 | 13.50 A |
|  | King Solomon's Mines–H. Rider Haggard | | | A |
| 19 | Trek East–Talbot Mundy; aka The Ivory Trail | 4.50 | 9.00 | 13.50 A |
| 20 | Full Moon–Talbot Mundy | 30.00 | 60.00 | 90.00 E |
|  | High Priest of California–Charles Willeford; orig. 1953 | | | E |
| 21 | Highway Episode–George Weller; aka Clutch and Differential. Note: Same cover as Beacon B109 and B200 | 3.00 | 6.00 | 9.00 E |
| 22 | Gonzaga's Woman–John Jakes; orig. 1953 | 4.50 | 9.00 | 13.50 A |
|  | Affair in Araby–Talbot Mundy; aka The King in Check | | | A |
| 23 | The Case of Sergeant Grischa–Arnold Zweig | 2.50 | 5.00 | 7.50 C |
| 24 | Roxana–Daniel Defoe | 2.50 | 5.00 | 7.50 E |
| 25 | Mademoiselle De Maupin–Theophile Gautier | 3.00 | 6.00 | 9.00 E |
|  | Candide–Voltaire | | | E |
| 26 | The Harem of Hsi Men–anthology | 7.50 | 15.00 | 22.50 E |
| 27 | Confessions of a Psychiatrist–Henry Lewis Nixon; orig. 1954. Note: Same cover as Beacon B118 | 4.50 | 9.00 | 13.50 E |
|  | The Woman He Wanted–Daoma Winston; orig. 1954. | 4.50 | 9.00 | 13.50 E |

Royal Giant 18, Royal Giant 20, Royal Giant 28.

| | | V/Good | Fine | N/Mint | |
|---|---|---|---|---|---|

**ROYAL GIANT EDITION,** *continued*

| 28 | The Unnatural Son–Mark Twain; aka Pudd'n'head Wilson | 3.00 | 6.00 | 9.00 | F |
| | A Connecticut Yankee in King Arthur's Court–Mark Twain | | | | F |
| 29 | The Way of All Flesh–Samuel Butler | 3.00 | 6.00 | 9.00 | E |

# RUTLEDGE BOOKS
## Scholastic Book Services
### Digest Size

| RP10 | The Buccaneer–Iris Vinton; 1959; movie tie-in | 1.50 | 3.00 | 4.50 | A |
| RB13 | Victory at Sea: The Submarine–Thomas D. Parrish; 1959; TV tie-in | 2.00 | 4.00 | 6.00 | C |
| RB18 | Victory at Sea: Flattops–Christopher Douglas; 1959; TV tie-in | 2.00 | 4.00 | 6.00 | C |

# (R.W.)
## The R.W. Company
### Digest Size

| nn | The Vice Czar Murders–Franklin Charles | 2.50 | 5.00 | 7.50 | M |

# SABER BOOKS
## Sunset Enterprises/Saber Books

| SA1 | Call Girl–R. Lewis | 1.00 | 2.00 | 3.00 | X |
| SA2 | Karla–Vern Wade; 1957 | 1.00 | 2.00 | 3.00 | X |
| SA3 | Turbulent Daughters–Reese Hayes; 1958 | 1.00 | 2.00 | 3.00 | X |
| SA4 | Desperate Moments–G. Roberts | 1.00 | 2.00 | 3.00 | X |
| SA5 | Love Princess–Orrie Hitt; 1958 | 1.50 | 3.00 | 4.50 | X |
| SA6 | Society Daughter–Wilson C. Gilman | 1.00 | 2.00 | 3.00 | X |
| SA7 | I Am a Lesbian–Lora Sela | 1.50 | 3.00 | 4.50 | X |
| SA8 | Never Enough–Byron Woolfe | 1.00 | 2.00 | 3.00 | X |
| SA9 | Out of Darkness–Lonny Bass; 1959 | 1.00 | 2.00 | 3.00 | X |
| SA10 | Bold Desires–Byron Woolfe | 1.00 | 2.00 | 3.00 | X |
| SA11 | Sex Life of a Cop–Oscar Peck | 1.00 | 2.00 | 3.00 | X |
| SA12 | Deception–Jock Spruill | 1.00 | 2.00 | 3.00 | X |
| SA13 | Camera Bait–Lora Sela | 1.00 | 2.00 | 3.00 | X |
| SA14 | The Right Bed–Lee Walters; 1959 | 1.00 | 2.00 | 3.00 | X |
| SA15 | Bachelor Husband–Lee Walters; 1960 | 1.00 | 2.00 | 3.00 | X |
| SA16 | I Peddle Jazz–Pat Bunyan | 1.00 | 2.00 | 3.00 | X |
| SA17 | Ruthless Fraternity–Arnold Marmor | 1.00 | 2.00 | 3.00 | X |
| SA18 | The Gay Detective–Lou Rand | 1.50 | 3.00 | 4.50 | M |
| SA19 | The Odd Switch–Lynda Parker | 1.00 | 2.00 | 3.00 | X |
| SA20 | Unknown Tomorrows–Lora Sela; 1961 | 1.00 | 2.00 | 3.00 | X |
| SA21 | Office Wife–Arnold Kane | 1.00 | 2.00 | 3.00 | X |

| | | V/Good | Fine | N/Mint | |
|---|---|---|---|---|---|
| SA22 | Two of a Kind–Brady Hampton | 1.00 | 2.00 | 3.00 | X |
| SA23 | Hutch Creek Girl–Mary S. Gooch | 1.00 | 2.00 | 3.00 | X |
| SA24 | Vicious Vixen–Byron Woolfe; 1962 | 1.00 | 2.00 | 3.00 | X |
| SA25 | The Way of the Flesh–Charles Wayne | 1.00 | 2.00 | 3.00 | X |
| SA26 | The Awakening of Cindy–Edwin Shell | 1.50 | 3.00 | 4.50 | X |
| SA27 | Blind Date–Ralph Brandon | 1.50 | 3.00 | 4.50 | X |
| SA28 | Depraved Debutante–Roger Blake; 1962 | 1.00 | 2.00 | 3.00 | X |
| SA29 | Hard Way Back–Jack Woodford; 1963 | 1.25 | 2.50 | 3.75 | X |
| SA30 | Slum Virgin–Richard Geis | 1.50 | 3.00 | 4.50 | X |
| SA31 | Hell Is for Hammons–Jannet Anderson | 1.50 | 3.00 | 4.50 | X |
| SA32 | Carnal Frenzy–Adam Coulter | 1.50 | 3.00 | 4.50 | X |
| SA33 | Call of the Flesh–Jack Moore | 1.50 | 3.00 | 4.50 | X |
| SA34 | Nympho Mania–Don Bartell | 1.50 | 3.00 | 4.50 | X |
| SA35 | His Sisters Were Call Girls–Ralph Brandon | 1.00 | 2.00 | 3.00 | X |
| SA36 | The Girls of Club Sappho–Joy Taylor | 3.00 | 6.00 | 9.00 | X |
| SA37 | Mike Addison–Frank G. Harris | 1.00 | 2.00 | 3.00 | X |
| SA38 | Embrace the Storm–Del Rio; 1963 | 1.50 | 3.00 | 4.50 | X |
| SA39 | Rape Included–Jack Moore | 1.00 | 2.00 | 3.00 | X |
| SA40 | Call Boy–Frank G. Harris | 1.00 | 2.00 | 3.00 | X |
| SA41 | A Town in Heat–Lee Walters | 1.00 | 2.00 | 3.00 | X |
| SA42 | Brenda Caldwell–Jack Moore; 1963 | 1.00 | 2.00 | 3.00 | X |
| SA43 | The Emerald Bikini–Robert B. Ford | 1.00 | 2.00 | 3.00 | X |
| SA44 | Third Paradise–Roberta Everhart | 1.00 | 2.00 | 3.00 | X |
| SA45 | 6 Were with Him–Sayre Tremain; 1964 | 1.00 | 2.00 | 3.00 | X |
| SA46 | Summer of Sex–Ann Carroll | 1.00 | 2.00 | 3.00 | X |
| SA47 | Love's Final Act–Mark Daniels | 1.00 | 2.00 | 3.00 | X |
| SA48 | Untamed Desires–Rex Weldon | 1.00 | 2.00 | 3.00 | X |
| SA49 | The Women Were Willing–Sheldon Abbott | 1.00 | 2.00 | 3.00 | X |
| SA50 | A Wife to Lend–Frank G. Harris | 1.00 | 2.00 | 3.00 | X |
| SA51 | Lust of a Wanton–Mark Daniels; 1964 | 1.00 | 2.00 | 3.00 | X |
| SA52 | Hot Angel–Byron Woolfe | 1.00 | 2.00 | 3.00 | X |
| SA53 | Moments of Passion–Drew Palmer | 1.00 | 2.00 | 3.00 | X |
| SA54 | Strands of Lust–Byron Woolfe | 1.00 | 2.00 | 3.00 | X |
| SA55 | Girls of Carnation House–Robert Vaughn | 1.00 | 2.00 | 3.00 | X |
| SA56 | We Poor Sinners–Joseph Devon | 1.00 | 2.00 | 3.00 | X |
| SA57 | The Swingers–Rex Nevins | 1.00 | 2.00 | 3.00 | X |
| SA58 | House of the Damned–James Harvey | 1.00 | 2.00 | 3.00 | X |
| SA59 | Virgin Stripper–Wyn Blue; 1964 | 1.00 | 2.00 | 3.00 | X |
| SA60 | The Bold and the Innocent–Larry Tuttle | 1.00 | 2.00 | 3.00 | X |
| SA61 | The Beauty Contest–Frank G. Harris | 1.00 | 2.00 | 3.00 | X |
| SA62 | Sin Switch–Drew Palmer | 1.00 | 2.00 | 3.00 | X |
| SA63 | Sexmates–Rex Weldon | 1.00 | 2.00 | 3.00 | X |
| SA64 | Fraternity of Lust–Wilton Grady | 1.00 | 2.00 | 3.00 | X |
| SA65 | Lust Has No Mercy–Frank G. Harris | 1.50 | 3.00 | 4.50 | X |
| SA66 | She Offered Her Body–Jack Moore | 1.00 | 2.00 | 3.00 | X |
| SA67 | Sin without Shame–Frank G. Harris | 1.00 | 2.00 | 3.00 | X |
| SA68 | His Second Wife–Sheldon Abbott | 1.50 | 3.00 | 4.50 | X |
| SA69 | Joy Wives–Drew Palmer | 1.00 | 2.00 | 3.00 | X |
| SA70 | Too Ready for Love–James De Marco | 1.00 | 2.00 | 3.00 | X |
| SA71 | The Shared Wife–Douglas Dee | 1.00 | 2.00 | 3.00 | X |
| SA72 | Passion–Their Pastime–Drew Palmer | 1.00 | 2.00 | 3.00 | X |
| SA73 | The Adulteress–Jack Moore | 1.00 | 2.00 | 3.00 | X |
| SA74 | Strange Lovers–Adam Coulter | 1.00 | 2.00 | 3.00 | X |
| SA75 | Lust Has No Bounds–Henry Martin | 1.00 | 2.00 | 3.00 | X |
| SA76 | The Way with Women–Rick Rand; 1965 | 1.00 | 2.00 | 3.00 | X |
| SA77 | The Sex Seekers–Arnold Marmor | 1.00 | 2.00 | 3.00 | X |
| SA78 | Suzanne–Mark Lucas | 1.00 | 2.00 | 3.00 | X |
| SA79 | When Lesbians Strike–Frank G. Harris | 1.00 | 2.00 | 3.00 | X |
| SA80 | Lust at the Waterfront–Byron Woolfe | 1.00 | 2.00 | 3.00 | X |
| SA81 | Party Girl–Jack Moore | 1.00 | 2.00 | 3.00 | X |
| SA82 | Double-Crossed Beds–Richard Pauvre | 1.00 | 2.00 | 3.00 | X |
| SA83 | Twisted Passions–Drew Palmer; 1965 | 1.00 | 2.00 | 3.00 | X |
| SA84 | Backwoods Daughters–Reese Haynes | 1.00 | 2.00 | 3.00 | X |
| SA85 | Wanted: Broad-Minded Couples–Randall Williams | 1.00 | 2.00 | 3.00 | X |
| SA86 | Pay Off the Damned–Angelo DiSpaldo | 1.00 | 2.00 | 3.00 | X |
| SA87 | The Tricked and the Wicked–Jay Roberts | 1.00 | 2.00 | 3.00 | X |
| SA88 | The Left Hand of Satan–Mark Lucas | 1.00 | 2.00 | 3.00 | X |
| SA89 | Woman in the Window–Jack Moore | 1.00 | 2.00 | 3.00 | X |
| SA90 | Immorality in Three Dimension–Drew Palmer | 1.50 | 3.00 | 4.50 | X |
| SA91 | Passion's Outer Limits–Mark Lucas; 1965 | 1.00 | 2.00 | 3.00 | X |
| SA92 | Long Way Home–Virginia Harris | 1.00 | 2.00 | 3.00 | X |
| SA93 | Lesbian in Retreat–Ben Daniels | 1.00 | 2.00 | 3.00 | X |
| SA94 | In Rooms of Sin–Kip Madigan | 1.00 | 2.00 | 3.00 | X |

Saint Novel K103, Saber SA104, Saber SA161.

## SABER READER

### Saber Books

## SABER-TROPIC–see TROPIC BOOKS/ SABER-TROPIC BOOKS

## SAINT MYSTERY LIBRARY

### Great American Publications, Inc.

Saint Mystery Library 123, Saint Mystery Library 128, Shooting Script nn.

| | | V/Good | Fine | N/Mint |
|---|---|---|---|---|

**SAINT MYSTERY LIBRARY,** *continued*

| | | V/Good | Fine | N/Mint | |
|---|---|---|---|---|---|
| 128 | Let Her Kill Herself—ed. Leslie Charteris; orig. 1960; title story by Rufus King, also includes Harlan Ellison & John Jakes | 5.00 | 10.00 | 15.00 | M |
| 129 | Innocent Bystander—ed. Leslie Charteris; 1960; title story by Craig Rice | 3.00 | 6.00 | 9.00 | M |
| 130 | Death Walks in Marble Halls—ed. Leslie Charteris; orig. 1960; title story by Lawrence G. Blochman, also includes Frederic Brown, Cornell Woolrich, John Jakes | 3.00 | 6.00 | 9.00 | M |
| 131 | The Rum and Coca-Cola Murders—ed. Leslie Charteris; orig. 1960; title story by Wenzell Brown | 2.50 | 5.00 | 7.50 | M |

## SAINT NOVEL
## Fiction Publishing Company

| | | V/Good | Fine | N/Mint | |
|---|---|---|---|---|---|
| K101 | The Saint Steps In—Leslie Charteris; 1967; TV tie-in | 2.00 | 4.00 | 6.00 | M |
| K102 | The Saint Sees It Through—Leslie Charteris; nd; TV tie-in | 2.00 | 4.00 | 6.00 | M |
| K103 | The Saint Closes the Case—Leslie Charteris; nd; TV tie-in | 2.00 | 4.00 | 6.00 | M |
| K104 | The Avenging Saint—Leslie Charteris; nd; TV tie-in | 2.00 | 4.00 | 6.00 | M |
| K105 | Saint's Getaway—Leslie Charteris; nd; TV tie-in | 2.00 | 4.00 | 6.00 | M |
| K106 | The Saint in New York—Leslie Charteris; nd; TV tie-in | 2.00 | 4.00 | 6.00 | M |
| K107 | Enter the Saint—Leslie Charteris; nd; TV tie-in | 2.00 | 4.00 | 6.00 | M |
| K108 | The Saint Meets His Match—Leslie Charteris; nd; TV tie-in | 2.00 | 4.00 | 6.00 | M |
| K109 | Featuring the Saint—Leslie Charteris; nd; TV tie-in | 2.00 | 4.00 | 6.00 | M |
| K110 | Alias the Saint—Leslie Charteris; nd; TV tie-in | 2.00 | 4.00 | 6.00 | M |
| K111 | The Saint Overboard—Leslie Charteris; nd; TV tie-in | 2.00 | 4.00 | 6.00 | M |
| K112 | The Saint—The Brighter Buccaneer—Leslie Charteris; nd; TV tie-in | 2.00 | 4.00 | 6.00 | M |
| K113 | The Saint vs. Scotland Yard—Leslie Charteris; nd; TV tie-in | 2.00 | 4.00 | 6.00 | M |
| K114 | The Saint and Mr. Teal—Leslie Charteris; 1969; TV tie-in | 2.00 | 4.00 | 6.00 | M |

## (SCIENCE SERVICE)
## Science Service

| | | V/Good | Fine | N/Mint | |
|---|---|---|---|---|---|
| nn | Science from Shipboard—What to Do Aboard the Transport; 1943 | 1.50 | 3.00 | 4.50 | NF |

| | | V/Good | Fine | N/Mint |
|---|---|---|---|---|

## SHOOTING SCRIPT
## Catechetical Guild

| | | V/Good | Fine | N/Mint |
|---|---|---|---|---|
| nn | Guilty of Treason—Emmet Lavery; 1950; movie tie-in | 4.00 | 8.00 | 12.00 |

## SIGNET
## New American Library of World Literature, Inc.

**(See also Penguin; some issued as Penguin Signet)**

| | | V/Good | Fine | N/Mint | |
|---|---|---|---|---|---|
| 660 | 100 American Poems—Selden Rodman; 1948 | 1.75 | 3.50 | 5.25 | |
| 661 | Tragic Ground—Erskine Caldwell | 1.75 | 3.50 | 5.25 | |
| 662 | Invitation to the Waltz—Rosamond Lehman | 1.75 | 3.50 | 5.25 | |
| 663 | As Good As Dead—Thomas B. Dewey | 2.00 | 4.00 | 6.00 | M |
| 664 | Portrait of the Artist As a Young Man—James Joyce | 1.75 | 3.50 | 5.25 | |
| 665 | Strange Fruit—Lillian Smith | 1.75 | 3.50 | 5.25 | |
| 666 | The Valley of Hunted Men—Paul Evan Lehman | 1.75 | 3.50 | 5.25 | W |
| 667 | The Pinkerton Case Book—ed. Alan Hynd | 2.00 | 4.00 | 6.00 | M |
| 668 | The Dim View—Basil Heatter | 1.75 | 3.50 | 5.25 | M |
| 669 | The Caballero—Johnston McCulley | 1.75 | 3.50 | 5.25 | W |
| 670 | They Shoot Horses, Don't They?—Horace McCoy | 3.50 | 7.00 | 10.50 | |
| 671 | Darkness at Noon—Arthur Koestler | 1.75 | 3.50 | 5.25 | |
| 672 | Cattle Kingdom—Alan LeMay | 1.75 | 3.50 | 5.25 | W |
| 673 | Sons of the Saddle—William MacLeod Raine | 1.75 | 3.50 | 5.25 | W |
| 674 | Mine Own Executioner—Nigel Balchin | 1.75 | 3.50 | 5.25 | |
| 675 | About the Kinsey Report—Enid Curie & Donald Porter Geddes | .75 | 1.50 | 2.25 | NF |
| 676 | Ariane—Claude Anet | 1.75 | 3.50 | 5.25 | E |
| 677 | Guilty Bystander—Wade Miller | 2.50 | 5.00 | 7.50 | M |
| 678 | The Signet Crossword Puzzle Book—Albert Morehead & Geoffrey Mott-Smith | 3.00 | 6.00 | 9.00 | NF |
| 679 | Laramie Rides Again—Will Ermine | 1.75 | 3.50 | 5.25 | W |
| 680 | Past All Dishonor—James M. Cain | 1.75 | 3.50 | 5.25 | |
| 681 | Contract Bridge for Everyone—Ely Culbertson | .75 | 1.50 | 2.25 | NF |
| 682 | Blood of the West—Paul Evan Lehman | 1.75 | 3.50 | 5.25 | W |
| 683 | The Lost Weekend—Charles Jackson; movie tie-in | 2.00 | 4.00 | 6.00 | |
| 684 | Slay the Murderer—Hugh Holman | 1.75 | 3.50 | 5.25 | M |
| 685 | Lobo Law—Will Ermine | 1.75 | 3.50 | 5.25 | W |
| 686 | A House in the Uplands—Erskine Caldwell | 1.75 | 3.50 | 5.25 | |
| 687 | Shore Leave—Frederic Wakeman | 1.75 | 3.50 | 5.25 | |
| 688 | High Pockets—Herbert Shappiro | 1.75 | 3.50 | 5.25 | |
| 689 | The Silver Tombstone—Frank Gruber | 2.00 | 4.00 | 6.00 | M |
| 690 | No Pockets in a Shroud—Horace McCoy | 3.00 | 6.00 | 9.00 | M |
| 691 | All the Girls We Loved—Prudencio De Pereda | 1.75 | 3.50 | 5.25 | |
| 692 | The Old Man—William Faulkner | 1.75 | 3.50 | 5.25 | |
| 693 | I Love You, I Love You, I Love You—Ludwig Bemelmans | 1.75 | 3.50 | 5.25 | |
| 694 | Lawless Range—Charles N. Heckelmann | 1.75 | 3.50 | 5.25 | W |
| 695 | Fatal Step—Wade Miller | 2.50 | 5.00 | 7.50 | M |
| 696 | The Snake Pit—Mary Jane Ward; movie tie-in | 1.75 | 3.50 | 5.25 | |
| 697 | Look Homeward, Angel, Part II—Thomas Wolfe | 1.75 | 3.50 | 5.25 | |
| 698 | Black Sombrero—William Colt MacDonald | 1.75 | 3.50 | 5.25 | W |
| 699 | I, the Jury—Mickey Spillane; used in Parade of Pleasure, pg. 172 | 5.00 | 10.00 | 15.00 | W |
| 700 | Other Voices, Other Rooms—Truman Capote; 1949 | 2.50 | 5.00 | 7.50 | |
| 701 | Finnley Wren—Philip Wylie | 1.75 | 3.50 | 5.25 | |
| 702 | The Vehement Flame—Ludwig Lewisohn | 1.75 | 3.50 | 5.25 | |

*Signet 707, Signet 721, Signet 722.*

| | V/Good | Fine | N/Mint | |
|---|---|---|---|---|

SIGNET, *continued*

| | | V/Good | Fine | N/Mint | |
|---|---|---|---|---|---|
| 703 | Find My Killer–Manly Wade Wellman | 2.50 | 5.00 | 7.50 | M |
| 704 | Gold of Smoky Mesa–Johnston McCulley | 1.75 | 3.50 | 5.25 | W |
| 705 | A Woman in the House–Erskine Caldwell | 1.75 | 3.50 | 5.25 | |
| 706 | Last of the Conquerors–William Gardner Smith | 1.75 | 3.50 | 5.25 | |
| 707 | The Honest Dealer–Frank Gruber | 1.75 | 3.50 | 5.25 | M |
| 708 | The Texan–Herbert Shapiro | 1.75 | 3.50 | 5.25 | W |
| 709 | Deadlier Than the Male–James E. Gunn | 2.00 | 4.00 | 6.00 | M |
| 710 | The Street–Ann Petry | 1.75 | 3.50 | 5.25 | |
| 711 | Love in Dishevelment–David Greenhood | 1.75 | 3.50 | 5.25 | |
| 712 | The Fighting Tenderfoot–William MacLeod Raine | 1.75 | 3.50 | 5.25 | W |
| 713 | Murder As a Fine Art–Francis Bonnamy | 1.75 | 3.50 | 5.25 | M |
| 714 | The Gilded Hearse–Charles Gorham | 2.00 | 4.00 | 6.00 | M |
| 715 | The Fall of Valor–Charles Jackson | 1.75 | 3.50 | 5.25 | |
| 716 | We Were Strange–Robert Sylvester | 1.75 | 3.50 | 5.25 | |
| 717 | A Son of Arizona–Charles Alden Seltzer | 1.75 | 3.50 | 5.25 | W |
| 718 | Another Man's Poison–Hugh Holman | 1.75 | 3.50 | 5.25 | |
| 719 | Baseball for Everyone–Joe Di Maggio | 3.00 | 6.00 | 9.00 | S |
| 720 | The Butterfly–James M. Cain | 2.00 | 4.00 | 6.00 | |
| 721 | Night of Flame–Warren Desmond | 1.75 | 3.50 | 5.25 | |
| 722 | Uneasy Street–Wade Miller | 2.50 | 5.00 | 7.50 | M |
| 723 | The Crimson Quirt–William Colt MacDonald | 1.75 | 3.50 | 5.25 | W |
| 724 | The Golden Sleep–Vivian Connell | 1.75 | 3.50 | 5.25 | |
| 725 | At Heaven's Gate–Robert Penn Warren; 1949 | 1.75 | 3.50 | 5.25 | |
| 726 | The Whispering Master–Frank Gruber | 2.00 | 4.00 | 6.00 | M |
| 727 | Trigger Justice–Leslie Ernenwein | 1.75 | 3.50 | 5.25 | W |
| 728 | Lona Hanson–Thomas Savage | 1.75 | 3.50 | 5.25 | |
| 729 | Stranger in Town–Howard Hunt | 2.00 | 4.00 | 6.00 | M |
| 730 | The Body in the Bed–Bill S. Ballinger | 2.00 | 4.00 | 6.00 | M |
| 731 | Montana Man–Paul Evan Lehman | 1.75 | 3.50 | 5.25 | W |
| 732 | The Sure Hand of God–Erskine Caldwell | 1.75 | 3.50 | 5.25 | E |
| 733 | Crime and Punishment–Fyodor Dostoyevsky | 1.50 | 3.00 | 4.50 | |
| 734 | Meet the Girls–James T. Farrell | 2.00 | 4.00 | 6.00 | |
| 735 | Everybody Slept Here–Elliott Arnold | 1.75 | 3.50 | 5.25 | |
| 736 | Draw the Curtain Close–Thomas B. Dewey | 2.00 | 4.00 | 6.00 | M |
| 737 | Brave in the Saddle–Will Ermine | 1.75 | 3.50 | 5.25 | W |
| 738 | Nightmare Alley–William Lindsay Gresham | 2.50 | 5.00 | 7.50 | E |
| 739 | Beyond the Forest–Stuart Engstrand | 1.75 | 3.50 | 5.25 | E |
| 740 | Whistling Lead–Eugene Cunningham | 1.75 | 3.50 | 5.25 | W |
| 741 | Life in a Putty Knife Factory–H. Allen Smith | .75 | 1.50 | 2.25 | H |
| 742 | Kill or Cure–William Francis | 2.00 | 4.00 | 6.00 | M |
| 743 | Intruder in the Dust–William Faulkner | 1.75 | 3.50 | 5.25 | |
| 744 | The Christian Demand for Social Justice–William Scarlett | .75 | 1.50 | 2.25 | NF |
| 745 | The Ox-Bow Incident–Walter Van Tilburg Clark | 2.50 | 5.00 | 7.50 | W |
| 746 | Human Destiny–Pierre Lecomte du Nouy | 1.75 | 3.50 | 5.25 | NF |
| 747 | Walden–Henry David Thoreau | 2.00 | 4.00 | 6.00 | |
| 748 | Mistress Glory–Susan Morley | 1.75 | 3.50 | 5.25 | E |
| 749 | For Ever Wilt Thou Love–Ludwig Lewisohn | 1.75 | 3.50 | 5.25 | E |
| 750 | Devil in the Flesh–Raymond Radiguet; 1949 | 1.75 | 3.50 | 5.25 | |
| 751 | Love without Fear–Eustace Chesser | .75 | 1.50 | 2.25 | NF |
| 752 | The Future Mr. Dolan–Charles Gorham | 1.75 | 3.50 | 5.25 | JD |
| 753 | The Gamecock Murders–Frank Gruber | 2.00 | 4.00 | 6.00 | M |
| 754 | Kiss Tomorrow Good-bye–Horace McCoy | 3.00 | 6.00 | 9.00 | E |
| 755 | An American Tragedy–Theodore Dreiser | 1.75 | 3.50 | 5.25 | |
| 756 | If He Hollers Let Him Go–Chester Himes | 3.00 | 6.00 | 9.00 | |
| 757 | Brother of the Cheyennes–Max Brand | 1.75 | 3.50 | 5.25 | W |
| 758 | Clattering Hoofs–William MacLeod Raine | 1.75 | 3.50 | 5.25 | W |
| 759 | Everybody Does It and the Embezzler–James M. Cain; aka Career in C Major | 2.00 | 4.00 | 6.00 | |
| 760 | Georgia Boy–Erskine Caldwell; 1950 | 1.75 | 3.50 | 5.25 | |
| 761 | Country Place–Ann Petry | 1.75 | 3.50 | 5.25 | |
| 762 | You Can Change the World–James Keller | 1.50 | 3.00 | 4.50 | NF |
| 763 | The Weeper and the Blackmailer–Richard H. Rovere | 1.75 | 3.50 | 5.25 | |
| 764 | Six-Shooter Showdown–William Colt MacDonald | 1.75 | 3.50 | 5.25 | W |
| 765 | Murder All Over–Cleve F. Adams; aka Up Jumped the Devil | 2.50 | 5.00 | 7.50 | M |
| 766 | Appointment in Samarra–John O'Hara | 1.75 | 3.50 | 5.25 | |
| 767 | Alien Land–Willard Savoy | 1.75 | 3.50 | 5.25 | E |
| 768 | Dark Encounter–Howard Hunt; aka Maelstrom | 2.00 | 4.00 | 6.00 | M |
| 769 | Margaret–Caroline Slade | 1.75 | 3.50 | 5.25 | E |
| 770 | Two Loves–Elliott Arnold | 1.75 | 3.50 | 5.25 | |
| 771 | Killer's Choice–Wade Miller; aka Devil on Two Sticks | 2.50 | 5.00 | 7.50 | M |
| 772 | Three Musketeers and a Lady–Tiffany Thayer | 1.75 | 3.50 | 5.25 | A |
| 773 | The City and the Pillar–Gore Vidal | 1.75 | 3.50 | 5.25 | |
| 774 | The Body Beautiful–Bill S. Ballinger | 2.00 | 4.00 | 6.00 | M |
| 775 | Vengeance Trail–Charles N. Heckelmann; 1950 | 1.75 | 3.50 | 5.25 | W |
| 776 | Now I Lay Me Down to Sleep–Ludwig Bemelmans | 1.75 | 3.50 | 5.25 | |
| 777 | Laughter in the Dark–Vladimir Nabokov | 1.75 | 3.50 | 5.25 | |
| 778 | I Am Thinking of My Darling–Vincent McHugh | 1.75 | 3.50 | 5.25 | |
| 779 | Ellen Rogers–James T. Farrell | 2.00 | 4.00 | 6.00 | E |
| 780 | The Restless Hands–Bruno Fischer | 2.50 | 5.00 | 7.50 | M |
| 781 | The Outer Edges–Charles Jackson | 1.75 | 3.50 | 5.25 | E |
| 782 | The Buckaroo–Burt Arthur | 1.75 | 3.50 | 5.25 | E |
| 783 | The Saxon Charm–Frederic Wakeman | 1.75 | 3.50 | 5.25 | E |
| 784 | Double Indemnity–James M. Cain | 2.00 | 4.00 | 6.00 | M |
| 785 | Horseback Hellion–George Owen Baxter | 1.75 | 3.50 | 5.25 | W |
| 786 | The Sling and the Arrow–Stuart Engstrand | 1.75 | 3.50 | 5.25 | E |
| 787 | The Hanging Heiress–Richard Wormser | 2.00 | 4.00 | 6.00 | M |
| 788 | Having a Baby–Alan F. Guttmacher | 1.75 | 3.50 | 5.25 | NF |

*Signet 758, Signet 801, Signet 816.*

287

| | | V/Good | Fine | N/Mint | |
|---|---|---|---|---|---|

**SIGNET,** *continued*

| 789 | The Love-Making of Max–Robert–Robert Shaplen; aka Corner of the World | 1.75 | 3.50 | 5.25 | |
|---|---|---|---|---|---|
| 790 | Lily Henry–Mae Cooper | 1.75 | 3.50 | 5.25 | |
| 791 | My Gun Is Quick–Mickey Spillane | 2.50 | 5.00 | 7.50 | M |
| 792 | The Shadow Rider–William Colt MacDonald | 1.75 | 3.50 | 5.25 | W |
| 793 | Kitty Foyle–Christopher Morley | 1.75 | 3.50 | 5.25 | |
| S794 | Native Son–Richard Wright | 3.00 | 6.00 | 9.00 | |
| 795 | Healthy Babies Are Happy Babies–Josephine H. Kenyon & Ruth K. Russell | 1.00 | 2.00 | 3.00 | NF |
| S796 | Arch of Triumph–Erich Maria Remarque | 1.75 | 3.50 | 5.25 | |
| 797 | A Tale of Poor Lovers–Vasco Pratolini | 1.75 | 3.50 | 5.25 | |
| 798 | 1984–George Orwell | 3.00 | 6.00 | 9.00 | SF |
| 799 | The Fourth Letter–Frank Gruber | 2.00 | 4.00 | 6.00 | M |
| 800 | Fannie Farmer's Handy Cook Book; 1950 | 1.75 | 3.50 | 5.25 | NF |
| 801 | The Track of the Cat–Walter Van Tilburg Clark | 1.75 | 3.50 | 5.25 | W |
| 802AB | Knock on Any Door–Willard Motley | 3.00 | 6.00 | 9.00 | JD |
| 803 | World Full of Strangers–David Alman | 1.75 | 3.50 | 5.25 | |
| 804 | Night Rider–Robert Penn Warren | 1.75 | 3.50 | 5.25 | |
| 805 | The Runaways–Carl Bottume; aka The Hills around Havana | 1.75 | 3.50 | 5.25 | E |
| 806 | Powdersmoke Feud–William MacLeod Raine | 1.75 | 3.50 | 5.25 | W |
| 807 | The Bandaged Nude–Robert Finnegan | 2.50 | 5.00 | 7.50 | M |
| 808 | The New American Webster Dictionary | 1.25 | 2.50 | 3.75 | NF |
| 809AB | Forever Amber–Kathleen Winsor | 3.00 | 6.00 | 9.00 | E |
| 810 | The Young Manhood of Studs Lonigan–James T. Farrell | 2.50 | 5.00 | 7.50 | |
| 811 | The Moth–James M. Cain | 2.00 | 4.00 | 6.00 | |
| 812 | Beyond the Moon–Edmond Hamilton | 2.50 | 5.00 | 7.50 | SF |
| 813 | The World Next Door–Fritz Peters | 1.75 | 3.50 | 5.25 | |
| 814 | Room for Murder–Thomas B. Dewey | 2.00 | 4.00 | 6.00 | M |
| 815 | Wanted–Dead or Alive–Gordon Young | 1.75 | 3.50 | 5.25 | W |
| 816 | Tortilla Flat–John Steinbeck | 2.50 | 5.00 | 7.50 | |
| 817AB | The Young Lions–Irwin Shaw | 2.00 | 4.00 | 6.00 | |
| 818 | A Swell-Looking Girl–Erskine Caldwell; aka American Earth | 1.75 | 3.50 | 5.25 | E |
| 819 | The Lonely–Paul Gallico | 1.75 | 3.50 | 5.25 | |
| 820 | Shriek with Pleasure–Toni Howard | 1.75 | 3.50 | 5.25 | E |
| 821 | Sleep No More–Sam S. Taylor | 1.75 | 3.50 | 5.25 | |
| 822 | Trigger Man–Burt Arthur | 1.75 | 3.50 | 5.25 | W |
| 823 | The Wastrel–Frederic Wakeman | 1.75 | 3.50 | 5.25 | |
| 824 | State Fair–Phil Stong | 2.00 | 4.00 | 6.00 | |
| 825 | Knight's Gambit–William Faulkner; 1950 | 1.75 | 3.50 | 5.25 | |
| 826 | Son of the Giant–Stuart Engstrand | 1.75 | 3.50 | 5.25 | |
| 827 | A Job of Murder–Frank Gruber | 2.00 | 4.00 | 6.00 | M |
| 828 | Gunsmoke–Leslie Ernenwein | 1.75 | 3.50 | 5.25 | W |
| 829 | Lilly Crackell–Caroline Slade | 1.75 | 3.50 | 5.25 | |
| 830 | Night unto Night–Philip Wylie | 1.75 | 3.50 | 5.25 | E |
| 831 | Saturday Night–James T. Farrell | 2.00 | 4.00 | 6.00 | E |
| 832 | Love Knows No Barriers–Will Thomas; aka God Is for White Folks | 2.00 | 4.00 | 6.00 | E |
| 833 | The Flesh Was Cold–Bruno Fischer | 2.50 | 5.00 | 7.50 | M |
| 834 | Heart of Darkness and the Secret Sharer–Joseph Conrad | 2.50 | 5.00 | 7.50 | |
| 835 | Dead Man's Gold–William Colt MacDonald | 1.75 | 3.50 | 5.25 | W |
| 836 | Montana Riders!–Evan Evans (Max Brand); 1951 | 1.75 | 3.50 | 5.25 | W |
| 837AB | The Naked and the Dead–Norman Mailer | 2.00 | 4.00 | 6.00 | |
| 838 | This Very Earth–Erskine Caldwell | 1.75 | 3.50 | 5.25 | |
| 839 | Limbo Tower–William Lindsay Gresham | 1.75 | 3.50 | 5.25 | |
| 840 | The Sheltering Sky–Paul Bowles | 1.75 | 3.50 | 5.25 | E |
| 841 | Black Boy–Richard Wright | 3.00 | 6.00 | 9.00 | |
| 842 | Two-Bit Rancher–Charles N. Heckelmann | 1.75 | 3.50 | 5.25 | W |
| 843 | Calamity Fair–Wade Miller | 2.50 | 5.00 | 7.50 | M |
| S844 | The Woman of Rome–Alberto Moravia | 1.75 | 3.50 | 5.25 | E |
| 845 | Tiger in the Garden–Speed Lamkin | 1.75 | 3.50 | 5.25 | E |
| 846 | The Short Cut–Ennio Flaiano | 1.75 | 3.50 | 5.25 | E |
| 847 | The Man Who Sold the Moon–Robert A. Heinlein | 2.50 | 5.00 | 7.50 | SF |
| 848 | The Conquest of Happiness–Bertrand Russell | 1.75 | 3.50 | 5.25 | |

*Signet 820, Signet 834, Signet 841.*

| | | V/Good | Fine | N/Mint | |
|---|---|---|---|---|---|
| 849 | Brother of the Kid–Paul Evan Lehman | 1.75 | 3.50 | 5.25 | W |
| 850 | The Private Eye–Cleve F. Adams; 1951 | 2.50 | 5.00 | 7.50 | M |
| S851 | The Strange Land–Ned Calmer | 1.75 | 3.50 | 5.25 | |
| 852 | Vengeance Is Mine–Mickey Spillane; used in Parade of Pleasure, pp. 180–182 | 2.50 | 5.00 | 7.50 | M |
| 853 | Black Gold–Jewel Gibson | 2.00 | 4.00 | 6.00 | E |
| 854 | Memory and Desire–Leonora Hornblow | 1.75 | 3.50 | 5.25 | |
| 855 | The Snow Was Black–Georges Simenon | 1.75 | 3.50 | 5.25 | M |
| 856 | Mean As Hell–Dee Harkey | 1.75 | 3.50 | 5.25 | W |
| 857 | Meg–Theodora Keogh | 1.75 | 3.50 | 5.25 | |
| 858 | Dirty Eddie–Ludwig Bemelmans | 1.75 | 3.50 | 5.25 | |
| 859 | The Consumer's Guide to Better Buying–Sidney Margolius | .75 | 1.50 | 2.25 | NF |
| 860 | Follow Me Down–Shelby Foote | 2.50 | 5.00 | 7.50 | E |
| 861 | Prettiest Girl in Town–Thomas Fall | 1.75 | 3.50 | 5.25 | E |
| 862 | Courage and Confidence from the Bible–Walter L. Moore | 1.75 | 3.50 | 5.25 | NF |
| 863 | Pylon–William Faulkner | 1.75 | 3.50 | 5.25 | |
| 864 | Strangers and Lovers–Edwin Gran Gerry | 1.75 | 3.50 | 5.25 | E |
| 865 | I.O.U.–Murder–William Francis; aka Rough on Rats | 2.00 | 4.00 | 6.00 | M |
| 866 | Trouble Town–Burt Arthur | 1.75 | 3.50 | 5.25 | W |
| 867 | They Sought for Paradise–Stuart Engstrand | 1.75 | 3.50 | 5.25 | |
| 868AB | Star Money–Kathleen Winsor | 1.25 | 2.50 | 3.75 | |
| 869 | Kneel to the Rising Sun–Erskine Caldwell | 1.75 | 3.50 | 5.25 | |
| 870 | Time for Love–Margaret Lee Runbeck | 1.75 | 3.50 | 5.25 | E |
| 871 | The Dog Star–Donald Windham | 1.75 | 3.50 | 5.25 | E |
| 872 | There's No Home–Alexander Baron; aka The Wine of Etna | 1.25 | 2.50 | 3.75 | E |
| 873 | Appointment with Fear–Donald Stokes | 1.75 | 3.50 | 5.25 | |
| 874 | Hell for Leather–Leslie Ernenwein | 1.75 | 3.50 | 5.25 | W |
| S875 | Judgment Day–James T. Farrell; 1951 | 2.00 | 4.00 | 6.00 | |
| 876 | A Stretch on the River–Richard Bissell | 1.75 | 3.50 | 5.25 | |
| 877 | Cry of Violence–Joseph Kessel; aka Sirrocco | 1.75 | 3.50 | 5.25 | |
| 878 | A Tree of Night–Truman Capote | 2.00 | 4.00 | 6.00 | |
| 879 | No Luck for a Lady–Floyd Mahannah; aka The Yellow Hearse | 2.50 | 5.00 | 7.50 | M |
| 880 | Gunsight Range–William Colt MacDonald | 1.75 | 3.50 | 5.25 | W |
| 881 | Fertility in Marriage–Louis Portnoy & Jules Saltman | 1.25 | 2.50 | 3.75 | NF |
| 882 | The Day after Tomorrow–Robert A. Heinlein | 2.50 | 5.00 | 7.50 | SF |
| 883 | Stone Cold Blonde–Adam Knight | 2.50 | 5.00 | 7.50 | M |
| 884 | I Should Have Stayed Home–Horace McCoy | 3.00 | 6.00 | 9.00 | |
| 885 | Buckskin Marshal–Will Ermine | 1.75 | 3.50 | 5.25 | W |
| 886 | The Daughter–Arthur Markowitz | 1.75 | 3.50 | 5.25 | |
| 887 | Soldier's Pay–William Faulkner | 1.75 | 3.50 | 5.25 | |
| 888 | One Lonely Night–Mickey Spillane; used in Parade of Pleasure, pg. 175 | 3.00 | 6.00 | 9.00 | M |
| 889 | Your Way to Popularity and Personal Power–James Bender & Lee Graham | .75 | 1.50 | 2.25 | NF |
| 890 | The Invaders–Stuart Engstrand | 1.75 | 3.50 | 5.25 | |
| 891 | Gunplay Valley–Joseph Wayne | 1.75 | 3.50 | 5.25 | W |
| 892 | The Silent Dust–Bruno Fischer | 2.50 | 5.00 | 7.50 | M |
| S893 | Bernard Carr–James T. Farrell | 2.00 | 4.00 | 6.00 | E |

Signet 892, Signet 899, Signet 1084.

| | | V/Good | Fine | N/Mint | |
|---|---|---|---|---|---|
| **SIGNET,** *continued* | | | | | |
| 894 | Cornbread Aristocrat–Claud Garner | 1.75 | 3.50 | 5.25 | E |
| 895 | The Triumph of Willie Pond–Caroline Slade | 1.75 | 3.50 | 5.25 | E |
| 896 | Jubel's Children–Lenard Kaufman | 1.75 | 3.50 | 5.25 | E |
| 897 | Portrait in Smoke–Bill S. Ballinger | 1.50 | 3.00 | 4.50 | M |
| 898 | A Texas Cowboy–Charles A. Siringo | 1.75 | 3.50 | 5.25 | W |
| 899 | The Humorous Side of Erskine Caldwell–Erskine Caldwell | 1.75 | 3.50 | 5.25 | |
| 900 | A Wind Is Rising–William Russell; 1951 | 1.75 | 3.50 | 5.25 | |
| 901 | Good Is for Angels–Christopher Clark | 1.75 | 3.50 | 5.25 | E |
| 902 | Contraband–Cleve Adams; illus. in Parade of Pleasure | 2.50 | 5.00 | 7.50 | M |
| 903 | High, Wide and Handsome–Curt Brandon | 1.75 | 3.50 | 5.25 | |
| 904AB | The Rains Came–Louis Bromfield | 1.75 | 3.50 | 5.25 | |
| 905 | Thunder Mountain–Theodore Pratt | 1.75 | 3.50 | 5.25 | |
| 906 | Love Is the One with Wings–Philip van Doren Stern | 1.75 | 3.50 | 5.25 | |
| 907 | Anger at Innocence–William Gardner Smith | 1.75 | 3.50 | 5.25 | |
| 908 | Murder Charge–Wade Miller | 2.50 | 5.00 | 7.50 | M |
| 909 | Butcher's Dozen–John Bartlow Martin | 1.75 | 3.50 | 5.25 | NF |
| 910 | Let the Guns Roar!–Charles N. Heckelmann | 1.75 | 3.50 | 5.25 | W |
| 911 | The Young Lovers–Meyor Levin | 1.75 | 3.50 | 5.25 | |
| 912 | A Family Romance–Elizabeth Pollet | 1.75 | 3.50 | 5.25 | |
| 913 | They Don't Dance Much–James Ross | 1.75 | 3.50 | 5.25 | E |
| 914 | Mission: Interplanetary–A.E. Van Vogt | 2.50 | 5.00 | 7.50 | SF |
| 915 | The Big Kill–Mickey Spillane; used in Parade of Pleasure, pg. 178 | 2.50 | 5.00 | 7.50 | M |
| 916 | Bugles in the Night–Arthur Herbert; 1952 | 1.75 | 3.50 | 5.25 | |
| 917 | A Streetcar Named Desire–Tennessee Williams; movie tie-in | 2.50 | 5.00 | 7.50 | |
| 918 | A Place Called Estherville–Erskine Caldwell | 1.75 | 3.50 | 5.25 | E |
| 919 | The Delicate Prey–Paul Bowles | 1.75 | 3.50 | 5.25 | |
| 920 | Murder for Madame–Adam Knight | 2.50 | 5.00 | 7.50 | M |
| 921AB | Moulin Rouge–Pierre LaMure | 1.75 | 3.50 | 5.25 | |
| 922 | Conjugal Love–Alberto Moravia | 1.75 | 3.50 | 5.25 | |
| 923 | Laird's Choice–Rosamond Marshall | 1.75 | 3.50 | 5.25 | |
| S924 | The Promising Young Men–George Sklar | 1.50 | 3.00 | 4.50 | |
| 925 | The Killer Brand–William Colt MacDonald; 1952 | 1.75 | 3.50 | 5.25 | W |
| D926 | A World I Never Made–James T. Farrell | 2.00 | 4.00 | 6.00 | F |
| 927 | Renee–H.R. Lenormand | 1.75 | 3.50 | 5.25 | |
| 928 | Deadly Weapon–Wade Miller | 2.50 | 5.00 | 7.50 | M |
| D929 | The Seven Storey Mountain–Thomas Merton | 1.75 | 3.50 | 5.25 | |
| 930 | Finistere–Fritz Peters | 1.75 | 3.50 | 5.25 | E |
| S931 | The Troubled Air–Irwin Shaw | 1.75 | 3.50 | 5.25 | |
| 932 | The Long Wait–Mickey Spillane; used in Parade of Pleasure, pg. 179 | 2.50 | 5.00 | 7.50 | M |
| 933 | Southways–Erskine Caldwell | 1.75 | 3.50 | 5.25 | |
| T934 | The Fountainhead–Ayn Rand | 3.00 | 6.00 | 9.00 | |
| 935 | Montana Rides Again–Evan Evans (Max Brand) | 1.75 | 3.50 | 5.25 | W |
| 936 | Sabotage–Cleve F. Adams | 2.50 | 5.00 | 7.50 | M |
| 937 | Goodbye to Berlin–Christopher Isherwood | 2.00 | 4.00 | 6.00 | |
| 938 | Where Town Begins–Richard R. Werry | 2.00 | 4.00 | 6.00 | M |
| 939 | China Station–Donald R. Morris | 1.75 | 3.50 | 5.25 | |
| 940 | Walk on the Water–Ralph Leveridge | 1.75 | 3.50 | 5.25 | |
| 941 | There's One in Every Town–James Aswell | 1.75 | 3.50 | 5.25 | |
| 942 | Pressure–Charles Francis Coe | 1.75 | 3.50 | 5.25 | |
| 943 | The Green Hills of Earth–Robert A. Heinlein | 2.50 | 5.00 | 7.50 | SF |
| 944 | The Loved and the Lost–Morley Callaghan | 1.75 | 3.50 | 5.25 | |
| 945 | Rock Wagram–William Saroyan | 1.75 | 3.50 | 5.25 | |
| D946 | No Star Is Lost–James T. Farrell | 2.00 | 4.00 | 6.00 | |
| 947 | See How They Run–Don M. Mankiewicz | 1.75 | 3.50 | 5.25 | |
| 948 | The Girl in His Past–Georges Simenon | 1.75 | 3.50 | 5.25 | M |
| 949 | The Kiss-Off–Douglas Heyes | 1.75 | 3.50 | 5.25 | |
| 950 | Only the Dead Know Brooklyn–Thomas Wolfe; 1952 | 2.00 | 4.00 | 6.00 | |
| 951 | Elinda–Frances Clippinger | 1.75 | 3.50 | 5.25 | |
| 952 | Stirrups in the Dust–Burt Arthur | 1.75 | 3.50 | 5.25 | W |
| 953 | A Grove of Fever Trees–Daphne Rooke | 1.75 | 3.50 | 5.25 | |
| S954 | Mister Smith–Louis Bromfield | 1.75 | 3.50 | 5.25 | |
| 955 | The Roman Spring of Mrs. Stone–Tennessee Williams | 1.75 | 3.50 | 5.25 | |
| S956 | The Stubborn Heart–Frank G. Slaughter | 1.75 | 3.50 | 5.25 | |
| 957 | The Broken Body–Floyd Mahannah | 2.50 | 5.00 | 7.50 | M |
| 958 | The Double Door–Theodora Keogh | 1.75 | 3.50 | 5.25 | |
| 959 | The Revolt of Mamie Stover–William Bradford Huie; movie tie-in | 1.75 | 3.50 | 5.25 | E |
| 960 | Two Adolescents–Alberto Moravia | 1.75 | 3.50 | 5.25 | |
| S961 | Back Street–Fannie Hurst | 1.75 | 3.50 | 5.25 | |
| 962 | The Face of Innocence–William Sansom | 1.75 | 3.50 | 5.25 | |
| 963 | The Caravan Passes–George Tabori | 1.75 | 3.50 | 5.25 | E |
| 964 | The Heart of a Man–Georges Simenon | 1.75 | 3.50 | 5.25 | |
| 965 | Fighting Ramrod–Charles N. Heckelmann | 1.75 | 3.50 | 5.25 | W |
| 966 | Death Is a Round Black Ball–Mike Roscoe | 2.00 | 4.00 | 6.00 | M |
| D967 | Lie Down in Darkness–William Styron | 1.75 | 3.50 | 5.25 | |
| 968 | The Long November–James Benson Nablo | 1.75 | 3.50 | 5.25 | |
| 969 | A Hero of Our Time–Vasco Pratolini | 1.75 | 3.50 | 5.25 | |
| 970 | Love in a Dry Season–Shelby Foote | 2.50 | 5.00 | 7.50 | |
| S971 | The Sky Is Red–Guiseppe Berto | 1.75 | 3.50 | 5.25 | |
| 972 | Those Devils in Baggy Pants–Ross Carter | 1.75 | 3.50 | 5.25 | C |
| 973 | The Six-Gun Kid–William MacLeod Raine | 1.75 | 3.50 | 5.25 | W |
| 974 | Who Walk in Darkness–Chandler Brossard | 1.75 | 3.50 | 5.25 | |
| D975 | World Enough and Time–Robert Penn Warren; 1952 | 1.75 | 3.50 | 5.25 | |
| 976 | The Temptress–Rosamond Marshall | 1.75 | 3.50 | 5.25 | |
| 977 | The Unvanquished–William Faulkner | 1.75 | 3.50 | 5.25 | |
| 978 | Tobacco Road–Jack Kirkland | 1.75 | 3.50 | 5.25 | E |
| S979 | Possession–Louis Bromfield | 1.75 | 3.50 | 5.25 | |
| 980 | The Puppet Masters–Robert A. Heinlein | 2.50 | 5.00 | 7.50 | SF |
| 981 | The Lonely Hearts Murders–Wenzell Brown; aka Introduction to Murder | 2.00 | 4.00 | 6.00 | NF |
| 982 | Gunhawk Harvest–Leslie Ernenwein | 1.75 | 3.50 | 5.25 | W |
| 983 | Episode in Palmetto–Erskine Caldwell; 1953 | 1.75 | 3.50 | 5.25 | E |
| 984 | The Unwanted–Dante Arfelli | 1.75 | 3.50 | 5.25 | |
| S985 | The Age of Longing–Arthur Koestler | 1.75 | 3.50 | 5.25 | |
| 986 | Your Body and Your Mind–Frank G. Slaughter | 1.75 | 3.50 | 5.25 | |
| 987 | Reach to the Stars–Calder Willingham | 1.75 | 3.50 | 5.25 | |
| 988 | Stripped for Murder–Bruno Fischer; illus. in Parade of Pleasure | 2.50 | 5.00 | 7.50 | M |
| 989 | Trouble in Tombstone–Tom J. Hopkins | 1.75 | 3.50 | 5.25 | W |
| 990 | Sailor's Choice–Carl Bottume | 1.75 | 3.50 | 5.25 | |
| 991 | Moulded in Earth–Richard Vaughan | 1.75 | 3.50 | 5.25 | |
| D992 | We Fished All Night–Willard Motley | 3.00 | 6.00 | 9.00 | |
| 993 | Act of Passion–Georges Simenon | 1.50 | 3.00 | 4.50 | |
| 994 | When Boyhood Dreams Came True–James T. Farrell | 2.00 | 4.00 | 6.00 | |
| 995 | Night at the Vulcan–Ngaio Marsh | 1.50 | 3.00 | 4.50 | M |
| 996 | Doubtful Valley–George Garland | 1.75 | 3.50 | 5.25 | W |

| | V/Good | Fine | N/Mint | |
|---|---|---|---|---|

| No. | Title | V/Good | Fine | N/Mint | |
|---|---|---|---|---|---|
| 997 | Leopard in the Grass–Desmond Stewart | 1.75 | 3.50 | 5.25 | |
| 998 | Moira–Julian Green | 1.75 | 3.50 | 5.25 | |
| S999 | The Hoods–Harry Gray | 3.00 | 6.00 | 9.00 | M |
| 1000 | Kiss Me, Deadly–Mickey Spillane; illus. in Parade of Pleasure | 2.50 | 5.00 | 7.50 | M |
| 1001 | The Catcher in the Rye–J.D. Salinger | 2.50 | 5.00 | 7.50 | |
| 1002 | Let It Come Down–Paul Bowles | 1.75 | 3.50 | 5.25 | |
| 1003 | Dangerous Voyage–Gore Vidal | 1.75 | 3.50 | 5.25 | |
| 1004 | Sybil–Louis Auchincloss | 1.75 | 3.50 | 5.25 | |
| 1005 | Blind Cartridges–William Colt MacDonald | 1.75 | 3.50 | 5.25 | W |
| 1006 | Captive in the Night–Donald Stokes | 1.75 | 3.50 | 5.25 | |
| 1007 | Destination: Universe!–A.E. Van Vogt | 2.50 | 5.00 | 7.50 | SF |
| 1008 | You and Your Heart–H.M. Marvin | 1.00 | 2.00 | 3.00 | NF |
| D1009 | Down All Your Streets–Leonard Bishop | 1.75 | 3.50 | 5.25 | |
| S1010 | Back of Town–Maritta Wolff | 1.75 | 3.50 | 5.25 | |
| 1011 | Dream of Eden–Winston Brebner; aka The Second Circle | 1.75 | 3.50 | 5.25 | |
| 1012 | The Blessing–Nancy Mitford | 1.75 | 3.50 | 5.25 | |
| 1013 | Shoot to Kill–Wade Miller | 2.50 | 5.00 | 7.50 | M |
| 1014 | They Lived by Their Guns–ed. anon. | 2.00 | 4.00 | 6.00 | W |
| 1015 | Song of the Whip–Evan Evans (Max Brand) | 1.75 | 3.50 | 5.25 | W |
| 1016 | The Courting of Susie Brown–Erskine Caldwell | 1.75 | 3.50 | 5.25 | |
| S1017 | Scalpel–Horace McCoy | 3.50 | 7.00 | 10.50 | |
| S1018 | Dream of Innocence–Turnley Walker | 1.75 | 3.50 | 5.25 | |
| 1019 | Barbary Shore–Norman Mailer | 1.75 | 3.50 | 5.25 | E |
| 1020 | The Glass Harp–Truman Capote | 1.75 | 3.50 | 5.25 | |
| 1021 | Mittee–Daphne Rooke | 1.75 | 3.50 | 5.25 | |
| 1022 | Knife at My Back–Adam Knight | 1.50 | 3.00 | 4.50 | M |
| S1023 | Spark of Life–Erich Maria Remarque | 1.75 | 3.50 | 5.25 | E |
| 1024 | A Husband in the House–Stuart Engstrand | .75 | 1.50 | 2.25 | |
| S1025 | The Green Bay Tree–Louis Bromfield; 1953 | 1.75 | 3.50 | 5.25 | |
| 1026 | Frail Barrier–Philip Gillon | 1.75 | 3.50 | 5.25 | |
| 1027 | The Devil's Passkey–Jimmy Shannon | 1.75 | 3.50 | 5.25 | |
| 1028 | The Snake Stomper–Joseph Wayne | 1.75 | 3.50 | 5.25 | W |
| 1029 | Wise Blood–Flannery O'Connor | 1.75 | 3.50 | 5.25 | |
| D1030 | Invisible Man–Ralph Ellison | 4.00 | 8.00 | 12.00 | |
| 1031 | An American Dream Girl–James T. Farrell | 2.00 | 4.00 | 6.00 | |
| S1032 | Sartoris–William Faulkner | 1.75 | 3.50 | 5.25 | |
| 1033 | My Life in Crime–John Bartlow Martin | 1.75 | 3.50 | 5.25 | NF |
| 1034 | I Take This Woman–George Simenon | 1.75 | 3.50 | 5.25 | M |
| 1035 | To End the Night–Alex Gaby | 1.75 | 3.50 | 5.25 | |
| 1036 | Death in the Fifth Position–Edgar Box | 2.00 | 4.00 | 6.00 | M |
| 1037 | Bugle's Wake–Curt Brandon | 1.75 | 3.50 | 5.25 | W |
| S1038 | Rage of the Soul–Vincent Sheean | 1.75 | 3.50 | 5.25 | |
| S1039 | Sons and Lovers–D.H. Lawrence | 1.75 | 3.50 | 5.25 | |
| 1040 | The Darkening Door–Bill S. Ballinger | 1.75 | 3.50 | 5.25 | M |
| S1041 | This Dear Encounter–Catherine Hutter | 1.75 | 3.50 | 5.25 | |
| 1042 | The Red Carnation–Elio Vittorini | 1.75 | 3.50 | 5.25 | |
| S1043 | Submarine!–Edward L. Beach | 1.75 | 3.50 | 5.25 | C |
| 1044 | Tomorrow, the Stars–Robert A. Heinlein | 2.50 | 5.00 | 7.50 | SF |
| 1045 | Trigger Vengeance–B.M. Bower | 1.75 | 3.50 | 5.25 | W |
| 1046 | Brother of the Cheyennes–Max Brand | 1.75 | 3.50 | 5.25 | W |
| 1047 | Wives and Husbands–David Duncan; c-Maguire | 1.75 | 3.50 | 5.25 | E |
| 1048 | By Any Other Name–Roy Michaels | 1.75 | 3.50 | 5.25 | |
| 1049 | Street Music–Theodora Keogh | 1.75 | 3.50 | 5.25 | |
| 1050 | Pistol Pete–Frank Eaton; 1953 | 1.75 | 3.50 | 5.25 | W |
| S1051 | Scollay Square–Pearl Schiff | 1.75 | 3.50 | 5.25 | |
| S1052 | Heaven Pays No Dividends–Richard Kaufmann; c-Maguire | 1.75 | 3.50 | 5.25 | |
| 1053 | The Brigand–Giuseppe Berto | 1.75 | 3.50 | 5.25 | |
| 1054 | Naked to Mine Enemies–Susan Yorke | 1.75 | 3.50 | 5.25 | |
| S1055 | The Consumer's Guide to Better Buying–Sidney Margolius | .75 | 1.50 | 2.25 | NF |
| 1056 | The Mistress–H.C. Branner | 1.50 | 3.00 | 4.50 | |
| 1057 | No Head for Her Pillow–Sam S. Taylor | 1.50 | 3.00 | 4.50 | |
| 1058 | Ashes–Charles Francis Coe | 1.50 | 3.00 | 4.50 | |
| 1059 | Ranger Man–William Colt MacDonald | 1.75 | 3.50 | 5.25 | W |
| 1060 | Riddle Me This–Mike Roscoe | 2.50 | 5.00 | 7.50 | M |
| 1061 | The Naked Streets–Vasco Pratolini | 1.50 | 3.00 | 4.50 | |
| S1062 | Natural Child–Calder Willingham | 1.50 | 3.00 | 4.50 | |
| 1063 | Home Is Upriver–Brian Horwin | 1.50 | 3.00 | 4.50 | |
| 1064 | The Descent–Fritz Peters | 1.50 | 3.00 | 4.50 | |
| 1065 | A Funeral for Sabella–Robert Travers | 1.75 | 3.50 | 5.25 | |
| D1066 | Father and Son–James T. Farrell | 2.00 | 4.00 | 6.00 | |
| 1067 | Crime without Punishment–Guenther Reinhardt | 1.75 | 3.50 | 5.25 | |
| D1068 | Confessors of the Name–Gladys Schmitt; c-Maguire | 1.75 | 3.50 | 5.25 | |
| 1069 | Justice Comes to Tomahawk–William MacLeod Raine | 1.75 | 3.50 | 5.25 | W |
| S1070 | The Best Thing That Ever Happened–Warren Leslie | 1.50 | 3.00 | 4.50 | |
| S1071 | The Conformist–Alberto Moravia | 1.50 | 3.00 | 4.50 | |
| 1072 | A Cow Is Too Much Trouble in Los Angeles–Joseph Foster | 1.50 | 3.00 | 4.50 | |
| 1073 | Four Days in a Lifetime–Georges Simenon | 1.75 | 3.50 | 5.25 | M |
| S1074 | Strange Fruit–Lillian Smith | 1.75 | 3.50 | 5.25 | |
| T1075 | From Here to Eternity–James Jones; 1953 | 2.50 | 5.00 | 7.50 | C |
| 1076 | The Big Sin–Jack Webb | 1.75 | 3.50 | 5.25 | M |
| 1077 | By Gun and Spur–Joseph Wayne | 1.75 | 3.50 | 5.25 | W |
| S1078 | The Curve and the Tusk–Stuart Cloete | 1.75 | 3.50 | 5.25 | A |
| S1079 | Sanctuary and Requiem for a Nun–William Faulkner | 1.50 | 3.00 | 4.50 | |
| S1080 | Caesar's Angel–Mary Anne Amsbary | 1.50 | 3.00 | 4.50 | |
| 1081 | The Disguises of Love–Robie Macauley | 1.50 | 3.00 | 4.50 | |
| 1082 | The Currents of Space–Isaac Asimov | 2.50 | 5.00 | 7.50 | SF |
| 1083 | The Day I Died–Lawrence Lariar | 2.00 | 4.00 | 6.00 | M |
| 1084 | Deadlier Than the Male–James E. Gunn | 1.75 | 3.50 | 5.25 | M |
| 1085 | The Saga of Billy the Kid–Walter Noble Burns | 1.75 | 3.50 | 5.25 | B |
| S1086 | Lady Chatterley's Lover–D.H. Lawrence | 1.75 | 3.50 | 5.25 | |
| 1087 | Appointment in Samarra–John O'Hara | 1.75 | 3.50 | 5.25 | |
| 1088 | Young Man with a Horn–Dorothy Baker | 1.75 | 3.50 | 5.25 | |
| 1089 | Guilty Bystander–Wade Miller; 1954 | 1.50 | 3.00 | 4.50 | M |
| S1090 | The Mountain and the Valley–Ernest Buckler | 1.50 | 3.00 | 4.50 | |
| 1091 | A Lamp for Nightfall–Erskine Caldwell | 1.50 | 3.00 | 4.50 | |
| 1092 | Depends What You Mean by Love–Nicholas Monsarrat | 1.50 | 3.00 | 4.50 | |
| 1093 | Death before Bedtime–Edgar Box | 1.50 | 3.00 | 4.50 | M |
| S1094 | Amazon Head-Hunters–Lewis Cotlow | 2.50 | 5.00 | 7.50 | A |
| 1095 | Uncle Tom's Children–Richard Wright | 2.50 | 5.00 | 7.50 | |
| 1096 | Gigi and Julie de Carneilhan–Sidonie Colette | 1.75 | 3.50 | 5.25 | |
| 1097 | The Waitress–William Fisher | 1.50 | 3.00 | 4.50 | |
| S1098 | The Skin–Curzio Malaparte | 1.50 | 3.00 | 4.50 | |
| 1099 | The Center of the Stage–Gerald Sykes | 1.50 | 3.00 | 4.50 | |
| 1100 | The Tatooed Heart–Theodora Keogh; 1954 | 1.75 | 3.50 | 5.25 | |
| 1101 | The Big Dry–George Garland | 1.50 | 3.00 | 4.50 | W |
| D1102 | Night Shift–Maritta Wolff | 1.50 | 3.00 | 4.50 | |
| 1103 | The Sunburned Corpse–Adam Knight | 1.50 | 3.00 | 4.50 | M |
| 1104 | Shiloh–Shelby Foote | 2.00 | 4.00 | 6.00 | |
| 1105 | The Demolished Man–Alfred Bester | 2.00 | 4.00 | 6.00 | SF |
| 1106 | A Breed Apart–Fleming MacLiesh | 1.50 | 3.00 | 4.50 | |
| D1107 | Days of My Love–Leonard Bishop | 1.50 | 3.00 | 4.50 | |
| 1108 | Hell in His Holsters–Charles N. Heckelmann | 1.75 | 3.50 | 5.25 | W |
| 1109 | The Brother Rico–Georges Simenon | 1.75 | 3.50 | 5.25 | M |
| 1110 | Portrait of the Damned–Richard McKaye; c-Maguire | 1.75 | 3.50 | 5.25 | |
| 1111 | Nine Stories–J.D. Salinger | 1.75 | 3.50 | 5.25 | |
| 1112 | The Double Shuffle–James Hadley Chase | 1.75 | 3.50 | 5.25 | M |
| 1113 | The Execution of Private Slovik–William Bradford Hule | 1.75 | 3.50 | 5.25 | C |
| S1114 | The Outsider–Richard Wright | 2.00 | 4.00 | 6.00 | |
| 1115 | The Lost Year–Robert Hazel | 1.50 | 3.00 | 4.50 | |
| 1116 | Morning, Winter and Night–John Nairne Michaelson | 1.50 | 3.00 | 4.50 | |
| 1117 | The Moon and the Bonfires–Cesare Pavese | 1.50 | 3.00 | 4.50 | |
| S1118 | My Days of Anger–James T. Farrell | 2.00 | 4.00 | 6.00 | |
| 1119 | Murder, Madness and the Law–Louis H. Cohen, M.D.; c-Maguire | 2.00 | 4.00 | 6.00 | NF |
| 1120 | Smoke Bellew–Jack London | 1.75 | 3.50 | 5.25 | A |
| 1121 | The Birds and the Bees–James Aswell | 1.50 | 3.00 | 4.50 | |
| 1122 | The Fancy Dress Party–Alberto Moravia | 1.50 | 3.00 | 4.50 | |
| S1123 | The Street–Ann Petry | 1.75 | 3.50 | 5.25 | E |
| 1124 | Belle–Georges Simenon | 1.75 | 3.50 | 5.25 | M |

*Signet 1104, Signet 1120, Signet 1172.*

|  | V/Good | Fine | N/Mint |  |
|---|---|---|---|---|
| **SIGNET,** *continued* | | | | |
| 1125 may not exist | | | | |
| 1126 The Naked Heart–John Lee Weldon; 1954 | 1.50 | 3.00 | 4.50 | |
| 1127 The Time Masters–Wilson Tucker | 1.50 | 3.00 | 4.50 | SF |
| 1128 The Long Wind–Joseph Wayne | 1.50 | 3.00 | 4.50 | W |
| 1129 Pajama–Richard Bissell | 1.50 | 3.00 | 4.50 | |
| D1130 Trial by Darkness–Charles Gorham | 1.50 | 3.00 | 4.50 | |
| S1131 Cancel All Our Vows–John D. MacDonald | 3.00 | 6.00 | 9.00 | M |
| 1132 The Face of the Deep–Jacob Twersky | 1.25 | 2.50 | 3.75 | |
| S1133 The Time of Man–Elizabeth Madox Roberts | 1.25 | 2.50 | 3.75 | |
| 1134 The Beautiful Trap–Bill S. Ballinger | 1.75 | 3.50 | 5.25 | M |
| 1135 The Texan–Burt Arthur | 1.75 | 3.50 | 5.25 | W |
| 1136 We Are the Living–Erskine Caldwell | 1.50 | 3.00 | 4.50 | |
| S1137 A House of Her Own–Robert F. Mirvish | 1.25 | 2.50 | 3.75 | |
| 1138 Go Tell It on the Mountain–James Baldwin | 3.00 | 6.00 | 9.00 | |
| 1139 Kiss and Kill–Adam Knight | 1.75 | 3.50 | 5.25 | M |
| 1140 Guns of the Frontier–William MacLeod Raine | 1.75 | 3.50 | 5.25 | W |
| 1141 may not exist | | | | |
| 1142 Branded–A.C. Abbott | 1.75 | 3.50 | 5.25 | W |
| S1143 A Law for the Lion–Louis Auchincloss | 1.50 | 3.00 | 4.50 | |
| 1144 The Bottom of the Bottle–Georges Simenon | 1.75 | 3.50 | 5.25 | M |
| 1145 The Money Song–Arnold Shaw | 1.25 | 2.50 | 3.75 | |
| 1146 The Wayward Ones–Sara Harris | 1.75 | 3.50 | 5.25 | E |
| 1147 A Kiss before Dying–Ira Levin | 1.25 | 2.50 | 3.75 | |
| S1148 The Wild Palms and the Old Man–William Faulkner | 1.75 | 3.50 | 5.25 | |
| 1149 The Naked Angel–Jack Webb; c-Maguire | 1.75 | 3.50 | 5.25 | M |
| S1150 Portrait of the Artist As a Young Man–James Joyce; 1955 | 2.00 | 4.00 | 6.00 | |
| 1151 Mafia–Ed Reid | 1.75 | 3.50 | 5.25 | |
| 1152 Galatea–James M. Cain | 2.00 | 4.00 | 6.00 | |
| 1153 Serenade–James M. Cain | 2.00 | 4.00 | 6.00 | |
| 1154 Requiem for a Redhead–Lindsay Hardy | 2.00 | 4.00 | 6.00 | M |
| 1155 Awakening–Jean-Baptiste Rossi | 1.25 | 2.50 | 3.75 | |
| D1156 The Chain in the Heart–Hubert Creekmore | 1.25 | 2.50 | 3.75 | |
| S1157 The Hive–Camilo Jose Cela | 1.25 | 2.50 | 3.75 | |
| 1158 This Man and This Woman–James T. Farrell | 2.00 | 4.00 | 6.00 | |
| 1159 The Scattered Seed–Stuart Engstrand | 1.25 | 2.50 | 3.75 | |
| 1160 The Ox-Bow Incident–Walter Van Tilburg Clark | 1.75 | 3.50 | 5.25 | W |
| 1161 Assignment in Eternity–Robert A. Heinlein | 2.50 | 5.00 | 7.50 | SF |
| S1162 Mud on the Stars–William Bradford Huie | 1.25 | 2.50 | 3.75 | |
| 1163 The General's Wench–Rosamond Marshall | 1.75 | 3.50 | 5.25 | |
| 1164 The Black City–M.F. Caulfield | 1.75 | 3.50 | 5.25 | |
| 1165 The Color of His Blood–Marris Murray | 1.75 | 3.50 | 5.25 | |
| 1166 The Young and Hungry-Hearted–James Aswell | 1.50 | 3.00 | 4.50 | |
| 1167 Let the Night Cry–Charles Wells; c-Maguire | 1.75 | 3.50 | 5.25 | |

|  | V/Good | Fine | N/Mint |  |
|---|---|---|---|---|
| 1168 Law and Order, Unlimited–William Colt MacDonald | 1.75 | 3.50 | 5.25 | W |
| D1169 Forever Amber–Kathleen Winsor | 1.25 | 2.50 | 3.75 | R |
| 1170 Time for Love–Margaret Lee Runbeck | 1.25 | 2.50 | 3.75 | |
| S1171 Search for the Sun–Charles Furcolowe | 1.25 | 2.50 | 3.75 | |
| 1172 A Private Stair–David Loughlin; 1955 | 1.25 | 2.50 | 3.75 | |
| 1173 The Spider in the Cup–Norman Hales | 1.25 | 2.50 | 3.75 | |
| 1174 Texas Hellion–J.H. Plenn | 1.75 | 3.50 | 5.25 | W |
| 1175 Devil in the Flesh–Raymond Radiguet | 1.75 | 3.50 | 5.25 | |
| 1176 The Sling and the Arrow–Stuart Engstrand | 1.75 | 3.50 | 5.25 | |
| 1177 Proud Youth–Alexander Eliot | 1.25 | 2.50 | 3.75 | |
| S1178 The Housewarming–George Sklar | 1.25 | 2.50 | 3.75 | |
| 1179 The Lie–Peggy Goodin | 1.25 | 2.50 | 3.75 | |
| 1180 Fatal Step–Wade Miller | 1.75 | 3.50 | 5.25 | M |
| 1181 Six-Shooter Showdown–William Colt MacDonald | 1.75 | 3.50 | 5.25 | W |
| 1182 The Snake Pit–Mary Jane Ward | 1.25 | 2.50 | 3.75 | |
| D1183 A Many-Splendored Thing–Suyin Han | 1.25 | 2.50 | 3.75 | |
| 1184 Thunder in the Heart–John Lee Weldon | 1.25 | 2.50 | 3.75 | |
| 1185 Room Clerk–Herbert Gold | 1.25 | 2.50 | 3.75 | |
| 1186 All the Way Home–Walter Freeman | 1.25 | 2.50 | 3.75 | |
| 1187 I'll Bury My Dead–James Hadley Chase | 1.75 | 3.50 | 5.25 | M |
| 1188 Inspector Maigret and the Strangled Stripper–Georges Simenon; c-Maguire | 1.75 | 3.50 | 5.25 | M |
| S1189 Cheri and the Last of Cheri–Sidonie Colette | 1.75 | 3.50 | 5.25 | |
| 1190 Kitty–Rosamond Marshall | 1.25 | 2.50 | 3.75 | |
| 1191 The Final Hours–Jose Suarez Carreno | 1.75 | 3.50 | 5.25 | |
| 1192 A Texas Cowboy–Charles A. Siringo | 1.75 | 3.50 | 5.25 | W |
| 1193 River in My Blood–Richard Bissell; aka The Monongahela | 1.75 | 3.50 | 5.25 | |
| 1194 Revolt in 2100–Robert A. Heinlein | 2.50 | 5.00 | 7.50 | SF |
| 1195 The Butterfly–James M. Cain | 2.00 | 4.00 | 6.00 | |
| 1196 Mean As Hell–Dee Harkey | 1.25 | 2.50 | 3.75 | W |
| S1197 Street of the Barefoot Lovers–Joseph Foster | 1.25 | 2.50 | 3.75 | |
| D1198 Love Is a Bridge–Charles Bracelen Flood | 1.25 | 2.50 | 3.75 | |
| D1199 The Complete Stories of Erskine Caldwell–Erskine Caldwell | 1.50 | 3.00 | 4.50 | |
| S1200 The Jungle Seas–Arthur A. Ageton; 1955 | 1.50 | 3.00 | 4.50 | |
| 1201 Bamboo–Robert O. Bowen | 1.25 | 2.50 | 3.75 | |
| 1202 Out of the Red Brush–Kermit Daugherty | 1.25 | 2.50 | 3.75 | |
| 1203 Win, Place and Die!–Lawrence Lariar | 1.75 | 3.50 | 5.25 | M |
| 1204 Love Trap–Lionel White; orig. 1955 | 2.50 | 5.00 | 7.50 | M |
| S1205 Tombstone–Walter Noble Burns | 1.25 | 2.50 | 3.75 | NF |
| D1206 The Cry and the Covenant–Morton Thompson | 1.25 | 2.50 | 3.75 | |
| 1207 Three Sinners in Paris–Toni Howard | 1.25 | 2.50 | 3.75 | |
| 1208 Live for Today–Vincent Sheean; c-Maguire | 1.75 | 3.50 | 5.25 | |
| 1209 The Fascinator–Theodora Keogh | 1.75 | 3.50 | 5.25 | |
| 1210 My Husband Keeps Telling Me to Go to Hell–Ella Bentley Arthur | 1.25 | 2.50 | 3.75 | |
| D1211 The Hoods–Harry Grey | 2.50 | 5.00 | 7.50 | |
| T1212 A Child of the Century–Ben Hecht | 1.25 | 2.50 | 3.75 | |
| S1213 The Time of Indifference–Alberto Moravia | 1.25 | 2.50 | 3.75 | |

*Signet 1194, Signet 1216, Signet 1283.*

| | V/Good | Fine | N/Mint | |
|---|---|---|---|---|

SIGNET, *continued*

| No. | Title | V/Good | Fine | N/Mint | |
|---|---|---|---|---|---|
| S1214 | Life of Davy Crockett–Davy Crockett | 1.75 | 3.50 | 5.25 | B |
| S1215 | Lost Island–Graham McInnes | 1.25 | 2.50 | 3.75 | F |
| 1216 | Slice of Hell–Mike Roscoe; c-Maguire | 2.50 | 5.00 | 7.50 | M |
| 1217 | Death Likes It Hot–Edgar Box | 1.50 | 3.00 | 4.50 | M |
| 1218 | The City and the Pillar–Gore Vidal | 1.75 | 3.50 | 5.25 | |
| 1219 | Cattle Kingdom–Alan LeMay | 1.75 | 3.50 | 5.25 | W |
| S1220 | Darkness at Noon–Arthur Koestler | 1.25 | 2.50 | 3.75 | |
| 1221 | The Black Donnellys–Thomas P. Kelley | 1.50 | 3.00 | 4.50 | NF |
| S1222 | The Eternal Voyagers–Robert F. Mirvish | 1.25 | 2.50 | 3.75 | |
| 1223 | First Affair–Raffaele LaCapria | 1.25 | 2.50 | 3.75 | |
| 1224 | The Space Frontiers–Roger Lee Vernon | 1.50 | 3.00 | 4.50 | SF |
| 1225 | The Last Kill–Charles Wells; 1955; c-Maguire | 1.75 | 3.50 | 5.25 | M |
| 1226 | Violent Streets–Dale Kramer | 1.75 | 3.50 | 5.25 | |
| D1227 | The Lovers–Kathleen Winsor | 1.25 | 2.50 | 3.75 | |
| 1228 | Sons of the Saddle–William MacLeod Raine | 1.25 | 2.50 | 3.75 | W |
| D1229 | Moby Dick–Herman Melville | 2.00 | 4.00 | 6.00 | A |
| 1230 | High Water–Richard Bissell | 1.75 | 3.50 | 5.25 | |
| 1231 | The Farmer's Bride–Robert Hazel | 1.25 | 2.50 | 3.75 | |
| 1232 | Hard Man with a Gun–Charles N. Heckelmann | 1.25 | 2.50 | 3.75 | W |
| 1233 | The Damned Lovely–Jack Webb; c-Maguire | 1.75 | 3.50 | 5.25 | M |
| 1234 | This Thing Called Love–Harve Breit & Marc Slonim | 1.25 | 2.50 | 3.75 | |
| 1235 | Killer's Choice–Wade Miller | 1.50 | 3.00 | 4.50 | M |
| 1236 | The Rose Tattoo–Tennessee Williams | 1.25 | 2.50 | 3.75 | |
| D1237 | The Lying Days–Nadine Gordimer | 1.25 | 2.50 | 3.75 | |
| S1238 | Everything Happens at Night–Bernard Wolfe | 1.25 | 2.50 | 3.75 | |
| 1239 | Warrior's Return–Ted Pittenger | 1.25 | 2.50 | 3.75 | |
| S1240 | The Caves of Steel–Isaac Asimov | 2.50 | 5.00 | 7.50 | SF |
| 1241 | To Find a Killer–Lionel White; c-Maguire | 2.50 | 5.00 | 7.50 | M |
| 1242 | Web of Gunsmoke–Will Hickok | 1.25 | 2.50 | 3.75 | W |
| 1243 | The Body in the Bed–Bill S. Ballinger | 1.50 | 3.00 | 4.50 | M |
| D1244 | The Gold of Their Bodies–Charles Gorham | 2.00 | 4.00 | 6.00 | |
| S1245 | Satchmo–Louis Armstrong | 1.75 | 3.50 | 5.25 | B |
| 1246 | Nights of Love and Laughter–Henry Miller | 2.50 | 5.00 | 7.50 | |
| 1247 | So Cold, My Bed–Sam S. Taylor; c-Maguire | 2.50 | 5.00 | 7.50 | |
| 1248 | Inspector Maigret and the Killers–Georges Simenon | 1.50 | 3.00 | 4.50 | M |
| S1249 | The Sheltering Sky–Paul Bowles | 1.25 | 2.50 | 3.75 | |
| 1250 | The Golden Sleep–Vivian Connell; 1955 | 1.25 | 2.50 | 3.75 | |
| 1251 | Laramie Rides Alone–Will Ermine | 1.25 | 2.50 | 3.75 | W |
| S1252 | Goodbye to Berlin–Christopher Isherwood | 1.75 | 3.50 | 5.25 | |
| S1253 | Intruder in the Dust–William Faulkner | 1.25 | 2.50 | 3.75 | |
| S1254 | Heart of Darkness and the Secret Sharer–Joseph Conrad | 1.50 | 3.00 | 4.50 | |
| 1255 | The Unholy Three and Other Stories–Louis Auchincloss | 1.25 | 2.50 | 3.75 | |
| 1256 | The Bleeding Scissors–Bruno Fischer; c-Maguire | 2.50 | 5.00 | 7.50 | M |
| 1257 | Uneasy Street–Wade Miller | 1.50 | 3.00 | 4.50 | M |
| 1258 | Montana Man–Paul Evan Lehman | 1.25 | 2.50 | 3.75 | W |
| T1259 | The Narrows–Ann Petry | 1.25 | 2.50 | 3.75 | |
| D1260 | The Farm–Louis Bromfield | 1.25 | 2.50 | 3.75 | E |
| 1261 | How Green Was My Sex Life–Lawrence Lariar | 1.50 | 3.00 | 4.50 | H |
| S1262 | A Streetcar Named Desire–Tennessee Williams | 1.75 | 3.50 | 5.25 | |
| D1263 | The Rains Came–Louis Bromfield; 1956 | 1.25 | 2.50 | 3.75 | |
| 1264 | The Primitive–Chester Himes | 3.50 | 7.00 | 10.50 | |
| T1265 | Not as a Stranger–Morton Thompson | 1.25 | 2.50 | 3.75 | |
| S1266 | The Soft Voice of the Serpent–Nadine Gordimer | 1.25 | 2.50 | 3.75 | |
| 1267 | Margaret–Caroline Slade | 1.25 | 2.50 | 3.75 | |
| 1268 | Stopover for Murder–Floyd Mahannah; c-Maguire | 2.50 | 5.00 | 7.50 | M |
| 1269 | Whistling Lead–Eugene Cunningham | 1.25 | 2.50 | 3.75 | W |
| 1270 | Calamity Fair–Wade Miller; c-Maguire | 1.75 | 3.50 | 5.25 | M |
| S1271 | Fifty Roads to Town–Earl Hammer, Jr | 1.75 | 3.50 | 5.25 | |
| 1272 | Love and Money–Erskine Caldwell | 1.25 | 2.50 | 3.75 | |
| S1273 | The Blue Hussar–Roger Nimier | 1.25 | 2.50 | 3.75 | |
| 1274 | The Body Beautiful–Bill S. Ballinger | 1.50 | 3.00 | 4.50 | M |

| No. | Title | V/Good | Fine | N/Mint | |
|---|---|---|---|---|---|
| 1275 | The Face of Time–James T. Farrell; 1956; c-Maguire | 1.50 | 3.00 | 4.50 | |
| 1276 | I'll Kill You Next!–Adam Knight; c-Maguire | 1.75 | 3.50 | 5.25 | M |
| 1277 | Bunch Grass–Joseph Wayne | 1.25 | 2.50 | 3.75 | W |
| 1278 | Dirty Eddie–Ludwig Bemelmans | 1.25 | 2.50 | 3.75 | |
| S1279 | Making of a Mistress–Susan Morley | 1.25 | 2.50 | 3.75 | |
| S1280 | General Billy Mitchell–Roger Burlingame | 1.25 | 2.50 | 3.75 | B |
| S1281 | Adventures in the Skin Trade–Dylan Thomas | 1.75 | 3.50 | 5.25 | |
| S1282 | I, Robot–Isaac Asimov | 2.50 | 5.00 | 7.50 | SF |
| 1283 | The Nightshade Ring–Lindsay Hardy | 1.25 | 2.50 | 3.75 | M |
| 1284 | Meg–Theodora Keogh | 1.25 | 2.50 | 3.75 | |
| S1285 | No Time for Sergeants–Mac Hyman | 1.25 | 2.50 | 3.75 | H |
| 1286 | The Big Steal–Earle Basinsky | 1.50 | 3.00 | 4.50 | M |
| 1287 | Lobo Law–Will Ermine | 1.25 | 2.50 | 3.75 | W |
| 1288 | Conjugal Love–Alberto Moravia | 1.25 | 2.50 | 3.75 | |
| 1289 | Animal Farm–George Orwell | 3.50 | 7.00 | 10.50 | SF |
| S1290 | Too Late the Phalarope–Alan Paton | 1.00 | 2.00 | 3.00 | |
| D1291 | The Royal Box–Frances Parkinson Keyes | 1.25 | 2.50 | 3.75 | |
| S1292 | The Enemy–Wirt Williams | 1.25 | 2.50 | 3.75 | C |
| 1293 | I Stole $16,000,000–Thomas P. Kelley & Herbert Emerson Wilson | 1.75 | 3.50 | 5.25 | NF |
| 1294 | Violence in Velvet–Michael Avallone; c-Maguire | 2.50 | 5.00 | 7.50 | M |
| 1295 | The Lonely–Paul Gallico | 1.25 | 2.50 | 3.75 | |
| 1296 | The Delicate Prey–Paul Bowles | 1.25 | 2.50 | 3.75 | |
| 1297 | The Valley of Hunted Men–Paul Evan Lehman | 1.25 | 2.50 | 3.75 | W |
| 1298 | Contraband–Cleve F. Adams | 1.50 | 3.00 | 4.50 | |
| D1299 | The Third Generation–Chester Himes | 3.50 | 7.00 | 10.50 | |
| 1300 | Washington Lowdown–Larston Farrar; 1956 | 1.25 | 2.50 | 3.75 | |
| 1301 | The Secret of Mary Magdalene–Paul Ilton | 1.25 | 2.50 | 3.75 | E |
| 1302 | Gunplay Valley–Joseph Wayne | 1.25 | 2.50 | 3.75 | W |
| 1303 | The Six-Gun Kid–William MacLeod Raine | 1.25 | 2.50 | 3.75 | W |
| 1304 | Winesburg, Ohio–Sherwood Anderson | 1.25 | 2.50 | 3.75 | |
| D1305 | Boswell's London Journal–James Boswell | 1.25 | 2.50 | 3.75 | |
| S1306 | A Ghost at Noon–Alberto Moravia | 1.25 | 2.50 | 3.75 | |
| S1307 | Murder in Paradise–Richard Gehman | 1.25 | 2.50 | 3.75 | M |
| S1308 | The Girl in the Dogwood Cabin–Calder Willingham | 1.25 | 2.50 | 3.75 | |
| S1309 | The Whispers of Love–Marguerite Duras | 1.25 | 2.50 | 3.75 | |
| 1310 | The Killing–Lionel White; c-Maguire; movie tie-in | 2.50 | 5.00 | 7.50 | M |
| 1311 | The Broken Doll–Jack Webb; c-Maguire | 1.75 | 3.50 | 5.25 | M |
| 1312 | The Fastest Gun in Texas–C.J. LaRoche & J.H. Plenn | 1.75 | 3.50 | 5.25 | W |
| 1313 | The Tent of the Wicked–Robert Switzer | 1.25 | 2.50 | 3.75 | |
| 1314 | There's One in Every Town–James Aswell | 1.25 | 2.50 | 3.75 | |
| 1315 | Knight's Gambit–William Faulkner | 1.25 | 2.50 | 3.75 | |
| 1316 | The Glass Playpen–Edwin Fadiman, Jr; c-Maguire | 1.75 | 3.50 | 5.25 | |
| 1317 | A Devil in Paradise–Henry Miller | 1.25 | 2.50 | 3.75 | |

*Signet 1322, Signet 1335, Signet 1349.*

292

SIGNET, *continued*

| | | V/Good | Fine | N/Mint | |
|---|---|---|---|---|---|
| S1318 | The Black Prince and Other Stories–Shirley Ann Grau | 1.75 | 3.50 | 5.25 | |
| 1319 | The Tooth and the Nail–Bill S. Ballinger; c-Maguire | 1.75 | 3.50 | 5.25 | M |
| 1320 | Shore Leave–Frederic Wakeman | 1.25 | 2.50 | 3.75 | |
| 1321 | Portrait in Smoke–Bill S. Ballinger | 1.75 | 3.50 | 5.25 | M |
| 1322 | Stone Cold Blonde–Adam Knight; c-Maguire | 2.00 | 4.00 | 6.00 | M |
| 1323 | Buckskin Marshal–Will Ermine | 1.25 | 2.50 | 3.75 | W |
| 1324 | Delay en Route–Jerry Weil; c-Maguire | 2.00 | 4.00 | 6.00 | |
| 1325 | The Navigator–Jules Roy; 1956 | 1.25 | 2.50 | 3.75 | |
| 1326 | Nightmare Alley–William Lindsay Gresham | 1.25 | 2.50 | 3.75 | |
| 1327 | The Snow Was Black–Georges Simenon | 1.25 | 2.50 | 3.75 | M |
| D1328 | The New American Handy College Dictionary–Albert H. Morehead & Loy Morehead | 1.00 | 2.00 | 3.00 | NF |
| 1329 | The Kiss-off–Douglas Heyes | 1.25 | 2.50 | 3.75 | |
| D1330 | Band of Angels–Robert Penn Warren | 1.25 | 2.50 | 3.75 | |
| 1331 | Black Sombrero–William Colt MacDonald | 1.25 | 2.50 | 3.75 | W |
| 1332 | Julie–Andrew L. Stone; c-Maguire; movie tie-in | 2.00 | 4.00 | 6.00 | |
| S1333 | The Glass Harp and A Tree of Night–Truman Capote | 1.25 | 2.50 | 3.75 | |
| 1334 | Baby Doll–Tennessee Williams; movie tie-in | 3.00 | 6.00 | 9.00 | |
| 1335 | The Living Idol–Robert Switzer; c-Maguire; movie tie-in | 3.00 | 6.00 | 9.00 | |
| S1336 | Nectar in a Sieve–Kamala Markandaya | 1.25 | 2.50 | 3.75 | |
| S1337 | The Alien Heart–Catherine Hutter | 1.25 | 2.50 | 3.75 | |
| 1338 | Inspector Maigret in New York's Underworld–Georges Simenon; c-Maguire | 2.00 | 4.00 | 6.00 | M |
| 1339 | Return of the Texan–Burt Arthur | 1.25 | 2.50 | 3.75 | W |
| 1340 | Trigger Justice–Leslie Ernenwein | 1.25 | 2.50 | 3.75 | W |
| 1341 | The Wayward Ones–Sara Harris | 1.50 | 3.00 | 4.50 | E |
| 1342 | Gretta–Erskine Caldwell | 1.25 | 2.50 | 3.75 | |
| 1343 | Tea and Sympathy–Robert Anderson; movie tie-in | 1.25 | 2.50 | 3.75 | |
| 1344 | Good Night, Sailor–J. Inchardi | 1.25 | 2.50 | 3.75 | |
| S1345 | A Good Man Is Hard to Find–Flannery O'Connor | 1.25 | 2.50 | 3.75 | |
| S1346 | Operation: Outer Space–Murray Leinster | 2.50 | 5.00 | 7.50 | SF |
| S1347 | Girl Running–Adam Knight | 1.50 | 3.00 | 4.50 | M |
| S1348 | The Teahouse of the August Moon–Vern Sneider; movie tie-in | 2.00 | 4.00 | 6.00 | |
| 1349 | French Girls Are Vicious–James T. Farrell | 2.00 | 4.00 | 6.00 | |
| 1350 | Office Wife–Jerry Weil; 1957 | 1.25 | 2.50 | 3.75 | |
| 1351 | Death Is a Cold, Keen Edge–Earle Basinsky; c-Maguire | 2.50 | 5.00 | 7.50 | M |
| 1352 | Blood of the West–Paul Evan Lehman | 1.25 | 2.50 | 3.75 | W |
| 1353 | The Slander of Witches–Richard Gehman | 1.25 | 2.50 | 3.75 | |
| 1354 | Night Flight–Antoine de Saint Exupery | 1.25 | 2.50 | 3.75 | |
| D1355 | The Strangeland–Ned Calmer | 1.25 | 2.50 | 3.75 | |
| S1356 | Anastasia–Marcelle Maurette; movie tie-in | 1.25 | 2.50 | 3.75 | |
| 1357 | A Stranger in Eden–Desmond Stewart | 1.25 | 2.50 | 3.75 | |
| 1358 | One Tear for My Grave–Mike Roscoe; c-Maguire | 2.00 | 4.00 | 6.00 | M |
| 1359 | Desire Me–Leonhard Frank | 1.25 | 2.50 | 3.75 | |
| 1360 | Brave in the Saddle–Will Ermine | 1.25 | 2.50 | 3.75 | W |
| 1361 | Ever since Adam and Eve–Alfred Andriola & Mel Casson | 1.25 | 2.50 | 3.75 | H |
| S1362 | Quicksand–William Brinkley | 1.25 | 2.50 | 3.75 | |
| S1363 | The Tyranny of Sex–Ludwig Lewisohn | 1.25 | 2.50 | 3.75 | |
| S1364 | The Girl He Left Behind–Marion Hargrove | 1.25 | 2.50 | 3.75 | |
| S1365 | The Angry Hills–Leon Uris | 1.25 | 2.50 | 3.75 | C |
| 1366 | Death Rider–J.O. Barnwell; 1957 | 1.25 | 2.50 | 3.75 | |
| S1367 | Gift from the Sea–Anne Morrow Lindbergh | 1.25 | 2.50 | 3.75 | |
| D1368 | 1,000,000 Delinquents–Benjamin Fine | 2.50 | 5.00 | 7.50 | JD |
| 1369 | Shoot to Kill–Wade Miller | 1.50 | 3.00 | 4.50 | M |
| S1370 | The Short Cut–Ennio Flaiano | 1.25 | 2.50 | 3.75 | |
| S1371 | I Leap over the Wall–Monica Baldwin | 1.25 | 2.50 | 3.75 | |
| 1372 | Two Adolescents–Alberto Moravia | 1.25 | 2.50 | 3.75 | |
| 1373 | Bullet Law–Charles N. Heckelmann | 1.25 | 2.50 | 3.75 | W |
| 1374 | An Act of Violence–Edwin Fadiman, Jr | 1.25 | 2.50 | 3.75 | |
| D1375 | The Deer Park–Norman Mailer; 1957 | 1.25 | 2.50 | 3.75 | |
| 1376 | Strangers in the House–Georges Simenon | 1.50 | 3.00 | 4.50 | M |
| 1377 | The Life, the Loves, the Adventures of Omar Khayyam–Manuel Komroff; movie tie-in | 2.00 | 4.00 | 6.00 | A |
| 1378 | Flight into Terror–Lionel White; c-Maguire | 1.50 | 3.00 | 4.50 | M |
| 1379 | The Bandaged Nude–Robert Finnegan | 1.50 | 3.00 | 4.50 | M |
| 1380 | Tortilla Flat–John Steinbeck | 1.75 | 3.50 | 5.25 | |
| 1381 | The Story of Sandy–Susan Stanhope Wexler | 1.25 | 2.50 | 3.75 | |
| 1382 | What Am I Doing Here?–Abner Dean | 1.25 | 2.50 | 3.75 | |
| 1383 | Killer in the House–Borden Deal | 1.50 | 3.00 | 4.50 | M |
| 1384 | The Return of the Kid–Joseph Wayne | 1.25 | 2.50 | 3.75 | W |
| S1385 | The Bachelor Party–Paddy Chayefsky; movie tie-in | 1.50 | 3.00 | 4.50 | |
| D1386 | End as a Man–Calder Willingham | 1.25 | 2.50 | 3.75 | |
| S1387 | Look Not upon Me–Denys Jones | 1.25 | 2.50 | 3.75 | |
| T1388 | Andersonville–MacKinlay Kantor | 1.75 | 3.50 | 5.25 | NF |
| S1389 | The Stars, My Destination–Alfred Bester | 1.50 | 3.00 | 4.50 | SF |
| 1390 | The Wastrel–Frederic Wakeman | 1.25 | 2.50 | 3.75 | |
| D1391 | The Long Ships–Frans G. Bengtsson | 1.75 | 3.50 | 5.25 | A |
| S1392 | The Girl He Left Behind–Marion Hargrove; special edition revised for Teen-Age Book Club | 1.25 | 2.50 | 3.75 | |
| 1393 | Paint on Their Faces–Jerry Weil; c-Maguire | 1.50 | 3.00 | 4.50 | |
| 1394 | may not exist | | | | |
| 1395 | Murder for Madame–Adam Knight | 1.50 | 3.00 | 4.50 | M |
| 1396 | Clattering Hoofs–William MacLeod Raine | 1.25 | 2.50 | 3.75 | W |
| 1397 | In a Summer Season–Ludwig Lewisohn | 1.25 | 2.50 | 3.75 | |
| 1398 | Montana Rides!–Evan Evans (Max Brand) | 1.25 | 2.50 | 3.75 | W |
| 1399 | The Last Days of Sodom and Gomorrah–Paul Ilton; c-Maguire | 2.50 | 5.00 | 7.50 | E |
| S1400 | Lizzie–Shirley Jackson; 1957; movie tie-in | 1.25 | 2.50 | 3.75 | |
| 1401 | Trigger Man–Burt Arthur | 1.25 | 2.50 | 3.75 | W |
| 1402 | Ripening Seed–Sidonie Colette | 1.25 | 2.50 | 3.75 | |
| 1403 | Quick-Trigger Country–Clem Colt | 1.25 | 2.50 | 3.75 | W |
| 1404 | Love in the Afternoon–Claude Anet | 1.25 | 2.50 | 3.75 | |
| 1405 | The Private Eye–Cleve F. Adams; c-Maguire | 1.75 | 3.50 | 5.25 | M |
| 1406 | may not exist | | | | |
| D1407 | Beyond Desire–Pierre LaMure | 1.25 | 2.50 | 3.75 | |
| S1408 | More Deaths Than One–Stuart Engstrand | 1.25 | 2.50 | 3.75 | |
| S1409 | The Prince and the Showgirl–Terence Rattigan; movie tie-in | 3.00 | 6.00 | 9.00 | E |
| D1410 | Heart of Darkness and the Secret Sharer–Joseph Conrad | 1.25 | 2.50 | 3.75 | |
| D1411 | Confessions of Felix Krull, Confidence Man–Thomas Mann | 1.50 | 3.00 | 4.50 | NF |
| S1412 | A Hatful of Rain–Michael Vincente Gazzo; movie tie-in | 1.25 | 2.50 | 3.75 | |
| S1413 | Sweet Smell of Success–Ernest Lehman; movie tie-in | 1.25 | 2.50 | 3.75 | |
| 1414 | Flint–Gil Dodge | 1.25 | 2.50 | 3.75 | W |
| S1415 | The Night before Chancellorsville–Shelby Foote | 2.00 | 4.00 | 6.00 | |
| 1416 | The Killer Brand–William Colt MacDonald | 1.25 | 2.50 | 3.75 | W |
| 1417 | This Very Earth–Erskine Caldwell | 1.25 | 2.50 | 3.75 | |
| 1418 | Doubtful Valley–George Garland | 1.25 | 2.50 | 3.75 | |
| 1419 | Sabotage–Cleve F. Adams | 1.75 | 3.50 | 5.25 | M |
| S1420 | The Deliverance of Sister Cecilia–William Brinkley & Sister Cecilia | 1.25 | 2.50 | 3.75 | |
| 1421 | The Hitchhiker–Georges Simenon | 1.50 | 3.00 | 4.50 | M |
| 1422 | The Bad Blonde–Jack Webb; c-Maguire | 1.75 | 3.50 | 5.25 | M |
| 1423 | The Manhunter–Matthew Gant | 1.25 | 2.50 | 3.75 | |
| S1424 | This Is the West–Robert West Howard | 1.25 | 2.50 | 3.75 | NF |
| S1425 | Pajama–Richard Bissell; 1957 | 1.25 | 2.50 | 3.75 | |
| S1426 | Country Place–Ann Petry | 1.25 | 2.50 | 3.75 | |
| 1427 | Double Indemnity–James M. Cain; c-Maguire | 1.75 | 3.50 | 5.25 | M |
| D1428 | Lady Chatterley's Lover–D.H. Lawrence | 1.25 | 2.50 | 3.75 | |
| 1429 | The Unfaithful Wife–Jules Roy | 1.25 | 2.50 | 3.75 | |

| | | V/Good | Fine | N/Mint | |
|---|---|---|---|---|---|
| S1430 | Gulf Coast Stories–Erskine Caldwell | 1.25 | 2.50 | 3.75 | |
| D1431 | New American Roget's College Thesaurus in Dictionary Form | 1.00 | 2.00 | 3.00 | NF |
| 1432 | The Hard Guys–John B. Sanford | 1.25 | 2.50 | 3.75 | |
| S1433 | The Martian Way and Other Stories–Isaac Asimov | 1.50 | 3.00 | 4.50 | SF |
| 1434 | The Tight Corner–Sam Ross | 1.25 | 2.50 | 3.75 | |
| 1435 | The Man from Yesterday–John S. Daniels | 1.25 | 2.50 | 3.75 | W |
| 1436 | Montana Rides Again–Evan Evans (Max Brand) | 1.25 | 2.50 | 3.75 | W |
| S1437 | Appointment in Samarra–John O'Hara | 1.25 | 2.50 | 3.75 | |
| D1438 | Lucy Crown–Irwin Shaw | 1.25 | 2.50 | 3.75 | |
| S1439 | Ruby McCollum–William Bradford Huie | 1.25 | 2.50 | 3.75 | |
| 1440 | Coral Comes High–George P. Hunt | 1.25 | 2.50 | 3.75 | C |
| 1441 | The Mountain Boys–Paul Webb | 1.25 | 2.50 | 3.75 | |
| 1442 | The House Next Door–Lionel White; c-Maguire | 1.50 | 3.00 | 4.50 | M |
| 1443 | Gunsmoke in Nevada–Burt Arthur | 1.25 | 2.50 | 3.75 | W |
| S1444 | Double Star–Robert A. Heinlein | 2.50 | 5.00 | 7.50 | SF |
| 1445 | Love's Lovely Counterfeit–James M. Cain | 1.50 | 3.00 | 4.50 | |
| 1446 | The Comedian and Other Stories–Ernest Lehman; TV tie-in for Playhouse 90 | 1.25 | 2.50 | 3.75 | |
| 1447 | Secret of Hidden Valley–Loring Hutchinson | 1.25 | 2.50 | 3.75 | |
| 1448 | Find My Killer–Manly Wade Wellman; c-Maguire | 2.00 | 4.00 | 6.00 | M |
| 1449 | Nobody Dies in Paris–Jerry Weil | 1.25 | 2.50 | 3.75 | |
| 1450 | Shore Leave–Frederic Wakeman; 1957; 10th printing is movie tie-in | 1.25 | 2.50 | 3.75 | |
| S1451 | Comfort Me with Apples–Peter De Vries | 1.25 | 2.50 | 3.75 | |
| S1452 | I'm Owen Harrison Harding–James Whitfield Ellison | 1.25 | 2.50 | 3.75 | |
| S1453 | Tip on a Dead Jockey–Irwin Shaw; movie tie-in | 1.25 | 2.50 | 3.75 | |
| T1454 | Marjorie Morningstar–Herman Wouk | 1.25 | 2.50 | 3.75 | |
| D1455 | The Field of Vision–Wright Morris | 1.25 | 2.50 | 3.75 | |
| 1456 | A House in the Uplands–Erskine Caldwell | 1.25 | 2.50 | 3.75 | |
| S1457 | A Dangerous Woman–James T. Farrell | 1.25 | 2.50 | 3.75 | |
| D1458 | Don't Go Near the Water–William Brinkley; movie tie-in | 1.25 | 2.50 | 3.75 | |
| S1459 | Submarine!–Edward L. Beach | 1.50 | 3.00 | 4.50 | C |
| S1460 | This Is Goggle–Bentz Plagemann | 1.25 | 2.50 | 3.75 | |
| 1461 | Wild Town–Jim Thompson; orig. 1957; c-Maguire | 12.50 | 25.00 | 37.50 | |
| S1462 | Bitter Victory–Rene Hardy | 1.25 | 2.50 | 3.75 | |
| S1463 | Modern Sex Life–Edwin Hirsch | 1.00 | 2.00 | 3.00 | |
| S1464 | The City and the Stars–Arthur C. Clarke | 1.50 | 3.00 | 4.50 | SF |
| 1465 | The Fugitive–Georges Simenon | 1.50 | 3.00 | 4.50 | M |
| S1466 | Those Devils in Baggy Pants–Ross Carter | 1.25 | 2.50 | 3.75 | C |
| S1467 | A Walk in the Sun–Harry Brown | 1.25 | 2.50 | 3.75 | |
| T1468 | The Fountainhead–Ayn Rand | 1.50 | 3.00 | 4.50 | |
| D1469 | The Amazing Crime and Trial of Leopold and Loeb–Maureen McKernan | 1.25 | 2.50 | 3.75 | NF |
| S1470 | The Ox-Bow Incident–Walter Van Tilburg Clark | 1.25 | 2.50 | 3.75 | W |
| 1471 | Old Soldiers Never Die–Wolf Mankowitz | 1.25 | 2.50 | 3.75 | |
| 1472 | Kill Once, Kill Twice–Kyle Hunt; c-Maguire | 2.00 | 4.00 | 6.00 | M |
| 1473 | Bandido–Nelson Nye | 1.25 | 2.50 | 3.75 | W |
| 1474 | The Flesh Was Cold–Bruno Fischer; c-Maguire | 2.00 | 4.00 | 6.00 | M |
| 1475 | Death in the Fifth Position–Edgar Box; 1957 | 1.50 | 3.00 | 4.50 | M |
| S1476 | The FBI in Action–Ken Jones | 1.25 | 2.50 | 3.75 | NF |
| D1477 | Raquel–Lion Feuchtwanger | 1.25 | 2.50 | 3.75 | |
| S1478 | War!–Alex Austin | 1.25 | 2.50 | 3.75 | C |
| 1479 | A Place Called Estherville–Erskine Caldwell | 1.25 | 2.50 | 3.75 | |
| 1480 | The Sins of Sandra Shaw–Larston Farrar; 1958 | 1.25 | 2.50 | 3.75 | |
| 1481 | Thirty Notches–Brad Ward | 1.25 | 2.50 | 3.75 | W |
| 1482 | Guilty Bystander–Wade Miller | 1.25 | 2.50 | 3.75 | M |

*Signet 1351, Signet S1495, Signet 1556.*

| | | V/Good | Fine | N/Mint | |
|---|---|---|---|---|---|
| 1483 | Powdersmoke Feud–William MacLeod Raine | 1.25 | 2.50 | 3.75 | W |
| 1484 | Death Likes It Hot–Edgar Box | 1.50 | 3.00 | 4.50 | M |
| S1485 | Pylon–William Faulkner; movie tie-in | 1.25 | 2.50 | 3.75 | |
| D1486 | Sanctuary and Requiem for a Nun–William Faulkner | 1.25 | 2.50 | 3.75 | |
| D1487 | The Last Parallel–Martin Russ | 1.25 | 2.50 | 3.75 | |
| T1488 | The Brothers Karamazov–Fyodor Dostoyevsky | 1.25 | 2.50 | 3.75 | |
| 1489 | Sing, Boy, Sing–Richard Vincent; movie tie-in | 2.00 | 4.00 | 6.00 | |
| D1490 | Too Much, Too Soon–Diana Barrymore & Gerold Frank | 1.25 | 2.50 | 3.75 | |
| S1491 | Kitty Foyle–Christopher Morley | 1.25 | 2.50 | 3.75 | |
| 1492 | Violent Hours–Robert Walsh | 1.25 | 2.50 | 3.75 | M |
| S1493 | The End of Eternity–Isaac Asimov | 1.75 | 3.50 | 5.25 | SF |
| 1494 | The Wife of the Red-haired Man–Bill S. Ballinger | 1.25 | 2.50 | 3.75 | M |
| S1495 | Last of the Great Outlaws–Homer Croy | 1.50 | 3.00 | 4.50 | NF |
| T1496 | The Young Lions–Irwin Shaw | 1.25 | 2.50 | 3.75 | |
| S1497 | The Sacrilege of Alan Kent–Erskine Caldwell | 1.25 | 2.50 | 3.75 | |
| D1498 | Nine Stories–J.D. Salinger | 1.25 | 2.50 | 3.75 | |
| S1499 | Cat Man–Edward Hoagland | 1.25 | 2.50 | 3.75 | E |
| S1500 | Mafia–Ed Reid; 1958 | 1.25 | 2.50 | 3.75 | NF |
| S1501 | The Long Hot Summer–William Faulkner; movie tie-in | 1.75 | 3.50 | 5.25 | E |
| S1502 | Desire under the Elms–Eugene O'Neill; movie tie-in | 1.25 | 2.50 | 3.75 | |
| D1503 | Grandfather Stories–Samuel Hopkins Adams | 1.25 | 2.50 | 3.75 | |
| 1504 | West Side Jungle–Jason Ridgway | 2.50 | 5.00 | 7.50 | JD |
| 1505 | Smoke of the Gun–John S. Daniels | 1.25 | 2.50 | 3.75 | W |
| D1506 | Able Company–D.J. Hollands | 1.25 | 2.50 | 3.75 | C |
| S1507 | The Tunnel of Love–Peter De Vries | 1.25 | 2.50 | 3.75 | |
| 1508 | Cry Terror–Andrew L. Stone; c-Maguire; movie tie-in | 2.00 | 4.00 | 6.00 | M |
| D1509 | Sons and Lovers–D.H. Lawrence | 1.25 | 2.50 | 3.75 | |
| D1510 | The Conformist–Alberto Moravia | 1.25 | 2.50 | 3.75 | |
| S1511 | Intruder in the Dust–William Faulkner | 1.25 | 2.50 | 3.75 | |
| S1512 | The Invisible Flag–Peter Bamm | 1.25 | 2.50 | 3.75 | |
| S1513 | The Barbarian and the Geisha–Robert Payne; movie tie-in | 2.50 | 5.00 | 7.50 | A |
| S1514 | The Assistant–Bernard Malamud | 1.25 | 2.50 | 3.75 | |
| 1515 | Hang by Your Neck–Henry Kane | 1.50 | 3.00 | 4.50 | M |
| 1516 | Maverick Marshal–Nelson Nye | 1.25 | 2.50 | 3.75 | W |
| S1517 | Duchess Hotspur–Rosamond Marshall | 1.00 | 2.00 | 3.00 | |
| T1518 | Studs Lonigan–James T. Farrell | 1.25 | 2.50 | 3.75 | |
| D1519 | Gallery of Women–Bernard Glemser | 1.25 | 2.50 | 3.75 | |
| S1520 | Bitter Honeymoon–Alberto Moravia | 1.25 | 2.50 | 3.75 | |
| S1521 | Soldier's Three–Humphrey Slater | 1.25 | 2.50 | 3.75 | C |
| S1522 | Company K–William March | 1.25 | 2.50 | 3.75 | C |
| 1523 | Edge of Panic–Henry Kane | 1.75 | 3.50 | 5.25 | M |
| S1524 | Starburst–Alfred Bester | 1.50 | 3.00 | 4.50 | SF |
| S1525 | Gigi and Julie de Carneilhan–Sidonie Colette; 1958 | 1.25 | 2.50 | 3.75 | |
| 1526 | Death before Bedtime–Edgar Box; c-Maguire | 2.00 | 4.00 | 6.00 | M |
| 1527 | The Body–Carter Brown | 1.25 | 2.50 | 3.75 | M |
| 1528 | The Nightwalkers–Beverley Cross | 1.25 | 2.50 | 3.75 | |
| D1529 | A Streetcar Named Desire–Tennessee Williams | 1.25 | 2.50 | 3.75 | |

Signet S1563, Signet 1584, Signet S1590.

|  |  | V/Good | Fine | N/Mint |  |
|---|---|---|---|---|---|
| SIGNET, *continued* | | | | | |
| D1530 | No Time for Sergeants–Mac Hyman | 1.25 | 2.50 | 3.75 | H |
| S1531 | Love among the Cannibals–Wright Morris | 1.25 | 2.50 | 3.75 | |
| S1532 | Some Inner Fury–Kamala Markandaya | 1.25 | 2.50 | 3.75 | |
| S1533 | Branded West–Don Ward | 1.25 | 2.50 | 3.75 | W |
| S1534 | 43,000 Years Later–Horace Coon | 1.25 | 2.50 | 3.75 | SF |
| S1535 | A Thirsty Evil–Gore Vidal | 1.25 | 2.50 | 3.75 | |
| 1536 | A Texan Came Riding–Frank O'Rourke | 1.25 | 2.50 | 3.75 | W |
| S1537 | The Green Hills of Earth–Robert A. Heinlein | 1.50 | 3.00 | 4.50 | SF |
| 1538 | Dame in Danger–Thomas B. Dewey; c-Maguire | 2.00 | 4.00 | 6.00 | M |
| 1539 | The Case of the Dead Divorcee– William Holder | 1.75 | 3.50 | 5.25 | M |
| 1540 | No Luck for a Lady–Floyd Mahannah; c-Maguire | 1.50 | 3.00 | 4.50 | |
| 1541 | The Restless Gun–Will Hickok; TV tie-in | 2.50 | 5.00 | 7.50 | W |
| D1542 | Whispers of the Flesh–Fletcher Flora | 1.25 | 2.50 | 3.75 | |
| S1543 | Silent Grow the Guns–MacKinlay Kantor | 1.25 | 2.50 | 3.75 | |
| S1544 | The Puppet Masters–Robert A. Heinlein | 1.75 | 3.50 | 5.25 | SF |
| D1545 | Bread and Wine–Ignazio Silone | 1.25 | 2.50 | 3.75 | |
| D1546 | Bon Voyage!–Joseph Hayes & Marrijane Hayes | 1.25 | 2.50 | 3.75 | |
| T1547 | A Dictionary of American-English Usage–Margaret Nicholson | 1.00 | 2.00 | 3.00 | NF |
| D1548 | The Love-Seekers–Leonora Hornblow | 1.25 | 2.50 | 3.75 | |
| T1549 | The Naked and the Dead–Norman Mailer | 1.25 | 2.50 | 3.75 | |
| D1550 | Birdman of Alcatraz–Thomas E. Gaddis; 1958 | 1.50 | 3.00 | 4.50 | |
| S1551 | My Fair Lady–Alan Jay Lerner; movie tie-in | 1.75 | 3.50 | 5.25 | |
| D1552 | The World of Suzie Wong–Richard Mason; movie tie-in | 1.75 | 3.50 | 5.25 | |
| S1553 | Selected Stories–Liam O'Flaherty | 1.25 | 2.50 | 3.75 | |
| 1554 | Escapade–Jerry Weil | 1.25 | 2.50 | 3.75 | |
| 1555 | Hell to Pay–William R. Cox | 3.00 | 6.00 | 9.00 | JD |
| 1556 | The Brass Halo–Jack Webb; c-Maguire | 2.00 | 4.00 | 6.00 | M |
| S1557 | The Wild Bunch–James D. Horan | 1.25 | 2.50 | 3.75 | NF |
| S1558 | Destination: Universe–A.E. Van Vogt | 1.50 | 3.00 | 4.50 | SF |
| S1559 | Giovanni's Room–James Baldwin | 1.25 | 2.50 | 3.75 | |
| S1560 | My Name Is Rose–Theodora Keogh | 1.50 | 3.00 | 4.50 | |
| D1561 | The Girl with the Swansdown Seat– Cyril Pearl | 1.25 | 2.50 | 3.75 | |
| D1562 | On the Beach–Nevil Shute | 2.50 | 5.00 | 7.50 | SF |
| S1563 | From Russia, with Love–Ian Fleming | 3.00 | 6.00 | 9.00 | |
| S1564 | This Very Earth–Erskine Caldwell | 1.25 | 2.50 | 3.75 | |
| 1565 | The Blonde–Carter Brown | 1.25 | 2.50 | 3.75 | M |
| 1566 | Damaron's Gun–Wesley Ray | 1.25 | 2.50 | 3.75 | |
| T1567 | Forever Amber–Kathleen Winsor | 1.25 | 2.50 | 3.75 | R |
| S1568 | Certain Women–Erskine Caldwell | 1.25 | 2.50 | 3.75 | |
| S1569 | Room at the Top–John Braine | 1.00 | 2.00 | 3.00 | |
| S1570 | Nine Miles to Reno–Jill Stern | 1.25 | 2.50 | 3.75 | |
| S1571 | Henry the Last–Giuseppe Puzza | 1.25 | 2.50 | 3.75 | |
| S1572 | Portrait of a Mobster–Harry Grey | 2.00 | 4.00 | 6.00 | |
| 1573 | Kill a Wicked Man–Kyle Hunt | 1.25 | 2.50 | 3.75 | |
| D1574 | Moulin Rouge–Pierre LaMure | 1.25 | 2.50 | 3.75 | |
| D1575 | The Hoods–Harry Grey; 1959 | 1.25 | 2.50 | 3.75 | |
| D1576 | Knock on Any Door–Willard Motley | 1.50 | 3.00 | 4.50 | |
| S1577 | The Day after Tomorrow–Robert A. Heinlein | 1.50 | 3.00 | 4.50 | SF |
| T1578 | Remember Me to God–Myron S. Kaufmann | 1.25 | 2.50 | 3.75 | |
| S1579 | Not Yet . . .–Tereska Torres | 1.25 | 2.50 | 3.75 | |
| S1580 | Subways Are for Sleeping–Edmund Love | 1.25 | 2.50 | 3.75 | |
| 1581 | The Heart of a Stranger–Lionel Olay | 1.25 | 2.50 | 3.75 | |
| 1582 | The Doll's Smile–Eva Boros | 1.25 | 2.50 | 3.75 | |
| S1583 | The Deep Range–Arthur C. Clarke | 1.50 | 3.00 | 4.50 | SF |
| 1584 | The Getaway–Jim Thompson; orig. 1959 | 12.00 | 24.00 | 36.00 | M |
| 1585 | Formula for Murder–Bill S. Ballinger | 1.50 | 3.00 | 4.50 | M |
| 1586 | The Case of the Strangled Starlet– James Hadley Chase | 1.50 | 3.00 | 4.50 | M |
| S1587 | I Want to Live!–Tabor Rawson; movie tie-in | 1.00 | 2.00 | 3.00 | |
| 1588 | The Crimson Quirt–William Colt MacDonald | 1.25 | 2.50 | 3.75 | W |

|  |  | V/Good | Fine | N/Mint |  |
|---|---|---|---|---|---|
| S1589 | The Sure Hand of God–Erskine Caldwell | 1.25 | 2.50 | 3.75 | |
| S1590 | Cat on a Hot Tin Roof–Tennessee Williams; movie tie-in | 1.50 | 3.00 | 4.50 | |
| D1591 | The American Woman–Eric J. Dingwall | 1.25 | 2.50 | 3.75 | |
| S1592 | Journeyman–Erskine Caldwell | 1.25 | 2.50 | 3.75 | |
| S1593 | The Demolished Man–Alfred Bester | 1.50 | 3.00 | 4.50 | SF |
| 1594 | The Mistress–Carter Brown | 1.25 | 2.50 | 3.75 | M |
| 1595 | The Decks Ran Red–Andrew L. Stone; movie tie-in | 1.25 | 2.50 | 3.75 | C |
| D1596 | The Woman of Rome–Alberto Moravia | 1.25 | 2.50 | 3.75 | |
| S1597 | Sigrid and the Sergeant–Robert Buckner | 1.25 | 2.50 | 3.75 | |
| S1598 | Episode in Palmetto–Erskine Caldwell | 1.25 | 2.50 | 3.75 | |
| S1599 | The Knife–Theon Wright | 1.25 | 2.50 | 3.75 | |
| D1600 | America, with Love–Kathleen Winsor; 1958 | 1.25 | 2.50 | 3.75 | |
| D1601 | The Called and the Chosen–Monica Baldwin | 1.25 | 2.50 | 3.75 | |
| S1602 | Summer in Salandar–H.E. Bates | 1.25 | 2.50 | 3.75 | |
| S1603 | A Restless Breed–J. William Terry | 1.25 | 2.50 | 3.75 | |
| S1604 | Fortune Is a Woman–Hermes Nye | 1.25 | 2.50 | 3.75 | |
| 1605 | Ute Country–John S. Daniels | 1.25 | 2.50 | 3.75 | W |
| 1606 | The Corpse–Carter Brown | 1.25 | 2.50 | 3.75 | M |
| 1607 | Gunsmoke Men–L.L. Foreman | 1.25 | 2.50 | 3.75 | W |
| S1608 | Trouble in July–Erskine Caldwell | 1.25 | 2.50 | 3.75 | |
| S1609 | Separate Tables–Terence Rattigan; 1959; movie tie-in | 1.25 | 2.50 | 3.75 | |
| S1610 | Expense Account–Joe Morgan | 1.25 | 2.50 | 3.75 | |
| S1611 | Tragic Ground–Erskine Caldwell | 1.25 | 2.50 | 3.75 | |
| S1612 | Roman Tales–Alberto Moravia | 1.25 | 2.50 | 3.75 | |
| S1613 | Nobody Cares for Me–Sara Harris | 1.25 | 2.50 | 3.75 | |
| D1614 | Sartoris–William Faulkner | 1.25 | 2.50 | 3.75 | |
| S1615 | Animal Farm–George Orwell | 1.25 | 2.50 | 3.75 | SF |
| S1616 | The Unvanquished–William Faulkner | 1.25 | 2.50 | 3.75 | |
| D1617 | Man of Montmartre–Ethel Longstreet & Stephen Longstreet | 1.25 | 2.50 | 3.75 | |
| 1618 | Texas Hellion–J.H. Plenn | 1.25 | 2.50 | 3.75 | W |
| D1619 | On the Road–Jack Kerouac | 2.50 | 5.00 | 7.50 | |
| 1620 | The Lover–Carter Brown | 1.25 | 2.50 | 3.75 | M |
| S1621 | The Courting of Susie Brown–Erskine Caldwell | 1.25 | 2.50 | 3.75 | |
| S1622 | The Seedling Star–James Blish | 1.25 | 2.50 | 3.75 | SF |
| S1623 | A Place Called Estherville–Erskine Caldwell | 1.25 | 2.50 | 3.75 | |
| S1624 | Saturday Night–James T. Farrell | 1.50 | 3.00 | 4.50 | |
| S1625 | The Blessing–Nancy Mitford; 1959 | 1.25 | 2.50 | 3.75 | |
| S1626 | Last Train from Gun Hill–Gordon D. Shirreffs; movie tie-in | 1.50 | 3.00 | 4.50 | W |
| D1627 | Grandfather Stories–Samuel Hopkins Adams | 1.25 | 2.50 | 3.75 | |
| D1628 | The Sound and the Fury–William Faulkner; movie tie-in | 1.25 | 2.50 | 3.75 | |
| D1629 | Soldier's Pay–William Faulkner | 1.25 | 2.50 | 3.75 | |
| D1630 | Arch of Triumph–Erich Maria Remarque | 1.25 | 2.50 | 3.75 | |
| 1631 | The Overlanders–Nelson Nye | 1.25 | 2.50 | 3.75 | W |
| 1632 | The Caballero–Johnston McCulley | 1.25 | 2.50 | 3.75 | W |
| 1633 | The Victim–Carter Brown | 1.25 | 2.50 | 3.75 | M |
| 1634 | The Last Blitzkrieg–Walter Freeman | 1.25 | 2.50 | 3.75 | |
| 1635 | The Fastest Gun in Texas–C.J. LaRoche & J.H. Plenn | 1.25 | 2.50 | 3.75 | W |

**SIGNET,** *continued*

| | | V/Good | Fine | N/Mint | |
|---|---|---|---|---|---|
| 1636 | The Whispering Master–Frank Gruber | 1.25 | 2.50 | 3.75 | M |
| T1637 | Some Came Running–James Jones | 1.25 | 2.50 | 3.75 | |
| D1638 | Darkness at Noon–Arthur Koestler | 1.25 | 2.50 | 3.75 | |
| S1639 | The Door into Summer–Robert A. Heinlein | 1.50 | 3.00 | 4.50 | SF |
| D1640 | 1984–George Orwell | 1.25 | 2.50 | 3.75 | SF |
| D1641 | The Shadow and the Peak–Raymond Mason | 1.25 | 2.50 | 3.75 | |
| 1642 | An Eye for an Eye–John B. West | 1.25 | 2.50 | 3.75 | M |
| D1643 | The Wild Palms and the Old Man–William Faulkner | 1.25 | 2.50 | 3.75 | |
| S1644 | The Man Who Sold the Moon–Robert A. Heinlein | 1.25 | 2.50 | 3.75 | SF |
| T1645 | Never So Few–Tom T. Chamales | 1.25 | 2.50 | 3.75 | |
| 1646 | Dormitory Women–R.V. Cassill; c-Maguire | 2.00 | 4.00 | 6.00 | |
| S1647 | The Bedside Mad–William M. Gaines | 2.50 | 5.00 | 7.50 | H |
| S1648 | The Mackerel Plaza–Peter De Vries | 1.25 | 2.50 | 3.75 | |
| S1649 | The Darling Buds of May–H.E. Bates | 1.25 | 2.50 | 3.75 | |
| S1650 | Miri–Peter Sourian; 1959 | 1.25 | 2.50 | 3.75 | |
| S1651 | Wolf Whistle and Other Stories–William Bradford Huie | 1.25 | 2.50 | 3.75 | |
| S1652 | Beat, Beat, Beat–William F. Brown | 1.25 | 2.50 | 3.75 | H |
| D1653 | The Intimate Henry Miller–Henry Miller | 2.00 | 4.00 | 6.00 | |
| 1654 | The Loving and the Dead–Carter Brown | 1.25 | 2.50 | 3.75 | M |
| 1655 | Slattery's Range–Richard Wormser | 1.25 | 2.50 | 3.75 | |
| S1656 | Some Like It Hot!–I.A.L. Diamond & Billy Wilder; movie tie-in | 3.00 | 6.00 | 9.00 | |
| D1657 | Two Women–Alberto Moravia | 1.25 | 2.50 | 3.75 | |
| S1658 | The Silent Service–William C. Chambliss | 2.00 | 4.00 | 6.00 | C |
| S1659 | Something about a Soldier–Mark Harris | 1.25 | 2.50 | 3.75 | |
| 1660 | Night Ward–Noah Gordon | 1.25 | 2.50 | 3.75 | |
| T1661 | And Quiet Flows the Don–Mikhail Sholokhov | 1.25 | 2.50 | 3.75 | |
| 1662 | Kiss Her Goodbye–Wade Miller | 1.25 | 2.50 | 3.75 | M |
| 1663 | Walk Softly, Witch–Carter Brown | 1.25 | 2.50 | 3.75 | M |
| S1664 | The Roman Spring of Mrs. Stone–Tennessee Williams | 1.25 | 2.50 | 3.75 | |
| S1665 | Cancel All Our Vows–John D. MacDonald | 1.50 | 3.00 | 4.50 | M |
| S1666 | Georgia Boy–Erskine Caldwell | 1.00 | 2.00 | 3.00 | |
| D1667 | The Catcher in the Rye–J.D. Salinger | 1.25 | 2.50 | 3.75 | |
| T1668 | The Time of the Dragons–Alice Ekert-Rotholz | 1.25 | 2.50 | 3.75 | |
| D1669 | Safe Conduct–Boris Pasternak | 1.50 | 3.00 | 4.50 | |
| S1670 | Doctor No–Ian Fleming | 3.00 | 6.00 | 9.00 | |
| S1671 | The Dangerous American–A.E. Hotchner | 1.25 | 2.50 | 3.75 | |
| S1672 | A Lamp for Nightfall–Erskine Caldwell | 1.25 | 2.50 | 3.75 | |
| S1673 | The Black Cloud–Fred Hoyle | 1.25 | 2.50 | 3.75 | SF |
| 1674 | The Passionate–Carter Brown | 1.25 | 2.50 | 3.75 | M |
| 1675 | Trail of the Restless Gun–Will Hickok; 1959; TV tie-in | 2.50 | 5.00 | 7.50 | W |
| 1676 | may not exist | | | | |
| 1677 | The Silver Tombstone Mystery–Frank Gruber | 1.50 | 3.00 | 4.50 | M |
| D1678 | Lola–Dario Fernandez-Florez | 1.25 | 2.50 | 3.75 | |
| D1679 | They Came to Cordura–Glendon Swarthout; movie tie-in | 1.25 | 2.50 | 3.75 | A |
| D1680 | Chiara–Gene d'Olive | 1.25 | 2.50 | 3.75 | |
| D1681 | Ben-Hur–Lew Wallace | 1.25 | 2.50 | 3.75 | A |
| S1682 | The Slot–John Clagett | 1.25 | 2.50 | 3.75 | |
| S1683 | No Time like Tomorrow–Brian W. Aldiss | 1.25 | 2.50 | 3.75 | SF |
| S1684 | The Wounds of Hunger–Luis Spota | 1.25 | 2.50 | 3.75 | |
| S1685 | Follow Me Down–Shelby Foote | 1.25 | 2.50 | 3.75 | |
| 1686 | Gun Code–Philip Ketchum | 1.25 | 2.50 | 3.75 | W |
| 1687 | Violent Streets–Dale Kramer | 1.25 | 2.50 | 3.75 | |
| 1688 | Wake Up with a Stranger–Fletcher Flora | 1.25 | 2.50 | 3.75 | |
| S1689 | The Loved and the Lost–Morley Callaghan | 1.25 | 2.50 | 3.75 | |
| S1690 | The Roman and the Slave Girl–John Medford Morgan | 1.25 | 2.50 | 3.75 | |
| S1691 | Crow Killer–Robert Bunker & Raymond Thorp | 1.25 | 2.50 | 3.75 | W |
| D1692 | Nautilus 90 North–William R. Anderson & Clay Blair, Jr | 1.25 | 2.50 | 3.75 | NF |
| D1693 | Let No Man Write My Epitaph–Willard Motley | 3.50 | 7.00 | 10.50 | |
| 1694 | None But the Lethal Heart–Carter Brown | 1.25 | 2.50 | 3.75 | M |
| 1695 | Brand of a Man–Thomas Thompson | 1.25 | 2.50 | 3.75 | W |
| 1696 | Shock Treatment–James Hadley Chase | 1.50 | 3.00 | 4.50 | M |
| 1697 | Stirrups in the Dust–Burt Arthur | 1.25 | 2.50 | 3.75 | W |
| S1698 | No But I Saw the Movie–Peter DeVries | 1.25 | 2.50 | 3.75 | |
| S1699 | Revolt in 2100–Robert A. Heinlein | 1.50 | 3.00 | 4.50 | SF |
| S1700 | The Big Kill–Mickey Spillane; 1959 | 1.25 | 2.50 | 3.75 | M |
| S1701 | Son of Mad–William M. Gaines | 2.50 | 5.00 | 7.50 | H |
| Q1702 | Atlas Shrugged–Ayn Rand | 4.00 | 8.00 | 12.00 | |
| S1703 | Frontier–MacKinlay Kantor | 1.25 | 2.50 | 3.75 | |
| 1704 | Manuela–William Woods | 1.25 | 2.50 | 3.75 | |
| S1705 | The Long Wait–Mickey Spillane | 1.25 | 2.50 | 3.75 | M |
| S1706 | The Eighth Day of the Week–Marek Hasko | 1.25 | 2.50 | 3.75 | |
| 1707 | Invitation to Violence–Lionel White | 1.50 | 3.00 | 4.50 | M |
| S1708 | You Tell My Son–Rex Pratt | 1.25 | 2.50 | 3.75 | |
| D1709 | Around the World with Auntie Mame–Patrick Dennis | 1.25 | 2.50 | 3.75 | |
| S1710 | Vengeance Is Mine–Mickey Spillane | 1.25 | 2.50 | 3.75 | M |
| S1711 | Summer of the Seventeenth Doll–Ray Lawler; movie tie-in | 1.25 | 2.50 | 3.75 | |
| S1712 | Entry E–Richard Frede | 1.25 | 2.50 | 3.75 | |
| 1713 | The Wanton–Carter Brown | 1.25 | 2.50 | 3.75 | M |
| 1714 | Apache Warpath–George Garland | 1.25 | 2.50 | 3.75 | W |
| 1715 | Ambuscade–Frank O'Rourke | 1.25 | 2.50 | 3.75 | W |
| 1716 | The 21" Scream–Edwin Fadiman, Jr | 1.25 | 2.50 | 3.75 | |
| T1717 | The Mountain Is Young–Suyin Han | 1.25 | 2.50 | 3.75 | |
| D1718 | The Dharma Bums–Jack Kerouac | 1.75 | 3.50 | 5.25 | |
| S1719 | Galactic Cluster–James Blish | 1.25 | 2.50 | 3.75 | SF |
| S1720 | The Blue Angel–Heinrich Mann; movie tie-in | 3.00 | 6.00 | 9.00 | |
| S1721 | Devil in the Flesh–Raymond Radiguet | 1.25 | 2.50 | 3.75 | |
| 1722 | Suddenly by Violence–Carter Brown | 1.25 | 2.50 | 3.75 | M |
| S1723 | Live and Let Die–Ian Fleming | 3.00 | 6.00 | 9.00 | |
| 1724 | Triple Slay–Adam Knight | 1.50 | 3.00 | 4.50 | M |
| D1725 | Star Money–Kathleen Winsor; 1959 | 1.00 | 2.00 | 3.00 | |
| T1726 | The Hard Blue Sky–Shirley Ann Grau | 1.25 | 2.50 | 3.75 | |
| D1727 | Breakfast at Tiffany's–Truman Capote | 1.25 | 2.50 | 3.75 | |
| S1728 | One Lonely Night–Mickey Spillane | 1.25 | 2.50 | 3.75 | M |
| S1729 | The Other Side of the Sky–Arthur C. Clarke | 1.25 | 2.50 | 3.75 | SF |
| 1730 | The Longest Second–Bill S. Ballinger | 1.25 | 2.50 | 3.75 | M |
| S1731 | A Stretch on the River–Richard Bissell | 1.25 | 2.50 | 3.75 | |
| S1732 | The Incident–Marc Rivette | 1.25 | 2.50 | 3.75 | |
| S1733 | Kneel to the Rising Sun–Erskine Caldwell | 1.25 | 2.50 | 3.75 | |
| S1734 | Southways–Erskine Caldwell | 1.25 | 2.50 | 3.75 | |
| S1735 | We Are the Living–Erskine Caldwell | 1.25 | 2.50 | 3.75 | |
| D1736 | Lady Chatterley's Lover–D.H. Lawrence | 1.25 | 2.50 | 3.75 | |
| S1737 | Tortilla Flat–John Steinbeck | 1.25 | 2.50 | 3.75 | |
| 1738 | The Dame–Carter Brown | 1.25 | 2.50 | 3.75 | M |
| S1739 | A Swell-Looking Girl–Erskine Caldwell | 1.25 | 2.50 | 3.75 | |
| D1740 | The Rainbow and the Rose–Nevil Shute | 1.25 | 2.50 | 3.75 | |
| T1741 | The Memoirs of Field-Marshall Montgomery–Bernard Law; The Viscount Montgomery of Alamein | 1.25 | 2.50 | 3.75 | NF |

*Signet 1675, Signet S1701, Signet S1720.*

SIGNET, *continued*

| Code | Title | V/Good | Fine | N/Mint | |
|---|---|---|---|---|---|
| Q1742 | A Child of the Century–Ben Hecht | 1.25 | 2.50 | 3.75 | |
| S1743 | The Girl in the Freudian Slip–William F. Brown | 1.25 | 2.50 | 3.75 | |
| 1744 | The Dead-Shot Kid–Philip Ketchum | 1.25 | 2.50 | 3.75 | W |
| S1745 | The Fugitive Kind–Tennessee Williams; 1960; movie tie-in | 1.25 | 2.50 | 3.75 | |
| D1746 | Strike Heaven on the Face–Charles Calitri | 1.25 | 2.50 | 3.75 | |
| S1747 | The Lovely Lady–D.H. Lawrence | 1.25 | 2.50 | 3.75 | |
| 1748 | Desperate Rider–Frank O'Rourke | 1.25 | 2.50 | 3.75 | W |
| 1749 | The Guilty Are Afraid–James Hadley Chase | 1.50 | 3.00 | 4.50 | M |
| 1750 | Terror Comes Creeping–Carter Brown | 1.25 | 2.50 | 3.75 | M |
| S1751 | The Strange Ordeal of S.S. Normandier–H.L. Tredree | 1.25 | 2.50 | 3.75 | NF |
| S1752 | Methuselah's Children–Robert A. Heinlein; 1960 | 1.25 | 2.50 | 3.75 | SF |
| S1754 | The Land Beyond–Bill Gulick | 1.25 | 2.50 | 3.75 | W |
| 1755 | Cobra Venom–John B. West | 1.25 | 2.50 | 3.75 | M |
| D1756 | The Irish Genius–ed. Devin A. Garrity | 1.25 | 2.50 | 3.75 | |
| S1757 | Suddenly Last Summer–Tennessee Williams; movie tie-in | 1.25 | 2.50 | 3.75 | |
| S1762 | Casino Royale–Ian Fleming; 1960 | 3.00 | 6.00 | 9.00 | M |
| S1763 | Seidman and Son–Elick Moll | 1.25 | 2.50 | 3.75 | |
| 1764 | The Desired–Carter Brown; 1960 | 1.25 | 2.50 | 3.75 | M |
| D1765 | A Place without Twilight–Peter S. Feibleman | 1.25 | 2.50 | 3.75 | |
| 1767 | The Bombshell–Carter Brown | 1.25 | 2.50 | 3.75 | M |
| 1768 | The Restless Lovers–Robert Dundee | 1.25 | 2.50 | 3.75 | E |
| S1769 | Islands in the Sky–Arthur C. Clarke; 1960 | 1.25 | 2.50 | 3.75 | SF |
| D1772 | Jephta and His Daughter–Léon Feuchtwanger; 1960 | 1.25 | 2.50 | 3.75 | A |
| T1773 | The Don Flows Home to the Sea–Mikhail Sholokhov | 1.25 | 2.50 | 3.75 | |
| S1776 | The Alamo–Lon Tinkle; aka 13 Days to Glory; 1960; movie tie-in | 1.25 | 2.50 | 3.75 | A |
| S1777 | The Pledge–Friedrich Duerrenmatt | 1.25 | 2.50 | 3.75 | |
| S1778 | Claudelle Inglish–Erskine Caldwell | 1.25 | 2.50 | 3.75 | |
| S1779 | Starship–Brian Aldiss; 1960 | 1.25 | 2.50 | 3.75 | SF |
| D1780 | Band of Brothers–Ernest Frankel | 1.25 | 2.50 | 3.75 | C |
| 1782 | The Feudists–Ernest Haycox; 1960 | 1.25 | 2.50 | 3.75 | W |
| S1783 | Murder in Vegas–William R. Cox | 1.25 | 2.50 | 3.75 | M |
| 1784 | The Wayward Wahine–Carter Brown | 1.25 | 2.50 | 3.75 | M |
| S1785 | The Mantrackers–William Mulvihill | 1.25 | 2.50 | 3.75 | A |
| S1788 | Visit to a Small Planet–Gore Vidal; 1960; movie tie-in | 2.00 | 4.00 | 6.00 | SF |
| T1790 | The Caretakers–Dariel Telfer | 1.25 | 2.50 | 3.75 | |
| T1791 | We the Living–Ayn Rand | 1.50 | 3.00 | 4.50 | |
| D1792 | Wild River–William Bradford Huie; aka Mud on the Stars; movie tie-in | 1.25 | 2.50 | 3.75 | |
| D1793 | The Mountain Road–Theodore Harold White; movie tie-in | 1.25 | 2.50 | 3.75 | C |
| S1794 | Beacon in the Night–Bill Ballinger; 1960 | 1.25 | 2.50 | 3.75 | M |
| S1795 | The Organization Mad–William M. Gaines; 1960 | 2.00 | 4.00 | 6.00 | H |
| T1796 | Tenderloin–Samuel Hopkins Adams | 1.25 | 2.50 | 3.75 | |
| S1797 | A Real Cool Cat–Jerry Weil; 1960 | 2.00 | 4.00 | 6.00 | |
| S1799 | The Wayward Comrade and the Commissars–Yumi Karlovich Olesha | 1.25 | 2.50 | 3.75 | H |
| S1801 | Graves, I Dig!–Carter Brown | 1.25 | 2.50 | 3.75 | M |
| S1806 | Tomorrow Is Murder–Carter Brown | 1.25 | 2.50 | 3.75 | M |
| S1807 | Violent Country–Frank O'Rourke; 1960 | 1.25 | 2.50 | 3.75 | W |
| S1810 | The Long, Long Love–Walter Sullivan | 1.25 | 2.50 | 3.75 | |
| D1811 | Danger! Marines at Work–Robert G. Fuller | 1.25 | 2.50 | 3.75 | C |
| S1812 | The Beach Bums–Jack Owen | 1.25 | 2.50 | 3.75 | |
| D1813 | . . . and the Rain My Drink–Suyin Han | 1.25 | 2.50 | 3.75 | |
| S1815 | Galaxies like Grains of Sand–Brian Aldiss | 1.25 | 2.50 | 3.75 | SS |
| S1816 | The Delicate Darlings–Jack Webb | 1.25 | 2.50 | 3.75 | M |
| S1817 | The Temptress–Carter Brown; 1960 | 1.25 | 2.50 | 3.75 | M |
| S1822 | Goldfinger–Ian Fleming; 1960 | 3.00 | 6.00 | 9.00 | M |
| T1823 | Invisible Man–Ralph Ellison | 1.25 | 2.50 | 3.75 | |
| S1825 | The Americanization of Emily–William Bradford Huie | 1.25 | 2.50 | 3.75 | |
| T1826 | The Manchurian Candidate–Richard Condon; 1960 | 2.50 | 5.00 | 7.50 | |
| D1827 | The Tents of Wickedness–Peter deVries | 1.25 | 2.50 | 3.75 | |
| D1829 | Sons and Lovers–D.H. Lawrence; movie tie-in | 1.25 | 2.50 | 3.75 | |
| T1831 | One Hour–Lillian Smith; 1960 | 1.25 | 2.50 | 3.75 | |
| D1832 | New Face in the Mirror–Yael Dayan | 1.25 | 2.50 | 3.75 | |
| S1833 | Harry Vernon at Prep–Franc Smith (Francis Dennis Smith) | 1.25 | 2.50 | 3.75 | H |
| S1834 | The Dark Corners of the Night–Lionel Olay | 1.25 | 2.50 | 3.75 | M |
| S1836 | The Brazen–Carter Brown; 1960 | 1.25 | 2.50 | 3.75 | M |
| S1839 | When You Think of Me–Erskine Caldwell | 1.25 | 2.50 | 3.75 | |
| S1840 | The Status Civilization–Robert Sheckley; 1960 | 1.25 | 2.50 | 3.75 | SF |
| D1842 | Saturday Night and Sunday Morning–Alan Sillitoe; 1960 | 1.25 | 2.50 | 3.75 | |
| S1845 | The Dream Is Deadly–Carter Brown | 1.25 | 2.50 | 3.75 | M |
| S1850 | Moonraker–Ian Fleming; 1960 | 2.50 | 5.00 | 7.50 | M |
| S1851 | Those Crazy Mixed-up Kids–Harold Dunn; 1961 | 1.25 | 2.50 | 3.75 | H |
| D1853 | Add a Dash of Pity–Peter Ustinov; 1961 | 1.25 | 2.50 | 3.75 | |
| S1854 | The Mind of an Assassin–Isaac Don Levine | 1.25 | 2.50 | 3.75 | NF |
| S1856 | Lament for a Lousy Lover–Carter Brown; 1960 | 1.25 | 2.50 | 3.75 | M |
| T1861 | Flaming Feather–Laurens van der Post | 1.25 | 2.50 | 3.75 | |
| T1864 | The Search–Sir Charles Percy Snow | 1.25 | 2.50 | 3.75 | |
| D1865 | Naked in Babylon–Gwen Davis | 1.25 | 2.50 | 3.75 | |
| T1866 | The Cave–Robert Penn Warren; 1960 | 1.25 | 2.50 | 3.75 | |
| T1867 | The Watch That Ends the Night–Hugh MacLennan | 1.25 | 2.50 | 3.75 | |
| D1868 | Sunrise at Campobello–Dore Schary; movie tie-in | .75 | 1.50 | 2.25 | |
| D1870 | A Long Way from Home–Vern Sneider | 1.25 | 2.50 | 3.75 | |
| D1876 | I'm All Right, Jack–Alan Hackney; aka Private Life; movie tie-in | 1.25 | 2.50 | 3.75 | |
| T1877 | Diamond Head–Peter Gilman; movie tie-in | 1.25 | 2.50 | 3.75 | |
| T1878 | Go Naked in the World–Tom T. Chamales; movie tie-in | 1.25 | 2.50 | 3.75 | |
| T1881 | The Asiatics–Frederic Prokosch; 1960 | 1.25 | 2.50 | 3.75 | |
| S1883 | Death on the Rocks–John B. West; 1961 | 1.25 | 2.50 | 3.75 | M |
| D1890 | Where the Boys Are–Glendon Swarthout; 1961; movie tie-in | 1.25 | 2.50 | 3.75 | |
| T1892 | Two Weeks in Another Town–Irwin Shaw | 1.25 | 2.50 | 3.75 | |
| S1894 | The Girl in the Gold Leather Dress–Victoria Morhaim; 1961 | 1.25 | 2.50 | 3.75 | |
| S1896 | The Savage Salome–Carter Brown | 1.25 | 2.50 | 3.75 | M |
| S1897 | Westering–Irwin R. Blacker; 1961 | 1.25 | 2.50 | 3.75 | |
| T1900 | Sanctuary/Requiem for a Nun–William Faulkner; movie tie-in | 1.25 | 2.50 | 3.75 | |
| D1901 | A Raisin in the Sun–L. Hansberry; movie tie-in | 1.25 | 2.50 | 3.75 | |
| D1905 | The Outsiders–Alexander Trocchi | 1.25 | 2.50 | 3.75 | |
| D1906 | The African–William Conton; 1961 | 1.25 | 2.50 | 3.75 | |
| S1908 | Scandale–Floyd Miller | 1.25 | 2.50 | 3.75 | |
| S1909 | The Million Dollar Babe–Carter Brown | 1.25 | 2.50 | 3.75 | M |
| S1910 | Rawhide–Frank C. Robertson; TV tie-in | 1.50 | 3.00 | 4.50 | W |
| S1913 | The New American Crossword Puzzle Book–Jack Luzzatto | 2.00 | 4.00 | 6.00 | NF |
| D1915 | The Dud Avocado–Elaine Dundy | 1.25 | 2.50 | 3.75 | |
| D1917 | Parktilden Village–George P. Elliott | 1.25 | 2.50 | 3.75 | |
| S1918 | Hot Seat–W.E. Butterworth | 1.25 | 2.50 | 3.75 | |
| S1919 | The Ever-Loving Blues–Carter Brown | 1.25 | 2.50 | 3.75 | M |
| S1920 | Law of the Gun–Lewis B. Patten; 1961 | 1.25 | 2.50 | 3.75 | W |
| S1924 | The Myopic Mermaid–Carter Brown | 1.25 | 2.50 | 3.75 | M |
| D1927 | The Raven and the Sword–Matthew Gant; 1961 | 1.25 | 2.50 | 3.75 | |
| D1928 | The Loneliness of the Long-Distance Runner–Alan Sillitoe | 1.25 | 2.50 | 3.75 | |
| S1929 | Never Kill a Cop–John B. West; 1961 | 1.25 | 2.50 | 3.75 | M |
| D1934 | Cat on a Hot Tin Roof–Tennessee Williams; movie tie-in | 1.25 | 2.50 | 3.75 | |
| T1935 | The Chapman Report–Irving Wallace | 1.25 | 2.50 | 3.75 | |
| Q1936 | Peter the First–Alexey Tolstoy; 1961 | 1.25 | 2.50 | 3.75 | |
| D1937 | The Violent Bear It Away–Flannery O'Connor | 1.25 | 2.50 | 3.75 | |
| S1938 | The Strip–Aben Kandel | 1.25 | 2.50 | 3.75 | |
| S1939 | Skyport–Curt Siodmak; 1961 | 1.25 | 2.50 | 3.75 | SF |
| S1940 | Death of a Flack–Henny Kane; 1961 | 1.25 | 2.50 | 3.75 | M |

**SIGNET,** *continued*

| No. | Title | V/Good | Fine | N/Mint | |
|---|---|---|---|---|---|
| P1941 | The Patch–Kathleen Hampton | 1.25 | 2.50 | 3.75 | |
| S1943 | Those Who Prey Together Slay Together–Don Von Elsner | 1.25 | 2.50 | 3.75 | M |
| Q1944 | Set This House on Fire–William Styron | 1.25 | 2.50 | 3.75 | |
| T1945 | Short Term–Jay Kennedy | 1.25 | 2.50 | 3.75 | |
| D1946 | If It Moves, Salute It–Bob Duncan | 1.25 | 2.50 | 3.75 | H |
| S1948 | For Your Eyes Only–Ian Fleming; 1961 | 2.50 | 5.00 | 7.50 | M |
| S1949 | Season of Desire–Augusta W. Lyons | 1.25 | 2.50 | 3.75 | E |
| S1950 | The Unorthodox Corpse–Carter Brown; 1961 | 1.25 | 2.50 | 3.75 | M |
| S1951 | Company of Cowards–Jack Schaefer; 1961 | 1.50 | 3.00 | 4.50 · | W |
| T1954 | The View from the Fortieth Floor–Theodore White | 1.25 | 2.50 | 3.75 | |
| T1955 | Three Novels–Alberto Moravia | 1.25 | 2.50 | 3.75 | |
| D1956 | Level 7–Mordecai Roshwald | 1.25 | 2.50 | 3.75 | SF |
| T1957 | I Can Take It All–Anthony Glyn (Sir Geoffrey Dauson) | 1.25 | 2.50 | 3.75 | |
| S1958 | The Deceivers–Richard Goldhurst | 1.25 | 2.50 | 3.75 | |
| D1959 | Welcome to Hard Times–E.L. Doctorow | 1.25 | 2.50 | 3.75 | W |
| T1960 | The Leopard–Giuseppe Di Lampedusa | 1.25 | 2.50 | 3.75 | A |
| S1961 | Comanche Moon–William R. Cox | 1.25 | 2.50 | 3.75 | W |
| T1963 | Peaceable Lane–Keith Wheeler | 1.25 | 2.50 | 3.75 | |
| S1971 | The Girls in Rome–Chandler Brossard | 1.25 | 2.50 | 3.75 | |
| S1973 | The Brothers Brannagan–Henry E. Helseth; 1961; TV tie-in | 1.25 | 2.50 | 3.75 | |
| S1976 | Fighting Mad–William M. Gaines; 1961 | 1.50 | 3.00 | 4.50 | H |
| T1977 | The Man with a Certain Talent–Pierre Sichel; aka The Sapbucket Genius | 1.25 | 2.50 | 3.75 | |
| D1978 | The Sins of Philip Fleming–Irving Wallace | 1.25 | 2.50 | 3.75 | |
| S1979 | The New American 2nd Crossword Puzzle Book–Jack Luzzatto & Albert H. Morehead | 2.00 | 4.00 | 6.00 | NF |
| S1980 | Pandora's Box–Robert Dundee | 1.25 | 2.50 | 3.75 | M |
| S1981 | The Stripper–Carter Brown | 1.25 | 2.50 | 3.75 | M |
| S1982 | Wanted: Dead or Alive–Frank C. Robertson; 1961; TV tie-in | 2.00 | 4.00 | 6.00 | W |
| T1984 | The Love Pavilion–Paul Scott | 1.25 | 2.50 | 3.75 | |
| D1985 | Anthem–Ayn Rand | 1.25 | 2.50 | 3.75 | SF |
| D1986 | The Walls of Jolo–Alan Caillou | 1.25 | 2.50 | 3.75 | |
| D1987 | Starship Troopers–Robert A. Heinlein | 1.50 | 3.00 | 4.50 | SF |
| S1988 | The Deadly Sex–Jack Webb | 1.25 | 2.50 | 3.75 | M |
| S1989 | The Tigress–Carter Brown | 1.25 | 2.50 | 3.75 | M |
| S2000 | Daughter of Evil–Jerry Weil; 1961 | 1.25 | 2.50 | 3.75 | |
| P2008 | Are You Hungry, Are You Cold–Ludwig Bemelmans | 1.25 | 2.50 | 3.75 | |
| S2009 | The Exotic–Carter Brown | 1.25 | 2.50 | 3.75 | M |
| D2010 | The Life and Death of Clay Allison–Ray Hogan | 1.25 | 2.50 | 3.75 | W |
| T2013 | Mistaken Ambitions–Alberto Moravia | 1.25 | 2.50 | 3.75 | |
| P2016 | Trustee from the Toolroom–Nevil Shute | 1.25 | 2.50 | 3.75 | |
| P2017 | The Inhabitants–Julius Horwitz | 1.25 | 2.50 | 3.75 | |
| D2018 | The Long Afternoon of Earth–Brian Aldiss | 1.50 | 3.00 | 4.50 | SF |
| D2019 | Summer and Smoke–Tennessee Williams; movie tie-in | 1.25 | 2.50 | 3.75 | |
| T2020 | The Years with Ross–James Thurber | 1.25 | 2.50 | 3.75 | H |
| S2022 | Aloha Nurse–Ethel Hamill | .75 | 1.50 | 2.25 | R |
| S2023 | The Sad-eyed Seductress–Carter Brown | 1.25 | 2.50 | 3.75 | M |
| D2024 | Rodeo: Last Frontier of the Old West–Oren Arnold & Robert W. Howard | 1.25 | 2.50 | 3.75 | NF |
| D2025 | Judgement at Nuremberg–Abby Mann; movie tie-in | 1.25 | 2.50 | 3.75 | |
| S2026 | Hit the Beach–Arthur A. Ageton | 1.25 | 2.50 | 3.75 | C |
| D2027 | The Roman Spring of Mrs. Stone–Tennessee Williams; movie tie-in | 1.25 | 2.50 | 3.75 | |
| D2028 | Rebel against the Light–Alexander Ramati | 1.25 | 2.50 | 3.75 | |
| D2029 | Diamonds Are Forever–Ian Fleming; 1961 | 2.50 | 5.00 | 7.50 | M |
| 2030 | From Russia with Love–Ian Fleming; 1961 | 1.25 | 2.50 | 3.75 | M |
| D2031 | King of the Mountain–George Garrett | 1.25 | 2.50 | 3.75 | |
| D2032 | Arsenic and Red Tape–Edmund G. Love | 1.25 | 2.50 | 3.75 | |
| S2033 | Zelda–Carter Brown | 1.25 | 2.50 | 3.75 | M |
| S2034 | The Transgressors–Jim Thompson; 1st ed. 1961 | 35.00 | 70.00 | 105.00 | M |
| D2035 | The Evil That Men Do–Ben Simcoe | 1.25 | 2.50 | 3.75 | |
| 2036 | Dr. No–Ian Fleming; 1963; 9th–11th printings are movie tie-ins | 1.25 | 2.50 | 3.75 | M |
| S2039 | Forced March–Morton Warnow | 1.25 | 2.50 | 3.75 | C |
| S2040 | Just Not Making Mayhem Like They Used To–Don Von Elsner | 1.25 | 2.50 | 3.75 | M |
| T2041 | Vangel Griffen–Herbert Lobsenz | 1.25 | 2.50 | 3.75 | |
| D2044 | The Deep–Mickey Spillane | 1.25 | 2.50 | 3.75 | M |
| P2045 | There Must Be a Pony!–Jim Kirkwood | 1.25 | 2.50 | 3.75 | |
| S2047 | Second-Chance Nurse–Jane Converse | .75 | 1.50 | 2.25 | R |
| S2048 | Murder Wears a Mantilla–Carter Brown | 1.25 | 2.50 | 3.75 | M |
| D2052 | Goldfinger–Ian Fleming | 1.25 | 2.50 | 3.75 | M |
| S2055 | The Gunfighters–John S. Daniels | 1.25 | 2.50 | 3.75 | W |
| D2058 | I Love You, Mary Fatt–Russell F. Davis | 1.25 | 2.50 | 3.75 | |
| P2059 | The Night of the Tiger–Al Dewlen; 1962 | 1.25 | 2.50 | 3.75 | |
| P2060 | The Loser–Peter Ustinov; 1962 | 1.25 | 2.50 | 3.75 | |
| P2061 | Combat Soldier–Dennis Lynds | 1.25 | 2.50 | 3.75 | C |
| D2062 | The Girl Who Had Everything–Victoria Morhaim | 1.25 | 2.50 | 3.75 | |
| S2063 | The Kilroy Gambit–Irwin R. Blacker | 1.25 | 2.50 | 3.75 | |
| S2064 | New American 3rd Crossword Puzzle Book–Jack Luzzatto & Albert H. Morehead | 2.00 | 4.00 | 6.00 | NF |
| D2076 | Where We Go from Here–W.E. Butterworth | 1.25 | 2.50 | 3.75 | |
| D2077 | The General–Alan Sillitoe; 1962 | 1.25 | 2.50 | 3.75 | |
| S2078 | The Mercy Heroes–Shane Douglas | 1.25 | 2.50 | 3.75 | |
| S2079 | Emergency Nurse–Jane Converse | .75 | 1.50 | 2.25 | R |
| S2080 | Run for Doom–Henry Kane | 1.25 | 2.50 | 3.75 | M |
| T2089 | Harvest on the Don–Mikhali Sholokhov | 1.25 | 2.50 | 3.75 | |
| 2092 | The Birdman of Alcatraz–; movie tie-in | 1.25 | 2.50 | 3.75 | |
| D2095 | Sweet Bird of Youth–Tennessee Williams; movie tie-in | 1.25 | 2.50 | 3.75 | |
| S2096 | Alias Miss Saunders, R.N.–Jane Converse | .75 | 1.50 | 2.25 | R |
| S2097 | Air Surgeon–Shane Douglas | .75 | 1.50 | 2.25 | R |
| P2101 | The Seeker–Allen Wheelis | 1.25 | 2.50 | 3.75 | |
| P2102 | Through the Fields of Clover–Peter De Vries | 1.25 | 2.50 | 3.75 | |
| S2103 | The Confession of Alma Quartier–David Robinson | 1.25 | 2.50 | 3.75 | |
| D2104 | The Other One–Colette; 1962 | 1.25 | 2.50 | 3.75 | |
| D2105 | The Menace from Earth–Robert A. Heinlein | 1.25 | 2.50 | 3.75 | SF |
| S2108 | Adventures in a Cold-Water Flat–Jerry Weil; 1962 | 1.25 | 2.50 | 3.75 | |
| S2109 | This Man Dawson–Henry E. Helseth; TV tie-in | 1.25 | 2.50 | 3.75 | M |
| S2110 | The Ice-Cold Nude–Carter Brown; 1962 | 1.25 | 2.50 | 3.75 | M |
| D2118 | Kick Me in the Traditions–Leif Panduro | 1.25 | 2.50 | 3.75 | |
| D2119 | A Breath of French Air–Herbert Ernest Bates | 1.25 | 2.50 | 3.75 | |
| D2120 | The Plotters–Alan Caillou | 1.25 | 2.50 | 3.75 | |
| D2121 | Jenny by Nature–Erskine Caldwell | 1.25 | 2.50 | 3.75 | |
| S2122 | The Hellcat–Carter Brown | 1.25 | 2.50 | 3.75 | M |
| P2125 | The Violent Season–Robert Goulet | 1.00 | 2.00 | 3.00 | |
| D2126 | Thunderball–Ian Fleming; 1962 | 2.50 | 5.00 | 7.50 | M |
| S2127 | Big Red–Burt Arthur; 1962 | 1.25 | 2.50 | 3.75 | W |
| D2129 | The Children's Hour–Lillian Hellman; movie tie-in | 1.25 | 2.50 | 3.75 | |
| T2131 | Three: Williwaw, A Thirsty Evil, Julian the Apostate–Gore Vidal | 1.25 | 2.50 | 3.75 | |
| S2134 | Don't Just Stand There, Do Someone–Don Von Elsner | 1.25 | 2.50 | 3.75 | M |
| T2136 | Two Adolescents; the Time of Indifference–Alberto Moravia | 1.25 | 2.50 | 3.75 | |
| T2138 | The Mill–Bradley Robinson | 1.25 | 2.50 | 3.75 | |
| S2139 | Sky Doctor–Shane Douglas | .75 | 1.50 | 2.25 | R |
| S2140 | Murder in the Key Club–Carter Brown; 1962 | 1.25 | 2.50 | 3.75 | M |
| S2141 | Someone to Hate–Jack Donahue | 1.25 | 2.50 | 3.75 | |
| P2145 | Pale Horse, Pale Rider: Three Short Novels–Katherine Anne Porter | 1.25 | 2.50 | 3.75 | |
| P2146 | The Teahouse of the August Moon–Vern Sneider; movie tie-in | 1.25 | 2.50 | 3.75 | |
| S2148 | The Lady Is Transparent–Carter Brown | 1.25 | 2.50 | 3.75 | M |
| S2149 | The New American 4th Crossword Puzzle Book–Jack Luzzatto & Albert H. Morehead | 2.00 | 4.00 | 6.00 | NF |
| D2150 | When Time Stood Still–Ben Orkow; 1962 | 1.25 | 2.50 | 3.75 | SF |
| D2151 | The Court-Martial–W.E. Butterworth | 1.25 | 2.50 | 3.75 | |

**SIGNET,** *continued*

| | V/Good | Fine | N/Mint | |
|---|---|---|---|---|
| P2153 Special People–Jacques Serguine | 1.25 | 2.50 | 3.75 | |
| T2155 The Young Texans–Claud Garner | 1.25 | 2.50 | 3.75 | |
| S2158 Death on Location–William R. Cox | 1.25 | 2.50 | 3.75 | M |
| S2159 Inferno–Robert Dundee | 1.25 | 2.50 | 3.75 | |
| D2160 17 Royal Palms Drive–Evans Wakeman | 1.25 | 2.50 | 3.75 | |
| D2161 The Dark Side of Love–Jerry Weil | 1.25 | 2.50 | 3.75 | |
| P2163 Cleopatra–Carlo Maria Franzero; movie tie-in, 1962 | 1.50 | 3.00 | 4.50 | A |
| T2165 Jason–Henry Treece | 1.25 | 2.50 | 3.75 | A |
| S2166 Assistant Surgeon–Shane Douglas | .75 | 1.50 | 2.25 | R |
| P2167 The Olympians–Guy Bolton | 1.00 | 2.00 | 3.00 | |
| S2169 Bamboo Ward–Noah Gordon | 1.00 | 2.00 | 3.00 | |
| D2170 The Presence of Mine Enemies–Turnley Walker | 1.00 | 2.00 | 3.00 | |
| D2172 The 300 Spartans–John Burke; 1962; movie tie-in | 1.25 | 2.50 | 3.75 | A |
| D2178 The Golden Platter–Joe Greene | 1.00 | 2.00 | 3.00 | |
| S2180 The Hong Kong Caper–Carter Brown | 1.00 | 2.00 | 3.00 | M |
| P2182 Ceremony in Lone Tree–Wright Morris | 1.00 | 2.00 | 3.00 | |
| D2186 A Very Private Island–Z.Z. Smith | 1.00 | 2.00 | 3.00 | |
| T2188 A Climate of Violence–Russell O'Neil | 1.00 | 2.00 | 3.00 | |
| S2190 Doctor at Fault–Shane Douglas | .75 | 1.50 | 2.25 | R |
| D2193 The Race West: Boom Town to Ghost Town–Robert West Howard; 1962 | 1.25 | 2.50 | 3.75 | NF |
| Q2194 Spirit Lake–MacKinlay Kantor | 1.00 | 2.00 | 3.00 | |
| S2195 Nurse in Danger–Jane Converse | .75 | 1.50 | 2.25 | R |
| S2196 The Dumdum Murder–Carter Brown; 1962 | 1.00 | 2.00 | 3.00 | M |
| T2198 The Empty Canvas–Alberto Moravia | 1.00 | 2.00 | 3.00 | |
| P2199 The Valley–Clifford Irving; 1962 | 1.00 | 2.00 | 3.00 | |
| S2200 The Duke–William R. Cox; 1962 | 1.00 | 2.00 | 3.00 | |
| S2205 The Hundred-Dollar Girl–William Campbell Gault | 2.00 | 4.00 | 6.00 | M |
| T2206 Capitol Hill–Andrew Tully; 1962 | 1.00 | 2.00 | 3.00 | |
| D2208 The End of It–Mitchell Goodman | 1.00 | 2.00 | 3.00 | |
| D2210 Period of Adjustment–Tennessee Williams; movie tie-in | 1.25 | 2.50 | 3.75 | |
| D2213 Lau-Lau–Harry Roskolenko; 1962 | 1.00 | 2.00 | 3.00 | |
| S2214 You Can't Do Business with Murder–Don Von Elsner | 1.00 | 2.00 | 3.00 | M |
| S2216 Lobo Gray–L.L. Foreman | 1.00 | 2.00 | 3.00 | W |
| D2219 Men and Women–Erskine Caldwell | 1.00 | 2.00 | 3.00 | |
| S2220 The Guilt-Edged Cage–Carter Brown | 1.00 | 2.00 | 3.00 | M |
| D2223 Journey beyond Tomorrow–Robert Sheckley | 1.25 | 2.50 | 3.75 | SF |
| D2224 Taras Bulba–Nikolai Gogol; 1962 | 1.00 | 2.00 | 3.00 | A |
| D2225 Palmetto Springs–Paul Hackett | 1.00 | 2.00 | 3.00 | |
| S2227 Surgeon on Call–Shane Douglas | .75 | 1.50 | 2.25 | R |
| S2228 A Murderer among Us–Carter Brown | 1.00 | 2.00 | 3.00 | M |
| P2231 Wilderness–Robert Penn Warren; 1962 | 1.00 | 2.00 | 3.00 | A |
| S2233 The Border Guidon–Gordon D. Shirreffs; 1963 | 1.00 | 2.00 | 3.00 | W |
| D2236 Give Me Myself–Susan Sherman | .75 | 1.50 | 2.25 | R |
| P2237 Take a Girl like You–Kingsley Amis | 1.00 | 2.00 | 3.00 | |
| S2238 Emergency Surgeon–Shane Douglas | .75 | 1.50 | 2.25 | R |
| T2240 One Flew over the Cuckoo's Nest–Ken Kesey | 1.25 | 2.50 | 3.75 | |
| S2241 Don't Betray Me–John Berry; 1963 | 1.00 | 2.00 | 3.00 | |
| S2242 The Doctor's Pledge–Shane Douglas | .75 | 1.50 | 2.25 | R |
| S2244 The Lady Is Available–Carter Brown | 1.00 | 2.00 | 3.00 | M |
| Q2246 The Agony and the Ecstasy–Irving Stone; 1963 | 1.00 | 2.00 | 3.00 | |
| T2248 Portrait of a Young Man Drowning–Charles Perry | 1.00 | 2.00 | 3.00 | |
| P2252 Haste to Succeed–Jason Striker | 1.00 | 2.00 | 3.00 | |
| S2255 The New American Library 5th Crossword Puzzle Book–Jack Luzatto & Albert H. Morehead | 1.50 | 3.00 | 4.50 | NF |
| T2257 Twilight of Honor–Al Dewlen | 1.00 | 2.00 | 3.00 | |
| S2258 Masquerade Nurse–Jane Converse | .75 | 1.50 | 2.25 | R |
| S2259 The Passionate Pagan–Carter Brown | 1.00 | 2.00 | 3.00 | M |
| D2262 Wand of Noble Wood–Onuora Nzekwu; 1963 | 1.00 | 2.00 | 3.00 | |
| D2266 The Girl Hunters–Mickey Spillane; 1963 | 1.25 | 2.50 | 3.75 | M |
| D2267 Uptown Downtown–Dennis Lynds; 1963 | 1.25 | 2.50 | 3.75 | |
| D2269 The Ballad of Cat Ballou–Roy Chanslor | 1.00 | 2.00 | 3.00 | W |
| T2274 Delta Wedding–Eudora Welty | .75 | 1.50 | 2.25 | R |
| S2275 The White Bikini–Carter Brown | 1.00 | 1.00 | 1.00 | M |
| D2276 The Voodoo Mad–William M. Gaines; 1963 | 1.50 | 3.00 | 4.50 | H |

| | V/Good | Fine | N/Mint | |
|---|---|---|---|---|
| T2277 Charley Is My Darling–Joyce Cary | 1.00 | 2.00 | 3.00 | |
| S2278 How to Succeed at Murder without Really Trying–Don Von Elsner | 1.00 | 2.00 | 3.00 | M |
| D2280 The Spy Who Loved Me–Ian Fleming; 1963 | 2.50 | 5.00 | 7.50 | M |
| T2281 The Fox in the Attic–Richard Hughes | 1.00 | 2.00 | 3.00 | |
| D2282 The Sleeping Woman–Polan Banks | 1.00 | 2.00 | 3.00 | |
| D2284 Close to Home–Erskine Caldwell | 1.00 | 2.00 | 3.00 | |
| T2288 Horseshoe Bend–Bruce Palmer & John Clifford Giles | 1.00 | 2.00 | 3.00 | W |
| G2291 The Girl Who Was Possessed–Carter Brown | 1.00 | 2.00 | 3.00 | M |
| D2293 The Outlawed–William R. Cox; 1963 | 1.00 | 2.00 | 3.00 | W |
| D2296 Always Go First Class–Laurence Marks | 1.00 | 2.00 | 3.00 | |
| T2297 Key to the Door–Alan Sillitoe; 1963 | 1.00 | 2.00 | 3.00 | |
| T2298 At Heaven's Gate–Robert Penn Warren | 1.00 | 2.00 | 3.00 | |
| P2300 Goodbye, I Guess–Michael Blankfort | 1.00 | 2.00 | 3.00 | |
| G2301 The Crumpled Cop–Henry Kane; 1963 | 1.00 | 2.00 | 3.00 | M |
| D2304 Mister Will You Marry Me?–Frederick Kohner | 1.00 | 2.00 | 3.00 | |
| Q2305 The Prize–Irving Wallace | 1.00 | 2.00 | 3.00 | |
| P2306 The Blood of the Lamb–Peter De Vries; 1963 | 1.00 | 2.00 | 3.00 | |
| S2307 The Doctor's Past–Shane Douglas; 1964 | .75 | 1.50 | 2.25 | R |
| T2310 The Love Riddle–Claire Kenneth; 1963 | .75 | 1.50 | 2.25 | R |
| G2311 The Life and Death of Johnny Ringo–Ray Hogan; 1964 | 1.25 | 2.50 | 3.75 | W |
| P2315 A Ticket to the Stars–Vasili Aksenov (trans. Andrew MacAndrew) | 1.00 | 2.00 | 3.00 | |
| Y2325 Youngblood Hawke–Herman Wouk; 1963 | 1.00 | 2.00 | 3.00 | |
| T2326 The Love Thieves–Peter Packer | 1.00 | 2.00 | 3.00 | |
| G2327 Dr. Holland's Nurse–Jane Converse | .75 | 1.50 | 2.25 | R |
| P2330 Contract Bridge Summary–Albert H. Morehead | .50 | 1.00 | 1.50 | NF |
| Q2333 Ship of Fools–Katherine Anne Porter | 1.00 | 2.00 | 3.00 | |
| G2334 The Tarnished Star–Lewis B. Patten; 1963 | 1.00 | 2.00 | 3.00 | W |
| P2340 The Ides of March–Thornton Wilder; 1963 | 1.00 | 2.00 | 3.00 | |
| G2344 Girl in a Shroud–Carter Brown | 1.00 | 2.00 | 3.00 | M |
| G2345 The Crossing–John S. Daniels | 1.00 | 2.00 | 3.00 | W |
| P2352 Luther–John Osborne | 1.00 | 2.00 | 3.00 | |
| Q2364 The Thin Red Line–James Jones; 1964 | 1.00 | 2.00 | 3.00 | C |
| G2365 The Scarlet Flush–Carter Brown | 1.00 | 2.00 | 3.00 | M |
| D2368 The Teleman Touch–William Haggard | 1.00 | 2.00 | 3.00 | |
| G2369 Good-bye Wisconsin–Glenway Wescott | 1.00 | 2.00 | 3.00 | |
| P2371 Rampage–Alan Caillou | 1.00 | 2.00 | 3.00 | A |
| T2372 The Groves of Academe–Mary McCarthy | 1.00 | 2.00 | 3.00 | |
| T2380 Cast a Cold Eye–Mary McCarthy | 1.00 | 2.00 | 3.00 | |
| P2386 The Late Risers–Bernard Wolfe; aka Everything Happens at Night | 1.00 | 2.00 | 3.00 | |
| T2387 In Harm's Way–James E. Bassett; aka Harm's Way; movie tie-in | 1.50 | 3.00 | 4.50 | C |
| D2390 Vessel of Dishonor–Paul Roche | 1.00 | 2.00 | 3.00 | |
| G2391 Psychiatric Nurse–Jane Converse | .75 | 1.50 | 2.25 | R |
| G2394 Charlie Sent Me!–Carter Brown; 1964 | 1.00 | 2.00 | 3.00 | M |
| D2398 The Face of Innocence–William Sansom | 1.00 | 2.00 | 3.00 | |
| P2399 Trial at Odawara–Robert Eunson | 1.00 | 2.00 | 3.00 | |
| G2400 The Silken Nightmare–Carter Brown; 1964 | 1.00 | 2.00 | 3.00 | M |
| P2401 Cross to Bear Proudly–Rex Barley | 1.00 | 2.00 | 3.00 | C |
| G2407 Who Says a Corpse Has to Be Dull–Don von Elsner | 1.00 | 2.00 | 3.00 | M |
| T2410 The Voice at the Back Door–Elizabeth Spencer | .75 | 1.50 | 2.25 | |
| T2416 A Charmed Life–Mary McCarthy | 1.00 | 2.00 | 3.00 | |
| P2417 A Wreath for the Enemy–Pamela Frankau | 1.00 | 2.00 | 3.00 | |
| P2426 Field of Women–Alan Caillou; 1964 | 1.00 | 2.00 | 3.00 | |
| P2431 Cards of Identity–Nigel Dennis | 1.00 | 2.00 | 3.00 | SF |
| D2436 Night Must Fall–William Drummond; movie tie-in | 1.00 | 2.00 | 3.00 | |
| P2437 Lord Grizzly–Frederick Manfred; 1964 | 1.50 | 3.00 | 4.50 | W |
| D2438 Racers to the Sun–James B. Hall | 1.00 | 2.00 | 3.00 | |
| T2440 The Birthday King–Gabriel Fielding (Alan Gabriel Barnsley) | 1.00 | 2.00 | 3.00 | |
| D2447 Trot–David Ely; 1964 | 1.00 | 2.00 | 3.00 | M |
| D2836 The Wild Wild West–Richard Wormser; TV tie-in | 3.00 | 6.00 | 9.00 | W |

## SIGNET, *continued*

| | | V/Good | Fine | N/Mint | |
|---|---|---|---|---|---|
| D2939 | Batman–Bob Kane; 1966. Note Contains DC comic reprints; TV tie-in | 4.00 | 8.00 | 12.00 | A |
| D2940 | Batman vs. Three Villains of Doom–Winston Lyon; 1st ed. 1966; TV tie-in | 5.00 | 10.00 | 15.00 | A |
| D2969 | Batman vs. The Joker–. Note: Comic book reprints; 1966; TV tie-in | 4.00 | 8.00 | 12.00 | A |
| D2970 | Batman vs. The Penguin–. Note: Comic book reprints; 1966; TV tie-in | 4.00 | 8.00 | 12.00 | A |

# SIGNET CLASSICS
## New American Library of World Literature, Inc.

| | | V/Good | Fine | N/Mint | |
|---|---|---|---|---|---|
| CD1 | Adolphe and the Red Notebook–Benjamin Constant; 1959 | .75 | 1.50 | 2.25 | |
| CD2 | The Adventures of Tom Sawyer–Mark Twain | .75 | 1.50 | 2.25 | |
| CD3 | Animal Farm–George Orwell | .75 | 1.50 | 2.25 | SF |
| CD4 | Heart of Darkness and the Secret Sharer–Joseph Conrad | .75 | 1.50 | 2.25 | |
| CD5 | The Adventures of Huckleberry Finn–Mark Twain | .75 | 1.50 | 2.25 | A |
| CD6 | Kidnapped–Robert Louis Stevenson | .75 | 1.50 | 2.25 | A |
| CD7 | The Return of the Native–Thomas Hardy | .75 | 1.50 | 2.25 | |
| CD8 | The Scarlet Letter–Nathaniel Hawthorne | .75 | 1.50 | 2.25 | |
| CD9 | The Unvanquished–William Faulkner | .75 | 1.50 | 2.25 | |
| CD10 | Wuthering Heights–Emily Bronte | .75 | 1.50 | 2.25 | R |

# SIGNET KEY
## New American Library of World Literature, Inc.

| | | V/Good | Fine | N/Mint | |
|---|---|---|---|---|---|
| K300 | Gandhi: His Life and Message for the World–Louis Fischer; 1954 | .50 | 1.00 | 1.50 | B |
| K301 | How to Make a Success of Your Marriage–Dr. Eustace Chesser | .50 | 1.00 | 1.50 | NF |
| K302 | Speak Better–Write Better–English–Horace Coon | .50 | 1.00 | 1.50 | NF |
| K303 | The United States Political System and How It Works–David Cushman Coyle | .50 | 1.00 | 1.50 | NF |
| K304 | A Brief History of the United States–Franklin Escher, Jr | .50 | 1.00 | 1.50 | NF |
| K305 | Flower Arrangements Anyone Can Do Anywhere–Matilda Rogers | .50 | 1.00 | 1.50 | NF |
| K306 | Lives of Destiny as Told for the Reader's Digest–Donald Culross Peattie | .50 | 1.00 | 1.50 | B |
| Ks307 | Hoyle's Rules of Games–Albert H. Morehead & Geoffrey Mott-Smith | .50 | 1.00 | 1.50 | NF |
| K308 | How the Great Religions Began–Joseph Gaer | .50 | 1.00 | 1.50 | NF |
| K309 | Diet to Suit Yourself–Walter Ross | .50 | 1.00 | 1.50 | NF |
| Ks310 | A Treasury of Wisdom and Inspiration–David St. Leger | .50 | 1.00 | 1.50 | |
| Ks311 | Andy's Everyday Encyclopedia–Ellen Wales | .50 | 1.00 | 1.50 | NF |
| K312 | The Householder's Manual–Richard Kent | .50 | 1.00 | 1.50 | NF |
| K313 | Your Way to Popularity and Personal Power–James Bender & Lee Graham | .50 | 1.00 | 1.50 | |
| Ks314 | How to Help Your Child in School–Lawrence K. Frank & Mary Frank | .50 | 1.00 | 1.50 | NF |
| KD315 | God's Wonderful World–Agnes Lockie Mason & Phyllis Brown Ohanian | .50 | 1.00 | 1.50 | NF |
| Ks316 | How to Land the Job You Want–Jules Z. Willing | .50 | 1.00 | 1.50 | NF |
| Ks317 | Flight into Space–Jonathan N. Leonard | .50 | 1.00 | 1.50 | NF |
| Ks318 | Hobbies for Pleasure and Profit–Horace Coon; 1955 | .50 | 1.00 | 1.50 | NF |
| KD319 | The Life of Abraham Lincoln–Stefan Lorant Lorant | .50 | 1.00 | 1.50 | B |
| Ks320 | Science in Our Lives–Ritchie Calder | .50 | 1.00 | 1.50 | NF |
| K321 | Benjamin Franklin–Roger Burlingame | .50 | 1.00 | 1.50 | B |

| | | V/Good | Fine | N/Mint | |
|---|---|---|---|---|---|
| Ks322 | The Conquest of Happiness–Bertrand Russell | .50 | 1.00 | 1.50 | |
| Ks323 | The Handy Book of Gardening–Victor A. Tiedjens & Albert E. Wilkinson | .50 | 1.00 | 1.50 | NF |
| Ks324 | The United Nations and How It Works–David Cushman Coyle | .50 | 1.00 | 1.50 | NF |
| Ks325 | Your Guide to Financial Security–Sidney Margolius | .50 | 1.00 | 1.50 | NF |
| Ks326 | The Nature of Living Things–C. Brooke Worth & Robert K. Enders | .50 | 1.00 | 1.50 | NF |
| Ks327 | Machines That Built America–Roger Burlingame | .50 | 1.00 | 1.50 | NF |
| KD328 | How to Know American Antiques–Alice Winchester | .50 | 1.00 | 1.50 | NF |
| Ks329 | Fifty Years a Surgeon–Robert T. Morris | .50 | 1.00 | 1.50 | NF |
| Ks330 | The Crust of the Earth–Samuel Rapport & Helen Wright | .50 | 1.00 | 1.50 | NF |
| KD331 | Stories of Famous Operas–Harold Vincent Milligan | .50 | 1.00 | 1.50 | NF |
| Ks332 | Having a Baby–Alan F. Guttmacher | .50 | 1.00 | 1.50 | NF |
| Ks333 | The Web of Life–John H. Storer; 1956 | .50 | 1.00 | 1.50 | |
| Ks334 | The American Presidency–Clinton Rossiter | .50 | 1.00 | 1.50 | NF |
| K335 | How to Live without Liquor–Ralph A. Habas | .50 | 1.00 | 1.50 | |
| K336 | The Unknown–Is It Nearer?–Eric J. Dingwall & John Langdon-Davies; c-Powers | .50 | 1.00 | 1.50 | |
| K337 | Henry Ford–Roger Burlingame | .50 | 1.00 | 1.50 | B |
| Ks338 | Live without Fear–T.V. Smith | .50 | 1.00 | 1.50 | |
| Ks339 | The Meaning of the Dead Sea Scrolls–A. Powell Davies | .50 | 1.00 | 1.50 | NF |
| KD340 | American Folk Tales and Songs–Richard Chase | .50 | 1.00 | 1.50 | NF |
| Ks341 | How to Be a Better Member–Horace Coon | .50 | 1.00 | 1.50 | NF |
| Ks342 | Sight without Glasses–Harold M. Peppard | .50 | 1.00 | 1.50 | NF |
| Ks343 | The Ten Commandments–A. Powell Davies | .50 | 1.00 | 1.50 | NF |
| Ks344 | Call It Experience–Erskine Caldwell | .50 | 1.00 | 1.50 | |
| Ks345 | Seeds of Life–John Langdon-Davies; 1957 | .50 | 1.00 | 1.50 | NF |
| KD346 | How to Know the Minerals and Rocks–Richard M. Pearl | .75 | 1.50 | 2.25 | NF |
| KD347 | How to Know the Birds–Roger Tory Peterson | .75 | 1.50 | 2.25 | NF |
| Ks348 | The Eloquence of Winston Churchill–Winston Churchill | .50 | 1.00 | 1.50 | NF |
| KD349 | How to Know the American Mammals–Ivan T. Sanderson | .75 | 1.50 | 2.25 | NF |
| Ks350 | Here's How! A Round-the-World Bar Guide–Lawrence G. Blochman | .50 | 1.00 | 1.50 | NF |
| KD351 | Electronics for Everyone–Monroe Upton | .50 | 1.00 | 1.50 | NF |
| Ks352 | The Shape of Tomorrow–George Soule | .50 | 1.00 | 1.50 | NF |
| KD353 | How to Know and Predict the Weather–Robert Moore Fisher | .50 | 1.00 | 1.50 | NF |
| K354 | Speak Better–Write Better–English–Horace Coon | .50 | 1.00 | 1.50 | NF |
| KD355 | The Human Body and How It Works–Elbert Tokay | .50 | 1.00 | 1.50 | NF |
| KD356 | You and Your Heart–H.M. Marvin | .50 | 1.00 | 1.50 | NF |
| KD357 | Gods, Heroes and Men of Ancient Greece–W.H.D. Rouse | .50 | 1.00 | 1.50 | |
| KD358 | Pregnancy and Birth–Alan F. Guttmacher; 1958 | .50 | 1.00 | 1.50 | NF |
| KD359 | How the Great Religions Began–Joseph Gaer | .50 | 1.00 | 1.50 | NF |
| Ks360 | Satellites, Rockets and Outer Space–Willy Ley | .50 | 1.00 | 1.50 | NF |
| K361 | Magic House of Numbers–Irving Adler | .50 | 1.00 | 1.50 | NF |
| KD362 | Buffalo Bill and the Wild West–Henry Blackman Sell & Victor Weybright | .75 | 1.50 | 2.25 | B |
| KD363 | Hoyle's Rules of Games–Albert H. Morehead & Geoffrey Mott-Smith | .50 | 1.00 | 1.50 | NF |
| K364 | The Stars–Irving Adler | .50 | 1.00 | 1.50 | NF |
| KD365 | Your Body and Your Mind–Frank G. Slaughter | .50 | 1.00 | 1.50 | NF |
| K366 | may not exist | | | | |
| Ks367 | A Brief History of the United States–Franklin Escher, Jr; 1959 | .50 | 1.00 | 1.50 | NF |

| | | V/Good | Fine | N/Mint |
|---|---|---|---|---|

**SIGNET KEY**, *continued*

| | | V/Good | Fine | N/Mint | |
|---|---|---|---|---|---|
| KD368 | The Complete Italian System of Winning Bridge–Edgar Kaplan | .50 | 1.00 | 1.50 | NF |
| Ks369 | How Life Began–Irving Adler | .50 | 1.00 | 1.50 | NF |
| Ks370 | How to Spell and Increase Your Word Power–Horace Coon | .50 | 1.00 | 1.50 | NF |
| KD371 | The Bible Was Right–Hugh J. Schonfield | .50 | 1.00 | 1.50 | |
| KD372 | Your Adolescent at Home and in School–Lawrence K. Frank & Mary Frank | .50 | 1.00 | 1.50 | NF |
| KD373 | The New American Guide to Colleges–Gene R. Hawes | .50 | 1.00 | 1.50 | NF |

*Stanley Library SL72, Star Book 11, Star Novel (unlisted).*

# SIGNET STUDENT EDITIONS
## New American Library
### Special 10-Cent Editions of Signet Titles

| | | V/Good | Fine | N/Mint | |
|---|---|---|---|---|---|
| nn | Machines That Built America–Roger Burlingame; 1953 | .50 | 1.00 | 1.50 | NF |
| nn | American Capitalism–John Kenneth Galbraith | .50 | 1.00 | 1.50 | |
| nn | Basic Selections from Emerson–ed. Edward C. Lindeman | .50 | 1.00 | 1.50 | |
| nn | Education and Liberty–James Bryant Conant | .50 | 1.00 | 1.50 | |
| nn | The Prospects for Communist China–W.W. Roslow | .50 | 1.00 | 1.50 | |
| nn | The Grass Harp–Truman Capote | .50 | 1.00 | 1.50 | |
| nn | The Track of the Cat–Walter Van tilburg Clark | .50 | 1.00 | 1.50 | W |
| nn | Lenin–David Shub; special abridged edition | .50 | 1.00 | 1.50 | B |

# STALLION BOOKS
## Stallion Books/Universal Publishing and Distributing Corporation
### Digest Size

| 203 | Three Bad Girls–Steve Harragan | 4.00 | 8.00 | 12.00 | E |
|---|---|---|---|---|---|
| 204 | Marijuana Girl–H.R. de Mexico | 8.00 | 16.00 | 24.00 | E |
| 205 | Tramp Girl–Thomas Stone | 4.00 | 8.00 | 12.00 | E |
| 206 | The Queer Sisters–Steve Harragan | 4.00 | 8.00 | 12.00 | M |
| 207 | Miami Widow–Gene Harvey | 4.00 | 8.00 | 12.00 | E |
| 209 | Ship's Doctor–Henry Lewis Nixon; c-Walter Popp | 4.00 | 8.00 | 12.00 | E |
| 210 | Gutter Star–D.B. Clark; orig. 1951. Note: Same cover as Intimate 52 and Beacon B135 and B377 | 4.00 | 8.00 | 12.00 | E |
| 211 | Trailer-Camp Girl–Doug Dupperault | 4.00 | 8.00 | 12.00 | E |
| 212 | Side-Show Girl–Steve Harragan | 4.00 | 8.00 | 12.00 | E |
| 213 | Reefer Club–Luke Roberts. Note: Same cover as Intimate 32 and virtually identical to Beacon B260 | 8.00 | 16.00 | 24.00 | E |
| 214 | Another Man's Wife–Margaret Carruthers; aka Bondage | 4.00 | 8.00 | 12.00 | E |
| 216 | Cracker Girl–Harry Whittington | 4.00 | 8.00 | 12.00 | E |

# STANLEY LIBRARY
## Stanley Library, Inc.

| SL67 | The Oldest Profession–Jean Campbell; orig. 1958 | 2.50 | 5.00 | 7.50 | E |
|---|---|---|---|---|---|
| SL68 | So Nice, So Wild–Max Day; orig. 1959 | 2.50 | 5.00 | 7.50 | E |
| SL69 | Quarry Road–A.R. Dispaldo; orig. 1959 | 2.50 | 5.00 | 7.50 | E |
| SL70 | Love Doctor–Florence Stonebraker | 2.50 | 5.00 | 7.50 | E |
| SL71 | Lover Boy–John B. Flint | | | | |
| SL72 | Strictly for the Boys–Harry Whittington; orig. 1959 | 2.50 | 5.00 | 7.50 | E |
| SL73 | Strange Sinner–Florence Stonebraker | 2.50 | 5.00 | 7.50 | E |
| SL74 | Bed of Fear–Doug Duperault; orig. 1959 | 2.50 | 5.00 | 7.50 | E |

# STAR BOOKS
## Publication House, Inc.
### Digest Size

| | | V/Good | Fine | N/Mint | |
|---|---|---|---|---|---|
| 750 | Boy-Crazy–Albert L. Quandt; 1955. Note: Same cover as Original No. 721 | 4.00 | 8.00 | 12.00 | JD |
| 751 | Babysitter–Albert L. Quandt; 1955 | 3.00 | 6.00 | 9.00 | E |
| 752 | French Alley–Matthew Clay | 3.00 | 6.00 | 9.00 | E |
| 754 | Cellar Club–Albert L. Quandt | 5.00 | 10.00 | 15.00 | JD |
| 756 | Shanty Road–Whit Harrison (Harry Whittington) | 3.00 | 6.00 | 9.00 | E |
| 758 | Sinners Club–Harry Whittington; 1956 | 3.00 | 6.00 | 9.00 | E |
| 759 | City Girl–Hallam Whitney (Harry Whittington) | 3.00 | 6.00 | 9.00 | E |
| 760 | Waterfront Girl–Amos Hatter | 3.00 | 6.00 | 9.00 | E |
| 761 | Native Girl–Whit Harrison (Harry Whittington); aka Savage Love | 3.00 | 6.00 | 9.00 | E |
| 762 | Backwoods Hussy–Hallam Whitney (Harry Whittington) | 3.00 | 6.00 | 9.00 | E |
| 763 | Motel Mistress–Norman Bligh | 3.00 | 6.00 | 9.00 | E |
| 765 | River Boat Girl–Norman Bligh | 3.00 | 6.00 | 9.00 | E |
| 768 | Ward Nurse–M. Coleman | 3.00 | 6.00 | 9.00 | E |

# STAR BOOKS
## Star Guidance, Inc.
### Digest Size

| 1 | Texas Gun Slinger–Murray Leinster; aka Fighting Horse Valley | 5.00 | 10.00 | 15.00 | W |
|---|---|---|---|---|---|
| 2 | Bachelor Bait–Peggy Gaddis | 2.00 | 4.00 | 6.00 | E |
| 3 | Outlaw Guns–Murray Leinster; aka Wanted Dead or Alive | 5.00 | 10.00 | 15.00 | W |
| 4 | Hell Cat!–Martin Gregor; aka Bodies Are Different | 2.00 | 4.00 | 6.00 | E |
| 5 | Outlaw Deputy–Murray Leinster; 1950 | 5.00 | 10.00 | 15.00 | W |
| 6 | The Flaming Guns–Burt Arthur | 2.00 | 4.00 | 6.00 | W |
| 7 | Bad Hombre–Archie Joscelyn; orig. 1950; c-Gross | 2.00 | 4.00 | 6.00 | W |
| 8 | Range Justice–Paul Evan Lehman; orig. 1950; c-Gross | 2.00 | 4.00 | 6.00 | W |
| 9 | Border Wolves–Archie Joscelyn; c-Gross | 2.00 | 4.00 | 6.00 | W |
| 10 | Law of the .45–Paul Evan Lehman | 2.00 | 4.00 | 6.00 | W |
| 11 | Killer's Moon–Burt Arthur; orig. 1950; c-Gross | 2.00 | 4.00 | 6.00 | W |
| 12 | The Black Rider–Burt Arthur; orig. 1950; c-Gross | 2.00 | 4.00 | 6.00 | W |
| 13 | Gun-Thunder Valley–Archie Joscelyn; c-Gross | 2.00 | 4.00 | 6.00 | W |
| 14 | The Vengeance Trail–Archie Joscelyn | 2.00 | 4.00 | 6.00 | W |
| 15 | The Long Trail North–Lee Floren; orig. 1951. Note: Same cover as Star No. 27 | 2.00 | 4.00 | 6.00 | W |
| 16 | The Sheep Killers–Paul Evan Lehman; orig. 1951 | 2.00 | 4.00 | 6.00 | W |
| 17 | Two-Gun Trail–Lee Floren; orig. 1951; c-Gross | 2.00 | 4.00 | 6.00 | W |

STAR BOOKS, *continued*

| 18 | Wyoming Outlaw–Archie Joscelyn | 2.00 | 4.00 | 6.00 W |
|---|---|---|---|---|
| 19 | Duel on the Range–Burt Arthur | 2.00 | 4.00 | 6.00 W |
| 20 | Rustler's Trail–Lee Floren; orig. 1951 | 2.00 | 4.00 | 6.00 W |
| 21 | Black Gunsmoke–Lee Floren; orig. 1951; c-Gross | 2.00 | 4.00 | 6.00 W |
| 22 | Texas Vengeance–Paul Evan Lehman; c-Gross | 2.00 | 4.00 | 6.00 W |
| 23 | The Black Rider–Burt Arthur | 2.00 | 4.00 | 6.00 W |
| 24 | Gun-Thunder Valley–Archie Joscelyn | 2.00 | 4.00 | 6.00 W |
| 25 | Law of the '45–Paul Evan Lehman; 1952 | 2.00 | 4.00 | 6.00 W |
| 26 | Killers Moon–Burth Arthur | 2.00 | 4.00 | 6.00 W |
| 27 | Deputy's Revenge–Lee Floren; 1952; aka The Long Trail North. Note: Same cover as Star No. 15 | 2.00 | 4.00 | 6.00 W |
| 28 | Texas Guns–Paul Evan Lehman; aka Range Justice; c-Gross | 2.00 | 4.00 | 6.00 W |
| 29 | Duel at Killman Creek–Archie Joscelyn; aka Border Wolves; c-Gross | 2.00 | 4.00 | 6.00 W |
| 30 | Texas Outlaw–Archie Joscelyn; 1952; aka Bad Hombre; c-Gross | 2.00 | 4.00 | 6.00 W |
| 31 | Range War at Keno–Paul Evan Lehman | 2.00 | 4.00 | 6.00 W |
| 32 | Ambush on Satan's Hill–Archie Joscelyn; aka The Vengeance Trail; c-Gross | 2.00 | 4.00 | 6.00 W |
| 33 | Outlaw Fury–Burt Arthur; 1952 | 2.00 | 4.00 | 6.00 W |
| 34 | Action at Spanish Flat–Burt Arthur; 1952 | 2.00 | 4.00 | 6.00 W |
| 35 | Rustlers of Rio Grande–Paul Evan Lehman | 2.00 | 4.00 | 6.00 W |
| 36 | Two-Gun Outlaw–Burt Arthur | 2.00 | 4.00 | 6.00 W |
| 37 | The Texans Revenge–Archie Joscelyn | 2.00 | 4.00 | 6.00 W |
| 38 | Gun-Law on the Range–Burt Arthur | 2.00 | 4.00 | 6.00 W |
| 39 | Texas Showdown–Archie Joscelyn | 2.00 | 4.00 | 6.00 W |
| 41 | The Way of a Texan–Walt Coburn | 2.00 | 4.00 | 6.00 W |
| 42 | Two-Gun Vengeance–Archie Joscelyn | 2.00 | 4.00 | 6.00 W |
| 43 | Duel on the Range–Burt Arthur | 2.00 | 4.00 | 6.00 W |
| 44 | Texas Vengeance–Paul Evan Lehman; c-Gross | 2.00 | 4.00 | 6.00 W |
| 46 | Two-Gun Trail–Lee Floren | 2.00 | 4.00 | 6.00 W |
| 47 | Wyoming Outlaw–Archie Joscelyn; c-Gross | 2.00 | 4.00 | 6.00 W |
| 48 | Texas Revenge–Archie Joscelyn | 2.00 | 4.00 | 6.00 W |

## (STAR STORIES)
### Star Stories Inc.

| nn | Great Civil War Stories–Curtis Blackerby; orig. 1961 | 1.50 | 3.00 | 4.50 NF |
|---|---|---|---|---|

## STORK ORIGINAL NOVEL
### Star Guidance, Inc.
#### Digest Size

| nn | Lust for Love–Wright Williams; c-Cole | 4.00 | 8.00 | 12.00 E |
|---|---|---|---|---|
| nn | Life of Passion–Gordon Semple; orig. 1949; c-Rodewald | 4.00 | 8.00 | 12.00 E |
| 3 | Sinful Life–Glen Watkins | 4.00 | 8.00 | 12.00 E |
| 4 | Soul of Passion–Richard Himmel | 4.00 | 8.00 | 12.00 E |
| 5 | Passionate Lover–Gail Jordan (Peggy Gaddis); c-Rodewald | 4.00 | 8.00 | 12.00 E |
| 6 | The Sins of Donna Kenyon–Ralph Carter | 3.00 | 6.00 | 9.00 E |
| 7 | Raging Passions–Thomas Stone; orig. 1950; c-Cole | 4.00 | 8.00 | 12.00 E |
| 8 | Two Sinners–Lee Jackquin; c-Cole | 4.00 | 8.00 | 12.00 E |

## (STOVEL-ADVOCATE)
### Stovel-Advocate Press Ltd.
#### (Canadian)

| nn | Grey Cup or Bust–Tony Allan; 1954 | 2.50 | 5.00 | 7.50 S |
|---|---|---|---|---|
| nn | Curling to Win–Ken Watson; 1955 | 2.50 | 5.00 | 7.50 S |

## STREAMLINE
### Streamline Publishing
#### (Canadian)

| nn | Whispering City–Horace Brown; 1947; movie tie-in | 3.00 | 6.00 | 9.00 |
|---|---|---|---|---|

## (STUART)
### Stuart Art Gallery, Inc.

| nn | Precious Rubbish–Theodore L. Shaw; orig. 1956 | 1.25 | 2.50 | 3.75 NF |
|---|---|---|---|---|
| nn | Critical Quackery–Theodore L. Shaw | 1.25 | 2.50 | 3.75 NF |
| nn | Hypocrisy About Art–Theodore L. Shaw | 1.00 | 2.00 | 3.00 NF |
| nn | Don't Get Taught Art This Way– Theodore L. Shaw; orig. 1967 | 1.00 | 2.00 | 3.00 NF |

## STUDIO POCKET EDITION
### Studio Publications
#### (Canadian)

| 4 | Sins of the Fathers–James (Jim) Thompson; 1952; aka Heed the Thunder | 40.00 | 80.00 | 120.00 |
|---|---|---|---|---|
| 105 | Werewolf of Paris–Guy Endore; 1952 | 9.00 | 18.00 | 27.00 HO |
| 107 | Flee the Night in Anger–Dan Keller | 2.50 | 5.00 | 7.50 M |
| 108 | Hotel Berlin–Vicki Baum | 2.50 | 5.00 | 7.50 |
| 109 | The Man in the Iron Mask–Alexander Dumas; movie tie-in | 4.00 | 8.00 | 12.00 A |
| 110 | The Brick Foxhole–R. Brooks | 2.50 | 5.00 | 7.50 C |
| 111 | Rebecca–Daphne du Maurier | 2.50 | 5.00 | 7.50 R |
| 112 | The Parasites–Daphne du Maurier | 2.50 | 5.00 | 7.50 |
| 113 | The Great Escape–Paul Brickhill; movie tie-in for The Wooden Horse | 3.00 | 6.00 | 9.00 C |

## SUPERIOR DETECTIVE NOVEL
### Superior Publishers/Duchess Printing and Publishing Co., Ltd./ Duchess Publishing Company
#### Digest Size
#### (Canadian)

| nn | The Stuffed Men–Anthony Rud | 25.00 | 50.00 | 75.00 M |
|---|---|---|---|---|
| nn | Bedroom Eyes–Maurice Dekobra | 6.00 | 12.00 | 18.00 E |
| nn | Guns of Wrath–Cliff Campbell | 6.00 | 12.00 | 18.00 W |
| nn | True Canadian Detective Stories | 6.00 | 12.00 | 18.00 NF |
| nn | True Mysteries and Murders–Robert Henry Todd & Lloyd C. Steele; 1945 | 4.00 | 8.00 | 12.00 NF |
| nn | Prize True Detective Stories. Note: Same cover as Double Action Detective No. 2 and Big Green Detective Novel No. 2 | 6.00 | 12.00 | 18.00 NF |
| nn | Brigands of the Moon–John Campbell; nd. Note: Miscredited, actually written by Ray Cummings | 25.00 | 50.00 | 75.00 SF |

## SUPERIOR REPRINTS
### The Military Service Publishing Company

| M637 | White Magic–Faith Baldwin; 1944 | 1.50 | 3.00 | 4.50 R |
|---|---|---|---|---|
| M638 | Ol' Man Adam an' His Chillun–Roark Bradford | 1.50 | 3.00 | 4.50 |
| M639 | Unexpected Night–Elizabeth Daly | 1.50 | 3.00 | 4.50 M |
| M640 | An April Afternoon–Philip Wylie | 1.50 | 3.00 | 4.50 |
| M641 | Family Affair–Ione Sundberg Shriber | 1.50 | 3.00 | 4.50 |

| | V/Good | Fine | N/Mint | |
|---|---|---|---|---|

**SUPERIOR REPRINTS,** *continued*

| | | V/Good | Fine | N/Mint | |
|---|---|---|---|---|---|
| M642 | The Rynox Murder Mystery–Philip MacDonald | 2.00 | 4.00 | 6.00 | M |
| M643 | Cartoons by George Price–George Price; 1945 | 2.50 | 5.00 | 7.50 | H |
| M644 | Embarrassment of Riches–Marjorie Fischer | 1.50 | 3.00 | 4.50 | |
| M645 | Murder in Mink–Robert George Dean | 1.50 | 3.00 | 4.50 | M |
| M646 | The Love Nest, and Other Stories–Ring Lardner | 1.50 | 3.00 | 4.50 | H |
| M647 | Inquest–Percival Wilde | 1.50 | 3.00 | 4.50 | |
| M648 | One Foot in Heaven–Hartzell Spence | 1.50 | 3.00 | 4.50 | |
| M649 | The Navy Colt–Frank Gruber | 2.50 | 5.00 | 7.50 | |
| M650 | The Informer–Liam O'Flaherty | 1.50 | 3.00 | 4.50 | |
| M651 | Mr. Angel Comes Aboard–Charles G. Booth | 1.50 | 3.00 | 4.50 | |
| M652 | This Gun for Hire–Graham Greene | 2.00 | 4.00 | 6.00 | |
| M653 | The House without the Door–Elizabeth Daly | 1.50 | 3.00 | 4.50 | M |
| M654 | On Ice–Robert George Dean | 1.50 | 3.00 | 4.50 | M |
| M655 | The Mighty Blockhead–Frank Gruber | 2.50 | 5.00 | 7.50 | |
| M656 | Saki Sampler–H.H. Munro | 2.00 | 4.00 | 6.00 | F |
| M657 | Good Night, Sheriff–Harrison R. Steeves | 1.50 | 3.00 | 4.50 | |

## SUSPENSE NOVELS
### Farrell Publishing Corporation
**Digest Size**

| | | V/Good | Fine | N/Mint | |
|---|---|---|---|---|---|
| 1 | Strange Pursuit–N.R. De Mexico | 2.50 | 5.00 | 7.50 | M |
| 2 | The Case of the Lonely Lovers–Will Daemer; 1951 | 2.50 | 5.00 | 7.50 | M |
| 3 | Naked Villainy–Carl G. Hodges | 2.50 | 5.00 | 7.50 | M |

## SWAN
### Swan Publishing Co. Inc.

| | | V/Good | Fine | N/Mint | |
|---|---|---|---|---|---|
| 1 | Stag Party Humor–ed. anon.; 1st ed. 1966 | 1.50 | 3.00 | 4.50 | H |
| S102 | Ian Fleming: Man with the Golden Pen–Eleanor Pelrine & Dennis Pelrine; orig. 1966 | 3.00 | 6.00 | 9.00 | B |

## SWAN
### Swan Publishing Co., Ltd.
**(Canadian)**

| | | V/Good | Fine | N/Mint | |
|---|---|---|---|---|---|
| 112 | Ian Fleming: Man with the Golden Pen–Eleanor Pelrine & Dennis Pelrine; virtually identical to U.S. ed., also identified as both orig. and 1st ed., exact publishing sequence unknown | 3.00 | 6.00 | 9.00 | B |

## TECH MYSTERY
### Tech Mysteries, Inc.
**Digest Size**

| | | V/Good | Fine | N/Mint | |
|---|---|---|---|---|---|
| 1 | The Candle–Linton C. Hopkins | 2.00 | 4.00 | 6.00 | M |
| 2 | Murder Is My Racket–Robert H. Leitfred | 2.00 | 4.00 | 6.00 | M |
| nn | Murder Man–William Bogart | 2.00 | 4.00 | 6.00 | M |

## TECH WESTERN
### Tech Books, Inc.
**Digest Size**

| | | V/Good | Fine | N/Mint | |
|---|---|---|---|---|---|
| 1 | The Black Rider–Herbert Shapiro | 2.00 | 4.00 | 6.00 | W |
| 2 | Rainbow Trail–Herbert Shapiro | 2.00 | 4.00 | 6.00 | W |

## TEMPO BOOKS
### Grosset and Dunlap, Inc.

| | | V/Good | Fine | N/Mint | |
|---|---|---|---|---|---|
| 5320 | Grove of Doom–Walter B. Gibson; 1966 | 2.00 | 4.00 | 6.00 | M |
| 5368 | The Best of Creepy–1971; c-Frazetta. Note: Comic story reprints include art by Williamson, Wood & Adkins, Torres, Crandall, Frazetta, Toth, and Ditko. | 3.00 | 6.00 | 9.00 | |
| 17311 | Star Hawks–Gil Kane & Ron Goulart; 1st ed. 1979; contains comic strip reprints | 1.50 | 3.00 | 4.50 | SF |

## (THEODORE ROOSEVELT)
### Theodore Roosevelt Association

| | | V/Good | Fine | N/Mint | |
|---|---|---|---|---|---|
| nn | A Theodore Roosevelt Round-Up– Herman Hagedorn & Sidney Wallach; 1st ed. 1958 | 1.00 | 2.00 | 3.00 | NF |

## THREE STAR BOOKS
### Novel Books, Inc.

| | | V/Good | Fine | N/Mint | |
|---|---|---|---|---|---|
| 101 | In the Lion's Den–Jerry Cotton; 1st U.S. ed. 1965 | 1.50 | 3.00 | 4.50 | M |
| 102 | Great Science Fiction–ed. Tony Licata | 1.00 | 2.00 | 3.00 | SF |
| 104 | Ian Fleming's Incredible Creation–Paul Antony & Jacquelyn Friedman; 1965 | 3.00 | 6.00 | 9.00 | NF |

## A THRILLER BOOK
### Lev Gleason Publications, Inc.
**Size–3½" x 5¾"**

| | | V/Good | Fine | N/Mint | |
|---|---|---|---|---|---|
| nn | Big Shot Gangsters, Their Crimes, Careers and Deaths–Stanford Quayle; 1947; c-Cole | 5.00 | 10.00 | 15.00 | NF |
| nn | The Greatest Prison Breaks of All Time–Michael Finn; c-Cole | 5.00 | 10.00 | 15.00 | NF |
| nn | How Detectives Catch Crooks–Stanford Quayle; c-Cole | 5.00 | 10.00 | 15.00 | NF |
| nn | 10 Most Terrible Crimes of All Time– Stanford Quayle; c-Cole | 5.00 | 10.00 | 15.00 | NF |
| nn | Mysteries of Magic, Mind Reading and Hypnotism Explained–Hamilton Holt; c-Cole | 5.00 | 10.00 | 15.00 | NF |

## THRILLER NOVEL CLASSIC
### Novel Selections, Inc.
**Digest Size**

| | | V/Good | Fine | N/Mint | |
|---|---|---|---|---|---|
| 1 | Secret Agent No. 1–Frederick Frost | 3.00 | 6.00 | 9.00 | M |
| 2 | Bulldog Drummond on Dartmoor– Gerald Fairlie | 3.00 | 6.00 | 9.00 | M |
| 3 | The Yellow Strangler–Colin Robertson | 4.00 | 8.00 | 12.00 | M |
| 4 | The Insidious Dr. Fu-Manchu–Sax Rohmer | 4.00 | 8.00 | 12.00 | M |
| 5 | Lord of Terror–Sidney Horler | 3.50 | 7.00 | 10.50 | M |
| 6 | Murder and the Secret Weapon– George F. Worts | 3.00 | 6.00 | 9.00 | M |
| 7 | Spy Meets Spy–Frederick Frost | 3.00 | 6.00 | 9.00 | |
| 8 | Jimmy Dale and the Phantom Clue– Frank L. Packard | 3.00 | 6.00 | 9.00 | M |
| 9 | The Golden Scorpion–Sax Rohmer | 4.00 | 8.00 | 12.00 | M |
| 10 | The White Wolf–Franklin Gregory | 4.00 | 8.00 | 12.00 | SF |
| 11 | Death in Four Letters–Francis Beeding | 3.00 | 6.00 | 9.00 | M |
| 12 | The Bamboo Whistle–Frederick Frost | 3.00 | 6.00 | 9.00 | |
| 13 | Invasion–Whitman Chambers | 5.00 | 10.00 | 15.00 | SF |
| 14 | Bulldog Drummond Meets a Murderess–H.C. McNeile | 3.00 | 6.00 | 9.00 | M |
| 15 | Terror by Night–Lee Crosby | 3.00 | 6.00 | 9.00 | M |

| | | V/Good | Fine | N/Mint | |
|---|---|---|---|---|---|

THRILLER NOVEL CLASSIC, *continued*

| 16 | The Saint in Miami–Leslie Charteris | 3.00 | 6.00 | 9.00 | M |
|---|---|---|---|---|---|
| 17 | Trial by Murder–Elisabeth Sanxay Holding | 3.00 | 6.00 | 9.00 | M |
| 18 | Murder Greets Jean Holton–Kathleen Moore Knight | 3.00 | 6.00 | 9.00 | M |
| 19 | Eleven Were Brave–Francis Beeding | 3.00 | 6.00 | 9.00 | M |
| 20 | Night Attack–Lee Crosby | 3.00 | 6.00 | 9.00 | |
| 21 | Design in Evil–Rufus King | 3.00 | 6.00 | 9.00 | M |
| 22 | Cradled in Fear–Anita Boutell | 3.00 | 6.00 | 9.00 | |
| 23 | Poison in Jest–John Dickson Carr | 3.00 | 6.00 | 9.00 | M |
| 24 | Deadline for Destruction–Charles L. Leonard | 3.00 | 6.00 | 9.00 | |
| 25 | Doors to Death–Lee Crosby; aka Too Many Doors | 3.00 | 6.00 | 9.00 | M |
| 26 | Deep Lay the Dead–Frederick C. Davis | 3.00 | 6.00 | 9.00 | M |
| 27 | Assignment to Death–Charles L. Leonard | 3.00 | 6.00 | 9.00 | M |
| 28 | Death at Dakar–Kerry O'Neill | 3.00 | 6.00 | 9.00 | A |
| 29 | The Black Path of Fear–Cornell Woolrich | 4.00 | 8.00 | 12.00 | M |
| 30 | The Secret of the Spa–Charles A. Leonard | 4.00 | 8.00 | 12.00 | M |
| 31 | Fear Came First–Vera Kelsey | 3.00 | 6.00 | 9.00 | M |
| 32 | Death Goes Fishing–Edward Lee | 3.00 | 6.00 | 9.00 | M |
| 33 | Murder for Empire–Kathleen Moore Knight | 3.00 | 6.00 | 9.00 | SF |
| 34 | Action at World's End–Whitman Chambers | 3.00 | 6.00 | 9.00 | |
| 35 | Death at Abu Mina–Peter William; aka The Affair at Abu Mina | 3.00 | 6.00 | 9.00 | M |
| 36 | Death and Bitters–Kit Christian | 3.00 | 6.00 | 9.00 | M |
| 37 | Murder in Silence–George Selmark | 3.00 | 6.00 | 9.00 | M |
| 38 | Under a Cloud–Van Siller | 3.00 | 6.00 | 9.00 | |
| 39 | A Shroud for Shylock–Stephen Ransome | 3.00 | 6.00 | 9.00 | M |

## THRILLING BOOKS/NOVELS
## Popular Library, Inc.
### Digest Size

| 11 | Trail Dust–Clarence E. Mulford | 2.50 | 5.00 | 7.50 | W |
|---|---|---|---|---|---|
| 12 | Texas Man–William MacLeod Raine | 2.50 | 5.00 | 7.50 | W |
| 13 | Holster Law–Gordon Young | 2.50 | 5.00 | 7.50 | W |
| 14 | Square Deal Sanderson–Charles Alden Seltzer | 2.50 | 5.00 | 7.50 | W |
| 15 | The Quirt–B.M. Bower | 2.50 | 5.00 | 7.50 | W |
| 16 | Cow Country Law–Frank C. Robertson | 2.50 | 5.00 | 7.50 | W |
| 17 | Man to Man–Jackson Gregory | 2.50 | 5.00 | 7.50 | W |
| 18 | Guns of Paradise Bend–William White | 2.50 | 5.00 | 7.50 | W |
| 19 | Two Rangers from Texas–Caddo Cameron | 2.50 | 5.00 | 7.50 | W |
| 20 | Rustler's Valley–Clarence E. Mulford | 2.50 | 5.00 | 7.50 | W |
| 21 | Trigger Gospel–Harry Sinclair Drago | 2.50 | 5.00 | 7.50 | W |
| 22 | Hot Lead Trail–Charles Alden Seltzer; aka The Red Brand | 2.50 | 5.00 | 7.50 | W |
| 23 | Gunman from Abilene–Gordon Young; aka Red Clark to the Rescue | 2.50 | 5.00 | 7.50 | W |
| 24 | Heart of the Range–William Patterson White | 2.50 | 5.00 | 7.50 | W |
| 25 | Longhorns of Hate–Frank C. Robertson | 2.50 | 5.00 | 7.50 | W |
| 26 | Dead-End Trail–Norman A. Fox | 2.50 | 5.00 | 7.50 | W |
| 27 | It's Hell to Be a Ranger–Caddo Cameron | 2.50 | 5.00 | 7.50 | W |
| 28 | Riders of the Rocker K–S. Payne | 2.50 | 5.00 | 7.50 | W |
| 29 | Bring Me His Ears–Clarence E. Mulford | 2.50 | 5.00 | 7.50 | W |
| 30 | Thorson of Thunder Gulch–Norman A. Fox | 2.50 | 5.00 | 7.50 | W |
| 31 | Guardians of the Sage–Harry Sinclair Drago | 2.50 | 5.00 | 7.50 | W |
| 32 | Hidden Trails–William Patterson White | 2.50 | 5.00 | 7.50 | W |

## THRILLING MYSTERY NOVEL
## Sphere Publications
### Digest Size

| nn | Final Appearance–Jeannette Covert Nolan | 3.00 | 6.00 | 9.00 | M |
|---|---|---|---|---|---|

*Thrilling Novel 20, Toby unnumbered, Travellers Pocket Library 102.*

| | | V/Good | Fine | N/Mint | |
|---|---|---|---|---|---|

## TIGER–see POWELL/TIGER

## TOBY
## Toby Press, Inc./Modern Living Council, Inc.
### Digest Size

| nn | Dangerous People; orig. 1952 | 2.00 | 4.00 | 6.00 | NF |
|---|---|---|---|---|---|
| nn | Space Pirate–Jack Vance; orig. 1953 | 6.00 | 12.00 | 18.00 | SF |
| nn | Escape; orig. 1953 | 2.00 | 4.00 | 6.00 | A |
| nn | Sunset Showdown–Steve Frazee; orig. 1953 | 2.00 | 4.00 | 6.00 | W |
| nn | Private Lives–Ellis Whitfield | 2.00 | 4.00 | 6.00 | NF |
| nn | The Lil Abner Square Dance Book– F. Leifer | 2.00 | 4.00 | 6.00 | NF |
| nn | You'll Die Now–Raymond Drennen | 2.00 | 4.00 | 6.00 | M |
| nn | 10 Ways to Win Peace of Mind–Dr. David Harold Fink, Dr. Robert Goldenson, & others; 1953 | 1.50 | 3.00 | 4.50 | NF |
| nn | How to Run a Successful Party–Maggi McNellis, Hubie Boscowitz, Louise Price Bell | 1.50 | 3.00 | 4.50 | NF |

## TODAY'S CROSSWORDS
## Today's Crosswords, Inc.

| nn | Today's Crossword Dictionary–ed. David Shulman; 1955 | 1.25 | 2.50 | 3.75 | NF |
|---|---|---|---|---|---|

## TOWER
## Tower Publications, Inc.

**Note: Two-digit prefix is price code, and last three numbers are stock number.**

| 42-405 | Love a La Carte–George St. George; movie tie-in | 2.00 | 4.00 | 6.00 | E |
|---|---|---|---|---|---|
| 42-407 | Before I Die–Lionel White | 1.50 | 3.00 | 4.50 | M |
| 43-430 | Catharine the Great–Kevin Matthews (Gardner F. Fox) | 1.50 | 3.00 | 4.50 | A |
| 42-431 | The Killing–Lionel White | 1.50 | 3.00 | 4.50 | M |
| 43-444 | Hemingway's Paris–Morrill Cody | 1.50 | 3.00 | 4.50 | NF |
| 43-460 | Can a Mermaid Kill?–Thomas B. Dewey; 1965 | 1.50 | 3.00 | 4.50 | M |
| 43-475 | Helen of Troy–Kevin Matthews (Gardner F. Fox) | 1.50 | 3.00 | 4.50 | A |
| 42-502 | Five Day Nightmare–Fredric Brown | 6.00 | 12.00 | 18.00 | M |
| 43-530 | Flight into Terror–Lionel White | 1.50 | 3.00 | 4.50 | M |
| 43-531 | Dragon's Island–Jack Williamson; 1965 | 1.50 | 3.00 | 4.50 | SF |
| 43-543 | Rebels in the Streets–Kitty Hanson | 2.00 | 4.00 | 6.00 | JD |
| 42-593 | Mistress of Farrondale–Dorothea Nile (Michael Avallone) | 1.50 | 3.00 | 4.50 | |
| 42-658 | The Evil Men Do–Dorothea Nile (Michael Avallone) | 1.50 | 3.00 | 4.50 | |
| 42-660 | Dynamo–Larry Ivie; 1st ed. 1966; c-Wood. Note: Contains comic book reprints | 2.00 | 4.00 | 6.00 | A |

Triple Nickel Library 8, Trophy Book 402, Uni-Book 15.

| | | V/Good | Fine | N/Mint | |
|---|---|---|---|---|---|
| **TOWER,** *continued* | | | | | |
| 42-672 | Noman–Larry Ivie; 1st ed. 1966; c-Wood. Note: Contains comic book reprints | 2.00 | 4.00 | 6.00 | A |
| 42-674 | Menthor–Larry Ivie; 1st ed. 1966; c-Wood. Note: Contains comic book reprints | 2.00 | 4.00 | 6.00 | A |
| 42-687 | The Terrific Trio–Larry Ivie; 1st ed. 1966; c-Wood. Note: Contains comic book reprints | 2.00 | 4.00 | 6.00 | A |
| 43-735 | Operation: Sky Drop–Dan Brennan; 1st ed. 1966 | 1.50 | 3.00 | 4.50 | C |
| 42-778 | Murder Las Vegas Style–W.T. Ballard; 1967 | 1.50 | 3.00 | 4.50 | M |
| 43-878 | The President's Right Hand–Dan Brennan | 1.50 | 3.00 | 4.50 | |
| 43-970 | Dracula's Curse and the Jewel of Seven Stars–Bram Stoker | 1.50 | 3.00 | 4.50 | HO |

## TRAVELLERS POCKET LIBRARY BEST-SELLER
### Ward-Hill Books

| | | V/Good | Fine | N/Mint | |
|---|---|---|---|---|---|
| 100 | Passion Is a Gentle Whip–Milton H. Gropper; 1949 | 3.00 | 6.00 | 9.00 | E |
| 102 | Lady Chatterley's Lover–D.H. Lawrence | 3.00 | 6.00 | 9.00 | E |
| 103 | Venus in Furs–Leopold Sacher-Masoch; 1949. Note: Two cover variants exist. | 3.00 | 6.00 | 9.00 | E |
| 104 | Pagan in Silk–Irving Sinclair | 3.00 | 6.00 | 9.00 | E |
| 106 | Speak the Sin Softly–Virginia Thomas | 3.00 | 6.00 | 9.00 | E |

## TRIPLE NICKEL LIBRARY
### Solomon & Gelman, Inc.
**Digest Size**

**Note: Premiums for Bazooka bubble gum.**

| | | | | | |
|---|---|---|---|---|---|
| 1 | The Adventures of Davy Crockett–Nat Wilson | 3.50 | 7.00 | 10.50 | A |
| 2 | Davy Crockett and Danger from the Mountain–Nat Wilson | 3.50 | 7.00 | 10.50 | A |
| 3 | The Life of Wild Bill Hickok | 3.50 | 7.00 | 10.50 | W |
| 5 | Barbie Lane and Mystery of the Egyptian Museum–Lucy Carlton; 1955 | 3.50 | 7.00 | 10.50 | M |
| 6 | The Power Boys and the Riddle of the Sunken Ship–Arthur Benwood; 1956 | 3.50 | 7.00 | 10.50 | M |
| 7 | The Power Boys in the Castle of Curious Creatures–Arthur Benwood; 1956 | 3.50 | 7.00 | 10.50 | M |
| 8 | The Power Boys and the Mystery of the Marble Face–Arthur Benwood | 3.50 | 7.00 | 10.50 | M |
| 21 | The Mystery of the Marlow Mansion–Arthur Benwood | 3.50 | 7.00 | 10.50 | M |
| 22 | The Secret of Crazy Cavern–Arthur Benwood | 3.50 | 7.00 | 10.50 | M |

## TROPIC BOOKS/SABER-TROPIC BOOKS
### West Coast News Co., Inc.

| | | V/Good | Fine | N/Mint | |
|---|---|---|---|---|---|
| 901 | Devil's Playmate–Earl Mead | 1.00 | 2.00 | 3.00 | X |
| 902 | Bartered Sin–Mark Savage; 1962 | 1.00 | 2.00 | 3.00 | X |
| 903 | Girls of Chance–Nina Sands | 1.00 | 2.00 | 3.00 | X |
| 904 | Price of Passion–George Jade; 1962 | 1.00 | 2.00 | 3.00 | X |
| 905 | Hell Is for Hammons–Jannet Anderson | 1.00 | 2.00 | 3.00 | X |
| 906 | Carnal Frenzy–Adam Coulter | 1.00 | 2.00 | 3.00 | X |
| 907 | Wings of Sin–Cameron Howley | 1.00 | 2.00 | 3.00 | X |
| 908 | Patterns of Passion–Leonard Jackson; 1963 | 1.00 | 2.00 | 3.00 | X |
| 909 | The Errant Wife–Don King | 1.00 | 2.00 | 3.00 | X |
| 910 | Web of Lust–Adam Coulter; 1965 | 1.00 | 2.00 | 3.00 | X |
| 911 | Project Girl–Mark Lucas | 1.00 | 2.00 | 3.00 | X |
| 912 | The Mirrored Orgy–Douglas Dee | 3.00 | 6.00 | 9.00 | X |
| 914 | Frustrations of Judy–Frank G. Harris; 1965 | 1.00 | 2.00 | 3.00 | X |
| 915 | In Search of Sin–Gil McDonald | 1.00 | 2.00 | 3.00 | X |
| 916 | The Wide Bed–Brenda Porter | 1.00 | 2.00 | 3.00 | X |
| 917 | Candidate for Seduction–Drew Palmer | 1.00 | 2.00 | 3.00 | X |
| 918 | Lust and His Daughter–Sharon L. Thompson | 1.00 | 2.00 | 3.00 | X |
| 919 | Punished Passions–Steve Davis | 1.00 | 2.00 | 3.00 | X |
| 920 | Sex in White–Kimberly Marchand; 1966 | 1.00 | 2.00 | 3.00 | X |
| 921 | Sin Moved In–Rick Rand | 1.00 | 2.00 | 3.00 | X |
| 922 | Patterns of Sin–Dave Patrick | 1.00 | 2.00 | 3.00 | X |
| 923 | Female Spoilers–Frank G. Harris; 1966 | 1.00 | 2.00 | 3.00 | X |
| 925 | Pleasure Came Hither–Drew Palmer | 1.00 | 2.00 | 3.00 | X |
| 926 | 3 Months of Sin–Drew Palmer | 1.00 | 2.00 | 3.00 | X |
| 927 | Exploiting the Innocent–John Nemec | 1.50 | 3.00 | 4.50 | X |
| 928 | Sex Racket–Mark Lucas; 1966 | 1.00 | 2.00 | 3.00 | X |
| 929 | Nurse on the Beach–Mary Fletcher | 1.00 | 2.00 | 3.00 | X |
| 931 | Hell in Paradise–Mark Lucas | 1.00 | 2.00 | 3.00 | X |
| 933 | Passion's Greatest Trap–Jack Vast | 3.00 | 6.00 | 9.00 | X |
| 937 | None Said Maybe–Leucerne | 1.00 | 2.00 | 3.00 | X |
| 938 | One Adam and Five Eves–A.J. Davis | 1.00 | 2.00 | 3.00 | X |
| 939 | The Flesh Is Wild–Jack Moore; 1966 | 1.00 | 2.00 | 3.00 | X |
| 940 | Inroad to Immorality–Drew Palmer; 1967 | 1.00 | 2.00 | 3.00 | X |
| 941 | Man in Demand–A.J. Davis | 1.50 | 3.00 | 4.50 | X |
| 942 | Obsession–Frank G. Harris | 1.00 | 2.00 | 3.00 | X |
| 943 | Love? Thank You!–Sharon L. Thompson | 1.00 | 2.00 | 3.00 | X |
| 945 | The Sin Goddess–Frank G. Harris | 1.00 | 2.00 | 3.00 | X |
| 946 | White Trash–Mark Lucas | 1.50 | 3.00 | 4.50 | X |
| 948 | Queen of the Surf–Dee Douglas; 1967 | 1.00 | 2.00 | 3.00 | X |

## TROPHY BOOKS
### Royce Publishers

| | | V/Good | Fine | N/Mint | |
|---|---|---|---|---|---|
| 401 | Smile, Brother, Smile–anthology | 15.00 | 30.00 | 45.00 | H |
| 402 | The Pilditch Puzzle–W.B.M. Ferguson; 1946 | 12.50 | 25.00 | 37.50 | M |

## 20TH CENTURY THRILLER
## (see WHITMAN)

## UNI-BOOKS
### Universal Publishing and Distributing Corp.
**Digest Size**

| | | V/Good | Fine | N/Mint | |
|---|---|---|---|---|---|
| 3 | Unfaithful Wives–Peggy Gaddis; aka Wives in Scarlet | 3.00 | 6.00 | 9.00 | E |
| 4 | Wicked–Eleanor Gates | 3.00 | 6.00 | 9.00 | E |
| 5 | Sins of a Paris Doctor–Karen Bramson | 3.00 | 6.00 | 9.00 | E |
| 6 | Man Bait–Richard Grant; aka Man Hater | 3.00 | 6.00 | 9.00 | E |
| 7 | Male for Sale–Florenz Branch | 3.00 | 6.00 | 9.00 | E |
| 8 | Backstage Sin–Dana Lewis | 3.00 | 6.00 | 9.00 | E |
| 9 | Warped Women–Janet Pritchard | 3.00 | 6.00 | 9.00 | E |
| 10 | Without Consent–M. Pill Grilli | 3.00 | 6.00 | 9.00 | E |
| 13 | Tormented–Richard Meeker | 3.00 | 6.00 | 9.00 | E |

UNI-BOOKS, *continued*

| | | V/Good | Fine | N/Mint | |
|---|---|---|---|---|---|
| 14 | Stripper–Wright Williams | 3.00 | 6.00 | 9.00 | E |
| 15 | The Thing That Made Love–David V. Reed | 6.00 | 12.00 | 18.00 | SF |
| 16 | Raw Passion–Charles Martin | 3.00 | 6.00 | 9.00 | E |
| 17 | Scandalous Affair–Florenz Branch | 3.00 | 6.00 | 9.00 | E |
| 18 | Love Cheat–William Arthur | 3.00 | 6.00 | 9.00 | E |
| 19 | Marijuana Girl–N.R. de Mexico | 8.00 | 16.00 | 24.00 | E |
| 20 | Side Street–Wright Williams | 3.00 | 6.00 | 9.00 | E |
| 21 | Hideaway–Peggy Gaddis | 3.00 | 6.00 | 9.00 | E |
| 22 | Tainted Passions–H.M. Appel | 3.00 | 6.00 | 9.00 | E |
| 23 | Sin Ship–Janet Pritchard | 3.00 | 6.00 | 9.00 | E |
| 24 | Badge of Shame–A. Abram | 3.00 | 6.00 | 9.00 | E |
| 25 | River Barge Virgin–Wright Williams | 3.00 | 6.00 | 9.00 | E |
| 26 | The Fiend–Gerald Foster; aka Lust | 3.00 | 6.00 | 9.00 | E |
| 27 | Jezebel's Daughter–Ann Lawrence | 3.00 | 6.00 | 9.00 | E |
| 28 | Unleashed Woman–Gail Jordan (Peggy Gaddis); aka Dark Passion | 3.00 | 6.00 | 9.00 | E |
| 29 | Brutal Kisses–H.M. Appel; aka The Farmer's Daughter. Note: Same cover as Beacon B177 | 3.00 | 6.00 | 9.00 | E |
| 30 | Eurasian Girl–Richard Grant | 3.00 | 6.00 | 9.00 | E |
| 31 | Dr. Prescott's Secret–Peggy Gaddis. Note: Same cover as Beacon B184 | 3.00 | 6.00 | 9.00 | E |
| 32 | Loves of a Girl Wrestler–Ben West. Note: Virtually same cover as Beacon B112 | 3.50 | 7.00 | 10.50 | E |
| 33 | White Trash–Beulan Poynter; orig. 1952 | 3.50 | 7.00 | 10.50 | E |
| 34 | Resort Hostess–Gordon Semple. Note: Same cover as Beacon B168 | 3.00 | 6.00 | 9.00 | E |
| 35 | Slave Ship–H.B. Drake | 3.50 | 7.00 | 10.50 | E |
| 36 | Hoyden of the Hills–Ann Lawrence; aka She Wanted More. Note: Same cover as Beacon B125 | 3.50 | 7.00 | 10.50 | E |
| 37 | Student Nurse–Gail Jordan (Peggy Gaddis) | 3.00 | 6.00 | 9.00 | E |
| 38 | Secrets of a Co-ed–Ben West. Note: Same cover as Beacon B131 | 3.00 | 6.00 | 9.00 | E |
| 39 | Pleasure Resort Women–Gordon Semple | 3.00 | 6.00 | 9.00 | E |
| 40 | Ike, Man of the Hour–Rudolph Field | 3.00 | 6.00 | 9.00 | B |
| 41 | She Devil–John Saxon. Note: Same cover as Beacon B111 | 3.00 | 6.00 | 9.00 | E |
| 42 | Side-Show Girl–Steve Harragan | 3.50 | 7.00 | 10.50 | M |
| 43 | The Queer Sisters–Steve Harragan | 3.50 | 7.00 | 10.50 | M |
| 44 | Sin Is a Redhead–Steve Harragan. Note: Same cover as Beacon B139 and B380 | 3.50 | 7.00 | 10.50 | M |
| 45 | Bad Sister–Evans Wall. Note: Same cover as Beacon B146 | 3.00 | 6.00 | 9.00 | E |
| 46 | Smuggled Sin–Steve Harragan | 3.50 | 7.00 | 10.50 | M |
| 47 | Kiss of the Damned–Steve Harragan | 3.50 | 7.00 | 10.50 | M |
| 48 | Women of Paris–L.H. Brenning | 3.00 | 6.00 | 9.00 | E |
| 49 | Reefer Club–Luke Roberts | 8.00 | 16.00 | 24.00 | E |
| 50 | River Woman–Evans Wall | 3.00 | 6.00 | 9.00 | E |
| 51 | Dirt Farm–Francis Mitchell | 3.00 | 6.00 | 9.00 | E |
| 52 | The Shayne Dame–Steve Harragan | 3.50 | 7.00 | 10.50 | M |
| 53 | Wild Body–Manning Clay | 3.00 | 6.00 | 9.00 | E |
| 54 | Carney's Burlesque–Steve Harragan | 3.50 | 7.00 | 10.50 | M |
| 55 | Mountain Woman | 3.00 | 6.00 | 9.00 | E |
| 56 | Her Last Lover–Kelsey Freeman; aka Last Lover | 3.00 | 6.00 | 9.00 | E |
| 57 | Three Bad Girls–Bart Frame | 3.00 | 6.00 | 9.00 | M |
| 58 | Cracker Girl–Harry Whittington; orig. 1953 | 3.50 | 7.00 | 10.50 | E |
| 59 | Another Man's Wife–Margaret Carruthers | 3.00 | 6.00 | 9.00 | E |
| 60 | Savage Eve–Jack Woodford. Note: Same cover as Beacon B127 | 3.00 | 6.00 | 9.00 | E |
| 61 | Runaway Blonde–Daoma Winston | 3.00 | 6.00 | 9.00 | E |
| 62 | Hungry for Love–George Willis; aka Wild Faun | 3.00 | 6.00 | 9.00 | E |
| 63 | Passion in the Pines–Jack Woodford. Note: Same cover as Beacon B123 | 3.00 | 6.00 | 9.00 | E |
| 64 | Cuban Heel–Steve Harragan; orig. nd. Note: Same cover as Beacon B124 | 3.50 | 7.00 | 10.50 | M |
| 65 | Hillbilly in High Heels–Jeff Bogar | 3.50 | 7.00 | 10.50 | E |
| 66 | Witch on Wheels–Bill Bolton | 3.50 | 7.00 | 10.50 | E |
| 67 | Male Virgin–Jack Woodford | 3.00 | 6.00 | 9.00 | E |
| 68 | Country Club Cheat–Janet Pritchard | 3.00 | 6.00 | 9.00 | E |
| 69 | Confessions of a Chinatown Moll–Jeff Bogar | 5.00 | 10.00 | 15.00 | M |

| | | V/Good | Fine | N/Mint | |
|---|---|---|---|---|---|
| 70 | Wild Oats–Harry Whittington; orig. 1954 | 3.50 | 7.00 | 10.50 | E |
| 71 | Swamp Hoyden–Jack Woodford & John B. Thompson. Note: Same cover as Beacon B125 | 3.50 | 7.00 | 10.50 | E |
| 72 | Honey–Jack Woodford & John Thompson | 3.50 | 7.00 | 10.50 | E |
| 73 | Cabin Fever–Orrie Hitt; orig. 1954 | 3.50 | 7.00 | 10.50 | E |
| 74 | Gang Girl–Leo Rifkin | 6.00 | 12.00 | 18.00 | E |
| 75 | Harlem Doctor–Luke Roberts; orig. 1953 | 6.00 | 12.00 | 18.00 | E |
| 76 | Below the Belt–Robert Lucas | 3.00 | 6.00 | 9.00 | E |
| 77 | Bayou Girl–John B. Thompson. Note: Same cover as Beacon B129 | 3.50 | 7.00 | 10.50 | E |
| 78 | Out of Bounds–Ernest L. Matthews, Jr | 3.00 | 6.00 | 9.00 | E |

# (UNICORN)
## Unicorn Press
### Digest Size

| | | V/Good | Fine | N/Mint | |
|---|---|---|---|---|---|
| nn | Everything's a Puzzle; 1953 | 1.50 | 3.00 | 4.50 | NF |

# (UNITED STATES PLAYING CARD COMPANY)
## United States Playing Card Co./ Whitman Publishing Company

| | | V/Good | Fine | N/Mint | |
|---|---|---|---|---|---|
| nn | Poker; 1941 | 1.00 | 2.00 | 3.00 | NF |
| 3768 | 50 Card Games for Children–Vernon Quinn; 1946 | .50 | 1.00 | 1.50 | NF |

# (UNITED STATES SALES COMPANY)
## United States Sales Company

| | | V/Good | Fine | N/Mint | |
|---|---|---|---|---|---|
| nn | Judge Priest Turns Detective–Irvin S. Cobb; nd | 2.50 | 5.00 | 7.50 | M |

# UNIVERSAL GIANT EDITION
## Universal Publishing and Distributing Corporation
### Digest Size
### (See also Royal Giant Edition)

| | | V/Good | Fine | N/Mint | |
|---|---|---|---|---|---|
| 1 | Prime Sucker–Harry Whittington; orig. 1952 | 6.00 | 12.00 | 18.00 | E |
| | The Hussy–Idabel Williams. Note: Same cover as Beacon B117 | | | | E |
| 2 | Paprika–Erich von Stroheim. Note: Same cover as Beacon B157 | 7.50 | 15.00 | 22.50 | E |
| 3 | His Majesty O'Keefe–Lawrence Klingman and Gerald Green | 4.50 | 9.00 | 13.50 | A |
| 4 | Dope Doll–Steve Harragan | 10.00 | 20.00 | 30.00 | E |
| | The Bigamy Kiss–Steve Harragan | | | | E |
| 5 | Bulls, Blood and Passion–David Williams; orig. | 7.50 | 15.00 | 22.50 | E |
| | The Sinful Ones–Fritz Leiber; 1st ed. 1953 | | | | SF |
| 6 | The Private Life of Julius Caesar– William Marston | 4.50 | 9.00 | 13.50 | E |
| 7 | Savage Mistress–Jon Hartt Concubine–Elsie Dean | 4.50 | 9.00 | 13.50 | E |
| 8 | The Lusty Land–Valerie Taylor | 4.50 | 9.00 | 13.50 | E |
| | Forbidden Fruit–Curtis Lucas | | | | E |
| 9 | Aphrodite's Lover–Arthur MacArthur. Note: Same cover as Beacon B156 | 4.50 | 9.00 | 13.50 | E |
| 10 | The Memoirs of Casanova–Jacques Casanova | 4.50 | 9.00 | 13.50 | E |
| 11 | The Queen's Warrant–Talbot Mundy; 1st ed. 1953 | 6.00 | 12.00 | 18.00 | A |
| | Paths of Glory–Humphrey Cobb | | | | C |

# UNIVERSAL ROMANCE
## Universal Publishing and Distributing Corporation
### Digest Size

| | | V/Good | Fine | N/Mint | |
|---|---|---|---|---|---|
| nn | Any Man's Woman–Cecil Barr; aka It's Hard to Sin | 2.50 | 5.00 | 7.50 | E |
| nn | Red Hot–Ray Booth. Note: Same cover as No Imprint/Universal Publishing | 2.50 | 5.00 | 7.50 | E |

# VALUE BOOKS
## Value Books, Inc.

| 101 | The Young Adventurer–Horatio Alger | 2.00 | 4.00 | 6.00 | A |
|---|---|---|---|---|---|
| 102 | Strive and Succeed–Horatio Alger | 2.00 | 4.00 | 6.00 | A |
| 103 | Do and Dare–Horatio Alger | 2.00 | 4.00 | 6.00 | A |
| 104 | Brave and Bold–Horatio Alger | 2.00 | 4.00 | 6.00 | A |
| 105 | Making His Way–Horatio Alger | 2.00 | 4.00 | 6.00 | A |

# VANITAS
## The Harvard Lampoon, Inc.

| V4402 | Alligator–I*n Fl*m*ng; 1st ed. 1962. Note: James Bond spoof, all copies seen are indicated as 2nd printings. | 7.50 | 15.00 | 22.50 | H |
|---|---|---|---|---|---|

# VEGA BOOKS
## Vega Books, Inc.

| V1 | The Animal Urge–Byron Woolfe; 1960 | 1.50 | 3.00 | 4.50 | X |
|---|---|---|---|---|---|
| V4 | Joy Killer–Brandon | 1.00 | 2.00 | 3.00 | X |
| V8 | Included Out–Mary Gooch | 1.00 | 2.00 | 3.00 | X |
| V10 | The Opposite Six–Marie Turni; 1961 | 1.50 | 3.00 | 4.50 | M |
| V12 | Murder Is So Easy–Willo L. Roberts | 1.50 | 3.00 | 4.50 | M |
| V14 | Destination: Death–George Bishop | 1.00 | 2.00 | 3.00 | M |
| V15 | The Elusive Clue–Dave Stephens | 1.00 | 2.00 | 3.00 | M |
| V16 | Frame Up–Stephen Gregory | 1.00 | 2.00 | 3.00 | M |
| V17 | Vice Town–Ennis Willie | 1.00 | 2.00 | 3.00 | M |
| V18 | The Suspected Four–Willo L. Roberts | 1.00 | 2.00 | 3.00 | M |
| V19 | Knock on Any Head–Frank S. Miller | 1.50 | 3.00 | 4.50 | M |
| V20 | All for One–Arnold Marmor | 1.00 | 2.00 | 3.00 | X |
| V21 | Hayseed–Herbert L. Moore | 1.00 | 2.00 | 3.00 | X |
| V22 | Beauty Can Kill–Michael McCretton | 2.50 | 5.00 | 7.50 | M |
| V23 | The River Is Cold–Duane Rimel | 1.00 | 2.00 | 3.00 | M |
| V24 | The Suckers–James Fullilove | 1.00 | 2.00 | 3.00 | X |
| V25 | Savage Summer–Guy Vance; 1962 | 1.00 | 2.00 | 3.00 | X |
| V26 | The Pagans Three–Wilson Gilman; 1963 | 1.50 | 3.00 | 4.50 | X |
| V27 | Reaching High–Bunny Strand | 1.00 | 2.00 | 3.00 | X |
| V28 | I Wanted the Killer–Arthur A. Howe | 1.00 | 2.00 | 3.00 | M |
| V29 | Weekend to Danger–Thomas Vail | 1.50 | 3.00 | 4.50 | M |
| V30 | Murder by Proxy–Jook Spruill | 1.00 | 2.00 | 3.00 | M |
| V31 | Satan in Malibu–Frank Cannon | 1.00 | 2.00 | 3.00 | M |

Universal Giant 4, Universal Giant 5, Universal Giant 11.

Value Books 101, Value Books 102, Vanitas V4402.

| | | V/Good | Fine | N/Mint | |
|---|---|---|---|---|---|
| V32 | All Killers Aren't Ugly–Thomas K. Makagon; 1963 | 1.50 | 3.00 | 4.50 | M |
| V33 | The Fat Boy Must Die–Robert E. Pearson | 1.50 | 3.00 | 4.50 | M |
| V34 | Press Agent for Murder–Martin Ryerson | 1.00 | 2.00 | 3.00 | M |
| V35 | Stalk the Killer–Steve Davis | 1.50 | 3.00 | 4.50 | M |
| V36 | Jackasses of Los Causes–Edwin C. Groh; 1964 | 2.50 | 5.00 | 7.50 | M |
| V40 | Doctor vs. Murder–Martin Ryerson | 1.50 | 3.00 | 4.50 | M |
| V41 | Hide in Hell–Frank Cannon; 1964 | 1.00 | 2.00 | 3.00 | M |
| V42 | Twice a Fool–Bunny Strand | 1.00 | 2.00 | 3.00 | X |
| V43 | Cousin Jess–Marie Turni | 1.00 | 2.00 | 3.00 | X |

# VEGA SCIENCE FICTION LIBRARY
## Vega Books, Inc.

| VSF1 | Walk Through Tomorrow–Karl Zeigfreid | 2.00 | 4.00 | 6.00 | SF |
|---|---|---|---|---|---|
| VSF2 | Space Fury–R.L. Fanthorpe | 2.00 | 4.00 | 6.00 | SF |
| VSF3 | The Day the World Died–John Muller | 2.00 | 4.00 | 6.00 | SF |
| VSF4 | Radar Alert–Karl Zeigfreid | 2.00 | 4.00 | 6.00 | SF |
| VSF5 | Plan for Conquest–A.A. Glynn | 2.00 | 4.00 | 6.00 | SF |
| VSF6 | In the Beginning–John Muller | 2.00 | 4.00 | 6.00 | SF |
| VSF7 | The Planet Seekers–Erle Barton | 2.00 | 4.00 | 6.00 | SF |
| VSF8 | Special Mission–John Muller | 1.50 | 3.00 | 4.50 | SF |
| VSF9 | Suspension–Bron Fane | 1.50 | 3.00 | 4.50 | SF |
| VSF10 | The Return–Pel Torro | 1.50 | 3.00 | 4.50 | SF |
| VSF11 | The Venus Venture–John Muller | 2.00 | 4.00 | 6.00 | SF |
| VSF12 | Projection Infinity–Karl Zeigfreid | 2.00 | 4.00 | 6.00 | SF |
| VSF13 | A Ticket to Nowhere–Don Becker | 2.00 | 4.00 | 6.00 | SF |
| VSF14 | Star Trail–Thomas W. Crumley | 2.00 | 4.00 | 6.00 | SF |

# VEGA WESTERN LIBRARY
## Vega Books, Inc.

| VW100 | Blood on Big Sandy–Benny Runnels; 1962 | 1.00 | 2.00 | 3.00 | W |
|---|---|---|---|---|---|
| VW101 | Uncertain Destiny–Wade Pierce | 1.00 | 2.00 | 3.00 | W |
| VW102 | Trail of Vengeance–Al Clark | 1.00 | 2.00 | 3.00 | W |
| VW103 | War at Bluestem Basin–John Nemec | 1.00 | 2.00 | 3.00 | W |
| VW104 | Bloody Wyoming–Robert E. Pearson; 1963 | 1.00 | 2.00 | 3.00 | W |
| VW105 | Dangerous Guns–Marvin Tuma; 1963 | 1.00 | 2.00 | 3.00 | W |
| VW106 | Trouble Trail–William Cuthbert | 1.00 | 2.00 | 3.00 | W |
| VW107 | Trigger Justice–Arthur A. Howe | 1.00 | 2.00 | 3.00 | W |
| VW108 | Showdown at Devil's Fork–Martin Ryerson; 1964 | 1.00 | 2.00 | 3.00 | W |
| VW109 | Gun-fire at Big Needles–Martin Ryerson | 1.00 | 2.00 | 3.00 | W |
| VW110 | Frontier Scout–Nelson Nye | 1.00 | 2.00 | 3.00 | W |
| VW111 | Come A-Smokin'–Nelson Nye | 1.00 | 2.00 | 3.00 | W |
| VW112 | Storm Ross–Arthur A. Howe | 1.00 | 2.00 | 3.00 | W |
| VW113 | Two Gun Law–Allen Stark | 1.00 | 2.00 | 3.00 | W |
| VW115 | Sudden Rage at War Rim–Martin Ryerson; 1964 | 1.00 | 2.00 | 3.00 | W |

# VENUS BOOKS

## Star Guidance, Inc.

### Digest Size

| # | Title | V/Good | Fine | N/Mint | |
|---|---|---|---|---|---|
| 101 | Girl with My Past–Peggy Gaddis | 4.00 | 8.00 | 12.00 | E |
| 102 | She Wanted Love–Joan Sherman (Peggy Gaddis) | 4.00 | 8.00 | 12.00 | E |
| 103 | Mazie–Any Man's Girl–Gerald Foster | 4.00 | 8.00 | 12.00 | E |
| 104 | Beach Party–Peggy Gaddis; aka Lovers No More | 4.00 | 8.00 | 12.00 | E |
| 105 | Take My Love!–Peggy Gaddis; aka Shameless | 4.00 | 8.00 | 12.00 | E |
| 106 | Overnight–Norman Bligh; aka Harlot in Her Heart | 4.00 | 8.00 | 12.00 | E |
| 107 | Play Girl–Norman Bligh | 4.00 | 8.00 | 12.00 | E |
| 108 | Cutie–Gene Harvey; aka Passion's Slave | 4.00 | 8.00 | 12.00 | E |
| 109 | Lover Boy–Harmon Bellamy; aka Sacrifice; c-Gross | 4.50 | 9.00 | 13.50 | E |
| 110 | Hard-Boiled–Harmon Bellamy; 1950; aka Struggle | 4.50 | 9.00 | 13.50 | E |
| 111 | Pick-Up Alley–Albert L. Quandt | 4.50 | 9.00 | 13.50 | E |
| 112 | Temptation–Peggy Gaddis | 4.00 | 8.00 | 12.00 | E |
| 113 | Reckless–James Clayford (Peggy Gaddis) | 4.00 | 8.00 | 12.00 | E |
| 114 | Confessions of a Carnival Dancer–Gene Harvey | 4.00 | 8.00 | 12.00 | E |
| 115 | Journey into Ecstacy–Albert L. Quandt | 4.00 | 8.00 | 12.00 | E |
| 116 | One Wild Night–Peggy Gaddis | 4.00 | 8.00 | 12.00 | E |
| 117 | Desire Is a Woman–Gene Harvey | 4.00 | 8.00 | 12.00 | E |
| 118 | Honey–Broadway Playgirl–Peggy Gaddis | 4.00 | 8.00 | 12.00 | E |
| 119 | No Time for Marriage–David Charlson | 4.00 | 8.00 | 12.00 | E |
| 120 | The Naked Night–Norman Bligh; orig. 1951 | 4.00 | 8.00 | 12.00 | E |
| 121 | Girl of the Slum–Albert L. Quandt | 4.00 | 8.00 | 12.00 | E |
| 122 | Pleasure at Midnight–Peggy Gaddis | 4.00 | 8.00 | 12.00 | E |
| 123 | Emotions of Fire–Peggy Gaddis | 4.00 | 8.00 | 12.00 | E |
| 124 | She Couldn't Be Good–Gene Harvey | 4.00 | 8.00 | 12.00 | E |
| 125 | Thrill Me Again!–Albert L. Quandt; orig. 1951 | 4.00 | 8.00 | 12.00 | E |
| 126 | No Time for Sleep–Amos Hatter | 4.00 | 8.00 | 12.00 | E |
| 127 | Painted Lips–Peggy Gaddis; orig. 1951 | 4.00 | 8.00 | 12.00 | E |
| 128 | She Had What It Takes–Kermit Welles | 4.00 | 8.00 | 12.00 | E |
| 129 | Big-Time Girl–Albert L. Quandt | 4.00 | 8.00 | 12.00 | E |
| 130 | The Men She Knew–Norman Bligh | 4.00 | 8.00 | 12.00 | E |
| 131 | Tough Doll–Peggy Gaddis | 4.00 | 8.00 | 12.00 | E |
| 132 | Lady with a Past–Amos Hatter | 4.00 | 8.00 | 12.00 | E |
| 133 | She Tried to Be Good–Florence Stonebraker; orig. 1951 | 4.00 | 8.00 | 12.00 | E |
| 134 | The Doctor's Wife–Arthur Marin | 4.00 | 8.00 | 12.00 | E |
| 135 | Night Nurse–David Charlson; orig. 1951 | 4.00 | 8.00 | 12.00 | E |
| 136 | Torch Singer–William Arnold | 4.00 | 8.00 | 12.00 | E |
| 137 | Lost to Desire–Peggy Gaddis; orig. 1952 | 4.00 | 8.00 | 12.00 | E |
| 138 | Reckless–Joan Sherman (Peggy Gaddis); orig. 1952 | 4.00 | 8.00 | 12.00 | E |
| 139 | The Naked Canvas–William Arnold; orig. 1952; c-Gross | 4.50 | 9.00 | 13.50 | E |
| 140 | Oriental Nights–Florence Stonebraker; orig. 1952 | 5.00 | 10.00 | 15.00 | E |
| 141 | Strip Street–Gene Harvey; orig. 1952 | 4.00 | 8.00 | 12.00 | E |
| 142 | Unfaithful–Peggy Gaddis | 4.00 | 8.00 | 12.00 | E |
| 143 | Lovers in the Sun–Joan Sherman (Peggy Gaddis); orig. 1952 | 4.00 | 8.00 | 12.00 | E |
| 144 | The Innocent Wanton–Kermit Welles; orig. 1952 | 4.00 | 8.00 | 12.00 | E |
| 145 | Frenchie–David Charlson; orig. 1952 | 4.00 | 8.00 | 12.00 | E |
| 146 | Call It Marriage–Gail Jordan (Peggy Gaddis); orig. 1952 | 4.00 | 8.00 | 12.00 | E |
| 147 | Weekend of Madness–Joan Tucker | 4.00 | 8.00 | 12.00 | E |
| 148 | Remembered Moment–Norman Bligh; orig. 1952 | 4.00 | 8.00 | 12.00 | E |
| 149 | Runaway Lovers–Peggy Gaddis; orig. 1952 | 4.00 | 8.00 | 12.00 | E |
| 150 | The Affairs of a Leading Lady–Jane Manning; orig. 1952 | 4.00 | 8.00 | 12.00 | E |
| 151 | Young Wife–Norman Bligh | 4.00 | 8.00 | 12.00 | E |

| # | Title | V/Good | Fine | N/Mint | |
|---|---|---|---|---|---|
| 152 | Passion Is a Woman–Kate Nickerson | 4.00 | 8.00 | 12.00 | E |
| 153 | Sailor's Weekend–Whit Harrison (Harry Whittington); orig. 1952 | 4.50 | 9.00 | 13.50 | E |
| 154 | Hired Girl–Amos Hatter; orig. 1953 | 4.00 | 8.00 | 12.00 | E |
| 155 | Night Nurse–David Charlson | 4.00 | 8.00 | 12.00 | E |
| 156 | The Doctor's Wife–A. Marin | 4.00 | 8.00 | 12.00 | E |
| 157 | Women's Doctor–Frank Haskell; c-Nappi | 4.00 | 8.00 | 12.00 | E |
| 158 | Girl on Parole–Harry Whittington; orig. 1953; aka Man Crazy | 4.50 | 9.00 | 13.50 | E |
| 159 | Shanty Girl–Joan Tucker; c-Belarski | 5.00 | 10.00 | 15.00 | E |
| 160 | Farmer's Wife–Peggy Gaddis | 4.00 | 8.00 | 12.00 | E |
| 161 | Army Girl–Whit Harrison (Harry Whittington); c-Belarski | 5.00 | 10.00 | 15.00 | E |
| 162 | Wayward Nurse–Norman Bligh; c-Belarski | 5.00 | 10.00 | 15.00 | E |
| 163 | Private Nurse–David Charlson | 4.00 | 8.00 | 12.00 | E |
| 164 | Hired Girl–Amos Hatter | 4.00 | 8.00 | 12.00 | E |
| 165 | Passion Is a Woman–Kate Nickerson; c-Belarski | 5.00 | 10.00 | 15.00 | E |
| 166 | Sailor's Weekend–Whit Harrison (Harry Whittington) | 4.50 | 9.00 | 13.50 | E |
| 167 | Young Secretary–Joan Tucker; orig. 1954 | 4.00 | 8.00 | 12.00 | E |
| 168 | Backwoods Girl–Peggy Gaddis | 4.00 | 8.00 | 12.00 | E |
| 169 | Strip Street–Gene Harvey | 4.00 | 8.00 | 12.00 | E |
| 170 | Male Ward–M. Coleman; c-Belarski | 5.00 | 10.00 | 15.00 | E |
| 171 | Beach Girl–Joan Sherman (Peggy Gaddis); aka Lovers in the Sun | 4.00 | 8.00 | 12.00 | E |
| 172 | Farmer's Woman–Peggy Gaddis; orig. 1954 | 4.00 | 8.00 | 12.00 | E |
| 173 | Young Doctor–Frank Haskell; orig. 1954; c-Belarski | 5.00 | 10.00 | 15.00 | E |
| 174 | Night Nurse–David Charlson | 4.00 | 8.00 | 12.00 | E |
| 177 | Young Wife–Norman Bligh | 4.00 | 8.00 | 12.00 | E |
| 178 | Wild Sister–Kermit Welles | 4.00 | 8.00 | 12.00 | E |
| 179 | Hotel Doctor–Frank Haskell | 4.00 | 8.00 | 12.00 | E |
| 180 | Beach Girl–Joan Sherman (Peggy Gaddis); aka Lovers in the Sun | 4.00 | 8.00 | 12.00 | E |
| 181 | Hired Girl–Amos Hatter | 4.00 | 8.00 | 12.00 | E |
| 184 | Hotel Doctor–Frank Haskell | 4.00 | 8.00 | 12.00 | E |
| 186 | Wayward Nurse–Norman Bligh; c-Belarski | 5.00 | 10.00 | 15.00 | E |
| 188 | Young Wife–Norman Bligh | 4.00 | 8.00 | 12.00 | E |
| 190 | Farmer's Woman–Peggy Gaddis | 4.00 | 8.00 | 12.00 | E |
| 191 | Young Doctor–Frank Haskell; c-Belarski | 5.00 | 10.00 | 15.00 | E |
| 193 | Waterfront Club–Joan Tucker | 4.00 | 8.00 | 12.00 | E |
| 194 | Army Girl–Whit Harrison (Harry Whittington); orig. 1953; c-Belarski | 5.00 | 10.00 | 15.00 | E |
| 195 | Young Bride–George Jordan | 4.00 | 8.00 | 12.00 | E |
| 196 | Cabin Hostess–Peggy Gaddis | 4.00 | 8.00 | 12.00 | E |
| 197 | Professional Model–William Arnold | 4.00 | 8.00 | 12.00 | E |

# VENUS FREEWAY PRESS–see FREEWAY PRESS

*Vital Book 4, Vulcan Mystery unnumbered, The West in Action 3.*

# VITAL BOOK
## Vital Publications, Inc.
### Digest Size

| | | V/Good | Fine | N/Mint | |
|---|---|---|---|---|---|
| 1 | Empire of Crime–Nicholas Carter (Richard Wormser); aka Crook's Empire | 4.00 | 8.00 | 12.00 | M |
| 2 | Murder Unlimited–Nicholas Carter (Richard Wormser); aka Bid for a Railroad | 4.00 | 8.00 | 12.00 | M |
| 3 | Death Has Green Eyes–Nicholas Carter (Richard Wormser) | 4.00 | 8.00 | 12.00 | M |
| 4 | Park Avenue Murder–Nicholas Carter (Richard Wormser); aka Death on Park Avenue | 4.00 | 8.00 | 12.00 | M |

Western Action Novel 1, Western Novel Classic 25, Western Novel Classic 42.

# VULCAN MYSTERY
## Vulcan Publishing, Inc.
### Digest Size

| | | V/Good | Fine | N/Mint | |
|---|---|---|---|---|---|
| nn | The Maori Murder Case–Andrew I. Albert; orig. 1944; c-Hoffman | 3.00 | 6.00 | 9.00 | M |
| nn | Death Meets the Deadline–David Robinson George; orig. 1944 | 3.00 | 6.00 | 9.00 | M |
| 3 | The Laughing Buddha Murder–Richard Foster; orig. 1944 | 3.00 | 6.00 | 9.00 | M |
| 4 | Murder for a Hollow Shell–Andrew I. Albert; orig. 1945 | 3.00 | 6.00 | 9.00 | M |
| 5 | The Case of the Phantom Fingerprints–Kendall Foster Crossen; orig. 1945 | 3.00 | 6.00 | 9.00 | M |
| 6 | Curtain Call for Murder–Peter Yates; orig. 1945 | 3.00 | 6.00 | 9.00 | M |

# WARNER BOOKS
## Warner Books, Inc.

| | | V/Good | Fine | N/Mint | |
|---|---|---|---|---|---|
| 88-107 | The Giant Rat of Sumatra–Richard L. Boyer; 1st ed. 1976; authorized Sherlock Holmes sequel. | 7.50 | 15.00 | 22.50 | M |

# WASHINGTON SQUARE PRESS
## Washington Square Press, Inc./Pocket Books, Inc.

| | | V/Good | Fine | N/Mint | |
|---|---|---|---|---|---|
| W1 | English Through Pictures–Book 1–Christine Gibson & I.A. Richards; 1959 | .75 | 1.50 | 2.25 | NF |
| W2 | First Steps in Reading English–Christine Gibson & I.A. Richards | .75 | 1.50 | 2.25 | NF |
| W4 | English Through Pictures–Book 2–Christine Gibson & I.A. Richards | .75 | 1.50 | 2.25 | NF |
| W8 | French Through Pictures–Book 1–I.A. Richards & others | .75 | 1.50 | 2.25 | NF |
| W18 | A First Workbook of French–Christine Gibson & I.A. Richards | .75 | 1.50 | 2.25 | NF |
| W15 | German Through Pictures–Book 1–I.A. Richards & others | .75 | 1.50 | 2.25 | NF |
| W22 | Italian Through Pictures–Book 1–I.A. Richards & others | .75 | 1.50 | 2.25 | NF |
| W30 | Spanish Through Pictures–Book 1–I.A. Richards & others | .75 | 1.50 | 2.25 | NF |
| W38 | Hebrew Through Pictures–Book 1–I.A. Richards & others | .75 | 1.50 | 2.25 | NF |
| W39 | Hebrew Reader–I.A. Richards & others | .75 | 1.50 | 2.25 | NF |
| W99 | Oedipus the King–Sophocles | .75 | 1.50 | 2.25 | |
| W100 | Doctor Faustus–Christopher Marlowe | .75 | 1.50 | 2.25 | |
| W101 | The Duchess of Malfi–John Webster | .75 | 1.50 | 2.25 | |
| W115 | Macbeth–William Shakespeare | .75 | 1.50 | 2.25 | |
| W121 | Romeo and Juliet–William Shakespeare | .75 | 1.50 | 2.25 | |
| W550 | Collected Lyrics–Edna St. Vincent Millay | .75 | 1.50 | 2.25 | |

| | | V/Good | Fine | N/Mint | |
|---|---|---|---|---|---|
| W551 | Collected Sonnets–Edna St. Vincent Millay | .75 | 1.50 | 2.25 | |
| W561 | The Way of All Flesh–Samuel Butler | .75 | 1.50 | 2.25 | |
| W571 | The Return of the Native–Thomas Hardy; 1959 | .75 | 1.50 | 2.25 | |

# WESTERN ACTION NOVEL
## Hillman Periodicals, Inc./Novel Selections
### Digest Size

| | | V/Good | Fine | N/Mint | |
|---|---|---|---|---|---|
| 1 | Round-up in the River–Frank C. Robertson | 2.00 | 4.00 | 6.00 | W |
| 2 | The Riddle of Ramrod Ridge–William Colt MacDonald | 2.00 | 4.00 | 6.00 | W |
| 3 | Powdersmoke Range–Bennett Foster | 2.00 | 4.00 | 6.00 | W |
| 4 | Donovan Rides–Arthur Henry Gooden | 2.00 | 4.00 | 6.00 | W |

# WESTERN NOVEL CLASSIC
## Hillman Periodicals, Inc./Novel Selections
### Digest Size

| | | V/Good | Fine | N/Mint | |
|---|---|---|---|---|---|
| 22 | The Sheriff's Son–William MacLeod Raine | 2.00 | 4.00 | 6.00 | W |
| 23 | Brothers on the Trail–Max Brand | 2.00 | 4.00 | 6.00 | W |
| 24 | Thunder on the Range–Frank C. Robertson | 2.00 | 4.00 | 6.00 | W |
| 25 | Wild Blood–Robert Crane | 2.00 | 4.00 | 6.00 | W |
| 26 | Hopalong Cassidy and the Eagle's Brood–Clarence Mulford | 3.00 | 6.00 | 9.00 | W |
| 27 | Bluffer's Luck–W.C. Tuttle | 2.00 | 4.00 | 6.00 | W |
| 28 | Ironheart–William MacLeod Raine | 2.00 | 4.00 | 6.00 | W |
| 30 | Hell's Hip Pocket–Dane Coolidge | 2.00 | 4.00 | 6.00 | W |
| 31 | Hunted Riders–Max Brand | 2.00 | 4.00 | 6.00 | W |
| 32 | Thunder Ranch–Clarence E. Mulford; aka Me an' Shorty | 2.00 | 4.00 | 6.00 | W |
| 33 | Tumbling River Range–W.C. Tuttle | 2.00 | 4.00 | 6.00 | W |
| 34 | Riders of Buck River–William MacLeod Raine | 2.00 | 4.00 | 6.00 | W |
| 35 | Murder Range–Alan LeMay | 2.00 | 4.00 | 6.00 | W |
| 36 | Raiders of the Rimrock–Luke Short | 2.00 | 4.00 | 6.00 | W |
| 37 | Black Sombrero–William Colt MacDonald | 2.00 | 4.00 | 6.00 | W |
| 38 | Red Range–Eugene Cunningham | 2.00 | 4.00 | 6.00 | W |
| 39 | Trail's End–William MacLeod Raine | 2.00 | 4.00 | 6.00 | W |
| 40 | War on the Cimarron–Luke Short | 2.00 | 4.00 | 6.00 | W |
| 41 | The Keeper of Red Horse Pass–W.C. Tuttle | 2.00 | 4.00 | 6.00 | W |
| 42 | Tall in the Saddle–Gordon Young; movie tie-in | 6.00 | 12.00 | 18.00 | W |
| 43 | Whistling Lead–Eugene Cunningham | 2.00 | 4.00 | 6.00 | W |

**WESTERN NOVEL CLASSIC,** *continued*

| | | V/Good | Fine | N/Mint | |
|---|---|---|---|---|---|
| 44 | Roaring River Range–Arthur Henry Gooden | 2.00 | 4.00 | 6.00 | W |
| 45 | The Feud at Single Shot–Luke Short | 2.00 | 4.00 | 6.00 | W |
| 46 | The Tin God of Twisted River–W.C. Tuttle | 2.00 | 4.00 | 6.00 | W |
| 47 | On the Dodge–William MacLeod Raine | 2.00 | 4.00 | 6.00 | W |
| 48 | Texas Triggers–Eugene Cunningham | 2.00 | 4.00 | 6.00 | W |
| 49 | Murder at Two Rivers–Frederick R. Bechdolt | 2.00 | 4.00 | 6.00 | W |
| 50 | The Dead-Line–W.C. Tuttle | 2.00 | 4.00 | 6.00 | W |
| 51 | The Noose Hangs High–Frank C. Robertson | 2.00 | 4.00 | 6.00 | W |
| 52 | Outlaw River–Bliss Lomax (Harry Sinclair Drago) | 2.00 | 4.00 | 6.00 | W |
| 53 | Bear Paw–Dane Coolidge | 2.00 | 4.00 | 6.00 | W |
| 54 | Cartridge Carnival–William Colt MacDonald | 2.00 | 4.00 | 6.00 | W |
| 55 | Hash Knife of the Double Bar 8–W.C. Tuttle | 2.00 | 4.00 | 6.00 | W |
| 56 | Bushwack Basin–Tom West | 2.00 | 4.00 | 6.00 | W |
| 57 | Rusty Guns–Bliss Lomax (Harry Sinclair Drago) | 2.00 | 4.00 | 6.00 | W |
| 58 | Hell in Paradise Valley–Dane Coolidge | 2.00 | 4.00 | 6.00 | W |
| 59 | Hopalong Serves a Writ–Clarence E. Mulford | 3.00 | 6.00 | 9.00 | W |
| 60 | Trouble Trail–Tom West | 2.00 | 4.00 | 6.00 | W |
| 61 | Long Rope–Dane Coolidge | 2.00 | 4.00 | 6.00 | W |
| 63 | Horse Thief Creek–Bliss Lomax (Harry Sinclair Drago) | 2.00 | 4.00 | 6.00 | W |
| 65 | Windy Range–George W. Ogden | 2.00 | 4.00 | 6.00 | W |
| 66 | Saddle Hawks–Bliss Lomax (Harry Sinclair Drago) | 2.00 | 4.00 | 6.00 | W |
| 67 | Sudden Takes Charge–O. Strange | 2.00 | 4.00 | 6.00 | W |
| 68 | Rough Mesa–John Trace | 2.00 | 4.00 | 6.00 | W |
| 69 | South to Sonora–Ryerson Johnson | 2.00 | 4.00 | 6.00 | W |
| 70 | Death in the Saddle–Archie Joscelyn | 2.00 | 4.00 | 6.00 | W |
| 71 | Range of Golden Hoofs–John Trace | 2.00 | 4.00 | 6.00 | W |
| 72 | Gunsmoke in the Hills–Ray Palmer Tracy | 2.00 | 4.00 | 6.00 | W |
| 73 | Gunsight Range–Frank R. Adams | 2.00 | 4.00 | 6.00 | W |
| 74 | Renegade Range–Tom West | 2.00 | 4.00 | 6.00 | W |
| 75 | Horsethief Trail–Frederick Bechdolt | 2.00 | 4.00 | 6.00 | W |
| 76 | Trigger Vengeance–John Trace | 2.00 | 4.00 | 6.00 | W |
| 77 | Guns of Ghost Valley–Claude Rister | 2.00 | 4.00 | 6.00 | W |
| 78 | Come Out and Fight–Allan V. Elston | 2.00 | 4.00 | 6.00 | W |
| 79 | The Prodigal Bandit–Randolph Hale | 2.00 | 4.00 | 6.00 | W |
| 80 | Red River Gunman–Claude Rister | 2.00 | 4.00 | 6.00 | W |
| 81 | Black Gold Stampede–Ed Moore | 2.00 | 4.00 | 6.00 | W |
| 82 | Flame of Forgotten Guns–Ralph Page | 2.00 | 4.00 | 6.00 | W |
| 83 | The Firebrand from Burnt Creek–Frank C. Robertson | 2.00 | 4.00 | 6.00 | W |
| 84 | Blood on the Sage–Louis E. Legner | 2.00 | 4.00 | 6.00 | W |
| 85 | Black River Ranch–Lynn Westland | 2.00 | 4.00 | 6.00 | W |
| 86 | The Brand Stealer–Charles H. Snow | 2.00 | 4.00 | 6.00 | W |
| 88 | Poison the Valley–Frank C. Robertson | 2.00 | 4.00 | 6.00 | W |
| 89 | Marked Man–Harold Channing Wire. Note: Same cover as Hillman No. 28 | 2.00 | 4.00 | 6.00 | W |
| 90 | Gunsmoke Galoot–Leslie Ernenwein | 2.00 | 4.00 | 6.00 | W |
| 91 | Meddling Maverick–Tom West | 2.00 | 4.00 | 6.00 | W |
| 92 | Bury Me Not–Allan R. Bosworth | 2.00 | 4.00 | 6.00 | W |
| 93 | Lead Law–Amos Moore | 2.00 | 4.00 | 6.00 | W |
| 94 | The Deuce of Diamonds–Charles M. Martin | 2.00 | 4.00 | 6.00 | W |
| 95 | Badland Bill–Ranger Lee | 2.00 | 4.00 | 6.00 | W |
| 96 | Closed Range–Bliss Lomax (Harry Sinclair Drago) | 2.00 | 4.00 | 6.00 | W |
| 97 | The Lightning Kid–J.E. Grinstead | 2.00 | 4.00 | 6.00 | W |
| 98 | The Shootin' Sheriff–Tex Riley | 2.00 | 4.00 | 6.00 | W |
| 99 | Horsethief Pass–Charles H. Snow | 2.00 | 4.00 | 6.00 | W |
| 100 | Barbed Wire Empire–Will Ermine | 2.00 | 4.00 | 6.00 | W |
| 101 | Painted Post Rustlers–Tom Gunn | 2.00 | 4.00 | 6.00 | W |
| 102 | Colt Lightnin'–Kirk Deming | 2.00 | 4.00 | 6.00 | W |
| 104 | The Hard Riders–Tom J. Hopkins | 2.00 | 4.00 | 6.00 | W |
| 105 | Dakota Marshal–Lynn Westland | 2.00 | 4.00 | 6.00 | W |
| 106 | Lawless Legion–Will Ermine | 2.00 | 4.00 | 6.00 | W |
| 107 | Poison Springs–Eli Colter | 2.00 | 4.00 | 6.00 | W |
| 108 | The Vultures of Vacaville–W.C. Tuttle | 2.00 | 4.00 | 6.00 | W |
| 109 | Blow, Desert Winds–William Corcoran | 2.00 | 4.00 | 6.00 | W |
| 110 | Both Sides of the Law–B.W. Sinclair | 2.00 | 4.00 | 6.00 | W |
| 111 | Hell for Leather–Archie Joscelyn | 2.00 | 4.00 | 6.00 | W |
| 112 | Room for the Rolling M–B.W. Sinclair | 2.00 | 4.00 | 6.00 | W |

# WESTERN NOVEL OF THE MONTH

## Hillman Periodicals, Inc./Novel Selections

### Digest Size

| | | V/Good | Fine | N/Mint | |
|---|---|---|---|---|---|
| nn | Rancho Bonita–Dan James | 2.00 | 4.00 | 6.00 | W |
| nn | Gunsmoke in Sunset Valley–D. Bardwell | 2.00 | 4.00 | 6.00 | W |
| 3 | Guns at Lazy River–S. Adams | 2.00 | 4.00 | 6.00 | W |
| 4 | Hell on the Pecos–Ed Earl Repp | 2.00 | 4.00 | 6.00 | W |
| 5 | The Gun Tamer–Max Brand | 2.00 | 4.00 | 6.00 | W |
| 6 | Quick Triggers–Eugene Cunningham | 2.00 | 4.00 | 6.00 | W |
| 7 | Border Breed–William MacLeod Raine | 2.00 | 4.00 | 6.00 | W |
| 8 | Gunpowder Heritage–George B. Rodney | 2.00 | 4.00 | 6.00 | W |
| 9 | Rustler's Range–Max Brand | 2.00 | 4.00 | 6.00 | W |
| 10 | Roaring River–William MacLeod Raine | 2.00 | 4.00 | 6.00 | W |
| 11 | Brand of the Outlaw–Paul Evan Lehman | 2.00 | 4.00 | 6.00 | W |
| 12 | Ranger Two-Rifles–Dane Coolidge | 2.00 | 4.00 | 6.00 | W |
| 13 | The Outlaw Trail–Max Brand | 2.00 | 4.00 | 6.00 | W |
| 14 | Riders of the Night–Eugene Cunningham | 2.00 | 4.00 | 6.00 | W |
| 15 | The Outlaw of Antler–Frank C. Robertson | 2.00 | 4.00 | 6.00 | W |
| 16 | Badman of Elk Head–Robert Claiborne Pitzer | 2.00 | 4.00 | 6.00 | W |
| 17 | Comanche Chaser–Dane Coolidge | 2.00 | 4.00 | 6.00 | W |
| 18 | The Seven of Diamonds–Max Brand | 2.00 | 4.00 | 6.00 | W |
| 19 | Suicide Ranch–Ed Earl Repp | 2.00 | 4.00 | 6.00 | W |
| 20 | Stormy Range–Robert Crane | 2.00 | 4.00 | 6.00 | W |
| 21 | Pistol Passport–Eugene Cunningham | 2.00 | 4.00 | 6.00 | W |

# (WESTERN PRINTING AND LITHOGRAPHING)

## Western Printing and Lithographing

| | | V/Good | Fine | N/Mint | |
|---|---|---|---|---|---|
| nn | Your Power as a Woman–Alma Archer; 1957 | .50 | 1.00 | 1.50 | |

# WESTERN THRILLER

## Vital Publications, Inc.

### Digest Size

| | | V/Good | Fine | N/Mint | |
|---|---|---|---|---|---|
| 4 | Open Land Renegades–Tom J. Hopkins; 1948; abridged version of Slash G Hombre. Note: It is strongly suspected that this book corresponds to missing book of Atlas Mystery (Vital Publications) series. | 3.00 | 6.00 | 9.00 | W |

# THE WEST IN ACTION

## Astro Distributing Corporation

### Digest Size

| | | V/Good | Fine | N/Mint | |
|---|---|---|---|---|---|
| 1 | Outlaw Sheriff–Murray Leinster; 1948 | 5.00 | 10.00 | 15.00 | W |
| 2 | Guns along the Western Trail–Murray Leinster | 5.00 | 10.00 | 15.00 | W |
| 3 | Kid Deputy–Murray Leinster; 1948 | 5.00 | 10.00 | 15.00 | W |
| 4 | Two-Gun Showdown–Murray Leinster | 5.00 | 10.00 | 15.00 | W |

# WHITMAN

## Whitman Publishing Company

| | | V/Good | Fine | N/Mint | |
|---|---|---|---|---|---|
| 347 | 100 Games of Solitaire–Helen L. Coops | 1.25 | 2.50 | 3.75 | NF |
| 556 | Pinocchio: 1939; movie tie-in (Disney) | 25.00 | 50.00 | 75.00 | |
| 630 | Universal Dream Book; 1940 | 3.00 | 6.00 | 9.00 | NF |

*Whitman 556, Wisdom House W104, Yogi Mysteries unnumbered.*

| | | V/Good | Fine | N/Mint | |
|---|---|---|---|---|---|
| **WHITMAN,** *continued* | | | | | |
| 790 | Murder C.O.D.–Donald Ross (Fred MacIsaac) | 4.00 | 8.00 | 12.00 | M |
| | With dust jacket | 20.00 | 40.00 | 60.00 | |
| 790 | The Alligator Ring–Donald Ross (Fred MacIsaac) | 4.00 | 8.00 | 12.00 | A |
| | With dust jacket | 20.00 | 40.00 | 60.00 | A |
| 790 | The Wild Man of Cape Cod–Fred MacIsaac | 4.00 | 8.00 | 12.00 | A |
| | With dust jacket | 20.00 | 40.00 | 60.00 | A |
| 790 | M.D.–Doctor of Murder–Fred MacIsaac | 4.00 | 8.00 | 12.00 | M |
| | With dust jacket | 20.00 | 40.00 | 60.00 | |
| 790 | The Devil Was Kind–Donald Ross (Fred MacIsaac) | 4.00 | 8.00 | 12.00 | |
| | With dust jacket | 20.00 | 40.00 | 60.00 | |
| 790 | Dead Men Tell Tales–Donald Ross (Fred MacIsaac) | 4.00 | 8.00 | 12.00 | |
| | With dust jacket | 20.00 | 40.00 | 60.00 | |
| 790 | The Gleaming Blade–Kaspar Kane (Fred MacIsaac) | 4.00 | 8.00 | 12.00 | A |
| | With dust jacket | 20.00 | 40.00 | 60.00 | |
| 790 | Five Keys to Mystery–Francis Moore | 4.00 | 8.00 | 12.00 | M |
| | With dust jacket | 20.00 | 40.00 | 60.00 | |
| 2060 | Superman Smashes the Secret of the Mad Director–George S. Elrick; 1st ed. 1966 | 3.00 | 6.00 | 9.00 | A |

# WIDE WORLD
## Peters Publishing Company

| | | V/Good | Fine | N/Mint | |
|---|---|---|---|---|---|
| 1 | A World in Crisis?–Allan Forester; 1952 | 1.50 | 3.00 | 4.50 | NF |
| 2 | Republicans Today–Philip Arthur; 1952 | 1.50 | 3.00 | 4.50 | NF |
| 3 | Democrats Today–Philip Arthur; 1952 | 2.00 | 4.00 | 6.00 | NF |
| 5 | Cold War Politics–John Breamer; 1953 | 1.50 | 3.00 | 4.50 | NF |

# WISDOM HOUSE
## Wisdom House, Inc.

| | | V/Good | Fine | N/Mint | |
|---|---|---|---|---|---|
| G1 | The Day the Communists Took Over America–Isabel Moore; 1961 | 1.50 | 3.00 | 4.50 | F |
| G2 | God in Hollywood–Alyce Canfield; 1961; Note: Marilyn Monroe on cover. | 2.00 | 4.00 | 6.00 | NF |
| W101 | Sex Crimes and Sex Criminals–Alan Bentham; 1961 | 1.50 | 3.00 | 4.50 | NF |
| W102 | I Confess . . . –Intimate Stories of True Confessions | 1.50 | 3.00 | 4.50 | NF |
| W103 | Those Fabulous Kennedy Women–William H.A. Carr | 1.50 | 3.00 | 4.50 | NF |
| W104 | The Life and Loves of Lana Turner–Jacqueline Wright | 1.50 | 3.00 | 4.50 | B |
| W105 | Sexual Behavior among Teenagers–Shailer Upton Lawton, MD | 1.25 | 2.50 | 3.75 | |
| W106 | Secrets of Famous Mistresses–Jay Simpson; 1961 | 1.50 | 3.00 | 4.50 | E |
| W107 | Peeping Tom–Orrie Hitt | 1.50 | 3.00 | 4.50 | E |

| | | V/Good | Fine | N/Mint | |
|---|---|---|---|---|---|
| W108 | All the Sad Young Men–anon. | 1.25 | 2.50 | 3.75 | NF |
| W109 | Splendors of Love–John Burton Thompson; 1962 | 1.25 | 2.50 | 3.75 | E |

# YOGI MYSTERIES
## Wiegers Publishing Company
### Digest Size

| | | V/Good | Fine | N/Mint | |
|---|---|---|---|---|---|
| nn | Death from Nowhere–Stuart Towne (Clayton Rawson) | 60.00 | 120.00 | 180.00 | M |
| nn | Man about Broadway–Herbert Crooker | 4.00 | 8.00 | 12.00 | M |

# ZENITH
## Zenith Books, Inc.

| | | V/Good | Fine | N/Mint | |
|---|---|---|---|---|---|
| ZB1 | The Sisters–Charles Jackson; 1958 | 2.00 | 4.00 | 6.00 | E |
| ZB2 | All Over Town–George Milburn | 2.00 | 4.00 | 6.00 | |
| ZB3 | Johnny Purple–John Wyllie | 2.00 | 4.00 | 6.00 | M |
| ZB4 | Die Screaming–Jo Pagano; aka The Condemned | 2.00 | 4.00 | 6.00 | M |
| ZB5 | The Best Cartoons from Argosy | 5.00 | 10.00 | 15.00 | H |
| ZB6 | The Oral Roberts Reader–Oral Roberts | 2.00 | 4.00 | 6.00 | |
| ZB7 | The Girl from Hateville–Gil Brewer | 2.50 | 5.00 | 7.50 | E |
| ZB8 | Adventure in Paradise–Emile C. Schurmacher | 2.00 | 4.00 | 6.00 | A |
| ZB9 | The Man without a Face–John Eugene Hasry | 2.00 | 4.00 | 6.00 | |
| ZB10 | Rawhiders–Tom Roan | 2.00 | 4.00 | 6.00 | W |
| ZB11 | The Long Desire–Max Weatherly; 1959 | 2.00 | 4.00 | 6.00 | E |
| ZB12 | The Rascal's Guide–Bruce Jay Friedman | 2.00 | 4.00 | 6.00 | |
| ZB13 | The Three Legions–Gregory Solon | 2.00 | 4.00 | 6.00 | |
| ZB14 | The People Maker–Damon Knight | 3.00 | 6.00 | 9.00 | SF |
| ZB15 | Etched in Murder–Ken Jones | 2.00 | 4.00 | 6.00 | M |
| ZB16 | Lysistrata–Fletcher Flora | 2.00 | 4.00 | 6.00 | E |
| ZB17 | Death of the Party–Ruth Fenisong | 2.00 | 4.00 | 6.00 | M |
| ZB18 | Blonde Bait–Ed Lacy | 3.00 | 6.00 | 9.00 | M |
| ZB19 | The Deadly Doll–Henry Kane | 2.00 | 4.00 | 6.00 | M |
| ZB20 | Fall Girl–Richard Deming | 2.00 | 4.00 | 6.00 | M |
| ZB21 | Young Sinner–Elisabeth Gill | 2.00 | 4.00 | 6.00 | E |
| ZB22 | Georgia Girl–Bart Frame | 2.00 | 4.00 | 6.00 | E |
| ZB23 | A Fine and Private Place–Ann Hebson | 2.00 | 4.00 | 6.00 | E |
| ZB24 | Moran's Woman–Day Keene; orig. 1959 | 3.00 | 6.00 | 9.00 | E |
| ZB25 | The Sweet Blonde Trap–William Campbell Gault; 1st ed. 1959 | 4.00 | 8.00 | 12.00 | M |
| ZB26 | Nurse's Quarters–Sylvia Erskine | 2.00 | 4.00 | 6.00 | E |
| ZB27 | Wayward Nymph–Elisabeth Gill | 2.00 | 4.00 | 6.00 | E |
| ZB28 | Your Body and Its Care–Richard E. Winter | 2.00 | 4.00 | 6.00 | NF |
| ZB29 | Sweet and Deadly–A. Boyd Correll & Philip MacDonald | 2.00 | 4.00 | 6.00 | M |
| ZB30 | Strangers on Friday–Harry Whittington | 2.50 | 5.00 | 7.50 | M |
| ZB31 | Too Black for Heaven–Day Keene; orig. 1960 | 3.00 | 6.00 | 9.00 | E |
| ZB32 | Rita–Ray Gaulden | 2.00 | 4.00 | 6.00 | E |

*Zenith ZB2, Zenith ZB6, Zenith ZB12.*

Zenith ZB25, Zenith ZB31, Zenith ZB33.

| | | V/Good | Fine | N/Mint | |
|---|---|---|---|---|---|
| ZENITH, *continued* | | | | | |
| ZB33 | The Gray Flannel Shroud—Henry Slesar | 2.00 | 4.00 | 6.00 | M |
| ZB34 | Frenchie—David Charlson | 2.00 | 4.00 | 6.00 | E |
| ZB36 | Kiss and Tell—Richard Deming | 2.00 | 4.00 | 6.00 | |

| | | V/Good | Fine | N/Mint | |
|---|---|---|---|---|---|
| ZB37 | The Girl Who Killed Things—Talmage Powell | 2.00 | 4.00 | 6.00 | |
| ZB38 | French Alley—Matthew Clay | 2.00 | 4.00 | 6.00 | E |
| ZB39 | The Blonde on Borrowed Time—B.X. Sanborn; 1960, aka The Doom-Maker | 2.00 | 4.00 | 6.00 | M |
| ZB40 | Corpus Earthling—Louis Charbonneau; orig. 1960 | 2.50 | 5.00 | 7.50 | SF |
| ZB42 | The Violated One—Jack Hanley; aka City Streets | 2.00 | 4.00 | 6.00 | E |
| ZB43 | The Hot Sand of Hell—Christopher Landon; 1960; aka Ice Cold in Alex; movie tie-in | 2.50 | 5.00 | 7.50 | C |
| ZB44 | Black Satin Jungle—Bart Frame; aka Indiscretions of a French Model | 2.50 | 5.00 | 7.50 | E |

# (ZIEGELHEIM)
# Ziegelheim
## Digest Size

| | | V/Good | Fine | N/Mint | |
|---|---|---|---|---|---|
| nn | Fun, Inc.—anon; 1945 | 3.00 | 6.00 | 9.00 | H |

# AUTHOR INDEX

## ABBREVIATIONS IN INDEX

LOVE ROMANCE SERIES LoveRS
(LUCOM) Luc
MACFADDEN BOOKS McF
MAGABOOKS Maga
(MAGAZINE VILLAGE) MagV
(MANHATTAN) Man
(MASTHEAD) Mast
MENTOR BOOKS Ment
MENTOR GUIDES MentG
MERCURY LIBRARY MercL
MERCURY MYSTERY MM
MERIT BOOKS;em1st SERIES MeritF
MERIT BOOKS;em2nd SERIES MeritS
MERIT BOOKS Merit
(METRO) Metro
MIDWOOD Midw
MIDWOOD-TOWER MidT
MODERN LIVING COUNCIL ModLC
MONARCH AMERICANA MonA
MONARCH BOOKS MonB
MONARCH HUMAN BEHAVIOR SERIES MonHBS
MONARCH K-SERIES MonK
MONARCH LANGUAGE SERIES MonLS
MONARCH MOVIE SERIES MonMS
MONARCH SELECT MonS
MYSTERY NOVEL CLASSIC MNC
MYSTERY NOVEL OF THE MONTH MNM
MYSTERY PUZZLE OF THE MONTH MyPM
(NATIONAL DAIRY) NatD
NEW CLASSICS HOUSE NCH
NEWS STAND LIBRARY;em1st SERIES NSLF
NEWS STAND LIBRARY;em2nd SERIES NSLS
NEWSSTAND LIBRARY;em1st SERIES NSLF
NEWSSTAND LIBRARY;em2nd SERIES NSLS
NO IMPRINT NOI
NOVEL BOOKS;em1st SERIES NovF
NOVEL BOOKS;em2nd SERIES Novs
NOVEL LIBRARY NovL
NOVEL SELECTIONS NovSl
(NOVELS INC.) Novl
OLYMPIC FOTO-READERS OIFR
OMNIBUS Omni
$1,000 PRIZE MYSTERY NOVELS PriMN
ORIGINAL NOVELS OrigN
PADELL Pad
PAPERBACK LIBRARY;em1ST SERIES PapLF
PAPERBACK LIBRARY;em2ND SERIES PapLS
PAPILLON BOOKS Papi
(PARENTS INSTITUTE) Parl
PELICAN BOOKS PelB
PENGUIN Pen
PENGUIN GUIDES PenG
PENGUIN SPECIALS PenS
PENNANT Penn
PENNANT MYSTERY PennM
PENNANT STUDENT EDITIONS PennSE
PERMA BOOKS Perma
PERMA BOOKS (Hardbound) PermaH
PERMA BOOKS (Softbound) PermaS

(PETERS) Peters
PHANTOM BOOKS Phan
PHANTOM MYSTERY PhanM
PHOENIX Phoe
PITMAN EDITION Pit
POCKET BOOK Pock
POCKET BOOK (BRITISH) PockB
POCKET BOOK COLLECTOR'S EDITION PBCE
POCKET BOOK JR. PocJr
POCKET BOOK;emSPECIAL EDITION PocSp
POCKET BOOK SPECIAL PocSp
POCKET LIBRARY PocL
POCKET LIBRARY OF GREAT ART PocLGA
PONY BOOKS Pony
POPULAR LIBRARY Pop
POPULAR LIBRARY EAGLE PopLE
POPULAR LIBRARY G-SERIES PopLG
POPULAR LIBRARY PC-SERIES PopPC
POPULAR LIBRARY SP-SERIES PopSP
POPULAR LIBRARY W-SERIES PopW
POWELL/TIGER Powe
(PREFERRED BOOKS) Pre
PREMIER BOOKS Prem
PRIVATE EDITIONS Priv
PRIZE Prize
PRIZE LOVE NOVELS PrizeLN
PRIZE MYSTERY NOVELS PrizeMN
PRIZE SCIENCE FICTION NOVELS PSFN
PRIZE WESTERN NOVELS PrizeWN
(PUTNAM) Putn
PYRAMID BOOKS Pyr
PYRAMID ROYAL (PR/PG-SERIES) PyrPR
PYRAMID STUDENT EDITION PyrSE
PYTHON Pyth
QUARTER BOOKS QB
QUICK READER QR
(QUINN) Quinn
RAINBOW Rain
RAINBOW BOOKS RB
READERS CHOICE LIBRARY RCL
(READER'S LEAGUE) ReaL
RED ARROW BOOKS RA
RED CIRCLE RC
RED DAGGER MYSTERY RDM
RED SEAL BOOKS RSB
REGENCY Regy
(RETAIL DISTRIBUTORS) RetD
REX STOUT MYSTERY Rex
ROMANTIC NOVELS RomN
ROYAL GIANT EDITION RoyG
RUTLEDGE BOOKS Rutl
(R.W.) RW
SABER BOOKS Saber
SABER READER SabR
SAINT MYSTERY LIBRARY SML
SAINT NOVEL SN
(SCIENCE SERVICE) SS
SHOOTING SCRIPT Shoot
SIGNET Signet
SIGNET CLASSICS SigC

SIGNET KEY SigK
SIGNET STUDENT EDITIONS SigSE
STALLION BOOKS Stall
STANLEY LIBRARY StanL
STAR BOOKS Star
(STAR STORIES) StarSt
STORK ORIGINAL NOVEL StorON
(STOVEL-ADVOCATE) StovA
STREAMLINE Strl
(STUART) Stuart
STUDIO POCKET EDITION SPE
SUPERIOR DETECTIVE NOVEL SDN
SUPERIOR REPRINTS SupR
SUSPENSE NOVELS SusN
SWAN Swan
TECH MYSTERY TechM
TECH WESTERN TechW
TEMPO BOOKS Tempo
(THEODORE ROOSEVELT) TR
THREE STAR BOOKS TSB
A THRILLER BOOK Thrill
THRILLER NOVEL CLASSIC TNC
THRILLING BOOKS/NOVELS ThrillBN
THRILLING MYSTERY NOVEL ThrillMN
TOBY Toby
TODAY'S CROSSWORDS TC
TOWER Tower
TRAVELLERS POCKET LIBRARY BEST-SELLER TPLBS
TRIPLE NICKEL LIBRARY TNL
TROPIC BOOKS/SABER-TROPIC BOOKS TBSTB
TROPHY BOOKS Trophy
UNI-BOOKS Uni
(UNICORN) Unic
(UNITED STATES PLAYING CARD COMPANY) USPCC
(UNITED STATES SALES COMPANY) USSC
UNIVERSAL GIANT EDITION UGE
UNIVERSAL ROMANCE UR
VALUE BOOKS Value
VANITAS Vanit
VEGA BOOKS Vega
VEGA SCIENCE FICTION LIBRARY VegaSFL
VEGA WESTERN LIBRARY VWL
VENUS BOOKS Venus
VITAL BOOK Vital
VULCAN MYSTERY VulM
WARNER BOOKS War
WASHINGTON SQUARE PRESS WSP
WESTERN ACTION NOVEL WAN
WESTERN NOVEL CLASSIC WNC
WESTERN NOVEL OF THE MONTH WNM
(WESTERN PRINTING AND LITHOGRAPHING) WPL
WESTERN THRILLER WT
THE WEST IN ACTION WIA
WHITMAN Whit
WIDE WORLD WW
WISDOM HOUSE WH
YOGI MYSTERIES Yogi
ZENITH Zenith
(ZIEGELHEIM) Zieg

Aadland, Mrs. Florence—Lan (72-)607
Aaron, Daniel—AvDYD D7; AvWYX W103
Aaron, Sam W.—Perma M4065
Aarons, Edward S.—GM 258, 280, 362, 424, 491, 568,
    621, 666, 707, 749, 799, 834, 863, 895, 906, s911,
    923, 971, 979, 1023, S1036, S1073, S1091, S1118,
    S1152, S1164, S1189, S1237, S1270, K1304, K1307,
    K1370, K1372, K1373, K1398, K1423, K1442, K1455,
    K1456, K1481, K1495, K1497, K1505, K1515, K1525,
    K1534, K1535, K1539, K1556, K1559, K1570, D1583,
    D1612, D1613, D1630, D1631, D1640, D1653, D1654,
    D1656, D1660, D1661, D1672, D1692, D1695, D1703,
    D1707; GMB 36, 52; MM 143
Abbey, Edward—Pock 1185
Abbey, Kieran—Dell 93
Abbot, Anthony—AvMMM 25; Dell 88; GreD 27; Pop 159,
    286
Abbott, A.C.—GM 208; GMB 32; Signet 1142
Abbott, Anita—CreB s204
Abbott, E.C.—ASE N8, 756
Abbott, Sheldon—Saber SA49, SA68
Abby, Alain—AvG G1110
Abell, Elizabeth—Bal 19, 75; BB 503, 742, A914
Abrahams, Robert D.—HH 19
Abram, A.—Uni 24
Abrams, Ted E.—NSLS U173
Abro, Ben—CreB D790
Abzug, Martin—BerkG G58
Ackerman, Forrest J.—PapLF 52-290, 52-504, 52-813
Ackworth, Robert C.—Hill 129; Lan 71-308
Acton, Harold—AceD D26
Adamic, Louis—ASE B54
Adams, Caswell—Pony 61 Signet 902
Adams, Cleve F.—AceD D115; Dell 104; Han nn(2), nn(7),
    33, 112; Harl 256; MNC 43; MNM 31, 36; Pen 522;
    Pop 426, 456; PrizeMN 5; Signet 765, 850, 902, 936,
    1298, 1405, 1419
Adams, Clifford—Dell 224
Adams, Clifton—AceF F262, F404; AceG G628, G708; AvFS
    F234; Bal 569; DellFE A199; GM 121, 168, 230, 291,
    422, 483, 533, 593, 674, 683, S1274, S1375, K1705;
    GMB 5, 16
Adams, Eustace L.—ANC 31
Adams, Evangeline—PermaH P36
Adams, Fay—GM 228, 333; RSB 19
Adams, Frank R.—Dell 413; WNC 73
Adams, Franklin P.—ASE H231
Adams, Henry—ASE Q40
Adams, Herbert—CWC 65, 93, 279, 281
Adams, Joey—Av 202; AvS S285; Pock 1130; Pop 285, 504;
    PopLG G216, G371
Adams, Sir John—CreB D454, R844
Adams, John Paul—Av 295, 645; AvT T123; Berk 376; Pop
    223
Adams, Samuel Hopkins—ASE R40, 931; BB A1107; Dell 20,
    130; DellF F51; DellTC 3; Signet D1503, D1627, T1796;
    WNM 3
Adams, Tracy—AceD D549, D583; AvFS F190
Aday, Sanford—Fab Z102; FabR Z6
Addams, Charles—BB 37
Addams, Kay—Bea B259, B289, B308; NovF 6026, 6085,
    6088, 60103; Novs 6N253
Addis, Hugh—Han 37
Addy, Ted—MonA MA320
Adkins, Cleo—Harl 479
Adler, Alfred—PermaH P57; Prem d52
Adler, Bill—AvFS F225
Adler, Edward—AceD S114, D399
Adler, Irving—Ment MD281; SigK K361, Ks364, Ks369
Adler, Polly—PopLG G140; PopSP SP36
Adlon, Arthur—CHARf CB116, CB120, CB127, CB134,
    CB144, CB154, CB155, CB157, CB159, CB179, CB204,
    CB210, CB216; CHARs CB1602, CB1607; Lan 72-698,
    72-757, 72-905, 72-921, 72-962, 72-975
Advisory Board,—DellM M101
Agar, Brian—MonB 195
Agar, Herbert—ASE A21
Agee, James—AvG G1034; AvNS NS18; AvS S133; AvVS
    VS12
Ageton, Arthur A.—Signet S1200, S2026
Ahern, Helen—Ast 11; Crow 28
Aherne, Owen—AvT T177, T182
Ahlswede, Ann—Bal 405K, 448K, F620
Ahriman, Seth—Fran F3
Aiken, Henry O.—Ment MD185
Aiken, Joan—AceK K219, K294
Aiken, Maj. W.A.—ASE S1
Aikens, Kate—CWC 445
Ainsworth, Ed—ASE 1237
Airlie, Catherine—Harl 511, 789
Aitken, Kate—CWC 528; Harl 768
Aksenov, Vasili    (trans. Andrew MacAndrew)—Signet P2315
Alain,—Pyr X659
Alan, Jan—Harl 924
Albee, George Sumner—AvFS F102; DellFE 4, B131
Albert, Andrew I.—VulM nn, 4
Albert, Jay—AceD D144
Albert, Marvin H.—CardE C389; CreB D551; DellFE K101; GM
    519, 553, 696, 756, 760, 808, 826, 846, 856, 902,

918, S1167, S1193, S1345, S1387, K1410, K1666;
    Prem d66; Pyr G532
Albert, Sim—BerkG G244; Croy 44, 56, 73, 77, 81, 87, 93
Albert, Simms—Bea B287; IN 45
Albrand, Martha—AceG G542, G559, G563; ASE D96; Dell
    396, 544, 651; Lan 73-548, 73-556; Pock 247
Alcott, Louisa May—Dell 296; Pock 75
Ald, Roy—Lan 74-956, 75-021, 75-024
Alden, Troy—MonHBS MB523
Aldiss, Brian W.—AceD D369, D443; AceF F382; Bal F555;
    Bea 305; Lan 74-677; Signet S1683, S1779, S1815,
    D2018
Aldrich, Ann—GM 509, s727, s774, D1009, D1196, 1266,
    K1313, D1553
Aldrich, Bess Streeter—Pock 470
Aldrich, D.B.—PermaH P45
Aldridge, James—Dell 657
Aldridge, John W.—CardE C80
Alen, Kevin—Powe PP117
Alexander, David—AceD D59; BB 1315, 1408, 1534, 1601,
    1655, 1736; CreB D557, D757; DellD D362; Regy
    RB114
Alexander, Jan—Lan 74-648, 74-670, 74-745
Alfred, Gordon T.—Bal 317K
Alger, Horatio—Value 101, 102, 103, 104, 105
Algren, Nelson—Av 185, 222, 419, 424; AvT T108, T125,
    T185, T223, T394; CardE C31; CreB d157, D377,
    D496, T727, T890; Lan 73-409; NCH 7N730; Pock 757
Aliandro, Hygino—CardGC GC750
Alighieri, Dante—Ment Ms113
Allan, Bette—Harl 308
Allan, Dennis—DNC 19
Allan, Frederick Lewis—BB 27
Allan, Jack—NSLS U148, U155
Allan, John B.    (Donald Westlake)—MonK K55
Allan, Tony—Harl 480, 622, 694; StovA nn
Alleg, Henri—Bel 202
Allen, Barbara—Harl 416
Allen, Edward Frank—CreB s284, D521; Prem S13
Allen, Eric—AceG G687; Lan 70-016, 73-757, 74-796; MonB
    345, 359, 420; Pyr G329
Allen, Francis—BB 34
Allen, Frederick Lewis—BantB FB402; BantC FC15; BB
    A1069, F1620
Allen, Hervey—ASE L23, A28, C83, 849; Dell 281, 283, 285;
    DellD D110, D128; DellF F105; Pock 370
Allen, Jane—Av 345; Cent 103
Allen, Johannes—CreB S345
Allen, John Houghton—BB 1167
Allen, Leslie    (Horace Brown)—FSM 45
Allen, Ralph—AvN N138; Harl 706
Allen, Robert S.—BerkG BG90
Allen, Steve—DellD D172; PopLG G377
Allen, T.D.—CreB 152; Harl 251
Allen, Warner H.—Pen 510
Allingham, Margery—AvG G1238; Av nn(29); AvFS F114;
    AvMMM 17, 35; AvT T493, T530; BM B33, B51, B56;
    BondM 12; Dell 777; DellD D234; JonM J32; MM 49,
    112, 132; Pen 276, 503, 534; Pock 329, 665; Pony 56
Allison, Carlyle—Harl 453
Allison, Clyde—Midw 64, 73
Allison, Sam—Lion 183; LionLL LB157
Allred, Gordon T.—Bal 693; BEDN 244
Alman, David—Signet 803
Alman, E.A.—AceD D412
Alpert, Hollis—AvG G1102; BB A1954
Alter, Robert Edmond—AvG G1312; AvS S325; GM S1095,
    D1611
Alth, Max—DellF G161
Alvarez, Walter C.—DellD D146
Amado, Jorge—CardB T704
Amberg, George—Ment M42, Ms123
Ambler, Eric—BB 1327, A1671, A1772; DellD D201, D238,
    D343; Pen 511; Penn P3; Pock 193, 232, 286, 887
Ames, Clyde—Lan 73-607, 73-826
Ames, Delano—AceH H93, H97, H109; Dell 493, 552, 579
Ames, Francis—AceK K247
Ames, H.P.—Bea B163
Ames, Jennifer—AceD D524; CWC 241, 263, 326, 389, 417
Ames, Louise Bates—DellD D180; DellLE LC120
Ames, Robert—GM 269, 435, 518
Amis, Kingsley—Bal 479K; Signet P2237
Amory, Richard—FPVFP FP2006, FP2032
Amos, Alan—ANC 24
Amsbary, Mary Anne—Signet S1080
Anders, Curt—BB A1908
Andersch, Alfred—PopSP SP169
Anderson,—MonB 267
Anderson, Alston—Pyr G538
Anderson, Ben—CHARf CB178
Anderson, Brad—MonB 109; Pop 795
Anderson, Chester—GM K1374
Anderson, Clifford—AceD D404
Anderson, Edward—BB 350; BerkG G130; Lion 8; LionLL
    LL51; MM 5; Pyr G456
Anderson, Frank W. Jr.—DellLE LB116
Anderson, Jannet—Fab Z154; Saber SA31; TBSTB 905
Anderson, Jerry—EHO 0130
Anderson, M.—NSLS U134
Anderson, Marian—AvB Bard 5; AvS S165; AvZS ZS129
Anderson, Oliver—Av 391; Harl 243

Anderson, Poul—AceD D110, D199, D255, D303, D335,
    D407, D479, D550, D568; AceF F104, F139, F209,
    F425; AceG G634, G697; AvG G1127; AvT T388, T472;
    AvZS ZS166; Bal 80, 393K, 422K, 483K, 579; BalAF
    02107, 23526, 23562; BalU U2342; Bea 270; BerkG
    G289; Lan 73-505, 73-677, 74-536, 74-698, 74-742,
    75-185, 75-319, 75-374, 75-388; MonS MS15; Pyr
    F818, G615
Anderson, Robert—Signet 1343
Anderson, Sherwood—ASE Q9; Pen 585; Pock 878; Signet
    1304
Anderson, Thomas—BB A1570
Anderson, U.S.—CardE C140; PopLE EB72
Anderson, W.W.—AtM nn
Anderson, William C.—AceD D467
Anderson, William R.—Signet D1692
Anderton, Russ—PermaS 308
Andors, Lisa—CreB s204
Andrews, John Paul—ASE 1018
Andrews, Ned—PocJr J56
Andrews, Robert Hardy—AceD D206
Andrews, Roy Chapman—ASE F168, 1160; Harl 291
Andreyev, Leonid—Av 655
Andrezel, Pierre    (Isak Dinesen)—AceK K167
Andriola, Alfred—Signet 1361
Anet, Claude—DB 3; Signet 676, 1404
Angelo, Tony—ArB 6, 12; LeiL 17
Angus, Douglas—CreB D427
anon.,    (H.S. Drago)—NovL 21
Anslinger, Harry J.—AvV V2064
Antholz, Peyson—AceD D306
Anthony, Bill—NovF 5085, 5088, 5091; Novs 6N222, 6N224
Anthony, Edward—Pock 47
Anthony, Evelyn—Hill 134
Anthony, Jed—IN 6
Anthony, John J.—Hill 21
Anthony, Joseph—BB A1760
Anthony, Norman—CWC 331
Anthony, Piers—AceA A19; AvWYX W166; Las 44
Anton, Cal—Bea B266
Antony, Paul—TSB 104
Anvil, Christopher—MonB 478
Apollinaire, Guillaume—HollH HH145
Appel, Benjamin—AvT T101, T162, T468; Bal 345K; BerkG
    G152; DellF F81; GM 266, 385, s642, s809; Lion 39,
    95, 166; LionLL LB116, LL151
Appel, David—Prem S28, d84
Appel, H.M.—QB 54; Uni 22, 29
Appell, George C.—AvT T549; Bal 185; Dell 892; DellFE 74;
    Lion 139, 199; LionLL LL57, LL161; Perma M3013,
    M3112; Pock 1232
Appleby, John—Dell 663, 751, 994
April, Jack—Pyr G239, F775
Apuleius, Madaurensis—CardE C62
Aradi, Zsolt—MonHBS MB509
Arana, Ric—Powe PP125, PP187
Arbor, Jane—Harl 423, 454, 474, 482, 489, 498, 513, 524,
    576, 646, 690, 701, 780, 801, 832, 858, 887, 919,
    950
Archer, Alma—WPL nn
Archer, C.S.—CWC 454, 473
Archer, Jules—BerkG G2, G200; RC 1
Archer, Robert—Han 10
Arcone, Sonya—CreB D705
Ard, William—BerkD D2037; Dell 991; DellD D364; DellFE
    B145; MonB 124, 147, 152, 172; Pop 416, 477, 502,
    526, 569, 591, 639, 723, 756; PopLG G236, G328
Ard, William    (John Jakes)—MonB 215, 231, 269
Arden, Leon—DellF F64
Arfelli, Dante—BerkG G113; Signet 984
Ariosto, Ludovico—BalAF 03057
Aristotle,—PocL PL519
Ariot, John—PockB B39
Armitage, Angus—Ment M65
Armour, Tommy—CreB D505, D803
Armstrong, Charlotte—AceG G501, G510, G511, G512,
    G513, G514, G521, G526, G533, G540; CreB 191,
    247, 382, 383, K679; MM 85; Pock 427, 444, 575,
    805, 880, 1034, 1058, 1095
Armstrong, Donald—Pock 220
Armstrong, John—GM S1038
Armstrong, Juliet—Harl 681, 689, 892, 938
Armstrong, Louis—Signet S1245
Armstrong, Margaret—ASE 1048; BM B16, B30; DNC 12
Army Weekly, The—Bea B113
Arnaldi, Jean—PopSP SP202
Arnaud, Georges—Av 531, 804
Arno, Peter—Pock 417, 1087
Arnold,—Novs 7N714
Arnold, A.F.—Bal 105
Arnold, Edwin L.—AceF F296
Arnold, Elliot—Harl 175
Arnold, Elliott—ASE 681, 1273; BB A918, F1379, F1500,
    A1770; CWC 79, 225, 379; Pock 839; Pop 620; Signet
    735, 770
Arnold, Oren—MeritF 354; Perma M3081; Signet D2024
Arnold, Pauline—Perma M4084
Arnold, W.—Lan 72-629
Arnold, William—Cam 302, 314, 355; OrigN 717, 719, 724,
    734; Venus 136, 139, 197
Arnothy, Christine—PopLE EB95; PopLG G226

315

Arowitz,—Lan 72-611
Arquette, Cliff—DelID D347
Arthur, Bert—BCW 33
Arthur, Budd—AvFS F213, F229, F230
Arthur, Burt—AceD D92; Av 770, 785; AvFS F116, F132, F173, F187, F213, F229, F230, F237, F239, F245; AvT T198; BerkD D2021, D2033, D2039; BerkG G242; Cent 128; Lion 168, 189; LionLL LB85; Pop 425; PrizeWN 37; Signet 782, 822, 866, 952, 1135, 1339, 1401, 1443, 1697, S2127; Star 6, 11, 12, 19, 23, 26, 33, 34, 36, 38, 43
Arthur, Ella Bentley—Signet 1210
Arthur, Eric—EtB E117
Arthur, Philip—WW 2, 3
Arthur, Phyllis—Cent 84; Prize 58
Arthur, Robert—AceD D489
Arthur, William—Bea B166; Cent 79, 106, 111, 115, 120, 130; DB 2, 7; Knick nn; Novl nn; Prize 55; Uni 18
Artzybasheff, Mikhail—Lion 64
Arvonen, Helen—AceG G757; AceK K225, K278
Asbury, Herbert—AceK K148; ASE K26; Av 263; CardE C195, C251; Pock 474, 565
Asch, Sholem—ASE J299; CardE C255; CardGC GC36, GC38, GC43, GC49
Ash, Pauline—Harl 833, 916, 970
Ashabrannar, Brent—Penn P64
Ashbrook, H.—GreD 8, 18
Ashbrook, Harriette—ArM 6; Pen 626
Ashburn, Wade—PopLG G359
Ashe, Gordon—AceD D71, D221
Ashley, Luthar—HollH HH106
Ashton, Blair—AceD D314
Ashton, Helen—CWC 246
Asimov, Isaac—AceD D84, D110, D125, D538; AceF F216; AceN N4; AvG G1248; AvNS NS25; AvS S127, S224, S234, S237; AvT T232, T287; BB A1646, A1731, A1978; GSFN 14; Lan 72-103, 72-104, 72-107, 72-108, 72-753, 73-504, 73-701, 73-702, 73-703, 73-704, 74-504, 74-545, 74-644, 74-815, 74-816, 74-818, 74-930, 74-986, 74-996, 75-315; Pyr F784; Signet 1082, S1240, S1282, S1433, S1493
Asquith, Nan—Harl 699, 898
Astor, Mary—DellF F92
Astrachan, Sam—BB A1739
Aswell, James—Av 247; Signet 941, 1121, 1166, 1314
Aswell, Mary Louise—Bal 63
Athanas, Verne—DellFE A115; Pock 936, 999
Athas, Daphne—Pyr G267
Athens, Christopher—CPH A102
Atholl, Justin—PockB B55
Atiyah, Edward—Av 510, 786
Atkinson, D.T.—Prem d69
Atkinson, Oriana—Pop 307; PopLG G400
Atlee, Philip—GM K1321, K1489, D1632, D1634, D1694, D1702; Lion 188; LionLL LL66
Attaway, William—Lion 86; LionLL LL77; Pop 491
Atwater, Montgomery—PocJr J35
Auchincloss, Louis—BB F1722; CreB D750, R817, R825; Lan 73-434, 73-437, 74-844, 74-885, 74-925; Signet 1004, S1143, 1255
Auchircloss, Louis—CreB s320
Audett, Blackie—BB A1440
Auerbach, Arnold "Red"—CardE C289; Pock 933
August, John—Pop 65, 133
Augustine, Aurelius—CardE C27; PocL PL45
Augustus, Albert Jr (Charles Nuetzel)—Powe PP179, PP189
Austen, Jane—BantC FC10; CardE C37; DelLE LC122, LC128; PBCE nn(14); PocL PL9
Austin, Alex—BelLB L92-580; Hill 110; LionLL LL53, LL88, LL111, LL141; Pyr R896; Signet S1478
Austin, Brett—Han 121; Lion 20
Austin, Frank—Dell 636; Pop 784; PopLG G515
Austin, Gene—Perma M3001; PermaS 257
Austin, Jane—Pock 63
Austin, William A.—NSLS U165
Autry, Gene—Dell 153, 217
Avallone, Michael—AceD D259; AceG G553; AvG G1307; Bel 90-276, 90-293, 90-297, 90-318; BelLB B50-736, L92-570; GM 703, 718, 1024; Lan 74-636, 74-942; Midw 60, Y168; Perma M3012; PermaS 244, 289; Signet 1294
Avallone, Mike—Midw 120, F132, Y135, F146, Y184, F189, F202, F205
Averbuch, Bernard—Bal 141
Avery, A.A.—BB 38
Avery, Anderson—MonB 274
Avery, Kevin Quinn—FPVFP FP2042
Avery, Robert—DH 3; GreD 4; MNM 37
Avner,—Pyr G516
Axelrod, George—BB 403, 1371, A1653; GM 248
Ayers, Ruby M.—AvRNM 1; Dell 336
Aylesworth, John—AvG G1166
Ayling, Keith—ASE I242
Ayme, Marcel—CreB s250
Azoy, A.C.M.—FFS nn
Baarslag, Karl—ASE I258
Babcock, Dwight V.—Av nn(30), 68, 320, 332; AvMMM 10, 38
Babington-Smith, Constance—Bal F307K
Baccante, Leonora—Pop 423; PopLG G336

Bach, George R.—AvWYX W186
Bachmann, Lawrence—BM B46; CreB s237; Dell 122, 356
Backus, Jim—HollH HH115
Bacon, Peggy—MM 183
Badrig, Robert H.—Novs 6N273
Bagby, George—BB 1197, 1226, 1308; BDSM 4; BerkG G84; BM B87, B113, B200; Cent 13; Dell 848, 904, 949, 997; DellD D392; JonM J67, J71, J73, J87; MM 156; Pock 736
Bagnold, Enid—Pock 66
Bailey, H.C.—BondM 8, 16; Pock 190; Pony 52, 60, 64
Bailey, John—LionLL LL58
Bailey, Seth—BartH nn(1)
Bailey, Temple—BartH 31; Dell 178, 245
Bailey, Tom—MonA MA321, MA357
Bainton, Roland H.—AvWYX W109; Ment MD127
Baird, Jack—GM 557; PermaH P76
Baker, Asa (Brett Halliday)—ArM 8
Baker, Brenda—Fab Z136; FabF Z164
Baker, Carlotta—Cent 90; Knick nn; NSLF 29; Prize 64
Baker, Charles Jr—Dell 492
Baker, Denys Val—BelLB L92-589; CreB 122; Pyr G341, F681, R955
Baker, Dorothy—ASE S10; AvG G1118; AvS S173; Pen 561, 604; Signet 1088
Baker, Sgt. George—ASE 719
Baker, Ledru Jr—AceD S122; GM 183, 244, 841; NovF 5033
Baker, Rachel—Pop 712
Baker, Samm Sinclair—BB A1746; Grap 97, 135
Baker, W. Howard—Lan 73-628, 73-646, 73-659, 73-671, 74-511
Balch, Glenn—AceD D208, D372; Com 31; PocJr J50
Balchin, Nigel—CWC 206, 231; Lan 73-625; Lion 31; Signet 674
Baldwin, Bates—AvT T72; Pock 884; PopLG G186; PopSP SP134
Baldwin, Faith—BB 411, 455, 471; Dell 12, 73, 116, 138, 163, 196, 236, 255, 288, 318, 368, 445, 475, 532, 574; DellD D317, D399, D402, D415 7, 5, 30; Pock 150, 311, 380, 445, 456, 513, 603, 613, 658; PockB B41; Pony 51; SupR M637
Baldwin, Hanson W.—AvWYX W117
Baldwin, James—Signet 1138, S1559
Baldwin, Linton—Lion 227
Baldwin, Monica—Signet S1371, D1601
Baldwin, Peter—Pyr F828
Ball, John—AvS S308
Ballard, P.D.—GM D1352, D1486
Ballard, Willis Todhunter—AceA A9; Bann B40-105; BB A1600; BDSM 9; CardE C277; CWC 496, 525; GM 259; Grap 18, 26, 65, 72; MonB 134, 356; Pen 566; Pop 454, 476, 492, 524, 552, 617, 638, 680, 735, 772; PopLE EB83, EB93; PopLG G249, G255, G309, G320, G335, G411, G440; PopSP SP259; Tower 42-778
Ballinger, Bill S.—GM K1529; Signet 730, 774, 897, 1040, 1134, 1243, 1274, 1319, 1321, 1494, 1585, 1730, S1794
Ballinger, W.A.—Lan 73-669, 74-513
Balmer, Edwin—ASE 801; Dell 627
Balmer, Jon—ExNM 19; Rain 104
Bamm, Peter—Signet S1512
Banigan,—FFS nn
Bankhead, Tallulah—DelID D132
Banks, Harold—AvV V2173
Banks, Polan—Pop 319; Signet D2282
Banks, Raymond—PopLG G495, G547
Banks, Rosie M.—Perma MA4153; Pock 1243
Bannett, Dorothy—Chec 11
Bannett, Fifi—Chec 11
Banning, Margaret Culkin—Dell 381
Bannion, Della—NovF 5028
Bannister, Pat—GM K1418
Bannon, Ann—GM s653, d833, s919, S965, S977, S1066, D1195, D1224, D1411, D1434
Barber,—ASE 1130
Barber, Rowland—AvS S102; AvV V2050; CardE C210; Dell 671
Barber, W.A.—Pen 524, 531, 542
Barbera, Joe—DellFE B199
Barbette, Jay—BB 1076, 1349
Bard, Daniel—PopLG G516
Bardon, Minna—MNC 42
Bardwell, Denver—FWN 5; GWN 10; WNM nn
Barker, R.S.—FFS nn
Barker, Richard—Dell 733
Barker, Shirley—DelID D107
Barkley, John—MonB 238
Barksdale, Bob—NSLS U184
Barlay, Bennett—Eers 4
Barley, Rex—Signet P2401
Barnard, Allan—Dell 414, 797
Barnard, Charles N.—Barn nn; CreB d256
Barnes, Margaret Ayer—AvV V2067
Barnes, Margaret Campbell—Dell 563; Harl 169
Barnet, Cybelle—Lan 74-975
Barnet, Sylvan—Ment MD195, MD216, MT287
Barnett, Lincoln—Ment M71, MD231
Barnhart, Clarence—BB F1299; PermaS P130
Barns, Glenn M.—AceD S142; BM B162, B175; JonM J94; Perma M3114
Barnwell, J.O.—Signet 1366

Baron, Alexander—BB A1634; PopLG G243; Signet 872
Baron, Stanley—AceD S91; Bal 3
Baroni, Nick—Fie 1
Barr, Cecil—Bea B133; IN 2; UR nn
Barr, George—PopLG G426
Barr, Tyrone C.—CHARf CB150
Barrett, Gloria—Lan 75-014
Barrett, Michael—CreB 153; GM S1206, K1577
Barrett, Monte—ASE 807; Croy nn; Pop 224, 270, 311, 630; PopLG G137, G207, G445
Barrett, Neal Jr—Lan 74-721, 75-133
Barrett, William E.—CardE C247; Penn P54; Pock 924
Barrie, Alexander—Bal X553
Barrie, Susan—Harl 572, 580, 587, 628, 687, 730, 765, 779, 792, 831, 904, 926, 967
Barrington, Lowell—Pop 670
Barron, Dave—PopLE EB19
Barron, Mike "Pitcher"—BelLB L92-544
Barrows, Marjorie—ASE H234
Barrows, R.M.—Best 592
Barry, Iris—MonB 424
Barry, Jack—Pyr G322
Barry, Jane—AvN N129
Barry, Jerome—DellD D369; MNC 83, 86
Barry, Joe—AceD D47; FMS 2; Han 42, 52, 63, 106; Harl 43, 83, 84, 101; Phan 500; PrizeMN 12
Barry, Peter—GM K1349
Barry, Philip—Pock 102
Barry, Winchell—Bea B290; IN 33
Barrymore, Diana—Signet D1490
Barstow, Stan—AvG G1136
Bartdorf, Steve—Fran F13
Bartell, Don—Novs 6N228; Saber SA34
Barth, Alan—CardE C32
Barth, John—AvGS GS2; AvNS NS40; AvT T481; AvVS VS5, VS18
Bartimeus,—CWC 52
Bartlett, George H.—PelB P18
Bartlett, John—Perma M5002; PermaS P205S
Bartlett, Sy—BB 743
Bartly, Jack—Saber SA99
Bartolini, Elio—LionLL LB163
Barton, Bruce—ASE N4, I250; PermaH P49; Pock 40
Barton, Erle—VegaSFL VSF7
Barton, Fred B.—PermaH P32
Barton, Jacques—Pop 498, 611, 659, 708, 729, 768, 793, 826; PopLG G322; PopSP SP253
Barton, Jack (Joseph Chadwick)—PopLG G433, G446, g504
Barton, Minna—BK 24; BIH 14
Baruch, Bernard—CardGC GC4
Basinsky, Earle—Signet 1286, 1351
Bass, Frank—Pock 1247
Bass, Lonny—Saber SA9
Bassett, J.K.—PockB B88
Bassett, Jack—Perma M3054
Bassett, James E.—Signet T2387
Bassett, Marjorie—Harl 538
Bassing, Eileen—BB F1807
Bassler, Dr. Anthony—Av 227
Basso, Hamilton—CardE C229; PopSP SP89
Bast, William—Bal 180
Batchelor, Paula—AvT T171
Bates, H.E.—BB 820; PockB B78; Pop 550, 654, 683; PopLG G127, G192, G565; PopSP SP37, SP204; Signet D2119, S1602, S1649
Bates, Marsha—FabR Z1
Bauer, W.W.—DellFE B101
Baum, L. Frank—AvZS ZS12; CreB S395, K674
Baum, Vicki—Av 64, 265; BartH 28; Dell 524; DelID D239; DellF F83; PermaS P109, P208; Pyr G328; SPE 108
Baumann, Margaret—Harl 641, 671, 778, 827, 842, 947
Baume, Eric—ASE 805; Harl 296; PermaS P235
Bawden, Nina—Lan 74-552, 75-064, 75-430
Bax, Roger—Dell 634; MM 176; Pock 606, 716
Baxter, George Owen—Signet 785
Baxter, John—AceG G588; Av 647, 836; AvT T78
Baxter, Walter—PopLG G121, G151; PopSP SP41
Bayard, James—MonS MS14
Bayer, Oliver Weld—ASE 983
Bayer, Sanford—Bal S601
Bayley, James—PocL PL518
Bayliss, Marguerite F.—ASE S32
Bayliss, Raymond—AceH H68
Bayne, Jessica—Lan 72-755
Baynes, Jack—CreB 195, 224, 234, 325, 344
Bazin, Hervée—Hill 167
Beach,—AceK K128S
Beach, Edward L.—Perma M4061; Signet S1043, S1459
Beach, Rex—ASE 1195; BLA 19; Harl 241
Beagle, Peter S.—BalAF 01503, 02892
Beal, Sam—Lan 70-041
Beam,—DiaL nn
Beard, Charles A.—ASE P29
Beard, James A.—DellX X1; Perma M4030; Pyr R494
Beasley, Norman—BantA A3
Beater, Jack—DellFE B113
Beatty, Jerome Jr—BB 1523
Beatty, Betty—Harl 737, 790, 824
Beaty, David—Perma M4093; PopLG G168
Beauchamp, D.D.—ASE 900

316

Beauchamp, Loren (Robert Silverberg)—Midw 7, 18, 21, 29, 30, 65, 70, 74, 86, F102, F145, F206, F276, F292
Beaumont, Charles—Bal F641; BB A1759, A1917, A2087; DellF F94; GM D1586; NCH 7N730
Bechdolt, F.M.—Cent 81
Bechdolt, Frederick R.—ANC 28; ASE J275; Cent 52, 102; Penn P30, P57; WNC 49, 75
Beck, Calvin T.—Bal F680
Becker, Belle—DellF F57
Becker, Beril—Pyr G86
Becker, Don—VegaSFL VSF13
Becker, Edwin J.—Lion 84
Becker, Stephen—DellFE C101; DSSE nn; GM 994
Beckford, William—BalAF 02279
Beckhard, Arthur—AvB Bard 9
Beckhardt, Israel—Pop 734
Beckman, Charles Jr—Fal 44
Bedford, James H.—ASE 1081
Bedwell, Harry—ASE M17
Bee, Clair—AceT T137
Beebe, William—ASE F161
Beech, Jane—Harl 575
Beech, Webb—GM S1212, K1431, K1467, D1548
Beeding, Francis—Av nn(37); Pen 544; Pop 42, 57, 71, 268, 381; RA 9; TNC 11, 19
Beely, James—Fab Z145
Beer, Thomas—ASE S13, 668
Beerbohm, Max—ASE C67
Begner, Edith P.—AvV V2182; CreB D483, D519; Lan 75-184, 75-360
Behan, Brendan—AvSS SS2, SS22; AvV V2033; AvWYX W182
Behan, Leslie—Dom 84700; Lan 72-764, 72-930
Bekker, C.D.—Bal 183; BalU U2210
Belbenoit, Rene—BB 728
Belinkie, Helen—AvV V2190
Bell, Joseph N.—AvG G1075
Bell, Josephine—AceK K198; Bal F706, F727, F767; BalU U2154, U2155, U2156, U2157, U2158, U2159
Bell, Steve—NSLS U176
Bell, Thomas—ASE 1007, 1020
Bell, Vereen—ASE C68, 743; BB 97, 1225; Dell 582
Bell, Wyatt—GM S1149
Bellah, James Warner—Bal 44, 352K; BalU U1054; GM 155, S1218; Lion 43; Pop 195, 380, 404; PopLE EB3; PopLG G350; Regy RB323
Bellaman, H.—Lan 73-402
Bellaman, Henry—ASE E150
Bellaman, K.—Lan 73-402
Bellamy, Henry—AceK K187; CardE C2; CardGC GC55; CreB M660
Bellamy, Francis Rufus—AceD D79; ASE 1303
Bellamy, Harmon—Crow 30, 38, 44; QB 39, 41, 66; Venus 109, 110
Bellamy, Jean—Lan 74-520, 74-597
Bellem, Robert Leslie—Han 118; Harl 106
Beller, William—AB A1765
Bellow, Saul—CreB M780, R857, M868, M879; PopLG G289; PopSP SP 2, SP56
Bellus, Jean—CreB 266
Belmont, Jack—Powe PP132
Belmonte, Juan—BB A1160
Bemelmans, Ludwig—ASE S3, P4; Pen 637; Pock 306; Signet 693, 776, 858, 1278, P2008
Benchley, Nathaniel—CreB S448; PopSP SP178; Pyr G431
Benchley, Robert—ASE M4, R5, T13, B39, G192, 865; Pock 449
Bender, James—SigK K313; Signet 889
Bender, William Jr—AceD S198
Benedict, Gerald—Edell nn
Benedict, Jack—NSLS 7A
Benedict, Ruth—Ment M89; PelB P2
Benefield, Barry—ASE M10, 710, 1127; BB 24
Benet, James—BB 825; BM B146
Benét, Rosemary—ASE L1
Benét, Stephen Vincent—ASE L1, N3, C77, H215, 855, 1114; Pen 546; Pock 360
Bengtsson, Frans G.—Signet D1391
Benjamin, Elda—Cent 12
Benjamin, Lois—AvS S123
Benjamin, Philip—AvS S168
Bennett, Adrian—AvG G1101
Bennett, Alan—Croy 40, 94
Bennett, Arnold—ASE H214, 830
Bennett, Dorothea—CreB K802
Bennett, Dorothy—BDM 1
Bennett, Dwight—BB 1001, 1141; Lan 70-075, 73-734, 73-764, 75-334; Penn P21; Perma M3023, M3045
Bennett, Edna—LionLL LL17; Pop 777
Bennett, George—DellLE LB126
Bennett, Hall—Cent 97; Hanro 4; IN 19; Knick nn; Pyr 14
Bennett, Hall (on cover)/ Thomas Stone—Priv 2
Bennett, Harry—AM 185
Bennett, James O'Donnell—Prem d81
Bennett, Jay—CreB S524
Bennett, Margot—CreB s332
Bennett, Moll—NSLF 104
Bennett, William—Fab Z126; FabR Z4
Benney, Mark—Av 470
Benoit, Pierre—AceF F281
Bensen, D.R.—Pyr R851, R962

Benson, Ben—BB 1014, 1070, 1271, 1323, 1359, 1421, 1468, 1552, A1698, 1909, 1910, 1974, 2001; GM s583; Penn P4, P16
Benson, Ezra Taft—MonS MS11
Benson, G.R.—ReaL nn
Benson, O.G.—DellFE A200
Benson, Sally—ASE 699; BB 15, A1891; Pock 332
Bentham, Alan—WH W101
Bentley, E.C.—Bal F690; Dell 704; Pen 510; Pock 269
Bentley, Patricia—Lan 75-028
Bentley, Phyllis—AceK K183
Benton, Jesse James—ASE I256, 708
Benton, John L.—GreD 14
Benuto, Rita—HollN HH152
Benwood, Arthur—TNL 6, 7, 8, 21, 22
Benzoni, Juliette—AvV V2176
Beran, A.J.—AvT T150
Berckman, Evelyn—AceF F175, F202; Dell 841, 936; DellD D268, D345
Berczeller, Richard—AvV V2129
Berenstain, Janice—BB 1074; Dell 998; DellD D427, D447; DellFE 50, B143, B166
Berenstain, Stanley—BB 1074; Dell 998; DellD D427, D447; DellFE 50, B143, B166
Beresford-Howe, Constance—Bal 112
Berg, Louis—BB 427, A2008; Harl 191, 258
Berg, Pierre—HollH HH182
Bergamini, David—PopSP SP138
Bergaust, Erik—BB A1765
Berger, Meyer—ASE K17, 757
Berger, Thomas—CreB M851
Bergman, Lee—Pyr G443
Bergner, Edith—AvS S150
Bergquist, Lillian—Grap 84
Berkeley, Anthony—Pock 307, 814
Berle, Milton—BB 550; CreB S414
Berlin, Isaiah—Ment MD172, M198
Berman, Harold—Pock 187
Bernard—Lan 75-036
Bernard, Ronald—CHARf CB114
Bernard, William—Lan 74-859; Pop 392, 743; PopLG G321
Bernhard, Hubert J.—Ment M52, Ms114
Bernstein, Abraham—Chec 8
Bernstein, Morey—CardGC GC37; Lan 75-042
Bernstein, Walter—ASE 903
Berrill, N.J.—CardE C169; Prem d50, d80
Berrill, N.S.—Prem S26
Berry, Don—AceK K133
Berry, James R.—Las 31
Berry, John—Hill F202; Signet S2241
Berryman, Oral Leigh—NSLS U168
Berson, Fred—PopLG G122
Berto, Giuseppe—Signet S971, 1053
Berzen, A.H.—AceD S126
Besnard, Marie—AvG G1215
Bessie, Oscar—Lan 72-799, 72-960
Best, Herbert—ASE R28; CardE C184
Best, Winfield—Bal F532
Best, Winifred—BalU U2136
Bester, Alfred—BerkG G19; Signet 1105, S1389, S1524, S1593
Beston, Henry—ASE K12, 660
Beveridge, Elizabeth—Pock 217
Beverley-Giddings, A.R.—ASE M20; Pock 946
Beyer, William—BartH 24
Beymer, William Gilmore—ASE 1258
Bezzerides, A.I.—BB 750, A1768; Dell 416; Lion 153
Bickham, Jack M.—AceD D308, D384, D442, D462, D510; AceF F120
Bickham, John M.—AceG G754
Biddle, Livingston Jr—Pop 402
Bienvenue, Harold—Av N126
Bier, Jesse—AvV V2082
Bierce, Ambrose—Av 628
Bierstadt, Edward Hale—PopLE EB16
Biggers, Earl Derr—ASE E130; Av nn(17), 337, 344, 350; Dell 47; Pock 50, 133, 168, 191, 207; PockB B57, B68; Pop 132; QR 131; ReaL nn
Biggle, Lloyd Jr—AceD D485
Billany, Dan—BCD 9
Billings, Buck—Harl 226; Pyr 182
Binder, Eando—BelLB B50-852
Binder, Otto—BB F3569
Bingham, Carson—Bel 203; MonB 194, 227, 283, 372, 487; MonMS MM603, MM606
Bingham, John—Dell 813, 873, 941; DellD D351
Binns, Archie—ASE L31, B47
Bird, Brandon—Dell 531, 857
Bird, Horace V.—BB A1340
Birkenfeld, Gunther—Av 675
Birkley, Dolan—BartH 8
Birmingham, Frederic A.—BB F1688
Birmingham, Stephen—CardE C342; CreB T878
Birney, Earle—CWC 534
Birney, Hoffman—BB A1017; Perma M4073
Birren, Faber—Pyr G423
Bisch, Dr. Louis E.—CreB D432, D642; Perma M4013; PermaH P60; Prem d57
Bischoff, David—Las 30
Bishop, Curtis—ASE 1192, 1275; BB 108; Pyr 230

Bishop, George—Vega V14
Bishop, Jim—BB F1428, F2035; CardGC GC73; GM 351; MonHBS MB504
Bishop, John Peale—AvNS NS17
Bishop, Leonard—GM D1125, K1247; MonK K53; PopSP SP11, SP106; Pyr G206; Signet D1009, D1107
Bishop, Malden Grange—AceD D40
Bishop, Sheila—AceK K192, K212
Bishop, Lt. Col. William A.—AceA A24
Bissell, Betty—BB A1897
Bissell, Richard—BB F1740; Signet 876, 1129, 1193, 1230, S1425, S1731
Bixby, Jerome—BalU U2203
Black, Edgar—MonK K56
Black, Gavin—Bann B60-102
Black, Hillel—Perma M4103
Black, Ian Stuart—CreB s322
Black, Lucy—BB F1558
Black, Tedd—Fran F9
Black, Thomas B.—BB 1448; BM B138, B151; JonM J37, J41; MM 123, 187
Blackburn, Barbara—AceK K258
Blackburn, John—Lan 73-583
Blackburn, Thomas W.—BB 207, 958, 1164, A1798; DellFE A171; DellTC 20; Penn P1
Blacker, Irwin R.—Signet D1897, S2063
Blackerby, Curtis—StarSt nn
Blackmore, Jane—AceK K264, K289, K303; CWC 409; Lan 74-528, 75-479
Blackmore, R.D.—PocL PL508
Blackstock, Charity—BalU U2123, U2124, U2125, U2126, U2127, U2128, U2129
Blackstock, Lee—DellD D301
Blackstone, Harry—PermaH P15
Blackwood, Algernon—ASE S26
Blair, Clay Jr—Bal 134; Signet D1692
Blair, Joan—Harl 648, 672, 703, 811, 907
Blair, Kathryn—Harl 633, 650, 667, 682, 700, 717, 749, 766, 785, 805, 823, 843, 861, 878, 893, 920, 941, 954, 972
Blair, Lyle—PockB B12
Blair, Raymond—Carn 914, 948
Blair, Walter—ASE 716
Blaisdell, Ann—CreB S518
Blaisdell, Anne—Lan 73-653
Blake, Andrea—Harl 755, 864, 944, 974
Blake, Bud—AvFS F170
Blake, Eleanor—Pen 571
Blake, Fredric—Powe PP122
Blake, Forrester—BB 989, A1808, A1809
Blake, Nicholas—ASE 1031; BCD 7; BM B193; CreB S388; CWC nn, 66, 202, 268, 450; DellD D227, D339; MM 147; Pen 543, 592; Pock 548, 742; Pop 30, 41, 60, 123
Blake, Rodger—CrAS FB1011
Blake, Roger—Fab Z151, Z155, Z157; Fran F57; Saber SA28
Blake, Steve—MeritS 7M810, 7M813
Blake, Walker E.—MonB 279, 419, 556
Blake, William—ASE 1145
Blanc, Suzanne—Lan 74-578
Blanco, Antonio de Fierro—ASE K19
Bland, Margot—PopLE EB9; PopLG G368
Blankfort, Michael—Lan 1256; Dell 686; MM 185; Signet P2300
Blanton, Smiley MD—CreB R832
Blassingame, Wyatt—BartH 5; PopLG G438
Blatty, William Peter—CreB D763; Lan 70-001
Blayne, Sebastian—VFS 175, 325; GMB 46
Blechman, Burt—AvG G1228
Bleiler, Everett F.—BB 1328; BerkG G233
Bligh, Norman—Cam 303, 313, 316, 344, 357; Crow 39, 42; EcsNM nn(3), nn(5), nn(9); ExNM nn; NSLF 155; OrigN 702, 727, 740, 741; QB 47, 78, 79, 81, 84, 89, 94; Star 763, 765; Venus 106, 107, 120, 130, 148, 151, 162, 177, 186, 188
Blish, James—AceA A29; AvFS F122; AvG G1268, G1280; AvS S210, S218, S221, S313, S337; AvT T193, T225, T238, T268, T279; AvWYX W187; Bal 197, 465K, F647; BalU U2251, U2331; BEDN 256; BelLB 92-612; GSFN 16, 19; Lan 73-580; Signet S1622, S1719
Bliss, Arthur—CHARf CB160
Bliss, Tip—Chec 2
Blizard, Marie—GreD 29, 32
Bloch, Blanche—MM 90
Bloch, Robert—AceD D59, S67, D265; Av 211, 494; AvMN 9; AvSp nn; Bel 233, 90-275; BelLB B50-787, L92-527, L92-530, L92-537; CreB S385, K615; GM S1192, S1231; Lan 73-615; Lion 185; NCH 7N730; PopLG G532; Pyr F839; Regy RB101
Blochman, Lawrence G.—BM B140; Dell 7, 43, 134, 156, 311, 488, 638, 740, 833; DellTC 19; Han 128; Pock 793; SigK Ks350
Block, Anita Rowe—PopLG G298
Block, Eugene B.—AvT T398
Block, Lawrence—Bel 236; GM S1085, S1162, K1555, D1722
Block, Libbie—Dell 344
Blond, Georges—Pyr R318
Blood, Matthew—GM 235, 423, 924
Bloodstone, John (Stuart J. Byrne)—Powe PP205
Bloom, Murray Teigh—Bal F435K

Brock, Stuart—AceD D23, D166, D573; Dell 337; Grap 136; Pyr 255, 333, F927; RCL 38
Broderick, Gerry P.—Pyr 33, 148, G481, F897
Brodman, John—Lan 75-343
Brodrick, Alan H.—ASE R16
Brogan, D.W.—ASE R16
Bromberg, Lester—RetD nn
Brome, Vincent—Pyr G379, R616
Bromfield, Louis—ASE L7, S31, T32, Q34, I265, 811, 845; Av 52; AvMSS 13, 24; BB 28, 462, A869, A910, 957; BerkG G36; BM B6; CardE C138; Lan 70-003; Pen 512; Pock 56; PopLG G179; Pyr R305; X968; Signet 904AB, S954, S979, S1025, D1260, D1263
Bromley, Joseph—ASE F158
Bronson, F.W.—MM 148
Bronstein, Yetta—AvS S250
Bronte, Anne—Lan 74-854
Bronte, Charlotte—ASE I268; CardE C88; PocL PL44; QR 110
Bronte, Emily—CardE C33; PBCE nn(20); Pock 7; PocL PL10; QR 122; SigC CD10
Broocks, Schuyler—DHM 28
Brook, Ian—PopSP SP171
Brook, Peter—AvDYD D11
Brooke, Rupert—ASE 776
Brooker, Clark—Bal 121, 198
Brooks, George S.—ASE 1064
Brooks, Grant R.—NSLS 10A
Brooks, John—BerkG G187; CardE C340; Pock 767
Brooks, R.—SPE 110
Brooks, Richard—CardE C84
Brooks, Van Wyck—AvNS NS34; AvVS VS2
Brooks, William Allan—Knick nn
Brooks, Win—Pock 984
Brophy, John—CWC 51, 91
Brossard, Chandler—DellD D137; GM D1670; PocSp 10139; Pop 626; Pyr G260, G592; Regy RB302; Signet 974, S1971
Brothers, Joyce—Perma M4125
Brothers, William—GM s403; Hill 111
Brough, James—Pyr T934
Broward, Donn—AceD D432
Browd, Victor L.—CreB T783
Brower, Millicent—BEDN 286K
Brower, Reuben A.—DellLE LB157
Brown,—NSLS 17A; PocSp 10012
Brown, Alan MD—Harl 415
Brown, Beth—Av 97; BelLB L92-545, L92-554; CLN 26; Fed 2; Harl 224; IN 38; PrizeLN 28; RomN nn
Brown, Carter—Signet 1527, 1565, 1594, 1606, 1620, 1633, 1654, 1663, 1674, 1694, 1713, 1722, 1738, 1740, 1764, 1767, 1784, S1801, S1806, S1817, S1836, S1845, S1856, S1896, S1909, S1919, S1924, S1950, S1981, S1989, S2009, S2023, S2033, S2048, S2110, S2122, S2140, S2148, S2180, S2196, S2220, S2228, S2244, S2259, S2275, S2291, S2344, S2365, S2394, G2400
Brown, Dee—Bal 202; Perma M3101
Brown, Douglas (Walter Gibson)—MonA MA320
Brown, Elwood—Pony 127
Brown, Eugene—Pock 964, 1212
Brown, Francis—Ment M104
Brown, Fredric—BB 302, 361, 735, 783, 831, 835, 876, 943, 990, 1040, 1077, 1133, 1134, 1176, 1215, 1216, 1253, 1285, 1312, 1423, 1436, A1546, 1565, 1566, 1567, A1615, A1701, 1712, 1757, A1812, 1990, 2030, A2135, A2187, J2587; DellFE 2E; DellTC 33; GM S1132; Lan 73-727; Penn P59; Tower 42-502
Brown, Gerald—BCD 20; HH 7
Brown, Harry—ASE 941; Lion 76; Signet S1467
Brown, Helen Evans—Pyr R494
Brown, Helen Gurley—AvV V2147
Brown, Horace—Strl nn
Brown, J.—NSLS 19A
Brown, Joe David—CardC C315; Pock 645, 810, 1162
Brown, Joe E.—ASE S19
Brown, Joy—Harl 72
Brown, Lyle—Pock 996
Brown, Marion—CardE C85
Brown, Marion Marsh—AvFS F157; AvG G1320
Brown, Pete—DellD D155
Brown, Rosel George—Bal F703; Lan 75-278
Brown, Russell S.—Novs 6N274
Brown, Dr. Walter C.—MonHBS MB515
Brown, Warren—ASE 1197
Brown, Wenzell—Av 560, 722; AvT T235; Bel 90-265; FSM 6, 38; GM 292, s522, 640, s734, s897, s917, S1013, S1042, S1160; Lan 72-769, 74-897, 75-026; MonB 276, 293, 403, 460; MonHBS MB510; PermaS P186; Pop 374, 549, 581, 685, 732, 734; PopLG G228, G317; Pyr G345, G439, G609; Signet 981
Brown, Will C.—Dell 878, 986; DellFE A183, B194; Pop 715; PopLE EB91; PopLG G624
Brown, William F.—Signet S1652, S1743
Brown-Burnham, Creighton—Pyr G414
Browne, Eleanore—Lion 73; NovL 26
Browne, Howard—Dell 894
Browne, Lewis—Av 54
Browning, Elizabeth Barrett—ASE 939; Av 251; AvB Bard 11; AvGS GS11
Browning, Robert—ASE 939
Bruce, Eva—ASE M19

Bruce, Jean—CreB K795, K806
Bruce, Robert—Lion 226
Brucker, Margaretta—DHM 20
Bruff, Nancy—ASE 1104; Harl 1; Pyr 24
Brunini, John Gilland—GM s312
Brunner, John—AceD D335, D362, D385, D391, D421, D457, D465, D471, D507, D547; AceF F133, F161, F215, F227, F242, F277, F299, F361; AceG G592, G649, G664, G709, G761; AceM M115, M123; AvS S323; BalU U2219, U2329; Lan 73-797, 75-346; Pyr F829
Brunner, Lousene Rousseau—AvS S104, S253
Bruno, Mike—HollH HH117
Brush, Katharine—Av nn(22), 154, 192, 239; AvMN 12; AvMSS 48; DellTC 18
Brussel, J.—Bru nn
Bryan, C.D.B.—CreB T891
Bryan, George S.—ASE D103
Bryan, Joseph III—Bal 67, 228, 692
Bryan, Michael—DellFE 88, A145
Bryant, Arthur Herbert—Berk 317; Harl 4
Bryant, Rear Adm. Ben—Bal F447K
Bryant, Matt—Berk 333
Bryant, Peter—AceD D350, D551; AceF F210
Bryson, Leigh—Han 60
Buchan, John—ANC 1, 4; BB 31, 71, 1143; Pock 69, 94; PopLG G531
Buchan, William—Lan 73-522
Büchner, Georg Jr—AvWYX YW172
Buchwald, Art—CardE C350; CreB D571, D662, D762; LionLL LL80
Buck, Frank—Pock 47
Buck, Pearl S.—ASE nn; AvMSS 23; BartH 21; CardE C46, C105, C108, C111, C114, C308, C334, C372; CardGC GC35, GC41, GC46; DellTC 8; MM 19; Pen 505; Pock nn, 11, 359, 642, 679, 951, 993
Buckingham, Nancy—AceG G676; AceK X283, X302; Lan 74-507
Buckler, Ernest—Signet S1090
Buckley, David—PopLG G227
Buckmaster, Henrietta—ASE R39
Buckner, Robert—Perma M4185; Signet S1597
Budd, Lillian—Pock 994
Budrys, Algis—Bal 388K; BEDN 243; GM S1057, L1474; Lan 73-810; Lion 230; Pyr G339, G416, F693; Regy RB110
Buel, J.W.—AmFH nn(2)
Buell, John—CreB 408
Bugbee, Emma—Com 6
Bukowski, Charles—EHO 0115
Bulfinch, Thomas—DellLE LX111
Bull, Lois—DPN 1; Harl 314; MagV 6, 7; NovL 14, 23
Bull, Terry—FFS nn
Bullett, Gerald—PockB B24
Bullitt, William—AvWYX W119
Bullock, Alan—BB F1896
Bulmer, Kenneth—AceD D255, D331, D369, D453, D507; AceF F104, F209, F285, F289, F396; AceG G625, G680; AceH H20, H65; AceM M111, M131
Bulosan, Carlos—BB 48
Bunce, Frank—Pock 777; PockB B53
Bunch, A.—Saber SA158, SA160
Bunin, Ed—Regy RB316
Bunker, Robert—Signet S1691
Bunyan, John—PockB B32; PocL PL53
Bunyan, Pat—NSLS U103; Saber SA16
Burch, Guy I.—PelB P17
Burchardt, Bill—AceF F214
Burchell, Mary—Harl 409, 422, 461, 468, 478, 494, 521, 528, 533, 546, 565, 603, 605, 616, 627, 658, 686, 712, 746, 782, 813, 837, 844, 871, 895, 915, 956
Burdick, Eugene—CreB D365, R546, M880, T889; DellF F60
Burgan, John—AvT T265
Burgess,—Lan 74-852
Burgess, Alan—BB A1800
Burgess, Ann Marie—Bel 226; MonHBS MB539
Burgess, Eric—CWC 480
Burgess, Michael—Bel 226; MonHBS MB539
Burghley, Rose—Harl 617, 928, 960
Burke, Jack—BB 1311
Burke, James Wakefield—Berk 106; BerkG G164; LionLL LL135; Pop 1060; PopLG G126; Pyr 164, G263
Burke, John—AvS S304; Signet D2172
Burke, Noel—BartH 7
Burke, Richard—ArM 5; Croy 9; Dell 204, 260; Han 64; Pop 310
Burke, Thomas—NSLF 68
Burleson, Terry—Rain 122
Burlingame, Roger—AvFS F113; AvG G1274; SigK K321, Ks327, K337; Signet S1280; SigSE nn
Burman, Ben Lucien—ASE T27, 999, 1096; BB A1439; Pock 363
Burnett, Constance Buel—PyrPR PG34
Burnett, David—Bal S383K, S473K, S572, S695
Burnett, Hallie—Bal 466K; BB A1550; DellD D237; Pop 541; PopLE EB28; PopLG G352
Burnett, Hugh—CreB S663
Burnett, Stan—MonHBS MB532
Burnett, W.R.—ASE 019, 1161; Av 66, 212, 329; AvMMM 33, 40; AvS S222; BB 826, 888, 942, 998, 1124, A1331, 1547, A1819, A1871, 1973; GM 106,

S1145; GMB 3; Hill 20; Lan 71-307; Penn P7; Pock 714; PopLG G538
Burnett, Whit—ASE 848; AvAn nn(1); Bal 466K, F598; BB A1550; Perma M3094; Pock 276; PopLE EB28; PopLG G352; Pyr G361
Burns, Elizabeth—PopSP SP35
Burns, Eugene—DellD D148; Prem d23
Burns, James MacGreger—AvG G1063; AvNS NS14
Burns, John Horne—BB A807, A1146, 1147; PopLG G194
Burns, Robert E.—Pyr 45
Burns, Vincent G. (as told to)—Pyr 58, 191, G377, G549
Burns, Walter Noble—ASE 1108; Pen 514, 520; Signet 1085, S1205
Burroughs, Edgar Rice—AceA A25; AceF F156, F157, F158, F159, F168, F169, F170, F171, F179, F180, F181, F182, F189, F190, F193, F194, F203, F204, F205, F206, F212, F213, F220, F221, F232, F233, F234, F235, F245, F247, F256, F258, F268, F270, F280, F282; AceG G733, G734, G735, G736, G737, G738, G739, G745, G748; ASE M16, 022; Bal F701, F702, F711, F728, F739, F745, F746, F747, F748, F749, F750, F751, F752, F753, F754, F762, F770, F772, F776, F777; BalU U2001, U2002, U2003, U2004, U2005, U2006, U2007, U2008, U2009, U2010, U2011, U2012, U2013, U2014, U2015, U2016, U2017, U2018, U2019, U2020, U2021, U2022, U2023, U2024, U2031, U2032, U2033, U2034, U2036, U2037, U2038, U2039, U2040, U2041, U2045, U2046, U2048, U6039; BLA 23; ChB 18900, 28903; Dell 320, 536
Burroughs, John Coleman—Bal U6035
Burroughs, William—AceK X202
Burstela, Joseph PhD—MeritS 7M811
Burt, Katharine Newlin—Dell 191
Burt, Kendal—BEDN F262
Burt, Struthers—ASE B53
Burtis, Thomas—Harl 312, 315
Burton, Carl D.—BB 1517
Burton, Miles—CWC nn, 55, 100, 200, 252, 289, 415
Burtt, Edwin A.—Ment MD131
Busbee, James Jr—AvT AT64, T73
Busch, Fritz-Otto—BerkG G115
Busch, Harald—Bal 120, F678
Busch, Niven—ASE N17; BB 777, 1204; Pop 102, 489, 770; PopLE EB94; PopSP SP200
Bush, Raymond—PelB P9
Bushnell, O.A.—AceK K114
Butcher, Capt. Harry C.—ASE 1102
Butcher, Margaret Just—Ment MD206
Butler, Gerald—Dell 197, 242, 511, 726; Lion 81
Butler, Ivan—PapLS 66-627
Butler, Penelope—Harl 660
Butler, Samuel—JL nn(4); Pock 8; QR 129; RoyG 29; WSP W561
Butterworth, W.E.—Signet S1918, D2076, D2151
Byram, George—AvFS F199; MonB 117
Byrd, Richard E.—AceK K102T, K188
Byrne, Brendan—BB A1414
Byrne, Donn—ASE N21, F151; AvG G1140; Pen 611
Byrne, Jack—Pop 449
Byrne, Stuart J.—Powe PP165
Byron, James—AceD D197
Cabell, James Branch—AvVS VS7; BalAF 01678, 01763, 01855, 02067, 02364, 02545; Pen 601
Cabot, Isabel—AceD D532
Cadell, Elizabeth—BerkG G209; Harl 448, 473
Cadwallader, Clyde T.—Hill S188
Caen, Herb—PermaS P261
Caesar, Gene—MonA MA338; Pop 614
Cahill, Holger—ASE 1249
Cahn, Robert—AvG G1066
Caidin, Martin—Bal F201, F322K, F323K, F359K, F404K, F425K, F467K, F514K, F549, F583, F737, F764; BEDN F248; PyrPR PR35
Caillou, Alan—AvS S279; Signet D1986, D2120, P2371, P2426
Cain, James M.—ASE Q2, 766, 1058; Av 60, 99, 137, 141, 161, 174, 348, 421, 455, 479, 581, 599, 768; AvMMM 6, 16, 20, 44; AvMN 1, 17; AvMSS 22; AvT T285; MM 1; Pen 591, 621; Pock 443; PockB B11, B30; Signet 680, 720, 759, 784, 811, 1152, 1153, 1195, 1427, 1445
Cain, Paul—Av 178, 268, 496; Bond 10; Chart 21
Caird, Janet—AceH H50, H106
Cairns, David—ASE MM 170
Calahan, H.A.—PocJr J69
Calder, Ritchie—Ment MD217; SigK Ks320
Caldwell, John—Carn 902, 936, 945; Crow 36; QB 40, 42
Caldwell, Erskine—AAP nn; ASE P19, 866, 945; Av 134, 151, 177, 309, 340; AvMSS 14, 30; CardE C270; CWC 257, 335, 346; NovSl 51, 52; Pen 567, 581, 627, 646; Pock 392; SigK Ks344; Signet 661, 686, 705, 732, 760, 818, 838, 869, 899, 918, 933, 983, 1016, 1091, 1136, D1199, 1272, 1342, 1417, S1430, 1456, 1479, S1497, S1564, S1568, S1589, S1592, S1598, S1608, S1611, S1621, S1623, S1666, S1672, S1733, S1734, S1735, S1739, S1778, S1839, D2121, D2219, D2284
Caldwell, Jay Thomas—Lion 220
Caldwell, Taylor—BB A760, A956, A1139, F1702, S1879; CardE C202, C245, C252, C274, C311; CreB K706, D737, M745, R848; GM 288, 525; GMB 25; PopLG

325

Gordon, Leo—HollH HH175
Gordon, Luther—Ast 4; Crow 29, 34, 37; EcsNM 10, 11; ExNM nn(1), nn(2); Lan 72-637; QB 14, 21, 22, 24, 29, 31, 33, 34, 35, 36, 37, 38, 67, 70, 71
Gordon, Noah—Signet 1660, S2169
Gordon, Rex—AceD D233, D405; AceF F174, F416
Gordon, Richard (Gordon Ostlere)—AvT T424, T490
Gordon, Russell—Av 283; JonM J44
Gordon, Stewart—CreB 164
Gordon, William E.—Carn 903, 908, 921, 935
Gordons, The—BB 1273, 1348, 1455, 1475, 1782; BM B153, B170
Gore, Michael—Dou nn
Goren, Charles H.—BB A1953; Perma M4016; PermaH P58, P71, P100; PermaS P184
Gorham, Charles—BerkD D2022; BerkG G83, G199; CreB d285, S373, D587; Pop 555, 593; Pyr G197, G449; Signet 714, 752, D1130, D1244
Gorham, Nicholas (Noel B. Gerson)—AceD D342; MonB 474; PopLG G559
Gorkin, Julian—Lion 122
Gorky, Maxim—AvT T154
Gorn, Lester—PopSP SP51
Goscinny, Rene—LionLL LL38, LB99
Gosling, John—Hill 184
Gotlieb, Phyllis—GM K1488
Gotshall, Jack—CreB s257; GM 358
Gottehrer, Barry—Pyr F913
Gottscho, Samuel—Pock 788
Goudge, Elizabeth—ASE S39; CreB R756; Lan 74-806; PermaS P178S; Pock 564, 672
Goulart, Ron—Lan 75-420; Tempo 17311
Gould, Chester—DellUN nn
Gould, John—Pock 496
Gould, Lawrence—Av 200
Gould, R.E.—BB 456
Gould, Stephen—Eers 8; Metro 7
Goulet, Robert—Signet P2125
Gourse, R. Leslie—AvV V2052
Govan, Christine Noble—Croy 8
Govoni, Albert—Lan 74-614
Gowen, Emmett—Dell 572
Gowen, Vincent—Pyr R942
Gowland, J.S.—Harl 455
Goyne, Richard—BEDN 2
Grabach, John R.—DellLE LC115, LX120
Grabendike, Barbara—AceD D586
Grace, Alicia (Irving Greenfield)—Lan 73-541, 73-758, 74-565, 74-682, 74-765, 75-295
Grace, Edward—Berk 106; BerkG G164
Grady, Lester—CreB 118, s331
Grady, Tex—Pop 493
Grady, Wilton—Saber SA64
Graeme, G.A.—NSLS U107, U114, U123
Graffis, Herb—ASE 965
Grafton, C.W.—ASE 1284; Dell 180, 232; MM 97; Pock 752
Grafton, Samuel—Pock 1102
Graham, Alice Walworth—DellD D105
Graham, Billy—Perma M4003
Graham, Carroll—BRNM 7; Dell 625
Graham, Frank—ASE T24, J277, 781, 846, 963, 1170
Graham, Garrett—BRNM 7
Graham, Gwethalyn—ASE R27; BB 460
Graham, Kenneth—AvZS ZS101
Graham, Lee—Pop 692; SigK K313; Signet 889
Graham, Lewis—Han 85; Harl 151
Graham, Sheilah—BB F2033
Graham, Shirley—ASE 1283
Graham, Virginia—AvV V2153
Graham, Winston—BM B209; CreB D500, R736; PermaS P128
Grahame, Kenneth—AvSS SS4
Grainger, Boine—RCL 22
Gramling, Oliver—ASE K29
Grange, Red—Dell 862
Granger, K.R.G.—Lan 74-760, 74-998; Perma M3018; Pop 505
Grant,—PocSp 10004, 10005, 10006
Grant, Ambrose—CWC 355
Grant, E.S.—BelLB L92-553
Grant, Joan—AceK K246
Grant, Maxwell—BB H4056, H4463, H4688, H4770, H4884, H5413; BLA 21
Grant, Maxwell (Dennis Lynds)—BelLB B50-647, B50-683, B50-709, B50-725, B50-737, 92-602, 92-615, 92-624
Grant, Ozro—AceD D50
Grant, Richard—IN 22; Knick nn; Uni 6, 30
Grantland, Keith (Charles Beaumont)—GM 701, 1062
Grass, Günter—CreB M691
Grau, Shirley Ann—CreB R799; Signet S1318, T1726
Graves, Ralph—CardE C225
Graves, Robert—ASE L27; AvG G1037; AvT AT68; AvV V2062, V2075
Gray, Angela—Lan 74-744, 75-197, 75-366, 75-377, 75-456, 75-469
Gray, Berkeley—CWC 267; CWC nn, 60, 85, 105, 227, 244, 291, 344, 360, 383, 442, 465, 486, 512, 527
Gray, Eunice—Bea B216
Gray, George W.—ASE L22
Gray, Harriet—AvT T126, T156
Gray, Harry—Signet S999

Gray, Hugh—ASE Q4, 1060
Gray, Russell (Bruno Fischer)—Lion 38
Grayson, Capt. Charles—AceD D49, D207; ASE M28, E136; BB F1441; PermaH P30; PermaS P122
Grayson, Harry—ASE O4
Graziano, Rocky—AceF C210
Green, Abel—PermaS P217S
Green, Alan—ASE 896; Dell 483, 701
Green, Chalmers—GM 246
Green, F.L.—Pock 472
Green, Gerald—CardGC GC84, GC757; UGE 3
Green, Gordon—NSLF 131
Green, Graham—LionLL LL31
Green, Joseph I.—Bal 19; BB A914
Green, Joseph L.—BalU U2233
Green, Julian—AvT T91; Signet 998
Green, Roger L.—BalAF 02420
Green, Shoshone—GW 51
Green, Ward—LionLL LL55
Greenberg, Clement—PocLGA A10
Greenberg, David B.—ASE 1095
Greenberg, Martin—Pyr G234, F852
Greene, Felix—Bal N628
Greene, Graham—ASE A22, 873; BB 315, 355, 797, 971, 1217, A1306, 1316, 1333, A1424, A1480, A1669, A1773, F2004, A2018, F2039; BerkG G146; Pen 515, 530; SupR M652
Greene, Joe—Signet D2178
Greene, Joseph I.—BB 503, 742
Greene, Josiah E.—Green 8; PermaS P150
Greene, Laurence—Lan 182
Greene, Ward—Av 190, 266, 664; Lion 89, 115; MM 14
Greenfield, Irving A.—Lan 73-624, 73-672, 74-539, 74-655, 74-994
Greenhood, David—CreB 119; Signet 711
Greenshade, Ted—NSLF 111; NSLS 26A
Greenwald, Dr. Harold—Bal F333K, F399K, F428K, Bal F613; BalU U2165, U2166; BEDN F280K
Greer, David—AvG G1126
Gregg, Alan—Com 7; PocJr J47
Gregg, Jess—AvS S138
Greggson, Dale—Dom 82113; Lan 72-794, 72-922, 72-939
Gregor, Manfred—AvT T532
Gregor, Martin—Star 4
Gregory, Dan—Grap 143
Gregory, Dick—AvS S129
Gregory, F.L.—HH 15
Gregory, Franklin—TNC 10
Gregory, Horace—Ment MD189
Gregorcz, J.—BLA 6
Gregory, Jackson—Av nn(13); Pop 95, 140, 160, 184, 226, 255, 313, 337, 383, 430, 545, 597, 789; PopLE EB10, EB17, EB103; PopLG 257, G380, G396, G474; ThrillBN 17
Gregory, James—Hill 130
Gregory, Stephen—Vega V16
Gregory, Susan—Lan 75-141
Greig, Maysie—BB 110; CWC 260, 312; Dell 170, 239, 309, 446, 496; Pock 463, 541, 574
Gresham, William Lindsay—Signet 738, 839, 1326
Grew, David—PocJr J72
Grew, Joseph C.—ASE A2
Grew, William—Grap 105; Perma M3019
Grey, Harry—GrapG G215; Signet D1211, S1572, D1575
Grey, Robin—BartH 29
Grey, Zane—ASE Q19, 678, 722, 797, 842, 883, 997, 1107, 1294; BB 3, 73, 1067, 1298, A1717, A1718; CardE C231, C239, C264, C333, C351, C385; Penn P2; Pock 161, 371
Grider, George—Pyr G406
Grieg, Maysie—CWC 280, 321, 342, 406; RCL 21
Grierson, Edward—BB A1525
Grierson, Francis—PockB B92
Grierson, Linden—Lan 73-449, 73-450
Griffen, Buford—Lan 75-076
Griffen, Warren—AvT T506
Griffin, Gwyn—AvG G1061; AvS S170; AvV V2053, V2133; PopLG G465
Griffin, John Howard—CardGC GC14
Griffith, Beatrice—Penn P39
Griffith, Corinne—AceA A21
Griffith, Maxwell—CardE C215; PermaS P197
Grilli, M. Pill—Uni 10
Grinioff, Vladimir B.—Pyr G424
Grinnell, David—AceD D286, D362, D465; AceF F161; AceG G728; AceH H85; AceM M162
Grinstead, J.E.—Av 829; BCW 32; Cent 82; FWN 14; GWN 36; Han 103, 115, 123; Harl 75, 119, 411, 417; WNC 97
Grisman, Arnold E.—BerkG G198
Griswold, Francis—ASE 1262
Groh, Edwin C.—Vega V36
Grombach, John V.—AvG G1208; Bal 161, F386K
Gronowicz, Antoni—Bel 219
Gropper, Milton Herbert—BRNM 3, 6; TPLBS 100
Grose, Helena—CWC 77, 226, 234, 330, 345, 348, 387, 390
Gross, Fred—CardE C260; Pock 1057
Gross, Gerald—AvV V2152
Gross, Milton—AvG G1117
Gross, Nancy E.—Ment M109

Grosser, Maurice—Ment M159
Grossman, Alfred—AvVS VS13
Grote, William—AceD D203
Grove, Fred—Bal 324K, 560, 671, Y769; BalU U1010; BEDN 251; Pyr G313
Grove, Gene—GM D1141
Grove, Walt—DellFE 1E, D81, B136; GM 120, 134, 545, s649, s801; GMB 30
Grubb, Davis—AvV V2169; CreB d160, D578, D814; DellD D149
Gruber, Frank—AceD D39, D196; ASE S6, A12; Av 91; AvMMM 4, 12, 23; BB 2, 50, 144, 151, 212, 1198, 1287, 1347, 1488, 1527, A1598, 1666, 1726, 1741, 1742, 1743, 1934, A1998, A2021; BelLB L92-586, L92-592, 92-607; Cent nn(60), 64, 72; Chart 25; CreB 115; Grap 119; JonM J66, J72, J76, J85, J89; Lion 157, 163; LionLL LB93, LB117; MM 191; MonB 432; Pen 538, 545, 562, 623, 651; Penn P43; Pop 188, 761; RCL 2, 13, 15, 16, 19; Signet 689, 707, 726, 753, 799, 827, 1636, 1677; SupR M649, M655
Gruenberg, Sidonie Matsner (ed. Frances Ullman)—GM 112
Guareschi, Giovanni—Pock 1000, 1067
Guderian, Heinz—Bal F225, S485K
Guedalla, Phillip—ASE F177
Guenther, John—Pyr G373
Guerard, Albert—CreB s328
Guerard, Arthur Rose—Av 148
Guild, Leo—Av 513; AvSp nn; AvT T118, T346; CreB 369; GM K1379; HollH HH105, HH168, HH173, HH180; Pock 636
Guin, Wyman—AvS S298
Guinn, William—GM 503
Gulick, Bill—BB 906, 1094; Pop 701, 755; PopLG G247, G429, G526; Signet S1754
Gunn, James E.—AceD D169, D223; AceF F241; ASE 946; BB A1825; BerkG G232; Chart 18; CWC 339; Signet 709, 1084
Gunn, Tom—BCW 37; GWN 27; Harl 24; Pock 808, 841, 942, 1002; WNC 101
Gunn, Victor (Berkeley Gray)—CWC nn, 61, 81, 205, 271, 410, 436
Gunther, John—AvT T239; BB A1033, A1034; PopSP SP165, SP209; Pyr R243
Guralnik, David B.—PopSP SP15
Gurney, Gene—Bal F488K
Gutheil, Emil A.—Prem S46
Guthrie, A.B. Jr.—ASE 1297; CardE C30, C52, C267; Pock 600, 780; PocL PL17, PL513; Pop 376; PopLG G274
Guttmacher, Alan F.—AvG G1065; Bal F532; BalU U2136; PelB P12; SigK Ks332, KD358; Signet 788
Gutwillig, Robert—CreB S367; PopLG G330
Guyon, Rene—FranE E3
Gwaltney, Francis Irby—CreB D379; Pop 699; PopSP SP 5, SP27, SP107
Gwinn, William—Lion 209, 225
Haas, Ben—Regy RB319
Haase, John—AvT T251, T454; CreB S447
Habas, Ralph A.—SigK K335
Habe, Hans—AvN N136; Bea B106, B147; CreB s207, s270, S364
Haber, Heinz—DellFE B104; DellLE LB117
Hachiya, Michihiko—AvT T259
Hackett, Francis—ASE S37; BantB FB401; BantC FC9
Hackett, Paul—Signet 2225
Hackney, Alan—Signet D1876
Haden, Allen—Dell 595
Hadida, Sophie C.—PermaH P75
Hadley, Franklin—MonB 431
Hadley, Harold—Pyr G242
Hadrian, Philip (Philip Ketchum)—MonB 278
Haedrich, Marcel—DellFE B160
Hagedorn, Herman—TR nn
Hagen, Miriam-Ann—MM 157
Haggard, H. Rider—ASE 795, 881; Bal X733, X743; BalAF 02467, 23660, 23927; Dell 339, 433; Lan 72-140, 72-614, 72-925, 74-899; RoyG 18
Haggard, Howard W.—CardE C101; CardGC GC70; Pock 379
Haggard, Paul—MNM nn
Haggard, William—AvG G1197; Signet D2368
Hahn, Emily—Av 217; BB 858, 1479; BerkG G274; CreB 121, s203; Lion 57
Hahn, Steve—Las 51
Haig-Brown, Roderick—Com 21; CWC 265
Haight, Anne Lyon—Bow nn
Haines, Donal Hamilton—ASE Q23; Com 16
Haines, William Wister—ASE D115, I249, 1243; BB A1901, F1902, A1964; Pock 412, 502, 571
Haislip, Harvey—PopSP SP240, SP263
Halacy, D.S. Jr.—MonA MA316; MonB 479; MonK K69, K73
Hale, Arlene—AceD D540, D563, D569, D580, D585, D587, D596, D598; AceF F339, F352, F368, F371, F385, F387, F410, F424, F430; AceG G653, G672, G696, G750; Bann B50-109, B50-121
Hale, Christopher—BarH 32; Dell 150; DNC 34, 39, 51
Hale, Laura—ExNM 20; Fal 37; Rain 103, 118
Hale, Nancy—AvN N119; PermaS P199S
Hale, Randolph—WNC 79
Haleck, Oscar—LionLL LL67
Hales, Carol—BerkG G95
Hales, Norman—Signet 1173

Halevy, Julian—DellD D170
Hall, Austin—AceF F318; AceG G547
Hall, Bennie C.—DellD D413
Hall, Calvin S.—DellD D287; Ment M147, MD271
Hall, Desmond—Pop 413
Hall, Donald—DellLE LB148
Hall, Evan—LionLL LB132
Hall, Geoffrey Holiday—Pock 776
Hall, Gramm—Lan 75-157
Hall, James B.—Signet D2438
Hall, James Norman—ASE P5, T10, F179, H238, 725, 905;
    CardE C34; MonB 141; Perma M4001; Pock 188, 216,
    358, 457; Pyr R928
Hall, Marcia—NovF 5016; Novs 6N255
Hall, O.M.—Harl 103
Hall, Oakley—BB 908, A1898, F1980; Perma M4006, M4042;
    Pock 828
Hall, Radclyffe—Perma M4024, M5010; PermaS P112
Hall, Warner—DellFE B122
Hallas, Richard—Dell 510
Halleran, E.E.—ANC 38; ASE Q11, 951, 1206; Av 367, 507,
    522; AvFS F120; Bal 142, 153, 170, 205, 219, 396K,
    471K, 502K, 635, 682, 710, Y759; BalU U1031,
    U1035, U2256, U2257; BB 1004, 1385; Dell 616, 755;
    GM 1056; GWN 28; Harl 58, 61; Lan 71-321, 73-737;
    Lion 134; Pock 703, 783, 876; RCL 33
Halliburton, Richard—Pock 147
Halliday, Brett—ASE 663; Dell 23, 64, 78, 112, 128, 168,
    184, 222, 268, 280, 323, 324, 325, 326, 385, 386,
    387, 388, 426, 427, 428, 429, 458, 459, 503, 533,
    578, 590, 617, 668, 723, 743, 768, 803, 829, 842,
    865, 866, 867, 891, 905, 914, 934, 946, 957, 958,
    960, 965, 978, 981, 987, 988, 989; DellD D248,
    D269, D283, D291, D292, D293, D314, D327, D331,
    D342, D355, D358, D359, D374, D379, D381, D387,
    D391, D401, D416, D423, D424, D425, D437, D446,
    D463; DellTC 15; DNC 21, 26, 31; Han 15; Hill 143,
    193; Pop 98, 192
Halliday, Dean—AvUn nn
Hallock, Grace T.—Pock 220
Halper, Albert—BelLB L92-555, L92-577; DellFE 94
Halsey, Ashley Jr—CreB S444, D671; GM S1185
Halsey, Margaret—AvFS F101
Ham, Roswell G. Jr—Av 512; AvG G1082; AvT T139; Perma
    M4098
Hamblen, Charles—GM D1582; Lan 72-646
Hamill,—Lan 72-611
Hamill, Ethel—AceD D554; BB 1841; Hill 173, 204; Signet
    S2022
Hamilton, Bruce—Hill 15; PockB B2, B29
Hamilton, Donald—Dell 375, 473, 577; DellFE 18, 27, 46,
    91, B115, A123, B170; GM 957, 1025, 1035, S1082,
    S1194, S1246, K1333, K1334, K1335, K1336, K1386,
    K1391, K1392, K1452, K1472, K1480, K1491, K1500,
    K1551, D1602, D1608, D1617, D1623, D1641, D1646,
    D1673, D1687, D1696, D1697
Hamilton, Edith—Ment M32, Ms86, MD213
Hamilton, Edmond—AceD D351; AceF F271, F319; AceG
    G639, G701, G766; AceM M111; CreB s184, s329,
    S494, L758; GSFN 18; Lan 72-721, 73-577, 74-612;
    Pyr R698; Signet 812
Hamilton, Harry—ASE 839; PermaS P260
Hamilton, Kay—Harl 348, 357, 363
Hamilton, Trudy—EcsNM nn(1)
Hamilton, Wade—Harl 398; Pyr 396, 403
Hammer, Earl Jr—Signet S1271
Hammett, Catherine T.—CardE C180; PocJr J46; Pock 893
Hammett, Dashiell—ASE nn; Bel 230, 239; BM B40, B50,
    B62, B81; Dell 53, 90, 129, 154, 223, 308, 379, 411,
    421, 452, 486, 538; JonM J17, J29, J36, J40, J48,
    J59; MM 120, 131, 233; Perma M3043, M3074,
    M4200, M4201, M4202; Pock 196, 211, 241, 268,
    295; ReaL nn
Hampshire, Stuart—Ment MD158
Hampton, Brady—Saber SA22
Hampton, Kathleen—Signet P1941
Hampton, Stella—Fab Z117
Han, Suyin—Signet D1183, T1717, D1813
Hancock, Alfred—PenS s214
Hancock, Frances Dean—Lan 73-873; MonB 235
Hancock, Lucy Agnes—BB 408, 1433; CWC 295; Harl 235,
    264, 284, 292, 302, 313, 324, 332, 333, 338, 339,
    344, 346, 347, 356, 372, 397, 496, 502, 562; Pock
    520, 692
Hancock, W.K.—PenS s213
Handley, Alan—Harl 27; Pyr 20
Hankins, R.M.—BB 214, 259, 757
Hanley, Gerald—CreB D638; Pyr G120, R211
Hanley, Glen—FWN 29
Hanley, Jack—Av 417, 580; AvbD 2; AvMN 21; Bea B296;
    BerkG G171, G252, G261; Hill nn(1), 120; IN 18, 26,
    30, 37; Zenith ZB42
Hanlin, Tom—BB 978
Hanline, M.H.—AvMN 14
Hanna, William—DellFE B199
Hano, Arnold—BB 200, 256
Hansberry, L.—Signet D1901
Hansen, Alvin H.—PelB P10
Hansen, Eva Hemmer—Pop 825
Hansen, Robert P.—BB 1469; Perma M3066; Pop 774
Hansen, Zora—CPH A106

Hanser, Richard—CreB D579
Hanson, Kitty—Tower 43-543
Hanson, Robert P.—BB 1188
Hanson, V.J.—PrizeWN 38
Hara, Capt.—Bal SA457K
Harben, Philip—PockB B38
Hardin, Clement—AceD D56, D248; AceF F116, F144; AceG
    G584, G622, G659, G732; AceM M130
Hardin, Dave—Bal 57
Hardin, Peter—BB 1030; Dell 922
Harding, Lee—Las 41
Harding, Matt—Lan 72-694, 72-728
Hardwick, Richard—BelLB B50-741; MonS MS17
Hardy, J.L.—MM 2, 26
Hardy, Lindsay—Pop 709; Pyr R661; Signet 1154, 1283
Hardy, Rene—Signet S1462
Hardy, Ronald—BerkG G23
Hardy, Stuart—GWN 30, 37; PockB B106; PrizeWN 26
Hardy, T.A.—FFS nn
Hardy, Thomas—CardE C42, C47; DellLE LX108; JL nn(11);
    PBCE nn(15); Pock 20; PocL PL23, PL25, PL52; SigC
    CD7; WSP W571
Hardy, William M.—AvT AT70; Dell 995; DellD D360; Harl
    201, 215; Pop 464; PopLG G189; PopSP SP31
Hare, Cyril—AvFS F134; MM 190
Hargest, Brigadier James—PockB B6
Hargitay, Mickey—HollH HH110
Hargrove, Marion—Pock 206; Pop 222; Signet S1364, S1392
Harkary, Dr. Myron—AceF F136
Harkey, Dee—Signet 856, 1196
Harkins, Philip—Com 29; PocJr J55
Harlow, Alvin F.—Pyr 123
Harlow, James—CLN 22
Harman, Carter—DellFE C102
Harmon, Bob—Pock 1080
Harmon, Jim—AceA A27; Fran F21, F30
Harmon, Robert W.—Carn 901
Harness, Charles L.—AceD D118
Harper, Daniel—Av 591; EtB E122; Lan 72-634, 72-669
Harper, E.M.—BerkD D2027
Harragan, Steve—Dell 203, 206, 212; UGE 4; Uni 42, 43,
    44, 46, 47, 52, 54, 64
Harre, Everett—Pyr G64, G146
Harrey, Gene—QB 74
Harriman, John—AceD D246
Harriman, Margaret Case—ASE Q26
Harrington, Alan—AvNS NS20
Harrington, Joseph D.—Bal S600
Harrington, William—AvS S199; AvV V2148
Harris, Colver—MNM nn
Harris, Eleanor—Bal 78
Harris, Frank G.—Saber SA37, SA40, SA50, SA61, SA65,
    SA67, SA79, SA95, SA117, SA146; TBSTB 914, 923,
    942, 945
Harris, H.E.—Pock 892
Harris, John—Bann B60-101; BB A1289; Pock 1061; PopSP
    SP188
Harris, John Beynon (John Wyndham)—Lan 72-155, 72-701
Harris, Kathleen  (Adelaide Humphries)—PopLG G453,
    G497, G566; Pyr G561
Harris, Larry M.—Bea 263
Harris, Margaret—Pock 995, 1061; PopSP SP188
Harris, Mark—PermaS P299; Signet S1659
Harris, Mel—BerkG G9
Harris, Merv—Lan 75-406
Harris, Sara—Bel 205, 223; CardE C286; CreB S352; PermaS
    P300; Signet 1146, 1341, S1613
Harris, Timothy—Lan 75-171
Harris, Victor—Fran F65
Harris, Virginia—Saber SA92
Harris, William Howard—BerkG G151
Harrison, C. William—AvFS F135; Bal 394K; BB 1926; GM
    560; Lion 88, 103, 181; LionLL LB123; Perma M3030
Harrison, G.B.—PelB P14
Harrison, George Russell—ASE 1008
Harrison, Harry—Pyr F672, F771
Harrison, Joan—AvFS F152
Harrison, Whit   (Harry Whittington)—Bea B350, B392; Carn
    918, 924, 934, 952; Harl 240; OrigN 714, 718, 742; Phan 508,
    511; Star 756, 761; Venus 153, 161, 166, 194
Harrison, William—Perma M3093
Harsh, James—NSLS U110
Hart, B.H. Liddell—BerkG BG135
Hart, Constance—DellFE D40, C106
Hart, Frances Noyes—BM B7; DellD D233; Pock 264
Hart, Francis Russell—ASE 938
Hart, Harold—ASE 1171
Hart, Henry—BantB FB403
Hart, Johnny—CreB S478, S684, K767, K876
Hart, Moss—Av 58; Pock 143
Harte, Bret—ASE F162; Av 446
Hartley, William E.—Pop 765
Hartt, Frederick—PocLGA A9
Hartt, Jon—UGE 7
Harvey, Doug—MeritF 626
Harvey, Frank—Bal 116, 329K, 691
Harvey, Gene—Cam 301, 305, 309, 334, 336, 353; Carn
    920; CLN 21; ExNM nn(6), nn(10); IN 44; Novl 9; NSLF
    148; OrigN 744; Pyr R634; Rain 101; RC 3; Stall 207;
    Venus 108, 114, 117, 124, 141, 169
Harvey, James—Midw 42, 50, 59; NSLF 515; Saber SA58

Harvin, Emily—Av 276
Harwin, Brian—MonB 110
Harwood, Ronald—AvG G1138
Hasek, Jaroslav—Pen 572; PenS s211
Hashimoto, Mochitsura—AvT T246
Haskell, Frank—Bel 245; Cam 331, 348, 365; Carn 926;
    Venus 157, 173, 179, 184, 191
Hasko, Marek—Signet S1706
Haslip, Joan—AceK K150
Hasry, John Eugene—Zenith ZB9
Hassel, Sven—CreB s217; GM D1176, R1368, R1644; Lan
    75-117, 75-120
Hastings, MacDonald—MM 177
Hastings, March—Bea B190, B198, B207; Midw 37, 53, 80,
    D231; NSLS U106, U109, U116, U118, U152, U157
Hastings, Phyllis—Pop 672, 762; PopLG G177
Hastings, Roderic—AvT T267
Hasty, John Eugene—GM S1142, S1269
Hatch, Alden—PopLG G164
Hatch, Eric—ASE S12; BartH nn(2); BB 121, 414, 453, 476,
    1694; GM 176, 213, 690; GMB 13
Hatch, Gerald—MonB 354
Hatch, Richard Warren—DellD D114
Hatcher, Harlan—ASE S30
Hatlo, Jimmy—Av 366, 524, 612, 652, 707, 789, 826, 857;
    AvT T501; DellFE 78; Pock 298
Hatten, Homer—GM 157, 215, 352, 416, 492, 541; RSB 15
Hatter, Amos—Cam 308, 312, 318, 320, 350; Carn 956;
    OrigN 701, 705, 730; QB 88; Star 760; Venus 126,
    132, 154, 164, 181
Haupt, Enid A.—PopLG G522
Hauser, Gayelord—AvG G1044; CreB R560, T598, R644,
    R839; Pop 559; Prem S18
Havemann, Ernest—MonHBS MB546
Haven,—FFS nn
Haviland, Monica—MonB 373, 438
Hawes, Gene R.—SigK KD373
Hawkins, Dean—GreD 28
Hawkins, John—AceD D289; ANC 22, 29, 35; ASE Q20, 998;
    Pop 824
Hawkins, Ward—AceD D289; ANC 22, 29, 35; ASE Q20,
    998; CreB S393; Han 41; Pop 824
Hawley, Cameron—Bal 1, X516K; BalSSE S2; CardE C313;
    CardGC GC751
Hawthorne, Nathaniel—ASE 863; CardE C65; Keep 2; PBCE
    nn(8), nn(16); Pock 52, 551; PocL PL15, PL26, PL59;
    SigC CD8
Hawton, Hector—Prem S20, d75
Haycox, Ernest—AceM M144; ASE N9, M13, K14, P16, Q16,
    E129, F164, I254, 683, 706, 748, 791, 837, 867, 916,
    1094, 1164, 1267; AvFS F231; BB 25, 261, 788, A980,
    1115, A1627, 1628, F1872, F2058; CardE C97, C204,
    C370; Dell 120, 227, 317, 347, 450, 598, 618, 748,
    945, 952, 975; DellID D290; MonB 108; Pock 301, 466,
    531, 573, 594, 608, 640, 790, 864, 983, 1011, 1028,
    1069, 1148; Pop 85, 143, 171, 199, 235, 271, 360,
    398, 442, 450, 460, 484, 499, 588, 590, 616,
    644, 700, 728, 767, 796, 804, 831; PopLE EB4;
    PopLG G218, G237, G261, G283, G300, G318, G326,
    G347, G351, G367, G402, G418, G439, G461, G478,
    G535; Pyr F952; Signet 1782
Hayden, Eric Rhodes—RCL 39
Haydn, Hiram—Perma M4007
Haye, Jan—Harl 758, 897
Hayes, Alfred—BB A1880; Lion 40; LionLL LL68; Pock 666,
    1019; Pyr G365
Hayes, Bob—NovF 5044, 60106
Hayes, Joseph—BB 1948; CreB T816; Perma M3007; Signet
    D1546
Hayes, Leal—AceG G612
Hayes, Marrijane—Signet D1546
Hayes, Reese—Fab Z109, Z115; FabR Z7; Saber SA3; SabR
    1
Hayes, Robert—NSLS U129
Haynes, Floyd—Fab Z123
Haynes, Reese—Saber SA84
Haynes, William—ASE G203
Hays, H.R.—ASE P11
Haystead, Ladd—ASE 1089
Hayward, Richard—GM 242, 479, 558
Hazel, Robert—Signet 1115, 1231
Hazlitt, Henry—Pock 553
Head, Matthew—AvG G1229, G1252, G1261; Dell 158, 219,
    346, 390, 605; MM 96
Heal, Edith—PocJr J68
Healey, Ben—Lan 73-518
Healy, Eugene—Harl 55
Healy, Raymond J.—BB 1310; CardE C319; Penn P44; Pock
    908
Healy, Wayne—AvG G1133
Heard, H.F.—AceM M142; Av 108, 625, 808; BB 1079; Dell
    44; Lan 72-752, 72-754, 73-647, 74-605; MM 70
Hearne, L.A.—GM 656
Hearst, Mike—NovF 5054
Heath, Eric—MNM nn
Heath, Peter—Lan 73-600, 73-631, 73-783
Heath, Sharon—AceF C369; F381, F413; AceM M161
Heath, William L.—BB 1438; Hill 114
Heatter, Basil—GM 1037, S1126, S1238, K1310; Lion 170,
    228; Pop 266, 602, 771; PopLE EB1; Signet 668
Heber, William E.—BB 1476

Heberden, M.V.—BM B181; Dell 401; DNC 48; MNC 80
Hebson, Ann—Zenith ZB23
Hechinger, Fred M.—CreB D705
Hechinger, Grace—CreB D705
Hechler, Ken—Bal F234
Hecht, Ben—ASE 921; Av nn(11); AvMSS 11, 26, 37; BartH 25; Chec 9; DellD D294; Harl 32; QR 107, 117; Signet T1212, Q1742
Heckelmann, Charles N.—BB 128, 206; GrapG G202, G221; Harl 198; Lan 73-867; Lion 34; PrizeWN 21; Signet 694, 775, 842, 910, 965, 1108, 1232, 1373
Hedden, Worth Tuttle—BB 463, 1192
Heffner, Richard D.—Ment M78
Heggen, Thomas—ASE 1203; Pock 550
Heiden, Konrad—ASE M30
Heiman, Judith—CreB D562, D797
Heimer, Mel—ASE Q6; GM 458
Heimler, Eugene—Pyr R625
Heinlein, Robert A.—AceF F375; AvG G1211; AvS S335; AvT T261; AvV V2056, V2102, V2191; DellTC 36; Pyr G642, F859, F910; Signet 847, 882, 943, 980, 1044, 1161, 1194, S1444, S1537, S1544, S1577, S1639, S1644, S1699, S1752, D1987, D2105
Heinrich, Willi—BB F1599, F1913
Heinz, W.C.—BerkG BG197; CreB R692
Heise, Jack—BelLB L92-531
Heise, Jack G.—CreB D715
Helbrant, Maurice—AceD D15
Held, John Jr—Dell 477
Held, Julius S.—PocLGA A17
Held, Peter   (Jack Vance)—Pyr G327
Heller, David—MonA MA312; MonB 458; MonK K54; MonS MS2, MS8, MS23
Heller, Deane—MonA MA312; MonB 458; MonK K54; MonS MS8, MS23
Heller, Jack—Bel 218
Heller, Larry—Pop 760; Pyr F751
Heller, Marcus Van—FPVFP FP2002
Heller, Mike—GM 664
Hellman,—ASE M23
Hellman, Lillian—Signet D2129
Helmericks, Constance—ASE O26
Helseth, Henry Edward—Pock 484; Signet S1973, S2109
Hemingway, Ernest—ASE K9, 667; AvG G1006; BB 467, 717, A883, A1240, A1249; BelLB L506; BerkG S127; DellD D117; Perma M3041, M3056; PermaS 253, P296
Hemingway, Leicester—CreB T593
Henderson, Donald—MM 101
Henderson, G.H.—NSLF 67
Henderson, George C.—Harl 134; RCL 26
Henderson, George Wylie—Av 400, 577; BerkG G218
Henderson, J.Y.—BB 992
Henderson, James Leal—CWC 396; Pop 399
Henderson, John—BB F1365, F1665
Henderson, Zenna—AvG G1185; AvS S243, S328
Hendricks, George D.—AceD G500; AceG G500
Hendryx, James B.—ANC 10, 17, 41; ASE 1073, 1230; Dell 587, 876; Harl 156; Pony 66; Pop 314
Henius, Frank—FFS nn
Henkin, Leo J.—Perma MA018; PermaS P98
Henkin, Prof. Louis—BalSSE S10
Hennessey, Caroline—Lan 75-132
Henning, William E.—BB 724, A1708
Henri, Florette—AvT AT60
Henry, Alan—GM 344
Henry, Joan—PermaS 239
Henry, Lewis C.—PermaH P3; Prem S15
Henry,—ASE K16, 944; BM B94; Pen 595; Pock 65, 510
Henry, Thomas R.—AceK K155
Henry, Will—BB 946, 1168, A1411, A1481, A1482, A1483, 1855, A1935
Hensley, Joe L.—AceD D452; Las 17
Hepburn, Andrew—Av G440
Heppenstall, Rayner—BerkG G27, G204
Herber, William E.—BB 1589, F1969
Herbert, A.P.—Harl 273
Herbert, Arthur—Signet 916
Herbert, Frank—AceF F379; AceN N3; AvG G1092; AvS S290, S319; AvT T146
Herbert, Hugh—Han 97
Hergesheimer, Joseph—ASE O24, D102
Heriat, Philippe—PopLE EB86
Herlihy, James Leo—BA A1957; Lan 75-110
Herling, Gustaw—Ment M75
Herman, Fred—ASE B32
Herman, William—BB 1584
Hermann, Walter—Av 706
Herndon, Booton—GM D1514
Heron, Joseph—NSLS U126, U159
Heron, Nora—NovF 6007, 6098
Herries, Norman—AceD S97, D147
Herring, Hubert—ASE B57
Herrington, Lee—Dell 641
Herrnstein, Barbara—AvWYX W142
Herron, Edward A.—ASE 1278
Hersey, John—AvG G1043; AvS S134; BantC AC26; BB 45, 404, 1219, 1529; CardGC GC12; DellD D263; DellTC 25; Pock 225, 279; PopLG G475
Hershfield, Harry—Av 65, 158; AvUn nn; BalU U2200; BartH 39
Hershfield, Harry   (Walter B. Gibson)—BartH 102

Hertzler, Arthur E.—ASE F169; BalLE L7; Lad L7; Pock 356
Hervey, Harry—Pyr 89, G301
Hervey, Michael—AceK K259, K300
Herzberg, Max J.—ASE A23; Pock 730
Herzog, Dorothy—Ast 12
Hespro, Herbert—PermaH P26
Hess, Dean E.—PyrSE nn
Heth, Edward Harris—BB 553
Heuman, William—AceD D380; AceF F254; Av 569, 855; AvFS F144; AvT T386, T433, T486; GM 131, 146, 187, 216, 267, 287, 310, 322, 330, 414, 429, 631, 681, 705, 842, 944, 992, S1180, K1536; GMB 27,31,59,61; Hill 104; Pock 1112
Hewes, Henry—DellLE LX119
Heyan, Evan Lee—PopLG G554
Heyer, Georgette—AceH H23, H44, H45, H75, H76, H101; AceK K174, K179, K201, K226, K235, K265; AvV V2157; Pen 519
Heyerdahl, Thor—CardGC GC758; Perma M4062; PermaS P243
Heyes, Douglas—Signet 949, 1329
Heygate, John—CWC 464
Heym, Stefan—ASE R34, B56
Heyman, Evan Lee—AvS S233, S354; AvT T531
Heyn, Ernest—Pock 545
Heyward, Du Bose—ASE L5, C74; BB A1689; Pen 558
Heywood, Victor D.—Papi OSF-503
Hibbs, Ben—BB 555
Hickerson, Clayton—NSLS U142
Hickey, H.B.—Cent 73; Prize 53
Hickok, Will—Signet 1242, 1541, 1675
Higgins, Jack—Lan 74-604, 74-730, 75-396
Higgins, Marguerite—Lan 82
Higgins, Russell—QB 44, 49
High, Philip E.—AceF F255, F275; AceG G609, G623; AceH H59, H85; AceM M135
Highsmith, David—Midw F90
Highsmith, Patricia—BB 905; DellD D282; PopLE EB58
Hiken, Nat—Bal 229
Hill,—FFS nn
Hill, Doreen—Saber SA155
Hill, Douglas—AvS S389
Hill, Ernest—AceH H56
Hill, Ernestine—ASE C80; PermaS P247
Hill, Evan—Av G1072
Hill, Janet McKenzie—Dell 798
Hill, Katharine—MNC 74
Hill, Katharine St.—FPVFP FP2035
Hill, Kendall—Fran F36
Hill, Napoleon—CreB D389, R536, T864, T872
Hill, Pamela—PopSP SP100
Hill, Pati—AvH H105
Hill, Paull—AvT T514
Hill, Weldon—CreB T592; PopSP SP13
Hillary, Richard—DellD D244
Hilliard, Jan—AceK K203
Hilliard, Nerina—Harl 557, 840, 927
Hills, L. Rust—PopSP SP129
Hills, Tynette—CreB s269; Prem S39
Hilton, Conrad—PopPC PC400
Hilton, Francis W.—Dell 250, 451, 509; FWN 37
Hilton, Hilary—CHARf CB107
Hilton, James—ASE D91, E138, 966; Av nn(4), nn(39), 42, 79, 223, 301, 325, 381; AvMSS 5; AvT T427; AvV V2181, V2191; BB A1636; Bob nn; CardE C70; CWC 404; Pock 1, 89, 93, 118, 136, 275, 630, 1046; Pyr R956; ReaL nn
Hilton, Joseph—AvT T178, T230; CreB S424; GM 278, 475, s913; Lan 70-050, 75-398
Himes, Chester—AvG G1244; AvT T328, T357, T384, T434; BerkG G6, G139; GM 717; Signet 756, 1264, D1299
Himmel, Ralph—Croy 75
Himmel, Richard—AvT T329; Croy 22; GM 104, 143, 179, 234, 274, 373, 460, 488, 543, 566, s735, 800, s859; GMB 22; NSLF 151; StorON 4
Hinckley, Julian—GW 55
Hinds, Arthur—Pock 291
Hine, Al—AvV V2054; BB A1073; GM K1433; PopSP SP65, SP187
Hines, Duncan—CardE C188
Hines, Jack—PocJr J75
Hinkle, Thomas C.—Com 4, 14; PocJr J41, J58, J70
Hinsdale, Harriet—PermaS P170
Hinshaw, Les—MeritF 512
Hirsch, Edwin W.—PermaH P21; PermaS P21; Signet S1463
Hirsch, Lee—HH 20
Hirsch, Richard—Harl 154
Hirsch, W. Phil—Pyr G496, G550, G583, G598, G662, F721, F902
Hirschberg, Cornelius—AvG G1240
Hirschfeld, Burt—Lan 70-055, 72-917, 73-884, 73-888, 74-706
Hirshberg, Al—BB A1582; PopLG G342
Hitchcock, Alfred—Dell 92, 143, 206, 262, 264, 367; DellD D231, D281
Hitchcock, Alfred   (Henry Slesar)—AvFS F121; AvT T485
Hitchens, Bert—Perma M3051, M3100; Pock 1230
Hitchens, Dolores—BM B177, B184; Dell 659, 779; Lan 73-778; Perma M3040, M3051, M3100; Pock 1230, 1239
Hitrec, Joseph—BB 1029

Hitt, Orrie—Av 554; Bea B101, B104, B126, B132, B137, B139, B142, B146, B151, B153, B158, B159, B164, B168, B169, B174, B176, B180, B186, B191, B194, B195, B197, B203, B206, B209, B211, B212, B222, B227, B232, B238, B239, B250, B254, B261, B267, B274, B288, B294, B304, B314, B325; CHARf CB153, CB158, CB163, CB167, CB187, CB195; CHARs CB1604, CB1610, CB1619, CB1620; Dom 82107; Lan 72-670, 72-703, 72-707, 72-712, 72-726, 72-963, 73-411; Midw 10, 12, 16, 23, 34, 38, 45, 115, 150, F225; NovF 5065, 5082, 5089, 6006, 6008, 6014, 6026, 6054, 6085, 6088, 6091, 6096, 6097, 60103, 60116; Novs 6N252, 6N253, 6N256, 7N751, 7N758; Saber SA5; SabR 3; Uni 73; WH W107
Hitti, Phillip K.—ASE A18
Hives, Frank—Bal F575
Hix, Elsie—BB 1334
Hoagland, Edward—Signet S1499
Hobart, Alice Tisdale—ASE 1049; BB 20; DellF F80; Pyr X848
Hobart, Donald Bayne—Pony 125
Hobbs, Lisa—AvS S245
Hobhouse, Adam—MM 118
Hobson, Burton—GM D1554
Hobson, Laura Z.—ASE 1268; PermaS P154, P190
Hoch, Edward D.—Lan 74-525
Hodapp, William—Berk 101; BerkG G12
Hodges, Carl G.—AceD D33; Harl 182, 279; Phan 506; SusN 3
Hodgins, Eric—Pock 505; PopSP SP174
Hodgson, William Hope—AceD D553; BalAF 02145, 02669, 02670; FPVFP FP2038
Hoehling, A.A.—AceK K115; PopLG G184
Hoff, Syd—PocSp 10007; Pop 698
Hoffe, Arthur—AvS S368
Hoffenberg, Jack—AvN N107, N114, N123, N140, N146; AvV V2183
Hoffer, Eric—Ment MD228
Hoffman, Betty Hannah—AvT T510
Hoffman, Lee—AceF F380; AceG G587, G721, G726; AvS S417; BalU U2333; BelLB B50-779
Hoffman, W.D.—GWN 24
Hoffman, William—CreB s156, d278, D384, T526, R733
Hoffmann, H.—GM 351
Hofman, Von—Fab Z156
Hogan, Ben—CardE C358; Pock 928
Hogan, Ray—AceD D186, D220, D236, D248, D260, D346, D368, D430, D450, D484; AceF F110, F126, F160, F176, F230, F244, F257; AceG G577, G601, G615, G668, G698, G747; AceM M102, M136, M163; AvFS F131, F178, F205, F227; AvT T411, T463, T523; BalU U2237; GM 843, 892; Lan 73-845, 73-847; Pyr G498, G540; Signet D2010, G2311
Hogan, Robert J.—Av 454, 469, 550, 674, 820; AvT T540, T542; BerkM X1734, X1746, X1764, X2002, X2004, X2023, X2043, X2058; Lan 73-774, 73-789, 73-796, 73-807, 73-863
Hogarth, Emmett—BondM 1; DNC 3
Hoke, Helen—BB F1854
Hoke, Newton Wilson—Pock 1160
Holbrook, Marion—MNC 57, 63
Holbrook, Stewart H.—ASE K13, H224
Holden, Curry—PopLG G508
Holden, Genevieve—AceG G554, G558; BM B172
Holden, Larry—EtB E132; Pyr G306, G429
Holden, Richard—Perma M3034
Holder, William—Signet 1539
Holding, Elisabeth Sanxay—AceG G509, G511, G512, G519, G524, G530, G534; BB 26; BCD 14; BM B167; BondM 14; Dell 103, 194; Harl 54, 60; MM 175; MNC 58; Pock 662; Pop 189, 302; TNC 17
Holiday, Billie—Lan 74-839, 75-081
Holk, Agnete—Pyr G170, R863
Holland, Marty—Av 181; AvBD 5; AvLBM 1; AvMN 2, 15; Cent 26; DivPN 4; NovL 45
Holland, W. Bob—PermaH P94
Hollander, John—DellLE LB152
Hollands, D.J.—Signet D1506
Holley, H.—RDM 29
Holliday, Billy—PopLG G208
Holliday, Don—Midw 25, 39, 66, F109
Hollingshead, Kyle—AceG G642, G698
Hollis, Jim—Av 725
Hollister, Paul—CBS nn
Holloway, Elizabeth—Dell 133
Holly, Joan Hunter—AceG G636; AvG G1231;Las 22, 55; MonB 213, 240, 260, 342
Holman, Hugh—HH 8; Signet 684, 718
Holmes, Clellon—AceD D238; CreB s307
Holmes, David—Pyr G493, F792
Holmes, David C.—Perma M3122
Holmes, Geoffrey—Av nn(18)
Holmes, H.H.   (Anthony Boucher)—Pen 553; PhanM 1
Holmes, L.P.—AceD D597; AceF F142, F208, F384; BB 823, 898, 968, 1048, 1103, 1384, 1514, 1822, 1873, 2031; Grap 77, 144; Lan 74-789, 74-790, 75-347; Penn P13, P25; Pock 514, 675; RCL 18
Holmes, Rick—MonB 262, 346, 557, 563
Holmgren, Virginia C.—Lan 73-883
Holt, Allison—RDM 21
Holt, Felix—Dell 750; DellD D202
Holt, Hamilton—Thrill nn

Holt, Henry—CWC nn, 70, 98, 106
Holt, L. Emmett Jr—PopSP SP42
Holt, Rackham—ASE A25
Holt, Tex—Han 117, 136; Harl 155; PrizeWN 22, 24, 33
Holt, Victoria—CreB D468, R618, D629, R778, R855, T885
Holtman, Jerry—HollH HH159
Holzer, Hans—AceH H16, H47, H100; AceK K210, K272
Homer, Dale—BB 1838
Homerus—Ment M46, M92, Ms110; PelB P21; Pen 613
Homes, Geoffrey—AceD D185; BB 12, 52, 89, 117, 309, 701, 779; Cent 10; Dell 14, 41, 86; JonM J35
Honig, Donald—AvT T512; Pyr G359; Regy RB105
Hood, Margaret Page—Dell 602, 880; DellD D365
Hood, Matthew—AvG G1193
Hoopes, Roy Jr—EtB E129
Hooton, Barbara—PopSP SP16
Hoover, J. Edgar—CardGC GC39
Hoover, P.A.—AceD S168, S219, D290, D428
Hope, Anthony—BB 33; Pyr G595
Hope, Bob—ASE O14; AvV V2203; CardE C205
Hope, Edward—BB 66
Hope, Emerson—Pock 1014
Hope, Fielding—BelLB L92-598
Hopkins, Linton C.—TechM 1
Hopkins, Mary A.—AceK K182
Hopkins, Stanley—BM B72
Hopkins, Tom J.—Av 474; BB 208; Hill 30, 47; Perma M3008; PermaS 238, 271; Pop 390; Signet 989; WNC 104; WT 4
Hopley, George    (Cornell Woolrich)—PapLF 54-438
Hopley, George    (William Irish)—Pop 424
Hopper, Hedda—Pyr T934
Hopper, Millard—Pock 239
Hopson, William—AceD D68, D128, D272, D320, D430, D492; Av 414, 516, 687, 709, 723, 824, 837, 875; AvFS F161; AvT T508, T533, T553; AvWNM 2, 3; BB 1117, 1180, 1461; Berk 107, 324, 341, 347, 366; BerkD D2014; BerkG G87, G230; Cent 74, 88, 118, 129; GM 501, 569, S1265, K1715; GWN 50; Han 137; Harl 110, 158, 236, 275, 304, 309, 360; Lan 70-044, 70-047, 70-051; Lion 65, 66, 195; LionLL LB156; Prize 88; Pyr 225
Horan, James D.—Av 330; BB A1402; Perma M4118; PopLG G381; Signet S1557
Horgan, Paul—CreB M475, D503, M559, M720; Perma M4108
Horikoshi, Jiro—Bal S467K
Horikoshi, Okumiya—Bal F201
Horler, Sydney—Harl 307, 322, 400, 410, 425, 488; MNM 18; TNC 5
Horman, Richard E.—AvQS QS16
Horn, Allan—Meritf S21, 680; NovF 5032; Saber SA153
Hornay, Norton—Powe PP137
Hornblow, Leonora—Signet 854, D1548
Horner, Lance—CreB D422, R655, T809; GM M1698
Hornes, Larry—CHARf CB169
Hornstein, Lillian Herlands—Ment MD179
Horowitz, David—Bal F603
Horowitz, Irving Louis—Bal S705
Horowitz, Robert S.—MonB 484
Horstein, Lillian Herlands—Ment MT232
Horton,—NSLF 47
Horwin, Brian—Signet 1063
Horwitz, Julius—BelLB L522; Signet P2017
Hoskins, Robert—Lan 75-108, 75-166, 75-320, 75-387, 75-477; Las 40
Hostovsky, Egon—BB 1161
Hotchner, A.E.—Signet S1671
Hough, Donald—ASE N12, S17, 870
Hough, Emerson—Pock 410, 429
Hough, Henry Beetle—ASE M21
Hough, Richard B.—Bal 451K, 513K
Hough, S.B.—AvG G1205
Houghton, Elizabeth—Harl 485, 556, 594, 664, 726, 835
Houghton, Norris—DellLE LC110
Hougron, Jean—Dell 1006; DellD D135, D190
House, Brant—AceD S116, S132, S145, S165, S179, S188, D268, S275, D307, D323; AceK K142, K152, K176, K224; Cor CR122, CR126, CR130, CR134, CR138, CR142, CR146; Pop 777
House, O.T.—Pyr F749
Household, Geoffrey—ASE I248, I165; BB 9, 1019; BM B207; Com 12; DellTC 29; Penn P11; Pyr R930, R944, R957, R967, R979
Housepian, Marjorie—DellD D229
Housman, A.E.—ASE M1, 1015; Av 246; AvB Bard 8; AvGS GS7
Houston, Jack—AceD D35; Av 412, 492; AvT T294
Howarath, David—Pyr R486
Howard, Elizabeth Metzger—PermaS P153
Howard, Hartley—CWC 530
Howard, Ivan—BelLB L92-557, L92-564, L92-567, L92-571, L92-575, L92-582
Howard, James A.—AceF F130; Pock 1255; PopLE EB30, EB46, EB70, EB90; PopLG G346
Howard, John Tasker—Ment MD212
Howard, Leigh—AvT T404
Howard, Mark—DellFE B171
Howard, Mary—CWC 254, 444, 461, 502
Howard, Peter—GSB IL7-67

Howard, Robert E.—AceD D36; AceF F305; Lan 73-526, 73-549, 73-572, 73-599, 73-650, 73-685, 73-721, 73-780, 73-800, 74-561, 74-958, 74-963, 74-976, 75-072, 75-102, 75-103, 75-104, 75-119, 75-136, 75-137, 75-148, 75-149, 75-265, 75-299, 75-371
Howard, Robert West—Signet S1424, D2024, D2193
Howard, Toni—Pyr G157; Signet 820, 1207
Howard, Vechel—GM 685, 789, 854, 878, 943, S1121, S1281, K1627, K1668
Howarth, David—AceD D228; AceF F228; AceG G569; BEDN 283K
Howatch, Susan—AceK K220, K240, K280
Howe, Arthur A.—Fab Z150, Z152; Vega V28; VWL VW107, VW112
Howe, Cliff—AceD D271, D282
Howe, George—Pock 748
Howe, Helen—AvG G1153; DellD D115; Perma M4104
Howe, Margaret—AceD D521; AceF F101; AvT T537; BB 1711, 2002; Pock 1236
Howe, Quincy—Pock 127
Howells, J. Harvey—AceD G376
Howells, William—ASE 729
Howes, Royce—MNC 73
Howley, Cameron—TBSTB 907
Hoy, Elizabeth—Harl 433, 449, 472, 483, 491, 497, 501, 507, 526, 532, 542, 573, 577, 903, 925, 959
Hoyer, Niels—PopSP SP00
Hoyle, Fred—CreB D773; Ment M125, MD200; Signet S1673
Hoyle, Geoffrey—CreB D812
Hoyt, Don—Powe 1009N
Hubbard, L. Ron—AceD S66; GSFN 29; Lan 73-573
Hubbard, P.M.—BalU U2217
Hubler, Richard Gibson—Av 504; Pop 594; PopLG G427, G457; PopSP SP229
Hudiburg, Edward—LionLL LB137
Hudson, Jan    (George H. Smith)—Fran F24
Hudson, W.H.—ASE O5, C71, G196, 721; BB 63, F1878; JL nn(3); Pock 16
Hueston, Ethel—Av 362
Huff, Darrell—ASE 1002
Huff, Frances—ASE 1002
Huffaker, Clair—CreB 158, 167, 193, 222, 398, S421; GM 733, 736, S1459
Huggins, Roy—ASE 1088; Av 282; DellFE A176; Pock 524, 602
Hughes, Cledwyn—NSLF 60
Hughes, Dorothy B.—ASE N11, 785, 828, 869; AvS S161; BondM 11; Dell 31, 48, 100, 149, 210, 853; DellD D225; Harl 44; JonM J70; Pock 394, 422, 454, 587, 845
Hughes, Helen MacGill—MonB 459
Hughes, Isabelle—CWC 412
Hughes, Lawrence—Pyr R922
Hughes, Richard—ASE J282; Pen 536, 628; Signet T2281
Hughes, Thomas—Pock 58
Hughes, Zach—Las 49
Hugo, Victor—AvT T190; BB F1526, F1678; Pock 31, 32
Huie, William Bradford—Signet 959, 1113, S1162, S1439, S1651, D1792, S1825
Hulbert, Archer Butler—ASE J301
Hulburd, David—Pop 495
Hull, E. Mayne—Dell 174, 279, 342, 402; PapLG 52-979; Powe PP128
Hull, Helen—PopLG G564
Hull, Richard—CWC nn, 56, 237, 298; MM 98; MNM 25; Pen 526; Pock 381
Hulme, Kathryn—CardGC GC54
Hultman, Helen Joan—FGM nn; HH 10
Hume, David—CWC nn, 53, 94, 107, 243, 272, 286, 322, 333, 380
Hume, Doris—DellFE K104
Humphrey, William—AvV V2097; Perma M4128
Humphries, Adelaide—AvFS F172; BB 422, 1496; BerkG G288; DellD D419; MonB 198, 223
Humphries, John R.—DellFE 61
Humphries, Rolfe—Bal 39, 226
Huneker, James—AvT T71, T260
Hunger, Anna—AceD D162
Hunt, Charlotte—AceH H37, H98
Hunt, George P.—Signet 1440
Hunt, Harrison—BM 108
Hunt, Howard—Av 457; Berk 345; BerkD D2001; GM 113, 167, 268, 297, 738, s869; GMB 23; Harl 3; Signet 729, 768
Hunt, Kyle—CreB 334; Signet 1472, 1573
Hunt, Peter—Dell 42; PrizeMN 19
Hunter, Alan B.—Bal F645
Hunter, Anson—MonA MA325
Hunter, Edward—Pyr R340, R612
Hunter, Elizabeth—Harl 654
Hunter, Evan—CardF C187, C236; CardGC GC56, GC94; Fal 41; Pock 1126; Pop 478; PopLG G277
Hunter, Georgiana—Pyr 200, G334
Hunter, Hall    (Edison Marshall)—PermaS P223
Hunter, J.A.—BB A1391
Hunter, John—Bal 65; Perma M3092, M3123; Pock 1249
Hunter, Kristin—AvN N215
Hunter, Robert—NSLS U184
Hunter, Samuel—DellFE FE98; DellLE LY102; PocLGA A3
Huntington, Ellsworth—Ment MT248
Hunton, Mary—Harl 611, 729

Hurd, Florence—GM D1709
Hurk, Nick—HollH HH171
Hurley, Gene—Croy nn
Hurley, Victor—AvS S112; AvV V2135
Hurley, William—Lan 75-097
Hurst, Fannie—AvMSS 14; DellTC 14; Pen 589; Perma M4124; Pop 101; Signet S961
Hurwood, Bernhardt J.—AceH H83; AceK K276; BelLB B50-735; GM D1544; Lan 72-656, 75-085
Huston, H.C.—PermaS 277
Hutchins, Maude—CreB 138; Pyr 49, 130, G436, F782, F793
Hutchinson, A.S.M.—Pock 486
Hutchinson, Loring—Signet 1447
Hutschnecker, Arnold A.—Perma M4059; PermaS P276
Hutter, Catherine—Signet S1041, S1337
Hutter, Ernie—MonB 370
Hutton, Brett—BLA 22
Hutton, J.F.—AceD D29; MM 142
Huxley, Aldous—ASE 926; Av AT435; AvG G1020, G1027, G1031, G1059 G2001; AvSS SS1; AvT T75, T160; AvV V2031; AvVS VS1; BantC AC1, AC22; BB A1071, 1142, F1233, A1260, A1369, A1490, A1560, F1622, A1793; BelLB L516; BerkG BG66; LionLL LL114
Huxley, Elspeth—Pop 100; PrizeMN 10
Huxley, Julian—Ment M31, MD148, MD204, MD244
Huxley, Laura Archera—CreB R815
Hye, Celia—Bea B188
Hyland, Raymond—Saber SA108
Hyman, Dr. Harold T.—AvN N103; AvWYX W106
Hyman, Mac—Signet S1285, D1530
Hynd, Alan—Av 604; BerkG G75; GM 101, 473; Pen 641; Pyr G304; Signet 667
Hytes, Jason—Midw D231, S277, 34-395, 34-612
Iams, Jack—ASE N20, 276; Dell 139, 274, 384, 457, 514, 631, 722; Lion 22, 46
Ibanez, Vincente Blasco—Dell 500
Ibsen, Henrik—AvGS GS3, GS8; AvS YS418, YS421; BantC FC23; DellLE LC123
Idell, Albert—GM S953, D1479; RSB 9
Iles, Francis—DellD D215; Pock 419, 432; PockB B48
Ilg, Frances L.—DellD D180; DellLE LC120
Ilton, Paul—DellFE B105; Signet 1301, 1399
Inchardi, J.—Signet 1344
Ingalls, Edna—PermaH P2
Inge, William—BB 1457, 1518
Ingersoll, Major Ralph—FFS nn; LionLL LL48; PenS s226; Pop 248, 401
Ingles, James Wesley—Pop 299
Ingram, Hunter—BalU U2332, U2350
Innes, Hammond—Bal F614, F615, F642, F661, F696, F734, F768; BB 364, 741, 890, 1024, 1058, 1125, 1516; CWC nn, 358, 381, 408, 434, 514, 544; JonM J60; Perma M4079
Innes, Michael—Av 752; AvG G1247, G1273; AvT T351; Pock 741
Irish, William—AceD D40; ASE S20, 878, 1173; Av 104, 220; AvMMM 31, 42; BM B90; Dell 679; DellD D207; DellTC 11, 26; Grap 16, 20, 31, 81, 108; JonM J31; MM 82, 135; Pock 253; Pop 137, 258, 309, 431, 473; RCL 12; ReaL nn
Irving, Alexander—Dell 289
Irving, Clifford—PopLG G187, G311; Signet P2199
Irving, Washington—AvSS SS9; Lad L8
Irwin, Margaret—ASE 843
Irwin, Theodore D.—Hill 18
Isaksson, Ulla—Bal F444K
Isherwood, Christopher—ASE 1115; Av 448; BerkG G153; DellLE LC102; Lan 74-943, 75-127; Pop 710; Signet 937, S1252
Ishloan, Deborah—AvT T503
Ishmael,—PocSp 10047, 10058
Israel, Charles E.—CreB 313, T517
Iverson, Andrina—Hill 172
Ives, Averil—Harl 624, 632, 683, 872
Ives, Burl—Bal 48, 146, X525K, X774; BEDN F295K
Ives, Morgan    (Marion Zimmer Bradley)—MonB 335
Ivie, Larry—Tower 42-660, 42-672, 42-674, 42-687
Jablonski, Edward—MonK K72
Jackquin, Lee—StorON 8
Jackson, Charles—ASE O19, 1041; Bal 36; BelLB L505; BerkG G1; Dell 504; LionLL LL35, LL143; PockB B3; Signet 683, 715, 781; Zenith ZB1
Jackson, Delmar—Pop 599; PopLG G279
Jackson, Félix—BB A1462; PopLG G281
Jackson, Giles—Han 25, 82
Jackson, Howard—Powe PP116
Jackson, Joseph Henry—BB 354; GM s688
Jackson, Leonard—TBSTB 908
Jackson, Norman—Lan 73-798, 73-809, 73-828, 73-837, 74-989, 75-090, 75-092, 75-099
Jackson, O.T.—Lan 74-577, 74-739
Jackson, Ralph—AceD S137
Jackson, Shirley—AceH H96; AceK K166, K185; AvS S197; AvT T449; AvVS VS29; Bal 337K, 342K; Lion 14, 36; Perma M3004; Pyr G212; Signet S1400
Jackson, W. Warner—NSLF 519; NSLS U143
Jacobs,—PocSp 10046
Jacobs, Bruce—Lion 23, 125, 172, 194; LionLL LL12, LL74, LL150
Jacobs, Jesse—CP nn
Jacobs, T.C.H.—BEDN 1

Jacobs, William H.—MonB 163
Jacobson,—PocSp 10044
Jacobson, Edmund—Pock 330
Jacobson, Sid—Lan 74-523
Jacoby, Oswald—CreB R873; PermaH P33
Jacquin, Lee—Croy 106; Knick nn; PrizeLN 24
Jade, George—MeritF 535, 688; MeritS 6M410; TBSTB 904
Jaediker, Kermit—Lion 51, 156
Jaffe, Bernard—ASE 809; Prem S49
Jaffe, Frederick S.—Bal F532; BalU U2136
Jaffe, Michael—BDSM 3
Jaffe, Rona—CardGC GC68; CreB R462, T770
Jakes, John—AceD D209, D220; AceG G656; AvS S363; Bea
    B115; Bel 204, 90-261, 90-289; BelLB B50-762; Lan
    75-113, 75-415; MonB 339; NovF 6001; PapLS 63-089,
    63-184; RoyG 22
James, Al—NovF 5048; Novs 7N708
James, Barbara—AceG G598, G684
James, C.L.R.—Jam nn
James, D.—AvV V2039
James, Dan—FWN 7, 10; Pyr 269; WNM nn
James, Daniel—AvG G1083
James, Don—MonB 101, 183, 237, 258, 358, 456; MonHBS
    MB502, MB506, MB512, MB534
James, Griffith—Knick nn; LevGL 103
James, Henry—ASE T18; BantC AC38; Dell 800; DellD D181;
    DellLE LC117, LC121, LC136; Pen 625
James, Jerry—GSB IL7-75, IL7-76
James, Les—Powe PP102
James, M.E. Clifton—Av 692
James, M.R.—ASE O28
James, Marquis—ASE K23, 1144
James, Martin MD—MonHBS MB528, MB536
James, Maryl—Lan 73-822
James, Stuart—Lan 71-309; Midw F77; MonB 143; MonMS
    MM601
James, Vincent—Pop 800
James, Walter S.—DellD D418
James, Will—BB 47
James, William—Ment MD221
James, William H.—Powe PP188
Jameson, Keith—MonK K65
Jameson, Malcolm—Bond 10A; GSFN 27
Jamieson, Leland—AceD S262
Janeway, Elizabeth—Pock 393
Janifer, Laurence M.—AceH H91; Lan 72-789, 73-611, 73-
    752; Pyr F840, F963
Janney, Russell—Dell 474
Jansen, Laura Mae—Lan 73-586
Janson, Hank—Chec 10; GSB IL7-11, IL7-12, IL7-13, IL7-
    14, IL7-15, IL7-16, IL7-17, IL7-18, IL7-20, IL7-22,
    IL7-28, IL7-32, IL7-48, IL7-57, IL7-63, IL7-68, IL7-70;
    Pony 126
Jantzen, Fritz—Eur 1101
January, Steve—Av 553; AvT T359
Jarrett, Cora—ASE H220
Jarrett, Kay—Bann B60-107
Jarvis, D.C. MD—CreB D438, D537
Jason, Stuart  (Oscar Wilson)—Lan 75-095, 75-100, 75-
    111, 75-146, 75-165
Jasper, Robert—Av 487
Jastrow, Joseph—Perma M4134; Pock 522
Javellana, Stevan—Pop 435
Jay, Charlotte—Av 623, 670, 736; AvG G1281; AvS S182;
    AvT T376
Jay, Willa—Lan 73-613
Jeans, James—Prem d70
Jeffers, Albert—BIH 12
Jefferson, Lara—Crow 21
Jellett, Dr. Henry—MM 79
Jenison, Dan P.—AceG G721
Jenkins, Dorothy H.—BB A1418
Jenkins, Elizabeth—BB 64
Jenkins, Geoffrey—AvG G1052; AvS S158, S183, S196,
    S242
Jenkins, Will F.  (Murray Leinster)—GM 126, 161, 346;
    GMB 4; Han 62; HH 4; NSLF 141
Jennings, Dean—Pock 831
Jennings, John—ASE Q36, 1226, 1306; CardE C22, C137;
    DellD D267; Perma M3071; PermaS P125, P133, P141,
    P157, P256, P293; Pock 1047; PopSP PP19, SP72
Jepson, Selwyn—BB 803; MM 73
Jerome, E.J.—Croy 12
Jerome, Owen Fox—BCD 13; Han 58; Harl 77, 86
Jessel, George—AvG G1119; Friars nn
Jessup, M.K.—BB A1374
Jessup, Richard—DellFE 92, 109, B118, A194; GM s440,
    s515, 647, s660, 672, 699, 771, s1105, S1159,
    S1172, S1273, S1404, K1530, K1642
Jeter, K.W.—Las 7, 33
Joesten, Joachim—AceD S58; Av 538; PopLG G155
Johnen, Wilhelm—AceD D326
Johns, Veronica Parker—AtM nn; MM 197
Johnson,—FFS nn
Johnson, Annabel—CreB s201
Johnson, Crockett—Pock 366
Johnson, David—Powe PP112
Johnson, Dorothy M.—Bal 29, 402K, 610; BalU U1045;
    BEDN 241, 274K
Johnson, Frank—GM S1267

Johnson, George—GM S1263; MonK K57, K61, K64; MonS
    MS20
Johnson, George Clayton—CardE C412
Johnson, Gerald—BantB FB408
Johnson, Gerald W.—ASE 735
Johnson, Grady—DellFE B128
Johnson, Hope—GM S1230
Johnson, Capt. J.E.—Bal F195
Johnson, Jack—GM 517
Johnson, James Weldon—Ment M29
Johnson, Josephine—AvG G1109; AvS S214
Johnson, Katrina—Harl 183
Johnson, Martin—ASE 1124
Johnson, Nora—AvG G1222
Johnson, Osa—ASE L32, E141
Johnson, Pyke Jr—BB F1558
Johnson, Robert S.—Bal F323K, F514K, F764
Johnson, Ryerson—GM 459; RSB 10, 28; WNC 69
Johnson, Thomas M.—FFS nn
Johnson, Victor H.—CWC 427; Grap 101; Pyr 125, 229
Johnston, Alexander—ASE I263
Johnston, Bill—NovF 60105
Johnston, George Henry—Pock 818
Johnston, Mary—CardE C322; Pock 354
Johnston, Stanley—MonB 98
Johnston, William—AceG G702, G725; Lan 70-006, 70-043,
    70-049, 73-205, 73-206, 73-838, 73-849, 73-864, 73-
    872, 73-876, 73-889, 73-891, 74-582, 75-463; MonB
    243, 275, 284, 336, 355, 411, 442
Johnstone, Lane—PopLG G383
Jonas, Carl—DellD D120, D124
Jones, Arthur Frederick—CardE C304; Pock 629
Jones, Constance—Pock 503
Jones, Denys—Signet S1387
Jones, Evan—BB 1313
Jones, George—Bea B134; Novs 6N227
Jones, George E.—Grap 106
Jones, Gregory—AceD D147
Jones, Guy Pearce—Pen 506
Jones, H.—QB 63
Jones, H. Bedford—Cent 133; Harl 228, 232
Jones, H. Spencer—Ment M39, MD144
Jones, Howard—PockB B42
Jones, Idwal—ASE 1310
Jones, Inigo—MNM nn, 33
Jones, James—Signet T1075, T1637, Q2364
Jones, Jennifer—Dell 3; RA 2
Jones, Ken—Lion 142; Signet S1476; Zenith ZB15
Jones, Nard—AvT T79, T164; GM 388, 512
Jones, Nathaniel—AceD D201
Jones, Neil R.—AceF F420; AceG G631, G650, G681, G719
Jones, Philip—AvG G1311
Jones, Raymond F.—Bea 242; BelLB L92-588; GSFN 6; Las
    1, 12, 54; Pyr F941
Jones, Robert Page—MonB 396
Jones, Tom—AvWYX W121
Jones, X.X.—AceG G760
Joneway, Elizabeth—Pock 442
Jordan, Cathy—Dom 82106
Jordan, David—Prem S32
Jordan, Gail  (Peggy Gaddis)—Cam 311, 328, 341; Cent
    119; Croy 19, 23, 109; DB 10; Harl 26; Knick nn, 15,
    16; Novl nn; NSLF 17, 22, 103; Pyr 15; QB 46; StorON
    5; Uni 28, 37; Venus 146
Jordan, George—Venus 195
Jordan, Holly—NovF 7502
Jordan, J.J.—NovF 5071, 6070, 60112
Jordan, Valerie—MonHBS MB526
Jorgensen, Ivar  (Paul Fairman)—AceD D351; BelLB B50-
    849; MonB 297, 362
Joscelyn, Archie—AceD D304, D392; Av 739, 788, 791, 798,
    813, 819; AvFS F200; BCW 31, 40, 41, 45; Cent 71,
    134; GWN 39, 47; Han 89, 109; Harl 73, 244, 263,
    374; PrizeWN 28; Pyr 259, G618; Star 7, 9, 13, 14,
    18, 24, 29, 30, 32, 37, 39, 42, 47, 48; WNC 70, 111
Joseph, George—PopLE EB44; PopLG G265
Joseph, Jennie—Fab Z153; FabR nn
Joseph, Richard—Dou nn
Joseph, Robert—Harl 137
Joseph, Stephen M.—AvNS NS29
Josephs, Carla—Lan 72-902
Josephs, Ira M.—Lan 72-154
Joswick, Jerry J.—Pyr R800
Jourdan, Eric—Pyr G415
Joyce, Carlton—MonB 366, 463
Joyce, James—Signet 664, S1150
Joyeux, Odette—Pyr G415
Judah, Charles B.—Perma M4075; PermaS P146
Judd, Cyril—AceD D227; Bea 312; Dell 760
Judd, Harrison—GM S1124
Judson, Jeanne—AceF F112; BB 1614, 1667, 1751
Julian, Peter—LionLL LL174
Jung, C.G.—Ment MD259
Kades, Hans—DellD D265
Kahler, Jack—Novs 6N250
Kahn,—Metro nn
Kahn, Herman—AvNS NS3; AvWYX W135
Kahn, Lawrence H.—Pock 1202
Kahn, Steve—McF 50-114
Kainen, Ray—FPVFP FP2005
Kains, M.G.—ASE 889; Pock 543

Kalashnikoff, Nicholas—ASE 1062
Kale, Susan—AvG G1069
Kalman, Victor—Perma M4147
Kamal, Ahmad—BB 716
Kamm, Jacob O. PhD—AceF F118
Kandel, Aben—Harl 23, 144; Signet S1938
Kandel, H.—BelLB L92-574
Kandel, Howard—Kan K102
Kane, Arnold—Saber SA21
Kane, Bob—Signet D2939
Kane, Frank—AceD D33; Bea B111; Dell 665, 749, 785, 822,
    886, 901, 918, 973; DellD D226, D264, D280, D333,
    D451; DellFE A117, B123, B125, A126, C127, B137,
    A142, B150, B159, B173, B174, B187, B197, B226;
    Han 72; Harl 126; JonM J56, J64; Pop 400; RCL 8
Kane, Frank E.—Fed 3, 4
Kane, Gil—BB S5871; Tempo 17311
Kane, Harnett Thomas—AceK K132; ASE J294; Perma
    M4071; PopSP SP90
Kane, Henry—Av 572, 602, 618, 646, 672, 703, 733, 745,
    751, 761, 790, 796; AvFS F165; AvG G1207; AvT
    T264, T276, T291, T460; BelLB 92-623; Dell 231, 316,
    330, 348, 455, 535, 580, 735; DellFE A144, B155,
    B198; Lan 70-048, 71-304, 73-817, 73-823, 73-835,
    73-839, 73-858, 74-559, 74-562, 74-595, 74-610, 74-
    643, 74-646, 74-664, 74-694, 75-158, 75-180, 75-
    261, 75-407, 75-409, 75-410, 75-412; MidT
    F330; Pop 806; Pyr G284, G432, G569; Signet 1515,
    1523, S1940, S2080, G2301; Zenith ZB19
Kane, Irene—DellFE A179, B200
Kane, Joseph Nathan—Perma M3039, M4101
Kane, Kaspar  (Fred MacIsaac)—Whit 790
Kanigher, Robert—CamH nn
Kanin, Fay—BB 1780
Kanin, Garson—CardE C401
Kanin, Michael—BB 1780
Kannon, Jackie—Kan K101
Kanto, Peter—Lan 74-673
Kantor, MacKinlay—ASE K6, T14, B38, G202, 813, 1233; BB
    753, 809, 900, A965, A1008, 1038, 1175, 1237,
    1238, 1351, A1625, F2029; GM 122, 675, S1181; Pen
    636; PennSE nn; Pock 135; Pop 183; PopLE EB13;
    PopLG G161, G241, G379, G540; PopSP SP176; Signet
    T1388, S1543, S1703, Q2194
Kapelner, Allan—Bel 224; LionLL LB92; PopSP SP126
Kaplan, Arthur—AvG G1130
Kaplan, Edgar—SigK KD368
Karelitz, Samuel—Perma M5008
Karig, Comm. Walter—ASE T31, 734; BB A1340; CardE C56;
    Pop 419; PopSP SP24
Karloff, Boris—AvG G1254
Karlova, Irina—Dell 125
Karmel, Alex—Bel 212
Karneke, Joseph Sidney—AceK K196
Karney, Jack—AceD D101, D373 MonB 116, 157; Pock 898;
    PopLG G212, G304; Pyr 31, 99, G444
Karney, Louis—NSLF 506
Karp, Daniel—Lion 93
Karp, David—AvT T504; Bann B50-105, B50-107, B50-110,
    B50-111, B50-113; Lion 105, 119, 132; LionLL LL10,
    LL86
Karp, Ivan C.—Lan 73-588
Karpman, Benjamin MD—Lan 75-010
Karr, David—Bal 157
Karr, Madeline—Pop 820
Karsell, Tom—AvG G1141
Karson, Arlene—MonB 376
Kasner, Edward—ASE N25
Kastle, Herbert D.—AvT T355; CreB d271, S491; GM L1494,
    D1591; Pop 823
Kastner, Erich—MM 21
Katcha, Vahé—Pyr G547
Katcher, Leo—Pock 1197
Katkov, Norman—AvN N127; Pop 251
Ka-Tzetnik,—Pyr G326
Kauffmann, Lane—AvG G1243; AvN N120; AvS S289 LionLL
    LL64
Kauffmann, Sidney—AvV V2123
Kauffmann, Stanley—Pop 520, 705; PopLG G183; PopSP
    SP30
Kaufman, Bel—AvN N130
Kaufman, Bob—GM S1115
Kaufman, Eve—Pock 143
Kaufman, George S.—Pock 143
Kaufman, Joseph J. MD—CreB D621
Kaufman, Lenard—AceD D202; Av 433; AvT T105, T217; Dell
    444; Signet 896
Kaufman, Maxine—Pyr R289
Kaufman, Robert—GM K1349
Kaufman, Stanley—Bal 118
Kaufman, Theodore N.—Arg nn
Kaufmann, Myron S.—Signet T1578
Kaufmann, Richard—Signet S1052
Kaufmann, Stanley—Bal 461K
Kavinoky, Bernice—PopLG G185, G297, G375, G487
Kay, Cameron—GM 311
Kaye, H.R.—HollH HH153
Kaye, M.M.—PopSP SP18
Kaye, Philip B.—Av 377
Kaye, Tom—PopLG G573
Kaylin, Walter—GM K1284

333

Lucas, Bob—Lan 70-009
Lucas, Cary—Dell 366
Lucas, Curtis—Bea B119, B173; Lion 80, 91, 162; LionLL LL14; UGE 8
Lucas, George—PapLS 64-624
Lucas, Joe—NovF 60110
Lucas, Mark—Saber SA78, SA88, SA91, SA103, SA110, SA118, SA119, SA126; TBSTB 911, 928, 931, 946
Lucas, Rick—Bea B279, B303, B309; BerkG G228
Lucas, Robert—Uni 76
Lucas-Dubreton, J.—BantB FB407
Lucchese, John A.—AvG.G1084
Lucchesi, Aldo—Midw 44
Luce, Gay Gaer—Lan 74-874
Luck, Barry—EHO 0142
Ludwig, Emil—AceK K141; BantB FB400; BantC FC27; CardGC GC11; Prem d34, d55
Lueddecke, W.J.—GM D1562
Lumbard, C.G.—Pop 640
Lund, Robert—BB F1393; CardE C39
Lundin, John Philip PhD—Lan 75-008, 75-025
Lupoff, Richard A.—AceN N6; Lan 74-892
Lupton, Leonard—Grap 149
Lurie, Alison—AvN N159
Lurton, Douglas—CreB s241, S506; Prem S12
Lurton, Douglas E.—ASE 1032
Lustgarten, Edgar—Av 179; BB 360, 861; CWC 374, 449; DellD D299; PockB B33
Lutz, E.H.G.—AceK K157
Lutz, Giles A.—AceD D408, D436, D492; AceF F172; AvFS F174, F209, F238; AvG G1294; AvH H100; BalU U1053; CreB 170, 181; GM 548, 567, 741, 804, 877, S1148, S1229, S1314, K1538, K1542, K1615; Lan 73-874; PopLE EB12
Luzzatto, Jack—AvG G1236; Pyr 221, G485, G582; Signet S1913, S1979, S2064, S2149, S2255
Lyall, Gavia—AvS S281
Lymington, John—Lan 74-741
Lynch, Dan (actually writtenby Robert Silverberg)—GM S1240
Lynch, James C.—Pop 476; PopLG G335
Lynch, Miriam—Lan 74-609, 74-661, 74-689, 74-726, 74-746, 74-747
Lynch, William—Lion 25; NSLF 113
Lyndon, Barre—AvT T362
Lynds, Dennis—Signet P2061, D2267
Lynn, David—Saber SA130
Lynn, Jack—NovF 3501, 5002, 5006, 5007, 5014, 5027, 5034, 5038, 5049, 5056, 5063, 5066, 5083, 6019, 6060, 6071, 6072, 6082, 6083, 60100; Novs 6N230, 6N263, 7N712, 7N734
Lynn, Margaret—AceK K180
Lyon, Dana—AceG G525, G535, G545; MM 158; PrizeMN 27; Pyr G393; QR 132
Lyon, Peter—AvG G1156
Lyon, Winston—Signet D2940
Lyons, Augusta W.—Signet S1949
Lyons, Delphine C.—Lan 72-932, 74-654, 74-929, 75-354, 75-355, 75-358
Lyons, Gwen—EcsNLW 116
Lyons, Herbert—PermaS P229
Lyons, James—Ment MD212
Lyons, Ruth—LevGL 101
Lytle, H.M.—Pad nn
Lytton, David—AvS S107
Maas, Carl—MentG G2; PenG G1
Macao, Marshall—FPVFV FP2001, FP2008, FP2015, FP2022, FP2029, FP2037, FP2055
Macardle, Dorothy—ASE B51, 1185; BB 90, 915
MacArthur, Arthur—UGE 9
MacArthur, Douglas—CreB M850
Macauley, C.B.F.—ASE 978
Macauley, Robie—Signet 1081
MacBrian, James—MonB 382, 429
MacCampbell, Donald—PermaH P88
MacCormac, John—Dell 32
MacCuish, David—CreB T552, T751
MacDonald,—Fran F62
MacDonald, Betty—ASE 1100; AvS S180; AvZS ZS102; Bal F356K; Pock 566, 1119
MacDonald, Charles B.—Bal S529
MacDonald, Fred—Powe PP107
MacDonald, George—BalAF 01711, 01902, 02874, 23528
MacDonald, John D.—CreB s295, S359, S400, S464, S520, R661, K788; DellFE 12, 62, 85, B112, A113, K116, B117, B121, B127, A130, B134, B141, B146, A152, B167; GM 124, 164, 186, 200, 240, 298, 323, 420, 481, 482, 724, 737, 767, s777, 782, s790, 792, 884, 894, s907, S961, S962, 963, S1015, S1061, S1069, S1076, S1112, S1165, S1177, S1198, S1259, K1291, K1292, K1302, K1318, S1354, D1389, K1394, K1405, K1406, K1421, K1451, K1461, K1464, K1469, K1496, D1499, K1513, D1528, K1537, D1543, K1547, D1552, D1563, K1566, D1573, D1579, K1580, K1587, D1588, D1590, D1599, D1606, D1609, D1610, D1621, D1633, D1635, D1636, R1649, D1659, D1674, D1682, T1684, D1690, D1699, D1712; GMB 41, 57, 72; Pock 943; Pop 675, 697, 737, 750, 830; PopLG G271, G507; Signet S1113, S1665
MacDonald, John Ross—BB 1295, 1360, 1613, 1839, A2024; Pock 680, 821, 907, 971, 1020

MacDonald, Philip—AvG G1256, G1257, G1264; BB 146; BM B195; BondM 13; CWC 207, 228; DellD D194, D247; MM 181; Pen 79, 586; Pock 70, 328; PopSP SP248; SupR M642; Zenith ZB29
MacDonald, William Colt—AceD D2, D52, D216; AceF F389, F428; AceG G746; ASE 712, 956, 1208, 1304; Av 343, 491, 498, 514, 536, 579, 586, 592, 678, 689, 765, 769, 799, 865; AvFS F241, F242; AvT T353, T369, T396, T409, T421, T428, T443, T522; Cent 16, 56, 61, 65, 69, 76; CreB 134, 149; EtB E127; Grap 25, 50; GWN 8, 11, 14, 17, 19, 22, 26; Hill 19, 25, 31, 34, 102; PermaH P96; Pyr 95, 101, 115, 172, 231, G276, 286, 294, G363, G451; Signet 698, 723, 764, 792, 835, 880, 925, 1005, 1059, 1168, 1181, 1331, 1416, 1588; WAN 2; WNC 37, 54
MacDonald, W.R.—Cents CB1611
MacDonald, Wilson—CHARf CB149
MacDonald, Zillah K.—BB 1562; BerkG G159
MacDonnell, J.E.—Pyr G450, G473
MacDougall, Curtis D.—AceK K136
MacDougall, Michael—ASE H223
Mace, Merida—BCD 15, 17, 28; Harl 25
MacFadyen, Ralph—CreB D666; Prem d68
MacGowan, Kenneth—DellLE LX116
MacGowan, Norman—GM R1550
MacGregor, James—AceD D460
MacHaug, William—Pop 340
Machen, Arthur—ASE 940; BalAF 02643
Machiavelli, Niccolo—Ment M69; Prem d72
Machlin, Milt—PapLF 52-128
MacInnes, Helen—ASE M32; CreB d300, R476, R568, T631, T746, T748, R801, M886; Pock 186, 235; Pop 453
MacIntyre, Donald—AvT T205
MacIsaac, Fred—BLA 18; Whit 790
MacIver, Joyce—Lan 75-091
MacKenzie, Donald—AvG G1214; AvS S202; DellD D328; PopLG G245
MacKenzie, Richard Charlton—PermaH P1
Mackersey, Ian—Perma M4081
Mackey, Joe—Bel 207
MacKinnon, Allan—CWC 351, 441, 497; Dell 237
Macklin, John—AceH H81, H89, H94, H108; AceK K222, K279, K292, K297, K305
Macklin, Mark—AceD D149
MacLean, Alistair—CreB R761; Perma M4067, M4089, M4116
MacLean, Katherine—AceF F149; AvG G1143
MacLean, Robinson—Dell 508
MacLennan, Hugh—ASE 932; CWC nn, 75, 529, 540; Signet T1867
MacLeod, Jean S.—Harl 431, 434, 451, 516, 517, 541, 543, 545, 547, 586, 597, 599, 606, 630, 638, 651, 674, 711, 748, 797, 853, 939, 966
MacLeod, Richard—GM D1720
MacLeod, Robert—GM S1330
MacLeod, Ruth—AceD D556, D595
MacLiesh, Fleming—Signet 1106
MacMillan, Don—Harl 78, 408
MacNeil, Neil—GM 807, s844, 898, 964, 1055, S1182, K1484, D1658
MacPherson, Michael—EHO 0105
MacRoss, Ross—GM 386
MacTyre, Paul—AceF F201
MacVeigh, Sue—Hill 10; MNM 27
Madaurensis, Apuleius—PocL PL6
Madden, Joe—ASE 936
Madden, Mary Ann—Lan 75-303
Maddock, Larry—AceG G605, G620, G644
Maddock, Stephen—CWC nn, 63, 83, 108, 109, 320, 422, 439, 492
Maddox, Gaynor—AvG G1167
Maddox, Harry—CreB R753
Madigan, Kip—Fab Z107, Z114; FabR Z8; Saber SA94, SA154
Maeterlinck, Maurice—Ment M111
Magee, Martin—MonHBS MB545
Magee, N.H.—CardC C90; CardGC GC13, GC19
Mager, Sylvia K.—CardE C90, C232; CardGC GC13, GC19; Pock 890
Mahan, Patte W.—AvS S240
Mahannah, Floyd—Perma M3087; Pock 1231; Signet 879, 957, 1268, 1663
Mahler, Conrad—AvV V2125
Mahler, Helen A.—BB A1157
Maier, William—BB 785
Mailer, Norman—Signet 837AB, 1019, D1375, T1549
Maine, Charles Eric—AceD D274; AvT T524; Bal 218, 360K; BB A1470; BEDN 290K
Maine, Conrad—Pop 679
Maine, Harold—PermaS P156
Maisel, Albert Q.—ASE A20
Majdalany, Fred—Bal 23; BEDN F252, 253
Majors, Simon (Gardner F. Fox)—PapLS 63-359
Makagon, Thomas K.—Vega V32
Makow, Henry—AceF F219
Makris, John N.—AceD D21
Malachy, Frank—Perma M3059
Malamud, Bernard—Dell 712; Signet S1514
Malaparte, Curzio—AvN N117, N135, N145; Signet S1098
Malcolm, Donald—Las 19, 29

Malcolm, Margaret—Harl 584, 592, 596, 600, 613, 634, 723, 777, 809, 923, 945
Malcolm-Smith, George—BB 410; Dell 999; Grap 104
Malina, Fred—Harl 36
Mallery, Richard D.—PermaH P61
Mallet, Francoise—Pop 508; PopLE EB84; PopLG G215
Mallette, Gertrude E.—BerkG G208
Malley, Louis—AceD D257; Av 551; AvT T394; Bel 243; MonB 105; Pock 894
Malloy, Fred—Bea B103, B171, B185, B218, B235, B310; BerkG G170, G185
Malloy, Paul—AvG G1269
Malm, Dorothea—AceA K173; Lan 74-594, 74-858
Malmar, McKnight—PrizeMN 23
Malo, Vincent Gaspard—CreB s327
Malone, Dorothy—AceA A20; AceD D32
Malone, Ted—Pock 308
Maloney, Ralph—AvS S137; CreB S485
Maloney, Russell—ASE 1159
Malston, Alan—NSLF 110; NSLS 25A
Maltz, Albert—ASE 733
Maltz, Maxwell MD—AvFS F142; Avg G1329; AvT T475; Perma M4107
Malzberg, Barry N.—Lan 75-345, 75-486
Manceron, Genevieve—DellD D417
Manchester, Harland—ASE 1044
Manchester, William—Bal 26; Pock 1252
Mandel, George—AvN N147; AvT T489; BB F1165; Lan 74-864
Mandel, Paul—AvV V2076
Manfred, Frederick—CardE C192, C301; Signet P2437
Manis, Harry—NovF 60104, 60109
Mankiewicz, Don M.—DellD D160; Signet 947
Mankowitz, Wolf—Signet 1471
Mann, Abby—PopSP SP212; Signet D2025
Mann, E.B.—ASE 947; BelLB B50-754, B50-784; Dell 333; Lion 27; Pock 694, 987, 1022, 1194; RCL 6
Mann, Heinrich—Signet S1720
Mann, Peggy—PopLG G167
Mann, Thomas—ASE L28; CardE C60; CardGC GC3; Signet D1411
Manners, David X.—HH 18
Manners, Dorine—Pyr 21, G249
Manners, Margaret—DellFE B183
Manners, Martin—Pyr 165, G241, G521, F938
Manners, William—BB A1392; Lion 165, 219
Mannes, Marya—Dell 515
Mannin, Ethel—Pop 438
Manning,—Bea B276
Manning, Bruce—H 14, 25, 48
Manning, Jane—Cam 330; Carn 919, 933, 939; Venus 150
Manning, Lee—Pop 341
Manning, Roy—AceD D20, D46, D86, D192, D308; FWN 16, 18; GWN 31; Pock 663
Manning, Tom—Cam 360
Mannix, Daniel P.—AceD G402; Bal 302K, 354K, 355K, 452K, F765, F766; BalU U2225; BB 1006; BEDN 275K
Mannix, Jule—Bal 348K
Mannon, M.M.—Croy nn
Manor, Jason—Perma M3002; Pop 794; PopLE EB42, EB56; PopLG G362
Mansfield, Harold—Bal F375K
Mansfield, Jayne—HollH HH110
Mansfield, Katharine—ASE 1252
Manson, John—CreB S218
Mantle, Burns—ASE T25
Mantley, John—CreB s209; Perma M4146
Manus, Max—ASE 1272
Manus, William—AceD D232
Manvell, Roger—Pyr R587
Mara, Bernard (Brian Moore)—GM 402, 472, 562
Marais, Claude—Lion 116
Marais, Miranda—Bal F432K; BalU U2204
Marbie, M.S.—Grap 102
Marcelle, Denise—Croy 41, 96
March, Sheldon—CHARs CB1616
March, William—ASE 775; BB A1084; Dell 847; Lion 111; LionLL LB62, LL121; MM 4; Pyr R367, X768; Signet S1522
Marchal, Lucie—BB 862, 1923
Marchant, Kimberly—TBSTB 920
Marchant, Catherine—Lan 72-796, 72-944, 72-984, 73-436, 73-443, 74-716, 74-904, 74-992, 74-995
Marcus, A.A.—Grap 21, 35, 64, 67, 115; Harl 90
Marcus, Alan—AvS S151; Pop 422
Marcus, Carl—NSLF 501; NSLS U132
Marcus, Jerry—DellFE B161
Marcus, Margaret Fairbanks—PocLGA A24
Marcus, Paul—GM 185
Marcus, Robert B.—Las 57
Marcus, Tony—Saber SA141, SA166
Maresca, James—BB 419, 1471, 1756
Marge,—DellFE A125
Margolies, Joseph A.—ASE 1223
Margolius, Sidney—AvV V2111; GM 191; SigK Ks325; Signet 859, S1055
Margroff, Robert—AceA A19
Margulies, Leo—CreB s245, s254, s272, s282, S362, 419, L728; DellFE K109; Grap 76, D1324, D1680; Pock 1007; Pop 156, 187; Pyr G244, G271, G386, G504, G531, G590, G665, F899, R921

337

Mari, Isa—Bel 211
Marin, Arthur—Cam 368; Venus 134, 156
Marina, Vic—CPH B110
Marino, Nick—Pyr 159, G315, F887
Mario, Queena—BartH 11
Marion, Frances—DivPN 3
Maritain, Jacques—PocLGA A14
Mark, David—DellD D300; PopLG G437
Mark, Edwina—BerkG G44, G141, G245; Hill 121
Mark, Stephen—NSLS 24A
Mark, Ted—Lan 72-918, 72-958, 72-989, 72-996, 73-446, 73-461, 73-477, 73-485, 73-487, 73-488, 73-489, 73-490, 73-508, 73-515, 73-527, 73-546, 73-563, 74-541, 74-542, 74-543, 74-544, 74-566, 74-567, 74-569, 74-570, 74-571, 74-572, 75-101, 75-205, 75-210, 75-214
Markandaya, Kamala—Signet S1336, S1532
Marke, Julius J.—Doc 1
Markel, Robert—Perma M4133
Markey, Gene—Bal 18; Perma M4078; PopSP SP96
Markey, Morris—Pony 53
Markham, Beryl—ASE F166
Markham, Virgil—BartH 10
Marko, Zekial—GM K1569
Markowitz, Arthur—Pyr G295, G603; Signet 886
Marks, Jason—GM D1234
Marks, Laurence—Signet D2296
Markson, David—DellFE B189, A193; Pyr R860
Marlett, Melba—AceG G568
Marlot, Melba—MNC 72
Marlow, Edwina—AceG G707
Marlow, Stephen (Milton Lesser)—AceD D77
Marlowe, Alan S.—EHO 0127
Marlowe, Christopher—WSP W100
Marlowe, Dan J.—Avt T307, T349, T392, T452, T491; GM S1184, K1340, K1441, K1524, D1625
Marlowe, Hugh—AvG G1289
Marlowe, Stephen (Milton Lesser)—AceD D89, D189; AvT T330; BerkD D2023; CreB 296; GM S523, 575, 627, 658, 693, 769, 813, 880, 914, d926, 986, 1003, 1018, S1078, S1098, S1116, S1214, K1285, D1288, K1413, K1420, K1508, K1527, R1560, D1686; Grap 94
Marmor, Arnold—MeritF 351, 353, 505, 531, 627, 639; Saber SA17, SA77; Vega V20
Marmur, Jacland—ASE R9
Marnay, Jane—Harl 955, 969
Marquand, John P.—ASE L26, D120, E146, G208, 852, 1084, 1225; AvV V2189; BB A805, 881, A919, A987, F1087, 1200, F1453, F1454, F1675, A1690, A1691, A1781, 1810, S2013; BM B12, B124; DellTC 13; JonM J49, J52, J54; MM 139; Pock 59, 258; PockB B1, B34; Pyr R873
Marquis, Don—ASE K2; MercL L1
Marr, Reed—GM 576, 638
Marric, J.J.—BerkG G122, G278; Pyr G323, G335, R872, R947
Marsh, Ellen—PopLG G399
Marsh, Irving T.—ASE 913
Marsh, Ngaio—ASE 727, 760, 882, 1269; AvT T254; BM B23, B64, B68; CreB S452; CWC nn, 76, 96, 113, 114, 117, 300, 371, 474; JonM J3; MM 79, 203; Pock 113, 137, 221, 297, 351, 437, 475, 527, 626, 762; ReaL nn; Signet 995
Marsh, Peter—Lion 16; NSLF 109
Marsh, Ronald—BB 778, A2009
Marsh, Willard—AvS S247
Marshack, Alexander—DellLE LB111; DSSE nn
Marshall, Alan—Midw 15, 17, 20, 22, 28, 31, 36, 41, 48, 51, 62
Marshall, Alan (Donald Westlake)—Midw F259
Marshall, Bruce—ASE 942; BB 84; PermaS P275; Pock 435; Pyr R576
Marshall, Catherine—CreB T729, T769
Marshall, D.J.—Saber SA157
Marshall, Edison—ASE C87, 689, 841; AvN N204, N214; CardE C194, C233; Dell 144, 188, 233, 341, 353, 364, 422, 431, 468, 487, 530; DellD D102, D103, D119, D122, D139, D157, D173; DellF F67, F72, F87, F98; Harl 200, 239; Pop 128, 208, 242, 272, 345; PopSP SP55, SP69; Pyr X868
Marshall, Frank W.—NovF 5058
Marshall, Gary—CWC 307, 317, 352, 356, 385, 393
Marshall, George C.—FFS nn, F14
Marshall, Joseph R.—GM S1173
Marshall, Marguerite Mooers—BB 464, 1434, 1575, 1645; Pock 746
Marshall, Raymond—Harl 255, 265, 300, 310, 317, 340, 341, 382
Marshall, Rosamond—BB A1724; CWC 99, 313, 435; Dell 382; Eag nn(2), E3; Perma M4114; Pock 469; Pop 527, 717; PopLG G176, G219, G258; PopSP SP104; Pyr G201, G428, R936, R966, R981, R982; Signet 923, 976, 1163, 1190, S1517
Marshall, S.L.A.—FFS nn; PenS s240; Perma M4115
Marshall, Sidney—Green 6
Marshe, Richard—BerkG G196, G236
Marsten, Richard—CreB 139, s178, D581; GM 415, 507; Perma M3097, M3117; Pock 1235
Marston, William—UGE 6
Martin, A.E.—BM B84; Dell 840; MM 116
Martin, Andrew—Saber SA147, SA156

Martin, Aylwin Lee—GM 170, 214, 253; GMB 28; Grap 45
Martin, Charles—Uni 16
Martin, Charles M. (Chuck)—AceD D42, D46; Av 654, 822, 828, 841, 863; AvFS F167; BerkD D2011; BerkG G247; Chec 4; Grap 74, 86, 128; Harl 389; Hill 122; WNC 94
Martin, Cort—Powe PP184; Saber SA145
Martin, Don—RC 4
Martin, Edgar A.—NSLS U163
Martin, Fred—Midw 13
Martin, George Victor—AvMN 10; BB 103, 1595; BerkG G162; EtB E120; NovL 35; NSLF 1
Martin, Gerry—NSLF 117; NSLS 28A
Martin, Hansford—AvT T88, T206
Martin, Henriette—Pock 770
Martin, Henry—Saber SA75
Martin, Jay—Lan 73-634, 73-753, 73-803, 74-522
Martin, Kay—AvT T495; Hill 158, ,190; Pyr F701, F750
Martin, L.—BLA 11
Martin, Pete—BB 721; CardE C248; DellD D266; PenS s230
Martin, Ralph G.—ASE 1227
Martin, Robert—AceD D451; AceF F111; BB 1372, 1397, 1577; Dell 794; Pock 913
Martin, Thom—NSLF 508
Marvin, H.M.—SigK KD356; Signet 1008
Marvin, Ronn—Regy RB103
Marvin, Susan—Lan 74-991
Marx, Groucho—DellF F112
Marx, Harpo—AvV V2050
Maschke, T.A.—NSLS U167
Masefield, John—ASE 820
Masin, Herman L.—BerkG G89; LionLL LL29; Pyr G331; PyrPR PG18
Mason, A.E.W.—Harl 460
Mason, Agnes Lockie—SigK KD315
Mason, David—Lan 74-564, 74-628, 75-217, 75-361, 75-372
Mason, Ernst—Bal 361K
Mason, F. Van Wyck—ASE M31, D119,1234; BB 311, F1744; BM B27, B57, B63; CardE C4, C23, C57, C165, C211, C242, C365; CardGC GC2, GC6, GC9, GC17; Cent 21, 32, nn(70); DNC9; Han 98; Harl 74; Pock 129, 799, 929, 977, 1024, 1076 1115, 1143, 1176, 1201, 1219, 1223; RA 10
Mason, Frank (Algis Budrys)—Regy RB314
Mason, Gregory—Lion 59
Mason, Margot—GSB IL7-56, IL7-62, IL7-69, IL7-72
Mason, Raymond—GM S1248; Hill 175; Signet D1641
Mason, Richard—BB A1003, A1779; GM 395, 468, 589; Signet D1552
Mason, Sara Elizabeth—BB 770; Dell 207
Massie, Chris—BB 54; BerkG G256
Massiker, Frances—AvN N131
Masson, Rene—BB 1054
Masters, John—BB A1072, 1187, A1335, F1381, F1416, F1714, F1805, F2040
Masterson, Whit—AvG G1217; AvS S212; BB 1487, 1543, A1699
Masur, Harold A.—AvG G1194
Masur, Harold Q.—AvG G1233, G1258, G1259; Dell 874, 944; DellD D232, D250, D298, D329, D383; LionLL LB152; Pock 558, 704, 860, 998; Pyr F720
Matcha, Jack—GM 873; Powe 1011N
Mather, Anne—Lan 74-999
Mather, Melissa—AvS S346
Mathers, Edward Powys—Av 682; CreB d199
Matheson, Richard—Bal 301K; BB 1294, A1571, F2281, J2467; CreB s308; DellFE B195; GM 417, s577, 643, D1203; Lion 137, 180
Mathison, Richard—Bal F450K
Matson, Norman—Pop 200
Mattersdorf, Leo—Prem S27
Matthewman, Phyllis—Harl 825
Matthews, Allen R.—PermaS 258; Pock 1207
Matthews, Clayton—MonB 164, 207, 253, 289, 461, 551; Powe PP194, PP202, 1005N
Matthews, Ernest L. Jr—Uni 78
Matthews, John D.—Av 847
Matthews, John F.—PocLGA A2
Matthews, John L.—BelLB L92-551
Matthews, Kevin (Gardner F. Fox)—Hill 140, 205; MidT F348; PopLE EB54, EB78; PopLG G293; Tower 43-430, 43-475
Matthews, Leone—Lan 72-773
Matthews, T.S.—Pop 514
Matthiessen, Peter—Av 753; BB A1578
Mattimore, Clarke—AceA A22
Mattimore, Jenn—AceA A22
Maugham, Robin—Av 233, 333, 428, 464, 695; AvFS F211; MonB 412
Maugham, W. Somerset—ASE N14, L30, Q31, E128, I260, 971; Av nn(24), 41, 50, 56, 129, 139, 188, 203, 331, 364; AvB Bard 4; AvG G1224; AvMSS 1, 8, 18, 35, 38, 43, 51; AvS S216; AvT T119, T412, T420; Bal S663; BantC AC25; BB 136, 423, 810, 852, 909, 949, A1339, A1399, 1489, A1930, A1931; BelLB L511; BerkG BG149, BG213, G268; CardE C19, C63, C161, C261, C273; CreB d276; DellD D106, D176; DellTC 2, 16; Harl 266; Lan (72-)605, 74-889; Ment M60, MD203; Pen 597; Perma M4056; PermaH P74; Pock 262, 418, 581, 700, 1158; PopSP SP75; Prem S30; Pyr R881

Maughan, A.M.—BB F1604
Mauldin, Bill—ASE 822; BB 83, 461, 855; Lan 73-408
Maule, Harry E.—DellD D367; Pock 293
Maund, Alfred—BEDN 250; Lan 74-837
Maurel, Micheline—Bel 208
Maurer, David W.—Pock 618
Maurette, Marcelle—Signet S1356
Mauriac, Francois—AvG G1058; GoldM nn
Maurino, Ferdinando D. PhD—MonB 493
Maurois, Andrée—ASE 864; AvQS QS4; AvWYX W111; Bel 201; Pyr R232
Mausert, Pete—Powe PP105, PP123
Mawrence, Col. Mel—AvG G1107
Mawson, Christopher—CardE C13; Pock 383
Maxey, W. de Ortega—Fab Z125
Maxfield, Henry S.—AvS S171, S341; CreB s288
Maxim, Hiram Percy—ASE 778
Maxon, P.B.—BartH 9; Pony 123
Maxwell, Gavin—CreB R567, R800
Maxwell, Malcolm—Lan 72-924
Maxwell, Nicole—AceK K208
Maxwell, William—ASE 919
May, Daniel—GM 875
Maybury, Anne—AceK K191, K211, K227, K232, K238, K248, K251, K257, K263, K271, K277; CWC 278, 511; Lan 74-977
Mayer, Frederick—AvG G1098
Mayer, Martin—CardGC GC66; Pock 1110
Mayer, N.H.—Perma M4066, M4148
Mayer, S.K.—Perma M4066, M4148
Mayfield, Julian—Pock 1229; Pyr G461
Mayo, Dallas—Midw 85, 98, 100
Mayo, Jim (Louis L'amour)—AceD D38, D48
Mayse, Arthur—Pock 727
Mazo, Earl—AvT T416
McAllister, Robert—PopLG G252
McArthur, A.—Harl 216
McBain, Ed—DellD D306; Perma M3037, M3055, M3061, M3062, M3108, M3113, M3119, M4150
McCaffery, J.K.M.—AvV V2041
McCague, James—AceD D184
McCaig, Robert—AceD D320, D424; AceF F316; BB 1435; Dell 884; Penn P53
McCarthy, Sen. Eugene J.—AvG G1145
McCarthy, Justin—Pock 1242
McCarthy, Mary—Dell 824; DellD D184, D214; Signet T2372, T2380, T2416
McCary, Reed—Av 797; Harl 297; OrigN 713
McCauley, Elfrieda—DellFE 38
McCauley, Leon—DellFE 38, B106
McClary, Thomas Calvert—AceD D176; BartH 6
McClellan, W.—Grif nn
McClintock, Marshall—DellFE D72; NOI D1920; Pyr 118, G483
McCloy, Helen—AceG G562; ASE 1034; BM B152, B203, B208; Dell 33, 72, 107, 151, 212, 261, 295, 355, 369, 430, 519; DellD D228; DellTC 34; Grap 113; Hill 193
McClusky, Thorp—PyrPR PR39
McCollum, R.R.—Rain 108
McComas, J. Francis—AceD D422; AceG G712; BB 1310; Penn P44
McComb, Katherine—AceD D571; Lan 73-861
McCombs, R.L.F.—MNM 20
McConnaughey, James—Pock 1050
McConnaughey, Susanne—BB 1398; PopLG G112
McConnor, Vincent—AvS S215
McCord, David—Pock 388
McCord, Joseph—Pock 388
McCormick, Charles P.—BantA A5
McCoy, Horace—AvSS SS10; AvV V2127; Berk 108, 328; BerkG G134; DellFE A188; Signet 670, 690, 754, 884, S1017
McCoy, John Pleasant—Av 601; AvT T350; PermaS P227; Pock 802
McCrea, E.R.—Harl 391
McCready, Jack—MonB 229
McCretion, Michael—Vega V22
McCroskey, Jacob—Lan P37
McCullers, Carson—BB 821, 822, A1091, A1156, A1235, F1761, F1762, F1763, F1764; Pen 596
McCulley, Johnston—ASE 803; Av 748, 779, 795, 856; AvFS F159; AvT T395; Cent 131; Dell 553; DellD D204; FWN 1, 8, 12, 43; GWN 49; Harl 260; Pyr 187; Signet 669, 704, 1632
McCully, Walbridge—DNC 47, 53; MNC 84
McDaniel, David—AceG G571, G590, G600, G613, G667, G670, G729
McDermid, Finlay—BM B102
McDermott, C.L.—Pop 417
McDonald, Angus—ASE M12
McDonald, Gil—TBSTB 915
McDonald, K.—Bal 175, 312K, 499K
McDonell, Gordon—BB 795
McDonnell, Virginia B.—AceD D589
McDougald, Roman—BartH 17
McDougall, Colin—CreB D489
McDow, Joe—Lan 72-717
McDowell, Emmett—AceD D51, D329, D445
McElfresh, Adeline—BB 1498, 1776, 1929, 1951; DellFE K110, K115, B168, B177, B185, A187, B201, A206; Perma M3099

McErlean, Sheila—Lan 73-799
McEvoy, J.P.—GoldM nn
McFeatters, Dale—Berk 349
McFee, William—ASE F178, 765; GrapG G207
McGee, George—Midw F97
McGerr, Pat—ASE 1255; Dell 307, 412, 612
McGerr, Patricia—AvG G1283
McGivern, William P.—CardE C316; CreB S499; Dell 599;
    Pock 693, 786, 870, 961, 981, 1030, 1062, 1105,
    1156, 1193
McGoldrick, Edward J. Jr—MonHBS MB503
McGovern, Ann—CreB s324, K754
McGovern, James—Hill 160; PopLG G181; Pyr G651
McGowan, Frank J. MD—GM D1204
McGrath, Lt. Tom—Harl 299
McGreevey, John—AceD D120
McGuire, Atha—GM 502
McGuire, Don—HollH HH149, HH165
McGuire, John J.—AceD D227, D299
McGuire, Paul—Pen 631
McHugh, Vincent—Bal 53; Signet 778
McIlvaine, Jane S.—BerkG G285
McInnes, Graham—Signet S1215
McIntosh, Georgia—AceD D113; AceF F113; AvS S347; AvT
    T249; CreB 150; Las 24; Perma M3027; Pyr F898
McIntyre, Marjorie—Pock 1117
McIntyre, William—CreB 239, 394, S488
McKay, Claude—Av 376
McKaye, Richard—Signet 1110
McKee, A.—AvS S131
McKee, Alexander—Lan 73-568, 75-067
McKee, Douglas—DellFE 21, 64, B184; GM S1254
McKenna, Edward L.—ASE 788
McKenna, George—CreB s221
McKenna, Richard—CreB M689
McKenney, Ruth—ASE 695; BerkG G284; Pock 189
McKenzie, A.R.—HH 5
McKernan, Maureen—Signet D1469
McKie, Ronald—Pop 609
McKimmey, James—AvS S257; BalU U2239; DellFE B157,
    A159, B169, A185, B192, B211, B230
McKimmey, James Jr—MonB 173
McKnight, Bob—AceD D217, D279, D387, D411, D419,
    D447, D469, D511; AceF F102, F143, F229; MeritF 650
McKnight, Evans—Bea B324
McKown, Robin—AvFS F212
McLane, B.V. Jr—NSLS U161
McLaughlin, Dean—Lan 73-441, 74-949; Pyr F763, F923
McLaughlin, Robert—ASE 1308; CreB S380
McLean, Beth Bailey—Pock 852
McLeod, Ken—Harl 283
McLoughlin, E.U.—CardE C61
McMeekin, Clark—Ace M27, Q30, H226, 1001; CWC 411
McMillen, V.A.—GM 353
McMullen, Larry—Novs 6N239
McMullen, Mary—Dell 713
McMullen, Richard—NSLF 26; Pop 212, 572; PopLG G229,
    G385
McMurtry, Larry—PopSP SP218
McNair-Wilson, Michael—BelLB L520
McNamara, Lena Brooke—AceG G635
McNaughton, Charles Jr—EHO 0120
McNeile, H.C.—TNC 14
McNeilly, Mildred Masterson—CardE C116; Pock 844
McNellis, Maggi—Toby nn
McNichols, Charles L.—ASE O16; BB 1272
McNulty, John—ASE 1180; BB 1232
McPartland, John—BerkG BG128; CardE C298; GM 263, 336,
    354, 393, 406, 571, 574, 596, 732, 881, 909, S1090,
    K1343; GMB 60, 69
McShane, Mark—CreB K781, K846
McSorley, Edward—PopLG G462
McVeigh, Sue—AtM nn; MNC 49
Mead, Earl—TBSTB 901
Mead, Harold—Bal 147
Mead, Margaret—ASE 826; Ment M44, M56, M91, MD133,
    MD134, MD150, MD153, MD255
Mead, Shepherd—AvG G1116, G1129; AvV V2107; Bal 127,
    174, F558, F576; BEDN 287K; Pop 228
Meade, Richard—Lan 70-012
Meany, Tom—BB 505, 763; Dell 839
Meares, Ainslie MD—AceA A30
Mechem, Philip—Croy nn
Medearis, Mary—PyrPR PG28
Meeker, Richard—Uni 13
Mehling, Harold—AceK K125T
Meier, Frank—ASE C79; Dell 265
Meier, Frederick—PermaH P39
Meissner, Hans-Otto—AceD D319
Meiter, Walter—OIFR F111
Melick, Weldon—ASE T9
Meline, Frank—Fran F1
Mell,—PyrPR PF42
Mellett, Lowell—Pen 593
Mellne, Frank—Fran F11
Melman, Seymour—Bal F564
Melnicove, Bettye F.—CreB D654, D811
Meloney, William Brown—Pop 391; PopLG G154; Pyr 37,
    G154, G460, F816

Meltzer, David—EHO 0102, 0104, 0107, 0111, 0116, 0117,
    0122, 0129, 0134
Melville, Herman—ASE L15, A24, G209; AvT T117; BantC
    FC16; BB F1803; DellLE LX105; Pock 612; PocL PL28;
    PopSP SP142; Signet D1229
Memmi, Albert—AvFS F153
Mencer, Dorothy—Fab Z130
Mencken, H.L.—ASE A13, F159
Mende, Robert—Av 382; AvT T99
Menen, AuGray—Pock 1188
Menke, Frank G.—Barn nn
Meoni, Armando—Pop 534; PopLG G434
Mercer, Charles—AvS S305; BB F1723, F1818
Meredith, Anne—Dell 588
Meredith, George—BalAF 01958
Meredith, Scott—Perma M3035, M3082, M3111, M3116
Meredith, Sidney—Perma M3111
Meredith, William—DellLE LB156
Mergendahl, Charles—BB F1968; CreB s302; DellD D240;
    DellFE C112; Hill 116; Pop 304, 351, 484; PopLE EB18;
    PopLG G275, G372, G424; PopSP SP97, SP241
Merimee, Prosper—Pock 559
Merriam, Robert E.—Bal 190, F697
Merriam-Webster,—ASE 717, 718
Merrick, Clyde—Midw 93
Merrick, Elliott—ASE 1314
Merrick, Gordon—Ace 1266; Pop 446, 703; PopLG G158,
    G344
Merril, Judith—BB 751; DellF F118; DellFE B103, B110,
    B119, B129; Lion 205; LionLL LL25; Penn P56; Pyr
    G397, G499, G502, F806, F830
Merrill,—FFS nn
Merrill, Mark—Pyr R210, G227
Merriman, Chad—Bal 315K, 343K, 438K, 544, 640; BalU
    U1001, U1002, U1003, U2314; BEDN 282K, 289K; GM
    271, 305, 381
Merritt, A.A.—Av nn(26), 43, 117, 214, 235, 315, 324, 370,
    392, 413; AvG G1192; AvMMM 5, 11, 18, 24, 29, 34,
    41; AvMur 1; AvT T135, T152, T161, T172,
    T208; AvS S229, S231, S271
Merserau, John—AtM nn
Mertes, Jack—NSLF 516
Merton, Thomas—Dell 725; DellD D189, D208, D256, D313;
    DellF F155; Signet D929
Merwin, Sam Jr—AceD D121; BCD 19; Bea 284; Cent
    nn(63); GM 227; GreD 30; GSFN 12, 22; Han 12, 44;
    Harl 62, 70, 87, 122; Lan 74-776; Midw 170; PrizeMN
    22
Meservey, Russ—GM 302
Meskil, Paul—Lion 198; Pyr R667
Mesta, Perle—AvG G1066
Metalious, Grace—DellF F61, F91
Metzelthin, Pearl V.—Av 101, 261
Meyer, J.A.—AceD D366
Meyer, Jerome S.—AvS S223; CreB d262, D437; Lan 72-
    612; Perma M4138; Pock 580; Prem d56
Meyer, Karl E.—Bal F593
Meyer, Lewis—AvV V2100, V2178; DellD D430
Meyers, Bart—Fran F19
Meyers, David—DellFE 55
Meyers, Harold—Av 133, 230, 359, 627, 633, 637, 643,
    649, 662, 681, 698, 860; AvT T92, T95, T227, T282
Meyers, Lester—CardGC GC67
Meyerson, Charlotte—AvSS SS16
Meynell, Laurence—AvG G1295; CWC nn, 201, 325, 392,
    397, 471, 413
Meynier, Gil—CreB 117
Meyrick, Gordon—Han 43
Mezzrow, Mezz—DellD D118
Mialoca, Pat—FPVFP FP2021
Michael, D.J.—Lion 208
Michael, Jan—MonS MS13
Michael, Marjorie—PyrPR PR14
Michaels, Bart—Lan 72-743, 72-971
Michaels, Dale—GM S1154
Michaels, Rea—Dom 82103; Lan 72-680, 72-705, 72-714,
    72-727, 72-735, 72-741, 72-750, 72-785, 72-793, 72-
    900, 72-913, 72-961, 72-972
Michaels, Roy—Signet 1048
Michaels, Steve   (Michael Avallone)—BelLB L92-565
Michaelson, John Nairne—BerkG G166; Signet 1116
Michaud, Don—NSLF 509
Michel, M. Scott—BK 27; Han 30, 47, 61; Harl 42, 64; NSLF
    129
Michelfelder, William—AvFS F107; BerkG G7, G65; MonHBS
    MB514
Michener, James A.—ASE 1248; BB A884, A999, A1000,
    1269, A1318, F1350, A1641, A1650, F1674, F1705,
    F1844; CardE C226; Pock 516
Middleton, Ted—Av 731
Miers, Earl Schenck—ASE 1027
Mik,—Grap 107
Milburn, George—ASE 1301; Dell 608, 676; Lion 159, 202;
    LionLL LL82, LL160; Pyr G491; Zenith ZB2
Miles, John—AceD D489
Miles, Julie-Shirley—OIFR F109
Miles, Shirley—OIFR F113
Miles, Truxton—Saber SA159, SA165
Miles, William E.—MonHBS MB540; Regy RB310
Miles, X—Eur 804
Miles, Yukon—GM 201; GMB 17

Milieu, Pierre du—Hill 195
Millar, George—BB F1591
Millar, Kenneth   (Ross MacDonald)—Dell 363, 408, 497;
    Lion 47, 48; LionLL LL40, LL52
Millar, Margaret—BB 1542, A1979; Dell 110, 157, 209, 558,
    730, 920; Lan 72-968, 72-976, 72-986, 72-994, 73-
    531, 74-890, 74-966, 74-969
Millard, Joseph—CreB D458; GM 129, 404, s590; MonA
    MA402; MonB 414; Regy RB324
Millay, Edna St. Vincent—ASE 857; WSP W550, W551
Millburn, Cynthia—PrizeLN 20
Millen, Gilmore—Pyr G59, G142
Miller,—Powe PP158
Miller, Arthur—AvS S185; BantC AC31; BB 952, A1322;
    DellD D273; DellF F115; PockB B37; Pop 230
Miller, Ben E.—Powe PP186, PP195
Miller, Bill—Grap 11, 54; Harl 99
Miller, Caroline—AvG G1088; AvV V2131
Miller, Diane Disney—DellD D266
Miller, Douglas—Pock 139
Miller, Floyd—Pop 746, 787; PopLE EB96; PopLG G252;
    Signet S1908
Miller, Frank—BB 1576
Miller, Frank S.—Vega V19
Miller, Harry—BantUn nn; BB A1528
Miller, Helen Topping—Av 210, 254; Dell 462; Harl 20, 33;
    Pock 653
Miller, Henry—AvV V2038; Signet 1246, 1317, D1653
Miller, Joe—Pad nn
Miller, John A.—BantA A1
Miller, John J.—MonB 454
Miller, Lee—BB A1098
Miller, Lee O.—Powe PP178
Miller, Llewellyn—Bal 72
Miller, Margery—ASE 1118
Miller, Max—MM 12
Miller, Merle—AvV V2049; Lan 74-883, 74-939; Pop 210,
    277; PopSP SP125
Miller, Nolan—AceD S87, D398; BB F1367, F1649
Miller, Paul
    Eduard—ASE 676, 1000
Miller, R. DeWitt—AceD D162; AceF F137; AceK K168, K229,
    K255; BB 1507
Miller, Sigmund—GM S1106
Miller, Tevis—EtB E118
Miller, Wade—AceD D518; GM 108, 139, 152, 173, 257,
    279, 331, 469, 513, 521, 682, 758, s791, 810, s845,
    s936, 945, 1001, 1027, S1155, S1221, K1355, K1363,
    K1490, D1639; GMB 55; Han 65; LionLL LL96; Pen
    648; Pyr G495; Signet 677, 695, 722, 771, 843, 908,
    928, 1013, 1089, 1180, 1235, 1257, 1270, 1369,
    1482, 1662
Miller, Walter M. Jr—Bal F626; BalU U2212
Miller, Warren—CreB s299, S386, D463, D542, R653, K700,
    D749, R793, R833
Miller, William—DellLE LX101
Miller, William Robert—AvQS QS9
Millhauser, Bertram—BB 554
Milligan, Harold Vincent—PermaH P66; SigK KD331
Millis, Walter—Ment MD208
Mills, Arthur—CWC nn
Mills, C. Wright—Bal F420K, F454K, F568
Mills, Carley—Pyr R730
Mills, John—ASE 824
Mills, Mervyn—AvT T201
Mills, Robert P.—AceF F267; AceM M116, M137; DellX X12
Milne, A.A.—AvZS ZS103; DellD D321; Pock 81
Milner, Michael—CardE C437; Lan 70-059
Miloradovich, Milo—BA A1378
Milton, George Fort—FFS nn
Milton, Henry A.—Bann B60-105
Milton, Joseph—Lan 74-881
Minton, Paula—Lan 72-780, 72-956, 72-978, 73-
    605, 74-880, 74-882, 74-950, 75-516, 75-521
Mirabelli, Eugene—PopLG G425
Mirbeau, Octave—AvT T94, T145; Berk 111; BerkG G39; Lan
    74-840
Mirrlees, Hope—BalAF 01880
Mirvish, Robert F.—Pop 647, 690; PopLG G174; Signet
    S1137, S1222
Mishima, Yukio—AvV V2078
Mitchell, Albert—Pyr G296
Mitchell, Anthea—Pop 601; PopLG G470
Mitchell, Edwin Valentine—PermaH P82
Mitchell, Francis—AvT T84, T132; Uni 51
Mitchell, Gladys—MM 119
Mitchell, Gordon—Midw 11
Mitchell, J. Leslie—GSFN 15
Mitchell, Joseph—ASE D108; CWC 208; Harl 210; Pen 557
Mitchell, Margaret—Perma M7500; PermaS P294
Mitchell, Ruth Comfort—AceK K242
Mitchell, Will—GM 118
Mitford, Jessica—AvV V2091; CreB T735
Mitford, Nancy—BantB FB409; Pock 506; PopSP SP148,
    SP219; Signet 1012, S1625
Mitgang, Herbert—Hill 174
Mitsuko, Iolana—HollH HH163
Mittelholzer, Edgar—CreB d305, R566, T845; DellD D151;
    DellF F97; Pock 918
Miyoshi, Tami—HollH HH164
Moberley, Leeds—RetD 102

339

Mock, Elizabeth B.—PelB P20
Mockridge, Norton—GM 177, s704, D1662
Modell, Merriam—BB 425; Pyr G181
Modley, Rudolf—PenS s216
Moessinger, David—Lan 74-540
Moffett, Cleveland—Bal F637
Mokray, William G.—Pyr G570, F675, F945
Mole, William—DellD D272
Moll, Elick—BB 926; CreB K652; Signet S1763
Molnar, Louis—DNC 29
Monaghan, Jay—BB A1145
Monahan, John    (W.R. Burnett)—GM 355
Monash, Paul—Av 405, 595, 622; AvT T342
Monath, Norman—Perma M3054
Monig, Christopher—Dell 992
Mons, H.M.—Pop 564
Monsarrat, Nicholas—Bal F592, F773; CardGC GC10, GC755; Dell 327; Pock 1043, 1139; Pyr R943; Signet 1092
Monsey, Derek—AvT T505
Montagu, Ashley—Lan 74-824; Ment MD239; Perma M4141
Montague, Ewen—Av 640
Montague, Joseph F.—PermaS P106
Montana, Duke—Lion 78
Monte, Jill—Lan 72-749
Monteleone, Thomas F.—Las nn
Montgomery, Herb—MeritT 550, 629
Montgomery, Ione—AtM nn
Montgomery, L.M.—Pock 72
Montgomery, Marlon—PopSP SP201
Montgomery, Ruth—AvS S136, S155
Montrose, David—CWC 516, 539; Harl 262
Moon, Bucklin—BB 737; Lion 229; Pock 697
Mooney, Belle S.—PermaH P11
Mooney, Booth—AceD D292; AvS S148; GM 218, 781
Mooney, Martin—Harl 28
Moorcock, Michael—AceH H36; AvS S351; Lan 73-545, 73-579, 73-688, 73-707, 73-761, 73-824, 74-668, 74-736, 75-199, 75-375, 75-376
Moore, Amos—GWN 13; Harl 66, 399; WNC 93
Moore, Arthur—Powe PP212, 1009N
Moore, Brian—DellD D205; Harl 102, 117; Pyr 94
Moore, C.L.—AceD D69; AceF F306; AvS S378; AvT T297; Bal 122; GSFN 26, 31; PapLS 63-166
Moore, Dan Tyler—BerkG G169
Moore, Ed—WNC 81
Moore, Edward—AceD D446
Moore, Frances Sarah—AceD D577; AvRNM 2
Moore, Francis—Whit 790
Moore, Hal R.—Bea B183; IN 56; NSLS U135
Moore, Herbert L.—Vega V21
Moore, Irving—Grap 84
Moore, Isabelle—AceD D567; BB 706; Lan 75-125; WH G1
Moore, Jack—Saber SA33, SA39, SA42, SA66, SA73, SA81, SA89, SA105; TBSTB 939
Moore, John—CWC 343
Moore, Lucia B.—Bal 15
Moore, Marjorie—Harl 446, 459, 492, 500, 504, 508, 509, 520, 589, 609, 659
Moore, Mary Furlong—Berk 384
Moore, Olga—RA 11
Moore, Pamela—Bal A1630
Moore, Robin—AvN N128, N134; PopLG G211
Moore, Rosalind—DellFE 60
Moore, Ruth—Pock 508, 938, 1051
Moore, Walter L.—Signet 862
Moore, Ward—Saber SA148
Moore, William—Bal 38, 527; Pyr F805
Moorehead, Alan—Bal S416K; BB F2070; DellX X15
Morac, Jules-Jean—ArB 33; LeiL 1, 6, 12
Moran, Mike—Pop 494
Moravia, Alberto—Signet S844, 922, 960, S1071, 1122, S1213, 1288, S1306, 1372, S1510, S1520, S1596, S1612, D1657, T1955, T2013, T2136, T2198
Moray, Helga—BelL L92-593; Dell 484, 630; MonK K52; PopLG G130; PopSP SP25, SP44
Morehead, Albert H.—CreB R740; Pen 614, 652; Pock 260, 925, 955; SigK Ks307, KD363; Signet 678, D1328, S2064, S2255, P2330
Morehead, James—Pock 925, 955
Morehead, Loy—Signet D1328
Morehouse, Ward—ASE J287
Morell, Lee—Bea B275, B316
Morell, Parker—MM 7
Morella, Jane—Lan 74-727
Morelli, Spike    (William Simpson Newton)—ArB 3, 8, 11; LeiL 2, 7
Moretti, Al—Pop 585
Morgan, Al—AvS S141; CardE C223, C306
Morgan, Claire—BB 1148, A1831
Morgan, Henry—Av 673
Morgan, Jason—Lan 73-785, 74-967
Morgan, Joe—Signet S1610
Morgan, John Medford—Signet S1690
Morgan, Mark—Lion 136; LionLL LB70
Morgan, Michael—AceD D9; Lion 11; Pyr 116
Morgan, Murray—Lad E36
Morgan, Nancy—GM 433, s453, d839; RSB 12
Morgan, William J.—Pock 1204
Morhaim, Victoria—Signet S1894, D2062
Morheim, Lou—GM S1115

Morino, Nick—Pyr 65
Morison, Samuel Eliot—Ment M181
Morland, Nigel    (John Donavan)—MNM nn
Morley, Christopher—ASE R25; Pen 529, 582; Pock 51; Signet 793, S1491
Morley, Susan—Signet 748, S1279
Morningside, Mee—GM 450
Moroso, John—RC 2
Morressy, John—Las 21, 52
Morrill, George—PopLG G473
Morris, Alice—AvNS NS4
Morris, Donald R.—BerkG G25; Perma M4132; Signet 939
Morris, Robert T.—SigK Ks329
Morris, William—BalAF O1652, O1982, O2015, O2421, O2995, O2996, O3261, 23515, 23516, 23730
Morris, Wright—Signet D1455, S1531, P2182
Morrison, Emmeline—PockB B59
Morrison, Ray—AvT T417; BB 794
Morro, Don—Bea B244
Morros, Boris—DellF F99
Morse, Dr. Benjamin—Lan 74-813, 74-817, 74-822, 75-049; MonB 436; MonHBS MB513, MB518, MB527, MB531, MB535, MB537, MB543
Morse, James—BB F1788
Mortimer, John—BB 977
Mortimer, Lee—Dell 400, 440, 534; DellD D101, D108
Mortimer, Penelope—Lan 72-748
Mortimer, Peter—DHM 24
Morton, Frederic—CreB T591
Morton, Patricia—Bann B50-114; Lan 72-977
Morton, Stanley—Pyr G54, G140
Mosel, Tad—AvV V2074
Moseley, Wendell F.—AceD D519
Mosely, Dana—Dell 953
Mosher, J.S.—MNM nn
Mosley, Leonard—AvN N163; Bel 225
Moss, W. Stanley—Harl 165
Motley, Willard—Signet 802AB, D992, D1576, D1693
Mott, Lucretia—AvN N163
Mott-Smith, Geoffrey—FFS nn; Pen 614, 652; PermaH P34, P55; SigK Ks307; Signet 678
Moulton, Powers—Perma M3060, M4014; PermaH P8; PermaS P8
Mowat, Farley—Bal F387K; PyrPR PR20
Mowery, William Byron—Pop 103, 127, 179, 214
Moyes, Patricia—BalU U2240, U2241, U2242, U2243, U2244
Moyzisch, L.C.—BB 982; PockB B58; Pyr B337
Mozes, Eugene B. MD—MonHBS MB505
Muir, Denis—GreD 19
Mulford, Clarence E.—ASE D72, F163, H227, I257, 759, 834, 918, 1072, 1141; Dell 246; DellUN nn; Grap 15, 23, 28, 53, 91; GWN 7; Harl 107, 131; Pock 337; Pop 104, 146, 198; Pyr 25; ThrillBN 11, 20, 29; WNC 26, 32, 59
Mulholland, John—ASE O3
Mulholland, P.J.—Av 781
Mullady, Detective—BelLB L507
Mullally, Frederic—Lan 73-582
Mullen, Clarence—HH 16
Muller, Herbert J.—Ment Ms112
Muller, John—VegaSFL VSF3, VSF6, VSF8, VSF11
Muller, Julius—Keep 1, 3, 4
Mulvihill, William P.—Bal 189; CreB D457, D701, D861; Signet S1785
Mundy, Talbot—AceK K149; AvS S303, S309, S316, S318; Bea B105; RoyG 12, 19, 20, 22; UGE 11
Munn, H. Warner—AceG G618; AceM M152; BalAF 24010
Munro, W. Carroll—Av 383, 501; BerkG BG238
Munroe, Val—Rain 115, 125
Munson, Gorham—FPVFP FP2047
Munson, E.L.—FFS nn
Munves, Elizabeth—DellFE D53; DellLE LC124
Murdoch, Iris—AvS S193; AvV V2092, V2145, V2154, V2159, V2170
Murger, Henri—Av 163
Muriac, Francois—BB 1039
Murphy, Audie—Perma M4029; PermaS P119, P214
Murphy, Bill—PopLG G201
Murphy, Dennis—CreB s291
Murphy, Francis X.—AvG G1093
Murphy, John D.—DellD D243
Murphy, L.E.    (H.G. Lewis)—Novs 7N710
Murphy, Robert—AvS S174, S294, S312; AvZS ZS107
Murray, A.A.—Bel 213
Murray, Chalmers S.—BB 1193
Murray, James F. Jr.—LionLL LL67
Murray, Katherine—AvT T510
Murray, Ken—AceD D34, D62
Murray, Marris—Signet 1165
Murray, Max—BB 358; CWC 402, 459, 506; Dell 485, 560, 639; MM 138; Pyr G362
Murray, William—Pop 726; PopLG G251
Murry, William—AvFS F105
Murtagh, Judge John—Bel 205
Murtagh, John M.—CardE C286
Musprat, Eric—RA 6
Musselman, M.M.—ASE 1153
Myers,—AvS S226
Myers, Bernard—BantC NC33; BB 1171, S1692
Myers, Beth—BB 1936

Myers, Harriet Kathryn—AceD D543, D564
Myers, John Myers—AceA A8; ASE 1285; Hill 115
Myers, Roy—Las 56
Myers, Russell—Lan 73-217
Myers, Virginia—GM 320
Myrer, Anton—BB F1707
Nabarro, Derrick—PopLE EB34
Nablo, James Benson—NSLF 15; NSLS 2A; Signet 968
Nabokov, Vladimir—AvNS NS41; AvT T323; BerkG G156; CreB d338, S412; Lan 72-661, 75-009; PopLG G365; Signet 777
Nafziger,—ASE T28
Naidish, Theodore—ASE Q12, 952
Nake, Matt—NovF 6076
Narayan, R.K.—PockB B31
Narcejac, Thomas—Dell 977
Nasatir, Mort—Bal F363K
Nash, Anne—BartH 19
Nash, Eleanor—NovL 33
Nash, Jay—NCH 7N760
Nash, N. Richard—BB 1559
Nash, Ogden—ASE A3, 981, 1151; CardE C158; Pock 251
Nathan, Leonard—Pop 664
Nathan, Robert—ASE R3, 655, 737, 800; BB 19; BM B2; Pen 638; Pyr G438, R772
Nathan, Simon—CreB s223
Naylor, F.L.—CHARs CB1624
Neal, Hilary—Harl 662, 812, 931
Nebel, Frederick—Av 264; Cent 30; MM 33
Nebel, Long John—Lan 72-644
Nefesh, Holly—OIFR F112
Neher, Fred—Berk 383, 385
Neider, Charles—BB A1452; CreB 368
Neill, Robert—AvS S377
Neimark, Paul—NCH 7N730, 7N760
Neitzel, Neal—MeritF 529, 6102
Nelkin, Sandy—Lion 213; LionLL LL24, LL119; Pyr G346
Nelms, Paul—Saber SA131, SA139
Nelson, Al P.—Lan 73-887, 74-638
Nelson, Hugh Lawrence—BM B116; Dell 520
Nelson, Klondy—PyrPR PG24
Nelson, R. Faraday—Las 13, 32, 53
Nelson, Ray—AceG G637
Nelson, Valerie K.—Harl 714, 744, 764, 793, 818, 834, 852, 890, 940, 961
Nemec, Jack—NovF 6077
Nemec, John—MeritF 544; NovF 5062, 5069; TBSTB 927; VWL VW103
Nemerov, Howard—AvT T415
Ness, Eliot—PopLG G403; PopSP SP258
Neubauer, William—AvFS F129, F175
Neumann, Alfred—Bal 88
Neville, Kris—BelLB 92-611
Neville, Margot—Pock 829
Neville, Myles Jr—MeritF 602; MeritS 7M809
Nevins, Allan—ASE A17; PocL PL512
Nevins, Rex—FabF Z161; Saber SA57, SA106
Nevius, Alan—Pock 195
Newborough, Lady—Pyr G462
Newbury, Will—MonB 226, 347
Newcomb, Richard F.—Perma M4143
Newell, Audrey—MNC 44
Newell, Berger F.—MonB 161
Newhouse, Edward—Berk 323
Newland, N.M.—CHARt CB200; GWN 23
Newman, Bernard—Ment nn
Newman, Edwin S.—Doc 2
Newman, Frank—FPVFP FP2023
Newman, Frank Eaton—Perma M4021; PermaH P89; PermaS P89
Newman, James—ASE N25
Newman, Robert—MonK K60
Newman, Stanley—Bal X655
Newmeyer, Sarah
    —Ment MD211
Newsom, Ed—BB A1685
Newsom, John D.—Dell 165
Newton, D.B.—GM 357, 534; MonB 271; Pock 563; Pop 367, 437; PrizeWN 29
Nezelof, N.P.—AvT T166; RCL 30
Niall, Michael—GM 451; MonB 421
Nichols, Beverly—PockB B16
Nichols, C. Maynard—AvFS F143
Nichols, Fan—AceD D503; Av 346; Bea B102, B114, B122, B220; BerkD D2008; BerkG G243, G253; GM 251; MonB 103; NSLF 4; Pop 409, 483, 536, 586, 642, 706, 791; PopLG G231, G325
Nichols, John Treadwell—AvN N233; AvV V2143
Nichols, Margaret—Harl 5, 30
Nichols, Maynard—AvT T534
Nicholson, Margaret—Signet T1547
Nickerson, Kate—Cam 359; Carn 927, 937, 951, 957; OrigN 725, 729; Venus 152, 165
Nickles, Marione R.—BB 1364
Nickson, Hilda—Harl 555, 670, 702, 735, 745, 776, 794, 820, 836, 882
Nielsen, Greg—FPVFP FP2043
Nielsen, Helen—AceF F121; Bal 310K; BalU U2150; Dell 649, 747, 806, 837, 900, 971
Nielsen, Lou—Dell 77

Schurmacher, Emile C.—Zenith ZB8
Schuster, M. Lincoln—ASE M24
Schwartz,—PocSp 10529
Schwartz, Alan—AceH H20
Schwartz, Irving—Pock 904
Schweitzer, Albert—Ment M83
Schweitzer, Gertrude—GM 125, 754
Schwob, Marcel—AvG G1162
Scortia, Thomas N.—Regy RB111
Scotland, Jay  (John Jakes)—AceD D523; AceF F146; AceG
  G520, G532; AvFS F123; AvT T375
Scott, Ann—Pyr G371
Scott, Anthony—EcsNM 12; ExNM 17; Fal 21; NovL 27; QB
  95; RC 13
Scott, Bradford  (Leslie Scott)—Harl 133, 259; Pyr 34,
  178, 186, 190, 199, 209, 219, 220, 238, 258, 264,
  282, 293, 308, 319, 409, 420, 426, 435, 442, 455,
  G475, G492, G507, G523, G542, G573, G591, G602,
  G610, G637, G674, G684, G704, G714, G734, G745,
  G765, G773, G796, G807, G819, G831, G842, G854,
  G865, G876, G888, G889, G901, G911, G926, G939,
  G951, G953, G975, F988
Scott, Dennis—Croy 6
Scott, Eve—Dom 82112
Scott, George Ryley—AceH H2
Scott, Glenn—Pop 665
Scott, J.M.—CreB 162; Dell 854; Lan 73-819
Scott, Jay—MonA MA314, MA329, MA363
Scott, L.K.—Pyr 103, F850
Scott, Les—Bea B156, B179
Scott, Leslie—AceD D10, D22; NSLF 102; NSLS 23A; Pyr
  251, 302
Scott, Mary Semple—Dell 34
Scott, Natalie Anderson—ASE 1319; Pock 597; Pop 633
Scott, Paul—BerkG G32; Signet T1984
Scott, R.T.M.—BerkM X1735, nn(1774); Green 13
Scott, Roney—Lan 75-124
Scott, Gen. Robert L. Jr—AceD D234; AceH H46; Bal 145,
  217, 306K, 314K, 477K, 694; BalU U0001
Scott, Roney  (William Campbell Gault)—AceD D17
Scott, Sir Walter—CardE C79
Scott, Sutherland—MNM 28
Scott, Tarn—GM 668
Scott, Thurston—Pop 452; PopLG G287
Scott, Virgil—Pop 296, 576; PopLG G319
Scott, Walter—PocL PL19, PL502
Scott, Warwick—Lion 140, 148; Pop 648
Scott, William R.—DellFE 63; GM S1378
Scully, Frank—Pock 504; Pop 326
Seabrook, William—BB 106; Dell 802; Lan 75-038
Seager, Allan—AvG G1097; CardE C250; Pyr G48, G145
Seagrave, Dr. Gordon—ASE D104; Bal F374K; FFS nn
Seale, Sara—Harl 469, 560, 583, 645, 657, 661, 692, 719,
  747, 781, 816, 838, 870, 896, 918, 949, 973
Seaman, Augusta—Com 19
Searles, Len—AceD D590; AceF F284, F409; AceM M134
Searls, Hank—CreB R798
Sears, Jane L.—AceD D559; AvFS F179, F180
Sears, Paul B.—ASE I247, 790
Seaton, George John—Pop 444; Pyr G291
Secondari, John H.—PermaS P246; PopLG G178
Secrist, Kelliher—GreD 1, 25
Sedgwick, Anne Douglas—Pock 30
Sedillot, Rene—Ment M88
Seeger, Alan—MonHBS MB532
Seeley, Clinton—PopLE EB60
Seeley, E.S. Jr—Bea B241, B277; CHARf CB164, CB174,
  CB177, CB194, CB199
Seeley, Mabel—BB A806; BM B37, B80; MM 45, 74, 209;
  Pock 862; Pop 51, 69, 231, 370; Pyr R823
Seeman, Bernard—PyrPR PG29
Segal, Julius—Lan 74-874
Seghers, Anna—ASE Q33
Segre, Alfredo—ASE 1035
Seidman, Dr. Theodore R.—CreB D551; Prem d66
Seifert, Elizabeth—BB 122, 458, 1585; CreB s251, S387,
  K707; CWC 324; DellID D344, D412, D428, D436,
  D443; Harl 326, 364, 369, 375, 379, 392, 401; Pock
  1245
Seilaz, Aileen—AceK K209
Sela, Lora—Fab Z121; Saber SA7, SA13, SA20; SabR 5
Selby, John—ASE C86, 732
Seldes, Gilbert—BB 936
Self, Edwin B.—NSLF 36
Seifert, Elizabeth—Pock 302
Seligman, Selig—Pock 1004
Selinko, Annemarie—CardGC GC22
Sell, Henry Blackman—SigK KD362
Sellers, Con—NCH 7N760; NovF 5016, 5022, 5025, 5028,
  5031, 5039, 5045, 5057, 5060, 6002, 6004, 6007,
  6034, 6048, 6081, 6084, 6089, 6092, 6094, 6098,
  7502, 7504; Novs 6N255, 6N282, 7N718; Papi OSF-
  502
Sellers, Connie—NovF 5019; NSLS U120
Sellings, Arthur—Bal F609
Selmark, George—TNC 37
Seltzer, Charles Alden—ANC 13; ASE T16, 833, 917, 949,
  987, 1030, 1071, 1101; FWN 6; Pop 151, 204; Signet
  717; ThrillBN 14, 22
Seltzer, Nadine—Berk 320, 360, 381

Semple, Gordon—Bea B297; Cent 80, 86, 94, 99, 109, 113;
  Croy 16, 18, 21, 27, 36, 53, 57, 61, 63, 65, 74, 76,
  91, 92, 103, 110; DB 11; IN 4, 36, 40; Lan 72-671;
  LoveRS 1; NSLF 38; Prize 56, 60; RomN nn; StorON
  nn; Uni 34, 39
Serguine, Jacques—Signet P2153
Serling, Robert J.—Bal F623
Serling, Rod—BB F1832, A2046, A2227, A2412
Serra, William 84
Service, Robert W.—ARL 4
Serviss, Garrett P.—Powe PP173
Seton, Anya—AceK K177; ASE P27; BalSSE S6; CardE C64,
  C339; CardGC GC77, GC752; Lan 73-405; Pock 365,
  534, 723, 850
Seton, E. Thompson—BB 59
Seton, Ernest Thompson—BB A1676
Seton, Gerald—Merit B14
Settel, Irving—AceD D175; Bal 235
Sevareid, Eric—ASE 1250
Severin, John—PocSp 10043
Seward, Florence A.—AceH H6
Sewell, Anna—PocJr J43
Sewell, W. Stuart—PermaH P24
Shafer, Robert—Pop 686
Shaffer, Eugene Carl—Papi OSF-501
Shakespeare, Henry—DellM M102
Shakespeare, William—CardE C1, C14, C15, C55; DellLE
  LB113, LB114, LB115, LB118, LB119, LB124,
  LB125, LB129, LB130, LB133, LB134, LB137, LB139,
  LB141, LB144, LB149, LB150, LB153, LB154, LB159,
  LB159; JL nn(5); Pock 3, 114, 532, 533; PocL PL30,
  PL31, PL57, PL60, PL61, PL64, PL66, PL67, PL70;
  PyrPR T37; WSP W115, W121
Shalett, Sidney—AvV V2032
Shallit, James—Av 461, 490, 528, 558; AvT T170; JonM
  J42
Shane, Mark—Fab Z103
Shane, Ted—Dell 152; GM 135, 337, D1605, D1713
Shann, Renee—CWC 214, 269, 285, 340, 349, 373, 416,
  469, 476; Dell 234; DellD D260
Shannon, Carl—Harl 91; HH 21
Shannon, Duke—Fran F2, F12
Shannon, Jimmy—Signet 1027
Shannon, Lytle—PockB B54, B82
Shannon, Steve—CreB 189; GM S1390
Shapiro, Herbert—Signet 708; TechW 1, 2
Shapiro, Lionel—BB 357, 932, F1459; Lan 73-406
Shaplen, Robert—Signet 789
Shapley, Harlow—ASE P31
Shappiro, Herbert—FWN 3; PrizeWN 20, 25, 27; Signet 688
Sharkey, Jack—AceD D471; AceM M117
Sharon, Sylvia—Dom 82101, 82104; Lan 72-718, 72-729,
  72-765, 72-782, 72-792, 72-912, 72-923, 72-931, 72-
  948, 72-951, 74-831, 74-843, 75-058
Sharp, Margery—ASE T12, R22; Av 165, 624; CWC nn, 215,
  224, 304; Pock 169, 395
Sharpe, William—BEDN 292K
Shattuck, Richard—ASE 821; MM 180, 194; Pop 125
Shaw—ASE T28
Shaw, Larry T.—Lan 72-139
Shaw, Arnold—Dor 1; Fei nn; Pyr R556; Signet 1145
Shaw, Bob—AceH H79; AvS S398
Shaw, Carolyn Hagner—CreB D371, D569, R840
Shaw, Charles B.—Ment M26, MD137; Pop 543; PopLE
  EB88; PopSP SP233; Pyr G292
Shaw, Floyd—Av 570, 740
Shaw, Frederick L.—AceG G614
Shaw, George Bernard—ASE 1005; AvGS GS13; AvS YS426;
  BantC FC52; DellLE LC101; Pen 502, 607, 608, 609
Shaw, Howard—CreB S466
Shaw, Irwin—AvMSS 32; Bel 232; Signet 817AB, S931,
  D1438, S1453, T1496, T1892
Shaw, Joseph T.—PermaS P126; Pock 875
Shaw, Larry T.—Lan 72-697, 73-740, 74-944
Shaw, Lau—ASE 968
Shaw, Robert—AvG G1056
Shaw, Sam—Bal 108
Shaw, T.E.—ASE 925
Shaw, Theodore L.—Stuart nn
Shaw, Wilene—AceD D50, S74, S80, S263, D378, D464,
  D520
Shay, Frank—Pyr G75, G517
Shayne, Mike—DellFE 77; MyPM 1
Shea, J. Vernon—Lion 191; LionLL LL47; Pyr R635
Shearing, Joseph—ASE P23, L24, D111, 850, 923; Dell 818;
  MM 99; Pock 560, 592
Sheckley, Robert—Bal 73, 126, 437K, F648; BB A1672,
  A1991, A2003; Regy RB112; Signet S1840, D2223
Shedd, Robert K.—NSLS U141
Sheean, Vincent—CreB T776; Signet S1038, 1208
Sheen, Bishop Fulton J.—CreB s168, s283, D473, D474,
  D607; DellID D141; Perma M1000, M4033; Pop 613,
  682, 786; PocGG 209, G273
Sheers, James C.—DellFE B186
Sheff, Alexander L.—PermaH P2
Shefter, Harry—CardE C145, C190; CardGC GC50
Sheldon, Charles M.—PermaH P29; Pyr G574
Sheldon, Walt—Bann B50-106; BB 1221, A1656; GM K1546
Sheldon, Walter J.—PopLG G518
Shell, Edwin—Saber SA26

Shellabarger, Samuel—ASE 854, 1321; BB A860, A973,
  A1131, F1284, F1720
Shelley, David—AceF F340; AceG G763
Shelley, John L.—AceD D348; AceF F340; AceG G601, G610,
  G763; Bal 366K, 455K; Grap 124
Shelley, Mary Wollstonecraft—ASE 909; Lion 146; Pyr R290
Shelley, Paul—GM 315; GMB 71
Shelley, Percy Bysshe—ASE Q1
Shelley, Peter—Lion 15; NSLF 106
Shelly, Bruce—Meritf 681
Shelly, Gordon—PopLG G239
Shelton, Jess—AceG G604; CreB D434, D470
Shelton, Lola—BalSSE S14
Shepard, Craig—Cent 95
Shepard, Fern—AvFS F186; Lan 73-622
Shepard, Lee—CHARf CB205
Shepard, Odell—ASE 1224
Shepard, Willard—ASE 1224
Shepherd, Eric—Dell 951
Shepherd, Jean—Bal 165
Shepherd, Joan—Av 578
Shepherd, John—Bel 215
Sheridan, Clare—CWC 332
Sheridan, Jack—DellFE B147; GM 184, 356, s946; Pop 312;
  RSB 20
Sheridan, Juanita—BM B150, B155
Sheridan, Lee—Lan 71-303
Sheridan, Michael—Lan 71-319
Sherlock, John—AvS S266
Sherman, Hal—AceF F288; AvFS F115, F158
Sherman, Harold—Cent 104; CreB s145, D544; Prem S22,
  d73, d77
Sherman, Joan  (Peggy Gaddis)—Ast 31; Crow 24; Croy
  26, 32, 86, 107; ExNM nn, nn(11), nn(12); Han 91; QB
  86, 93; Venus 102, 138, 143, 171, 180
Sherman, Richard—BB 124
Sherman, Robert—Lan 72-123
Sherman, Susan—Signet D2236
Sherrod, Robert—Pock 273
Sherry, Edna—Dell 604, 933, 1004
Sherry, John Olden—Pop 606
Sherwood, John—BM B144; MM 161, 198
Sherwood, Robert E.—BantUn nn
Shiff, Nathan D. MD—Lan 74-876
Shiffrin, A.B.—Pop 485
Shiflet, Kenneth E.—DellFE B126
Shikes, Ralph—AceD S75
Shipman, Natalie—BB 451
Shipwreck, Matt—NovF 5061
Shiras, Wilmar H.—AvT T221
Shir-Cliff, Bernard W.—Bal 171
Shirer, William L.—AvV V2035; CreB A522; Pop 363; PopSP
  SP110
Shirley, Glenn—MonA MA303, MA393
Shirreffs, Gordon D.—AceD D400, D412, D514; AceF F134,
  F152, F238, F292; Av 862; AvFS F185; AvS S395; AvT
  T312, T352, T515; CreB 146; GM 580, 639, 714, 876,
  1071, S1476, K1512; Pop 808, 832; PopLG G288; Pyr
  192; Signet S1626, S2233
Sholokhov, Mikhail—Signet T1661, T1773
Sholokhov, Mikhail—Signet T2089
Shore, Julian—AtM nn
Shore, Juliet—Harl 518, 531, 535, 549, 564, 568, 647, 707,
  757, 876, 929
Shore, William—Pock 811
Short, Betty—Fab Z112, Z116, Z122; FabR Z9
Short, Dorothy—Prem d85
Short, Luke  (Frederick Glidden)—ANC 23; ASE R11, G195,
  670, 874, 1184; Bal 4, 43; BB 82, 112, 139, 140, 204,
  209, 258, 702, 703, 747, 748, 791, 792, 853, 854,
  911, 1063, 1075, 1104, 1105, 1293, 1346, 1356,
  1373, A1401, F1417, 1446, 1466, 1485, 1531, 1532,
  1533, 1564, 1588, 1652, 1668, 1680, 1710, 1755,
  1821, 1865, 1866, 1916, A1959, A1989, A2006,
  A2036; Cent 50; Dell 562, 606, 647, 702, 769, 826,
  869, 895, 962, 963; DellD D289, D350, D457; DellFE
  7, 31, 68, 70, A122, B130, A134, A151, A154; DellTC
  1; GM 159, 720, S1080; GMB 39; Pop 114, 346, 792;
  PopLG G421; WNC 36, 40, 45
Shorten, Harry—Grap 52, 61, 85, 109; Midw nn, 4, 68
Shott, Abel—Harl 194
Showers, Paul—PermaH P16
Shrake, Edwin—AvN N116, N143
Shriber, Ione Sandberg—ASE 798; BB 320; MM 113; SupR
  M641
Shub, David—Ment M57, MD140; SigSE nn
Shubin, Seymour—Perma M4004
Shugg, Roger W.—FFS nn
Shulman, David—TC nn
Shulman, Davis—CP nn
Shulman, Irving—Av 169, 244, 300, 372; AvG G1009,
  G1023; AvT T124, T138, T303, T334; GM S1005,
  S1197; Lan 73-433, 74-887; Pop 817; PopLG G145,
  G175, G436; PopSP SP29
Shulman, Max—ASE Q5, 657, 1119; BB F1791, A1939,
  A1940, A2012, F2041; CardGC GC122; Pock 728, 840
Shurtleff, Bertrand—PocJr J36
Shute, Nevil—AvG G1104; AvV V2128; Bal X688, X689,
  X720, X757; CWC 407; Dell 516; DellID D109, D123,
  D130, D175; Lan 72-645, 73-427, 73-432, 74-633, 74-

Stanley, Ellin—AvG G1199
Stanley, Fay Grissom—Dell 662
Stanton, Elaine—HollH HH162
Stanton, Will—Lan 75-472
Stanwell-Fletcher, Theodora C.—ASE 1212
Stapledon, Olaf—Bea 236; GSFN 8
Stapleton, Douglas—FSM 44; Pony 122
Star, Clav—PrizeWN 32
Star, Hedy Jo—NovF 7501; Novs 7N723
Stark, Allen—VWL VW113
Stark, James—AvFS F139
Stark, Michael—AceD D55; Han 70; Harl 121
Stark, Sheldon—AceD D81
Starling, Trudy—Lan 72-795
Starnes, Richard—Pock 779, 858, 917
Starr, Jimmy—BartH 15
Starr, John—CreB D529
Starr, Kate—Harl 679, 828, 951
Starrett, Vincent—BB A1403; PriMN nn(1)
Stead, Christina—ASE 1145; AvNS NS9; AvWYX YW170
Stearn, Jess—PopLG G196
Stearns, Marshall—Ment MD240
Stechow, Wolfgang—PocLGA A21
Sted, Don—Lan 73-719
Sted, Richard—BM B186
Steel, Kurt—AtM nn; CrNS 1, 2, 4; Dell 244
Steele, Curtis—Cor CR116, CR120, CR124, CR128, CR132, CR136, CR140, CR144; FPVFP FP2041, FP2046, FP2056
Steele, Jaclen—GM 221
Steele, Tedd—NSLF nn
Steele, Wilbur Daniel—ASE 1146, 1213; Dell 548
Steelman, Robert—AceD D172; Bal 334K; BalU U1046, U1049, U1052; BEDN 294K
Steen, Marguerite—AvN N115, N151; PermaS P110; RoyG 14
Steeves, Harrison R.—BB 149; MM 60; SupR M657
Stefani, Livia de—Hill 148
Steffensen, James L. Jr—AvDYD D9; AvQS QS5; AvWYX W101
Stefferud, Alfred—Ment M48, M82, MD157
Steger, Shelby—AceD D224
Stegner, Mary—DellLE LC103; DSSE nn
Stegner, Wallace—ASE N32; DellLE LC103; DellTC 17; DSSE nn; Harl 149
Steichen, Edward—CardGC GC51
Steig, Henry—AvG G1012
Steiger, Brad—AceK K241, K268, K291, K307; BellB B50-727; Lan 74-952, 75-060, 75-332; MeritS 7M814, 7M816, 7M817, 7M820
Stein, Aaron Marc—BM B132, B158; MNC 82
Stein, Jess—DellLE LC104
Stein, Leopold MD—PopSP SP63
Stein, Samuel—PocJr J63
Steinbeck, John—ASE T5, A9, C90, 690, 703, 750, 794, 1232; Av 77, 132; AvMSS 9; BantC AC12, AC18; BB 7, 75, 131, 402, 752, A868, 899, 953, 1065, 1066, 1184, 1266, F1267, F1301, A1324, A1329, 1406, A1412, A1478, 1544, A1555, A1753, F1895; Dell 358, 407; MM 20; Pen 509, 599; PenS s219; Pock 243; Pop 216; Signet 816, 1380, S1737
Steinberg, Saul—Pen 640
Steincrohn, Dr. Peter J.—AceA A26; AceD D213; GrapG G204
Steiner, Lee R.—ASE 1143
Steiner, Paul—BB A1358; LionLL LL105, LL168
Steinman, D.B.—ASE 1051
Stekel, Wilhelm—AvB Bard 2; EtB ET105
Stendahl,—BantC SC40; BB S1734
Stephens, Dave—Vega V15
Stephens, James—ASE L4, N5, 1121
Stephenson, J.L.—Av 225
Stephenson, S.L.—AvB Bard 3
Sterens, Dan J.—MonB 135
Sterling, Anthony—MonA MA300, MA310
Sterling, Hank—RB 103
Sterling, Sandra—Lan 72-788
Sterling, Stewart—AceD D415, D463, D515; Av 685, 762, 835; AvT T320; Dell 275, 314, 420, 513, 583, 693, 816; DNC 45; Han 23; Pyr 139, G261, G644
Sterling, Thomas—DellID D270; Pock 774
Stern,—PocSp 10014, 10015, 10027, 10506, 10583
Stern, Bill—Hill 194; Pock 416, 494, 555, 572
Stern, Daniel—AvV V2184; Bal 114; Perma M4010; PopLG G464
Stern, David—ASE 1228; Dell 507
Stern, G.B.—ASE R1, K4
Stern, Jill—Signet S1570
Stern, Philip Van Doren—ASE nn; Berk 334; BerkD D2040; CardE C156; DellID D159; PocL PL24; Pock 108, 142, 182, 238, 284, 384, 586; ReaL nn; Signet 906
Stern, Richard Martin—Bal 331K, F707; BEDN 288K; CreB D532; Lan 73-581
Sterne, Laurence—ASE K31; PocL PL511
Steuer, Arthur—AceD D250
Stevens, Dan J.—AceD D12; AceF F176; AceG G591, G633, G687; AceM M104; Lion 50; LionLL LL36; MonB 383; Perma M3033
Stevens, Edmund—EtB ET108
Stevens, Gus—Novs 7N737

Stevens, James—ASE M8
Stevens, William Oliver—BB F1442
Stevenson, Burton—MNM 40
Stevenson, D.E.—AvG G1226, G1245, G1253, G1260, G1265, G1271, G1303; CWC 452
Stevenson, Eleanor—PenS s230
Stevenson, Robert Louis—ASE N13, 885; BB 142; CardE C48; CWC nn; DellLE LB135, LC140; JL nn(1); PocJr J57; Pock 25, 123; PocL PL34, PL49; PopSP SP265; QR 130, 142; SigC CD6
Stever, Arthur—DellFE A124
Steward, Davenport—Hill 123; PermaS P181; Pop 578, 669; PopLG G200, G256; PopSP SP78
Stewart, Desmond—Signet 997, 1357
Stewart, Donald—DellID D368
Stewart, George R.—AceK K127, K138, K154; ASE C81, E134, G210, 929, 1045; BB 155, 802; PenS s238
Stewart, Logan—GM 137, 182, 193, 243, 313, 327, 367; GMB 20, 35, 66
Stewart, Mary—CreB D351, D446, D472, D508, D550, D563, R590, D609, D688, D702, R717, R774, T823, T837, R853, R862, R893, R894
Stewart, Ramona—AvS S306; Pock 526
Stewart, Sidney—GM 377; PopLG G233
Sticker, Henry—PermaH P90
Stiles, Bert—Bal 216
Stilwell, Hart—BB 765; Pop 331
Stimpson, George—Prem S29
Stine, G. Harry—AceD D239
Stine, Hank—EHO 0112, 0141
Stinetorf, Louise A.—Pock 851
Stirling, Peter—BK 33
Stix, Thomas L.—ASE 832
Stockbridge, Grant—BerkM X1782
Stockton, J. Roy—ASE 1172; BB 552
Stoddard, Charles—Harl 414
Stoker, Bram—ASE L25, 851; BalU U2271; Lan 75-442; Perma M4088; Pock 452; Tower 43-970
Stokes, Donald—CreB 126; Signet 873, 1006
Stokes, Manning Lee—APM nn; AvS S274; BK 29; DellD D420; DellFE A163; Grap 40, 98, 117; Harl 432; MM 124; PrizeMN 21
Stokley, James—ASE 682
Stone, Abraham—CardE C179
Stone, Andrew L.—Signet 1332, 1508, 1595
Stone, Elna—Lan 75-426
Stone, Ezra—ASE T9
Stone, Gladys—NSLF 16, 21
Stone, Grace Zaring (Ethel Vance)—ASE A29, H229, 1125, 1152; BB 44; Pop 169
Stone, Hampton—BM B173; Dell 464, 790, 883, 943; DellID D278; MM 149
Stone, Hannah—CardE C179
Stone, Harriet—Lan 72-955
Stone, Irving—ASE L29, 693; AvS S103; AvV V2151; BantB FB418; CardE C10; CardGC GC32; PermaS P228; Pock 344; PopSP SP68, SP179; Signet Q2246
Stone, Patti—AceF F122; Hill 185
Stone, Peter—GM K1358
Stone, Philip Alston—DellID D363
Stone, Scott—Bea B246, B248, B315; BerkG G227
Stone, Thomas—Bea B285; Cent 87, 110, 117; Croy 102; CWC 484; Gem 102; Grif nn; Hanro 1; Harl 142; IN 21, 23, 27, 35, 47; Knick nn; LevGL 104; NovL 41; Priv 1; Prize 61; PrizeLN 25; Pyr 18; Stanl 205; StorON 7
Stone, Tom—ExNM 16; Rain 106, 112
Stonebraker, Florence—Bea B321; Bel 234; BellB B50-800; Cam 300, 304, 315; CLN 23; Croy 24, 38, 52, 53, 55, 64, 70, 89, 95; ExNM nn(8); IN 13, 16; Lan 72-637, 72-654, 72-666; NSLF 139; OrigN 706; QB 73, 80, 83, 85, 90, 92; Rain 102; StanL SL70, SL73; Venus 133, 140
Stong, Phil.—AvT AT57; Signet 824
Stoopnagle, Col.—ASE R8
Stopes, Dr. Marie C.—Eug 100; PermaH P99
Storer, Doug—GM D1359, D1655
Storer, John H.—SigK Ks333
Storey, David—AvN N118; PopSP SP122, SP173
Storey, Ed—NovF 5053
Storey, Philip—NSLS U177
Storm, Elliot—RC 7
Storme, Michael—ArB 5, 71, 84; LeiL 4, 5, 11, 15, 19, 23
Storme, Peter—BondM 6; MNM 22
Stout, Rex—ASE P6, 906, 1222; Av nn(20), 62, 82, 95, 103, 256, 714, 738; AvFS F192; AvG G1285; AvMMM 9; AvT T216, T296, T374; BB 308, 722, 824, 925, 1032, 1173, 1252, 1326, 1386, 1387, 1388, 1394, 1395, A1631, A1632, A1633, A1795, A1796, A1797, A1961, A2016, A2023; BLA A1; BM B31, B44; Cent 28; Dell 9, 28, 45, 70, 115, 146, 177, 235, 267, 299, 495, 540, 626, 674; DellD D223, D252; DellTC 21; Hill 136; JonM J2, J6, J9, J15, J27, J33; LionLL LL23; MM 37, 48, 72; Pock 112, 208; Pyr R588, R822, R870, R894, R917, R919, R931, R960, R970, R983
Stover, Herbert E.—AvT AT62; PopLE EB26; PopLG G349
Stowe, Elizabeth—DellFE B179
Stowe, Perry—DellTC 35
Strabel, Thelma—Penn P19
Strachey, Lytton—ASE L20, I261; Pock 26
Strand, Bunny—Fab Z140; Vega V27, V42

Strange, John Stephen—AL 1; BM B107, B161; Cent 27; Dell 438; MM 95; MNC 53, 59
Strange, O.—WNC 67
Stratton, Ted—GM 443
Stratton, Thomas—AceG G645, G663
Strauss, Theodore—BB 857, 889
Street, James—ASE 840; CardE C26, C74; CardGC GC8; Perma M4005; PermaS P255; Pock 819
Street, Leroy—Pyr 122
Street, Robert—Lan 74-804, 74-853, 75-040
Streeter, Edward—Hill 48; PopSP SP162
Stribling, T.S.—ASE 1028; AvV V2046
Striker, Fran—BLA 14
Striker, Jason—Signet P2252
Striker, Willis—Peters 4
Strindberg, August—AvGS GS9; AvS YS422
Stringer, Arthur—Harl 328
Strong, Charles—CLN 25
Strong, Charles S.—Knick nn
Strong, L.A.G.—CWC 221, 524
Strong, Phil—ASE E121, 961
Strunsky, Robert—CBS nn
Struther, Jan—Pock 159
Strutton, Bill—AceD D355
Stuart, Alex—Harl 430, 436, 438, 464, 481, 506, 527, 598, 614, 639, 640, 669, 684, 705, 810
Stuart, E.B.—Pop 671
Stuart, E.R.—Lan 75-107
Stuart, Florence—AceD D557; AvFS F166; Lan 70-080
Stuart, Ian (Alistair MacLean)—PopSP SP208, SP231
Stuart, Jeb—Pyr 106
Stuart, Jesse—ASE G188, 888; Pock 357
Stuart, Lyle—Av 305
Stuart, Matt—BB 924, 1018, 1095, 1419, 1696; GSB IL7-30; Lan 73-635, 73-833, 74-793; Penn P8, P18, P42; Perma M3109; Pock 726; Pop 407
Stuart, Sidney (Michael Avallone)—BelLB 92-636
Stuart, Vivian—Harl 558, 566, 574, 678
Stuart, W.J.—BB A1443
Stuart, William L.—AceD D11; Av 186, 597, 801
Stump, Al—CreB D709
Sturdy, Carl—Grif nn; Harl 47; MagV 5
Sturgeon, Theodore—AvT T304, T439; Bal 46, 119, 165, 179, 458K, 462K, 506K, F562; BalU U2231, U2247, U2253; BerkG G280; DellFE B120, A128; GM D1626; Maga 3; Pyr G247, G544, G622, G636, F673, F732, F974
Sturgeon, Theodore (ed. by Groff Conklin)—Pyr G184
Sturgis, Robert—ASE O23
Styles, Showell—Bal F713
Styron, William—Signet D967, Q1944
Sublette, C.M.—ASE N30
Sudak, Eunice—Lan 70-015, 70-034, 70-052, 71-325
Suehsdorf, Adie—CreB D376; Perma M4106
Suess, Dr.—Pock 110
Sugar, Andrew—Lan 75-443, 75-461, 75-473
Sugrue, Thomas—DellF F56
Su-Ling—HollH HH143
Sullivan, Arthur—Av 228
Sullivan, Frank—ASE S11, 1193
Sullivan, J.W.N.—Ment M35, M45
Sullivan, Katherine—CreB G182
Sullivan, Reese—AceG G596, G732, G760; AceM M106, M128, M140
Sullivan, Scott—AceK K169
Sullivan, Walter—Signet S1810
Summers, Charline—Saber SA128
Summers, Erick—Saber SA102, SA138
Summers, Essie—Harl 625, 668, 724, 742, 774, 784, 802, 822, 847, 862, 886, 910, 933, 957
Summers, Hollis—BB 727
Summers, Joseph H.—DellLE LB151
Summers, Richard—BB 1025; CWC 466; Dell 471
Summersby, Kay—Dell 286
Summerskill, Shirley—Harl 763
Summerton, Margaret—AceG G575, G589; AceK K181, K194
Sumner, Cid Ricketts—BB 126
Sumner, Earl—PrizeWN 39
Sumner, Nick—BB 1551; Dell 979; Penn P52
Sundgaard, Arnold—Pyr G213; PyrPR PR22
Surdez, Georges—Dell 501
Surrency, Erwin C.—Doc 3
Suskind, Richard—Bal F573
Sutcliff, Rosemary—CreB M713
Sutter, Larabie—GM 255, 630; GMB 53
Sutton, Jeff—AceD D377, D478; AceF F222, F374; AceH H18, H95
Sutton, Stack—Powe 1003N
Svensson, Robert—AvV V2118
Swados, Felice—Av 298, 430; BerkG G240; DivRN 1
Swados, Harvey—BB A2042
Swain, Dwight V.—AceD D113
Swanberg, W.A.—AceK K104; Dell 332
Swann,—Lan 73-564
Swann, Francis—Lan 73-472, 73-777
Swann, Thomas Burnett—AceF F407; AceG G640, G694, G758
Swanson, Gregory—Bea B320
Swanson, Neil H.—BB A1016, F1041, A1159; DellID D113; PermaS P108
Swarthout, Glendon—CreB T625; Signet D1679, D1890

348

Wall, William—Papi OSM-901, OSM-904
Wallace, Claire—Harl 271, 550
Wallace, Edgar—Av 112, 125, 173; AvMMM 3, 45; BB
F3093; BM B71; CWC nn, 255, 545; Dell 49; Harl 334,
349, 352, 361, 378, 387, 395, 418, 420, 428, 444,
447, 456, 466, 475, 484, 493
Wallace, F.L.—AceD D209, D357; GSFN 32
Wallace, Francis—ASE 746, 1092; BB 133; DNC 24; PockB
B20
Wallace, Irving—CreB M841; Signet T1935, D1978, Q2305
Wallace, J.H.—Pop 385
Wallace, Lew—BB A1450, F1903; CardGC GC75; DellF F79;
Signet D1681
Wallace, Mary—AvS S262
Wallace, Robert—Cor CR101, CR102, CR103, CR104,
CR105, CR106, CR107, CR108, CR109, CR110,
CR111, CR112, CR113, CR114, CR115, CR117,
CR119, CR123, CR127, CR131, CR135, CR139
Wallace, Ruth Sawtell—Dell 123
Wallace, William—Saber SA112
Wallach, Ira—AvFS F100; DellD D357
Wallach, Sidney—TR nn
Wallbank, T. Walter—Ment MD224
Wallenstein, Marcel—Av AT447; EtB E124
Waller, Leslie—GM K1319; Pop 393; PopLE EB76
Walling, R.A.J.—ASE Q15; Av nn(8), nn(16); Pock 24; Pony
49; Pop 106, 139
Wallis, G. McDonald—AceF F108, F187
Wallis, J.H.—ASE 723; MM 81
Wallis, Ruth Sawtell—BB 72, 109
Wallop, Douglass—AvS S307; CardE C144, C328; Pock 1146
Walpole, Hugh—ASE 928; Av 204
Walsh, J.M.—CWC nn, 64, 89, 294, 305, 334, 503
Walsh, Maurice—Penn P28
Walsh, Paul E.—Av 742, 767, 802
Walsh, Penelope—Harl 968
Walsh, Robert—Signet 1492
Walsh, Ruth M.—Bea B229
Walsh, Thomas—BB 895, 1150, 1840
Waltari, Mika—CardE C244, C263, C287; CardGC GC31,
GC34
Walters, Hank—NovF 3505, 5047, 6050, 60107
Walters, Lee—Saber SA14, SA15, SA41
Walton, Bryce—Fal 42
Walton, Evangeline—BalAF 01959, 02332, 02773, 24209,
24233; MonB 264
Walz, Audrey—BB 1182; Harl 157
Walz, Jay—BB 1182
Wand, Della—NSLS U140, U149
Ward, Arch—ASE 1037
Ward, Brad (Samuel Peeples)—AceD D18, D30, D48, S60,
S148, D475; AceF F370; BB 1596; Grap 129; Penn
P76; Signet 1481
Ward, Don—Bal 236, 364K; BB F1972; Signet S1533
Ward, Jonas (William Ard)—GM 604, 662, 742, 803, 951,
1021, 1026, K1574, K1575, K1576, K1622, K1651,
K1689
Ward, Mary Jane—Signet 696, 1182
Ward, Steve—AceD D451
Ware, Harlan—BB A1097
Warner, Douglas—Hill 184
Warner, Rex—Ment MD226, MD254, MD280
Warnow, Morton—Signet S2039
Warren, Charles M.—BB 732, 776, 1068
Warren, Charles Marquis—JonM J47
Warren, Doug—AceD D373
Warren, James—BM B83; CWC 54, 233, 238
Warren, Jay—Midw 72
Warren, John T.—Lan 72-102
Warren, Laura—NSLS 13A
Warren, Paul—DellFE nn
Warren, Paulette—Lan 72-945, 72-985, 73-649, 73-834, 73-
842, 73-877, 74-530, 74-836, 75-427, 75-470
Warren, Robert Penn—ASE 1201; BantC FC34; BB A939,
F1338, F1556; BerkG BG35; DellF F82; DellFE F16,
FE69; DellLE LX102, LC109, LX110; Signet 725, 804,
D975, D1330, T1866, P2231, T2298
Warwick, Chester—AceF F107
Warwick, Jarvis (Hugh Garner)—NSLS 27A
Washburn, Charles—BelLB L518
Washington, Booker T.—BantB FB406; BantC FC37; Pock 80
Washington, Kipp—HollH HH122
Waskow, Arthur I.—Bal X655
Wassam, Rosqua—CrAS FB1010
Waters, Ethel—BB F1976
Waters, Ethel (with Charles Samuels)—BB A985
Waters, Frank—ASE 1236; Berk 104; DellD D127; RCL 32
Waters, Harold—AvT T130
Waters, T.A.—Lan 73-623, 73-656, 73-713, 73-769, 74-563,
74-618, 74-629, 75-200
Watkin, Lawrence Edward—ASE 779; DellFE A181; Pock 317
Watkins, Glen (on cover)/ Eliot Brewster)—NSLF 31
Watkins, Glen—Croy 13, 20; Knick nn; NSLF 42; Pyr 17;
StorON 3
Watkins, Peter—AvNS NS23
Watson, Betty—ASE C78
Watson, John—Pock 734
Watson, Ken—Harl 442, 635; StovA nn
Watson, Lilian E.—BB F1747
Watson, Will—Harl 396; Lion 61
Watts, Alan W.—Ment MD273

Watts, Franklin—CardE C152, C160, C200
Waugh, Alec—BB F1568
Waugh, Evelyn—Dell 771, 807; DellD D163, D222; DellF F68,
F74; DellLE LX104, LB146
Waugh, Hillary—AvG G1212, G1239, G1288; CreB 172, 292;
CWC 483; DellD D338; Grap 12; Han 88; Pock 988,
1075
Way, Frederick Jr—DellF P14
Way, Isabel Stewart—AvFS F145, F168, F207
Way, Wayne—DB 9; IN 29
Wayman, Tony Russell—AceH H21
Wayne, Anderson—PopLG G123, G310
Wayne, Arlo—BerkG G195
Wayne, Charles—Saber SA25
Wayne, Ernie—Pop 512
Wayne, Joseph—AceG G741; AvFS F148, F204, F220; AvS
S425; DellFE A138, A201; Signet 891, 1028, 1077,
1128, 1277, 1302, 1384
Wayne, Rick—Rain 113
Weale, Anne—Harl 537, 553, 578, 582, 644, 716, 743, 767,
798, 830, 855, 870, 901, 914, 948
Weatherall, Ernie—Bea B131, B150
Weatherly, Max—Zenith ZB11
Weaver, John D.—ASE 879, 902
Weaver, Ward (F. Van Wyck Mason)—ASE J289; Pop 342,
388; PopLG G180, G303
Webb, Jack—AvG G1277; CreB s341; Regy RB311; Signet
1076, 1149, 1233, 1311, 1422, 1556, S1816, S1988
Webb, Jean Francis—Dell 331
Webb, Jon Edgar—BB 1179
Webb, Lionel—Lan 75-052, 75-061
Webb, Mary—Dell 436; Pock 535
Webb, Nancy—Perma M3102
Webb, Paul—Signet 1441
Webber, Everett—Pock 681; Pop 303; PopLG G159
Webber, Gordon—BB 1345
Webber, Olga—Pock 681; Pop 303
Weber, Lenora Mattingly—BerkG G223, G293
Weber, Rubin—AvG G1282
Webster, Doris—AceK K182
Webster, John—WSP W101
Webster, M. Coates—Harl 293
Webster, Margaret—Prem d54
Webster, Noah—Books 107
Webster, Sam—MonB 234, 245, 268, 385, 404
Wechsberg, Josef—ASE 749; Lion 33; Pen 622
Wechsler, Herman J.—CardE C28; PBCE nn(6); Pock 578,
661; PocLGA A7
Weegee—BerkG G9
Weekley, William George—PermaS P111
Weeks, Edward—Pock 397
Weeks, Jack—DellFE D20
Weeks, Joseph—PopLG G165
Weeks, William Rawle—BB A1706
Weenolsen, Hebe—BB A1052
Wees, Frances Shelley—BB 418; Harl 2, 8, 295
Weidman, Jerome—Av 226, 241, 279, 322, 356, 429, 442;
AvG G1026, G1032, G1049; AvT AT63, T82, T97,
T103, T131, T153, T207, T240, T425; AvV V2104;
BerkG G49; CardGC GC79; CreB M633; EtB E114
Weigall, Arthur—BRNM 1; NovL 24
Weil, Jerry—Signet 1324, 1350, 1393, 1449, 1554, S1797,
S2000, S2108, D2161
Weinbaum, Stanley G.—Harl 205; Lan 72-146, 74-808, 75-
399
Weinberg, Meyer—AceD S622
Weiner, Ed—Pop 220
Weiner, Henri—MNM nn
Weiner, Joan—Lan 75-183
Weinreb, Nathaniel Norsen—PermaS P305; PopLG G356
Weinsott, Genevieve—NSLF 91
Weinstein, Alfred A. MD—Lan 74-838, 75-147
Weinstein, Sol—PocSp 10081, 10094, 10172
Weir, Ruth—Dell 38, 89
Weirauch, Anna Elisabet—AvT AT58; CreB s214, S392, K710
Weisinger, Mort—BB 1309, 1606, A2017
Weiss, David B.—HollH HH117
Weiss, Joe—Av 582, 717; AvT T332; Bea B141, B145, B148,
B155; Fal 28; Lan 74-836
Weiss, Martin L.—AceD D45, D214
Weissman, Sidney—AceD S130
Welch, Douglass—ASE 1109
Welch, Maud McCurdy—Lan 71-306; MonB 177
Weldman, Jerome—AvG G1017
Weldon, John Lee—Signet 1126, 1184
Weldon, Rex—NovF 6086, 60115; Novs 6N223, 6N243;
Saber SA48, SA63
Wellard, James Howard—AvT T188; CreB R417; Dell 812;
Han 35
Weller, George—RoyG 21
Welles, Kermit—AceD D332; Cam 307, 310, 338; Carn 925;
OrigN 704, 710; Venus 128, 144, 178
Welles, Orson—Dell 305; PockB B77; Pyr G357
Welles, Sumner—ASE R35
Wellman, Manly Wade—AceD D443; BalU U2222; Cent 68;
DellFE 52; GSFN 34; PSFN 11; Signet 703, 1448
Wellman, Paul I.—ASE 1262; BB F1915; CardE C96, C141,
C278; CardGC GC20; PermaS P115, P129, P142, P240,
263; Pock 794; PockB B71; Pyr R855, R867
Wells, Anna Mary—Dell 66, 126
Wells, Barry—Bal F602

Wells, Caroline—DNC nn, 5
Wells, Carolyn—AtM nn
Wells, Charles—Signet 1167, 1225
Wells, Evelyn—ASE 1286; Pock 637
Wells, H.G.—AceD D309, D388, D537; AceF F240; ASE T2,
698, 745, 958, 1091; Bal S414K, F687, F725, S742,
F761; BalU U2232; Berk 380; CHARf CB128; Dell 201,
269; Pock 119, 947, 1140; PopSP SP170
Wells, John Warren—Lan 75-029, 75-041
Wells, Lee E.—AceD D264; AceF F110; AceG G579; Av 529,
573, 620, 754; AvT T315, T327, T378, T457; Dell 906;
Pock 865
Wells, Michael—AceD D243; Hill 186
Wells, Susan—BondM 15
Wellsley, Julie—Lan 73-674, 73-841, 73-882, 74-550, 74-
758, 75-271, 75-369, 75-481
Welty, Eudora—Dell 887; Signet T2274
Wendt, Gerald—AvB Bard 6
Wendt, Stephen—Pop 458
Wenner, Sim—DellFE K107
Wentworth, Patricia—ASE 1166; BM B75; CWC 423; Dell 2;
DNC 4; Pop 29, 39, 66, 79, 105, 131, 197, 232, 283,
333, 382; Pyr R895, R932
Wentworth, Rick—CHARf CB129
Wenzell, Isabel D'Este—Lan 73-619
Werfel, Franz—CardE C67; DellF F78; MM 29; Pock 433
Werner, Alfred—PocLGA A5, A12
Werner, George—GSB IL7-27
Werner, M.R.—ASE M26
Werper, Barton—GSB IL7-42, IL7-49, IL7-54, IL7-60, IL7-65
Werry, Richard R.—BB 1506; Signet 938
Werstein, Irving—AceD D325
Wertenbaker, Lael Tucker—BB A1693
Werth, Alexander—AvDYD D1; CreB T540
Wertham, Fredric—EtB ET106
Wescott, Glenway—ASE 792; BB 69, 87; Signet P2369
Wesley, Elizabeth (Adeline McElfresh)—AvT T525; BB
1607, A1962
West,—Powe PP106, PP124, PP161
West, Alice N.—Lan 74-753
West, Anthony—CardE C235; CreB T490, T725
West, Ben—IN 17; Uni 32, 38
West, Edwin—MonB 165, 189, 199, 232, 334, 410
West, Elliot—AceK K116
West, Gloria—Saber SA134
West, Jessamyn—BB A995; CreB R456, T665; Pock 1073
West, John B.—Signet 1642, 1755, S1883, S1929
West, Kingsley—Bann B40-102, B40-103
West, Mae—AvG G1047; Dell 525
West, Morris L.—DellF F178; DellFE A116; Perma M4155
West, Nathanael—Av 634; AvGS GS1; AvNS NS39; AvSS
SS6, SS13; AvT T634 BantC AC14; BB 1093, A1704
West, Roger—Powe PP190
West, Ruth—BB 1592, A1784, A1924
West, Token—Bea B182; BerkG G237; RC 12
West, Tom—AceD D8, D24, D78, D240, D276, D328, D356,
D392, D418, D436, D450, D476, D496; AceF F106,
F128, F148, F172, F200, F230, F250, F264, F292;
AceG G573, G591, G607, G622, G648, G682, G710,
G742; AceM M104, M110, M118, M124, M134; ASE
1240; FWN 11, 20, 31; GWN 35; Pock 733; Pyr 216;
WNC 56, 60, 74, 91
West, Wallace—AceF F114
West, Ward—Dell 527; Pock 972
Westcott, Edward Noyes—BB 41
Westcott, Jan—CardE C136, C157; Dell 439; GrapG G101,
G201, G211; Harl 164; Pock 827, 932
Westheimer, David—AvFS F141; Pop 395; Pyr G52, G233,
G601
Westlake, Donald E.—Lan 73-591, 75-156; Midw 48
Westland, Lynn—Av 838; BCW 30, 34, 38; FWN 26, 28, 40;
GWN 44; Han 132; Harl 146, 148, 212, 248; WNC 85,
105
Westley, Kirk—BerkG G260; Cam 361; Carn 949
Weston, Carolyn—BerkG G132
Weston, Christine—ASE M25; BB 723; DellD D158
Weston, Clay—Han 133
Weston, Garnett—Harl 48, 125; MM 106
Weston, Marc—Lan 75-065
Weston, Paul B.—Regy RB117, RB304
Westwood, Perry—GM 299
Wetherell, June Pat—Lan 73-632, 74-576, 74-671, 74-690,
75-367; Pop 557; PopLG G109, G129, G348; PopSP
SP64
Wexler, Susan Stanhope—Signet 1381
Weybright, Victor—SigK KD362
Weymouth, Anthony—PockB B45, B47
Wharton, Edith—ASE B34
Wharton, John F.—ASE 1105
Whatmough, Joshua—Ment MD209
Wheeler, Elmer—Av 517
Wheeler, Keith—Pop 403; Signet T1963
Wheelis, Allen—Signet P2101
Wheelock, Dorothy—Bard nn
Whelan, Ron—NovF 5001, 6036
Whelton, Paul—CWC 490, 522; Grap 13, 17, 19, 24, 37, 49,
71, 95; Pony 63
Whipple, Chandler—AceD D64; FWN 2
Whipple, Dorothy—PockB B8
Whitaker, David—AvG G1322

351

# OTHER TOPICS COVERED BY WALLACE-HOMESTEAD

All the following books can be purchased from your local book store, antiques dealer, or can be borrowed from your public library. Books can also be purchased directly from **Chilton Book Company, Chilton Way, Radnor, PA 19089**. Include code number, title, and price when ordering. Add applicable sales tax and **$2.00** postage and handling for the first book plus $ .50 for each additional book shipped to the same address. VISA/Mastercard orders call **1-800-345-1214** and ask for Customer Service Department (AK, HI, & PA residents call **215-964-4000** and ask for Customer Service Department). Prices and availability are subject to change without notice. Please call for a current Wallace-Homestead catalog.

## COLLECTOR'S GUIDE SERIES

| Code | Title/Author | Price |
|------|-------------|-------|
| W5339 | Collector's Guide to Baseball Cards, *Troy Kirk* | $12.95 |
| W5479 | Collector's Guide to Early Photographs, *O. Henry Mace* | $16.95 |
| W5320 | Collector's Guide to American Toy Trains, *Susan & Al Bagdade* | $16.95 |
| W5568 | Collector's Guide to Autographs, *George Sanders, Helen Sanders, and Ralph Roberts* | $16.95 |
| W5487 | Collector's Guide to Comic Books, *John Hegenberger* | $12.95 |

## COLLECTIBLES

| Code | Title/Author | Price |
|------|-------------|-------|
| W5258 | American Clocks and Clockmakers, *Robert W. & Harriett Swedberg* | $16.95 |
| W4529 | British Royal Commemoratives with Prices, *Audrey Zeder* | $24.95 |
| W4464 | Check the Oil: Gas Station Collectibles with Prices, *Scott Anderson* | $18.95 |
| W4723 | Clock Guide Identification with Prices, *Robert W. Miller* | $14.95 |
| W3786 | Cocoa-Cola Collectibles, Wallace-Homestead Price Guide to, *Deborah Goldstein Hill* | $15.95 |
| W4235 | Collectible Clothing with Prices, *Sheila Malouff* | $14.95 |
| W0175 | Collecting Antique Marbles, *Paul Baumann* | $12.95 |
| W5460 | Commercial Aviation Collectibles: An Illustrated Price Guide, *Richard Wallin* | $15.95 |
| W5177 | Contemporary Fast-Food and Drinking Glass Collectibles, *Mark E. Chase & Michael Kelly* | $16.95 |
| W4731 | Dolls, Wallace-Homestead Price Guide to, *Robert W. Miller* | $16.95 |
| W4936 | Dr. Records' Original 78 RPM Pocket Price Guide, *Peter A. Soderbergh Ph.D.* | $12.95 |
| W5118 | Food and Drink Containers and Their Prices, *Al Bergevin* | $16.95 |
| W4901 | Girl Scout Collector's Guide: 75 Years of Uniforms, Insignia, Publications & Keepsakes, *Mary Degenhardt and Judy Kirsch* | $21.95 |
| W5185 | Guide to Old Radios: Pointers, Pictures, and Prices, *David & Betty Johnson* | $16.95 |
| W5436 | Herron's Price Guide to Dolls, *R. Lane Herron* | $16.95 |
| W0060* | Illustrated Radio Premium Catalof and Price Guide, *Tom Tumbusch* | $34.95 |
| W5371 | Jigsaw Puzzles: An Illustrated History and Price Guide, *Anne D. Williams* | $24.95 |
| W121X* | Oil Lamps: The Kerosene Era in North America, *Catherine M. V. Thuro* | $38.95 |
| W5312* | Petretti's Coca-Cola Collectibles Price Guide, *Allan Petretti* | $29.95 |
| W4944 | Plastic Collectibles, Wallace-Homestead Price Guide to, *Lyndi Stewart McNulty* | $17.95 |
| W5169 | Presidential and Campaign Memorabilia with Prices, Second Edition, *Stan Gores* | $18.95 |
| W541X | Psychedelic Collectibles of the 1960s and 1970s: An Illustrated Price Guide, *Susanne White* | $21.95 |
| W5657 | Space Adventure Collectibles, *T. N. Tumbusch* | $19.95 |
| W4154 | Steiff Teddy Bears, Dolls, and Toys with Prices, *Shirley Conway & Jean Wilson* | $17.95 |
| W538X | Steiff Toys Revisited, *Jean Wilson* | $18.95 |
| W4847* | Thimble Collector's Encyclopedia: New International Edition, *John von Hoelle* | $35.95 |
| W1236 | Thimble Treasury, *Myrtle Lundquist* | $12.95 |
| W3972 | Tins 'N' Bins, *Robert W. & Harriett Swedberg* | $16.95 |
| W4642 | Tobacco Tins and Their Prices, *Al Bergevin* | $16.95 |
| W5584 | Tomart's Illustrated Disneyana Catalog and Price Guide, Condensed Edition, *Tom Tumbusch* | $19.95 |
| W5576 | Warman's Americana & Collectibles, *Edited by Harry L. Rinker* | $14.95 |
| W5606 | Warman's Antiques and Their Prices, 24th Edition, *Edited by Harry L. Rinker* | $13.95 |
| W0140* | Zalkin's Handbook of Thimbles & Sewing Implements, *Estelle Zalkin* | $24.95 |
| W4383 | Yesterday's Toys with Today's Prices, *Fred and Marilyn Fintel* | $14.95 |

## COUNTRY

| Code | Title/Author | Price |
|------|--------------|-------|
| W524X | American Country Antiques, Wallace-Homestead Price Guide to, Ninth Edition, *Don & Carol Raycraft* | $14.95 |
| W4499 | Antiques From the Country Kitchen, *Frances Thompson* | $16.95 |
| W5428 | Baskets, Wallace-Homestead Price Guide to, Second Edition, *Frances Thompson* | $16.95 |
| W5002 | Country Sourcebook, Second Edition, *Elaine Hawley* | $19.95 |
| W3956 | Country Store 'N' More, *Robert W. & Harriett Swedberg* | $17.95 |
| W3263 | Graniteware Collector's Guide with Prices, *Vernagene Vogelzang & Evelyn Welch* | $16.95 |
| W4588 | Granite Ware, Book II, *Vernagene Vogelzang & Evelyn Welch* | $18.95 |
| W3581 | Kitchens and Gadgets: 1920 to 1950, *Jane Celehar* | $16.95 |
| W4251 | Kitchens and Kitchenware: 1900 to 1950, *Jane Celehar* | $15.95 |
| W443X | Shaker: A Collector's Source Book II, *Don & Carol Raycraft* | $15.95 |

## FURNITURE

| Code | Title/Author | Price |
|------|--------------|-------|
| W4758 | American Oak Furniture, Revised Edition, *Robert W. & Harriett Swedberg* | $16.95 |
| W4243 | American Oak Furniture, Volume II, *Robert W. & Harriett Swedberg* | $16.95 |
| W4928 | American Oak Furniture, Volume III, *Robert W. & Harriett Swedberg* | $16.95 |
| W4111 | Country Furniture and Accessories with Prices, *Robert W. & Harriett Swedberg* | $16.95 |
| W376X | Country Furniture and Accessories with Prices, Book II, *Robert W. & Harriett Swedberg* | $16.95 |
| W3883 | Country Pine Furniture, Revised Edition, *Robert W. & Harriett Swedberg* | $14.95 |
| W5401* | Macdonald Guide to Buying Antique Furniture, *Rachael Feild* | $25.00 |
| W393X | Victorian Furniture, Book I, Revised, *Robert W. & Harriett Swedberg* | $16.95 |
| W3875 | Victorian Furniture, Book II, *Robert W. & Harriett Swedberg* | $16.95 |
| W3964 | Victorian Furniture, Book III, *Robert W. & Harriett Swedberg* | $16.95 |
| W5207 | Wicker Furniture: Styles and Prices, Revised, *Robert W. & Harriett Swedberg* | $14.95 |

## GENERAL

| Code | Title/Author | Price |
|------|--------------|-------|
| W4189 | Antique Radios: Restoration and Price Guide, *Betty & David Johnson* | $14.95 |
| W3921 | Antiques, Wallace-Homestead Price Guide to, Eleventh Edition, *Dan D'Imperio* | $14.95 |
| W5274 | Antiquing in England: A Guide to Antique Centres, *Robert W. & Harriett Swedberg* | $16.95 |
| W5126 | The Complete Collector's Guide to Fakes and Forgeries, *Colin Haynes* | $15.95 |
| W5592 | Flea Market Handbook: Making Money in Antiques, Second Edition, *Robert G. Miner* | $12.95 |
| W3913 | Flea Market Price Guide, Fifth Edition, *Robert G. Miller* | $12.95 |
| W4618 | Joy of Collecting, *Harry Rinker & Frank Hill* | $ 6.95 |
| W4855 | Oriental Antiques & Art: An Identification and Value Guide, *Sandra Andacht* | $17.95 |
| W5266 | Rinker on Collectibles, *Harry L. Rinker* | $14.95 |

## GLASS

| Code | Title/Author | Price |
|------|--------------|-------|
| W4308* | American Cut and Engraved Glass of the Brilliant Period, *Martha Louise Swan* | $35.00 |
| W5452* | Early American Pattern Glass – 1850 to 1910: Major Collectible Table Settings with Prices, *Bill Jenks & Jerry Luna* | $29.95 |
| W4626 | Glass Signatures, Trademarks, and Trade Names, *Anne Geffken Pullen* | $16.95 |
| W4421 | Pattern Glass, Wallace-Homestead Price Guide to, Eleventh Edition, *Robert W. Miller & Dori Miles* | $15.95 |
| W5444* | Perfume and Scent Bottle Collecting with Prices, Second Edition, *Jean Sloan* | $35.00 |

## JEWELRY

| Code | Title/Author | Price |
|------|--------------|-------|
| W3697 | Antique Jewelry with Prices, *Doris J. Snell* | $14.95 |
| W5231* | Ladies' Compacts of The 19th and 20th Centuries, *Roselyn Gerson* | $34.95 |

## PAPER EPHEMERA

| Code | Title/Author | Price |
|------|--------------|-------|
| W460X | A Collector's Guide to Autographs with Prices, *Bob Bennett* | $14.95 |
| W4987 | Currier & Ives: An Illustrated Value Guide, *Craig McClain* | $16.95 |
| W5363 | Hancer's Price Guide to Paperback Books, Third Edition, *Kevin Hancer* | $16.95 |
| W5029 | Military Postcards, 1870 to 1945, *Jack H. Smith* | $19.95 |
| W5193* | Postcard Companion: The Collector's Reference, *Jack H. Smith* | $39.95 |
| W5053 | The Price Guide to Autographs, *George Sanders, Helen Sanders, & Ralph Roberts* | $18.95 |

## POTTERY & PORCELAIN

| Code | Title/Author | Price |
|------|-------------|-------|
| 80038* | British Studio Ceramics in the 20th Century, *Paul Rice and Christopher Gowing* | $45.00 |
| 7982X | A History of World Pottery, Revised and Updated Edition, *Emmanuel Cooper* | $24.95 |
| W5398* | Macdonald Guide to Buying Antique Pottery & Porcelain, *Rachael Feild* | $25.00 |
| W0116 | Warman's English & Continental Pottery & Porcelain, *Susan & Al Bagdade* | $18.95 |

* Denotes hardcover, all others are paperback.